CPT® Expert

2006

6th edition

Notice

The *2006 CPT Expert* is designed to be an accurate and authoritative source of information about this coding system. Every effort has been made to verify the accuracy of the listings, and all information is believed reliable at the time of publication. Absolute accuracy cannot be guaranteed, however. This publication is made available with the understanding that the publisher is not engaged in rendering legal or other services that require a professional license. If you identify a correction or wish to share information, please email the Ingenix customer service department at customerservice@ingenix.com or fax us at 801.982.4033.

American Medical Association Notice

CPT codes, descriptions, and other CPT material only are copyright 2004 American Medical Association (AMA). All Rights Reserved. No fee schedules, basic units, relative values or related listings are included in CPT. AMA does not directly or indirectly practice medicine or dispense medical services. AMA assumes no liability for data contained or not contained herein.

The responsibility for the content of any '*National Correct Coding Policy*' included in this product is with the Centers for Medicare & Medicaid Services (CMS) and no endorsement by the AMA is intended or should be implied. The AMA disclaims responsibility for any consequences or liability attributable to or related to any use, nonuse or interpretation of information contained in this product.

CPT is a registered trademark of the American Medical Association.

Our Commitment to Accuracy

Ingenix is committed to producing accurate and reliable materials. To report corrections, please visit www.ingenixonline.com/accuracy or email accuracy@ingenix.com. You can also reach customer service by calling 1.800.INGENIX (464.3649), option 1.

Copyright

ISBN 1-56337-683-0

Continuing Education Units for Certified Members of the American Academy of Professional Coders

This publication has prior approval by the American Academy of Professional Coders for continuing education units (CEUs). Granting of prior approval in no way constitutes endorsement by the Academy of the publication content nor the publisher. Instructions to submit CEUs are available within the "Preapproved CEU Vendor List" file at www.aapc.com/education/CEUs/ceus.html.

Acknowledgments

Brad Ericson, MPC, *Product Manager*
Sheri Poe Bernard, CPC, CPC-H, CPC-P, *Senior Director, Product Management*
Lynn Speirs, *Senior Director, Editorial/Desktop Publishing*
Karen Schmidt, BSN, *Technical Director*
Stacy Perry, *Manager, Desktop Publishing*
Lisa Singley, *Project Manager*
Wendy Gabbert-McConkie, CPC, CPC-H, *Clinical/Technical Editor*
Karen Kachur, RN, CPC, *Clinical/Technical Editor*
Kerrie Hornsby, *Desktop Publishing Specialist*
Irene Day, *Desktop Publishing Specialist*
Kate Holden, *Editor*

About the Contributors

Wendy Gabbert-McConkie, CPC, CPC-H
Clinical/Technical Editor

Ms. Gabbert-McConkie has more than 20 years of experience in the health care field. She has extensive background in CPT/HCPCS and ICD-9-CM coding. She served several years as a coding consultant. Her areas of expertise include physician and hospital CPT coding assessments, chargemaster reviews, and the Outpatient Prospective Payment System (OPPS). She is a member of the American Academy of Professional Coders (AAPC).

Karen H. Kachur, RN, CPC
Clinical/Technical Editor

Ms. Kachur is a Clinical/Technical Editor for Ingenix with expertise in CPT/HCPCS and ICD-9-CM coding, in addition to physician billing, compliance, and fraud and abuse. Prior to joining Ingenix, she worked for many years as a staff RN in a variety of clinical settings including medicine, surgery, intensive care, psychiatry, and geriatrics. Ms Kachur has served as assistant director of a hospital utilization management and quality assurance department. She also has extensive experience as a nurse reviewer for Blue Cross/Blue Shield.

CONTENTS

© 2005 Ingenix, Inc

Introduction

Welcome to the Ingenix *CPT Expert*, the definitive procedure coding source that combines the work of the American Medical Association (AMA) with the technical components you need for proper reimbursement and coding accuracy. *CPT Expert* not only provides you with the most recent version of the AMA's Physicians' Current Procedural Terminology (CPT®), but also with detailed coding instructions, clinical guidelines, lay definitions of complex procedures and medical terms, and summaries of the coverage policies used by federal and commercial payers.

CPT Expert includes the information needed to submit claims to commercial payers or federal intermediaries and carriers, and is correct at the time of printing. However, commercial payers and CMS may change payment rules at any time throughout the year. Commercial payers will announce changes through monthly news or information posted on their Web sites. CMS will post changes in policy on its website at http://www.cms.hhs.gov/manuals/transmittals/comm_date_dsc.asp. Local coverage determinations (LCDs) provide individual carrier guidelines for specific services. The existence of a procedure code does not imply coverage under any given insurance plan.

CPT Expert is based on the American Medical Association's Physicians' Current Procedural Terminology (CPT) coding system, which is copyrighted and owned by the physician organization. CPT is the nation's official, HIPAA compliant code set for procedures and services provided by physicians, ambulatory surgical centers, and hospital outpatient services, as well as laboratories, imaging centers, physical therapy clinics, urgent care centers, and others. **CPT Expert is not intended to be a replacement for the official AMA CPT manual**.

GETTING STARTED WITH *CPT EXPERT*

CPT Expert combines the most current material at publication time from the American Medical Association's CPT 2006, the Centers for Medicare and Medicaid Services online manual system, the Correct Coding Initiative, CMS fee schedules and rules, and Ingenix's own coding expertise.

Designed to be easy to use and full of information, this product is an excellent companion to your AMA CPT book, Medicare, Ingenix, or other resources. These are presented in black text or through use of an easy-to-spot color bar or icon. Coding guidelines, annotations and tips from Ingenix technical experts are designated in blue ink.

Icons derived from AMA guidelines or coding conventions are presented as circles. Icons derived from federal guidelines, data, or rules are square.

Blue Color Bar—Not Covered by Medicare
Services and procedures identified by this color bar are never a covered benefit under Medicare. Services and procedures that are not covered may be billed directly to the patient at the time of the service.

11975 Insertion, implantable contraceptive capsules ♀ Ⓔ

Yellow Color Bar—Unlisted Procedure
Unlisted CPT codes report procedures that have not been assigned a specific code number. An unlisted code delays payment due to the extra time necessary for review. When using an unlisted procedure code, include cover notes, documentation of medical necessity, and operative reports.

20999 Unlisted procedure, musculoskeletal system, general Ⓣ ⑧⓪

Ⓣ **Technical Component Only**
Codes with this icon represent only the technical component (staff and equipment costs) of a procedure or service. Do not use either modifier 26 or TC with these codes.

77520 Proton treatment delivery; simple, without compensation Ⓢ Ⓣ

---

26 Professional Component
Only codes with this icon represent the physician's work or professional component of a procedure or service. Do not use either modifier 26 or TC with these codes.

77427 Radiation treatment management, five treatments E 26 ◨

50 Bilateral Procedure
This icon identifies codes that can be reported bilaterally when the same surgeon provides the service for the same patient on the same date. Medicare allows payment for both procedures at 150 percent of the usual amount for one procedure. The modifier does not apply to bilateral procedures inclusive to one code.

27235 Percutaneous skeletal fixation of femoral fracture, proximal end, neck T 50 ◨

80 Assist-at-Surgery Allowed
Services noted by this icon are allowed an assist at surgery with payment equal to 16 percent of the allowed amount for the global surgery for that procedure. No documentation is required.

30460 Rhinoplasty for nasal deformity secondary to congenital cleft lip and/or palate, including columellar lengthening; tip only 7 T 80 ◨

80 Assist-at-Surgery Allowed with Documentation
Services noted by this icon are allowed an assistant at surgery with payment equal to 16 percent of the allowed amount for the global surgery for that procedure. Documentation is required.

30400 Rhinoplasty, primary; lateral and alar cartilages and/or elevation of nasal tip 4 T 80 ◨

+ Add-on Codes
This icon identifies procedures reported in addition to the primary procedure. The icon "+" denotes add-on codes. An add-on code is neither a stand-alone code nor subject to multiple procedure rules since it describes work in addition to the primary procedure.

22216 each additional vertebral segment (List separately in addition to primary procedure) C ◨

⊘ Modifier 51 Exempt
Codes identified by this icon indicate that the procedure does not meet the definition of an add-on procedure and is not subject to multiple procedure rules.

50327 Backbench reconstruction of cadaver or living donor renal allograft prior to transplantation; venous anastomosis, each C 80 ◨

◧ Correct Coding Initiative (CCI)
CPT Expert identifies those codes with a corresponding CCI edit in Version 11.3, effective October 1, 2005. The CCI edits define correct coding practices that now serve as the basis of the national Medicare policy for paying claims. The code noted is the column 1 (comprehensive) code.

12051 Layer closure of wounds of face, ears, eyelids, nose, lips and/or mucous membranes; 2.5 cm or less T ◧

✕ CLIA Waived Test
This icon identifies laboratory services that are not subject to the latest available Clinical Laboratory Improvement Amendments (CLIA) regulations.

84830 Ovulation tests, by visual color comparison methods for human luteinizing hormone ♀ A ✕

63 Modifier 63 Exempt
This icon identifies procedures performed on infants that weigh less than 4 kg. Because of the complexity of performing procedures on infants less than 4 kg, this modifier may be added to the surgical codes to inform the payers of the special circumstance.

44055 Correction of malrotation by lysis of duodenal bands and/or reduction of midgut volvulus (eg, Ladd procedure) C 80 ◨ 63

INTRODUCTION

1–9 ASC Group
This icon identifies a service that is on the latest available list of Medicare covered ASC procedures, and identifies the ASC group, effective July 1, 2005.

50393 Introduction of ureteral catheter or stent into ureter through renal pelvis for drainage and/or injection, percutaneous **1 T 50 ⚡**

⊙ Conscious Sedation
This icon identifies procedures that include conscious sedation. Conscious sedation codes should not be reported with these procedures.

⊙ 92986 Percutaneous balloon valvuloplasty; aortic valve **T 80 ⚡**

A Age Edit
This icon denotes codes intended for use with a specific age group, such as neonate, newborn, pediatric, and adult. Carefully review the code description to assure the code you report most appropriately reflects the patient's age.

49580 Repair umbilical hernia, under age 5 years;reducible **A 4 T 80 ⚡**

M Maternity
This icon identifies procedures that by definition should only be used for maternity patients generally between 12 and 55 years of age.

59871 Removal of cerclage suture under anesthesia (other than local) **M ♀ 5 T 80 ⚡**

♀ Female Only
This icon identifies procedures that should only be reported for female patients.

57220 Plastic operation on urethral sphincter, vaginal approach (eg, Kelly urethral plication) **♀ 3 T 80 ⚡**

♂ Male Only
This icon identifies procedures that should only be reported for male patients.

52500 Transurethral resection of bladder neck (separate procedure) **♂ 3 T ⚡**

MED: This notation precedes an instruction pertaining to this code in the Centers for Medicare and Medicaid Services' (CMS) new Publication 100 (Pub 100) electronic manual or in a National Coverage Decision (NCD). These CMS sources, formerly called the Medicare Carriers Manual (MCM) and Coverage Issues Manual (CIM), present the rules for submitting these services to the federal government or its contractors and are included in the appendix of this book.

46615 with ablation of tumor(s), polyp(s), or other lesion(s) not amenable to removal by hot biopsy forceps, bipolar cautery or snare technique **2 T 80 ⚡**
MED: 100-2, 15, 260; 100-3, 100.2; 100-4, 12, 90.3; 100-4, 14, 10

AMA: This indicates discussion of the code in the American Medical Association's (AMA) CPT Assistant newsletter. Use the citation to find the correct issue.

46083 Incision of thrombosed hemorrhoid, external **T ⚡**
AMA: 1997, Jun, 10

⁄ Drug Not Approved by FDA
The AMA CPT Editorial Panel is publishing new vaccine product codes prior to FDA approval. This symbol indicates which of these codes are pending FDA approval at press time. Check the Ingenix OnLine Web site (http://www.ingenixonline.com/content/pn/) or AMA Web site (http://www.ama-assn.org/ama/pub/category/3113.html) for updates to these codes as they pass through the FDA process.

⁄▲90680 Rotavirus vaccine, pentavalent, 3 dose schedule, live, for oral use **N**

A–Y APC Status Indicators

Status indicators identify how individual CPT codes are paid or not paid under the latest available hospital outpatient prospective payment system (OPPS). The same status indicator is assigned to all the codes within an Ambulatory Payment Classification (APC). Consult your payer or resource to learn which CPT codes fall within various APCs.

A Indicates services that are paid under some other method such as the DMEPOS fee schedule or the physician fee schedule

B Indicates codes that should not be used on an OPPS hospital outpatient bill (types 12X, 13X, and 14X). Codes may be allowable on other types of bills.

C Indicates inpatient services that are not paid under the OPPS

E Indicates services for which payment is not allowed under the OPPS. In some instances, the service is not covered by Medicare. In other instances, Medicare does not use the code in question, but does use another code to describe the service

F Indicates corneal tissue acquisition costs, which are paid separately

G Indicates a current drug or biological for which payment is made under the transitional pass-through

H Indicates a device for which payment is made under the transitional pass-through

K Indicates non-pass-through drugs and biologicals. Effective July 1, 2001, co-payments for these items and the service for the administration of the administration of the items are aggregated and may not exceed the inpatient hospital deductible

L Indicates influenza or pneumonia vaccine paid as reasonable cost with no deductible or coinsurance

M Services not billable to the fiscal intermediary and not payable under OPPS

N Indicates services that are incidental, with payment packaged into another service or APC group

P Indicates services paid only in partial hospitalization programs

S Indicates significant procedures for which payment is allowed under the hospital OPPS but to which the multiple procedure reduction does not apply

T Indicates surgical services for which payment is allowed under the hospital OPPS. Services with this payment indicator are the only service to which the multiple procedure payment reduction applies

V Indicates medical visits for which payment is allowed under the hospital OPPS

X Indicates ancillary services for which payment is allowed under the hospital OPPS

Y Indicates nonimplantable durable medical equipment (DME) that is not paid under OPPS. True DME. Providers other than home health agencies bill to the DMERC.

50393 Introduction of ureteral catheter or stent into ureter through renal pelvis for drainage and/or injection, percutaneous ① Ⓣ ⑤⓪ ☒

Current as of 10/31/2005

For more information about ongoing development of the CPT coding system, consult the AMA Web site at URL http://www.ama-assn.org/

You may subscribe to an e-mail service to receive special reports when information in this book changes. Contact customer service at 1-800-INGENIX, option 1.

A

3D Rendering, 76376-76377
Abbe-Estlander Procedure, 40527
Abdomen, Abdominal
  Abdominal Wall
    Reconstruction, 49905
    Removal
      Mesh, 11008
      Prosthesis, 11008
    Repair
      Hernia, 49491-49525, 49590
      by Laparoscopy, 49650, 49651
    Tumor
      Excision, 22900
      Unlisted Services and Procedures, 22999
  Abscess
    Drainage, 49020, 49040
      Fluid, 49080, 49081
      Peritoneal
        Open, 49020
        Percutaneous, 49021
      Peritonitis, localized, 49020
      Retroperitoneal
        Open, 49060
        Percutaneous, 49061
      Skin and Subcutaneous Tissue
        Complicated, 10061
        Multiple, 10061
        Simple, 10060
        Single, 10060
      Subdiaphragmatic
        Open, 49040
        Percutaneous, 49041
      Subphrenic, 49040
    Incision and drainage
      Open, 49040
      Pancreatitis, 48000
      Peritoneal, 49020
      Peritonitis, Localized, 49020
      Retroperitoneal, 49060
      Skin and Subcutaneous Tissue
        Complicated, 10061
        Multiple, 10061
        Simple, 10060
        Single, 10060
      Subdiaphragmatic, 49040
      Subphrenic, 49040
  Angiography, 74175, 75635
  Anorectal Exam with Anesthesia, 45990
  Aorta
    Aneurysm, 0078T-0081T, 34800-34805,
      34825-34832, 35081-35103, 75952,
      75953
    Thromboendarterectomy, 35331
  Aortic Aneurysm, 0078T-0081T, 34800-34805,
    34825-34832, 35081-35103, 75952,
    75953
  Artery
    Ligation, 37617
  Biopsy
    Open, 49000
    Percutaneous, 49180
    Skin and Subcutaneous Tissue, 11100,
      11101
  Bypass Graft, 35907
  Cannula/catheter
    Insertion, 49420, 49421
    Removal, 49422
  Celiotomy
    for Staging, 49220

Abdomen, Abdominal — *continued*
  CT Scan, 74150-74175, 75635
  Cyst
    Destruction/Excision, 49200, 49201
  Delivery
    with Hysterectomy, 59525
    After Attempted Vaginal Delivery, 59618
      Delivery Only, 59620
      Postpartum Care, 59622
      Routine Care, 59618
    Delivery Only, 59514
    Postpartum Care, 59515
    Routine Care, 59510
    Tubal Ligation at Time of, 58611
  Drainage
    Fluid, 49080, 49081
  Ectopic Pregnancy, 59130
  Endometrioma
    Destruction
      Excision, 49200, 49201
  Excision
    Excess Skin, 15831
    Tumor, Abdominal Wall, 22900
  Exploration, 49000, 49002
    Blood Vessel, 35840
    Staging, 58960
  Hernia Repair, 49495-49525, 49560-49587
  Incision, 49000
    Staging, 58960
  Incision and Drainage
    Pancreatitis, 48000
  Injection
    Air, 49400
    Contrast Material, 49400
  Insertion
    Catheter, 49419-49421
    Venous Shunt, 49425
  Intraperitoneal
    Catheter Removal, 49422
    Shunt
      Ligation, 49428
      Removal, 49429
  Laparotomy
    with Biopsy, 49000
    Exploration, 47015, 49000-49002, 58960
    Hemorrhage Control, 49002
    Second Look, 58960
    Staging, 49220, 58960
  Magnetic Resonance Imaging (MRI), 74181-
    74183
  Needle Biopsy
    Mass, 49180
  Peritoneocentesis, 49080, 49081
  Radical Resection, 51597
  Repair
    Blood Vessel, 35221
    with
      Other Graft, 35281
      Vein Graft, 35251
    Hernia, 49491-49525, 49560-49587
    Suture, 49900
  Revision
    Venous Shunt, 49426
  Suture, 49900
  Tumor
    Destruction/Excision, 49200, 49201
  Ultrasound, 76700, 76705
  Unlisted Services and Procedures, 49999
  Wound Exploration
    Penetrating, 20102
  X-ray, 74000-74022

Abdominal Lymphangiogram
  See Lymphangiography, Abdomen
Abdominal Paracentesis
  See Abdomen, Drainage
Abdominal Radiographies
Abdominal Wall
  See Abdomen, X-Ray
  Debridement
    Infected, 11005-11006
  Reconstruction, 49905
  Removal
    Mesh, 11008
    Prosthesis, 11008
  Surgery, 22999
  Tumor
    Excision, 22900
Abdominohysterectomy
  See Hysterectomy, Abdominal
Abdominopelvic Amputation
  See Amputation, Interpelviabdominal
Abdominoplasty, 15831
ABG, 82803, 82805
Ablation
  Anal
    Polyp, 46615
    Tumor, 46615
  Bone tumor, 20982
  Colon
    Tumor, 45339
  Cryosurgical
    Fibroadenoma, 0120T
    Renal mass, 50250
    Renal Tumor
      Percutaneous, 0135T
  CT Scan Guidance, 76362
  Endometrial, 58353, 58356, 58563
  Endometrium
    Ultrasound Guidance, 58356
  Heart
    Arrhythmogenic Focus, 93650-93652
    Intracardiac Pacing and Mapping, 93631
      follow-up Study, 93624
      Stimulation and Pacing, 93623
  Liver
    Tumor, 47380-47382
      Laparoscopic, 47370, 47371
      Open, 47380-47382
  Magnetic Resonance Guidance, 76394
  Prostate, 55873
  Renal
    Cyst, 50541
    Mass, 50542
      Radiofrequency, 50592
    Tumor
      Cryotherapy
        Percutaneous, 0135T
  Turbinate Mucosa, 30801, 30802
  Ultrasound
    Guidance, 76940
    Ultrasound Focused, 0071T-0072T
    Uterine Tumor, 0071T-0072T
  Uterine Leiomyomata, 0071T, 0072T
  Vein
    Endovenous
ABO, 86900
Abortion
  See Obstetrical Care
  Incomplete, 59812
  Induced by
    with Hysterotomy, 59100, 59852, 59857

Abortion — *continued*
  Induced by — *continued*
    Amniocentesis Injection, 59850-59852
    Dilation and Curettage, 59840
    Dilation and Evacuation, 59841
    Saline, 59850, 59851
    Vaginal Suppositories, 59855, 59856
  Missed
    First Trimester, 59820
    Second Trimester, 59821
  Septic, 59830
  Spontaneous, 59812
  Therapeutic, 59840-59852
    by Saline, 59850
      with Dilatation and Curettage, 59851
      with Hysterotomy, 59852
Abrasion, Skin
  Chemical Peel, 15788-15793
  Dermabrasion, 15780-15783
  Lesion, 15786, 15787
ABS, 86255, 86403, 86850
Abscess
  Abdomen, 49040, 49041
    Drainage, 49020, 49040
      Peritoneal
        Open, 49020
        Percutaneous, 49021
      Peritonitis, localized, 49020
      Retroperitoneal
        Open, 49060
        Percutaneous, 49061
      Skin and Subcutaneous Tissue
        Complicated, 10061
        Multiple, 10061
        Simple, 10060
        Single, 10060
      Subdiaphragmatic, 49040
        Open, 49040
        Percutaneous, 49041
      Subphrenic, 49040
  Anal
    Incision and Drainage, 46045, 46050
  Ankle
    Incision and Drainage, 27603
  Appendix
    Incision and Drainage, 44900
      Open, 44900
      Percutaneous, 44901
  Arm, Lower, 25028
    Excision, 25145
    Incision and Drainage, 25035
  Arm, Upper
    Incision and Drainage, 23930-23935
  Auditory Canal, External, 69020
  Bartholin's Gland
    Incision and Drainage, 56420
  Bladder
    Incision and Drainage, 51080
  Brain
    Drainage by
      Burrhole, 61150, 61151
      Craniotomy/Craniectomy, 61320, 61321
    Excision, 61514, 61522
  Breast
    Incision and Drainage, 19020
  Carpals
    Incision, Deep, 25035
  Clavicle
    Sequestrectomy, 23170
  Drainage
    with X-ray, 75989, 76080

Abscess — *continued*
  Thoracostomy, 32020
  Thorax
    Incision and Drainage, 21501, 21502
  Throat
    Incision and Drainage, 42700-42725
  Tongue
    Incision and Drainage, 41000-41006
  Tonsil
    Incision and Drainage, 42700
  Ulna
    Incision, Deep, 25035
  Urethra
    Incision and Drainage, 53040
  Uvula
    Incision and Drainage, 42000
  Vagina
    Incision and Drainage, 57010
  Vulva
    Incision and Drainage, 56405
  Wrist
    Excision, 25145
    Incision and Drainage, 25028, 25035
  X-ray, 76080
Absorptiometry
  Dual Energy
    Body Composition, 0028T
    Bone
      Appendicular, 76076
      Axial Skeleton, 76075
      Vertebral, 76077
  Dual Photon
    Bone, 78351
  Radiographic
    Photodensity, 76078
  Single Photon
    Bone, 78350
Absorption Spectrophotometry, 82190
  Absorption Spectrophotometry, 82190
Accessory Nerve
  Incision, 63191
  Section, 63191
  Spinal — *See* Nerves, Spinal Accessory
Accessory, Toes, 28344
ACD, 63075, 63076
ACE (Angiotensin Converting Enzyme), 82164
Acellular Immunization, 90700
Acetabuloplasty, 27120, 27122
Acetabulum
  Fracture
    with Manipulation, 27222
    without Manipulation, 27220
    Closed Treatment, 27220, 27222
    Open Treatment, 27226-27228
  Reconstruction, 27120
    with Resection, Femoral Head, 27122
  Tumor
    Excision, 27076
Acetaldehyde
  Blood, 82000
Acetaminophen
  Urine, 82003
Acetic Anhydrides, 84600
Acetone
  Blood or Urine, 82009, 82010
Acetone Body, 82009, 82010
Acetylcholinesterase
  Blood or Urine, 82013
AcG, 85220

Achilles Tendon
  Incision, 27605, 27606
  Lengthening, 27612
  Repair, 27650-27654
Achillotomy, 27605-27606
Acid
  Gastric, 82926, 82928
Acid, Adenylic, 82030
Acid, Aminolevulinic
  Urine or Blood, 82135
Acid, Ascorbic
  Blood, 82180
Acid, Deoxyribonucleic
  Antibody, 86225-86226
Acid Diethylamide, Lysergic, 80102, 80103,
    80299
Acid Fast Bacilli (AFB)
  Culture, 87116
Acid Fast Stain, 88312
Acid, Folic, 82746
  RBC, 82747
Acid, Glycoholic
  Blood, 82240
Acidity/Alkalinity
  See pH
Acid, Lactic, 83605
Acid, N-Acetylneuraminic, 84275
Acid Perfusion Test
  Esophagus, 91012, 91030
Acid, Phenylethylbarbituric, 82205
  Assay, 80184
Acid Phosphatase, 84060-84066
Acid Probes, Nucleic
  See Nucleic Acid Probe
Acid Reflux Test
  Esophagus, 91034-91038
Acids, Amino
  Blood or Urine, 82127-82139
Acids, Bile, 82239
  Blood, 82240
Acids, Fatty
  Blood, 82725
  Very Long Chain, 82726
Acids, Guanylic, 83008
Acids, N-Acetylneuraminic, 84275
Acid, Uric
  Blood, 84550
  Other Source, 84560
  Urine, 84560
ACL Repair
  Arthroscopy aided, 29888
  Open, 27407, 27409
Acne Surgery
  Incision and Drainage
    Abscess, 10060, 10061
      Puncture Aspiration, 10160
    Bulla
      Puncture Aspiration, 10160
    Comedones, 10040
    Cyst, 10040
      Puncture Aspiration, 10160
    Milia, Multiple, 10040
    Pustules, 10040
Acne Treatment
  Abrasion, 15786, 15787
  Chemical Peel, 15788-15793
  Cryotherapy, 17340

Acne Treatment — *continued*
Dermabrasion, 15780-15783
Exfoliation
Chemical, 17360
Acoustic Evoked Brain Stem Potential, 92585, 92586
Acoustic Heart Sound Recording, 0068T, 0069T, 0070T
Acoustic Neuroma
Brainstem
Biopsy, 61575, 61576
Decompression, 61575, 61576
Evoked Potentials, 92585
Lesion Excision, 61575, 61576
Brain Tumor Excision, 61510, 61518, 61520, 61521, 61526, 61530, 61545
Mesencephalon
Tractotomy, 61480
Skull Base Surgery
Anterior Cranial Fossa
Bicoronal Approach, 61586
Craniofacial Approach, 61580-61583
Extradural, 61600, 61601
LeFort I Osteotomy Approach, 61586
Orbitocranial Approach, 61584, 61585
Transzygomatic Approach, 61586
Carotid Aneurysm, 61613
Carotid Artery, 61610
Transection
Ligation, 61609-61612
Craniotomy, 62121
Dura
Repair of Cerebrospinal
Fluid Leak, 61618, 61619
Middle Cranial Fossa
Extradural, 61605-61607
Infratemporal Approach, 61590, 61591
Intradural, 61606-61608
Orbitocranial Zygomatic Approach, 61592
Posterior Cranial Fossa
Extradural, 61615
Intradural, 61616
Transcondylar Approach, 61596, 61597
Transpetrosal Approach, 61598
Transtemporal Approach, 61595
Acoustic Recording
Heart Sounds
with Computer Analysis, 0068T-0070T
ACP, 84060-84066
Acromioclavicular Joint
Arthrocentesis, 20605
Arthrotomy, 23044
with Biopsy, 23101
Dislocation, 23540-23552
Open Treatment, 23550, 23552
X-ray, 73050
Acromion
Excision
Shoulder, 23130
Acromionectomy
Partial, 23130
Acromioplasty, 23415, 23420
Partial, 23130
ACTH (Adrenocorticotropic Hormone), 80400-80406, 80412, 80418, 82024
ACTH Releasing Factor, 80412
Actigraphy
Sleep Study, 0089T

Actinomyces
Antibody, 86602
Actinomycosis, 86000
Actinomycotic Infection
See Actinomycosis
Actinotherapy, 96900
See Dermatology
Activated Factor X, 85260
Activated Partial Thromboplastin Time, 85730, 85732
Activation, Lymphocyte, 86353
Activities of Daily Living (ADL)
See Physical Medicine/Therapy/ Occupational Therapy
Training, 97535, 97537
Activity, Glomerular Procoagulant
See Thromboplastin
Acupuncture
One or More Needles
with Electrical Stimulation, 97813-97814
without Electrical Stimulation, 97810-97811
Acute Poliomyelitis
See Polio
Acylcarnitines, 82016, 82017
Adamantinoma, Pituitary
See Craniopharyngioma
Addam Operation, 26040, 26045
Adductor Tenotomy of Hip
See Tenotomy, Hip, Adductor
Adelson
Crosby Immersion Method, 85999
Adenoidectomy
with Tonsillectomy, 42820, 42821
Primary
Age 12 or Over, 42831
Under Age 12, 42830
Secondary
Age 12 or Over, 42836
Under Age 12, 42835
Adenoids
Excision, 42830-42836
with Tonsillectomy, 42820, 42821
Unlisted Services and Procedures, 42999
Adenoma
Pancreas
Excision, 48120
Thyroid Gland
Excision, 60200
Adenosine 3', 5' Monophosphate, 82030
Adenosine Diphosphate
Blood, 82030
Adenosine Monophosphate (AMP)
Blood, 82030
Adenovirus
Antibody, 86603
Antigen Detection
Enzyme Immunoassay, 87301-87451
Immunofluorescence, 87260
Adenovirus Vaccine, 90476-90477
ADH (Antidiuretic Hormone), 84588
Adhesion, Adhesions
Epidural, 0027T, 62263, 62264
Eye
Corneovitreal, 65880
Incision
Anterior Segment, 65860-65870
Posterior Segment, 65875

Index

Adhesion, Adhesions — Alcohol

Adhesion, Adhesions — *continued*
  Intermarginal
    Construction, 67880
      Transposition of Tarsal Plate, 67882
  Intestinal
    Enterolysis, 44005
      Laparoscopic, 44180
  Intracranial
    Lysis, 62161
  Intrauterine
    Lysis, 58559
  Labial
    Lysis, 56441
  Lungs
    Lysis, 32124
  Pelvic
    Lysis, 58660, 58662, 58740
  Penile
    Lysis
      Post-circumcision, 54162
  Preputial
    Lysis, 54450
  Urethral
    Lysis, 53500
Adipectomy
  See Lipectomy
ADL
  Activities of Daily Living, 97535, 97537
Administration
  Immunization
    Each Additional Vaccine/Toxoid, 90472,
      90474
      with Counseling, 90466, 90468
    One (single) Vaccine/Toxoid, 90471, 90473
      with Counseling, 90465, 90467
  Injection
    Intramuscular Antibiotic, 90772
    Therapeutic, Diagnostic, Prophylactic
      Intra-arterial, 90773
      Intramuscular, 90772
      Intravenous, 90774
      Subcutaneous, 90772
ADP, 82030
ADP Phosphocreatine Phosphotransferase
  See CPK
Adrenal Cortex Hormone
  See Corticosteroids
Adrenalectomy, 60540
  with Excision Retroperitoneal Tumor, 60545
  Laparoscopic, 50545
Adrenal Gland
  Biopsy, 60540, 60545
  Excision
    Laparoscopy, 60650
    Retroperitoneal, 60545
  Exploration, 60540, 60545
  Nuclear Medicine
    Imaging, 78075
Adrenalin
  Blood, 82383, 82384
  Fractionated, 82384
  Urine, 82382, 82384
Adrenaline or Noradrenaline
  Testing, 82382-82384
Adrenal Medulla
  See Medulla
Adrenocorticotropic Hormone (ACTH), 80400-
    80406, 80412, 80418, 82024
  Blood or Urine, 82024

Adrenocorticotropic Hormone (ACTH) — *continued*
  Stimulation Panel, 80400-80406
Adrenogenital Syndrome, 56805, 57335
Adult T Cell Leukemia Lymphoma Virus I
  See HTLV I
Advanced Life Support
  Emergency Department Services, 99281-99288
  Physician Direction, 99288
Advancement
  Tendon
    Foot, 28238
    Genioglossus, 21199
Advancement Flap
  Skin, Adjacent Tissue Transfer, 14000-14350
AEP, 92585, 92586
Aerosol Inhalation
  Inhalation Treatment, 94640, 94664
  Pentamidine, 94642
AFB (Acid Fast Bacilli), 87116
AFBG, 35546, 35646
Afferent Nerve
  See Sensory Nerve
AFGE, 66020
AFP, 82105, 82106
After Hours Medical Services, 99050-99060
Agents, Anticoagulant
  See Clotting Inhibitors
Agglutinin
  Cold, 86156, 86157
  Febrile, 86000
Aggregation
  Platelet, 85576
AGTT, 82951, 82952
AHG (Antihemophilic Globulin), 85240
AICD (Pacing Cardioverter-Defibrillator), 33223,
    93741-93744
  Heart
    Defibrillator, 33240-33249, 93741-93744
    Pacemaker, 33200-33210, 33212-33214,
      33233-33237
Aid, Hearing
  See Hearing Aid
AIDS Antibodies
  See Antibody, HIV
AIDS Virus
  See HIV-1
A-II (Angiotensin II), 82163
Akin Operation
  See Bunion Repair
ALA (Aminolevulinic Acid), 82135
Alanine 2 Oxoglutarate Aminotransferase
  See Transaminase, Glutamic Pyruvic
Alanine Amino (ALT), 84460
Alanine Transaminase
  See Transaminase, Glutamic Pyruvic
Albarran Test
  Water Load Test, 89235
Albumin
  Ischemia Modified, 82045
  Serum, 82040
  Urine, 82042-82044
Alcohol
  Breath, 82075
  Ethyl
    Blood, 82055
    Urine, 82055
  Ethylene Glycol, 82693

Alveolar Ridge
Fracture
Closed Treatment, 21440
Open Treatment, 21445
Alveolectomy, 41830
Alveoli
Fracture
Closed Treatment, 21421
Open Treatment, 21422, 21423
Alveoloplasty, 41874
Alveolus
Excision, 41830
Amide, Procaine, 80190-80192
Amikacin
Assay, 80150
Amine
Vaginal Fluid, 82120
Amino Acids
Blood or Urine, 82127-82139
Aminolevulinic Acid (ALA)
Blood or Urine, 82135
Aminotransferase
Alanine (SGPT), 84460
Aspartate (SGOT), 84450
Amitriptyline
Assay, 80152
Ammonia
Blood, 82140
Urine, 82140
Amniocentesis, 59000
with Amniotic Fluid Reduction, 59001
See Chromosome Analysis
Induced Abortion, 59850
with Dilation and Curettage, 59851
with Dilation and Evacuation, 59851
with Hysterotomy, 59852
Amnioinfusion
Transabdominal, 59070
Amnion
Amniocentesis, 59000
with Amniotic Fluid Reduction, 59001
Amniotic Fluid
Alpha-Fetoprotein, 82106
Scan, 82143
Testing, 83661, 83663, 83664
Amniotic Membrane
See Amnion
Amobarbital, 82205
AMP (Adenosine Monophosphate), 82030
AMP, Cyclic, 82030
Amphetamine
Blood or Urine, 82145
Amputation
Ankle, 27888
Arm and Shoulder, 23900-23921
Arm, Lower, 25900, 25905, 25915
with Implant, 24931, 24935
Cineplasty, 24940
Revision, 25907, 25909
Arm, Upper, 24900, 24920
with Implant, 24931, 24935
and Shoulder, 23900-23921
Revision, 24925, 24930
Cervix
Total, 57530
Ear
Partial, 69110
Total, 69120

Amputation — *continued*
Finger, 26910-26952
Foot, 28800, 28805
Hand
at Metacarpals, 25927
at Wrist, 25920
Revision, 25922
Revision, 25924, 25929, 25931
Interpelviabdominal, 27290
Interthoracoscapular, 23900
Knee joint Disarticulation, 27598
Leg, Lower, 27598, 27880-27882
Revision, 27884, 27886
Leg, Upper, 27590-27592
at Hip, 27290, 27295
Revision, 27594, 27596
Metacarpal, 26910
Metatarsal, 28810
Penis
Partial, 54120
Radical, 54130, 54135
Total, 54125
Thumb, 26910-26952
Toe, 28810-28825
Tuft of Distal Phalanx, 11752
Upper Extremity
Cineplasty, 24940
Amputation, Nose
See Resection, Nose
Amputation through Hand
See Hand, Amputation
Amylase
Blood, 82150
Urine, 82150
ANA (Antinuclear Antibodies), 86038, 86039
Anabolic Steroid
Androstenedione, 82160
Anal
Polyp, 46615
Tumor, 46615
Anal Abscess
See Abscess, Anal
Anal Bleeding
See Anus, Hemorrhage
Anal Fistula
See Fistula, Anal
Anal Fistulectomy
See Excision, Fistula, Anal
Anal Fistulotomy
See Fistulotomy, Anal
Analgesia, 99143-99150
See also Anesthesia, Sedation
Analgesic Cutaneous Electrostimulation
See Application, Neurostimulation
Anal Sphincter
Dilation, 45905
Incision, 46080
Anal Ulceration
See Anus, Fissure
Analysis
Computer Data, 99090
Electroencephalogram
Digital, 95957
Electronic
Antitachycardia Pacemaker, 93724
Cardiac Event Recorder, 93727
Cardioverter-Defibrillator, 93741-93744
Drug Infusion Pump, 62367, 62368
Pacemaker, 93731-93736

Anesthesia — *continued*
  Amputation — *continued*
    Forequarter, 01636
    Interthoracoscapular, 01636
    Penis
      Complete, 00932
      Radical with Bilateral Inguinal and Iliac
        Lymphadenectomy, 00936
      Radical with Bilateral Inguinal
        Lymphadenectomy, 00934
  Aneurysm
    Axillary-Brachial, 01652
    Knee, 01444
    Popliteal Artery, 01444
  Angiography, 01920
  Angioplasty, 01924-01926
  Ankle, 00400, 01462-01522
    Achilles Tendon, 01472
    Nerves, Muscles, Tendons, 01470
    Skin, 00400
  Anorectal Procedure, 00902
  Anus, 00902
  Arm
    Lower, 00400, 01810-01860
      Arteries, 01842
      Bones, Closed, 01820
      Bones, Open, 01830
      Cast Application, 01860
      Cast Removal, 01860
      Embolectomy, 01842
      Nerves, Muscle, Tendons, 01810
      Phleborrhaphy, 01852
      Shunt Revision, 01844
      Skin, 00400
      Total Wrist, 01832
      Veins, 01850
    Upper Arm, and Elbow, 00400, 01710-01782
      Nerves, Muscles, Tendons, 01710
        Tenodesis, 01716
        Tenoplasty, 01714
        Tenotomy, 01712
      Skin, 00400
  Arrhythmias, 00410
  Arteriograms, 01916
  Arteriography, 01916
  Arteriovenous (AV) Fistula, 01432
  Arthroplasty
    Hip, 01214, 01215
    Knee, 01402
  Arthroscopic Procedures
    Ankle, 01464
    Elbow, 01732
    Foot, 01464
    Hip, 01202
    Knee, 01382, 01464
    Shoulder, 01622-01630
    Wrist, 01829-01830
  Auditory Canal, External
    Removal Foreign Body, 69205
  Axilla, 00400, 01610-01682
  Back Skin, 00300
  Batch-Spittler-McFaddin Operation, 01404
  Biopsy
    Anorectal, 00902
    Clavicle, 00454
    External ear, 00120
    Inner ear, 00120
    Intraoral, 00170
    Liver, 00702
    Middle ear, 00120
    Nose, 00164

Anesthesia — *continued*
  Biopsy — *continued*
    Parotid gland, 00100
    Salivary gland, 00100
    Sinuses, accessory, 00164
    Sublingual gland, 00100
    Submandibular gland, 00100
  Bladder, 00870, 00912
  Blepharoplasty, 00103
  Brain, 00210-00218, 00220-00222
  Breast, 00402-00406
    Augmentation Mammoplasty, 00402
    Breast Reduction, 00402
    Muscle Flaps, 00402
  Bronchi, 00542
    Intrathoracic Repair of Trauma, 00548
    Reconstruction, 00539
  Bronchoscopy, 00520
  Burns
    Debridement and/or Excision, 01951-01953
    Dressings and/or Debridement, 16020-16030
  Burr Hole, 00214
  Bypass Graft
    with pump oxygenator, under one year of age, 00561
    Coronary Artery without Pump Oxygenator, 00566
    Leg
      Lower, 01500
      Upper, 01270
    Shoulder, Axillary, 01654, 01656
  Cardiac Catheterization, 01920
  Cardioverter, 00534, 00560
  Cast
    Application
      Body Cast, 01130
      Forearm, 01860
      Hand, 01860
      Knee Joint, 01420
      Lower Leg, 01490
      Pelvis, 01130
      Shoulder, 01680
      Shoulder Spica, 01682
      Wrist, 01860
    Removal
      Forearm, 01860
      Hand, 01860
      Knee Joint, 01420
      Lower Leg, 01490
      Shoulder, 01680
      Shoulder Spica, 01682
    Repair
      Forearm, 01860
      Hand, 01860
      Knee Joint, 01420
      Lower Leg, 01490
      Shoulder, 01680
      Shoulder Spica, 01682
  Central Venous Circulation, 00532
  Cervical Cerclage, 00948
  Cervix, 00948
  Cesarean Section, 01961, 01963, 01968, 01969
  Chemonucleolysis, 00634
  Chest, 00400-00410, 00470-00474, 00522, 00530-00539, 00542, 00546-00550
  Chest Skin, 00400
  Childbirth
    Cesarean Delivery, 01961, 01963, 01968, 01969
    External Cephalic Version, 01958
    Vaginal Delivery, 01960, 01967

Index

Anesthesia — Anesthesia

Anesthesia — *continued*
  Radical Surgery, Procedures, Resections — *continued*
    Breast with Internal Mammary Node Dissection, 00406
    Clavicle, 00452
    Elbow, 01756
    Facial Bones, 00192
    Femur, 01234
    Foot Resection, 01482
    Hip Joint Resection, 01234
    Humeral Head and Neck Resection, 01632
    Humerus, 01756
    Hysterectomy, 00846
    Intraoral Procedures, 00176
    Lower Leg Bone Resection, 01482
    Nose, 00162
    Orchiectomy, Abdominal, 00928
    Orchiectomy, Inguinal, 00926
    Pectus Excavatum, 00474
    Pelvis, 01150
    Penis Amputation with Bilateral Inguinal and Iliac Lymphadenectomy, 00936
    Penis Amputation with Bilateral Inguinal Lymphadenectomy, 00934
    Perineal, 00904
    Prognathism, 00192
    Prostatectomy, 00865
    Scapula, 00452
    Shoulder Joint Resection, 01632
    Sinuses, Accessory, 00162
    Sternoclavicular Joint resection, 01632
    Testes
      Abdominal, 00928
      Inguinal, 00926
  Radiologic Procedures, 01905-01922
    Arterial
      Therapeutic, 01924-01926
    Arteriograms
      Needle, Carotid, Vertebral, 01916
      Retrograde, Brachial, Femoral, 01916
    Cardiac Catheterization, 01920
    Diskography Lumbar, 01905
    Injection Hysterosalpingography, 00952
    Venous/Lymphatic, 01930-01933
      Therapeutic, 01930-01933
  Reconstructive Procedures
    Blepharoplasty, 00103
    Breast, 00402
    Ptosis Surgery, 00103
  Renal Procedures, 00862
  Repair
    Achilles Tendon, Ruptured, with or without Graft, 01472
    Cast
      Forearm, 01860
      Hand, 01860
      Knee Joint, 01420
      Lower Leg, 01490
      Shoulder, 01680
      Shoulder Spica, 01682
      Wrist, 01860
    Cleft Lip, 00102
    Cleft Palate, 00172
    Humerus
      Malunion, 01744
      Nonunion, 01744
    Knee Joint, 01420
  Repair, Plastic
    Cleft Lip, 00102
    Cleft Palate, 00172

Anesthesia — *continued*
  Replacement
    Ankle, 01486
    Elbow, 01760
    Hip, 01212-01215
    Knee, 01402
    Shoulder, 01638
    Wrist, 01832
  Restriction
    Gastric
      for Obesity, 00797
  Retropharyngeal Tumor Excision, 00174
  Rib Resection, 00470-00474
  Sacroiliac Joint, 01160, 01170, 27096
  Salivary Glands, 00100
  Scheie Procedure, 00147
  Second Degree Burn, 01953
  Sedation
    Moderate, 99148-99150
      with Independent Observation, 99143-99145
  Seminal Vesicles, 00922
  Shoulder, 00400-00454, 01610-01682
  Shunt
    Spinal Fluid, 00220
  Sinuses
    Accessory, 00160-00164
      Biopsy, Soft Tissue, 00164
      Radical Surgery, 00162
  Skin
    Anterior Chest, 00400
    Anterior Pelvis, 00400
    Arm, Upper, 00400
    Axilla, 00400
    Elbow, 00400
    Forearm, 00400
    Hand, 00400
    Head, 00300
    Knee, 00400
    Leg, Lower, 00400
    Leg, Upper, 00400
    Neck, 00300
    Perineum, 00400
    Popliteal Area, 00400
    Posterior Chest, 00300
    Posterior Pelvis, 00300
    Shoulder, 00400
    Wrist, 00400
  Skull, 00190
  Skull Fracture
    Elevation, 00215
  Special Circumstances
    Emergency, 99140
    Extreme Age, 99100
    Hypotension, 99135
    Hypothermia, 99116
  Spinal Instrumentation, 00670
  Spine and Spinal Cord, 00600-00670
    Cervical, 00600-00604, 00640, 00670
    Injection, 62310-62319
    Lumbar, 00630-00635, 00640, 00670
    Thoracic, 00620-00622, 00640, 00670
    Vascular, 00670
  Sternoclavicular Joint, 01620
  Sternum, 00550
  Stomach
    Restriction
      for Obesity, 00797
  Strayer Procedure, 01474
  Subcutaneous Tissue
    Anterior Chest, 00400
    Anterior Pelvis, 00400

Angel Dust, 83992

Anginal Symptoms and Level of Acivity Assessment, 1002F

Angiocardiographies
See Heart, Angiography

Angiography
Abdomen, 74175, 74185, 75635, 75726
Abdominal Aorta, 0080T-0081T, 75635, 75952, 75953
Adrenal Artery, 75731, 75733
Aortography, 75600-75630
   Injection, 93544
Arm Artery, 73206, 75710, 75716
Arteriovenous Shunt, 75790
Brachial Artery, 75658
Brain, 70496
Carotid Artery, 75660, 75671
   Cervical
      Bilateral, 75680
      Unilateral, 75676
Chest, 71275, 71555
Coronary Artery, 93556
   Flow Velocity Measurement During Angiography, 93571, 93572
Coronary Bypass, 93556
Endovascular Repair, 0080T-0081T, 75952, 75953
Extremity, Lower, 73725
Extremity, Upper, 73225
Fluorescein, 92235
Head, 70496, 70544-70546
   Artery, 75650
Heart
   with Catheterization, 93543-93545
Heart Vessels
   with Catheterization, 93510
   Aortocoronary Bypass, 93539, 93540
   Injection, 93545
Indocyanine-Green, 92240
Left Heart
   Injection, 93543
Leg Artery, 73706, 75635, 75710, 75716
Lung
   Injection, 93541
      See Cardiac Catheterization, Injection
Mammary Artery, 75756
Neck, 70498, 70547-70549
   Artery, 75650
Nuclear Medicine, 78445
Other Artery, 75774
Pelvic Artery, 72198, 75736
Pelvis, 72191
Pulmonary Artery, 75741-75746
Renal Artery, 75722, 75724
Right Heart
   Injection, 93542
Spinal Artery, 75705
Spinal Canal, 72159
Thorax, 71275
Transcatheter Therapy
   Embolization, 75894, 75898
   Infusion, 75896, 75898
Vertebral, 75685

Angioma
See Lesion, Skin

Angioplasties, Coronary Balloon
See Percutaneous Transluminal Angioplasty

Angioplasty
Aorta
   Intraoperative, 35452
   Percutaneous, 35472

Angioplasty — continued
Axillary Artery
   Intraoperative, 35458
Brachiocephalic Artery
   Intraoperative, 35458
   Percutaneous, 35475
Coronary Artery
   Percutaneous Transluminal, 92982, 92984
Femoral Artery
   Intraoperative, 35456
   Percutaneous, 35474
Iliac Artery
   Intraoperative, 35454
   Percutaneous, 35473
Intracranial, 61630, 61635
   Percutaneous Transluminal Angioplasty, 92982, 92984, 92997, 92998
Popliteal Artery
   Intraoperative, 35456
   Percutaneous, 35474
Pulmonary Artery
   Percutaneous Transluminal, 92997, 92998
Renal or Visceral Artery
   Intraoperative, 35450
   Percutaneous, 35471
Subclavian Artery
   Intraoperative, 35458
Tibioperoneal Artery
   Intraoperative, 35459
   Percutaneous, 35470
Transluminal
   Arterial, 75962-75968
   Venous, 75978
Venous
   Intraoperative, 35460
   Percutaneous, 35476
Visceral Artery
   Intraoperative, 35450
   Percutaneous, 35471

Angioscopy
Noncoronary vessels, 35400

Angiotensin Converting Enzyme (ACE), 82164

Angiotensin Forming Enzyme
See Renin

Angiotensin I, 84244
Riboflavin, 84252

Angiotensin II
Blood or Urine, 82163

Angle Deformity
See Carbon Dioxide
Reconstruction
   Toe, 28313

Anhyrides, Acetic
See Acetic Anhydrides

Animal Inoculation, 87001, 87003, 87250

Ankle
See also Fibula, Leg, Lower; Tibia, Tibiofibular
   Joint
Abscess
   Incision and Drainage, 27603
Amputation, 27888
Arthrocentesis, 20605
Arthrodesis, 27870
Arthrography, 73615
Arthroplasty, 27700, 27702, 27703
Arthroscopy
   Surgical, 29891-29898
Arthrotomy, 27610, 27612, 27620-27626
Biopsy, 27613, 27614, 27620

Ankle — *continued*
Bursa
Incision and Drainage, 27604
Disarticulation, 27889
Dislocation
Closed Treatment, 27840, 27842
Open Treatment, 27846, 27848
Exploration, 27610, 27620
Fracture
Lateral, 27786-27814
Medial, 27760-27766, 27808-27814
Trimalleolar, 27816-27823
Fusion, 27870
Hematoma
Incision and Drainage, 27603
Incision, 27607
Injection
Radiologic, 27648
Lesion
Excision, 27630
Magnetic Resonance Imaging (MRI), 73721-73723
Manipulation, 27860
Removal
Foreign Body, 27610, 27620
Implant, 27704
Loose Body, 27620
Repair
Achilles Tendon, 27650-27654
Ligament, 27695-27698
Tendon, 27612, 27680-27687
Strapping, 29540
Synovium
Excision, 27625, 27626
Tenotomy, 27605, 27606
Tumor
Excision, 27615-27619
Unlisted Services and Procedures, 27899
X-ray, 73600, 73610
with Contrast, 73615

Ankylosis (Surgical)
See Arthrodesis

Annuloplasty
Percutaneous, Intradiscal, 0062T-0063T

Anogenital Region
See Perineum

Anoplasty
Stricture, 46700, 46705

Anorectal Myomectomy, 45108

Anorectal Procedure
Biofeedback, 90911

Anorectovaginoplasty, 46744, 46746

Anoscopy
Ablation
Polyp, 46615
Tumor, 46615
Biopsy, 46606
Dilation, 46604
Exploration, 46600
Hemorrhage, 46614
Removal
Foreign Body, 46608
Polyp, 46610-46612
Tumor, 46610-46612

Antebrachium
See Forearm

Antecedent, Plasma Thromboplastin, 85270

Antepartum Care
Antepartum Care Only, 59425, 59426

Antepartum Care — *continued*
Included with
Cesarean Delivery, 59510
Failed NSVD, Previous C-Section, 59618
Vaginal Delivery, 59400
Previous C-Section, 59610

Anterior Ramus of Thoracic Nerve
See Intercostal Nerve

Antesternal Esophagostomy, 43499

Anthrax Vaccine, 90581

Anthrogon, 80418, 80426, 83001

Anti Australia Antigens
See Antibody, Hepatitis B

Antibiotic Administration
Injection, 90772

Antibiotic Sensitivity, 87181, 87184, 87188
Enzyme Detection, 87185
Minimum Bactericidal Concentration, 87187
Minimum Inhibitory Concentration, 87186

Antibodies, Thyroid-Stimulating, 84445
See Immunoglobulin, Thyroid Stimulating

Antibodies, Viral
See Viral Antibodies

Antibody
Actinomyces, 86602
Adenovirus, 86603
Antinuclear, 86038, 86039
Anti-Phosphatidylserine (Phospholipid), 86148
Antiprothrombin, 0030T
Antistreptolysin 0, 86060, 86063
Aspergillus, 86606
Bacterium, 86609
Bartonella, 86611
Beta 2 Glycoprotein I, 86146
Blastomyces, 86612
Blood Crossmatch, 86920-86922
Bordetella, 86615
Borrelia, 86618, 86619
Brucella, 86622
Campylobacter, 86625
Candida, 86628
Cardiolipin, 86147
Chlamydia, 86631, 86632
Coccidioides, 86635
Coxiella Burnetii, 86638
Cryptococcus, 86641
Cytomegalovirus, 86644, 86645
Cytotoxic Screen, 86807, 86808
Deoxyribonuclease, 86215
Deoxyribonucleic Acid (DNA), 86225, 86226
Diphtheria, 86648
Ehrlichia, 86666
Encephalitis, 86651-86654
Enterovirus, 86658
Epstein-Barr Virus, 86663-86665
Fluorescent, 86255, 86256
Francisella Tularensis, 86668
Fungus, 86671
Giardia Lamblia, 86674
Growth Hormone, 86277
Helicobacter Pylori, 86677
Helminth, 86682
Hemoglobin, Fecal, 82274
Hemophilus Influenza, 86684
Hepatitis A, 86708, 86709
Hepatitis B
Core, 86704
IgM, 86705
Surface, 86706
Hepatitis Be, 86707

Aorta — *continued*
Excision
Coarctation, 33840-33851
Insertion
Balloon Device, 33967
Graft, 33330-33335
Intracatheter, 36160
Needle, 36160
Removal
Balloon Assist Device, 33968, 33971
Repair, 33320-33322, 33802, 33803
Aortic Anomalies, 33800-33803
Coarctation, 33840-33851
Graft, 33860-33877
Hypoplastic or Interrupted Aortic Arch
with Cardiopulmonary Bypass, 33853
without Cardiopulmonary Bypass, 33852
Sinus of Valsalva, 33702-33720
Thoracic Aneurysm with Graft, 33860-33877
Endovascular, 33880-33891, 75956-75959
Transposition of the Great Vessels, 33770-33781
Suspension, 33800
Suture, 33320-33322
Thoracic
Aneurysm, 33880-33889, 75956-75959
Ultrasound, 76770, 76775
Valve
Incision, 33415
Repair, 33400-33403
Left Ventricle, 33414
Supravalvular Stenosis, 33417
Replacement, 33405-33413
X-ray with Contrast, 75600-75630
Aorta-Pulmonary ART Transposition
See Transposition, Great Arteries
Aortic Sinus
See Sinus of Valsalva
Aortic Stenosis
Repair, 33415
Supravalvular, 33417
Aortic Valve
See Heart, Aortic Valve
Aortic Valve Replacement
See Replacement, Aortic Valve
Aortocoronary Bypass
See Coronary Artery Bypass Graft (CABG)
Aortocoronary Bypass for Heart Revascularization
See Artery, Coronary, Bypass
Aortography, 75600, 75605, 75630, 93544
with Ileofemoral Artery, 75630
See Angiography
Serial, 75625
Aortoiliac
Embolectomy, 34151, 34201
Thrombectomy, 34151, 34201
Aortopexy, 33800
Aortoplasty
Supravalvular Stenosis, 33417
AP, 51797
Apert-Gallais Syndrome
See Adrenogenital Syndrome
Apexcardiogram, 93799
Aphasia Testing, 96105
Apheresis
Therapeutic, 36511-36516
Apical-Aortic Conduit, 33404

Apicectomy
with Mastoidectomy, 69530, 69605
Petrous, 69530
Apicoectomy, 41899
Apoaminotransferase, Aspartate, 84550
Apolipoprotein
Blood or Urine, 82172
Appendectomy, 44950-44960
Laparoscopic, 44970
Appendiceal Abscess
See Abscess, Appendix
Appendico-Stomy, 44799
Appendico-Vesicostomy
Cutaneous, 50845
Appendix
Abscess
Incision and Drainage, 44900
Open, 44900
Percutaneous, 44901
Excision, 44950-44960
Application
Allergy Tests, 95044
Bone Fixation Device
Multiplane, 20692
Uniplane, 20690
Caliper, 20660
Cranial Tongs, 20660
Fixation Device
Shoulder, 23700
Halo
Cranial, 20661
Thin Skull Osteology, 20664
Femoral, 20663
Maxillofacial Fixation, 21100
Pelvic, 20662
Interdental Fixation Device, 21110
Neurostimulation, 64550
Radioelement, 77761-77778
with Ultrasound, 76965
Surface, 77789
Stereotactic Frame, 20660
Application of External Fixation Device
See Fixation (Device), Application, External
APPT
See Thromboplastin, Partial, Time
APPY, 44950-44960
APTT
See Thromboplastin, Partial, Time
Aquatic Therapy
with Exercises, 97113
Aqueous Shunt
to Extraocular Reservoir, 66180
Revision, 66185
Arch, Zygomatic
See Zygomatic Arch
Arm
See Radius; Ulna; Wrist
Excision
Bone, 25145
Excess Skin, 15836
Lipectomy, Suction Assisted, 15878
Removal
Foreign Body
Forearm or Wrist, 25248
Repair
Muscle, 24341
Tendon, 24341
Skin Graft
Delay of Flap, 15610

Index

Arm — Arteriovenous Anastomosis

Arm — *continued*
  Skin Graft — *continued*
    Full Thickness, 15220, 15221
    Muscle, Myocutaneous, or Fasciocutaneous Flaps, 15736
    Pedicle Flap, 15572
    Split, 15100-15111
  Tissue Transfer, Adjacent, 14020, 14021
Arm, Lower
  Abscess, 25028
    Excision, 25145
    Incision and Drainage Bone, 25035
  Amputation, 24900, 24920, 25900, 25905, 25915
    Cineplasty, 24940
    Revision, 25907, 25909
  Angiography, 73206
  Artery
    Ligation, 37618
  Biopsy, 25065, 25066
  Bursa
    Incision and Drainage, 25031
  Bypass Graft, 35903
  Cast, 29075
  CT Scan, 73200-73206
  Decompression, 25020-25025
  Exploration
    Blood Vessel, 35860
  Fasciotomy, 24495, 25020-25025
  Hematoma, 25028
  Incision and Drainage, 23930
  Lesion, Tendon Sheath
    Excision, 25110
  Magnetic Resonance Imaging (MRI), 73218-73220, 73223
  Reconstruction
    Ulna, 25337
  Removal
    Foreign Body, 25248
  Repair
    Blood Vessel with Other Graft, 35266
    Blood Vessel with Vein Graft, 35236
    Decompression, 24495
    Muscle, 25260, 25263, 25270
      Secondary, 25265
    Secondary
      Muscle or Tendon, 25272, 25274
    Tendon, 25260-25274, 25280-25295, 25310-25316
      Secondary, 25265
    Tendon Sheath, 25275
  Replantation, 20805
  Splint, 29125, 29126
  Tenotomy, 25290
  Tumor
    Excision, 25075-25077
  Ultrasound, 76880
  Unlisted Services and Procedures, 25999
  X-ray, 73090
    with Upper Arm, 73092
Arm, Upper
  Abscess
    Incision and Drainage, 23930
      See Elbow; Humerus
  Amputation, 23900-23921, 24900, 24920
    with Implant, 24931, 24935
    Cineplasty, 24940
    Revision, 24925, 24930
  Angiography, 73206
  Artery
    Ligation, 37618

Arm, Upper — *continued*
  Biopsy, 24065, 24066
  Bypass Graft, 35903
  Cast, 29065
  CT Scan, 73200-73206
  Exploration
    Blood Vessel, 35860
  Hematoma
    Incision and Drainage, 23930
  Magnetic Resonance Imaging (MRI), 73218-73220, 73223
  Muscle Revision, 24330, 24331
  Removal
    Cast, 29705
    Foreign Body, 24200, 24201
  Repair
    Blood Vessel with Other Graft, 35266
    Blood Vessel with Vein Graft, 35236
    Muscle Revision, 24301, 24320
    Muscle Transfer, 24301, 24320
    Tendon, 24332
    Tendon Lengthening, 24305
    Tendon Revision, 24320
    Tendon Transfer, 24301
    Tenotomy, 24310
  Replantation, 20802
  Splint, 29105
  Tumor
    Excision, 24075-24077
  Ultrasound, 76880
  Unlisted Services and Procedures, 24999
  Wound Exploration, 20103
  X-ray, 73060
  X-ray with Lower Arm
    Infant, 73092
Arnold-Chiari Malformation Repair, 61343
AROM, 95851, 95852, 97110, 97530
Arrest, Epiphyseal
  See Epiphyseal Arrest
Arrhythmias
  Electrical Conversion Anesthesia, 00410
  Induction, 93618
Arrhythmogenic Focus
  Heart
    Catheter Ablation, 93650-93652
    Destruction, 33250, 33251
Arsenic, 82175
  Heavy Metal Screen, 83015
ART, 86592, 86593
Arterial Catheterization
  See Cannulation, Arterial
Arterial Dilatation, Transluminal
  See Angioplasty, Transluminal
Arterial Grafting for Coronary Artery Bypass
  See Bypass Graft, Coronary Artery, Arterial
Arterial Pressure
  See Blood Pressure
Arterial Puncture, 36600
Arteriography, Aorta
  See Aortography
Arteriosus, Ductus
  See Ductus Arteriosus
Arteriosus, Truncus
  See Truncus Arteriosus
Arteriotomy
  See Incision, Artery; Transection, Artery
Arteriovenous Anastomosis, 36818-36820

Arteriovenous Fistula
Cannulization
Vein, 36815
Repair
Abdomen, 35182
Acquired or Traumatic, 35189
Head, 35180
Acquired or Traumatic, 35188
Lower Extremity, 35184
Acquired or Traumatic, 35190
Neck, 35180
Acquired or Traumatic, 35188
Thorax, 35182
Acquired or Traumatic, 35189
Upper Extremity, 35184
Acquired or Traumatic, 35190
Revision
Hemodialysis Graft or Fistula
with Thrombectomy, 36833
without Thrombectomy, 36832
Thrombectomy
Dialysis Graft
without Revision, 36831
Graft, 36870
Arteriovenous Malformation
Cranial
Repair, 61680-61692, 61705, 61708
Spinal
Excision, 63250-63252
Injection, 62294
Repair, 63250-63252
Arteriovenous Shunt
Angiography, 75790
Catheterization, 36145
Artery
Abdomen
Angiography, 75726
Catheterization, 36245-36248
Ligation, 37617
Adrenal
Angiography, 75731, 75733
Anastomosis
Cranial, 61711
Angiography, Visceral, 75726
Angioplasty, 75962-75968
Aorta
Angioplasty, 35452
Atherectomy, 35481, 35491
Aortoiliac
Embolectomy, 34151, 34201
Thrombectomy, 34151, 34201
Aortoiliofemoral, 35363
Arm
Angiography, 75710, 75716
Harvest of Artery for Coronary Artery Bypass
Graft, 35600
Atherectomy
Open, 35480-35485
Percutaneous, 35490-35495, 92995, 92996
Axillary
Aneurysm, 35011, 35013
Angioplasty, 35458
Bypass Graft, 35516-35522, 35533, 35616-
35623, 35650, 35654
Embolectomy, 34101
Thrombectomy, 34101
Thromboendarterectomy, 35321
Basilar
Aneurysm, 61698, 61702
Biopsy
Transcatheter, 75970

Artery — *continued*
Brachial
Aneurysm, 35011, 35013
Angiography, 75658
Bypass Graft, 35510, 35512, 35522, 35525
Catheterization, 36120
Embolectomy, 34101
Exploration, 24495
Exposure, 34834
Thrombectomy, 34101
Thromboendarterectomy, 35321
Brachiocephalic
Angioplasty, 35458
Atherectomy, 35484, 35494, 75992, 75993
Catheterization, 36215-36218
Bypass Graft
with Composite Graft, 35681-35683
Autogenous
Three or More Segments
Two Locations, 35683
Two Segments
Two Locations, 35682
Cannulization
for Extra Corporeal Circulation, 36823
to Vein, 36810-36821
Carotid
Aneurysm, 35001-35005, 61697-61705
Vascular Malformation or Carotid
Cavernous Fistula, 61710
Angiography, 75660-75680
Bypass Graft, 35500-35510, 35526, 35601-
35606, 35626, 35642
Catheterization, 36100
Decompression, 61590, 61591, 61595,
61596
Embolectomy, 34001
Exploration, 35701
Ligation, 37600-37606, 61611, 61612
Thrombectomy, 34001
Thromboendarterectomy, 35301, 35390
Transection, 61611, 61612
Carotid, Common Intima-Media Thickness
Study, 0126T
Celiac
Aneurysm, 35121, 35122
Bypass Graft, 35531, 35631
Embolectomy, 34151
Thrombectomy, 34151
Thromboendarterectomy, 35341
Chest
Ligation, 37616
Coronary
Angiography, 93556
X-ray, Artery (Atherectomy), 75992-75996
Atherectomy, 92995, 92996
Bypass, 33517-33519
Arterial, 33533-33536
Bypass Venous Graft, 33510-33516
Graft, 33503-33505
Ligation, 33502
Repair, 33500-33506
Thrombectomy
Percutaneous, 92973
Digital
Sympathectomy, 64820
Ethmoidal
Ligation, 30915
Extra Corporeal Circulation
for Regional Chemotherapy of Extremity,
36823

Artery — *continued*
  Extracranial
    Vascular Studies
      Non-invasive, Physiologic, 93875
  Extremities
    Vascular Studies, 93922, 93923
  Extremity
    Bypass Graft Revision, 35879, 35881
    Catheterization, 36140
    Ligation, 37618
  Femoral
    Aneurysm, 35141, 35142
    Angioplasty, 35456
    Atherectomy, 35483, 35493
    Bypass Graft, 35521, 35533, 35546, 35551-35558, 35566, 35621, 35646, 35647, 35651-35661, 35666, 35700
    Bypass In Situ, 35583-35585
    Embolectomy, 34201
    Exploration, 35721
    Exposure, 34812, 34813
    Thrombectomy, 34201
    Thromboendarterectomy, 35371-35381
  Great Vessel Repair, 33770-33781
  Head
    Angiography, 75650
  Hepatic
    Aneurysm, 35121, 35122
  Iliac
    Aneurysm, 35131, 35132
    Angioplasty, 35454
    Atherectomy, 35482, 35492
    Bypass Graft, 35541, 35563, 35641, 35663
    Embolectomy, 34151, 34201
    Exposure, 34820, 34833
    Graft, 34900
    Occlusion Device, 34808
    Thrombectomy, 34151, 34201
    Thromboendarterectomy, 35351, 35361, 35363
  Iliofemoral
    Bypass Graft, 35548, 35549, 35565, 35665
    Thromboendarterectomy, 35355, 35363
    X-ray with Contrast, 75630
  Innominate
    Aneurysm, 35021, 35022
    Embolectomy, 34001, 34101
    Thrombectomy, 34001, 34101
    Thromboendarterectomy, 35311
  Leg
    Angiography, 75710, 75716
    Catheterization, 36245-36248
  Mammary
    Angiography, 75756
  Maxillary
    Ligation, 30920
  Mesenteric
    Aneurysm, 35121, 35122
    Bypass Graft, 35331, 35631
    Embolectomy, 34151
    Thrombectomy, 34151
    Thromboendarterectomy, 35341
  Middle Cerebral Artery, Fetal Vascular Studies, 76821
  Neck
    Angiography, 75650
    Ligation, 37615
  Nose
    Incision, 30915, 30920
  Other Angiography, 75774
  Other Artery
    Exploration, 35761

Artery — *continued*
  Pelvic
    Angiography, 75736
    Catheterization, 36245-36248
  Peripheral Arterial Rehabilitation, 93668
  Peroneal
    Bypass Graft, 35566, 35571, 35666, 35671
    Bypass In Situ, 35585, 35587
    Embolectomy, 34203
    Thrombectomy, 34203
    Thromboendarterectomy, 35381
  Popliteal
    Aneurysm, 35151, 35152
    Angioplasty, 35456
    Atherectomy, 35483, 35493
    Bypass Graft, 35551, 35556, 35571, 35623, 35651, 35656, 35671, 35700
    Bypass In Situ, 35583, 35587
    Embolectomy, 34203
    Exploration, 35741
    Thrombectomy, 34203
    Thromboendarterectomy, 35381
  Pulmonary
    Anastomosis, 33606
    Angiography, 75741-75746
    Repair, 33690
  Radial
    Aneurysm, 35045
    Embolectomy, 34111
    Sympathectomy, 64821
    Thrombectomy, 34111
  Rehabilitation, 93668
  Reimplantation
    Carotid, 35691, 35694, 35695
    Subclavian, 35693-35695
    Vertebral, 35691-35693
    Visceral, 35697
  Renal
    Aneurysm, 35121, 35122
    Angiography, 75722, 75724
    Angioplasty, 35450
    Atherectomy, 35480, 35490
    Bypass Graft, 35536, 35560, 35631, 35636
    Embolectomy, 34151
    Thrombectomy, 34151
    Thromboendarterectomy, 35341
  Repair
    with Other Graft, 35261-35286
    with Vein Graft, 35231-35256
    Aneurysm, 36834, 61697-61708
    Angioplasty, 75962-75968
    Direct, 35201-35226
  Revision
    Hemodialysis Graft or Fistula
      with Thrombectomy, 36833
      without Thrombectomy, 36832
  Spinal
    Angiography, 75705
  Splenic
    Aneurysm, 35111, 35112
    Angioplasty, 35458
    Bypass Graft, 35536, 35636
  Subclavian
    Aneurysm, 35001-35002, 35021-35022
    Angioplasty, 35458
    Bypass Graft, 35506, 35507, 35511-35516, 35526, 35606-35616, 35626, 35645
    Embolectomy, 34001-34101
    Thrombectomy, 34001-34101
    Thromboendarterectomy, 35301, 35311
    Unlisted Services and Procedures, 37799

Artery — *continued*
Superficial Palmar Arch
  Sympathectomy, 64823
Temporal
  Biopsy, 37609
  Ligation, 37609
Thoracic
  Catheterization, 36215-36218
Thrombectomy
  Hemodialysis Graft or Fistula, 36831
  Other than Hemodialysis Graft or Fistula, 35875, 36870
Tibial
  Bypass Graft, 35566, 35571, 35623, 35666, 35671
  Bypass In Situ, 35585, 35587
  Embolectomy, 34203
  Thrombectomy, 34203
  Thromboendarterectomy, 35381
Tibioperoneal
  Angioplasty, 35459, 35470
  Atherectomy, 35485, 35495
Transcatheter Therapy, 75894, 75896
  with Angiography, 75898
Transposition
  Carotid, 33889, 35691, 35694, 35695
  Subclavian, 33889, 35693-35695
  Vertebral, 35691, 35693
Ulnar
  Aneurysm, 35045
  Embolectomy, 34111
  Sympathectomy, 64822
  Thrombectomy, 34111
Unlisted Services and Procedures, 37799
Vascular Study
  Extremities, 93922, 93923
Vertebral
  Aneurysm, 35005, 61698, 61702
  Angiography, 75685
  Bypass Graft, 35508, 35515, 35642, 35645
  Catheterization, 36100
  Decompression, 61597
  Thromboendarterectomy, 35301
Visceral
  Angioplasty, 35450, 35471
  Atherectomy, 35480, 35490
  Reimplantation, 35697
Artery Catheterization, Pulmonary
  See Catheterization, Pulmonary Artery
Artherectomies, Coronary
  See Artery, Coronary, Atherectomy
Arthrectomy
  Elbow, 24155
Arthrocentesis
  Intermediate Joint, 20605
  Large Joint, 20610
  Small Joint, 20600
Arthrodesis
  Ankle, 27870
    Tibiotalar and Fibulotalar Joints, 29899
  Carpometacarpal Joint
    Hand, 26843, 26844
    Thumb, 26841, 26842
  Cervical Anterior
    with Discectomy, 22554
  Elbow, 24800, 24802
  Finger Joint, 26850-26863
    Interphalangeal, 26860-26863
    Metacarpophalangeal, 26850
  Foot Joint, 28705-28735, 28740
    with Advancement, 28737

Arthrodesis — *continued*
  Foot Joint — *continued*
    with Lengthening, 28737
    Pantalar, 28705
    Subtalar, 28725
    Triple, 28715
  Hand Joint, 26843, 26844
  Hip Joint, 27284, 27286
  Intercarpal Joint, 25820
    with Autograft, 25825
    Great Toe, 28755
      with Tendon Transfer, 28760
  Knee, 27580
  Metacarpophalangeal Joint, 26850, 26852
    Great Toe, 28750
  Pubic Symphysis, 27282
  Radioulnar Joint, Distal, 25830
    with Resection of Ulna, 25830
  Sacroiliac Joint, 27280
  Shoulder Joint, 23800
    with Autogenous Graft, 23802
  Talus
    Pantalar, 28705
    Subtalar, 28725
    Triple, 28715
  Tarsal Joint, 28730, 28735, 28740
    with Advancement, 28737
    with Lengthening, 28737
  Tarsometatarsal Joint, 28730, 28735, 28740
  Thumb Joint, 26841, 26842
  Tibiofibular Joint, 27871
  Vertebra
    Additional Interspace
      Anterior/Anterolateral Approach, 22585
      Lateral Extracavitary, 22534
      Posterior/Posterolateral and/or Lateral Transverse Process, 22632
    Cervical
      Anterior/Anterolateral Approach, 22548
      Posterior/Posterolateral and/or Lateral Transverse Process, 22590-22600
    Lumbar
      Anterior/Anterolateral Approach, 22558
      Lateral Extracavitary, 22533
      Posterior/Interbody, 22630
      Posterior/Posterolateral and/or Lateral Transverse Process, 22612, 22630
    Spinal Deformity
      Anterior Approach, 22808-22812
      Posterior Approach, 22800, 22802, 22804
    Spinal Fusion
      Exploration, 22830
    Thoracic
      Anterior/Anterolateral Approach, 22556
      Lateral Extracavitary, 22532
      Posterior/Posterolateral and/or Lateral Traverse Process, 22610
  Vertebrae
    Posterior, 22614
  Wrist, 25800
    with Graft, 25810
    with Sliding Graft, 25805
    Radioulnar Joint, Distal, 25830
Arthrography
  Ankle, 73615
    Injection, 27648
  Elbow, 73085
    Injection, 24220
  Hip, 73525
    Injection, 27093, 27095
  Knee, 73580
    Injection, 27370

Artery — Arthrography

Arthrography — *continued*
  Sacroiliac Joint, 73542
    Injection, 27096
  Shoulder, 73040
    Injection, 23350
  Temporomandibular Joint (TMJ), 70328-70332
    Injection, 21116
  Wrist, 73115
    Injection, 25246
Arthroplasties, Knee Replacement
  See Prosthesis, Knee
Arthroplasty
  Ankle, 27700-27703
  Cervical, 0090T, 0092T
  Elbow, 24360
    with Implant, 24361, 24362
    Total Replacement, 24363
  Hip, 27132
    Partial Replacement, 27125
    Revision, 27134-27138
    Total Replacement, 27130
  Interphalangeal Joint, 26535, 26536
  Knee, 27437-27443, 27446, 27447
    with Prosthesis, 27438, 27445
    Implantation, 27445
    Revision, 27486, 27487
  Lumbar, 0091T, 0092T
  Metacarpophalangeal Joint, 26530, 26531
  Radius, 24365
    with Implant, 24366
  Reconstruction
    Prosthesis
      Hip, 27125
  Removal
    Cervical, 0093T
    Each Additional Interspace, 0095T
    Lumbar, 0094T
  Revision
    Cervical, 0096T
    Each Additional Interspace, 0098T
    Lumbar, 0097T
  Shoulder Joint
    with Implant, 23470, 23472
  Spine
    Cervical, 0090T
    Each Additional Interspace, 0092T
    Lumbar, 0091T
  Temporomandibular Joint, 21240-21243
  Wrist, 25332, 25441-25447
    with Implant, 25441-25445
    Carpal, 25443
    Lunate, 25444
    Navicular, 25443
    Pseudarthrosis Type, 25332
    Radius, 25441
    Revision, 25449
    Total Replacement, 25446
    Trapezium, 25445
    Ulna, 25442
Arthroplasty, Hip, Total
  See Hip, Total Replacement
Arthropods
  Examination, 87168
Arthroscopy
  Diagnostic
    Elbow, 29830
    Hip, 29860
    Knee, 29870, 29871
    Metacarpophalangeal Joint, 29900
    Shoulder, 29805
    Temporomandibular Joint, 29800
    Wrist, 29840

Arthroscopy — *continued*
  Surgical
    Ankle, 29891-29899
    Elbow, 29834-29838
    Foot, 29999
    Hip, 29861-29863
    Knee, 29871-29889
      Cartilage Allograft, 29867
      Cartilage Autograft, 29866
      Meniscal Transplantation, 29868
    Metacarpophalangeal Joint, 29901, 29902
    Shoulder, 29806-29827
    Temporomandibular Joint, 29804
    Toe, 29999
    Wrist, 29843-29848
  Unlisted Services and Procedures, 29999
Arthroscopy of Ankle
  See Ankle, Arthroscopy
Arthrotomy
  with Biopsy
    Acromioclavicular Joint, 23101
    Glenohumeral Joint, 23100
    Hip Joint, 27052
    Knee Joint, 27330
    Sacroiliac Joint
      Hip Joint, 27050
    Sternoclavicular Joint, 23101
  with Synovectomy
    Glenohumeral Joint, 23105
    Sternoclavicular Joint, 23106
  Acromioclavicular Joint, 23044, 23101
  Ankle, 27610, 27612, 27620
  Ankle Joint, 27625, 27626
  Carpometacarpal Joint, 26070, 26100
    with Synovial Biopsy, 26100
  Elbow, 24000
    with Joint Exploration, 24101
    with Synovectomy, 24102
    with Synovial Biopsy, 24100
    Capsular Release, 24006
  Finger Joint, 26075
    Interphalangeal with Synovial Biopsy, 26110
    Metacarpophalangeal with Biopsy,
      Synovium, 26105
  Glenohumeral Joint, 23040
  Hip, 27033
    with Synovectomy, 27054
    for Infection with Drainage, 27030
  Interphalangeal Joint, 26080, 26110
    Toe, 28024, 28054
  Intertarsal Joint, 28020, 28050
  Knee, 27310, 27330-27335, 27403, 29868
  Metacarpophalangeal Joint, 26075, 26105
  Metatarsophalangeal Joint, 28022, 28052
  Sacroiliac Joint, 27050
  Shoulder, 23044, 23105-23107
  Shoulder Joint, 23100, 23101
    Exploration and/or Removal of Loose
      Foreign Body, 23107
  Sternoclavicular Joint, 23044, 23101
  Tarsometatarsal Joint, 28020, 28050, 28052
  Temporomandibular Joint, 21010
  Wrist, 25040, 25100-25107
Arthrotomy for Removal of Prosthesis of Ankle
  See Ankle, Removal, Implant
Arthrotomy for Removal of Prosthesis of Hip
  See Hip, Removal, Prosthesis
Arthrotomy for Removal of Prosthesis of Wrist
  See Prosthesis, Wrist, Removal
Articular Ligament
  See Ligament

Ataxy, Telangiectasia, 88248
Atherectomy
  See X-Ray, Artery
  Open
    Aorta, 35481
    Brachiocephalic, 35484
    Femoral, 35483
    Iliac, 35482
    Popliteal, 35483
    Renal, 35480
    Tibioperoneal, 35485
    Visceral, 35480
  Percutaneous
    Aorta, 35491
    Brachiocephalic, 35494
    Coronary, 92995, 92996
      See Artery, Coronary
    Femoral, 35493
    Iliac, 35492
    Popliteal, 35493
    Renal, 35490
    Tibioperoneal, 35495
    Visceral, 35490
  X-ray
    Peripheral Artery, 75992, 75993
    Renal Artery, 75994
    Visceral Artery, 75995, 75996
ATLV
  See HTLV-1
ATLV Antibodies
  See Antibody, HTLV-1
Atomic Absorption Spectroscopy, 82190
ATP Creatine Phosphotransferase
  See CPK
Atresia, Choanal
  See Choanal Atresia
Atresia, Congenital
  Auditory Canal, External
    Reconstruction, 69320
Atria
  Reconstruction, 33253
Atrial Electrogram
  See Cardiology, Diagnostic
  Esophageal Recording, 93615, 93616
Atrial Fibrillation
  See Fibrillation, Atrial
Atrioseptopexy
  See Heart, Repair, Atrial Septum
Atrioseptoplasty
  See Heart, Repair, Atrial Septum
Attachment
  See Fixation
Atticotomy, 69631, 69635
Audiologic Function Tests
  See Ear, Nose and Throat; Hearing Evaluation
  Acoustic Reflex, 92568
  Acoustic Reflex Decay, 92569
  Audiometry
    Bekesy, 92560, 92561
    Comprehensive, 92557
    Conditioning Play, 92582
    Groups, 92559
    Pure Tone, 92552, 92553
    Select Picture, 92583
    Speech, 92555, 92556
    Visual ReinForcement, 92579
  Central Auditory Function, 92620, 92621
  Electrocochleography, 92584
  Evoked Otoacoustic Emissions, 92587, 92588

Audiologic Function Tests — *continued*
  Filtered Speech, 92571
  Lombard Test, 92573
  Loudness Balance, 92562
  Screening, 92551
  Sensorineural Acuity, 92575
  Short Increment Sensitivity Index, 92564
  Staggered Spondaic Word Test, 92572
  Stenger Test, 92565, 92577
  Synthetic Sentence Test, 92576
  Tinnitus Assessment, 92625
  Tone Decay, 92563
Audiometry
  Bekesy, 92560, 92561
  Brainstem Evoked Response, 92585, 92586
  Comprehensive, 92557
  Conditioning Play, 92582
  Groups, 92559
  Pure Tone, 92552, 92553
  Select Picture, 92583
  Speech, 92555, 92556
  Tympanometry, 92567
Auditory Brain Stem Evoked Response
  See Evoked Potential, Auditory Brainstem
Auditory Canal
  Decompression, 61591
  External
    Abscess
      Incision and Drainage, 69020
    Atresia, Congenital, 69320
    Biopsy, 69105
    Lesion
      Excision, 69140-69155
    Reconstruction, 69310, 69320
      for Congenital Atresia, 69320
      for Stenosis, 69310
    Removal
      Cerumen, 69210
      Ear Wax, 69210
      Foreign Body, 69200, 69205
  Internal
    Decompression, 69960
Auditory Canal Atresia, External
  See Atresia, Congenital, Auditory Canal,
    External
Auditory Evoked Otoacoustic Emission, 92587,
  92588
Auditory Evoked Potentials, 92585, 92586
Auditory Labyrinth
  See Ear, Inner
Auditory Meatus
  X-ray, 70134
Auditory Tube
  See Eustachian Tube
Augmentation
  Chin, 21120, 21123
  Malar, 21270
  Mandibular Body
    with Bone Graft, 21127
    with Prosthesis, 21125
  Osteoplasty
    Facial Bones, 21208
  Vertebral, 22523-22525
Augmentation Mammoplasty
  See Breast, Augmentation
Augmented Histamine Test, 91052
  Gastric Analysis Test, 91052
Aural Rehabilitation Test, 92626-92633

Bile Duct
  See Gallbladder
  Anastomosis
    with Intestines, 47760, 47780, 47785
    Cyst, 47716
  Biopsy
    Endoscopy, 47553
  Catheterization, 75982
  Change Catheter Tube, 75984
  Cyst
    Excision, 47715
    Repair, 47716
  Destruction
    Calculi (Stone), 43265
  Dilation
    Endoscopic, 43271, 47555, 47556
  Drainage
    Transhepatic, 75980
  Endoscopy
    Biopsy, 47553
    Destruction
      Calculi (Stone), 43265
      Tumor, 43272
    Dilation, 43271, 47555, 47556
    Exploration, 47552
    Intraoperative, 47550
    Removal
      Calculi, 43264, 47554
      Foreign Body, 43269
      Stent, 43269
    Specimen Collection, 43260
    Sphincterotomy, 43262
    Sphincter Pressure, 43263
    Tube Placement, 43267, 43268
  Exploration
    Atresia, 47700
    Endoscopy, 47552
  Incision
    Sphincter, 43262, 47460
  Incision and Drainage, 47420, 47425
  Insertion
    Catheter, 47510, 47525, 75982
      Revision, 47530
    Stent, 47511, 47801
  Nuclear Medicine
    Imaging, 78223
  Reconstruction
    Anastomosis, 47800
  Removal
    Calculi (Stone), 43264, 47420, 47425, 47554
      Percutaneous, 47630
    Foreign Body, 43269
    Stent, 43269
  Repair, 47701
    with Intestines, 47760, 47780
    Cyst, 47716
    Gastrointestinal Tract, 47785
  Tube Placement
    Nasobiliary, 43267
    Stent, 43268
  Tumor
    Destruction, 43271
    Excision, 47711, 47712
  Unlisted Services and Procedures, Biliary Tract, 47999
  X-ray
    with Contrast, 74300-74320
      Calculus Removal, 74327
      Guide Catheter, 74328, 74330
    Guide Dilation, 74360

Bile Duct, Common, Cystic Dilatation
  See Cyst, Choledochal
Bilirubin
  Blood, 82247, 82248
  Feces, 82252
  Total
    Direct, 82247, 82248
    Transcutaneous, 88400
  Total Blood, 82247, 82248
Billroth I or II, 43631-43634
Bilobectomy, 32482
Bimone
  See Testosterone
Binding Globulin, Testosterone Estradiol
  See Globulin, Sex Hormone Binding
Binet-Simon Test, 96101-96103
Binet Test, 96101-96103
Binocular Microscopy, 92504
Biofeedback
  Anorectal, 90911
  Blood-flow, 90901
  Blood Pressure, 90901
  Brainwaves, 90901
  EEG (Electroencephalogram), 90901
  Electromyogram, 90901
  Electro-Oculogram, 90901
  EMG (with Anorectal), 90911
  Eyelids, 90901
  Nerve Conduction, 90901
  Other (unlisted) biofeedback, 90901
  Perineal Muscles, 90911
  Psychiatric Treatment, 90875, 90876
  Urethral Sphincter, 90911
Bioimpedance
  Breast, 0060T
  Thorax, 93701
Biological Skin Grafts
  See Allograft, Skin
Biometry
  Eye, 76516, 76519, 92136
Biopsies, Needle
  See Needle Biopsy
Biopsy
  with Arthrotomy
    Acromioclavicular Joint, 23101
    Glenohumeral Joint, 23100
    Sternoclavicular Joint, 23101
  with Cystourethroscopy, 52354
  See also Brush Biopsy; Needle Biopsy
  Abdomen, 49000
  Adenoids (and Tonsils), 42999
  Adrenal Gland
    Laparoscopic, 60650
    Open, 60540, 60545, 60699
    Percutaneous, 49180
  Alveolus, 41899
  Anal
    Endoscopy, 46606
  Ankle, 27613, 27614, 27620
  Arm, Lower, 25065, 25066
  Arm, Upper, 24065, 24066
  Artery
    Temporal, 37609
  Auditory Canal, External, 69105
  Back/Flank, 21920, 21925
  Bile Duct
    Endoscopic, 47553
    Open, 47999

Biopsy — *continued*
  Perivesical Tissue, 53899
  Pharynx, 42800-42806
  Pineal Gland, 60699
  Pituitary Gland, 60699
  Pleura
    Needle, 32400, 32402
    Thoracotomy, 32095, 32100
  Pleural
    Open, 32402
  Prostate, 0137T, 55700, 55705
  Rectum, 45100
  Retroperitoneal Area, 49010
  Sacroiliac Joint, 27050
  Salivary Gland, 42405
  Seminal Vesicles, 54699, 55899
  Shoulder
    Deep, 23066
    Joint, 23100, 23101
    Soft Tissue, 23065
  Sinus
    Sphenoid, 31050, 31051
  Skin Lesion, 11100, 11101
  Spinal Cord, 63275-63290
    Percutaneous, 62269
    Stereotactic, 63615
  Spleen, 38999
  Stomach, 43600, 43605
  Tarsometatarsal Joint
    Synovial, 28050
  Testis, 54500, 54505
  Thorax, 21550
  Throat, 42800-42806
  Thymus, 38999, 60699
  Thyroid Gland, 60699
  Tongue, 41100, 41105
  Tonsils (and Adenoids), 42999
  Transcatheter, 37200
  Tunica Vaginalis, 54699, 55899
  Ureter, 52354
    Endoscopic, 50955-50957, 50974-50976
    Open, 53899
  Urethra, 52204, 52354, 53200
  Uterus
    Endometrial, 58100
    Endoscopic, 58558
  Uvula, 42100
  Vagina, 57100, 57105, 57421
    Endocervical, 57454
  Vertebral Body, 20250, 20251
  Vulva, 56605, 56606, 56821
  Wrist, 25065, 25066, 25100, 25101
Biopsy, Skin
  See Skin, Biopsy
Biopsy, Vein
  See Vein, Biopsy
Biostatistics
  See Biometry
Biosterol
  See Vitamin, A
Biotinidase, 82261
Birthing Room
  Newborn Care, 99431
Bischof Procedure
  Laminectomy, Surgical, 63170, 63172
Bismuth, 83015
Bizzozero's Corpuscle/Cell
  See Blood, Platelet
BKA, 27598, 27880-27882

Bladder
  Abscess
    Incision and Drainage, 51080
  Anastomosis
    with Intestine, 51960
  Anesthesia, 00864, 00870, 00912
  Aspiration, 51000-51010
  Biopsy
    by Cystourethroscopy, 52204
  Catheterization, 51045, 51701-51703
  Change Tube, 51705, 51710
  Creation/Stoma, 51980
  Cyst
    Urachal
      Excision, 51500
  Destruction
    Endoscopic, 52214-52240, 52354
  Dilation
    Ureter, 52260, 52265, 52341, 52342, 52344, 52345
  Diverticulum
    Excision, 51525
    Incision, 52305
    Resection, 52305
  Endoscopy, 52000
    with Urethrotomy, 52270-52276
    Biopsy, 52204, 52354
    Catheterization, 52005, 52010
    Destruction, 52214, 52224, 52400
    Dilation, 52260, 52265
      Urethra, 52281
    Diverticulum, 52305
    Evacuation
      Clot, 52001
    Excision
      Tumor, 52234-52240, 52355
    Exploration, 52351
    Injection, 52283
    Insertion of Stent, 52332, 52334
    Lithotripsy, 52353
    Radiotracer, 52250
    Removal
      Calculus, 52310, 52315, 52352
      Foreign Body, 52310, 52315
    Sphincter Surgery, 52277
    Tumor
      Excision, 52355
    Ureter Surgery, 52290, 52300
    Urethral Syndrome, 52285
  Excision
    Partial, 51550-51565
    Total, 51570, 51580, 51590-51597
      with Nodes, 51575, 51585, 51595
    Transurethral of Neck, 52640
    Tumor, 52234-52240
  Incision
    with
      Cryosurgery, 51030
      Destruction, 51020, 51030
      Fulguration, 51020
      Insertion Radioactive, 51020
      Radiotracer, 51020
    Catheter or Stent, 51045
  Incision and Drainage, 51040
  Injection
    Radiologic, 51600-51610
  Insertion
    Stent, 51045, 52282, 52334
  Instillation
    Drugs, 51720
  Irrigation, 51700

Bladder — *continued*
  Lesion
    Destruction, 51030
  Neck
    Endoscopy
      Injection of Implant Material, 51715
    Excision, 51520
  Nuclear Medicine
    Residual Study, 78730
  Radiotracer, 52250
  Reconstruction
    with Intestines, 51960
    with Urethra, 51800, 51820
  Removal
    Calculus, 51050, 52310, 52315
    Foreign Body, 52310, 52315
    Urethral Stent, 52310, 52315
  Repair
    Diverticulum, 52305
    Exstrophy, 51940
    Fistula, 44660, 44661, 45800, 45805,
      51880-51925
    Neck, 51845
    Wound, 51860, 51865
  Resection, 52500
  Residual Study, 78730
  Sphincter Surgery, 52277
  Suspension, 51990
  Suture
    Fistula, 44660, 44661, 45800, 45805,
      51880-51925
    Wound, 51860, 51865
  Tumor
    Excision, 51530
  Unlisted Services and Procedures, 53899
  Urethrocystography, 74450, 74455
  Urethrotomy, 52270-52276
  Urinary Incontinence Procedures
    Laparoscopy, 51990, 51992
    Pulsed Magnetic Neuromodulation, 0029T
  X-ray, 74430
    with Contrast, 74450, 74455
Bladder Neck
  Endoscopy
    Injection of Implant Material, 51715
Bladder Voiding Pressure Studies, 51795
Blalock-Hanlon Procedure, 33735-33737
  See Septostomy, Atrial
Blalock-Taussig Procedure, 33750
Blastocyst Transfer
  See Embryo Transfer
Blastogenesis, 86353
Blastomyces
  Antibody, 86612
Blastomycosis, European
  See Cryptococcus
Blast Transformation
  See Blastogenesis
Bleeding
  See Hemorrhage
Bleeding, Anal
  See Anus, Hemorrhage
Bleeding Disorder
  See Coagulopathy
Bleeding Time, 85002
Bleeding Tube, 91100
Bleeding, Uterine
  See Hemorrhage, Uterus

Bleeding, Vaginal
  See Hemorrhage, Vagina
Blepharoplasty, 15820-15823
  See Canthoplasty
  Anesthesia, 00103
  Ectropion
    Excision Tarsal Wedge, 67916
    Extensive, 67917
  Entropion
    Excision Tarsal Wedge, 67923
    Extensive, 67924
Blepharoptosis
  Repair, 67901-67909
    Frontalis Muscle Technique, 67901
      with Fascial Sling, 67902
    Superior Rectus Technique with Fascial
      Sling, 67906
    Tarso Levator Resection
      Advancement
        External Approach, 67904
        Internal Approach, 67903
Blepharorrhaphy
  See Tarsorrhaphy
Blepharospasm
  Chemodenervation, 64612
Blepharotomy, 67700
Blister
  See Bulla
Blom-Singer Prosthesis, 31611
Blood
  Bleeding Time, 85002
  Collection, for Autotransfusion
    Intraoperative, 86891
    Preoperative, 86890
  Feces, 82270, 82272
    by Hemoglobin Immunoassay, 82274
  Gastric Contents, 82271
  Harvesting of Stem Cells, 38205-38206
  Nuclear Medicine
    Flow Imaging, 78445
    Plasma Iron, 78160
    Red Cell, 78140
    Red Cell Survival, 78130, 78135
  Occult, 82270
  Osmolality, 83930
  Other Sources, 82271
  Plasma
    Exchange, 36514-36516
  Platelet
    Aggregation, 85576
    Automated Count, 85049
    Count, 85008
    Manual Count, 85032
  Reticulocyte, 85046
  Stem Cell
    Donor Search, 38204
    Harvesting, 38205-38206
    Transplantation, 38240-38242
      Cell Concentration, 38215
      Cryopreservation, 38207, 88240
      Plasma Depletion, 38214
      Platelet Depletion, 38213
      Red Blood Cell Depletion, 38212
      T-cell Depletion, 38210
      Thawing, 38208, 88241
      Tumor Cell Depletion, 38211
      Washing, 38209
  Transfusion, 36430, 36440
    Exchange, 36455
      Newborn, 36450

Blood — *continued*
  Transfusion — *continued*
    Fetal, 36460
    Push
      Infant, 36440
    Unlisted Services and Procedures, 85999
    Urine, 83491
    Viscosity, 85810
Blood Banking
  Frozen Blood Preparation, 86930-86932
  Frozen Plasma Preparation, 86927
  Physician Services, 86077-86079
Blood Cell
  CD4 and CD8
    Including Ratio, 86360
  Enzyme Activity, 82657
  Exchange, 36511-36513
  Sedimentation Rate
    Automated, 85652
    Manual, 85651
Blood Cell Count
  Automated, 85049
  B-Cells, 86355
  Blood Smear, 85007, 85008
  Differential WBC Count, 85004-85007, 85009
  Hematocrit, 85014
  Hemoglobin, 85018
  Hemogram
    Added Indices, 85025-85027
    Automated, 85025-85027
    Manual, 85032
  Microhematocrit, 85013
  Natural Killer (NK) Cells, 86357
  Red
    See Red Blood Cell (RBC), Count
  Red Blood Cell, 85041
  Reticulocyte, 85044, 85045
  Stem Cells, 86367
  T Cell, 86359-86361
  White
    See White Blood Cell, Count
  White Blood Cell, 85032, 85048, 89055
Blood Clot
  Assay, 85396
  Clot Lysis Time, 85175
  Clot Retraction, 85170
  Clotting Factor, 85250-85293
  Clotting Factor Test, 85210-85244
  Clotting Inhibitors, 85300-85302, 85305, 85307
  Coagulation Time, 85345-85348
  Factor Inhibitor Test, 85335
Blood Coagulation
  Factor I, 85384, 85385
  Factor II, 85210
  Factor III, 85730, 85732
  Factor IV, 82310
  Factor IX, 85250
  Factor V, 85220
  Factor VII, 85230
  Factor VIII, 85244, 85247
  Factor X, 85260
  Factor XI, 85270
  Factor XIII, 85290, 85291
Blood Coagulation Defect
  See Coagulopathy
Blood Coagulation Disorders
  See Clot
Blood Coagulation Test
  See Coagulation

Blood Component Removal
  See Apheresis
Blood Count, Complete
  See Complete Blood Count (CBC)
Blood Flow Check, Graft, 15860, 90940
Blood Gases
  02, 82803-82810
  by Pulse Oximetry, 94760
  CO2, 82803
  HCO3, 82803
  Hemoglobin-Oxygen Affinity, 82820
  O2 Saturation, 82805, 82810
  p02, 82803
  pCO2, 82803
  pH, 82800, 82803
Blood Letting
  See Phlebotomy
Blood Lipoprotein
  See Lipoprotein
Blood, Occult
  See Occult Blood
Blood Pool Imaging, 78472, 78473, 78481, 78483, 78494, 78496
Blood Pressure
  140/90 mm Hg, 3000F
  >140/90 mm Hg, 3002F
  Left Ventricular Filling, 0086T
  Monitoring, 24 hour, 93784-93790
  Venous, 93770
Blood Products
  Irradiation, 86945
  Pooling, 86965
  Splitting, 86985
Blood Sample
  Fetal, 59030
Blood Serum
  See Serum
Blood Smear, 85060
Blood Syndrome
  Chromosomal Analysis, 88245, 88248
Blood Test(s)
  Nuclear Medicine
    Plasma Volume, 78110, 78111
    Platelet Survival, 78190, 78191
    Red Cell Volume, 78120, 78121
    Whole Blood Volume, 78122
  Panels
    Electrolyte, 80051
    General Health Panel, 80050
    Hepatic Function, 80076
    Hepatitis, Acute, 80074
    Lipid Panel, 80061
    Metabolic
      Basic, 80048
      Comprehensive, 80053
    Obstetric Panel, 80055
    Renal Function, 80069
  Volume Determination, 78122
Blood Transfusion, Autologous
  See Autotransfusion
Blood Typing
  ABO Only, 86900
  Antigen Screen, 86903, 86904
  Crossmatch, 86920-86922
  Other RBC Antigens, 86905
  Paternity Testing, 86910, 86911
  Rh(D), 86901
  Rh Phenotype, 86906
Blood Urea Nitrogen, 84520, 84525

Bone — *continued*
Fixation — *continued*
Pin
Wire, 20650
Skeletal
Humeral Epicondyle
Percutaneous, 24566
Stereotactic Frame, 20660
Uniplane, 20690
Insertion
Needle, 36680
Osseointegrated Implant
for External Speech Processor/Cochlear
Stimulator, 69714-69718
Nuclear Medicine
Density Study, 78350, 78351
Imaging, 78300-78320
SPECT, 78320
Unlisted Services and Procedures, 78399
Protein, 83937
Removal
Fixation Device, 20670, 20680
Replacement
Osseointegrated Implant
for External Speech Processor/Cochlear
Stimulator, 69714-69718
X-ray
Age Study, 76020
Dual Energy Absorptiometry, 76075-76077
Length Study, 76040
Osseous Survey, 76061-76065
Bone 4-Carboxyglutamic Protein
See Osteocalcin
Bone, Carpal
See Carpal Bone
Bone, Cheek
See Cheekbone
**Bone Conduction Hearing Device,
Electromagnetic**
Implantation
Replacement, 69710
Removal
Repair, 69711
Bone Density Study
Appendicular Skeleton, 76071, 76076
Axial Skeleton, 76070, 76075
Ultrasound, 76977
Vertebral Fracture Assessment, 76077
Bone, Facial
See Facial Bone
Bone Graft
Allograft
Morselized, 20930
Structural, 20931
Augmentation
Mandibular Body, 21127
Autograft, 20936
Morselized, 20937
Structural, 20938
Femur, 27170
Fracture
Orbit, 21408
Harvesting, 20900, 20902
Malar Area, 21210
Mandible, 21215
Mandibular Ramus, 21194
Maxilla, 21210
Microvascular Anastomosis
Fibula, 20955
Iliac Crest, 20956

Bone Graft — *continued*
Microvascular Anastomosis — *continued*
Metatarsal Bone, 20957
Other, 20962
Rib, 20962
Nasal Area, 21210
Nasomaxillary Complex Fracture, 21348
Open Treatment
Craniofacial Separation, 21436
Osteocutaneous Flap, 20969-20973
Patella, 27599
Reconstruction
Mandibular Ramis, 21194
Midface, 21145-21160
Skull, 61316
Excision, 62148
Spine Surgery
Allograft
Morselized, 20930
Structural, 20931
Autograft
Local, 20936
Morselized, 20937
Structural, 20938
Vascular Pedicle, 25430
Bone Healing
Electrical Stimulation
Invasive, 20975
Noninvasive, 20974
Ultrasound Stimulation, 20979
Bone, Hyoid
See Hyoid Bone
Bone Infection
See Osteomyelitis
Bone Marrow
Aspiration, 38220
Harvesting, 38230
Magnetic Resonance Imaging (MRI), 76400
Needle Biopsy, 38221
Nuclear Medicine
Imaging, 78102-78104
Smear, 85097
T-Cell
Transplantation, 38240, 38241, 38242
Trocar Biopsy, 38221
Bone, Metatarsal
See Metatarsal
Bone, Nasal
See Nasal Bone
Bone, Navicular
See Navicular
Bone Osseous Survey, 76061-76065
Bone Plate
Mandible, 21244
Bone, Scan
See Bone, Nuclear Medicine; Nuclear Medicine
Bone, Semilunar
See Lunate
Bone, Sesamoid
See Sesamoid Bone
Bone Spur
See Exostosis
Bone, Tarsal
See Ankle Bone
Bone, Temporal
See Temporal, Bone
Bone Wedge Reversal
Osteotomy, 21122

Bordetella
　Antibody, 86615
　Antigen Detection
　　Direct Fluorescent Antibody, 87265
Borrelia
　Antibody, 86618, 86619
　Antigen, 87475-87477
Borrelia burgdorferi ab
　See Antibody, Lyme Disease
Borreliosis, Lyme
　See Lyme Disease
Borthen Operation
　See Iridotasis
Bost Fusion
　Arthrodesis, Wrist, 25800-25810
Bosworth Operation, 23550, 23552
Bottle Type Procedure, 55060
Botulinum Toxin
　Chemodenervation
　　Extraocular Muscle, 67345
　　Facial Muscle, 64612
　　Neck Muscle, 64613
Boutonniere Deformity, 26426, 26428
Bowel
　See Intestine(s)
Bowleg Repair, 27455, 27457
Boyce Operation, 50040, 50045
Boyd Hip Disarticulation, 27590
Brace
　See Cast
　for Leg Cast, 29358
Brachial Arteries
　See Artery, Brachial
Brachial Plexus
　Decompression, 64713
　Injection
　　Anesthetic, 64415, 64416
　Neuroplasty, 64713
　Release, 64713
　Repair
　　Suture, 64861
Brachiocephalic Artery
　See Artery, Brachiocephalic
Brachycephaly, 21175
Brachytherapy, 77761-77778, 77789
　Dose Plan, 77326-77328
　Remote Afterloading
　　1-4 Positions, 77781
　　5-8 Positions, 77782
　　9-12 Positions, 77783
　　over 12 Positions, 77784
　Unlisted Services and Procedures, 77799
Bradykinin
　Blood or Urine, 82286
Brain
　See Brainstem; Mesencephalon; Skull Base
　　Surgery
　Abscess
　　Drainage, 61150, 61151
　　Excision, 61514, 61522
　　Incision and Drainage, 61320, 61321
　Adhesions
　　Lysis, 62161
　Angiography, 70496
　Biopsy, 61140
　　Stereotactic, 61750, 61751
　Catheter
　　Irrigation, 62194, 62225

Brain — *continued*
　Catheter — *continued*
　　Replacement, 62160, 62194, 62225
　Cisternography, 70015
　Computer Assisted
　　Surgery, 61795
　Cortex
　　Magnetic Stimulation, 0018T
　Craniopharyngioma, 61545
　CT Scan, 0042T, 70450-70470, 70496
　Cyst
　　Drainage, 61150, 61151, 62161, 62162
　　Excision, 61516, 61524, 62162
　Doppler Transcranial, 93886-93893
　Epileptogenic Focus
　　Excision, 61534, 61536
　Excision
　　Amygdala, 61566
　　Choroid Plexus, 61544
　　Hemispherectomy, 61542, 61543
　　Hippocampus, 61566
　　Other Lobe, 61323, 61539, 61540
　　Temporal Lobe, 61537, 61538
　Exploration
　　Infratentorial, 61305
　　Supratentorial, 61304
　Hematoma
　　Drainage, 61154
　　Incision and Drainage, 61312-61315
　Implantation
　　Chemotherapeutic Agent, 61517
　　Electrode, 61850-61875
　　Pulse Generator, 61885, 61886
　　Receiver, 61885, 61886
　　Thermal Perfusion Probe, 0077T
　Incision
　　Corpus Callosum, 61541
　　Frontal Lobe, 61490
　　Mesencephalic Tract, 61480
　　Subpial, 61567
　Insertion
　　Catheter, 61210
　　Electrode, 61531, 61533, 61850-61875
　　Pulse Generator, 61885, 61886
　　Receiver, 61885, 61886
　　Reservoir, 61210, 61215
　Lesion
　　Aspiration, Stereotactic, 61750, 61751
　　Excision, 61534, 61536, 61600-61608,
　　　61615, 61616
　Magnetic Resonance Imaging (MRI), 70551-
　　70553
　　Intraoperative, 70557-70559
　Meningioma
　　Excision, 61512, 61519
　Myelography, 70010
　Nuclear Medicine
　　Blood Flow, 78610, 78615
　　Cerebrospinal Fluid, 78630-78650
　　Imaging, 78600-78607
　　　Vascular Flow, 78610
　　Shunt Evaluation, 78645
　Positron Emission Tomography (PET), 78608,
　　78609
　Removal
　　Electrode, 61535, 61880
　　Foreign Body, 61570, 62163
　　Pulse Generator, 61888
　　Receiver, 61888
　　Shunt, 62256, 62258
　Repair
　　Dura, 61618

Breath Test — *continued*
Hydrogen, 91065
Bricker Operation
Intestines Anastomosis, 50820
Bristow Procedure, 23450-23462
Capsulorrhaphy, Anterior, 23450-23462
Brock Operation, 33470-33475
Valvotomy, Pulmonary Valve, 33470-33474
Broken, Nose
See Fracture, Nasal Bone
Bronchi
Aspiration
Catheter, 31720-31725
Endoscopic, 31645-31646
Biopsy
Endoscopic, 31625-31629, 31632, 31633
Brushing
Protected Brushing, 31623
Catheterization
with Bronchial Brush Biopsy, 31717
Insertion, 31710
with Intracavitary Radioelement, 31643
Endoscopy
Aspiration, 31645, 31646
Biopsy, 31625, 31628, 31629, 31632, 31633
Destruction
Tumor, 31641
Dilation, 31630-31631, 31636-31638
Excision
Lesion, 31640
Exploration, 31622
Foreign Body Removal, 31635
Fracture, 31630
Injection, 31656
Lesion, 31640, 31641
Stenosis, 31641
Tumor, 31640, 31641
Ultrasound, 31620
Exploration
Endoscopic, 31622
Fracture
Endoscopy, 31630
Injection
X-ray, 31656, 31715
Instillation
Contrast Material, 31708
Needle Biopsy, 31629, 31633
Reconstruction
Graft Repair, 31770
Stenosis, 31775
Removal
Foreign Body, 31635
Repair
Fistula, 32815
Stenosis
Endoscopic Treatment, 31641
Stent
Placement, 31636-31637
Revision, 31638
Tumor
Excision, 31640
Ultrasound, 31620
Unlisted Services and Procedures, 31899
X-ray
with Contrast, 71040, 71060
Bronchial Allergen Challenge
See Bronchial Challenge Test
Bronchial Alveolar Lavage, 31624
Bronchial Brush Biopsy
with Catheterization, 31717

Bronchial Brushings
Protected Brushing, 31623
Bronchial Challenge Test
with Antigens or Gases, 95071
with Chemicals, 95070
See also Allergy Tests
Bronchial Provocation Test
See Allergy Tests, Challenge Test, Bronchial
Bronchoalveolar Lavage, 31624
Broncho-Bronchial Anastomosis, 32486
Bronchography, 71040, 71060
Catheterization, 31710
Injection
Transtracheal, 31715
Instillation
Contrast Material, 31708
Segmental
Injection, 31656
Bronchoplasty
Excision Stenosis and Anastomosis, 31775
Graft Repair, 31770
Reconstruction, Bronchi, 32501
Graft Repair, 31770
Stenosis, 31775
Bronchopneumonia, Hiberno-Vernal
See Q Fever
Bronchopulmonary Lavage, 31624
Bronchoscopy
Alveolar Lavage, 31624
Aspiration, 31645, 31646
Biopsy, 31625-31629, 31632, 31633
Brushing, Protected Brushing, 31623
Catheter Placement
Intracavity Radioelement, 31643
Diagnostic, 31622-31624, 31643
Dilation, 31630-31631, 31636-31638
Exploration, 31622
Fracture, 31630
Injection, 31656
Needle Biopsy, 31629, 31633
Removal
Foreign Body, 31635
Tumor, 31640, 31641
Stenosis, 31641
Stent Placement, 31631, 31636-31637
Stent Revision, 31638
Ultrasound, 31620
X-ray Contrast, 31656
Bronchospasm Evaluation, 94060, 94070
Pulmonology, Diagnostic, Spirometry, 94010-94070
Bronkodyl
See Theophylline
Brow Ptosis
Repair, 67900
Brucella, 86000
Antibody, 86622
Bruise
See Hematoma
Brunschwig Operation, 58240
Pelvis, Exenteration, 58240
Brush Biopsy
Bronchi, 31717
Brush Border ab
See Antibody, Heterophile
BSO, 58720
Bucca
See Cheek

Buccal Mucosa
See Mouth, Mucosa
Bulbourethral Gland
Excision, 53250
Bulla
Incision and Drainage
Puncture Aspiration, 10160
Lung
Excision-Plication, 32141
Endoscopic, 32655
BUN, 84520-84545
Bunion Repair
with Implant, 28293
Bunionectomy, 28290-28299
Chevron Procedure, 28296
Concentric Procedure, 28296
Joplin Procedure, 28294
Keller Procedure, 28292
Lapidus Procedure, 28297
Mayo Procedure, 28292
McBride Procedure, 28292
Mitchell Procedure, 28296
Silver Procedure, 28290
Burch Operation
Laparoscopic, 58152
Burgess Amputation
Disarticulation, Ankle, 27889
Burhenne Procedure, 43500
Bile Duct, Removal of Calculus, 43264, 47420,
47425, 47554
Percutaneous, 47630
Burkitt Herpevirus
See Epstein-Barr Virus
Burns
Allograft, 15300-15321, 15330-15336
Anesthesia, 01951-01953
Debridement, 15000-15001, 16020-16030
Dressing, 16020-16030
Escharotomy, 16035, 16036
Excision, 15000, 15001
Initial Treatment, 16000
Tissue Culture Skin Grafts, 15100-15157
Xenograft, 15400-15431
Burr Hole
Skull
with Injection, 61120
Biopsy, Brain, 61140
Catheterization, 61210
Drainage
Abscess, 61150, 61151
Cyst, 61150, 61151
Hematoma, 61154, 61156
Exploration
Infratentorial, 61253
Supratentorial, 61250
Implant
Cerebral Thermal Perfusion Probe, 0077T
Neurostimulator Array, 61863-61868
Insertion
Catheter, 61210
Reservoir, 61210
Burrow's Operation, 14000-14350
Bursa
Ankle, 27604
Arm, Lower, 25031
Elbow
Excision, 24105
Incision and Drainage, 23931
Femur
Excision, 27062

Bursa — *continued*
Foot
Incision and Drainage, 28001
Hip
Incision and Drainage, 26991
Injection, 20600-20610
Ischial
Excision, 27060
Joint
Aspiration, 20600-20610
Drainage, 20600-20610
Injection, 20600-20610
Knee
Excision, 27340
Leg, Lower, 27604
Palm
Incision and Drainage, 26025, 26030
Pelvis
Incision and Drainage, 26991
Shoulder
Drainage, 23031
Wrist, 25031
Excision, 25115, 25116
Incision and Drainage, 25020
Infected Bursa, 25031
Bursectomy
of Hand, 26989
Bursitis, Radiohumeral
See Tennis Elbow
Bursocentesis
See Aspiration, Bursa
Buttock
Excision
Excess Skin, 15835
Button
Nasal Septal Prosthesis
Insertion, 30220
Butyrylcholine Esterase
See Cholinesterase
B Vitamins
B-1 (Thiamine), 84425
B-12 (Cyanocobalamin), 82607, 82608
Absorption Study, 78270-78272
B-2 (Riboflavin), 84252
B-6 (Pyridoxal Phosphate), 84207
Bypass, Cardiopulmonary
See Cardiopulmonary Bypass
Bypass Graft
with Composite Graft, 35681-35683
Autogenous
Three or More Segments
Two Locations, 35683
Two Segments
Two Locations, 35682
Axillary Artery, 35516-35522, 35533, 35616-35623, 35650, 35654
Brachial Artery, 35510, 35512, 35522-35525
Carotid Artery, 33891, 35501-35510, 35526, 35601, 35606, 35626, 35642
Celiac Artery, 35331, 35631
Coronary Artery
Angiography, 93556
Arterial, 33533-33536
Venous Graft, 33510-33516
Excision
Abdomen, 35907
Extremity, 35903
Neck, 35901
Thorax, 35905

Index

Bypass Graft — Caldwell-Luc Procedure(s)

Bypass Graft — *continued*
  Femoral Artery, 35521, 35533, 35546, 35551-
      35558, 35566, 35621, 35646, 35647,
      35651-35661, 35666, 35700
  Harvest
    Endoscopic, 33508
    Upper Extremity Vein, 35500
  Iliac Artery, 35541, 35563, 35641, 35663
  Iliofemoral Artery, 35548, 35549, 35565, 35665
  Mesenteric Artery, 35531, 35631
  Peroneal Artery, 35566, 35571, 35666, 35671
  Placement
    Vein Patch, 35685
  Popliteal Artery, 35551-35558, 35571, 35623,
      35651, 35656, 35671, 35700
  Renal Artery, 35536, 35560, 35631, 35636
  Reoperation, 35700
  Repair
    Abdomen, 35907
    Extremity, 35903
      Lower Extremity
        with Composite Graft, 35681-35683
    Neck, 35901
    Thorax, 35905
  Revascularization
    Extremity, 35903
    Neck, 35901
    Thorax, 35905
  Revision
    Lower Extremity
      with Angioplasty, 35879
      with Vein Interposition, 35881
  Secondary Repair, 35870
  Splenic Artery, 35536, 35636
  Subclavian Artery, 35506, 35507, 35511-
      35516, 35526, 35606-35616, 35626,
      35645, 35693
  Thrombectomy, 35875, 35876
  Tibial Artery, 35566, 35571, 35623, 35666,
      35671
  Vertebral Artery, 35508, 35515, 35642, 35645
Bypass In Situ
  Femoral Artery, 35583-35585
  Peroneal Artery, 35585, 35587
  Popliteal Artery, 35583, 35587
  Tibial Artery, 35585, 35587

C

C-13
  Urea Breath Test, 83013, 83014
  Urease Activity, 83013, 83014
C-14
  Urea Breath Test, 78267, 78268
  Urease Activity, 83013, 83014
CA, 82310-82340
CABG, 33503-33505, 33510-33536
Cadmium
  Urine, 82300
Caffeine Halothane Contracture Test (CHCT),
  89049
Calcaneus
  Craterization, 28120
  Cyst
    Excision, 28100-28103
  Diaphysectomy, 28120
  Excision, 28118-28120
  Fracture
    with Manipulation, 28405, 28406
    without Manipulation, 28400
    Open Treatment, 28415, 28420

Calcaneus — *continued*
  Fracture — *continued*
    Percutaneous Fixation, 28406
    Repair
      Osteotomy, 28300
    Saucerization, 28120
    Tumor
      Excision, 27647, 28100-28103
    X-ray, 73650
Calcareous Deposits
  Subdeltoid
    Removal, 23000
Calcifediol
  Blood or Urine, 82306
Calcifediol Assay
  See Calciferol
Calciferol
  Blood or Urine, 82307
Calcification
  See Calcium, Deposits
Calciol
  See Calcifediol
Calcitonin
  Blood or Urine, 82308
  Stimulation Panel, 80410
Calcium
  Blood
    Infusion Test, 82331
  Deposits
    Removal, Calculi-Stone
      Bile Duct, 43264, 47420, 47425, 47554,
        47630
      Bladder, 51050, 52310-52318
      Gallbladder, 47480
      Hepatic Duct, 47400
      Kidney, 50060-50081, 50130, 50561,
        50580
      Pancreas, 48020
      Pancreatic Duct, 43264
      Salivary Gland, 42330-42340
      Ureter, 50610-50630, 50961, 50980,
        51060, 51065, 52320-52330
      Urethra, 52310, 52315
  Ionized, 82330
  Total, 82310
  Urine, 82340
Calcium-Binding Protein, Vitamin K-Dependent
  See Osteocalcin
Calcium-Pentagastrin Stimulation, 80410
Calculus
  Analysis, 82355-82370
  Destruction
    Bile Duct, 43265
    Pancreatic Duct, 43265
  Removal
    Bile Duct, 43264, 47554, 74327
    Bladder, 51050, 52310-52318, 52352
    Kidney, 50060-50081, 50130, 50561, 50580,
      52352
    Pancreatic Duct, 43264
    Ureter, 50610-50630, 50961, 50980, 51060,
      51065, 52320, 52325, 52352
    Urethra, 52310, 52315, 52352
Calculus of Kidney
  See Calculus, Removal, Kidney
Caldwell-Luc Procedure(s), 21385, 31030, 31032
  Orbital Floor Blowout Fracture, 21385
  Sinusotomy, 31030, 31032

Caliper
Application
Removal, 20660
Callander Knee Disarticulation, 27598
Callosum, Corpuss
See Corpus Callosum
Calmette Guerin Bacillus Vaccine
See BCG Vaccine
Caloric Vestibular Test, 92533, 92543
Calycoplasty, 50405
Camey Enterocystoplasty, 50825
CAMP
See Cyclic AMP
Campbell Procedure, 27422
Campylobacter
Antibody, 86625
Antigen, 86628
Skin Test, 86485
Canal, Ear
See Auditory Canal
Canaloplasty, 69631, 69635
Canal, Semicircular
See Semicircular Canal
Candida
Antibody, 86628
Antigen, 87480-87482
Skin Test, 86485
Cannulation
Arterial, 36620, 36625
Pancreatic Duct, 48999
Sinus
Maxillary, 31000
Sphenoid, 31002
Thoracic Duct, 38794
Cannulation, Renoportal
See Anastomosis, Renoportal
Cannulization
See Catheterization
Arteriovenous (AV), 36145, 36810, 36815
Chemotherapy, 36823
Declotting, 36550, 36860, 36861
ECMO, 36822
Isolated with Chemotherapy Perfusion, 36823
Vas Deferens, 55200
Vein to Vein, 36800
Canthocystostomy
See Conjunctivorhinostomy
Canthopexy
Lateral, 21282
Medial, 21280
Canthoplasty, 67950
Canthorrhaphy, 67880, 67882
Canthotomy, 67715
Canthus
Reconstruction, 67950
Cap, Cervical
See Cervical Cap
CAPD, 90945, 90947
Capsule
See Capsulodesis
Elbow
Arthrotomy, 24006
Excision, 24006
Foot, 28260-28264
Interphalangeal Joint
Excision, 26525

Capsule — continued
Interphalangeal Joint — continued
Incision, 26525
Knee, 27435
Metacarpophalangeal Joint
Excision, 26520
Incision, 26520
Metatarsophalangeal Joint Release, 28289
Shoulder, Incision, 23020
Wrist
Excision, 25320
Capsulectomy
Breast, Periprosthetic, 19371
Capsulodesis
Metacarpophalangeal Joint, 26516-26518
Capsulorrhaphy
Anterior, 23450-23462
Multi-Directional Instability, 23466
Posterior, 23465
Wrist, 25320
Capsulotomy
Breast
Periprosthetic, 19370
Foot, 28260-28262
Hip with Release, Flexor Muscles, 27036
Interphalangeal Joint, 28272
Knee, 27435
Metacarpophalangeal Joint, 26520
Metatarsophalangeal Joint, 28270
Toe, 28270, 28272
Wrist, 25085
Captopril, 80416, 80417
Carbamazepine
Assay, 80156, 80157
Carbazepin
See Carbamazepine
Carbinol
See Methanol
Carbohydrate Deficient Transferin, 82373
Carbon Dioxide
Blood or Urine, 82374
Carbon Monoxide
Blood, 82375, 82376
Carbon Tetrachloride, 84600
Carboxycathepsin
See Angiotensin Converting Enzyme (ACE)
Carboxyhemoglobin, 82375, 82376
Carbuncle
Incision and Drainage, 10060, 10061
Carcinoembryonal Antigen
See Antigen, Carcinoembryonic
Carcinoembryonic Antigen, 82378
Cardiac Arrhythmia, Tachycardia
See Tachycardia
Cardiac Atria
See Atria
Cardiac Catheterization
Combined Left and Right Heart, 93526-93529
Flow Directed, 93503
for Biopsy, 93505
for Congenital Anomalies
Right and Retrograde Left, 93531
Transseptal and Retrograde Left, 93532, 93533
for Dilution Studies, 93561, 93562
Imaging, 93555, 93556
Injection, 93539-93545
Left Heart, 93510-93529

Cardiac Catheterization — *continued*
Pacemaker, 33210
Right Heart, 93501, 93503
for Congenital Anomalies, 93530
Cardiac Electroversion
See Cardioversion
Cardiac Event Recorder
Implantation, 33282
Removal, 33284
Cardiac Magnetic Resonance Imaging (CMRI)
Complete Study, 75554
Limited Study, 75555
Morphology, 75553
Velocity Flow Mapping, 75556
Cardiac Massage
Thoracotomy, 32160
Cardiac Output Measurement
by Indicator Dilution, 93561, 93562
Inert Gas Rebreathing
During Exercise, 0105T
During Rest, 0104T
Cardiac Pacemaker
See Heart, Pacemaker
Cardiac Rehabilitation, 93797, 93798
Cardiac Septal Defect
See Septal Defect
Cardiac Transplantation
See Heart, Transplantation
Cardiectomy
Donor, 33930, 33940
Cardioassist, 0049T, 92970, 92971
Cardiolipin Antibody, 86147
Cardiology
See Electrocardiography
Diagnostic
Acoustic Recording with Computer Analysis
Heart Sounds, 0068T-0070T
Atrial Electrogram
Esophageal Recording, 93615, 93616
Cardioverter-Defibrillator
Evaluation and Testing, 93640-93642,
93741-93744
Echocardiography
Doppler, 93303-93321, 93662
Intracardiac, 93662
Transesophageal, 93318
Transthoracic, 93303-93317, 93350
Electrocardiogram
Evaluation, 93000, 93010, 93014
Microvolt T-wave, Alternans, 93025
Monitoring, 93224-93237
Patient-Demand, Single Event, 93268-
93272
Rhythm, 93040-93042
Tracing, 93005
Transmission, 93012
Electrophysiologic
Follow-Up Study, 93624
Ergonovine Provocation Test, 93024
Evaluation
Heart Device, 93640
Heart
Stimulation and Pacing, 93623
Hemodynamic Monitoring Non-invasive,
0086T
Implantable Loop Recorder System, 93727
Intracardiac Pacing and Mapping, 93631
3-D Mapping, 93613
Follow-up Study, 93624
Stimulation and Pacing, 93623

Cardiology — *continued*
Intracardiac Pacing and Recording
Arrhythmia Induction, 93618-93620
Bundle of His, 93600
Comprehensive, 93619-93622
Intra-Atrial, 93602, 93610
Right Ventricle, 93603
Tachycardia Sites, 93609
Ventricular, 93612
Intravascular Ultrasound, 92978, 92979
Left Ventricular Pressure Measurement,
0086T
M Mode and Real Time, 93307-93321
Pacemaker Testing, 93642
Antitachycardia System, 93724
Dual Chamber, 93731-93733
Leads, 93641
Single Chamber, 93734-93736
Perfusion Imaging, 78460, 78461
See Nuclear Medicine
Stress Tests
Cardiovascular, 93015-93018
Drug Induced, 93024
MUGA (Multiple Gated Acquisition),
78483
Tilt Table Evaluation, 93660
Vectorcardiogram
Evaluation, 93799
Tracing, 93799
Therapeutic
Angioplasty
Percutaneous, Transluminal, 92982,
92984
Cardioassist, 92970, 92971
Cardio Defibrillator Initial Set-up and
Programming, 93745
Cardiopulmonary Resuscitation, 92950
Cardioversion, 92960, 92961
Intravascular Ultrasound, 92978, 92979
Pacing
Transcutaneous, Temporary, 92953
Thrombolysis
Coronary Vessel, 92975, 92977
Thrombolysis, Coronary, 92977
Valvuloplasty
Percutaneous, 92986, 92990
Cardiomyotomy
See Esophagomyotomy
Cardioplasty, 43320
Cardioplegia, 33999
Cardiopulmonary Bypass
with Prosthetic Valve Repair, 33496
Lung Transplant with
Double, 32854
Single, 32852
Cardiopulmonary Resuscitation, 92950
Cardiotomy, 33310, 33315
Cardiovascular Stress Test
See Exercise Stress Tests
Cardioversion, 92960, 92961
Care, Custodial
See Nursing Facility Services
Care, Intensive
See Intensive Care
Care, Neonatal Intensive
See Intensive Care, Neonatal
Care Plan Oversight Services
Home Health Agency Care, 99374, 99375
Hospice, 99377, 99378
Nursing Facility, 99379, 99380

Care, Self
See Self Care
Carneous Mole
See Abortion
Carnitine Total and Free, 82379
Carotene, 82380
Carotid Artery
Aneurysm Repair
    Vascular Malformation or Carotid Cavernous
      Fistula, 61710
Excision, 60605
Ligation, 37600-37606
Stent, Transcatheter Placement, 0075T-0076T
Transection
    with Skull Base Surgery, 61609
Carotid Body
Lesion
    Carotid Artery, 60605
    Excision, 60600
Carotid, Common, 0126T
Carotid Pulse Tracing
with ECG Lead, 93799
Carpal Bone
See Wrist
Arthroplasty
    with Implant, 25443
Cyst
    Excision, 25130-25136
Dislocation
    Closed Treatment, 25690
    Open Treatment, 25695
Excision, 25210, 25215
    Partial, 25145
Fracture, 25622-25628
    with Manipulation, 25624, 25635
    without Manipulation, 25630
    Closed Treatment, 25622, 25630
    Open Treatment, 25628, 25645
Incision and Drainage, 26034
Insertion
    Vascular Pedicle, 25430
Osteoplasty, 25394
Repair, 25431-25440
Sequestrectomy, 25145
Tumor
    Excision, 25130-25136
Carpals
Incision and Drainage, 25035
Carpal Tunnel
Injection
    Therapeutic, 20526
Carpal Tunnel Syndrome
Decompression, 64721
Carpectomy, 25210, 25215
Carpometacarpal Joint
Arthrodesis
    Hand, 26843, 26844
    Thumb, 26841, 26842
Arthrotomy, 26070, 26100
Biopsy
    Synovium, 26100
Dislocation
    Closed Treatment, 26670
      with Manipulation, 26675, 26676
    Open Treatment, 26685, 26686
Exploration, 26070
Fusion
    Hand, 26843, 26844
    Thumb, 26841, 26842

Carpometacarpal Joint — *continued*
Removal
    Foreign Body, 26070
Repair, 25447
Synovectomy, 26130
Cartilage, Arytenoid
See Arytenoid
Cartilage, Ear
See Ear Cartilage
Cartilage Graft
Ear to Face, 21235
Harvesting, 20910, 20912
Rib to Face, 21230
Cartilaginous Exostosis
See Exostosis
Case Management Services
Team Conferences, 99361-99362
Telephone Calls, 99371-99373
Cast
See Brace; Splint
Body
    Halo, 29000
    Risser Jacket, 29010, 29015
    Turnbuckle Jacket, 29020, 29025
    Upper Body and Head, 29040
    Upper Body and Legs, 29046
    Upper Body and One Leg, 29044
    Upper Body Only, 29035
Clubfoot, 29450
Cylinder, 29365
Finger, 29086
Hand, 29085
Hip, 29305, 29325
Leg
    Rigid Total Contact, 29445
Long Arm, 29065
Long Leg, 29345, 29355, 29365, 29450
Long Leg Brace, 29358
Patellar Tendon Bearing (PTB), 29435
Removal, 29700-29715
Repair, 29720
Short Arm, 29075
Short Leg, 29405-29435, 29450
Shoulder, 29049-29058
Unlisted Services and Procedures, 29799
Walking, 29355, 29425
    Revision, 29440
Wedging, 29740, 29750
Windowing, 29730
Wrist, 29085
Casting
Unlisted Services and Procedures, 29799
Castration
See Orchiectomy
Castration, Female
See Oophorectomy
Cataract
Excision, 66830
Incision, 66820, 66821
    Laser, 66821
    Stab Incision, 66820
Removal
    Extraction
      Extracapsular, 66982, 66984
      Intracapsular, 66983
Catecholamines, 80424, 82382-82384
Blood, 82383
Urine, 82382
Cathepsin-D, 82387

Catheter
See Cannulization; Venipuncture
Aspiration
  Nasotracheal, 31720
  Tracheobronchial, 31725
Bladder, 51701-51703
  Irrigation, 51700
Breast
  Cytology, 0046T, 0047T
  for interstitial Radioelement Application, 19296-19298
Bronchus for Intracavitary Radioelement Application, 31643
Central Venous
  Repair, 36575
  Replacement, 36580, 36581, 36584
  Repositioning, 36597
Coronary Artery without Concomitant Left Heart Catheterization, 93508
  Venous Coronary Bypass Graft without Concomitant Left Heart Catheterization, 93508
Declotting, 36550
Exchange
  Drainage, 49423
  Intravascular, 37209, 75900
Intracatheter
  Irrigation, 99507
  Obstruction Clearance, 36596
Pericatheter
  Obstruction Clearance, 36595
Placement
  Arterial Coronary Conduit without Concomitant Left Heart Catheterization, 93508
Removal
  Central Venous, 36589
  Peritoneum, 49422
  Spinal Cord, 62355

Catheterization
Abdomen, 49420, 49421
Abdominal Artery, 36245-36248
Aorta, 36160-36215
Arterial
  Cutdown, 36625
  Intracatheter/Needle, 36100-36140
  Percutaneous, 36620
Arteriovenous Shunt, 36145
Bile Duct, 47510, 47530
  Change, 47525
  Percutaneous, 47510
Bladder, 51010, 51045
Brachiocephalic Artery, 36215-36218
Brain, 61210
  Replacement, 62160, 62194, 62225
Bronchography, 31710
  with Bronchial Brush Biopsy, 31717
Cardiac
  Combined Left and Right Heart, 93526-93529
  Flow Directed, 93503
  for Biopsy, 93505
  for Congenital Anomalies
    Right and Retrograde Left, 93531
    Transseptal and Retrograde Left, 93532, 93533
  for Dilution Studies, 93561, 93562
  Imaging, 93555, 93556
  Injection, 93539-93545
  Left Heart, 93510-93529
  Pacemaker, 33210

Catheterization — *continued*
Cardiac — *continued*
  Right Heart, 36013, 93501, 93503
    for Congenital Cardiac Anomalies, 93530
  Central, 36555-36566
  Cerebral Artery, 36215
  Cystourethroscopy
    Ejaculatory Duct, 52010
    Urethral, 52005
  Ear, Middle, 69405
  Eustachian Tube, 69405
  Fallopian Tube, 58345, 74742
  Intracardiac
    Ablation, 93650-93652
  Jejunum
    for Enteral Therapy, 44015
  Kidney
    with Ureter, 50393
    Drainage, 50392
  Legs, 36245-36248
  Nasotracheal, 31720
  Nasotracheobronchi, 31720
  Newborn
    Umbilical Vein, 36510
  Pelvic Artery, 36245-36248
  Peripheral, 36568-36571
  Placement
    Arterial Coronary Conduit without Concomitant Left Heart Catheterization, 93508
    Coronary Artery without Concomitant Left Heart Catheterization, 93508
    Venous Coronary Bypass Graft without Concomitant Left Heart Catheterization, 93508
  Pleural Cavity, 32019
  Portal Vein, 36481
  Pulmonary Artery, 36013-36015
  Radioelement Application, 55859
  Removal
    Fractured Catheter, 75961
    Obstructive Material
      Intracatheter, 36596
      Pericatheter, 36595
  Salivary Duct, 42660
  Skull, 61107
  Spinal Cord, 62350, 62351
  Spinal Epidural or Intrathecal, 62350, 62351, 62360-62362
    Removal, 62355
  Thoracic Artery, 36215-36218
  Tracheobronchi, 31725
  Transglottic, 31700
  Umbilical Artery, 36660
  Umbilical Vein, 36510
  Ureter
    Endoscopic, 50553, 50572, 50953, 50972, 52005
    Injection, 50394, 50684
    Manometric Studies, 50396, 50686
  Uterus, 58340
    Radiology, 58340
  Vena Cava, 36010
  Venous
    Central-Line, 36555, 36556, 36568, 36569, 36580, 36584
    First Order, 36011
    Intracatheter, 36000
    Needle, 36000
    Organ Blood, 36500
    Second Order, 36012

Chemical Exfoliation, 15788-15793, 17360
Chemical Peel, 15788-15793
Chemiluminescent Assay, 82397
Chemistry Tests
  Organ or Disease Oriented Panel
    Electrolyte, 80051
    General Health Panel, 80050
    Hepatic Function Panel, 80076
    Hepatitis Panel, Acute, 80074
    Lipid Panel, 80061
    Metabolic
      Basic, 80048
      Comprehensive, 80053
    Obstetric Panel, 80055
  Unlisted Services and Procedures, 84999
Chemocauterization
  Corneal Epithelium, 65435
    with Chelating Agent, 65436
Chemodenervation
  Eccrine Glands, 64650, 64653
  Electrical Stimulation for Guidance, 95873
  Extraocular Muscle, 67345
  Extremity Muscle, 64614
  Facial Muscle, 64612
  Internal Anal Sphincter, 46505
  Neck Muscle, 64613
  Trunk Muscle, 64614
Chemonucleolysis, 62292
Chemosurgery
  Mohs Technique, 17304-17310
  Skin Lesion, 17004, 17110, 17270, 17280
Chemotaxis Assay, 86155
Chemotherapy
  Arterial Catheterization, 36640
  Bladder Instillation, 51720
  Central Nervous System, 61517, 96450
  Extracorporeal Circulation Membrane
      Oxygenation, 36822
    Isolated with Chemotherapy Perfusion,
      36823
  Home Infusion Procedures, 99601, 99602
  Intra-Arterial, 96420-96425
  Intralesional, 96405, 96406
  Intramuscular, 96401-96402
  Intravenous, 96409-96417
  Kidney Instillation, 50391
  Peritoneal Cavity, 96445
  Pleural Cavity, 96440
  Pump Services
    Implantable, 96530
    Initiation, 96416
    Maintenance, 95990-95991, 96521-96522
    Portable, 96520
  Reservoir Filling, 96542
  Subcutaneous, 96401-96402
  Supply of Agent, 96545
  Unlisted Services and Procedures, 96549
  Ureteral Instillation, 50391
Chest
  See Mediastinum; Thorax
  Angiography, 71275
  Artery
    Ligation, 37616
  CT Scan, 71250-71275
  Exploration
    Blood Vessel, 35820
  Magnetic Resonance Imaging (MRI), 71550-
      71552

Chest — *continued*
  Repair
    Blood Vessel, 35211, 35216
      with Other Graft, 35271, 35276
      with Vein Graft, 35241, 35246
  Ultrasound, 76604
  Wound Exploration
    Penetrating, 20101
  X-ray, 71010-71035
    Complete (four views) with Fluoroscopy,
      71034
    Insertion Pacemaker, 71090
    Partial (two views) with Fluoroscopy, 71023
    Stereo, 71015
Chest Cavity
  Bypass Graft, 35905
  Endoscopy
    Exploration, 32601-32606
    Surgical, 32650-32665
    Therapeutic, 32654-32665
Chest, Funnel
  See Pectus Excavatum Repair
Chest Wall
  Manipulation, 94667, 94668
  Reconstruction, 49904
    Trauma, 32820
  Repair, 32905
    Closure, 32810
    Fistula, 32906
  Tumor
    Excision, 19260-19272
  Unlisted Services and Procedures, 32999
Chest Wall Fistula
  See Fistula, Chest Wall
Chevron Procedure, 28296
Chiari Osteotomy of the Pelvis
  See Osteotomy, Pelvis
Chicken Pox (Varicella)
  Immunization, 90716
Child Procedure, 48146
  See also Excision, Pancreas, Partial
Chin
  Repair
    Augmentation, 21120
    Osteotomy, 21121-21123
  Rhytidectomy, 15828
  Skin Graft
    Delay of Flap, 15620
    Full Thickness, 15240, 15241
    Pedicle Flap, 15574
    Split, 15120-15121
  Tissue Transfer, Adjacent, 14040, 14041
Chinidin, 80194
Chiropractic Manipulation
  See Manipulation, Chiropractic
Chiropractic Treatment
  Spinal
    Extraspinal, 98940-98943
Chlamydia
  Antibody, 86631, 86632
  Antigen Detection
    Direct
      Optical Observation, 87810
    Direct Fluorescent, 87270
    Enzyme Immunoassay, 87320
    Nucleic Acid, 87485-87492
  Culture, 87110
Chloramphenicol, 82415
Chlorhydrocarbon, 82441

Chloride
Blood, 82435
Other Source, 82438
Spinal Fluid, 82438
Urine, 82436

Chloride, Methylene
See Dichloromethane

Chlorinated Hydrocarbons, 82441

Chlorpromazine, 84022

Choanal Atresia
Repair, 30540, 30545

CHOL, 82465, 83718-83721

Cholangiogram
Intravenous, 76499

Cholangiography
with Cholecystectomy, 47563, 47605
Injection, 47500, 47505
Intraoperative, 74300, 74301
Percutaneous, 74320
with Laparoscopy, 47560, 47561
with Peritoneoscopy, 47560, 47561
Postoperative, 74305
Repair
with Bile Duct Exploration, 47700
with Cholecystectomy, 47620

Cholangiopancreatography, 43260
with Biopsy, 43261
with Surgery, 43262-43267, 43269
See Bile Duct, Pancreatic Duct

Cholangiostomy
See Hepaticostomy

Cholangiotomy
See Hepaticostomy

Cholecalciferol, 82306

Cholecystectomy
Laparoscopic, 47562-47570
with Cholangiography, 47563
with Exploration Common Duct, 47564
Open Approach, 47600-47620
with Cholangiography, 47605, 47620
with Exploration Common Duct, 47610

Cholecystenterostomy, 47570, 47720-47741

Cholecystography, 74290, 74291

Cholecystostomy, 47480

Cholecystotomy, 47480, 48001
Percutaneous, 47490

Choledochoplasty
See Bile Duct, Repair

Choledochoscopy, 47550

Choledochostomy, 47420, 47425

Choledochotomy, 47420, 47425

Choledochus, Cyst
See Cyst, Choledochal

Cholera Vaccine
Injectable, 90725

Cholesterol
Measurement, 83721
Serum, 82465
Testing, 83718, 83719

Choline Esterase I, 82013

Choline Esterase II, 82480, 82482

Cholinesterase
Blood, 82480, 82482

Cholyglycine
Blood, 82240

Chondroitin Sulfate, 82485

Chondromalacia Patella
Repair, 27418

Chondropathia Patellae
See Chondromalacia Patella

Chondroplasty, 29877, 29879

Chondrosteoma
See Exostosis

Chopart Procedure, 28800
Amputation, Foot, 28800, 28805

Chordotomies
See Cordotomy

Chorioangioma
See Lesion, Skin

Choriomeningitides, Lymphocytic, 86727

Chorionic Gonadotropin, 80414, 84702, 84703
Stimulation, 80414, 80415

Chorionic Growth Hormone, 83632

Chorionic Tumor
See HydatidiForm Mole

Chorionic Villus
Biopsy, 59015

Choroid
Destruction
Lesion, 0016T, 67220-67225

Choroidopathy, 67208-67218

Choroid Plexus
Excision, 61544

Christmas Factor, 85250

Chromaffionoma, Medullary
See Pheochromocytoma

Chromatin, Sex
See Barr Bodies

Chromatography
Column
Mass Spectrometry, 82541-82544
Gas-Liquid or HPLC, 82486, 82491, 82492
Paper, 82487, 82488
Thin-Layer, 82489

Chromium, 82495

Chromogenic Substrate Assay, 85130

Chromosome Analysis
Added Study, 88280-88289
Amniotic Fluid, 88267, 88269
Culture, 88235
Biopsy Culture
Tissue, 88233
Bone Marrow Culture, 88237
Chorionic Villus, 88267
5 Cells, 88261
15-20 Cells, 88262
20-25 Cells, 88264
45 Cells, 88263
Culture, 88235
for Breakage Syndromes, 88245-88249
Fragile-X, 88248
Lymphocyte Culture, 88230
Pregnancy Associated Plasma Protein A, 84163
Skin Culture
Tissue, 88233
Tissue Culture, 88239
Unlisted Services and Procedures, 88299

Chromotubation
Oviduct, 58350

Chronic Erection
See Priapism

Chronic Interstitial Cystitides
See Cystitis, Interstitial

Ciliary Body
 Cyst
  Destruction
   Cryotherapy, 66720
   Cyclodialysis, 66740
   Cyclophotocoagulation, 66710-66711
   Diathermy, 66700
   Nonexcisional, 66770
 Destruction
  Cyclophotcoagulation, 66710, 66711
  Endoscopic, 66711
 Lesion
  Destruction, 66770
 Repair, 66680
Cimino Type Procedure, 36821
Cinefluorographies
 See Cineradiography
Cineplasty
 Arm, Lower, 24940
 Arm, Upper, 24940
Cineradiography
 Esophagus, 74230
 Pharynx, 70371, 74230
 Speech Evaluation, 70371
 Swallowing Evaluation, 74230
 Unlisted Services and Procedures, 76120, 76125
Cingulotomy, 61490
Circulation Assist
 Aortic, 33967, 33970
 Balloon Counterpulsation, 33967, 33970
  Removal, 33971
 Cardioassist Method
  External, 92971
  Internal, 92970
 External, 33960, 33961
Circulation, Extracorporeal
 See Extracorporeal Circulation
Circumcision
 with Clamp or Other Device, 54152
  Newborn, 54150
 Repair, 54163
 Surgical Excision, 54161
  Newborn, 54160
Cisternal Puncture, 61050, 61055
Cisternography, 70015
 Nuclear, 78630
Citrate
 Blood or Urine, 82507
CK, 82550-82554
 Total, 82550
Cl, 82435-82438
Clagett Procedure
 Chest Wall, Repair, Closure, 32810
Clavicle
 Craterization, 23180
 Cyst
  Excision, 23140
   with Allograft, 23146
   with Autograft, 23145
 Diaphysectomy, 23180
 Dislocation
  without Manipulation, 23540
  Acromioclavicular Joint
   Closed Treatment, 23540, 23545
   Open Treatment, 23550, 23552
  Sternoclavicular Joint
   Closed Treatment, 23520, 23525
   Open Treatment, 23530, 23532

Clavicle — *continued*
 Excision, 23170
  Partial, 23120, 23180
  Total, 23125
 Fracture
  Closed Treatment
   with Manipulation, 23505
   without Manipulation, 23500
  Open Treatment, 23515
 Osteotomy, 23480, 23485
 Pinning, Wiring, Etc., 23490
 Prophylactic Treatment, 23490
 Repair Osteotomy, 23480, 23485
 Saucerization, 23180
 Sequestrectomy, 23170
 Tumor
  Excision, 23140, 23146, 23200
   with Allograft, 23146
   with Autograft, 23145
   Radical Resection, 23200
 X-ray, 73000
Clavicula
 See Clavicle
Claviculectomy
 Partial, 23120
 Total, 23125
Claw Finger Repair, 26499
Clayton Procedure, 28114
Cleft, Branchial
 See Branchial Cleft
Cleft Cyst, Branchial
 See Branchial Cleft, Cyst
Cleft Foot
 Reconstruction, 28360
Cleft Hand
 Repair, 26580
Cleft Lip
 Repair, 40700-40761
 Rhinoplasty, 30460, 30462
Cleft Palate
 Repair, 42200-42225
 Rhinoplasty, 30460, 30462
Clinical Act of Insertion
 See Insertion
Clitoroplasty
 for Intersex State, 56805
Closed [Transurethral] Biopsy of Bladder
 See Biopsy, Bladder , Cystourethroscopy
Clostridial Tetanus
 See Tetanus
Clostridium Botulinum Toxin
 See Chemodenervation
Clostridium Difficile Toxin
 Antigen Detection
  Enzyme Immunoassay, 87324
 by Immunoassay
  with Direct Optical Observation, 87803
Clostridium Tetani ab
 See Antibody, Tetanus
Closure, 12001-13160
 Anal Fistula, 46288
 Appendiceal Fistula, 44799
 Atrioventricular Valve, 33600
 Cardiac Valve, 33600, 33602
 Cystostomy, 51880
 Diaphragm
  Fistula, 39599
 Enterostomy, 44620-44626

Closure — *continued*
Lacrimal Fistula, 68770
Lacrimal Punctum
  Plug, 68761
  Thermocauterization, Ligation, or Laser
    Surgery, 68760
Rectovaginal Fistula, 57300-57308
Semilunar Valve, 33602
Septal Defect, 33615
Skin
  Abdomen
    Complex, 13100-13102
    Intermediate, 12031-12037
    Layered, 12031-12037
    Simple, 12001-12007
    Superficial, 12001-12007
  Arm, Arms
    Complex, 13120-13122
    Intermediate, 12031-12037
    Layered, 12031-12037
    Simple, 12001-12007
    Superficial, 12001-12007
  Axilla, Axillae
    Complex, 13131-13133
    Intermediate, 12031-12037
    Layered, 12031-12037
    Simple, 12001-12007
    Superficial, 12001-12007
  Back
    Complex, 13100-13102
    Intermediate, 12031-12037
    Layered, 12031-12037
    Simple, 12001-12007
    Superficial, 12001-12007
  Breast
    Complex, 13100-13102
    Intermediate, 12031-12037
    Layered, 12031-12037
    Simple, 12001-12007
    Superficial, 12001-12007
  Buttock
    Complex, 13100-13102
    Intermediate, 12031-12037
    Layered, 12031-12037
    Simple, 12001-12007
    Superficial, 12001-12007
  Cheek, Cheeks
    Complex, 13131-13133
    Intermediate, 12051-12057
    Layered, 12051-12057
    Simple, 12011-12018
    Superficial, 12011-12018
  Chest
    Complex, 13100-13102
    Intermediate, 12031-12037
    Layered, 12031-12037
    Simple, 12001-12007
    Superficial, 12001-12007
  Chin
    Complex, 13131-13133
    Intermediate, 12051-12057
    Layered, 12051-12057
    Simple, 12011-12018
    Superficial, 12011-12018
  Ear, Ears
    Complex, 13150-13153
    Intermediate, 12051-12057
    Layered, 12051-12057
      2.5 cm or less, 12051
    Simple, 12011-12018
    Superficial, 12011-12018

Closure — *continued*
Skin — *continued*
  External
    Genitalia
      Intermediate, 12041-12047
      Layered, 12041-12047
      Simple, 12001-12007
      Superficial, 12001-12007
  Extremity, Extremities
    Intermediate, 12031-12037
    Layered, 12031-12037
    Simple, 12001-12007
    Superficial, 12001-12007
  Eyelid, Eyelids
    Complex, 13150-13153
    Intermediate, 12051-12057
    Layered, 12051-12057
    Simple, 12011-12018
    Superficial, 12011-12018
  Face
    Complex, 13131-13133
    Intermediate, 12051-12057
    Layered, 12051-12057
    Simple, 12011-12018
    Superficial, 12011-12018
  Feet
    Complex, 13131-13133
    Intermediate, 12041-12047
    Layered, 12041-12047
    Simple, 12001-12007
    Superficial, 12001-12007
  Finger, Fingers
    Complex, 13131-13133
    Intermediate, 12041-12047
    Layered, 12041-12047
    Simple, 12001-12007
    Superficial, 12001-12007
  Foot
    Complex, 13131-13133
    Intermediate, 12041-12047
    Layered, 12041-12047
    Simple, 12001-12007
    Superficial, 12001-12007
  Forearm, Forearms
    Complex, 13120-13122
    Intermediate, 12031-12037
    Layered, 12031-12037
    Simple, 12001-12007
    Superficial, 12001-12007
  Forehead
    Complex, 13131-13133
    Intermediate, 12051-12057
    Layered, 12051-12057
    Simple, 12011-12018
    Superficial, 12011-12018
  Genitalia
    Complex, 13131-13133
    External
      Intermediate, 12041-12047
      Layered, 12041-12047
      Simple, 12001-12007
      Superficial, 12001-12007
  Hand, Hands
    Complex, 13131-13133
    Intermediate, 12041-12047
    Layered, 12041-12047
    Simple, 12001-12007
    Superficial, 12001-12007
  Leg, Legs
    Complex, 13120-13122
    Intermediate, 12031-12037
    Layered, 12031-12037

Closure — *continued*
  Skin — *continued*
    Leg, Legs — *continued*
      Simple, 12001-12007
      Superficial, 12001-12007
    Lip, Lips
      Complex, 13150-13153
      Intermediate, 12051-12057
      Layered, 12051-12057
      Simple, 12011-12018
      Superficial, 12011-12018
    Lower
      Arm, Arms
        Complex, 13120-13122
        Intermediate, 12031-12037
        Layered, 12031-12037
        Simple, 12001-12007
        Superficial, 12001-12007
      Extremity, Extremities
        Intermediate, 12031-12037
        Layered, 12031-12037
        Simple, 12001-12007
        Superficial, 12001-12007
      Leg, Legs
        Complex, 13120-13122
        Intermediate, 12031-12037
        Layered, 12031-12037
        Simple, 12001-12007
        Superficial, 12001-12007
    Mouth
      Complex, 13131-13133
    Mucous Membrane, Mucous Membranes
      Intermediate, 12051-12057
      Layered, 12051-12057
      Simple, 12011-12018
      Superficial, 12011-12018
    Neck
      Complex, 13131-13133
      Intermediate, 12041-12047
      Layered, 12041-12047
      Simple, 12001-12007
      Superficial, 12001-12007
    Nose
      Complex, 13150-13153
      Intermediate, 12051-12057
      Layered, 12051-12057
      Simple, 12011-12018
      Superficial, 12011-12018
    Palm, Palms
      Complex, 13131-13133
      Intermediate, 12041-12047
      Layered, 12041-12047
      Simple, 12001-12007
      Superficial, 12001-12007
    Scalp
      Complex, 13120-13122
      Intermediate, 12031-12037
      Layered, 12031-12037
      Simple, 12001-12007
      Superficial, 12001-12007
    Toe, Toes
      Complex, 13131-13133
      Intermediate, 12041-12047
      Layered, 12041-12047
      Simple, 12001-12007
      Superficial, 12001-12007
    Trunk
      Complex, 13100-13102
      Intermediate, 12031-12037
      Layered, 12031-12037
      Simple, 12001-12007
      Superficial, 12001-12007

Closure — *continued*
  Skin — *continued*
    Upper
      Arm, Arms
        Complex, 13120-13122
        Intermediate, 12031-12037
        Layered, 12031-12037
        Simple, 12001-12007
        Superficial, 12001-12007
      Extremity
        Intermediate, 12031-12037
        Layered, 12031-12037
        Simple, 12001-12007
        Superficial, 12001-12007
      Leg, Legs
        Complex, 13120-13122
        Intermediate, 12031-12037
        Layered, 12031-12037
        Simple, 12001-12007
        Superficial, 12001-12007
    Sternotomy, 21750
    Ventricular Tunnel, 33722
Closure, Atrial Septal Defect
  See Heart, Repair, Atrial Septum
Closure, Cranial Sutures, Premature
  See Craniosynostosis
Closure, Fistula, Vesicouterine
  See Fistula, Vesicouterine, Closure
Closure, Meningocele, Spinal
  See Meningocele Repair
Closure of Esophagostomy
  See Esophagostomy, Closure
Closure of Gastrostomy
  See Gastrostomy, Closure
Closure, Vagina
  See Vagina, Closure
Clot, 34001-34490, 35875, 35876, 50230
Clot Lysis Time, 85175
Clot Retraction, 85170
Clotting Disorder
  See Coagulopathy
Clotting Factor, 85210-85293
Clotting Inhibitors, 85300-85305, 85307
Clotting Operation
  Excision, Nail Fold, 11765
Clotting Test
  Protein C, 85303, 85307
  Protein S, 85306
Clotting Time
  See Coagulation
Cloverleaf Skull
  Suture of, 61558
Clubfoot Cast, 29450
  Wedging, 29750
CMG (Cystometrogram), 51725, 51726
CMRI (Cardiac Magnetic Resonance Imaging)
  Complete Study, 75554
  Limited Study, 75555
  Velocity Flow Mapping, 75556
CMV (Cytomegalovirus)
  Antibody, 86644, 86645
  Antigen Detection
    Enzyme Immunoassay, 87332
    Nucleic Acid, 87495-87497
CNP, 94662
CNPB (Continuous Negative Pressure Breathing), 94662

Index

Closure — CNPB (Continuous Negative Pressure Breathing)

CO2
  See Carbon Dioxide
Coagulation
  Factor I, 85384, 85385
  Factor II, 85210
  Factor III, 85730, 85732
  Factor IV, 82310
  Factor IX, 85250
  Factor V, 85220
  Factor VII, 85230
  Factor VIII, 85244, 85247
  Factor X, 85260
  Factor XI, 85270
  Factor XII, 85280
  Factor XIII, 85290, 85291
  Time, 85345-85348
  Unlisted Services and Procedures, 85999
Coagulin
  See Thromboplastin
Coagulopathy, 85390
  Assay, 85130
Cocaine
  Blood or Urine, 82520
  Screen, 82486
Coccidioides
  Antibody, 86635
Coccidioidin Test
  Streptokinase, Antibody, 86590
Coccidioidomycosis
  Skin Test, 86490
Coccygeal Spine Fracture
  See Coccyx, Fracture
Coccygectomy, 15920, 15922, 27080
Coccyx
  Excision, 27080
  Fracture
    Closed Treatment, 27200
    Open Treatment, 27202
  Pressure Ulcer, 15920, 15922
  Tumor
    Excision, 49215
  X-ray, 72220
Cochlear Device
  Insertion, 69930
  Programming, 92601-92604
Codeine
  Alkaloid Screening, 82101
Codeine Screen, 82486
Co-Factor I, Heparin
  See Antithrombin III
Cofactor Protein S
  See Protein S
Coffey Operation
  Uterus, Repair, Suspension, 58400
    with Presacral Sympathectomy, 58410
Cognitive Function Tests, 96116
  See Neurology, Diagnostic
Cognitive Skills Development, 97532
  See Physical Medicine/Therapy/Occupational
    Therapy
COHB, 82375, 82376
Cold Agglutinin, 86156, 86157
Cold Pack Treatment, 97010
Cold Preservation
  See Cryopreservation
Cold Therapies
  See Cryotherapy

Colectomy
  Partial, 44140
    with
      Anastomosis, 44140
        Laparoscopic, 44204, 44207, 44208
      Coloproctostomy, 44145, 44146
      Colostomy, 44141-44144
        Laparoscopic, 44206, 44208
      Ileocolostomy
        Laparoscopic, 44205
      Ileostomy, 44144
      Ileum Removal, 44160
      Transcanal Approach, 44147
  Total
    Laparoscopic
      with
        Proctectomy and Ileostomy, 44211,
          44212
      without
        Proctectomy, 44210
    Open
      with
        Anastomosis, 44152
        Ileal Reservoir, 44153
        Ileostomy, 44150, 44151
        Proctectomy, 44155, 44156, 45121
Collagen Cross Links, 82523
Collagen Injection, 11950-11954
Collar Bone
  Craterization, 23180
  Cyst
    Excision, 23140
      with
        Allograft, 23146
        Autograft, 23145
  Diaphysectomy, 23180
  Dislocation
    with Manipulation, 23540
    Acromioclavicular Joint
      Closed Treatment, 23540, 23545
      Open Treatment, 23550, 23552
    Sternoclavicular Joint
      Closed Treatment, 23520, 23525
      Open Treatment, 23530, 23532
  Excision
    Partial, 23120, 23180
    Total, 23125
  Fracture
    Closed Treatment
      with Manipulation, 23505
      without Manipulation, 23500
    Open Treatment, 23515
  Osteotomy, 23480, 23485
  Pinning, Wiring, Etc., 23490
  Prophylactic Treatment, 23490
  Repair Osteotomy, 23480, 23485
  Saucerization, 23180
  Sequestrectomy, 23170
  Tumor
    Excision, 23140
      with Allograft, 23146
      with Autograft, 23145
    Radical Resection, 23200
  X-ray, 73000
Collateral Ligament
  Ankle
    Repair, 27695-27698
  Interphalangeal Joint, 26545
  Knee Joint
    Repair, 27409
  Knee Repair, 27405

Colonoscopy — *continued*
  via Stoma, 44388-44390
    Biopsy, 44393
    Destruction
      of Lesion, 44393
      of Tumor, 44393
    Exploration, 44388
    Hemorrhage, 44391
    Placement
      Stent, 44397
    Removal
      Foreign Body, 44390
      Polyp, 44392, 44394
      Tumor, 44392, 44394
  Virtual, 0066T-0067T
Colon-Sigmoid
  See Colon
  Biopsy
    Endoscopy, 45331
  Endoscopy
    Ablation
      Polyp, 45339
      Tumor, 45339
    Biopsy, 45331
    Dilation, 45340
    Exploration, 45330, 45335
    Hemorrhage, 45334
    Needle Biopsy, 45342
    Placement
      Stent, 45327, 45345
    Removal
      Foreign Body, 45332
      Polyp, 45333, 45338
      Tumor, 45333, 45338
    Ultrasound, 45341, 45342
    Volvulus, 45337
  Exploration
    Endoscopy, 45330, 45335
  Hemorrhage
    Endoscopy, 45334
  Needle Biopsy
    Endoscopy, 45342
  Removal
    Foreign Body, 45332
  Repair
    Volvulus
      Endoscopy, 45337
  Ultrasound
    Endoscopy, 45341, 45342
Colorrhaphy, 44604
Color Vision Examination, 92283
Colostomy, 44320, 45563
  Abdominal
    Establishment, 50810
  Delayed Opening, 44799
  Home Visit, 99505
  Intestine, Large
    with Suture, 44605
  Perineal
    Establishment, 50810
  Revision, 44340
    Paracolostomy Hernia, 44345, 44346
Colotomy, 44025
Colpectomy
  with Hysterectomy, 58275
    with Repair of Enterocele, 58280
  Partial, 57106
  Total, 57110
Colpoceliocentesis
  See Colpocentesis

Colpocentesis, 57020
Colpocleisis, 57120
Colpocleisis Complete
  See Vagina, Closure
Colpohysterectomies
  See Excision, Uterus, Vaginal
Colpoperineorrhaphy, 57210
Colpopexy, 57280
  Extra-peritoneal, 57282
  Intraperitoneal, 57283
  Laparoscopic, 57425
Colpoplasty
  See Repair, Vagina
Colporrhaphy
  Anterior, 57240, 57289
    with Insertion of Mesh, 57267
    with Insertion of Prosthesis, 57267
  Anteroposterior, 57260, 57265
    with Enterocele Repair, 57265
    with Insertion of Mesh, 57267
    with Insertion of Prosthesis, 57267
  Nonobstetrical, 57200
  Posterior, 57250
Colposcopy
  Biopsy, 56821, 57421, 57454-57455, 57460
    Endometrial, 58110
  Cervix, 57421, 57452-57461
  Exploration, 57452
  Loop Electrode Biopsy, 57460
  Loop Electrode Conization, 57461
  Perineum, 99170
  Vagina, 57420-57421
  Vulva, 56820
    Biopsy, 56821
Colpotomy
  Drainage
    Abscess, 57010
  Exploration, 57000
Colpo-Urethrocystopexy, 58152, 58267, 58293
  Marshall-Marchetti-Krantz procedure, 58152,
    58267, 58293
  Pereyra Procedure, 58267, 58293
Colprosterone
  See Progesterone
CO₂
  See Carbon Dioxide
Columna Vertebralis
  See Spine
Column Chromatography/Mass Spectrometry,
  82541-82544
Combined Heart-Lung Transplantation
  See Transplantation, Heart-Lung
Combined Right and Left Heart Cardiac
  Catheterization
  See Cardiac Catheterization, Combined Left and
    Right Heart
Combined Vaccine, 90710
Comedones
  Opening or Removal of (Incision and Drainage)
    Acne Surgery, 10040
Commando-Type Procedure, 41155
Commissurotomy
  Right Ventricular, 33476, 33478
Common Sensory Nerve
  Repair, Suture, 64834
Common Truncus
  See Truncus, Arteriosus

Concentration Test for Renal Function
Water Load Test, 89235
Concentric Procedure, 28296
Concha Bullosa Resection
with Nasal/Sinus Endoscopy, 31240
Conchae Nasale
See Nasal Turbinate
Conduction, Nerve
See Nerve Conduction
Conduit, Ileal
See Ileal Conduit
Condyle
Humerus
Fracture
Closed Treatment, 24576, 24577
Open Treatment, 24579
Percutaneous, 24582
Metatarsal
Excision, 28288
Phalanges
Toe
Excision, 28126
Condylectomy
with Skull Base Surgery, 61596, 61597
Temporomandibular Joint, 21050
Condyle, Mandibular
See Mandibular Condyle
Condyloma
Destruction
Anal, 46900-46924
Penis, 54050-54065
Vagina, 57061, 57065
Vulva, 56501, 56515
Conference
Medical
with Interdisciplinary Team, 99361-99373
Telephone
Brief, 99371
Complex, 99373
Intermediate, 99372
Confirmation
Drug, 80102
Congenital Arteriovenous Malformation
See Arteriovenous Malformation
Congenital Elevation of Scapula
See Sprengal's Deformity
Congenital Heart Septum Defect
See Septal Defect
Congenital Kidney Abnormality
Nephrolithotomy, 50070
Pyeloplasty, 50405
Pyelotomy, 50135
Congenital Laryngocele
See Laryngocele
Congenital Vascular Anomaly
See Vascular Malformation
Conisation
See Cervix, Conization
Conization
Cervix, 57461, 57520, 57522
Conjoint Psychotherapy, 90847
Conjunctiva
Biopsy, 68100
Cyst
Incision and Drainage, 68020
Fistulize for Drainage
with Tube, 68750
without Tube, 68745

Conjunctiva — continued
Insertion Stent, 68750
Lesion
Destruction, 68135
Excision, 68110-68130
with Adjacent Sclera, 68130
over 1 cm, 68115
Reconstruction, 68320-68335
with Flap
Bridge or Partial, 68360
Total, 68362
Symblepharon
with Graft, 68335
without Graft, 68330
Total, 68362
Repair
Symblepharon
with Graft, 68335
without Graft, 68330
Division, 68340
Wound
Direct Closure, 65270
Mobilization and Rearrangement, 65272, 65273
Unlisted Services and Procedure, 68399
Conjunctivoccystorhinostomy
See Conjunctivorhinostomy
Conjunctivodacryocystostomy
See Conjunctivorhinostomy
Conjunctivoplasty, 68320-68330
with Extensive Rearrangement, 68320
with Graft, 68320
Buccal Mucous Membrane, 68325
Reconstruction Cu-de-Sac
with Extensive Rearrangement, 68326
with Graft, 68326
Buccal Mucous Membrane, 68328
Conjunctivorhinostomy
with Tube, 68750
without Tube, 68745
Conjunctivo-Tarso-Levator
Resection, 67908
Conjunctivo-Tarso-Muller Resection, 67908
Conscious Sedation
See Sedation
Construction
Finger
Toe to Hand Transfer, 26551-26556
Neobladder, 51596
Vagina
with Graft, 57292
without Graft, 57291
Consultation
See Second Opinion; Third Opinion
Clinical Pathology, 80500, 80502
Initial Inpatient
New or Established Patient, 99251-99255
Office and/or Other Outpatient
New or Established Patient, 99241-99245
Pathology
During Surgery, 88333-88334
Psychiatric, with Family, 90887
Radiation Therapy
Radiation Physics, 77336, 77370
Surgical Pathology, 88321-88325
Intraoperation, 88329-88332
X-ray, 76140
Consumption Test, Antiglobulin
See Coombs Test

Coronary Artery Bypass Graft — *continued*
(CABG) Reoperation, 33530
Venous, 33510-33516
Coronary Endarterectomy, 33572
Coroner's Exam, 88045
Coronoidectomy
Temporomandibular Joint, 21070
Corpectomy, 63101-63103
Corpora Cavernosa
Corpus Spongiosum Shunt, 54430
Glans Penis Fistulization, 54435
Injection, 54235
Irrigation
Priapism, 54220
Saphenous Vein Shunt, 54420
X-ray with Contrast, 74445
Corpora Cavernosa, Plastic Induraton
See Peyronie Disease
Corpora Cavernosography, 74445
Corpus Callosum
Transection, 61541
Corpus Uteri, 58100-58285
Corpus Vertebrae (Vertebrale)
See Vertebral Body
Correction of Cleft Palate
See Cleft Palate, Repair
Correction of Lid Retraction
See Repair, Eyelid, Retraction
Correction of Malrotation of Duodenum
See Ladd Procedure
Correction of Ureteropelvic Junction
See Pyeloplasty
Cortex Decortication, Cerebral
See Decortication
Cortical Mapping
Transection by Electric Stimulation, 95961, 95962
Corticoids
See Corticosteroids
Corticoliberin
See Corticotropic Releasing Hormone (CRH)
Corticosteroid Binding Protein, 84449
Corticosteroids
Blood, 83491
Urine, 83491
Corticosterone
Blood or Urine, 82528
Corticotropic Releasing Hormone (CRH), 80412
Cortisol, 80400-80406, 80418, 80420, 80436, 82530
Stimulation Panel, 80412
Total, 82533
Cortisol Binding Globulin, 84449
Costectomy
See Resection, Ribs
Costen Syndrome
See Temporomandibular
Costotransversectomy, 21610
Cothromboplastin
See Proconvertin
Cotte Operation, 58400, 58410
Repair, Uterus, Suspension, 58400, 58410
Cotting Operation
Excision, Nail Fold, 11765
Cotton (Bohler) Procedure, 28405
Cotton Scoop Procedure, 28118

Counseling and/or Risk Factor Reduction Intervention - Preventive Medicine, Individual Counseling
See Preventive Medicine, Counseling and/or Risk Factor Reduction Intervention, Individual Counseling
Counseling, Preventive
Group, 99411, 99412
Individual, 99401-99404
Other, 99420, 99429
Count, Blood Cell
See Blood Cell Count
Count, Blood Platelet
See Blood, Platelet, Count
Count, Cell
See Cell Count
Count, Complete Blood
See Complete Blood Count (CBC)
Counterimmunoelectrophoresis, 86185
Counters, Cell
See Cell Count
Countershock, Electric
See Cardioversion
Count, Erythrocyte
See Red Blood Cell (RBC), Count
Count, Leukocyte
See White Blood Cell, Count
Count, Reticulocyte
See Reticulocyte, Count
Coventry Tibial Wedge Osteotomy
See Osteotomy, Tibia
Cowper's Gland
Excision, 53250
Coxa
See Hip
Coxiella Brunetii
Antibody, 86638
Coxsackie
Antibody, 86658
CPAP (Continuous Positive Airway Pressure), 94660
CPB, 32852, 32854, 33496, 33503-33505, 33510-33523, 33533-33536
C-Peptide, 80432, 84681
CPK
Blood, 82550, 82552
CPR (Cardiopulmonary Resuscitation), 92950
CR, 82565-82575
Cranial Bone
Halo
for Thin Skull Osteology, 20664
Reconstruction
Extracranial, 21181-21184
Tumor
Excision, 61563, 61564
Cranial Halo, 20661
Cranial Nerve
Avulsion, 64732-64760, 64771
Decompression, 61458, 64716
Implantation
Electrode, 64553, 64573
Incision, 64732-64752, 64760, 65771
Injection
Anesthetic, 64400-64408, 64412
Neurolytic, 64600-64610
Insertion
Electrode, 64553, 64573

Craterization — *continued*
- Humerus, 23184, 24140
- Ileum, 27070, 27071
- Metacarpal, 26230
- Metatarsal, 28122
- Olecranon Process, 24147
- Phalanges
  - Finger, 26235, 26236
  - Toe, 28124
- Pubis, 27070, 27071
- Radius, 24145, 25151
- Scapula, 23182
- Talus, 28120
- Tarsal, 28122
- Tibia, 27360, 27640
- Ulna, 24147, 25150

C-Reactive Protein, 86140, 86141

Creatine, 82553, 82554
- Blood or Urine, 82540

Creatine Kinase (Total), 82550

Creatine Phosphokinase
- Blood, 82552
- Total, 82550

Creatinine
- Blood, 82565
- Clearance, 82575
- Other Source, 82570
- Urine, 82570, 82575

Creation
- Arteriovenous
  - Fistula/Autogenous Graft, 36825
- Colonic Reservoir, 45119
- Complete Heart Block, 93650
- Cutaneoperitoneal Fistula, 49999
- Defect, 40720
- Ileal Reservoir, 44153, 45113
- Lesion, 61790, 63600
  - Gasserian Ganglion, 61790
  - Spinal Cord, 63600
  - Trigeminal Tract, 61791
- Mucofistula, 44144
- Pericardial Window, 32659
- Recipient Site, 15000
- Shunt
  - Cerebrospinal Fluid, 62200
  - Subarachnoid
    - Lumbar-Peritoneal, 63740
  - Subarachnoid-Subdural, 62190
  - Ventriculo, 62220
- Sigmoid Bladder, 50810
- Speech Prosthesis, 31611
- Stoma
  - Bladder, 51980
  - Kidney, 50395
  - Renal Pelvis, 50395
  - Tympanic Membrane, 69433, 69436
  - Ureter, 50860
- Ventral Hernia, 39503

CRF
- *See* Corticotropic Releasing Hormone (CRH)

CRH (Corticotropic Releasing Hormone), 80412

Cricoid Cartilage Split, 31587

Cricothyroid Membrane
- Incision, 31605

Cristobalite
- *See* Silica

CRIT, 85013

Critical Care Services, 99289-99292
- *See* Emergency Department Services; Prolonged Attendance
- Evaluation and Management, 99291-99292
- Gastric Intubation, 91105
- Interfacility Transport, 99289, 99290
- Ipecac Administration for Poison, 99175
- Neonatal
  - Initial, 99295
  - Low Birth Weight Infant, 99298-99299
  - Subsequent, 99296
- Pediatric
  - Initial, 99293
  - Interfacility Transport, 99289, 99290
  - Subsequent, 99294, 99299

Cross Finger Flap, 15574

Crossmatch, 86920-86922

Crossmatching, Tissue
- *See* Tissue Typing

CRP, 86140

Cruciate Ligament
- Arthroscopic Repair, 29888, 29889
- Repair, 27407, 27409
  - Knee with Collateral Ligament, 27409

Cryoablation
- *See* Cryosurgery

Cryofibrinogen, 82585

Cryoglobulin, 82595

Cryopreservation
- Cells, 38207-38208, 88240, 88241
- Embryo, 89258
- Freezing and Storage, 38207, 88240
- Oocyte, 0059T
- Ovarian Tissue, 0058T
- Sperm, 89259
- Testes, 89335
  - Embryo, 89352
  - Oocytes, 89353
  - Reproductive Tissue, 89354
  - Sperm, 89356
  - Thawing

Cryosurgery, 17000-17286, 47371, 47381
- *See* Destruction
- Cervix, 57511
- Labyrinthotomy, 69801
- Lesion
  - Anus, 46916, 46924
  - Mouth, 40820
  - Penis, 54056, 54065
  - Skin
    - Benign, 17000-17004
    - Malignant, 17260-17286
    - Pre Malignant, 17000-17004
- Vagina, 57061-57065
- Vulva, 56501-56515
- Warts, flat, 17110, 17111

Cryotherapy
- Acne, 17340
- Destruction
  - Ciliary body, 66720
- Lesion
  - Cornea, 65450
  - Retina, 67208, 67227
- Retinal Detachment
  - Prophylaxis, 67141
  - Repair, 67101
- Trichiasis
  - Correction, 67825

Cryptectomy, 46210, 46211

Cryptococcus
Antibody, 86641
Antigen Detection
Enzyme Immunoassay, 87327
Cryptococcus NeoFormans
Antigen Detection
Enzyme Immunoassay, 87327
Cryptorchism
See Testis, Undescended
Cryptosporidium
Antigen Detection
Direct Fluorescent Antibody, 87272
Enzyme Immunoassay, 87328
Crystal Identification
Any Body Fluid, 89060
CS, 99143-99150
C-Section, 59510-59515, 59618-59622
See also Cesarean Delivery
CSF, 86325, 89050, 89051
CST, 59020
CTS, 29848, 64721
CT Scan
with Contrast
Abdomen, 74160
Arm, 73201
Brain, 70460
Ear, 70481
Face, 70487
Head, 70460
Leg, 73701
Maxilla, 70487
Neck, 70491
Orbit, 70481
Pelvis, 72193
Sella Turcica, 70481
Spine
Cervical, 72126
Lumbar, 72132
Thoracic, 72129
Thorax, 71260
without Contrast
Abdomen, 74150
Arm, 73200
Brain, 70450
Ear, 70480
Face, 70486
Head, 70450
Leg, 73700
Maxilla, 70486
Neck, 70490
Orbit, 70480
Pelvis, 72192
Sella Turcica, 70480
Spine
Cervical, 72125
Lumbar, 72131
Thoracic, 72128
Thorax, 71250
without Contrast, followed by Contrast
Abdomen, 74170, 74175, 75635
Arm, 73202, 73206, 73220, 73223
Brain, 70470, 70496
Chest, 71275
Ear, 70482
Face, 70488
Head, 70470, 70496
Leg, 73702, 73706, 75635
Maxilla, 70488
Neck, 70492, 70498
Orbit, 70482

CT Scan — *continued*
without Contrast, followed by Contrast —
continued
Pelvis, 72191, 72194
Sella Turcica, 70482
Spine
Cervical, 72127
Lumbar, 72133
Thoracic, 72130
Thorax, 71270, 71275
3D Rendering, 76376-76377
Bone
Density Study, 76070
Colon
Diagnostic, 0067T
Screening, 0066T
Drainage, 75989
Follow-up Study, 76380
Guidance
Localization, 76355
Needle Biopsy, 76360
Radiation Therapy, 76370
Tissue Ablation, 76362
Vertebroplasty, 76013
CT Scan, Radionuclide
See Emission Computerized Tomography
Cuff, Rotator
See Rotator Cuff
Culdocentesis, 57020
Culdoscopy, 57452
Culdotomy, 57000
Culture
Acid Fast Bacilli, 87116
Amniotic Fluid
Chromosome Analysis, 88235
Bacteria
Additional Methods, 87077
Aerobic, 87040-87070
Anaerobic, 87073-87076
Blood, 87040
Feces, 87045, 87046
Other, 87070-87073
Screening, 87081
Urine, 87086, 87088
Bone Marrow
Chromosome Analysis, 88237
Chlamydia, 87110
Chorionic Villus
Chromosome Analysis, 88235
Fertilized Oocyte
for In Vitro Fertilization, 89250
with Co-Culture of Embryo, 89251
Assisted Microtechnique, 89280, 89281
Fungus
Blood, 87103
Hair, 87101
Identification, 87106
Nail, 87101
Other, 87102
Skin, 87101
Lymphocyte
Chromosome Analysis, 88230
Mold, 87107
Mycobacteria, 87116-87118
Mycoplasma, 87109
Oocyte/Embryo
Extended Culture, 89272
for In Vitro Fertilization, 89250
with Co-Culture of Embryo, 89251
Pathogen
by Kit, 87084

Index

Cryptococcus — Culture

Culture — *continued*
Skin
Chromosome Analysis, 88233
Tissue
Toxin
Antitoxin, 87230
Toxin Virus, 87252, 87253
Tubercle Bacilli, 87116
Typing, 87140-87158
Unlisted Services and Procedures, 87999
Yeast, 87106
Curettage
See Dilation and Curettage
Cervix
Endocervical, 57454, 57456, 57505
Cornea, 65435, 65436
Chelating Agent, 65436
HydatidiForm Mole, 59870
Postpartum, 59160
Curettage, Uterus
See Uterus, Curettage
Curettement
Skin Lesion, 11055-11057, 17004, 17110, 17270, 17280
Curietherapy
See Brachytherapy
Custodial Care
See Domiciliary Services; Nursing Facility Services
Cutaneolipectomy
See Lipectomy
Cutaneous Electrostimulation, Analgesic
See Application, Neurostimulation
Cutaneous Tag
See Skin, Tags
Cutaneous Tissue
See Integumentary System
Cutaneous-Vesicostomy
See Vesicostomy, Cutaneous
CVS, 59015
CXR, 71010-71035, 71090
Cyanide
Blood, 82600
Tissue, 82600
Cyanocobalamin, 82607, 82608
Cyclic AMP, 82030
Cyclic Citrullinated Peptide (CCP), Antibody, 86200
Cyclic GMP, 83008
Cyclic Somatostatin
See Somatostatin
Cyclocryotherapy
See Cryotherapy, Destruction, Ciliary Body
Cyclodialysis
Destruction
Ciliary Body, 66740
Cyclophotocoagulation
Destruction
Ciliary Body, 66710, 66711
Cyclosporine
Assay, 80158
Cyst
Abdomen
Destruction
Excision, 49200, 49201
Ankle
Capsule, 27630
Tendon Sheath, 27630

Cyst — *continued*
Bartholin's Gland
Excision, 56740
Repair, 56440
Bile Duct
Excision, 47715, 47716
Bladder
Excision, 51500
Bone
Drainage, 20615
Injection, 20615
Brain
Drainage, 61150, 61151, 61156, 62161, 62162
Excision, 61516, 61524, 62162
Branchial Cleft
Excision, 42810, 42815
Breast
Incision and Drainage, 19020
Puncture Aspiration, 19000, 19001
Calcaneus, 28100-28103
Carpal, 25130-25136
Choledochal
Excision, 47715, 47716
Ciliary Body
Destruction, 66770
Clavicle
Excision, 23140-23146
Conjunctiva, 68020
Dermoid
Nose
Excision, 30124, 30125
Drainage
Contrast Injection, 49424
with X-ray, 76080
Excision
Cheekbone, 21030
Clavicle, 23140
with Allograft, 23146
with Autograft, 23145
Femur, 27355, 27357, 27358
Ganglion
See Ganglion
Humerus
with Allograft, 23156
with Autograft, 23155
Hydatid
See Echinococcosis
Lymphatic
See Lymphocele
Maxilla, 21030
Mediastinum, 32662
Olecranon Process
with Allograft, 24126
with Autograft, 24125
Pericardial, 32661
Pilonidal, 11770-11772
Radius
with Allograft, 24126
with Autograft, 24125
Scapula, 23140
with Allograft, 23146
with Autograft, 23145
Ulna
with Allograft, 24126
with Autograft, 24125
Zygoma, 21030
Facial Bones
Excision, 21030
Femur
Excision, 27065-27067, 27355-27358
Fibula, 27635-27638

Cyst — *continued*
  Ganglion
    Aspiration/Injection, 20612
  Gums
    Incision and Drainage, 41800
  Hip, 27065-27067
  Humerus
    Excision, 23150-23156, 24110
      with Allograft, 24116
      with Autograft, 24115
  Ileum, 27065-27067
  Incision and Drainage, 10060, 10061
    Pilonidal, 10080, 10081
    Puncture Aspiration, 10160
  Iris
    Destruction, 66770
  Kidney
    Ablation, 50541
    Aspiration, 50390
    Excision, 50280, 50290
    Injection, 50390
    X-ray, 74470
  Knee
    Baker's, 27345
    Excision, 27347
  Leg, Lower
    Capsule, 27630
    Tendon Sheath, 27630
  Liver
    Incision and Drainage
      Open, 47010
      Percutaneous, 47011
    Repair, 47300
  Lung
    Incision and Drainage, 32200
    Removal, 32140
  Lymph Node
    Axillary
    Cervical
      Excision, 38550, 38555
  Mandible
    Excision, 21040, 21046, 21047
  Mediastinal
    Excision, 39200
  Metacarpal, 26200, 26205
  Metatarsal, 28104-28107
  Mouth, 41005-41009, 41015-41018
    Incision and Drainage, 40800, 40801
  Mullerian Duct
    Excision, 55680
  Nose
    Excision, 30124, 30125
  Olecranon, 24120
  Opening or Removal of (Incision and Drainage)
    Acne Surgery, 10040
  Ovarian
    Excision, 58925
    Incision and Drainage, 58800, 58805
  Pancreas, 48500
    Anastomosis, 48520, 48540
    Excision, 48120
  Pelvis
    Aspiration, 50390
    Injection, 50390
  Pericardial
    Excision, 33050
  Phalanges
    Finger, 26210, 26215
    Toe, 28108
  Pilonidal
    Excision, 11770-11772
    Incision and Drainage, 10080, 10081

Cyst — *continued*
  Pubis, 27065-27067
  Radius
    Excision, 24120, 25120-25126
  Rathke's Pouch
    See Craniopharyngioma
  Removal
    Skin, 10040
  Retroperitoneum
    Destruction, 49200, 49201
    Excision, 49200, 49201
  Salivary Gland
    Drainage, 42409
    Excision, 42408
  Scapula
    Excision, 23140-23146
  Seminal Vesicles
    Excision, 55680
  Skin
    Puncture Aspiration, 10160
  Spinal Cord
    Aspiration, 62268
    Incision and Drainage, 63172, 63173
  Sublingual Gland
    Drainage, 42409
    Excision, 42408
  Talus, 28100-28103
  Tarsal, 28104-28107
  Thyroglossal Duct
    Excision, 60280, 60281
    Incision and Drainage, 60000
  Thyroid Gland
    Aspiration, 60001
    Excision, 60200
    Injection, 60001
  Tibia
    Excision, 27635-27638
  Tongue
    Incision and Drainage, 41000-41006, 41015
  Ulna, 24120, 25120-25126
  Urachal
    Bladder
      Excision, 51500
  Vaginal
    Excision, 57135
  Wrist, 25130-25136
    Excision, 25111, 25112
  Zygoma
    Excision, 21030

Cystatins, Kininogen
  See Kininogen

Cystectomy
  Complete, 51570
    with Bilateral Pelvic Lymphadenectomy, 51575, 51585, 51595
    with Continent Diversion, 51596
    with Ureteroileal Conduit, 51590
    with Ureterosigmoidostomy, 51580
  Ovarian
    Laparoscopic, 58661
    Open, 58925
  Partial, 51550
    Complicated, 51555
    Reimplantation of Ureters, 51565
    Simple, 51550

Cystic Hygroma
  See Hygroma

Cystine
  Urine, 82615

Cystitis
  Interstitial, 52260, 52265

Cystography, 74430
  Injection, 52281
    Radiologic, 51600
Cystolithotomy, 51050
Cystometrogram, 51725, 51726
Cystoplasty, 51800
Cystorrhaphy, 51860, 51865
Cystoscopy, 52000
Cystoscopy, with Biopsy
  See Biopsy, Bladder, Cystourethroscopy
Cystostomy
  with Fulgration, 51020
  with Insertion
    Radioactive Material, 51020
  with Urethrectomy
    Female, 53210
    Male, 53215
  Change Tube, 51705, 51710
  Closure, 51880
  Home Visit, 99505
Cystotomy
  with Calculus Basket Extraction, 51065
  with Destruction Intravesical Lesion, 51030
  with Drainage, 51040
  with Fulgration, 51020
  with Insertion
    Radioactive Material, 51020
    Urethral Catheter, 51045
  with Removal Calculus, 51050, 51065
  Excision
    Bladder Diverticulum, 51525
    Bladder Tumor, 51530
    Diverticulum, 51525
    Repair of Ureterocele, 51535
    Vesical Neck, 51520
  Repair Ureterocele, 51535
Cystourethroplasty, 51800, 51820
Cystourethroscopy, 52000, 52351, 52601,
    52647, 52648, 53500
  with Direct Vision Internal Urethrotomy, 52276
  with Ejaculatory Duct Catheterization, 52010
  with Fulgration, 52214, 52354
    Lesion, 52224
    Tumor, 52234-52240
  with Internal Urethrotomy
    Female, 52270
    Male, 52275
  with Steroid Injection, 52283
  with Urethral Catheterization, 52005
  with Urethral Meatotomy, 52290, 52300, 52305
  Biopsy, 52204, 52354
    Brush, 52007
  Calibration and/or Dilation Urethral Stricture
    or Stenosis, 52281
  Catheterization
    Ejaculatory Duct, 52010
    Ureteral, 52005
  Destruction
    Lesion, 52400
  Dilation
    Bladder, 52260, 52265
    Intra-Renal Stricture, 52343, 52346
    Ureter, 52341, 52342, 52344, 52345
    Urethra, 52281
  Evacuation
    Clot, 52001
  Female Urethral Syndrome, 52285
  Incision
    Ejaculatory Duct, 52402
  Injection of Implant Material, 52327

Cystourethroscopy — *continued*
  Insertion
    Indwelling Urethral Stent, 50947, 52332
    Radioactive Substance, 52250
    Ureteral Guide Wire, 52334
    Urethral Stent, 52282
  Lithotripsy, 52353
  Manipulation of Ureteral Calculus, 52330
  Meatotomy
    Urethral, 52290-52305
  Removal
    Calculus, 52310, 52315, 52320, 52325,
      52352
    Foreign Body, 52310, 52315
    Urethral Stent, 52310, 52315
  Resection
    Ejaculatory Duct, 52402
    External Sphincter, 52277
    Tumor, 52355
  Urethral Syndrome, 52285
  Vasectomy
    Transurethral, 52402
  Vasotomy
    Transurethral, 52402
Cyst, Ovary
  See Ovary, Cyst
Cytochrome, Reductase, Lactic
  See Lactic Dehydrogenase
Cytogenetic Study
  Molecular DNA Probe, 88271-88275, 88291,
    88365
  Unlisted Services and Procedures, 88299
Cytomegalovirus
  Antibody, 86644, 86645
  Antigen Detection
    Direct Fluorescence, 87271
    Enzyme Immunoassay, 87332
    Nucleic Acid, 87495-87497
Cytometries, Flow
  See Flow Cytometry
Cytopathology
  Cervical or Vaginal
    Requiring Interpretation by Physician, 88141
    Thin Layer Prep, 88142-88143, 88174-
      88175
  Concentration Technique, 88108
  Evaluation, 88172
  Fluids, Washings, Brushings, 88104-88108
  Forensic, 88125
  Other Source, 88160-88162
  Smears
    Cervical or Vaginal, 88141-88155, 88164-
      88167, 88174-88175
    Other Source, 88160-88162
  Unlisted Services and Procedures, 88199
Cytoscopy
  See Bladder, Endoscopy
Cytotoxic Screen
  Lymphocyte, 86805, 86806
  Percent Reactive Antibody (PRA), 86807, 86808
  Serum Antibodies, 86807, 86808

D

Discharge Instruction
Discharge Instructions
D2, Vitamin
  See Calciferol
Dacrocystogram
  See Dacrocystography

Dacryoadenectomy
Partial, 68505
Total, 68500

Dacryocystectomy, 68520

Dacryocystography, 68850, 70170
with Nuclear Imaging, 78660

Dacryocystorhinostomy, 68720
Total
with Nasal
Sinus Endoscopy, 31239

Dacryocystostomy, 68420

Daily Living Activities
See Activities of Daily Living

D&C Yellow No. 7
See Fluorescein

Damus-Kaye-Stansel Procedure, 33606

Dana Operation, 63185, 63190
Rhizotomy, 63185, 63190

D and C (Dilation and Curettage), 59840

D and E (Dilation and Evacuation), 59841-59851

Dandy Operation, 62200

Dark Adaptation Examination, 92284

Dark Field Examination, 87164, 87166

Darkroom Test, 92140

Darrach Procedure, 25240
See Excision, Ulna, Partial

Day Test, 82270

DCR, 31239, 68720

DDST, 96101-96103

Death, Brain
See Brain Death

Debridement
Brain, 62010
Burns, 16020-16030
Anesthesia, 01951-01953
Mastoid Cavity
Complex, 69222
Simple, 69220
Metatarsophalangeal Joint, 28289
Muscle
Infected, 11004-11006
Nails, 11720, 11721
Necrotizing Soft Tissue, 11004-11008
Nose
Endoscopic, 31237
Pancreatic Tissue, 48005
Skin, 11040-11041
with Open Fracture and/or Dislocation,
11010-11012
Eczematous, 11000, 11001
Full Thickness, 11041
Infected, 11000, 11001
Partial Thickness, 11040
Subcutaneous Tissue, 11042-11044
Infected, 11004-11006
Sternum, 21627
Wound
Non-Selective, 97602
Selective, 97597-97598

Debulking Procedure
Ovary
Pelvis, 58952-58954

Decapsulation
of Kidney, 53899

Decompression
with Nasal
Sinus Endoscopy
Optic Nerve, 31294
Orbit Wall, 31292, 31293
Arm, Lower, 24495, 25020-25025
Auditory Canal, Internal, 69960
Brainstem, 61575, 61576
Carpal Tunnel, 64721
Cauda Equina, 63011, 63017, 63047, 63048,
63056, 63057, 63087-63091
Cranial Nerves, 61458
Esophagogastric Varices, 37181
Facial Nerve, 61590
Intratemporal
Lateral to Geniculate Ganglion, 69720,
69740
Medial to Geniculate Ganglion, 69725,
69745
Total, 69955
Finger, 26035
Gasserian Ganglion
Sensory Root, 61450
Gill Type procedure, 63012
Hand, 26035, 26037
Intestines
Small, 44021
Jejunostomy
Laparoscopic, 44186
Leg
Fasciotomy, 27600-27602
Nerve, 64702-64727
Root, 63020-63048, 63055-63103
Nucleus of Disk
Lumbar, 62287
Optic Nerve, 67570
Orbit, 61330
Removal of Bone, 67414, 67445
Posterior Tibial Nerve, 28035
Skull, 61322-61323, 61340-61345
Spinal Cord, 63001-63017, 63045-63103
Anterolateral Approach, 63075-63091
Posterior Approach, 63001-63048
Cauda Equina, 63001-63017
Cervical, 63001, 63015, 63020, 63035,
63045, 63048
Gill Type Procedure, 63012
Lumbar, 63005, 63017, 63030, 63042,
63047, 63048
Sacral, 63011
Thoracic, 63003, 63016, 63046, 63048
Transpedicular or Costovertebral Approach,
63055-63066
Tarsal Tunnel Release, 28035
Volvulus, 45321, 45337
Wrist, 25020-25025

Decortication
Lung
with Parietal Pleurectomy, 32320
Endoscopic, 32651, 32652
Partial, 32225
Total, 32220

Decubiti
See Pressure Ulcer (Decubitus)

Decubitus Ulcers
See Debridement; Pressure Ulcer (Decubitus);
Skin Graft and Flap

Deetjen's Body
See Blood, Platelet

Defect, Coagulation
See Coagulopathy

Index

Defect, Heart Septal — Dermatology

Defect, Heart Septal
  See Septal Defect
Defect, Septal Closure, Atrial
  See Heart, Repair, Atrial Septum
Deferens, Ductus
  See Vas Deferens
Defibrillation
  See Cardioversion
Defibrillator, Heart
  See Pacemaker, Heart
  Evaluation and Testing, 93640-93642, 93741-93744
  Insertion, 33240
    Pads, 33245, 33246
  Insertion Single/Dual Chamber
    Electrodes, 33216, 33217, 33224-33225, 33245-33249
    Pulse Generator, 33240, 33246
    Removal, 33243, 33244
      Pulse Generator Only, 33241
  Repair
    Leads, Dual Chamber, 33220
    Leads, Single Chamber, 33218
  Repositioning Single/Dual Chamber
    Electrodes, 33215, 33226
  Revise Pocket Chest, 33223
  Wearable Device, 93741-93742, 93745
Deformity, Boutonniere
  See Boutonniere Deformity
Deformity, Sprengel's
  See Sprengel's Deformity
Degenerative, Articular Cartilage, Patella
  See Chondromalacia Patella
Degradation Products, Fibrin
  See Fibrin Degradation Products
Dehiscence
  Suture
    Abdominal Wall, 49900
    Skin and Subcutaneous Tissue
      Complex, 13160
      Complicated, 13160
      Extensive, 13160
    Skin and Subcutaneous Tissue
      Simple, 12020
        with Packing, 12021
      Superficial, 12020
        with Packing, 12021
  Wound
    Abdominal Wall, 49900
    Skin and Subcutaneous Tissue
      Complex, 13160
      Complicated, 13160
      Extensive, 13160
    Skin and Subcutaneous Tissue
      Simple, 12020
        with Packing, 12021
      Superficial, 12020
        with Packing, 12021
Dehydroepiandrosterone, 82626
Dehydroepiandrosterone-Sulfate, 82627
Dehydrogenase, 6-Phosphogluconate
  See Phosphogluconate-6, Dehydrogenase
Dehydrogenase, Alcohol
  See Antidiuretic Hormone
Dehydrogenase, Glucose-6-Phosphate
  See Glucose-6-Phosphate, Dehydrogenase
Dehydrogenase, Glutamate
  See Glutamate Dehydrogenase

Dehydrogenase, Isocitrate
  See Isocitric Dehydrogenase
Dehydrogenase, Lactate
  See Lactic Dehydrogenase
Dehydrogenase, Malate
  See Malate Dehydrogenase
Dehydroisoandrosterone Sulfate
  See Dehydroepiandrosterone Sulfate
Delay of Flap, 15600-15630
Deligation
  Ureter, 50940
Deliveries, Abdominal
  See Cesarean Delivery
Delivery
  See Cesarean Delivery, Vaginal Delivery
Delorme Operation, 33030
Denervation
  Hip
    Femoral Nerve, 27035
    Obturator Nerve, 27035
    Sciatic Nerve, 27035
Denervation, Sympathetic
  See Excision, Nerve, Sympathetic
Denis-Browne Splint, 29590
Dens Axis
  See Odontoid Process
Denver Developmental Screening Test, 96101-96103
Denver Krupin Procedure
  Aqueous Shunt, to Extraocular
    Reservoir, 66180
    Revision, 66185
Denver Shunt
  Patency Test, 78291
Deoxycorticosterone, 82633
Deoxycortisol, 80436, 82634
Deoxyephedrine
  See Methamphetamine
Deoxyribonuclease
  Antibody, 86215
Deoxyribonuclease I
  See DNAse
Deoxyribonucleic Acid
  Antibody, 86225, 86226
Depilation
  See Removal, Hair
Depletion
  Plasma, 38214
  Platelet, 38213
  T-Cell, 38210
  Tumor Cell, 38211
Deposit Calcium
  See Calcium, Deposits
Depth Electrode
  Insertion, 61760
DeQuervain's Disease Treatment, 25000
Dermabrasion, 15780-15783
Derma-Fat-Fascia Graft, 15770
Dermatology
  Actinotherapy, 96900
  Examination of Hair
    Microscopic, 96902
  Ultraviolet A Treatment, 96912
  Ultraviolet B Treatment, 96910-96913
  Ultraviolet Light Treatment, 96900-96913
  Unlisted Services and Procedures, 96999

Destruction — *continued*
Sinus
    Frontal, 31080-31085
Skene's Gland, 53270
Skin Lesion
    Benign, 17000-17004
        Fifteen or More Lesions, 17004
        Two to Fourteen Lesions, 17003
    Malignant, 17260-17286
        by Photodynamic Therapy, 96567
    Premalignant, 17000-17004
        by Photodynamic Therapy, 96567
        Fifteen or More Lesions, 17004
        Two to Fourteen Lesions, 17003
Skin Tags, 11200, 11201
Tonsil
    Lingual, 42870
Tumor
    Abdomen, 49200, 49201
    Bile Duct, 43272
    Breast, 0061T
    Chemosurgery, 17304-17310
    Colon, 45383
    Intestines
        Large, 44393
        Small, 44369
    Pancreatic Duct, 43272
    Rectum, 45190, 45320, 46937, 46938
    Retroperitoneal, 49200, 49201
    Urethra, 53220
Tumor or Polyp
    Rectum, 45320
Turbinate Mucosa, 30801, 30802
Unlisted Services and Procedures, 17999
Ureter
    Endoscopic, 50957, 50976
Urethra, 52214, 52224, 52354
    Prolapse, 53275
Warts
    Flat, 17110, 17111
Determination, Blood Pressure
See Blood Pressure
Developmental Testing
Evaluation
    Extended, 96111
    Limited, 96110
Device
Contraceptive, Intrauterine
    Insertion, 58300
    Removal, 58301
Iliac Artery Occlusion Device
    Insertion, 34808
Venous Access
    Collection of Blood Specimen, 36540
    Fluoroscopic Guidance, 75998
    Insertion
        Catheter, 36578
        Central, 36560-36566
        Imaging, 75901, 75902
        Obstruction Clearance, 36595, 36596
        Peripheral, 36570, 36571
        Removal, 36590
        Repair, 36576
        Replacement, 36582, 36583, 36585
    Ventricular Assist
        Extracorporeal Removal, 0050T
Device Handling, 99002
Device, Orthotic
See Orthotics
Dexamethasone
Suppression Test, 80420

D Galactose
See Galactose
D Glucose
See Glucose
DHA Sulfate
See Dehydroepiandrosterone Sulfate
DHEA (Dehydroepiandrosterone), 82626
DHEAS, 82627
DHT (Dihydrotestosterone), 82651
Diagnosis, Psychiatric
See Psychiatric Diagnosis
Diagnostic Amniocentesis
See Amniocentesis
Diagnostic Aspiration of Anterior Chamber of Eye
See Eye, Paracentesis, Anterior Chamber, with Diagnostic Aspiration of Aqueous
Dialysis
Arteriovenous Fistula
    Revision
        without Thrombectomy, 36832
Arteriovenous Shunt, 36145
    Revision
        with Thrombectomy, 36833
End Stage Renal Disease, 90918-90925
Hemodialysis, 90935, 90937
    Blood Flow Study, 90940
Hemoperfusion, 90997
Patient Training
    Completed Course, 90989
    Per Session, 90993
Peritoneal, 90945, 90947
Unlisted Procedures, 90999
Dialysis, Extracorporeal
See Hemodialysis
DI-Amphetamine
See Amphetamine
Diaphragm
Anesthesia, 00540
    Hernia Repair, 00756
Repair
    for Eventration, 39545
    Hernia, 39502-39541
    Laceration, 39501
Resection, 39560, 39561
Unlisted Procedures, 39599
Vagina
    Fitting, 57170
Diaphragm Contraception, 57170
Diaphysectomy
Calcaneus, 28120
Clavicle, 23180
Femur, 27360
Fibula, 27360, 27641
Humerus, 23184, 24140
Metacarpal, 26230
Metatarsal, 28122
Olecranon Process, 24147
Phalanges
    Finger, 26235, 26236
    Toe, 28124
Radius, 24145, 25151
Scapula, 23182
Talus, 28120
Tarsal, 28122
Tibia, 27360, 27640
Ulna, 24147, 25150
Diastase
See Amylase

Diastasis
See Separation
Diathermy, 97024
See Physical Medicine/ Therapy/Occupational
Destruction
Ciliary Body, 66700
Lesion
Retina, 67208, 67227
Retinal Detachment
Prophylaxis, 67141
Repair, 67101
Diathermy, Surgical
See Electrocautery
Dibucaine Number, 82638
Dichloride, Methylene
See Dichloromethane
Dichlorides, Ethylene
See Dichloroethane
Dichloroethane, 84600
Dichloromethane, 84600
Diethylamide, Lysergic Acid
See Lysergic Acid Diethylamide
Diethylether, 84600
Differential Count
White Blood Cell Count, 85007, 85009, 85540
Differentiation Reversal Factor
See Prothrombin
Diffusion Test, Gel
See Immunodiffusion
Digestive Tract
See Gastrointestinal Tract
Digit(s)
See also Finger, Toe
Pinch Graft, 15050
Replantation, 20816, 20822
Skin Graft
Split, 15120, 15121
Digital Artery Sympathectomy, 64820
Digital Slit-Beam Radiograph
See Scanogram
Digoxin
Assay, 80162
Blood or Urine, 80162
Dihydrocodeinone, 82646
Dihydrocodeinone Screen, 82486
Dihydrohydroxycodeinone
See Oxycodinone
Dihydromorphinone, 82486, 82649
Dihydrotestosterone, 82651
Dihydroxyethanes
See Ethylene Glycol
Dihydroxyvitamin D, 82652
Dilatation, Transluminal Arterial
See Angioplasty, Transluminal
Dilation
See Dilation and Curettage
Anal
Endoscopic, 46604
Sphincter, 45905
Bile Duct
Endoscopic, 43271, 47555, 47556
Bladder
Cystourethroscopy, 52260, 52265
Bronchi
Endoscopy, 31630, 31636-31638
Cervix
Canal, 57800

Dilation — continued
Cervix — continued
Stump, 57820
Colon
Endoscopy, 45386
Colon-Sigmoid
Endoscopy, 45340
Curettage, 57820
Enterostomy Stoma, 44799
Esophagus, 43450-43458
Endoscopic Balloon, 43249
Endoscopy, 43220-43226, 43249
Surgical, 43510
Frontonasal Duct, 30999
Intestines, Small
Endoscopy, 44370
Intracranial Vasospasm, 61640-61642
Kidney, 50395
Intra-Renal Stricture, 52343, 52346
Lacrimal Punctum, 68801
Larynx
Endoscopy, 31528, 31529
Pancreatic Duct
Endoscopy, 43271
Rectum
Endoscopy, 45303
Sphincter, 45910
Salivary Duct, 42650, 42660
Trachea
Endoscopic, 31630, 31631, 31636-31638
Ureter, 50395, 52341, 52342, 52344, 52345
Endoscopic, 50553, 50572, 50953, 50972
Urethra, 52260, 52265
General, 53665
Suppository and/or Instillation, 53660,
53661
Urethral
Stenosis, 52281
Stricture, 52281, 53600-53621
Vagina, 57400
Dilation and Curettage
See Curettage; Dilation
Cervical Stump, 57820
Cervix, 57800, 57820
Corpus Uteri, 58120
Hysteroscopy, 58558
Induced Abortion, 59840
with Amniotic Injections, 59851
with Vaginal Suppositories, 59856
Postpartum, 59160
Dilation and Evacuation, 59841
with Amniotic Injections, 59851
Dimethadione, 82654
Dioxide, Carbon
See Carbon Dioxide
Dioxide Silicon
See Silica
Dipeptidyl Peptidase A
See Angiotensin Converting Enzyme (ACE)
Diphenylhydantoin
See Phenytoin
Diphosphate, Adenosine
See Adenosine Diphosphate
Diphtheria
Antibody, 86648
Immunization, 90698, 90700-90702, 90714-
90715, 90718-90723
Dipropylacetic Acid
Assay, 80164

Direct Pedicle Flap
  Formation, 15570-15576

Disability Evaluation Services
  Basic Life and/or Disability Evaluation, 99450
  Work-Related or Medical Disability Evaluation, 99455, 99456

Disarticulation
  Ankle, 27889
  Elbow, 20999
  Hip, 27295
  Knee, 27598
  Shoulder, 23920, 23921
  Wrist, 25920, 25924
    Revision, 25922

Disarticulation of Shoulder
  See Shoulder, Disarticulation

Discectomies
  See Diskectomy

Discectomies, Percutaneous
  See Diskectomy, Percutaneous

Discharge, Body Substance
  See Drainage

Discharge Instructions
  Heart Failure, 4014F

Discharge Services
  See Hospital Services
  Hospital, 99238, 99239
  Nursing Facility, 99315, 99316
  Observation Care, 99234-99236

Disc, Intervertebral
  See Intervertebral Disc

Discission
  Cataract
    Laser Surgery, 66821
    Stab Incision, 66820
  Vitreous Strands, 67030

Discography
  See Diskography

Discolysis
  See Chemonucleolysis

Disease
  Durand-Nicolas-Favre
    See Lymphogranuloma Venereum
  Erb-Goldflam
    See Myasthenia Gravis
  Heine-Medin
    See Polio
  Hydatid
    See Echinococcosis
  Lyme
    See Lyme Disease
  Ormond
    See Retroperitoneal Fibrosis
  Peyronie
    See Peyronie Disease
  Posada-Wernicke
    See Coccidioidomycosis

Disease/Organ Panel
  See Organ/Disease Panel

Disk Chemolyses, Intervertebral
  See Chemonucleolysis

Diskectomy
  Anterior with Decompression
    Cervical Interspace, 63075
      Each Additional, 63076
    Thoracic Interspace, 63077
      Each Additional, 63078

Diskectomy — *continued*
  Arthrodesis
    Additional Interspace, 22534, 22585
    Lumbar, 22533, 22558, 22630
    Thoracic, 22532, 22556
    Vertebra
      Cervical, 22554
  Cervical, 22220
  Lumbar, 22224, 22630
  Percutaneous, 62287
  Thoracic, 22222
    Additional Segment, 22226

Diskography
  Cervical Disk, 72285
  Injection, 62290, 62291
  Lumbar Disk, 72295
  Thoracic, 72285

Dislocated Elbow
  See Dislocation, Elbow

Dislocated Hip
  See Dislocation, Hip Joint

Dislocated Jaw
  See Dislocation, Temporomandibular Joint

Dislocated Joint
  See Dislocation

Dislocated Shoulder
  See Dislocation, Shoulder

Dislocation
  Acromioclavicular Joint
    Open Treatment, 23550, 23552
  Ankle Joint
    Closed Treatment, 27840, 27842
    Open Treatment, 27846, 27848
  Carpal, 25690
    Closed Treatment, 25690
    Open Treatment, 25695
  Carpometacarpal Joint
    Closed Treatment, 26641, 26645, 26670
      with Anesthesia, 26675
    Open Treatment, 26665, 26685, 26686
    Percutaneous Fixation, 26676
  Clavicle
    with Manipulation, 23545
    without Manipulation, 23540
    Closed Treatment, 23540, 23545
    Open Treatment, 23550, 23552
  Elbow
    with Manipulation, 24620, 24640
    Closed Treatment, 24600, 24605, 24640
    Open Treatment, 24586, 24615
  Hip Joint
    without Trauma, 27265, 27266
    Closed Treatment, 27250, 27252, 27265, 27266
    Congenital, 27256-27259
    Open Treatment, 27253, 27254, 27258, 27259
  Interphalangeal Joint
    Finger(s)/Hand
      Closed Treatment, 26770, 26775
      Open Treatment, 26785
      Percutaneous Fixation, 26776
    Toe(s)/Foot, 28660-28675
      Closed Treatment, 28660, 28665
      Open Treatment, 28675
      Percutaneous Fixation, 28666
  Knee
    Closed Treatment, 27550, 27552
    Open Treatment, 27556-27558, 27566, 27730
    Recurrent, 27420-27424

Dislocation — *continued*
Lunate, 25690-25695
  with Manipulation, 25690, 26670-26676,
    26700-26706
  Closed Treatment, 25690
  Open Treatment, 25695
Metacarpophalangeal Joint
  Closed Treatment, 26700-26706
  Open Treatment, 26715
Metatarsophalangeal Joint
  Closed Treatment, 28630, 28635
  Open Treatment, 28645
  Percutaneous Fixation, 28636
Patella
  Closed Treatment, 27560, 27562
  Open Treatment, 27566
  Recurrent, 27420-27424
Pelvic Ring
  Closed Treatment, 27193, 27194
  Open Treatment, 27217, 27218
  Percutaneous Fixation, 27216
Percutaneous Fixation
  Metacarpophalangeal, 26705
Peroneal Tendons, 27675, 27676
Radioulnar Joint
  Closed Treatment, 25675
    with Radial Fracture, 25520
  Open Treatment, 25676
    with Radial Fracture, 25525, 25526
Radius
  with Fracture, 24620, 24635
    Closed Treatment, 24620
    Open Treatment, 24635
  Closed Treatment, 24640
Shoulder
  Closed Treatment
    with Manipulation, 23650, 23655
      with Fracture of Greater Humeral
        Tuberosity, 23665
      Open Treatment, 23670
      with Surgical or Anatomical Neck
        Fracture, 23675
      Open Treatment, 25680
  Open Treatment, 23660
  Recurrent, 23450-23466
Sternoclavicular Joint
  Closed Treatment
    with Manipulation, 23525
    without Manipulation, 23520
  Open Treatment, 23530, 23532
Talotarsal Joint
  Closed Treatment, 28570, 28575
  Open Treatment, 28546
  Percutaneous Fixation, 28576
Tarsal
  Closed Treatment, 28540, 28545
  Open Treatment, 28555
  Percutaneous Fixation, 28545, 28546
Tarsometatarsal Joint
  Closed Treatment, 28600, 28605
  Open Treatment, 28615
  Percutaneous Fixation, 28606
Temporomandibular Joint
  Closed Treatment, 21480, 21485
  Open Treatment, 21490
Thumb
  with Fracture, 26645
    Open Treatment, 26665
    Percutaneous Fixation, 26650, 26665
  with Manipulation, 26641-26650
    Closed Treatment, 26641, 26645

Dislocation — *continued*
Thumb — *continued*
  Open Treatment, 26665
  Percutaneous Fixation, 26650
Tibiofibular Joint
  Closed Treatment, 27830, 27831
  Open Treatment, 27832
Vertebrae
  Additional Segment, Any Level
    Open Treatment, 22328
  Cervical
    Open Treatment, 22326
  Closed Treatment
    with Manipulation, Casting and/or
      Bracing, 22315
    without Manipulation, 22310
  Lumbar
    Open Treatment, 22325
  Thoracic
    Open Treatment, 22327
Wrist
  with Fracture
    Closed Treatment, 25680
    Open Treatment, 25685
  Intercarpal
    Closed Treatment, 25660
    Open Treatment, 25670
  Percutaneous, 25671
  Radiocarpal
    Closed Treatment, 25660
    Open Treatment, 25670
  Radioulnar
    Closed Treatment, 25675
    Open Treatment, 25676
    Percutaneous Fixation, 25671

Dislocation, Radiocarpal Joint
See Radiocarpal Joint, Dislocation
Disorder
Blood Coagulation
  See Coagulopathy
Penis
  See Penis
Retinal
  See Retina
Displacement Therapy
Nose, 30210
Dissection
Hygroma, Cystic
  Axillary, 38550, 38555
  Cervical, 38550, 38555
Lymph Nodes, 38542
Dissection, Neck, Radical
See Radical Neck Dissection
Distention
See Dilation
Diverticulectomy, 44800
Esophagus, 43130, 43135
Diverticulectomy, Meckel's
See Meckel's Diverticulum, Excision
Diverticulopexy
Esophagus, 43499
Pharynx, 43499
Diverticulum
Bladder
  See Bladder, Diverticulum
Meckel's
  Excision, 44800
Repair
  Urethra, 53400, 53405

Division
  Muscle
    Foot, 28250
  Plantar Fascia
    Foot, 28250
Division, Isthmus, Horseshoe Kidney
  See Symphysiotomy, Horseshoe Kidney
Division, Scalenus Anticus Muscle
  See Muscle Division, Scalenus Anticus
DMO
  See Dimethadione
DNA Antibody, 86225, 86226
DNA Endonuclease
  See DNAse
DNA Probe
  See Cytogenetics Studies; Nucleic Acid Probe
DNAse, 86215
DNAse Antibody, 86215
Domiciliary Services
  See Nursing Facility Services
  Assisted Living, 99339-99340
  Care Plan Oversight, 99339-99340
  Discharge Services, 99315, 99316
  Established Patient, 99334-99337
  New Patient, 99324-99328
Donor Procedures
  Backbench Preparation Prior to Transplantation
    Intestine, 44715-44721
    Kidney, 50323-50329
    Liver, 47143-47147
    Pancreas, 48551-48552
  Conjunctival Graft, 68371
  Heart Excision, 33940
  Heart-Lung Excision, 33930
  Liver Segment, 47140-47142
  Stem Cells
    Donor Search, 38204
Dopamine
  See Catecholamines
  Blood, 82383, 82384
  Urine, 82382, 82384
Doppler Echocardiography, 76827, 76828,
    93320-93350
  Extracranial, 93875
  Hemodialysis Access, 93990
  Intracardiac, 93662
Doppler Scan
  Arterial Studies, Extremities, 93922-93924
  Fetal
    Middle Cerebral Artery, 76821
    Umbilical Artery, 76820
  Extremities, 93965
  Intracranial Arteries, 93886, 93888
Dorsal Vertebra
  See Vertebra, Thoracic
Dose Plan
  Radiation Therapy, 77300, 77331, 77399
    Brachytherapy, 77326-77328
    Teletherapy, 77305-77321
Dosimetry
  Radiation Therapy, 77300, 77331, 77399
    Brachytherapy, 77326-77328
    Intensity Modulation, 77301
    Teletherapy, 77305-77321
Double-J Stent, 52332
  Cystourethroscopy, 52000, 52601, 52647,
    52648

Double-Stranded DNA
  See Deoxyribonucleic Acid
Douglas-Type Procedure, 41510
Doxepin
  Assay, 80166
DPH
  See Phenytoin
DPT, 90701
Drainage
  See Excision; Incision; Incision and Drainage
  Abdomen
    Abdominal Fluid, 49080, 49081
    Paracentesis, 49080, 49081
    Peritoneal, 49020
    Peritoneal Lavage, 49080, 49081
    Peritonitis, Localized, 49020
    Retroperitoneal, 49060
    Subdiaphragmatic, 49040
    Subphrenic, 49040
  Wall
    Skin and Subcutaneous Tissue, 10060,
      10061
      Complicated, 10061
      Multiple, 10061
      Simple, 10060
      Single, 10060
  Abscess
    Abdomen, 49040, 49041
      Fluid, 49080, 49081
      Peritoneal
        Open, 49020
          Percutaneous, 49021
        Peritonitis, localized, 49020
      Retroperitoneal
        Open, 49060
          Percutaneous, 49061
      Skin and Subcutaneous Tissue
        Complicated, 10061
        Multiple, 10061
        Simple, 10060
        Single, 10060
      Subdiaphragmatic, 49040
        Open, 49040
          Percutaneous, 49041
      Subphrenic, 49040
    Anal
      Incision and Drainage, 46045, 46050
    Ankle
      Incision and Drainage, 27603
    Appendix
      Incision and Drainage, 44900
        Open, 44900
        Percutaneous, 44901
    Arm, Lower, 25028
      Incision and Drainage, 25035
    Arm, Upper
      Incision and Drainage, 23930-23935
    Auditory Canal, External, 69020
    Bartholin's Gland
      Incision and Drainage, 56420
    Bladder
      Incision and Drainage, 51080
    Brain
      by
        Burrhole, 61150, 61151
        Craniotomy/Craniectomy, 61320,
          61321
    Breast
      Incision and Drainage, 19020
    Carpals
      Incision, Deep, 25035

Drainage — *continued*
  Abscess — *continued*
    Clavicle
      Sequestrectomy, 23170
    Contrast Injection, 49424
      with X-ray, 75989, 76080
    Ear, External
      Complicated, 69005
      Simple, 69000
    Elbow
      Incision and Drainage, 23930-23935
    Epididymis
      Incision and Drainage, 54700
    Eyelid
      Incision and Drainage, 67700
    Facial Bone(s)
      Excision, 21026
    Finger
      Incision and Drainage, 26010, 26011,
        26034
    Foot
      Incision, 28005
    Ganglion Cyst, 20600-20605
    Gums
      Incision and Drainage, 41800
    Hand
      Incision and Drainage, 26034
    Hematoma
      Brain, 61154-61156
      Incision and Drainage, 27603
      Vagina, 57022, 57023
    Hip
      Incision and Drainage, 26990-26992
    Humeral Head, 23174
    Humerus
      Incision and Drainage, 23935
    Kidney
      Incision and Drainage, 50020
        Open, 50020
        Percutaneous, 50021
    Leg, Lower, 27603
      Incision and Drainage, 27603
    Liver
      Incision and Drainage
        Open, 47010
        Percutaneous, 47011
      Injection, 47015
      Repair, 47300
    Localization
      Nuclear Medicine, 78806, 78807
    Lung
      Percutaneous Drainage, 32200, 32201
    Lymph Node, 38300, 38305
    Lymphocele, 49062
    Mandible
      Excision, 21025
    Mouth
      Incision and Drainage, 40800, 40801,
        41005-41009, 41015-41018
    Nasal Septum
      Incision and Drainage, 30020
    Neck
      Incision and Drainage, 21501, 21502
    Nose
      Incision and Drainage, 30000, 30020
    Ovary
      Incision and Drainage
        Abdominal Approach, 58822
        Percutaneous, 58823
        Vaginal Approach, 58820

Drainage — *continued*
  Abscess — *continued*
    Palate
      Incision and Drainage, 42000
    Paraurethral Gland
      Incision and Drainage, 53060
    Parotid Gland, 42300, 42305
    Pelvic
      Percutaneous, 58823
    Pelvis, 26990
      Incision and Drainage, 26990-26992,
        45000
      Percutaneous, 58823
    Pericolic
      Percutaneous, 58823
    Perineum
      Incision and Drainage, 56405
    Perirenal or Renal
      Open, 50020
      Percutaneous, 50021
    Peritoneum, 49020
      Open, 49020
      Percutaneous, 49021
    Prostate
      Incision and Drainage
        Prostatotomy, 55720, 55725
        Transurethral, 52700
    Radius
      Incision, Deep, 25035
    Rectum
      Incision and Drainage, 45005, 45020,
        46040, 46060
    Retroperitoneal
      Open, 49060
      Percutaneous, 49061
    Salivary Gland, 42300-42320
    Scapula
      Sequestrectomy, 23172
    Scrotum
      Incision and Drainage, 54700, 55100
    Shoulder
      Incision and Drainage, 23030
    Skene's Gland
      Incision and Drainage, 53060
    Skin
      Incision and Drainage
        Complicated, 10061
        Multiple, 10061
        Simple, 10060
        Single, 10060
      Puncture Aspiration, 10160
    Soft Tissue
      Incision, 20000, 20005
    Subdiaphragmatic
      Incision and Drainage
        Open, 49040
        Percutaneous, 49041
    Sublingual Gland, 42310, 42320
    Submaxillary Gland, 42310, 42320
    Subphrenic, 49040, 49041
    Testis
      Incision and Drainage, 54700
    Thoracostomy, 32020
    Thorax
      Incision and Drainage, 21501, 21502
    Throat
      Incision and Drainage, 42700-42725
    Tongue
      Incision and Drainage, 41000-41006,
        41015-41018
    Tonsil
      Incision and Drainage, 42700

Drainage — *continued*
  Abscess — *continued*
    Ulna
      Incision, Deep, 25035
    Urethra
      Incision and Drainage, 53040
    Uvula
      Incision and Drainage, 42000
    Vagina
      Incision and Drainage, 57010
    Vulva
      Incision and Drainage, 56405
    Wrist
      Incision and Drainage, 25028, 25035
    X-ray, 76080
  Amniotic Fluid
    Diagnostic Aspiration, 59000
    Therapeutic Aspiration, 59001
  Bile Duct
    Transhepatic, 47510
  Brain Fluid, 61070
  Bursa, 20600-20610
  Cerebrospinal Fluid, 61000-61020, 61050,
    61070, 62272
  Cervical Fluid, 61050
  Cisternal Fluid, 61050
  Cyst
    Bone, 20615
    Brain, 61150, 61151, 62161, 62162
    Breast, 19000, 19001
    Ganglion, 20612
    Liver, 47010, 47011
      Percutaneous, 47011
    Salivary Gland, 42409
    Sublingual Gland, 42409
  Extraperitoneal Lymphocele
    Laparoscopic, 49323
    Open, 49062
  Eye
    Anterior Chamber
      Paracentesis
        with Diagnostic Aspiration of Aqueous,
          65800
        with Therapeutic Release of Aqueous,
          65805
      Removal Blood, 65815
      Removal Vitreous and/or Discission
        Anterior Hyaloid Membrane, 65810
  Fetal Fluid, 59074
  Ganglion Cyst, 20612
  Hematoma
    Brain, 61154, 61156
    Subungual, 11740
    Vagina, 57022, 57023
  Joint, 20600-20610
  Liver
    Abscess or Cyst, 47010, 47011
      Percutaneous, 47011
  Lymphocele
    Endoscopic, 49323
  Onychia, 10060, 10061
  Orbit, 67405, 67440
  Pancreas
    See Anastomosis, Pancreas to Intestines
    Pseudocyst, 48510, 48511
      Percutaneous, 48511
  Paronychia, 10060, 10061
  Pericardial Sac, 32659
  Pericardium
    See Aspiration, Pericardium
  Pseudocyst
    Gastrointestinal, Upper
      Transmural Endoscopic, 43240

Drainage — *continued*
  Pseudocyst — *continued*
    Pancreas, 48510
      Open, 48510
      Percutaneous, 48511
  Puncture
    Chest, 32000, 32002
  Skin, 10040-10180
  Spinal Cord
    Cerebrospinal Fluid, 62272
    Subdural Fluid, 61000, 61001
  Urethra
    Extravasation, 53080, 53085
  Ventricular Fluid, 61020

Drainage Implant, Glaucoma
  See Aqueous Shunt

Dressings
  Burns, 16020-16030
  Change under Anesthesia, 15852

DREZ Procedure, 63170

Drill Hole
  Skull
    Catheter, 61107
    Drain Hematoma, 61108
    Exploration, 61105
    Implant Electrode, 61850
      Twist Drill Hole, 61105
    Surgery, 61105-61108

Drinking Test for Glaucoma
  Glaucoma Provocative Test, 92140

Drug
  See also Drug Assay
  Confirmation, 80102
  Implant Infusion Device, 62360-62362
  Screening, 80100, 80101
  Tissue Preparation, 80103

Drug Assay
  Amikacin, 80150
  Amitriptyline, 80152
  Benzodiazepine, 80154
  Carbamazepine, 80156, 80157
  Cyclosporine, 80158
  Desipramine, 80160
  Digoxin, 80162
  Dipropylacetic Acid, 80164
  Doxepin, 80166
  Ethosuximide, 80168
  Gentamicin, 80170
  Gold, 80172
  Haloperidol, 80173
  Imipramine, 80174
  Lidocaine, 80176
  Lithium, 80178
  Nortriptyline, 80182
  Phenobarbital, 80184
  Phenytoin, 80185, 80186
  Primidone, 80188
  Procainamide, 80190, 80192
  Quantitative
    Other, 80299
  Quinidine, 80194
  Salicylate, 80196
  Tacrolimus, 80197
  Theophylline, 80198
  Tobramycin, 80200
  Topiramate, 80201
  Vancomycin, 80202

Drug Confirmation, 80102

Drug Delivery Implant
  Insertion, 11981
  Maintenance
    Brain, 95990, 95991
    Epidural, 95990, 95991
    Intra-arterial, 96530
    Intrathecal, 95990, 95991
    Intravenous, 96530
    Intraventricular, 95990, 95991
  Removal, 11982, 11983
    with Reinsertion, 11983
Drug Instillation
  See Instillation, Drugs
Drug Management
  Psychiatric, 90862
Drugs, Anticoagulant
  See Clotting Inhibitors
Drug Screen, 80100, 80101, 82486
DST, 80420
DT, 90702
DTaP, 90700
DTaP-HepB-IPV Immunization, 90723
DTaP with Hib, 90721
DTP, 90701
DTP with Hib, 90720
DT Shots, 90702
Dual Photon Absorptiometry
Dual X-ray Absorptiometry (DXA)
  See Absorptiometry, Dual Photon
  Appendicular, 76076
  Axial Skeleton, 76075
  Body Composition, 0028T
  Vertebral Fracture, 76077
Duct, Bile
  See Bile Duct
Duct, Hepatic
  See Hepatic Duct
Duct, Nasolacrimal
  See Nasolacrimal Duct
Ductogram, Mammary
  See Galactogram
Duct, Omphalomesenteric
  See Omphalomesenteric Duct
Duct, Pancreatic
  See Pancreatic Duct
Duct, Salivary
  See Salivary Duct
Duct, Stensen's
  See Parotid Duct
Duct, Thoracic
  See Thoracic Duct
Ductus Arteriosus
  Repair, 33820-33824
Ductus Deferens
  See Vas Deferens
Duhamel Procedure, 45120
Dunn Operation, 28725
Duodenectomy
  Near Total, 48153, 48154
  Total, 48150, 48152
Duodenography, 74260
Duodenotomy, 44010
Duodenum
  Biopsy, 44010
  Exclusion, 48547
  Exploration, 44010

Duodenum — *continued*
  Incision, 44010
  Removal/Foreign Body, 44010
  X-ray, 74260
Duplex Scan
  See Vascular Studies
  Arterial Studies
    Aorta, 93978, 93979
    Extracranial, 93880, 93882
    Lower Extremity, 93925, 93926
    Penile, 93980, 93981
    Upper Extremity, 93930, 93931
    Visceral, 93975-93979
  Hemodialysis Access, 93990
  Venous Studies
    Extremity, 93970, 93971
    Penile, 93980, 93981
Dupuy-Dutemp Operation, 67971
Dupuytren's Contracture, 26040, 26045
Durand-Nicolas-Favre Disease
  See Lymphogranuloma Venereum
Dust, Angel
  See Phencyclidine
Duvries Operation
  See Tenoplasty
D Vitamin
  See Vitamin, D
Dwyer Procedure, 28300
DXA (Dual Energy X-ray Absorptiometry),
  76075, 76076, 76077
D-Xylose Absorption Test, 84620
Dynamometry
  See Osteotomy, Calcaneus
  Venous Studies
    with Ophthalmoscopy, 92260

E

E1
  See Estrone
E2
  See Estradiol
E3
  See Estriol
E Antigens
  See Hepatitis Antigen, Be
Ear
  Collection of Blood from, 36415, 36416
  Drum, 69420, 69421, 69433, 69436, 69450,
    69610, 69620
    See Tympanic Membrane
  External
    Abscess
      Incision and Drainage
        Complicated, 69005
        Simple, 69000
    Biopsy, 69100
    Excision
      Partial, 69110
      Total, 69120
    Hematoma
      Incision and Drainage, 69000, 69005
    Reconstruction, 69300
    Unlisted Services and Procedures, 69399
  Inner
    CT Scan, 70480-70482
    Excision
      Labyrinth, 69905, 69910
    Exploration
      Endolymphatic Sac, 69805, 69806

Electrophoresis
Counterimmuno-, 86185
Immuno-, 86320-86327
Immunofixation, 86334-86335
Protein, 84165-84166
Unlisted Services and Procedures, 82664
Electrophysiology Procedure, 93600-93660
Electroretinography, 92275
Electrostimulation, Analgesic Cutaneous
See Application, Neurostimulation
Electrosurgery
Skin Lesion, 17000-17111, 17260-17286
Skin Tags, 11200, 11201
Trichiasis
Correction, 67825
Electroversion, Cardiac
See Cardioversion
Elevation, Scapula, Congenital
See Sprengel's Deformity
Elliot Operation, 66130
Excision, Lesion, Sclera, 66130
Eloesser Procedure, 32035, 32036
Eloesser Thoracoplasty, 32905
Embolectomy
Aortoiliac Artery, 34151, 34201
Axillary Artery, 34101
Brachial Artery, 34101
Carotid Artery, 34001
Celiac Artery, 34151
Femoral, 34201
Iliac, 34151, 34201
Innominate Artery, 34001-34101
Mesentery Artery, 34151
Peroneal Artery, 34203
Popliteal Artery, 34203
Pulmonary Artery, 33910-33916
Radial Artery, 34111
Renal Artery, 34151
Subclavian Artery, 34001-34101
Tibial Artery, 34203
Ulnar Artery, 34111
Embryo
Biopsy, 89290, 89291
Cryopreservation, 89258
Cryopreserved
Preparation/Thawing, 89352
Culture, 89250
with Co-Culture Oocyte, 89251
Hatching
Assisted Microtechnique, 89253
Preparation for Transfer, 89255
Storage, 89342
Embryo/Fetus Monitoring
See Monitoring, Fetal
Embryo Implantation
See Implantation
Embryonated Eggs
Inoculation, 87250
Embryo Transfer
In Vitro Fertilization, 58974, 58976
Intrafallopian Transfer, 58976
Intrauterine Transfer, 58974
Emergency Department Services, 99281-99288
See Critical Care; Emergency Department
Anesthesia, 99140
in Office, 99058
Physician Direction of Advanced Life Support,
99288

Emesis Induction, 99175
EMG (Electromyography, Needle), 51784, 51785,
92265, 95860-95872
EMI Scan
See CT Scan
Emission Computerized Tomography, 78607,
78647
**Emission Computerized Tomography, Single-
Photon**
See SPECT
Emmet Operation
Perineum, Repair, 56810
Vagina, Repair, 56800
Empyema
Closure
Chest Wall, 32810
Thoracostomy, 32020, 32035, 32036
Empyema, Lung
See Abscess, Thorax
Empyemectomy, 32540
EMS, 99288
Encephalitis
Antibody, 86651-86654
Encephalitis Virus Vaccine, 90735
Encephalocele
Repair, 62120
Craniotomy, 62121
Encephalography, A-Mode, 76506
Encephalon
See Brain
Endarterectomy
Coronary Artery, 33572
Pulmonary, 33916
Endemic Flea-Borne Typhus
See Murine Typhus
End-Expiratory Pressure, Positive
See Pressure Breathing, Positive
Endobronchial Challenge Tests
See Bronchial Challenge Test
Endocavitary Fulguration
See Electrocautery
Endocrine System
Unlisted Services and Procedures, 60699,
78099
Endolymphatic Sac
Exploration
with Shunt, 69806
without Shunt, 69805
Endometrial Ablation, 58353, 58356
Curettage, 58356
Exploration via Hysteroscopy, 58563
Endometrioma
Abdomen
Destruction
Excision, 49200, 49201
Retroperitoneal
Destruction
Excision, 49200, 49201
Endometriosis, Adhesive
See Adhesions, Intrauterine
Endometrium
Ablation, 58356
Biopsy, 58100, 58558
Endonuclease, DNA
See DNAse
Endopyelotomy, 50575

Endorectal Pull-Through
  Proctectomy, Total, 45110, 45112, 45120, 45121
Endoscopic Retrograde Cannulation of Pancreatic Duct (ERCP)
  See Cholangiopancreatography
Endoscopies, Pleural
  See Thoracoscopy
Endoscopy
  See Arthroscopy; Thoracoscopy
  Adrenal Gland
    Biopsy, 60650
    Excision, 60650
  Anal
    Biopsy, 46606
    Dilation, 46604
    Exploration, 46600
    Hemorrhage, 46614
    Removal
      Foreign Body, 46608
      Polyp, 46610, 46612
      Tumor, 46610, 46612
  Bile Duct
    Biopsy, 47553
    Destruction
      Calculi (Stone), 43265
      Tumor, 43272
    Dilation, 43271, 47555, 47556
    Exploration, 47552
    Intraoperative, 47550
    Percutaneous, 47552-47555
    Removal
      Calculi (Stone), 43264, 47554
      Foreign Body, 43269
      Stent, 43269
    Specimen Collection, 43260
    Sphincterotomy, 43262
    Sphincter Pressure, 43263
    Tube Placement, 43267, 43268
  Bladder
    Biopsy, 52007, 52204, 52354
    Catheterization, 52005, 52010
    Destruction, 52354
      Lesion, 52400
    Diagnostic, 52000
    Evacuation
      Clot, 52001
    Excision
      Tumor, 52355
    Exploration, 52351
    Lithotripsy, 52353
    Removal
      Calculus, 52352
    Urethral Stent Insertion, 0084T, 52282
  Bladder Neck
    Injection of Implant Material, 51715
  Brain
    Shunt Creation, 62201
  Bronchi
    Aspiration, 31645, 31646
    Biopsy, 31625-31629, 31632, 31633
    Destruction
      Lesion, 31641
    Dilation, 31630, 31631, 31636-31638
    Exploration, 31622
    Injection, 31656
    Lesion, 31641
      Destruction, 31641
    Needle Biopsy, 31629, 31633
    Placement
      Stent, 31631, 31636-31637

Endoscopy — *continued*
  Bronchi — *continued*
    Revision
      Stent, 31638
    Stenosis, 31641
    Tumor
    Ultrasound, 31620
      Destruction, 31641
      Excision, 31640
  Cervix
    Biopsy, 57454, 57455, 57460
    Curettage, 57454, 57456
    Exploration, 57452
    Loop Electrode Biopsy, 57460
    Loop Electrode Conization, 57461
  Chest Cavity
    Exploration, 32601-32606
    Surgical, 32650-32665
  Colon
    Biopsy, 44389, 45380
    Destruction
      Lesion, 44393, 45383
      Tumor, 44393, 45383
    Exploration, 44388, 45378
    Hemorrhage, 44391, 45382
    Injection, 45381
    Placement
      Stent, 45387
    Removal
      Foreign Body, 44390, 45379
      Polyp, 44392, 45384, 45385
      Tumor, 44392, 45384, 45385
    Specimen Collection, 45380
    Ultrasound, 45391-45392
    via Colotomy, 45355
    via Stoma (Colostomy), 44388-44393, 44397
    Virtual, 0066T-0067T
  Colon-Sigmoid
    Ablation
      Polyp, 45339
      Tumor, 45339
    Biopsy, 45331
    Dilation, 45340
    Exploration, 45330
      Specimen Collection, 45331
    Hemorrhage, 45334
    Injection, 45335
    Needle Biopsy, 45342
    Placement
      Stent, 45327, 45345
    Removal
      Foreign Body, 45332
      Polyp, 45333, 45338
      Tumor, 45333, 45338
    Specimen Collection, 45331
    Ultrasound, 45341, 45342
    Volvulus, 45337
  Esophagus
    Biopsy, 43202
    Dilation, 43220, 43226
    Exploration, 43200
    Hemorrhage, 43227
    Injection, 43201, 43204
    Insertion Stent, 43219
    Needle Biopsy, 43232
    Removal
      Foreign Body, 43215
      Polyp, 43216, 43217, 43228
      Tumor, 43216, 43228
    Ultrasound, 43231-43232
    Vein Ligation, 43205
  Eye, 66990

Endoscopy — *continued*
Foot
  Plantar Fasciotomy, 29893
Gastrointestinal
  Upper
    Biopsy, 43239
    Catheterization, 43241
    Destruction of Lesion, 43258
    Dilation, 43245, 43248, 43249
    Drainage of Pseudocyst, 43240
    Exploration, 43234, 43235
    Foreign Body, 43247
    Gastric Bypass, 43644-43645
    Gastroenterostomy, 43644-43645
    Hemorrhage, 43255
    Injection, 0133T, 43236
    Inject Varices, 43243
    Needle Biopsy, 43232, 43238
    Removal, 43247, 43250, 43251
    Roux-En-Y, 43644
    Stent Placement, 43256
    Suturing, 0008T
    Thermal Radiation, 43257
    Tube Placement, 43246
    Ultrasound, 43237-43242, 43259, 76975
    Vein Ligation, 43244
Ileum
  via Stoma, 44383
Intestines, Small
  Biopsy, 44361, 44377
  Destruction
    Lesion, 44369
    Tumor, 44369
  Diagnostic, 44376
  Exploration, 44360
  Hemorrhage, 44366, 44378
  Insertion
    Stent, 44370, 44379
    Tube, 44379
  Pelvic Pouch, 44385, 44386
  Removal
    Foreign Body, 44363
    Lesion, 44365
    Polyp, 44364, 44365
    Tumor, 44364, 44365
  Tube Placement, 44372
  Tube Revision, 44373
  via Stoma, 44380, 44382
  Tumor, 44364, 44365
Intracranial, 62160-62165
Kidney
  Biopsy, 50555, 50574-50576, 52354
  Catheterization, 50553, 50572
  Destruction, 50557, 50576, 52354
  Dilation of Ureter, 50553
  Excision
    Tumor, 52355
  Exploration, 52351
  Lithotripsy, 52353
  Removal
    Calculus, 50561, 50580, 52352
    Foreign Body, 50561, 50580
  via Incision, 50562-50576, 50580
  via Stoma, 50551-50557, 50561
Larynx
  with Injection, 31570
  Biopsy, 31510, 31535, 31536
  Direct, 31515-31571
  Exploration, 31505, 31520-31526, 31575
  Fiberoptic, 31575-31579
  Indirect, 31505-31513
  Operative, 31530-31561

Endoscopy — *continued*
Larynx — *continued*
  Removal
    Foreign Body, 31530, 31531
    Lesion, 31511, 31545-31546
Lysis
  Device, 0027T
Mediastinoscopy
  Biopsy, 39400
  Exploration, 39400
Nose
  Diagnostic, 31231-31235
  Surgical, 31237-31294
  Unlisted Procedure, Accessory Sinuses, 31299
Pancreatic Duct
  Destruction
    Stone, 43265
    Tumor, 43272
  Dilation, 43271
  Removal
    Calculi (Stone), 43264
    Foreign Body, 43269
    Stent, 43269
  Specimen Collection, 43260
  Sphincterotomy, 43262
  Sphincter Pressure, 43263
  Tube Placement, 43267, 43268
Pelvis
  Aspiration, 49322
  Destruction of Lesions, 58662
  Lysis of Adhesions, 58660
  Oviduct Surgery, 58670, 58671
  Removal of Adnexal Structures, 58661
Peritoneum
  Biopsy, 47561
  Drainage Lymphocele, 49323, 54690
  Radiologic, 47560
Rectum
  Biopsy, 45305
  Destruction
    Tumor, 45320
  Dilation, 45303
  Exploration, 45300
  Hemorrhage, 45317
  Removal
    Foreign Body, 45307
    Polyp, 45308-45315
    Tumor, 45308-45315
  Volvulus, 45321
Spleen
  Removal, 38120
Testis
  Removal, 54690
Trachea
  Dilation, 31630-31631, 31636-31638
  via Tracheostomy, 31615
Ureter
  Biopsy, 50955-50957, 50974-50976, 52354
  Catheterization, 50953, 50972
  Destruction, 50957, 50976, 52354
  Excision
    Tumor, 52355
  Exploration, 52351
  Injection of Implant Material, 52327
  Lithotripsy, 52353
  Manipulation of Ureteral Calculus, 52330
  Placement
    Stent, 50947
  Removal
    Calculus, 50961, 50980, 52352
    Foreign Body, 50961, 50980

Endoscopy — *continued*
  Ureter — *continued*
    Resection, 52355
      via Incision, 50970-50976, 50980
      via Stoma, 50951-50957, 50961
      via Ureterotomy, 50970-50980
  Ureteral
    Biopsy, 52007
    Catheterization, 52005
  Urethra, 52000, 52010
    Biopsy, 52007, 52204, 52354
    Catheterization, 52005, 52010
    Destruction, 52354
      Lesion, 52400
    Evacuation
      Clot, 52001
    Excision
      Tumor, 52355
    Exploration, 52351
    Incision
      Ejaculatory Duct, 52402
    Injection of Implant Material, 51715
    Lithotripsy, 52353
    Removal
      Calculus, 52352
    Resection
      Ejaculatory Duct, 52402
    Vasectomy, 52402
    Vasotomy, 52402
  Uterus
    Anesthesia, 00952
    Hysteroscopy
      with Division
        Resection Intrauterine Septum, 58560
      with Lysis of Intrauterine Adhesions, 58559
      Diagnostic, 58555
      Placement
        Fallopian Tube, 58565
      Removal
        Endometrial, 58563
        Impacted Foreign Body, 58562
        Leiomyomata, 58561
      Surgical with Biopsy, 58558
  Vagina
    Biopsy, 57454
    Exploration, 57452
  Vascular
    Surgical, 33508, 37500, 37501
  Virtual
    Colon, 0066T-0067T
Endosteal Implant
  Reconstruction
    Mandible, 21248, 21249
    Maxilla, 21248, 21249
Endothelioma, Dural
  See Meningioma
Endotoxin
  Bacteria, 87176
Endotracheal Tube
  Intubation, 31500
Endovascular Repair, 0078T-0081T, 33880-33891, 34800-34805, 34812-34826, 34833-34900, 75952-75959
  Angiography, 75952-75954
  Imaging Neck, 75956-75959
Endovascular Therapy
  Ablation
    Vein, 36475-36479
  Occlusion, 61623

Endrocrine, Pancreas
  See Islet Cell
End Stage Renal Disease Services, 90918-90925
Enema
  Diagnostic, 74000, 74280
  Home Visit for Fecal Impaction, 99511
  Therapeutic
    for Intussusception, 74283
Energies, Electromagnetic
  See Irradiation
ENG, 92541, 92542, 92544
ENT
  See Ear, Nose, and Throat;
      Otorhinolaryngology, Diagnostic
  Therapeutic
    See Otorhinolaryngology
Entamoeba Histolytica
  Antigen Detection
    Enzyme Immunoassay, 87336, 87337
Enterectomy, 44126-44128, 44137, 44202
  with Enterostomy, 44125
  Donor, 44132, 44133
  Resection, 44120, 44121
Enterocele
  Repair, 57556
    Hysterectomy
      with Colpectomy, 58280
      with Colpo-Urethrocystopexy, 58270
Enterocystoplasty, 51960
  Camey, 50825
Enteroenterostomy, 44130
Enterolysis, 44005
  Laparoscopic, 44180
Enteropancreatostomy
  See Anastomosis, Pancreas to Intestines
Enterorrhaphy, 44602, 44603, 44615
Enteroscopy
  Intestines, Small
    Biopsy, 44361, 44377
    Control of Bleeding, 44378
    Destruction
      Lesion, 44369
      Tumor, 44369
    Diagnostic, 44376
    Exploration, 44360
    Hemorrhage, 44366
    Pelvic Pouch, 44385, 44386
    Removal
      Foreign Body, 44363
      Lesion, 44364, 44365
      Polyp, 44365
      Tumor, 44364, 44365
    Tube Placement, 44372
    Tube Revision, 44373
    via Stoma, 44380, 44382
    Tumor, 44364, 44365
Enterostomy, 44300
  with Enterectomy
    Intestine, Small, 44125
  Closure, 44625, 44626
Enterotomy, 44615
Enterovirus
  Antibody, 86658
  Antigen Detection
    Direct Fluorescence, 87265-87272, 87276, 87278, 87280, 87285-87290

Entropion
Repair, 67921-67924
 Blepharoplasty
  Excision Tarsal Wedge, 67923
  Extensive, 67923
  Suture, 67921
  Thermocauterization, 67922
Enucleation
Eye
 with Implant, 65103
  Muscles Attached, 65105
 without Implant, 65101
Pleural, 32540
Enucleation, Cyst, Ovarian
See Cystectomy, Ovarian
Environmental Intervention
for Psychiatric Patients, 90882
Enzyme Activity, 82657
Radioactive Substrate, 82658
Enzyme, Angiotensin Converting
See Angiotensin Converting Enzyme (ACE)
Enzyme, Angiotensin-Forming
See Renin
EOG (Electro-Oculography), 92270
Eosinocyte
See Eosinophils
Eosinophils
Nasal Smear, 89190
Epiandrosterone, 82666
Epicondylitis, 24350
Epidemic Parotitis
See Mumps
Epididymectomy
Bilateral, 54861
Unilateral, 54860
Epididymis
Abscess
 Incision and Drainage, 54700
Anastomosis
 to Vas Deferens
  Bilateral, 54901
  Unilateral, 54900
Biopsy, 54800, 54820
Epididymography, 74440
Excision
 Bilateral, 54861
 Unilateral, 54860
Exploration
 Biopsy, 54820
Hematoma
 Incision and Drainage, 54700
Lesion
 Excision
  Local, 54830
  Spermatocele, 54840
Needle Biopsy, 54800
Repair, 54900, 54901
Spermatocele
 Excision, 54840
Unlisted Procedures, Male Genital, 54699, 55899
X-ray with Contrast, 74440
Epididymograms, 55300
Epididymography, 74440
Epididymoplasty
See Repair, Epididymis

Epididymovasostomy
Bilateral, 54901
Unilateral, 54900
Epidural
Analgesia
 Continuous, 01967-01969
 Drug Administration, 01996
Electrode
 Insertion, 61531
 Removal, 61535
Injection, 62281, 62282, 62310-62319, 64479-64484
Lysis, 0027T, 62263, 62264
Epidurography, 72275
Epigastric
Hernia Repair, 49572
Epiglottidectomy, 31420
Epiglottis
Excision, 31420
Epikeratoplasty, 65767
Epilation
See Removal, Hair
Epinephrine
See Catecholamines
Blood, 82383, 82384
Urine, 82384
Epiphyseal Arrest
Femur, 20150, 27185, 27475, 27479, 27485, 27742
Fibula, 20150, 27477-27485, 27730-27742
Radius, 20150, 25450, 25455
Tibia, 20150, 27477-27485, 27730, 27734-27742
Ulna, 20150, 25450, 25455
Epiphyseal Separation
Radius
 Closed Treatment, 25600
 Open Treatment, 25620
Epiphysiodesis
See Epiphyseal Arrest
Epiphysis
See Bone; Specific Bone
Epiploectomy, 49255
EPIS, 59300, 92585, 95925-95930
Episiotomy, 59300
Epispadias
Penis
 Reconstruction, 54385
 Repair, 54380-54390
  with Exstrophy of Bladder, 54390
  with Incontinence, 54380, 54385
Epistaxis
with Nasal
 Sinus Endoscopy, 31238
Control, 30901-30906
EPO
See Erythropoietin
EPS, 93600-93660
Epstein-Barr Virus
Antibody, 86663-86665
Equina, Cauda
See Cauda Equina
ER, 99281-99288
ERCP (Cholangiopancreatography), 43260-43272
ERG (Electroretinography), 92275

Ergocalciferol
See Calciferol

Ergocalciferols
See Calciferol

Ergonovine Provocation Test, 93024

Erythrocyte
See Red Blood Bell (RBC)

Erythrocyte ab
See Antibody, Red Blood Cell

Erythrocyte Count
See Red Blood Cell (RBC), Count

Erythropoietin, 82668

Escharotomy
Burns, 16035, 16036

Escherichia Coli 0157
Antigen Detection
Enzyme Immunoassay, 87335

ESD
See Endoscopy, Gastrointestinal, Upper

Esophageal Acid Infusion Test, 91012, 91030

Esophageal Polyp
See Polyp, Esophagus

Esophageal Tumor
See Tumor, Esophagus

Esophageal Varices
Ligation, 43205, 43400
Transection and Repair, 43401

Esophagectomy
Partial, 43116-43124
Total, 43107-43113, 43124

Esophagoenterostomy
with Total Gastrectomy, 43260

Esophagogastroduodenoscopies
See Endoscopy, Gastrointestinal, Upper

Esophagogastrostomy, 43320

Esophagojejunostomy, 43340, 43341

Esophagomyotomy, 32665, 43330, 43331

Esophagoplasty, 43300-43312

Esophagorrphaphy
See Esophagus, Suture

Esophagoscopies
See Endoscopy, Esophagus

Esophagoscopy
Operative By Incision, 43499
Through Artificial Stoma, 43499

Esophagostomy, 43350-43352
Closure, 43420, 43425

Esophagotomy, 43020, 43045

Esophagotracheal Fistula
See Fistula, Tracheoesophageal

Esophagus
Acid Perfusion Test, 91012, 91030
Acid Reflux Tests, 91034-91035, 91037-91038
Balloon Distension
Provocation Study, 91040
Biopsy
Endoscopy, 43202
Cineradiography, 74230
Dilation, 43450-43458
Endoscopic, 43220, 43226, 43248, 43249
Surgical, 43510
Endoscopy
Biopsy, 43202
Dilation, 43220, 43226
Exploration, 43200
Hemorrhage, 43227
Injection, 43201, 43204

Esophagus — continued
Endoscopy — continued
Insertion Stent, 43219
Needle Biopsy, 43232
Removal
Foreign Body, 43215
Polyp, 43216, 43217, 43228
Tumor, 43216, 43228
Ultrasound, 43231, 43232
Vein Ligation, 43205
Excision
Diverticula, 43130, 43135
Partial, 43116-43124
Total, 43107-43113, 43124
Exploration
Endoscopy, 43200
Hemorrhage, 43227
Incision, 43020, 43045
Muscle, 43030
Injection
Sclerosis Agent, 43204
Submucosal, 43201
Insertion
Stent, 43219
Tamponade, 43460
Tube, 43510
Intubation with Specimen Collection, 91000
Lesion
Excision, 43100, 43101
Ligation, 43405
Motility Study, 78258, 91010-91012
Needle Biopsy
Endoscopy, 43232
Nuclear Medicine
Imaging (Motility), 78258
Reflux Study, 78262
Reconstruction, 43300, 43310, 43313
Creation
Stoma, 43350-43352
Esophagostomy, 43350
Fistula, 43305, 43312, 43314
Gastrointestinal, 43360, 43361
Removal
Foreign Bodies, 43020, 43045, 43215,
74235
Lesion, 43216
Polyp, 43216, 43217, 43228
Repair, 43300, 43310, 43313
Esophagogastric Fundoplasty, 43324, 43325
Laparoscopic, 43280
Esophagogastrostomy, 43320
Esophagojejunostomy, 43340, 43341
Fistula, 43305, 43312, 43314, 43420, 43425
Muscle, 43330, 43331
Pre-existing Perforation, 43405
Varices, 43401
Wound, 43410, 43415
Stapling Gastroesophageal Junction, 43405
Suture
Gastroesophageal Junction, 43405
Wound, 43410, 43415
Ultrasound, 43231, 43232
Unlisted Services and Procedures, 43289,
43499
Vein
Ligation, 43205, 43400
Video, 74230
X-ray, 74220

Esophagus Neoplasm
See Tumor, Esophagus

Excision — *continued*
  Destruction of the Vestibule of the Mouth
    See Mouth, Vestibule of, Excision,
      Destruction
  Diverticulum, Meckel's
    See Meckel's Diverticulum, Excision
  Ear, External
    Partial, 69110
    Total, 69120
  Elbow Joint, 24155
  Electrode, 57522
  Embolectomy/Thrombectomy
    Aortoiliac Artery, 34151, 34201
    Axillary Artery, 34101
    Brachial Artery, 34101
    Carotid Artery, 34001
    Celiac Artery, 34151
    Femoral Artery, 34201
    Iliac Artery, 34151, 34201
    Innominate Artery, 34001-34101
    Mesentery Artery, 34151
    Peroneal Artery, 34203
    Popliteal Artery, 34203
    Radial Artery, 34111
    Renal Artery, 34151
    Subclavian Artery, 34001-34101
    Tibial Artery, 34203
    Ulnar Artery, 34111
  Embolism
    Pulmonary Artery, 33910-33916
  Empyema
    Lung, 32540
    Pleural, 32540
  Epididymis
    Bilateral, 54861
    Unilateral, 54860
  Epiglottis, 31420
  Epikeratoplasty, 65767
  Epiphyseal Bar, 20150
  Esophagus
    Diverticulum, 43130, 43135
    Partial, 43116-43124
    Total, 43107-43113, 43124
  Excess Skin
    Abdomen, 15831
  Eye
    See Enucleation, Eye
  Fallopian Tubes
    Salpingectomy, 58700
    Salpingo-Oophorectomy, 58720
  Fascia
    See Fasciectomy
  Femur, 27360
    Partial, 27070, 27071
  Fibula, 27360, 27455, 27457, 27641
  Fistula
    Anal, 46270-46285
  Foot
    Fasciectomy, 28060
      Radical, 28060, 28062
  Gallbladder
    Open, 47600-47620
    via Laparoscopy
      Cholecystectomy, 47562, 47563
        with Cholangiography, 47563
        with Exploration Common Duct, 47564
  Ganglion Cyst
    Knee, 27347
    Wrist, 25111, 25112
  Gingiva, 41820

Excision — *continued*
  Gums, 41820
    Alveolus, 41830
    Operculum, 41821
  Heart
    Donor, 33940
  Lung
    Donor, 33930
  Hemangioma, 11400-11446
  Hemorrhoids, 46221, 46250
    with Fissurectomy, 46257, 46258
    Clot, 46320
    Complex, 46260-46262
    Simple, 46255
  Hip
    Partial, 27070, 27071
  Hippocampus, 61566
  Humeral Head
    Resection, 23195
    Sequestrectomy, 23174
  Humerus, 23184, 23220-23222, 24134, 24140,
    24150, 24151
  Hydrocele
    Spermatic Cord, 55500
    Tunica Vaginalis, 55040, 55041
      Bilateral, 55041
      Unilateral, 55040
  Hygroma, Cystic
    Axillary
    Cervical, 38550, 38555
  Hymenotomy, 56700
    See Hymen, Excision
  Ileum
    Ileoanal Reservoir, 45136
    Partial, 27070, 27071
  Inner Ear
    See Ear, Inner, Excision
  Interphalangeal Joint
    Toe, 28160
  Intervertebral Disk
    Decompression, 63075-63078
    Hemilaminectomy, 63040, 63043, 63044
    Herniated, 63020-63044, 63055-63066
  Intestine
    Laparoscopic
      with Anastomosis, 44202, 44203
  Intestines
    Donor, 44132, 44133
  Intestines, Small, 44120-44128
    Transplantation, 44137
  Iris
    Iridectomy
      with Corneoscleral or Corneal Section,
        66600
      with Cyclectomy, 66605
      Optical, 66635
      Peripheral, 66625
      Sector, 66630
  Kidney
    with Ureters, 50220-50236
    Donor, 50300, 50320, 50547
    Partial, 50240
    Recipient, 50340
    Transplantation, 50370
  Kneecap, 27350
  Labyrinth
    with Mastoidectomy, 69910
    Transcanal, 69905
  Lacrimal Gland
    Partial, 68505
    Total, 68500

Excision — *continued*
  Lacrimal Sac, 68520
  Laparoscopy
    Adrenalectomy, 60650
  Larynx
    with Pharynx, 31390, 31395
    Endoscopic, 31545-31546
  Leg, Lower, 27630
  Meniscus, 27347
  Mesentery, 44820
  Mouth, 40810-40816, 41116
  Nasopharynx, 61586, 61600
  Nerve, 64774-64792
  Neuroma, 64778
  Nose
    Intranasal, 30117, 30118
  Orbit, 61333
    Lateral Approach, 67420
    Removal, 67412
  Palate, 42104-42120
  Pancreas, 48120
  Partial, 31367-31382
  Penis, 54060
    Surgical Excision Penile Plaque, 54110-54112
  Pharynx, 42808
  Rectum, 45108
  Sclera, 66130
  Skin
    Benign, 11400-11471
    Malignant, 11600-11646
  Skull, 61500, 61615, 61616
  Spermatic Cord, 55520
  Spinal Cord, 63300-63308
  Stomach, 43611
  Talus
    Arthroscopic, 29891
  Tendon Sheath
    Arm, Lower, 25110
  Testis, 54512
  Tibia
    Arthroscopic, 29891
  Toe, 28092
  Tongue, 41110-41114
  Total, 31360, 31365
  Urethra, 52224, 53265
  Uterus, 59100
    Leiomyomata, 58140, 58545, 58546, 58561
  Uvula, 42104-42107
  Wrist Tendon, 25110
Lesion
  Anal, 45108, 46922
  Ankle, 27630
    Arthroscopic, 29891
  Arm, Lower, 25110
  Auditory Canal, External
    Exostosis, 69140
    Radical with Neck Dissection, 69155
    Radical without Neck Dissection, 69150
    Soft Tissue, 69145
  Bladder, 52224
  Brain, 61534, 61536-61540
  Brainstem, 61575, 61576
  Carotid Body, 60600, 60605
  Colon, 44110, 44111
  Conjunctiva, 68110-68130
    with Adjacent Sclera, 68130
    over One Centimeter, 68115

Excision — *continued*
  Lesion — *continued*
    Cornea, 65400
      without Graft, 65420
    Ear, Middle, 69540
    Epididymis
      Local, 54830
      Spermatocele, 54840
    Esophagus, 43100, 43101
    Eye, 65900
    Eyelid
      without Closure, 67840
      Multiple, Different Lids, 67805
      Multiple, Same Lid, 67801
      Single, 67800
      under Anesthesia, 67808
    Femur, 27062
    Finger, 26160
    Foot, 28080, 28090
    Gums, 41822-41828
    Hand, 26160
    Intestines, 44110
      Small, 43250, 44111
    Intraspinal, 63265-63273
    Knee, 27347
  Lesion, Arthroscopic
    Ankle, 29891
    Talus, 29891
    Tibia, 29891
  Lesion, Tendon Sheath
    Arm, Lower, 25110
  Lip, 40500-40530
    Frenum, 40819
  Liver
    Allotransplantation, 47135
      Heterotopic, 47136
    Biopsy, wedge, 47100
    Donor, 47133
    Partial
    Extensive, 47122
      Lobectomy, total
        Left, 47125
        Right, 47130
    Resection
      Partial, 47120, 47125, 47140-47142
      Total, 47133
    Trisegmentectomy, 47122
  Lung, 32440-32445, 32488
    Bronchus Resection, 32486
    Bullae
      Endoscopic, 32655
    Completion, 32488
    Emphysematous, 32491
    Heart
      Donor, 33930
    Lobe, 32480, 32482
    Segment, 32484
    Total, 32440-32445
    Wedge Resection, 32500
      Endoscopic, 32657
  Lymph Nodes, 38500, 38510-38530
    Abdominal, 38747
    Axillary, 38740
      Complete, 38745
    Cervical, 38720, 38724
    Cloquet's node, 38760
    Deep
      Axillary, 38525
      Cervical, 38510, 38520
      Mammary, 38530
    Inguinofemoral, 38760, 38765

Excision — *continued*
Radical Synovium
Wrist, 25115, 25116
Radius, 24130, 24136, 24145, 24152, 24153, 25145
Styloid Process, 25230
Rectum
with Colon, 45121
Partial, 45111, 45113-45116, 45123
Prolapse, 45130, 45135
Stricture, 45150
Total, 45119, 45120
Redundant Skin of Eyelid
See Blepharoplasty
Ribs, 21600-21616, 32900
Scapula
Ostectomy, 23190
Partial, 23182
Sequestrectomy, 23172
Tumor
Radical Resection, 23210
Sclera, 66160
Scrotum, 55150
Semilunar Cartilage of Knee
See Knee, Meniscectomy
Seminal Vesicle, 55650
Sesamoid Bone
Foot, 28315
Sinus
Ethmoid, 31200-31205
Endoscopic, 31254, 31255
Frontal
Endoscopic, 31276
Maxillary, 31225, 31230
Maxillectomy, 31230, 31255
Endoscopic, 31267
Unlisted Procedure, Accessory Sinuses, 31299
Skene's Gland, 53270
Skin
Excess, 15831-15839
Lesion
Benign, 11400-11471
Malignant, 11600-11646
Nose, 30120
Skin Graft
Preparation of Site, 15000, 15001
Skull, 61501
Spermatic Veins, 55530-55540
with Hernia Repair, 55540
Abdominal Approach, 55535
Spleen, 38100-38102
Laparoscopic, 38120
Stapes
with Footplate Drill Out, 69661
without Foreign Material, 69660
Sternum, 21620, 21630, 21632
Stomach
Partial, 43631-43635, 43845
Total, 43620-43622, 43634
Sublingual Gland, 42450
Submandibular Gland, 42440, 42508
Sweat Glands
Axillary, 11450, 11451
Inguinal, 11462, 11463
Perianal, 11470, 11471
Perineal, 11470, 11471
Umbilical, 11470, 11471
Synovium
Ankle, 27625, 27626
Carpometacarpal Joint, 26130

Excision — *continued*
Synovium — *continued*
Elbow, 24102
Hip Joint, 27054
Interphalangeal Joint, Finger, 26140
Intertarsal Joint, 28070
Knee Joint, 27334, 27335
Metacarpophalangeal Joint, 26135
Metatarsophalangeal Joint, 28072
Shoulder, 23105, 23106
Tarsometatarsal Joint, 28070
Wrist, 25105, 25115-25119
Talus, 28120, 28130
Tarsal, 28116, 28122
Temporal Bone, 69535
Temporal, Petrous
Apex, 69530
Tendon
Finger, 26180, 26390, 26415
Hand, 26390, 26415
Palm, 26170
Tendon Sheath
Finger, 26145
Foot, 28086, 28088
Palm, 26145
Wrist, 25115, 25116
Testis
Laparoscopic, 54690
Partial, 54522
Radical, 54530, 54535
Simple, 54520
Tumor, 54530, 54535
Thrombectomy
Axillary Vein, 34490
Bypass Graft, 35875, 35876
Femoropopliteal Vein, 34401-34451
Iliac Vein, 34401-34451
Subclavian Vein, 34471, 34490
Vena Cava, 34401-34451
Thromboendarterectomy
Aorta, Abdominal, 35331
Aortoiliac, 35361
Aortoiliofemoral, 35363
Axillary Artery, 35321
Brachial Artery, 35321
Carotid Artery, 35301, 35390
Celiac Artery, 35341
Femoral Artery, 35371-35381
Iliac, 35361, 35363
Iliac Artery, 35351
Iliofemoral Artery, 35355, 35363
Innominate Artery, 35311
Mesenteric Artery, 35341
Peroneal Artery, 35381
Popliteal Artery, 35381
Renal Artery, 35341
Subclavian Artery, 35301, 35311, 35331, 35390
Tibial Artery, 35381
Vertebral Artery, 35301, 35390
Thymus Gland, 60521
Thyroid Gland
for Malignancy, 60252, 60254
Limited Neck Dissection, 60252
Radical Neck Dissection, 60254
Partial, 60210-60225
Removal All Thyroid Tissue, 60260
Secondary, 60260
Total, 60240
Cervical Approach, 60271
Sternal Split
Transthoracic, 60270

Index

Excision — Excision

Excision — *continued*
  Tumor — *continued*
    Thorax, 21555-21557
    Thyroid, 60200
    Tibia
      Benign, 27635
        with Allograft, 27638
        with Autograft, 27637
      Radical, 27645
    Trachea
      Cervical, 31785
      Thoracic, 31786
    Ulna
      Excluding Olecranon Process
        with Allograft, 25126
        with Autograft, 25125
        Benign, 25120
      Olecranon Process
        with Allograft, 25126
        with Autograft, 25125
        Benign, 25120
      Radical Resection, 25170
    Ureter, 52355
    Urethra, 52234, 52235, 52240, 52355, 53220
    Uterus
      Abdominal Approach, 58140, 58146
      Vaginal Approach, 58145
    Vagina, 57135
    Vertebra
      Lumbar, 22102
      Thoracic, 22101
    Wrist, 25075, 25077
    Zygoma, 21030, 21034
  Turbinate, 30130, 30140
  Tympanic Nerve, 69676
  Ulcer
    Stomach, 43610
  Ulna, 24147, 25145
    Complete, 25240
    Partial, 24147, 25150, 25240
    Radical, 25170
  Umbilicus, 49250
  Ureter
    See Ureterectomy
  Ureterocele, 51535
  Urethra
    Diverticulum, 53230, 53235
    Prolapse, 53275
    Total
      Female, 53210
      Male, 53215
  Uterus
    with Colo-urethrocystopexy, 58267, 58293
    with Colpectomy, 58275-58280
    with Repair of Enterocele, 58270, 58292, 58294
    Laparoscopic, 58550
    Leiomyomata, 58546
    Partial, 58180
    Radical, 58210, 58285
    Removal Tubes and/or Ovaries, 58262-58263, 58291, 58552, 58554
    Total, 58150, 58152, 58200
    Vaginal, 58260, 58290-58294, 58550, 58553
      with Colpectomy, 58275-58280
      with Colpo-Urethrocystopexy, 58267, 58293
      with Repair of Enterocele, 58270, 58292, 58294
      Removal Tubes and or Ovaries, 58262, 58263, 58291, 58552, 58554

Excision — *continued*
  Uvula, 42140, 42145
  Vagina
    with Hysterectomy, 58275, 58280
      with Colpectomy, 58275
      Repair of Enterocele, 58280
    Closure, 57120
    Complete
      with Removal of Paravaginal Tissue with Lymphadenectomy, 57112
      with Removal of Paravaginal Tissue, 57111
      with Removal of Vaginal Wall, 57110
    Partial
      with Removal of Paravaginal Tissue with Lymphadenectomy, 57109
      with Removal of Paravaginal Tissue, 57107
      with Removal of Vaginal Wall, 57106
    Septum, 57130
    Total, 57110
  Varicocele
    Spermatic Cord, 55530-55540
      with Hernia Repair, 55540
      Abdominal Approach, 55535
  Vascular Malformation
    Finger, 26115
    Hand, 26115
  Vas Deferens, 55250
  Vein
    Varicose, 37765, 37766
  Vertebra
    Additional Segment, 22103, 22116
    Cervical, 22110
      for Tumor, 22100, 22110
    Lumbar, 22102
      for Tumor, 22114
    Thoracic, 22112
      for Tumor, 22101
  Vertebral Body
    Decompression, 63081-63091
    Lesion, 63300-63308
  Vitreous, 67039
    with Retinal Surgery, 67038
    Total
      with Epiretinal Membrane Stripping, 67038
      Pars Plana Approach, 67036
  Vulva
    Radical
      Complete, 56633-56640
      Partial, 56630-56632
    Simple
      Complete, 56625
      Partial, 56620

Exclusion
  Duodenum, 48547
  Small Bowel, 44700

Exenteration
  Eye
    with Muscle or Myocutaneous Flap, 65114
    Removal Orbital Contents, 65110
    Therapeutic Removal of Bone, 65112
  Pelvis, 45126, 58240
    for Colorectal Malignancy, 45126

Exercise Stress Tests, 93015-93018

Exercise Test
  See Electromyography, Needle
  Ischemic Limb, 95875

Exercise Therapy, 97110-97113
  See Physical Medicine/ Therapy/Occupational

Exfoliation
Chemical, 17360
Exhaled Breath Condensate pH, 0140T
Exocrine, Pancreas
See Pancreas
Exomphalos
See Omphalocele
Exostectomy, 28288, 28290
Exostoses, Cartilaginous
See Exostosis
Exostosis
Excision, 69140
Expander, Skin, Inflatable
See Tissue, Expander
Expired Gas Analysis, 94680-94690, 94770
See Pulmonology, Diagnostic
Carbon Monoxide Breath Test, 0043T
Spectroscopic, 0064T
Exploration
Abdomen, 49000, 49002
Blood Vessel, 35840
Penetrating Wound, 20102
Staging, 58960
Adrenal Gland, 60540, 60545
Anal
Endoscopy, 46600
Ankle, 27610, 27620
Arm, Lower, 25248
Artery
Brachial, 24495
Carotid, 35701
Femoral, 35721
Other, 35761
Popliteal, 35741
Unlisted Services and Procedures, 35761
Back, Penetrating Wound, 20102
Bile Duct
Atresia, 47700
Endoscopy, 47552, 47553
Blood Vessel
Abdomen, 35840
Chest, 35820
Extremity, 35860
Neck, 35800
Brain
Infratentorial, 61305
Supratentorial, 61304
via Burr Hole
Infratentorial, 61253
Supratentorial, 61250
Breast, 19020
Bronchi
Endoscopy, 31622
Bronchoscopy, 31622
Cauda Equina, 63005, 63011, 63017
Chest, Penetrating Wound, 20101
Colon
Endoscopic, 44388, 45378
Colon, Sigmoid
Endoscopy, 45330, 45335
Common Bile Duct
with Cholecystectomy, 47610
Duodenum, 44010
Ear, Inner
Endolymphatic Sac
with Shunt, 69806
without Shunt, 69805
Ear, Middle, 69440
Elbow, 24000-24101
Epididymis, 54820

Exploration — *continued*
Esophagus
Endoscopy, 43200
Extremity
Penetrating Wound, 20103
Finger Joint, 26075, 26080
Flank
Penetrating Wound, 20102
Gallbladder, 47480
Gastrointestinal Tract, Upper
Endoscopy, 43234, 43235
Hand Joint, 26070
Heart, 33310, 33315
Hepatic Duct, 47400
Hip, 27033
Interphalangeal Joint
Toe, 28024
Intertarsal Joint, 28020
Intestines, Small
Endoscopy, 43360
Enterotomy, 44020
Kidney, 50010, 50045, 50120, 50135
Knee, 27310, 27331
Lacrimal Duct, 68810
with Anesthesia, 68811
with Insertion Tube or Stent, 68815
Canaliculi, 68840
Laryngoscopy, 31575
Larynx, 31320, 31505, 31520-31526, 31575
Liver
Wound, 47361, 47362
Mediastinum, 39000, 39010
Metatarsophalangeal Joint, 28022
Nasolacrimal Duct, 68810
with Anesthesia, 68811
with Insertion Tube or Stent, 68815
Neck
Lymph Nodes, 38542
Penetrating Wound, 20100
Nipple, 19110
Nose
Endoscopy, 31231-31235
Orbit, 61332-61334
without Bone Flap, 67400
with/without Biopsy, 67450
Parathyroid Gland, 60500-60505
Pelvis, 49320
Peritoneum
Endoscopic, 49320
Prostate, 55860
with Nodes, 55862, 55865
Pterygomaxillary Fossa, 31040
Rectum
Endoscopic, 45300
Injury, 45562, 45563
Retroperitoneal Area, 49010
Scrotum, 55110
Shoulder Joint, 23040, 23044, 23107
Sinus
Frontal, 31070, 31075
Endoscopic, 31276
Transorbital, 31075
Maxillary, 31020, 31030
Sphenoid, 31050
Skull, Drill Hole, 61105
Spinal Cord, 63001-63011, 63015-63017, 63040-63044
Facetectomy, Foraminotomy
Partial Cervical, 63045
Additional Segments, 63048
Partial Lumbar, 63047
Additional Segments, 63048

Exploration — *continued*

Spinal Cord — *continued*

Facetectomy, Foraminotomy — *continued*

Partial Thoracic, 63046

Additional Segments, 63048

Fusion, 22830

Hemilaminectomy (including partial Facetectomy, Foraminotomy)

Cervical, 63045

Additional Segments, 63048

Lumbar, 63047

Additional Segments, 63048

Thoracic, 63046

Additional Segments, 63048

Laminectomy

Cervical, 63001, 63015

Lumbar, 63005, 63017

Thoracic, 63003, 63016

Laminotomy

Initial

Cervical, 63020

Each Additional Space, 63035

Lumbar, 63030

Reexploration

Cervical, 63040

Each Additional Space, 63043

Lumbar, 63042

Each Additional Interspace, 63044

Stomach, 43500

Tarsometatarsal Joint, 28020

Testis

Undescended, 54550, 54560

Toe Joint, 28024

Ureter, 50600, 50650, 50660

Vagina, 57000

Endoscopic Endocervical, 57452

Wrist, 25101, 25248

Joint, 25040

Exploration, Larynx by Incision

See Laryngotomy, Diagnostic

Exploratory Laparotomy

See Abdomen, Exploration

Expression

Lesion

Conjunctiva, 68040

Exteriorization, Small Intestine

See Enterostomy

External Auditory Canal

See Auditory Canal

External Cephalic Version, 59412

External Ear

See Ear, External

External Extoses

See Exostosis

External Fixation (System)

Adjustment/Revision, 20693

Application, 20690, 20692

Mandibular Fracture

Open Treatment, 21454

Percutaneous Treatment, 21452

Removal, 20694

Extirpation, Lacrimal Sac

See Dacryocystectomy

Extracorporeal Circulation, 33960, 33961

Regional Chemotherapy

Extremity, 36823

Extracorporeal Dialyses

See Hemodialysis

Extracorporeal Membrane Oxygenation

Cannulization, 36822

Extracorporeal Photochemotherapies

See Photopheresis

Extracorporeal Shock Wave Therapy

See Lithotripsy

Lateral Humeral Epicondyle, 0102T

Musculoskeletal, 0019T, 0101T

Plantar Fascia, 28890

Extraction

Lens

Extracapsular, 66940

Intracapsular, 66920

Dislocated Lens, 66930

Extraction, Cataract

See Cataract, Excision

Extradural Anesthesia

See Anesthesia, Epidural

Extradural Injection

See Epidural, Injection

Extraocular Muscle

See Eye Muscles

Extrauterine Pregnancy

See Ectopic Pregnancy

Extravasation Blood

See Hemorrhage

Extremity

Lower

Harvest of Vein for Bypass Graft, 35500

Harvest of Vein for Vascular Reconstruction, 35572

Repair of Blood Vessel, 35286

Revision, 35879, 35881

Penetrating Wound, 20103

Upper

Harvest of Artery for Coronary Artery Bypass Graft, 35600

Harvest of Vein for Bypass Graft, 35500

Repair of Blood Vessel, 35206

Extremity Testing

Physical Therapy, 97750

Vascular Diagnostics, 93924

Eye

with Muscle or Myocutaneous Flap, 65114

Muscles Attached, 65105

Ocular Contents

with Implant, 65093

without Implant, 65091

Orbital Contents, 65110

without Implant, 65101

See Ciliary Body; Cornea; Iris; Lens; Retina; Sclera; Vitreous

Biometry, 76516, 76519, 92136

Drainage

with Removal of Vitreous and/or Discission of Anterior Hyaloid Membrane, 65810

with Therapeutic Release of Aqueous, 65805

Anterior Chamber, 65800-65815

with Diagnostic Aspiration of Aqueous, 65800

with Removal of Blood, 65815

Endoscopy, 66990

Goniotomy, 65820

Incision

Adhesions

Anterior Synechiae, 65860, 65870

Corneovitreal Adhesions, 65880

Goniosynechiae, 65865

Posterior Synechiae, 65875

Eye — *continued*
  Incision — *continued*
    Anterior Chamber, 65820
    Trabecula, 65850
  Injection
    Air, 66020
    Medication, 66030
  Insertion
    Implantation
      Drug Delivery System, 67027
      Foreign Material for ReinForcement, 65155
      Muscles Attached, 65140
      Muscles Not Attached, 65135
      Reinsertion, 65150
      Scleral Shell, 65130
  Interferometry
    Biometry, 92136
  Lesion
    Excision, 65900
  Nerve
    Destruction, 67345
  Paracentesis
    Anterior Chamber
      with Diagnostic Aspiration of Aqueous, 65800
      with Removal of Blood, 65815
    Removal of Vitreous and/or Discission
      Anterior Hyaloid Membrane, 65810
      with Therapeutic Release of Aqueous, 65805
  Radial Keratotomy, 65771
  Reconstruction
    Amniotic Membrane, 65780
    Conjunctiva, 65782
  Removal
    Blood Clot, 65930
    Bone, 65112
    Foreign Body
      Conjunctival Embedded, 65210
      Conjunctival Superficial, 65205
      Corneal without Slit Lamp, 65220
      Corneal with Slit Lamp, 65222
      Intraocular, 65235-65265
    Implant, 65175
      Anterior Segment, 65920
      Muscles not Attached, 65103
      Posterior Segment, 67120, 67121
  Repair
    Conjunctiva
      by Mobilization and Rearrangement with Hospitalization, 65273
      by Mobilization and Rearrangement without Hospitalization, 65272
      Direct Closure, 65270
    Cornea
      NonperForating, 65275
      Perforating, 65280, 65285
    Muscles, 65290
    Sclera
      with Graft, 66225
      with Tissue Glue, 65286
      without Graft, 66220
      Anterior Segment, 66250
    Trabeculae, 65855
    Wound
      by Mobilization and Rearrangement, 65272, 65273
      Direct Closure, 65270
  Shunt, Aqueous
    to Extraocular Reservoir, 66180

Eye — *continued*
  Ultrasound, 76510-76514
    Biometry, 76516, 76519
    Foreign Body, 76529
  Unlisted Services and Procedures
    Anterior Segment, 66999
    Posterior Segment, 67299
  X-ray, 70030
Eye Allergy Test, 95060
  See Allergy Tests
Eyebrow
  Repair
    Ptosis, 67900
Eye Evisceration
  See Evisceration, Ocular Contents
Eye Exam
  with Anesthesia, 92018, 92019
  Established Patient, 92012, 92014
  New Patient, 92002, 92004
  Radiologic, 70030
Eye Exercises
  Training, 92065
Eyeglasses
  See Spectacle Services
Eyelashes
  Repair Trichiasis
    Epilation
      by Forceps Only, 67820
      by Other than Forceps, 67825
    Incision of Lid Margin, 67830
      with Free Mucous Membrane Graft, 67835
Eyelid
  Abscess
    Incision and Drainage, 67700
  Biopsy, 67810
  Blepharoplasty, 15820-15823
  Chalazion
    Excision
      with Anesthesia, 67808
      Multiple, 67801, 67805
      Single, 67800
  Closure by Suture, 67875
  Incision
    Canthus, 67715
  Injection
    Subconjunctival, 68200
    Sutures, 67710
  Lesion
    Destruction, 67850
    Excision
      with Anesthesia, 67808
      without Closure, 67840
      Multiple, 67801, 67805
      Single, 67800
  Reconstruction
    Canthus, 67950
    Total Eyelid
      Conjunctivo-Tarso-Muller's Muscle-Levator Resection, 67908
      Lower, 67973
        Second Stage, 67975
      Upper, 67974
        Second Stage, 67975
    Transfer of Tarsoconjunctival Flap from Opposing Eyelid, 67971
  Removal
    Foreign Body, 67938

Eyelid — *continued*
Repair, 21280, 21282
  Blepharoptosis
    Reduction Overcorrection of Ptosis, 67909
    Superior Rectus Technique with Fascial
      Sling, 67906
  Ectropion
    Excision Tarsal Wedge, 67916
    Extensive, 67917
    Suture, 67914
    Thermocauterization, 67915
  Entropion
    Excision Tarsal Wedge, 67923
    Extensive, 67924
    Frontalis Muscle Technique, 67901-
      67904
    Suture, 67921
    Thermocauterization, 67922
  Excisional, 67961
    over One-Fourth of Lid Margin, 67966
  Lagophthalmos, 67912
  Lashes
    Epilation, by Forceps Only, 67820
    Epilation by Other than Forceps, 67825
    Lid Margin, 67830, 67835
  Wound
    Full Thickness, 67935
    Partial Thickness, 67930
Repair with Graft
  Retraction, 67911
Skin Graft
  Delay of Flap, 15630
  Full Thickness, 15260, 15261, 67961
  Pedicle Flap, 15576
  Split, 15120, 15121, 67961
Suture, 67880
  with Transposition of Tarsal Plate, 67882
Tissue Transfer, Adjacent, 14060, 14061,
  67961
Unlisted Services and Procedures, 67999
Eyelid Ptoses
See Blepharoptosis
Eye Muscles
Biopsy, 67350
Repair
  Strabismus
    with Scarring Extraocular Muscles, 67332
    with Superior Oblique Muscle, 67318
    Adjustable Sutures, 67335
    Exploration and/or Repair Detached
      Extraocular Muscle, 67340
    One Vertical Muscle, 67314
    on Patient with Previous Surgery, 67331
    Posterior Fixation Suture, 67334
    Recession or Resection, 67311, 67312
    Release of Scar Tissue without Detaching
      Extraocular Muscle, 67343
    Two or More Vertical Muscles, 67316
  Transposition, 67320
  Unlisted Procedure, Ocular Muscle, 67399
Eye Prosthesis
See Prosthesis
Eye Socket
See Orbit; Orbital Contents; Orbital Floor;
  Periorbital Region

F

Face
CT Scan, 70486-70488
Lesion
  Destruction, 17000-17108, 17280-17286

Face — *continued*
Magnetic Resonance Imaging (MRI), 70540-
  70543
Skin Graft
  Split, 15120, 15121
Tumor Resection, 21015
Face Lift, 15824-15828
Facial Asymmetries
See Hemifacial Microsomia
Facial Bone
See Mandible; Maxilla
Tumor
  Excision, 21034
Facial Bones
Abscess
  Excision, 21026
Anesthesia, 00190, 00192
Reconstruction
  Secondary, 21275
Repair, 21208, 21209
Tumor
  Excision, 21029, 21030, 21034
  Resection
    Radical, 21015
X-ray
  Complete, Minimum Three Views, 70150
  Less than Three Views, 70140
  Nasal Bones, 70160
Facial Nerve
Anastomosis
  to Hypoglossal Nerve, 64868
  to Phrenic Nerve, 64870
  to Spinal Accessory Nerve, 64866
Avulsion, 64742
Decompression, 61590, 61596
  Intratemporal
    Lateral to Geniculate Ganglion, 69720,
      69740
    Medial to Geniculate Ganglion, 69725,
      69745
  Total, 69955
Function Study, 92516
Incision, 64742
Injection
  Anesthetic, 64402
Mobilization, 61590
Paralysis Repair, 15840-15845
Repair
  Lateral to Geniculate Ganglion, 69740
  Medial to Geniculate Ganglion, 69745
  Suture with or without Graft, 64864, 64865
Suture
  Lateral to Geniculate Ganglion, 69740
  Medial to Geniculate Ganglion, 69745
Transection, 64742
Facial Nerve Paralysis
Graft, 15840-15845
Repair, 15840-15845
Facial Prosthesis, 21088
Facial Rhytidectomy
See Face Lift
Factor
I, 85384, 85385
II, 85210
III, 85730, 85732
IV, 82310
IX, 85250
V, 85220
VII, 85230
VIII, 85244, 85247

Femoral Vein
See Vein, Femoral
Femur
See Hip; Knee; Leg, Upper
Bursa
Excision, 27062
Craterization, 27070, 27071, 27360
Cyst
Excision, 27065-27067, 27355-27358
Diaphysectomy, 27360
Drainage, 27303
Excision, 27070, 27071, 27360
Epiphyseal Bar, 20150
Fracture
Closed Treatment, 27501-27503
Distal, 27508, 27510, 27514
Distal, Medial or Lateral Condyle, 27509
Epiphysis, 27516-27519
Intertrochanteric, 27238-27245
with Implant, 27245
with Manipulation, 27240
Closed Treatment, 27238
Open Treatment, 27244
Neck, 27230-27236
Closed Treatment, 27230, 27232
Open Treatment, 27236
Percutaneous Fixation, 27235
Open Treatment, 27244, 27245, 27506,
27507, 27511, 27513
Percutaneous Fixation, 27509
Pertrochanteric, 27238-27245
with Implant, 27245
with Manipulation, 27240
Closed Treatment, 27238
Open Treatment, 27244
Shaft, 27500, 27502, 27506, 27507
Subtrochanteric, 27238-27245
with Implant, 27245
with Manipulation, 27240
Closed Treatment, 27238
Open Treatment, 27244
Supracondylar, 27501-27503, 27509, 27511,
27513
Transcondylar, 27501-27503, 27509, 27511,
27513
Trochanteric, 27246, 27248
with Manipulation, 27503
without Manipulation, 27501
Closed Treatment, 27246
Open Treatment, 27248
Halo, 20663
Lesion
Excision, 27062
Osteoplasty
Lengthening, 27466, 27468
Shortening, 27465, 27468
Osteotomy
without Fixation, 27448
Prophylactic Treatment, 27187, 27495
Realignment on Intramedullary Rod, 27454
Reconstruction, 27468
at Knee, 27442, 27443, 27446
Lengthening, 27466, 27468
Shortening, 27465, 27468
Repair, 27470, 27472
with Graft, 27170
Epiphysis, 27181, 27742
Arrest, 27185, 27475, 27479
Muscle Transfer, 27110
Osteotomy, 27448, 27450
with Open Reduction, Hip, 27156

Femur — continued
Repair — continued
Osteotomy — continued
and Transfer of Greater Trochanter,
27140
as part of other, 27151
Femoral Neck, 27161
Intertrochanteric or Subtrochanteric,
27165
Multiple, Shaft, 27454
Shaft or Supracondylar, 27448
Saucerization, 27070, 27071, 27360
Tumor
Excision, 27065-27067, 27355-27358,
27365
X-ray, 73550
Fenestration, Pericardium
See Pericardiostomy
Fenestration Procedure
Semicircular Canal, 69820
Revision, 69840
Tracheostomy, 31610
Fern Test
Smear and Stain, Wet Mount, 87210
Ferric Chloride
Urine, 81005
Ferrihemoglobin
See Methemoglobin
Ferritin
Blood or Urine, 82728
Ferroxidase
See Ceruloplasmin
Fertility Control
See Contraception
Fertility Test
Semen Analysis, 89300-89321
Sperm Evaluation
Cervical Mucus Penetration Test, 89330
Hamster Penetration, 89329
Hyaluronan Binding Assay, 0087T
Fertilization
Oocytes (Eggs)
In Vitro, 89250-89251
with Co-Culture of Embryo, 89251
Assisted (Microtechnique), 89280, 89281
Fertilization in Vitro
See In Vitro Fertilization
Fetal Biophysical Profile, 76818, 76819
Fetal Contraction Stress Test, 59020
Fetal Hemoglobin, 83030, 83033, 85460, 85461
**Fetal Lung Maturity Assessment, Lecithin
Sphingomyelin Ratio**, 83661
Fetal Monitoring
See Monitoring, Fetal
Fetal Non-Stress Test, 59025
Ultrasound, 76818
Fetal Procedure
Amnioinfusion, 59070
Cord Occlusion, 59072
Fluid Drainage, 59074
Shunt Placement, 59076
Unlisted Procedure, 59897
Fetal Testing
Biophysical Profile, 76818-76819
Lung Maturity, 83661, 83663, 83664
Heart, 76825, 76826
Doppler
Complete, 76827
Follow-up or Repeat Study, 76828

Finger — *continued*
Bone
  Incision and Drainage, 26034
Cast, 29086
Collection of Blood, 36415, 36416
Decompression, 26035
Excision
  Constricting Ring, 26596
  Tendon, 26180, 26390, 26415
Insertion
  Tendon Graft, 26392
Magnetic Resonance Imaging (MRI), 73221
Reconstruction
  Extra Digit, 26587
  Toe to Hand Transfer, 26551-26554, 26556
Removal
  Implantation, 26320
  Tube, 26392, 26416
Repair
  Blood Vessel, 35207
  Claw Finger, 26499
  Extra Digit, 26587
  Macrodactylia, 26590
  Tendon
    Dorsum, 26418, 26420
    Extensor, 26415-26434, 26445, 26449,
      26460
      Central Slip, 26426, 26428
      Distal Insertion, 26432, 26433
      Excision with Implantation, 26415
      Hand, 26410
        with Graft, 26412
      Realignment, Hand, 26437
    Flexor, 26356-26358, 26440, 26442,
      26455
    Flexor Excision with Implantation, 26390
    Lengthening, 26476, 26478
    Opponensplasty, 26490-26496
    Profundus, 26370-26373
    Removal Tube or Rod
      Extensor, 26416
      Flexor, 26392
    Shortening, 26477, 26479
    Tenodesis, 26471, 26474
    Tenolysis, 26440-26449
    Tenotomy, 26450-26460
    Transfer or Transplant, 26485, 26489,
      26497, 26498
    Volar Plate, 26548
    Web Finger, 26560-26562
Replantation, 20816, 20822
Reposition, 26555
Sesamoidectomy, 26185
Splint, 29130, 29131
Strapping, 29280
Tendon Sheath
  Excision, 26145
  Incision, 26055
  Incision and Drainage, 26020
  Tenotomy, 26060, 26460
    Flexor, 26455
Tumor
  Excision, 26115-26117
Unlisted Services and Procedures/Hands or
  Fingers, 26989
X-ray, 73140
Finger Flap
Tissue Transfer, 14350
Finger Joint
See Intercarpal Joint
Finney Operation, 43850

FISH, 88365
Fishberg Concentration Test
Water Load Test, 89235
Fissurectomy, 46200
Fissure in Ano
See Anus, Fissure
Fistula
Anal
  Repair, 46288, 46706
Arteriovenous, 36831-36833
  Revision
    with Thrombectomy, 36831
    without Thrombectomy, 36832
  Thrombectomy without revision, 36831
Autogenous Graft, 36825
Bronchi
  Repair, 32815
Carotid-Cavernous Repair, 61710
Chest Wall
  Repair, 32906
Conjunctiva
  with Tube or Stent, 68750
  without Tube, 68745
Enterovesical
  Closure, 44660, 44661
Kidney, 50520-50526
Lacrimal Gland
  Closure, 68770
  Dacryocystorhinostomy, 68720
Nose
  Repair, 30580, 30600
    Window, 69666
Oval Window, 69666
Postauricular, 69700
Rectovaginal
  with Concomitant Colostomy, 57307
  Abdominal Approach, 57305
  Transperineal Approach, 57308
Round Window, 69667
Sclera
  Iridencleisis or Iridotasis, 66165
  Sclerectomy with Punch or Scissors with
    Iridectomy, 66160
  Thermocauterization with Iridectomy, 66155
  Trabeculectomy ab Externo in Absence
    Previous Surgery, 66170
  Trabeculectomy ab Externo with Scarring,
    66172
  Trephination with Iridectomy, 66150
Suture
  Kidney, 50520-50526
  Ureter, 50920, 50930
Trachea, 31755
Tracheoesophageal
  Repair, 43305, 43312, 43314
  Speech Prothesis, 31611
Transperineal Approach, 57308
Ureter, 50920, 50930
Urethra, 53400, 53405
Urethrovaginal, 57310
  with Bulbocavernosus Transplant, 57311
Vesicouterine
  Closure, 51920, 51925
Vesicovaginal
  Closure, 51900
  Transvesical and Vaginal Approach, 57330
  Vaginal Approach, 57320
X-ray, 76080
Fistula Arteriovenous
See Arteriovenous Fistula

Fistulectomy
See Hemorrhoids
Anal, 46060, 46270-46285

Fistulization
Conjunction to Nasal Cavity, 68745
Esophagus, 43350-43352
Intestines, 44300-44346
Lacrimal Sac to Nasal Cavity, 68720
Penis, 54435
Pharynx, 42955
Sclera, 0123T
Tracheopharyngeal, 31755

Fistulization, Interatrial
See Septostomy, Atrial

Fistulotomy
Anal, 46270, 46280

Fitting
Cervical Cap, 57170
Contact Lens, 92070, 92310-92313
See Contact Lens Services
Diaphragm, 57170
Low Vision Aid, 92354, 92355
See Spectacle Services
Spectacle Prosthesis, 92352, 92353
Spectacles, 92340-92342

Fitzgerald Factor, 85293

Fixation (Device)
See Application; Bone; Fixation; Spinal
Instrumentation
Application, External, 20690, 20692
Insertion, 22841-22844
Prosthetic, 22851
Reinsertion, 22849
Interdental without Fracture, 21497
Pelvic
Insertion, 22848
Removal
External, 20694
Internal, 20670, 20680
Sacrospinous Ligament
Vaginal Prolapse, 57282
Shoulder, 23700
Skeletal
Humeral Epicondyle
Percutaneous, 24566
Spinal
Insertion, 22841-22847
Prosthetic, 22851
Reinsertion, 22849

Fixation, External
See External Fixation

Fixation, Kidney
See Nephropexy

Fixation, Rectum
See Proctopexy

Fixation Test Complement
See Complement, Fixation Test

Fixation, Tongue
See Tongue, Fixation

Flank
See Back/Flank

Flap
See Skin Graft and Flap
Delay of Flap at Trunk, 15600
at Eyelids, Nose Ears, or Lips, 15630
at Forehead, Cheeks, Chin, Neck, Axillae,
Genitalia, Hands, Feet, 15620
at Scalp, Arms, or Legs, 15610
Section Pedicle of Cross Finger, 15620

Flap — continued
Free
Breast Reconstruction, 19364
Microvascular Transfer, 15756-15758
Grafts, 15574-15650, 15842
Composite, 15760
Derma-Fat-Fascia, 15770
Cross Finger Flap, 15574
Punch for Hair Transplant
Less than 15, 15775
More than 15, 15776
Island Pedicle, 15740
Neurovascular Pedicle, 15750
Latissimus Dorsi
Breast Reconstruction, 19361
Omentum
Free
with Microvascular Anastomosis, 49906
Transfer
Intermediate of Any Pedicle, 15650
Transverse Rectus Abdominis Myocutaneous
Breast Reconstruction, 19367-19369

Flatfoot Correction, 28735

Flea Typhus
See Murine Typhus

Fletcher Factor, 85292

Flow Cytometry, 88182-88189

Flow Volume Loop/Pulmonary, 94375
See Pulmonology, Diagnostic

Fluid, Amniotic
See Amniotic Fluid

Fluid, Body
See Body Fluid

Fluid, Cerebrospinal
See Cerebrospinal Fluid

Fluid Collection
Incision and Drainage
Skin, 10140

Fluid Drainage
Abdomen, 49080, 49081

Fluorescein
Angiography, Ocular, 92287
Intravenous Injection
Vascular Flow Check, Graft, 15860

Fluorescein, Angiography
See Angiography, Fluorescein

Fluorescent Antibody, 86255, 86256

Fluorescent In Situ Hybridization, 88365

Fluoride
Blood, 82735
Urine, 82735

Fluoroscopy
Bile Duct
Calculus Removal, 74327
Guide for Catheter, 74328, 74330
Chest
Bronchoscopy, 31622-31646
Complete (four views), 71034
Partial (two views), 71023
Drain Abscess, 75989
GI Tract
Guidance Intubation, 74340
Hourly, 76000, 76001
Introduction
GI Tube, 74340
Larynx, 70370
Nasogastric, 43752
Needle Biopsy, 76003

Fluoroscopy — *continued*
　Pancreatic Duct
　　Catheter, 74329, 74330
　Pharynx, 70370
　Renal
　　Guide Catheter, 74475
　Spine/Paraspinous
　　Guide Catheter
　　　Needle, 76005
　Unlisted Procedure, 76496
　Ureter
　　Guidance Catheter, 74480
　Vertebra
　　Osteoplasty, 76012
　X-ray with Contrast
　　Guidance Catheter, 74475
Flurazepam
　Blood or Urine, 82742
Flush Aortogram, 75722, 75724
Flu Vaccines, 90645-90660
FNA
　See Fine Needle Aspiration
Foam Stability Test, 83662
Fold, Vocal
　See Vocal Cords
Foley Operation Pyeloplasty
　See Pyeloplasty
Foley Y-Pyeloplasty, 50400, 50405
Folic Acid, 82747
　RBC, 82746
Follicle Stimulating Hormone (FSH), 80418,
　　80426, 83001
Folliculin
　See Estrone
Follitropin
　See Follicle Stimulating Hormone (FSH)
Follow-Up Services
　See Hospital Services; Office and/or Other
　　　Outpatient Services
　Post-Op, 99024
Fontan Procedure, 33615, 33617
Food Allergy Test, 95075
　See Allergy Tests
Foot
　See Metatarsal; Tarsal
　Amputation, 28800, 28805
　Bursa
　　Incision and Drainage, 28001
　Capsulotomy, 28260-28264
　Cast, 29450
　Cock Up Fifth Toe, 28286
　Fasciectomy, 28060
　　Radical, 28060, 28062
　Fasciotomy, 28008
　　Endoscopic, 29893
　Hammertoe Operation, 28285
　Incision, 28002-28005
　Joint
　　See Talotarsal Joint; Tarsometatarsal Joint
　　Magnetic Resonance Imaging (MRI), 73721-
　　　73723
　Lesion
　　Excision, 28080, 28090
　Magnetic Resonance Imaging (MRI), 73718-
　　73720
　Nerve
　　Excision, 28030
　　Incision, 28035

Foot — *continued*
　Neuroma
　　Excision, 28080
　Ostectomy, Metatarsal Head, 28288
　Reconstruction
　　Cleft Foot, 28360
　Removal
　　Foreign Body, 28190-28193
　Repair
　　Muscle, 28250
　　Tendon
　　　Advancement Posterior Tibial, 28238
　　　Capsulotomy; Metatarsophalangeal,
　　　　28270
　　　　Interphalangeal, 28272
　　　Capsulotomy, Midfoot; Medial Release,
　　　　26820
　　　Capsulotomy, Midtarsal (Heyman Type),
　　　　28264
　　　Extensor, Single, 28208
　　　　Secondary with Free Graft, 28210
　　　Flexor, Single, with Free Graft, 28200
　　　　Secondary with Free Graft, 28202
　　　Tenolysis, Extensor
　　　　Multiple through Same Incision, 28226
　　　Tenolysis, Flexor
　　　　Multiple through Same Incision, 28222
　　　　Single, 28220
　　　Tenotomy, Open, Extensor
　　　　Foot or Toe, 28234
　　　Tenotomy, Open, Flexor, 28230
　　　　Toe, Single Procedure, 28232
　Replantation, 20838
　Sesamoid
　　Excision, 28315
　Skin Graft
　　Delay of Flap, 15620
　　Full Thickness, 15240, 15241
　　Pedicle Flap, 15574
　　Split, 15100, 15101
　Splint, 29590
　Strapping, 29540, 29590
　Suture
　　Tendon, 28200-28210
　Tendon Sheath
　　Excision, 28086, 28088
　Tenolysis, 28220-28226
　Tenotomy, 28230-28234
　Tissue Transfer, Adjacent, 14040, 14041
　Tumor
　　Excision, 28043-28046
　Unlisted Services and Procedures, 28899
　X-ray, 73620, 73630
Foot Abscess
　See Abscess, Foot
Foot Navicular Bone
　See Navicular
Forearm
　See Arm, Lower
Forehead
　Reconstruction, 21179-21180, 21182-21184
　　Midface, 21159, 21160
　Reduction, 21137-21139
　Rhytidectomy, 15824, 15826
　Skin Graft
　　Delay of Flap, 15620
　　Full Thickness, 15240, 15241
　　Pedicle Flap, 15574
　Tissue Transfer, Adjacent, 14040, 14041
Forehead and Orbital Rim
　Reconstruction, 21172-21180

Index

Fracture, Treatment — Fracture, Treatment

Fracture, Treatment — *continued*
  Humerus — *continued*
    Greater Tuberosity Fracture
      Closed Treatment with Manipulation, 23625
      Closed Treatment without Manipulation, 23620
      Open Treatment, 23630
    Open Treatment, 23615, 23616
    Shaft, 24500
      Open Treatment, 24515, 24516
    Supracondylar
      Closed Treatment, 24530, 24535
      Open Treatment, 24545, 24546
      Percutaneous Fixation, 24538
    Transcondylar
      Closed Treatment, 24530, 24535
      Open Treatment, 24545, 24546
      Percutaneous Fixation, 24538
  Hyoid Bone
    Open Treatment, 21495
  Ilium
    Open Treatment, 27215, 27218
    Percutaneous Fixation, 27216
  Knee, 27520
    Arthroscopic Treatment, 29850, 29851
    Open Treatment, 27524
  Larynx
    Open Treatment, 31584
  Leg
    Femur
      Closed Treatment
        With manipulation, 27502, 27503, 27510, 27516
        Without manipulation, 27500, 27501, 27508, 27517
      Open Treatment, 27506, 27507, 27511-27514, 27519
      Percutaneous fixation, 27509
    Fibula
      Closed Treatment
        With manipulation, 27752, 27781, 27788
        Without manipulation, 27750, 27780, 27786
      Open Treatment, 27758, 27759, 27784, 27792, 27826-27832
    Tibia
      Closed Treatment
        With manipulation, 27752, 27825
        Without manipulation, 27750, 27824, 27830, 27831
      Open Treatment, 27758, 27759, 27826-27829, 27832
      Percutaneous fixation, 27756
  Malar Area
    with Bone Graft, 21366
    with Manipulation, 21355
    Open Treatment, 21360-21366
  Mandible
    Closed Treatment
      with Manipulation, 21451
      without Manipulation, 21450
      Interdental Fixation, 21453
    Open Treatment, 21454-21470
      with Interdental Fixation, 21462
      without Interdental Fixation, 21461
      External Fixation, 21454
    Percutaneous Treatment, 21452
  Maxilla
    Closed Treatment, 21421
    Open Treatment, 21422, 21423

Fracture, Treatment — *continued*
  Metacarpal
    with Manipulation, 26605, 26607
    without Manipulation, 26600
    Closed Treatment, 26600, 26605
      with Fixation, 26607
    Open Treatment, 26615
    Percutaneous Fixation, 26608
  Metatarsal
    with Manipulation, 28475, 28476
    without Manipulation, 28450, 28470
    Closed Treatment, 28470, 28475
    Open Treatment, 28485
    Percutaneous Fixation, 28476
  Monteggia
    See Fracture, Ulna; Monteggia Fracture
  Nasal Bone
    with Manipulation, 21315, 21320
    without Manipulation, 21310
    Closed Treatment, 21310-21320
    Open Treatment, 21325-21335
  Nasal Septum
    Closed Treatment, 21337
    Open Treatment, 21336
  Nasal Turbinate
    Therapeutic, 30930
  Nasoethmoid
    with Fixation, 21340
    Open Treatment, 21338, 21339
    Percutaneous Treatment, 21340
  Nasomaxillary
    with Bone Grafting, 21348
    with Fixation, 21345-21347
    Closed Treatment, 21345
    Open Treatment, 21346-21348
  Navicular
    with Manipulation, 25624
    Closed Treatment, 25622
    Open Treatment, 25628
  Odontoid
    Open Treatment
      with Graft, 22319
      without Graft, 22318
  Orbit
    Closed Treatment, 21400
      with Manipulation, 21401
      without Manipulation, 21400
    Open Treatment, 21406-21408
      Blowout Fracture, 21385-21395
  Orbital Floor
    Blow Out, 21385-21395
  Palate
    Closed Treatment, 21421
    Open Treatment, 21422, 21423
  Patella
    Closed Treatment
      without Manipulation, 27520
    Open Treatment, 27524
  Pelvic Ring
    Closed Treatment, 27193, 27194
      without Manipulation, 27193, 27194
    Open Treatment
      Anterior, 27217
      Posterior, 27218
    Percutaneous Fixation, 27216
  Phalanges
    Finger(s)
      Articular
        with Manipulation, 26742
        Closed Treatment, 26740
        Open Treatment, 26746

Fracture, Treatment — *continued*
    Phalanges — *continued*
        Finger(s — *continued*
            Closed Treatment
                with Manipulation, 26725, 26742,
                    26755
                without Manipulation, 26720, 26740,
                    26750
            Distal, 26755, 26756
                Closed Treatment, 26750
                Open Treatment, 26765
                Percutaneous Fixation, 26756
            Finger/Thumb
                with Manipulation, 26725, 26727
                Bennett Fracture, 26650, 26665
                Closed Treatment, 26720, 26725
                Percutaneous Fixation, 26650, 26727,
                    26756
                Shaft, 26720-26727
            Great Toe, 28490
                Closed Treatment, 28490, 28495
                Open Treatment, 28505
                Percutaneous Fixation, 28496
                without Manipulation, 28496
            Open Treatment, 26735, 26746
                Distal, 26765
            Shaft
                Closed Treatment, 26725
                Open Treatment, 26735
                Percutaneous Fixation, 26727
            Toe
                with Manipulation, 28515
                without Manipulation, 28510
                Closed Treatment, 28515
                Open Treatment, 28525
    Radius
        with Manipulation, 25565, 25605
        with Ulna, 25560, 25565
            Open Treatment, 25575
        without Manipulation, 25560, 25600
        Closed Treatment, 24650, 24655, 25500,
            25505, 25520, 25560, 25565, 25600,
            25605
        Colles, 25600, 25605
        Distal, 25600-25611
            Open Treatment, 25620
            Smith, 25600-25620
        Head/Neck
            Closed Treatment, 24650, 24655
            Open Treatment, 24665, 24666
        Open Treatment, 25515, 25620
        Percutaneous Fixation, 25611
        Shaft, 25500, 25525, 25526
            Closed Treatment, 25500, 25505, 25520
            Open Treatment, 25515, 25525, 25526,
                25574
    Rib
        Closed Treatment, 21800
        External Fixation, 21810
        Open Treatment, 21805
    Scaphoid
        with Dislocation
            Closed Treatment, 25680
            Open Treatment, 25685
        with Manipulation, 25624
        Closed Treatment, 25622
        Open Treatment, 25628
    Scapula
        Closed Treatment
            with Manipulation, 23575
            without Manipulation, 23570
        Open Treatment, 23585

Fracture, Treatment — *continued*
    Sesamoid
        Closed Treatment, 28530
        Foot, 28530, 28531
        Open Treatment, 28531
    Shoulder
        Closed Treatment
            with Greater Tuberosity Fracture, 23620,
                23655
            with Surgical or Anatomical Neck
                Fracture, 23600, 23675
        Open Treatment, 23630, 23680
    Skull, 62000-62010
        Closed Treatment, 21300
    Sternum
        Closed Treatment, 21820
        Open Treatment, 21825
    Talus
        with Manipulation, 28435, 28436
        without Manipulation, 28430
        Closed Treatment, 28430, 28435
        Open Treatment, 28445
    Tarsal
        with Manipulation, 28455, 28456
        without Manipulation, 28450
        Open Treatment, 28465
        Percutaneous Fixation, 28456
    Thigh
        Femur
            Closed Treatment
                with manipulation, 27502, 27503,
                    27510, 27517
                Without manipulation, 27500, 27501,
                    27508, 27516, 27520
            Open Treatment, 27506, 27507, 27511,
                27513, 27514, 27519, 27524
            Percutaneous fixation, 27509
    Thumb
        with Dislocation, 26645, 26650
            Open Treatment, 26665
        Closed Treatment, 26645, 26650
        Percutaneous Fixation, 26650
    Tibia
        with Manipulation, 27752, 27762, 27810
        without Manipulation, 27530, 27750, 27760,
            27808, 27825
        Arthroscopic Treatment, 29855, 29856
        Closed Treatment, 27530, 27532, 27538,
            27750, 27752, 27760, 27762, 27808,
            27810, 27824, 27825
            with Traction, 27532, 27825
        Distal, 27824-27828
        Intercondylar Spines, 27538, 27540
        Malformation, 27810
        Malleolus, 27760-27766, 27808-27814
        Open Treatment, 27535, 27536, 27540,
            27758, 27759, 27766, 27814, 27826-
            27828
        Percutaneous Fixation, 27756
            Bimalleolar
                Closed Treatment, 27808
                    with Manipulation, 27810
                Open Treatment, 27814
            Lateral
                Closed Treatment, 27786
                    with Manipulation, 27788
                Open Treatment, 27792
            Medial
                Closed Treatment, 27760
                    with Manipulation, 27762
                Open Treatment, 27766

Fracture, Treatment — *continued*
Tibia — *continued*
Percutaneous Fixation — *continued*
Trimalleolar
Closed Treatment, 27816
with Manipulation, 27818
Open Treatment, 27822
with Fixation, 27823
Plateau, 27530-27536, 29855, 29856
Shaft, 27750-27759
with Manipulation, 27752, 27762, 27825
without Manipulation, 27530, 27750,
27760, 27824
Tibia and Fibula
Malleolar, 27808-27814
Trachea
Endoscopy Repair, 31630
Turbinate
Therapeutic, 30930
Ulna
with Dislocation, 24620, 24635
Closed Treatment, 24620
Monteggia, 24620, 24635
Open Treatment, 24635
with Manipulation, 25535, 25565
with Radius, 25560, 25565
Open Treatment, 25575
without Manipulation, 25530, 25560
See Elbow; Humerus; Radius
Closed Treatment, 25560, 25565
Monteggia type, 24620
of Shaft, 25530, 25535
with Manipulation, 25535
and Radial, 25560
with Manipulation, 25565
Proximal end, 24670
with Manipulation, 24675
Ulnar Styloid, 25650
Olecranon
Closed Treatment, 24670, 24675
with Manipulation, 24675
Open Treatment, 24685
Open Treatment, 25574, 25575
Proximal End, 24685
Radial AND Ulnar Shaft, 25574, 25575
Shaft, 25545
Shaft
Closed Treatment, 25530, 25535
Open Treatment, 25545, 25574
Styloid Process
Closed Treatment, 25650
Open Treatment, 25652
Percutaneous Fixation, 25651
Vertebra
Additional Segment
Open Treatment, 22328
Cervical
Open Treatment, 22326
Closed Treatment
with Manipulation, Casting and/or
Bracing, 22315
without Manipulation, 22310
Lumbar
Open Treatment, 22325
Posterior
Open Treatment, 22325-22327
Thoracic
Open Treatment, 22327
Vertebral Process
Closed Treatment, 22305

Fracture, Treatment — *continued*
Wrist
with Dislocation, 25680, 25685
Closed Treatment, 25680
Open Treatment, 25685
Zygomatic Arch
Open Treatment, 21356, 21360-21366
with Manipulation, 21355
Fragile-X
Chromosome Analysis, 88248
Fragility
Red Blood Cell
Mechanical, 85547
Osmotic, 85555, 85557
Frames, Stereotactic
See Stereotactic Frame
Francisella, 86000
Antibody, 86668
Fredet-Ramstedt Procedure, 43520
Free E3
See Estriol
Free Skin Graft
See Skin, Grafts, Free
Free T4
See Thyroxine, Free
Frei Disease
See Lymphogranuloma Venereum
Frenectomy, 40819, 41115
Frenectomy, Lingual
See Excision, Tongue, Frenum
Frenoplasty, 41520
Frenotomy, 40806, 41010
Frenulectomy, 40819
Frenuloplasty, 41520
Frenum
See Lip
Lip
Incision, 40806
Frenumectomy, 40819
Frickman Operation, 45550
See Proctopexy
Frontal Craniotomy, 61556
Frontal Sinus
See Sinus, Frontal
Frontal Sinusotomy
See Exploration, Sinus, Frontal
Frost Suture
Eyelid
Closure by Suture, 67875
Frozen Blood Preparation, 86930-86932
Fructose, 84375
Semen, 82757
Fructose Intolerance Breath Test, 91065
Fruit Sugar
See Fructose
FSF, 85290, 85291
FSH, 83001
with Additional Tests, 80418, 80426
FSP, 85362-85380
FT-4, 84439
FTG, 15200-15261
FTI, 84439
FTSG, 15200-15261

Fulguration
See Destruction
Bladder, 51020
Cystourethroscopy with, 52214
Lesion, 52224
Tumor, 52234-52240
Ureter, 50957, 50976
Ureterocele
Ectopic, 52301
Orthotopic, 52300
Fulguration, Endocavitary
See Electrocautery
Full Thickness Graft, 15200-15261
Functional Ability
See Activities of Daily Living
Function, Study, Nasal
See Nasal Function Study
Function Test, Lung
See Pulmonology, Diagnostic
Function Test, Vestibular
See Vestibular Function Tests
Fundoplasty
Esophagogastric, 43324, 43325
with Gastroplasty, 43326
Laparoscopic, 43280
Fundoplication
See Fundoplasty, Esophagogastric
Fungus
Antibody, 86671
Culture
Blood, 87103
Hair, 87101
Identification, 87106
Nail, 87101
Other, 87102
Skin, 87101
Tissue Exam, 87220
Funnel Chest
See Pectus Excavatum
Furuncle
Incision and Drainage, 10060, 10061
Furuncle, Vulva
See Abscess, Vulva
Fusion
See Arthrodesis
Pleural Cavity, 32005
Thumb
in Opposition, 26820
Fusion, Epiphyseal-Diaphyseal
See Epiphyseal Arrest
Fusion, Joint
See Arthrodesis
Fusion, Joint, Ankle
See Ankle, Arthrodesis
Fusion, Joint, Interphalangeal, Finger
See Arthrodesis, Finger Joint, Interphalangeal

G

GA, 91052
Gago Procedure
Repair, Tricuspid Valve, 33463-33465
Gait Training, 97116
Galactogram, 76086, 76088
Injection, 19030
Galactokinase
Blood, 82759

Galactose
Blood, 82760
Urine, 82760
Galactose-1-Phosphate
Uridyl Transferase, 82775-82776
Galeazzi Dislocation
Fracture
Closed Treatment, 25520
Open Treatment, 25525, 25526
Gallbladder
See Bile Duct
Anastomosis
with Intestines, 47720-47741
Cholecystectomy, 47600
Laparoscopic, 47562
with Cholangiogram, 47564
Open, 47600
with Cholangiogram, 47605
with Choledochoenterostomy, 47612
with Exploration Common Duct, 47610
with Transduodenal Sphincterotomy or
Sphincteroplasty, 47620
Cholecystostomy
for Drainage, 47480
for Exploration, 47480
for Removal of Stone, 47480
Percutaneous, 47490
Excision, 47562-47564, 47600-47620
Exploration, 47480
Incision, 47490
Incision and Drainage, 47480
Nuclear Medicine
Imaging, 78223
Removal Calculi, 47480
Repair
with Gastroenterostomy, 47741
with Intestines, 47720-47740
Unlisted Services and Procedures, 47999
X-ray with Contrast, 74290, 74291
Galvanocautery
See Electrocautery
Galvanoionization
See Iontophoresis
Gamete Intrafallopian Transfer (GIFT), 58976
Gamete Transfer
In Vitro Fertilization, 58976
Gamma Camera Imaging
See Nuclear Medicine
Gammacorten
See Dexamethasone
Gammaglobulin
Blood, 82784-82787
Gamma Glutamyl Transferase, 82977
Gamma Seminoprotein
See Antigen, Prostate Specific
Gamulin Rh
See Imune Globulins, Rho (D)
Ganglia, Trigeminal
See Gasserian Ganglion
Ganglion
See Gasserian Ganglion
Cyst
Aspiration/Injection, 20612
Drainage, 20612
Wrist
Excision, 25111, 25112
Injection
Anesthetic, 64505, 64510

Ganglion Cervicothoracicum
See Stellate Ganglion

Ganglion, Gasser's
See Gasserian Ganglion

Ganglion Pterygopalatinum
See Sphenopalatine Ganglion

Gardnerella Vaginalis Detection, 87510-87512

Gardner Operation, 63700, 63702

Gasser Ganglion
See Gasserian Ganglion

Gasserian Ganglion
Sensory Root
Decompression, 61450
Section, 61450
Stereotactic, 61790

Gastrectomy
Partial, 43631
with Gastroduodenostomy, 43631
with Roux-en-Y Reconstruction, 43633
with Gastrojejunostomy, 43632
with Intestinal Pouch, 43634
Distal with Vagotomy, 43635
Total, 43621, 43622
with Esophagoenterostomy, 43620
with Intestinal Pouch, 43622

Gastric Acid, 82926, 82928

Gastric Analysis Test, 91052

Gastric Intubation, 89130-89141, 91105

Gastric Lavage
Therapeutic, 91105

Gastric Restrictive Procedure
Laparoscopy, 43770-43774
Open, 43886-43888

Gastric Tests
Manometry, 91020

Gastric Ulcer Disease
See Stomach, Ulcer

Gastrin, 82938, 82941

Gastrocnemius Recession
Leg, Lower, 27687

Gastroduodenostomy, 43810
with Gastrectomy, 43631, 43632
Revision of Anastomosis with Reconstruction, 43850
with Vagotomy, 43855

Gastroenterology, Diagnostic
Breath Hydrogen Test, 91065
Esophagus Tests
Acid Perfusion, 91030
Acid Reflux Test, 91034-91038
Balloon Distension Provocation Study, 91040
Intubation with Specimen Collection, 91000
Manometry, 91020
Motility Study, 91010-91012
Gastric Tests
Manometry, 91020
Gastroesophageal Reflux Test
See Acid Reflux, 91034-91038
Intestine
Bleeding Tube, 91100
Manometry, 91020
Rectum
Manometry, 91122
Sensation, Tone, and Compliance Test, 91120
Stomach
Intubation with Specimen Prep, 91055

Gastroenterology, Diagnostic — continued
Stomach — continued
Manometry, 91020
Saline Load Test, 91060
Stimulation of Secretion, 91052
Unlisted Services and Procedures, 91299

Gastroenterostomy
for Obesity, 43644-43645, 43842-43848

Gastroesophageal Reflux Test, 91034-91038

Gastrointestinal Endoscopies
See Endoscopy, Gastrointestinal

Gastrointestinal Exam
Nuclear Medicine
Blood Loss Study, 78278
Protein Loss Study, 78282
Shunt Testing, 78291
Unlisted Services and Procedures, 78299

Gastrointestinal Prophylaxis for NSAID Use Prescribed, 4017F

Gastrointestinal Tract
Imaging Intraluminal, 91110
Reconstruction, 43360, 43361
Upper
Dilation, 43249
X-ray, 74240-74245
with Contrast, 74246-74249
Guide Dilator, 74360
Guide Intubation, 74340, 74350

Gastrointestinal, Upper
Biopsy
Endoscopy, 43239
Dilation
Endoscopy, 43245
Esophagus, 43248
Endoscopy
Catheterization, 43241
Destruction
Lesion, 43258
Dilation, 43245
Drainage
Pseudocyst, 43240
Exploration, 43234, 43235
Hemorrhage, 43255
Inject Varices, 43243
Needle Biopsy, 43238, 43242
Removal
Foreign Body, 43247
Lesion, 43251
Polyp, 43251
Tumor, 43251
Stent Placement, 43256
Suturing
Esophagogastric Junction, 0008T
Thermal Radiation, 43257
Tube Placement, 43246
Ultrasound, 43237, 43238, 43242, 76975
Exploration
Endoscopy, 43234, 43235
Hemorrhage
Endoscopic Control, 43255
Injection
Submucosal, 43236
Varices, 43243
Lesion
Destruction, 43258
Ligation of Vein, 43244
Needle Biopsy
Endoscopy, 43238, 43242
Removal
Foreign body, 43247

Gastrointestinal, Upper — *continued*
Removal — *continued*
   Lesion, 43250
   Polyp, 43250, 43251
   Tumor, 43250
  Stent Placement, 43256
  Suturing
   Esophagogastric Junction, 0008T
  Tube Placement
   Endoscopy, 43237, 43238, 43246
  Ultrasound
   Endoscopy, 43237, 43238, 43242, 43259,
    76975
Gastrojejunostomy, 43860, 43865
  with Duodenal Exclusion, 48547
  with Partial Gastrectomy, 43632
  with Vagotomy, 43825
  without Vagotomy, 43820
  Revision, 43860
   with Vagotomy, 43865
Gastroplasty
  with Esophagogastric Fundoplasty, 43326
  for Obesity, 43644-43645, 43842-43848
  Restrictive for Obesity, 43842
   Other than Vertical Banded, 43843
Gastrorrhaphy, 43840
Gastroschisis, 49605
Gastrostomy
  with Pancreatic Drain, 48001
  with Pyloroplasty, 43640
  with Vagotomy, 43640
  Closure, 43870
  Laparoscopic
   Permanent, 43832
   Temporary, 43653
  Temporary, 43830
   Laparoscopic, 43653
   Neonatal, 43831
Gastrostomy Tube
  Change of, 43760
  Directed Placement
   Endoscopic, 43246
  Insertion
   Percutaneous, 43750
  Percutaneous, 43750
  Repositioning, 43761
Gastrotomy, 43500, 43501, 43510
GDH, 82965
GE
  Reflux, 78262
Gel Diffusion, 86331
Gene Product
  See Protein
Genioplasty, 21120-21123
  Augmentation, 21120, 21123
  Osteotomy, 21121-21123
Genitalia
  Female
   Anesthesia, 00940-00952
  Male
   Anesthesia, 00920-00938
  Skin Graft
   Delay of Flap, 15620
   Full Thickness, 15240, 15241
   Pedicle Flap, 15574
   Split, 15120, 15121
  Tissue Transfer, Adjacent, 14040, 14041
Genitourinary Sphincter, Artificial
  See Prosthesis, Urethral Sphincter

Genotype Analysis
  by Nucleic Acid
   Infectious Agent
    Hepatitis C Virus, 87902
    HIV-1 Protease/Reverse Transcriptase,
     87901
Gentamicin, 80170
  Assay, 80170
Gentiobiase, 82963
Genus: Human Cytomegalovirus Group
  See Cytomegalovirus
GERD
  See Gastroesophageal Reflux Test
German Measles
  See Rubella
Gestational Trophoblastic Tumor
  See HydatidiForm Mole
GGT, 82977
GH, 83003
GHb, 83036
Giardia
  Antigen Detection
   Enzyme Immunoassay, 87329
   Immunofluorescence, 87269
Giardia Lamblia
  Antibody, 86674
Gibbons Stent, 52332
GIF, 84307
GIFT, 58976
Gillies Approach
  Fracture
   Zygomatic Arch, 21356
Gill Operation, 63012
Gingiva
  See Gums
Gingiva, Abscess
  See Abscess
  Fracture
   See Abscess, Gums; Gums
   Zygomatic Arch
    See Abscess, Gums; Gums, Abscess
Gingivectomy, 41820
Gingivoplasty, 41872
Girdlestone Laminectomy
  See Laminectomy
Girdlestone Procedure
  Acetabulum, Reconstruction, 27120, 27122
GI Tract
  See Gastrointestinal Tract
  X-Rays, 74240-74249, 74340, 74350, 74360
Glabellar Frown Lines
  Rhytidectomy, 15826
Gland
  See Specific Gland
Gland, Adrenal
  See Adrenal Gland
Gland, Bartholin's
  See Bartholin's Gland
Gland, Bulbourethral
  See Bulbourethral Gland
Gland, Lacrimal
  See Lacrimal Gland
Gland, Mammary
  See Breast
Gland, Parathyroid
  See Parathyroid Gland

Great Vessel(s) — *continued*
  Shunt — *continued*
    Vena Cava to Pulmonary Artery, 33766, 33767
    Unlisted Services and Procedures, 33999
Great Vessels Transposition
  See Transposition, Great Arteries
Green Operation
  See Scapulopexy
Gridley Stain, 88312
Grippe, Balkan
  See Q Fever
Gritti Operation, 27590-27592
  See Amputation, Leg, Upper; Radical Resection; Replantation
Groin Area
  Repair
    Hernia, 49550-49557
Gross Type Procedure, 49610, 49611
Group Health Education, 99078
Grouping, Blood
  See Blood Typing
Growth Factors, Insulin-Like
  See Somatomedin
Growth Hormone, 83003
  with Arginine Tolerance Test, 80428
  Human, 80418, 80428, 80430, 86277
Growth Hormone Release Inhibiting Factor
  See Somatostatin
GTT, 82951, 82952
Guaiac Test
  Blood in Feces, 82270
Guanosine Monophosphate, 83008
Guanosine Monophosphate, Cyclic
  See Cyclic GMP
Guanylic Acids
  See Guanosine Monophosphate
Guard Stain, 88313
Gullet
  See Esophagus
Gums
  Abscess
    Incision and Drainage, 41800
  Alveolus
    Excision, 41830
  Cyst
    Incision and Drainage, 41800
  Excision
    Gingiva, 41820
    Operculum, 41821
  Graft
    Mucosa, 41870
  Hematoma
    Incision and Drainage, 41800
  Lesion
    Destruction, 41850
    Excision, 41822-41828
  Mucosa
    Excision, 41828
  Reconstruction
    Alveolus, 41874
    Gingiva, 41872
  Removal
    Foreign Body, 41805
  Tumor
    Excision, 41825-41827
  Unlisted Services and Procedures, 41899
Gunning-Lieben Test, 82009, 82010
Guthrie Test, 84030

H

HAA (Hepatitis Associated Antigen), 87340-87380, 87515-87527
  See Hepatitis Antigen, B Surface
HAAb (Antibody, Hepatitis), 86708, 86709
Haemoglobin F
  See Fetal Hemoglobin
Haemorrhage
  See Hemorrhage
Haemorrhage Rectum
  See Hemorrhage, Rectum
Hageman Factor, 85280
  Clotting Factor, 85210-85293
HAI (Hemagglutination Inhibition Test), 86280
Hair
  Electrolysis, 17380
  KOH Examination, 87220
  Microscopic Evaluation, 96902
  Transplant
    Punch Graft, 15775, 15776
    Strip Graft, 15220, 15221
Hair Removal
  See Removal, Hair
Hallux
  See Great Toe
Hallux Rigidus
  Correction with Cheilectomy, 28289
Halo
  Body Cast, 29000
  Cranial, 20661
    for Thin Skull Osteology, 20664
  Femur, 20663
  Maxillofacial, 21100
  Pelvic, 20662
  Removal, 20665
Haloperidol
  Assay, 80173
Halsted Mastectomy, 19200, 19220
Halsted Repair
  Hernia, 49495
Hammertoe Repair, 28285, 28286
Hamster Penetration Test, 89329
Ham Test
  Hemolysins, 85475
    with Agglutinins, 86940, 86941
Hand
  See Carpometacarpal Joint; Intercarpal Joint
  Amputation
    at Metacarpal, 25927
    at Wrist, 25920
      Revision, 25922
    Revision, 25924, 25929, 25931
  Arthrodesis
    Carpometacarpal Joint, 26843, 26844
    Intercarpal Joint, 25820, 25825
  Bone
    Incision and Drainage, 26034
  Cast, 29085
  Decompression, 26035, 26037
  Excision
    Excess Skin, 15837
  Fracture
    Metacarpal, 26600
  Implantation
    Removal, 26320
      Tube/Rod, 26392, 26416
    Tube/Rod, 26390

Hand — *continued*
 Insertion
  Tendon Graft, 26392
 Magnetic Resonance Imaging (MRI), 73218-73223
 Reconstruction
  Tendon Pulley, 26500-26504
 Repair
  Blood Vessel, 35207
  Cleft Hand, 26580
  Muscle, 26591, 26593
   Release, 26593
  Tendon
   Extensor, 26410-26416, 26426, 26428, 26433-26437
   Flexor, 26350-26358, 26440
   Profundus, 26370-26373
 Replantation, 20808
 Skin Graft
  Delay of Flap, 15620
  Full Thickness, 15240, 15241
  Pedicle Flap, 15574
  Split, 15100, 15101
 Strapping, 29280
 Tendon
  Excision, 26390
   Extensor, 26415
 Tenotomy, 26450, 26460
 Tissue Transfer, Adjacent, 14040, 14041
 Tumor
  Excision, 26115-26117
 Unlisted Services and Procedures, 26989
 X-ray, 73120, 73130
Hand Abscess
 See Abscess, Hand
Hand(s) Dupuytren's Contracture(s)
 See Dupuytren's Contracture
Handling
 Device, 99002
 Radioelement, 77790
 Specimen, 99000, 99001
Hand Phalange
 See Finger, Bone
Hanganutziu Deicher Antibodies
 See Antibody, Heterophile
Haptoglobin, 83010, 83012
Hard Palate
 See Palate
Harelip Operation
 See Cleft Lip, Repair
Harii Procedure (Carpal Bone), 25430
Harrington Rod
 Insertion, 22840
 Removal, 22850
Hartmann Procedure, 44143
 Laparoscopy
  Partial Colectomy with Colostomy, 44206
 Open, 44143
Harvesting
 Bone Graft, 20900, 20902
 Bone Marrow, 38230
 Cartilage, 20910, 20912
 Conjunctival Graft, 68371
 Eggs for In Vitro Fertilization, 58970
 Endoscopic
  Vein for Bypass Graft, 33508
 Fascia Lata Graft, 20920, 20922
 Intestines, 44132, 44133
 Kidney, 50300, 50320, 50547

Harvesting — *continued*
 Liver, 47133, 47140-47142
 Lower Extremity Vein for Vascular Reconstruction, 35572
 Skin, 15040
 Stem Cell, 38205, 38206
 Tendon Graft, 20924
 Tissue Grafts, 20926
 Upper Extremity Artery
  for Coronary Artery Bypass Graft, 35600
 Upper Extremity Vein
  for Bypass Graft, 35500
Hauser Procedure
 Reconstruction, Patella, for Instability, 27420
Hayem's Elementary Corpuscle
 See Blood, Platelet
Haygroves Procedure, 27120, 27122
HBcAb, 86704, 86705
HBeAb, 86707
HBeAg, 87350
HBsAb, 86706
HBsAg (Hepatitis B Surface Antigen), 87340
HCG, 84702, 84703
HCO3
 See Bicarbonate
Hct, 85013, 85014
HCV Antibodies
 See Antibody, Hepatitis C
HD, 27295
HDL (High Density Lipoprotein), 83718
Head
 Angiography, 70496, 70544-70546
 CT Scan, 70450-70470, 70496
 Excision, 21015-21070
 Fracture and/or Dislocation, 21300-21497
 Incision, 21010, 61316, 62148
 Introduction, 21076-21116
 Lipectomy, Suction Assisted, 15876
 Magnetic Resonance Angiography (MRA), 70544-70546
 Nerve
  Graft, 64885, 64886
 Other Procedures, 21299, 21499
 Repair
  Revision and/or Reconstruction, 21120-21296
 Ultrasound Examination, 76506, 76536
 Unlisted Services and Procedures, 21499
 X-ray, 70350
Headbrace
 Application, 21100
  Removal, 20661
Head Rings, Stereotactic
 See Stereotactic Frame
Heaf Test
 TB Test, 86580
Health Behavior
 See Evaluation and Management, Health Behavior
Health Risk Assessment Instrument, 99420
Hearing Aid
 Bone Conduction
  Implant, 69710
  Removal, 69711
  Repair, 69711
  Replace, 69710
 Check, 92592, 92593

Index

Hearing Aid Services — Heart

Hearing Aid Services
Electroacoustic Test, 92594, 92595
Examination, 92590, 92591
Hearing Evaluation, 92506
Hearing Tests
See Audiologic Function Tests; Hearing
   Evaluation
Hearing Therapy, 92507, 92601-92604
Heart
Ablation
   Ventricular Septum
      Non-surgical, 0024T
Accoustic Sound Recording, 0068T, 0069T,
   0070T
Allograft Preparation, 33933, 33944
Angiocardiography, 93555
Angiography
   Injection, 93542, 93543
      See Cardiac Catheterization; Injection
Aortic Arch
   with Cardiopulmonary Bypass, 33853
   without Cardiopulmonary Bypass, 33852
Aortic Valve
   Repair, Left Ventricle, 33414
   Replacement, 33405-33413
Arrhythmogenic Focus
   Catheter Ablation, 93650-93652
   Destruction, 33250, 33251, 33261
Atria
   See Atria
Biopsy, 93505
   Radiologic Guidance, 76932
Blood Vessel
   Repair, 33320-33322
Cardiac Output Measurements, 93561, 93562
Cardiac Rehabilitation, 93797, 93798
Cardioassist, 92970, 92971
   Ventricular Assist Device Extracorporeal,
      0049T
Cardiopulmonary Bypass
   with Lung Transplant, 32852, 32854
Cardioverter-Defibrillator
   Evaluation and Testing, 93641, 93642
Catheterization, 93501, 93510-93533
   Combined Right and Retrograde Left for
      Congenital Cardiac Anomalies, 93531
   Combined Right and Transseptal Left for
      Congenital Cardiac Anomalies, 93532,
      93533
   Flow-Directed, 93503
   Right for Congenital Cardiac Anomalies,
      93530
      See Catheterization, Cardiac
Closure
   Septal Defect, 33615
   Valve
      Atrioventricular, 33600
      Semilunar, 33602
Commissurotomy, Right Ventricle, 33476,
   33478
Defibrillator
   Insertion, 33240
      Pads, 33245, 33246
   Removal, 33243, 33244
      Pulse Generator Only, 33241
   Repair, 33218, 33220
   Replacement, Leads, 33216, 33217, 33249
Destruction
   Arrhythmogenic Focus, 33250, 33261

Heart — continued
Electrical Recording
   3-D Mapping, 93613
   Acoustic Heart Sound, 0068T-0070T
   Atria, 93602
   Atrial Electrogram, Esophageal (or Trans-
      esophageal), 93615, 93616
   Bundle of His, 93600
   Comprehensive, 93619, 93620
   Right Ventricle, 93603
   Tachycardia Sites, 93609
Electroconversion, 92960, 92961
Electrophysiologic Follow-Up Study, 93624
Evaluation of Device, 93640
Excision
   Donor, 33930, 33940
   Tricuspid Valve, 33460, 33465
Exploration, 33310, 33315
Fibrillation
   Atrial, 33253
Great Vessels
   See Great Vessels
Heart-Lung Bypass
   See Cardiopulmonary Bypass
Heart-Lung Transplantation
   See Tranplantation, Heart-Lung
Hemodynamic Monitoring
   Non-invasive, 0086T
Implantation
   Artificial Heart, Intracorporeal, 0051T
   Total Replacement Heart System,
      Intracorporeal, 0051T
   Ventricular Assist Device, 33976
      Extracorporeal, 0048T
Incision
   Atrial, 33253
   Exploration, 33310, 33315
Injection
   Radiologic, 93542, 93543
      See Cardiac Catheterization, Injection
Insertion
   Balloon Device, 33973
   Defibrillator, 33212, 33246
   Electrode, 33210, 33211, 33214-33217,
      33224-33225
   Pacemaker, 33200-33208, 33212, 33213
      Catheter, 33210
   Pulse Generator, 33212-33214
   Ventricular Assist Device, 33975
Intraoperative Pacing and Mapping, 93631
Ligation
   Fistula, 37607
Magnetic Resonance Imaging (MRI)/with
      Contrast Material, 75553
   without Contrast Material, 75552
Mitral Valve
   See Mitral Valve
Muscle
   See Myocardium
Myocardium
   Imaging, Nuclear, 78466-78469
   Perfusion Study, 78460-78465
Nuclear Medicine
   Blood Flow Study, 78414
   Blood Pool Imaging, 78472, 78473, 78481,
      78483, 78494, 78496
   Myocardial Imaging, 78466-78469
   Myocardial Perfusion, 78460-78465, 78491,
      78492
   Shunt Detection (Test), 78428
   Unlisted Services and Procedures, 78499
Open Chest Massage, 32160

Hemoglobin, Glycosylated, 83036-83037

Hemogram
Added Indices, 85025-85027
Automated, 85025-85027
Manual, 85014, 85018, 85032

Hemolysins, 85475
with Agglutinins, 86940, 86941

Hemolytic Complement
See Complement, Hemolytic

Hemolytic Complement, Total
See Complement, Hemolytic, Total

Hemoperfusion, 90997

Hemophil
See Clotting Factor

Hemophilus Influenza
Antibody, 86684
B Vaccine, 90645-90648, 90720-90721, 90748

Hemorrhage
Abdomen, 49002
Anal
Endoscopic Control, 46614
Bladder
Postoperative, 52606
Chest Cavity
Endoscopic Control, 32654
Colon
Endoscopic Control, 44391, 45382
Colon-Sigmoid
Endoscopic Control, 45334
Esophagus
Endoscopic Control, 43227
Gastrointestinal, Upper
Endoscopic Control, 43255
Intestines, Small
Endoscopic Control, 44366, 44378
Liver
Control, 47350
Lung, 32110
Nasal
Cauterization, 30901-30906
Endoscopic Control, 31238
Nasopharynx, 42970-42972
Nose
Cauterization, 30901-30906
Oropharynx, 42960-42962
Rectum
Endoscopic Control, 45317
Throat, 42960-42962
Uterus
Postpartum, 59160
Vagina, 57180

Hemorrhoidectomy
Complex, 46260
with Fissurectomy, 46261, 46262
External Complete, 46250
Ligature, 46221
Simple, 46255
with Fissurectomy, 46257, 46258

Hemorrhoidopexy, 46947

Hemorrhoids
Destruction, 46934-46936
Incision
External, 46083
Injection
Sclerosing Solution, 46500
Ligation, 46945, 46946
Stapling, 46947
Suture, 46945, 46946

Hemosiderin, 83070, 83071

Hemothorax
Thoracostomy, 32020

Heparin, 85520
Clotting Inhibitors, 85300-85305
Neutralization, 85525
Protamine Tolerance Test, 85530

Heparin Cofactor I
See Antithrombin III

Hepatectomy
Extensive, 47122
Left Lobe, 47125
Partial
Donor, 47140-47142
Lobe, 47120
Right Lobe, 47130
Total
Donor, 47133

Hepatic Abscess
See Abscess, Liver

Hepatic Arteries
See Artery, Hepatic

Hepatic Artery Aneurysm
See Artery, Hepatic, Aneurysm

Hepatic Duct
Anastomosis
with Intestines, 47765, 47802
Exploration, 47400
Incision and Drainage, 47400
Nuclear Medicine
Imaging, 78223
Removal
Calculi (Stone), 47400
Repair
with Intestines, 47765, 47802
Unlisted Services and Procedures, 47999

Hepatic Haemorrhage
See Hemorrhage, Liver

Hepaticodochotomy
See Hepaticostomy

Hepaticoenterostomy, 47802

Hepaticostomy, 47400

Hepaticotomy, 47400

Hepatic Portal Vein
See Vein, Hepatic Portal

Hepatic Portoenterostomies
See Hepaticoenterostomy

Hepatic Transplantation
See Liver, Transplantation

Hepatitis A and Hepatitis B, 90636

Hepatitis Antibody
A, 86708, 86709
B core, 86704, 86705
Be, 86707
B Surface, 86706
C, 86803, 86804
Delta Agent, 86692
IgG, 86704, 86708
IgM, 86704, 86705, 86708, 86709

Hepatitis Antigen
B, 87515-87517
Be, 87350
B Surface, 87340, 87341
C, 87520-87522
Delta Agent, 87380
G, 87525-87527

HIV Detection — *continued*
  Confirmation Test, 86689
HK3 Kallikrein
  See Antigen, Prostate Specific
HLA, 86812-86817
HLA Typing, 86812-86817
HMRK
  See Fitzgerald Factor
Hoffman Apparatus, 20690
Hofmeister Operation, 43632
Holotranscobalamin
  Quantitative, 0103T
Holten Test, 82575
Home Services
  Activities of Daily Living, 99509
  Catheter Care, 99507
  Enema Administration, 99511
  Established Patient, 99347-99350
  Hemodialysis, 99512
  Home Infusion Procedures, 99601, 99602
  Individual or Family Counseling, 99510
  Intramuscular Injections, 99506
  Mechanical Ventilation, 99504
  Newborn Care, 99502
  New Patient, 99341-99345
  Postnatal Assessment, 99501
  Prenatal Monitoring, 99500
  Respiratory Therapy., 99503
  Sleep Studies, 95805-95811
  Stoma Care, 99505
  Unlisted Services and Procedures, 99600
Homocystine, 83090
  Urine, 82615
Homogenization, Tissue, 87176
Homograft
  Skin, 15300-15336
Homologous Grafts
  See Graft
Homologous Transplantation
  See Homograft
Homovanillic Acid
  Urine, 83150
Hormone Adrenocorticotrophic
  See Adrenocorticotrophic Hormone (ACTH)
Hormone Assay
  ACTH, 82024
  Aldosterone
    Blood or Urine, 82088
  Androstenedione
    Blood or Urine, 82157
  Androsterone
    Blood or Urine, 82160
  Angiotensin II, 82163
  Corticosterone, 82528
  Cortisol
    Total, 82533
  Dehydroepiandrosterone, 82626-82627
  Dihydroelestosterone, 82651
  Dihydrotestosterone, 82651
  Epiandrosterone, 82666
  Estradiol, 82670
  Estriol, 82677
  Estrogen, 82671, 82672
  Estrone, 82679
  Follicle Stimulating Hormone, 83001
  Growth Hormone, 83003
    Suppression Panel, 80430
  Hydroxyprogesterone, 83498, 83499
  Luteinizing Hormone, 83002

Hormone Assay — *continued*
  Somatotropin, 80430, 83003
  Testosterone, 84403
  Vasopressin, 84588
Hormone-Binding Globulin, Sex
  See Globulin, Sex Hormone Binding
Hormone, Corticotropin-Releasing
  See Corticotropic Releasing Hormone (CRH)
Hormone, Growth
  See Growth Hormone
Hormone, Human Growth
  See Gowth Hormone, Human
Hormone, Interstitial Cell-Stimulation
  See Luteinizing Hormone (LH)
Hormone, Parathyroid
  See Parathormone
Hormone Pellet Implantation, 11980
Hormone, Pituitary Lactogenic
  See Prolactin
Hormone, Placental Lactogen
  See Lactogen, Human Placental
Hormones, Adrenal Cortex
  See Corticosteroids
Hormones, Antidiuretic
  See Antidiuretic Hormone
Hormone, Somatotropin Release-Inhibiting
  See Somatostatin
Hormone, Thyroid-Stimulating
  See Thyroid Stimulating Hormone (TSH)
Hospital Discharge Services
  See Discharge Services, Hospital
Hospital Services
  Inpatient Services
    Discharge Services, 99238, 99239
    Initial Care New or Established Patient,
      99221-99223
    Initial Hospital Care, 99221-99223
    Newborn, 99431-99433
    Prolonged Services, 99356, 99357
    Subsequent Hospital Care, 99231-99233
  Normal Newborn, 99432
  Observation
    Discharge Services, 99234-99236
    Initial Care, 99218-99220
      New or Established Patient, 99218-99220
  Same Day Admission
    Discharge Services, 99234-99236
  Subsequent Newborn Care, 99433
Hot Pack Treatment, 97010
  See Physical Medicine and Rehabilitation
House Calls, 99341-99350
Howard Test
  Cystourethroscopy, Catheterization, Ureter,
    52005
HP, 83010, 83012
HPL, 83632
H-Reflex Study, 95934, 95936
HSG, 58340, 74740
HTLV I
  Antibody
    Confirmatory Test, 86689
    Detection, 86687
HTLV-II
  Antibody, 86688
HTLV III
  See HIV

Hydrocele — *continued*
Excision
   Bilateral, Tunica Vaginalis, 55041
   Unilateral
     Spermatic Cord, 55500
     Tunica Vaginalis, 55040
Repair, 55060

Hydrocelectomy, 49495-49501

Hydrocele, Tunica Vaginalis
See Tunica Vaginalis, Hydrocele

Hydrochloric Acid, Gastric
See Acid, Gastric

Hydrochloride, Vancomycin
See Vancomycin

Hydrocodon
See Dihydrocodeinone

Hydrogen Ion Concentration
See pH

Hydrolase, Acetylcholine
See Acetylcholinesterase

Hydrolases, Phosphoric Monoester
See Phosphatase

Hydrolase, Triacylglycerol
See Lipase

Hydrotherapy (Hubbard Tank), 97036
with Exercises, 97036, 97113
See Physical Medicine/Therapy/ Occupational Therapy

Hydrotubation, 58350

Hydroxyacetanilide
See Acetaminophen

Hydroxycorticosteroid, 83491

Hydroxyindolacetic Acid, 83497
Urine, 83497

Hydroxypregnenolone, 80406, 84143

Hydroxyprogesterone, 80402, 80406, 83498, 83499

Hydroxyproline, 83500, 83505

Hydroxytyramine
See Dopamine

Hygroma, Cystic
Axillary
   Cervical
     Excision, 38550, 38555

Hymen
Excision, 56700
Incision, 56720

Hymenal Ring
Revision, 56700

Hymenectomy, 56700

Hymenotomy, 56720

Hyoid Bone
Fracture
   Open Treatment, 21495

Hyperbaric Oxygen Pressurization, 99183

Hypercycloidal X-ray, 76101, 76102

Hyperdactylies
See Supernumerary Digit

Hyperglycemic Glycogenolytic Factor
See Glucagon

Hypertelorism of Orbit
See Orbital Hypertelorism

Hyperthermia Therapy
See Thermotherapy

Hyperthermia Treatment, 77600-77620

Hypnotherapy, 90880

Hypodermis
See Subcutaneous Tissue

Hypogastric Plexus
Destruction, 64681
Injection
   Anesthetic, 64517
   Neurolytic, 64681

Hypoglossal-Facial Anastomosis
See Anastomosis, Nerve, Facial to Hypoglossal

Hypoglossal Nerve
Anastomosis
   to Facial Nerve, 64868

Hypopharynges
See Hypopharynx

Hypopharynx
Biopsy, 42802

Hypophysectomy, 61546, 61548, 62165

Hypophysis
See Pituitary Gland

Hypopyrexia
See Hypothermia

Hypospadias
Repair, 54300, 54352
   Complications, 54340-54348
   First Stage, 54304
     Meatal Advancement, 54322
     Perineal, 54336
     Proximal Penile or Penoscrotal, 54332
   One Stage
     Meatal Advancement, 54322
     Perineal, 54336
   Urethroplasty by
     Local Skin Flaps, 54324
     Local Skin Flaps and Mobilization of Urethra, 54326
     Local Skin Flaps, Skin Graft Patch and/or Island Flap, 54328
   Urethroplasty for Second Stage, 54308-54316
     Free Skin Graft, 54316
   Urethroplasty for Third Stage, 54318

Hypothermia, 99185, 99186

Hypoxia
Breathing Response, 94450
High Altitude Simulation Test, 94452-94453

Hysterectomy
Abdominal
   Radical, 58210
   Resection of Ovarian Malignancy, 58951, 58953, 58983-58956
   Supracervical, 58180
   Total, 58150, 58200
     with Colpo-Urethrocystopexy, 58152
     with Omentectomy, 58956
     with Partial Vaginectomy, 58200
Cesarean
   with Closure of Vesicouterine Fistula, 51925
   After Cesarean Section, 59525
Removal
   Lesion, 59100
Vaginal, 58260-58270, 58290-58294, 58550-58554
   with Colpectomy, 58275, 58280
   with Colpo-Urethrocystopexy, 58267, 58293
   See Lysis, Adhesions, Uterus
   Laparoscopic, 58550
   Radical, 58285

Hysterectomy — *continued*
Vaginal — *continued*
Removal Tubes
Ovaries, 52402, 58262, 58263, 58291-58292, 58552-58554
Repair of Enterocele, 58263, 58292, 58294
Hysterolysis
Hysteroplasty, 58540
Hysterorrhaphy, 58520, 59350
Hysterosalpingography, 74740
Catheterization, 58345
Introduction of Contrast, 58340
Hysterosalpingostomy
See Implantation, Tubouterine
Hysteroscopy
with Endometrial Ablation, 58563
with Lysis of Adhesions, 58559
Ablation
Endometrial, 58563
Diagnostic, 58555
Lysis
Adhesions, 58559
Placement
Fallopian Tube Implants, 58565
Removal
Impacted Foreign Body, 58562
Leiomyomata, 58561
Resection
of Intrauterine Septum, 58560
Surgical with Biopsy, 58558
Unlisted Services and Procedures, 58579
Hysterosonography, 76831
See Ultrasound
Hysterotomy, 59100
See Ligation, Uterus
Induced Abortion
with Amniotic Injections, 59852
with Vaginal Suppositories, 59857
Hysterotrachelectomy
See Amputation, Cervix

I

IA, 36100-36140, 36260, 90773
IAB, 33970-33974
IABP, 33970-33974
IAC, 33970-33974
I, Angiotensin
See Angiotensin I
I Antibodies, HTLV
See Antibody, HTLV-I
IBC, 83550
ICCE, 66920, 66930
See Extraction, Lens, Intracapsular
Ichthyosis, Sex-Linked
See Syphilis Test
I Coagulation Factor
See Fibrinogen
ICSH
See Luteinizing Hormone
Identification
Oocyte from Follicular Fluid, 89254
Sentinel Node from Injection, 38792
Sperm
from Aspiration, 89257
from Tissue, 89264
IDH (Isocitric Dehydrogenase, Blood), 83570

IG, 82787, 84445, 86023
IgA, Gammaglobulin, 82784
IgD, Gammaglobulin, 82784
IgE
Allergen Specific, 86003, 86005
Gammaglobulin, 82785
IgG
Allergen Specific, 86001
Gammaglobulin, 82784
IgM, Gammaglobulin, 82784
I, Heparin Co-Factor
See Antithrombin III
II, Coagulation Factor
See Prothrombin
II, CranialNerve
See Optic Nerve
Ileal Conduit
Visualization, 50690
Ileocolostomy, 44160
Ileoproctostomy, 44150
Ileoscopy, 44380, 44382
via Stoma, 44383
Ileostomy, 44310, 45136
Continent (Kock Pouch), 44316
Revision, 44312, 44314
Iliac Arteries
See Artery, Iliac
Iliac Crest
Free Osteocutaneous flap with Microvascular Anastomosis, 20970
Iliohypogastric Nerve
Injection
Anesthetic, 64425
Ilioinguinal Nerve
Injection
Anesthetic, 64425
Ilium
Craterization, 27070, 27071
Cyst, 27065-27067
Excision, 27070, 27071
Fracture, 27215, 27218
Saucerization, 27070, 27071
Tumor, 27065-27067
Ilizarov Procedure
Application, Bone Fixation Device, 20690, 20692
Monticelli Type, 20692
IM, 90772
Imaging
See Vascular Studies
Imaging, Gamma Camera
See Nuclear Medicine
Imaging, Magnetic Resonance
See Magnetic Resonance Imaging (MRI)
Imaging, Ultrasonic
See Echography
Imbrication
Diaphragm, 39545
Imidobenzyle
See Imipramine
IM Injection
See Injection, Intramuscular
Imipramine
Assay, 80174
Immune Complex Assay, 86332

Implantation — *continued*
  Cerebral Thermal Perfusion Probe, 0077T
  Contraceptive Capsules, 11975, 11977
  Corneal Ring Segment
    Intrastomal, 0099T
  Drug Delivery Device, 11981, 11983, 61517
  Electrode
    Brain, 61850-61875
    Nerve, 64553-64581
    Spinal Cord, 63650, 63655
  Eye
    Anterior Segment, 65920
    Aqueous Shunt to Extraocular Reservoir, 66180
    Placement or Replacement of Pegs, 65125
    Posterior Segment
      Extraocular, 67120
      Intraocular, 67121
    Reservoir, 66180
    Vitreous
      Drug Delivery System, 67027
  Fallopian Tube, 58565
  Hearing Aid
    Bone Conduction, 69710
  Hip Prosthesis
    See Arthroplasty, Hip
  Hormone Pellet, 11980
  Intraocular Lens
    See Insertion, Intraocular Lens
  Intraocular Retinal Electrode Array, 0100T
  Intrastomal Corneal Ring Segments, 0099T
  Joint
    See Arthroplasty
  Mesh
    Hernia Repair, 49568
    Vaginal Repair, 57267
  Nerve
    into Bone, 64787
    into Muscle, 64787
  Neurostimulators
    Pulse Generator, 61885
    Receiver, 61886
  Ovum, 58976
  Pulsatile Heart Assist System, 33999
  Pulse Generator
    Brain, 61885, 61886
    Spinal Cord, 63685
  Receiver
    Brain, 61885, 61886
    Nerve, 64590
    Spinal Cord, 63685
  Removal, 20670, 20680
    Anesthesia, External Fixation, 20694
    Elbow, 24164
    Radius, 24164
    Wire, Pin, Rod, 20670
    Wire, Pin, Rod/Deep, 20680
  Reservoir Vascular Access Device
    Declotting, 36550
  Total Replacement Heart System,
    Intracorporeal, 0051T
  Tubouterine, 58752
  Ventricular Assist Device, 33976
    Extracorporeal, 0048T
    Intracorporeal, 33979
Implant, Breast
  See Breast,Implants
Implant, Glaucoma Drainage
  See Aqueous Shunt

Implant, Orbital
  See Orbital Implant
Implant, Penile
  See Penile Prosthesis
Implant,Penile Prosthesis, Inflatable
  See Penile Prosthesis, Insertion, Inflatable
Implant Removal
  See Specific Anatomical Site
Implant, Subperiosteal
  See Subperiosteal Implant
Implant, Ureters into, Bladder
  See Anastomosis, Ureter, to Bladder
Impression, Maxillofacial, 21076-21089
  Auricular Prosthesis, 21086
  Definitive Obturator Prosthesis, 21080
  Facial Prosthesis, 21088
  Interim Obturator, 21079
  Mandibular Resection Prosthesis, 21081
  Nasal Prosthesis, 21087
  Oral Surgical Splint, 21085
  Orbital Prosthesis, 21077
  Palatal Augmentation Prosthesis, 21082
  Palatal Lift Prosthesis, 21083
  Speech Aid Prosthesis, 21084
  Surgical Obturator, 21076
Incision
  See Incision and Drainage
  Abdomen, 49000
    Exploration, 58960
  Abscess
    Soft Tissue, 20000, 20005
  Accessory Nerve, 63191
  Anal
    Fistula, 46270, 46280
    Septum, 46070
    Sphincter, 46080
  Ankle, 27607
    Tendon, 27605, 27606
  Anus
    See Anus, Incision
  Aortic Valve, 33401, 33403
    for Stenosis, 33415
  Artery
    Nose, 30915, 30920
  Atrial Septum, 33735-33737
  Bile Duct
    Sphincter, 43262, 47460
  Bladder
    with Destruction, 51020, 51030
    with Radiotracer, 51020
    Catheterization, 51045
  Bladder Diverticulum, 52305
  Brachial Artery
    Exposure, 34834
  Brain
    Amygdalohippocampectomy, 61566
    Subpial, 61567
  Breast
    Capsules, 19370
  Bronchus, 31899
  Burn Scab, 16035, 16036
  Cataract
    Secondary
      Laser Surgery, 66821
      Stab Incision Technique, 66820
  Chest
    Biopsy, 32095, 32100
  Colon
    Exploration, 44025

Incision — *continued*
Colon — *continued*
Stoma
Creation, 44320, 44322
Revision, 44340-44346
Cornea
for Astigmatism, 65772
Corpus Callosum, 61541
Cricothyroid Membrane, 31605
Dentate Ligament, 63180, 63182
Duodenum, 44010
Ear, Inner
Labyrinth
with Mastoidectomy, 69802
with or without Cryosurgery, 69801
Elbow, 24000
Esophagus, 43020, 43045
Esophageal Web, 43499
Muscle, 43030
Exploration
Kidney, 50010
Eye
Adhesions, 65880
Anterior Segment, 65860, 65865
Anterior Synechiae, 65870
Corneovitreal, 65880
Posterior, 65875
Anterior Chamber, 65820
Trabecular, 65850
Eyelid
Canthus, 67715
Sutures, 67710
Femoral Artery
Exposure, 34812, 34813
Fibula, 27607
Finger
Decompression, 26035
Tendon, 26060, 26455, 26460
Tendon Sheath, 26055, 26060, 26455, 26460
Foot, 28005
Capsule, 28260-28264
Fascia, 28008
for Infection, 28002, 28003
Tendon, 28230, 28234
Frontal Lobe, 61490
Gallbladder, 47490
Hand Decompression, 26035, 26037
Tendon, 26450, 26460
Heart
Exploration, 33310, 33315
Incision, Not Specified, 33999
Hemorrhoid
External, 46083
Hepatic Ducts
See Hepaticostomy
Hip
Denervation, 27035
Exploration, 27033
Fasciotomy, 27025
Joint Capsule for Flexor Release, 27036
Tendon
Abductor, 27006
Adductor, 27000-27003
Iliopsoas, 27005
Hymen
See Hymen, Incision
Hymenotomy, 56720
Hyoid, Muscle, 21685
Iliac Artery
Exposure, 34820, 34833

Incision — *continued*
Intercarpal Joint
Dislocation, 25670
Interphalangeal Joint
Capsule, 26525
Intestines (Except Rectum)
See Enterotomy
Intestines, Small, 44010
Biopsy, 44020
Creation
Pouch, 44316
Stoma, 44300, 44310, 44314
Decompression, 44021
Exploration, 44020
Incision, 44020
Removal
Foreign Body, 44020
Revision
Stoma, 44312
Intracranial Vessels, 37799
Iris, 66500, 66505
Kidney, 50010, 50045
Calculus Removal, 50130
Complicated, 50135
Exploration, 50010
Nephrotomy, with Exploration, 50045
Pyelotomy, with exploration, 50120
Knee
Capsule, 27435
Exploration, 27310
Fasciotomy, 27305
Removal of Foreign Body, 27310
Lacrimal Punctum, 68440
Lacrimal Sac
See Dacryocystotomy
Larynx, 31300, 31320
Leg, Lower
Fasciotomy, 27600-27602
Leg, Upper
Fasciotomy, 27025, 27305
Tenotomy, 27306, 27307, 27390-27392
Lip
Frenum, 40806
Liver
See Hepatotomy
Lung
Biopsy, 32095, 32100
Decortication
Partial, 32225
Total, 32220
Lymphatic Channels, 38308
Mastoid
See Mastoidotomy
Medullary Tract, 61470
Mesencephalic Tract, 61480
Metacarpophalangeal Joint
Capsule, 26520
Mitral Valve, 33420, 33422
Muscle
See Myotomy
Nerve, 64573-64580, 64585-64772
Foot, 28035
Root, 63185, 63190
Sacral, 64581
Vagus, 43640, 43641
Nose
See Rhinotomy
Orbit
See Orbitotomy
Palm
Fasciotomy, 26040, 26045

Incision — *continued*
Pancreas
  Sphincter, 43262
Penis
  Prepuce, 54000, 54001
    Newborn, 54000
Pericardium, 33030, 33031
  with Clot Removal, 33020
  with Foreign Body Removal, 33020
  with Tube Insertion, 33015
Pharynx
  Stoma, 42955
Pleura, 32320
  Biopsy, 32095, 32100
Pleural Cavity
  Empyema, 32035, 32036
  Pneumothorax, 32020
Prostate
  Exposure
    Bilateral Pelvic Lymphadenectomy, 55865
    Insertion Radioactive Substance, 55860
    Lymph Node Biopsy, 55862
  Transurethral, 52450
Pterygomaxillary Fossa, 31040
Pulmonary Valve, 33470-33474
Pyloric Sphincter, 43520
Retina
  Encircling Material, 67115
Sclera
  Fistulization
    with Iridectomy, 66160
    Iridencleisis or Iridotasis, 66165
    Sclerectomy with Punch or Scissors with
      Iridectomy, 66160
    Thermocauterization with Iridectomy,
      66155
    Trabeculectomy ab Externo in Absence
      Previous Surgery, 66170
    Trephination with Iridectomy, 66150
Semicircular Canal Revision, 69840
  Fenestration, 69820
Seminal Vesicle, 55600-55605
  Complicated, 55605
Shoulder
  Bone, 23035
  Capsule Contracture Release, 23020
  Removal
    Calcareous Deposits, 23000
  Tenomyotomy, 23405-23406
Shoulder Joint, 23040, 23044
Sinus
  Frontal, 31070-31087
  Maxillary, 31020-31032
    Endoscopic, 31256, 31267
  Multiple, 31090
  Sphenoid
    Sinusotomy, 31050, 31051
Skin, 10040-10180
Skull, 61316, 62148
  Suture, 61550, 61552
Spinal Cord, 63200
  Tract, 63170, 63194-63199
Stomach
  Creation
    Stoma, 43830-43832
  Exploration, 43500
  Pyloric Sphincter, 43520
Synovectomy, 26140
Temporomandibular Joint, 21010-21070
Tendon
  Arm, Upper, 24310

Incision — *continued*
Thigh
  Fasciotomy, 27025
Thorax
  Empyema, 32035, 32036
  Pneumothorax, 32020
Thyroid Gland
  See Thyrotomy
Tibia, 27607
Toe
  Capsule, 28270, 28272
  Fasciotomy, 28008
  Tendon, 28232, 28234
  Tenotomy, 28010, 28011
Tongue
  Frenum, 41010
Trachea
  with Flaps, 31610
  Emergency, 31603, 31605
  Planned, 31600
    Under Two Years, 31601
Tympanic Membrane, 69420
  with Anesthesia, 69421
Ureter, 50600
Ureterocele, 51535
Urethra, 53000, 53010
  Meatus, 53020, 53025
Uterus
  Remove Lesion, 59100
Vagina
  Exploration, 57000
Vas Deferens, 55200
  for X-ray, 55300
Vestibule of Mouth
  See Mouth, Vestibule of, Incision
Vitreous Strands
  Laser Surgery, 67031
  Pars Plana Approach, 67030
Wrist, 25100-25105
  Capsule, 25085
  Decompression, 25020-25025
  Tendon Sheath, 25000, 25001

Incisional Hernia Repair
  See Hernia, Repair, Incisional

Incision and Drainage
  See Drainage; Incision
Abscess
  Abdomen, Abdominal
    Open, 49040
    Pancreatitis, 48000
    Peritoneal, 49020
    Peritonitis, Localized, 49020
    Retroperitoneal, 49060
    Skin and Subcutaneous Tissue
      Complicated, 10061
      Multiple, 10061
      Simple, 10060
      Single, 10060
    Subdiaphragmatic, 49040
    Subphrenic, 49040
  Acne Surgery
    Comedones, 10040
    Cysts, 10040
    Marsupialization, 10040
    Milia, Multiple, 10040
    Pustules, 10040
  Anal, 46045, 46050
  Ankle, 27603
  Appendix
    Open, 44900
    Percutaneous, 44901
  Arm, Lower, 25028, 25035

Incision and Drainage — *continued*
  Hematoma — *continued*
    Neck, 21501, 21502
    Nose, 30000, 30020
    Pelvis, 26990
    Scrotum, 54700
    Shoulder, 23030
    Skin, 10140
      Puncture Aspiration, 10160
    Skull, 61312-61315
    Testis, 54700
    Thorax, 21501, 21502
    Tongue, 41000-41006, 41015
    Vagina, 57022, 57023
    Wrist, 25028
  Hepatic Duct, 47400
  Hip
    Bone, 26992, 27030
  Humerus
    Abscess, 23935
  Interphalangeal Joint
    Toe, 28024
  Intertarsal Joint, 28020
  Kidney, 50040, 50125
  Knee, 27303, 27310
  Lacrimal Gland, 68400
  Lacrimal Sac, 68420
  Liver
    Abscess or Cyst, 47010, 47011
    Percutaneous, 47011
  Mediastinum, 39000, 39010
  Metatarsophalangeal Joint, 28022
  Milia, Multiple, 10040
  Onychia, 10060, 10061
  Orbit, 67405, 67440
  Paronychia, 10060, 10061
  Pelvic/Bone, 26992
  Penis, 54015
  Pericardium, 33025
  Phalanges
    Finger, 26034
  Pilonidal Cyst, 10080, 10081
  Pustules
    Skin, 10040
  Radius, 25035
  Seroma
    Skin, 10140
  Shoulder
    Abscess, 23030
    Arthrotomy
      Acromioclavicular Joint, 23044
      Glenohumeral Joint, 23040
      Sternoclavicular Joint, 23044
    Bursa, 23031
    Hematoma, 23030
  Shoulder Joint
    Arthrotomy, Glenohumeral Joint, 23040
  Tarsometatarsal Joint, 28020
  Tendon Sheath
    Finger, 26020
    Palm, 26020
  Thorax
    Deep, 21510
  Toe, 28024
  Ulna, 25035
  Ureter, 50600
  Vagina, 57020
  Wound Infection
    Skin, 10180
  Wrist, 25028, 25040
Inclusion Bodies
  Fluid, 88106

Incomplete
  Abortion, 59812
Indicator Dilution Studies, 93561, 93562
Induced
  Abortion
    with Hysterotomy, 59100, 59852, 59857
    by Dilation and Curettage, 59840
    by Dilation and Evacuation, 59841
    by Saline, 59850, 59851
    by Vaginal Suppositories, 59855, 59856
Induced Hyperthermia
  See Thermotherapy
Induced Hypothermia
  See Hypothermia
Induratio Penis Plastica
  See Peyronie Disease
Infantile Paralysis
  See Polio
Infant, Newborn, Intensive Care
  See Intensive Care, Neonatal
Infection
  Immunoassay, 86317, 86318
  Rapid Test, 86403, 86406
Infection, Actinomyces
  See Actinomycosis
Infection, Bone
  See Osteomyelitis
Infection, Filarioidea
  See Filariasis
Infection, Postoperative Wound
  See Postoperative Wound Infection
Infection, Wound
  See Wound, Infection
Infectious Agent Detection
  Antigen Detection
    Direct Fluorescence
      Bordetella, 87265
      Chlamydia Trachomatis, 87270
      Cryptosporidium, 87272
      Cytomegalovirus, 87271
      Enterovirus, 87267
      Giardia, 87269
      Influenza A, 87276
      Legionella Pneumophila, 87278
      Pertussis, 87265
      Respiratory Syncytial Virus, 87280
      Treponema Pallidum, 87285
      Varicella Zoster, 87290
    Enzyme Immunoassay
      Adenovirus, 87301
      Chlamydia Trachomatis, 87320
      Clostridium Difficile Toxin A, 87324
      Cryptococcus NeoFormans, 87327
      Cryptosporidium, 87328
      Cytomegalovirus, 87332
      Entamoeba Histolytica Dispar Group, 87336
      Entamoeba Histolytica Group, 87337
      Escherichia coli 0157, 87335
      Giardia, 87329
      Helicobacter Pylori, 87338, 87339
      Hepatitis Be Antigen (HBeAg), 87350
      Hepatitis B Surface Antigen (HBsAg), 87340
      Hepatitis B Surface Antigen (HBsAg) Neutralization, 87341
      Hepatitis, Delta Agent, 87380
      Histoplasma Capsulatum, 87385
      HIV-1, 87390

Infectious Agent Detection — *continued*
  Antigen Detection — *continued*
    Enzyme Immunoassay — *continued*
      HIV-2, 87391
      Influenza A, 87400
      Influenza B, 87400
      Multiple Step Method, 87301-87449,
        87451
        See specific agent
      Not Otherwise Specified, 87449-87451
      Respiratory Syncytial Virus, 87420
      Rotavirus, 87425
      Shiga-like Toxin, 87427
      Single Step Method, 87450
      Streptococcus, Group A, 87430
    Immunofluorescence
      Adenovirus, 87260
      Herpes Simplex, 87273, 87274
      Influenza B, 87275
      Legionella Micdadei, 87277
      Not otherwise Specified, 87299
      Parainfluenza Virus, 87279
      Pneumocystis Carinii, 87281
      Polyvalent, 87300
      Rubeola, 87283
  Concentration, 87015
  Detection
    by Immunoassay with Direct Optical
      Observation, 87802-87899
    Chlamydia Trachomatis, 87810
    Clostridium difficile, 87803
    Influenza, 87804
    Neisseria Gonorrhoeae, 87850
    Not Otherwise Specified, 87899
    Respiratory Syncytial Virus, 87807
    Streptococcus, Group A, 87880
    Streptococcus, Group B, 87802
    by Nucleic Acid
      Bartonella Henselae, 87470-87472
      Bartonella Quintana, 87470-87472
      Borrelia Burgdorferi, 87475-87477
      Candida Species, 87480-87482
      Chlamydia Pneumoniae, 87485-87487
      Chlamydia Trachomatis, 87490-87492
      Cytomegalovirus, 87495-87497
      Gardnerella Vaginalis, 87510-87512
      Hepatitis B Virus, 87515-87517
      Hepatitis C, 87520-87522
      Hepatitis G, 87525-87527
      Herpes Simplex Virus, 87528-87530
      Herpes Virus-6, 87531-87533
      HIV-1, 87534-87536
      HIV-2, 87537-87539
      Intracellulare, 87560-87562
      Legionella Pneumophila, 87540-87542
      Multiple Organisms, 87800, 87801
      Mycobacteria Species, 87550-87552
      Mycobacteria Tuberculosis, 87555-87557
      Mycoplasma Pneumoniae, 87580-87582
      Neisseria Gonorrhoeae, 87590-87592
      Not Otherwise Specified, 87797-87799
      Papillomavirus, Human, 87620-87622
      Streptococcus, Group A, 87650-87652
      Trichomonas Vaginalis, 87660
    Urinalysis, 0041T
  Genotype Analysis
    by Nucleic Acid
      Hepatitis C Virus, 87902
      HIV-1 Protease/Reverse Transcriptase,
        87901

Infectious Agent Detection — *continued*
  Phenotype Analysis
    by Nucleic Acid
      HIV-1 Drug Resistance, 87903, 87904
      HIV-1 Drug Resistance, 87900
Infectious Mononucleosis Virus
  See Epstein-Barr Virus
Inflammatory Process
  Localization
    Nuclear Medicine, 78805-78807
Inflation
  Ear, Middle
    Eustachian Tube
      with Catheterization, 69400
      without Catheterization, 69401
    Eustachian Tube
      Myringotomy, 69420
        Anesthesia, 69424
Influenza A
  Antigen Detection
    Direct Fluorescent, 87276
    Enzyme Immunoassay, 87400
Influenza B
  Antigen Detection
    Enzyme Immunoassay, 87400
    Immunofluorescence, 87275
Influenza B Vaccine, 90645-90648, 90720-
  90721, 90748
Influenza Vaccine
  See Vaccines
Influenza Virus
  Antibody, 86710
    Vaccine, 90657-90660
  by Immunoassay
    with Direct Optical Observation, 87804
Infraorbital Nerve
  Avulsion, 64734
  Incision, 64734
  Transection, 64734
Infrared Light Treatment, 97026
  See Physical Medicine/Therapy/ Occupational
    Therapy
Infratentorial Craniotomy, 61520, 61521
Infusion
  Amnion, Transabdominal, 59072
  Cerebral
    Intravenous for Thrombolysis, 37195
  Intraosseous, 36680
  Radioelement, 77750
  Transcatheter Therapy, 37201, 37202
Infusion Pump
  Electronic Analysis
    Spinal Cord, 62367, 62368
  Insertion
    Intraarterial, 36260
  Intraarterial
    Removal, 36262
    Revision, 36261
  Intravenous
    Insertion, 36563
    Removal, 36590
    Revision, 36576, 36578
  Maintenance, 95990, 96520, 96530
    Chemotherapy, Pump Services, 96520,
      96530
  Spinal Cord, 62361, 62362
  Ventricular Catheter, 61215
Infusion Therapy, 62350, 62351, 62360-62362
  See Injection, Chemotherapy

Infusion Therapy — *continued*
- Arterial Catheterization, 36640
- Chemotherapy, 96401-96542
- Home Infusion Procedures, 99601-99602
- Intravenous, 90760-90761, 90765-90768
- Pain, 62360-62362, 62367-62368
- Transcatheter Therapy, 75896

Ingestion Challenge Test, 95075
- *See* Allergy Tests

Inguinal Hernia Repair
- *See* Hernia, Repair, Inguinal

INH
- *See* Drug Assay

Inhalation
- Pentamidine, 94642

Inhalation Provocation Tests
- *See* Bronchial Challenge Test

Inhalation Treatment, 94640, 94664, 99503
- *See* Pulmonology, Therapeutic

Inhibin A, 86336

Inhibition, Fertilization
- *See* Contraception

Inhibition Test, Hemagglutination
- *See* Hemagglutination Inhibition Test

Inhibitor, Alpha 1-Protease
- *See* Alpha-1 Antitrypsin

Inhibitor, Alpha 2-Plasmin
- *See* Alpha-2 Antiplasmin

Inhibitory Concentration, Minimum
- *See* Minimum Inhibitory Concentration

Initial Inpatient Consultations
- *See* Consultation, Initial Inpatient

Injection
- *See* Allergen Immunotherapy, Infusion
- Abdomen
  - Air, 49400
  - Contrast Material, 49400
- Angiography
  - Coronary, 93556
  - Pulmonary, 75746
- Ankle
  - Radial, 27648
- Antibiotic Administration, 90772
- Antigen (Allergen), 95115-95125, 95145-95170
- Aorta (Aortography)
  - Radiologic, 93544
- Aponeurosis, 20550
- Bladder
  - Radiologic, 51600-51610
- Bone Marrow, into, 38999
- Brain Canal, 61070
- Breast
  - Radiologic, 19030
- Bronchography
  - Segmental, 31656
- Bursa, 20600-20610
- Cardiac Catheterization, 93539-93545
- Carpal Tunnel
  - Therapeutic, 20526
- Chemotherapy, 96401-96402, 96450, 96542
- Cistern
  - Medication or Other, 61055
- Contrast
  - Central Venous Access Device, 36598
  - via Peritoneal Catheter, 49424
- Corpora Cavernosa, 54235
- Cyst
  - Bone, 20615
  - Kidney, 50390

Injection — *continued*
- Cyst — *continued*
  - Pelvis, 50390
  - Thyroid, 60001
- Elbow
  - Arthrography, Radiologic, 24220
- Epidural
  - *See* Epidural, Injection
- Esophageal Varices
  - Endoscopy, 43243
- Esophagus
  - Sclerosing Agent, 43204
  - Sphincter, 0133T
  - Submucosal, 43201
- Extremity
  - Pseudoaneurysm, 36002
- Eye
  - Air, 66020
  - Medication, 66030
- Eyelid
  - Subconjunctival, 68200
- Ganglion
  - Anesthetic, 64505, 64510
- Ganglion Cyst, 20612
- Gastric Secretion Stimulant, 91052
- Gastric Varices
  - Endoscopy, 43243
- Heart
  - Therapeutic Substance into Pericardium, 33999
- Heart Vessels
  - Cardiac Catheterization, 93539-93545
    - *See* Catheterization, Cardiac
  - Radiologic, 93545
- Hemorrhoids
  - Sclerosing Solution, 46500
- Hip
  - Radiologic, 27093, 27095
- Insect Venom, 95130-95134
- Intervertebral Disk
  - Chemonucleolysis Agent, 62292
  - Radiological, 62290, 62291
- Intra-amniotic, 59850-59852
- Intraarterial
  - Diagnostic, 90773
  - Therapeutic, 90773
- Intradermal, Tattooing, 11920-11922
- Intralesional, Skin, 11900, 11901
- Intramuscular, 90772
  - Diagnostic, 90772
  - Therapeutic, 90772, 99506
- Intravenous
  - Diagnostic, 90774
  - Therapeutic, 90774
  - Vascular Flow Check, Graft, 15860
- Joint, 20600-20610
- Kidney
  - Drugs, 50391
  - Radiologic, 50394
- Knee
  - Radiologic, 27370
- Lacrimal Gland
  - Radiologic, 68850
- Left Heart
  - Radiologic, 93543
- Lesion, Skin, 11900, 11901
- Ligament, 20550
- Liver, 47015
  - Radiologic, 47500, 47505
- Lungs
  - Radiologic, 93541
- Lymphangiography, 38790

Injection — *continued*
Mammary Ductogram
Galactogram, 19030
Muscle Endplate
Cervical Spinal, 64613
Extremity, 64614
Facial, 64612
Trunk, 64614
Nerve
Anesthetic, 64400-64530
Neurolytic Agent, 64600-64680
Orbit
Retrobulbar
Alcohol, 67505
Medication, 67500
Tenon's Capsule, 67515
Pancreatography, 48400
Paravertebral Facet Joint
Nerve, 64470-64476
Penis
for Erection, 54235
Peyronie Disease, 54200
with Surgical Exposure of Plaque, 54205
Radiology, 54230
Vasoactive Drugs, 54231
Pericardium
Injection of Therapeutic Substance, 33999
Peritoneal Cavity Air
See Pneumoperitoneum
Radiologic
Breast, 19030
Rectum
Sclerosing Solution, 45520
Right Heart
See Cardiac Catheterization, Injection
Injection of Radiologic Substance, 93542
Sacroiliac Joint
for Arthrography, 27096
Salivary Duct, 42660
Salivary Gland
Radiologic, 42550
Sclerosing Agent
Esophagus, 43204
Intravenous, 36470, 36471
Sentinel Node Identification, 38792
Shoulder
Arthrography, Radiologic, 23350
Shunt
Peritoneal
Venous, 49427
Sinus Tract, 20500
Diagnostic, 20501
Spider Veins
Telangiectasia, 36468, 36469
Spinal Artery, 62294
Spinal Cord
Anesthetic, 62310-62319
Blood, 62273
Neurolytic Agent, 62280-62282
Other, 62310, 62311
Radiologic, 62284
Spleen
Radiologic, 38200
Steroids for Urethral Stricture, 52283
Subcutaneous
Diagnostic, 90772
Silicone, 11950-11954
Therapeutic, 90772
Temporomandibular Joint
Arthrography, 21116
Tendon Origin, Insertion, 20551
Tendon Sheath, 20550

Injection — *continued*
Therapeutic
Extremity Pseudoaneurysm, 36002
Lung, 32960
Thyroid, 60001
Turbinate, 30200
Thoracic Cavity
See Pleurodesis, Chemical
Trachea
Puncture, 31612
Transtracheal
Bronchography, 31715
Trigger Point(s)
One or Two Muscle Groups, 20552
Three or More Muscle Groups, 20553
Turbinate, 30200
Unlisted, 90779
Unlisted Services and Procedures, 90779
Ureter
Drugs, 50391
Radiologic, 50684
Ureteropyelography, 50690
Venography, 36005
Ventricular
Dye, 61120
Medication or Other, 61026
Vitreous, 67028
Fluid Substitute, 67025
Vocal Cords
Therapeutic, 31513, 31570, 31571
Wrist
Carpal Tunnel
Therapeutic, 20526
Radiologic, 25246
Inkblot Test, 96101-96103
Inner Ear
See Ear, Inner
Innominate
Tumor
Excision, 27077
Innominate Arteries
See Artery, Brachiocephalic
Inorganic Sulfates
See Sulfate
Insemination
Artificial, 58321, 58322, 89268
Insertion
See Implantation; Intubation; Transplantation
Balloon
Intra-Aortic, 33967, 33973
Breast
Implants, 19340, 19342
Cannula
Arteriovenous, 36810, 36815
ECMO, 36822
Extra Corporeal Circulation for Regional
Chemotherapy of Extremity, 36823
Thoracic Duct, 38794
Vein to Vein, 36800
Catheter
Abdomen, 49420, 49421
Abdominal Artery, 36245-36248
Aorta, 36200
Bile Duct, 47525, 47530, 75982
Percutaneous, 47510
Bladder, 51045, 51701-51703
Brachiocephalic Artery, 36215-36218
Brain, 61210, 61770
Breast
for Interstitial Radioelement Application,
19296-19298

Insertion — *continued*
Catheter — *continued*
Bronchi, 31710, 31717
Bronchus
for Intracavity Radioelement Application, 31643
Cardiac
See Catheterization, Cardiac
Flow Directed, 93503
Ear, Middle, 69405
Eustachian Tube, 69405
Flow Directed, 93503
Gastrointestinal, Upper, 43241
Jejunum, 44015
Kidney, 50392
Lower Extremity Artery, 36245-36248
Nasotracheal, 31720
Pelvic Artery, 36245-36248
Pleural Cavity, 32019
Portal Vein, 36481
Prostate, 55859
Pulmonary Artery, 36013-36015
Right Heart, 36013
Skull, 61107
Spinal Cord, 62350, 62351
Suprapubic, 51010
Thoracic Artery, 36215-36218
Trachea, 31700
Tracheobronchial, 31725
Ureter via Kidney, 50393
Urethra, 51701-51703
Vena Cava, 36010
Venous, 36011, 36012, 36400-36425, 36500, 36510, 36555-36558, 36568-36569
Cervical Dilator, 59200
Cochlear Device, 69930
Contraceptive Capsules, 11975, 11977
Defibrillator
Heart, 33212, 33245, 33246
Leads, 33216, 33217
Pads, 33245, 33246
Pulse Generator Only, 33240
Drug Delivery Implant, 11981, 11983
Electrode
Brain, 61531, 61533, 61760, 61850-61875
Heart, 33210-33217, 33224, 33225, 93620-93622
Nerve, 64553-64581
Sphenoidal, 95830
Spinal Cord, 63650, 63655
Endotracheal Tube, 31500
FiliForm
Urethra, 53620
Gastrostomy Tube
Laparoscopic, 43653
Percutaneous, 43750
Graft
Aorta, 33330-33335
Heart Vessel, 33330-33335
Guide
Kidney, Pelvis, 50395
Guide Wire
Endoscopy, 43248
Esophagoscopy, 43248
with Dilation, 43226
Heyman Capsule
Uterus
for Brachytherapy, 58346
Iliac Artery
Occlusion Device, 34808

Insertion — *continued*
Implant
Bone
for External Speech Processor/Cochlear Stimulator, 69714-69718
Infusion Pump
Intraarterial, 36260
Intravenous, 36563
Spinal Cord, 62361, 62362
Intracatheter/Needle
Aorta, 36160
Arteriovenous Shunt, 36145
Intraarterial, 36100-36140
Intravenous, 36000
Kidney, 50392
Venous, 36000
Intraocular Lens, 66983
Manual or Mechanical Technique, 66982, 66984
not Associated with Concurrent Cataract Removal, 66985
Intrauterine Device (IUD), 58300
IVC Filter, 75940
Jejunostomy Tube
Endoscopy, 44372
Keel
Laryngoplasty, 31580
Laminaria, 59200
Mesh
Pelvic Floor, 57267
Nasobiliary Tube
Endoscopy, 43267
Nasopancreatic Tube
Endoscopy, 43267
Needle
Bone, 36680
Intraosseous, 36680
Prostate, 55859
Needle Wire Dilator
Stent
Trachea, 31730
Transtracheal for Oxygen, 31720
Neurostimulator
Pulse Generator, 64590
Receiver, 64590
Nose
Septal Prosthesis, 30220
Obturator/Larynx, 31527
Ocular Implant
with Foreign Material, 65155
with or without Conjunctival Graft, 65150
in Scleral Shell, 65130, 67550
Muscles Attached, 65140
Muscles not Attached, 65135
Orbital Transplant, 67550
Oviduct
Chromotubation, 58350
Hydrotubation, 58350
Ovoid
Vagina
for Brachytherapy, 57155
Pacemaker
Fluoroscopy
Radiography, 71090
Heart, 33200-33208, 33212, 33213
Pacing Cardio-Defibrillator
Electrodes, 33245, 33246
Leads, 33216-33220, 33224, 33225, 33243-33245
Pulse Generator Only, 33240, 33241
Packing
Vagina, 57180

Insertion — *continued*
  Penile Prosthesis Inflatable
    See Penile Prosthesis, Insertion, Inflatable
  Pessary
    Vagina, 57160
  Pin
    Skeletal Traction, 20650
  Probe
    Brain, 61770
  Prostaglandin, 59200
  Prostate
    Radioactive Substance, 55860
  Prosthesis
    Knee, 27438, 27445
    Nasal Septal, 30220
    Palate, 42281
    Pelvic Floor, 57267
    Penis
      Inflatable, 54401-54405
      Non-inflatable, 54400
    Speech, 31611
    Testis, 54660
    Urethral Sphincter, 53444-53445
  Pulse Generator
    Brain, 61885, 61886
    Heart, 33212, 33213
    Spinal Cord, 63685
  Radioactive Material
    Bladder, 51020
    Cystourethroscopy, 52250
    Interstitial Brachytherapy, 77776-77778
    Intracavitary Brachytherapy, 77761, 77762
    Prostate, 55859, 55860
    Remote Afterloading Brachytherapy, 77781-
      77784
  Receiver
    Brain, 61885, 61886
    Spinal Cord, 63685
  Reservoir
    Brain, 61210, 61215
    Spinal Cord, 62360
    Subcutaneous, 49419
  Sensor, Fetal Oximetry
    Cervix, 0021T
    Vagina, 0021T
  Shunt, 36835
    Abdomen
      Vein, 49425
      Venous, 49426
    Intrahepatic Portosystemic, 37182
  Spinal Instrument, 22849
    Spinous Process, 22841
  Spinal Instrumentation
    Anterior, 22845-22847
    Internal Spinal Fixation, 22841
    Pelvic Fixation, 22848
    Posterior Non-segmental
      Harrington Rod Technique, 22840
    Posterior Segmental, 22842-22844
    Prosthetic Device, 22851
  Stent
    Bile Duct, 43268, 47801
      Percutaneous, 47511
    Bladder, 51045
    Conjunctiva, 68750
    Coronary, 92980, 92981
    Esophagus, 43219
    Gastrointestinal, Upper, 43256
    Ileum, 44383
    Indwelling, 50605
    Intracoronary, 92980, 92981
    Lacrimal Duct, 68810-68815

Insertion — *continued*
  Stent — *continued*
    Pancreatic Duct, 43268
    Small Intestines, 44370, 44379
    Ureteral, 50947, 52332
    Ureter via Kidney, 50393
    Urethral, 0084T, 52282
  Tamponade
    Esophagus, 43460
  Tandem
    Uterus
      for Brachytherapy, 57155
  Tendon Graft
    Finger, 26392
    Hand, 26392
  Testicular Prosthesis
    See Prosthesis, Testicular, Insertion
  Tissue Expanders, Skin, 11960-11971
  Tube
    Bile Duct, 43268
    Esophagus, 43510
    Gastrointestinal, Upper, 43241
    Ileum, 44383
    Kidney, 50398
    Pancreatic Duct, 43268
    Small Intestines, 44379
    Trachea, 31730
    Ureter, 50688
  Urethral Guide Wire, 52334
  Vascular Pedicle
    Carpal Bone, 25430
  Venous Access Device
    Central, 36560-36566
    Peripheral, 36570, 36571
  Venous Shunt
    Abdomen, 49425
  Ventilating Tube, 69433
  Ventricular Assist Device, 33975
  Wire
    Skeletal Traction, 20650
In Situ Hybridization
    See Nucleic Acid Probe, Cytogenic Studies,
      Morphometric Analysis
Inspiratory Positive Pressure Breathing
    See Intermittent Positive Pressure Breathing
      (IPPB)
Instillation
  Contrast Material
    Bronchography, 31708
    Laryngography, 31708
  Drugs
    Bladder, 51720
    Kidney, 50391
    Ureter, 50391
Instillation, Bladder
    See Bladder, Instillation
Instrumentation
    See Application; Bone; Fixation; Spinal
      Instrumentation
  Spinal
    Insertion, 22840-22848, 22851
    Reinsertion, 22849
    Removal, 22850, 22852, 22855
Insufflation, Eustachian Tube
    See Eustachian Tube, Inflation
Insulin, 80422, 80432-80435
  Antibody, 86337
  Blood, 83525
  Free, 83527

Interphalangeal Joint — *continued*
Fracture — *continued*
  Open Treatment, 26746
Fusion, 26860-26863
Great Toe
  Arthrodesis, 28755
    with Tendon Transfer, 28760
  Fusion, 28755
    with Tendon Transfer, 28760
Removal
  Foreign Body, 26080
  Loose Body, 28024
Repair
  Collateral Ligament, 26545
  Volar Plate, 26548
Synovectomy, 26140
Synovial
  Biopsy, 28054
Toe, 28272
  Arthrotomy, 28024
  Biopsy
    Synovial, 28054

Interruption
Vein
  Femoral, 37650
  Iliac, 37660
  Vena Cava, 37620

Intersex State
Clitoroplasty, 56805
Vaginoplasty, 57335

Intersex Surgery
Female to Male, 55980
Male to Female, 55970

Interstitial Cell Stimulating Hormone
See Luteinizing Hormone (LH)

Interstitial Cystitides, Chronic
See Cystitis, Interstitial

Interstitial Cystitis
See Cystitis, Interstitial

Interstitial Fluid Pressure
Monitoring, 20950

Interstitual Cell Stimulating Hormone
See Luteinizing Hormone (LH)

Intertarsal Joint
Arthrotomy, 28020, 28050
Biopsy
  Synovial, 28050
Exploration, 28020
Removal
  Foreign Body, 28020
  Loose Body, 28020
Synovial
  Biopsy, 28050
  Excision, 28070

Interthoracoscapular Amputation
See Amputation, Interthoracoscapular

Intertrochanteric Femur Fracture
See Femur, Fracture,Intertrochanteric

Intervertebral Chemonucleolysis
See Chemonucleolysis

Intervertebral Disk
Diskography
  Cervical, 72285
  Lumbar, 72295
  Thoracic, 72285
Excision
  Decompression, 63075-63078
  Herniated, 63020-63044, 63055-63066
Injection
  Chemonucleolysis Agent, 62292

Intervertebral Disk — *continued*
Injection — *continued*
  X-ray, 62290, 62291
X-ray with Contrast
  Cervical, 72285
  Lumbar, 72295

Intestinal Anastomosis
See Anastomosis, Intestines

Intestinal Invagination
See Intussusception

Intestinal Peptide, Vasoconstrictive
See Vasoactive Intestinal Peptide

Intestine(s)
Allotransplantation, 44135, 44136
  Removal, 44137
Anastomosis, 44625, 44626
Biopsy, 44100
Bleeding Tube, 91100
Closure
  Enterostomy
    Large or Small, 44625, 44626
  Stoma, 44620, 44625
Excision
  Donor, 44132, 44133
Exclusion, 44700
Laparoscopic Resection with Anastomosis,
    44202, 44203, 44207, 44208
Lesion
  Excision, 44110, 44111
Lysis of Adhesions
  Laparoscopic, 44180
Nuclear Medicine
  Imaging, 78290
Reconstruction
  Bladder, 50820
  Colonic Reservoir, 45119
Repair
  Diverticula, 44605
  Obstruction, 44615
  Ulcer, 44605
  Wound, 44605
Suture
  Diverticula, 44605
  Stoma, 44620, 44625
  Ulcer, 44605
  Wound, 44605
Transplantation
  Allograft Preparation, 44715-44721
  Donor Enterectomy, 44132, 44133
  Removal of Allograft, 44137
Unlisted Laparoscopic Procedure, 44238

Intestines, Large
See Anus; Cecum; Colon; Rectum

Intestines, Small
Anastomosis, 43845, 44130
Biopsy, 44020, 44100
  Endoscopy, 44361
Catheterization
  Jejunum, 44015
Closure
  Stoma, 44620, 44625
Decompression, 44021
Destruction
  Lesion, 44369
  Tumor, 44369
Endoscopy, 44360
  Biopsy, 44361, 44377
  Control of Bleeding, 44366, 44378
    via Stoma, 44382
  Destruction
    Lesion, 44369

Intestines, Small — *continued*
  Endoscopy — *continued*
    Destruction — *continued*
      Tumor, 44369
    Diagnostic, 44376
    Exploration, 44360
    Hemorrhage, 44366
    Insertion
      Stent, 44370, 44379
      Tube, 44379
    Pelvic Pouch, 44385, 44386
    Place Tube, 44372
    Removal
      Foreign Body, 44363
      Lesion, 44365
      Polyp, 44364, 44365
      Tumor, 44364, 44365
    Tube Placement, 44372
    Tube Revision, 44373
    via Stoma, 44380, 44382
  Enterostomy, 44300, 44620-44626
  Excision, 44120-44128
    Partial with Anastomosis, 44140
  Exclusion, 44700
  Exploration, 44020
  Gastrostomy Tube, 44373
  Hemorrhage, 44378
  Hemorrhage Control, 44366
  Ileostomy, 44310-44314, 44316
    Continent, 44316
  Incision, 44010, 44020
    Creation
      Pouch, 44316
      Stoma, 44300-44314
    Decompression, 44021
    Exploration, 44020
    Revision
      Stoma, 44312
      Stoma Closure, 44620-44626
  Insertion
    Catheter, 44015
    Jejunostomy Tube, 44015, 44372
  Jejunostomy, 44310
    Laparoscopic, 44186
  Lesion
    Excision, 44110, 44111
  Lysis
    Adhesions, 44005
  Removal
    Foreign Body, 44020, 44363
  Repair
    Diverticula, 44602-44605
    Enterocele
      Abdominal Approach, 57270
      Vaginal Approach, 57268
    Fistula, 44640-44661
    Hernia, 44050
    Malrotation, 44055
    Obstruction, 44050, 44615
    Ulcer, 44602, 44603, 44605
    Volvulus, 44050
    Wound, 44602, 44603, 44605
  Revision
    Jejunostomy Tube, 44373
  Specimen Collection, 89100, 89105
  Suture
    Diverticula, 44602, 44603, 44605
    Fistula, 44640-44661
    Plication, 44680
    Stoma, 44620, 44625
    Ulcer, 44602, 44603, 44605
    Wound, 44602, 44603, 44605

Intestines, Small — *continued*
  Unlisted Services and Procedures, 44799
  X-ray, 74245, 74249-74251
    Guide Intubation, 74355
Intestinovesical Fistula
  See Fistula, Enterovesical
Intimectomy
  See Endarterectomy
Intra-Abdominal Manipulation
  Intestines, 44799
Intra-Abdominal Voiding Pressure Studies,
  51797
Intra Arterial Injections
  See Injection, Intraarterial
Intracapsular Extraction of Lens
  See Extraction,Lens, Intracapsular
Intracardiac Echocardiography, 93662
Intracranial
  Biopsy, 61140
  Microdissection, 69990
    with Surgical Microscope, 69990
Intracranial Arterial Perfusion
  Thrombolysis, 61624
Intracranial Neoplasm, Acoustic Neuroma
  See Brain, Tumor, Excision
Intracranial Neoplasm, Craniopharyngioma
  See Craniopharyngioma
Intracranial Neoplasm, Meningioma
  See Meningioma
Intracranial Nerve
  Electrocoagulation
    Anesthesia, 00222
Intracranial Procedures
  Anesthesia, 00190, 00210-00222
Intrafallopian Transfer, Gamete
  See GIFT
Intraluminal Angioplasty
  See Angioplasty
Intramuscular Injection
  See Injection, Intramuscular
Intraocular Lens
  Exchange, 66986
  Insertion, 66983
    Manual or Mechanical Technique, 66982, 66984
    not Associated with Concurrent Cataract Removal, 66985
Intraoperative Manipulation of Stomach, 43659, 43999
Intraoral
  Skin Graft
    Pedicle Flap, 15576
Intra-Osseous Infusion
  See Infusion, Intraosseous
Intrathoracic Esophagoesophagostomy, 43499
Intrathoracic System
  Anesthesia, 00500-00580
Intratracheal Intubation
  See Insertion, Endotracheal Tube
Intrauterine Contraceptive Device
  See Intrauterine Device (IUD)
Intrauterine Device (IUD)
  Insertion, 58300
  Removal, 58301
Intrauterine Synechiae
  See Adhesions, Intrauterine

Iris — *continued*
  Suture
    with Ciliary Body, 66682
Iron, 83540
Iron Binding Capacity, 83550
Iron Hematoxylin Stain, 88312
Iron Stain, 85536, 88313
Irradiation
  Blood Products, 86945
Irrigation
  Bladder, 51700
  Caloric Vestibular Test, 92533, 92543
  Catheter
    Brain, 62194, 62225
  Corpora Cavernosa
    Priapism, 54220
  Penis
    Priapism, 54220
  Peritoneal
    See Peritoneal Lavage
  Rectum
    for Fecal Impaction, 91123
  Shunt
    Spinal Cord, 63744
  Sinus
    Maxillary, 31000
    Sphenoid, 31002
  Vagina, 57150
  Venous Access Device
Irving Sterilization
  Ligation, Fallopian Tube, Oviduct, 58600-58611, 58670
Ischial
  Excision
    Bursa, 27060
    Tumor, 27078, 27079
Ischiectomy, 15941
Ischium
  Pressure Ulcer, 15940-15946
ISG Immunization, 90281, 90283
Island Pedicle Flaps, 15740
Islands of Langerhans
  See Islet Cell
Islet Cell
  Antibody, 86341
Isocitrate Dehydrogenase
  See Isocitric Dehydrogenase
Isocitric Dehydrogenase
  Blood, 83570
Isolation
  Sperm, 89260, 89261
Isomerase, Glucose 6 Phophate
  See Phosphohexose Isomerase
Isopropanol
  See Isopropyl Alcohol
Isopropyl Alcohol, 84600
Isthmusectomy
  Thyroid Gland, 60210-60225
IUD, 58300, 58301
  Insertion, 58300
  Removal, 58301
IV, 90760-90761, 90765-90768, 90774-90775
IVC Filter
  Placement, 75940
IV, Coagulation Factor
  See Calcium

IVF (In Vitro Fertilization), 58970-58976, 89250-89255
IV Infusion Therapy
  See Allergen Immunotherapy; Chemotherapy; Infusion
  Injection, Chemotherapy, 96409, 96411, 96413-96417, 96542
IV Injection
  Injection, Intravenous, 90774-90775
Ivor Lewis, 43117
IVP, 50394, 74400
Ivy Bleeding Time, 85002
IX Complex, Factor
  See Christmas Factor

J

Jaboulay Operation
  Gastroduodenostomy, 43810, 43850, 43855
Jannetta Procedure
  Decompression, Cranial Nerves, 61458
Japanese, River Fever
  See Scrub Typhus
Jatene Procedure
  Repair, Great Arteries, 33770-33781
Jaw Joint
  See Facial Bones; Mandible; Maxilla
Jaws
  Muscle Reduction, 21295, 21296
  X-ray
    for Orthodontics, 70355
Jejunostomy
  with Pancreatic Drain, 48001
  Catheterization, 44015
  Insertion
    Catheter, 44015
  Laparoscopic, 44186
  Non-Tube, 44310
Jejunum
  Transfer with Microvascular Anastomosis, Free, 43496
Johannsen Procedure, 53400
Johanson Operation
  See Reconstruction, Urethra
Joint
  See Specific Joint
  Acromioclavicular
    See Acromioclavicular Joint
  Arthrocentesis, 20600-20610
  Aspiration, 20600-20610
  Dislocation
    See Dislocation
  Drainage, 20600-20610
  Finger
    See Intercarpal Joint
  Fixation (Surgical)
    See Arthrodesis
  Foot
    See Foot, Joint
  Hip
    See Hip, Joint
  Injection, 20600-20610
  Intertarsal
    See Intertarsal Joint
  Knee
    See Knee Joint
  Ligament
    See Ligament
  Metacarpophalangeal
    See Metacarpophalangeal Joint

Joint — *continued*
  Metatarsophalangeal
    See Metatarsophalangeal Joint
  Mobilization, 97140
  Nuclear Medicine
    Imaging, 78300-78315
  Radiology
    Stress Views, 76006
  Sacroiliac
    See Sacroiliac Joint
  Shoulder
    See Glenohumeral Joint
  Sternoclavicular
    See Sternoclavicular Joint
  Survey, 76066
  Temporomandibular
    See Temporomandibular Joint (TMJ)
    Dislocation Temporomandibular
      See Dislocation, Temporomandibular
        Joint
    Implant
      See Prosthesis, Temporomandibular Joint
  Wrist
    See Radiocarpal Joint
Joint Syndrome, Temporomandibular
  See Temporomandibular Joint (TMJ)
Jones and Cantarow Test
  Clearance, Urea Nitrogen, 84545
Jones Procedure
  Arthrodesis, Interphalangeal Joint, Great Toe,
    28760
Joplin Procedure, 28294
Jugal Bone
  See Cheekbone
Jugular Vein
  See Vein, Jugular

K

K+, 84132
Kader Operation
  Incision, Stomach, Creation of Stoma, 43830-
    43832
Kala Azar Smear, 87207
Kallidin I /Kallidin 9
  See Bradykinin
Kallidrein HK3
  See Antigen, Prostate Specific
Kallikreinogen
  See Fletcher Factor
Kasai Procedure, 47701
Keel
  Insertion
    Removal
      Laryngoplasty, 31580
Keen Operation, 63198
  Laminectomy, 63600
Kelikian Procedure, 28280
Keller Procedure, 28292
Kelly Urethral Plication, 57220
Keratectomy
  Partial
    for Lesion, 65400
Keratomileusis, 65760
Keratophakia, 65765
Keratoplasty
  Lamellar, 65710
    in Aphakia, 65750
    in Pseudophakia, 65755

Keratoplasty — *continued*
  Lamellar — *continued*
    Penetrating, 65730
Keratoprosthesis, 65770
Keratotomy
  Radial, 65771
Ketogenic Steroids, 83582
Ketone Body
  Acetone, 82009, 82010
Ketosteroids, 83586, 83593
Kidner Procedure, 28238
Kidney
  Abscess
    Incision and Drainage
      Open, 50020
      Percutaneous, 50021
  Allograft Preparation, 50323-50329
    Donor Nephrectomy, 50300, 50320, 50547
    Implantation of Graft, 50360
    Recipient Nephrectomy, 50340, 50365
    Reimplantation Kidney, 50380
    Removal Transplant Renal Autograft, 50370
  Anesthesia
    Donor, 00862
    Recipient, 00868
  Biopsy, 50200, 50205
    Endoscopic, 50555-50557, 52354
  Catheterization
    Endoscopic, 50572
  Cyst
    Ablation, 50541
    Aspiration, 50390
    Excision, 50280, 50290
    Injection, 50390
    X-ray, 74470
  Destruction
    Calculus, 50590
    Endoscopic, 50557, 50576, 52354
  Dilation, 50395
  Endoscopy
    with Endopyelotomy, 50575
    Biopsy, 50555, 50574-50576, 52354
    Catheterization, 50553, 50572
    Destruction, 50557, 50576, 52354
    Dilation
      Intra-Renal Stricture, 52343, 52346
      Ureter, 50553
    Excision
      Tumor, 52355
    Exploration, 52351
    Lithotripsy, 52353
    Removal
      Calculus, 50561, 50580, 52352
      Foreign Body, 50561, 50580
    via Incision, 50570-50580
    via Stoma, 50551-50561
  Excision
    with Ureters, 50220-50236
    Donor, 50300, 50320, 50547
    Partial, 50240
    Recipient, 50340
    Transplantation, 50370
  Exploration, 50010, 50045, 50120
  Incision, 50010, 50045, 50120, 50130, 50135
  Incision and Drainage, 50040, 50125
  Injection
    Drugs, 50391
    Radiologic, 50394
  Insertion
    Catheter, 50392, 50393

Laminectomy, 63600
Decompression
Cervical, 63001, 63015
with Facetectomy and Foraminotomy, 63045, 63048
Laminotomy
Initial
Cervical, 63020
Each Additional Space, 63035
Lumbar, 63030
Reexploration
Cervical, 63040
Each Additional Interspace, 63043
Lumbar, 63042
Each Additional Interspace, 63044
Lumbar, 63005, 63017
with Facetectomy and Foraminotomy, 63046, 63048
Sacral, 63011
Thoracic, 63003, 63016
with Facetectomy and Foraminotomy, 63047, 63048
Excision
Lesion, 63250-63273
Neoplasm, 63275-63290
Surgical, 63170-63200
Laminoplasty
Cervical, 63050-63051
Laminotomy
Cervical, One Interspace, 63020
Lumbar, 63042
One Interspace, 63030
Each Additional, 63035
Re-exploration, Cervical, 63040
Langerhans Islands
See Islet Cell
Language Evaluation, 92506
Language Therapy, 92507, 92508
LAP, 83670
Laparoscopic Appendectomy
See Appendectomy, Laparoscopic
Laparoscopic Biopsy of Ovary
See Biopsy, Ovary, Laparoscopic
Laparoscopy
with X-ray, 47560
Abdominal, 49320-49329
Adrenalectomy, 50545
Adrenal Gland
Biopsy, 60650
Excision, 60650
Appendectomy, 44970
Aspiration, 49322
Biopsy, 47561, 49321
Lymph Nodes, 38570
Cecostomy, 44188
Cholangiography, 47560, 47561
Cholecystectomy, 47562-47564
Cholecystoenterostomy, 47570
Closure
Enterostomy, 44227
Colectomy
Partial, 44204-44208, 44213
Total, 44210-44212
Colostomy, 44188
Destruction
Lesion, 58662
Diagnostic, 49320
Drainage
Extraperitoneal Lymphocele, 49323

Laparoscopy — *continued*
Ectopic Pregnancy, 59150
with Salpingectomy and/or Oophorectomy, 59151
Enterolysis, 44180
Esophagogastric Fundoplasty, 43280
Fimbrioplasty, 58672
Gastric Restrictive Procedures, 43644-43645, 43770-43774
Gastrostomy
Temporary, 43653
Hernia Repair
Initial, 49650
Recurrent, 49651
Ileostomy, 44187
Incontinence Repair, 51990, 51992
In Vitro Fertilization, 58976
Retrieve Oocyte, 58970
Transfer Embryo, 58974
Transfer Gamete, 58976
Jejunostomy, 44186
Kidney
Ablation, 50541-50542
Ligation
Veins, Spermatic, 55500
Liver
Ablation
Tumor, 47370, 47371
Lymphadenectomy, 38571-38572
Lymphatic, 38570-38589
Lysis of Adhesions, 58660
Lysis of Intestinal Adhesions, 44180
Mobilization
Splenic Flexure, 44213
Nephrectomy, 50545-50548
Partial, 50543
Orchiectomy, 54690
Orchiopexy, 54692
Ovary
Reimplantation, 59898
Suture, 59898
Oviduct Surgery, 58670, 58671, 58679
Pancreatic Islet Cell Transplantation, 0143T
Pelvis, 49320
Proctectomy, 45395, 45397
Proctopexy, 45400, 45402
Prostatectomy, 55866
Pyloplasty, 50544
Removal
Fallopian Tubes, 58661
Leiomyomata, 58545-58546
Ovaries, 58661
Spleen, 38120
Testis, 54690
Resection
Intestines
with Anastomosis, 44202, 44203
Salpingostomy, 58673
Splenectomy, 38120, 38129
Stomach, 43651-43659
Gastric Bypass, 43644-43645
Gastroenterostomy, 43644-43645
Roux-en-Y, 43644
Surgical, 38570-38572, 43651-43653, 44180-44188, 44212, 44213, 44227, 44970, 45395-45402, 47370, 47371, 49321-49323, 49650, 49651, 50541, 50543, 50545, 50945-50948, 51992, 54690, 54692, 55550, 55866, 57425, 58545, 58546, 58552, 58554
with Guided Transhepatic Cholangiography, 47560-47561

Index

Leg — Lesion

Leg — *continued*
   Upper — *continued*
      X-ray, 73592
      Wound Exploration
         Penetrating, 20103

Legionella
   Antibody, 86713
   Antigen, 87277, 87278, 87540-87542

Legionella Micdadei
   Immunofluorescence, 87277

Legionella Pneumophilia
   Antigen Detection
      Direct Fluorescence, 87278

Leg Length Measurement X-Ray
   See Scanogram

Leiomyomata
   Removal, 58140, 58545-58546, 58561

Leishmania
   Antibody, 86717

Lengthening, Tendon
   See Tendon, Lengthening

Lens
   Extracapsular, 66940
   Intracapsular, 66920
      Dislocated, 66930
   Intraocular
      Exchange, 66986
      Reposition, 66825
   Prosthesis
      Insertion, 66983
         Manual or Mechanical Technique, 66982, 66984
         not Associated with Concurrent Cataract Removal, 66985
   Removal
      Lens Material
         Aspiration Technique, 66840
         Extracapsular, 66940
         Intracapsular, 66920, 66930
         Pars Plana Approach, 66852
         Phacofragmentation Technique, 66850

Lens Material
   Aspiration Technique, 66840
   Pars Plana Approach, 66852
   Phacofragmentation Technique, 66850

Leptomeningioma
   See Meningioma

Leptospira
   Antibody, 86720

Leriche Operation
   Sympathectomy, Thoracolumbar, 64809

Lesion
   See Tumor
   Anal
      Destruction, 46900-46917, 46924
      Excision, 45108, 46922
   Ankle
      Tendon Sheath, 27630
   Arm, Lower
      Tendon Sheath Excision, 25110
   Auditory Canal, External
      Excision
         Exostosis, 69140
         Radical with Neck Dissection, 69155
         Radical without Neck Dissection, 69150
         Soft Tissue, 69145
   Bladder
      Destruction, 51030

Lesion — *continued*
   Brain
      Excision, 61534, 61536, 61600-61608, 61615, 61616
      Radiation Treatment, 77432
   Brainstem
      Excision, 61575, 61576
   Breast
      Excision, 19120-19126
   Carotid Body
      Excision, 60600, 60605
   Chemotherapy, 96405, 96406
      Destruction, 67220-67225
   Choroid
      Destruction, 0016T
   Ciliary Body
      Destruction, 66770
   Colon
      Destruction, 44393, 45383
      Excision, 44110, 44111
   Conjunctiva
      Destruction, 68135
      Excision, 68110-68130
         with Adjacent Sclera, 68130
         over 1cm, 68115
      Expression, 68040
   Cornea
      Destruction, 65450
      Excision, 65400
         of Pterygium, 65420, 65426
   Destruction
      Ureter, 52341, 52342, 52344, 52345, 52354
   Ear, Middle
      Excision, 69540
   Epididymis
      Excision, 54830
   Esophagus
      Ablation, 43228
      Excision, 43100, 43101
      Removal, 43216
   Excision, 59100
      Bladder, 52224
      Urethra, 52224, 53265
   Eye
      Excision, 65900
   Eyelid
      Destruction, 67850
      Excision
         without Closure, 67840
         Multiple, Different Lids, 67805
         Multiple, Same Lid, 67801
         Single, 67800
         under Anesthesia, 67808
   Facial
      Destruction, 17000-17108, 17280-17286
   Femur
      Excision, 27062
   Finger
      Tendon Sheath, 26160
   Foot
      Excision, 28080, 28090
   Gums
      Destruction, 41850
      Excision, 41822-41828
   Hand
      Tendon Sheath, 26160
   Intestines
      Excision, 44110
   Intestines, Small
      Destruction, 44369
      Excision, 44111

Lesion — *continued*
Iris
  Destruction, 66770
Larynx
  Excision, 31545-31546
Leg, Lower
  Tendon Sheath, 27630
Lymph Node
  Incision and Drainage, 38300, 38305
Mesentery
  Excision, 44820
Mouth
  Destruction, 40820
  Excision, 40810-40816, 41116
  Vestibule
    Destruction, 40820
    Repair, 40830
Nasopharynx
  Excision, 61586, 61600
Nerve
  Excision, 64774-64792
Nose
  Intranasal
    External Approach, 30118
    Internal Approach, 30117
Orbit
  Excision, 61333, 67412
Palate
  Destruction, 42160
  Excision, 42104-42120
Pancreas
  Excision, 48120
Pelvis
  Destruction, 58662
Penis
  Destruction
    Any Method, 54065
    Cryosurgery, 54056
    Electrodesiccation, 54055
    Extensive, 54065
    Laser Surgery, 54057
    Simple, 54050-54060
    Surgical Excision, 54060
  Excision, 54060
    Penile Plaque, 54110-54112
Pharynx
  Destruction, 42808
  Excision, 42808
Rectum
  Excision, 45108
Removal
  Larynx, 31512, 31578
Resection, 52354
Retina
  Destruction
    Extensive, 67227, 67228
    Localized, 0017T, 67208, 67210
    Radiation by Implantation of Source, 67218
Sclera
  Excision, 66130
Skin
  Abrasion, 15786, 15787
  Biopsy, 11100, 11101
  Destruction
    Benign, 17000-17250
    Malignant, 17260-17286
      by Photodynamic Therapy, 96567
  Excision
    Benign, 11400-11471
    Malignant, 11600-11646
  Injection, 11900, 11901

Lesion — *continued*
Skin — *continued*
  Paring or Curettement, 11055-11057
    Benign Hyperkeratotic, 11055-11057
  Shaving, 11300-11313
Skin Tags
  Removal, 11200, 11201
Skull
  Excision, 61500, 61600-61608, 61615, 61616
Spermatic Cord
  Excision, 55520
Spinal Cord
  Destruction, 62280-62282
  Excision, 63265-63273
Stomach
  Excision, 43611
Testis
  Excision, 54512
Toe
  Excision, 28092
Tongue
  Excision, 41110-41114
Uvula
  Destruction, 42145
  Excision, 42104-42107
Vagina
  Destruction, 57061, 57065
Vulva
  Destruction
    Extensive, 56515
    Simple, 56501
Wrist Tendon
  Excision, 25110
Lesion of Sciatic Nerve
  See Sciatic Nerve, Lesion
Leu 2 Antigens
  See CD8
Leucine Aminopeptidase, 83670
Leukemia Lymphoma Virus I, Adult T Cell
  See HTLV-I
Leukemia Lymphoma Virus I Antibodies, Human T Cell
  See Antibody, HTLV-I
Leukemia Lymphoma Virus II Antibodies, Human T Cell
  See Antibody, HTLV-II
Leukemia Virus II, Hairy Cell Associated, Human T Cell
  See HTLV-II
Leukoagglutinins, 86021
Leukocyte
  See White Blood Cell
  Alkaline Phosphatase, 85540
  Antibody, 86021
  Histamine Release Test, 86343
  Phagocytosis, 86344
  Transfusion, 86950
Leukocyte Count
  See White Blood Cell, Count
Leukocyte Histamine Release Test, 86343
Levarterenol
  See Noradrenalin
Levator Muscle Rep
  Blepharoptosis, Repair, 67901-67909
LeVeen Shunt
  Insertion, 49425
  Patency Test, 78291
  Revision, 49426

Levulose
See Fructose

L Glutamine
See Glutamine

LH (Luteinizing Hormone), 80418, 80426, 83002

LHR (Leukocyte Histamine Release Test), 86343

Lidocaine
Assay, 80176

Lid Suture
Blepharoptosis, Repair, 67901-67909

Life Support
Organ Donor, 01990

Lift, Face
See Face Lift

Ligament
See Specific Site
Collateral
Repair, Knee with Cruciate Ligament, 27409
Dentate
Incision, 63180, 63182
Section, 63180, 63182
Injection, 20550
Release
Coracoacromial, 23415
Transverse Carpal, 29848
Repair
Elbow, 24343-24346
Knee Joint, 27405-27409

Ligation
Appendage
Dermal, 11200
Artery
Abdomen, 37617
Carotid, 37600-37606
Chest, 37616
Coronary, 33502
Coronary Artery, 33502
Ethmoidal, 30915
Extremity, 37618
Fistula, 37607
Maxillary, 30920
Neck, 37615
Temporal, 37609
Bronchus, 31899
Esophageal Varices, 43204, 43400
Fallopian Tube
Oviduct, 58600-58611, 58670
Gastroesophageal, 43405
Hemorrhoids, 46945, 46946
Oviducts, 59100
Salivary Duct, 42665
Shunt
Aorta
Pulmonary, 33924
Peritoneal
Venous, 49428
Thoracic Duct, 38380
Abdominal Approach, 38382
Thoracic Approach, 38381
Thyroid Vessels, 37615
Ureter, 53899
Vas Deferens, 55450
Vein
Clusters, 37785
Esophagus, 43205, 43244, 43400
Femoral, 37650
Gastric, 43244
Iliac, 37660
Jugular, Internal, 37565
Perforate, 37760

Ligation — continued
Vein — continued
Saphenous, 37700-37735, 37780
Vena Cava, 37620

Ligature Strangulation
Skin Tags, 11200, 11201

Light Coagulation
See Photocoagulation

Light Scattering Measurement
See Nephelometry

Light Therapy, UV
See Actinotherapy

Limb
See Extremity

Limited Lymphadenectomy for Staging
See Lymphadenectomy, Limited, for Staging

Limited Neck Dissection
with Thyroidectomy, 60252

Limited Resection Mastectomies
See Breast, Excision, Lesion

Lindholm Operation
See Tenoplasty

Lingual Bone
See Hyoid Bone

Lingual Frenectomy
See Excision, Tongue, Frenum

Lingual Nerve
Avulsion, 64740
Incision, 64740
Transection, 64740

Lingual Tonsil
See Tonsils, Lingual

Linton Procedure, 37760

Lip
Biopsy, 40490
Excision, 40500-40530
Frenum, 40819
Incision
Frenum, 40806
Reconstruction, 40525, 40527
Repair, 40650-40654
Cleft Lip, 40700-40761
Fistula, 42260
Unlisted Services and Procedures, 40799

Lipase, 83690

Lip, Cleft
See Cleft Lip

Lipectomies, Aspiration
See Liposuction

Lipectomy, 15831-15839
Suction Assisted, 15876-15879

Lipids
Feces, 82705, 82710

Lipo-Lutin
See Progesterone

Lipolysis, Aspiration
See Liposuction

Lipophosphodiesterase I
See Tissue Typing

Lipoprotein, 83695
Blood, 0026T, 83700-83701, 83704, 83718-83719
LDL, 83700-83701, 83721

Lipoprotein, Alpha
See Lipoprotein

Lipoprotein, Pre-Beta
See Lipoprotein, Blood

Liposuction — Lower Extremities

Lower GI Series
See Barium Enema
Low Vision Aids
Fitting, 92354, 92355
LP, 62270
LRH (Luteinizing Releasing Hormone), 83727
L/S, 83661
LSD (Lysergic Acid Diethylamide), 80100-80103, 80299
L/S Ratio
Amniotic Fluid, 83661
LTH
See Prolactin
Lumbar
See Spine
Aspiration, Disk
Percutaneous, 62287
Lumbar Plexus
Decompression, 64714
Injection, Anesthetic, 64449
Neuroplasty, 64714
Release, 64714
Repair
Suture, 64862
Lumbar Puncture
See Spinal Tap
Lumbar Spine Fracture
See Fracture, Vertebra, Lumbar
Lumbar Sympathectomy
See Sympathectomy, Lumbar
Lumbar Vertebra
See Vertebra, Lumbar
Lumen Dilation, 74360
Lumpectomy, 19160-19162
Lunate
Arthroplasty
with Implant, 25444
Dislocation
Closed Treatment, 25690
Open Treatment, 25695
Lung
Abscess
Incision and Drainage
Open, 32200
Percutaneous Drainage, 32200, 32201
Angiography
Injection, 93541
Aspiration, 32420
Biopsy, 32095, 32100
Bullae
Excision, 32141
Endoscopic, 32655
Cyst
Incision and Drainage
Open, 32200
Percutaneous, 32201
Removal, 32140
Decortication
with Parietal Pleurectomy, 32320
Endoscopic, 32651, 32652
Partial, 32225
Total, 32220
Empyema
Excision, 32540
Excision
Bronchus Resection, 32486
Completion, 32488
Donor, 33930
Heart Lung, 33930

Lung — *continued*
Excision — *continued*
Donor — *continued*
Lung, 32850
Emphysematous, 32491
Lobe, 32480, 32482
Segment, 32484
Total, 32440-32445
Wedge Resection, 32500
Endoscopic, 32657
Foreign Body
Removal, 32151
Hemorrhage, 32110
Injection
Radiologic, 93541
Lavage
Bronchial, 31624
Total, 32997
Lysis
Adhesions, 32124
Needle Biopsy, 32405
Nuclear Medicine
Imaging, Perfusion, 78580-78585
Imaging, Ventilation, 78586-78594
Unlisted Services and Procedures, 78599
Pneumocentesis, 32420
Pneumolysis, 32940
Pneumothorax, 32960
Puncture, 32420
Removal
Bronchoplasty, 32501
Completion Pneumonectomy, 32488
Extrapleural, 32445
Single Lobe, 32480
Single Segment, 32484
Sleeve Lobectomy, 32486
Sleeve Pneumonectomy, 32442
Total Pneumonectomy, 32440-32445
Two Lobes, 32482
Volume Reduction, 32491
Wedge Resection, 32500
Repair
Hernia, 32800
Segmentectomy, 32484
Tear
Repair, 32110
Thoracotomy, 32110-32160
with Excision-Plication of Bullae, 32141
with Open Intrapleural Pneumonolysis, 32124
Biopsy, 32095, 32100
Cardiac Massage, 32160
for Post-Operative Complications, 32120
Removal
Bullae, 32141
Cyst, 32140
Intrapleural Foreign Body, 32150
Intrapulmonary Foreign Body, 32151
Repair, 32110
Transplantation, 32851-32854, 33935
Allograft Preparation, 32855-32856, 33933
Donor Pneumonectomy
Heart-Lung, 33930
Lung, 32850
Unlisted Services and Procedures, 32999
Lung Function Tests
See Pulmonology, Diagnostic
Lung Volume Reduction
Emphysematous, 32491
Lupus Anticoagulant Assay, 85705

Lupus Band Test
  Immunofluorescent Study, 88346, 88347
Luschke Procedure, 45120
Luteinizing Hormone (LH), 80418, 80426, 83002
Luteinizing Release Factor, 83727
Luteotropic Hormone
  See Prolactin
Luteotropin
  See Prolactin
Luteotropin, Placental
  See Lactogen, Human Placental
Lyme Disease, 86617, 86618
Lyme Disease ab
  See Antibody, Lyme Disease
Lyme Disease Vaccine, 90665
Lymphadenectomy
  Abdominal, 38747
  Bilateral Inguinofemoral, 54130, 56632, 56637
  Bilateral Pelvic, 51575, 51585, 51595, 54135,
    55845, 55865
    Total, 38571, 38572, 57531, 58210
  Diaphragmatic Assessment, 58960
  Gastric, 38747
  Inguinofemoral, 38760, 38765
  Inguinofemoral, Iliac and Pelvic, 56640
  Injection
    Sentinel Node, 38792
  Limited, for Staging
    Para-Aortic, 38562
    Pelvic, 38562
    Retroperitoneal, 38564
  Limited Para-Aortic, Resection of Ovarian
    Malignancy, 58951
  Limited Pelvic, 55842, 55862, 58954
  Malignancy, 58951, 58954
  Mediastinal, 21632
  Peripancreatic, 38747
  Portal, 38747
  Radical
    Axillary, 38740, 38745
    Cervical, 38720, 38724
    Groin Area, 38760, 38765
    Pelvic, 54135, 55845
    Suprahyoid, 38700
  Regional, 50230
  Retroperitoneal Transabdominal, 38780
  Thoracic, 38746
  Unilateral Inguinofemoral, 56631, 56634
Lymphadenitis
  Incision and Drainage, 38300, 38305
Lymphadenopathy Associated Antibodies
  See Antibody, HIV
Lymphadenopathy Associated Virus
  See HIV
Lymphangiogram, Abdominal
  See Lymphangiography, Abdomen
Lymphangiography
  Abdomen, 75805, 75807
  Arm, 75801, 75803
  Injection, 38790
  Leg, 75801, 75803
  Pelvis, 75805, 75807
Lymphangioma, Cystic
  See Hygroma
Lymphangiotomy, 38308
Lymphatic Channels
  Incision, 38308

Lymphatic System
  Anesthesia, 00320
  Unlisted Procedure, 38999
Lymph Duct
  Injection, 38790
Lymphedema Debulking, 15831
Lymph Node(s)
  Abscess
    Incision and Drainage, 38300, 38305
  Biopsy, 38500, 38510-38530, 38570
    Needle, 38505
  Dissection, 38542
  Excision, 38500, 38510-38530
    Abdominal, 38747
    Inguinofemoral, 38760, 38765
    Laparoscopic, 38571, 38572
    Limited, for Staging
      Para-Aortic, 38562
      Pelvic, 38562
      Retroperitoneal, 38564
    Pelvic, 38770
    Radical
      Axillary, 38740, 38745
      Cervical, 38720, 38724
      Suprahyoid, 38720, 38724
    Retroperitoneal Transabdominal, 38780
    Thoracic, 38746
  Exploration, 38542
  Hygroma, Cystic
    Axillary
      Cervical
        Excision, 38550, 38555
  Nuclear Medicine
    Imaging, 78195
  Removal
    Abdominal, 38747
    Inguinofemoral, 38760, 38765
    Pelvic, 38747, 38770
    Retroperitoneal Transabdominal, 38780
    Thoracic, 38746
Lymphoblast Transformation
  See Blastogenesis
Lymphocele
  Drainage
    Laparoscopic, 49323
  Extraperitoneal
    Open Drainage, 49062
Lymphocyte
  Culture, 86821, 86822
  Toxicity Assay, 86805, 86806
  Transformation, 86353
Lymphocytes, CD4
  See CD4
Lymphocytes, CD8
  See CD8
Lymphocyte, Thymus-Dependent
  See T-Cells
Lymphocytic Choriomeningitis
  Antibody, 86727
Lymphocytotoxicity, 86805, 86806
Lymphogranuloma Venereum
  Antibody, 86729
Lymphoma Virus, Burkitt
  See Epstein-Barr Virus
Lymph Vessel(s)
  Abdomen
    Lymphangiography, 75805, 75807
  Arm
    Lymphangiography, 75801, 75803

Lymph Vessel(s) — *continued*
Leg
Lymphangiography, 75801, 75803
Nuclear Medicine
Imaging, 78195
Pelvis
Lymphangiography, 75805, 75807
Lynch Procedure, 31075
Lysergic Acid Diethylamide, 80102, 80103, 80299
Lysis
Adhesions
Bladder
Intraluminal, 53899
Comeovitreal, 65880
Epidural, 0027T, 62263, 62264
Fallopian Tube, 58740
Foreskin, 54450
Intestinal, 44005
Labial, 56441
Lung, 32124
Nose, 30560
Ovary, 58740
Oviduct, 58740
Penile
Post-circumcision, 54162
Spermatic Cord, 54699, 55899
Tongue, 41599
Ureter, 50715-50725
Intraluminal, 53899
Uterus, 58559
Euglobulin, 85360
Eye
Goniosynechiae, 65865
Synechiae
Anterior, 65870
Posterior, 65875
Labial
Adhesions, 56441
Nose
Intranasal Synechia, 30560
Transurethral
Adhesions, 53899
Lysozyme, 85549

M

MacEwen Operation
Hernia Repair, Inguinal, 49495-49500, 49505
Incarcerated, 49496, 49501, 49507, 49521
Laparoscopic, 49650, 49651
Recurrent, 49520
Sliding, 49525
Machado Test
Complement, Fixation Test, 86171
MacLean-De Wesselow Test
Clearance, Urea Nitrogen, 84540, 84545
Macrodactylia
Repair, 26590
Maculopathy, 67208-67218
Madlener Operation, 58600
Magnesium, 83735
Magnetic Resonance Angiography (MRA)
Abdomen, 74185
Arm, 73225
Chest, 71555
Head, 70544-70546
Leg, 73725
Neck, 70547
Pelvis, 72198
Spine, 72159

Magnetic Resonance Imaging (MRI)
Abdomen, 74181-74183
Ankle, 73721-73723
Arm, 73218-73220, 73223
Bone Marrow Study, 76400
Brain, 70551-70553
Intraoperative, 70557-70559
Breast, 76093, 76094
Chest, 71550-71552
Elbow, 73221
Face, 70540-70543
Finger Joint, 73221
Foot, 73718, 73719
Foot Joints, 73721-73723
Guidance
Needle Placement, 76393
Tissue Ablation, 76394
Hand, 73218-73220, 73223
Heart, 75552
with Contrast Material, 75553
Complete Study, 75554
Flow Mapping, 75556
Limited Study, 75555
Morphology, 75553
Joint
Lower Extremity, 73721-73723
Upper Extremity, 73221-73223
Knee, 73721-73723
Leg, 73718-73720
Neck, 70540-70543
Orbit, 70540-70543
Pelvis, 72195-72197
Radiology
Unlisted Diagnostic Procedure, 76499
Spectroscopy, 76390
Spine
Cervical, 72141, 72142, 72156-72158
Lumbar, 72148-72158
Thoracic, 72146, 72147, 72156-72158
Temporomandibular Joint (TMJ), 70336
Toe, 73721-73723
Wrist, 73221
Magnetic Resonance Spectroscopy, 76390
Magnetic Stimulation
Brain Cortex, 0018T
Magnetoencephalography (MEG), 95965-95967
Magnet Operation
Eye, Removal of Foreign Body
Conjunctival Embedded, 65210
Conjunctival Superficial, 65205
Corneal without Slit Lamp, 65220
Corneal with Slit Lamp, 65222
Intraocular, 65235-65265
Magnuson Procedure, 23450
Magpi Procedure, 54322
Major Vestibular Gland
See Bartholin's Gland
Malar Area
Augmentation, 21270
Bone Graft, 21210
Fracture
with Bone Grafting, 21366
with Manipulation, 21355
Open Treatment, 21360-21366
Reconstruction, 21270
Malar Bone
See Cheekbone
Malaria Antibody, 86750
Malaria Smear, 87207

Mastoidectomy — *continued*
  with Tympanoplasty, 69604, 69641-69646
    Ossicular Chain Reconstruction, 69636
    and Synthetic Prosthesis, 69636
  Cochlear Device Implantation, 69930
  Complete, 69502
    Revision, 69601-69605
  Osseointegrated Implant
    for External Speech Processor/Cochlear
      Stimulator, 69715, 69718
  Ossicular Chain Reconstruction, 69605
  Radical, 69511
    Modified, 69505
    Revision, 69602, 69603
  Simple, 69501
Mastoidotomy, 69635-69637
  with Tympanoplasty, 69635
    Ossicular Chain Reconstruction, 69636
    and Synthetic Prosthesis, 69637
Mastoids
  Polytomography, 76101, 76102
  X-ray, 70120, 70130
Mastopexy, 19316
Mastotomy, 19020
Maternity Care and Delivery, 0500F-0502F,
  0503F, 59400-59898
  See also Abortion, Cesarean Delivery, Ectopic
    Pregnancy, Vaginal Delivery
Maxilla
  See Facial Bones; Mandible
  Bone Graft, 21210
  CT Scan, 70486-70488
  Cyst, Excision, 21048, 21049
  Excision, 21030, 21032-21034
  Fracture
    with Fixation, 21345-21347
    Closed Treatment, 21345, 21421
    Open Treatment, 21346-21348, 21422,
      21423
  Osteotomy, 21206
  Reconstruction
    with Implant, 21245, 21246, 21248, 21249
  Tumor
    Excision, 21048-21049
Maxillary Arteries
  See Artery, Maxillary
Maxillary Sinus
  See Sinus, Maxillary
Maxillary Torus Palatinus
  Tumor Excision, 21032
Maxillectomy, 31225, 31230
Maxillofacial Fixation
  Application
    Halo Type Appliance, 21100
Maxillofacial Impressions
  Auricular Prosthesis, 21086
  Definitive Obturator Prosthesis, 21080
  Facial Prosthesis, 21088
  Interim Obturator Prosthesis, 21079
  Mandibular Resection Prosthesis, 21081
  Nasal Prosthesis, 21087
  Oral Surgical Splint, 21085
  Orbital Prosthesis, 21077
  Palatal Augmentation Prosthesis, 21082
  Palatal Lift Prosthesis, 21083
  Speech Aid Prosthesis, 21084
  Surgical Obturator Prosthesis, 21076
Maxillofacial Procedures
  Unlisted Services and Procedures, 21299

Maxillofacial Prosthetics, 21076-21088
  Unlisted Services and Procedures, 21089
Maydl Operation, 45563, 50810
Mayo Hernia Repair, 49580-49587
Mayo Operation
  Varicose Vein Removal, 37700-37735, 37780,
    37785
Mayo Procedure, 28292
Maze Procedure, 33253
MBC, 87181-87190
McBride Procedure, 28292
McBurney Operation
  Hernia Repair, Inguinal, 49495-49500, 49505
    Incarcerated, 49496, 49501, 49507, 49521
    Recurrent, 49520
    Sliding, 49525
McCannel Procedure, 66682
McCauley Procedure, 28240
McDonald Operation, 57700
McKissock Surgery, 19318
McIndoe Procedure, 57291
McVay Operation
  Hernia Repair, Inguinal, 49495-49500, 49505
    Incarcerated, 49496, 49501, 49507, 49521
    Laparoscopic, 49650, 49651
    Recurrent, 49520
    Sliding, 49525
Measles, German
  See Rubella
Measles Immunization, 90705, 90707-90708,
  90710
Measles Uncomplicated
Measurement
  See Rubeola
  Left Ventricular Filling Pressure, 0086T
Meat Fibers
  Feces, 89160
Meatoplasty, 69310
Meatotomy, 53020, 53025
  Contact Laser Vaporization with/without
    Transurethral Resection of Prostate,
    52648
  with Cystourethroscopy, 52281
  Infant, 53025
  Non-Contact Laser Coagulation Prostate, 52647
  Transurethral Electrosurgical Resection
    Prostate, 52601
  Ureter, 52290
  Urethral
    Cystourethroscopy, 52290-52305
Meckel's Diverticulum
  Excision, 44800
  Unlisted Services and Procedures, 44899
Median Nerve
  Decompression, 64721
  Neuroplasty, 64721
  Release, 64721
  Repair
    Suture
      Motor, 64835
  Transposition, 64721
Median Nerve Compression
  See Carpal Tunnel Syndrome
Mediastinal Cyst
  See Cyst, Mediastinal
Mediastinoscopy, 39400

Mediastinotomy
Cervical Approach, 39000
Transthoracic Approach, 39010
Mediastinum
See Chest; Thorax
Cyst
Excision, 32662, 39200
Endoscopy
Biopsy, 39400
Exploration, 39400
Exploration, 39000, 39010
Incision and Drainage, 39000, 39010
Needle Biopsy, 32405
Removal
Foreign Body, 39000, 39010
Tumor
Excision, 32662, 39220
Unlisted Procedures, 39499
Medical Disability Evaluation Services, 99455, 99456
Medical Testimony, 99075
Medication Therapy Management
By a Pharmacist
Initial Encounter, 0115T
Subsequent Encounter, 0116T
Each Additional 15 Minutes, 0117T
Medicine, Preventive
See Preventive Medicine
Medicine, Pulmonary
See Pulmonology
Medulla
Tractotomy, 61470
Medullary Tract
Incision, 61470
Section, 61470
Meibomian Cyst
See Chalazion
Membrane, Mucous
See Mucosa
Membrane Oxygenation, Extracorporeal
See Extracorporeal Membrane Oxygenation
Membrane, Tympanic
See Ear, Drum
Meninges
Tumor
Excision, 61512, 61519
Meningioma
Excision, 61512, 61519
Tumor
Excision, 61512, 61519
Meningitis, Lymphocytic Benign
See Lymphocytic Choriomeningitis
Meningocele Repair, 63700, 63702
Meningococcal Vaccine
Conjugate, serogroups A, C, Y, W-135, 90734
Polysaccharide, any groups, 90733
Meningococcus
See Neisseria Meningitidis
Meningomyelocele
See Myelomeningocele
Meniscectomy
Knee Joint, 27332, 27333
Temporomandibular Joint, 21060
Meniscus
Knee
Excision, 27332, 27333
Repair, 27403
Transplantation, 29868

Mental Nerve
Avulsion, 64736
Incision, 64736
Transection, 64736
Meprobamate, 83805
Mercury, 83015, 83825
Merskey Test
Fibrin Degradation Products, 85362-85379
Mesencephalic Tract
Incision, 61480
Section, 61480
Mesencephalon
Tractotomy, 61480
Mesenteric Arteries
See Artery, Mesenteric
Mesentery
Lesion
Excision, 44820
Repair, 44850
Suture, 44850
Unlisted Services and Procedures, 44899
Metabisulfite Test
Red Blood Cell, Sickling, 85660
Metabolite, 82520
Metacarpal
Amputation, 26910
Craterization, 26230
Cyst
Excision, 26200, 26205
Diaphysectomy, 26230
Excision, 26230
Radical for Tumor, 26250, 26255
Fracture
with Manipulation, 26605, 26607
without Manipulation, 26600
Closed Treatment, 26605
with Fixation, 26607
Open Treatment, 26615
Percutaneous Fixation, 26608
Ostectomy
Radical
for Tumor, 26250, 26255
Repair
Lengthening, 26568
Nonunion, 26546
Osteotomy, 26565
Saucerization, 26230
Tumor
Excision, 26200, 26205
Metacarpophalangeal Joint
Arthrodesis, 26850, 26852
Arthroplasty, 26530, 26531
Arthroscopy
Diagnostic, 29900
Surgical, 29901, 29902
Arthrotomy, 26075
Biopsy
Synovium, 26105
Capsule
Excision, 26520
Incision, 26520
Capsulodesis, 26516-26518
Dislocation
with Manipulation, 26340
Closed Treatment, 26700
Open Treatment, 26715
Percutaneous Fixation, 26705, 26706
Exploration, 26075
Fracture
with Manipulation, 26742

Metacarpophalangeal Joint — *continued*
  Fracture — *continued*
    Closed Treatment, 26740
    Open Treatment, 26746
  Fusion, 26516-26518, 26850, 26852
  Removal of Foreign Body, 26075
  Repair
    Collateral Ligament, 26540-26542
  Synovectomy, 26135
Metadrenaline
  See Metanephrines
Metals, Heavy
  See Heavy Metal
Metamfetamine
  See Methamphetamine
Metanephrine, 83835
Metatarsal
  See Foot
  Amputation, 28810
  Condyle
    Excision, 28288
  Craterization, 28122
  Cyst
    Excision, 28104-28107
  Diaphysectomy, 28122
  Excision, 28110-28114, 28122, 28140
  Fracture
    Closed Treatment
      with Manipulation, 28475, 28476
      without Manipulation, 28470
    Open Treatment, 28485
    Percutaneous Fixation, 28476
  Free Osteocutaneous Flap with Microvascular
    Anastomosis, 20972
  Repair, 28322
    Lengthening, 28306, 28307
    Osteotomy, 28306-28309
  Saucerization, 28122
  Tumor
    Excision, 28104-28107, 28173
Metatarsectomy, 28140
Metatarsophalangeal Joint
  Arthrotomy, 28022, 28052
  Cheilectomy, 28289
  Dislocation, 28630, 28635, 28645
    Percutaneous Fixation, 28636
  Exploration, 28022
  Great Toe
    Arthrodesis, 28750
    Fusion, 28750
  Release, 28289
  Removal
    of Foreign Body, 28022
    of Loose Body, 28022
  Repair
    Hallux Rigidus, 28289
  Synovial
    Biopsy, 28052
    Excision, 28072
  Toe, 28270
Methadone, 83840
Methaemoglobin
  See Methemoglobin
Methamphetamine
  Blood or Urine, 82145
Methanol, 84600
Methbipyranone
  See Metyrapone
Methemalbumin, 83857

Methemoglobin, 83045, 83050
Methenamine Silver Stain, 88312
Methopyrapone
  See Metyrapone
Methoxyhydroxymandelic Acid
  See Vanillylmandelic Acid
Methsuximide, 83858
Methyl Alcohol
  See Methanol
Methylamphetamine
  See Methamphetamine
Methylene Bichloride
  See Dichloromethane
Methylfluorprednisolone
  See Dexamethasone
Methylmorphine
  See Codeine
Metroplasty
  See Hysteroplasty
Metyrapone, 80436
Mg, 83735
MIC (Minimum Inhibitory Concentration),
  87186
Microalbumin
  Urine, 82043, 82044
Microbiology, 87001-87999
Microdissection, 88380
Microfluorometries, Flow
  See Flow Cytometry
Microglobulin, Beta 2
  Blood, 82232
  Urine, 82232
Micrographic Surgery
  Mohs Technique, 17304-17310
Micro-Ophthalmia
  Orbit Reconstruction, 21256
Micropigmentation
  Correction, 11920-11922
Microscope, Surgical
  See Operating Microscope
Microscopic Evaluation
  Hair, 96902
Microscopies, Electron
  See Electron Microscopy
Microscopy
  Ear Exam, 92504
Microsomal Antibody, 86376
Microsomia, Hemifacial
  See Hemifacial Microsomia
Microsurgery
  Operating Microscope, 69990
Microvascular Anastomosis
  Bone Graft
    Fibula, 20955
    Other, 20962
  Facial Flap, Free, 15758
  Muscle Flap, Free, 15756
  Osteocutaneous Flap with, 20969-20973
  Skin Flap, Free, 15757
Microvite A
  See Vitamin A
Microwave Therapy, 97024
  See Physical Medicine/Therapy/Occupational
    Therapy
Midbrain
  See Brain; Brainstem; Mesencephalon; Skull
    Base Surgery

Moschcowitz Operation
Repair, Hernia, Femoral, 49550-49557
Mosenthal Test, 81002
Mother Cell
See Stem Cell
Motility Study
Duodenal, 91022
Esophagus, 91010-91012
Motion Analysis
by Video and 3-D Kinematics, 96000, 96004
Computer-based, 96000, 96004
Mousseaux-Barbin Procedure, 43510
Mouth
Abscess
Incision and Drainage, 40800, 40801, 41005-41009, 41015-41018
Biopsy, 40808, 41108
Cyst
Incision and Drainage, 40800, 40801, 41005-41009, 41015
Excision
Frenum, 40819
Hematoma
Incision and Drainage, 40800, 40801, 41005-41009, 41015-41018
Lesion
Destruction, 40820
Excision, 40810-40816, 41116
Vestibule of
Destruction, 40820
Repair, 40830
Mucosa
Excision, 40818
Reconstruction, 40840-40845
Removal
Foreign Body, 40804, 40805
Repair
Laceration, 40830, 40831
Skin Graft
Full Thickness, 15240, 15241
Pedicle Flap, 15574
Split, 15120, 15121
Tissue Transfer, Adjacent, 14040, 14041
Unlisted Services and Procedures, 40899, 41599
Vestibule
Excision
Destruction, 40808-40820
Incision, 40800-40806
Other Procedures, 40899
Removal
Foreign Body, 40804
Repair, 40830-40845
Move
See Transfer
Finger, 26555
Toe Joint, 26556
Toe to Hand, 26551-26554
Moynihan Test
Gastrointestinal Tract, X-ray, with Contrast, 74246-74249
MPR (Multifetal Pregnancy Reduction), 59866
MRA (Magnetic Resonance Angiography), 71555, 72159, 72198, 73225, 73725, 74185
MRI, 70336, 70540, 70551-70553, 71550, 72141-72158, 72196, 73220, 73221, 73720, 73721, 74181, 75552-75556, 76093, 76094, 76400
MSLT, 95805

Mucin
Synovial Fluid, 83872
Mucocele
Sinusotomy
Frontal, 31075
Mucopolysaccharides, 83864, 83866
Mucormycoses
See Mucormycosis
Mucormycosis
Antibody, 86732
Mucosa
Ectopic Gastric Imaging, 78290
Excision of Lesion
Alveolar, Hyperplastic, 41828
Vestibule of Mouth, 40810-40818
via Esophagoscopy, 43228
via Small Intestinal Endoscopy, 44369
via Upper GI Endoscopy, 43258
Periodontal Grafting, 41870
Urethra, Mucosal Advancement, 53450
Vaginal Biopsy, 57100, 57105
Mucosa, Buccal
See Mouth, Mucosa
Mucosectomy
Rectal, 44152, 44153, 45113
Mucous Cyst
Antibody
Hand or Finger, 26160
Mucous Membrane
See Mouth, Mucosa
Cutaneous
Biopsy, 11100, 11101
Excision
Benign Lesion, 11440-11446
Malignant, 11640-11646
Layer Closure, Wounds, 12051-12057
Simple Repair, Wounds, 12011-12018
Excision
Sphenoid Sinus, 31288
Lid Margin
Correction of Trichiasis, 67835
Nasal Test, 95065
Ophthalmic Test, 95060
Rectum
Proctoplasty for Prolapse, 45505
Mucus Cyst
See Mucous Cyst
MUGA (Multiple Gated Acquisition), 78472-78478, 78483
Muller Procedure
Attended, 95806
Unattended, 95807
Multifetal Pregnancy Reduction, 59866
Multiple Sleep Latency Testing (MSLT), 95805
Multiple Valve Procedures
See Valvuloplasty
MumFord Procedure, 29824
Mumps
Antibody, 86735
Immunization, 90704, 90707, 90710
Vaccine, 90704
MMR, 90707
MMRV, 90710
Muramidase, 85549
Murine Typhus, 86000
Muscle
See Specific Muscle
Abdomen
See Abdominal Wall

Muscle — *continued*
Biofeedback Training, 90911
Biopsy, 20200-20206
Debridement
Infected, 11004-11006
Heart
See Myocardium
Neck
See Neck Muscle
Removal
Foreign Body, 20520, 20525
Repair
Extraocular, 65290
Forearm, 25260-25274
Wrist, 25260-25274
Revision
Arm, Upper, 24330, 24331
Elbow, 24301
Transfer
Arm, Upper, 24301, 24320
Elbow, 24301
Femur, 27110
Hip, 27100-27105, 27111
Shoulder, 23395, 23397, 24301, 24320

Muscle Compartment Syndrome
Detection, 20950

Muscle Denervation
See Denervation

Muscle Division
Scalenus Anticus, 21700, 21705
Sternocleidomastoid, 21720, 21725

Muscle Flaps, 15732-15738
Free, 15756

Muscle Grafts, 15841-15845

Muscle, Oculomotor
See Eye Muscles

Muscles
Repair
Extraocular, 65290

Muscle Testing
Dynamometry, Eye, 92260
Extraocular Multiple Muscles, 92265
Manual, 95831-95834

Musculoplasty
See Muscle, Repair

Musculoskeletal System
Unlisted Services and Procedures, 20999,
21499, 24999, 25999, 26989, 27299,
27599, 27899

Musculotendinous (Rotator) Cuff
Repair, 23410, 23412

Mustard Procedure, 33774-33777

Mutation Identification, 83914

MVR, 33430

Myasthenia Gravis
Tensilon Test, 95857

Myasthenic, Gravis
See Myasthenia Gravis

Mycobacteria
Culture, 87116
Identification, 87118
Detection, 87550-87562
Sensitivity Studies, 87190

Mycoplasma
Antibody, 86738
Culture, 87109
Detection, 87580-87582

Mycota
See Fungus

Myectomy, Anorectal
See Myomectomy, Anorectal

Myelencephalon
See Medulla

Myelin Basic Protein
Cerebrospinal Fluid, 83873

Myelography
Brain, 70010
Spine
Cervical, 72240
Lumbosacral, 72265
Thoracic, 72255
Total, 72270

Myelomeningocele
Repair, 63704, 63706
Stereotaxis
Creation Lesion, 63600

Myelotomy, 63170

Myocardial
Imaging, 78466, 78468, 78469
Perfusion Imaging, 78460-78465, 78478, 78480
See Nuclear Medicine
Positron Emission Tomography (PET), 78459,
78491, 78492
Repair
Postinfarction, 33542

Myocutaneous Flaps, 15732-15738, 15756

Myofascial Pain Dysfunction Syndrome
See Temporomandibular Joint (TMJ)

Myofascial Release, 97140

Myofibroma
See Leiomyomata

Myoglobin, 83874

Myomectomy
Anorectal, 45108
Uterus, 58140-58146, 58545, 58546

Myoplasty
See Muscle, Repair

Myotomy
Esophagus, 43030
Hyoid, 21685
Sigmoid Colon
Intestine, 44799
Rectum, 45999

Myringoplasty, 69620

Myringostomy
See Myringotomy

Myringotomy, 69420, 69421

Myxoid Cyst
See Ganglion

N

Na, 84295

Naffziger Operation, 61330

Nagel Test, 92283

Nail Bed
Reconstruction, 11762
Repair, 11760

Nail Fold
Excision
Wedge, 11765

Nail Plate Separation
See Onychia

Nails
Avulsion, 11730, 11732
Biopsy, 11755
Debridement, 11720, 11721

Nails — *continued*
Evacuation
Hematoma, Subungual, 11740
Excision, 11750, 11752
Cyst
Pilonidal, 11770-11772
KOH Examination, 87220
Removal, 11730, 11732, 11750, 11752
Trimming, 11719
Narcosynthesis
Diagnostic and Therapeutic, 90865
Nasal Abscess
See Nose, Abscess
Nasal Area
Bone Graft, 21210
Nasal Bleeding
See Epistaxis
Nasal Bone
Fracture
with Manipulation, 21315, 21320
without Manipulation, 21310
Closed Treatment, 21310-21320
Open Treatment, 21325-21335
X-ray, 70160
Nasal Deformity
Repair, 40700-40761
Nasal Function Study, 92512
Nasal Polyp
See Nose, Polyp
Nasal Prosthesis
Impression, 21087
Nasal Septum
Abscess
Incision and Drainage, 30020
Fracture
Closed Treatment, 21337
Open Treatment, 21336
Hematoma
Incision and Drainage, 30020
Repair, 30630
Submucous Resection, 30520
Nasal Sinuses
See Sinus; Sinuses
Nasal Smear
Eosinophils, 89190
Nasal Turbinate
Fracture
Therapeutic, 30930
Nasoethmoid Complex
Fracture
Open Treatment, 21338, 21339
Percutaneous Treatment, 21340
Reconstruction, 21182-21184
Nasogastric Tube
Placement, 43752
Nasolacrimal Duct
Exploration, 68810
with Anesthesia, 68811
Insertion
Stent, 68815
X-ray
with Contrast, 70170
Nasomaxillary
Fracture
with Bone Grafting, 21348
Closed Treatment, 21345
Open Treatment, 21346-21348
Nasopharynges
See Nasopharynx

Nasopharyngoscopy, 92511
Nasopharynx
See Pharynx
Biopsy, 42804, 42806
Hemorrhage, 42970-42972
Unlisted Services and Procedures, 42999
Natriuretic Peptide, 83880
Natural Killer Cells (NK)
Total Count, 86357
Natural Ostium
Sinus
Maxillary, 31000
Sphenoid, 31002
Navicular
Arthroplasty
with Implant, 25443
Fracture
with Manipulation, 25624
Closed Treatment, 25622
Open Treatment, 25628
Repair, 25440
Neck
Angiography, 70498, 70547-70549
Artery
Ligation, 37615
Biopsy, 21550
Bypass Graft, 35901
CT Scan, 70490-70492, 70498
Dissection, Radical
See Radical Neck Dissection
Exploration
Blood Vessels, 35800
Lymph Nodes, 38542
Incision and Drainage
Abscess, 21501, 21502
Hematoma, 21501, 21502
Lipectomy, Suction Assisted, 15876
Magnetic Resonance Angiography (MRA),
70547-70549
Magnetic Resonance Imaging (MRI), 70540-
70543
Nerve
Graft, 64885, 64886
Repair
with Other Graft, 35261
with Vein Graft, 35231
Blood Vessel, 35201
Rhytidectomy, 15825, 15828
Skin
Revision, 15819
Skin Graft
Delay of Flap, 15620
Full Thickness, 15240, 15241
Pedicle Flap, 15574
Split, 15120, 15121
Surgery, Unlisted, 21899
Tissue Transfer, Adjacent, 14040, 14041
Tumor
Excision, 21555, 21556
Excision/Resection, 21557
Ultrasound Exam, 76536
Unlisted Services and Procedures, 21899
Urinary Bladder
See Bladder, Neck
Wound Exploration
Penetrating, 20100
X-ray, 70360
Neck, Humerus
Fracture
with Shoulder Dislocation
Closed Treatment, 23680
Open Treatment, 23675

Nerve — *continued*
  Spinal
    See Spinal Nerve
  Tibial
    See Tibial Nerve
  Ulnar
    See Ulnar Nerve
  Vestibular
    See Vestibular Nerve
Nerve Conduction
  Motor Nerve, 95900, 95903
  Sensory Nerve, 95904
Nerve II, Cranial
  See Optic Nerve
Nerve Root
  See Cauda Equina; Spinal Cord
  Decompression, 63020-63048, 63055-63103
  Incision, 63185, 63190
  Section, 63185, 63190
Nerves
  Anastomosis
    Facial to Hypoglossal, 64868
    Facial to Phrenic, 64870
    Facial to Spinal Accessory, 64866
  Avulsion, 64732-64772
  Biopsy, 64795
  Decompression, 64702-64727
  Destruction, 64600-64680
    Laryngeal, Recurrent, 31595
  Foot
    Excision, 28030
    Incision, 28035
  Graft, 64885-64907
  Implantation
    Electrode, 64553-64581
    to Bone, 64787
    to Muscle, 64787
  Incision, 43640, 43641, 64732-64772
  Injection
    Anesthetic, 64400-64530
    Neurolytic Agent, 64600-64680
  Insertion
    Electrode, 64553-64581
  Lesion
    Excision, 64774-64792
  Neurofibroma
    Excision, 64788-64792
  Neurolemmoma
    Excision, 64788-64792
  Neurolytic
    Internal, 64727
  Neuroma
    Excision, 64774-64786
  Neuroplasty, 64702-64721
  Nuclear Medicine
    Unlisted Services and Procedures, 78699
  Removal
    Electrode, 64585
  Repair
    Graft, 64885-64907
    Microdissection
      with Surgical Microscope, 69990
    Suture, 64831-64876
  Spinal Accessory
    Incision, 63191
    Section, 63191
  Suture, 64831-64876
  Sympathectomy
    Excision, 64802-64818
  Transection, 43640, 43641, 64732-64772
  Transposition, 64718-64721
  Unlisted Services and Procedures, 64999

Nerve Stimulation, Transcutaneous
  See Application, Neurostimulation
Nerve Teasing, 88362
Nerve V, Cranial
  See Trigeminal Nerve
Nerve VII, Cranial
  See Facial Nerve
Nerve X, Cranial
  See Vagus Nerve
Nerve XI, Cranial
  See Accessory Nerve
Nerve XII, Cranial
  See Hypoglossal Nerve
Nervous System
  Nuclear Medicine
    Unlisted Services and Procedures, 78699
Nesidioblast
  See Islet Cell
Neural Conduction
  See Nerve Conduction
Neural Ganglion
  See Ganglion
Neurectasis, 64999
Neurectomy
  Foot, 28030
  Gastrocnemius, 27320
  Hamstring Muscle, 27315
  Leg, Upper, 27315, 27320
  Popliteal, 27320
  Tympanic, 69676
Neuroendoscopy
  Intracranial, 62160-62165
Neurofibroma
  Cutaneous Nerve
    Excision, 64788
  Extensive
    Excision, 64792
  Peripheral Nerve
    Excision, 64790
Neurolemmoma
  Cutaneous Nerve
    Excision, 64788
  Extensive
    Excision, 64792
  Peripheral Nerve
    Excision, 64790
Neurologic System
  See Nervous System
Neurology
  Central Motor
    Electrocorticogram
      Intraoperative, 95829
    Electroencephalogram (EEG)
      Brain Death, 95824
      Electrode Placement, 95830
      Intraoperative, 95955
      Monitoring, 95812, 95813, 95950-95953, 95956
      Physical or Drug Activation, 95954
      Sleep, 95808, 95810, 95822, 95827
        Attended, 95806, 95807
        Standard, 95819
      WADA activation, 95958
    Electroencephalography (EEG)
      Digital Analysis, 95957
    Electromyography
      See Electromyography
    Fine Wire
      Dynamic, 96004

Index

Nerve — Neurology

Neurology — *continued*
　Central Motor — *continued*
　　Electromyography — *continued*
　　　Ischemic Limb Exercise Test, 95875
　　　Needle, 51785, 95860-95872
　　　Surface
　　　　Dynamic, 96002-96004
　　Higher Cerebral Function
　　　Aphasia Test, 96105
　　　Cognitive Function Tests, 96116
　　　Developmental Tests, 96110, 96111
　　　Magnetoencephalography (MEG), 95965-
　　　　95967
　　Motion Analysis
　　　by Video and 3-D Kinematics, 96000,
　　　　96004
　　　Computer-based, 96000, 96004
　　Muscle Testing
　　　Manual, 95831-95834
　　Nerve Conduction
　　　Motor Nerve, 95900, 95903
　　　Sensory Nerve, 95904
　　Neuromuscular Junction Tests, 95937
　　Neurophysiological Testing
　　　Intraoperative, 95920
　　Neuropsychological Testing, 96118-96120
　　Plantar Pressure Measurements
　　　Dynamic, 96001, 96004
　　Polysomnography, 95808-95811
　　Range of Motion Test, 95851, 95852
　　Reflex
　　　H-Reflex, 95933, 95934
　　Reflex Test
　　　Blink Reflex, 95933
　　Sleep Study, 95808, 95810
　　　Attended, 95806
　　　Unattended, 95807
　　Somatosensory Testing, 95925-95927
　　Tensilon Test, 95857
　　Transcranial Motor Stimulation, 95928-
　　　95929
　　Unlisted Services and Procedures, 95999
　　Urethral Sphincter, 51785
　　Visual Evoked Potential, CNS, 95930
　Diagnostic
　　Anal Sphincter, 51785
　　Autonomic Nervous Function
　　　Heart Rate Response, 95921-95923
　　　Pseudomotor Response, 95921-95923
　　　Sympathetic Function, 95921-95923
　　Brain Cortex Magnetic Stimulation, 0018T
　　Brain Surface Electrode Stimulation, 95961,
　　　95962

Neurolysis
　Nerve, 64704, 64708
　　Internal, 64727

Neuroma
　Acoustic
　　See Brain, Tumor, Excision
　Cutaneous Nerve
　　Excision, 64774
　Digital Nerve
　　Excision, 64776, 64778
　Excision, 64774
　Foot Nerve
　　Excision, 28080, 64782, 64783
　Hand Nerve
　　Excision, 64782, 64783
　Interdigital
　　See Morton's Neuroma

Neuroma — *continued*
　Peripheral Nerve
　　Excision, 64784
　Sciatic Nerve
　　Excision, 64786
Neuromuscular Junction Tests, 95937
Neuromuscular Pedicle
　Reinnervation
　　Larynx, 31590
Neuromuscular Reeducation, 97112
　See Physical Medicine/Therapy/Occupational
　　Therapy
　Intraoperative, Per Hour, 95920
Neurophysiological Testing, 96118-96120
Neurophysiologic Testing
　Autonomic Nervous Function
　　Heart Rate Response, 95921-95923
　　Pseudomotor Response, 95921-95923
　　Sympathetic Function, 95921-95923
　Intraoperative, Per Hour, 95920
Neuroplasty, 64712
　Cranial Nerve, 64716
　Digital Nerve, 64702, 64704
　Peripheral Nerve, 64708-64714, 64718-64721
Neuropsychological Testing, 96118-96120
Neurorrhaphy, 64831-64876
　Peripheral Nerve
　　with Graft, 64885-64907
Neurostimulation
　Application, 64550
Neurostimulators
　Analysis, 95970-95975
　Insertion
　　Pulse Generator, 61885-61886, 64590
　　Receiver, 61885-61886, 64590
　Removal
　　Electrodes, 61880
　　Pulse Generator, 61888, 64595
　　Receiver, 61888, 64595
　Replacement, 61885
Neurotomy, Sympathetic
　See Gasserian Ganglion, Sensory Root,
　　Decompression
Neurovascular Pedicle Flaps, 15750
Neutralization Test
　Virus, 86382
Newborn Care, 99431-99440, 99502
　Attendance at Delivery, 99436
　Birthing Room, 99431
　Blood Transfusion, 36450
　　See Neonatal Intensive Care
　Circumcision
　　Clamp or Other Device, 54150
　　Surgical Excision, 54160
　History and Examination, 99431, 99435
　Intermittent Positive Pressure Breathing (IPPB)
　Laryngoscopy, 31520
　Normal, 99431-99433
　Prepuce Slitting, 54000
　Preventive
　　Office, 99432
　Resuscitation, 99440
　Standby for C-Section, 99360
　Subsequent Hospital Care, 99433
　Umbilical Artery Catheterization, 36660
New Patient
　Domiciliary or Rest Home Visit, 99324-99328
　Emergency Department Services, 99281-99288
　Home Services, 99341-99345

New Patient — *continued*
  Hospital Inpatient Services, 99221-99239
  Hospital Observation Services, 99217-99220
  Initial Inpatient Consultations, 99251-99255
  Initial Office Visit, 99201-99205
    See Evaluation and Management, Office and
      Other Outpatient
  Office and/or Other Outpatient Consultations,
    99241-99245
  Outpatient Visit, 99211-99215
Nickel, 83885
Nicolas-Durand-Favre Disease
  See Lymphogranuloma Venerum
Nicotine, 83887
Nidation
  See Implantation
Nipples
  See Breast
  Inverted, 19355
  Reconstruction, 19350
Nissen Operation
  See Fundoplasty, Esophagogastric
Nissen Procedure, 43324
  Laparoscopic, 43280
Nitrate Reduction Test
  Urinalysis, 81000-81099
Nitroblue Tetrazolium Dye Test, 86384
Nitrogen, Blood Urea
  See Blood Urea Nitrogen
N. Meningitidis
  See Neisseria Meningitidis
NMR Imaging
  See Magnetic Resonance Spectroscopy
NMR Spectroscopies
  See Magnetic Resonance Spectroscopy
Noble Procedure, 44680
Nocardia
  Antibody, 86744
Nocturnal Penile Rigidity Test, 54250
Nocturnal Penile Tumescence Test, 54250
Node Dissection, Lymph
  See Dissection, Lymph Nodes
Node, Lymph
  See Lymph Nodes
Nodes
  See Lymph Nodes
No Man's Land
  Tendon Repair, 26356-26358
Non-Invasive Vascular Imaging
  See Vascular Studies
Non-Office Medical Services, 99056
Non-Stress Test, Fetal, 59025
Nonunion Repair
  Femur
    with Graft, 27472
    without Graft, 27470
  Metatarsal, 28322
  Tarsal Joint, 28320
Noradrenalin
  Blood, 82383, 82384
  Urine, 82382
Norchlorimipramine
  See Imipramine
Norepinephrine
  See Catecholamines
  Blood, 82383, 82384
  Urine, 82382

Nortriptyline
  Assay, 80182
Norwood Procedure, 33611, 33612, 33619
  See Repair, Heart, Ventricle; Revision
Nose
  Abscess
    Incision and Drainage, 30000, 30020
  Artery
    Incision, 30915, 30920
  Biopsy
    Intranasal, 30100
  Dermoid Cyst
    Excision
      Complex, 30125
      Simple, 30124
  Displacement Therapy, 30210
  Endoscopy
    Diagnostic, 31231-31235
    Surgical, 31237-31294
  Excision
    Rhinectomy, 30150, 30160
  Fracture
    with Fixation, 21330, 21340, 21345-21347
    Closed Treatment, 21345
    Open Treatment, 21325-21336, 21338,
      21339, 21346, 21347
    Percutaneous Treatment, 21340
  Hematoma
    Hemorrhage
      Cauterization, 30901-30906
    Incision and Drainage, 30000, 30020
  Insertion
    Septal Prosthesis, 30220
  Intranasal
    Lesion
      External Approach, 30118
      Internal Approach, 30117
  Lysis of Adhesions, 30560
  Polyp
    Excision
      Extensive, 30115
      Simple, 30110
  Reconstruction
    Cleft Lip
      Cleft Palate, 30460, 30462
    Dermatoplasty, 30620
    Primary, 30400-30420
    Secondary, 30430-30450
    Septum, 30520
  Removal
    Foreign Body, 30300
      with Anesthesia, 30310
      by Lateral Rhinotomy, 30320
  Repair
    Adhesions, 30560
    Cleft Lip, 40700-40761
    Fistula, 30580, 30600, 42260
    Rhinophyma, 30120
    Septum, 30540, 30545, 30630
    Synechia, 30560
    Vestibular Stenosis, 30465
  Skin
    Excision, 30120
    Surgical Planing, 30120
  Skin Graft
    Delay of Flap, 15630
    Full Thickness, 15260, 15261
    Pedicle Flap, 15576
  Submucous Resection Turbinate
    Excision, 30140
  Tissue Transfer, Adjacent, 14060, 14061

Index

Nose — Nuclear Medicine

O

O2 Saturation
See Oxygen Saturation

Ober-Yount Procedure, 27025
See Fasciotomy, Hip

Obliteration
Mastoid, 69670
Vaginal
Total, 57110-57112
Vault, 57120

Obliteration, Total Excision of Vagina
See Excision, Vagina, Complete

Obliteration, Vaginal Vault
See Vagina, Closure

Oblongata, Medulla
See Medulla

Observation, 99234-99236
See Evaluation and Management, Hospital
Services
Initial, 99218-99220
Same Date Admit/Discharge, 99234-99236

Obstetrical Care
Abortion
Induced
by Amniocentesis Injection, 59850-59852
See Abortion, Cesarean Delivery,
Ectopic Pregnancy
by Dilation and Curettage, 59840
by Dilation and Evaluation, 59841
Missed
First Trimester, 59820
Second Trimester, 59821
Spontaneous, 59812
Therapeutic, 59840-59852
Antepartum Care, 59425, 59426
Cesarean Section
with Hysterectomy, 59525
with Postpartum Care, 59515
for Failed VBAC
with Postpartum Care, 59622
Only, 59620
Routine (Global), 59618
Only, 59514
Routine (Global), 59510
Curettage
HydatidiForm Mole, 59870
Evacuation
HydatidiForm Mole, 59870
External Cephalic Version, 59412
Miscarriage
Surgical Completion, 59812-59821
Placenta Delivery, 59414
Postpartum Care, 59430
Septic Abortion, 59830
Total (Global), 59400, 59510, 59610, 59618
Unlisted Services and Procedures, 59898,
59899
Vaginal Delivery
with Postpartum Care, 59410
After C/S-VBAC (Global), 59610
with Postpartum Care, 59614
Delivery Only, 59612
Only, 59409
Routine (Global), 59400

Obstetric Tamponade
Uterus, 59899
Vagina, 59899

Obstruction
See Occlusion

Obstruction Clearance
Venous Access Device, 36595, 36596

Obstruction Colon
See Colon, Obstruction

Obturator Nerve
Avulsion, 64763, 64766
Incision, 64763, 64766
Transection, 64763, 64766

Obturator Prosthesis
Definitive, 21080
Impression, 21076
Insertion
Larynx, 31527
Interim, 21079

Occipital Nerve, Greater
Avulsion, 64744
Incision, 64744
Injection
Anesthetic, 64405
Transection, 64744

Occlusion
Extracranial/Intracranial, 61623
Fallopian Tubes
Oviduct, 58565, 58615
Penis
Vein, 37790
Umbilical Cord, 59072

Occlusive Disease of Artery
See Repair, Artery, Revision

Occult Blood, 82270-82272
by Hemoglobin Immunoassay, 82274

Occupational Therapy
Evaluation, 97003, 97004

Ocular Implant
See Orbital Implant
Insertion
in Scleral Shell, 65130
Muscles Attached, 65140
Muscles not Attached, 65135
Modification, 65125
Reinsertion, 65150
with Foreign Material, 65155
Removal, 65175

Ocular Muscle
See Eye Muscles

Ocular Orbit
See Orbit
Ocular Photoscreening, 0065T

Ocular Prostheses
See Prosthesis, Ocular

Oculomotor Muscle
See Eye Muscles

Oddi Sphincter
See Sphincter of Oddi

ODM, 92260

Odontoid Dislocation
Open Treatment
Reduction, 22318
with Grafting, 22319

Odontoid Fracture
Open Treatment
Reduction, 22318
With Grafting, 22319

Odontoid Process
Excisions, 22548

Oesophageal Neoplasm
See Tumor, Esophagus

Oesophageal Varices
See Esophageal Varices

Oesophagus
See Esophagus

Oestradiol
See Estradiol

Office and/or Other Outpatient Visits
with Surgical Procedure
See History and Physical
Consultation, 99241-99245
Established Patient, 99211-99215
New Patient, 99201-99205
Normal Newborn, 99432
Office Visit
Established Patient, 99211-99215
New Patient, 99201-99205
Outpatient Visit
Established Patient, 99211-99215
New Patient, 99201-99205
Prolonged Service, 99354, 99355

Office Medical Services
After Hours, 99050
Emergency Care, 99058
Extended Hours, 99051

Office or Other Outpatient Consultations
See Consultation, Office and/or Other
Outpatient

Olecranon
See Elbow; Humerus; Radius; Ulna
Bursa
Arthrocentesis, 20605
Cyst
Excision, 24125, 24126
Tumor
Cyst, 24120
Excision, 24125, 24126

Olecranon Process
Craterization, 24147
Diaphysectomy, 24147
Excision, 24147
Abscess, 24138
Fracture
See Elbow; Humerus; Radius
Closed Treatment, 24670, 24675
Open Treatment, 24685
Osteomyelitis, 24138, 24147
Saucerization, 24147
Sequestrectomy, 24138

Oligoclonal Immunoglobulin
Cerebrospinal Fluid, 83916

Omentectomy, 49255, 58950-58956
Laparotomy, 58960
Oophorectomy, 58943
Resection Ovarian Malignancy, 58950-58952
Resection Peritoneal Malignancy, 58950-58956
Resection Tubal Malignancy, 58950-58956

Omentum
Excision, 49255, 58950-58954
Flap, 49904, 49905
Free
with Microvascular Anastomosis, 49906
Unlisted Services and Procedures, 49999

Omphalectomy, 49250

Omphalocele
Repair, 49600-49611

Omphalomesenteric Duct
Excision, 44800

Omphalomesenteric Duct, Persistent
See Diverticulum, Meckel's

OMT, 98925-98929

Oncoprotein
HER-2/neu, 83950

One Stage Prothrombin Time, 85610, 85611
See Prothrombin Time

ONSD, 67570

Onychectomy
See Excision, Nails

Onychia
Drainage, 10060, 10061

Oocyte
Assisted Fertilization, Microtechnique, 89280, 89281
Biopsy, 89290, 89291
Cryopreservation, 0059T
Culture
with Co-Culture, 89251
Extended, 89272
Less than 4 days, 89250
Identification, Follicular Fluid, 89254
Insemination, 89268
Retrieval
for In Vitro Fertilization, 58970
Storage, 89346
Thawing, 89356

Oophorectomy, 58262, 58263, 58291, 58292, 58552, 58554, 58661, 58940, 58943
Ectopic Pregnancy
Laparoscopic Treatment, 59120
Surgical Treatment, 59120

Oophorectomy, Partial
See Excision, Ovary, Partial

Oophorocystectomy
See Cystectomy, Ovarian

Open Biopsy, Adrenal Gland
See Adrenal Gland, Biopsy

Opening (Incision and Drainage)
Acne
Comedones, 10040
Cysts, 10040
Milia, Multiple, 10040
Pustules, 10040

Operating Microscope, 69990

Operation
Blalock-Hanlon
See Septostomy, Atrial
Blalock-Taussig Subclavian-Pulmonary
Anastomosis
See Pulmonary Artery, Shunt, Subclavian
Borthen
See Iridotasis
Dana
See Rhizotomy
Dunn
See Arthrodesis, Foot Joint
Duvries
See Tenoplasty
Estes
See Ovary, Transposition
Foley Pyeloplasty
See Pyeloplasty
Fontan
See Repair, Heart, Anomaly
Fox
See Fox Operation
Gardner
See Meningocele Repair
Green
See Scapulopexy

Index

Operation — Orbit

Operation — *continued*
Harelip
    See Cleft Lip, Repair
Heine
    See Cyclodialysis
Heller
    See Esophagomyotomy
Iris, Inclusion
    See Iridencleisis
Jaboulay Gastroduodenostomy
    See Gastroduodenostomy
Johanson
    See Reconstruction, Urethra
Keller
    See Keller Procedure
Krause
    See Gasserian Ganglion, Sensory Root,
        Decompression
Kuhnt-Szymanowski
    See Ectropion, Repair, Blepharoplasty
MumFord
    See Calviculectomy, Partial
Nissen
    See Fundoplasty, Esophagogastric
Peet
    See Nerves, Sympathectomy, Excision
Ramstedt
    See Pyloromyotomy
Richardson Hysterectomy
    See Hysterectomy, Abdominal, Total
Schanz
    See Femur, Osteotomy
Schlatter Total Gastrectomy
    See Excision, Stomach, Total
Smithwick
    See Excision, Nerve, Sympathetic
Winiwarter Cholecystoenterostomy
    See Anastomosis, Gallbladder to Intestines
Operation Microscopes
    See Operating Microscope
Operculectomy, 41821
Operculum
    See Gums
Ophthalmic Mucous Membrane Test, 95060
    See Allergy Tests
Ophthalmology
    Unlisted Services and Procedures, 92499
    See Opthalmology, Diagnostic
Ophthalmology, Diagnostic
    Color Vision Exam, 92283
    Computerized Scanning, 92135
    Computerized Screening, 0065T, 99172
    Dark Adaptation, 92284
    Electromyography, Needle, 92265
    Electro-oculography, 92270
    Electroretinography, 92275
    Endoscopy, 66990
    Eye Exam
        with Anesthesia, 92018, 92019
        Established Patient, 92012, 92014
        New Patient, 92002, 92004
    Glaucoma Provocative Test, 92140
    Gonioscopy, 92020
    Ocular Photography
        External, 92285
        Internal, 92286, 92287
    Ophthalmoscopy, 92225, 92226
        with Angiography, 92235
        with Angioscopy, 92230
        with Dynamometry, 92260
        with Fluorescein Angiography, 92235

Ophthalmology, Diagnostic — *continued*
Ophthalmoscopy — *continued*
        with Fluorescein Angioscopy, 92230
        with Fundus Photography, 92250
        with Indocyanine-Green Angiography, 92240
    Photoscreening, 0065T
    Refractive Determination, 92015
    Rotation Tests, 92499
    Sensorimotor Exam, 92060
    Tonography, 92120
        with Provocation, 92130
    Tonometry
        Serial, 92100
    Ultrasound, 76510-76529
    Visual Acuity Screen, 99173
    Visual Field Exam, 92081-92083
    Visual Function Screen, 0065T, 99172
Ophthalmoscopy, 92225, 92226
    See Ophthalmology, Diagnostic
Opiates, 83925
Opinion, Second
    See Confirmatory Consultations
Optic Nerve
    Decompression, 67570
        with Nasal/Sinus Endoscopy, 31294
Optokinectic Nystagmus Test
    See Nystagmus Tests, Optokinetic
OPV, 90712
Oral Lactose Tolerance Test, 82951-82953
    See Glucose, Tolerance Test
Oral Mucosa
    See Mouth, Mucosa
Oral Surgical Splint, 21085
Orbit
    See Orbital Contents; Orbital Floor; Periorbital
        Region
    Biopsy, 61332
        Exploration, 67450
        Fine Needle Aspiration or Orbital Contents,
            67415
        Orbitotomy without Bone Flap, 67400
    CT Scan, 70480-70482
    Decompression, 61330
        Bone Removal, 67414, 67445
    Exploration, 61332, 67400, 67450
        Lesion
            Excision, 61333
    Fracture
        Closed Treatment
            with Manipulation, 21401
            without Manipulation, 21400
        Open Treatment, 21406-21408
            Blowout Fracture, 21385-21395
    Incision and Drainage, 67405, 67440
    Injection
        Retrobulbar, 67500, 67505
        Tenon's Capsule, 67515
    Insertion
        Implant, 67550
    Lesion
        Excision, 67412, 67420
    Magnetic Resonance Imaging (MRI), 70540-
        70543
    Removal
        Decompression, 67445
        Exploration, 61334
        Foreign Body, 61334, 67413, 67430
        Implant, 67560
    Sella Turcica, 70482
    Unlisted Services and Procedures, 67599

Orbit — *continued*
X-ray, 70190, 70200
Orbital Contents
Aspiration, 67415
Orbital Floor
See Orbit; Periorbital Region
Fracture
Blow-Out, 21385-21395
Orbital Hypertelorism
Osteotomy
Periorbital, 21260-21263
Orbital Implant
See Ocular Implant
Insertion, 67550
Removal, 67560
Orbital Prosthesis, 21077
Orbital Rim and Forehead
Reconstruction, 21172-21180
Orbital Rims
Reconstruction, 21182-21184
Orbital Transplant, 67560
Orbit Area
Reconstruction
Secondary, 21275
Orbitocraniofacial Reconstruction, 21275
Orbitotomy
with Bone Flap
with Drainage, 67440
with Drainage Only, 67405
with Removal Foreign Body, 67430
with Removal lesion, 67412
with Removal of Bone for Decompression, 67445
for Exploration, 67450
Lateral Approach, 67420
with Removal of Foreign Body, 67413
Orbits
Skin Graft
Split, 15120, 15121
Orbit Wall
Decompression
with Nasal
Sinus Endoscopy, 31292, 31293
Orbit Walls
Reconstruction, 21182-21184
Orchidectomies
See Excision, Testis
Orchidopexy
See Orchiopexy
Orchidoplasty
See Repair, Testis
Orchiectomy
Laparoscopic, 54690
Partial, 54522
Radical
Abdominal Exploration, 54535
Inguinal Approach, 54530
Simple, 54520
Orchiopexy
Abdominal Approach, 54650
Inguinal Approach, 54640
Intra-Abdominal Testis, 54692
Orchioplasty
See Repair, Testis
Organ Donor
Life Support, 01990
Organ Grafting
See Transplantation

Organic Acids, 83918-83921
Organ or Disease Oriented Panel
Electrolyte, 80051
General Health Panel, 80050
Hepatic Function Panel, 80076
Hepatitis Panel, 80074
Lipid Panel, 80061
Metabolic
Basic, 80048
Comprehensive, 80053
Obstetric Panel, 80055
Renal Function, 80069
Organ System, Neurologic
See Nervous System
ORIF
Dislocation
Ankle, 27848
Bennett, 26685, 26686
Bennett Thumb, 26665
Carpometacarpal, 26685, 26686
Thumb, 26665
Elbow, 24635
Monteggia, 24635
Galeazzi, 25525, 25526
with
Repair
Triangular Cartilage, 25526
Hip
Spontaneous, 27258
with
Femoral Shaft Shortening, 27259
Traumatic, 27254
with
Fracture
Acetabular Wall, 27254
Femoral Head, 27254
Interphalangeal
Foot, 28675
Hand, 26785
Knee, 27556
with
Ligament, Ligamentous
Augmentation, 27558
Reconstruction, 27558
Repair, 27557, 27558
Lunate, 25695
Metacarpophalangeal, 26715
Metatarsophalangeal Joint, 28645
Monteggia, 24635
Odontoid, 22318, 22319
Pelvic, Pelvis
Ring
Anterior
Open, 27217
Pubis Symphysis, 27217
Rami, 27217
Posterior
Open, 27218
Sacroiliac joint
Open, 27218
Radioulnar
Distal, 25676
Sacroiliac Joint, 27218
Sacrum, 27218
Shoulder
with
Fracture
Humeral, Humerus
Anatomical Neck, 23680
Surgical Neck, 23680
Tuberosity, 23670
Talotarsal Joint, 28585

ORIF — *continued*
  Dislocation — *continued*
    Tarsal, 28555
    Tarsometatarsal Joint, 28615
    Temporomandibular, 21490
    Tibiofibular Joint, 27832
      with
        Excision
          Proximal
            Fibula, 27832
    TMJ, 21490
    Trans-Scaphoperilunar, 25685
  Fracture
    Acetabulum, Acetabular
      Column
        Anterior, 27227, 27228
        Posterior, 27227, 27228
      T-fracture, 27228
      Wall
        Anterior, 27226, 27228
        Posterior, 27226, 27228
      Traumatic, 27254
        with
          Dislocation of Hip, 27254
    Alveolar Ridge, 21445
    Ankle
      Bimalleolar, 27814
      Trimalleolar, 27822
        with
          Fixation
            Posterior Lip, 27823
          Malleolus Fracture
            Lateral, 27822, 27823
            Medial, 27822, 27823
    Calcaneal, Calcaneus, 28415
      with
        Bone Graft, 28420
    Capitate, 25645
    Carpal (Other), 25645
      Navicular, 25628
      Scaphoid, 25628
    Clavicle, 23515
    Clavicular, 23515
    Coccyx, Coccygeal, 27202
    Colles, 25620
    Craniofacial, 21432-21436
    Cuboid, 28465
    CuneiForms, 28465
    Elbow
      Monteggia, 24635
      Periarticular, 24586, 24587
    Epiphysis, Epiphyseal, 27519
    Femur, Femoral
      Condyle
        Lateral, 27514
        Medial, 27514
      Distal, 27514
        Lateral Condyle, 27514
        Medial Condyle, 27514
      Epiphysis, Epiphyseal, 27519
      Head, 27254
        Traumatic, 27254
          with
            Dislocation Hip, 27254
      Intertrochanteric, Intertrochanter, 27244, 27245
        with/Intermedullary Implant, 27245
      Lateral condyle, 27514
      Medial condyle, 27514
      Pertrochanteric, Pertrochanter, 27244, 27245
        with
          Intermedullary Implant, 27245

ORIF — *continued*
  Fracture — *continued*
    Femur, Femoral — *continued*
      Proximal End, 27236
        with
          Prosthetic Replacement, 27236
      Proximal Neck, 27236
        with
          Prosthetic Replacement, 27236
      Shaft, 27506, 27507
        with
          Intermedullary Implant, 27245
      Subtrochanteric, Subtrochanter, 27244, 27245
      Supracondylar, 27511, 27513
        with
          Intercondylar Extension, 27513
      Transcondylar, 27511, 27513
        with
          Intercondylar Extension, 27513
      Trochanteric, Trochanter
        Greater, 27248
        Intertrochanteric, Intertrochanter, 27244, 27245
          with
            Intermedullary Implant, 27245
        Petrochanteric, Pertrochanter, 27244, 27245
          with
            Intermedullary implant, 27245
        Subtrochanteric, Subtrochanter, 27244, 27245
          with
            Intermedullary Implant, 27245
    Fibula and Tibia, 27828
      Distal
        with
          Tibia Fracture, 27826
    Fibula, Fibular
      Distal, 27792
      Malleolus
        Lateral, 27792
      Proximal, 27784
      Shaft, 27784
    Foot
      Sesamoid, 28531
    Frontal Sinus, 21343, 21344
    Galeazzi, 25525, 25526
      with
        Fracture
          Radial Shaft, 25525, 25526
        Repair
          Triangular Cartilage, 25526
    Great Toe, 28505
    Hamate, 25645
    Heel, 28415
      with
        Bone Graft, 28420
    Humeral, Humerus
      Anatomical Neck, 23615, 23616
      Condylar
        Lateral, 24579
        Medial, 24579
      Epicondylar
        Lateral, 24575
        Medial, 24575
      Proximal, 23615, 23616
      Shaft, 24515, 24516
      Supracondylar, 24545, 24546
        with
          Intercondylar Extension, 24546
      Surgical neck, 23615, 23616

ORIF — *continued*
  Fracture — *continued*
    Humeral, Humerus — *continued*
      Transcondylar, 24545, 24546
      with
        Intercondylar Extension, 24546
      Tuberosity, 23630
    Hyoid, 21495
    Interphalangeal, 26746
    Knee
      Intercondylar Spine, 27540
      Tuberosity, 27540
    Larynx, Laryngeal, 31584
    LeFort I, 21422, 21423
    LeFort II, 21346-21348
    LeFort III, 21432-21436
    Lunate, 25645
    Malar, 21365, 21366
      with Malar Tripod, 21365, 21366
      with Zygomatic Arch, 21365, 21366
    Malar Area, 21365, 21366
      with Malar Tripod, 21365, 21366
      with Zygomatic Arch, 21365, 21366
    Malar Tripod, 21365, 21366
      with Malar area, 21365, 21366
      with Zygomatic Arch, 21365, 21366
    Malleolus
      Lateral, 27792
      with
        Ankle Fracture
          Trimalleolar, 27822, 27823
      Medial, 27766
      with
        Ankle Fracture
          Trimalleolar, 27822, 27823
    Mandibular, Mandible, 21462, 21470
      Alveolar Ridge, 21445
      Condylar, Condyle, 21465
    Maxillary
      Alveolar Ridge, 21445
    Maxillary, Maxilla, 21422, 21423
    Metacarpal, 26615
    Metacarpophalangeal, 26715
    Metatarsal, 28485
    Monteggia, 24635
    Nasal Bone, 21330, 21335
      with Nasal Septum, 21335
    Nasal Septum, 21335
    Nasoethmoid, 21339
    Nasomaxillary, 21346-21348
    Navicular
      Foot, 28465
      Hand, 25628
    Odontoid, 22318, 22319
    Olecranon process, 24685
    Orbit, 21406-21408
    Palate, Palatal, 21422, 21423
    Patella, Patellar, 27524
      with
        Patellectomy
          Complete, 27524
          Partial, 27524
        Repair
          Soft Tissue, 27524
    Phalange, Phalangeal
      Foot, 28525
        Great Toe, 28505
      Hand, 26735
        Distal, 26765
    PisiForm, 25645

ORIF — *continued*
  Fracture — *continued*
    Radial, Radius
      and
        Ulnar, Ulna, 25575
      Distal, 25620
        with Fracture
          Ulnar Styloid, 25620
      Head, 24665, 24666
      Neck, 24665, 24666
      or
        Ulnar, Ulna, 25574
      Shaft, 25515, 25525, 25526
        with Dislocation
          Distal
            Radio-Ulnar Joint, 25525, 25526
        with Repair
          Triangular Cartilage, 25526
    Rib, 21810
    Scaphoid, 25628
    Scapula, Scapular, 23585
    Sesamoid, 28531
    Smith, 25620
    Sternum, 21825
    Talar, Talus, 28445
    Tarsal
      Calcaneal, 28415
        with Bone Graft, 28420
      Cuboid, 28465
      CuneiForms, 28465
      Navicular, 28465
      Talus, 28445
    T-Fracture, 27228
    Thigh
      Femur, Femoral
        Condyle
          Lateral, 27514
          Medial, 27514
        Distal, 27514
          Lateral Condyle, 27514
          Medial Condyle, 27514
        Epiphysis, Epiphyseal, 27519
        Head, 27254
          Traumatic, 27254
            with Dislocation Hip, 27254
        Intertrochanteric, Intertrochanter, 27244, 27245
          with Intermedullary Implant, 27245
        Lateral Condyle, 27514
        Medial Condyle, 27514
        Pertrochanteric, Pertrochanter, 27244, 27245
          with Intermedullary Implant, 27245
        Proximal End, 27236
          with Prosthetic Replacement, 27236
        Proximal Neck, 27236
          with Prosthetic Replacement, 27236
        Shaft, 27506, 27507
          with Intermedullary Implant, 27245
        Subtrochanteric, Subtrochanter, 27244, 27245
        Supracondylar, 27511, 27513
          with Intercondylar Extension, 27513
        Transcondylar, 27511, 27513
          with Intercondylar Extension, 27513

ORIF — *continued*
  Fracture — *continued*
    Thigh — *continued*
      Femur, Femoral — *continued*
        Trochanteric, Trochanter
          Greater, 27248
          Intertrochanteric, Intertrochanter, 27244, 27245
            with Intermedullary Implant, 27245
          Pertrochanteric, Pertrochanter, 27244, 27245
            with Intermedullary Implant, 27245
          Subtrochanteric, Subtrochanter, 27244, 27245
            with Intermedullary Implant, 27245
  Thumb, 26665
  Tibia and Fibula, 27828
  Tibia, Tibial
    Articular Surface, 27827
      with Fibula, Fibular Fracture, 27828
    Bicondylar, 27536
    Condylar
      Bicondylar, 27536
      Unicondylar, 27535
    Distal, 27826
    Pilon, 27827
      with Fibula, Fibular Fracture, 27828
    Plafond, 27827
      with Fibula, Fibular Fracture, 27828
    Plateau, 27535, 27536
    Proximal, 27535, 27536
    Shaft, 27758, 27759
      with Fibula, Fibular Fracture, 27758, 27759
      with Intermedullary Implant, 27759
    Unicondylar, 27535
  Toe, 28525
    Great, 28505
  Trapezium, 25645
  Trapezoid, 25645
  Triquetral, 25645
  Ulna, Ulnar
    and Radial, Radius, 25575
    Monteggia, 24635
    Proximal, 24635, 24685
    Shaft, 25545
      or Radial, Radius, 25574
  Vertebral, 22325-22328
  Zygomatic Arch, 21365, 21366
Ormond Disease
  See Retroperitoneal Fibrosis
Orogastric Tube
  Placement, 43752
Oropharynx
  Biopsy, 42800
Orthodontic Cephalogram, 70350
Orthomyxoviridae
  See Influenza Virus
Orthomyxovirus
  See Influenza Virus
Orthopantogram, 70355
Orthopedic Cast
  See Cast

Orthopedic Surgery
  Computer Assisted Navigation, 0054T-0056T
  Stereotaxis
    Computer Assisted, 0054T-0056T
Orthoptic Training, 92065
Orthoroentgenogram, 76040
Orthosis
  See Orthotics
Orthotics
  Check-Out, 97762
  Training and Fitting, 97760
Os Calcis Fracture
  See Calcaneus, Fracture
Osmolality
  Blood, 83930
  Urine, 83935
Osseous Survey, 76061-76065
Osseous Tissue
  See Bone
Ossicles
  Excision
    Stapes
      with Footplate Drill Out, 69661
      without Foreign Material, 69660, 69661
  Reconstruction
    Ossicular Chain
      Tympanoplasty with Antrotomy or Mastoidectomy, 69636, 69637
      Tympanoplasty with Mastoidectomy, 69642-69646
      Tympanoplasty without Mastoidectomy, 69632, 69633
  Release
    Stapes, 69650
  Replacement
    with Prosthesis, 69633, 69637
OST, 59020
Ostectomy
  Carpal, 25215
  Femur, 27365
  Humerus, 24999
  Metacarpal, 26250, 26255
  Metatarsal, 28288
  Phalanges
    Fingers, 26260-26262
  Pressure Ulcer
    Ischial, 15941, 15945
    Sacral, 15933, 15935, 15937
    Trochanteric, 15951, 15953, 15958
  Radius, 25999
  Scapula, 23190
  Sternum, 21620
  Ulna, 25999
Osteocalcin, 83937
Osteocartilaginous Exostoses
  See Exostosis
Osteochondroma
  See Exostosis
Osteoclasis
  Carpal, 26989
  Clavicle, 23929
  Femur, 27599
  Humerus, 24999
  Metacarpal, 26989
  Metatarsal, 28899
  Patella, 27599
  Radius, 26989
  Scapula, 23929
  Tarsal, 28899

Other Nonoperative Measurements and Examinations, Fetal

Index

P

Pacemaker, Heart
See Defibrillator, Heart
Conversion, 33214
Electronic Analysis, 93641, 93642
  Antitachycardia System, 93724
  Dual Chamber, 93731, 93732, 93743-93744
  Single Chamber, 93734, 93735, 93741-93742
  Wearable Device, 93741-93742, 93745
Insertion, 33200-33208
  Electrode(s), 33210, 33211, 33216, 33217, 33224, 33225
  Pulse Generator Only, 33212, 33213
Removal
  Cardioverter-Defibrillator Pulse Generator, 33212, 33213
  Electrodes, Transvenous, 33238
  Pacemaker Pulse Generator, 33241-33244
    via Thoracotomy, 33236, 33237
Repair
  Electrode, 33218, 33220
  Leads, 33218, 33220
Replacement
  Catheter, 33210
  Electrode, 33210, 33211, 33217
  Insertion, 33206-33208
  Leads, 33216, 33217, 33249
  Pulse Generator, 33212, 33213
Repositioning
  Electrodes, 33215, 33226
Revise Pocket
  Chest, 33222, 33223
Telephonic Analysis, 93733, 93736
Upgrade, 33214
P-Acetamidophenol
See Acetaminophen
Pachymetry
Eye, 76514
Packing
Nasal Hemorrhage, 30901-30906
Pain Management
See Injection, Chemotherapy
Epidural, 62350-62351, 62360-62362, 99601-99602
Intrathecal, 62350-62351, 62360-62362, 99601-99602
Intravenous Therapy, 90760-90761, 90765-90766, 90774, 90775
Pain Therapy, 62350-62365
Palatal Augmentation Prosthesis, 21082
Palatal Lift Prosthesis, 21083
Palate
Abscess
  Incision and Drainage, 42000
Biopsy, 42100
Excision, 42120, 42145
Fracture
  Closed Treatment, 21421
  Open Treatment, 21422, 21423
Lesion
  Destruction, 42160
  Excision, 42104-42120
Prosthesis, 42280, 42281
Reconstruction
  Lengthening, 42226, 42227
Repair
  Cleft Palate, 42200-42225
  Laceration, 42180, 42182

Palate — continued
Repair — continued
  Vomer Flap, 42235
  Unlisted Services and Procedures, 42299
Palate, Cleft
See Cleft Palate
Palatopharyngoplasty, 42145
Palatoplasty, 42200-42225
Palatoschisis
See Cleft Palate
Palm
Bursa
  Incision and Drainage, 26025, 26030
Fasciectomy, 26121-26125
Fasciotomy, 26040, 26045
Tendon
  Excision, 26170
Tendon Sheath
  Excision, 26145
  Incision and Drainage, 26020
Palsy, Seventh Nerve
See Facial Nerve Paralysis
P&P, 85230
Pancoast Tumor Resection, 32503-32504
Pancreas
Anastomosis
  with Intestines, 48520, 48540
  to Intestines, 48180
Biopsy, 48100
  Needle Biopsy, 48102
Cyst
  Anastomosis, 48520, 48540
  Repair, 48500
Debridement
  Peripancreatic Tissue, 48005
Excision
  Ampulla of Vater, 48148
  Duct, 48148
  Partial, 48140-48146, 48150-48154, 48160
  Peripancreatic Tissue, 48005
  Total, 48155, 48160
Lesion
  Excision, 48120
Needle Biopsy, 48102
Placement
  Drainage, 48001
Pseudocyst
  Drainage
    Open, 48510
    Percutaneous, 48511
Removal
  Calculi (Stone), 48020
  Removal Transplanted Allograft, 48556
Repair
  Cyst, 48500
Suture, 48545
Transplantation, 48160, 48550, 48554-48556
  Allograft Preparation, 48550-48552
Unlisted Services and Procedures, 48999
X-ray with Contrast, 74300-74305
  Injection Procedure, 48400
Pancreas, Endocrine Only
See Islet Cell
Pancreatectomy
with Transplantation, 48160
Donor, 48550
Partial, 48140-48146, 48150-48154, 48160
Total, 48155, 48160
Pancreatic DNAse
See DNAse

Pancreatic Duct
Destruction
Calculi (Stone), 43265
Dilation
Endoscopy, 43271
Drainage
of Cyst, 48999
Endoscopy
Collection
Specimen, 43260
Destruction
Calculi (Stone), 43265
Tumor, 43272
Dilation, 43271
Removal (Endoscopic)
Calculi (Stone), 43264
Foreign Body, 43269
Stent, 43269
Sphincterotomy, 43262
Sphincter Pressure, 43263
Tube Placement, 43267, 43268
Incision
Sphincter, 43262
Removal
Calculi (Stone), 43264
Foreign Body, 43269
Stent, 43269
Tube Placement
Nasopancreatic, 43267
Stent, 43268
Tumor
Destruction, 43272
X-ray with Contrast
Guide Catheter, 74329, 74330
Pancreatic Elastase 1 (PE1), 82656
Pancreatic Islet Cell AB
See Antibody, Islet Cell
Pancreaticojejunostomy, 48180
Pancreatitis
Incision and Drainage, 48000
Pancreatography
Injection Procedure, 48400
Intraoperative, 74300, 74301
Postoperative, 74305
Pancreatojejunostomies
See Pancreaticojejunostomy
Pancreatorrhaphy, 48545
Pancreatotomy
See Incision, Pancreas
Pancreozymin-Secretin Test, 82938
Panel
See Organ or Disease Oriented panel
Panniculectomy
See Lipectomy
PAP, 88141-88167, 88174-88175
Paper Chromatographies
See Chromatography, Paper
Paper, Chromatography
See Chromatography, Paper
Papilla, Interdental
See Gums
Papillectomy, 46220
Papilloma
Destruction, 54050-54065
Papillotomy, 43262
Destruction
Anus, 46900-46924
Penis, 54050-54065

PAPP D
See Lactogen, Human Placental
Pap Smears, 88141-88155, 88164-88167, 88174-88175
Paracentesis
Abdomen, 49080-49081
Eye
Anterior Chamber
with Diagnostic Aspiration of Aqueous, 65800
with Removal of Blood, 65815
with Removal Vitreous and
or Discission of Anterior Hyaloid
Membrane, 65810
with Therapeutic Release of Aqueous, 65805
Thorax, 32000-32002
Paracentesis, Abdominal
See Abdomen, Drainage
Paracentesis, Thoracic
See Thoracentesis
Paracervical Nerve
Injection
Anesthetic, 64435
Paraffin Bath Therapy, 97018
See Physical Medicine/Therapy/Occupational Therapy
Paraganglioma, Medullary
See Pheochromocytoma
Parainfluenza Virus
Antigen Detection
Immunofluorescence, 87279
Paralysis, Facial Nerve
See Facial Nerve Paralysis
Paralysis, Infantile
See Polio
Paranasal Sinuses
See Sinus
Parasites
Blood, 87207
Concentration, 87015
Examination, 87169
Smear, 87177
Parasitic Worms
See Helminth
Parathormone, 83970
Parathyrin
See Parathormone
Parathyroid Autotransplantation, 60512
Parathyroidectomy, 60500-60505
Parathyroid Gland
Autotransplant, 60512
Biopsy, 60699
Excision, 60500, 60502
Exploration, 60500-60505
Nuclear Medicine
Imaging, 78070
Parathyroid Hormone, 83970
Parathyroid Hormone Measurement
See Parathormone
Parathyroid Transplantation
See Transplantation, Parathyroid
Para-Tyrosine
See Tyrosine
Paraurethral Gland
Abscess
Incision and Drainage, 53060

Paravertebral Nerve
  Destruction, 64622-64627
  Injection
    Anesthetic, 64470-64484
    Neurolytic, 64622-64627
Parietal Cell Vagotomies
  See Vagotomy, Highly Selective
Parietal Craniotomy, 61556
Paring
  Skin Lesion
    Benign Hyperkeratotic
      More than Four Lesions, 11057
      Single Lesion, 11055
      Two to Four Lesions, 11056
Park Posterior Anal Repair, 46761
Paronychia
  Incision and Drainage, 10060, 10061
Parotid Duct
  Diversion, 42507-42510
  Reconstruction, 42507-42510
Parotidectomy, 61590
Parotid Gland
  Abscess
    Incision and Drainage, 42300, 42305
  Calculi (Stone)
    Excision, 42330, 42340
  Excision
    Partial, 42410, 42415
    Total, 42420-42426
  Tumor
    Excision, 42410-42426
Parotitides, Epidemic
  See Mumps
Pars Abdominalis Aortae
  See Aorta, Abdominal
Partial Colectomy
  See Colectomy, Partial
Partial Cystectomy
  See Cystectomy, Partial
Partial Esophagectomy
  See Esophagectomy, Partial
Partial Gastrectomy
  See Excision, Stomach, Partial
Partial Glossectomy
  See Excision, Tongue, Partial
Partial Hepatectomy
  See Excision, Liver, Partial
Partial Mastectomies
  See Breast, Excision, Lesion
Partial Nephrectomy
  See Excision, Kidney, Partial
Partial Pancreatectomy
  See Pancreatectomy, Partial
Partial Splenectomy
  See Splenectomy, Partial
Partial Thromboplastin Time
  See Thromboplastin, Partial, Time
Partial Ureterectomy
  See Ureterectomy, Partial
Particle Agglutination, 86403, 86406
Parvovirus
  Antibody, 86747
Patch
  Allergy Tests, 95044
    See Allergy Tests
Patella
  See Knee

Patella — *continued*
  Dislocation, 27560-27566
  Excision, 27350
    with Reconstruction, 27424
  Fracture, 27520, 27524
  Reconstruction, 27437, 27438
  Repair
    Chondromalacia, 27418
    Instability, 27420-27424
Patella, Chondromalacia
  See Chondromalacia Patella
Patellar Tendon Bearing (PTB) Cast, 29435
Patellectomy, 27350, 27524, 27566
  with Reconstruction, 27424
Paternity Testing, 86910, 86911
Patey's Operation
  Mastectomy, Radical, 19200, 19220
Pathologic Dilatation
  See Dilation
Pathology
  Clinical
    Consultation, 80500, 80502
  Surgical
    Consultation, 88321-88325
      Intraoperative, 88329-88332
    Decalcification Procedure, 88311
    Electron Microscopy, 88348, 88349
    Gross and Micro Exam
      Level II, 88302
      Level III, 88304
      Level IV, 88305
      Level V, 88307
      Level VI, 88309
    Gross Exam
      Level I, 88300
    Histochemistry, 88318, 88319
    Immunocytochemistry, 88342
    Immunofluorescent Study, 88346, 88347
    Morphometry
      Nerve, 88356
      Skeletal Muscle, 88355
      Tumor, 88358, 88361
    Nerve Teasing, 88362
    Special Stain, 88312-88314
    Staining, 88312-88314
    Tissue Hybridization, 88365
    Unlisted Services and Procedures, 88399,
      89240
Patient
  Dialysis Training
    Completed Course, 90989
  Education
    Heart Failure, 4003F
Patterson's Test
  Blood Urea Nitrogen, 84520, 84525
Paul-Bunnell Test
  See Antibody; Antibody Identification;
    Microsomal Antibody
P B Antibodies
  See Antibody, Heterophile
PBG
  See Porphobilinogen
PCL, 27407, 29889
PCP, 83992
PCR (Polymerase Chain Reaction), 83898-
  83902, 83904-83912
Peak Flow Rate, 94150
Pean's Operation
  Amputation, Leg, Upper, at Hip, 27290

Index

Pectoral Cavity — Penis

Pectoral Cavity
See Chest Cavity
Pectus Carinatum
Reconstructive Repair, 21740-21742
with Thoracoscopy, 21743
Pectus Excavatum Repair
Anesthesia, 00474
Reconstructive Repair, 21740-21742
with Thoracoscopy, 21743
Pediatric Critical Care
Initial, 99293
Subsequent, 99294
Pedicle Fixation, 22842-22844
Pedicle Flap
Formation, 15570-15576
Island, 15740
Neurovascular, 15750
Transfer, 15650
PEEP
See Pressure Breathing, Positive
Peet Operation
See Nerves, Sympathectomy, Excision
PEG, 43246
Pelvic Adhesions
See Adhesions, Pelvic
Pelvic Bone
Drainage, 26990
Pelvic Exam, 57410
Pelvic Exenteration, 51597
for Colorectal Malignancy, 45126
Pelvic Fixation
Insertion, 22848
Pelvic Lymphadenectomy, 58240
Pelvimetry, 74710
Pelviolithotomy, 50130
Pelvis
See Hip
Abscess
Incision and Drainage, 26990, 45000
Angiography, 72191
Biopsy, 27040, 27041
Bone
Drainage, 26992
Brace Application, 20662
Bursa
Incision and Drainage, 26991
CT Scan, 72191-72194
Cyst
Aspiration, 50390
Injection, 50390
Destruction
Lesion, 58662
Endoscopy
Destruction of Lesions, 58662
Lysis of Adhesions, 58660
Oviduct Surgery, 58670, 58671
Exclusion
Small Intestine, 44700
Exenteration, 58240
for Colorectal Malignancy, 45126
Halo, 20662
Hematoma
Incision and Drainage, 26990
Lysis
Adhesions, 58660
Magnetic Resonance Angiography, 72198
Magnetic Resonance Imaging (MRI), 72195-
72197

Pelvis — *continued*
Removal
Foreign Body, 27086, 27087
Repair
Osteotomy, 27158
Tendon, 27098
Ring
Dislocation, 27193, 27194, 27216-27218
Fracture, 27216-27218
Closed Treatment, 27193, 27194
Tumor
Excision, 27047-27049
Ultrasound, 76856, 76857
Unlisted Services and Procedures, 27299
X-ray, 72170, 72190, 73540
Manometry, 74710
Pelvi-Ureteroplasty
See Pyeloplasty
Pemberton Osteotomy of Pelvis
See Osteotomy, Pelvis
Penectomy
See Amputation, Penis
Penetrating Keratoplasties
See Keratoplasty, Penetrating
Penile Induration
See Peyronie Disease
Penile Prosthesis
Insertion
Inflatable, 54401, 54405
Noninflatable, 54400
Removal
Inflatable, 54406, 54410-54417
Semi-Rigid, 54415-54417
Repair
Inflatable, 54408
Replacement
Inflatable, 54410-54411, 54416, 54417
Semi-Rigid, 54416, 54417
Penile Rigidity Test, 54250
Penile Tumescence Test, 54250
Penis
Amputation
Partial, 54120
Radical, 54130, 54135
Total, 54125-54135
Biopsy, 54100, 54105
Circumcision
with Clamp or Other Device, 54152
Newborn, 54150
Repair, 54163
Surgical Excision, 54161
Newborn, 54160
Excision
Partial, 54120
Prepuce, 54150-54161, 54163
Total, 54125-54135
Frenulum
Excision, 54164
Incision
Prepuce, 54000, 54001
Incision and Drainage, 54015
Injection
for Erection, 54235
Peyronie Disease, 54200
Surgical Exposure Plaque, 54205
Vasoactive Drugs, 54231
X-ray, 54230
Insertion
Prosthesis
Inflatable, 54401-54405
Noninflatable, 54400

Penis — *continued*
Irrigation
   Priapism, 54220
Lesion
   Destruction
      Any Method
         Extensive, 54065
      Cryosurgery, 54056
      Electrodesiccation, 54055
      Laser Surgery, 54057
      Simple, 54050-54060
      Surgical Excision, 54060
   Excision, 54060
      Penile Plaque, 54110, 54112
Nocturnal Tumescence Test, 54250
Occlusion
   Vein, 37790
Plaque
   Excision, 54110-54112
Plethysmography, 54240
Prepuce
   Stretch, 54450
Reconstruction
   Angulation, 54360
   Chordee, 54300, 54304, 54328
   Complications, 54340-54348
   Epispadias, 54380-54390
   Hypospadias, 54328-54352
   Injury, 54440
Removal
   Foreign Body, 54115
   Prosthesis
      Inflatable, 54406, 54410-54417
      Semi-Rigid, 54415-54417
Repair
   Fistulization, 54435
   Priapism with Shunt, 54420, 54430
   Prosthesis
      Inflatable, 54408
Replacement
   Prosthesis
      Inflatable, 54410, 54411, 54416, 54417
      Semi-Rigid, 54416, 54417
Revascularization, 37788
Rigidity Test, 54250
Test Erection, 54250
Unlisted Services and Procedures, 54699,
   55899
Venous Studies, 93980, 93981
Penis Adhesions
Lysis
   Post-circumcision, 54162
Penis Prostheses
See Penile Prosthesis
Pentagastrin Test
Gastric Analysis Test, 91052
Pentamidine
Inhalation Treatment, 94640, 94642, 94664
Peptidase P
See Angiotensin Converting Enzyme (ACE)
Peptidase S
See Leucine Aminopeptidase
Peptide, Connecting
See C-Peptide
Peptide, Vasoactive Intestinal
See Vasoactive Intestinal Peptide
Peptidyl Dipeptidase A
See Angiotensin Converting Enzyme (ACE)
Percutaneous Abdominal Paracentesis
See Abdomen, Drainage

Percutaneous Aspiration
Bartholin's Gland, 58999
Gallbladder, 47999
Seminal Vesicle, 54699, 55899
Percutaneous Atherectomies
See Artery, Atherectomy
Percutaneous Biopsy, Gallbladder/Bile Ducts
See Bile Duct, Biopsy
Percutaneous Cardiopulmonary Bypass, 33999
Percutaneous Cystostomy, 53899
Percutaneous Discectomies
See Diskectomy, Percutaneous
Percutaneous Electric Nerve Stimulation
See Application, Neurostimulation
Percutaneous Intradiscal Annuloplasty, 0062T,
   0063T
Percutaneous Lumbar Diskectomy, 62287
See Aspiration, Nucleus of Disk, Lumbar;
   Puncture Aspiration
Percutaneous Lysis, 62263, 62264
Percutaneous Nephrostomies
See Nephrostomy, Percutaneous
Percutaneous Transluminal Angioplasty
Artery
   Aortic, 35472
   Brachiocephalic, 35475
   Coronary, 92982, 92984
   Femoral-Popliteal, 35474
   Iliac, 35473
   Pulmonary, 92997, 92998
   Renal, 35471
   Tibioperoneal, 35470
   Visceral, 35471
Venous, 35476
Percutaneous Transluminal Coronary
   Angioplasty
See Percutaneous Transluminal Angioplasty
Pereyra Procedure, 51845, 57289, 58267, 58293
Performance Measures
ACE Inhibitor Therapy, 4009F
Anginal Symptom Assessment, 1002F
Antiplatelet Therapy, 4011F
Beta-Blocker Therapy, 4006F
Blood Pressure, 2000F
   Postpartum Care Visit, 0503F
   Prenatal Care Visit Initial, 0500F
   Prenatal Care Visit Subsequent, 0502F
   Prenatal Flow Sheet, 0501F
Statin Therapy, 4002F
Tobacco Use
   Assessment, 1000F-1001F
   Counseling, 4000F
   Pharmacologic Therapy, 4001F
Performance Test
See Physical Medicine/Therapy/Occupational
   Therapy
Performance Test Physical Therapy, 97750
Psychological Test, 96101-96103
Perfusion
Brain
   Imaging, 0042T
Myocardial, 78460-78465, 78478, 78480
   Imaging, 78466-78469
Positron Emission Tomography (PET)
   Myocardial Imaging, 78491, 78492
Perfusion, Intracranial Arterial
Thrombolysis, 61624
Perfusion Pump
See Infusion Pump

Pericardectomies
See Excision, Pericardium
Pericardial Cyst
See Cyst, Pericardial
Pericardial Sac
Drainage, 32659
Pericardial Window
for Drainage, 33025
Pericardiectomy
Complete, 33030, 33031
Subtotal, 33030, 33031
Total
Endoscopic, 32660
Pericardiocentesis, 33010, 33011
Ultrasound Guidance, 76930
Pericardiostomy
Tube, 33015
Pericardiotomy
Removal
Clot, 33020
Foreign Body, 33020
Pericardium
Cyst
Excision, 32661, 33050
Excision, 32659, 33030, 33031
Incision, 33030, 33031
with Tube, 33015
Removal
Clot, 33020
Foreign Body, 33020
Incision and Drainage, 33025
Lung
Pneumonocentesis, 32420
Puncture Aspiration, 33010, 33011
Removal
Clot
Endoscopic, 32658
Foreign Body
Endoscopic, 32658
Tumor
Excision, 32661, 33050
Peridural Anesthesia
See Anesthesia, Epidural
Peridural Injection
See Epidural, Injection
Perineal Prostatectomy
See Proastatectomy, Perineal
Perineoplasty, 56810
Perineorrhaphy
Repair
Rectocele, 57250
Perineum
Abscess
Incision and Drainage, 56405
Biopsy, 56605, 56606
Colposcopy, 99170
Debridement
Infected, 11004, 11006
Removal
Prosthesis, 53442
Repair, 56810
X-ray with Contrast, 74775
Perionychia
See Paronychia
Periorbital Region
Reconstruction-Osteotomy
with Graft, 21267, 21268
Repair-Osteotomy, 21260-21263

Peripheral Artery Disease (PAD) Rehabilitation, 93668
Peripheral Nerve
Repair/Suture
Major, 64856, 64859
Periprosthetic Capsulotomy
Breast, 19371
Peristaltic Pumps
See Infusion Pump
Peritoneal Dialysis, 90945, 90947
Training
Counseling, 90989, 90993
Peritoneal Free Air
See Pneumoperitoneum
Peritoneal Lavage, 49080
Peritoneocentesis, 49080, 49081
Peritoneoscopy
Biopsy, 47561, 49321
Exploration, 49320
Radiologic, 47560
Peritoneum
Abscess
Incision and Drainage, 49020
Percutaneous, 49021
Chemotherapy Administration, 96445
See Chemotherapy
Endoscopy
Biopsy, 47561
Drainage
Lymphocele, 49323
X-ray, 47560
Exchange
Drainage Catheter, 49423
Injection
Contrast
Via Catheter, 49424
Ligation
Shunt, 49428
Removal
Cannula
Catheter, 49422
Foreign Body, 49085
Shunt, 49429
Tumor
Resection, 58950-58954
Unlisted Services and Procedures, 49999
Venous Shunt, 49427
X-ray, 74190
Persistent, Omphalomesenteric Duct
See Diverticulum, Meckel's
Persistent Truncus Arteriosus
See Truncus Arteriosus
Personal Care
See Self Care
Pertussis Immunization, 90698-90701, 90715, 90720-90723
Pessary
Insertion, 57160
Pesticides
Chlorinated Hydrocarbons, 82441
PET, 78459, 78491, 78492, 78608, 78811-78816
Petrous Temporal
Excision
Apex, 69530
Peyreva Procedure, 51845
Peyronie Disease
with Graft, 54110-54112
Injection, 54200

Peyronie Disease — *continued*
Surgical Exposure, 54205
PG, 84081, 84150
pH
See Blood
Blood Gases, 82800, 82803, 82805, 82810
Body Fluid (Other), 83986
Phacoemulsification
Removal
Extracapsular Cataract, 66982, 66984
Secondary Membranous Cataract, 66850
Phagocytosis
White Blood Cells, 86344
Phalangectomy
Toe, 28150
Partial, 28160
Phalanges (Hand)
See Finger, Bone
Phalanx, Finger
Craterization, 26235, 26236
Cyst
Excision, 26210, 26215
Diaphysectomy, 26235, 26236
Excision, 26235, 26236
Radical
for Tumor, 26260-26262
Fracture
Articular
with Manipulation, 26742
Closed Treatment, 26740
Open Treatment, 26746
Distal, 26755, 26756
Closed Treatment, 26750
Open Treatment, 26765
Percutaneous, 26756
Open Treatment, 26735
Distal, 26765
Percutaneous Fixation, 26756
Shaft, 26720-26727
Open Treatment, 26735
Incision and Drainage, 26034
Ostectomy
Radical
for Tumor, 26260-26262
Repair
Lengthening, 26568
Nonunion, 26546
Osteotomy, 26567
Saucerization, 26235, 26236
Thumb
Fracture
Shaft, 26720-26727
Tumor
Excision, 26210, 26215
Phalanx, Great Toe
See Phalanx, Toe
Fracture
Closed Treatment, 28490
with Manipulation, 28495, 28496
Percutaneous Fixation, 28496
Open Treatment, 28505
Phalanx, Toe
Condyle
Excision, 28126
Craterization, 28124
Cyst
Excision, 28108
Diaphysectomy, 28124
Excision, 28124, 28150-28160

Phalanx, Toe — *continued*
Fracture
with Manipulation, 28515
without Manipulation, 28510
Open Treatment, 28525
Repair
Osteotomy, 28310, 28312
Saucerization, 28124
Tumor
Excision, 28108, 28175
Pharmaceutic Preparations
See Drug
Pharmacotherapies
See Chemotherapy
Pharyngeal Tonsil
See Adenoids
Pharyngectomy
Partial, 42890
Pharyngolaryngectomy, 31390, 31395
Pharyngoplasty, 42950
Pharyngorrhaphy
See Suture, Pharynx
Pharyngostomy, 42955
Pharyngotomy
See Incision, Pharynx
Pharyngotympanic Tube
See Eustachian Tube
Pharynx
See Nasopharynx; Throat
Biopsy, 42800-42806
Cineradiography, 70371, 74230
Creation
Stoma, 42955
Excision, 42145
with Larynx, 31390, 31395
Partial, 42890
Resection, 42892, 42894
Hemorrhage, 42960-42962
Lesion
Destruction, 42808
Excision, 42808
Reconstruction, 42950
Removal, Foreign Body, 42809
Repair
with Esophagus, 42953
Unlisted Services and Procedures, 42999
Video, 70371, 74230
X-ray, 70370, 74210
Phencyclidine, 83992
Phenobarbital, 82205
Assay, 80184
Phenothiazine, 84022
Phenotype Analysis
by Nucleic Acid
Infectious Agent
HIV-1 Drug Resistance, 87903, 87904
Phenotype Prediction
by Generic Database
HIV-1
Drug Resistance, 87900
Using Regularly Updated Genotypic
BioinFormatics, 87900
Phenylalanine, 84030
Phenylalanine-Tyrosine Ratio, 84030
Phenylketones, 84035
Phenylketonuria
See Phenylalanine

Index

Phenytoin — Physical Medicine/Therapy/Occupational Therapy

Phenytoin
Assay, 80185, 80186
Pheochromocytoma, 80424
Pheresis
See Apheresis
Phlebectasia
See Varicose Vein
Phlebectomy
Varicose Veins, 37765, 37766
Phlebographies
See Venography
Phlebography, 76499
Phleborheography, 93965
Phleborrhaphy
See Suture, Vein
Phlebotomy
Therapeutic, 99195
Phonocardiogram
Evaluation, 93799
Intracardiac, 93799
Tracing, 93799
Phoria
See Strabismus
Phosphatase
Alkaline, 84075, 84080
Blood, 84078
Forensic Examination, 84061
Phosphatase, Acid, 84060
Blood, 84066
Phosphate, Pyridoxal
See Pyridoxal Phosphate
Phosphatidylcholine Cholinephosphohydrolase
See Tissue Typing
Phosphatidylglycerol, 84081
Phosphatidyl Glycerol
See Phosphatidylglycerol
Phosphocreatine Phosphotransferase, ADP
See CPK
Phosphogluconate-6
Dehydrogenase, 84085
Phosphoglycerides, Glycerol
See Phosphatidylglycerol
Phosphohexose Isomerase, 84087
Phosphohydrolases
See Phosphatase
Phosphokinase, Creatine
See CPK
Phospholipase C
See Tissue Typing
Phospholipid Antibody, 86147, 86148
Phospholipid Cofactor Antibody, 0030T
Phosphomonoesterase
See Phosphatase
Phosphoric Monoester Hydrolases
See Phosphatase
Phosphorous, 84100
Urine, 84105
Phosphotransferase, ADP Phosphocreatine
See CPK
Photochemotherapies, Extracorporeal
See Photopheresis
Photochemotherapy, 96910-96913
See Dermatology
Endoscopic Light, 96570, 96571

Photocoagulation
Endolaser Panretinal
Vitrectomy, 67040
Focal Endolaser
Vitrectomy, 67040
Iridoplasty, 66762
Lesion
Cornea, 65450
Retina, 0017T, 67210, 67227, 67228
Retinal Detachment
Prophylaxis, 67145
Repair, 67105
Photodensity
Radiographic Absorptiometry, 76078
Photodynamic Therapy
External, 96567
Photography
Ocular
External, 92285
Internal, 92286, 92287
Skin, Diagnostic, 0044T-0045T
Photo Patch
Allergy Test, 95052
See Allergy Tests
Photopheresis
Extracorporeal, 36522
Photophoresis
See Actinotherapy; Photochemotherapy
Photoradiation Therapies
See Actinotherapy
Photoscreen
Ocular, 0065T
Photosensitivity Testing, 95056
See Allergy Tests
Phototherapies
See Actinotherapy
Phototherapy, Ultraviolet
See Actinotherapy
Phrenic Nerve
Anastomosis
to Facial Nerve, 64870
Avulsion, 64746
Incision, 64746
Injection
Anesthetic, 64410
Transection, 64746
Physical Examination
Office and/or Other Outpatient Services,
99201-99205
**Physical Medicine/Therapy/Occupational
Therapy**
See Neurology, Diagnostic
Activities of Daily Living, 97535, 99509
Aquatic Therapy
with Exercises, 97113
Athletic Training
Evaluation, 97005
Re-evaluation, 97006
Check-Out
Orthotics/Prosthetics
ADL, 97762
Cognitive Skills Development, 97532
Community/Work Reintegration, 97537
Evaluation, 97001, 97002
Hydrotherapy
Hubbard Tank, 97036
Pool with Exercises, 97036, 97113
Joint Mobilization, 97140
Kinetic Therapy, 97530

Physical Medicine/Therapy/Occupational Therapy — *continued*
Manipulation, 97140
Modalities
    Contrast Baths, 97034
    Diathermy Treatment, 97024
    Electric Stimulation
        Attended, Manual, 97032
        Unattended, 97014
    Hot or Cold Pack, 97010
    Hydrotherapy (Hubbard Tank), 97036
    Infrared Light Treatment, 97026
    Iontophoresis, 97033
    Microwave Therapy, 97024
    Paraffin Bath, 97018
    Traction, 97012
    Ultrasound, 97035
    Ultraviolet Light, 97028
    Unlisted Services and Procedures, 97039
    Vasopneumatic Device, 97016
    Whirlpool Therapy, 97022
Orthotics Training, 97760
Osteopathic Manipulation, 98925-98929
Procedures
    Aquatic Therapy, 97113
    Gait Training, 97116
    Group Therapeutic, 97150
    Massage Therapy, 97124
    Neuromuscular Reeducation, 97112
    Physical Performance Test, 97750
    Therapeutic Exercises, 4018F, 97110
    Traction Therapy, 97140
    Work Hardening, 97545, 97546
Prosthetic Training, 97761
Sensory Integration, 97533
Therapeutic Activities, 97530
Unlisted Services and Procedures, 97139, 97799
Wheelchair Management, 97542
Work Reintegration, 97537
Physical Therapy
See Physical Medicine/Therapy/Occupational Therapy
Physician Services
Care Plan Oversight Services, 99374-99380
    Home Health Agency Care, 99374
    Hospice, 99377, 99378
    Nursing Facility, 99379, 99380
Direction, Advanced Life Support, 99288
Prolonged
    with Direct Patient Contact, 99354-99357
        Outpatient Office, 99354, 99355
    with Direct Patient Services
        Inpatient, 99356, 99357
    without Direct Patient Contact, 99358, 99359
Standby, 99360
Supervision, Care Plan Oversight Services, 99374-99380
Pierce Ears, 69090
Piercing of Ear Lobe, 69090
Piles
See Hemorrhoids
Pilon Fracture Treatment, 27824
Pilonidal Cyst
Excision, 11770-11772
Incision and Drainage, 10080, 10081

Pin
See Wire
Insertion
Removal
    Skeletal Traction, 20650
Prophylactic Treatment
    Femur, 27187
    Humerus, 24498
    Shoulder, 23490, 23491
Pinch Graft, 15050
Pineal Gland
Excision
    Partial, 60699
    Total, 60699
Incision, 60699
Pinna
See Ear, External
Pinworms
Examination, 87172
Pirogoff Procedure, 27888
Pituitary Epidermoid Tumor
See Craniopharyngioma
Pituitary Fossa
Exploration, 60699
Pituitary Gland
Excision, 61546, 61548
Incision, 60699
Tumor
    Excision, 61546, 61548, 62165
Pituitary Growth Hormone
See Growth Hormone
Pituitary Lactogenic Hormone
See Prolactin
Pituitectomy
See Excision, Pituitary Gland
PKP, 65730-65755
PKU, 84030
PL, 80418, 80440, 84146
Placement
Bronchial Stent, 31636-31637
Catheter
    Bile Duct, 75982
    Breast
        for Interstitial Radioelement Application, 19296-19298
    Bronchus
        for Intracavitary Radioelement Application, 31643
        See Catheterization
Catheter, Cardiac, 93503
    See Catheterization, Cardiac
Colonic Stent, 44397, 45327, 45345, 45387
Drainage
    Pancreas, 48001
IVC Filter, 75940
Jejunostomy Tube
    Endoscopic, 44372
Metallic Localization Clip
    Breast, 19295
Nasogastric Tube, 43752
Needle
    Bone, 36680
Needle Wire
    Breast, 19290, 19291
Orogastric Tube, 43752
Pharmacological Agent
    Posterior Juxtascleral, 0124T
Radiation Delivery Device
    Intracoronary Artery, 92974

Placement — *continued*
Seton
Anal, 46020
Subconjunctival Retinal Prosthesis Receiver,
0100T
Tracheal Stent, 31631
Transcatheter
Extracranial, 0075T-0076T
Ureteral Stent, 50947
Placenta
Delivery, 59414
Placental Lactogen
See Lactogen, Human Placental
Placental Villi
See Chorionic Villus
Plafond Fracture Treatment
Tibial, 27824
Plagiocephaly, 21175
Plague Vaccine, 90727
Planing
Nose
Skin, 30120
Plantar Digital Nerve
Decompression, 64726
Plantar Pressure Measurements
Dynamic, 96001, 96004
Plasma
Frozen Preparation, 86927
Volume Determination, 78110, 78111
Plasma Prokallikrein
See Fletcher Factor
Plasma Protein-A, Pregnancy Associated (PAPP-A), 84163
Plasma Test
Volume Determination, 78110-78111
Plasma Thromboplastin
Antecedent, 85270
Component, 85250
Frozen Preparation, 86927
Plasmin, 85400
Plasmin Antiactivator
See Alpha-2 Antiplasmin
Plasminogen, 85420, 85421
Plasmodium
Antibody, 86750
Plastic Repair of Mouth
See Mouth, Repair
Plate, Bone
See Bone Plate
Platelet
Aggregation, 85576
Antibody, 86022, 86023
Assay, 85055
Blood, 85025
Count, 85032, 85049
Neutralization, 85597
Platelet Cofactor I
See Clotting Factor
Platelet Test
Survival Test, 78190, 78191
Platelet Thromboplastin Antecedent, 85270
Platysmal Flap, 15825
PLC, 86822
Pleoptic Training, 92065

Plethysmography
See Vascular Studies
Extremities, 93922, 93923
Veins, 93965
Penis, 54240
Total Body, 93720-93722
Pleura
Biopsy, 32095, 32100, 32400, 32402
Decortication, 32320
Empyema
Excision, 32540
Excision, 32310, 32320
Endoscopic, 32656
Foreign Body
Removal, 32150, 32151
Incision, 32320
Needle Biopsy, 32400
Removal
Foreign Body, 32150, 32653
Repair, 32215
Thoracotomy, 32095, 32100
Unlisted Services and Procedures, 32999
Pleural Cavity
Aspiration, 32000, 32002
Catheterization, 32019
Chemotherapy Administration, 96440
See Chemotherapy
Fusion, 32005
Incision
Empyema, 32035, 32036
Pneumothorax, 32020
Puncture and Drainage, 32000, 32002
Thoracostomy, 32035, 32036
Pleural Endoscopies
See Thoracoscopy
Pleural Scarification
for Repeat Pneumothorax, 32215
Pleural Tap
See Thoracentesis
Pleurectomy
Parietal, 32310, 32320
Endoscopic, 32656
Pleuritis, Purulent
See Abscess, Thorax
Pleurocentesis
See Thoracentesis
Pleurodesis
Chemical, 32005
Endoscopic, 32650
Pleurosclerosis
See Pleurodesis
Pleurosclerosis, Chemical
See Pleurodesis, Chemical
Plexectomy, Choroid
See Choroid Plexus, Excision
Plexus Brachialis
See Brachial Plexus
Plexus Cervicalis
See Cervical Plexus
Plexus, Choroid
See Choroid Plexus
Plexus Coeliacus
See Celiac Plexus
Plexus Lumbalis
See Lumbar Plexus
PLGN
See Plasminogen
Plication
Diaphragm, 39599

Index

Plication, Sphincter, Urinary Bladder — Postmortem

Plication, Sphincter, Urinary Bladder
See Bladder, Repair, Neck

Pneumocentesis
Lung, 32420

Pneumocisternogram
See Cisternography

Pneumococcal Vaccine, 90669, 90732

Pneumocystis Carinii
Antigen Detection, 87281

Pneumoencephalogram, 78635

Pneumoencephalography
Anesthesia, 01905

Pneumogastric Nerve
See Vagus Nerve

Pneumogram
Pediatric, 94772

Pneumolysis, 32940

Pneumonectomy, 32440-32500
Completion, 32488
Donor, 32850, 33930
Sleeve, 32442
Total, 32440-32445

Pneumonology
See Pulmonology

Pneumonolysis, 32940
Intrapleural, 32652
Open Intrapleural, 32124

Pneumonostomy, 32200-32201

Pneumonotomy
See Incision, Lung

Pneumoperitoneum, 49400

Pneumoplethysmography
Ocular, 93875

Pneumothorax
Chemical Pleurodesis, 32005
Pleural Scarification for Repeat, 32215
Therapeutic
Injection Intrapleural Air, 32960
Thoracentesis with Tube Insertion, 32002

Polio
Antibody, 86658
Vaccine, 90698, 90712, 90713

Poliovirus Vaccine, Inactivated
See Vaccines

Pollicization
Digit, 26550

Polya Gastrectomy
See Gastrectomy, Partial

Polydactylism
See Supernumerary Digit

Polydactylous Digit
Reconstruction, 26587
Repair, 26587

Polydactyly, Toes, 28344

Polymerase Chain Reaction, 83898

Polyp
Antrochoanal
Removal, 31032
Esophagus
Ablation, 43228
Nose
Excision
Endoscopic, 31237-31240
Extensive, 30115
Simple, 30110
Removal
Sphenoid Sinus, 31051

Polyp — continued
Urethra
Excision, 53260

Polypectomy
Nose
Endoscopic, 31237
Uterus, 58558

Polypeptide, Vasoactive Intestinal
See Vasoactive Intestinal Peptide

Polysomnography, 95808-95811

Polyuria Test
Water Load Test, 89235

Pomeroy's Operation
Tubal Ligation, 58600

Pooling
Blood Products, 86965

Pool Therapy with Exercises, 97036, 97113

Popliteal Arteries
See Artery, Popliteal

Popliteal Synovial Cyst
See Baker's Cyst

Poradenitistras
See Lymphogranuloma Venereum

PORP (Partial Ossicular Replacement Prosthesis), 69633, 69637

Porphobilinogen
Urine, 84106, 84110

Porphyrin Precursors, 82135

Porphyrins
Feces, 84126, 84127
Urine, 84119, 84120

Port
Venous Access
Insertion
Removal
Revision

Portal Vein
See Vein, Hepatic Portal

Porter-Silber Test
Corticosteroid, Blood, 82528

Port Film, 77417

Portoenterostomies, Hepatic
See Hepaticoenterostomy

Portoenterostomy, 47701

Posadas-Wernicke Disease
See Coccidioidomycosis

Positional Nystagmus Test
See Nystagmus Test, Positional

Positive End Expiratory Pressure
See Pressure Breathing, Positive

Positive-Pressure Breathing, Inspiratory
See Intermittent Positive Pressure Breathing (IPPB)

Positron Emission Tomography (PET)
Brain, 78608, 78609
Heart, 78459
Myocardial Imaging
Perfusion Study, 78491, 78492
Tumor, 78814-78816

Postauricular Fistula
See Fistula, Postauricular

Postcaval Ureter
See Retrocaval Ureter

Postmortem
See Autopsy

Prescription
Contact Lens, 92310-92317
See Contact Lens Services

Pressure, Blood
See Blood Pressure

Pressure Breathing
See Pulmonology, Therapeutic
Negative
Continuous (CNP), 94662
Positive
Continuous (CPAP), 94660
Intermittent (IPPB)

Pressure Measurement of Sphincter of Oddi
See Sphincter of Oddi, Pressure Measurement

Pressure Trousers
Application, 99199

Pressure Ulcer (Decubitus)
See Debridement; Skin Graft and Flap
Excision, 15920-15999
Coccygeal, 15920, 15922
Ischial, 15940-15946
Sacral, 15931-15937
Trochanter, 15950-15958
Unlisted Procedures and Services, 15999

Pressure, Venous
See Blood Pressure, Venous

Pretreatment
Red Blood Cell
Antibody Identification, 86970-86972
Serum
Antibody Identification, 86975-86978

Prevention & Control
See Prophylaxis

Preventive Medicine, 99381-99387
See Immunization; Newborn Care, Normal;
Office and/or Other Outpatient Services;
Prophylactic Treatment
Administration and Interpretation of Health
Risk Assessment, 99420
Counseling and/or Risk Factor Reduction
Intervention, 99401-99429
Established Patient, 99382-99397
Established Patient Exam, 99391-99397
Intervention, 99401-99429
Group Counseling, 99411, 99412
Individual Counseling, 99401-99404
Newborn Care, 99432
New Patient Exam, 99381-99387
Respiratory Pattern Recording, 94772
Unlisted Services and Procedures, 99429

Priapism
Repair
with Shunt, 54420, 54430
Fistulization, 54435

Primidone
Assay, 80188

PRL
See Prolactin

Proalbumin
See Prealbumin

Probes, DNA
See Nucleic Acid Probe

Probes, Nucleic Acid
See Nucleic Acid Probe

Procainamide
Assay, 80190, 80192

Procedure, Fontan
See Repair, Heart, Anomaly

Procedure, Maxillofacial
See Maxillofacial Procedures

Process
See anatomic Term (e.g., coracoid, odontoid)

Process, Odontoid
See Odontoid Process

Procidentia
Rectal
Excision, 45130, 45135
Repair, 45900

Procoagulant Activity, Glomerular
See Thromboplastin

Proconvertin, 85230

Proctectasis
See Dilation, Rectum

Proctectomy
with Ileostomy, 44212
Partial, 45111, 45113-45116, 45123
Total, 45110, 45112, 45119, 45120
with Colon, 45121

Proctocele
See Rectocele

Proctopexy, 45540, 45541
with Sigmoid Excision, 45550

Proctoplasty, 45500, 45505

Proctorrhaphy
See Rectum, Suture

Proctoscopies
See Anoscopy

Proctosigmoidoscopy
Ablation
Polyp or Lesion, 45320
Biopsy, 45305
Destruction
Tumor, 45320
Dilation, 45303
Exploration, 45300
Hemorrhage Control, 45317
Placement
Stent, 45327
Removal
Foreign Body, 45307
Polyp, 45308-45315
Tumor, 45315
Stoma
through Artificial, 45999
Volvulus Repair, 45321

Proctostomy
Closure, 45999

Proctotomy, 45160

Products, Gene
See Protein

Proetz Therapy, 30210

Profibrinolysin
See Plasminogen

Progenitor Cell
See Stemm Cell

Progesterone, 84144

Progesterone Receptors, 84234

Progestin Receptors
See Progesterone Receptors

Proinsulin, 84206

Pro-Insulin C Peptide
See C-Peptide

Projective Test, 96101-96103

Prokallikrein
See Fletcher Factor

Prokallikrein, Plasma
See Fletcher Factor
Prokinogenase
See Fletcher Factor
Prolactin, 80418, 80440, 84146
Prolapse
See procidentia
Prolapse, Rectal
See Procidentia, Rectum
Prolastin
See Alpha-1 Antitrypsin
Prolonged Services
with Direct Patient Contact, 99354-99357
without Direct Patient Contact, 99358, 99359
Physician Standby Services, 99360
PROM, 95851, 95852, 97110, 97530
Prophylactic Treatment
See Preventive Medicine
Clavicle, 23490
Femoral Neck and Proximal Femur
  Nailing, 27187
  Pinning, 27187
  Wiring, 27187
Femur, 27495
  Nailing, 27495
  Pinning, 27495
Humerus, 23491
  Pinning, Wiring, 24498
Radius, 25490, 25492
  Nailing, 25490, 25492
  Pinning, 25490, 25492
  Plating, 25490, 25492
  Wiring, 25490, 25492
Shoulder
  Clavicle, 23490
  Humerus, 23491
Tibia, 27745
Ulna, 25491, 25492
  Nailing, 25491, 25492
  Pinning, 25491, 25492
  Plating, 25491, 25492
  Wiring, 25491, 25492
Prophylaxis
Retina
  Detachment
    Cryotherapy, Diathermy, 67141
    Photocoagulation, 67145
Prostaglandin, 84150
Insertion, 59200
Prostanoids
See Prostaglandin
Prostate
Ablation
  Cryosurgery, 55873
Abscess
  Drainage, 52700
  Incision and Drainage, 55720, 55725
Biopsy, 0137T, 55700, 55705
Brachytherapy
  Needle Insertion, 55859
Coagulation
  Laser, 52647
Destruction
  Cryosurgery, 55873
  Thermotherapy, 53850-53853
    Microwave, 53850
    Radio Frequency, 53852
Excision
  Partial, 55801, 55821, 55831
  Perineal, 55801-55815

Prostate — continued
Excision — continued
  Radical, 55810-55815, 55840-55845
  Retropubic, 55831-55845
  Suprapubic, 55821
  Transurethral, 52402, 52601, 52612, 52614
Exploration
  with Nodes, 55862, 55865
  Exposure, 55860
Incision
  Exposure, 55860-55865
  Transurethral, 52450
Insertion
  Radioactive Substance, 55860
Needle Biopsy, 55700
Thermotherapy
  Transurethral, 53850-53853
Ultrasound, 76872, 76873
Unlisted Services and Procedures, 54699,
  55899
Urinary System, 53899
Urethra
  Stent Insertion, 0084T
  Transurethral Balloon Dilation, 52510
Vaporization
  Laser, 52648
Prostatectomy, 52601
Laparoscopic, 55866
Perineal
  Partial, 55801
  Radical, 55810, 55815
Retropubic
  Partial, 55831
  Radical, 55840-55845, 55866
Suprapubic
  Partial, 55821
Transurethral, 52612, 52614
Prostate Specific Antigen
Complexed, 84152
Free, 84154
Total, 84153
Prostatic Abscess
See Abscess, Prostate
Prostatotomy, 55720, 55725
Prosthesis
Augmentation
  Mandibular Body, 21125
Auricular, 21086
Breast
  Insertion, 19340, 19342
  Removal, 19328, 19330
  Supply, 19396
Check-Out, 97762
  See Physical Medicine/Therapy/
    Occupational Therapy
Cornea, 65770
Facial, 21088
Hernia
  Mesh, 49568
Hip
  Removal, 27090, 27091
Intestines, 44700
Knee
  Insertion, 27438, 27445
Lens
  Insertion, 66982-66985
  Manual or Mechanical Technique, 66982-
    66984
  not Associated with Concurrent Cataract
    Removal, 66985
Mandibular Resection, 21081

Prosthesis — *continued*
Nasal, 21087
Nasal Septum
Insertion, 30220
Obturator, 21076
Definitive, 21080
Interim, 21079
Ocular, 21077, 65770, 66982-66985, 92358
Fitting and Prescription, 92002-92014
Loan, 92358
Prescription, 92002-92014
Orbital, 21077
Ossicle Reconstruction
Chain
Partial or Total, 69633, 69637
Palatal Augmentation, 21082
Palatal Lift, 21083
Palate, 42280, 42281
Penile
Fitting, 54699, 55899
Insertion, 54400-54405
Removal, 54406, 54410-54417
Repair, 54408
Replacement, 54410, 54411, 54416, 54417
Perineum
Removal, 53442
Skull Plate
Removal, 62142
Replacement, 62143
Spectacle
Fitting, 92352, 92353
Repair, 92371
Speech Aid, 21084
Spinal
Insertion, 22851
Synthetic, 69633, 69637
Temporomandibular Joint
Arthroplasty, 21243
Testicular
Insertion, 54660
Training, 97761
Urethral Sphincter
Insertion, 53444, 53445
Removal, 53446, 53447
Repair, 53449
Replacement, 53448
Vagina
Insertion, 57267
Wrist
Removal, 25250, 25251
Protease F, 85400
Protein
C-Reactive, 86140, 86141
Glycated, 82985
Myelin Basic, 83873
Osteocalcin, 83937
Other Source, 84157
Prealbumin, 84134
Serum, 84155
Total, 84155
Urine, 84156
by Dipstick, 81000-81003
Western Blot, 84181, 84182, 88372
Protein Analysis, Tissue
See Western Blot
Protein C Activator, 85337
Protein C Antigen, 85302
Protein C Assay, 85303
Protein C Resistance Assay, 85307

Protein S
Assay, 85306
Total, 85305
Prothrombase
See Thrombokinase
Prothrombin, 85210
Prothrombinase
See Thromboplastin
Prothrombin Time, 85610, 85611
Prothrombokinase, 85230
Protime
See Prothrombin Time
Proton Treatment Delivery
Complex, 77525
Intermediate, 77523
Simple, 77520, 77522
Protoporphyrin, 84202, 84203
Protozoa
Antibody, 86753
Provitamin A
See Vitamin, A
Provocation Test
for Allergies, 95078
See Allergy Tests
for Glaucoma, 92140
Provocation Tonography, 92130
Prower Factor
See Stuart-Prower Factor
PRP, 67040
PSA, 84152
Free, 84154
Total, 84153
Pseudocyst, Pancreas
See Pancreas, Pseudocyst
PSG
See Polysomnography
Psoriasis Treatment, 96910-96922
See Dermatology; Photochemotherapy
Psychiatric Diagnosis
Evaluation of Records, Reports, and Tests, 90885
Interview and Evaluation, 90801, 90802
Interactive, 90802
Narcosynthesis, 90865
Psychological Testing, 96101-96103
Unlisted Services and Procedures, 90899
Psychiatric Treatment
See Psychotherapy
Biofeedback Training, 90875, 90876
Consultation with Family, 90887
Drug Management, 90862
Electroconvulsive Therapy, 90870
Environmental Intervention, 90882
Family, 90846-90849, 99510
Group, 90853, 90857
Hypnotherapy, 90880
Individual
Insight-Oriented
Home Visit, 99510
Hospital or Residential Care, 90816-90822
Office or Outpatient, 90804-90809
Interactive
Home Visit, 99510
Hospital or Residential Care, 90823-90829
Office or Outpatient, 90810-90815

Radical Resection — *continued*
  Ovarian Tumor — *continued*
    Bilateral Salpingo-Oophorectomy-
      Omentectomy, 58950-58954
    Omentectomy, 58950-58956
  Pelvis
    Soft Tissue, 27049
  Peritoneal Tumor
    with Radical Dissection for Debulking,
      58952-58954
    Bilateral Salpingo-Oophorectomy-
      Omentectomy, 58952-58954
  Phalanges
    Fingers, 26260-26262
    Toes, 28175
  Radius, 25170
  Scalp, 21015
  Scapula, 23210
  Shoulder, 23077
  Sternum, 21630, 21632
  Talus
    Tumor
      Calcaneus, 27647
  Tarsal, 28171
  Tibia, 27645
  Tonsil, 42842-42845
  Tumor
    Back/Flank, 21935
    Femur, 27365
    Knee, 27329, 27365
    Leg, Upper, 27329
    Neck, 21557
    Thorax, 21557
  Ulna, 25170
  Wrist, 25077
Radical Vaginal Hysterectomy
  See Hysterectomy, Vaginal, Radical
Radical Vulvectomy
  See Vulvectomy, Radical
Radioactive Colloid Therapy, 79300
Radioactive Substance
  Insertion
    Prostate, 55860
Radiocarpal Joint
  Arthrotomy, 25040
  Dislocation
    Closed Treatment, 25660
Radio-Cobalt B12 Schilling Test
  Vitamin B12 Absorption Study, 78270-78272
Radioelement
  Application, 77761-77778
    with Ultrasound, 76965
    Surface, 77789
  Handling, 77790
  Infusion, 77750
Radioelement Substance
  Catheterization, 55859
  Catheter Placement
    Breast, 19296-19298
    Bronchus, 31643
  Needle Placement
    Prostate, 55859
Radiography
  See Radiology, Diagnostic; X-Ray
Radioimmunosorbent Test
  Gamma-globulin, Blood, 82784, 82785
Radioisotope Brachytherapy
  See Brachytherapy
Radioisotope Scan
  See Nuclear Medicine

Radiological Marker
  Preoperative Placement
    Excision of Breast Lesion, 19125, 19126
Radiology
  See Nuclear Medicine, Radiation Therapy, X-
    Ray, Ultrasound
  Diagnostic
    Unlisted Services and Procedures, 76499
    Examination, 70030
      Stress Views, 76006
    Joint Survey, 76066
  Therapeutic
    Field Set-Up, 77280-77290
    Planning, 77261-77263, 77299
    Port Film, 77417
Radionuclide Therapy
  See Radiopharmaceutical Therapy
  Heart, 7944
  Inter-arterial, 79445
  Interstitial, 79300
  Intra-articular, 79440
  Intracavitary, 79200
  Intravascular, 79101
  Intravenous, 79101, 79403
  Intravenous Infusion, 79101, 79403
  Oral, 79005
  Unlisted Services and Procedures, 79999
Radionuclide Tomography, Single-Photon
  Emission-Computed
  See SPECT
Radiopharmaceutical Therapy
  Heart, 79440
  Inter-arterial particulate, 79445
  Interstitial, 79300
    Colloid Administration, 79300
  Intra-articular, 79440
  Intracavitary, 79200
  Intravascular, 79101
  Intravenous Infusion, 79403
  Oral, 79005
  Unlisted Services and Procedures, 79999
Radiotherapeutic
  See Radiation Therapy
Radiotherapies
  See Irradiation
Radiotherapy, Surface
  See Application, Radioelement, Surface
Radioulnar Joint
  Arthrodesis, 25830
  Dislocation
    Closed Treatment, 25675
    Open Treatment, 25676
    Percutaneous Fixation, 25671
Radius
  See Arm, Lower; Elbow; Ulna
  Arthroplasty, 24365
    with Implant, 24366, 25441
  Craterization, 24145, 25151
  Cyst
    Excision, 24125, 24126, 25120-25126
  Diaphysectomy, 24145, 25151
  Dislocation
    with Fracture
      Closed Treatment, 24620
      Open Treatment, 24635
    Partial, 24640
    Subluxate, 24640
  Excision, 24130, 24136, 24145, 24152, 24153
    Epiphyseal Bar, 20150
    Partial, 25145

Radius — *continued*
  Excision — *continued*
    Styloid Process, 25230
  Fracture, 25605
    with Ulna, 25560, 25565
      Open Treatment, 25575
      Closed Treatment, 25500, 25505, 25520,
        25600, 25605
        with Manipulation, 25605
        without Manipulation, 25600
    Distal, 25600-25611
      Open Treatment, 25620
    Head/Neck
      Closed Treatment, 24650, 24655
      Open Treatment, 24665, 24666
    Open Treatment, 25515, 25525, 25526,
      25574
    Percutaneous Fixation, 25611
    Shaft, 25500-25526
      Open Treatment, 25574
  Implant
    Removal, 24164
  Incision and Drainage, 25035
  Osteomyelitis, 24136, 24145
  Osteoplasty, 25390-25393
  Prophylactic Treatment, 25490, 25492
  Repair
    with Graft, 25405, 25420-25426
    Epiphyseal Arrest, 25450, 25455
    Epiphyseal Separation
      Closed, 25600
        Closed with Manipulation, 25605
      Open Treatment, 25620
      Percutaneous Fixation, 25611
    Malunion or Nonunion, 25400, 25415
    Osteotomy, 25350, 25355, 25370, 25375
      and Ulna, 25365
  Saucerization, 24145, 25151
  Sequestrectomy, 24136, 25145
  Subluxation, 24640
  Tumor
    Cyst, 24120
    Excision, 24125, 24126, 25120-25126,
      25170

RA Factor
  Qualitative, 86430
  Quantitative, 86431
Ramstedt Operation
  Pyloromyotomy, 43520
Ramus Anterior, Nervus Thoracicus
  See Intercostal Nerve
Range of Motion Test
  Extremities, 95851
  Eye, 92018, 92019
  Hand, 95852
  Rectum
    Biofeedback, 90911
  Trunk, 97530
Ranula
  Treatment of, 42408
Rapid Heart Rate
  See Tachycardia
Rapid Plasma Reagin Test, 86592, 86593
Rapid Test for Infection, 86308, 86403, 86406
  Monospot Test, 86308
Rapoport Test, 52005
Raskind Procedure, 33735-33737
Rastelli Procedure, 33786
Rathke Pouch Tumor
  See Craniopharyngioma

Rat Typhus
  See Murine Typhus
Rays, Roentgen
  See X-Ray
Raz Procedure, 51845
  See Repair, Bladder, Neck
RBC, 78120, 78121, 78130-78140, 85007, 85014,
    85041, 85547, 85555, 85557, 85651-85660,
    86850-86870, 86970-86978
RBC ab
  See Antibody, Red Blood Cell
Reaction
  Lip
    without Reconstruction, 40530
Reaction, Polymerase Chain
  See Polymerase Chain Reaction
Realignment
  Femur, with Osteotomy, 27454
  Knee, Extensor, 27422
  Muscle, 20999
    Hand, 26989
  Tendon, Extensor, 26437
Reattachment
  Muscle, 20999
  Thigh, 27599
Receptor
  See CD4; Estrogen Receptor; FC Receptor;
    Progesterone Receptors
Receptor Assay
  Hormone, 84233
  Non-Hormone, 84238
Recession
  Gastrocnemius
    Leg, Lower, 27687
  Tendon
    Hand, 26989
Reconstruction
  See Revision
  Abdominal Wall
    Ometal Flap, 49905
  Acetabulum, 27120, 27122
  Anal
    with Implant, 46762
    Congenital Absence, 46730-46740
    Fistula, 46742
    Graft, 46753
    Sphincter, 46750, 46751, 46760-46762
  Ankle, 27700-27703
  Apical-Aortic Conduit, 33404
  Atrial, 33253
  Auditory Canal, External, 69310, 69320
  Bile Duct
    Anastomosis, 47800
  Bladder
    with Urethra, 51800, 51820
    from Colon, 50810
    from Intestines, 50820, 51960
  Breast
    with Free Flap, 19364
    with Latissimus Dorsi Flap, 19361
    with Other Techniques, 19366
    with Tissue Expander, 19357
    Augmentation, 19324, 19325
    Mammoplasty, 19318-19325
    Nipple, 19350, 19355
    Revision, 19380
    Transverse Rectus Abdominis Myocutaneous
      Flap, 19367-19369

Reconstruction — Reconstruction

Reduction — *continued*
  Dislocation — *continued*
    Lunate — *continued*
      Open Treatment, 25695
    Metacarpophalangeal Joint
      Closed Treatment, 26700-26706
      Open Treatment, 26715
    Metatarsophalangeal joint
      Closed Treatment, 28630, 28635
      Open Treatment, 28645
      Percutaneous Fixation, 28636
    Monteggia, 24635
    Odontoid
      Open Treatment, 22318, 22319
    Patella, Patellar
      Acute
        Closed Treatment, 27560, 27562
        Open Treatment, 27566
          Partial, 27566
          Total, 27566
      Recurrent, 27420-27424
        with Patellectomy, 27424
    Pelvic, Ring
      Closed Treatment, 27193, 27194
      Open Treatment, 27217, 27218
      Percutaneous Fixation, 27216
    Radiocarpal
      Closed Treatment, 25660
      Open Treatment, 25670
    Radio-ulnar Joint
      Closed Treatment, 25675
        with Radial Fracture, 25520
      Open Treatment, 25676
        with Radial Fracture, 25525, 25526
    Radius
      with Fracture
        Closed Treatment, 24620
        Open Treatment, 24635
      Closed Treatment, 24640
    Sacrum, 27218
    Shoulder
      Closed Treatment with Manipulation, 23650, 23655
        with Fracture of Greater Humeral Tuberosity, 23665
        with Surgical or Anatomical Neck Fracture, 23675
      Open Treatment, 23660
      Recurrent, 23450-23466
    Sternoclavicular
      Closed Treatment, 23525
      Open Treatment, 23530, 23532
    Talotarsal joint
      Closed Treatment, 28570, 28575
      Open Treatment, 28585
      Percutaneous Fixation, 28576
    Tarsal
      Closed Treatment, 28540, 28545
      Open Treatment, 28555
      Percutaneous Fixation, 28546
    Tarsometatarsal joint
      Closed Treatment, 28600
      Open Treatment, 28615
      Percutaneous Fixation, 28606
    Temporomandibular
      Closed Treatment, 21480, 21485
      Open Treatment, 21490
    Tibiofibular Joint
      Closed Treatment, 27830, 27831
      Open Treatment, 27832
    TMJ
      Closed Treatment, 21480, 21485
      Open Treatment, 21490

Reduction — *continued*
  Dislocation — *continued*
    Vertebral
      Closed Treatment, 22315
      Open Treatment, 22326-22328
  Forehead, 21137-21139
  Fracture
    Acetabulum, Acetabular
      Closed Treatment, 27222
      Open Treatment, 27227, 27228
      with Dislocation hip, 27254
    Alveolar Ridge
      Closed Treatment, 21440
      Open Treatment, 21445
    Ankle
      Bimalleolar
        Closed Treatment, 27810
        Open Treatment, 27814
      Trimalleolar
        Closed Treatment, 27818
        Open Treatment, 27822
          with Fixation
            Posterior Lip, 27823
          with Malleolus Fracture
            Lateral, 27822, 27823
            Medial, 27822, 27823
    Bennett
      Closed Treatment, 26670, 26675
      Open Treatment, 26665, 26685, 26686
      Percutaneous Fixation, 26650, 26676
    Blowout
      Open Treatment, 21385-21395
    Bronchi, Bronchus
      Closed
        Endoscopic Treatment, 31630
    Calcaneal, Calcaneus
      Closed Treatment, 28405
      Open Treatment, 28415
        with
          Bone graft, 28420
      Percutaneous Fixation, 28406
    Carpal Bone(s)
      Closed Treatment, 25624, 25635
        Capitate, 25635
        Hamate, 25635
        Lunate, 25635
        Navicular, 25624
        PisiForm, 25635
        Scaphoid, 25624
        Trapezium, 25635
        Trapezoid, 25635
        Triquetral, 25635
      Open Treatment, 25628, 25645
        Capitate, 25645
        Hamate, 25645
        Lunate, 25645
        Navicular, 25628
        PisiForm, 25645
        Scaphoid, 25628
        Trapezium, 25645
        Trapezoid, 25645
        Triquetral, 25645
    Carpometacarpal
      Closed Treatment, 26645
      Open Treatment, 26665
      Percutaneous Fixation, 26650
    Cheek
      Percutaneous, 21355
    Clavicle
      Closed Treatment, 23505
      Open Treatment, 23515

Index

Reduction — Reduction

Reduction — *continued*
Fracture — *continued*
Coccyx, Coccygeal
Open Treatment, 27202
Colles
Closed Treatment, 25605
Open Treatment, 25620
Percutaneous Fixation, 25611
Craniofacial
Open Treatment, 21432-21436
Cuboid
Closed Treatment, 28455
Open Treatment, 28465
CuneiForms
Closed Treatment, 28455
Open Treatment, 28465
Elbow
Closed Treatment, 24620
Open Treatment, 24586, 24587
Epiphysis, Epiphyseal
Closed Treatment, 27517
Open Treatment, 27519
Femur, Femoral
Condyle
Lateral
Closed Treatment, 27510
Open Treatment, 27514
Medial
Closed Treatment, 27510
Open Treatment, 27514
Distal
Closed Treatment, 27510
Lateral condyle, 27510
Medial condyle, 27510
Open Treatment, 27514
Lateral condyle, 27514
Medial condyle, 27514
Epiphysis, Epiphyseal
Closed Treatment, 27517
Open Treatment, 27519
Greater Trochanteric
Open Treatment, 27248
Head
Traumatic, 27254
with Dislocation Hip, 27254
with Greater Trochanteric
Open Treatment, 27248
Intertrochanteric, Intertrochanter
Closed Treatment, 27238, 27240
Open Treatment, 27244, 27245
with Intermedullary Implant, 27245
Pertrochanteric, Pertrochanter
Closed Treatment, 27240
Open Treatment, 27244, 27245
with Intermedullary Implant, 27245
Proximal End
Closed Treatment, 27232
Open Treatment, 27236
with Prosthetic Replacement, 27236
Proximal Neck
Closed, 27232
Open Treatment, 27236
with Prosthetic Replacement, 27236
Shaft
Closed Treatment, 27502
Open Treatment, 27506, 27507
with Intermedullary Implant, 27245
Subtrochanteric, Subtrochanter
Closed Treatment, 27240
Open Treatment, 27244, 27245

Reduction — *continued*
Fracture — *continued*
Femur, Femoral — *continued*
Supracondylar
Closed Treatment, 27503
with Intercondylar Extension,
27503
Open Treatment, 27511, 27513
with Intercondylar Extension,
27513
Transcondylar
Closed Treatment, 27503
Open Treatment, 27511, 27513
with Intercondylar Extension,
27513
Fibula and Tibia, 27828
Fibula, Fibular
Distal
Closed Treatment, 27788
Open Treatment, 27792
with Fracture
Tibia, 27828
Malleolus
Lateral
Closed Treatment, 27788
Open Treatment, 27792
Proximal
Closed Treatment, 27781
Open Treatment, 27784
Shaft
Closed Treatment, 27781
Open Treatment, 27784
Foot
Sesamoid
Open Treatment, 28531
Frontal Sinus
Open Treatment, 21343, 21344
Great Toe
Closed Treatment, 28495
Open Treatment, 28505
Percutaneous Fixation, 28496
Heel
Closed Treatment, 28405
Open Treatment, 28415
with Bone graft, 28420
Humeral, Humerus
Anatomical neck
Closed Treatment, 23605
Open Treatment, 23615, 23616
Condylar
Lateral
Closed Treatment, 24577
Open Treatment, 24579
Percutaneous Fixation, 24582
Medial
Closed Treatment, 24577
Open Treatment, 24579
Percutaneous Fixation, 24566
Epicondylar
Lateral
Closed Treatment, 24565
Open Treatment, 24575
Percutaneous Fixation, 24566
Medial
Closed Treatment, 24565
Open, 24575
Percutaneous Fixation, 24566
Proximal
Closed Treatment, 23605
Open Treatment, 23615, 23616

Reduction — *continued*
  Fracture — *continued*
    Orbital Floor
      Blowout, 21385-21395
      Open Treatment, 21385-21395
    Palate, Palatal
      Open Treatment, 21422, 21423
    Patella, Patellar
      Open Treatment, 27524
    Pelvic, Pelvis
      Iliac, Ilium
        Open Treatment
          Spine, 27215
          Tuberosity, 27215
          Wing, 27215
    Pelvic Ring
      Closed Treatment, 27194
      Open Treatment, 27217, 27218
      Percutaneous Fixation, 27216
    Phalange, Phalanges, Phalangeal
      Foot
        Closed Treatment, 28515
          Great Toe, 28495, 28505
        Open Treatment, 28525
          Great Toe, 28505
        Percutaneous Fixation, 28496
          Great Toe, 28496
      Hand
        Closed Treatment, 26725
          Distal, 26755
        Open Treatment, 26735
          Distal, 26765
        Percutaneous Fixation, 26727, 26756
    PisiForm
      Closed Treatment, 25635
      Open Treatment, 25645
    Radial, Radius
      Colles
        Closed Treatment, 25605
        Open Treatment, 25620
        Percutaneous Fixation, 25611
      Distal
        Closed Treatment, 25605
          with Fracture
            Ulnar Styloid, 25605, 25620
        Open Treatment, 25620
      Head
        Closed Treatment, 24655
        Open Treatment, 24665, 24666
      Neck
        Closed Treatment, 24655
        Open Treatment, 24665, 24666
      Shaft
        Closed Treatment, 25505
          with Dislocation
            Radio-Ulnar Joint, Distal, 25520
        Open Treatment, 25515
          with Dislocation
            Radio-Ulnar Joint, Distal, 25525,
              25526
            Repair, Triangular Cartilage,
              25526
      Smith
        Closed Treatment, 25605
        Open Treatment, 25620
        Percutaneous Fixation, 25611
    Rib
      Open Treatment, 21805, 21810
    Sacroiliac Joint, 27218
    Sacrum, 27218
    Scaphoid
      Closed Treatment, 25624
      Open Treatment, 25628

Reduction — *continued*
  Fracture — *continued*
    Scapula, Scapular
      Closed Treatment, 23575
      Open Treatment, 23585
    Sesamoid
      Open Treatment, 28531
    Sternum
      Open Treatment, 21825
    Talar, Talus
      Closed Treatment, 28435
      Open Treatment, 28445
      Percutaneous Fixation, 28436
    Tarsal
      Calcaneal
        Closed Treatment, 28405
        Open Treatment, 28415
          With Bone Graft, 28420
        Percutaneous Fixation, 28456
      Cuboid
        Closed Treatment, 28455
        Open Treatment, 28465
        Percutaneous Fixation, 28456
      CuneiForms
        Closed Treatment, 28455
        Open Treatment, 28465
        Percutaneous Fixation, 28456
      Navicular
        Closed Treatment, 28465
        Open Treatment, 28465
        Percutaneous Fixation, 28456
      Navicular Talus
        Closed Treatment, 28435
        Open Treatment, 28445
        Percutaneous Fixation, 28436
    T-Fracture, 27228
    Thigh
      Femur, Femoral
        Condyle
          Lateral
            Closed Treatment, 27510
            Open Treatment, 27514
          Medial
            Closed Treatment, 27510
            Open Treatment, 27514
        Distal
          Closed Treatment, 27510
            Lateral condyle, 27510
            Medial condyle, 27510
          Open, 27514
            Lateral condyle, 27514
            Medial condyle, 27514
        Epiphysis, Epiphyseal
          Closed, 27517
          Open, 27519
        Greater Trochanteric
          Open Treatment, 27248
        Head
          Traumatic, 27254
            with Dislocation Hip, 27254
        Intertrochanter
          Closed Treatment, 27240
          Open Treatment, 27244, 27245
            with Intermedullary Implant,
              27245
        Pertrochanteric, Pertrochanter
          Closed Treatment, 27240
          Open Treatment, 27244, 27245
            with Intermedullary Implant,
              27245

Index

Reduction — Reduction

Reduction — *continued*
  Fracture — *continued*
    Thigh — *continued*
      Femur, Femoral — *continued*
        Proximal End
          Closed Treatment, 27232
          Open Treatment, 27236
            with Prosthetic Replacement,
              27236
        Proximal Neck
          Closed Treatment, 27232
          Open Treatment, 27236
            with Prosthetic Replacement,
              27236
        Shaft
          Closed Treatment, 27502
          Open Treatment, 27506, 27507
            with Intermedullary Implant,
              27245
        Subtrochanteric, Subtrochanter
          Closed Treatment, 27240
          Open Treatment, 27244, 27245
        Supracondylar
          Closed Treatment, 27503
            with Intercondylar Extension,
              27503
        Transcondylar
          Closed Treatment, 27503
            with Intercondylar Extension,
              27503
          Open Treatment, 27511
            with Intercondylar Extension,
              27513
    Thumb
      Bennett, 26645
      Closed Treatment, 26645
      Open Treatment, 26665
      Percutaneous Fixation, 26650
    Tibia and Fibula, 27828
    Tibia, Tibial
      Articular Surface
        Closed Treatment, 27825
        Open Treatment, 27827
          with Fibula, Fibular
            Fracture, 27828
      Condylar
        Bicondylar, 27536
        Unicondylar, 27535
      Distal
        Closed Treatment, 27825
        Open Treatment, 27826
      Pilon
        Closed Treatment, 27825
        Open Treatment, 27827
          with Fibula, Fibular
            Fracture, 27828
      Plafond
        Closed Treatment, 27825
        Open Treatment, 27827
          with Fibula, Fibular
            Fracture, 27828
      Plateau
        Closed Treatment, 27532
        Open Treatment, 27535, 27536
      Proximal Plateau
        Closed Treatment, 27532
        Open Treatment, 27535, 27536
      Shaft
        Closed Treatment, 27752
          with Fibula, Fibular
            Fracture, 27752

Reduction — *continued*
  Fracture — *continued*
    Tibia, Tibial — *continued*
      Shaft — *continued*
        Open Treatment, 27758, 27759
          with Fibula, Fibular
            Fracture, 27758, 27759
          with Intermedullary Implant, 27759
        Percutaneous Fixation, 27756
    Toe
      Closed Treatment, 28515
        Great, 28495
      Open Treatment, 28525
        Great, 28505
      Percutaneous Fixation, 28496
        Great, 28496
    Trachea, Tracheal
      Closed
        Endoscopic Treatment, 31630
    Trans-Scaphoperilunar
      Closed Treatment, 25680
      Open Treatment, 25685
    Trapezium
      Closed Treatment, 25635
      Open Treatment, 25645
    Trapezoid
      Closed Treatment, 25635
      Open Treatment, 25645
    Triquetral
      Closed Treatment, 25635
      Open Treatment, 25645
    Ulna, Ulnar
      Proximal
        Closed Treatment, 24675
        Open Treatment, 24685
          with Dislocation
            Radial Head, 24635
          Monteggia, 24635
      Shaft
        Closed Treatment, 25535
          And
            Radial, Radius, 25565
        Open Treatment, 25545
          and
            Radial, Radius, 25574, 25575
        Styloid, 25650
    Vertebral
      Closed Treatment, 22315
      Open Treatment, 22325-22328, 63081-
        63091
    Zygomatic Arch, 21356-21366
      Open Treatment, 21356-21366
        with Malar Area, 21360
        with Malar Tripod, 21360
      Percutaneous, 21355
  Lung Volume, 32491
  Mammoplasty, 19318
  Masseter Muscle/Bone, 21295, 21296
  Osteoplasty
    Facial Bones, 21209
  Pregnancy
    Multifetal, 59866
  Renal Pedicle
    Torsion, 53899
  Separation
    Craniofacial
      Open, 21432-21436
  Skull
    Craniomegalic, 62115-62117
  Subluxation
    Pelvic ring
      Closed, 27194

Removal — *continued*
  Drug Delivery Implant, 11982, 11983
  Ear Wax
    Auditory Canal, External, 69210
  Electrode
    Brain, 61535, 61880
    Heart, 33238
    Nerve, 64585
    Spinal Cord, 63660
  External Fixation System, 20694
  Eye
    with Bone, 65112
    with Implant
      Muscles Attached, 65105
      Muscles not Attached, 65103
    with Muscle or Myocutaneous Flap, 65114
    without Implant, 65101
    Bone, 67414, 67445
    Ocular Contents
      with Implant, 65093
      without Implant, 65091
    Orbital Contents Only, 65110
  Fallopian Tube
    Laparoscopy, 58661
  Fat
    Lipectomy, 15876-15879
  Fecal Impaction
    Rectum, 45915
  Fibrin Deposit, 32150
  Fixation Device, 20670, 20680
  Foreign Bodies
    Adenoid, 42999
    Anal, 46608
    Ankle Joint, 27610, 27620
    Arm
      Lower, 25248
      Upper, 24200, 24201
    Auditory Canal, External, 69200
      with Anesthesia, 69205
    Bile Duct, 43269
    Bladder, 52310, 52315
    Brain, 61570, 62163
    Bronchi, 31635
    Colon, 44025, 44390, 45379
    Colon-Sigmoid, 45332
    Conjunctival Embedded, 65210
    Cornea
      with Slip Lamp, 65222
      without Slit Lamp, 65220
    Duodenum, 44010
    Elbow, 24000, 24101, 24200, 24201
    Esophagus, 43020, 43045, 43215, 74235
    External Eye, 65205
    Eyelid, 67938
    Finger, 26075, 26080
    Foot, 28190-28193
    Gastrointestinal, Upper, 43247
    Gum, 41805
    Hand, 26070
    Hip, 27033, 27086, 27087
    Hysteroscopy, 58562
    Interphalangeal Joint
      Toe, 28024
    Intertarsal Joint, 28020
    Intestines, Small, 44020, 44363
    Intraocular, 65235
    Kidney, 50561, 50580
    Knee Joint, 27310, 27331, 27372
    Lacrimal Duct, 68530
    Lacrimal Gland, 68530
    Larynx, 31511, 31530, 31531, 31577
    Leg, Upper, 27372

Removal — *continued*
  Foreign Bodies — *continued*
    Lung, 32151
    Mandible, 41806
    Maxillary Sinus, 31299
    Mediastinum, 39000, 39010
    Metatarsophalangeal Joint, 28022
    Mouth, 40804, 40805
    Muscle, 20520, 20525
      Stimulator
        Skeletal, 20999
    Nose, 30300
      Anesthesia, under, 30310
      Lateral Rhinotomy, 30320
    Orbit, 61334, 67413, 67430
      with Bone Flap, 67430
      without Bone Flap, 67413
    Pancreatic Duct, 43269
    Patella
      See Patellectomy
    Pelvis, 27086, 27087
    Penile Tissue, 54115
    Penis, 54115
    Pericardium, 33020
      Endoscopic, 32658
    Peritoneum, 49085
    Pharynx, 42809
    Pleura, 32150, 32151
      Endoscopic, 32653
    Posterior Segment
      Magnetic Extraction, 65260
      Nonmagnetic Extraction, 65265
    Rectum, 45307, 45915
    Scrotum, 55120
    Shoulder, 23040, 23044
      Complicated, 23332
      Deep, 23331
      Subcutaneous, 23330
    Skin
      with Debridement, 11010-11012
    Stomach, 43500
    Subcutaneous, 10120, 10121
      with Debridement, 11010-11012
    Tarsometatarsal Joint, 28020
    Tendon Sheath, 20520, 20525
    Toe, 28022
    Ureter, 50961, 50980
    Urethra, 52310, 52315
    Uterus, 58562
    Vagina, 57415
    Wrist, 25040, 25101, 25248
  Hair
    by Electrolysis, 17380
  Halo, 20665
  Hearing Aid
    Bone Conduction, 69711
  Hematoma
    Brain, 61312-61315
  Implant, 20670, 20680
    Ankle, 27704
    Contraceptive Capsules, 11976, 11977
    Elbow, 24160
    Eye, 67120, 67121
    Finger, 26320
    Hand, 26320
    Pin, 20670, 20680
    Radius, 24164
    Rod, 20670, 20680
    Screw, 20670, 20680
    Wrist, 25449
  Infusion Pump
    Intra-Arterial, 36262

Removal — *continued*
Tissue
Vaginal, Partial, 57107
Tissue Expanders, 11971
Transplant Intestines, 44137
Transplant Kidney, 50370
Tube
Ear, Middle, 69424
Finger, 26392, 26416
Hand, 26392, 26416
Nephrostomy, 50389
Tumor
Temporal Bone, 69970
Ureter
Ligature, 50940
Stent, 50382-50387
Urethral Stent
Bladder, 52310, 52315
Urethra, 52310, 52315
Vagina
Partial
with Nodes, 57109
Tissue, 57106
Wall, 57107, 57110, 57111
Vein
Clusters, 37785
Perforation, 37760
Saphenous, 37718-37735, 37780
Secondary, 37785
Varicose, 37765, 37766
Venous Access Device
Obstruction, 75901-75902
Ventilating Tube
Ear, Middle, 69424
Ventricular Assist Device, 33977, 33978
Intracorporeal, 33980
Vitreous
Partial, 67005, 67010
Wire
Anal, 46754
Renal Abscess
See Abscess, Kidney
Renal Arteries
See Artery, Renal
Renal Autotransplantation
See Autotransplantation, Renal
Renal Calculus
See Calculus, Removal, Kidney
Renal Cyst
See Cyst, Kidney
Renal Dialyses
See Hemodialysis
Renal Disease Services
Arteriovenous Fistula
Revision
without Thrombectomy, 36833
Arteriovenous Shunt
Revision with Thrombectomy, 36833
Thrombectomy, 36831
End Stage Renal Disease, 90918-90925
Hemodialysis, 90935, 90937
Blood Flow Study, 90940
Hemoperfusion, 90997
Patient Training, 90989, 90993
Peritoneal Dialysis, 90945-90947
Renal Transplantation
See Kidney, Transplantation
Renin, 80408, 80416, 84244
Peripheral Vein, 80417
Renin-Converting Enzyme, 82164

Reoperation
Carotid
Thromboendarterectomy, 35390
Coronary Artery Bypass
Valve Procedure, 33530
Distal Vessel Bypass, 35700
Repair
See Revision
Abdomen, 49900
Hernia, 49491-49525, 49565, 49570, 49582-49590
Omphalocele, 49600-49611
Suture, 49900
Abdominal Wall, 15831
Anal
Anomaly, 46744-46748
Fistula, 46288, 46706-46716
Stricture, 46700, 46705
Anastomosis
Cyst, 47716
Aneurysm
Aorta, 33877, 33880-33886, 34800-34805, 34825-34832, 75952, 75953
Arteriovenous, 36834
Intracranial Artery, 61697-61708
Ankle
Ligament, 27695-27698
Tendon, 27612, 27650-27654, 27680-27687
Aorta, 33320-33322, 33802, 33803
Coarctation, 33840-33851
Graft, 33860-33877
Sinus of Valsalva, 33702-33720
Thoracic
Endovascular 33880-33891
Prosthesis Placement, 33886
Radiological Supervison and Interpretation, 75956-75959
Aortic Arch
with Cardiopulmonary Bypass, 33853
without Cardiopulmonary Bypass, 33852
Aortic Valve, 33400-33403
Obstruction
Outflow Tract, 33414
Septal Hypertrophy, 33416
Stenosis, 33415
Valvuloplasty, 33400-33403
Arm
Lower, 25260, 25263, 25270
Fasciotomy, 24495
Secondary, 25265, 25272, 25274
Tendon, 25290
Tendon Sheath, 25275
Muscle, 24341
Tendon, 24332, 24341, 25280, 25295, 25310-25316
Upper
Muscle Revision, 24330, 24331
Muscle Transfer, 24301, 24320
Tendon Lengthening, 24305
Tendon Revision, 24320
Tendon Transfer, 24301
Tenotomy, 24310
Arteriovenous Aneurysm, 36834
Arteriovenous Fistula
Abdomen, 35182
Acquired or Traumatic, 35189
Head, 35180
Acquired or Traumatic, 35188
Lower Extremity, 35184
Acquired or Traumatic, 35190
Neck, 35180
Acquired or Traumatic, 35188

Repair — *continued*
  Arteriovenous Fistula — *continued*
    Thorax, 35182
      Acquired or Traumatic, 35189
    Upper Extremity, 35184
      Acquired or Traumatic, 35190
  Arteriovenous Malformation
    Intracranial, 61680-61692
    Intracranial Artery, 61705, 61708
    Spinal Artery, 62294
    Spinal Cord, 63250-63252
  Artery
    Angioplasty, 75962-75968
    Aorta, 35452, 35472
    Axillary, 35458
    Brachiocephalic, 35458, 35475
    Bypass Graft, 35500-35571, 35601-35683, 35691-35700
    Bypass In-Situ, 35583-35587
    Bypass Venous Graft, 33510-33516, 35510-35525
    Coronary, 33502, 33505, 33506-33507
    Femoral, 35456, 35474
    Iliac, 34900, 35454, 35473
    Occlusive Disease, 35001, 35005-35021, 35045, 35081, 35091, 35102, 35111, 35121, 35131, 35141, 35151
    Popliteal, 35456, 35474
    Pulmonary, 33690, 33925-33926
    Renal, 35450
    Renal or Visceral, 35471
    Subclavian, 35458
    Thromboendarterectomy, 35301-35321, 35341-35390
    Tibioperoneal, 35459, 35470
    Venous Graft, 33510-33516, 35510-35525
    Viscera, 35450, 35471
  Arytenoid Cartilage, 31400
  Atrial Fibrillation, 33253
  Bile Duct, 47701
    with Intestines, 47760, 47780, 47785
    Cyst, 47716
    Wound, 47900
  Bladder
    Exstrophy, 51940
    Fistula, 44660, 44661, 45800, 45805, 51880-51925
    Neck, 51845
    Resection, 52500
    Wound, 51860, 51865
  Blepharoptosis
    Frontalis Muscle Technique
      with Fascial Sling, 67902
  Blood Vessel(s)
    Abdomen, 35221
      with Other Graft, 35281
      with Vein Graft, 35251
    Chest, 35211, 35216
      with Other Graft, 35271, 35276
      with Vein Graft, 35241, 35246
    Finger, 35207
    Graft Defect, 35870
    Hand, 35207
    Kidney, 50100
    Lower Extremity, 35226
      with Other Graft, 35286
      with Vein Graft, 35256
    Neck, 35201
      with Other Graft, 35261
      with Vein Graft, 35231
    Upper Extremity, 35206
      with Other Graft, 35266
      with Vein Graft, 35236

Repair — *continued*
  Body Cast, 29720
  Brain
    Wound, 61571
  Breast
    Suspension, 19316
  Bronchi
    Fistula, 32815
  Brow Ptosis, 67900
  Bunion, 28290-28299
  Bypass Graft, 35901-35907
    Fistula, 35870
  Calcaneus
    Osteotomy, 28300
  Cannula, 36860, 36861
  Carpal, 25440
  Carpal Bone, 25431
  Cervix
    Cerclage, 57700
      Abdominal, 59320, 59325
    Suture, 57720
  Chest Wall, 32905
    Closure, 32810
    Fistula, 32906
    Pectus Excavatum, 21740
  Chin
    Augmentation, 21120, 21123
    Osteotomy, 21121-21123
  Clavicle
    Osteotomy, 23480, 23485
  Cleft Hand, 26580
  Cleft Lip, 40525, 40527, 40700-40761
    Nasal Deformity, 40700, 40701, 40720, 40761
  Cleft Palate
    See Cleft Palate Repair
  Colon
    Fistula, 44650-44661
    Hernia, 44050
    Malrotation, 44055
    Obstruction, 44050
  Cornea
    See Cornea, Repair
  Coronary Chamber Fistula, 33500, 33501
  Cyst
    Bartholin's Gland, 56440
    Choledochal, 47716
    Liver, 47300
  Defibrillator, Heart, 33218, 33220
  Diaphragm
    for Eventration, 39545
    Hernia, 39502-39541
    Lacerations, 39501
  Ductus Arteriosus, 33820-33824
  Ear, Middle
    Oval Window Fistula, 69666
    Round Window Fistula, 69667
  Elbow
    Fasciotomy, 24350-24356
    Hemiepiphyseal Arrest, 24470
    Ligament, 24343-24346
    Muscle, 24341
    Muscle Transfer, 24301
    Tendon, 24340-24342
      Each, 24341
    Tendon Lengthening, 24305
    Tendon Transfer, 24301
    Tennis Elbow, 24350-24356
  Encephalocele, 62121
  Enterocele
    Hysterectomy, 58270, 58294
    Epididymis, 54900, 54901

Repair — *continued*
  Epispadias, 54380-54390
  Esophagus, 43300, 43310, 43313
    Esophagogastrostomy, 43320
    Esophagojejunostomy, 43340, 43341
    Fistula, 43305, 43312, 43314, 43420, 43425
    Fundoplasty, 43324, 43325
    Muscle, 43330, 43331
    Preexisting Perforation, 43405
    Varices, 43401
    Wound, 43410, 43415
  Eye
    Ciliary Body, 66680
      Suture, 66682
    Conjunctiva, 65270-65273
      Wound, 65270-65273
    Cornea, 65275
      with Glue, 65286
      Astigmatism, 65772, 65775
      Wound, 65275-65285
        Dehiscence, 66250
    Fistula
      Lacrimal Gland, 68770
    Iris
      with Ciliary Body, 66680
      Suture, 66682
    Lacrimal Duct
      Canaliculi, 68700
    Lacrimal Punctum, 68705
    Retina
      Detachment, 67101-67112
    Sclera
      with Glue, 65286
      with Graft, 66225
      ReinForcement, 67250, 67255
      Staphyloma, 66220, 66225
      Wound, 65286, 66250
    Strabismus
      Chemodenervation, 67345
    Symblepharon
      with Graft, 68335
      without Graft, 68330
      Division, 68340
    Trabeculae, 65855
  Eyebrow
    Ptosis, 67900
  Eyelashes
    Epilation
      by Forceps, 67820
      by Other than Forceps, 67825
    Incision of Lid Margin, 67830
      with Free Mucous Membrane Graft, 67835
  Eyelid, 21280, 21282
    Ectropion
      Blepharoplasty, 67916, 67917
      Suture, 67914
      Thermocauterization, 67915
    Entropion
      Blepharoplasty, 67923, 67924
      Suture, 67921-67924
      Thermocauterization, 67922
    Excisional, 67961, 67966
    Lagophthalmos, 67912
    Ptosis
      Conjunctivo-Tarso-Muller's Muscle-Levator Resection, 67908
      Frontalis Muscle Technique, 67901, 67902
      Levator Resection, 67903, 67904
      Reduction of Overcorrection, 67909
      Superior Rectus Technique, 67906

Repair — *continued*
  Eyelid — *continued*
    Retraction, 67911
    Wound
      Suture, 67930, 67935
  Eye Muscles
    Strabismus
      Adjustable Sutures, 67335
      One Horizontal Muscle, 67311
      One Vertical Muscle, 67314
      Posterior Fixation Suture Technique, 67334, 67335
      Previous Surgery not Involving Extraocular Muscles, 67331
      Release Extensive Scar Tissue, 67343
      Superior Oblique Muscle, 67318
      Two Horizontal Muscles, 67312
      Two or More Vertical Muscles, 67316
    Wound
      Extraocular Muscle, 65290
  Facial Bones, 21208, 21209
  Facial Nerve
    Paralysis, 15840-15845
    Suture
      Intratemporal, Lateral to Geniculate Ganglion, 69740
      Intratemporal, Medial to Geniculate Ganglion, 69745
  Fallopian Tube, 58752
    Anastomosis, 58750
    Create Stoma, 58770
  Fascial Defect, 50728
  Femur, 27470, 27472
    with Graft, 27170
    Epiphysis, 27475-27485, 27742
      Arrest, 27185
      by Pinning, 27176
      by Traction, 27175
      Open Treatment, 27177, 27178
      Osteoplasty, 27179
      Osteotomy, 27181
    Muscle Transfer, 27110
    Osteotomy, 27140, 27151, 27450, 27454
      with Fixation, 27165
      with Open Reduction, 27156
      Femoral Neck, 27161
  Fibula
    Epiphysis, 27477-27485, 27730-27742
    Osteotomy, 27707-27712
  Finger
    Claw Finger, 26499
    Macrodactyly, 26590
    Polydactylous, 26587
    Syndactyly, 26560-26562
    Tendon
      Extensor, 26415-26434, 26445, 26449, 26455
      Flexor, 26356-26358, 26440, 26442
      Joint Stabilization, 26474
      PIP Joint, 26471
      Toe Transfer, 26551-26556
      Trigger, 26055
      Volar Plate, 26548
      Web Finger, 26560
  Fistula
    Carotid-Cavernous, 61710
    Ileoanal Pouch, 46710, 46712
    Mastoid, 69700
    Rectovaginal, 57308
  Foot
    Fascia, 28250
    Muscles, 28250
    Tendon, 28200-28226, 28238

Repair — *continued*
  Laceration, Skin — *continued*
    Hand, Hands — *continued*
      Superficial, 12001-12007
    Leg, Legs
      Complex, 13120-13122
      Intermediate, 12031-12037
      Layered, 12031-12037
      Simple, 12001-12007
      Superficial, 12001-12007
    Lip, Lips
      Complex, 13150-13153
      Intermediate, 12051-12057
      Layered, 12051-12057
      Simple, 12011-12018
      Superficial, 12011-12018
    Lower
      Arm, Arms
        Complex, 13120-13122
        Intermediate, 12031-12037
        Layered, 12031-12037
        Simple, 12001-12007
        Superficial, 12001-12007
      Extremity, Extremities
        Complex, 13120-13122
        Intermediate, 12031-12037
        Layered, 12031-12037
        Simple, 12001-12007
        Superficial, 12001-12007
      Leg, Legs
        Complex, 13120-13122
        Intermediate, 12031-12037
        Layered, 12031-12037
        Simple, 12001-12007
        Superficial, 12001-12007
    Mouth
      Complex, 13131-13133
    Mucous Membrane
      Complex/Intermediate, 12051-12057
      Layered, 12051-12057
      Simple, 12011-12018
      Superficial, 12011-12018
    Neck
      Complex, 13131-13133
      Intermediate, 12041-12047
      Layered, 12041-12047
      Simple, 12001-12007
      Superficial, 12001-12007
    Nose
      Complex, 13150-13153
      Complex/Intermediate, 12051-12057
      Layered, 12051-12057
      Simple, 12011-12018
      Superficial, 12011-12018
    Palm, Palms
      Complex, 13131-13133
      Intermediate, 12041-12047
      Layered, 12041-12047
      Layered Simple, 12001-12007
      Superficial, 12001-12007
    Scalp
      Complex, 13120-13122
      Intermediate, 12031-12037
      Layered, 12031-12037
      Simple, 12001-12007
      Superficial, 12001-12007
    Toe, Toes
      Complex, 13131-13133
      Intermediate, 12041-12047
      Layered, 12041-12047
      Simple, 12001-12007
      Superficial, 12001-12007

Repair — *continued*
  Laceration, Skin — *continued*
    Trunk
      Complex, 13100-13102
      Intermediate, 12031-12037
      Layered, 12031-12037
      Simple, 12001-12007
      Superficial, 12001-12007
    Upper
      Arm, Arms
        Complex, 13120-13122
        Intermediate, 12031-12037
        Layered, 12031-12037
        Simple, 12001-12007
        Superficial, 12001-12007
      Extremity
        Complex, 13120-13122
        Intermediate, 12031-12037
        Layered, 12031-12037
        Simple, 12001-12007
        Superficial, 12001-12007
      Leg, Legs
        Complex, 13120-13122
        Intermediate, 12031-12037
        Layered, 12031-12037
        Simple, 12001-12007
        Superficial, 12001-12007
  Larynx
    Reinnervation
      Neuromuscular Pedicle, 31590
  Leg
    Lower
      Fascia, 27656
      Tendon, 27658-27692
    Upper
      Muscles, 27385, 27386, 27400, 27430
      Tendon, 27393-27400
  Ligament
    See Ligament, Repair
  Lip, 40650-40654
    Cleft Lip, 40700-40761
    Fistula, 42260
  Liver
    Abscess, 47300
    Cyst, 47300
    Wound, 47350-47361
  Lung
    Hernia, 32800
    Pneumolysis, 32940
    Tear, 32110
  Mastoidectomy
    with Apicectomy, 69605
    with Tympanoplasty, 69604
    Complete, 69601
    Modified Radical, 69602
    Radical, 69603
  Maxilla
    Osteotomy, 21206
  Mesentery, 44850
  Metacarpal
    Lengthen, 26568
    Nonunion, 26546
    Osteotomy, 26565
  Metacarpophalangeal Joint
    Capsulodesis, 26516-26518
    Collateral Ligament, 26540-26542
    Fusion, 26516-26518
  Metatarsal, 28322
    Osteotomy, 28306-28309
  Microsurgery, 69990
  Mitral Valve, 33420-33427

Index

Repair — Repair

Repair — *continued*
  Wrist — *continued*
    Tendon, 25280-25316
      Sheath, 25275
    Total Replacement, 25446
Repeat Surgeries
  See Reoperation
Replacement
  Acellular Dermal, 15170-15176
  Aortic Valve, 33405-33413
  Artificial Heart
    Intracorporeal, 0052T-0053T
  Cerebrospinal Fluid Shunt, 62160, 62194,
      62225, 62230
  Contact Lens, 92326
    See Contact Lens Services
  Elbow
    Total, 24363
  Electrode
    Heart, 33210, 33211, 33216, 33217
  Eye
    Drug Delivery System, 67121
  Gastrostomy Tube, 43760
  Hearing Aid
    Bone Conduction, 69710
  Heart
    Defibrillator
      Leads, 33249
  Hip, 27130, 27132
    Revision, 27134-27138
  Implant
    Bone
      for External Speech Processor/Cochlear
          Stimulator, 69717, 69718
  Knee
    Total, 27447
  Mitral Valve, 33430
  Nerve, 64726
  Neurostimulator
    Pulse Generator/Receiver
      Intracranial, 61885
      Peripheral Nerve, 64590
      Spinal, 63685
  Ossicles
    with Prosthesis, 69633, 69637
  Ossicular Replacement
    See TORP (Total Ossicular Replacement
        Prosthesis)
  Pacemaker, 33206-33208
    Catheter, 33210
    Electrode, 33210, 33211, 33216, 33217
  Pacing Cardioverter-Defibrillator
    Leads, 33243, 33244
    Pulse Generator Only, 33241
  Penile
    Prosthesis, 54410, 54411, 54416, 54417
  Prosthesis
    Skull, 62143
    Urethral Sphincter, 53448
  Pulmonary Valve, 33475
  Pulse Generator
    Brain, 61885
    Peripheral Nerve, 64590
    Spinal Cord, 63685
  Receiver
    Brain, 61885
    Peripheral Nerve, 64590
    Spinal Cord, 63685
  Skull Plate, 62143
  Spinal Cord
    Reservoir, 62360

Replacement — *continued*
  Stent
    Ureteral, 50382, 50387
  Tissue Expanders
    Skin, 11970
  Total Replacement
    See Hip, Total Replacement
  Total Replacement Heart System
    Intracorporeal, 0052T-0053T
  Tricuspid Valve, 33465
  Ureter
    with Intestines, 50840
    Electronic Stimulator, 53899
  Uterus
    Inverted, 59899
  Venous Access Device, 36582, 36583, 36585
    Catheter, 36578
  Venous Catheter
    Central, 36580, 36581, 36584
Replantation, Reimplantation
  Adrenal Tissue, 60699
  Arm, Upper, 20802
  Digit, 20816, 20822
  Foot, 20838
  Forearm, 20805
  Hand, 20808
  Scalp, 17999
  Thumb, 20824, 20827
Report Preparation
  Extended, Medical, 99080
  Psychiatric, 90889
Reposition
  Toe to Hand, 26551-26556
Repositioning
  Central Venous Catheter, Previously Placed,
      36597
  Electrode
    Heart, 33215, 33216, 33217, 33226
  Gastrostomy Tube, 43761
  Heart
    Defibrillator
      Leads, 33215, 33216, 33226, 33249
  Intraocular Lens, 66825
  Tricuspid Valve, 33468
Reproductive Tissue
  Cryopreserved
  Preparation
    Thawing, 89354
  Storage, 89344
Reprogramming
  Shunt
    Brain, 62252
Reptilase Test, 85635
  Time, 85635
Reptilase Time
  See Thrombin Time
Resection
  Abdomen, 51597
  Aortic Valve Stenosis, 33415
  Bladder Diverticulum, 52305
  Bladder Neck
    Transurethral, 52500
  Brain Lobe
    See Lobectomy, Brain
  Chest Wall, 19260-19272
  Diaphragm, 39560, 39561
  Humeral Head, 23195
  Intestines, Small
    Laparoscopic, 44202, 44203

Schlatter Operation Total Gastrectomy
See Excision, Stomach, Total

Schlicter Test, 87197

Schocket Procedure, 66180
See Aqueous Shunt

Schuchard Procedure
Osteotomy
Maxilla, 21206

Schwannoma, Acoustic
See Brain, Tumor, Excision

Sciatic Nerve
Decompression, 64712
Injection
Anesthetic, 64445, 64446
Lesion
Excision, 64786
Neuroma
Excision, 64786
Neuroplasty, 64712
Release, 64712
Repair
Suture, 64858

Scintigraphy
See Computed Tomographic Scintigraphy
See Emission Computerized Tomography
See Nuclear Medicine

Scissoring
Skin Tags, 11200, 11201

Sclera
Excision, 66130
Sclerectomy with Punch or Scissors, 66160
Fistulization
Iridencleisis or Iridotasis, 66165
Sclerectomy with Punch or Scissors with
Iridectomy, 66160
Thermocauterization with Iridectomy, 66155
Trabeculectomy ab Externo in Absence of
Previous Surgery, 66170
Trephination with Iridectomy, 66150
Incision
Iridencleisis or Iridotasis, 66165
Sclerectomy with Punch or Scissors with
Iridectomy, 66160
Thermocauterization with Iridectomy, 66155
Trabeculectomy ab Externo in Absence of
Previous Surgery, 66170
Trephination with Iridectomy, 66150
Lesion
Excision, 66130
Repair
with Glue, 65286
ReinForcement
with Graft, 67255
without Graft, 67250
Staphyloma
with Graft, 66225
without Graft, 66220
Wound (Operative), 66250
Tissue Glue, 65286

Scleral Buckling Operation
Retina, Repair, Detachment, 67107-67112

Scleral Ectasia
See Staphyloma, Sclera

Sclerectomy, 66160

Sclerotherapy
Venous, 36468-36471

Sclerotomy
See Incision, Sclera

Screening, Drug
See Drug, Screen

Scribner Cannulization, 36810

Scrotal Varices
See Varicocele

Scrotoplasty, 55175, 55180

Scrotum
Abscess
Incision and Drainage, 54700, 55100
Excision, 55150
Exploration, 55110
Hematoma
Incision and Drainage, 54700
Removal
Foreign Body, 55120
Repair, 55175, 55180
Ultrasound, 76870
Unlisted Services and Procedures, 55899

Scrub Typhus, 86000

Second Look Surgery
See Reoperation

Section
See Decompression
Cesarean
See Cesarean Delivery
Cranial Nerve, 61460
Spinal Access, 63191
Dentate Ligament, 63180, 63182
Gasserian Ganglion
Sensory Root, 61450
Medullary Tract, 61470
Mesencephalic Tract, 61480
Nerve Root, 63185, 63190
Spinal Accessory Nerve, 63191
Spinal Cord Tract, 63194-63199
Tentorium Cerebelli, 61440
Vestibular Nerve
Transcranial Approach, 69950
Translabyrinthine Approach, 69915

Sedation
Conscious (Moderate), 99143-99150

Seddon-Brookes Procedure, 24320

Sedimentation Rate
Blood Cell
Automated, 85652
Manual, 85651

Segmentectomy
Breast, 19160-19162
Lung, 32484

Selenium, 84255

Self Care
See Physical Medicine/ Therapy/Occupational
Therapy
Training, 97535, 99509

Sella Turcica
CT Scan, 70480-70482
X-ray, 70240

Semen Analysis, 89300-89321
with Sperm Isolation, 89260-89261
Sperm Analysis
Antibodies, 89325
Hyaluronan Binding Assay, 0087T

Semenogelase
See Antigen, Prostate Specific

Semicircular Canal
Incision
Fenestration, 69820
Revised, 69840

Semilunar
Bone
　See Lunate
Ganglion
　See Gasserian Ganglion
Seminal Vesicle
Cyst
　Excision, 55680
Excision, 55650
Incision, 55600, 55605
Mullerian Duct
　Excision, 55680
Unlisted Services and Procedures, 55899
Seminal Vesicles
Vesiculography, 74440
X-ray with Contrast, 74440
Seminin
　See Antigen, Prostate Specific
Semiquantitative, 81005
Sengstaaken Tamponade
Esophagus, 43460
Senning Procedure
　See Repair, Great Arteries; Revision
Repair, Great Arteries, 33774-33777
Senning Type, 33774-33777
Sensitivity Study
Antibiotic
　Agar, 87181
　Disc, 87184
　Enzyme Detection, 87185
　Macrobroth, 87188
　MIC, 87186
　Microtiter, 87186
　MLC, 87187
　Mycobacteria, 87190
Antiviral Drugs
　HIV-1
　　Tissue Culture, 87904
Sensor, Fetal Oximetry
Insertion
　Cervix, 0021T
　Vagina, 0021T
Sensorimotor Exam, 92060
Sensory Nerve
Common
　Repair/Suture, 64834
Sensory Testing
Quantitative (QST), Per Extremity
　Cooling Stimuli, 0108T
　Heat-Pain Stimuli, 0109T
　Touch Pressure Stimuli, 0106T
　Using Other Stimuli, 0110T
　Vibration Stimuli, 0107T
Sentinel Node
Injection Procedure, 38792
Separation
Craniofacial
　Closed Treatment, 21431
　Open Treatment, 21432-21436
Septal Defect
Repair, 33813, 33814
Septectomy
Atrial, 33735-33737
　Balloon Type, 92992
　Blade Method, 92993
Closed
　See Septostomy, Atrial
Submuccous Nasal
　See Nasal Septum, Submuccous Resection

Septic Abortion
　See Abortion, Septic
Septoplasty, 30520
Septostomy
Atrial, 33735-33737
　Balloon Type, 92992
　Blade Method, 92993
Septum, Nasal
　See Nasal Septum
Sequestrectomy
with Alveolectomy, 41830
Calcaneus, 28120
Carpal, 25145
Clavicle, 23170
Forearm, 25145
Humeral Head, 23174
Humerus, 24134
Olecranon Process, 24138
Radius, 24136, 25145
Scapula, 23172
Skull, 61501
Talus, 28120
Ulna, 24138, 25145
Wrist, 25145
Serialography
Aorta, 75625
Serodiagnosis, Syphilis
　See Serologic Test for Syphilis
Serologic Test for Syphilis, 86592, 86593
Seroma, 10140
Incision and Drainage
　Skin, 10140
Serotonin, 84260
Serum
Albumin
　See Albumin, Serum
Antibody Identification
　Pretreatment, 86975-86978
CPK
　See Creatine Kinase, Total
Serum Immune Globulin, 90281-90283
Serum Globulin Immunization, 90281, 90283
Sesamoid Bone
Excision, 28315
Finger
　Excision, 26185
Foot
　Fracture, 28530, 28531
Thumb
　Excision, 26185
Sesamoidectomy
Toe, 28315
Severing of Blepharorrhaphy
　See Tarsorrhaphy, Severing
Sever Procedure, 23020
Sex Change Operation
Female to Male, 55980
Male to Female, 55970
Sex Chromatin
See Barr Bodies
Sex Chromatin Identification, 88130, 88140
Sex Hormone Binding Globulin, 84270
Sex-Linked Ichthyoses
　See Syphilis Test
SG, 84315, 93503
SGOT, 84450
SGPT, 84460

Shunt(s) — *continued*
  Brain
    Creation, 62180-62223
    Removal, 62256, 62258
    Replacement, 62160, 62194, 62225, 62230, 62258
    Reprogramming, 62252
  Cerebrospinal Fluid, 62200
    See Cerebrospinal Fluid Shunt
    Thomas Shunt, 36835
  Creation
    Arteriovenous
      with Bypass Graft, 35686
      with Graft, 36825, 36830
      Direct, 36821
      ECMO, 36822
        Isolated with Chemotherapy Perfusion, 36823
      Thomas Shunt, 36835
      Transposition, 36820
  Fetal, 59076
  Great Vessel
    Aorta
      Pulmonary, 33924
    Aortic Pulmonary Artery
      Ascending, 33755
      Descending, 33762
    Central, 33764
    Subclavian-Pulmonary Artery, 33750
    Vena Cava to Pulmonary Artery, 33766, 33767
  Intra-atrial, 33735-33737
  LeVeen
    See LeVeen Shunt
  Nonvascular
    X-ray, 75809
  Peritoneal
    Venous
      Injection, 49427
      Ligation, 49428
      Removal, 49429
    X-ray, 75809
  Pulmonary Artery
    See Pulmonary Artery, Shunt
  Revision
    Arteriovenous, 36832
  Spinal Cord
    Creation, 63740, 63741
    Irrigation, 63744
    Removal, 63746
    Replacement, 63744
  Superior Mesenteric-Cavel
    See Anastomosis, Caval to Mesenteric
  Ureter to Colon, 50815
  Ventriculocisternal with Valve
    See Ventriculocisternostomy
Shuntogram, 75809
Sialic Acid, 84275
Sialodochoplasty, 42500, 42505
Sialogram
  See Sialography
Sialography, 70390
Sialolithotomy, 42330, 42340
Sickling
  Electrophoresis, 83020
Siderocytes, 85536
Siderophilin
  See Transferrin
Sigmoid
  See Colon-Sigmoid

Sigmoid Bladder
  Cystectomy, 51590
Sigmoidoscopy
  Ablation
    Polyp, 45339
    Tumor, 45339
  Biopsy, 45331
  Collection
    Specimen, 45331
  Exploration, 45330
  Hemorrhage Control, 45334
  Injection
    Submucosal, 45335
  Needle Biopsy, 45342
  Placement
    Stent, 45345
  Removal
    Foreign Body, 45332
    Polyp, 45333, 45338
    Tumor, 45333, 45338
  Repair
    Volvulus, 45337
  Ultrasound, 45341, 45342
Signal-Averaged Electrocardiography
  See Electrocardiogram
Silica, 84285
Silicon Dioxide
  See Silica
Silicone
  Contouring Injections, 11950-11954
Silver Procedure, 28290
Simple Mastectomies
  See Mastectomy
Single Photon Absorptiometry
  See Absorptiometry, Single Photon
Single Photon Emission Computed Tomography
  See SPECT
Sinogram, 76080
Sinus
  Ethmoidectomy
    Excision, 31254
  Pilonidal
    See Cyst, Pilonidal
Sinusectomy, Ethmoid
  See Ethmoidectomy
Sinuses
  Ethmoid
    with Nasal
      Sinus Endoscopy, 31254, 31255
    Excision, 31200-31205
    Repair of Cerebrospinal Leak, 31290
  Frontal
    Destruction, 31080-31085
    Exploration, 31070, 31075
      with Nasal
        Sinus Endoscopy, 31276
    Fracture
      Open Treatment, 21343, 21344
    Incision, 31070-31087
  Injection, 20500
    Diagnostic, 20501
  Maxillary
    Antrostomy, 31256, 31267
    Excision, 31225, 31230
    Exploration, 31020-31033
      with Nasal/Sinus Endoscopy, 31233
    Incision, 31020-31032, 31256, 31267
    Irrigation, 31000
    Skull Base Surgery, 61581

Skin — *continued*
  Wound Repair — *continued*
    Lip, Lips — *continued*
      Superficial, 12011-12018
    Lower
      Arm, Arms
        Complex, 13120-13122
        Intermediate, 12031-12037
        Layered, 12031-12037
        Simple, 12001-12007
        Superficial, 12001-12007
      Extremity, Extremities
        Complex, 13120-13122
        Intermediate, 12031-12037
        Layered, 12031-12037
        Simple, 12001-12007
        Superficial, 12001-12007
      Leg, Legs
        Complex, 13120-13122
        Intermediate, 12031-12037
        Layered, 12031-12037
        Simple, 12001-12007
        Superficial, 12001-12007
    Mouth
      Complex, 13131-13133
    Mucous Membrane
      Complex/Intermediate, 12051-12057
      Layered, 12051-12057
      Simple, 12011-12018
      Superficial, 12011-12018
    Neck
      Complex, 13131-13133
      Intermediate, 12041-12047
      Layered, 12041-12047
      Simple, 12001-12007
      Superficial, 12001-12007
    Nose
      Complex, 13150-13153
      Intermediate, 12051-12057
      Layered, 12051-12057
      Simple, 12011-12018
      Superficial, 12011-12018
    Palm, Palms
      Complex, 13131-13133
      Intermediate, 12041-12047
      Layered, 12041-12047
      Simple, 12001-12007
      Superficial, 12001-12007
    Scalp
      Complex, 13120-13122
      Intermediate, 12031-12057
      Layered, 12031-12037
      Simple, 12001-12007
      Superficial, 12001-12007
    Toe, Toes
      Complex, 13131-13133
      Intermediate, 12041-12047
      Layered, 12041-12047
      Simple, 12001-12007
      Superficial, 12001-12007
    Trunk
      Complex, 13100-13102
      Intermediate, 12031-12037
      Layered, 12031-12037
      Simple, 12001-12007
      Superficial, 12001-12007
    Upper
      Arm, Arms
        Complex, 13120-13122
        Intermediate, 12031-12037
        Layered, 12031-12037
        Simple, 12001-12007
        Superficial, 12001-12007

Skin — *continued*
  Wound Repair — *continued*
    Upper — *continued*
      Extremity
        Complex, 13120-13122
        Intermediate, 12031-12037
        Layered, 12031-12037
        Simple, 12001-12007
        Superficial, 12001-12007
      Leg, Legs
        Complex, 13120-13122
        Intermediate, 12031-12037
        Layered, 12031-12037
        Simple, 12001-12007
        Superficial, 12001-12007
Skin Graft and Flap
  Allograft, 15300-15336
  Composite Graft, 15760, 15770
  Cross Finger Flap, 15574
  Delay of Flap, 15600-15630
  Derma-Fat-Fascia Graft, 15770
  Fascial
    Free, 15758
  Fasciocutaneous Flap, 15732-15738
  Formation, 15570-15576
  Free
    Microvascular Anastomosis, 15756-15758
  Free Skin Graft
    Full Thickness, 15200-15261
  Island Pedicle Flap, 15740
  Muscle, 15732-15738, 15732
    Free, 15756
  Myocutaneous, 15732-15738
  Pedicle Flap
    Formation, 15570-15576
    Island, 15740
    Neurovascular, 15750
    Transfer, 15650
  Pinch Graft, 15050
  Platysmal, 15825
  Punch Graft for Hair Transplant, 15775, 15776
  Recipient Site Preparation, 15000, 15001
  Skin
    Free, 15757
  Split Graft, 15100-15121
  Superficial Musculoaponeurotic System, 15829
  Tissue-Cultured, 15150-15157
  Tissue Transfer, 14000-14350
  Transfer, 15650
  Vascular Flow Check, 15860
  Xenograft, 15400-15421
    Acellular Implant, 15430-15431
Skull
  Burr Hole
    with Injection, 61120
    Biopsy Brain, 61140
    Drainage
      Abscess, 61150, 61151
      Cyst, 61150, 61151
      Hematoma, 61154, 61156
    Exploration
      Infratentorial, 61253
      Supratentorial, 61250
    Insertion
      Catheter, 61210
      EEG Electrode, 61210
      Reservoir, 61210
    Intracranial Biopsy, 61140
  Decompression, 61322-61323, 61340-61345
  Orbit, 61330

Index

Skull — Special Services

Skull — *continued*
Drill Hole
    Catheter, 61107
    Drainage Hematoma, 61108
    Exploration, 61105
Excision, 61501
Exploration Drill Hole, 61105
Fracture, 62000-62010
    Closed Treatment, 21300
Hematoma Drainage, 61108
Incision
    Suture, 61550, 61552
Insertion
    Catheter, 61107
Lesion
    Excision, 61500, 61600-61608, 61615,
        61616
Orbit
    Biopsy, 61332
    Excision
        Lesion, 61333
    Exploration, 61332-61334
    Removal of Foreign Body, 61334
Puncture
    Cervical, 61050
    Cisternal, 61050
    Drain Fluid, 61070
    Injection, 61070
    Subdural, 61000, 61001
    Ventricular Fluid, 61020
Reconstruction, 21172-21180
    Defect, 62140, 62141, 62145
Reduction
    Craniomegalic, 62115-62117
Removal
    Plate, 62142
    Prosthesis, 62142
Repair
    Cerebrospinal Fluid Leak, 62100
    Encephalocele, 62120
Replacement
    Plate, 62143
    Prosthesis, 62143
Tumor
    Excision, 61500
X-ray, 70250, 70260
Skull Base Surgery
Anterior Cranial Fossa
    Bicoronal Approach, 61586
    Craniofacial Approach, 61580-61583
    Extradural, 61600, 61601
    LeFort I Osteotomy Approach, 61586
    Orbitocranial Approach, 61584, 61585
    Transzygomatic Approach, 61586
Carotid Aneurysm, 61613
Carotid Artery, 61610
    Transection
        Ligation, 61609-61612
Craniotomy, 62121
Dura
    Repair of Cerebrospinal Fluid Leak, 61618,
        61619
Middle Cranial Fossa
    Extradural, 61605, 61607
    Infratemporal Approach, 61590, 61591
    Intradural, 61606, 61608
    Orbitocranial Zygomatic Approach, 61592
Posterior Cranial Fossa
    Extradural, 61615
    Intradural, 61616
    Transcondylar Approach, 61596, 61597

Skull Base Surgery — *continued*
Posterior Cranial Fossa — *continued*
    Transpetrosal Approach, 61598
    Transtemporal Approach, 61595
Sleep Study, 0089T, 95805-95807
    Polysomnography, 95808-95811
Sliding Inlay Graft, Tibia
    Tibia, Repair, 27720-27725
Sling Operation
    Incontinence, 53440
        Removal, 53442
    Stress Incontinence, 51992, 57287
    Vagina, 57287, 57288
SMAS Flap, 15829
Smear and Stain
    Cornea, 65430
    Fluorescent, 87206
    Gram or Giesma, 87205
    Intracellular Parasites, 87207
    Ova
        Parasite, 87177, 87209
    Parasites, 87207
    Wet Mount, 87210
Smith Fracture, 25600-25620
Smith-Robinson Operation
    Arthrodesis, Vertebra, 22614
Smooth Muscle Antibody, 86255
Soave Procedure, 45120
Sodium, 84295, 84302
    Urine, 84300
Sofield Procedure, 24410
Somatomammotropin, Chorionic, 83632
Somatomedin, 84305
Somatosensory Testing
    Lower Limbs, 95926
    Trunk or Head, 95927
    Upper Limbs, 95925
Somatostatin, 84307
Somatotropin, 83003
Sonography
    See Echography
Sonohysterography, 76831
    Saline Infusion
        Injection Procedure, 58340
Sore, Bed
    See Pressure Ulcer (Decubitus)
Spasm, Eyelid
    See Blepharospasm
Special Services
    After Hours Medical Services, 99050
    Analysis
        Remote Physiologic Data, 99091
    Computer Data Analysis, 99090
    Device Handling, 99002
    Emergency Care in Office, 99058
        Out of Office, 99060
    Extended Hours, 99051-99053
    Group Education, 99078
    Hyperbaric Oxygen, 99183
    Hypothermia, 99185, 99186
    Medical Testimony, 99075
    Non-Office Medical Services, 99056
    On Call, Hospital Mandated, 99026, 99027
    Phlebotomy, 99199
    Postoperative Visit, 99024
    Prolonged Attendance, 99354-99360
    Psychiatric, 90889
    Pump Services, 99190-99192

Spine — *continued*
  Fusion — *continued*
    Lateral Extracavitary, 22532-22534
    Posterior Approach, 22590-22802
  Insertion
    Instrumentation, 22840-22848, 22851
  Kyphectomy, 22818, 22819
  Magnetic Resonance Angiography, 72159
  Magnetic Resonance Imaging
    Cervical, 72141, 72142, 72156-72158
    Lumbar, 72148-72158
    Thoracic, 72146, 72147, 72156-72158
  Manipulation
    Anesthesia, 22505
  Myelography
    Cervical, 72240
    Lumbosacral, 72265
    Thoracic, 72255
    Total, 72270
  Reconstruction
    Dorsal Spine Elements, 63295
  Reinsertion Instrumentation, 22849
  Removal Instrumentation, 22850, 22852,
    22855
  Repair, Osteotomy
    Anterior, 22220-22226
    Posterior, 22210-22214
      Cervical Laminoplasty, 63050-63051
      Posterolateral, 22216
  Standing X-ray, 72069
  Ultrasound, 76800
  Unlisted Services and Procedures, 22899
  X-ray, 72020, 72090
    with Contrast
      Cervical, 72240
      Lumbosacral, 72265
      Thoracic, 72255
      Total, 72270
    Absorptiometry, 76075, 76077
    Cervical, 72040-72052
    Lumbosacral, 72100-72120
    Standing, 72069
    Thoracic, 72070-72074
    Thoracolumbar, 72080
    Total, 72010

Spine Chemotherapy
  Administration, 96450
  See Chemotherapy

Spirometry, 94010-94070
  See Pulmonology, Diagnostic
  Patient Initiated, 94014-94016

Splanchnicectomy
  See Nerves, Sympathectomy, Excision

Spleen
  Excision, 38100-38102
    Laparoscopic, 38120
  Injection
    Radiologic, 38200
  Nuclear Medicine
    Imaging, 78185, 78215, 78216
  Repair, 38115

Splenectomy
  Laparoscopic, 38120
  Partial, 38101
  Partial with Repair, Ruptured Spleen, 38115
  Total, 38100
    En Bloc, 38102

Splenoplasty
  See Repair, Spleen

Splenoportography, 75810
  Injection Procedures, 38200

Splenorrhaphy, 38115

Splenotomy, 38999

Splint
  See Casting; Strapping
  Arm
    Long, 29105
    Short, 29125, 29126
  Finger, 29130, 29131
  Foot, 29590
  Leg
    Long, 29505
    Short, 29515
  Oral Surgical, 21085
  Ureteral
    See Ureteral Splinting

Split Grafts, 15100-15121

Split Renal Function Test
  See Cystourethroscopy, Catheterization,
    Ureteral

Splitting
  Blood Products, 86985

Sprengel's Deformity, 23400

Spring Water Cyst
  See Cyst, Pericardial

Spur, Bone
  See Exostosis
  Calcaneal
    See Heel Spur

Sputum Analysis

SQ, 90772

SRH
  See Somatostatin

Ssabanejew-Frank Operation
  Incision, Stomach, Creation of Stoma, 43830-
    43832

Stabilizing Factor, Fibrin
  See Fibrin Stabilizing Factor

Stable Factor, 85230

Stallard Procedure
  See Conjunctivorhinostomy

Stamey Procedure, 51845

Standby Services, 99360

Standing X-ray, 72069, 73564, 73565

Stanftan
  See Binet Test

Stapedectomy
  with Footplate Drill Out, 69661
  without Foreign Material, 69660
  Revision, 69662

Stapedotomy
  with Footplate Drill Out, 69661
  without Foreign Material, 69660
  Revision, 69662

Stapes
  Excision
    with Footplate Drill Out, 69661
    without Foreign Material, 69660
  Mobilization
    See Mobilization, Stapes
  Release, 69650
  Revision, 69662

Staphyloma
  Sclera
    Repair
      with Graft, 66225
      without Graft, 66220

Starch Granules
Feces

State Operation
Proctectomy
Partial, 45111, 45113-45116, 45123
Total, 45110, 45112, 45120
with Colon, 45121

Statin Therapy, 4002F

Statistics/Biometry
See Biometry

Steindler Stripping, 28250

Steindler Type Advancement, 24330

Stellate Ganglion
Injection
Anesthetic, 64510

Stem, Brain
See Brainstem

Stem Cell
Cell Concentration, 38215
Count, 86367
Total Count, 86367
Cryopreservation, 38207, 88240
Donor Search, 38204
Harvesting, 38205-38206
Limbal
Allograft, 65781
Plasma Depletion, 38214
Platelet Depletion, 38213
Red Blood Cell Depletion, 38212
T-cell Depletion, 38210
Thawing, 38208, 38209, 88241
Transplantation, 38240-38242
Tumor Cell Depletion, 38211
Washing, 38209

Stenger Test, 92565, 92577
See Audiologic Function Test; Ear, Nose and
Throat

Stenosis
Aortic
See Aortic Stenosis
Bronchi, 31641
Reconstruction, 31775
Excision
Trachea, 31780, 31781
Laryngoplasty, 31582
Reconstruction
Auditory Canal, External, 69310
Repair
Trachea, 31780, 31781
Tracheal
See Trachea Stenosis
Urethral Stenosis
See Urethral Stenosis

Stenson Duct
See Parotid Duct

Stent
Indwelling
Insertion
Ureter, 50605
Placement
Bronchoscopy, 31631, 31636-31637
Colonoscopy, 45387
via Stoma, 44397
Endoscopy
Gastrointestinal, Upper, 43256
Enteroscopy, 44370
Proctosigmoidoscopy, 45327
Sigmoidoscopy, 45345

Stent — continued
Placement — continued
Transcatheter
Intravascular, 37205-37208, 37215,
37216
Extracranial, 0075T-0076T
Ureteroneocystomy, 50947, 50948
Revision
Bronchoscopy, 31638
Urethra, 52282
Insertion, 52282
Prostatic, 0084T

Stent, Intravascular
See Transcatheter, Placement, Intravascular
Stents

Stents, Tracheal
See Tracheal Stent

Stereotactic Frame
Application
Removal, 20660

Stereotaxis
Aspiration
Brain Lesion, 61750
with CT Scan and/or MRI, 61751
Spinal Cord, 63615
Biopsy
Aspiration
Brain Lesion, 61750
Brain, 61750
Brain with CT Scan and/or MRI, 61751
Breast, 76095
Spinal Cord, 63615
Computer Assisted
Brain Surgery, 61795
Orthopedic Surgery, 0054T-0056T
Creation Lesion
Brain
Deep, 61720, 61735
Percutaneous, 61790
Gasserian Ganglion, 61790
Spinal Cord, 63600
Trigeminal Tract, 61791
CT Scan
Aspiration, 61751
Biopsy, 61751
Excision Lesion
Brain, 61750
Spinal Cord, 63615
Focus Beam
Radiosurgery, 61793
Localization
Brain, 61770
Radiation Therapy, 0082T-0083T, 77432
Stimulation
Spinal Cord, 63610

Sterile Coverings
See Dressings

Sternal Fracture
See Fracture, Sternum

Sternoclavicular Joint
Arthrotomy, 23044
with Biopsy, 23101
with Synovectomy, 23106
Dislocation
Closed Treatment
with Manipulation, 23525
without Manipulation, 23520
Open Treatment, 23530, 23532
with Fascial Graft, 23532

Sternocleidomastoid
Division, 21720, 21725

Sternotomy
Closure, 21750

Sternum
Debridement, 21627
Excision, 21620, 21630, 21632
Fracture
Closed Treatment, 21820
Open Treatment, 21825
Ostectomy, 21620
Radical Resection, 21630, 21632
Reconstruction, 21740-21742, 21750
with Thoracoscoy, 21743
X-ray, 71120, 71130

Steroid-Binding Protein, Sex
See Globulin, Sex Hormonee Binding

Steroids
Anabolic
See Androstenedione
Injection
Urethral Stricture, 52283
Ketogenic
Urine, 83582

STG, 15100-15121

STH
See Growth Hormone

Stimulating Antibody, Thyroid
See Immunoglobulin, Thyroid Stimulating

Stimulation
Electric
See Electrical Stimulation
Lymphoccyte
See Blastogenesis
Spinal Cord
Stereotaxis, 63610
Transcutaneous Electric
See Application, Neurostimulation

Stimulator, Long-Acting Thyroid
See Thyrotropin Releasing Hormone (TRH)

Stimulators, Cardiac
See Heart, Pacemaker

Stimulus Evoked Response, 51792

Stoffel Operation
Rhizotomy, 63185, 63190

Stoma
Closure
Intestines, 44620
Creation
Bladder, 51980
Kidney, 50551-50561
Stomach
Neonatal, 43831
Permanent, 43832
Temporary, 43830, 43831
Ureter, 50860
Revision
Colostomy, 44345
Ileostomy
Complicated, 44314
Simple, 44312
Ureter
Endoscopy via, 50951-50961

Stomach
Anastomosis
with Duodenum, 43810, 43850, 43855
with Jejunum, 43820, 43825, 43860, 43865
Biopsy, 43600, 43605

Stomach — *continued*
Creation
Stoma
Permanent, 43832
Temporary, 43830, 43831
Temporary Stoma
Laparoscopic, 43653
Electrogastrography, 91132, 91133
Excision
Partial, 43631-43635, 43845
Total, 43620-43622
Exploration, 43500
Gastric Bypass, 43644-43645, 43846
Revision, 43848
Gastropexy, 43659, 43999
Incision, 43830-43832
Exploration, 43500
Pyloric Sphincter, 43520
Removal
Foreign Body, 43500
Intubation with Specimen Prep, 91055
Nuclear Medicine
Blood Loss Study, 78278
Emptying Study, 78264
Imaging, 78261
Protein Loss Study, 78282
Reflux Study, 78262
Vitamin B-12
Absorption, 78270-78272
Reconstruction
for Obesity, 43644-43645, 43842-43847
Roux-en-Y, 43644, 43846
Removal
Foreign Body, 43500
Repair, 48547
Fistula, 43880
Fundoplasty, 43324, 43325
Laparoscopic, 43280
Laceration, 43501, 43502
Stoma, 43870
Ulcer, 43501
Saline Load Test, 91060
Specimen Collection, 89130-89141
Stimulation of Secretion, 91052
Suture
Fistula, 43880
for Obesity, 43842, 43843
Stoma, 43870
Ulcer, 43840
Wound, 43840
Tumor
Excision, 43610, 43611
Ulcer
Excision, 43610
Unlisted Services and Procedures, 43659,
43999

Stomatoplasty
See Mouth, Repair

Stone
Calculi
Bile Duct, 43264, 47420, 47425
Percutaneous, 47554, 47630
Bladder, 51050, 52310-52318, 52352
Gallbladder, 47480
Hepatic Duct, 47400
Kidney, 50060-50081, 50130, 50561, 50580,
52352
Pancreas, 48020
Pancreatic Duct, 43264
Salivary Gland, 42330-42340

Stone — *continued*
  Calculi — *continued*
      Ureter, 50610-50630, 50961, 50980, 51060,
          51065, 52320-52330, 52352
      Urethra, 52310, 52315, 52352
Stone, Kidney
  See Calculus, Removal, Kidney
Stookey-Scarff Procedure
  Ventriculocisternostomy, 62200
Stool Blood
  See Blood, Feces
Storage
  Embryo, 89342
  Oocyte, 89346
  Reproductive Tissue, 89344
  Sperm, 89343
Strabismus
  Chemodenervation, 67345
  Repair
      Adjustable Sutures, 67335
      Extraocular Muscles, 67340
      One Horizontal Muscle, 67311
      One Vertical Muscle, 67314
      Posterior Fixation Suture Technique, 67334,
          67335
      Previous Surgery not Involving Extraocular
          Muscles, 67331
      Release Extensive Scar Tissue, 67343
      Superior Oblique Muscle, 67318
      Transposition, 67320
      Two Horizontal Muscles, 67312
      Two or More Vertical Muscles, 67316
Strapping
  See Cast; Splint
  Ankle, 29540
  Back, 29220
  Chest, 29200
  Elbow, 29260
  Finger, 29280
  Foot, 29540, 29590
  Hand, 29280
  Hip, 29520
  Knee, 29530
  Shoulder, 29240
  Thorax, 29200
  Toes, 29550
  Unlisted Services and Procedures, 29799
  Unna Boot, 29580
  Wrist, 29260
Strassman Procedure, 58540
Strayer Procedure, 27687
Strep Quick Test, 86403
Streptococcus, Group A
  Antigen Detection
      Enzyme Immunoassay, 87430
      Nucleic Acid, 87650-87652
  Direct Optical Observation, 87880
Streptococcus, Group B
  by Immunoassay
      with Direct Optical Observation, 87802
Streptococcus pneumoniae Vaccine
  See Vaccines
Streptokinase, Antibody, 86590
Stress Tests
  Cardiovascular, 93015-93024
  Multiple Gated Acquisition (MUGA), 78472,
      78473
  Myocardial Perfusion Imaging, 78460-78465
  Pulmonary, 94620, 94621
      See Pulmonology, Diagnostic

Stricture
  Repair
      Urethra, 53400, 53405
  Urethra
      See Urethral Stenosis
Stricturoplasty
  Intestines, 44615
Stroboscopy
  Larynx, 31579
STS, 86592, 86593
  See Syphilis Test
STSG, 15100-15121
Stuart-Prower Factor, 85260
Study
  Color Vision, 92283
  Common Carotid Intima-media Thickness (IMT),
      0126T
  Implanted Wireless Pressure Sensor, 0154T
Sturmdorf Procedure, 57520
Styloidectomy
  Radial, 25230
Styloid Process
  Fracture, 25645, 25650
  Radial
      Excision, 25230
Stypven Time
  See Russell Viper Venom Time
Subacromial Bursa
  Arthrocentesis, 20610
Subarachnoid Drug Administration, 01996
Subclavian Arteries
  See Artery, Subclavian
Subcutaneous Injection
  See Injecton, Subcutaneous
Subcutaneous Mastectomies
  See Mastectomy, Subcutaneous
Subcutaneous Tissue
  Excision, 15831-15839
  Repair
      Complex, 13100-13160
      Intermediate, 12031-12057
      Simple, 12020, 12021
Subdiaphragmatic Abscess
  See Abscess, Subdiaphragmatic
Subdural Electrode
  Insertion, 61531, 61533
  Removal, 61535
Subdural Hematoma
  See Hematoma, Subdural
Subdural Puncture, 61105-61108
Subdural Tap, 61000, 61001
Sublingual Gland
  Abscess
      Incision and Drainage, 42310, 42320
  Calculi
      Excision, 42330
  Cyst
      Drainage, 42409
      Excision, 42408
  Excision, 42450
Subluxation
  Elbow, 24640
Submandibular Gland
  Calculi
      Excision, 42330, 42335
  Excision, 42440

Submaxillary Gland
Abscess
Incision and Drainage, 42310, 42320
Submental Fat Pad
Excision
Excess Skin, 15838
Submucous Resection of Nasal Septum
See Nasal Septum, Submucous Resection
Subperiosteal Implant
Reconstruction
Mandible, 21245, 21246
Maxilla, 21245, 21246
Subphrenic Abscess
See Abscess, Subdiaphragmatic
Substance S, Reichstein's
See Deoxycortisol
Subtrochanteric Fracture
See Femur, Fracture, Subtrochanteric
Sucrose Hemolysis Test
Sucrose Hemolysis Test
See Red Blood Cell (RBC), Fragility, Osmotic
Red Blood Cell, Fragility, Osmotic, 85555, 85557
Suction Lipectomies
See Liposuction
Sudiferous Gland
See Sweat Glands
Sugars, 84375-84379
Sugiura Procedure
Esophagus, Repair, Varices, 43401
Sulfate
Chondroitin
See Chondroitin Sulfate
DHA
See Dehydroepiandrosterone Sulfate
Urine, 84392
Sulfation Factor
See Somatomedin
Sulphates
See Sulfate
Sumatran Mite Fever
See Scrub Typhus
Superficial Musculoaponeurotic Systems (SMAS) Flap
Rhytidectomy, 15829
Supernumerary Digit
Reconstruction, 26587
Repair, 26587
Supply
Chemotherapeutic Agent, 96545
See Chemotherapy
Educational Materials, 99071
Materials, 99070
Prosthesis
Breast, 19396
Suppositories, Vaginal
See Pessary
Suppression, 80400-80408
Suppression/Testing
See Evocative/Suppression Test
Suppressor T Lymphocyte Marker
See CD8
Suppurative Hidradenitides
See Hidradenitis, Suppurative
Suprahyoid
Lymphadenectomy, 38700

Supraorbital Nerve
Avulsion, 64732
Incision, 64732
Transection, 64732
Supraorbital Rim and Forehead
Reconstruction, 21179, 21180
Suprapubic Prostatectomies
See Prostatectomy, Suprapubic
Suprarenal
Gland
See Adrenal Gland
Vein
See Vein, Adrenal
Suprascapular Nerve
Injection
Anesthetic, 64418
Suprasellar Cyst
See Craniopharyngioma
Surface CD4 Receptor
See CD4
Surface Radiotherapy
See Application, Radioelement, Surface
Surgeries
Breast-Conserving
See Breast, Excision, Lesion
Conventional
See Celiotomy
Laser
See Laser Surgery
Mohs
See Mohs Micrographic Surgery
Repeat
See Reoperation
Surgical
Avulsion
See Avulsion
Cartilage
Excision, 21060
Cataract Removal
See Cataract, Excision
Collapse Therapy, Thoracoplasty
See Thoracoplasty
Diathermy
See Electrocautery
Galvanism
See Electrolysis
Incision
See Incision
Meniscectomy, 21060
Microscopes
See Operating Microscope
Pathology
See Pathology, Surgical
Planing
Nose
Skin, 30120
Pneumoperitoneum
See Pneumoperitoneum
Removal, Eye
See Enucleation, Eye
Revision
See Reoperation
Surgical Correction
Uterus
Inverted, 59899
Surgical Services
Post-Operative Visit, 99024
Surveillance
See Monitoring

Suspension
Aorta, 33800
Kidney
   See Nephropexy
Muscle
   Hyoid, 21685
Vagina
   See Colpexy
Suture
See Repair
Abdomen, 49900
Anus, 46999
Aorta, 33320, 33321
Bile Duct
   Wound, 47900
Bladder
   Fistulization, 44660, 44661, 45800, 45805,
      51880-51925
      Vesicouterine, 51920, 51925
      Vesicovaginal, 51900
   Wound, 51860, 51865
Cervix, 57720
Colon
   Diverticula, 44604, 44605
   Fistula, 44650-44661
   Plication, 44680
   Stoma, 44620, 44625
   Ulcer, 44604, 44605
   Wound, 44604, 44605
Esophagus
   Wound, 43410, 43415
Eyelid, 67880
   with Transposition of Tarsal Plate, 67882
   Closure of, 67875
   Wound
      Full Thickness, 67935
      Partial Thickness, 67930
Facial Nerve
   Intratemporal
      Lateral to Geniculate Ganglion, 69740
      Medial to Geniculate Ganglion, 69745
Fallopian Tube
   Simple, 58999
Foot
   Tendon, 28200-28210
Gastroesophageal, 0008T, 43405
Great Vessel, 33320-33322
Hemorrhoids, 46945, 46946
Intestines
   Large
      Diverticula, 44604, 44605
      Ulcer, 44604, 44605
      Wound, 44604, 44605
   Small
      Diverticula, 44602, 44603
      Fistula, 44640-44661
      Plication, 44680
      Stoma, 44620, 44625
      Ulcer, 44602, 44603
      Wound, 44602, 44603
      Stoma, 44620, 44625
Iris
   with Ciliary Body, 66682
Kidney
   Fistula, 50520-50526
   Horseshoe, 50540
   Wound, 50500
Leg, Lower
   Tendon, 27658-27665
Leg, Upper
   Muscles, 27385, 27386

Suture — *continued*
Liver
   Wound, 47350-47361
Mesentery, 44850
Nerve, 64831-64876
Pancreas, 48545
Pharynx
   Wound, 42900
Rectum
   Fistula, 45800-45825
   Prolapse, 45540, 45541
Removal
   Anesthesia, 15850, 15851
Spleen
   See Splenorrhaphy
Stomach
   Fistula, 43880
   Laceration, 43501, 43502
   Stoma, 43870
   Ulcer, 43501, 43840
   Wound, 43840
Tendon
   Foot, 28200-28210
   Knee, 27380, 27381
Testis
   Injury, 54670
   Suspension, 54620, 54640
Thoracic Duct
   Abdominal Approach, 38382
   Cervical Approach, 38380
   Thoracic Approach, 38381
Throat
   Wound, 42900
Tongue
   to Lip, 41510
Trachea
   Fistula, 31825
      with Plastic Repair, 31825
      without Plastic Repair, 31820
   Stoma, 31825
      with Plastic Repair, 31825
      without Plastic Repair, 31820
   Wound
      Cervical, 31800
      Intrathoracic, 31805
Ulcer, 44604, 44605
Ureter, 50900, 50940
   Deligation, 50940
   Fistula, 50920, 50930
Urethra
   Fistula, 45820, 45825, 53520
   Stoma, 53520
   to Bladder, 51840, 51841
   Wound, 53502-53515
Uterus
   Fistula, 51920, 51925
   Rupture, 58520, 59350
   Suspension, 58400, 58410
Vagina
   Cystocele, 57240, 57260
   Enterocele, 57265
   Fistula
      Rectovaginal, 57300-57307
      Transvesical and Vaginal Approach,
         57330
      Urethrovaginal, 57310, 57311
      Vesicovaginal, 51900, 57320, 57330
   Rectocele, 57250, 57260
   Suspension, 57280
   Wound, 57200, 57210
Vas Deferens, 55400

Suture — *continued*
- Vein
  - Femoral, 37650
  - Iliac, 37660
  - Vena Cava, 37620
- Wound, 44604, 44605
  - Skin
    - Complex, 13100-13160
    - Intermediate, 12031-12057
    - Simple, 12020, 12021

Swallowing
- Cine, 74230
- Evaluation, 92610-92613, 92616-92617
- Therapy, 92526
- Video, 74230

Swanson Procedure
- Repair, Metatarsal, 28322
  - Osteotomy, 28306-28309

Sweat Collection
- Iontophoresis, 89230

Sweat Glands
- Excision
  - Axillary, 11450, 11451
  - Inguinal, 11462, 11463
  - Perianal, 11470, 11471
  - Perineal, 11470, 11471
  - Umbilical, 11470, 11471

Sweat Test
- Chloride, Blood, 82435

Swenson Procedure, 45120

Syme Procedure, 27888

Sympathectomy
- with Rib Excision, 21616
- Artery
  - Digital, 64820
  - Radial, 64821
  - Superficial Palmar Arch, 64823
  - Ulnar, 64822
- Cervical, 64802
- Cervicothoracic, 64804
- Digital Artery with Magnification, 64820
- Lumbar, 64818
- Presacral, 58410
- Thoracic, 32664
- Thoracolumbar, 64809

Sympathetic Nerve
- Excision, 64802-64818
- Injection
  - Anesthetic, 64508, 64520, 64530

Sympathins
- *See* Catecholamines

Symphysiotomy
- Horseshoe Kidney, 50540

Symphysis, Pubic
- *See* Pubic Symphysis

Syncytial Virus, Respiratory
- *See* Respiratory Syncytial Virus

Syndactylism, Toes
- *See* Webbed, Toe

Syndactyly
- Repair, 26560-26562

Syndesmotomy
- *See* Ligament, Release

Syndrome
- Adrenogenital
  - *See* Adrenogenital Syndrome
- Ataxia-Telangiectasia
  - *See* Ataxia Telangiectasia

Syndrome — *continued*
- Bloom
  - *See* Bloom Syndrome
- Carpal Tunnel
  - *See* Carpal Tunnel Syndrome
- Costen's
  - *See* Temporomandibular Joint (TMJ)
- Erb-Goldflam
  - *See* Myasthenia Gravis
- Ovarian Vein
  - *See* Ovarian Vein Syndrome
- Synechiae, Intrauterine
  - *See* Adhesions, Intrauterine
- Treacher Collins
  - *See* Treacher-Collins Syndrome
- Urethral
  - *See* Urethral Syndrome

Syngesterone
- *See* Progesterone

Synostosis (Cranial)
- *See* Craniosynostosis

Synovectomy
- Arthrotomy with
  - Glenohumeral Joint, 23105
  - Sternoclavicular Joint, 23106
- Elbow, 24102
- Excision
  - Carpometacarpal Joint, 26130
  - Finger Joint, 26135, 26140
  - Hip Joint, 27054
  - Interphalangeal Joint, 26140
  - Knee Joint, 27334-27335
  - Metacarpophalangeal Joint, 26135
  - Palm, 26145
- Wrist, 25105, 25115-25119
  - Radical, 25115, 25116

Synovial
- Bursa
  - *See* Bursa
- Cyst
  - *See* Ganglion
- Membrane
  - *See* Synovium
- Popliteal Space
  - *See* Baker's Cyst

Synovium
- Biopsy
  - Carpometacarpal Joint, 26100
  - Interphalangeal Joint, 26110
  - Knee Joint, 27330
  - Metacarpophalangeal Joint
    - with Synovial Biopsy, 26105
- Excision
  - Carpometacarpal Joint, 26130
  - Finger Joint, 26135-26140
  - Hip Joint, 27054
  - Interphalangeal Joint, 26140
  - Knee Joint, 27334-27335

Syphilis ab
- *See* Antibody, Treponema Pallidum

Syphilis Test, 86592, 86593

Syrinx
- Spinal Cord
  - Aspiration, 62268

System
- Endocrine
  - *See* Endocrine System
- Hemic
  - *See* Hemic System

System — *continued*
Lymphatic
   See Lymphatic System
Nervous
   See Nervous System

T

T-3, 84480
T3 Free
   See Triiodothyronine, Free
T-4
   T Cells, 86360, 86361
   Thyroxine, 84436-84439
T4 Molecule
   See CD4
T4 Total
   See Thyroxine, Total
T-7 Index
   Thyroxine, Total, 84436
   Triiodothyronine, 84480-84482
T-8, 86360
Taarnhoj Procedure
   Decompression, Gasserian Ganglion, Sensory
     Root, 61450
Tachycardia
   Heart
     Recording, 93609
Tacrolimus
   Drug Assay, 80197
Tag, Skin
   See Skin, Tags
TAH, 51925, 58150, 58152, 58200-58240, 58951,
   59525
TAHBSO, 58150, 58152, 58200-58240, 58951
Tail Bone
   Excision, 27080
   Fracture, 27200, 27202
Takeuchi Procedure, 33505
Talectomy
   See Astragalectomy
Talotarsal Joint
   Dislocation, 28570, 28575, 28585
   Percutaneous Fixation, 28576
Talus
   Arthrodesis
     Pantalar, 28705
     Subtalar, 28725
     Triple, 28715
   Arthroscopy
     Surgical, 29891, 29892
   Craterization, 28120
   Cyst
     Excision, 28100-28103
   Diaphysectomy, 28120
   Excision, 28120, 28130
   Fracture
     with Manipulation, 28435, 28436
     without Manipulation, 28430
     Open Treatment, 28445
     Percutaneous Fixation, 28436
   Repair
     Osteochondritis Dissecans, 29892
     Osteotomy, 28302
   Saucerization, 28120
   Tumor
     Excision, 27647, 28100-28103

Tap
   Cisternal
     See Cisternal Puncture
   Lumbar Diagnostic
     See Spinal Tap
Tarsal
   Fracture
     Percutaneous Fixation, 28456
Tarsal Bone
   See Ankle Bone
Tarsal Joint
   See Foot
   Arthrodesis, 28730, 28735, 28740
     with Advancement, 28737
     with Lengthening, 28737
   Craterization, 28122
   Cyst
     Excision, 28104-28107
   Diaphysectomy, 28122
   Dislocation, 28540, 28545, 28555
     Percutaneous Fixation, 28545, 28546
   Excision, 28116, 28122
   Fracture
     with Manipulation, 28455, 28456
     without Manipulation, 28450
     Open Treatment, 28465
   Fusion, 28730, 28735, 28740
     with Advancement, 28737
     with Lengthening, 28737
   Repair, 28320
     Osteotomy, 28304, 28305
   Saucerization, 28122
   Tumor
     Excision, 28104-28107, 28171
Tarsal Strip Procedure, 67917, 67924
Tarsal Tunnel Release, 28035
Tarsal Wedge Procedure, 67916, 67923
Tarsometatarsal Joint
   Arthrodesis, 28730, 28735, 28740
   Arthrotomy, 28020, 28050
   Biopsy
     Synovial, 28050, 28052
   Dislocation, 28600, 28605, 28615
     Percutaneous Fixation, 28606
   Exploration, 28020
   Fusion, 28730, 28735, 28740
   Removal
     Foreign Body, 28020
     Loose Body, 28020
   Synovial
     Biopsy, 28050
     Excision, 28070
Tarsorrhaphy, 67875
   Median, 67880
   Severing, 67710
     with Transposition of Tarsal Plate, 67882
Tattoo
   Cornea, 65600
   Skin, 11920-11922
TB, 87015, 87116, 87190
TBG, 84442
TBS, 88164, 88166
TB Test
   Antigen Response, 86480
   Cell Mediated Immunity Measurement, 86480
   Skin Test, 86580
T Cell Leukemia Virus I Antibodies, Adult
   See Antibody, HTLV-I

Tendon Origin
Insertion
Injection, 20551
Tendon Pulley Reconstruction of Hand
See Hand, Reconstruction, Tendon Pulley
Tendon Sheath
Arm
Lower
Repair, 25275
Finger
Incision, 26055
Incision and Drainage, 26020
Lesion, 26160
Foot
Excision, 28086, 28088
Hand
Lesion, 26160
Injection, 20550
Palm
Incision and Drainage, 26020
Removal
Foreign Body, 20520, 20525
Wrist
Excision, 25115, 25116
Incision, 25000, 25001
Repair, 25275
Tendon Shortening
Ankle, 27685, 27686
Leg, Lower, 27685, 27686
Tenectomy, Tendon Sheath
See Excision, Lesion, Tendon Sheath
Tennis Elbow
Repair, 24350-24356
Tenodesis
Biceps Tendon
at Elbow, 24340
at Shoulder, 23430
Finger, 26471, 26474
Wrist, 25300, 25301
Tenolysis
Ankle, 27680, 27681
Arm, Lower, 25295
Arm, Upper, 24332
Finger
Extensor, 26445, 26449
Flexor, 26440, 26442
Foot, 28220-28226
Hand
Extensor, 26445, 26449
Flexor, 26440, 26442
Leg, Lower, 27680, 27681
Wrist, 25295
Tenomyotomy, 23405, 23406
Tenon's Capsule
Injection, 67515
Tenoplasty
Anesthesia, 01714
Tenorrhaphy
See Suture, Tendon
Tenosuspension
See Tenodesis
Tenosuture
See Suture, Tendon
Tenosynovectomy, 26145, 27626
Tenotomy
Achilles Tendon, 27605, 27606
Anesthesia, 01712
Ankle, 27605, 27606
Arm, Lower, 25290

Tenotomy — continued
Arm, Upper, 24310
Finger, 26060, 26455, 26460
Foot, 28230, 28234
Hand, 26450, 26460
Hip
Abductor, 27006
Adductor, 27000-27003
Iliopsoas Tendon, 27005
Leg, Upper, 27306, 27307, 27390-27392
Toe, 28010, 28011, 28232, 28234, 28240
Wrist, 25290
TENS, 64550, 97014, 97032
Tensilon Test, 95857
Tentorium Cerebelli
Section, 61440
Terman-Merrill Test, 96101-96103
Termination, Pregnancy
See Abortion
Tester, Color Vision
See Color Vision Examination
Testes
Cryopreservation, 89335
Nuclear Medicine
Imaging, 78760, 78761
Undescended
See Testis, Undescended
Testicular Vein
See Spermatic Veins
Testimony, Medical, 99075
Testing
Actigraphy, 0089T
Neurobehavioral, 96116
Neuropsychological, 96118-96120
Intraoperative, 95920
Psychological, 96101-96103
Range of Motion
Extremities, 95851
Eye, 92018-92019
Hand, 95852
Rectum
Biofeedback, 90911
Trunk, 97530
Rectum
Testing, Histocompatibility
See Tissue Typing
Testis
Abscess
Incision and Drainage, 54700
Biopsy, 54500, 54505
Cryopreservation, 89335
Excision
Laparoscopic, 54690
Partial, 54522
Radical, 54530, 54535
Simple, 54520
Hematoma
Incision and Drainage, 54700
Insertion
Prosthesis, 54660
Lesion
Excision, 54512
Needle Biopsy, 54500
Nuclear Medicine
Imaging, 78760, 78761
Repair
Injury, 54670
Suspension, 54620, 54640
Torsion, 54600

Testis — Thin Layer Chromatographies

Thrombectomy — *continued*
Femoropopliteal Vein, 34421, 34451
Iliac Artery, 34151, 34201
Iliac Vein, 34401-34451
Innominate Artery, 34001-34101
Mesenteric Artery, 34151
Percutaneous
  Coronary Artery, 92973
  Noncoronary, 37184-37186
  Vein, 37187-37188
Peroneal Artery, 34203
Popliteal Artery, 34203
Radial Artery, 34111
Renal Artery, 34151
Subclavian Artery, 34001-34101
Subclavian Vein, 34471, 34490
Tibial Artery, 34203
Ulnar Artery, 34111
Vena Cava, 34401-34451
Vena Caval, 50230
Venous, Mechanical, 37187-37188

Thrombin Inhibitor I
See Antithrombin III

Thrombin Time, 85670, 85675

Thrombocyte (Platelet)
See Blood, Platelet

Thrombocyte ab
See Antibody, Platelet

Thromboendarterectomy
See Thrombectomy
Aorta, Abdominal, 35331
Aortoiliofemoral Artery, 35363
Axillary Artery, 35321
Brachial Artery, 35321
Carotid Artery, 35301, 35390
Celiac Artery, 35341
Femoral Artery, 35371-35381
Iliac Artery, 35351, 35361, 35363
Iliofemoral Artery, 35355, 35363
Innominate Artery, 35311
Mesenteric Artery, 35341
Peroneal Artery, 35381
Popliteal Artery, 35381
Renal Artery, 35341
Subclavian Artery, 35301, 35311
Tibial Artery, 35381
Vertebral Artery, 35301

Thrombokinase, 85260

Thrombolysin
See Plasmin

Thrombolysis
Catheter Exchange
  Arterial, 37209, 75900
Cerebral
  Intravenous Infusion, 37195
Coronary Vessels, 92975, 92977
Cranial Vessels, 37195

Thrombolysis Biopsy Intracranial
Arterial Perfusion, 61624

Thrombolysis Intracranial, 65205
See Ciliary Body; Cornea; Eye; Lens; Retina; Sclera;
  Foreign Body; Iris; Lens; Retina; Sclera;
  Vitreous

Thrombomodulin, 85337

Thromboplastin
Inhibition, 85705
Inhibition Test, 85347
Partial Time, 85730, 85732

Thromboplastin Antecedent, Plasma
See Plasma Thromboplastin, Antecedent

Thromboplastinogen
See Clotting Factor

Thromboplastinogen B
See Christmas Factor
See Pharynx
Amputation, 26910-26952
Arthrodesis
  Carpometacarpal Joint, 26841, 26842
Dislocation
  with Fracture, 26645, 26650
    Open Treatment, 26665
  with Manipulation, 26641
Fracture
  with Dislocation, 26645, 26650
    Open Treatment, 26665
Fusion
  in Opposition, 26820
Reconstruction
  from Finger, 26550
  Opponensplasty, 26490-26496
Repair
  Muscle, 26508
  Muscle Transfer, 26494
  Tendon Transfer, 26510
Replantation, 20824, 20827
Sesamoidectomy, 26185
Unlisted Services and Procedures, 26989

Thymectomy, 60520, 60521
Sternal Split
  Transthoracic Approach, 60521, 60522
Transcervical Approach, 60520

Thymotaxin
See Beta-2-Microglobulin

Thymus Gland, 60520
Excision, 60520, 60521
Exploration
  Thymus Field, 60699
Incision, 60699
Other Operations, 60699
Repair, 60699
Transplantation, 60699

Thyramine
See Amphetamine

Thyrocalcitonin
See Calcitonin

Thyroglobulin, 84432
Antibody, 86800

Thyroglossal Duct
Cyst
  Excision, 60280, 60281

Thyroidectomy
Partial, 60210-60225
Secondary, 60260
Total, 60240, 60271
  Cervical Approach, 60271
    for Malignancy
      Limited Neck Dissection, 60252
      Radical Neck Dissection, 60254
  Removal All Thyroid Tissue, 60260
  Sternal Split
    Transthoracic Approach, 60270

Thyroid Gland
Biopsy
  Open, 60699
Cyst
  Aspiration, 60001
  Excision, 60200
  Incision and Drainage, 60000

Thyroid Gland — *continued*
  Cyst — *continued*
    Injection, 60001
  Excision
    for Malignancy
      Limited Neck Dissection, 60252
      Radical Neck Dissection, 60254
    Partial, 60210-60225
    Secondary, 60260
    Total, 60240, 60271
      Cervical Approach, 60271
      Removal All Thyroid Tissue, 60260
      Sternal Split
        Transthoracic Approach, 60270
      Transcervical Approach, 60520
  Metastatic Cancer
    Nuclear Imaging, 78015-78018
  Needle Biopsy, 60100
  Nuclear Medicine
    Imaging, 78010
    Imaging for Metastases, 78015-78018
    Imaging with Flow, 78011
    Imaging with Uptake, 78006, 78007
    Metastases Uptake, 78020
    Uptake, 78000-78003
  Suture, 60699
  Tissue
    Reimplantation, 60699
  Tumor
    Excision, 60200
Thyroid Hormone Binding Ratio, 84479
Thyroid Hormone Uptake, 84479
Thyroid Isthmus
  Transection, 60200
Thyroid Simulator, Long Acting
  See Thyrotropin Releasing Hormone (TRH)
Thyroid Stimulating Hormone (TSH), 80418,
  80438-80440, 84443
Thyroid Stimulating Hormone Receptor ab
  See Thyrotropin Releasing Hormone (TRH)
Thyroid Stimulating Immune Globulins (TSI),
  84445
Thyroid Suppression Test
  Nuclear Medicine, Thyroid Uptake, 78000-
    78003
Thyrolingual Cyst
  See Cyst, Thyroglossal Duct
Thyrotomy, 31300
Thyrotropin Receptor ab
  See Thyrotropin Releasing Hormone (TRH)
Thyrotropin Releasing Hormone (TRH), 80438,
  80439
Thyrotropin Stimulating Immunoglobulins,
  84445
Thyroxine
  Free, 84439
  Neonatal, 84437
  Total, 84436
  True, 84436
Thyroxine Binding Globulin, 84442
TIBC, 83550
Tibia
  See Ankle
  Arthroscopy Surgical, 29891, 29892
  Craterization, 27360, 27640
  Cyst
    Excision, 27635-27638
  Diaphysectomy, 27360, 27640

Tibia — *continued*
  Excision, 27360, 27640
    Epiphyseal Bar, 20150
  Fracture
    with Manipulation, 27825
    without Manipulation, 27824
      Incision, 27607
    Arthroscopic Treatment, 29855, 29856
      Plafond, 29892
    Closed Treatment, 27824, 27825
      with Manipulation, 27825
      without Manipulation, 27824
    Distal, 27824-27828
    Intercondylar, 27538, 27540
    Malleolus, 27760-27766, 27808-27814
    Open Treatment, 27535, 27536, 27758,
      27759, 27826-27828
    Plateau, 29855, 29856
      Closed Treatment, 27530, 27532
    Shaft, 27752-27759
  Osteoplasty
    Lengthening, 27715
  Prophylactic Treatment, 27745
  Reconstruction, 27418
    at Knee, 27440-27443, 27446
  Repair, 27720-27725
    Epiphysis, 27477-27485, 27730-27742
    Osteochondritis Dissecans Arthroscopy,
      29892
    Osteotomy, 27455, 27457, 27705, 27709,
      27712
    Pseudoarthrosis, 27727
  Saucerization, 27360, 27640
  Tumor
    Excision, 27635-27638, 27645
  X-ray, 73590
Tibial
  Arteries
    See Artery, Tibial
  Nerve
    Repair/Suture
      Posterior, 64840
Tibiofibular Joint
  Arthrodesis, 27871
  Dislocation, 27830-27832
  Disruption
    Open Treatment, 27829
  Fusion, 27871
TIG
  See Immune Globulins, Tetanus
Time
  Bleeding
    See Bleeding Time
  Prothrombin
    See Prothrombin Time
  Reptilase
    See Thrombin Time
Tinnitus
  Assessment, 92625
Tissue
  Culture
    Chromosome Analysis, 88230-88239
    Homogenization, 87176
    Non-neoplastic Disorder, 88230, 88237
    Skin Grafts, 15040-15157
    Solid tumor, 88239
    Toxin/Antitoxin, 87230
    Virus, 87252, 87253
  Enzyme Activity, 82657
  Examination for Ectoparasites, 87220
  Examination for Fungi, 87220

Tissue Adhesives — *continued*
  Closure, Skin with — *continued*
    Forehead — *continued*
      Layered, 12051-12057
      Simple, 12011-12018
      Superficial, 12011-12018
    Genitalia
      Complex, 13131-13133
      External
        Complex/Intermediate, 12041-12047
        Layered, 12041-12047
        Simple, 12001-12007
        Superficial, 12001-12007
    Hand, Hands
      Complex, 13131-13133
      Intermediate, 12041-12047
      Layered, 12041-12047
      Simple, 12001-12007
      Superficial, 12001-12007
    Leg, Legs
      Complex, 13120-13122
      Intermediate, 12031-12037
      Layered, 12031-12037
      Simple, 12001-12007
      Superficial, 12001-12007
    Lip, Lips
      Complex, 13150-13153
      Intermediate, 12051-12057
      Layered, 12051-12057
      Simple, 12011-12018
      Superficial, 12011-12018
    Lower
      Arm, Arms
        Complex, 13120-13122
        Intermediate, 12031-12037
        Layered, 12031-12037
        Simple, 12001-12007
        Superficial, 12001-12007
      Extremity, Extremities
        Complex, 13120-13122
        Intermediate, 12031-12037
        Layered, 12031-12037
        Simple, 12001-12007
        Superficial, 12001-12007
      Leg, Legs
        Complex, 13120-13122
        Intermediate, 12031-12037
        Layered, 12031-12037
        Simple, 12001-12007
        Superficial, 12001-12007
    Mouth
      Complex, 13131-13133
    Mucous Membrane
      Complex/Intermediate, 12051-12057
      Layered, 12051-12057
      Simple, 12011-12018
      Superficial, 12011-12018
    Neck
      Complex, 13131-13133
      Intermediate, 12041-12047
      Layered, 12041-12047
      Simple, 12001-12007
      Superficial, 12001-12007
    Nose
      Complex, 13150-13153
      Intermediate, 12051-12057
      Layered, 12051-12057
      Simple, 12011-12018
      Superficial, 12011-12018
    Palm, Palms
      Complex, 13131-13133
      Intermediate, 12041-12047

Tissue Adhesives — *continued*
  Closure, Skin with — *continued*
    Palm, Palms — *continued*
      Layered, 12041-12047
      Simple, 12001-12007
      Superficial, 12001-12007
    Scalp
      Complex, 13120-13122
      Intermediate, 12031-13133
      Layered, 12031-12037
      Simple, 12001-12007
      Superficial, 12001-12007
    Skin/Eyelid, Eyelids
      Complex, 13150-13153
      Intermediate, 12051-12057
      Layered, 12051-12057
      Simple, 12011-12018
      Superficial, 12011-12018
    Toe, Toes
      Complex, 13131-13133
      Intermediate, 12041-12047
      Layered, 12041-12047
      Simple, 12001-12007
      Superficial, 12001-12007
    Trunk
      Complex, 13100-13102
      Intermediate, 12031-12037
      Layered, 12031-12037
      Simple, 12001-12007
      Superficial, 12001-12007
    Upper
      Arm, Arms
        Complex, 13120-13122
        Intermediate, 12031-12037
        Layered, 12031-12037
        Simple, 12001-12007
        Superficial, 12001-12007
      Extremity
        Complex, 13120-13122
        Intermediate, 12031-12037
        Layered, 12031-12037
        Simple, 12001-12007
        Superficial, 12001-12007
      Leg, Legs
        Complex, 13120-13122
        Intermediate, 12031-12037
        Layered, 12031-12037
        Simple, 12001-12007
        Superficial, 12001-12007
  Subcutaneous Tissue
    Abdomen
      Complex, 13100-13102
      Intermediate, 12031-12037
      Layered, 12031-12037
      Simple, 12001-12007
      Superficial, 12001-12007
    Arm, Arms
      Complex, 13120-13122
      Intermediate, 12031-12037
      Layered, 12031-12037
      Simple, 12001-12007
      Superficial, 12001-12007
    Axilla, Axillae
      Complex, 13131-13133
      Intermediate, 12031-12037
      Layered, 12031-12037
      Simple, 12001-12007
      Superficial, 12001-12007
    Back
      Complex, 13100-13102
      Intermediate, 12031-12037
      Layered, 12031-12037

Toe — *continued*
Repair — *continued*
Muscle, 28240
Tendon, 28232, 28234, 28240
Webbed, 28280, 28345
Webbed Toe, 28345
Reposition, 20973, 26551-26554
Strapping, 29550
Tenotomy, 28010, 28011, 28232, 28234
Unlisted Services and Procedures, 28899
X-ray, 73660
Toe Flap
Tissue Transfer, 14350
Toes
Arthrocentesis, 20600
Dislocation
See Specific Joint
Magnetic Resonance Imaging (MRI), 73721-73723
Reconstruction
Extra Digit, 26587
Repair
Extra Digit, 26587
Macrodactylia, 26590
Reposition to Hand, 26551-26554, 26556
Strapping, 29550
X-Ray, 73660
Tolbutamide Tolerance Test, 82953
Tolerance Test(s)
Glucagon, 82946
Glucose, 82951, 82952
with Tolbutamide, 82953
Heparin-Protamine, 85530
Insulin, 80434, 80435
Maltose, 82951, 82952
Tolbutamide, 82953
Tomodensitometries
See CT Scan
Tomographic Scintigraphy, Computed
See Emission Computerized Tomography
Tomographic SPECT
Myocardial Imaging, 78469
Tomographies, Computed X-Ray
See CT Scan
Tomography, Computed
Abdomen
See Abdomen, CT Scan
Head
See Head, CT Scan
Tomography, Emission Computed
See Positron Emission Tomography
Single Photon
See SPECT
Tompkins Metroplasty
Uterus Reconstruction, 58540
Tongue
Abscess
Incision and Drainage, 41000-41006, 41015
Biopsy, 41100, 41105
Cyst
Incision and Drainage, 41000-41006, 41015, 60000
Excision
with Mouth Resection, 41150, 41153
with Radical Neck, 41135, 41145, 41153, 41155
Base
Radiofrequency, 0088T
Complete, 41140-41155

Tongue — *continued*
Excision — *continued*
Frenum, 41115
Partial, 41120-41135
Fixation, 41500
Hematoma
Incision and Drainage, 41000-41006, 41015
Incision
Frenum, 41010
Lesion
Excision, 41110-41114
Reconstruction
Frenum, 41520
Reduction for Sleep Apnea, 0088T
Repair
Laceration, 41250-41252
Suture, 41510
Unlisted Services and Procedures, 41599
Tonography, 92120
with Provocation, 92130
Tonometry, Serial, 92100
Tonsillectomy, 42820-42826
with Adenoidectomy
Age 12 or Over, 42821
Under Age 12, 42820
Primary
Age 12 or Over, 42826
Under Age 12, 42825
Secondary
Age 12 or Over, 42826
Under Age 12, 42825
Tonsil, Pharyngeal
See Adenoids
Tonsils
Abscess
Incision and Drainage, 42700
Excision, 42825, 42826
Excision with Adenoids, 42820, 42821
Lingual, 42870
Radical, 42842-42845
Tag, 42860
Lingual
Destruction, 42870
Removal
Foreign Body, 42999
Unlisted Services and Procedures, 42999
Topiramate
Assay, 80201
Torek Procedure
Orchiopexy, 54650
Torkildsen Procedure, 62180
TORP (Total Ossicular Replacement Prosthesis), 69633, 69637
Torsion Swing Test, 92546
Torula
See Cryptococcus
Torus Mandibularis
Tumor Excision, 21031
Total
Abdominal Hysterectomy
See Hysterectomy, Abdominal, Total
Bilirubin Level
See Bilirubin, Total
Catecholamines
See Catecholamines, Urine
Cystectomy
See Bladder, Excision, Total
Dacryoadenectomy
See Dacryoadenectomy, Total

Index

Toe — Total

Tractotomy
  Medulla, 61470
  Mesencephalon, 61480
Tract, Urinary
  See Urinary Tract
Training
  Activities of Daily Living, 97535, 99509
  Biofeedback, 90901, 90911
  Cognitive Skills, 97532
  Community
    Work Reintegration, 97537
  Home Management, 97535, 99509
  Management
    Propulsion, 97542
  Orthoptic
    Pleoptic, 92065
  Orthotics, 97760
  Prosthetics, 97761
  Seeing Impaired, 97799
    Braille, or Moon, 97799
    Lead Dog, Use of, 97799
  Self Care, 97535, 99509
  Sensory Integration, 97533
  Walking (Physical Therapy), 97116
  Wheelchair Management
    Propulsion, 97542
TRAM Flap
  Breast Reconstruction, 19367-19369
Transabdominal Endoscopy
  Intestine, Large, 45355
Transaminase
  Glutamic Oxaloacetic, 84450
  Glutamic Pyruvic, 84460
Transcatheter
  Biopsy, 37200
  Closure
    Percutaneous, Heart, 93580, 93581
  Embolization
    Percutaneous, 37204
      Cranial, 61624, 61626
  Occlusion
    Percutaneous, 37204
      Cranial, 61624, 61626
  Placement
    Intravascular Stent(s), 0075T-0076T, 37205-
      37208, 37215-37216
    Wireless Physiologic Sensor, 0153T
  Therapy
    Embolization, 75894
    Infusion, 37201, 37202, 75896, 75898
    Perfusion
      Cranial, 61624, 61626
    Retrieval, 75961
Transcatheter Foreign Body
  Retrieval, 37203
Transcortin, 84449
Transcranial
  Doppler Study (TCP), 93886-93893
  Stimulation, Motor, 95928-95929
Transcutaneous Electric Nerve Stimulation
  See Application, Neurostimulation
Transdermal Electrostimulation
  See Application, Neurostimulation
Transection
  Artery
    Carotid, 61610, 61612
  Blood Vessel
    Kidney, 50100

Transection — *continued*
  Brain
    Subpial, 61597
  Carotid
    with Skull Base Surgery, 61609
  Nerve, 64732-64772
    Vagus, 43640, 43641
  Pulmonary Artery, 33922
Transesophageal
  Echocardiography, 93312-93318
Transfer
  Blastocyst
    See Embryo Transfer
  Cryopreserved, 89352
  Finger Position, 26555
  Gamete Intrafallopian
    See GIFT
  Jejunum
    with Microvascular Anastomosis
      Preparation/Embryo, 89255
    Free, 43496
  Toe Joint, 26556
  Toe to Hand, 26551-26554, 26556
Transferase
  Aspartate Amino, 84450
  Glutamic Oxaloacetic, 84450
Transferrin, 84466
Transformation
  Lymphocyte, 86353
Transfusion
  Blood, 36430
    Exchange, 36450, 36455
    Fetal, 36460
    Push
      Infant, 36440
  Blood Parts
    Exchange
  Unlisted Services and Procedures, 86999
  White Blood Cells, 86950
Transfusion of, Blood, Autologous
  See Autotransfusion
Transillumination
  Skull
    Newborn, 95999
Transluminal
  Angioplasty
    Arterial, 75962-75968
  Atherectomies
    See Artery, Atherectomy
  Coronary Balloon Dilatation
    See Percutaneous Transluminal Angioplasty
Transmyocardial Laser Revascularization,
  33140, 33141
Transosteal Bone Plate
  Reconstruction
    Mandible, 21244
Transpeptidase, Gamma-Glutamyl
  See Gamma Glutamyl Transferase
Transplant
  See Graft
  Bone
    See Bone Graft
  Hair
    See Hair, Transplant
Transplantation
  See Graft
  Allogenic
    See Homograft

Trendelenburg Operation
See Varicose Vein, Removal, Secondary
Varicosity

Trephine Procedure
Sinusotomy
Frontal, 31070

Treponema Pallidum
Antibody
Confirmation Test, 86781
Antigen Detection
Direct Fluorescent Antibody, 87285

TRH, 80438, 80439

Triacylglycerol, 84478

Triacylglycerol Hydrolase, 83690

Triangular Cartilage
Repair with Fracture
Radial shaft, 25526

Triangular Fibrocartilage
Excision, 29846

Tributyrinase, 83690

Trichiasis
Repair, 67825
Epilation, by Forceps, 67820
Epilation, by Other than Forceps, 67825
Incision of Lid Margin, 67830
with Free Mucous Membrane Graft,
67835

Trichina
See Trichinella

Trichinella
Antibody, 86784

Trichogram, 96902

Trichomonas Vaginalis
Antigen Detection
Nucleic Acid, 87660

Trichrome Stain, 88313

Tricuspid Valve
Excision, 33460
Repair, 33463-33465
Replace, 33465
Repositioning, 33468

Tridymite
See Silica

Trigeminal Ganglia
See Gasserian Ganglion

Trigeminal Nerve
Destruction, 64600-64610
Injection
Anesthetic, 64400
Neurolytic, 64600, 64605

Trigeminal Tract
Stereotactic
Create Lesion, 61791

Trigger Finger Repair, 26055

Trigger Point
Injection
One or Two Muscle Groups, 20552
Two or More Muscle Groups, 20553

Triglyceridase
See Lipase

Triglyceride Lipase
See Lipase

Triglycerides, 84478

Trigonocephaly, 21175

Triiodothyronine
Free, 84481
Resin Uptake, 84479

Triiodothyronine — *continued*
Reverse, 84482
Total, 84480
True, 84480

Triolean Hydrolase
See Lipase

Trioxopurine
See Uric Acid

Tripcellim
See Trypsin

Trisegmentectomy, 47122

Trocar Biopsy
Bone Marrow, 38221

Trochanter
Pressure Ulcer, 15950-15958

Trochanteric Femur Fracture
See Femur, Fracture, Trochanteric

Trophoblastic Tumor GTT
See HydatidiForm Mole

Troponin
Qualitative, 84512
Quantitative, 84484

Truncal Vagotomies
See Vagotomy, Truncal

Truncus Arteriosus
Repair, 33786

Truncus Brachiocephalicus
See Artery, Brachiocephalic

Trunk
Lipectomy, Suction Assisted, 15877
Skin Graft
Delay of Flap, 15600
Full Thickness, 15200
Muscle, Myocutaneous, or Fasciocutaneous
Flaps, 15734
Split, 15100, 15101
Tissue Transfer, Adjacent, 14001

Trypanosomiases
See Trypanosomiasis

Trypanosomiasis, 86171, 86280

Trypsin
Duodenum, 84485
Feces, 84488, 84490

Trypure
See Trypsin

Trysin Inhibitor, Alpha 1-Antitrypsin
See Alpha-1 Antitrypsin

TSA, 86316

Tsalicylate Intoxication
See Salicylate

TSH, 80418, 80438-80440, 84443

TSI, 84445

Tsutsugamushi Disease
See Scrub Typhus

TT
See Thrombin Time

TT-3
See Triiodothyronine, True

TT-4
See Thyroxine, True

Tuba, Auditoria (Auditiva)
See Eustachian Tube

Tubal Embryo Stage Transfer
See Embryo Transfer

Tubal Ligation, 58600
  with Cesarean Section, 58611
  Laparoscopic, 58670
  Postpartum, 58605
Tubal Occlusion
  with Cesarean Delivery
    See Fallopian tube, Occlusion; Occlusion
    Create Lesion
      See Fallopian Tube, Occlusion;
        Occlusion, Fallopian Tube
  See Fallopian Tube
Tubal Pregnancy, 59121
  with Salpingectomy and/or Oophorectomy,
    59120
Tube Change
  Tracheotomy, 31502
Tubectomy
  See Excision, Fallopian Tube
Tubed Pedicle Flap
  Formation, 15570-15576
  Walking Tube, 15650
Tube, Fallopian
  See Fallopian Tube
Tube Placement
  Endoscopic
    Bile Duct, Pancreatic Duct, 43268
    Nasobiliary, Nasopancreatic for Drainage,
      43267
  Gastrostomy Tube, 43750
  Nasogastric Tube, 43752
  Orogastric Tube, 43752
Tubercle Bacilli
  Culture, 87116
Tubercleplasty, Anterior Tibial, 27418
Tuberculin Test
  See Skin, Tests, Tuberculosis
Tuberculosis
  Antigen Response Test, 86480
  Culture, 87116
  Skin Test, 86580
Tuberculosis Vaccine (BCG), 90585, 90586
Tubes
  Endotracheal
    See Endotracheal Tube
  Gastrostomy
    See Gastrostomy Tube
Tudor "Rabbit Ear"
  Urethra, Repair
    Diverticulum, 53240, 53400, 53405
    Fistula, 45820, 45825, 53400, 53405, 53520
    Sphincter, 57220
    Stricture, 53400, 53405
    Urethrocele, 57230
    Wound, 53502-53515
Tuffier Vaginal Hysterectomy
  See Hysterectomy, Vaginal
Tumor
  See Craniopharyngioma
  See Lesion
  Abdomen
    Destruction
      Excision, 49200, 49201
  Abdominal Wall
    Excision, 22900
  Acetabulum
    Excision, 27076
  Ankle, 27615-27619
  Arm, Lower, 25075-25077
  Arm, Upper, 24075-24077

Tumor — *continued*
  Back
    Flank
      Excision, 21930
      Radical Resection, 21935
  Bile Duct
    Destruction, 43272
    Extrahepatic, 47711
    Intrahepatic, 47712
  Bladder, 52234-52240
    Excision, 51530, 52355
  Brain, 61510
    Excision, 61518, 61520, 61521, 61526,
      61530, 61545, 62164
  Breast
    Excision, 19120-19126
  Bronchi
    Excision, 31640
  Calcaneus, 28100-28103
    Excision, 27647
  Carpal, 25130-25136
  Chest Wall
    Excision, 19260-19272
  Clavicle
    Excision, 23140, 23200
      with Allograft, 23146
      with Autograft, 23145
  Coccyx, 49215
  Colon
    Destruction, 44393, 45383
  Cranial Bone
    Reconstruction, 21181, 21182
  Destruction
    Abdomen, 49200, 49201
    Chemosurgery, 17304-17310
    Urethra, 53220
  Ear, Middle
    Extended, 69554
    Transcanal, 69550
    Transmastoid, 69552
  Elbow
    Excision, 24075-24077
  Esophagus
    Ablation, 43228
  Excision
    Femur, 27355-27358
    Facial Bones, 21029, 21030, 21034
  Fallopian Tube
    Resection, 58950, 58952-58956
  Femoral, 27355-27358
    Excision, 27365
  Femur, 27065-27067
    Excision, 27365
  Fibula, 27635-27638
    Excision, 27646
  Finger
    Excision, 26115-26117
    Foot, 28043, 28045, 28046
  Forearm
    Radical Resection, 25077
  Gums
    Excision, 41825-41827
  Hand, 26115-26117
  Heart
    Excision, 33120, 33130
  Hip, 27047-27049, 27065-27067
    Excision, 27075, 27076
  Humerus
    with Allograft, 23156
    with Autograft, 23155

Tumor — *continued*
  Humerus — *continued*
    Excision, 23150, 23220-23222, 24110
      with Allograft, 23156, 24116
      with Autograft, 23155, 24115
  Ileum, 27065-27067
  Immunoassay for Antigen, 86294, 86316
    CA 125, 86304
    CA 15-3, 86300
    CA 19-9, 86301
  Innominate
    Excision, 27077
  Intestines, Small
    Destruction, 44369
  Ischial
    Excision, 27078, 27079
  Kidney
    Excision, 52355
  Knee
    Excision, 27327-27329, 27365
  Lacrimal Gland
    Excision
      with Osteotomy, 68550
      Frontal Approach, 68540
  Larynx, 31540, 31541
    Excision, 31300
      Endoscopic, 31540, 31541, 31578
    Incision, 31300
  Leg, Lower, 27615-27619
  Leg, Upper
    Excision, 27327-27329
  Localization
    with Nuclear Medicine, 78800-78803
  Mandible, 21040-21045
  Maxillary Torus Palatinus, 21032
  Mediastinal
    Excision, 39220
  Mediastinum, 32662
  Meningioma
    Excision, 61519
  Metacarpal, 26200, 26205, 26250, 26255
  Metatarsal, 28104-28107
    Excision, 28173
  Neck
    Excision, 21555, 21556
    Radical Resection, 21557
  Olecranon Process
    with Allograft, 24126
    with Autograft, 24125
    Excision, 24120
  Ovary
    Resection, 58950, 58952-58954
  Pancreatic Duct
    Destruction, 43272
  Parotid Gland
    Excision, 42410-42426
  Pelvis, 27047-27049
  Pericardial
    Endoscopic, 32661
    Excision, 33050
  Peritoneum
    Resection, 58950-58956
  Phalanges
    Finger, 26210, 26215, 26260-26262
    Toe, 28108
      Excision, 28175
  Pituitary Gland
    Excision, 61546, 61548
  Positron Emission Tomography (PET), 78811-78816
  Pubis, 27065-27067
  Radiation Therapy, 77295

Tumor — *continued*
  Radius, 25120-25126, 25170
    with Allograft, 24126
    with Autograft, 24125
    Excision, 24120
  Rectum
    Destruction, 45190, 45320, 46937, 46938
    Excision, 45160, 45170
  Resection
    with Cystourethroscopy, 52355
    Face, 21015
    Scalp, 21015
  Retroperitoneal
    Destruction
      Excision, 49200, 49201
  Sacrum, 49215
  Scapula, 23140
    Excision, 23140, 23210
      with Allograft, 23146
      with Autograft, 23145
  Shoulder
    Excision, 23075-23077
  Skull
    Excision, 61500
  Soft Tissue
    Elbow
      Excision, 24075
    Finger
      Excision, 26115
    Forearm
      Radical Resection, 25077
    Hand
      Excision, 26115
  Spinal Cord
    Excision, 63275-63290
  Stomach
    Excision, 43610, 43611
  Talus, 28100-28103
    Excision, 27647
  Tarsal, 28104-28107
    Excision, 28171
  Temporal Bone
    Removal, 69970
  Testis
    Excision, 54530, 54535
  Thorax
    Excision, 21555, 21556
    Radical Resection, 21557
  Thyroid
    Excision, 60200
  Tibia, 27365, 27635-27638
    Excision, 27645
  Torus Mandibularis, 21031
  Trachea
    Excision
      Cervical, 31785
      Thoracic, 31786
  Ulna, 25120-25126, 25170
    with Allograft
      Excision, 24126
    with Autograft
      Excision, 24125
    Excision, 24120
  Ureter
    Excision, 52355
  Urethra, 52234-52240, 53220
    Excision, 52355
  Uterus
    Excision, 58140, 58145
  Vagina
    Excision, 57135

Tumor — *continued*
Vertebra
  Additional Segment
    Excision, 22103, 22116
  Cervical
    Excision, 22100
  Lumbar, 22102
  Thoracic
    Excision, 22101
Wrist, 25075-25077, 25135, 25136
  Excision, 25075
  Radical Resection, 25077

Tunica Vaginalis
Hydrocele
  Aspiration, 55000
  Excision, 55040, 55041
  Repair, 55060

Turbinate
Excision, 30130, 30140
Fracture
  Therapeutic, 30930
Injection, 30200
Submucous Resection
  Nose
    Excision, 30140

Turbinate Mucosa
Ablation, 30801, 30802
Cauterization, 30801, 30802

Turcica, Sella
See Sella Turcica

Turnbuckle Jacket, 29020, 29025
Removal, 29715

TURP, 52601, 52612-52630

Tylectomy
See Breast, Excision, Lesion

Tylenol
Urine, 82003

Tympanic Membrane
Create Stoma, 69433, 69436
Incision, 69420, 69421
Reconstruction, 69620
Repair, 69450, 69610

Tympanic Nerve
Excision, 69676

Tympanolysis, 69450

Tympanometry, 92567
See Audiologic Function Tests

Tympanoplasty
with Antrotomy or Mastoidectomy, 69635
  with Ossicular Chain Reconstruction, 69636
    and Synthetic Prosthesis, 69637
with Mastoidectomy, 69641
  with Intact or Reconstructed Wall
    without Ossicular Chain Reconstruction,
      69643
    and Ossicular Chain Reconstruction,
      69644
  and Ossicular Chain Reconstruction, 69644
without Mastoidectomy, 69631
  with Ossicular Chain Reconstruction, 69632
  and Synthetic Prosthesis, 69633
See Myringoplasty
Radical or Complete, 69645
  with Ossicular Chain Reconstruction, 69646

Tympanostomy, 69433, 69436

Tympanotomy
See Myringotomy

Typhoid Vaccine, 90690-90693
AKD, 90693
H-P, 90692
Oral, 90690
Polysaccharide, 90691

Typhus
Endemic
  See Murine Typhus
Mite-Bone
  See Scrub Typhus
Sao Paulo
  See Rocky Mountain Spotted Fever
Tropical
  See Scrub Typhus

Typing, Blood
See Blood Typing

Typing, HLA
See HLA Typing

Typing, Tissue
See Tissue Typing

Tyrosine, 84510

Tzank Smear, 87207

U

UAC, 36660

Uchida Procedure
Tubal Ligation, 58600

UDP Galactose Pyrophysphorylase
See Galactose-1-Phosphate, Uridyl Transferase

UFR, 51736, 51741

Ulcer
Anal
  See Anus, Fissure
Decubitus
  See Debridement, Pressure Ulcer
    (Decubitus); Skin Graft and Flap
Pinch Graft, 15050
Pressure, 15920-15999
Stomach
  Excision, 43610

Ulcerative, Cystitis
See Cystitis, Interstitial

Ulna
See Arm, Lower; Elbow; Humerus; Radius
Arthrodesis
  Radioulnar Joint
    with Resection, 25830
Arthroplasty
  with Implant, 25442
Centralization of Wrist, 25335
Craterization, 24147, 25150, 25151
Cyst
  Excision, 24125, 24126, 25120-25126
Diaphysectomy, 24147, 25150, 25151
Excision, 24147
  Abscess, 24138
  Complete, 25240
  Epiphyseal Bar, 20150
  Partial, 25145-25151, 25240
Fracture, 25605
  with Dislocation
    Closed Treatment, 24620
    Open Treatment, 24635
  with Manipulation, 25535
  with Radius, 25560, 25565
    Open Treatment, 25575
  without Manipulation, 25530
    Closed Treatment, 25530, 25535

Ultraviolet Light Therapy
Dermatology, 96900
  Ultraviolet A, 96912
  Ultraviolet B, 96910
for Physical Medicine, 97028
Umbilectomy, 49250
Umbilical
Artery Ultrasound, 76820
Hernia
  See Omphalocele
Vein Catheterization
  See Catheterization, Umbilical Vein
Umbilical Cord
Occlusion, 59072
Umbilicus
Excision, 49250
Repair
  Hernia, 49580-49587
  Omphalocele, 49600-49611
Undescended Testicle
See Testis, Undescended
Unfertilized Egg
See Ova
Unguis
See Nails
Unilateral Simple Mastectomy
See Mastectomy
Unlisted Services or Procedures, 99499
Abdomen, 22999, 49329, 49999
Allergy
  Immunology, 95199
Anal, 46999
Anesthesia, 01999
Arm, Upper, 24999
Arthroscopy, 29999
Autopsy, 88099
Bile Duct, 47999
Bladder, 53899
Brachytherapy, 77799
Breast, 19499
Bronchi, 31899
Cardiac, 33999
Cardiovascular Studies, 93799
Casting, 29799
Cervix, 58999
Chemistry Procedure, 84999
Chemotherapy, 96549
Chest, 32999
Coagulation, 85999
Colon, 44799
Conjunctiva Surgery, 68399
Craniofacial, 21299
CT Scan, 76497
Cytogenetic Study, 88299
Cytopathology, 88199
Dermatology, 96999
Dialysis, 90999
Diaphragm, 39599
Ear
  External, 69399
  Inner, 69949
  Middle, 69799
Endocrine System, 60699
Epididymis, 55899
Esophagus, 43289, 43499
Evaluation and Management Services, 99499
Eyelid, 67999
Eye Muscle, 67399
Eye Surgery
  Anterior Segment, 66999
  Posterior Segment, 67299

Unlisted Services or Procedures — *continued*
Forearm, 25999
Gallbladder Surgery, 47999
Gastroenterology Test, 91299
Gum Surgery, 41899
Hand, 26989
Hemic System, 38999
Hepatic Duct, 47999
Hip Joint, 27299
Home Services
Hysteroscopy, 58579
Immunization, 90749
Immunology, 86849
Intestine, 44799
Kidney, 49659
Lacrimal System, 68899
Laparoscopy, 38129, 38589, 43289, 43659,
  44979, 47379, 47579, 49329, 49659,
  50549, 50949, 54699, 55559, 58578,
  58679, 59898, 60659
Larynx, 31599
Lip, 40799
Liver, 47379, 47399
Lungs, 32999
Lymphatic System, 38999
Maxillofacial, 21299
Maxillofacial Prosthetics, 21089
Meckel's Diverticulum, 44899
Mediastinum, 39499
Mesentery Surgery, 44899
Microbiology, 87999
Mouth, 40899, 41599
Musculoskeletal, 25999, 26989
Musculoskeletal Surgery
  Abdominal Wall, 22999
  Neck, 21899
  Spine, 22899
  Thorax, 21899
Musculoskeletal System, 20999
  Ankle, 27899
  Arm, Upper, 24999
  Elbow, 24999
  Head, 21499
  Knee, 27599
  Leg, Lower, 27899
  Leg, Upper, 27599
Necropsy, 88099
Nervous System Surgery, 64999
Neurology
  Neuromuscular Testing, 95999
Nose, 30999
Nuclear Medicine, 78999
  Blood, 78199
  Bone, 78399
  Endocrine Procedure, 78099
  Genitourinary System, 78799
  Heart, 78499
  Hematopoietic System, 78199
  Lymphatic System, 78199
  Musculoskeletal System, 78399
  Nervous System, 78699
  Therapeutic, 79999
Obstetric Care, 59898, 59899
Omentum, 49329, 49999
Ophthalmology, 92499
Orbit, 67599
Otorhinolaryngology, 92700
Ovary, 58679, 58999
Oviduct, 58679, 58999

Urethral Stent — *continued*
Removal
Bladder, 52310, 52315
Urethra, 52310, 52315
Urethral Stricture
Dilation, 52281, 53600, 53621
Injection
Steroids, 52283
Urethral Syndrome
Cystourethroscopy, 52285
Urethrectomy, 50650, 50660
Partial, 50220
Total
Female, 53210
Male, 53215
Urethrocele
See Urethra, Prolapse
Urethrocystography, 74450, 74455
Contrast and/or Chain, 51605
Retrograde, 51610
Voiding, 51600
Urethrocystopexy
See Vesicourethropexy
Urethromeatoplasty, 53450, 53460
Urethropexy, 51840, 51841
Urethroplasty, 46744, 46746
First Stage, 53400
Hypospadias, 54322-54328
Reconstruction
Female Urethra, 53430
Male Anterior Urethra, 53410
Prostatic
Membranous Urethra
First Stage, 53420
One Stage, 53415
Second Stage, 53425
Second Stage, 53405
Hypospadias, 54308-54316
Third Stage
Hypospadias, 54318
Urethrorrhaphy, 53502-53515
Urethroscopy
with Cystourethroscopy, 52351
See Endoscopy, Urethra
Perineal, 53899
Urethrostomy, 53000, 53010
Urethrotomy, 53000, 53010
with Cystourethroscopy
Female, 52270
Male, 52275
Direct Vision
with Cystourethroscopy, 52276
Internal, 52601, 52647, 52648
Uric Acid
Blood, 84550
Other Source, 84560
Urine, 84560
Uridyltransferase, Galactose-1-Phosphate
See Galactose-1-Phosphate, Uridyl Transferase
Uridylyltransferase, Galactosephophate
See Galactose-1-Phosphate, Uridyl Transferase
Urinalysis, 0041T, 81000-81099
without Microscopy, 81002
Automated, 81001, 81003
Glass Test, 81020
Microalbumin, 82043, 82044
Microscopic, 81015
Pregnancy Test, 81025

Urinalysis — *continued*
Qualitative, 81005
Routine, 81002
Screen, 81007
Semiquantitative, 0041T, 81005
Unlisted Services and Procedures, 81099
Volume Measurement, 81050
Water Load Test, 89235
Urinary Bladder
See Bladder
Urinary Catheter Irrigation
See Irrigation, Catheter
Urinary Concentration Test
See Water Load Test
Urinary Sphincter, Artificial
See Prosthesis, Urethral Sphincter
Urinary Tract
X-ray with Contrast, 74400-74425
Urine
Albumin
See Albumin, Urine
Blood
See Blood, Urine
Colony Count, 87086
Pregnancy Test, 81025
Tests, 81000-81099
Urobilinogen
Feces, 84577
Urine, 84578-84583
Urodynamic Tests
Bladder Capacity
Ultrasound, 51798
Cystometrogram, 51725, 51726
Electromyography Studies
Needle, 51785
Residual Urine
Ultrasound, 51798
Stimulus Evoked Response, 51792
Urethra Pressure Profile, 51772
Uroflowmetry, 51736, 51741
Voiding Pressure Studies
Bladder, 51795
Intra-Abdominal, 51797
Uroflowmetry, 51736, 51741
Urography
Antegrade, 74425
Infusion, 74410, 74415
Intravenous, 74400-74415
Retrograde, 74420
Uroporphyrin, 84120
Urostomy, 50727, 50728
Urothromboplastin
See Thromboplastin
Uterine
Adhesion
See Adhesions, Intruterine
Cervix
See Cervix
Endoscopies
See Endoscopy, Uterus
Hemorrhage
See Hemorrhage, Uterus
Uterus
Ablation
Endometrium, 58353-58356
Tumor
Ultrasound Focused, 0071T-0072T

Uterus — *continued*
Biopsy
Endometrium, 58100
Endoscopy, 58558
Catheterization
X-ray, 58340
Chromotubation, 58350
Curettage, 58356
Postpartum, 59160
Dilation and Curettage, 58120
Postpartum, 59160
Ectopic Pregnancy
Interstitial
Partial Resection Uterus, 59136
Total Hysterectomy, 59135
Endoscopy
Endometrial Ablation, 58563
Exploration, 58555
Surgery, 58558-58565
Treatment, 58558-58565
Excision
Laparoscopic, 58550
Partial, 58180
Radical, 58210, 58285
Removal of Tubes and/or Ovaries, 58262,
58263, 58291-58293, 58552, 58554
Sonohysterography, 76831
Total, 58150-58152, 58200, 58953-58956
Vaginal, 58260-58270, 58290-58294, 58550-
58554
with Colpectomy, 58275, 58280
with Colpo-Urethrocystopexy, 58267
with Repair of Enterocele, 58270, 58294
Hemorrhage
Postpartum, 59160
HydatidiForm Mole
Excision, 59100
Hydrotubation, 58350
Hysterosalpingography, 74740
Hysterosonography, 76831
Incision
Removal of Lesion, 59100
Insertion
Heyman Capsule
for Brachytherapy, 58346
Intrauterine Device, 58300
Tandem
for Brachytherapy, 57155
Laparoscopy, 58578
Lesion
Excision, 58545, 58546, 59100
Reconstruction, 58540
Removal
Intrauterine Device (IUD), 58301
Repair
Fistula, 51920, 51925
Rupture, 58520, 59350
Suspension, 58400
with Presacral Sympathectomy, 58410
Suture
Rupture, 59350
Tumor
Excision
Abdominal Approach, 58140, 58146
Vaginal Approach, 58145
Unlisted Services and Procedures, 58578,
58999
X-ray with Contrast, 74740
UTP Hexose 1 Phosphate Uridylyltransferase
See Galactose-1-Phosphate, Uridyl Transferase
UVC, 36510

UV Light Therapy
See Actinotherapy
Uvula
Abscess
Incision and Drainage, 42000
Biopsy, 42100
Excision, 42140, 42145
Lesion
Destruction, 42145
Excision, 42104-42107
Unlisted Services and Procedures, 42299
Uvulectomy, 42140
Uvulopalatopharyngoplasty, 42145
Uvulopharyngoplasty, 42145

V

Vaccination
See Allergen Immunotherapy; Immunization;
Vaccines
Vaccines
Adenovirus, 90476, 90477
Anthrax, 90581
Chicken Pox, 90716
Cholera Injectable, 90725
Diphtheria, Tetanus (DT), 90702
Diphtheria, Tetanus, Acellular Pertussis (DTaP),
90700
Diphtheria, Tetanus, Acellular Pertussis and
Hemophilus Influenza B (Hib) (DtaP-Hib),
90721
Diphtheria, Tetanus, Acellular Pertussis,
Hemophilus Influenza B, and Poliovirus
Inactivated (DTaP-Hib-IPV), 90698
Diphtheria, Tetanus, Acellular Pertussis,
Hepatitis B, and Inactivated Poliovirus
(DTaP-HepB-IPV), 90723
Diphtheria, Tetanus, and Acellular Pertussis,
(Tdap), 90715
Diphtheria, Tetanus, Whole Cell Pertussis
(DTP), 90701
Diphtheria, Tetanus, Whole Cell Pertussis and
Hemophilus Influenza B (DTP-Hib), 90720
Diphtheria Toxoid, 90719
Encephalitis, Japanese, 90735
Hemophilus Influenza b, 90645-90648
Hepatitis A, 90632-90634
Hepatitis A and Hepatitis B, 90636
Hepatitis B, 90740-90747
Hepatitis B and Hemophilus Influenza B (HepB-
Hib), 90748
Human Papilloma Virus (HPV), 90649
Influenza, 90655-90660
Lyme Disease, 90665
Measles, 90705
Measles and Rubella, 90708
Measles, Mumps and Rubella (MMR), 90707
Measles, Mumps, Rubella and Varicella
(MMRV), 90710
Meningococcal, 90733, 90734
Mumps, 90704
Plague, 90727
Pneumococcal, 90669, 90732
Poliovirus, Inactivated
Intramuscular, 90713
Subcutaneous, 90713
Poliovirus, Live
Oral, 90712
Rabies, 90675, 90676
Rotavirus, 90680
Rubella, 90706

Vaginal Suppositories
Induced Abortion, 59855
   with Dilation and Curettage, 59856
   with Hysterotomy, 59857

Vaginal Tissue
Removal, Partial, 57106

Vaginal Wall
Removal, Partial, 57107

Vaginectomy
Partial, 57109
   with Nodes, 57109

Vaginoplasty
Intersex State, 57335

Vaginorrhaphy
See Coporrhaphy

Vaginoscopy
Biopsy, 57454
Exploration, 57452

Vaginotomy
See Colpotomy

Vagotomy
With Gastroduodenostomy
   Revision/Reconstruction, 43855
With Gastrojejunostomy
   Revision/Reconstruction, 43865
With Partial Distal Gastrectomy, 43635
   Abdominal, 64760
Highly Selective, 43641
Parietal Cell, 43641, 64755
Reconstruction, 43855
   with Gastroduodenostomy Revision, 43855
   with Gastrojejunostomy Revision,
     Reconstruction, 43865
Selective, 43640
Transthoracic, 64752
Truncal, 43640

Vagus Nerve
Avulsion
   Abdominal, 64760
   Selective, 64755
   Thoracic, 64752
Incision, 43640, 43641
   Abdominal, 64760
   Selective, 64755
   Thoracic, 64752
Injection
   Anesthetic, 64408
Transection, 43640, 43641
   Abdominal, 64760
   Selective, 43652, 64755
   Thoracic, 64752
   Truncal, 43651

Valentine's Test
Urinalysis, Glass Test, 81020

Valproic Acid
See Dipropylacetic Acid

Valproic Acid Measurement
See Dipropylacetic Acid

Valsalva Sinus
See Sinus of Valsalva

Valva Atrioventricularis Sinistra (Valva Mitralis)
See Mitral Valve

Valve
Aortic
   See Heart, Aortic Valve
Bicuspid
   See Mitral Valve
Mitral
   See Mitral Valve

Valve — *continued*
Pulmonary
   See Pulmonary Valve
Tricuspid
   See Tricuspid Valve

Valvectomy
Tricuspid Valve, 33460

Valve Stenoses, Aortic
See Aortic Stenosis

Valvotomy
Mitral Valve, 33420, 33422
Pulmonary Valve, 33470-33474
Reoperation, 33530

Valvuloplasty
Aortic Valve, 33400-33403
Femoral Vein, 34501
Mitral Valve, 33425-33427
Percutaneous Balloon
   Aortic Valve, 92986
   Mitral Valve, 92987
   Pulmonary Valve, 92990
Prosthetic Valve, 33496
Reoperation, 33530
Tricuspid Valve, 33460-33465

Vancomycin
Assay, 80202

Van Den Bergh Test, 82247, 82248

Vanillymandelic Acid
Urine, 84585

Vanilmandelic Acid
See Vanillylmandelic Acid

Varicella (Chicken Pox)
Immunization, 90710, 90716

Varicella-Zoster
Antibody, 86787
Antigen Detection
   Direct Fluorescent Antibody, 87290

Varices Esophageal
See Esophageal Varices

Varicocele
Spermatic Cord
   Excision, 55530-55540

Varicose Vein
with Tissue Excision, 37735, 37760
Ablation, 36475-36479
Removal, 37718, 37722, 37735, 37765-37785
Secondary Varicosity, 37785

Vascular Flow Check, Graft, 15860

Vascular Injection
Unlisted Services and Procedures, 36299

Vascular Lesion
Cranial
   Excision, 61600-61608, 61615, 61616
Cutaneous
   Destruction, 17106-17108

Vascular Malformation
Cerebral
   Repair, 61710
Finger
   Excision, 26115
Hand
   Excision, 26115

Vascular Procedure
Brachytherapy
   Intracoronary Artery, 92974
Intravascular Ultrasound
   Coronary Vessels, 92978, 92979
Stent
   Intracoronary, 92980, 92981

Vein — *continued*
Extremity
Non-Invasive Studies, 93965-93971
Femoral
Repair, 34501
Femoropopliteal
Thrombectomy, 34421, 34451
Guidance
Fluoroscopic, 75998
Ultrasound, 76937
Hepatic Portal
Splenoportography, 75810
Venography, 75885, 75887
Iliac
Thrombectomy, 34401, 34421, 34451
Injection
Sclerosing Agent, 36468-36471
Insertion
IVC Filter, 75940
Interrupt
Femoral Vein, 37650
Iliac, 37660
Vena Cava, 37620
Jugular
Venography, 75860
Leg
Harvest for Vascular Reconstruction, 35572
Venography, 75820, 75822
Ligation
Clusters, 37785
Esophagus, 43205
Jugular, 37565
Perforation, 37760
Saphenous, 37700-37735, 37780
Secondary, 37785
Liver
Venography, 75860, 75889, 75891
Neck
Venography, 75860
Nuclear Medicine
Thrombosis Imaging, 78456-78458
Orbit
Venography, 75880
Placement
IVC Filter, 75940
Portal
Catheterization, 36481
Pulmonary
Repair, 33730
Removal
Clusters, 37785
Saphenous, 37700-37735, 37780
Varicose, 37765, 37766
Renal
Venography, 75831, 75833
Repair
Aneurysm, 36834
Angioplasty, 75978
Graft, 34520
Sampling
Venography, 75893
Sinus
Venography, 75870
Skull
Venography, 75870, 75872
Spermatic
Excision, 55530-55540
Ligation, 55500
Splenic
Splenoportography, 75810
Stripping
Saphenous, 37720-37735, 37780

Vein — *continued*
Subclavian
Thrombectomy, 34471, 34490
Thrombectomy
Other than Hemodialysis Graft or Fistula, 35875, 35876
Unlisted Services and Procedures, 37799
Valve Transposition, 34510
Varicose
See Varicose Vein
Vena Cava
Thrombectomy, 34401-34451
Venography, 75825, 75827
Velpeau Cast, 29058
Vena Cava
Catheterization, 36010
Reconstruction, 34502
Resection with Reconstruction, 37799
Vena Caval
Thrombectomy, 50230
Venereal Disease Research Laboratory
See VDRL
Venipuncture
See Cannulation; Catheterization
Breast
Cytology, 0045T
Child/Adult
Cutdown, 36425
Percutaneous, 36410
Infant
Cutdown, 36420
Percutaneous, 36400-36406
Routine, 36415
Venography
Adrenal, 75840, 75842
Arm, 75820, 75822
Epidural, 75872
Hepatic Portal, 75885, 75887
Injection, 36005
Jugular, 75860
Leg, 75820, 75822
Liver, 75889, 75891
Neck, 75860
Nuclear Medicine, 78445, 78457, 78458
Orbit, 75880
Renal, 75831, 75833
Sagittal Sinus, 75870
Thoracic, 22520-22522
Vena Cava, 75825, 75827
Venous Sampling, 75893
Venorrhaphy
See Suture, Vein
Venotomy
See Phlebotomy
Venous Access Device
Fluoroscopic Guidance, 75998
Insertion
Central, 36560-36566
Peripheral, 36570, 36571
Obstruction Clearance, 36595, 36596
Guidance, 75901, 75902
Removal, 36590
Repair, 36576
Replacement, 36582, 36583, 36585
Catheter Only, 36578
Venous Blood Pressure
See Blood Pressure, Venous
Venovenostomy
See Anastomosis, Vein

Index

Ventilating Tube — Vestibular Function Tests

Vestibular Function Tests — *continued*
Nystagmus
Optokinetic, 92534, 92544
Positional, 92532, 92542
Spontaneous, 92531, 92541
Posturography, 92548
Sinusoidal Rotational Testing, 92546
Torsion Swing Test, 92546
Tracking Test, 92545

Vestibular Nerve
Section
Transcranial Approach, 69950
Translabyrinthine Approach, 69915

Vestibule of Mouth
See Mouth, Vestibule of

Vestibuloplasty, 40840-40845

VF, 92081-92083

V-Flap Procedure
One Stage Distal Hypospadias Repair, 54322
One Stage Distal Hypospadias Repair, 54322

Vidal Procedure
See Varicocele, Spermatic Cord, Excision
Varicocele, Spermatic Cord, Excision, 55530-55540

Video
Esophagus, 74230
Pharynx, 70371-74230
Speech Evaluation, 70371
Swallowing Evaluation, 74230

Video-Assisted Thoracoscopic Surgery
See Thoracoscopy

Videoradiography
Unlisted Services and Procedures, 76120-76125

VII, Coagulation Factor
See Proconvertin

VII, Cranial Nerve
See Facial Nerve

VIII, Coagulation Factor
See Clotting Factor

Villus, Chorionic
See Chorionic Villus

Villusectomy
See Synovectomy

VIP, 84586

Viral
AIDS
See HIV-1
Burkitt Lymphoma
See Epstein-Barr Virus
Human Immunodeficiency
See HIV
Influenza
See Influenza Virus
Respiratory Syncytial
See Respiratory Syncytial Virus
Salivary Gland
See Cytomegalovirus

Viral Antibodies, 86280

Viral Warts
See Warts

Virtual Colonoscopy
Diagnostic, 0067T
Screening, 0066T

Virus Identification
Immunofluorescence, 87254

Virus Isolation, 87250-87255

Visceral Larval Migrans, 86280

Viscosities, Blood
See Blood, Viscosity

Visit, Home
See House Calls

Visual Acuity Screen, 99172, 99173

Visual Field Exam, 92081-92083

Visualization
Ideal Conduit, 50690

Visual ReinForcement Audiometry, 92579
See Audiologic Function Tests

Vital Capacity Measurement, 94150

Vitamin
A, 84590
B-1, 84425
B-12, 82607, 82608
Absorption Study, 78270-78272
B-2, 84252
B-6, 84207
B-6 Measurement
See Pyridoxal Phophate
BC
See Folic Acid
B Complex
See B Complex Vitamins
C, 82180
D, 82307, 82652
D-2
See Calciferol
D, 25-Hydroxy Measurement
See Calcifediol
D-3, 82306
E, 84446
K, 84597
K Dependent Bone Protein
See Osteocalcin
K-Dependent Protein S
See Protein S

Vitelline Duct
See Omphalomesenteric Duct

Vitrectomy
with Endolaser Panretinal Photocoagulation, 67040
with Epiretinal Membrane Stripping, 67038
with Focal Endolaser Photocoagulation, 67039
with Implantation of Intra-ocular Retinal Electrode Array, 0100T
with Implantation or Replacement Drug Delivery System, 67027
with Placement of Subconjunctival Retinal Prosthesis Receiver, 0100T
Anterior Approach
Partial, 67005
Pars Plana Approach, 67036
Partial, 67005, 67010
Subtotal, 67010

Vitreous
Aspiration, 67015
Excision
with Epiretinal Membrane Stripping, 67038
with Focal Endolaser Photocoagulation, 67039
Pars Plana Approach, 67036
Implantation
Drug Delivery System, 67027
Incision
Strands, 67030, 67031
Injection
Fluid Substitute, 67025
Pharmacologic Agent, 67028

Wound — *continued*
  Secondary — *continued*
    Skin and subcutaneous tissue — *continued*
      Simple with packing, 12021
      Superficial, 12020
        with packing, 12021
  Suture
    Bladder, 51860, 51865
    Kidney, 50500
    Trachea
      Cervical, 31800
      Intrathoracic, 31805
    Urethra, 53502-53515
  Vagina
    Repair, 57200, 57210
W-Plasty
  See Skin, Adjacent Tissue Transfer
  Skin Surgery, Adjacent Tissue Transfer, 14000-
    14350
Wrist
  See Arm, Lower; Carpal Bone
  Abscess, 25028
  Arthrocentesis, 20605
  Arthrodesis, 25800
    with Graft, 25810
    with Sliding Graft, 25805
  Arthrography, 73115
  Arthroplasty, 25332, 25443, 25447
    with Implant, 25441, 25442, 25444, 25445
    Revision, 25449
    Total Replacement, 25446
  Arthroscopy
    Diagnostic, 29840
    Surgical, 29843-29848
  Arthrotomy, 25040, 25100-25105
    for Repair, 25107
  Biopsy, 25065, 25066, 25100, 25101
  Bursa
    Excision, 25115, 25116
      Incision and Drainage, 25031
  Capsule
    Incision, 25085
  Cast, 29085
  Cyst, 25130-25136
  Decompression, 25020, 25023
  Disarticulation, 25920
    Reamputation, 25924
    Revision, 25922
  Dislocation
    with Fracture
      Closed Treatment, 25680
      Open Treatment, 25685
    with Manipulation, 25259, 25660, 25675
      Closed Treatment, 25660
    Intercarpal, 25660
      Open Treatment, 25670
    Open Treatment, 25660, 25670, 25676
    Percutaneous Fixation, 25671
    Radiocarpal, 25660
      Open Treatment, 25670
    Radioulnar
      Closed Treatment, 25675
      Percutaneous Fixation, 25671
  Excision
    Carpal, 25210, 25215
    Cartilage, 25107
    Tendon Sheath, 25115, 25116
  Exploration, 25040, 25101
  Fasciotomy, 25020-25025
  Fracture, 25645
    with Dislocation, 25680, 25685

Wrist — *continued*
  Fracture — *continued*
    with Manipulation, 25259, 25624, 25635
    Closed Treatment, 25622, 25630
    Open Treatment, 25628
  Ganglion Cyst
    Excision, 25111, 25112
  Hematoma, 25028
  Incision, 25040, 25100-25105
    Tendon Sheath, 25000, 25001
  Injection
    Carpal Tunnel
      Therapeutic, 20526
    X-ray, 25246
  Joint
    See Radiocarpal Joint
  Lesion
    Excision, 25110
    Tendon Sheath, 25000
  Magnetic Resonance Imaging, 73221
  Reconstruction
    Capsulectomy, 25320
    Capsulorrhaphy, 25320
    Carpal Bone, 25394, 25430
    Realign, 25335
  Removal
    Foreign Body, 25040, 25101, 25248
    Implant, 25449
    Loose Body, 25101
    Prosthesis, 25250, 25251
  Repair, 25447
    Bone, 25440
    Carpal Bone, 25431
    Muscle, 25260, 25270
      Secondary, 25263, 25265, 25272, 25274
    Tendon, 25260, 25270, 25280-25316
      Secondary, 25263, 25265, 25272, 25274
    Tendon Sheath, 25275
  Strapping, 29260
  Synovium
    Excision, 25105, 25115-25119
  Tendon Sheath
    Excision, 25115, 25116
  Tenodesis, 25300, 25301
  Tenotomy, 25290
  Tumor, 25130-25136
    Excision, 25075-25077
  Unlisted Services and Procedures, 25999
  X-ray, 73100, 73110
    with Contrast, 73115

X

Xa, Coagulation Factor
  See Thrombokinase
X, Coagulation Factor
  See Stuart-Prower Factor
X, Cranial Nerve
  See Vagus Nerve
Xenoantibodies
  See Antibody, Heterophile
Xenograft, 15400, 15401, 15420-15421, 15430-
    15431
Xenotransplantation
  See Heterograft
Xerography, 76150
Xerography
  See Xeroradiography
Xeroradiography, 76150
XI, Coagulation Factor
  See Plasma Thromboplastin, Antecedent

XI, Cranial Nerve
  See Accessory Nerve
XII, Coagulation Factor
  See Hageman Factor
XII, Cranial Nerve
  See Hypoglossal Nerve
XIII, Coagulation Factor
  See Fibrin Stabilizing Factor
X-Linked Ichthyoses
  See Syphilis Test
X-ray
  with Contrast
    Ankle, 73615
    Aorta, 0080T-0081T, 75600-75630, 75952,
      75953
    Artery
      with Additional Vessels, 75774
      Abdominal, 75726
      Adrenal, 75731, 75733
      Arm, 75710, 75716
      Arteriovenous Shunt, 75790
      Brachial, 75658
      Carotid, 75660-75680
      Coronary, 93556
      Coronary Bypass, 93556
      Head and Neck, 75650
      Leg, 75710, 75716
      Mammary, 75756
      Pelvic, 75736
      Pulmonary, 75741-75746
      Renal, 75722, 75724
      Spine, 75705
      Transcatheter Therapy, 75894-75898
        Angiogram, 75898
        Embolization, 75894
        Infusion, 75896
      Vertebral, 75685
    Bile Duct, 74300-74320
      Calculus Removal, 74327
      Catheterization, 75982, 75984
      Drainage, 75980, 75982
      Guide Catheter, 74328, 74330
    Bladder, 74430, 74450, 74455
    Brain, 70010, 70015
    Bronchi, 71040, 71060
    Colon
      Barium Enema, 74270, 74280
    Corpora Cavernosa, 74445
    Elbow, 73085
    Epididymis, 74440
    Gallbladder, 74290, 74291
    Gastrointestinal Tract, 74246-74249
    Hip, 73525
    Iliofemoral Artery, 75630
    Intervertebral Disk
      Cervical, 72285
      Lumbar, 72295
      Thoracic, 72285
    Kidney
      Cyst, 74470
      Guide Catheter, 74475
    Knee, 73560-73564, 73580
    Lacrimal Duct, 70170
    Larynx, 70373
    Lymph Vessel, 75805, 75807
      Abdomen, 75805, 75807
      Arm, 75801, 75803
      Leg, 75801, 75803
    Mammary Duct, 76086, 76088
    Nasolacrimal Duct, 70170
      Guide Dilation, 74485

X-ray — *continued*
  with Contrast — *continued*
    Oviduct, 74740
    Pancreas, 74300, 74301, 74305
    Pancreatic Duct
      Guide Catheter, 74329, 74330
    Perineum, 74775
    Peritoneum, 74190
    Salivary Gland, 70390
    Seminal Vesicles, 74440
    Shoulder, 73040
    Spine
      Cervical, 72240
      Lumbosacral, 72265
      Thoracic, 72255
      Total, 72270
    Subtraction Method, 76350
    Temporomandibular Joint (TMJ), 70328-
      70332
    Ureter
      Guide Catheter, 74480
      Guide Dilation, 74485
    Urethra, 74450, 74455
    Urinary Tract, 74400-74425
    Uterus, 74740
    Vas Deferens, 74440
    Vein
      Adrenal, 75840, 75842
      Arm, 75820, 75822
        Hepatic Portal, 75810, 75885, 75887
      Jugular, 75860
      Leg, 75820, 75822
      Liver, 75889, 75891
      Neck, 75860
      Orbit, 75880
      Renal, 75831, 75833
      Sinus, 75870
      Skull, 75870, 75872
      Splenic, 75810
      Vena Cava, 75825, 75827
    Wrist, 73115
  Abdomen, 74000-74022
  Abscess, 76080
  Acromioclavicular Joint, 73050
  Ankle, 73600, 73610
  Arm, Lower, 73090
  Arm, Upper, 73092
  Artery
    Atherectomy, 75992-75996
      Transluminal, 75992
        Additional, 75993
        Renal, 75994
        Visceral, 75995
  Auditory Meatus, 70134
  Bile Duct
    Guide Dilation, 74360
  Body Composition
    Dual Energy Absorptiometry, 0028T
  Body Section, 76100
    Motion, 76101, 76102
  Bone
    Age Study, 76020
    Dual Energy Absorptiometry, 76075-76077
    Length Study, 76040
    Osseous Survey, 76061-76065
      Complete, 76062
      Infant, 76065
      Limited, 76061
  Breast, 76090-76092
    with Computer-aided Detection, 76082-
      76083
    Localization Nodule, 76096

Y

Z

Index

X-ray — Zygomatic Arch

Evaluation and Management

The following information is taken directly from the AMA's *Physicians' Current Procedural Terminology.*

CLASSIFICATION OF EVALUATION AND MANAGEMENT (E/M) SERVICES

The E/M section is divided into broad categories such as office visits, hospital visits, and consultations. Most of the categories are further divided into two or more subcategories of E/M services. For example, there are two subcategories of office visits (new patient and established patient) and there are two subcategories of hospital visits (initial and subsequent). The subcategories of E/M services are further classified into levels of E/M services that are identified by specific codes. This classification is important because the nature of physician work varies by type of service, place of service, and the patient's status.

The basic format of the levels of E/M services is the same for most categories. First, a unique code number is listed. Second, the place and/or type of service are specified (e.g., office consultation). Third, the content of the service is defined (e.g., comprehensive history and comprehensive examination). (See "Levels of E/M Services," for details on the content of E/M services.) Fourth, the nature of the presenting problem(s) usually associated with a given level is described. Fifth, the time typically required to provide the service is specified. (A detailed discussion of time begins on page 2.)

DEFINITIONS OF COMMONLY USED TERMS

Certain key words and phrases are used throughout the E/M section. The following definitions are intended to reduce the potential for differing interpretations and to increase the consistency of reporting by physicians in differing specialties.

NEW AND ESTABLISHED PATIENT

Solely for the purposes of distinguishing between new and established patients, professional services are those face-to-face services rendered by a physician and reported by a specific CPT code(s). A new patient is one who has not received any professional services from the physician, or another physician of the same specialty who belongs to the same group practice, within the past three years.

An established patient is one who has received professional services from the physician, or another physician of the same specialty who belongs to the same group practice, within the past three years.

In the instance where a physician is on call for or covering for another physician, the patient's encounter will be classified as it would have been by the physician who is not available.

No distinction is made between new and established patients in the emergency department. E/M services in the emergency department category may be reported for any new or established patient who presents for treatment in the emergency department.

CHIEF COMPLAINT

A concise statement describing the symptom, problem, condition, diagnosis or other factor that is the reason for the encounter, usually stated in the patient's words.

CONCURRENT CARE

Concurrent care is the provision of similar services, e.g., hospital visits, to the same patient by more than one physician on the same day. When concurrent care is provided, no special reporting is required.

COUNSELING

Counseling is a discussion with a patient and/or family concerning one or more of the following areas:

- Diagnostic results, impressions, and/or recommended diagnostic studies

- Prognosis

- Risks and benefits of management (treatment) options

- Instructions for management (treatment) and/or follow-up

- Importance of compliance with chosen management (treatment) options

- Risk factor reduction

- Patient and family education

(For psychotherapy, see 90804–90857.)

FAMILY HISTORY

A review of medical events in the patient's family that includes significant information about:

- The health status or cause of death of parents, siblings, and children
- Specific diseases related to problems identified in the Chief Complaint or History of the Present Illness, and/or System Review
- Diseases of family members which may be hereditary or place the patient at risk

HISTORY OF PRESENT ILLNESS

The history of present illness is a chronological description of the development of the patient's present illness from the first sign and/or symptom to the present. This includes a description of location, quality, severity, timing, context, modifying factors and associated signs and symptoms significantly related to the presenting problem(s).

LEVELS OF E/M SERVICES

Within each category or subcategory of E/M service, there are three to five levels of E/M services available for reporting purposes. Levels of E/M services are not interchangeable among the different categories or subcategories of service. For example, the first level of E/M services in the subcategory of office visit, new patient, does not have the same definition as the first level of E/M services in the subcategory of office visit, established patient.

The levels of E/M services include examinations, evaluations, treatments, conferences with or concerning patients, preventive pediatric and adult health supervision, and similar medical services, such as the determination of the need and/or location for appropriate care. Medical screening includes the history, examination, and medical decision-making required to determine the need and/or location for appropriate care and treatment of the patient (e.g., office and other outpatient setting, emergency department, nursing facility, etc.). The levels of E/M services encompass the wide variations in skill, effort, time, responsibility and medical knowledge required for the prevention or diagnosis and treatment of illness or injury and the promotion of optimal health. All physicians may use each level of E/M services.

The descriptors for the levels of E/M services recognize seven components, six of which are used in defining the levels of E/M services. These components are:

- History
- Examination
- Medical decision making
- Counseling

- Coordination of care
- Nature of presenting problem
- Time

The first three of these components (history, examination, and medical decision making) are considered the key components in selecting a level of E/M services. (See "Determine the Extent of History Obtained.")

The next three components (counseling, coordination of care, and the nature of the presenting problem) are considered contributory factors in the majority of encounters. Although the first two of these contributory factors are important E/M services, it is not required that these services be provided at every patient encounter.

Coordination of care with other providers or agencies without a patient encounter on that day is reported using the case management codes.

The final component, time, is discussed in detail below.

Any specifically identifiable procedure (i.e., identified with a specific CPT code) performed on or subsequent to the date of initial or subsequent E/M services should be reported separately.

The actual performance and/or interpretation of diagnostic tests/studies ordered during a patient encounter are not included in the levels of E/M services. Physician performance of diagnostic tests/studies for which specific CPT codes are available may be reported separately, in addition to the appropriate E/M code. The physician's interpretation of the results of diagnostic tests/studies (i.e., professional component) with preparation of a separate distinctly identifiable signed written report may also be reported separately, using the appropriate CPT code with the modifier 26 appended.

The physician may need to indicate that on the day a procedure or service identified by a CPT code was performed, the patient's condition required a significant separately identifiable E/M service above and beyond other services provided or beyond the usual preservice and postservice care associated with the procedure that was performed. The E/M service may be caused or prompted by the symptoms or condition for which the procedure and/or service was provided. This circumstance may be reported by adding the modifier 25 to the appropriate level of E/M service. As such, different diagnoses are not required for reporting of the procedure and the E/M services on the same date.

NATURE OF PRESENTING PROBLEM

A presenting problem is a disease, condition, illness, injury, symptom, sign, finding, complaint, or other reason for encounter, with or without a diagnosis being established at the time of the encounter. The E/M codes recognize five types of presenting problems that are defined as follows:

Minimal: A problem that may not require the presence of the physician, but service is provided under the physician's supervision.

Self-limited or minor: A problem that runs a definite and prescribed course, is transient in nature, and is not likely to permanently alter health status OR has a good prognosis with management/compliance.

Low severity: A problem where the risk of morbidity without treatment is low; there is little to no risk of mortality without treatment; full recovery without functional impairment is expected.

Moderate severity: A problem where the risk of morbidity without treatment is moderate; there is moderate risk of mortality without treatment; uncertain prognosis OR increased probability of prolonged functional impairment.

High severity: A problem where the risk of morbidity without treatment is high to extreme; there is a moderate to high risk of mortality without treatment OR high probability of severe, prolonged functional impairment.

PAST HISTORY

A review of the patient's past experiences with illnesses, injuries, and treatments that includes significant information about:

- Prior major illnesses and injuries
- Prior operations
- Prior hospitalizations
- Current medications
- Allergies (e.g., drug, food)
- Age appropriate immunization status
- Age appropriate feeding/dietary status

SOCIAL HISTORY

An age appropriate review of past and current activities that includes significant information about:

- Marital status and/or living arrangements
- Current employment
- Occupational history
- Use of drugs, alcohol, and tobacco
- Level of education

- Sexual history
- Other relevant social factors

SYSTEM REVIEW (REVIEW OF SYSTEMS)

An inventory of body systems obtained through a series of questions seeking to identify signs and/or symptoms which the patient may be experiencing or has experienced. For the purposes of the CPT coding system, the following elements of a system review have been identified:

- Constitutional symptoms (fever, weight loss, etc.)
- Eyes
- Ears, nose, mouth, throat
- Cardiovascular
- Respiratory
- Gastrointestinal
- Genitourinary
- Musculoskeletal
- Integumentary (skin and/or breast)
- Neurological
- Psychiatric
- Endocrine
- Hematologic/lymphatic
- Allergic/immunologic

The review of systems helps define the problem, clarify the differential diagnosis, identify needed testing, or serves as baseline data on other systems that might be affected by any possible management options.

TIME

The inclusion of time in the definitions of levels of E/M services has been implicit in prior editions of the CPT book. The inclusion of time as an explicit factor beginning in *CPT 1992* is done to assist physicians in selecting the most appropriate level of E/M services. It should be recognized that the specific times expressed in the visit code descriptors are averages, and therefore represent a range of times which may be higher or lower depending on actual clinical circumstances.

Time is not a descriptive component for the emergency department levels of E/M services because emergency department services are typically provided on a variable intensity basis, often involving multiple encounters with several patients over an extended period of time. Therefore, it is often difficult for physicians to provide accurate estimates of the time spent face-to-face with the patient.

Studies to establish levels of E/M services employed surveys of practicing physicians to obtain data on the amount of time and work associated with typical E/M services. Since "work" is not easily quantifiable, the codes must rely on other objective, verifiable measures that correlate with physicians' estimates of their "work". It has been demonstrated that physicians' estimations of intraservice time (as explained on the next page), both within and across specialties, is a variable that is predictive of the "work" of E/M services. This same research has shown there is a strong relationship between intra-service time and total time for E/M services. Intra-service time, rather than total time, was chosen for inclusion with the codes because of its relative ease of measurement and because of its direct correlation with measurements of the total amount of time and work associated with typical E/M services. Intra-service times are defined as face-to-face time for office and other outpatient visits and as unit/floor time for hospital and other inpatient visits. This distinction is necessary because most of the work of typical office visits takes place during the face-to-face time with the patient, while most of the work of typical hospital visits takes place during the time spent on the patient's floor or unit.

Face-to-face time (office and other outpatient visits and office consultations): For coding purposes, face-to-face time for these services is defined as only that time that the physician spends face-to-face with the patient and/or family. This includes the time in which the physician performs such tasks as obtaining a history, performing an examination, and counseling the patient.

Physicians also spend time doing work before or after the face-to-face time with the patient, performing such tasks as reviewing records and tests, arranging for further services, and communicating further with other professionals and the patient through written reports and telephone contact.

This non-face-to-face time for office services—also called pre- and post-encounter time—is not included in the time component described in the E/M codes. However, the pre- and post-face-to-face work associated with an encounter was included in calculating the total work of typical services in physician surveys.

Thus, the face-to-face time associated with the services described by any E/M code is a valid proxy for the total work done before, during, and after the visit.

Unit/floor time (hospital observation services, inpatient hospital care, and nursing facility): For reporting purposes, intra-service time for these services is defined as unit/floor time, which includes the time that the physician is present on the patient's hospital unit and at the bedside rendering services for that patient. This includes the time in which the physician establishes and/or reviews the patient's chart, examines the patient, writes notes and communicates with other professionals and the patient's family.

In the hospital, pre- and post-time includes time spent off the patient's floor performing such tasks as reviewing pathology and radiology findings in another part of the hospital.

This pre- and post-visit time is not included in the time component described in these codes. However, the pre- and post-work performed during the time spent off the floor or unit was included in calculating the total work of typical services in physician surveys.

Thus, the unit/floor time associated with the services described by any code is a valid proxy for the total work done before, during, and after the visit.

UNLISTED SERVICE

An E/M service may be provided that is not listed in this section of the CPT book. When reporting such a service, the appropriate "Unlisted" code may be used to indicate the service, identifying it by "Special Report," as discussed in the following paragraph. The "unlisted services" and accompanying codes for the E/M section are as follows:

99429 Unlisted preventive medicine service

99499 Unlisted evaluation and management service

SPECIAL REPORT

An unlisted service or one that is unusual, variable, or new may require a special report demonstrating the medical appropriateness of the service. Pertinent information should include an adequate definition or description of the nature, extent, and need for the procedure; and the time, effort, and equipment necessary to provide the service. Additional items which may be included are complexity of symptoms, final diagnosis, pertinent physical findings, diagnostic and therapeutic procedures, concurrent problems, and follow-up care.

CLINICAL EXAMPLES

Clinical examples of the codes for E/M services are provided to assist physicians in understanding the meaning of the descriptors and selecting the correct code. The clinical examples are listed in Appendix C (of *CPT 2005*). Each example was developed by physicians in the specialties shown.

The same problem, when seen by physicians in different specialties, may involve different amounts of work. Therefore, the appropriate level of encounter should be reported using the descriptors rather than the examples.

The examples have been tested for validity and approved by the CPT Editorial Panel. Physicians were given the examples and asked to assign a code or assess the amount of time and work involved. Only those examples that were rated consistently have been included in Appendix C (of CPT 2006).

INSTRUCTIONS FOR SELECTING A LEVEL OF E/M SERVICE

IDENTIFY THE CATEGORY AND SUBCATEGORY OF SERVICE

The categories and subcategories of codes available for reporting E/M services are shown in table 1.

REVIEW THE REPORTING INSTRUCTIONS FOR THE SELECTED CATEGORY OR SUBCATEGORY

Most of the categories and many of the subcategories of service have special guidelines or instructions unique to that category or subcategory. Where these are indicated, e.g., "Inpatient Hospital Care," special instructions will be presented preceding the levels of E/M services.

REVIEW THE LEVEL OF E/M SERVICE DESCRIPTORS AND EXAMPLES IN THE SELECTED CATEGORY OR SUBCATEGORY

The descriptors for the levels of E/M services recognize seven components, six of which are used in defining the levels of E/M services. These components are:

- History
- Examination
- Medical decision making
- Counseling
- Coordination of care
- Nature of presenting problem
- Time

The first three of these components (i.e., history, examination, and medical decision making) should be considered the key components in selecting the level of E/M services. An exception to this rule is in the case of visits which consist predominantly of counseling or coordination of care. (See numbered paragraph 3, page 6.)

The nature of the presenting problem and time are provided in some levels to assist the physician in determining the appropriate level of E/M service.

DETERMINE THE EXTENT OF HISTORY OBTAINED

The extent of the history is dependent upon clinical judgment and on the nature of the presenting problem(s). The levels of E/M services recognize four types of history that are defined as follows:

Problem focused: Chief complaint; brief history of present illness or problem.

Expanded problem focused: Chief complaint; brief history of present illness; problem pertinent system review.

Detailed: Chief complaint; extended history of present illness; problem pertinent system review extended to include a review of a limited number of additional systems; pertinent past, family, and/or social history directly related to the patient's problems.

Comprehensive: Chief complaint; extended history of present illness; review of systems which is directly related to the problem(s) identified in the history of the present illness plus a review of all additional body systems; complete past, family, and social history.

The comprehensive history obtained as part of the preventive medicine evaluation and management service is not problem-oriented and does not involve a chief complaint or present illness. It does, however, include a comprehensive system review and comprehensive or interval past, family, and social history as well as a comprehensive assessment/history of pertinent risk factors.

DETERMINE THE EXTENT OF EXAMINATION PERFORMED

The extent of the examination performed is dependent on clinical judgment and on the nature of the presenting problem(s). The levels of E/M services recognize four types of examination that are defined as follows:

Problem focused: A limited examination of the affected body area or organ system.

Expanded problem focused: A limited examination of the affected body area or organ system and other symptomatic or related organ system(s).

Detailed: An extended examination of the affected body area(s) and other symptomatic or related organ system(s).

Comprehensive: A general multisystem examination or a complete examination of a single organ system. Note: The comprehensive examination performed as part of the preventive medicine evaluation and management service is multisystem, but its extent is based on age and risk factors identified.

For the purposes of these CPT definitions, the following body areas are recognized:

- Head, including the face
- Neck
- Chest, including breasts and axilla
- Abdomen
- Genitalia, groin, buttocks
- Back
- Each extremity

For the purposes of these CPT definitions, the following organ systems are recognized:

- Eyes
- Ears, nose, mouth, and throat
- Cardiovascular
- Respiratory
- Gastrointestinal
- Genitourinary
- Musculoskeletal
- Skin
- Neurologic
- Psychiatric
- Hematologic/lymphatic/immunologic

DETERMINE THE COMPLEXITY OF MEDICAL DECISION MAKING

Medical decision making refers to the complexity of establishing a diagnosis and/or selecting a management option as measured by:

- The number of possible diagnoses and/or the number of management options that must be considered
- The amount and/or complexity of medical records, diagnostic tests, and/or other information that must be obtained, reviewed, and analyzed
- The risk of significant complications, morbidity, and/or mortality, as well as comorbidities, associated with the patient's presenting problem(s), the diagnostic procedure(s) and/or the possible management options

Four types of medical decision making are recognized: straightforward; low complexity; moderate complexity; and high complexity. To qualify for a given type of decision making, two of the three elements in Table 2 must be met or exceeded.

Comorbidities/underlying diseases, in and of themselves, are not considered in selecting a level of E/M services unless their presence significantly increases the complexity of the medical decision making.

SELECT THE APPROPRIATE LEVEL OF E/M SERVICES BASED ON THE FOLLOWING

1. For the following categories/subcategories, all of the key components, i.e., history, examination, and medical decision making, must meet or exceed the stated requirements to qualify for a particular level of E/M service: office, new patient; hospital observation services; initial hospital care; office consultations; initial inpatient consultations; emergency department services; initial nursing facility care; domiciliary care, new patient; and home, new patient.

2. For the following categories/subcategories, two of the three key components (i.e., history, examination, and medical decision making) must meet or exceed the stated requirements to qualify for a particular level of E/M services: office, established patient; subsequent hospital care; subsequent nursing facility care; domiciliary care, established patient; and home, established patient.

3. When counseling and/or coordination of care dominates (more than 50%) the physician/patient and/or family encounter (face-to-face time in the office or other outpatient setting or floor/unit time in the hospital or nursing facility), then time may be considered the key or controlling factor to qualify for a particular level of E/M services. This includes time spent with parties who have assumed responsibility for the care of the patient or decision making whether or not they are family members (e.g., foster parents, person acting in locum parentis, legal guardian). The extent of counseling and/or coordination of care must be documented in the medical record.

DOCUMENTATION GUIDELINES

Originally jointly developed by the American Medical Association (AMA) and the Health Care Financing Administration (HCFA) in 1995, the documentation guidelines for E/M services experienced substantial revision in 1997. These documentation guidelines are not included in CPT guidelines and AMA policy does not endorse them. For the time being, physicians may use either the 1995 or 1997 guidelines for Medicare purposes. These can be found on the Internet at http://www.cms.hhs.gov/medlearn/emdoc.asp. A comparison of the two systems can be found at http://www.cms.hhs.gov/medlearn/appndix1.pdf.

COMPONENTS

HISTORY COMPONENT GUIDELINES

- The chief complaint, review of systems, and the past, family, and/or social history may be included as separate elements of the history. Or, this information may be included in the description of the history of the present illness.

- A review of systems and/or a past, family, and/or social history obtained during an earlier encounter does not need to be re-recorded if there is evidence that the physician reviewed and updated the previous information. This may occur when a physician updates his or her own record, or in an institutional setting or group practice where many physicians use a common record. The review and update may be documented by describing any new review of systems and/or past, family, and/or social history information or noting there has been no change in the information and indicating the date and location of the earlier review of systems and/or past, family, and/or social history.

- The review of systems and/or past, family, and/or social history may be recorded by ancillary staff or on a form completed by the patient. To document that the physician reviewed the information, there must be a notation supplementing or confirming the information recorded by others.

- If the physician cannot obtain a history from the patient or other source, the record should describe the patient's condition or other circumstance that precludes obtaining this information.

- The medical record should clearly reflect the chief complaint.

- To qualify for brief history of present illness, the medical record should describe one to three elements of the present illness.

- To qualify for extended history of present illness, the medical record should describe

four or more elements of the present illness or associated comorbidities.

- To qualify for problem pertinent review of systems, the patient's positive responses and pertinent negatives for the system related to the problem should be documented.

- To qualify for extended review of systems, the patient's positive responses and pertinent negatives for two to nine systems should be documented.

- To qualify for complete review of systems, at least 10 organ systems must be reviewed. Those systems with positive or pertinent negative responses must be individually documented. For the remaining systems, a notation indicating all other systems are negative is permissible.

- At least one specific item from any of the three history areas must be documented for a pertinent past, family, and/or social history.

- At least one specific item from two of the three history areas must be documented for a complete past, family, and/or social history for the following categories of E/M services: office or other outpatient services, established patient; emergency department; subsequent nursing facility care; domiciliary care, established patient; and home care, established patient.

- At least one specific item from each of the three history areas must be documented for a complete past, family, and/or social history for the following categories of E/M services: office or other outpatient services, new patient; hospital observation services; hospital inpatient services, initial care; consultations; comprehensive nursing facility assessments; domiciliary care, new patient; and home care, new patient.

EXAMINATION COMPONENT GUIDELINES

- Specific abnormal findings and relevant negative findings of the examination of the affected or symptomatic body area(s) or organ system(s) should be documented. A notation of "abnormal" without elaboration is insufficient.

- Abnormal or unexpected findings of the examination of the unaffected or asymptomatic body area(s) or organ system(s) should be described.

- A brief statement or notation indicated "negative" or "normal" is sufficient to document normal findings related to unaffected area(s) or asymptomatic organ system(s).

- Examinations are divided into two different types, general multi-system examinations or single organ system examinations. Any physician can perform either type of examination in any specialty. The type is based upon clinical judgment, the patient's history, and the nature of presenting problems.

- Specific elements have been identified for each type of examination and for each specialty. The elements for each are not included in this book as the tables are too lengthy to be reproduced here. Obtain a copy of the complete documentation guidelines for specific details about each type of examination.

MEDICAL DECISION MAKING COMPONENT GUIDELINES

Make sure the following components are documented:

- Number of diagnoses or management options

- An assessment, clinical impression, or diagnosis for each encounter. This information may be explicitly stated or implied in documented decisions regarding management plans and/or further evaluation.

- The initiation of, or changes in, treatment. Treatment includes a wide range of management options including patient instructions, nursing instructions, therapies, and medications.

- Amount/complexity of data reviewed

TABLE 1

CATEGORIES AND SUBCATEGORIES OF SERVICE

Category/Subcategory	Code Numbers
Office or Other Outpatient Services	
New Patient	99201–99205
Established Patient	99211–99215
Hospital Observation Services	
Hospital Observation Discharge Services	99217
Initial Hospital Observation Services	99218–99220
Hospital Observation or Inpatient Care Services (Including Admission and Discharge Services)	99234–99236
Hospital Inpatient Services	
Initial Hospital Care	99221–99223
Subsequent Hospital Care	99231–99233
Hospital Discharge Services	99238–99239
Consultations	
Office Consultations	99241–99245
Initial Inpatient Consultations	99251–99255
Emergency Department Services	99281–99288
Pediatric Patient Transport	99289–99290
Critical Care Services	
Adult (over 24 months of age)	99291–99292
Pediatric	99293–99294
Neonatal	99295–99296
Continuing Intensive Care Services	99298–99299
Nursing Facility Services	
Initial Nursing Facility Care	99304–99306
Subsequent Nursing Facility Care	99307–99310
Nursing Facility Discharge Services	99315–99316
Other Nursing Facility Services	99318

- In cases of referrals or consultations, who requests the advice, and to which provider the referral or consultation is made.

- If a diagnostic service is ordered, planned, scheduled, or performed at the time of the E/M encounter, the type of service (e.g., lab or x-ray).

- The review of lab, radiology, and/or other diagnostic tests. An entry in a progress note such as "WBC elevated" or "chest x-ray unremarkable" is acceptable.

- A decision to obtain old records or a decision to obtain additional history from the family, caretaker, or other source to supplement that obtained from the patient.

- Relevant findings from the review of old records, and/or the receipt of additional history from the family, caretaker, or other source. If there is no relevant information

beyond that already obtained, that fact should be documented. A notation of "old records reviewed" or "additional history obtained from family" without elaboration is insufficient.

- The results of discussion of laboratory, radiology, or other diagnostic test with the physician who performed or interpreted the study.

- The direct visualization and independent interpretation of an image, tracing, or specimen previously or subsequently interpreted by another physician.

- Risks of complications, morbidity, mortality

- Comorbidities, underlying diseases, or other factors that increase the complexity of medical decision making by increasing

CATEGORIES AND SUBCATEGORIES OF SERVICE

Category/Subcategory	Code Numbers
Domiciliary, Rest Home or Custodial Care Services	
New Patient	99324-99328
Established Patient	99334-33337
Domiciliary, Rest Home (e.g., Assisted Living Facility), or Home Care Plan Oversight Services	99339-99340
Home Services	
New Patient	99341-99345
Established Patient	99347-99350
Prolonged Services	
With Direct Patient Contact	99354-99357
Without Direct Patient Contact	99358-99359
Standby Services	99360
Case Management Services	
Team Conferences	99361-99362
Telephone Calls	99371-99373
Care Plan Oversight Services	99374-99380
Preventive Medicine Services	
New Patient	99381-99387
Established Patient	99391-99397
Individual Counseling	99401-99404
Group Counseling	99411-99412
Other	99420-99429
Newborn Care	99431-99440
Special E/M Services	99450-99456
Other E/M Services	99499

TABLE 2

COMPLEXITY OF MEDICAL DECISION MAKING

NUMBER OF DIAGNOSES OR MANAGEMENT OPTIONS	AMOUNT AND/OR COMPLEXITY OF DATA TO BE REVIEWED	RISK OF COMPLICATIONS AND/OR MORBIDITY OR MORTALITY	TYPE OF DECISION MAKING
minimal	minimal or none	minimal	straightforward
limited	limited	low	low complexity
multiple	moderate	moderate	moderate complexity
extensive	extensive	high	high complexity

the risk of complications, morbidity, and/or mortality.

- If a surgical or invasive diagnostic procedure is ordered, planned, or scheduled at the time of the E/M encounter, the type of procedure (e.g., laparoscopy).

- The specific procedure if performed at the time of the E/M encounter

- The referral for, or decision to perform, a surgical or invasive diagnostic procedure on an urgent basis.

CONTRIBUTING FACTORS

If the physician elects to report the level of service based on counseling and/or coordination of care, the total length of time of the encounter (face-to-face or floor time, as appropriate) as well as the time spent counseling should be documented. The record should describe the counseling and/or activities to coordinate care.

SUMMARY

- Clarify that a code may be selected and documented based on counseling/coordination of care, without reference needed to any other dimension of code selection (i.e., history, exam, and medical decision making).

- Emphasize that for established patients, only two of the three key components need be performed (i.e., history, examination, complexity of medical decision making).

- Simplify history selection by allowing documentation of two of the three history areas (HPI, ROS, and PFSH) instead of requiring all three to be documented.

- Add a note that, when a history cannot be obtained due to the patient's condition (e.g., inability to communicate, urgent, emergent situation), the history is deemed

"comprehensive" for coding and documentation purposes.

- Simplify examination criteria by eliminating confusing instructions, while enhancing clinical flexibility by eliminating rigid distinctions between general multi-system vs. single system examinations.

- Simplify the medical decision making component by eliminating one level of complexity (straightforward)—the proposed levels are: low, moderate, and high complexity.

- Simplify the medical decision making component by allowing the highest complexity element (i.e., the number of diagnoses/risk of complications, diagnostic procedures/tests and or data to be reviewed, or management options) to drive the level of medical decision making selection. In addition to the noted changes in the glossary, clarifications in the proposed guidelines also include the following:

— These documentation guidelines are not applicable to the preventive medicine services, critical care, or neonatal intensive care codes.

— Any record format for documenting history (including preprinted history forms completed by the patient and reviewed by the physician) is acceptable.

— The chief complaint and reason for the encounter requirements are not applicable to subsequent inpatient hospital services.

— Definitions of chief complaint, reason for encounter, and brief/extended history of present illness have been added.

Evaluation and Management

PLACE-OF-SERVICE DISTINCTIONS

The E/M code section is divided into subsections by type and place of service. Keep the following in mind when coding each service setting:

- A patient is considered an outpatient at a health care facility until formal inpatient admission occurs.

- Physicians, regardless of specialty, may use 99281–99285 for reporting emergency department services within hospital-based emergency facilities. Other Emergency Services (99288) is reserved for physician directed emergency care provided by the physician in a hospital emergency or critical care department in two-way communication with ambulance or rescue personnel outside the hospital.

- Consultation codes are linked to location.

- Initial hospital inpatient and hospital observation codes as well as initial nursing facility visit codes include evaluation and management services provided elsewhere (office visit codes or emergency department) by the admitting physician on the same day.

DOCUMENTING THE PATIENT RECORD

Physicians and staff members have developed numerous methods to document professional services, and there is no single "right" way as long as all pertinent components of the codes are documented. Some physicians check off a CPT code on an encounter form, while others make clinical notations in the patient's chart for the coding personnel to translate into codes.

E/M SUBCATEGORIES

E/M codes are intended to standardize the way physicians, coders, and claims processors code patient visits. The varied choices presented by E/M codes result in more consistent billing patterns.

OFFICE OR OTHER OUTPATIENT SERVICES

Use codes (99201–99215) to report the services for office or outpatient visits. The CPT book does not provide instructions for reporting multiple office or outpatient visits provided by the same physician on the same calendar date. The most common practice is to report a single visit code per day, evaluating all services provided during that day to arrive at the correct level of service. Prolonged service codes may be used to report services beyond the usual.

HOSPITAL OBSERVATION SERVICES

Codes 99217–99220 report E/M services provided to patients designated or admitted as "observation status" in a hospital. It is not necessary that the patient be located in an observation area designated by the hospital to use these codes; however, whenever a patient is placed in a separately designated observation area of the hospital or emergency department, these codes should be used.

INITIAL OBSERVATION CARE

When a patient is admitted to observation status in the course of an encounter in another site of service (e.g., hospital emergency department, physician's office, nursing facility). All related E/M services provided by that physician on the same day are included in the admission for hospital observation. Only one physician can report initial observation services. Do not use these observation codes for post-recovery of a procedure that is considered a global surgical service.

OBSERVATION CARE DISCHARGE SERVICES

Use 99217 only if discharge from observation status occurs on a date other than the initial date of observation status. The code includes final examination of the patient, discussion of the hospital stay, instructions for continuing care, and preparation of discharge records. If a patient is admitted to and subsequently discharged from observation status on the same date, report the service observation/inpatient hospital care codes 99234–99236.

HOSPITAL INPATIENT SERVICES

The codes for hospital inpatient services report admission to a hospital setting, follow-up care provided in a hospital setting, observation or inpatient care for same day admission and discharge, and hospital discharge day management. For inpatient care, the time component includes not only face-to-face time with the patient, but also any unit/floor time related to the patient's care. This time may include family counseling or discussing the patient's condition with the family, establishing and reviewing the patient's record, documenting within the chart, and communicating with other health care professionals, such as other physicians, nursing staff, and respiratory therapists.

Initial hospital care codes (99221–99223) are used by the admitting physician to report the first hospital inpatient encounter. All evaluation and management services provided by the admitting physician in conjunction with the admission regardless of the site of the encounter are included in the initial hospital care service. Services provided in the emergency room, observation room, physician's office, or nursing facility specifically related to the admission cannot be reported separately. Physicians, other than the admitting physician, should not use initial hospital care codes, but should report their services with the appropriate consultation or subsequent hospital care codes.

Codes 99238 and 99239 report hospital discharge day management, but exclude discharge of a patient from observation status. Discharge services for newborns or neonates may be reported with 99238 or 99239 for lengths of stay of more than one day. When a physician other than the attending physician provides concurrent care on discharge day, report these services using subsequent hospital care codes.

Observation or inpatient care services, which include admission and discharge services for the same date of service, are reported with 99234–99236. These codes are reported once and include all care provided by the admitting physician whether initiated at another site, within the observation unit, or on an inpatient basis.

CONSULTATIONS

Consultations are provided at the request of another physician or other appropriate source for the purpose of rendering an opinion or advice regarding the evaluation and management of a specific problem. Consultations in the CPT book fall under two subcategories: office or other outpatient consultations and inpatient consultations. If counseling dominates the encounter, time determines the correct code.

The general rules and requirements of a consultation are as follows:

- Requests for consultation must come from an attending physician or other appropriate source, and the necessity for this service must be documented in the patient's record.

- The consulting physician should provide communication regarding his/her findings to the requesting physician.

- The consultant may initiate diagnostic and/or therapeutic services, such as writing orders or prescriptions and initiating treatment plans.

- The opinion rendered and services ordered or performed and the physician ID number must be documented in the patient's medical record and a report of this information communicated to the requesting provider.

- Report separately any identifiable procedure or service performed on, or subsequent to, the date of the initial consultation.

- When the consultant assumes responsibility for the management of any or all of the patient's care subsequent to the consultation encounter, consult codes are no longer appropriate. Depending on the location, identify the correct subsequent or established patient codes.

- A consultation initiated by the patient or family rather than by a physician is reported with the appropriate office visit code.

- A consultation mandated by a third-party payer should be appended with modifier 32.

OFFICE OR OTHER OUTPATIENT SERVICES

NEW PATIENT

99201 Office or other outpatient visit for the evaluation and management of a new patient, which requires these three key components: a problem focused history; a problem focused examination; straightforward medical decision making. Counseling and/or coordination of care with other providers or agencies are provided consistent with the nature of the problem(s) and the patient's and/or family's needs. Usually, the presenting problem(s) are self limited or minor. Physicians typically spend 10 minutes face-to-face with the patient and/or family. Ⓥ 80 🔁

MED: 100-3, 10.4; 100-3, 130.2; 100-3, 130.3; 100-3, 130.4; 100-3, 130.5; 100-3, 130.6; 100-3, 130.7; 100-3, 160.2; 100-3, 160.7.1; 100-3, 230.1; 100-3, 250.1; 100-3, 250.4; 100-3, 270.4; 100-3, 40.50; 100-3, 70.1; 100-3, 70.2; 100-4, 12, 6.7

AMA: 2000, Feb, 3, 9, 11; 1999, Jun, 8; 1998, Jul, 9; 1995, Summer, 4; 1995, Spring, 1; 1995, Fall, 9; 1993, Summer, 2; 1993, Spring, 34; 1993, Fall, 9; 1992, Summer, 1, 24; 1992, Spring, 9, 24; 1991, Winter, 11

99202 Office or other outpatient visit for the evaluation and management of a new patient, which requires these three key components: an expanded problem focused history; an expanded problem focused examination; straightforward medical decision making. Counseling and/or coordination of care with other providers or agencies are provided consistent with the nature of the problem(s) and the patient's and/or family's needs. Usually, the presenting problem(s) are of low to moderate severity. Physicians typically spend 20 minutes face-to-face with the patient and/or family. Ⓥ 80 🔁

MED: 100-3, 10.4; 100-3, 130.2; 100-3, 130.3; 100-3, 130.4; 100-3, 130.5; 100-3, 130.6; 100-3, 130.7; 100-3, 160.2; 100-3, 160.7.1; 100-3, 230.1; 100-3, 250.1; 100-3, 250.4; 100-3, 270.4; 100-3, 40.50; 100-3, 70.1; 100-3, 70.2; 100-4, 12, 6.7

AMA: 2000, Feb, 11; 1998, Jul, 9; 1995, Summer, 4; 1995, Spring, 1; 1995, Fall, 9; 1993, Summer, 2; 1993, Spring, 34; 1993, Fall, 9; 1992, Summer, 1, 24; 1992, Spring, 9, 24; 1991, Winter, 11

99203 Office or other outpatient visit for the evaluation and management of a new patient, which requires these three key components: a detailed history; a detailed examination; medical decision making of low complexity. Counseling and/or coordination of care with other providers or agencies are provided consistent with the nature of the problem(s) and the patient's and/or family's needs. Usually, the presenting problem(s) are of moderate severity. Physicians typically spend 30 minutes face-to-face with the patient and/or family. Ⓥ 80 🔁

MED: 100-3, 10.4; 100-3, 130.2; 100-3, 130.3; 100-3, 130.4; 100-3, 130.5; 100-3, 130.6; 100-3, 130.7; 100-3, 160.2; 100-3, 160.7.1; 100-3, 230.1; 100-3, 250.1; 100-3, 250.4; 100-3, 270.4; 100-3, 40.50; 100-3, 70.1; 100-3, 70.2; 100-4, 12, 6.7

AMA: 2000, Feb, 11; 1998, Jul, 9; 1995, Summer, 4; 1995, Spring, 1; 1995, Fall, 9; 1993, Summer, 2; 1993, Spring, 34; 1993, Fall, 9; 1992, Summer, 1, 24; 1992, Spring, 9, 24; 1991, Winter, 11

99204   Office or other outpatient visit for the evaluation and management of a new patient, which requires these three key components: a comprehensive history; a comprehensive examination; medical decision making of moderate complexity. Counseling and/or coordination of care with other providers or agencies are provided consistent with the nature of the problem(s) and the patient's and/or family's needs. Usually, the presenting problem(s) are of moderate to high severity. Physicians typically spend 45 minutes face-to-face with the patient and/or family.   Ⓥ 80 🔾

MED: 100-3, 10.4; 100-3, 130.2; 100-3, 130.3; 100-3, 130.4; 100-3, 130.5; 100-3, 130.6; 100-3, 130.7; 100-3, 160.2; 100-3, 160.7.1; 100-3, 230.1; 100-3, 250.1; 100-3, 250.4; 100-3, 270.4; 100-3, 40.50; 100-3, 70.1; 100-3, 70.2; 100-4, 12, 6.7

AMA: 2000, Feb, 11; 1998, Jul, 9; 1995, Summer, 4; 1995, Spring, 1; 1995, Fall, 9; 1993, Summer, 2; 1993, Spring, 34; 1993, Fall, 9; 1992, Summer, 1, 24; 1992, Spring, 9, 24; 1991, Winter, 11

99205   Office or other outpatient visit for the evaluation and management of a new patient, which requires these three key components: a comprehensive history; a comprehensive examination; medical decision making of high complexity. Counseling and/or coordination of care with other providers or agencies are provided consistent with the nature of the problem(s) and the patient's and/or family's needs. Usually, the presenting problem(s) are of moderate to high severity. Physicians typically spend 60 minutes face-to-face with the patient and/or family.   Ⓥ 80 🔾

MED: 100-3, 10.4; 100-3, 130.2; 100-3, 130.3; 100-3, 130.4; 100-3, 130.5; 100-3, 130.6; 100-3, 130.7; 100-3, 160.2; 100-3, 160.7.1; 100-3, 230.1; 100-3, 250.1; 100-3, 250.4; 100-3, 270.4; 100-3, 40.50; 100-3, 70.1; 100-3, 70.2; 100-4, 12, 6.7

AMA: 2000, Feb, 11; 1998, Jul, 9; 1995, Summer, 4; 1995, Spring, 1; 1995, Fall, 9; 1993, Summer, 2; 1993, Spring, 34; 1993, Fall, 9; 1992, Summer, 1, 24; 1992, Spring, 9, 24; 1991, Winter, 11

ESTABLISHED PATIENT

99211   Office or other outpatient visit for the evaluation and management of an established patient, that may not require the presence of a physician. Usually, the presenting problem(s) are minimal. Typically, 5 minutes are spent performing or supervising these services.   Ⓥ 80 🔾

MED: 100-3, 10.4; 100-3, 130.2; 100-3, 130.3; 100-3, 130.4; 100-3, 130.5; 100-3, 130.6; 100-3, 130.7; 100-3, 160.2; 100-3, 160.7.1; 100-3, 230.1; 100-3, 250.1; 100-3, 250.4; 100-3, 270.4; 100-3, 40.50; 100-3, 70.1; 100-3, 70.2; 100-4, 12, 6.7

AMA: 2000, Feb, 11; 1999, Oct, 9; 1998, Jul, 9; 1997, Feb, 9; 1996, Oct, 10; 1995, Summer, 4; 1995, Spring, 1; 1995, Fall, 9; 1993, Summer, 2; 1993, Spring, 34; 1993, Fall, 9; 1992, Summer, 1, 24; 1992, Spring, 9, 24; 1991, Winter, 11

99212   Office or other outpatient visit for the evaluation and management of an established patient, which requires at least two of these three key components: a problem focused history; a problem focused examination; straightforward medical decision making. Counseling and/or coordination of care with other providers or agencies are provided consistent with the nature of the problem(s) and the patient's and/or family's needs. Usually, the presenting problem(s) are self limited or minor. Physicians typically spend 10 minutes face-to-face with the patient and/or family.   Ⓥ 80 🔾

MED: 100-3, 10.4; 100-3, 130.2; 100-3, 130.3; 100-3, 130.4; 100-3, 130.5; 100-3, 130.6; 100-3, 130.7; 100-3, 160.2; 100-3, 160.7.1; 100-3, 230.1; 100-3, 250.1; 100-3, 250.4; 100-3, 270.4; 100-3, 40.50; 100-3, 70.1; 100-3, 70.2; 100-4, 12, 6.7

AMA: 2002, May, 17; 2000, Jun, 11; 2000, Feb, 11; 1998, Jul, 9; 1995, Summer, 4; 1995, Spring, 1; 1995, Fall, 9; 1993, Summer, 2; 1993, Spring, 34; 1993, Fall, 9; 1992, Summer, 1, 24; 1992, Spring, 9, 24; 1991, Winter, 11

26/TC Professional/Technical Component   80/80 Assist-at-Surgery Allowed/With Documentation   ⊙ Conscious Sedation
Unlisted   Not Covered   **MED:** Pubs 100/NCD Reference   1-9 ASC Group   63 Modifier 63 Exempt

99213   Office or other outpatient visit for the evaluation and management of an
         established patient, which requires at least two of these three key
         components: an expanded problem focused history; an expanded problem
         focused examination; medical decision making of low complexity.
         Counseling and coordination of care with other providers or agencies are
         provided consistent with the nature of the problem(s) and the patient's
         and/or family's needs. Usually, the presenting problem(s) are of low to
         moderate severity. Physicians typically spend 15 minutes face-to-face with
         the patient and/or family.   V 80 ◪
         MED: 100-3, 10.4; 100-3, 130.2; 100-3, 130.3; 100-3, 130.4; 100-3, 130.5; 100-3, 130.6; 100-3,
         130.7; 100-3, 160.2; 100-3, 160.7.1; 100-3, 230.1; 100-3, 250.1; 100-3, 250.4; 100-3, 270.4; 100-
         3, 40.50; 100-3, 70.1; 100-3, 70.2; 100-4, 12, 6.7

         AMA: 1998, Jul, 9; 1997, Jan, 10; 1995, Summer, 4; 1995, Spring, 1; 1995, Fall, 9; 1993,
         Summer, 2; 1993, Spring, 34; 1993, Fall, 9; 1992, Summer, 1, 24; 1992, Spring, 9, 24; 1991,
         Winter, 11

99214   Office or other outpatient visit for the evaluation and management of an
         established patient, which requires at least two of these three key
         components: a detailed history; a detailed examination; medical decision
         making of moderate complexity. Counseling and/or coordination of care
         with other providers or agencies are provided consistent with the nature of
         the problem(s) and the patient's and/or family's needs. Usually, the
         presenting problem(s) are of moderate to high severity. Physicians typically
         spend 25 minutes face-to-face with the patient and/or family.   V 80 ◪
         MED: 100-3, 10.4; 100-3, 130.2; 100-3, 130.3; 100-3, 130.4; 100-3, 130.5; 100-3, 130.6; 100-3,
         130.7; 100-3, 160.2; 100-3, 160.7.1; 100-3, 230.1; 100-3, 250.1; 100-3, 250.4; 100-3, 270.4; 100-
         3, 40.50; 100-3, 70.1; 100-3, 70.2; 100-4, 12, 6.7

         AMA: 1998, Jul, 9; 1995, Summer, 4; 1995, Spring, 1; 1995, Fall, 9; 1993, Summer, 2; 1993,
         Spring, 34; 1993, Fall, 9; 1992, Summer, 1, 24; 1992, Spring, 9, 24; 1991, Winter, 11

99215   Office or other outpatient visit for the evaluation and management of an
         established patient, which requires at least two of these three key
         components: a comprehensive history; a comprehensive examination;
         medical decision making of high complexity. Counseling and/or
         coordination of care with other providers or agencies are provided
         consistent with the nature of the problem(s) and the patient's and/or
         family's needs. Usually, the presenting problem(s) are of moderate to high
         severity. Physicians typically spend 40 minutes face-to-face with the
         patient and/or family.   V 80 ◪
         MED: 100-3, 10.4; 100-3, 130.2; 100-3, 130.3; 100-3, 130.4; 100-3, 130.5; 100-3, 130.6; 100-3,
         130.7; 100-3, 160.2; 100-3, 160.7.1; 100-3, 230.1; 100-3, 250.1; 100-3, 250.4; 100-3, 270.4; 100-
         3, 40.50; 100-3, 70.1; 100-3, 70.2; 100-4, 12, 6.7

         AMA: 1998, Jul, 9; 1997, Jan, 10; 1995, Summer, 4; 1995, Spring, 1; 1995, Fall, 9; 1993,
         Summer, 2; 1993, Spring, 34; 1993, Fall, 9; 1992, Summer, 1, 24; 1992, Spring, 9, 24; 1991,
         Winter, 11

HOSPITAL OBSERVATION SERVICES

OBSERVATION CARE DISCHARGE SERVICES

If the patient is admitted to the hospital on the same day as admission to the observation area, consult CPT codes for Hospital Admission (99221-99223).

Consult CPT codes 99234-99236 for admission and discharge to observation area on same date.

99217   Observation care discharge day management (This code is to be utilized by the physician to report all services provided to a patient on discharge from "observation status" if the discharge is on other than the initial date of "observation status." To report services to a patient designated as "observation status" or "inpatient status" and discharged on the same date, use the codes for Observation or Inpatient Care Services [including Admission and Discharge Services, 99234-99236 as appropriate.]) B 80 🗨

MED: 100-1, 5, 70; 100-2, 15, 30; 100-4, 11, 40.1.3.1; 100-4, 12, 10; 100-4, 12, 100; 100-4, 12, 100.1.7; 100-4, 12, 100.1.8; 100-4, 12, 30.6; 100-4, 12, 30.6.8

AMA: 1998, May, 1; 1998, Mar, 1; 1997, Nov, 2

INITIAL OBSERVATION CARE

NEW OR ESTABLISHED PATIENT

99218   Initial observation care, per day, for the evaluation and management of a patient which requires these three key components: a detailed or comprehensive history; a detailed or comprehensive examination; and medical decision making that is straightforward or of low complexity. Counseling and/or coordination of care with other providers or agencies are provided consistent with the nature of the problem(s) and the patient's and/or family's needs. Usually, the problem(s) requiring admission to observation status are of low severity. B 80 🗨

MED: 100-1, 5, 70; 100-2, 15, 30; 100-4, 11, 40.1.3.1; 100-4, 12, 10; 100-4, 12, 100; 100-4, 12, 100.1.7; 100-4, 12, 100.1.8; 100-4, 12, 30.6; 100-4, 12, 30.6.8

AMA: 1998, Mar, 1; 1995, Fall, 9; 1993, Spring, 34

99219   Initial observation care, per day, for the evaluation and management of a patient, which requires these three key components: a comprehensive history; a comprehensive examination; and medical decision making of moderate complexity. Counseling and/or coordination of care with other providers or agencies are provided consistent with the nature of the problem(s) and the patient's and/or family's needs. Usually, the problem(s) requiring admission to observation status are of moderate severity. B 80 🗨

MED: 100-1, 5, 70; 100-2, 15, 30; 100-4, 11, 40.1.3.1; 100-4, 12, 10; 100-4, 12, 100; 100-4, 12, 100.1.7; 100-4, 12, 100.1.8; 100-4, 12, 30.6; 100-4, 12, 30.6.8

AMA: 1998, Mar, 1; 1995, Fall, 16; 1993, Spring, 34

99220   Initial observation care, per day, for the evaluation and management of a patient, which requires these three key components: a comprehensive history; a comprehensive examination; and medical decision making of high complexity. Counseling and/or coordination of care with other providers or agencies are provided consistent with the nature of the problem(s) and the patient's and/or family's needs. Usually, the problem(s) requiring admission to observation status are of high severity. B 80 🗨

MED: 100-1, 5, 70; 100-2, 15, 30; 100-4, 11, 40.1.3.1; 100-4, 12, 10; 100-4, 12, 100; 100-4, 12, 100.1.7; 100-4, 12, 100.1.8; 100-4, 12, 30.6; 100-4, 12, 30.6.8

AMA: 1998, Mar, 1; 1995, Fall, 16; 1993, Spring, 34

HOSPITAL INPATIENT SERVICES

INITIAL HOSPITAL CARE

99221   Initial hospital care, per day, for the evaluation and management of a patient, which requires these three key components: a detailed or comprehensive history; a detailed or comprehensive examination; and medical decision making that is straightforward or of low complexity. Counseling and/or coordination of care with other providers or agencies are provided consistent with the nature of the problem(s) and the patient's and/or family's needs. Usually, the problem(s) requiring admission are of low severity. Physicians typically spend 30 minutes at the bedside and on the patient's hospital floor or unit. E 80 ▣

MED: 100-3, 10.3; 100-3, 130.1; 100-3, 130.7; 100-3, 70.1; 100-3, 70.2; 100-4, 12, 100; 100-4, 12, 100.1.7; 100-4, 12, 100.1.8; 100-4, 12, 30.6; 100-4, 12, 30.6.9; 100-4, 8, 140; 100-4, 8, 170

AMA: 1998, Mar, 1; 1996, Sep, 10; 1996, Jul, 11; 1995, Spring, 1; 1995, Fall, 9; 1993, Spring, 34; 1992, Summer, 1, 24; 1992, Spring, 13, 24; 1992, Fall, 1; 1991, Winter, 11

99222   Initial hospital care, per day, for the evaluation and management of a patient, which requires these three key components: a comprehensive history; a comprehensive examination; and medical decision making of moderate complexity. Counseling and/or coordination of care with other providers or agencies are provided consistent with the nature of the problem(s) and the patient's and/or family's needs. Usually, the problem(s) requiring admission are of moderate severity. Physicians typically spend 50 minutes at the bedside and on the patient's hospital floor or unit. E 80 ▣

MED: 100-3, 10.3; 100-3, 130.1; 100-3, 130.7; 100-3, 70.1; 100-3, 70.2; 100-4, 12, 100; 100-4, 12, 100.1.7; 100-4, 12, 100.1.8; 100-4, 12, 30.6; 100-4, 12, 30.6.9; 100-4, 8, 140; 100-4, 8, 170

AMA: 1998, Mar, 1; 1996, Sep, 10; 1996, Jul, 11; 1995, Spring, 1; 1995, Fall, 9; 1993, Spring, 34; 1992, Summer, 1, 24; 1992, Spring, 13, 24; 1992, Fall, 1; 1991, Winter, 11

99223   Initial hospital care, per day, for the evaluation and management of a patient, which requires these three key components: a comprehensive history; a comprehensive examination; and medical decision making of high complexity. Counseling and/or coordination of care with other providers or agencies are provided consistent with the nature of the problem(s) and the patient's and/or family's needs. Usually, the problem(s) requiring admission are of high severity. Physicians typically spend 70 minutes at the bedside and on the patient's hospital floor or unit. E 80 ▣

MED: 100-3, 10.3; 100-3, 130.1; 100-3, 130.7; 100-3, 70.1; 100-3, 70.2; 100-4, 12, 100; 100-4, 12, 100.1.7; 100-4, 12, 100.1.8; 100-4, 12, 30.6; 100-4, 12, 30.6.9; 100-4, 8, 140; 100-4, 8, 170

AMA: 1998, Mar, 1; 1996, Sep, 10; 1996, Jul, 11; 1995, Spring, 1; 1995, Fall, 9; 1993, Spring, 34; 1992, Summer, 1, 24; 1992, Spring, 13, 24; 1992, Fall, 1; 1991, Winter, 11

SUBSEQUENT HOSPITAL CARE

99231   Subsequent hospital care, per day, for the evaluation and management of a patient, which requires at least two of these three key components: a problem focused interval history; a problem focused examination; medical decision making that is straightforward or of low complexity. Counseling and/or coordination of care with other providers or agencies are provided consistent with the nature of the problem(s) and the patient's and/or family's needs. Usually, the patient is stable, recovering or improving. Physicians typically spend 15 minutes at the bedside and on the patient's hospital floor or unit. E 80 ▣

MED: 100-3, 10.3; 100-3, 130.1; 100-3, 130.7; 100-4, 12, 100; 100-4, 12, 100.1.7; 100-4, 12, 100.1.8; 100-4, 12, 30.6; 100-4, 12, 30.6.15; 100-4, 12, 30.6.9; 100-4, 8, 140; 100-4, 8, 170

AMA: 1995, Spring, 1; 1995, Fall, 16; 1993, Spring, 34; 1992, Summer, 1, 24; 1992, Spring, 13, 24; 1992, Fall, 1; 1991, Winter, 11

Evaluation and Management

99232 — 99234

99232   Subsequent hospital care, per day, for the evaluation and management of a patient, which requires at least two of these three key components: an expanded problem focused interval history; an expanded problem focused examination; medical decision making of moderate complexity. Counseling and/or coordination of care with other providers or agencies are provided consistent with the nature of the problem(s) and the patient's and/or family's needs. Usually, the patient is responding inadequately to therapy or has developed a minor complication. Physicians typically spend 25 minutes at the bedside and on the patient's hospital floor or unit.   E 80 ▶

MED: 100-3, 10.3; 100-3, 130.1; 100-3, 130.7; 100-4, 12, 100; 100-4, 12, 100.1.7; 100-4, 12, 100.1.8; 100-4, 12, 30.6; 100-4, 12, 30.6.15; 100-4, 12, 30.6.9; 100-4, 8, 140; 100-4, 8, 170

AMA: 2000, Jan, 11; 1995, Spring, 1; 1995, Fall, 16; 1993, Spring, 34; 1992, Summer, 1, 24; 1992, Spring, 13, 24; 1992, Fall, 1; 1991, Winter, 11

99233   Subsequent hospital care, per day, for the evaluation and management of a patient, which requires at least two of these three key components: a detailed interval history; a detailed examination; medical decision making of high complexity. Counseling and/or coordination of care with other providers or agencies are provided consistent with the nature of the problem(s) and the patient's and/or family's needs. Usually, the patient is unstable or has developed a significant complication or a significant new problem. Physicians typically spend 35 minutes at the bedside and on the patient's hospital floor or unit.   E 80 ▶

MED: 100-3, 10.3; 100-3, 130.1; 100-3, 130.7; 100-4, 12, 100; 100-4, 12, 100.1.7; 100-4, 12, 100.1.8; 100-4, 12, 30.6; 100-4, 12, 30.6.15; 100-4, 12, 30.6.9; 100-4, 8, 140; 100-4, 8, 170

AMA: 1995, Spring, 1; 1995, Fall, 16; 1993, Spring, 34; 1992, Summer, 1, 24; 1992, Spring, 13, 24; 1992, Fall, 1; 1991, Winter, 11

OBSERVATION OR INPATIENT CARE SERVICES (INCLUDING ADMISSION AND DISCHARGE SERVICES)

Consult CPT codes 99217-99220 for patients that are admitted and discharged from observation on different dates. Consult CPT codes 99221-99223 and 99238-99239 for patients admitted for inpatient care and discharged on different dates.

99234   Observation or inpatient hospital care, for the evaluation and management of a patient including admission and discharge on the same date which requires these three key components: a detailed or comprehensive history; a detailed or comprehensive examination; and medical decision making that is straightforward or of low complexity. Counseling and/or coordination of care with other providers or agencies are provided consistent with the nature of the problem(s) and the patient's and/or family's needs. Usually the presenting problem(s) requiring admission are of low severity.   B 80 ▶

MED: 100-1, 5, 70; 100-2, 15, 30; 100-3, 10.3; 100-3, 130.1; 100-3, 130.7; 100-4, 11, 40.1.3.1; 100-4, 12, 10; 100-4, 12, 100; 100-4, 12, 100.1.7; 100-4, 12, 100.1.8; 100-4, 12, 30.6; 100-4, 12, 30.6.9

AMA: 2002, Jun, 10; 2000, Jan, 11; 1998, May, 1; 1998, Mar, 1

99235　　Observation or inpatient hospital care, for the evaluation and management of a patient including admission and discharge on the same date which requires these three key components: a comprehensive history; a comprehensive examination; and medical decision making of moderate complexity. Counseling and/or coordination of care with other providers or agencies are provided consistent with the nature of the problem(s) and the patient's and/or family's needs. Usually the presenting problem(s) requiring admission are of moderate severity. 　　　　　　　　　B 80 □

MED: 100-1, 5, 70; 100-2, 15, 30; 100-3, 10.3; 100-3, 130.1; 100-3, 130.7; 100-4, 11, 40.1.3.1; 100-4, 12, 10; 100-4, 12, 100; 100-4, 12, 100.1.7; 100-4, 12, 100.1.8; 100-4, 12, 30.6; 100-4, 12, 30.6.9

AMA: 2002, Jun, 10; 2000, Jan, 11; 1998, May, 1; 1998, Mar, 1

99236　　Observation or inpatient hospital care, for the evaluation and management of a patient including admission and discharge on the same date which requires these three key components: a comprehensive history; a comprehensive examination; and medical decision making of high complexity. Counseling and/or coordination of care with other providers or agencies are provided consistent with the nature of the problem(s) and the patient's and/or family's needs. Usually the presenting problem(s) requiring admission are of high severity. 　　　　　　　　B 80 □

MED: 100-1, 5, 70; 100-2, 15, 30; 100-3, 10.3; 100-3, 130.1; 100-3, 130.7; 100-4, 11, 40.1.3.1; 100-4, 12, 10; 100-4, 12, 100; 100-4, 12, 100.1.7; 100-4, 12, 100.1.8; 100-4, 12, 30.6; 100-4, 12, 30.6.9

AMA: 2002, Jun, 10; 2000, Jan, 11; 1998, May, 1; 1998, Mar, 1

HOSPITAL DISCHARGE SERVICES

99238　　Hospital discharge day management; 30 minutes or less 　　　　E 80 □

MED: 100-3, 10.3; 100-3, 130.1; 100-3, 130.7; 100-4, 12, 100; 100-4, 12, 100.1.7; 100-4, 12, 100.1.8; 100-4, 12, 30.6; 100-4, 12, 30.6.9; 100-4, 12, 70; 100-4, 13, 20; 100-4, 13, 90; 100-4, 8, 140; 100-4, 8, 170

AMA: 1999, Jan, 10; 1998, May, 1; 1998, Mar, 1, 11; 1997, Nov, 4; 1993, Spring, 4; 1992, Fall, 1

These codes are to be utilized by the physician to report all services provided to a patient on the date of discharge, if other than the initial date of inpatient status. To report concurrent care services provided by a physician(s) other than the attending physician, use subsequent hospital care codes (99231-99233) on the day of discharge. For Observation Care Discharge, consult CPT code 99217. For observation or inpatient hospital care including the admission and discharge of the patient on the same date, consult CPT codes 99234-99236. For Nursing Facility Care Discharge, consult CPT codes 99315 and 99316. If discharge services are provided to newborns admitted and discharged on the same date, consult CPT code 99435.

99239　　more than 30 minutes 　　　　　　　　　　　　　　　　E 80 □

MED: 100-1, 5, 70; 100-2, 15, 30; 100-3, 10.3; 100-3, 130.1; 100-3, 130.7; 100-4, 11, 40.1.3.1; 100-4, 12, 10; 100-4, 12, 100; 100-4, 12, 100.1.7; 100-4, 12, 100.1.8; 100-4, 12, 30.6; 100-4, 12, 30.6.9; 100-4, 8, 140; 100-4, 8, 170

AMA: 1999, Jan, 10; 1998, May, 1; 1998, Mar, 1, 11; 1997, Nov, 4

Evaluation and Management

99241 — 99244

CONSULTATIONS

OFFICE OR OTHER OUTPATIENT CONSULTATIONS

NEW OR ESTABLISHED PATIENT

99241   Office consultation for a new or established patient, which requires these three key components: a problem focused history; a problem focused examination; and straightforward medical decision making. Counseling and/or coordination of care with other providers or agencies are provided consistent with the nature of the problem(s) and the patient's and/or family's needs. Usually, the presenting problem(s) are self limited or minor. Physicians typically spend 15 minutes face-to-face with the patient and/or family.   [V] [80] [🔲]

MED: 100-1, 5, 70; 100-2, 15, 30; 100-4, 11, 40.1.3.1; 100-4, 12, 10; 100-4, 12, 100; 100-4, 12, 100.1.7; 100-4, 12, 100.1.8; 100-4, 12, 30.6; 100-4, 12, 30.6.10; 100-4, 12, 30.6.15

AMA: 2002, Sep, 11; 2002, Jul, 2; 2001, Aug, 1; 2000, Apr, 10; 1999, Jun, 10; 1997, Oct, 1; 1995, Spring, 1; 1993, Spring, 1, 34; 1992, Summer, 1; 1992, Spring, 1, 13, 24; 1991, Winter, 11

99242   Office consultation for a new or established patient, which requires these three key components: an expanded problem focused history; an expanded problem focused examination; and straightforward medical decision making. Counseling and/or coordination of care with other providers or agencies are provided consistent with the nature of the problem(s) and the patient's and/or family's needs. Usually, the presenting problem(s) are of low severity. Physicians typically spend 30 minutes face-to-face with the patient and/or family.   [V] [80] [🔲]

MED: 100-1, 5, 70; 100-2, 15, 30; 100-4, 11, 40.1.3.1; 100-4, 12, 10; 100-4, 12, 100; 100-4, 12, 100.1.7; 100-4, 12, 100.1.8; 100-4, 12, 30.6; 100-4, 12, 30.6.10; 100-4, 12, 30.6.15

AMA: 2002, Sep, 11; 2002, Jul, 2; 2001, Aug, 1; 1995, Spring, 1; 1993, Spring, 1, 34; 1992, Summer, 1; 1992, Spring, 1, 13, 24; 1991, Winter, 11

99243   Office consultation for a new or established patient, which requires these three key components: a detailed history; a detailed examination; and medical decision making of low complexity. Counseling and/or coordination of care with other providers or agencies are provided consistent with the nature of the problem(s) and the patient's and/or family's needs. Usually, the presenting problem(s) are of moderate severity. Physicians typically spend 40 minutes face-to-face with the patient and/or family.   [V] [80] [🔲]

MED: 100-1, 5, 70; 100-2, 15, 30; 100-4, 11, 40.1.3.1; 100-4, 12, 10; 100-4, 12, 100; 100-4, 12, 100.1.7; 100-4, 12, 100.1.8; 100-4, 12, 30.6; 100-4, 12, 30.6.10; 100-4, 12, 30.6.15

AMA: 2002, Sep, 11; 2002, Jul, 2; 2001, Aug, 1; 1995, Spring, 1; 1993, Spring, 1, 34; 1992, Summer, 1; 1992, Spring, 1, 13, 24; 1991, Winter, 11

99244   Office consultation for a new or established patient, which requires these three key components: a comprehensive history; a comprehensive examination; and medical decision making of moderate complexity. Counseling and/or coordination of care with other providers or agencies are provided consistent with the nature of the problem(s) and the patient's and/or family's needs. Usually, the presenting problem(s) are of moderate to high severity. Physicians typically spend 60 minutes face-to-face with the patient and/or family.   [V] [80] [🔲]

MED: 100-1, 5, 70; 100-2, 15, 30; 100-4, 11, 40.1.3.1; 100-4, 12, 10; 100-4, 12, 100; 100-4, 12, 100.1.7; 100-4, 12, 100.1.8; 100-4, 12, 30.6; 100-4, 12, 30.6.10; 100-4, 12, 30.6.15

AMA: 2002, Sep, 11; 2002, Jul, 2; 2001, Aug, 1; 1995, Spring, 1; 1993, Spring, 1, 34; 1992, Summer, 1; 1992, Spring, 1, 13, 24; 1991, Winter, 11

99245   Office consultation for a new or established patient, which requires these three key components: a comprehensive history; a comprehensive examination; and medical decision making of high complexity. Counseling and/or coordination of care with other providers or agencies are provided consistent with the nature of the problem(s) and the patient's and/or family's needs. Usually, the presenting problem(s) are of moderate to high severity. Physicians typically spend 80 minutes face-to-face with the patient and/or family.   V 80 🗗

MED: 100-1, 5, 70; 100-2, 15, 30; 100-4, 11, 40.1.3.1; 100-4, 12, 10; 100-4, 12, 100; 100-4, 12, 100.1.7; 100-4, 12, 100.1.8; 100-4, 12, 30.6; 100-4, 12, 30.6.10; 100-4, 12, 30.6.15; 100-4, 12, 30.6.15.1

AMA: 2002, Sep, 11; 2002, Jul, 2; 2001, Aug, 1; 1997, Oct, 1; 1995, Spring, 1; 1993, Spring, 1, 34; 1992, Summer, 1; 1992, Spring, 1, 13, 24; 1991, Winter, 11

INITIAL INPATIENT CONSULTATIONS

NEW OR ESTABLISHED PATIENT

99251   Initial inpatient consultation for a new or established patient, which requires these three key components: a problem focused history; a problem focused examination; and straightforward medical decision making. Counseling and/or coordination of care with other providers or agencies are provided consistent with the nature of the problem(s) and the patient's and/or family's needs. Usually, the presenting problem(s) are self limited or minor. Physicians typically spend 20 minutes at the bedside and on the patient's hospital floor or unit.   C 80 🗗

MED: 100-3, 10.3; 100-3, 130.1; 100-3, 130.7; 100-3, 160.7.1; 100-3, 70.1; 100-3, 70.2; 100-4, 12, 100; 100-4, 12, 100.1.7; 100-4, 12, 100.1.8; 100-4, 12, 30.6; 100-4, 12, 30.6.10; 100-4, 8, 140; 100-4, 8, 170

AMA: 2002, Sep, 11; 2001, Aug, 1; 1997, Oct, 1; 1995, Spring, 1; 1993, Spring, 34; 1992, Summer, 1; 1992, Spring, 1, 13, 24; 1991, Winter, 11

99252   Initial inpatient consultation for a new or established patient, which requires these three key components: an expanded problem focused history; an expanded problem focused examination; and straightforward medical decision making. Counseling and/or coordination of care with other providers or agencies are provided consistent with the nature of the problem(s) and the patient's and/or family's needs. Usually, the presenting problem(s) are of low severity. Physicians typically spend 40 minutes at the bedside and on the patient's hospital floor or unit.   C 80 🗗

AMA: 2002, Sep, 11; 2001, Aug, 1; 1995, Spring, 1; 1993, Summer, 34; 1992, Summer, 1; 1992, Spring, 1, 13, 24; 1991, Winter, 11

99253   Initial inpatient consultation for a new or established patient, which requires these three key components: a detailed history; a detailed examination; and medical decision making of low complexity. Counseling and/or coordination of care with other providers or agencies are provided consistent with the nature of the problem(s) and the patient's and/or family's needs. Usually, the presenting problem(s) are of moderate severity. Physicians typically spend 55 minutes at the bedside and on the patient's hospital floor or unit.   C 80 🗗

MED: 100-3, 10.3; 100-3, 130.1; 100-3, 130.7; 100-3, 160.7.1; 100-3, 70.1; 100-3, 70.2; 100-4, 12, 100; 100-4, 12, 100.1.7; 100-4, 12, 100.1.8; 100-4, 12, 30.6; 100-4, 12, 30.6.10; 100-4, 8, 140; 100-4, 8, 170

AMA: 2002, Sep, 11; 2001, Aug, 1; 1995, Spring, 1; 1993, Summer, 34; 1992, Summer, 1; 1992, Spring, 1, 13, 24; 1991, Winter, 11

99254   Initial inpatient consultation for a new or established patient, which requires these three key components: a comprehensive history; a comprehensive examination; and medical decision making of moderate complexity. Counseling and/or coordination of care with other providers or agencies are provided consistent with the nature of the problem(s) and the patient's and/or family's needs. Usually, the presenting problem(s) are of moderate to high severity. Physicians typically spend 80 minutes at the bedside and on the patient's hospital floor or unit.   C 80 ▣

> MED: 100-3, 10.3; 100-3, 130.1; 100-3, 130.7; 100-3, 160.7.1; 100-3, 70.1; 100-3, 70.2; 100-4, 12, 100; 100-4, 12, 100.1.7; 100-4, 12, 100.1.8; 100-4, 12, 30.6; 100-4, 12, 30.6.10; 100-4, 8, 140; 100-4, 8, 170

> AMA: 2002, Sep, 11; 2001, Aug, 1; 1995, Spring, 1; 1993, Summer, 34; 1992, Summer, 1; 1992, Spring, 1, 13, 24; 1991, Winter, 11

99255   Initial inpatient consultation for a new or established patient, which requires these three key components: a comprehensive history; a comprehensive examination; and medical decision making of high complexity. Counseling and/or coordination of care with other providers or agencies are provided consistent with the nature of the problem(s) and the patient's and/or family's needs. Usually, the presenting problem(s) are of moderate to high severity. Physicians typically spend 110 minutes at the bedside and on the patient's hospital floor or unit.   C 80 ▣

> MED: 100-3, 10.3; 100-3, 130.1; 100-3, 130.7; 100-3, 160.7.1; 100-3, 70.1; 100-3, 70.2; 100-4, 12, 100; 100-4, 12, 100.1.7; 100-4, 12, 100.1.8; 100-4, 12, 30.6; 100-4, 12, 30.6.10; 100-4, 8, 140; 100-4, 8, 170

> AMA: 2002, Sep, 11; 2001, Aug, 1; 1995, Spring, 1; 1993, Summer, 34; 1992, Summer, 1; 1992, Spring, 1, 13, 24; 1991, Winter, 11

FOLLOW-UP INPATIENT CONSULTATIONS

ESTABLISHED PATIENT

~~99261~~   ~~Follow-up inpatient consultation for an established patient, which requires at least two of these three key components: a problem focused interval history; a problem focused examination; medical decision making that is straightforward or of low complexity. Counseling and/or coordination of care with other providers or agencies are provided consistent with nature of the problem(s) and the patient's and/or family's needs. Usually, the patient is stable, recovering or improving. Physicians typically spend 10 minutes at the bedside and on the patient's hospital floor or unit.~~

~~99262~~   ~~Follow-up inpatient consultation for an established patient which requires at least two of these three key components: an expanded problem focused interval history; an expanded problem focused examination; medical decision making of moderate complexity. Counseling and/or coordination of care with other providers or agencies are provided consistent with the nature of the problem(s) and the patient's and/or family's needs. Usually, the patient is responding inadequately to therapy or has developed a minor complication. Physicians typically spend 20 minutes at the bedside and on the patient's hospital floor or unit.~~

~~99263~~   ~~Follow-up inpatient consultation for an established patient which requires at least two of these three key components: a detailed interval history; a detailed examination; medical decision making of high complexity. Counseling and/or coordination of care with other providers or agencies are provided consistent with the nature of the problem(s) and the patient's and/or family's needs. Usually, the patient is unstable or has developed a significant complication or a significant new problem. Physicians typically spend 30 minutes at the bedside and on the patient's hospital floor or unit.~~

CONFIRMATORY CONSULTATIONS

NEW OR ESTABLISHED PATIENT

99271 ~~Confirmatory consultation for a new or established patient, which requires these three key components: a problem focused history; a problem focused examination; and straightforward medical decision making. Counseling and/or coordination of care with other providers or agencies are provided consistent with the nature of the problem(s) and the patient's and/or family's needs. Usually, the presenting problem(s) are self limited or minor.~~

99272 ~~Confirmatory consultation for a new or established patient, which requires these three key components: an expanded problem focused history; an expanded problem focused examination; and straightforward medical decision making. Counseling and/or coordination of care with other providers or agencies are provided consistent with the nature of the problem(s) and the patient's and/or family's needs. Usually, the presenting problem(s) are of low severity.~~

99273 ~~Confirmatory consultation for a new or established patient, which requires these three key components: a detailed history; a detailed examination; and medical decision making of low complexity. Counseling and/or coordination of care with other providers or agencies are provided consistent with the nature of the problem(s) and the patient's and/or family's needs. Usually, the presenting problem(s) are of moderate severity.~~

99274 ~~Confirmatory consultation for a new or established patient, which requires these three key components: a comprehensive history; a comprehensive examination; and medical decision making of moderate complexity. Counseling and/or coordination of care with other providers or agencies are provided consistent with the nature of the problem(s) and the patient's and/or family's needs. Usually, the presenting problem(s) are of moderate to high severity.~~

99275 ~~Confirmatory consultation for a new or established patient, which requires these three key components: a comprehensive history; a comprehensive examination; and medical decision making of high complexity. Counseling and/or coordination of care with other providers or agencies are provided consistent with the nature of the problem(s) and the patient's and/or family's needs. Usually, the presenting problem(s) are of moderate to high severity.~~

EMERGENCY DEPARTMENT SERVICES

Emergency department (ED) service codes do not differentiate between new and established patients and are used by hospital-based and nonhospital-based physicians.

Time is not a descriptive component for the emergency department levels of E/M services since services are on a variable basis and usually involve multiple encounters with several patients over extended periods of time.

Use 99217–99220 to report evaluation and management services provided in the observation area of a hospital. Use 99291 and 99292 to report critical care provided in the emergency department.

An E/M service can be billed by a physician in addition to a surgical procedure when a separately identifiable E/M service is rendered. For example, if a physician sutures a scalp wound and performs a full neurological exam for a patient with head trauma, it would be proper to bill the surgery and the E/M service. This circumstance would be reported by adding modifier 25 to the appropriate E/M code. It would not be correct, however, if the evaluation only required identifying the need for sutures and confirming immunization status.

Associated with ED services is 99288 Physician direction of emergency medical systems (EMS) emergency care, advanced life support. The physician must be located in the ED or critical care department; be in two-way voice communication with the ambulance or rescue personnel outside the hospital; and direct the performance of necessary medical procedures.

NEW OR ESTABLISHED PATIENT

99281   Emergency department visit for the evaluation and management of a patient, which requires these three key components: a problem focused history; a problem focused examination; and straightforward medical decision making. Counseling and/or coordination of care with other providers or agencies are provided consistent with the nature of the problem(s) and the patient's and/or family's needs. Usually, the presenting problem(s) are self limited or minor.   Ⓥ 80 ▣

MED: 100-1, 5, 70; 100-2, 15, 30; 100-3, 70.1; 100-3, 70.2; 100-4, 11, 40.1.3.1; 100-4, 12, 10; 100-4, 12, 100; 100-4, 12, 100.1.7; 100-4, 12, 100.1.8; 100-4, 12, 30.6; 100-4, 12, 30.6.11; 100-4, 12, 70; 100-4, 13, 20; 100-4, 13, 90

AMA: 2002, Jul, 2; 2000, Jan, 11; 2000, Feb, 11; 1995, Spring, 1; 1993, Spring, 34; 1992, Summer, 1; 1992, Spring, 24; 1991, Winter, 11

99282   Emergency department visit for the evaluation and management of a patient, which requires these three key components: an expanded problem focused history; an expanded problem focused examination; and medical decision making of low complexity. Counseling and/or coordination of care with other providers or agencies are provided consistent with the nature of the problem(s) and the patient's and/or family's needs. Usually, the presenting problem(s) are of low to moderate severity.   Ⓥ 80 ▣

MED: 100-1, 5, 70; 100-2, 15, 30; 100-3, 70.1; 100-3, 70.2; 100-4, 11, 40.1.3.1; 100-4, 12, 10; 100-4, 12, 100; 100-4, 12, 100.1.7; 100-4, 12, 100.1.8; 100-4, 12, 30.6; 100-4, 12, 30.6.11; 100-4, 12, 70; 100-4, 13, 20; 100-4, 13, 90

AMA: 2002, Jul, 2; 2000, Jan, 11; 2000, Feb, 11; 1995, Summer, 1; 1995, Spring, 1; 1993, Spring, 34; 1992, Summer, 1, 18; 1992, Spring, 24; 1991, Winter, 11

99283   Emergency department visit for the evaluation and management of a patient, which requires these three key components: an expanded problem focused history; an expanded problem focused examination; and medical decision making of moderate complexity. Counseling and/or coordination of care with other providers or agencies are provided consistent with the nature of the problem(s) and the patient's and/or family's needs. Usually, the presenting problem(s) are of moderate severity.   Ⓥ 80 ▣

MED: 100-1, 5, 70; 100-2, 15, 30; 100-3, 70.1; 100-3, 70.2; 100-4, 11, 40.1.3.1; 100-4, 12, 10; 100-4, 12, 100; 100-4, 12, 100.1.7; 100-4, 12, 100.1.8; 100-4, 12, 30.6; 100-4, 12, 30.6.11; 100-4, 12, 70; 100-4, 13, 20; 100-4, 13, 90

AMA: 2002, Jul, 2; 2000, Jan, 11; 2000, Feb, 11; 1995, Summer, 1; 1995, Spring, 1; 1993, Spring, 34; 1992, Summer, 1, 18; 1992, Spring, 24; 1991, Winter, 11

99284   Emergency department visit for the evaluation and management of a patient, which requires these three key components: a detailed history; a detailed examination; and medical decision making of moderate complexity. Counseling and/or coordination of care with other providers or agencies are provided consistent with the nature of the problem(s) and the patient's and/or family's needs. Usually, the presenting problem(s) are of high severity, and require urgent evaluation by the physician but do not pose an immediate significant threat to life or physiologic function. Ⓥ 80 ▣

MED: 100-1, 5, 70; 100-2, 15, 30; 100-3, 70.1; 100-3, 70.2; 100-4, 11, 40.1.3.1; 100-4, 12, 10; 100-4, 12, 100; 100-4, 12, 100.1.7; 100-4, 12, 100.1.8; 100-4, 12, 30.6; 100-4, 12, 30.6.11; 100-4, 12, 70; 100-4, 13, 20; 100-4, 13, 90

AMA: 2002, Jul, 2; 2000, Jan, 11; 2000, Feb, 11; 1995, Summer, 1; 1995, Spring, 1; 1993, Spring, 34; 1992, Summer, 1, 18; 1992, Spring, 24; 1991, Winter, 11

99285   **Emergency department visit for the evaluation and management of a patient, which requires these three key components within the constraints imposed by the urgency of the patient's clinical condition and/or mental status: a comprehensive history; a comprehensive examination; and medical decision making of high complexity. Counseling and/or coordination of care with other providers or agencies are provided consistent with the nature of the problem(s) and the patient's and/or family's needs. Usually, the presenting problem(s) are of high severity and pose an immediate significant threat to life or physiologic function.** Ⅴ 80 ◨

MED: 100-1, 5, 70; 100-2, 15, 30; 100-3, 70.1; 100-3, 70.2; 100-4, 11, 40.1.3.1; 100-4, 12, 10; 100-4, 12, 100; 100-4, 12, 100.1.7; 100-4, 12, 100.1.8; 100-4, 12, 30.6; 100-4, 12, 30.6.11; 100-4, 12, 70; 100-4, 13, 20; 100-4, 13, 90

AMA: 2002, Sep, 11; 2002, Jul, 2; 2000, Jan, 11; 2000, Feb, 11; 1999, Nov, 2-3; 1995, Summer, 1; 1995, Spring, 1; 1993, Spring, 34; 1992, Summer, 1, 18; 1992, Spring, 24; 1991, Winter, 11

OTHER EMERGENCY SERVICES

99288   **Physician direction of emergency medical systems (EMS) emergency care, advanced life support**   Ⓑ

MED: 100-1, 5, 70; 100-2, 15, 30; 100-4, 11, 40.1.3.1; 100-4, 12, 10; 100-4, 12, 100; 100-4, 12, 100.1.7; 100-4, 12, 100.1.8; 100-4, 12, 30.6; 100-4, 12, 30.6.11

AMA: 1992, Summer, 18

PEDIATRIC CRITICAL CARE PATIENT TRANSPORT

CPT codes 99289 and 99290 are reported for physical attendance and direct face-to-face care provided by a physician during interfacility transport of a critically ill or critically injured pediatric patient. Patient must be 24 months of age or younger.

The following procedures are included in CPT codes 99289 and 99290: the interpretation of cardiac output measurements (93561, 93562), chest x-rays (71010, 71015, 71020), pulse oximetry (94760, 94761, 94762), computer stored information (99090), gastric intubation (43752, 91105), temporary transcutaneous pacing (92953), ventilation management (94656, 94660, 94662), and vascular access procedures (36000, 36400, 36405, 36406, 36410, 36415, 36540, 36600). Any other services performed should be reported separately.

CRITICAL CARE SERVICES GUIDELINES

- Critical care codes include evaluation and management of the critically ill or injured patient, requiring direct delivery of medical care.

- Care provided to a patient who is not critically ill but happens to be in a critical care unit should be identified using subsequent hospital care codes or inpatient consultation codes as appropriate.

- Critical care of less than 30 minutes should be reported using an appropriate E/M code.

- Critical care codes identify the duration of time spent by a physician on a given date, even if the time is not continuous. Code 99291 reports the first hour and is used only once per date. Code 99292 reports each additional 30 minutes of critical care per date.

- Critical care of less than 15 minutes beyond the first hour or less than 15 minutes beyond the final 30 minutes should not be reported.

99289   **Critical care services delivered by a physician, face-to-face, during an interfacility transport of critically ill or critically injured pediatric patient, 24 months of age or less; first 30-74 minutes of hands on care during transport**   Ⓐ Ⓝ 80 ◨

MED: 100-1, 5, 70; 100-2, 15, 30; 100-4, 11, 40.1.3.1; 100-4, 12, 10; 100-4, 12, 100; 100-4, 12, 100.1.7; 100-4, 12, 100.1.8; 100-4, 12, 30.6; 100-4, 12, 30.6.12

Evaluation and Management

99290 — 99292

+   99290   **Critical care services delivered by a physician, face-to-face, during an interfacility transport of critically ill or critically injured pediatric patient, 24 months of age or less; each additional 30 minutes (List separately in addition to code for primary service)** A N 80 ☑

MED: 100-1, 5, 70; 100-2, 15, 30; 100-4, 11, 40.1.3.1; 100-4, 12, 10; 100-4, 12, 100; 100-4, 12, 100.1.7; 100-4, 12, 100.1.8; 100-4, 12, 30.6; 100-4, 12, 30.6.12

Note that 99290 is an add-on code and must be used in conjuction with 99289.

Do not report these codes for pediatric critical care transport services of less than 30 minutes duration, in these instances, report the appropriate E/M code.

CRITICAL CARE SERVICES

Critical care is not specific to a location such as an ICU or CCU. Rather it is determined by the patient's critical condition requiring this type of physician care. Therefore, routine visits to a stabilized patient in an ICU are not necessarily critical care.

Services such as endotracheal intubation (31500) and the insertion and placement of a flow directed catheter (e.g., Swan-Ganz, 93503) may be reported separately. Append modifier 25 to the critical care code to indicate a separate service was performed.

The following CPT codes are considered part of critical care services and should not be separately reported: the interpretation of chest x-rays (71010-71020), cardiac output measurements (93561-93562), pulse oximetry (94760-94762), blood gases and other information stored in computers (e.g., blood pressures, hematologic date, ECGs (99090)), gastric intubation (43752 and 91105), ventilation management (94656-94662), temporary transcutaneous pacing (92953), and vascular procedures (36000, 36410, 36415, 36540, and 36600).

   99291   **Critical care, evaluation and management of the critically ill or critically injured patient; first 30-74 minutes** S 80 ☑

MED: 100-1, 5, 70; 100-2, 15, 30; 100-4, 11, 40.1.3.1; 100-4, 12, 10; 100-4, 12, 100; 100-4, 12, 100.1.7; 100-4, 12, 100.1.8; 100-4, 12, 30.6; 100-4, 12, 30.6.12

AMA: 2003, Feb, 15; 2002, Jul, 2; 2000, Apr, 6; 1999, Nov, 3-5; 1998, Dec, 6; 1996, Jan, 7; 1995, Summer, 1; 1993, Summer, 1; 1992, Summer, 18

+   99292   **each additional 30 minutes (List separately in addition to code for primary service)** N 80 ☑

MED: 100-1, 5, 70; 100-2, 15, 30; 100-4, 11, 40.1.3.1; 100-4, 12, 10; 100-4, 12, 100; 100-4, 12, 100.1.7; 100-4, 12, 100.1.8; 100-4, 12, 30.6; 100-4, 12, 30.6.12

AMA: 2003, Feb, 15; 2000, Dec, 15; 2000, Apr, 6; 1998, Dec, 6; 1996, Jan, 7; 1995, Summer, 1; 1993, Summer, 1; 1992, Summer, 18

Note that 99292 is an add-on code and must be used in conjunction with 99291.

INPATIENT NEONATAL AND PEDIATRIC CRITICAL CARE SERVICES

CPT codes 99295, 99296 are used to report services provided by a physician for a critically ill baby through the first 28 days of life. Code 99295 is for the date of admission and 99296 should be reported for subsequent days. Each code may only be reported once per day per patient.

CPT codes 99293, 99294 are used to report services provided by a physician for a critically ill infant or child from 29 days through 24 months of age. Code 99293 is for the date of admission and 99294 should be reported for subsequent days. Each code may only be reported once per day per patient. Services for critically ill or injured patients older than 24 months would be reported with codes 99291, 99292.

Report critical care services provided in the outpatient setting (e.g., emergency department or office) for neonates and pediatric patients up through 24 months of age with the Critical Care codes 99291, 99292. If the same physician provides critical care on both an inpatient and outpatient basis, report

---

only the appropriate Neonatal or Pediatric Critical Care code 99295-99296 for all critical care services provided on that day.

The pediatric and neonatal critical care codes include all the procedures listed in the hourly critical care codes plus these procedures: umbilical venous (36510) and umbilical arterial catheters (36660), other arterial catheters (36140, 36620), central (36555) or peripheral vessel catheterization (36000), vascular access procedures (36400, 36405, 36406), vascular punctures (36420, 36600), oral or nasogastric tube placement (43752), endotracheal intubation (31500), lumbar puncture (62270), suprapubic bladder aspiration (51000), bladder catheterization (51701, 51702), initiation and management of mechanical ventilation (94656, 94657) or continuous positive airway pressure (CPAP) (94660), surfactant administration, intravascular fluid administration (90760–90761), transfusion of blood components (36430, 36440), invasive or non-invasive electronic monitoring of vital signs, bedside pulmonary function testing (94375), and/or monitoring or interpretation of blood gases or oxygen saturation (94760–94762). Any services not contained in this list should be reported separately.

Initial NICU critical care does not include physician standby services (99360), attendance at delivery and initial stabilization (99436), or newborn resuscitation (99440) when the physician's presence for the delivery and resuscitation is required prior to transfer of the infant to the NICU. In addition, codes for prolonged physician services (99356 and 99357) may be used if prolonged, face-to-face services are required, prior to admission to NICU.

99293 **Initial inpatient pediatric critical care, per day, for the evaluation and management of a critically ill infant or young child, 29 days through 24 months of age** A C 80 ↻
MED: 100-4, 12, 100; 100-4, 12, 100.1.7; 100-4, 12, 100.1.8; 100-4, 12, 30.6.12

AMA: 2003, Feb, 15

99294 **Subsequent inpatient pediatric critical care, per day, for the evaluation and management of a critically ill infant or young child, 29 days through 24 months of age** A C 80 ↻
MED: 100-4, 12, 100; 100-4, 12, 100.1.7; 100-4, 12, 100.1.8; 100-4, 12, 30.6.12

AMA: 2003, Feb, 15

INPATIENT NEONATAL CRITICAL CARE

99295 **Initial inpatient neonatal critical care, per day, for the evaluation and management of a critically ill neonate, 28 days of age or less** A C 80 ↻
MED: 100-1, 5, 70; 100-2, 15, 30; 100-4, 11, 40.1.3.1; 100-4, 12, 10; 100-4, 12, 100; 100-4, 12, 100.1.7; 100-4, 12, 100.1.8; 100-4, 12, 30.6; 100-4, 12, 30.6.12

AMA: 2003, Feb, 15; 2000, Dec, 14; 1999, Nov, 5-6; 1998, Mar, 11; 1997, Nov, 4-5; 1993, Summer, 1

99296 **Subsequent inpatient neonatal critical care, per day, for the evaluation and management of a critically ill neonate, 28 days of age or less** A C 80 ↻
MED: 100-1, 5, 70; 100-2, 15, 30; 100-4, 11, 40.1.3.1; 100-4, 12, 10; 100-4, 12, 100; 100-4, 12, 100.1.7; 100-4, 12, 100.1.8; 100-4, 12, 30.6; 100-4, 12, 30.6.12

AMA: 2003, Feb, 15; 2000, Dec, 14; 1999, Nov, 5-6; 1998, Mar, 11; 1997, Nov, 4-5; 1993, Summer, 1

INTENSIVE (NON-CRITICAL) LOW BIRTH WEIGHT SERVICES

CPT codes 99299–99300 are used to report services rendered subsequent to the date of admission for very low birth weight (VLBW), low birth weight (LBW), or normal weight infant that is not critically ill but needs intensive observation. Very low birth weight is defined as less than 1500 grams present body weight, low body weight is 1500–2500 grams present body weight, and normal body weight is 2501–5000 grams present body weight. These codes may be reported only once per day, per patient. These codes are global codes and the same codes are included as described in codes 99293–99296.

99298   Subsequent intensive care, per day, for the evaluation and management of the recovering very low birth weight infant (present body weight less than 1500 grams)   A C 80 ↵

> MED: 100-1, 5, 70; 100-2, 15, 30; 100-4, 11, 40.1.3.1; 100-4, 12, 10; 100-4, 12, 100; 100-4, 12, 100.1.7; 100-4, 12, 100.1.8; 100-4, 12, 30.6; 100-4, 12, 30.6.12
>
> AMA: 2000, Dec, 15; 1998, Nov, 2-3

99299   Subsequent intensive care, per day, for the evaluation and management of the recovering low birth weight infant (present body weight of 1500-2500 grams)   A C 80 ↵

> MED: 100-4, 12, 100; 100-4, 12, 100.1.7; 100-4, 12, 100.1.8; 100-4, 12, 30.6; 100-4, 12, 30.6.12

● **99300**   Subsequent intensive care, per day, for the evaluation and management of the recovering infant (present body weight of 2501-5000 grams)

NURSING FACILITY SERVICES

INITIAL NURSING FACILITY CARE

Two main subcategories for these codes are Initial Facility Care and Subsequent Nursing Facility Care. Both apply to either new or established patients.

Physicians are responsible for ensuring that patients receive a multi-disciplinary plan of care, provide input in to the Resident Assessment Instrument (RAI) which includes the Minimum Data Set (MDS), Resident Assessment Protocols (RAPs) and utilization guidelines.

NEW OR ESTABLISHED PATIENT

Typical times have not been established for 99304–99306.

~~99301~~   ~~Evaluation and management of a new or established patient involving an annual nursing facility assessment which requires these three key components: a detailed interval history; a comprehensive examination; and medical decision making that is straightforward or of low complexity. Counseling and/or coordination of care with other providers or agencies are provided consistent with the nature of the problem(s) and the patient's and/or family's needs. Usually, the patient is stable, recovering or improving. The review and affirmation of the medical plan of care is required. Physicians typically spend 30 minutes at the bedside and on the patient's facility floor or unit.~~

~~99302~~   ~~Evaluation and management of a new or established patient involving a nursing facility assessment which requires these three key components: a detailed interval history; a comprehensive examination; and medical decision making of moderate to high complexity. Counseling and/or coordination of care with other providers or agencies are provided consistent with the nature of the problem(s) and the patient's and/or family's needs. Usually, the patient has developed a significant complication or a significant new problem and has had a major permanent change in status. The creation of a new medical plan of care is required. Physicians typically spend 40 minutes at the bedside and on the patient's facility floor or unit.~~

26 / TC Professional/Technical Component   **80 / 80** Assist-at-Surgery Allowed/With Documentation   ⊙ Conscious Sedation

Unlisted   Not Covered   **MED:** Pubs 100/NCD Reference   **1 - 9** ASC Group   63 Modifier 63 Exempt

28 — E/M   CPT only © 2005 American Medical Association. All Rights Reserved. *(Black Ink)*   © 2005 Ingenix, Inc. *(Blue Ink)*

~~99303~~ ~~Evaluation and management of a new or established patient involving a nursing facility assessment at the time of initial admission or readmission to the facility, which requires these three key components: a comprehensive history; a comprehensive examination; and medical decision making of moderate to high complexity. Counseling and/or coordination of care with other providers or agencies are provided consistent with the nature of the problem(s) and the patient's and/or family's needs. The creation of a medical plan of care is required. Physicians typically spend 50 minutes at the bedside and on the patient's facility floor or unit.~~

● 99304 Initial nursing facility care, per day, for the evaluation and management of a patient which requires these three key components: a detailed or comprehensive history; a detailed or comprehensive examination; and medical decision making that is straightforward or of low complexity. Counseling and/or coordination of care with other providers or agencies are provided consistent with the nature of the problem(s) and the patients and/or familys needs. Usually, the problem(s) requiring admission are of low severity.

● 99305 Initial nursing facility care, per day, for the evaluation and management of a patient which requires these three key components: a comprehensive history; a comprehensive examination; and medical decision making of moderate complexity. Counseling and/or coordination of care with other providers or agencies are provided consistent with the nature of the problem(s) and the patients and/or familys needs. Usually, the problem(s) requiring admission are of moderate severity.

● 99306 Initial nursing facility care, per day, for the evaluation and management of a patient, which requires these three key components: a comprehensive history; a comprehensive examination; and medical decision making of high complexity. Counseling and/or coordination of care with other providers or agencies are provided consistent with the nature of the problem(s) and the patients and/or familys needs. Usually, the problem(s) requiring admission are of high severity.

SUBSEQUENT NURSING FACILITY CARE

Subsequent nursing facility care codes include reviewing medical records, tests, patient condition, response to treatment and any changes in the patient's staus since the patient's last assessment.

● 99307 Subsequent nursing facility care, per day, for the evaluation and management of a patient, which requires at least two of these three key components: a problem focused interval history; a problem focused examination; straightforward medical decision making. Counseling and/or coordination of care with other providers or agencies are provided consistent with the nature of the problem(s) and the patients and/or familys needs. Usually, the patient is stable, recovering, or improving.

● 99308 Subsequent nursing facility care, per day, for the evaluation and management of a patient, which requires at least two of these three key components: an expanded problem focused interval history; an expanded problem focused examination; medical decision making of low complexity. Counseling and/or coordination of care with other providers or agencies are provided consistent with the nature of the problem(s) and the patients and/or familys needs. Usually, the patient is responding inadequately to therapy or has developed a minor complication.

Evaluation and Management

99309 — 99315

- 99309 Subsequent nursing facility care, per day, for the evaluation and management of a patient, which requires at least two of these three key components: a detailed interval history; a detailed examination; medical decision making of moderate complexity. Counseling and/or coordination of care with other providers or agencies are provided consistent with the nature of the problem(s) and the patients and/or familys needs. Usually, the patient has developed a significant complication or a significant new problem.

- 99310 Subsequent nursing facility care, per day, for the evaluation and management of a patient, which requires at least two of these three key components: a comprehensive interval history; a comprehensive examination; medical decision making of high complexity. Counseling and/or coordination of care with other providers or agencies are provided consistent with the nature of the problem(s) and the patients and/or familys needs. The patient may be unstable or may have developed a significant new problem requiring immediate physician attention.

SUBSEQUENT NURSING FACILITY CARE

Subsequent nursing facility care codes include reviewing medical records, tests, patient condition, response to treatment, and any changes in the patient's status since the patient's last assessment.

99311 Subsequent nursing facility care, per day, for the evaluation and management of a new or established patient, which requires at least two of these three key components: a problem focused interval history; a problem focused examination; medical decision making that is straightforward or of low complexity. Counseling and/or coordination of care with other providers or agencies are provided consistent with the nature of the problem(s) and the patient's and/or family's needs. Usually, the patient is stable, recovering or improving. Physicians typically spend 15 minutes at the bedside and on the patient's facility floor or unit.

99312 Subsequent nursing facility care, per day, for the evaluation and management of a new or established patient, which requires at least two of these three key components: an expanded problem focused interval history; an expanded problem focused examination; medical decision making of moderate complexity. Counseling and/or coordination of care with other providers or agencies are provided consistent with the nature of the problem(s) and the patient's and/or family's needs. Usually, the patient is responding inadequately to therapy or has developed a minor complication. Physicians typically spend 25 minutes at the bedside and on the patient's facility floor or unit.

99313 Subsequent nursing facility care, per day, for the evaluation and management of a new or established patient, which requires at least two of these three key components: a detailed interval history; a detailed examination; medical decision making of moderate to high complexity. Counseling and/or coordination of care with other providers or agencies are provided consistent with the nature of the problem(s) and the patient's and/or family's needs. Usually, the patient has developed a significant complication or a significant new problem. Physicians typically spend 35 minutes at the bedside and on the patient's facility floor or unit.

NURSING FACILITY DISCHARGE SERVICES

99315 Nursing facility discharge day management; 30 minutes or less Ⓑ 80 🄽

MED: 100-1, 5, 70; 100-2, 15, 30; 100-4, 11, 40.1.3.1; 100-4, 12, 10; 100-4, 12, 100; 100-4, 12, 100.1.7; 100-4, 12, 100.1.8; 100-4, 12, 30.6; 100-4, 12, 30.6.13

AMA: 2002, Nov, 11; 2002, May, 19; 1998, May, 1; 1997, Nov, 5-6

99316   **more than 30 minutes**   B 80

MED: 100-1, 5, 70; 100-2, 15, 30; 100-4, 11, 40.1.3.1; 100-4, 12, 10; 100-4, 12, 100; 100-4, 12, 100.1.7; 100-4, 12, 100.1.8; 100-4, 12, 30.6; 100-4, 12, 30.6.13

AMA: 2002, Nov, 11; 2002, May, 19; 1998, May, 1; 1997, Nov, 5-6

OTHER NURSING FACILITY SERVICES

● 99318   Evaluation and management of a patient involving an annual nursing facility assessment, which requires these three key components: a detailed interval history; a comprehensive examination; and medical decision making that is of low to moderate complexity. Counseling and/or coordination of care with other providers or agencies are provided consistent with the nature of the problem(s) and the patients and/or familys needs. Usually, the patient is stable, recovering, or improving.

DOMICILIARY, REST HOME (EG, BOARDING HOME), OR CUSTODIAL CARE SERVICES

Domiciliary, Rest Home, or Custodial Care Service codes are used to report services provided for the evaluation and management of patients in a facility which provides room and board and long-term personal assistance such as an assisted living facility. Medical services are not part of the facility's services.

NEW PATIENT

99321   ~~Domiciliary or rest home visit for the evaluation and management of a new patient which requires these three key components: a problem focused history; a problem focused examination; and medical decision making that is straightforward or of low complexity. Counseling and/or coordination of care with other providers or agencies are provided consistent with the nature of the problem(s) and the patient's and/or family's needs. Usually, the presenting problem(s) are of low severity.~~

99322   ~~Domiciliary or rest home visit for the evaluation and management of a new patient, which requires these three key components: an expanded problem focused history; an expanded problem focused examination; and medical decision making of moderate complexity. Counseling and/or coordination of care with other providers or agencies are provided consistent with the nature of the problem(s) and the patient's and/or family's needs. Usually, the presenting problem(s) are of moderate severity.~~

99323   ~~Domiciliary or rest home visit for the evaluation and management of a new patient, which requires these three key components: a detailed history; a detailed examination; and medical decision making of high complexity. Counseling and/or coordination of care with other providers or agencies are provided consistent with the nature of the problem(s) and the patient's and/or family's needs. Usually, the presenting problem(s) are of high complexity.~~

● 99324   Domiciliary or rest home visit for the evaluation and management of a new patient, which requires these three key components: a problem focused history; a problem focused examination; and straightforward medical decision making. Counseling and/or coordination of care with other providers or agencies are provided consistent with the nature of the problem(s) and the patients and/or familys needs. Usually, the presenting problem(s) are of low severity. Physicians typically spend 20 minutes with the patient and/or family or caregiver.

Evaluation and Management

99325 — 99332

● 99325 Domiciliary or rest home visit for the evaluation and management of a new patient, which requires these three key components: an expanded problem focused history; an expanded problem focused examination; and medical decision making of low complexity. Counseling and/or coordination of care with other providers or agencies are provided consistent with the nature of the problem(s) and the patients and/or familys needs. Usually, the presenting problem(s) are of moderate severity. Physicians typically spend 30 minutes with the patient and/or family or caregiver.

● 99326 Domiciliary or rest home visit for the evaluation and management of a new patient, which requires these three key components: a detailed history; a detailed examination; and medical decision making of moderate complexity. Counseling and/or coordination of care with other providers or agencies are provided consistent with the nature of the problem(s) and the patients and/or familys needs. Usually, the presenting problem(s) are of moderate to high severity. Physicians typically spend 45 minutes with the patient and/or family or caregiver.

● 99327 Domiciliary or rest home visit for the evaluation and management of a new patient, which requires these three key components: a comprehensive history; a comprehensive examination; and medical decision making of moderate complexity. Counseling and/or coordination of care with other providers or agencies are provided consistent with the nature of the problem(s) and the patients and/or familys needs. Usually, the presenting problem(s) are of high severity. Physicians typically spend 60 minutes with the patient and/or family or caregiver.

● 99328 Domiciliary or rest home visit for the evaluation and management of a new patient, which requires these three key components: a comprehensive history; a comprehensive examination; and medical decision making of high complexity. Counseling and/or coordination of care with other providers or agencies are provided consistent with the nature of the problem(s) and the patients and/or familys needs. Usually, the patient is unstable or has developed a significant new problem requiring immediate physician attention. Physicians typically spend 75 minutes with the patient and/or family or caregiver.

ESTABLISHED PATIENT

~~99331~~ ~~Domiciliary or rest home visit for the evaluation and management of an established patient, which requires at least two of these three key components: a problem focused interval history; a problem focused examination; medical decision making that is straightforward or of low complexity. Counseling and/or coordination of care with other providers or agencies are provided consistent with the nature of the problem(s) and the patient's and/or family's needs. Usually, the patient is stable, recovering or improving.~~

~~99332~~ ~~Domiciliary or rest home visit for the evaluation and management of an established patient, which requires at least two of these three key components: an expanded problem focused interval history; an expanded problem focused examination; medical decision making of moderate complexity. Counseling and/or coordination of care with other providers or agencies are provided consistent with the nature of the problem(s) and the patient's and/or family's needs. Usually, the patient is responding inadequately to therapy or has developed a minor complication.~~

~~99333~~ ~~Domiciliary or rest home visit for the evaluation and management of an established patient, which requires at least two of these three key components: a detailed interval history; a detailed examination; medical decision making of high complexity. Counseling and/or coordination of care with other providers or agencies are provided consistent with the nature of the problem(s) and the patient's and/or family's needs. Usually, the patient is unstable or has developed a significant complication or a significant new problem.~~

● 99334   Domiciliary or rest home visit for the evaluation and management of an established patient, which requires at least two of these three key components: a problem focused interval history; a problem focused examination; straightforward medical decision making. Counseling and/or coordination of care with other providers or agencies are provided consistent with the nature of the problem(s) and the patients and/or familys needs. Usually, the presenting problem(s) are self-limited or minor. Physicians typically spend 15 minutes with the patient and/or family or caregiver.

● 99335   Domiciliary or rest home visit for the evaluation and management of an established patient, which requires at least two of these three key components: an expanded problem focused interval history; an expanded problem focused examination; medical decision making of low complexity. Counseling and/or coordination of care with other providers or agencies are provided consistent with the nature of the problem(s) and the patients and/or familys needs. Usually, the presenting problem(s) are of low to moderate severity. Physicians typically spend 25 minutes with the patient and/or family or caregiver.

● 99336   Domiciliary or rest home visit for the evaluation and management of an established patient, which requires at least two of these three key components: a detailed interval history; a detailed examination; medical decision making of moderate complexity. Counseling and/or coordination of care with other providers or agencies are provided consistent with the nature of the problem(s) and the patients and/or familys needs. Usually, the presenting problem(s) are of moderate to high severity. Physicians typically spend 40 minutes with the patient and/or family or caregiver.

● 99337   Domiciliary or rest home visit for the evaluation and management of an established patient, which requires at least two of these three key components: a comprehensive interval history; a comprehensive examination; and medical decision making of moderate to high complexity. Counseling and/or coordination of care with other providers or agencies are provided consistent with the nature of the problem(s) and the patients and/or familys needs. Usually, the presenting problem(s) are of moderate to high severity. The patient may be unstable or may have developed a significant new problem requiring immediate physician attention. Physicians typically spend 60 minutes with the patient and/or family or caregiver.

DOMICILIARY, REST HOME, (E.G., ASSISTED LIVING FACILITY) OR HOME CARE PLAN OVERSIGHT SERVICES

These codes are to report care plan oversight services provided under the individual supervision of a physician to a patient in a rest home, (e.g., assisted living facility), home, or in domiciliary care.

●   **99339**   Individual physician supervision of a patient (patient not present) in home, domiciliary or rest home (eg, assisted living facility) requiring complex and multidisciplinary care modalities involving regular physician development and/or revision of care plans, review of subsequent reports of patient status, review of related laboratory and other studies, communication (including telephone calls) for purposes of assessment or care decisions with health care professional(s), family member(s), surrogate decision maker(s) (eg, legal guardian) and/or key caregiver(s) involved in patient's care, integration of new information into the medical treatment plan and/or adjustment of medical therapy, within a calendar month; 15-29 minutes

●   **99340**   Individual physician supervision of a patient (patient not present) in home, domiciliary or rest home (eg, assisted living facility) requiring complex and multidisciplinary care modalities involving regular physician development and/or revision of care plans, review of subsequent reports of patient status, review of related laboratory and other studies, communication (including telephone calls) for purposes of assessment or care decisions with health care professional(s), family member(s), surrogate decision maker(s) (eg, legal guardian) and/or key caregiver(s) involved in patient's care, integration of new information into the medical treatment plan and/or adjustment of medical therapy, within a calendar month; 30 minutes or more

HOME SERVICES

Services and care provided at the patient's home or other private residence are reported from this subcategory. While not all payers will reimburse for physician home services, it is important to document home visits and submit a claim.

NEW PATIENT

     99341   Home visit for the evaluation and management of a new patient, which requires these three key components: a problem focused history; a problem focused examination; and straightforward medical decision making. Counseling and/or coordination of care with other providers or agencies are provided consistent with the nature of the problem(s) and the patient's and/or family's needs. Usually, the presenting problem(s) are of low severity. Physicians typically spend 20 minutes face-to-face with the patient and/or family.   B 80 🔲

             MED: 100-1, 5, 70; 100-2, 15, 30; 100-4, 11, 40.1.3.1; 100-4, 12, 10; 100-4, 12, 30.6; 100-4, 12, 30.6.14; 100-4, 12, 30.6.14.1; 100-4, 12, 30.6.15

             AMA: 1998, Oct, 6; 1997, Nov, 6-8; 1997, Jun, 6; 1995, Spring, 1; 1993, Spring, 34; 1992, Summer, 1; 1992, Spring, 24; 1991, Winter, 11

     99342   Home visit for the evaluation and management of a new patient, which requires these three key components: an expanded problem focused history; an expanded problem focused examination; and medical decision making of low complexity. Counseling and/or coordination of care with other providers or agencies are provided consistent with the nature of the problem(s) and the patient's and/or family's needs. Usually, the presenting problem(s) are of moderate severity. Physicians typically spend 30 minutes face-to-face with the patient and/or family.   B 80 🔲

             MED: 100-1, 5, 70; 100-2, 15, 30; 100-4, 11, 40.1.3.1; 100-4, 12, 10; 100-4, 12, 30.6; 100-4, 12, 30.6.14; 100-4, 12, 30.6.14.1; 100-4, 12, 30.6.15

             AMA: 1998, Oct, 6; 1997, Nov, 6-8; 1997, Jun, 6; 1995, Spring, 1; 1993, Spring, 34; 1992, Summer, 1; 1992, Spring, 24; 1991, Winter, 11

26 / **TC** Professional/Technical Component   **80** / **80** Assist-at-Surgery Allowed/With Documentation   ⊙ Conscious Sedation

Unlisted   Not Covered   **MED:** Pubs 100/NCD Reference   **1** - **9** ASC Group   63 Modifier 63 Exempt

34 — E/M   CPT only © 2005 American Medical Association. All Rights Reserved. *(Black Ink)*   © 2005 Ingenix, Inc. *(Blue Ink)*

99343   Home visit for the evaluation and management of a new patient, which requires these three key components: a detailed history; a detailed examination; and medical decision making of moderate complexity. Counseling and/or coordination of care with other providers or agencies are provided consistent with the nature of the problem(s) and the patient's and/or family's needs. Usually, the presenting problem(s) are of moderate to high severity. Physicians typically spend 45 minutes face-to-face with the patient and/or family.   B 80 ◨

MED: 100-1, 5, 70; 100-2, 15, 30; 100-4, 11, 40.1.3.1; 100-4, 12, 10; 100-4, 12, 30.6; 100-4, 12, 30.6.14; 100-4, 12, 30.6.14.1; 100-4, 12, 30.6.15

AMA: 1998, Oct, 6; 1997, Nov, 6-8; 1997, Jun, 6; 1995, Spring, 1; 1993, Spring, 34; 1992, Summer, 1; 1992, Spring, 24; 1991, Winter, 11

99344   Home visit for the evaluation and management of a new patient, which requires these three key components: a comprehensive history; a comprehensive examination; and medical decision making of moderate complexity. Counseling and/or coordination of care with other providers or agencies are provided consistent with the nature of the problem(s) and the patient's and/or family's needs. Usually, the presenting problem(s) are of high severity. Physicians typically spend 60 minutes face-to-face with the patient and/or family.   B 80 ◨

MED: 100-1, 5, 70; 100-2, 15, 30; 100-4, 11, 40.1.3.1; 100-4, 12, 10; 100-4, 12, 30.6; 100-4, 12, 30.6.14; 100-4, 12, 30.6.14.1; 100-4, 12, 30.6.15

AMA: 1998, Oct, 6; 1997, Nov, 6-8

99345   Home visit for the evaluation and management of a new patient, which requires these three key components: a comprehensive history; a comprehensive examination; and medical decision making of high complexity. Counseling and/or coordination of care with other providers or agencies are provided consistent with the nature of the problem(s) and the patient's and/or family's needs. Usually, the patient is unstable or has developed a significant new problem requiring immediate physician attention. Physicians typically spend 75 minutes face-to-face with the patient and/or family.   B 80 ◨

MED: 100-1, 5, 70; 100-2, 15, 30; 100-4, 11, 40.1.3.1; 100-4, 12, 10; 100-4, 12, 30.6; 100-4, 12, 30.6.14; 100-4, 12, 30.6.14.1; 100-4, 12, 30.6.15

AMA: 1998, Oct, 6; 1997, Nov, 6-8

ESTABLISHED PATIENT

99347   Home visit for the evaluation and management of an established patient, which requires at least two of these three key components: a problem focused interval history; a problem focused examination; straightforward medical decision making. Counseling and/or coordination of care with other providers or agencies are provided consistent with the nature of the problem(s) and the patient's and/or family's needs. Usually, the presenting problem(s) are self-limited or minor. Physicians typically spend 15 minutes face-to-face with the patient and/or family.   B 80 ◨

MED: 100-1, 5, 70; 100-2, 15, 30; 100-4, 11, 40.1.3.1; 100-4, 12, 10; 100-4, 12, 30.6; 100-4, 12, 30.6.14; 100-4, 12, 30.6.14.1; 100-4, 12, 30.6.15

AMA: 1998, Oct, 6; 1997, Nov, 6-8

99348   Home visit for the evaluation and management of an established patient, which requires at least two of these three components: an expanded problem focused interval history; an expanded problem focused examination; medical decision making of low complexity. Counseling and/or coordination of care with other providers or agencies are provided consistent with the nature of the problem(s) and the patient's and/or family's needs. Usually, the presenting problem(s) are of low to moderate severity. Physicians typically spend 25 minutes face-to-face with the patient and/or family.   B 80 ▣

MED: 100-1, 5, 70; 100-2, 15, 30; 100-4, 11, 40.1.3.1; 100-4, 12, 10; 100-4, 12, 30.6; 100-4, 12, 30.6.14; 100-4, 12, 30.6.14.1; 100-4, 12, 30.6.15

AMA: 1998, Oct, 6; 1997, Nov, 6-8

99349   Home visit for the evaluation and management of an established patient, which requires at least two of these three key components: a detailed interval history; a detailed examination; medical decision making of moderate complexity. Counseling and/or coordination of care with other providers or agencies are provided consistent with the nature of the problem(s) and the patient's and/or family's needs. Usually, the presenting problem(s) are moderate to high severity. Physicians typically spend 40 minutes face-to-face with the patient and/or family.   B 80 ▣

MED: 100-1, 5, 70; 100-2, 15, 30; 100-4, 11, 40.1.3.1; 100-4, 12, 10; 100-4, 12, 30.6; 100-4, 12, 30.6.14; 100-4, 12, 30.6.14.1; 100-4, 12, 30.6.15

AMA: 1998, Oct, 6; 1997, Nov, 6-8

99350   Home visit for the evaluation and management of an established patient, which requires at least two of these three key components: a comprehensive interval history; a comprehensive examination; medical decision making of moderate to high complexity. Counseling and/or coordination of care with other providers or agencies are provided consistent with the nature of the problem(s) and the patient's and/or family's needs. Usually, the presenting problem(s) are of moderate to high severity. The patient may be unstable or may have developed a significant new problem requiring immediate physician attention. Physicians typically spend 60 minutes face-to-face with the patient and/or family.   B 80 ▣

MED: 100-1, 5, 70; 100-2, 15, 30; 100-4, 11, 40.1.3.1; 100-4, 12, 10; 100-4, 12, 30.6; 100-4, 12, 30.6.14; 100-4, 12, 30.6.14.1; 100-4, 12, 30.6.15

AMA: 1998, Oct, 6; 1997, Nov, 6-8

PROLONGED SERVICES

PROLONGED PHYSICIAN SERVICE WITH DIRECT (FACE-TO-FACE) PATIENT CONTACT

These codes report services involving direct patient contact beyond the usual service, with separate codes for office or outpatient encounters (99354 and 99355) and for inpatient encounters (99356 and 99357). Prolonged physician services are add-on services and should be listed separately in addition to the E/M service. The codes report the total duration of face-to-face time spent by the physician on a given date, even if the time is not continuous.

Code 99354 or 99356 reports the first hour of prolonged service on a given date, depending on the place of service, with 99355 or 99357 used to report each additional 30 minutes for that date. Services lasting less than 30 minutes are not reportable in this category, and the services must extend 15 minutes or more into the next time period to be reportable. For example, services lasting one hour and 12 minutes are reported by 99354 or 99356 alone. Services lasting one hour and 17 minutes are reported by the code for the first hour plus the code for an additional 30 minutes.

+ 99354 **Prolonged physician service in the office or other outpatient setting requiring direct (face-to-face) patient contact beyond the usual service (eg, prolonged care and treatment of an acute asthmatic patient in an outpatient setting); first hour (List separately in addition to code for office or other outpatient Evaluation and Management service)** N 80 CCI
MED: 100-1, 5, 70; 100-2, 15, 30; 100-4, 11, 40.1.3.1; 100-4, 12, 10; 100-4, 12, 100; 100-4, 12, 100.1.7; 100-4, 12, 100.1.8; 100-4, 12, 30.6; 100-4, 12, 30.6.15

AMA: 2000, Sep, 1; 1994, Spring, 30, 32

Note that 99354 is an add-on code and must be used in conjunction with 99201-99215, 99241-99245, and 99301-99350.

+ 99355 **each additional 30 minutes (List separately in addition to code for prolonged physician service)** N 80 CCI
MED: 100-1, 5, 70; 100-2, 15, 30; 100-4, 11, 40.1.3.1; 100-4, 12, 10; 100-4, 12, 100; 100-4, 12, 100.1.7; 100-4, 12, 100.1.8; 100-4, 12, 30.6; 100-4, 12, 30.6.15

AMA: 2000, Sep, 1; 1994, Spring, 30, 32

Note that 99355 is an add-on code and must be used in conjunction with 99354.

+ 99356 **Prolonged physician service in the inpatient setting, requiring direct (face-to-face) patient contact beyond the usual service (eg, maternal fetal monitoring for high risk delivery or other physiological monitoring, prolonged care of an acutely ill inpatient); first hour (List separately in addition to code for inpatient Evaluation and Management service)** C 80 CCI
MED: 100-1, 5, 70; 100-2, 15, 30; 100-4, 11, 40.1.3.1; 100-4, 12, 10; 100-4, 12, 100; 100-4, 12, 100.1.7; 100-4, 12, 100.1.8; 100-4, 12, 30.6; 100-4, 12, 30.6.15

AMA: 1994, Spring, 30, 32

Note that 99356 is an add-on code and must be used in conjunction with 99221-99233, 99251-99255, and 99261-99263.

+ 99357 **each additional 30 minutes (List separately in addition to code for prolonged physician service)** C 80 CCI
MED: 100-1, 5, 70; 100-2, 15, 30; 100-4, 11, 40.1.3.1; 100-4, 12, 10; 100-4, 12, 100; 100-4, 12, 100.1.7; 100-4, 12, 100.1.8; 100-4, 12, 30.6; 100-4, 12, 30.6.15

Note that 99357 is an add-on code and must be used in conjunction with 99356.

PROLONGED PHYSICIAN SERVICE WITHOUT DIRECT (FACE-TO-FACE) PATIENT CONTACT

These prolonged physician services without direct patient contact are used before and/or after face-to-face patient care and may include review of extensive records and tests, and communication (other than telephone calls, 99371–99373) with other professionals and/or the patient and family. These are beyond the usual services and include both inpatient and outpatient settings. Report these services in addition to other services provided, including any level of E/M service.

Use 99358 to report the first hour and 99359 for each additional 30 minutes. All aspects of time reporting are the same as explained above for direct patient contact services.

+ 99358 **Prolonged evaluation and management service before and/or after direct (face-to-face) patient care (eg, review of extensive records and tests, communication with other professionals and/or the patient/family); first hour (List separately in addition to code(s) for other physician service(s) and/or inpatient or outpatient Evaluation and Management service)** N
MED: 100-1, 5, 70; 100-2, 15, 30; 100-4, 11, 40.1.3.1; 100-4, 12, 10; 100-4, 12, 100; 100-4, 12, 100.1.7; 100-4, 12, 100.1.8; 100-4, 12, 30.6; 100-4, 12, 30.6.15

AMA: 1998, Nov, 3; 1994, Spring, 32

Note that 99358 is an add-on code and must be used in conjunction with other physician services, including E/M services at any level.

If telephone calls need to be reported, consult CPT codes 99371-99373.

+   **99359**   **each additional 30 minutes (List separately in addition to code for prolonged physician service)**   Ⓝ
MED: 100-1, 5, 70; 100-2, 15, 30; 100-4, 11, 40.1.3.1; 100-4, 12, 10; 100-4, 12, 100; 100-4, 12, 100.1.7; 100-4, 12, 100.1.8; 100-4, 12, 30.6; 100-4, 12, 30.6.15

Note that 99359 is an add-on code and must be used in conjunction with 99358.

PHYSICIAN STANDBY SERVICES

Report code 99360 for physician standby services requested by another physician. The standby physician has no direct patient contact. The standby physician may not provide services to other patients or be proctoring another physician for the time to be reportable. Also, if the standby physician ultimately provides services subject to a surgical package, the standby is not separately reportable.

This code reports cumulative standby time by date of service. Less than 30 minutes is not reportable and a full 30 minutes must be spent for each unit of service reported. For example, 25 minutes is not reportable and 50 minutes is reported as one unit (99360 x 1).

99360   **Physician standby service, requiring prolonged physician attendance, each 30 minutes (eg, operative standby, standby for frozen section, for cesarean/high risk delivery, for monitoring EEG)**   Ⓑ ⬛
MED: 100-1, 5, 70; 100-1, 5, 90.2; 100-2, 15, 30; 100-2, 15, 80; 100-2, 15, 80.1; 100-4, 11, 40.1.3.1; 100-4, 12, 10; 100-4, 12, 30.6; 100-4, 12, 30.6.15; 100-4, 16, 10; 100-4, 16, 10.1; 100-4, 16, 110.4

AMA: 1997, Nov, 8; 1997, Aug, 18; 1997, Apr, 10; 1994, Spring, 32

To report hospital mandated on-call services, consult CPT codes 99026-99027.

Note that 99360 may be reported in addition to 99431 or 99440 as appropriate. However, 99360 cannot be reported in addition to 99436.

CASE MANAGEMENT SERVICES

Physician case management is a process of involving direct patient care as well as coordinating and controlling access to the patient or initiating and/or supervising other necessary health care services. Case management services include team conferences (99361–99362) and telephone calls (99371–99373).

TEAM CONFERENCES

99361   **Medical conference by a physician with interdisciplinary team of health professionals or representatives of community agencies to coordinate activities of patient care (patient not present); approximately 30 minutes** Ⓔ
MED: 100-1, 5, 70; 100-2, 15, 30; 100-4, 11, 40.1.3.1; 100-4, 12, 10; 100-4, 12, 30.6; 100-4, 12, 30.6.16

99362   **approximately 60 minutes**   Ⓔ
MED: 100-1, 5, 70; 100-2, 15, 30; 100-4, 11, 40.1.3.1; 100-4, 12, 10; 100-4, 12, 30.6; 100-4, 12, 30.6.16

TELEPHONE CALLS

99371   **Telephone call by a physician to patient or for consultation or medical management or for coordinating medical management with other health care professionals (eg, nurses, therapists, social workers, nutritionists, physicians, pharmacists); simple or brief (eg, to report on tests and/or laboratory results, to clarify or alter previous instructions, to integrate new information from other health professionals into the medical treatment plan, or to adjust therapy)**   Ⓑ
MED: 100-1, 5, 70; 100-2, 15, 30; 100-4, 11, 40.1.3.1; 100-4, 12, 10; 100-4, 12, 30.6; 100-4, 12, 30.6.16; 100-4, 12, 70; 100-4, 13, 20; 100-4, 13, 90

AMA: 2000, May, 11

99372   intermediate (eg, to provide advice to an established patient on a new problem, to initiate therapy that can be handled by telephone, to discuss test results in detail, to coordinate medical management of a new problem in an established patient, to discuss and evaluate new information and details, or to initiate new plan of care)   ⊞

MED: 100-1, 5, 70; 100-2, 15, 30; 100-4, 11, 40.1.3.1; 100-4, 12, 10; 100-4, 12, 30.6; 100-4, 12, 30.6.16; 100-4, 12, 70; 100-4, 13, 20; 100-4, 13, 90

AMA: 2000, May, 11

99373   complex or lengthy (eg, lengthy counseling session with anxious or distraught patient, detailed or prolonged discussion with family members regarding seriously ill patient, lengthy communication necessary to coordinate complex services of several different health professionals working on different aspects of the total patient care plan)   ⊞

MED: 100-1, 5, 70; 100-2, 15, 30; 100-4, 11, 40.1.3.1; 100-4, 12, 10; 100-4, 12, 30.6; 100-4, 12, 30.6.16; 100-4, 12, 70; 100-4, 13, 20; 100-4, 13, 90

AMA: 2000, May, 11

CARE PLAN OVERSIGHT SERVICES

Codes 99374–99380 report the services of a physician providing ongoing review and revision of a patient's care plan involving complex or multidisciplinary care modalities. Care plan oversight services are reported separately from any necessary office/outpatient, hospital, home, nursing facility, or domiciliary services. Only one physician may report these codes per patient per 30-day period. Also, low intensity and infrequent supervision services are not reported separately.

99374   Physician supervision of a patient under care of home health agency (patient not present) in home, domiciliary or equivalent environment (eg, Alzheimer's facility) requiring complex and multidisciplinary care modalities involving regular physician development and/or revision of care plans, review of subsequent reports of patient status, review of related laboratory and other studies, communication (including telephone calls) for purposes of assessment or care decisions with health care professional(s), family member(s), surrogate decision maker(s) (eg, legal guardian) and/or key caregiver(s) involved in patient's care, integration of new information into the medical treatment plan and/or adjustment of medical therapy, within a calendar month; 15-29 minutes   ⊞

MED: 100-1, 5, 70; 100-2, 15, 30; 100-4, 11, 40.1.3.1; 100-4, 12, 10; 100-4, 12, 30.6

AMA: 1997, Nov, 8-9; 1994, Summer, 9

99375   30 minutes or more   🅴

MED: 100-1, 5, 70; 100-2, 15, 30; 100-4, 11, 40.1.3.1; 100-4, 12, 10; 100-4, 12, 30.6

AMA: 1997, Nov, 8-9; 1994, Summer, 9

99377   Physician supervision of a hospice patient (patient not present) requiring complex and multidisciplinary care modalities involving regular physician development and/or revision of care plans, review of subsequent reports of patient status, review of related laboratory and other studies, communication (including telephone calls) for purposes of assessment or care decisions with health care professional(s), family member(s), surrogate decision maker(s) (eg, legal guardian) and/or key caregiver(s) involved in patient's care, integration of new information into the medical treatment plan and/or adjustment of medical therapy, within a calendar month; 15-29 minutes   ⊞

MED: 100-1, 5, 70; 100-2, 15, 30; 100-4, 11, 10; 100-4, 11, 40.1.3; 100-4, 11, 40.1.3.1; 100-4, 12, 10; 100-4, 12, 30.6

AMA: 1997, Nov, 8-9

99378   30 minutes or more   [E]
MED: 100-1, 5, 70; 100-2, 15, 30; 100-4, 11, 10; 100-4, 11, 40.1.3; 100-4, 11, 40.1.3.1; 100-4, 12, 10; 100-4, 12, 30.6

AMA: 1997, Nov, 8-9

99379   Physician supervision of a nursing facility patient (patient not present)
requiring complex and multidisciplinary care modalities involving regular
physician development and/or revision of care plans, review of subsequent
reports of patient status, review of related laboratory and other studies,
communication (including telephone calls) for purposes of assessment or
care decisions with health care professional(s), family member(s), surrogate
decision maker(s) (eg, legal guardian) and/or key caregiver(s) involved in
patient's care, integration of new information into the medical treatment
plan and/or adjustment of medical therapy, within a calendar month; 15-29
minutes   [B]
MED: 100-1, 5, 70; 100-2, 15, 30; 100-4, 11, 40.1.3.1; 100-4, 12, 10; 100-4, 12, 30.6

99380   30 minutes or more   [B]
MED: 100-1, 5, 70; 100-2, 15, 30; 100-4, 11, 40.1.3.1; 100-4, 12, 10; 100-4, 12, 30.6
AMA: 1997, Nov, 8-9

PREVENTIVE MEDICINE SERVICES

Preventive medicine codes are used to report periodic preventive medicine evaluation and
management of infants, children, adolescents, and adults. Examples of services reported with these
codes include well-child exams, annual gynecologic exams, and other annual or periodic exams
specifically focused on promoting health and preventing illness.

Preventive medicine evaluation and management services can be reported with problem-oriented
evaluation and management services (99201–99215) if the abnormality encountered or the pre-
existing condition addressed during the preventive medicine exam requires significant additional
work. Report with modifier 25 to indicate that a separately identifiable evaluation and management
service was provided.

Codes 99381–99397 include counseling, anticipatory guidance, and risk factor reduction provided at
the time of the preventive medicine service. Use 99401–99429 only when reporting counseling and
risk factor reduction provided at a separate encounter. Report all ancillary lab, x-ray, and other
procedures additionally.

NEW PATIENT

99381   Initial comprehensive preventive medicine evaluation and management of
an individual including an age and gender appropriate history, examination,
counseling/anticipatory guidance/risk factor reduction interventions, and
the ordering of appropriate immunization(s), laboratory/diagnostic
procedures, new patient; infant (age under 1 year)   [A][E]
MED: 100-1, 5, 70; 100-2, 15, 30; 100-2, 16, 90; 100-4, 11, 40.1.3.1; 100-4, 12, 10; 100-4, 12, 30.6

AMA: 2002, May, 1; 1998, Nov, 3-4; 1998, Jul, 9; 1997, Aug, 1; 1995, Spring, 1; 1993, Spring,
14, 34; 1992, Summer, 1; 1992, Spring, 24; 1991, Winter, 11

If counseling/anticipatory guidance/risk factor reduction interventions are
provided at an encounter separate from the preventive medicine examination,
consult CPT codes 99401-99412.

99382   early childhood (age 1 through 4 years)   [A][E]
MED: 100-1, 5, 70; 100-2, 15, 30; 100-2, 16, 90; 100-4, 11, 40.1.3.1; 100-4, 12, 10; 100-4, 12, 30.6

AMA: 2002, May, 1; 1998, Nov, 3-4; 1998, Jul, 9; 1997, Aug, 1; 1995, Spring, 1; 1993, Spring,
14, 34; 1992, Summer, 1; 1992, Spring, 24; 1991, Winter, 11

99383   **late childhood (age 5 through 11 years)**   A E
MED: 100-1, 5, 70; 100-2, 15, 30; 100-2, 16, 90; 100-4, 11, 40.1.3.1; 100-4, 12, 10; 100-4, 12, 30.6

AMA: 2002, May, 1; 1998, Nov, 3-4; 1998, Jul, 9; 1997, Aug, 1; 1995, Spring, 1; 1993, Spring, 14, 34; 1992, Summer, 1; 1992, Spring, 24; 1991, Winter, 11

99384   **adolescent (age 12 through 17 years)**   A E
MED: 100-1, 5, 70; 100-2, 15, 30; 100-2, 16, 90; 100-4, 11, 40.1.3.1; 100-4, 12, 10; 100-4, 12, 30.6

AMA: 2002, May, 1; 1998, Nov, 3-4; 1998, Jul, 9; 1997, Aug, 1; 1995, Spring, 1; 1993, Spring, 14, 34; 1992, Summer, 1; 1992, Spring, 24; 1991, Winter, 11

99385   **18-39 years**   A E
MED: 100-1, 5, 70; 100-2, 15, 30; 100-2, 16, 90; 100-4, 11, 40.1.3.1; 100-4, 12, 10; 100-4, 12, 30.6

AMA: 2002, May, 1; 1998, Nov, 3-4; 1998, Jul, 9; 1997, Aug, 1; 1995, Spring, 1; 1993, Spring, 14, 34; 1992, Summer, 1; 1992, Spring, 24; 1991, Winter, 11

99386   **40-64 years**   A E
MED: 100-1, 5, 70; 100-2, 15, 30; 100-2, 16, 90; 100-4, 11, 40.1.3.1; 100-4, 12, 10; 100-4, 12, 30.6

AMA: 2002, May, 1; 1998, Nov, 3-4; 1998, Jul, 9; 1997, Aug, 1; 1995, Spring, 1; 1993, Spring, 14, 34; 1992, Summer, 1; 1992, Spring, 24; 1991, Winter, 11

99387   **65 years and over**   A E
MED: 100-1, 5, 70; 100-2, 15, 30; 100-2, 16, 90; 100-4, 11, 40.1.3.1; 100-4, 12, 10; 100-4, 12, 30.6

AMA: 2002, May, 1; 1998, Nov, 3-4; 1998, Jul, 9; 1997, Aug, 1; 1995, Spring, 1; 1993, Spring, 14, 34; 1992, Summer, 1; 1992, Spring, 24; 1991, Winter, 11

ESTABLISHED PATIENT

99391   **Periodic comprehensive preventive medicine reevaluation and management of an individual including an age and gender appropriate history, examination, counseling/anticipatory guidance/risk factor reduction interventions, and the ordering of appropriate immunization(s), laboratory/diagnostic procedures, established patient; infant (age under 1 year)**   A E
MED: 100-1, 5, 70; 100-2, 15, 30; 100-2, 16, 90; 100-4, 11, 40.1.3.1; 100-4, 12, 10; 100-4, 12, 30.6

AMA: 2002, May, 1; 1998, Nov, 3-4; 1998, Jul, 9; 1997, Aug, 1; 1995, Spring, 1; 1993, Spring, 14, 34; 1992, Summer, 1; 1992, Spring, 24; 1991, Winter, 11

99392   **early childhood (age 1 through 4 years)**   A E
MED: 100-1, 5, 70; 100-2, 15, 30; 100-2, 16, 90; 100-4, 11, 40.1.3.1; 100-4, 12, 10; 100-4, 12, 30.6

AMA: 2002, May, 1; 1998, Nov, 3-4; 1998, Jul, 9; 1997, Aug, 1; 1995, Spring, 1; 1993, Spring, 14, 34; 1992, Summer, 1; 1992, Spring, 24; 1991, Winter, 11

99393   **late childhood (age 5 through 11 years)**   A E
MED: 100-1, 5, 70; 100-2, 15, 30; 100-2, 16, 90; 100-4, 11, 40.1.3.1; 100-4, 12, 10; 100-4, 12, 30.6

AMA: 2002, May, 1; 1998, Nov, 3-4; 1998, Jul, 9; 1997, Aug, 1; 1995, Spring, 1; 1993, Spring, 14, 34; 1992, Summer, 1; 1992, Spring, 24; 1991, Winter, 11

99394   **adolescent (age 12 through 17 years)**   A E
MED: 100-1, 5, 70; 100-2, 15, 30; 100-2, 16, 90; 100-4, 11, 40.1.3.1; 100-4, 12, 10; 100-4, 12, 30.6

AMA: 2002, May, 1; 1998, Nov, 3-4; 1998, Jul, 9; 1997, Aug, 1; 1995, Spring, 1; 1993, Spring, 14, 34; 1992, Summer, 1; 1992, Spring, 24; 1991, Winter, 11

99395   **18-39 years**   A E
MED: 100-1, 5, 70; 100-2, 15, 30; 100-2, 16, 90; 100-4, 11, 40.1.3.1; 100-4, 12, 10; 100-4, 12, 30.6

AMA: 2002, May, 1; 1998, Nov, 3-4; 1998, Jul, 9; 1997, Aug, 1; 1995, Spring, 1; 1993, Spring, 14, 34; 1992, Summer, 1; 1992, Spring, 24; 1991, Winter, 11

Evaluation and Management

99396 — 99429

99396	**40-64 years** A E

MED: 100-1, 5, 70; 100-2, 15, 30; 100-2, 16, 90; 100-4, 11, 40.1.3.1; 100-4, 12, 10; 100-4, 12, 30.6

AMA: 2002, May, 1; 1998, Nov, 3-4; 1998, Jul, 9; 1997, Aug, 1; 1995, Spring, 1; 1993, Spring, 14, 34; 1992, Summer, 1; 1992, Spring, 24; 1991, Winter, 11

99397	**65 years and over** A E

MED: 100-1, 5, 70; 100-2, 15, 30; 100-2, 16, 90; 100-4, 11, 40.1.3.1; 100-4, 12, 10; 100-4, 12, 30.6

AMA: 2002, May, 1; 1998, Nov, 3-4; 1998, Jul, 9; 1997, Aug, 1; 1995, Spring, 1; 1993, Spring, 14, 34; 1992, Summer, 1; 1992, Spring, 24; 1991, Winter, 11

COUNSELING AND/OR RISK FACTOR REDUCTION INTERVENTION

PREVENTIVE MEDICINE, INDIVIDUAL COUNSELING

99401	**Preventive medicine counseling and/or risk factor reduction intervention(s) provided to an individual (separate procedure); approximately 15 minutes** E

MED: 100-1, 5, 70; 100-2, 15, 30; 100-2, 16, 90; 100-4, 11, 40.1.3.1; 100-4, 12, 10; 100-4, 12, 30.6

AMA: 1998, Jan, 12; 1997, Aug, 1

99402	**approximately 30 minutes** E

MED: 100-1, 5, 70; 100-2, 15, 30; 100-2, 16, 90; 100-4, 11, 40.1.3.1; 100-4, 12, 10; 100-4, 12, 30.6

AMA: 1997, Aug, 1

99403	**approximately 45 minutes** E

MED: 100-1, 5, 70; 100-2, 15, 30; 100-2, 16, 90; 100-4, 11, 40.1.3.1; 100-4, 12, 10; 100-4, 12, 30.6

AMA: 1997, Aug, 1

99404	**approximately 60 minutes** E

MED: 100-1, 5, 70; 100-2, 15, 30; 100-2, 16, 90; 100-4, 11, 40.1.3.1; 100-4, 12, 10; 100-4, 12, 30.6

AMA: 1997, Aug, 1

PREVENTIVE MEDICINE, GROUP COUNSELING

99411	**Preventive medicine counseling and/or risk factor reduction intervention(s) provided to individuals in a group setting (separate procedure); approximately 30 minutes** E

MED: 100-1, 5, 70; 100-2, 15, 30; 100-2, 16, 90; 100-4, 11, 40.1.3.1; 100-4, 12, 10; 100-4, 12, 30.6

AMA: 1997, Aug, 1

99412	**approximately 60 minutes** E

MED: 100-1, 5, 70; 100-2, 15, 30; 100-2, 16, 90; 100-4, 11, 40.1.3.1; 100-4, 12, 10; 100-4, 12, 30.6

AMA: 1998, Jan, 12; 1997, Aug, 1

OTHER PREVENTIVE MEDICINE SERVICES

99420	**Administration and interpretation of health risk assessment instrument (eg, health hazard appraisal)** E

MED: 100-1, 5, 70; 100-2, 15, 30; 100-2, 16, 90; 100-4, 11, 40.1.3.1; 100-4, 12, 10; 100-4, 12, 30.6

99429	**Unlisted preventive medicine service** E

MED: 100-1, 5, 70; 100-2, 15, 30; 100-2, 16, 90; 100-4, 11, 40.1.3.1; 100-4, 12, 10; 100-4, 12, 30.6

NEWBORN CARE

Codes 99431–99440 describe care provided to normal or high-risk newborns in several different settings. The codes identify specific locations, such as the hospital or birthing room, or other than hospital or birthing room.

Discharge services provided to newborns admitted and discharged on the same date should be reported with 99435. Discharge services to newborns discharged on a date subsequent to the admission date should be reported with 99238–99239.

99431   **History and examination of the normal newborn infant, initiation of diagnostic and treatment programs and preparation of hospital records. (This code should also be used for birthing room deliveries.)** A V 80 🗗
MED: 100-1, 5, 70; 100-2, 15, 30; 100-4, 11, 40.1.3.1; 100-4, 12, 10; 100-4, 12, 30.6

AMA: 1997, Apr, 10

99432   **Normal newborn care in other than hospital or birthing room setting, including physical examination of baby and conference(s) with parent(s)** A N 80 🗗
MED: 100-1, 5, 70; 100-2, 15, 30; 100-4, 11, 40.1.3.1; 100-4, 12, 10; 100-4, 12, 30.6

AMA: 1999, May, 11

99433   **Subsequent hospital care, for the evaluation and management of a normal newborn, per day** A C 80 🗗

99435   **History and examination of the normal newborn infant, including the preparation of medical records (this code should only be used for newborns assessed and discharged from the hospital or birthing room on the same date)** A E 80 🗗
MED: 100-1, 5, 70; 100-2, 15, 30; 100-4, 11, 40.1.3.1; 100-4, 12, 10; 100-4, 12, 30.6

99436   **Attendance at delivery (when requested by delivering physician) and initial stabilization of newborn** A N 80 🗗
MED: 100-1, 5, 70; 100-2, 15, 30; 100-4, 11, 40.1.3.1; 100-4, 12, 10; 100-4, 12, 30.6

AMA: 1997, Nov, 9-10

Note that this procedure may be reported in addition to 99431. However, this procedure cannot be reported in addition to 99440.

99440   **Newborn resuscitation: provision of positive pressure ventilation and/or chest compressions in the presence of acute inadequate ventilation and/or cardiac output** A S 80 🗗
MED: 100-1, 5, 70; 100-2, 15, 30; 100-4, 11, 40.1.3.1; 100-4, 12, 10; 100-4, 12, 30.6

AMA: 1996, Mar, 10; 1993, Summer, 1

SPECIAL EVALUATION AND MANAGEMENT SERVICES

This group of codes (99450–99456) covers any purely evaluative services provided by a physician when no active management of the patient's problem is undertaken during the encounter.

Use these codes to report evaluations for life or disability insurance eligibility certificates and work-related medical disability. These services can be performed in the office or other setting, and no distinction is made between new or established patient.

These codes should not be used to indicate any active management of problems or conditions. If other E/M services and/or procedures are performed on the same date, report them with the appropriate E/M code in addition to the special evaluation code.

Code 99450 is a basic life or disability examination that includes a medical history; height, weight, and blood pressure measurement; collecting blood and urine specimens; and filling out the necessary forms and reports.

Codes 99455 and 99456 are used for work-related or medical disability. They include history, exam, formulation of a diagnosis, assessment of disability, impairment, and capabilities, development of future medical treatment plans, and completion of necessary forms and reports. Use 99455 for the treating physician and 99456 for other than the treating physician.

BASIC LIFE AND/OR DISABILITY EVALUATION SERVICES

99450   **Basic life and/or disability examination that includes: measurement of height, weight and blood pressure; completion of a medical history following a life insurance pro forma; collection of blood sample and/or urinalysis complying with "chain of custody" protocols; and completion of necessary documentation/certificates.**   E

       MED: 100-1, 5, 70; 100-2, 15, 30; 100-4, 11, 40.1.3.1; 100-4, 12, 10; 100-4, 12, 30.6

       AMA: 1995, Summer, 14

WORK RELATED OR MEDICAL DISABILITY EVALUATION SERVICES

99455   **Work related or medical disability examination by the treating physician that includes: •completion of a medical history commensurate with the patient's condition; •performance of an examination commensurate with the patient's condition; •formulation of a diagnosis, assessment of capabilities and stability, and calculation of impairment; •development of future medical treatment plan; and •completion of necessary documentation/certificates and report.**   B 80 ▣

       MED: 100-1, 5, 70; 100-2, 15, 30; 100-4, 11, 40.1.3.1; 100-4, 12, 10; 100-4, 12, 30.6

       AMA: 1995, Summer, 14

       When completing Workman's Compensation forms, do not report CPT code 99080 with 99455.

99456   **Work related or medical disability examination by other than the treating physician that includes: •completion of a medical history commensurate with the patient's condition; •performance of an examination commensurate with the patient's condition; •formulation of a diagnosis, assessment of capabilities and stability, and calculation of impairment; •development of future medical treatment plan; and •completion of necessary documentation/certificates and report.**   B 80 ▣

       MED: 100-1, 5, 70; 100-2, 15, 30; 100-4, 11, 40.1.3.1; 100-4, 12, 10; 100-4, 12, 30.6

       AMA: 1995, Summer, 14

       When completing Workman's Compensation forms, do not report CPT code 99080 with 99456.

OTHER EVALUATION AND MANAGEMENT SERVICES

Code 99499 is an unlisted code to report other E/M services not specifically defined in the CPT manual.

99499   **Unlisted evaluation and management service**   B 80

       MED: 100-4, 12, 30.6

       AMA: 1996, Apr, 10

Anesthesia

CODING INFORMATION

Two organizations are responsible for developing anesthesia codes and guidelines: the American Medical Association (AMA) and the American Society of Anesthesiologists (ASA). The AMA includes a section on anesthesia codes (00100–01999) in the CPT book immediately following the evaluation and management (E/M) section. In addition, the CPT book includes four codes (99100–99140) to report qualifying circumstances for anesthesia. Although categorized as medicine codes, the four codes can be found in the anesthesia section as part of the guidelines, as well as in the medicine section. The ASA publishes a Relative Value Guide (RVG) that contains codes from the anesthesia section of the CPT book but also includes 1) codes to supplement those in the CPT anesthesia section and 2) codes from other sections of the CPT book for services frequently provided by anesthesiologists.

The CPT book and ASA guidelines are similar. Guidelines are as follows:

1. Both specify that reporting of anesthesia services is appropriate when provided by or under the medical supervision of a physician. The ASA further specifies that a physician anesthesiologist should supervise anesthesia services.

2. According to both sets of guidelines, anesthesia services include but are not limited to general, regional, supplementation of local anesthesia, and other supportive services required to afford the patient optimal anesthesia care. The ASA includes monitored anesthesia care in the service and also states that you report any professional anesthesia services as if an anesthetic was administered.

3. The ASA publication is a relative value guide. A relative value is a numeric ranking assigned to a procedure in relation to other procedures in terms of work and cost. Therefore, in addition to codes and descriptions, the ASA relative value guide provides information on the value of each anesthesia service. The ASA relative value guide is not a fee schedule, but only a guide intended to assist physicians in developing consistent and equitable fees for their services.

ORGANIZATION OF ANESTHESIA CODES

THE CPT BOOK

The anesthesia section of the CPT book is organized into 15 anatomical sites followed by four additional categories for radiological and other procedures. Codes are organized by type of procedure (open, closed, endoscopic, etc.), and each code relates to specific surgical procedures, though there is no direct one-to-one correspondence. One anesthesia code may be used to report several surgical procedures that share similar anesthesia requirements.

Example

01202 **Anesthesia for arthroscopic procedures of hip joint**

This procedure code would be selected to report anesthesia services related to the following surgical procedures:

29860 **Arthroscopy, hip, diagnostic with or without synovial biopsy (separate procedure)**

29861 **Arthroscopy, hip, surgical; with removal of loose body or foreign body**

29862 **with debridement/shaving of articular cartilage (chondroplasty), abrasion arthroplasty, and/or resection of labrum**

29863 **with synovectomy**

ASA RELATIVE VALUE GUIDE

The codes in the main section of the ASA Relative Value Guide (RVG) are the same as those in the CPT book with two exceptions: The ASA includes a few codes not found in the CPT book and excludes a few codes found in the CPT book. In addition, some of the narrative descriptions used by the ASA differ slightly from those found in the CPT book.

The ASA RVG also lists codes for other services frequently provided by anesthesiologists. These codes are CPT codes found in the evaluation and management, medicine, and surgery sections of the CPT book. The services include: pulmonary function testing, evaluation and management services, pain management and nerve blocks, and placement of venous catheters and monitoring devices. In all cases, the ASA provides a relative value designation for each code.

REPORTING ANESTHESIA SERVICES

The anesthesia codes should be used only by physicians not performing the surgical procedures. Reporting anesthesia services differs from reporting other types of physician services. Reporting other physician services typically involves selecting the correct CPT code and submitting a specific fee for that CPT code. The fee is the same every time the service is provided. For example, a problem focused established patient exam and history is reported with code 99212 and the fee assigned to that procedure by a given physician is $30. The physician submits the fee of $30 every time he or she performs procedure 99212.

However, anesthesia billing is based on several variables specific to the particular anesthesia service. The fee submitted for a specific anesthesia code varies each time the code is reported.

The key terms described next are essential to the correct reporting of anesthesia services.

KEY TERMS

Basic value or base unit: the basic value, also referred to as the base unit or relative value, has two components. One component reflects all usual services included in the anesthesia service. Usual services include: pre-operative and postoperative visits, administration of fluids and/or blood products incident to the procedure, and interpretation of non-invasive monitoring (ECG, temperature, blood pressure, oximetry, capnography, and mass spectrometry). The second component reflects the relative work or cost of the specific anesthesia service. Cost in this context refers to the physician's cost of doing business. For anesthesiologists, the majority of the cost goes to malpractice insurance. For example, the basic value for the anesthesia service related to a closed reduction of a radius fracture might be three, as it has a relatively low level of work or cost. The basic value for an anesthesia service associated with an intrathoracic coronary artery bypass graft procedure might be 20, reflecting a high level of work or cost.

The ASA lists two exceptions to using the basic value listed in the RVG. A minimum basic value of five is allowed for all procedures of the head, neck or shoulder girdle, requiring field avoidance. In addition, any procedure performed in any position other than lithotomy or supine has a minimum basic value of five. If the anesthesia code associated with the surgical procedure carries a basic value greater than five the higher basic value is reported.

Base units for anesthesia listed in the RVG are widely accepted across the United States by both physicians and payers. However, some payers, especially government agency payers, may use different relative value scales developed exclusively for their use. Other payers may use national relative value guides based on the RVG, with some modification.

Time: Time is the actual time spent providing the anesthesia service. Time begins as the anesthesiologist prepares the patient for anesthesia care. Time ends when the personal attendance of the anesthesiologist is no longer required and the patient can be safely placed in post-anesthesia recovery under the supervision of nursing or other trained personnel.

Time is reported in units based on defined time increments. The most commonly used time increment is 15 minutes, with one unit being reported for each 15-minute increment. However, time units for anesthesia vary across the country. Both ASA and the CPT book suggest reporting time increments as customary in the geographic area.

The same holds for reporting fractions of time units. For example, a procedure requiring 65 minutes of anesthesia time, reported in 15-minute time increments, results in total time units of 4.33. In some areas, this is reported as the fractional amount 4.33; other areas might round to the nearest whole number four; or another geographical area might allow reporting of another full unit for any fractional amount to five.

For some anesthesia services, time is not reported additionally. The ASA RVG designates a +TM after the base unit for procedures requiring time reported separately. Do not list time separately for procedures without the designation.

Physical status modifiers: Physical status modifiers reflect the patient's state of health. Individuals undergoing surgery may be healthy or may have varying degrees of systemic disease. A patient's health status affects the work related to providing the anesthesia service. The CPT book states that physical status modifiers reflect the level of complexity associated with the anesthesia service.

Physical status modifiers in the CPT book and ASA RVG are represented with the letter P followed by a single digit (e.g., P1, P2). ASA RVG lists the number of additional anesthesia units allowed with each physical status modifier to the right in the column titled "units."

ANESTHESIA

MODIFIER	DESCRIPTION	UNITS
P1	Normal healthy patient	0
P2	Patient with mild systemic disease	0
P3	Patient with severe systemic disease	1
P4	Patient with severe systemic disease that is a constant threat to life	2
P5	Moribund patient who is not expected to survive without the operation	3
P6	A declared brain-dead patient whose organs are being removed for donor purposes	0

Qualifying circumstances: Many anesthesia services are provided under particularly difficult circumstances depending on factors such as extraordinary condition of patient, notable operative conditions, and unusual risk factors. The information provided by both the CPT book and the ASA RVG includes a list of important qualifying circumstances that significantly impact the character of the anesthesia service provided. These procedures are not be reported alone but as additional procedure numbers to qualify an anesthesia procedure or service. The ASA provides modifying units that may be added to the basic unit values, as follows:

CODE	DESCRIPTION	ASA RVG UNITS
99100	**Anesthesia for patient of extreme age, under one year and over seventy**	1
99116	**Anesthesia complicated by utilization of total body hypothermia**	5
99135	**Anesthesia complicated by utilization of controlled hypotension**	5
99140	**Anesthesia complicated by emergency conditions (specify)**	2

An emergency exists when a delay in treatment poses a significant increase in the threat to the patient's life or to a body part, as defined in both the CPT book and ASA RVG.

Conversion factor: Anesthesia charges must be calculated by means of a conversion factor since the charges are not based on fixed amounts. A conversion factor is the dollar value associated with each unit of anesthesia. The dollar conversion factor is multiplied by the total number of anesthesia units for a given anesthesia service to arrive at the total charges for the anesthesia service.

The dollar conversion factor may vary significantly between geographical regions and to a lesser degree between physicians in a given geographic area. However, the standard formula to calculate total anesthesia units and anesthesia fees is basically the same both among regions and physicians as illustrated in the examples below.

Standard formula: Now that the basic elements of the anesthesia service have been defined, total anesthesia units for a given anesthesia service can be determined. Using the total units and the conversion factor, the fee for a specific anesthesia service can then be calculated.

The total charge for a specific anesthesia service is calculated by means of the following formula:

Basic Value + Time Units + Modifying Units = Total Units

Total Units X Conversion Factor = Total Fee

Example

A closed reduction of a distal radius fracture is accomplished under general anesthesia. The patient is a healthy 10-year-old. The procedure is not performed on an emergency basis. The anesthesiologist reports procedure 01820 that has a basic value of three. Total time for the procedure is 45 minutes. The anesthesiologist reports time units in 15-minute increments. The total units reported for the procedure are as follows:

Basic Value	
3	
Time Units (45 divided by 15)	+
3	
Physical Status (P1)	+
0	
Qualifying Circumstances (none)	+
0	
Total Units	=
6	

The anesthesiologist uses a conversion factor of $45 per unit of anesthesia.

Total Units	
6	
Conversion Factor	x
$45	
Total Fee	=
$270	

SPECIAL CODING SITUATIONS

MULTIPLE PROCEDURES

When multiple surgical procedures are performed during a single anesthetic administration, the

ASA recommends reporting only the anesthesia procedure with the highest unit value. In other words, only one basic value is assigned per single surgical session. The time reported should be the combined total for all procedures performed.

ADDITIONAL PROCEDURES

Services not included in the usual anesthesia services may be reported separately. These services include unusual forms of monitoring, prolonged physician services, and provision of additional anesthesia services such as postoperative pain management. These additional services are reported in terms of units with the appropriate CPT or ASA codes under the designation "other procedures." They are calculated as an additional variable in the standard formula.

Unusual monitoring: Unusual forms of monitoring anesthesia are reported by most anesthesiologists and many payers allow benefits beyond the basic anesthesia service. For example, codes 36555–36558, 36568–36569 for insertion of a central venous catheter; 36620–36625 for insertion of an intra-arterial catheter, and 93503 Swan-Ganz insertion, represent unusual forms of monitoring that may be rendered by an anesthesiologist.

Prolonged physician services: Extended pre- or postoperative care provided to a patient whose condition requires services beyond the usual may be reported additionally. These services would be billed with prolonged service codes (99354–99359).

Moderate (conscious) sedation: To report moderate sedation provided by the same physician performing the procedure, consult codes 99143–99145.

When a physician other than a physician performing the procedure administers the moderate sedation in the facility setting, the second physician reports his/her services with codes 99148–99150. In the non-facility setting, codes 99148–99150 would not be used. Moderate sedation does not include minimal sedation (anxiolysis), deep sedation, or monitored anesthesia care (00100–01999).

Postoperative pain management: Normally postoperative pain management is provided or supervised by the surgeon by oral, intramuscular or intravenous medications. Postoperative pain management provided by the surgeon is included in the global fee for the surgical procedure. Some procedures and/or patients require more than the usual type of postoperative pain management, and this is frequently provided or supervised by

an anesthesiologist. These services are additional procedures and are reported as follows:

- Epidural or subarachnoid pain management is reported with procedure codes 62310–62319 for placement of the epidural or subarachnoid catheter that includes the initial day of pain management. Subsequent management is reported with 01996 and is reported per day.

- Patient-controlled analgesia is reported with 01997 on a per day basis. Code 01997 is included only in the ASA Relative Value Guide not in the CPT book, but is recognized by most payers as a valid code for this anesthesia service.

- Postoperative pain management services are not calculated based on time. These services are reported as a single, daily charge.

MONITORED (STAND-BY) ANESTHESIA

Monitored anesthesia care is defined in the ASA RVG as those instances when an anesthesiologist has been requested to provide specific services to a patient undergoing a planned procedure. The patient receives either local anesthesia or no anesthesia. However, the anesthesiologist is required to provide pre-operative assessment, to remain in attendance during the procedure to monitor the patient and to administer additional anesthetics should they be required, and to provide postoperative services as required.

Monitored care, as described above, is reported as is customary for any other anesthesia procedure. The procedure should be assigned the applicable anesthesia code with time and modifying units being added as is customary in the local area.

OBSTETRICAL ANESTHESIA

The formula for reporting of epidural analgesia for labor and delivery may differ from the standard formula in some geographical areas. When epidural analgesia is administered, an anesthesiologist may attend to more than one patient. The anesthesiologist may insert the epidural catheter, start the continuous anesthetic, and leave the patient's bedside. The anesthesiologist periodically returns to check on the patient or to increase the amount of anesthetic while attending to other patients who are also receiving epidurals for vaginal deliveries. For this reason epidural analgesia for labor and delivery may be reimbursed at a reduced rate.

The following are some variations in reporting anesthesia services when the anesthesiologist is not required to be in constant attendance:

ANESTHESIA

1. Basic value and modifying units are reported as usual. The first hour of anesthesia is reported at the usual rate, but subsequent hours are reported at a reduced rate. For example, total units for the first hour would be reported in full, but units for the second hour would be reported at 50 percent and units for all subsequent hours at 25 percent. If 15-minute time increments were being used the first hour units would be reported as four units, the second hour as two, and third and subsequent hours as one unit each.

2. A flat rate may be established and reported regardless of the actual epidural time. Basic value units are included in the flat rate. For example, the anesthesiologist may bill $500 for anesthesia services provided at every vaginal delivery. Modifying units may or may not be reported separately.

3. Basic value and modifying units are reported as usual. Actual time spent in attendance of the patient may be used and reported at the usual rate. For example, a patient who received epidural analgesia for four hours might have required the anesthesiologist's presence for only two hours of the total time. If 15-minute time increments were used, the anesthesiologist would report eight units.

These are examples of possible variations and should not be adopted without evaluating current practices in the geographic area. Payers should be queried as to their rules for reporting anesthesia services related to obstetrical care.

REGIONAL ANESTHESIA

Disagreement regarding the correct method of reporting regional IV anesthesia centers on code 01995 that has been assigned for regional IV administration of local anesthetic agent (upper or lower extremity). This procedure has no time units associated with it. In practice, anesthesiologists rarely report this service, and instead report regional anesthesia with the anesthesia code that describes the surgical procedure performed. For example regional anesthesia for repair of a tendon injury of the hand is reported with 01810, not 01995. Applicable time and modifying units are also reported.

If the anesthesiologist performs regional anesthesia with the usual pre- and postoperative care and monitors the patient throughout the procedure, the anesthesia code that describes the surgical procedure should be reported along with time and modifying units. However, if the anesthesiologist provides no service other than the initial administration of regional anesthetic, it may be appropriate to report code 01995 instead.

UNUSUAL ANESTHESIA

The CPT book defines unusual anesthesia as follows:

23 Unusual anesthesia: Occasionally, a procedure that usually requires either no anesthesia or local anesthesia must be done under general anesthesia due to unusual circumstances. This circumstance may be reported by adding modifier 23 to the procedure code of the basic service.

Although it is generally inappropriate to report anesthesia with some E/M, medicine, surgery, and radiology codes, there are situations where medical necessity requires anesthesia (e.g. a baby, small child, or hard-to-control patient needing dressings and/or debridement). Under these unusual circumstances, payers will usually allow the anesthesia charge. Submit an operative report and cover letter with the claim explaining the need for any unusual anesthesia.

CHRONIC PAIN MANAGEMENT SERVICES

Chronic pain management services are not anesthesia services. These are distinct services frequently performed by anesthesiologists who have additional training in pain management procedures. Pain management services are reported following the same rules as those for surgical procedures.

Pain management services include initial and subsequent evaluation and management (E/M) services, trigger point injections, spine and spinal cord injections, and nerve blocks.

E/M services may be reported with outpatient/office codes 99201–99215 or outpatient consultation codes 99241–99245 depending on the nature of the E/M service.

Tendon injections are reported with codes 20550 and 20551 Trigger point injections are reported with codes 20552 and 20553 for injections of single or multiple points in one or two, or three or more muscles, respectively. Codes 62280–62284 and 62290–62319 are used to report spine and spinal cord injections.

Nerve blocks are reported with codes 64400–64530. Nerve blocks are defined as the introduction or injection of an anesthetic agent into a nerve or nerve branch.

Home infusion procedures (99601–99602) report home infusion for pain therapy. Use 99601 for the first two hours and 99602 for each additional hour.

Each code for pain management services should have a specific fee and the fee should be the same each time that specific code is reported. In other words, no adjustments are made based on time, physical status, or qualifying circumstances.

SPECIAL REPORT

A service that is rarely provided, unusual, variable, or new may require a special report to help the payer determine the medical appropriateness of the service. Pertinent information should include an adequate definition or description of the nature, extent, and need for the procedure; and the time, effort, and equipment necessary to provide the service.

COMMON BILLING ERRORS

Incorrect ICD-9-CM or CPT coding is a frequent problem encountered in anesthesia reporting. The code may be incorrect because it does not match the diagnosis or procedure reported by the surgeon. Claims must reflect the same diagnosis and procedure by the anesthesiologist and surgeon, with the exception of listing a global surgery code when only part of the service is provided.

There are codes in the surgery section of the CPT book designated as "add on" codes. These add-on codes, however, are not used for coding anesthesia services.

For example, 11001 is an "add on" code. The primary procedure code is 11000 Debridement of extensive eczematous or infected skin; up to 10% of body surface. Always report 11001 with "in addition to" code 11000 because its description states each additional 10 percent of the body surface. In this case, the appropriate CPT code for determining anesthesia base units and guidelines is 11000.

HEAD

00100   **Anesthesia for procedures on salivary glands, including biopsy**   N ▪
     MED: 100-4, 12, 140; 100-4, 12, 140.2; 100-4, 12, 140.3.2; 100-4, 12, 50

     AMA: 1999, Nov, 6; 1997, Feb, 4

00102   **Anesthesia for procedures involving plastic repair of cleft lip**   N ▪
     MED: 100-4, 12, 140; 100-4, 12, 140.2; 100-4, 12, 140.3.2; 100-4, 12, 50

     AMA: 1999, Nov, 6

00103   **Anesthesia for reconstructive procedures of eyelid (eg, blepharoplasty, ptosis surgery)**   N ▪
     MED: 100-4, 12, 140; 100-4, 12, 140.2; 100-4, 12, 140.3.2; 100-4, 12, 50

     AMA: 1999, Nov, 6

00104   **Anesthesia for electroconvulsive therapy**   N ▪
     MED: 100-4, 12, 140; 100-4, 12, 140.2; 100-4, 12, 140.3.2; 100-4, 12, 50

00120   **Anesthesia for procedures on external, middle, and inner ear including biopsy; not otherwise specified**   N ▪
     MED: 100-4, 12, 140; 100-4, 12, 140.2; 100-4, 12, 140.3.2; 100-4, 12, 50

00124   **otoscopy**   N ▪
     MED: 100-4, 12, 140; 100-4, 12, 140.2; 100-4, 12, 140.3.2; 100-4, 12, 50

     AMA: 1999, Nov, 7

00126   **tympanotomy**   N ▪
     MED: 100-4, 12, 140; 100-4, 12, 140.2; 100-4, 12, 140.3.2; 100-4, 12, 50

00140   **Anesthesia for procedures on eye; not otherwise specified**   N ▪
     MED: 100-4, 12, 140; 100-4, 12, 140.2; 100-4, 12, 140.3.2; 100-4, 12, 50

00142   **lens surgery**   N ▪
     MED: 100-3, 10.1; 100-4, 12, 140; 100-4, 12, 140.2; 100-4, 12, 140.3.2; 100-4, 12, 50

00144   **corneal transplant**   N ▪
     MED: 100-4, 12, 140; 100-4, 12, 140.2; 100-4, 12, 140.3.2; 100-4, 12, 50

00145   **vitreoretinal surgery**   N ▪
     MED: 100-4, 12, 140; 100-4, 12, 140.2; 100-4, 12, 140.3.2; 100-4, 12, 50

00147   **iridectomy**   N ▪
     MED: 100-4, 12, 140; 100-4, 12, 140.2; 100-4, 12, 140.3.2; 100-4, 12, 50

00148   **ophthalmoscopy**   N ▪
     MED: 100-4, 12, 140; 100-4, 12, 140.2; 100-4, 12, 140.3.2; 100-4, 12, 50

00160   **Anesthesia for procedures on nose and accessory sinuses; not otherwise specified**   N ▪
     MED: 100-4, 12, 140; 100-4, 12, 140.2; 100-4, 12, 140.3.2; 100-4, 12, 50

00162   **radical surgery**   N ▪
     MED: 100-4, 12, 140; 100-4, 12, 140.2; 100-4, 12, 140.3.2; 100-4, 12, 50

00164   **biopsy, soft tissue**   N ▪
     MED: 100-4, 12, 140; 100-4, 12, 140.2; 100-4, 12, 140.3.2; 100-4, 12, 50

00170   **Anesthesia for intraoral procedures, including biopsy; not otherwise specified**   N ▪
     MED: 100-4, 12, 140; 100-4, 12, 140.2; 100-4, 12, 140.3.2; 100-4, 12, 50

Anesthesia

00100 — 00170

Anestheisa

00172 — 00322

00172	repair of cleft palate	N ↻

MED: 100-4, 12, 140; 100-4, 12, 140.2; 100-4, 12, 140.3.2; 100-4, 12, 50

00174	excision of retropharyngeal tumor	N ↻

MED: 100-4, 12, 140; 100-4, 12, 140.2; 100-4, 12, 140.3.2; 100-4, 12, 50

00176	radical surgery	C ↻

MED: 100-4, 12, 140; 100-4, 12, 140.2; 100-4, 12, 140.3.2; 100-4, 12, 50

00190	Anesthesia for procedures on facial bones or skull; not otherwise specified	N ↻

MED: 100-4, 12, 140; 100-4, 12, 140.2; 100-4, 12, 140.3.2; 100-4, 12, 50

00192	radical surgery (including prognathism)	C ↻

MED: 100-4, 12, 140; 100-4, 12, 140.2; 100-4, 12, 140.3.2; 100-4, 12, 50

00210	Anesthesia for intracranial procedures; not otherwise specified	N ↻

MED: 100-4, 12, 140; 100-4, 12, 140.2; 100-4, 12, 140.3.2; 100-4, 12, 50

00212	subdural taps	N ↻

MED: 100-4, 12, 140; 100-4, 12, 140.2; 100-4, 12, 140.3.2; 100-4, 12, 50

00214	burr holes, including ventriculography	C ↻

MED: 100-4, 12, 140; 100-4, 12, 140.2; 100-4, 12, 140.3.2; 100-4, 12, 50

AMA: 1999, Nov, 7

00215	cranioplasty or elevation of depressed skull fracture, extradural (simple or compound)	C ↻

MED: 100-4, 12, 140; 100-4, 12, 140.2; 100-4, 12, 140.3.2; 100-4, 12, 50

00216	vascular procedures	N ↻

MED: 100-4, 12, 140; 100-4, 12, 140.2; 100-4, 12, 140.3.2; 100-4, 12, 50

00218	procedures in sitting position	N ↻

MED: 100-4, 12, 140; 100-4, 12, 140.2; 100-4, 12, 140.3.2; 100-4, 12, 50

00220	cerebrospinal fluid shunting procedures	N ↻

MED: 100-4, 12, 140; 100-4, 12, 140.2; 100-4, 12, 140.3.2; 100-4, 12, 50

00222	electrocoagulation of intracranial nerve	N ↻

MED: 100-4, 12, 140; 100-4, 12, 140.2; 100-4, 12, 140.3.2; 100-4, 12, 50

NECK

00300	Anesthesia for all procedures on the integumentary system, muscles and nerves of head, neck, and posterior trunk, not otherwise specified	N ↻

MED: 100-4, 12, 140; 100-4, 12, 140.2; 100-4, 12, 140.3.2; 100-4, 12, 50

AMA: 1999, Nov, 7

00320	Anesthesia for all procedures on esophagus, thyroid, larynx, trachea and lymphatic system of neck; not otherwise specified, age 1 year or older	N ↻

MED: 100-4, 12, 140; 100-4, 12, 140.2; 100-4, 12, 140.3.2; 100-4, 12, 50

00322	needle biopsy of thyroid	N ↻

MED: 100-4, 12, 140; 100-4, 12, 140.2; 100-4, 12, 140.3.2; 100-4, 12, 50

To report anesthesia for procedures on the cervical spine and cord, consult CPT codes 00600, 00604, 00670.

00326	Anesthesia for all procedures on the larynx and trachea in children less than 1 year of age	Ⓐ Ⓝ ⚑

Note that code 00326 cannot be reported with CPT code 99100.

00350	Anesthesia for procedures on major vessels of neck; not otherwise specified	Ⓝ ⚑
	MED: 100-4, 12, 140; 100-4, 12, 140.2; 100-4, 12, 140.3.2; 100-4, 12, 50	

00352	simple ligation	Ⓝ ⚑
	MED: 100-4, 12, 140; 100-4, 12, 140.2; 100-4, 12, 140.3.2; 100-4, 12, 50	

To report anesthesia for arteriograms, consult CPT code 01916.

THORAX (CHEST WALL AND SHOULDER GIRDLE)

00400	Anesthesia for procedures on the integumentary system on the extremities, anterior trunk and perineum; not otherwise specified	Ⓝ ⚑
	MED: 100-4, 12, 140; 100-4, 12, 140.2; 100-4, 12, 140.3.2; 100-4, 12, 50	

00402	reconstructive procedures on breast (eg, reduction or augmentation mammoplasty, muscle flaps)	Ⓝ ⚑
	MED: 100-4, 12, 140; 100-4, 12, 140.2; 100-4, 12, 140.3.2; 100-4, 12, 50	

00404	radical or modified radical procedures on breast	Ⓒ ⚑
	MED: 100-4, 12, 140; 100-4, 12, 140.2; 100-4, 12, 140.3.2; 100-4, 12, 50	

00406	radical or modified radical procedures on breast with internal mammary node dissection	Ⓒ ⚑
	MED: 100-4, 12, 140; 100-4, 12, 140.2; 100-4, 12, 140.3.2; 100-4, 12, 50	

00410	electrical conversion of arrhythmias	Ⓝ ⚑
	MED: 100-4, 12, 140; 100-4, 12, 140.2; 100-4, 12, 140.3.2; 100-4, 12, 50	

00450	Anesthesia for procedures on clavicle and scapula; not otherwise specified	Ⓝ ⚑
	MED: 100-4, 12, 140; 100-4, 12, 140.2; 100-4, 12, 140.3.2; 100-4, 12, 50	

00452	radical surgery	Ⓒ ⚑
	MED: 100-4, 12, 140; 100-4, 12, 140.2; 100-4, 12, 140.3.2; 100-4, 12, 50	

00454	biopsy of clavicle	Ⓝ ⚑
	MED: 100-4, 12, 140; 100-4, 12, 140.2; 100-4, 12, 140.3.2; 100-4, 12, 50	

00470	Anesthesia for partial rib resection; not otherwise specified	Ⓝ ⚑
	MED: 100-4, 12, 140; 100-4, 12, 140.2; 100-4, 12, 140.3.2; 100-4, 12, 50	

00472	thoracoplasty (any type)	Ⓝ ⚑
	MED: 100-4, 12, 140; 100-4, 12, 140.2; 100-4, 12, 140.3.2; 100-4, 12, 50	

00474	radical procedures (eg, pectus excavatum)	Ⓒ ⚑
	MED: 100-4, 12, 140; 100-4, 12, 140.2; 100-4, 12, 140.3.2; 100-4, 12, 50	

INTRATHORACIC

00500	Anesthesia for all procedures on esophagus	Ⓝ ⚑
	MED: 100-4, 12, 140; 100-4, 12, 140.2; 100-4, 12, 140.3.2; 100-4, 12, 50	

00520	Anesthesia for closed chest procedures; (including bronchoscopy) not otherwise specified	Ⓝ ⚑
	MED: 100-4, 12, 140; 100-4, 12, 140.2; 100-4, 12, 140.3.2; 100-4, 12, 50	
	AMA: 1999, Nov, 7	

Anestheisa

00522 — 00563

00522	**needle biopsy of pleura** MED: 100-4, 12, 140; 100-4, 12, 140.2; 100-4, 12, 140.3.2; 100-4, 12, 50	N

00524	**pneumocentesis** MED: 100-4, 12, 140; 100-4, 12, 140.2; 100-4, 12, 140.3.2; 100-4, 12, 50	C

00528　**mediastinoscopy and diagnostic thoracoscopy not utilizing one lung ventilation**　N
MED: 100-4, 12, 140; 100-4, 12, 140.2; 100-4, 12, 140.3.2; 100-4, 12, 50

AMA: 1999, Nov, 7

To report anesthesia for tracheobronchial reconstruction, consult CPT code 00539.

00529　**mediastinoscopy and diagnostic thoracoscopy utilizing one lung ventilation**　N

00530　**Anesthesia for permanent transvenous pacemaker insertion**　N
MED: 100-3, 20.8.3; 100-4, 12, 140; 100-4, 12, 140.2; 100-4, 12, 140.3.2; 100-4, 12, 50

00532　**Anesthesia for access to central venous circulation**　N
MED: 100-4, 12, 140; 100-4, 12, 140.2; 100-4, 12, 140.3.2; 100-4, 12, 50

00534　**Anesthesia for transvenous insertion or replacement of pacing cardioverter-defibrillator**　N
MED: 100-3, 20.8.3; 100-4, 12, 140; 100-4, 12, 140.2; 100-4, 12, 140.3.2; 100-4, 12, 50

To report anesthesia in transthoracic approach, consult CPT code 00560.

00537　**Anesthesia for cardiac electrophysiologic procedures including radiofrequency ablation**　N

00539　**Anesthesia for tracheobronchial reconstruction**　N

00540　**Anesthesia for thoracotomy procedures involving lungs, pleura, diaphragm, and mediastinum (including surgical thoracoscopy); not otherwise specified**　C
MED: 100-4, 12, 140; 100-4, 12, 140.2; 100-4, 12, 140.3.2; 100-4, 12, 50

00541　**utilizing one lung ventilation**　N

00542　**decortication**　C
MED: 100-4, 12, 140; 100-4, 12, 140.2; 100-4, 12, 140.3.2; 100-4, 12, 50

00546　**pulmonary resection with thoracoplasty**　C
MED: 100-4, 12, 140; 100-4, 12, 140.2; 100-4, 12, 140.3.2; 100-4, 12, 50

00548　**intrathoracic procedures on the trachea and bronchi**　N
MED: 100-4, 12, 140; 100-4, 12, 140.2; 100-4, 12, 140.3.2; 100-4, 12, 50

AMA: 1997, Nov, 10

00550　**Anesthesia for sternal debridement**　N

00560　**Anesthesia for procedures on heart, pericardial sac, and great vessels of chest; without pump oxygenator**　C
MED: 100-3, 160.8; 100-3, 160.9; 100-4, 12, 140; 100-4, 12, 140.2; 100-4, 12, 140.3.2; 100-4, 12, 50

00561　**with pump oxygenator, under one year of age**　A C
Do not report 00561 with 99100, 99115, and 99135.

00562　**with pump oxygenator**　C
MED: 100-3, 160.8; 100-3, 160.9; 100-4, 12, 140; 100-4, 12, 140.2; 100-4, 12, 140.3.2; 100-4, 12, 50

00563　**with pump oxygenator with hypothermic circulatory arrest**　N
MED: 100-3, 160.8; 100-3, 160.9

00566   **Anesthesia for direct coronary artery bypass grafting without pump oxygenator**   N ⚑
MED: 100-3, 160.9

00580   **Anesthesia for heart transplant or heart/lung transplant**   C ⚑
MED: 100-4, 12, 140; 100-4, 12, 140.2; 100-4, 12, 140.3.2; 100-4, 12, 50

SPINE AND SPINAL CORD

00600   **Anesthesia for procedures on cervical spine and cord; not otherwise specified**   N ⚑
MED: 100-4, 12, 140; 100-4, 12, 140.2; 100-4, 12, 140.3.2; 100-4, 12, 50

To report anesthesia for myelography, diskography, or vertebroplasty, consult CPT code 01905.

00604   **procedures with patient in the sitting position**   C ⚑
MED: 100-4, 12, 140; 100-4, 12, 140.2; 100-4, 12, 140.3.2; 100-4, 12, 50

00620   **Anesthesia for procedures on thoracic spine and cord; not otherwise specified**   N ⚑
MED: 100-4, 12, 140; 100-4, 12, 140.2; 100-4, 12, 140.3.2; 100-4, 12, 50

To report anesthesia for myelography, diskography, or vertebroplasty, consult CPT code 01905.

00622   **thoracolumbar sympathectomy**   C ⚑
MED: 100-4, 12, 140; 100-4, 12, 140.2; 100-4, 12, 140.3.2; 100-4, 12, 50

00630   **Anesthesia for procedures in lumbar region; not otherwise specified**   N ⚑
MED: 100-4, 12, 140; 100-4, 12, 140.2; 100-4, 12, 140.3.2; 100-4, 12, 50

To report anesthesia for myelography, diskography, or vertebroplasty, consult CPT code 01905.

00632   **lumbar sympathectomy**   C ⚑
MED: 100-4, 12, 140; 100-4, 12, 140.2; 100-4, 12, 140.3.2; 100-4, 12, 50

00634   **chemonucleolysis**   N ⚑
MED: 100-4, 12, 140; 100-4, 12, 140.2; 100-4, 12, 140.3.2; 100-4, 12, 50

00635   **diagnostic or therapeutic lumbar puncture**   N ⚑

00640   **Anesthesia for manipulation of the spine or for closed procedures on the cervical, thoracic or lumbar spine**   N ⚑

00670   **Anesthesia for extensive spine and spinal cord procedures (eg, spinal instrumentation or vascular procedures)**   C ⚑
MED: 100-4, 12, 140; 100-4, 12, 140.2; 100-4, 12, 140.3.2; 100-4, 12, 50

UPPER ABDOMEN

00700   **Anesthesia for procedures on upper anterior abdominal wall; not otherwise specified**   N ⚑
MED: 100-4, 12, 140; 100-4, 12, 140.2; 100-4, 12, 140.3.2; 100-4, 12, 50

Note 0070T must be used with code 93010.

00702   **percutaneous liver biopsy**   N ⚑
MED: 100-4, 12, 140; 100-4, 12, 140.2; 100-4, 12, 140.3.2; 100-4, 12, 50

00730   **Anesthesia for procedures on upper posterior abdominal wall**   N ⚑
MED: 100-4, 12, 140; 100-4, 12, 140.2; 100-4, 12, 140.3.2; 100-4, 12, 50

Anestheisa

00740 — 00830

00740	**Anesthesia for upper gastrointestinal endoscopic procedures, endoscope introduced proximal to duodenum**	N ↻

MED: 100-4, 12, 140; 100-4, 12, 140.2; 100-4, 12, 140.3.2; 100-4, 12, 50

AMA: 1999, Nov, 7

00750	**Anesthesia for hernia repairs in upper abdomen; not otherwise specified**	N ↻

MED: 100-4, 12, 140; 100-4, 12, 140.2; 100-4, 12, 140.3.2; 100-4, 12, 50

00752	**lumbar and ventral (incisional) hernias and/or wound dehiscence**	N ↻

MED: 100-4, 12, 140; 100-4, 12, 140.2; 100-4, 12, 140.3.2; 100-4, 12, 50

00754	**omphalocele**	N ↻

MED: 100-4, 12, 140; 100-4, 12, 140.2; 100-4, 12, 140.3.2; 100-4, 12, 50

00756	**transabdominal repair of diaphragmatic hernia**	N ↻

MED: 100-4, 12, 140; 100-4, 12, 140.2; 100-4, 12, 140.3.2; 100-4, 12, 50

00770	**Anesthesia for all procedures on major abdominal blood vessels**	N ↻

MED: 100-4, 12, 140; 100-4, 12, 140.2; 100-4, 12, 140.3.2; 100-4, 12, 50

00790	**Anesthesia for intraperitoneal procedures in upper abdomen including laparoscopy; not otherwise specified**	N ↻

MED: 100-4, 12, 140; 100-4, 12, 140.2; 100-4, 12, 140.3.2; 100-4, 12, 50

00792	**partial hepatectomy or management of liver hemorrhage (excluding liver biopsy)**	C ↻

MED: 100-4, 12, 140; 100-4, 12, 140.2; 100-4, 12, 140.3.2; 100-4, 12, 50

00794	**pancreatectomy, partial or total (eg, Whipple procedure)**	C ↻

MED: 100-4, 12, 140; 100-4, 12, 140.2; 100-4, 12, 140.3.2; 100-4, 12, 50

00796	**liver transplant (recipient)**	C ↻

MED: 100-4, 12, 140; 100-4, 12, 140.2; 100-4, 12, 140.3.2; 100-4, 12, 50

To report anesthesia for harvesting of the liver, consult CPT code 01990.

00797	**gastric restrictive procedure for morbid obesity**	N ↻

LOWER ABDOMEN

00800	**Anesthesia for procedures on lower anterior abdominal wall; not otherwise specified**	N ↻

MED: 100-4, 12, 140; 100-4, 12, 140.2; 100-4, 12, 140.3.2; 100-4, 12, 50

00802	**panniculectomy**	C ↻

MED: 100-4, 12, 140; 100-4, 12, 140.2; 100-4, 12, 140.3.2; 100-4, 12, 50

00810	**Anesthesia for lower intestinal endoscopic procedures, endoscope introduced distal to duodenum**	N ↻

MED: 100-4, 12, 140; 100-4, 12, 140.2; 100-4, 12, 140.3.2; 100-4, 12, 50

AMA: 1999, Nov, 7

00820	**Anesthesia for procedures on lower posterior abdominal wall**	N ↻

MED: 100-4, 12, 140; 100-4, 12, 140.2; 100-4, 12, 140.3.2; 100-4, 12, 50

00830	**Anesthesia for hernia repairs in lower abdomen; not otherwise specified**	N ↻

MED: 100-4, 12, 140; 100-4, 12, 140.2; 100-4, 12, 140.3.2; 100-4, 12, 50

00832   **ventral and incisional hernias**   N ⟲
MED: 100-4, 12, 140; 100-4, 12, 140.2; 100-4, 12, 140.3.2; 100-4, 12, 50

To report anesthesia for hernia repairs, infant age 1 year or less, consult CPT codes 00834, 00836.

00834   **Anesthesia for hernia repairs in the lower abdomen not otherwise specified, under 1 year of age**   A N ⟲
Note that code 00834 cannot be reported with CPT code 99100.

00836   **Anesthesia for hernia repairs in the lower abdomen not otherwise specified, infants less than 37 weeks gestational age at birth and less than 50 weeks gestational age at time of surgery**   A N ⟲
Note that code 00836 cannot be reported with CPT code 99100.

00840   **Anesthesia for intraperitoneal procedures in lower abdomen including laparoscopy; not otherwise specified**   N ⟲
MED: 100-4, 12, 140; 100-4, 12, 140.2; 100-4, 12, 140.3.2; 100-4, 12, 50

00842   **amniocentesis**   M ♀ N ⟲
MED: 100-4, 12, 140; 100-4, 12, 140.2; 100-4, 12, 140.3.2; 100-4, 12, 50

00844   **abdominoperineal resection**   C ⟲
MED: 100-4, 12, 140; 100-4, 12, 140.2; 100-4, 12, 140.3.2; 100-4, 12, 50

00846   **radical hysterectomy**   ♀ C ⟲
MED: 100-4, 12, 140; 100-4, 12, 140.2; 100-4, 12, 140.3.2; 100-4, 12, 50

00848   **pelvic exenteration**   C ⟲
MED: 100-4, 12, 140; 100-4, 12, 140.2; 100-4, 12, 140.3.2; 100-4, 12, 50

00851   **tubal ligation/transection**   ♀ N ⟲

00860   **Anesthesia for extraperitoneal procedures in lower abdomen, including urinary tract; not otherwise specified**   N ⟲
MED: 100-4, 12, 140; 100-4, 12, 140.2; 100-4, 12, 140.3.2; 100-4, 12, 50

00862   **renal procedures, including upper 1/3 of ureter, or donor nephrectomy**   N ⟲
MED: 100-4, 12, 140; 100-4, 12, 140.2; 100-4, 12, 140.3.2; 100-4, 12, 50

00864   **total cystectomy**   C ⟲
MED: 100-4, 12, 140; 100-4, 12, 140.2; 100-4, 12, 140.3.2; 100-4, 12, 50

00865   **radical prostatectomy (suprapubic, retropubic)**   ♂ C ⟲

00866   **adrenalectomy**   C ⟲
MED: 100-4, 12, 140; 100-4, 12, 140.2; 100-4, 12, 140.3.2; 100-4, 12, 50

00868   **renal transplant (recipient)**   C ⟲
MED: 100-4, 12, 140; 100-4, 12, 140.2; 100-4, 12, 140.3.2; 100-4, 12, 50

To report anesthesia for donor nephrectomy, consult CPT code 00862. To report anesthesia for harvesting a kidney from a brain-dead patient, consult CPT code 01990.

00870   **cystolithotomy**   N ⟲
MED: 100-4, 12, 140; 100-4, 12, 140.2; 100-4, 12, 140.3.2; 100-4, 12, 50

00872   **Anesthesia for lithotripsy, extracorporeal shock wave; with water bath**   N ⟲
MED: 100-4, 12, 140; 100-4, 12, 140.2; 100-4, 12, 140.3.2; 100-4, 12, 50

00873   **without water bath**   N ⟲
MED: 100-4, 12, 140; 100-4, 12, 140.2; 100-4, 12, 140.3.2; 100-4, 12, 50

Anestheisa

00880 — 00932

00880 Anesthesia for procedures on major lower abdominal vessels; not otherwise specified N ▣
    MED: 100-4, 12, 140; 100-4, 12, 140.2; 100-4, 12, 140.3.2; 100-4, 12, 50

00882   inferior vena cava ligation C ▣
    MED: 100-4, 12, 140; 100-4, 12, 140.2; 100-4, 12, 140.3.2; 100-4, 12, 50

PERINEUM

00902 Anesthesia for; anorectal procedure N ▣
    MED: 100-4, 12, 140; 100-4, 12, 140.2; 100-4, 12, 140.3.2; 100-4, 12, 50

00904   radical perineal procedure C ▣
    MED: 100-4, 12, 140; 100-4, 12, 140.2; 100-4, 12, 140.3.2; 100-4, 12, 50

00906   vulvectomy ♀ N ▣
    MED: 100-4, 12, 140; 100-4, 12, 140.2; 100-4, 12, 140.3.2; 100-4, 12, 50

00908   perineal prostatectomy ♂ C ▣
    MED: 100-4, 12, 140; 100-4, 12, 140.2; 100-4, 12, 140.3.2; 100-4, 12, 50

00910 Anesthesia for transurethral procedures (including urethrocystoscopy); not otherwise specified N ▣
    MED: 100-4, 12, 140; 100-4, 12, 140.2; 100-4, 12, 140.3.2; 100-4, 12, 50

00912   transurethral resection of bladder tumor(s) N ▣
    MED: 100-4, 12, 140; 100-4, 12, 140.2; 100-4, 12, 140.3.2; 100-4, 12, 50

00914   transurethral resection of prostate ♂ N ▣
    MED: 100-4, 12, 140; 100-4, 12, 140.2; 100-4, 12, 140.3.2; 100-4, 12, 50

00916   post-transurethral resection bleeding N ▣
    MED: 100-4, 12, 140; 100-4, 12, 140.2; 100-4, 12, 140.3.2; 100-4, 12, 50

00918   with fragmentation, manipulation and/or removal of ureteral calculus N ▣
    MED: 100-4, 12, 140; 100-4, 12, 140.2; 100-4, 12, 140.3.2; 100-4, 12, 50
    AMA: 1999, Nov, 8

00920 Anesthesia for procedures on male genitalia (including open urethral procedures); not otherwise specified ♂ N ▣
    MED: 100-4, 12, 140; 100-4, 12, 140.2; 100-4, 12, 140.3.2; 100-4, 12, 50

00921   vasectomy, unilateral or bilateral ♂ N ▣

00922   seminal vesicles ♂ N ▣
    MED: 100-4, 12, 140; 100-4, 12, 140.2; 100-4, 12, 140.3.2; 100-4, 12, 50

00924   undescended testis, unilateral or bilateral ♂ N ▣
    MED: 100-4, 12, 140; 100-4, 12, 140.2; 100-4, 12, 140.3.2; 100-4, 12, 50

00926   radical orchiectomy, inguinal ♂ N ▣
    MED: 100-4, 12, 140; 100-4, 12, 140.2; 100-4, 12, 140.3.2; 100-4, 12, 50

00928   radical orchiectomy, abdominal ♂ N ▣
    MED: 100-4, 12, 140; 100-4, 12, 140.2; 100-4, 12, 140.3.2; 100-4, 12, 50

00930   orchiopexy, unilateral or bilateral ♂ N ▣
    MED: 100-4, 12, 140; 100-4, 12, 140.2; 100-4, 12, 140.3.2; 100-4, 12, 50

00932   complete amputation of penis ♂ C ▣
    MED: 100-4, 12, 140; 100-4, 12, 140.2; 100-4, 12, 140.3.2; 100-4, 12, 50

---

26 / TC Professional/Technical Component   80 / 80 Assist-at-Surgery Allowed/With Documentation   ⊙ Conscious Sedation

Unlisted   Not Covered   MED: Pubs 100/NCD Reference   1 - 9 ASC Group   63 Modifier 63 Exempt

00934   radical amputation of penis with bilateral inguinal lymphadenectomy   ♂ C 🔄
MED: 100-4, 12, 140; 100-4, 12, 140.2; 100-4, 12, 140.3.2; 100-4, 12, 50

00936   radical amputation of penis with bilateral inguinal and iliac lymphadenectomy   ♂ C 🔄
MED: 100-4, 12, 140; 100-4, 12, 140.2; 100-4, 12, 140.3.2; 100-4, 12, 50

00938   insertion of penile prosthesis (perineal approach)   ♂ N 🔄
MED: 100-4, 12, 140; 100-4, 12, 140.2; 100-4, 12, 140.3.2; 100-4, 12, 50

00940   Anesthesia for vaginal procedures (including biopsy of labia, vagina, cervix or endometrium); not otherwise specified   ♀ N 🔄
MED: 100-4, 12, 140; 100-4, 12, 140.2; 100-4, 12, 140.3.2; 100-4, 12, 50

00942   colpotomy, vaginectomy, colporrhaphy, and open urethral procedures   ♀ N 🔄
MED: 100-4, 12, 140; 100-4, 12, 140.2; 100-4, 12, 140.3.2; 100-4, 12, 50

00944   vaginal hysterectomy   ♀ C 🔄
MED: 100-4, 12, 140; 100-4, 12, 140.2; 100-4, 12, 140.3.2; 100-4, 12, 50

00948   cervical cerclage   ♀ N 🔄
MED: 100-4, 12, 140; 100-4, 12, 140.2; 100-4, 12, 140.3.2; 100-4, 12, 50

00950   culdoscopy   ♀ N 🔄
MED: 100-4, 12, 140; 100-4, 12, 140.2; 100-4, 12, 140.3.2; 100-4, 12, 50

00952   hysteroscopy and/or hysterosalpingo- graphy   ♀ N 🔄
MED: 100-4, 12, 140; 100-4, 12, 140.2; 100-4, 12, 140.3.2; 100-4, 12, 50

AMA: 1999, Nov, 8

PELVIS (EXCEPT HIP)

01112   Anesthesia for bone marrow aspiration and/or biopsy, anterior or posterior iliac crest   N 🔄
MED: 100-1, 5, 90.2; 100-2, 15, 80; 100-2, 15, 80.1; 100-4, 16, 10; 100-4, 16, 10.1; 100-4, 16, 110.4

01120   Anesthesia for procedures on bony pelvis   N 🔄
MED: 100-4, 12, 140; 100-4, 12, 140.2; 100-4, 12, 140.3.2; 100-4, 12, 50

01130   Anesthesia for body cast application or revision   N 🔄
MED: 100-4, 12, 140; 100-4, 12, 140.2; 100-4, 12, 140.3.2; 100-4, 12, 50

01140   Anesthesia for interpelviabdominal (hindquarter) amputation   C 🔄
MED: 100-4, 12, 140; 100-4, 12, 140.2; 100-4, 12, 140.3.2; 100-4, 12, 50

01150   Anesthesia for radical procedures for tumor of pelvis, except hindquarter amputation   C 🔄
MED: 100-4, 12, 140; 100-4, 12, 140.2; 100-4, 12, 140.3.2; 100-4, 12, 50

01160   Anesthesia for closed procedures involving symphysis pubis or sacroiliac joint   N 🔄
MED: 100-4, 12, 140; 100-4, 12, 140.2; 100-4, 12, 140.3.2; 100-4, 12, 50

01170   Anesthesia for open procedures involving symphysis pubis or sacroiliac joint   N 🔄
MED: 100-4, 12, 140; 100-4, 12, 140.2; 100-4, 12, 140.3.2; 100-4, 12, 50

01173   Anesthesia for open repair of fracture disruption of pelvis or column fracture involving acetabulum   N 🔄

01180	Anesthesia for obturator neurectomy; extrapelvic	N ↕
	MED: 100-4, 12, 140; 100-4, 12, 140.2; 100-4, 12, 140.3.2; 100-4, 12, 50	
01190	intrapelvic	N ↕
	MED: 100-4, 12, 140; 100-4, 12, 140.2; 100-4, 12, 140.3.2; 100-4, 12, 50	

UPPER LEG (EXCEPT KNEE)

01200	Anesthesia for all closed procedures involving hip joint	N ↕
	MED: 100-4, 12, 140; 100-4, 12, 140.2; 100-4, 12, 140.3.2; 100-4, 12, 50	
01202	Anesthesia for arthroscopic procedures of hip joint	N ↕
	MED: 100-4, 12, 140; 100-4, 12, 140.2; 100-4, 12, 140.3.2; 100-4, 12, 50	
01210	Anesthesia for open procedures involving hip joint; not otherwise specified	N ↕
	MED: 100-4, 12, 140; 100-4, 12, 140.2; 100-4, 12, 140.3.2; 100-4, 12, 50	
01212	hip disarticulation	C ↕
	MED: 100-4, 12, 140; 100-4, 12, 140.2; 100-4, 12, 140.3.2; 100-4, 12, 50	
01214	total hip arthroplasty	C ↕
	MED: 100-4, 12, 140; 100-4, 12, 140.2; 100-4, 12, 140.3.2; 100-4, 12, 50	
01215	revision of total hip arthroplasty	N ↕
01220	Anesthesia for all closed procedures involving upper 2/3 of femur	N ↕
	MED: 100-4, 12, 140; 100-4, 12, 140.2; 100-4, 12, 140.3.2; 100-4, 12, 50	
01230	Anesthesia for open procedures involving upper 2/3 of femur; not otherwise specified	N ↕
	MED: 100-4, 12, 140; 100-4, 12, 140.2; 100-4, 12, 140.3.2; 100-4, 12, 50	
01232	amputation	C ↕
	MED: 100-4, 12, 140; 100-4, 12, 140.2; 100-4, 12, 140.3.2; 100-4, 12, 50	
01234	radical resection	C ↕
01250	Anesthesia for all procedures on nerves, muscles, tendons, fascia, and bursa of upper leg	N ↕
	MED: 100-4, 12, 140; 100-4, 12, 140.2; 100-4, 12, 140.3.2; 100-4, 12, 50	
01260	Anesthesia for all procedures involving veins of upper leg, including exploration	N ↕
	MED: 100-4, 12, 140; 100-4, 12, 140.2; 100-4, 12, 140.3.2; 100-4, 12, 50	
01270	Anesthesia for procedures involving arteries of upper leg, including bypass graft; not otherwise specified	N ↕
01272	femoral artery ligation	C ↕
01274	femoral artery embolectomy	C ↕
	MED: 100-4, 12, 140; 100-4, 12, 140.2; 100-4, 12, 140.3.2; 100-4, 12, 50	

KNEE AND POPLITEAL AREA

Diagnostic endoscopy/arthroscopy is always included in surgical endoscopy/arthroscopy, do not report separately.

01320	Anesthesia for all procedures on nerves, muscles, tendons, fascia, and bursa of knee and/or popliteal area	N ↕
	MED: 100-4, 12, 140; 100-4, 12, 140.2; 100-4, 12, 140.3.2; 100-4, 12, 50	
01340	Anesthesia for all closed procedures on lower 1/3 of femur	N ↕
	MED: 100-4, 12, 140; 100-4, 12, 140.2; 100-4, 12, 140.3.2; 100-4, 12, 50	

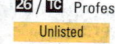 

01360	**Anesthesia for all open procedures on lower 1/3 of femur** MED: 100-4, 12, 140; 100-4, 12, 140.2; 100-4, 12, 140.3.2; 100-4, 12, 50	N ↻
01380	**Anesthesia for all closed procedures on knee joint** MED: 100-4, 12, 140; 100-4, 12, 140.2; 100-4, 12, 140.3.2; 100-4, 12, 50	N ↻
01382	**Anesthesia for diagnostic arthroscopic procedures of knee joint** MED: 100-4, 12, 140; 100-4, 12, 140.2; 100-4, 12, 140.3.2; 100-4, 12, 50	N ↻
01390	**Anesthesia for all closed procedures on upper ends of tibia, fibula, and/or patella** MED: 100-4, 12, 140; 100-4, 12, 140.2; 100-4, 12, 140.3.2; 100-4, 12, 50	N ↻
01392	**Anesthesia for all open procedures on upper ends of tibia, fibula, and/or patella** MED: 100-4, 12, 140; 100-4, 12, 140.2; 100-4, 12, 140.3.2; 100-4, 12, 50	N ↻
01400	**Anesthesia for open or surgical arthroscopic procedures on knee joint; not otherwise specified** MED: 100-4, 12, 140; 100-4, 12, 140.2; 100-4, 12, 140.3.2; 100-4, 12, 50	N ↻
01402	**total knee arthroplasty** MED: 100-4, 12, 140; 100-4, 12, 140.2; 100-4, 12, 140.3.2; 100-4, 12, 50	C ↻
01404	**disarticulation at knee** MED: 100-4, 12, 140; 100-4, 12, 140.2; 100-4, 12, 140.3.2; 100-4, 12, 50	C ↻
01420	**Anesthesia for all cast applications, removal, or repair involving knee joint** MED: 100-4, 12, 140; 100-4, 12, 140.2; 100-4, 12, 140.3.2; 100-4, 12, 50	N ↻
01430	**Anesthesia for procedures on veins of knee and popliteal area; not otherwise specified**	N ↻
01432	**arteriovenous fistula**	N ↻
01440	**Anesthesia for procedures on arteries of knee and popliteal area; not otherwise specified** MED: 100-4, 12, 140; 100-4, 12, 140.2; 100-4, 12, 140.3.2; 100-4, 12, 50	N ↻
01442	**popliteal thromboendarterectomy, with or without patch graft** MED: 100-4, 12, 140; 100-4, 12, 140.2; 100-4, 12, 140.3.2; 100-4, 12, 50	C ↻
01444	**popliteal excision and graft or repair for occlusion or aneurysm**	C ↻

LOWER LEG (BELOW KNEE, INCLUDES ANKLE AND FOOT)

Diagnostic endoscopy/arthroscopy is always included in surgical endoscopy/arthroscopy; do not report separately.

01462	**Anesthesia for all closed procedures on lower leg, ankle, and foot**	N ↻
01464	**Anesthesia for arthroscopic procedures of ankle and/or foot** MED: 100-4, 12, 140; 100-4, 12, 140.2; 100-4, 12, 140.3.2; 100-4, 12, 50	N ↻
01470	**Anesthesia for procedures on nerves, muscles, tendons, and fascia of lower leg, ankle, and foot; not otherwise specified** MED: 100-4, 12, 140; 100-4, 12, 140.2; 100-4, 12, 140.3.2; 100-4, 12, 50	N ↻
01472	**repair of ruptured Achilles tendon, with or without graft** MED: 100-4, 12, 140; 100-4, 12, 140.2; 100-4, 12, 140.3.2; 100-4, 12, 50	N ↻
01474	**gastrocnemius recession (eg, Strayer procedure)** MED: 100-4, 12, 140; 100-4, 12, 140.2; 100-4, 12, 140.3.2; 100-4, 12, 50	N ↻

↻ CCI Comp   50 Bilateral Procedure   + CPT Add-on Code   ⊘ Modifier -51 Exempt   ♂ Male   ♀ Female
● New Code   ▲ Revised Code   M Maternity Edit   A Age Edit   A–Y APC Status Ind.   **AMA:** CPT Assistant

© 2005 Ingenix, Inc. *(Blue Ink)*   CPT only © 2005 American Medical Association. All Rights Reserved. *(Black Ink)*   Anesthesia — 61

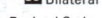

Anestheisa

01480 — 01636

01480	Anesthesia for open procedures on bones of lower leg, ankle, and foot; not otherwise specified	N ⌐
	MED: 100-4, 12, 140; 100-4, 12, 140.2; 100-4, 12, 140.3.2; 100-4, 12, 50	
01482	radical resection (including below knee amputation)	N ⌐
	MED: 100-4, 12, 140; 100-4, 12, 140.2; 100-4, 12, 140.3.2; 100-4, 12, 50	
01484	osteotomy or osteoplasty of tibia and/or fibula	N ⌐
	MED: 100-4, 12, 140; 100-4, 12, 140.2; 100-4, 12, 140.3.2; 100-4, 12, 50	
01486	total ankle replacement	C ⌐
	MED: 100-4, 12, 140; 100-4, 12, 140.2; 100-4, 12, 140.3.2; 100-4, 12, 50	
01490	Anesthesia for lower leg cast application, removal, or repair	N ⌐
	MED: 100-4, 12, 140; 100-4, 12, 140.2; 100-4, 12, 140.3.2; 100-4, 12, 50	
01500	Anesthesia for procedures on arteries of lower leg, including bypass graft; not otherwise specified	N ⌐
	MED: 100-4, 12, 140; 100-4, 12, 140.2; 100-4, 12, 140.3.2; 100-4, 12, 50	
01502	embolectomy, direct or with catheter	C ⌐
	MED: 100-4, 12, 140; 100-4, 12, 140.2; 100-4, 12, 140.3.2; 100-4, 12, 50	
01520	Anesthesia for procedures on veins of lower leg; not otherwise specified	N ⌐
	MED: 100-4, 12, 140; 100-4, 12, 140.2; 100-4, 12, 140.3.2; 100-4, 12, 50	
01522	venous thrombectomy, direct or with catheter	N ⌐
	MED: 100-4, 12, 140; 100-4, 12, 140.2; 100-4, 12, 140.3.2; 100-4, 12, 50	

SHOULDER AND AXILLA

Diagnostic endoscopy/arthroscopy is always included in surgical endoscopy/arthroscopy; do not report separately.

These codes include procedures performed on the humeral head and neck, sternoclavicular, acromioclavicular, and shoulder joints.

01610	Anesthesia for all procedures on nerves, muscles, tendons, fascia, and bursa of shoulder and axilla	N ⌐
	MED: 100-4, 12, 140; 100-4, 12, 140.2; 100-4, 12, 140.3.2; 100-4, 12, 50	
01620	Anesthesia for all closed procedures on humeral head and neck, sternoclavicular joint, acromioclavicular joint, and shoulder joint	N ⌐
	MED: 100-4, 12, 140; 100-4, 12, 140.2; 100-4, 12, 140.3.2; 100-4, 12, 50	
01622	Anesthesia for diagnostic arthroscopic procedures of shoulder joint	N ⌐
	MED: 100-4, 12, 140; 100-4, 12, 140.2; 100-4, 12, 140.3.2; 100-4, 12, 50	
01630	Anesthesia for open or surgical arthroscopic procedures on humeral head and neck, sternoclavicular joint, acromioclavicular joint, and shoulder joint; not otherwise specified	N ⌐
	MED: 100-4, 12, 140; 100-4, 12, 140.2; 100-4, 12, 140.3.2; 100-4, 12, 50	
01632	radical resection	C ⌐
	MED: 100-4, 12, 140; 100-4, 12, 140.2; 100-4, 12, 140.3.2; 100-4, 12, 50	
01634	shoulder disarticulation	C ⌐
	MED: 100-4, 12, 140; 100-4, 12, 140.2; 100-4, 12, 140.3.2; 100-4, 12, 50	
01636	interthoracoscapular (forequarter) amputation	C ⌐
	MED: 100-4, 12, 140; 100-4, 12, 140.2; 100-4, 12, 140.3.2; 100-4, 12, 50	

01638	total shoulder replacement	C 🔲	
	MED: 100-4, 12, 140; 100-4, 12, 140.2; 100-4, 12, 140.3.2; 100-4, 12, 50		
01650	Anesthesia for procedures on arteries of shoulder and axilla; not otherwise specified	N 🔲	
	MED: 100-4, 12, 140; 100-4, 12, 140.2; 100-4, 12, 140.3.2; 100-4, 12, 50		
01652	axillary-brachial aneurysm	C 🔲	
	MED: 100-4, 12, 140; 100-4, 12, 140.2; 100-4, 12, 140.3.2; 100-4, 12, 50		
01654	bypass graft	C 🔲	
	MED: 100-4, 12, 140; 100-4, 12, 140.2; 100-4, 12, 140.3.2; 100-4, 12, 50		
01656	axillary-femoral bypass graft	C 🔲	
	MED: 100-4, 12, 140; 100-4, 12, 140.2; 100-4, 12, 140.3.2; 100-4, 12, 50		
01670	Anesthesia for all procedures on veins of shoulder and axilla	N 🔲	
	MED: 100-4, 12, 140; 100-4, 12, 140.2; 100-4, 12, 140.3.2; 100-4, 12, 50		
01680	Anesthesia for shoulder cast application, removal or repair; not otherwise specified	N 🔲	
	MED: 100-4, 12, 140; 100-4, 12, 140.2; 100-4, 12, 140.3.2; 100-4, 12, 50		
01682	shoulder spica	N 🔲	
	MED: 100-4, 12, 140; 100-4, 12, 140.2; 100-4, 12, 140.3.2; 100-4, 12, 50		

UPPER ARM AND ELBOW

Diagnostic endoscopy/arthroscopy is always included in surgical endoscopy/arthroscopy; do not report separately.

01710	Anesthesia for procedures on nerves, muscles, tendons, fascia, and bursa of upper arm and elbow; not otherwise specified	N 🔲	
	MED: 100-4, 12, 140; 100-4, 12, 140.2; 100-4, 12, 140.3.2; 100-4, 12, 50		
01712	tenotomy, elbow to shoulder, open	N 🔲	
	MED: 100-4, 12, 140; 100-4, 12, 140.2; 100-4, 12, 140.3.2; 100-4, 12, 50		
01714	tenoplasty, elbow to shoulder	N 🔲	
	MED: 100-4, 12, 140; 100-4, 12, 140.2; 100-4, 12, 140.3.2; 100-4, 12, 50		
01716	tenodesis, rupture of long tendon of biceps	N 🔲	
	MED: 100-4, 12, 140; 100-4, 12, 140.2; 100-4, 12, 140.3.2; 100-4, 12, 50		
01730	Anesthesia for all closed procedures on humerus and elbow	N 🔲	
	MED: 100-4, 12, 140; 100-4, 12, 140.2; 100-4, 12, 140.3.2; 100-4, 12, 50		
01732	Anesthesia for diagnostic arthroscopic procedures of elbow joint	N 🔲	
	MED: 100-4, 12, 140; 100-4, 12, 140.2; 100-4, 12, 140.3.2; 100-4, 12, 50		
01740	Anesthesia for open or surgical arthroscopic procedures of the elbow; not otherwise specified	N 🔲	
	MED: 100-4, 12, 140; 100-4, 12, 140.2; 100-4, 12, 140.3.2; 100-4, 12, 50		
01742	osteotomy of humerus	N 🔲	
	MED: 100-4, 12, 140; 100-4, 12, 140.2; 100-4, 12, 140.3.2; 100-4, 12, 50		
01744	repair of nonunion or malunion of humerus	N 🔲	
	MED: 100-4, 12, 140; 100-4, 12, 140.2; 100-4, 12, 140.3.2; 100-4, 12, 50		
01756	radical procedures	C 🔲	
	MED: 100-4, 12, 140; 100-4, 12, 140.2; 100-4, 12, 140.3.2; 100-4, 12, 50		

01758	excision of cyst or tumor of humerus	N ♦
	MED: 100-4, 12, 140; 100-4, 12, 140.2; 100-4, 12, 140.3.2; 100-4, 12, 50	
01760	total elbow replacement	N
	MED: 100-4, 12, 140; 100-4, 12, 140.2; 100-4, 12, 140.3.2; 100-4, 12, 50	
01770	Anesthesia for procedures on arteries of upper arm and elbow; not otherwise specified	N ♦
	MED: 100-4, 12, 140; 100-4, 12, 140.2; 100-4, 12, 140.3.2; 100-4, 12, 50	
01772	embolectomy	N ♦
	MED: 100-4, 12, 140; 100-4, 12, 140.2; 100-4, 12, 140.3.2; 100-4, 12, 50	
01780	Anesthesia for procedures on veins of upper arm and elbow; not otherwise specified	N ♦
	MED: 100-4, 12, 140; 100-4, 12, 140.2; 100-4, 12, 140.3.2; 100-4, 12, 50	
01782	phleborrhaphy	N ♦
	MED: 100-4, 12, 140; 100-4, 12, 140.2; 100-4, 12, 140.3.2; 100-4, 12, 50	

FOREARM, WRIST, AND HAND

Diagnostic endoscopy/arthroscopy is always included in surgical endoscopy/arthroscopy; do not report separately.

01810	Anesthesia for all procedures on nerves, muscles, tendons, fascia, and bursa of forearm, wrist, and hand	N ♦
	MED: 100-4, 12, 140; 100-4, 12, 140.2; 100-4, 12, 140.3.2; 100-4, 12, 50	
01820	Anesthesia for all closed procedures on radius, ulna, wrist, or hand bones	N ♦
	MED: 100-4, 12, 140; 100-4, 12, 140.2; 100-4, 12, 140.3.2; 100-4, 12, 50	
01829	Anesthesia for diagnostic arthroscopic procedures on the wrist	N ♦
01830	Anesthesia for open or surgical arthroscopic/endoscopic procedures on distal radius, distal ulna, wrist, or hand joints; not otherwise specified	N ♦
	MED: 100-4, 12, 140; 100-4, 12, 140.2; 100-4, 12, 140.3.2; 100-4, 12, 50	
01832	total wrist replacement	N ♦
	MED: 100-4, 12, 140; 100-4, 12, 140.2; 100-4, 12, 140.3.2; 100-4, 12, 50	
01840	Anesthesia for procedures on arteries of forearm, wrist, and hand; not otherwise specified	N ♦
	MED: 100-4, 12, 140; 100-4, 12, 140.2; 100-4, 12, 140.3.2; 100-4, 12, 50	
01842	embolectomy	N ♦
	MED: 100-4, 12, 140; 100-4, 12, 140.2; 100-4, 12, 140.3.2; 100-4, 12, 50	
01844	Anesthesia for vascular shunt, or shunt revision, any type (eg, dialysis)	N ♦
	MED: 100-4, 12, 140; 100-4, 12, 140.2; 100-4, 12, 140.3.2; 100-4, 12, 50	
01850	Anesthesia for procedures on veins of forearm, wrist, and hand; not otherwise specified	N ♦
	MED: 100-4, 12, 140; 100-4, 12, 140.2; 100-4, 12, 140.3.2; 100-4, 12, 50	
01852	phleborrhaphy	N ♦
	MED: 100-4, 12, 140; 100-4, 12, 140.2; 100-4, 12, 140.3.2; 100-4, 12, 50	

Anesthesia

| 01860 | Anesthesia for forearm, wrist, or hand cast application, removal, or repair N |
| | MED: 100-4, 12, 140; 100-4, 12, 140.2; 100-4, 12, 140.3.2; 100-4, 12, 50 |

RADIOLOGICAL PROCEDURES

01905   Anesthesia for myelography, diskography, vertebroplasty N

01916   Anesthesia for diagnostic arteriography/ venography N
MED: 100-3, 20.17; 100-4, 12, 140; 100-4, 12, 140.2; 100-4, 12, 140.3.2; 100-4, 12, 50

Note that code 01916 cannot be reported with therapeutic codes 01924-01926, 01930-01933.

01920   Anesthesia for cardiac catheterization including coronary angiography and ventriculography (not to include Swan-Ganz catheter) N
MED: 100-4, 12, 140; 100-4, 12, 140.2; 100-4, 12, 140.3.2; 100-4, 12, 50

01922   Anesthesia for non-invasive imaging or radiation therapy N
MED: 100-4, 12, 140; 100-4, 12, 140.2; 100-4, 12, 140.3.2; 100-4, 12, 50

01924   Anesthesia for therapeutic interventional radiologic procedures involving the arterial system; not otherwise specified N

01925   carotid or coronary N

01926   intracranial, intracardiac, or aortic N

01930   Anesthesia for therapeutic interventional radiologic procedures involving the venous/lymphatic system (not to include access to the central circulation); not otherwise specified N

01931   intrahepatic or portal circulation (eg, transcutaneous porto-caval shunt (TIPS)) N

01932   intrathoracic or jugular N

01933   intracranial N

BURN EXCISIONS OR DEBRIDEMENT

01951   Anesthesia for second and third degree burn excision or debridement with or without skin grafting, any site, for total body surface area (TBSA) treated during anesthesia and surgery; less than four percent total body surface area N
MED: 100-3, 270.5

01952   between four and nine percent of total body surface area N

+ 01953   each additional nine percent total body surface area or part thereof (List separately in addition to code for primary procedure) N

Note that 01953 is an add-on code and must be used in conjunction with code 01952.

OBSTETRIC

01958   Anesthesia for external cephalic version procedure M ♀ N

01960   Anesthesia for vaginal delivery only M ♀ N

01961   Anesthesia for cesarean delivery only M ♀ N

01962   Anesthesia for urgent hysterectomy following delivery M ♀ N

01963   Anesthesia for cesarean hysterectomy without any labor analgesia/anesthesia care M ♀ N

~~01964~~   ~~Anesthesia for abortion procedures~~

(Use 01965, 01966)

01860 — 01964

Anestheisa

01965 — 01999

● 01965 Anesthesia for incomplete or missed abortion procedures

● 01966 Anesthesia for induced abortion procedures

01967 Neuraxial labor analgesia/anesthesia for planned vaginal delivery (this includes any repeat subarachnoid needle placement and drug injection and/or any necessary replacement of an epidural catheter during labor) Ⓜ ♀ Ⓝ ⤴

+ 01968 Anesthesia for cesarean delivery following neuraxial labor analgesia/anesthesia (List separately in addition to code for primary procedure performed) Ⓜ ♀ Ⓝ ⤴

Note that 01968 is an add-on code and must be used in conjunction with code 01967.

+ 01969 Anesthesia for cesarean hysterectomy following neuraxial labor analgesia/anesthesia (List separately in addition to code for primary procedure performed) Ⓜ ♀ Ⓝ ⤴

Note that 01969 is an add-on code and must be used in conjunction with code 01967.

OTHER PROCEDURES

01990 Physiological support for harvesting of organ(s) from brain-dead patient Ⓒ ⤴

MED: 100-4, 12, 140; 100-4, 12, 140.2; 100-4, 12, 140.3.2; 100-4, 12, 50

01991 Anesthesia for diagnostic or therapeutic nerve blocks and injections (when block or injection is performed by a different provider); other than the prone position Ⓝ ⤴

Note that code 01991 cannot be reported with CPT code 99141.

01992 Anesthesia for diagnostic or therapeutic nerve blocks and injections (when block or injection is performed by a different provider); prone position Ⓝ ⤴

Note that code 01992 cannot be reported with CPT code 99141.

01995 Regional intravenous administration of local anesthetic agent or other medication (upper or lower extremity) Ⓝ ⤴
MED: 100-4, 12, 140; 100-4, 12, 140.2; 100-4, 12, 140.3.2; 100-4, 12, 50

To report an intra-arterial or intravenous therapeutic, prophylactic or diagnostic injection, consult CPT codes 90783 and 90784.

01996 Daily hospital management of epidural or subarachnoid continuous drug administration Ⓝ ⤴
MED: 100-4, 12, 140; 100-4, 12, 140.2; 100-4, 12, 140.3.2; 100-4, 12, 50

AMA: 1997, Nov, 10

Use code 01996 to report services performed after insertion of an epidural or subarachnoid catheter placed primarily for anesthesia administration during an operative session, but retained for post-operative pain management.

01999 Unlisted anesthesia procedure(s) Ⓝ
MED: 100-4, 12, 140; 100-4, 12, 140.2; 100-4, 12, 140.3.2; 100-4, 12, 50

AMA: 1997, Feb, 4

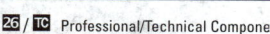 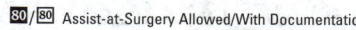

QUALIFYING CIRCUMSTANCES FOR ANESTHESIA

If an explanation is needed for these services, consult the Anesthesia guidelines.

+   99100   **Anesthesia for patient of extreme age, under 1 year and over 70 (List separately in addition to code for primary anesthesia procedure)**   Ⓑ ↴
MED: 100-4, 12, 140; 100-4, 12, 140.2; 100-4, 12, 140.3.2; 100-4, 12, 50

To report anesthesia for hernia repairs in the lower abdomen, infant one year of age or younger, consult CPT codes 00834, 00836.

+   99116   **Anesthesia complicated by utilization of total body hypothermia (List separately in addition to code for primary anesthesia procedure)**   Ⓑ ↴
MED: 100-4, 12, 140; 100-4, 12, 140.2; 100-4, 12, 140.3.2; 100-4, 12, 50

+   99135   **Anesthesia complicated by utilization of controlled hypotension (List separately in addition to code for primary anesthesia procedure)**   Ⓑ ↴
MED: 100-4, 12, 140; 100-4, 12, 140.2; 100-4, 12, 140.3.2; 100-4, 12, 50

+   99140   **Anesthesia complicated by emergency conditions (specify) (List separately in addition to code for primary anesthesia procedure)**   Ⓑ ↴
MED: 100-4, 12, 140; 100-4, 12, 140.2; 100-4, 12, 140.3.2; 100-4, 12, 50

AMA: 2001, Mar, 10

An emergency exists when a delay in treatment would lead to a significant increase in the threat to life or body part.

Surgery Services

CODING INFORMATION

ORGANIZATION

The surgery section (10021–69990) is the largest section of the CPT book. It is divided into 18 subsections by body system (e.g., integumentary, endocrine), procedure site (e.g., mediastinum and diaphragm), or type of service (e.g., maternity care and delivery). The subsections are as follows:

General

Integumentary System

Musculoskeletal System

Respiratory System

Cardiovascular System

Hemic and Lymphatic Systems

Mediastinum and Diaphragm

Digestive System

Urinary System

Male Genital System

Intersex Surgery

Female Genital System

Maternity Care and Delivery

Endocrine System

Nervous System

Eye and Ocular Adnexa

Auditory System

Operating Microscope

Instructions that apply to all surgical codes are found at the beginning of the surgery section. In addition, information or notes, specific to subsections, groups of codes and single codes are found throughout the surgery section. Guidelines, including terms and concepts, important to all surgical codes will be explained first. Then guidelines and notes specific to subsections or codes will be reviewed.

FORMAT OF THE TERMINOLOGY

CPT guidelines state that some of the procedures are not printed in their entirety but refer back to a common portion of the procedure listed in a preceding entry. This space-saving format means that many "indented" codes within a code range repeat some common portion of a procedure's description.

While some procedures presented in this indented form are mutually exclusive (i.e., cannot be billed together), others are not. For procedures that are not mutually exclusive, payers may make special allowances. Knowing which procedures are mutually exclusive, however, is the key to avoiding unbundling.

GENERAL INFORMATION

Surgical procedures can generally be divided into two categories: diagnostic and therapeutic.

SURGICAL PACKAGE

The majority of the CPT surgery codes are "package" services. According to the CPT book, they include the actual surgical procedure, local infiltration, metacarpal, or digital block or topical anesthesia, writing orders, postanesthesia recovery evaluation and typical follow-up care such as talking with the family and writing orders. Also included is the evaluation and management service on the day of or the day prior to surgery unless that is the visit that led to the decision for surgery. When a patient is seen for a routine follow-up postoperative visit within the normal follow-up period, code 99024 may be reported for normal uncomplicated postoperative care. However, additional payment will not be provided for this service since normal postoperative care is included in the surgical package.

Post-procedure care for diagnostic procedures includes only the care related to recover from the procedure itself. Care for the condition that required the procedure and any other conditions is not included and should be reported separately.

Many payers have strict guidelines related to reimbursement for preoperative services. Additional reimbursement for preoperative evaluation and management services is usually allowed prior to the decision for surgery or to establish the need for surgery. Reimbursement may be denied for any care provided after the decision for surgical intervention However, some payers may identify a specific preoperative period (24 hours to 30 days), during which no additional reimbursement will be made for evaluation and management services. Because of these differing payer policies, it is important for individual providers to establish a policy related to the reporting of preoperative services. Patients should be made aware of this policy. Review contractual arrangements with payers to verify that your policy is not in violation of those contracts.

Postoperative complications, exacerbations, and recurrences are not included in the surgical package and should be reported separately. Postoperative complications include conditions such as wound dehiscence, infection, and bleeding. A diagnosis code should be assigned to reflect the nature of the complication when billing for services rendered to treat the complication.

Unrelated care is always coded. Report services unrelated to the operative problem, such as care for other diseases or injuries, with an appropriate inpatient or outpatient level of service modifier and a corresponding diagnostic code that identifies a problem other than the surgical diagnosis.

FRAGMENTATION AND UNBUNDLING

Understanding unbundling and fragmentation can be accomplished by first defining the term, "bundle." A bundle is a defined set of items or services wrapped together in a group, bunch, or package. The items in the bundle can be related or unrelated, but all defined elements must be present to make a specific bundle. Unbundling or fragmentation occurs primarily two ways.

First, unbundling occurs when minor integral services are reported separately or in addition to a major procedure. Unfortunately, since all minor components of a procedure may not be listed explicitly, it is sometimes difficult to determine which services are integral to a given procedure. One way to approach this is to ask what services are normally performed with a given procedure. A simple example is an excision of a skin lesion. To excise the skin lesion, an incision must be made. An incision is always integral to an excision of a lesion and should not be billed separately. However, an incision is not described in the excision of skin lesion codes. It is implicit because it must be performed with every excision.

Second, unbundling occurs when a single procedure with two or more explicitly described components is broken into its component parts and reported with several CPT codes instead of the single CPT code for the combined service. A simple example of this type of unbundle can be illustrated with the procedure for a combined abdominal hysterectomy with colpo-urethrocystopexy. Since the two components of this procedure are frequently performed together, a combined code 58152 has been assigned to describe this service. However, it is also possible to perform each of the components separately (abdominal hysterectomy 58150 and colpo-urethrocystopexy 51840 or 51845). When the combined procedure is performed during a single surgical session, it must be reported with the bundled CPT code 58152. If it is reported with code 58150 in conjunction with 51840 or 58145, it is considered unbundled or fragmented.

Unbundling, whether intentional or not, is considered by payers to be a form of fraudulent or reckless billing. The rationale is simple.

Unbundled services will frequently net more reimbursement than reporting the single bundled CPT code.

The Centers for Medicare and Medicaid Services (CMS) has adopted the Correct Coding Initiative (CCI) unbundling guidelines, an evolving list of codes that cannot be reported in combination with other codes for Medicare claims. The CPT book does not have a specific guideline for unbundling. Instead, payers and other interested parties have developed guidelines for bundled procedures from information that is listed in the CPT book. The most common areas of the CPT book used for these interpretations are the format of the listed surgical procedures, separate procedures, and subsection information in the surgery guidelines.

PREVENTION TIPS

Your office can take some easy steps to avoid problems with fragmentation or unbundling.

- Use a current CPT book as well as the current rules, regulations, and provider manuals for Medicare and for the private payers with whom you have a contractual arrangement.

- Educate everyone on CPT guidelines as well as the rules and regulations of your payers. Educational sessions should occur any time changes are made.

- When using a preprinted charge ticket or routing sheet, specify the exact CPT code and description. Always have an area on the charge ticket for the physician to indicate that a service should be coded by hand and code from the operative report or medical record. Many providers feel reimbursement is better by coding directly from the record or operative report.

- Date the charge ticket and update codes annually.

- Create your charge tickets or routing sheets to avoid fragmented billing. Adding the abbreviation "SP" to separate procedure codes alerts the coder that a separate procedure should not be reported when related to, or integral to, a major procedure.

- Make sure physicians provide coders with complete documentation and concise information. Query the physician if documentation is not adequate to support the codes selected.

- Use the correct modifiers as appropriate to clarify or append circumstances that can arise within global package time periods.

Surgery—69

SEPARATE PROCEDURES

Separate procedures are services that are commonly carried out as an integral part of a larger service, and as such do not warrant separate identification. These services are noted in the CPT book with the parenthetical phrase "separate procedure." When this phrase appears before the semicolon, all indented descriptions that follow include it.

Separate procedures are often improperly reported as related procedures, which are performed for the same diagnosis and within the same operative area. Reporting a separate procedure in addition to the larger procedure to which it is related is incorrect. A separate procedure can be a component of, or incidental to, a larger, related procedure.

DIAGNOSTIC PROCEDURES

Diagnostic procedures are performed to evaluate the patient's complaints or symptoms. These procedures help the physician establish the nature of the patient's disease or condition so that definitive care can be provided. Diagnostic procedures include endoscopy, arthroscopy, injection procedures, and biopsies. Follow-up care for diagnostic procedures includes only care directly related to recovery from the diagnostic procedure itself. Care of the condition identified by the diagnostic procedures or other concomitant conditions is not included and may be listed separately.

THERAPEUTIC SERVICES

Therapeutic services are performed for treatment of a specific diagnosis. These services include performance of the procedure, various incidental elements, and normal, related follow-up care.

SEQUENCING

The code with the highest dollar value is always sequenced first when reporting multiple procedures. The second and subsequent codes are ordered and listed in decreasing dollar values with the correct modifier appended. When reporting multiple procedures, do not reduce the amount of secondary codes. However, if overpaid, reimburse the payer for the overpayment. Set a ceiling on nonactionable overpayments in policy or contracts (e.g., up to $10 need not be refunded). Overpayments that are not returned to the payer may target an office for an audit.

MATERIALS SUPPLIED BY A PHYSICIAN

Many payers reimburse only for supplies that are excessive or extraordinarily expensive. Do not report supplies that are customarily included in surgical packages, such as gauze, sponges, applicators, or Steri-strips. Surgical services do not include the supply of medications, which may be coded and billed separately. Applicable CPT codes are the following:

- 99070 for supplies, including reusable and disposable items. Specify the supply, and the amount that was provided
- 96545 for the provision of chemotherapy agent
- 92330 and 92335 for ocular prostheses; additional supplies relating to the eye (including contact lenses and spectacles) are identified with 92390–92396. HCPCS Level II codes also can report ocular prostheses
- Many payers prefer or require the use of HCPCS Level II codes for reporting supplies and drugs as they provide greater specificity.

SURGICAL PROCEDURES

Several subsections of the CPT book contain guidelines, notes, definitions, and special instructions. Following is a list of some of the subsections:

Fine Needle Aspiration

Removal of Skin Tags

Shaving of Epidermal/Dermal Lesions

Excision of Benign and Malignant Lesions

Repair of Wounds

Adjacent Tissue Transfers

Skin grafts and Flaps

Destruction of Lesions

Fracture Care

Cast and Splint Application

Spine Surgeries

Pacemaker/Defibrillator Care

Coronary Artery Bypass Grafts

Vascular Catheterization/Injection

Gastrointestinal Endoscopy

Hernia Repair

Urodynamics

Cystoscopy, Urethroscopy, and Cystourethroscopy

Vulvectomy

Maternity Care and Delivery

Surgery of Skull Base

GENERAL

10021   **Fine needle aspiration; without imaging guidance**   T 80 CCI
          AMA: 2002, Aug, 10

10022   **with imaging guidance**   T 80 CCI

          If radiological supervision and interpretation is performed, consult CPT codes 76003, 76360, 76393, 76942.

          If percutaneous needle biopsy, other than fine needle aspiration, is performed, consult CPT code 20206 for muscle, 32400 for pleura, 32405 for lung or mediastinum, 42400 for salivary gland, 47000, 47001 for liver, 48102 for pancreas, 49180 for abdominal or retroperitoneal mass, 60100 for thyroid, 62269 for spinal cord.

          If evaluation of fine needle aspirate is performed, consult CPT codes 88172, 88173.

INTEGUMENTARY SYSTEM

SKIN, SUBCUTANEOUS AND ACCESSORY STRUCTURES

INCISION AND DRAINAGE
To report excision procedures, consult CPT code 11400 and subsequent codes.

10040   **Acne surgery (eg, marsupialization, opening or removal of multiple milia, comedones, cysts, pustules)**   T CCI
          AMA: 1992, Fall, 1

10060   **Incision and drainage of abscess (eg, carbuncle, suppurative hidradenitis, cutaneous or subcutaneous abscess, cyst, furuncle, or paronychia); simple or single**   T CCI

10061   **complicated or multiple**   T CCI

10080   **Incision and drainage of pilonidal cyst; simple**   T CCI

10081   **complicated**   T CCI

          If an excision of a pilonidal cyst or sinus is performed, consult CPT codes 11770-11772.

10120   **Incision and removal of foreign body, subcutaneous tissues; simple**   T CCI

10121   **complicated**   2 T CCI
          MED: 100-2, 15, 260; 100-4, 12, 90.3; 100-4, 14, 10

          If exploration of a penetrating wound, not requiring thoracotomy or laparotomy, is performed, consult CPT codes 20100-20103. If debridement related to an open fracture(s) and/or dislocation(s) is performed, consult CPT codes 11010-11012.

10140   **Incision and drainage of hematoma, seroma or fluid collection**   T CCI

          To report imaging guidance, consult CPT codes 76030, 76393, 76942.

10160   **Puncture aspiration of abscess, hematoma, bulla, or cyst**   T CCI

          To report imaging guidance, consult CPT codes 76030, 76393, 76942.

10180   **Incision and drainage, complex, postoperative wound infection**   2 T CCI
          MED: 100-2, 15, 260; 100-4, 12, 90.3; 100-4, 14, 10

          If secondary closure of surgical wound is performed, consult CPT codes 12020, 12021, 13160.

Integumentary System

11000 — 11011

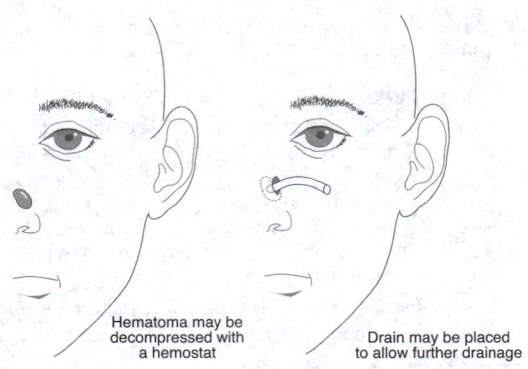

Hematoma may be decompressed with a hemostat

Drain may be placed to allow further drainage

EXCISION — DEBRIDEMENT

If dermabrasions are performed, consult CPT codes 15780-15811. If nail debridement is performed, consult CPT codes 11720-11721. If burns are being treated, consult CPT codes 16000-16035.

11000   **Debridement of extensive eczematous or infected skin; up to 10% of body surface**   T ▶

+ 11001   **each additional 10% of the body surface (List separately in addition to code for primary procedure)**   T

Note that 11001 is an add-on code and must be used in conjunction with 11000.

11004   **Debridement of skin, subcutaneous tissue, muscle and fascia for necrotizing soft tissue infection; external genitalia and perineum**   C ▶

11005   **abdominal wall, with or without fascial closure**   C 80 ▶

11006   **external genitalia, perineum and abdominal wall, with or without fascial closure**   C ▶

+ 11008   **Removal of prosthetic material or mesh, abdominal wall for necrotizing soft tissue infection (List separately in addition to code for primary procedure)**   C 80

Note that 11008 must be used in conjunction with 11004-11006.

Do not report 11000-11001 and 11010-11044 together with 11008.

When skin grafts or flaps are performed separately for closure at the same session as 11004-11008, consult the relevant graft and flap codes.

For orchiectomy consult CPT code 54520.

For testicular transplantation consult CPT code 54680.

11010   **Debridement including removal of foreign material associated with open fracture(s) and/or dislocation(s); skin and subcutaneous tissues**   2 T ▶
MED: 100-2, 15, 260; 100-4, 12, 90.3; 100-4, 14, 10

AMA: 1997, Mar, 1; 1997, Aug, 6; 1997, Apr, 10

11011   **skin, subcutaneous tissue, muscle fascia, and muscle**   2 T ▶
MED: 100-2, 15, 260; 100-4, 12, 90.3; 100-4, 14, 10

AMA: 1997, Mar, 1; 1997, Aug, 6; 1997, Apr, 10

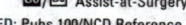

11012 skin, subcutaneous tissue, muscle fascia, muscle, and bone
MED: 100-2, 15, 260; 100-4, 12, 90.3; 100-4, 14, 10

AMA: 1997, Mar, 1; 1997, Aug, 6; 1997, Apr, 10

11040 **Debridement; skin, partial thickness**
AMA: 1997, Feb, 7; 1997, Aug, 6; 1996, May, 6; 1993, Fall, 21

11041 skin, full thickness
AMA: 1997, Feb, 7; 1997, Aug, 6; 1996, May, 6; 1993, Fall, 21

11042 skin, and subcutaneous tissue
MED: 100-2, 15, 260; 100-4, 12, 90.3; 100-4, 14, 10

AMA: 2000, Aug, 5; 1997, Feb, 7; 1997, Aug, 6; 1996, May, 6; 1992, Winter, 10

11043 skin, subcutaneous tissue, and muscle
MED: 100-2, 15, 260; 100-4, 12, 90.3; 100-4, 14, 10

AMA: 1997, Feb, 7; 1997, Aug, 6; 1997, Apr, 11; 1996, May, 6

11044 subcutaneous tissue, muscle, and bone
MED: 100-2, 15, 260; 100-4, 12, 90.3; 100-4, 14, 10

AMA: 1997, Feb, 7; 1997, Aug, 6; 1997, Apr, 11; 1996, May, 6; 1996, Mar, 10; 1993, Fall, 21

Do not report 11040-11044 with 97597-97602.

PARING OR CUTTING
To report lesion destruction, consult CPT codes 17000-17004.

11055 **Paring or cutting of benign hyperkeratotic lesion (eg, corn or callus); single lesion**
AMA: 1999, Jan, 11; 1997, Nov, 11

11056 two to four lesions
AMA: 1999, Jan, 11; 1997, Nov, 11

11057 more than four lesions
AMA: 1999, Jan, 11; 1997, Nov, 11

BIOPSY
Often tissue obtained during certain skin procedures, such as excisions, destructions or removals is sent to pathology. This is considered a component of such procedures and should not be reported with codes 11100 or 11101.

Biopsies performed at different sites or on different lesions on the same date should be reported separately, append modifier 59.

11100 **Biopsy of skin, subcutaneous tissue and/or mucous membrane (including simple closure), unless otherwise listed; single lesion**
AMA: 1997, Mar, 4; 1997, Jun, 5; 1994, Fall, 18

If the conjunctiva is biopsied, consult CPT code 68100; if the eyelid is biopsied, consult CPT code 67810.

+ **11101** **each separate/additional lesion (List separately in addition to code for primary procedure)**
AMA: 2000, Apr, 6; 1994, Fall, 18

Note that 11101 is an add-on code and must be used in conjunction with 11100.

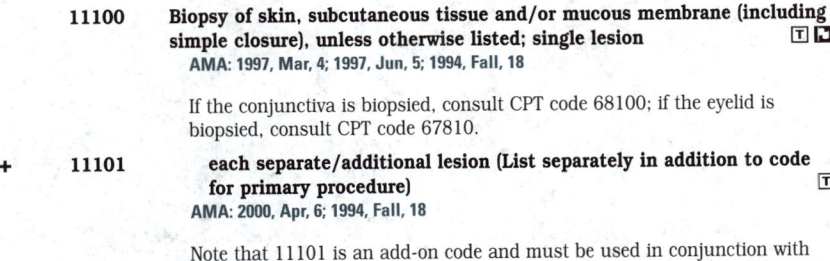

Integumentary System

11200 — 11306

REMOVAL OF SKIN TAGS

CPT codes 11200 and 11201 identify the use of scissors or any sharp methods, ligature strangulation, electrosurgical destruction or any combination of treatment methods including electrosurgical techniques or the use of chemicals. Local anesthesia is included in these services.

11200   **Removal of skin tags, multiple fibrocutaneous tags, any area; up to and including 15 lesions**   T ⬥
        AMA: 2002, Nov, 11; 1997, Nov, 11-12

+   **11201**   **each additional ten lesions (List separately in addition to code for primary procedure)**   T
        AMA: 2002, Nov, 11; 1997, Nov, 11-12

        Note that 11201 is an add-on code and must be used in conjunction with 11200.

SHAVING OF EPIDERMAL OR DERMAL LESIONS

Shaving is the removal of epidermal or dermal skin lesions without a full-thickness dermal excision by use of a transverse incision or horizontal slicing technique. Administration of local anesthesia and any chemical or electrocautery is included.

CPT codes 11300-11313, include local anesthesia, chemical or electrocauterization of the wound. These wounds do not require suture closure.

11300   **Shaving of epidermal or dermal lesion, single lesion, trunk, arms or legs; lesion diameter 0.5 cm or less**   T 80 ⬥
        AMA: 2002, Nov, 11; 2000, Feb, 11

11301   **lesion diameter 0.6 to 1.0 cm**   T 80 ⬥
        AMA: 2000, Feb, 11

11302   **lesion diameter 1.1 to 2.0 cm**   T 80 ⬥
        AMA: 2000, Feb, 10

11303   **lesion diameter over 2.0 cm**   T 80 ⬥
        AMA: 2000, Feb, 10

11305   **Shaving of epidermal or dermal lesion, single lesion, scalp, neck, hands, feet, genitalia; lesion diameter 0.5 cm or less**   T 80 ⬥
        AMA: 2000, Feb, 10

11306   **lesion diameter 0.6 to 1.0 cm**   T 80 ⬥
        AMA: 2000, Feb, 10

Shave excision of an elevated lesion; technique also used to biopsy

Eliptical excision is often used when tissue removal is larger than 4 mm or when deep pathology is suspected

A punch biopsy cuts a core of tissue as the tool is twisted downward

The skin is the largest organ of the human body and accounts for about 20 percent of total body weight. It serves mainly as a protective barrier, a temperature regulator, and as a sensory device. The epidermis is outermost and is the thinnest of the skin layers; the major part of the dermis is high in collagen and is notable for its great elasticity and strength; the major blood and nerve network is found in the middermis. Adnexal structures are the hair follicles, sebaceous glands, sweat glands, and the follicles that produce fingernails and toenails. Lesions are small areas of skin disease and may be solitary or multiple

| 11307 | lesion diameter 1.1 to 2.0 cm | T 80 |
| | AMA: 2000, Feb, 10 | |

| 11308 | lesion diameter over 2.0 cm | T 80 |
| | AMA: 2000, Feb, 10 | |

| 11310 | Shaving of epidermal or dermal lesion, single lesion, face, ears, eyelids, nose, lips, mucous membrane; lesion diameter 0.5 cm or less | T 80 |
| | AMA: 2000, Feb, 10 | |

| 11311 | lesion diameter 0.6 to 1.0 cm | T 80 |
| | AMA: 2000, Feb, 10 | |

| 11312 | lesion diameter 1.1 to 2.0 cm | T 80 |
| | AMA: 2000, Feb, 10 | |

| 11313 | lesion diameter over 2.0 cm | T 80 |
| | AMA: 2000, Feb, 10 | |

EXCISION — BENIGN LESIONS

In the CPT book excision of benign lesions is defined as a full thickness removal of the lesion, including margins. Benign lesions may include neoplasms, cysts and growths caused by inflammation, fibrous tissue, and tissues present since birth. The lesions may occur in the skin or tissues below the skin. Non-layered closure and local anesthesia are included.

Layered, intermediate or complex closure of the defect created by the excision of the lesion is separately reported.

If an excision of a benign lesion(s) requiring more than simple closure (e.g., requiring intermediate, or complex closure) is performed, report the appropriate closure CPT codes (12031-12057 for intermediate, 13100-13153 for complex) in addition to appropriate lesion removal code (11400-11446). For reconstructive closure report CPT codes 14000-14300, 15000-15261, and 15570-15770 in addition to appropriate lesion removal code. If electrosurgery, cryosurgery, laser, or chemical treatment is used, consult CPT codes 17000 and subsequent codes.

Each benign lesion excised should be reported separately. If the excision is unusual or complicated, append modifier 22 or 09922.

Code selection is based on excised diameter, which is defined as lesion diameter plus most narrow margins required to completely excise the lesion. Measurements should be taken prior to excision.

| 11400 | Excision, benign lesion including margins, except skin tag (unless listed elsewhere), trunk, arms or legs; excised diameter 0.5 cm or less | T |
| | AMA: 2002, Nov, 5; 1996, May, 11; 1995, Fall, 3; 1993, Fall, 7 | |

| 11401 | excised diameter 0.6 to 1.0 cm | T |
| | AMA: 2002, Nov, 5; 1996, May, 11; 1995, Fall, 3; 1993, Fall, 7 | |

| 11402 | excised diameter 1.1 to 2.0 cm | T |
| | AMA: 2002, Nov, 5; 1996, May, 11; 1995, Fall, 3; 1993, Fall, 7 | |

| 11403 | excised diameter 2.1 to 3.0 cm | T |
| | AMA: 2002, Nov, 5; 1996, May, 11; 1995, Fall, 3; 1993, Fall, 7 | |

11404	excised diameter 3.1 to 4.0 cm	1 T
	MED: 100-2, 15, 260; 100-4, 12, 90.3; 100-4, 14, 10	
	AMA: 2002, Nov, 5; 1996, May, 11; 1995, Fall, 3; 1993, Fall, 7	

11406	excised diameter over 4.0 cm	2 T
	MED: 100-2, 15, 260; 100-4, 12, 90.3; 100-4, 14, 10	
	AMA: 2002, Nov, 5; 1996, May, 11; 1995, Fall, 3; 1993, Fall, 7	

11420   **Excision, benign lesion including margins, except skin tag (unless listed elsewhere), scalp, neck, hands, feet, genitalia; excised diameter 0.5 cm or less**   Ⓣ 🡔
          AMA: 1995, Fall, 3

11421   **excised diameter 0.6 to 1.0 cm**   Ⓣ 🡔
               AMA: 1996, May, 11; 1995, Fall, 3

11422   **excised diameter 1.1 to 2.0 cm**   Ⓣ 🡔
               AMA: 1996, May, 11; 1995, Fall, 3

11423   **excised diameter 2.1 to 3.0 cm**   Ⓣ 🡔
               AMA: 1996, May, 11; 1995, Fall, 3

11424   **excised diameter 3.1 to 4.0 cm**   ② Ⓣ 🡔
               MED: 100-2, 15, 260; 100-4, 12, 90.3; 100-4, 14, 10

               AMA: 1996, May, 11; 1995, Fall, 3

11426   **excised diameter over 4.0 cm**   ② Ⓣ 🡔
               MED: 100-2, 15, 260; 100-4, 12, 90.3; 100-4, 14, 10

               AMA: 1996, May, 11; 1995, Fall, 3

▲ 11440   **Excision, other benign lesion including margins, except skin tag (unless listed elsewhere), face, ears, eyelids, nose, lips, mucous membrane; excised diameter 0.5 cm or less**   Ⓣ 🡔
             AMA: 1996, May, 11; 1995, Fall, 3

▲ 11441   **excised diameter 0.6 to 1.0 cm**   Ⓣ 🡔
                  AMA: 1996, May, 11; 1995, Fall, 3

▲ 11442   **excised diameter 1.1 to 2.0 cm**   Ⓣ 🡔
                  AMA: 2000, Aug, 5; 1996, May, 11; 1995, Fall, 3

▲ 11443   **excised diameter 2.1 to 3.0 cm**   Ⓣ 🡔
                  AMA: 1996, May, 11; 1995, Fall, 3

▲ 11444   **excised diameter 3.1 to 4.0 cm**   ① Ⓣ 🡔
                  MED: 100-2, 15, 260; 100-4, 12, 90.3; 100-4, 14, 10

                  AMA: 1996, May, 11; 1995, Fall, 3

▲ 11446   **excised diameter over 4.0 cm**   ② Ⓣ 🡔
                  MED: 100-2, 15, 260; 100-4, 12, 90.3; 100-4, 14, 10

                  AMA: 1996, May, 11; 1995, Fall, 3

If the excision on the eyelids involves more than skin, consult CPT code 67800 and subsequent codes.

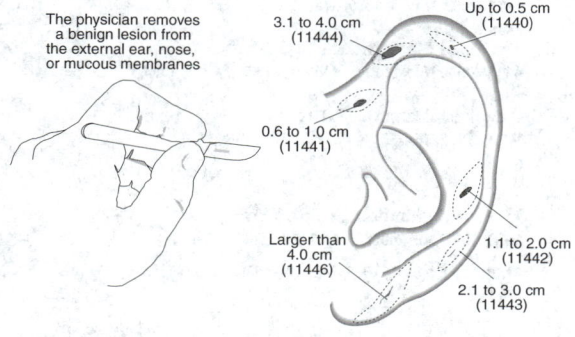

The physician removes a benign lesion from the external ear, nose, or mucous membranes

Up to 0.5 cm (11440)

3.1 to 4.0 cm (11444)

0.6 to 1.0 cm (11441)

Larger than 4.0 cm (11446)

1.1 to 2.0 cm (11442)

2.1 to 3.0 cm (11443)

26 / TC Professional/Technical Component   80 / 80 Assist-at-Surgery Allowed/With Documentation   ⊙ Conscious Sedation
Unlisted   Not Covered   **MED:** Pubs 100/NCD Reference   1 - 9 ASC Group   63 Modifier 63 Exempt
76 — Surgery   CPT only © 2005 American Medical Association. All Rights Reserved. *(Black Ink)*   © 2005 Ingenix, Inc. *(Blue Ink)*

11450   **Excision of skin and subcutaneous tissue for hidradenitis, axillary; with simple or intermediate repair**   2 T 🔲
          MED: 100-2, 15, 260; 100-4, 12, 90.3; 100-4, 14, 10

11451   **with complex repair**   2 T 80 🔲
          MED: 100-2, 15, 260; 100-4, 12, 90.3; 100-4, 14, 10

          If a skin graft or flap is used for closure, consult the appropriate CPT code and use in addition to 11451.

11462   **Excision of skin and subcutaneous tissue for hidradenitis, inguinal; with simple or intermediate repair**   2 T 80 🔲
          MED: 100-2, 15, 260; 100-4, 12, 90.3; 100-4, 14, 10

11463   **with complex repair**   2 T 80 🔲
          MED: 100-2, 15, 260; 100-4, 12, 90.3; 100-4, 14, 10

          If a skin graft or flap is used for closure, consult the appropriate CPT code and use in addition to 11463.

11470   **Excision of skin and subcutaneous tissue for hidradenitis, perianal, perineal, or umbilical; with simple or intermediate repair**   2 T 🔲
          MED: 100-2, 15, 260; 100-4, 12, 90.3; 100-4, 14, 10

11471   **with complex repair**   2 T 80 🔲
          MED: 100-2, 15, 260; 100-4, 12, 90.3; 100-4, 14, 10

          If codes 11450-11471 are performed bilaterally, append modifier 50 or 09950.

          If a skin graft or flap is used for closure, consult the appropriate CPT code and use in addition to 11471.

EXCISION — MALIGNANT LESIONS

Excision is defined as a full-thickness removal of lesion including simple closure of the wound. Excision codes are selected on the basis of the type of lesion (benign or malignant), anatomic site, and lesion diameter. Benign lesions include those described as cicatricial, fibrous, inflammatory, congenital and cystic as well as any other lesion that is noninvasive or nonmalignant. Malignant lesions are typically invasive or have the potential to metastasize. Examples of malignant lesions are basal cell carcinomas and melanomas of the skin.

Layered, intermediate or complex closure of the defect created by the excision of the lesion is separately reported.

If an excision of a malignant lesion(s) requiring more than simple closure (e.g., requiring intermediate, or complex closure) is performed, report the appropriate closure CPT codes (12031-12057 for intermediate, 13100-13153 for complex) in addition to appropriate lesion removal code (11600-11646). For reconstructive closure report CPT codes14000-14300, 15000-15261, and 15570-15770 in addition to appropriate lesion removal code.

Code selection is based on excised diameter, which is defined as lesion diameter plus most narrow margins required to completely excise the lesion. Measurements should be taken prior to excision.

If pathology shows margins were not large enough for complete lesion removal and an additional excision is performed at the same session, report only one code based on the greatest excised diameter. For re-excision at subsequent sessions, consult CPT codes 11600-11646, and append modifier 58 when appropriate.

11600   **Excision, malignant lesion including margins, trunk, arms, or legs; excised diameter 0.5 cm or less**   T 🔲
          AMA: 2002, Nov, 5; 1996, May, 11; 1995, Fall, 3

11601   **excised diameter 0.6 to 1.0 cm**   T 🔲
          AMA: 1996, May, 11; 1995, Fall, 3

Integumentary System

11602 — 11646

11602	excised diameter 1.1 to 2.0 cm AMA: 1996, May, 11; 1995, Fall, 3	T ↻
11603	excised diameter 2.1 to 3.0 cm AMA: 1996, May, 11; 1995, Fall, 3	T ↻
11604	excised diameter 3.1 to 4.0 cm MED: 100-2, 15, 260; 100-4, 12, 90.3; 100-4, 14, 10 AMA: 1996, May, 11; 1995, Fall, 3	2 T ↻
11606	excised diameter over 4.0 cm MED: 100-2, 15, 260; 100-4, 12, 90.3; 100-4, 14, 10 AMA: 1996, May, 11; 1995, Fall, 3; 1991, Fall, 6	2 T ↻
11620	**Excision, malignant lesion including margins, scalp, neck, hands, feet, genitalia; excised diameter 0.5 cm or less** AMA: 2002, Nov, 5; 1995, Fall, 3	T ↻
11621	excised diameter 0.6 to 1.0 cm AMA: 1996, May, 11; 1995, Fall, 3	T ↻
11622	excised diameter 1.1 to 2.0 cm AMA: 1996, May, 11; 1995, Fall, 3	T ↻
11623	excised diameter 2.1 to 3.0 cm AMA: 1996, May, 11; 1995, Fall, 3	T ↻
11624	excised diameter 3.1 to 4.0 cm MED: 100-2, 15, 260; 100-4, 12, 90.3; 100-4, 14, 10 AMA: 1996, May, 11; 1995, Fall, 3	2 T ↻
11626	excised diameter over 4.0 cm MED: 100-2, 15, 260; 100-4, 12, 90.3; 100-4, 14, 10 AMA: 1996, May, 11; 1995, Fall, 3	2 T ↻
11640	**Excision, malignant lesion including margins, face, ears, eyelids, nose, lips; excised diameter 0.5 cm or less** AMA: 2002, Nov, 5; 1996, May, 11; 1995, Fall, 3	T ↻
11641	excised diameter 0.6 to 1.0 cm AMA: 1996, May, 11; 1995, Fall, 3	T ↻
11642	excised diameter 1.1 to 2.0 cm AMA: 1996, May, 11; 1995, Fall, 3	T ↻
11643	excised diameter 2.1 to 3.0 cm AMA: 1996, May, 11; 1995, Fall, 3	T ↻
11644	excised diameter 3.1 to 4.0 cm MED: 100-2, 15, 260; 100-4, 12, 90.3; 100-4, 14, 10 AMA: 1996, May, 11; 1995, Fall, 3	2 T ↻
11646	excised diameter over 4.0 cm MED: 100-2, 15, 260; 100-4, 12, 90.3; 100-4, 14, 10 AMA: 1996, May, 11; 1995, Fall, 3	2 T ↻

If the excision on the eyelids involves more than skin, consult CPT code 67800 and subsequent codes.

26 / **TC** Professional/Technical Component   **80**/**80** Assist-at-Surgery Allowed/With Documentation   ☉ Conscious Sedation

Unlisted   Not Covered   **MED:** Pubs 100/NCD Reference   **1**-**9** ASC Group   ⑥③ Modifier 63 Exempt

78 — Surgery   CPT only © 2005 American Medical Association. All Rights Reserved. *(Black Ink)*   © 2005 Ingenix, Inc. *(Blue Ink)*

NAILS

If drainage of a paronychia or onychia is performed, consult CPT codes 10060 and 10061.

11719   **Trimming of nondystrophic nails, any number**   T ⟳
MED: 100-2, 16, 100; 100-3, 1, 70.2.1

AMA: 2002, Nov, 5; 2002, Dec, 4; 1997, Nov, 12

11720   **Debridement of nail(s) by any method(s); one to five**   T ⟳
MED: 100-2, 16, 100; 100-3, 1, 70.2.1

AMA: 2002, Nov, 5; 2002, Dec, 4

11721   **six or more**   T ⟳
MED: 100-2, 16, 100; 100-3, 1, 70.2.1

AMA: 2002, Nov, 5; 2002, Dec, 4

11730   **Avulsion of nail plate, partial or complete, simple; single**   T ⟳
MED: 100-2, 16, 100; 100-3, 1, 70.2.1

AMA: 2002, Nov, 5; 2002, Dec, 4; 1996, Mar, 10

+   **11732**   **each additional nail plate (List separately in addition to code for primary procedure)**   T ⟳
MED: 100-2, 16, 100; 100-3, 1, 70.2.1

AMA: 2002, Nov, 5; 2002, Dec, 4

Note that 11732 is an add-on code and must be used in conjunction with 11730.

11740   **Evacuation of subungual hematoma**   T ⟳
AMA: 2002, Nov, 5; 2002, Dec, 4

11750   **Excision of nail and nail matrix, partial or complete, (eg, ingrown or deformed nail) for permanent removal;**   T ⟳
MED: 100-2, 16, 100; 100-3, 1, 70.2.1

AMA: 2002, Nov, 5; 2002, Dec, 4

11752   **with amputation of tuft of distal phalanx**   T ⟳
AMA: 2002, Nov, 5

If a skin graft is performed, consult CPT code 15050.

11755   **Biopsy of nail unit (eg, plate, bed, matrix, hyponychium, proximal and lateral nail folds) (separate procedure)**   T 80 ⟳
AMA: 2002, Nov, 5; 1996, Mar, 11

11760   **Repair of nail bed**   T ⟳
AMA: 2002, Nov, 5; 2002, Dec, 4

11762   **Reconstruction of nail bed with graft**   T ⟳
AMA: 2002, Nov, 5; 2002, Dec, 4

11765   **Wedge excision of skin of nail fold (eg, for ingrown toenail)**   T ⟳
AMA: 2002, Nov, 5; 2002, Dec, 4

Cotting's operation

PILONIDAL CYST

11770   **Excision of pilonidal cyst or sinus; simple**   3 T ⟳
MED: 100-2, 15, 260; 100-4, 12, 90.3; 100-4, 14, 10

If a pilonidal cyst is incised, consult CPT codes 10080 and 10081.

| ⟳ CCI Comp | 50 Bilateral Procedure | + CPT Add-on Code | ⊘ Modifier -51 Exempt | ♂ Male | ♀ Female |
| ● New Code | ▲ Revised Code | M Maternity Edit | A Age Edit | A–Y APC Status Ind. | AMA: CPT Assistant |

© 2005 Ingenix, Inc. *(Blue Ink)*   CPT only © 2005 American Medical Association. All Rights Reserved. *(Black Ink)*   Surgery — 79

Integumentary System

11771 — 11977

11771	extensive	3 T ▣

MED: 100-2, 15, 260; 100-4, 12, 90.3; 100-4, 14, 10

11772	complicated	3 T ▣

MED: 100-2, 15, 260; 100-4, 12, 90.3; 100-4, 14, 10

INTRODUCTION

11900   **Injection, intralesional; up to and including seven lesions**   T ▣
       AMA: 2000, Feb, 11; 1998, May, 10; 1996, Sep, 5

11901   **more than seven lesions**   T ▣
       AMA: 2000, Feb, 11; 1998, May, 10; 1996, Sep, 5

If the injection of sclerosing solution is for a vein, consult CPT codes 36470-36471. If intralesional chemotherapy is administered, consult CPT codes 96405-96406.

Do not report 11900, 11901 for preoperative local anesthetic injections.

11920   **Tattooing, intradermal introduction of insoluble opaque pigments to correct color defects of skin, including micropigmentation;**
       6.0 sq. cm or less   T 80 ▣
       MED: 100-2, 16, 10; 100-2, 16, 120; 100-2, 16, 180; 100-4, 12, 70; 100-4, 13, 20; 100-4, 13, 90

11921   **6.1 to 20.0 sq. cm**   T 80 ▣
       MED: 100-2, 16, 10; 100-2, 16, 120; 100-2, 16, 180; 100-4, 12, 70; 100-4, 13, 20; 100-4, 13, 90

+ **11922**   **each additional 20.0 sq. cm (List separately in addition to code**
       for primary procedure)   T 80
       MED: 100-2, 16, 10; 100-2, 16, 120; 100-2, 16, 180

Note that 11922 is an add-on code and must be used in conjunction with 11921.

11950   **Subcutaneous injection of filling material (eg, collagen); 1 cc or less** T 80 ▣
       MED: 100-2, 16, 10; 100-2, 16, 120; 100-2, 16, 180; 100-3, 230.10

11951   **1.1 to 5.0 cc**   T 80 ▣
       MED: 100-2, 16, 10; 100-2, 16, 120; 100-2, 16, 180; 100-3, 230.10

11952   **5.1 to 10.0 cc**   T 80 ▣
       MED: 100-2, 16, 10; 100-2, 16, 120; 100-2, 16, 180; 100-3, 230.10

11954   **over 10.0 cc**   T 80 ▣
       MED: 100-2, 16, 10; 100-2, 16, 120; 100-2, 16, 180; 100-3, 230.10

11960   **Insertion of tissue expander(s) for other than breast, including subcutaneous expansion**   2 T ▣
       MED: 100-2, 15, 260; 100-4, 12, 90.3; 100-4, 14, 10

If the breast is reconstructed with a tissue expander(s), consult CPT code 19357.

11970   **Replacement of tissue expander with permanent prosthesis**   3 T ▣
       MED: 100-2, 15, 260; 100-4, 12, 90.3; 100-4, 14, 10

11971   **Removal of tissue expander(s) without insertion of prosthesis**   1 T 80 ▣
       MED: 100-2, 15, 260; 100-4, 12, 90.3; 100-4, 14, 10

11975   **Insertion, implantable contraceptive capsules**   ♀ E

11976   **Removal, implantable contraceptive capsules**   ♀ T 80 ▣

11977   **Removal with reinsertion, implantable contraceptive capsules**   ♀ E

11980	**Subcutaneous hormone pellet implantation (implantation of estradiol and/or testosterone pellets beneath the skin)** ☒ 🔗	
	AMA: 1999, Nov, 8	
11981	**Insertion, non-biodegradable drug delivery implant** ☒ 80 🔗	
11982	**Removal, non-biodegradable drug delivery implant** ☒ 80 🔗	
11983	**Removal with reinsertion, non-biodegradable drug delivery implant** ☒ 80 🔗	

REPAIR (CLOSURE)

Repair is the surgical closure of a wound. The wound may be a result of injury/trauma or it may be a surgically created defect. Repairs can be any of the following:

- Stand alone procedures

- Separately reportable services when performed with certain other procedures as in the case of excisions requiring intermediate or complex repair

- An integral part of a more complex procedure and not separately reportable

Repairs are divided into three categories: simple, intermediate, and complex. They are further described by anatomic site and wound size.

Simple repair is performed when the wound is superficial, e.g., involving partial or full-thickness damage to the skin and/or subcutaneous tissues. There is no significant involvement of deeper structures and only simple, one layer, primary suturing is required. This procedure includes local anesthetic and chemical or electrocauterization of wounds not closed. Wounds closed with adhesive strips should be reported using the appropriate evaluation and management code.

Intermediate repair is performed for wounds and lacerations in which one or more of the deeper layers of subcutaneous tissue and non-muscle fascia are repaired in addition to the skin and subcutaneous tissue. Single-layer closure can also be coded as an intermediate repair if the wound is heavily contaminated and requires extensive cleaning or removal of particulate matter.

Complex repair includes repair of wounds requiring more than layered closure. Wounds coded from this category include those requiring revision, debridement, extensive undermining, and placement of stents or retention sutures. Complex repairs also include those requiring creation of a defect (e.g., extending excision) and special preparation of the site.

The following rules should be followed when reporting repairs:

1. Measure the length of the repaired wound or wounds and report in centimeters. A centimeter is 0.39 inches.

2. Add together the lengths of multiple wounds in the same classification and report as a single item.

   For example, a simple repair of a 2-centimeter scalp wound and a simple repair of a 1.5-centimeter wound of the forearm would be reported with a single code.

   12002   Simple repair of superficial wounds of scalp, neck, axillae, external genitalia, trunk and/or extremities (including hands and feet); 2.6 cm to 7.5 cm

   This procedure is coded with a single procedure code because both wounds are classified as simple and both are in the same group of simple repairs (12001–12007). Total length of the two wounds is 3.5 centimeters so 12002 is reported.

3. Wounds in more than one classification should be listed separately with the more complicated service listed as the primary procedure and the less complicated listed as the secondary procedure with modifier 51 Multiple procedures appended.

4. Decontamination and debridement are considered integral to wound repair except when gross contamination requires prolonged cleansing or when appreciable amounts of devitalized contaminated tissue must be removed.

5. Repair of nerves, blood vessels, and tendons should be reported under the appropriate system. Repair of associated skin wounds is considered integral to the repair of nerves, blood vessels, and tendons and is not reported separately unless the wound repair qualifies as complex. In these instances report the complex repair code.

6. Simple exploration of nerves, blood vessels, and tendons exposed in an open wound is considered integral to the repair and should not be reported separately.

7. Wounds resulting from penetrating trauma that require exploration, enlargement, extension, dissection, removal of foreign body, and/or ligation or coagulation of minor blood vessels of subcutaneous tissue, muscle fascia, or muscle should be reported with 20100–20103 as indicated.

REPAIR — SIMPLE

12001   **Simple repair of superficial wounds of scalp, neck, axillae, external genitalia, trunk and/or extremities (including hands and feet); 2.5 cm or less**   T ⏁
AMA: 2002, Jan, 10; 2000, Jul, 10; 2000, Jan, 11; 2000, Apr, 8; 1998, Feb, 11; 1996, Jun, 7

12002   **2.6 cm to 7.5 cm**   T ⏁
AMA: 2002, Jan, 10

12004   **7.6 cm to 12.5 cm**   T ⏁
AMA: 2002, Jan, 10

12005   **12.6 cm to 20.0 cm**   2 T ⏁
MED: 100-2, 15, 260; 100-4, 12, 90.3; 100-4, 14, 10

AMA: 2002, Jan, 10

12006   **20.1 cm to 30.0 cm**   2 T ⏁
MED: 100-2, 15, 260; 100-4, 12, 90.3; 100-4, 14, 10

AMA: 2002, Jan, 10; 1998, Feb, 11

12007   **over 30.0 cm**   2 T ⏁
MED: 100-2, 15, 260; 100-4, 12, 90.3; 100-4, 14, 10

AMA: 2002, Jan, 10

12011   **Simple repair of superficial wounds of face, ears, eyelids, nose, lips and/or mucous membranes; 2.5 cm or less**   T ⏁
AMA: 2002, Jan, 10; 2000, May, 8

12013   **2.6 cm to 5.0 cm**   T ⏁
AMA: 2002, Jan, 10

12014   **5.1 cm to 7.5 cm**   T ⏁
AMA: 2002, Jan, 10

12015   **7.6 cm to 12.5 cm**   T ⏁
AMA: 2002, Jan, 10

12016   **12.6 cm to 20.0 cm**   2 T ⏁
MED: 100-2, 15, 260; 100-4, 12, 90.3; 100-4, 14, 10

AMA: 2002, Jan, 10

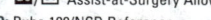

12017	**20.1 cm to 30.0 cm**	2 T 80 ⏎
	MED: 100-2, 15, 260; 100-4, 12, 90.3; 100-4, 14, 10	
	AMA: 2002, Jan, 10	

12018	**over 30.0 cm**	2 T 80 ⏎
	MED: 100-2, 15, 260; 100-4, 12, 90.3; 100-4, 14, 10	
	AMA: 2002, Jan, 10	

12020	**Treatment of superficial wound dehiscence; simple closure**	1 T ⏎
	MED: 100-2, 15, 260; 100-4, 12, 90.3; 100-4, 14, 10	
	AMA: 2002, Jan, 10	

12021	**with packing**	1 T ⏎
	MED: 100-2, 15, 260; 100-4, 12, 90.3; 100-4, 14, 10	
	AMA: 2002, Jan, 10	

If the secondary wound closure is extensive or complicated, consult CPT code 13160.

REPAIR — INTERMEDIATE

| 12031 | **Layer closure of wounds of scalp, axillae, trunk and/or extremities (excluding hands and feet); 2.5 cm or less** | T ⏎ |
| | AMA: 2002, Jan, 10; 2000, Apr, 8; 1997, Sep, 11 | |

| 12032 | **2.6 cm to 7.5 cm** | T ⏎ |
| | AMA: 2002, Jan, 10; 1996, Jun, 8 | |

12034	**7.6 cm to 12.5 cm**	2 T ⏎
	MED: 100-2, 15, 260; 100-4, 12, 90.3; 100-4, 14, 10	
	AMA: 2002, Jan, 10; 1991, Fall, 6	

12035	**12.6 cm to 20.0 cm**	2 T ⏎
	MED: 100-2, 15, 260; 100-4, 12, 90.3; 100-4, 14, 10	
	AMA: 2002, Jan, 10	

12036	**20.1 cm to 30.0 cm**	2 T ⏎
	MED: 100-2, 15, 260; 100-4, 12, 90.3; 100-4, 14, 10	
	AMA: 2002, Jan, 10	

12037	**over 30.0 cm**	2 T 80 ⏎
	MED: 100-2, 15, 260; 100-4, 12, 90.3; 100-4, 14, 10	
	AMA: 2002, Jan, 10	

| 12041 | **Layer closure of wounds of neck, hands, feet and/or external genitalia; 2.5 cm or less** | T ⏎ |
| | AMA: 2002, Jan, 10; 2000, Apr, 8; 1997, Sep, 11 | |

| 12042 | **2.6 cm to 7.5 cm** | T ⏎ |
| | AMA: 2002, Jan, 10 | |

12044	**7.6 cm to 12.5 cm**	2 T ⏎
	MED: 100-2, 15, 260; 100-4, 12, 90.3; 100-4, 14, 10	
	AMA: 2002, Jan, 10	

12045	**12.6 cm to 20.0 cm**	2 T ⏎
	MED: 100-2, 15, 260; 100-4, 12, 90.3; 100-4, 14, 10	
	AMA: 2002, Jan, 10	

Integumentary System

12017 — 12045

Integumentary System

12046 — 13121

12046	**20.1 cm to 30.0 cm**	2 T 80 ⬚

MED: 100-2, 15, 260; 100-4, 12, 90.3; 100-4, 14, 10

AMA: 2002, Jan, 10

12047	**over 30.0 cm**	2 T 80 ⬚

MED: 100-2, 15, 260; 100-4, 12, 90.3; 100-4, 14, 10

AMA: 2002, Jan, 10

12051	**Layer closure of wounds of face, ears, eyelids, nose, lips and/or mucous membranes; 2.5 cm or less**	T ⬚

AMA: 2002, Jan, 10; 2000, Apr, 8; 1997, Sep, 11

12052	**2.6 cm to 5.0 cm**	T ⬚

AMA: 2002, Jan, 10

12053	**5.1 cm to 7.5 cm**	T ⬚

AMA: 2002, Jan, 10

12054	**7.6 cm to 12.5 cm**	2 T ⬚

MED: 100-2, 15, 260; 100-4, 12, 90.3; 100-4, 14, 10

AMA: 2002, Jan, 10

12055	**12.6 cm to 20.0 cm**	2 T ⬚

MED: 100-2, 15, 260; 100-4, 12, 90.3; 100-4, 14, 10

AMA: 2002, Jan, 10

12056	**20.1 cm to 30.0 cm**	2 T 80 ⬚

MED: 100-2, 15, 260; 100-4, 12, 90.3; 100-4, 14, 10

AMA: 2002, Jan, 10

12057	**over 30.0 cm**	2 T 80 ⬚

MED: 100-2, 15, 260; 100-4, 12, 90.3; 100-4, 14, 10

AMA: 2002, Jan, 10

REPAIR — COMPLEX

13100	**Repair, complex, trunk; 1.1 cm to 2.5 cm**	2 T ⬚

MED: 100-2, 15, 260; 100-4, 12, 90.3; 100-4, 14, 10

AMA: 2000, Apr, 8; 1999, Nov, 9-10; 1998, Dec, 5; 1997, Sep, 11

If the repair is 1.0 cm or less, see simple or intermediate repairs.

13101	**2.6 cm to 7.5 cm**	3 T ⬚

MED: 100-2, 15, 260; 100-4, 12, 90.3; 100-4, 14, 10

AMA: 1999, Nov, 9-10; 1998, Dec, 5

+ 13102	**each additional 5 cm or less (List separately in addition to code for primary procedure)**	T ⬚

AMA: 1999, Nov, 9-10

Note that 13102 is an add-on code and must be used in conjunction with 13101.

13120	**Repair, complex, scalp, arms, and/or legs; 1.1 cm to 2.5 cm**	2 T ⬚

MED: 100-2, 15, 260; 100-4, 12, 90.3; 100-4, 14, 10

AMA: 2000, Apr, 8; 1999, Nov, 9-10; 1999, Apr, 11; 1997, Sep, 11

If the repair is 1.0 cm or less, see simple or intermediate repairs.

13121	**2.6 cm to 7.5 cm**	3 T ⬚

MED: 100-2, 15, 260; 100-4, 12, 90.3; 100-4, 14, 10

AMA: 2000, Feb, 10; 1999, Nov, 9-10; 1998, Dec, 5

+   **13122**   **each additional 5 cm or less (List separately in addition to code for primary procedure)**   T ↻
                         AMA: 1999, Nov, 10

                Note that 13122 is an add-on code and must be used in conjunction with 13121.

13131   **Repair, complex, forehead, cheeks, chin, mouth, neck, axillae, genitalia, hands and/or feet; 1.1 cm to 2.5 cm**   2 T ↻
                         MED: 100-2, 15, 260; 100-4, 12, 90.3; 100-4, 14, 10

                         AMA: 2000, Apr, 8; 1999, Nov, 10; 1998, Dec, 5; 1997, Sep, 11; 1993, Fall, 7

                If the repair is 1.0 cm or less, see simple or intermediate repairs.

13132   **2.6 cm to 7.5 cm**   3 T ↻
                         MED: 100-2, 15, 260; 100-4, 12, 90.3; 100-4, 14, 10

                         AMA: 1999, Nov, 10; 1999, Dec, 10; 1998, Dec, 5; 1993, Fall, 7

+   **13133**   **each additional 5 cm or less (List separately in addition to code for primary procedure)**   T ↻
                         AMA: 1998, Nov, 10

                Note that 13133 is an add-on code and must be used in conjunction with 13132.

13150   **Repair, complex, eyelids, nose, ears and/or lips; 1.0 cm or less**   3 T ↻
                         MED: 100-2, 15, 260; 100-4, 12, 90.3; 100-4, 14, 10

                         AMA: 2000, Apr, 8; 1999, Nov, 10; 1998, Dec, 5; 1997, Sep, 11

                Consult also CPT codes 40650-40654, and 67961-67975.

13151   **1.1 cm to 2.5 cm**   3 T ↻
                         MED: 100-2, 15, 260; 100-4, 12, 90.3; 100-4, 14, 10

                         AMA: 1999, Nov, 10; 1998, Dec, 5

13152   **2.6 cm to 7.5 cm**   3 T ↻
                         MED: 100-2, 15, 260; 100-4, 12, 90.3; 100-4, 14, 10

                         AMA: 1999, Nov, 10; 1998, Dec, 5

+   **13153**   **each additional 5 cm or less (List separately in addition to code for primary procedure)**   T ↻
                         AMA: 1999, Nov, 10

                If full thickness repair of the lip or the eyelid is required, consult relevant anatomical subsections.

                Note that 13153 is an add-on code and must be used in conjunction with 13152.

13160   **Secondary closure of surgical wound or dehiscence, extensive or complicated**   2 T ↻
                         MED: 100-2, 15, 260; 100-4, 12, 90.3; 100-4, 14, 10

                         AMA: 2000, Apr, 8; 1998, Dec, 5; 1997, Sep, 11

                To report packing or simple secondary wound closure, consult CPT codes 12020 and 12021.

ADJACENT TISSUE TRANSFER OR REARRANGEMENT

Anatomic site and size of the defect defines adjacent tissue transfer or rearrangement. Adjacent tissue transfers include excision of the defect or lesion so excision codes should not be reported additionally. For code selection, the term defect includes both primary and secondary defects. The primary defect results from the excision and the secondary defect results from the creation of the flap design. Measure both defects together to determine code selection.

Terms used to describe transfer or rearrangement procedures include: Z-plasty, W-plasty, V-Y-plasty, rotation flap, advancement flap, double pedicle flap. When applied to primary traumatic wound closure, the configuration listed must be developed by the surgeon to accomplish the repair. Transfer and rearrangement codes should not be applied when traumatic wounds incidentally result in these configurations.

Tissue transfer or rearrangement codes describe moving normal tissue from the donor site to the recipient site. The donor site is adjacent or next to the affected area, allowing the tissue to remain attached to its original location and blood supply, ensuring survival of the graft.

A skin graft that is needed to close a secondary defect is an additional procedure.

Refer to the specific anatomical subsections for CPT codes for full-thickness repairs of the lips and eyelids.

14000   **Adjacent tissue transfer or rearrangement, trunk; defect 10 sq. cm or less**   ② T ▣
MED: 100-2, 15, 260; 100-4, 12, 90.3; 100-4, 14, 10

AMA: 2000, Jul, 10; 1999, Jul, 3; 1996, Sep, 11

Burrow's operation

14001   **defect 10.1 sq. cm to 30.0 sq. cm**   ③ T ▣
MED: 100-2, 15, 260; 100-4, 12, 90.3; 100-4, 14, 10

AMA: 1999, Jul, 3

14020   **Adjacent tissue transfer or rearrangement, scalp, arms and/or legs; defect 10 sq. cm or less**   ③ T ▣
MED: 100-2, 15, 260; 100-4, 12, 90.3; 100-4, 14, 10

AMA: 1999, Jul, 3

14021   **defect 10.1 sq. cm to 30.0 sq. cm**   ③ T ▣
MED: 100-2, 15, 260; 100-4, 12, 90.3; 100-4, 14, 10

AMA: 1999, Jul, 3

14040   **Adjacent tissue transfer or rearrangement, forehead, cheeks, chin, mouth, neck, axillae, genitalia, hands and/or feet; defect 10 sq. cm or less**   ② T ▣
MED: 100-2, 15, 260; 100-4, 12, 90.3; 100-4, 14, 10

AMA: 2000, Jul, 10; 1999, Jul, 3

Krimer's palatoplasty

14041   **defect 10.1 sq. cm to 30.0 sq. cm**   ③ T ▣
MED: 100-2, 15, 260; 100-4, 12, 90.3; 100-4, 14, 10

AMA: 1999, Jul, 3

14060   **Adjacent tissue transfer or rearrangement, eyelids, nose, ears and/or lips; defect 10 sq. cm or less**   ③ T ▣
MED: 100-2, 15, 260; 100-4, 12, 90.3; 100-4, 14, 10

AMA: 1999, Jul, 3; 1999, Dec, 10; 1993, Fall, 7

Denonvillier's operation

14061   **defect 10.1 sq. cm to 30.0 sq. cm**   ③ T ▣
MED: 100-2, 15, 260; 100-4, 12, 90.3; 100-4, 14, 10

AMA: 1999, Jul, 3

14300   Adjacent tissue transfer or rearrangement, more than 30 sq. cm, unusual or complicated, any area   4 T ▨
MED: 100-2, 15, 260; 100-4, 12, 90.3; 100-4, 14, 10

AMA: 1996, Sep, 11

14350   Filleted finger or toe flap, including preparation of recipient site   3 T 80 ▨
MED: 100-2, 15, 260; 100-4, 12, 90.3; 100-4, 14, 10

SKIN REPLACEMENT SURGERY AND SKIN SUBSTITUTE

The site where the tissue originates is referred to as the donor site, while the site where the tissue is being relocated is referred to as the recipient site.

Skin replacement surgery and skin substitute codes are chosen by the size and location of the defect (recipient site) and the type of graft or skin substitute. The codes include uncomplicated debridement of granulation tissue or recent avulsion.

Surgical preparation of the recipient site should be reported separately with codes 15000–15001. These codes should also be used for burn and wound preparation or incisional or excisional scar contracture release that requires a skin graft.

Use 100 square cm for children age 10 and older and percentages of body surface area for infants and children under the age of 10.

Report codes 15100–15261 by recipient site for autologous skin grafts. For autologous tissue-cultured epidermal grafts, consult 15150–15157. Report 15040 for harvesting of autologous keratinocytes and dermal tissue for tissue-cultured skin grafts. Report 15170–15176 for acellular dermal replacement. Add modifier 58 for staged application procedures.

These codes require that the graft be anchored and not just stabilized with dressings.

SURGICAL PREPARATION

▲ **15000**   Surgical preparation or creation of recipient site by excision of open wounds, burn eschar, or scar (including subcutaneous tissues), or incisional release of scar contracture; first 100 sq cm or one percent of body area of infants and children   2 T ▨
MED: 100-2, 15, 260; 100-3, 270.5; 100-4, 12, 90.3; 100-4, 14, 10

AMA: 2002, Nov, 5; 1999, May, 10; 1999, Jan, 4; 1999, Apr, 10; 1998, Nov, 5; 1997, Sep, 1; 1997, Aug, 6; 1997, Apr, 4; 1993, Fall, 7

To report skin grafts or replacements, consult 15050-15261, 15330-15336. List the graft or replacement separately by procedure code number when the graft, immediate or delayed, is applied.

+ ▲ **15001**   each additional 100 sq cm or each additional one percent of body area of infants and children (List separately in addition to code for primary procedure)   T 1 80
AMA: 1999, May, 10; 1999, Jan, 4; 1998, Nov, 5-6

Note that 15001 is an add-on code and must be used in conjunction with 15000.

Use 15000-15001 only for excision to prepare or create a recipient site with materials or dressings not listed in codes 15040-15431.

Use codes 15000-15001 in conjunction with 15050-15261 for excision with immediate placement of an allograft.

Use codes 15000-15001 in conjunction with 15300-15366 for excision with immediate placement of xenogeneic dermis.

GRAFTS

AUTOGRAFT/TISSUE CULTURED AUTOGRAFT

● **15040** Harvest of skin for tissue cultured skin autograft, 100 sq cm or less

15050 Pinch graft, single or multiple, to cover small ulcer, tip of digit, or other minimal open area (except on face), up to defect size 2 cm diameter   **2** T
MED: 100-2, 15, 260; 100-4, 12, 90.3; 100-4, 14, 10
AMA: 1998, Nov, 6; 1997, Sep, 1; 1997, Apr, 4

▲ **15100** Split-thickness autograft, trunk, arms, legs; first 100 sq cm or less, or one percent of body area of infants and children (except 15050)   **2** T
MED: 100-2, 15, 260; 100-4, 12, 90.3; 100-4, 14, 10
AMA: 2002, Sep, 3; 1998, Nov, 6; 1997, Sep, 1; 1997, Aug, 6; 1997, Apr, 4; 1993, Fall, 7

+ ▲ **15101**   each additional 100 sq cm, or each additional one percent of body area of infants and children, or part thereof (List separately in addition to code for primary procedure)   **3** T
MED: 100-2, 15, 260; 100-4, 12, 90.3; 100-4, 14, 10
AMA: 2002, Sep, 3; 1998, Nov, 6; 1997, Apr, 4

Note that 15101 is an add-on code and must be used in conjunction with 15100.

● **15110** Epidermal autograft, trunk, arms, legs; first 100 sq cm or less, or one percent of body area of infants and children

+ ● **15111**   each additional 100 sq cm, or each additional one percent of body area of infants and children, or part thereof (List separately in addition to code for primary procedure)

Note that 15111 is an add-on code and must be used in conjunction with 15110.

● **15115** Epidermal autograft, face, scalp, eyelids, mouth, neck, ears, orbits, genitalia, hands, feet, and/or multiple digits; first 100 sq cm or less, or one percent of body area of infants and children

+ ● **15116**   each additional 100 sq cm, or each additional one percent of body area of infants and children, or part thereof (List separately in addition to code for primary procedure)

Note that 15116 is an add-on code and must be used in conjunction with 15115.

▲ **15120** Split-thickness autograft, face, scalp, eyelids, mouth, neck, ears, orbits, genitalia, hands, feet, and/or multiple digits; first 100 sq cm or less, or one percent of body area of infants and children (except 15050)   **2** T
MED: 100-2, 15, 260; 100-4, 12, 90.3; 100-4, 14, 10
AMA: 2002, Sep, 3; 1999, Jan, 4; 1998, Nov, 6; 1997, Sep, 1; 1997, Aug, 6; 1997, Apr, 4

+ ▲ **15121**   each additional 100 sq cm, or each additional one percent of body area of infants and children, or part thereof (List separately in addition to code for primary procedure)   **3** T
MED: 100-2, 15, 260; 100-4, 12, 90.3; 100-4, 14, 10
AMA: 2002, Sep, 3; 1999, Jan, 4; 1998, Nov, 6; 1997, Sep, 1; 1997, Aug, 6; 1997, Apr, 4

Note that 15121 is an add-on code and must be used in conjunction with 15120. If the split graft is performed on the eyelids, consult also CPT codes 67961 and subsequent codes.

● **15130** Dermal autograft, trunk, arms, legs; first 100 sq cm or less, or one percent of body area of infants and children

+ ● **15131**   each additional 100 sq cm, or each additional one percent of body area of infants and children, or part thereof (List separately in addition to code for primary procedure)

Note that 15131 is an add-on code and must be used in conjunction with 15130.

● **15135**   Dermal autograft, face, scalp, eyelids, mouth, neck, ears, orbits, genitalia, hands, feet, and/or multiple digits; first 100 sq cm or less, or one percent of body area of infants and children

+ ● **15136**   each additional 100 sq cm, or each additional one percent of body area of infants and children, or part thereof (List separately in addition to code for primary procedure)

Note that 15136 is an add-on code and must be used in conjunction with 15135.

● **15150**   Tissue cultured epidermal autograft, trunk, arms, legs; first 25 sq cm or less

+ ● **15151**   additional 1 sq cm to 75 sq cm (List separately in addition to code for primary procedure)

Code 15151 cannot be reported more than once per session.

Note that 15151 is an add-on code and must be used in conjunction with 15150.

+ ● **15152**   each additional 100 sq cm, or each additional one percent of body area of infants and children, or part thereof (List separately in addition to code for primary procedure)

Note that 15152 is an add-on code and must be used in conjunction with 15151.

● **15155**   Tissue cultured epidermal autograft, face, scalp, eyelids, mouth, neck, ears, orbits, genitalia, hands, feet, and/or multiple digits; first 25 sq cm or less

+ ● **15156**   additional 1 sq cm to 75 sq cm (List separately in addition to code for primary procedure)

Code 15156 should not be reported more than once per session.

Note that 15156 is an add-on code and must be used in conjunction with 15155.

+ ● **15157**   each additional 100 sq cm, or each additional one percent of body area of infants and children, or part thereof (List separately in addition to code for primary procedure)

Note that 15157 is an add-on code and must be used in conjunction with 15156.

ACELLULAR DERMAL REPLACEMENT

● **15170**   Acellular dermal replacement, trunk, arms, legs; first 100 sq cm or less, or one percent of body area of infants and children

+ ● **15171**   each additional 100 sq cm, or each additional one percent of body area of infants and children, or part thereof (List separately in addition to code for primary procedure)

Note that 15171 is an add-on code and must be used in conjunction with 15170.

● **15175**   Acellular dermal replacement, face, scalp, eyelids, mouth, neck, ears, orbits, genitalia, hands, feet, and/or multiple digits; first 100 sq cm or less, or one percent of body area of infants and children

Integumentary System

15176 — 15260

+ ● **15176** each additional 100 sq cm, or each additional one percent of body area of infants and children, or part thereof (List separately in addition to code for primary procedure)

Note that 15176 is an add-on code and must be used in conjunction with 15175.

15200 Full thickness graft, free, including direct closure of donor site, trunk; 20 sq. cm or less 3 T ♦
MED: 100-2, 15, 260; 100-4, 12, 90.3; 100-4, 14, 10

AMA: 1997, Sep, 1; 1997, Aug, 6; 1996, Aug, 11

+ **15201** each additional 20 sq. cm (List separately in addition to code for primary procedure) 2 T 80
MED: 100-2, 15, 260; 100-4, 12, 90.3; 100-4, 14, 10

AMA: 1997, Sep, 1; 1997, Aug, 6; 1997, Apr, 4

Note that 15201 is an add-on code and must be used in conjunction with 15200.

15220 Full thickness graft, free, including direct closure of donor site, scalp, arms, and/or legs; 20 sq. cm or less 2 T ♦
MED: 100-2, 15, 260; 100-4, 12, 90.3; 100-4, 14, 10

AMA: 1997, Sep, 1; 1997, Aug, 6; 1997, Apr, 4

+ **15221** each additional 20 sq. cm (List separately in addition to code for primary procedure) 2 T
MED: 100-2, 15, 260; 100-4, 12, 90.3; 100-4, 14, 10

AMA: 1997, Sep, 1; 1997, Aug, 6; 1997, Apr, 4

Note that 15221 is an add-on code and must be used in conjunction with 15220.

15240 Full thickness graft, free, including direct closure of donor site, forehead, cheeks, chin, mouth, neck, axillae, genitalia, hands, and/or feet; 20 sq. cm or less 3 T ♦
MED: 100-2, 15, 260; 100-4, 12, 90.3; 100-4, 14, 10

AMA: 2000, Nov, 10; 1997, Sep, 1; 1997, Aug, 6; 1997, Apr, 4

If the flap is microvascular, consult CPT codes 15756-15758.

If the graft is performed on the fingertip, consult CPT code 15050. If the repair is performed on a web finger (syndactyly), consult CPT codes 26560-26562.

+ **15241** each additional 20 sq. cm (List separately in addition to code for primary procedure) 3 T
MED: 100-2, 15, 260; 100-4, 12, 90.3; 100-4, 14, 10

AMA: 1997, Sep, 1; 1997, Aug, 6; 1997, Apr, 4

Note that 15241 is an add-on code and must be used in conjunction with 15240.

15260 Full thickness graft, free, including direct closure of donor site, nose, ears, eyelids, and/or lips; 20 sq. cm or less 2 T ♦
MED: 100-2, 15, 260; 100-4, 12, 90.3; 100-4, 14, 10

AMA: 1999, Jul, 3; 1997, Sep, 1; 1997, Aug, 6; 1997, Apr, 4; 1993, Fall, 7; 1991, Fall, 7

+   **15261**   **each additional 20 sq. cm (List separately in addition to code for primary procedure)**   **2** **T**

MED: 100-2, 15, 260; 100-4, 12, 90.3; 100-4, 14, 10

AMA: 1997, Sep, 1; 1997, Aug, 6; 1997, Apr, 4; 1991, Fall, 7

Note that 15261 is an add-on code and must be used in conjunction with 15260. If a full-thickness graft is performed on the eyelids, consult also 67961 and subsequent codes. If the donor site repair requires a skin graft or local flaps, the procedure is to be added as an additional separate procedure.

AUTOGRAFT/TISSUE CULTURED ALLOGENIC SKIN SUBSTITUTE

●   **15300**   **Allograft skin for temporary wound closure, trunk, arms, legs; first 100 sq cm or less, or one percent of body area of infants and children**

+ ●   **15301**   **each additional 100 sq cm, or each additional one percent of body area of infants and children, or part thereof (List separately in addition to code for primary procedure)**

Note that 15301 is an add-on code and must be used in conjunction with 15300.

●   **15320**   **Allograft skin for temporary wound closure, face, scalp, eyelids, mouth, neck, ears, orbits, genitalia, hands, feet, and/or multiple digits; first 100 sq cm or less, or one percent of body area of infants and children**

+ ●   **15321**   **each additional 100 sq cm, or each additional one percent of body area of infants and children, or part thereof (List separately in addition to code for primary procedure)**

Note that 15321 is an add-on code and must be used in conjunction with 15320.

●   **15330**   **Acellular dermal allograft, trunk, arms, legs; first 100 sq cm or less, or one percent of body area of infants and children**

+ ●   **15331**   **each additional 100 sq cm, or each additional one percent of body area of infants and children, or part thereof (List separately in addition to code for primary procedure)**

Note that 15331 is an add-on code and must be used in conjunction with 15330.

●   **15335**   **Acellular dermal allograft, face, scalp, eyelids, mouth, neck, ears, orbits, genitalia, hands, feet, and/or multiple digits; first 100 sq cm or less, or one percent of body area of infants and children**

+ ●   **15336**   **each additional 100 sq cm, or each additional one percent of body area of infants and children, or part thereof (List separately in addition to code for primary procedure)**

Note that 15336 is an add-on code and must be used in conjunction with 15335.

●   **15340**   **Tissue cultured allogeneic skin substitute; first 25 sq cm or less**

+ ●   **15341**   **each additional 25 sq cm**

Note that 15341 is an add-on code and must be used in conjunction with 15340.

Codes 15340 and 15341 should not be reported with 11040-11042, 15000.

~~15342~~   ~~Application of bilaminate skin substitute/neodermis; 25 sq. cm~~

(Use 15170, 15175, 15340, 15360, 15365)

~~15343~~   ~~each additional 25 sq. cm (List separately in addition to code for primary procedure)~~

(Use 15171, 15176, 15341, 15361, 15366)

Integumentary System

15350 — 15431

~~15350~~   ~~Application of allograft, skin; 100 sq. cm or less~~

(Use 15300, 15320, 15330, 15335)

~~15351~~   ~~each additional 100 sq. cm (List separately in addition to code for primary procedure)~~

(Use 15301, 15321, 15331, 15336)

● **15360** **Tissue cultured allogeneic dermal substitute; trunk, arms, legs; first 100 sq cm or less, or one percent of body area of infants and children**

+ ● **15361** **each additional 100 sq cm, or each additional one percent of body area of infants and children, or part thereof (List separately in addition to code for primary procedure)**

Note that 15361 is an add-on code and must be used in conjunction with 15360.

● **15365** **Tissue cultured allogeneic dermal substitute, face, scalp, eyelids, mouth, neck, ears, orbits, genitalia, hands, feet, and/or multiple digits; first 100 sq cm or less, or one percent of body area of infants and children**

+ ● **15366** **each additional 100 sq cm, or each additional one percent of body area of infants and children, or part thereof (List separately in addition to code for primary procedure)**

Note that 15366 is an add-on code and must be used in conjunction with 15365.

XENOGRAFT

▲ **15400** **Xenograft, skin (dermal), for temporary wound closure; trunk, arms, legs; first 100 sq cm or less, or one percent of body area of infants and children**   2 T ▶

MED: 100-2, 15, 260; 100-4, 12, 90.3; 100-4, 14, 10

AMA: 2001, Apr, 10; 1999, Jan, 4; 1998, Nov, 6; 1997, Sep, 1; 1997, Apr, 4

+ ▲ **15401** **each additional 100 sq cm, or each additional one percent of body area of infants and children, or part thereof (List separately in addition to code for primary procedure)**   2 T

MED: 100-2, 15, 260; 100-4, 12, 90.3; 100-4, 14, 10

AMA: 1999, Jan, 4; 1998, Nov, 6

Note that 15401 is an add-on code and must be used in conjunction with 15440.

● **15420** **Xenograft skin (dermal), for temporary wound closure, face, scalp, eyelids, mouth, neck, ears, orbits, genitalia, hands, feet, and/or multiple digits; first 100 sq cm or less, or one percent of body area of infants and children**

+ ● **15421** **each additional 100 sq cm, or each additional one percent of body area of infants and children, or part thereof (List separately in addition to code for primary procedure)**

Note that 15421 is an add-on code and must be used in conjunction with 15420.

● **15430** **Acellular xenograft implant; first 100 sq cm or less, or one percent of body area of infants and children**

+ ● **15431** **each additional 100 sq cm, or each additional one percent of body area of infants and children, or part thereof (List separately in addition to code for primary procedure)**

Note that 15431 is an add-on code and must be used in conjunction with 15430.

Codes 15430 and 15431 cannot be reported with 11040-11042, 15000.

FLAPS (SKIN AND/OR DEEP TISSUES)

If the physician is attaching the flap in transfer or to a final site, select these codes by recipient site. If the physician is forming a tube for later or there will be a delay of the flap, report these codes by donor site.

If repair of the donor site requires skin grafts or local flaps, code as an additional procedure.

If the flap is microvascular, consult CPT codes 15756-15758.

Extensive immobilization (e.g., large casts and other devices) is not included in CPT codes 15570-15738 and should be reported separately.

15570	**Formation of direct or tubed pedicle, with or without transfer; trunk**	**3** T ↻
	MED: 100-2, 15, 260; 100-4, 12, 90.3; 100-4, 14, 10	
	AMA: 2002, Nov, 5	
15572	**scalp, arms, or legs**	**3** T ↻
	MED: 100-2, 15, 260; 100-4, 12, 90.3; 100-4, 14, 10	
15574	**forehead, cheeks, chin, mouth, neck, axillae, genitalia, hands or feet**	**3** T ↻
	MED: 100-2, 15, 260; 100-4, 12, 90.3; 100-4, 14, 10	
15576	**eyelids, nose, ears, lips, or intraoral**	**3** T ↻
	MED: 100-2, 15, 260; 100-4, 12, 90.3; 100-4, 14, 10	
15600	**Delay of flap or sectioning of flap (division and inset); at trunk**	**3** T 80 ↻
	MED: 100-2, 15, 260; 100-4, 12, 90.3; 100-4, 14, 10	
	AMA: 1999, Nov, 10	
15610	**at scalp, arms, or legs**	**3** T 80 ↻
	MED: 100-2, 15, 260; 100-4, 12, 90.3; 100-4, 14, 10	
15620	**at forehead, cheeks, chin, neck, axillae, genitalia, hands (except 15625), or feet**	**4** T ↻
	MED: 100-2, 15, 260; 100-4, 12, 90.3; 100-4, 14, 10	
15630	**at eyelids, nose, ears, or lips**	**3** T ↻
	MED: 100-2, 15, 260; 100-4, 12, 90.3; 100-4, 14, 10	

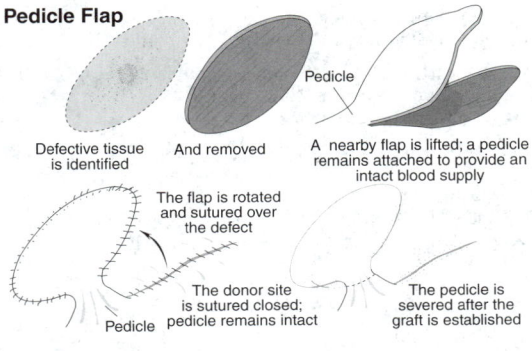

Pedicle Flap

Defective tissue is identified

And removed

A nearby flap is lifted; a pedicle remains attached to provide an intact blood supply

Pedicle

The flap is rotated and sutured over the defect

The donor site is sutured closed; pedicle remains intact

Pedicle

The pedicle is severed after the graft is established

Integumentary System

15650 — 15770

15650   **Transfer, intermediate, of any pedicle flap (eg, abdomen to wrist, Walking tube), any location**   5 T 80
MED: 100-2, 15, 260; 100-4, 12, 90.3; 100-4, 14, 10

If the transfer is performed on the eyelids, nose, ears, or lips, consult also the anatomical area.

If a pedicle flap or skin graft is revised, defatted, or rearranged, consult CPT codes 13100-14300.

15732   **Muscle, myocutaneous, or fasciocutaneous flap; head and neck (eg, temporalis, masseter muscle, sternocleidomastoid, levator scapulae)**   3 T 80
MED: 100-2, 15, 260; 100-4, 12, 90.3; 100-4, 14, 10

15734   **trunk**   3 T 80
MED: 100-2, 15, 260; 100-4, 12, 90.3; 100-4, 14, 10

15736   **upper extremity**   3 T
MED: 100-2, 15, 260; 100-4, 12, 90.3; 100-4, 14, 10

15738   **lower extremity**   3 T 80
MED: 100-2, 15, 260; 100-4, 12, 90.3; 100-4, 14, 10

OTHER FLAPS AND GRAFTS

If repair of the donor site requires skin grafts or local flaps, code as an additional procedure.

15740   **Flap; island pedicle**   2 T
MED: 100-2, 15, 260; 100-4, 12, 90.3; 100-4, 14, 10

15750   **neurovascular pedicle**   2 T 80
MED: 100-2, 15, 260; 100-4, 12, 90.3; 100-4, 14, 10

15756   **Free muscle or myocutaneous flap with microvascular anastomosis**   C 80
AMA: 1998, Nov, 6; 1997, Nov, 12; 1997, Apr, 5

Do not report 69990 in addition to code 15756 as the operating microscope is considered an inclusive component of the surgery.

15757   **Free skin flap with microvascular anastomosis**   C 80
AMA: 1998, Nov, 6; 1997, Apr, 5

Do not report 69990 in addition to code 15757 as the operating microscope is considered an inclusive component of the surgery.

15758   **Free fascial flap with microvascular anastomosis**   C 80
AMA: 1998, Nov, 6; 1997, Apr, 5

Do not report 69990 in addition to code 15758 as the operating microscope is considered an inclusive component of the surgery.

15760   **Graft; composite (eg, full thickness of external ear or nasal ala), including primary closure, donor area**   2 T
MED: 100-2, 15, 260; 100-4, 12, 90.3; 100-4, 14, 10

AMA: 1997, Sep, 1

15770   **derma-fat-fascia**   3 T 80
MED: 100-2, 15, 260; 100-4, 12, 90.3; 100-4, 14, 10

AMA: 1997, Sep, 1

 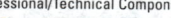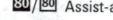

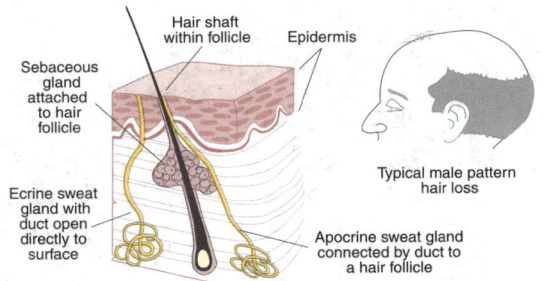

Alopecia means hair loss and the condition is separated into two major categories: that which occurs with associated, visable scalp disease, and that which occurs in the absence of visible disease. Male and female pattern hair loss is of the latter category. Hirsutism is excess hair growth, particularly in women, and is often a sign of a systemic medical syndrome

15775   **Punch graft for hair transplant; 1 to 15 punch grafts**   3 T 80 ▣
                MED: 100-2, 15, 260; 100-2, 16, 10; 100-2, 16, 120; 100-2, 16, 180; 100-4, 12, 90.3; 100-4, 14, 10

                AMA: 1997, Sep, 1

15776   **more than 15 punch grafts**   3 T 80 ▣
                MED: 100-2, 15, 260; 100-2, 16, 10; 100-2, 16, 120; 100-2, 16, 180; 100-4, 12, 90.3; 100-4, 14, 10

                AMA: 1997, Sep, 1

             If the procedure is a strip transplant, consult CPT code 15220.

OTHER PROCEDURES

15780   **Dermabrasion; total face (eg, for acne scarring, fine wrinkling,**
             rhytids, general keratosis)   T 80 ▣

15781   **segmental, face**   T ▣

15782   **regional, other than face**   T 80 ▣

15783   **superficial, any site, (eg, tattoo removal)**   T 80 ▣

15786   **Abrasion; single lesion (eg, keratosis, scar)**   T ▣

+ **15787**   **each additional four lesions or less (List separately in addition to**
             code for primary procedure)   T

             Note that 15787 is an add-on code and must be used in conjunction with 15786.

15788   **Chemical peel, facial; epidermal**   T ▣

15789   **dermal**   T ▣

15792   **Chemical peel, nonfacial; epidermal**   T 80 ▣

15793   **dermal**   T 80 ▣

~~15810~~   ~~Salabrasion; 20 sq. cm or less~~

~~15811~~   ~~over 20 sq. cm~~

15819   **Cervicoplasty**   T 80 ▣

15820   **Blepharoplasty, lower eyelid;**   3 T 50 80 ▣
             MED: 100-2, 15, 260; 100-4, 12, 90.3; 100-4, 14, 10

15821   **with extensive herniated fat pad**   3 T 50 80 ▣
             MED: 100-2, 15, 260; 100-4, 12, 90.3; 100-4, 14, 10

15822   **Blepharoplasty, upper eyelid;**   3 T 50 ▣
             MED: 100-2, 15, 260; 100-4, 12, 90.3; 100-4, 14, 10

Integumentary System

15823 — 15837

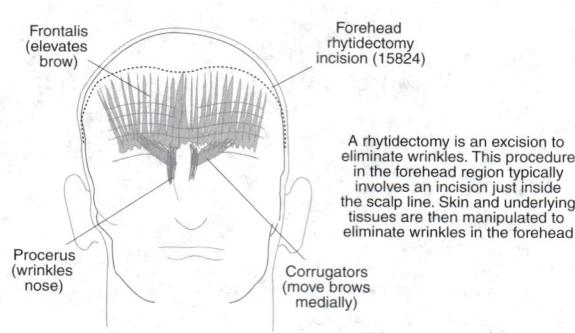

Frontalis (elevates brow)

Forehead rhytidectomy incision (15824)

A rhytidectomy is an excision to eliminate wrinkles. This procedure in the forehead region typically involves an incision just inside the scalp line. Skin and underlying tissues are then manipulated to eliminate wrinkles in the forehead

Procerus (wrinkles nose)

Corrugators (move brows medially)

15823　　　**with excessive skin weighting down lid**　　　⑤ Ⓣ ⑤⓪ ⬍
MED: 100-2, 15, 260; 100-4, 12, 90.3; 100-4, 14, 10

AMA: 2000, Sep, 7

If procedures 15820-15823 are performed bilaterally, append modifier 50 or 09950.

15824　　　**Rhytidectomy; forehead**　　　③ Ⓣ ⑤⓪ ⑧⓪ ⬍
MED: 100-2, 15, 260; 100-2, 16, 10; 100-2, 16, 120; 100-2, 16, 180; 100-4, 12, 90.3; 100-4, 14, 10

If the brow ptosis is repaired, consult CPT code 67900.

15825　　　**neck with platysmal tightening (platysmal flap, P-flap)**　　　③ Ⓣ ⑤⓪ ⑧⓪ ⬍
MED: 100-2, 15, 260; 100-2, 16, 10; 100-2, 16, 120; 100-2, 16, 180; 100-4, 12, 90.3; 100-4, 14, 10

15826　　　**glabellar frown lines**　　　③ Ⓣ ⑤⓪ ⑧⓪ ⬍
MED: 100-2, 15, 260; 100-4, 12, 90.3; 100-4, 14, 10

15828　　　**cheek, chin, and neck**　　　③ Ⓣ ⑤⓪ ⑧⓪ ⬍
MED: 100-2, 15, 260; 100-2, 16, 10; 100-2, 16, 120; 100-2, 16, 180; 100-4, 12, 90.3; 100-4, 14, 10

15829　　　**superficial musculoaponeurotic system (SMAS) flap**　　　⑤ Ⓣ ⑤⓪ ⑧⓪ ⬍
MED: 100-2, 15, 260; 100-2, 16, 10; 100-2, 16, 120; 100-2, 16, 180; 100-4, 12, 90.3; 100-4, 14, 10

If rhytidectomy is performed bilaterally, append modifier 50.

15831　　　**Excision, excessive skin and subcutaneous tissue (including lipectomy); abdomen (abdominoplasty)**　　　③ Ⓣ ⑧⓪ ⬍
MED: 100-2, 15, 260; 100-4, 12, 90.3; 100-4, 14, 10

AMA: 2001, May, 11

15832　　　**thigh**　　　③ Ⓣ ⑧⓪ ⬍
MED: 100-2, 15, 260; 100-4, 12, 90.3; 100-4, 14, 10

15833　　　**leg**　　　③ Ⓣ ⑧⓪ ⬍
MED: 100-2, 15, 260; 100-4, 12, 90.3; 100-4, 14, 10

15834　　　**hip**　　　③ Ⓣ ⑧⓪ ⬍
MED: 100-2, 15, 260; 100-4, 12, 90.3; 100-4, 14, 10

15835　　　**buttock**　　　③ Ⓣ ⑧⓪ ⬍
MED: 100-2, 15, 260; 100-4, 12, 90.3; 100-4, 14, 10

15836　　　**arm**　　　③ Ⓣ ⑧⓪ ⬍

15837　　　**forearm or hand**　　　Ⓣ ⑧⓪ ⬍

15838	**submental fat pad**	T 80 🔁
15839	**other area**	3 T 80 🔁

MED: 100-2, 15, 260; 100-4, 12, 90.3; 100-4, 14, 10

If procedures 15831-15839 are performed bilaterally, append modifier 50.

15840   **Graft for facial nerve paralysis; free fascia graft (including obtaining fascia)**   4 T 🔁

If the facial nerve graft is performed bilaterally, append modifier 50.

15841   **free muscle graft (including obtaining graft)**   4 T 80 🔁
MED: 100-2, 15, 260; 100-4, 12, 90.3; 100-4, 14, 10

15842   **free muscle flap by microsurgical technique**   T 80 🔁

Do not report CPT code 69990 together with 15842.

15845   **regional muscle transfer**   4 T 80 🔁
MED: 100-2, 15, 260; 100-4, 12, 90.3; 100-4, 14, 10

15850   **Removal of sutures under anesthesia (other than local), same surgeon**   T
AMA: 1993, Spring, 34

15851   **Removal of sutures under anesthesia (other than local), other surgeon**   T 🔁
AMA: 1993, Spring, 34

15852   **Dressing change (for other than burns) under anesthesia (other than local)**   X 🔁

15860   **Intravenous injection of agent (eg, fluorescein) to test vascular flow in flap or graft**   X 80 🔁

15876   **Suction assisted lipectomy; head and neck**   3 T 80 🔁
MED: 100-2, 15, 260; 100-2, 16, 10; 100-2, 16, 120; 100-2, 16, 180; 100-3, 140.4; 100-4, 12, 90.3; 100-4, 14, 10

15877   **trunk**   3 T 80 🔁
MED: 100-2, 15, 260; 100-2, 16, 10; 100-2, 16, 120; 100-2, 16, 180; 100-4, 12, 90.3; 100-4, 14, 10

AMA: 1999, Oct, 10

15878   **upper extremity**   3 T 80 🔁
MED: 100-2, 15, 260; 100-2, 16, 10; 100-2, 16, 120; 100-2, 16, 180; 100-4, 12, 90.3; 100-4, 14, 10

15879   **lower extremity**   3 T 80 🔁
MED: 100-2, 15, 260; 100-2, 16, 10; 100-2, 16, 120; 100-2, 16, 180; 100-4, 12, 90.3; 100-4, 14, 10

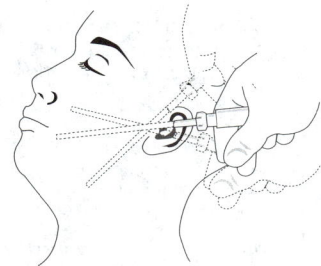

Cannula typically
inserted through
incision in front of ear

In 15876, a liposuction cannula is inserted
through fat deposits creating tunnels
and removing excess deposits

Integumentary System

15920 — 15951

PRESSURE ULCERS (DECUBITUS ULCERS)

15920   **Excision, coccygeal pressure ulcer, with coccygectomy; with primary suture**   3 T 80 ↵
MED: 100-2, 15, 260; 100-3, 270.5; 100-4, 12, 90.3; 100-4, 14, 10

If a free skin graft is used to close an ulcer or the donor site, consult CPT codes 15000 and subsequent codes.

15922   **with flap closure**   4 T 80 ↵
MED: 100-2, 15, 260; 100-3, 270.5; 100-4, 12, 90.3; 100-4, 14, 10

15931   **Excision, sacral pressure ulcer, with primary suture;**   3 T ↵
MED: 100-2, 15, 260; 100-3, 270.5; 100-4, 12, 90.3; 100-4, 14, 10

15933   **with ostectomy**   3 T 80 ↵
MED: 100-2, 15, 260; 100-3, 270.5; 100-4, 12, 90.3; 100-4, 14, 10

15934   **Excision, sacral pressure ulcer, with skin flap closure;**   3 T ↵
MED: 100-2, 15, 260; 100-3, 270.5; 100-4, 12, 90.3; 100-4, 14, 10

15935   **with ostectomy**   4 T 80 ↵
MED: 100-2, 15, 260; 100-3, 270.5; 100-4, 12, 90.3; 100-4, 14, 10

15936   **Excision, sacral pressure ulcer, in preparation for muscle or myocutaneous flap or skin graft closure;**   4 T ↵
MED: 100-2, 15, 260; 100-3, 270.5; 100-4, 12, 90.3; 100-4, 14, 10

AMA: 1998, Nov, 6-7

15937   **with ostectomy**   4 T 80 ↵
MED: 100-2, 15, 260; 100-3, 270.5; 100-4, 12, 90.3; 100-4, 14, 10

If a defect is repaired using a muscle or a myocutaneous flap, consult CPT code(s) 15734 and/or 15738 in addition to 15936 and 15937. If a defect is repaired using a split skin graft, consult CPT code(s) 15100 and/or 15101 in addition to 15936 and 15937.

15940   **Excision, ischial pressure ulcer, with primary suture;**   3 T ↵
MED: 100-2, 15, 260; 100-3, 270.5; 100-4, 12, 90.3; 100-4, 14, 10

15941   **with ostectomy (ischiectomy)**   3 T 80 ↵
MED: 100-2, 15, 260; 100-4, 12, 90.3; 100-4, 14, 10

15944   **Excision, ischial pressure ulcer, with skin flap closure;**   3 T 80 ↵
MED: 100-2, 15, 260; 100-3, 270.5; 100-4, 12, 90.3; 100-4, 14, 10

15945   **with ostectomy**   4 T 80 ↵
MED: 100-2, 15, 260; 100-3, 270.5; 100-4, 12, 90.3; 100-4, 14, 10

15946   **Excision, ischial pressure ulcer, with ostectomy, in preparation for muscle or myocutaneous flap or skin graft closure**   4 T 80 ↵
MED: 100-2, 15, 260; 100-3, 270.5; 100-4, 12, 90.3; 100-4, 14, 10

AMA: 2003, Jan, 23; 2002, Jun, 10; 1998, Nov, 6-7

If a defect is repaired using a muscle or a myocutaneous flap, consult CPT code(s) 15734 and/or 15738 in addition to 15946. If a defect is repaired using a split skin graft, consult CPT code(s) 15100 and/or 15101 in addition to 15946.

15950   **Excision, trochanteric pressure ulcer, with primary suture;**   3 T ↵
MED: 100-2, 15, 260; 100-3, 270.5; 100-4, 12, 90.3; 100-4, 14, 10

15951   **with ostectomy**   4 T 80 ↵
MED: 100-2, 15, 260; 100-3, 270.5; 100-4, 12, 90.3; 100-4, 14, 10

 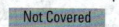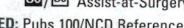

15952	**Excision, trochanteric pressure ulcer, with skin flap closure;**		3 T 80 ↵

MED: 100-2, 15, 260; 100-3, 270.5; 100-4, 12, 90.3; 100-4, 14, 10

15953	**with ostectomy**		4 T ↵

MED: 100-2, 15, 260; 100-3, 270.5; 100-4, 12, 90.3; 100-4, 14, 10

15956	**Excision, trochanteric pressure ulcer, in preparation for muscle or myocutaneous flap or skin graft closure;**		3 T ↵

MED: 100-2, 15, 260; 100-3, 270.5; 100-4, 12, 90.3; 100-4, 14, 10

AMA: 1998, Nov, 6-7

15958	**with ostectomy**		4 T 80 ↵

MED: 100-2, 15, 260; 100-3, 270.5; 100-4, 12, 90.3; 100-4, 14, 10

AMA: 1998, Nov, 6-7

If a defect is repaired using a muscle or a myocutaneous flap, consult CPT codes 15734 and/or 15738 in addition to 15956 and 15958. If a defect is repaired using a split skin graft, consult CPT codes 15100 and/or 15101 in addition to 15956 and 15958.

15999	**Unlisted procedure, excision pressure ulcer**		T 80

MED: 100-3, 270.5

If a free skin graft is used to close an ulcer or the donor site, consult CPT codes 15000 and subsequent codes.

BURNS, LOCAL TREATMENT

CPT codes 16000-16036 identify local treatment of burned surface only. For management of burn patients (e.g., prolonged detention, hospital visits) and related medical services, consult appropriate services in the Medicine or Evaluation and Management chapters.

Codes 16020–16030 include the application of materials such as Biobrane® and other dressings that are not described in codes 15100–15431.

If the application of skin grafts or skin substitutes is performed, consult CPT codes 15100–15650.

The percentage of body surface and the depth of the burn should be listed.

16000	**Initial treatment, first degree burn, when no more than local treatment is required**		T ↵

MED: 100-4, 12, 70; 100-4, 13, 20; 100-4, 13, 90

AMA: 1997, Aug, 6

~~**16010**~~	~~**Dressings and/or debridement, initial or subsequent; under anesthesia, small**~~	

(Use 16020-16030)

~~**16015**~~	~~**under anesthesia, medium or large, or with major debridement**~~	

(Use 16020-16030)

▲	**16020**	**Dressings and/or debridement of partial-thickness burns, initial or subsequent; small (less than 5% total body surface area)**	T ↵

MED: 100-3, 270.5; 100-4, 12, 70; 100-4, 13, 20; 100-4, 13, 90

AMA: 1997, Aug, 6

▲	**16025**	**medium (eg, whole face or whole extremity, or 5% to 10% total body surface area)**	T ↵

MED: 100-3, 270.5; 100-4, 12, 70; 100-4, 13, 20; 100-4, 13, 90

AMA: 1997, Aug, 6

Rule of Nines for Burns

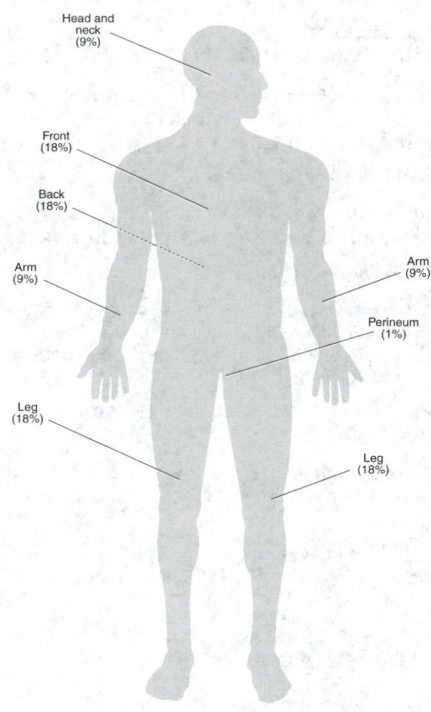

▲   **16030**   **large (eg, more than one extremity, or greater than 10% total body surface area)**   Ⓣ 🔁

MED: 100-3, 270.5; 100-4, 12, 70; 100-4, 13, 20; 100-4, 13, 90

AMA: 1997, Aug, 6

16035   **Escharotomy; initial incision**   Ⓒ 🔁

AMA: 1997, Aug, 6

+   **16036**   **each additional incision (List separately in addition to code for primary procedure)**   Ⓒ

If a debridement, curettement of burn wound is performed, consult CPT codes 16020-16030.

Note that 16036 is an add-on code and must be used in conjunction with 16035.

DESTRUCTION

Destruction is defined as the ablation of benign, premalignant, or malignant tissue by any of the following methods used alone or in combination: electrosurgery, cryosurgery, laser, and chemical treatment. Lesions include condylomata, papillomata, molluscum contagiosum, herpetic lesions, warts, milia, actinic keratosis, or other benign, premalignant or malignant lesions. Destruction includes administration of local anesthesia. Codes from this section should not be used when a more specific destruction code is listed under the particular anatomical site. For example, code 40820 should be used for destruction of lesions of the vestibule of the mouth.

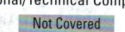 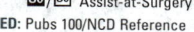

Consult CPT codes 40820, 46900-46917, 46924, 54050-54057, 54065, 56501, 56515, 57061, 57065, 67850, and 68135 for destruction of lesion(s) of specified anatomical sites.

To report the paring or cutting of benign hyperkeratotic lesions (e.g., corns or calluses), consult CPT codes 11055-11057. To report sharp removal or electrosurgical destruction of skin tags and fibrocutaneous tags, consult CPT codes 11200 and 11201. If cryotherapy is used for acne, consult CPT code 17340. If destruction is performed on malignant skin lesions, consult CPT codes 17260-17286. If epidermal or dermal lesions are shaved, consult CPT codes 11300-11313. To report the initiation or follow-up care of topical chemotherapy (e.g., 5-FU or comparable agents), consult the appropriate evaluation and management codes.

BENIGN OR PREMALIGNANT LESIONS

17000   **Destruction (eg, laser surgery, electrosurgery, cryosurgery, chemosurgery, surgical curettement), all benign or premalignant lesions (eg, actinic keratoses) other than skin tags or cutaneous vascular proliferative lesions; first lesion** Ⓣ ▣

MED: 100-3, 140.5; 100-4, 12, 40.6

AMA: 1999, Jun, 10; 1997, Nov, 12

+ **17003**   **second through 14 lesions, each (List separately in addition to code for first lesion)** Ⓣ

MED: 100-3, 140.5; 100-4, 12, 40.6

AMA: 1999, Jun, 10; 1997, Nov, 12

Note that 17003 is an add-on code and must be used in conjunction with 17000.

⊘ **17004**   **Destruction (eg, laser surgery, electrosurgery, cryosurgery, chemosurgery, surgical curettement), all benign or premalignant lesions (eg, actinic keratoses) other than skin tags or cutaneous vascular proliferative lesions, 15 or more lesions** Ⓣ ▣

MED: 100-3, 140.5; 100-4, 12, 40.6

AMA: 1999, Jun, 10; 1998, Nov, 7; 1997, Nov, 12

Do not report 17004 with 17000-17003.

17106   **Destruction of cutaneous vascular proliferative lesions (eg, laser technique); less than 10 sq. cm** Ⓣ ▣

MED: 100-3, 140.5

17107   **10.0 - 50.0 sq. cm** Ⓣ ▣

MED: 100-3, 140.5

17108   **over 50.0 sq. cm** Ⓣ 80 ▣

MED: 100-3, 140.5

17110   **Destruction (eg, laser surgery, electrosurgery, cryosurgery, chemosurgery, surgical curettement), of flat warts, molluscum contagiosum, or milia; up to 14 lesions** Ⓣ ▣

MED: 100-3, 140.5

AMA: 1997, Nov, 13

17111   **15 or more lesions** Ⓣ ▣

MED: 100-3, 140.5

AMA: 1997, Nov, 13

To report the destruction of common or plantar warts, consult CPT codes 17000, 17003, and 17004.

Integumentary System

17250 — 17284

17250 Chemical cauterization of granulation tissue (proud flesh, sinus or fistula) ☐T☐ ☐
AMA: 1997, Nov, 14

Do not report this service with removal/excision codes of the same lesion.

MALIGNANT LESIONS, ANY METHOD

17260 Destruction, malignant lesion (eg, laser surgery, electrosurgery, cryosurgery, chemosurgery, surgical curettement), trunk, arms or legs; lesion diameter 0.5 cm or less ☐T☐ ☐
MED: 100-3, 140.5

17261 lesion diameter 0.6 to 1.0 cm ☐T☐ ☐
MED: 100-3, 140.5

17262 lesion diameter 1.1 to 2.0 cm ☐T☐ ☐
MED: 100-3, 140.5

17263 lesion diameter 2.1 to 3.0 cm ☐T☐ ☐
MED: 100-3, 140.5

17264 lesion diameter 3.1 to 4.0 cm ☐T☐ ☐
MED: 100-3, 140.5

17266 lesion diameter over 4.0 cm ☐T☐ ☐
MED: 100-3, 140.5

17270 Destruction, malignant lesion (eg, laser surgery, electrosurgery, cryosurgery, chemosurgery, surgical curettement), scalp, neck, hands, feet, genitalia; lesion diameter 0.5 cm or less ☐T☐ ☐
MED: 100-3, 140.5

17271 lesion diameter 0.6 to 1.0 cm ☐T☐ ☐
MED: 100-3, 140.5

17272 lesion diameter 1.1 to 2.0 cm ☐T☐ ☐
MED: 100-3, 140.5

17273 lesion diameter 2.1 to 3.0 cm ☐T☐ ☐
MED: 100-3, 140.5

17274 lesion diameter 3.1 to 4.0 cm ☐T☐ ☐
MED: 100-3, 140.5

17276 lesion diameter over 4.0 cm ☐T☐ ☐
MED: 100-3, 140.5

17280 Destruction, malignant lesion (eg, laser surgery, electrosurgery, cryosurgery, chemosurgery, surgical curettement), face, ears, eyelids, nose, lips, mucous membrane; lesion diameter 0.5 cm or less ☐T☐ ☐
MED: 100-3, 140.5

17281 lesion diameter 0.6 to 1.0 cm ☐T☐ ☐
MED: 100-3, 140.5

17282 lesion diameter 1.1 to 2.0 cm ☐T☐ ☐
MED: 100-3, 140.5

17283 lesion diameter 2.1 to 3.0 cm ☐T☐ ☐
MED: 100-3, 140.5

17284 lesion diameter 3.1 to 4.0 cm ☐T☐ ☐
MED: 100-3, 140.5

26 / **TC** Professional/Technical Component **80**/**80** Assist-at-Surgery Allowed/With Documentation ⊙ Conscious Sedation
Unlisted Not Covered MED: Pubs 100/NCD Reference **1**-**9** ASC Group 63 Modifier 63 Exempt
102 — Surgery CPT only © 2005 American Medical Association. All Rights Reserved. *(Black Ink)* © 2005 Ingenix, Inc. *(Blue Ink)*

17286	lesion diameter over 4.0 cm	T
	MED: 100-3, 140.5	

MOHS MICROGRAPHIC SURGERY

Mohs micrographic surgery must be kept is listed in the destruction subsection. This is a special technique used to treat complex or ill-defined skin cancer and requires a single physician to provide two distinct services. The first service is surgical and involves the removal of the lesion without trying to remove a margin of normal tissue. This is often called debulking the lesion. The second service is that of a pathologist and includes mapping, color coding of specimens, microscopic examination of specimens, and complete histopathologic preparation. Mohs microsurgery surgery codes should be used only when one physician is functioning as both the surgeon and the pathologist.

If a single physician is not acting as both the surgeon and the pathologist for these procedures, this group of CPT codes should not be used. When repair is performed, consult appropriate CPT codes for the type of repair (e.g., graft, wound repair).

If this is an initiation or a follow-up care of topical chemotherapy (e.g., 5-FU or similar agents), consult appropriate office visits.

If a skin biopsy is performed on the same day, and there was not prior pathology confirmation of a diagnosis, consult CPT codes 11100, 11101, and 88331 to report frozen section pathology performed on the same day with modifier 59.

⊘ **17304** **Chemosurgery (Mohs micrographic technique), including removal of all gross tumor, surgical excision of tissue specimens, mapping, color coding of specimens, microscopic examination of specimens by the surgeon, and complete histopathologic preparation including the first routine stain (eg, hematoxylin and eosin, toluidine blue); first stage, fresh tissue technique, up to 5 specimens** T

AMA: 2002, Nov, 5; 1999, Mar, 11; 1999, Jun, 10; 1994, Winter, 19

To report additional special pathology services, consult CPT codes 88311-88314 and 88342.

⊘ **17305** **second stage, fixed or fresh tissue, up to 5 specimens** T

AMA: 2002, Nov, 5; 1999, Mar, 11; 1999, Jun, 10; 1994, Winter, 19

⊘ **17306** **third stage, fixed or fresh tissue, up to 5 specimens** T

AMA: 2002, Nov, 5; 1999, Mar, 11; 1999, Jun, 10; 1994, Winter, 19

⊘ **17307** **additional stage(s), up to 5 specimens, each stage** T

AMA: 2002, Nov, 5; 1999, Mar, 11; 1999, Jun, 10; 1994, Winter, 19

+ **17310** **each additional specimen, after the first 5 specimens, fixed or fresh tissue, any stage (List separately in addition to code for primary procedure)** T

AMA: 2002, Nov, 5; 1999, Mar, 11; 1999, Jun, 10; 1994, Winter, 19

Note that 17310 is an add-on code and must be used in conjunction with 17304-17307.

OTHER PROCEDURES

17340	Cryotherapy (CO_2 slush, liquid N_2) for acne	T
17360	Chemical exfoliation for acne (eg, acne paste, acid)	T
17380	Electrolysis epilation, each 1/2 hour	T 80
	MED: 100-2, 16, 10; 100-2, 16, 120; 100-2, 16, 180	

To report actinotherapy, consult CPT code 96900.

17999 **Unlisted procedure, skin, mucous membrane and subcutaneous tissue** T 80

AMA: 1998, Dec, 9

Integumentary System

19000 — 19030

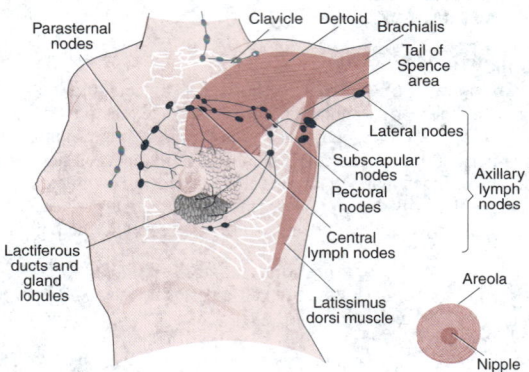

BREAST

INCISION

| | 19000 | **Puncture aspiration of cyst of breast;** | T ↵ |

AMA: 1994, Fall, 18

| + | 19001 | **each additional cyst (List separately in addition to code for primary procedure)** | T ↵ |

AMA: 1994, Fall, 18

Note that 19001 is an add-on code and must be used in conjunction with 19000.

To report imaging guidance, consult CPT codes 76095, 76096, 76393, 76942.

| | 19020 | **Mastotomy with exploration or drainage of abscess, deep** | 2 T 50 ↵ |

MED: 100-2, 15, 260; 100-4, 12, 90.3; 100-4, 14, 10

| | 19030 | **Injection procedure only for mammary ductogram or galactogram** | N 50 ↵ |

To report radiological supervision and interpretation, consult CPT codes 76086 and 76088.

To report catheter lavage of mammary ducts for cytology specimen collection, consult CPT Category III codes 0046T and 0047T.

EXCISION

Breast biopsies include excision of cysts, tumors or lesions and may involve different amounts of tissue removed for evaluation or treatment.

Excisional breast procedures may include biopsy and may be open or percutaneous. This includes the excision of cysts, benign or malignant lesions of the breast and chest wall.

A biopsy is a procedure in which a lesion is removed without regard for surgical margins and is reported with codes 19100-19103.

Partial mastectomy procedures include lumpectomy, tylectomy, segmentectomy and quadrantectomy.

Partial mastectomy codes are reported with codes 19160 or 19162. A partial mastectomy should be reported when the surgeon pays particular attention to assuring adequate surgical margins surrounding the lesion are excised.

Total mastectomy procedures are reported with codes 19180, 19182, 19200, 19220 or 19240. These procedures include simple mastectomy, complete mastectomy, subcutaneous mastectomy, modified radical mastectomy, radical mastectomy, and more extensive procedures.

26 / TC	Professional/Technical Component	80 / 80 Assist-at-Surgery Allowed/With Documentation	⊙ Conscious Sedation
Unlisted	Not Covered	MED: Pubs 100/NCD Reference	1 - 9 ASC Group	63 Modifier 63 Exempt
104 — Surgery	CPT only © 2005 American Medical Association. All Rights Reserved. *(Black Ink)*	© 2005 Ingenix, Inc. *(Blue Ink)*

Codes 19260, 19271 or 19272 are used to report excision or resection of chest wall tumors. This includes ribs with or without reconstruction and with or without mediastinal lymphadenectomy. Codes 19260-19272 are not only to report breast tumors. Use these codes to report resection of chest wall tumors that originate from any chest wall component. (To report lung or pleural excisions , consult 32310 et seq.) To report bilateral procedures, append modifier 50.

19100   **Biopsy of breast; percutaneous, needle core, not using imaging guidance (separate procedure)**   1 T 50
      MED: 100-2, 15, 260; 100-3, 20.7; 100-3, 220.13; 100-4, 12, 90.3; 100-4, 14, 10

      AMA: 2002, May, 18; 2001, Jan, 8; 1998, Nov, 7; 1997, Mar, 4; 1996, Apr, 8; 1994, Fall, 18

      To report fine needle aspiration, consult CPT code 10021.

      To report image guided breast biopsy, consult CPT codes 10022, 19102, 19103.

19101   **open, incisional**   2 T 50
      MED: 100-2, 15, 260; 100-3, 20.7; 100-3, 220.13; 100-4, 12, 90.3; 100-4, 14, 10

      AMA: 2002, May, 18; 2001, Jan, 8; 1994, Fall, 19

19102   **percutaneous, needle core, using imaging guidance**   2 T 50
      MED: 100-2, 15, 260; 100-3, 20.7; 100-3, 220.13; 100-4, 12, 90.3; 100-4, 14, 10

      AMA: 2002, May, 18; 2001, Jan, 8

      To report placement of percutaneous localization clip, report 19295 in conjunction with 19102.

      To report the radiologic guidance in conjunction with a breast biopsy, consult CPT codes 76095, 76096, 76360, 76393, and 76942.

19103   **percutaneous, automated vacuum assisted or rotating biopsy device, using imaging guidance**   2 T 50
      MED: 100-2, 15, 260; 100-3, 20.7; 100-3, 220.13; 100-4, 12, 90.3; 100-4, 14, 10

      AMA: 2002, May, 18; 2001, Jan, 8

      To report the radiologic guidance in conjunction with a breast biopsy, consult CPT codes 76095, 76096, 76360, 76393, and 76942.

      For placement of percutaneous localization clip, report 19295 in conjunction with 19103.

19110   **Nipple exploration, with or without excision of a solitary lactiferous duct or a papilloma lactiferous duct**   2 T 50
      MED: 100-2, 15, 260; 100-4, 12, 90.3; 100-4, 14, 10

19112   **Excision of lactiferous duct fistula**   3 T 50 80
      MED: 100-2, 15, 260; 100-4, 12, 90.3; 100-4, 14, 10

19120   **Excision of cyst, fibroadenoma, or other benign or malignant tumor aberrant breast tissue, duct lesion, nipple or areolar lesion (except 19140), open, male or female, one or more lesions**   3 T 80
      MED: 100-2, 15, 260; 100-4, 12, 90.3; 100-4, 14, 10

      AMA: 2001, May, 10; 2001, Jan, 8; 1997, Nov, 14; 1996, Feb, 9

19125   **Excision of breast lesion identified by preoperative placement of radiological marker, open; single lesion**   3 T 80
      MED: 100-2, 15, 260; 100-4, 12, 90.3; 100-4, 14, 10

      AMA: 2001, Jan, 8; 1998, Mar, 10; 1994, Fall, 18

Integumentary System

19126 — 19272

+ 19126 **each additional lesion separately identified by a preoperative radiological marker (List separately in addition to code for primary procedure)** 3 T ▣
MED: 100-2, 15, 260; 100-4, 12, 90.3; 100-4, 14, 10

AMA: 2001, Jan, 8; 1998, Mar, 10; 1994, Fall, 18

Note that 19126 is an add-on code and must be used in conjunction with 19125.

19140 **Mastectomy for gynecomastia** ♂ 4 T 50 ▣
MED: 100-2, 15, 260; 100-4, 12, 90.3; 100-4, 14, 10

AMA: 1996, Feb, 9

19160 **Mastectomy, partial (eg, lumpectomy, tylectomy, quadrantectomy, segmentectomy);** 3 T 50 80 ▣
MED: 100-2, 15, 260; 100-4, 12, 90.3; 100-4, 14, 10

19162 **with axillary lymphadenectomy** 7 T 50 80 ▣
MED: 100-2, 15, 260; 100-4, 12, 90.3; 100-4, 14, 10

AMA: 2000, Jun, 11

To report placement of radiotherapy afterloading balloon/brachytherapy catheters consult CPT codes 19296-19298.

19180 **Mastectomy, simple, complete** 4 T 50 80 ▣
MED: 100-2, 15, 260; 100-4, 12, 90.3; 100-4, 14, 10

To report immediate or delayed implant insertion, consult CPT code 19340 or 19342. If the mastectomy is for gynecomastia, consult CPT code 19140.

19182 **Mastectomy, subcutaneous** 4 T 50 80 ▣
MED: 100-2, 15, 260; 100-4, 12, 90.3; 100-4, 14, 10

To report the immediate or delayed insertion of an implant, consult CPT code 19340 or 19342.

19200 **Mastectomy, radical, including pectoral muscles, axillary lymph nodes** C 50 80 ▣
Halsted mastectomy

To report the immediate or delayed insertion of an implant, consult CPT code 19340 or 19342.

19220 **Mastectomy, radical, including pectoral muscles, axillary and internal mammary lymph nodes (Urban type operation)** C 50 80 ▣

To report the immediate or delayed insertion of an implant, consult CPT code 19340 or 19342.

19240 **Mastectomy, modified radical, including axillary lymph nodes, with or without pectoralis minor muscle, but excluding pectoralis major muscle** T 50 80 ▣

Patey's mastectomy

To report the immediate or delayed insertion of an implant, consult CPT code 19340 or 19342.

19260 **Excision of chest wall tumor including ribs** T 80 ▣

19271 **Excision of chest wall tumor involving ribs, with plastic reconstruction; without mediastinal lymphadenectomy** C 80 ▣

19272 **with mediastinal lymphadenectomy** C 80 ▣

Codes 19260, 19271, and 19272 should not be reported in conjunction with code 32002, 32020, 32100, 32503, or 32504.

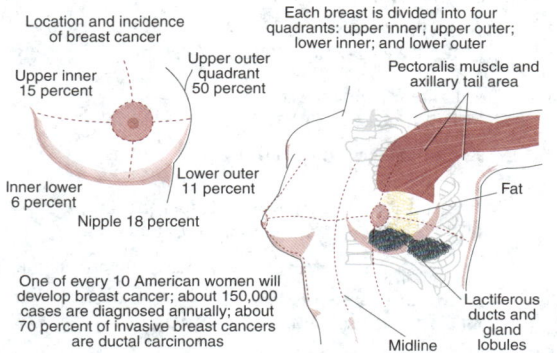

Location and incidence of breast cancer

Each breast is divided into four quadrants: upper inner; upper outer; lower inner; and lower outer

Upper inner 15 percent

Upper outer quadrant 50 percent

Pectoralis muscle and axillary tail area

Inner lower 6 percent

Lower outer 11 percent

Nipple 18 percent

Fat

One of every 10 American women will develop breast cancer; about 150,000 cases are diagnosed annually; about 70 percent of invasive breast cancers are ductal carcinomas

Lactiferous ducts and gland lobules

Midline

INTRODUCTION

19290   **Preoperative placement of needle localization wire, breast;**
MED: 100-2, 15, 260; 100-4, 12, 90.3; 100-4, 14, 10

AMA: 1994, Fall, 19

To report radiological supervision and interpretation, consult CPT codes 76095, 76096, 76942.

+   **19291**   **each additional lesion (List separately in addition to code for primary procedure)**
MED: 100-2, 15, 260; 100-4, 12, 90.3; 100-4, 14, 10

AMA: 1994, Fall, 19

Note that 19291 is an add-on code and must be used in conjunction with 19290.

+   **19295**   **Image guided placement, metallic localization clip, percutaneous, during breast biopsy (List separately in addition to code for primary procedure)**
AMA: 2001, Jan, 8

Note that 19295 is an add-on code and must be used in conjunction with 19102, 19103.

19296   **Placement of radiotherapy afterloading balloon catheter into the breast for interstitial radioelement application following partial mastectomy, includes imaging guidance; on date separate from partial mastectomy**

+   **19297**   **concurrent with partial mastectomy (List separately in addition to code for primary procedure)**

Note that 19297 must be used with 19160 or 19162.

⊙   **19298**   **Placement of radiotherapy afterloading brachytherapy catheters (multiple tube and button type) into the breast for interstitial radioelement application following (at the time of or subsequent to) partial mastectomy, includes imaging guidance**

Integumentary System

19316 — 19364

REPAIR AND/OR RECONSTRUCTION

19316 **Mastopexy** `4` `T` `50` `80` ↵
MED: 100-2, 15, 260; 100-4, 12, 90.3; 100-4, 14, 10

19318 **Reduction mammaplasty** ♀ `4` `T` `50` `80` ↵
MED: 100-2, 15, 260; 100-4, 12, 90.3; 100-4, 14, 10

Aries-Pitanguy mammaplasty

19324 **Mammaplasty, augmentation; without prosthetic implant** `4` `T` `50` `80` ↵
MED: 100-2, 15, 260; 100-4, 12, 90.3; 100-4, 14, 10

If a flap or graft is needed, consult also appropriate number.

19325 **with prosthetic implant** `9` `T` `50` `80` ↵
MED: 100-2, 15, 260; 100-4, 12, 90.3; 100-4, 14, 10

Consult CPT code 99070 for supply of implant.

If a flap or graft is needed, consult also appropriate number.

19328 **Removal of intact mammary implant** `1` `T` `50` ↵
MED: 100-2, 15, 260; 100-4, 12, 90.3; 100-4, 14, 10

19330 **Removal of mammary implant material** `1` `T` `50` ↵
MED: 100-2, 15, 260; 100-4, 12, 90.3; 100-4, 14, 10

AMA: 2001, Nov, 11

19340 **Immediate insertion of breast prosthesis following mastopexy, mastectomy or in reconstruction** `2` `T` `50` ↵
MED: 100-2, 15, 260; 100-3, 140.2; 100-4, 12, 90.3; 100-4, 14, 10

AMA: 1996, Aug, 8

19342 **Delayed insertion of breast prosthesis following mastopexy, mastectomy or in reconstruction** ♀ `3` `T` `50` `80` ↵
MED: 100-2, 15, 260; 100-3, 140.2; 100-4, 12, 90.3; 100-4, 14, 10

AMA: 1996, Aug, 8

Consult CPT code 99070 for supply of implant. If a custom breast implant is prepared, consult CPT code 19396.

19350 **Nipple/areola reconstruction** `4` `T` `50` ↵
MED: 100-2, 15, 260; 100-3, 140.2; 100-4, 12, 90.3; 100-4, 14, 10

AMA: 1996, Aug, 11

19355 **Correction of inverted nipples** `4` `T` `50` `80` ↵
MED: 100-2, 15, 260; 100-3, 140.2; 100-4, 12, 90.3; 100-4, 14, 10

19357 **Breast reconstruction, immediate or delayed, with tissue expander, including subsequent expansion** ♀ `5` `T` `50` `80` ↵
MED: 100-2, 15, 260; 100-3, 140.2; 100-4, 12, 90.3; 100-4, 14, 10

19361 **Breast reconstruction with latissimus dorsi flap, with or without prosthetic implant** ♀ `C` `50` `80` ↵
MED: 100-3, 140.2

19364 **Breast reconstruction with free flap** `C` `50` `80` ↵
MED: 100-3, 140.2

AMA: 1998, Nov, 7; 1996, Aug, 8

Do not report 69990 in addition to code 19364 as the operating microscope is considered an inclusive component of the surgery. Note that 19364 includes harvesting of the flap, microvascular transfer, closure of the donor site, and inset shaping the flap into a breast.

19366   **Breast reconstruction with other technique**   5 T 50 80 🗗
MED: 100-2, 15, 260; 100-3, 140.2; 100-4, 12, 90.3; 100-4, 14, 10

AMA: 1998, Nov, 7; 1996, Aug, 8

If an operating microscope is used, consult CPT code 69990. If a prosthesis is inserted, consult also CPT code 19340 or 19342.

19367   **Breast reconstruction with transverse rectus abdominis myocutaneous flap (TRAM), single pedicle, including closure of donor site;**   ♀ C 50 80 🗗
MED: 100-3, 140.2

AMA: 1998, Nov, 7

19368   **with microvascular anastomosis (supercharging)**   ♀ C 50 80 🗗
MED: 100-3, 140.2

AMA: 1998, Nov, 7

Do not report 69990 in addition to code 19368 as the operating microscope is considered an inclusive component of the surgery.

19369   **Breast reconstruction with transverse rectus abdominis myocutaneous flap (TRAM), double pedicle, including closure of donor site**   ♀ C 50 80 🗗
MED: 100-3, 140.2

AMA: 2000, Oct, 1

19370   **Open periprosthetic capsulotomy, breast**   4 T 50 🗗
MED: 100-2, 15, 260; 100-3, 140.2; 100-4, 12, 90.3; 100-4, 14, 10

AMA: 1996, Aug, 8

19371   **Periprosthetic capsulectomy, breast**   4 T 50 🗗
MED: 100-2, 15, 260; 100-3, 140.2; 100-4, 12, 90.3; 100-4, 14, 10

AMA: 2001, Nov, 11; 1996, Aug, 8

19380   **Revision of reconstructed breast**   5 T 50 🗗
MED: 100-2, 15, 260; 100-3, 140.2; 100-4, 12, 90.3; 100-4, 14, 10

19396   **Preparation of moulage for custom breast implant**   T 50 80 🗗
MED: 100-3, 140.2

AMA: 2003, Jan, 1

OTHER PROCEDURES

To report microwave thermotherapy of breast, consult CPT Category III code 0061T.

19499   **Unlisted procedure, breast**   T 50 80

Musculoskeletal System

MUSCULOSKELETAL SYSTEM

Codes listed in the Musculoskeletal chapter include the application and removal of the first cast or traction device. Replacement of casts and/or traction devices subsequent to the first should be reported separately. CPT codes for other additional procedures, such as obtaining grafts and external fixation, should only be used if the procedure is not already listed as included as part of the basic procedure. Consult the glossary for terms and definitions and the front matter of this chapter for additional information.

To report computer assisted musculoskeletal surgical navigational orthopedic procedures, consult CPT Category III codes 0054T-0056T.

FRACTURE CARE

Fracture management codes are package services and include percutaneous pinning and open or closed treatment of the fracture, application and removal of the initial cast or splint, and normal, uncomplicated follow-up care.

Two types of fixation—internal and external—are described in the CPT book. Internal skeletal fixation involves wires, pins, screws, and/or plates placed through or within the fractured area to stabilize and immobilize the injury. This procedure is generally accomplished through an incision over the fracture site. It is commonly described as an open reduction with internal fixation (ORIF). Internal fixation may also be accomplished by percutaneous technique. In this case, a pin is inserted through the skin without an incision. Deep internal devices are usually left in place even after the fracture has healed. If the hardware is removed, report codes 20670 or 20680. Use modifier 78 Return to the operating room for a related procedure, or modifier 58 Staged or related procedure by the same physician during the postoperative period, if removal is performed during the initial hospital care or during the postoperative follow-up period. The ICD-9-CM code is assigned according to the reason for the removal (e.g., pain, infection). The codes describing internal fixation are placed throughout the fracture care codes according to anatomical site.

External fixation (20690–20694) is hardware passing through bone and skin and held rigid by cross-braces outside the body. External fixation is always removed after the fracture has healed and removal usually is considered part of the global service. However, if required to remain in place beyond the usual postoperative period, its removal should be reported (20694).

INCISION

20000	**Incision of soft tissue abscess (eg, secondary to osteomyelitis); superficial**	T
20005	**deep or complicated**	2 T
	MED: 100-2, 15, 260; 100-4, 12, 90.3; 100-4, 14, 10	

WOUND EXPLORATION — TRAUMA (EG, PENETRATING GUNSHOT, STAB WOUND)

Use these codes to describe the physician's surgical treatment of a traumatic penetrating wound resulting from knives, guns, or other sources. The physician may explore or enlarge the wound, dissect the wound to determine penetration, remove foreign bodies, debridement, and repair minor blood vessels. When a thoracotomy or laparotomy is necessary to repair major structures or blood vessels, the code for that procedure is used instead of the 20100-20103 series.

20100	**Exploration of penetrating wound (separate procedure); neck**	T 50 80
	AMA: 1996, Jun, 7; 1996, Aug, 10	
20101	**chest**	T
	AMA: 1996, Jun, 7	
20102	**abdomen/flank/back**	T 80
	AMA: 1996, Jun, 7	
20103	**extremity**	T 80
	AMA: 1996, Jun, 7; 1996, Aug, 10	

EXCISION

To report sequestrectomy, osteomyelitis, or drainage of bone abscess, consult CPT codes for appropriate anatomical area.

20150   **Excision of epiphyseal bar, with or without autogenous soft tissue graft obtained through same fascial incision**   T 50 80 ⬛

If bone marrow is aspirated, consult CPT code 38220.

20200   **Biopsy, muscle; superficial**   2 T ⬛
MED: 100-2, 15, 260; 100-4, 12, 90.3; 100-4, 14, 10

If excision of a muscle tumor, deep, is included, consult specific anatomical section.

20205   **deep**   3 T ⬛
MED: 100-2, 15, 260; 100-4, 12, 90.3; 100-4, 14, 10

20206   **Biopsy, muscle, percutaneous needle**   1 T ⬛
MED: 100-2, 15, 260; 100-4, 12, 90.3; 100-4, 14, 10

To report imaging guidance, consult CPT codes 76360, 76393, 76942.

To report fine needle aspiration, consult CPT codes 10021 or 10022.

To report evaluation of fine needle aspirate, consult CPT codes 88172-88173.

20220   **Biopsy, bone, trocar, or needle; superficial (eg, ilium, sternum, spinous process, ribs)**   1 T ⬛
MED: 100-2, 15, 260; 100-3, 150.3; 100-4, 12, 90.3; 100-4, 14, 10

AMA: 1998, Jul, 4; 1992, Winter, 17

20225   **deep (eg, vertebral body, femur)**   2 T ⬛
MED: 100-2, 15, 260; 100-3, 150.3; 100-4, 12, 90.3; 100-4, 14, 10

AMA: 1998, Jul, 4; 1992, Winter, 17

If bone marrow is biopsied, consult CPT code 38221.

To report radiologic supervision and interpretation, see 76003, 76360, 76393.

20240   **Biopsy, bone, open; superficial (eg, ilium, sternum, spinous process, ribs, trochanter of femur)**   2 T ⬛
MED: 100-2, 15, 260; 100-3, 150.3; 100-4, 12, 90.3; 100-4, 14, 10

AMA: 1998, Jul, 4; 1992, Winter, 17

20245   **deep (eg, humerus, ischium, femur)**   3 T ⬛
MED: 100-2, 15, 260; 100-3, 150.3; 100-4, 12, 90.3; 100-4, 14, 10

AMA: 1998, Jul, 4; 1992, Winter, 17

20250   **Biopsy, vertebral body, open; thoracic**   3 T ⬛
MED: 100-2, 15, 260; 100-4, 12, 90.3; 100-4, 14, 10

AMA: 1998, Jul, 4; 1992, Winter, 17

20251   **lumbar or cervical**   3 T 80 ⬛
MED: 100-2, 15, 260; 100-4, 12, 90.3; 100-4, 14, 10

AMA: 1998, Jul, 4; 1992, Winter, 17

INTRODUCTION OR REMOVAL

If an injection procedure for arthrography is performed, consult appropriate anatomical area.

20500	**Injection of sinus tract; therapeutic (separate procedure)**	T ↰
20501	**diagnostic (sinogram)**	N ↰

To report radiologic supervision and interpretation, consult CPT code 76080.

20520	**Removal of foreign body in muscle or tendon sheath; simple**	T ↰
20525	**deep or complicated**	3 T ↰

MED: 100-2, 15, 260; 100-4, 12, 90.3; 100-4, 14, 10

20526	**Injection, therapeutic (eg, local anesthetic, corticosteroid), carpal tunnel**	T 50 ↰

AMA: 2002, Mar, 7

TRIGGER POINT AND TENDON INJECTIONS

Trigger point injections are reported with code 20552 and 20553 for injections into one or more trigger points in one or two, or three or more muscles, respectively. Tendon injections are reported using codes 20550 (single tendon sheath, ligament, or aponeurosis) or 20551(single tendon origin/insertion). These codes should be reported one time for multiple or single injections to a single tendon sheath, ligament, tendon origin, or tendon insertion performed.

20550	**Injection(s); single tendon sheath, or ligament, aponeurosis (eg, plantar "fascia")**	T ↰

MED: 100-3, 150.7

AMA: 2002, Mar, 7; 1998, Jun, 10; 1996, Jan, 7

20551	**single tendon origin/insertion**	T ↰

MED: 100-3, 150.7

AMA: 2002, Mar, 7

20552	**single or multiple trigger point(s), one or two muscle(s)**	T ↰

MED: 100-3, 150.7

AMA: 2002, Mar, 7

20553	**single or multiple trigger point(s), three or more muscle(s)**	T ↰

MED: 100-3, 150.7

AMA: 2002, Mar, 7

To report imaging guidance, consult CPT codes 76003, 76393, 76942.

20600	**Arthrocentesis, aspiration and/or injection; small joint or bursa (eg, fingers, toes)**	T 50 ↰

MED: 100-3, 150.6; 100-3, 150.7

20605	**intermediate joint or bursa (eg, temporomandibular, acromioclavicular, wrist, elbow or ankle, olecranon bursa)**	T 50 ↰

MED: 100-3, 150.6; 100-3, 150.7

20610	**major joint or bursa (eg, shoulder, hip, knee joint, subacromial bursa)**	T 50 ↰

MED: 100-3, 150.6; 100-3, 150.7

AMA: 2001, Mar, 10; 1992, Spring, 8

To report imaging guidance, consult CPT codes 76003, 76350, 76393, 76942.

To report procedure performed on ganglion cyst, consult CPT code 20612.

20612	**Aspiration and/or injection of ganglion cyst(s) any location**	T 🔾

To report procedure performed on multiple cysts, append modifier 59.

20615	**Aspiration and injection for treatment of bone cyst**	T 🔾

20650	**Insertion of wire or pin with application of skeletal traction, including removal (separate procedure)**	3 T 🔾

MED: 100-2, 15, 260; 100-4, 12, 90.3; 100-4, 14, 10

⊘   **20660**   **Application of cranial tongs, caliper, or stereotactic frame, including removal (separate procedure)**   C 🔾

AMA: 1997, Nov, 14; 1996, Jun, 10

20661	**Application of halo, including removal; cranial**	C 🔾
20662	pelvic	T 80 🔾
20663	femoral	T 80 🔾

20664	**Application of halo, including removal, cranial, 6 or more pins placed, for thin skull osteology (eg, pediatric patients, hydrocephalus, osteogenesis imperfecta), requiring general anesthesia**	C 🔾
20665	**Removal of tongs or halo applied by another physician**	X 80 🔾
20670	**Removal of implant; superficial, (eg, buried wire, pin or rod) (separate procedure)**	1 T 🔾

MED: 100-2, 15, 260; 100-4, 12, 90.3; 100-4, 14, 10

20680	deep (eg, buried wire, pin, screw, metal band, nail, rod or plate)	3 T 80 🔾

MED: 100-2, 15, 260; 100-4, 12, 90.3; 100-4, 14, 10

AMA: 1992, Spring, 11

⊘   **20690**   **Application of a uniplane (pins or wires in one plane), unilateral, external fixation system**   2 T 50 🔾

MED: 100-2, 15, 260; 100-4, 12, 90.3; 100-4, 14, 10

AMA: 1999, Oct, 4; 1993, Fall, 21

⊘   **20692**   **Application of a multiplane (pins or wires in more than one plane), unilateral, external fixation system (eg, Ilizarov, Monticelli type)**   3 T 80 🔾

MED: 100-2, 15, 260; 100-4, 12, 90.3; 100-4, 14, 10

AMA: 2000, Jul, 11; 1999, Oct, 4; 1993, Fall, 21

20693	**Adjustment or revision of external fixation system requiring anesthesia (eg, new pin(s) or wire(s) and/or new ring(s) or bar(s))**	3 T 🔾

MED: 100-2, 15, 260; 100-4, 12, 90.3; 100-4, 14, 10

AMA: 2000, Jul, 11; 1999, Oct, 4; 1993, Fall, 21

20694	**Removal, under anesthesia, of external fixation system**	1 T 🔾

MED: 100-2, 15, 260; 100-4, 12, 90.3; 100-4, 14, 10

AMA: 2000, Jul, 11; 1999, Oct, 4; 1993, Fall, 21; 1992, Winter, 10

REPLANTATION

To report repair of bone(s), ligament(s), tendon(s), nerve(s), or blood vessel(s) with replantation, consult appropriate anatomic area, and append modifier 52.

20802	**Replantation, arm (includes surgical neck of humerus through elbow joint), complete amputation**	C 50 80 🔾
20805	**Replantation, forearm (includes radius and ulna to radial carpal joint), complete amputation**	C 50 80 🔾

Musculoskeletal System

20808 — 20930

20808	**Replantation, hand (includes hand through metacarpophalangeal joints), complete amputation** C 50 80 ↰
20816	**Replantation, digit, excluding thumb (includes metacarpophalangeal joint to insertion of flexor sublimis tendon), complete amputation** C 80 ↰
	AMA: 1996, Oct, 11
20822	**Replantation, digit, excluding thumb (includes distal tip to sublimis tendon insertion), complete amputation** T 80 ↰
20824	**Replantation, thumb (includes carpometacarpal joint to MP joint), complete amputation** C 50 80 ↰
20827	**Replantation, thumb (includes distal tip to MP joint), complete amputation** C 50 80 ↰
20838	**Replantation, foot, complete amputation** C 50 80 ↰

GRAFTS (OR IMPLANTS)

If spinal surgery bone graft(s) is needed, consult CPT codes 20930-20938. If needle aspiration of bone marrow for the purpose of bone grafting is needed, consult CPT code 38220. Do not report modifier 62 with any codes in range 20900-20938.

The harvesting of grafts through separate incisions should be reported separately unless the primary procedure code narrative states that it already includes obtaining grafts.

⊘ **20900** **Bone graft, any donor area; minor or small (eg, dowel or button)** 3 T 80 ↰
MED: 100-2, 15, 260; 100-4, 12, 90.3; 100-4, 14, 10

AMA: 2000, Dec, 15

⊘ **20902** **major or large** 4 T 80 ↰
MED: 100-2, 15, 260; 100-4, 12, 90.3; 100-4, 14, 10

AMA: 2000, Dec, 15

⊘ **20910** **Cartilage graft; costochondral** 3 T 80 ↰
MED: 100-2, 15, 260; 100-4, 12, 90.3; 100-4, 14, 10

⊘ **20912** **nasal septum** 3 T 80 ↰
MED: 100-2, 15, 260; 100-4, 12, 90.3; 100-4, 14, 10

To report ear cartilage, consult CPT code 21235.

⊘ **20920** **Fascia lata graft; by stripper** 4 T ↰
MED: 100-2, 15, 260; 100-4, 12, 90.3; 100-4, 14, 10

AMA: 1999, Aug, 5

⊘ **20922** **by incision and area exposure, complex or sheet** 3 T 80 ↰
MED: 100-2, 15, 260; 100-4, 12, 90.3; 100-4, 14, 10

⊘ **20924** **Tendon graft, from a distance (eg, palmaris, toe extensor, plantaris)** 4 T 80 ↰
MED: 100-2, 15, 260; 100-4, 12, 90.3; 100-4, 14, 10

⊘ **20926** **Tissue grafts, other (eg, paratenon, fat, dermis)** 4 T ↰
MED: 100-2, 15, 260; 100-4, 12, 90.3; 100-4, 14, 10

AMA: 1999, Nov, 10; 1999, Aug, 5; 1991, Summer, 12

CPT states that codes 20930-20938 should be reported, without modifier 51, in addition to the definitive procedure. Individual payer policies may differ, check with your specific payer.

⊘ **20930** **Allograft for spine surgery only; morselized** C
AMA: 1999, Nov, 10; 1997, Sep, 8; 1996, Mar, 4; 1996, Feb, 6

⊘ **20931**   structural   [C] [≈]
AMA: 1996, Feb, 6

⊘ **20936**   Autograft for spine surgery only (includes harvesting the graft); local (eg, ribs, spinous process, or laminar fragments) obtained from same incision   [C]
AMA: 1997, Sep, 8; 1996, Feb, 6

⊘ **20937**   morselized (through separate skin or fascial incision)   [C] [≈]
AMA: 1999, Dec, 2; 1997, Sep, 8; 1996, Feb, 6

⊘ **20938**   structural, bicortical or tricortical (through separate skin or fascial incision)   [C]
AMA: 1997, Sep, 8; 1996, Mar, 5; 1996, Feb, 6

OTHER PROCEDURES

20950   Monitoring of interstitial fluid pressure (includes insertion of device, eg, wick catheter technique, needle manometer technique) in detection of muscle compartment syndrome   [T] [80] [≈]

> Do not report 69990 in addition to codes 20955-20962 as the operating microscope is considered an inclusive component of these procedures.

20955   Bone graft with microvascular anastomosis; fibula   [C] [80] [≈]
AMA: 1997, Apr, 4

20956   iliac crest   [C] [80] [≈]
AMA: 1997, Apr, 4

20957   metatarsal   [C] [80] [≈]
AMA: 1997, Apr, 4

20962   other than fibula, iliac crest, or metatarsal   [C] [80] [≈]
AMA: 1997, Apr, 4

> Do not report 69990 in addition to codes 20969-20973 as the operating microscope is considered an inclusive component of these procedures.

20969   Free osteocutaneous flap with microvascular anastomosis; other than iliac crest, metatarsal, or great toe   [C] [80] [≈]
AMA: 1997, Apr, 4

20970   iliac crest   [C] [80] [≈]
AMA: 1997, Apr, 4

20972   metatarsal   [T] [80] [≈]
AMA: 1997, Apr, 4

20973   great toe with web space   [T] [80] [≈]
MED: 100-3, 150.2

AMA: 1997, Apr, 4

> If a great toe wrap-around procedure is performed, consult CPT code 26551.

⊘ **20974**   Electrical stimulation to aid bone healing; noninvasive (nonoperative)   [A] [≈]
MED: 100-3, 150.2

AMA: 1996, Sep, 11

⊘ **20975**   invasive (operative)   [2] [X] [80] [≈]
MED: 100-2, 15, 260; 100-3, 150.2; 100-4, 12, 90.3; 100-4, 14, 10

20979   Low intensity ultrasound stimulation to aid bone healing, noninvasive (nonoperative)   [A] [≈]
MED: 100-3, 220.5

AMA: 2000, Nov, 8; 1999, Nov, 10

[≈] CCI Comp	[50] Bilateral Procedure	✚ CPT Add-on Code	⊘ Modifier -51 Exempt	♂Male	♀ Female
● New Code	▲ Revised Code	[M] Maternity Edit	[A] Age Edit	[A]–[Y] APC Status Ind.	AMA: CPT Assistant

© 2005 Ingenix, Inc. *(Blue Ink)*   CPT only © 2005 American Medical Association. All Rights Reserved. *(Black Ink)*   Surgery — 115

Musculoskeletal System

20982 — 21029

⊙   20982   **Ablation, bone tumor(s) (eg, osteoid osteoma, metastasis) radiofrequency, percutaneous, including computed tomographic guidance**   T 50 80 ⟳

     20999   **Unlisted procedure, musculoskeletal system, general**   T 80

HEAD

Codes listed in the Musculoskeletal chapter include the application and removal of the first cast or traction device. Replacement of casts and/or traction devices subsequent to the first should be reported separately. CPT codes for other additional procedures, such as obtaining grafts and external fixation, should only be used if the procedure is not already listed as included as part of the basic procedure. Consult the glossary for terms and definitions and the front matter of this chapter for additional information.

This section includes the skull, facial bones and the temporomandibular joint.

INCISION

     21010   **Arthrotomy, temporomandibular joint**   2 T 50 80 ⟳
              MED: 100-2, 15, 260; 100-4, 12, 90.3; 100-4, 14, 10

              If a superficial abscess and hematoma is drained, consult CPT code 20000. If an embedded foreign body is removed from dentoalveolar structures, consult CPT codes 41805 and 41806.

              If procedure 21010 is performed bilaterally, append modifier 50.

EXCISION

     21015   **Radical resection of tumor (eg, malignant neoplasm), soft tissue of face or scalp**   3 T ⟳
              MED: 100-2, 15, 260; 100-4, 12, 90.3; 100-4, 14, 10

              If only a biopsy is done, consult CPT codes 20220 and 20240.

              Consult CPT code 61501 for the excision of a skull tumor for osteomyelitis.

     21025   **Excision of bone (eg, for osteomyelitis or bone abscess); mandible**   2 T ⟳
              MED: 100-2, 15, 260; 100-4, 12, 90.3; 100-4, 14, 10

     21026   **facial bone(s)**   2 T ⟳
              MED: 100-2, 15, 260; 100-4, 12, 90.3; 100-4, 14, 10

     21029   **Removal by contouring of benign tumor of facial bone (eg, fibrous dysplasia)**   2 T 80 ⟳
              MED: 100-2, 15, 260; 100-4, 12, 90.3; 100-4, 14, 10

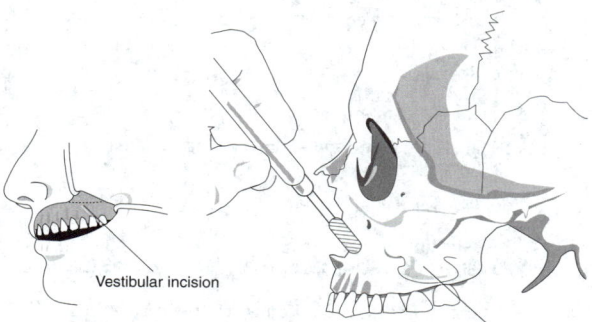

Vestibular incision

Burs, files, and osteotomes used to remove bone   Area of benign bone growth

21030	Excision of benign tumor or cyst of maxilla or zygoma by enucleation and curettage	T ↻
21031	Excision of torus mandibularis	T ↻
21032	Excision of maxillary torus palatinus	T ↻
21034	Excision of malignant tumor of maxilla or zygoma MED: 100-2, 15, 260; 100-4, 12, 90.3; 100-4, 14, 10	3 T 80 ↻
21040	Excision of benign tumor or cyst of mandible, by enucleation and/or curettage MED: 100-2, 15, 260; 100-4, 12, 90.3; 100-4, 14, 10	2 T ↻

To report excision requiring osteotomy, consult CPT codes 21046, 21047.

21044	Excision of malignant tumor of mandible; MED: 100-2, 15, 260; 100-4, 12, 90.3; 100-4, 14, 10	2 T 80 ↻
21045	radical resection	C 80 ↻

If a bone graft is done, consult CPT code 21215.

21046	Excision of benign tumor or cyst of mandible; requiring intra-oral osteotomy (eg, locally aggressive or destructive lesion(s)) MED: 100-2, 15, 260; 100-4, 12, 90.3; 100-4, 14, 10	2 T 80 ↻
21047	requiring extra-oral osteotomy and partial mandibulectomy (eg, locally aggressive or destructive lesion(s)) MED: 100-2, 15, 260; 100-4, 12, 90.3; 100-4, 14, 10	2 T 80 ↻
21048	Excision of benign tumor or cyst of maxilla; requiring intra-oral osteotomy (eg, locally aggressive or destructive lesion(s))	T 80 ↻
21049	requiring extra-oral osteotomy and partial maxillectomy (eg, locally aggressive or destructive lesion(s))	66 80 ↻
21050	Condylectomy, temporomandibular joint (separate procedure) MED: 100-2, 15, 260; 100-4, 12, 90.3; 100-4, 14, 10	3 T 50 80 ↻

If procedure 21050 is performed bilaterally, append modifier 50.

21060	Meniscectomy, partial or complete, temporomandibular joint (separate procedure) MED: 100-2, 15, 260; 100-4, 12, 90.3; 100-4, 14, 10	2 T 50 80 ↻

If procedure 21060 is performed bilaterally, append modifier 50.

21070	Coronoidectomy (separate procedure) MED: 100-2, 15, 260; 100-4, 12, 90.3; 100-4, 14, 10	3 T 50 80 ↻

If procedure 21070 is performed bilaterally, append modifier 50.

INTRODUCTION OR REMOVAL

Codes listed in the Musculoskeletal chapter include the application and removal of the first cast or traction device. Replacement of casts and/or traction devices subsequent to the first should be reported separately. CPT codes for other additional procedures, such as obtaining grafts and external fixation, should only be used if the procedure is not already listed as included as part of the basic procedure. Consult the glossary for terms and definitions.

CPT codes 21076-21089 are reported only if the physician (not an outside lab) actually designs, prepares, and supplies the prosthesis.

21076	Impression and custom preparation; surgical obturator prosthesis	T 80 ↻
21077	orbital prosthesis	T 50 80 ↻
21079	interim obturator prosthesis	T ↻

21080	definitive obturator prosthesis	T ↻
21081	mandibular resection prosthesis	T 80 ↻
21082	palatal augmentation prosthesis	T 80 ↻
21083	palatal lift prosthesis	T 80 ↻
21084	speech aid prosthesis	T 80 ↻
21085	oral surgical splint	T 80 ↻
21086	auricular prosthesis	T 50 80 ↻
21087	nasal prosthesis	T 80 ↻
21088	facial prosthesis	T 80 ↻
21089	**Unlisted maxillofacial prosthetic procedure**	T

21100 Application of halo type appliance for maxillofacial fixation, includes
removal (separate procedure) 2 T 80 ↻
MED: 100-2, 15, 260; 100-4, 12, 90.3; 100-4, 14, 10

21110 Application of interdental fixation device for conditions other than fracture
or dislocation, includes removal T ↻
AMA: 1997, Mar, 10

If another physician removes an interdental fixation, consult CPT codes
20670-20680.

21116 Injection procedure for temporomandibular joint arthrography N ↻

If radiological supervision and interpretation is performed, consult CPT code
70332. Code 76003 cannot be reported in addition to 70332.

REPAIR, REVISION, AND/OR RECONSTRUCTION
If cranioplasty is performed, consult CPT codes 21179, 21180, 62116, 62120, and 62140-62147.

21120 Genioplasty; augmentation (autograft, allograft, prosthetic material) 7 T ↻

21121 sliding osteotomy, single piece 7 T 80 ↻
MED: 100-2, 15, 260; 100-4, 12, 90.3; 100-4, 14, 10

21122 sliding osteotomies, two or more osteotomies (eg, wedge excision or
bone wedge reversal for asymmetrical chin) 7 T 80 ↻
MED: 100-2, 15, 260; 100-4, 12, 90.3; 100-4, 14, 10

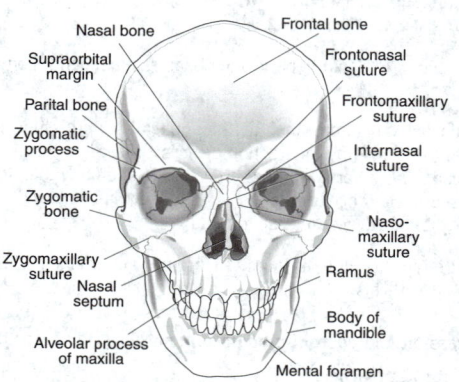

Nasal bone
Frontal bone
Supraorbital margin
Frontonasal suture
Parital bone
Frontomaxillary suture
Zygomatic process
Internasal suture
Zygomatic bone
Naso-maxillary suture
Zygomaxillary suture
Nasal septum
Ramus
Alveolar process of maxilla
Body of mandible
Mental foramen

21123   sliding, augmentation with interpositional bone grafts (includes obtaining autografts) **7** T 80 ▣
   MED: 100-2, 15, 260; 100-4, 12, 90.3; 100-4, 14, 10

21125   Augmentation, mandibular body or angle; prosthetic material **7** T 80 ▣

21127   with bone graft, onlay or interpositional (includes obtaining autograft) **9** T 80 ▣
   MED: 100-2, 15, 260; 100-4, 12, 90.3; 100-4, 14, 10

21137   Reduction forehead; contouring only   T 80 ▣
   MED: 100-2, 16, 10; 100-2, 16, 120; 100-2, 16, 180

21138   contouring and application of prosthetic material or bone graft (includes obtaining autograft)   T 80 ▣

21139   contouring and setback of anterior frontal sinus wall   T 80 ▣

21141   Reconstruction midface, LeFort 1; single piece, segment movement in any direction (eg, for Long Face Syndrome), without bone graft   C 80 ▣

21142   two pieces, segment movement in any direction, without bone graft   C 80 ▣

21143   three or more pieces, segment movement in any direction, without bone graft   C 80 ▣

21145   single piece, segment movement in any direction, requiring bone grafts (includes obtaining autografts)   C 80 ▣

21146   two pieces, segment movement in any direction, requiring bone grafts (includes obtaining autografts) (eg, ungrafted unilateral alveolar cleft)   C 80 ▣

21147   three or more pieces, segment movement in any direction, requiring bone grafts (includes obtaining autografts) (eg, ungrafted bilateral alveolar cleft or multiple osteotomies)   C 80 ▣

21150   Reconstruction midface, LeFort II; anterior intrusion (eg, Treacher-Collins Syndrome)   T 80 ▣

21151   any direction, requiring bone grafts (includes obtaining autografts)   C 80 ▣

21154   Reconstruction midface, LeFort III (extracranial), any type, requiring bone grafts (includes obtaining autografts); without LeFort I   C 80 ▣

21155   with LeFort I   C 80 ▣

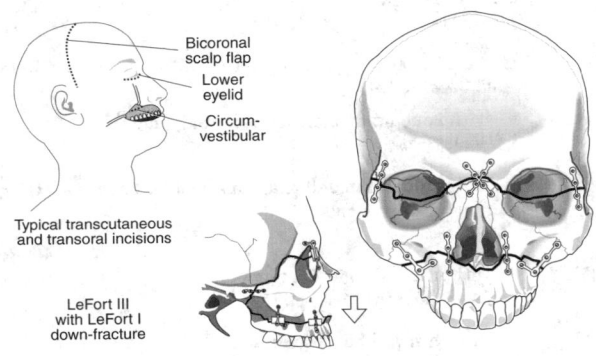

Bicoronal scalp flap
Lower eyelid
Circum-vestibular

Typical transcutaneous and transoral incisions

LeFort III with LeFort I down-fracture

Musculoskeletal System

21159 — 21199

21159 Reconstruction midface, LeFort III (extra and intracranial) with forehead advancement (eg, mono bloc), requiring bone grafts (includes obtaining autografts); without LeFort I ⒸⒶⓇ

21160 with LeFort I ⒸⒶⓇ

21172 Reconstruction superior-lateral orbital rim and lower forehead, advancement or alteration, with or without grafts (includes obtaining autografts) ⒸⒶⓇ

If frontal or parietal craniotomy is performed for craniosynostosis, consult CPT code 61556.

21175 Reconstruction, bifrontal, superior-lateral orbital rims and lower forehead, advancement or alteration (eg, plagiocephaly, trigonocephaly, brachycephaly), with or without grafts (includes obtaining autografts) ⓉⒶⓇ

If bifrontal craniotomy is performed for craniosynostosis, consult CPT code 61557.

21179 Reconstruction, entire or majority of forehead and/or supraorbital rims; with grafts (allograft or prosthetic material) ⒸⒶⓇ

21180 with autograft (includes obtaining grafts) ⒸⒶⓇ

If an extensive craniectomy for multiple suture craniosynostosis is performed, consult CPT code 61558 or 61559.

21181 Reconstruction by contouring of benign tumor of cranial bones (eg, fibrous dysplasia), extracranial ⑦ⓉⒶⓇ
MED: 100-2, 15, 260; 100-4, 12, 90.3; 100-4, 14, 10

21182 Reconstruction of orbital walls, rims, forehead, nasoethmoid complex following intra- and extracranial excision of benign tumor of cranial bone (eg, fibrous dysplasia), with multiple autografts (includes obtaining grafts); total area of bone grafting less than 40 sq. cm ⒸⒶⓇ

21183 total area of bone grafting greater than 40 sq. cm but less than 80 sq. cm ⒸⒶⓇ

21184 total area of bone grafting greater than 80 sq. cm ⒸⒶⓇ

If a benign tumor of the cranial bones is excised, consult CPT codes 61563 and 61564.

21188 Reconstruction midface, osteotomies (other than LeFort type) and bone grafts (includes obtaining autografts) ⒸⒶⓇ

21193 Reconstruction of mandibular rami, horizontal, vertical, C, or L osteotomy; without bone graft ⒸⒶⓇ
AMA: 1996, Apr, 11

If cranioplasty is performed, consult CPT codes 21179, 21180, 62116, 62120, and 62140-62147.

21194 with bone graft (includes obtaining graft) ⒸⒶⓇ
AMA: 1996, Apr, 11

21195 Reconstruction of mandibular rami and/or body, sagittal split; without internal rigid fixation ⓉⒶⓇ
AMA: 1996, Apr, 11

21196 with internal rigid fixation ⒸⒶⓇ
AMA: 1997, Mar, 11; 1996, Apr, 11

21198 Osteotomy, mandible, segmental; ⓉⒶⓇ

21199 with genioglossus advancement ⓉⒶⓇ

21206 Osteotomy, maxilla, segmental (eg, Wassmund or Schuchard) **5** **T** **80** **⌘**
MED: 100-2, 15, 260; 100-4, 12, 90.3; 100-4, 14, 10

21208 Osteoplasty, facial bones; augmentation (autograft, allograft, or prosthetic implant) **7** **T** **80** **⌘**
MED: 100-2, 15, 260; 100-4, 12, 90.3; 100-4, 14, 10

21209   reduction **5** **T** **80** **⌘**
MED: 100-2, 15, 260; 100-4, 12, 90.3; 100-4, 14, 10

21210 Graft, bone; nasal, maxillary or malar areas (includes obtaining graft) **7** **T** **⌘**
MED: 100-2, 15, 260; 100-4, 12, 90.3; 100-4, 14, 10

If cleft palate is repaired, consult CPT codes 42200-42225.

21215   mandible (includes obtaining graft) **7** **T** **⌘**
MED: 100-2, 15, 260; 100-4, 12, 90.3; 100-4, 14, 10

21230 Graft; rib cartilage, autogenous, to face, chin, nose or ear (includes obtaining graft) **7** **T** **80** **⌘**
MED: 100-2, 15, 260; 100-4, 12, 90.3; 100-4, 14, 10

21235   ear cartilage, autogenous, to nose or ear (includes obtaining graft) **7** **T** **⌘**
MED: 100-2, 15, 260; 100-4, 12, 90.3; 100-4, 14, 10

21240 Arthroplasty, temporomandibular joint, with or without autograft (includes obtaining graft) **4** **T** **50** **80** **⌘**
MED: 100-2, 15, 260; 100-4, 12, 90.3; 100-4, 14, 10

21242 Arthroplasty, temporomandibular joint, with allograft **5** **T** **50** **80** **⌘**
MED: 100-2, 15, 260; 100-4, 12, 90.3; 100-4, 14, 10

21243 Arthroplasty, temporomandibular joint, with prosthetic joint replacement **5** **T** **50** **80** **⌘**
MED: 100-2, 15, 260; 100-4, 12, 90.3; 100-4, 14, 10

21244 Reconstruction of mandible, extraoral, with transosteal bone plate (eg, mandibular staple bone plate) **7** **T** **80** **⌘**
MED: 100-2, 15, 260; 100-4, 12, 90.3; 100-4, 14, 10

21245 Reconstruction of mandible or maxilla, subperiosteal implant; partial **7** **T** **80** **⌘**
MED: 100-2, 15, 260; 100-4, 12, 90.3; 100-4, 14, 10

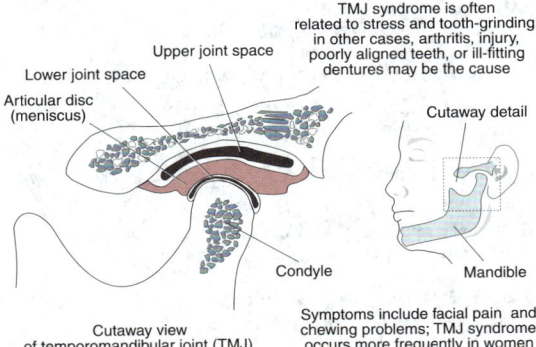

TMJ syndrome is often related to stress and tooth-grinding; in other cases, arthritis, injury, poorly aligned teeth, or ill-fitting dentures may be the cause

Upper joint space
Lower joint space
Articular disc (meniscus)
Cutaway detail
Condyle
Mandible
Cutaway view of temporomandibular joint (TMJ)
Symptoms include facial pain and chewing problems; TMJ syndrome occurs more frequently in women

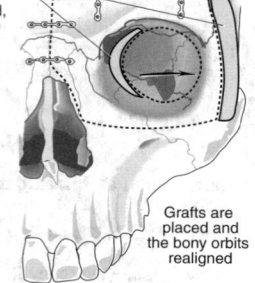

In 21263, a frontal craniotomy is performed, the brain retracted, and the orbit approached from inside the skull; frontal bone is advanced and secured

Grafts

Osteotomies are cut 360 degrees around the orbit; portions of nasal and ethmoid bones are removed

Grafts are placed and the bony orbits realigned

21246　　　**complete**　　　　　　　　　　　　　7 T 80 ↻
　　　　　MED: 100-2, 15, 260; 100-4, 12, 90.3; 100-4, 14, 10

21247　　Reconstruction of mandibular condyle with bone and cartilage autografts (includes obtaining grafts) (eg, for hemifacial microsomia)　C 80 ↻

21248　　Reconstruction of mandible or maxilla, endosteal implant (eg, blade, cylinder); partial　　　　　　　　　　　　　7 T ↻
　　　　　MED: 100-2, 15, 260; 100-4, 12, 90.3; 100-4, 14, 10

21249　　　**complete**　　　　　　　　　　　　　7 T 80 ↻
　　　　　MED: 100-2, 15, 260; 100-4, 12, 90.3; 100-4, 14, 10

　　　　If a reconstruction of the midface is performed, consult CPT codes 21141–21160.

21255　　Reconstruction of zygomatic arch and glenoid fossa with bone and cartilage (includes obtaining autografts)　　　　　　　C 80 ↻

21256　　Reconstruction of orbit with osteotomies (extracranial) and with bone grafts (includes obtaining autografts) (eg, micro-ophthalmia)　C 80 ↻

21260　　Periorbital osteotomies for orbital hypertelorism, with bone grafts; extracranial approach　　　　　　　　　　　T 80 ↻

21261　　　combined intra- and extracranial approach　　　T 80 ↻

21263　　　with forehead advancement　　　　　　　T 80 ↻

21267　　Orbital repositioning, periorbital osteotomies, unilateral, with bone grafts; extracranial approach　　　　　　　　　7 T 80 ↻
　　　　　MED: 100-2, 15, 260; 100-4, 12, 90.3; 100-4, 14, 10

21268　　　combined intra- and extracranial approach　　　C 80 ↻

21270　　Malar augmentation, prosthetic material　　　5 T 80 ↻
　　　　　MED: 100-2, 15, 260; 100-4, 12, 90.3; 100-4, 14, 10

　　　　If malar augmentation with a bone graft is performed, consult CPT code 21210.

21275　　Secondary revision of orbitocraniofacial reconstruction　7 T 80 ↻
　　　　　MED: 100-2, 15, 260; 100-4, 12, 90.3; 100-4, 14, 10

21280　　Medial canthopexy (separate procedure)　　5 T 50 80 ↻
　　　　　MED: 100-2, 15, 260; 100-4, 12, 90.3; 100-4, 14, 10

　　　　If medial canthoplasty is performed, consult CPT code 67950.

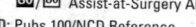

21282   Lateral canthopexy   5 T 50 ⏹
      MED: 100-2, 15, 260; 100-4, 12, 90.3; 100-4, 14, 10

21295   Reduction of masseter muscle and bone (eg, for treatment of benign
      masseteric hypertrophy); extraoral approach   1 T 80 ⏹
      MED: 100-2, 15, 260; 100-4, 12, 90.3; 100-4, 14, 10

21296   intraoral approach   1 T 80 ⏹
      MED: 100-2, 15, 260; 100-4, 12, 90.3; 100-4, 14, 10

OTHER PROCEDURES

21299   Unlisted craniofacial and maxillofacial procedure   T 80

FRACTURE AND/OR DISLOCATION

21300   Closed treatment of skull fracture without operation   2 T 80 ⏹
      MED: 100-2, 15, 260; 100-4, 12, 90.3; 100-4, 14, 10

      If operative repair is needed, consult CPT codes 62000-62010.

21310   Closed treatment of nasal bone fracture without manipulation   2 T ⏹
      MED: 100-2, 15, 260; 100-4, 12, 90.3; 100-4, 14, 10

21315   Closed treatment of nasal bone fracture; without stabilization   2 T ⏹
      MED: 100-2, 15, 260; 100-4, 12, 90.3; 100-4, 14, 10

21320   with stabilization   2 T ⏹
      MED: 100-2, 15, 260; 100-4, 12, 90.3; 100-4, 14, 10

21325   Open treatment of nasal fracture; uncomplicated   4 T 80 ⏹
      MED: 100-2, 15, 260; 100-4, 12, 90.3; 100-4, 14, 10

21330   complicated, with internal and/or external skeletal fixation   5 T 80 ⏹
      MED: 100-2, 15, 260; 100-4, 12, 90.3; 100-4, 14, 10

21335   with concomitant open treatment of fractured septum   7 T ⏹
      MED: 100-2, 15, 260; 100-4, 12, 90.3; 100-4, 14, 10

21336   Open treatment of nasal septal fracture, with or without
      stabilization   4 T 80 ⏹
      MED: 100-2, 15, 260; 100-4, 12, 90.3; 100-4, 14, 10

21337   Closed treatment of nasal septal fracture, with or without
      stabilization   2 T 80 ⏹
      MED: 100-2, 15, 260; 100-4, 12, 90.3; 100-4, 14, 10

21338   Open treatment of nasoethmoid fracture; without external
      fixation   4 T 80 ⏹
      MED: 100-2, 15, 260; 100-4, 12, 90.3; 100-4, 14, 10

21339   with external fixation   5 T 80 ⏹
      MED: 100-2, 15, 260; 100-4, 12, 90.3; 100-4, 14, 10

21340   Percutaneous treatment of nasoethmoid complex fracture, with splint, wire
      or headcap fixation, including repair of canthal ligaments and/or the
      nasolacrimal apparatus   4 T 80 ⏹
      MED: 100-2, 15, 260; 100-4, 12, 90.3; 100-4, 14, 10

21343   Open treatment of depressed frontal sinus fracture   C 80 ⏹

21344   Open treatment of complicated (eg, comminuted or involving posterior wall)
      frontal sinus fracture, via coronal or multiple approaches   C 80 ⏹

Musculoskeletal System

21345 — 21433

21345   Closed treatment of nasomaxillary complex fracture (LeFort II type), with interdental wire fixation or fixation of denture or splint **7** T 80
MED: 100-2, 15, 260; 100-4, 12, 90.3; 100-4, 14, 10

21346   Open treatment of nasomaxillary complex fracture (LeFort II type); with wiring and/or local fixation C

21347   requiring multiple open approaches C 80

21348   with bone grafting (includes obtaining graft) C 80

21355   Percutaneous treatment of fracture of malar area, including zygomatic arch and malar tripod, with manipulation **3** T 80
MED: 100-2, 15, 260; 100-4, 12, 90.3; 100-4, 14, 10

21356   Open treatment of depressed zygomatic arch fracture (eg, Gilles approach) T 80

21360   Open treatment of depressed malar fracture, including zygomatic arch and malar tripod C 80

21365   Open treatment of complicated (eg, comminuted or involving cranial nerve foramina) fracture(s) of malar area, including zygomatic arch and malar tripod; with internal fixation and multiple surgical approaches C 80

21366   with bone grafting (includes obtaining graft) C 80

21385   Open treatment of orbital floor blowout fracture; transantral approach (Caldwell-Luc type operation) C 80

21386   periorbital approach C 80

21387   combined approach C 80

21390   periorbital approach, with alloplastic or other implant T 80

21395   periorbital approach with bone graft (includes obtaining graft) C 80

21400   Closed treatment of fracture of orbit, except blowout; without manipulation **2** T 80
MED: 100-2, 15, 260; 100-4, 12, 90.3; 100-4, 14, 10

21401   with manipulation **3** T 80
MED: 100-2, 15, 260; 100-4, 12, 90.3; 100-4, 14, 10

21406   Open treatment of fracture of orbit, except blowout; without implant T 80

21407   with implant T 80

21408   with bone grafting (includes obtaining graft) T 80

21421   Closed treatment of palatal or maxillary fracture (LeFort I type), with interdental wire fixation or fixation of denture or splint **4** T 80
MED: 100-2, 15, 260; 100-4, 12, 90.3; 100-4, 14, 10

21422   Open treatment of palatal or maxillary fracture (LeFort I type); C 80

21423   complicated (comminuted or involving cranial nerve foramina), multiple approaches C 80

21431   Closed treatment of craniofacial separation (LeFort III type) using interdental wire fixation of denture or splint C 80

21432   Open treatment of craniofacial separation (LeFort III type); with wiring and/or internal fixation C 80

21433   complicated (eg, comminuted or involving cranial nerve foramina), multiple surgical approaches C 80

21435   complicated, utilizing internal and/or external fixation techniques (eg, head cap, halo device, and/or intermaxillary fixation)   C 80 ⬚

> If an internal or an external fixation device is removed, consult CPT code 20670.

21436   complicated, multiple surgical approaches, internal fixation, with bone grafting (includes obtaining graft)   C 80 ⬚

21440   **Closed treatment of mandibular or maxillary alveolar ridge fracture (separate procedure)**   T 80 ⬚
     MED: 100-2, 15, 260; 100-4, 12, 90.3; 100-4, 14, 10

21445   **Open treatment of mandibular or maxillary alveolar ridge fracture (separate procedure)**   4 T 80 ⬚
     MED: 100-2, 15, 260; 100-4, 12, 90.3; 100-4, 14, 10

21450   **Closed treatment of mandibular fracture; without manipulation**   3 T 80 ⬚
     MED: 100-2, 15, 260; 100-4, 12, 90.3; 100-4, 14, 10

21451   **with manipulation**   4 T 80 ⬚
     MED: 100-2, 15, 260; 100-4, 12, 90.3; 100-4, 14, 10

21452   **Percutaneous treatment of mandibular fracture, with external fixation**   2 T 80 ⬚
     MED: 100-2, 15, 260; 100-4, 12, 90.3; 100-4, 14, 10

21453   **Closed treatment of mandibular fracture with interdental fixation**   3 T 80 ⬚
     MED: 100-2, 15, 260; 100-4, 12, 90.3; 100-4, 14, 10

21454   **Open treatment of mandibular fracture with external fixation**   5 T 80 ⬚
     MED: 100-2, 15, 260; 100-4, 12, 90.3; 100-4, 14, 10

21461   **Open treatment of mandibular fracture; without interdental fixation**   4 T 80 ⬚
     MED: 100-2, 15, 260; 100-4, 12, 90.3; 100-4, 14, 10

21462   **with interdental fixation**   5 T 80 ⬚
     MED: 100-2, 15, 260; 100-4, 12, 90.3; 100-4, 14, 10

21465   **Open treatment of mandibular condylar fracture**   4 T 80 ⬚
     MED: 100-2, 15, 260; 100-4, 12, 90.3; 100-4, 14, 10

21470   **Open treatment of complicated mandibular fracture by multiple surgical approaches including internal fixation, interdental fixation, and/or wiring of dentures or splints**   T 80 ⬚
     AMA: 2002, Nov, 10

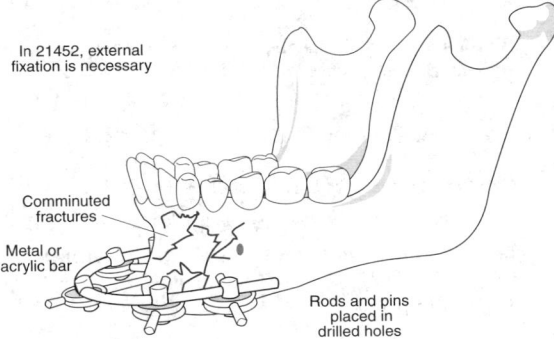

In 21452, external fixation is necessary

Comminuted fractures

Metal or acrylic bar

Rods and pins placed in drilled holes

21480   **Closed treatment of temporomandibular dislocation; initial or
        subsequent**   1 T 50 ▣
        MED: 100-2, 15, 260; 100-4, 12, 90.3; 100-4, 14, 10

21485   **complicated (eg, recurrent requiring intermaxillary fixation or
            splinting), initial or subsequent**   2 T 50 80 ▣
            MED: 100-2, 15, 260; 100-4, 12, 90.3; 100-4, 14, 10

21490   **Open treatment of temporomandibular dislocation**   3 T 50 80 ▣
        MED: 100-2, 15, 260; 100-4, 12, 90.3; 100-4, 14, 10

        To report interdental wire fixation, consult CPT code 21497.

~~21493~~ ~~Closed treatment of hyoid fracture; without manipulation~~

~~21494~~   ~~with manipulation~~

21495   **Open treatment of hyoid fracture**   T 80 ▣

        If laryngoplasty with open reduction of a fracture is performed, consult CPT
        code 31584. For treatment of a closed fracture of the larynx, consult the
        appropriate evaluation and management codes.

21497   **Interdental wiring, for condition other than fracture**   2 T 80 ▣
        MED: 100-2, 15, 260; 100-4, 12, 90.3; 100-4, 14, 10

        AMA: 1997, Mar, 10

OTHER PROCEDURES

21499   **Unlisted musculoskeletal procedure, head**   T 80

        If a craniofacial or a maxillofacial procedure is unlisted, consult CPT code
        21299.

NECK (SOFT TISSUES) AND THORAX

If these procedures are being performed on the cervical spine and back, consult CPT codes 21920 et
seq. If an injection is needed at the fracture site or trigger point, consult CPT code 20550.

INCISION

If a superficial abscess or hematoma is incised and drained, consult CPT codes 10060 and 10140.

21501   **Incision and drainage, deep abscess or hematoma, soft tissues of
        neck or thorax;**   2 T ▣
        MED: 100-2, 15, 260; 100-4, 12, 90.3; 100-4, 14, 10

        If a subfascial incision and drainage is performed on the posterior spine,
        consult CPT codes 22010-22015.

21502   **with partial rib ostectomy**   2 T 80 ▣
            MED: 100-2, 15, 260; 100-4, 12, 90.3; 100-4, 14, 10

21510   **Incision, deep, with opening of bone cortex (eg, for osteomyelitis
        or bone abscess), thorax**   C 80 ▣

EXCISION

If bone biopsy is needed, consult CPT codes 20220-20251.

21550   **Biopsy, soft tissue of neck or thorax**   T ▣

        If a needle biopsy of soft tissue is needed, consult CPT code 20206.

21555   **Excision tumor, soft tissue of neck or thorax; subcutaneous**   2 T ▣
        MED: 100-2, 15, 260; 100-4, 12, 90.3; 100-4, 14, 10

        AMA: 2002, Oct, 11

| 21556 | deep, subfascial, intramuscular | 2 T ◪ |
| | MED: 100-2, 15, 260; 100-4, 12, 90.3; 100-4, 14, 10 | |

| 21557 | Radical resection of tumor (eg, malignant neoplasm), soft tissue of neck or thorax | T 80 ◪ |

| 21600 | Excision of rib, partial | 2 T 80 ◪ |
| | MED: 100-2, 15, 260; 100-4, 12, 90.3; 100-4, 14, 10 | |

If a radical resection for a tumor is performed, consult CPT code 19260.

If radical debridement due to injury is performed, consult CPT codes 11040-11044.

| 21610 | Costotransversectomy (separate procedure) | 2 T 80 ◪ |
| | MED: 100-2, 15, 260; 100-4, 12, 90.3; 100-4, 14, 10 | |

21615	Excision first and/or cervical rib;	C 50 80 ◪
21616	with sympathectomy	C 50 80 ◪
21620	Ostectomy of sternum, partial	C 80 ◪
21627	Sternal debridement	C 80 ◪

If both debridement and closure are performed, consult CPT code 21750.

| 21630 | Radical resection of sternum; | C 80 ◪ |
| 21632 | with mediastinal lymphadenectomy | C 80 ◪ |

REPAIR, REVISION, AND/OR RECONSTRUCTION
If the wound is superficial, consult the Integumentary System section under Repair, Simple.

21685	Hyoid myotomy and suspension	T 80 ◪
21700	Division of scalenus anticus; without resection of cervical rib	2 T 80 ◪
	MED: 100-2, 15, 260; 100-4, 12, 90.3; 100-4, 14, 10	

21705	with resection of cervical rib	C 80 ◪
21720	Division of sternocleidomastoid for torticollis, open operation; without cast application	3 T 80 ◪
	MED: 100-2, 15, 260; 100-4, 12, 90.3; 100-4, 14, 10	

If nerve transsection is performed, consult CPT codes 63191 and 64722.

| 21725 | with cast application | 3 T 80 ◪ |
| | MED: 100-2, 15, 260; 100-4, 12, 90.3; 100-4, 14, 10 | |

21740	Reconstructive repair of pectus excavatum or carinatum; open	C 80 ◪
21742	minimally invasive approach (Nuss procedure), without thoracoscopy	T 80 ◪
21743	minimally invasive approach (Nuss procedure), with thoracoscopy	T 80 ◪
21750	Closure of median sternotomy separation with or without debridement (separate procedure)	C 80 ◪

FRACTURE AND/OR DISLOCATION

| 21800 | Closed treatment of rib fracture, uncomplicated, each | 1 T ◪ |
| | MED: 100-2, 15, 260; 100-4, 12, 90.3; 100-4, 14, 10 | |

| 21805 | Open treatment of rib fracture without fixation, each | 2 T 80 ◪ |
| | MED: 100-2, 15, 260; 100-4, 12, 90.3; 100-4, 14, 10 | |

| 21810 | Treatment of rib fracture requiring external fixation (flail chest) | C 80 ◪ |

Musculoskeletal System

21820 — 21935

| 21820 | Closed treatment of sternum fracture | 1 T ▣ |

MED: 100-2, 15, 260; 100-4, 12, 90.3; 100-4, 14, 10

| 21825 | Open treatment of sternum fracture with or without skeletal fixation | C 80 ▣ |

> If a sternoclavicular dislocation is treated, consult CPT codes 23520-23532.

OTHER PROCEDURES

| 21899 | Unlisted procedure, neck or thorax | T 80 |

BACK AND FLANK, EXCISION

| 21920 | Biopsy, soft tissue of back or flank; superficial | T ▣ |
| 21925 | deep | 2 T ▣ |

MED: 100-2, 15, 260; 100-4, 12, 90.3; 100-4, 14, 10

> If soft tissue needle biopsy is performed, consult CPT code 20206.

| 21930 | Excision, tumor, soft tissue of back or flank | 2 T ▣ |

MED: 100-2, 15, 260; 100-4, 12, 90.3; 100-4, 14, 10

| 21935 | Radical resection of tumor (eg, malignant neoplasm), soft tissue of back or flank | 3 T ▣ |

MED: 100-2, 15, 260; 100-4, 12, 90.3; 100-4, 14, 10

SPINE (VERTEBRAL COLUMN)

SPINAL SURGERY

Procedure codes for reporting spine surgeries are found in two sections of the CPT book. Fracture/dislocation, spinal fusion/instrumentation, and treatment of scoliosis/kyphosis are reported with codes from the musculoskeletal section. Procedures of the spine with spinal cord involvement are reported with codes from the nervous system section (62263–63746). It is not unusual for procedures to require a procedure from the musculoskeletal section (arthrodesis, instrumentation) with a procedure from the nervous system section (laminectomy, hemilaminectomy, diskectomy), and it is appropriate to report both procedures separately.

Arthrodesis is a joint fusion and spinal arthrodesis is reported with 22548–22632. These codes are assigned based on technique (anterior/anterolateral, posterior/posterolateral, or lateral). Codes 22548–22558, 22590–22612, and 22630 are for single interspace arthrodesis—two adjacent vertebral segments. When the surgery is performed on more than one interspace, each additional interspace is reported with 22585, 22614, or 22632. These procedures are considered "add on" services and are not reported with modifier 51.

Procedures for scoliosis and kyphosis (22800–22819) also include arthrodesis procedures. The arthrodesis procedures in this section differ since they involve multiple vertebral segments, and the code is assigned based on the number of segments treated.

Spinal instrumentation (22840–22855) involves placement of rods, hooks, and/or wires to stabilize the fusion or fracture. Instrumentation codes are assigned based on the type of instrumentation (segmental, non-segmental), the approach (anterior, posterior) and the number of vertebral segments involved. Instrumentation codes are exempt from modifier 51 and are reported in addition to the definitive procedure. However, if instrumentation reinsertion or removal or exploration of fusion is performed in conjunction with other definitive procedures including arthrodesis, modifier 51 should be appended.

Bone allografts and autografts should be reported separately with codes 20930–20938. These codes are exempt from modifier 51 and are reported in addition to the definitive procedure. Procedures of the spine with spinal cord are found in the nervous system section (62263–63746).

Diskectomy is the excision of intervertebral disk material. Codes 63075–63078 are specific to this surgery; however, many other codes from this section of the nervous system include diskectomies as a component of the procedure. Laminectomy is the removal of the entire lamina on both sides, inclusive of the spinous process. Hemilaminectomy is the excision of the right or left lamina, the posterior bony covering of the spinal cord. Laminotomy is the process of creating a hole in the lamina to achieve the required result, for example, excising a herniated intervertebral disk.

For the injection procedure of a myelography, consult CPT code 62284. For the injection procedure of a diskography, consult CPT codes 62290 and 62291. For the injection procedure for chemonucleolysis, single or multiple levels, consult CPT code 62292. For the injection procedure of facet joints, consult CPT codes 64470-64476 and 64622-64627.

For needle or trocar biopsy, consult CPT codes 20220-20225.

For bone biopsy, consult CPT code 20220-20251.

Report bone grafting procedure separately in addition to spinal arthrodesis. Consult codes 20930–20938. Do not use modifier 51 with these codes. Do not report modifier 62 with codes 20900–20938.

Spinal instrumentation codes are reported separately in addition to spinal arthrodesis. Consult codes 22840–22855 for spinal instrumentation codes performed with definitive vertebral procedures. Do not report modifier 51 with codes 22840–22848 and 22851. Do not report modifier 62 with instrumentation codes 22840–22848 and 22850–22852.

In some instances vertebral procedures are followed by arthrodesis and may also include bone grafts and instrumentation.

When arthrodesis is performed with another procedure, the arthrodesis should be reported in addition to the vertebral procedure with modifier 51. Because bone grafts and instrumentation are never performed without arthrodesis, modifier 51 is not used.

If arthrodesis is performed without other procedures and is combined with another definitive procedure, use modifier 51.

Surgeons that work together, each performing distinct parts of a single surgery, should report the procedure code and use modifier 62.

INCISION

- **22010**   **Incision and drainage, open, of deep abscess (subfascial), posterior spine; cervical, thoracic, or cervicothoracic**

- **22015**   **lumbar, sacral, or lumbosacral**

  Code 22015 cannot be reported with 22010.

  Code 22015 cannot be reported with instrumentation removal, codes 10180, 22850, and 22852.

  To report incision and drainage of a superficial abscess or hematoma, consult codes 10060 and 10140.

EXCISION

Surgeons, each performing distinct parts of a single surgery, should report the procedure code and use modifier 62. Modifier 62 may be used with code(s) 22100–22102, 22110–22114 and as appropriate to the related additional vertebral segment add-on code(s) 22103 and 22116 when both surgeons continue to perform distinct components of the surgery, working together as primary surgeons.

22100	**Partial excision of posterior vertebral component (eg, spinous process, lamina or facet) for intrinsic bony lesion, single vertebral segment;**
	cervical
22101	**thoracic**
22102	**lumbar**

22100 cervical — T 80 ⊡
22101 thoracic — T 80 ⊡
22102 lumbar — T 80 ⊡

Musculoskeletal System

22103 — 22222

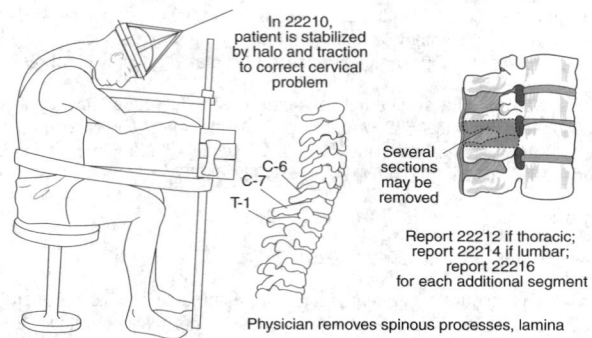

In 22210,
patient is stabilized
by halo and traction
to correct cervical
problem

Several
sections
may be
removed

C-6
C-7
T-1

Report 22212 if thoracic;
report 22214 if lumbar;
report 22216
for each additional segment

Physician removes spinous processes, lamina

+ **22103**   **each additional segment (List separately in addition to code for primary procedure)**   T 80 ⚑

> Note that 22103 is an add-on code and must be used in conjunction with 22100, 22101, and 22102.

22110   **Partial excision of vertebral body for intrinsic bony lesion, without decompression of spinal cord or nerve root(s), single vertebral segment; cervical**   C 80 ⚑

22112   **thoracic**   C 80 ⚑

22114   **lumbar**   C 80 ⚑

+ **22116**   **each additional vertebral segment (List separately in addition to code for primary procedure)**   C 80 ⚑

> Note that 22116 is in add-on code and must be used in conjunction with 22110, 22112 and 22114.

OSTEOTOMY

Surgeons each performing distinct parts of a single surgery when working together as primary surgeons should report the procedure code and use modifier 62. Modifier 62 may be used with code(s) 22210–22214, 22220–22224 and, as appropriate to the related segment, add-on code(s) 22216 and 22226 if both surgeons continue to perform distinct components of the surgery. Modifier 62 should not be reported with codes 20900–20938.

Additional procedures, such as arthrodesis (CPT codes 22590-22632), bone grafting (CPT codes 20930-20938), and instrumentation (CPT codes 22840-22855), are reported in addition to the CPT codes for the definitive procedure. Do not report modifier 51 with instrumentation procedures, codes 22840–22855, or with bone graft procedures, codes 20930–20938.

22210   **Osteotomy of spine, posterior or posterolateral approach, one vertebral segment; cervical**   C 80 ⚑

22212   **thoracic**   C 80 ⚑

22214   **lumbar**   C 80 ⚑

+ **22216**   **each additional vertebral segment (List separately in addition to primary procedure)**   C ⚑

> Note that 22216 is an add-on code and must be used in conjunction with 22210, 22212, and 22214.

22220   **Osteotomy of spine, including diskectomy, anterior approach, single vertebral segment; cervical**   C 80 ⚑

22222   **thoracic**   T 80 ⚑

26 / TC Professional/Technical Component   **80 / 80** Assist-at-Surgery Allowed/With Documentation   ⊙ Conscious Sedation

Unlisted   Not Covered   **MED:** Pubs 100/NCD Reference   **1 - 9** ASC Group   ⑥³ Modifier 63 Exempt

130 — Surgery   CPT only © 2005 American Medical Association. All Rights Reserved. *(Black Ink)*   © 2005 Ingenix, Inc. *(Blue Ink)*

	22224	lumbar	[C] [80] [↰]
+	22226	each additional vertebral segment (List separately in addition to code for primary procedure)	[C] [↰]

> Note that 22226 is an add-on code and must be used in conjunction with 22220, 22222, and 22224.

FRACTURE AND/OR DISLOCATION

Surgeons, each performing distinct parts of a single surgery, when working together as primary surgeons should report the procedure code and use modifier 62. Modifier 62 may be used with code(s) 22318–22327 and, as appropriate to the related additional fractured vertebra or dislocated segment, add-on code 22328 if both surgeons continue to perform distinct components of the surgery.

Additional procedures, such as arthrodesis (CPT codes 22590–22632), bone grafting (CPT codes 20930–20938), and instrumentation (CPT codes 22840–22855), are reported in addition to the CPT codes for the definitive procedure. Do not append modifier 51 with instrumentation procedures, codes 22840–22855, or with bone graft procedures, codes 20930–20938.

22305   **Closed treatment of vertebral process fracture(s)**   [1] [T] [↰]
      MED: 100-2, 15, 260; 100-4, 12, 90.3; 100-4, 14, 10

22310   **Closed treatment of vertebral body fracture(s), without manipulation, requiring and including casting or bracing**   [1] [T] [↰]
      MED: 100-2, 15, 260; 100-4, 12, 90.3; 100-4, 14, 10

22315   **Closed treatment of vertebral fracture(s) and/or dislocations(s) requiring casting or bracing, with and including casting and/or bracing, with or without anesthesia, by manipulation or traction**   [2] [T] [↰]
      MED: 100-2, 15, 260; 100-4, 12, 90.3; 100-4, 14, 10

> If spinal subluxation is performed, consult CPT code 97140.

22318   **Open treatment and/or reduction of odontoid fracture(s) and or dislocation(s) (including os odontoideum), anterior approach, including placement of internal fixation; without grafting**   [C] [80] [↰]
      AMA: 1999, Nov, 11

22319   **with grafting**   [C] [80] [↰]
      AMA: 1999, Nov, 11

22325   **Open treatment and/or reduction of vertebral fracture(s) and/or dislocation(s); posterior approach, one fractured vertebrae or dislocated segment; lumbar**   [C] [80] [↰]
      AMA: 1997, Sep, 8

22326   **cervical**   [C] [80] [↰]
      AMA: 1997, Sep, 8

22327   **thoracic**   [C] [80] [↰]
      AMA: 1997, Sep, 8

+   **22328**   **each additional fractured vertebrae or dislocated segment (List separately in addition to code for primary procedure)**   [C] [80] [↰]

> Note that 22328 is an add-on code and must be used in conjunction with 22325, 22326, and 22327.

> For anterior approach, consult CPT codes 63081-63091, and appropriate arthrodesis, bone graft and instrumentation codes.

[↰] CCI Comp	[50] Bilateral Procedure	✛ CPT Add-on Code	⊘ Modifier -51 Exempt	♂ Male	♀ Female
● New Code	▲ Revised Code	[M] Maternity Edit	[A] Age Edit	[A]–[Y] APC Status Ind.	AMA: CPT Assistant

© 2005 Ingenix, Inc. *(Blue Ink)*   CPT only © 2005 American Medical Association. All Rights Reserved. *(Black Ink)*   Surgery — 131

Musculoskeletal System

22505 — 22525

MANIPULATION

22505   **Manipulation of spine requiring anesthesia, any region**   ▣ Ⓣ ▣
           MED: 100-2, 15, 260; 100-4, 12, 90.3; 100-4, 14, 10

           AMA: 1999, Jan, 11; 1997, Mar, 11

           For manipulation of the spine without anesthesia, consult CPT code 97140.

VERTEBRAL BODY, EMBOLIZATION OR INJECTION
These CPT codes describe the injection of a fixative into the vertebral body to bond bone fragments.

22520   **Percutaneous vertebroplasty, one vertebral body, unilateral or bilateral injection; thoracic**   Ⓣ ▣
           AMA: 2001, Mar, 1

22521   **lumbar**   Ⓣ ▣
           AMA: 2001, Mar, 1

+   **22522**   **each additional thoracic or lumbar vertebral body (List separately in addition to code for primary procedure)**   Ⓣ ▣
           AMA: 2001, Mar, 1

           Note that 22522 is an add-on code and must be used in conjunction with 22520 and 22521.

           To report radiological supervision and interpretation, consult CPT codes 76012 and 76013.

●   **22523**   **Percutaneous vertebral augmentation, including cavity creation (fracture reduction and bone biopsy included when performed) using mechanical device, one vertebral body, unilateral or bilateral cannulation (eg, kyphoplasty); thoracic**

●   **22524**   **lumbar**

+ ●   **22525**   **each additional thoracic or lumbar vertebral body (List separately in addition to code for primary procedure)**

           Code 22525 cannot be reported with 20225 when performed at the same level as 22523-22525.

           Note that 22525 is an add-on code and must be used in conjunction with 22523 and 22524.

           To report radiological supervision and interpretation, consult CPT codes 76012 and 76013.

ARTHRODESIS
Arthrodesis may be performed without other procedures so when it is performed in addition to other procedures such as osteotomy, fracture care, vertebral corpectomy or laminectomy, append modifier 51. Codes 22585, 22614 and 22632 are add-on procedures and should not be reported with the 51 modifier.

Instrumentation procedures should be reported with codes 22840-22855. Report codes 22840-22848 and 22851 with the code(s) for the definitive procedure(s) without appending modifier 51. Report modifier 51 with codes 22849, 22850, 22852 and 22855 when instrumentation reinsertion or removal codes are used with the other definitive procedures. This includes arthrodesis, decompression, and exploration of fusion. Do not report modifier 62, to spinal instrumentation codes 22840-22848 and 22850-22852.

Bone graft codes, 20930–20938, are reported in addition to the code for the definitive procedure without modifier 51. Modifier 62 should not be appended to codes 20900–20938.

LATERAL EXTRACAVITARY APPROACH TECHNIQUE

22532   Arthrodesis, lateral extracavitary technique, including minimal diskectomy to prepare interspace (other than for decompression); thoracic   C 80 🔲

22533   lumbar   C 80 🔲

+ 22534   thoracic or lumbar, each additional vertebral segment (List separately in addition to code for primary procedure)   C 80 🔲

> Note that 22534 is an add-on code and must be used in conjunction with 22532 and 22533.

ANTERIOR OR ANTEROLATERAL APPROACH TECHNIQUE

These codes address surgical approaches to the spine from the front or to the side of the front. CPT codes 22554-22558 are used to report arthrodesis of a single vertebral interspace. Consult CPT code 22585 for additional interspaces. The non-bony compartment between two adjacent vertebral bodies that contain the intervertebral disk, the nucleus pulposus, annulus fibrosus and two cartilagenous endplates is considered the vertebral interspace.

22548   Arthrodesis, anterior transoral or extraoral technique, clivus-C1-C2 (atlas-axis), with or without excision of odontoid process   C 80 🔲
MED: 100-3, 150.2

AMA: 2000, Sep, 10; 1997, Sep, 8; 1996, Feb, 7; 1993, Spring, 36

> To report the injection procedure for myelography and/or computed tomography, consult CPT code 62284. To report the injection procedure of a diskography, consult CPT codes 62290 and 62291. To report the injection procedure To report chemonucleolysis, single or multiple levels, consult CPT code 62292. To report the injection procedure of facet joints, consult CPT codes 64470-64476 and 64622-64627.

22554   Arthrodesis, anterior interbody technique, including minimal diskectomy to prepare interspace (other than for decompression); cervical below C2   C 80 🔲

MED: 100-3, 150.2

AMA: 2002, Feb, 4; 2001, Jan, 12; 2000, Sep, 10; 1997, Sep, 8; 1993, Spring, 36

22556   thoracic   C 80 🔲
MED: 100-3, 150.2

AMA: 2002, Feb, 4; 2000, Sep, 10; 1997, Sep, 8; 1996, Jul, 7; 1993, Spring, 36

22558   lumbar   C 80 🔲
MED: 100-3, 150.2

AMA: 2000, Sep, 10; 1997, Sep, 8; 1996, Mar, 6; 1996, Jul, 7; 1993, Spring, 36

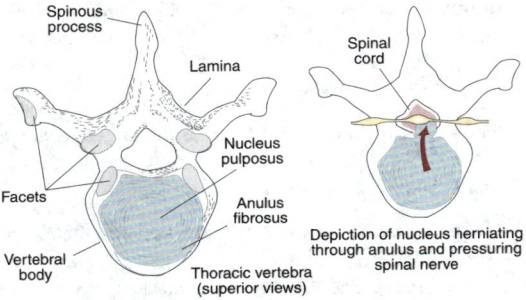

Spinous process
Lamina
Spinal cord
Nucleus pulposus
Facets
Anulus fibrosus
Vertebral body
Thoracic vertebra (superior views)
Depiction of nucleus herniating through anulus and pressuring spinal nerve

Intervertebral disc displacement and prolapse are major causes of disability among working people. When a disc prolapses, nuclear material bursts through the anulus fibrosus damaging ligaments, nerve roots, and other structures. The herniated matter usually fibroses and shrinks over time

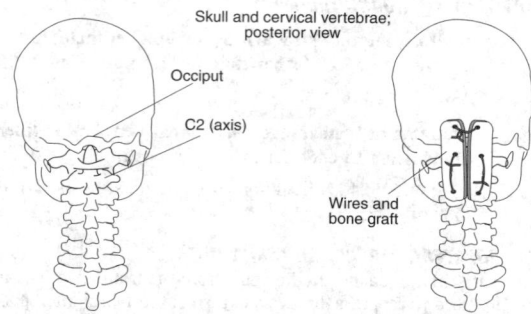

In 22590, the physician fuses skull to C2 (axis) to stabilize cervical vertebrae; anchor holes are drilled in the occiput of the skull

+   22585   **each additional interspace (List separately in addition to code for primary procedure)**   C 80 ⟲
                         MED: 100-3, 150.2

                         AMA: 2000, Sep, 10; 1997, Sep, 8; 1996, Mar, 6; 1993, Spring, 36

                         Note that 22585 is an add-on code and must be used in conjunction with 22554, 22556, and 22558.

ARTHRODESIS — POSTERIOR, POSTEROLATERAL OR LATERAL TRANSVERSE PROCESS TECHNIQUE

These codes address surgical approaches to the spine from the back and side. The non-bony compartment between two adjacent vertebral bodies that contain the intervertebral disk, the nucleus pulposus, annulus fibrosus, and two cartilagenous endplates is considered the vertebral interspace.

Additional procedures, such as bone grafting (CPT codes 20930-20938) and instrumentation (CPT codes 22840-22855), are reported in addition to the CPT codes for the definitive procedure. Do not append modifier 51.

22590   **Arthrodesis, posterior technique, craniocervical (occiput-C2)**   C 80 ⟲
                   MED: 100-3, 150.2

                   AMA: 1997, Sep, 8; 1993, Spring, 36

22595   **Arthrodesis, posterior technique, atlas-axis (C1-C2)**   C 80 ⟲
                   MED: 100-3, 150.2

                   AMA: 1997, Sep, 8; 1993, Spring, 36

22600   **Arthrodesis, posterior or posterolateral technique, single level; cervical below C2 segment**   C 80 ⟲
                   MED: 100-3, 150.2

                   AMA: 1997, Sep, 8; 1993, Spring, 36

22610   **thoracic (with or without lateral transverse technique)**   C 80 ⟲
                   MED: 100-3, 150.2

                   AMA: 1997, Sep, 8; 1993, Spring, 36

22612   **lumbar (with or without lateral transverse technique)**   T 80 ⟲
                   MED: 100-3, 150.2

                   AMA: 1997, Sep, 8, 11; 1996, Mar, 7; 1993, Spring, 36

26 / TC Professional/Technical Component   80 / 80 Assist-at-Surgery Allowed/With Documentation   ☉ Conscious Sedation
  Unlisted   Not Covered   MED: Pubs 100/NCD Reference   1 - 9 ASC Group   63 Modifier 63 Exempt
134 — Surgery   CPT only © 2005 American Medical Association. All Rights Reserved. *(Black Ink)*   © 2005 Ingenix, Inc. *(Blue Ink)*

+   **22614**   **each additional vertebral segment (List separately in addition to code for primary procedure)**   T 80 ▣
MED: 100-3, 150.2

AMA: 1996, Mar, 7

Note that 22614 is an add-on code and must be used in conjunction with 22600, 22610, and 22612.

22630   **Arthrodesis, posterior interbody technique, including laminectomy and/or diskectomy to prepare interspace (other than for decompression), single interspace; lumbar**   C 80 ▣
MED: 100-3, 150.2

AMA: 2001, Jan, 12; 1999, Nov, 11; 1999, Dec, 2; 1997, Sep, 8; 1993, Spring, 36

+   **22632**   **each additional interspace (List separately in addition to code for primary procedure)**   C 80 ▣
MED: 100-3, 150.2

AMA: 1999, Dec, 2; 1997, Sep, 8

Note that 22632 is an add-on code and must be used in conjunction with 22630.

SPINE DEFORMITY (EG, SCOLIOSIS, KYPHOSIS)

To report bone graft procedures, consult CPT codes 20930–20938. Bone graft codes should be reported in addition to code(s) for the definitive procedure(s) without modifier 51. Modifier 62 should not be used with bone graft codes 20900–20938.

A vertebral segment describes the basic element into which the spine may be divided. It represents one complete vertebral bone and its associated articular processes and laminae.

Surgeons, each performing distinct parts of an arthrodesis for spinal deformity, when working together as primary surgeons, should report the procedure code and use modifier 62. Modifier 62 may be used with code(s) 22800–22819 if both surgeons continue to perform distinct components of the surgery.

Additional procedures, such as bone grafting (CPT codes 20930-20938) and instrumentation (CPT codes 22840-22855), are reported in addition to the CPT codes for the definitive procedure. Do not append modifier 51.

22800   **Arthrodesis, posterior, for spinal deformity, with or without cast; up to 6 vertebral segments**   C 80 ▣
MED: 100-3, 150.2

22802   **7 to 12 vertebral segments**   C 80 ▣
MED: 100-3, 150.2

AMA: 1996, Mar, 10

22804   **13 or more vertebral segments**   C 80 ▣
MED: 100-3, 150.2

22808   **Arthrodesis, anterior, for spinal deformity, with or without cast; 2 to 3 vertebral segments**   C 80 ▣
MED: 100-3, 150.2

Smith-Robinson arthrodesis

22810   **4 to 7 vertebral segments**   C 80 ▣
MED: 100-3, 150.2

AMA: 1997, Sep, 8; 1996, Mar, 10

Musculoskeletal System

22812 — 22830

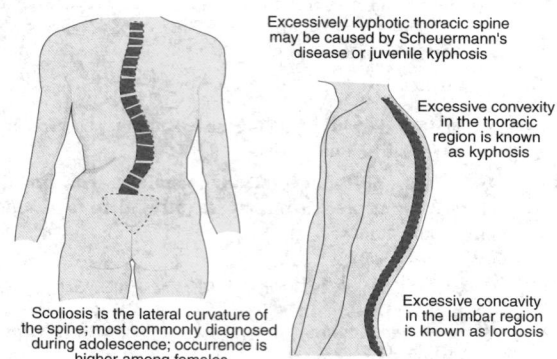

Excessively kyphotic thoracic spine may be caused by Scheuermann's disease or juvenile kyphosis

Excessive convexity in the thoracic region is known as kyphosis

Excessive concavity in the lumbar region is known as lordosis

Scoliosis is the lateral curvature of the spine; most commonly diagnosed during adolescence; occurrence is higher among females

22812   **8 or more vertebral segments**   C 80 ↻
             MED: 100-3, 150.2

22818   **Kyphectomy, circumferential exposure of spine and resection of vertebral segment(s) (including body and posterior elements); single or 2 segments**   C 80 ↻
             MED: 100-3, 150.2

             AMA: 1997, Nov, 14

22819   **3 or more segments**   C 80 ↻
             MED: 100-3, 150.2

             AMA: 1997, Nov, 14

             If arthrodesis is performed, consult CPT codes 22800-22804 and append modifier 51.

EXPLORATION

For instrumentation procedures, consult codes 22840-22855. Report 22840-22848 and 22851 with the codes(s) for the definitive procedure(s) without appending modifier 51. Report modifier 51 with 22849, 22850, 22852 and 22855 when instrumentation reinsertion or removal is reported with other definitive procedures such as arthrodesis, decompression, and exploration of fusion. For exploration of fusion, consult 22830. Report modifier 51 with code 22830 when exploration is reported with other definitive procedures such as arthrodesis and decompression.

22830   **Exploration of spinal fusion**   C 80 ↻
             MED: 100-3, 150.2

             AMA: 1997, Sep, 11

SPINAL INSTRUMENTATION

This section describes the instruments affixed to the spine to correct defects resulting from injury or deformity. The instrumentation may correct the spine's anatomic position or help support injured vertebrae. Instrumentation is divided into segmental and non-segmental. Segmental instrumentation connects to each or most vertebra(e) it spans. Non-segmental instrumentation may span several vertebrae between fixation.

Spinal instrumentation and additional procedures, such as bone grafting (CPT codes 20930-20938) are reported in addition to the CPT code(s) for the primary procedure. Do not append modifier 51.

Report codes 22840-22855 when used with code(s) for fracture dislocation, arthrodesis or exploration of fusion of spine 22325-22328, 22548-22812, and 22830. Do not append modifier 51 to codes 22840-22848, 22851 when reported with code(s) for the definitive procedure(s).Report modifier 51 to codes 22849, 22850, 22852, and 22855 if they are used with other definitive procedure(s). This includes arthrodesis, decompression, and exploration of fusion. Do not report code 22849 with CPT codes 22850, 22852, and 22855 at the same spinal levels.

⊘ **22840** Posterior non-segmental instrumentation (eg, Harrington rod technique, pedicle fixation across one interspace, atlantoaxial transarticular screw fixation, sublaminar wiring at C1, facet screw fixation) C 80 ⌐
AMA: 1999, Nov, 12; 1997, Sep, 8; 1996, Jul, 10; 1996, Feb, 6

⊘ **22841** Internal spinal fixation by wiring of spinous processes C
AMA: 1997, Sep, 8; 1996, Feb, 6

Hibb's fusion

⊘ **22842** Posterior segmental instrumentation (eg, pedicle fixation, dual rods with multiple hooks and sublaminal wires); 3 to 6 vertebral segments C 80 ⌐
AMA: 1997, Sep, 8; 1996, Mar, 7; 1996, Feb, 6

⊘ **22843**   7 to 12 vertebral segments C 80 ⌐
AMA: 1997, Sep, 8; 1996, Feb, 6

⊘ **22844**   13 or more vertebral segments C 80 ⌐
AMA: 1997, Sep, 8; 1996, Feb, 6

⊘ **22845** Anterior instrumentation; 2 to 3 vertebral segments C 80 ⌐
AMA: 1997, Sep, 8; 1996, Mar, 10; 1996, Jul, 7,10; 1996, Feb, 6

Dwyer instrumentation technique

⊘ **22846**   4 to 7 vertebral segments C 80 ⌐
AMA: 1997, Sep, 8; 1996, Feb, 6

⊘ **22847**   8 or more vertebral segments C 80 ⌐
AMA: 1997, Sep, 8; 1996, Feb, 6

⊘ **22848** Pelvic fixation (attachment of caudal end of instrumentation to pelvic bony structures) other than sacrum C 80 ⌐
AMA: 1997, Sep, 8; 1996, Feb, 6

22849 Reinsertion of spinal fixation device C 80 ⌐
AMA: 2002, Nov, 1; 1997, Sep, 8; 1996, Feb, 6

22850 Removal of posterior nonsegmental instrumentation (eg, Harrington rod) C 80 ⌐
AMA: 1997, Sep, 8; 1996, Feb, 6

⊘ **22851** Application of intervertebral biomechanical device(s) (eg, synthetic cage(s), threaded bone dowel(s), methylmethacrylate) to vertebral defect or interspace C 80 ⌐
AMA: 2001, Mar, 1; 1999, Nov, 12; 1999, Dec, 2; 1997, Sep, 8; 1996, Feb, 6

22852 Removal of posterior segmental instrumentation C 80 ⌐
AMA: 1997, Sep, 8; 1996, Feb, 6

22855 Removal of anterior instrumentation C 80 ⌐
AMA: 2002, Nov, 1; 1997, Sep, 8; 1996, Feb, 6

OTHER PROCEDURES

22899 Unlisted procedure, spine T 80
AMA: 2000, Sep, 10; 2000, May, 11

ABDOMEN

Replacement of casts and/or traction devices subsequent to the first should be reported separately. CPT codes for other additional procedures, such as obtaining grafts and external fixation, should only be used if the procedure is not already listed as included as part of the basic procedure. Consult the glossary for terms and definitions and the front matter of this chapter for additional information.

EXCISION

22900   **Excision, abdominal wall tumor, subfascial (eg, desmoid)**   4 T 80
MED: 100-2, 15, 260; 100-4, 12, 90.3; 100-4, 14, 10

OTHER PROCEDURES

22999   **Unlisted procedure, abdomen, musculoskeletal system**   T 80

SHOULDER

Codes listed in the Musculoskeletal chapter include the application and removal of the first cast or traction device. Replacement of casts and/or traction devices subsequent to the first should be reported separately. CPT codes for other additional procedures, such as obtaining grafts and external fixation, should only be used if the procedure is not already listed as included as part of the basic procedure. Consult the glossary for terms and definitions.

This section includes the acromioclavicular joint, clavicle, head and neck of the humerus, shoulder joint, and sternoclavicular joint.

INCISION

23000   **Removal of subdeltoid calcareous deposits, open**   2 T 80
MED: 100-2, 15, 260; 100-4, 12, 90.3; 100-4, 14, 10

To report arthroscopic removal of bursal deposits, consult CPT code 29999.

23020   **Capsular contracture release (eg, Sever type procedure)**   2 T 50 80
MED: 100-2, 15, 260; 100-4, 12, 90.3; 100-4, 14, 10

If superficial incision and drainage is performed, consult CPT codes 10040-10160.

23030   **Incision and drainage, shoulder area; deep abscess or hematoma**   1 T
MED: 100-2, 15, 260; 100-4, 12, 90.3; 100-4, 14, 10

23031   **infected bursa**   3 T 50
MED: 100-2, 15, 260; 100-4, 12, 90.3; 100-4, 14, 10

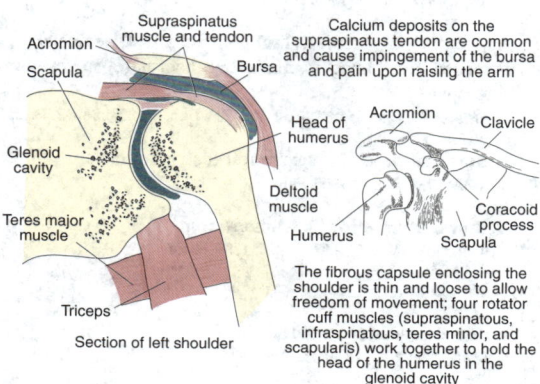

Supraspinatus muscle and tendon
Acromion
Scapula
Bursa
Calcium deposits on the supraspinatus tendon are common and cause impingement of the bursa and pain upon raising the arm
Glenoid cavity
Head of humerus
Acromion
Clavicle
Deltoid muscle
Teres major muscle
Humerus
Coracoid process
Scapula
Triceps
Section of left shoulder
The fibrous capsule enclosing the shoulder is thin and loose to allow freedom of movement; four rotator cuff muscles (supraspinatous, infraspinatous, teres minor, and scapularis) work together to hold the head of the humerus in the glenoid cavity

23035 Incision, bone cortex (eg, osteomyelitis or bone abscess), shoulder area ③ T 50 80 �
  MED: 100-2, 15, 260; 100-4, 12, 90.3; 100-4, 14, 10

23040 Arthrotomy, glenohumeral joint, including exploration, drainage, or removal of foreign body ③ T 50 80 ▐
  MED: 100-2, 15, 260; 100-4, 12, 90.3; 100-4, 14, 10

  AMA: 1998, Nov, 8

23044 Arthrotomy, acromioclavicular, sternoclavicular joint, including exploration, drainage, or removal of foreign body ④ T 50 ▐
  MED: 100-2, 15, 260; 100-4, 12, 90.3; 100-4, 14, 10

  AMA: 1998, Nov, 8

EXCISION

23065 Biopsy, soft tissue of shoulder area; superficial T 50 ▐
23066   deep ② T 50 ▐
  MED: 100-2, 15, 260; 100-4, 12, 90.3; 100-4, 14, 10

  If a needle biopsy of soft tissue is performed, consult CPT code 20206.

23075 Excision, soft tissue tumor, shoulder area; subcutaneous ② T 50 ▐
  MED: 100-2, 15, 260; 100-4, 12, 90.3; 100-4, 14, 10

  AMA: 1998, Nov, 8; 1992, Summer, 22

23076   deep, subfascial or intramuscular ② T 50 ▐
  MED: 100-2, 15, 260; 100-4, 12, 90.3; 100-4, 14, 10

  AMA: 1992, Summer, 22

23077 Radical resection of tumor (eg, malignant neoplasm), soft tissue of shoulder area ③ T 50 80 ▐
  MED: 100-2, 15, 260; 100-4, 12, 90.3; 100-4, 14, 10

23100 Arthrotomy, glenohumeral joint, including biopsy ② T 50 80 ▐
  MED: 100-2, 15, 260; 100-4, 12, 90.3; 100-4, 14, 10

  AMA: 1998, Nov, 8

23101 Arthrotomy, acromioclavicular joint or sternoclavicular joint, including biopsy and/or excision of torn cartilage ⑦ T 50 ▐
  MED: 100-2, 15, 260; 100-4, 12, 90.3; 100-4, 14, 10

  AMA: 1998, Nov, 8

23105 Arthrotomy; glenohumeral joint, with synovectomy, with or without biopsy ④ T 50 80 ▐
  MED: 100-2, 15, 260; 100-4, 12, 90.3; 100-4, 14, 10

  AMA: 1998, Nov, 8

23106   sternoclavicular joint, with synovectomy, with or without biopsy ④ T 50 ▐
  MED: 100-2, 15, 260; 100-4, 12, 90.3; 100-4, 14, 10

23107 Arthrotomy, glenohumeral joint, with joint exploration, with or without removal of loose or foreign body ④ T 50 80 ▐
  MED: 100-2, 15, 260; 100-4, 12, 90.3; 100-4, 14, 10

23120 Claviculectomy; partial [5] [T] [80] [►]
MED: 100-2, 15, 260; 100-4, 12, 90.3; 100-4, 14, 10

If performed arthroscopically consult CPT code 29824.
Mumford claviculectomy

23125 total [5] [T] [50] [80] [►]
MED: 100-2, 15, 260; 100-4, 12, 90.3; 100-4, 14, 10

23130 Acromioplasty or acromionectomy, partial, with or without coracoacromial ligament release [5] [T] [50] [►]
MED: 100-2, 15, 260; 100-4, 12, 90.3; 100-4, 14, 10

AMA: 2001, Aug, 11

23140 Excision or curettage of bone cyst or benign tumor of clavicle or scapula; [4] [T] [50] [►]
MED: 100-2, 15, 260; 100-4, 12, 90.3; 100-4, 14, 10

23145 with autograft (includes obtaining graft) [5] [T] [50] [80] [►]
MED: 100-2, 15, 260; 100-4, 12, 90.3; 100-4, 14, 10

23146 with allograft [5] [T] [50] [80] [►]
MED: 100-2, 15, 260; 100-4, 12, 90.3; 100-4, 14, 10

23150 Excision or curettage of bone cyst or benign tumor of proximal humerus; [4] [T] [50] [80] [►]
MED: 100-2, 15, 260; 100-4, 12, 90.3; 100-4, 14, 10

23155 with autograft (includes obtaining graft) [5] [T] [50] [80] [►]
MED: 100-2, 15, 260; 100-4, 12, 90.3; 100-4, 14, 10

23156 with allograft [5] [T] [50] [80] [►]
MED: 100-2, 15, 260; 100-4, 12, 90.3; 100-4, 14, 10

23170 Sequestrectomy (eg, for osteomyelitis or bone abscess), clavicle [2] [T] [50] [►]
MED: 100-2, 15, 260; 100-4, 12, 90.3; 100-4, 14, 10

23172 Sequestrectomy (eg, for osteomyelitis or bone abscess), scapula [2] [T] [50] [80] [►]
MED: 100-2, 15, 260; 100-4, 12, 90.3; 100-4, 14, 10

23174 Sequestrectomy (eg, for osteomyelitis or bone abscess), humeral head to surgical neck [2] [T] [50] [80] [►]
MED: 100-2, 15, 260; 100-4, 12, 90.3; 100-4, 14, 10

23180 Partial excision (craterization, saucerization, or diaphysectomy) bone (eg, osteomyelitis), clavicle [4] [T] [50] [►]
MED: 100-2, 15, 260; 100-4, 12, 90.3; 100-4, 14, 10

AMA: 1998, Nov, 9

23182 Partial excision (craterization, saucerization, or diaphysectomy) bone (eg, osteomyelitis), scapula [4] [T] [50] [80] [►]
MED: 100-2, 15, 260; 100-4, 12, 90.3; 100-4, 14, 10

AMA: 1998, Nov, 9

23184 Partial excision (craterization, saucerization, or diaphysectomy) bone (eg, osteomyelitis), proximal humerus [4] [T] [50] [80] [►]
MED: 100-2, 15, 260; 100-4, 12, 90.3; 100-4, 14, 10

AMA: 1998, Nov, 9

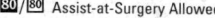

| 23190 | Ostectomy of scapula, partial (eg, superior medial angle) | **4** T 50 80 |
| | MED: 100-2, 15, 260; 100-4, 12, 90.3; 100-4, 14, 10 | |

| 23195 | Resection humeral head | **5** T 50 80 |
| | MED: 100-2, 15, 260; 100-4, 12, 90.3; 100-4, 14, 10 | |

If replacement is needed with an implant, consult CPT code 23470.

23200	Radical resection for tumor; clavicle	C 50 80
23210	scapula	C 50 80
23220	Radical resection of bone tumor, proximal humerus;	C 50 80
	AMA: 1998, Nov, 8	

| 23221 | with autograft (includes obtaining graft) | C 50 80 |
| 23222 | with prosthetic replacement | C 50 80 |

INTRODUCTION OR REMOVAL

If arthrocentesis or needling of bursa is needed, consult CPT code 20610. If a K-wire or a pin is inserted or removed, consult CPT codes 20650, 20670, and 20680.

23330	Removal of foreign body, shoulder; subcutaneous	**1** T 50 80
	MED: 100-2, 15, 260; 100-4, 12, 90.3; 100-4, 14, 10	
	AMA: 1999, Aug, 3	

23331	deep (eg, Neer hemiarthroplasty removal)	**1** T 50 80
	MED: 100-2, 15, 260; 100-4, 12, 90.3; 100-4, 14, 10	
	AMA: 1999, Aug, 3	

| 23332 | complicated (eg, total shoulder) | C 50 80 |
| | AMA: 1999, Aug, 3; 1998, Nov, 8; 1996, Jun, 10 | |

| 23350 | Injection procedure for shoulder arthrography or enhanced CT/MRI shoulder arthrography | N 50 |
| | AMA: 2001, Jul, 3 | |

If radiological supervision and interpretation is performed, consult CPT code 73040. Fluoroscopy (76003) is included in 73040, and not reported separately.

If fluoroscopic guided injection is performed for enhanced CT arthrography, use codes 23350, 76003, and 73201 or 73202. For enhanced MR arthrography, consult CPT codes 23350, 76003 and either 73222 or 73223.

To report biopsy of the shoulder and joint, consult 29805-29826.

REPAIR, REVISION, AND/OR RECONSTRUCTION

| 23395 | Muscle transfer, any type, shoulder or upper arm; single | **5** T 80 |
| | MED: 100-2, 15, 260; 100-4, 12, 90.3; 100-4, 14, 10 | |

| 23397 | multiple | **7** T 80 |
| | MED: 100-2, 15, 260; 100-4, 12, 90.3; 100-4, 14, 10 | |

| 23400 | Scapulopexy (eg, Sprengel's deformity or for paralysis) | **7** T 50 80 |
| | MED: 100-2, 15, 260; 100-4, 12, 90.3; 100-4, 14, 10 | |

23405	Tenotomy, shoulder area; single tendon	**2** T 80
	MED: 100-2, 15, 260; 100-4, 12, 90.3; 100-4, 14, 10	
	AMA: 1998, Nov, 8	

23406	multiple tendons through same incision	**2** T 80
	MED: 100-2, 15, 260; 100-4, 12, 90.3; 100-4, 14, 10	
	AMA: 1998, Nov, 8	

CCI Comp   50 Bilateral Procedure   + CPT Add-on Code   ⊘ Modifier -51 Exempt   ♂ Male   ♀ Female
● New Code   ▲ Revised Code   M Maternity Edit   A Age Edit   A−Y APC Status Ind.   AMA: CPT Assistant

© 2005 Ingenix, Inc. *(Blue Ink)*   CPT only © 2005 American Medical Association. All Rights Reserved. *(Black Ink)*   Surgery — 141

23410   **Repair of ruptured musculotendinous cuff (eg, rotator cuff) open;
              acute**   5 T 50
              MED: 100-2, 15, 260; 100-4, 12, 90.3; 100-4, 14, 10

              AMA: 2002, Feb, 11; 2001, Aug, 11

23412   **chronic**   7 T 50 80
              MED: 100-2, 15, 260; 100-4, 12, 90.3; 100-4, 14, 10

              AMA: 2002, Feb, 11

              To report arthroscopic procedure, consult CPT code 29827.

23415   **Coracoacromial ligament release, with or without acromioplasty** 5 T 50
              MED: 100-2, 15, 260; 100-4, 12, 90.3; 100-4, 14, 10

              If performed arthroscopically consult CPT code 29826.

23420   **Reconstruction of complete shoulder (rotator) cuff avulsion, chronic
              (includes acromioplasty)**   7 T 50 80
              MED: 100-2, 15, 260; 100-4, 12, 90.3; 100-4, 14, 10

              AMA: 2002, Feb, 11

23430   **Tenodesis of long tendon of biceps**   4 T 50 80
              MED: 100-2, 15, 260; 100-4, 12, 90.3; 100-4, 14, 10

23440   **Resection or transplantation of long tendon of biceps** 4 T 50 80
              MED: 100-2, 15, 260; 100-4, 12, 90.3; 100-4, 14, 10

23450   **Capsulorrhaphy, anterior; Putti-Platt procedure or Magnuson type
              operation**   5 T 50 80
              MED: 100-2, 15, 260; 100-4, 12, 90.3; 100-4, 14, 10

              If arthroscopic thermal capsulorrhaphy is performed, consult CPT code 29999.

23455   **with labral repair (eg, Bankart procedure)**   7 T 50 80
              MED: 100-2, 15, 260; 100-4, 12, 90.3; 100-4, 14, 10

              AMA: 1998, Nov, 8

              If performed arthroscopically, consult CPT code 29806.

23460   **Capsulorrhaphy, anterior, any type; with bone block** 5 T 50 80
              MED: 100-2, 15, 260; 100-4, 12, 90.3; 100-4, 14, 10

              Bristow procedure

23462   **with coracoid process transfer**   7 T 50 80
              MED: 100-2, 15, 260; 100-4, 12, 90.3; 100-4, 14, 10

              If open thermal capsulorrhaphy is performed, consult CPT code 23929.

23465   **Capsulorrhaphy, glenohumeral joint, posterior, with or without
              bone block**   5 T 50 80
              MED: 100-2, 15, 260; 100-4, 12, 90.3; 100-4, 14, 10

              AMA: 1998, Nov, 8

              If sternoclavicular and acromioclavicular reconstruction is performed, consult
              CPT codes 23530 and 23550.

23466   **Capsulorrhaphy, glenohumeral joint, any type multi-directional
              instability**   7 T 50 80
              MED: 100-2, 15, 260; 100-4, 12, 90.3; 100-4, 14, 10

              AMA: 1998, Nov, 8

23470   **Arthroplasty, glenohumeral joint; hemiarthroplasty**   T 50 80
              AMA: 1998, Nov, 8

---

26 / TC Professional/Technical Component   80 / 80 Assist-at-Surgery Allowed/With Documentation   ⊙ Conscious Sedation
    Unlisted   Not Covered   **MED:** Pubs 100/NCD Reference   1 - 9 ASC Group   63 Modifier 63 Exempt

Musculoskeletal System

23472 — 23552

| 23472 | total shoulder (glenoid and proximal humeral replacement (eg, total shoulder))   C 50 80 |

AMA: 1998, Nov, 8; 1996, Jun, 10

If the total shoulder implant is removed, consult CPT codes 23331 and 23332. If an osteotomy of the proximal humerus is needed, consult CPT code 24400.

| 23480 | Osteotomy, clavicle, with or without internal fixation;   4 T 50 |

MED: 100-2, 15, 260; 100-4, 12, 90.3; 100-4, 14, 10

| 23485 | with bone graft for nonunion or malunion (includes obtaining graft and/or necessary fixation)   7 T 50 80 |

MED: 100-2, 15, 260; 100-4, 12, 90.3; 100-4, 14, 10

| 23490 | Prophylactic treatment (nailing, pinning, plating or wiring) with or without methylmethacrylate; clavicle   3 T 50 80 |

MED: 100-2, 15, 260; 100-4, 12, 90.3; 100-4, 14, 10

| 23491 | proximal humerus   3 T 50 80 |

MED: 100-2, 15, 260; 100-4, 12, 90.3; 100-4, 14, 10

AMA: 1998, Nov, 8

FRACTURE AND/OR DISLOCATION

| 23500 | Closed treatment of clavicular fracture; without manipulation   1 T 50 |

MED: 100-2, 15, 260; 100-4, 12, 90.3; 100-4, 14, 10

| 23505 | with manipulation   1 T 50 |

MED: 100-2, 15, 260; 100-4, 12, 90.3; 100-4, 14, 10

| 23515 | Open treatment of clavicular fracture, with or without internal or external fixation   3 T 50 80 |

MED: 100-2, 15, 260; 100-4, 12, 90.3; 100-4, 14, 10

| 23520 | Closed treatment of sternoclavicular dislocation; without manipulation   1 T 50 80 |

MED: 100-2, 15, 260; 100-4, 12, 90.3; 100-4, 14, 10

| 23525 | with manipulation   1 T 50 80 |

MED: 100-2, 15, 260; 100-4, 12, 90.3; 100-4, 14, 10

| 23530 | Open treatment of sternoclavicular dislocation, acute or chronic;   3 T 50 80 |

MED: 100-2, 15, 260; 100-4, 12, 90.3; 100-4, 14, 10

| 23532 | with fascial graft (includes obtaining graft)   4 T 50 80 |

MED: 100-2, 15, 260; 100-4, 12, 90.3; 100-4, 14, 10

| 23540 | Closed treatment of acromioclavicular dislocation; without manipulation   1 T 50 |

MED: 100-2, 15, 260; 100-4, 12, 90.3; 100-4, 14, 10

| 23545 | with manipulation   1 T 50 80 |

MED: 100-2, 15, 260; 100-4, 12, 90.3; 100-4, 14, 10

| 23550 | Open treatment of acromioclavicular dislocation, acute or chronic;   3 T 50 80 |

MED: 100-2, 15, 260; 100-4, 12, 90.3; 100-4, 14, 10

| 23552 | with fascial graft (includes obtaining graft)   4 T 50 80 |

MED: 100-2, 15, 260; 100-4, 12, 90.3; 100-4, 14, 10

Musculoskeletal System

23570 — 23570

23570	Closed treatment of scapular fracture; without manipulation	**1** T 50 ▣
	MED: 100-2, 15, 260; 100-4, 12, 90.3; 100-4, 14, 10	
23575	with manipulation, with or without skeletal traction (with or without shoulder joint involvement)	**1** T 50 80 ▣
	MED: 100-2, 15, 260; 100-4, 12, 90.3; 100-4, 14, 10	
23585	Open treatment of scapular fracture (body, glenoid or acromion) with or without internal fixation	**3** T 50 80 ▣
	MED: 100-2, 15, 260; 100-4, 12, 90.3; 100-4, 14, 10	
23600	Closed treatment of proximal humeral (surgical or anatomical neck) fracture; without manipulation	T 50 ▣
	MED: 100-2, 15, 260; 100-4, 12, 90.3; 100-4, 14, 10	
23605	with manipulation, with or without skeletal traction	**2** T 50 ▣
	MED: 100-2, 15, 260; 100-4, 12, 90.3; 100-4, 14, 10	
23615	Open treatment of proximal humeral (surgical or anatomical neck) fracture, with or without internal or external fixation, with or without repair of tuberosity(s);	**4** T 50 80 ▣
	MED: 100-2, 15, 260; 100-4, 12, 90.3; 100-4, 14, 10	
23616	with proximal humeral prosthetic replacement	**4** T 50 80 ▣
	MED: 100-2, 15, 260; 100-4, 12, 90.3; 100-4, 14, 10	
23620	Closed treatment of greater humeral tuberosity fracture; without manipulation	T 50 ▣
	MED: 100-2, 15, 260; 100-4, 12, 90.3; 100-4, 14, 10	
	AMA: 1998, Nov, 8	
23625	with manipulation	**2** T 50 ▣
	MED: 100-2, 15, 260; 100-4, 12, 90.3; 100-4, 14, 10	
23630	Open treatment of greater humeral tuberosity fracture, with or without internal or external fixation	**5** T 50 80 ▣
	MED: 100-2, 15, 260; 100-4, 12, 90.3; 100-4, 14, 10	
	AMA: 1998, Nov, 8	
23650	Closed treatment of shoulder dislocation, with manipulation; without anesthesia	**1** T 50 ▣
	MED: 100-2, 15, 260; 100-4, 12, 90.3; 100-4, 14, 10	
23655	requiring anesthesia	**1** T 50 ▣
	MED: 100-2, 15, 260; 100-4, 12, 90.3; 100-4, 14, 10	
23660	Open treatment of acute shoulder dislocation	**3** T 50 80 ▣
	MED: 100-2, 15, 260; 100-4, 12, 90.3; 100-4, 14, 10	
	AMA: 1996, Feb, 5	

If recurrent dislocations are repaired, consult CPT codes 23450-23466.

23665	Closed treatment of shoulder dislocation, with fracture of greater humeral tuberosity, with manipulation	**2** T 50 ▣
	MED: 100-2, 15, 260; 100-4, 12, 90.3; 100-4, 14, 10	
	AMA: 1998, Nov, 8	
23670	Open treatment of shoulder dislocation, with fracture of greater humeral tuberosity, with or without internal or external fixation	**3** T 50 80 ▣
	MED: 100-2, 15, 260; 100-4, 12, 90.3; 100-4, 14, 10	
	AMA: 1998, Nov, 8	

23675   Closed treatment of shoulder dislocation, with surgical or anatomical neck fracture, with manipulation   2 T 50 ⬚
> MED: 100-2, 15, 260; 100-4, 12, 90.3; 100-4, 14, 10

23680   Open treatment of shoulder dislocation, with surgical or anatomical neck fracture, with or without internal or external fixation   3 T 50 80 ⬚
> MED: 100-2, 15, 260; 100-4, 12, 90.3; 100-4, 14, 10

MANIPULATION

23700   Manipulation under anesthesia, shoulder joint, including application of fixation apparatus (dislocation excluded)   1 T ⬚
> MED: 100-2, 15, 260; 100-4, 12, 90.3; 100-4, 14, 10

> AMA: 1999, Jan, 1

ARTHRODESIS

23800   Arthrodesis, glenohumeral joint;   4 T 50 80 ⬚
> MED: 100-2, 15, 260; 100-4, 12, 90.3; 100-4, 14, 10

> AMA: 1998, Nov, 8

23802   with autogenous graft (includes obtaining graft)   7 T 80 ⬚
> MED: 100-2, 15, 260; 100-4, 12, 90.3; 100-4, 14, 10

AMPUTATION

23900   Interthoracoscapular amputation (forequarter)   C 80 ⬚

23920   Disarticulation of shoulder;   C 80 ⬚

23921   secondary closure or scar revision   3 T ⬚
> MED: 100-2, 15, 260; 100-4, 12, 90.3; 100-4, 14, 10

OTHER PROCEDURES

23929   Unlisted procedure, shoulder   T 80

HUMERUS (UPPER ARM) AND ELBOW

Codes listed in the Musculoskeletal chapter include the application and removal of the first cast or traction device. Replacement of casts and/or traction devices subsequent to the first should be reported separately. CPT codes for other additional procedures, such as obtaining grafts and external fixation, should only be used if the procedure is not already listed as included as part of the basic procedure. Consult the glossary for terms and definitions and the front matter of this chapter for additional information.

The elbow is considered to include the olecranon process and the radius head and neck.

INCISION

If superficial incision and drainage procedures are performed, consult CPT codes 10040-10160.

23930   Incision and drainage, upper arm or elbow area; deep abscess or hematoma   1 T 50 ⬚
> MED: 100-2, 15, 260; 100-4, 12, 90.3; 100-4, 14, 10

23931   bursa   2 T 50 ⬚
> MED: 100-2, 15, 260; 100-4, 12, 90.3; 100-4, 14, 10

> AMA: 1998, Nov, 8

23935   Incision, deep, with opening of bone cortex (eg, for osteomyelitis or bone abscess), humerus or elbow   2 T 50 80 ⬚
> MED: 100-2, 15, 260; 100-4, 12, 90.3; 100-4, 14, 10

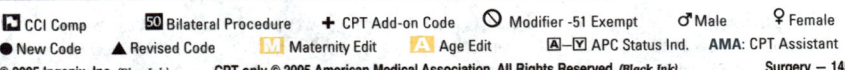

Musculoskeletal System

24000 — 24130

24000 Arthrotomy, elbow, including exploration, drainage, or removal of foreign body 4 T 50 80 🔲
MED: 100-2, 15, 260; 100-4, 12, 90.3; 100-4, 14, 10

AMA: 1998, Nov, 8-9

24006 Arthrotomy of the elbow, with capsular excision for capsular release (separate procedure) 4 T 50 80 🔲
MED: 100-2, 15, 260; 100-4, 12, 90.3; 100-4, 14, 10

EXCISION

24065 Biopsy, soft tissue of upper arm or elbow area; superficial T 50 🔲

24066 deep (subfascial or intramuscular) 2 T 50 🔲
MED: 100-2, 15, 260; 100-4, 12, 90.3; 100-4, 14, 10

If needle biopsy of soft tissue is performed, consult CPT code 20206.

24075 Excision, tumor, soft tissue of upper arm or elbow area; subcutaneous 2 T 50 🔲
MED: 100-2, 15, 260; 100-4, 12, 90.3; 100-4, 14, 10

24076 deep, subfascial or intramuscular 2 T 50 🔲
MED: 100-2, 15, 260; 100-4, 12, 90.3; 100-4, 14, 10

24077 Radical resection of tumor (eg, malignant neoplasm), soft tissue of upper arm or elbow area 3 T 50 80 🔲
MED: 100-2, 15, 260; 100-4, 12, 90.3; 100-4, 14, 10

24100 Arthrotomy, elbow; with synovial biopsy only 1 T 50 80 🔲
MED: 100-2, 15, 260; 100-4, 12, 90.3; 100-4, 14, 10

24101 with joint exploration, with or without biopsy, with or without removal of loose or foreign body 4 T 50 80 🔲
MED: 100-2, 15, 260; 100-4, 12, 90.3; 100-4, 14, 10

24102 with synovectomy 4 T 50 80 🔲
MED: 100-2, 15, 260; 100-4, 12, 90.3; 100-4, 14, 10

24105 Excision, olecranon bursa 3 T 50 🔲
MED: 100-2, 15, 260; 100-4, 12, 90.3; 100-4, 14, 10

24110 Excision or curettage of bone cyst or benign tumor, humerus; 2 T 50 🔲
MED: 100-2, 15, 260; 100-4, 12, 90.3; 100-4, 14, 10

24115 with autograft (includes obtaining graft) 3 T 50 80 🔲
MED: 100-2, 15, 260; 100-4, 12, 90.3; 100-4, 14, 10

24116 with allograft 3 T 50 80 🔲
MED: 100-2, 15, 260; 100-4, 12, 90.3; 100-4, 14, 10

24120 Excision or curettage of bone cyst or benign tumor of head or neck of radius or olecranon process; 3 T 50 80 🔲
MED: 100-2, 15, 260; 100-4, 12, 90.3; 100-4, 14, 10

24125 with autograft (includes obtaining graft) 3 T 50 80 🔲
MED: 100-2, 15, 260; 100-4, 12, 90.3; 100-4, 14, 10

24126 with allograft 3 T 50 80 🔲
MED: 100-2, 15, 260; 100-4, 12, 90.3; 100-4, 14, 10

24130 Excision, radial head 3 T 50 🔲
MED: 100-2, 15, 260; 100-4, 12, 90.3; 100-4, 14, 10

If replacement is performed with an implant, consult CPT code 24366.

24134   Sequestrectomy (eg, for osteomyelitis or bone abscess), shaft or distal humerus   2 ⊤ 50 80 ⬛
MED: 100-2, 15, 260; 100-4, 12, 90.3; 100-4, 14, 10

24136   Sequestrectomy (eg, for osteomyelitis or bone abscess), radial head or neck   2 ⊤ 50 ⬛
MED: 100-2, 15, 260; 100-4, 12, 90.3; 100-4, 14, 10

24138   Sequestrectomy (eg, for osteomyelitis or bone abscess), olecranon process   2 ⊤ 50 80 ⬛
MED: 100-2, 15, 260; 100-4, 12, 90.3; 100-4, 14, 10

24140   Partial excision (craterization, saucerization, or diaphysectomy) bone (eg, osteomyelitis), humerus   3 ⊤ 50 80 ⬛
MED: 100-2, 15, 260; 100-4, 12, 90.3; 100-4, 14, 10

AMA: 1998, Nov, 9

24145   Partial excision (craterization, saucerization, or diaphysectomy) bone (eg, osteomyelitis), radial head or neck   3 ⊤ 50 ⬛
MED: 100-2, 15, 260; 100-4, 12, 90.3; 100-4, 14, 10

AMA: 1998, Nov, 9

24147   Partial excision (craterization, saucerization, or diaphysectomy) bone (eg, osteomyelitis), olecranon process   2 ⊤ 50 ⬛
MED: 100-2, 15, 260; 100-4, 12, 90.3; 100-4, 14, 10

AMA: 1998, Nov, 9

24149   Radical resection of capsule, soft tissue, and heterotopic bone, elbow, with contracture release (separate procedure)   ⊤ 50 80 ⬛

If only capsular and soft tissue is released, consult CPT code 24006.

24150   Radical resection for tumor, shaft or distal humerus;   ⊤ 50 80 ⬛

24151   with autograft (includes obtaining graft)   ⊤ 50 80 ⬛

24152   Radical resection for tumor, radial head or neck;   ⊤ 50 80 ⬛

24153   with autograft (includes obtaining graft)   ⊤ 50 80 ⬛

24155   Resection of elbow joint (arthrectomy)   3 ⊤ 50 80 ⬛
MED: 100-2, 15, 260; 100-4, 12, 90.3; 100-4, 14, 10

INTRODUCTION OR REMOVAL
If a K-wire or a pin is inserted or removed, consult CPT codes 20650, 20670, and 20680. If arthrocentesis or needling of a bursa or a joint is performed, consult CPT code 20605.

24160   Implant removal; elbow joint   2 ⊤ 50 ⬛
MED: 100-2, 15, 260; 100-4, 12, 90.3; 100-4, 14, 10

24164   radial head   3 ⊤ 50 ⬛
MED: 100-2, 15, 260; 100-4, 12, 90.3; 100-4, 14, 10

24200   Removal of foreign body, upper arm or elbow area; subcutaneous   ⊤ 50 80 ⬛

24201   deep (subfascial or intramuscular)   2 ⊤ 50 ⬛
MED: 100-2, 15, 260; 100-4, 12, 90.3; 100-4, 14, 10

AMA: 1998, Nov, 8

24220   Injection procedure for elbow arthrography   N 50 80 ⬛

If radiological supervision and interpretation is performed, consult CPT code 73085. Do not report 76003 with 73085.

If an injection is performed for tennis elbow, consult CPT code 20550.

Musculoskeletal System

24300 — 24354

REPAIR, REVISION, AND/OR RECONSTRUCTION

24300   **Manipulation, elbow, under anesthesia**   T 50 ⟲
        If external fixation is applied, consult CPT codes 20690 or 20692.

24301   **Muscle or tendon transfer, any type, upper arm or elbow, single (excluding 24320-24331)**   4 T 80 ⟲
        MED: 100-2, 15, 260; 100-4, 12, 90.3; 100-4, 14, 10

24305   **Tendon lengthening, upper arm or elbow, each tendon**   4 T 80 ⟲
        MED: 100-2, 15, 260; 100-4, 12, 90.3; 100-4, 14, 10
        AMA: 1998, Nov, 8

24310   **Tenotomy, open, elbow to shoulder, each tendon**   3 T 80 ⟲
        MED: 100-2, 15, 260; 100-4, 12, 90.3; 100-4, 14, 10
        AMA: 1998, Nov, 8

24320   **Tenoplasty, with muscle transfer, with or without free graft, elbow to shoulder, single (Seddon-Brookes type procedure)**   3 T 80 ⟲
        MED: 100-2, 15, 260; 100-4, 12, 90.3; 100-4, 14, 10

24330   **Flexor-plasty, elbow (eg, Steindler type advancement);**   3 T 50 80 ⟲
        MED: 100-2, 15, 260; 100-4, 12, 90.3; 100-4, 14, 10

24331   **with extensor advancement**   3 T 50 80 ⟲
        MED: 100-2, 15, 260; 100-4, 12, 90.3; 100-4, 14, 10

24332   **Tenolysis, triceps**   T 50 ⟲

24340   **Tenodesis of biceps tendon at elbow (separate procedure)**   3 T 50 80 ⟲
        MED: 100-2, 15, 260; 100-4, 12, 90.3; 100-4, 14, 10

24341   **Repair, tendon or muscle, upper arm or elbow, each tendon or muscle, primary or secondary (excludes rotator cuff)**   3 T 50 80 ⟲
        MED: 100-2, 15, 260; 100-4, 12, 90.3; 100-4, 14, 10

24342   **Reinsertion of ruptured biceps or triceps tendon, distal, with or without tendon graft**   3 T 50 80 ⟲
        MED: 100-2, 15, 260; 100-4, 12, 90.3; 100-4, 14, 10

24343   **Repair lateral collateral ligament, elbow, with local tissue**   T 50 80 ⟲

24344   **Reconstruction lateral collateral ligament, elbow, with tendon graft (includes harvesting of graft)**   T 50 80 ⟲

24345   **Repair medial collateral ligament, elbow, with local tissue**   2 T 50 80 ⟲
        MED: 100-2, 15, 260; 100-4, 12, 90.3; 100-4, 14, 10

24346   **Reconstruction medial collateral ligament, elbow, with tendon graft (includes harvesting of graft)**   T 50 80 ⟲

24350   **Fasciotomy, lateral or medial (eg, tennis elbow or epicondylitis);**   3 T 50 80 ⟲
        MED: 100-2, 15, 260; 100-4, 12, 90.3; 100-4, 14, 10

24351   **with extensor origin detachment**   3 T 50 80 ⟲
        MED: 100-2, 15, 260; 100-4, 12, 90.3; 100-4, 14, 10

24352   **with annular ligament resection**   3 T 50 80 ⟲
        MED: 100-2, 15, 260; 100-4, 12, 90.3; 100-4, 14, 10

24354   **with stripping**   3 T 50 ⟲
        MED: 100-2, 15, 260; 100-4, 12, 90.3; 100-4, 14, 10

24356   with partial ostectomy   ③ T 50 80 ⌐
MED: 100-2, 15, 260; 100-4, 12, 90.3; 100-4, 14, 10

24360   Arthroplasty, elbow; with membrane (eg, fascial)   ⑤ T 50 80 ⌐
MED: 100-2, 15, 260; 100-4, 12, 90.3; 100-4, 14, 10

AMA: 1998, Nov, 8

24361   with distal humeral prosthetic replacement   ⑤ T 50 80 ⌐
MED: 100-2, 15, 260; 100-4, 12, 90.3; 100-4, 14, 10

24362   with implant and fascia lata ligament reconstruction   ⑤ T 50 80 ⌐
MED: 100-2, 15, 260; 100-4, 12, 90.3; 100-4, 14, 10

24363   with distal humerus and proximal ulnar prosthetic replacement
(eg, total elbow)   ⑦ T 50 80 ⌐
MED: 100-2, 15, 260; 100-4, 12, 90.3; 100-4, 14, 10

24365   Arthroplasty, radial head;   ⑤ T 50 80 ⌐
MED: 100-2, 15, 260; 100-4, 12, 90.3; 100-4, 14, 10

24366   with implant   ⑤ T 50 80 ⌐
MED: 100-2, 15, 260; 100-4, 12, 90.3; 100-4, 14, 10

24400   Osteotomy, humerus, with or without internal fixation   ④ T 50 80 ⌐
MED: 100-2, 15, 260; 100-4, 12, 90.3; 100-4, 14, 10

24410   Multiple osteotomies with realignment on intramedullary rod, humeral
shaft (Sofield type procedure)   ④ T 50 80 ⌐
MED: 100-2, 15, 260; 100-4, 12, 90.3; 100-4, 14, 10

24420   Osteoplasty, humerus (eg, shortening or lengthening)
(excluding 64876)   ③ T 50 80 ⌐
MED: 100-2, 15, 260; 100-4, 12, 90.3; 100-4, 14, 10

24430   Repair of nonunion or malunion, humerus; without graft (eg, compression
technique)   ③ T 50 80 ⌐
MED: 100-2, 15, 260; 100-4, 12, 90.3; 100-4, 14, 10

24435   with iliac or other autograft (includes obtaining graft)   ④ T 50 80 ⌐
MED: 100-2, 15, 260; 100-4, 12, 90.3; 100-4, 14, 10

If a nonunion or malunion repair of the proximal radius and/or ulna is
performed, consult CPT codes 25400-25420.

24470   Hemiepiphyseal arrest (eg, cubitus varus or valgus, distal
humerus)   ③ T 50 80 ⌐
MED: 100-2, 15, 260; 100-4, 12, 90.3; 100-4, 14, 10

24495   Decompression fasciotomy, forearm, with brachial artery
exploration   ② T 50 80 ⌐
MED: 100-2, 15, 260; 100-4, 12, 90.3; 100-4, 14, 10

24498   Prophylactic treatment (nailing, pinning, plating or wiring), with or without
methylmethacrylate, humeral shaft   ③ T 50 80 ⌐
MED: 100-2, 15, 260; 100-4, 12, 90.3; 100-4, 14, 10

AMA: 1998, Nov, 8

FRACTURE AND/OR DISLOCATION

24500   Closed treatment of humeral shaft fracture; without
manipulation   ① T 50 ⌐
MED: 100-2, 15, 260; 100-4, 12, 90.3; 100-4, 14, 10

Musculoskeletal System

24505 — 24582

24505   with manipulation, with or without skeletal traction   **1** T 50
MED: 100-2, 15, 260; 100-4, 12, 90.3; 100-4, 14, 10

24515   Open treatment of humeral shaft fracture with plate/screws, with or without cerclage   **4** T 50 80
MED: 100-2, 15, 260; 100-4, 12, 90.3; 100-4, 14, 10

24516   Treatment of humeral shaft fracture, with insertion of intramedullary implant, with or without cerclage and/or locking screws   **4** T 50 80
MED: 100-2, 15, 260; 100-4, 12, 90.3; 100-4, 14, 10

AMA: 1996, Feb, 4

24530   Closed treatment of supracondylar or transcondylar humeral fracture, with or without intercondylar extension; without manipulation   **1** T 50
MED: 100-2, 15, 260; 100-4, 12, 90.3; 100-4, 14, 10

24535   with manipulation, with or without skin or skeletal traction   **1** T 50
MED: 100-2, 15, 260; 100-4, 12, 90.3; 100-4, 14, 10

24538   Percutaneous skeletal fixation of supracondylar or transcondylar humeral fracture, with or without intercondylar extension   **2** T 50
MED: 100-2, 15, 260; 100-4, 12, 90.3; 100-4, 14, 10

AMA: 1992, Winter, 10

24545   Open treatment of humeral supracondylar or transcondylar fracture, with or without internal or external fixation; without intercondylar extension   **4** T 50 80
MED: 100-2, 15, 260; 100-4, 12, 90.3; 100-4, 14, 10

24546   with intercondylar extension   **5** T 50 80
MED: 100-2, 15, 260; 100-4, 12, 90.3; 100-4, 14, 10

24560   Closed treatment of humeral epicondylar fracture, medial or lateral; without manipulation   **1** T 50
MED: 100-2, 15, 260; 100-4, 12, 90.3; 100-4, 14, 10

24565   with manipulation   **2** T 50
MED: 100-2, 15, 260; 100-4, 12, 90.3; 100-4, 14, 10

24566   Percutaneous skeletal fixation of humeral epicondylar fracture, medial or lateral, with manipulation   **2** T 50
MED: 100-2, 15, 260; 100-4, 12, 90.3; 100-4, 14, 10

24575   Open treatment of humeral epicondylar fracture, medial or lateral, with or without internal or external fixation   **3** T 50 80
MED: 100-2, 15, 260; 100-4, 12, 90.3; 100-4, 14, 10

24576   Closed treatment of humeral condylar fracture, medial or lateral; without manipulation   **1** T 50
MED: 100-2, 15, 260; 100-4, 12, 90.3; 100-4, 14, 10

24577   with manipulation   **1** T 50
MED: 100-2, 15, 260; 100-4, 12, 90.3; 100-4, 14, 10

24579   Open treatment of humeral condylar fracture, medial or lateral, with or without internal or external fixation   **3** T 50 80
MED: 100-2, 15, 260; 100-4, 12, 90.3; 100-4, 14, 10

24582   Percutaneous skeletal fixation of humeral condylar fracture, medial or lateral, with manipulation   **2** T 50
MED: 100-2, 15, 260; 100-4, 12, 90.3; 100-4, 14, 10

24586   **Open treatment of periarticular fracture and/or dislocation of the elbow (fracture distal humerus and proximal ulna and/or proximal radius);**   4 T 50 80 ⬚
MED: 100-2, 15, 260; 100-4, 12, 90.3; 100-4, 14, 10

24587   **with implant arthroplasty**   5 T 50 80 ⬚
MED: 100-2, 15, 260; 100-4, 12, 90.3; 100-4, 14, 10

Consult also CPT code 24361.

24600   **Treatment of closed elbow dislocation; without anesthesia**   1 T 50 ⬚
MED: 100-2, 15, 260; 100-4, 12, 90.3; 100-4, 14, 10

24605   **requiring anesthesia**   2 T 50 ⬚
MED: 100-2, 15, 260; 100-4, 12, 90.3; 100-4, 14, 10

24615   **Open treatment of acute or chronic elbow dislocation**   3 T 50 80 ⬚
MED: 100-2, 15, 260; 100-4, 12, 90.3; 100-4, 14, 10

24620   **Closed treatment of Monteggia type of fracture dislocation at elbow (fracture proximal end of ulna with dislocation of radial head), with manipulation**   2 T 50 80 ⬚
MED: 100-2, 15, 260; 100-4, 12, 90.3; 100-4, 14, 10

24635   **Open treatment of Monteggia type of fracture dislocation at elbow (fracture proximal end of ulna with dislocation of radial head), with or without internal or external fixation**   3 T 50 80 ⬚
MED: 100-2, 15, 260; 100-4, 12, 90.3; 100-4, 14, 10

24640   **Closed treatment of radial head subluxation in child, nursemaid elbow, with manipulation**   A T 50 80 ⬚

24650   **Closed treatment of radial head or neck fracture; without manipulation**   T 50 ⬚

24655   **with manipulation**   1 T 50 ⬚
MED: 100-2, 15, 260; 100-4, 12, 90.3; 100-4, 14, 10

24665   **Open treatment of radial head or neck fracture, with or without internal fixation or radial head excision;**   4 T 50 80 ⬚
MED: 100-2, 15, 260; 100-4, 12, 90.3; 100-4, 14, 10

24666   **with radial head prosthetic replacement**   4 T 50 80 ⬚
MED: 100-2, 15, 260; 100-4, 12, 90.3; 100-4, 14, 10

24670   **Closed treatment of ulnar fracture, proximal end (olecranon process); without manipulation**   1 T 50 ⬚
MED: 100-2, 15, 260; 100-4, 12, 90.3; 100-4, 14, 10

24675   **with manipulation**   1 T 50 ⬚
MED: 100-2, 15, 260; 100-4, 12, 90.3; 100-4, 14, 10

24685   **Open treatment of ulnar fracture proximal end (olecranon process), with or without internal or external fixation**   3 T 50 80 ⬚
MED: 100-2, 15, 260; 100-4, 12, 90.3; 100-4, 14, 10

ARTHRODESIS

24800   **Arthrodesis, elbow joint; local**   4 T 50 80 ⬚
MED: 100-2, 15, 260; 100-4, 12, 90.3; 100-4, 14, 10

24802   **with autogenous graft (includes obtaining graft)**   5 T 50 80 ⬚
MED: 100-2, 15, 260; 100-4, 12, 90.3; 100-4, 14, 10

Musculoskeletal System

24900 — 25028

AMPUTATION

24900	Amputation, arm through humerus; with primary closure	© 50 80 ↱
24920	open, circular (guillotine)	© 50 80 ↱
24925	secondary closure or scar revision	3 T 50 80 ↱
	MED: 100-2, 15, 260; 100-4, 12, 90.3; 100-4, 14, 10	
24930	re-amputation	© 50 80 ↱
24931	with implant	© 50 80 ↱
24935	Stump elongation, upper extremity	T 50 80 ↱
24940	Cineplasty, upper extremity, complete procedure	© 50 80 ↱

OTHER PROCEDURES

24999	Unlisted procedure, humerus or elbow	T 50 80

FOREARM AND WRIST

Codes listed in the Musculoskeletal chapter include the application and removal of the first cast or traction device. Replacement of casts and/or traction devices subsequent to the first should be reported separately. CPT codes for other additional procedures, such as obtaining grafts and external fixation, should only be used if the procedure is not already listed as included as part of the basic procedure. Consult the glossary for terms and definitions and the front matter of this chapter for additional information.

Forearm and wrist procedures include those performed on the radius, ulna, carpal bones, and joints.

INCISION

25000 Incision, extensor tendon sheath, wrist (eg, deQuervain's disease) 3 T 50 ↱
MED: 100-2, 15, 260; 100-4, 12, 90.3; 100-4, 14, 10
AMA: 1998, Nov, 8

If decompression of a median nerve is performed or for carpal tunnel syndrome, consult CPT code 64721.

25001 Incision, flexor tendon sheath, wrist (eg, flexor carpi radialis) T 50 ↱

25020 Decompression fasciotomy, forearm and/or wrist, flexor OR extensor compartment; without debride-ment of nonviable muscle and/or nerve 3 T 50 ↱
MED: 100-2, 15, 260; 100-4, 12, 90.3; 100-4, 14, 10

25023 with debridement of nonviable muscle and/or nerve 3 T 50 80 ↱
MED: 100-2, 15, 260; 100-4, 12, 90.3; 100-4, 14, 10

For superficial incision and drainage procedures, consult codes 10060-10160. If debridement is performed, consult also CPT codes 11000-11044.

If decompression fasciotomy with brachial artery exploration is performed, consult CPT code 24495.

25024 Decompression fasciotomy, forearm and/or wrist, flexor AND extensor compartment; without debridement of nonviable muscle and/or nerve 3 T 50 ↱
MED: 100-2, 15, 260; 100-4, 12, 90.3; 100-4, 14, 10

25025 with debridement of nonviable muscle and/or nerve 3 T 50 80 ↱
MED: 100-2, 15, 260; 100-4, 12, 90.3; 100-4, 14, 10

25028 Incision and drainage, forearm and/or wrist; deep abscess or hematoma 1 T 50 ↱
MED: 100-2, 15, 260; 100-4, 12, 90.3; 100-4, 14, 10

| 25031 | bursa | ② T 50 80 🖸 |

MED: 100-2, 15, 260; 100-4, 12, 90.3; 100-4, 14, 10

AMA: 1998, Nov, 9

| 25035 | Incision, deep, bone cortex, forearm and/or wrist (eg, osteomyelitis or bone abscess) | ② T 50 80 🖸 |

MED: 100-2, 15, 260; 100-4, 12, 90.3; 100-4, 14, 10

| 25040 | Arthrotomy, radiocarpal or midcarpal joint, with exploration, drainage, or removal of foreign body | ⑤ T 50 80 🖸 |

MED: 100-2, 15, 260; 100-4, 12, 90.3; 100-4, 14, 10

EXCISION

| 25065 | Biopsy, soft tissue of forearm and/or wrist; superficial | T 50 🖸 |
| 25066 | deep (subfascial or intramuscular) | ② T 50 🖸 |

MED: 100-2, 15, 260; 100-4, 12, 90.3; 100-4, 14, 10

AMA: 1998, Nov, 8

If a needle biopsy of soft tissue is needed, consult CPT code 20206.

| 25075 | Excision, tumor, soft tissue of forearm and/or wrist area; subcutaneous | ② T 50 🖸 |

MED: 100-2, 15, 260; 100-4, 12, 90.3; 100-4, 14, 10

| 25076 | deep, (subfascial or intramuscular) | ③ T 50 🖸 |

MED: 100-2, 15, 260; 100-4, 12, 90.3; 100-4, 14, 10

| 25077 | Radical resection of tumor (eg, malignant neoplasm), soft tissue of forearm and/or wrist area | ③ T 50 🖸 |

MED: 100-2, 15, 260; 100-4, 12, 90.3; 100-4, 14, 10

| 25085 | Capsulotomy, wrist (eg, contracture) | ③ T 50 80 🖸 |

MED: 100-2, 15, 260; 100-4, 12, 90.3; 100-4, 14, 10

| 25100 | Arthrotomy, wrist joint; with biopsy | ② T 50 80 🖸 |

MED: 100-2, 15, 260; 100-4, 12, 90.3; 100-4, 14, 10

| 25101 | with joint exploration, with or without biopsy, with or without removal of loose or foreign body | ③ T 50 80 🖸 |

MED: 100-2, 15, 260; 100-4, 12, 90.3; 100-4, 14, 10

| 25105 | with synovectomy | ④ T 50 80 🖸 |

MED: 100-2, 15, 260; 100-4, 12, 90.3; 100-4, 14, 10

| 25107 | Arthrotomy, distal radioulnar joint including repair of triangular cartilage, complex | ③ T 50 80 🖸 |

MED: 100-2, 15, 260; 100-4, 12, 90.3; 100-4, 14, 10

| 25110 | Excision, lesion of tendon sheath, forearm and/or wrist | ③ T 50 🖸 |

MED: 100-2, 15, 260; 100-4, 12, 90.3; 100-4, 14, 10

| 25111 | Excision of ganglion, wrist (dorsal or volar); primary | ③ T 50 🖸 |

MED: 100-2, 15, 260; 100-4, 12, 90.3; 100-4, 14, 10

If this procedure involves the hand or finger, consult CPT code 26160.

| 25112 | recurrent | ④ T 50 🖸 |

MED: 100-2, 15, 260; 100-4, 12, 90.3; 100-4, 14, 10

If this procedure involves the hand or finger, consult CPT code 26160.

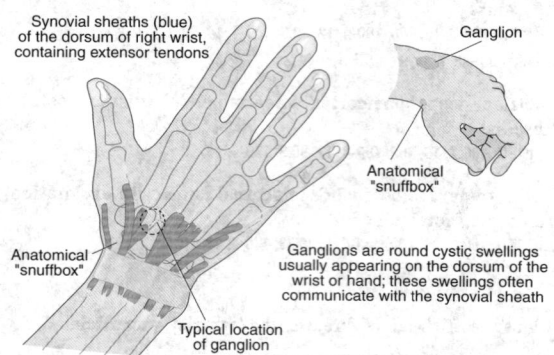

Synovial sheaths (blue) of the dorsum of right wrist, containing extensor tendons

Ganglion

Anatomical "snuffbox"

Anatomical "snuffbox"

Ganglions are round cystic swellings usually appearing on the dorsum of the wrist or hand; these swellings often communicate with the synovial sheath

Typical location of ganglion

25115 **Radical excision of bursa, synovia of wrist, or forearm tendon sheaths (eg, tenosynovitis, fungus, Tbc, or other granulomas, rheumatoid arthritis); flexors** **4** T 50 ↳
MED: 100-2, 15, 260; 100-4, 12, 90.3; 100-4, 14, 10

25116   **extensors, with or without transposition of dorsal retinaculum** **4** T 50 80 ↳
MED: 100-2, 15, 260; 100-4, 12, 90.3; 100-4, 14, 10

If finger synovectomies are performed, consult CPT code 26145.

25118 **Synovectomy, extensor tendon sheath, wrist, single compartment;** **2** T 50 ↳
MED: 100-2, 15, 260; 100-4, 12, 90.3; 100-4, 14, 10

25119   **with resection of distal ulna** **3** T 50 80 ↳
MED: 100-2, 15, 260; 100-4, 12, 90.3; 100-4, 14, 10

25120 **Excision or curettage of bone cyst or benign tumor of radius or ulna (excluding head or neck of radius and olecranon process);** **3** T 50 80 ↳
MED: 100-2, 15, 260; 100-4, 12, 90.3; 100-4, 14, 10

If this procedure involves the head or the neck of the radius or the olecranon process, consult CPT codes 24120-24126.

25125   **with autograft (includes obtaining graft)** **3** T 50 80 ↳
MED: 100-2, 15, 260; 100-4, 12, 90.3; 100-4, 14, 10

25126   **with allograft** **3** T 50 80 ↳
MED: 100-2, 15, 260; 100-4, 12, 90.3; 100-4, 14, 10

25130 **Excision or curettage of bone cyst or benign tumor of carpal bones;** **3** T 50 80 ↳
MED: 100-2, 15, 260; 100-4, 12, 90.3; 100-4, 14, 10

25135   **with autograft (includes obtaining graft)** **3** T 50 80 ↳
MED: 100-2, 15, 260; 100-4, 12, 90.3; 100-4, 14, 10

25136   **with allograft** **3** T 50 80 ↳
MED: 100-2, 15, 260; 100-4, 12, 90.3; 100-4, 14, 10

25145 **Sequestrectomy (eg, for osteomyelitis or bone abscess), forearm and/or wrist** **2** T 50 80 ↳
MED: 100-2, 15, 260; 100-4, 12, 90.3; 100-4, 14, 10

25150   Partial excision (craterization, saucerization or diaphysectomy) of bone (eg, for osteomyelitis); ulna   ☑ Ⓣ 50 🔾
         MED: 100-2, 15, 260; 100-4, 12, 90.3; 100-4, 14, 10

25151   radius   ☑ Ⓣ 50 80 🔾
            MED: 100-2, 15, 260; 100-4, 12, 90.3; 100-4, 14, 10

            If this procedure involves the head or the neck of the radius or the olecranon process, consult CPT codes 24145 and 24147.

25170   Radical resection for tumor, radius or ulna   Ⓣ 50 80 🔾

25210   Carpectomy; one bone   ☑ Ⓣ 80 🔾
         MED: 100-2, 15, 260; 100-4, 12, 90.3; 100-4, 14, 10

            If carpectomy is performed with an implant, consult CPT codes 25441-25445.

25215   all bones of proximal row   ☑ Ⓣ 80 🔾
            MED: 100-2, 15, 260; 100-4, 12, 90.3; 100-4, 14, 10

25230   Radial styloidectomy (separate procedure)   ☑ Ⓣ 50 🔾
         MED: 100-2, 15, 260; 100-4, 12, 90.3; 100-4, 14, 10

25240   Excision distal ulna partial or complete (eg, Darrach type or matched resection)   ☑ Ⓣ 50 80 🔾
         MED: 100-2, 15, 260; 100-4, 12, 90.3; 100-4, 14, 10

            If an implant replacement is performed for the distal ulna, consult CPT code 25442. If obtaining fascia for interposition, consult CPT codes 20920 and 20922.

INTRODUCTION OR REMOVAL
If a K-wire, a pin, or a rod is inserted or removed, consult CPT codes 20650, 20670, and 20680.

25246   Injection procedure for wrist arthrography   Ⓝ 50 🔾

            If radiological supervision and interpretation is needed, consult CPT code 73115. Code 76003 cannot be reported in addition to 73115.

            If a superficial foreign body is removed, consult CPT code 20520.

25248   Exploration with removal of deep foreign body, forearm or wrist ☑ Ⓣ 50 🔾
         MED: 100-2, 15, 260; 100-4, 12, 90.3; 100-4, 14, 10

25250   Removal of wrist prosthesis; (separate procedure)   ☑ Ⓣ 50 80 🔾
         MED: 100-2, 15, 260; 100-4, 12, 90.3; 100-4, 14, 10

25251   complicated, including total wrist   ☑ Ⓣ 80 🔾
            MED: 100-2, 15, 260; 100-4, 12, 90.3; 100-4, 14, 10

25259   Manipulation, wrist, under anesthesia   Ⓣ 50 🔾

            If external fixation is applied, consult CPT code 20690 or 20692.

REPAIR, REVISION, AND/OR RECONSTRUCTION

25260   Repair, tendon or muscle, flexor, forearm and/or wrist; primary, single, each tendon or muscle   ☑ Ⓣ 🔾
         MED: 100-2, 15, 260; 100-4, 12, 90.3; 100-4, 14, 10

25263   secondary, single, each tendon or muscle   ☑ Ⓣ 80 🔾
            MED: 100-2, 15, 260; 100-4, 12, 90.3; 100-4, 14, 10

25265   secondary, with free graft (includes obtaining graft), each tendon or muscle   ☑ Ⓣ 80 🔾
            MED: 100-2, 15, 260; 100-4, 12, 90.3; 100-4, 14, 10

Musculoskeletal System

25270 — 25332

25270   **Repair, tendon or muscle, extensor, forearm and/or wrist; primary, single, each tendon or muscle**   4 T 80 ▶
MED: 100-2, 15, 260; 100-4, 12, 90.3; 100-4, 14, 10

25272   **secondary, single, each tendon or muscle**   3 T 80 ▶
MED: 100-2, 15, 260; 100-4, 12, 90.3; 100-4, 14, 10

25274   **secondary, with free graft (includes obtaining graft), each tendon or muscle**   4 T 80 ▶
MED: 100-2, 15, 260; 100-4, 12, 90.3; 100-4, 14, 10

25275   **Repair, tendon sheath, extensor, forearm and/or wrist, with free graft (includes obtaining graft) (eg, for extensor carpi ulnaris subluxation)**   4 T 50 80 ▶
MED: 100-2, 15, 260; 100-4, 12, 90.3; 100-4, 14, 10

25280   **Lengthening or shortening of flexor or extensor tendon, forearm and/or wrist, single, each tendon**   4 T 80 ▶
MED: 100-2, 15, 260; 100-4, 12, 90.3; 100-4, 14, 10

25290   **Tenotomy, open, flexor or extensor tendon, forearm and/or wrist, single, each tendon**   3 T ▶
MED: 100-2, 15, 260; 100-4, 12, 90.3; 100-4, 14, 10

25295   **Tenolysis, flexor or extensor tendon, forearm and/or wrist, single, each tendon**   3 T ▶
MED: 100-2, 15, 260; 100-4, 12, 90.3; 100-4, 14, 10
AMA: 1998, Aug, 10; 1997, Apr, 11

25300   **Tenodesis at wrist; flexors of fingers**   3 T 50 80 ▶
MED: 100-2, 15, 260; 100-4, 12, 90.3; 100-4, 14, 10

25301   **extensors of fingers**   3 T 50 80 ▶
MED: 100-2, 15, 260; 100-4, 12, 90.3; 100-4, 14, 10

25310   **Tendon transplantation or transfer, flexor or extensor, forearm and/or wrist, single; each tendon**   3 T 80 ▶
MED: 100-2, 15, 260; 100-4, 12, 90.3; 100-4, 14, 10
AMA: 2002, Jun, 11

25312   **with tendon graft(s) (includes obtaining graft), each tendon**   4 T 80 ▶
MED: 100-2, 15, 260; 100-4, 12, 90.3; 100-4, 14, 10

25315   **Flexor origin slide (eg, for cerebral palsy, Volkmann contracture), forearm and/or wrist;**   3 T 50 80 ▶
MED: 100-2, 15, 260; 100-4, 12, 90.3; 100-4, 14, 10

25316   **with tendon(s) transfer**   3 T 50 80 ▶
MED: 100-2, 15, 260; 100-4, 12, 90.3; 100-4, 14, 10

25320   **Capsulorrhaphy or reconstruction, wrist, open (eg, capsulodesis, ligament repair, tendon transfer or graft) (includes synovectomy, capsulotomy and open reduction) for carpal instability**   3 T 50 80 ▶
MED: 100-2, 15, 260; 100-4, 12, 90.3; 100-4, 14, 10

25332   **Arthroplasty, wrist, with or without interposition, with or without external or internal fixation**   5 T 50 80 ▶
MED: 100-2, 15, 260; 100-4, 12, 90.3; 100-4, 14, 10

If obtaining fascia for interposition, consult CPT codes 20920 and 20992. If arthroplasty with a prosthetic replacement is performed, consult CPT codes 25441-25446.

Musculoskeletal System

25335 — 25426

25335	Centralization of wrist on ulna (eg, radial club hand)	⬛3 T 50 80 ⬚
	MED: 100-2, 15, 260; 100-4, 12, 90.3; 100-4, 14, 10	
25337	Reconstruction for stabilization of unstable distal ulna or distal radioulnar joint, secondary by soft tissue stabilization (eg, tendon transfer, tendon graft or weave, or tenodesis) with or without open reduction of distal radioulnar joint	⬛5 T 50 ⬚
	MED: 100-2, 15, 260; 100-4, 12, 90.3; 100-4, 14, 10	

If a fascia lata graft is harvested, consult CPT codes 20920 and 20922.

25350	Osteotomy, radius; distal third	⬛3 T 50 80 ⬚
	MED: 100-2, 15, 260; 100-4, 12, 90.3; 100-4, 14, 10	
25355	middle or proximal third	⬛3 T 50 80 ⬚
	MED: 100-2, 15, 260; 100-4, 12, 90.3; 100-4, 14, 10	
25360	Osteotomy; ulna	⬛3 T 50 80 ⬚
	MED: 100-2, 15, 260; 100-4, 12, 90.3; 100-4, 14, 10	
25365	radius AND ulna	⬛3 T 50 80 ⬚
	MED: 100-2, 15, 260; 100-4, 12, 90.3; 100-4, 14, 10	
25370	Multiple osteotomies, with realignment on intramedullary rod (Sofield type procedure); radius OR ulna	⬛3 T 50 80 ⬚
	MED: 100-2, 15, 260; 100-4, 12, 90.3; 100-4, 14, 10	
25375	radius AND ulna	⬛4 T 50 80 ⬚
	MED: 100-2, 15, 260; 100-4, 12, 90.3; 100-4, 14, 10	
25390	Osteoplasty, radius OR ulna; shortening	⬛3 T 50 80 ⬚
	MED: 100-2, 15, 260; 100-4, 12, 90.3; 100-4, 14, 10	
25391	lengthening with autograft	⬛4 T 50 80 ⬚
	MED: 100-2, 15, 260; 100-4, 12, 90.3; 100-4, 14, 10	
25392	Osteoplasty, radius AND ulna; shortening (excluding 64876)	⬛3 T 50 80 ⬚
	MED: 100-2, 15, 260; 100-4, 12, 90.3; 100-4, 14, 10	
25393	lengthening with autograft	⬛4 T 50 80 ⬚
	MED: 100-2, 15, 260; 100-4, 12, 90.3; 100-4, 14, 10	
25394	Osteoplasty, carpal bone, shortening	T 50 80 ⬚
25400	Repair of nonunion or malunion, radius OR ulna; without graft (eg, compression technique)	⬛3 T 50 80 ⬚
	MED: 100-2, 15, 260; 100-4, 12, 90.3; 100-4, 14, 10	
25405	with autograft (includes obtaining graft)	⬛4 T 50 80 ⬚
	MED: 100-2, 15, 260; 100-4, 12, 90.3; 100-4, 14, 10	
25415	Repair of nonunion or malunion, radius AND ulna; without graft (eg, compression technique)	⬛3 T 50 80 ⬚
	MED: 100-2, 15, 260; 100-4, 12, 90.3; 100-4, 14, 10	
25420	with autograft (includes obtaining graft)	⬛4 T 50 80 ⬚
	MED: 100-2, 15, 260; 100-4, 12, 90.3; 100-4, 14, 10	
25425	Repair of defect with autograft; radius OR ulna	⬛3 T 50 80 ⬚
	MED: 100-2, 15, 260; 100-4, 12, 90.3; 100-4, 14, 10	
25426	radius AND ulna	⬛4 T 50 80 ⬚
	MED: 100-2, 15, 260; 100-4, 12, 90.3; 100-4, 14, 10	

Musculoskeletal System

25430 — 25505

25430	Insertion of vascular pedicle into carpal bone (eg, Hori procedure)	T 50 ⟲
25431	Repair of nonunion of carpal bone (excluding carpal scaphoid (navicular)) (includes obtaining graft and necessary fixation), each bone	T 50 80 ⟲
25440	Repair of nonunion, scaphoid carpal (navicular) bone, with or without radial styloidectomy (includes obtaining graft and necessary fixation) 4 T 50 80 ⟲	

MED: 100-2, 15, 260; 100-4, 12, 90.3; 100-4, 14, 10

25441	Arthroplasty with prosthetic replacement; distal radius	5 T 50 80 ⟲

MED: 100-2, 15, 260; 100-4, 12, 90.3; 100-4, 14, 10

25442	distal ulna	5 T 50 80 ⟲

MED: 100-2, 15, 260; 100-4, 12, 90.3; 100-4, 14, 10

25443	scaphoid carpal (navicular)	5 T 50 80 ⟲

MED: 100-2, 15, 260; 100-4, 12, 90.3; 100-4, 14, 10

25444	lunate	5 T 50 80 ⟲

MED: 100-2, 15, 260; 100-4, 12, 90.3; 100-4, 14, 10

25445	trapezium	5 T 50 ⟲

MED: 100-2, 15, 260; 100-4, 12, 90.3; 100-4, 14, 10

25446	distal radius and partial or entire carpus (total wrist)	7 T 50 80 ⟲

MED: 100-2, 15, 260; 100-4, 12, 90.3; 100-4, 14, 10

25447	Arthroplasty, interposition, intercarpal or carpometacarpal joints	5 T 50 80 ⟲

MED: 100-2, 15, 260; 100-4, 12, 90.3; 100-4, 14, 10

AMA: 1998, Nov, 8

If wrist arthroplasty is performed, consult CPT code 25332.

25449	Revision of arthroplasty, including removal of implant, wrist joint	5 T 50 80 ⟲

MED: 100-2, 15, 260; 100-4, 12, 90.3; 100-4, 14, 10

25450	Epiphyseal arrest by epiphysiodesis or stapling; distal radius OR ulna	3 T 50 ⟲

MED: 100-2, 15, 260; 100-4, 12, 90.3; 100-4, 14, 10

25455	distal radius AND ulna	3 T 50 ⟲

MED: 100-2, 15, 260; 100-4, 12, 90.3; 100-4, 14, 10

25490	Prophylactic treatment (nailing, pinning, plating or wiring) with or without methylmethacrylate; radius	3 T 50 80 ⟲

MED: 100-2, 15, 260; 100-4, 12, 90.3; 100-4, 14, 10

25491	ulna	3 T 50 80 ⟲

MED: 100-2, 15, 260; 100-4, 12, 90.3; 100-4, 14, 10

25492	radius AND ulna	3 T 50 80 ⟲

MED: 100-2, 15, 260; 100-4, 12, 90.3; 100-4, 14, 10

FRACTURE AND/OR DISLOCATION

25500	Closed treatment of radial shaft fracture; without manipulation	T 50 ⟲
25505	with manipulation	1 T 50 ⟲

MED: 100-2, 15, 260; 100-4, 12, 90.3; 100-4, 14, 10

25515   Open treatment of radial shaft fracture, with or without internal or external fixation   3 T 50 80 ▮
MED: 100-2, 15, 260; 100-4, 12, 90.3; 100-4, 14, 10

25520   Closed treatment of radial shaft fracture and closed treatment of dislocation of distal radioulnar joint (Galeazzi fracture/dislocation)   1 T 50 ▮
MED: 100-2, 15, 260; 100-4, 12, 90.3; 100-4, 14, 10

25525   Open treatment of radial shaft fracture, with internal and/ or external fixation and closed treatment of dislocation of distal radioulnar joint (Galeazzi fracture/dislocation), with or without percutaneous skeletal fixation   4 T 50 80 ▮
MED: 100-2, 15, 260; 100-4, 12, 90.3; 100-4, 14, 10

25526   Open treatment of radial shaft fracture, with internal and/or external fixation and open treatment, with or without internal or external fixation of distal radioulnar joint (Galeazzi fracture/dislocation), includes repair of triangular fibrocartilage complex   5 T 50 80 ▮
MED: 100-2, 15, 260; 100-4, 12, 90.3; 100-4, 14, 10

25530   Closed treatment of ulnar shaft fracture; without manipulation   T 50 ▮

25535   with manipulation   1 T 50 ▮
MED: 100-2, 15, 260; 100-4, 12, 90.3; 100-4, 14, 10

25545   Open treatment of ulnar shaft fracture, with or without internal or external fixation   3 T 50 80 ▮
MED: 100-2, 15, 260; 100-4, 12, 90.3; 100-4, 14, 10

AMA: 1999, Oct, 4; 1993, Fall, 23

25560   Closed treatment of radial and ulnar shaft fractures; without manipulation   T 50 ▮

25565   with manipulation   2 T 50 ▮
MED: 100-2, 15, 260; 100-4, 12, 90.3; 100-4, 14, 10

25574   Open treatment of radial AND ulnar shaft fractures, with internal or external fixation; of radius OR ulna   3 T 50 80 ▮
MED: 100-2, 15, 260; 100-4, 12, 90.3; 100-4, 14, 10

AMA: 1999, Oct, 4; 1993, Fall, 23

25575   of radius AND ulna   3 T 50 80 ▮
MED: 100-2, 15, 260; 100-4, 12, 90.3; 100-4, 14, 10

25600   Closed treatment of distal radial fracture (eg, Colles or Smith type) or epiphyseal separation, with or without fracture of ulnar styloid; without manipulation   T 50 ▮

25605   with manipulation   3 T 50 ▮
MED: 100-2, 15, 260; 100-4, 12, 90.3; 100-4, 14, 10

25611   Percutaneous skeletal fixation of distal radial fracture (eg, Colles or Smith type) or epiphyseal separation, with or without fracture of ulnar styloid, requiring manipulation, with or without external fixation   3 T 50 ▮
MED: 100-2, 15, 260; 100-4, 12, 90.3; 100-4, 14, 10

AMA: 1999, Oct, 4; 1993, Fall, 23

25620   Open treatment of distal radial fracture (eg, Colles or Smith type) or epiphyseal separation, with or without fracture of ulnar styloid, with or without internal or external fixation   5 T 50 80 ▮
MED: 100-2, 15, 260; 100-4, 12, 90.3; 100-4, 14, 10

Musculoskeletal System

25622 — 25800

25622   Closed treatment of carpal scaphoid (navicular) fracture; without
manipulation   T 50 🔲

25624   with manipulation   2 T 50 80 🔲
     MED: 100-2, 15, 260; 100-4, 12, 90.3; 100-4, 14, 10

25628   Open treatment of carpal scaphoid (navicular) fracture, with or without
internal or external fixation   3 T 50 80 🔲
     MED: 100-2, 15, 260; 100-4, 12, 90.3; 100-4, 14, 10

25630   Closed treatment of carpal bone fracture (excluding carpal scaphoid
(navicular)); without manipulation, each bone   T 50 🔲

25635   with manipulation, each bone   1 T 50 80 🔲
     MED: 100-2, 15, 260; 100-4, 12, 90.3; 100-4, 14, 10

25645   Open treatment of carpal bone fracture (other than carpal scaphoid
(navicular)), each bone   3 T 50 80 🔲
     MED: 100-2, 15, 260; 100-4, 12, 90.3; 100-4, 14, 10

25650   Closed treatment of ulnar styloid fracture   T 50 🔲

25651   Percutaneous skeletal fixation of ulnar styloid fracture   T 50 80 🔲

25652   Open treatment of ulnar styloid fracture   T 50 🔲

25660   Closed treatment of radiocarpal or intercarpal dislocation, one or more
bones, with manipulation   1 T 50 80 🔲
     MED: 100-2, 15, 260; 100-4, 12, 90.3; 100-4, 10

25670   Open treatment of radiocarpal or intercarpal dislocation, one or
more bones   3 T 50 80 🔲
     MED: 100-2, 15, 260; 100-4, 12, 90.3; 100-4, 14, 10

25671   Percutaneous skeletal fixation of distal radioulnar dislocation   1 T 50 🔲
     MED: 100-2, 15, 260; 100-4, 12, 90.3; 100-4, 14, 10

25675   Closed treatment of distal radioulnar dislocation with
manipulation   1 T 50 80 🔲
     MED: 100-2, 15, 260; 100-4, 12, 90.3; 100-4, 14, 10

25676   Open treatment of distal radioulnar dislocation, acute or
chronic   2 T 50 80 🔲
     MED: 100-2, 15, 260; 100-4, 12, 90.3; 100-4, 14, 10

25680   Closed treatment of trans-scaphoperilunar type of fracture dislocation, with
manipulation   2 T 50 80 🔲
     MED: 100-2, 15, 260; 100-4, 12, 90.3; 100-4, 14, 10

25685   Open treatment of trans-scaphoperilunar type of fracture
dislocation   3 T 50 80 🔲
     MED: 100-2, 15, 260; 100-4, 12, 90.3; 100-4, 14, 10

25690   Closed treatment of lunate dislocation, with manipulation   1 T 50 80 🔲
     MED: 100-2, 15, 260; 100-4, 12, 90.3; 100-4, 14, 10

25695   Open treatment of lunate dislocation   2 T 50 80 🔲
     MED: 100-2, 15, 260; 100-4, 12, 90.3; 100-4, 14, 10

ARTHRODESIS

25800   Arthrodesis, wrist; complete, without bone graft (includes radiocarpal
and/or intercarpal and/or carpometacarpal joints)   4 T 50 80 🔲
     MED: 100-2, 15, 260; 100-4, 12, 90.3; 100-4, 14, 10
     AMA: 1998, Nov, 8

25805	with sliding graft	5 T 50 80 ↩
	MED: 100-2, 15, 260; 100-4, 12, 90.3; 100-4, 14, 10	
25810	with iliac or other autograft (includes obtaining graft)	5 T 50 80 ↩
	MED: 100-2, 15, 260; 100-4, 12, 90.3; 100-4, 14, 10	
25820	Arthrodesis, wrist; limited, without bone graft (eg, intercarpal or radiocarpal)	4 T 50 80 ↩
	MED: 100-2, 15, 260; 100-4, 12, 90.3; 100-4, 14, 10	
	AMA: 1998, Nov, 8	
25825	with autograft (includes obtaining graft)	5 T 50 80 ↩
	MED: 100-2, 15, 260; 100-4, 12, 90.3; 100-4, 14, 10	
25830	Arthrodesis, distal radioulnar joint with segmental resection of ulna, with or without bone graft (eg, Sauve-Kapandji procedure)	5 T 50 80 ↩
	MED: 100-2, 15, 260; 100-4, 12, 90.3; 100-4, 14, 10	
	AMA: 1998, Nov, 8	

AMPUTATION

25900	Amputation, forearm, through radius and ulna;	C 50 80 ↩
25905	open, circular (guillotine)	C 50 80 ↩
25907	secondary closure or scar revision	3 T 50 80 ↩
	MED: 100-2, 15, 260; 100-4, 12, 90.3; 100-4, 14, 10	
25909	re-amputation	C 50 80 ↩
25915	Krukenberg procedure	C 50 80 ↩
25920	Disarticulation through wrist;	C 50 80 ↩
25922	secondary closure or scar revision	3 T 50 80 ↩
	MED: 100-2, 15, 260; 100-4, 12, 90.3; 100-4, 14, 10	
25924	re-amputation	C 50 80 ↩
25927	Transmetacarpal amputation;	C 50 80 ↩
25929	secondary closure or scar revision	3 T 50 80 ↩
	MED: 100-2, 15, 260; 100-4, 12, 90.3; 100-4, 14, 10	
25931	re-amputation	C 50 ↩

OTHER PROCEDURES

25999	Unlisted procedure, forearm or wrist	T 50 80

HAND AND FINGERS

Codes listed in the Musculoskeletal chapter include the application and removal of the first cast or traction device. Replacement of casts and/or traction devices subsequent to the first should be reported separately. CPT codes for other additional procedures, such as obtaining grafts and external fixation, should only be used if the procedure is not already listed as included as part of the basic procedure. Consult the glossary for terms and definitions and the front matter of this chapter for additional information.

INCISION

26010	Drainage of finger abscess; simple	T ↩
26011	complicated (eg, felon)	1 T ↩
	MED: 100-2, 15, 260; 100-4, 12, 90.3; 100-4, 14, 10	
	AMA: 1998, Nov, 8	

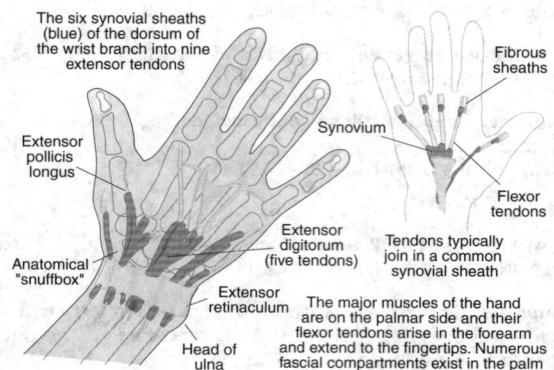

The six synovial sheaths (blue) of the dorsum of the wrist branch into nine extensor tendons

Fibrous sheaths

Extensor pollicis longus

Synovium

Flexor tendons

Extensor digitorum (five tendons)

Tendons typically join in a common synovial sheath

Anatomical "snuffbox"

Extensor retinaculum

The major muscles of the hand are on the palmar side and their flexor tendons arise in the forearm and extend to the fingertips. Numerous fascial compartments exist in the palm

Head of ulna

26020 **Drainage of tendon sheath, digit and/or palm, each** 2 T
MED: 100-2, 15, 260; 100-4, 12, 90.3; 100-4, 14, 10

26025 **Drainage of palmar bursa; single, bursa** 1 T 80
MED: 100-2, 15, 260; 100-4, 12, 90.3; 100-4, 14, 10

AMA: 1998, Nov, 8

26030 **multiple bursa** 2 T 80
MED: 100-2, 15, 260; 100-4, 12, 90.3; 100-4, 14, 10

AMA: 1998, Nov, 8

26034 **Incision, bone cortex, hand or finger (eg, osteomyelitis or bone abscess)** 2 T
MED: 100-2, 15, 260; 100-4, 12, 90.3; 100-4, 14, 10

AMA: 1998, Nov, 8

26035 **Decompression fingers and/or hand, injection injury (eg, grease gun)** T 80

26037 **Decompressive fasciotomy, hand (excludes 26035)** T 80

If decompression of the fingers and/or hand for an injection injury is performed, consult CPT code 26035.

26040 **Fasciotomy, palmar (eg, Dupuytrens contracture); percutaneous** 4 T 50
MED: 100-2, 15, 260; 100-4, 12, 90.3; 100-4, 14, 10

26045 **open, partial** 3 T 50
MED: 100-2, 15, 260; 100-4, 12, 90.3; 100-4, 14, 10

If a fasciectomy is performed, consult CPT codes 26121-26125.

26055 **Tendon sheath incision (eg, for trigger finger)** 2 T
MED: 100-2, 15, 260; 100-4, 12, 90.3; 100-4, 14, 10

26060 **Tenotomy, percutaneous, single, each digit** 2 T 80
MED: 100-2, 15, 260; 100-4, 12, 90.3; 100-4, 14, 10

26070 **Arthrotomy, with exploration, drainage, or removal of loose or foreign body; carpometacarpal joint** 2 T 50
MED: 100-2, 15, 260; 100-4, 12, 90.3; 100-4, 14, 10

AMA: 1998, Nov, 10

26075 **metacarpophalangeal joint, each** 4 T 50
MED: 100-2, 15, 260; 100-4, 12, 90.3; 100-4, 14, 10

| 26080 | interphalangeal joint, each | 4 T ⟂ |

MED: 100-2, 15, 260; 100-4, 12, 90.3; 100-4, 14, 10

EXCISION

| 26100 | Arthrotomy with biopsy; carpometacarpal joint, each | 2 T 50 80 ⟂ |

MED: 100-2, 15, 260; 100-4, 12, 90.3; 100-4, 14, 10

| 26105 | metacarpophalangeal joint, each | 1 T 50 80 ⟂ |

MED: 100-2, 15, 260; 100-4, 12, 90.3; 100-4, 14, 10

| 26110 | interphalangeal joint, each | 1 T ⟂ |

MED: 100-2, 15, 260; 100-4, 12, 90.3; 100-4, 14, 10

| 26115 | Excision, tumor or vascular malformation, soft tissue of hand or finger; subcutaneous | 2 T ⟂ |

MED: 100-2, 15, 260; 100-4, 12, 90.3; 100-4, 14, 10

| 26116 | deep (subfascial or intramuscular) | 2 T ⟂ |

MED: 100-2, 15, 260; 100-4, 12, 90.3; 100-4, 14, 10

| 26117 | Radical resection of tumor (eg, malignant neoplasm), soft tissue of hand or finger | 3 T ⟂ |

MED: 100-2, 15, 260; 100-4, 12, 90.3; 100-4, 14, 10

| 26121 | Fasciectomy, palm only, with or without Z-plasty, other local tissue rearrangement, or skin grafting (includes obtaining graft) | 4 T 50 ⟂ |

MED: 100-2, 15, 260; 100-4, 12, 90.3; 100-4, 14, 10

If a fasciotomy is performed, consult CPT codes 26040 and 26045.

| 26123 | Fasciectomy, partial palmar with release of single digit including proximal interphalangeal joint, with or without Z-plasty, other local tissue rearrangement, or skin grafting (includes obtaining graft); | 4 T 50 ⟂ |

MED: 100-2, 15, 260; 100-4, 12, 90.3; 100-4, 14, 10

If a fasciotomy is performed, consult CPT codes 26040 and 26045.

| + | 26125 | each additional digit (List separately in addition to code for primary procedure) | 4 T ⟂ |

MED: 100-2, 15, 260; 100-4, 12, 90.3; 100-4, 14, 10

If a fasciotomy is performed, consult CPT codes 26040 and 26045.

Note that 26125 is an add-on code and must be used in conjunction with 26123.

| 26130 | Synovectomy, carpometacarpal joint | 3 T 50 ⟂ |

MED: 100-2, 15, 260; 100-4, 12, 90.3; 100-4, 14, 10

| 26135 | Synovectomy, metacarpophalangeal joint including intrinsic release and extensor hood reconstruction, each digit | 4 T 80 ⟂ |

MED: 100-2, 15, 260; 100-4, 12, 90.3; 100-4, 14, 10

| 26140 | Synovectomy, proximal interphalangeal joint, including extensor reconstruction, each interphalangeal joint | 2 T ⟂ |

MED: 100-2, 15, 260; 100-4, 12, 90.3; 100-4, 14, 10

| 26145 | Synovectomy, tendon sheath, radical (tenosynovectomy), flexor tendon, palm and/or finger, each tendon | 3 T ⟂ |

MED: 100-2, 15, 260; 100-4, 12, 90.3; 100-4, 14, 10

AMA: 1998, Nov, 8

If a tendon sheath synovectomy is performed at the wrist, consult CPT codes 25115 and 25116.

Musculoskeletal System

26160 — 26262

26160   **Excision of lesion of tendon sheath or joint capsule (eg, cyst, mucous cyst, or ganglion), hand or finger**   3 T
MED: 100-2, 15, 260; 100-4, 12, 90.3; 100-4, 14, 10

For a wrist ganglion, consult CPT codes 25111 and 25112. If this procedure is performed on a trigger digit, consult CPT code 26055.

26170   **Excision of tendon, palm, flexor, single (separate procedure), each**   3 T 80
MED: 100-2, 15, 260; 100-4, 12, 90.3; 100-4, 14, 10

26180   **Excision of tendon, finger, flexor (separate procedure), each tendon**   3 T 80
MED: 100-2, 15, 260; 100-4, 12, 90.3; 100-4, 14, 10

AMA: 1998, Nov, 8

26185   **Sesamoidectomy, thumb or finger (separate procedure)**   4 T 50 80
MED: 100-2, 15, 260; 100-4, 12, 90.3; 100-4, 14, 10

26200   **Excision or curettage of bone cyst or benign tumor of metacarpal;** 2 T 80
MED: 100-2, 15, 260; 100-4, 12, 90.3; 100-4, 14, 10

26205   **with autograft (includes obtaining graft)**   3 T
MED: 100-2, 15, 260; 100-4, 12, 90.3; 100-4, 14, 10

26210   **Excision or curettage of bone cyst or benign tumor of proximal, middle or distal phalanx of finger;**   2 T
MED: 100-2, 15, 260; 100-4, 12, 90.3; 100-4, 14, 10

26215   **with autograft (includes obtaining graft)**   3 T
MED: 100-2, 15, 260; 100-4, 12, 90.3; 100-4, 14, 10

26230   **Partial excision (craterization, saucerization, or diaphysectomy) bone (eg, osteomyelitis); metacarpal**   7 T 80
MED: 100-2, 15, 260; 100-4, 12, 90.3; 100-4, 14, 10

26235   **proximal or middle phalanx of finger**   3 T 80
MED: 100-2, 15, 260; 100-4, 12, 90.3; 100-4, 14, 10

26236   **distal phalanx of finger**   3 T
MED: 100-2, 15, 260; 100-4, 12, 90.3; 100-4, 14, 10

26250   **Radical resection, metacarpal (eg, tumor);**   3 T 80
MED: 100-2, 15, 260; 100-4, 12, 90.3; 100-4, 14, 10

AMA: 1998, Nov, 8

26255   **with autograft (includes obtaining graft)**   3 T 80
MED: 100-2, 15, 260; 100-4, 12, 90.3; 100-4, 14, 10

26260   **Radical resection, proximal or middle phalanx of finger (eg, tumor);**   3 T 80
MED: 100-2, 15, 260; 100-4, 12, 90.3; 100-4, 14, 10

AMA: 1998, Nov, 8

26261   **with autograft (includes obtaining graft)**   3 T 80
MED: 100-2, 15, 260; 100-4, 12, 90.3; 100-4, 14, 10

26262   **Radical resection, distal phalanx of finger (eg, tumor)**   2 T 80
MED: 100-2, 15, 260; 100-4, 12, 90.3; 100-4, 14, 10

AMA: 1998, Nov, 8

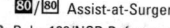

INTRODUCTION OR REMOVAL

26320   **Removal of implant from finger or hand**   2 T ⟲
MED: 100-2, 15, 260; 100-4, 12, 90.3; 100-4, 14, 10

If a foreign body is removed in the hand or the finger, consult CPT codes 20520 and 20525.

REPAIR, REVISION, AND/OR RECONSTRUCTION

26340   **Manipulation, finger joint, under anesthesia, each joint**   T 50 ⟲
AMA: 2002, Nov, 10

If external fixation is applied, consult CPT code 20690 or 20692.

26350   **Repair or advancement, flexor tendon, not in zone 2 digital flexor tendon sheath (eg, no man's land); primary or secondary without free graft, each tendon**   1 T ⟲
MED: 100-2, 15, 260; 100-4, 12, 90.3; 100-4, 14, 10

AMA: 1998, Nov, 8

26352   secondary with free graft (includes obtaining graft), each tendon   4 T 80 ⟲
MED: 100-2, 15, 260; 100-4, 12, 90.3; 100-4, 14, 10

26356   **Repair or advancement, flexor tendon, in zone 2 digital flexor tendon sheath (eg, no man's land); primary, without free graft, each tendon**   4 T ⟲
MED: 100-2, 15, 260; 100-4, 12, 90.3; 100-4, 14, 10

AMA: 1998, Nov, 8; 1998, Dec, 9

26357   secondary, without free graft, each tendon   4 T 80 ⟲
MED: 100-2, 15, 260; 100-4, 12, 90.3; 100-4, 14, 10

26358   secondary, with free graft (includes obtaining graft), each tendon   4 T 80 ⟲
MED: 100-2, 15, 260; 100-4, 12, 90.3; 100-4, 14, 10

26370   **Repair or advancement of profundus tendon, with intact superficialis tendon; primary, each tendon**   4 T 80 ⟲
MED: 100-2, 15, 260; 100-4, 12, 90.3; 100-4, 14, 10

AMA: 1998, Nov, 8

26372   secondary with free graft (includes obtaining graft), each tendon   4 T 80 ⟲
MED: 100-2, 15, 260; 100-4, 12, 90.3; 100-4, 14, 10

AMA: 1998, Nov, 8

26373   secondary without free graft, each tendon   3 T 80 ⟲
MED: 100-2, 15, 260; 100-4, 12, 90.3; 100-4, 14, 10

26390   **Excision flexor tendon, with implantation of synthetic rod for delayed tendon graft, hand or finger, each rod**   4 T 80 ⟲
MED: 100-2, 15, 260; 100-4, 12, 90.3; 100-4, 14, 10

AMA: 1998, Nov, 8

26392   **Removal of synthetic rod and insertion of flexor tendon graft, hand or finger (includes obtaining graft), each rod**   3 T 80 ⟲
MED: 100-2, 15, 260; 100-4, 12, 90.3; 100-4, 14, 10

AMA: 1998, Nov, 8

26410   **Repair, extensor tendon, hand, primary or secondary; without free graft, each tendon**   3 T 🔲
MED: 100-2, 15, 260; 100-4, 12, 90.3; 100-4, 14, 10

AMA: 1998, Nov, 8

26412   **with free graft (includes obtaining graft), each tendon**   3 T 80 🔲
MED: 100-2, 15, 260; 100-4, 12, 90.3; 100-4, 14, 10

AMA: 1998, Nov, 8

26415   **Excision of extensor tendon, with implantation of synthetic rod for delayed tendon graft, hand or finger, each rod**   4 T 80 🔲
MED: 100-2, 15, 260; 100-4, 12, 90.3; 100-4, 14, 10

AMA: 1998, Nov, 8

26416   **Removal of synthetic rod and insertion of extensor tendon graft (includes obtaining graft), hand or finger, each rod**   3 T 🔲
MED: 100-2, 15, 260; 100-4, 12, 90.3; 100-4, 14, 10

AMA: 1999, Nov, 12

26418   **Repair, extensor tendon, finger, primary or secondary; without free graft, each tendon**   4 T 🔲
MED: 100-2, 15, 260; 100-4, 12, 90.3; 100-4, 14, 10

AMA: 2000, Dec, 14; 1999, Dec, 10; 1998, Nov, 8

26420   **with free graft (includes obtaining graft) each tendon**   4 T 80 🔲
MED: 100-2, 15, 260; 100-4, 12, 90.3; 100-4, 14, 10

26426   **Repair of extensor tendon, central slip, secondary (eg, boutonniere deformity); using local tissue(s), including lateral band(s), each finger**   3 T 🔲
MED: 100-2, 15, 260; 100-4, 12, 90.3; 100-4, 14, 10

AMA: 1998, Nov, 8

26428   **with free graft (includes obtaining graft), each finger**   3 T 80 🔲
MED: 100-2, 15, 260; 100-4, 12, 90.3; 100-4, 14, 10

26432   **Closed treatment of distal extensor tendon insertion, with or without percutaneous pinning (eg, mallet finger)**   3 T 🔲
MED: 100-2, 15, 260; 100-4, 12, 90.3; 100-4, 14, 10

AMA: 1998, Nov, 8

26433   **Repair of extensor tendon, distal insertion, primary or secondary; without graft (eg, mallet finger)**   3 T 🔲
MED: 100-2, 15, 260; 100-4, 12, 90.3; 100-4, 14, 10

AMA: 1998, Nov, 8

26434   **with free graft (includes obtaining graft)**   3 T 80 🔲
MED: 100-2, 15, 260; 100-4, 12, 90.3; 100-4, 14, 10

If a tenovaginotomy is performed on the trigger finger, consult CPT code 26055.

26437   **Realignment of extensor tendon, hand, each tendon**   3 T 🔲
MED: 100-2, 15, 260; 100-4, 12, 90.3; 100-4, 14, 10

AMA: 1998, Nov, 8

26440   **Tenolysis, flexor tendon; palm OR finger, each tendon**   3 T 🔲
MED: 100-2, 15, 260; 100-4, 12, 90.3; 100-4, 14, 10

AMA: 2002, Apr, 18

26442	palm AND finger, each tendon	3 T 🔲

MED: 100-2, 15, 260; 100-4, 12, 90.3; 100-4, 14, 10

26445	Tenolysis, extensor tendon, hand OR finger, each tendon	3 T 🔲

MED: 100-2, 15, 260; 100-4, 12, 90.3; 100-4, 14, 10

AMA: 2002, Dec, 11; 1998, Nov, 8

26449	Tenolysis, complex, extensor tendon, finger, including forearm, each tendon	3 T 80 🔲

MED: 100-2, 15, 260; 100-4, 12, 90.3; 100-4, 14, 10

AMA: 1998, Nov, 8

26450	Tenotomy, flexor, palm, open, each tendon	3 T 80 🔲

MED: 100-2, 15, 260; 100-4, 12, 90.3; 100-4, 14, 10

AMA: 1998, Nov, 8

26455	Tenotomy, flexor, finger, open, each tendon	3 T 80 🔲

MED: 100-2, 15, 260; 100-4, 12, 90.3; 100-4, 14, 10

AMA: 1998, Nov, 8

26460	Tenotomy, extensor, hand or finger, open, each tendon	3 T 🔲

MED: 100-2, 15, 260; 100-4, 12, 90.3; 100-4, 14, 10

AMA: 1998, Nov, 8

26471	Tenodesis; of proximal interphalangeal joint, each joint	2 T 80 🔲

MED: 100-2, 15, 260; 100-4, 12, 90.3; 100-4, 14, 10

AMA: 1998, Nov, 8

26474	of distal joint, each joint	2 T 80 🔲

MED: 100-2, 15, 260; 100-4, 12, 90.3; 100-4, 14, 10

AMA: 1998, Nov, 8

26476	Lengthening of tendon, extensor, hand or finger, each tendon	1 T 🔲

MED: 100-2, 15, 260; 100-4, 12, 90.3; 100-4, 14, 10

AMA: 1998, Nov, 8

26477	Shortening of tendon, extensor, hand or finger, each tendon	1 T 🔲

MED: 100-2, 15, 260; 100-4, 12, 90.3; 100-4, 14, 10

AMA: 1998, Nov, 8

26478	Lengthening of tendon, flexor, hand or finger, each tendon	1 T 80 🔲

MED: 100-2, 15, 260; 100-4, 12, 90.3; 100-4, 14, 10

AMA: 1998, Nov, 8

26479	Shortening of tendon, flexor, hand or finger, each tendon	1 T 80 🔲

MED: 100-2, 15, 260; 100-4, 12, 90.3; 100-4, 14, 10

AMA: 1998, Nov, 8

26480	Transfer or transplant of tendon, carpometacarpal area or dorsum of hand; without free graft, each tendon	3 T 80 🔲

MED: 100-2, 15, 260; 100-4, 12, 90.3; 100-4, 14, 10

AMA: 1998, Nov, 8

26483	with free tendon graft (includes obtaining graft), each tendon	3 T 80 🔲

MED: 100-2, 15, 260; 100-4, 12, 90.3; 100-4, 14, 10

Musculoskeletal System

26485 — 26517

26485 Transfer or transplant of tendon, palmar; without free tendon graft, each tendon 2 T 80 ✎
MED: 100-2, 15, 260; 100-4, 12, 90.3; 100-4, 14, 10

AMA: 1998, Nov, 8

26489 with free tendon graft (includes obtaining graft), each tendon 3 T 80 ✎
MED: 100-2, 15, 260; 100-4, 12, 90.3; 100-4, 14, 10

26490 Opponensplasty; superficialis tendon transfer type, each tendon 3 T 80 ✎
MED: 100-2, 15, 260; 100-4, 12, 90.3; 100-4, 14, 10

26492 tendon transfer with graft (includes obtaining graft), each tendon 3 T 80 ✎
MED: 100-2, 15, 260; 100-4, 12, 90.3; 100-4, 14, 10

26494 hypothenar muscle transfer 3 T 80 ✎
MED: 100-2, 15, 260; 100-4, 12, 90.3; 100-4, 14, 10

26496 other methods 3 T 80 ✎
MED: 100-2, 15, 260; 100-4, 12, 90.3; 100-4, 14, 10

If thumb fusion in opposition is performed, consult CPT code 26820.

26497 Transfer of tendon to restore intrinsic function; ring and small finger 3 T 80 ✎
MED: 100-2, 15, 260; 100-4, 12, 90.3; 100-4, 14, 10

AMA: 1998, Nov, 8

26498 all four fingers 4 T 80 ✎
MED: 100-2, 15, 260; 100-4, 12, 90.3; 100-4, 14, 10

26499 Correction claw finger, other methods 3 T 80 ✎
MED: 100-2, 15, 260; 100-4, 12, 90.3; 100-4, 14, 10

26500 Reconstruction of tendon pulley, each tendon; with local tissues (separate procedure) 4 T 80 ✎
MED: 100-2, 15, 260; 100-4, 12, 90.3; 100-4, 14, 10

AMA: 1998, Nov, 8

26502 with tendon or fascial graft (includes obtaining graft) (separate procedure) 4 T 80 ✎
MED: 100-2, 15, 260; 100-4, 12, 90.3; 100-4, 14, 10

26504 with tendon prosthesis (separate procedure) 4 T 80 ✎
MED: 100-2, 15, 260; 100-4, 12, 90.3; 100-4, 14, 10

26508 Release of thenar muscle(s) (eg, thumb contracture) 3 T 80 ✎
MED: 100-2, 15, 260; 100-4, 12, 90.3; 100-4, 14, 10

AMA: 1998, Nov, 8

26510 Cross intrinsic transfer, each tendon 3 T 80 ✎
MED: 100-2, 15, 260; 100-4, 12, 90.3; 100-4, 14, 10

26516 Capsulodesis, metacarpophalangeal joint; single digit 1 T 80 ✎
MED: 100-2, 15, 260; 100-4, 12, 90.3; 100-4, 14, 10

AMA: 1998, Nov, 8

26517 two digits 3 T 80 ✎
MED: 100-2, 15, 260; 100-4, 12, 90.3; 100-4, 14, 10

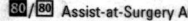

26518   **three or four digits**   `3` `T` `80` `↻`
MED: 100-2, 15, 260; 100-4, 12, 90.3; 100-4, 14, 10

26520   **Capsulectomy or capsulotomy; metacarpophalangeal joint,**
each joint   `3` `T` `↻`
MED: 100-2, 15, 260; 100-4, 12, 90.3; 100-4, 14, 10

AMA: 1998, Nov, 8

26525   **interphalangeal joint, each joint**   `3` `T` `↻`
MED: 100-2, 15, 260; 100-4, 12, 90.3; 100-4, 14, 10

AMA: 2002, Apr, 18; 1998, Nov, 8

To report a carpometacarpal joint arthroplasty, consult CPT code 25447.

26530   **Arthroplasty, metacarpophalangeal joint; each joint**   `3` `T` `80` `↻`
MED: 100-2, 15, 260; 100-4, 12, 90.3; 100-4, 14, 10

AMA: 1998, Nov, 8

26531   **with prosthetic implant, each joint**   `7` `T` `80` `↻`
MED: 100-2, 15, 260; 100-4, 12, 90.3; 100-4, 14, 10

AMA: 1998, Nov, 8

26535   **Arthroplasty, interphalangeal joint; each joint**   `5` `T` `↻`
MED: 100-2, 15, 260; 100-4, 12, 90.3; 100-4, 14, 10

AMA: 1998, Nov, 8

26536   **with prosthetic implant, each joint**   `5` `T` `80` `↻`
MED: 100-2, 15, 260; 100-4, 12, 90.3; 100-4, 14, 10

AMA: 1998, Nov, 8

26540   **Repair of collateral ligament, metacarpophalangeal or interphalangeal**
joint   `4` `T` `80` `↻`
MED: 100-2, 15, 260; 100-4, 12, 90.3; 100-4, 14, 10

26541   **Reconstruction, collateral ligament, metacarpophalangeal joint, single, with**
tendon or fascial graft (includes obtaining graft)   `7` `T` `80` `↻`
MED: 100-2, 15, 260; 100-4, 12, 90.3; 100-4, 14, 10

AMA: 1997, Jan, 3

26542   **with local tissue (eg, adductor advancement)**   `4` `T` `80` `↻`
MED: 100-2, 15, 260; 100-4, 12, 90.3; 100-4, 14, 10

AMA: 1997, Jan, 3

26545   **Reconstruction, collateral ligament, interphalangeal joint, single, including**
graft, each joint   `4` `T` `80` `↻`
MED: 100-2, 15, 260; 100-4, 12, 90.3; 100-4, 14, 10

26546   **Repair non-union, metacarpal or phalanx, (includes obtaining bone graft**
with or without external or internal fixation)   `4` `T` `50` `80` `↻`
MED: 100-2, 15, 260; 100-4, 12, 90.3; 100-4, 14, 10

26548   **Repair and reconstruction, finger, volar plate, interphalangeal**
joint   `4` `T` `80` `↻`
MED: 100-2, 15, 260; 100-4, 12, 90.3; 100-4, 14, 10

26550   **Pollicization of a digit**   `2` `T` `80` `↻`
MED: 100-2, 15, 260; 100-4, 12, 90.3; 100-4, 14, 10

Musculoskeletal System

26551 — 26590

26551   **Transfer, toe-to-hand with microvascular anastomosis; great toe wrap-around with bone graft**   C 80
AMA: 1998, Nov, 8, 10-11; 1997, Jun, 9; 1997, Apr, 7

Do not report 69990 in addition to 26551-26554 as the operating microscope is considered an inclusive component of these procedures.

If a free osteocutaneous flap with microvascular anastomosis is performed on the great toe with web space, consult CPT code 20973.

26553   **other than great toe, single**   C 80
AMA: 1998, Nov, 8, 10-11; 1997, Jun, 9; 1997, Apr, 7

26554   **other than great toe, double**   C 80
AMA: 1998, Nov, 8, 10-11; 1997, Jun, 9; 1997, Apr, 7

26555   **Transfer, finger to another position without microvascular anastomosis**   3 T 80
MED: 100-2, 15, 260; 100-4, 12, 90.3; 100-4, 14, 10

AMA: 1998, Nov, 8, 10-11

26556   **Transfer, free toe joint, with microvascular anastomosis**   C 80
AMA: 1998, Nov, 8; 1997, Jun, 9; 1997, Apr, 7

Do not report 69990 in addition to 26556 as the operating microscope is considered an inclusive component of the surgery. If a great toe-to-hand transfer is performed, consult CPT code 20973.

26560   **Repair of syndactyly (web finger) each web space; with skin flaps**   2 T 80
MED: 100-2, 15, 260; 100-4, 12, 90.3; 100-4, 14, 10

26561   **with skin flaps and grafts**   3 T 80
MED: 100-2, 15, 260; 100-4, 12, 90.3; 100-4, 14, 10

26562   **complex (eg, involving bone, nails)**   4 T 80
MED: 100-2, 15, 260; 100-4, 12, 90.3; 100-4, 14, 10

26565   **Osteotomy; metacarpal, each**   5 T 80
MED: 100-2, 15, 260; 100-4, 12, 90.3; 100-4, 14, 10

AMA: 1998, Nov, 9

26567   **phalanx of finger, each**   5 T 80
MED: 100-2, 15, 260; 100-4, 12, 90.3; 100-4, 14, 10

26568   **Osteoplasty, lengthening, metacarpal or phalanx**   3 T 80
MED: 100-2, 15, 260; 100-4, 12, 90.3; 100-4, 14, 10

26580   **Repair cleft hand**   5 T 80
MED: 100-2, 15, 260; 100-4, 12, 90.3; 100-4, 14, 10

Barsky's procedure

26587   **Reconstruction of polydactylous digit, soft tissue and bone**   5 T 80
MED: 100-2, 15, 260; 100-4, 12, 90.3; 100-4, 14, 10

AMA: 2001, Oct, 10

If an excision is performed on the supernumerary digit, soft tissue only, consult CPT code 11200.

26590   **Repair macrodactylia, each digit**   5 T 80
MED: 100-2, 15, 260; 100-4, 12, 90.3; 100-4, 14, 10

AMA: 2001, Oct, 10

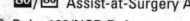

26591	Repair, intrinsic muscles of hand, each muscle ③ T 80 ↻
	MED: 100-2, 15, 260; 100-4, 12, 90.3; 100-4, 14, 10
	AMA: 1998, Nov, 8, 11; 1998, May, 11; 1998, Jul, 11

26593	Release, intrinsic muscles of hand, each muscle ③ T ↻
	MED: 100-2, 15, 260; 100-4, 12, 90.3; 100-4, 14, 10
	AMA: 1998, Nov, 8, 11

| 26596 | Excision of constricting ring of finger, with multiple Z-plasties   ② T 80 ↻ |
| | MED: 100-2, 15, 260; 100-4, 12, 90.3; 100-4, 14, 10 |

To report the release of scar contracture or graft repairs, consult CPT codes 11041-11042, 14040-14041, or 15120 and 15240.

FRACTURE AND/OR DISLOCATION

| 26600 | Closed treatment of metacarpal fracture, single; without manipulation, each bone   T ↻ |

| 26605 | with manipulation, each bone   ② T ↻ |
| | MED: 100-2, 15, 260; 100-4, 12, 90.3; 100-4, 14, 10 |

| 26607 | Closed treatment of metacarpal fracture, with manipulation, with external fixation, each bone   ② T 80 ↻ |
| | MED: 100-2, 15, 260; 100-4, 12, 90.3; 100-4, 14, 10 |

| 26608 | Percutaneous skeletal fixation of metacarpal fracture, each bone   ④ T 80 ↻ |
| | MED: 100-2, 15, 260; 100-4, 12, 90.3; 100-4, 14, 10 |

| 26615 | Open treatment of metacarpal fracture, single, with or without internal or external fixation, each bone   ④ T ↻ |
| | MED: 100-2, 15, 260; 100-4, 12, 90.3; 100-4, 14, 10 |

| 26641 | Closed treatment of carpometacarpal dislocation, thumb, with manipulation   T 80 ↻ |

| 26645 | Closed treatment of carpometacarpal fracture dislocation, thumb (Bennett fracture), with manipulation   ① T 80 ↻ |
| | MED: 100-2, 15, 260; 100-4, 12, 90.3; 100-4, 14, 10 |

| 26650 | Percutaneous skeletal fixation of carpometacarpal fracture dislocation, thumb (Bennett fracture), with manipulation, with or without external fixation   ② T ↻ |
| | MED: 100-2, 15, 260; 100-4, 12, 90.3; 100-4, 14, 10 |

| 26665 | Open treatment of carpometacarpal fracture dislocation, thumb (Bennett fracture), with or without internal or external fixation   ④ T ↻ |
| | MED: 100-2, 15, 260; 100-4, 12, 90.3; 100-4, 14, 10 |

| 26670 | Closed treatment of carpometacarpal dislocation, other than thumb, with manipulation, each joint; without anesthesia   T 80 ↻ |

| 26675 | requiring anesthesia   ② T 80 ↻ |
| | MED: 100-2, 15, 260; 100-4, 12, 90.3; 100-4, 14, 10 |

| 26676 | Percutaneous skeletal fixation of carpometacarpal dislocation, other than thumb, with manipulation, each joint   ② T ↻ |
| | MED: 100-2, 15, 260; 100-4, 12, 90.3; 100-4, 14, 10 |

| 26685 | Open treatment of carpometacarpal dislocation, other than thumb; with or without internal or external fixation, each joint   ③ T ↻ |
| | MED: 100-2, 15, 260; 100-4, 12, 90.3; 100-4, 14, 10 |

Musculoskeletal System

26686 — 26776

26686	complex, multiple or delayed reduction	3 T 80 ⟳

MED: 100-2, 15, 260; 100-4, 12, 90.3; 100-4, 14, 10

26700 Closed treatment of metacarpophalangeal dislocation, single, with manipulation; without anesthesia   T ⟳

26705 requiring anesthesia   2 T 80 ⟳

MED: 100-2, 15, 260; 100-4, 12, 90.3; 100-4, 14, 10

26706 Percutaneous skeletal fixation of metacarpophalangeal dislocation, single, with manipulation   2 T ⟳

MED: 100-2, 15, 260; 100-4, 12, 90.3; 100-4, 14, 10

26715 Open treatment of metacarpophalangeal dislocation, single, with or without internal or external fixation   4 T 80 ⟳

MED: 100-2, 15, 260; 100-4, 12, 90.3; 100-4, 14, 10

26720 Closed treatment of phalangeal shaft fracture, proximal or middle phalanx, finger or thumb; without manipulation, each   T ⟳

26725 with manipulation, with or without skin or skeletal traction, each   T ⟳

26727 Percutaneous skeletal fixation of unstable phalangeal shaft fracture, proximal or middle phalanx, finger or thumb, with manipulation, each   7 T ⟳

MED: 100-2, 15, 260; 100-4, 12, 90.3; 100-4, 14, 10

26735 Open treatment of phalangeal shaft fracture, proximal or middle phalanx, finger or thumb, with or without internal or external fixation, each   4 T ⟳

MED: 100-2, 15, 260; 100-4, 12, 90.3; 100-4, 14, 10

26740 Closed treatment of articular fracture, involving metacarpophalangeal or interphalangeal joint; without manipulation, each   T ⟳

26742 with manipulation, each   2 T ⟳

MED: 100-2, 15, 260; 100-4, 12, 90.3; 100-4, 14, 10

26746 Open treatment of articular fracture, involving metacarpophalangeal or interphalangeal joint, with or without internal or external fixation, each   5 T ⟳

MED: 100-2, 15, 260; 100-4, 12, 90.3; 100-4, 14, 10

26750 Closed treatment of distal phalangeal fracture, finger or thumb; without manipulation, each   T ⟳

26755 with manipulation, each   T ⟳

26756 Percutaneous skeletal fixation of distal phalangeal fracture, finger or thumb, each   2 T 80 ⟳

MED: 100-2, 15, 260; 100-4, 12, 90.3; 100-4, 14, 10

26765 Open treatment of distal phalangeal fracture, finger or thumb, with or without internal or external fixation, each   4 T ⟳

MED: 100-2, 15, 260; 100-4, 12, 90.3; 100-4, 14, 10

26770 Closed treatment of interphalangeal joint dislocation, single, with manipulation; without anesthesia   T ⟳

26775 requiring anesthesia   T ⟳

26776 Percutaneous skeletal fixation of interphalangeal joint dislocation, single, with manipulation   2 T ⟳

MED: 100-2, 15, 260; 100-4, 12, 90.3; 100-4, 14, 10

26785   Open treatment of interphalangeal joint dislocation, with or without internal or external fixation, single   2️⃣ T 🔳
MED: 100-2, 15, 260; 100-4, 12, 90.3; 100-4, 14, 10

ARTHRODESIS

26820   Fusion in opposition, thumb, with autogenous graft (includes obtaining graft)   5️⃣ T 80 🔳
MED: 100-2, 15, 260; 100-4, 12, 90.3; 100-4, 14, 10

26841   Arthrodesis, carpometacarpal joint, thumb, with or without internal fixation;   4️⃣ T 80 🔳
MED: 100-2, 15, 260; 100-4, 12, 90.3; 100-4, 14, 10

26842   with autograft (includes obtaining graft)   4️⃣ T 80 🔳
MED: 100-2, 15, 260; 100-4, 12, 90.3; 100-4, 14, 10

26843   Arthrodesis, carpometacarpal joint, digit, other than thumb, each; 3️⃣ T 80 🔳
MED: 100-2, 15, 260; 100-4, 12, 90.3; 100-4, 14, 10

26844   with autograft (includes obtaining graft)   3️⃣ T 80 🔳
MED: 100-2, 15, 260; 100-4, 12, 90.3; 100-4, 14, 10

26850   Arthrodesis, metacarpophalangeal joint, with or without internal fixation;   4️⃣ T 80 🔳
MED: 100-2, 15, 260; 100-4, 12, 90.3; 100-4, 14, 10

26852   with autograft (includes obtaining graft)   4️⃣ T 80 🔳
MED: 100-2, 15, 260; 100-4, 12, 90.3; 100-4, 14, 10

26860   Arthrodesis, interphalangeal joint, with or without internal fixation; 3️⃣ T 🔳
MED: 100-2, 15, 260; 100-4, 12, 90.3; 100-4, 14, 10

+ 26861   each additional interphalangeal joint (List separately in addition to code for primary procedure)   2️⃣ T 🔳
MED: 100-2, 15, 260; 100-4, 12, 90.3; 100-4, 14, 10

Note that 26861 is an add-on code and must be used in conjunction with 26860.

26862   with autograft (includes obtaining graft)   4️⃣ T 80 🔳
MED: 100-2, 15, 260; 100-4, 12, 90.3; 100-4, 14, 10

+ 26863   with autograft (includes obtaining graft), each additional joint (List separately in addition to code for primary procedure)   3️⃣ T 80 🔳
MED: 100-2, 15, 260; 100-4, 12, 90.3; 100-4, 14, 10

Note that 26863 is an add-on code and must be used in conjunction with 26862.

AMPUTATION
If the amputation is on the hand through metacarpal bones, consult CPT code 25927

26910   Amputation, metacarpal, with finger or thumb (ray amputation), single, with or without interosseous transfer   3️⃣ T 🔳
MED: 100-2, 15, 260; 100-4, 12, 90.3; 100-4, 14, 10

If repositioning is performed, consult CPT codes 26550 and 26555.

26951   Amputation, finger or thumb, primary or secondary, any joint or phalanx, single, including neurectomies; with direct closure   2️⃣ T 🔳
MED: 100-2, 15, 260; 100-4, 12, 90.3; 100-4, 14, 10

Musculoskeletal System

26952 — 27033

| 26952 | with local advancement flaps (V-Y, hood) | 4 T ↻ |

MED: 100-2, 15, 260; 100-4, 12, 90.3; 100-4, 14, 10

If repair of a soft tissue defect requiring a split or a full thickness graft or other pedicle flaps is performed, consult CPT codes 15050-15758.

OTHER PROCEDURES

| 26989 | Unlisted procedure, hands or fingers | T |

PELVIS AND HIP JOINT

Codes listed in the Musculoskeletal chapter include the application and removal of the first cast or traction device. Replacement of casts and/or traction devices subsequent to the first should be reported separately. CPT codes for other additional procedures, such as obtaining grafts and external fixation, should only be used if the procedure is not already listed as included as part of the basic procedure. Consult the glossary for terms and definitions and the front matter of this chapter for additional information.

This section includes procedures performed on the head and neck of the femur.

INCISION

If superficial incision and drainage procedures are performed, consult CPT codes 10040-10160.

| 26990 | Incision and drainage, pelvis or hip joint area; deep abscess or hematoma | 1 T ↻ |

MED: 100-2, 15, 260; 100-4, 12, 90.3; 100-4, 14, 10

| 26991 | infected bursa | 1 T 80 ↻ |

MED: 100-2, 15, 260; 100-4, 12, 90.3; 100-4, 14, 10

| 26992 | Incision, bone cortex, pelvis and/or hip joint (eg, osteomyelitis or bone abscess) | C 80 ↻ |

AMA: 2002, Jan, 10

| 27000 | Tenotomy, adductor of hip, percutaneous (separate procedure) | 2 T 50 ↻ |

MED: 100-2, 15, 260; 100-4, 12, 90.3; 100-4, 14, 10

| 27001 | Tenotomy, adductor of hip, open | 3 T 50 80 ↻ |

MED: 100-2, 15, 260; 100-4, 12, 90.3; 100-4, 14, 10

| 27003 | Tenotomy, adductor, subcutaneous, open, with obturator neurectomy | 3 T 50 80 ↻ |

MED: 100-2, 15, 260; 100-4, 12, 90.3; 100-4, 14, 10

| 27005 | Tenotomy, hip flexor(s), open (separate procedure) | C 50 80 ↻ |

| 27006 | Tenotomy, abductors and/or extensor(s) of hip, open (separate procedure) | C 50 80 ↻ |

| 27025 | Fasciotomy, hip or thigh, any type | C 50 80 ↻ |

| 27030 | Arthrotomy, hip, with drainage (eg, infection) | C 50 80 ↻ |

AMA: 1998, Nov, 8

| 27033 | Arthrotomy, hip, including exploration or removal of loose or foreign body | 3 T 50 80 ↻ |

MED: 100-2, 15, 260; 100-4, 12, 90.3; 100-4, 14, 10

AMA: 1992, Spring, 11

27035   **Denervation, hip joint, intrapelvic or extrapelvic intra-articular branches of sciatic, femoral, or obturator nerves**   4 T 50 ⟲
MED: 100-2, 15, 260; 100-3, 160.1; 100-4, 12, 90.3; 100-4, 14, 10

AMA: 1998, Nov, 8

If an obturator neurectomy is performed, consult CPT codes 64763 and 64766.

27036   **Capsulectomy or capsulotomy, hip, with or without excision of heterotopic bone, with release of hip flexor muscles (ie, gluteus medius, gluteus minimus, tensor fascia latae, rectus femoris, sartorius, iliopsoas)**   C 50 80 ⟲

EXCISION

27040   **Biopsy, soft tissue of pelvis and hip area; superficial**   1 T 50 ⟲
MED: 100-2, 15, 260; 100-4, 12, 90.3; 100-4, 14, 10

27041   **deep, subfascial or intramuscular**   2 T 50 ⟲
MED: 100-2, 15, 260; 100-4, 12, 90.3; 100-4, 14, 10

AMA: 1998, Nov, 8

If a needle biopsy of the soft tissue is performed, consult CPT code 20206.

27047   **Excision, tumor, pelvis and hip area; subcutaneous tissue**   2 T 50 ⟲
MED: 100-2, 15, 260; 100-4, 12, 90.3; 100-4, 14, 10

AMA: 1998, Nov, 8

27048   **deep, subfascial, intramuscular**   3 T 50 80 ⟲
MED: 100-2, 15, 260; 100-4, 12, 90.3; 100-4, 14, 10

27049   **Radical resection of tumor, soft tissue of pelvis and hip area (eg, malignant neoplasm)**   3 T 50 80 ⟲
MED: 100-2, 15, 260; 100-4, 12, 90.3; 100-4, 14, 10

AMA: 1998, Nov, 8

27050   **Arthrotomy, with biopsy; sacroiliac joint**   3 T 50 80 ⟲
MED: 100-2, 15, 260; 100-4, 12, 90.3; 100-4, 14, 10

27052   **hip joint**   3 T 50 80 ⟲
MED: 100-2, 15, 260; 100-4, 12, 90.3; 100-4, 14, 10

27054   **Arthrotomy with synovectomy, hip joint**   C 50 80 ⟲

27060   **Excision; ischial bursa**   5 T 50 ⟲
MED: 100-2, 15, 260; 100-4, 12, 90.3; 100-4, 14, 10

27062   **trochanteric bursa or calcification**   5 T 50 ⟲
MED: 100-2, 15, 260; 100-4, 12, 90.3; 100-4, 14, 10

27065   **Excision of bone cyst or benign tumor; superficial (wing of ilium, symphysis pubis, or greater trochanter of femur) with or without autograft**   5 T 50 80 ⟲
MED: 100-2, 15, 260; 100-4, 12, 90.3; 100-4, 14, 10

27066   **deep, with or without autograft**   5 T 50 80 ⟲
MED: 100-2, 15, 260; 100-4, 12, 90.3; 100-4, 14, 10

27067   **with autograft requiring separate incision**   5 T 50 80 ⟲
MED: 100-2, 15, 260; 100-4, 12, 90.3; 100-4, 14, 10

27070   **Partial excision (craterization, saucerization) (eg, osteomyelitis or bone abscess); superficial (eg, wing of ilium, symphysis pubis, or greater trochanter of femur)**   C 50 80 ⟲

27071   **deep (subfascial or intramuscular)**   C 50 80 ⟲

| 27075 | Radical resection of tumor or infection; wing of ilium, one pubic or ischial ramus or symphysis pubis | C 80 ⬚ |

27076   ilium, including acetabulum, both pubic rami, or ischium and acetabulum — C 80 ⬚

27077   innominate bone, total — C 80 ⬚

27078   ischial tuberosity and greater trochanter of femur — C 80 ⬚

27079   ischial tuberosity and greater trochanter of femur, with skin flaps — C 80 ⬚

27080   Coccygectomy, primary — 2 T 80 ⬚
MED: 100-2, 15, 260; 100-4, 12, 90.3; 100-4, 14, 10

If this procedure involves a pressure (decubitus) ulcer, consult CPT codes 15920, 15922, and 15931-15958.

INTRODUCTION OR REMOVAL

27086   Removal of foreign body, pelvis or hip; subcutaneous tissue — 1 T 50 80 ⬚
MED: 100-2, 15, 260; 100-4, 12, 90.3; 100-4, 14, 10

AMA: 1998, Jul, 8

27087   deep (subfascial or intramuscular) — 3 T 50 80 ⬚
MED: 100-2, 15, 260; 100-4, 12, 90.3; 100-4, 14, 10

AMA: 1998, Nov, 8

27090   Removal of hip prosthesis; (separate procedure) — C 50 80 ⬚

27091   complicated, including total hip prosthesis, methylmethacrylate with or without insertion of spacer — C 50 80 ⬚

27093   Injection procedure for hip arthrography; without anesthesia — N 50 ⬚

To report radiological supervision and interpretation of procedure, consult CPT code 73525. Do not report 76003 with 73525.

27095   with anesthesia — N 50 ⬚

To report radiological supervision and interpretation of procedure, consult CPT code 73525. Do not report 76003 in addition to 73525.

27096   Injection procedure for sacroiliac joint, arthrography and/or anesthetic/steroid — B 50 ⬚
AMA: 1999, Nov, 12

Report 27096 only with imaging confirmation of intraarticular needle positioning.

To report radiological supervision and interpretation of sacroiliac joint arthrography, consult CPT code 73542.

To report fluoroscopic guidance without formal arthrography, use 76005.

Code 27096 is a unilateral procedure. For bilateral procedure, append modifier 50.

REPAIR, REVISION, AND/OR RECONSTRUCTION

27097   Release or recession, hamstring, proximal — 3 T 50 80 ⬚
MED: 100-2, 15, 260; 100-4, 12, 90.3; 100-4, 14, 10

AMA: 1998, Nov, 8

27098   Transfer, adductor to ischium — 3 T 50 80 ⬚
MED: 100-2, 15, 260; 100-4, 12, 90.3; 100-4, 14, 10

AMA: 1998, Nov, 8

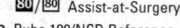

27100   Transfer external oblique muscle to greater trochanter including fascial or tendon extension (graft)   [4] [T] [50] [80] [↘]
MED: 100-2, 15, 260; 100-4, 12, 90.3; 100-4, 14, 10

Eggers procedure

27105   Transfer paraspinal muscle to hip (includes fascial or tendon extension graft)   [4] [T] [50] [80] [↘]
MED: 100-2, 15, 260; 100-4, 12, 90.3; 100-4, 14, 10

27110   Transfer iliopsoas; to greater trochanter of femur   [4] [T] [50] [80] [↘]
MED: 100-2, 15, 260; 100-4, 12, 90.3; 100-4, 14, 10

27111   to femoral neck   [4] [T] [50] [80] [↘]
MED: 100-2, 15, 260; 100-4, 12, 90.3; 100-4, 14, 10

27120   Acetabuloplasty; (eg, Whitman, Colonna, Haygroves, or cup type)   [C] [50] [80] [↘]

27122   resection, femoral head (eg, Girdlestone procedure)   [C] [50] [80] [↘]

27125   Hemiarthroplasty, hip, partial (eg, femoral stem prosthesis, bipolar arthroplasty)   [C] [50] [80] [↘]
AMA: 1998, Nov, 8; 1998, Feb, 11; 1992, Spring, 8

If prosthetic replacement follows a fracture of the hip, consult CPT code 27236.

27130   Arthroplasty, acetabular and proximal femoral prosthetic replacement (total hip arthroplasty), with or without autograft or allograft   [C] [50] [80] [↘]
AMA: 1992, Spring, 8

27132   Conversion of previous hip surgery to total hip arthroplasty, with or without autograft or allograft   [C] [50] [80] [↘]
AMA: 1992, Spring, 11

27134   Revision of total hip arthroplasty; both components, with or without autograft or allograft   [C] [50] [80] [↘]

27137   acetabular component only, with or without autograft or allograft   [C] [50] [80] [↘]

27138   femoral component only, with or without allograft   [C] [50] [80] [↘]

27140   Osteotomy and transfer of greater trochanter of femur (separate procedure)   [C] [50] [80] [↘]

27146   Osteotomy, iliac, acetabular or innominate bone;   [C] [50] [80] [↘]
AMA: 1999, Feb, 10

Salter osteotomy

27147   with open reduction of hip   [C] [50] [80] [↘]
Pemberton osteotomy

27151   with femoral osteotomy   [C] [50] [80] [↘]

27156   with femoral osteotomy and with open reduction of hip   [C] [50] [80] [↘]
Chiari osteotomy

27158   Osteotomy, pelvis, bilateral (eg, congenital malformation)   [C] [80] [↘]

27161   Osteotomy, femoral neck (separate procedure)   [C] [50] [80] [↘]

27165   Osteotomy, intertrochanteric or subtrochanteric including internal or external fixation and/or cast   [C] [80] [↘]
AMA: 1992, Spring, 11

| [↘] CCI Comp | [50] Bilateral Procedure | + CPT Add-on Code | ○ Modifier -51 Exempt | ♂ Male | ♀ Female |
| ● New Code | ▲ Revised Code | [M] Maternity Edit | [A] Age Edit | [A]–[Y] APC Status Ind. | AMA: CPT Assistant |

© 2005 Ingenix, Inc. *(Blue Ink)*   CPT only © 2005 American Medical Association. All Rights Reserved. *(Black Ink)*   Surgery — 177

Musculoskeletal System

27170 — 27228

| 27170 | Bone graft, femoral head, neck, intertrochanteric or subtrochanteric area (includes obtaining bone graft) | C 50 80 ⏹ |
| | AMA: 1992, Spring, 11 | |

| 27175 | Treatment of slipped femoral epiphysis; by traction, without reduction | C 50 80 ⏹ |

| 27176 | by single or multiple pinning, in situ | C 50 80 ⏹ |

| 27177 | Open treatment of slipped femoral epiphysis; single or multiple pinning or bone graft (includes obtaining graft) | C 50 80 ⏹ |

| 27178 | closed manipulation with single or multiple pinning | C 50 80 ⏹ |

| 27179 | osteoplasty of femoral neck (Heyman type procedure) | C 50 80 ⏹ |

| 27181 | osteotomy and internal fixation | C 50 80 ⏹ |

| 27185 | Epiphyseal arrest by epiphysiodesis or stapling, greater trochanter of femur | C 50 ⏹ |

| 27187 | Prophylactic treatment (nailing, pinning, plating or wiring) with or without methylmethacrylate, femoral neck and proximal femur | C 50 80 ⏹ |

FRACTURE AND/OR DISLOCATION

| 27193 | Closed treatment of pelvic ring fracture, dislocation, diastasis or subluxation; without manipulation | 1 T 50 ⏹ |
| | MED: 100-2, 15, 260; 100-4, 12, 90.3; 100-4, 14, 10 | |

| 27194 | with manipulation, requiring more than local anesthesia | 2 T 80 ⏹ |
| | MED: 100-2, 15, 260; 100-4, 12, 90.3; 100-4, 14, 10 | |

| 27200 | Closed treatment of coccygeal fracture | T ⏹ |

| 27202 | Open treatment of coccygeal fracture | 2 T 80 ⏹ |
| | MED: 100-2, 15, 260; 100-4, 12, 90.3; 100-4, 14, 10 | |

| 27215 | Open treatment of iliac spine(s), tuberosity avulsion, or iliac wing fracture(s) (eg, pelvic fracture(s) which do not disrupt the pelvic ring), with internal fixation | C 80 ⏹ |

| 27216 | Percutaneous skeletal fixation of posterior pelvic ring fracture and/or dislocation (includes ilium, sacroiliac joint and/or sacrum) | T 80 ⏹ |

| 27217 | Open treatment of anterior ring fracture and/or dislocation with internal fixation, (includes pubic symphysis and/or rami) | C 80 ⏹ |

| 27218 | Open treatment of posterior ring fracture and/or dislocation with internal fixation (includes ilium, sacroiliac joint and/or sacrum) | C 80 ⏹ |

| 27220 | Closed treatment of acetabulum (hip socket) fracture(s); without manipulation | T 50 ⏹ |

| 27222 | with manipulation, with or without skeletal traction | C 50 ⏹ |

| 27226 | Open treatment of posterior or anterior acetabular wall fracture, with internal fixation | C 50 80 ⏹ |

| 27227 | Open treatment of acetabular fracture(s) involving anterior or posterior (one) column, or a fracture running transversely across the acetabulum, with internal fixation | C 50 80 ⏹ |

| 27228 | Open treatment of acetabular fracture(s) involving anterior and posterior (two) columns, includes T-fracture and both column fracture with complete articular detachment, or single column or transverse fracture with associated acetabular wall fracture, with internal fixation | C 50 80 ⏹ |

27230	Closed treatment of femoral fracture, proximal end, neck; without manipulation ▣ T 50 ◪
	MED: 100-2, 15, 260; 100-4, 12, 90.3; 100-4, 14, 10

27232	with manipulation, with or without skeletal traction C 50 ◪

27235	Percutaneous skeletal fixation of femoral fracture, proximal end, neck T 50 ◪

27236	Open treatment of femoral fracture, proximal end, neck, internal fixation or prosthetic replacement C 50 80 ◪
	AMA: 1998, Feb, 11; 1992, Spring, 10

27238	Closed treatment of intertrochanteric, pertrochanteric, or subtrochanteric femoral fracture; without manipulation ▣ T 50 ◪
	MED: 100-2, 15, 260; 100-4, 12, 90.3; 100-4, 14, 10

27240	with manipulation, with or without skin or skeletal traction C 50 ◪

27244	Treatment of intertrochanteric, pertrochanteric, or subtrochanteric femoral fracture; with plate/screw type implant, with or without cerclage C 50 80 ◪

27245	with intramedullary implant, with or without interlocking screws and/or cerclage C 50 80 ◪

27246	Closed treatment of greater trochanteric fracture, without manipulation ▣ T 50 ◪
	MED: 100-2, 15, 260; 100-4, 12, 90.3; 100-4, 14, 10

27248	Open treatment of greater trochanteric fracture, with or without internal or external fixation C 50 80 ◪

27250	Closed treatment of hip dislocation, traumatic; without anesthesia ▣ T 50 ◪
	MED: 100-2, 15, 260; 100-4, 12, 90.3; 100-4, 14, 10

27252	requiring anesthesia ▣ T 50 ◪
	MED: 100-2, 15, 260; 100-4, 12, 90.3; 100-4, 14, 10

27253	Open treatment of hip dislocation, traumatic, without internal fixation C 50 80 ◪

27254	Open treatment of hip dislocation, traumatic, with acetabular wall and femoral head fracture, with or without internal or external fixation C 50 80 ◪

27256	Treatment of spontaneous hip dislocation (developmental, including congenital or pathological), by abduction, splint or traction; without anesthesia, without manipulation T 50 80 ◪

27257	with manipulation, requiring anesthesia ▣ T 50 80 ◪
	MED: 100-2, 15, 260; 100-4, 12, 90.3; 100-4, 14, 10

27258	Open treatment of spontaneous hip dislocation (developmental, including congenital or pathological), replacement of femoral head in acetabulum (including tenotomy, etc.); C 50 80 ◪
	Lorenz's operation

27259	with femoral shaft shortening C 50 80 ◪

27265	Closed treatment of post hip arthroplasty dislocation; without anesthesia ▣ T 50 ◪
	MED: 100-2, 15, 260; 100-4, 12, 90.3; 100-4, 14, 10

27266	requiring regional or general anesthesia ▣ T 50 ◪
	MED: 100-2, 15, 260; 100-4, 12, 90.3; 100-4, 14, 10

Musculoskeletal System

27275 — 27307

MANIPULATION

27275	Manipulation, hip joint, requiring general anesthesia	2 T ↻
	MED: 100-2, 15, 260; 100-4, 12, 90.3; 100-4, 14, 10	

ARTHRODESIS

27280	Arthrodesis, sacroiliac joint (including obtaining graft)	C 50 80 ↻
27282	Arthrodesis, symphysis pubis (including obtaining graft)	C 80 ↻
27284	Arthrodesis, hip joint (including obtaining graft);	C 50 80 ↻
27286	with subtrochanteric osteotomy	C 50 80 ↻

AMPUTATION

27290	Interpelviabdominal amputation (hindquarter amputation) **Pean's amputation**	C 80 ↻
27295	Disarticulation of hip	C 80 ↻

OTHER PROCEDURES

27299	Unlisted procedure, pelvis or hip joint	T 50 80

FEMUR (THIGH REGION) AND KNEE JOINT

Codes listed in the Musculoskeletal chapter include the application and removal of the first cast or traction device. Replacement of casts and/or traction devices subsequent to the first should be reported separately. CPT codes for other additional procedures, such as obtaining grafts and external fixation, should only be used if the procedure is not already listed as included as part of the basic procedure. Consult the glossary for terms and definitions and the front matter of this chapter for additional information.

This section includes procedures performed on tibial plateaus.

INCISION

If a superficial abscess or hematoma is incised and drained, consult CPT codes 10040-10160.

27301	Incision and drainage, deep abscess, bursa, or hematoma, thigh or knee region	3 T 50 ↻
	MED: 100-2, 15, 260; 100-4, 12, 90.3; 100-4, 14, 10	
	AMA: 1998, Nov, 9	
27303	Incision, deep, with opening of bone cortex, femur or knee (eg, osteomyelitis or bone abscess)	C 50 80 ↻
	AMA: 1998, Nov, 8	
27305	Fasciotomy, iliotibial (tenotomy), open	2 T 50 80 ↻
	MED: 100-2, 15, 260; 100-4, 12, 90.3; 100-4, 14, 10	
	If a combined Ober-Yount fasciotomy is performed, consult CPT code 27025.	
27306	Tenotomy, percutaneous, adductor or hamstring; single tendon (separate procedure)	3 T 50 80 ↻
	MED: 100-2, 15, 260; 100-4, 12, 90.3; 100-4, 14, 10	
	AMA: 1998, Nov, 8	
27307	multiple tendons	3 T 50 80 ↻
	MED: 100-2, 15, 260; 100-4, 12, 90.3; 100-4, 14, 10	
	AMA: 1998, Nov, 8	

| 27310 | Arthrotomy, knee, with exploration, drainage, or removal of foreign body (eg, infection) 4 T 50 80 □ |

MED: 100-2, 15, 260; 100-4, 12, 90.3; 100-4, 14, 10

AMA: 1998, Nov, 8

| 27315 | Neurectomy, hamstring muscle 2 T 50 80 □ |

MED: 100-2, 15, 260; 100-4, 12, 90.3; 100-4, 14, 10

| 27320 | Neurectomy, popliteal (gastrocnemius) 2 T 50 80 □ |

MED: 100-2, 15, 260; 100-4, 12, 90.3; 100-4, 14, 10

EXCISION

| 27323 | Biopsy, soft tissue of thigh or knee area; superficial 1 T 50 □ |

MED: 100-2, 15, 260; 100-4, 12, 90.3; 100-4, 14, 10

AMA: 1997, Jun, 12

If a needle biopsy of soft tissue is performed, consult CPT code 20206.

| 27324 | deep (subfascial or intramuscular) 1 T 50 □ |

MED: 100-2, 15, 260; 100-4, 12, 90.3; 100-4, 14, 10

AMA: 1998, Nov, 8; 1997, Mar, 4

| 27327 | Excision, tumor, thigh or knee area; subcutaneous 2 T 50 □ |

MED: 100-2, 15, 260; 100-4, 12, 90.3; 100-4, 14, 10

| 27328 | deep, subfascial, or intramuscular 3 T 50 □ |

MED: 100-2, 15, 260; 100-4, 12, 90.3; 100-4, 14, 10

| 27329 | Radical resection of tumor (eg, malignant neoplasm), soft tissue of thigh or knee area 4 T 50 80 □ |

MED: 100-2, 15, 260; 100-4, 12, 90.3; 100-4, 14, 10

| 27330 | Arthrotomy, knee; with synovial biopsy only 4 T 50 □ |

MED: 100-2, 15, 260; 100-4, 12, 90.3; 100-4, 14, 10

| 27331 | including joint exploration, biopsy, or removal of loose or foreign bodies 4 T 50 80 □ |

MED: 100-2, 15, 260; 100-4, 12, 90.3; 100-4, 14, 10

AMA: 1998, Nov, 8

| 27332 | Arthrotomy, with excision of semilunar cartilage (meniscectomy) knee; medial OR lateral 4 T 50 80 □ |

MED: 100-2, 15, 260; 100-4, 12, 90.3; 100-4, 14, 10

AMA: 1998, Nov, 8

| 27333 | medial AND lateral 4 T 50 80 □ |

MED: 100-2, 15, 260; 100-4, 12, 90.3; 100-4, 14, 10

| 27334 | Arthrotomy, with synovectomy, knee; anterior OR posterior 4 T 50 80 □ |

MED: 100-2, 15, 260; 100-4, 12, 90.3; 100-4, 14, 10

AMA: 1998, Nov, 8

| 27335 | anterior AND posterior including popliteal area 4 T 50 80 □ |

MED: 100-2, 15, 260; 100-4, 12, 90.3; 100-4, 14, 10

| 27340 | Excision, prepatellar bursa 3 T 50 □ |

MED: 100-2, 15, 260; 100-4, 12, 90.3; 100-4, 14, 10

| 27345 | Excision of synovial cyst of popliteal space (eg, Bakers cyst) 4 T 50 80 □ |

MED: 100-2, 15, 260; 100-4, 12, 90.3; 100-4, 14, 10

Musculoskeletal System

27347 — 27370

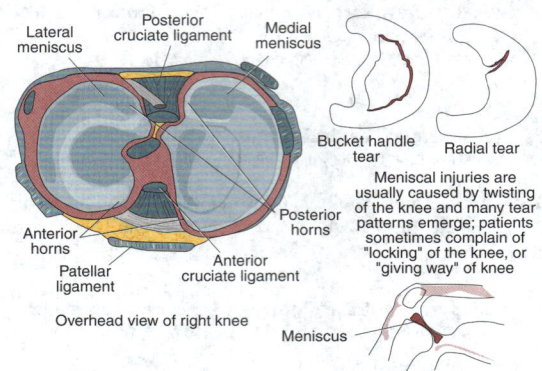

Lateral meniscus · Posterior cruciate ligament · Medial meniscus · Bucket handle tear · Radial tear · Posterior horns · Anterior horns · Patellar ligament · Anterior cruciate ligament

Meniscal injuries are usually caused by twisting of the knee and many tear patterns emerge; patients sometimes complain of "locking" of the knee, or "giving way" of knee

Overhead view of right knee

Meniscus

27347	**Excision of lesion of meniscus or capsule (eg, cyst, ganglion), knee**	4 T 50 80 ⤴
	MED: 100-2, 15, 260; 100-4, 12, 90.3; 100-4, 14, 10	
	AMA: 1998, Nov, 11	
27350	**Patellectomy or hemipatellectomy**	4 T 50 80 ⤴
	MED: 100-2, 15, 260; 100-4, 12, 90.3; 100-4, 14, 10	
27355	**Excision or curettage of bone cyst or benign tumor of femur;**	3 T 50 80 ⤴
	MED: 100-2, 15, 260; 100-4, 12, 90.3; 100-4, 14, 10	
27356	**with allograft**	4 T 50 80 ⤴
	MED: 100-2, 15, 260; 100-4, 12, 90.3; 100-4, 14, 10	
27357	**with autograft (includes obtaining graft)**	5 T 50 80 ⤴
	MED: 100-2, 15, 260; 100-4, 12, 90.3; 100-4, 14, 10	
	AMA: 2002, Dec, 11	
+ **27358**	**Excision or curettage of bone cyst or benign tumor of femur; with internal fixation (List in addition to code for primary procedure)**	5 T ⤴
	MED: 100-2, 15, 260; 100-4, 12, 90.3; 100-4, 14, 10	

Note that 27358 is an add-on code and must be used in conjunction with 27355, 27356, or 27357.

27360	**Partial excision (craterization, saucerization, or diaphysectomy) bone, femur, proximal tibia and/or fibula (eg, osteomyelitis or bone abscess)**	5 T 50 80 ⤴
	MED: 100-2, 15, 260; 100-4, 12, 90.3; 100-4, 14, 10	
	AMA: 1998, Nov, 8	
27365	**Radical resection of tumor, bone, femur or knee**	C 50 80 ⤴

If a radical resection of a tumor, soft tissue, is performed, consult CPT code 27329.

INTRODUCTION OR REMOVAL

27370	**Injection procedure for knee arthrography**	N 50 ⤴

If radiological supervision and interpretation is performed, consult CPT code 73580. Code 76003 cannot be reported in addition to 73580.

27372 **Removal of foreign body, deep, thigh region or knee area**   7 T 50 80 ⏎
MED: 100-2, 15, 260; 100-4, 12, 90.3; 100-4, 14, 10

> If a knee prosthesis, including total knee, is removed, consult CPT code 27488. For arthroscopic knee procedures, consult CPT codes 29870-29887.

REPAIR, REVISION, AND/OR RECONSTRUCTION

27380 **Suture of infrapatellar tendon; primary**   1 T 50 80 ⏎
MED: 100-2, 15, 260; 100-4, 12, 90.3; 100-4, 14, 10

27381   **secondary reconstruction, including fascial or tendon graft**   3 T 50 80 ⏎
MED: 100-2, 15, 260; 100-4, 12, 90.3; 100-4, 14, 10

27385 **Suture of quadriceps or hamstring muscle rupture; primary**   3 T 50 80 ⏎
MED: 100-2, 15, 260; 100-4, 12, 90.3; 100-4, 14, 10

27386   **secondary reconstruction, including fascial or tendon graft**   3 T 50 80 ⏎
MED: 100-2, 15, 260; 100-4, 12, 90.3; 100-4, 14, 10

27390 **Tenotomy, open, hamstring, knee to hip; single tendon**   1 T 80 ⏎
MED: 100-2, 15, 260; 100-4, 12, 90.3; 100-4, 14, 10

AMA: 1998, Nov, 8

27391   **multiple tendons, one leg**   2 T 80 ⏎
MED: 100-2, 15, 260; 100-4, 12, 90.3; 100-4, 14, 10

AMA: 1998, Nov, 8

27392   **multiple tendons, bilateral**   3 T 80 ⏎
MED: 100-2, 15, 260; 100-4, 12, 40.7; 100-4, 12, 90.3; 100-4, 14, 10

AMA: 1998, Nov, 8

27393 **Lengthening of hamstring tendon; single tendon**   2 T 80 ⏎
MED: 100-2, 15, 260; 100-4, 12, 90.3; 100-4, 14, 10

AMA: 1998, Nov, 8

27394   **multiple tendons, one leg**   3 T 80 ⏎
MED: 100-2, 15, 260; 100-4, 12, 90.3; 100-4, 14, 10

AMA: 1998, Nov, 8

27395   **multiple tendons, bilateral**   3 T 80 ⏎
MED: 100-2, 15, 260; 100-4, 12, 40.7; 100-4, 12, 90.3; 100-4, 14, 10

AMA: 1998, Nov, 8

27396 **Transplant, hamstring tendon to patella; single tendon**   3 T 80 ⏎
MED: 100-2, 15, 260; 100-4, 12, 90.3; 100-4, 14, 10

AMA: 1998, Nov, 8

27397   **multiple tendons**   3 T 80 ⏎
MED: 100-2, 15, 260; 100-4, 12, 90.3; 100-4, 14, 10

AMA: 1998, Nov, 8

27400 **Transfer, tendon or muscle, hamstrings to femur (eg, Egger's type procedure)**   3 T 50 80 ⏎
MED: 100-2, 15, 260; 100-4, 12, 90.3; 100-4, 14, 10

AMA: 1998, Nov, 8

27403 **Arthrotomy with meniscus repair, knee** ⓸ Ⓣ 50 80 🔽
MED: 100-2, 15, 260; 100-4, 12, 90.3; 100-4, 14, 10

AMA: 1998, Nov, 8

If arthroscopic repair is performed, consult CPT code 29882.

27405 **Repair, primary, torn ligament and/or capsule, knee; collateral** ⓸ Ⓣ 50 80 🔽
MED: 100-2, 15, 260; 100-4, 12, 90.3; 100-4, 14, 10

27407 **cruciate** ⓸ Ⓣ 50 80 🔽
MED: 100-2, 15, 260; 100-4, 12, 90.3; 100-4, 14, 10

27409 **collateral and cruciate ligaments** ⓸ Ⓣ 50 80 🔽
MED: 100-2, 15, 260; 100-4, 12, 90.3; 100-4, 14, 10

To report ligament reconstruction, consult CPT codes 27427-27429

27412 **Autologous chondrocyte implantation, knee** Ⓣ 50 80 🔽
Code 27412 cannot be reported with CPT codes 20926, 27331, or 27570.

For harvesting of chondrocytes, consult CPT code 29870.

27415 **Osteochondral allograft, knee, open** Ⓣ 50 80 🔽
To report arthroscopic implant of osteochondral allograft, consult CPT code 29867.

27418 **Anterior tibial tubercleplasty (eg, Maquet type procedure)** ⓷ Ⓣ 50 80 🔽
MED: 100-2, 15, 260; 100-4, 12, 90.3; 100-4, 14, 10

27420 **Reconstruction of dislocating patella; (eg, Hauser type procedure)** ⓷ Ⓣ 50 80 🔽
MED: 100-2, 15, 260; 100-4, 12, 90.3; 100-4, 14, 10

27422 **with extensor realignment and/or muscle advancement or release (eg, Campbell, Goldwaite type procedure)** ⓻ Ⓣ 50 80 🔽
MED: 100-2, 15, 260; 100-4, 12, 90.3; 100-4, 14, 10

27424 **with patellectomy** ⓷ Ⓣ 50 80 🔽
MED: 100-2, 15, 260; 100-4, 12, 90.3; 100-4, 14, 10

27425 **Lateral retinacular release, open** ⓻ Ⓣ 50 🔽
MED: 100-2, 15, 260; 100-4, 12, 90.3; 100-4, 14, 10

AMA: 2000, Nov, 11

To report arthroscopic lateral release, consult CPT code 29873.

27427 **Ligamentous reconstruction (augmentation), knee; extra-articular** ⓷ Ⓣ 50 80 🔽
MED: 100-2, 15, 260; 100-4, 12, 90.3; 100-4, 14, 10

AMA: 1999, Nov, 13

If a primary repair of ligament(s) is performed in addition to reconstruction, report CPT code 27405, 27407, or 27409 in addition to 27427, 27428, or 27429.

27428 **intra-articular (open)** ⓸ Ⓣ 50 80 🔽
MED: 100-2, 15, 260; 100-4, 12, 90.3; 100-4, 14, 10

AMA: 1999, Nov, 13

If a primary repair of ligament(s) is performed in addition to reconstruction, report CPT code 27405, 27407, or 27409 in addition to 27427, 27428, or 27429.

27429   **intra-articular (open) and extra-articular**   4️⃣ T 50 80 ⮐
MED: 100-2, 15, 260; 100-4, 12, 90.3; 100-4, 14, 10

AMA: 1999, Nov, 13

If a primary repair of ligament(s) is performed in addition to reconstruction, report CPT code 27405, 27407, or 27409 in addition to 27427, 27428, or 27429.

27430   **Quadricepsplasty (eg, Bennett or Thompson type)**   4️⃣ T 50 80 ⮐
MED: 100-2, 15, 260; 100-4, 12, 90.3; 100-4, 14, 10

27435   **Capsulotomy, posterior capsular release, knee**   4️⃣ T 50 80 ⮐
MED: 100-2, 15, 260; 100-4, 12, 90.3; 100-4, 14, 10

AMA: 1998, Nov, 8

27437   **Arthroplasty, patella; without prosthesis**   4️⃣ T 50 ⮐
MED: 100-2, 15, 260; 100-4, 12, 90.3; 100-4, 14, 10

27438   **with prosthesis**   5️⃣ T 50 80 ⮐
MED: 100-2, 15, 260; 100-4, 12, 90.3; 100-4, 14, 10

27440   **Arthroplasty, knee, tibial plateau;**   T 50 80 ⮐

27441   **with debridement and partial synovectomy**   5️⃣ T 50 80 ⮐
MED: 100-2, 15, 260; 100-4, 12, 90.3; 100-4, 14, 10

27442   **Arthroplasty, femoral condyles or tibial plateau(s), knee;**   5️⃣ T 50 80 ⮐
MED: 100-2, 15, 260; 100-4, 12, 90.3; 100-4, 14, 10

AMA: 1999, Nov, 13

27443   **with debridement and partial synovectomy**   5️⃣ T 50 80 ⮐
MED: 100-2, 15, 260; 100-4, 12, 90.3; 100-4, 14, 10

27445   **Arthroplasty, knee, hinge prosthesis (eg, Walldius type)**   C 50 80 ⮐
AMA: 1998, Nov, 8

27446   **Arthroplasty, knee, condyle and plateau; medial OR lateral compartment**   T 50 80 ⮐

27447   **medial AND lateral compartments with or without patella resurfacing (total knee arthroplasty)**   C 50 80 ⮐

If a total knee arthroplasty is revised, consult CPT code 27487. If a total knee prosthesis is removed, consult CPT code 27488.

27448   **Osteotomy, femur, shaft or supracondylar; without fixation**   C 50 80 ⮐

27450   **with fixation**   C 50 80 ⮐

27454   **Osteotomy, multiple, with realignment on intramedullary rod, femoral shaft (eg, Sofield type procedure)**   C 50 80 ⮐
AMA: 1998, Nov, 8

27455   **Osteotomy, proximal tibia, including fibular excision or osteotomy (includes correction of genu varus (bowleg) or genu valgus (knock-knee)); before epiphyseal closure**   C 50 80 ⮐

27457   **after epiphyseal closure**   C 50 80 ⮐

27465   **Osteoplasty, femur; shortening (excluding 64876)**   C 50 80 ⮐

27466   **lengthening**   C 50 80 ⮐

27468   **combined, lengthening and shortening with femoral segment transfer**   C 50 80 ⮐

Musculoskeletal System

27470 — 27502

27470　Repair, nonunion or malunion, femur, distal to head and neck; without graft (eg, compression technique)　C 50 80

27472　　with iliac or other autogenous bone graft (includes obtaining graft)　C 50 80

27475　Arrest, epiphyseal, any method (eg, epiphysiodesis); distal femur　T 50
　　　AMA: 1998, Nov, 8

27477　　tibia and fibula, proximal　C 50

27479　　combined distal femur, proximal tibia and fibula　C 50 80

27485　Arrest, hemiepiphyseal, distal femur or proximal tibia or fibula (eg, genu varus or valgus)　C 50
　　　AMA: 1998, Nov, 8

27486　Revision of total knee arthroplasty, with or without allograft; one component　C 50 80

27487　　femoral and entire tibial component　C 50 80
　　　AMA: 1998, Nov, 8

27488　Removal of prosthesis, including total knee prosthesis, methylmethacrylate with or without insertion of spacer, knee　C 50 80
　　　AMA: 1998, Nov, 8

27495　Prophylactic treatment (nailing, pinning, plating or wiring) with or without methylmethacrylate, femur　C 50 80

27496　Decompression fasciotomy, thigh and/or knee, one compartment (flexor or extensor or adductor);　5 T 50
　　　MED: 100-2, 15, 260; 100-4, 12, 90.3; 100-4, 14, 10

27497　　with debridement of nonviable muscle and/or nerve　3 T 50 80
　　　MED: 100-2, 15, 260; 100-4, 12, 90.3; 100-4, 14, 10

27498　Decompression fasciotomy, thigh and/or knee, multiple compartments;　3 T 50 80
　　　MED: 100-2, 15, 260; 100-4, 12, 90.3; 100-4, 14, 10

27499　　with debridement of nonviable muscle and/or nerve　3 T 50 80
　　　MED: 100-2, 15, 260; 100-4, 12, 90.3; 100-4, 14, 10

FRACTURE AND/OR DISLOCATION

If arthroscopic treatment of the intercondylar spine(s) and tuberosity fracture(s) of the knee is performed, consult CPT codes 29850 and 29851. If arthroscopic treatment of tibial fracture(s) is performed, consult CPT codes 29855 and 29856.

27500　Closed treatment of femoral shaft fracture, without manipulation　1 T 50
　　　MED: 100-2, 15, 260; 100-4, 12, 90.3; 100-4, 14, 10

27501　Closed treatment of supracondylar or transcondylar femoral fracture with or without intercondylar extension, without manipulation　2 T 50 80
　　　MED: 100-2, 15, 260; 100-4, 12, 90.3; 100-4, 14, 10

27502　Closed treatment of femoral shaft fracture, with manipulation, with or without skin or skeletal traction　2 T 50
　　　MED: 100-2, 15, 260; 100-4, 12, 90.3; 100-4, 14, 10

　　　AMA: 1999, Oct, 4; 1993, Fall, 22

27503   Closed treatment of supracondylar or transcondylar femoral fracture with or without intercondylar extension, with manipulation, with or without skin or skeletal traction   3 T 50 80 ⏎
MED: 100-2, 15, 260; 100-4, 12, 90.3; 100-4, 14, 10

27506   Open treatment of femoral shaft fracture, with or without external fixation, with insertion of intramedullary implant, with or without cerclage and/or locking screws   C 50 80 ⏎
AMA: 1992, Winter, 10

27507   Open treatment of femoral shaft fracture with plate/screws, with or without cerclage   C 50 80 ⏎

27508   Closed treatment of femoral fracture, distal end, medial or lateral condyle, without manipulation   1 T 50 ⏎
MED: 100-2, 15, 260; 100-4, 12, 90.3; 100-4, 14, 10

27509   Percutaneous skeletal fixation of femoral fracture, distal end, medial or lateral condyle, or supracondylar or transcondylar, with or without intercondylar extension, or distal femoral epiphyseal separation   3 T 50 80 ⏎
MED: 100-2, 15, 260; 100-4, 12, 90.3; 100-4, 14, 10

27510   Closed treatment of femoral fracture, distal end, medial or lateral condyle, with manipulation   1 T 50 ⏎
MED: 100-2, 15, 260; 100-4, 12, 90.3; 100-4, 14, 10

27511   Open treatment of femoral supracondylar or transcondylar fracture without intercondylar extension, with or without internal or external fixation   C 50 80 ⏎

27513   Open treatment of femoral supracondylar or tran-scondylar fracture with intercondylar extension, with or without internal or external fixation   C 50 80 ⏎

27514   Open treatment of femoral fracture, distal end, medial or lateral condyle, with or without internal or external fixation   C 50 80 ⏎

27516   Closed treatment of distal femoral epiphyseal separation; without manipulation   1 T 50 ⏎
MED: 100-2, 15, 260; 100-4, 12, 90.3; 100-4, 14, 10

27517   with manipulation, with or without skin or skeletal traction   1 T 50 80 ⏎
MED: 100-2, 15, 260; 100-4, 12, 90.3; 100-4, 14, 10

27519   Open treatment of distal femoral epiphyseal separation, with or without internal or external fixation   C 50 80 ⏎

27520   Closed treatment of patellar fracture, without manipulation   1 T 50 ⏎
MED: 100-2, 15, 260; 100-4, 12, 90.3; 100-4, 14, 10

27524   Open treatment of patellar fracture, with internal fixation and/or partial or complete patellectomy and soft tissue repair   T 50 80 ⏎

27530   Closed treatment of tibial fracture, proximal (plateau); without manipulation   1 T 50 ⏎
MED: 100-2, 15, 260; 100-4, 12, 90.3; 100-4, 14, 10

27532   with or without manipulation, with skeletal traction   1 T 50 ⏎
MED: 100-2, 15, 260; 100-4, 12, 90.3; 100-4, 14, 10

If arthroscopic treatment of a tibial fracture is performed, consult CPT codes 29855 and 29856.

Musculoskeletal System

27535 — 27598

| 27535 | Open treatment of tibial fracture, proximal (plateau); unicondylar, with or without internal or external fixation | C 50 80 |
| 27536 | bicondylar, with or without internal fixation | C 50 80 |

If arthroscopic treatment of a tibial fracture is performed, consult CPT codes 29855 and 29856.

| 27538 | Closed treatment of intercondylar spine(s) and/or tuberosity fracture(s) of knee, with or without manipulation | 1 T 50 80 |

MED: 100-2, 15, 260; 100-4, 12, 90.3; 100-4, 14, 10

If treated arthroscopically, consult CPT codes 29850 and 29851.

| 27540 | Open treatment of intercondylar spine(s) and/or tuberosity fracture(s) of the knee, with or without internal or external fixation | C 50 80 |
| 27550 | Closed treatment of knee dislocation; without anesthesia | 1 T 50 80 |

MED: 100-2, 15, 260; 100-4, 12, 90.3; 100-4, 14, 10

| 27552 | requiring anesthesia | 1 T 50 80 |

MED: 100-2, 15, 260; 100-4, 12, 90.3; 100-4, 14, 10

27556	Open treatment of knee dislocation, with or without internal or external fixation; without primary ligamentous repair or augmentation/reconstruction	C 50 80
27557	with primary ligamentous repair	C 50 80
27558	with primary ligamentous repair, with augmentation/reconstruction	C 50 80
27560	Closed treatment of patellar dislocation; without anesthesia	1 T 50

MED: 100-2, 15, 260; 100-4, 12, 90.3; 100-4, 14, 10

If this is a recurrent dislocation, consult CPT codes 27420-27424.

| 27562 | requiring anesthesia | 1 T 50 80 |

MED: 100-2, 15, 260; 100-4, 12, 90.3; 100-4, 14, 10

| 27566 | Open treatment of patellar dislocation, with or without partial or total patellectomy | 2 T 50 80 |

MED: 100-2, 15, 260; 100-4, 12, 90.3; 100-4, 14, 10

MANIPULATION

| 27570 | Manipulation of knee joint under general anesthesia (includes application of traction or other fixation devices) | 1 T |

MED: 100-2, 15, 260; 100-4, 12, 90.3; 100-4, 14, 10

ARTHRODESIS

| 27580 | Arthrodesis, knee, any technique | C 50 80 |
| | Albert's operation | |

AMPUTATION

27590	Amputation, thigh, through femur, any level;	C 50 80
27591	immediate fitting technique including first cast	C 50 80
27592	open, circular (guillotine)	C 50 80
27594	secondary closure or scar revision	3 T 50

MED: 100-2, 15, 260; 100-4, 12, 90.3; 100-4, 14, 10

27596	re-amputation	C 50
27598	Disarticulation at knee	C 50 80
	Batch-Spittler-McFaddin operation	

26 / TC Professional/Technical Component   **80 / 80** Assist-at-Surgery Allowed/With Documentation   ⊙ Conscious Sedation

Unlisted   Not Covered   **MED:** Pubs 100/NCD Reference   **1 - 9** ASC Group   63 Modifier 63 Exempt

188 — Surgery   CPT only © 2005 American Medical Association. All Rights Reserved. *(Black Ink)*   © 2005 Ingenix, Inc. *(Blue Ink)*

OTHER PROCEDURES

27599   Unlisted procedure, femur or knee   T 50 80

LEG (TIBIA AND FIBULA) AND ANKLE JOINT

Codes listed in the Musculoskeletal chapter include the application and removal of the first cast or traction device. Replacement of casts and/or traction devices subsequent to the first should be reported separately. CPT codes for other additional procedures, such as obtaining grafts and external fixation, should only be used if the procedure is not already listed as included as part of the basic procedure. Consult the glossary for terms and definitions and the front matter of this chapter for additional information.

INCISION

27600   **Decompression fasciotomy, leg; anterior and/or lateral compartments only**   3 T 50
MED: 100-2, 15, 260; 100-4, 12, 90.3; 100-4, 14, 10

If a decompression fasciotomy is performed with debridement, consult CPT codes 27892-27894. If superficial incision and drainage procedures are performed, consult CPT codes 10040-10160.

27601   **posterior compartment(s) only**   3 T 50
MED: 100-2, 15, 260; 100-4, 12, 90.3; 100-4, 14, 10

27602   **anterior and/or lateral, and posterior compartment(s)**   3 T 50 80
MED: 100-2, 15, 260; 100-4, 12, 90.3; 100-4, 14, 10

27603   **Incision and drainage, leg or ankle; deep abscess or hematoma**   2 T 50
MED: 100-2, 15, 260; 100-4, 12, 90.3; 100-4, 14, 10

27604   **infected bursa**   2 T 50 80
MED: 100-2, 15, 260; 100-4, 12, 90.3; 100-4, 14, 10

27605   **Tenotomy, percutaneous, Achilles tendon (separate procedure); local anesthesia**   1 T 50 80
MED: 100-2, 15, 260; 100-4, 12, 90.3; 100-4, 14, 10

27606   **general anesthesia**   1 T 50
MED: 100-2, 15, 260; 100-4, 12, 90.3; 100-4, 14, 10

27607   **Incision (eg, osteomyelitis or bone abscess), leg or ankle**   2 T 50
MED: 100-2, 15, 260; 100-4, 12, 90.3; 100-4, 14, 10

27610   **Arthrotomy, ankle, including exploration, drainage, or removal of foreign body**   2 T 50
MED: 100-2, 15, 260; 100-4, 12, 90.3; 100-4, 14, 10
AMA: 1998, Nov, 9

27612   **Arthrotomy, posterior capsular release, ankle, with or without Achilles tendon lengthening**   3 T 50 80
MED: 100-2, 15, 260; 100-4, 12, 90.3; 100-4, 14, 10
AMA: 1998, Nov, 8

Consult also CPT code 27685.

EXCISION

27613   **Biopsy, soft tissue of leg or ankle area; superficial**   T 50
If a needle biopsy is performed on soft tissue, consult CPT code 20206.

27614   **deep (subfascial or intramuscular)**   2 T 50
MED: 100-2, 15, 260; 100-4, 12, 90.3; 100-4, 14, 10
AMA: 1998, Nov, 8

Musculoskeletal System

27615 — 27650

27615 Radical resection of tumor (eg, malignant neoplasm), soft tissue of leg or ankle area
MED: 100-2, 15, 260; 100-4, 12, 90.3; 100-4, 14, 10

27618 Excision, tumor, leg or ankle area; subcutaneous tissue
MED: 100-2, 15, 260; 100-4, 12, 90.3; 100-4, 14, 10

27619 deep (subfascial or intramuscular)
MED: 100-2, 15, 260; 100-4, 12, 90.3; 100-4, 14, 10

27620 Arthrotomy, ankle, with joint exploration, with or without biopsy, with or without removal of loose or foreign body
MED: 100-2, 15, 260; 100-4, 12, 90.3; 100-4, 14, 10

27625 Arthrotomy, with synovectomy, ankle;
MED: 100-2, 15, 260; 100-4, 12, 90.3; 100-4, 14, 10

AMA: 1998, Nov, 8

27626 including tenosynovectomy
MED: 100-2, 15, 260; 100-4, 12, 90.3; 100-4, 14, 10

27630 Excision of lesion of tendon sheath or capsule (eg, cyst or ganglion), leg and/or ankle
MED: 100-2, 15, 260; 100-4, 12, 90.3; 100-4, 14, 10

27635 Excision or curettage of bone cyst or benign tumor, tibia or fibula;
MED: 100-2, 15, 260; 100-4, 12, 90.3; 100-4, 14, 10

27637 with autograft (includes obtaining graft)
MED: 100-2, 15, 260; 100-4, 12, 90.3; 100-4, 14, 10

27638 with allograft
MED: 100-2, 15, 260; 100-4, 12, 90.3; 100-4, 14, 10

27640 Partial excision (craterization, saucerization, or diaphysectomy) bone (eg, osteomyelitis or exostosis); tibia
MED: 100-2, 15, 260; 100-4, 12, 90.3; 100-4, 14, 10

27641 fibula
MED: 100-2, 15, 260; 100-4, 12, 90.3; 100-4, 14, 10

27645 Radical resection of tumor, bone; tibia
27646 fibula
27647 talus or calcaneus
MED: 100-2, 15, 260; 100-4, 12, 90.3; 100-4, 14, 10

INTRODUCTION OR REMOVAL

27648 Injection procedure for ankle arthrography

If radiological supervision and interpretation is performed, consult CPT code 73615. Do not report 76003 with 73615.

If ankle arthroscopy is performed, consult CPT codes 29894-29898.

REPAIR, REVISION, AND/OR RECONSTRUCTION

27650 Repair, primary, open or percutaneous, ruptured Achilles tendon;

MED: 100-2, 15, 260; 100-4, 12, 90.3; 100-4, 14, 10

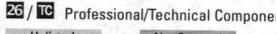 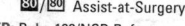 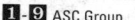

27652 with graft (includes obtaining graft) ▣ T 50 ⇱
MED: 100-2, 15, 260; 100-4, 12, 90.3; 100-4, 14, 10

27654 Repair, secondary, Achilles tendon, with or without graft ▣ T 50 80 ⇱
MED: 100-2, 15, 260; 100-4, 12, 90.3; 100-4, 14, 10

27656 Repair, fascial defect of leg ▣ T 50 80 ⇱
MED: 100-2, 15, 260; 100-4, 12, 90.3; 100-4, 14, 10

27658 Repair, flexor tendon, leg; primary, without graft, each tendon ▣ T 80 ⇱
MED: 100-2, 15, 260; 100-4, 12, 90.3; 100-4, 14, 10

AMA: 1998, Nov, 8

27659 secondary, with or without graft, each tendon ▣ T 80 ⇱
MED: 100-2, 15, 260; 100-4, 12, 90.3; 100-4, 14, 10

27664 Repair, extensor tendon, leg; primary, without graft, each tendon ▣ T 80 ⇱
MED: 100-2, 15, 260; 100-4, 12, 90.3; 100-4, 14, 10

AMA: 1998, Nov, 8

27665 secondary, with or without graft, each tendon ▣ T 80 ⇱
MED: 100-2, 15, 260; 100-4, 12, 90.3; 100-4, 14, 10

AMA: 1998, Nov, 8

27675 Repair, dislocating peroneal tendons; without fibular
osteotomy ▣ T 50 80 ⇱
MED: 100-2, 15, 260; 100-4, 12, 90.3; 100-4, 14, 10

27676 with fibular osteotomy ▣ T 50 80 ⇱
MED: 100-2, 15, 260; 100-4, 12, 90.3; 100-4, 14, 10

27680 Tenolysis, flexor or extensor tendon, leg and/or ankle; single,
each tendon ▣ T ⇱
MED: 100-2, 15, 260; 100-4, 12, 90.3; 100-4, 14, 10

AMA: 1998, Nov, 8

27681 multiple tendons (through separate incision(s)) ▣ T ⇱
MED: 100-2, 15, 260; 100-4, 12, 90.3; 100-4, 14, 10

AMA: 1998, Nov, 8

27685 Lengthening or shortening of tendon, leg or ankle; single tendon (separate
procedure) ▣ T 80 ⇱
MED: 100-2, 15, 260; 100-4, 12, 90.3; 100-4, 14, 10

AMA: 1998, Nov, 8

27686 multiple tendons (through same incision), each ▣ T ⇱
MED: 100-2, 15, 260; 100-4, 12, 90.3; 100-4, 14, 10

AMA: 1998, Nov, 8

27687 Gastrocnemius recession (eg, Strayer procedure) ▣ T 50 80 ⇱
MED: 100-2, 15, 260; 100-4, 12, 90.3; 100-4, 14, 10

Toe extensors as a group are considered a single tendon when transplanted
into midfoot.

27690 Transfer or transplant of single tendon (with muscle redirection or
rerouting); superficial (eg, anterior tibial extensors into
midfoot) ▣ T 50 80 ⇱
MED: 100-2, 15, 260; 100-4, 12, 90.3; 100-4, 14, 10

Musculoskeletal System

27652 — 27690

Musculoskeletal System

27691 — 27730

| 27691 | deep (eg, anterior tibial or posterior tibial through interosseous space, flexor digitorum longus, flexor hallicus longus, or peroneal tendon to midfoot or hindfoot) | 4 T 50 80 ⟲ |

MED: 100-2, 15, 260; 100-4, 12, 90.3; 100-4, 14, 10

Barr procedure

| + 27692 | each additional tendon (List in addition to code for primary procedure) | 3 T |

MED: 100-2, 15, 260; 100-4, 12, 90.3; 100-4, 14, 10

Note that 27692 is an add-on code and must be used in conjunction with 27690 and 27691.

| 27695 | **Repair, primary, disrupted ligament, ankle; collateral** | 2 T 50 ⟲ |

MED: 100-2, 15, 260; 100-4, 12, 90.3; 100-4, 14, 10

| 27696 | both collateral ligaments | 2 T 50 ⟲ |

MED: 100-2, 15, 260; 100-4, 12, 90.3; 100-4, 14, 10

| 27698 | **Repair, secondary, disrupted ligament, ankle, collateral (eg, Watson-Jones procedure)** | 2 T 50 80 ⟲ |

MED: 100-2, 15, 260; 100-4, 12, 90.3; 100-4, 14, 10

| 27700 | **Arthroplasty, ankle;** | 5 T 50 80 ⟲ |

MED: 100-2, 15, 260; 100-4, 12, 90.3; 100-4, 14, 10

27702	with implant (total ankle)	C 50 80 ⟲
27703	revision, total ankle	C 50 80 ⟲
27704	**Removal of ankle implant**	2 T 50 ⟲

MED: 100-2, 15, 260; 100-4, 12, 90.3; 100-4, 14, 10

| 27705 | **Osteotomy; tibia** | 2 T 50 80 ⟲ |

MED: 100-2, 15, 260; 100-4, 12, 90.3; 100-4, 14, 10

| 27707 | fibula | 2 T 50 ⟲ |

MED: 100-2, 15, 260; 100-4, 12, 90.3; 100-4, 14, 10

| 27709 | tibia and fibula | 2 T 50 80 ⟲ |

MED: 100-2, 15, 260; 100-4, 12, 90.3; 100-4, 14, 10

| 27712 | multiple, with realignment on intramedullary rod (eg, Sofield type procedure) | C 50 80 ⟲ |

If an osteotomy is performed to correct genu varus (bowleg) or genu valgus (knock-knee), consult CPT codes 27455-27457.

| 27715 | **Osteoplasty, tibia and fibula, lengthening or shortening** | C 50 80 ⟲ |

Anderson tibial lengthening

27720	**Repair of nonunion or malunion, tibia; without graft, (eg, compression technique)**	C 50 80 ⟲
27722	with sliding graft	C 50 80 ⟲
27724	with iliac or other autograft (includes obtaining graft)	C 50 80 ⟲
27725	by synostosis, with fibula, any method	C 50 80 ⟲
27727	**Repair of congenital pseudarthrosis, tibia**	C 50 80 ⟲
27730	**Arrest, epiphyseal (epiphysiodesis), open; distal tibia**	2 T 50 ⟲

MED: 100-2, 15, 260; 100-4, 12, 90.3; 100-4, 14, 10

AMA: 1998, Nov, 8

27732   **distal fibula**   2 T 50 ⬒
MED: 100-2, 15, 260; 100-4, 12, 90.3; 100-4, 14, 10

27734   **distal tibia and fibula**   2 T 50 ⬒
MED: 100-2, 15, 260; 100-4, 12, 90.3; 100-4, 14, 10

27740   **Arrest, epiphyseal (epiphysiodesis), any method, combined, proximal and distal tibia and fibula;**   2 T 50 80 ⬒
MED: 100-2, 15, 260; 100-4, 12, 90.3; 100-4, 14, 10

AMA: 1998, Nov, 8

27742   **and distal femur**   2 T 50 80 ⬒
MED: 100-2, 15, 260; 100-4, 12, 90.3; 100-4, 14, 10

If epiphyseal arrest of proximal tibia and fibula is performed, consult CPT code 27477.

27745   **Prophylactic treatment (nailing, pinning, plating or wiring) with or without methylmethacrylate, tibia**   3 T 50 80 ⬒
MED: 100-2, 15, 260; 100-4, 12, 90.3; 100-4, 14, 10

FRACTURE AND/OR DISLOCATION

27750   **Closed treatment of tibial shaft fracture (with or without fibular fracture); without manipulation**   1 T 50 ⬒
MED: 100-2, 15, 260; 100-4, 12, 90.3; 100-4, 14, 10

AMA: 1996, Mar, 10; 1993, Fall, 21; 1992, Winter, 10

27752   **with manipulation, with or without skeletal traction**   1 T 50 ⬒
MED: 100-2, 15, 260; 100-4, 12, 90.3; 100-4, 14, 10

AMA: 1996, Mar, 10; 1996, Feb, 3; 1993, Fall, 21; 1992, Winter, 10

27756   **Percutaneous skeletal fixation of tibial shaft fracture (with or without fibular fracture) (eg, pins or screws)**   3 T 50 80 ⬒
MED: 100-2, 15, 260; 100-4, 12, 90.3; 100-4, 14, 10

AMA: 1992, Winter, 10

27758   **Open treatment of tibial shaft fracture, (with or without fibular fracture) with plate/screws, with or without cerclage**   4 T 50 80 ⬒
MED: 100-2, 15, 260; 100-4, 12, 90.3; 100-4, 14, 10

AMA: 2000, Mar, 11; 1992, Winter, 10

27759   **Treatment of tibial shaft fracture (with or without fibular fracture) by intramedullary implant, with or without interlocking screws and/or cerclage**   4 T 50 80 ⬒
MED: 100-2, 15, 260; 100-4, 12, 90.3; 100-4, 14, 10

AMA: 1992, Winter, 10

27760   **Closed treatment of medial malleolus fracture; without manipulation**   1 T 50 ⬒
MED: 100-2, 15, 260; 100-4, 12, 90.3; 100-4, 14, 10

27762   **with manipulation, with or without skin or skeletal traction**   1 T 50 ⬒
MED: 100-2, 15, 260; 100-4, 12, 90.3; 100-4, 14, 10

27766   **Open treatment of medial malleolus fracture, with or without internal or external fixation**   3 T 50 ⬒
MED: 100-2, 15, 260; 100-4, 12, 90.3; 100-4, 14, 10

Musculoskeletal System

27780 — 27825

27780 Closed treatment of proximal fibula or shaft fracture; without manipulation ▮1▮ T 50 ▯
MED: 100-2, 15, 260; 100-4, 12, 90.3; 100-4, 14, 10

AMA: 1992, Winter, 11

27781 with manipulation ▮1▮ T 50 ▯
MED: 100-2, 15, 260; 100-4, 12, 90.3; 100-4, 14, 10

27784 Open treatment of proximal fibula or shaft fracture, with or without internal or external fixation ▮3▮ T 50 ▯
MED: 100-2, 15, 260; 100-4, 12, 90.3; 100-4, 14, 10

AMA: 2000, Mar, 11

27786 Closed treatment of distal fibular fracture (lateral malleolus); without manipulation ▮1▮ T 50 ▯
MED: 100-2, 15, 260; 100-4, 12, 90.3; 100-4, 14, 10

27788 with manipulation ▮1▮ T 50 ▯
MED: 100-2, 15, 260; 100-4, 12, 90.3; 100-4, 14, 10

27792 Open treatment of distal fibular fracture (lateral malleolus), with or without internal or external fixation ▮3▮ T 50 ▯
MED: 100-2, 15, 260; 100-4, 12, 90.3; 100-4, 14, 10

27808 Closed treatment of bimalleolar ankle fracture, (including Potts); without manipulation ▮1▮ T 50 ▯
MED: 100-2, 15, 260; 100-4, 12, 90.3; 100-4, 14, 10

27810 with manipulation ▮1▮ T 50 ▯
MED: 100-2, 15, 260; 100-4, 12, 90.3; 100-4, 14, 10

27814 Open treatment of bimalleolar ankle fracture, with or without internal or external fixation ▮3▮ T 50 80 ▯
MED: 100-2, 15, 260; 100-4, 12, 90.3; 100-4, 14, 10

27816 Closed treatment of trimalleolar ankle fracture; without manipulation ▮1▮ T 50 ▯
MED: 100-2, 15, 260; 100-4, 12, 90.3; 100-4, 14, 10

27818 with manipulation ▮1▮ T 50 ▯
MED: 100-2, 15, 260; 100-4, 12, 90.3; 100-4, 14, 10

27822 Open treatment of trimalleolar ankle fracture, with or without internal or external fixation, medial and/or lateral malleolus; without fixation of posterior lip ▮3▮ T 50 80 ▯
MED: 100-2, 15, 260; 100-4, 12, 90.3; 100-4, 14, 10

27823 with fixation of posterior lip ▮3▮ T 50 80 ▯
MED: 100-2, 15, 260; 100-4, 12, 90.3; 100-4, 14, 10

27824 Closed treatment of fracture of weight bearing articular portion of distal tibia (eg, pilon or tibial plafond), with or without anesthesia; without manipulation ▮1▮ T 50 ▯
MED: 100-2, 15, 260; 100-4, 12, 90.3; 100-4, 14, 10

27825 with skeletal traction and/or requiring manipulation ▮2▮ T 50 80 ▯
MED: 100-2, 15, 260; 100-4, 12, 90.3; 100-4, 14, 10

27826 Open treatment of fracture of weight bearing articular surface/portion of distal tibia (eg, pilon or tibial plafond), with internal or external fixation; of fibula only 3 T 50 80 ⬁
MED: 100-2, 15, 260; 100-4, 12, 90.3; 100-4, 14, 10

27827 of tibia only 3 T 50 80 ⬁
MED: 100-2, 15, 260; 100-4, 12, 90.3; 100-4, 14, 10

27828 of both tibia and fibula 4 T 50 80 ⬁
MED: 100-2, 15, 260; 100-4, 12, 90.3; 100-4, 14, 10

27829 Open treatment of distal tibiofibular joint (syndesmosis) disruption, with or without internal or external fixation 2 T 50 80 ⬁
MED: 100-2, 15, 260; 100-4, 12, 90.3; 100-4, 14, 10

AMA: 1992, Winter, 11

27830 Closed treatment of proximal tibiofibular joint dislocation; without anesthesia 1 T 50 80 ⬁
MED: 100-2, 15, 260; 100-4, 12, 90.3; 100-4, 14, 10

27831 requiring anesthesia 1 T 50 80 ⬁
MED: 100-2, 15, 260; 100-4, 12, 90.3; 100-4, 14, 10

27832 Open treatment of proximal tibiofibular joint dislocation, with or without internal or external fixation, or with excision of proximal fibula 2 T 50 80 ⬁
MED: 100-2, 15, 260; 100-4, 12, 90.3; 100-4, 14, 10

27840 Closed treatment of ankle dislocation; without anesthesia 1 T 50 ⬁
MED: 100-2, 15, 260; 100-4, 12, 90.3; 100-4, 14, 10

27842 requiring anesthesia, with or without percutaneous skeletal fixation 1 T 50 ⬁
MED: 100-2, 15, 260; 100-4, 12, 90.3; 100-4, 14, 10

27846 Open treatment of ankle dislocation, with or without percutaneous skeletal fixation; without repair or internal fixation 3 T 50 80 ⬁
MED: 100-2, 15, 260; 100-4, 12, 90.3; 100-4, 14, 10

27848 with repair or internal or external fixation 3 T 50 80 ⬁
MED: 100-2, 15, 260; 100-4, 12, 90.3; 100-4, 14, 10

MANIPULATION

27860 Manipulation of ankle under general anesthesia (includes application of traction or other fixation apparatus) 1 T 80 ⬁
MED: 100-2, 15, 260; 100-4, 12, 90.3; 100-4, 14, 10

ARTHRODESIS

27870 Arthrodesis, ankle, open 4 T 50 80 ⬁
MED: 100-2, 15, 260; 100-4, 12, 90.3; 100-4, 14, 10

To report arthroscopic ankle arthrodesis, consult CPT code 29899.

27871 Arthrodesis, tibiofibular joint, proximal or distal 4 T 50 80 ⬁
MED: 100-2, 15, 260; 100-4, 12, 90.3; 100-4, 14, 10

AMPUTATION

27880 Amputation, leg, through tibia and fibula; C 50 80 ⬁
Burgess amputation

Musculoskeletal System

27881 — 28003

27881	with immediate fitting technique including application of first cast	C 50 80 ↰
27882	open, circular (guillotine)	C 50 80 ↰
27884	secondary closure or scar revision	3 T 50 ↰
	MED: 100-2, 15, 260; 100-4, 12, 90.3; 100-4, 14, 10	
27886	re-amputation	C 50 ↰
27888	Amputation, ankle, through malleoli of tibia and fibula (eg, Syme, Pirogoff type procedures), with plastic closure and resection of nerves	C 50 80 ↰
27889	Ankle disarticulation	3 T 50 ↰
	MED: 100-2, 15, 260; 100-4, 12, 90.3; 100-4, 14, 10	

OTHER PROCEDURES

27892	Decompression fasciotomy, leg; anterior and/or lateral compartments only, with debridement of nonviable muscle and/or nerve	3 T 50 80 ↰
	MED: 100-2, 15, 260; 100-4, 12, 90.3; 100-4, 14, 10	

If decompression fasciotomy without debridement, is performed on the leg, consult CPT code 27600.

27893	posterior compartment(s) only, with debridement of nonviable muscle and/or nerve	3 T 50 80 ↰
	MED: 100-2, 15, 260; 100-4, 12, 90.3; 100-4, 14, 10	

If decompression fasciotomy without debridement, is performed on the leg, consult CPT code 27601.

27894	anterior and/or lateral, and posterior compartment(s), with debridement of nonviable muscle and/or nerve	3 T 50 80 ↰
	MED: 100-2, 15, 260; 100-4, 12, 90.3; 100-4, 14, 10	

If decompression fasciotomy without debridement, is performed on the leg, consult CPT code 27602.

27899	Unlisted procedure, leg or ankle	T 50 80
	AMA: 2000, Aug, 11	

FOOT AND TOES

Codes listed in the Musculoskeletal chapter include the application and removal of the first cast or traction device. Replacement of casts and/or traction devices subsequent to the first should be reported separately. CPT codes for other additional procedures, such as obtaining grafts and external fixation, should only be used if the procedure is not already listed as included as part of the basic procedure. Consult the glossary for terms and definitions and the front matter of this chapter for additional information.

INCISION

If superficial incision and drainage procedures are performed, consult CPT codes 10040-10160

28001	Incision and drainage, bursa, foot	T ↰
	AMA: 1998, Nov, 9	
28002	Incision and drainage below fascia, with or without tendon sheath involvement, foot; single bursal space	3 T ↰
	MED: 100-2, 15, 260; 100-4, 12, 90.3; 100-4, 14, 10	
	AMA: 1998, Nov, 8	
28003	multiple areas	3 T ↰
	MED: 100-2, 15, 260; 100-4, 12, 90.3; 100-4, 14, 10	
	AMA: 1998, Nov, 9	

28005 Incision, bone cortex (eg, osteomyelitis or bone abscess), foot **3** T 🔃
MED: 100-2, 15, 260; 100-4, 12, 90.3; 100-4, 14, 10

AMA: 1998, Nov, 9

28008 Fasciotomy, foot and/or toe **3** T 50 🔃
MED: 100-2, 15, 260; 100-4, 12, 90.3; 100-4, 14, 10

Consult also CPT codes 28060, 28062, and 28250.

28010 Tenotomy, percutaneous, toe; single tendon T 🔃
AMA: 1998, Nov, 8

28011   multiple tendons **3** T 🔃
MED: 100-2, 15, 260; 100-4, 12, 90.3; 100-4, 14, 10

AMA: 1998, Nov, 8

If an open tenotomy is performed, consult CPT codes 28230-28234.

28020 Arthrotomy, including exploration, drainage, or removal of loose or foreign body; intertarsal or tarsometatarsal joint **2** T 🔃
MED: 100-2, 15, 260; 100-4, 12, 90.3; 100-4, 14, 10

28022   metatarsophalangeal joint **2** T 🔃
MED: 100-2, 15, 260; 100-4, 12, 90.3; 100-4, 14, 10

28024   interphalangeal joint **2** T 🔃
MED: 100-2, 15, 260; 100-4, 12, 90.3; 100-4, 14, 10

28030 Neurectomy, intrinsic musculature of foot **4** T 80 🔃
MED: 100-2, 15, 260; 100-4, 12, 90.3; 100-4, 14, 10

28035 Release, tarsal tunnel (posterior tibial nerve decompression) **4** T 🔃
MED: 100-2, 15, 260; 100-4, 12, 90.3; 100-4, 14, 10

AMA: 1998, Nov, 8

If other nerves are entrapped, consult CPT codes 64704 and 64722.

EXCISION

28043 Excision, tumor, foot; subcutaneous tissue **2** T 50 🔃
MED: 100-2, 15, 260; 100-4, 12, 90.3; 100-4, 14, 10

28045   deep, subfascial, intramuscular **3** T 50 80 🔃
MED: 100-2, 15, 260; 100-4, 12, 90.3; 100-4, 14, 10

28046 Radical resection of tumor (eg, malignant neoplasm), soft tissue of foot **3** T 50 🔃
MED: 100-2, 15, 260; 100-4, 12, 90.3; 100-4, 14, 10

28050 Arthrotomy with biopsy; intertarsal or tarsometatarsal joint **2** T 50 🔃
MED: 100-2, 15, 260; 100-4, 12, 90.3; 100-4, 14, 10

28052   metatarsophalangeal joint **2** T 50 🔃
MED: 100-2, 15, 260; 100-4, 12, 90.3; 100-4, 14, 10

28054   interphalangeal joint **2** T 50 80 🔃
MED: 100-2, 15, 260; 100-4, 12, 90.3; 100-4, 14, 10

28060 Fasciectomy, plantar fascia; partial (separate procedure) **2** T 50 🔃
MED: 100-2, 15, 260; 100-4, 12, 90.3; 100-4, 14, 10

28062   radical (separate procedure) **3** T 🔃
MED: 100-2, 15, 260; 100-4, 12, 90.3; 100-4, 14, 10

If a plantar fasciotomy is performed, consult CPT codes 28008 and 28250.

Musculoskeletal System

28070 — 28107

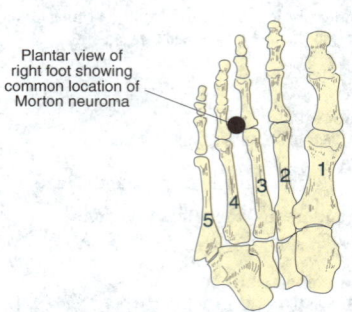

Plantar view of
right foot showing
common location of
Morton neuroma

Morton neuroma is a chronic inflammation or irritation of the nerves in
the web space between the heads of the metatarsals and phalanges

28070	**Synovectomy; intertarsal or tarsometatarsal joint, each**	3 T ⌐
	MED: 100-2, 15, 260; 100-4, 12, 90.3; 100-4, 14, 10	
28072	**metatarsophalangeal joint, each**	3 T ⌐
	MED: 100-2, 15, 260; 100-4, 12, 90.3; 100-4, 14, 10	
28080	**Excision, interdigital (Morton) neuroma, single, each**	3 T 80 ⌐
	MED: 100-2, 15, 260; 100-4, 12, 90.3; 100-4, 14, 10	
28086	**Synovectomy, tendon sheath, foot; flexor**	2 T 50 80 ⌐
	MED: 100-2, 15, 260; 100-4, 12, 90.3; 100-4, 14, 10	
28088	**extensor**	2 T 50 80 ⌐
	MED: 100-2, 15, 260; 100-4, 12, 90.3; 100-4, 14, 10	
28090	**Excision of lesion, tendon, tendon sheath, or capsule (including synovectomy) (eg, cyst or ganglion); foot**	3 T 50 ⌐
	MED: 100-2, 15, 260; 100-4, 12, 90.3; 100-4, 14, 10	
	AMA: 1998, Nov, 8	
28092	**toe(s), each**	3 T ⌐
	MED: 100-2, 15, 260; 100-4, 12, 90.3; 100-4, 14, 10	
28100	**Excision or curettage of bone cyst or benign tumor, talus or calcaneus;**	2 T 50 80 ⌐
	MED: 100-2, 15, 260; 100-4, 12, 90.3; 100-4, 14, 10	
28102	**with iliac or other autograft (includes obtaining graft)**	3 T 50 80 ⌐
	MED: 100-2, 15, 260; 100-4, 12, 90.3; 100-4, 14, 10	
28103	**with allograft**	3 T 50 80 ⌐
	MED: 100-2, 15, 260; 100-4, 12, 90.3; 100-4, 14, 10	
28104	**Excision or curettage of bone cyst or benign tumor, tarsal or metatarsal, except talus or calcaneus;**	2 T 80 ⌐
	MED: 100-2, 15, 260; 100-4, 12, 90.3; 100-4, 14, 10	
28106	**with iliac or other autograft (includes obtaining graft)**	3 T 80 ⌐
	MED: 100-2, 15, 260; 100-4, 12, 90.3; 100-4, 14, 10	
28107	**with allograft**	3 T 80 ⌐
	MED: 100-2, 15, 260; 100-4, 12, 90.3; 100-4, 14, 10	

26 / **TC** Professional/Technical Component   **80** / **80** Assist-at-Surgery Allowed/With Documentation   ⊙ Conscious Sedation

Unlisted   Not Covered   **MED:** Pubs 100/NCD Reference   **1**-**9** ASC Group   63 Modifier 63 Exempt

198 — Surgery   CPT only © 2005 American Medical Association. All Rights Reserved. *(Black Ink)*   © 2005 Ingenix, Inc. *(Blue Ink)*

28108 Excision or curettage of bone cyst or benign tumor, phalanges of foot   2 T ↻

If a partial ostectomy (e.g., hallux valgus, Silver type procedure) is performed, consult CPT code 28290.

28110 Ostectomy, partial excision, fifth metatarsal head (bunionette) (separate procedure)   3 T 50 ↻
MED: 100-2, 15, 260; 100-4, 12, 90.3; 100-4, 14, 10

AMA: 2000, Sep, 9; 1998, Oct, 10

28111 Ostectomy, complete excision; first metatarsal head   3 T 50 ↻
MED: 100-2, 15, 260; 100-4, 12, 90.3; 100-4, 14, 10

28112 other metatarsal head (second, third or fourth)   3 T 50 ↻
MED: 100-2, 15, 260; 100-4, 12, 90.3; 100-4, 14, 10

28113 fifth metatarsal head   3 T 50 80 ↻
MED: 100-2, 15, 260; 100-4, 12, 90.3; 100-4, 14, 10

28114 all metatarsal heads, with partial proximal phalangectomy, excluding first metatarsal (eg, Clayton type procedure)   3 T 50 80 ↻
MED: 100-2, 15, 260; 100-4, 12, 90.3; 100-4, 14, 10

28116 Ostectomy, excision of tarsal coalition   3 T 50 ↻
MED: 100-2, 15, 260; 100-4, 12, 90.3; 100-4, 14, 10

28118 Ostectomy, calcaneus;   4 T 50 80 ↻
MED: 100-2, 15, 260; 100-4, 12, 90.3; 100-4, 14, 10

28119 for spur, with or without plantar fascial release   4 T 50 ↻
MED: 100-2, 15, 260; 100-4, 12, 90.3; 100-4, 14, 10

28120 Partial excision (craterization, saucerization, sequestrectomy, or diaphysectomy) bone (eg, osteomyelitis or bossing); talus or calcaneus   7 T 50 ↻
MED: 100-2, 15, 260; 100-4, 12, 90.3; 100-4, 14, 10

Barker operation

28122 tarsal or metatarsal bone, except talus or calcaneus   3 T 50 80 ↻
MED: 100-2, 15, 260; 100-4, 12, 90.3; 100-4, 14, 10

AMA: 1998, Nov, 11

If a partial excision of talus or calcaneus is performed, consult CPT code 28120. If a cheilectomy is performed for hallux rigidus, consult CPT code 28289.

28124 phalanx of toe   T 50 ↻

28126 Resection, partial or complete, phalangeal base, each toe   3 T ↻
MED: 100-2, 15, 260; 100-4, 12, 90.3; 100-4, 14, 10

AMA: 1998, Nov, 8

28130 Talectomy (astragalectomy)   3 T 50 80 ↻
MED: 100-2, 15, 260; 100-4, 12, 90.3; 100-4, 14, 10

Whitman astragalectomy

28140 Metatarsectomy   3 T ↻
MED: 100-2, 15, 260; 100-4, 12, 90.3; 100-4, 14, 10

28150	**Phalangectomy, toe, each toe**	3 T
	MED: 100-2, 15, 260; 100-4, 12, 90.3; 100-4, 14, 10	
	AMA: 1998, Nov, 8	

28153	**Resection, condyle(s), distal end of phalanx, each toe**	3 T
	MED: 100-2, 15, 260; 100-4, 12, 90.3; 100-4, 14, 10	
	AMA: 1998, Nov, 8	

28160	**Hemiphalangectomy or interphalangeal joint excision, toe, proximal end of phalanx, each**	3 T
	MED: 100-2, 15, 260; 100-4, 12, 90.3; 100-4, 14, 10	
	AMA: 1998, Nov, 8	

| 28171 | **Radical resection of tumor, bone; tarsal (except talus or calcaneus)** | 3 T 80 |
| | MED: 100-2, 15, 260; 100-4, 12, 90.3; 100-4, 14, 10 | |

| 28173 | **metatarsal** | 3 T |
| | MED: 100-2, 15, 260; 100-4, 12, 90.3; 100-4, 14, 10 | |

| 28175 | **phalanx of toe** | 3 T |
| | MED: 100-2, 15, 260; 100-4, 12, 90.3; 100-4, 14, 10 | |

If a radical resection of a talus or a calcaneus tumor is performed, consult CPT code 27647.

INTRODUCTION OR REMOVAL

28190	**Removal of foreign body, foot; subcutaneous**	T 50
28192	**deep**	2 T 50
	MED: 100-2, 15, 260; 100-4, 12, 90.3; 100-4, 14, 10	

| 28193 | **complicated** | 4 T 50 |
| | MED: 100-2, 15, 260; 100-4, 12, 90.3; 100-4, 14, 10 | |

REPAIR, REVISION, AND/OR RECONSTRUCTION

28200	**Repair, tendon, flexor, foot; primary or secondary, without free graft, each tendon**	3 T
	MED: 100-2, 15, 260; 100-4, 12, 90.3; 100-4, 14, 10	
	AMA: 1998, Nov, 8	

| 28202 | **secondary with free graft, each tendon (includes obtaining graft)** | 3 T 80 |
| | MED: 100-2, 15, 260; 100-4, 12, 90.3; 100-4, 14, 10 | |

28208	**Repair, tendon, extensor, foot; primary or secondary, each tendon**	3 T
	MED: 100-2, 15, 260; 100-4, 12, 90.3; 100-4, 14, 10	
	AMA: 1998, Nov, 8	

| 28210 | **secondary with free graft, each tendon (includes obtaining graft)** | 3 T 80 |
| | MED: 100-2, 15, 260; 100-4, 12, 90.3; 100-4, 14, 10 | |

| 28220 | **Tenolysis, flexor, foot; single tendon** | T |
| | AMA: 1998, Nov, 8 | |

28222	**multiple tendons**	1 T
	MED: 100-2, 15, 260; 100-4, 12, 90.3; 100-4, 14, 10	
	AMA: 1998, Nov, 8	

28225 Tenolysis, extensor, foot; single tendon ■T ▯
MED: 100-2, 15, 260; 100-4, 12, 90.3; 100-4, 14, 10

AMA: 1998, Nov, 8

28226 multiple tendons ■T ▯
MED: 100-2, 15, 260; 100-4, 12, 90.3; 100-4, 14, 10

AMA: 1998, Nov, 8

28230 Tenotomy, open, tendon flexor; foot, single or multiple tendon(s) (separate procedure) T ▯
AMA: 1998, Nov, 8

28232 toe, single tendon (separate procedure) T ▯
AMA: 1998, Nov, 8

28234 Tenotomy, open, extensor, foot or toe, each tendon ❷T ▯
MED: 100-2, 15, 260; 100-4, 12, 90.3; 100-4, 14, 10

AMA: 1998, Nov, 8

28238 Reconstruction (advancement), posterior tibial tendon with excision of accessory tarsal navicular bone (eg, Kidner type procedure) ❸T 50 80 ▯
MED: 100-2, 15, 260; 100-4, 12, 90.3; 100-4, 14, 10

If a subcutaneous tenotomy is performed, consult CPT codes 28010 and 28011. If a transfer or transplant of a tendon with muscle redirection or rerouting is performed, consult CPT codes 27690-27692. If an extensor hallucis longus transfer with a great toe IP fusion (Jones procedure) is performed, consult CPT code 28760.

28240 Tenotomy, lengthening, or release, abductor hallucis muscle ❷T 50 ▯
MED: 100-2, 15, 260; 100-4, 12, 90.3; 100-4, 14, 10

28250 Division of plantar fascia and muscle (eg, Steindler stripping) (separate procedure) ❸T 50 80 ▯
MED: 100-2, 15, 260; 100-4, 12, 90.3; 100-4, 14, 10

28260 Capsulotomy, midfoot; medial release only (separate procedure)❸T 50 80 ▯
MED: 100-2, 15, 260; 100-4, 12, 90.3; 100-4, 14, 10

28261 with tendon lengthening ❸T 50 80 ▯
MED: 100-2, 15, 260; 100-4, 12, 90.3; 100-4, 14, 10

28262 extensive, including posterior talotibial capsulotomy and tendon(s) lengthening (eg, resistant clubfoot deformity) ❹T 50 80 ▯
MED: 100-2, 15, 260; 100-4, 12, 90.3; 100-4, 14, 10

Cuneiform bones
Metatarsals
Phalanges
Cuboid
Metatarso-phalangeal joint
Metatarso-phalangeal joint
Tenorrhaphy
Interphalangeal joints

Tarsals, metatarsals, and phalanges

The metatarsophalangeal joint capsule is incised (capsulotomy)

28264   **Capsulotomy, midtarsal (eg, Heyman type procedure)**   ■ T 50 80 ↺
MED: 100-2, 15, 260; 100-4, 12, 90.3; 100-4, 14, 10

28270   **Capsulotomy; metatarsophalangeal joint, with or without tenorrhaphy, each joint (separate procedure)**   ■ T 50 ↺
MED: 100-2, 15, 260; 100-4, 12, 90.3; 100-4, 14, 10

28272   **interphalangeal joint, each joint (separate procedure)**   T 50 ↺
AMA: 2002, Dec, 11

28280   **Syndactylization, toes (eg, webbing or Kelikian type procedure)** ■ T 50 80 ↺
MED: 100-2, 15, 260; 100-4, 12, 90.3; 100-4, 14, 10

AMA: 1998, Nov, 8

28285   **Correction, hammertoe (eg, interphalangeal fusion, partial or total phalangectomy)**   ■ T 50 ↺
MED: 100-2, 15, 260; 100-4, 12, 90.3; 100-4, 14, 10

AMA: 1998, Nov, 8

28286   **Correction, cock-up fifth toe, with plastic skin closure (eg, Ruiz-Mora type procedure)**   ■ T ↺
MED: 100-2, 15, 260; 100-4, 12, 90.3; 100-4, 14, 10

AMA: 1998, Nov, 8

28288   **Ostectomy, partial, exostectomy or condylectomy, metatarsal head, each metatarsal head**   ■ T ↺
MED: 100-2, 15, 260; 100-4, 12, 90.3; 100-4, 14, 10

28289   **Hallux rigidus correction with cheilectomy, debridement and capsular release of the first metatarsophalangeal joint**   ■ T 50 80 ↺
MED: 100-2, 15, 260; 100-4, 12, 90.3; 100-4, 14, 10

AMA: 1998, Nov, 11

28290   **Correction, hallux valgus (bunion), with or without sesamoidectomy; simple exostectomy (eg, Silver type procedure)**   ■ T 50 ↺
MED: 100-2, 15, 260; 100-4, 12, 90.3; 100-4, 14, 10

AMA: 1996, Dec, 5

28292   **Keller, McBride or Mayo type procedure**   ■ T 50 80 ↺
MED: 100-2, 15, 260; 100-4, 12, 90.3; 100-4, 14, 10

AMA: 2000, Sep, 9; 1996, Dec, 5

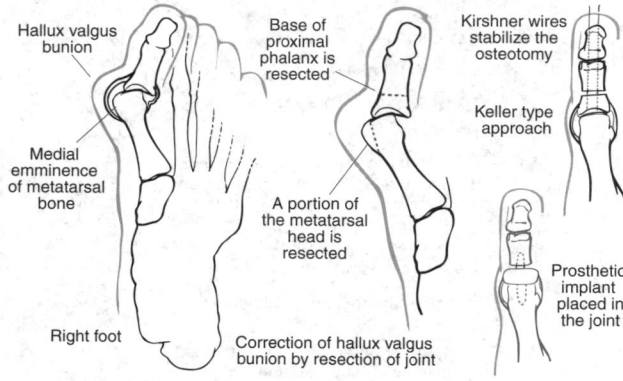

Hallux valgus bunion

Base of proximal phalanx is resected

Kirshner wires stabilize the osteotomy

Keller type approach

Medial emminence of metatarsal bone

A portion of the metatarsal head is resected

Prosthetic implant placed in the joint

Right foot

Correction of hallux valgus bunion by resection of joint

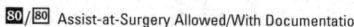

28293   resection of joint with implant   3 T 50 80 🗗
MED: 100-2, 15, 260; 100-4, 12, 90.3; 100-4, 14, 10
AMA: 1996, Dec, 6

28294   with tendon transplants (eg, Joplin type procedure)   3 T 50 80 🗗
MED: 100-2, 15, 260; 100-4, 12, 90.3; 100-4, 14, 10
AMA: 1996, Dec, 6

28296   with metatarsal osteotomy (eg, Mitchell, Chevron, or concentric type procedures)   3 T 50 80 🗗
MED: 100-2, 15, 260; 100-4, 12, 90.3; 100-4, 14, 10
AMA: 1997, Jan, 10; 1996, Dec, 6

▲ **28297**   Lapidus-type procedure
MED: 100-2, 15, 260; 100-4, 12, 90.3; 100-4, 14, 10
AMA: 1996, Dec, 6

28298   by phalanx osteotomy   3 T 50 80 🗗
MED: 100-2, 15, 260; 100-4, 12, 90.3; 100-4, 14, 10
AMA: 1996, Dec, 7

28299   by double osteotomy   5 T 50 80 🗗
MED: 100-2, 15, 260; 100-4, 12, 90.3; 100-4, 14, 10
AMA: 1996, Dec, 7

28300   Osteotomy; calcaneus (eg, Dwyer or Chambers type procedure), with or without internal fixation   2 T 50 80 🗗
MED: 100-2, 15, 260; 100-4, 12, 90.3; 100-4, 14, 10

28302   talus   2 T 50 80 🗗
MED: 100-2, 15, 260; 100-4, 12, 90.3; 100-4, 14, 10

28304   Osteotomy, tarsal bones, other than calcaneus or talus;   2 T 50 🗗
MED: 100-2, 15, 260; 100-4, 12, 90.3; 100-4, 14, 10
AMA: 1998, Nov, 8

28305   with autograft (includes obtaining graft) (eg, Fowler type)   3 T 50 🗗
MED: 100-2, 15, 260; 100-4, 12, 90.3; 100-4, 14, 10

28306   Osteotomy, with or without lengthening, shortening or angular correction, metatarsal; first metatarsal   4 T 50 🗗
MED: 100-2, 15, 260; 100-4, 12, 90.3; 100-4, 14, 10
AMA: 1999, Dec, 7; 1998, Nov, 8

28307   first metatarsal with autograft (other than first toe)   4 T 50 🗗
MED: 100-2, 15, 260; 100-4, 12, 90.3; 100-4, 14, 10
AMA: 1998, Nov, 9

28308   other than first metatarsal, each   2 T 50 🗗
MED: 100-2, 15, 260; 100-4, 12, 90.3; 100-4, 14, 10

28309   multiple (eg, Swanson type cavus foot procedure)   4 T 50 80 🗗
MED: 100-2, 15, 260; 100-4, 12, 90.3; 100-4, 14, 10
AMA: 1999, Dec, 7; 1998, Nov, 8

28310   Osteotomy, shortening, angular or rotational correction; proximal phalanx, first toe (separate procedure)   3 T 🗗
MED: 100-2, 15, 260; 100-4, 12, 90.3; 100-4, 14, 10

28312　　　　other phalanges, any toe　　　　　　　3 T ⟲
　　　　　MED: 100-2, 15, 260; 100-4, 12, 90.3; 100-4, 14, 10

28313　　Reconstruction, angular deformity of toe, soft tissue procedures only (eg, overlapping second toe, fifth toe, curly toes)　2 T ⟲
　　　　　MED: 100-2, 15, 260; 100-4, 12, 90.3; 100-4, 14, 10

　　　　　AMA: 1998, Nov, 8

28315　　Sesamoidectomy, first toe (separate procedure)　　4 T 50 ⟲
　　　　　MED: 100-2, 15, 260; 100-4, 12, 90.3; 100-4, 14, 10

28320　　Repair, nonunion or malunion; tarsal bones　　　4 T 80 ⟲
　　　　　MED: 100-2, 15, 260; 100-4, 12, 90.3; 100-4, 14, 10

　　　　　AMA: 1998, Nov, 9

28322　　　　metatarsal, with or without bone graft (includes obtaining graft)　　　　　　　　　　　　　　　　　4 T 80 ⟲
　　　　　MED: 100-2, 15, 260; 100-4, 12, 90.3; 100-4, 14, 10

28340　　Reconstruction, toe, macrodactyly; soft tissue resection　4 T ⟲
　　　　　MED: 100-2, 15, 260; 100-4, 12, 90.3; 100-4, 14, 10

28341　　　　requiring bone resection　　　　　　　　4 T ⟲
　　　　　MED: 100-2, 15, 260; 100-4, 12, 90.3; 100-4, 14, 10

28344　　Reconstruction, toe(s); polydactyly　　　　　4 T ⟲
　　　　　MED: 100-2, 15, 260; 100-4, 12, 90.3; 100-4, 14, 10

28345　　　　syndactyly, with or without skin graft(s), each web　4 T 80 ⟲
　　　　　MED: 100-2, 15, 260; 100-4, 12, 90.3; 100-4, 14, 10

28360　　Reconstruction, cleft foot　　　　　　　　　T 80 ⟲

FRACTURE AND/OR DISLOCATION

28400　　Closed treatment of calcaneal fracture; without manipulation　1 T 50 ⟲
　　　　　MED: 100-2, 15, 260; 100-4, 12, 90.3; 100-4, 14, 10

28405　　　　with manipulation　　　　　　　　2 T 50 80 ⟲
　　　　　MED: 100-2, 15, 260; 100-4, 12, 90.3; 100-4, 14, 10

　　　　　Bohler reduction

28406　　Percutaneous skeletal fixation of calcaneal fracture, with manipulation
　　　　　　　　　　　　　　　　　　　　　2 T 50 80 ⟲
　　　　　MED: 100-2, 15, 260; 100-4, 12, 90.3; 100-4, 14, 10

28415　　Open treatment of calcaneal fracture, with or without internal or external fixation;　　　　　　　　　　　　3 T 50 80 ⟲
　　　　　MED: 100-2, 15, 260; 100-4, 12, 90.3; 100-4, 14, 10

28420　　　　with primary iliac or other autogenous bone graft (includes obtaining graft)　　　　　　　　　　　　　　4 T 50 80 ⟲
　　　　　MED: 100-2, 15, 260; 100-4, 12, 90.3; 100-4, 14, 10

28430　　Closed treatment of talus fracture; without manipulation　T 50 ⟲

28435　　　　with manipulation　　　　　　　　2 T 50 80 ⟲
　　　　　MED: 100-2, 15, 260; 100-4, 12, 90.3; 100-4, 14, 10

28436　　Percutaneous skeletal fixation of talus fracture, with manipulation　　　　　　　　　　　　　　　　2 T 50 ⟲
　　　　　MED: 100-2, 15, 260; 100-4, 12, 90.3; 100-4, 14, 10

28445	Open treatment of talus fracture, with or without internal or external fixation 3 T 50 80 ◪
	MED: 100-2, 15, 260; 100-4, 12, 90.3; 100-4, 14, 10

28450	Treatment of tarsal bone fracture (except talus and calcaneus); without manipulation, each T ◪
	AMA: 2001, Dec, 7

28455	with manipulation, each T 80 ◪

28456	Percutaneous skeletal fixation of tarsal bone fracture (except talus and calcaneus), with manipulation, each 2 T ◪
	MED: 100-2, 15, 260; 100-4, 12, 90.3; 100-4, 14, 10

28465	Open treatment of tarsal bone fracture (except talus and calcaneus), with or without internal or external fixation, each 3 T ◪
	MED: 100-2, 15, 260; 100-4, 12, 90.3; 100-4, 14, 10

28470	Closed treatment of metatarsal fracture; without manipulation, each T ◪

28475	with manipulation, each T ◪

28476	Percutaneous skeletal fixation of metatarsal fracture, with manipulation, each 2 T 80 ◪
	MED: 100-2, 15, 260; 100-4, 12, 90.3; 100-4, 14, 10

28485	Open treatment of metatarsal fracture, with or without internal or external fixation, each 4 T ◪
	MED: 100-2, 15, 260; 100-4, 12, 90.3; 100-4, 14, 10

28490	Closed treatment of fracture great toe, phalanx or phalanges; without manipulation T ◪

28495	with manipulation T ◪

28496	Percutaneous skeletal fixation of fracture great toe, phalanx or phalanges, with manipulation 2 T ◪
	MED: 100-2, 15, 260; 100-4, 12, 90.3; 100-4, 14, 10

28505	Open treatment of fracture great toe, phalanx or phalanges, with or without internal or external fixation 3 T ◪
	MED: 100-2, 15, 260; 100-4, 12, 90.3; 100-4, 14, 10

28510	Closed treatment of fracture, phalanx or phalanges, other than great toe; without manipulation, each T ◪

28515	with manipulation, each T ◪

28525	Open treatment of fracture, phalanx or phalanges, other than great toe, with or without internal or external fixation, each 3 T 80 ◪
	MED: 100-2, 15, 260; 100-4, 12, 90.3; 100-4, 14, 10

28530	Closed treatment of sesamoid fracture T 80 ◪

28531	Open treatment of sesamoid fracture, with or without internal fixation 3 T ◪
	MED: 100-2, 15, 260; 100-4, 12, 90.3; 100-4, 14, 10

28540	Closed treatment of tarsal bone dislocation, other than talotarsal; without anesthesia T 80 ◪

28545	requiring anesthesia 1 T 80 ◪
	MED: 100-2, 15, 260; 100-4, 12, 90.3; 100-4, 14, 10

28546 Percutaneous skeletal fixation of tarsal bone dislocation, other than talotarsal, with manipulation 2 T 80
MED: 100-2, 15, 260; 100-4, 12, 90.3; 100-4, 14, 10

28555 Open treatment of tarsal bone dislocation, with or without internal or external fixation 2 T 80
MED: 100-2, 15, 260; 100-4, 12, 90.3; 100-4, 14, 10

28570 Closed treatment of talotarsal joint dislocation; without anesthesia T 80

28575 requiring anesthesia 1 T 80
MED: 100-2, 15, 260; 100-4, 12, 90.3; 100-4, 14, 10

28576 Percutaneous skeletal fixation of talotarsal joint dislocation, with manipulation 3 T 80
MED: 100-2, 15, 260; 100-4, 12, 90.3; 100-4, 14, 10

28585 Open treatment of talotarsal joint dislocation, with or without internal or external fixation 3 T 80
MED: 100-2, 15, 260; 100-4, 12, 90.3; 100-4, 14, 10

28600 Closed treatment of tarsometatarsal joint dislocation; without anesthesia T 80

28605 requiring anesthesia 1 T 80
MED: 100-2, 15, 260; 100-4, 12, 90.3; 100-4, 14, 10

28606 Percutaneous skeletal fixation of tarsometatarsal joint dislocation, with manipulation 2 T
MED: 100-2, 15, 260; 100-4, 12, 90.3; 100-4, 14, 10

28615 Open treatment of tarsometatarsal joint dislocation, with or without internal or external fixation 3 T 80
MED: 100-2, 15, 260; 100-4, 12, 90.3; 100-4, 14, 10

28630 Closed treatment of metatarsophalangeal joint dislocation; without anesthesia T 80

28635 requiring anesthesia 1 T 80
MED: 100-2, 15, 260; 100-4, 12, 90.3; 100-4, 14, 10

28636 Percutaneous skeletal fixation of metatarsophalangeal joint dislocation, with manipulation 3 T
MED: 100-2, 15, 260; 100-4, 12, 90.3; 100-4, 14, 10

28645 Open treatment of metatarsophalangeal joint dislocation, with or without internal or external fixation 3 T
MED: 100-2, 15, 260; 100-4, 12, 90.3; 100-4, 14, 10

28660 Closed treatment of interphalangeal joint dislocation; without anesthesia T

28665 requiring anesthesia 1 T 80
MED: 100-2, 15, 260; 100-4, 12, 90.3; 100-4, 14, 10

28666 Percutaneous skeletal fixation of interphalangeal joint dislocation, with manipulation 3 T
MED: 100-2, 15, 260; 100-4, 12, 90.3; 100-4, 14, 10

28675 Open treatment of interphalangeal joint dislocation, with or without internal or external fixation 3 T
MED: 100-2, 15, 260; 100-4, 12, 90.3; 100-4, 14, 10

ARTHRODESIS

28705	**Arthrodesis; pantalar**	4 T 80 ⬓
	MED: 100-2, 15, 260; 100-4, 12, 90.3; 100-4, 14, 10	
28715	**triple**	4 T 80 ⬓
	MED: 100-2, 15, 260; 100-4, 12, 90.3; 100-4, 14, 10	
28725	**subtalar**	4 T 80 ⬓
	MED: 100-2, 15, 260; 100-4, 12, 90.3; 100-4, 14, 10	
	Dunn arthrodesis	
28730	**Arthrodesis, midtarsal or tarsometatarsal, multiple or transverse;**	4 T 80 ⬓
	MED: 100-2, 15, 260; 100-4, 12, 90.3; 100-4, 14, 10	
	Lambrinudi arthrodesis	
28735	**with osteotomy (eg, flatfoot correction)**	4 T 80 ⬓
	MED: 100-2, 15, 260; 100-4, 12, 90.3; 100-4, 14, 10	
28737	**Arthrodesis, with tendon lengthening and advancement, midtarsal, tarsal navicular-cuneiform (eg, Miller type procedure)**	5 T 80 ⬓
	MED: 100-2, 15, 260; 100-4, 12, 90.3; 100-4, 14, 10	
28740	**Arthrodesis, midtarsal or tarsometatarsal, single joint**	4 T 80 ⬓
	MED: 100-2, 15, 260; 100-4, 12, 90.3; 100-4, 14, 10	
28750	**Arthrodesis, great toe; metatarsophalangeal joint**	4 T 50 80 ⬓
	MED: 100-2, 15, 260; 100-4, 12, 90.3; 100-4, 14, 10	
	AMA: 1996, Dec, 7	
28755	**interphalangeal joint**	4 T 50 ⬓
	MED: 100-2, 15, 260; 100-4, 12, 90.3; 100-4, 14, 10	
28760	**Arthrodesis, with extensor hallucis longus transfer to first metatarsal neck, great toe, interphalangeal joint (eg, Jones type procedure)**	4 T 50 80 ⬓
	MED: 100-2, 15, 260; 100-4, 12, 90.3; 100-4, 14, 10	
	AMA: 1998, Nov, 8	

If a hammertoe operation or interphalangeal joint fusion is performed, consult CPT code 28285.

AMPUTATION

28800	**Amputation, foot; midtarsal (eg, Chopart type procedure)**	C 50 80 ⬓
28805	**transmetatarsal**	C 50 80 ⬓
28810	**Amputation, metatarsal, with toe, single**	2 T 80 ⬓
	MED: 100-2, 15, 260; 100-4, 12, 90.3; 100-4, 14, 10	
28820	**Amputation, toe; metatarsophalangeal joint**	2 T ⬓
	MED: 100-2, 15, 260; 100-4, 12, 90.3; 100-4, 14, 10	
28825	**interphalangeal joint**	2 T ⬓
	MED: 100-2, 15, 260; 100-4, 12, 90.3; 100-4, 14, 10	

If the tuft of the distal phalanx is amputated, consult CPT code 11752.

Musculoskeletal System

28890 — 28899

OTHER PROCEDURES

To report extracorporeal shock wave therapy involving musculoskeletal system not otherwise specified, consult Category III codes 0019T, 0101T, 0102T.

● **28890**   **Extracorporeal shock wave, high energy, performed by a physician, requiring anesthesia other than local, including ultrasound guidance, involving the plantar fascia**

   To report extracorporeal shock wave therapy involving musculoskeletal system not otherwise specified, consult Category III codes 0019T, 0101T, 0102T.

28899   **Unlisted procedure, foot or toes**   T 80

APPLICATION OF CASTS AND STRAPPING

Codes listed in the Musculoskeletal chapter include the application and removal of the first cast or traction device. Replacement of casts and/or traction devices subsequent to the first should be reported separately. CPT codes for other additional procedures, such as obtaining grafts and external fixation, should only be used if the procedure is not already listed as included as part of the basic procedure.

Codes found in the application of casts and strapping section (29000–29799) should be reported separately when:

- The cast application or strapping is a replacement procedure used during or after the period of follow-up care.

- The cast application or strapping is an initial service performed without restorative treatment or procedures to stabilize or protect a fracture, injury, or dislocation and/or to afford comfort to a patient.

- An initial casting or strapping when no other treatment or procedure is performed or will be performed by the same physician.

- A physician performs the initial application of a cast or strapping subsequent to another physician having performed a restorative treatment or procedure.

- A physician who applies the initial cast, strap, or splint and also assumes all of the subsequent fracture, dislocation, or injury care cannot use the application of casts and strapping codes as an initial service. The first cast, splint, or strap application is included in the treatment of the fracture and/or dislocation codes.

- A temporary cast, splint, or strap is not condisered to be a part of the preoperative care. It is not necessary to use modifier 56.

- Report evaluation and management services only if they are separately identifiable from the application of the cast, splint, or strap.

- Do not report removal of the cast or strap separately.

Use these codes when replacing a cast or strap during or after follow-up care. They also apply when the application is an initial service without treatment or procedure to protect an injury.

Casts are rigid dressings, often made of fiberglass or plaster. Strapping is the application of tape to bind, correct, or protect an anatomical part.

If orthotics management and training are necessary, consult CPT code 97760–97762.

26 / **TC** Professional/Technical Component   **80**/**80** Assist-at-Surgery Allowed/With Documentation   ⊙ Conscious Sedation

Unlisted   Not Covered   **MED:** Pubs 100/NCD Reference   **1**-**9** ASC Group   ⑥③ Modifier 63 Exempt

208 — Surgery   CPT only © 2005 American Medical Association. All Rights Reserved. *(Black Ink)*   © 2005 Ingenix, Inc. *(Blue Ink)*

BODY AND UPPER EXTREMITY — CASTS

29000	Application of halo type body cast (see 20661-20663 for insertion)	S 80 ⬑
	AMA: 2002, Apr, 13; 1996, Feb, 3, 5	

29010	Application of Risser jacket, localizer, body; only	S 80 ⬑
	AMA: 2002, Apr, 13; 1996, Feb, 3	

29015	including head	S 80 ⬑
	AMA: 2002, Apr, 13; 1996, Feb, 3	

29020	Application of turnbuckle jacket, body; only	S 80 ⬑
	AMA: 2002, Apr, 13; 1996, Feb, 3	

29025	including head	S 80 ⬑
	AMA: 2002, Apr, 13; 1996, Feb, 3	

29035	Application of body cast, shoulder to hips;	S 80 ⬑
	AMA: 2002, Apr, 13; 1996, Feb, 3	

29040	including head, Minerva type	S 80 ⬑
	AMA: 2002, Apr, 13; 1996, Feb, 3	

29044	including one thigh	S 80 ⬑
	AMA: 2002, Apr, 13; 1996, Feb, 3	

29046	including both thighs	S 80 ⬑
	AMA: 2002, Apr, 13; 1996, Feb, 3	

29049	Application, cast; figure-of-eight	S 80 ⬑
	MED: 100-2, 15, 100	
	AMA: 2002, Apr, 13; 1996, Feb, 3	

29055	shoulder spica	S 80 ⬑
	MED: 100-2, 15, 100	
	AMA: 2002, Apr, 13; 1996, Feb, 3	

29058	plaster Velpeau	S 80 ⬑
	MED: 100-2, 15, 100	
	AMA: 2002, Apr, 13; 1996, Feb, 3	

29065	shoulder to hand (long arm)	S 50 ⬑
	MED: 100-2, 15, 100	
	AMA: 2002, Apr, 13; 1996, Feb, 3	

29075	elbow to finger (short arm)	S 50 ⬑
	MED: 100-2, 15, 100	
	AMA: 2002, Apr, 13; 1996, Feb, 3, 4	

29085	hand and lower forearm (gauntlet)	S 50 ⬑
	MED: 100-2, 15, 100	
	AMA: 2002, Dec, 11; 2002, Apr, 13; 1996, Feb, 3	

29086	finger (eg, contracture)	S 50 ⬑
	MED: 100-2, 15, 100	
	AMA: 2002, Apr, 13	

Musculoskeletal System

29105 — 29345

BODY AND UPPER EXTREMITY — SPLINTS

29105   **Application of long arm splint (shoulder to hand)**   S 50 ⬓
MED: 100-2, 15, 100

AMA: 2002, Apr, 13; 1996, Feb, 3

29125   **Application of short arm splint (forearm to hand); static**   S 50 ⬓
MED: 100-2, 15, 100

AMA: 2002, Apr, 13; 1996, Feb, 3, 4

29126   **dynamic**   S 50 ⬓
MED: 100-2, 15, 100

AMA: 2002, Apr, 13; 1996, Feb, 3

29130   **Application of finger splint; static**   S 50 ⬓
MED: 100-2, 15, 100

AMA: 2002, Apr, 13; 1996, Feb, 3

29131   **dynamic**   S 50 ⬓
MED: 100-2, 15, 100

AMA: 2002, Apr, 13; 1996, Feb, 3

BODY AND UPPER EXTREMITY — STRAPPING — ANY AGE

29200   **Strapping; thorax**   S ⬓
MED: 100-2, 15, 100

AMA: 2002, Apr, 13; 1996, Feb, 3

29220   **low back**   S ⬓
MED: 100-2, 15, 100

AMA: 2002, Apr, 13; 1996, Feb, 3

29240   **shoulder (eg, Velpeau)**   S ⬓
MED: 100-2, 15, 100

AMA: 2002, Apr, 13; 1996, Feb, 3

29260   **elbow or wrist**   S 50 ⬓
MED: 100-2, 15, 100

AMA: 2002, Apr, 13; 1996, Feb, 3

29280   **hand or finger**   S 50 ⬓
MED: 100-2, 15, 100

AMA: 2002, Apr, 13; 1996, Feb, 3

LOWER EXTREMITY — CASTS

29305   **Application of hip spica cast; one leg**   S 80 ⬓
AMA: 2002, Apr, 13; 1996, Feb, 3

29325   **one and one-half spica or both legs**   S 80 ⬓
AMA: 2002, Apr, 13; 1996, Feb, 3

To report the application of a hip spica (body) cast, including thighs only, consult CPT code 29046.

29345   **Application of long leg cast (thigh to toes);**   S 50 ⬓
AMA: 2002, Apr, 13; 1996, Feb, 3

29355   **walker or ambulatory type**   S 50 ⬓
AMA: 2002, Apr, 13; 1996, Feb, 3

---

26 / TC Professional/Technical Component   **80/80** Assist-at-Surgery Allowed/With Documentation   ⊙ Conscious Sedation

Unlisted   Not Covered   **MED:** Pubs 100/NCD Reference   **1**-**9** ASC Group   63 Modifier 63 Exempt

210 — Surgery   CPT only © 2005 American Medical Association. All Rights Reserved. *(Black Ink)*   © 2005 Ingenix, Inc. *(Blue Ink)*

29358	Application of long leg cast brace	S 50 ⟳
	AMA: 2002, Apr, 13; 1996, Feb, 3	
29365	Application of cylinder cast (thigh to ankle)	S 50 ⟳
	AMA: 2002, Apr, 13; 1996, Feb, 3	
29405	Application of short leg cast (below knee to toes);	S 50 ⟳
	MED: 100-2, 15, 100	
	AMA: 2002, Apr, 13; 1996, Feb, 3	
29425	walking or ambulatory type	S 50 ⟳
	MED: 100-2, 15, 100	
	AMA: 2002, Apr, 13; 1996, Feb, 3	
29435	Application of patellar tendon bearing (PTB) cast	S 50 ⟳
	AMA: 2002, Apr, 13; 1996, Feb, 3	
29440	Adding walker to previously applied cast	S 50 ⟳
	MED: 100-2, 15, 100	
	AMA: 2002, Apr, 13; 1996, Feb, 3	
29445	Application of rigid total contact leg cast	S 50 ⟳
	AMA: 2002, Apr, 13; 1996, Feb, 3	
29450	Application of clubfoot cast with molding or manipulation, long or short leg	S 50 ⟳
	AMA: 2002, Apr, 13; 1996, Feb, 3	

LOWER EXTREMITY — SPLINTS

29505	Application of long leg splint (thigh to ankle or toes)	S 50 ⟳
	MED: 100-2, 15, 100	
	AMA: 2002, Apr, 13; 1996, Feb, 3	
29515	Application of short leg splint (calf to foot)	S 50 ⟳
	MED: 100-2, 15, 100	
	AMA: 2002, Apr, 13; 1996, Feb, 3	

LOWER EXTREMITY — STRAPPING — ANY AGE

29520	Strapping; hip	S 80 ⟳
	MED: 100-2, 15, 100	
	AMA: 2002, Apr, 13; 1996, Feb, 3	
29530	knee	S ⟳
	MED: 100-2, 15, 100	
	AMA: 2002, Apr, 13; 1996, Feb, 3	
29540	ankle and/or foot	S ⟳
	MED: 100-2, 15, 100	
	AMA: 2002, Apr, 13; 1996, Feb, 3	
29550	toes	S ⟳
	MED: 100-2, 15, 100	
	AMA: 2002, Apr, 13; 1996, Feb, 3	
29580	Unna boot	S 50 ⟳
	MED: 100-2, 15, 100	
	AMA: 2002, Apr, 13; 1999, Jul, 10; 1996, Feb, 3	

29590   **Denis-Browne splint strapping**   S ↵
        AMA: 2002, Apr, 13; 1996, Feb, 3

REMOVAL OR REPAIR

These codes are only used for casts applied by another physician.

29700   **Removal or bivalving; gauntlet, boot or body cast**   S ↵
        AMA: 2002, Apr, 13

29705   **full arm or full leg cast**   S 50 ↵
        AMA: 2002, Apr, 13

29710   **shoulder or hip spica, Minerva, or Risser jacket, etc.**   S 50 80 ↵
        AMA: 2002, Apr, 13

29715   **turnbuckle jacket**   S 80 ↵
        AMA: 2002, Apr, 13

29720   **Repair of spica, body cast or jacket**   S ↵
        AMA: 2002, Apr, 13

29730   **Windowing of cast**   S ↵
        AMA: 2002, Apr, 13

29740   **Wedging of cast (except clubfoot casts)**   S ↵
        AMA: 2002, Apr, 13

29750   **Wedging of clubfoot cast**   S 50 80 ↵
        AMA: 2002, Apr, 13

OTHER PROCEDURES

29799   **Unlisted procedure, casting or strapping**   S 80

ENDOSCOPY/ARTHROSCOPY

When arthrotomy is performed in addition to the arthroscopy, append with modifier 51.

Diagnostic endoscopy/arthroscopy is always included in surgical endoscopy/arthroscopy; do not report separately.

29800   **Arthroscopy, temporomandibular joint, diagnostic, with or without synovial biopsy (separate procedure)**   3 T 50 80 ↵
        MED: 100-2, 15, 260; 100-3, 100.2; 100-4, 12, 90.3; 100-4, 14, 10

29804   **Arthroscopy, temporomandibular joint, surgical**   3 T 50 80 ↵
        MED: 100-2, 15, 260; 100-3, 100.2; 100-4, 12, 90.3; 100-4, 14, 10

        To report open procedure, consult CPT code 21010.

29805   **Arthroscopy, shoulder, diagnostic, with or without synovial biopsy (separate procedure)**   3 T 50 ↵
        MED: 100-2, 15, 260; 100-3, 100.2; 100-4, 12, 90.3; 100-4, 14, 10

        To report open procedure, consult CPT codes 23065-23066, 23100-23101.

29806   **Arthroscopy, shoulder, surgical; capsulorrhaphy**   3 T 50 ↵
        MED: 100-2, 15, 260; 100-3, 100.2; 100-4, 12, 90.3; 100-4, 14, 10

        If an open procedure is performed, consult CPT codes 23450-23466.
        If thermal capsulorrhaphy is performed, consult CPT code 29999.

29807   **repair of SLAP lesion**   3 T 50 ↵
        MED: 100-2, 15, 260; 100-3, 100.2; 100-4, 12, 90.3; 100-4, 14, 10

29819 **Arthroscopy, shoulder, surgical; with removal of loose body or foreign body** ③ T 50 📄
MED: 100-2, 15, 260; 100-3, 100.2; 100-4, 12, 90.3; 100-4, 14, 10

To report open procedure, consult CPT codes 23040-23044, 23107.

29820 **synovectomy, partial** ③ T 50 80 📄
MED: 100-2, 15, 260; 100-3, 100.2; 100-4, 12, 90.3; 100-4, 14, 10

To report open procedure, consult CPT code 23105.

29821 **synovectomy, complete** ③ T 50 80 📄
MED: 100-2, 15, 260; 100-3, 100.2; 100-4, 12, 90.3; 100-4, 14, 10

To report open procedure, consult CPT code 23105.

29822 **debridement, limited** ③ T 50 80 📄
MED: 100-2, 15, 260; 100-3, 100.2; 100-4, 12, 90.3; 100-4, 14, 10

AMA: 2001, May, 8

To report open procedure, consult the specific open shoulder procedure performed.

29823 **debridement, extensive** ③ T 50 80 📄
MED: 100-2, 15, 260; 100-3, 100.2; 100-4, 12, 90.3; 100-4, 14, 10

To report open procedure, consult the specific open shoulder procedure performed.

29824 **distal claviculectomy including distal articular surface (Mumford procedure)** ⑤ T 50 80 📄
MED: 100-2, 15, 260; 100-3, 100.2; 100-4, 12, 90.3; 100-4, 14, 10

To report open procedure, consult CPT code 23120.

29825 **with lysis and resection of adhesions, with or without manipulation** ③ T 50 80 📄
MED: 100-2, 15, 260; 100-3, 100.2; 100-4, 12, 90.3; 100-4, 14, 10

To report open procedure, consult the specific open shoulder procedure performed.

29826 **decompression of subacromial space with partial acromioplasty, with or without coracoacromial release** ③ T 50 80 📄
MED: 100-2, 15, 260; 100-3, 100.2; 100-4, 12, 90.3; 100-4, 14, 10

AMA: 2001, May, 8

To report open procedure, consult CPT code 23130 or 23415.

29827 **Arthroscopy, shoulder, surgical; with rotator cuff repair** ⑤ T 50 80 📄
MED: 100-2, 15, 260; 100-3, 100.2; 100-4, 12, 90.3; 100-4, 14, 10

To report open or mini-open repair, consult CPT code 23412.

If arthroscopic subacromial decompression is performed at the same time, consult CPT code 29826, and append modifier 51.

If arthroscopic distal clavicle resection is performed at the same time, consult CPT code 29824, and append modifier 51.

29830 **Arthroscopy, elbow, diagnostic, with or without synovial biopsy (separate procedure)** ③ T 50 📄
MED: 100-2, 15, 260; 100-3, 100.2; 100-4, 12, 90.3; 100-4, 14, 10

29834 **Arthroscopy, elbow, surgical; with removal of loose body or foreign body** ③ T 50 80 📄
MED: 100-2, 15, 260; 100-3, 100.2; 100-4, 12, 90.3; 100-4, 14, 10

29835   synovectomy, partial   **3** T 50 80 ↻
MED: 100-2, 15, 260; 100-3, 100.2; 100-4, 12, 90.3; 100-4, 14, 10

29836   synovectomy, complete   **3** T 50 80 ↻
MED: 100-2, 15, 260; 100-3, 100.2; 100-4, 12, 90.3; 100-4, 14, 10

29837   debridement, limited   **3** T 50 80 ↻
MED: 100-2, 15, 260; 100-3, 100.2; 100-4, 12, 90.3; 100-4, 14, 10

29838   debridement, extensive   **3** T 50 80 ↻
MED: 100-2, 15, 260; 100-3, 100.2; 100-4, 12, 90.3; 100-4, 14, 10

29840   Arthroscopy, wrist, diagnostic, with or without synovial biopsy (separate procedure)   **3** T 50 80 ↻
MED: 100-2, 15, 260; 100-3, 100.2; 100-4, 12, 90.3; 100-4, 14, 10

29843   Arthroscopy, wrist, surgical; for infection, lavage and drainage   **3** T 50 80 ↻
MED: 100-2, 15, 260; 100-3, 100.2; 100-4, 12, 90.3; 100-4, 14, 10

29844   synovectomy, partial   **3** T 50 80 ↻
MED: 100-2, 15, 260; 100-3, 100.2; 100-4, 12, 90.3; 100-4, 14, 10

29845   synovectomy, complete   **3** T 50 80 ↻
MED: 100-2, 15, 260; 100-3, 100.2; 100-4, 12, 90.3; 100-4, 14, 10

29846   excision and/or repair of triangular fibrocartilage and/or joint debridement   **3** T 50 80 ↻
MED: 100-2, 15, 260; 100-3, 100.2; 100-4, 12, 90.3; 100-4, 14, 10

29847   internal fixation for fracture or instability   **3** T 50 80 ↻
MED: 100-2, 15, 260; 100-3, 100.2; 100-4, 12, 90.3; 100-4, 14, 10

29848   Endoscopy, wrist, surgical, with release of transverse carpal ligament   **9** T 50 ↻
MED: 100-2, 15, 260; 100-3, 100.2; 100-4, 12, 90.3; 100-4, 14, 10

AMA: 1999, Dec, 7

If this is an open procedure, consult CPT code 64721.

29850   Arthroscopically aided treatment of intercondylar spine(s) and/or tuberosity fracture(s) of the knee, with or without manipulation; without internal or external fixation (includes arthroscopy)   **4** T 50 80 ↻
MED: 100-2, 15, 260; 100-3, 100.2; 100-4, 12, 90.3; 100-4, 14, 10

29851   with internal or external fixation (includes arthroscopy)   **4** T 50 80 ↻
MED: 100-2, 15, 260; 100-3, 100.2; 100-4, 12, 90.3; 100-4, 14, 10

If a bone graft is performed, consult CPT codes 20900 and 20902.

29855   Arthroscopically aided treatment of tibial fracture, proximal (plateau); unicondylar, with or without internal or external fixation (includes arthroscopy)   **4** T 50 80 ↻
MED: 100-2, 15, 260; 100-3, 100.2; 100-4, 12, 90.3; 100-4, 14, 10

If a bone graft is performed, consult CPT codes 20900 and 20902.

29856   bicondylar, with or without internal or external fixation (includes arthroscopy)   **4** T 50 80 ↻
MED: 100-2, 15, 260; 100-3, 100.2; 100-4, 12, 90.3; 100-4, 14, 10

29860   **Arthroscopy, hip, diagnostic with or without synovial biopsy (separate procedure)** 4 T 50 80 ▶
> MED: 100-2, 15, 260; 100-3, 100.2; 100-4, 12, 90.3; 100-4, 14, 10
>
> AMA: 1998, Jul, 8; 1997, Nov, 15

29861   **Arthroscopy, hip, surgical; with removal of loose body or foreign body** 4 T 50 80 ▶
> MED: 100-2, 15, 260; 100-3, 100.2; 100-4, 12, 90.3; 100-4, 14, 10
>
> AMA: 1998, Jul, 8; 1997, Nov, 15

29862   **Arthroscopy, hip, surgical; with debridement/shaving of articular cartilage (chondroplasty), abrasion arthroplasty, and/or resection of labrum** 9 T 50 80 ▶
> MED: 100-2, 15, 260; 100-3, 100.2; 100-4, 12, 90.3; 100-4, 14, 10
>
> AMA: 1998, Jul, 8; 1997, Nov, 15

29863   **Arthroscopy, hip, surgical; with synovectomy** 4 T 50 80 ▶
> MED: 100-2, 15, 260; 100-3, 100.2; 100-4, 12, 90.3; 100-4, 14, 10
>
> AMA: 1998, Jul, 8; 1997, Nov, 15

29866   **Arthroscopy, knee, surgical; osteochondral autograft(s) (eg, mosaicplasty) (includes harvesting of the autograft)** T 50 80 ▶
> Code 29866 cannot be reported with CPT codes 29870, 29871, 29875, 29884 when performed at the same session and/or CPT codes 29874, 29877, 29879, 29885-29887 when performed in the same compartment.

29867   **osteochondral allograft (eg, mosaicplasty)** T 50 80 ▶
> Code 29867 cannot be reported with CPT codes 27570, 29870, 29871, 29875, and 29884 when performed at the same session and/or CPT codes 29874, 29877, 29879, 29885-29887 when performed in the same compartment.
>
> Code 29867 cannot be reported with CPT code 27415.

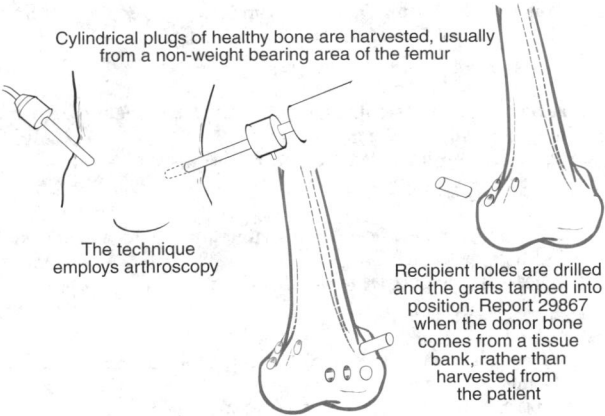

Cylindrical plugs of healthy bone are harvested, usually from a non-weight bearing area of the femur

The technique employs arthroscopy

Recipient holes are drilled and the grafts tamped into position. Report 29867 when the donor bone comes from a tissue bank, rather than harvested from the patient

29868   **meniscal transplantation (includes arthrotomy for meniscal insertion), medial or lateral** T 50 80 ▶

| ▶ CCI Comp | 50 Bilateral Procedure | + CPT Add-on Code | ⊘ Modifier -51 Exempt | ♂ Male | ♀ Female |
| ● New Code | ▲ Revised Code | M Maternity Edit | A Age Edit | A–Y APC Status Ind. | AMA: CPT Assistant |

© 2005 Ingenix, Inc. *(Blue Ink)*   CPT only © 2005 American Medical Association. All Rights Reserved. *(Black Ink)*   Surgery — 215

Musculoskeletal System

29868 — 29881

Code 29868 cannot be reported with CPT codes 29870, 29871, 29875, 29880, 29883, 29884 when performed at the same session or CPT code 29874, 29877, 29881, or 29882 when performed in the same compartment.

29870 **Arthroscopy, knee, diagnostic, with or without synovial biopsy (separate procedure)** 3 T 50 ↻
MED: 100-2, 15, 260; 100-3, 100.2; 100-4, 12, 90.3; 100-4, 14, 10

To report open autologous chondrocyte implantation of the knee, consult CPT code 27412.

29871 **Arthroscopy, knee, surgical; for infection, lavage and drainage** 3 T 50 ↻
MED: 100-2, 15, 260; 100-3, 100.2; 100-4, 12, 90.3; 100-4, 14, 10

AMA: 2001, Aug, 5

To report implantation of osteochondral graft to treat an articular surface defect, consult CPT codes 27412, 27415, 29866, and 29867.

29873 **Arthroscopy, knee, surgical; with lateral release** 3 T 50 ↻
MED: 100-3, 100.2

To report open lateral release, consult CPT code 27425.

29874 **for removal of loose body or foreign body (eg, osteochondritis dissecans fragmentation, chondral fragmentation)** 3 T 50 80 ↻
MED: 100-2, 15, 260; 100-3, 100.2; 100-4, 12, 90.3; 100-4, 14, 10

AMA: 2001, Aug, 5

29875 **synovectomy, limited (eg, plica or shelf resection) (separate procedure)** 4 T 50 80 ↻
MED: 100-2, 15, 260; 100-3, 100.2; 100-4, 12, 90.3; 100-4, 14, 10

AMA: 2001, Aug, 5

29876 **synovectomy, major, two or more compartments (eg, medial or lateral)** 4 T 50 ↻
MED: 100-2, 15, 260; 100-3, 100.2; 100-4, 12, 90.3; 100-4, 14, 10

AMA: 2001, Aug, 5

29877 **debridement/shaving of articular cartilage (chondroplasty)** 4 T 50 80 ↻
MED: 100-2, 15, 260; 100-3, 100.2; 100-4, 12, 90.3; 100-4, 14, 10

AMA: 2001, Aug, 5; 1999, Jun, 11; 1996, Feb, 9

29879 **abrasion arthroplasty (includes chondroplasty where necessary) or multiple drilling or microfracture** 3 T 50 80 ↻
MED: 100-2, 15, 260; 100-3, 100.2; 100-4, 12, 90.3; 100-4, 14, 10

AMA: 2001, Aug, 5; 1999, Nov, 13

29880 **with meniscectomy (medial AND lateral, including any meniscal shaving)** 4 T 50 80 ↻
MED: 100-2, 15, 260; 100-3, 100.2; 100-4, 12, 90.3; 100-4, 14, 10

AMA: 2001, Aug, 5; 1999, Jun, 11

29881 **with meniscectomy (medial OR lateral, including any meniscal shaving)** 4 T 50 80 ↻
MED: 100-2, 15, 260; 100-3, 100.2; 100-4, 12, 90.3; 100-4, 14, 10

AMA: 2001, Aug, 5; 1999, Jun, 11; 1996, Feb, 9

29882 **with meniscus repair (medial OR lateral)** 3 T 50 ↻
MED: 100-2, 15, 260; 100-3, 100.2; 100-4, 12, 90.3; 100-4, 14, 10

AMA: 2001, Aug, 5

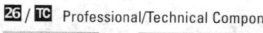 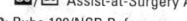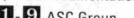

29883   **with meniscus repair (medial AND lateral)**   3️⃣ T 50 80 🔾
MED: 100-2, 15, 260; 100-3, 100.2; 100-4, 12, 90.3; 100-4, 14, 10

AMA: 2001, Aug, 5

To report meniscal transplantation, medial or lateral, knee, consult CPT code 29868.

29884   **with lysis of adhesions, with or without manipulation (separate procedure)**   3️⃣ T 50 80 🔾
MED: 100-2, 15, 260; 100-3, 100.2; 100-4, 12, 90.3; 100-4, 14, 10

AMA: 2001, Aug, 5

29885   **drilling for osteochondritis dissecans with bone grafting, with or without internal fixation (including debridement of base of lesion)**   3️⃣ T 50 80 🔾
MED: 100-2, 15, 260; 100-3, 100.2; 100-4, 12, 90.3; 100-4, 14, 10

AMA: 2001, Aug, 5

29886   **drilling for intact osteochondritis dissecans lesion**   3️⃣ T 50 🔾
MED: 100-2, 15, 260; 100-3, 100.2; 100-4, 12, 90.3; 100-4, 14, 10

AMA: 2001, Aug, 5

29887   **drilling for intact osteochondritis dissecans lesion with internal fixation**   3️⃣ T 50 80 🔾
MED: 100-2, 15, 260; 100-3, 100.2; 100-4, 12, 90.3; 100-4, 14, 10

AMA: 2001, Aug, 5

29888   **Arthroscopically aided anterior cruciate ligament repair/augmentation or reconstruction**   3️⃣ T 50 80 🔾
MED: 100-2, 15, 260; 100-3, 100.2; 100-4, 12, 90.3; 100-4, 14, 10

Note that 29888 and 29889 should not be reported in conjunction with reconstructive procedures 27427-27429.

29889   **Arthroscopically aided posterior cruciate ligament repair/augmentation or reconstruction**   3️⃣ T 50 80 🔾
MED: 100-2, 15, 260; 100-3, 100.2; 100-4, 12, 90.3; 100-4, 14, 10

AMA: 2001, Aug, 8; 1998, Oct, 11; 1996, Sep, 9

29891   **Arthroscopy, ankle, surgical, excision of osteochondral defect of talus and/or tibia, including drilling of the defect**   3️⃣ T 50 80 🔾
MED: 100-2, 15, 260; 100-3, 100.2; 100-4, 12, 90.3; 100-4, 14, 10

29892   **Arthroscopically aided repair of large osteochondritis dissecans lesion, talar dome fracture, or tibial plafond fracture, with or without internal fixation (includes arthroscopy)**   3️⃣ T 50 80 🔾
MED: 100-2, 15, 260; 100-3, 100.2; 100-4, 12, 90.3; 100-4, 14, 10

AMA: 1997, Nov, 15

29893   **Endoscopic plantar fasciotomy**   9️⃣ T 50 80 🔾
MED: 100-2, 15, 260; 100-3, 100.2; 100-4, 12, 90.3; 100-4, 14, 10

AMA: 1997, Nov, 15

29894   **Arthroscopy, ankle (tibiotalar and fibulotalar joints), surgical; with removal of loose body or foreign body**   3️⃣ T 50 80 🔾
MED: 100-2, 15, 260; 100-3, 100.2; 100-4, 12, 90.3; 100-4, 14, 10

29895   **synovectomy, partial**   3️⃣ T 50 80 🔾
MED: 100-2, 15, 260; 100-3, 100.2; 100-4, 12, 90.3; 100-4, 14, 10

29897	**debridement, limited**	3 T 50 80 ▶
	MED: 100-2, 15, 260; 100-3, 100.2; 100-4, 12, 90.3; 100-4, 14, 10	
29898	**debridement, extensive**	3 T 50 80 ▶
	MED: 100-2, 15, 260; 100-3, 100.2; 100-4, 12, 90.3; 100-4, 14, 10	
29899	**with ankle arthrodesis**	3 T 50 80 ▶
	MED: 100-2, 15, 260; 100-3, 100.2; 100-4, 12, 90.3; 100-4, 14, 10	

To report open ankle arthrodesis, consult CPT code 27870.

29900	**Arthroscopy, metacarpophalangeal joint, diagnostic, includes synovial biopsy**	3 T 50 80 ▶
	MED: 100-2, 15, 260; 100-3, 100.2; 100-4, 12, 90.3; 100-4, 14, 10	

Code 29900 should not be reported with CPT codes 29901, 29902.

29901	**Arthroscopy, metacarpophalangeal joint, surgical; with debridement**	3 T 50 80 ▶
	MED: 100-2, 15, 260; 100-3, 100.2; 100-4, 12, 90.3; 100-4, 14, 10	
29902	**with reduction of displaced ulnar collateral ligament (eg, Stenar lesion)**	3 T 50 80 ▶
	MED: 100-2, 15, 260; 100-3, 100.2; 100-4, 12, 90.3; 100-4, 14, 10	
29999	**Unlisted procedure, arthroscopy**	T 50 80 ▶
	MED: 100-3, 100.2	

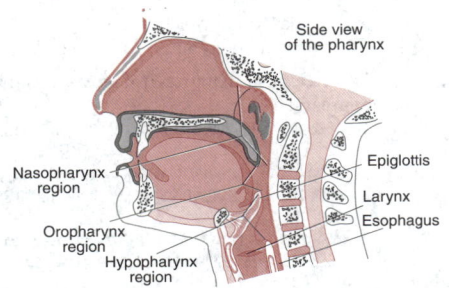

Side view
of the pharynx

Nasopharynx
region

Oropharynx
region

Hypopharynx
region

Epiglottis

Larynx

Esophagus

The nasopharynx is the membranous passage above the level of the soft
palate; the oropharynx is the region between the soft palate and the upper
edge of the epiglottis; the hypopharynx is the region of the epiglottis to the
juncture of the larynx and esophagus; the three regions are collectively
known as the pharynx

RESPIRATORY SYSTEM

NOSE

INCISION

30000 **Drainage abscess or hematoma, nasal, internal approach** T 80

If this procedure requires an external approach, consult CPT codes 10060 and
10140.

30020 **Drainage abscess or hematoma, nasal septum** T

If a lateral rhinotomy is performed, consult specific application (eg, 30118,
30320).

EXCISION

30100 **Biopsy, intranasal** T

If the skin of the nose is biopsied, consult CPT codes 11100 and 11101.

30110 **Excision, nasal polyp(s), simple** T 50

Note that 30110 is generally performed in an office setting. If a bilateral
procedure is performed, append modifier 50.

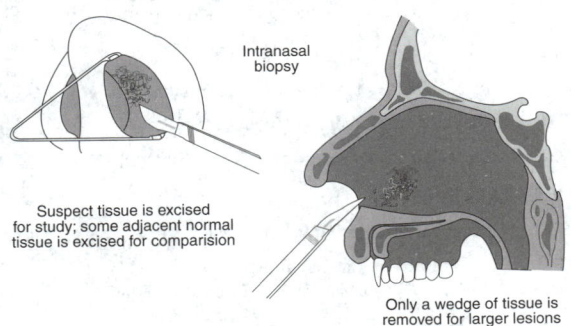

Intranasal
biopsy

Suspect tissue is excised
for study; some adjacent normal
tissue is excised for comparision

Only a wedge of tissue is
removed for larger lesions

Respiratory System

30115 — 30320

30115   **Excision, nasal polyp(s), extensive**
MED: 100-2, 15, 260; 100-4, 12, 90.3; 100-4, 14, 10

Note that 30115 generally requires the facilities available in a hospital setting. If a bilateral procedure is performed, append modifier 50.

30117   **Excision or destruction (eg, laser), intranasal lesion; internal approach**
MED: 100-2, 15, 260; 100-3, 140.5; 100-4, 12, 90.3; 100-4, 14, 10

30118   **external approach (lateral rhinotomy)**
MED: 100-2, 15, 260; 100-3, 140.5; 100-4, 12, 90.3; 100-4, 14, 10

30120   **Excision or surgical planing of skin of nose for rhinophyma**
MED: 100-2, 15, 260; 100-4, 12, 90.3; 100-4, 14, 10

30124   **Excision dermoid cyst, nose; simple, skin, subcutaneous**

30125   **complex, under bone or cartilage**
MED: 100-2, 15, 260; 100-4, 12, 90.3; 100-4, 14, 10

▲ **30130**   **Excision inferior turbinate, partial or complete, any method**
MED: 100-2, 15, 260; 100-4, 12, 90.3; 100-4, 14, 10

AMA: 2001, Sep, 10; 1998, Nov, 11; 1998, Feb, 11

To report excision of superior or middle turbinate, consult 30999.

▲ **30140**   **Submucous resection inferior turbinate, partial or complete, any method**
MED: 100-2, 15, 260; 100-4, 12, 90.3; 100-4, 14, 10

AMA: 2002, Dec, 10; 1998, Nov, 11

Codes 30130 and 30140 cannot be reported with 30801, 30802, 30930. If a submucous resection of the superior or middle turbinate is performed, consult CPT code 30999. If an endoscopic resecion of the concha bullosa of the middle turbinate is performed, consult CPT code 31240.

30150   **Rhinectomy; partial**
MED: 100-2, 15, 260; 100-4, 12, 90.3; 100-4, 14, 10

If primary or delayed closure and/or reconstruction is performed, consult the Integumentary System (13150-13152, 14060-14300, 15120, 15121, 15260, 15261, 15760, and 20900-20912).

30160   **total**
MED: 100-2, 15, 260; 100-4, 12, 90.3; 100-4, 14, 10

If primary or delayed closure and/or reconstruction is needed, consult the Integumentary System codes (13150-13160, 14060-14300, 15120, 15121, 15260, 15261, 15760, and 20900-20912).

INTRODUCTION

30200   **Injection into turbinate(s), therapeutic**

30210   **Displacement therapy (Proetz type)**

30220   **Insertion, nasal septal prosthesis (button)**

REMOVAL OF FOREIGN BODY

30300   **Removal foreign body, intranasal; office type procedure**

30310   **requiring general anesthesia**
MED: 100-2, 15, 260; 100-4, 12, 90.3; 100-4, 14, 10

30320   **by lateral rhinotomy**
MED: 100-2, 15, 260; 100-4, 12, 90.3; 100-4, 14, 10

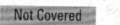 **26** / **TC** Professional/Technical Component   **80** / **80** Assist-at-Surgery Allowed/With Documentation   ⊙ Conscious Sedation

Unlisted   Not Covered   **MED:** Pubs 100/NCD Reference   **1** - **9** ASC Group   ⑥③ Modifier 63 Exempt

220 — Surgery   CPT only © 2005 American Medical Association. All Rights Reserved. *(Black Ink)*   © 2005 Ingenix, Inc. *(Blue Ink)*

REPAIR

If obtaining tissues for a graft, consult CPT codes 20900-20926 and 21210.

30400   **Rhinoplasty, primary; lateral and alar cartilages and/or elevation of nasal tip**   4 T 80 �
   MED: 100-2, 15, 260; 100-4, 12, 90.3; 100-4, 14, 10

   If columellar reconstruction is performed, consult CPT codes 13150-13153.
   Carpue's operation

30410   **complete, external parts including bony pyramid, lateral and alar cartilages, and/or elevation of nasal tip**   5 T 80 �
      MED: 100-2, 15, 260; 100-4, 12, 90.3; 100-4, 14, 10

30420   **including major septal repair**   5 T �
      MED: 100-2, 15, 260; 100-4, 12, 90.3; 100-4, 14, 10

30430   **Rhinoplasty, secondary; minor revision (small amount of nasal tip work)**   3 T 80 �
   MED: 100-2, 15, 260; 100-4, 12, 90.3; 100-4, 14, 10

30435   **intermediate revision (bony work with osteotomies)**   5 T 80 �
      MED: 100-2, 15, 260; 100-4, 12, 90.3; 100-4, 14, 10

30450   **major revision (nasal tip work and osteotomies)**   7 T 80 �
      MED: 100-2, 15, 260; 100-4, 12, 90.3; 100-4, 14, 10

30460   **Rhinoplasty for nasal deformity secondary to congenital cleft lip and/or palate, including columellar lengthening; tip only**   7 T 80 �
   MED: 100-2, 15, 260; 100-4, 12, 90.3; 100-4, 14, 10

30462   **tip, septum, osteotomies**   9 T 80 �
      MED: 100-2, 15, 260; 100-4, 12, 90.3; 100-4, 14, 10

30465   **Repair of nasal vestibular stenosis (eg, spreader grafting, lateral nasal wall reconstruction)**   9 T 80 �
   MED: 100-2, 15, 260; 100-4, 12, 90.3; 100-4, 14, 10

   Code 30465 is used to report a bilateral procedure. if the procedure is done as a unilateral procedure, append with modifier 52. If a graft procedure is performed, consult CPT codes 20900-20926 and 21210.

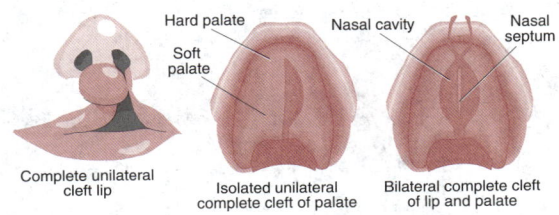

Cleft lip and cleft palate are described according to length of cleft and whether bilateral or unilateral

Hard palate   Nasal cavity   Nasal septum
Soft palate

Complete unilateral cleft lip

Isolated unilateral complete cleft of palate

Bilateral complete cleft of lip and palate

Cleft lip with or without cleft palate is a common birth defect and is seen once or twice per 1000 live births; the condition is twice as common among boys than girls; isolated cleft palate is distinct from cleft lip with or without cleft palate and occurs about once in 2000 births; the condition is more common among girls than boys

---

Respiratory System

30520 — 30802

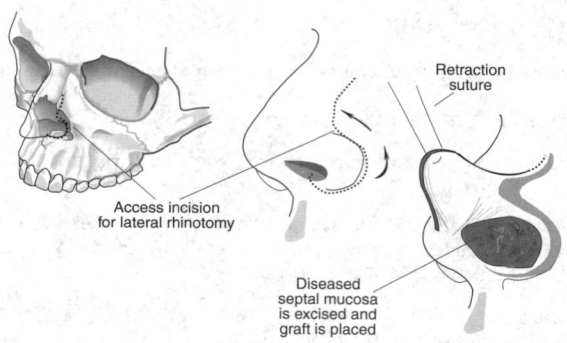

Retraction
suture

Access incision
for lateral rhinotomy

Diseased
septal mucosa
is excised and
graft is placed

30520	**Septoplasty or submucous resection, with or without cartilage scoring, contouring or replacement with graft**	4 T ↻

MED: 100-2, 15, 260; 100-4, 12, 90.3; 100-4, 14, 10

AMA: 2002, Dec, 10; 1997, Oct, 11

If submucous resection of the turbinates is performed, consult CPT code 30140.

30540	**Repair choanal atresia; intranasal**	5 T 80 ↻

MED: 100-2, 15, 260; 100-4, 12, 90.3; 100-4, 14, 10

30545	**transpalatine**	5 T 80 ↻ 63

MED: 100-2, 15, 260; 100-4, 12, 90.3; 100-4, 14, 10

30560	**Lysis intranasal synechia**	2 T ↻

MED: 100-2, 15, 260; 100-4, 12, 90.3; 100-4, 14, 10

30580	**Repair fistula; oromaxillary (combine with 31030 if antrotomy is included)**	4 T ↻

MED: 100-2, 15, 260; 100-4, 12, 90.3; 100-4, 14, 10

30600	**oronasal**	4 T 80 ↻

MED: 100-2, 15, 260; 100-4, 12, 90.3; 100-4, 14, 10

30620	**Septal or other intranasal dermatoplasty (does not include obtaining graft)**	7 T ↻

MED: 100-2, 15, 260; 100-4, 12, 90.3; 100-4, 14, 10

30630	**Repair nasal septal perforations**	7 T 80 ↻

MED: 100-2, 15, 260; 100-4, 12, 90.3; 100-4, 14, 10

DESTRUCTION

▲ **30801**	**Cautery and/or ablation, mucosa of inferior turbinates, unilateral or bilateral, any method; superficial**	1 T ↻

MED: 100-2, 15, 260; 100-4, 12, 90.3; 100-4, 14, 10

To report cautery and ablation of the superior or middle turbinates, consult 30999.

▲ **30802**	**intramural**	1 T ↻

MED: 100-2, 15, 260; 100-4, 12, 90.3; 100-4, 14, 10

Codes 30801 and 30802, and 30930 cannot be reported with 30130 or 30140. Consult CPT codes 30901-30906 for cautery to control nasal hemorrhage.

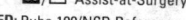

OTHER PROCEDURES

30901   Control nasal hemorrhage, anterior, simple (limited cautery and/or packing) any method   [T] [50] [↻]

30903   Control nasal hemorrhage, anterior, complex (extensive cautery and/or packing) any method   [1] [T] [50] [↻]
   MED: 100-2, 15, 260; 100-4, 12, 90.3; 100-4, 14, 10

30905   Control nasal hemorrhage, posterior, with posterior nasal packs and/or cautery, any method; initial   [1] [T] [↻]
   MED: 100-2, 15, 260; 100-4, 12, 90.3; 100-4, 14, 10

30906   subsequent   [1] [T] [↻]
   MED: 100-2, 15, 260; 100-4, 12, 90.3; 100-4, 14, 10

30915   Ligation arteries; ethmoidal   [2] [T] [↻]
   MED: 100-2, 15, 260; 100-4, 12, 90.3; 100-4, 14, 10

   If the external carotid artery is ligated, consult CPT code 37600.

30920   internal maxillary artery, transantral   [3] [T] [↻]
   MED: 100-2, 15, 260; 100-4, 12, 90.3; 100-4, 14, 10

   If the external carotid artery is ligated, consult CPT code 37600.

▲ **30930**   Fracture nasal inferior turbinate(s), therapeutic   [4] [T] [50] [↻]
   MED: 100-2, 15, 260; 100-4, 12, 90.3; 100-4, 14, 10

   AMA: 2002, Dec, 10; 2001, Jul, 11

   Codes 30801, 30802, 30930 cannot be reported with 30130 or 30140.

   To report fracture of superior or middle turbinate(s), consult 30999.

30999   Unlisted procedure, nose   [T] [80]

ACCESSORY SINUSES

INCISION

31000   Lavage by cannulation; maxillary sinus (antrum puncture or natural ostium)   [T] [50] [↻]

   If a bilateral procedure is performed, append modifier 50.

31002   sphenoid sinus   [T] [50] [80] [↻]

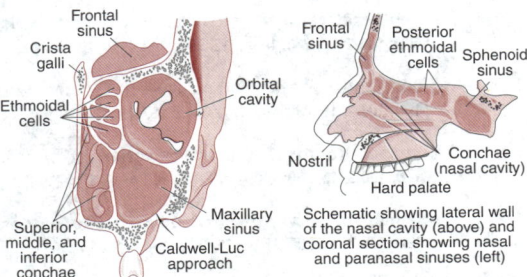

Frontal sinus
Crista galli
Ethmoidal cells
Orbital cavity
Superior, middle, and inferior conchae
Maxillary sinus
Caldwell-Luc approach

Frontal sinus
Posterior ethmoidal cells
Sphenoid sinus
Nostril
Conchae (nasal cavity)
Hard palate

Schematic showing lateral wall of the nasal cavity (above) and coronal section showing nasal and paranasal sinuses (left)

The nasal sinuses are air filled cavities in the cranial bones that bear their names; all are lined with mucous membrane continuous with the nasal cavity and all drain fluids into the nasal cavity. The ethmoid cells vary in size and number and feature very thin septa, or walls. The maxillary sinuses are the largest and are the most frequently infected.

Respiratory System

31020 — 31090

31020   **Sinusotomy, maxillary (antrotomy); intranasal**   ② T 50 ⟳
MED: 100-2, 15, 260; 100-4, 12, 90.3; 100-4, 14, 10

If a bilateral procedure is performed, append modifier 50.

31030   **radical (Caldwell-Luc) without removal of antrochoanal polyps**   ③ T 50 ⟳
MED: 100-2, 15, 260; 100-4, 12, 90.3; 100-4, 14, 10

If a bilateral procedure is performed, append modifier 50.

31032   **radical (Caldwell-Luc) with removal of antrochoanal polyps**   ④ T 50 ⟳
MED: 100-2, 15, 260; 100-4, 12, 90.3; 100-4, 14, 10

If a bilateral procedure is performed, append modifier 50.

31040   **Pterygomaxillary fossa surgery, any approach**   T ⟳

If a transantral ligation of the internal maxillary artery is performed, consult CPT code 30920.

31050   **Sinusotomy, sphenoid, with or without biopsy;**   ② T 50 ⟳
MED: 100-2, 15, 260; 100-4, 12, 90.3; 100-4, 14, 10

31051   **with mucosal stripping or removal of polyp(s)**   ④ T 50 ⟳
MED: 100-2, 15, 260; 100-4, 12, 90.3; 100-4, 14, 10

31070   **Sinusotomy frontal; external, simple (trephine operation)**   ② T 50 ⟳
MED: 100-2, 15, 260; 100-4, 12, 90.3; 100-4, 14, 10

If a frontal intranasal sinusotomy is performed, consult CPT code 31726.
Killian operation

31075   **transorbital, unilateral (for mucocele or osteoma, Lynch type)**   ④ T 50 80 ⟳
MED: 100-2, 15, 260; 100-4, 12, 90.3; 100-4, 14, 10

31080   **obliterative without osteoplastic flap, brow incision (includes ablation)**   ④ T 50 80 ⟳
MED: 100-2, 15, 260; 100-4, 12, 90.3; 100-4, 14, 10

Ridell sinusotomy

31081   **obliterative, without osteoplastic flap, coronal incision (includes ablation)**   ④ T 50 80 ⟳
MED: 100-2, 15, 260; 100-4, 12, 90.3; 100-4, 14, 10

31084   **obliterative, with osteoplastic flap, brow incision**   ④ T 50 80 ⟳
MED: 100-2, 15, 260; 100-4, 12, 90.3; 100-4, 14, 10

31085   **obliterative, with osteoplastic flap, coronal incision**   ④ T 50 80 ⟳
MED: 100-2, 15, 260; 100-4, 12, 90.3; 100-4, 14, 10

31086   **nonobliterative, with osteoplastic flap, brow incision**   ④ T 50 80 ⟳
MED: 100-2, 15, 260; 100-4, 12, 90.3; 100-4, 14, 10

31087   **nonobliterative, with osteoplastic flap, coronal incision**   ④ T 50 80 ⟳
MED: 100-2, 15, 260; 100-4, 12, 90.3; 100-4, 14, 10

31090   **Sinusotomy, unilateral, three or more paranasal sinuses (frontal, maxillary, ethmoid, sphenoid)**   ⑤ T 50 ⟳
MED: 100-2, 15, 260; 100-4, 12, 90.3; 100-4, 14, 10

AMA: 1998, Nov, 11; 1997, Nov, 15

EXCISION

31200   **Ethmoidectomy; intranasal, anterior**   2️⃣ T 50 🔲
MED: 100-2, 15, 260; 100-4, 12, 90.3; 100-4, 14, 10

31201   **intranasal, total**   5️⃣ T 50 🔲
MED: 100-2, 15, 260; 100-4, 12, 90.3; 100-4, 14, 10

31205   **extranasal, total**   3️⃣ T 50 80 🔲
MED: 100-2, 15, 260; 100-4, 12, 90.3; 100-4, 14, 10

31225   **Maxillectomy; without orbital exenteration**   C 50 80 🔲

31230   **with orbital exenteration (en bloc)**   C 50 80 🔲

If only orbital exenteration is performed, consult CPT codes 65110 and subsequent codes. If skin grafts are necessary, consult CPT codes 15120 and subsequent codes.

ENDOSCOPY

Sinus endoscopies include the examination of all parts of the sinuses, including the nasal cavity to the turbinates, and the spheno-ethmoid recess. Any sinusotomy performed during the examination is included in these codes.

Unless otherwise stated, CPT codes 31231-31294 report unilateral procedures. If these procedures are performed bilaterally, append modifier 50.

31231   **Nasal endoscopy, diagnostic, unilateral or bilateral (separate procedure)**   T 🔲
MED: 100-3, 100.2; 100-4, 12, 40.6

AMA: 1997, Jan, 4

31233   **Nasal/sinus endoscopy, diagnostic with maxillary sinusoscopy (via inferior meatus or canine fossa puncture)**   2️⃣ T 50 🔲
MED: 100-2, 15, 260; 100-3, 100.2; 100-4, 12, 40.6; 100-4, 12, 90.3; 100-4, 14, 10

AMA: 1997, Jan, 4

31235   **Nasal/sinus endoscopy, diagnostic with sphenoid sinusoscopy (via puncture of sphenoidal face or cannulation of ostium)**   1️⃣ T 50 🔲
MED: 100-2, 15, 260; 100-3, 100.2; 100-4, 12, 40.6; 100-4, 12, 90.3; 100-4, 14, 10

AMA: 1997, Jan, 4

31237   **Nasal/sinus endoscopy, surgical; with biopsy, polypectomy or debridement (separate procedure)**   2️⃣ T 50 🔲
MED: 100-2, 15, 260; 100-3, 100.2; 100-4, 12, 40.6; 100-4, 12, 90.3; 100-4, 14, 10

AMA: 2001, Dec, 6; 1997, Jan, 4

31238   **with control of nasal hemorrhage**   1️⃣ T 50 80 🔲
MED: 100-2, 15, 260; 100-4, 12, 40.6; 100-4, 12, 90.3; 100-4, 14, 10

AMA: 1997, Jan, 4

31239   **with dacryocystorhinostomy**   4️⃣ T 50 80 🔲
MED: 100-2, 15, 260; 100-4, 12, 40.6; 100-4, 12, 90.3; 100-4, 14, 10

AMA: 1997, Jan, 4

31240   **with concha bullosa resection**   2️⃣ T 50 80 🔲
MED: 100-2, 15, 260; 100-4, 12, 40.6; 100-4, 12, 90.3; 100-4, 14, 10

AMA: 1997, Jan, 4

Respiratory System

31254 — 31267

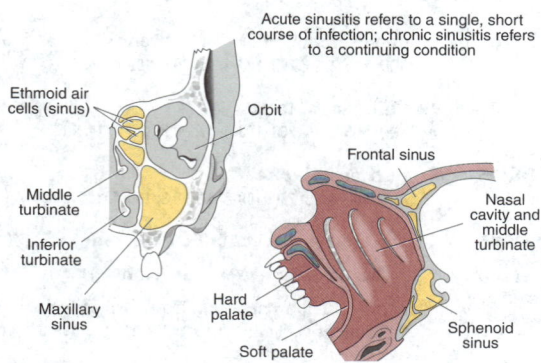

Acute sinusitis refers to a single, short course of infection; chronic sinusitis refers to a continuing condition

Ethmoid air cells (sinus)
Orbit
Frontal sinus
Middle turbinate
Nasal cavity and middle turbinate
Inferior turbinate
Maxillary sinus
Hard palate
Sphenoid sinus
Soft palate

If an endoscopic osteomeatal complex (OMC) resection with antrostomy and/or anterior ethmoidectomy, with or without polyp removal is performed, consult CPT codes 31254 and 31256. For OMC resection with antrostomy, removal of antral mucosal disease, and/or anterior ethmoidectomy, with or without polyp removal, consult codes 31254 and 31267, For endoscopic frontal sinus exploration, OMC resection and/or anterior ethmoidectomy, with or without polyp removal, consult codes 31254 and 31276; and when antrostomy is also performed, consult codes 31254, 31256, and 31276. Consult codes 31231-31235 for an endoscopic nasal diagnostic endoscopy. For OMC resection, frontal sinus exploration, antrostomy, removal of antral mucosal disease, and/or anterior ethmoidectomy, with or without the removal of polyps, consult CPT codes 31254, 31267, and 31276.

31254 **Nasal/sinus endoscopy, surgical; with ethmoidectomy, partial (anterior)** 3 T 50 ⬛

MED: 100-2, 15, 260; 100-3, 100.2; 100-4, 12, 40.6; 100-4, 12, 90.3; 100-4, 14, 10

AMA: 2001, Dec, 6; 1997, Sep, 10; 1997, Oct, 5; 1997, Jan, 4

31255 **with ethmoidectomy, total (anterior and posterior)** 5 T 50 ⬛

MED: 100-2, 15, 260; 100-4, 12, 40.6; 100-4, 12, 90.3; 100-4, 14, 10

AMA: 2002, Dec, 10; 1997, Jan, 4

31256 **Nasal/sinus endoscopy, surgical, with maxillary antrostomy;** 3 T 50 ⬛

MED: 100-2, 15, 260; 100-3, 100.2; 100-4, 12, 40.6; 100-4, 12, 90.3; 100-4, 14, 10

AMA: 1997, Jan, 4

If an endoscopic anterior and posterior ethmoidectomy (APE), and antrostomy with or without polyp(s) removal is performed, consult CPT codes 31255 and 31256. When APE, antrostomy and removal of antral mucosal disease, with or without polyp(s) removal is performed, consult CPT codes 31255 and 31267. When APE, frontal sinus exploration, with or without polyp(s) removal is performed, consult CPT codes 31255 and 31276.

31267 **with removal of tissue from maxillary sinus** 3 T 50 ⬛

MED: 100-2, 15, 260; 100-4, 12, 40.6; 100-4, 12, 90.3; 100-4, 14, 10

AMA: 2001, Dec, 6; 1997, Jan, 4

If an endoscopic anterior and posterior ethmoidectomy (APE), frontal sinus exploration, and antrostomy, with or without polyp(s) removal is performed, consult CPT codes 31255, 31256,and 31276. When APE, frontal sinus exploration, antrostomy and removal of antral mucosal disease, with or without polyp(s) removal is performed, consult CPT codes 31255, 31267, and 31276.

31276 **Nasal/sinus endoscopy, surgical with frontal sinus exploration, with or without removal of tissue from frontal sinus** 3 T 50 ⌂
MED: 100-2, 15, 260; 100-3, 100.2; 100-4, 12, 40.6; 100-4, 12, 90.3; 100-4, 14, 10

AMA: 1997, Jan, 4

Consult CPT codes 31231-31235 for unilateral endoscopy of two or more sinuses. If an endoscopic anterior and posterior ethmoidectomy and spenoidotomy (APS), with or without polyp(s) removal is performed, consult CPT codes 31255, 31287, or 31288. For APS and antrostomy, with or without polyp(s) removal, consult codes 31255, 31256, and 31287 or 31288. For APS, antrostomy and removal of antral mucosal disease, without without polyp(s) removal, consult codes 31255, 31267 and 31287 or 31288. For APS and frontal sinus exploration with or without polyp(s) removal, consult codes 31255, 31287, or 31288, and 31276. For APS with or without polyp(s) removal, with frontal sinus exploration and antrostomy, consult codes 31255, 31256, 31287 or 31288, and 31276. For APS with frontal sinus exploration, antrostomy and removal of antral mucosal disease, with or without polyp(s) removal, consult codes 31255, 31267, 31287 or 31288, and 31276.

31287 **Nasal/sinus endoscopy, surgical, with sphenoidotomy;** 3 T 50 80 ⌂
MED: 100-2, 15, 260; 100-3, 100.2; 100-4, 12, 40.6; 100-4, 12, 90.3; 100-4, 14, 10

AMA: 1997, Jan, 4

31288 **with removal of tissue from the sphenoid sinus** 3 T 50 80 ⌂
MED: 100-2, 15, 260; 100-4, 12, 40.6; 100-4, 12, 90.3; 100-4, 14, 10

AMA: 1997, Jan, 4

31290 **Nasal/sinus endoscopy, surgical, with repair of cerebrospinal fluid leak; ethmoid region** C 50 80 ⌂
MED: 100-3, 100.2; 100-4, 12, 40.6

AMA: 1997, Jan, 4

31291 **sphenoid region** C 50 80 ⌂
MED: 100-4, 12, 40.6

AMA: 1997, Jan, 4

31292 **Nasal/sinus endoscopy, surgical; with medial or inferior orbital wall decompression** T 50 80 ⌂
MED: 100-3, 100.2; 100-4, 12, 40.6

AMA: 1997, Jan, 4

31293 **with medial orbital wall and inferior orbital wall decompression** T 50 80 ⌂
MED: 100-4, 12, 40.6

AMA: 1997, Jan, 4

31294 **with optic nerve decompression** T 50 80 ⌂
MED: 100-4, 12, 40.6

AMA: 1997, Jan, 4

OTHER PROCEDURES

31299 **Unlisted procedure, accessory sinuses** T 80
MED: 100-4, 12, 40.6

If a hypophysectomy is performed using a transantral or a transeptal approach, consult CPT code 61548. If a transcranial hypophysectomy is performed, consult CPT code 61546.

Respiratory System

31300 — 31502

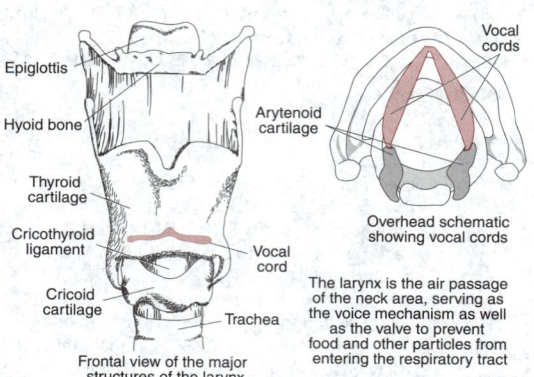

Epiglottis

Hyoid bone

Thyroid cartilage

Cricothyroid ligament

Cricoid cartilage

Vocal cord

Trachea

Frontal view of the major structures of the larynx

Vocal cords

Arytenoid cartilage

Vocal cord

Overhead schematic showing vocal cords

The larynx is the air passage of the neck area, serving as the voice mechanism as well as the valve to prevent food and other particles from entering the respiratory tract

LARYNX

EXCISION

31300	**Laryngotomy (thyrotomy, laryngofissure); with removal of tumor or laryngocele, cordectomy** 5 T 80	
	MED: 100-2, 15, 260; 100-4, 12, 90.3; 100-4, 14, 10	
31320	diagnostic 2 T 80	
	MED: 100-2, 15, 260; 100-4, 12, 90.3; 100-4, 14, 10	
31360	**Laryngectomy; total, without radical neck dissection** C 80	
31365	total, with radical neck dissection C 80	
	AMA: 2001, Oct, 10	
31367	subtotal supraglottic, without radical neck dissection C 80	
31368	subtotal supraglottic, with radical neck dissection C 80	
31370	**Partial laryngectomy (hemilaryngectomy); horizontal** C 80	
31375	laterovertical C 80	
31380	anterovertical C 80	
31382	antero-latero-vertical C 80	
31390	**Pharyngolaryngectomy, with radical neck dissection; without reconstruction** C 80	
31395	with reconstruction C 80	
31400	**Arytenoidectomy or arytenoidopexy, external approach** 2 T 80	
	MED: 100-2, 15, 260; 100-4, 12, 90.3; 100-4, 14, 10	

If performed endoscopically, consult CPT code 31560.

31420	**Epiglottidectomy** 2 T 80	
	MED: 100-2, 15, 260; 100-4, 12, 90.3; 100-4, 14, 10	

INTRODUCTION

⊘ 31500	**Intubation, endotracheal, emergency procedure** S	
	If an injection procedure is used for bronchography, consult CPT codes 31656, 31708, and 31710.	
31502	**Tracheotomy tube change prior to establishment of fistula tract** T	

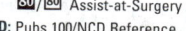

Respiratory System

31505 — 31527

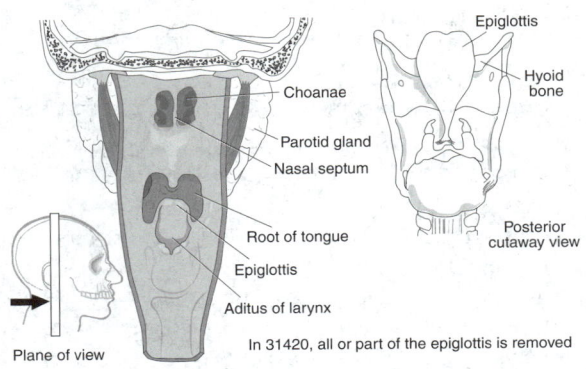

Choanae

Epiglottis

Hyoid bone

Parotid gland

Nasal septum

Posterior cutaway view

Root of tongue

Epiglottis

Aditus of larynx

Plane of view

In 31420, all or part of the epiglottis is removed

ENDOSCOPY
Code each anatomic site examined via endoscope.

31505	**Laryngoscopy, indirect; diagnostic (separate procedure)**	T 🔁
	MED: 100-3, 100.2; 100-4, 12, 40.6	
	AMA: 1999, Nov, 13	
31510	**with biopsy**	2 T 80 🔁
	MED: 100-2, 15, 260; 100-3, 100.2; 100-4, 12, 40.6; 100-4, 12, 90.3; 100-4, 14, 10	
	AMA: 1999, Nov, 13	
31511	**with removal of foreign body**	2 T 🔁
	MED: 100-2, 15, 260; 100-3, 100.2; 100-4, 12, 40.6; 100-4, 12, 90.3; 100-4, 14, 10	
	AMA: 1999, Nov, 13	
31512	**with removal of lesion**	2 T 80 🔁
	MED: 100-2, 15, 260; 100-3, 100.2; 100-4, 12, 40.6; 100-4, 12, 90.3; 100-4, 14, 10	
	AMA: 1999, Nov, 13	
31513	**with vocal cord injection**	2 T 80 🔁
	MED: 100-2, 15, 260; 100-3, 100.2; 100-4, 12, 40.6; 100-4, 12, 90.3; 100-4, 14, 10	
	AMA: 1999, Nov, 13	
31515	**Laryngoscopy direct, with or without tracheoscopy; for aspiration**	1 T 🔁
	MED: 100-2, 15, 260; 100-3, 100.2; 100-4, 12, 40.6; 100-4, 12, 90.3; 100-4, 14, 10	
31520	**diagnostic, newborn**	A T 80 🔁 63
	MED: 100-3, 100.2; 100-4, 12, 40.6	
31525	**diagnostic, except newborn**	1 T 🔁
	MED: 100-2, 15, 260; 100-3, 100.2; 100-4, 12, 40.6; 100-4, 12, 90.3; 100-4, 14, 10	
▲ **31526**	**diagnostic, with operating microscope or telescope**	2 T 🔁
	MED: 100-2, 15, 260; 100-3, 100.2; 100-4, 12, 40.6; 100-4, 12, 90.3; 100-4, 14, 10	
	AMA: 1998, Nov, 11-12	

Do not report 69990 in addition to 31526 as the operating microscope is considered an inclusive component of the surgery.

31527	**with insertion of obturator**	1 T 80 🔁
	MED: 100-2, 15, 260; 100-3, 100.2; 100-4, 12, 40.6; 100-4, 12, 90.3; 100-4, 14, 10	

Respiratory System

31528 — 31571

| 31528 | with dilation, initial | ② Ⓣ 80 Ⓚ |

MED: 100-2, 15, 260; 100-3, 100.2; 100-4, 12, 40.6; 100-4, 12, 90.3; 100-4, 14, 10

| 31529 | with dilation, subsequent | ② Ⓣ 80 Ⓚ |

MED: 100-2, 15, 260; 100-3, 100.2; 100-4, 12, 40.6; 100-4, 12, 90.3; 100-4, 14, 10

| 31530 | **Laryngoscopy, direct, operative, with foreign body removal;** | ② Ⓣ Ⓚ |

MED: 100-2, 15, 260; 100-3, 100.2; 100-4, 12, 40.6; 100-4, 12, 90.3; 100-4, 14, 10

▲ | 31531 | with operating microscope or telescope | ③ Ⓣ 80 Ⓚ |

MED: 100-2, 15, 260; 100-3, 100.2; 100-4, 12, 40.6; 100-4, 12, 90.3; 100-4, 14, 10

AMA: 1998, Nov, 11-12

Do not report 69990 in addition to 31531 as the operating microscope or telescope is considered an inclusive component of the surgery.

| 31535 | **Laryngoscopy, direct, operative, with biopsy;** | ② Ⓣ Ⓚ |

MED: 100-2, 15, 260; 100-3, 100.2; 100-4, 12, 40.6; 100-4, 12, 90.3; 100-4, 14, 10

▲ | 31536 | with operating microscope or telescope | ③ Ⓣ Ⓚ |

MED: 100-2, 15, 260; 100-3, 100.2; 100-4, 12, 40.6; 100-4, 12, 90.3; 100-4, 14, 10

AMA: 1998, Nov, 11-12

Do not report 69990 in addition to 31536 as the operating microscope or telescope is considered an inclusive component of the surgery.

| 31540 | **Laryngoscopy, direct, operative, with excision of tumor and/or stripping of vocal cords or epiglottis;** | ③ Ⓣ Ⓚ |

MED: 100-2, 15, 260; 100-3, 100.2; 100-4, 12, 40.6; 100-4, 12, 90.3; 100-4, 14, 10

▲ | 31541 | with operating microscope or telescope | ④ Ⓣ Ⓚ |

MED: 100-2, 15, 260; 100-3, 100.2; 100-4, 12, 40.6; 100-4, 12, 90.3; 100-4, 14, 10

AMA: 1998, Nov, 11-12

Do not report 69990 in addition to 31541 as the operating microscope or telescope is considered an inclusive component of the surgery.

| 31545 | **Laryngoscopy, direct, operative, with operating microscope or telescope, with submucosal removal of non-neoplastic lesion(s) of vocal cord; reconstruction with local tissue flap(s)** | ④ Ⓣ Ⓚ |

| 31546 | reconstruction with graft(s) (includes obtaining autograft) | ④ Ⓣ Ⓚ |

Code 31546 cannot be reported with CPT code 20926 for graft harvest.

For reconstruction of vocal cord with allograft consult CPT code 31599.

Code 31545 or 31546 cannot be reported with CPT codes 31540, 31541, and 69990.

| 31560 | **Laryngoscopy, direct, operative, with arytenoidectomy;** | ⑤ Ⓣ 80 Ⓚ |

MED: 100-2, 15, 260; 100-3, 100.2; 100-4, 12, 40.6; 100-4, 12, 90.3; 100-4, 14, 10

▲ | 31561 | with operating microscope or telescope | ⑤ Ⓣ 80 Ⓚ |

MED: 100-2, 15, 260; 100-3, 100.2; 100-4, 12, 40.6; 100-4, 12, 90.3; 100-4, 14, 10

AMA: 1998, Nov, 11-12

Do not report 69990 in addition to 31561 as the operating microscope or telescope is considered an inclusive component of the surgery.

| 31570 | **Laryngoscopy, direct, with injection into vocal cord(s), therapeutic;** ② Ⓣ Ⓚ |

MED: 100-2, 15, 260; 100-3, 100.2; 100-4, 12, 40.6; 100-4, 12, 90.3; 100-4, 14, 10

▲ | 31571 | with operating microscope or telescope | ② Ⓣ Ⓚ |

MED: 100-2, 15, 260; 100-3, 100.2; 100-4, 12, 40.6; 100-4, 12, 90.3; 100-4, 14, 10

AMA: 1998, Nov, 11-12

Do not report 69990 in addition to 31571 as the operating microscope or telescope is considered an inclusive component of the surgery.

31575	Laryngoscopy, flexible fiberoptic; diagnostic	T 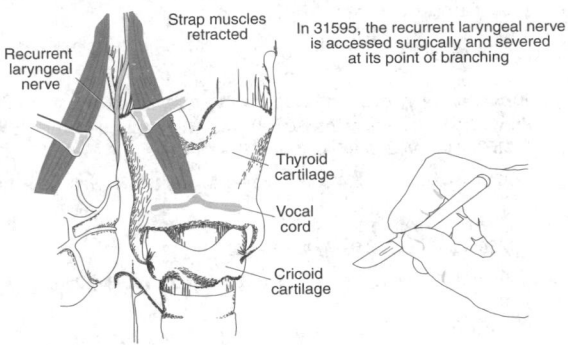
31576	with biopsy	2 T
	MED: 100-2, 15, 260; 100-4, 12, 90.3; 100-4, 14, 10	
31577	with removal of foreign body	2 T 80
	MED: 100-2, 15, 260; 100-4, 12, 90.3; 100-4, 14, 10	
31578	with removal of lesion	2 T 80
	MED: 100-2, 15, 260; 100-4, 12, 90.3; 100-4, 14, 10	

If flexible fiberoptic endoscopic evaluation of swallowing is performed, consult CPT codes 92612-92613; for sensory testing, consult CPT code 92614-92615; for swallowing with sensory testing, consult CPT codes 92616-92617.

To report flexible fiberoptic laryngoscopy performed as part of a flexible fiberoptic endoscopic evaluation of swallowing and/or laryngeal sensory testing by cine or video recording, consult CPT codes 92612-92617.

31579	Laryngoscopy, flexible or rigid fiberoptic, with stroboscopy	T

REPAIR

31580	Laryngoplasty; for laryngeal web, two stage, with keel insertion and removal	5 T 80
	MED: 100-2, 15, 260; 100-4, 12, 90.3; 100-4, 14, 10	
31582	for laryngeal stenosis, with graft or core mold, including tracheotomy	5 T
	MED: 100-2, 15, 260; 100-4, 12, 90.3; 100-4, 14, 10	
31584	with open reduction of fracture	C 80
~~31585~~	~~Treatment of closed laryngeal fracture; without manipulation~~	
~~31586~~	~~with closed manipulative reduction~~	
31587	Laryngoplasty, cricoid split	C 80
31588	Laryngoplasty, not otherwise specified (eg, for burns, reconstruction after partial laryngectomy)	5 T 80
	MED: 100-2, 15, 260; 100-4, 12, 90.3; 100-4, 14, 10	
31590	Laryngeal reinnervation by neuromuscular pedicle	5 T 80

DESTRUCTION

31595	Section recurrent laryngeal nerve, therapeutic (separate procedure), unilateral	2 T 80
	MED: 100-2, 15, 260; 100-4, 12, 90.3; 100-4, 14, 10	
	MED: 100-2, 15, 260; 100-4, 12, 90.3; 100-4, 14, 10	

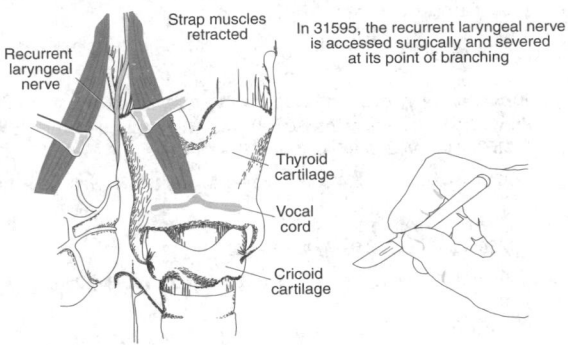

Strap muscles retracted

Recurrent laryngeal nerve

In 31595, the recurrent laryngeal nerve is accessed surgically and severed at its point of branching

Thyroid cartilage

Vocal cord

Cricoid cartilage

Respiratory System

31599 — 31623

OTHER PROCEDURES

31599   Unlisted procedure, larynx   T 80

TRACHEA AND BRONCHI

INCISION

31600   Tracheostomy, planned (separate procedure);   T ⬛

If endotracheal intubation is necessary, consult CPT code 31500.

31601   under two years   A T 80 ⬛

31603   Tracheostomy, emergency procedure; transtracheal   1 T ⬛

31605   cricothyroid membrane   T ⬛

31610   Tracheostomy, fenestration procedure with skin flaps   T ⬛

31611   Construction of tracheoesophageal fistula and subsequent insertion of an
alaryngeal speech prosthesis (eg, voice button, Blom-Singer
prosthesis)   3 T 80 ⬛
MED: 100-2, 15, 260; 100-4, 12, 90.3; 100-4, 14, 10

31612   Tracheal puncture, percutaneous with transtracheal aspiration and/or
injection   1 T 80 ⬛
MED: 100-2, 15, 260; 100-4, 12, 90.3; 100-4, 14, 10

If tracheal aspiration under direct vision is performed, consult CPT code
31515.

31613   Tracheostoma revision; simple, without flap rotation   2 T ⬛
MED: 100-2, 15, 260; 100-4, 12, 90.3; 100-4, 14, 10

31614   complex, with flap rotation   2 T ⬛
MED: 100-2, 15, 260; 100-4, 12, 90.3; 100-4, 14, 10

ENDOSCOPY

Code each anatomic site examined via endoscope. Diagnostic bronchoscopy is always included in
surgical bronchoscopy when performed by the same physician.

Fluoroscopic guidance, when performed with CPT codes 31622-31646, should not be reported
separately.

If a tracheoscopy is performed, consult laryngoscopy codes 31515-31578.

⊙   **31615**   Tracheobronchoscopy through established tracheostomy incision 1 T ⬛
MED: 100-2, 15, 260; 100-4, 12, 90.3; 100-4, 14, 10

+⊙ **31620**   Endobronchial ultrasound (EBUS) during bronchoscopic diagnostic or
therapeutic intervention(s) (List separately in addition to code for primary
procedure(s))   S

Note that code 31620 is an add-on code and must be used in conjunction with
31622-31646.

⊙   **31622**   Bronchoscopy, rigid or flexible, with or without fluoroscopic guidance;
diagnostic, with or without cell washing (separate procedure)   1 T ⬛
MED: 100-2, 15, 260; 100-4, 12, 90.3; 100-4, 14, 10

AMA: 2002, Jan, 10; 2001, Jun, 10; 1999, Mar, 3; 1998, Nov, 12; 1998, Dec, 8; 1996, Jul, 11

⊙   **31623**   with brushing or protected brushings   2 T ⬛
MED: 100-2, 15, 260; 100-4, 12, 90.3; 100-4, 14, 10

AMA: 2002, Jun, 10; 1999, Nov, 13; 1999, Mar, 3; 1998, Nov, 12

⊙ 31624   **with bronchial alveolar lavage** ▣▣▣
MED: 100-2, 15, 260; 100-4, 12, 90.3; 100-4, 14, 10

AMA: 2002, Jan, 10; 1999, Mar, 3; 1999, Feb, 9; 1998, Nov, 12

⊙ 31625   **with bronchial or endobronchial biopsy(s), single or multiple sites** ▣▣▣
MED: 100-2, 15, 260; 100-4, 12, 90.3; 100-4, 14, 10

AMA: 2002, Jun, 10; 1991, Spring, 2

⊙ 31628   **with transbronchial lung biopsy(s), single lobe** ▣▣▣
MED: 100-2, 15, 260; 100-4, 12, 90.3; 100-4, 14, 10

Code 31628 should only be reported once regardless of how many biopsy specimens are taken from the lobe. To report transbronchial lung biopsies performed on an additional lobe, consult also CPT code 31632.

To report transbronchial needle aspiration biopsies, consult CPT codes 31629 and 31633.

⊙ 31629   **with transbronchial needle aspiration biopsy(s), trachea, main stem and/or lobar bronchus(i)** ▣▣▣
MED: 100-2, 15, 260; 100-4, 12, 90.3; 100-4, 14, 10

AMA: 2000, Apr, 10

Code 31629 should only be reported once regardless of how many biopsy specimens are taken from the upper airway or lobe. To report transbronchial needle aspiration lung biopsies performed on an additional lobe, consult CPT code 31633.

To report transbronchial lung biopsies, consult CPT codes 31628 and 31632. Code 31629 includes conscious sedation.

31630   **with tracheal/bronchial dilation or closed reduction of fracture** ▣▣▣
MED: 100-2, 15, 260; 100-4, 12, 90.3; 100-4, 14, 10

31631   **with placement of tracheal stent(s) (includes tracheal/bronchial dilation as required)** ▣▣▣
MED: 100-2, 15, 260; 100-4, 12, 90.3; 100-4, 14, 10

To report placement of bronchial stent, consult CPT codes 31636, 31637.

To report revision of tracheal/bronchial stent, consult CPT code 31638.

+ 31632   **with transbronchial lung biopsy(s), each additional lobe (List separately in addition to code for primary procedure)** ▣▣
Note that 31632 is an add-on code and must be used in conjunction with 31628.

Code 31632 should only be reported once regardless of how many biopsy specimens are taken from the additional lobe.

+ 31633   **with transbronchial needle aspiration biopsy(s), each additional lobe (List separately in addition to code for primary procedure)** ▣▣
Note that 31633 is an add-on code and must be used in conjunction with 31629.

Code 31633 should only be reported once regardless of how many needle aspiration biopsy specimens are taken from the additional lobe or trachea.

⊙ 31635   **with removal of foreign body** ▣▣▣
MED: 100-2, 15, 260; 100-4, 12, 90.3; 100-4, 14, 10

AMA: 2002, Jun, 10

Respiratory System

31636 — 31700

	31636	**with placement of bronchial stent(s) (includes tracheal/bronchial dilation as required), initial bronchus** ②ⓉⓅ
+	31637	**each additional major bronchus stented (List separately in addition to code for primary procedure)** ❶Ⓣ

Note that 31637 must be used with 31636.

31638   **with revision of tracheal or bronchial stent inserted at previous session (includes tracheal/bronchial dilation as required)** ②ⓉⓅ

31640   **with excision of tumor** ②ⓉⓅ
MED: 100-2, 15, 260; 100-4, 12, 90.3; 100-4, 14, 10

31641   **Bronchoscopy, (rigid or flexible); with destruction of tumor or relief of stenosis by any method other than excision (eg, laser therapy, cryotherapy)** ②ⓉⓅ
MED: 100-2, 15, 260; 100-4, 12, 90.3; 100-4, 14, 10

AMA: 2000, Sep, 5; 1999, Nov, 13

If bronchoscopic photodynamic therapy is performed, report CPT code 31641 in addition to 96570 and 96571 as appropriate.

31643   **with placement of catheter(s) for intracavitary radioelement application** ②ⓉⓅ
MED: 100-2, 15, 260; 100-4, 12, 90.3; 100-4, 14, 10

AMA: 1999, Mar, 3; 1998, Nov, 12

If intracavitary radioelement application is performed, consult CPT codes 77761-77763 and 77781-77784.

⊙ **31645**   **with therapeutic aspiration of tracheobronchial tree, initial (eg, drainage of lung abscess)** ❶ⓉⓅ
MED: 100-2, 15, 260; 100-4, 12, 90.3; 100-4, 14, 10

If catheter aspiration of the tracheobronchial tree at bedside is performed, consult CPT code 31725. Code 31645 includes conscious sedation.

⊙ **31646**   **with therapeutic aspiration of tracheobronchial tree, subsequent** ❶ⓉⓅ
MED: 100-2, 15, 260; 100-4, 12, 90.3; 100-4, 14, 10

If catheter aspiration of the tracheobronchial tree at bedside is performed, consult CPT code 31725. Code 31646 includes conscious sedation.

⊙ **31656**   **with injection of contrast material for segmental bronchography (fiberscope only)** ❶Ⓣ⑧⓪Ⓟ
MED: 100-2, 15, 260; 100-4, 12, 90.3; 100-4, 14, 10

To report radiological supervision and interpretation, consult CPT codes 71040 and 71060.

INTRODUCTION

If endotracheal intubation is performed, consult CPT code 31500. If tracheal aspiration under direct vision is performed, consult CPT code 31515.

31700   **Catheterization, transglottic (separate procedure)** ❶Ⓣ⑧⓪Ⓟ
MED: 100-2, 15, 260; 100-4, 12, 90.3; 100-4, 14, 10

AMA: 2001, Feb, 11

31708	**Instillation of contrast material for laryngography or bronchography, without catheterization** N 50 80 ◪	

MED: 100-2, 15, 260; 100-4, 12, 90.3; 100-4, 14, 10

To report radiological supervision interpretation, consult CPT codes 70373, 71040, and 71060.

31710 **Catheterization for bronchography, with or without instillation of contrast material** N 50 80 ◪

If bronchoscopic catheterization is performed for bronchography, fiberscope only, consult CPT code 31656. If radiological supervision and interpretation is performed, consult CPT codes 71040 and 71060.

31715 **Transtracheal injection for bronchography** N 50 80 ◪

To report radiological supervision and interpretation, consult CPT codes 71040 and 71060. If prolonged services are necessary, consult CPT codes 99354-99360.

31717 **Catheterization with bronchial brush biopsy** 1 T ◪

MED: 100-2, 15, 260; 100-4, 12, 90.3; 100-4, 14, 10

AMA: 2001, Feb, 11

31720 **Catheter aspiration (separate procedure); nasotracheal** 1 T ◪

MED: 100-2, 15, 260; 100-4, 12, 90.3; 100-4, 14, 10

⊙ 31725   **tracheobronchial with fiberscope, bedside** C ◪

31730 **Transtracheal (percutaneous) introduction of needle wire dilator/stent or indwelling tube for oxygen therapy** 1 T ◪

MED: 100-2, 15, 260; 100-4, 12, 90.3; 100-4, 14, 10

REPAIR

31750 **Tracheoplasty; cervical** 5 T 80 ◪

MED: 100-2, 15, 260; 100-4, 12, 90.3; 100-4, 14, 10

31755   **tracheopharyngeal fistulization, each stage** 2 T 80 ◪

MED: 100-2, 15, 260; 100-4, 12, 90.3; 100-4, 14, 10

31760   **intrathoracic** C 80 ◪

31766 **Carinal reconstruction** C 80 ◪

31770 **Bronchoplasty; graft repair** C 80 ◪

If a lobectomy and bronchoplasty are performed, consult CPT code 32501.

31775   **excision stenosis and anastomosis** C 80 ◪

31780 **Excision tracheal stenosis and anastomosis; cervical** C 80 ◪

31781   **cervicothoracic** C 80 ◪

31785 **Excision of tracheal tumor or carcinoma; cervical** T 80 ◪

31786   **thoracic** C 80 ◪

31800 **Suture of tracheal wound or injury; cervical** C 80 ◪

31805   **intrathoracic** C 80 ◪

31820 **Surgical closure tracheostomy or fistula; without plastic repair** 1 T 80 ◪

MED: 100-2, 15, 260; 100-4, 12, 90.3; 100-4, 14, 10

If a tracheoesophageal fistula is repaired, consult CPT codes 43305 and 43312.

31825   **with plastic repair** 2 T 80 ◪

MED: 100-2, 15, 260; 100-4, 12, 90.3; 100-4, 14, 10

Respiratory System

31708 — 31825

Respiratory System

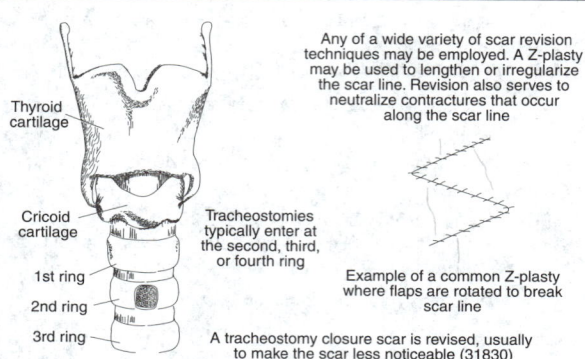

Any of a wide variety of scar revision techniques may be employed. A Z-plasty may be used to lengthen or irregularize the scar line. Revision also serves to neutralize contractures that occur along the scar line

Thyroid cartilage

Cricoid cartilage

Tracheostomies typically enter at the second, third, or fourth ring

1st ring

2nd ring

3rd ring

Example of a common Z-plasty where flaps are rotated to break scar line

A tracheostomy closure scar is revised, usually to make the scar less noticeable (31830)

31830 **Revision of tracheostomy scar** 2 T 80 ↵
MED: 100-2, 15, 260; 100-4, 12, 90.3; 100-4, 14, 10

OTHER PROCEDURES

31899 **Unlisted procedure, trachea, bronchi** T 80

LUNGS AND PLEURA

INCISION

⊘ **32000** **Thoracentesis, puncture of pleural cavity for aspiration, initial or subsequent** 1 T 50 ↵
MED: 100-2, 15, 260; 100-4, 12, 90.3; 100-4, 14, 10

AMA: 1991, Spring, 4

To report imaging guidance, consult CPT codes 76003, 76360, and 76942. Consult CPT code 32997 for total lung lavage.

⊘ **32002** **Thoracentesis with insertion of tube with or without water seal (eg, for pneumothorax) (separate procedure)** T 50 ↵

Code 32002 cannot be reported with 19260, 19271, 19272, 32503, or 32504.

To report imaging guidance, consult CPT codes 76003, 76360, and 76942.

32005 **Chemical pleurodesis (eg, for recurrent or persistent pneumothorax)** T ↵

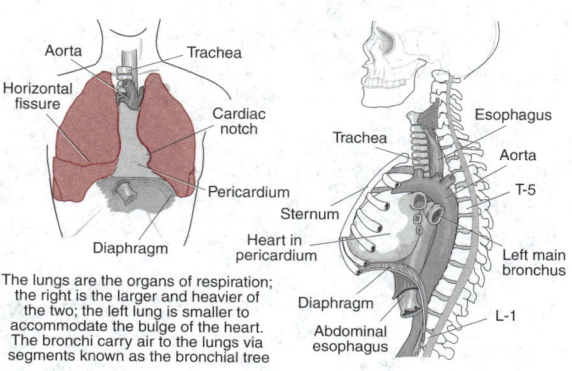

Aorta

Trachea

Horizontal fissure

Cardiac notch

Esophagus

Trachea

Aorta

T-5

Pericardium

Sternum

Heart in pericardium

Left main bronchus

Diaphragm

Diaphragm

L-1

Abdominal esophagus

The lungs are the organs of respiration; the right is the larger and heavier of the two; the left lung is smaller to accommodate the bulge of the heart. The bronchi carry air to the lungs via segments known as the bronchial tree

26 / TC Professional/Technical Component   80 / 80 Assist-at-Surgery Allowed/With Documentation   ☉ Conscious Sedation

Unlisted   Not Covered   MED: Pubs 100/NCD Reference   1 - 9 ASC Group   63 Modifier 63 Exempt

236 — Surgery   CPT only © 2005 American Medical Association. All Rights Reserved. *(Black Ink)*   © 2005 Ingenix, Inc. *(Blue Ink)*

⊙   **32019**   **Insertion of indwelling tunneled pleural catheter with cuff**   T ▸
       Code 32019 cannot be reported with CPT codes 32000-32005, 32020, 36000, 36410, 62318, 62319, 64450, 64470, 64475.
       If imaging guidance is performed, consult 75989.

⊘ ⊙   **32020**   **Tube thoracostomy with or without water seal (eg, for abscess, hemothorax, empyema) (separate procedure)**   T 50 ▸
       To report imaging guidance, consult CPT code 75989. Code 32020 includes conscious sedation.

   32035   **Thoracostomy; with rib resection for empyema**   C 80 ▸

   32036   **with open flap drainage for empyema**   C 80 ▸

   32095   **Thoracotomy, limited, for biopsy of lung or pleura**   C 80 ▸
       If wound exploration without thoracotomy is performed due to penetrating trauma, consult CPT code 20102.

   32100   **Thoracotomy, major; with exploration and biopsy**   C 80 ▸

   32110   **with control of traumatic hemorrhage and/or repair of lung tear** C 80 ▸

   32120   **for postoperative complications**   C 80 ▸

   32124   **with open intrapleural pneumonolysis**   C 80 ▸

   32140   **with cyst(s) removal, with or without a pleural procedure**   C 80 ▸
       If segmental or other resections of the lung are performed, consult CPT codes 32480-32525.

   32141   **with excision-plication of bullae, with or without any pleural procedure**   C 80 ▸
       If lung volume reduction is performed, consult CPT code 32491.

   32150   **with removal of intrapleural foreign body or fibrin deposit**   C 80 ▸

   32151   **with removal of intrapulmonary foreign body**   C 80 ▸

   32160   **with cardiac massage**   C 80 ▸
       To report segemental or other resections of lung, consult CPT codes 32480-32504.

   32200   **Pneumonostomy; with open drainage of abscess or cyst**   C 80 ▸

⊙   **32201**   **with percutaneous drainage of abscess or cyst**   T 80 ▸
       AMA: 1998, Mar, 8; 1997, Nov, 15-16
       To report radiological supervision and interpretation, consult CPT code 75989.

   32215   **Pleural scarification for repeat pneumothorax**   C 80 ▸

   32220   **Decortication, pulmonary, (separate procedure); total**   C 80 ▸

   32225   **Decortication, pulmonary (separate procedure); partial**   C 80 ▸

EXCISION

   32310   **Pleurectomy, parietal (separate procedure)**   C 80 ▸

   32320   **Decortication and parietal pleurectomy**   C 80 ▸

   32400   **Biopsy, pleura; percutaneous needle**   1 T ▸
       MED: 100-2, 15, 260; 100-4, 12, 90.3; 100-4, 14, 10

       AMA: 1994, Fall, 1, 2

       To report imaging guidance, consult CPT codes 76003, 76360, 76393, and 76942.
       To report fine needle aspiration, consult CPT code 10021 or 10022.
       To report evaluation of fine needle aspirate, consult CPT codes 88172, 88173.

Respiratory System

32402 — 32484

32402   open   [C] [80] [▶]
AMA: 1994, Fall, 1, 2

32405   **Biopsy, lung or mediastinum, percutaneous needle**   [1] [T] [▶]
MED: 100-2, 15, 260; 100-4, 12, 90.3; 100-4, 14, 10

AMA: 2002, Aug, 10; 1997, Mar, 4; 1994, Fall, 1, 2

To report radiological supervision and interpretation, consult CPT codes 76003, 76360, 76393, 76942.

To report fine needle aspiration, consult CPT code 10022.

To report evaluation of fine needle aspirate, consult CPT codes 88172, 88173.

32420   **Pneumocentesis, puncture of lung for aspiration**   [1] [T] [▶]
MED: 100-2, 15, 260; 100-4, 12, 90.3; 100-4, 14, 10

AMA: 1994, Fall, 1, 2

32440   **Removal of lung, total pneumonectomy;**   [C] [80] [▶]
AMA: 1994, Fall, 1

32442   **with resection of segment of trachea followed by broncho-tracheal anastomosis (sleeve pneumonectomy)**   [C] [80] [▶]
AMA: 1994, Fall, 1, 3

32445   **extrapleural**   [C] [80] [▶]
AMA: 1994, Fall, 1, 3

For extrapleural pneumonectomy with empyemectomy consult CPT codes 32445 and 32540.

To report lung resection performed with a chest wall tumor resection, report the code for the chest wall tumor resection, 19260-19272, as appropriate, in addition to the code for the lung resection, 32480-32500.

32480   **Removal of lung, other than total pneumonectomy; single lobe (lobectomy)**   [C] [80] [▶]
AMA: 1994, Fall, 1, 4; 1991, Spring, 5

32482   **two lobes (bilobectomy)**   [C] [80] [▶]
AMA: 1994, Fall, 1, 4

32484   **single segment (segmentectomy)**   [C] [80] [▶]
AMA: 1994, Fall, 1, 4

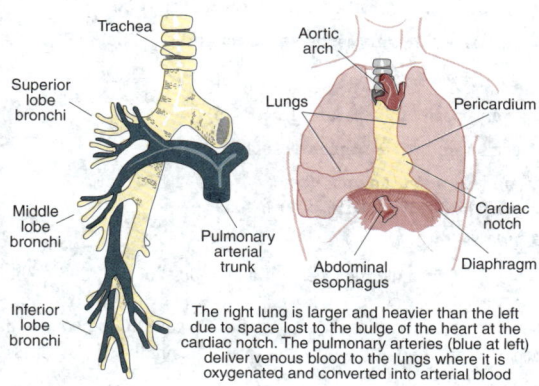

Trachea

Aortic arch

Superior lobe bronchi

Lungs

Pericardium

Middle lobe bronchi

Cardiac notch

Pulmonary arterial trunk

Abdominal esophagus

Diaphragm

Inferior lobe bronchi

The right lung is larger and heavier than the left due to space lost to the bulge of the heart at the cardiac notch. The pulmonary arteries (blue at left) deliver venous blood to the lungs where it is oxygenated and converted into arterial blood

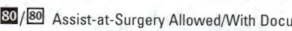

| 32486 | with circumferential resection of segment of bronchus followed by broncho-bronchial anastomosis (sleeve lobectomy) | C 80 ⮐ |
| | AMA: 1994, Fall, 1, 4 | |

| 32488 | all remaining lung following previous removal of a portion of lung (completion pneumonectomy) | C 80 ⮐ |
| | AMA: 1994, Fall, 1, 4 | |

| 32491 | excision-plication of emphysematous lung(s) (bullous or non-bullous) for lung volume reduction, sternal split or transthoracic approach, with or without any pleural procedure | C 50 80 ⮐ |

| 32500 | wedge resection, single or multiple | C 80 ⮐ |
| | AMA: 1997, Mar, 4; 1994, Fall, 1, 5 | |

To report lung resection performed with a chest wall tumor resection, report the code for the chest wall tumor resection, 19260-19272, as appropriate, in addition to the code for the lung resection, 32440-32445.

+ **32501**   **Resection and repair of portion of bronchus (bronchoplasty) when performed at time of lobectomy or segmentectomy (List separately in addition to code for primary procedure)**   C

Note that 32501 is an add-on code and must be used in conjunction with 32480, 32482, and 32484. Note also that 32501 is to be used when a portion of the bronchus is removed in order to preserve the lung and consequently requires plastic closure to maintain function of that preserved lung. This code is not to be used when the proximal end of a resected bronchus is closed.

● **32503**   **Resection of apical lung tumor (eg, Pancoast tumor), including chest wall resection, rib(s) resection(s), neurovascular dissection, when performed; without chest wall reconstruction(s)**

● **32504**   **with chest wall reconstruction**

Codes 32503, 32504 cannot be reported with 19260, 19271, 19272, 32002, 32020, 32100.

To report performance of lung resection in conjunction with chest wall resection, consult 19260, 19271, 19272 and 32480-32500, 32503, 32504.

~~32520~~	~~Resection of lung; with resection of chest wall~~	
~~32522~~	~~with reconstruction of chest wall, without prosthesis~~	
~~32525~~	~~with major reconstruction of chest wall, with prosthesis~~	

| 32540 | Extrapleural enucleation of empyema (empyemectomy) | C 80 ⮐ |

ENDOSCOPY
Surgical thoracoscopy always includes diagnostic thoracoscopy.

Code each anatomic site examined via endoscope.

32601	Thoracoscopy, diagnostic (separate procedure); lungs and pleural space, without biopsy	T 80 ⮐
	MED: 100-3, 100.2; 100-4, 12, 40.6	
	AMA: 1994, Fall, 1, 4	

32602	lungs and pleural space, with biopsy	T 80 ⮐
	MED: 100-3, 100.2; 100-4, 12, 40.6	
	AMA: 1997, Jun, 5; 1994, Fall, 1, 4	

32603	pericardial sac, without biopsy	T 80 ⮐
	MED: 100-3, 100.2; 100-4, 12, 40.6	
	AMA: 1994, Fall, 1, 4	

⮐ CCI Comp   50 Bilateral Procedure   + CPT Add-on Code   ⊘ Modifier -51 Exempt   ♂ Male   ♀ Female
● New Code   ▲ Revised Code   M Maternity Edit   A Age Edit   A–Y APC Status Ind.   AMA: CPT Assistant
© 2005 Ingenix, Inc. *(Blue Ink)*   CPT only © 2005 American Medical Association. All Rights Reserved. *(Black Ink)*   Surgery — 239

32604	pericardial sac, with biopsy	T 80 ⊡

MED: 100-3, 100.2; 100-4, 12, 40.6

AMA: 1994, Fall, 1, 4

32605	mediastinal space, without biopsy	T 80 ⊡

MED: 100-3, 100.2; 100-4, 12, 40.6

AMA: 1994, Fall, 1, 4

32606	mediastinal space, with biopsy	T 80 ⊡

MED: 100-3, 100.2; 100-4, 12, 40.6

AMA: 1994, Fall, 1, 5

32650	Thoracoscopy, surgical; with pleurodesis (eg, mechanical or chemical)	C 80 ⊡

MED: 100-3, 100.2; 100-4, 12, 40.6

AMA: 1994, Fall, 1, 6

32651	with partial pulmonary decortication	C 80 ⊡

MED: 100-3, 100.2; 100-4, 12, 40.6

AMA: 1994, Fall, 1, 6

32652	with total pulmonary decortication, including intrapleural pneumonolysis	C 80 ⊡

MED: 100-3, 100.2; 100-4, 12, 40.6

AMA: 1994, Fall, 1, 6

32653	with removal of intrapleural foreign body or fibrin deposit	C 80 ⊡

MED: 100-3, 100.2; 100-4, 12, 40.6

AMA: 1994, Fall, 1, 6

32654	with control of traumatic hemorrhage	C 80 ⊡

MED: 100-3, 100.2; 100-4, 12, 40.6

AMA: 1994, Fall, 1, 6

32655	with excision-plication of bullae, including any pleural procedure	C 80 ⊡

MED: 100-3, 100.2; 100-4, 12, 40.6

AMA: 1994, Fall, 1, 6

32656	with parietal pleurectomy	C 80 ⊡

MED: 100-3, 100.2; 100-4, 12, 40.6

AMA: 1994, Fall, 1, 6

32657	with wedge resection of lung, single or multiple	C 80 ⊡

MED: 100-3, 100.2; 100-4, 12, 40.6

AMA: 1994, Fall, 1, 6

32658	with removal of clot or foreign body from pericardial sac	C 80 ⊡

MED: 100-3, 100.2; 100-4, 12, 40.6

AMA: 1994, Fall, 1, 6

32659	with creation of pericardial window or partial resection of pericardial sac for drainage	C 80 ⊡

MED: 100-3, 100.2; 100-4, 12, 40.6

AMA: 1994, Fall, 1, 6

32660	with total pericardiectomy	C 80 ↰

MED: 100-3, 100.2; 100-4, 12, 40.6

AMA: 1994, Fall, 1, 6

32661	with excision of pericardial cyst, tumor, or mass	C 80 ↰

MED: 100-3, 100.2; 100-4, 12, 40.6

AMA: 1994, Fall, 1, 6

32662	with excision of mediastinal cyst, tumor, or mass	C 80 ↰

MED: 100-3, 100.2; 100-4, 12, 40.6

AMA: 1994, Fall, 1, 6

32663	with lobectomy, total or segmental	C 80 ↰

MED: 100-3, 100.2; 100-4, 12, 40.6

AMA: 1994, Fall, 1, 6

32664	with thoracic sympathectomy	C 50 80 ↰

MED: 100-3, 100.2; 100-4, 12, 40.6

AMA: 1994, Fall, 1, 6

32665	with esophagomyotomy (Heller type)	C 80 ↰

MED: 100-3, 100.2; 100-4, 12, 40.6

AMA: 1994, Fall, 1, 6

REPAIR

32800	Repair lung hernia through chest wall	C 80 ↰

MED: 100-3, 100.2; 100-4, 12, 40.6

32810	Closure of chest wall following open flap drainage for empyema (Clagett type procedure)	C 80 ↰

MED: 100-3, 100.2; 100-4, 12, 40.6

32815	Open closure of major bronchial fistula	C 80 ↰

MED: 100-3, 100.2; 100-4, 12, 40.6

32820	Major reconstruction, chest wall (post-traumatic)	C 80 ↰

MED: 100-3, 100.2; 100-4, 12, 40.6

LUNG TRANSPLANTATION

Lung transplantation involves three different components:

- Harvesting of the lung and cold preservation (See 32850).

- Backbench work consists of preparation of cadaver donor single lung or both lungs prior to transplantation. This includes dissection of the lung from tissue around it and preparation of the pulmonary venous/atrial cuff, pulmonary artery and bronchus bilaterally (see codes 32855, 32856).

- Recipient transplantation which includes transplanting a single lung or both lungs into the patient (See 32851-32854).

32850	Donor pneumonectomy(s) (including cold preservation), from cadaver donor	C ↰

MED: 100-3, 100.2; 100-4, 12, 40.6

32851	Lung transplant, single; without cardiopulmonary bypass	C 80 ↰

MED: 100-3, 100.2; 100-4, 12, 40.6

Respiratory System

32852 — 32999

32852	with cardiopulmonary bypass		C 80 ↻
	MED: 100-3, 100.2; 100-4, 12, 40.6		

32853	Lung transplant, double (bilateral sequential or en bloc); without cardiopulmonary bypass		C 80 ↻
	MED: 100-3, 100.2; 100-4, 12, 40.6		

32854	with cardiopulmonary bypass		C 80 ↻
	MED: 100-3, 100.2; 100-4, 12, 40.6		

32855	Backbench standard preparation of cadaver donor lung allograft prior to transplantation, including dissection of allograft from surrounding soft tissues to prepare pulmonary venous/atrial cuff, pulmonary artery, and bronchus; unilateral		C 50 ↻

32856	bilateral		C 50 ↻

To report resection or repair procedures on the donor lung, consult CPT codes 32491, 32500, 35216, or 35278.

SURGICAL COLLAPSE THERAPY; THORACOPLASTY

Consult also CPT codes 32503 and 32504

32900	Resection of ribs, extrapleural, all stages		C 80 ↻
	MED: 100-3, 100.2; 100-4, 12, 40.6		

32905	Thoracoplasty, Schede type or extrapleural (all stages);		C 80 ↻
	MED: 100-3, 100.2; 100-4, 12, 40.6		

32906	with closure of bronchopleural fistula		C 80 ↻
	MED: 100-3, 100.2; 100-4, 12, 40.6		

If the first rib for thoracic outer compression is resected, consult CPT codes 21615 and 21616.

If the major bronchial fistula required open closure, consult CPT code 32815.

32940	Pneumonolysis, extraperiosteal, including filling or packing procedures		C 80 ↻
	MED: 100-3, 100.2; 100-4, 12, 40.6		

32960	Pneumothorax, therapeutic, intrapleural injection of air		T ↻
	MED: 100-3, 100.2; 100-4, 12, 40.6		

OTHER PROCEDURES

32997	Total lung lavage (unilateral)		C ↻
	MED: 100-3, 100.2; 100-4, 12, 40.6		
	AMA: 1999, Nov, 14; 1998, Nov, 13		

If a bronchoscopic bronchial alveolar lavage is performed, consult CPT code 31624.

32999	Unlisted procedure, lungs and pleura		T 80
	MED: 100-3, 100.2; 100-4, 12, 40.6		
	AMA: 2002, Jan, 11		

CARDIOVASCULAR SYSTEM

HEART AND PERICARDIUM

Code vascular catheterization to include introduction and all lesser order catheterization used in the approach. Consult 36218 and 36248 to report additional second and third order arterial catheterization within the same family of arteries. Code separately catheterization in first order vessels different from the family originally coded.

If monitoring and the operation of pump and other nonsurgical services are performed, consult CPT codes 99190-99192, 99291, 99292, and 99354-99360. If other medical or laboratory related services are performed, consult the appropriate section of CPT. If radiological supervision and interpretation are performed, consult CPT codes 75600-75978.

PERICARDIUM

⊙　33010　**Pericardiocentesis; initial**　　　　　　　2 T 🔁
　　　　　　MED: 100-2, 15, 260; 100-4, 12, 90.3; 100-4, 14, 10

　　　　　　If radiological supervision and interpretation is performed, consult CPT code 76930.

⊙　33011　　**subsequent**　　　　　　　　　　2 T 80 🔁
　　　　　　MED: 100-2, 15, 260; 100-4, 12, 90.3; 100-4, 14, 10

　　　　　　If radiological supervision and interpretation is performed, consult CPT code 76930.

　　33015　**Tube pericardiostomy**　　　　　　　　C 🔁

　　33020　**Pericardiotomy for removal of clot or foreign body (primary procedure)**　　　　　　　　　　　　C 80 🔁

　　33025　**Creation of pericardial window or partial resection for drainage**　　C 80 🔁

　　33030　**Pericardiectomy, subtotal or complete; without cardiopulmonary bypass**　　　　　　　　　　　　C 80 🔁
　　　　　　Delorme pericardiectomy

　　33031　　**with cardiopulmonary bypass**　　　　C 80 🔁

　　33050　**Excision of pericardial cyst or tumor**　　　C 80 🔁

CARDIAC TUMOR

　　33120　**Excision of intracardiac tumor, resection with cardiopulmonary bypass**　　　　　　　　　　　C 80 🔁

　　33130　**Resection of external cardiac tumor**　　　C 80 🔁

TRANSMYOCARDIAL REVASCULARIZATION

　　33140　**Transmyocardial laser revascularization, by thoracotomy (separate procedure)**　　　　　　　　　　C 80 🔁
　　　　　　MED: 100-3, 20.6

　　　　　　AMA: 2001, Apr, 7; 2000, Nov, 5; 1999, Nov, 14

+　　33141　　**performed at the time of other open cardiac procedure(s) (List separately in addition to code for primary procedure)**　　　C
　　　　　　MED: 100-3, 20.6

　　　　　　AMA: 2001, Apr, 7

　　　　　　Note that 33141 is an add-on code and must be used in conjunction with 33400-33496, 33510-33536, and 33542.

Cardiovascular System

33200–33208

PACEMAKER OR PACING CARDIOVERTER-DEFIBRILLATOR

Pacemakers differ from pacing cardioverter-defibrillator pulse generators. In their simplicity, pacemakers maintain the rhythm of the heart through electrodes placed on the heart or in an artery. The electronics within stimulate one or more chambers in the heart. Pacing cardioverter-defibrillators also include a generator that stimulates the heart but also applies defibrillating shocks to treat ventricular tachycardia or ventricular fibrillation. Most are placed in a subcutaneous "pocket" below the clavicle or below the ribcage.

Pacemaker and defibrillator systems include a pulse generator and electrodes. Electrodes are inserted through a vein (transvenous) or on the surface of the heart (epicardial). Pacemaker systems are either single or dual chamber systems. In a single chamber system a single electrode is placed in either the atrium or ventricle. In a dual chamber system two electrodes are placed, one into the atrium and one into the ventricle.

Repositioning or replacement procedures performed during the first 14 days after the initial insertion or reportable replacement are included in the code for the initial procedure and should not be reported separately. Repositioning and replacement procedures performed after 14 days are considered new, not repeat, services and modifiers 76 and 77 should not be used.

Replacement of a pulse generator requires assignment of two codes, one for the removal and another for the insertion. This may also be referred to as a pacemaker battery change.

When an additional electrode is required to achieve left ventricular pacing, report CPT code 33224 or 33225.

Repositioning of a previously implanted electrode should be reported with CPT code 33215 or 33226.

If an electronic, telephonic analysis of the internal pacemaker system is performed, consult CPT codes 93731-93736.

If radiological supervision and interpretation with insertion of pacemaker is performed, consult CPT code 71090.

33200   **Insertion of permanent pacemaker with epicardial electrode(s); by thoracotomy** 　　　　　　　　　　　　　　　　　　　　　　　　　ⓒ ⏎
     MED: 100-3, 20.8; 100-3, 20.8.1

     AMA: 2000, Jun, 5; 1994, Summer, 10, 17

33201   **by xiphoid approach** 　　　　　　　　　　　　　　　ⓒ ⏎
     MED: 100-3, 20.8; 100-3, 20.8.1; 100-3, 20.8.3

     AMA: 1994, Summer, 10, 17

⊙ **33206**   **Insertion or replacement of permanent pacemaker with transvenous electrode(s); atrial** 　　　　　　　　　　　　　　　　　Ⓣ ⏎
     MED: 100-3, 20.8; 100-3, 20.8.1; 100-3, 20.8.3

     AMA: 1999, Nov, 15; 1996, Oct, 9; 1994, Summer, 10, 17

⊙ **33207**   **ventricular** 　　　　　　　　　　　　　　　　　　　Ⓣ ⏎
     MED: 100-3, 20.8; 100-3, 20.8.1; 100-3, 20.8.3

     AMA: 1999, Nov, 15; 1996, Oct, 9; 1994, Summer, 10, 17

⊙ **33208**   **atrial and ventricular** 　　　　　　　　　　　　　　Ⓣ ⏎
     MED: 100-3, 20.8; 100-3, 20.8.1; 100-3, 20.8.3

     AMA: 1999, Nov, 15; 1996, Jul, 10; 1994, Summer, 10, 17

     Subcutaneous insertion of pulse generator and transvenous placement of electrode(s) are included in codes 33206-33208, do not report separately.

⊙ 33210 **Insertion or replacement of temporary transvenous single chamber cardiac electrode transvenous single chamber cardiac electrode or pacemaker catheter (separate procedure)** Ⓣ ⌷
MED: 100-3, 20.25; 100-3, 20.8; 100-3, 20.8.1; 100-3, 20.8.3
AMA: 1994, Summer, 10, 17

⊙ 33211 **Insertion or replacement of temporary transvenous dual chamber pacing electrodes (separate procedure)** Ⓣ ⌷
MED: 100-3, 20.8; 100-3, 20.8.1; 100-3, 20.8.3
AMA: 1994, Summer, 10, 17

⊙ 33212 **Insertion or replacement of pacemaker pulse generator only; single chamber, atrial or ventricular** ③ Ⓣ ⌷
MED: 100-3, 20.8; 100-3, 20.8.1
AMA: 1994, Summer, 10, 18; 1994, Fall, 24

⊙ 33213 **dual chamber** ③ Ⓣ ⌷
MED: 100-3, 20.8; 100-3, 20.8.1
AMA: 1998, Feb, 11; 1996, Oct, 10; 1994, Summer, 10, 18

⊙ 33214 **Upgrade of implanted pacemaker system, conversion of single chamber system to dual chamber system (includes removal of previously placed pulse generator, testing of existing lead, insertion of new lead, insertion of new pulse generator)** Ⓣ ⑧⓪ ⌷
MED: 100-3, 20.8; 100-3, 20.8.1
AMA: 1994, Summer, 10, 18; 1994, Fall, 24

33215 **Repositioning of previously implanted transvenous pacemaker or pacing cardioverter-defibrillator (right atrial or right ventricular) electrode** Ⓣ ⌷
MED: 100-3, 20.8; 100-3, 20.8.1

⊙ 33216 **Insertion of a transvenous electrode; single chamber (one electrode) permanent pacemaker or single chamber pacing cardioverter-defibrillator** Ⓣ ⌷
MED: 100-3, 20.8; 100-3, 20.8.1; 100-3, 20.8.3
AMA: 1999, Nov, 15-16; 1996, Jul, 10; 1994, Summer, 10, 18

⊙ 33217 **dual chamber (two electrodes) permanent pacemaker or dual chamber pacing cardioverter-defibrillator** Ⓣ ⌷
MED: 100-3, 20.8; 100-3, 20.8.1; 100-3, 20.8.3
AMA: 1999, Nov, 15-16; 1996, Jul, 10; 1994, Summer, 10, 18

Codes 33216-33217 should not be reported with 33214.

⊙ 33218 **Repair of single transvenous electrode for a single chamber, permanent pacemaker or single chamber pacing cardioverter-defibrillator** Ⓣ ⌷
MED: 100-3, 20.8; 100-3, 20.8.1; 100-3, 20.8.3
AMA: 1999, Nov, 15-16; 1996, Oct, 1, 9; 1994, Summer, 10, 19

If atrial or ventricular single chamber single transvenous electrode is repaired with the replacement of a pulse generator, consult CPT codes 33212 or 33213 and 33218 or 33220.

⊙ 33220 **Repair of two transvenous electrodes for a dual chamber permanent pacemaker or dual chamber pacing cardioverter-defibrillator** Ⓣ ⌷
MED: 100-3, 20.8; 100-3, 20.8.1; 100-3, 20.8.3
AMA: 1999, Nov, 15-16; 1996, Oct, 9; 1994, Summer, 10, 19

⊙ 33222 **Revision or relocation of skin pocket for pacemaker** ② T ▣
MED: 100-2, 15, 260; 100-3, 20.8; 100-3, 20.8.1; 100-3, 20.8.3; 100-4, 12, 90.3; 100-4, 14, 10

AMA: 1999, Nov, 15-16; 1994, Summer, 10; 1994, Spring, 30

⊙ 33223 **Revision of skin pocket for single or dual chamber pacing cardioverter-defibrillator** ② T 80 ▣
MED: 100-2, 15, 260; 100-3, 20.8; 100-3, 20.8.1; 100-4, 12, 90.3; 100-4, 14, 10

AMA: 1999, Nov, 15-16; 1994, Summer, 10, 19

33224 **Insertion of pacing electrode, cardiac venous system, for left ventricular pacing, with attachment to previously placed pacemaker or pacing cardioverter-defibrillator pulse generator (including revision of pocket, removal, insertion and/or replacement of generator)** T ▣
MED: 100-3, 20.8; 100-3, 20.8.1

+ 33225 **Insertion of pacing electrode, cardiac venous system, for left ventricular pacing, at time of insertion of pacing cardioverter-defibrillator or pacemaker pulse generator (including upgrade to dual chamber system) (List separately in addition to code for primary procedure)** T ▣
MED: 100-3, 20.8; 100-3, 20.8.1

Note that 33225 is an add-on code and must be used in conjunction with 33206-33208, 33212-33214, 33216-33217, 33222, 33233-33235, 33240, and 33249.

33226 **Repositioning of previously implanted cardiac venous system (left ventricular) electrode (including removal, insertion and/or replacement of generator)** T ▣
MED: 100-3, 20.8; 100-3, 20.8.1

⊙ 33233 **Removal of permanent pacemaker pulse generator** ② T ▣
MED: 100-3, 20.8; 100-3, 20.8.1

AMA: 1996, Oct, 10; 1994, Summer, 10, 19; 1994, Fall, 24

⊙ 33234 **Removal of transvenous pacemaker electrode(s); single lead system, atrial or ventricular** T ▣
MED: 100-3, 20.8; 100-3, 20.8.1; 100-3, 20.8.3

AMA: 1999, Nov, 16; 1994, Summer, 10, 19

⊙ 33235 **dual lead system** T ▣
MED: 100-3, 20.8; 100-3, 20.8.1; 100-3, 20.8.3

AMA: 1999, Nov, 16; 1994, Summer, 10, 19

33236 **Removal of permanent epicardial pacemaker and electrodes by thoracotomy; single lead system, atrial or ventricular** C 80 ▣
MED: 100-3, 20.8; 100-3, 20.8.1; 100-3, 20.8.3

AMA: 1999, Nov, 16; 1994, Summer, 10, 19

33237 **dual lead system** C 80 ▣
MED: 100-3, 20.8; 100-3, 20.8.1; 100-3, 20.8.3

AMA: 1999, Nov, 16; 1994, Summer, 10, 19

33238 **Removal of permanent transvenous electrode(s) by thoracotomy** C 80 ▣
MED: 100-3, 100.9; 100-3, 20.4; 100-3, 20.8; 100-3, 20.8.1

AMA: 1999, Nov, 16; 1994, Summer, 10, 19

⊙ **33240** **Insertion of single or dual chamber pacing cardioverter-defibrillator pulse generator** B [🔺]

MED: 100-3, 100.9; 100-3, 20.4; 100-3, 20.8; 100-3, 20.8.1

AMA: 2000, Jul, 5; 1999, Nov, 16-17; 1996, Jun, 10; 1994, Summer, 40

⊙ **33241** **Subcutaneous removal of single or dual chamber pacing cardioverter-defibrillator pulse generator** T 80 [🔺]

MED: 100-3, 100.9; 100-3, 20.4; 100-3, 20.8; 100-3, 20.8.1

AMA: 1999, Nov, 16-17; 1994, Summer, 40

If an electrode(s) is removed by thoracotomy, consult CPT code 33243 in conjunction with 33241.

If an electrode(s) is removed transvenously, report 33244 in conjunction with 33241.

If the complete pacing defibrillator system is removed and replaced, report 33241 and 33243 or 33244 and 33249. If the implantable cardioverter-defibrillator pulse gnerator and/or leads are repaired, consult CPT codes 33218 and 33220.

33243 **Removal of single or dual chamber pacing cardioverter-defibrillator electrode(s); by thoracotomy** C 80 [🔺]

MED: 100-3, 100.9; 100-3, 20.4; 100-3, 20.8; 100-3, 20.8.1

AMA: 1999, Nov, 16-17; 1994, Summer, 40

⊙ **33244** **by transvenous extraction** T [🔺]

MED: 100-3, 100.9; 100-3, 20.4; 100-3, 20.8; 100-3, 20.8.1

AMA: 2000, Jul, 5; 1999, Nov, 16-17; 1994, Summer, 40

To report subcutaneous removal of pulse generator, consult CPT code 33241, report in conjunction with 33243 or 33244.

33245 **Insertion of epicardial single or dual chamber pacing cardioverter-defibrillator electrodes by thoracotomy;** C 80 [🔺]

MED: 100-3, 100.9; 100-3, 20.4; 100-3, 20.8; 100-3, 20.8.1

AMA: 1999, Nov, 16-17; 1994, Summer, 21

33246 **with insertion of pulse generator** C 80 [🔺]

MED: 100-3, 100.9; 100-3, 20.4; 100-3, 20.8; 100-3, 20.8.1

AMA: 1999, Nov, 16-17; 1994, Summer, 21

⊙ **33249** **Insertion or repositioning of electrode lead(s) for single or dual chamber pacing cardioverter-defibrillator and insertion of pulse generator** B [🔺]

MED: 100-3, 100.9; 100-3, 20.4; 100-3, 20.8; 100-3, 20.8.1

AMA: 1999, Nov, 16-17; 1994, Summer, 21

To report removal and reinsertion of a complete pacing cardioverter-defibrillator system, consult CPT codes 33241 and 33243 or 33244 and 33249.

ELECTROPHYSIOLOGIC OPERATIVE PROCEDURES

33250 **Operative ablation of supraventricular arrhythmogenic focus or pathway (eg, Wolff-Parkinson-White, atrioventricular node re-entry), tract(s) and/or focus (foci); without cardiopulmonary bypass** C 80 [🔺]

AMA: 1999, Nov, 17-18; 1994, Summer, 16

33251 **with cardiopulmonary bypass** C 80 [🔺]

AMA: 1999, Nov, 17-18; 1994, Summer, 16

Cardiovascular System

33253–33406

33253　　Operative incisions and reconstruction of atria for treatment of atrial fibrillation or atrial flutter (eg, maze procedure)　　© 80 🔲

33261　　Operative ablation of ventricular arrhythmogenic focus with cardiopulmonary bypass　　© 80 🔲
　　　　　AMA: 1994, Summer, 16

PATIENT-ACTIVATED EVENT RECORDER

Note that initial implantation includes programming. If subsequent electronic analysis and/or reprogramming are performed, consult CPT code 93727.

33282　　Implantation of patient-activated cardiac event recorder　　Ⓢ 🔲
　　　　　AMA: 2000, Jul, 5; 1999, Nov, 17-18

33284　　Removal of an implantable, patient-activated cardiac event recorder　　Ⓣ 🔲
　　　　　AMA: 2000, Jul, 5; 1999, Nov, 17-18

WOUNDS OF THE HEART AND GREAT VESSELS

33300　　Repair of cardiac wound; without bypass　　© 80 🔲

33305　　　　with cardiopulmonary bypass　　© 80 🔲

33310　　Cardiotomy, exploratory (includes removal of foreign body, atrial or ventricular thrombus); without bypass　　© 80 🔲

33315　　　　with cardiopulmonary bypass　　© 80 🔲

　　　　　Unless a separate incision in the heart is made to remove the atrial or ventricular thrombus do not report CPT codes 33310 or 33315 in conjunction with other cardiac procedures.

　　　　　If a separate heart incision is made to remove the thrombus append modifier 59 to code 33315 when reported with 33120, 33130, 33420-33468, 33496, 33542, 33545, 33641-33647, 33670, 33681, or 33975-33980.

33320　　Suture repair of aorta or great vessels; without shunt or cardiopulmonary bypass　　© 80 🔲

33321　　　　with shunt bypass　　© 80 🔲

33322　　　　with cardiopulmonary bypass　　© 80 🔲

33330　　Insertion of graft, aorta or great vessels; without shunt, or cardiopulmonary bypass　　© 80 🔲

33332　　　　with shunt bypass　　© 80 🔲

33335　　　　with cardiopulmonary bypass　　© 80 🔲

CARDIAC VALVES — AORTIC VALVE

33400　　Valvuloplasty, aortic valve; open, with cardiopulmonary bypass　　© 80 🔲

33401　　　　open, with inflow occlusion　　© 80 🔲 ⊙

33403　　　　using transventricular dilation, with cardiopulmonary bypass　　© 80 🔲 ⊙

33404　　Construction of apical-aortic conduit　　© 80 🔲

33405　　Replacement, aortic valve, with cardiopulmonary bypass; with prosthetic valve other than homograft or stentless valve　　© 80 🔲
　　　　　AMA: 1999, Nov, 18

33406　　　　with allograft valve (freehand)　　© 80 🔲
　　　　　AMA: 1999, Nov, 18

33410　　　　with stentless tissue valve　　© 80 🔲
　　　　　AMA: 1999, Nov, 18

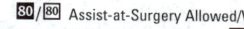

33411	Replacement, aortic valve; with aortic annulus enlargement, noncoronary cusp	C 80 ⤴
33412	with transventricular aortic annulus enlargement (Konno procedure)	C 80 ⤴
33413	by translocation of autologous pulmonary valve with allograft replacement of pulmonary valve (Ross procedure)	C 80 ⤴
33414	Repair of left ventricular outflow tract obstruction by patch enlargement of the outflow tract	C 80 ⤴
33415	Resection or incision of subvalvular tissue for discrete subvalvular aortic stenosis	C 80 ⤴
33416	Ventriculomyotomy (-myectomy) for idiopathic hypertrophic subaortic stenosis (eg, asymmetric septal hypertrophy)	C 80 ⤴
33417	Aortoplasty (gusset) for supravalvular stenosis	C 80 ⤴

CARDIAC VALVES — MITRAL VALVE

33420	Valvotomy, mitral valve; closed heart	C ⤴
33422	open heart, with cardiopulmonary bypass	C 80 ⤴
33425	Valvuloplasty, mitral valve, with cardiopulmonary bypass;	C 80 ⤴
33426	with prosthetic ring	C 80 ⤴
33427	radical reconstruction, with or without ring	C 80 ⤴
33430	Replacement, mitral valve, with cardiopulmonary bypass	C 80 ⤴

CARDIAC VALVES — TRICUSPID VALVE

33460	Valvectomy, tricuspid valve, with cardiopulmonary bypass	C 80 ⤴
33463	Valvuloplasty, tricuspid valve; without ring insertion	C 80 ⤴
33464	with ring insertion	C 80 ⤴
33465	Replacement, tricuspid valve, with cardiopulmonary bypass	C 80 ⤴
33468	Tricuspid valve repositioning and plication for Ebstein anomaly	C 80 ⤴

CARDIAC VALVES — PULMONARY VALVE

33470	Valvotomy, pulmonary valve, closed heart; transventricular	C 80 ⤴

Note that modifier 63 cannot be reported with CPT code 33470.
Brock's operation

33471	via pulmonary artery	C 80 ⤴

If percutaneous valvuloplasty of the pulmonary valve is performed, consult CPT code 92990.
Brock's operation

33472	Valvotomy, pulmonary valve, open heart; with inflow occlusion	C 80 ⤴ 63

Brock's operation

33474	with cardiopulmonary bypass	C 80 ⤴

Brock's operation

33475	Replacement, pulmonary valve	C 80 ⤴
33476	Right ventricular resection for infundibular stenosis, with or without commissurotomy	C 80 ⤴

Brock's operation

Cardiovascular System

33476–33508

33478   **Outflow tract augmentation (gusset), with or without commissurotomy or infundibular resection**   C 80 ▸

> If a cavopulmonary anastomosis to a second superior vena cava is performed, report code 33478 in conjunction with 33768.

OTHER VALVULAR PROCEDURES

33496   **Repair of non-structural prosthetic valve dysfunction with cardiopulmonary bypass (separate procedure)**   C 80 ▸
AMA: 1997, Nov, 16

> If this procedure is a reoperation, use CPT code 33530 in addition to 33496.

CORONARY ARTERY ANOMALIES

Codes in this section include endarterectomy or angioplasty.

33500   **Repair of coronary arteriovenous or arteriocardiac chamber fistula; with cardiopulmonary bypass**   C 80 ▸

33501   **without cardiopulmonary bypass**   C 80 ▸

▲ 33502   **Repair of anomalous coronary artery from pulmonary artery origin; by ligation**   C 80 ▸ 63

▲ 33503   **by graft, without cardiopulmonary bypass**   C 80 ▸ 63

> Modifier 63 should not be reported with codes 33502 and 33503.

▲ 33504   **by graft, with cardiopulmonary bypass**   C 80 ▸

▲ 33505   **with construction of intrapulmonary artery tunnel (Takeuchi procedure)**   C 80 ▸ 63

▲ 33506   **by translocation from pulmonary artery to aorta**   C 80 ▸ 63

● 33507   **Repair of anomalous (eg, intramural) aortic origin of coronary artery by unroofing or translocation**

ENDOSCOPY

Diagnostic endoscopy is always included in surgical endoscopy, do not report separately.

+ 33508   **Endoscopy, surgical, including video-assisted harvest of vein(s) for coronary artery bypass procedure (List separately in addition to code for primary procedure)**   N ▸

> Note that 33508 is an add-on code and must be used in conjunction with 33510-33523.
>
> To report harvest of upper extremity vein, open procedure, consult CPT code 35500.

CORONARY ARTERY BYPASS GRAFTS

Coronary artery bypass grafts (CABG) are coded by type of graft. Venous grafting alone is reported with 33510–33516. Arterial grafting alone is reported with 33533–33545. Combined arterial–venous grafting is reported with 33517–33523 in combination with 33533–33535. Codes 33517–33523 cannot be reported alone.

Procurement of saphenous vein grafts is included in CABG procedures and should not be reported separately. If a second surgeon procures the graft, report the services as assistant surgeon services with modifier 80 Assistant surgeon appended to the applicable CABG code.

To report harvesting of an upper extremity vein, consult CPT code 35500. To report harvesting of a femoropopliteal vein segment, consult CPT code 35572. These services should be reported in addition to the appropriate CABG procedure code.

VENOUS GRAFTING ONLY FOR CORONARY ARTERY BYPASS

Use the following codes to report coronary artery bypass procedures using venous grafts only. Do not use these codes to report coronary artery bypass procedures using arterial grafts and venous grafts during the same surgery. For combined arterial-venous graft surgery, consult CPT codes 33517–33523 and 33533–33536.

CPT codes 33510-33516 include the harvesting of the saphenous vein graft and it should not be reported separately. Harvesting of an upper extremity vein may be reported separately, consult CPT code 35500. Harvesting of a femoropopliteal vein segment may be reported separately, consult CPT code 35572. These codes report bypass procedures using venous grafts only.

33510   **Coronary artery bypass, vein only; single coronary venous graft**   C 80 🔁
AMA: 2001, Apr, 7; 1999, Jul, 11; 1992, Winter, 12; 1991, Fall, 5

33511   **two coronary venous grafts**   C 80 🔁
AMA: 2001, Apr, 7; 1999, Jul, 11; 1992, Winter, 12; 1991, Fall, 5

33512   **three coronary venous grafts**   C 80 🔁
AMA: 2001, Apr, 7; 1992, Winter, 12; 1991, Fall, 5

33513   **four coronary venous grafts**   C 80 🔁
AMA: 2001, Apr, 7; 1992, Winter, 12; 1991, Fall, 5

33514   **five coronary venous grafts**   C 80 🔁
AMA: 2001, Apr, 7; 1992, Winter, 12; 1991, Fall, 5

33516   **six or more coronary venous grafts**   C 80 🔁
AMA: 2001, Apr, 7; 1999, Jul, 11; 1992, Winter, 12; 1991, Fall, 5

COMBINED ARTERIAL-VENOUS GRAFTING FOR CORONARY BYPASS

Use these codes to report coronary artery bypass procedures using both venous and arterial grafts during the same procedure, but do not use them alone. They must be reported with a code from range 33533-33536. Harvesting of an upper extremity vein may be reported separately, consult CPT code 35500. Harvesting of a femoropopliteal vein segment may be reported separately, consult CPT code 35572.

Two codes must be used to report arterial-venous grafts:

1.   33517–33523 for the combined arterial-venous graft code

2.   33533–33536 for the appropriate arterial graft code

Harvesting the artery for grafting is included in 33533–33536 and should not be reported separately except when an upper extremity artery is used. To report harvesting of an upper extremity artery, consult 35600. When a surgical assistant harvests the venous or arterial graft, add modifier 80 to codes 33517–33523, 33533–33536, as appropriate.

CPT codes 33517-33523 include the harvesting of the saphenous vein graft and it should not be reported separately.

⊘   **33517**   **Coronary artery bypass, using venous graft(s) and arterial graft(s); single vein graft (list separately in addition to code for arterial graft)**   C 80 🔁
AMA: 2001, Apr, 7; 1999, Nov, 18; 1992, Winter, 13; 1991, Fall, 5

⊘   **33518**   **two venous grafts (list separately in addition to code for arterial graft)**   C 80 🔁
AMA: 2001, Apr, 7; 1992, Winter, 13; 1991, Fall, 5

⊘   **33519**   **three venous grafts (list separately in addition to code for arterial graft)**   C 80 🔁
AMA: 2001, Apr, 7; 1992, Winter, 13; 1991, Fall, 5

Cardiovascular System

33519–33545

⊘   33521   **four venous grafts (list separately in addition to code for arterial graft)**   C 80 ⬚
AMA: 2001, Apr, 7; 1992, Winter, 13; 1991, Fall, 5

⊘   33522   **five venous grafts (list separately in addition to code for arterial graft)**   C 80 ⬚
AMA: 2001, Apr, 7; 1992, Winter, 13; 1991, Fall, 5

⊘   33523   **six or more venous grafts (list separately in addition to code for arterial graft)**   C 80 ⬚
AMA: 2001, Apr, 7; 1992, Winter, 13; 1991, Fall, 5

+   33530   **Reoperation, coronary artery bypass procedure or valve procedure, more than one month after original operation (list separately in addition to code for primary procedure)**   C 80 ⬚
AMA: 2001, Jul, 11; 2001, Apr, 7; 1992, Winter, 13; 1991, Fall, 5

Note that 33530 is an add-on code and must be used in conjunction with 33400-33496, 33510-33536, and 33863.

ARTERIAL GRAFTING FOR CORONARY ARTERY BYPASS

Use the following codes to report coronary artery bypass surgeries using either arterial grafts only or a combination of arterial-venous grafts. The codes include using the internal mammary artery, gastroepiploic artery, epigastric artery, radial artery, and arterial conduits procured from other sites.

Two codes must be used to report arterial-venous grafts:

1.   33533–33536 for the arterial graft code

2.   33517–33523 for the appropriate arterial-venous graft code

Harvesting the artery for grafting is included in the description for 33533–33536 and should not be reported separately except when an upper extremity artery is harvested. Harvesting of an upper extremity artery may be reported using code 35600. Report the harvesting of an upper extremity vein with code 35500. When a surgical assistant harvests the venous or arterial graft, add modifier 80 to codes 33517–33523, 33533–33536, as appropriate.

Harvesting of a femoropopliteal vein segment may be reported separately, consult CPT code 35572.

33533   **Coronary artery bypass, using arterial graft(s); single arterial graft**   C 80 ⬚
AMA: 2001, Apr, 7; 1999, Nov, 18; 1992, Winter, 12

33534   **two coronary arterial grafts**   C 80 ⬚
AMA: 2001, Apr, 7; 1992, Winter, 12

33535   **three coronary arterial grafts**   C 80 ⬚
AMA: 2001, Apr, 7; 1992, Winter, 12

33536   **four or more coronary arterial grafts**   C 80 ⬚
AMA: 2001, Apr, 7; 1992, Winter, 12

33542   **Myocardial resection (eg, ventricular aneurysmectomy)**   C 80 ⬚

33545   **Repair of postinfarction ventricular septal defect, with or without myocardial resection**   C 80 ⬚

●   33548   **Surgical ventricular restoration procedure, includes prosthetic patch, when performed (eg, ventricular remodeling, SVR, SAVER, DOR procedures)**

Code 33548 cannot be reported with 32020, 33210, 33211, 33310, 33315.

To report Batista procedure or pachopexy, consult 33999.

CORONARY ENDARTERECTOMY

+   **33572**   Coronary endarterectomy, open, any method, of left anterior descending, circumflex, or right coronary artery performed in conjunction with coronary artery bypass graft procedure, each vessel (list separately in addition to primary procedure)   C 80 ↵

> Note that 33572 is an add-on code and must be used in conjunction with 33510-33516 and 33533-33536.

SINGLE VENTRICLE AND OTHER COMPLEX CARDIAC ANOMALIES

33600   Closure of atrioventricular valve (mitral or tricuspid) by suture or patch   C 80 ↵

33602   Closure of semilunar valve (aortic or pulmonary) by suture or patch   C 80 ↵

33606   Anastomosis of pulmonary artery to aorta (Damus-Kaye-Stansel procedure)   C 80 ↵

33608   Repair of complex cardiac anomaly other than pulmonary atresia with ventricular septal defect by construction or replacement of conduit from right or left ventricle to pulmonary artery   C 80 ↵

> If pulmonary artery arborization anomalies are repaired by unifocalization, consult CPT codes 33925-33926.

33610   Repair of complex cardiac anomalies (eg, single ventricle with subaortic obstruction) by surgical enlargement of ventricular septal defect   C 80 ↵ ⑬

33611   Repair of double outlet right ventricle with intraventricular tunnel repair;   C 80 ↵ ⑬

33612   with repair of right ventricular outflow tract obstruction   C 80 ↵

33615   Repair of complex cardiac anomalies (eg, tricuspid atresia) by closure of atrial septal defect and anastomosis of atria or vena cava to pulmonary artery (simple Fontan procedure)   C 80 ↵

33617   Repair of complex cardiac anomalies (eg, single ventricle) by modified Fontan procedure   C 80 ↵

> If a cavopulmonary anastomosis to a second superior vena cava is performed, report code 33617 in conjunction with 33768.

33619   Repair of single ventricle with aortic outflow obstruction and aortic arch hypoplasia (hypoplastic left heart syndrome) (eg, Norwood procedure)   C 80 ↵ ⑬

SEPTAL DEFECT

33641   Repair atrial septal defect, secundum, with cardiopulmonary bypass, with or without patch   C 80 ↵

33645   Direct or patch closure, sinus venosus, with or without anomalous pulmonary venous drainage   C 80 ↵

33647   Repair of atrial septal defect and ventricular septal defect, with direct or patch closure   C 80 ↵ ⑬

> Consult CPT code 33615 for the repair of tricuspid atresia.

33660   Repair of incomplete or partial atrioventricular canal (ostium primum atrial septal defect), with or without atrioventricular valve repair   C 80 ↵

33665   Repair of intermediate or transitional atrioventricular canal, with or without atrioventricular valve repair   C 80 ↵

33670   Repair of complete atrioventricular canal, with or without prosthetic valve   C 80 ↵ ⑬

33681   Closure of ventricular septal defect, with or without patch   C 80 ↵

Cardiovascular System

33665–33768

33684	with pulmonary valvotomy or infundibular resection (acyanotic) Ⓒ 80 ↵
33688	with removal of pulmonary artery band, with or without gusset Ⓒ 80 ↵
33690	Banding of pulmonary artery Ⓒ 80 ↵ 63
33692	Complete repair tetralogy of Fallot without pulmonary atresia; Ⓒ 80 ↵
33694	with transannular patch Ⓒ 80 ↵ 63
33697	Complete repair tetralogy of Fallot with pulmonary atresia including construction of conduit from right ventricle to pulmonary artery and closure of ventricular septal defect Ⓒ 80 ↵

SINUS OF VALSALVA

33702	Repair sinus of Valsalva fistula, with cardiopulmonary bypass; Ⓒ 80 ↵
33710	with repair of ventricular septal defect Ⓒ 80 ↵
33720	Repair sinus of Valsalva aneurysm, with cardiopulmonary bypass Ⓒ 80 ↵
33722	Closure of aortico-left ventricular tunnel Ⓒ 80 ↵

TOTAL ANOMALOUS PULMONARY VENOUS DRAINAGE

| 33730 | Complete repair of anomalous venous return (supracardiac, intracardiac, or infracardiac types)   Ⓒ 80 ↵ 63 |

To code a partial anomalous return, consult atrial septal defect.

| 33732 | Repair of cor triatriatum or supravalvular mitral ring by resection of left atrial membrane   Ⓒ 80 ↵ 63 |

SHUNTING PROCEDURES

33735	Atrial septectomy or septostomy; closed heart (Blalock-Hanlon type operation) Ⓒ 80 ↵ 63
33736	open heart with cardiopulmonary bypass Ⓒ 80 ↵ 63
33737	open heart, with inflow occlusion Ⓒ 80 ↵
33750	Shunt; subclavian to pulmonary artery (Blalock-Taussig type operation) Ⓒ 80 ↵ 63
33755	ascending aorta to pulmonary artery (Waterston type operation) Ⓒ 80 ↵ 63
33762	descending aorta to pulmonary artery (Potts-Smith type operation) Ⓒ 80 ↵ 63
33764	central, with prosthetic graft Ⓒ 80 ↵
33766	superior vena cava to pulmonary artery for flow to one lung (classical Glenn procedure) Ⓒ 80 ↵
33767	superior vena cava to pulmonary artery for flow to both lungs (bidirectional Glenn procedure) Ⓒ 80 ↵
+ ● 33768	Anastomosis, cavopulmonary, second superior vena cava (List separately in addition to primary procedure)

Report code 33768 with 33478, 33617, 33767.

Code 33768 cannot be reported with 32020, 33210, 33211.

TRANSPOSITION OF THE GREAT VESSELS

| 33770 | Repair of transposition of the great arteries with ventricular septal defect and subpulmonary stenosis; without surgical enlargement of ventricular septal defect   Ⓒ 80 ↵ |
| 33771 | with surgical enlargement of ventricular septal defect   Ⓒ 80 ↵ |

33774	Repair of transposition of the great arteries, atrial baffle procedure (eg, Mustard or Senning type) with cardiopulmonary bypass;	C 80 🔁
33775	with removal of pulmonary band	C 80 🔁
33776	with closure of ventricular septal defect	C 80 🔁
33777	with repair of subpulmonic obstruction	C 80 🔁
33778	Repair of transposition of the great arteries, aortic pulmonary artery reconstruction (eg, Jatene type);	C 80 🔁 63
33779	with removal of pulmonary band	C 80 🔁
33780	with closure of ventricular septal defect	C 80 🔁
33781	with repair of subpulmonic obstruction	C 80 🔁

TRUNCUS ARTERIOSUS

33786	Total repair, truncus arteriosus (Rastelli type operation)	C 80 🔁 63
33788	Reimplantation of an anomalous pulmonary artery	C 80 🔁

If banding of the pulmonary artery is performed, consult CPT code 33690.

AORTIC ANOMALIES

33800	Aortic suspension (aortopexy) for tracheal decompression (eg, for tracheomalacia) (separate procedure)	C 80 🔁
33802	Division of aberrant vessel (vascular ring);	C 80 🔁
33803	with reanastomosis	C 80 🔁
33813	Obliteration of aortopulmonary septal defect; without cardiopulmonary bypass	C 80 🔁
33814	with cardiopulmonary bypass	C 80 🔁
33820	Repair of patent ductus arteriosus; by ligation	C 80 🔁
33822	by division, under 18 years	A C 80 🔁
33824	by division, 18 years and older	C 80 🔁
33840	Excision of coarctation of aorta, with or without associated patent ductus arteriosus; with direct anastomosis	C 80 🔁
33845	with graft	C 80 🔁
33851	repair using either left subclavian artery or prosthetic material as gusset for enlargement	C 80 🔁
33852	Repair of hypoplastic or interrupted aortic arch using autogenous or prosthetic material; without cardiopulmonary bypass	C 80 🔁
33853	with cardiopulmonary bypass	C 80 🔁

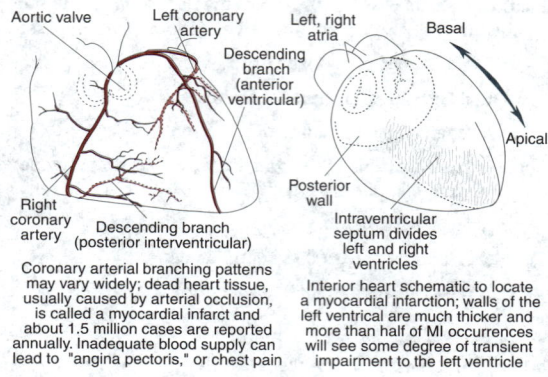

Coronary arterial branching patterns may vary widely; dead heart tissue, usually caused by arterial occlusion, is called a myocardial infarct and about 1.5 million cases are reported annually. Inadequate blood supply can lead to "angina pectoris," or chest pain

Interior heart schematic to locate a myocardial infarction; walls of the left ventrical are much thicker and more than half of MI occurrences will see some degree of transient impairment to the left ventricle

THORACIC AORTIC ANEURYSM

Codes 33880–33891 are used to report placement of an endovascular graft for repair of the descending thoracic aorta. These codes include all the device introduction, manipulation, positioning, and deployment. Do not report balloon angioplasty and/or stent deployment separately. Report open arterial exposure and associated closure of the arteriotomy sites (34812, 34820, 34833, 34834), introduction of guidewires and catheters (36140, 36200–36218), and extensive repair or replacement of an artery (35226, 35286), and transposition of subclavian artery to carotid, and carotid–carotid bypass performed in conjunction with endovascular repair of the descending thoracic aorta (33889, 33891) separately. Codes 33880 and 33881 include placement of all distal extensions. However, if proximal extensions are needed, they should be reported separately.

Consult 75956–75959 for fluoroscopic guidance.

Report other interventional procedures performed at the time of the endovascular repair separately.

33860	**Ascending aorta graft, with cardiopulmonary bypass, with or without valve suspension;**	C 80 ↻
33861	**with coronary reconstruction**	C 80 ↻
33863	**with aortic root replacement using composite prosthesis and coronary reconstruction**	C 80 ↻
33870	**Transverse arch graft, with cardiopulmonary bypass**	C 80 ↻
33875	**Descending thoracic aorta graft, with or without bypass**	C 80 ↻
33877	**Repair of thoracoabdominal aortic aneurysm with graft, with or without cardiopulmonary bypass**	C 80 ↻

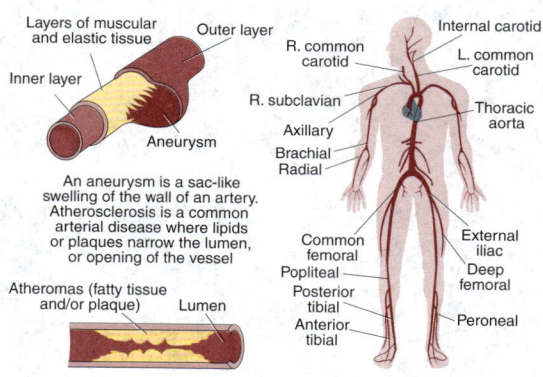

An aneurysm is a sac-like swelling of the wall of an artery. Atherosclerosis is a common arterial disease where lipids or plaques narrow the lumen, or opening of the vessel

ENDOVASCULAR REPAIR OF DESCENDING THORACIC AORTA

● **33880** **Endovascular repair of descending thoracic aorta (eg, aneurysm, pseudoaneurysm, dissection, penetrating ulcer, intramural hematoma, or traumatic disruption); involving coverage of left subclavian artery origin, initial endoprosthesis plus descending thoracic aortic extension(s), if required, to level of celiac artery origin**

To report radiological supervision and interpretation, use 75956 with 33880.

● **33881** **not involving coverage of left subclavian artery origin, initial endoprosthesis plus descending thoracic aortic extension(s), if required, to level of celiac artery origin**

To report radiological supervision and interpretation, use 75957 with 33881.

● **33883** **Placement of proximal extension prosthesis for endovascular repair of descending thoracic aorta (eg, aneurysm, pseudoaneurysm, dissection, penetrating ulcer, intramural hematoma, or traumatic disruption); initial extension**

To report radiological supervision and interpretation, use 75958 with 33883.

Codes 33881, 33883 cannot be reported when extension placement converts repair to cover left subclavian origin. Use only 33880.

+ ● **33884** **each additional proximal extension (List separately in addition to code for primary procedure)**

Note that 33884 is an add-on code and must be used in conjunction with 33883.

To report radiological supervision and interpretation, report 75958 with 33884.

● **33886** **Placement of distal extension prosthesis(s) delayed after endovascular repair of descending thoracic aorta**

Code 33886 cannot be reported with 33880, 33881.

Code 33886 can be reported only once, regardless of the number of modules deployed.

To report radiological supervision and interpretation, report 75959 with 33886.

● **33889** **Open subclavian to carotid artery transposition performed in conjunction with endovascular repair of descending thoracic aorta, by neck incision, unilateral**

Code 33889 cannot be reported with 35694.

● **33891** **Bypass graft, with other than vein, transcervical retropharyngeal carotid-carotid, performed in conjunction with endovascular repair of descending thoracic aorta, by neck incision**

Code 33891 cannot be reported with 35509, 35601.

PULMONARY ARTERY

● **33910** **Pulmonary artery embolectomy; with cardiopulmonary bypass** Ⓒ 80 ⬚
   MED: 100-3, 240.6

  33915 **without cardiopulmonary bypass** Ⓒ 80 ⬚
   MED: 100-3, 240.6

  33916 **Pulmonary endarterectomy, with or without embolectomy, with cardiopulmonary bypass** Ⓒ 80 ⬚
   MED: 100-3, 240.6

Cardiovascular System

33917–33933

33917   **Repair of pulmonary artery stenosis by reconstruction with patch or graft**   C 80 ⚕
       MED: 100-3, 240.6

~~**33918** Repair of pulmonary atresia with ventricular septal defect, by unifocalization of pulmonary arteries; without cardiopulmonary bypass~~

(Use 33925, 33926)

~~**33919** with cardiopulmonary bypass~~

(Use 33925, 33926)

33920   **Repair of pulmonary atresia with ventricular septal defect, by construction or replacement of conduit from right or left ventricle to pulmonary artery**   C 80 ⚕
       MED: 100-3, 240.6

       If other complex cardiac anomalies by construction of right or left ventricle to pulmonary artery conduit are repaired, consult CPT code 33608.

33922   **Transection of pulmonary artery with cardiopulmonary bypass**   C 80 ⚕ 63
       MED: 100-3, 240.6

+   **33924**   **Ligation and takedown of a systemic-to-pulmonary artery shunt, performed in conjunction with a congenital heart procedure (List separately in addition to code for primary procedure)**   C 80 ⚕
       MED: 100-3, 240.6

       Note that 33924 is an add-on code and must be used in conjunction with 33470-33475, 33600-33619, 33684-33688, 33692-33697, 33735-33767, 33770-33781, 33786, and 33920-33922.

●   **33925**   **Repair of pulmonary artery arborization anomalies by unifocalization; without cardiopulmonary bypass**

●   **33926**   **with cardiopulmonary bypass**

       Codes 33925, 33926 cannot be reported with 33697.

HEART/LUNG TRANSPLANTATION

Heart with or without lung transplantation involves three different components:

- Cadaver donor cardiectomy with or without pneumonectomy consists of harvesting and cold preservation of the graft prior to transport (see 33930, 33940).

- Backbench work includes dissection of the tissue around the heart and lungs and preparation of aorta, superior vena cava, inferior vena cava, and trachea for transplantation (see 33933, 33944). Repair or resection procedures of the donor heart should be reported using codes 33300, 33310, 33320, 33320, 33400, 33463, 33464, 33510, 33641, 35216, 35276, and 35685, as appropriate.

- Recipient transplantation which includes transplanting the heart/lungs into the patient (see 33935, 33945). To report implantation of an artificial heart system with recipient cardiectomy or heart replacement system components, consult CPT Category III codes 0051T-0053T.

33930   **Donor cardiectomy-pneumonectomy (including cold preservation)**   C ⚕
       MED: 100-2, 15, 50.5; 100-2, 16, 180; 100-3, 260.9

33933   **Backbench standard preparation of cadaver donor heart/lung allograft prior to transplantation, including dissection of allograft from surrounding soft tissues to prepare aorta, superior vena cava, inferior vena cava, and trachea for implantation**   C 80 ⚕

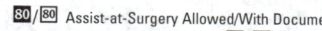

33935 Heart-lung transplant with recipient cardiectomy-pneumonectomy C 80 🗗
MED: 100-2, 15, 50.5; 100-2, 15, 60.3; 100-3, 260.9; 100-4, 8, 120.1

33940 Donor cardiectomy (including cold preservation) C 🗗

33944 Backbench standard preparation of cadaver donor heart allograft prior to transplantation, including dissection of allograft from surrounding soft tissues to prepare aorta, superior vena cava, inferior vena cava, pulmonary artery, and left atrium for implantation C 80 🗗

To report resection or repair of the donor heart, consult CPT codes 33300, 33310, 33320, 33400, 33463, 33464, 33510, 33641, 35216, 35276, 35685.

33945 Heart transplant, with or without recipient cardiectomy C 80 🗗
MED: 100-2, 15, 50.5; 100-2, 15, 60.3; 100-3, 260.9; 100-4, 8, 120.1

CARDIAC ASSIST

To report percutaneous implantation of extracorporeal ventricular assist device or for removal of percutaneously implanted extracorporeal ventricular assist device, consult CPT Category III codes 0048T-0050T.

33960 Prolonged extracorporeal circulation for cardiopulmonary insufficiency; initial 24 hours C 80 🗗 ⑥

If an insertion of a cannula is performed for prolonged extracorporeal circulation, consult CPT code 36822.

+ 33961 each additional 24 hours (List separately in addition to code for primar procedure) C 80 🗗 ⑥

If an insertion of a cannula is performed for prolonged extracorporeal circulation, consult CPT code 36822.

Note that 33961 is an add-on code and must be used in conjunction with 33960.

33967 Insertion of intra-aortic balloon assist device, percutaneous C 80 🗗
AMA: 2002, Feb, 1

33968 Removal of intra-aortic balloon assist device, percutaneous C 🗗
AMA: 2000, Jan, 10; 1999, Nov, 19

33970 Insertion of intra-aortic balloon assist device through the femoral artery, open approach C 80 🗗
AMA: 1999, Nov, 19

If the insertion is performed percutaneously, consult CPT code 33967.

33971 Removal of intra-aortic balloon assist device including repair of femoral artery, with or without graft C 🗗

33973 Insertion of intra-aortic balloon assist device through the ascending aorta C 80 🗗

33974 Removal of intra-aortic balloon assist device from the ascending aorta, including repair of the ascending aorta, with or without graft C 🗗

33975 Insertion of ventricular assist device; extracorporeal, single ventricle C 80 🗗
AMA: 2002, Feb, 1

33976 extracorporeal, biventricular C 80 🗗
AMA: 2002, Feb, 1

33977 Removal of ventricular assist device; extracorporeal, single ventricle C 80 🗗
AMA: 2002, Feb, 1

Cardiovascular System

33978	extracorporeal, biventricular	C 80 ⊡

AMA: 2002, Feb, 1

33979	Insertion of ventricular assist device, implantable intracorporeal, single ventricle	C 80 ⊡

AMA: 2002, Feb, 1

33980	Removal of ventricular assist device, implantable intracorporeal, single ventricle	C 80 ⊡

AMA: 2002, Feb, 1

OTHER PROCEDURES

33999	Unlisted procedure, cardiac surgery	T 80

MED: 100-3, 20.6

AMA: 1999, Oct, 11

ARTERIES AND VEINS

Primary vascular procedures include the establishment of both inflow and outflow. Also included is the portion of the operative arteriogram performed by the surgeon. When performed, sympathectomy is included in the listed aortic procedures. Report 37799 for unlisted vascular procedures.

EMBOLECTOMY/THROMBECTOMY — ARTERIAL, WITH OR WITHOUT CATHETER

34001	Embolectomy or thrombectomy, with or without catheter; carotid, subclavian or innominate artery, by neck incision	C 50 80 ⊡

MED: 100-3, 160.8

34051	innominate, subclavian artery, by thoracic incision	C 50 80 ⊡
34101	axillary, brachial, innominate, subclavian artery, by arm incision	T 50 80 ⊡
34111	radial or ulnar artery, by arm incision	T 50 80 ⊡
34151	renal, celiac, mesentery, aortoiliac artery, by abdominal incision	C 50 80 ⊡
34201	femoropopliteal, aortoiliac artery, by leg incision	T 50 80 ⊡
34203	popliteal-tibio-peroneal artery, by leg incision	T 50 80 ⊡

EMBOLECTOMY/THROMBECTOMY — VENOUS, DIRECT OR WITH CATHETER

34401	Thrombectomy, direct or with catheter; vena cava, iliac vein, by abdominal incision	C 50 80 ⊡
34421	vena cava, iliac, femoropopliteal vein, by leg incision	T 50 80 ⊡

AMA: 1994, Spring, 30

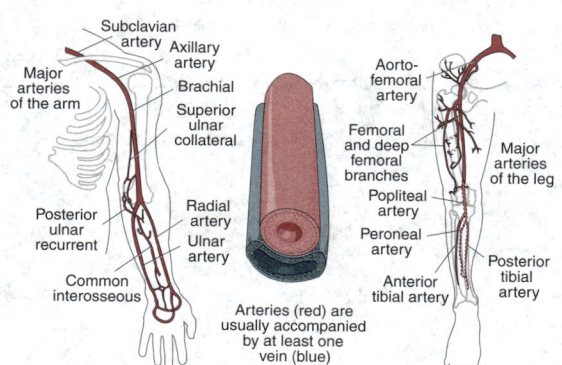

Subclavian artery
Axillary artery
Major arteries of the arm
Brachial
Superior ulnar collateral
Posterior ulnar recurrent
Radial artery
Ulnar artery
Common interosseous
Arteries (red) are usually accompanied by at least one vein (blue)
Aorto-femoral artery
Femoral and deep femoral branches
Major arteries of the leg
Popliteal artery
Peroneal artery
Posterior tibial artery
Anterior tibial artery

34451	vena cava, iliac, femoropopliteal vein, by abdominal and leg incision	C 50 80 ↱
34471	subclavian vein, by neck incision	T 50 ↱
34490	axillary and subclavian vein, by arm incision	T 50 ↱

VENOUS RECONSTRUCTION

34501	Valvuloplasty, femoral vein	T 50 80 ↱
34502	Reconstruction of vena cava, any method	C 80 ↱
34510	Venous valve transposition, any vein donor	T 50 80 ↱
34520	Cross-over vein graft to venous system	T 50 80 ↱
34530	Saphenopopliteal vein anastomosis	T 50 80 ↱

ENDOVASCULAR REPAIR OF ABDOMINAL AORTIC ANEURYSM

CPT codes 38000-34834 address the repair of a weakness of the aorta with an endovascular graft under fluoroscopic guidance. These codes include open femoral or iliac artery exposure, device manipulation and deployment, balloon angioplasty, stent deployment, and closure. Report introduction of guidewires and catheters separately.

If extensive repair or replacement of an artery is required, report as an additional procedure.

If fluoroscopic guidance is performed with endovascular aneurysm repair, consult 75952 or 75953. Angiography of the aorta and its branches for diagnostic imaging before deployment of the endovascular device, fluoroscopic guidance in the delivery of the endovascular components, and arterial angiography during the procedure are included in code 75952.

Report other interventional procedures such as renal transluminal angioplasty, arterial embolization, or intravascular ultrasound separately.

	34800	Endovascular repair of infrarenal abdominal aortic aneurysm or dissection; using aorto-aortic tube prosthesis	C 80 ↱
		AMA: 2002, Sep, 3; 2000, Dec, 1	
	34802	using modular bifurcated prosthesis (one docking limb)	C 80 ↱
		AMA: 2002, Sep, 3; 2000, Dec, 1	
	34803	using modular bifurcated prosthesis (two docking limbs)	C 80 ↱

To report endovascular repair of abdominal aortic aneurysm or dissection involving visceral vessels using a fenestrated modular bifurcated prosthesis with two docking limbs, consult Category III codes 0078T, 0079T.

	34804	using unibody bifurcated prosthesis	C 80 ↱
		AMA: 2002, Sep, 3; 2000, Dec, 1	
	34805	using aorto-uniiliac or aorto-unifemoral prosthesis	C 80 ↱
+	34808	Endovascular placement of iliac artery occlusion device (List separately in addition to code for primary procedure)	C 80 ↱
		AMA: 2002, Sep, 3; 2000, Dec, 1	

Note that 34808 is an add-on code and must be used in conjunction with codes 34800, 34805, 34813, 34825 and 34826.

To report radiological supervision and interpretation, consult CPT code 75952, report with codes 34800-34808.

To report open arterial exposure, consult CPT codes 34812, 34820, 34833, or 34834, in addition to codes 34800-34808.

| ↱ CCI Comp | 50 Bilateral Procedure | + CPT Add-on Code | ⊘ Modifier -51 Exempt | ♂ Male | ♀ Female |
| ● New Code | ▲ Revised Code | M Maternity Edit | A Age Edit | A—Y APC Status Ind. | AMA: CPT Assistant |

© 2005 Ingenix, Inc. (Blue Ink)   CPT only © 2005 American Medical Association. All Rights Reserved. (Black Ink)   Surgery — 261

34812   **Open femoral artery exposure for delivery of endovascular prosthesis, by groin incision, unilateral**   C 50 80 ↰
AMA: 2003, Feb, 1; 2002, Sep, 3; 2000, Dec, 1

To report a procedure performed bilaterally, append modifier 50.

+   34813   **Placement of femoral-femoral prosthetic graft during endovascular aortic aneurysm repair (List separately in addition to code for primary procedure)**   C 80 ↰
AMA: 2002, Sep, 3; 2000, Dec, 1

Note that 34813 is an add-on code and must be used in conjunction with 34812.

If femoral artery grafting is performed, consult CPT codes 35521, 35533, 35546, 35551-35558, 35566, 35621, 35646, 35651-35661, 35666 and 35700.

34820   **Open iliac artery exposure for delivery of endovascular prosthesis or iliac occlusion during endovascular therapy, by abdominal or retroperitoneal incision, unilateral**   C 50 80 ↰
AMA: 2003, Feb, 1; 2002, Sep, 3; 2000, Dec, 1

34825   **Placement of proximal or distal extension prosthesis for endovascular repair of infrarenal abdominal aortic or iliac aneurysm, false aneurysm, or dissection; initial vessel**   C 80 ↰
AMA: 2003, Feb, 1; 2002, Sep, 3; 2000, Dec, 1

Report codes 34825 and 34826 with codes 34800-34808 and 34900, when appropriate.

To report a staged procedure, append modifier 58.

To report radiological supervision and interpretation, consult CPT code 75953.

+   34826   **each additional vessel (List separately in addition to code for primary procedure)**   C 80 ↰
AMA: 2003, Feb, 1; 2002, Sep, 3; 2000, Dec, 1

Note that 34826 is an add-on code and must be reported in conjunction with 34825.

34830   **Open repair of infrarenal aortic aneurysm or dissection, plus repair of associated arterial trauma, following unsuccessful endovascular repair; tube prosthesis**   C 80 ↰
AMA: 2002, Sep, 3; 2000, Dec, 1

34831   **aorto-bi-iliac prosthesis**   C 80 ↰
AMA: 2002, Sep, 3; 2000, Dec, 1

34832   **aorto-bifemoral prosthesis**   C 80 ↰
AMA: 2002, Sep, 3; 2000, Dec, 1

▲   34833   **Open iliac artery exposure with creation of conduit for delivery of aortic or iliac endovascular prosthesis, by abdominal or retroperitoneal incision, unilateral**   C 50 80 ↰
AMA: 2003, Feb, 1

Do not report 34833 in conjunction with CPT code 34820.

To report procedure performed bilaterally, append modifier 50.

▲   34834   **Open brachial artery exposure to assist in the deployment of aortic or iliac endovascular prosthesis by arm incision, unilateral**   C 50 80 ↰
AMA: 2003, Feb, 1

To report procedure performed bilaterally, append modifier 50.

ENDOVASCULAR REPAIR OF ILIAC ANEURYSM

Code 34900 includes angioplasty and/or stent placements within the target treatment zone either before or after endograft vascular graft replacement, do not report separately. The following services should be reported in addition to 34900 when appropriate; open femoral or iliac artery exposure (34812, 34820), introduction of guidewires or catheters (36200, 36215-36218), extensive repair or artery replacement (35206-35286).

If fluoroscopic guidance is performed with endovascular iliac aneurysm repair, consult 75954. Angiography of the aorta and iliac arteries for diagnostic imaging before deployment of the endovascular device, fluoroscopic guidance in the delivery of the endovascular components, and angiography to verify for correct placement of the graft, check for endoleaks, and assess the status of the runoff vessels is included in 75954.

Report other interventional procedures performed at the time of the endovascular aortic aneurysm repair separately when appropriate.

34900   **Endovascular graft placement for repair of iliac artery (eg, aneurysm, pseudoaneurysm, arteriovenous malformation, trauma)**   Ⓒ 50 🔃
          AMA: 2003, Feb, 1

              To report radiological supervision and interpretation, consult CPT code 75954.

              To report placement of extension prosthesis during endovascular iliac artery repair, consult CPT code 34825.

              To report procedure performed bilaterally, append modifier 50.

DIRECT REPAIR OF ANEURYSM OR EXCISION (PARTIAL OR TOTAL) AND GRAFT INSERTION FOR ANEURYSM, FALSE ANEURYSM, RUPTURED ANEURYSM, AND ASSOCIATED OCCLUSIVE DISEASE

Preparation of the artery for anastomosis, including endarterectomy is included in CPT codes 35001-35152.

If direct repairs associated with occlusive disease only are performed, consult CPT codes 35201-35286.

If a thoracic aortic aneurysm is repaired, consult CPT codes 33860-33875.

If an intracranial aneurysm is repaired, consult CPT code 61700 and subsequent codes.

To report endovascular repair of abdominal aortic aneurysm, consult CPT codes 34800-34826; of iliac artery aneurysm, consult CPT code 34900; thoracic aortic aneurysm, consult code 33880.

35001   **Direct repair of aneurysm, pseudoaneurysm, or excision (partial or total) and graft insertion, with or without patch graft; for aneurysm and associated occlusive disease, carotid, subclavian artery, by neck incision**   Ⓒ 50 80 🔃

35002   **for ruptured aneurysm, carotid, subclavian artery, by neck incision**   Ⓒ 50 80 🔃

35005   **for aneurysm, pseudoaneurysm, and associated occlusive disease, vertebral artery**   Ⓒ 50 80 🔃

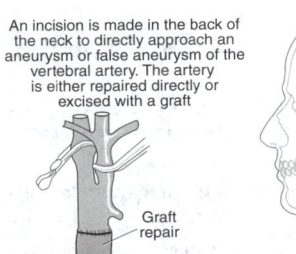
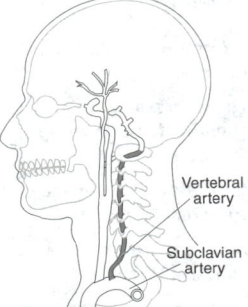

An incision is made in the back of the neck to directly approach an aneurysm or false aneurysm of the vertebral artery. The artery is either repaired directly or excised with a graft

Graft repair

Vertebral artery

Subclavian artery

Cardiovascular System

35011–35152

35011	for aneurysm and associated occlusive disease, axillary-brachial artery, by arm incision	T 50 80
35013	for ruptured aneurysm, axillary-brachial artery, by arm incision	C 50 80
35021	for aneurysm, pseudoaneurysm, and associated occlusive disease, innominate, subclavian artery, by thoracic incision	C 50 80
35022	for ruptured aneurysm, innominate, subclavian artery, by thoracic incision	C 50 80
35045	for aneurysm, pseudoaneurysm, and associated occlusive disease, radial or ulnar artery	C 50 80
35081	for aneurysm, pseudoaneurysm, and associated occlusive disease, abdominal aorta	C 80

MED: 100-3, 20.23

AMA: 2001, Dec, 7; 2000, Dec, 1

| 35082 | for ruptured aneurysm, abdominal aorta | C 80 |

MED: 100-3, 20.23

| 35091 | for aneurysm, pseudoaneurysm, and associated occlusive disease, abdominal aorta involving visceral vessels (mesenteric, celiac, renal) | C 50 80 |

MED: 100-3, 20.23

AMA: 2000, Dec, 1

35092	for ruptured aneurysm, abdominal aorta involving visceral vessels (mesenteric, celiac, renal)	C 50 80
35102	for aneurysm, pseudoaneurysm, and associated occlusive disease, abdominal aorta involving iliac vessels (common, hypogastric, external)	C 50 80
35103	for ruptured aneurysm, abdominal aorta involving iliac vessels (common, hypogastric, external)	C 50 80
35111	for aneurysm, pseudoaneurysm, and associated occlusive disease, splenic artery	C 50 80
35112	for ruptured aneurysm, splenic artery	C 50 80
35121	for aneurysm, pseudoaneurysm, and associated occlusive disease, hepatic, celiac, renal, or mesenteric artery	C 50 80
35122	for ruptured aneurysm, hepatic, celiac, renal, or mesenteric artery	C 50 80
35131	for aneurysm, pseudoaneurysm, and associated occlusive disease, iliac artery (common, hypogastric, external)	C 50 80

AMA: 2003, Feb, 1

35132	for ruptured aneurysm, iliac artery (common, hypogastric, external)	C 50 80
35141	for aneurysm, pseudoaneurysm, and associated occlusive disease, common femoral artery (profunda femoris, superficial femoral)	C 50 80
35142	for ruptured aneurysm, common femoral artery (profunda femoris, superficial femoral)	C 50 80
35151	for aneurysm, pseudoaneurysm, and associated occlusive disease, popliteal artery	C 50 80
35152	for ruptured aneurysm, popliteal artery	C 50 80

REPAIR ARTERIOVENOUS FISTULA

35180	Repair, congenital arteriovenous fistula; head and neck	T 80 ▯
35182	thorax and abdomen	C 80 ▯
35184	extremities	T 80 ▯
35188	Repair, acquired or traumatic arteriovenous fistula; head and neck	4 T 80 ▯
	MED: 100-2, 15, 260; 100-4, 12, 90.3; 100-4, 14, 10	
35189	thorax and abdomen	C 80 ▯
35190	extremities	T 80 ▯

REPAIR BLOOD VESSEL OTHER THAN FOR FISTULA, WITH OR WITHOUT PATCH ANGIOPLASTY

If an AV fistula is repaired, consult CPT codes 35180-35190.

35201	Repair blood vessel, direct; neck	T 50 80 ▯
35206	upper extremity	T 50 80 ▯
	AMA: 2000, Oct, 1	
35207	hand, finger	4 T 50 ▯
	MED: 100-2, 15, 260; 100-4, 12, 90.3; 100-4, 14, 10	
35211	intrathoracic, with bypass	C 50 80 ▯
35216	intrathoracic, without bypass	C 50 80 ▯
35221	intra-abdominal	C 50 80 ▯
35226	lower extremity	T 50 80 ▯
35231	Repair blood vessel with vein graft; neck	T 50 80 ▯
35236	upper extremity	T 50 80 ▯
35241	intrathoracic, with bypass	C 50 80 ▯
35246	intrathoracic, without bypass	C 50 80 ▯
35251	intra-abdominal	C 50 80 ▯
35256	lower extremity	T 50 80 ▯
35261	Repair blood vessel with graft other than vein; neck	T 50 80 ▯
35266	upper extremity	T 50 80 ▯
35271	intrathoracic, with bypass	C 50 80 ▯
35276	intrathoracic, without bypass	C 50 80 ▯
35281	intra-abdominal	C 50 80 ▯
35286	lower extremity	T 50 80 ▯

THROMBOENDARTERECTOMY

If a coronary artery bypass is performed, consult CPT codes 33510-33536 and 33572.

35301	Thromboendarterectomy, with or without patch graft; carotid, vertebral, subclavian, by neck incision	C 50 80 ▯
	MED: 100-3, 160.8; 100-3, 20.1	
35311	subclavian, innominate, by thoracic incision	C 50 80 ▯
	MED: 100-3, 20.1	
35321	axillary-brachial	T 50 80 ▯
35331	abdominal aorta	C 50 80 ▯
35341	mesenteric, celiac, or renal	C 50 80 ▯

▯ CCI Comp   50 Bilateral Procedure   ✚ CPT Add-on Code   ⊘ Modifier -51 Exempt   ♂Male   ♀ Female
● New Code   ▲ Revised Code   M Maternity Edit   A Age Edit   A—Y APC Status Ind.   AMA: CPT Assistant

© 2005 Ingenix, Inc. *(Blue Ink)*    CPT only © 2005 American Medical Association. All Rights Reserved. *(Black Ink)*    Surgery — 265

Cardiovascular System

35180–35341

35351	iliac	C 50 80 ⬛
35355	iliofemoral	C 50 80 ⬛
35361	combined aortoiliac	C 50 80 ⬛
35363	combined aortoiliofemoral	C 50 80 ⬛
35371	common femoral	C 50 80 ⬛
35372	deep (profunda) femoral	C 50 80 ⬛
35381	femoral and/or popliteal, and/or tibioperoneal	C 50 80 ⬛

+   **35390**   **Reoperation, carotid, thromboendarterectomy, more than one month after original operation (List separately in addition to code for primary procedure)**   C ⬛
          AMA: 1997, Nov, 16

> Note that 35390 is an add-on code and must be used in conjunction with 35301.

ANGIOSCOPY

+   **35400**   **Angioscopy (non-coronary vessels or grafts) during therapeutic intervention (List separately in addition to code for primary procedure)**   C 80 ⬛

> Note that 35400 is an add-on code and must be used in conjunction with a code for the therapeutic intervention.

TRANSLUMINAL ANGIOPLASTY — OPEN

For radiological supervision and interpretation, consult CPT codes 75962-75968 and 75978.

When performed as part of another procedure, append modifier 51 or 52 as appropriate.

35450   **Transluminal balloon angioplasty, open; renal or other visceral artery**   C 50 80 ⬛
          MED: 100-3, 20.7; 100-3, 220.13

          AMA: 2000, Dec, 1; 1997, Feb, 2, 3

35452   **aortic**   C 50 80 ⬛
          AMA: 1997, Feb, 2, 3

35454   **iliac**   C 50 80 ⬛
          AMA: 2003, Feb, 1; 2000, Dec, 1; 1997, Feb, 2, 3

35456   **femoral-popliteal**   C 50 80 ⬛
          AMA: 1997, Feb, 2, 3

35458   **brachiocephalic trunk or branches, each vessel**   T 50 80 ⬛
          AMA: 2001, May, 11; 1997, Feb, 2, 3

35459   **tibioperoneal trunk and branches**   T 50 80 ⬛
          AMA: 1997, Feb, 2, 3

35460   **venous**   T 50 ⬛
          AMA: 1997, Feb, 2, 3

26 / TC Professional/Technical Component   80 / 80 Assist-at-Surgery Allowed/With Documentation   ☉ Conscious Sedation
Unlisted   Not Covered   MED: Pubs 100/NCD Reference   1 - 9 ASC Group   63 Modifier 63 Exempt
266 — Surgery   CPT only © 2005 American Medical Association. All Rights Reserved. *(Black Ink)*   © 2005 Ingenix, Inc. *(Blue Ink)*
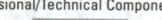

TRANSLUMINAL ANGIOPLASTY — PERCUTANEOUS

For radiological supervision and interpretation, consult CPT codes 75962-75968 and 75978.

Codes for catheter placement should also be reported.

⊙	**35470**	**Transluminal balloon angioplasty, percutaneous; tibioperoneal trunk or branches, each vessel**	T 50 ⏎
		MED: 100-3, 20.7; 100-3, 220.13	
		AMA: 1997, Feb, 2, 3; 1996, Aug, 3	
⊙	**35471**	**renal or visceral artery**	T 50 ⏎
		MED: 100-3, 20.7; 100-3, 220.13	
		AMA: 1997, Feb, 2, 3; 1996, Aug, 3	
⊙	**35472**	**aortic**	T 50 80 ⏎
		MED: 100-3, 20.7; 100-3, 220.13	
		AMA: 1997, Feb, 2, 3; 1996, Aug, 3	
⊙	**35473**	**iliac**	T 50 ⏎
		MED: 100-3, 20.7; 100-3, 220.13	
		AMA: 2003, Feb, 1; 2001, May, 1; 1997, Feb, 2, 3; 1996, Aug, 3; 1993, Fall, 11	
⊙	**35474**	**femoral-popliteal**	T 50 ⏎
		MED: 100-3, 20.7; 100-3, 220.13	
		AMA: 2001, May, 1; 1997, Feb, 2, 3; 1996, Aug, 3	
⊙	**35475**	**brachiocephalic trunk or branches, each vessel**	T 50 ⏎
		MED: 100-3, 20.7; 100-3, 220.13	
		AMA: 2001, May, 1; 1997, Feb, 2, 3; 1996, Aug, 3	
⊙	**35476**	**venous**	T 50 ⏎
		MED: 100-3, 20.7; 100-3, 220.13	
		AMA: 2001, May, 1; 1997, Feb, 2, 3; 1996, Aug, 3	

TRANSLUMINAL ATHERECTOMY — OPEN

If radiological supervision and interpretation is needed, consult CPT codes 75992-75996.

When performed as part of another procedure, append modifier 51 or 52 as appropriate.

	35480	**Transluminal peripheral atherectomy, open; renal or other visceral artery** C 80 ⏎	
		AMA: 1997, Feb, 2, 3	

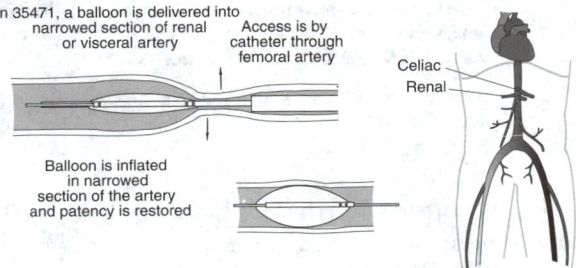

In 35471, a balloon is delivered into narrowed section of renal or visceral artery

Access is by catheter through femoral artery

Celiac
Renal

Balloon is inflated in narrowed section of the artery and patency is restored

A balloon angioplasty is performed on the renal or visceral artery in a percutaneous procedure

| 35481 | aortic | C 80 ▸ |
| | AMA: 1997, Feb, 2 | |

| 35482 | iliac | C 80 ▸ |
| | AMA: 1997, Feb, 2 | |

| 35483 | femoral-popliteal | C 80 ▸ |
| | AMA: 1997, Feb, 2 | |

| 35484 | brachiocephalic trunk or branches, each vessel | T 80 ▸ |
| | AMA: 1997, Feb, 2 | |

| 35485 | tibioperoneal trunk and branches | T 80 ▸ |
| | AMA: 1997, Feb, 2 | |

TRANSLUMINAL ATHERECTOMY — PERCUTANEOUS

For radiological supervision and interpretation, consult CPT codes 75992-75996.

Codes for catheter placement should also be reported.

| 35490 | Transluminal peripheral atherectomy, percutaneous; renal or other visceral artery | T 80 ▸ |
| | AMA: 1997, Feb, 2 | |

| 35491 | aortic | T 80 ▸ |
| | AMA: 1997, Feb, 2 | |

| 35492 | iliac | T 80 ▸ |
| | AMA: 1997, Feb, 2 | |

| 35493 | femoral-popliteal | T ▸ |
| | AMA: 1997, Feb, 2 | |

| 35494 | brachiocephalic trunk or branches, each vessel | T ▸ |
| | AMA: 1997, Feb, 2 | |

| 35495 | tibioperoneal trunk and branches | T 80 ▸ |
| | AMA: 1997, Feb, 2 | |

BYPASS GRAFT — VEIN

Harvesting of the saphenous vein graft is included in codes 35501-35587 and not reported separately or as co-surgery. To report vein harvesting: upper extremity, consult CPT code 35500; femoropopliteal vein segment, consult CPT code 35572; two segments from two distant sites, consult CPT code 35682; three or more segments from distant sites, consult CPT code 35683. These should be reported in addition to the bypass graft procedure.

| + 35500 | Harvest of upper extremity vein, one segment, for lower extremity or coronary artery bypass procedure (List separately in addition to code for primary procedure) | T ▸ |
| | AMA: 1999, Nov, 19; 1999, Mar, 6; 1998, Nov, 13 | |

Note that 35500 is an add-on code and must be used in conjunction with CPT codes 33510-33536, 35556, 35566, 35571, 35583-35587.

If more than one vein segment is harvested, consult CPT codes 35682 and 35683.

To report endoscopic procedure, consult CPT code 35508.

| 35501 | Bypass graft, with vein; carotid | C 50 80 ▸ |
| | AMA: 1999, Apr, 11 | |

| 35506 | carotid-subclavian | C 50 80 ▸ |

35507	subclavian-carotid	C 50 80 ⬀
35508	carotid-vertebral MED: 100-3, 20.1	C 50 80 ⬀
35509	carotid-carotid	C 50 80 ⬀
35510	carotid-brachial	C 50 80 ⬀
35511	subclavian-subclavian	C 50 80 ⬀
35512	subclavian-brachial	C 50 80 ⬀
35515	subclavian-vertebral MED: 100-3, 20.1	C 50 80 ⬀
35516	subclavian-axillary	C 50 80 ⬀
35518	axillary-axillary	C 50 80 ⬀
35521	axillary-femoral	C 50 80 ⬀

If a bypass graft is performed with a synthetic graft, consult CPT code 35621.

35522	axillary-brachial	C 50 80 ⬀
35525	brachial-brachial	C 50 80 ⬀
35526	aortosubclavian or carotid	C 50 80 ⬀

If a bypass graft is performed with a synthetic graft, consult CPT code 35626.

35531	aortoceliac or aortomesenteric	C 50 80 ⬀
35533	axillary-femoral-femoral	C 50 80 ⬀

If a bypass graft is performed with a synthetic graft, consult CPT code 35654.

35536	splenorenal AMA: 1999, Jun, 10	C 50 80 ⬀
35541	aortoiliac or bi-iliac	C 80 ⬀

If a bypass graft is performed with a synthetic graft, consult CPT code 35641.

35546	aortofemoral or bifemoral	C 50 80 ⬀

If a bypass graft is performed with a synthetic graft, consult CPT code 35646.

35548	aortoiliofemoral, unilateral	C 80 ⬀

If a bypass graft is performed with a synthetic graft, consult CPT code 37799.

35549	aortoiliofemoral, bilateral	C 80 ⬀

If a bypass graft is performed with a synthetic graft, consult CPT code 37799.

35551	aortofemoral-popliteal	C 50 80 ⬀
35556	femoral-popliteal	C 50 80 ⬀
35558	femoral-femoral	C 50 80 ⬀
35560	aortorenal AMA: 1999, Jun, 10	C 50 80 ⬀
35563	ilioiliac	C 50 80 ⬀
35565	iliofemoral	C 50 80 ⬀
35566	femoral-anterior tibial, posterior tibial, peroneal artery or other distal vessels	C 50 80 ⬀
35571	popliteal-tibial, -peroneal artery or other distal vessels	C 50 80 ⬀

Cardiovascular System

35572–35626

\+   **35572**   **Harvest of femoropopliteal vein, one segment, for vascular reconstruction procedure (eg, aortic, vena caval, coronary, peripheral artery) (List separately in addition to code for primary procedure)**   N 80 ⤵

Note that 35572 is an add-on code and must be used in conjunction with 33510-33516, 33517-33523, 33533-33536, 34502, 34520, 35001-35002, 35011-35022, 35102-35103, 35121-35152, 35231-35256, 35501-35587, 35879-35907.

To report procedure performed bilaterally, append modifier 50.

BYPASS GRAFT — IN-SITU VEIN

35583   **In-situ vein bypass; femoral-popliteal**   C 50 80 ⤵

To report aortobifemoral bypass using synthetic conduit, and femoral-popliteal bypass with vein conduit in-situ, consult CPT codes 35646 and 35583. To report aorto(uni)femoral bypass with synthetic conduit, and femoral-popliteal bypass with vein conduit in-situe, consult CPT codes 35647 and 35583. To report aortofemoral bypass using vein conduit, and femoral-popliteal bypass with vein conduit in-situ, consult CPT codes 35546 and 35583.

35585   **femoral-anterior tibial, posterior tibial, or peroneal artery**   C 50 80 ⤵

35587   **popliteal-tibial, peroneal**   C 50 80 ⤵
       AMA: 1999, Apr, 11

BYPASS GRAFT — OTHER THAN VEIN

⊘   **35600**   **Harvest of upper extremity artery, one segment, for coronary artery bypass procedure**   C ⤵

35601   **Bypass graft, with other than vein; carotid**   C 50 80 ⤵
       MED: 100-3, 20.1

35606   **carotid-subclavian**   C 50 80 ⤵
       MED: 100-3, 20.1

Report code 33891 for an open transcervical common carotid-common carotid bypass performed with the endovascular repair of the descending thoracic aorta.

Report code 33889 for an open subclavian to carotid artery transposition performed with an endovascular thoracic aneurysm repair by neck incision.

35612   **subclavian-subclavian**   C 50 80 ⤵

35616   **subclavian-axillary**   C 50 80 ⤵

35621   **axillary-femoral**   C 50 80 ⤵

35623   **axillary-popliteal or -tibial**   C 50 80 ⤵

35626   **aortosubclavian or carotid**   C 50 80 ⤵

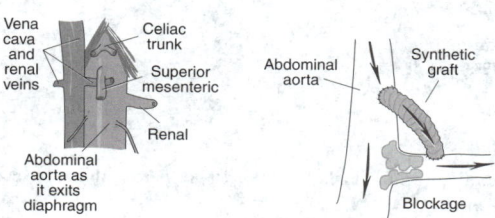

In 35631, a bypass graft of material other than vein is surgically installed from the aorta to the celiac, mesenteric, or renal arteries. The graft is typically placed in an end-to-side fashion on both the aorta and the recipient vessel downstream from the blockage

35631	aortoceliac, aortomesenteric, aortorenal	C 50 80 ↰
35636	splenorenal (splenic to renal arterial anastomosis)	C 50 80 ↰
35641	aortoiliac or bi-iliac	C 80 ↰

AMA: 2001, Dec, 7

To report open placement of aorto-bi-iliac prosthesis, post unsuccessful endovascular repair, consult CPT code 34831.

35642	carotid-vertebral	C 50 80 ↰

MED: 100-3, 20.1

35645	subclavian-vertebral	C 50 80 ↰

MED: 100-3, 20.1

35646	aortobifemoral	C 80 ↰

To report open placment of aortobifemoral prosthesis post unsuccessful endovascular repair, consult CPT code 34832.

35647	aortofemoral	C 50 80 ↰
35650	axillary-axillary	C 50 80 ↰
35651	aortofemoral-popliteal	C 50 80 ↰
35654	axillary-femoral-femoral	C 80 ↰
35656	femoral-popliteal	C 50 80 ↰
35661	femoral-femoral	C 50 80 ↰
35663	ilioiliac	C 50 80 ↰
35665	iliofemoral	C 50 80 ↰
35666	femoral-anterior tibial, posterior tibial, or peroneal artery	C 50 80 ↰
35671	popliteal-tibial or -peroneal artery	C 50 80 ↰

COMPOSITE GRAFTS

Use the following codes to report harvest and anastomosis of two or more vein segments from sites distant to that where the bypass is being performed.

+	35681	Bypass graft; composite, prosthetic and vein (List separately in addition to code for primary procedure)	C ↰

AMA: 1999, Mar, 6; 1999, Apr, 11; 1998, Nov, 13-14

Note that 35681 is not to be reported in addition to 35682 and 35683.

+	35682	autogenous composite, two segments of veins from two locations (List separately in addition to code for primary procedure)	C 80 ↰

AMA: 2002, Sep, 3; 1999, Mar, 6; 1999, Apr, 11; 1998, Nov, 13-14

Note that 35682 is not to be reported in addition to 35681 and 35683.

+	35683	autogenous composite, three or more segments of vein from two or more locations (List separately in addition to code for primary procedure)	C 80 ↰

AMA: 2002, Sep, 3; 1999, Mar, 6; 1999, Apr, 11; 1998, Nov, 13-14

Note that 35683 is not to be reported in addition to 35681 and 35682.

ADJUVANT TECHNIQUES

To report composite graft(s), consult CPT codes 35681-35683.

+   **35685**   **Placement of vein patch or cuff at distal anastomosis of bypass graft, synthetic conduit (List separately in addition to code for primary procedure)**   T ↱

          AMA: 2002, Sep, 3

          Note that 35685 is an add-on code and must be used in conjunction with CPT codes 35656, 35666, or 35671.

+   **35686**   **Creation of distal arteriovenous fistula during lower extremity bypass surgery (non-hemodialysis) (List separately in addition to code for primary procedure)**   T ↱

          AMA: 2002, Sep, 3

          Note that 35686 is an add-on code and must be used in conjunction with CPT codes 35556, 35566, 35571, 35583-35587, 35656, 35666, or 35671.

ARTERIAL TRANSPOSITION

   35691   **Transposition and/or reimplantation; vertebral to carotid artery** C 50 80 ↱

   35693   **vertebral to subclavian artery**   C 50 80 ↱

   35694   **subclavian to carotid artery**   C 50 80 ↱

          Report code 33889 for an open subclavian to carotid artery transposition performed with an endovascular repair of the descending thoracic aorta.

   35695   **carotid to subclavian artery**   C 50 80 ↱

+   **35697**   **Reimplantation, visceral artery to infrarenal aortic prosthesis, each artery (List separately in addition to code for primary procedure)**   C 80 ↱

          Code 35697 should not be reported with CPT code 33877

EXPLORATION/REVISION

+   **35700**   **Reoperation, femoral-popliteal or femoral (popliteal) -anterior tibial, posterior tibial, peroneal artery or other distal vessels, more than one month after original operation (List separately in addition to code for primary procedure)**   C ↱

          Note that 35700 is an add-on code and must be used in conjunction with 35556, 35566, 35571, 35583, 35585, 35587, 35656, 35666, and 35671.

   35701   **Exploration (not followed by surgical repair), with or without lysis of artery; carotid artery**   C 50 80 ↱

   35721   **femoral artery**   C 50 80 ↱
          AMA: 1996, Jun, 8

   35741   **popliteal artery**   C 50 80 ↱

   35761   **other vessels**   T 50 80 ↱

   35800   **Exploration for postoperative hemorrhage, thrombosis or infection; neck**   C 80 ↱

   35820   **chest**   C 80 ↱

   35840   **abdomen**   C 80 ↱

   35860   **extremity**   T 80 ↱

   35870   **Repair of graft-enteric fistula**   C 80 ↱

   35875   **Thrombectomy of arterial or venous graft (other than hemodialysis graft or fistula);**   9 T ↱
          MED: 100-2, 15, 260; 100-4, 12, 90.3; 100-4, 14, 10

          AMA: 2000, Apr, 10; 1999, Mar, 6; 1999, Feb, 6; 1998, Nov, 14

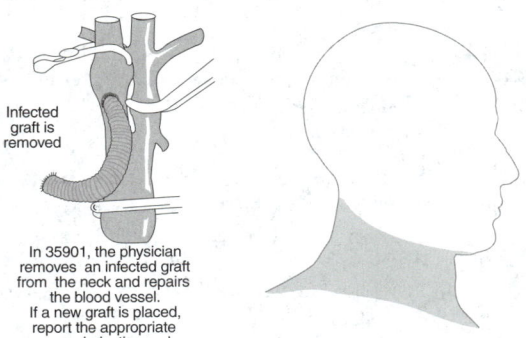

In 35901, the physician removes an infected graft from the neck and repairs the blood vessel. If a new graft is placed, report the appropriate revascularization code

35876 **with revision of arterial or venous graft** 9 T 80 ↰

MED: 100-2, 15, 260; 100-4, 12, 90.3; 100-4, 14, 10

AMA: 1998, Nov, 14

If thrombectomy of hemodialysis graft of fistula is performed, consult CPT codes 36831 and 36833.

If thrombectomy with revision of any non-coronary arterial or venous graft, including those of the lower extremity (other than hemodialysis graft of fistula) of a lower extremity blood vessel (with or without patch angioplasty), consult CPT code 35226. For repair (other than for a fistula) for a lower extremity blood vessel using a vein graft, consult CPT code 35256.

35879 **Revision, lower extremity arterial bypass, without thrombectomy, open; with vein patch angioplasty** T 50 80 ↰

AMA: 1999, Nov, 19

35881 **with segmental vein interposition** T 50 80 ↰

AMA: 1999, Nov, 19

To report open revision of previous autogenous vein bypass graft of lower extremity, use CPT code 35879 or 35881. Consult CPT codes 35901-35907 and the appropriate revascularization code for the excision of infected grafts.

35901 **Excision of infected graft; neck** C 80 ↰

35903 **extremity** T 80 ↰

35905 **thorax** C 80 ↰

35907 **abdomen** C 80 ↰

VASCULAR INJECTION PROCEDURES

Vascular catheterization/injection services include local anesthesia, introduction of needle or catheter, injection of contrast media, and use of power injections. Since these are diagnostic procedures, only the pre-injection and post-injection care directly related to the procedure is included. Catheters, drugs, and contrast media should be reported separately.

Selective vascular catheterization codes include introduction and all lesser order vessels catheterized used in the approach. Selective catheterization of the right middle cerebral artery includes the introduction and placement catheterization of the right common and internal carotid arteries. Only code 36217 for the third order branch would be reported. Additional second or third order vessels supplied by the same first order branch are reported with "add on" procedure codes 36012, 36218, and 36248.

These procedures are reported by vascular family and, as such, any procedure performed on more than one vascular family is reported separately using the conventions described above. Bilateral procedures are reported as separate vascular families.

To report injection procedures with cardiac catheterizations, consult CPT codes 93541-93545.

To report chemotherapy administration for malignant disease, consult CPT codes 96401-96549.

INTRAVENOUS

36000   **Introduction of needle or intracatheter, vein**   Ⓝ 50 🔾
             MED: 100-4, 12, 30.6.12

             AMA: 1998, Jul, 1; 1998, Apr, 1, 3, 7

36002   **Injection procedures (eg, thrombin) for percutaneous treatment of
             extremity pseudoaneurysm**   Ⓢ 50 🔾

             To report imaging guidance, consult CPT codes 76003, 76360, 76393, or
             76942.

             To report ultrasound guided compression repair of pseudoaneurysms, consult
             CPT code 76936.

             Code 36002 should not be used to report vascular sealant of an arteriotomy
             site.

36005   **Injection procedure for extremity venography (including introduction of
             needle or intracatheter)**   Ⓝ 50 🔾

             To report radiological supervision and interpretation, consult CPT codes 75820
             and 75822.

36010   **Introduction of catheter, superior or inferior vena cava**   Ⓝ 50 🔾
             AMA: 2001, May, 10; 2000, Sep, 11; 1998, Apr, 1; 1996, Aug, 2

36011   **Selective catheter placement, venous system; first order branch (eg, renal
             vein, jugular vein)**   Ⓝ 50 🔾
             AMA: 1998, Apr, 1; 1996, Aug, 11

36012   **second order, or more selective, branch (eg, left adrenal vein, petrosal
             sinus)**   Ⓝ 50 🔾
             AMA: 1996, Aug, 11

36013   **Introduction of catheter, right heart or main pulmonary artery** Ⓝ 🔾
             AMA: 1996, Aug, 11

36014   **Selective catheter placement, left or right pulmonary artery** Ⓝ 50 🔾
             AMA: 1998, Apr, 1; 1996, Aug, 11

36015   **Selective catheter placement, segmental or subsegmental pulmonary
             artery**   Ⓝ 50 🔾
             AMA: 2000, Sep, 11; 1996, Aug, 11

             If a flow directed catheter is inserted (eg. Swan-Ganz), consult CPT code
             93503. If venous catheterization is performed for selective organ blood
             sampling, consult CPT code 36500.

INTRA-ARTERIAL — INTRA-AORTIC

If angioplasty is performed, consult CPT codes 35470-35475. If transcatheter therapies are
performed, consult CPT codes 37200-37208, 61624, and 61626.

If radiological supervision and interpretation is needed, see the Radiology section of CPT. If
angiography is performed, consult CPT codes 75600-75790.

36100   **Introduction of needle or intracatheter, carotid or vertebral artery** Ⓝ 50 🔾
             AMA: 1996, Aug, 11

36120   **Introduction of needle or intracatheter; retrograde brachial artery** Ⓝ 🔾
             AMA: 1996, Aug, 3; 1993, Fall, 16

36140   **extremity artery**   N ↴
AMA: 1996, Aug, 3; 1993, Fall, 16

36145   **arteriovenous shunt created for dialysis (cannula, fistula, or graft)** N ↴
AMA: 2001, May, 1; 1997, Feb, 2; 1996, Aug, 3

To report insertion of arteriovenous cannula, consult CPT codes 36810-36821.

36160   **Introduction of needle or intracatheter, aortic, translumbar**   N ↴
AMA: 1996, Aug, 3

36200   **Introduction of catheter, aorta**   N 50 ↴
AMA: 2003, Feb, 1; 1996, Aug, 3; 1993, Fall, 16

36215   **Selective catheter placement, arterial system; each first order thoracic or brachiocephalic branch, within a vascular family** N ↴
AMA: 2003, Feb, 1; 2000, Sep, 11; 1998, Apr, 1; 1997, Nov, 16; 1996, Aug, 3; 1993, Fall, 15

To report catheter placement for coronary angiography, consult CPT code 93508.

36216   **initial second order thoracic or brachiocephalic branch, within a vascular family**   N ↴
AMA: 2000, Oct, 4; 1996, Aug, 3; 1993, Fall, 15

36217   **initial third order or more selective thoracic or brachiocephalic branch, within a vascular family**   N ↴
AMA: 2000, Oct, 4; 1996, Aug, 3; 1993, Fall, 15

+   36218   **additional second order, third order, and beyond, thoracic or brachiocephalic branch, within a vascular family (List in addition to code for initial second or third order vessel as appropriate)** N ↴
AMA: 2000, Oct, 4; 1996, Aug, 3; 1993, Fall, 15

Note that 36218 is an add-on code and must be used in conjunction with 36216 and 36217.

36245   **Selective catheter placement, arterial system; each first order abdominal, pelvic, or lower extremity artery branch, within a vascular family**   N 50 ↴
AMA: 2001, Jan, 14; 1996, Aug, 3; 1993, Fall, 15

36246   **initial second order abdominal, pelvic, or lower extremity artery branch, within a vascular family**   N 50 ↴
AMA: 2001, Jan, 14; 1996, Aug, 3; 1993, Fall, 15

36247   **initial third order or more selective abdominal, pelvic, or lower extremity artery branch, within a vascular family**   N 50 ↴
AMA: 2001, Jan, 14; 1996, Aug, 3; 1993, Fall, 15

+   36248   **additional second order, third order, and beyond, abdominal, pelvic, or lower extremity artery branch, within a vascular family (List in addition to code for initial second or third order vessel as appropriate)** N ↴
AMA: 2001, Jan, 14; 1998, Apr, 1, 7; 1996, Aug, 3; 1993, Fall, 15

Note that 36248 is an add-on code and must be used in conjunction with 36246 and 36247.

36260   **Insertion of implantable intra-arterial infusion pump (eg, for chemotherapy of liver)**   3 T ↴
MED: 100-2, 15, 260; 100-3, 110.6; 100-3, 280.14; 100-4, 12, 90.3; 100-4, 14, 10

AMA: 1995, Fall, 5

Cardiovascular System

36261–36470

36261 Revision of implanted intra-arterial infusion pump 2 T 80 ↻
MED: 100-2, 15, 260; 100-3, 280.14; 100-4, 12, 90.3; 100-4, 14, 10

36262 Removal of implanted intra-arterial infusion pump 1 T ↻
MED: 100-2, 15, 260; 100-3, 280.14; 100-4, 12, 90.3; 100-4, 14, 10

36299 Unlisted procedure, vascular injection N 80

VENOUS

36400 Venipuncture, under age 3 years, necessitating physicians skill, not to be used for routine venipuncture; femoral or jugular vein A N ↻

36405   scalp vein A N ↻

36406   other vein A N ↻

36410 Venipuncture, age 3 years or older, necessitating physician's skill (separate procedure), for diagnostic or therapeutic purposes (not to be used for routine venipuncture) N ↻
MED: 100-4, 12, 30.6.12

AMA: 2001, May, 11

If venipuncture is performed as part of critical care services (99291-99292) do not report separately.

36415 Collection of venous blood by venipuncture A 63
MED: 100-4, 12, 30.6.12

AMA: 1999, Oct, 11; 1998, Mar, 10; 1997, Feb, 9; 1996, Jun, 10

36416 Collection of capillary blood specimen (eg, finger, heel, ear stick) N

36420 Venipuncture, cutdown; under age 1 year A T 80 ↻ 63

36425   age 1 or over T ↻
MED: 100-3, 110.5; 100-3, 110.7; 100-3, 20.18; 100-4, 12, 70; 100-4, 13, 20; 100-4, 13, 90

36430 Transfusion, blood or blood components S ↻
MED: 100-1, 3, 20.5; 100-1, 3, 20.5.2; 100-3, 110.16; 100-3, 110.5; 100-3, 110.7; 100-3, 110.8

AMA: 2001, Mar, 10; 1997, Aug, 18

36440 Push transfusion, blood, 2 years or under A S 80 ↻
MED: 100-1, 3, 20.5; 100-1, 3, 20.5.2; 100-3, 110.5; 100-3, 110.7; 100-3, 110.8

36450 Exchange transfusion, blood; newborn A S 80 ↻ 63
MED: 100-1, 3, 20.5; 100-1, 3, 20.5.2; 100-3, 110.5; 100-3, 110.7; 100-3, 110.8

36455   other than newborn S ↻
MED: 100-1, 3, 20.5.2; 100-3, 110.5; 100-3, 110.7

36460 Transfusion, intrauterine, fetal A ♀ S 80 ↻ 63
MED: 100-1, 3, 20.5.2; 100-3, 110.5; 100-3, 110.7; 100-3, 110.8

If radiological supervision and interpretation is performed, consult CPT code 76941.

36468 Single or multiple injections of sclerosing solutions, spider veins (telangiectasia); limb or trunk T 80 ↻
MED: 100-2, 16, 10; 100-2, 16, 120; 100-2, 16, 180

36469   face T 80 ↻
MED: 100-2, 16, 10; 100-2, 16, 120; 100-2, 16, 180

36470 Injection of sclerosing solution; single vein T 50 ↻
MED: 100-2, 16, 10; 100-2, 16, 120; 100-2, 16, 180; 100-3, 150.7

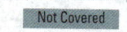

36471   **multiple veins, same leg**   ☐T☐ ☐50☐ ☐◪☐
MED: 100-2, 16, 10; 100-2, 16, 120; 100-2, 16, 180; 100-3, 150.7

ARTERIES AND VEINS

36475   **Endovenous ablation therapy of incompetent vein, extremity, inclusive of all imaging guidance and monitoring, percutaneous, radiofrequency; first vein treated**   ☐3☐☐T☐ ☐50☐ ☐◪☐

+ 36476   **second and subsequent veins treated in a single extremity, each through separate access sites (List separately in addition to code for primary procedure)**   ☐3☐ ☐50☐ ☐T☐

Note that 36476 must be used with 36475.

Codes 36475, 36476 cannot be reported with CPT codes 36000-36005, 36410, 36425, 36478, 36479, 37204, 75894, 76000-76003, 76937, 76942, 93970, 93971.

36478   **Endovenous ablation therapy of incompetent vein, extremity, inclusive of all imaging guidance and monitoring, percutaneous, laser; first vein treated**   ☐3☐☐T☐ ☐50☐ ☐◪☐

+ 36479   **second and subsequent veins treated in a single extremity, each through separate access sites (List separately in addition to code for primary procedure)**   ☐3☐ ☐50☐ ☐T☐

Note that 36479 must be used with 36478.

Codes 36478, 36479 cannot be reported with CPT codes 36000-36005, 36410, 36425, 36475, 36476, 37204, 75894, 76000-76003, 76937, 76942, 93970, 93971.

VASCULAR INJECTION PROCEDURES

36481   **Percutaneous portal vein catheterization by any method**   ☐N☐ ☐◪☐
AMA: 2002, Mar, 10; 1996, Oct, 1

To report radiological supervision and interpretation, consult CPT codes 75885 and 75887.

36500   **Venous catheterization for selective organ blood sampling**   ☐N☐ ☐◪☐

If the superior or inferior vena cava is catheterized, consult CPT code 36010. If radiological supervision and interpretation is performed, consult CPT code 75893.

36510   **Catheterization of umbilical vein for diagnosis or therapy, newborn**   ☐A☐ ☐N☐ ☐80☐ ☐◪☐ ㉓
MED: 100-3, 110.14

Modifier 63 should not be reported with code 36510.

36511   **Therapeutic apheresis; for white blood cells**   ☐S☐ ☐◪☐
MED: 100-1, 3, 20.5.2; 100-3, 110.14

36512   **for red blood cells**   ☐S☐ ☐◪☐
MED: 100-1, 3, 20.5.2; 100-3, 110.14

36513   **for platelets**   ☐S☐ ☐◪☐
MED: 100-1, 3, 20.5.2; 100-3, 110.14

36514   **for plasma pheresis**   ☐S☐ ☐◪☐
MED: 100-1, 3, 20.5.2; 100-3, 110.14

36515   **with extracorporeal immunoadsorption and plasma reinfusion**   ☐S☐ ☐◪☐
MED: 100-1, 3, 20.5.2; 100-3, 110.14

Cardiovascular System

36471–36515

Cardiovascular System

36516–36555

36516   **with extracorporeal selective adsorption or selective filtration and
plasma reinfusion**   Ⓢ ◪
MED: 100-1, 3, 20.5.2; 100-3, 110.14

To report physician evaluation, append modifier 26.

36522   **Photopheresis, extracorporeal**   Ⓢ ◪
MED: 100-3, 110.4; 100-3, 20.5

AMA: 1993, Fall, 25

36540   **Collection of blood specimen from a completely implantable venous access
device**   Ⓝ
AMA: 2002, Nov, 1; 2002, Jan, 11

Note that 36540 cannot be used in conjunction with CPT codes 36415, 36416.

To report venous blood specimen collection by venipuncture, consult CPT code
36415.

To report capillary blood specimen collection, consult CPT code 36416.

36550   **Declotting by thrombolytic agent of implanted vascular access device or
catheter**   Ⓣ 80 ◪
AMA: 1999, Nov, 20

VENOUS — CENTRAL VENOUS ACCESS PROCEDURES

For coding purposes to qualify as a central venous access catheter or device, the tip must end in the
subclavian, brachiocephalic (innominate) or iliac veins, the superior or inferior vena cava, or right
atrium. The venous access device may be inserted centrally (jugular, subclavian, femoral vein or
inferior vena cava) or peripherally (e.g., basilic or cephalic). There is no longer a coding distinction
made between percutaneous venous access and that achieved via cutdown.

Procedures for the insertion of central venous access fall into the following categories:

- **Insertion:** Placement through a newly established venous access.

- **Repair:** Fixing of device without replacement of any components.

- **Partial replacement:** Replacement of only the catheter component, not the entire device.

- **Complete replacement:** Replacement of entire (all components) device via same access
site.

- **Removal:** Removal of entire (all components) device.

- **Removal of obstruction:** Mechanical removal of obstructive material from device.

For the above categories of service rendered on a dual catheter system placed from separate venous
access sites, report the appropriate procedure code with a frequency of two. If an existing device is
entirely removed and a new device placed via a separate venous access site, then report both the
removal and insertion.

To report refilling and maintenance of an implantable pump or reservoir for intravenous or intra-
arterial drug delivery, consult CPT code 96530.

To report radiological imaging used during these procedures, consult CPT codes 76937 and 75998.

INSERTION OF CENTRAL VENOUS ACCESS DEVICE

⊙   36555   **Insertion of non-tunneled centrally inserted central venous catheter; under
5 years of age**   Ⓐ ❶ Ⓣ ◪

To report peripherally inserted non-tunneled central venous catheter, under 5
years of age, consult CPT code 36568.

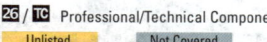 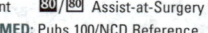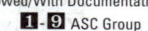

| 36556 | age 5 years or older | ◼ 1 T 🔁 |

To report peripherally inserted non-tunneled central venous catheter, age 5 years or older, consult CPT code 36569.

⊙ | 36557 | **Insertion of tunneled centrally inserted central venous catheter, without subcutaneous port or pump; under 5 years of age** | A 2 T 50 80 🔁

⊙ | 36558 | age 5 years or older | 2 T 50 80 🔁

To report peripherally inserted central venous catheter with port, 5 years or older, consult CPT code 36571.

⊙ | 36560 | **Insertion of tunneled centrally inserted central venous access device, with subcutaneous port; under 5 years of age** | A 3 T 50 80 🔁

To report peripherally inserted central venous access device with subcutaneous port, under 5 years of age, consult CPT code 36570.

⊙ | 36561 | age 5 years or older | 3 T 50 80 🔁

To report peripherally inserted central venous catheter with subcutaneous port, 5 years or older, consult CPT code 36571.

⊙ | 36563 | **Insertion of tunneled centrally inserted central venous access device with subcutaneous pump** | 3 T 80 🔁

⊙ | 36565 | **Insertion of tunneled centrally inserted central venous access device, requiring two catheters via two separate venous access sites; without subcutaneous port or pump (eg, Tesio type catheter)** | 3 T 50 80 🔁

⊙ | 36566 | with subcutaneous port(s) | 3 T 50 80 🔁

⊙ | 36568 | **Insertion of peripherally inserted central venous catheter (PICC), without subcutaneous port or pump; under 5 years of age** | A 1 T 🔁

To report placement of centrally inserted non-tunneled central venous catheter, without subcutaneous port or pump, under 5 years of age, consult CPT code 36555.

| 36569 | age 5 years or older | 1 T 🔁

To report placement of centrally inserted non-tunneled central venous catheter, without subcutaneous port or pump, age 5 years or older, consult CPT code 36556.

⊙ | 36570 | **Insertion of peripherally inserted central venous access device, with subcutaneous port; under 5 years of age** | A 3 T 50 80 🔁

To report insertion of tunneled centrally inserted central venous access device with subcutaneous port, under 5 years of age, consult CPT code 36560.

⊙ | 36571 | age 5 years or older | 3 T 50 80 🔁

To report insertion of tunneled centrally inserted central venous access device with subcutaneous port, age 5 years or older, consult CPT code 36561.

REPAIR OF CENTRAL VENOUS ACCESS DEVICE

To report mechanical removal of pericatheter obstructive material, consult CPT code 36595.

To report mechanical removal of intracatheter obstructive material, consult CPT code 36596.

| 36575 | **Repair of tunneled or non-tunneled central venous access catheter, without subcutaneous port or pump, central or peripheral insertion site** | 2 T 80 🔁

⊙ | 36576 | **Repair of central venous access device, with subcutaneous port or pump, central or peripheral insertion site** | 2 T 80 🔁

Cardiovascular System

36578–36597

PARTIAL REPLACEMENT OF CENTRAL VENOUS ACCESS DEVICE (CATHETER ONLY)

⊙   **36578**   **Replacement, catheter only, of central venous access device, with subcutaneous port or pump, central or peripheral insertion site** ② Ⓣ ⑧⓪ ⬛

To report replacement of entire device through same venous access site, consult CPT codes 36582 or 36583.

COMPLETE REPLACEMENT OF CENTRAL VENOUS ACCESS DEVICE THROUGH SAME VENOUS ACCESS SITE

36580   **Replacement, complete, of a non-tunneled centrally inserted central venous catheter, without subcutaneous port or pump, through same venous access** ① Ⓣ ⬛

⊙   **36581**   **Replacement, complete, of a tunneled centrally inserted central venous catheter, without subcutaneous port or pump, through same venous access** ② Ⓣ ⑧⓪ ⬛

⊙   **36582**   **Replacement, complete, of a tunneled centrally inserted central venous access device, with subcutaneous port, through same venous access** ③ Ⓣ ⑧⓪ ⬛

⊙   **36583**   **Replacement, complete, of a tunneled centrally inserted central venous access device, with subcutaneous pump, through same venous access** ③ Ⓣ ⑧⓪ ⬛

36584   **Replacement, complete, of a peripherally inserted central venous catheter (PICC), without subcutaneous port or pump, through same venous access** ① Ⓣ ⬛

⊙   **36585**   **Replacement, complete, of a peripherally inserted central venous access device, with subcutaneous port, through same venous access** ③ Ⓣ ⑧⓪ ⬛

REMOVAL OF CENTRAL VENOUS ACCESS DEVICE

36589   **Removal of tunneled central venous catheter, without subcutaneous port or pump** ① Ⓣ ⑤⓪ ⑧⓪ ⬛

⊙   **36590**   **Removal of tunneled central venous access device, with subcutaneous port or pump, central or peripheral insertion** ① Ⓣ ⑧⓪ ⬛

Codes 36589 and 36590 cannot be reported for removal of non-tunneled central venous catheters.

MECHANICAL REMOVAL OF OBSTRUCTIVE MATERIAL

36595   **Mechanical removal of pericatheter obstructive material (eg, fibrin sheath) from central venous device via separate venous access** Ⓣ ⬛

Code 36550 cannot be reported in addition to 36595.

To report venous catheterization, consult CPT codes 36010-36012.

To report radiological supervision and interpretation, consult CPT code 75901.

36596   **Mechanical removal of intraluminal (intracatheter) obstructive material from central venous device through device lumen** Ⓣ ⬛

Code 36550 cannot be reported in addition to 36596.

To report venous catheterization, consult CPT codes 36010-36012.

To report radiological supervision and interpretation, consult CPT code 75902.

OTHER CENTRAL VENOUS ACCESS PROCEDURES

36597   **Repositioning of previously placed central venous catheter under fluoroscopic guidance** Ⓣ ⬛

To report fluoroscopic guidance, consult CPT code 76000.

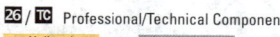 **26** / **TC** Professional/Technical Component   **80**/**80** Assist-at-Surgery Allowed/With Documentation   ⊙ Conscious Sedation

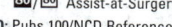 Unlisted   Not Covered   **MED:** Pubs 100/NCD Reference   **1**-**9** ASC Group   ㊛ Modifier 63 Exempt

280 — Surgery   CPT only © 2005 American Medical Association. All Rights Reserved. *(Black Ink)*   © 2005 Ingenix, Inc. *(Blue Ink)*

● **36598** **Contrast injection(s) for radiologic evaluation of existing central venous access device, including fluoroscopy, image documentation and report**

Code 36598 cannot be reported with 36595, 36596, or 76000.

To report complete diagnostic studies, consult 75820, 75825, 75827.

ARTERIAL

36600 **Arterial puncture, withdrawal of blood for diagnosis** 🅽 ▣
MED: 100-4, 12, 30.6.12

AMA: 1995, Fall, 7

If arterial puncture is performed as part of critical care services (99291-99292) do not report separately.

⊘ **36620** **Arterial catheterization or cannulation for sampling, monitoring or transfusion (separate procedure); percutaneous** 🅽 ▣
MED: 100-3, 110.5; 100-3, 110.7; 100-3, 110.8

AMA: 1998, Apr, 3; 1995, Fall, 7

36625 **cutdown** 🅽 ▣
MED: 100-3, 110.5; 100-3, 110.8

AMA: 1995, Fall, 7

36640 **Arterial catheterization for prolonged infusion therapy (chemotherapy), cutdown** ❶ Ⓣ ▣
MED: 100-2, 15, 260; 100-3, 110.6; 100-4, 12, 90.3; 100-4, 14, 10

AMA: 1995, Fall, 7

Consult also 96420-96425. If arterial catheterization is performed for occlusion therapy, consult CPT code 75894.

⊘ **36660** **Catheterization, umbilical artery, newborn, for diagnosis or therapy** 🅰 Ⓒ 80 ▣ 63
AMA: 1995, Fall, 8

INTRAOSSEOUS

36680 **Placement of needle for intraosseous infusion** Ⓣ 80 ▣

HEMODIALYSIS ACCESS, INTERVASCULAR CANNULATION FOR EXTRACORPOREAL CIRCULATION, OR SHUNT INSERTION

36800 **Insertion of cannula for hemodialysis, other purpose (separate procedure); vein to vein** ❸ Ⓣ ▣
MED: 100-2, 15, 260; 100-4, 12, 90.3; 100-4, 14, 10

AMA: 1993, Fall, 3

36810 **arteriovenous, external (Scribner type)** ❸ Ⓣ ▣
MED: 100-2, 15, 260; 100-4, 12, 90.3; 100-4, 14, 10

AMA: 1993, Fall, 3

36815 **arteriovenous, external revision, or closure** ❸ Ⓣ ▣
MED: 100-2, 15, 260; 100-4, 12, 90.3; 100-4, 14, 10

AMA: 1993, Fall, 3

36818 **Arteriovenous anastomosis, open; by upper arm cephalic vein transposition** Ⓣ 80 ▣

Code 36818 cannot be reported with CPT codes 36819, 36820, 36821, and 36830 during a unilateral upper extremity procedure. For an open arteriovenous anastomoses performed at the same operative session on both extremities, report modifier 50 or 59 as required.

36819   **Arteriovenous anastomosis, open; by upper arm basilic vein transposition**   `3` `T` `80` `↵`

MED: 100-2, 15, 260; 100-4, 12, 90.3; 100-4, 14, 10

AMA: 1999, Nov, 20

Code 36819 cannot be reported with CPT codes 36818, 36820, 36821, and 36830 during a unilateral upper extremity procedure. For an open arteriovenous anastomoses performed at the same operative session on both extremities, report modifier 50 or 59 as required.

36820   **by forearm vein transposition**   `T` `50` `80` `↵`

MED: 100-2, 15, 260; 100-4, 12, 90.3; 100-4, 14, 10

36821   **direct, any site (eg, Cimino type) (separate procedure)**   `3` `T` `80` `↵`

MED: 100-2, 15, 260; 100-4, 12, 90.3; 100-4, 14, 10

AMA: 1999, Nov, 20; 1997, Feb, 2; 1993, Fall, 3

36822   **Insertion of cannula(s) for prolonged extracorporeal circulation for cardiopulmonary insufficiency (ECMO) (separate procedure)**   `C` `↵`

AMA: 1997, Feb, 11; 1993, Fall, 3

If maintenance is performed for prolonged extracorporal circulation, consult CPT codes 33960 and 33961.

36823   **Insertion of arterial and venous cannula(s) for isolated extracorporeal circulation including regional chemotherapy perfusion to an extremity, with or without hyperthermia, with removal of cannula(s) and repair of arteriotomy and venotomy sites**   `C` `↵`

MED: 100-3, 110.6

AMA: 1998, Nov, 14-15

Code 36823 includes chemotherapy perfusion supported by a membrane oxygenator/perfusion pump. Do not report 96408-96425 with 36823.

36825   **Creation of arteriovenous fistula by other than direct arteriovenous anastomosis (separate procedure); autogenous graft**   `4` `T` `80` `↵`

MED: 100-2, 15, 260; 100-4, 12, 90.3; 100-4, 14, 10

AMA: 1997, Feb, 1; 1993, Fall, 3

If direct arteriovenous anastomosis is performed, consult CPT code 36821.

36830   **nonautogenous graft (eg, biological collagen, thermoplastic graft)**   `4` `T` `80` `↵`

MED: 100-2, 15, 260; 100-4, 12, 90.3; 100-4, 14, 10

AMA: 1997, Feb, 1; 1993, Fall, 3

If direct arteriovenous anastomosis is performed, consult CPT code 36821.

36831   **Thrombectomy, open, arteriovenous fistula without revision, autogenous or nonautogenous dialysis graft (separate procedure)**   `9` `T` `80` `↵`

MED: 100-2, 15, 260; 100-4, 12, 90.3; 100-4, 14, 10

AMA: 1999, Mar, 6; 1999, Feb, 6; 1999, Apr, 11; 1998, Nov, 14-15

36832   **Revision, open, arteriovenous fistula; without thrombectomy, autogenous or nonautogenous dialysis graft (separate procedure)**   `4` `T` `80` `↵`

MED: 100-2, 15, 260; 100-4, 12, 90.3; 100-4, 14, 10

AMA: 1999, Nov, 20; 1999, Mar, 6; 1999, Feb, 6; 1999, Apr, 11; 1998, Nov, 15; 1997, Feb, 2; 1993, Fall, 3

36833 with thrombectomy, autogenous or nonautogenous dialysis graft (separate procedure) ▣ Ⓣ 80 ▣

MED: 100-2, 15, 260; 100-4, 12, 90.3; 100-4, 14, 10

AMA: 1999, Feb, 6; 1999, Apr, 11; 1998, Nov, 15

36834 Plastic repair of arteriovenous aneurysm (separate procedure) ③ Ⓣ 80 ▣

AMA: 1993, Fall, 3

36835 Insertion of Thomas shunt (separate procedure) ④ Ⓣ ▣

MED: 100-2, 15, 260; 100-4, 12, 90.3; 100-4, 14, 10

36838 Distal revascularization and interval ligation (DRIL), upper extremity hemodialysis access (steal syndrome) Ⓣ 50 80 ▣

Code 36838 cannot be reported with CPT codes 35512, 35522, 36832, 37607, 37618.

36860 External cannula declotting (separate procedure); without balloon catheter ② Ⓣ ▣

MED: 100-2, 15, 260; 100-4, 12, 90.3; 100-4, 14, 10

AMA: 2001, May, 1; 1999, Feb, 6; 1998, Nov, 15; 1997, Feb, 2; 1993, Fall, 3

36861 with balloon catheter ③ Ⓣ ▣

MED: 100-2, 15, 260; 100-4, 12, 90.3; 100-4, 14, 10

AMA: 2001, May, 1; 1997, Feb, 2; 1993, Fall, 3

To report imaging guidance is performed, consult CPT code 76000.

⊙ **36870** Thrombectomy, percutaneous, arteriovenous fistula, autogenous or nonautogenous graft (includes mechanical thrombus extraction and intra-graft thrombolysis) ⑨ Ⓣ 50 ▣

MED: 100-2, 15, 260; 100-4, 12, 90.3; 100-4, 14, 10

AMA: 2001, May, 1

Do not report code 36550 with 36870. For catheterization, report code 36145.

To report radiological supervision and interpretation, consult CPT code 75790.

PORTAL DECOMPRESSION PROCEDURES

37140 Venous anastomosis, open; portocaval Ⓒ ▣

If peritoneal-venous shunt is inserted, consult CPT code 49425.

37145 renoportal Ⓒ 80 ▣

37160 caval-mesenteric Ⓒ 80 ▣

37180 splenorenal, proximal Ⓒ 80 ▣

37181 splenorenal, distal (selective decompression of esophagogastric varices, any technique) Ⓒ 80 ▣

To report percutaneous procedure, consult CPT code 37182.

37182 Insertion of transvenous intrahepatic portosystemic shunt(s) (TIPS) (includes venous access, hepatic and portal vein catheterization, portography with hemodynamic evaluation, intrahepatic tract formation/dilatation, stent placement and all associated imaging guidance and documentation) Ⓒ 80 ▣

To report open procedure, consult CPT code 37140.

Note that 75885 and 75887 cannot be reported with CPT code 37182.

Cardiovascular System

37183–37185

37183 **Revision of transvenous intrahepatic portosystemic shunt(s) (TIPS) (includes venous access, hepatic and portal vein catheterization, portography with hemodynamic evaluation, intrahepatic tract recanulization/dilatation, stent placement and all associated imaging guidance and documentation)** 〔T〕〔80〕〔▣〕

Note that 75885 and 75887 cannot be reported with CPT code 37183.

TRANSCATHETER PROCEDURES

The appropriate CPT codes for placement of catheters and radiological supervision and interpretation should be reported in addition to the following therapeutic procedures.

MECHANICAL THROMBECTOMY

Report separately code(s) for catheter placement(s), diagnostic studies, and other percutaneous interventions.

Codes 37184–37188 include radiological supervision and interpretation during the procedure.

Injection(s) of a thrombolytic substance during the procedure is included and not separately reportable with a mechanical thrombectomy. However, continuous infusion before and after the procedure is not included and may be reported with codes 37201, 75896, 75989.

For coronary mechanical thrombectomy, consult 92973.

For mechanical thrombectomy for dialysis fistula, consult 36870.

ARTERIAL MECHANICAL THROMBECTOMY

Arterial mechanical thrombectomy may be performed as a "primary" transcatheter procedure with planning before the procedure, the procedure itself, and evaluation after the procedure. Primary mechanical thrombectomy is reported per vascular family. Report 37184 for the initial vessel treated and 37185 for the second and all succeeding vessel(s) in the same vascular family. Report mechanical thrombectomy of an additional vascular family treated through a separate access site, by appending modifier 51 to 37184–37185, as appropriate.

Do not report 37184–37185 for mechanical thrombectomy performed for the treatment of a thrombus or embolus that complicates other percutaneous interventional procedures. Consult CPT code 37186 for these procedures.

Arterial mechanical thrombectomy is considered a "secondary" transcatheter procedure for taking out short segments of thrombus or embolus when performed either before or after another percutaneous procedure. Report secondary mechanical thrombectomy with 37186. Do not report 37186 with 37184–37185.

VENOUS MECHANICAL THROMBECTOMY

Report the initial application of venous mechanical thrombectomy with code 37188. Use modifier 50 to report a bilateral procedure.

⊙ ● **37184** **Primary percutaneous transluminal mechanical thrombectomy, noncoronary, arterial or arterial bypass graft, including fluoroscopic guidance and intraprocedural pharmacological thrombolytic injection(s); initial vessel**

Code 37184 cannot be reported with 76000, 76001, 90774, 99143-99150.

⊙+● **37185** **second and all subsequent vessel(s) within the same vascular family (List separately in addition to code for primary mechanical thrombectomy procedure)**

Code 37185 cannot be reported with 76000, 76001, 90775.

⊙+● 37186 **Secondary percutaneous transluminal thrombectomy (eg, nonprimary mechanical, snare basket, suction technique), noncoronary, arterial or arterial bypass graft, including fluoroscopic guidance and intraprocedural pharmacological thrombolytic injections, provided in conjunction with another percutaneous intervention other than primary mechanical thrombectomy (List separately in addition to code for primary procedure)**

> Code 37186 cannot be reported with 76000, 76001, 90775.

⊙ ● 37187 **Percutaneous transluminal mechanical thrombectomy, vein(s), including intraprocedural pharmacological thrombolytic injections and fluoroscopic guidance**

> Code 37187 cannot be reported with 76000, 76001, 90775.

⊙ ● 37188 **Percutaneous transluminal mechanical thrombectomy, vein(s), including intraprocedural pharmacological thrombolytic injections and fluoroscopic guidance, repeat treatment on subsequent day during course of thrombolytic therapy**

> Code 37188 cannot be reported with 76000, 76001, 90775.

OTHER PROCEDURES

37195 **Thrombolysis, cerebral, by intravenous infusion** Ⓣ 🔲
AMA: 1997, Nov, 16

37200 **Transcatheter biopsy** Ⓣ 🔲

> To report radiological supervision and interpretation, consult CPT code 75970.

37201 **Transcatheter therapy, infusion for thrombolysis other than coronary** Ⓣ 🔲
AMA: 2001, May, 1; 2001, Feb, 10; 1997, Feb, 2

> To report radiological supervision and interpretation, consult CPT code 75896.

> If thrombolysis of the coronary vessels is performed, consult CPT codes 92975 and 92977.

37202 **Transcatheter therapy, infusion other than for thrombolysis, any type (eg, spasmolytic, vasoconstrictive)** Ⓣ 🔲
AMA: 1998, Jan, 11; 1998, Apr, 3, 9; 1996, Oct, 11

> To report radiological supervision and interpretation, consult CPT code 75896.

⊙ 37203 **Transcatheter retrieval, percutaneous, of intravascular foreign body (eg, fractured venous or arterial catheter)** Ⓣ 🔲
MED: 100-3, 20.28

> To report radiological supervision and interpretation, consult CPT code 75961.

37204 **Transcatheter occlusion or embolization (eg, for tumor destruction, to achieve hemostasis, to occlude a vascular malformation), percutaneous, any method, non-central nervous system, non-head or neck** Ⓣ 🔲
MED: 100-3, 20.28

AMA: 1998, Sep, 7; 1998, Oct, 10

> To report radiological supervision and interpretation, consult CPT code 75894.

> Consult also CPT codes 61624 and 61626.

37205 **Transcatheter placement of an intravascular stent(s), (except coronary, carotid, and vertebral vessel), percutaneous; initial vessel** Ⓣ 80 🔲
AMA: 2003, Feb, 1; 2001, May, 1; 1993, Fall, 18

> To report radiological supervision and interpretation, consult CPT code 75960.

🔲 CCI Comp   50 Bilateral Procedure   + CPT Add-on Code   ⊘ Modifier -51 Exempt   ♂ Male   ♀ Female
● New Code   ▲ Revised Code   Ⓜ Maternity Edit   Ⓐ Age Edit   Ⓐ–Ⓨ APC Status Ind.   **AMA:** CPT Assistant
© 2005 Ingenix, Inc. *(Blue Ink)*   CPT only © 2005 American Medical Association. All Rights Reserved. *(Black Ink)*   Surgery — 285

Cardiovascular System

37206–37216

+ **37206**   **each additional vessel (List separately in addition to code for primary procedure)** [T] [80] [↖]
AMA: 2003, Feb, 1; 1993, Fall, 18

Note that 37206 is an add-on code and must be used in conjunction with 37205.

To report transcatheter placement of intravascular cervical carotid artery stent(s), consult CPT codes 37215, 37216.

To report transcatheter placement of extracranial vertebral or intrathoracic carotid artery stent(s), consult Category III codes 0075T, 0076T.

For radiological supervision and interpretation, consult CPT code 75960.

37207   **Transcatheter placement of an intravascular stent(s), (non-coronary vessel), open; initial vessel** [T] [50] [80] [↖]
AMA: 2003, Feb, 1

To report radiological supervision and interpretation, consult CPT code 75960.

To report catheterizations, consult CPT codes 36215-36248.

To report transcatheter placement of intracoronary stent(s), consult CPT codes 92980, 92981.

+ **37208**   **each additional vessel (List separately in addition to code for primary procedure)** [T]
AMA: 2003, Feb, 1

To report radiological supervision and interpretation, consult CPT code 75960.

To report catheterizations, consult CPT codes 36215-36248.

To report transcatheter placement of intracoronary stent(s), consult CPT codes 92980, 92981.

Note that 37208 is an add-on code and must be used in conjunction with 37207.

▲ **37209**   **Exchange of a previously placed intravascular catheter during thrombolytic therapy** [T] [↖]

To report radiological supervision and interpretation consult CPT code 75900.

⊙ **37215**   **Transcatheter placement of intravascular stent(s), cervical carotid artery, percutaneous; with distal embolic protection** [C] [80] [↖]

⊙ **37216**   **without distal embolic protection** [C] [80] [↖]

All diagnostic imaging for ipsilateral, cervical and cerebral carotid arteriography, all related radiological supervision and interpretation, and all ipsilateral selective carotid catheterization are included in 37215 and 37216. Codes 37215 and 37216 include stenting when ipsilateral carotid arteriogram verifies the need for the procedure. Report the appropriate code for catheterization and imaging if stenting is not required rather than 37215 and 37216.

Codes 37215 and 37216 cannot be reported with CPT codes 75671 and 75680.

For transcatheter placement of extracranial vertebral or intrathoracic carotid artery stent(s), consult Category III codes 0075T and 0076T.

For percutaneous transcatheter placement of intravascular stents other than coronary, carotid or vertebral, consult CPT codes 37205 and 37206.

INTRAVASCULAR ULTRASOUND SERVICES

Includes all manipulations and repositioning of the transducer with the specific vessel being examined, before and after treatment.

+ 37250 **Intravascular ultrasound (non-coronary vessel) during diagnostic evaluation and/or therapeutic intervention; initial vessel (List separately in addition to code for primary procedure)** S 80 ☐

MED: 100-3, 220.5

AMA: 1999, Nov, 20; 1997, Nov, 17

If catheterization is performed, consult CPT codes 36215-36248. If transcatheter therapies are performed, consult CPT codes 37200-37208, 61624, and 61626. For radiological supervision and interpretation, consult CPT codes 75945 and 75946.

Note that 37250 is an add-on code and must be used in conjunction with the appropriate CPT code for the diagnostic or therapeutic procedure performed.

+ 37251 **each additional vessel (List separately in addition to code for primary procedure)** S 80

AMA: 1999, Nov, 20; 1997, Nov, 17

Note that 37251 is an add-on code and must be used in conjunction with 37250.

ENDOSCOPY

Diagnostic endoscopy is always included in surgical endoscopy.

37500 **Vascular endoscopy, surgical, with ligation of perforator veins, subfascial (SEPS)** 3 T 50 ☐

To report open procedure, consult CPT code 37760.

37501 **Unlisted vascular endoscopy procedure** T 50

LIGATION AND OTHER PROCEDURES

37565 **Ligation, internal jugular vein** T 80 ☐

MED: 100-3, 160.8

37600 **Ligation; external carotid artery** T 80 ☐

MED: 100-3, 160.8

If ligation is used to treat an intracranial aneurysm, consult CPT code 61703.

37605 **internal or common carotid artery** T 80 ☐

MED: 100-3, 160.8

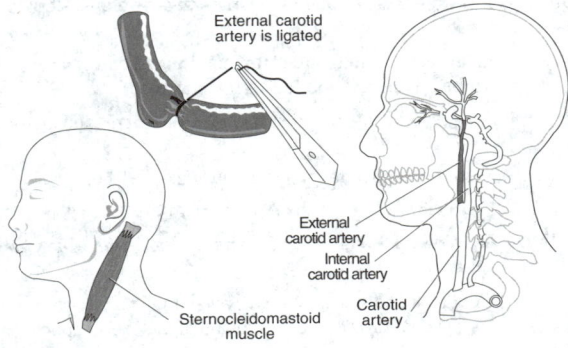

External carotid artery is ligated

External carotid artery

Internal carotid artery

Carotid artery

Sternocleidomastoid muscle

Cardiovascular System

37606–37730

37606   **internal or common carotid artery, with gradual occlusion, as with Silverstone or Crutchfield clamp**   T 80
MED: 100-3, 160.8

To report permanent transcatheter arterial occlusion or embolization, consult CPT codes 31624-31626.

To report temporary endovascular arterial balloon occlusion, consult CPT code 61623.

37607   **Ligation or banding of angioaccess arteriovenous fistula**   3 T
MED: 100-2, 15, 260; 100-4, 12, 90.3; 100-4, 14, 10

37609   **Ligation or biopsy, temporal artery**   2 T 50
MED: 100-2, 15, 260; 100-4, 12, 90.3; 100-4, 14, 10

37615   **Ligation, major artery (eg, post-traumatic, rupture); neck**   T 80
Touroff ligation

37616   **chest**   C 80
Bardenheurer operation

37617   **abdomen**   C 80

37618   **extremity**   C 80

37620   **Interruption, partial or complete, of inferior vena cava by suture, ligation, plication, clip, extravascular, intravascular (umbrella device)**   T
AMA: 2001, May, 10; 2000, Nov, 10

To report radiological supervision and interpretation, consult CPT code 75940.

37650   **Ligation of femoral vein**   2 T 50
MED: 100-2, 15, 260; 100-4, 12, 90.3; 100-4, 14, 10

37660   **Ligation of common iliac vein**   C 80

37700   **Ligation and division of long saphenous vein at saphenofemoral junction, or distal interruptions**   2 T 50
MED: 100-2, 15, 260; 100-4, 12, 90.3; 100-4, 14, 10

AMA: 1996, Aug, 10

Code 37700 should not be reported with 37718, 37722.

● 37718   **Ligation, division, and stripping, short saphenous vein**

To report bilateral procedure, use modifier 50.

Code 37718 cannot be reported with 37735, 37780.

~~37720~~   ~~Ligation and division and complete stripping of long or short saphenous veins~~

● 37722   **Ligation, division, and stripping, long (greater) saphenous veins from saphenofemoral junction to knee or below**

To report ligation and stripping of the short saphenous vein, consult CPT code 37718.

To report bilateral procedure, use modifier 50.

Code 37722 cannot be reported with 37700, 37735.

~~37730~~   ~~Ligation and division and complete stripping of long and short saphenous veins~~

(For ligation, division, and stripping of the greater saphenous vein, use 37722. For ligation, division, and stripping of the short saphenous vein, use 37718.)

37735	**Ligation and division and complete stripping of long or short saphenous veins with radical excision of ulcer and skin graft and/or interruption of communicating veins of lower leg, with excision of deep fascia** 3 T 50 80 ⌐	

MED: 100-2, 15, 260; 100-4, 12, 90.3; 100-4, 14, 10

Code 37735 cannot be reported with 37700, 37718, 37722, 37780.

37760	**Ligation of perforator veins, subfascial, radical (Linton type), with or without skin graft, open** 3 T 80 ⌐	

MED: 100-2, 15, 260; 100-4, 12, 90.3; 100-4, 14, 10

To report endoscopic procedure, consult CPT code 37500.

37765	**Stab phlebectomy of varicose veins, one extremity; 10-20 stab incisions** T 50 ⌐	

To report less than 10 incisions, use CPT code 37799. To report more than 20 incisions, use CPT code 37766.

37766	**more than 20 incisions** T 50 ⌐	
37780	**Ligation and division of short saphenous vein at saphenopopliteal junction (separate procedure)** 3 T 50 ⌐	

MED: 100-2, 15, 260; 100-4, 12, 90.3; 100-4, 14, 10

AMA: 1996, Aug, 10

37785	**Ligation, division, and/or excision of varicose vein cluster(s), one leg** 3 T 50 ⌐	

MED: 100-2, 15, 260; 100-4, 12, 90.3; 100-4, 14, 10

37788	**Penile revascularization, artery, with or without vein graft** ♂ C 80 ⌐	
37790	**Penile venous occlusive procedure** ♂ 3 T 80 ⌐	

MED: 100-2, 15, 260; 100-4, 12, 90.3; 100-4, 14, 10

37799	**Unlisted procedure, vascular surgery** T 80	

AMA: 2001, May, 11; 1997, Sep, 10; 1997, Feb, 10; 1993, Spring, 12; 1993, Fall, 3

HEMIC AND LYMPHATIC SYSTEMS

SPLEEN

EXCISION

38100	**Splenectomy; total (separate procedure)** C 80 ⌐	
38101	**partial (separate procedure)** C 80 ⌐	
+ 38102	**total, en bloc for extensive disease, in conjunction with other procedure (List in addition to code for primary procedure)** C 80 ⌐	

REPAIR

38115	**Repair of ruptured spleen (splenorrhaphy) with or without partial splenectomy** C 80 ⌐	

LAPAROSCOPY

Surgical laparoscopy always includes diagnostic laparoscopy.

To report diagnostic laparoscopy, consult CPT code 49320.

38120	**Laparoscopy, surgical, splenectomy** T 80 ⌐	

AMA: 2000, Mar, 5; 1999, Nov, 20-21

38129	**Unlisted laparoscopy procedure, spleen** T 80	

AMA: 2000, Mar, 5; 1999, Nov, 20-21

Hemic and Lymphatic Systems

38200–38241

INTRODUCTION

38200   Injection procedure for splenoportography   N 80 ▣

To report radiological supervision and interpretation, consult CPT code 75810.

GENERAL

BONE MARROW OR STEM CELL SERVICES/PROCEDURES

CPT codes 38207-38215 should be reported only once per day.

38204   Management of recipient hematopoietic progenitor cell donor search and cell acquisition   E

38205   Blood-derived hematopoietic progenitor cell harvesting for transplantation, per collection; allogenic   S 80 ▣

38206   autologous   S 80 ▣
MED: 100-3, 110.8.1

38207   Transplant preparation of hematopoietic progenitor cells; cryopreservation and storage   E

To report diagnostic cryopreservation and storage, consult CPT code 88240.

38208   thawing of previously frozen harvest, without washing   E

To report diagnostic thawing and expansion of frozen cells, consult CPT code 88241.

38209   thawing of previously frozen harvest, with washing   E

38210   specific cell depletion within harvest, T-cell depletion   E

38211   tumor cell depletion   E

38212   red blood cell removal   E

38213   platelet depletion   E

38214   plasma (volume) depletion   E

38215   cell concentration in plasma, mononuclear, or buffy coat layer   E

Codes 38207-38215 cannot be reported with CPT codes 88182, 88184-88189.

38220   Bone marrow; aspiration only   T 50 80 ▣
MED: 100-1, 5, 90.2; 100-2, 15, 80; 100-2, 15, 80.1; 100-4, 16, 10; 100-4, 16, 10.1; 100-4, 16, 110.4

38221   biopsy, needle or trocar   T 50 80 ▣
MED: 100-1, 5, 90.2; 100-2, 15, 80; 100-2, 15, 80.1; 100-4, 16, 10; 100-4, 16, 10.1; 100-4, 16, 110.4

To report bone marrow biopsy interpretation, consult CPT code 88305.

38230   Bone marrow harvesting for transplantation   S 80 ▣
MED: 100-1, 5, 90.2; 100-2, 15, 80; 100-2, 15, 80.1; 100-3, 190.1; 100-4, 16, 10; 100-4, 16, 10.1; 100-4, 16, 110.4

38240   Bone marrow or blood-derived peripheral stem cell transplantation; allogenic   S 80 ▣
MED: 100-2, 15, 80; 100-2, 15, 80.1; 100-3, 110.8.1; 100-3, 190.1

AMA: 1999, Nov, 21; 1998, Nov, 15; 1996, Apr, 1

38241   autologous   S 80 ▣
MED: 100-2, 15, 80; 100-2, 15, 80.1; 100-3, 110.8.1

AMA: 1999, Nov, 21; 1998, Nov, 15; 1996, Apr, 1

38242   **allogeneic donor lymphocyte infusions**   S 80 🔁
MED: 100-3, 190.1

If bone marrow aspiration is performed, consult CPT code 38220.

If modification, treatment, and processing of bone marrow or blood-derived stem cell specimens is performed for transplantation, consult CPT code 38210-38213.

If compatibility studies are performed, consult CPT codes 86812-86822.

If cryopreservation, freezing, and storage of blood-derived stem cells is performed for transplantation, consult CPT code 88240. If thawing and expansion of blood-derived stem cells is performed for transplantation, consult CPT code 88241.

LYMPH NODES AND LYMPHATIC CHANNELS

INCISION

38300   **Drainage of lymph node abscess or lymphadenitis; simple**   1 T 🔁
MED: 100-2, 15, 260; 100-4, 12, 90.3; 100-4, 14, 10

38305   **extensive**   2 T 🔁
MED: 100-2, 15, 260; 100-4, 12, 90.3; 100-4, 14, 10

38308   **Lymphangiotomy or other operations on lymphatic channels**   2 T 80 🔁
MED: 100-2, 15, 260; 100-4, 12, 90.3; 100-4, 14, 10

38380   **Suture and/or ligation of thoracic duct; cervical approach**   C 80 🔁

38381   **thoracic approach**   C 80 🔁

38382   **abdominal approach**   C 80 🔁

EXCISION

If injection is performed for sentinel node identification, consult CPT code 38792.

38500   **Biopsy or excision of lymph node(s); open, superficial**   2 T 50 🔁
MED: 100-2, 15, 260; 100-4, 12, 90.3; 100-4, 14, 10

AMA: 1999, Jul, 6; 1997, Jun, 5

Do not report code 38500 in conjunction with 38700-38780.

To report imaging guidance, consult CPT codes 76360, 76393, 76942.

If fine needle aspiration is performed, consult CPT code 10021 or 10022.

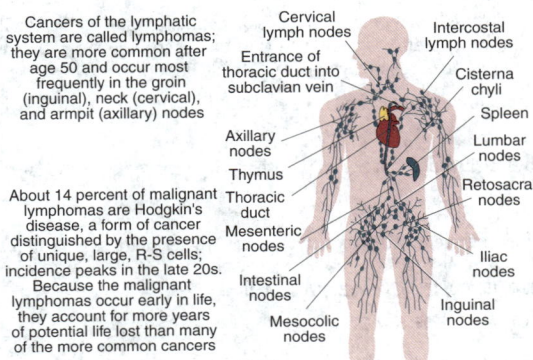

Cancers of the lymphatic system are called lymphomas; they are more common after age 50 and occur most frequently in the groin (inguinal), neck (cervical), and armpit (axillary) nodes

About 14 percent of malignant lymphomas are Hodgkin's disease, a form of cancer distinguished by the presence of unique, large, R-S cells; incidence peaks in the late 20s. Because the malignant lymphomas occur early in life, they account for more years of potential life lost than many of the more common cancers

Cervical lymph nodes
Intercostal lymph nodes
Entrance of thoracic duct into subclavian vein
Cisterna chyli
Axillary nodes
Spleen
Thymus
Lumbar nodes
Thoracic duct
Retosacral nodes
Mesenteric nodes
Iliac nodes
Intestinal nodes
Inguinal nodes
Mesocolic nodes

38505   **by needle, superficial (eg, cervical, inguinal, axillary)**   ⬛1 Ⓣ 50 🔧
MED: 100-2, 15, 260; 100-4, 12, 90.3; 100-4, 14, 10

To report evaluation of fine needle aspirate, consult CPT codes 88172, 88173.

38510   **open, deep cervical node(s)**   ⬛2 Ⓣ 50 🔧
MED: 100-2, 15, 260; 100-4, 12, 90.3; 100-4, 14, 10

AMA: 1998, May, 10

38520   **open, deep cervical node(s) with excision scalene fat pad**   ⬛2 Ⓣ 50 🔧
MED: 100-2, 15, 260; 100-4, 12, 90.3; 100-4, 14, 10

AMA: 1998, May, 10

38525   **open, deep axillary node(s)**   ⬛2 Ⓣ 50 🔧
MED: 100-2, 15, 260; 100-4, 12, 90.3; 100-4, 14, 10

AMA: 1999, Jul, 6; 1998, May, 10

38530   **open, internal mammary node(s)**   ⬛2 Ⓣ 50 80 🔧
MED: 100-2, 15, 260; 100-4, 12, 90.3; 100-4, 14, 10

AMA: 1998, May, 10

If percutaneous needle biopsy is performed on a retroperitoneal lymph node or mass, consult CPT code 49180; if fine needle aspiration is performed, consult CPT code 10022.

Do not report CPT code 38530 in conjuction with 38720-38746.

38542   **Dissection, deep jugular node(s)**   ⬛2 Ⓣ 50 80 🔧
MED: 100-2, 15, 260; 100-4, 12, 90.3; 100-4, 14, 10

AMA: 1999, Jul, 6

If radical cervical neck dissection is performed, consult CPT code 38720.

38550   **Excision of cystic hygroma, axillary or cervical; without deep neurovascular dissection**   ⬛3 Ⓣ 80 🔧
MED: 100-2, 15, 260; 100-4, 12, 90.3; 100-4, 14, 10

38555   **with deep neurovascular dissection**   ⬛4 Ⓣ 80 🔧
MED: 100-2, 15, 260; 100-4, 12, 90.3; 100-4, 14, 10

LIMITED LYMPHADENECTOMY FOR STAGING

38562   **Limited lymphadenectomy for staging (separate procedure); pelvic and para-aortic**   Ⓒ 80 🔧
AMA: 2001, Mar, 10

If this procedure is combined with prostatectomy, consult CPT code 55812 or 55842. If this procedure is combined with the insertion of a radioactive substance into the prostate, consult CPT code 55862.

38564   **retroperitoneal (aortic and/or splenic)**   Ⓒ 80 🔧

LAPAROSCOPY

Diagnostic laparoscopy is always included in surgical laparoscopy. To report diagnostic laparoscopy, consult CPT code 49320.

38570   **Laparoscopy, surgical; with retroperitoneal lymph node sampling (biopsy), single or multiple**   ⬛9 Ⓣ 80 🔧
MED: 100-2, 15, 260; 100-4, 12, 90.3; 100-4, 14, 10

AMA: 2000, Mar, 5; 1999, Nov, 21

If drainage of a lymphocele to the peritoneal cavity is performed, consult CPT code 49323.

38571	**with bilateral total pelvic lymphadenectomy** 9 T 80 ↰
	MED: 100-2, 15, 260; 100-4, 12, 90.3; 100-4, 14, 10
	AMA: 2000, Mar, 5; 1999, Nov, 21
38572	**with bilateral total pelvic lymphadenectomy and peri-aortic lymph node sampling (biopsy), single or multiple** 9 T 80 ↰
	MED: 100-2, 15, 260; 100-4, 12, 90.3; 100-4, 14, 10
	AMA: 1999, Nov, 21
38589	**Unlisted laparoscopy procedure, lymphatic system** T 50 80
	AMA: 2000, Mar, 5; 1999, Nov, 21

RADICAL LYMPHADENECTOMY (RADICAL RESECTION OF LYMPH NODES)

If limited pelvic and retroperitoneal lymphadenectomies are performed, consult CPT codes 38562 and 38564.

38700	**Suprahyoid lymphadenectomy** T 50 80 ↰
	AMA: 2002, Aug, 8
	To report a bilateral procedure, append modifier 50 to code 38700.
38720	**Cervical lymphadenectomy (complete)** T 50 80 ↰
	AMA: 2002, Aug, 8; 2001, Oct, 10
	To report a bilateral procedure, append modifier 50 to code 38720.
38724	**Cervical lymphadenectomy (modified radical neck dissection)** C 50 80 ↰
	AMA: 2002, Aug, 8; 2001, Jan, 13
38740	**Axillary lymphadenectomy; superficial** 2 T 80 ↰
	MED: 100-2, 15, 260; 100-4, 12, 90.3; 100-4, 14, 10
38745	**complete** 4 T 80 ↰
	MED: 100-2, 15, 260; 100-4, 12, 90.3; 100-4, 14, 10
+ **38746**	**Thoracic lymphadenectomy, regional, including mediastinal and peritracheal nodes (List in addition to code for primary procedure)** C 80 ↰
	Note that 38746 is an add-on code that must be used in conjunction with the appropriate code for the primary procedure. This code cannot be reported alone.
+ **38747**	**Abdominal lymphadenectomy, regional, including celiac, gastric, portal, peripancreatic, with or without para-aortic and vena caval nodes (List separately in addition to code for primary procedure)** C 80 ↰
	AMA: 1998, Nov, 15
	Note that 38747 is an add-on code that must be used in conjunction with the appropriate code for the primary procedure. This code cannot be reported alone.
38760	**Inguinofemoral lymphadenectomy, superficial, including Cloquet's node (separate procedure)** 2 T 50 80 ↰
	MED: 100-2, 15, 260; 100-4, 12, 90.3; 100-4, 14, 10
	To report a bilateral procedure, append modifier 50 to code 38760.
38765	**Inguinofemoral lymphadenectomy, superficial, in continuity with pelvic lymphadenectomy, including external iliac, hypogastric, and obturator nodes (separate procedure)** C 50 80 ↰
	To report a bilateral procedure, append modifier 50 to code 38765.

| 38770 | **Pelvic lymphadenectomy, including external iliac, hypogastric, and obturator nodes (separate procedure)** | C 50 80 ⬏ |

To report a bilateral procedure, append modifier 50 to code 38770.

| 38780 | **Retroperitoneal transabdominal lymphadenectomy, extensive, including pelvic, aortic, and renal nodes (separate procedure)** | C 80 ⬏ |

If lymphedematous skin and subcutaneous tissue are excised and repaired, consult CPT codes 15000 and 15570-15650.

INTRODUCTION

| 38790 | **Injection procedure; lymphangiography** | N 50 ⬏ |

If radiological supervision and interpretation is performed, consult CPT codes 75801-75807.

| ⊘ | 38792 | **for identification of sentinel node** | N 50 ⬏ |
| | | AMA: 1999, Jul, 6; 1998, Nov, 15 | |

If the sentinel node is excised, consult CPT codes 38500-38542. If nuclear medicine lymphatics and lymph gland imaging is performed, consult CPT code 78195.

| 38794 | **Cannulation, thoracic duct** | N 80 ⬏ |

OTHER PROCEDURES

| 38999 | **Unlisted procedure, hemic or lymphatic system** | S 80 |
| | AMA: 1998, May, 10 | |

MEDIASTINUM AND DIAPHRAGM

MEDIASTINUM

INCISION

| 39000 | **Mediastinotomy with exploration, drainage, removal of foreign body, or biopsy; cervical approach** | C 80 ⬏ |
| 39010 | **transthoracic approach, including either transthoracic or median sternotomy** | C 80 ⬏ |

EXCISION

| 39200 | **Excision of mediastinal cyst** | C 80 ⬏ |
| 39220 | **Excision of mediastinal tumor** | C 80 ⬏ |

If a substernal thyroidectomy is performed, consult CPT code 60270. If a thymectomy is performed, consult CPT code 60520.

ENDOSCOPY

| 39400 | **Mediastinoscopy, with or without biopsy** | T ⬏ |

OTHER PROCEDURES

| 39499 | **Unlisted procedure, mediastinum** | C 80 |

DIAPHRAGM

REPAIR

To report a transabdominal repair of diaphragmatic (esophageal hiatal) hernia, consult 43324, 43325.

| 39501 | **Repair, laceration of diaphragm, any approach** | C 80 ⬏ |
| | AMA: 2000, Nov, 3 | |

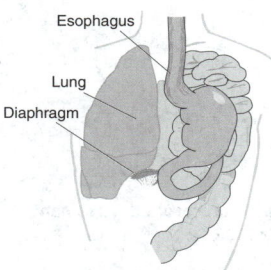

Esophagus

Lung

Diaphragm

A defect of the diaphragm
can allow abdominal contents
to herniate into the thoracic cavity

Code 39503 reports the repair of a
diaphragmatic hernia in a neonate.
The nature of the repair may
necessitate the creation of a ventral
hernia (an opening in the anterior
abdomen to accommodate the
viscera). A chest tube may or
may not be required

The code is reserved for
procedures on neonates

39502	**Repair, paraesophageal hiatus hernia, transabdominal, with or without fundoplasty, vagotomy, and/or pyloroplasty, except neonatal**	C 80 ↰
39503	**Repair, neonatal diaphragmatic hernia, with or without chest tube insertion and with or without creation of ventral hernia**	A C 80 ↰ 63
39520	**Repair, diaphragmatic hernia (esophageal hiatal); transthoracic**	C 80 ↰
39530	**combined, thoracoabdominal**	C 80 ↰
39531	**combined, thoracoabdominal, with dilation of stricture (with or without gastroplasty)**	C 80 ↰
39540	**Repair, diaphragmatic hernia (other than neonatal), traumatic; acute** AMA: 2000, Nov, 3	C 80 ↰
39541	**chronic**	C 80 ↰
39545	**Imbrication of diaphragm for eventration, transthoracic or transabdominal, paralytic or nonparalytic** AMA: 2000, Nov, 3	C 80 ↰
39560	**Resection, diaphragm; with simple repair (eg, primary suture)** AMA: 2000, Nov, 3; 1999, Nov, 21	C 80 ↰
39561	**with complex repair (eg, prosthetic material, local muscle flap)** AMA: 2000, Nov, 3; 1999, Nov, 21	C 80 ↰

OTHER PROCEDURES

39599	**Unlisted procedure, diaphragm**	C 80

↰ CCI Comp   50 Bilateral Procedure   ✚ CPT Add-on Code   ⊘ Modifier -51 Exempt   ♂ Male   ♀ Female
● New Code   ▲ Revised Code   M Maternity Edit   A Age Edit   A–Y APC Status Ind.   AMA: CPT Assistant
© 2005 Ingenix, Inc. *(Blue Ink)*   CPT only © 2005 American Medical Association. All Rights Reserved. *(Black Ink)*   Surgery — 295

Digestive System

40490 — 40702

DIGESTIVE SYSTEM

LIPS

To report procedures performed on the skin of the lips, consult CPT code 10040 and subsequent codes.

EXCISION

40490   **Biopsy of lip**   ⊤ ▣

40500   **Vermilionectomy (lip shave), with mucosal advancement**   ② ⊤ ▣
MED: 100-2, 15, 260; 100-4, 12, 90.3; 100-4, 14, 10

40510   **Excision of lip; transverse wedge excision with primary closure**   ② ⊤ ▣
MED: 100-2, 15, 260; 100-4, 12, 90.3; 100-4, 14, 10

If mucous lesions are excised, consult CPT codes 40810-40816.

40520   **V-excision with primary direct linear closure**   ② ⊤ ▣
MED: 100-2, 15, 260; 100-4, 12, 90.3; 100-4, 14, 10

If mucous lesions are excised, consult CPT codes 40810-40816.

40525   **full thickness, reconstruction with local flap (eg, Estlander or fan)**   ② ⊤ ▣
MED: 100-2, 15, 260; 100-4, 12, 90.3; 100-4, 14, 10

40527   **full thickness, reconstruction with cross lip flap (Abbe-Estlander)**   ② ⊤ 80 ▣
MED: 100-2, 15, 260; 100-4, 12, 90.3; 100-4, 14, 10

40530   **Resection of lip, more than one-fourth, without reconstruction**   ② ⊤ ▣
MED: 100-2, 15, 260; 100-4, 12, 90.3; 100-4, 14, 10

If reconstruction is performed, consult CPT codes 13131 and subsequent codes.

REPAIR (CHEILOPLASTY)

If the cleft palate is repaired, consult CPT codes 42200 and subsequent codes. If other reconstructive procedures are performed, consult CPT codes 14060, 14061, 15120-15261, 15574, 15576, and 15630.

40650   **Repair lip, full thickness; vermilion only**   ③ ⊤ 80 ▣
MED: 100-2, 15, 260; 100-4, 12, 90.3; 100-4, 14, 10
AMA: 2000, Jul, 10

40652   **up to half vertical height**   ③ ⊤ 80 ▣
MED: 100-2, 15, 260; 100-4, 12, 90.3; 100-4, 14, 10
AMA: 2000, Jul, 10

40654   **over one-half vertical height, or complex**   ③ ⊤ ▣
MED: 100-2, 15, 260; 100-4, 12, 90.3; 100-4, 14, 10

40700   **Plastic repair of cleft lip/nasal deformity; primary, partial or complete, unilateral**   ⑦ ⊤ 80 ▣
MED: 100-2, 15, 260; 100-4, 12, 90.3; 100-4, 14, 10

40701   **primary bilateral, one stage procedure**   ⑦ ⊤ 80 ▣
MED: 100-2, 15, 260; 100-4, 12, 90.3; 100-4, 14, 10

40702   **primary bilateral, one of two stages**   ⊤ 80 ▣

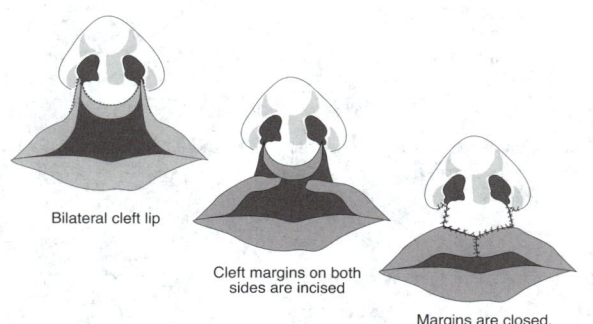

Bilateral cleft lip

Cleft margins on both sides are incised

Margins are closed, correcting cleft

| 40720 | secondary, by recreation of defect and reclosure | 7 T 50 80 ↩ |

MED: 100-2, 15, 260; 100-4, 12, 90.3; 100-4, 14, 10

If rhinoplasty only is performed for nasal deformity secondary to a congenital cleft lip, consult CPT codes 30460 and 30462.

To report a bilateral procedure, append modifier 50 to code 40720. To report repair of a cleft lip, with cross pedicle flap (Abbe-Estlander types), consult 40527.

| 40761 | with cross lip pedicle flap (Abbe-Estlander type), including sectioning and inserting of pedicle | 3 T ↩ |

MED: 100-2, 15, 260; 100-4, 12, 90.3; 100-4, 14, 10

OTHER PROCEDURES

| 40799 | Unlisted procedure, lips | T 80 |

VESTIBULE OF MOUTH

INCISION

Part of the oral cavity outside the dentoalveolar structures includes the mucosal and submucosal tissue of lips and cheeks.

| 40800 | Drainage of abscess, cyst, hematoma, vestibule of mouth; simple | T ↩ |
| 40801 | complicated | 2 T ↩ |

MED: 100-2, 15, 260; 100-4, 12, 90.3; 100-4, 14, 10

40804	Removal of embedded foreign body, vestibule of mouth; simple	X 80 ↩
40805	complicated	T 80 ↩
40806	Incision of labial frenum (frenotomy)	T 80 ↩

EXCISION, DESTRUCTION

40808	Biopsy, vestibule of mouth	T ↩
40810	Excision of lesion of mucosa and submucosa, vestibule of mouth; without repair	T ↩
40812	with simple repair	T ↩
40814	with complex repair	2 T ↩

MED: 100-2, 15, 260; 100-4, 12, 90.3; 100-4, 14, 10

| 40816 | complex, with excision of underlying muscle | 2 T ↩ |

MED: 100-2, 15, 260; 100-4, 12, 90.3; 100-4, 14, 10

☐ CCI Comp　50 Bilateral Procedure　✛ CPT Add-on Code　⊘ Modifier -51 Exempt　♂ Male　♀ Female
● New Code　▲ Revised Code　M Maternity Edit　A Age Edit　A—Y APC Status Ind.　AMA: CPT Assistant
© 2005 Ingenix, Inc. *(Blue Ink)*　CPT only © 2005 American Medical Association. All Rights Reserved. *(Black Ink)*　Surgery — 297

Digestive System

40818 — 41005

40818	Excision of mucosa of vestibule of mouth as donor graft	1 T 80 ☍

MED: 100-2, 15, 260; 100-4, 12, 90.3; 100-4, 14, 10

40819	Excision of frenum, labial or buccal (frenumectomy, frenulectomy, frenectomy)	1 T 80 ☍

MED: 100-2, 15, 150; 100-2, 15, 260; 100-4, 12, 90.3; 100-4, 14, 10

40820	Destruction of lesion or scar of vestibule of mouth by physical methods (eg, laser, thermal, cryo, chemical)	T ☍

MED: 100-3, 140.5

REPAIR

40830	Closure of laceration, vestibule of mouth; 2.5 cm or less	T 80 ☍
40831	over 2.5 cm or complex	1 T 80 ☍

MED: 100-2, 15, 260; 100-4, 12, 90.3; 100-4, 14, 10

40840	Vestibuloplasty; anterior	2 T 80 ☍

MED: 100-2, 15, 260; 100-4, 12, 90.3; 100-4, 14, 10

40842	posterior, unilateral	3 T 80 ☍

MED: 100-2, 15, 260; 100-4, 12, 90.3; 100-4, 14, 10

40843	posterior, bilateral	3 T 80 ☍

MED: 100-2, 15, 260; 100-4, 12, 90.3; 100-4, 14, 10

40844	entire arch	5 T 80 ☍

MED: 100-2, 15, 260; 100-4, 12, 90.3; 100-4, 14, 10

40845	complex (including ridge extension, muscle repositioning)	5 T 80 ☍

MED: 100-2, 15, 260; 100-4, 12, 90.3; 100-4, 14, 10

If skin grafts are performed, consult CPT codes 15000 and subsequent codes.

OTHER PROCEDURES

40899	Unlisted procedure, vestibule of mouth	T 80

TONGUE AND FLOOR OF MOUTH

INCISION

41000	Intraoral incision and drainage of abscess, cyst, or hematoma of tongue or floor of mouth; lingual	T ☍
41005	sublingual, superficial	1 T 80 ☍

MED: 100-2, 15, 260; 100-4, 12, 90.3; 100-4, 14, 10

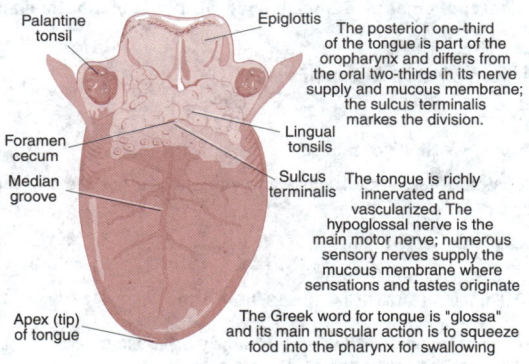

Palantine tonsil

Epiglottis

The posterior one-third of the tongue is part of the oropharynx and differs from the oral two-thirds in its nerve supply and mucous membrane; the sulcus terminalis markes the division.

Foramen cecum

Lingual tonsils

Median groove

Sulcus terminalis

The tongue is richly innervated and vascularized. The hypoglossal nerve is the main motor nerve; numerous sensory nerves supply the mucous membrane where sensations and tastes originate

Apex (tip) of tongue

The Greek word for tongue is "glossa" and its main muscular action is to squeeze food into the pharynx for swallowing

---

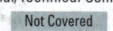 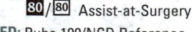

41006	sublingual, deep, supramylohyoid MED: 100-2, 15, 260; 100-4, 12, 90.3; 100-4, 14, 10	1 T 80 ◪
41007	submental space MED: 100-2, 15, 260; 100-4, 12, 90.3; 100-4, 14, 10	1 T 80 ◪
41008	submandibular space MED: 100-2, 15, 260; 100-4, 12, 90.3; 100-4, 14, 10	1 T 80 ◪
41009	masticator space MED: 100-2, 15, 260; 100-4, 12, 90.3; 100-4, 14, 10	1 T 80 ◪
41010	**Incision of lingual frenum (frenotomy)** MED: 100-2, 15, 260; 100-4, 12, 90.3; 100-4, 14, 10	1 T 80 ◪
41015	**Extraoral incision and drainage of abscess, cyst, or hematoma of floor of mouth; sublingual** MED: 100-2, 15, 260; 100-4, 12, 90.3; 100-4, 14, 10	1 T 80 ◪
41016	submental MED: 100-2, 15, 260; 100-4, 12, 90.3; 100-4, 14, 10	1 T 80 ◪
41017	submandibular MED: 100-2, 15, 260; 100-4, 12, 90.3; 100-4, 14, 10	1 T 80 ◪
41018	masticator space MED: 100-2, 15, 260; 100-4, 12, 90.3; 100-4, 14, 10	1 T 80 ◪

If a frenoplasty is performed, consult CPT code 41520.

EXCISION

41100	**Biopsy of tongue; anterior two-thirds**	T ◪
41105	posterior one-third	T ◪
41108	**Biopsy of floor of mouth**	T ◪
41110	**Excision of lesion of tongue without closure**	T ◪
41112	**Excision of lesion of tongue with closure; anterior two-thirds** MED: 100-2, 15, 260; 100-4, 12, 90.3; 100-4, 14, 10	2 T ◪
41113	posterior one-third MED: 100-2, 15, 260; 100-4, 12, 90.3; 100-4, 14, 10	2 T ◪

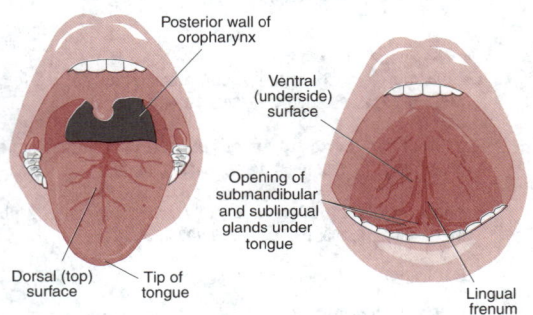

Posterior wall of oropharynx

Ventral (underside) surface

Opening of submandibular and sublingual glands under tongue

Dorsal (top) surface

Tip of tongue

Lingual frenum

Anterior (front) two-thirds of tongue comprises most of easily visible portions; the base, or root, comprises the remainder of tongue

Digestive System

41114 — 41599

41114	**with local tongue flap** MED: 100-2, 15, 260; 100-4, 12, 90.3; 100-4, 14, 10	2 T 80 ↵

Note that 41114 must be listed in addition to 41112 or 41113.

41115	**Excision of lingual frenum (frenectomy)** MED: 100-2, 15, 150	T 80 ↵
41116	**Excision, lesion of floor of mouth** MED: 100-2, 15, 260; 100-4, 12, 90.3; 100-4, 14, 10	1 T ↵
41120	**Glossectomy; less than one-half tongue** MED: 100-2, 15, 260; 100-4, 12, 90.3; 100-4, 14, 10	5 T 80 ↵
41130	**hemiglossectomy**	C 80 ↵
41135	**partial, with unilateral radical neck dissection**	C 80 ↵
41140	**complete or total, with or without tracheostomy, without radical neck dissection** **Regnolli's excision**	C 80 ↵
41145	**complete or total, with or without tracheostomy, with unilateral radical neck dissection**	C 80 ↵
41150	**composite procedure with resection floor of mouth and mandibular resection, without radical neck dissection**	C 80 ↵
41153	**composite procedure with resection floor of mouth, with suprahyoid neck dissection**	C 80 ↵
41155	**composite procedure with resection floor of mouth, mandibular resection, and radical neck dissection (Commando type)** AMA: 2001, Jan, 13	C 80 ↵

REPAIR

41250	**Repair of laceration 2.5 cm or less; floor of mouth and/or anterior two-thirds of tongue** MED: 100-2, 15, 260; 100-4, 12, 90.3; 100-4, 14, 10	2 T 80 ↵
41251	**posterior one-third of tongue** MED: 100-2, 15, 260; 100-4, 12, 90.3; 100-4, 14, 10	2 T 80 ↵
41252	**Repair of laceration of tongue, floor of mouth, over 2.6 cm or complex** MED: 100-2, 15, 260; 100-4, 12, 90.3; 100-4, 14, 10	2 T 80 ↵

OTHER PROCEDURES

41500	**Fixation of tongue, mechanical, other than suture (eg, K-wire)** MED: 100-2, 15, 260; 100-4, 12, 90.3; 100-4, 14, 10	1 T 80 ↵
41510	**Suture of tongue to lip for micrognathia (Douglas type procedure)** MED: 100-2, 15, 260; 100-4, 12, 90.3; 100-4, 14, 10	1 T 80 ↵
41520	**Frenoplasty (surgical revision of frenum, eg, with Z-plasty)** MED: 100-2, 15, 260; 100-4, 12, 90.3; 100-4, 14, 10	2 T 80 ↵

If a frenotomy is performed, consult CPT codes 40806 and 41010.

41599	**Unlisted procedure, tongue, floor of mouth** AMA: 2000, Dec, 14	T 80

DENTOALVEOLAR STRUCTURES

INCISION

41800 Drainage of abscess, cyst, hematoma from dentoalveolar structures ▣▣▣
 MED: 100-2, 15, 260; 100-4, 12, 90.3; 100-4, 14, 10

41805 Removal of embedded foreign body from dentoalveolar structures; soft tissues ▣▣▣

41806 bone ▣▣▣

EXCISION, DESTRUCTION

41820 Gingivectomy, excision gingiva, each quadrant ▣▣▣

41821 Operculectomy, excision pericoronal tissues ▣▣▣

41822 Excision of fibrous tuberosities, dentoalveolar structures ▣▣▣

41823 Excision of osseous tuberosities, dentoalveolar structures ▣▣▣

41825 Excision of lesion or tumor (except listed above), dentoalveolar structures; without repair ▣▣

41826 with simple repair ▣▣

41827 with complex repair ▣▣▣
 MED: 100-2, 15, 260; 100-4, 12, 90.3; 100-4, 14, 10

If the destruction of lesion is nonexcisional, consult CPT code 41850.

41828 Excision of hyperplastic alveolar mucosa, each quadrant (specify) ▣▣▣

41830 Alveolectomy, including curettage of osteitis or sequestrectomy ▣▣▣

41850 Destruction of lesion (except excision), dentoalveolar structures ▣▣▣

OTHER PROCEDURES

41870 Periodontal mucosal grafting ▣▣▣

41872 Gingivoplasty, each quadrant (specify) ▣▣▣

41874 Alveoloplasty, each quadrant (specify) ▣▣▣
 MED: 100-2, 15, 150

If laceration closure is performed, consult CPT codes 40830 and 40831. If a segmental osteotomy is performed, consult CPT code 21206. If fractures are reduced, consult CPT codes 21421-21490.

41899 Unlisted procedure, dentoalveolar structures ▣▣

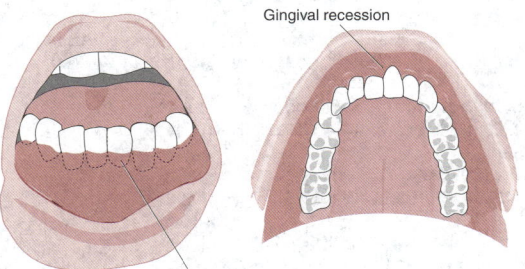

Gingival recession

Excessive mucosal growth

Gingivitis is an inflammatory response to bacteria on the teeth; it is characterized by tender, red, swollen gums and can lead to gingival recession

PALATE AND UVULA

INCISION

42000	**Drainage of abscess of palate, uvula**	▣ T 80 ◪
	MED: 100-2, 15, 260; 100-4, 12, 90.3; 100-4, 14, 10	

EXCISION, DESTRUCTION

42100	**Biopsy of palate, uvula**	T ◪
42104	**Excision, lesion of palate, uvula; without closure**	T ◪
42106	**with simple primary closure**	T ◪
42107	**with local flap closure**	▣ T ◪
	MED: 100-2, 15, 260; 100-4, 12, 90.3; 100-4, 14, 10	

If a skin graft is performed, consult CPT codes 14040-14300. If a mucosal graft is performed, consult CPT code 40818.

42120	**Resection of palate or extensive resection of lesion**	▣ T 80 ◪
	MED: 100-2, 15, 260; 100-4, 12, 90.3; 100-4, 14, 10	

If reconstruction of palate with extraoral tissue is performed, consult CPT codes 14040-14300, 15050, 15120, 15240, and 15576.

42140	**Uvulectomy, excision of uvula**	▣ T ◪
	MED: 100-2, 15, 260; 100-4, 12, 90.3; 100-4, 14, 10	
42145	**Palatopharyngoplasty (eg, uvulopalatopharyngoplasty, uvulopharyngoplasty)**	▣ T ◪
	MED: 100-2, 15, 260; 100-4, 12, 90.3; 100-4, 14, 10	
42160	**Destruction of lesion, palate or uvula (thermal, cryo or chemical)**	T 80 ◪

REPAIR

42180	**Repair, laceration of palate; up to 2 cm**	▣ T 80 ◪
	MED: 100-2, 15, 260; 100-4, 12, 90.3; 100-4, 14, 10	
42182	**over 2 cm or complex**	▣ T 80 ◪
	MED: 100-2, 15, 260; 100-4, 12, 90.3; 100-4, 14, 10	
42200	**Palatoplasty for cleft palate, soft and/or hard palate only**	▣ T 80 ◪
	MED: 100-2, 15, 260; 100-4, 12, 90.3; 100-4, 14, 10	
42205	**Palatoplasty for cleft palate, with closure of alveolar ridge; soft tissue only**	▣ T 80 ◪
	MED: 100-2, 15, 260; 100-4, 12, 90.3; 100-4, 14, 10	
42210	**with bone graft to alveolar ridge (includes obtaining graft)**	▣ T 80 ◪
	MED: 100-2, 15, 260; 100-4, 12, 90.3; 100-4, 14, 10	
42215	**Palatoplasty for cleft palate; major revision**	▣ T 80 ◪
	MED: 100-2, 15, 260; 100-4, 12, 90.3; 100-4, 14, 10	
42220	**secondary lengthening procedure**	▣ T 80 ◪
	MED: 100-2, 15, 260; 100-4, 12, 90.3; 100-4, 14, 10	
42225	**attachment pharyngeal flap**	T 80 ◪
	AMA: 1997, Aug, 18	
42226	**Lengthening of palate, and pharyngeal flap**	▣ T 80 ◪
	MED: 100-2, 15, 260; 100-4, 12, 90.3; 100-4, 14, 10	

Digestive System

42000 — 42226

42227	**Lengthening of palate, with island flap**	T 80 ↵
42235	**Repair of anterior palate, including vomer flap**	5 T 80 ↵
	MED: 100-2, 15, 260; 100-4, 12, 90.3; 100-4, 14, 10	
42260	**Repair of nasolabial fistula**	4 T 80 ↵
	MED: 100-2, 15, 260; 100-4, 12, 90.3; 100-4, 14, 10	

If a cleft lip is repaired, consult CPT codes 40700 and subsequent codes.

| 42280 | **Maxillary impression for palatal prosthesis** | T 80 ↵ |
| 42281 | **Insertion of pin-retained palatal prosthesis** | T 80 ↵ |

OTHER PROCEDURES

| 42299 | **Unlisted procedure, palate, uvula** | T 80 |

SALIVARY GLAND AND DUCTS

INCISION

42300	**Drainage of abscess; parotid, simple**	1 T ↵
	MED: 100-2, 15, 260; 100-4, 12, 90.3; 100-4, 14, 10	
42305	**parotid, complicated**	2 T 80 ↵
	MED: 100-2, 15, 260; 100-4, 12, 90.3; 100-4, 14, 10	
42310	**Drainage of abscess; submaxillary or sublingual, intraoral**	1 T 80 ↵
	MED: 100-2, 15, 260; 100-4, 12, 90.3; 100-4, 14, 10	
42320	**submaxillary, external**	1 T 80 ↵
	MED: 100-2, 15, 260; 100-4, 12, 90.3; 100-4, 14, 10	
~~42325~~	~~Fistulization of sublingual salivary cyst (ranula);~~	
~~42326~~	~~with prosthesis~~	
42330	**Sialolithotomy; submandibular (submaxillary), sublingual or parotid, uncomplicated, intraoral**	T ↵
42335	**submandibular (submaxillary), complicated, intraoral**	T ↵
42340	**parotid, extraoral or complicated intraoral**	2 T 80 ↵
	MED: 100-2, 15, 260; 100-4, 12, 90.3; 100-4, 14, 10	

EXCISION

| 42400 | **Biopsy of salivary gland; needle** | T ↵ |

To report fine needle aspiration, consult CPT codes 10021, 10022.

To report evaluation of fine needle aspirate, consult CPT codes 88172, 88173.

If imaging guidance is performed, see 76003, 76360, 76393, 76942.

| 42405 | **incisional** | 2 T ↵ |
| | MED: 100-2, 15, 260; 100-4, 12, 90.3; 100-4, 14, 10 | |

If imaging guidance is performed, see 76003, 76360, 76393, 76942.

42408	**Excision of sublingual salivary cyst (ranula)**	3 T 80 ↵
	MED: 100-2, 15, 260; 100-4, 12, 90.3; 100-4, 14, 10	
42409	**Marsupialization of sublingual salivary cyst (ranula)**	3 T 80 ↵
	MED: 100-2, 15, 260; 100-4, 12, 90.3; 100-4, 14, 10	

If fistulization of a sublingual salivary cyst is performed, consult CPT code 42325.

Digestive System

42410 — 42510

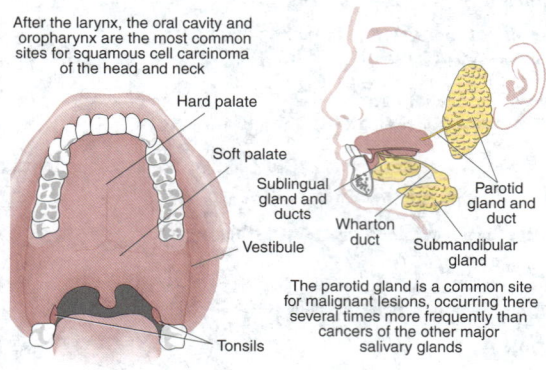

After the larynx, the oral cavity and oropharynx are the most common sites for squamous cell carcinoma of the head and neck

- Hard palate
- Soft palate
- Sublingual gland and ducts
- Wharton duct
- Vestibule
- Parotid gland and duct
- Submandibular gland
- Tonsils

The parotid gland is a common site for malignant lesions, occurring there several times more frequently than cancers of the other major salivary glands

42410 **Excision of parotid tumor or parotid gland; lateral lobe, without nerve dissection** 3 T 80 🔲
MED: 100-2, 15, 260; 100-4, 12, 90.3; 100-4, 14, 10

42415 **lateral lobe, with dissection and preservation of facial nerve** 7 T 80 🔲
MED: 100-2, 15, 260; 100-4, 12, 90.3; 100-4, 14, 10

42420 **total, with dissection and preservation of facial nerve** 7 T 80 🔲
MED: 100-2, 15, 260; 100-4, 12, 90.3; 100-4, 14, 10

42425 **total, en bloc removal with sacrifice of facial nerve** 7 T 80 🔲
MED: 100-2, 15, 260; 100-4, 12, 90.3; 100-4, 14, 10

42426 **total, with unilateral radical neck dissection** C 80 🔲

If suture or grafting of a facial nerve is performed, consult CPT codes 64864, 64865, 69740, and 69745.

42440 **Excision of submandibular (submaxillary) gland** 3 T 80 🔲
MED: 100-2, 15, 260; 100-4, 12, 90.3; 100-4, 14, 10

42450 **Excision of sublingual gland** 2 T 80 🔲
MED: 100-2, 15, 260; 100-4, 12, 90.3; 100-4, 14, 10

REPAIR

42500 **Plastic repair of salivary duct, sialodochoplasty; primary or simple** 3 T 80 🔲
MED: 100-2, 15, 260; 100-4, 12, 90.3; 100-4, 14, 10

42505 **secondary or complicated** 4 T 🔲
MED: 100-2, 15, 260; 100-4, 12, 90.3; 100-4, 14, 10

42507 **Parotid duct diversion, bilateral (Wilke type procedure);** 3 T 80 🔲
MED: 100-2, 15, 260; 100-4, 12, 90.3; 100-4, 14, 10

42508 **with excision of one submandibular gland** 4 T 80 🔲
MED: 100-2, 15, 260; 100-4, 12, 90.3; 100-4, 14, 10

42509 **with excision of both submandibular glands** 4 T 80 🔲
MED: 100-2, 15, 260; 100-4, 12, 90.3; 100-4, 14, 10

42510 **with ligation of both submandibular (Wharton's) ducts** 4 T 80 🔲
MED: 100-2, 15, 260; 100-4, 12, 90.3; 100-4, 14, 10

OTHER PROCEDURES

42550   Injection procedure for sialography   N ⟲

     If radiological supervision and interpretation is performed, consult CPT code 70390.

42600   Closure salivary fistula   1 T 80 ⟲
     MED: 100-2, 15, 260; 100-4, 12, 90.3; 100-4, 14, 10

42650   Dilation salivary duct   T ⟲

42660   Dilation and catheterization of salivary duct, with or without injection   T 80 ⟲

42665   Ligation salivary duct, intraoral   7 T 80 ⟲

42699   Unlisted procedure, salivary glands or ducts   T 80

PHARYNX, ADENOIDS, AND TONSILS

INCISION

42700   Incision and drainage abscess; peritonsillar   1 T ⟲
     MED: 100-2, 15, 260; 100-4, 12, 90.3; 100-4, 14, 10

42720   retropharyngeal or parapharyngeal, intraoral approach   1 T 80 ⟲
     MED: 100-2, 15, 260; 100-4, 12, 90.3; 100-4, 14, 10

42725   retropharyngeal or parapharyngeal, external approach   2 T 80 ⟲
     MED: 100-2, 15, 260; 100-4, 12, 90.3; 100-4, 14, 10

EXCISION, DESTRUCTION

42800   Biopsy; oropharynx   T ⟲

42802   hypopharynx   1 T ⟲
     MED: 100-2, 15, 260; 100-4, 12, 90.3; 100-4, 14, 10

42804   nasopharynx, visible lesion, simple   1 T ⟲
     MED: 100-2, 15, 260; 100-4, 12, 90.3; 100-4, 14, 10

42806   nasopharynx, survey for unknown primary lesion   2 T ⟲
     MED: 100-2, 15, 260; 100-4, 12, 90.3; 100-4, 14, 10

     If a laryngoscopic biopsy is performed, consult CPT codes 31510, 31535, and 31536.

42808   Excision or destruction of lesion of pharynx, any method   2 T ⟲
     MED: 100-2, 15, 260; 100-4, 12, 90.3; 100-4, 14, 10

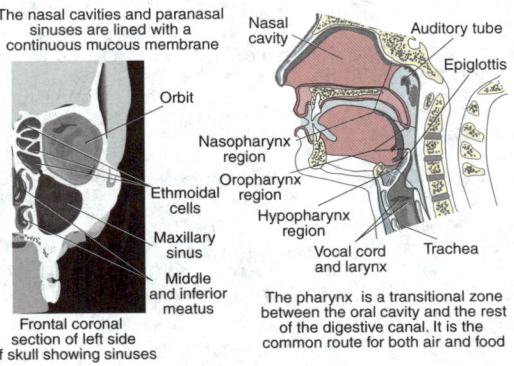

The nasal cavities and paranasal sinuses are lined with a continuous mucous membrane

Nasal cavity — Auditory tube — Epiglottis

Orbit

Nasopharynx region

Ethmoidal cells

Oropharynx region

Maxillary sinus

Hypopharynx region

Middle and inferior meatus

Vocal cord and larynx — Trachea

Frontal coronal section of left side of skull showing sinuses

The pharynx is a transitional zone between the oral cavity and the rest of the digestive canal. It is the common route for both air and food

Digestive System

42809 — 42890

42809	**Removal of foreign body from pharynx**	X ↵
42810	**Excision branchial cleft cyst or vestige, confined to skin and subcutaneous tissues**	3 T 80 ↵
	MED: 100-2, 15, 260; 100-4, 12, 90.3; 100-4, 14, 10	
42815	**Excision branchial cleft cyst, vestige, or fistula, extending beneath subcutaneous tissues and/or into pharynx**	5 T 80 ↵
	MED: 100-2, 15, 260; 100-4, 12, 90.3; 100-4, 14, 10	
42820	**Tonsillectomy and adenoidectomy; under age 12**	A 3 T 80 ↵
	MED: 100-2, 15, 260; 100-4, 12, 90.3; 100-4, 14, 10	
	AMA: 1998, Feb, 11; 1997, Aug, 18	
42821	**age 12 or over**	5 T 80 ↵
	MED: 100-2, 15, 260; 100-4, 12, 90.3; 100-4, 14, 10	
	AMA: 1997, Aug, 18	
42825	**Tonsillectomy, primary or secondary; under age 12**	A 4 T 80 ↵
	MED: 100-2, 15, 260; 100-4, 12, 90.3; 100-4, 14, 10	
	AMA: 1997, Aug, 18	
42826	**age 12 or over**	4 T ↵
	MED: 100-2, 15, 260; 100-4, 12, 90.3; 100-4, 14, 10	
	AMA: 1997, Aug, 18	
42830	**Adenoidectomy, primary; under age 12**	A 4 T 80 ↵
	MED: 100-2, 15, 260; 100-4, 12, 90.3; 100-4, 14, 10	
42831	**age 12 or over**	4 T 80 ↵
	MED: 100-2, 15, 260; 100-4, 12, 90.3; 100-4, 14, 10	
42835	**Adenoidectomy, secondary; under age 12**	A 4 T 80 ↵
	MED: 100-2, 15, 260; 100-4, 12, 90.3; 100-4, 14, 10	
42836	**age 12 or over**	4 T 80 ↵
	MED: 100-2, 15, 260; 100-4, 12, 90.3; 100-4, 14, 10	
	AMA: 1998, Feb, 11	
42842	**Radical resection of tonsil, tonsillar pillars, and/or retromolar trigone; without closure**	T 80 ↵
42844	**closure with local flap (eg, tongue, buccal)**	T 80 ↵
42845	**closure with other flap**	C 80 ↵

If closure is performed with another flap(s), consult the appropriate CPT code for the flap(s). If this procedure is combined with a radical neck dissection, consult also CPT code 38720.

42860	**Excision of tonsil tags**	3 T 80 ↵
	MED: 100-2, 15, 260; 100-4, 12, 90.3; 100-4, 14, 10	
42870	**Excision or destruction lingual tonsil, any method (separate procedure)**	3 T 80 ↵
	MED: 100-2, 15, 260; 100-4, 12, 90.3; 100-4, 14, 10	

If the nasopharynx is resected by bicoronal and/or transzygomatic approach, consult CPT codes 61586 and 61600.

42890	**Limited pharyngectomy**	7 T 80 ↵
	MED: 100-2, 15, 260; 100-4, 12, 90.3; 100-4, 14, 10	

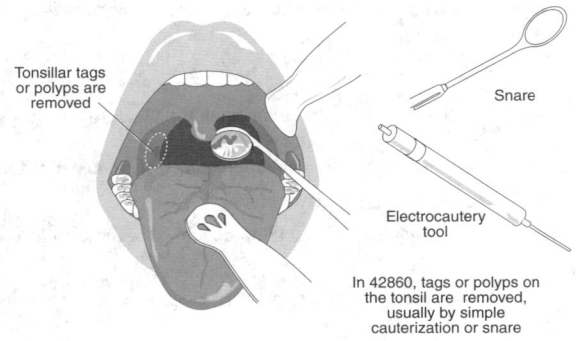

Tonsillar tags
or polyps are
removed

Snare

Electrocautery
tool

In 42860, tags or polyps on
the tonsil are removed,
usually by simple
cauterization or snare

42892 **Resection of lateral pharyngeal wall or pyriform sinus, direct closure by advancement of lateral and posterior pharyngeal walls** 7 T 80 🗗
MED: 100-2, 15, 260; 100-4, 12, 90.3; 100-4, 14, 10

If this procedure is combined with a radical neck dissection, consult CPT code 38720.

42894 **Resection of pharyngeal wall requiring closure with myocutaneous flap** C 80 🗗

If this procedure is combined with a radical neck dissection, consult CPT code 38720.

REPAIR

42900 **Suture pharynx for wound or injury** 1 T 80 🗗
MED: 100-2, 15, 260; 100-4, 12, 90.3; 100-4, 14, 10

42950 **Pharyngoplasty (plastic or reconstructive operation on pharynx)** 2 T 80 🗗
MED: 100-2, 15, 260; 100-4, 12, 90.3; 100-4, 14, 10

If this procedure involves the pharyngeal flap, consult CPT code 42225.

42953 **Pharyngoesophageal repair** C 80 🗗

If closure with myocutaneous or other flap is performed, use the appropriate CPT code in addition to 42953.

OTHER PROCEDURES

42955 **Pharyngostomy (fistulization of pharynx, external for feeding)** 2 T 80 🗗
MED: 100-2, 15, 260; 100-4, 12, 90.3; 100-4, 14, 10

42960 **Control oropharyngeal hemorrhage, primary or secondary (eg, posttonsillectomy); simple** 1 T 80 🗗
MED: 100-2, 15, 260; 100-4, 12, 90.3; 100-4, 14, 10

42961 **complicated, requiring hospitalization** C 80 🗗

42962 **with secondary surgical intervention** 2 T 80 🗗
MED: 100-2, 15, 260; 100-4, 12, 90.3; 100-4, 14, 10

42970 **Control of nasopharyngeal hemorrhage, primary or secondary (eg, postadenoidectomy); simple, with posterior nasal packs, with or without anterior packs and/or cautery** T 🗗

42971 **complicated, requiring hospitalization** C 80 🗗

42972 **with secondary surgical intervention** 3 T 80 🗗
MED: 100-2, 15, 260; 100-4, 12, 90.3; 100-4, 14, 10

Digestive System

42999 — 43124

42999   Unlisted procedure, pharynx, adenoids, or tonsils   T 80

ESOPHAGUS

INCISION

If esophageal intubation is performed with a laparotomy, consult CPT code 43510.

43020   Esophagotomy, cervical approach, with removal of foreign body   T 80 ▷

43030   Cricopharyngeal myotomy   T 80 ▷

43045   Esophagotomy, thoracic approach, with removal of foreign body   C 80 ▷

EXCISION

To report gastrointestinal reconstruction for previous esophagectomy, consult CPT codes 43360, 43361.

43100   **Excision of lesion, esophagus, with primary repair; cervical approach**   C 80 ▷

43101   **thoracic or abdominal approach**   C 80 ▷

43107   **Total or near total esophagectomy, without thoracotomy; with pharyngogastrostomy or cervical esophagogastrostomy, with or without pyloroplasty (transhiatal)**   C 80 ▷

43108   **with colon interposition or small intestine reconstruction, including intestine mobilization, preparation and anastomosis(es)**   C 80 ▷

43112   **Total or near total esophagectomy, with thoracotomy; with pharyngogastrostomy or cervical esophagogastrostomy, with or without pyloroplasty**   C 80 ▷

43113   **with colon interposition or small intestine reconstruction, including intestine mobilization, preparation, and anastomosis(es)**   C 80 ▷

43116   **Partial esophagectomy, cervical, with free intestinal graft, including microvascular anastomosis, obtaining the graft and intestinal reconstruction**   C 80 ▷
         AMA: 1998, Nov, 16; 1997, Nov, 17

         Do not report 69990 in addition to 43116 as the operating microscope is considered an inclusive component of the surgery. If another physician performs an intestinal or a free jejunal graft with microvascular anastomosis, append modifier 52 to this code. If a free jejunal graft with microvascular anastomosis is performed alone, consult CPT code 43496.

43117   **Partial esophagectomy, distal two-thirds, with thoracotomy and separate abdominal incision, with or without proximal gastrectomy; with thoracic esophagogastrostomy, with or without pyloroplasty (Ivor Lewis)**   C 80 ▷

43118   **with colon interposition or small intestine reconstruction, including intestine mobilization, preparation, and anastomosis(es)**   C 80 ▷

43121   **Partial esophagectomy, distal two-thirds, with thoracotomy only, with or without proximal gastrectomy, with thoracic esophagogastrostomy, with or without pyloroplasty**   C 80 ▷

43122   **Partial esophagectomy, thoracoabdominal or abdominal approach, with or without proximal gastrectomy; with esophagogastrostomy, with or without pyloroplasty**   C 80 ▷

43123   **with colon interposition or small intestine reconstruction, including intestine mobilization, preparation, and anastomosis(es)**   C 80 ▷

43124   **Total or partial esophagectomy, without reconstruction (any approach), with cervical esophagostomy**   C 80 ▷

| 43130 | Diverticulectomy of hypopharynx or esophagus, with or without myotomy; cervical approach | T 80 ⟳ |
| 43135 | thoracic approach | C 80 ⟳ |

ENDOSCOPY

GASTROINTESTINAL ENDOSCOPY

Gastrointestinal endoscopy codes are reported by site and are listed as follows: esophagus (43200–43232), upper gastrointestinal (43234–43259), endoscopic retrograde cholangiopancreatography (ERCP) (43260–43272), other small intestine or stomal (44360–44397), and large intestine (45300–45392).

Endoscopic procedures may be diagnostic or surgical. The procedure is considered diagnostic when performed to visualize an abnormality or determine the extent of disease. When anything more than visualization is performed, the procedure is considered to be a surgical procedure. A surgical endoscopy always includes a diagnostic endoscopy.

For example, if the patient is to have a diagnostic flexible sigmoidoscopy with biopsy of a lesion during the same surgical session, the diagnostic portion of the procedure (45330) would not be reported separately. Only the surgical portion of the procedure (45331) would be reported.

Diagnostic endoscopic procedures can be reported with open or incisional procedures.

Diagnostic endoscopy is always included in surgical endoscopy.

⊙ **43200** **Esophagoscopy, rigid or flexible; diagnostic, with or without collection of specimen(s) by brushing or washing (separate procedure)** 1 T ⟳
MED: 100-2, 15, 260; 100-3, 100.2; 100-4, 12, 90.3; 100-4, 14, 10

AMA: 1999, Nov, 21; 1998, Jun, 10; 1994, Spring, 1

⊙ **43201** **with directed submucosal injection(s), any substance** 1 T ⟳
MED: 100-2, 15, 260; 100-4, 12, 90.3; 100-4, 14, 10

To report injection sclerosis of esophageal varices, consult CPT code 43204.

⊙ **43202** **with biopsy, single or multiple** 1 T ⟳
MED: 100-2, 15, 260; 100-3, 100.2; 100-4, 12, 40.6; 100-4, 12, 90.3; 100-4, 14, 10

AMA: 1994, Spring, 1

⊙ **43204** **with injection sclerosis of esophageal varices** 1 T ⟳
MED: 100-2, 15, 260; 100-3, 100.10; 100-3, 100.2; 100-4, 12, 90.3; 100-4, 14, 10

AMA: 1994, Spring, 1

⊙ **43205** **with band ligation of esophageal varices** 1 T 80 ⟳
MED: 100-2, 15, 260; 100-3, 100.2; 100-4, 12, 90.3; 100-4, 14, 10

AMA: 1994, Spring, 1

⊙ **43215** **with removal of foreign body** 1 T ⟳
MED: 100-2, 15, 260; 100-3, 100.2; 100-4, 12, 90.3; 100-4, 14, 10

AMA: 1994, Spring, 1

To report radiological supervision and interpretation, consult CPT code 74235.

⊙ **43216** **with removal of tumor(s), polyp(s), or other lesion(s) by hot biopsy forceps or bipolar cautery** 1 T 80 ⟳
MED: 100-2, 15, 260; 100-3, 100.2; 100-4, 12, 90.3; 100-4, 14, 10

AMA: 1994, Spring, 1

Digestive System

43217 — 43234

⊙ **43217**   **with removal of tumor(s), polyp(s), or other lesion(s) by snare technique**   🔟 Ⓣ ▶️
MED: 100-2, 15, 260; 100-3, 100.2; 100-4, 12, 40.6; 100-4, 12, 90.3; 100-4, 14, 10

AMA: 1994, Spring, 1

⊙ **43219**   **with insertion of plastic tube or stent**   🔟 Ⓣ ▶️
MED: 100-2, 15, 260; 100-3, 100.2; 100-4, 12, 90.3; 100-4, 14, 10

AMA: 1994, Spring, 2

⊙ **43220**   **with balloon dilation (less than 30 mm diameter)**   🔟 Ⓣ ▶️
MED: 100-2, 15, 260; 100-3, 100.2; 100-4, 12, 90.3; 100-4, 14, 10

AMA: 1997, Jan, 10; 1994, Spring, 2

If an endoscopic dilation is performed with a balloon 30 mm in diameter or larger, consult CPT code 43458. If dilation is performed without visualization, consult CPT codes 43450-43453.

If the procedure is performed with imaging guidance consult CPT code 74360.

⊙ **43226**   **with insertion of guide wire followed by dilation over guide wire**🔟 Ⓣ ▶️
MED: 100-2, 15, 260; 100-3, 100.2; 100-4, 12, 90.3; 100-4, 14, 10

AMA: 1994, Spring, 2

To report radiological supervision and interpretation, consult CPT code 74360.

⊙ **43227**   **with control of bleeding (eg, injection, bipolar cautery, unipolar cautery, laser, heater probe, stapler, plasma coagulator)**   ②️ Ⓣ ▶️
MED: 100-2, 15, 260; 100-3, 100.2; 100-4, 12, 90.3; 100-4, 14, 10

AMA: 1994, Spring, 2

⊙ **43228**   **with ablation of tumor(s), polyp(s), or other lesion(s), not amenable to removal by hot biopsy forceps, bipolar cautery or snare technique**   ②️ Ⓣ ▶️
MED: 100-2, 15, 260; 100-3, 100.2; 100-4, 12, 90.3; 100-4, 14, 10

AMA: 1998, Nov, 21; 1994, Spring, 2

If esophagoscopic photodynamic therapy is performed, report 43228 in addition to CPT codes 96570 and 96571 as appropriate.

⊙ **43231**   **with endoscopic ultrasound examination**   ②️ Ⓣ 🔠 ▶️
MED: 100-2, 15, 260; 100-3, 220.5; 100-4, 12, 90.3; 100-4, 14, 10

AMA: 2001, Oct, 4

Do not report CPT code 76975 when reporting 43231.

⊙ **43232**   **with transendoscopic ultrasound-guided intramural or transmural fine needle aspiration/biopsy(s)**   ②️ Ⓣ 🔠 ▶️
MED: 100-2, 15, 260; 100-3, 220.5; 100-4, 12, 90.3; 100-4, 14, 10

AMA: 2001, Oct, 4

To report interpretation of specimen, consult CPT codes 88172 and 88173.

Code 76975 cannot be reported with CPT code 43232.

Code 43232 cannot be reported with CPT code 76942.

⊙ **43234**   **Upper gastrointestinal endoscopy, simple primary examination (eg, with small diameter flexible endoscope) (separate procedure)**   🔟 Ⓣ ▶️
MED: 100-2, 15, 260; 100-3, 100.2; 100-4, 12, 90.3; 100-4, 14, 10

⊙   **43235**   **Upper gastrointestinal endoscopy including esophagus, stomach, and either the duodenum and/or jejunum as appropriate; diagnostic, with or without collection of specimen(s) by brushing or washing (separate procedure)**   **1** T **⌐**
        MED: 100-2, 15, 260; 100-3, 100.2; 100-4, 12, 90.3; 100-4, 14, 10

        AMA: 1997, Dec, 11; 1994, Spring, 4

⊙   **43236**   **with directed submucosal injection(s), any substance**   **2** T **⌐**
        MED: 100-2, 15, 260; 100-4, 12, 90.3; 100-4, 14, 10

        To report injection sclerosis of esophageal an/or gastric varices, consult CPT code 43243.

   43237   **with endoscopic ultrasound examination limited to the esophagus**   **2** T 80 **⌐**

        Code 43237 cannot be reported with CPT code 76975.

   43238   **with transendoscopic ultrasound-guided intramural or transmural fine needle aspiration/biopsy(s), esophagus (includes endoscopic ultrasound examination limited to the esophagus)**   **2** T 80 **⌐**

        Code 43238 cannot be reported with CPT codes 76942 or 76975.

⊙   **43239**   **with biopsy, single or multiple**   **2** T **⌐**
        MED: 100-2, 15, 260; 100-3, 100.2; 100-4, 12, 90.3; 100-4, 14, 10

        AMA: 2001, Oct, 4; 1999, Feb, 11; 1998, Apr, 14; 1994, Spring, 4

        To report upper gastrointestinal endoscopy with suturing of the esophagogastric junction, consult CPT Category III code 0008T.

        To report upper gastrointestinal endoscopy with injection of implant material into and along the muscle of the lower esophageal sphincter, Category III code 0133T should be reported.

⊙   **43240**   **with transmural drainage of pseudocyst**   **2** T **⌐**
        MED: 100-2, 15, 260; 100-4, 12, 90.3; 100-4, 14, 10

        AMA: 2001, Oct, 4

⊙   **43241**   **with transendoscopic intraluminal tube or catheter placement**   **2** T **⌐**
        MED: 100-2, 15, 260; 100-3, 100.2; 100-4, 12, 90.3; 100-4, 14, 10

        AMA: 2001, Nov, 7; 1994, Spring, 4

⊙   **43242**   **with transendoscopic ultrasound-guided intramural or transmural fine needle aspiration/biopsy(s) (includes endoscopic ultrasound examination of the esophagus, stomach, and either the duodenum and/or jejunum as appropriate)**   **2** T 80 **⌐**
        MED: 100-2, 15, 260; 100-3, 220.5; 100-4, 12, 90.3; 100-4, 14, 10

        AMA: 2001, Oct, 4

        To report interpretation of specimen, consult CPT codes 88172, 88173.

        Code 43242 cannot be reported with CPT codes 76942 or 76975.

        To report this procedure limited to the esophagus, consult CPT code 43238.

⊙   **43243**   **with injection sclerosis of esophageal and/or gastric varices**   **2** T **⌐**
        MED: 100-2, 15, 260; 100-3, 100.2; 100-4, 12, 90.3; 100-4, 14, 10

        AMA: 1994, Spring, 4

⊙   **43244**   **with band ligation of esophageal and/or gastric varices**   **2** T 80 **⌐**
        MED: 100-2, 15, 260; 100-3, 100.2; 100-4, 12, 90.3; 100-4, 14, 10

        AMA: 1994, Spring, 4

Digestive System

43245 — 43258

⊙ 43245 **with dilation of gastric outlet for obstruction (eg, balloon, guide wire, bougie)** 2 T
MED: 100-2, 15, 260; 100-3, 100.2; 100-4, 12, 90.3; 100-4, 14, 10

AMA: 2001, Oct, 4; 1994, Spring, 4

Code 43245 cannot be reported with CPT code 43256.

⊙ 43246 **with directed placement of percutaneous gastrostomy tube** 2 T 80
MED: 100-2, 15, 260; 100-3, 100.2; 100-4, 12, 90.3; 100-4, 14, 10; 100-4, 20, 100.2.2; 100-4, 20, 100.2.2.3; 100-4, 20, 50.3

AMA: 1997, Feb, 10; 1994, Spring, 4

To report radiological supervision and interpretation, consult CPT code 74350.

⊙ 43247 **with removal of foreign body** 2 T
MED: 100-2, 15, 260; 100-3, 100.2; 100-4, 12, 90.3; 100-4, 14, 10

AMA: 1994, Spring, 4

To report radiological supervision and interpretation, consult CPT code 74235.

⊙ 43248 **with insertion of guide wire followed by dilation of esophagus over guide wire** 2 T
MED: 100-2, 15, 260; 100-3, 100.2; 100-4, 12, 90.3; 100-4, 14, 10

AMA: 1997, Dec, 11; 1994, Spring, 4

⊙ 43249 **with balloon dilation of esophagus (less than 30 mm diameter)** 2 T
MED: 100-2, 15, 260; 100-3, 100.2; 100-4, 12, 90.3; 100-4, 14, 10

⊙ 43250 **with removal of tumor(s), polyp(s), or other lesion(s) by hot biopsy forceps or bipolar cautery** 2 T
MED: 100-2, 15, 260; 100-3, 100.2; 100-4, 12, 90.3; 100-4, 14, 10

AMA: 1999, Feb, 11; 1994, Spring, 4

⊙ 43251 **with removal of tumor(s), polyp(s), or other lesion(s) by snare technique** 2 T
MED: 100-2, 15, 260; 100-3, 100.2; 100-4, 12, 90.3; 100-4, 14, 10

AMA: 1994, Spring, 4

⊙ 43255 **with control of bleeding, any method** 2 T
MED: 100-2, 15, 260; 100-3, 100.2; 100-4, 12, 90.3; 100-4, 14, 10

AMA: 1994, Spring, 4

⊙ 43256 **with transendoscopic stent placement (includes predilation)** 3 T
MED: 100-2, 15, 260; 100-4, 12, 90.3; 100-4, 14, 10

⊙ 43257 **with delivery of thermal energy to the muscle of lower esophageal sphincter and/or gastric cardia, for treatment of gastroesophageal reflux disease** T

⊙ 43258 **with ablation of tumor(s), polyp(s), or other lesion(s) not amenable to removal by hot biopsy forceps, bipolar cautery or snare technique** 3 T
MED: 100-2, 15, 260; 100-3, 100.2; 100-4, 12, 90.3; 100-4, 14, 10

AMA: 1994, Spring, 4

If injection sclerosis of esophageal varices is performed, consult CPT code 43204 or 43243.

⊙   43259   **with endoscopic ultrasound examination, including the esophagus, stomach, and either the duodenum and/or jejunum as appropriate**   3 T 80 ⏺
MED: 100-2, 15, 260; 100-3, 100.2; 100-3, 220.5; 100-4, 12, 30.1; 100-4, 12, 90.3; 100-4, 14, 10
AMA: 1994, Spring, 4

     Code 43259 cannot be reported with CPT code 76975.

⊙   43260   **Endoscopic retrograde cholangiopancreatography (ERCP); diagnostic, with or without collection of specimen(s) by brushing or washing (separate procedure)**   2 T ⏺
MED: 100-2, 15, 260; 100-3, 100.2; 100-4, 12, 90.3; 100-4, 14, 10
AMA: 1994, Spring, 5

     To report radiological supervision and interpretation performed with codes 46260-43272, consult CPT codes 74328, 74329 and 74330.

⊙   43261   **with biopsy, single or multiple**   2 T ⏺
MED: 100-2, 15, 260; 100-3, 100.2; 100-4, 12, 90.3; 100-4, 14, 10
AMA: 1994, Spring, 5

⊙   43262   **with sphincterotomy/papillotomy**   2 T ⏺
MED: 100-2, 15, 260; 100-3, 100.2; 100-4, 12, 90.3; 100-4, 14, 10
AMA: 1994, Spring, 5

⊙   43263   **with pressure measurement of sphincter of Oddi (pancreatic duct or common bile duct)**   2 T ⏺
MED: 100-2, 15, 260; 100-3, 100.2; 100-4, 12, 90.3; 100-4, 14, 10
AMA: 1994, Spring, 5

     To report radiological supervision and interpretation, consult CPT codes 74328, 74329, and 74330.

⊙   43264   **with endoscopic retrograde removal of calculus/calculi from biliary and/or pancreatic ducts**   2 T ⏺
MED: 100-2, 15, 260; 100-3, 100.2; 100-4, 12, 90.3; 100-4, 14, 10
AMA: 1994, Spring, 5

     If these procedures (43264-43271) are performed with a sphincterotomy, consult also CPT code 43262.

⊙   43265   **with endoscopic retrograde destruction, lithotripsy of calculus/calculi, any method**   2 T ⏺
MED: 100-2, 15, 260; 100-3, 100.2; 100-4, 12, 90.3; 100-4, 14, 10
AMA: 1994, Spring, 5

⊙   43267   **with endoscopic retrograde insertion of nasobiliary or nasopancreatic drainage tube**   2 T ⏺
MED: 100-2, 15, 260; 100-3, 100.2; 100-4, 12, 90.3; 100-4, 14, 10
AMA: 1994, Spring, 6

⊙   43268   **with endoscopic retrograde insertion of tube or stent into bile or pancreatic duct**   2 T ⏺
MED: 100-2, 15, 260; 100-3, 100.2; 100-4, 12, 90.3; 100-4, 14, 10
AMA: 1994, Spring, 6

⊙   43269   **with endoscopic retrograde removal of foreign body and/or change of tube or stent**   2 T ⏺
MED: 100-2, 15, 260; 100-3, 100.2; 100-4, 12, 90.3; 100-4, 14, 10
AMA: 1994, Spring, 6

Digestive System

43271 — 43340

⊙ 43271 **with endoscopic retrograde balloon dilation of ampulla, biliary and/or pancreatic duct(s)** [2][T][↕]
MED: 100-2, 15, 260; 100-3, 100.2; 100-4, 12, 90.3; 100-4, 14, 10

AMA: 1994, Spring, 6

⊙ 43272 **with ablation of tumor(s), polyp(s), or other lesion(s) not amenable to removal by hot biopsy forceps, bipolar cautery or snare technique** [2][T][80][↕]
MED: 100-2, 15, 260; 100-3, 100.2; 100-4, 12, 90.3; 100-4, 14, 10

LAPAROSCOPY

Diagnostic laparoscopy is always included in surgical laparoscopy.

To report only a diagnostic laparoscopy (peritoneoscopy), consult CPT code 49320.

43280 **Laparoscopy, surgical, esophagogastric fundoplasty (eg, Nissen, Toupet procedures)** [T][80][↕]
AMA: 2002, Dec, 1; 2000, Mar, 5; 1999, Nov, 22

If an open approach is used, consult CPT code 43324.

43289 **Unlisted laparoscopy procedure, esophagus** [T][50][80]
AMA: 2000, Mar, 5; 1999, Nov, 22

REPAIR

43300 **Esophagoplasty (plastic repair or reconstruction), cervical approach; without repair of tracheoesophageal fistula** [C][80][↕]

43305 **with repair of tracheoesophageal fistula** [C][80][↕]

43310 **Esophagoplasty (plastic repair or reconstruction), thoracic approach; without repair of tracheoesophageal fistula** [C][80][↕]

43312 **with repair of tracheoesophageal fistula** [C][80][↕]

43313 **Esophagoplasty for congenital defect (plastic repair or reconstruction), thoracic approach; without repair of congenital tracheoesophageal fistula** [C][80][↕][63]

43314 **with repair of congenital tracheoesophageal fistula** [C][80][↕][63]

43320 **Esophagogastrostomy (cardioplasty), with or without vagotomy and pyloroplasty, transabdominal or transthoracic approach** [C][80][↕]

43324 **Esophagogastric fundoplasty (eg, Nissen, Belsey IV, Hill procedures)** [C][80][↕]
AMA: 1999, Nov, 22; 1996, Sep, 10

If a laparoscopic approach is used, consult CPT code 43280.

43325 **Esophagogastric fundoplasty; with fundic patch (Thal-Nissen procedure)** [C][80][↕]
If a cricopharyngeal myotomy is performed, consult CPT code 43030.

43326 **with gastroplasty (eg, Collis)** [C][80][↕]

43330 **Esophagomyotomy (Heller type); abdominal approach** [C][80][↕]
AMA: 1999, Nov, 22

43331 **thoracic approach** [C][80][↕]
AMA: 1999, Nov, 22

If a thoracoscopic esophagomyotomy is performed, consult CPT code 32665.

43340 **Esophagojejunostomy (without total gastrectomy); abdominal approach** [C][80][↕]

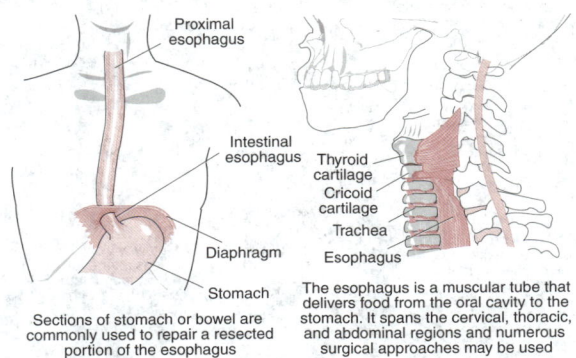

Proximal esophagus

Intestinal esophagus

Diaphragm

Stomach

Sections of stomach or bowel are commonly used to repair a resected portion of the esophagus

Thyroid cartilage
Cricoid cartilage
Trachea
Esophagus

The esophagus is a muscular tube that delivers food from the oral cavity to the stomach. It spans the cervical, thoracic, and abdominal regions and numerous surgical approaches may be used

43341	thoracic approach	C 80
43350	Esophagostomy, fistulization of esophagus, external; abdominal approach	C 80
43351	thoracic approach	C 80
43352	cervical approach	C 80
43360	Gastrointestinal reconstruction for previous esophagectomy, for obstructing esophageal lesion or fistula, or for previous esophageal exclusion; with stomach, with or without pyloroplasty	C 80
43361	with colon interposition or small intestine reconstruction, including intestine mobilization, preparation, and anastomosis(es)	C 80
43400	Ligation, direct, esophageal varices	C 80
43401	Transection of esophagus with repair, for esophageal varices	C 80
43405	Ligation or stapling at gastroesophageal junction for pre-existing esophageal perforation	C 80
43410	Suture of esophageal wound or injury; cervical approach	C 80

        AMA: 1996, Jun, 7

43415	transthoracic or transabdominal approach	C 80
43420	Closure of esophagostomy or fistula; cervical approach	C 80
43425	transthoracic or transabdominal approach	C 80

If an esophageal hiatal hernia is repaired, consult CPT codes 39520 and subsequent codes.

MANIPULATION

If an associated esophagogram is performed, consult CPT code 74220.

43450	Dilation of esophagus, by unguided sound or bougie, single or multiple passes	1 T

        MED: 100-2, 15, 260; 100-4, 12, 90.3; 100-4, 14, 10

        AMA: 1998, Jun, 10; 1998, Apr, 14; 1997, Jan, 10; 1994, Spring, 1

⊙ **43453**	Dilation of esophagus, over guide wire	1 T

        MED: 100-2, 15, 260; 100-4, 12, 90.3; 100-4, 14, 10

        AMA: 1997, Jan, 10; 1997, Dec, 11; 1994, Spring, 1

If dilation is performed with direct visualization, consult CPT code 43220.

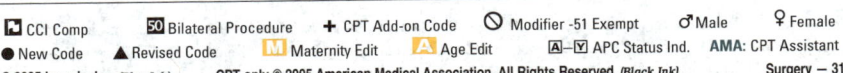

Digestive System

43456 — 43520

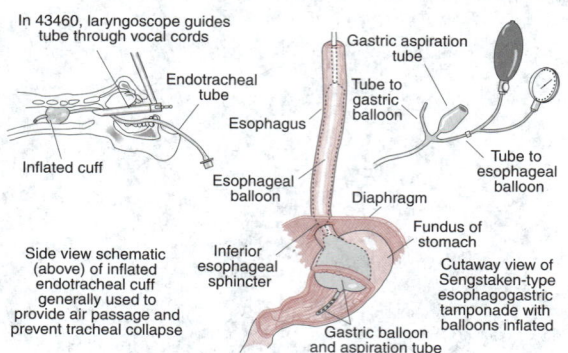

In 43460, laryngoscope guides tube through vocal cords

Endotracheal tube

Inflated cuff

Esophagus

Esophageal balloon

Side view schematic (above) of inflated endotracheal cuff generally used to provide air passage and prevent tracheal collapse

Inferior esophageal sphincter

Gastric aspiration tube

Tube to gastric balloon

Tube to esophageal balloon

Diaphragm

Fundus of stomach

Cutaway view of Sengstaken-type esophagogastric tamponade with balloons inflated

Gastric balloon and aspiration tube

⊙ 43456 **Dilation of esophagus, by balloon or dilator, retrograde** ②ⓉⓁ
MED: 100-2, 15, 260; 100-4, 12, 90.3; 100-4, 14, 10

AMA: 1997, Jan, 10; 1994, Spring, 3

⊙ 43458 **Dilation of esophagus with balloon (30 mm diameter or larger) for achalasia** ②ⓉⓁ
MED: 100-2, 15, 260; 100-4, 12, 90.3; 100-4, 14, 10

AMA: 1997, Jan, 10; 1994, Spring, 3

If dilation is performed with a balloon less than 30 mm in diameter, consult CPT code 43220. If radiological supervision and interpretation is performed, consult CPT code 74360.

43460 **Esophagogastric tamponade, with balloon (Sengstaaken type)** ⒸⓁ

If an esophageal foreign body is removed by balloon catheter, consult CPT codes 43215, 43247, and 74235.

OTHER PROCEDURES

43496 **Free jejunum transfer with microvascular anastomosis** Ⓒ⑧⓪Ⓛ
AMA: 1998, Nov, 16; 1997, Nov, 17; 1997, Jun, 10; 1997, Apr, 4

Do not report 69990 in addition to 43496 as the operating microscope is considered an inclusive component of the surgery.

43499 **Unlisted procedure, esophagus** Ⓣ⑧⓪

STOMACH

INCISION

43500 **Gastrotomy; with exploration or foreign body removal** Ⓒ⑧⓪Ⓛ

43501 **with suture repair of bleeding ulcer** Ⓒ⑧⓪Ⓛ

43502 **with suture repair of pre-existing esophagogastric laceration (eg, Mallory-Weiss)** Ⓒ⑧⓪Ⓛ

43510 **with esophageal dilation and insertion of permanent intraluminal tube (eg, Celestin or Mousseaux-Barbin)** Ⓣ⑧⓪Ⓛ

43520 **Pyloromyotomy, cutting of pyloric muscle (Fredet-Ramstedt type operation)** Ⓒ⑧⓪Ⓛ⑥③

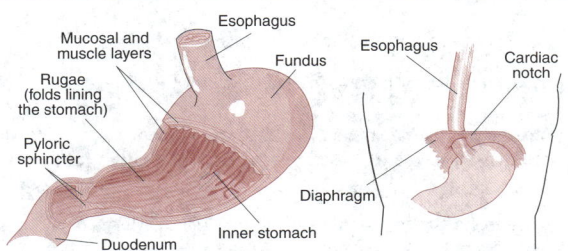

The stomach is a highly distensible organ that serves as a reservoir to mix food and break it down with digestive juices. The esophagus pierces the diaphragm at the cardiac notch, where the stomach begins. The pyloric sphincter marks the inferior border of the stomach. The vagal nerve trunks run down the front and back of the esophagus and serve the stomach by controlling secretion of digestive acids

EXCISION

43600   **Biopsy of stomach; by capsule, tube, peroral (one or more specimens)**   1 T
MED: 100-2, 15, 260; 100-4, 12, 90.3; 100-4, 14, 10

43605   **by laparotomy**   C 80

43610   **Excision, local; ulcer or benign tumor of stomach**   C 80

43611   **malignant tumor of stomach**   C 80

43620   **Gastrectomy, total; with esophagoenterostomy**   C 80

43621   **with Roux-en-Y reconstruction**   C 80

43622   **with formation of intestinal pouch, any type**   C 80

43631   **Gastrectomy, partial, distal; with gastroduodenostomy**   C 80
Billroth operation

43632   **with gastrojejunostomy**   C 80
Polya anastomosis

43633   **with Roux-en-Y reconstruction**   C 80

43634   **with formation of intestinal pouch**   C 80

+ **43635**   **Vagotomy when performed with partial distal gastrectomy (List separately in addition to code(s) for primary procedure)**   C 80
AMA: 1997, Nov, 17

Note that 43635 is an add-on code and must be used in conjunction with 43631, 43632, 43633, and 43634.

~~43638~~   ~~Gastrectomy, partial, proximal, thoracic or abdominal approach including esophagogastrostomy, with vagotomy;~~

~~43639~~   ~~with pyloroplasty or pyloromyotomy~~

43640   **Vagotomy including pyloroplasty, with or without gastrostomy; truncal or selective**   C 80

If pyloroplasty is performed, consult CPT code 43800. If a vagotomy is performed, consult CPT codes 64752-64760.

43641   **parietal cell (highly selective)**   C 80

If an upper gastrointestinal endoscopy is performed, consult CPT codes 43234-43259.

Digestive System

43644 — 43761

LAPAROSCOPY

Diagnostic laparoscopy is always included in surgical endoscopy.

To report only a diagnostic laparoscopy (peritoneoscopy), consult CPT code 49320.

43644   **Laparoscopy, surgical, gastric restrictive procedure; with gastric bypass and Roux-en-Y gastroenterostomy (roux limb 150 cm or less)**   `C` `80` `↵`

Code 43644 cannot be reported with CPT codes 43846, 49320.

Report Esophagogastroduodenoscopy (EGD) performed for a different condition with modifier 59.

43645   **with gastric bypass and small intestine reconstruction to limit absorption**   `C` `80` `↵`

Code 43645 cannot be reported with CPT codes 49320, 43847.

43651   **Laparoscopy, surgical; transection of vagus nerves, truncal**   `T` `80` `↵`
AMA: 2000, Mar, 5; 1999, Nov, 22

43652   **transection of vagus nerves, selective or highly selective**   `T` `80` `↵`
AMA: 2000, Mar, 5; 1999, Nov, 22

43653   **gastrostomy, without construction of gastric tube (eg, Stamm procedure) (separate procedure)**   `9` `T` `80` `↵`
MED: 100-2, 15, 260; 100-4, 12, 90.3; 100-4, 14, 10
AMA: 2000, Mar, 5; 1999, Nov, 22

43659   **Unlisted laparoscopy procedure, stomach**   `T` `50` `80`
AMA: 2000, Mar, 5; 1999, Nov, 22

INTRODUCTION

43750   **Percutaneous placement of gastrostomy tube**   `2` `T` `↵`
MED: 100-2, 15, 260; 100-4, 12, 90.3; 100-4, 14, 10; 100-4, 20, 100.2.2; 100-4, 20, 100.2.2.3; 100-4, 20, 50.3
AMA: 1994, Spring, 1

To report radiological supervision and interpretation, consult CPT code 74350.

43752   **Naso- or oro-gastric tube placement, requiring physician's skill and fluoroscopic guidance (includes fluoroscopy, image documentation and report)**   `X` `↵`
MED: 100-4, 20, 100.2.2; 100-4, 20, 100.2.2.3; 100-4, 20, 50.3
AMA: 2002, Jan, 11

To report enteric tube placement, consult CPT codes 44500, 74340.

Code 43752 cannot be reported with CPT codes 99291-99292, 99293-99294, 99295-99296 or 99298-99299.

43760   **Change of gastrostomy tube**   `1` `T` `↵`
MED: 100-2, 15, 260; 100-4, 12, 90.3; 100-4, 14, 10; 100-4, 20, 100.2.2; 100-4, 20, 100.2.2.3; 100-4, 20, 50.3

If an endoscopic placement of a gastrostomy tube is performed, consult CPT code 43246. For radiological supervision and interpretation, consult CPT code 75984.

43761   **Repositioning of the gastric feeding tube, any method, through the duodenum for enteric nutrition**   `T` `↵`
MED: 100-4, 20, 100.2.2; 100-4, 20, 50.3
AMA: 1999, Nov, 22; 1996, Oct, 9

If imaging guidance is performed, consult CPT code 75984.

BARIATRIC SURGERY

Bariatric surgery may include the stomach, duodenum, jejunum, and/or the ileum.

Band adjustments are included during the postoperative period after gastric restriction that utilizes the adjustable gastric band technique. Band adjustment refers to changing the gastric band diameter by injection or aspiration of fluid through the subcutaneous port component.

● **43770**   **Laparoscopy, surgical, gastric restrictive procedure; placement of adjustable gastric band (gastric band and subcutaneous port components)**

> To report replacement of an individual component, use 43770 with modifier 52.

● **43771**   **revision of adjustable gastric band component only**

● **43772**   **removal of adjustable gastric band component only**

● **43773**   **removal and replacement of adjustable gastric band component only**

> Code 43773 cannot be reported with 43772.

● **43774**   **removal of adjustable gastric band and subcutaneous port components**

> To report removal and replacement of both gastric band and subcutaneous port components, consult CPT code 43659.

OTHER PROCEDURES

43800   **Pyloroplasty**   C 80 ▶

> If pyloroplasty and vagotomy are performed, consult CPT code 43640.

43810   **Gastroduodenostomy**   C 80 ▶

43820   **Gastrojejunostomy; without vagotomy**   C 80 ▶

43825   **with vagotomy, any type**   C 80 ▶

43830   **Gastrostomy, open; without construction of gastric tube (eg, Stamm procedure) (separate procedure)**   T 80 ▶
   AMA: 1999, Nov, 22

43831   **neonatal, for feeding**   A T 80 ▶ 63
   AMA: 1999, Nov, 22

> If a gastrostomy tube is changed, consult CPT code 43760.

43832   **with construction of gastric tube (eg, Janeway procedure)**   C 80 ▶
   AMA: 1999, Nov, 22

43840   **Gastrorrhaphy, suture of perforated duodenal or gastric ulcer, wound, or injury**   C 80 ▶
   MED: 100-3, 100.12

43842   **Gastric restrictive procedure, without gastric bypass, for morbid obesity; vertical-banded gastroplasty**   C 80 ▶
   MED: 100-3, 100.8; 100-3, 130.5; 100-3, 130.6; 100-3, 160.2; 100-3, 230.1; 100-3, 250.1; 100-3, 250.4; 100-3, 270.4; 100-3, 40.50

   AMA: 1998, May, 5

43843   **other than vertical-banded gastroplasty**   C 80 ▶
   MED: 100-3, 100.1; 100-3, 100.8; 100-3, 130.5; 100-3, 130.6; 100-3, 160.2; 100-3, 230.1; 100-3, 250.1; 100-3, 250.4; 100-3, 270.4; 100-3, 40.50

   AMA: 1998, May, 5

Digestive System

43845 — 43999

43845   **Gastric restrictive procedure with partial gastrectomy, pylorus-preserving duodenoileostomy and ileoileostomy (50 to 100 cm common channel) to limit absorption (biliopancreatic diversion with duodenal switch)** C 80 ↰

> Code 43845 cannot be reported with CPT codes 43633, 43847, 44130, and 49000.

43846   **Gastric restrictive procedure, with gastric bypass for morbid obesity; with short limb (150 cm or less) Roux-en-Y gastroenterostomy** C 80 ↰
MED: 100-3, 100.1; 100-3, 100.8; 100-3, 130.5; 100-3, 130.6; 100-3, 160.2; 100-3, 230.1; 100-3, 250.1; 100-3, 250.4; 100-3, 270.4; 100-3, 40.50

AMA: 1998, May, 5

> To report greater than 150 cm, consult CPT code 43847.

> To report laparoscopic procedure, consult CPT code 43644.

43847   **with small intestine reconstruction to limit absorption** C 80 ↰
MED: 100-3, 100.1; 100-3, 100.8; 100-3, 130.5; 100-3, 130.6; 100-3, 160.2; 100-3, 230.1; 100-3, 250.1; 100-3, 250.4; 100-3, 270.4; 100-3, 40.50

AMA: 1998, May, 5

▲ **43848**   **Revision, open, of gastric restrictive procedure for morbid obesity, other than adjustable gastric band (separate procedure)** C 80 ↰
MED: 100-3, 100.1; 100-3, 100.8; 100-3, 130.5; 100-3, 130.6; 100-3, 160.2; 100-3, 230.1; 100-3, 250.1; 100-3, 250.4; 100-3, 270.4; 100-3, 40.50

AMA: 1998, May, 5

> For adjustable gastric band procedures, consult CPT codes 43770-43774, 43886-43888.

43850   **Revision of gastroduodenal anastomosis (gastroduodenostomy) with reconstruction; without vagotomy** C 80 ↰

43855   **with vagotomy** C 80 ↰

43860   **Revision of gastrojejunal anastomosis (gastrojejunostomy) with reconstruction, with or without partial gastrectomy or intestine resection; without vagotomy** C 80 ↰
MED: 100-3, 100.1

43865   **with vagotomy** C 80 ↰
MED: 100-3, 100.1

43870   **Closure of gastrostomy, surgical** 1 T 80 ↰
MED: 100-2, 15, 260; 100-4, 12, 90.3; 100-4, 14, 10

43880   **Closure of gastrocolic fistula** C 80 ↰

● **43886**   **Gastric restrictive procedure, open; revision of subcutaneous port component only**

● **43887**   **removal of subcutaneous port component only**

● **43888**   **removal and replacement of subcutaneous port component only**

> Code 43888 cannot be reported with 43774, 43887.

> To report the laparoscopic removal of both gastric band and subcutaneous port components, consult CPT code 43774.

> To report removal and replacement of both gastric band and subcutaneous port components, consult code 43659.

43999   **Unlisted procedure, stomach** T 80

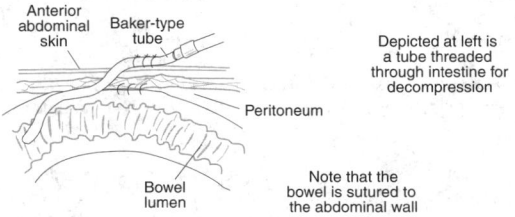

Anterior abdominal skin
Baker-type tube

Depicted at left is a tube threaded through intestine for decompression

Peritoneum

Bowel lumen

Note that the bowel is sutured to the abdominal wall

In 44021, a select portion of intestine is surgically approached and incised. A tube is inserted into the bowel lumen and threaded distally, often to a point of obstruction. The tube is used to decompress the bowel segment it passes through, often during or immediately following surgery for bowel obstruction

INTESTINES (EXCEPT RECTUM)

INCISION

44005   **Enterolysis (freeing of intestinal adhesion) (separate procedure)**   C 80 ⬛
AMA: 2000, Jan, 11; 2000, Apr, 10; 1999, Nov, 23; 1997, Nov, 17

Code 44005 is not to be used with CPT code 45136.

If a laparoscopic approach is used, consult CPT code 44180.

44010   **Duodenotomy, for exploration, biopsy(s), or foreign body removal**   C 80 ⬛

+   **44015**   **Tube or needle catheter jejunostomy for enteral alimentation, intraoperative, any method (List separately in addition to primary procedure)**   C 80 ⬛
AMA: 2002, Mar, 10

Note that 44015 is an add-on code that must be used in conjunction with the appropriate code for the primary procedure. This code cannot be reported alone.

44020   **Enterotomy, small intestine, other than duodenum; for exploration, biopsy(s), or foreign body removal**   C 80 ⬛

44021   **for decompression (eg, Baker tube)**   C 80 ⬛

44025   **Colotomy, for exploration, biopsy(s), or foreign body removal**   C 80 ⬛
Amussat's operation

44050   **Reduction of volvulus, intussusception, internal hernia, by laparotomy**   C 80 ⬛

44055   **Correction of malrotation by lysis of duodenal bands and/or reduction of midgut volvulus (eg, Ladd procedure)**   C 80 ⬛ ⊚

EXCISION

Intestinal transplantation involves three different components:

- Cadaver or living donor enterectomy which consists of harvesting and cold preparation of the graft prior to transplantation and care of the donor (44132, 44133).

- Backbench work consists of preparation of donor intestine prior to transplantation. This includes mobilizing and developing the superior mesenteric artery and vein (44715). Also included is any additional reconstruction of graft including venous and arterial anastomosis(es) (44720-44721) prior to transplantation.

- Recipient transplantation which includes transplanting the intestine into the patient (codes 44135 and 44136).

44100   **Biopsy of intestine by capsule, tube, peroral (one or more specimens)**   ⬛ Ⓣ ⧉
       MED: 100-2, 15, 260; 100-4, 12, 90.3; 100-4, 14, 10

44110   **Excision of one or more lesions of small or large intestine not requiring anastomosis, exteriorization, or fistulization; single enterotomy**   Ⓒ 80 ⧉

44111   **multiple enterotomies**   Ⓒ 80 ⧉

44120   **Enterectomy, resection of small intestine; single resection and anastomosis**   Ⓒ 80 ⧉

       Code 44120 is not to be used with code 45136.

+   **44121**   **each additional resection and anastomosis (List separately in addition to code for primary procedure)**   Ⓒ 80 ⧉

       Note that 44121 is an add-on code and must be used in conjunction with 44120.

44125   **with enterostomy**   Ⓒ 80 ⧉

44126   **Enterectomy, resection of small intestine for congenital atresia, single resection and anastomosis of proximal segment of intestine; without tapering**   Ⓒ 80 ⧉ ⑥③

44127   **with tapering**   Ⓒ 80 ⧉ ⑥③

+   **44128**   **each additional resection and anastomosis (List separately in addition to code for primary procedure)**   Ⓒ 80 ⧉ ⑥③

       Note that 44128 is an add-on code and must be used in conjunction with codes 44126 and 44127.

44130   **Enteroenterostomy, anastomosis of intestine, with or without cutaneous enterostomy (separate procedure)**   Ⓒ 80 ⧉

44132   **Donor enterectomy (including cold preservation), open; from cadaver donor**   Ⓒ 80 ⧉

       To report backbench intestinal graft preparation or reconstruction, consult CPT codes 44715, 44720, 44721.

44133   **partial, from living donor**   Ⓒ 80 ⧉

44135   **Intestinal allotransplantation; from cadaver donor**   Ⓒ 80 ⧉

44136   **from living donor**   Ⓒ 80 ⧉

44137   **Removal of transplanted intestinal allograft, complete**   Ⓒ 80 ⧉

       To report partial removal of transplant allograft, consult CPT codes 44120, 44121, and 44140.

+   **44139**   **Mobilization (take-down) of splenic flexure performed in conjunction with partial colectomy (List separately in addition to primary procedure)** Ⓒ 80 ⧉

       Note that 44139 is an add-on code and must be used in conjunction with 44140-44147.

44140   **Colectomy, partial; with anastomosis**   Ⓒ 80 ⧉

       If procedure is performed laparoscopically, consult CPT code 44204.

44141   **with skin level cecostomy or colostomy**   Ⓒ 80 ⧉

44143   **with end colostomy and closure of distal segment (Hartmann type procedure)**   Ⓒ 80 ⧉

       To report laparoscopic procedure, consult CPT code 44206.

44144   **with resection, with colostomy or ileostomy and creation of mucofistula**   Ⓒ 80 ⧉

44145   **with coloproctostomy (low pelvic anastomosis)**   Ⓒ 80 ⧉

       To report laparoscopic procedure, consult CPT code 44207.

44146	with coloproctostomy (low pelvic anastomosis), with colostomy C 80 ⬀	

To report laparoscopic procedure, consult CPT code 44208.

44147	abdominal and transanal approach	C 80 ⬀
44150	Colectomy, total, abdominal, without proctectomy; with ileostomy or ileoproctostomy	C 80 ⬀

To report laparoscopic procedure, consult CPT code 44210.
Lane's operation

44151	with continent ileostomy	C 80 ⬀
44152	with rectal mucosectomy, ileoanal anastomosis, with or without loop ileostomy	C 80 ⬀

To report laparoscopic procedure, consult CPT code 44211.

44153	with rectal mucosectomy, ileoanal anastomosis, creation of ileal reservoir (S or J), with or without loop ileostomy	C 80 ⬀

To report laparoscopic procedure, consult CPT code 44211.

44155	Colectomy, total, abdominal, with proctectomy; with ileostomy	C 80 ⬀

To report laparoscopic procedure, consult CPT code 44212.
Miles' colectomy

44156	with continent ileostomy	C 80 ⬀
44160	Colectomy, partial, with removal of terminal ileum with ileocolostomy	C 80 ⬀

To report laparoscopic procedure (peritoneoscopy), consult CPT code 44205.

LAPAROSCOPY

Diagnostic laparoscopy is always included in a surgical laparoscopy. To report only diagnostic laparoscopy, consult CPT code 49320.

● 44180   **Laparoscopy, surgical, enterolysis (freeing of intestinal adhesion) (separate procedure)**

● 44186   **Laparoscopy, surgical; jejunostomy (eg, for decompression or feeding)**

● 44187   **ileostomy or jejunostomy, non-tube**

To report open procedure, consult CPT code 44310.

● 44188   **Laparoscopy, surgical, colostomy or skin level cecostomy**

To report open procedure, consult CPT code 44320.

Do not report 44188 in conjunction with 44970.

~~44200~~   ~~Laparoscopy, surgical; enterolysis (freeing of intestinal adhesion) (separate procedure)~~

(Use 44180)

~~44201~~   ~~jejunostomy (eg, for decompression or feeding)~~

(Use 44186)

▲ 44202   **Laparoscopy, surgical; enterectomy, resection of small intestine, single resection and anastomosis** C 80 ⬀
       AMA: 2000, Mar, 5; 1999, Nov, 23

Digestive System

44203 — 44300

+   **44203**   **each additional small intestine resection and anastomosis (List separately in addition to code for primary procedure)**   [C] [80] [↵]

Note that 44203 is an add-on code and must be used in conjunction with CPT code 44202.

To report open procedure, consult CPT codes 44120, 44121.

   44204   **colectomy, partial, with anastomosis**   [C] [80] [↵]

To report open procedure, consult CPT code 44140.

   44205   **colectomy, partial, with removal of terminal ileum with ileocolostomy**   [C] [80] [↵]

To report open procedure, consult CPT code 44160.

   44206   **colectomy, partial, with end colostomy and closure of distal segment (Hartmann type procedure)**   [T] [80] [↵]

To report open procedure, consult CPT code 44143.

   44207   **colectomy, partial, with anastomosis, with coloproctostomy (low pelvic anastomosis)**   [T] [80] [↵]

To report open procedure, consult CPT code 44145.

   44208   **colectomy, partial, with anastomosis, with coloproctostomy (low pelvic anastomosis) with colostomy**   [T] [80] [↵]

To report open procedure, consult CPT code 44146.

   44210   **colectomy, total, abdominal, without proctectomy, with ileostomy or ileoproctostomy**   [C] [80] [↵]

To report open procedure, consult CPT code 44150.

   44211   **colectomy, total, abdominal, with proctectomy, with ileoanal anastomosis, creation of ileal reservoir (S or J), with loop ileostomy, with or without rectal mucosectomy**   [C] [80] [↵]

To report open procedure, consult CPT codes 44152, 44153.

   44212   **colectomy, total, abdominal, with proctectomy, with ileostomy** [C] [80] [↵]

To report open procedure, consult CPT code 44155.

+ ●   **44213**   **Laparoscopy, surgical, mobilization (take-down) of splenic flexure performed in conjunction with partial colectomy (List separately in addition to primary procedure)**

Note that 44213 is an add-on code and must be reported in conjunction with 44204-44208.

To report open procedure, consult CPT code 44139.

●   **44227**   **Laparoscopy, surgical, closure of enterostomy, large or small intestine, with resection and anastomosis**

To report open procedure, consult CPT codes 44625, 44626.

   44238   **Unlisted laparoscopy procedure, intestine (except rectum)**   [T] [50] [80] [↵]

   ~~44239~~   ~~Unlisted laparoscopy procedure, rectum~~

(Use 45499)

ENTEROSTOMY — EXTERNAL FISTULIZATION OF INTESTINES

   44300   **Enterostomy or cecostomy, tube (eg, for decompression or feeding) (separate procedure)**   [C] [80] [↵]
AMA: 2002, Mar, 10

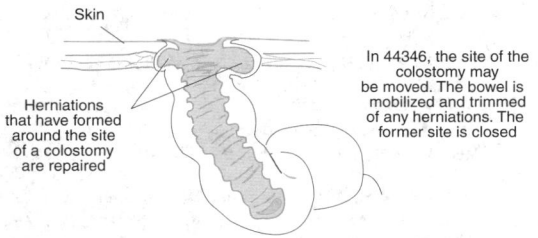

Skin

Herniations that have formed around the site of a colostomy are repaired

In 44346, the site of the colostomy may be moved. The bowel is mobilized and trimmed of any herniations. The former site is closed

The colon is mobilized, trimmed if necessary, and a new stoma is often created

▲ **44310**   **Ileostomy or jejunostomy, non-tube**   ⓒ 80 🗗
AMA: 2002, Mar, 10

To report laparoscopic procedure, consult CPT code 44187.

Code 44310 cannot be reported with 44144, 44150-44153, 44155, 44156, 45113, 45119, 45136.

44312   **Revision of ileostomy; simple (release of superficial scar) (separate procedure)**   ❶ T 80 🗗
MED: 100-2, 15, 260; 100-4, 12, 90.3; 100-4, 14, 10

44314   **complicated (reconstruction in-depth) (separate procedure)**   ⓒ 80 🗗

44316   **Continent ileostomy (Kock procedure) (separate procedure)**   ⓒ 80 🗗

If a fiberoptic evaluation is performed, consult CPT code 44385.

▲ **44320**   **Colostomy or skin level cecostomy;**   ⓒ 80 🗗
Mikulicz resection

To report laparoscopic procedure, consult CPT code 44188.

Code 44320 cannot be reported with 44141, 44144, 44146, 44605, 45110, 45119, 45126, 45563, 45805, 45825, 50810, 51597, 57307, or 58240.

44322   **with multiple biopsies (eg, for congenital megacolon) (separate procedure)**   ⓒ 80 🗗
Mikulicz resection

44340   **Revision of colostomy; simple (release of superficial scar) (separate procedure)**   ❸ T 🗗
MED: 100-2, 15, 260; 100-4, 12, 90.3; 100-4, 14, 10

44345   **complicated (reconstruction in-depth) (separate procedure)**   ⓒ 80 🗗

44346   **with repair of paracolostomy hernia (separate procedure)**   ⓒ 80 🗗

ENDOSCOPY, SMALL INTESTINE AND STOMAL
Diagnostic endoscopy is always included in surgical endoscopy.

⊙ **44360**   **Small intestinal endoscopy, enteroscopy beyond second portion of duodenum, not including ileum; diagnostic, with or without collection of specimen(s) by brushing or washing (separate procedure)**   ❷ T 🗗
MED: 100-2, 15, 260; 100-3, 100.2; 100-4, 12, 90.3; 100-4, 14, 10
AMA: 1994, Spring, 7

⊙ **44361**   **with biopsy, single or multiple**   ❷ T 🗗
MED: 100-2, 15, 260; 100-3, 100.2; 100-4, 12, 90.3; 100-4, 14, 10

⊙ **44363**   **with removal of foreign body**   ❷ T 80 🗗
MED: 100-2, 15, 260; 100-3, 100.2; 100-4, 12, 90.3; 100-4, 14, 10

Digestive System

44364 — 44383

⊙ **44364**   with removal of tumor(s), polyp(s), or other lesion(s) by snare technique   2️⃣ T 80 🔾
MED: 100-2, 15, 260; 100-3, 100.2; 100-4, 12, 90.3; 100-4, 14, 10

⊙ **44365**   with removal of tumor(s), polyp(s), or other lesion(s) by hot biopsy forceps or bipolar cautery   2️⃣ T 80 🔾
MED: 100-2, 15, 260; 100-3, 100.2; 100-4, 12, 90.3; 100-4, 14, 10

⊙ **44366**   with control of bleeding (eg, injection, bipolar cautery, unipolar cautery, laser, heater probe, stapler, plasma coagulator)   2️⃣ T 🔾
MED: 100-2, 15, 260; 100-3, 100.2; 100-4, 12, 90.3; 100-4, 14, 10

⊙ **44369**   with ablation of tumor(s), polyp(s), or other lesion(s) not amenable to removal by hot biopsy forceps, bipolar cautery or snare technique   2️⃣ T 80 🔾
MED: 100-2, 15, 260; 100-3, 100.2; 100-4, 12, 90.3; 100-4, 14, 10

⊙ **44370**   with transendoscopic stent placement (includes predilation) 9️⃣ T 80 🔾
MED: 100-2, 15, 260; 100-4, 12, 90.3; 100-4, 14, 10

AMA: 2001, Nov, 7

⊙ **44372**   with placement of percutaneous jejunostomy tube   2️⃣ T 🔾
MED: 100-2, 15, 260; 100-3, 100.2; 100-4, 12, 90.3; 100-4, 14, 10

AMA: 1994, Spring, 7

⊙ **44373**   with conversion of percutaneous gastrostomy tube to percutaneous jejunostomy tube   2️⃣ T 🔾
MED: 100-2, 15, 260; 100-3, 100.2; 100-4, 12, 90.3; 100-4, 14, 10

AMA: 1994, Spring, 7

⊙ **44376**   **Small intestinal endoscopy, enteroscopy beyond second portion of duodenum, including ileum; diagnostic, with or without collection of specimen(s) by brushing or washing (separate procedure)**   2️⃣ T 80 🔾
MED: 100-2, 15, 260; 100-3, 100.2; 100-4, 12, 90.3; 100-4, 14, 10

AMA: 1994, Spring, 7

⊙ **44377**   with biopsy, single or multiple   2️⃣ T 80 🔾
MED: 100-2, 15, 260; 100-3, 100.2; 100-4, 12, 90.3; 100-4, 14, 10

AMA: 1994, Spring, 7

⊙ **44378**   with control of bleeding (eg, injection, bipolar cautery, unipolar cautery, laser, heater probe, stapler, plasma coagulator)   2️⃣ T 80 🔾
MED: 100-2, 15, 260; 100-3, 100.2; 100-4, 12, 90.3; 100-4, 14, 10

AMA: 1994, Spring, 7

⊙ **44379**   with transendoscopic stent placement (includes predilation) 9️⃣ T 80 🔾
MED: 100-2, 15, 260; 100-4, 12, 90.3; 100-4, 14, 10

AMA: 2001, Nov, 7

⊙ **44380**   **Ileoscopy, through stoma; diagnostic, with or without collection of specimen(s) by brushing or washing (separate procedure)**   1️⃣ T 🔾
MED: 100-2, 15, 260; 100-3, 100.2; 100-4, 12, 90.3; 100-4, 14, 10

⊙ **44382**   with biopsy, single or multiple   1️⃣ T 🔾
MED: 100-2, 15, 260; 100-3, 100.2; 100-4, 12, 90.3; 100-4, 14, 10

⊙ **44383**   with transendoscopic stent placement (includes predilation) 9️⃣ T 🔾
MED: 100-2, 15, 260; 100-4, 12, 90.3; 100-4, 14, 10

AMA: 2001, Nov, 7

⊙ **44385** Endoscopic evaluation of small intestinal (abdominal or pelvic) pouch; diagnostic, with or without collection of specimen(s) by brushing or washing (separate procedure) 〔1〕〔T〕〔↻〕
MED: 100-2, 15, 260; 100-3, 100.2; 100-4, 12, 90.3; 100-4, 14, 10

⊙ **44386** with biopsy, single or multiple 〔1〕〔T〕〔80〕〔↻〕
MED: 100-2, 15, 260; 100-3, 100.2; 100-4, 12, 90.3; 100-4, 14, 10

⊙ **44388** Colonoscopy through stoma; diagnostic, with or without collection of specimen(s) by brushing or washing (separate procedure) 〔1〕〔T〕〔↻〕
MED: 100-2, 15, 260; 100-3, 100.2; 100-4, 12, 90.3; 100-4, 14, 10

If colonoscopy is performed via rectum, consult CPT codes 45330-45385.

⊙ **44389** with biopsy, single or multiple 〔1〕〔T〕〔↻〕
MED: 100-2, 15, 260; 100-3, 100.2; 100-4, 12, 90.3; 100-4, 14, 10

⊙ **44390** with removal of foreign body 〔1〕〔T〕〔80〕〔↻〕
MED: 100-2, 15, 260; 100-3, 100.2; 100-4, 12, 90.3; 100-4, 14, 10

⊙ **44391** with control of bleeding (eg, injection, bipolar cautery, unipolar cautery, laser, heater probe, stapler, plasma coagulator) 〔1〕〔T〕〔80〕〔↻〕
MED: 100-2, 15, 260; 100-3, 100.2; 100-4, 12, 90.3; 100-4, 14, 10

⊙ **44392** with removal of tumor(s), polyp(s), or other lesion(s) by hot biopsy forceps or bipolar cautery 〔1〕〔T〕〔↻〕
MED: 100-2, 15, 260; 100-3, 100.2; 100-4, 12, 90.3; 100-4, 14, 10

⊙ **44393** with ablation of tumor(s), polyp(s), or other lesion(s) not amenable to removal by hot biopsy forceps, bipolar cautery or snare technique 〔1〕〔T〕〔↻〕
MED: 100-2, 15, 260; 100-3, 100.2; 100-4, 12, 90.3; 100-4, 14, 10

⊙ **44394** with removal of tumor(s), polyp(s), or other lesion(s) by snare technique 〔1〕〔T〕〔↻〕
MED: 100-2, 15, 260; 100-3, 100.2; 100-4, 12, 90.3; 100-4, 14, 10

⊙ **44397** with transendoscopic stent placement (includes predilation) 〔1〕〔T〕〔↻〕
AMA: 2001, Nov, 7

INTRODUCTION

⊙ ⃠ **44500** Introduction of long gastrointestinal tube (eg, Miller-Abbott) (separate procedure) 〔T〕〔80〕〔↻〕
To report radiological supervision and interpretation, consult CPT code 74340.
To report placement of naso- or oro-gastric tube, consult CPT code 43752.

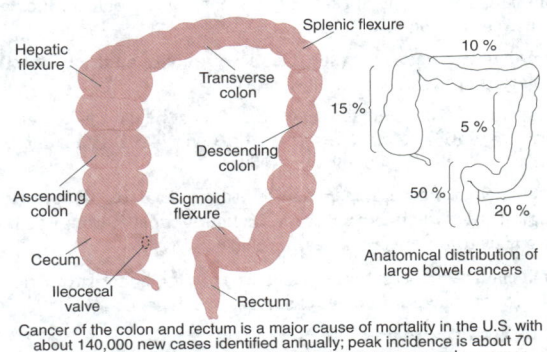

Splenic flexure

Hepatic flexure

Transverse colon

Descending colon

Ascending colon

Sigmoid flexure

Cecum

Ileocecal valve

Rectum

10 %

15 %

5 %

50 %

20 %

Anatomical distribution of large bowel cancers

Cancer of the colon and rectum is a major cause of mortality in the U.S. with about 140,000 new cases identified annually; peak incidence is about 70 years of age; rectal cancer is more common among men, colon cancer among women

Digestive System

44602 — 44721

REPAIR

44602 **Suture of small intestine (enterorrhaphy) for perforated ulcer, diverticulum, wound, injury or rupture; single perforation** [C] [80] [►]

44603 multiple perforations [C] [80] [►]

44604 **Suture of large intestine (colorrhaphy) for perforated ulcer, diverticulum, wound, injury or rupture (single or multiple perforations); without colostomy** [C] [80] [►]

44605 with colostomy [C] [80] [►]

44615 **Intestinal stricturoplasty (enterotomy and enterorrhaphy) with or without dilation, for intestinal obstruction** [C] [80] [►]

44620 **Closure of enterostomy, large or small intestine;** [C] [80] [►]
AMA: 1997, Nov, 17

44625 with resection and anastomosis other than colorectal [C] [80] [►]
AMA: 1997, Nov, 17

44626 with resection and colorectal anastomosis (eg, closure of Hartmann type procedure) [C] [80] [►]
AMA: 1997, Nov, 17

To report laparoscopic procedure, consult CPT code 44188.

44640 **Closure of intestinal cutaneous fistula** [C] [80] [►]

44650 **Closure of enteroenteric or enterocolic fistula** [C] [80] [►]

44660 **Closure of enterovesical fistula; without intestinal or bladder resection** [C] [80] [►]

44661 with intestine and/or bladder resection [C] [80] [►]

If closure of a renocolic fistula is performed, consult CPT codes 50525 and 50526. If closure of a gastrocolic fistula is performed, consult CPT code 43880. If closure of a rectovesical fistula is performed, consult CPT codes 45800 and 45805.

44680 **Intestinal plication (separate procedure)** [C] [80] [►]
Noble intestinal plication

OTHER PROCEDURES

44700 **Exclusion of small intestine from pelvis by mesh or other prosthesis, or native tissue (eg, bladder or omentum)** [C] [80] [►]
AMA: 1997, Nov, 18

If therapeutic radiation clinical treatment is given, consult the Radiation Oncology section.

+ 44701 **Intraoperative colonic lavage (List separately in addition to code for primary procedure)** [N] [80] [►]

Note that 44701 is an add-on code and must be used in conjunction with CPT codes 44140, 44145, 44150, or 44604. Code 44701 should not be reported with CPT codes 44300, 44950-44960.

44715 **Backbench standard preparation of cadaver or living donor intestine allograft prior to transplantation, including mobilization and fashioning of the superior mesenteric artery and vein** [C] [80] [►]

⊘ **44720** **Backbench reconstruction of cadaver or living donor intestine allograft prior to transplantation; venous anastomosis, each** [C] [80] [►]

⊘ **44721** arterial anastomosis, each [C] [80] [►]

44799 Unlisted procedure, intestine ⊤ 80

> To report unlisted laparoscopy procedure, intestine except rectum, consult CPT code 44238.

MECKEL'S DIVERTICULUM AND THE MESENTERY

EXCISION

44800 Excision of Meckel's diverticulum (diverticulectomy) or omphalomesenteric duct C 80 ☒

44820 Excision of lesion of mesentery (separate procedure) C 80 ☒

> If this procedure is performed with an intestine resection, consult CPT codes 44120 or 44140 and subsequent codes.

SUTURE

44850 Suture of mesentery (separate procedure) C 80 ☒

> If an internal hernia is reduced and repaired, consult CPT code 44050.

OTHER PROCEDURES

44899 Unlisted procedure, Meckel's diverticulum and the mesentery C 80

APPENDIX

INCISION

44900 Incision and drainage of appendiceal abscess; open C 80 ☒
AMA: 1997, Nov, 18

⊙ **44901** percutaneous ⊤ 80 ☒
AMA: 1998, Mar, 8; 1997, Nov, 18

> To report radiological supervision and interpretation, consult CPT code 75989.

EXCISION

44950 Appendectomy; C 80 ☒
AMA: 1996, Sep, 4

> An incidental appendectomy during intra-abdominal surgery does not usually warrant a separate identification. However, if it is necessary to report, append modifier 52.
>
> **Battle's operation**

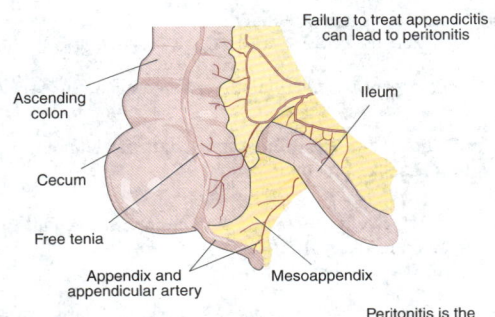

Failure to treat appendicitis can lead to peritonitis

Ascending colon

Ileum

Cecum

Free tenia

Appendix and appendicular artery

Mesoappendix

Appendicitis, the inflammation and infection of the appendix, is most prevalent between the ages of 15 and 24

Peritonitis is the inflammation of the lining of the abdominal cavity

Digestive System

44955 — 45113

+   **44955**   **when done for indicated purpose at time of other major procedure (not as separate procedure) (List separately in addition to code for primary procedure)**   `C` `80` `🔁`
AMA: 1996, Sep, 4

Note that 44955 is an add-on code that must be used in conjunction with the appropriate code for the primary procedure. This code cannot be reported alone.

44960   **for ruptured appendix with abscess or generalized peritonitis**   `C` `80` `🔁`
Battle's operation

LAPAROSCOPY

Diagnostic laparoscopy is always include in surgical laparoscopy.

To report only diagnostic laparoscopy, consult CPT code 49320.

44970   **Laparoscopy, surgical, appendectomy**   `T` `80` `🔁`
AMA: 2000, Mar, 5; 1999, Nov, 23

44979   **Unlisted laparoscopy procedure, appendix**   `T` `50` `80`
AMA: 2000, Mar, 5; 1999, Nov, 23

RECTUM

INCISION

45000   **Transrectal drainage of pelvic abscess**   `1` `T` `🔁`
MED: 100-2, 15, 260; 100-4, 12, 90.3; 100-4, 14, 10

45005   **Incision and drainage of submucosal abscess, rectum**   `2` `T` `🔁`
MED: 100-2, 15, 260; 100-4, 12, 90.3; 100-4, 14, 10

45020   **Incision and drainage of deep supralevator, pelvirectal, or retrorectal abscess**   `2` `T` `🔁`
MED: 100-2, 15, 260; 100-4, 12, 90.3; 100-4, 14, 10

Consult also CPT codes 46050 and 46060.

EXCISION

45100   **Biopsy of anorectal wall, anal approach (eg, congenital megacolon)** `1` `T` `🔁`
MED: 100-2, 15, 260; 100-4, 12, 90.3; 100-4, 14, 10

If an endoscopic biopsy is performed, consult CPT code 45305.

45108   **Anorectal myomectomy**   `2` `T` `🔁`
MED: 100-2, 15, 260; 100-4, 12, 90.3; 100-4, 14, 10

45110   **Proctectomy; complete, combined abdominoperineal, with colostomy**   `C` `80` `🔁`

45111   **partial resection of rectum, transabdominal approach**   `C` `80` `🔁`
Luschka proctectomy

45112   **Proctectomy, combined abdominoperineal, pull-through procedure (eg, colo-anal anastomosis)**   `C` `80` `🔁`
AMA: 1997, Nov, 18

If a colo-anal anastomosis is performed with the creation of a colonic reservoir or pouch, consult CPT code 45119.

45113   **Proctectomy, partial, with rectal mucosectomy, ileoanal anastomosis, creation of ileal reservoir (S or J), with or without loop ileostomy**   `C` `80` `🔁`

`26` / `TC` Professional/Technical Component   `80`/`80` Assist-at-Surgery Allowed/With Documentation   ⊙ Conscious Sedation

Unlisted   Not Covered   **MED:** Pubs 100/NCD Reference   `1`-`9` ASC Group   `63` Modifier 63 Exempt

330 — Surgery   CPT only © 2005 American Medical Association. All Rights Reserved. *(Black Ink)*   © 2005 Ingenix, Inc. *(Blue Ink)*

45114	Proctectomy, partial, with anastomosis; abdominal and transsacral approach ⓒ 80 🔁
45116	transsacral approach only (Kraske type) ⓒ 80 🔁

▲ 45119   Proctectomy, combined abdominoperineal pull-through procedure (eg, colo-anal anastomosis), with creation of colonic reservoir (eg, J-pouch), with diverting enterostomy when performed   ⓒ 80 🔁
AMA: 1997, Nov, 18

To report laparoscopic procedure, consult CPT code 45397.

45120	Proctectomy, complete (for congenital megacolon), abdominal and perineal approach; with pull-through procedure and anastomosis (eg, Swenson, Duhamel, or Soave type operation) ⓒ 80 🔁
45121	with subtotal or total colectomy, with multiple biopsies ⓒ 80 🔁
45123	Proctectomy, partial, without anastomosis, perineal approach ⓒ 80 🔁

45126   Pelvic exenteration for colorectal malignancy, with proctectomy (with or without colostomy), with removal of bladder and ureteral transplantations, and/or hysterectomy, or cervicectomy, with or without removal of tube(s), with or without removal of ovary(s), or any combination thereof   ⓒ 80 🔁
AMA: 1998, Nov, 16

45130   Excision of rectal procidentia, with anastomosis; perineal approach ⓒ 80 🔁
Altemeier procedure

45135	abdominal and perineal approach ⓒ 80 🔁
45136	Excision of ileoanal reservoir with ileostomy ⓒ 80 🔁

Code 45136 is not to be used with 44005, 44120, 44310.

45150   Division of stricture of rectum   2 T 80 🔁
MED: 100-2, 15, 260; 100-4, 12, 90.3; 100-4, 14, 10

45160   Excision of rectal tumor by proctotomy, transacral or transcoccygeal approach   2 T 80 🔁
MED: 100-2, 15, 260; 100-4, 12, 90.3; 100-4, 14, 10

45170   Excision of rectal tumor, transanal approach   2 T 80 🔁
MED: 100-2, 15, 260; 100-4, 12, 90.3; 100-4, 14, 10

DESTRUCTION

45190   Destruction of rectal tumor (eg, electrodessication, electrosurgery, laser ablation, laser resection, cryosurgery) transanal approach   9 T 80 🔁
MED: 100-2, 15, 260; 100-4, 12, 90.3; 100-4, 14, 10

ENDOSCOPY

Diagnostic endoscopy is included in surgical endoscopy.

45300   Proctosigmoidoscopy, rigid; diagnostic, with or without collection of specimen(s) by brushing or washing (separate procedure)   T 🔁
MED: 100-3, 100.2

AMA: 1997, Oct, 6; 1994, Spring, 8

⊙   45303   with dilation (eg, balloon, guide wire, bougie)   T 🔁
MED: 100-3, 100.2

AMA: 1997, Oct, 6; 1994, Spring, 8

If radiological supervision and interpretation is performed, consult CPT code 74360.

Digestive System

45305 — 45327

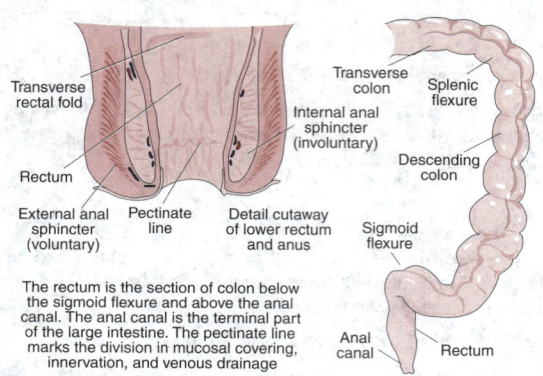

Transverse rectal fold

Rectum

External anal sphincter (voluntary)

Pectinate line

Detail cutaway of lower rectum and anus

Transverse colon

Splenic flexure

Internal anal sphincter (involuntary)

Descending colon

Sigmoid flexure

Anal canal

Rectum

The rectum is the section of colon below the sigmoid flexure and above the anal canal. The anal canal is the terminal part of the large intestine. The pectinate line marks the division in mucosal covering, innervation, and venous drainage

⊙ **45305**   **with biopsy, single or multiple**   1 T ↻
MED: 100-2, 15, 260; 100-3, 100.2; 100-4, 12, 90.3; 100-4, 14, 10

AMA: 1997, Oct, 6

⊙ **45307**   **with removal of foreign body**   1 T 80 ↻
MED: 100-2, 15, 260; 100-3, 100.2; 100-4, 12, 90.3; 100-4, 14, 10

AMA: 1997, Oct, 6; 1994, Spring, 8

⊙ **45308**   **with removal of single tumor, polyp, or other lesion by hot biopsy forceps or bipolar cautery**   1 T ↻
MED: 100-2, 15, 260; 100-3, 100.2; 100-4, 12, 90.3; 100-4, 14, 10

AMA: 1997, Oct, 6; 1994, Spring, 8

⊙ **45309**   **with removal of single tumor, polyp, or other lesion by snare technique**   1 T ↻
MED: 100-2, 15, 260; 100-3, 100.2; 100-4, 12, 90.3; 100-4, 14, 10

AMA: 1997, Oct, 6; 1994, Spring, 8

⊙ **45315**   **with removal of multiple tumors, polyps, or other lesions by hot biopsy forceps, bipolar cautery or snare technique**   1 T ↻
MED: 100-2, 15, 260; 100-3, 100.2; 100-4, 12, 90.3; 100-4, 14, 10

AMA: 1997, Oct, 6; 1994, Spring, 8

⊙ **45317**   **with control of bleeding (eg, injection, bipolar cautery, unipolar cautery, laser, heater probe, stapler, plasma coagulator)**   1 T ↻
MED: 100-2, 15, 260; 100-3, 100.2; 100-4, 12, 90.3; 100-4, 14, 10

AMA: 1997, Oct, 6; 1994, Spring, 8

⊙ **45320**   **with ablation of tumor(s), polyp(s), or other lesion(s) not amenable to removal by hot biopsy forceps, bipolar cautery or snare technique (eg, laser)**   1 T ↻
MED: 100-2, 15, 260; 100-3, 100.2; 100-4, 12, 90.3; 100-4, 14, 10

AMA: 1997, Oct, 6; 1994, Spring, 8

  45321   **with decompression of volvulus**   1 T ↻
MED: 100-2, 15, 260; 100-3, 100.2; 100-4, 12, 90.3; 100-4, 14, 10

AMA: 1997, Oct, 6; 1994, Spring, 8

⊙ **45327**   **with transendoscopic stent placement (includes predilation)**   1 T ↻
AMA: 2001, Nov, 7

45330 Sigmoidoscopy, flexible; diagnostic, with or without collection of specimen(s) by brushing or washing (separate procedure) T 🖸
MED: 100-3, 100.2; 100-4, 12, 30.1

AMA: 1994, Spring, 9

45331 with biopsy, single or multiple 1 T 🖸
MED: 100-2, 15, 260; 100-3, 100.2; 100-4, 12, 90.3; 100-4, 14, 10

AMA: 1996, Sep, 6; 1994, Spring, 9

⊙ 45332 with removal of foreign body 1 T 🖸
MED: 100-2, 15, 260; 100-3, 100.2; 100-4, 12, 90.3; 100-4, 14, 10

AMA: 1994, Spring, 9

⊙ 45333 with removal of tumor(s), polyp(s), or other lesion(s) by hot biopsy forceps or bipolar cautery 1 T 🖸
MED: 100-2, 15, 260; 100-3, 100.2; 100-4, 12, 90.3; 100-4, 14, 10

AMA: 1994, Spring, 9

⊙ 45334 with control of bleeding (eg, injection, bipolar cautery, unipolar cautery, laser, heater probe, stapler, plasma coagulator) 1 T 🖸
MED: 100-2, 15, 260; 100-3, 100.2; 100-4, 12, 90.3; 100-4, 14, 10

AMA: 1996, Sep, 6; 1994, Spring, 9

45335 with directed submucosal injection(s), any substance 1 T 🖸
MED: 100-2, 15, 260; 100-4, 12, 90.3; 100-4, 14, 10

⊙ 45337 with decompression of volvulus, any method 1 T 🖸
MED: 100-2, 15, 260; 100-3, 100.2; 100-4, 12, 90.3; 100-4, 14, 10

AMA: 1994, Spring, 9

⊙ 45338 with removal of tumor(s), polyp(s), or other lesion(s) by snare technique 1 T 🖸
MED: 100-2, 15, 260; 100-3, 100.2; 100-4, 12, 90.3; 100-4, 14, 10

AMA: 1994, Spring, 9

⊙ 45339 with ablation of tumor(s), polyp(s), or other lesion(s) not amenable to removal by hot biopsy forceps, bipolar cautery or snare technique 1 T 🖸
MED: 100-2, 15, 260; 100-3, 100.2; 100-4, 12, 90.3; 100-4, 14, 10

AMA: 1994, Spring, 9

⊙ 45340 with dilation by balloon, 1 or more strictures 1 T 🖸
MED: 100-2, 15, 260; 100-4, 12, 90.3; 100-4, 14, 10

Do not report 45340 with CPT code 45345.

⊙ 45341 with endoscopic ultrasound examination 1 T 🖸
MED: 100-3, 100.2; 100-3, 220.5

AMA: 2001, Oct, 4

To report transrectal ultrasound with rigid probe device, consult CPT code 76872.

Codes 76942 and 76975 cannot be reported with CPT code 45341.

Digestive System

45342 — 45385

⊙ 45342   **with transendoscopic ultrasound guided intramural or transmural fine needle aspiration/biopsy(s)** **1** T ⟁
MED: 100-3, 100.2; 100-3, 220.5

AMA: 2001, Oct, 4

To report transrectal ultrasound with rigid probe device, consult CPT code 76872.

To report the interpretation of specimen, consult CPT codes 88172-88173.

Codes 76942 and 76975 cannot be reported with CPT code 45342.

⊙ 45345   **with transendoscopic stent placement (includes predilation)** **1** T ⟁
AMA: 2001, Nov, 7

⊙ 45355   **Colonoscopy, rigid or flexible, transabdominal via colotomy, single or multiple** **1** T ⟁
MED: 100-2, 15, 260; 100-3, 100.2; 100-4, 12, 40.6; 100-4, 12, 90.3; 100-4, 14, 10

⊙ 45378   **Colonoscopy, flexible, proximal to splenic flexure; diagnostic, with or without collection of specimen(s) by brushing or washing, with or without colon decompression (separate procedure)** **2** T ⟁
MED: 100-2, 15, 260; 100-3, 100.2; 100-4, 12, 30.1; 100-4, 12, 40.6; 100-4, 12, 90.3; 100-4, 14, 10; 100-4, 18, 60

AMA: 1999, Aug, 3; 1994, Spring, 9

⊙ 45379   **with removal of foreign body** **2** T ⟁
MED: 100-2, 15, 260; 100-3, 100.2; 100-4, 12, 90.3; 100-4, 14, 10

AMA: 1999, Aug, 3; 1994, Spring, 9

⊙ 45380   **with biopsy, single or multiple** **2** T ⟁
MED: 100-2, 15, 260; 100-3, 100.2; 100-4, 12, 40.6; 100-4, 12, 90.3; 100-4, 14, 10

AMA: 1999, Feb, 11; 1999, Aug, 3; 1996, Jan, 7; 1994, Spring, 9

⊙ 45381   **with directed submucosal injection(s), any substance** **2** T ⟁
MED: 100-2, 15, 260; 100-4, 12, 90.3; 100-4, 14, 10

⊙ 45382   **with control of bleeding (eg, injection, bipolar cautery, unipolar cautery, laser, heater probe, stapler, plasma coagulator)** **2** T ⟁
MED: 100-2, 15, 260; 100-3, 100.2; 100-4, 12, 90.3; 100-4, 14, 10

AMA: 1999, Aug, 3; 1994, Spring, 9

⊙ 45383   **with ablation of tumor(s), polyp(s), or other lesion(s) not amenable to removal by hot biopsy forceps, bipolar cautery or snare technique** **2** T ⟁
MED: 100-2, 15, 260; 100-3, 100.2; 100-4, 12, 90.3; 100-4, 14, 10

AMA: 1999, Aug, 3; 1994, Spring, 9

⊙ 45384   **with removal of tumor(s), polyp(s), or other lesion(s) by hot biopsy forceps or bipolar cautery** **2** T ⟁
MED: 100-2, 15, 260; 100-3, 100.2; 100-4, 12, 90.3; 100-4, 14, 10

AMA: 1999, Feb, 11; 1999, Aug, 3; 1998, Jul, 10; 1994, Spring, 9

⊙ 45385   **with removal of tumor(s), polyp(s), or other lesion(s) by snare technique** **2** T ⟁
MED: 100-2, 15, 260; 100-3, 100.2; 100-4, 12, 40.6; 100-4, 12, 90.3; 100-4, 14, 10

AMA: 1999, Aug, 3; 1998, Jul, 10; 1996, Jan, 7; 1994, Spring, 9

If a small intestine and stomal endoscopy is performed, consult CPT codes 44360-44393.

⊙ **45386**   **with dilation by balloon, 1 or more strictures**   ② T ⏎
MED: 100-2, 15, 260; 100-4, 12, 90.3; 100-4, 14, 10

Note that 45386 is not be used in conjunction with 45387.

⊙ **45387**   **with transendoscopic stent placement (includes predilation)** ■ T ⏎
MED: 100-3, 100.2

AMA: 2001, Nov, 7

⊙ **45391**   **with endoscopic ultrasound examination**   ② T ⏎
Code 45391 cannot be reported with CPT codes 45330, 45341, 45342, 45378, 76872.

⊙ **45392**   **with transendoscopic ultrasound guided intramural or transmural fine needle aspiration/biopsy(s)**   ② T ⏎
Code 45392 cannot be reported with CPT codes 45330, 45341, 45342, 45378, 76872.

LAPAROSCOPY

EXCISION

● **45395**   **Laparoscopy, surgical; proctectomy, complete, combined abdominoperineal, with colostomy**

To report open procedure, consult CPT code 45110.

● **45397**   **proctectomy, combined abdominoperineal pull-through procedure (eg, colo-anal anastomosis), with creation of colonic reservoir (eg, J-pouch), with diverting enterostomy, when performed**

To report open procedure, consult CPT code 45119.

REPAIR

● **45400**   **proctopexy (for prolapse)**

To report open procedure, consult CPT codes 45540, 45541.

● **45402**   **proctopexy (for prolapse), with sigmoid resection**

To report open procedure, consult CPT code 45550.

● **45499**   **Unlisted laparoscopy procedure, rectum**

REPAIR

45500   **Proctoplasty; for stenosis**   ② T 80 ⏎
MED: 100-2, 15, 260; 100-4, 12, 90.3; 100-4, 14, 10

45505   **for prolapse of mucous membrane**   ② T ⏎
MED: 100-2, 15, 260; 100-4, 12, 90.3; 100-4, 14, 10

45520   **Perirectal injection of sclerosing solution for prolapse**   T ⏎
AMA: 2001, Jul, 11; 2001, Aug, 10

▲ **45540**   **Proctopexy (eg, for prolapse); abdominal approach**   C 80 ⏎
To report laparoscopic procedure, consult CPT code 45400.

▲ **45541**   **perineal approach**   T 80 ⏎

▲ **45550**   **with sigmoid resection, abdominal approach**   C 80 ⏎
Frickman proctopexy

To report laparoscopic procedure, consult CPT code 45402.

Digestive System

45560 — 45999

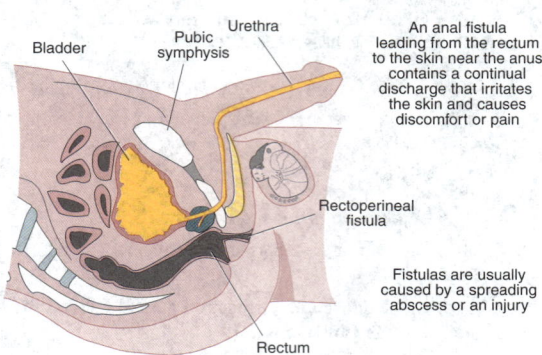

Bladder

Pubic symphysis

Urethra

An anal fistula leading from the rectum to the skin near the anus contains a continual discharge that irritates the skin and causes discomfort or pain

Rectoperineal fistula

Fistulas are usually caused by a spreading abscess or an injury

Rectum

45560 **Repair of rectocele (separate procedure)** `2` `T` `80` `↰`
MED: 100-2, 15, 260; 100-4, 12, 90.3; 100-4, 14, 10

If a rectocele is repaired with a posterior colporrhaphy, consult CPT code 57250.

45562 **Exploration, repair, and presacral drainage for rectal injury;** `C` `80` `↰`

45563 **with colostomy** `C` `80` `↰`
Maydl colostomy

45800 **Closure of rectovesical fistula;** `C` `80` `↰`

45805 **with colostomy** `C` `80` `↰`

45820 **Closure of rectourethral fistula;** `C` `80` `↰`

45825 **with colostomy** `C` `80` `↰`

If a rectovaginal fistula is closed, consult CPT codes 57300-57308.

MANIPULATION

45900 **Reduction of procidentia (separate procedure) under anesthesia** `1` `T` `80` `↰`
MED: 100-2, 15, 260; 100-4, 12, 90.3; 100-4, 14, 10

45905 **Dilation of anal sphincter (separate procedure) under anesthesia other than local** `1` `T` `↰`
MED: 100-2, 15, 260; 100-4, 12, 90.3; 100-4, 14, 10

45910 **Dilation of rectal stricture (separate procedure) under anesthesia other than local** `1` `T` `↰`
MED: 100-2, 15, 260; 100-4, 12, 90.3; 100-4, 14, 10

45915 **Removal of fecal impaction or foreign body (separate procedure) under anesthesia** `1` `T` `↰`
MED: 100-2, 15, 260; 100-4, 12, 90.3; 100-4, 14, 10

OTHER PROCEDURES

● **45990** **Anorectal exam, surgical, requiring anesthesia (general, spinal, or epidural), diagnostic**

Code 45990 cannot be reported with 45300-45327, 46600, 57410, 99170.

45999 **Unlisted procedure, rectum** `T` `80`

To report unlisted laparoscopic procedure, rectum, consult CPT code 45499.

`26`/`TC` Professional/Technical Component `80`/`80` Assist-at-Surgery Allowed/With Documentation ☉ Conscious Sedation
Unlisted   Not Covered   **MED:** Pubs 100/NCD Reference `1`-`9` ASC Group `63` Modifier 63 Exempt
336 — Surgery   CPT only © 2005 American Medical Association. All Rights Reserved. *(Black Ink)*   © 2005 Ingenix, Inc. *(Blue Ink)*

ANUS

INCISION

46020   **Placement of seton**   3 T ↵
MED: 100-2, 15, 260; 100-4, 12, 90.3; 100-4, 14, 10

Code 46020 is not to be used in conjunction with 46060, 46280, 46600.

46030   **Removal of anal seton, other marker**   1 T 80 ↵
MED: 100-2, 15, 260; 100-4, 12, 90.3; 100-4, 14, 10

46040   **Incision and drainage of ischiorectal and/or perirectal abscess (separate procedure)**   3 T ↵
MED: 100-2, 15, 260; 100-4, 12, 90.3; 100-4, 14, 10

46045   **Incision and drainage of intramural, intramuscular or submucosal abscess, transanal, under anesthesia**   2 T ↵
MED: 100-2, 15, 260; 100-4, 12, 90.3; 100-4, 14, 10

46050   **Incision and drainage, perianal abscess, superficial**   1 T ↵
MED: 100-2, 15, 260; 100-4, 12, 90.3; 100-4, 14, 10

Consult also CPT codes 45020 and 46060.

46060   **Incision and drainage of ischiorectal or intramural abscess, with fistulectomy or fistulotomy, submuscular, with or without placement of seton**   2 T ↵
MED: 100-2, 15, 260; 100-4, 12, 90.3; 100-4, 14, 10

Consult also CPT code 45020.

Code 46060 is not to be used in conjunction with 46020.

46070   **Incision, anal septum (infant)**   A T 80 ↵ 63
If anoplasty is performed, consult CPT codes 46700-46705.

46080   **Sphincterotomy, anal, division of sphincter (separate procedure)**   3 T ↵
MED: 100-2, 15, 260; 100-4, 12, 90.3; 100-4, 14, 10

46083   **Incision of thrombosed hemorrhoid, external**   T ↵
AMA: 1997, Jun, 10

EXCISION

46200   **Fissurectomy, with or without sphincterotomy**   2 T ↵
MED: 100-2, 15, 260; 100-4, 12, 90.3; 100-4, 14, 10

46210   **Cryptectomy; single**   2 T 80 ↵
MED: 100-2, 15, 260; 100-4, 12, 90.3; 100-4, 14, 10

46211   **multiple (separate procedure)**   2 T 80 ↵
MED: 100-2, 15, 260; 100-4, 12, 90.3; 100-4, 14, 10

46220   **Papillectomy or excision of single tag, anus (separate procedure)**   1 T ↵
MED: 100-2, 15, 260; 100-4, 12, 90.3; 100-4, 14, 10

46221   **Hemorrhoidectomy, by simple ligature (eg, rubber band)**   T ↵
AMA: 1997, Oct, 6

46230   **Excision of external hemorrhoid tags and/or multiple papillae**   1 T ↵

46250   **Hemorrhoidectomy, external, complete**   3 T ↵
MED: 100-2, 15, 260; 100-4, 12, 90.3; 100-4, 14, 10

46255   **Hemorrhoidectomy, internal and external, simple;**   3 T ↵
MED: 100-2, 15, 260; 100-4, 12, 90.3; 100-4, 14, 10

Digestive System

46257 — 46500

| 46257 | with fissurectomy | ③ T 🔲 |

MED: 100-2, 15, 260; 100-4, 12, 90.3; 100-4, 14, 10

| 46258 | with fistulectomy, with or without fissurectomy | ③ T 80 🔲 |

MED: 100-2, 15, 260; 100-4, 12, 90.3; 100-4, 14, 10

| 46260 | **Hemorrhoidectomy, internal and external, complex or extensive;** | ③ T 🔲 |

MED: 100-2, 15, 260; 100-4, 12, 90.3; 100-4, 14, 10

Whitehead hemorrhoidectomy

| 46261 | with fissurectomy | ④ T 🔲 |

MED: 100-2, 15, 260; 100-4, 12, 90.3; 100-4, 14, 10

| 46262 | with fistulectomy, with or without fissurectomy | ④ T 🔲 |

MED: 100-2, 15, 260; 100-4, 12, 90.3; 100-4, 14, 10

To report injection of hemorrhoids, consult CPT code 46500; to report destruction, consult CPT codes 46934-46936; to report ligation, consult CPT codes 46945, 46946; to report hemorrhoidopexy consult, CPT code 46947.

| 46270 | **Surgical treatment of anal fistula (fistulectomy/fistulotomy); subcutaneous** | ③ T 🔲 |

MED: 100-2, 15, 260; 100-4, 12, 90.3; 100-4, 14, 10

| 46275 | submuscular | ③ T 🔲 |

MED: 100-2, 15, 260; 100-4, 12, 90.3; 100-4, 14, 10

| 46280 | complex or multiple, with or without placement of seton | ④ T 🔲 |

MED: 100-2, 15, 260; 100-4, 12, 90.3; 100-4, 14, 10

Do not report 46280 in conjunction with CPT code 46020.

| 46285 | second stage | ① T 🔲 |

MED: 100-2, 15, 260; 100-4, 12, 90.3; 100-4, 14, 10

| 46288 | **Closure of anal fistula with rectal advancement flap** | ④ T 🔲 |

MED: 100-2, 15, 260; 100-4, 12, 90.3; 100-4, 14, 10

| 46320 | **Enucleation or excision of external thrombotic hemorrhoid** | T 🔲 |

INTRODUCTION

| 46500 | **Injection of sclerosing solution, hemorrhoids** | T 🔲 |

To report excision of hemorrhoids, consult CPT codes 46250-46262; to report destruction, consult CPT codes 46934-46936; to report ligation, consult CPT codes 46945, 46946; to report hemorrhoidopexy, consult CPT code 46947.

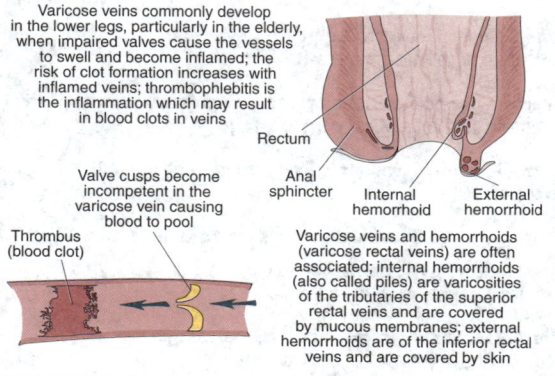

Varicose veins commonly develop in the lower legs, particularly in the elderly, when impaired valves cause the vessels to swell and become inflamed; the risk of clot formation increases with inflamed veins; thrombophlebitis is the inflammation which may result in blood clots in veins

Rectum

Valve cusps become incompetent in the varicose vein causing blood to pool

Anal sphincter

Internal hemorrhoid

External hemorrhoid

Thrombus (blood clot)

Varicose veins and hemorrhoids (varicose rectal veins) are often associated; internal hemorrhoids (also called piles) are varicosities of the tributaries of the superior rectal veins and are covered by mucous membranes; external hemorrhoids are of the inferior rectal veins and are covered by skin

- **46505**   **Chemodenervation of internal anal sphincter**

    To report chemodenervation of other muscles, consult CPT codes 64612-64614, 64640.

    Report the specific service in addition to the specific substance(s) or drug(s) provided.

ENDOSCOPY
Diagnostic endoscopy is always included in surgical endoscopy.

46600   **Anoscopy; diagnostic, with or without collection of specimen(s) by brushing or washing (separate procedure)**   ⊠ ◪
MED: 100-3, 100.2

AMA: 1997, Oct, 6; 1994, Spring, 9

Do not report 46600 in conjunction with CPT code 46020.

46604   **with dilation (eg, balloon, guide wire, bougie)**   Ⓣ ◪
MED: 100-3, 100.2

AMA: 1997, Oct, 6; 1994, Spring, 9

46606   **with biopsy, single or multiple**   Ⓣ ◪
MED: 100-3, 100.2; 100-4, 12, 40.6

AMA: 1997, Oct, 6; 1994, Spring, 9

46608   **with removal of foreign body**   ❶ Ⓣ 80 ◪
MED: 100-2, 15, 260; 100-3, 100.2; 100-4, 12, 40.6; 100-4, 12, 90.3; 100-4, 14, 10

AMA: 1997, Oct, 6; 1994, Spring, 9

46610   **with removal of single tumor, polyp, or other lesion by hot biopsy forceps or bipolar cautery**   ❶ Ⓣ ◪
MED: 100-2, 15, 260; 100-3, 100.2; 100-4, 12, 90.3; 100-4, 14, 10

AMA: 1997, Oct, 6; 1994, Spring, 10

46611   **with removal of single tumor, polyp, or other lesion by snare technique**   ❶ Ⓣ 80 ◪
MED: 100-2, 15, 260; 100-3, 100.2; 100-4, 12, 90.3; 100-4, 14, 10

AMA: 1997, Oct, 6; 1994, Spring, 10

46612   **with removal of multiple tumors, polyps, or other lesions by hot biopsy forceps, bipolar cautery or snare technique**   ❶ Ⓣ 80 ◪
MED: 100-2, 15, 260; 100-3, 100.2; 100-4, 12, 90.3; 100-4, 14, 10

AMA: 1997, Oct, 6; 1994, Spring, 10

46614   **with control of bleeding (eg, injection, bipolar cautery, unipolar cautery, laser, heater probe, stapler, plasma coagulator)**   Ⓣ ◪
MED: 100-3, 100.2

AMA: 1997, Oct, 6; 1994, Spring, 10

46615   **with ablation of tumor(s), polyp(s), or other lesion(s) not amenable to removal by hot biopsy forceps, bipolar cautery or snare technique**   ❷ Ⓣ 80 ◪
MED: 100-2, 15, 260; 100-3, 100.2; 100-4, 12, 90.3; 100-4, 14, 10

AMA: 1997, Oct, 6; 1994, Spring, 10

REPAIR
46700   **Anoplasty, plastic operation for stricture; adult**   ❸ Ⓣ ◪
MED: 100-2, 15, 260; 100-4, 12, 90.3; 100-4, 14, 10

46705	infant	C 80 ↵ 63

If a simple incision of the anal septum is performed, consult CPT code 46070.

46706	Repair of anal fistula with fibrin glue	1 T ↵
● 46710	Repair of ileoanal pouch fistula/sinus (eg, perineal or vaginal), pouch advancement; transperineal approach	
● 46712	combined transperineal and transabdominal approach	
46715	Repair of low imperforate anus; with anoperineal fistula (cut-back procedure)	C 80 ↵ 63
46716	with transposition of anoperineal or anovestibular fistula	C 80 ↵ 63
46730	Repair of high imperforate anus without fistula; perineal or sacroperineal approach	C 80 ↵ 63
46735	combined transabdominal and sacroperineal approaches	C 80 ↵ 63
46740	Repair of high imperforate anus with rectourethral or rectovaginal fistula; perineal or sacroperineal approach	C 80 ↵ 63
46742	combined transabdominal and sacroperineal approaches	C 80 ↵ 63
46744	Repair of cloacal anomaly by anorectovaginoplasty and urethroplasty, sacroperineal approach	♀ C 80 ↵ 63
46746	Repair of cloacal anomaly by anorectovaginoplasty and urethroplasty, combined abdominal and sacroperineal approach;	♀ C 80 ↵
46748	with vaginal lengthening by intestinal graft or pedicle flaps	♀ C 80 ↵
46750	Sphincteroplasty, anal, for incontinence or prolapse; adult	3 T 80 ↵
	MED: 100-2, 15, 260; 100-3, 230.10; 100-4, 12, 90.3; 100-4, 14, 10	
46751	child	A C 80 ↵
46753	Graft (Thiersch operation) for rectal incontinence and/or prolapse	3 T ↵
	MED: 100-2, 15, 260; 100-3, 230.10; 100-4, 12, 90.3; 100-4, 14, 10	
46754	Removal of Thiersch wire or suture, anal canal	2 T 80 ↵
	MED: 100-2, 15, 260; 100-4, 12, 90.3; 100-4, 14, 10	
46760	Sphincteroplasty, anal, for incontinence, adult; muscle transplant	2 T 80 ↵
	MED: 100-2, 15, 260; 100-3, 230.10; 100-4, 12, 90.3; 100-4, 14, 10	
46761	levator muscle imbrication (Park posterior anal repair)	3 T 80 ↵
	MED: 100-2, 15, 260; 100-4, 12, 90.3; 100-4, 14, 10	
46762	implantation artificial sphincter	7 T 80 ↵
	MED: 100-2, 15, 260; 100-4, 12, 90.3; 100-4, 14, 10	

DESTRUCTION

46900	Destruction of lesion(s), anus (eg, condyloma, papilloma, molluscum contagiosum, herpetic vesicle), simple; chemical	T ↵
46910	electrodesiccation	T ↵
46916	cryosurgery	T ↵
	MED: 100-3, 140.5	
46917	laser surgery	1 T ↵
	MED: 100-2, 15, 260; 100-3, 140.5; 100-4, 12, 90.3; 100-4, 14, 10	
46922	surgical excision	1 T ↵
	MED: 100-2, 15, 260; 100-4, 12, 90.3; 100-4, 14, 10	

46924	**Destruction of lesion(s), anus (eg, condyloma, papilloma, molluscum contagiosum, herpetic vesicle), extensive (eg, laser surgery, electrosurgery, cryosurgery, chemosurgery)**	**1** T ⟐

MED: 100-2, 15, 260; 100-4, 12, 90.3; 100-4, 14, 10

46934	**Destruction of hemorrhoids, any method; internal**	T ⟐
46935	**external**	T ⟐
46936	**internal and external**	T ⟐

To report excision of hemorrhoids, consult CPT codes 46250-46262; to report injection, consult CPT code 46500; to report ligation, consult CPT codes 46945, 46946; to report hemorrhoidopexy, consult CPT code 46947.

46937	**Cryosurgery of rectal tumor; benign**	**2** T 80 ⟐

MED: 100-2, 15, 260; 100-4, 12, 90.3; 100-4, 14, 10

46938	**malignant**	**2** T 80 ⟐

MED: 100-2, 15, 260; 100-4, 12, 90.3; 100-4, 14, 10

46940	**Curettage or cautery of anal fissure, including dilation of anal sphincter (separate procedure); initial**	T ⟐
46942	**subsequent**	T 80 ⟐

SUTURE

46945	**Ligation of internal hemorrhoids; single procedure**	T ⟐
46946	**multiple procedures**	T ⟐
46947	**Hemorrhoidopexy (eg, for prolapsing internal hemorrhoids) by stapling**	**3** T ⟐

To report excision of hemorrhoids, consult CPT codes 46250-46262; to report injection, consult CPT code 46500; to report destruction, consult CPT codes 46934-46936.

OTHER PROCEDURES

46999	**Unlisted procedure, anus**	T 80

AMA: 1997, Oct, 6

LIVER

INCISION

47000	**Biopsy of liver, needle; percutaneous**	**1** T ⟐

MED: 100-2, 15, 260; 100-4, 12, 90.3; 100-4, 14, 10

AMA: 1993, Fall, 12

To report imaging guidance, consult CPT codes 76003, 76360, 76393, and 76942.

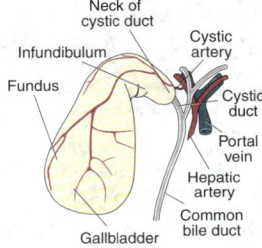

The liver is divided into four lobes for descriptive purposes, although the left and right halves are functionally separate, each receiving its own arterial supply and venous drainage. The liver is the largest gland in the body and serves many metabolic purposes including secretion of bile. The gallbladder is located on the visceral side of the quadrate lobe and stores bile between active phases of digestion; positions of the sac and its structures varies

⟐ CCI Comp	50 Bilateral Procedure	+ CPT Add-on Code	⊘ Modifier -51 Exempt	♂ Male	♀ Female
● New Code	▲ Revised Code	M Maternity Edit	A Age Edit	A—Y APC Status Ind.	AMA: CPT Assistant

© 2005 Ingenix, Inc. (*Blue Ink*)   CPT only © 2005 American Medical Association. All Rights Reserved. (*Black Ink*)   Surgery — 341

Digestive System

46924 — 47000

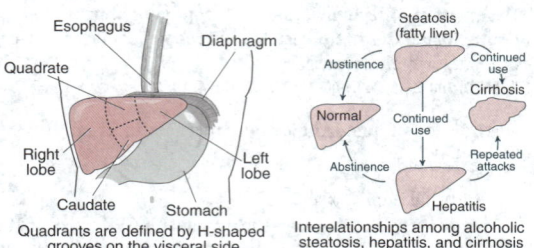

Quadrants are defined by H-shaped grooves on the visceral side

Interrelationships among alcoholic steatosis, hepatitis, and cirrhosis

The liver is the largest gland in the body and serves many metabolic purposes including secretion of bile. Chronic alcohol use leads to three similar forms of alcoholic liver disease: steatosis (fatty liver), hepatitis, and cirrhosis. The conditions have many overlapping features and each may occur without involvement of alcohol. Alcoholic cirrhosis accounts for about 60 percent of all cirrhosis cases and the risk appears to rise with the amount of alcohol consumed daily. The liver tends to shrink and become fibrotic

+ 47001 **when done for indicated purpose at time of other major procedure (List separately in addition to code for primary procedure)** N ⬚

To report imaging guidance, consult CPT codes 76003, 76942.

To report fine needle aspiration in conjunction with 47000, 47001, consult CPT codes 10021, 10022.

To report evaluation of fine needle aspirate consult CPT codes 88172, 88173.

Note that 47001 is an add-on code that must be used in conjunction with the appropriate code for the primary procedure. This code cannot be reported alone.

47010 **Hepatotomy; for open drainage of abscess or cyst, one or two stages** C 80 ⬚
AMA: 1997, Nov, 18

⊙ 47011 **for percutaneous drainage of abscess or cyst, one or two stages** T 80 ⬚
AMA: 1998, Mar, 8; 1997, Nov, 18

To report radiological supervision and interpretation, consult CPT code 75989.

47015 **Laparotomy, with aspiration and/or injection of hepatic parasitic (eg, amoebic or echinococcal) cyst(s) or abscess(es)** C 80 ⬚

EXCISION

47100 **Biopsy of liver, wedge** C 80 ⬚

47120 **Hepatectomy, resection of liver; partial lobectomy** C 80 ⬚
AMA: 1998, May, 10

47122 **trisegmentectomy** C 80 ⬚

47125 **total left lobectomy** C 80 ⬚

47130 **total right lobectomy** C 80 ⬚

LIVER TRANSPLANTATION

Liver transplantation involves three different components:

- Cadaver or living donor hepatectomy which consists of harvesting and cold preparation of the graft prior to transplantation and care of the donor, in the case of living donor hepatectomy, (see 47133, 47140-47142).

- Backbench work consists of preparation of donor liver prior to transplantation. This includes preparation of whole liver graft including dissection and removal of surrounding tissue and soft tissue, preparation of the vena cava, portal vein, hepatic artery and common bile duct. Also included is preparation of the whole liver with splitting of the liver for partial grafts. Additional reconstruction of the liver graft including venous and arterial anastomosis(es) may also be performed. (See 47143-47147).

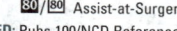

Digestive System

• Recipient transplantation which includes transplanting the liver into the patient and care of the recipient (see 47135-47136).

47133   **Donor hepatectomy (including cold preservation), from cadaver donor** C

47135   **Liver allotransplantation; orthotopic, partial or whole, from cadaver or living donor, any age**   C 80
MED: 100-2, 15, 50.5; 100-2, 15, 60.3; 100-3, 260.1; 100-3, 260.2; 100-4, 8, 120.1

47136   **heterotopic, partial or whole, from cadaver or living donor, any age**   C 80

MED: 100-2, 15, 50.5; 100-2, 15, 60.3; 100-3, 260.1; 100-3, 260.2; 100-4, 8, 120.1

47140   **Donor hepatectomy (including cold preservation), from living donor; left lateral segment only (segments II and III)**   C 80

47141   **total left lobectomy (segments II, III and IV)**   C 80

47142   **total right lobectomy (segments V, VI, VII and VIII)**   C 80

47143   **Backbench standard preparation of cadaver donor whole liver graft prior to allotransplantation, including cholecystectomy, if necessary, and dissection and removal of surrounding soft tissues to prepare the vena cava, portal vein, hepatic artery, and common bile duct for implantation; without trisegment or lobe split**   C 80

47144   **with trisegment split of whole liver graft into two partial liver grafts (ie, left lateral segment (segments II and III) and right trisegment (segments I and IV through VIII))**   C 80

47145   **with lobe split of whole liver graft into two partial liver grafts (ie, left lobe (segments II, III, and IV) and right lobe (segments I and V through VIII))**   C 80

⊘   **47146**   **Backbench reconstruction of cadaver or living donor liver graft prior to allotransplantation; venous anastomosis, each**   C 80

⊘   **47147**   **arterial anastomosis, each**   C 80

Codes 47143-47147 cannot be reported with CPT codes 47120-47125, 47600, 47610.

REPAIR

47300   **Marsupialization of cyst or abscess of liver**   C 80

47350   **Management of liver hemorrhage; simple suture of liver wound or injury**   C 80

47360   **complex suture of liver wound or injury, with or without hepatic artery ligation**   C 80

47361   **exploration of hepatic wound, extensive debridement, coagulation and/or suture, with or without packing of liver**   C 80

47362   **re-exploration of hepatic wound for removal of packing**   C 80

LAPAROSCOPY

Diagnostic laparoscopy is included in surgical laparoscopy. To report only a diagnostic laparoscopy, consult CPT code 49320.

47370   **Laparoscopy, surgical, ablation of one or more liver tumor(s); radiofrequency**   T 80
AMA: 2002, Oct, 1

To report imaging guidance, consult CPT code 76940.

47371   **cryosurgical**   T 80

47133 — 47371

Digestive System

47379 — 47505

47379	Unlisted laparoscopic procedure, liver	T 80

OTHER PROCEDURES

47380	**Ablation, open, of one or more liver tumor(s); radiofrequency** AMA: 2002, Oct, 1	C 80 ↵

To report imaging guidance, consult CPT code 76940.

47381	**cryosurgical**	C 80 ↵
47382	**Ablation, one or more liver tumor(s), percutaneous, radiofrequency** AMA: 2002, Oct, 1	T 80 ↵

To report imaging guidance and monitoring, consult CPT codes 76362, 76394, or 76940.

47399	Unlisted procedure, liver	T 80

BILIARY TRACT

INCISION

47400	**Hepaticotomy or hepaticostomy with exploration, drainage, or removal of calculus**	C 80 ↵
47420	**Choledochotomy or choledochostomy with exploration, drainage, or removal of calculus, with or without cholecystotomy; without transduodenal sphincterotomy or sphincteroplasty**	C 80 ↵
47425	**with transduodenal sphincterotomy or sphincteroplasty**	C 80 ↵
47460	**Transduodenal sphincterotomy or sphincteroplasty, with or without transduodenal extraction of calculus (separate procedure)**	C 80 ↵
47480	**Cholecystotomy or cholecystostomy with exploration, drainage, or removal of calculus (separate procedure)**	C 80 ↵
47490	**Percutaneous cholecystostomy**	T ↵

To report radiological supervision and interpretation, consult CPT code 75989.

INTRODUCTION

47500	**Injection procedure for percutaneous transhepatic cholangiography**	N ↵

To report radiological supervision and interpretation, consult CPT code 74320.

47505	**Injection procedure for cholangiography through an existing catheter (eg, percutaneous transhepatic or T-tube)**	N 80 ↵

To report radiological supervision and interpretation, consult CPT code 74305.

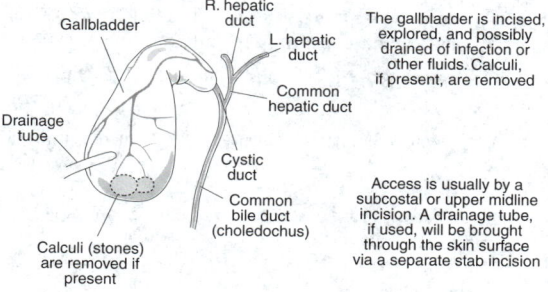

The gallbladder is incised, explored, and possibly drained of infection or other fluids. Calculi, if present, are removed

Access is usually by a subcostal or upper midline incision. A drainage tube, if used, will be brought through the skin surface via a separate stab incision

Gallbladder · R. hepatic duct · L. hepatic duct · Common hepatic duct · Drainage tube · Cystic duct · Common bile duct (choledochus) · Calculi (stones) are removed if present

---

47510 **Introduction of percutaneous transhepatic catheter for biliary drainage** ☐T☐
MED: 100-2, 15, 260; 100-4, 12, 90.3; 100-4, 14, 10

To report radiological supervision and interpretation, consult CPT code 75980.

47511 **Introduction of percutaneous transhepatic stent for internal and external biliary drainage** ☐T 50☐
MED: 100-2, 15, 260; 100-4, 12, 90.3; 100-4, 14, 10

To report radiological supervision and interpretation, consult CPT code 75982.

47525 **Change of percutaneous biliary drainage catheter** ☐T 50☐
MED: 100-2, 15, 260; 100-4, 12, 90.3; 100-4, 14, 10

To report radiological supervision and interpretation, consult CPT code 75984.

47530 **Revision and/or reinsertion of transhepatic tube** ☐T☐
MED: 100-2, 15, 260; 100-4, 12, 90.3; 100-4, 14, 10

To report radiological supervision and interpretation, consult CPT code 75984.

ENDOSCOPY

Diagnostic endoscopy is always included in surgical endoscopy.

+ **47550** **Biliary endoscopy, intraoperative (choledochoscopy) (List separately in addition to code for primary procedure)** C 80
MED: 100-3, 100.2

Note that 47550 is an add-on code that must be used in conjunction with the appropriate code for the primary procedure. This code cannot be reported alone.

47552 **Biliary endoscopy, percutaneous via T-tube or other tract; diagnostic, with or without collection of specimen(s) by brushing and/or washing (separate procedure)** ☐T☐
MED: 100-2, 15, 260; 100-3, 100.2; 100-4, 12, 90.3; 100-4, 14, 10

47553 **with biopsy, single or multiple** ☐T☐
MED: 100-2, 15, 260; 100-3, 100.2; 100-4, 12, 90.3; 100-4, 14, 10

47554 **with removal of calculus/calculi** ☐T☐
MED: 100-2, 15, 260; 100-3, 100.2; 100-4, 12, 90.3; 100-4, 14, 10

47555 **with dilation of biliary duct stricture(s) without stent** ☐T☐
MED: 100-2, 15, 260; 100-3, 100.2; 100-4, 12, 90.3; 100-4, 14, 10

If imaging guidance is provided, consult CPT codes 74363, 75982.

If an endoscopic retrograde cholangiopancreatography (ERCP) is performed, consult CPT codes 43260-43272 and 74363.

47556 **with dilation of biliary duct stricture(s) with stent** ☐T☐
MED: 100-2, 15, 260; 100-3, 100.2; 100-4, 12, 90.3; 100-4, 14, 10

If imaging guidance is provided, consult CPT codes 74363, 75982.

LAPAROSCOPY

Diagnostic laparoscopy is always included in surgical laparoscopy. To report only a diagnostic laparoscopy, consult CPT code 49320.

47560 **Laparoscopy, surgical; with guided transhepatic cholangiography, without biopsy** ☐T 80☐
MED: 100-2, 15, 260; 100-4, 12, 90.3; 100-4, 14, 10

AMA: 2000, Mar, 5; 1999, Nov, 23

Digestive System

47561 — 47620

47561   **with guided transhepatic cholangiography with biopsy**   3 T 80 ⟳
MED: 100-2, 15, 260; 100-3, 100.13; 100-4, 12, 90.3; 100-4, 14, 10
AMA: 2000, Mar, 5; 1999, Nov, 23

47562   **cholecystectomy**   T 80 ⟳
MED: 100-3, 100.13
AMA: 2000, Mar, 5; 1999, Nov, 23

47563   **cholecystectomy with cholangiography**   T 80 ⟳
MED: 100-3, 100.13
AMA: 2000, Mar, 5; 2000, Dec, 14; 1999, Nov, 23

47564   **cholecystectomy with exploration of common duct**   T 80 ⟳
MED: 100-3, 100.13
AMA: 2000, Mar, 5; 1999, Nov, 23

47570   **cholecystoenterostomy**   C 80 ⟳
AMA: 2000, Mar, 5; 1999, Nov, 23

47579   **Unlisted laparoscopy procedure, biliary tract**   T 50 80
AMA: 2000, Mar, 5; 1999, Nov, 23

EXCISION

47600   **Cholecystectomy;**   C 80 ⟳
AMA: 1999, Nov, 24

To report laparoscopic approach, consult CPT codes 47562-47564.

47605   **with cholangiography**   C 80 ⟳
AMA: 2002, Apr, 19; 1999, Nov, 24

47610   **Cholecystectomy with exploration of common duct;**   C 80 ⟳
AMA: 2002, Apr, 19

47612   **with choledochoenterostomy**   C 80 ⟳

47620   **with transduodenal sphincterotomy or sphincteroplasty, with or
without cholangiography**   C 80 ⟳

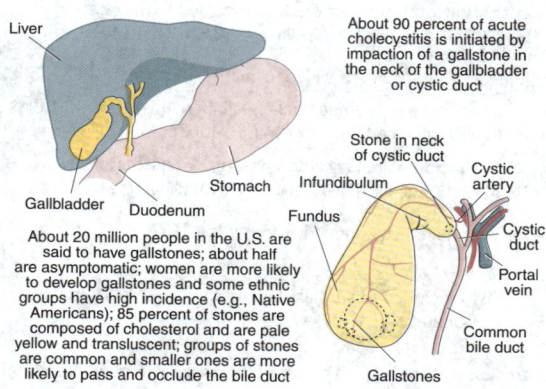

Liver

Gallbladder   Duodenum   Stomach

About 90 percent of acute cholecystitis is initiated by impaction of a gallstone in the neck of the gallbladder or cystic duct

Stone in neck of cystic duct
Infundibulum
Fundus
Cystic artery
Cystic duct
Portal vein
Common bile duct
Gallstones

About 20 million people in the U.S. are said to have gallstones; about half are asymptomatic; women are more likely to develop gallstones and some ethnic groups have high incidence (e.g., Native Americans); 85 percent of stones are composed of cholesterol and are pale yellow and transluscent; groups of stones are common and smaller ones are more likely to pass and occlude the bile duct

47630	**Biliary duct stone extraction, percutaneous via T-tube tract, basket or snare (eg, Burhenne technique)**	3 T 🗒

MED: 100-2, 15, 260; 100-4, 12, 90.3; 100-4, 14, 10

AMA: 1998, Jun, 10

To report radiological supervision and interpretation, consult CPT code 74327.

47700	**Exploration for congenital atresia of bile ducts, without repair, with or without liver biopsy, with or without cholangiography**	C 80 🗒 ⑱
47701	**Portoenterostomy (eg, Kasai procedure)**	C 80 🗒 ⑱
47711	**Excision of bile duct tumor, with or without primary repair of bile duct; extrahepatic**	C 80 🗒
47712	**intrahepatic**	C 80 🗒

If anastomosis is performed, consult CPT codes 47760-47800.

47715	**Excision of choledochal cyst**	C 80 🗒
47716	**Anastomosis, choledochal cyst, without excision**	C 80 🗒

REPAIR

47720	**Cholecystoenterostomy; direct**	C 80 🗒

AMA: 1999, Nov, 24

If a laparoscopic approach is used, consult CPT code 47570.

47721	**with gastroenterostomy**	C 80 🗒
47740	**Roux-en-Y**	C 80 🗒
47741	**Roux-en-Y with gastroenterostomy**	C 80 🗒
47760	**Anastomosis, of extrahepatic biliary ducts and gastrointestinal tract**	C 80 🗒
47765	**Anastomosis, of intrahepatic ducts and gastrointestinal tract** Longmire anastomosis	C 80 🗒
47780	**Anastomosis, Roux-en-Y, of extrahepatic biliary ducts and gastrointestinal tract**	C 80 🗒
47785	**Anastomosis, Roux-en-Y, of intrahepatic biliary ducts and gastrointestinal tract**	C 80 🗒
47800	**Reconstruction, plastic, of extrahepatic biliary ducts with end-to-end anastomosis**	C 80 🗒
47801	**Placement of choledochal stent**	C 80 🗒
47802	**U-tube hepaticoenterostomy**	C 80 🗒
47900	**Suture of extrahepatic biliary duct for pre-existing injury (separate procedure)**	C 80 🗒

OTHER PROCEDURES

47999	**Unlisted procedure, biliary tract**	T 80

PANCREAS

If peroral pancreatic endoscopic procedures are performed, consult CPT codes 43260-43272.

INCISION

48000	**Placement of drains, peripancreatic, for acute pancreatitis;**	C 80 🗒
48001	**with cholecystostomy, gastrostomy, and jejunostomy**	C 80 🗒
48005	**Resection or debridement of pancreas and peripancreatic tissue for acute necrotizing pancreatitis**	C 80 🗒

Digestive System

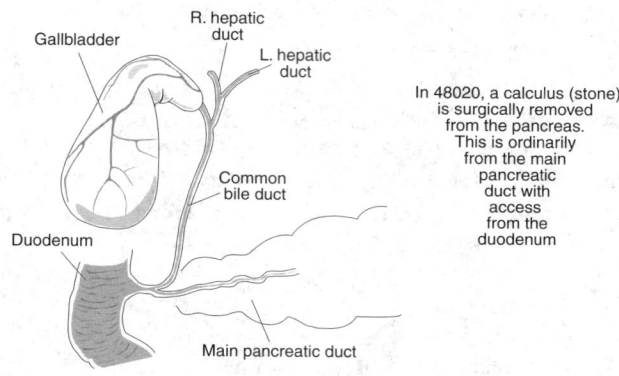

In 48020, a calculus (stone) is surgically removed from the pancreas. This is ordinarily from the main pancreatic duct with access from the duodenum

48020 — 48150

| | **48020** | **Removal of pancreatic calculus** | C 80 ⟲ |

EXCISION

| | **48100** | **Biopsy of pancreas, open (eg, fine needle aspiration, needle core biopsy, wedge biopsy)** | C 80 ⟲ |
| | **48102** | **Biopsy of pancreas, percutaneous needle**
MED: 100-2, 15, 260; 100-4, 12, 90.3; 100-4, 14, 10 | 1 T ⟲ |

To report radiological supervision and interpretation, consult CPT codes 76003, 76360, 76393, and 76942.

To report fine needle aspiration, consult CPT code 10022.

To report evaluation of fine needle aspirate, consult CPT codes 88172, 88173.

	48120	**Excision of lesion of pancreas (eg, cyst, adenoma)**	C 80 ⟲
	48140	**Pancreatectomy, distal subtotal, with or without splenectomy; without pancreaticojejunostomy**	C 80 ⟲
	48145	**with pancreaticojejunostomy**	C 80 ⟲
	48146	**Pancreatectomy, distal, near-total with preservation of duodenum (Child-type procedure)**	C 80 ⟲
	48148	**Excision of ampulla of Vater**	C 80 ⟲
	48150	**Pancreatectomy, proximal subtotal with total duodenectomy, partial gastrectomy, choledochoenterostomy and gastrojejunostomy (Whipple-type procedure); with pancreatojejunostomy**	C 80 ⟲

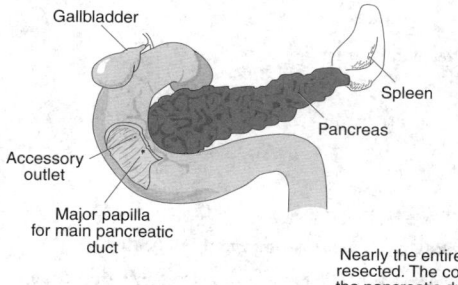

Nearly the entire pancreas is resected. The complex where the pancreatic ducts enter the duodenum is preserved (48146)

48152	without pancreatojejunostomy	C 80
48153	Pancreatectomy, proximal subtotal with near-total duodenectomy, choledochoenterostomy and duodenojejunostomy (pylorus-sparing, Whipple-type procedure); with pancreatojejunostomy	C 80
48154	without pancreatojejunostomy	C 80
48155	Pancreatectomy, total	C 80
48160	Pancreatectomy, total or subtotal, with autologous transplantation of pancreas or pancreatic islet cells	E
	MED: 100-3, 260.3	
48180	Pancreaticojejunostomy, side-to-side anastomosis (Puestow-type operation)	C 80

INTRODUCTION

+ 48400   Injection procedure for intraoperative pancreatography (List separately in addition to code for primary procedure)   C 80

> To report radiological supervision and interpretation, consult CPT codes 74300-74305.

> Note that 48400 is an add-on code that must be used in conjunction with the appropriate code To report the primary procedure. This code cannot be reported alone.

REPAIR

48500	Marsupialization of pancreatic cyst	C 80
48510	External drainage, pseudocyst of pancreas; open	C 80
	AMA: 1997, Nov, 18	
⊙ 48511	percutaneous	T 80
	AMA: 1998, Mar, 8; 1997, Nov, 18	

> To report radiological supervision and interpretation, consult CPT code 75989.

48520	Internal anastomosis of pancreatic cyst to gastrointestinal tract; direct	C 80
48540	Roux-en-Y	C 80
48545	Pancreatorrhaphy for injury	C 80
48547	Duodenal exclusion with gastrojejunostomy for pancreatic injury	C 80

PANCREAS TRANSPLANTATION

Pancreas transplantation involves three different components:

- Cadaver pancreatectomy which consists of harvesting and cold preparation of the graft prior to transplantation (see 48550).

- Backbench work consists of preparation of the donor pancreas prior to transplantation. This includes preparation of the pancreas by dissecting the soft tissues surrounding the pancreas, splenectomy, duodenotomy, ligation of the bile duct, ligation of the mesenteric vessels, and Y-graft arterial anastomoses from the iliac artery to the superior mesenteric artery and to the splenic artery. Venous anastomosis(es) may also be included in reconstruction of the donor pancreas. (See codes 48551 and 48552).

- Recipient transplantation which includes transplanting the pancreas into the patient (see 48554).

| CCI Comp | 50 Bilateral Procedure | + CPT Add-on Code | ⊘ Modifier -51 Exempt | ♂ Male | ♀ Female |
| ● New Code | ▲ Revised Code | M Maternity Edit | A Age Edit | A–Y APC Status Ind. | AMA: CPT Assistant |

© 2005 Ingenix, Inc. *(Blue Ink)*   CPT only © 2005 American Medical Association. All Rights Reserved. *(Black Ink)*   Surgery — 349

Digestive System

48550 — 49060

| | 48550 | Donor pancreatectomy (including cold preservation), with or without duodenal segment for transplantation 　E 🔼 |
| | | MED: 100-3, 260.3 |

48551　Backbench standard preparation of cadaver donor pancreas allograft prior to transplantation, including dissection of allograft from surrounding soft tissues, splenectomy, duodenotomy, ligation of bile duct, ligation of mesenteric vessels, and Y-graft arterial anastomoses from iliac artery to superior mesenteric artery and to splenic artery　C 80 🔼

⊘　48552　Backbench reconstruction of cadaver donor pancreas allograft prior to transplantation, venous anastomosis, each　C 80 🔼

> Codes 48551 and 48552 cannot be reported with CPT codes 35531, 35563, 35685, 38100-38102, 44010, 44820, 44850, 47460, 47505-47525, 47550-47556, 48100-48120, 48545.

48554　Transplantation of pancreatic allograft　E 80 🔼
　　　　MED: 100-3, 260.3

48556　Removal of transplanted pancreatic allograft　C 80 🔼
　　　　MED: 100-3, 260.3

OTHER PROCEDURES

48999　Unlisted procedure, pancreas　T 80

ABDOMEN, PERITONEUM, AND OMENTUM

INCISION

49000　Exploratory laparotomy, exploratory celiotomy with or without biopsy(s) (separate procedure)　C 80 🔼
　　　　AMA: 2001, Mar, 10

> If wound exploration due to a penetrating trauma without laparotomy is performed, consult CPT code 20102.

49002　Reopening of recent laparotomy　C 80 🔼

> If re-exploration is performed of a hepatic wound for removal of packing, consult CPT code 47362.

49010　Exploration, retroperitoneal area with or without biopsy(s) (separate procedure)　C 80 🔼

> If wound exploration is performed due to a penetrating trauma without a laparotomy, consult CPT code 20102.

49020　Drainage of peritoneal abscess or localized peritonitis, exclusive of appendiceal abscess; open　C 80 🔼

> If an appendiceal abscess is incised and drained, consult CPT code 44900.

⊙　49021　　percutaneous　T 🔼

> To report radiological supervision and interpretation, consult CPT code 75989.

49040　Drainage of subdiaphragmatic or subphrenic abscess; open　C 80 🔼
　　　　AMA: 1997, Nov, 18

⊙　49041　　percutaneous　T 80 🔼
　　　　AMA: 1998, Mar, 8; 1997, Nov, 18

> To report radiological supervision and interpretation, consult CPT code 75989.

49060　Drainage of retroperitoneal abscess; open　C 🔼
　　　　AMA: 2001, Jul, 11; 2001, Aug, 10; 1999, Nov, 24; 1997, Nov, 18

⊙ **49061**   **percutaneous**   T 80 ⌷
AMA: 2001, Jul, 11; 2001, Aug, 10; 1999, Nov, 24; 1998, Mar, 8; 1997, Nov, 18

If laparoscopic drainage is performed, consult CPT code 49323.

For radiological supervision and interpretation, consult CPT code 75989.

49062   **Drainage of extraperitoneal lymphocele to peritoneal cavity, open** C 80 ⌷
AMA: 2001, Jul, 11; 2001, Aug, 10; 1997, Nov, 19

49080   **Peritoneocentesis, abdominal paracentesis, or peritoneal lavage (diagnostic or therapeutic); initial** 2 T ⌷
MED: 100-2, 15, 260; 100-4, 12, 90.3; 100-4, 14, 10

49081   **subsequent** 2 T ⌷
MED: 100-2, 15, 260; 100-4, 12, 90.3; 100-4, 14, 10

To report imaging guidance, consult CPT codes 76360, 76942.

49085   **Removal of peritoneal foreign body from peritoneal cavity** 2 T ⌷
MED: 100-2, 15, 260; 100-4, 12, 90.3; 100-4, 14, 10

If lysis is performed on intestinal adhesions, consult CPT code 44005.

EXCISION, DESTRUCTION

49180   **Biopsy, abdominal or retroperitoneal mass, percutaneous needle** 1 T ⌷
MED: 100-2, 15, 260; 100-4, 12, 90.3; 100-4, 14, 10

AMA: 1993, Fall, 11

To report imaging guidance, consult CPT codes 76003, 76360, 76393, 76942.

To report fine needle aspiration, consult CPT code 10021 or 10022.

To report evaluation of fine needle aspirate, consult CPT codes 88172, 88173.

49200   **Excision or destruction, open, intra-abdominal or retroperitoneal tumors or cysts or endometriomas;** T 80 ⌷

49201   **extensive** C 80 ⌷

If open cryoablation of a renal tumor is performed, consult CPT code 50250.

If percutaneous cryotherapy ablation of renal tumors is performed, consult Category III code 0135T.

49215   **Excision of presacral or sacrococcygeal tumor** C 80 ⌷ ⊖

49220   **Staging laparotomy for Hodgkins disease or lymphoma (includes splenectomy, needle or open biopsies of both liver lobes, possibly also removal of abdominal nodes, abdominal node and/or bone marrow biopsies, ovarian repositioning)** C 80 ⌷
MED: 100-1, 5, 90.2; 100-2, 15, 80; 100-2, 15, 80.1; 100-4, 16, 10; 100-4, 16, 10.1; 100-4, 16, 110.4

49250   **Umbilectomy, omphalectomy, excision of umbilicus (separate procedure)** 4 T ⌷
MED: 100-2, 15, 260; 100-4, 12, 90.3; 100-4, 14, 10

49255   **Omentectomy, epiploectomy, resection of omentum (separate procedure)** C 80 ⌷
AMA: 1999, Nov, 24

Digestive System

49320 — 49423

LAPAROSCOPY

Surgical laparoscopy always includes diagnostic laparoscopy. To report only a diagnostic laparoscopy (peritoneoscopy), consult CPT code 49320. To report laparoscopic fulguration or excision of lesions of the ovary, pelvic viscera or peritoneal surface, consult CPT code 58662.

49320 **Laparoscopy, abdomen, peritoneum, and omentum, diagnostic, with or without collection of specimen(s) by brushing or washing (separate procedure)** ③ T 80 ☞
MED: 100-2, 15, 260; 100-4, 12, 90.3; 100-4, 14, 10

AMA: 2000, Mar, 5; 1999, Nov, 24

49321 **Laparoscopy, surgical; with biopsy (single or multiple)** ④ T 80 ☞
MED: 100-2, 15, 260; 100-4, 12, 90.3; 100-4, 14, 10

AMA: 2000, Mar, 5; 1999, Nov, 24

49322 **with aspiration of cavity or cyst (eg, ovarian cyst) (single or multiple)** ④ T 80 ☞
MED: 100-2, 15, 260; 100-4, 12, 90.3; 100-4, 14, 10

AMA: 2000, Mar, 5; 1999, Nov, 24

49323 **with drainage of lymphocele to peritoneal cavity** T 80 ☞
AMA: 2001, Jul, 11; 2001, Aug, 10; 2000, May, 4; 2000, Mar, 5; 1999, Nov, 24

If percutaneous or open drainage is performed, consult CPT codes 49060 and 49061.

49329 **Unlisted laparoscopy procedure, abdomen, peritoneum and omentum** T 50 80
AMA: 2000, Mar, 5; 1999, Nov, 24

INTRODUCTION, REVISION, AND/OR REMOVAL

49400 **Injection of air or contrast into peritoneal cavity (separate procedure)** N ☞
To report radiological supervision and interpretation, consult CPT code 74190.

49419 **Insertion of intraperitoneal cannula or catheter, with subcutaneous reservoir, permanent (ie, totally implantable)** ① T ☞
To report removal, consult CPT code 49422.

49420 **Insertion of intraperitoneal cannula or catheter for drainage or dialysis; temporary** ① T ☞
MED: 100-2, 15, 260; 100-4, 12, 90.3; 100-4, 14, 10

AMA: 1993, Fall, 2

49421 **permanent** ① T ☞
MED: 100-2, 15, 260; 100-4, 12, 90.3; 100-4, 14, 10

AMA: 1993, Fall, 2

49422 **Removal of permanent intraperitoneal cannula or catheter** ① T ☞
MED: 100-2, 15, 260; 100-4, 12, 90.3; 100-4, 14, 10

If a temporary catheter/cannula is removed, use the appropriate E/M code.

49423 **Exchange of previously placed abscess or cyst drainage catheter under radiological guidance (separate procedure)** T 80 ☞
AMA: 1998, Mar, 8; 1997, Nov, 19

To report radiological supervision and interpretation, consult CPT code 75984.

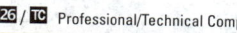 

49424   **Contrast injection for assessment of abscess or cyst via previously placed drainage catheter or tube (separate procedure)**   N 80 🔳

AMA: 1998, Mar, 8; 1997, Nov, 19

To report radiological supervision and interpretation, consult CPT code 76080.

49425   **Insertion of peritoneal-venous shunt**   C 80 🔳

49426   **Revision of peritoneal-venous shunt**   2 T 🔳

MED: 100-2, 15, 260; 100-4, 12, 90.3; 100-4, 14, 10

If a shunt patency test is performed, consult CPT code 78291.

49427   **Injection procedure (eg, contrast media) for evaluation of previously placed peritoneal-venous shunt**   N 80 🔳

To report radiological supervision and interpretation, consult CPT code 75809, 78291.

49428   **Ligation of peritoneal-venous shunt**   C 🔳

49429   **Removal of peritoneal-venous shunt**   T 🔳

REPAIR — HERNIOPLASTY, HERNIORRHAPHY, HERNIOTOMY

Hernia repair codes are categorized primarily by type of hernia (inguinal, femoral, incisional/ventral, epigastric, umbilical, spigelian). Some hernias are further categorized based on whether there has been a previous hernia repair (initial, or recurrent). Additional variables include patient age and clinical presentation (reducible, strangulated/incarcerated).

Implantation of mesh or prosthesis may be performed with hernia repairs. However, the implantation should only be reported separately when used for repair of incisional and ventral hernias (49560–49566). When used for repair of other types of hernias, it is not considered a separately reportable procedure. For laparoscopic repair of inguinal and other hernias, see codes 49650–49659.

Repair of strangulated organs or structures should be reported in addition to the hernia repair. Structures most often involved include intestine (44120), testicles (54520), and ovaries (58940).

49491   **Repair, initial inguinal hernia, preterm infant (less than 37 weeks gestation at birth), performed from birth up to 50 weeks postconception age, with or without hydrocelectomy; reducible**   A T 50 80 🔳 63

49492   **incarcerated or strangulated**   A T 50 80 🔳 63

Postconception age equals gestational age at birth plus age of infant in weeks at the time of the repair. To report initial inguinal hernia repairs that are performed on preterm infants who are over 50 weeks postconception age and under age 6 months at the time of surgery, consult CPT codes 49495, 49496.

49495   **Repair, initial inguinal hernia, full term infant under age 6 months, or preterm infant over 50 weeks postconception age and under age 6 months at the time of surgery, with or without hydrocelectomy; reducible**   A 4 T 50 80 🔳 63

MED: 100-2, 15, 260; 100-4, 12, 90.3; 100-4, 14, 10

AMA: 1994, Winter, 13; 1993, Winter, 6

Halsted repair

49496   **incarcerated or strangulated**   A 4 T 50 80 🔳 63

MED: 100-2, 15, 260; 100-4, 12, 90.3; 100-4, 14, 10

AMA: 1994, Winter, 13; 1993, Winter, 6

Postconception age equals gestational age at birth plus age in weeks at the time of ther hernia repair. To report initial inguinal hernia repairs that are performed on preterm infants who are under or up to 50 weeks postconception age but under 6 months of age since birth, should be consult CPT codes 49491, 49492. For inguinal hernia repairs on infants age 6 months to under 5 years consult CPT codes 49500-49501.

Digestive System

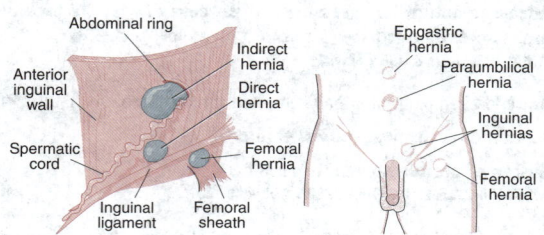

A hernia is a protrusion, usually through an abdominal wall containment. Often, hernias are congenital. Groin hernias are most common among both sexes and all age groups. In males, indirect hernias are often associated with incomplete closure of the path the testicle takes as it descends just prior to birth (the processus vaginalis). Direct hernias simply protrude through the wall. Femoral hernias occur below the inguinal ligament. Strangulation and necrosis of the protruding bowel section can occur. Umbilical hernias are often linked to incomplete closure of the umbilicus

49500 — 49550

49500   **Repair initial inguinal hernia, age 6 months to under 5 years, with or without hydrocelectomy; reducible**   A 4 T 50 80 ⬚
MED: 100-2, 15, 260; 100-4, 12, 90.3; 100-4, 14, 10

AMA: 1994, Winter, 13

49501   **incarcerated or strangulated**   A 9 T 50 80 ⬚
MED: 100-2, 15, 260; 100-4, 12, 90.3; 100-4, 14, 10

AMA: 1994, Winter, 13

49505   **Repair initial inguinal hernia, age 5 years or over; reducible**   4 T 50 80 ⬚
MED: 100-2, 15, 260; 100-4, 12, 90.3; 100-4, 14, 10

AMA: 2000, Sep, 10; 1994, Winter, 13

MacEwen hernia repair

49507   **incarcerated or strangulated**   A 9 T 50 80 ⬚
MED: 100-2, 15, 260; 100-4, 12, 90.3; 100-4, 14, 10

AMA: 1994, Winter, 13

49520   **Repair recurrent inguinal hernia, any age; reducible**   7 T 50 80 ⬚
MED: 100-2, 15, 260; 100-4, 12, 90.3; 100-4, 14, 10

AMA: 1994, Winter, 13

49521   **incarcerated or strangulated**   9 T 50 80 ⬚
MED: 100-2, 15, 260; 100-4, 12, 90.3; 100-4, 14, 10

AMA: 1994, Winter, 13

49525   **Repair inguinal hernia, sliding, any age**   4 T 50 80 ⬚
MED: 100-2, 15, 260; 100-4, 12, 90.3; 100-4, 14, 10

AMA: 1994, Winter, 14

49540   **Repair lumbar hernia**   2 T 50 80 ⬚
MED: 100-2, 15, 260; 100-4, 12, 90.3; 100-4, 14, 10

AMA: 1994, Winter, 14

49550   **Repair initial femoral hernia, any age, reducible;**   5 T 50 80 ⬚
MED: 100-2, 15, 260; 100-4, 12, 90.3; 100-4, 14, 10

AMA: 1994, Winter, 14

49553   incarcerated or strangulated   9 T 50 80 ⏎
MED: 100-2, 15, 260; 100-4, 12, 90.3; 100-4, 14, 10

AMA: 1994, Winter, 14

49555   Repair recurrent femoral hernia; reducible   5 T 50 80 ⏎
MED: 100-2, 15, 260; 100-4, 12, 90.3; 100-4, 14, 10

AMA: 1994, Winter, 14

49557   incarcerated or strangulated   9 T 50 80 ⏎
MED: 100-2, 15, 260; 100-4, 12, 90.3; 100-4, 14, 10

AMA: 1994, Winter, 14

49560   Repair initial incisional or ventral hernia; reducible   4 T 50 80 ⏎
MED: 100-2, 15, 260; 100-4, 12, 90.3; 100-4, 14, 10

AMA: 1997, Nov, 19; 1994, Winter, 14; 1993, Winter, 6

49561   incarcerated or strangulated   9 T 50 80 ⏎
MED: 100-2, 15, 260; 100-4, 12, 90.3; 100-4, 14, 10

AMA: 1994, Winter, 14

49565   Repair recurrent incisional or ventral hernia; reducible   4 T 50 80 ⏎
MED: 100-2, 15, 260; 100-4, 12, 90.3; 100-4, 14, 10

AMA: 1997, Nov, 19; 1994, Winter, 14

49566   incarcerated or strangulated   9 T 50 80 ⏎
MED: 100-2, 15, 260; 100-4, 12, 90.3; 100-4, 14, 10

AMA: 1994, Winter, 14

+   **49568**   Implantation of mesh or other prosthesis for incisional or ventral hernia repair (List separately in addition to code for the incisional or ventral hernia repair)   7 T ⏎
MED: 100-2, 15, 260; 100-4, 12, 90.3; 100-4, 14, 10

AMA: 2001, Sep, 11; 1997, Nov, 19; 1994, Winter, 14

Note that 49568 is an add-on code that must be used in conjunction with the code for the incisional or ventral hernia repair . This code cannot be reported alone.

49570   Repair epigastric hernia (eg, preperitoneal fat); reducible (separate procedure)   4 T 50 80 ⏎
MED: 100-2, 15, 260; 100-4, 12, 90.3; 100-4, 14, 10

AMA: 1994, Winter, 15

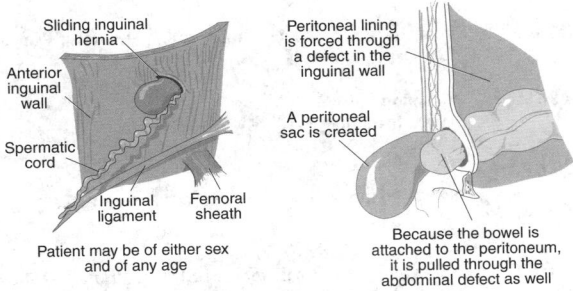

Sliding inguinal hernia

Anterior inguinal wall

Spermatic cord

Inguinal ligament

Femoral sheath

Patient may be of either sex and of any age

Peritoneal lining is forced through a defect in the inguinal wall

A peritoneal sac is created

Because the bowel is attached to the peritoneum, it is pulled through the abdominal defect as well

In 49525, a sliding inguinal hernia (depicted above, right) is repaired in a patient of any age

Digestive System

49572 — 49650

49572	incarcerated or strangulated	9 T 50 80 ↻
	MED: 100-2, 15, 260; 100-4, 12, 90.3; 100-4, 14, 10	
	AMA: 1994, Winter, 15	

49580	**Repair umbilical hernia, under age 5 years; reducible**	A 4 T 80 ↻
	MED: 100-2, 15, 260; 100-4, 12, 90.3; 100-4, 14, 10	
	AMA: 1994, Winter, 15	

49582	incarcerated or strangulated	A 9 T 80 ↻
	MED: 100-2, 15, 260; 100-4, 12, 90.3; 100-4, 14, 10	
	AMA: 1994, Winter, 15	

49585	**Repair umbilical hernia, age 5 years or over; reducible**	A 4 T 80 ↻
	MED: 100-2, 15, 260; 100-4, 12, 90.3; 100-4, 14, 10	
	AMA: 1994, Winter, 15	

Mayo hernia repair

49587	incarcerated or strangulated	A 9 T 80 ↻
	MED: 100-2, 15, 260; 100-4, 12, 90.3; 100-4, 14, 10	
	AMA: 1994, Winter, 15	

49590	**Repair spigelian hernia**	3 T 50 80 ↻
	MED: 100-2, 15, 260; 100-4, 12, 90.3; 100-4, 14, 10	
	AMA: 1994, Winter, 15	

49600	**Repair of small omphalocele, with primary closure**	4 T 80 ↻ 63
	MED: 100-2, 15, 260; 100-4, 12, 90.3; 100-4, 14, 10	
	AMA: 1994, Winter, 15	

If a diaphragmatic or hiatal hernia is repaired, consult CPT codes 39502-39541.

49605	**Repair of large omphalocele or gastroschisis; with or without prosthesis**	
	C 80 ↻ 63	
	AMA: 1994, Winter, 15	

If a diaphragmatic or hiatal hernia is repaired, consult CPT codes 39502-39541.

If an intra-abdominal hernia is reduced and repaired, consult CPT code 44050.

49606	**with removal of prosthesis, final reduction and closure, in operating room**	C 80 ↻ 63
	AMA: 1994, Winter, 15	

49610	**Repair of omphalocele (Gross type operation); first stage**	C 80 ↻ 63
	AMA: 1994, Winter, 15	

49611	**second stage**	C 80 ↻ 63
	AMA: 1994, Winter, 15	

LAPAROSCOPY

Surgical laparoscopy always includes diagnostic laparoscopy. To report only diagnostic laparoscopy, consult CPT code 49320.

49650	**Laparoscopy, surgical; repair initial inguinal hernia**	4 T 50 80 ↻
	MED: 100-2, 15, 260; 100-4, 12, 90.3; 100-4, 14, 10	
	AMA: 2000, Mar, 5; 1999, Nov, 24	

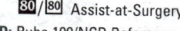

49651	**repair recurrent inguinal hernia**	7 T 50 80 ◪

MED: 100-2, 15, 260; 100-4, 12, 90.3; 100-4, 14, 10

AMA: 2000, Mar, 5; 1999, Nov, 24

49659   **Unlisted laparoscopy procedure, hernioplasty, herniorrhaphy, herniotomy**   T 50 80

AMA: 2001, Sep, 11; 2000, Mar, 5; 1999, Nov, 25

SUTURE

49900   **Suture, secondary, of abdominal wall for evisceration or dehiscence**   C 80 ◪

If a ruptured diaphragm is sutured, consult CPT codes 39540 and 39541. If debridement is performed on the abdominal wall, consult CPT codes 11042 and 11043.

OTHER PROCEDURES

49904   **Omental flap, extra-abdominal (eg, for reconstruction of sternal and chest wall defects)**   C ◪

Code 49904 includes both harvest and transplant. If a different surgeon harvests the flap, then both surgeons should report 49904 and append modifier 62.

+   **49905**   **Omental flap, intra-abdominal (List separately in addition to code for primary procedure)**   C 80 ◪

AMA: 2000, Nov, 11

Note that code 49905 should not be reported in conjunction with CPT code 47700.

Note that 48400 is an add-on code that must be used in conjunction with the appropriate code for the primary procedure. This code cannot be reported alone.

49906   **Free omental flap with microvascular anastomosis**   C ◪

AMA: 1998, Nov, 16; 1997, Apr, 8

Do not report 69990 in addition to 49906 as the operating microscope is considered an inclusive component of the surgery.

49999   **Unlisted procedure, abdomen, peritoneum and omentum**   T 80

Urinary System

50010 — 50070

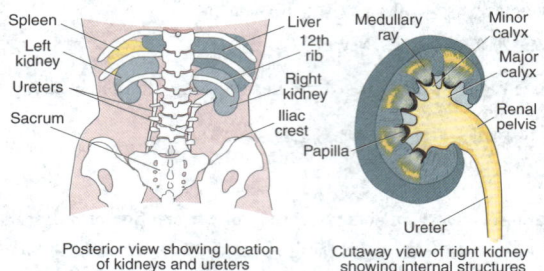

Posterior view showing location
of kidneys and ureters

Cutaway view of right kidney
showing internal structures

The kidneys remove waste products of protein metabolism and other excess materials and fluids from the blood. Variations in kidney anatomy are fairly common, though abnormalities can complicate procedures. "Pyelo" refers to the renal pelvis, an important access site to the inner kidney. Each kidney is imbedded in a mass of peritoneal fat that helps to enclose and position it

URINARY SYSTEM

KIDNEY

If retroperitoneal exploration is performed on an abscess, tumor, or cyst, consult CPT codes 49101, 49060, 49200, and 49201.

INCISION

50010 **Renal exploration, not necessitating other specific procedures** C 80 ↰

To report laparoscopic ablation of renal mass lesion(s), consult CPT code 50542.

50020 **Drainage of perirenal or renal abscess; open** T ↰
AMA: 2001, Oct, 8; 1997, Nov, 19

⊙ **50021** **percutaneous** T 80 ↰
AMA: 2001, Oct, 8; 1998, Mar, 8; 1997, Nov, 19

To report radiological supervision and interpretation, consult CPT code 75989.

50040 **Nephrostomy, nephrotomy with drainage** C ↰
AMA: 2001, Oct, 8

50045 **Nephrotomy, with exploration** C 80 ↰
AMA: 2001, Oct, 8

If renal endoscopy is performed in conjunction with this procedure, consult CPT codes 50570-50580.

50060 **Nephrolithotomy; removal of calculus** C 80 ↰
MED: 100-3, 130.5; 100-3, 130.6; 100-3, 160.2; 100-3, 230.1; 100-3, 250.1; 100-3, 250.4; 100-3, 270.4; 100-3, 40.50

AMA: 2001, Oct, 8

50065 **secondary surgical operation for calculus** C 80 ↰
MED: 100-3, 130.5; 100-3, 130.6; 100-3, 160.2; 100-3, 230.1; 100-3, 250.1; 100-3, 250.4; 100-3, 270.4; 100-3, 40.50

AMA: 2001, Oct, 8

50070 **complicated by congenital kidney abnormality** C 80 ↰
MED: 100-3, 130.5; 100-3, 130.6; 100-3, 160.2; 100-3, 230.1; 100-3, 250.1; 100-3, 250.4; 100-3, 270.4; 100-3, 40.50

AMA: 2001, Oct, 8

26 / TC Professional/Technical Component   **80 / 80** Assist-at-Surgery Allowed/With Documentation   ⊙ Conscious Sedation

Unlisted   Not Covered   **MED:** Pubs 100/NCD Reference   **1 - 9** ASC Group   63 Modifier 63 Exempt

358 — Surgery   CPT only © 2005 American Medical Association. All Rights Reserved. *(Black Ink)*   © 2005 Ingenix, Inc. *(Blue Ink)*

50075   removal of large staghorn calculus filling renal pelvis and calyces (including anatrophic pyelolithotomy)   C 80 ↴
MED: 100-3, 130.5; 100-3, 130.6; 100-3, 160.2; 100-3, 230.1; 100-3, 250.1; 100-3, 250.4; 100-3, 270.4; 100-3, 40.50

AMA: 2001, Oct, 8

50080   **Percutaneous nephrostolithotomy or pyelostolithotomy, with or without dilation, endoscopy, lithotripsy, stenting or basket extraction; up to 2 cm**   T 50 ↴
MED: 100-3, 100.2; 100-3, 130.5; 100-3, 130.6; 100-3, 160.2; 100-3, 230.1; 100-3, 250.1; 100-3, 250.4; 100-3, 270.4; 100-3, 40.50

AMA: 2001, Oct, 8

If nephrostomy is established without a nephrostolithotomy, consult CPT codes 50040, 50395, and 52334. If fluoroscopic guidance is used, consult CPT codes 76000 and 76001.

50081   **over 2 cm**   T 50 ↴
MED: 100-3, 130.5; 100-3, 130.6; 100-3, 160.2; 100-3, 230.1; 100-3, 250.1; 100-3, 250.4; 100-3, 270.4; 100-3, 40.50

AMA: 2001, Oct, 8

If nephrostomy is established without a nephrostolithotomy, consult CPT codes 50040, 50395, and 52334. If fluoroscopic guidance is used, consult CPT codes 76000 and 76001.

50100   **Transection or repositioning of aberrant renal vessels (separate procedure)**   C 80 ↴
AMA: 2001, Oct, 8

50120   **Pyelotomy; with exploration**   C 50 ↴
AMA: 2001, Oct, 8

If renal endoscopy is performed in conjunction with this procedure, consult CPT codes 50570-50580.
Gol-Vernet pyelotomy

50125   **with drainage, pyelostomy**   C 50 ↴
AMA: 2001, Oct, 8

If retroperitoneal exploration is performed on an abscess, tumor, or cyst, consult CPT codes 49101, 49060, 49200, and 49201.

50130   **with removal of calculus (pyelolithotomy, pelviolithotomy, including coagulum pyelolithotomy)**   C 50 ↴
MED: 100-3, 130.5; 100-3, 130.6; 100-3, 160.2; 100-3, 230.1; 100-3, 250.1; 100-3, 250.4; 100-3, 270.4; 100-3, 40.50

AMA: 2001, Oct, 8

50135   **complicated (eg, secondary operation, congenital kidney abnormality)**   C 50 ↴
AMA: 2001, Oct, 8

Report 99070 for supply of anticarcinogenic agents when used, in addition to primary procedure.

Urinary System

50200 — 50290

EXCISION

If a retroperitoneal tumor or cyst is excised, consult CPT codes 49200 and 49201.

To report laparoscopic ablation of renal mass lesion(s), consult CPT code 50542.

50200 **Renal biopsy; percutaneous, by trocar or needle** 🔳T 50 ↱
MED: 100-2, 15, 260; 100-3, 190.4; 100-4, 12, 90.3; 100-4, 14, 10

AMA: 2001, Oct, 8

To report radiological supervision and interpretation, consult CPT codes 76003, 76360, 76393, and 76942.

To report fine needle aspiration, consult CPT code 10022.

To report evaluation of fine needle aspirate, consult CPT codes 88172, 88173.

50205 **by surgical exposure of kidney** C 50 ↱
AMA: 2001, Oct, 8

50220 **Nephrectomy, including partial ureterectomy, any open approach including rib resection;** C 50 ↱
AMA: 2002, Nov, 1; 2001, Oct, 8

50225 **complicated because of previous surgery on same kidney** C 50 ↱
AMA: 2001, Oct, 8

50230 **radical, with regional lymphadenectomy and/or vena caval thrombectomy** C 50 ↱
AMA: 2001, Oct, 8

If vena caval resection with reconstruction is necessary, consult CPT code 37799.

50234 **Nephrectomy with total ureterectomy and bladder cuff; through same incision** C 80 ↱
AMA: 2001, Oct, 8

50236 **through separate incision** C 80 ↱
AMA: 2001, Oct, 8

50240 **Nephrectomy, partial** C 80 ↱
AMA: 2003, Jan, 19; 2002, Nov, 1; 2001, Oct, 8

To report laparoscopic partial nephrectomy, consult CPT code 50543.

● **50250** **Ablation, open, one or more renal mass lesion(s), cryosurgical, including intraoperative ultrasound, if performed**

To report laparoscopic ablation of renal mass lesions, consult CPT code 50542.

To report percutaneous cryotherapy ablation of renal tumors, consult CPT Category III code 0135T.

50280 **Excision or unroofing of cyst(s) of kidney** C 80 ↱
AMA: 2001, Oct, 8; 1999, Nov, 25

If laparoscopic ablation is performed on renal cysts, consult CPT code 50541.

50290 **Excision of perinephric cyst** C 80 ↱
AMA: 2001, Oct, 8

RENAL TRANSPLANTATION

Renal transplantation involves three different components:

- Cadaver or living donor nephrectomy which consists of harvesting and cold preparation of the graft prior to transplantation and care of the donor (see codes 50300, 50320, and 50547).

- Backbench work consists of preparation of the donor kidney prior to transplantation. This includes removal of perinephratic fat, diaphragmatic and retroperitoneal attachments, excision of adrenal gland; and preparation of ureter(s), renal vein(s), and renal artery(s), ligating branches as necessary. Other reconstruction procedures may involve venous, arterial, and/or ureteral anastomosis(es) necessary for the transplant (see codes 50323, 50325, 50327-50329).

- Recipient transplantation which includes transplanting the kidney into the patient (see 50360, 50365).

If dialysis is performed, consult CPT codes 90935-90999. If laparoscopic drainage of a lymphocele to peritoneal cavity is performed, consult CPT code 49323.

If a laparoscopic donor nephrectomy is performed, consult CPT code 50547.

50300   **Donor nephrectomy (including cold preservation); from cadaver donor, unilateral or bilateral**   C ⌐

     MED: 100-3, 110.16; 100-3, 190.1; 100-3, 20.3; 100-3, 230.12

     AMA: 1999, Nov, 25

50320   **open, from living donor**   C 50 80 ⌐

     AMA: 2000, May, 4; 1999, Nov, 25

50323   **Backbench standard preparation of cadaver donor renal allograft prior to transplantation, including dissection and removal of perinephric fat, diaphragmatic and retroperitoneal attachments, excision of adrenal gland, and preparation of ureter(s), renal vein(s), and renal artery(s), ligating branches, as necessary**   C 80 ⌐

     Code 50323 cannot be reported with CPT codes 60540, 60545.

50325   **Backbench standard preparation of living donor renal allograft (open or laparoscopic) prior to transplantation, including dissection and removal of perinephric fat and preparation of ureter(s), renal vein(s), and renal artery(s), ligating branches, as necessary**   C 80 ⌐

⊘ **50327**   **Backbench reconstruction of cadaver or living donor renal allograft prior to transplantation; venous anastomosis, each**   C 80 ⌐

⊘ **50328**   **arterial anastomosis, each**   C ⌐

⊘ **50329**   **ureteral anastomosis, each**   C ⌐

50340   **Recipient nephrectomy (separate procedure)**   C 50 80 ⌐

     MED: 100-3, 110.16; 100-3, 20.3; 100-4, 8, 120.1

50360   **Renal allotransplantation, implantation of graft; without recipient nephrectomy**   C 80 ⌐

     MED: 100-3, 190.1; 100-3, 260.3; 100-3, 260.7; 100-4, 8, 120.1

50365   **with recipient nephrectomy**   C 50 80 ⌐

     MED: 100-3, 260.3; 100-3, 260.7; 100-4, 8, 120.1

50370   **Removal of transplanted renal allograft**   C 80 ⌐

     MED: 100-3, 190.1; 100-3, 260.7

⌐ CCI Comp   50 Bilateral Procedure   + CPT Add-on Code   ⊘ Modifier -51 Exempt   ♂ Male   ♀ Female
● New Code   ▲ Revised Code   M Maternity Edit   A Age Edit   A—Y APC Status Ind.   AMA: CPT Assistant

© 2005 Ingenix, Inc. *(Blue Ink)*   CPT only © 2005 American Medical Association. All Rights Reserved. *(Black Ink)*   Surgery — 361

Urinary System

50380 — 50392

50380 **Renal autotransplantation, reimplantation of kidney** C 80 ▣
MED: 100-3, 110.16; 100-3, 20.3; 100-3, 260.7; 100-4, 8, 120.1

If renal autotransplantation extra-corporeal (bench) surgery is performed, report autotransplantation as the primary procedure and then add the secondary procedure (e.g., partial nephrectomy, nephrolithotomy) and append modifier 51.

INTRODUCTION

RENAL PELVIS CATHETER PROCEDURES—INTERNAL DWELLING

⊙ ● **50382** **Removal (via snare/capture) and replacement of internally dwelling ureteral stent via percutaneous approach, including radiological supervision and interpretation**

To report bilateral procedure, use modifier 50.

⊙ ● **50384** **Removal (via snare/capture) of internally dwelling ureteral stent via percutaneous approach, including radiological supervision and interpretation**

To report bilateral procedure, use modifier 50.

Codes 50382, 50384 cannot be reported with 50395.

RENAL PELVIS CATHETER PROCEDURES—EXTERNALLY ACCESSIBLE

⊙ ● **50387** **Removal and replacement of externally accessible transnephric ureteral stent (eg, external/internal stent) requiring fluoroscopic guidance, including radiological supervision and interpretation**

To report bilateral procedure, use modifier 50.

To report removal and replacement of an externally accessible ureteral stent via ureterostomy or ilieal conduit, consult CPT code 50688.

To report removal without replacement of an externally accessible ureteral stent not requiring fluoroscopic guidance, consult E/M services codes.

● **50389** **Removal of nephrostomy tube, requiring fluoroscopic guidance (eg, with concurrent indwelling ureteral stent)**

Removal of nephrostomy tube not requiring fluoroscopic guidance is included in the E/M services. Report the appropriate level of E/M service provided.

OTHER INTRODUCTION PROCEDURES

50390 **Aspiration and/or injection of renal cyst or pelvis by needle, percutaneous** 1 T 50 ▣
MED: 100-2, 15, 260; 100-4, 12, 90.3; 100-4, 14, 10

AMA: 2001, Oct, 8; 1997, Dec, 7; 1993, Fall, 14

To report radiological supervision and interpretation, consult CPT codes 74425, 74470, 76003, 76360, 76393, 76942.

To report evaluation of fine needle aspirate, consult CPT codes 88172, 88173.

50391 **Instillation(s) of therapeutic agent into renal pelvis and/or ureter through established nephrostomy, pyelostomy or ureterostomy tube (eg, anticarcinogenic or antifungal agent)** T ▣

50392 **Introduction of intracatheter or catheter into renal pelvis for drainage and/or injection, percutaneous** 1 T 50 ▣
MED: 100-2, 15, 260; 100-4, 12, 90.3; 100-4, 14, 10

AMA: 2001, Oct, 8; 1997, Dec, 7

To report radiological supervision and interpretation, consult CPT codes 74475, 76360, and 76942.

50393   **Introduction of ureteral catheter or stent into ureter through renal pelvis for drainage and/or injection, percutaneous** ① T 50 🔁
MED: 100-2, 15, 260; 100-4, 12, 90.3; 100-4, 14, 10

AMA: 2001, Oct, 8; 1993, Fall, 14

To report radiological supervision and interpretation, consult CPT codes 74480, 76003, 76360, and 76942.

50394   **Injection procedure for pyelography (as nephrostogram, pyelostogram, antegrade pyeloureterograms) through nephrostomy or pyelostomy tube, or indwelling ureteral catheter** N 50 🔁
AMA: 2001, Oct, 8; 1997, Dec, 7; 1993, Fall, 15

To report radiological supervision and interpretation, consult CPT code 74425.

50395   **Introduction of guide into renal pelvis and/or ureter with dilation to establish nephrostomy tract, percutaneous** ① T 50 🔁
MED: 100-2, 15, 260; 100-4, 12, 90.3; 100-4, 14, 10

AMA: 2001, Oct, 8

If a nephrostolithotomy is performed, consult CPT codes 50080 and 50081. If a retrograde percutaneous nephrostomy is performed, consult CPT code 52334. If endoscopic surgery is performed, consult CPT codes 50551-50561.

For radiolgical supervision and interpretation, consult CPT codes 74475, 74480, 74485.

50396   **Manometric studies through nephrostomy or pyelostomy tube, or indwelling ureteral catheter** ① T 50 80 🔁
MED: 100-2, 15, 260; 100-4, 12, 90.3; 100-4, 14, 10

AMA: 2001, Oct, 8; 1997, Dec, 7; 1993, Fall, 16

To report radiological supervision and interpretation, consult CPT codes 74425, 74475, and 74480.

50398   **Change of nephrostomy or pyelostomy tube** ① T 50 🔁
MED: 100-2, 15, 260; 100-4, 12, 90.3; 100-4, 14, 10

AMA: 2001, Oct, 8

If radiological supervision and interpretation is performed, consult CPT code 75984.

REPAIR

50400   **Pyeloplasty (Foley Y-pyeloplasty), plastic operation on renal pelvis, with or without plastic operation on ureter, nephropexy, nephrostomy, pyelostomy, or ureteral splinting; simple** C 80 🔁
AMA: 2001, Oct, 8; 2000, May, 4; 1999, Nov, 25

50405   **complicated (congenital kidney abnormality, secondary pyeloplasty, solitary kidney, calycoplasty)** C 80 🔁
AMA: 2001, Oct, 8; 2000, May, 4; 1999, Nov, 25

If a laparoscopic approach is used, consult CPT code 50544.

50500   **Nephrorrhaphy, suture of kidney wound or injury** C 80 🔁

50520   **Closure of nephrocutaneous or pyelocutaneous fistula** C 80 🔁

50525   **Closure of nephrovisceral fistula (eg, renocolic), including visceral repair; abdominal approach** C 80 🔁

50526   **thoracic approach** C 80 🔁

50540   **Symphysiotomy for horseshoe kidney with or without pyeloplasty and/or other plastic procedure, unilateral or bilateral (one operation)** C 80 🔁

Urinary System

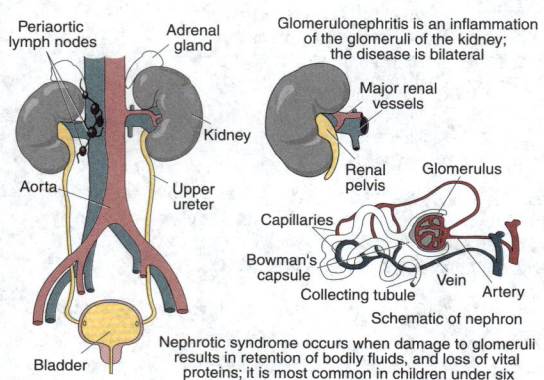

Periaortic lymph nodes

Adrenal gland

Glomerulonephritis is an inflammation of the glomeruli of the kidney; the disease is bilateral

Major renal vessels

Kidney

Aorta

Upper ureter

Renal pelvis

Glomerulus

Capillaries

Bowman's capsule

Collecting tubule

Vein

Artery

Schematic of nephron

Bladder

Nephrotic syndrome occurs when damage to glomeruli results in retention of bodily fluids, and loss of vital proteins; it is most common in children under six

LAPAROSCOPY

Diagnostic laparoscopy is always included in surgical laparoscopy.

To report only a diagnostic laparoscopy (peritoneoscopy), consult CPT code 49320.

50541   **Laparoscopy, surgical; ablation of renal cysts**   T 80
AMA: 2003, Jan, 19; 2001, Oct, 8; 2000, May, 4; 1999, Nov, 25

50542   **ablation of renal mass lesion(s)**   T 80
AMA: 2003, Jan, 19

To report open procedure, consult CPT codes 50220-50240.

If open cryoablation is performed, consult CPT code 50250.

If percutaneous cryotherapy ablation of renal tumors is performed, consult Category III code 0135T.

50543   **partial nephrectomy**   T 80
AMA: 2003, Jan, 19

To report open procedure, consult CPT code 50240.

50544   **pyeloplasty**   T 80
AMA: 2001, Oct, 8; 2000, May, 4; 1999, Nov, 25

50545   **radical nephrectomy (includes removal of Gerota's fascia and surrounding fatty tissue, removal of regional lymph nodes, and adrenalectomy)**   C 50 80
AMA: 2001, Oct, 8

Consult CPT code 50230 for open procedure.

50546   **nephrectomy, including partial ureterectomy**   C 80
AMA: 2001, Oct, 8; 2000, May, 4; 1999, Nov, 25

50547   **donor nephrectomy (including cold preservation), from living donor**   C 50 80
AMA: 2001, Oct, 8; 2000, May, 4; 1999, Nov, 25

Consult CPT code 50320 for open procedure.

For backbench renal allograft standard preparation before transplantation, consult CPT code 50325.

For backbench renal allograft reconstruction before transplantation, consult CPT code 50327-50329.

50548	**nephrectomy with total ureterectomy**	C 80 ↰

AMA: 2001, Oct, 8; 2000, May, 4; 1999, Nov, 25

Consult CPT codes 50234, 50236 for open procedure.

50549	**Unlisted laparoscopy procedure, renal**	T 50 80

AMA: 2000, May, 4; 2000, Mar, 5; 1999, Nov, 25

If laparoscopic drainage is performed of a lymphocele to the peritoneal cavity, consult CPT code 49323.

ENDOSCOPY

To report supplies and material, consult CPT code 99070.

50551	**Renal endoscopy through established nephrostomy or pyelostomy, with or without irrigation, instillation, or ureteropyelography, exclusive of radiologic service;**	1 T 50 80 ↰

MED: 100-2, 15, 260; 100-3, 100.2; 100-4, 12, 90.3; 100-4, 14, 10

AMA: 2003, Jan, 19; 2001, Oct, 8

50553	**with ureteral catheterization, with or without dilation of ureter**	1 T 50 ↰

MED: 100-2, 15, 260; 100-4, 12, 90.3; 100-4, 14, 10

AMA: 2001, Oct, 8

50555	**with biopsy**	1 T 50 80 ↰

MED: 100-2, 15, 260; 100-4, 12, 90.3; 100-4, 14, 10

AMA: 2001, Oct, 8

50557	**with fulguration and/or incision, with or without biopsy**	1 T 50 80 ↰

MED: 100-2, 15, 260; 100-4, 12, 90.3; 100-4, 14, 10

AMA: 2001, Oct, 8

50561	**with removal of foreign body or calculus**	1 T 50 80 ↰

MED: 100-2, 15, 260; 100-3, 130.5; 100-3, 130.6; 100-3, 160.2; 100-3, 230.1; 100-3, 250.1; 100-3, 250.4; 100-3, 270.4; 100-3, 40.50; 100-4, 12, 90.3; 100-4, 14, 10

AMA: 2003, Jan, 19; 2001, Oct, 8

50562	**with resection of tumor**	T 80 ↰

AMA: 2003, Jan, 19

If these procedures provide a significant identifiable service, they may be added to 50045 and 50120.

50570	**Renal endoscopy through nephrotomy or pyelotomy, with or without irrigation, instillation, or ureteropyelography, exclusive of radiologic service;**	T 50 80 ↰

MED: 100-3, 100.2

AMA: 2001, Oct, 8

If a nephrotomy is performed, consult CPT code 50045. If a pyelotomy is performed, consult CPT code 50120.

50572	**with ureteral catheterization, with or without dilation of ureter**	T 50 80 ↰

AMA: 2001, Oct, 8

50574	**with biopsy**	T 50 80 ↰

AMA: 2001, Oct, 8

Urinary System

50575 — 50610

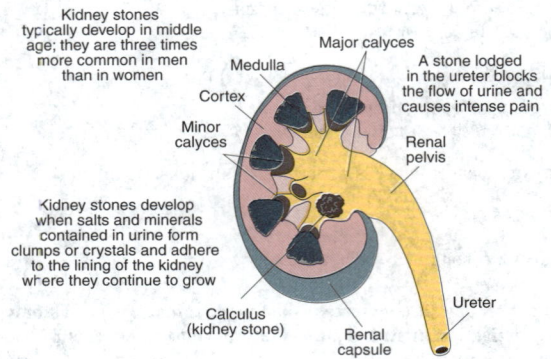

Kidney stones typically develop in middle age; they are three times more common in men than in women

Medulla

Major calyces

A stone lodged in the ureter blocks the flow of urine and causes intense pain

Cortex

Minor calyces

Renal pelvis

Kidney stones develop when salts and minerals contained in urine form clumps or crystals and adhere to the lining of the kidney where they continue to grow

Calculus (kidney stone)

Renal capsule

Ureter

50575 **with endopyelotomy (includes cystoscopy, ureteroscopy, dilation of ureter and ureteral pelvic junction, incision of ureteral pelvic junction and insertion of endopyelotomy stent)** T 50 ↵
AMA: 2002, Aug, 11; 2001, Oct, 8

50576 **with fulguration and/or incision, with or without biopsy** T 50 80 ↵
AMA: 2001, Oct, 8

50580 **with removal of foreign body or calculus** C 50 80 ↵
MED: 100-3, 130.5; 100-3, 130.6; 100-3, 160.2; 100-3, 230.1; 100-3, 250.1; 100-3, 250.4; 100-3, 270.4; 100-3, 40.50

AMA: 2001, Oct, 8

OTHER PROCEDURES

50590 **Lithotripsy, extracorporeal shock wave** T 50 ↵
MED: 100-3, 130.5; 100-3, 130.6; 100-3, 160.2; 100-3, 230.1; 100-3, 250.1; 100-3, 250.4; 100-3, 270.4; 100-3, 40.50

AMA: 2001, Oct, 8; 2001, Jul, 11; 2001, Aug, 10

⊙ ● **50592** **Ablation, one or more renal tumor(s), percutaneous, unilateral, radiofrequency**

Code 50592 is a unilateral procedure. To report a bilateral service, report 50592 with modifier 50.

To report imaging guidance and monitoring, consult CPT codes 76362, 76394, 76940.

To report percutaneous cryotherapy ablation of renal tumors, consult Category III code 0135T.

URETER

INCISION

50600 **Ureterotomy with exploration or drainage (separate procedure)** C 50 80 ↵

If ureteral endoscopy is performed in conjunction with this procedure, consult CPT codes 50970-50980.

50605 **Ureterotomy for insertion of indwelling stent, all types** C 50 80 ↵
AMA: 2001, Oct, 8

50610 **Ureterolithotomy; upper one-third of ureter** C 50 80 ↵
AMA: 2001, Oct, 8; 1999, Nov, 26

50620	**middle one-third of ureter**	C 50 80 ⬦
	AMA: 2001, Oct, 8; 1999, Nov, 26	

50630	**lower one-third of ureter**	C 50 80 ⬦
	AMA: 2001, Oct, 8; 1999, Nov, 26	

If a laparoscopic approach is used, consult CPT code 50945. If a transvesical ureterolithotomy is performed, consult CPT code 51060. If a cystotomy is performed with stone basket extraction of the ureteral calculus, consult CPT code 51065. If an endoscopic extraction or manipulation of the ureteral calculus is performed, consult CPT codes 50080, 50081, 50561, 50961, 50980, 52320-52330, 52352, and 52353.

EXCISION
For ureterocele, consult CPT codes 51535, 52300.

50650	**Ureterectomy, with bladder cuff (separate procedure)**	C 80 ⬦
50660	**Ureterectomy, total, ectopic ureter, combination abdominal, vaginal and/or perineal approach**	C 80 ⬦

INTRODUCTION

50684	**Injection procedure for ureterography or ureteropyelography through ureterostomy or indwelling ureteral catheter**	N 50 ⬦

To report radiological supervision and interpretation, consult CPT code 74425.

50686	**Manometric studies through ureterostomy or indwelling ureteral catheter**	T 80 ⬦

▲ 50688	**Change of ureterostomy tube or externally accessible ureteral stent via ileal conduit**	1 T ⬦
	MED: 100-2, 15, 260; 100-4, 12, 90.3; 100-4, 14, 10	

To report imaging guidance, consult CPT code 75984

50690	**Injection procedure for visualization of ileal conduit and/or ureteropyelography, exclusive of radiologic service**	N ⬦

To report radiological supervision and interpretation, consult CPT code 74425.

REPAIR

50700	**Ureteroplasty, plastic operation on ureter (eg, stricture)**	C 80 ⬦
50715	**Ureterolysis, with or without repositioning of ureter for retroperitoneal fibrosis**	C 50 80 ⬦

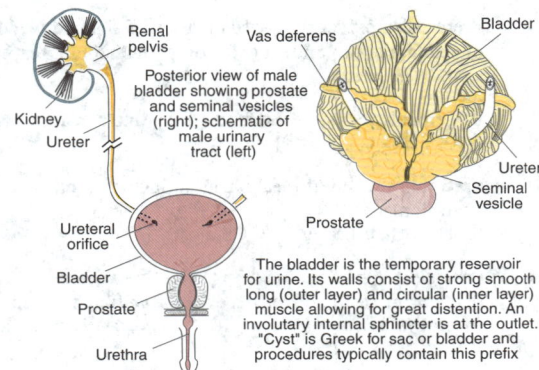

Renal pelvis

Kidney

Ureter

Ureteral orifice

Bladder

Prostate

Urethra

Posterior view of male bladder showing prostate and seminal vesicles (right); schematic of male urinary tract (left)

Vas deferens

Bladder

Ureter

Seminal vesicle

Prostate

The bladder is the temporary reservoir for urine. Its walls consist of strong smooth long (outer layer) and circular (inner layer) muscle allowing for great distention. An involuntary internal sphincter is at the outlet. "Cyst" is Greek for sac or bladder and procedures typically contain this prefix

50722   Ureterolysis for ovarian vein syndrome   ♀ C 80 ▣

50725   Ureterolysis for retrocaval ureter, with reanastomosis of upper urinary tract or vena cava   C 80 ▣

50727   Revision of urinary-cutaneous anastomosis (any type urostomy);   C 80 ▣

50728   with repair of fascial defect and hernia   C 80 ▣

50740   Ureteropyelostomy, anastomosis of ureter and renal pelvis   C 80 ▣
     AMA: 2001, Oct, 8

50750   Ureterocalycostomy, anastomosis of ureter to renal calyx   C 80 ▣
     AMA: 2001, Oct, 8

50760   Ureteroureterostomy   C 80 ▣
     AMA: 2001, Oct, 8

50770   Transureteroureterostomy, anastomosis of ureter to contralateral ureter   C 80 ▣

     Note that this procedure includes minor procedures to prevent vesicoureteral reflux.

50780   Ureteroneocystostomy; anastomosis of single ureter to bladder   C 50 80 ▣
     AMA: 2001, Oct, 8

     If this procedure is combined with a cystourethroplasty or a vesical neck revision, consult CPT code 51820.

50782   anastomosis of duplicated ureter to bladder   C 50 80 ▣
     AMA: 2001, Oct, 8

50783   with extensive ureteral tailoring   C 50 80 ▣
     AMA: 2001, Oct, 8

     Note that this procedure includes minor procedures to prevent vesicoureteral reflux.

50785   with vesico-psoas hitch or bladder flap   C 50 80 ▣
     AMA: 2001, Oct, 8

     Note that this procedure includes minor procedures to prevent vesicoureteral reflux.

50800   Ureteroenterostomy, direct anastomosis of ureter to intestine   C 50 80 ▣
     AMA: 2001, Oct, 8

     If procedures 50800-50820 are performed with a cystectomy, consult CPT codes 51580-51595.

50810   Ureterosigmoidostomy, with creation of sigmoid bladder and establishment of abdominal or perineal colostomy, including intestine anastomosis C 80 ▣
     AMA: 2001, Oct, 8

50815   Ureterocolon conduit, including intestine anastomosis   C 50 80 ▣
     AMA: 2001, Oct, 8

50820   Ureteroileal conduit (ileal bladder), including intestine anastomosis (Bricker operation)   C 50 80 ▣
     AMA: 2001, Oct, 8

50825   Continent diversion, including intestine anastomosis using any segment of small and/or large intestine (Kock pouch or Camey enterocystoplasty)   C 80 ▣
     AMA: 2001, Oct, 8

50830   **Urinary undiversion (eg, taking down of ureteroileal conduit, ureterosigmoidostomy or ureteroenterostomy with ureteroureterostomy or ureteroneocystostomy)**   `C` `80` `↰`
     AMA: 2001, Oct, 8

50840   **Replacement of all or part of ureter by intestine segment, including intestine anastomosis**   `C` `50` `80` `↰`
     AMA: 2001, Oct, 8

50845   **Cutaneous appendico-vesicostomy**   `C` `80` `↰`
     Mitrofanoff operation

50860   **Ureterostomy, transplantation of ureter to skin**   `C` `50` `80` `↰`

50900   **Ureterorrhaphy, suture of ureter (separate procedure)**   `C` `80` `↰`

50920   **Closure of ureterocutaneous fistula**   `C` `80` `↰`

50930   **Closure of ureterovisceral fistula (including visceral repair)**   `C` `80` `↰`

50940   **Deligation of ureter**   `C` `50` `80` `↰`

     If ureteroplasty or ureterolysis is performed, consult CPT codes 50700-50860.

LAPAROSCOPY

Diagnostic laparoscopy is always included with surgical laparoscopy

To report only a diagnostic laparoscopy (peritoneoscopy), consult CPT code 49320.

50945   **Laparoscopy, surgical; ureterolithotomy**   `T` `50` `80` `↰`
     AMA: 2001, Oct, 8; 2000, May, 4; 1999, Nov, 26

50947   **ureteroneocystostomy with cystoscopy and ureteral stent placement**   `9` `T` `50` `80` `↰`
     MED: 100-2, 15, 260; 100-4, 12, 90.3; 100-4, 14, 10

     AMA: 2001, Oct, 8

50948   **ureteroneocystostomy without cystoscopy and ureteral stent placement**   `9` `T` `50` `80` `↰`
     MED: 100-2, 15, 260; 100-4, 12, 90.3; 100-4, 14, 10

     AMA: 2001, Oct, 8

     To report open ureterocystostomy, consult CPT codes 50780-50785.

50949   **Unlisted laparoscopy procedure, ureter**   `T` `50` `80`
     AMA: 2001, Oct, 8

ENDOSCOPY

50951   **Ureteral endoscopy through established ureterostomy, with or without irrigation, instillation, or ureteropyelography, exclusive of radiologic service;**   `1` `T` `50` `80` `↰`
     MED: 100-2, 15, 260; 100-3, 100.2; 100-4, 12, 90.3; 100-4, 14, 10

     AMA: 2001, Oct, 8

50953   **with ureteral catheterization, with or without dilation of ureter**   `1` `T` `50` `80` `↰`
     MED: 100-2, 15, 260; 100-4, 12, 90.3; 100-4, 14, 10

     AMA: 2001, Oct, 8

50955   **with biopsy**   `1` `T` `50` `80` `↰`
     MED: 100-2, 15, 260; 100-4, 12, 90.3; 100-4, 14, 10

     AMA: 2001, Oct, 8

Urinary System

50957 — 51045

50957	**with fulguration and/or incision, with or without biopsy** ▪T 50 80 ↵
	MED: 100-2, 15, 260; 100-4, 12, 90.3; 100-4, 14, 10
	AMA: 2001, Oct, 8
50961	**with removal of foreign body or calculus** ▪T 50 80 ↵
	MED: 100-2, 15, 260; 100-4, 12, 90.3; 100-4, 14, 10
	AMA: 2001, Oct, 8

50970   **Ureteral endoscopy through ureterotomy, with or without irrigation, instillation, or ureteropyelography, exclusive of radiologic service;** ▪T 50 80 ↵

MED: 100-2, 15, 260; 100-3, 100.2; 100-4, 12, 90.3; 100-4, 14, 10

AMA: 2001, Oct, 8

If a ureterotomy is performed, consult CPT code 50600.

If these procedures (50970-50980) provide a significant identifiable service, they may be added to 50600.

50972   **with ureteral catheterization, with or without dilation of ureter** ▪T 50 80 ↵

MED: 100-2, 15, 260; 100-4, 12, 90.3; 100-4, 14, 10

AMA: 2001, Oct, 8

50974   **with biopsy** ▪T 50 80 ↵

MED: 100-2, 15, 260; 100-4, 12, 90.3; 100-4, 14, 10

AMA: 2001, Oct, 8

50976   **with fulguration and/or incision, with or without biopsy** ▪T 50 80 ↵

MED: 100-2, 15, 260; 100-4, 12, 90.3; 100-4, 14, 10

AMA: 2001, Oct, 8

50980   **with removal of foreign body or calculus** ▪T 50 80 ↵

MED: 100-2, 15, 260; 100-4, 12, 90.3; 100-4, 14, 10

AMA: 2001, Oct, 8

BLADDER

INCISION

51000	**Aspiration of bladder by needle** T ↵
51005	**Aspiration of bladder; by trocar or intracatheter** T ↵
51010	**with insertion of suprapubic catheter** ▪T ↵
	MED: 100-2, 15, 260; 100-4, 12, 90.3; 100-4, 14, 10

To report imaging guidance, consult CPT codes 76003, 76360, 76942.

51020   **Cystotomy or cystostomy; with fulguration and/or insertion of radioactive material** 4 T 80 ↵

MED: 100-2, 15, 260; 100-4, 12, 90.3; 100-4, 14, 10

51030   **with cryosurgical destruction of intravesical lesion** 4 T 80 ↵

MED: 100-2, 15, 260; 100-4, 12, 90.3; 100-4, 14, 10

51040   **Cystostomy, cystotomy with drainage** 4 T 80 ↵

MED: 100-2, 15, 260; 100-4, 12, 90.3; 100-4, 14, 10

51045   **Cystotomy, with insertion of ureteral catheter or stent (separate procedure)** 4 T 80 ↵

MED: 100-2, 15, 260; 100-4, 12, 90.3; 100-4, 14, 10

51050	Cystolithotomy, cystotomy with removal of calculus, without vesical neck resection ![4][T][80][CCI]	
	MED: 100-2, 15, 260; 100-4, 12, 90.3; 100-4, 14, 10	
51060	Transvesical ureterolithotomy ![C][80][CCI]	
51065	Cystotomy, with calculus basket extraction and/or ultrasonic or electrohydraulic fragmentation of ureteral calculus ![4][T][80][CCI]	
	MED: 100-2, 15, 260; 100-4, 12, 90.3; 100-4, 14, 10	
51080	Drainage of perivesical or prevesical space abscess ![1][T][80][CCI]	
	MED: 100-2, 15, 260; 100-4, 12, 90.3; 100-4, 14, 10	

EXCISION

51500   Excision of urachal cyst or sinus, with or without umbilical hernia repair   ![4][T][80][CCI]
MED: 100-2, 15, 260; 100-4, 12, 90.3; 100-4, 14, 10

51520   Cystotomy; for simple excision of vesical neck (separate procedure)   ![4][T][80][CCI]
MED: 100-2, 15, 260; 100-4, 12, 90.3; 100-4, 14, 10

51525   for excision of bladder diverticulum, single or multiple (separate procedure)   ![C][80][CCI]

51530   for excision of bladder tumor   ![C][80][CCI]

> If transurethral resection is performed, consult CPT codes 52234-52240 and 52305.

51535   Cystotomy for excision, incision, or repair of ureterocele   ![C][50][80][CCI]

> If a transurethral excision is performed, consult CPT code 52300.

51550   Cystectomy, partial; simple   ![C][80][CCI]

51555   complicated (eg, postradiation, previous surgery, difficult location)   ![C][80][CCI]

51565   Cystectomy, partial, with reimplantation of ureter(s) into bladder (ureteroneocystostomy)   ![C][80][CCI]

51570   Cystectomy, complete; (separate procedure)   ![C][80][CCI]

51575   with bilateral pelvic lymphadenectomy, including external iliac, hypogastric, and obturator nodes   ![C][80][CCI]

51580   Cystectomy, complete, with ureterosigmoidostomy or ureterocutaneous transplantations;   ![C][80][CCI]

51585   with bilateral pelvic lymphadenectomy, including external iliac, hypogastric, and obturator nodes   ![C][80][CCI]

51590   Cystectomy, complete, with ureteroileal conduit or sigmoid bladder, including intestine anastomosis;   ![C][80][CCI]

51595   with bilateral pelvic lymphadenectomy, including external iliac, hypogastric, and obturator nodes   ![C][80][CCI]

51596   Cystectomy, complete, with continent diversion, any open technique, using any segment of small and/or large intestine to construct neobladder ![C][80][CCI]

51597   Pelvic exenteration, complete, for vesical, prostatic or urethral malignancy, with removal of bladder and ureteral transplantations, with or without hysterectomy and/or abdominoperineal resection of rectum and colon and colostomy, or any combination thereof   ![C][80][CCI]

> If a pelvic exenteration is performed for gynecologic malignancy, consult CPT code 58240.

![CCI] CCI Comp	![50] Bilateral Procedure	✚ CPT Add-on Code ⊘ Modifier -51 Exempt ♂ Male ♀ Female
● New Code	▲ Revised Code	![M] Maternity Edit ![A] Age Edit ![A]–![Y] APC Status Ind. **AMA:** CPT Assistant
© 2005 Ingenix, Inc. *(Blue Ink)*		CPT only © 2005 American Medical Association. All Rights Reserved. *(Black Ink)* Surgery — 371

Urinary System

51600 — 51736

INTRODUCTION

If bladder catheterization is performed, consult CPT codes 53670 and 53675.

51600 **Injection procedure for cystography or voiding urethrocystography** N ↻
MED: 100-3, 230.2

> To report radiological supervision and interpretation, consult CPT codes 74430 and 74455.

51605 **Injection procedure and placement of chain for contrast and/or chain urethrocystography** N ↻

> To report radiological supervision and interpretation, consult CPT code 74430.

51610 **Injection procedure for retrograde urethrocystography** N ↻

> To report radiological supervision and interpretation, consult CPT code 74450.

51700 **Bladder irrigation, simple, lavage and/or instillation** T ↻

51701 **Insertion of non-indwelling bladder catheter (eg, straight catheterization for residual urine)** X ↻

> When catheter insertion is a component of another procedure, do not report CPT codes 51701 or 51702 separately.

51702 **Insertion of temporary indwelling bladder catheter; simple (eg, Foley)** X ↻

51703 **complicated (eg, altered anatomy, fractured catheter/balloon)** T ↻

51705 **Change of cystostomy tube; simple** T ↻

51710 **complicated** 1 T ↻
MED: 100-2, 15, 260; 100-4, 12, 90.3; 100-4, 14, 10

> Consult CPT code 75984 for imaging guidance.

51715 **Endoscopic injection of implant material into the submucosal tissues of the urethra and/or bladder neck** 3 T 80 ↻
MED: 100-2, 15, 260; 100-3, 230.10; 100-4, 12, 90.3; 100-4, 14, 10

51720 **Bladder instillation of anticarcinogenic agent (including detention time)** T ↻
AMA: 2002, Nov, 11

URODYNAMICS

Urodynamics is a diagnostic service performed to evaluate the storage of urine and urine flow through the urinary tract. All procedures in this section represent complete procedures (both the professional and technical components). Physicians reporting these services as complete procedures are expected to supply all instruments/equipment, supplies, and technician services. A physician performing only the operation of the equipment and interpretation of the report should report only the professional component by appending modifier 26 Professional component, to the procedure codes.

When multiple procedures are performed at the same operative session, append modifier 51.

51725 **Simple cystometrogram (CMG) (eg, spinal manometer)** T 80 ↻
AMA: 2002, Sep, 6

51726 **Complex cystometrogram (eg, calibrated electronic equipment)** 1 T ↻
MED: 100-2, 15, 260; 100-4, 12, 90.3; 100-4, 14, 10
AMA: 2002, Sep, 6

51736 **Simple uroflowmetry (UFR) (eg, stop-watch flow rate, mechanical uroflowmeter)** T 80 ↻
MED: 100-3, 230.2
AMA: 2002, Sep, 6

51741	Complex uroflowmetry (eg, calibrated electronic equipment)	T 🔼

MED: 100-3, 230.2

AMA: 2002, Sep, 6

51772	Urethral pressure profile studies (UPP) (urethral closure pressure profile), any technique	1 T 80 🔼

MED: 100-2, 15, 260; 100-4, 12, 90.3; 100-4, 14, 10

AMA: 2002, Sep, 6

Keitzer test

51784	Electromyography studies (EMG) of anal or urethral sphincter, other than needle, any technique	T 🔼

AMA: 2002, Sep, 6

51785	Needle electromyography studies (EMG) of anal or urethral sphincter, any technique	1 T 80 🔼

MED: 100-2, 15, 260; 100-4, 12, 90.3; 100-4, 14, 10

AMA: 2002, Sep, 6; 2002, Apr, 1

51792	Stimulus evoked response (eg, measurement of bulbocavernosus reflex latency time)	T 80 🔼

AMA: 2002, Sep, 6; 2002, Apr, 1

51795	Voiding pressure studies (VP); bladder voiding pressure, any technique	T 80 🔼

MED: 100-3, 230.2

AMA: 2002, Sep, 6; 2001, Dec, 7

51797	intra-abdominal voiding pressure (AP) (rectal, gastric, intraperitoneal)	T 80 🔼

MED: 100-3, 230.2

AMA: 2002, Sep, 6; 2001, Dec, 7

51798	Measurement of post-voiding residual urine and/or bladder capacity by ultrasound, non-imaging	X 80 🔼

REPAIR

51800	Cystoplasty or cystourethroplasty, plastic operation on bladder and/or vesical neck (anterior Y-plasty, vesical fundus resection), any procedure, with or without wedge resection of posterior vesical neck	C 80 🔼

51820	Cystourethroplasty with unilateral or bilateral ureteroneocystostomy	C 80 🔼

51840	Anterior vesicourethropexy, or urethropexy (eg, Marshall-Marchetti-Krantz, Burch); simple	C 80 🔼

AMA: 1998, Apr, 15; 1997, Nov, 19; 1997, Jan, 1

51841	complicated (eg, secondary repair)	C 80 🔼

AMA: 1997, Jan, 1

If urethropexy (Pereyra type) is performed, consult CPT code 57289.

51845	Abdomino-vaginal vesical neck suspension, with or without endoscopic control (eg, Stamey, Raz, modified Pereyra)	♀ C 80 🔼

AMA: 1997, Jan, 3

51860	Cystorrhaphy, suture of bladder wound, injury or rupture; simple	C 80 🔼
51865	complicated	C 80 🔼

Urinary System

51880 — 52001

51880	**Closure of cystostomy (separate procedure)**	▣ T 80 ⌐
	MED: 100-2, 15, 260; 100-4, 12, 90.3; 100-4, 14, 10	
51900	**Closure of vesicovaginal fistula, abdominal approach**	♀ C 80 ⌐
	If a vaginal approach is used, consult CPT codes 57320-57330.	
51920	**Closure of vesicouterine fistula;**	♀ C 80 ⌐
51925	**with hysterectomy**	♀ C 80 ⌐

If a vesicoenteric fistula is closed, consult CPT codes 44660 and 44661. If a rectovesical fistula is closed, consult CPT codes 45800-45805.

51940	**Closure, exstrophy of bladder**	C 80 ⌐
	Consult also CPT code 54390.	
51960	**Enterocystoplasty, including intestinal anastomosis**	C 80 ⌐
51980	**Cutaneous vesicostomy**	C 80 ⌐

LAPAROSCOPY

Diagnostic laparoscopy is always included in a surgical laparoscopy. For diagnostic laparoscopy only (peritoneoscopy), consult CPT code 49320.

51990   **Laparoscopy, surgical; urethral suspension for stress incontinence**   T 80 ⌐
                     MED: 100-3, 230.10

                     AMA: 2000, May, 4; 1999, Nov, 26

51992   **sling operation for stress incontinence (eg, fascia or synthetic)**   ♀ 5 T 80 ⌐
                     MED: 100-3, 230.10

                     AMA: 2000, May, 4; 1999, Nov, 26

                     Consult CPT code 57288 for open sling operation for stress incontinence. For removal or revision of sling operation consult CPT code 57287.

● **51999**   **Unlisted laparoscopy procedure, bladder**

ENDOSCOPY — CYSTOSCOPY, URETHROSCOPY, CYSTOURETHROSCOPY

Cystoscopy, urethroscopy, and cystourethroscopy are listed so that the main procedure can be identified without listing all minor related procedures performed. For example, a cystourethroscopy with dilation of a urethral stricture (52281) includes calibration, meatotomy, and the injection procedure for cystography, which are all explicitly described in the procedure.

Multiple procedures performed at the same operative session should be reported and modifier 51 Multiple procedures should be appended.. Many procedures on the ureter require placement of a temporary stent. Placement and removal of temporary stents are not reported separately. However, placement of more permanent, self-retaining, indwelling stents (52332) should be reported with the code for the primary procedure.

52000   **Cystourethroscopy (separate procedure)**   ▣ T ⌐
                     MED: 100-2, 15, 260; 100-4, 12, 90.3; 100-4, 14, 10

                     AMA: 2001, May, 5; 2000, Oct, 7

ENDOSCOPY — CYSTOSTOSCOPY, URETHROSCOPY, CYSTOURETHROSCOPY

52001   **Cystourethroscopy with irrigation and evacuation of multiple obstructing clots**   2 T ⌐
                     MED: 100-2, 15, 260; 100-4, 12, 90.3; 100-4, 14, 10

                     Do not report 52001 in conjunction with 52000.

---

26 / **TC** Professional/Technical Component   **80**/**80** Assist-at-Surgery Allowed/With Documentation   ⊙ Conscious Sedation

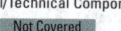 Unlisted    Not Covered   **MED:** Pubs 100/NCD Reference   **1**-**9** ASC Group   ⑥③ Modifier 63 Exempt

374 — Surgery   CPT only © 2005 American Medical Association. All Rights Reserved. *(Black Ink)*   © 2005 Ingenix, Inc. *(Blue Ink)*

ENDOSCOPY — CYSTOSCOPY, URETHROSCOPY, CYSTOURETHROSCOPY

52005 Cystourethroscopy, with ureteral catheterization, with or without irrigation, instillation, or ureteropyelography, exclusive of radiologic service; 2 T ▣

  MED: 100-2, 15, 260; 100-4, 12, 30.2; 100-4, 12, 90.3; 100-4, 14, 10

  AMA: 2001, Oct, 8; 2001, May, 5; 2001, Jan, 13; 2000, Sep, 11

  Howard test

52007 with brush biopsy of ureter and/or renal pelvis 2 T 50 ▣

  MED: 100-2, 15, 260; 100-4, 12, 90.3; 100-4, 14, 10

  AMA: 2001, Oct, 8; 2001, May, 5

52010 Cystourethroscopy, with ejaculatory duct catheterization, with or without irrigation, instillation, or duct radiography, exclusive of radiologic service ♂ 2 T ▣

  MED: 100-2, 15, 260; 100-4, 12, 90.3; 100-4, 14, 10

  AMA: 2001, May, 5

  To report radiological supervision and interpretation, consult CPT code 74440.

TRANSURETHRAL SURGERY — URETHRA AND BLADDER

52204 Cystourethroscopy, with biopsy 2 T ▣

  MED: 100-2, 15, 260; 100-4, 12, 90.3; 100-4, 14, 10

  AMA: 2001, Sep, 1; 2001, May, 5

52214 Cystourethroscopy, with fulguration (including cryosurgery or laser surgery) of trigone, bladder neck, prostatic fossa, urethra, or periurethral glands 2 T ▣

  MED: 100-2, 15, 260; 100-4, 12, 90.3; 100-4, 14, 10

  AMA: 2001, Sep, 1; 2001, May, 5

52224 Cystourethroscopy, with fulguration (including cryosurgery or laser surgery) or treatment of MINOR (less than 0.5 cm) lesion(s) with or without biopsy 2 T ▣

  MED: 100-2, 15, 260; 100-4, 12, 90.3; 100-4, 14, 10

  AMA: 2001, Sep, 1; 2001, May, 5

52234 Cystourethroscopy, with fulguration (including cryosurgery or laser surgery) and/or resection of; SMALL bladder tumor(s) (0.5 up to 2.0 cm) 2 T ▣

  MED: 100-2, 15, 260; 100-4, 12, 30.2; 100-4, 12, 90.3; 100-4, 14, 10

  AMA: 2003, Jan, 19; 2002, Oct, 12; 2001, Sep, 1; 2001, May, 5

52235 MEDIUM bladder tumor(s) (2.0 to 5.0 cm) 3 T ▣

  MED: 100-2, 15, 260; 100-4, 12, 30.2; 100-4, 12, 90.3; 100-4, 14, 10

  AMA: 2003, Jan, 19; 2002, Oct, 12; 2001, Sep, 1; 2001, May, 5

52240 LARGE bladder tumor(s) 3 T ▣

  MED: 100-2, 15, 260; 100-4, 12, 30.2; 100-4, 12, 90.3; 100-4, 14, 10

  AMA: 2001, Sep, 1; 2001, May, 5

52250 Cystourethroscopy with insertion of radioactive substance, with or without biopsy or fulguration 4 T ▣

  MED: 100-2, 15, 260; 100-3, 230.12; 100-4, 12, 90.3; 100-4, 14, 10

  AMA: 2001, Sep, 1; 2001, May, 5

Urinary System

52260 — 52300

52260 **Cystourethroscopy, with dilation of bladder for interstitial cystitis; general or conduction (spinal) anesthesia** ② T ↻
  MED: 100-2, 15, 260; 100-3, 230.12; 100-4, 12, 90.3; 100-4, 14, 10

  AMA: 2001, Sep, 1; 2001, May, 5

52265 **local anesthesia** T ↻
  MED: 100-3, 230.12

  AMA: 2001, Sep, 1; 2001, May, 5

52270 **Cystourethroscopy, with internal urethrotomy; female** ♀ ② T ↻
  MED: 100-2, 15, 260; 100-4, 12, 90.3; 100-4, 14, 10

  AMA: 2001, Sep, 1; 2001, May, 5

52275 **male** ♂ ② T ↻
  MED: 100-2, 15, 260; 100-4, 12, 90.3; 100-4, 14, 10

  AMA: 2001, Sep, 1; 2001, May, 5

52276 **Cystourethroscopy with direct vision internal urethrotomy** ③ T ↻
  MED: 100-2, 15, 260; 100-4, 12, 90.3; 100-4, 14, 10

  AMA: 2001, Sep, 1; 2001, May, 5

52277 **Cystourethroscopy, with resection of external sphincter (sphincterotomy)** ② T 80 ↻
  MED: 100-2, 15, 260; 100-4, 12, 90.3; 100-4, 14, 10

  AMA: 2001, Sep, 1; 2001, May, 5

52281 **Cystourethroscopy, with calibration and/or dilation of urethral stricture or stenosis, with or without meatotomy, with or without injection procedure for cystography, male or female** ② T ↻
  MED: 100-2, 15, 260; 100-4, 12, 90.3; 100-4, 14, 10

  AMA: 2001, Sep, 1; 2001, May, 5; 1997, Nov, 20

52282 **Cystourethroscopy, with insertion of urethral stent** ⑨ T ↻
  MED: 100-2, 15, 260; 100-4, 12, 90.3; 100-4, 14, 10

  AMA: 2001, Sep, 1; 2001, May, 5; 1997, Nov, 20

52283 **Cystourethroscopy, with steroid injection into stricture** ② T ↻
  MED: 100-2, 15, 260; 100-4, 12, 90.3; 100-4, 14, 10

  AMA: 2001, Sep, 1; 2001, May, 5

52285 **Cystourethroscopy for treatment of the female urethral syndrome with any or all of the following: urethral meatotomy, urethral dilation, internal urethrotomy, lysis of urethrovaginal septal fibrosis, lateral incisions of the bladder neck, and fulguration of polyp(s) of urethra, bladder neck, and/or trigone** ♀ ② T ↻
  MED: 100-2, 15, 260; 100-4, 12, 90.3; 100-4, 14, 10

  AMA: 2001, Sep, 1; 2001, May, 5

52290 **Cystourethroscopy; with ureteral meatotomy, unilateral or bilateral** ② T ↻
  MED: 100-2, 15, 260; 100-4, 12, 40.7; 100-4, 12, 90.3; 100-4, 14, 10

  AMA: 2001, Sep, 1; 2001, May, 5

52300 **with resection or fulguration of orthotopic ureterocele(s), unilateral or bilateral** ② T 80 ↻
  MED: 100-2, 15, 260; 100-4, 12, 40.7; 100-4, 12, 90.3; 100-4, 14, 10

  AMA: 2001, Sep, 1; 2001, May, 5

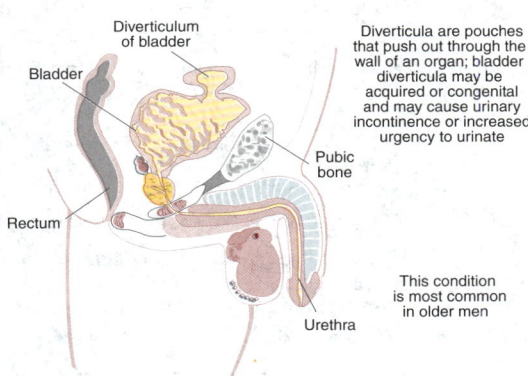

Diverticulum of bladder

Bladder

Diverticula are pouches that push out through the wall of an organ; bladder diverticula may be acquired or congenital and may cause urinary incontinence or increased urgency to urinate

Pubic bone

Rectum

This condition is most common in older men

Urethra

52301 **with resection or fulguration of ectopic ureterocele(s), unilateral or bilateral**
MED: 100-4, 12, 40.7

AMA: 2001, Sep, 1; 2001, May, 5

52305 **with incision or resection of orifice of bladder diverticulum, single or multiple**
MED: 100-2, 15, 260; 100-4, 12, 90.3; 100-4, 14, 10

AMA: 2001, Sep, 1; 2001, May, 5

52310 **Cystourethroscopy, with removal of foreign body, calculus, or ureteral stent from urethra or bladder (separate procedure); simple**
MED: 100-2, 15, 260; 100-4, 12, 90.3; 100-4, 14, 10

AMA: 2001, Sep, 1; 2001, May, 5

When reporting the removal of self-retaining, indwelling ureteral stent, append modifier 58 to code 52310 or 52315.

52315 **complicated**
MED: 100-2, 15, 260; 100-4, 12, 90.3; 100-4, 14, 10

AMA: 2001, Sep, 1; 2001, May, 5

52317 **Litholapaxy: crushing or fragmentation of calculus by any means in bladder and removal of fragments; simple or small (less than 2.5 cm)**
MED: 100-2, 15, 260; 100-4, 12, 90.3; 100-4, 14, 10

AMA: 2001, Sep, 1; 2001, May, 5

52318 **complicated or large (over 2.5 cm)**
MED: 100-2, 15, 260; 100-4, 12, 90.3; 100-4, 14, 10

AMA: 2001, Sep, 1; 2001, May, 5

URETER AND PELVIS

CPT codes 52320-52355 include the insertion and removal of a temporary stent during a therapeutic or diagnostic cystourethroscopy and should not be separately reported.

For insertion of a self-retaining, indwelling stent performed during a cystourethroscopic diagnostic or therapeutic proceudure(s) consult CPT code 52332 in addition to the primary procedure performed and add modifier 51. Code 52332 is used to report a unilateral procedure; add modifier 50 for insertion of a bilateral stent.

 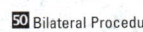

For the removal of a self-retaining indwelling ureteral stent, consult CPT codes 52310 and 52315 and add modifier 58.

Diagnostic cystourethroscopy is always included in surgical cystourethroscopy. To report only a diagnostic cystourethroscopy, consult CPT code 52351.

52320   **Cystourethroscopy (including ureteral catheterization); with removal of ureteral calculus**   5️⃣ Ⓣ 50 🔼
MED: 100-2, 15, 260; 100-4, 12, 90.3; 100-4, 14, 10

AMA: 2001, Sep, 1; 2001, Oct, 8; 2001, May, 5; 2001, Jan, 13; 1996, May, 11; 1996, Mar, 1

52325   **with fragmentation of ureteral calculus (eg, ultrasonic or electro-hydraulic technique)**   4️⃣ Ⓣ 50 🔼
MED: 100-2, 15, 260; 100-4, 12, 90.3; 100-4, 14, 10

AMA: 2001, Sep, 1; 2001, Oct, 8; 2001, May, 5; 1996, May, 11; 1996, Mar, 1

52327   **with subureteric injection of implant material**   2️⃣ Ⓣ 🔼
MED: 100-2, 15, 260; 100-3, 230.10; 100-4, 12, 90.3; 100-4, 14, 10

AMA: 2001, Sep, 1; 2001, Oct, 8; 2001, May, 5; 1996, May, 11; 1996, Mar, 1

52330   **with manipulation, without removal of ureteral calculus**   2️⃣ Ⓣ 50 🔼
MED: 100-2, 15, 260; 100-4, 12, 90.3; 100-4, 14, 10

AMA: 2001, Sep, 1; 2001, Oct, 8; 2001, May, 5; 2000, Sep, 11; 1996, May, 11; 1996, Mar, 1

52332   **Cystourethroscopy, with insertion of indwelling ureteral stent (eg, Gibbons or double-J type)**   2️⃣ Ⓣ 50 🔼
MED: 100-2, 15, 260; 100-4, 12, 90.3; 100-4, 14, 10

AMA: 2001, Sep, 1; 2001, Oct, 8; 2001, May, 5; 2001, Jan, 13; 1996, May, 11; 1996, Mar, 1

To report bilateral insertion, append modifier 50. If procedure is performed in addition to other diagnostic or therapeutic interventions, append modifier 51.

52334   **Cystourethroscopy with insertion of ureteral guide wire through kidney to establish a percutaneous nephrostomy, retrograde**   3️⃣ Ⓣ 50 🔼
MED: 100-2, 15, 260; 100-4, 12, 90.3; 100-4, 14, 10

AMA: 2001, Sep, 1; 2001, Oct, 8; 2001, May, 5; 1996, May, 11; 1996, Mar, 11

If percutaneous nephrostolithotomy is performed, consult CPT codes 50080 and 50081. If establishment of the nephrostomy tract is performed by itself, consult CPT code 50395.

52341   **Cystourethroscopy; with treatment of ureteral stricture (eg, balloon dilation, laser, electrocautery, and incision)**   3️⃣ Ⓣ 50 🔼
MED: 100-2, 15, 260; 100-4, 12, 90.3; 100-4, 14, 10

AMA: 2001, Sep, 1; 2001, Oct, 8; 2001, May, 5; 2001, Apr, 4

52342   **with treatment of ureteropelvic junction stricture (eg, balloon dilation, laser, electrocautery, and incision)**   3️⃣ Ⓣ 50 🔼
MED: 100-2, 15, 260; 100-4, 12, 90.3; 100-4, 14, 10

AMA: 2001, Sep, 1; 2001, Oct, 8; 2001, May, 5; 2001, Apr, 4

52343   **with treatment of intra-renal stricture (eg, balloon dilation, laser, electrocautery, and incision)**   3️⃣ Ⓣ 50 🔼
MED: 100-2, 15, 260; 100-4, 12, 90.3; 100-4, 14, 10

AMA: 2001, Sep, 1; 2001, Oct, 8; 2001, May, 5; 2001, Apr, 4

52344   **Cystourethroscopy with ureteroscopy; with treatment of ureteral stricture (eg, balloon dilation, laser, electrocautery, and incision)**   3️⃣ Ⓣ 50 🔼
MED: 100-2, 15, 260; 100-4, 12, 90.3; 100-4, 14, 10

AMA: 2001, Sep, 1; 2001, Oct, 8; 2001, May, 5; 2001, Apr, 4

52345   **with treatment of ureteropelvic junction stricture (eg, balloon dilation, laser, electrocautery, and incision)**   3 T 80

MED: 100-2, 15, 260; 100-4, 12, 90.3; 100-4, 14, 10

AMA: 2001, Sep, 1; 2001, Oct, 8; 2001, May, 5; 2001, Apr, 4

52346   **with treatment of intra-renal stricture (eg, balloon dilation, laser, electrocautery, and incision)**   3 T 80

MED: 100-2, 15, 260; 100-3, 230.3; 100-4, 12, 90.3; 100-4, 14, 10

AMA: 2001, Sep, 1; 2001, Oct, 8; 2001, May, 5; 2001, Apr, 4

To report transurethral resection or incision of ejaculatory ducts, consult CPT code 52402.

52351   **Cystourethroscopy, with ureteroscopy and/or pyeloscopy; diagnostic**   3 T

MED: 100-2, 15, 260; 100-4, 12, 90.3; 100-4, 14, 10

AMA: 2001, Sep, 1; 2001, Oct, 8; 2001, May, 5; 2001, Apr, 4

To report radiological supervision and interpretation, consult CPT code 74485.

Do not report CPT code 52351 when reporting 52341-52346, or 52352-52355.

52352   **with removal or manipulation of calculus (ureteral catheterization is included)**   4 T 50

MED: 100-2, 15, 260; 100-3, 130.5; 100-3, 130.6; 100-3, 160.2; 100-3, 230.1; 100-3, 250.1; 100-3, 250.4; 100-3, 270.4; 100-3, 40.50; 100-4, 12, 90.3; 100-4, 14, 10

AMA: 2001, Sep, 1; 2001, Oct, 8; 2001, May, 5; 2001, Apr, 4

52353   **with lithotripsy (ureteral catheterization is included)**   4 T 50

MED: 100-2, 15, 260; 100-3, 130.5; 100-3, 130.6; 100-3, 160.2; 100-3, 230.1; 100-3, 250.1; 100-3, 250.4; 100-3, 270.4; 100-3, 40.50; 100-4, 12, 90.3; 100-4, 14, 10

AMA: 2001, Sep, 1; 2001, Oct, 8; 2001, May, 5; 2001, Apr, 4

52354   **with biopsy and/or fulguration of ureteral or renal pelvic lesion**   4 T 50

MED: 100-2, 15, 260; 100-4, 12, 90.3; 100-4, 14, 10

AMA: 2001, Sep, 1; 2001, Oct, 8; 2001, May, 5; 2001, Apr, 4

52355   **with resection of ureteral or renal pelvic tumor**   4 T 50

MED: 100-2, 15, 260; 100-4, 12, 90.3; 100-4, 14, 10

AMA: 2001, Sep, 1; 2001, Oct, 8; 2001, May, 5; 2001, Apr, 4

VESICAL NECK AND PROSTATE

To report abdominal and perineal gangrene debridement, consult CPT codes 11004-11006.

52400   **Cystourethroscopy with incision, fulguration, or resection of congenital posterior urethral valves, or congenital obstructive hypertrophic mucosal folds**   3 T

MED: 100-2, 15, 260; 100-4, 12, 90.3; 100-4, 14, 10

AMA: 2001, Apr, 4

52402   **Cystourethroscopy with transurethral resection or incision of ejaculatory ducts**   ♂ 3 T 80

52450   **Transurethral incision of prostate**   ♂ 3 T

MED: 100-2, 15, 260; 100-4, 12, 90.3; 100-4, 14, 10

AMA: 2001, Apr, 4

For abdominal and perineal gangrene debridement, consult CPT codes 11004-11006.

Urinary System

52500 — 52648

52500   Transurethral resection of bladder neck (separate procedure)   ♂ 3 T 🔲
MED: 100-2, 15, 260; 100-4, 12, 90.3; 100-4, 14, 10

AMA: 2001, Apr, 4

52510   Transurethral balloon dilation of the prostatic urethra   ♂ 3 T 🔲
MED: 100-2, 15, 260; 100-4, 12, 90.3; 100-4, 14, 10

AMA: 2001, Apr, 4

52601   Transurethral electrosurgical resection of prostate, including control of postoperative bleeding, complete (vasectomy, meatotomy, cystourethroscopy, urethral calibration and/or dilation, and internal urethrotomy are included)   ♂ 4 T 🔲
MED: 100-2, 15, 260; 100-4, 12, 90.3; 100-4, 14, 10

AMA: 2001, Apr, 4

If other approaches are used, consult CPT codes 55801-55845.

52606   Transurethral fulguration for postoperative bleeding occurring after the usual follow-up time   ♂ 1 T 🔲
MED: 100-2, 15, 260; 100-4, 12, 90.3; 100-4, 14, 10

AMA: 2001, Apr, 4

52612   Transurethral resection of prostate; first stage of two-stage resection (partial resection)   ♂ 2 T 🔲
MED: 100-2, 15, 260; 100-4, 12, 90.3; 100-4, 14, 10

AMA: 2001, Apr, 4

52614   second stage of two-stage resection (resection completed)   ♂ 1 T 🔲
MED: 100-2, 15, 260; 100-4, 12, 90.3; 100-4, 14, 10

AMA: 2001, Apr, 4

52620   Transurethral resection; of residual obstructive tissue after 90 days postoperative   ♂ 1 T 🔲
MED: 100-2, 15, 260; 100-4, 12, 90.3; 100-4, 14, 10

AMA: 2001, Apr, 4

52630   of regrowth of obstructive tissue longer than one year postoperative   ♂ 2 T 🔲
MED: 100-2, 15, 260; 100-4, 12, 90.3; 100-4, 14, 10

AMA: 2001, Apr, 4

52640   of postoperative bladder neck contracture   ♂ 2 T 🔲
MED: 100-2, 15, 260; 100-4, 12, 90.3; 100-4, 14, 10

AMA: 2001, Apr, 4

▲ **52647**   Laser coagulation of prostate, including control of postoperative bleeding, complete (vasectomy, meatotomy, cystourethroscopy, urethral calibration and/or dilation, and internal urethrotomy are included if performed) ♂ 9 T 🔲
MED: 100-2, 15, 260; 100-4, 12, 90.3; 100-4, 14, 10

AMA: 2001, Apr, 4; 1998, Mar, 11

▲ **52648**   Laser vaporization of prostate, including control of postoperative bleeding, complete (vasectomy, meatotomy, cystourethroscopy, urethral calibration and/or dilation, internal urethrotomy and transurethral resection of prostate are included if performed)   ♂ 9 T 🔲
MED: 100-2, 15, 260; 100-4, 12, 90.3; 100-4, 14, 10

AMA: 2001, Apr, 4; 1998, Mar, 11

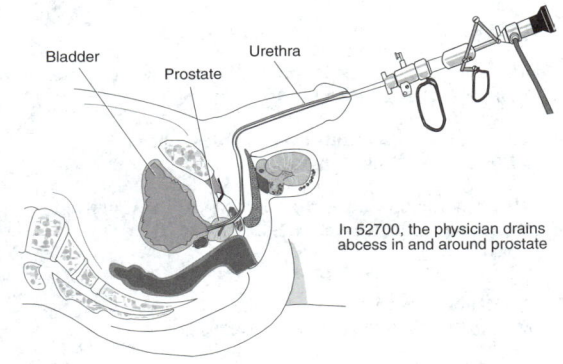

Bladder   Urethra

Prostate

In 52700, the physician drains abcess in and around prostate

52700   **Transurethral drainage of prostatic abscess**   ♂ 2 T 80 ↺
          MED: 100-2, 15, 260; 100-4, 12, 90.3; 100-4, 14, 10

          AMA: 2001, Apr, 4

URETHRA

If an endoscopy is performed, consult cystoscopy, urethroscopy, and cystourethroscopy procedures, 52000-52700. If an injection procedure is performed for urethrocystography, consult CPT codes 51600-51610.

INCISION

53000   **Urethrotomy or urethrostomy, external (separate procedure); pendulous urethra**   1 T ↺
          MED: 100-2, 15, 260; 100-4, 12, 90.3; 100-4, 14, 10

53010   **perineal urethra, external**   1 T ↺
          MED: 100-2, 15, 260; 100-4, 12, 90.3; 100-4, 14, 10

53020   **Meatotomy, cutting of meatus (separate procedure); except infant**   1 T ↺

53025   **infant**   A T 80 ↺ 63

53040   **Drainage of deep periurethral abscess**   2 T 80 ↺

          If a subcutaneous abscess is drained, consult CPT codes 10060 and 10061.

53060   **Drainage of Skene's gland abscess or cyst**   ♀ T ↺

53080   **Drainage of perineal urinary extravasation; uncomplicated (separate procedure)**   3 T ↺

53085   **complicated**   T 80 ↺

EXCISION

53200   **Biopsy of urethra**   1 T ↺

53210   **Urethrectomy, total, including cystostomy; female**   ♀ 5 T 80 ↺

53215   **male**   ♂ 5 T 80 ↺
          MED: 100-2, 15, 260; 100-4, 12, 90.3; 100-4, 14, 10

53220   **Excision or fulguration of carcinoma of urethra**   2 T 80 ↺
          MED: 100-2, 15, 260; 100-4, 12, 90.3; 100-4, 14, 10

53230   **Excision of urethral diverticulum (separate procedure); female**   ♀ 2 T 80 ↺
          MED: 100-2, 15, 260; 100-4, 12, 90.3; 100-4, 14, 10

Urinary System

53235 — 53442

53235   male   ♂ 3 T 80
MED: 100-2, 15, 260; 100-4, 12, 90.3; 100-4, 14, 10

53240 Marsupialization of urethral diverticulum, male or female   2 T
MED: 100-2, 15, 260; 100-4, 12, 90.3; 100-4, 14, 10

53250 Excision of bulbourethral gland (Cowper's gland)   ♂ 2 T
MED: 100-2, 15, 260; 100-4, 12, 90.3; 100-4, 14, 10

53260 Excision or fulguration; urethral polyp(s), distal urethra   2 T
MED: 100-2, 15, 260; 100-4, 12, 90.3; 100-4, 14, 10

If an endoscopic approach is used, consult CPT codes 52214 and 52224.

53265   urethral caruncle   2 T
MED: 100-2, 15, 260; 100-4, 12, 90.3; 100-4, 14, 10

53270   Skene's glands   ♀ 2 T
MED: 100-2, 15, 260; 100-4, 12, 90.3; 100-4, 14, 10

53275   urethral prolapse   ♀ 2 T
MED: 100-2, 15, 260; 100-4, 12, 90.3; 100-4, 14, 10

REPAIR

For hypospadias, consult CPT codes 54300-54352.

53400 Urethroplasty; first stage, for fistula, diverticulum, or stricture (eg, Johannsen type)   3 T 80
MED: 100-2, 15, 260; 100-4, 12, 90.3; 100-4, 14, 10

53405   second stage (formation of urethra), including urinary diversion   2 T 80
MED: 100-2, 15, 260; 100-4, 12, 90.3; 100-4, 14, 10

53410 Urethroplasty, one-stage reconstruction of male anterior urethra   ♂ 2 T 80
MED: 100-2, 15, 260; 100-4, 12, 90.3; 100-4, 14, 10

53415 Urethroplasty, transpubic or perineal, one stage, for reconstruction or repair of prostatic or membranous urethra   ♂ C 80
MED: 100-2, 15, 260; 100-4, 12, 90.3; 100-4, 14, 10

53420 Urethroplasty, two-stage reconstruction or repair of prostatic or membranous urethra; first stage   ♂ 3 T
MED: 100-2, 15, 260; 100-4, 12, 90.3; 100-4, 14, 10

53425   second stage   ♂ 2 T 80
MED: 100-2, 15, 260; 100-4, 12, 90.3; 100-4, 14, 10

53430 Urethroplasty, reconstruction of female urethra   ♀ 2 T 80
MED: 100-2, 15, 260; 100-4, 12, 90.3; 100-4, 14, 10

53431 Urethroplasty with tubularization of posterior urethra and/or lower bladder for incontinence (eg, Tenago, Leadbetter procedure)   2 T 80
MED: 100-2, 15, 260; 100-3, 230.10; 100-4, 12, 90.3; 100-4, 14, 10

53440 Sling operation for correction of male urinary incontinence (eg, fascia or synthetic)   ♂ 2 S 80
MED: 100-2, 15, 260; 100-3, 230.10; 100-4, 12, 90.3; 100-4, 14, 10

53442 Removal or revision of sling for male urinary incontinence (eg, fascia or synthetic)   ♂ 1 T 80
MED: 100-2, 15, 260; 100-4, 12, 90.3; 100-4, 14, 10

53444	**Insertion of tandem cuff (dual cuff)**	2 S 80 🔁

MED: 100-2, 15, 260; 100-4, 12, 90.3; 100-4, 14, 10

53445	**Insertion of inflatable urethral/bladder neck sphincter, including placement of pump, reservoir, and cuff**	1 S 80 🔁

MED: 100-2, 15, 260; 100-3, 230.10; 100-4, 12, 90.3; 100-4, 14, 10

53446	**Removal of inflatable urethral/bladder neck sphincter, including pump, reservoir, and cuff**	1 T 80 🔁

MED: 100-2, 15, 260; 100-4, 12, 90.3; 100-4, 14, 10

53447	**Removal and replacement of inflatable urethral/bladder neck sphincter including pump, reservoir, and cuff at the same operative session**	1 S 80 🔁

MED: 100-2, 15, 260; 100-3, 230.10; 100-4, 12, 90.3; 100-4, 14, 10

53448	**Removal and replacement of inflatable urethral/bladder neck sphincter including pump, reservoir, and cuff through an infected field at the same operative session including irrigation and debridement of infected tissue**	C 80 🔁

Do not report 11040-11043 in conjunction with CPT code 53448.

53449	**Repair of inflatable urethral/bladder neck sphincter, including pump, reservoir, and cuff**	1 T 80 🔁

MED: 100-2, 15, 260; 100-3, 230.10; 100-4, 12, 90.3; 100-4, 14, 10

53450	**Urethromeatoplasty, with mucosal advancement**	1 T 🔁

MED: 100-2, 15, 260; 100-4, 12, 90.3; 100-4, 14, 10

If a meatotomy is performed, consult CPT codes 53020 and 53025.

53460	**Urethromeatoplasty, with partial excision of distal urethral segment (Richardson type procedure)**	1 T 80 🔁

MED: 100-2, 15, 260; 100-4, 12, 90.3; 100-4, 14, 10

53500	**Urethrolysis, transvaginal, secondary, open, including cystourethroscopy (eg, postsurgical obstruction, scarring)**	♀ T 80 🔁

To report urethrolysis by retropubic approach, consult CPT code 53899.

Code 53500 cannot be reported with 52000.

53502	**Urethrorrhaphy, suture of urethral wound or injury, female**	♀ 2 T 🔁

MED: 100-2, 15, 260; 100-4, 12, 90.3; 100-4, 14, 10

53505	**Urethrorrhaphy, suture of urethral wound or injury; penile**	♂ 2 T 80 🔁

MED: 100-2, 15, 260; 100-4, 12, 90.3; 100-4, 14, 10

53510	**perineal**	2 T 80 🔁

MED: 100-2, 15, 260; 100-4, 12, 90.3; 100-4, 14, 10

53515	**prostatomembranous**	♂ 2 T 80 🔁

MED: 100-2, 15, 260; 100-4, 12, 90.3; 100-4, 14, 10

53520	**Closure of urethrostomy or urethrocutaneous fistula, male (separate procedure)**	♂ 2 T 🔁

MED: 100-2, 15, 260; 100-4, 12, 90.3; 100-4, 14, 10

If a urethrovaginal fistula is closed, consult CPT code 57310. If a urethrorectal fistula is closed, consult CPT codes 45820 and 45825.

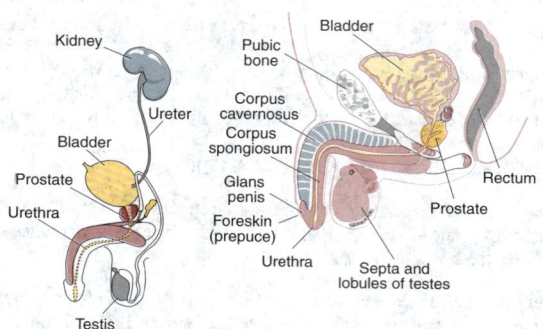

MANIPULATION
For radiological supervision and interpretation, consult CPT code 74485.

53600	**Dilation of urethral stricture by passage of sound or urethral dilator, male; initial**	♂ T
53601	**subsequent**	♂ T
53605	**Dilation of urethral stricture or vesical neck by passage of sound or urethral dilator, male, general or conduction (spinal) anesthesia**	♂ 2 T
	MED: 100-2, 15, 260; 100-4, 12, 90.3; 100-4, 14, 10	
53620	**Dilation of urethral stricture by passage of filiform and follower, male; initial**	♂ T
53621	**subsequent**	♂ T
53660	**Dilation of female urethra including suppository and/or instillation; initial**	♀ T
53661	**subsequent**	♀ T
53665	**Dilation of female urethra, general or conduction (spinal) anesthesia**	♀ 1 T
	MED: 100-2, 15, 260; 100-4, 12, 90.3; 100-4, 14, 10	

OTHER PROCEDURES

53850	**Transurethral destruction of prostate tissue; by microwave thermotherapy**	♂ 9 T
	MED: 100-2, 15, 260; 100-4, 12, 90.3; 100-4, 14, 10	
	AMA: 2001, Apr, 4; 1997, Nov, 20	
53852	**by radiofrequency thermotherapy**	♂ T
	AMA: 2001, Apr, 4; 1997, Nov, 20	
53853	**by water-induced thermotherapy**	♂ T
53899	**Unlisted procedure, urinary system**	T 80

MALE GENITAL SYSTEM

PENIS

INCISION

54000   **Slitting of prepuce, dorsal or lateral (separate procedure); newborn**   A ♂ 2 T 80 📋 63
     MED: 100-2, 15, 260; 100-4, 12, 90.3; 100-4, 14, 10

54001   **except newborn**   ♂ 2 T 📋
     MED: 100-2, 15, 260; 100-4, 12, 90.3; 100-4, 14, 10

54015   **Incision and drainage of penis, deep**   ♂ 4 T 80 📋
     MED: 100-2, 15, 260; 100-4, 12, 90.3; 100-4, 14, 10

     If a subcutaneous abscess is incised and drained, consult CPT codes 10060-10160.

DESTRUCTION

54050   **Destruction of lesion(s), penis (eg, condyloma, papilloma, molluscum contagiosum, herpetic vesicle), simple; chemical**   ♂ T 📋

54055   **electrodesiccation**   ♂ T 📋

54056   **cryosurgery**   ♂ T 📋

54057   **laser surgery**   ♂ 1 T 📋
     MED: 100-2, 15, 260; 100-3, 140.5; 100-4, 12, 90.3; 100-4, 14, 10

54060   **surgical excision**   ♂ 1 T 📋
     MED: 100-2, 15, 260; 100-4, 12, 90.3; 100-4, 14, 10

54065   **Destruction of lesion(s), penis (eg, condyloma, papilloma, molluscum contagiosum, herpetic vesicle), extensive (eg, laser surgery, electrosurgery, cryosurgery, chemosurgery)**   ♂ 1 T 📋
     MED: 100-2, 15, 260; 100-3, 140.5; 100-4, 12, 90.3; 100-4, 14, 10

     If destruction or an excision is performed on other lesions, see the Integumentary System.

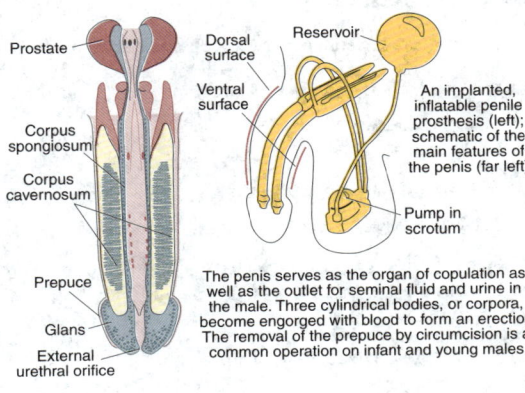

Prostate
Dorsal surface
Ventral surface
Reservoir
Corpus spongiosum
Corpus cavernosum
An implanted, inflatable penile prosthesis (left); schematic of the main features of the penis (far left)
Pump in scrotum
Prepuce
Glans
External urethral orifice

The penis serves as the organ of copulation as well as the outlet for seminal fluid and urine in the male. Three cylindrical bodies, or corpora, become engorged with blood to form an erection. The removal of the prepuce by circumcision is a common operation on infant and young males

Male Genital System

EXCISION

54100 **Biopsy of penis; (separate procedure)** ♂ **1** T ⌫
MED: 100-2, 15, 260; 100-4, 12, 90.3; 100-4, 14, 10

AMA: 1999, Nov, 26

54105   **deep structures** ♂ **1** T ⌫
MED: 100-2, 15, 260; 100-4, 12, 90.3; 100-4, 14, 10

54110 **Excision of penile plaque (Peyronie disease);** ♂ **2** T 80 ⌫
MED: 100-2, 15, 260; 100-4, 12, 90.3; 100-4, 14, 10

54111   **with graft to 5 cm in length** ♂ **2** T 80 ⌫
MED: 100-2, 15, 260; 100-4, 12, 90.3; 100-4, 14, 10

AMA: 1999, Aug, 5

54112   **with graft greater than 5 cm in length** ♂ **2** T 80 ⌫
MED: 100-2, 15, 260; 100-4, 12, 90.3; 100-4, 14, 10

54115 **Removal foreign body from deep penile tissue (eg, plastic implant)** ♂ **1** T 80 ⌫
MED: 100-2, 15, 260; 100-4, 12, 90.3; 100-4, 14, 10

54120 **Amputation of penis; partial** ♂ **2** T 80 ⌫
MED: 100-2, 15, 260; 100-4, 12, 90.3; 100-4, 14, 10

54125   **complete** ♂ C 80 ⌫

54130 **Amputation of penis, radical; with bilateral inguinofemoral lymphadenectomy** ♂ C 80 ⌫

54135   **in continuity with bilateral pelvic lymphadenectomy, including external iliac, hypogastric and obturator nodes** ♂ C 80 ⌫

If a lymphadenectomy (separate procedure) is performed, consult CPT codes 38760-38770.

54150 **Circumcision, using clamp or other device; newborn** A ♂ **1** T 80 ⌫ ⊛
MED: 100-2, 15, 260; 100-4, 12, 90.3; 100-4, 14, 10

AMA: 1998, May, 11; 1996, Sep, 11

54152   **except newborn** ♂ **1** T ⌫
MED: 100-2, 15, 260; 100-4, 12, 90.3; 100-4, 14, 10

AMA: 1998, May, 11; 1996, Sep, 11; 1996, Dec, 10

54160 **Circumcision, surgical excision other than clamp, device or dorsal slit; newborn** A ♂ **2** T ⌫ ⊛
MED: 100-2, 15, 260; 100-4, 12, 90.3; 100-4, 14, 10

AMA: 1998, May, 11; 1996, Sep, 11

54161   **except newborn** ♂ **2** T ⌫
MED: 100-2, 15, 260; 100-4, 12, 90.3; 100-4, 14, 10

AMA: 1998, May, 11; 1996, Sep, 11; 1996, Dec, 10

54162 **Lysis or excision of penile post-circumcision adhesions** ♂ **2** T ⌫
MED: 100-2, 15, 260; 100-4, 12, 90.3; 100-4, 14, 10

54163 **Repair incomplete circumcision** ♂ **2** T ⌫
MED: 100-2, 15, 260; 100-4, 12, 90.3; 100-4, 14, 10

54164	Frenulotomy of penis	♂ 2 T ▣

MED: 100-2, 15, 260; 100-4, 12, 90.3; 100-4, 14, 10

Do not use in conjunction with circumcision codes 54150-54161, 54162, 54163.

INTRODUCTION

54200	Injection procedure for Peyronie disease;	♂ T ▣
54205	with surgical exposure of plaque	♂ 4 T 80 ▣

MED: 100-2, 15, 260; 100-4, 12, 90.3; 100-4, 14, 10

54220	Irrigation of corpora cavernosa for priapism	♂ 1 T ▣

MED: 100-2, 15, 260; 100-4, 12, 90.3; 100-4, 14, 10

54230	Injection procedure for corpora cavernosography	♂ N ▣

To report radiological supervision and interpretation, consult CPT code 74445.

54231	Dynamic cavernosometry, including intracavernosal injection of vasoactive drugs (eg, papaverine, phentolamine)	♂ T ▣

54235	Injection of corpora cavernosa with pharmacologic agent(s) (eg, papaverine, phentolamine)	♂ T ▣

AMA: 1996, Sep, 10

54240	Penile plethysmography	♂ T 80 ▣

MED: 100-3, 20.14

If the physician only interprets the results and/or operates the equipment, modifier-26 should be appended to codes 54240 and 54250.

54250	Nocturnal penile tumescence and/or rigidity test	♂ T 80 ▣

If the physician only interprets the results and/or operates the equipment, modifier-26 should be appended to codes 54240 and 54250.

REPAIR

If other urethroplasties are performed, consult CPT codes 53400-53430. If penile revascularization is performed, consult CPT code 37788.

To report abdominal perineal gangrene debridement, consult 11004-11006.

54300	Plastic operation of penis for straightening of chordee (eg, hypospadias), with or without mobilization of urethra	♂ 3 T 80 ▣

MED: 100-2, 15, 260; 100-4, 12, 90.3; 100-4, 14, 10

54304	Plastic operation on penis for correction of chordee or for first stage hypospadias repair with or without transplantation of prepuce and/or skin flaps	♂ 3 T 80 ▣

MED: 100-2, 15, 260; 100-4, 12, 90.3; 100-4, 14, 10

54308	Urethroplasty for second stage hypospadias repair (including urinary diversion); less than 3 cm	♂ 3 T 80 ▣

MED: 100-2, 15, 260; 100-4, 12, 90.3; 100-4, 14, 10

54312	greater than 3 cm	♂ 3 T 80 ▣

MED: 100-2, 15, 260; 100-4, 12, 90.3; 100-4, 14, 10

54316	Urethroplasty for second stage hypospadias repair (including urinary diversion) with free skin graft obtained from site other than genitalia	♂ 3 T 80 ▣

MED: 100-2, 15, 260; 100-4, 12, 90.3; 100-4, 14, 10

Male Genital System

54318 — 54390

54318   **Urethroplasty for third stage hypospadias repair to release penis from scrotum (eg, third stage Cecil repair)**   ♂ 3 T 80 ▪
      MED: 100-2, 15, 260; 100-4, 12, 90.3; 100-4, 14, 10

54322   **One stage distal hypospadias repair (with or without chordee or circumcision); with simple meatal advancement (eg, Magpi, V-flap)**   ♂ 3 T 80 ▪
      MED: 100-2, 15, 260; 100-4, 12, 90.3; 100-4, 14, 10

54324   **with urethroplasty by local skin flaps (eg, flip-flap, prepucial flap)**   ♂ 3 T 80 ▪
      MED: 100-2, 15, 260; 100-4, 12, 90.3; 100-4, 14, 10

       Browne's operation

54326   **with urethroplasty by local skin flaps and mobilization of urethra**   ♂ 3 T 80 ▪
      MED: 100-2, 15, 260; 100-4, 12, 90.3; 100-4, 14, 10

54328   **with extensive dissection to correct chordee and urethroplasty with local skin flaps, skin graft patch, and/or island flap**   ♂ 3 T 80 ▪
      MED: 100-2, 15, 260; 100-4, 12, 90.3; 100-4, 14, 10

54332   **One stage proximal penile or penoscrotal hypospadias repair requiring extensive dissection to correct chordee and urethroplasty by use of skin graft tube and/or island flap**   ♂ C 80 ▪

54336   **One stage perineal hypospadias repair requiring extensive dissection to correct chordee and urethroplasty by use of skin graft tube and/or island flap**   ♂ C 80 ▪

54340   **Repair of hypospadias complications (ie, fistula, stricture, diverticula); by closure, incision, or excision, simple**   ♂ 3 T 80 ▪
      MED: 100-2, 15, 260; 100-4, 12, 90.3; 100-4, 14, 10

54344   **requiring mobilization of skin flaps and urethroplasty with flap or patch graft**   ♂ 3 T 80 ▪
      MED: 100-2, 15, 260; 100-4, 12, 90.3; 100-4, 14, 10

54348   **requiring extensive dissection and urethroplasty with flap, patch or tubed graft (includes urinary diversion)**   ♂ 3 T 80 ▪
      MED: 100-2, 15, 260; 100-4, 12, 90.3; 100-4, 14, 10

54352   **Repair of hypospadias cripple requiring extensive dissection and excision of previously constructed structures including re-release of chordee and reconstruction of urethra and penis by use of local skin as grafts and island flaps and skin brought in as flaps or grafts**   ♂ 3 T 80 ▪
      MED: 100-2, 15, 260; 100-4, 12, 90.3; 100-4, 14, 10

54360   **Plastic operation on penis to correct angulation**   ♂ 3 T 80 ▪
      MED: 100-2, 15, 260; 100-4, 12, 90.3; 100-4, 14, 10

54380   **Plastic operation on penis for epispadias distal to external sphincter;**   ♂ 3 T 80 ▪
      MED: 100-2, 15, 260; 100-4, 12, 90.3; 100-4, 14, 10

       Lowsley's operation

54385   **with incontinence**   ♂ 3 T 80 ▪
      MED: 100-2, 15, 260; 100-3, 230.10; 100-4, 12, 90.3; 100-4, 14, 10

54390   **with exstrophy of bladder**   ♂ C 80 ▪

Male Genital System

54400 — 54440

54400   Insertion of penile prosthesis; non-inflatable (semi-rigid)   ♂ 3 S ⟲
MED: 100-2, 15, 260; 100-3, 230.4; 100-4, 12, 90.3; 100-4, 14, 10

54401   inflatable (self-contained)   ♂ 3 S ⟲
MED: 100-2, 15, 260; 100-3, 230.4; 100-4, 12, 90.3; 100-4, 14, 10

54405   Insertion of multi-component, inflatable penile prosthesis, including placement of pump, cylinders, and reservoir   ♂ 3 S 80 ⟲
MED: 100-2, 15, 260; 100-3, 230.4; 100-4, 12, 90.3; 100-4, 14, 10

If service is reduced, report 54405 with modifier 52.

54406   Removal of all components of a multi-component, inflatable penile prosthesis without replacement of prosthesis   ♂ 3 T 80 ⟲
MED: 100-2, 15, 260; 100-3, 230.4; 100-4, 12, 90.3; 100-4, 14, 10

If service is reduced, report 54406 with modifier 52.

54408   Repair of component(s) of a multi-component, inflatable penile prosthesis   ♂ 3 T 80 ⟲
MED: 100-2, 15, 260; 100-3, 230.4; 100-4, 12, 90.3; 100-4, 14, 10

54410   Removal and replacement of all component(s) of a multi-component, inflatable penile prosthesis at the same operative session   ♂ 3 S 80 ⟲
MED: 100-2, 15, 260; 100-3, 230.4; 100-4, 12, 90.3; 100-4, 14, 10

54411   Removal and replacement of all components of a multi-component inflatable penile prosthesis through an infected field at the same operative session, including irrigation and debridement of infected tissue   ♂ C 80 ⟲
MED: 100-3, 230.4

If service is reduced, report 54411 with modifier 52.

Do not report 11040-11043 in conjunction with 54411.

54415   Removal of non-inflatable (semi-rigid) or inflatable (self-contained) penile prosthesis, without replacement of prosthesis   ♂ 3 T 80 ⟲
MED: 100-2, 15, 260; 100-3, 230.4; 100-4, 12, 90.3; 100-4, 14, 10

54416   Removal and replacement of non-inflatable (semi-rigid) or inflatable (self-contained) penile prosthesis at the same operative session   ♂ 3 S 80 ⟲
MED: 100-2, 15, 260; 100-3, 230.4; 100-4, 12, 90.3; 100-4, 14, 10

54417   Removal and replacement of non-inflatable (semi-rigid) or inflatable (self-contained) penile prosthesis through an infected field at the same operative session, including irrigation and debridement of infected tissue   ♂ C 80 ⟲
MED: 100-3, 230.4

Do not report 11040-11043 in conjunction with 54417.

54420   Corpora cavernosa-saphenous vein shunt (priapism operation), unilateral or bilateral   ♂ 4 T 80 ⟲
MED: 100-2, 15, 260; 100-4, 12, 90.3; 100-4, 14, 10

54430   Corpora cavernosa-corpus spongiosum shunt (priapism operation), unilateral or bilateral   ♂ C 80 ⟲

54435   Corpora cavernosa-glans penis fistulization (eg, biopsy needle, Winter procedure, rongeur, or punch) for priapism   ♂ 4 T ⟲
MED: 100-2, 15, 260; 100-4, 12, 90.3; 100-4, 14, 10

54440   Plastic operation of penis for injury   ♂ 4 T 80 ⟲
MED: 100-2, 15, 260; 100-4, 12, 90.3; 100-4, 14, 10

Male Genital System

MANIPULATION

54450   **Foreskin manipulation including lysis of preputial adhesions and stretching**   ♂ **1** T ↺
MED: 100-2, 15, 260; 100-4, 12, 90.3; 100-4, 14, 10

TESTIS

EXCISION

54500   **Biopsy of testis, needle (separate procedure)**   ♂ **1** T **50** **80** ↺
MED: 100-2, 15, 260; 100-4, 12, 90.3; 100-4, 14, 10

To report fine needle aspiration, consult CPT codes 10021, 10022.

To report evaluation of fine needle aspirate, consult CPT codes 88172, 88173.

54505   **Biopsy of testis, incisional (separate procedure)**   ♂ **1** T **50** **80** ↺
MED: 100-2, 15, 260; 100-4, 12, 90.3; 100-4, 14, 10

AMA: 2001, Oct, 8

If this procedure is combined with a vasogram, a seminal vesiculogram, or a epididymogram, consult CPT code 55300.

54512   **Excision of extraparenchymal lesion of testis**   ♂ **2** T **50** **80** ↺
MED: 100-2, 15, 260; 100-4, 12, 90.3; 100-4, 14, 10

AMA: 2001, Oct, 8

54520   **Orchiectomy, simple (including subcapsular), with or without testicular prosthesis, scrotal or inguinal approach**   ♂ **3** T **50** ↺
MED: 100-2, 15, 260; 100-3, 230.3; 100-4, 12, 90.3; 100-4, 14, 10

AMA: 2001, Oct, 8

Huggins' orchiectomy

54522   **Orchiectomy, partial**   ♂ **3** T **50** **80** ↺
MED: 100-2, 15, 260; 100-4, 12, 90.3; 100-4, 14, 10

AMA: 2001, Oct, 8

54530   **Orchiectomy, radical, for tumor; inguinal approach**   ♂ **4** T **50** **80** ↺
MED: 100-2, 15, 260; 100-3, 230.3; 100-4, 12, 90.3; 100-4, 14, 10

AMA: 2001, Oct, 8

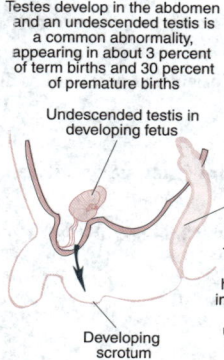

Testes develop in the abdomen and an undescended testis is a common abnormality, appearing in about 3 percent of term births and 30 percent of premature births

Undescended testis in developing fetus

Hypospadias   Glans penis

Penile raphe   Dorsum of penis

Scrotal raphe

Rectum   Epispadias

Developing scrotum

The penile raphe is the site where urogenital folds fuse during the fetal period and hypospadias results when fusion is absent or incomplete. Epispadias is when the dorsal wall of the urethra fails to fuse resulting in a urethral opening on the dorsum of the penis; occurrence in females usually results in a urethral opening into the vaginal canal

2G / **TC** Professional/Technical Component   **80** / **80** Assist-at-Surgery Allowed/With Documentation   ⊙ Conscious Sedation

Unlisted   Not Covered   **MED:** Pubs 100/NCD Reference   **1** - **9** ASC Group   ⑥③ Modifier 63 Exempt

390 — Surgery   CPT only © 2005 American Medical Association. All Rights Reserved. *(Black Ink)*   © 2005 Ingenix, Inc. *(Blue Ink)*

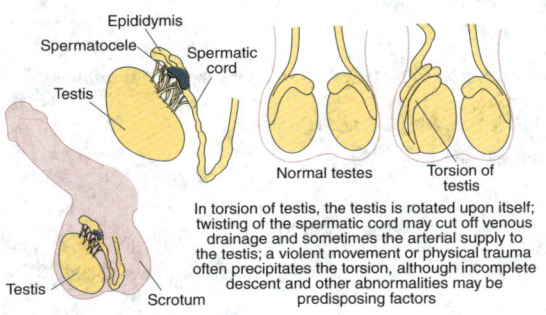

Spermatocele

Epididymis

Spermatic cord

Testis

Normal testes

Torsion of testis

In torsion of testis, the testis is rotated upon itself; twisting of the spermatic cord may cut off venous drainage and sometimes the arterial supply to the testis; a violent movement or physical trauma often precipitates the torsion, although incomplete descent and other abnormalities may be predisposing factors

Testis

Scrotum

A spermatocele is a cystic accumulation of semen, usually in the spermatic cord or at the head of the epididymis

54535   **with abdominal exploration**   ♂ C 50 80 ▶
MED: 100-3, 230.3

AMA: 2001, Oct, 8

If an orchiectomy is performed with repair of a hernia, consult CPT codes 49505 or 49507 and 54520. If a radical retroperitoneal lymphadenectomy is performed, consult CPT code 38780.

54550   **Exploration for undescended testis (inguinal or scrotal area)** ♂ 4 T 50 80 ▶
MED: 100-2, 15, 260; 100-4, 12, 90.3; 100-4, 14, 10

AMA: 2001, Oct, 8

54560   **Exploration for undescended testis with abdominal exploration** ♂ T 50 80 ▶
AMA: 2001, Oct, 8

REPAIR

54600   **Reduction of torsion of testis, surgical, with or without fixation of contralateral testis**   ♂ 4 T 50 ▶
MED: 100-2, 15, 260; 100-4, 12, 90.3; 100-4, 14, 10

54620   **Fixation of contralateral testis (separate procedure)**   ♂ 3 T 50 ▶
MED: 100-2, 15, 260; 100-4, 12, 90.3; 100-4, 14, 10

54640   **Orchiopexy, inguinal approach, with or without hernia repair** ♂ 4 T 80 ▶
MED: 100-2, 15, 260; 100-4, 12, 90.3; 100-4, 14, 10

AMA: 2001, Oct, 8

To report inguinal hernia repair performed with inguinal orchiopexy, consult CPT codes 49495-49525.

Bevan's operation

54650   **Orchiopexy, abdominal approach, for intra-abdominal testis (eg, Fowler-Stephens)**   ♂ C 50 80 ▶
AMA: 2001, Oct, 8; 2000, May, 4; 1999, Nov, 26

If a laparoscopic approach is used, consult CPT code 54692.

54660   **Insertion of testicular prosthesis (separate procedure)**   ♂ 2 T 50 80 ▶
MED: 100-2, 15, 260; 100-2, 16, 180; 100-4, 12, 90.3; 100-4, 14, 10

AMA: 2001, Oct, 8

Male Genital System

54670 — 54861

54670   **Suture or repair of testicular injury**   ♂ 3 T 50 80 🔁
MED: 100-2, 15, 260; 100-4, 12, 90.3; 100-4, 14, 10

AMA: 2001, Oct, 8

54680   **Transplantation of testis(es) to thigh (because of scrotal destruction)**   ♂ 3 T 50 80 🔁
MED: 100-2, 15, 260; 100-4, 12, 90.3; 100-4, 14, 10

AMA: 2001, Oct, 8

LAPAROSCOPY

Diagnostic laparoscopy is always included in surgical laparoscopy.

To report only a diagnostic laparoscopy (peritoneoscopy), consult CPT code 49320.

54690   **Laparoscopy, surgical; orchiectomy**   ♂ 9 T 50 80 🔁
MED: 100-2, 15, 260; 100-4, 12, 90.3; 100-4, 14, 10

AMA: 2001, Oct, 8; 2000, Mar, 5; 1999, Nov, 26

54692   **orchiopexy for intra-abdominal testis**   ♂ T 50 🔁
AMA: 2001, Oct, 8; 2000, May, 4; 1999, Nov, 27

54699   **Unlisted laparoscopy procedure, testis**   T 50 80
AMA: 2000, Mar, 5; 1999, Nov, 27

EPIDIDYMIS

INCISION

54700   **Incision and drainage of epididymis, testis and/or scrotal space (eg, abscess or hematoma)**   ♂ 2 T 🔁
MED: 100-2, 15, 260; 100-4, 12, 90.3; 100-4, 14, 10

AMA: 2001, Oct, 8

EXCISION

54800   **Biopsy of epididymis, needle**   ♂ 1 T 80 🔁
MED: 100-2, 15, 260; 100-4, 12, 90.3; 100-4, 14, 10

AMA: 2001, Oct, 8

To report fine needle aspiration, consult CPT codes 10021, 10022.

To report evaluation of fine needle aspirate, consult CPT codes 88172, 88173.

54820   **Exploration of epididymis, with or without biopsy**   ♂ 1 T 80 🔁
MED: 100-2, 15, 260; 100-4, 12, 90.3; 100-4, 14, 10

AMA: 2001, Oct, 8

54830   **Excision of local lesion of epididymis**   ♂ 3 T 80 🔁
MED: 100-2, 15, 260; 100-4, 12, 90.3; 100-4, 14, 10

AMA: 2001, Oct, 8

54840   **Excision of spermatocele, with or without epididymectomy**   ♂ 4 T 🔁
MED: 100-2, 15, 260; 100-4, 12, 90.3; 100-4, 14, 10

AMA: 2001, Oct, 8

54860   **Epididymectomy; unilateral**   ♂ 3 T 🔁
MED: 100-2, 15, 260; 100-4, 12, 90.3; 100-4, 14, 10

54861   **bilateral**   ♂ 4 T 80 🔁
MED: 100-2, 15, 260; 100-4, 12, 90.3; 100-4, 14, 10

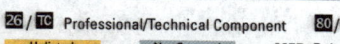 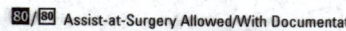 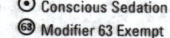

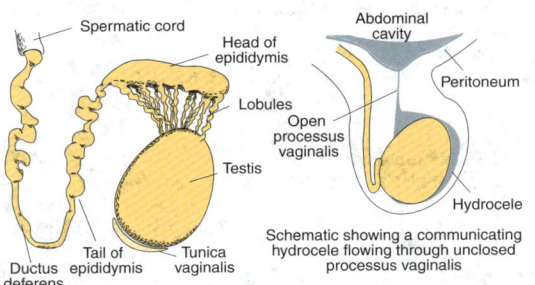

Schematic showing a communicating hydrocele flowing through unclosed processus vaginalis

The tunica vaginalis is a closed sac within the scrotum and is the lower remnant of the path taken by the testis as it descends from the abdomen just prior to birth. The presence of fluid in this pathway is called a hydrocele. The testes, or testicles, are the male reproductive organs. Each produces sperm and male sex hormones

REPAIR

54900 **Epididymovasostomy, anastomosis of epididymis to vas deferens; unilateral** ♂ 4 T 80 ↩
MED: 100-2, 15, 260; 100-4, 12, 90.3; 100-4, 14, 10

AMA: 1998, Nov, 16

54901 **bilateral** ♂ 4 T 80 ↩
MED: 100-2, 15, 260; 100-4, 12, 90.3; 100-4, 14, 10

AMA: 1998, Nov, 16

If an operating microscope is used, consult CPT code 69990.

TUNICA VAGINALIS

INCISION

55000 **Puncture aspiration of hydrocele, tunica vaginalis, with or without injection of medication** ♂ T ↩

EXCISION

55040 **Excision of hydrocele; unilateral** ♂ 3 T ↩
MED: 100-2, 15, 260; 100-4, 12, 90.3; 100-4, 14, 10

55041 **bilateral** ♂ 5 T ↩
MED: 100-2, 15, 260; 100-4, 12, 90.3; 100-4, 14, 10

If this procedure is performed with hernia repair, consult CPT codes 49495-49501.

REPAIR

55060 **Repair of tunica vaginalis hydrocele (Bottle type)** ♂ 4 T 50 80 ↩
MED: 100-2, 15, 260; 100-4, 12, 90.3; 100-4, 14, 10

SCROTUM

INCISION

55100 **Drainage of scrotal wall abscess** ♂ 1 T ↩
MED: 100-2, 15, 260; 100-4, 12, 90.3; 100-4, 14, 10

Consult also CPT code 54700.

Male Genital System

54900 — 55100

Male Genital System

55110 — 55450

55110	**Scrotal exploration**	♂ 🔲2 🔲T 🔲
	MED: 100-2, 15, 260; 100-4, 12, 90.3; 100-4, 14, 10	
55120	**Removal of foreign body in scrotum**	♂ 🔲2 🔲T 🔲80 🔲
	MED: 100-2, 15, 260; 100-4, 12, 90.3; 100-4, 14, 10	

EXCISION

55150	**Resection of scrotum**	♂ 🔲1 🔲T 🔲80 🔲
	MED: 100-2, 15, 260; 100-4, 12, 90.3; 100-4, 14, 10	

If a local lesion on the skin of the scrotum is excised, see the Integumentary System.

REPAIR

55175	**Scrotoplasty; simple**	♂ 🔲1 🔲T 🔲80 🔲
	MED: 100-2, 15, 260; 100-4, 12, 90.3; 100-4, 14, 10	
55180	**complicated**	♂ 🔲2 🔲T 🔲80 🔲
	MED: 100-2, 15, 260; 100-4, 12, 90.3; 100-4, 14, 10	

VAS DEFERENS

INCISION

55200	**Vasotomy, cannulization with or without incision of vas, unilateral or bilateral (separate procedure)**	♂ 🔲2 🔲T 🔲80 🔲
	MED: 100-2, 15, 260; 100-4, 12, 90.3; 100-4, 14, 10	

EXCISION

55250	**Vasectomy, unilateral or bilateral (separate procedure), including postoperative semen examination(s)**	♂ 🔲2 🔲T 🔲
	MED: 100-2, 15, 260; 100-3, 230.3; 100-4, 12, 90.3; 100-4, 14, 10	
	AMA: 1998, Jun, 10; 1998, Jul, 10	

INTRODUCTION

55300	**Vasotomy for vasograms, seminal vesiculograms, or epididymograms, unilateral or bilateral**	♂ 🔲N 🔲80 🔲

To report radiological supervision and interpretation, consult CPT code 74440. If this procedure is combined with a biopsy of the testis, consult CPT code 54505 and append modifier 51.

REPAIR

55400	**Vasovasostomy, vasovasorrhaphy**	♂ 🔲1 🔲T 🔲50 🔲80 🔲
	MED: 100-2, 15, 260; 100-4, 12, 90.3; 100-4, 14, 10	
	AMA: 2001, Oct, 8; 1998, Nov, 16	

If an operating microscope is used, consult CPT code 69990.

SUTURE

55450	**Ligation (percutaneous) of vas deferens, unilateral or bilateral (separate procedure)**	♂ 🔲T 🔲80 🔲

SPERMATIC CORD

EXCISION

Diagnostic laparosopy is always included in surgical laparoscopy.

55500   **Excision of hydrocele of spermatic cord, unilateral (separate procedure)**   ♂ 3 T 80 🔁
MED: 100-2, 15, 260; 100-4, 12, 90.3; 100-4, 14, 10

AMA: 2001, Oct, 8

55520   **Excision of lesion of spermatic cord (separate procedure)**   ♂ 4 T 80 🔁
MED: 100-2, 15, 260; 100-4, 12, 90.3; 100-4, 14, 10

AMA: 2001, Oct, 8; 2000, Sep, 10

55530   **Excision of varicocele or ligation of spermatic veins for varicocele; (separate procedure)**   ♂ 4 T 50 🔁
MED: 100-2, 15, 260; 100-4, 12, 90.3; 100-4, 14, 10

AMA: 2001, Oct, 8

55535   **abdominal approach**   ♂ 4 T 50 80 🔁
MED: 100-2, 15, 260; 100-4, 12, 90.3; 100-4, 14, 10

AMA: 2001, Oct, 8

55540   **with hernia repair**   ♂ 5 T 50 80 🔁
MED: 100-2, 15, 260; 100-4, 12, 90.3; 100-4, 14, 10

AMA: 2001, Oct, 8

LAPAROSCOPY

To report only a diagnostic laparoscopy (peritoneoscopy), consult CPT code 49320.

55550   **Laparoscopy, surgical, with ligation of spermatic veins for varicocele**   ♂ 9 T 50 80 🔁
MED: 100-2, 15, 260; 100-4, 12, 90.3; 100-4, 14, 10

AMA: 2001, Oct, 8; 2000, Mar, 5; 1999, Nov, 27

55559   **Unlisted laparoscopy procedure, spermatic cord**   T 50 80
AMA: 2000, Mar, 5; 1999, Nov, 27

SEMINAL VESICLES

INCISION

55600   **Vesiculotomy;**   ♂ T 50 80 🔁

55605   **complicated**   ♂ C 50 80 🔁

EXCISION

55650   **Vesiculectomy, any approach**   ♂ C 50 80 🔁

55680   **Excision of Mullerian duct cyst**   ♂ 1 T 80 🔁
MED: 100-2, 15, 260; 100-4, 12, 90.3; 100-4, 14, 10

If an injection procedure is performed, consult CPT codes 52010 and 55300.

Male Genital System

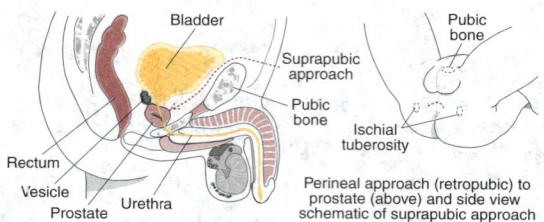

The walnut-sized prostate gland secretes a thin, milky fluid that mixes with spermatic fluids during ejaculation; its secretion constitutes about one-third of the volume of seminal fluid. The prostate is palpable via the rectum. Some procedures are via the urethra, which can be dilated to accommodate instruments. The seminal vesicles may also be palpated via the rectum. Each is a long, coiled tube which secretes a thick fluid that mixes with sperm as it passes along the ejaculatory ducts. The ejaculatory ducts are the union of the seminal vesicles and the sperm-carrying ductus deferens

PROSTATE

INCISION

55700   **Biopsy, prostate; needle or punch, single or multiple, any approach** ♂ 2 T ▸
MED: 100-2, 15, 260; 100-4, 12, 90.3; 100-4, 14, 10

AMA: 1996, May, 3

To report imaging guidance, consult CPT code 76942.

To report fine needle aspiration, consult CPT codes 10021, 10022.

To report evaluation of fine needle aspirate, consult CPT codes 88172, 88173.

55705   **incisional, any approach**   ♂ 2 T ▸
MED: 100-2, 15, 260; 100-4, 12, 90.3; 100-4, 14, 10

55720   **Prostatotomy, external drainage of prostatic abscess, any approach;**
simple   ♂ 1 T 80 ▸
MED: 100-2, 15, 260; 100-4, 12, 90.3; 100-4, 14, 10

55725   **complicated**   ♂ 2 T 80 ▸
MED: 100-2, 15, 260; 100-4, 12, 90.3; 100-4, 14, 10

If transurethral drainage is performed, consult CPT code 52700.

EXCISION

If transurethral removal of the prostate is performed, consult CPT codes 52601-52640. If transurethral destruction of the prostate is performed, consult CPT codes 53850-53852. If a limited pelvic lymphadenectomy is performed for staging (separate procedure), consult CPT code 38562. If an independent node is dissected, consult CPT codes 38770-38780.

55801   **Prostatectomy, perineal, subtotal (including control of postoperative**
bleeding, vasectomy, meatotomy, urethral calibration and/or dilation, and
internal urethrotomy)   ♂ C 80 ▸

55810   **Prostatectomy, perineal radical;**   ♂ C 80 ▸
Walsh modified radical prostatectomy

55812   **with lymph node biopsy(s) (limited pelvic lymphadenectomy)** ♂ C 80 ▸

55815   **with bilateral pelvic lymphadenectomy, including external iliac,**
hypogastric and obturator nodes   ♂ C 80 ▸

If this procedure is carried out on separate days, use CPT code 38770 and append modifier 50 and 55810.

55821	Prostatectomy (including control of postoperative bleeding, vasectomy, meatotomy, urethral calibration and/or dilation, and internal urethrotomy); suprapubic, subtotal, one or two stages	♂ C 80 ↩
55831	retropubic, subtotal	♂ C 80 ↩
55840	Prostatectomy, retropubic radical, with or without nerve sparing;	♂ C 80 ↩
55842	with lymph node biopsy(s) (limited pelvic lymphadenectomy)	♂ C 80 ↩
55845	with bilateral pelvic lymphadenectomy, including external iliac, hypogastric, and obturator nodes	♂ C 80 ↩

If this procedure is carried out on separate days, use CPT code 38770 and append modifier 50 and 55840.

To report laparoscopic retropubic radical prostectomy, consult CPT code 55866.

55859	Transperineal placement of needles or catheters into prostate for interstitial radioelement application, with or without cystoscopy	♂ 9 T 80 ↩

MED: 100-2, 15, 260; 100-4, 12, 90.3; 100-4, 14, 10

To report interstitial radioelement application, consult CPT codes 77776-77784.

To report ultrasonic guidance for interstitial radioelement application, consult CPT code 76965.

55860	Exposure of prostate, any approach, for insertion of radioactive substance;	♂ T ↩

To report interstitial radioelement application, consult CPT codes 77776-77778.

55862	with lymph node biopsy(s) (limited pelvic lymphadenectomy)	♂ C 80 ↩
55865	with bilateral pelvic lymphadenectomy, including external iliac, hypogastric and obturator nodes	♂ C 80 ↩

LAPAROSCOPY

Diagnostic laparoscopy is always included in surgical laparoscopy.

To report only a diagnostic laparoscopy (peritoneoscopy), consult CPT code 49320.

55866	Laparoscopy, surgical prostatectomy, retropubic radical, including nerve sparing	♂ C 80 ↩

To report open procedure, consult CPT code 55840.

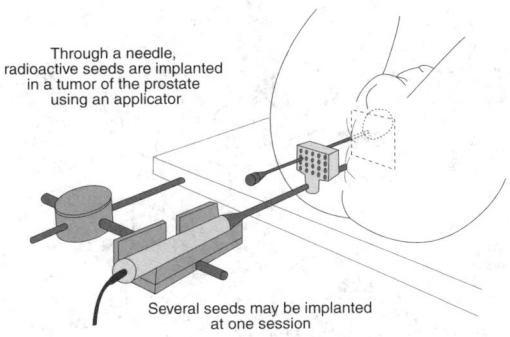

Through a needle, radioactive seeds are implanted in a tumor of the prostate using an applicator

Several seeds may be implanted at one session

Intersex Surgery

55870 — 55980

OTHER PROCEDURES
To report artificial insemination, consult CPT codes 58321, 58322.

55870	**Electroejaculation**	♂ T ▣
55873	**Cryosurgical ablation of the prostate (includes ultrasonic guidance for interstitial cryosurgical probe placement)**	♂ 9 T ▣

    MED: 100-3, 230.9

    AMA: 2002, Sep, 9; 2001, Apr, 4

55899	**Unlisted procedure, male genital system**	♂ T

INTERSEX SURGERY

55970	**Intersex surgery; male to female**	E

    MED: 100-3, 140.3

55980	**female to male**	E

    MED: 100-3, 140.3

FEMALE GENITAL SYSTEM

VULVA, PERINEUM AND INTROITUS

INCISION
The following definitions would be employed when selecting a vulvectomy code:

- Simple: Removal of skin and superficial subcutaneous tissues

- Radical: Removal of skin and deep subcutaneous tissues

- Partial: Removal of less than 80 percent of the vulvar area

- Complete: Removal of more than 80 percent of the vulvar area

If a pelvic laparotomy is performed, consult CPT code 49000. If excision or destruction is performed of endometriomas, open method, consult CPT codes 49200 and 49201. If paracentesis is performed, consult CPT codes 49080 and 49081. If secondary closure of the abdominal wall evisceration or disruption is performed, consult CPT code 49900. If fulguration or excision of lesions is performed through a laparoscopic approach, consult CPT code 58662. If chemotherapy is needed, consult CPT codes 96401-96549.

If a sebaceous cyst, furuncle, or abscess is incised and drained, consult CPT codes 10040, 10060, and 10061.

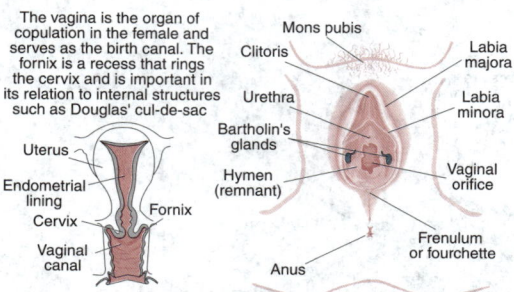

The external female genital region is collectively known as the vulva, or sometimes, the pudendum. A Bartholin's gland is located on either side of the orifice. The perineum is the space between the anus and the vagina, but is often generally defined as the entire pelvic floor and its related structures. Introitus is a general term for the vaginal entrance

---

 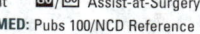 

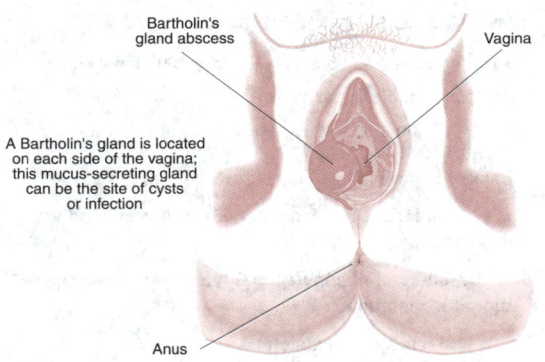

Bartholin's gland abscess

Vagina

A Bartholin's gland is located on each side of the vagina; this mucus-secreting gland can be the site of cysts or infection

Anus

56405	**Incision and drainage of vulva or perineal abscess**	♀ T
56420	**Incision and drainage of Bartholin's gland abscess**	♀ T
	To report incision and drainage of Skene's gland, consult CPT code 53060.	
56440	**Marsupialization of Bartholin's gland cyst** MED: 100-2, 15, 260; 100-4, 12, 90.3; 100-4, 14, 10	♀ 2 T
56441	**Lysis of labial adhesions** MED: 100-2, 15, 260; 100-4, 12, 90.3; 100-4, 14, 10	♀ 1 T 80

DESTRUCTION

If destruction is performed on a Skene's gland cyst or abscess, consult CPT code 53270. If cautery destruction of a urethral caruncle is performed, consult CPT code 53265.

56501	**Destruction of lesion(s), vulva; simple (eg, laser surgery, electrosurgery, cryosurgery, chemosurgery)**	♀ T
56515	**extensive (eg, laser surgery, electrosurgery, cryosurgery, chemosurgery)** MED: 100-2, 15, 260; 100-3, 140.5; 100-4, 12, 90.3; 100-4, 14, 10	♀ 3 T

EXCISION

If a pelvic laparotomy is performed, consult CPT code 49000. If excision or destruction is performed of endometriomas, open method, consult CPT codes 49200 and 49201. If paracentesis is performed, consult CPT codes 49080 and 49081. If secondary closure of the abdominal wall evisceration or disruption is performed, consult CPT code 49900. If fulguration or excision of lesions is performed through a laparoscopic approach, consult CPT code 58662. If chemotherapy is needed, consult CPT codes 96401-96549.

56605	**Biopsy of vulva or perineum (separate procedure); one lesion** AMA: 2000, Sep, 9	♀ T
+ 56606	**each separate additional lesion (List separately in addition to code for primary procedure)**	♀ T
	Note that 56606 is an add-on code and must be used in conjunction with 56605.	
	If a local lesion is excised, consult CPT codes 11420-11426 and 11620-11626.	
56620	**Vulvectomy simple; partial** MED: 100-2, 15, 260; 100-4, 12, 90.3; 100-4, 14, 10	♀ 5 T 80

Female Genital System

56405 — 56620

Female Genital System

56625 — 56805

| 56625 | complete | ♀ 7 T 80 ⬛ |

MED: 100-2, 15, 260; 100-4, 12, 90.3; 100-4, 14, 10

To report skin graft, consult CPT code 15000 and subsequent codes.

| 56630 | Vulvectomy, radical, partial; | ♀ C 80 ⬛ |

To report skin grafts, if necessary, consult CPT codes 15000, 15020, 15121, 15240, 15241.

Bassett's operation

| 56631 | with unilateral inguinofemoral lymphadenectomy | ♀ C 80 ⬛ |

Bassett's operation

| 56632 | with bilateral inguinofemoral lymphadenectomy | ♀ C 80 ⬛ |

Bassett's operation

| 56633 | Vulvectomy, radical, complete; | ♀ C 80 ⬛ |

Bassett's operation

| 56634 | with unilateral inguinofemoral lymphadenectomy | ♀ C 80 ⬛ |

Bassett's operation

| 56637 | with bilateral inguinofemoral lymphadenectomy | ♀ C 80 ⬛ |

Bassett's operation

| 56640 | Vulvectomy, radical, complete, with inguinofemoral, iliac, and pelvic lymphadenectomy | ♀ C 50 80 ⬛ |

If a lymphadenectomy is performed, consult CPT codes 38760-38780.

Bassett's operation

| 56700 | Partial hymenectomy or revision of hymenal ring | ♀ 1 T 80 ⬛ |

MED: 100-2, 15, 260; 100-4, 12, 90.3; 100-4, 14, 10

| 56720 | Hymenotomy, simple incision | ♀ 1 T 80 ⬛ |

MED: 100-2, 15, 260; 100-4, 12, 90.3; 100-4, 14, 10

| 56740 | Excision of Bartholin's gland or cyst | ♀ 3 T ⬛ |

MED: 100-2, 15, 260; 100-4, 12, 90.3; 100-4, 14, 10

If the Skene's gland is excised, consult CPT code 53270. If an excision is performed on the urethral caruncle, consult CPT code 53265. If excision or fulguration is performed on a urethral carcinoma, consult CPT code 53220. If excision or marsupialization is performed on the urethral diverticulum, consult CPT codes 53230 and 52340.

REPAIR

If a pelvic laparotomy is performed, consult CPT code 49000. If excision or destruction is performed of endometriomas, open method, consult CPT codes 49200 and 49201. If paracentesis is performed, consult CPT codes 49080 and 49081. If secondary closure of the abdominal wall evisceration or disruption is performed, consult CPT code 49900. If fulguration or excision of lesions is performed through a laparoscopic approach, consult CPT code 58662. If chemotherapy is needed, consult CPT codes 96401-96549.

If a repair of the urethra is performed for mucosal prolapse, consult CPT code 53275.

| 56800 | Plastic repair of introitus | ♀ 3 T 80 ⬛ |

MED: 100-2, 15, 260; 100-4, 12, 90.3; 100-4, 14, 10

Emmet's operation

| 56805 | Clitoroplasty for intersex state | ♀ T 80 ⬛ |

56810   **Perineoplasty, repair of perineum, non-obstetrical (separate procedure)** ♀ 5 T 80 ▣
MED: 100-2, 15, 260; 100-4, 12, 90.3; 100-4, 14, 10

To report repair of nonobstetrical recent injury, consult CPT code 57210. Consult also CPT code 56800. To report anal sphincteroplasty, consult CPT codes 46750, 46751.

To report wound repair of genitalia, consult CPT codes 12001-12007, 12041-12047 and 13131-13133.
Emmet's operation

ENDOSCOPY

56820   **Colposcopy of the vulva;** ♀ T ▣
AMA: 2003, Feb, 5

56821   **with biopsy(s)** ♀ T ▣
AMA: 2003, Feb, 5

To report colposcopic services involving the vagina, consult CPT codes 57420-57421; cervix, consult CPT codes 57452-57461.

VAGINA

INCISION
If a pelvic laparotomy is performed, consult CPT code 49000. If excision or destruction is performed of endometriomas, open method, consult CPT codes 49200 and 49201. If paracentesis is performed, consult CPT codes 49080 and 49081. If secondary closure of the abdominal wall evisceration or disruption is performed, consult CPT code 49900. If fulguration or excision of lesions is performed through a laparoscopic approach, consult CPT code 58662. If chemotherapy is needed, consult CPT codes 96401-96549.

57000   **Colpotomy; with exploration** ♀ 1 T 80 ▣
MED: 100-2, 15, 260; 100-4, 12, 90.3; 100-4, 14, 10

57010   **with drainage of pelvic abscess** ♀ 2 T 80 ▣
MED: 100-2, 15, 260; 100-4, 12, 90.3; 100-4, 14, 10

Laroyenne operation

57020   **Colpocentesis (separate procedure)** ♀ 2 T 80 ▣
MED: 100-2, 15, 260; 100-4, 12, 90.3; 100-4, 14, 10

57022   **Incision and drainage of vaginal hematoma; obstetrical/postpartum** ♀ T 80 ▣

57023   **non-obstetrical (eg, post-trauma, spontaneous bleeding)** ♀ 1 T 80 ▣
MED: 100-2, 15, 260; 100-4, 12, 90.3; 100-4, 14, 10

DESTRUCTION

57061   **Destruction of vaginal lesion(s); simple (eg, laser surgery, electrosurgery, cryosurgery, chemosurgery)** ♀ T ▣
MED: 100-3, 140.5

AMA: 1996, Apr, 11

57065   **extensive (eg, laser surgery, electrosurgery, cryosurgery, chemosurgery)** ♀ 1 T ▣
MED: 100-2, 15, 260; 100-3, 140.5; 100-4, 12, 90.3; 100-4, 14, 10

AMA: 1996, Apr, 11

Female Genital System

57100 — 57180

EXCISION

57100	Biopsy of vaginal mucosa; simple (separate procedure)	♀ T ◘
57105	extensive, requiring suture (including cysts) MED: 100-2, 15, 260; 100-4, 12, 90.3; 100-4, 14, 10	♀ 2 T ◘
57106	Vaginectomy, partial removal of vaginal wall; AMA: 1999, Oct, 4; 1998, Nov, 17	♀ T 80 ◘
57107	with removal of paravaginal tissue (radical vaginectomy) AMA: 1999, Oct, 4; 1998, Nov, 17	♀ T 80 ◘
57109	with removal of paravaginal tissue (radical vaginectomy) with bilateral total pelvic lymphadenectomy and para-aortic lymph node sampling (biopsy) AMA: 1999, Oct, 4; 1998, Nov, 17	♀ T 80 ◘
57110	Vaginectomy, complete removal of vaginal wall; AMA: 1999, Oct, 4; 1998, Nov, 17	♀ C 80 ◘
57111	with removal of paravaginal tissue (radical vaginectomy) AMA: 1999, Oct, 4; 1998, Nov, 17	♀ C 80 ◘
57112	with removal of paravaginal tissue (radical vaginectomy) with bilateral total pelvic lymphadenectomy and para-aortic lymph node sampling (biopsy) AMA: 1999, Oct, 4; 1998, Nov, 17	♀ C 80 ◘
57120	Colpocleisis (Le Fort type)	♀ T 80 ◘
57130	Excision of vaginal septum MED: 100-2, 15, 260; 100-4, 12, 90.3; 100-4, 14, 10	♀ 2 T 80 ◘
57135	Excision of vaginal cyst or tumor MED: 100-2, 15, 260; 100-4, 12, 90.3; 100-4, 14, 10	♀ 2 T ◘

INTRODUCTION

57150	Irrigation of vagina and/or application of medicament for treatment of bacterial, parasitic, or fungoid disease	♀ T ◘
57155	Insertion of uterine tandems and/or vaginal ovoids for clinical brachytherapy AMA: 2002, Feb, 7	♀ 2 T ◘

> To report insertion of radioelement sources of ribbons, consult CPT codes 77761-77763, 77781-77784.

57160	Fitting and insertion of pessary or other intravaginal support device AMA: 2000, Jun, 11; 1998, Oct, 11	♀ T ◘
57170	Diaphragm or cervical cap fitting with instructions	♀ T 80 ◘
57180	Introduction of any hemostatic agent or pack for spontaneous or traumatic nonobstetrical vaginal hemorrhage (separate procedure) MED: 100-2, 15, 260; 100-4, 12, 90.3; 100-4, 14, 10	♀ 1 T ◘

REPAIR

If an anterior vesicourethropexy or urethropexy is performed (e.g., Marshall-Marchetti-Krantz type), consult CPT codes 51840 and 51841. If laparoscopic suspension is performed on the ureter, consult CPT code 51990.

If a pelvic laparotomy is performed, consult CPT code 49000. If excision or destruction is performed of endometriomas, open method, consult CPT codes 49200 and 49201. If paracentesis is performed, consult CPT codes 49080 and 49081. If secondary closure of the abdominal wall evisceration or disruption is performed, consult CPT code 49900. If fulguration or excision of lesions is performed through a laparoscopic approach, consult CPT code 58662. If chemotherapy is needed, consult CPT codes 96401-96549.

57200 Colporrhaphy, suture of injury of vagina (nonobstetrical) ♀ **1** T 80 🔁
  MED: 100-2, 15, 260; 100-4, 12, 90.3; 100-4, 14, 10

57210 Colpoperineorrhaphy, suture of injury of vagina and/or perineum
  (nonobstetrical) ♀ **2** T 80 🔁
  MED: 100-2, 15, 260; 100-4, 12, 90.3; 100-4, 14, 10

57220 Plastic operation on urethral sphincter, vaginal approach (eg, Kelly urethral
  plication) ♀ **3** T 80 🔁
  MED: 100-2, 15, 260; 100-4, 12, 90.3; 100-4, 14, 10

57230 Plastic repair of urethrocele ♀ **3** T 80 🔁
  MED: 100-2, 15, 260; 100-4, 12, 90.3; 100-4, 14, 10

57240 Anterior colporrhaphy, repair of cystocele with or without repair of
  urethrocele ♀ **5** T 80 🔁
  MED: 100-2, 15, 260; 100-4, 12, 90.3; 100-4, 14, 10

  AMA: 2002, Jun, 4; 1997, Jan, 3

57250 Posterior colporrhaphy, repair of rectocele with or without
  perineorrhaphy ♀ **5** T 80 🔁
  MED: 100-2, 15, 260; 100-4, 12, 90.3; 100-4, 14, 10

  AMA: 2002, Jun, 4

  If rectocele is repaired without posterior colporrhaphy, consult CPT code 45560.

57260 Combined anteroposterior colporrhaphy; ♀ **5** T 80 🔁
  MED: 100-2, 15, 260; 100-4, 12, 90.3; 100-4, 14, 10

  AMA: 2002, Jun, 4

57265   with enterocele repair ♀ **7** T 80 🔁
  MED: 100-2, 15, 260; 100-4, 12, 90.3; 100-4, 14, 10

  AMA: 2002, Jun, 4

INTRODUCTION

+ **57267** Insertion of mesh or other prosthesis for repair of pelvic floor defect, each
  site (anterior, posterior compartment), vaginal approach (List separately in
  addition to code for primary procedure) ♀ T 80

  Note that 57267 must be used with 45560, 57240-57265.

REPAIR

57268 Repair of enterocele, vaginal approach (separate procedure) ♀ **3** T 80 🔁
  MED: 100-2, 15, 260; 100-4, 12, 90.3; 100-4, 14, 10

  AMA: 2002, Jun, 4

57270 Repair of enterocele, abdominal approach (separate procedure) ♀ C 80 🔁
  AMA: 2002, Jun, 4

57280 Colpopexy, abdominal approach ♀ C 80 🔁
  AMA: 2002, Jun, 4; 1997, Jan, 1

57282 Colpopexy, vaginal; extra-peritoneal approach (sacrospinous,
  iliococcygeus) ♀ C 80 🔁
  AMA: 2002, Jun, 4; 1997, Jan, 1

Female Genital System

57283 — 57410

57283	intra-peritoneal approach (uterosacral, levator myorrhaphy) ♀ C 80 ⚑	
57284	**Paravaginal defect repair (including repair of cystocele, stress urinary incontinence, and/or incomplete vaginal prolapse)** ♀ T 80 ⚑	
	MED: 100-3, 230.10	
	AMA: 2002, Jun, 4; 1997, Jan, 1	
57287	**Removal or revision of sling for stress incontinence (eg, fascia or synthetic)** ♀ T 80 ⚑	
	MED: 100-3, 230.10	
	AMA: 2002, Jun, 4	
57288	**Sling operation for stress incontinence (eg, fascia or synthetic)** ♀ 5 T 80 ⚑	
	AMA: 2002, Jun, 4; 2002, Apr, 18; 2000, Oct, 7; 2000, May, 4; 1999, Nov, 28	
	Millen-Read	
	If performed via laparoscope, consult CPT code 51992.	
57289	**Pereyra procedure, including anterior colporrhaphy** ♀ 5 T 80 ⚑	
	MED: 100-2, 15, 260; 100-4, 12, 90.3; 100-4, 14, 10	
	AMA: 2002, Jun, 4; 1997, Jan, 3	
57291	**Construction of artificial vagina; without graft** ♀ 5 T 80 ⚑	
	MED: 100-2, 15, 260; 100-4, 12, 90.3; 100-4, 14, 10	
	McIndoe vaginal construction	
57292	**with graft** ♀ C 80 ⚑	
● 57295	**Revision (including removal) of prosthetic vaginal graft, vaginal approach**	
57300	**Closure of rectovaginal fistula; vaginal or transanal approach** ♀ 3 T 80 ⚑	
	MED: 100-2, 15, 260; 100-4, 12, 90.3; 100-4, 14, 10	
	AMA: 1997, Nov, 21	
57305	**abdominal approach** ♀ C 80 ⚑	
	AMA: 1997, Nov, 21	
57307	**abdominal approach, with concomitant colostomy** ♀ C 80 ⚑	
	AMA: 1997, Nov, 21	
57308	**transperineal approach, with perineal body reconstruction, with or without levator plication** ♀ C 80 ⚑	
	AMA: 1997, Nov, 21	
57310	**Closure of urethrovaginal fistula;** ♀ T 80 ⚑	
57311	**with bulbocavernosus transplant** ♀ C 80 ⚑	
57320	**Closure of vesicovaginal fistula; vaginal approach** ♀ T 80 ⚑	
	To report concomitant cystostomy, consult CPT codes 51005-51040.	
57330	**transvesical and vaginal approach** ♀ T 80 ⚑	
	If performed via abdominal approach, consult CPT code 51900.	
57335	**Vaginoplasty for intersex state** ♀ C 80 ⚑	

MANIPULATION

57400	**Dilation of vagina under anesthesia** ♀ 2 T 80 ⚑	
	MED: 100-2, 15, 260; 100-4, 12, 90.3; 100-4, 14, 10	
57410	**Pelvic examination under anesthesia** ♀ 2 T ⚑	
	MED: 100-2, 15, 260; 100-4, 12, 90.3; 100-4, 14, 10	
	AMA: 1993, Spring, 34	

57415	**Removal of impacted vaginal foreign body (separate procedure) under anesthesia** ♀ 🔲T🔲80 🔲

MED: 100-2, 15, 260; 100-4, 12, 90.3; 100-4, 14, 10

> If removal of an impacted vaginal foreign body is performed without anesthesia, consult the appropriate E/M code.

ENDOSCOPY

To report speculoscopy, consult Category III codes 0031T and 0032T.

57420	**Colposcopy of the entire vagina, with cervix if present;** ♀ T🔲

AMA: 2003, Feb, 5

▲ 57421	**with biopsy(s) of vagina/cervix** ♀ T🔲

AMA: 2003, Feb, 5

> To report colposcopic visualization of cervix and adjacent upper vagina, consult CPT code 57452.
>
> To report colposcopies of multiple sites, append modifier 51 when appropriate.
>
> To report colposcopic services of the vulva, consult CPT codes 56820, 56821; of the cervix, consult CPT codes 57452-57461.
>
> To report endometrial sampling (biopsy) performed in conjunction with colposcopy, consult CPT code 58110.

57425	**Laparoscopy, surgical, colpopexy (suspension of vaginal apex)** ♀ T🔲80 🔲

CERVIX UTERI

To report cervicography, consult Category III code 0003T.

To report colposcopic services of the vulva, consult CPT codes 56820, 56821; of the vagina, consult CPT codes 57420, 57421.

57452	**Colposcopy of the cervix including upper/adjacent vagina;** ♀ T🔲

AMA: 2003, Feb, 5; 2000, Apr, 5

> Do not report 57452 in conjunction with CPT codes 57454-57461.

57454	**with biopsy(s) of the cervix and endocervical curettage** ♀ T🔲

AMA: 2003, Feb, 5; 2000, Apr, 5

57455	**with biopsy(s) of the cervix** ♀ T🔲

AMA: 2003, Feb, 5

57456	**with endocervical curettage** ♀ T🔲

AMA: 2003, Jan, 23; 2003, Feb, 5

57460	**with loop electrode biopsy(s) of the cervix** ♀ T🔲

AMA: 2003, Jan, 23; 2003, Feb, 5; 2000, Apr, 5

57461	**with loop electrode conization of the cervix** ♀ T🔲

AMA: 2003, Jan, 23; 2003, Feb, 5

> Do not report 57456 in conjunction with CPT code 57461.
>
> To report endometrial sampling (biopsy) performed in conjunction with colposcopy, consult CPT code 58110.

EXCISION

If radical surgical procedures are performed, consult CPT codes 58200-58240. If an intrauterine device is inserted, consult CPT code 58300.

If a pelvic laparotomy is performed, consult CPT code 49000. If excision or destruction is performed of endometriomas, open method, consult CPT codes 49200 and 49201. If paracentesis is performed,

Female Genital System

consult CPT codes 49080 and 49081. If secondary closure of the abdominal wall evisceration or disruption is performed, consult CPT code 49900. If fulguration or excision of lesions is performed through a laparoscopic approach, consult CPT code 58662. If chemotherapy is needed, consult CPT codes 96401-96549.

To report insertion of hemostatic agent or pack for non-obstetrical hemorrhage control, consult CPT code 57180.

57500 **Biopsy, single or multiple, or local excision of lesion, with or without fulguration (separate procedure)** ♀ Ⓣ ▯

57505 **Endocervical curettage (not done as part of a dilation and curettage)** ♀ Ⓣ ▯

57510 **Cautery of cervix; electro or thermal** ♀ Ⓣ ▯

57511 **cryocautery, initial or repeat** ♀ Ⓣ ▯

57513 **laser ablation** ♀ ②Ⓣ ▯
MED: 100-2, 15, 260; 100-4, 12, 90.3; 100-4, 14, 10

57520 **Conization of cervix, with or without fulguration, with or without dilation and curettage, with or without repair; cold knife or laser** ♀ ②Ⓣ ▯
MED: 100-2, 15, 260; 100-4, 12, 90.3; 100-4, 14, 10
AMA: 2000, Apr, 5

Consult also CPT code 58120.

57522 **loop electrode excision** ♀ ②Ⓣ ▯
MED: 100-2, 15, 260; 100-4, 12, 90.3; 100-4, 14, 10
AMA: 2000, Apr, 5

57530 **Trachelectomy (cervicectomy), amputation of cervix (separate procedure)** ♀ ③Ⓣ 80 ▯
MED: 100-2, 15, 260; 100-4, 12, 90.3; 100-4, 14, 10

57531 **Radical trachelectomy, with bilateral total pelvic lymphadenectomy and para-aortic lymph node sampling biopsy, with or without removal of tube(s), with or without removal of ovary(s)** ♀ Ⓒ 80 ▯
AMA: 1997, Nov, 21

If a radical abdominal hysterectomy is performed, consult CPT code 58210.

57540 **Excision of cervical stump, abdominal approach;** ♀ Ⓒ 80 ▯

57545 **with pelvic floor repair** ♀ Ⓒ 80 ▯

57550 **Excision of cervical stump, vaginal approach;** ♀ ③Ⓣ 80 ▯
MED: 100-2, 15, 260; 100-4, 12, 90.3; 100-4, 14, 10

57555 **with anterior and/or posterior repair** ♀ Ⓣ 80 ▯

57556 **with repair of enterocele** ♀ ⑤Ⓣ 80 ▯
MED: 100-2, 15, 260; 100-4, 12, 90.3; 100-4, 14, 10

REPAIR

57700 **Cerclage of uterine cervix, nonobstetrical** ♀ ①Ⓣ 80 ▯
MED: 100-2, 15, 260; 100-4, 12, 90.3; 100-4, 14, 10

McDonald cerclage

57720 **Trachelorrhaphy, plastic repair of uterine cervix, vaginal approach** ♀ ③Ⓣ 80 ▯
MED: 100-2, 15, 260; 100-4, 12, 90.3; 100-4, 14, 10

MANIPULATION

57800   Dilation of cervical canal, instrumental (separate procedure)   ♀ T ↵

57820   Dilation and curettage of cervical stump   ♀ 3 T ↵
MED: 100-2, 15, 260; 100-4, 12, 90.3; 100-4, 14, 10

CORPUS UTERI

If an endocervical curettage is performed by itself, consult CPT code 57505.

If a pelvic laparotomy is performed, consult CPT code 49000. If excision or destruction is performed of endometriomas, open method, consult CPT codes 49200 and 49201. If paracentesis is performed, consult CPT codes 49080 and 49081. If secondary closure of the abdominal wall evisceration or disruption is performed, consult CPT code 49900. If fulguration or excision of lesions is performed through a laparoscopic approach, consult CPT code 58662. If chemotherapy is needed, consult CPT codes 96401-96549.

If a postpartum curettage is performed, consult CPT code 59160.

EXCISION

58100   Endometrial sampling (biopsy) with or without endocervical sampling (biopsy), without cervical dilation, any method (separate procedure)   ♀ T ↵
MED: 100-3, 230.6

To report endometrial sampling (biopsy) performed in conjunction with colposcopy, consult CPT code 58110.

+ ● **58110**   Endometrial sampling (biopsy) performed in conjunction with colposcopy (List separately in addition to code for primary procedure)

Note that 58110 is an add-on code and must be used with 57420, 57421, 57452-57461.

58120   Dilation and curettage, diagnostic and/or therapeutic (nonobstetrical)   ♀ 2 T ↵
MED: 100-2, 15, 260; 100-4, 12, 90.3; 100-4, 14, 10

AMA: 1997, Nov, 21; 1995, Fall, 16

58140   Myomectomy, excision of fibroid tumor(s) of uterus, 1 to 4 intramural myoma(s) with total weight of 250 grams or less and/or removal of surface myomas; abdominal approach   ♀ C 80 ↵
AMA: 2003, Feb, 15

58145   Myomectomy, excision of fibroid tumor(s) of uterus, 1 to 4 intramural myoma(s) with total weight of 250 grams or less and/or removal of surface myomas; vaginal approach   ♀ 5 T 80 ↵
MED: 100-2, 15, 260; 100-4, 12, 90.3; 100-4, 14, 10

58146   Myomectomy, excision of fibroid tumor(s) of uterus, 5 or more intramural myomas and/or intramural myomas with total weight greater than 250 grams, abdominal approach   ♀ C 80 ↵
AMA: 2003, Feb, 15

Do not report 58146 in conjunction with CPT codes 58140-58145, 58150-58240.

58150   Total abdominal hysterectomy (corpus and cervix), with or without removal of tube(s), with or without removal of ovary(s);   ♀ C 80 ↵
MED: 100-3, 230.3

AMA: 2001, Aug, 11; 2000, Sep, 9; 1997, Nov, 21; 1997, Apr, 3; 1996, Dec, 10

Female Genital System

58152 — 58275

58152   with colpo-urethrocystopexy (eg, Marshall-Marchetti-Krantz, Burch)   ♀ C 80 ▷
MED: 100-3, 230.3

AMA: 1997, Nov, 22; 1997, Jan, 1

If a urethrocystopexy is performed without a hysterectomy, consult CPT codes 51840 and 51841.

58180   **Supracervical abdominal hysterectomy (subtotal hysterectomy), with or without removal of tube(s), with or without removal of ovary(s)**   ♀ C 80 ▷
MED: 100-3, 230.3

58200   **Total abdominal hysterectomy, including partial vaginectomy, with para-aortic and pelvic lymph node sampling, with or without removal of tube(s), with or without removal of ovary(s)**   ♀ C 80 ▷
MED: 100-3, 230.3

To report hysterectomy with pelvic lymphadenectomy, consult CPT code 58210.

58210   **Radical abdominal hysterectomy, with bilateral total pelvic lymphadenectomy and para-aortic lymph node sampling (biopsy), with or without removal of tube(s), with or without removal of ovary(s)**   ♀ C 80 ▷
MED: 100-3, 230.3

If a radical hysterectomy is performed with an ovarian transposition, consult also CPT code 58825.
Wertheim hysterectomy

58240   **Pelvic exenteration for gynecologic malignancy, with total abdominal hysterectomy or cervicectomy, with or without removal of tube(s), with or without removal of ovary(s), with removal of bladder and ureteral transplantations, and/or abdominoperineal resection of rectum and colon and colostomy, or any combination thereof**   ♀ C 80 ▷
MED: 100-3, 230.3

If pelvic exenteration is performed for a lower urinary tract or a male genital malignancy, consult CPT code 51597.

58260   **Vaginal hysterectomy, for uterus 250 grams or less;**   ♀ C 80 ▷
MED: 100-3, 230.3

58262   with removal of tube(s), and/or ovary(s)   ♀ C 80 ▷
MED: 100-3, 230.3

58263   with removal of tube(s), and/or ovary(s), with repair of enterocele   ♀ C 80 ▷
MED: 100-3, 230.3

Code 58263 cannot be reported with CPT code 57283.

58267   with colpo-urethrocystopexy (Marshall-Marchetti-Krantz type, Pereyra type) with or without endoscopic control   ♀ C 80 ▷
MED: 100-3, 230.3

58270   with repair of enterocele   ♀ C 80 ▷
MED: 100-3, 230.3

If an enterocele is repaired with removal of tubes and/or ovaries, consult CPT code 58263.

58275   **Vaginal hysterectomy, with total or partial vaginectomy;**   ♀ C 80 ▷
MED: 100-3, 230.3

58280	**with repair of enterocele** MED: 100-3, 230.3	♀ C 80
58285	**Vaginal hysterectomy, radical (Schauta type operation)** MED: 100-3, 230.3	♀ C 80
58290	**Vaginal hysterectomy, for uterus greater than 250 grams;**	♀ C 80
58291	**with removal of tube(s) and/or ovary(s)**	♀ C 80
58292	**with removal of tube(s) and/or ovary(s), with repair of enterocele**	♀ C 80
58293	**with colpo-urethrocystopexy (Marshall-Marchetti-Krantz type, Pereyra type) with or without endoscopic control**	♀ C 80
58294	**with repair of enterocele**	♀ C 80

INTRODUCTION

If implantable contraceptive capsules are inserted or removed, consult CPT codes 11975, 11976, and 11977.

If a pelvic laparotomy is performed, consult CPT code 49000. If excision or destruction is performed of endometriomas, open method, consult CPT codes 49200 and 49201. If paracentesis is performed, consult CPT codes 49080 and 49081. If secondary closure of the abdominal wall evisceration or disruption is performed, consult CPT code 49900. If fulguration or excision of lesions is performed through a laparoscopic approach, consult CPT code 58662. If chemotherapy is needed, consult CPT codes 96401-96549.

58300	**Insertion of intrauterine device (IUD)** AMA: 1998, Apr, 14	♀ E
58301	**Removal of intrauterine device (IUD)** AMA: 1998, Apr, 14	♀ T 80
58321	**Artificial insemination; intra-cervical**	♀ T 80
58322	**intra-uterine**	♀ T 80
58323	**Sperm washing for artificial insemination** AMA: 1998, Jan, 6	♀ T 80
58340	**Catheterization and introduction of saline or contrast material for saline infusion sonohysterography (SIS) or hysterosalpingography** AMA: 1999, Jul, 8; 1997, Nov, 22	♀ N

To report radiological supervision and interpretation of a saline infusion hysterosonography, consult CPT code 76831. To report radiological supervision and interpretation of hysterosalpingography, consult CPT code 74740.

To report cryoblation of endometrium with ultrasonic guidance, consult CPT Category III code 0009T.

58345	**Transcervical introduction of fallopian tube catheter for diagnosis and/or re-establishing patency (any method), with or without hysterosalpingography** AMA: 1997, Nov, 22	♀ T 50 80

To report radiological supervision and interpretation, consult CPT code 74742.

58346	**Insertion of Heyman capsules for clinical brachytherapy** AMA: 2002, Feb, 7	♀ 2 T

To report radioelement sources/ribbons insertion, consult CPT codes 77761-77763, 77781-77784.

Female Genital System

58350 — 58546

58350 **Chromotubation of oviduct, including materials** ♀ 3 T ▪
MED: 100-2, 15, 260; 100-4, 12, 90.3; 100-4, 14, 10

AMA: 2002, May, 19

To report physician supplied materials, consult CPT code 99070.

58353 **Endometrial ablation, thermal, without hysteroscopic guidance** ♀ 4 T 50 80 ▪
MED: 100-2, 15, 260; 100-3, 230.6; 100-4, 12, 90.3; 100-4, 14, 10

AMA: 2002, Mar, 11; 2002, Apr, 19

To report endometrial ablation with hysteroscopy consult CPT code 58563.

58356 **Endometrial cryoablation with ultrasonic guidance, including endometrial curettage, when performed** ♀ T 80 ▪

Code 58356 cannot be reported with CPT codes 58100, 58120, 58340, 76700, 76856.

REPAIR

If a pelvic laparotomy is performed, consult CPT code 49000. If excision or destruction is performed of endometriomas, open method, consult CPT codes 49200 and 49201. If paracentesis is performed, consult CPT codes 49080 and 49081. If secondary closure of the abdominal wall evisceration or disruption is performed, consult CPT code 49900. If fulguration or excision of lesions is performed through a laparoscopic approach, consult CPT code 58662. If chemotherapy is needed, consult CPT codes 96401-96549.

58400 **Uterine suspension, with or without shortening of round ligaments, with or without shortening of sacrouterine ligaments; (separate procedure)** ♀ C 80 ▪
Alexander's operation

58410 **with presacral sympathectomy** ♀ C 80 ▪
Alexander's operation

58520 **Hysterorrhaphy, repair of ruptured uterus (nonobstetrical)** ♀ C 80 ▪

58540 **Hysteroplasty, repair of uterine anomaly (Strassman type)** ♀ C 80 ▪

If a vesicouterine fistula is closed, consult CPT code 51920.
Tompkins metroplasty

LAPAROSCOPY/HYSTEROSCOPY

Diagnostic laparoscopy is always included in surgical laparoscopy. To report only a diagnostic laparoscopy, consult CPT code 49320.

For diagnostic hysteroscopy, consult CPT code 58555.

If a pelvic laparotomy is performed, consult CPT code 49000. If excision or destruction is performed of endometriomas, open method, consult CPT codes 49200 and 49201. If paracentesis is performed, consult CPT codes 49080 and 49081. If secondary closure of the abdominal wall evisceration or disruption is performed, consult CPT code 49900. If fulguration or excision of lesions is performed through a laparoscopic approach, consult CPT code 58662. If chemotherapy is needed, consult CPT codes 96400-96549.

58545 **Laparoscopy, surgical, myomectomy, excision; 1 to 4 intramural myomas with total weight of 250 grams or less and/or removal of surface myomas** ♀ 9 T 80 ▪
MED: 100-2, 15, 260; 100-4, 12, 90.3; 100-4, 14, 10

58546 **5 or more intramural myomas and/or intramural myomas with total weight greater than 250 grams** ♀ 9 T 80 ▪
MED: 100-2, 15, 260; 100-4, 12, 90.3; 100-4, 14, 10

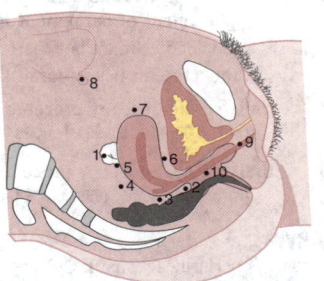

Some common sites
of endometriosis,
in descending order
of frequency:
(1) ovary,
(2) cul de sac,
(3) uterosacral ligaments,
(4) broad ligaments,
(5) fallopian tube,
(6) uterovesical fold,
(7) round ligament,
(8) vermiform appendix,
(9) vagina,
(10) rectovaginal septum

Endometriosis is a benign condition in which endometrial matter is present
outside of the endometrial cavity; it is estimated that 15 percent of women
have some degree of the disease; occurrence is most common in the
ovaries and about 60 percent of patients will have ovarian involvement,
many with cyst development

58550 **Laparoscopy surgical, with vaginal hysterectomy, for uterus 250 grams or less;** ♀ 9 T 80

MED: 100-2, 15, 260; 100-3, 230.3; 100-4, 12, 90.3; 100-4, 14, 10

AMA: 2000, Mar, 5; 1999, Nov, 28

58552 **with removal of tube(s) and/or ovary(s)** ♀ T 80

58553 **Laparoscopy, surgical, with vaginal hysterectomy, for uterus greater than 250 grams;** ♀ T 80

58554 **with removal of tube(s) and/or ovary(s)** ♀ T 80

58555 **Hysteroscopy, diagnostic (separate procedure)** ♀ 1 T 80
MED: 100-2, 15, 260; 100-4, 12, 90.3; 100-4, 14, 10

AMA: 2000, Mar, 5; 1999, Nov, 28

58558 **Hysteroscopy, surgical; with sampling (biopsy) of endometrium and/or polypectomy, with or without D & C** ♀ 3 T
MED: 100-2, 15, 260; 100-4, 12, 90.3; 100-4, 14, 10

AMA: 2003, Jan, 1; 2002, Sep, 10; 2000, Mar, 5; 1999, Nov, 28

58559 **with lysis of intrauterine adhesions (any method)** ♀ 2 T
MED: 100-2, 15, 260; 100-4, 12, 90.3; 100-4, 14, 10

AMA: 2000, Mar, 5; 1999, Nov, 28

58560 **with division or resection of intrauterine septum (any method)** ♀ 3 T 80
MED: 100-2, 15, 260; 100-4, 12, 90.3; 100-4, 14, 10

AMA: 2000, Mar, 5; 1999, Nov, 28

58561 **with removal of leiomyomata** ♀ 3 T 80
MED: 100-2, 15, 260; 100-4, 12, 90.3; 100-4, 14, 10

AMA: 2003, Jan, 1; 2000, Mar, 5; 1999, Nov, 28

58562 **with removal of impacted foreign body** ♀ 3 T
MED: 100-2, 15, 260; 100-4, 12, 90.3; 100-4, 14, 10

AMA: 2000, Mar, 5; 1999, Nov, 28

58563 **with endometrial ablation (eg, endometrial resection, electrosurgical ablation, thermoablation)** ♀ 4 T 80
MED: 100-2, 15, 260; 100-3, 230.6; 100-4, 12, 90.3; 100-4, 14, 10

AMA: 2003, Jan, 1; 2002, Mar, 11; 2002, Apr, 19; 2000, Mar, 5; 1999, Nov, 28

Female Genital System

58565 — 58615

| 58565 | with bilateral fallopian tube cannulation to induce occlusion by placement of permanent implants ♀ 4 T 🔷 |

Code 58565 cannot be reported with CPT code 58555 or 57800.

If this procedure is performed unilaterally, append modifier 52.

| 58578 | **Unlisted laparoscopy procedure, uterus** T 50 80 |

AMA: 2000, Mar, 5; 1999, Nov, 28

| 58579 | **Unlisted hysteroscopy procedure, uterus** T 50 80 |

AMA: 2000, Mar, 5; 1999, Nov, 28

OVIDUCT/OVARY

If a pelvic laparotomy is performed, consult CPT code 49000. If excision or destruction is performed of endometriomas, open method, consult CPT codes 49200 and 49201. If paracentesis is performed, consult CPT codes 49080 and 49081. If secondary closure of the abdominal wall evisceration or disruption is performed, consult CPT code 49900. If fulguration or excision of lesions is performed through a laparoscopic approach, consult CPT code 58662. If chemotherapy is needed, consult CPT codes 96400-96549.

INCISION

| 58600 | **Ligation or transection of fallopian tube(s), abdominal or vaginal approach, unilateral or bilateral** ♀ T 80 🔷 |

MED: 100-3, 230.3

AMA: 1999, Nov, 28

Madlener operation

| 58605 | **Ligation or transection of fallopian tube(s), abdominal or vaginal approach, postpartum, unilateral or bilateral, during same hospitalization (separate procedure)** ♀ C 80 🔷 |

MED: 100-3, 230.3

AMA: 1999, Nov, 28

If laparoscopic procedures are performed, consult CPT codes 58670 and 58371.

| + 58611 | **Ligation or transection of fallopian tube(s) when done at the time of cesarean delivery or intra-abdominal surgery (not a separate procedure) (List separately in addition to code for primary procedure)** ♀ C 80 🔷 |

MED: 100-3, 230.3

Note that 58611 is an add-on code that must be used in conjunction with the appropriate code for the primary procedure. This code cannot be reported alone.

| 58615 | **Occlusion of fallopian tube(s) by device (eg, band, clip, Falope ring) vaginal or suprapubic approach** ♀ T 80 🔷 |

MED: 100-3, 230.3

AMA: 1999, Nov, 28

If a laparoscopic approach is used, consult CPT code 58621.

LAPAROSCOPY

If a laparoscopic biopsy is performed of the ovary or fallopian tube, consult CPT code 49321.

If a pelvic laparotomy is performed, consult CPT code 49000. If excision or destruction is performed of endometriomas, open method, consult CPT codes 49200 and 49201. If paracentesis is performed, consult CPT codes 49080 and 49081. If secondary closure of the abdominal wall evisceration or disruption is performed, consult CPT code 49900. If fulguration or excision of lesions is performed through a laparoscopic approach, consult CPT code 58662. If chemotherapy is needed, consult CPT codes 96401-96549.

Diagnostic laparoscopy is always included in surgical laparoscopy. To report only diagnostic laparoscopy, consult CT code 49320.

58660	**Laparoscopy, surgical; with lysis of adhesions (salpingolysis, ovariolysis) (separate procedure)**	♀ 5 T 80 ⟲

MED: 100-2, 15, 260; 100-3, 230.3; 100-4, 12, 90.3; 100-4, 14, 10

AMA: 2000, Mar, 5; 1999, Nov, 28

58661	**with removal of adnexal structures (partial or total oophorectomy and/or salpingectomy)**	♀ 5 T 80 ⟲

MED: 100-2, 15, 260; 100-3, 230.3; 100-4, 12, 90.3; 100-4, 14, 10

AMA: 2002, Jan, 11; 2000, Mar, 5; 1999, Nov, 28

58662	**with fulguration or excision of lesions of the ovary, pelvic viscera, or peritoneal surface by any method**	♀ 5 T 80 ⟲

MED: 100-2, 15, 260; 100-3, 230.3; 100-4, 12, 90.3; 100-4, 14, 10

AMA: 2000, Mar, 5; 1999, Nov, 28

58670	**with fulguration of oviducts (with or without transection)**	♀ 3 T ⟲

MED: 100-2, 15, 260; 100-3, 230.3; 100-4, 12, 90.3; 100-4, 14, 10

AMA: 2000, Mar, 5; 1999, Nov, 29

58671	**with occlusion of oviducts by device (eg, band, clip, or Falope ring)**	♀ 3 T ⟲

MED: 100-2, 15, 260; 100-3, 230.3; 100-4, 12, 90.3; 100-4, 14, 10

AMA: 2000, Mar, 5; 1999, Nov, 29

58672	**with fimbrioplasty**	♀ 5 T 50 80 ⟲

MED: 100-2, 15, 260; 100-3, 230.3; 100-4, 12, 90.3; 100-4, 14, 10

AMA: 2000, Mar, 5; 1999, Nov, 29

58673	**with salpingostomy (salpingoneostomy)**	♀ 5 T 50 80 ⟲

MED: 100-2, 15, 260; 100-3, 230.3; 100-4, 12, 90.3; 100-4, 14, 10

AMA: 2000, Mar, 5; 1999, Nov, 29

Codes 58672 and 58673 describe unilateral procedures. If performed bilaterally, append modifier 50.

58679	**Unlisted laparoscopy procedure, oviduct, ovary**	T 50 80

AMA: 2000, Mar, 5; 1999, Nov, 29

EXCISION

58700	**Salpingectomy, complete or partial, unilateral or bilateral (separate procedure)**	♀ C 80 ⟲

58720	**Salpingo-oophorectomy, complete or partial, unilateral or bilateral (separate procedure)**	♀ C 80 ⟲

AMA: 2000, Sep, 9

REPAIR

If a pelvic laparotomy is performed, consult CPT code 49000. If excision or destruction is performed of endometriomas, open method, consult CPT codes 49200 and 49201. If paracentesis is performed, consult CPT codes 49080 and 49081. If secondary closure of the abdominal wall evisceration or disruption is performed, consult CPT code 49900. If fulguration or excision of lesions is performed through a laparoscopic approach, consult CPT code 58662. If chemotherapy is needed, consult CPT codes 96401-96549.

58740	**Lysis of adhesions (salpingolysis, ovariolysis)**	♀ C 80 ⟲

AMA: 1999, Nov, 29; 1996, Sep, 9

If a laparoscopic approach is used, consult CPT code 58660. If excision or destruction is performed of endometriomas, open method, consult CPT codes 49200 and 49201. If fulguration or excision of lesions is performed, laparoscopic approach, consult CPT code 58662.

Female Genital System

58750 — 58825

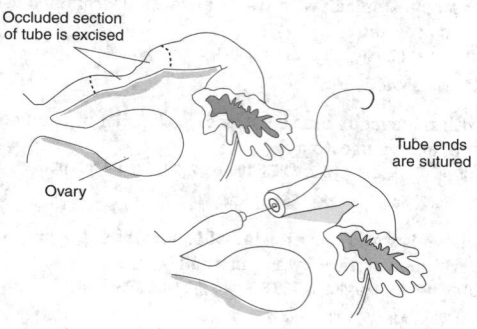

Occluded section
of tube is excised

Tube ends
are sutured

Ovary

58750	**Tubotubal anastomosis**	♀ C 80 ▣
58752	**Tubouterine implantation**	♀ C 80 ▣
58760	**Fimbrioplasty**	♀ C 50 80 ▣
	AMA: 1999, Nov, 29	

If a laparoscopic approach is used, consult CPT code 58672.

58770	**Salpingostomy (salpingoneostomy)**	♀ C 50 80 ▣
	AMA: 1999, Nov, 29	

If a laparoscopic approach is used, consult CPT code 58673.

OVARY

If a pelvic laparotomy is performed, consult CPT code 49000. If excision or destruction is performed of endometriomas, open method, consult CPT codes 49200 and 49201. If paracentesis is performed, consult CPT codes 49080 and 49081. If secondary closure of the abdominal wall evisceration or disruption is performed, consult CPT code 49900. If fulguration or excision of lesions is performed through a laparoscopic approach, consult CPT code 58662. If chemotherapy is needed, consult CPT codes 96401-96549.

INCISION

58800	**Drainage of ovarian cyst(s), unilateral or bilateral, (separate procedure); vaginal approach**	♀ 3 T ▣
	MED: 100-2, 15, 260; 100-4, 12, 90.3; 100-4, 14, 10	
58805	**abdominal approach**	♀ C 80 ▣
58820	**Drainage of ovarian abscess; vaginal approach, open**	♀ 3 T 80 ▣
	MED: 100-2, 15, 260; 100-4, 12, 90.3; 100-4, 14, 10	
	AMA: 1997, Nov, 22	
58822	**abdominal approach**	♀ C 80 ▣
	AMA: 1997, Nov, 22	
⊙ 58823	**Drainage of pelvic abscess, transvaginal or transrectal approach, percutaneous (eg, ovarian, pericolic)**	♀ T 80 ▣
	AMA: 1998, Mar, 8; 1997, Nov, 22	

To report radiological supervision and interpretation, consult CPT code 75989.

58825	**Transposition, ovary(s)**	♀ C 80 ▣

EXCISION

58900 Biopsy of ovary, unilateral or bilateral (separate procedure) ♀ ③ T 80 ◨
MED: 100-2, 15, 260; 100-4, 12, 90.3; 100-4, 14, 10

AMA: 1999, Nov, 29

If performed via laparoscope, consult CPT code 49321.

58920 Wedge resection or bisection of ovary, unilateral or bilateral ♀ T 80 ◨

58925 Ovarian cystectomy, unilateral or bilateral ♀ T 80 ◨

58940 Oophorectomy, partial or total, unilateral or bilateral; ♀ C 80 ◨
MED: 100-3, 230.3

58943 for ovarian, tubal or primary peritoneal malignancy, with para-aortic and pelvic lymph node biopsies, peritoneal washings, peritoneal biopsies, diaphragmatic assessments, with or without salpingectomy(s), with or without omentectomy ♀ C 80 ◨
MED: 100-3, 230.3

58950 Resection of ovarian, tubal or primary peritoneal malignancy with bilateral salpingo-oophorectomy and omentectomy; ♀ C 80 ◨

58951 with total abdominal hysterectomy, pelvic and limited para-aortic lymphadenectomy ♀ C 80 ◨
AMA: 2001, Aug, 11

58952 with radical dissection for debulking (ie, radical excision or destruction, intra-abdominal or retroperitoneal tumors) ♀ C 80 ◨
AMA: 2001, Aug, 11; 1996, Dec, 10

58953 Bilateral salpingo-oophorectomy with omentectomy, total abdominal hysterectomy and radical dissection for debulking; ♀ C 80 ◨
AMA: 2002, Feb, 7

58954 with pelvic lymphadenectomy and limited para-aortic lymphadenectomy ♀ C 80 ◨
AMA: 2002, Feb, 7

58956 Bilateral salpingo-oophorectomy with total omentectomy, total abdominal hysterectomy for malignancy ♀ C 80 ◨

Code 58956 cannot be reported with CPT codes 49255, 58150, 58180, 58262, 58263, 58550, 58661, 58700, 58720, 58900, 58925, 58940.

58960 Laparotomy, for staging or restaging of ovarian, tubal or primary peritoneal malignancy (second look), with or without omentectomy, peritoneal washing, biopsy of abdominal and pelvic peritoneum, diaphragmatic assessment with pelvic and limited para-aortic lymphadenectomy ♀ C 80 ◨

IN VITRO FERTILIZATION

58970 Follicle puncture for oocyte retrieval, any method ♀ ① T 80 ◨

To report radiological supervision and interpretation, consult CPT code 76948.

58974 Embryo transfer, intrauterine M ♀ ① T 80 ◨

58976 Gamete, zygote, or embryo intrafallopian transfer, any method M ♀ ① T 80 ◨
AMA: 1999, Nov, 29

OTHER PROCEDURES

58999 Unlisted procedure, female genital system (nonobstetrical) ♀ T 80

MATERNITY CARE AND DELIVERY

ANTEPARTUM SERVICES

Maternity care is outlined in the maternity care and delivery section. The codes for normal, uncomplicated care to the maternity patient (59400, 59510, 59610, 59618) include antepartum care, delivery, and postpartum care by the same physician.

Antepartum care includes the initial and routine subsequent history and physical exams, patient's weight, blood pressure, fetal heart tones, and routine urinalysis.

Delivery includes admission to the hospital, including the admitting history and exam, the management of uncomplicated labor, and either a vaginal or cesarean delivery.

Postpartum care includes the inpatient hospital care and any office visits following vaginal or cesarean delivery.

Codes for delivery following a previous cesarean delivery deserve some additional explanation. These codes report delivery after a previous cesarean delivery when an attempt is made to accomplish the delivery vaginally, also referred to as a VBAC.

When different physicians provide components of the total obstetric service, report the services separately using the codes designated for each component. Codes 59425 and 59426 identify a different physician providing four or more antepartum care visits. Use the appropriate E/M codes when a different physician provides one to three antepartum care visits. Use 59409, 59514, 59612, or 59620 when the physician performs vaginal or cesarean delivery only. Use 59410, 59515, 59614, or 59622 when the physician performs vaginal or cesarean delivery with postpartum care.

Services unrelated to the pregnancy should be reported with E/M codes or the procedure codes for the service. For example, a patient seen for a sore throat with a throat culture should have both the throat culture and E/M service reported separately. Clearly identify the reasons for the services as pharyngitis, not pregnancy.

Services directly related to the pregnancy, but not included in the global service, should be reported separately. Examples include ultrasound examination of pregnant uterus (76801–76817), glucose tolerance test (82951–82953), and Pap smear (88150). The neuraxial labor analgesia and anesthesia codes are reported in addition to the primary procedures.

Normal maternity care includes monthly visits up to 28 weeks gestation, biweekly visits to 36 weeks gestation, and weekly visits until delivery. For the patient at risk who is seen more frequently or for other medical/surgical intervention, report the additional services with a code representing the appropriate level of E/M service. The documentation must reflect the necessity of these visits as well as any additional laboratory or radiologic tests performed.

When the physician monitors the patient for a prolonged period, document the time spent in actual attendance and use prolonged services codes as appropriate. Codes 99356 and 99357 describe maternal-fetal monitoring, which is reported in addition to the delivery. Always include documentation to substantiate medical necessity.

59000	**Amniocentesis; diagnostic**	**M** ♀ T
	MED: 100-3, 220.5	
	AMA: 2002, Feb, 7; 1997, Apr, 2	

To report radiological supervision and interpretation, consult CPT code 76946.

59001	**therapeutic amniotic fluid reduction (includes ultrasound guidance)**	**M** ♀ T
	AMA: 2002, Feb, 7	

59012	**Cordocentesis (intrauterine), any method**	**M** ♀ T 80

To report radiological supervision and interpretation, consult CPT code 76941.

59015	**Chorionic villus sampling, any method**	M ♀ T 80 ⟲
	AMA: 1997, Apr, 2	

To report radiological supervision and interpretation, consult CPT code 76945.

59020	**Fetal contraction stress test**	M ♀ T 80 ⟲
	AMA: 1997, Apr, 2	

If the physician only interprets the results and/or operates the equipment, modifier 26 should be appended to 59020.

59025	**Fetal non-stress test**	M ♀ T 80 ⟲
	AMA: 1998, May, 10	

If the physician only interprets the results and/or operates the equipment, modifier 26 should be appended to 59025.

59030	**Fetal scalp blood sampling**	M ♀ T 80 ⟲
59050	**Fetal monitoring during labor by consulting physician (ie, non-attending physician) with written report; supervision and interpretation**	M ♀ E 80 ⟲
	AMA: 1997, Nov, 22	
59051	**interpretation only**	M ♀ B 80 ⟲
	AMA: 1997, Nov, 22	
59070	**Transabdominal amnioinfusion, including ultrasound guidance**	M ♀ T 80 ⟲
59072	**Fetal umbilical cord occlusion, including ultrasound guidance**	M ♀ T ⟲
59074	**Fetal fluid drainage (eg, vesicocentesis, thoracocentesis, paracentesis), including ultrasound guidance**	M ♀ T 80 ⟲
59076	**Fetal shunt placement, including ultrasound guidance**	M ♀ T 80 ⟲

To report unlisted fetal invasive procedure, consult CPT code 59897.

EXCISION

59100	**Hysterotomy, abdominal (eg, for hydatidiform mole, abortion)**	M ♀ T 80 ⟲

If tubal ligation is performed at the same time as the hysterotomy, consult CPT code 58611 and report in addition to 59100.

59120	**Surgical treatment of ectopic pregnancy; tubal or ovarian, requiring salpingectomy and/or oophorectomy, abdominal or vaginal approach**	M ♀ C 80 ⟲
	MED: 100-3, 230.3	
59121	**tubal or ovarian, without salpingectomy and/or oophorectomy**	M ♀ C 80 ⟲
59130	**abdominal pregnancy**	M ♀ C 80 ⟲
59135	**interstitial, uterine pregnancy requiring total hysterectomy**	M ♀ C 80 ⟲
	MED: 100-3, 230.3	
59136	**interstitial, uterine pregnancy with partial resection of uterus**	M ♀ C 80 ⟲
	MED: 100-3, 230.3	
59140	**cervical, with evacuation**	M ♀ C 80 ⟲
59150	**Laparoscopic treatment of ectopic pregnancy; without salpingectomy and/or oophorectomy**	M ♀ T 80 ⟲
	AMA: 1996, Sep, 9	

Maternity Care and Delivery

59151 — 59350

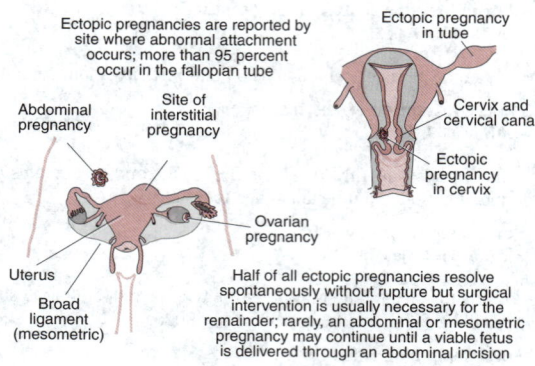

Ectopic pregnancies are reported by site where abnormal attachment occurs; more than 95 percent occur in the fallopian tube

Abdominal pregnancy

Site of interstitial pregnancy

Ectopic pregnancy in tube

Cervix and cervical canal

Ectopic pregnancy in cervix

Ovarian pregnancy

Uterus

Broad ligament (mesometric)

Half of all ectopic pregnancies resolve spontaneously without rupture but surgical intervention is usually necessary for the remainder; rarely, an abdominal or mesometric pregnancy may continue until a viable fetus is delivered through an abdominal incision

59151   **with salpingectomy and/or oophorectomy**   M ♀ T 80
                         MED: 100-3, 230.3

59160   **Curettage, postpartum**   M ♀ 3 T 80
                         MED: 100-2, 15, 260; 100-4, 12, 90.3; 100-4, 14, 10

                         AMA: 1997, Nov, 22

INTRODUCTION

59200   **Insertion of cervical dilator (eg, laminaria, prostaglandin) (separate procedure)**   M ♀ T
                         AMA: 1997, Apr, 3; 1993, Fall, 9

                         If intrauterine fetal transfusion is conducted, consult CPT code 36460. If a hypertonic solution and/or prostaglandins are introduced to initiate labor, consult CPT codes 59850-59857.

REPAIR

If tracheloplasty is performed, consult CPT code 57700.

59300   **Episiotomy or vaginal repair, by other than attending physician**   M ♀ T 80

59320   **Cerclage of cervix, during pregnancy; vaginal**   M ♀ 1 T 80
                         MED: 100-2, 15, 260; 100-4, 12, 90.3; 100-4, 14, 10

59325   **abdominal**   M ♀ C 80

59350   **Hysterorrhaphy of ruptured uterus**   M ♀ C 80

VAGINAL DELIVERY, ANTEPARTUM AND POSTPARTUM CARE

This section addresses antepartum care, delivery, and postpartum care. Antepartum care includes monthly visits up to 28 weeks gestation, biweekly visits up to 36 weeks gestation and weekly visits until delivery. Services included are history, examinations, recording of weight, blood pressures, fetal health, urinalysis, and other examinations pertinent to the health of mother and child. Delivery services include admission, management of labor and vaginal delivery, or cesarean delivery. Postpartum care includes hospital and office visits following vaginal or cesarean section delivery.

If the physician provides all or part of the antepartum care, but doesn't perform the delivery, consult CPT codes 59425-59426. If only one to three visits are provided, consult the appropriate Evaluation and Management Codes. For postpartum care only, consult CPT code 59430.

For insertion of transcervical or transvaginal fetal oximetry sensor, consult CPT Category III code 0021T.

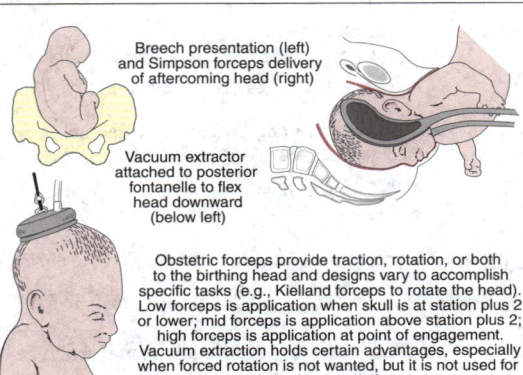

Breech presentation (left) and Simpson forceps delivery of aftercoming head (right)

Vacuum extractor attached to posterior fontanelle to flex head downward (below left)

Obstetric forceps provide traction, rotation, or both to the birthing head and designs vary to accomplish specific tasks (e.g., Kielland forceps to rotate the head). Low forceps is application when skull is at station plus 2 or lower; mid forceps is application above station plus 2; high forceps is application at point of engagement. Vacuum extraction holds certain advantages, especially when forced rotation is not wanted, but it is not used for breech presentations

59400 **Routine obstetric care including antepartum care, vaginal delivery (with or without episiotomy, and/or forceps) and postpartum care** M ♀ B ▣
MED: 100-2, 15, 180; 100-2, 15, 20.1
AMA: 2003, Feb, 15; 2002, Aug, 1; 1998, Jun, 10; 1998, Apr, 15; 1997, Feb, 11; 1997, Apr, 3; 1996, Mar, 11

59409 **Vaginal delivery only (with or without episiotomy and/or forceps);** M ♀ T 80 ▣
MED: 100-2, 15, 180; 100-2, 15, 20.1
AMA: 2002, Aug, 1; 1997, Feb, 11; 1997, Apr, 1; 1996, Sep, 4; 1996, Mar, 11; 1996, Jul, 11

59410 **including postpartum care** M ♀ B ▣
MED: 100-2, 15, 180; 100-2, 15, 20.1

59412 **External cephalic version, with or without tocolysis** M ♀ T 80 ▣
Report 59412 in conjunction with code(s) for delivery.

59414 **Delivery of placenta (separate procedure)** M ♀ T 80 ▣
AMA: 1998, Jun, 10; 1996, Jun, 10

59425 **Antepartum care only; 4-6 visits** M ♀ B 80 ▣
MED: 100-2, 15, 180; 100-2, 15, 20.1
AMA: 2002, Aug, 1; 1997, Apr, 11; 1994, Fall, 21

If 1-3 visits for antepartum care are provided, consult the appropriate Evaluation and Management code(s).

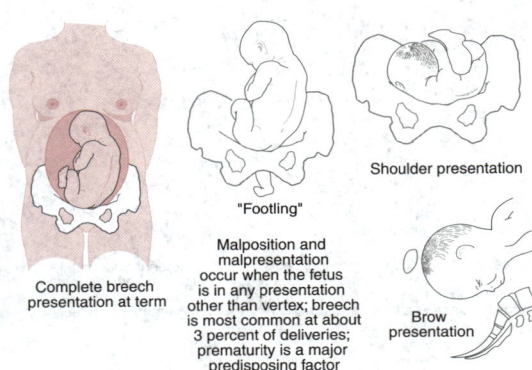

Complete breech presentation at term

"Footling"

Malposition and malpresentation occur when the fetus is in any presentation other than vertex; breech is most common at about 3 percent of deliveries; prematurity is a major predisposing factor

Shoulder presentation

Brow presentation

59426   **7 or more visits**   M ♀ B 80
MED: 100-2, 15, 180; 100-2, 15, 20.1

AMA: 2002, Aug, 1; 1997, Apr, 11; 1994, Fall, 21

59430   **Postpartum care only (separate procedure)**   M ♀ B
MED: 100-2, 15, 180; 100-2, 15, 20.1

AMA: 2002, Aug, 1; 1996, Jun, 10

CESAREAN DELIVERY

If a standby physician is present for an infant, consult CPT code 99360.

To report low cervical Cesarean section, consult 59510, 59515, 59525.

59510   **Routine obstetric care including antepartum care, cesarean delivery, and postpartum care**   M ♀ E
AMA: 2002, Aug, 1; 1997, Feb, 11; 1997, Apr, 2; 1996, Sep, 4; 1996, Oct, 10; 1996, Jul, 11

59514   **Cesarean delivery only;**   M ♀ C 80
AMA: 1997, Feb, 11; 1996, Oct, 10

59515   **including postpartum care**   M ♀ E

+ **59525**   **Subtotal or total hysterectomy after cesarean delivery (List separately in addition to code for primary procedure)**   M ♀ C 80

Note that 59525 is an add-on code and must be used in conjunction with 59510, 59514, 59515, 59618, 59620, and 59622.

DELIVERY AFTER PREVIOUS CESAREAN DELIVERY

If a standby physician is present for an infant, consult CPT code 99360.

Codes 59610-59622 are used to report delivery services rendered to a patient who has had a previous cesarean delivery and now presents with the expectation of a vaginal delivery.

For a successful vaginal delivery after a previous cesarean section, consult CPT codes 59610–59614. If the attempt is unsuccessful and the patient has another cesarean section, consult codes 59618–59622. For elective cesarean deliveries, consult code 59510, 59514, or 59515.

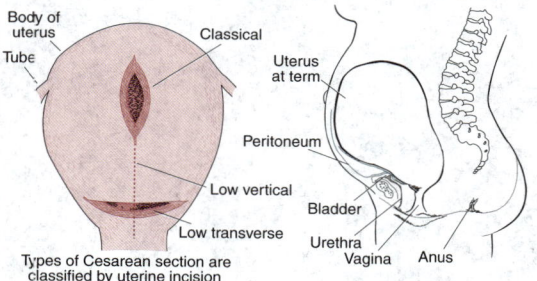

Types of Cesarean section are classified by uterine incision

Cesarean section is delivery through incisions in the anterior abdominal and uterine walls and is indicated for numerous conditions in both the fetus and the mother. Although other approaches may be warranted, low transverse is preferred to decrease chance of uterine rupture during future pregnancies

59610   **Routine obstetric care including antepartum care, vaginal delivery (with or without episiotomy, and/or forceps) and postpartum care, after previous cesarean delivery**   M ♀ E 80 ▣
 MED: 100-2, 15, 180; 100-2, 15, 20.1

 AMA: 2002, Aug, 1; 1997, Apr, 3; 1996, Feb, 2

 Codes 59610-59614 are reported for a successful vaginal delivery following a previous cesarean delivery.

59612   **Vaginal delivery only, after previous cesarean delivery (with or without episiotomy and/or forceps);**   M ♀ T 80 ▣
 MED: 100-2, 15, 180; 100-2, 15, 20.1

 AMA: 2002, Aug, 1; 1996, Feb, 2

59614   **including postpartum care**   M ♀ E 80 ▣
 MED: 100-2, 15, 180; 100-2, 15, 20.1

 AMA: 1996, Feb, 2

59618   **Routine obstetric care including antepartum care, cesarean delivery, and postpartum care, following attempted vaginal delivery after previous cesarean delivery**   M ♀ E 80 ▣
 AMA: 2002, Aug, 1; 1996, Feb, 2

 Codes 59618-59622 are reported for an attempted vaginal delivery that is unsuccessful following a previous cesarean delivery which again must be performed via cesarean delivery.

59620   **Cesarean delivery only, following attempted vaginal delivery after previous cesarean delivery;**   M ♀ C 80 ▣
 AMA: 1996, Feb, 2

59622   **including postpartum care**   M ♀ E 80 ▣
 AMA: 1996, Feb, 2

ABORTION

If medical treatment is needed for a spontaneous complete abortion, any trimester, consult E/M codes 99201-99233.

59812   **Treatment of incomplete abortion, any trimester, completed surgically**   M ♀ 5 T ▣
 MED: 100-2, 15, 20.1; 100-2, 15, 260; 100-4, 12, 90.3; 100-4, 14, 10

 AMA: 1995, Fall, 16; 1993, Fall, 9

59820   **Treatment of missed abortion, completed surgically; first trimester**   M ♀ 5 T ▣
 MED: 100-2, 15, 20.1; 100-2, 15, 260; 100-4, 12, 90.3; 100-4, 14, 10

 AMA: 1999, Feb, 10; 1995, Fall, 16; 1993, Fall, 9

59821   **second trimester**   M ♀ 5 T 80 ▣
 MED: 100-2, 15, 260; 100-4, 12, 90.3; 100-4, 14, 10

 AMA: 1995, Fall, 16; 1993, Fall, 9

59830   **Treatment of septic abortion, completed surgically**   M ♀ C 80 ▣
 AMA: 1993, Fall, 9

59840   **Induced abortion, by dilation and curettage**   M ♀ 5 T 80 ▣
 MED: 100-2, 15, 260; 100-3, 140.1; 100-4, 12, 90.3; 100-4, 14, 10

 AMA: 1993, Fall, 9

Endocrine System

59841 — 60000

59841   **Induced abortion, by dilation and evacuation**   M ♀ 5 T 80 ▣
MED: 100-2, 15, 260; 100-3, 140.1; 100-4, 12, 90.3; 100-4, 14, 10
AMA: 1993, Fall, 9

59850   **Induced abortion, by one or more intra-amniotic injections (amniocentesis-injections), including hospital admission and visits, delivery of fetus and secundines;**   M ♀ C 80 ▣
MED: 100-3, 140.1; 100-3, 230.3
AMA: 1993, Fall, 10

59851   **with dilation and curettage and/or evacuation**   M ♀ C 80 ▣
MED: 100-3, 140.1
AMA: 1993, Fall, 10

59852   **with hysterotomy (failed intra-amniotic injection)**   M ♀ C 80 ▣
MED: 100-3, 140.1; 100-3, 230.3
AMA: 1993, Fall, 10

If a cervical dilator is inserted, consult CPT code 59200.

59855   **Induced abortion, by one or more vaginal suppositories (eg, prostaglandin) with or without cervical dilation (eg, laminaria), including hospital admission and visits, delivery of fetus and secundines;**   M ♀ C 80 ▣
MED: 100-3, 140.1

59856   **with dilation and curettage and/or evacuation**   M ♀ C 80 ▣
MED: 100-3, 140.1

59857   **with hysterotomy (failed medical evacuation)**   M ♀ C 80 ▣
MED: 100-3, 140.1

OTHER PROCEDURES

59866   **Multifetal pregnancy reduction(s) (MPR)**   M ♀ T 80 ▣
MED: 100-3, 140.1

59870   **Uterine evacuation and curettage for hydatidiform mole**   M ♀ 5 T 80 ▣
MED: 100-2, 15, 260; 100-4, 12, 90.3; 100-4, 14, 10
AMA: 1999, Feb, 10

59871   **Removal of cerclage suture under anesthesia (other than local)**   M ♀ 5 T 80 ▣
MED: 100-2, 15, 260; 100-4, 12, 90.3; 100-4, 14, 10
AMA: 1997, Nov, 22

59897   **Unlisted fetal invasive procedure, including ultrasound guidance**   T ▣

59898   **Unlisted laparoscopy procedure, maternity care and delivery**   M ♀ T 50 80
AMA: 2000, Mar, 5; 1999, Nov, 29

59899   **Unlisted procedure, maternity care and delivery**   M ♀ T 80
AMA: 1997, Jun, 10

ENDOCRINE SYSTEM

If pituitary and pineal surgery is performed, consult the Nervous System section of the CPT book.

THYROID GLAND

INCISION

60000   **Incision and drainage of thyroglossal duct cyst, infected**   1 T 80 ▣
MED: 100-2, 15, 260; 100-4, 12, 90.3; 100-4, 14, 10

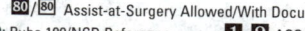

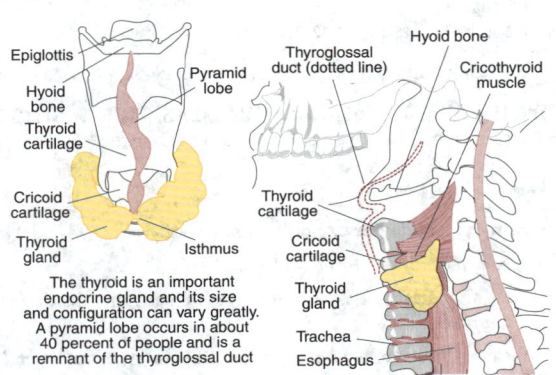

Epiglottis

Pyramid lobe

Hyoid bone

Thyroglossal duct (dotted line)

Cricothyroid muscle

Hyoid bone

Thyroid cartilage

Thyroid cartilage

Cricoid cartilage

Cricoid cartilage

Thyroid gland

Thyroid gland

Isthmus

Trachea

Esophagus

The thyroid is an important endocrine gland and its size and configuration can vary greatly. A pyramid lobe occurs in about 40 percent of people and is a remnant of the thyroglossal duct

EXCISION

60001   **Aspiration and/or injection, thyroid cyst**   T

To report fine needle aspiration, consult CPT codes 10020, 10021.

To report imaging guidance, consult CPT codes 76360, 76942

60100   **Biopsy thyroid, percutaneous core needle**   T
AMA: 1997, Jun, 5

To report imaging guidance, consult CPT codes 76003, 76360, 76393, and 76942. To report needle aspiration, consult CPT codes 10021, 10022. To report evaluation of fine needle aspirate, consult CPT codes 88172, 88173.

60200   **Excision of cyst or adenoma of thyroid, or transection of isthmus** 2 T 80
MED: 100-2, 15, 260; 100-4, 12, 90.3; 100-4, 14, 10

60210   **Partial thyroid lobectomy, unilateral; with or without isthmusectomy**   T 80

60212   **with contralateral subtotal lobectomy, including isthmusectomy** T 80
MED: 100-4, 12, 40.7

60220   **Total thyroid lobectomy, unilateral; with or without isthmusectomy** T 80

60225   **with contralateral subtotal lobectomy, including isthmusectomy** T 80
MED: 100-4, 12, 40.7

60240   **Thyroidectomy, total or complete**   T 80

60252   **Thyroidectomy, total or subtotal for malignancy; with limited neck dissection**   T 80
AMA: 2000, Nov, 10

60254   **with radical neck dissection**   C 80
AMA: 2000, Nov, 10

60260   **Thyroidectomy, removal of all remaining thyroid tissue following previous removal of a portion of thyroid**   T 50

60270   **Thyroidectomy, including substernal thyroid; sternal split or transthoracic approach**   C 80

60271   **cervical approach**   C 80

60280   **Excision of thyroglossal duct cyst or sinus;**   4 T 80
MED: 100-2, 15, 260; 100-4, 12, 90.3; 100-4, 14, 10

Endocrine System

60281 — 60545

60281	**recurrent**	4 T 80 ↵

MED: 100-2, 15, 260; 100-4, 12, 90.3; 100-4, 14, 10

If a thyroid ultrasonography is performed, consult CPT code 76536.

PARATHYROID, THYMUS, ADRENAL GLANDS, PANCREAS, AND CAROTID BODY

If pituitary and pineal surgery is performed, consult the Nervous System section of CPT.

EXCISION

60500	**Parathyroidectomy or exploration of parathyroid(s);**	T 80 ↵
60502	**re-exploration**	C 80 ↵
60505	**with mediastinal exploration, sternal split or transthoracic approach**	C 80 ↵
+ 60512	**Parathyroid autotransplantation (List separately in addition to code for primary procedure)**	T 80

> Note that 60512 is an add-on code and must be used in conjunction with 60500, 60502, 60505, 60212, 60225, 60240, 60252, 60254, 60260, 60270, and 60271.

60520	**Thymectomy, partial or total; transcervical approach (separate procedure)**	C 80 ↵
60521	**sternal split or transthoracic approach, without radical mediastinal dissection (separate procedure)**	C 80 ↵
60522	**sternal split or transthoracic approach, with radical mediastinal dissection (separate procedure)**	C 80 ↵
60540	**Adrenalectomy, partial or complete, or exploration of adrenal gland with or without biopsy, transabdominal, lumbar or dorsal (separate procedure);**	C 50 80 ↵

AMA: 1998, Nov, 17

60545	**with excision of adjacent retroperitoneal tumor**	C 80 ↵

AMA: 1998, Nov, 17

Code 60540, 60545 cannot be reported with CPT code 50323.

If 60540 is performed bilaterally report with modifier 50.

If a remote or disseminated pheochromocytoma is excised, consult CPT codes 49200 and 49201. If a laparoscopic approach is used, consult CPT code 60650.

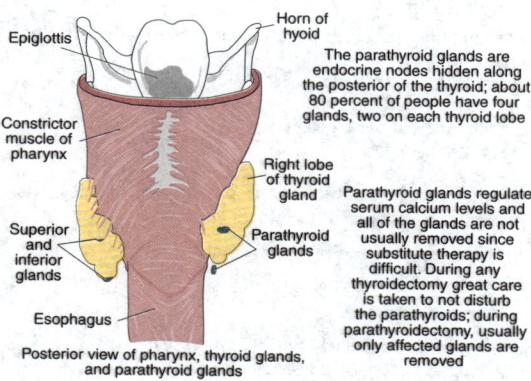

Horn of hyoid

Epiglottis

The parathyroid glands are endocrine nodes hidden along the posterior of the thyroid; about 80 percent of people have four glands, two on each thyroid lobe

Constrictor muscle of pharynx

Right lobe of thyroid gland

Superior and inferior glands

Parathyroid glands

Parathyroid glands regulate serum calcium levels and all of the glands are not usually removed since substitute therapy is difficult. During any thyroidectomy great care is taken to not disturb the parathyroids; during parathyroidectomy, usually only affected glands are removed

Esophagus

Posterior view of pharynx, thyroid glands, and parathyroid glands

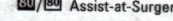

60600	**Excision of carotid body tumor; without excision of carotid artery** C 80 ▣
	MED: 100-3, 20.18
60605	**with excision of carotid artery** C 80 ▣
	MED: 100-3, 20.18

LAPAROSCOPY

Diagnostic laparoscopy is always included in surgical laparoscopy. To report diagnostic laparoscopy only, consult CPT code 49320.

60650	**Laparoscopy, surgical, with adrenalectomy, partial or complete, or exploration of adrenal gland with or without biopsy, transabdominal, lumbar or dorsal** C 50 80 ▣
	AMA: 2001, Nov, 8; 2000, Mar, 5; 1999, Nov, 30
60659	**Unlisted laparoscopy procedure, endocrine system** T 50 80
	AMA: 2000, Mar, 5; 1999, Nov, 30

OTHER PROCEDURES

60699	**Unlisted procedure, endocrine system** T 80

NERVOUS SYSTEM

SKULL, MENINGES, AND BRAIN

INJECTION, DRAINAGE, OR ASPIRATION

If an injection procedure is needed for cerebral angiography, consult CPT codes 36100-36218. If an injection procedure is needed for pneumoencephalography, consult CPT code 61055.

If an injection procedure is needed for ventriculography, consult CPT codes 61026, and 61120.

61000 **Subdural tap through fontanelle, or suture, infant, unilateral or bilateral; initial** A T

61001 **subsequent taps** A T

61020 **Ventricular puncture through previous burr hole, fontanelle, suture, or implanted ventricular catheter/reservoir; without injection** 1 T
MED: 100-2, 15, 260; 100-4, 12, 90.3; 100-4, 14, 10

61026 **with injection of medication or other substance for diagnosis or treatment** 1 T
MED: 100-2, 15, 260; 100-4, 12, 90.3; 100-4, 14, 10

61050 **Cisternal or lateral cervical (C1-C2) puncture; without injection (separate procedure)** 1 T 80
MED: 100-2, 15, 260; 100-4, 12, 90.3; 100-4, 14, 10

61055 **with injection of medication or other substance for diagnosis or treatment (eg, C1-C2)** 1 T
MED: 100-2, 15, 260; 100-4, 12, 90.3; 100-4, 14, 10

To report radiological supervision and interpretation, consult the Radiology section of the CPT book.

61070 **Puncture of shunt tubing or reservoir for aspiration or injection procedure** 1 T
MED: 100-2, 15, 260; 100-4, 12, 90.3; 100-4, 14, 10

To report radiological supervision and interpretation, consult CPT code 75809.

TWIST DRILL, BURR HOLE(S), OR TREPHINE

61105 **Twist drill hole for subdural or ventricular puncture;** C 80

⊘ **61107** **for implanting ventricular catheter or pressure recording device** C

To report intracranial neuroendoscopic ventricular catheter placement, consult CPT code 62160.

For twist drill or burr hole performed to place thermal perfusion probe, consult Category III code 0077T.

61108 **for evacuation and/or drainage of subdural hematoma** C

61120 **Burr hole(s) for ventricular puncture (including injection of gas, contrast media, dye, or radioactive material)** C 80

61140 **Burr hole(s) or trephine; with biopsy of brain or intracranial lesion** C 80

61150 **with drainage of brain abscess or cyst** C

61151 **with subsequent tapping (aspiration) of intracranial abscess or cyst** C

61154 **Burr hole(s) with evacuation and/or drainage of hematoma, extradural or subdural** C 50 80

61156 **Burr hole(s); with aspiration of hematoma or cyst, intracerebral** C 80

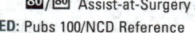

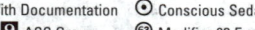

○ **61210** **for implanting ventricular catheter, reservoir, EEG electrode(s) or pressure recording device (separate procedure)** `C` `↵`

To report intracranial neuroendoscopic ventricular catheter placement, consult CPT code 62160.

61215 **Insertion of subcutaneous reservoir, pump or continuous infusion system for connection to ventricular catheter** `3` `T` `↵`
MED: 100-2, 15, 260; 100-3, 280.14; 100-4, 12, 90.3; 100-4, 14, 10

AMA: 1993, Spring, 13

If chemotherapy is administered, consult CPT code 96450.

To report refilling and maintenance of implantable infusion pump for spinal or brain drug therapy, consult CPT code 95990.

61250 **Burr hole(s) or trephine, supratentorial, exploratory, not followed by other surgery** `C` `50` `80` `↵`

61253 **Burr hole(s) or trephine, infratentorial, unilateral or bilateral** `C` `80` `↵`
AMA: 2002, Sep, 10

If a burr hole(s) or trephine are followed by a craniotomy at the same operative session, consult CPT codes 61304-61321; do not use 61250 or 61253.

CRANIECTOMY OR CRANIOTOMY

61304 **Craniectomy or craniotomy, exploratory; supratentorial** `C` `80` `↵`

61305 **infratentorial (posterior fossa)** `C` `80` `↵`

61312 **Craniectomy or craniotomy for evacuation of hematoma, supratentorial; extradural or subdural** `C` `80` `↵`
AMA: 2002, Sep, 10

61313 **intracerebral** `C` `80` `↵`

61314 **Craniectomy or craniotomy for evacuation of hematoma, infratentorial; extradural or subdural** `C` `80` `↵`

61315 **intracerebellar** `C` `80` `↵`

+ 61316 **Incision and subcutaneous placement of cranial bone graft (List separately in addition to code for primary procedure)** `C` `↵`

Note that 61316 is an add-on code and must be used in conjunction with 61304, 61312, 61313, 61322, 61323, 61340, 61570, 61571, 61680-61705.

61320 **Craniectomy or craniotomy, drainage of intracranial abscess; supratentorial** `C` `80` `↵`

61321 **infratentorial** `C` `80` `↵`

61322 **Craniectomy or craniotomy, decompressive, with or without duraplasty, for treatment of intracranial hypertension, without evacuation of associated intraparenchymal hematoma; without lobectomy** `C` `80` `↵`

To report subtemporal decompression, consult CPT code 61340. Do not report 61313 in conjunction with CPT code 61322.

61323 **with lobectomy** `C` `↵`

To report subtemporal decompression, consult CPT code 61340. Do not report 61313 in conjunction with CPT code 61323.

61330 **Decompression of orbit only, transcranial approach** `T` `50` `80` `↵`
Naffziger operation

61332 **Exploration of orbit (transcranial approach); with biopsy** `C` `80` `↵`

61333 **with removal of lesion** `C` `80` `↵`

Nervous System

61334 — 61524

61334	with removal of foreign body	T 80 ⬛
61340	Subtemporal cranial decompression (pseudotumor cerebri, slit ventricle syndrome)	C 50 80 ⬛

To report decompression craniotomy or craniectomy for intracranial hypertension, without hematoma evauation, consult CPT codes 61322, 61323.

61343	Craniectomy, suboccipital with cervical laminectomy for decompression of medulla and spinal cord, with or without dural graft (eg, Arnold-Chiari malformation)	C 80 ⬛
61345	Other cranial decompression, posterior fossa	C 80 ⬛

If an orbital decompression is performed by a lateral wall approach, Kroenlein type, consult CPT code 67445.

61440	Craniotomy for section of tentorium cerebelli (separate procedure)	C 80 ⬛
61450	Craniectomy, subtemporal, for section, compression, or decompression of sensory root of gasserian ganglion	C 80 ⬛

Frazier-Spiller procedure

61458	Craniectomy, suboccipital; for exploration or decompression of cranial nerves	C 80 ⬛

Jannetta decompression

61460	for section of one or more cranial nerves	C 80 ⬛
61470	for medullary tractotomy	C 80 ⬛
61480	for mesencephalic tractotomy or pedunculotomy	C 80 ⬛
61490	Craniotomy for lobotomy, including cingulotomy	C 50 80 ⬛
61500	Craniectomy; with excision of tumor or other bone lesion of skull	C 80 ⬛
61501	for osteomyelitis	C 80 ⬛
61510	Craniectomy, trephination, bone flap craniotomy; for excision of brain tumor, supratentorial, except meningioma	C 80 ⬛
61512	for excision of meningioma, supratentorial	C 80 ⬛
61514	for excision of brain abscess, supratentorial	C 80 ⬛
61516	for excision or fenestration of cyst, supratentorial	C 80 ⬛

If an excision is performed of a pituitary tumor or a craniopharyngioma, consult CPT codes 61545, 61546, and 61548.

+ 61517	Implantation of brain intracavitary chemotherapy agent (List separately in addition to code for primary procedure)	C ⬛

Note that 61517 is an add-on code and must be used in conjunction with 61510 or 61518. Do not use 61517 for brachytherapy insertion, consult CPT codes 77781-77784.

61518	Craniectomy for excision of brain tumor, infratentorial or posterior fossa; except meningioma, cerebellopontine angle tumor, or midline tumor at base of skull	C 80 ⬛
61519	meningioma	C 80 ⬛
61520	cerebellopontine angle tumor	C 80 ⬛
61521	midline tumor at base of skull	C 80 ⬛
61522	Craniectomy, infratentorial or posterior fossa; for excision of brain abscess	C 80 ⬛
61524	for excision or fenestration of cyst	C 80 ⬛

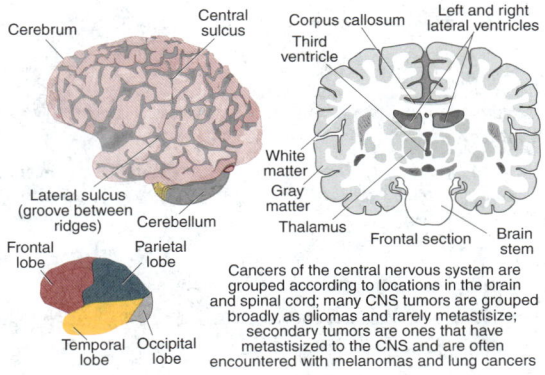

Cancers of the central nervous system are grouped according to locations in the brain and spinal cord; many CNS tumors are grouped broadly as gliomas and rarely metastisize; secondary tumors are ones that have metastisized to the CNS and are often encountered with melanomas and lung cancers

61526 **Craniectomy, bone flap craniotomy, transtemporal (mastoid) for excision of cerebellopontine angle tumor;** C ↻
  AMA: 1991, Summer, 8

61530 **combined with middle/posterior fossa craniotomy/craniectomy** C ↻

61531 **Subdural implantation of strip electrodes through one or more burr or trephine hole(s) for long term seizure monitoring** C 80 ↻
  MED: 100-3, 160.5

  If stereotactic implantation of electrodes is performed, consult CPT code 61760.

61533 **Craniotomy with elevation of bone flap; for subdural implantation of an electrode array, for long term seizure monitoring** C 80 ↻
  MED: 100-3, 160.5

  If continuous EEG monitoring is needed, consult CPT codes 95950-95954.

61534 **for excision of epileptogenic focus without electrocorticography during surgery** C 80 ↻

61535 **for removal of epidural or subdural electrode array, without excision of cerebral tissue (separate procedure)** C 80 ↻
  MED: 100-3, 160.5

61536 **for excision of cerebral epileptogenic focus, with electrocorticography during surgery (includes removal of electrode array)** C 80 ↻
  MED: 100-3, 160.5

61537 **for lobectomy, temporal lobe, without electrocorticography during surgery** C 80 ↻

61538 **for lobectomy, temporal lobe, with electrocorticography during surgery** C 80 ↻

61539 **for lobectomy, other than temporal lobe, partial or total, with electrocorticography during surgery** C 80 ↻

61540 **for lobectomy, other than temporal lobe, partial or total, without electrocorticography during surgery** C 80 ↻

61541 **for transection of corpus callosum** C 80 ↻

61542 **for total hemispherectomy** C 80 ↻

61543 **for partial or subtotal (functional) hemispherectomy** C 80 ↻

61544	for excision or coagulation of choroid plexus	C 80 ▶
61545	for excision of craniopharyngioma	C 80 ▶

To report craniotomy for selective amygdalohippocampectomy, consult CPT code 61566.

61546 **Craniotomy for hypophysectomy or excision of pituitary tumor, intracranial approach** C 80 ▶

61548 **Hypophysectomy or excision of pituitary tumor, transnasal or transseptal approach, nonstereotactic** C 80 ▶
AMA: 1998, Nov, 17

Do not report 69990 in addition to code 61548 as the operating microscope is considered an inclusive component of the surgery.

61550 **Craniectomy for craniosynostosis; single cranial suture** C 80 ▶

61552 **multiple cranial sutures** C 80 ▶

If cranial reconstruction is performed for orbital hypertelorism, consult CPT codes 21260-21263.

61556 **Craniotomy for craniosynostosis; frontal or parietal bone flap** C 80 ▶

61557 **bifrontal bone flap** C 80 ▶

61558 **Extensive craniectomy for multiple cranial suture craniosynostosis (eg, cloverleaf skull); not requiring bone grafts** C 80 ▶

61559 **recontouring with multiple osteotomies and bone autografts (eg, barrel-stave procedure) (includes obtaining grafts)** C 80 ▶

61563 **Excision, intra and extracranial, benign tumor of cranial bone (eg, fibrous dysplasia); without optic nerve decompression** C 80 ▶

61564 **with optic nerve decompression** C 80 ▶

If reconstruction is required, consult CPT codes 21181-21183.

61566 **Craniotomy with elevation of bone flap; for selective amygdalohippocampectomy** C 80 ▶

61567 **for multiple subpial transections, with electrocorticography during surgery** C 80 ▶

61570 **Craniectomy or craniotomy; with excision of foreign body from brain** C 80 ▶

61571 **with treatment of penetrating wound of brain** C 80 ▶

If a sequestrectomy is performed for osteomyelitis, consult CPT code 61501.

61575 **Transoral approach to skull base, brain stem or upper spinal cord for biopsy, decompression or excision of lesion;** C 80 ▶

61576 **requiring splitting of tongue and/or mandible (including tracheostomy)** C 80 ▶

If arthrodesis is performed, consult CPT code 22548.

SURGERY OF SKULL BASE, APPROACH PROCEDURES — ANTERIOR CRANIAL FOSSA

SURGERY OF SKULL BASE

Neurosurgical procedures of lesions involving the skull base often require the skills of several surgeons of different surgical specialties. These procedures have been broken into their component parts, categorized by the approach, definitive procedure, and repair/reconstruction of surgical defects following the definitive procedure.

The approach is defined as the portion of the procedure necessary to obtain adequate exposure of the lesion. It is described by anatomical area involved that includes anterior, middle, or posterior cranial fossa; brain stem; and upper spinal cord.

The definitive portion includes biopsy, excision, resection or repair of the lesion, and primary closure of the dura, mucous membrane and skin.

Repair/reconstruction is reported separately only when extensive dural grafting, cranioplasty, myocutaneous flaps, or extensive skin grafts are employed to close the surgical defect.

When different surgeons perform the component parts of skull base procedures, each reports only the code for the specific portion the physician has performed.

If one surgeon performs both the approach and definitive procedure, both codes should be reported, appending modifier 51 Multiple procedures to the secondary procedure.

Many physicians participate in the removal of lesions involving the skull base. Often working simultaneously, physicians from several specialties must work quickly to avoid infection. One physician may perform the approach procedure, another may perform the definitive procedure, and another may repair or reconstruct the dura, skull, and skin. Each must report the specific procedure performed.

61580   **Craniofacial approach to anterior cranial fossa; extradural, including lateral rhinotomy, ethmoidectomy, sphenoidectomy, without maxillectomy or orbital exenteration**   C 50 80 ⏣
         AMA: 1994, Spring, 11

61581   **extradural, including lateral rhinotomy, orbital exenteration, ethmoidectomy, sphenoidectomy and/or maxillectomy**   C 50 ⏣
         AMA: 1994, Spring, 11

61582   **extradural, including unilateral or bifrontal craniotomy, elevation of frontal lobe(s), osteotomy of base of anterior cranial fossa**   C 80 ⏣
         AMA: 1994, Spring, 11

61583   **intradural, including unilateral or bifrontal craniotomy, elevation or resection of frontal lobe, osteotomy of base of anterior cranial fossa**   C 80 ⏣
         AMA: 1994, Spring, 11

61584   **Orbitocranial approach to anterior cranial fossa, extradural, including supraorbital ridge osteotomy and elevation of frontal and/or temporal lobe(s); without orbital exenteration**   C 50 80 ⏣

61585   **with orbital exenteration**   C 50 80 ⏣

61586   **Bicoronal, transzygomatic and/or LeFort I osteotomy approach to anterior cranial fossa with or without internal fixation, without bone graft** C 80 ⏣

SURGERY OF SKULL BASE, APPROACH PROCEDURES — MIDDLE CRANIAL FOSSA

61590   **Infratemporal pre-auricular approach to middle cranial fossa (parapharyngeal space, infratemporal and midline skull base, nasopharynx), with or without disarticulation of the mandible, including parotidectomy, craniotomy, decompression and/or mobilization of the facial nerve and/or petrous carotid artery**   C 50 80 ⏣

61591   **Infratemporal post-auricular approach to middle cranial fossa (internal auditory meatus, petrous apex, tentorium, cavernous sinus, parasellar area, infratemporal fossa) including mastoidectomy, resection of sigmoid sinus, with or without decompression and/or mobilization of contents of auditory canal or petrous carotid artery**   C 50 80 ⏣

61592   **Orbitocranial zygomatic approach to middle cranial fossa (cavernous sinus and carotid artery, clivus, basilar artery or petrous apex) including osteotomy of zygoma, craniotomy, extra- or intradural elevation of temporal lobe**   C 50 80 ⏣

Nervous System

61595 — 61616

SURGERY OF SKULL BASE, APPROACH PROCEDURES — POSTERIOR CRANIAL FOSSA

61595   Transtemporal approach to posterior cranial fossa, jugular foramen or midline skull base, including mastoidectomy, decompression of sigmoid sinus and/or facial nerve, with or without mobilization   C 50 80

61596   Transcochlear approach to posterior cranial fossa, jugular foramen or midline skull base, including labyrinthectomy, decompression, with or without mobilization of facial nerve and/or petrous carotid artery   C 50 80

61597   Transcondylar (far lateral) approach to posterior cranial fossa, jugular foramen or midline skull base, including occipital condylectomy, mastoidectomy, resection of C1-C3 vertebral body(s), decompression of vertebral artery, with or without mobilization   C 50 80

61598   Transpetrosal approach to posterior cranial fossa, clivus or foramen magnum, including ligation of superior petrosal sinus and/or sigmoid sinus   C 80

SURGERY OF SKULL BASE, DEFINITIVE PROCEDURES — BASE OF ANTERIOR CRANIAL FOSSA

61600   Resection or excision of neoplastic, vascular or infectious lesion of base of anterior cranial fossa; extradural   C 80
         AMA: 1994, Spring, 12

61601   intradural, including dural repair, with or without graft   C 80
         AMA: 1994, Spring, 12

SURGERY OF SKULL BASE, DEFINITIVE PROCEDURES — BASE OF MIDDLE CRANIAL FOSSA

61605   Resection or excision of neoplastic, vascular or infectious lesion of infratemporal fossa, parapharyngeal space, petrous apex; extradural   C 80

61606   intradural, including dural repair, with or without graft   C 80

61607   Resection or excision of neoplastic, vascular or infectious lesion of parasellar area, cavernous sinus, clivus or midline skull base; extradural   C 80

61608   intradural, including dural repair, with or without graft   C 80

+   61609   Transection or ligation, carotid artery in cavernous sinus; without repair (List separately in addition to code for primary procedure)   C

         Note that 61609-61612 are reported in addition to code(s) for primary procedure(s) 61605-61608. Only one transection or ligation of carotid artery code should be reported per operative session.

+   61610   with repair by anastomosis or graft (List separately in addition to code for primary procedure)   C

+   61611   Transection or ligation, carotid artery in petrous canal; without repair (List separately in addition to code for primary procedure)   C

+   61612   with repair by anastomosis or graft (List separately in addition to code for primary procedure)   C

61613   Obliteration of carotid aneurysm, arteriovenous malformation, or carotid-cavernous fistula by dissection within cavernous sinus   C 50 80

SURGERY OF SKULL BASE, DEFINITIVE PROCEDURES — BASE OF POSTERIOR CRANIAL FOSSA

61615   Resection or excision of neoplastic, vascular or infectious lesion of base of posterior cranial fossa, jugular foramen, foramen magnum, or C1-C3 vertebral bodies; extradural   C 80

61616   intradural, including dural repair, with or without graft   C 80

SURGERY OF SKULL BASE, REPAIR AND/OR RECONSTRUCTION OF SURGICAL DEFECTS OF SKULL BASE

61618 **Secondary repair of dura for cerebrospinal fluid leak, anterior, middle or posterior cranial fossa following surgery of the skull base; by free tissue graft (eg, pericranium, fascia, tensor fascia lata, adipose tissue, homologous or synthetic grafts)** C 80
AMA: 2000, Mar, 11; 1994, Spring, 19

61619 **by local or regionalized vascularized pedicle flap or myocutaneous flap (including galea, temporalis, frontalis or occipitalis muscle)** C 80
AMA: 2000, Mar, 11; 1994, Spring, 19

ENDOVASCULAR THERAPY
Consult the glossary for terms and definitions and the front matter of this chapter for additional information.

61623 **Endovascular temporary balloon arterial occlusion, head or neck (extracranial/intracranial) including selective catheterization of vessel to be occluded, positioning and inflation of occlusion balloon, concomitant neurological monitoring, and radiologic supervision and interpretation of all angiography required for balloon occlusion and to exclude vascular injury post occlusion** T

If selective catheterization and angiography is performed on arteries other than the one being occluded, consult the appropriate CPT codes.

If complete angiography of artery to be occluded is performed immediately prior to temporary occlusion, consult the appropriate radiology supervision and interpretation CPT code only.

61624 **Transcatheter permanent occlusion or embolization (eg, for tumor destruction, to achieve hemostasis, to occlude a vascular malformation), percutaneous, any method; central nervous system (intracranial, spinal cord)** C
MED: 100-3, 20.28

AMA: 1999, Jun, 10

Consult also CPT code 37204. If radiological supervision and interpretation is needed, consult CPT code 75894.

61626 **Transcatheter permanent occlusion or embolization (eg, for tumor destruction, to achieve hemostasis, to occlude a vascular malformation), percutaneous, any method; non-central nervous system, head or neck (extracranial, brachiocephalic branch)** T
MED: 100-3, 20.28

Consult also CPT code 37204. If radiological supervision and interpretation is needed, consult CPT code 75894.

● **61630** **Balloon angioplasty, intracranial (eg, atherosclerotic stenosis), percutaneous**

● **61635** **Transcatheter placement of intravascular stent(s), intracranial (eg, atherosclerotic stenosis), including balloon angioplasty, if performed**

Codes 61630 and 61635 include all selective vascular catheterization of the target vascular family, all diagnostic imaging for arteriography of the target vascular family, and all radiological supervision and interpretation services related to the procedure. When a diagnostic arteriogram (including imaging and selective catheterization) confirms the need for an angioplasty or stent placement, codes 61630 and 61635 include these services. When angioplasty or stenting is not indicated, the appropriate codes for selective catheterization and imaging should be reported instead of 61630 and 61635.

Nervous System

61640 — 61702

● 61640   Balloon dilatation of intracranial vasospasm, percutaneous; initial vessel

+ ● 61641   **each additional vessel in same vascular family (List separately in addition to code for primary procedure)**

+ ● 61642   **each additional vessel in different vascular family (List separately in addition to code for primary procedure)**

Note that 61641 and 61642 are add-on codes and must be used in conjunction with 61640.

Codes 61640, 61641, and 61642 include all selective vascular catheterization of the target vessel, contrast injection(s), vessel measurement, roadmapping, postdilatation angiography, and fluoroscopic guidance for the balloon dilatation.

SURGERY FOR ANEURYSM, ARTERIOVENOUS MALFORMATION OR VASCULAR DISEASE

CPT codes 61680-61711 include craniotomy when it is appropriate for the procedure.

61680	**Surgery of intracranial arteriovenous malformation; supratentorial, simple**	C 80 ↵
61682	**supratentorial, complex**	C 80 ↵
61684	**infratentorial, simple**	C 80 ↵
61686	**infratentorial, complex**	C 80 ↵
61690	**dural, simple**	C 80 ↵
61692	**dural, complex**	C 80 ↵
61697	**Surgery of complex intracranial aneurysm, intracranial approach; carotid circulation**	C 80 ↵

CPT codes 61697, 61698 involve aneurysms that are larger than 15 mm or have calcification of the aneurysm neck, or if procedure requires temporary vessel occlusion, trapping or cardiopulmonary bypass to successfully treat the aneurysm.

61698	**vertebrobasilar circulation**	C 80 ↵
61700	**Surgery of simple intracranial aneurysm, intracranial approach; carotid circulation**	C 80 ↵
	AMA: 1999, Jun, 11; 1999, Jul, 10	
61702	**vertebrobasilar circulation**	C 80 ↵

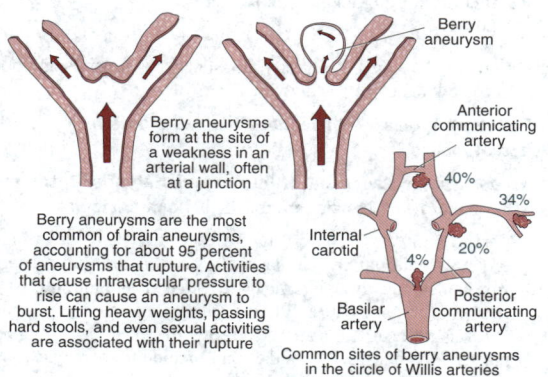

Berry aneurysm

Berry aneurysms form at the site of a weakness in an arterial wall, often at a junction

Berry aneurysms are the most common of brain aneurysms, accounting for about 95 percent of aneurysms that rupture. Activities that cause intravascular pressure to rise can cause an aneurysm to burst. Lifting heavy weights, passing hard stools, and even sexual activities are associated with their rupture

Anterior communicating artery

40%

34%

Internal carotid

20%

4%

Basilar artery

Posterior communicating artery

Common sites of berry aneurysms in the circle of Willis arteries

26/**TC** Professional/Technical Component   **80**/**80** Assist-at-Surgery Allowed/With Documentation   ⊙ Conscious Sedation

Unlisted   Not Covered   **MED**: Pubs 100/NCD Reference   **1**-**9** ASC Group   63 Modifier 63 Exempt

434 — Surgery   CPT only © 2005 American Medical Association. All Rights Reserved. *(Black Ink)*   © 2005 Ingenix, Inc. *(Blue Ink)*

Nervous System

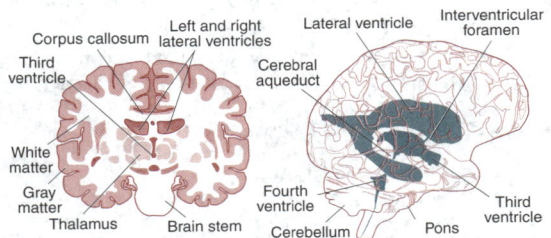

Frontal secion of the brain (left) and lateral view schematic
showing the ventricular system in blue (right)

Cerebral spinal fluid (CSF) is secreted in the ventricles and flows generally
from the laterals into the third ventricle via the interventricular foramina, and
into the fourth ventricle via the cerebral aqueduct. Many brain disorders
upset ventricular fluid pressures and shunts are employed to restore balance

61703 **Surgery of intracranial aneurysm, cervical approach by application of occluding clamp to cervical carotid artery (Selverstone-Crutchfield type)** C 80 ⏪

If direct ligation of the carotid artery is performed through a cervical approach, consult CPT codes 37600-37606.

61705 **Surgery of aneurysm, vascular malformation or carotid-cavernous fistula; by intracranial and cervical occlusion of carotid artery** C 80 ⏪

61708 **by intracranial electrothrombosis** C 80 ⏪

If ligation or gradual occlusion is performed on an internal/common carotid artery, consult CPT codes 37605 and 37606.

61710 **by intra-arterial embolization, injection procedure, or balloon catheter** C 80 ⏪

61711 **Anastomosis, arterial, extracranial-intracranial (eg, middle cerebral/cortical) arteries** C 80 ⏪

To report carotid or vertebral thomboendarterectomy, consult CPT code 35301.

STEREOTAXIS

61720 **Creation of lesion by stereotactic method, including burr hole(s) and localizing and recording techniques, single or multiple stages; globus pallidus or thalamus** C ⏪

61735 **subcortical structure(s) other than globus pallidus or thalamus** C ⏪
MED: 100-3, 160.4

61750 **Stereotactic biopsy, aspiration, or excision, including burr hole(s), for intracranial lesion;** C ⏪
AMA: 1999, Nov, 30

61751 **with computed tomography and/or magnetic resonance guidance** C ⏪
MED: 100-3, 220.1; 100-3, 220.13; 100-3, 220.3

AMA: 1999, Nov, 30; 1996, Jun, 10

If radiological supervision and interpretation of computerized tomography is needed, consult CPT codes 70450, 70460, and 70470 as appropriate. If radiological supervision and interpretation of magnetic resonance imaging is needed, consult CPT codes 70551, 70552, and 70553 as appropriate.

61760 **Stereotactic implantation of depth electrodes into the cerebrum for long term seizure monitoring** C ⏪
MED: 100-3, 160.5

61703 — 61760

Nervous System

61770 — 61864

61770　Stereotactic localization, including burr hole(s), with insertion of catheter(s) or probe(s) for placement of radiation source　[C] [▪]

61790　Creation of lesion by stereotactic method, percutaneous, by neurolytic agent (eg, alcohol, thermal, electrical, radiofrequency); gasserian ganglion　[3][T][▪]
　　　MED: 100-2, 15, 260; 100-4, 12, 90.3; 100-4, 14, 10

61791　　　trigeminal medullary tract　[3][T][80][▪]
　　　MED: 100-2, 15, 260; 100-4, 12, 90.3; 100-4, 14, 10

61793　Stereotactic radiosurgery (particle beam, gamma ray or linear accelerator), one or more sessions　[E][▪]
　　　AMA: 1997, Nov, 23

　　　To report intensity modulated beam delivery plan and treatment, see 77301, 77418.

+ 　**61795**　Stereotactic computer assisted volumetric (navigational) procedure, intracranial, extracranial, or spinal (List separately in addition to code for primary procedure)　[S][▪]
　　　AMA: 2001, Oct, 10; 1999, Nov, 30

　　　Note that 61795 is an add-on code that must be used in conjunction with the appropriate code for the primary procedure. This code cannot be reported alone.

NEUROSTIMULATORS (INTRACRANIAL)

Consult the glossary for terms and definitions and the front matter of this chapter for additional information.

For programming or electronic analysis of neurostimulator pulse generators, initial or subsequent, consult CPT codes 95970-95975.

If microelectrode recording is performed by the operating surgeon it should not be reported separately. If another physician participates in neurophysiological mapping during Deep brain stimulator implantation that physician may report 95961-95962.

61850　Twist drill or burr hole(s) for implantation of neurostimulator electrodes, cortical　[C][80][▪]
　　　MED: 100-3, 130.5; 100-3, 130.6; 100-3, 160.2; 100-3, 160.7; 100-3, 230.1; 100-3, 250.1; 100-3, 250.4; 100-3, 270.4; 100-3, 40.50

　　　AMA: 1999, Nov, 30

61860　Craniectomy or craniotomy for implantation of neurostimulator electrodes, cerebral, cortical　[C][80][▪]
　　　MED: 100-3, 130.5; 100-3, 130.6; 100-3, 160.2; 100-3, 160.7; 100-3, 230.1; 100-3, 250.1; 100-3, 250.4; 100-3, 270.4; 100-3, 40.50

　　　AMA: 1999, Nov, 30

61863　Twist drill, burr hole, craniotomy, or craniectomy with stereotactic implantation of neurostimulator electrode array in subcortical site (eg, thalamus, globus pallidus, subthalamic nucleus, periventricular, periaqueductal gray), without use of intraoperative microelectrode recording; first array　[C][50][80][▪]

+ 　**61864**　　　each additional array (List separately in addition to primary procedure)　[C][▪]

　　　Note that 61864 is an add-on code that must be used in conjunction with 61863.

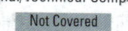
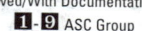

| 61867 | Twist drill, burr hole, craniotomy, or craniectomy with stereotactic implantation of neurostimulator electrode array in subcortical site (eg, thalamus, globus pallidus, subthalamic nucleus, periventricular, periaqueductal gray), with use of intraoperative microelectrode recording; first array 🄲 50 80 📵 |

+ 61868 **each additional array (List separately in addition to primary procedure)** 🄲 📵

> Note that 61868 is an add-on code that must be used in conjunction with 61867.

| 61870 | Craniectomy for implantation of neurostimulator electrodes, cerebellar; cortical 🄲 80 📵 |

MED: 100-3, 130.5; 100-3, 130.6; 100-3, 160.2; 100-3, 160.7; 100-3, 230.1; 100-3, 250.1; 100-3, 250.4; 100-3, 270.4; 100-3, 40.50

| 61875 | subcortical 🄲 80 📵 |

MED: 100-3, 130.5; 100-3, 130.6; 100-3, 160.2; 100-3, 160.7; 100-3, 230.1; 100-3, 250.1; 100-3, 250.4; 100-3, 270.4; 100-3, 40.50

| 61880 | Revision or removal of intracranial neurostimulator electrodes 🅣 50 80 📵 |

MED: 100-3, 130.5; 100-3, 130.6; 100-3, 160.2; 100-3, 160.7; 100-3, 230.1; 100-3, 250.1; 100-3, 250.4; 100-3, 270.4; 100-3, 40.50

| 61885 | Insertion or replacement of cranial neurostimulator pulse generator or receiver, direct or inductive coupling; with connection to a single electrode array 🄑 🅢 50 80 📵 |

MED: 100-2, 15, 260; 100-3, 130.5; 100-3, 130.6; 100-3, 160.2; 100-3, 160.7; 100-3, 230.1; 100-3, 250.1; 100-3, 250.4; 100-3, 270.4; 100-3, 40.50; 100-4, 12, 90.3; 100-4, 14, 10

AMA: 2001, Apr, 8; 2000, Jun, 3; 1999, Nov, 30

| 61886 | with connection to two or more electrode arrays 🄓 🅣 80 📵 |

MED: 100-2, 15, 260; 100-3, 130.5; 100-3, 130.6; 100-3, 160.2; 100-3, 160.7; 100-3, 230.1; 100-3, 250.1; 100-3, 250.4; 100-3, 270.4; 100-3, 40.50; 100-4, 12, 90.3; 100-4, 14, 10

AMA: 2001, Apr, 8; 2000, Jun, 3; 1999, Nov, 30

> If open placement of a cranial nerve (e.g., vagal, trigeminal) neurostimulator electrode(s) is performed, consult CPT code 64573. If percutaneous placement of a cranial nerve (eg, vagal, trigeminal) neurostimulator electrode(s) is performed, consult CPT code 65443. If revision or removal of a cranial nerve (eg, vagal, trigeminal) neurostimulator electrode(s) is performed, consult CPT code 64585.

| 61888 | Revision or removal of cranial neurostimulator pulse generator or receiver 🄖 🅣 50 📵 |

MED: 100-2, 15, 260; 100-3, 130.5; 100-3, 130.6; 100-3, 160.2; 100-3, 160.7; 100-3, 230.1; 100-3, 250.1; 100-3, 250.4; 100-3, 270.4; 100-3, 40.50; 100-4, 12, 90.3; 100-4, 14, 10

> Code 61888 cannot be reported with CPT code 61885 or 61886 for the same pulse generator.

REPAIR

62000	Elevation of depressed skull fracture; simple, extradural 🄲 📵
62005	compound or comminuted, extradural 🄲 80 📵
62010	with repair of dura and/or debridement of brain 🄲 80 📵
62100	Craniotomy for repair of dural/cerebrospinal fluid leak, including surgery for rhinorrhea/otorrhea 🄲 80 📵

> If a spinal dural/CSF leak is repaired, consult CPT codes 63707 and 63709.

Nervous System

62115 — 62200

62115	Reduction of craniomegalic skull (eg, treated hydrocephalus); not requiring bone grafts or cranioplasty	C 80 ⏎
62116	with simple cranioplasty	C 80 ⏎
62117	requiring craniotomy and reconstruction with or without bone graft (includes obtaining grafts)	C 80 ⏎
62120	Repair of encephalocele, skull vault, including cranioplasty	C 80 ⏎
62121	Craniotomy for repair of encephalocele, skull base	C 80 ⏎
62140	Cranioplasty for skull defect; up to 5 cm diameter	C 80 ⏎
62141	larger than 5 cm diameter	C 80 ⏎
62142	Removal of bone flap or prosthetic plate of skull	C 80 ⏎
62143	Replacement of bone flap or prosthetic plate of skull	C 80 ⏎
62145	Cranioplasty for skull defect with reparative brain surgery	C 80 ⏎
62146	Cranioplasty with autograft (includes obtaining bone grafts); up to 5 cm diameter	C 80 ⏎
62147	larger than 5 cm diameter	C 80 ⏎
+ 62148	Incision and retrieval of subcutaneous cranial bone graft for cranioplasty (List separately in addition to code for primary procedure)	C ⏎

Note that 62148 is an add-on code and must be used in conjunction with 62140-62147.

NEUROENDOSCOPY

Diagnostic endoscopy is always included in surgical endoscopy.

+ 62160	Neuroendoscopy, intracranial, for placement or replacement of ventricular catheter and attachment to shunt system or external drainage (List separately in addition to code for primary procedure)	T ⏎

Note that 62160 is an add-on code and must be used in conjunction with 61107, 61210, 62220, 62223, 62225, or 62230.

62161	Neuroendoscopy, intracranial; with dissection of adhesions, fenestration of septum pellucidum or intraventricular cysts (including placement, replacement, or removal of ventricular catheter)	C 80 ⏎
62162	with fenestration or excision of colloid cyst, including placement of external ventricular catheter for drainage	C 80 ⏎
62163	with retrieval of foreign body	C 80 ⏎
62164	with excision of brain tumor, including placement of external ventricular catheter for drainage	C 80 ⏎
62165	with excision of pituitary tumor, transnasal or trans-sphenoidal approach	C 80 ⏎

CSF SHUNT

62180	Ventriculocisternostomy (Torkildsen type operation)	C 80 ⏎
62190	Creation of shunt; subarachnoid/subdural-atrial, -jugular, -auricular	C ⏎
62192	subarachnoid/subdural-peritoneal, -pleural, other terminus	C 80 ⏎
62194	Replacement or irrigation, subarachnoid/subdural catheter	1 T 80 ⏎
	MED: 100-2, 15, 260; 100-4, 12, 90.3; 100-4, 14, 10	
62200	Ventriculocisternostomy, third ventricle;	C 80 ⏎
	Dandy ventriculocisternostomy	

| 62201 | stereotactic, neuroendoscopic method | C ↵ |

To report intracranial neuroendoscopic procedures, consult CPT codes 62161-62165.

| 62220 | Creation of shunt; ventriculo-atrial, -jugular, -auricular | C 80 ↵ |

To report intracranial neuroendoscopic ventricular catheter placement, consult CPT code 62160.

| 62223 | ventriculo-peritoneal, -pleural, other terminus | C 80 ↵ |

To report intracranial neuroendoscopic ventricular catheter placement, consult CPT code 62160.

| 62225 | Replacement or irrigation, ventricular catheter | 1 T ↵ |
MED: 100-2, 15, 260; 100-4, 12, 90.3; 100-4, 14, 10

To report intracranial neuroendoscopic ventricular catheter placement, consult CPT code 62160.

| 62230 | Replacement or revision of cerebrospinal fluid shunt, obstructed valve, or distal catheter in shunt system | 2 T 80 ↵ |
MED: 100-2, 15, 260; 100-4, 12, 90.3; 100-4, 14, 10

To report intracranial neuroendoscopic ventricular catheter placement, consult CPT code 62160.

| 62252 | Reprogramming of programmable cerebrospinal shunt | S 80 ↵ |

If the physician interprets the results and/or operates the equipment, modifier 26 should be appended to 62252.

| 62256 | Removal of complete cerebrospinal fluid shunt system; without replacement | C 80 ↵ |

| 62258 | with replacement by similar or other shunt at same operation | C 80 ↵ |

If percutaneous irrigation or aspiration of a shunt reservoir is performed, consult CPT code 61070.

For reprogramming of programmable CSF shunt, consult CPT code 62252.

SPINE AND SPINAL CORD

If application of caliper or tongs is performed, consult CPT code 20660. If a fracture or dislocation of the spine is treated, consult CPT codes 22305-22327. CPT codes 62263, 62264, 62270-62273, 62280-62282, and 62310-62319 include the injection of contrast during fluoroscopic guidance and localization; do not report separately.

INJECTION, DRAINAGE, OR ASPIRATION

Note that injection of contrast during fluoroscopic guidance and localization should not be reported separately with codes 62263–62264, 62270–62273, 62280–62282, 62310–62319, and 0027T. For fluoroscopic guidance consult code 76005 unless a complete study such as myelography, eipdurography, or arthrography is performed. If this is the case, the fluoroscopy is included in the more extensive procedure.

Report 62263 for a catheter-based treatment that involves targeted injections of various substances via an epidural catheter. This includes the insertion and removal of the catheter and the administration of one or more injections. This treatment may take more than one day. Adhesions or scarring may also be lysed during this treatment period. Do not report 62263 for each adhesiolysis treatment provided. This code should be reported only once for the entire series of treatment spanning two or more treatment days.

Report 62264 for multiple lysis of adhesions treatments performed on the same day. This may be performed by injection of neurolytic agent(s) or mechanically.

Both 62263 and 62264 include the injection of contrast material and fluoroscopy during all treatment sessions.

Nervous System

62263 — 62272

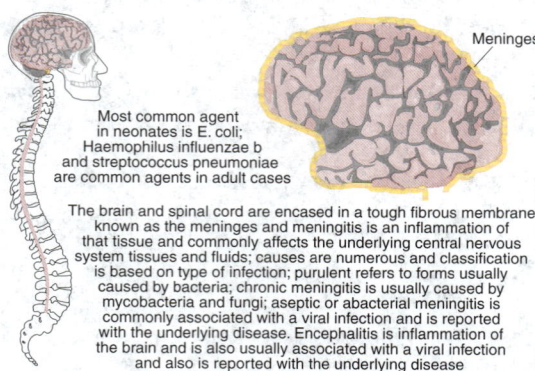

Meninges

Most common agent in neonates is E. coli; Haemophilus influenzae b and streptococcus pneumoniae are common agents in adult cases

The brain and spinal cord are encased in a tough fibrous membrane known as the meninges and meningitis is an inflammation of that tissue and commonly affects the underlying central nervous system tissues and fluids; causes are numerous and classification is based on type of infection; purulent refers to forms usually caused by bacteria; chronic meningitis is usually caused by mycobacteria and fungi; aseptic or abacterial meningitis is commonly associated with a viral infection and is reported with the underlying disease. Encephalitis is inflammation of the brain and is also usually associated with a viral infection and also is reported with the underlying disease

To report endoscopic lysis of adhesions, consult Catetory III code 0027T. To report daily management of continuous epidural or subarachnoid drug administration performed with 62318-62319, consult CPT code 01996.

62263   **Percutaneous lysis of epidural adhesions using solution injection (eg, hypertonic saline, enzyme) or mechanical means (eg, catheter) including radiologic localization (includes contrast when administered), multiple adhesiolysis sessions; 2 or more days**

MED: 100-2, 15, 260; 100-4, 12, 90.3; 100-4, 14, 10

AMA: 2002, Mar, 11; 1999, Nov, 33

62264   **1 day**

Codes 62263 and 62264 include 76005 and 72275; do not report separately.

Do not report 62264 in conjunction with code 62263.

62268   **Percutaneous aspiration, spinal cord cyst or syrinx**

MED: 100-2, 15, 260; 100-4, 12, 90.3; 100-4, 14, 10

To report radiological supervision and interpretation, consult CPT codes 76003, 76360, and 76942.

62269   **Biopsy of spinal cord, percutaneous needle**

MED: 100-2, 15, 260; 100-4, 12, 90.3; 100-4, 14, 10

To report radiological supervision and interpretation, consult CPT codes 76003, 76360, and 76942.

To report fine needle aspiration, consult CPT codes 10021, 10022. To report evaluation of fine needle aspirate, consult CPT codes 88172, 88173.

62270   **Spinal puncture, lumbar, diagnostic**

MED: 100-2, 15, 260; 100-4, 12, 90.3; 100-4, 14, 10

AMA: 1999, Nov, 32-33

62272   **Spinal puncture, therapeutic, for drainage of cerebrospinal fluid (by needle or catheter)**

MED: 100-2, 15, 260; 100-4, 12, 90.3; 100-4, 14, 10

AMA: 1999, Nov, 32-33

26 / **TC** Professional/Technical Component   **80** / **80** Assist-at-Surgery Allowed/With Documentation   ⊙ Conscious Sedation

Unlisted   Not Covered   **MED:** Pubs 100/NCD Reference   **1** - **9** ASC Group   ⑥ Modifier 63 Exempt

440 — Surgery   CPT only © 2005 American Medical Association. All Rights Reserved. *(Black Ink)*   © 2005 Ingenix, Inc. *(Blue Ink)*

62273   **Injection, epidural, of blood or clot patch**   ▮1▮T▮
MED: 100-2, 15, 260; 100-3, 10.5; 100-4, 12, 90.3; 100-4, 14, 10

AMA: 1999, Nov, 32-34

To report injection of diagnostic or therapeutic substance(s), consult 62310, 62311, 62318, 62319.

62280   **Injection/infusion of neurolytic substance (eg, alcohol, phenol, iced saline solutions), with or without other therapeutic substance;**
subarachnoid   ▮1▮T▮
MED: 100-2, 15, 260; 100-4, 12, 90.3; 100-4, 14, 10

AMA: 2000, Jan, 1; 1999, Nov, 32-34

62281   **epidural, cervical or thoracic**   ▮1▮T▮
MED: 100-2, 15, 260; 100-4, 12, 90.3; 100-4, 14, 10

AMA: 2000, Jan, 1; 1999, Nov, 32-34; 1996, Apr, 10

62282   **epidural, lumbar, sacral (caudal)**   ▮1▮T▮
MED: 100-2, 15, 260; 100-4, 12, 90.3; 100-4, 14, 10

AMA: 2000, Jan, 1; 1999, Nov, 32-34; 1996, Apr, 10

⊘ **62284**   **Injection procedure for myelography and/or computed tomography, spinal (other than C1-C2 and posterior fossa)**   ▮N▮
MED: 100-3, 220.1

AMA: 1993, Fall, 13

If an injection procedure is performed at C1-C2, consult CPT code 61055. For radiological supervision and interpretation, consult the Radiology section of the CPT book.

62287   **Aspiration or decompression procedure, percutaneous, of nucleus pulposus of intervertebral disk, any method, single or multiple levels, lumbar (eg, manual or automated percutaneous diskectomy, percutaneous laser diskectomy)**   ▮9▮T▮
MED: 100-2, 15, 260; 100-4, 12, 90.3; 100-4, 14, 10

AMA: 2002, Mar, 11; 1999, Nov, 34

If fluoroscopic guidance is performed, consult CPT code 76003.

62290   **Injection procedure for diskography, each level; lumbar**   ▮N▮
AMA: 1999, Nov, 35

62291   **cervical or thoracic**   ▮N▮
AMA: 1999, Nov, 35

To report radiological supervision and interpretation, consult CPT codes 72285 and 72295.

62292   **Injection procedure for chemonucleolysis, including diskography, intervertebral disk, single or multiple levels, lumbar**   ▮T▮80▮
AMA: 1999, Oct, 10

62294   **Injection procedure, arterial, for occlusion of arteriovenous malformation, spinal**   ▮3▮T▮
MED: 100-2, 15, 260; 100-4, 12, 90.3; 100-4, 14, 10

Nervous System

62310 — 62360

62310   Injection, single (not via indwelling catheter), not including neurolytic substances, with or without contrast (for either localization or epidurography), of diagnostic or therapeutic substance(s) (including anesthetic, antispasmodic, opioid, steroid, other solution), epidural or subarachnoid; cervical or thoracic   **1** T ↰
MED: 100-2, 15, 260; 100-4, 12, 90.3; 100-4, 14, 10

AMA: 2000, Jan, 1; 2000, Dec, 15; 1999, Nov, 32-35

62311   lumbar, sacral (caudal)   **1** T ↰
MED: 100-2, 15, 260; 100-4, 12, 90.3; 100-4, 14, 10

AMA: 2000, Jan, 1; 2000, Dec, 15; 1999, Nov, 32-35

62318   Injection, including catheter placement, continuous infusion or intermittent bolus, not including neurolytic substances, with or without contrast (for either localization or epidurography), of diagnostic or therapeutic substance(s) (including anesthetic, antispasmodic, opioid, steroid, other solution), epidural or subarachnoid; cervical or thoracic   **1** T ↰
MED: 100-2, 15, 260; 100-4, 12, 90.3; 100-4, 14, 10

AMA: 2001, Oct, 9; 2000, Jan, 1; 2000, Dec, 15; 1999, Nov, 32-35

62319   lumbar, sacral (caudal)   **1** T ↰
MED: 100-2, 15, 260; 100-4, 12, 90.3; 100-4, 14, 10

AMA: 2001, Oct, 9; 2000, Jan, 1; 2000, Dec, 15; 1999, Nov, 32-35

To report transforaminal epidural injections, consult CPT codes 64479-64484.

To report daily hospital management of continuous epidural or subarachnoid drug administration performed in conjunction with 62318-62319, consult CPT code 01996.

CATHETER IMPLANTATION

If an implantable infusion pump is refilled and maintained, consult CPT code 95990. If an intrathecal or epidural is place percutaneously, consult CPT codes 62270-62273, 62280-62284, and 62310-62319.

If application of caliper or tongs is performed, consult CPT code 20660. If a fracture or dislocation of the spine is treated, consult CPT codes 22305-22327.

62350   Implantation, revision or repositioning of tunneled intrathecal or epidural catheter, for long-term medication administration via an external pump or implantable reservoir/infusion pump; without laminectomy   **2** T ↰
MED: 100-2, 15, 260; 100-3, 280.14; 100-4, 12, 90.3; 100-4, 14, 10

AMA: 1999, Nov, 36

62351   with laminectomy   T 80 ↰
MED: 100-3, 280.14

AMA: 1999, Nov, 36

If an implantable pump for spinal or brain drug therapy is refilled or maintained, consult CPT code 95990.

62355   Removal of previously implanted intrathecal or epidural catheter **2** T 80 ↰
MED: 100-2, 15, 260; 100-4, 12, 90.3; 100-4, 14, 10

RESERVOIR/PUMP IMPLANTATION

62360   Implantation or replacement of device for intrathecal or epidural drug infusion; subcutaneous reservoir   **2** T 80 ↰
MED: 100-2, 15, 260; 100-3, 280.14; 100-4, 12, 90.3; 100-4, 14, 10

62361   **non-programmable pump**   2 T 80 🔲
MED: 100-2, 15, 260; 100-3, 280.14; 100-4, 12, 90.3; 100-4, 14, 10

62362   **programmable pump, including preparation of pump, with or without programming**   2 T 80 🔲
MED: 100-2, 15, 260; 100-4, 12, 90.3; 100-4, 14, 10

AMA: 1997, Mar, 11

62365   **Removal of subcutaneous reservoir or pump, previously implanted for intrathecal or epidural infusion**   2 T 80 🔲
MED: 100-2, 15, 260; 100-3, 280.14; 100-4, 12, 90.3; 100-4, 14, 10

62367   **Electronic analysis of programmable, implanted pump for intrathecal or epidural drug infusion (includes evaluation of reservoir status, alarm status, drug prescription status); without reprogramming**   S 80 🔲
MED: 100-3, 280.14

62368   **with reprogramming**   S 80 🔲
MED: 100-3, 280.14

AMA: 2002, Nov, 10

If an implantable pump for spinal or brain drug therapy is refilled or maintained, consult CPT code 95990.

POSTERIOR EXTRADURAL LAMINOTOMY OR LAMINECTOMY FOR EXPLORATION/DECOMPRESSION OF NEURAL ELEMENTS OR EXCISION OF HERNIATED INTERVERTEBRAL DISKS

If application of caliper or tongs is performed, consult CPT code 20660. If a fracture or dislocation of the spine is treated, consult CPT codes 22305-22327.

If these procedures are followed by arthrodesis, consult CPT codes 22590-22614.

63001   **Laminectomy with exploration and/or decompression of spinal cord and/or cauda equina, without facetectomy, foraminotomy or diskectomy, (eg, spinal stenosis), one or two vertebral segments; cervical**   T 80 🔲
AMA: 2001, Jan, 12

63003   **thoracic**   T 80 🔲
AMA: 2001, Jan, 12

63005   **lumbar, except for spondylolisthesis**   T 80 🔲
AMA: 2001, Jan, 12

63011   **sacral**   T 80 🔲
AMA: 2001, Jan, 12

63012   **Laminectomy with removal of abnormal facets and/or pars inter-articularis with decompression of cauda equina and nerve roots for spondylolisthesis, lumbar (Gill type procedure)**   T 80 🔲
AMA: 2001, Jan, 12

63015   **Laminectomy with exploration and/or decompression of spinal cord and/or cauda equina, without facetectomy, foraminotomy or diskectomy, (eg, spinal stenosis), more than 2 vertebral segments; cervical**   T 80 🔲
AMA: 2001, Jan, 12

63016   **thoracic**   T 80 🔲
AMA: 2001, Jan, 12

Nervous System

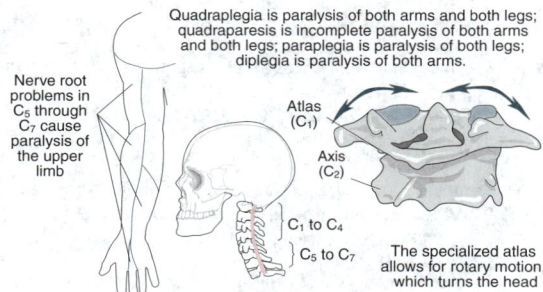

Quadraplegia is paralysis of both arms and both legs; quadraparesis is incomplete paralysis of both arms and both legs; paraplegia is paralysis of both legs; diplegia is paralysis of both arms.

Nerve root problems in C₅ through C₇ cause paralysis of the upper limb

Atlas (C₁)

Axis (C₂)

C₁ to C₄

C₅ to C₇

The specialized atlas allows for rotary motion, which turns the head

Cauda equina syndrome is a complex pattern of symptoms arising from spinal cord problems of the lower back (cauda equina); the bladder is often affected and pain usually occurs along the leg and buttock

63017 — 63044

63017	**lumbar**	T 80
	AMA: 2001, Jan, 12	

63020 **Laminotomy (hemilaminectomy), with decompression of nerve root(s), including partial facetectomy, foraminotomy and/or excision of herniated intervertebral disk; one interspace, cervical** T 50 80
AMA: 2001, Jan, 12; 1999, Nov, 36

Codes 63020, 63030, and 63035 are unilateral procedures. To report these procedures performed bilaterally, append modifier 50.

63030 **one interspace, lumbar (including open or endoscopically-assisted approach)** T 50 80
AMA: 2002, Sep, 10; 2001, Jan, 12; 2001, Feb, 10; 1999, Nov, 36; 1996, Mar, 7

+ **63035** **each additional interspace, cervical or lumbar (List separately in addition to code for primary procedure)** T
AMA: 2001, Jan, 12; 2001, Feb, 10; 1999, Nov, 36; 1996, Mar, 7

Note that 63035 is an add-on code and must be used in conjunction with 63020-63030.

63040 **Laminotomy (hemilaminectomy), with decompression of nerve root(s), including partial facetectomy, foraminotomy and/or excision of herniated intervertebral disk, reexploration, single interspace; cervical** T 50 80
AMA: 2001, Jan, 12; 1999, Jan, 11

Codes 63040-63044 are unilateral procedures. To report these procedures performed bilaterally, append modifier 50.

63042 **lumbar** T 50 80
AMA: 2001, Jan, 12; 1999, Jan, 11

+ **63043** **each additional cervical interspace (List separately in addition to code for primary procedure)** C
Note that CPT code 63043 is an add-on code and must be used in conjunction with 63040.

+ **63044** **each additional lumbar interspace (List separately in addition to code for primary procedure)** C
Note that CPT code 63044 is an add-on code and must be used in conjunction with 63042.

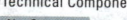 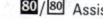

	63045	**Laminectomy, facetectomy and foraminotomy (unilateral or bilateral with decompression of spinal cord, cauda equina and/or nerve root(s), (eg, spinal or lateral recess stenosis), single vertebral segment; cervical** T 80 □

AMA: 2001, Jan, 12

63046   **thoracic**   T 80 □
AMA: 2001, Jan, 12; 1999, Jan, 11

63047   **lumbar**   T 80 □
AMA: 2002, Nov, 11; 2001, Jan, 12; 2001, Feb, 10; 1999, Jan, 11

+ **63048**   **each additional segment, cervical, thoracic, or lumbar (List separately in addition to code for primary procedure)** T 80 □
AMA: 2001, Jan, 12; 1999, Jan, 11

Note that 63048 is an add-on code and must be used in conjunction with 63045-63047.

63050   **Laminoplasty, cervical, with decompression of the spinal cord, two or more vertebral segments;** C 80 □

63051   **with reconstruction of the posterior bony elements (including the application of bridging bone graft and non-segmental fixation devices (eg, wire, suture, mini-plates), when performed)** C 80 □

Code 63050 or 63051 cannot be reported with CPT codes 22600, 22614, 22840-22842, 63001, 63015, 63045, 63048, 63295 for the same vertebral segment(s).

TRANSPEDICULAR OR COSTOVERTEBRAL APPROACH FOR POSTEROLATERAL EXTRADURAL EXPLORATION/DECOMPRESSION

If application of caliper or tongs is performed, consult CPT code 20660. If a fracture or dislocation of the spine is treated, consult CPT codes 22305-22327.

63055   **Transpedicular approach with decompression of spinal cord, equina and/or nerve root(s) (eg, herniated intervertebral disk), single segment; thoracic** T 80 □
AMA: 1999, Nov, 36

63056   **lumbar (including transfacet, or lateral extraforaminal approach) (eg, far lateral herniated intervertebral disk)** T 80 □
AMA: 1999, Nov, 36

+ **63057**   **each additional segment, thoracic or lumbar (List separately in addition to code for primary procedure)** T 80 □
AMA: 1999, Nov, 36

Note that 63057 is an add-on code and must be used in conjunction with 63055, 63056.

63064   **Costovertebral approach with decompression of spinal cord or nerve root(s), (eg, herniated intervertebral disk), thoracic; single segment** T 80 □

+ **63066**   **each additional segment (List separately in addition to code for primary procedure)** T 80 □

Note that 63066 is an add-on code and must be used in conjunction with 63064.

To report excision of thoracic intraspinal lesions by laminectomy, consult CPT codes 63266, 63271, 63276, 63281, 63286.

Nervous System

ANTERIOR OR ANTEROLATERAL APPROACH FOR EXTRADURAL EXPLORATION/DECOMPRESSION

When two surgeons work together as primary surgeons performing distinct part(s) of spinal cord exploration/decompression surgery, each surgeon should assign one of the following codes and append modifier 62, Two surgeons. Modifier 62 can be reported with CPT code(s) 63075, 63077, 63081, 63085, 63087, 63090, and, as appropriate associated additional interspace codes 63076, 63078, or additional segment add-on code(s) 63082, 63086, 63088, 63091 provided that both surgeons continue to work together as primary surgeons.

Do not report 69990 in addition to codes 63075-63078 as the operating microscope is considered an inclusive component of these procedures.

If application of caliper or tongs is performed, consult CPT code 20660. If a fracture or dislocation of the spine is treated, consult CPT codes 22305-22327.

63075   **Diskectomy, anterior, with decompression of spinal cord and/or nerve root(s), including osteophytectomy; cervical, single interspace** C 80 ⬚
AMA: 2001, Jan, 12; 1998, Nov, 18

+ **63076**   **cervical, each additional interspace (List separately in addition to code for primary procedure)** C 80 ⬚
AMA: 2001, Jan, 12; 1998, Nov, 18

Note that 63076 is an add-on code and must be used in conjunction with 63075.

63077   **thoracic, single interspace** C 80 ⬚
AMA: 2001, Jan, 12; 1998, Nov, 18

+ **63078**   **thoracic, each additional interspace (List separately in addition to code for primary procedure)** C 80 ⬚
AMA: 2001, Jan, 12; 1998, Nov, 18

Note that 63078 is an add-on code and must be used in conjunction with 63077.

63081   **Vertebral corpectomy (vertebral body resection), partial or complete, anterior approach with decompression of spinal cord and/or nerve root(s); cervical, single segment** C 80 ⬚
AMA: 1993, Spring, 37

+ **63082**   **cervical, each additional segment (List separately in addition to code for primary procedure)** C 80 ⬚
AMA: 1993, Spring, 37

Note that 63082 is an add-on code and must be used in conjunction with 63081.

If a transoral approach is used, consult CPT codes 61575 and 61576.

63085   **Vertebral corpectomy (vertebral body resection), partial or complete, transthoracic approach with decompression of spinal cord and/or nerve root(s); thoracic, single segment** C 80 ⬚
AMA: 1993, Spring, 37

+ **63086**   **thoracic, each additional segment (List separately in addition to code for primary procedure)** C 80 ⬚
AMA: 1993, Spring, 37

Note that 63086 is an add-on code and must be used in conjunction with 63085.

63087   **Vertebral corpectomy (vertebral body resection), partial or complete, combined thoracolumbar approach with decompression of spinal cord, cauda equina or nerve root(s), lower thoracic or lumbar; single segment** C 80 ⬚
AMA: 1993, Spring, 37

| + | **63088** | **each additional segment (List separately in addition to code for primary procedure)** ⒸⓐⓋ |
| | | AMA: 1993, Spring, 37 |

Note that 63088 is an add-on code and must be used in conjunction with 63087.

| | **63090** | **Vertebral corpectomy (vertebral body resection), partial or complete, transperitoneal or retroperitoneal approach with decompression of spinal cord, cauda equina or nerve root(s), lower thoracic, lumbar, or sacral; single segment** ⒸⓐⓋ |
| | | AMA: 1996, Mar, 6; 1993, Spring, 37 |

| + | **63091** | **each additional segment (List separately in addition to code for primary procedure)** ⒸⓐⓋ |
| | | AMA: 1996, Mar, 6; 1993, Spring, 37 |

Note that 63091 is an add-on code and must be used in conjunction with 63090.

LATERAL EXTRACAVITARY APPROACH FOR EXTRADURAL EXPLORATION/DECOMPRESSION

	63101	**Vertebral corpectomy (vertebral body resection), partial or complete, lateral extracavitary approach with decompression of spinal cord and/or nerve root(s) (eg, for tumor or retropulsed bone fragments); thoracic, single segment** ⒸⓐⓋ
	63102	**lumbar, single segment** ⒸⓐⓋ
+	**63103**	**thoracic or lumbar, each additional segment (List separately in addition to code for primary procedure)** ⒸⓐⓋ

Note that 63103 is an add-on code that must be used in conjunction with 63101 and 63102.

INCISION

If application of caliper or tongs is performed, consult CPT code 20660. If a fracture or dislocation of the spine is treated, consult CPT codes 22305-22327.

	63170	**Laminectomy with myelotomy (eg, Bischof or DREZ type), cervical, thoracic or thoracolumbar** ⒸⓐⓋ
	63172	**Laminectomy with drainage of intramedullary cyst/syrinx; to subarachnoid space** ⒸⓐⓋ
	63173	**to peritoneal or pleural space** ⒸⓐⓋ
	63180	**Laminectomy and section of dentate ligaments, with or without dural graft, cervical; one or two segments** ⒸⓐⓋ
	63182	**more than two segments** ⒸⓐⓋ
	63185	**Laminectomy with rhizotomy; one or two segments** ⒸⓐⓋ
		Dana rhizotomy
	63190	**more than two segments** ⒸⓐⓋ
	63191	**Laminectomy with section of spinal accessory nerve** ⒸⓣⓐⓋ

If resection of the sternocleidomastoid muscle is performed, consult CPT code 21720.

Code 63191 is a unilateral procedure. To report this procedure bilaterally, append modifier 50.

| | **63194** | **Laminectomy with cordotomy, with section of one spinothalamic tract, one stage; cervical** ⒸⓐⓋ |
| | **63195** | **thoracic** ⒸⓐⓋ |

Nervous System

63196 — 63295

63196	Laminectomy with cordotomy, with section of both spinothalamic tracts, one stage; cervical	C 80 ▸
63197	thoracic	C 80 ▸
63198	Laminectomy with cordotomy with section of both spinothalamic tracts, two stages within 14 days; cervical	C 80 ▸
	Keen laminectomy	
63199	thoracic	C 80 ▸
63200	Laminectomy, with release of tethered spinal cord, lumbar	C 80 ▸

EXCISION BY LAMINECTOMY OF LESION OTHER THAN HERNIATED DISK

63250	Laminectomy for excision or occlusion of arteriovenous malformation of spinal cord; cervical	C 80 ▸
63251	thoracic	C 80 ▸
63252	thoracolumbar	C 80 ▸
63265	Laminectomy for excision or evacuation of intraspinal lesion other than neoplasm, extradural; cervical	C 80 ▸
63266	thoracic	C 80 ▸
63267	lumbar	C 80 ▸
63268	sacral	C 80 ▸
63270	Laminectomy for excision of intraspinal lesion other than neoplasm, intradural; cervical	C 80 ▸
63271	thoracic	C 80 ▸
63272	lumbar	C 80 ▸
63273	sacral	C 80 ▸
63275	Laminectomy for biopsy/excision of intraspinal neoplasm; extradural, cervical	C 80 ▸
63276	extradural, thoracic	C 80 ▸
63277	extradural, lumbar	C 80 ▸
63278	extradural, sacral	C 80 ▸
63280	intradural, extramedullary, cervical	C 80 ▸
63281	intradural, extramedullary, thoracic	C 80 ▸
63282	intradural, extramedullary, lumbar	C 80 ▸
63283	intradural, sacral	C 80 ▸
63285	intradural, intramedullary, cervical	C 80 ▸
63286	intradural, intramedullary, thoracic	C 80 ▸
63287	intradural, intramedullary, thoracolumbar	C 80 ▸
63290	combined extradural-intradural lesion, any level	C 80 ▸

If an intramedullary cyst syrinx is drained, consult CPT codes 63172 and 63173.

+ 63295	Osteoplastic reconstruction of dorsal spinal elements, following primary intraspinal procedure (List separately in addition to code for primary procedure)	C 80

Note that 63295 is an add-on procedure and must be used in conjunction with 63172, 63173, 63185, 63190, 63200-63290. Code 63295 must not be used with 22590-22614, 22840-22844, 63050, 63051 for the same vertebral segment.

26 / TC Professional/Technical Component   **80 / 80** Assist-at-Surgery Allowed/With Documentation   ⊙ Conscious Sedation

Unlisted   Not Covered   **MED:** Pubs 100/NCD Reference   **1 - 9** ASC Group   ⑥③ Modifier 63 Exempt

448 — Surgery   CPT only © 2005 American Medical Association. All Rights Reserved. *(Black Ink)*   © 2005 Ingenix, Inc. *(Blue Ink)*

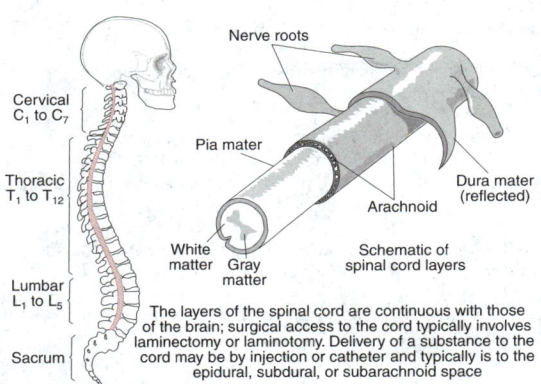

Nerve roots

Cervical
C_1 to C_7

Pia mater

Thoracic
T_1 to T_{12}

Dura mater
(reflected)

Arachnoid

White   Gray   Schematic of
matter   matter   spinal cord layers

Lumbar
L_1 to L_5

The layers of the spinal cord are continuous with those
of the brain; surgical access to the cord typically involves
laminectomy or laminotomy. Delivery of a substance to the
cord may be by injection or catheter and typically is to the
epidural, subdural, or subarachnoid space

Sacrum

EXCISION, ANTERIOR OR ANTEROLATERAL APPROACH, INTRASPINAL LESION

Surgeons working together as primary surgeons, each performing distinct parts of an anterior
approach for an intraspinal excision, should report the procedure with modifier 62.

If arthrodesis is performed, consult CPT codes 22548-22585. If the spine is reconstructed, consult
CPT codes 20930-20938.

63300   **Vertebral corpectomy (vertebral body resection), partial or complete, for
excision of intraspinal lesion, single segment; extradural, cervical** C 80 ⟐

63301   **extradural, thoracic by transthoracic approach** C 80 ⟐

63302   **extradural, thoracic by thoracolumbar approach** C 80 ⟐

63303   **extradural, lumbar or sacral by transperitoneal or retroperitoneal
approach** C 80 ⟐

63304   **intradural, cervical** C 80 ⟐

63305   **intradural, thoracic by transthoracic approach** C 80 ⟐

63306   **intradural, thoracic by thoracolumbar approach** C 80 ⟐

63307   **intradural, lumbar or sacral by transperitoneal or retroperitoneal
approach** C 80 ⟐

+   **63308**   **each additional segment (List separately in addition to codes for single
segment)** C 80 ⟐

Note that 63308 is an add-on code and must be used in conjunction with
63300-63307.

STEREOTAXIS

63600   **Creation of lesion of spinal cord by stereotactic method, percutaneous, any
modality (including stimulation and/or recording)** 2 T 80 ⟐
MED: 100-2, 15, 260; 100-4, 12, 90.3; 100-4, 14, 10

63610   **Stereotactic stimulation of spinal cord, percutaneous, separate procedure
not followed by other surgery** 1 T 80 ⟐
MED: 100-2, 15, 260; 100-4, 12, 90.3; 100-4, 14, 10

63615   **Stereotactic biopsy, aspiration, or excision of lesion, spinal cord** T ⟐

NEUROSTIMULATORS (SPINAL)

Codes 63650–63688 apply to both simple and complex neurostimulators.

For programming or electronic analysis of neurostimulator pulse generators, initial or subsequent, consult CPT codes 95970-95975.

Report codes 63650, 63655, and 63660, as appropriate, for the placement, revision, or removal of the spinal neurostimulator system components to provide spinal electrical stimulation. The neurostimulator system includes a neurostimulator, external controller, extension, and collection of contacts.

For codes 63650, 63660 the contacts are on a catheter-like lead. An array defines the collection of contacts on one catheter.

Consult 63655, 63660 for systems placed by open surgical exposure. These contacts are on a plate or paddle-shaped surface.

63650   **Percutaneous implantation of neurostimulator electrode array, epidural**   2 S ↻

MED: 100-2, 15, 260; 100-3, 130.5; 100-3, 130.6; 100-3, 160.2; 100-3, 160.7; 100-3, 230.1; 100-3, 250.1; 100-3, 250.4; 100-3, 270.4; 100-3, 40.50; 100-4, 12, 90.3; 100-4, 14, 10

AMA: 1999, Nov, 18; 1999, Mar, 11; 1999, Apr, 10; 1998, Jun, 1

63655   **Laminectomy for implantation of neurostimulator electrodes, plate/paddle, epidural**   S 80 ↻

MED: 100-3, 130.5; 100-3, 130.6; 100-3, 160.2; 100-3, 160.7; 100-3, 230.1; 100-3, 250.1; 100-3, 250.4; 100-3, 270.4; 100-3, 40.50

AMA: 1999, Sep, 1; 1998, Nov, 18; 1998, Jun, 1

63660   **Revision or removal of spinal neurostimulator electrode percutaneous array(s) or plate/paddle(s)**   1 T ↻

MED: 100-2, 15, 260; 100-3, 130.5; 100-3, 130.6; 100-3, 160.2; 100-3, 160.7; 100-3, 230.1; 100-3, 250.1; 100-3, 250.4; 100-3, 270.4; 100-3, 40.50; 100-4, 12, 90.3; 100-4, 14, 10

AMA: 1998, Nov, 18; 1998, Jun, 1

63685   **Insertion or replacement of spinal neurostimulator pulse generator or receiver, direct or inductive coupling**   2 T 80 ↻

MED: 100-2, 15, 260; 100-3, 160.7; 100-4, 12, 90.3; 100-4, 14, 10

AMA: 1998, Jun, 1

Code 63685 cannot be reported with CPT code 63688 for the same pulse generator or receiver.

63688   **Revision or removal of implanted spinal neurostimulator pulse generator or receiver**   1 T ↻

MED: 100-2, 15, 260; 100-3, 160.7; 100-4, 12, 90.3; 100-4, 14, 10

AMA: 1998, Jun, 1

REPAIR

63700   **Repair of meningocele; less than 5 cm diameter**   C 80 ↻ 63

63702   **larger than 5 cm diameter**   C 80 ↻ 63

63704   **Repair of myelomeningocele; less than 5 cm diameter**   C 80 ↻ 63

63706   **larger than 5 cm diameter**   C 80 ↻ 63

If this procedure involves complex skin closure, consult the Integumentary System section of the CPT book.

63707   **Repair of dural/cerebrospinal fluid leak, not requiring laminectomy**   C 80 ↻

Spina bifida results from the defective closure of the spinal column during early fetal development; classification is according to location along the spine

Degree of disability is related to location and type; mild spina bifida may include only a bony abnormality with no meningeal or nerve involvement

Cervical
Thoracic
Lumbar

A fluid-filled herniation that protrudes is spina bifida cystica, or meningocele

If nerves protrude into the defect, it is called rachischisis, or meningomyelocele

Dura mater

Most children with severe spina bifida also have hydrocephalus, which is excessive fluid in the skull

Spinal cord

Vertebra

63709	Repair of dural/cerebrospinal fluid leak or pseudomeningocele, with laminectomy	C 80
63710	Dural graft, spinal	C 80

If a cervical laminectomy and section of dentate ligaments are performed, with or without a dural graft, consult CPT codes 63180 and 63182.

SHUNT, SPINAL CSF

63740	Creation of shunt, lumbar, subarachnoid-peritoneal, -pleural, or other; including laminectomy	C 80
63741	percutaneous, not requiring laminectomy	T 80
63744	Replacement, irrigation or revision of lumbosubarachnoid shunt	3 T 80
	MED: 100-2, 15, 260; 100-4, 12, 90.3; 100-4, 14, 10	
63746	Removal of entire lumbosubarachnoid shunt system without replacement	2 T 80
	MED: 100-2, 15, 260; 100-4, 12, 90.3; 100-4, 14, 10	

EXTRACRANIAL NERVES, PERIPHERAL NERVES, AND AUTONOMIC NERVOUS SYSTEM

To report intracranial surgery on cranial nerves, consult CPT codes 61450, 61460, 61790.

INTRODUCTION/INJECTION OF ANESTHETIC AGENT (NERVE BLOCK), DIAGNOSTIC, OR THERAPEUTIC — SOMATIC NERVES

64400	Injection, anesthetic agent; trigeminal nerve, any division or branch	T
	AMA: 1999, Nov, 36; 1999, May, 8; 1998, Jul, 10	
64402	facial nerve	T
	AMA: 1998, Jul, 10	
64405	greater occipital nerve	T
	AMA: 1998, Jul, 10	
64408	vagus nerve	T 80
	AMA: 1998, Jul, 10	
64410	phrenic nerve	1 T 80
	MED: 100-2, 15, 260; 100-4, 12, 90.3; 100-4, 14, 10	
	AMA: 1998, Jul, 10	

| 64412 | **spinal accessory nerve** | T ↻ |
| | AMA: 1998, Jul, 10 | |

| 64413 | **cervical plexus** | T ↻ |
| | AMA: 1998, Jul, 10 | |

64415	**brachial plexus, single**	■1 T ↻
	MED: 100-2, 15, 260; 100-4, 12, 90.3; 100-4, 14, 10	
	AMA: 2001, Oct, 9; 1999, May, 8; 1998, Jul, 10	

64416   **brachial plexus, continuous infusion by catheter (including catheter placement) including daily management for anesthetic agent administration**   T ↻

Do not report 01996 in conjunction with CPT code 64416.

64417	**axillary nerve**	■1 T ↻
	MED: 100-2, 15, 260; 100-4, 12, 90.3; 100-4, 14, 10	
	AMA: 1998, Jul, 10	

| 64418 | **suprascapular nerve** | T ↻ |
| | AMA: 1998, Jul, 10 | |

64420	**intercostal nerve, single**	■1 T ↻
	MED: 100-2, 15, 260; 100-4, 12, 90.3; 100-4, 14, 10	
	AMA: 1998, Jul, 10	

64421	**intercostal nerves, multiple, regional block**	■1 T ↻
	MED: 100-2, 15, 260; 100-4, 12, 90.3; 100-4, 14, 10	
	AMA: 1998, Jul, 10	

| 64425 | **ilioinguinal, iliohypogastric nerves** | T ↻ |
| | AMA: 1998, Jul, 10 | |

64430	**pudendal nerve**	■1 T ↻
	MED: 100-2, 15, 260; 100-4, 12, 90.3; 100-4, 14, 10	
	AMA: 1998, Jul, 10	

| 64435 | **paracervical (uterine) nerve** | ♀ T ↻ |
| | AMA: 1998, Jul, 10 | |

| 64445 | **sciatic nerve, single** | T ↻ |
| | AMA: 1999, May, 8; 1998, Jul, 10 | |

64446   **sciatic nerve, continuous infusion by catheter, (including catheter placement) including daily management for anesthetic agent administration**   T ↻

Do not report 01996 in conjunction with CPT code 64446.

64447   **Injection, anesthetic agent; femoral nerve, single**   T ↻

Do not report 01996 in conjunction with CPT code 64447.

64448   **Injection, anesthetic agent; femoral nerve, continuous infusion by catheter (including catheter placement) including daily management for anesthetic agent administration**   T ↻

Do not report 01996 in conjunction with CPT code 64448.

64449   **lumbar plexus, posterior approach, continuous infusion by catheter (including catheter placement) including daily management for anesthetic agent administration**   T ↻

Do not report 01996 in conjunction with CPT code 64449.

Nervous System

64450   other peripheral nerve or branch   ⊤ 50 ↻
AMA: 2001, Oct, 9; 1999, Nov, 37; 1999, Dec, 7; 1998, Jul, 10

If phenol destruction is performed, consult CPT codes 64622-64627. If a subarachnoid or subdural injection is administered, consult CPT codes 62280, 62310-62319. If an epidural or a caudal injection is administered, consult CPT codes 62273, 62281-62282, 62310-62319.

64470   Injection, anesthetic agent and/or steroid, paravertebral facet joint or facet joint nerve; cervical or thoracic, single level   1 ⊤ 50 ↻
MED: 100-2, 15, 260; 100-4, 12, 90.3; 100-4, 14, 10
AMA: 2000, Feb, 4; 1999, Nov, 33, 37

If fluoroscopic guidance and localization for needle placement and injection is performed in conjunction with (64470-64484), consult CPT code 76005.

Codes 64470-64484 are unilateral procedures. To report these procedures performed bilaterally, append modifier 50.

\+ **64472**   cervical or thoracic, each additional level (List separately in addition to code for primary procedure)   1 ⊤ 50 ↻
MED: 100-2, 15, 260; 100-4, 12, 90.3; 100-4, 14, 10
AMA: 2000, Feb, 4; 1999, Nov, 33, 37

Note that 64472 is an add-on code and must be used in conjunction with 64470.

64475   lumbar or sacral, single level   1 ⊤ 50 ↻
MED: 100-2, 15, 260; 100-4, 12, 90.3; 100-4, 14, 10
AMA: 2000, Feb, 4; 1999, Nov, 33, 37

\+ **64476**   lumbar or sacral, each additional level (List separately in addition to code for primary procedure)   1 ⊤ 50 ↻
MED: 100-2, 15, 260; 100-4, 12, 90.3; 100-4, 14, 10
AMA: 2000, Feb, 4; 1999, Nov, 33, 37

Note that 64476 is an add-on code and must be used in conjunction with 64475.

64479   Injection, anesthetic agent and/or steroid, transforaminal epidural; cervical or thoracic, single level   1 ⊤ 50 ↻
MED: 100-2, 15, 260; 100-4, 12, 90.3; 100-4, 14, 10
AMA: 2000, Feb, 4; 1999, Nov, 33, 37

\+ **64480**   cervical or thoracic, each additional level (List separately in addition to code for primary procedure)   1 ⊤ ↻
MED: 100-2, 15, 260; 100-4, 12, 90.3; 100-4, 14, 10
AMA: 2000, Feb, 4; 1999, Nov, 33, 37

Note that 64480 is an add-on code and must be used in conjunction with 64479.

64483   lumbar or sacral, single level   1 ⊤ 50 ↻
MED: 100-2, 15, 260; 100-4, 12, 90.3; 100-4, 14, 10
AMA: 2000, Feb, 4; 1999, Nov, 33, 37

\+ **64484**   lumbar or sacral, each additional level (List separately in addition to code for primary procedure)   1 ⊤ ↻
MED: 100-2, 15, 260; 100-4, 12, 90.3; 100-4, 14, 10
AMA: 2000, Feb, 4; 1999, Nov, 33, 37

Note that 64484 is an add-on code and must be used in conjunction with 64483.

64450 — 64484

Nervous System

INTRODUCTION/INJECTION OF ANESTHETIC AGENT (NERVE BLOCK), DIAGNOSTIC, OR THERAPEUTIC — SYMPATHETIC NERVES

64505   **Injection, anesthetic agent; sphenopalatine ganglion**   T 🔲
       AMA: 1998, Jul, 10

64508   **carotid sinus (separate procedure)**   T 80 🔲
       AMA: 1998, Jul, 10

64510   **stellate ganglion (cervical sympathetic)**   1 T 🔲
       MED: 100-2, 15, 260; 100-4, 12, 90.3; 100-4, 14, 10

       AMA: 1998, Jul, 10

64517   **superior hypogastric plexus**   2 T 🔲

64520   **lumbar or thoracic (paravertebral sympathetic)**   1 T 🔲
       MED: 100-2, 15, 260; 100-4, 12, 90.3; 100-4, 14, 10

       AMA: 1998, Jul, 10

64530   **celiac plexus, with or without radiologic monitoring**   1 T 🔲
       MED: 100-2, 15, 260; 100-4, 12, 90.3; 100-4, 14, 10

       AMA: 1998, Jul, 10

NEUROSTIMULATORS (PERIPHERAL NERVE)

For programming or electronic analysis of neurostimulator pulse generators, initial or subsequent, consult CPT codes 95970-95975.

Consult the glossary for terms and definitions and the front matter of this chapter for additional information.

64550   **Application of surface (transcutaneous) neurostimulator**   A 🔲
       MED: 100-3, 10.2; 100-3, 130.5; 100-3, 130.6; 100-3, 160.2; 100-3, 160.7.1; 100-3, 230.1; 100-3, 250.1; 100-3, 250.4; 100-3, 270.4; 100-3, 280.13; 100-3, 40.50; 100-3, 45-25

       AMA: 2002, Apr, 18

64553   **Percutaneous implantation of neurostimulator electrodes; cranial nerve**   1 S 80 🔲
       MED: 100-2, 15, 260; 100-3, 130.5; 100-3, 130.6; 100-3, 160.2; 100-3, 160.7; 100-3, 230.1; 100-3, 250.1; 100-3, 250.4; 100-3, 270.4; 100-3, 40.50; 100-4, 12, 90.3; 100-4, 14, 10

       AMA: 2001, Apr, 18; 1999, Nov, 38

       If this procedure involves open placement of a cranial nerve (e.g., vagal, trigeminal) neurostimulator pulse generator or receiver, consult CPT codes 61885 and 61886, as appropriate.

64555   **peripheral nerve (excludes sacral nerve)**   S 🔲
       MED: 100-3, 130.5; 100-3, 130.6; 100-3, 160.2; 100-3, 160.7.1; 100-3, 230.1; 100-3, 250.1; 100-3, 250.4; 100-3, 270.4; 100-3, 30.1; 100-3, 30.1.1; 100-3, 40.50

64560   **autonomic nerve**   S 80 🔲
       MED: 100-3, 130.5; 100-3, 130.6; 100-3, 160.2; 100-3, 230.1; 100-3, 250.1; 100-3, 250.4; 100-3, 270.4; 100-3, 30.1; 100-3, 30.1.1; 100-3, 40.50

64561   **sacral nerve (transforaminal placement)**   3 S 🔲

64565   **neuromuscular**   S 🔲
       MED: 100-3, 130.5; 100-3, 130.6; 100-3, 160.12; 100-3, 160.2; 100-3, 230.1; 100-3, 250.1; 100-3, 250.4; 100-3, 270.4; 100-3, 30.1; 100-3, 30.1.1; 100-3, 40.50; 100-3, 45-25

       AMA: 2000, Jul, 11

+   **64623**   **lumbar or sacral, each additional level (List separately in addition to code for primary procedure)**   🔢 T 50 ↻

                   MED: 100-2, 15, 260; 100-3, 160.1; 100-4, 12, 90.3; 100-4, 14, 10

                   AMA: 2000, Mar, 4; 1999, Nov, 33, 39

                   Note that 64623 is an add-on code and must be used in conjunction with 64622.

   64626   **cervical or thoracic, single level**   🔢 T 50 ↻

                   MED: 100-2, 15, 260; 100-3, 160.1; 100-4, 12, 90.3; 100-4, 14, 10

                   AMA: 2000, Mar, 4; 1999, Nov, 33, 39

+   **64627**   **cervical or thoracic, each additional level (List separately in addition to code for primary procedure)**   🔢 T 50 ↻

                   MED: 100-2, 15, 260; 100-3, 160.1; 100-4, 12, 90.3; 100-4, 14, 10

                   AMA: 2000, Mar, 4; 1999, Nov, 33, 39

                   Note that 64627 is an add-on code and must be used in conjunction with 64626.

   64630   **Destruction by neurolytic agent; pudendal nerve**   2 T 80 ↻

                   MED: 100-2, 15, 260; 100-3, 160.1; 100-4, 12, 90.3; 100-4, 14, 10

   64640   **other peripheral nerve or branch**   T 50 ↻

                   MED: 100-3, 160.1

DESTRUCTION BY NEUROLYTIC AGENT (EG, CHEMICAL, THERMAL, ELECTRICAL, RADIOFREQUENCY) — SYMPATHETIC NERVES

The injection of other therapeutic agents (e.g., corticosteroids) is included in CPT codes 64680-64681. Do not report separately.

●   **64650**   **Chemodenervation of eccrine glands; both axillae**

●   **64653**   **other area(s) (eg, scalp, face, neck), per day**

                   Report the specific service in addition to the code(s) for the specific substance(s) or drug(s) provided.

                   To report chemodenervation of extremities (eg, hands or feet), consult CPT code 64999.

   64680   **Destruction by neurolytic agent, with or without radiologic monitoring; celiac plexus**   2 T ↻

                   MED: 100-2, 15, 260; 100-3, 160.1; 100-4, 12, 90.3; 100-4, 14, 10

                   AMA: 1999, Feb, 10

   64681   **superior hypogastric plexus**   3 T ↻

NEUROPLASTY (EXPLORATION, NEUROLYSIS OR NERVE DECOMPRESSION)

If facial nerve decompression is performed, consult CPT code 69720.

If internal neurolysis is performed and requires the use of an operating microscope, consult CPT code 64727.

   64702   **Neuroplasty; digital, one or both, same digit**   🔢 T ↻

                   MED: 100-2, 15, 260; 100-4, 12, 90.3; 100-4, 14, 10

                   AMA: 2001, Jun, 11

   64704   **nerve of hand or foot**   🔢 T 80 ↻

                   MED: 100-2, 15, 260; 100-4, 12, 90.3; 100-4, 14, 10

                   AMA: 2001, Jun, 11

 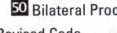

Nervous System

64708 — 64727

64708 **Neuroplasty, major peripheral nerve, arm or leg; other than specified**   2 T 80 ⬛
MED: 100-2, 15, 260; 100-4, 12, 90.3; 100-4, 14, 10

AMA: 2001, Jun, 11

64712   **sciatic nerve**   2 T 80 ⬛
MED: 100-2, 15, 260; 100-4, 12, 90.3; 100-4, 14, 10

AMA: 2001, Jun, 11

64713   **brachial plexus**   2 T 80 ⬛
MED: 100-2, 15, 260; 100-4, 12, 90.3; 100-4, 14, 10

AMA: 2001, Jun, 11

64714   **lumbar plexus**   2 T 80 ⬛
MED: 100-2, 15, 260; 100-4, 12, 90.3; 100-4, 14, 10

AMA: 2001, Jun, 11; 1997, Jun, 11

64716 **Neuroplasty and/or transposition; cranial nerve (specify)**   3 T 80 ⬛
MED: 100-2, 15, 260; 100-4, 12, 90.3; 100-4, 14, 10

AMA: 2001, Jun, 11

64718   **ulnar nerve at elbow**   2 T 80 ⬛
MED: 100-2, 15, 260; 100-4, 12, 90.3; 100-4, 14, 10

AMA: 2001, Jun, 11

64719   **ulnar nerve at wrist**   2 T ⬛
MED: 100-2, 15, 260; 100-4, 12, 90.3; 100-4, 14, 10

AMA: 2001, Jun, 11

64721   **median nerve at carpal tunnel**   2 T 50 ⬛
MED: 100-2, 15, 260; 100-4, 12, 90.3; 100-4, 14, 10

AMA: 2001, Jun, 11; 1997, Sep, 10

To report arthroscopic procedure, consult CPT code 29848.

64722 **Decompression; unspecified nerve(s) (specify)**   1 T 80 ⬛
MED: 100-2, 15, 260; 100-4, 12, 90.3; 100-4, 14, 10

AMA: 2001, Jun, 11; 1999, May, 11

64726   **plantar digital nerve**   1 T ⬛
MED: 100-2, 15, 260; 100-4, 12, 90.3; 100-4, 14, 10

AMA: 2001, Jun, 11

+ **64727** **Internal neurolysis, requiring use of operating microscope (list separately in addition to code for neuroplasty) (Neuroplasty includes external neurolysis)**   1 T ⬛
MED: 100-2, 15, 260; 100-4, 12, 90.3; 100-4, 14, 10

AMA: 2001, Jun, 11; 1998, Nov, 19

Do not report 69990 in addition to code 64727 as the operating microscope is considered an inclusive component of the surgery.

Note that 64727 is an add-on code that must be used in conjunction with the appropriate code for the primary procedure. This code cannot be reported alone.

TRANSECTION OR AVULSION

To report stereotactic lesion of gasserian ganglion, consult CPT code 61790.

64732   **Transection or avulsion of; supraorbital nerve**   2 T 80 ↰
MED: 100-2, 15, 260; 100-4, 12, 90.3; 100-4, 14, 10

AMA: 1999, Nov, 39

64734   **infraorbital nerve**   2 T 80 ↰
MED: 100-2, 15, 260; 100-4, 12, 90.3; 100-4, 14, 10

64736   **mental nerve**   2 T 80 ↰
MED: 100-2, 15, 260; 100-3, 160.1; 100-4, 12, 90.3; 100-4, 14, 10

64738   **inferior alveolar nerve by osteotomy**   2 T 80 ↰
MED: 100-2, 15, 260; 100-4, 12, 90.3; 100-4, 14, 10

64740   **lingual nerve**   2 T 80 ↰
MED: 100-2, 15, 260; 100-4, 12, 90.3; 100-4, 14, 10

64742   **facial nerve, differential or complete**   2 T 80 ↰
MED: 100-2, 15, 260; 100-4, 12, 90.3; 100-4, 14, 10

64744   **greater occipital nerve**   2 T 50 80 ↰
MED: 100-2, 15, 260; 100-4, 12, 90.3; 100-4, 14, 10

64746   **phrenic nerve**   2 T 80 ↰
MED: 100-2, 15, 260; 100-4, 12, 90.3; 100-4, 14, 10

To report section of a recurrent laryngeal nerve, consult CPT code 31595.

64752   **vagus nerve (vagotomy), transthoracic**   C 80 ↰

64755   **vagus nerves limited to proximal stomach (selective proximal vagotomy, proximal gastric vagotomy, parietal cell vagotomy, supra- or highly selective vagotomy)**   C 80 ↰
AMA: 1999, Nov, 39

If a laparoscopic approach is used, consult CPT code 43652.

64760   **vagus nerve (vagotomy), abdominal**   C 80 ↰
AMA: 1999, Nov, 39

If a laparoscopic approach is used, consult CPT code 43651.

64761   **pudendal nerve**   T 50 80 ↰

64763   **Transection or avulsion of obturator nerve, extrapelvic, with or without adductor tenotomy**   T 50 80 ↰

64766   **Transection or avulsion of obturator nerve, intrapelvic, with or without adductor tenotomy**   T 50 80 ↰
MED: 100-3, 160.1

64771   **Transection or avulsion of other cranial nerve, extradural**   2 T 80 ↰
MED: 100-2, 15, 260; 100-4, 12, 90.3; 100-4, 14, 10

64772   **Transection or avulsion of other spinal nerve, extradural**   2 T 80 ↰
MED: 100-2, 15, 260; 100-4, 12, 90.3; 100-4, 14, 10

If an excision is performed on a tender scar, skin, and subcutaneous tissue, with or without tiny neuroma, consult CPT codes 11400-11446 and 13100-13153.

Nervous System

64774 — 64820

EXCISION — SOMATIC NERVES

If a Morton Neurectomy is performed, consult CPT code 28080.

64774	**Excision of neuroma; cutaneous nerve, surgically identifiable**	26 T ⌐
	MED: 100-2, 15, 260; 100-4, 12, 90.3; 100-4, 14, 10	

64776	**digital nerve, one or both, same digit**	3 T 80 ⌐
	MED: 100-2, 15, 260; 100-4, 12, 90.3; 100-4, 14, 10	

+ 64778   **digital nerve, each additional digit (List separately in addition to code for primary procedure)**   26 T ⌐

MED: 100-2, 15, 260; 100-4, 12, 90.3; 100-4, 14, 10

Note that 64778 is an add-on code and must be used in conjunction with 64776.

64782	**hand or foot, except digital nerve**	3 T ⌐
	MED: 100-2, 15, 260; 100-4, 12, 90.3; 100-4, 14, 10	

+ 64783   **hand or foot, each additional nerve, except same digit (List separately in addition to code for primary procedure)**   26 T ⌐

MED: 100-2, 15, 260; 100-4, 12, 90.3; 100-4, 14, 10

Note that 64783 is an add-on code and must be used in conjunction with 64782.

64784	**major peripheral nerve, except sciatic**	3 T 80 ⌐
	MED: 100-2, 15, 260; 100-4, 12, 90.3; 100-4, 14, 10	

64786	**sciatic nerve**	3 T 80 ⌐
	MED: 100-2, 15, 260; 100-4, 12, 90.3; 100-4, 14, 10	

+ 64787   **Implantation of nerve end into bone or muscle (list separately in addition to neuroma excision)**   26 T 80 ⌐

MED: 100-2, 15, 260; 100-4, 12, 90.3; 100-4, 14, 10

Note that 64787 is an add-on code and must be used in conjunction with 64774-64786.

64788	**Excision of neurofibroma or neurolemmoma; cutaneous nerve**	3 T ⌐
	MED: 100-2, 15, 260; 100-4, 12, 90.3; 100-4, 14, 10	

64790	**major peripheral nerve**	3 T 80 ⌐
	MED: 100-2, 15, 260; 100-4, 12, 90.3; 100-4, 14, 10	

64792	**extensive (including malignant type)**	3 T 80 ⌐
	MED: 100-2, 15, 260; 100-4, 12, 90.3; 100-4, 14, 10	

64795	**Biopsy of nerve**	26 T ⌐
	MED: 100-2, 15, 260; 100-4, 12, 90.3; 100-4, 14, 10	

EXCISION — SYMPATHETIC NERVES

64802	**Sympathectomy, cervical**	26 T 50 80 ⌐
	MED: 100-2, 15, 260; 100-4, 12, 90.3; 100-4, 14, 10	

64804	**Sympathectomy, cervicothoracic**	C 50 80 ⌐

64809	**Sympathectomy, thoracolumbar**	C 50 80 ⌐
	Leriche sympathectomy	

64818	**Sympathectomy, lumbar**	C 50 80 ⌐

64820	**Sympathectomy; digital arteries, each digit**	T ⌐
	Code 69990 cannot be reported with 64820.	

64821	radial artery	4 T 50 ⟆

MED: 100-2, 15, 260; 100-4, 12, 90.3; 100-4, 14, 10

Code 69990 cannot be reported with 64821.

64822	ulnar artery	T 50 ⟆

Code 69990 cannot be reported with 64822.

64823	superficial palmar arch	T 50 ⟆

Code 69990 cannot be reported with 64823.

NEURORRHAPHY

64831	Suture of digital nerve, hand or foot; one nerve	4 T ⟆

MED: 100-2, 15, 260; 100-4, 12, 90.3; 100-4, 14, 10

+ 64832	each additional digital nerve (List separately in addition to code for primary procedure)	1 T 80 ⟆

MED: 100-2, 15, 260; 100-4, 12, 90.3; 100-4, 14, 10

AMA: 2000, Apr, 6

Note that 64832 is an add-on code and must be used in conjunction with 64831.

64834	Suture of one nerve, hand or foot; common sensory nerve	2 T 80 ⟆

MED: 100-2, 15, 260; 100-4, 12, 90.3; 100-4, 14, 10

64835	median motor thenar	3 T 80 ⟆

MED: 100-2, 15, 260; 100-4, 12, 90.3; 100-4, 14, 10

64836	ulnar motor	3 T 80 ⟆

MED: 100-2, 15, 260; 100-4, 12, 90.3; 100-4, 14, 10

+ 64837	Suture of each additional nerve, hand or foot (List separately in addition to code for primary procedure)	1 T 80 ⟆

MED: 100-2, 15, 260; 100-4, 12, 90.3; 100-4, 14, 10

Note that 64837 is an add-on code and must be used in conjunction with 64834-64836.

64840	Suture of posterior tibial nerve	2 T 80 ⟆

MED: 100-2, 15, 260; 100-4, 12, 90.3; 100-4, 14, 10

64856	Suture of major peripheral nerve, arm or leg, except sciatic; including transposition	2 T ⟆

MED: 100-2, 15, 260; 100-4, 12, 90.3; 100-4, 14, 10

64857	without transposition	2 T 80 ⟆

MED: 100-2, 15, 260; 100-4, 12, 90.3; 100-4, 14, 10

64858	Suture of sciatic nerve	2 T 80 ⟆

MED: 100-2, 15, 260; 100-4, 12, 90.3; 100-4, 14, 10

+ 64859	Suture of each additional major peripheral nerve (List separately in addition to code for primary procedure)	1 T 80 ⟆

MED: 100-2, 15, 260; 100-4, 12, 90.3; 100-4, 14, 10

Note that 64859 is an add-on code and must be used in conjunction with 64856 and 64857.

64861	Suture of; brachial plexus	3 T 80 ⟆

MED: 100-2, 15, 260; 100-4, 12, 90.3; 100-4, 14, 10

Nervous System

64862 — 64893

64862	**lumbar plexus** MED: 100-2, 15, 260; 100-4, 12, 90.3; 100-4, 14, 10	3 T 80
64864	**Suture of facial nerve; extracranial** MED: 100-2, 15, 260; 100-4, 12, 90.3; 100-4, 14, 10	3 T 80
64865	**infratemporal, with or without grafting** MED: 100-2, 15, 260; 100-4, 12, 90.3; 100-4, 14, 10	4 T 80
64866	**Anastomosis; facial-spinal accessory**	C 80
64868	**facial-hypoglossal** **Korte-Ballance anastomosis**	C 80
64870	**facial-phrenic** MED: 100-2, 15, 260; 100-4, 12, 90.3; 100-4, 14, 10	4 T 80

+ **64872**   **Suture of nerve; requiring secondary or delayed suture (list separately in addition to code for primary neurorrhaphy)**   2 T 80
MED: 100-2, 15, 260; 100-4, 12, 90.3; 100-4, 14, 10

Note that 64872 is an add-on code and must be used in conjunction with 64831-64865.

+ **64874**   **requiring extensive mobilization, or transposition of nerve (list separately in addition to code for nerve suture)**   3 T 80
MED: 100-2, 15, 260; 100-4, 12, 90.3; 100-4, 14, 10

Note that 64874 is an add-on code and must be used in conjunction with 64831-64865.

+ **64876**   **requiring shortening of bone of extremity (list separately in addition to code for nerve suture)**   3 T 80
MED: 100-2, 15, 260; 100-4, 12, 90.3; 100-4, 14, 10

Note that 64876 is an add-on code and must be used in conjunction with 64831-64865.

NEURORRHAPHY WITH NERVE GRAFT

64885	**Nerve graft (includes obtaining graft), head or neck;** **up to 4 cm in length** MED: 100-2, 15, 260; 100-4, 12, 90.3; 100-4, 14, 10 AMA: 2000, Nov, 11	2 T 80
64886	**more than 4 cm in length** MED: 100-2, 15, 260; 100-4, 12, 90.3; 100-4, 14, 10 AMA: 2000, Nov, 11	2 T 80
64890	**Nerve graft (includes obtaining graft), single strand, hand or foot;** **up to 4 cm length** MED: 100-2, 15, 260; 100-4, 12, 90.3; 100-4, 14, 10	2 T 80
64891	**more than 4 cm length** MED: 100-2, 15, 260; 100-4, 12, 90.3; 100-4, 14, 10	2 T 80
64892	**Nerve graft (includes obtaining graft), single strand, arm or leg;** **up to 4 cm length** MED: 100-2, 15, 260; 100-4, 12, 90.3; 100-4, 14, 10	2 T 80
64893	**more than 4 cm length** MED: 100-2, 15, 260; 100-4, 12, 90.3; 100-4, 14, 10	2 T 80

64895   **Nerve graft (includes obtaining graft), multiple strands (cable), hand or foot; up to 4 cm length** 3 T 80 ⬕
MED: 100-2, 15, 260; 100-4, 12, 90.3; 100-4, 14, 10

AMA: 2000, Nov, 11

64896   **more than 4 cm length** 3 T 80 ⬕
MED: 100-2, 15, 260; 100-4, 12, 90.3; 100-4, 14, 10

AMA: 2000, Nov, 11

64897   **Nerve graft (includes obtaining graft), multiple strands (cable), arm or leg; up to 4 cm length** 3 T 80 ⬕
MED: 100-2, 15, 260; 100-4, 12, 90.3; 100-4, 14, 10

AMA: 2000, Nov, 11

64898   **more than 4 cm length** 3 T 80 ⬕
MED: 100-2, 15, 260; 100-4, 12, 90.3; 100-4, 14, 10

AMA: 2000, Nov, 11

+   64901   **Nerve graft, each additional nerve; single strand (List separately in addition to code for primary procedure)** 2 T 80 ⬕
MED: 100-2, 15, 260; 100-4, 12, 90.3; 100-4, 14, 10

AMA: 2000, Nov, 11

Note that 64901 is an add-on code and must be used in conjunction with 64885-64893.

+   64902   **multiple strands (cable) (List separately in addition to code for primary procedure)** 2 T 80 ⬕
MED: 100-2, 15, 260; 100-4, 12, 90.3; 100-4, 14, 10

AMA: 2000, Nov, 11

Note that 64902 is an add-on code and must be used in conjunction with 64885, 64886, and 64895-64898.

64905   **Nerve pedicle transfer; first stage** 2 T 80 ⬕
MED: 100-2, 15, 260; 100-4, 12, 90.3; 100-4, 14, 10

64907   **second stage** 1 T 80 ⬕
MED: 100-2, 15, 260; 100-4, 12, 90.3; 100-4, 14, 10

OTHER PROCEDURES

64999   **Unlisted procedure, nervous system** T 80
AMA: 2000, Sep, 10; 2000, Jan, 10; 2000, Aug, 7; 1998, Sep, 16; 1998, Oct, 10; 1996, Apr, 10

EYE AND OCULAR ADNEXA

If a diagnostic and treatment program is initiated for ophthalmological services, consult the Medicine and Ophthalmology sections of CPT and CPT codes 92002 et seq. Do not report 69990 in addition to codes 65091-68850 as the operating microscope is considered an inclusive component of these procedures.

EYEBALL

REMOVAL OF EYE

65091   **Evisceration of ocular contents; without implant**   3 T 50 80 �lↄ
MED: 100-2, 15, 260; 100-4, 12, 90.3; 100-4, 14, 10

65093   **with implant**   3 T 50 �ↄ
MED: 100-2, 15, 260; 100-4, 12, 90.3; 100-4, 14, 10

65101   **Enucleation of eye; without implant**   3 T 50 ↄ
MED: 100-2, 15, 260; 100-4, 12, 90.3; 100-4, 14, 10

65103   **with implant, muscles not attached to implant**   3 T 50 ↄ
MED: 100-2, 15, 260; 100-4, 12, 90.3; 100-4, 14, 10

65105   **with implant, muscles attached to implant**   4 T 50 80 ↄ
MED: 100-2, 15, 260; 100-4, 12, 90.3; 100-4, 14, 10

If a conjunctivoplasty is performed after enucleation, consult CPT codes 68320 and subsequent codes.

65110   **Exenteration of orbit (does not include skin graft), removal of orbital contents; only**   5 T 50 80 ↄ
MED: 100-2, 15, 260; 100-4, 12, 90.3; 100-4, 14, 10

65112   **with therapeutic removal of bone**   7 T 50 80 ↄ
MED: 100-2, 15, 260; 100-4, 12, 90.3; 100-4, 14, 10

65114   **with muscle or myocutaneous flap**   7 T 50 80 ↄ
MED: 100-2, 15, 260; 100-4, 12, 90.3; 100-4, 14, 10

If a split skin graft is performed on the orbit, consult CPT codes 15120 and 15121. If a full thickness graft, free, is performed, consult CPT codes 15260 and 15261. If an eyelid, involving more than skin, is repaired, consult CPT codes 67930 and subsequent codes.

SECONDARY IMPLANT(S) PROCEDURES

Consult the glossary for terms and definitions and the front matter of this chapter for additional information.

If a diagnostic and treatment program is initiated for ophthalmological services, consult the Medicine and Ophthalmology sections of the CPT book and CPT codes 92002 and subsequent codes. Do not report 69990 in addition to codes 65091-68850 as the operating microscope is considered an inclusive component of these procedures.

65125   **Modification of ocular implant with placement or replacement of pegs (eg, drilling receptacle for prosthesis appendage) (separate procedure)**   T 50 ↄ

65130   **Insertion of ocular implant secondary; after evisceration, in scleral shell**   3 T 50 ↄ
MED: 100-2, 15, 260; 100-4, 12, 90.3; 100-4, 14, 10

65135   **after enucleation, muscles not attached to implant**   2 T 50 ↄ
MED: 100-2, 15, 260; 100-4, 12, 90.3; 100-4, 14, 10

65140	after enucleation, muscles attached to implant	3 T 50 ⟁

MED: 100-2, 15, 260; 100-4, 12, 90.3; 100-4, 14, 10

65150 Reinsertion of ocular implant; with or without conjunctival graft ⟁2 T 50 80 ⟁
MED: 100-2, 15, 260; 100-4, 12, 90.3; 100-4, 14, 10

65155 with use of foreign material for reinforcement and/or attachment of muscles to implant 3 T 50 ⟁
MED: 100-2, 15, 260; 100-4, 12, 90.3; 100-4, 14, 10

65175 Removal of ocular implant 1 T 50 ⟁
MED: 100-2, 15, 260; 100-4, 12, 90.3; 100-4, 14, 10

If an orbital implant (implant outside muscle cone) is inserted, consult CPT code 67550. If the implant is removed, consult CPT code 67560.

REMOVAL OF FOREIGN BODY

If a diagnostic and treatment program is initiated for ophthalmological services, consult the Medicine and Ophthalmology sections of the CPT book and CPT codes 92002 and subsequent codes. Do not report 69990 in addition to codes 65091-68850 as the operating microscope is considered an inclusive component of these procedures.

If implanted material is removed, consult the following CPT codes: ocular implant, see 56175; anterior segment implant, see 65920; posterior segment implant, see 67120; and orbital implant, see 67560. If a diagnostic x-ray is taken for a foreign body, consult CPT code 70030. If a diagnostic echography is needed for a foreign body, consult CPT code 76529. If a foreign body is removed from the orbit, consult the following CPT codes: frontal approach, see 67413; lateral approach, see 67430; and transcranial approach, see 61334. If an embedded foreign body is removed from the eyelid, consult CPT code 67938. If a foreign body is removed from the lacrimal system, consult CPT code 68530.

65205 Removal of foreign body, external eye; conjunctival superficial S 50 ⟁
65210 conjunctival embedded (includes concretions), subconjunctival, or scleral nonperforating S 50 ⟁
65220 corneal, without slit lamp S 50 ⟁
65222 corneal, with slit lamp S 50 ⟁

To report repair of corneal laceration with foreign body, consult CPT code 65275.

65235 Removal of foreign body, intraocular; from anterior chamber of eye or lens 2 T 50 80 ⟁
MED: 100-2, 15, 260; 100-4, 12, 90.3; 100-4, 14, 10

To report removal of implant material from anterior segment, consult CPT code 65920.

65260 from posterior segment, magnetic extraction, anterior or posterior route 3 T 50 80 ⟁
MED: 100-2, 15, 260; 100-4, 12, 90.3; 100-4, 14, 10

65265 from posterior segment, nonmagnetic extraction 4 T 50 80 ⟁
MED: 100-2, 15, 260; 100-4, 12, 90.3; 100-4, 14, 10

To report removal of implant material from posterior segment, consult CPT code 67120.

REPAIR OF LACERATION

If a diagnostic and treatment program is initiated for ophthalmological services, consult the Medicine and Ophthalmology sections of the CPT book and CPT codes 92002 and subsequent codes. Do not report 69990 in addition to codes 65091-68850 as the operating microscope is considered an inclusive component of these procedures.

If the orbit is fractured, consult CPT codes 21385 and subsequent codes. If a wound on the skin of the eyelid is repaired, linear, simple, consult CPT codes 12011-12018; intermediate, layered closure, consult CPT codes 12051-12057; linear, complex, consult CPT codes 13150-13153; and other, consult CPT codes 67930 and 67935. If a wound of the lacrimal system is repaired, consult CPT code 68700. If an operative wound is repaired, consult CPT code 66250.

65270 **Repair of laceration; conjunctiva, with or without nonperforating laceration sclera, direct closure** ② T 50 80 ▶
MED: 100-2, 15, 260; 100-4, 12, 90.3; 100-4, 14, 10

65272 **conjunctiva, by mobilization and rearrangement, without hospitalization** ② T 50 ▶
MED: 100-2, 15, 260; 100-4, 12, 90.3; 100-4, 14, 10

65273 **conjunctiva, by mobilization and rearrangement, with hospitalization** C 50 ▶

65275 **cornea, nonperforating, with or without removal foreign body** ④ T 50 80 ▶
MED: 100-2, 15, 260; 100-4, 12, 90.3; 100-4, 14, 10

65280 **cornea and/or sclera, perforating, not involving uveal tissue** ④ T 50 80 ▶
MED: 100-2, 15, 260; 100-4, 12, 90.3; 100-4, 14, 10

65285 **cornea and/or sclera, perforating, with reposition or resection of uveal tissue** ④ T 50 80 ▶
MED: 100-2, 15, 260; 100-4, 12, 90.3; 100-4, 14, 10

65286 **application of tissue glue, wounds of cornea and/or sclera** T 50 ▶
Note that this procedure includes use of a conjunctival flap and restoration of the anterior chamber, by air or saline injection when indicated. If the iris or ciliary body is repaired, consult CPT code 66680.

65290 **Repair of wound, extraocular muscle, tendon and/or Tenon's capsule** ③ T 50 ▶
MED: 100-2, 15, 260; 100-4, 12, 90.3; 100-4, 14, 10

ANTERIOR SEGMENT

If a diagnostic and treatment program is initiated for ophthalmological services, consult the Medicine and Ophthalmology sections of the CPT book and CPT codes 92002 and subsequent codes. Do not report 69990 in addition to codes 65091-68850 as the operating microscope is considered an inclusive component of these procedures.

CORNEA — EXCISION

65400 **Excision of lesion, cornea (keratectomy, lamellar, partial), except pterygium** ① T 50 ▶
MED: 100-2, 15, 260; 100-4, 12, 90.3; 100-4, 14, 10

65410 **Biopsy of cornea** ② T 50 80 ▶
MED: 100-2, 15, 260; 100-4, 12, 90.3; 100-4, 14, 10

65420 **Excision or transposition of pterygium; without graft** ② T 50 ▶
MED: 100-2, 15, 260; 100-4, 12, 90.3; 100-4, 14, 10

65426 with graft 5 T 50 CCI
MED: 100-2, 15, 260; 100-4, 12, 90.3; 100-4, 14, 10

CORNEA — REMOVAL OR DESTRUCTION

65430 **Scraping of cornea, diagnostic, for smear and/or culture** S 50 CCI

65435 **Removal of corneal epithelium; with or without chemocauterization (abrasion, curettage)** T 50 CCI

65436 **with application of chelating agent (eg, EDTA)** T 50 CCI

65450 **Destruction of lesion of cornea by cryotherapy, photocoagulation or thermocauterization** S 50 CCI

65600 **Multiple punctures of anterior cornea (eg, for corneal erosion, tattoo)** T 50 CCI

CORNEA — KERATOPLASTY

Corneal transplant procedures include the use of preserved or fresh grafts and the preparation of the donor material.

If refractive dermatoplasty procedures are performed in conjunction with this procedure, consult CPT codes 65760, 65765, and 65767.

If a diagnostic and treatment program is initiated for ophthalmological services, consult the Medicine and Ophthalmology sections of the CPT book and CPT codes 92002 and subsequent codes. Do not report 69990 in addition to codes 65091-68850 as the operating microscope is considered an inclusive component of these procedures.

65710 **Keratoplasty (corneal transplant); lamellar** 7 T 50 80 CCI
MED: 100-2, 15, 260; 100-3, 80.7; 100-4, 12, 90.3; 100-4, 14, 10
AMA: 2002, Oct, 8

65730 **penetrating (except in aphakia)** 7 T 50 80 CCI
MED: 100-2, 15, 260; 100-3, 80.7; 100-4, 12, 90.3; 100-4, 14, 10
AMA: 2002, Oct, 8

65750 **penetrating (in aphakia)** 7 T 50 80 CCI
MED: 100-2, 15, 260; 100-3, 80.7; 100-4, 12, 90.3; 100-4, 14, 10
AMA: 2002, Oct, 8

65755 **penetrating (in pseudophakia)** 7 T 50 80 CCI
MED: 100-2, 15, 260; 100-3, 80.7; 100-4, 12, 90.3; 100-4, 14, 10
AMA: 2002, Oct, 8

CORNEA — OTHER PROCEDURES

If a contact lens is fit for the treatment of a disease, consult CPT code 92070. If an unlisted procedure is performed on the cornea, consult CPT code 66999.

If a diagnostic and treatment program is initiated for ophthalmological services, consult the Medicine and Ophthalmology sections of the CPT book and CPT codes 92002 and subsequent codes. Do not report 69990 in addition to codes 65091-68850 as the operating microscope is considered an inclusive component of these procedures.

65760 **Keratomileusis** E
MED: 100-3, 80.7

65765 **Keratophakia** E
MED: 100-3, 80.7

Eye and Ocular Adnexa

65767 — 65855

| 65767 | **Epikeratoplasty** | E |
| | MED: 100-3, 80.7 | |

65770 **Keratoprosthesis** ⑦ T 50 80 ♥
MED: 100-2, 15, 260; 100-4, 12, 90.3; 100-4, 14, 10

65771 **Radial keratotomy** E
MED: 100-3, 80.7

65772 **Corneal relaxing incision for correction of surgically induced astigmatism** ④ T 50 ♥
MED: 100-2, 15, 260; 100-3, 80.7; 100-4, 12, 90.3; 100-4, 14, 10

65775 **Corneal wedge resection for correction of surgically induced astigmatism** ④ T 50 ♥
MED: 100-2, 15, 260; 100-3, 80.7; 100-4, 12, 90.3; 100-4, 14, 10

65780 **Ocular surface reconstruction; amniotic membrane transplantation** ⑤ T 50 80 ♥

65781 **limbal stem cell allograft (eg, cadaveric or living donor)** ⑤ T 50 80 ♥

65782 **limbal conjunctival autograft (includes obtaining graft)** ⑤ T 50 80 ♥

To report harvesting of conjunctival allograft, from a living donor, consult CPT 68371.

ANTERIOR CHAMBER — INCISION

If a diagnostic and treatment program is initiated for ophthalmological services, consult the Medicine and Ophthalmology sections of the CPT book and CPT codes 92002 and subsequent codes. Do not report 69990 in addition to codes 65091-68850 as the operating microscope is considered an inclusive component of these procedures.

65800 **Paracentesis of anterior chamber of eye (separate procedure); with diagnostic aspiration of aqueous** ① T 50 ♥
MED: 100-2, 15, 260; 100-4, 12, 90.3; 100-4, 14, 10

65805 **with therapeutic release of aqueous** ① T 50 ♥
MED: 100-2, 15, 260; 100-4, 12, 90.3; 100-4, 14, 10

65810 **with removal of vitreous and/or discission of anterior hyaloid membrane, with or without air injection** ③ T 50 ♥
MED: 100-2, 15, 260; 100-4, 12, 90.3; 100-4, 14, 10

65815 **with removal of blood, with or without irrigation and/or air injection** ② T 50 ♥
MED: 100-2, 15, 260; 100-4, 12, 90.3; 100-4, 14, 10

If an injection is needed, consult CPT codes 66020-66030.
To report removal of blood clot, consult CPT code 65930.

65820 **Goniotomy** ① T 50 80 ♥ ⑥³
Barkan's operation

65850 **Trabeculotomy ab externo** ④ T 50 ♥
MED: 100-2, 15, 260; 100-4, 12, 90.3; 100-4, 14, 10

65855 **Trabeculoplasty by laser surgery, one or more sessions (defined treatment series)** T 50 ♥
AMA: 1998, Mar, 7

If re-treatment is necessary after several months because of disease progression, a new treatment or treatment series should be reported with a modifier to indicate lesser or greater complexity. If a trabeculectomy is performed, consult CPT code 66170.

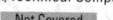

65860   **Severing adhesions of anterior segment, laser technique (separate procedure)** T 50 80

ANTERIOR CHAMBER — OTHER PROCEDURES

If a diagnostic and treatment program is initiated for ophthalmological services, consult the Medicine and Ophthalmology sections of the CPT book and CPT codes 92002 and subsequent codes. Do not report 69990 in addition to codes 65091-68850 as the operating microscope is considered an inclusive component of these procedures.

65865   **Severing adhesions of anterior segment of eye, incisional technique (with or without injection of air or liquid) (separate procedure); goniosynechiae** 1 T 50
MED: 100-2, 15, 260; 100-4, 12, 90.3; 100-4, 14, 10

If trabeculoplasty is performed by laser surgery, consult CPT code 65855.

65870   **anterior synechiae, except goniosynechiae** 4 T 50
MED: 100-2, 15, 260; 100-4, 12, 90.3; 100-4, 14, 10

65875   **posterior synechiae** 4 T 50
MED: 100-2, 15, 260; 100-4, 12, 90.3; 100-4, 14, 10

65880   **corneovitreal adhesions** 4 T 50
MED: 100-2, 15, 260; 100-4, 12, 90.3; 100-4, 14, 10

If laser surgery is performed, consult CPT code 66821.

65900   **Removal of epithelial downgrowth, anterior chamber of eye** 5 T 50 80
MED: 100-2, 15, 260; 100-4, 12, 90.3; 100-4, 14, 10

65920   **Removal of implanted material, anterior segment of eye** 7 T 50
MED: 100-2, 15, 260; 100-4, 12, 90.3; 100-4, 14, 10

65930   **Removal of blood clot, anterior segment of eye** 5 T 50
MED: 100-2, 15, 260; 100-4, 12, 90.3; 100-4, 14, 10

66020   **Injection, anterior chamber of eye (separate procedure); air or liquid** 1 T 50
MED: 100-2, 15, 260; 100-4, 12, 90.3; 100-4, 14, 10

66030   **medication** 1 T 50
MED: 100-2, 15, 260; 100-4, 12, 90.3; 100-4, 14, 10

If the procedure performed on the anterior segment is unlisted, consult CPT code 66999.

ANTERIOR SCLERA — EXCISION

If a diagnostic and treatment program is initiated for ophthalmological services, consult the Medicine and Ophthalmology sections of the CPT book and CPT codes 92002 and subsequent codes. Do not report 69990 in addition to codes 65091-68850 as the operating microscope is considered an inclusive component of these procedures.

If an intraocular foreign body is removed, consult CPT code 65235. If an operation is performed on the posterior sclera, consult CPT codes 67250 and 67255.

66130   **Excision of lesion, sclera** 7 T 50 80
MED: 100-2, 15, 260; 100-4, 12, 90.3; 100-4, 14, 10

66150   **Fistulization of sclera for glaucoma; trephination with iridectomy** 4 T 50
MED: 100-2, 15, 260; 100-4, 12, 90.3; 100-4, 14, 10

66155   **thermocauterization with iridectomy** 4 T 50
MED: 100-2, 15, 260; 100-4, 12, 90.3; 100-4, 14, 10

Eye and Ocular Adnexa

66160 — 66500

66160	**sclerectomy with punch or scissors, with iridectomy** 2 T 50

MED: 100-2, 15, 260; 100-4, 12, 90.3; 100-4, 14, 10

Knapp's operation

66165	**iridencleisis or iridotasis** 4 T 50 80

MED: 100-2, 15, 260; 100-4, 12, 90.3; 100-4, 10

66170	**trabeculectomy ab externo in absence of previous surgery** 4 T 50 80

MED: 100-2, 15, 260; 100-4, 12, 90.3; 100-4, 14, 10

If a trabeculotomy ab externo is performed, consult CPT code 65850. If an operative wound is repaired, consult CPT code 66250.

66172	**trabeculectomy ab externo with scarring from previous ocular surgery or trauma (includes injection of antifibrotic agents)** 4 T 50 80

MED: 100-2, 15, 260; 100-4, 12, 90.3; 100-4, 14, 10

To report transciliary body sclera fistulization, consult CPT Category III code 0123T.

66180	**Aqueous shunt to extraocular reservoir (eg, Molteno, Schocket, Denver-Krupin)** 5 T 50 80

MED: 100-2, 15, 260; 100-4, 12, 90.3; 100-4, 14, 10

66185	**Revision of aqueous shunt to extraocular reservoir** 2 T 50 80

MED: 100-2, 15, 260; 100-4, 12, 90.3; 100-4, 14, 10

If an implanted shunt is removed, consult CPT code 67120.

ANTERIOR SCLERA — REPAIR OR REVISION

If a diagnostic and treatment program is initiated for ophthalmological services, consult the Medicine and Ophthalmology sections of the CPT book and CPT codes 92002 and subsequent codes. Do not report 69990 in addition to codes 65091-68850 as the operating microscope is considered an inclusive component of these procedures.

If scleral procedures are performed in retinal surgery, consult CPT codes 67101 and subsequent codes.

66220	**Repair of scleral staphyloma; without graft** 3 T 50 80

MED: 100-2, 15, 260; 100-4, 12, 90.3; 100-4, 14, 10

66225	**with graft** 4 T 50 80

MED: 100-2, 15, 260; 100-4, 12, 90.3; 100-4, 14, 10

If scleral reinforcement is needed, consult CPT codes 67250 and 67255.

66250	**Revision or repair of operative wound of anterior segment, any type, early or late, major or minor procedure** 2 T 50

MED: 100-2, 15, 260; 100-4, 12, 90.3; 100-4, 14, 10

To report unlisted procedures on the anterior sclera, consult 66999.

IRIS, CILIARY BODY — INCISION

If a diagnostic and treatment program is initiated for ophthalmological services, consult the Medicine and Ophthalmology sections of the CPT book and CPT codes 92002 and subsequent codes. Do not report 69990 in addition to codes 65091-68850 as the operating microscope is considered an inclusive component of these procedures.

If an "iridotomy" is performed by photocoagulation, consult CPT code 66761.

66500	**Iridotomy by stab incision (separate procedure); except transfixion** 1 T 50

MED: 100-2, 15, 260; 100-4, 12, 90.3; 100-4, 14, 10

66505	with transfixion as for iris bombe	■ 1 T 50 ▣
	MED: 100-2, 15, 260; 100-4, 12, 90.3; 100-4, 14, 10	

IRIS, CILIARY BODY — EXCISION

If a diagnostic and treatment program is initiated for ophthalmological services, consult the Medicine and Ophthalmology sections of the CPT book and CPT codes 92002 and subsequent codes. Do not report 69990 in addition to codes 65091-68850 as the operating microscope is considered an inclusive component of these procedures.

If "coreoplasty" is performed by photocoagulation, consult CPT code 66762.

66600	Iridectomy, with corneoscleral or corneal section; for removal of lesion	3 T 50 ▣
	MED: 100-2, 15, 260; 100-4, 12, 90.3; 100-4, 14, 10	
66605	with cyclectomy	3 T 50 ▣
	MED: 100-2, 15, 260; 100-4, 12, 90.3; 100-4, 14, 10	
66625	peripheral for glaucoma (separate procedure)	3 T 50 ▣
	MED: 100-2, 15, 260; 100-4, 12, 90.3; 100-4, 14, 10	
66630	sector for glaucoma (separate proedure)	3 T 50 ▣
	MED: 100-2, 15, 260; 100-4, 12, 90.3; 100-4, 14, 10	
66635	optical (separate procedure)	3 T 50 ▣
	MED: 100-2, 15, 260; 100-4, 12, 90.3; 100-4, 14, 10	

IRIS, CILIARY BODY — REPAIR

If a diagnostic and treatment program is initiated for ophthalmological services, consult the Medicine and Ophthalmology sections of the CPT book and CPT codes 92002 and subsequent codes. Do not report 69990 in addition to codes 65091-68850 as the operating microscope is considered an inclusive component of these procedures.

If uveal tissue is repositioned or resected because of a perforating wound of the cornea or the sclera, consult CPT code 65285.

66680	Repair of iris, ciliary body (as for iridodialysis)	3 T 50 ▣
	MED: 100-2, 15, 260; 100-4, 12, 90.3; 100-4, 14, 10	
66682	Suture of iris, ciliary body (separate procedure) with retrieval of suture through small incision (eg, McCannel suture)	2 T 50 ▣
	MED: 100-2, 15, 260; 100-4, 12, 90.3; 100-4, 14, 10	

IRIS, CILIARY BODY — DESTRUCTION

If an iridectomy is performed for removal of a lesion, with corneoscleral or corneal section, consult CPT codes 66600 and 66605. If an epithelial downgrowth is removed from the anterior chamber of the eye, consult CPT code 65900. If a procedure performed on the iris or ciliary body is unlisted, consult CPT code 66999.

66700	Ciliary body destruction; diathermy	2 T 50 80 ▣
	MED: 100-2, 15, 260; 100-4, 12, 90.3; 100-4, 14, 10	
	Heine's operation	
66710	cyclophotocoagulation, transscleral	2 T 50 ▣
	MED: 100-2, 15, 260; 100-4, 12, 90.3; 100-4, 14, 10	
66711	cyclophotocoagulation, endoscopic	2 T 50 ▣
	Code 66711 cannot be reported with CPT code 66990.	

Eye and Ocular Adnexa

66720 — 66825

⊙ **66720** cryotherapy   [2] [T] [50] [▸]
MED: 100-2, 15, 260; 100-4, 12, 90.3; 100-4, 14, 10

66740 cyclodialysis   [2] [T] [50] [▸]
MED: 100-2, 15, 260; 100-4, 12, 90.3; 100-4, 14, 10

66761 **Iridotomy/iridectomy by laser surgery (eg, for glaucoma) (one or more sessions)**   [T] [50] [▸]
AMA: 1998, Mar, 7

66762 **Iridoplasty by photocoagulation (one or more sessions) (eg, for improvement of vision, for widening of anterior chamber angle)**   [T] [50] [▸]
AMA: 1998, Mar, 7

66770 **Destruction of cyst or lesion iris or ciliary body (nonexcisional procedure)**   [T] [50] [▸]

LENS — INCISION

If a diagnostic and treatment program is initiated for ophthalmological services, consult the Medicine and Ophthalmology sections of the CPT book and CPT codes 92002 and subsequent codes. Do not report 69990 in addition to codes 65091-68850 as the operating microscope is considered an inclusive component of these procedures.

66820 **Discission of secondary membranous cataract (opacified posterior lens capsule and/or anterior hyaloid); stab incision technique (Ziegler or Wheeler knife)**   [T] [50] [▸]

66821 laser surgery (eg, YAG laser) (one or more stages)   [2] [T] [50] [▸]
MED: 100-2, 15, 260; 100-4, 12, 90.3; 100-4, 14, 10

66825 **Repositioning of intraocular lens prosthesis, requiring an incision (separate procedure)**   [4] [T] [50] [80] [▸]
MED: 100-2, 15, 260; 100-4, 12, 90.3; 100-4, 14, 10

LENS — REMOVAL CATARACT

If a diagnostic and treatment program is initiated for ophthalmological services, consult the Medicine and Ophthalmology sections of the CPT book and CPT codes 92002 and subsequent codes. Do not report 69990 in addition to codes 65091-68850 as the operating microscope is considered an inclusive component of these procedures.

Anterior and/or posterior capsulotomy, iridotomy, iridectomy, lateral canthotomy, use of viscoelastic agents, enzymatic zonulysis, or the use of other pharmacologic agents, subconjunctival or sub-tenon injections, are all included as part of the CPT code(s) for extraction of lens.

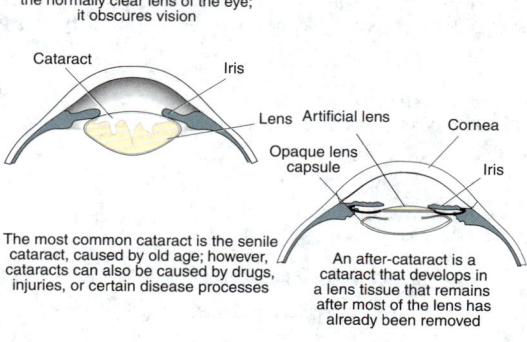

A cataract is a milky opacity on the normally clear lens of the eye; it obscures vision

Cataract   Iris   Lens   Artificial lens   Cornea

Opaque lens capsule   Iris

The most common cataract is the senile cataract, caused by old age; however, cataracts can also be caused by drugs, injuries, or certain disease processes

An after-cataract is a cataract that develops in a lens tissue that remains after most of the lens has already been removed

---

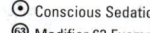

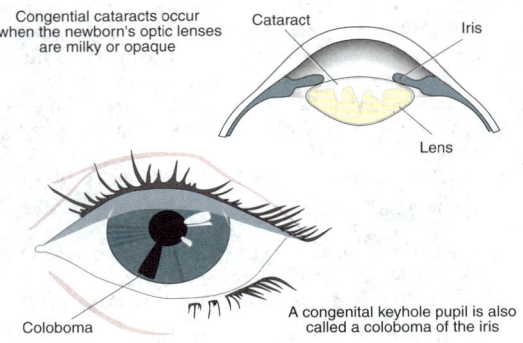

Congential cataracts occur when the newborn's optic lenses are milky or opaque

Cataract

Iris

Lens

Coloboma

A congenital keyhole pupil is also called a coloboma of the iris

66830   **Removal of secondary membranous cataract (opacified posterior lens capsule and/or anterior hyaloid) with corneo-scleral section, with or without iridectomy (iridocapsulotomy, iridocapsulectomy)**   4 T 50 ⊡
MED: 100-2, 15, 260; 100-3, 80.10; 100-3, 80.11; 100-4, 12, 90.3; 100-4, 14, 10

If implanted material from the anterior segment is removed, consult CPT code 65920.

Daviel's operation

66840   **Removal of lens material; aspiration technique, one or more stages**   4 T 50 ⊡
MED: 100-2, 15, 260; 100-3, 80.10; 100-3, 80.11; 100-4, 12, 90.3; 100-4, 14, 10

AMA: 1992, Fall, 4

If implanted material from the anterior segment is removed, consult CPT code 65920.

Fukala's operation

66850   **phacofragmentation technique (mechanical or ultrasonic) (eg, phacoemulsification), with aspiration**   7 T 50 ⊡
MED: 100-2, 15, 260; 100-3, 80.10; 100-3, 80.11; 100-4, 12, 90.3; 100-4, 14, 10

AMA: 1992, Fall, 6

66852   **pars plana approach, with or without vitrectomy**   4 T 50 80 ⊡
MED: 100-2, 15, 260; 100-3, 80.10; 100-3, 80.11; 100-4, 12, 90.3; 100-4, 14, 10

AMA: 1992, Fall, 8

66920   **intracapsular**   4 T 50 80 ⊡
MED: 100-2, 15, 260; 100-3, 80.10; 100-3, 80.11; 100-4, 12, 90.3; 100-4, 14, 10

AMA: 1992, Fall, 8

66930   **intracapsular, for dislocated lens**   5 T 50 80 ⊡
MED: 100-2, 15, 260; 100-3, 80.10; 100-3, 80.11; 100-4, 12, 90.3; 100-4, 14, 10

AMA: 1992, Fall, 8

66940   **extracapsular (other than 66840, 66850, 66852)**   5 T 50 80 ⊡
MED: 100-2, 15, 260; 100-3, 80.10; 100-3, 80.11; 100-4, 12, 90.3; 100-4, 14, 10

AMA: 1992, Fall, 4

To report removal of intralenticular foreign body without lens extraction, consult CPT code 65235. To report repair of operative wound, consult CPT code 66250.

Eye and Ocular Adnexa

66982 — 67005

66982   **Extracapsular cataract removal with insertion of intraocular lens prosthesis (one stage procedure), manual or mechanical technique (eg, irrigation and aspiration or phacoemulsification), complex, requiring devices or techniques not generally used in routine cataract surgery (eg, iris expansion device, suture support for intraocular lens, or primary posterior capsulorrhexis) or performed on patients in the amblyogenic developmental stage**   [S] [T] [50] [↰]
> MED: 100-2, 15, 260; 100-3, 80.10; 100-3, 80.11; 100-4, 12, 90.3; 100-4, 14, 10

> AMA: 2001, Feb, 7

66983   **Intracapsular cataract extraction with insertion of intraocular lens prosthesis (one stage procedure)**   [S] [T] [50] [↰]
> MED: 100-2, 15, 260; 100-3, 80.10; 100-3, 80.11; 100-4, 12, 90.3; 100-4, 14, 10

> AMA: 1992, Fall, 5, 8

66984   **Extracapsular cataract removal with insertion of intraocular lens prosthesis (one stage procedure), manual or mechanical technique (eg, irrigation and aspiration or phacoemulsification)**   [S] [T] [50] [↰]
> MED: 100-2, 15, 260; 100-3, 80.10; 100-3, 80.11; 100-4, 12, 90.3; 100-4, 14, 10

> AMA: 2001, Feb, 7; 1992, Fall, 5, 8

> To report complex cataract removal, consult CPT code 66982.

66985   **Insertion of intraocular lens prosthesis (secondary implant), not associated with concurrent cataract removal**   [6] [T] [50] [↰]
> MED: 100-2, 15, 260; 100-3, 80.10; 100-3, 80.11; 100-4, 12, 90.3; 100-4, 14, 10

> If an implant is performed at the time of a concurrent cataract surgery, consult CPT code 66982, 66983 or 66984. If a secondary fixation (separate procedure) is performed, consult CPT code 66682.

> To report intraocular lens prosthesis supplied by physician, consult CPT code 99070. To report removal of implant material from anterior segment, consult CPT code 65920. To report ultrasonic determination of intraocular lens power, consult CPT code 76519.

66986   **Exchange of intraocular lens**   [6] [T] [50] [↰]
> MED: 100-2, 15, 260; 100-3, 80.10; 100-3, 80.11; 100-4, 12, 90.3; 100-4, 14, 10

+   **66990**   **Use of ophthalmic endoscope (List separately in addition to code for primary procedure)**   [N] [↰]
> MED: 100-3, 80.10; 100-3, 80.11

> Note that 66990 is an add-on code and must be used in conjunction with 65820, 65875, 65920, 66985, 66986, 67038, 67039, 67040.

OTHER PROCEDURES

66999   **Unlisted procedure, anterior segment of eye**   [T] [50] [80]

POSTERIOR SEGMENT

If a diagnostic and treatment program is initiated for ophthalmological services, consult the Medicine and Ophthalmology sections of the CPT book and CPT codes 92002 and subsequent codes. Do not report 69990 in addition to codes 65091-68850 as the operating microscope is considered an inclusive component of these procedures.

VITREOUS

67005   **Removal of vitreous, anterior approach (open sky technique or limbal incision); partial removal**   [4] [T] [50] [↰]
> MED: 100-2, 15, 260; 100-3, 80.11; 100-4, 12, 90.3; 100-4, 14, 10

> AMA: 1992, Fall, 4

[26] / [TC] Professional/Technical Component   [80]/[80] Assist-at-Surgery Allowed/With Documentation   ⊙ Conscious Sedation

Unlisted   Not Covered   MED: Pubs 100/NCD Reference   [1]-[9] ASC Group   ⊛ Modifier 63 Exempt

474 — Surgery   CPT only © 2005 American Medical Association. All Rights Reserved. *(Black Ink)*   © 2005 Ingenix, Inc. *(Blue Ink)*

67010   subtotal removal with mechanical vitrectomy   4 T 50 80 ▣
MED: 100-2, 15, 260; 100-3, 80.11; 100-4, 12, 90.3; 100-4, 14, 10

AMA: 1992, Fall, 4

If a procedure performed on the vitreous is unlisted, consult CPT code 67299.

If paracentesis is performed on the anterior chamber of the eye, with removal of the vitreous, consult CPT code 65810. If corneovitreal adhesions are removed, consult CPT code 65880.

67015   Aspiration or release of vitreous, subretinal or choroidal fluid, pars plana approach (posterior sclerotomy)   1 T 50 ▣
MED: 100-2, 15, 260; 100-4, 12, 90.3; 100-4, 14, 10

67025   Injection of vitreous substitute, pars plana or limbal approach, (fluid-gas exchange), with or without aspiration (separate procedure)   1 T 50 ▣
MED: 100-2, 15, 260; 100-4, 12, 90.3; 100-4, 14, 10

67027   Implantation of intravitreal drug delivery system (eg, ganciclovir implant), includes concomitant removal of vitreous   4 T 50 80 ▣
MED: 100-2, 15, 260; 100-3, 80.11; 100-4, 12, 90.3; 100-4, 14, 10

AMA: 1998, Nov, 1; 1997, Nov, 23

If the implant is removed, consult CPT code 67121.

67028   Intravitreal injection of a pharmacologic agent (separate procedure) T 50 ▣

67030   Discission of vitreous strands (without removal), pars plana approach   1 T 50 80 ▣
MED: 100-2, 15, 260; 100-4, 12, 90.3; 100-4, 14, 10

67031   Severing of vitreous strands, vitreous face adhesions, sheets, membranes or opacities, laser surgery (one or more stages)   2 T 50 ▣
MED: 100-2, 15, 260; 100-4, 12, 90.3; 100-4, 14, 10

67036   Vitrectomy, mechanical, pars plana approach;   4 T 50 80 ▣
MED: 100-2, 15, 260; 100-3, 80.11; 100-4, 12, 90.3; 100-4, 14, 10

AMA: 1992, Fall, 6

67038   with epiretinal membrane stripping   5 T 50 80 ▣
MED: 100-2, 15, 260; 100-3, 80.11; 100-4, 12, 90.3; 100-4, 14, 10

67039   with focal endolaser photocoagulation   7 T 50 80 ▣
MED: 100-2, 15, 260; 100-3, 80.11; 100-4, 12, 90.3; 100-4, 14, 10

67040   with endolaser panretinal photocoagulation   7 T 50 80 ▣
MED: 100-2, 15, 260; 100-3, 80.11; 100-4, 12, 90.3; 100-4, 14, 10

If an associated lensectomy is performed, consult CPT code 66850. If the retinal detachment surgery includes a vitrectomy, consult CPT code 67108. If a foreign body is removed, consult CPT codes 65260 and 65265.

To report use of ophthalmic endoscope in conjunction with codes 67038, 67039 or 67040, consult CPT code 66990.

RETINA OR CHOROID — REPAIR

If a diagnostic and treatment program is initiated for ophthalmological services, consult the Medicine and Ophthalmology sections of CPT and CPT code 92002 and subsequent codes. Do not report 69990 in addition to codes 65091-68850 as the operating microscope is considered an inclusive component of these procedures.

If diathermy, cryotherapy, and/or photocoagulation are combined, report the procedure under the principal modality used.

Eye and Ocular Adnexa

67101 — 67112

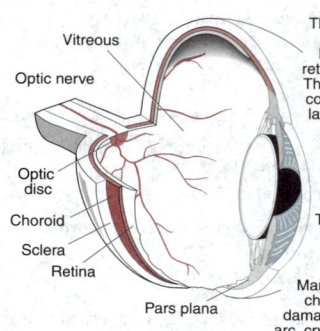

Vitreous

Optic nerve

Optic disc

Choroid

Sclera

Retina

Pars plana

Posterior chamber

The choroid is the vascular layer of the posterior chamber. It provides nourishment to the retina, to which it is firmly attached. The retina is a delicate membrane containing a light-sensitive neural layer fed by the optic nerve. This neural layer can delaminate (known as a detached retina). The optic nerve enters the chamber at the optic disc where the fibers spread throughout the retina. The vitreous is the transparent gel filling the interior of the posterior chamber.

Many surgeries to the posterior chamber center on repairing damage to the retina. Laser, zenon arc, cryoprobe, and diathermal probe are common techniques. Access to the retina is often via the pars plana

67101	**Repair of retinal detachment, one or more sessions; cryotherapy or diathermy, with or without drainage of subretinal fluid**　　T 50 ⬜	
	AMA: 1998, Mar, 7	
67105	**photocoagulation, with or without drainage of subretinal fluid** T 50 ⬜	
	AMA: 1998, Mar, 7	
67107	**Repair of retinal detachment; scleral buckling (such as lamellar scleral dissection, imbrication or encircling procedure), with or without implant, with or without cryotherapy, photocoagulation, and drainage of subretinal fluid**　　5 T 50 80 ⬜	
	MED: 100-2, 15, 260; 100-3, 140.5; 100-4, 12, 90.3; 100-4, 14, 10	
	Gonin's operation	
67108	**with vitrectomy, any method, with or without air or gas tamponade, focal endolaser photocoagulation, cryotherapy, drainage of subretinal fluid, scleral buckling, and/or removal of lens by same technique**　　7 T 50 80 ⬜	
	MED: 100-2, 15, 260; 100-3, 140.5; 100-3, 80.11; 100-4, 12, 90.3; 100-4, 14, 10	
67110	**by injection of air or other gas (eg, pneumatic retinopexy)**　　T 50 ⬜	
67112	**by scleral buckling or vitrectomy, on patient having previous ipsilateral retinal detachment repair(s) using scleral buckling or vitrectomy techniques**　　7 T 50 80 ⬜	
	MED: 100-2, 15, 260; 100-4, 12, 90.3; 100-4, 14, 10	

If subretinal or subchoroidal fluid is aspirated or drained, consult CPT code 67015.

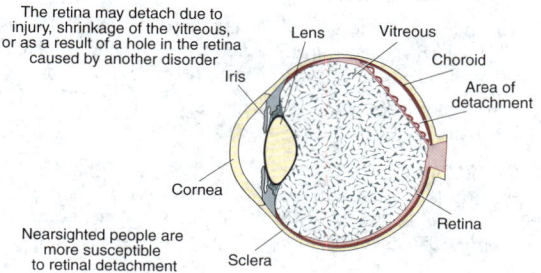

The retina may detach due to injury, shrinkage of the vitreous, or as a result of a hole in the retina caused by another disorder

Lens　Vitreous

Iris

Choroid

Area of detachment

Cornea

Retina

Nearsighted people are more susceptible to retinal detachment

Sclera

In retinal detachment, the photo-sensitive retinal layer of the eye separates from the blood-rich choroid layer; this can damage the retina and lead to blindness if not repaired

| 67115 | Release of encircling material (posterior segment) | 2 T 50 ⬛ |
| | MED: 100-2, 15, 260; 100-4, 12, 90.3; 100-4, 14, 10 | |

| 67120 | Removal of implanted material, posterior segment; extraocular | 2 T 50 ⬛ |
| | MED: 100-2, 15, 260; 100-4, 12, 90.3; 100-4, 14, 10 | |

67121	intraocular	2 T 50 80 ⬛
	MED: 100-2, 15, 260; 100-4, 12, 90.3; 100-4, 14, 10	
	AMA: 1998, Nov, 19; 1997, Nov, 23	

To report removal from anterior segment, consult CPT code 65920.
To report removal of foreign body, consult CPT codes 65260, 65265.

RETINA OR CHOROID — PROPHYLAXIS

If a diagnostic and treatment program is initiated for ophthalmological services, consult the Medicine and Ophthalmology sections of the CPT book and CPT codes 92002 and subsequent codes. Do not report 69990 in addition to codes 65091-68850 as the operating microscope is considered an inclusive component of these procedures.

Codes 67141-67145 are usually provided in multiple sessions or groups of sessions. These codes include all sessions in a defined treatment period.

67141	Prophylaxis of retinal detachment (eg, retinal break, lattice degeneration) without drainage, one or more sessions; cryotherapy, diathermy	2 T 50 ⬛
	MED: 100-2, 15, 260; 100-4, 12, 90.3; 100-4, 14, 10	
	AMA: 1998, Mar, 7	

67145	photocoagulation (laser or xenon arc)	T 50 ⬛
	MED: 100-3, 140.5	
	AMA: 1998, Mar, 7; 1992, Fall, 4	

RETINA OR CHOROID — DESTRUCTION

If a diagnostic and treatment program is initiated for ophthalmological services, consult the Medicine and Ophthalmology sections of the CPT book and CPT codes 92002 and subsequent codes. Do not report 69990 in addition to codes 65091-68850 as the operating microscope is considered an inclusive component of these procedures.

If a procedure performed on the retina is unlisted, consult CPT code 67299.

| 67208 | Destruction of localized lesion of retina (eg, macular edema, tumors), one or more sessions; cryotherapy, diathermy | T 50 ⬛ |
| | AMA: 1998, Nov, 19; 1998, Mar, 7 | |

67210	photocoagulation	T 50 ⬛
	MED: 100-3, 140.5	
	AMA: 1998, Nov, 19; 1998, Mar, 7	

67218	radiation by implantation of source (includes removal of source)	5 T 50 ⬛
	MED: 100-2, 15, 260; 100-4, 12, 90.3; 100-4, 14, 10	
	AMA: 1998, Mar, 7	

67220	Destruction of localized lesion of choroid (eg, choroidal neovascularization); photocoagulation (eg, laser), one or more sessions	T 50 ⬛
	MED: 100-3, 140.5	
	AMA: 2001, Feb, 7; 1999, Nov, 39; 1998, Nov, 19	

To report destruction of macular drusen, photocoagulation, consult CPT Category III code 0017T.
For destruction of localized lesion of choroid by transpupillary thermotherapy, consult CPT Category III code 0016T.

67221   **photodynamic therapy (includes intravenous infusion)**   T ▣

     MED: 100-3, 1, 80.2; 100-3, 45-30

     AMA: 2002, Jun, 10; 2001, Sep, 10; 2001, Feb, 7

+   67225   **photodynamic therapy, second eye, at single session (List separately in addition to code for primary eye treatment)**   T ▣

     MED: 100-3, 45-30

     AMA: 2002, Jun, 10

     Note that 67225 is an add-on code and must be used in conjunction with 67221.

67227   **Destruction of extensive or progressive retinopathy (eg, diabetic retinopathy), one or more sessions; cryotherapy, diathermy**   1 T 50 ▣

     MED: 100-2, 15, 260; 100-4, 12, 90.3; 100-4, 14, 10

     AMA: 1998, Mar, 7

67228   **photocoagulation (laser or xenon arc)**   T 50 ▣

     MED: 100-3, 140.5

     AMA: 1998, Mar, 7

SCLERA — REPAIR

If a diagnostic and treatment program is initiated for ophthalmological services, consult the Medicine and Ophthalmology sections of the CPT book and CPT codes 92002 and subsequent codes. Do not report 69990 in addition to codes 65091-68850 as the operating microscope is considered an inclusive component of these procedures.

If a procedure performed on the retina is unlisted, consult CPT code 67299.

To report excision of a lesion of the sclera, consult CPT code 66130.

67250   **Scleral reinforcement (separate procedure); without graft**   3 T 50 ▣

     MED: 100-2, 15, 260; 100-4, 12, 90.3; 100-4, 14, 10

67255   **with graft**   3 T 50 80 ▣

     MED: 100-2, 15, 260; 100-4, 12, 90.3; 100-4, 14, 10

     If a scleral staphyloma is repaired, consult CPT codes 66220 and 66225.

OTHER PROCEDURES

67299   **Unlisted procedure, posterior segment**   T 50 80

OCULAR ADNEXA

EXTRAOCULAR MUSCLES

If a diagnostic and treatment program is initiated for ophthalmological services, consult the Medicine and Ophthalmology sections of the CPT book and CPT codes 92002 and subsequent codes. Do not report 69990 in addition to codes 65091-68850 as the operating microscope is considered an inclusive component of these procedures.

If adjustable sutures are used, consult CPT code 67335 in addition to primary procedure (67311-67334) used that reflects the number of muscles operated on.

67311   **Strabismus surgery, recession or resection procedure; one horizontal muscle**   3 T 50 ▣

     MED: 100-2, 15, 260; 100-4, 12, 90.3; 100-4, 14, 10

     AMA: 2002, Sep, 10; 1998, Nov, 1; 1997, Mar, 5; 1993, Summer, 20

67312   **two horizontal muscles**   4 T 50 ▣

     MED: 100-2, 15, 260; 100-4, 12, 90.3; 100-4, 14, 10

     AMA: 1997, Mar, 5; 1993, Summer, 20

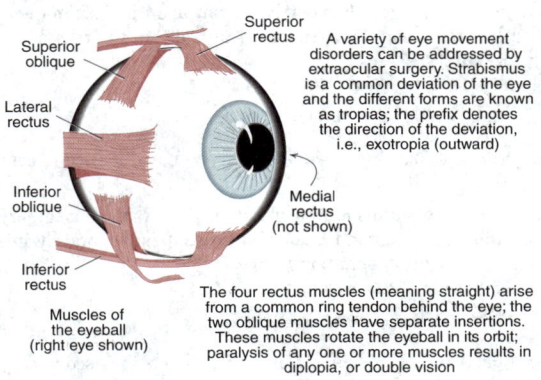

Superior
rectus

Superior
oblique

A variety of eye movement
disorders can be addressed by
extraocular surgery. Strabismus
is a common deviation of the eye
and the different forms are known
as tropias; the prefix denotes
the direction of the deviation,
i.e., exotropia (outward)

Lateral
rectus

Inferior
oblique

Medial
rectus
(not shown)

Inferior
rectus

Muscles of
the eyeball
(right eye shown)

The four rectus muscles (meaning straight) arise
from a common ring tendon behind the eye; the
two oblique muscles have separate insertions.
These muscles rotate the eyeball in its orbit;
paralysis of any one or more muscles results in
diplopia, or double vision

67314   one vertical muscle (excluding superior oblique)
MED: 100-2, 15, 260; 100-4, 12, 90.3; 100-4, 14, 10

AMA: 1997, Mar, 5; 1993, Summer, 20

67316   two or more vertical muscles (excluding superior oblique)
MED: 100-2, 15, 260; 100-4, 12, 90.3; 100-4, 14, 10

AMA: 1997, Mar, 5; 1993, Summer, 20

67318   Strabismus surgery, any procedure, superior oblique muscle
MED: 100-2, 15, 260; 100-4, 12, 90.3; 100-4, 14, 10

AMA: 1998, Nov, 19; 1997, Mar, 5; 1993, Summer, 20

+   67320   Transposition procedure (eg, for paretic extraocular muscle), any
extraocular muscle (specify) (List separately in addition to code for primary
procedure)
MED: 100-2, 15, 260; 100-4, 12, 90.3; 100-4, 14, 10

AMA: 1997, Mar, 5; 1993, Summer, 20

Note that 67320 is an add-on code and must be used in conjunction with
67311-67318.

+   67331   Strabismus surgery on patient with previous eye surgery or injury that did
not involve the extraocular muscles (List separately in addition to code for
primary procedure)
MED: 100-2, 15, 260; 100-4, 12, 90.3; 100-4, 14, 10

AMA: 1997, Mar, 5; 1993, Summer, 20

Note that 67331 is an add-on code and must be used in conjunction with
67311-67318.

+   67332   Strabismus surgery on patient with scarring of extraocular muscles (eg,
prior ocular injury, strabismus or retinal detachment surgery) or restrictive
myopathy (eg, dysthyroid ophthalmopathy) (List separately in addition to
code for primary procedure)
MED: 100-2, 15, 260; 100-4, 12, 90.3; 100-4, 14, 10

AMA: 1997, Mar, 5; 1993, Summer, 20

Note that 67332 is an add-on code and must be used in conjunction with
67311-67318.

\+ **67334** **Strabismus surgery by posterior fixation suture technique, with or without muscle recession (List separately in addition to code for primary procedure)** 4 T

MED: 100-2, 15, 260; 100-4, 12, 90.3; 100-4, 14, 10

AMA: 1997, Mar, 5; 1993, Summer, 20

Note that 67334 is an add-on code and must be used in conjunction with 67311-67318.

\+ **67335** **Placement of adjustable suture(s) during strabismus surgery, including postoperative adjustment(s) of suture(s) (List separately in addition to code for specific strabismus surgery)** 4 T

MED: 100-2, 15, 260; 100-4, 12, 90.3; 100-4, 14, 10

AMA: 1997, Mar, 5; 1993, Summer, 20

Note that 67335 is an add-on code and must be used in conjunction with codes 67311-67334.

\+ **67340** **Strabismus surgery involving exploration and/or repair of detached extraocular muscle(s) (List separately in addition to code for primary procedure)** 4 T

MED: 100-2, 15, 260; 100-4, 12, 90.3; 100-4, 14, 10

AMA: 1997, Mar, 5; 1993, Summer, 20

Note that 67340 is an add-on code and must be used in conjunction with 67311-67334.

Hummelshein operation

67343 **Release of extensive scar tissue without detaching extraocular muscle (separate procedure)** 7 T 50 80

AMA: 1997, Mar, 5; 1993, Summer, 20

Report 67343 in conjunction with 67311-67340, when performed other than on the affected muscle.

67345 **Chemodenervation of extraocular muscle** T 50

AMA: 1997, Mar, 5; 1993, Summer, 20

If chemodenervation is performed for blepharospasm and other neurological disorders, consult CPT codes 64612 and 64613.

EXTRAOCULAR MUSCLES — OTHER PROCEDURES

67350 **Biopsy of extraocular muscle** 1 T 50 80

MED: 100-2, 15, 260; 100-4, 12, 90.3; 100-4, 14, 10

If a wound of the extraocular muscle, tendon, and/or Tenon's capsule is repaired, consult CPT code 65290.

67399 **Unlisted procedure, ocular muscle** T 50 80

ORBIT — EXPLORATION, EXCISION, DECOMPRESSION

If a diagnostic and treatment program is initiated for ophthalmological services, consult the Medicine and Ophthalmology sections of the CPT book and CPT codes 92002 and subsequent codes. Do not report 69990 in addition to codes 65091-68850 as the operating microscope is considered an inclusive component of these procedures.

If an orbitotomy is performed through a transcranial approach, consult CPT codes 61330-61334. If an orbital implant is inserted, consult CPT codes 67550 and 67560. If an eyeball is removed or repaired after removal, consult CPT codes 65091-65175.

67400	**Orbitotomy without bone flap (frontal or transconjunctival approach); for exploration, with or without biopsy** ③ T 50 80 ◪	
	MED: 100-2, 15, 260; 100-4, 12, 90.3; 100-4, 14, 10	
67405	**with drainage only** ④ T 50 80 ◪	
	MED: 100-2, 15, 260; 100-4, 12, 90.3; 100-4, 14, 10	
67412	**with removal of lesion** ⑤ T 50 80 ◪	
	MED: 100-2, 15, 260; 100-4, 12, 90.3; 100-4, 14, 10	
67413	**with removal of foreign body** ⑤ T 50 80 ◪	
	MED: 100-2, 15, 260; 100-4, 12, 90.3; 100-4, 14, 10	
67414	**with removal of bone for decompression** T 50 80 ◪	
	AMA: 1999, Jul, 10	
67415	**Fine needle aspiration of orbital contents** ① T 50 80 ◪	
	MED: 100-2, 15, 260; 100-4, 12, 90.3; 100-4, 14, 10	

If exenteration, enucleation, and repair are performed, consult CPT codes 65101 and subsequent codes. If optic nerve decompression is performed, consult CPT code 67570.

67420	**Orbitotomy with bone flap or window, lateral approach (eg, Kroenlein); with removal of lesion** ⑤ T 50 80 ◪	
	MED: 100-2, 15, 260; 100-4, 12, 90.3; 100-4, 14, 10	
67430	**with removal of foreign body** ⑤ T 50 80 ◪	
	MED: 100-2, 15, 260; 100-4, 12, 90.3; 100-4, 14, 10	
67440	**with drainage** ⑤ T 50 80 ◪	
	MED: 100-2, 15, 260; 100-4, 12, 90.3; 100-4, 14, 10	
67445	**with removal of bone for decompression** ⑤ T 50 80 ◪	

If optic nerve sheath decompression is performed, consult CPT codes 67570.

67450	**for exploration, with or without biopsy** ⑤ T 50 80 ◪	
	MED: 100-2, 15, 260; 100-4, 12, 90.3; 100-4, 14, 10	

ORBIT — OTHER PROCEDURES

If a diagnostic and treatment program is initiated for ophthalmological services, consult the Medicine and Ophthalmology sections of the CPT book and CPT codes 92002 and subsequent codes. Do not report 69990 in addition to codes 65091-68850 as the operating microscope is considered an inclusive component of these procedures.

67500	**Retrobulbar injection; medication (separate procedure, does not include supply of medication)** S 50 ◪	
67505	**alcohol** T 50 ◪	
67515	**Injection of medication or other substance into Tenon's capsule** T 50 ◪	

If a subconjunctival injection is needed, consult CPT code 68200.

67550	**Orbital implant (implant outside muscle cone); insertion** ④ T 50 ◪	
	MED: 100-2, 15, 260; 100-4, 12, 90.3; 100-4, 14, 10	

If an ocular implant is needed (implant inside muscle cone), consult CPT codes 65093-65105 and 65130-65175. If treatment is needed for fractures of the malar area or orbit, consult CPT codes 21355 et seq.

67560	**removal or revision** ② T 50 80 ◪	
	MED: 100-2, 15, 260; 100-4, 12, 90.3; 100-4, 14, 10	

If an ocular implant is needed (implant inside muscle cone), consult CPT codes 65093-65105 and 65130-65175. If treatment is needed for fractures of the malar area or orbit, consult CPT codes 21355 et seq.

Eye and Ocular Adnexa

67570 — 67850

67570	Optic nerve decompression (eg, incision or fenestration of optic nerve sheath)	4 T 50 80 ↰
67599	Unlisted procedure, orbit	T 50 80

EYELIDS — INCISION

67700	Blepharotomy, drainage of abscess, eyelid	T 50 ↰
67710	Severing of tarsorrhaphy	T 50 ↰
67715	Canthotomy (separate procedure)	1 T 50 ↰
	MED: 100-2, 15, 260; 100-4, 12, 90.3; 100-4, 14, 10	

If canthoplasty is performed, consult CPT code 67950. If a division of the symblepharon is performed, consult CPT code 68340.

EYELIDS — EXCISION

These codes include the lid margin, palpebral conjunctiva, and tarsus.

If a diagnostic and treatment program is initiated for ophthalmological services, consult the Medicine and Ophthalmology sections of the CPT book and CPT codes 92002 and subsequent codes. Do not report 69990 in addition to codes 65091-68850 as the operating microscope is considered an inclusive component of these procedures.

If a lesion involving mainly the skin of the eyelid is removed, consult CPT codes 11310-11313, 11400-11446, 11640-11646, and 17000-17004.

To report repair of wounds, blepharoplasty, grafts and reconstructive surgery, consult CPT codes 67930-67975.

67800	Excision of chalazion; single	T ↰
	AMA: 1999, Sep, 10	
67801	multiple, same lid	T ↰
67805	multiple, different lids	T ↰
	AMA: 1999, Sep, 10	
67808	under general anesthesia and/or requiring hospitalization, single or multiple	2 T ↰
	MED: 100-2, 15, 260; 100-4, 12, 90.3; 100-4, 14, 10	
67810	Biopsy of eyelid	T 50 ↰
67820	Correction of trichiasis; epilation, by forceps only	S 50 ↰
	AMA: 1998, Jul, 1	
67825	epilation by other than forceps (eg, by electrosurgery, cryotherapy, laser surgery)	T 50 ↰
	AMA: 1998, Jul, 10	
67830	incision of lid margin	2 T 50 ↰
	MED: 100-2, 15, 260; 100-4, 12, 90.3; 100-4, 14, 10	
67835	incision of lid margin, with free mucous membrane graft	2 T 50 ↰
	MED: 100-2, 15, 260; 100-4, 12, 90.3; 100-4, 14, 10	
67840	Excision of lesion of eyelid (except chalazion) without closure or with simple direct closure	T 50 ↰

If an eyelid is excised and repaired by reconstructive surgery, consult CPT codes 67961 and 67966.

67850	Destruction of lesion of lid margin (up to 1 cm)	T 50 ↰

If Mohs micrographic surgery is performed, consult CPT codes 17304-17310. Report the appropriate E/M office visit codes for initiation or follow-up care of topical chemotherapy administration.

EYELIDS — TARSORRHAPHY

If a diagnostic and treatment program is initiated for ophthalmological services, consult the Medicine and Ophthalmology sections of the CPT book and CPT codes 92002 and subsequent codes. Do not report 69990 in addition to codes 65091-68850 as the operating microscope is considered an inclusive component of these procedures.

| 67875 | Temporary closure of eyelids by suture (eg, Frost suture) | T 50 CCI |
| 67880 | Construction of intermarginal adhesions, median tarsorrhaphy, or canthorrhaphy; | 3 T 50 CCI |

MED: 100-2, 15, 260; 100-4, 12, 90.3; 100-4, 14, 10

| 67882 | with transposition of tarsal plate | 3 T 50 CCI |

MED: 100-2, 15, 260; 100-4, 12, 90.3; 100-4, 14, 10

If severing of the tarsorrhaphy occurs, consult CPT codes 67710. If canthoplasty is performed for reconstruction of the canthus, consult CPTcode 67950. If a canthotomy is performed, consult CPT code 67715.

EYELIDS — REPAIR (BROW PTOSIS, BLEPHAROPTOSIS, LID RETRACTION, ECTROPION, ENTROPION)

If a diagnostic and treatment program is initiated for ophthalmological services, consult the Medicine and Ophthalmology sections of the CPT book and CPT codes 92002 and subsequent codes. Do not report 69990 in addition to codes 65091-68850 as the operating microscope is considered an inclusive component of these procedures.

| 67900 | Repair of brow ptosis (supraciliary, mid-forehead or coronal approach) | 4 T 50 CCI |

MED: 100-2, 15, 260; 100-4, 12, 90.3; 100-4, 14, 10

If a rhytidectomy is performed on the forehead, consult CPT code 15824.

▲ | 67901 | Repair of blepharoptosis; frontalis muscle technique with suture or other material (eg, banked fascia) | 5 T 50 CCI |

MED: 100-2, 15, 260; 100-4, 12, 90.3; 100-4, 14, 10

AMA: 2000, Sep, 7

▲ | 67902 | frontalis muscle technique with autologous fascial sling (includes obtaining fascia) | 5 T 50 CCI |

MED: 100-2, 15, 260; 100-4, 12, 90.3; 100-4, 14, 10

AMA: 2000, Sep, 7

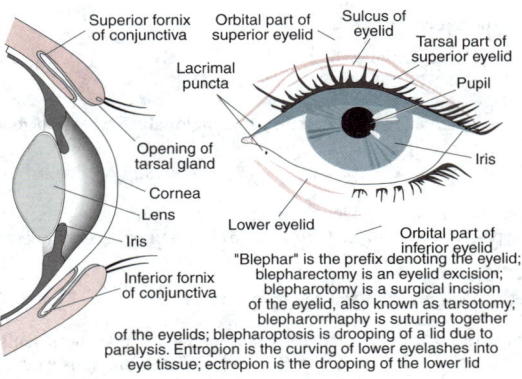

"Blephar" is the prefix denoting the eyelid; blepharectomy is an eyelid excision; blepharotomy is a surgical incision of the eyelid, also known as tarsotomy; blepharorrhaphy is suturing together of the eyelids; blepharoptosis is drooping of a lid due to paralysis. Entropion is the curving of lower eyelashes into eye tissue; ectropion is the drooping of the lower lid

67903   (tarso)levator resection or advancement, internal approach 4 T 50 ▣
MED: 100-2, 15, 260; 100-4, 12, 90.3; 100-4, 14, 10

AMA: 2000, Sep, 7

67904   (tarso)levator resection or advancement, external approach 4 T 50 ▣
MED: 100-2, 15, 260; 100-4, 12, 90.3; 100-4, 14, 10

AMA: 2000, Sep, 7

Everbusch's operation

67906   superior rectus technique with fascial sling (includes obtaining
fascia)   5 T 50 ▣
MED: 100-2, 15, 260; 100-4, 12, 90.3; 100-4, 14, 10

AMA: 2000, Sep, 7

67908   conjunctivo-tarso-Muller's muscle-levator resection (eg, Fasanella-
Servat type)   4 T 50 ▣
MED: 100-2, 15, 260; 100-4, 12, 90.3; 100-4, 14, 10

AMA: 2000, Sep, 7

67909 Reduction of overcorrection of ptosis   4 T 50 ▣
MED: 100-2, 15, 260; 100-4, 12, 90.3; 100-4, 14, 10

67911 Correction of lid retraction   3 T 50 ▣
MED: 100-2, 15, 260; 100-4, 12, 90.3; 100-4, 14, 10

67912 Correction of lagophthalmos, with implantation of upper eyelid lid load
(eg, gold weight)   3 T 50 ▣

67914 Repair of ectropion; suture   3 T 50 ▣
MED: 100-2, 15, 260; 100-4, 12, 90.3; 100-4, 14, 10

67915   thermocauterization   T 50 ▣

67916   excision tarsal wedge   4 T 50 ▣
MED: 100-2, 15, 260; 100-4, 12, 90.3; 100-4, 14, 10

67917   extensive (eg, tarsal strip operations)   4 T 50 ▣
MED: 100-2, 15, 260; 100-4, 12, 90.3; 100-4, 14, 10

To report correction of everted punctum, consult CPT code 68705.

67921 Repair of entropion; suture   3 T 50 ▣
MED: 100-2, 15, 260; 100-4, 12, 90.3; 100-4, 14, 10

67922   thermocauterization   T 50 ▣

67923   excision tarsal wedge   4 T 50 ▣
MED: 100-2, 15, 260; 100-4, 12, 90.3; 100-4, 14, 10

67924   extensive (eg, tarsal strip or capsulopalpebral fascia repairs
operation)   4 T 50 ▣
MED: 100-2, 15, 260; 100-4, 12, 90.3; 100-4, 14, 10

If a cicatricial ectropion or an entropion requiring scar excision or skin graft is
repaired, consult also CPT codes 67961 and subsequent codes.

EYELIDS — RECONSTRUCTION
These codes include the lid margin, palpebral conjunctiva, and tarsus.

If a diagnostic and treatment program is initiated for ophthalmological services, consult the Medicine
and Ophthalmology sections of the CPT book and CPT codes 92002 and subsequent codes. Do not

report 69990 in addition to codes 65091-68850 as the operating microscope is considered an inclusive component of these procedures.

If the skin of the eyelid is repaired, consult CPT codes 12011-12018, 12051-12057, 13150, and 13153. If tarsorrhaphy or canthorrhaphy is performed, consult CPT codes 67880 and 67882. If blepharoptosis and lid retraction is repaired, consult CPT codes 67901-67911.

To report blepharoplasty for entropion/ectropion, consult CPT codes 67916, 67917, 67923 and 67924. To report correction of blepharochalasis, consult CPT codes 15820-15823. To repair skin of eyelid with adjacent tissue transfer, consult CPT codes 14060, 14061; preparation of graft, see 15000; free graft, see 15120, 15121, 15260, and 15261.

To report excision of lesion of eyelid, consult CPT code 67800 and subsequent codes. To report repair of lacrimal canaliculi, consult CPT code 68700.

67930	**Suture of recent wound, eyelid, involving lid margin, tarsus, and/or palpebral conjunctiva direct closure; partial thickness**	T 50 ↵
67935	**full thickness**	2 T 50 ↵
	MED: 100-2, 15, 260; 100-4, 12, 90.3; 100-4, 14, 10	
67938	**Removal of embedded foreign body, eyelid**	S 50 ↵
67950	**Canthoplasty (reconstruction of canthus)**	2 T 50 ↵
	MED: 100-2, 15, 260; 100-4, 12, 90.3; 100-4, 14, 10	
67961	**Excision and repair of eyelid, involving lid margin, tarsus, conjunctiva, canthus, or full thickness, may include preparation for skin graft or pedicle flap with adjacent tissue transfer or rearrangement; up to one-fourth of lid margin**	3 T 50 ↵
	MED: 100-2, 15, 260; 100-4, 12, 90.3; 100-4, 14, 10	
67966	**over one-fourth of lid margin**	3 T 50 ↵
	MED: 100-2, 15, 260; 100-4, 12, 90.3; 100-4, 14, 10	
67971	**Reconstruction of eyelid, full thickness by transfer of tarsoconjunctival flap from opposing eyelid; up to two-thirds of eyelid, one stage or first stage**	3 T 50 ↵
	MED: 100-2, 15, 260; 100-4, 12, 90.3; 100-4, 14, 10	
	Dupuy-Dutemp reconstruction	
67973	**total eyelid, lower, one stage or first stage**	3 T 50 ↵
	MED: 100-2, 15, 260; 100-4, 12, 90.3; 100-4, 14, 10	
67974	**total eyelid, upper, one stage or first stage**	3 T 50 ↵
	MED: 100-2, 15, 260; 100-4, 12, 90.3; 100-4, 14, 10	
	Landboldt's operation	
67975	**second stage**	3 T 50 80 ↵
	MED: 100-2, 15, 260; 100-4, 12, 90.3; 100-4, 14, 10	
	Landboldt's operation	

EYELIDS — OTHER PROCEDURES

| 67999 | **Unlisted procedure, eyelids** | T 50 |

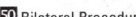

CONJUNCTIVA

INCISION AND DRAINAGE

If a foreign body is removed, consult CPT codes 65205 and subsequent codes.

If a diagnostic and treatment program is initiated for ophthalmological services, consult the Medicine and Ophthalmology sections of the CPT book and CPT codes 92002 and subsequent codes. Do not report 69990 in addition to codes 65091-68850 as the operating microscope is considered an inclusive component of these procedures.

| 68020 | Incision of conjunctiva, drainage of cyst | T 50 |
| 68040 | Expression of conjunctival follicles, eg, for trachoma | S 50 |

EXCISION AND/OR DESTRUCTION

If a diagnostic and treatment program is initiated for ophthalmological services, consult the Medicine and Ophthalmology sections of the CPT book and CPT codes 92002 and subsequent codes. Do not report 69990 in addition to codes 65091-68850 as the operating microscope is considered an inclusive component of these procedures.

68100	Biopsy of conjunctiva	T 50
68110	Excision of lesion, conjunctiva; up to 1 cm	T 50
68115	over 1 cm	2 T 50
	MED: 100-2, 15, 260; 100-4, 12, 90.3; 100-4, 14, 10	
68130	with adjacent sclera	2 T 50
	MED: 100-2, 15, 260; 100-4, 12, 90.3; 100-4, 14, 10	
68135	Destruction of lesion, conjunctiva	T 50

INJECTION

| 68200 | Subconjunctival injection | S 50 |

If an injection is made into the Tenon's capsule or if a retrobulbar injection is needed, consult CPT codes 67500-67515.

CONJUNCTIVOPLASTY

If a diagnostic and treatment program is initiated for ophthalmological services, consult the Medicine and Ophthalmology sections of the CPT book and CPT codes 92002 and subsequent codes. Do not report 69990 in addition to codes 65091-68850 as the operating microscope is considered an inclusive component of these procedures.

If a wound is repaired, consult CPT codes 65270-65273.

68320	Conjunctivoplasty; with conjunctival graft or extensive rearrangement	4 T 50
	MED: 100-2, 15, 260; 100-4, 12, 90.3; 100-4, 14, 10	
68325	with buccal mucous membrane graft (includes obtaining graft)	4 T 50
	MED: 100-2, 15, 260; 100-4, 12, 90.3; 100-4, 14, 10	
68326	Conjunctivoplasty, reconstruction cul-de-sac; with conjunctival graft or extensive rearrangement	4 T 50
	MED: 100-2, 15, 260; 100-4, 12, 90.3; 100-4, 14, 10	
68328	with buccal mucous membrane graft (includes obtaining graft)	4 T 50
	MED: 100-2, 15, 260; 100-4, 12, 90.3; 100-4, 14, 10	
68330	Repair of symblepharon; conjunctivoplasty, without graft	4 T 50
	MED: 100-2, 15, 260; 100-4, 12, 90.3; 100-4, 14, 10	

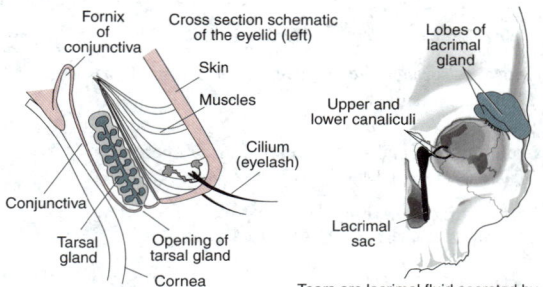

Fornix of conjunctiva

Cross section schematic of the eyelid (left)

Skin

Muscles

Cilium (eyelash)

Conjunctiva

Tarsal gland

Opening of tarsal gland

Cornea

Lobes of lacrimal gland

Upper and lower canaliculi

Lacrimal sac

The eyelid is a moveable fold covered by skin externally and highly vascularized conjunctiva internally. The tarsal glands secrete lubricant to the edges of the eyelid

Tears are lacrimal fluid secreted by the almond-sized lacrimal gland through ducts into the fornix of the conjunctiva; fluid is drained through the puncta and into the lacrimal sac and into the nose

| 68335 | with free graft conjunctiva or buccal mucous membrane (includes obtaining graft) | 4 T 50 |
| | MED: 100-2, 15, 260; 100-4, 12, 90.3; 100-4, 14, 10 | |

| 68340 | division of symblepharon, with or without insertion of conformer or contact lens | 4 T 50 |
| | MED: 100-2, 15, 260; 100-4, 12, 90.3; 100-4, 14, 10 | |

OTHER PROCEDURES

| 68360 | Conjunctival flap; bridge or partial (separate procedure) | 2 T 50 |
| | MED: 100-2, 15, 260; 100-4, 12, 90.3; 100-4, 14, 10 | |

| 68362 | total (such as Gunderson thin flap or purse string flap) | 2 T 50 |
| | MED: 100-2, 15, 260; 100-4, 12, 90.3; 100-4, 14, 10 | |

If a conjunctival flap is used for a perforating injury, consult CPT codes 65280 and 65285. If an operative wound is repaired, consult CPT code 66250. If a conjunctival foreign body is removed, consult CPT codes 65205 and 65210.

| 68371 | Harvesting conjunctival allograft, living donor | 2 T 50 |

| 68399 | Unlisted procedure, conjunctiva | T 50 |

LACRIMAL SYSTEM — INCISION

| 68400 | Incision, drainage of lacrimal gland | T 50 |

| 68420 | Incision, drainage of lacrimal sac (dacryocystotomy or dacryocystostomy) | T 50 |

| 68440 | Snip incision of lacrimal punctum | T 50 |

LACRIMAL SYSTEM — EXCISION

| 68500 | Excision of lacrimal gland (dacryoadenectomy), except for tumor; total | 3 T 50 |
| | MED: 100-2, 15, 260; 100-4, 12, 90.3; 100-4, 14, 10 | |

| 68505 | partial | 3 T 50 |
| | MED: 100-2, 15, 260; 100-4, 12, 90.3; 100-4, 14, 10 | |

| 68510 | Biopsy of lacrimal gland | 1 T 50 |
| | MED: 100-2, 15, 260; 100-4, 12, 90.3; 100-4, 14, 10 | |

| 68520 | Excision of lacrimal sac (dacryocystectomy) | 3 T 50 |
| | MED: 100-2, 15, 260; 100-4, 12, 90.3; 100-4, 14, 10 | |

Eye and Ocular Adnexa

68525 — 68850

68525	Biopsy of lacrimal sac	1 T 50
	MED: 100-2, 15, 260; 100-4, 12, 90.3; 100-4, 14, 10	
68530	Removal of foreign body or dacryolith, lacrimal passages	T 50
	Meller's excision	
68540	Excision of lacrimal gland tumor; frontal approach	3 T 50
	MED: 100-2, 15, 260; 100-4, 12, 90.3; 100-4, 14, 10	
68550	involving osteotomy	3 T 50
	MED: 100-2, 15, 260; 100-4, 12, 90.3; 100-4, 14, 10	

LACRIMAL SYSTEM — REPAIR

68700	Plastic repair of canaliculi	2 T 50
	MED: 100-2, 15, 260; 100-4, 12, 90.3; 100-4, 14, 10	
68705	Correction of everted punctum, cautery	T 50
68720	Dacryocystorhinostomy (fistulization of lacrimal sac to nasal cavity)	4 T 50
	MED: 100-2, 15, 260; 100-4, 12, 90.3; 100-4, 14, 10	
	AMA: 2001, Sep, 10	
68745	Conjunctivorhinostomy (fistulization of conjunctiva to nasal cavity); without tube	4 T 50
	MED: 100-2, 15, 260; 100-4, 12, 90.3; 100-4, 14, 10	
68750	with insertion of tube or stent	4 T 50
	MED: 100-2, 15, 260; 100-4, 12, 90.3; 100-4, 14, 10	
68760	Closure of the lacrimal punctum; by thermocauterization, ligation, or laser surgery	S 50
68761	by plug, each	S 50 80
	AMA: 1996, Jun, 1	
68770	Closure of lacrimal fistula (separate procedure)	4 T 50
	MED: 100-2, 15, 260; 100-4, 12, 90.3; 100-4, 14, 10	

LACRIMAL SYSTEM — PROBING AND/OR RELATED PROCEDURES

68801	Dilation of lacrimal punctum, with or without irrigation	S 50
68810	Probing of nasolacrimal duct, with or without irrigation;	1 S 50
	MED: 100-2, 15, 260; 100-4, 12, 90.3; 100-4, 14, 10	
	AMA: 2002, Nov, 11	
68811	requiring general anesthesia	2 T 50
	MED: 100-2, 15, 260; 100-4, 12, 90.3; 100-4, 14, 10	
	AMA: 2002, Nov, 11	
68815	with insertion of tube or stent	2 T 50
	MED: 100-2, 15, 260; 100-4, 12, 90.3; 100-4, 14, 10	
	AMA: 2002, Nov, 11	
	Consult also CPT code 92018.	
68840	Probing of lacrimal canaliculi, with or without irrigation	S 50
68850	Injection of contrast medium for dacryocystography	N 50
	AMA: 2001, Feb, 7	
	If radiological supervision and interpretation is needed, consult CPT codes 70170, 78660.	

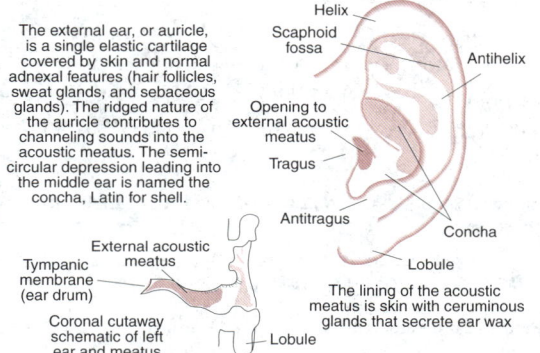

The external ear, or auricle, is a single elastic cartilage covered by skin and normal adnexal features (hair follicles, sweat glands, and sebaceous glands). The ridged nature of the auricle contributes to channeling sounds into the acoustic meatus. The semi-circular depression leading into the middle ear is named the concha, Latin for shell.

Helix
Scaphoid fossa
Antihelix
Opening to external acoustic meatus
Tragus
Antitragus
Concha
Lobule

The lining of the acoustic meatus is skin with ceruminous glands that secrete ear wax

Tympanic membrane (ear drum)
External acoustic meatus
Coronal cutaway schematic of left ear and meatus
Lobule

LACRIMAL SYSTEM — OTHER PROCEDURES

68899   **Unlisted procedure, lacrimal system**   S 50

AUDITORY SYSTEM

EXTERNAL EAR

INCISION

If diagnostic services are performed (e.g., audiometry, vestibular tests), consult CPT codes 92502 and subsequent codes.

69000   **Drainage external ear, abscess or hematoma; simple**   T ↻
AMA: 1999, Oct, 10; 1997, Oct, 11

69005   **complicated**   T ↻

69020   **Drainage external auditory canal, abscess**   T ↻
AMA: 1997, Oct, 11

69090   **Ear piercing**   E
MED: 100-2, 16, 10

EXCISION

69100   **Biopsy external ear**   T ↻

69105   **Biopsy external auditory canal**   T ↻

69110   **Excision external ear; partial, simple repair**   1 T ↻
MED: 100-2, 15, 260; 100-4, 12, 90.3; 100-4, 14, 10

69120   **complete amputation**   2 T ↻
MED: 100-2, 15, 260; 100-4, 12, 90.3; 100-4, 14, 10

If the ear is reconstructed, consult CPT codes 15120 and subsequent codes.

69140   **Excision exostosis(es), external auditory canal**   2 T 80 ↻
MED: 100-2, 15, 260; 100-4, 12, 90.3; 100-4, 14, 10

69145   **Excision soft tissue lesion, external auditory canal**   2 T ↻
MED: 100-2, 15, 260; 100-4, 12, 90.3; 100-4, 14, 10

69150   **Radical excision external auditory canal lesion; without neck dissection**   3 T ↻
MED: 100-2, 15, 260; 100-4, 12, 90.3; 100-4, 14, 10

Eye and Ocular Adnexa

69155 — 69420

69155	with neck dissection	C 80
	If skin grafting is necessary, consult CPT codes 15000-15261.	
	If the temporal bone is resected, consult CPT code 69535.	

REMOVAL OF FOREIGN BODY

If diagnostic services are performed (e.g., audiometry, vestibular tests), consult CPT codes 92502 and subsequent codes.

69200	**Removal foreign body from external auditory canal; without general anesthesia**	X
69205	**with general anesthesia**	1 T
	MED: 100-2, 15, 260; 100-4, 12, 90.3; 100-4, 14, 10	
69210	**Removal impacted cerumen (separate procedure), one or both ears**	X
69220	**Debridement, mastoidectomy cavity, simple (eg, routine cleaning)**	T 50
69222	**Debridement, mastoidectomy cavity, complex (eg, with anesthesia or more than routine cleaning)**	T 50

REPAIR

If a wound or injury of the external ear is sutured, consult CPT codes 12011-14300.

If diagnostic services are performed (e.g., audiometry, vestibular tests), consult CPT codes 92502 and subsequent codes.

69300	**Otoplasty, protruding ear, with or without size reduction**	3 T 50 80
	MED: 100-2, 15, 260; 100-4, 12, 90.3; 100-4, 14, 10	
69310	**Reconstruction of external auditory canal (meatoplasty) (eg, for stenosis due to injury, infection) (separate procedure)**	3 T
	MED: 100-2, 15, 260; 100-4, 12, 90.3; 100-4, 14, 10	
69320	**Reconstruction external auditory canal for congenital atresia, single stage**	7 T 80
	MED: 100-2, 15, 260; 100-4, 12, 90.3; 100-4, 14, 10	

To report procedure performed in conjunction with middle ear reconstruction, consult CPT codes 69631 and 69641. To report other reconstruction procedures with grafts, consult CPT codes 13150-15760 and 21230-21235.

OTHER PROCEDURES

If diagnostic services are performed (e.g., audiometry, vestibular tests), consult CPT codes 92502 and subsequent codes.

If otoscopy is performed under general anesthesia, consult CPT code 92502.

| 69399 | **Unlisted procedure, external ear** | T 80 |

MIDDLE EAR

INTRODUCTION

69400	**Eustachian tube inflation, transnasal; with catheterization**	T
69401	**without catheterization**	T
69405	**Eustachian tube catheterization, transtympanic**	T 80
~~69410~~	~~Focal application of phase control substance, middle ear (baffle technique)~~	

INCISION

| 69420 | **Myringotomy including aspiration and/or eustachian tube inflation** | T 50 |

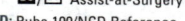 

69421 **Myringotomy including aspiration and/or eustachian tube inflation requiring general anesthesia** 〔3〕〔T〕〔50〕〔↩〕
MED: 100-2, 15, 260; 100-4, 12, 90.3; 100-4, 14, 10

69424 **Ventilating tube removal requiring general anesthesia** 〔T〕〔50〕〔↩〕

Do not report 69424 in addition to CPT codes 69205, 69210, 69420, 69421, 69433-69676, 69710-69745, 69801-69930.

This is a unilateral procedure. To report this procedure performed bilaterally, append modifier 50.

69433 **Tympanostomy (requiring insertion of ventilating tube), local or topical anesthesia** 〔T〕〔50〕〔↩〕

69436 **Tympanostomy (requiring insertion of ventilating tube), general anesthesia** 〔3〕〔T〕〔50〕〔↩〕
MED: 100-2, 15, 260; 100-4, 12, 90.3; 100-4, 14, 10

69440 **Middle ear exploration through postauricular or ear canal incision** 〔3〕〔T〕〔50〕〔↩〕
MED: 100-2, 15, 260; 100-4, 12, 90.3; 100-4, 14, 10

If an atticotomy is performed, consult CPT codes 69601 and subsequent codes.

69450 **Tympanolysis, transcanal** 〔1〕〔T〕〔50〕〔↩〕
MED: 100-2, 15, 260; 100-4, 12, 90.3; 100-4, 14, 10

EXCISION

69501 **Transmastoid antrotomy (simple mastoidectomy)** 〔7〕〔T〕〔50〕〔↩〕
MED: 100-2, 15, 260; 100-4, 12, 90.3; 100-4, 14, 10

69502 **Mastoidectomy; complete** 〔7〕〔T〕〔50〕〔↩〕
MED: 100-2, 15, 260; 100-4, 12, 90.3; 100-4, 14, 10

69505 **modified radical** 〔7〕〔T〕〔50〕〔↩〕
MED: 100-2, 15, 260; 100-4, 12, 90.3; 100-4, 14, 10

69511 **radical** 〔7〕〔T〕〔50〕〔↩〕
MED: 100-2, 15, 260; 100-4, 12, 90.3; 100-4, 14, 10

If a skin graft is needed, consult CPT codes 15000 and subsequent codes. If debridement is performed on the mastoidectomy cavity, consult CPT codes 69220 and 69222.

69530 **Petrous apicectomy including radical mastoidectomy** 〔7〕〔T〕〔50〕〔↩〕
MED: 100-2, 15, 260; 100-4, 12, 90.3; 100-4, 14, 10

69535 **Resection temporal bone, external approach** 〔C〕〔50〕〔↩〕

If a middle fossa approach is used, consult CPT codes 69950-69970.

69540 **Excision aural polyp** 〔T〕〔50〕〔↩〕

69550 **Excision aural glomus tumor; transcanal** 〔5〕〔T〕〔50〕〔↩〕
MED: 100-2, 15, 260; 100-4, 12, 90.3; 100-4, 14, 10

69552 **transmastoid** 〔7〕〔T〕〔50〕〔↩〕
MED: 100-2, 15, 260; 100-4, 12, 90.3; 100-4, 14, 10

69554 **extended (extratemporal)** 〔C〕〔50〕〔↩〕

Eye and Ocular Adnexa

69601 — 69633

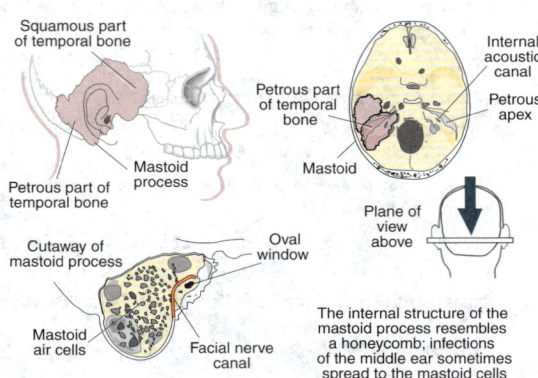

The internal structure of the mastoid process resembles a honeycomb; infections of the middle ear sometimes spread to the mastoid cells

REPAIR

69601   **Revision mastoidectomy; resulting in complete mastoidectomy** 7 T 50 ↻
MED: 100-2, 15, 260; 100-4, 12, 90.3; 100-4, 14, 10

69602   **resulting in modified radical mastoidectomy**   7 T 50 ↻
MED: 100-2, 15, 260; 100-4, 12, 90.3; 100-4, 14, 10

69603   **resulting in radical mastoidectomy**   7 T 50 ↻
MED: 100-2, 15, 260; 100-4, 12, 90.3; 100-4, 14, 10

69604   **resulting in tympanoplasty**   7 T 50 ↻
MED: 100-2, 15, 260; 100-4, 12, 90.3; 100-4, 14, 10

If a secondary tympanoplasty is planned after mastoidectomy, consult CPT codes 69631 and 69632.

69605   **with apicectomy**   7 T 50 ↻
MED: 100-2, 15, 260; 100-4, 12, 90.3; 100-4, 14, 10

If a skin graft is performed, consult CPT codes 15120, 15121, 15260, and 15261.

69610   **Tympanic membrane repair, with or without site preparation of perforation for closure, with or without patch**   T 50 ↻
AMA: 2001, Mar, 10

69620   **Myringoplasty (surgery confined to drumhead and donor area)** 2 T 50 ↻
MED: 100-2, 15, 260; 100-4, 12, 90.3; 100-4, 14, 10

AMA: 2001, Mar, 10

69631   **Tympanoplasty without mastoidectomy (including canalplasty, atticotomy and/or middle ear surgery), initial or revision; without ossicular chain reconstruction**   5 T 50 ↻
MED: 100-2, 15, 260; 100-4, 12, 90.3; 100-4, 14, 10

AMA: 2001, Mar, 10; 1998, Jul, 11

69632   **with ossicular chain reconstruction (eg, postfenestration)** 5 T 50 ↻
MED: 100-2, 15, 260; 100-4, 12, 90.3; 100-4, 14, 10

69633   **with ossicular chain reconstruction and synthetic prosthesis (eg, partial ossicular replacement prosthesis, (PORP), total ossicular replacement prosthesis (TORP))**   5 T 50 ↻
MED: 100-2, 15, 260; 100-4, 12, 90.3; 100-4, 14, 10

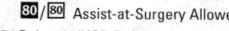

26 / TC Professional/Technical Component   80 / 80 Assist-at-Surgery Allowed/With Documentation   ⊙ Conscious Sedation
Unlisted   Not Covered   **MED:** Pubs 100/NCD Reference   1 - 9 ASC Group   63 Modifier 63 Exempt
492 — Surgery   CPT only © 2005 American Medical Association. All Rights Reserved. *(Black Ink)*   © 2005 Ingenix, Inc. *(Blue Ink)*

69635   **Tympanoplasty with antrotomy or mastoidotomy (including canalplasty, atticotomy, middle ear surgery, and/or tympanic membrane repair); without ossicular chain reconstruction**   7 T 50 ↻
MED: 100-2, 15, 260; 100-4, 12, 90.3; 100-4, 14, 10

69636   **with ossicular chain reconstruction**   7 T 50 ↻
MED: 100-2, 15, 260; 100-4, 12, 90.3; 100-4, 14, 10

69637   **with ossicular chain reconstruction and synthetic prosthesis (eg, partial ossicular replacement prosthesis, (PORP), total ossicular replacement prosthesis (TORP))**   7 T 50 ↻
MED: 100-2, 15, 260; 100-4, 12, 90.3; 100-4, 14, 10

69641   **Tympanoplasty with mastoidectomy (including canalplasty, middle ear surgery, tympanic membrane repair); without ossicular chain reconstruction**   7 T 50 ↻
MED: 100-2, 15, 260; 100-4, 12, 90.3; 100-4, 14, 10

69642   **with ossicular chain reconstruction**   7 T 50 ↻
MED: 100-2, 15, 260; 100-4, 12, 90.3; 100-4, 14, 10

69643   **with intact or reconstructed wall, without ossicular chain reconstruction**   7 T 50 ↻
MED: 100-2, 15, 260; 100-4, 12, 90.3; 100-4, 14, 10

69644   **with intact or reconstructed canal wall, with ossicular chain reconstruction**   7 T 50 ↻
MED: 100-2, 15, 260; 100-4, 12, 90.3; 100-4, 14, 10

69645   **radical or complete, without ossicular chain reconstruction**   7 T 50 ↻
MED: 100-2, 15, 260; 100-4, 12, 90.3; 100-4, 14, 10

69646   **radical or complete, with ossicular chain reconstruction**   7 T 50 ↻
MED: 100-2, 15, 260; 100-4, 12, 90.3; 100-4, 14, 10

69650   **Stapes mobilization**   7 T 50 ↻
MED: 100-2, 15, 260; 100-4, 12, 90.3; 100-4, 14, 10

69660   **Stapedectomy or stapedotomy with reestablishment of ossicular continuity, with or without use of foreign material;**   5 T 50 ↻
MED: 100-2, 15, 260; 100-4, 12, 90.3; 100-4, 14, 10

69661   **with footplate drill out**   5 T 50 ↻
MED: 100-2, 15, 260; 100-4, 12, 90.3; 100-4, 14, 10

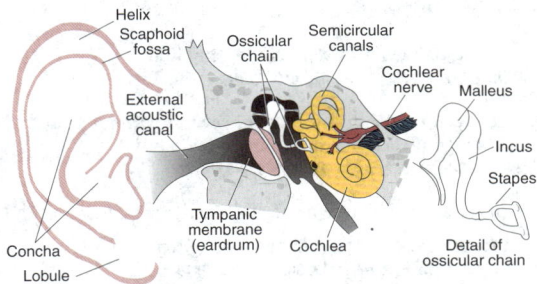

The tympanic membrane is a thin, sensitive tissue and is the gateway to the middle ear; the membrane vibrates in response to sound waves and the movement is transmitted via the ossicular chain to the internal ear. Many surgeries to the middle ear involve repair to the tympanic membrane and reconstruction to the various components of the ossicular chain

Eye and Ocular Adnexa

69662 — 69799

69662	**Revision of stapedectomy or stapedotomy** MED: 100-2, 15, 260; 100-4, 12, 90.3; 100-4, 14, 10	5 T 50
69666	**Repair oval window fistula** MED: 100-2, 15, 260; 100-4, 12, 90.3; 100-4, 14, 10	4 T 50
69667	**Repair round window fistula** MED: 100-2, 15, 260; 100-4, 12, 90.3; 100-4, 14, 10	4 T 50
69670	**Mastoid obliteration (separate procedure)** MED: 100-2, 15, 260; 100-4, 12, 90.3; 100-4, 14, 10	3 T 50
69676	**Tympanic neurectomy** MED: 100-2, 15, 260; 100-4, 12, 90.3; 100-4, 14, 10	3 T 50

OTHER PROCEDURES

69700	**Closure postauricular fistula, mastoid (separate procedure)** MED: 100-2, 15, 260; 100-4, 12, 90.3; 100-4, 14, 10	3 T 50
69710	**Implantation or replacement of electromagnetic bone conduction hearing device in temporal bone**	E

The replacement procedure includes the removal of the old device.

69711	**Removal or repair of electromagnetic bone conduction hearing device in temporal bone** MED: 100-2, 15, 260; 100-4, 12, 90.3; 100-4, 14, 10	1 T 50
69714	**Implantation, osseointegrated implant, temporal bone, with percutaneous attachment to external speech processor/cochlear stimulator; without mastoidectomy** MED: 100-2, 15, 260; 100-4, 12, 90.3; 100-4, 14, 10	9 T 50
69715	**with mastoidectomy** MED: 100-2, 15, 260; 100-4, 12, 90.3; 100-4, 14, 10	9 T 50
69717	**Replacement (including removal of existing device), osseointegrated implant, temporal bone, with percutaneous attachment to external speech processor/cochlear stimulator; without mastoidectomy** MED: 100-2, 15, 260; 100-4, 12, 90.3; 100-4, 14, 10	9 T 50
69718	**with mastoidectomy** MED: 100-2, 15, 260; 100-4, 12, 90.3; 100-4, 14, 10	9 T 50
69720	**Decompression facial nerve, intratemporal; lateral to geniculate ganglion** MED: 100-2, 15, 260; 100-4, 12, 90.3; 100-4, 14, 10	5 T 50
69725	**including medial to geniculate ganglion** MED: 100-2, 15, 260; 100-4, 12, 90.3; 100-4, 14, 10	T 50
69740	**Suture facial nerve, intratemporal, with or without graft or decompression; lateral to geniculate ganglion** MED: 100-2, 15, 260; 100-4, 12, 90.3; 100-4, 14, 10	5 T 50

If an extracranial suture of facial nerve is performed, consult CPT code 64864.

69745	**including medial to geniculate ganglion** MED: 100-2, 15, 260; 100-4, 12, 90.3; 100-4, 14, 10	5 T 50
69799	**Unlisted procedure, middle ear** AMA: 1999, Oct, 10	T 50

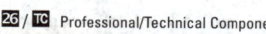 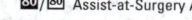

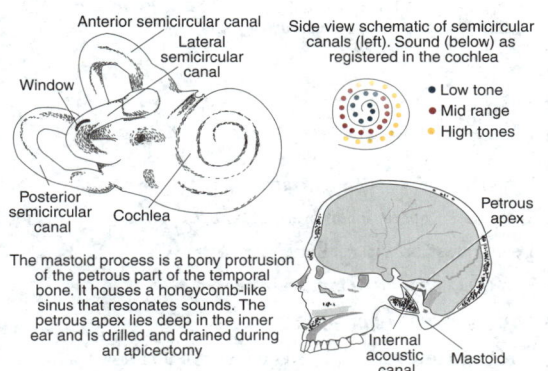

Anterior semicircular canal
Lateral semicircular canal
Window

Side view schematic of semicircular canals (left). Sound (below) as registered in the cochlea

● Low tone
● Mid range
● High tones

Posterior semicircular canal
Cochlea

Petrous apex

The mastoid process is a bony protrusion of the petrous part of the temporal bone. It houses a honeycomb-like sinus that resonates sounds. The petrous apex lies deep in the inner ear and is drilled and drained during an apicectomy

Internal acoustic canal
Mastoid

INNER EAR

INCISION AND/OR DESTRUCTION

69801 **Labyrinthotomy, with or without cryosurgery including other nonexcisional destructive procedures or perfusion of vestibuloactive drugs (single or multiple perfusions); transcanal** 5 T 50 ▸
MED: 100-2, 15, 260; 100-4, 12, 90.3; 100-4, 14, 10

This procedure includes all of the required infusions performed on initial and subsequent days of treatment.

69802 **with mastoidectomy** 7 T 50 ▸
MED: 100-2, 15, 260; 100-4, 12, 90.3; 100-4, 14, 10

69805 **Endolymphatic sac operation; without shunt** 7 T 50 ▸
MED: 100-2, 15, 260; 100-4, 12, 90.3; 100-4, 14, 10

69806 **with shunt** 7 T 50 ▸
MED: 100-2, 15, 260; 100-4, 12, 90.3; 100-4, 14, 10

69820 **Fenestration semicircular canal** 5 T 50 ▸
MED: 100-2, 15, 260; 100-4, 12, 90.3; 100-4, 14, 10

Lempert's fenestration

69840 **Revision fenestration operation** 5 T 50 ▸
MED: 100-2, 15, 260; 100-4, 12, 90.3; 100-4, 14, 10

EXCISION

69905 **Labyrinthectomy; transcanal** 7 T 50 ▸
MED: 100-2, 15, 260; 100-4, 12, 90.3; 100-4, 14, 10

69910 **with mastoidectomy** 7 T 50 ▸
MED: 100-2, 15, 260; 100-4, 12, 90.3; 100-4, 14, 10

69915 **Vestibular nerve section, translabyrinthine approach** 7 T 50 ▸
MED: 100-2, 15, 260; 100-4, 12, 90.3; 100-4, 14, 10

If a transcranial approach is used, consult CPT code 69950.

INTRODUCTION

69930 **Cochlear device implantation, with or without mastoidectomy** 7 T 50 ▸
MED: 100-2, 15, 260; 100-3, 50.3; 100-4, 12, 90.3; 100-4, 14, 10

Eye and Ocular Adnexa

69949 — 69990

OTHER PROCEDURES

69949	Unlisted procedure, inner ear	T 50

TEMPORAL BONE

MIDDLE FOSSA APPROACH
If an external approach is used, consult CPT code 69535.

69950	Vestibular nerve section, transcranial approach	C 50 ↰
69955	Total facial nerve decompression and/or repair (may include graft)	T 50 ↰
69960	Decompression internal auditory canal	T 50 ↰
69970	Removal of tumor, temporal bone	C 50 ↰

MIDDLE FOSSA APPROACH, OTHER PROCEDURES

69979	Unlisted procedure, temporal bone, middle fossa approach	T 50 80

OPERATING MICROSCOPE

+   69990   **Microsurgical techniques, requiring use of operating microscope (List separately in addition to code for primary procedure)**   N 80
             AMA: 2002, Oct, 8; 1999, Oct, 10; 1999, Jun, 11; 1999, Jul, 11; 1999, Apr, 11; 1998, Nov, 20

        Note that 69990 is an add-on code that must be used in conjunction with the appropriate code for the primary procedure. This code cannot be reported alone.

        Do not report 69990 with the following CPT codes 15756-15758, 15842, 19364, 19368, 20955-20962, 20969-20973, 26551-26554, 26556, 31526, 31531, 31536, 31541, 31545, 31546, 31561, 31571, 43116, 43496, 49906, 61548, 63075-63078, 64727, 64820-64823, 65091-68850.

Radiology Services

CODING INFORMATION

Radiology services regularly employ imaging, diagnostic, and therapeutic technologies developed only a few decades ago. Consequently, the radiology section (70010–79999) is under constant review to reflect current standards of service.

Radiological procedures are divided into four subsections in the CPT book: diagnostic radiology, including computed tomography (CT), magnetic resonance imaging (MRI), and interventional radiology procedures; diagnostic ultrasound; radiation oncology; and diagnostic and therapeutic nuclear medicine. Codes are ordered according to anatomic site (head, chest, abdomen), and body system (gastrointestinal, aorta, and arteries). The subject listings in the radiology section may be reported when a physician either performs or supervises the services.

Procedures are described by type of service (modality), specific body site, and are followed by additional information regarding the use of contrast material and the complexity of the procedure.

Procedures frequently performed by radiologists may be found outside the radiology section, such as noninvasive vascular diagnostic studies (93875–93990), which are found in the medicine section. Services involving the invasive or interventional component of interventional radiology services are found in the surgery section. These include percutaneous biopsies, injection procedures, and transcatheter procedures.

TECHNICAL AND PROFESSIONAL COMPONENTS

Radiology procedures are made up of two components: technical and professional. The technical component includes the provision of the equipment, supplies, technical personnel, and costs attendant to the performance of the procedure other than the professional services. The professional component encompasses the physician's work in providing the service, including supervision, interpretation, and report of the procedure. Education, malpractice insurance, and other expenses incident to maintaining a practice are also part of the professional component.

A common division for reimbursement of routine diagnostic procedures is 60 percent for the technical component and 40 percent for the professional component.

Coding radiology services has been difficult due to the technical component inherent to this area of medicine. The advent of freestanding medical facilities including physician offices capable of offering imaging services, catheterizations, and other diagnostic and therapeutic radiology services poses a challenge in securing reimbursement for both components. The CPT book reports the physician component of services rather than the technical. Coders will not find a modifier in the CPT book to reflect technical services. HCPCS Level II provides the modifier TC specifically for reporting the technical component. Unless instructed otherwise by payers, the professional component should be reported with modifier 26, the technical component with modifier TC.

GLOBAL SERVICE

A global service may be reported when one physician provides both components of the radiology procedure, such as owning the equipment, employing the technologist, and providing a written interpretation of the examination.

SUBSECTIONS

The radiology section of the CPT book is divided into four subsections. These are:

Diagnostic Radiology

Diagnostic Ultrasound

Radiation Oncology

Nuclear Medicine

DIAGNOSTIC RADIOLOGY

Procedures in diagnostic radiology subsection establish a diagnosis or follow the progression or remission of a disease process. However, also included in this section are procedures that are therapeutic. These therapeutic procedures are often referred to as interventional or invasive radiology services. Codes in this chapter of the CPT book report the radiological supervision and interpretation of these interventional and invasive procedures.

Diagnostic radiology uses different modalities, including x-rays, fluoroscopy, computed tomography (CT), and magnetic resonance imaging (MRI). Procedures in the diagnostic radiology section are ordered by anatomic site and described by type of service (modality), specific body site, number of views, and use of contrast materials.

TERMS AND INSTRUCTIONS

A radiological examination refers to plain films of specific sites. Other terms used to describe plain films include standard or conventional films. Services employing other modalities and additional techniques are described as such (i.e., radiography with fluoroscopy, computerized axial tomography, or magnetic resonance imaging).

Computed axial tomography (CT scan) is a type of imaging that employs basic tomographic technique enhanced by computer imaging. Computer enhancement synthesizes the images obtained from different directions in a given plane, effectively reconstructing a cross-sectional plane of the body.

Computed tomography angiography (CTA) provides multiple rapid thin section CT scans, a series of x-ray beams taken from different angles to create cross-sectional images of organs, bones, and tissues.

Magnetic resonance imaging (MRI) involves the application of an external magnetic field that forces a uniform alignment of hydrogen atom nuclei in the soft tissue. The nuclei emit radiofrequency signals that are converted into sets of tomographic images and displayed on a computer screen for three-dimensional visualization of the soft tissue structure.

Views describe the patient's position in relation to the camera. A code may specify a position, as in 71010 that describes a single frontal view of the chest. Other codes do not specify a position, but designate the number of views, as in 73610 that specifies a minimum of three views of the ankle.

Procedures performed with contrast material often do not specify the type of contrast, as in 74160 that reports computed axial tomography of the abdomen with contrast. However, other codes are more specific. Radiologic examination of the colon using barium enema contrast is reported with code 74270. An air contrast with specific high-density barium is reported with code 74280.

The radiological supervision and interpretation of many interventional and invasive procedures are reported with codes from diagnostic radiology. Interventional/invasive codes may be used to report procedures that are diagnostic in nature, such as fluoroscopic localization code 76003. Or, the codes may be used to report therapeutic procedures, such as radiologic supervision and interpretation of transcatheter embolization 75894.

ADMINISTRATION OF CONTRAST MATERIAL(S)

The phrases "with contrast" or "without contrast followed by contrast" appears within the code narrative of some radiology services codes. This represents contrast material administered intravascularly, intrathecally, or intra-articularly.

DIAGNOSTIC ULTRASOUND

Permanent records of ultrasound examinations such as description of anatomic region, measurements, obstructed view and site to be localized for a guided surgical procedure must be kept. A written report of the exam should be included in the patient's medical record. Ultrasound should not be reported unless there is image documentation and a final written report.

Procedures in the diagnostic ultrasound subsection are organized by anatomic site. However, when the ultrasound is part of an interventional radiology procedure for localization purposes, the procedure is listed under "Ultrasonic Guidance Procedures."

Codes for ultrasounds performed for diagnostic purposes are selected based on the technique or type of study (A-mode, B-scan), the extent of the study (limited, complete, follow-up), and additional services performed with certain ultrasounds (intraocular lens power calculation).

TECHNIQUE

A-mode (a-scan) is an ultrasonic scanning procedure providing one-dimensional measurement.

M-mode is an ultrasonic scanning procedure that measures the amplitude and velocity of moving echo-producing structures to allow one-dimensional viewing.

B-scan is a two-dimensional ultrasonic scanning procedure providing a two-dimensional display.

Real-time is a two-dimensional scanning procedure that displays both structure and movement in time.

Doppler is an ultrasonic scanning procedure that measures the velocity of moving objects and often applied in the study of blood flow.

EXTENT

"Complete" defines a complete procedure that implies a scan of the entire body area.

"Limited" defines a limited procedure that involves scanning a single organ, quadrant, or completing a partial examination.

"Follow-up/repeat" implies performing a limited study on an area previously scanned.

Ultrasound procedures may be found in other sections of the CPT book. For example, echocardiography procedures are in the medicine section under "Cardiovascular Services." Color mapping in conjunction with fetal echocardiography (76825–76826) is reported with 93325 in the medicine section. Duplex scans and Doppler studies of the vascular system are found in the medicine section under the heading "Noninvasive Vascular Diagnostic Studies."

RADIATION ONCOLOGY

Radiation oncology is a therapeutic method as opposed to a diagnostic service. The radiologist manages and prescribes treatment for patients who have malignant neoplasms responsive to radiation therapy.

Radiation oncology involves the following services: consultation, clinical treatment, planning, medical radiation physics, and treatment delivery and management.

Consultation codes from the evaluation and management (E/M) section of the CPT book report consultations conducted by radiation oncologists and the E/M guidelines must be followed when applying these codes. Office/outpatient consultations are reported with codes 99241–99245; codes 99251–99263 are reported for inpatient consultations.

Clinical treatment planning consists of two services, planning and simulation to determine the best course of treatment. Planning is reported with codes 77261–77263, depending on the extent or complexity of the process. Simulation is reported with codes 77280–77295, depending on the extent or complexity of the service.

- Report 77261 for simple planning that requires assessment of a single treatment area. No interpretation of special tests is required. The treatment site can be in a single port or simple parallel opposed ports with simple or no blocking.

- Report 77262 for an intermediate level of planning that requires interpretation of tests performed for tumor localization. The radiation oncologist may need to assess two separate treatment areas or protect sensitive organs.

- Report 77263 for the interpretation of complex testing procedures, including CT and MR localization and/or special laboratory tests. Planning requires complex blocks and/or custom shielding blocks for the protection of sensitive normal structures. Tangential ports may be required. Three or more areas may require treatment. In addition, complex treatment

planning often involves a combination of modalities such as brachytherapy, hyperthermia, chemotherapy and surgery.

- Simulation sets the treatment portals to specific treatment volumes. Simulation should be reported only once per time of set-up procedure.

- Simple simulation (77280) involves a single port or single pair of parallel ports on a single treatment area.

- Intermediate simulation (77285) involves three or more ports directed at a single treatment area. It also is required when two separate treatment areas are involved.

- Complex simulation (77290) involves a combination of multiple treatment areas, complex blocking rotation or arc therapy, multiple modalities, and use of contrast materials.

- Three-dimensional simulation (77295) involves computer-generated three-dimensional reconstruction of the tumor and surrounding critical structures.

- Medical radiation physics involves dosimetry calculation, the design and construction of treatment devices, and special services as defined below:

- Dosimetry calculation is the process a facility-based physicist uses to select the proper energy and modality to be used for each portal.

- Design and construction involves fabricating devices for the blocks. The physician must be involved in the design, selection, and placement of the devices and must document the involvement.

- Special services include hyperthermia or brachytherapy.

Treatment delivery and management (77401–77499) involves the delivery of radiation therapy and care of the patient during the course of therapy. While a nonphysician may deliver the treatment, the physician is responsible for checking and documenting the accuracy of the treatment. In addition, the physician responds to any adverse reactions to treatment and monitors the effects of the treatment on the tumor and surrounding tissues. Ongoing patient examinations are part of this service and not reported separately.

NUCLEAR MEDICINE

Nuclear medicine relies on radium or other radioelements for either diagnostic imaging or radiopharmaceutical therapy.

Radiopharmaceutical therapy destroys diseased tissues, usually malignant neoplasms, using radioelements. This subsection is organized first by the nature of the procedure, diagnostic or therapeutic. The diagnostic codes are organized by body system and defined by the extent or complexity of the service.

Procedures in nuclear medicine are independent services. Diagnostic work-up or follow-up care is reported separately, except when specifically noted as included in the service. These services do not include the provision of radium or other radioelements.

SPECIAL CODING SITUATIONS

INTERVENTIONAL RADIOLOGY

Interventional radiology services involve both an invasive component (such as a biopsy or injection) and a radiological component (radiological supervision and interpretation of the procedure). The invasive component, which may be either a diagnostic or therapeutic service, is reported with codes from the surgery section. Examples of the invasive component include injection procedure for shoulder arthrography (23350), percutaneous renal biopsy (50200), and transcatheter occlusion of a vascular malformation (61624–61626). The radiology component for supervision and interpretation is reported with codes from the diagnostic radiology and diagnostic ultrasound subsections.

Component coding was developed for services that can be performed by a single physician, usually an interventional radiologist or by two physicians, a surgeon and a radiologist. Whether performed by one or two physicians, an interventional radiology procedure must be documented as thoroughly as a surgical procedure. When two physicians perform an invasive procedure, each physician documents the portion of the service provided and references the other's involvement in the written report. Each physician reports only the CPT code for the portion of the service the respective physician provided.

The following diagnostic angiography procedures include the work provided in the interventional procedure and should not be reported separately:

- Contrast injections, angiography, roadmapping, and/or fluoroscopy

- Vessel measurement

- Post angiography or stent angiography

Diagnostic procedure codes may be used in addition to the interventional procedure only if the following criteria are met:

- No prior catheter-based angiographic study is available and a full diagnostic study is performed and the decision to intervene is based on the diagnostic study.

- A diagnostic study is documented in the medical records but the patient's condition has changed, there is not adequate visualization or there is a clinical change during the procedure that requires reevaluation.

- The diagnostic study is performed in a different area from the interventional surgery.

- Do not separately report a diagnostic angiography performed at the same time as an interventional procedure if it is specifically included in the interventional code procedure description.

The following venography diagnostic procedures include the work provided in the interventional procedure and should not be reported separately:

- Contrast injections, venography, roadmapping, and/or fluoroscopy

- Vessel measurement

- Post venography or stent venography

Diagnostic procedure codes may only be used in addition to the interventional procedure if the following are met:

- A full diagnostic study was done but is not available and a full diagnostic study and the basis for an interventional procedure was based on the diagnostic study.

- A diagnostic study is documented in the medical records but the patient's condition has changed, there is not adequate visualization, or there is a clinical change during the procedure that requires re-evaluation.

- The diagnostic study is performed in a different area from the interventional surgery.

- Do not separately report a diagnostic venography performed at the same time as an interventional procedure if it is specifically included in the interventional code procedure description.

The following procedures are included in a therapeutic transcatheter interventional procedure:

- Contrast injections, venography, roadmapping, and/or fluoroscopy

- Vessel measurement

- Except for services allowed by 75898, completion of angiography/venography

NONINVASIVE VASCULAR DIAGNOSTIC STUDIES

A description of noninvasive vascular diagnostic services (93875–93990) are mentioned here since radiologists frequently perform them also. Vascular study procedures are comprised of the following services: patient care required during performance of the study, supervision of the study, written interpretation of study results, a hard copy of output, and analysis of all data.

MODIFIERS

As in other specialties, modifiers in radiology denote circumstances that affect the performance of services and procedures. Radiologists most frequently apply modifier 26 Professional component which reports the physician (professional) component of a service separately from the technical portion. Other modifiers for radiology include, but are not limited to:

22   Unusual procedural services

52   Reduced services

59   Distinct procedural service

76   Repeat procedure by same physician

77   Repeat procedure by another physician

X-RAY CONSULTATIONS

Code 76140 Consultation on x-ray examination made elsewhere, written report is used by a physician providing a second interpretation and report on a radiologic procedure. The previous interpretation is usually from a source outside of the physician's practice and is provided at the request of another physician. Both written reports must be maintained as part of the patient's medical record. The initial report and the consultation must document the specific procedure reviewed and the complexity of the procedure, such as the number of views. Do not report 76140 for outside films that are reviewed in conjunction with evaluation and management services. The medical decision making component of E/M codes includes "amount and/or complexity of data to be reviewed."

DOCUMENTING RADIOLOGY SERVICES

Diagnostic coding is critical in establishing medical necessity, even though the radiologist may not have the information necessary to assign a definitive diagnosis. For example, many radiological services are performed to rule out a particular problem. Tests that are normal effectively rule out the suspected condition; however, the radiologist must be given sufficient information about the patient's clinical history to justify medical necessity. In instances of a rule-out diagnosis, the physician must provide the radiologist with information, regarding the patient's symptoms, signs, or complaints.

PHYSICIAN REQUIREMENTS

In general, the patient's physician orders the study and a radiologist performs and/or interprets the procedure. The radiologist sends a report to the referring physician who includes it in the overall assessment of the patient. For coding and reimbursement purposes, the radiologist's portion of the service is reported as a complete procedure or as the professional component of the study. The ordering physician evaluates the results of the study for consideration in the medical decision making but does not file a claim for any portion of the radiological study.

REQUESTING PHYSICIAN RESPONSIBILITIES

The physician should sign or initial the radiologist's report as evidence the information was reviewed and considered in medical decision making. While the actual film may be stored elsewhere, a written report should be incorporated into the patient's medical record to prove the study was medically necessary.

RADIOLOGIST RESPONSIBILITIES

Radiologists must complete a written report for every service claimed. The specific name or title of the study must appear on the report; for example, "Chest x-ray, PA and lateral." In addition to reporting the number and type of views taken, reports also must indicate any other circumstances that may affect the exam such as, a patient's state of fasting for a bowel study. Documentation should also include:

- Quality of the study (clear or blurry)

- Pertinent positive findings (abnormal)

- Pertinent negative findings (normal)

- Other aspects of the film such as incidental findings in other areas

- Radiologist's impression and diagnosis

- Recommendations for further studies or treatment

- Signature

Although the ordering physician must indicate the medical necessity, the radiologist must indicate the reason in the report. The complexity of the study dictates the depth of the radiology statement. Results from radiological studies done for urgent, acute problems must be communicated verbally by the radiologist to the physician as soon as they are available (and, also, documented later in the patient record).

REPORTS

Radiology reports are almost universally transcribed. For that reason, precautions must be taken to keep the patient's record current. Whenever possible, apply the rules for dictated operative reports to radiology reports. For example, a handwritten summary of the study should be placed in the chart until the transcription is available. The radiologist should read the transcription for accuracy and sign it before it is sent to the ordering physician or placed permanently in the patient's record.

Dictated reports should include the number and type of views taken, whether the study required a contrast medium, and the type and amount of contrast medium or radionuclide. This information plus other pertinent documentation is necessary to support CPT code selection and eliminate any extra time that could be necessary for verification.

Document all additional views beyond the usual number. Report with modifier 22 Unusual procedural services added to the CPT code that may qualify the service for higher reimbursement. This does not apply to codes that specify "minimum number of views" in their descriptions.

SECOND READINGS

The requesting physician may interpret a radiological study following the radiologist's interpretation. A second interpretation cannot be billed since it is part of the overall patient assessment. If the physician disagrees with the radiologist's findings, it should not be recorded in the patient chart. The physician should discuss

any differences of opinion with the radiologist and if a change in interpretation is made, a final corrected statement should be made in the chart. A brief note stating the reason for the change should be included. This clarifies the final diagnostic interpretation of the service that simplifies the process of assigning accurate codes.

ADDITIONAL STUDIES

Findings from a routine x-ray exam may warrant further studies. For example, a radiologist may elect to do tomograms on a patient whose chest x-ray revealed a mass. The documentation must indicate that the existence of the mass establishes the medical necessity for further studies. In such a situation, the radiologist usually is not required to check with the ordering physician before proceeding with additional studies.

STEPS FOR ACCURATE CODING AND DOCUMENTATION

The following procedures should be followed for complete and accurate coding and documentation:

1. Obtain sufficient history from the ordering physician to assign an accurate diagnosis code.

2. Document the exam in sufficient detail to allow complete and accurate procedure coding.

3. If the report is dictated, review the transcribed report for accuracy. Correct any error on the transcribed report and return to the transcriptionist to generate new and corrected hard copy.

Radiology

DIAGNOSTIC RADIOLOGY (DIAGNOSTIC IMAGING)

HEAD AND NECK

70010   **Myelography, posterior fossa, radiological supervision and interpretation**   S 80 ⬚
MED: 100-2, 15, 80; 100-4, 13, 10; 100-4, 13, 100

   To report procedure, consult CPT codes 61055, 62284.

70015   **Cisternography, positive contrast, radiological supervision and interpretation**   S 80 ⬚
MED: 100-2, 15, 80; 100-4, 13, 10; 100-4, 13, 100

   To report procedure, consult, CPT codes 61055, 62284.

70030   **Radiologic examination, eye, for detection of foreign body**   X
MED: 100-2, 15, 80; 100-4, 13, 10; 100-4, 13, 100

70100   **Radiologic examination, mandible; partial, less than four views**   X 80
MED: 100-2, 15, 80; 100-4, 13, 10; 100-4, 13, 100

70110   **complete, minimum of four views**   X 80 ⬚
MED: 100-2, 15, 80; 100-4, 13, 10; 100-4, 13, 100

70120   **Radiologic examination, mastoids; less than three views per side**   X
MED: 100-2, 15, 80; 100-4, 13, 10; 100-4, 13, 100

70130   **complete, minimum of three views perside**   X ⬚
MED: 100-2, 15, 80; 100-4, 13, 10; 100-4, 13, 100

70134   **Radiologic examination, internal auditory meati, complete**   X 80
MED: 100-2, 15, 80; 100-4, 13, 10; 100-4, 13, 100

70140   **Radiologic examination, facial bones; less than three views**   X 80
MED: 100-2, 15, 80; 100-4, 13, 10; 100-4, 13, 100

70150   **complete, minimum of three views**   X 80 ⬚
MED: 100-2, 15, 80; 100-4, 13, 10; 100-4, 13, 100

70160   **Radiologic examination, nasal bones, complete, minimum of three views**   X 80
MED: 100-2, 15, 80; 100-4, 13, 10; 100-4, 13, 100

70170   **Dacryocystography, nasolacrimal duct, radiological supervision and interpretation**   X 80 ⬚
MED: 100-2, 15, 80; 100-4, 13, 10; 100-4, 13, 100

   To report procedure, consult CPT code 68850.

70190   **Radiologic examination; optic foramina**   X
MED: 100-2, 15, 80; 100-4, 13, 10; 100-4, 13, 100

70200   **orbits, complete, minimum of four views**   X 80
MED: 100-2, 15, 80; 100-4, 13, 10; 100-4, 13, 100

70210   **Radiologic examination, sinuses, paranasal, less than three views**   X 80
MED: 100-2, 15, 80; 100-4, 13, 10; 100-4, 13, 100

70220   **Radiologic examination, sinuses, paranasal, complete, minimum of three views**   X 80 ⬚
MED: 100-2, 15, 80; 100-4, 13, 10; 100-4, 13, 100

70240   **Radiologic examination, sella turcica**   X 80
MED: 100-2, 15, 80; 100-4, 13, 10; 100-4, 13, 100

70010 — 70240

⬚ CCI Comp   50 Bilateral Procedure   + CPT Add-on Code   ⊘ Modifier -51 Exempt   ♂ Male   ♀ Female
● New Code   ▲ Revised Code   M Maternity Edit   A Age Edit   A–Y APC Status Ind.   AMA: CPT Assistant

Radiology

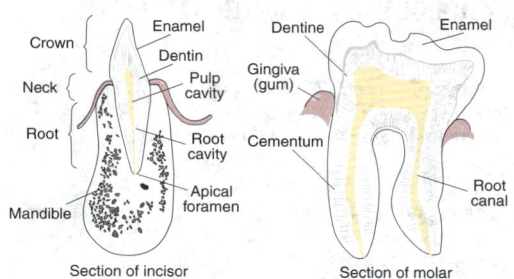

Normal dentition numbers 16 teeth in each jaw: two incisors, two canines, four premolars, and six molars. A common tooth eruption problem occurs with the third molars (wisdom teeth) which may be malposed and become impacted. Caries means "rotten" and is a decalcification of tooth enamel and sometimes penetration into the dentin and pulp. Disease processes may cause resorption of the dentin and cementum

70250 — 70360

70250 **Radiologic examination, skull; less than four views**   X 80
  MED: 100-2, 15, 80; 100-4, 13, 10; 100-4, 13, 100

70260 **complete, minimum of four views**   X 80 ⬏
  MED: 100-2, 15, 80; 100-4, 13, 10; 100-4, 13, 100

70300 **Radiologic examination, teeth; single view**   X 80
  MED: 100-2, 15, 80; 100-4, 13, 10; 100-4, 13, 100

70310 **partial examination, less than full mouth**   X 80 ⬏
  MED: 100-2, 15, 80; 100-4, 13, 10; 100-4, 13, 100

70320 **complete, full mouth**   X 80 ⬏
  MED: 100-2, 15, 80; 100-4, 13, 10; 100-4, 13, 100

70328 **Radiologic examination, temporomandibular joint, open and closed mouth; unilateral**   X 80
  MED: 100-2, 15, 80; 100-4, 13, 10; 100-4, 13, 100

70330 **bilateral**   X 80 ⬏
  MED: 100-2, 15, 80; 100-4, 13, 10; 100-4, 13, 100

70332 **Temporomandibular joint arthrography, radiological supervision and interpretation**   S ⬏
  MED: 100-2, 15, 80; 100-4, 13, 10; 100-4, 13, 100

  Code 76003 cannot be used with 70332.

  To report injection procedure, consult CPT code 21116.

70336 **Magnetic resonance (eg, proton) imaging, temporomandibular joint(s)** S ⬏
  MED: 100-2, 15, 80; 100-3, 220.2; 100-3, 220.3; 100-4, 13, 10; 100-4, 13, 100; 100-4, 13, 40

  AMA: 2001, Jul, 3; 1999, Jul, 11

70350 **Cephalogram, orthodontic**   X 80
  MED: 100-2, 15, 80; 100-4, 13, 10; 100-4, 13, 100

70355 **Orthopantogram**   X 80 ⬏
  MED: 100-2, 15, 80; 100-4, 13, 10; 100-4, 13, 100

70360 **Radiologic examination; neck, soft tissue**   X 80
  MED: 100-2, 15, 80; 100-4, 13, 10; 100-4, 13, 100

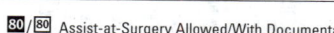

26 / **TC** Professional/Technical Component   **80** / **80** Assist-at-Surgery Allowed/With Documentation   ⊙ Conscious Sedation
  Unlisted   Not Covered   **MED:** Pubs 100/NCD Reference   **1**-**9** ASC Group   ⑥³ Modifier 63 Exempt
504 — Radiology   CPT only © 2005 American Medical Association. All Rights Reserved. *(Black Ink)*   © 2005 Ingenix, Inc. *(Blue Ink)*

70370   **pharynx or larynx, including fluoroscopy and/or magnification technique**   X 80 🔁
MED: 100-2, 15, 80; 100-4, 13, 10; 100-4, 13, 100

70371   **Complex dynamic pharyngeal and speech evaluation by cine or video recording**   X 80 🔁
MED: 100-2, 15, 80; 100-4, 13, 10; 100-4, 13, 100

70373   **Laryngography, contrast, radiological supervision and interpretation** X 80 🔁
MED: 100-2, 15, 80; 100-4, 13, 10; 100-4, 13, 100

       To report procedure, consult CPT code 31708.

70380   **Radiologic examination, salivary gland for calculus**   X 80
MED: 100-2, 15, 80; 100-4, 13, 10; 100-4, 13, 100

70390   **Sialography, radiological supervision and interpretation**   X 80 🔁
MED: 100-2, 15, 80; 100-4, 13, 10; 100-4, 13, 100

       To report procedure, consult CPT code 42550.

70450   **Computed tomography, head or brain; without contrast material**   S 80 🔁
MED: 100-2, 15, 80; 100-3, 220.1; 100-4, 13, 10; 100-4, 13, 100; 100-4, 13, 30

       AMA: 1996, Apr, 11

70460   **with contrast material(s)**   S 80 🔁
MED: 100-2, 15, 80; 100-3, 220.1; 100-4, 13, 10; 100-4, 13, 100; 100-4, 13, 30

       AMA: 1996, Apr, 11

70470   **Computed tomography, head or brain; without contrast material, followed by contrast material(s) and further sections**   S 80 🔁
MED: 100-2, 15, 80; 100-3, 220.1; 100-4, 13, 10; 100-4, 13, 100; 100-4, 13, 30

       AMA: 1996, Apr, 11

       If 3D rendering is performed, consult CPT codes 76376, 76377.

70480   **Computed tomography, orbit, sella, or posterior fossa or outer, middle, or inner ear; without contrast material**   S 80 🔁
MED: 100-2, 15, 80; 100-3, 220.1; 100-4, 13, 10; 100-4, 13, 100; 100-4, 13, 30

70481   **with contrast material(s)**   S 80 🔁
MED: 100-2, 15, 80; 100-3, 220.1; 100-4, 13, 10; 100-4, 13, 100; 100-4, 13, 30

70482   **without contrast material, followed by contrast material(s) and further sections**   S 80 🔁
MED: 100-2, 15, 80; 100-3, 220.1; 100-4, 13, 10; 100-4, 13, 100; 100-4, 13, 30

       If 3D rendering is performed, consult CPT codes 76376, 76377.

70486   **Computed tomography, maxillofacial area; without contrast material** S 80 🔁
MED: 100-2, 15, 80; 100-3, 220.1; 100-4, 13, 10; 100-4, 13, 100; 100-4, 13, 30

       AMA: 2002, Mar, 11

70487   **with contrast material(s)**   S 80 🔁
MED: 100-2, 15, 80; 100-3, 220.1; 100-4, 13, 10; 100-4, 13, 100; 100-4, 13, 30

70488   **without contrast material, followed by contrast material(s) and further sections**   S 80 🔁
MED: 100-2, 15, 80; 100-3, 220.1; 100-4, 13, 10; 100-4, 13, 100; 100-4, 13, 30

       If 3D rendering is performed, consult CPT codes 76376, 76377.

70490   **Computed tomography, soft tissue neck; without contrast material**   S 80 🔁
MED: 100-2, 15, 80; 100-3, 220.1; 100-4, 13, 10; 100-4, 13, 100; 100-4, 13, 30

🔁 CCI Comp   50 Bilateral Procedure   + CPT Add-on Code   ⊘ Modifier -51 Exempt   ♂ Male   ♀ Female
● New Code   ▲ Revised Code   M Maternity Edit   A Age Edit   A–Y APC Status Ind.   AMA: CPT Assistant

Radiology

70491 — 70547

70491   with contrast material(s)   S 80 ⟳
MED: 100-2, 15, 80; 100-3, 220.1; 100-4, 13, 10; 100-4, 13, 100; 100-4, 13, 30

70492   without contrast material followed by contrast material(s) and further
sections   S 80 ⟳
MED: 100-2, 15, 80; 100-3, 220.1; 100-4, 13, 10; 100-4, 13, 100; 100-4, 13, 30

If 3D rendering is performed, consult CPT codes 76376, 76377.

If computed axial axial tomography is performed on the cervical spine, consult
CPT codes 72125 and 72126.

70496   Computed tomographic angiography, head, without contrast material(s),
followed by contrast material(s) and further sections, including image post-
processing   S 80 ⟳
MED: 100-2, 15, 80; 100-3, 220.1; 100-4, 13, 10; 100-4, 13, 100; 100-4, 13, 30

AMA: 2001, Jul, 3

70498   Computed tomographic angiography, neck, without contrast material(s),
followed by contrast material(s) and further sections, including image post-
processing   S 80 ⟳
MED: 100-2, 15, 80; 100-3, 220.1; 100-4, 13, 10; 100-4, 13, 100; 100-4, 13, 30

AMA: 2001, Jul, 3

70540   Magnetic resonance (eg, proton) imaging, orbit, face, and neck; without
contrast material(s)   S 80 ⟳
MED: 100-2, 15, 80; 100-3, 220.2; 100-3, 220.3; 100-4, 13, 10; 100-4, 13, 100; 100-4, 13, 40

AMA: 2001, Jul, 3

70542   with contrast material(s)   S 80 ⟳
MED: 100-2, 15, 80; 100-3, 220.2; 100-3, 220.3; 100-4, 13, 10; 100-4, 13, 100; 100-4, 13, 40

AMA: 2001, Jul, 3

70543   without contrast material(s), followed by contrast material(s) and
further sequences   S 80 ⟳
MED: 100-2, 15, 80; 100-3, 220.2; 100-3, 220.3; 100-4, 13, 10; 100-4, 13, 100; 100-4, 13, 40

AMA: 2001, Jul, 3

70544   Magnetic resonance angiography, head; without contrast material(s) S 80 ⟳
MED: 100-2, 15, 80; 100-3, 220.2; 100-3, 220.3; 100-4, 13, 10; 100-4, 13, 100; 100-4, 13, 40.1;
100-4, 13, 40.1.1; 100-4, 18, 20.7

AMA: 2001, Sep, 4

70545   with contrast material(s)   S 80 ⟳
MED: 100-2, 15, 80; 100-3, 220.2; 100-3, 220.3; 100-4, 13, 10; 100-4, 13, 100; 100-4, 13, 40.1;
100-4, 13, 40.1.1; 100-4, 18, 20.7

AMA: 2001, Sep, 4

70546   without contrast material(s), followed by contrast material(s) and
further sequences   S 80 ⟳
MED: 100-2, 15, 80; 100-3, 220.2; 100-3, 220.3; 100-4, 13, 10; 100-4, 13, 100; 100-4, 13, 40.1;
100-4, 13, 40.1.1; 100-4, 18, 20.7

AMA: 2001, Sep, 4

70547   Magnetic resonance angiography, neck; without contrast material(s) S 80 ⟳
MED: 100-2, 15, 80; 100-3, 220.2; 100-3, 220.3; 100-4, 13, 10; 100-4, 13, 100; 100-4, 13, 40.1;
100-4, 13, 40.1.1; 100-4, 18, 20.7

AMA: 2001, Sep, 4

70548   **with contrast material(s)**   S 80 ▣
MED: 100-2, 15, 80; 100-3, 220.2; 100-3, 220.3; 100-4, 13, 10; 100-4, 13, 100; 100-4, 13, 40.1; 100-4, 13, 40.1.1; 100-4, 18, 20.7

AMA: 2001, Sep, 4

70549   **without contrast material(s), followed by contrast material(s) and further sequences**   S 80 ▣
MED: 100-2, 15, 80; 100-3, 220.2; 100-3, 220.3; 100-4, 13, 10; 100-4, 13, 100; 100-4, 13, 40.1; 100-4, 13, 40.1.1; 100-4, 18, 20.7

AMA: 2001, Sep, 4

70551   **Magnetic resonance (eg, proton) imaging, brain (including brain stem); without contrast material**   S 80 ▣
MED: 100-2, 15, 80; 100-3, 220.2; 100-3, 220.3; 100-4, 12, 70; 100-4, 13, 10; 100-4, 13, 100; 100-4, 13, 20; 100-4, 13, 40; 100-4, 13, 90

AMA: 1998, May, 10

70552   **with contrast material(s)**   S 80 ▣
MED: 100-2, 15, 80; 100-3, 220.2; 100-3, 220.3; 100-4, 13, 10; 100-4, 13, 100; 100-4, 13, 40

AMA: 2001, Jul, 3

70553   **without contrast material, followed by contrast material(s) and further sequences**   S 80 ▣
MED: 100-2, 15, 80; 100-3, 220.2; 100-3, 220.3; 100-4, 12, 70; 100-4, 13, 10; 100-4, 13, 100; 100-4, 13, 20; 100-4, 13, 40; 100-4, 13, 90

AMA: 2001, Jul, 3; 1997, Nov, 24

If magnetic spectroscopy is performed, consult CPT code 76390.

70557   **Magnetic resonance (eg, proton) imaging, brain (including brain stem and skull base), during open intracranial procedure (eg, to assess for residual tumor or residual vascular malformation); without contrast material** S 80 ▣

To report stereotactic biopsy of intracranial lesion with magnetic resonance guidance, use 61751.

Codes 70557, 70558 or 70559 can be reported only if a separate report is generated. Report only one of these codes once per operative session.

Do not report these codes in conjunction with 61751, 76393 or 76394.

70558   **with contrast material(s)**   S 80 ▣

70559   **without contrast material(s), followed by contrast material(s) and further sequences**   S 80 ▣

CHEST

71010   **Radiologic examination, chest; single view, frontal**   X 80
MED: 100-2, 15, 80; 100-2, 15, 80.4; 100-4, 12, 30.6.12; 100-4, 13, 10; 100-4, 13, 100; 100-4, 13, 90

If chest x-ray, single view, frontal is performed as part of critical care services do not report separately.

71015   **stereo, frontal**   X 80 ▣
MED: 100-2, 15, 80; 100-4, 12, 30.6.12; 100-4, 13, 10; 100-4, 13, 100

71020   **Radiologic examination, chest, two views, frontal and lateral;**   X 80 ▣
MED: 100-2, 15, 80; 100-2, 15, 80.4; 100-4, 12, 30.6.12; 100-4, 13, 10; 100-4, 13, 100; 100-4, 13, 90

If chest x-ray, two views, frontal and lateral is performed as part of critical care services do not report separately.

71021	**with apical lordotic procedure**	☒ 80 🔳

MED: 100-2, 15, 80; 100-2, 15, 80.4; 100-4, 13, 10; 100-4, 13, 100; 100-4, 13, 90

71022	**with oblique projections**	☒ 80

MED: 100-2, 15, 80; 100-4, 13, 10; 100-4, 13, 100

71023	**with fluoroscopy**	☒ 80 🔳

MED: 100-2, 15, 80; 100-4, 13, 10; 100-4, 13, 100

71030	**Radiologic examination, chest, complete, minimum of four views;**	☒ 80 🔳

MED: 100-2, 15, 80; 100-2, 15, 80.4; 100-4, 13, 10; 100-4, 13, 100; 100-4, 13, 90

71034	**with fluoroscopy**	☒ 80 🔳

MED: 100-2, 15, 80; 100-4, 13, 10; 100-4, 13, 100

If a separate chest fluoroscopy is performed, consult CPT code 76000.

71035	**Radiologic examination, chest, special views (eg, lateral decubitus, Bucky studies)**	☒ 80

MED: 100-2, 15, 80; 100-4, 13, 10; 100-4, 13, 100

71040	**Bronchography, unilateral, radiological supervision and interpretation**	☒ 80 🔳

MED: 100-2, 15, 80; 100-4, 13, 10; 100-4, 13, 100

To report procedure, consult CPT codes 31656, 31708, 31710, and 31715.

71060	**Bronchography, bilateral, radiological supervision and interpretation**	☒ 80 🔳

MED: 100-2, 15, 80; 100-4, 13, 10; 100-4, 13, 100

To report procedure, consult CPT codes 31656, 31708, 31710, and 31715.

71090	**Insertion pacemaker, fluoroscopy and radiography, radiological supervision and interpretation**	☒ 80 🔳

MED: 100-2, 15, 80; 100-4, 13, 10; 100-4, 13, 100

To report procedure, consult CPT for appropriate code.

71100	**Radiologic examination, ribs, unilateral; two views**	☒ 80 🔳

MED: 100-2, 15, 80; 100-4, 13, 10; 100-4, 13, 100

71101	**including posteroanterior chest, minimum of three views**	☒ 80 🔳

MED: 100-2, 15, 80; 100-4, 13, 10; 100-4, 13, 100

71110	**Radiologic examination, ribs, bilateral; three views**	☒ 80 🔳

MED: 100-2, 15, 80; 100-4, 13, 10; 100-4, 13, 100

71111	**including posteroanterior chest, minimum of four views**	☒ 80 🔳

MED: 100-2, 15, 80; 100-4, 13, 10; 100-4, 13, 100

71120	**Radiologic examination; sternum, minimum of two views**	☒ 80

MED: 100-2, 15, 80; 100-4, 13, 10; 100-4, 13, 100

71130	**sternoclavicular joint or joints, minimum of three views**	☒ 80

MED: 100-2, 15, 80; 100-4, 13, 10; 100-4, 13, 100

71250	**Computed tomography, thorax; without contrast material**	Ⓢ 80 🔳

MED: 100-2, 15, 80; 100-3, 220.1; 100-4, 13, 10; 100-4, 13, 100; 100-4, 13, 30

71260	**with contrast material(s)**	Ⓢ 80 🔳

MED: 100-2, 15, 80; 100-3, 220.1; 100-4, 13, 10; 100-4, 13, 100; 100-4, 13, 30

AMA: 2001, Jul, 3

71270   **without contrast material, followed by contrast material(s) and further sections**   Ⓢ 80 🔾
MED: 100-2, 15, 80; 100-3, 220.1; 100-4, 13, 10; 100-4, 13, 100; 100-4, 13, 30

AMA: 2001, Jun, 10

If 3D rendering is performed, consult CPT codes 76376, 76377.

71275   **Computed tomographic angiography, chest, without contrast material(s), followed by contrast material(s) and further sections, including image post-processing**   Ⓢ 80 🔾
MED: 100-2, 15, 80; 100-3, 220.1; 100-4, 13, 10; 100-4, 13, 100; 100-4, 13, 30

71550   **Magnetic resonance (eg, proton) imaging, chest (eg, for evaluation of hilar and mediastinal lymphadenopathy); without contrast material(s)**   Ⓢ 80 🔾
MED: 100-2, 15, 80; 100-3, 220.2; 100-3, 220.3; 100-4, 13, 10; 100-4, 13, 100; 100-4, 13, 40

AMA: 2001, Jul, 3

71551   **with contrast material(s)**   Ⓢ 80 🔾
MED: 100-2, 15, 80; 100-3, 220.2; 100-3, 220.3; 100-4, 13, 10; 100-4, 13, 100; 100-4, 13, 40

AMA: 2001, Jul, 3

71552   **without contrast material(s), followed by contrast material(s) and further sequences**   Ⓢ 80 🔾
MED: 100-2, 15, 80; 100-3, 220.2; 100-3, 220.3; 100-4, 13, 10; 100-4, 13, 100; 100-4, 13, 40

AMA: 2001, Jul, 3

If a breast MRI is performed, consult CPT codes 76093 and 76094.

71555   **Magnetic resonance angiography, chest (excluding myocardium), with or without contrast material(s)**   Ⓑ 80 🔾
MED: 100-2, 15, 80; 100-3, 220.2; 100-3, 220.3; 100-4, 13, 10; 100-4, 13, 100; 100-4, 13, 40.1; 100-4, 13, 40.1.1; 100-4, 18, 20.7

AMA: 1995, Fall, 2

SPINE AND PELVIS

72010   **Radiologic examination, spine, entire, survey study, anteroposterior and lateral**   Ⓧ 80 🔾
MED: 100-2, 15, 80; 100-4, 13, 10; 100-4, 13, 100

AMA: 2002, May, 18

72020   **Radiologic examination, spine, single view, specify level**   Ⓧ 80
MED: 100-2, 15, 80; 100-4, 13, 10; 100-4, 13, 100

72040   **Radiologic examination, spine, cervical; two or three views**   Ⓧ 80
MED: 100-2, 15, 80; 100-2, 15, 80.4; 100-4, 13, 10; 100-4, 13, 100; 100-4, 13, 90

AMA: 2001, Sep, 4

72050   **minimum of four views**   Ⓧ 80 🔾
MED: 100-2, 15, 80; 100-2, 15, 80.4; 100-4, 13, 10; 100-4, 13, 100; 100-4, 13, 90

72052   **complete, including oblique and flexion and/or extension studies**   Ⓧ 80 🔾
MED: 100-2, 15, 80; 100-2, 15, 80.4; 100-4, 13, 10; 100-4, 13, 100; 100-4, 13, 90

72069   **Radiologic examination, spine, thoracolumbar, standing (scoliosis)**   Ⓧ 80
MED: 100-2, 15, 80; 100-2, 15, 80.4; 100-4, 13, 10; 100-4, 13, 100; 100-4, 13, 90

72070 — 72132

72070	**Radiologic examination, spine; thoracic, two views**	X 80

MED: 100-2, 15, 80; 100-2, 15, 80.4; 100-4, 13, 10; 100-4, 13, 100; 100-4, 13, 90

AMA: 2001, Sep, 4

72072	**thoracic, three views**	X 80

MED: 100-2, 15, 80; 100-2, 15, 80.4; 100-4, 13, 10; 100-4, 13, 100; 100-4, 13, 90

AMA: 2001, Sep, 4

72074	**thoracic, minimum of four views**	X 80

MED: 100-2, 15, 80; 100-2, 15, 80.4; 100-4, 13, 10; 100-4, 13, 100; 100-4, 13, 90

AMA: 2001, Sep, 4

72080	**thoracolumbar, two views**	X 80

MED: 100-2, 15, 80; 100-2, 15, 80.4; 100-4, 13, 10; 100-4, 13, 100; 100-4, 13, 90

AMA: 2001, Sep, 4

72090	**scoliosis study, including supine and erect studies**	X 80

MED: 100-2, 15, 80; 100-4, 13, 10; 100-4, 13, 100

72100	**Radiologic examination, spine, lumbosacral; two or three views**	X 80

MED: 100-2, 15, 80; 100-4, 13, 10; 100-4, 13, 100

AMA: 2001, Sep, 4

72110	**minimum of four views**	X 80

MED: 100-2, 15, 80; 100-4, 13, 10; 100-4, 13, 100

AMA: 2001, Sep, 4

72114	**complete, including bending views**	X 80

MED: 100-2, 15, 80; 100-2, 15, 80.4; 100-4, 13, 10; 100-4, 13, 100; 100-4, 13, 90

72120	**Radiologic examination, spine, lumbosacral, bending views only, minimum of four views**	X 80

MED: 100-2, 15, 80; 100-4, 13, 10; 100-4, 13, 100

72125	**Computed tomography, cervical spine; without contrast material**	S 80

MED: 100-2, 15, 80; 100-3, 220.1; 100-4, 13, 10; 100-4, 13, 100; 100-4, 13, 30

72126	**with contrast material**	S 80

MED: 100-2, 15, 80; 100-3, 220.1; 100-4, 13, 10; 100-4, 13, 100; 100-4, 13, 30

72127	**without contrast material, followed by contrast material(s) and further sections**	S 80

MED: 100-2, 15, 80; 100-3, 220.1; 100-4, 13, 10; 100-4, 13, 100; 100-4, 13, 30

72128	**Computed tomography, thoracic spine; without contrast material**	S 80

MED: 100-2, 15, 80; 100-3, 220.1; 100-4, 13, 10; 100-4, 13, 100; 100-4, 13, 30

72129	**with contrast material**	S 80

MED: 100-2, 15, 80; 100-3, 220.1; 100-4, 13, 10; 100-4, 13, 100; 100-4, 13, 30

72130	**without contrast material, followed by contrast material(s) and further sections**	S 80

MED: 100-2, 15, 80; 100-3, 220.1; 100-4, 13, 10; 100-4, 13, 100; 100-4, 13, 30

72131	**Computed tomography, lumbar spine; without contrast material**	S 80

MED: 100-2, 15, 80; 100-3, 220.1; 100-4, 13, 10; 100-4, 13, 100; 100-4, 13, 30

72132	**with contrast material**	S 80

MED: 100-2, 15, 80; 100-3, 220.1; 100-4, 13, 10; 100-4, 13, 100; 100-4, 13, 30

AMA: 1993, Fall, 13

26 / **TC** Professional/Technical Component   **80**/**80** Assist-at-Surgery Allowed/With Documentation   ⊙ Conscious Sedation

Unlisted   Not Covered   MED: Pubs 100/NCD Reference   **1**-**9** ASC Group   63 Modifier 63 Exempt

510 — Radiology   CPT only © 2005 American Medical Association. All Rights Reserved. *(Black Ink)*   © 2005 Ingenix, Inc. *(Blue Ink)*

72133   **without contrast material, followed by contrast material(s) and further sections**   [S] [80] [⚑]
MED: 100-2, 15, 80; 100-3, 220.1; 100-4, 13, 10; 100-4, 13, 100; 100-4, 13, 30

If 3D rendering is performed, consult CPT codes 76376, 76377.

To report intrathecal injections, consult CPT codes 61055, 62284.

72141   **Magnetic resonance (eg, proton) imaging, spinal canal and contents, cervical; without contrast material**   [S] [80] [⚑]
MED: 100-2, 15, 80; 100-3, 220.2; 100-3, 220.3; 100-4, 13, 10; 100-4, 13, 100; 100-4, 13, 40

72142   **with contrast material(s)**   [S] [80] [⚑]
MED: 100-2, 15, 80; 100-3, 220.2; 100-3, 220.3; 100-4, 13, 10; 100-4, 13, 100; 100-4, 13, 40

If cervical spine canal imaging is performed first without contrast material followed by contrast material, consult CPT code 72156.

72146   **Magnetic resonance (eg, proton) imaging, spinal canal and contents, thoracic; without contrast material**   [S] [80] [⚑]
MED: 100-2, 15, 80; 100-3, 220.2; 100-3, 220.3; 100-4, 13, 10; 100-4, 13, 100; 100-4, 13, 40

AMA: 1999, May, 10

72147   **with contrast material(s)**   [S] [80] [⚑]
MED: 100-2, 15, 80; 100-3, 220.2; 100-3, 220.3; 100-4, 13, 10; 100-4, 13, 100; 100-4, 13, 40

AMA: 1999, May, 10

If thoracic spinal canal imaging is performed first without contrast material followed by contrast material, consult CPT code 72157.

72148   **Magnetic resonance (eg, proton) imaging, spinal canal and contents, lumbar; without contrast material**   [S] [80] [⚑]
MED: 100-2, 15, 80; 100-3, 220.2; 100-3, 220.3; 100-4, 13, 10; 100-4, 13, 100; 100-4, 13, 40

72149   **with contrast material(s)**   [S] [80] [⚑]
MED: 100-2, 15, 80; 100-3, 220.2; 100-3, 220.3; 100-4, 13, 10; 100-4, 13, 100; 100-4, 13, 40

If lumbar spinal canal imaging is performed first without contrast material followed by contrast material, consult CPT code 72158.

72156   **Magnetic resonance (eg, proton) imaging, spinal canal and contents, without contrast material, followed by contrast material(s) and further sequences; cervical**   [S] [80] [⚑]
MED: 100-2, 15, 80; 100-3, 220.2; 100-3, 220.3; 100-4, 12, 70; 100-4, 13, 10; 100-4, 13, 100; 100-4, 13, 20; 100-4, 13, 40; 100-4, 13, 90

72157   **thoracic**   [S] [80] [⚑]
MED: 100-2, 15, 80; 100-3, 220.2; 100-3, 220.3; 100-4, 12, 70; 100-4, 13, 10; 100-4, 13, 100; 100-4, 13, 20; 100-4, 13, 40; 100-4, 13, 90

72158   **lumbar**   [S] [80] [⚑]
MED: 100-2, 15, 80; 100-3, 220.2; 100-3, 220.3; 100-4, 12, 70; 100-4, 13, 10; 100-4, 13, 100; 100-4, 13, 20; 100-4, 13, 40; 100-4, 13, 90

72159   **Magnetic resonance angiography, spinal canal and contents, with or without contrast material(s)**   [E]
MED: 100-2, 15, 80; 100-3, 220.2; 100-3, 220.3; 100-4, 13, 10; 100-4, 13, 100; 100-4, 13, 40.1; 100-4, 13, 40.1.1; 100-4, 18, 20.7

72170   **Radiologic examination, pelvis; one or two views**   [X] [80]
MED: 100-2, 15, 80; 100-4, 13, 10; 100-4, 13, 100

AMA: 2001, Sep, 4

Radiology

72190 — 72240

72190	**complete, minimum of three views**	X 80 ⬚

MED: 100-2, 15, 80; 100-2, 15, 80.4; 100-4, 13, 10; 100-4, 13, 100; 100-4, 13, 90

If pelvimetry is performed, consult CPT code 74710.

72191 **Computed tomographic angiography, pelvis, without contrast material(s), followed by contrast material(s) and further sections, including image post-processing** S 80 ⬚

MED: 100-2, 15, 80; 100-3, 220.1; 100-4, 13, 10; 100-4, 13, 100; 100-4, 13, 30

AMA: 2001, Jul, 3

To report CTA aorto-iliofemoral runoff, consult CPT code 75635.

72192 **Computed tomography, pelvis; without contrast material** S 80 ⬚

MED: 100-2, 15, 80; 100-3, 220.1; 100-4, 13, 10; 100-4, 13, 100; 100-4, 13, 30

72193 **with contrast material(s)** S 80 ⬚

MED: 100-2, 15, 80; 100-3, 220.1; 100-4, 13, 10; 100-4, 13, 100; 100-4, 13, 30

72194 **without contrast material, followed by contrast material(s) and further sections** S 80 ⬚

MED: 100-2, 15, 80; 100-3, 220.1; 100-4, 13, 10; 100-4, 13, 100; 100-4, 13, 30

If 3D rendering is performed, consult CPT codes 76376, 76377.

For computed tomographic colonography, consult Category III codes 0066T, 0067T.

Codes 72192-72194 cannot be reported with Category III codes 0066T, 0067T.

72195 **Magnetic resonance (eg, proton) imaging, pelvis; without contrast material(s)** S 80 ⬚

MED: 100-2, 15, 80; 100-3, 220.1; 100-4, 13, 10; 100-4, 13, 100; 100-4, 13, 40

AMA: 2001, Jul, 3

72196 **with contrast material(s)** S 80 ⬚

MED: 100-2, 15, 80; 100-3, 220.1; 100-4, 13, 10; 100-4, 13, 100; 100-4, 13, 40

AMA: 2001, Jul, 3

72197 **without contrast material(s), followed by contrast material(s) and further sequences** S 80 ⬚

MED: 100-2, 15, 80; 100-3, 220.1; 100-4, 13, 10; 100-4, 13, 100; 100-4, 13, 40

AMA: 2001, Jul, 3

72198 **Magnetic resonance angiography, pelvis, with or without contrast material(s)** B 80 ⬚

MED: 100-2, 15, 80; 100-3, 220.2; 100-3, 220.3; 100-4, 13, 10; 100-4, 13, 100; 100-4, 13, 40.1; 100-4, 13, 40.1.1; 100-4, 18, 20.7

72200 **Radiologic examination, sacroiliac joints; less than three views** X 80

MED: 100-2, 15, 80; 100-4, 13, 10; 100-4, 13, 100

72202 **three or more views** X 80 ⬚

MED: 100-2, 15, 80; 100-4, 13, 10; 100-4, 13, 100

72220 **Radiologic examination, sacrum and coccyx, minimum of two views** X 80

MED: 100-2, 15, 80; 100-2, 15, 80.4; 100-4, 13, 10; 100-4, 13, 100; 100-4, 13, 90

72240 **Myelography, cervical, radiological supervision and interpretation** S 80 ⬚

MED: 100-2, 15, 80; 100-4, 13, 10; 100-4, 13, 100

AMA: 1993, Fall, 13

To report procedure, consult CPT codes 61055, 62284.

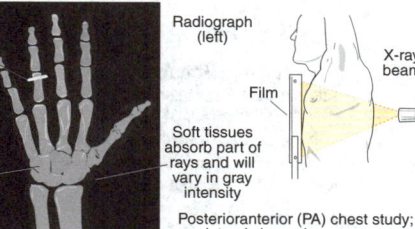

Traditional diagnostic radiography is defined by the x-ray. Radiographs, or x-rays, are "shadowgrams" of body structures and tissues and show radiopaque matter, such as bone, to be whiter and radiolucent substances, such as air, to be blacker. Each study is oriented by the direction path of the x-ray beam: e.g., PA, the most common, means the beam travels from posterior to anterior. Contrast agents are commonly used to highlight particular areas or structures

72255 **Myelography, thoracic, radiological supervision and interpretation** S 80 ⬛
MED: 100-2, 15, 80; 100-4, 13, 10; 100-4, 13, 100

To report procedure, consult CPT codes 61055, 62284.

72265 **Myelography, lumbosacral, radiological supervision and interpretation** S 80 ⬛
MED: 100-2, 15, 80; 100-4, 13, 10; 100-4, 13, 100

AMA: 2000, Aug, 7; 1993, Fall, 13

To report procedure, consult CPT codes 61055, 62284.

72270 **Myelography, two or more regions (eg, lumbar/thoracic, cervical/thoracic, lumbar/cervical, lumbar/thoracic/cervical), radiological supervision and interpretation** S 80 ⬛
MED: 100-2, 15, 80; 100-4, 13, 10; 100-4, 13, 100

To report procedure, consult CPT codes 61055, 62284.

72275 **Epidurography, radiological supervision and interpretation** S ⬛
MED: 100-2, 15, 80; 100-4, 13, 10; 100-4, 13, 100

AMA: 2000, Jan, 1; 2000, Aug, 7; 1999, Nov, 40

To report the injection procedure consult CPT codes 62280-62282, 62310-62319, 64479-64484, and 0027T.
Code 72275 includes code 76005.
Report 72275 only when an epidurogram is performed, images documented, and a formal radiology report is written.

72285 **Diskography, cervical or thoracic, radiological supervision and interpretation** S 80 ⬛
MED: 100-2, 15, 80; 100-4, 13, 10; 100-4, 13, 100

AMA: 1999, Nov, 35, 40

To report procedure, consult CPT code 62291.

72295 **Diskography, lumbar, radiological supervision and interpretation** S 80 ⬛
MED: 100-2, 15, 80; 100-4, 13, 10; 100-4, 13, 100

To report procedure, consult CPT code 62290.

UPPER EXTREMITIES

If a radiological examination of stress views is performed, any joint, consult CPT code 76006.

73000 **Radiologic examination; clavicle, complete** X
MED: 100-2, 15, 80; 100-4, 13, 10; 100-4, 13, 100

73010 **scapula, complete** X
MED: 100-2, 15, 80; 100-4, 13, 10; 100-4, 13, 100

Radiology

73020 — 73120

73020	**Radiologic examination, shoulder; one view**	☒
	MED: 100-2, 15, 80; 100-4, 13, 10; 100-4, 13, 100	
73030	**complete, minimum of two views**	☒ 🄳
	MED: 100-2, 15, 80; 100-4, 13, 10; 100-4, 13, 100	
73040	**Radiologic examination, shoulder, arthrography, radiological supervision and interpretation**	ⓈＣ 🄳
	MED: 100-2, 15, 80; 100-4, 13, 10; 100-4, 13, 100	
	AMA: 2001, Jul, 3	

Code 76003 cannot be reported with 73040.

To report inection procedure, consult CPT code 23350.

73050	**Radiologic examination; acromioclavicular joints, bilateral, with or without weighted distraction**	☒ 80
	MED: 100-2, 15, 80; 100-4, 13, 10; 100-4, 13, 100	
73060	**humerus, minimum of two views**	☒
	MED: 100-2, 15, 80; 100-4, 13, 10; 100-4, 13, 100	
73070	**Radiologic examination, elbow; two views**	☒
	MED: 100-2, 15, 80; 100-4, 13, 10; 100-4, 13, 100	
	AMA: 2001, Sep, 4	
73080	**complete, minimum of three views**	☒ 🄳
	MED: 100-2, 15, 80; 100-4, 13, 10; 100-4, 13, 100	
73085	**Radiologic examination, elbow, arthrography, radiological supervision and interpretation**	Ⓢ 🄳
	MED: 100-2, 15, 80; 100-4, 13, 10; 100-4, 13, 100	

Code 76003 cannot be reported with 73085.

To report injection procedure, consult CPT code 24220.

73090	**Radiologic examination; forearm, two views**	☒
	MED: 100-2, 15, 80; 100-4, 13, 10; 100-4, 13, 100	
	AMA: 2001, Sep, 4	
73092	**upper extremity, infant, minimum of two views**	Ⓐ ☒
	MED: 100-2, 15, 80; 100-4, 13, 10; 100-4, 13, 100	
73100	**Radiologic examination, wrist; two views**	☒
	MED: 100-2, 15, 80; 100-4, 13, 10; 100-4, 13, 100	
	AMA: 2001, Sep, 4	
73110	**complete, minimum of three views**	☒ 🄳
	MED: 100-2, 15, 80; 100-4, 13, 10; 100-4, 13, 100	
	AMA: 1997, Mar, 10	
73115	**Radiologic examination, wrist, arthrography, radiological supervision and interpretation**	Ⓢ 🄳
	MED: 100-2, 15, 80; 100-4, 13, 10; 100-4, 13, 100	

Code 76003 cannot be reported with 73115.

To report injection procedure, consult CPT code 25246.

73120	**Radiologic examination, hand; two views**	☒ 🄳
	MED: 100-2, 15, 80; 100-4, 13, 10; 100-4, 13, 100	

73130 minimum of three views ☒ ⬛
MED: 100-2, 15, 80; 100-4, 13, 10; 100-4, 13, 100

73140 Radiologic examination, finger(s), minimum of two views ☒
MED: 100-2, 15, 80; 100-4, 13, 10; 100-4, 13, 100

73200 Computed tomography, upper extremity; without contrast material ⬛⬛
MED: 100-2, 15, 80; 100-3, 220.1; 100-4, 13, 10; 100-4, 13, 100; 100-4, 13, 30

73201 with contrast material(s) ⬛⬛
MED: 100-2, 15, 80; 100-3, 220.1; 100-4, 13, 10; 100-4, 13, 100; 100-4, 13, 30

73202 without contrast material, followed by contrast material(s) and further sections ⬛⬛
MED: 100-2, 15, 80; 100-3, 220.1; 100-4, 13, 10; 100-4, 13, 100; 100-4, 13, 30

If 3D rendering is performed, consult CPT codes 76376, 76377.

73206 Computed tomographic angiography, upper extremity, without contrast material(s), followed by contrast material(s) and further sections, including image post-processing ⬛⬛⬛
MED: 100-2, 15, 80; 100-3, 220.1; 100-4, 13, 10; 100-4, 13, 100; 100-4, 13, 30

AMA: 2001, Jul, 3

73218 Magnetic resonance (eg, proton) imaging, upper extremity, other than joint; without contrast material(s) ⬛⬛⬛
MED: 100-2, 15, 80; 100-4, 13, 10; 100-4, 13, 100; 100-4, 13, 30

AMA: 2001, Jul, 3

73219 with contrast material(s) ⬛⬛⬛
MED: 100-2, 15, 80; 100-3, 220.2; 100-3, 220.3; 100-4, 13, 10; 100-4, 13, 100; 100-4, 13, 40

AMA: 2001, Jul, 3

73220 without contrast material(s), followed by contrast material(s) and further sequences ⬛⬛
MED: 100-2, 15, 80; 100-3, 220.2; 100-3, 220.3; 100-4, 13, 10; 100-4, 13, 100; 100-4, 13, 40

AMA: 2001, Jul, 3

73221 Magnetic resonance (eg, proton) imaging, any joint of upper extremity; without contrast material(s) ⬛⬛
MED: 100-2, 15, 80; 100-3, 220.2; 100-3, 220.3; 100-4, 13, 10; 100-4, 13, 100; 100-4, 13, 40

AMA: 2001, Jul, 3

73222 with contrast material(s) ⬛⬛⬛
MED: 100-2, 15, 80; 100-3, 220.2; 100-3, 220.3; 100-4, 13, 10; 100-4, 13, 100; 100-4, 13, 40

AMA: 2001, Jul, 3

73223 without contrast material(s), followed by contrast material(s) and further sequences ⬛⬛⬛
MED: 100-2, 15, 80; 100-3, 220.2; 100-3, 220.3; 100-4, 13, 10; 100-4, 13, 100; 100-4, 13, 40

AMA: 2001, Jul, 3

73225 Magnetic resonance angiography, upper extremity, with or without contrast material(s) ⬛
MED: 100-2, 15, 80; 100-3, 220.2; 100-3, 220.3; 100-4, 13, 10; 100-4, 13, 100; 100-4, 13, 40.1; 100-4, 13, 40.1.1; 100-4, 18, 20.7

LOWER EXTREMITIES

If a radiological examination of stress views is performed, any joint, consult CPT code 76006.

73500 **Radiologic examination, hip unilateral; one view** ☒ 80
MED: 100-2, 15, 80; 100-4, 13, 10; 100-4, 13, 100

73510 **complete, minimum of two views** ☒ 80 ↵
MED: 100-2, 15, 80; 100-4, 13, 10; 100-4, 13, 100
AMA: 2002, Apr, 19; 1999, May, 10; 1992, Spring, 9

73520 **Radiologic examination, hips, bilateral, minimum of two views of each hip, including anteroposterior view of pelvis** ☒ 80 ↵
MED: 100-2, 15, 80; 100-4, 13, 10; 100-4, 13, 100
AMA: 2002, Apr, 19

73525 **Radiologic examination, hip, arthrography, radiological supervision and interpretation** Ⓢ ↵
MED: 100-2, 15, 80; 100-4, 13, 10; 100-4, 13, 100

Code 76003 cannot be reported with 73525.

To report injection procedure, consult CPT codes 27093, 27095.

73530 **Radiologic examination, hip, during operative procedure** ☒
MED: 100-2, 15, 80; 100-4, 13, 10; 100-4, 13, 100

73540 **Radiologic examination, pelvis and hips, infant or child, minimum of two views** Ⓐ ☒ 80 ↵
MED: 100-2, 15, 80; 100-4, 13, 10; 100-4, 13, 100

73542 **Radiological examination, sacroiliac joint arthrography, radiological supervision and interpretation** Ⓢ ↵
MED: 100-2, 15, 80; 100-4, 13, 10; 100-4, 13, 100
AMA: 1999, Nov, 40-41

Code 76003 cannot be reported with 73542.

For injection procedure, use 27096. If formal arthrography is not performed, recorded, and a formal radiologic report is not issued, use 76005 for fluoroscopic guidance for sacroiliac joint injections.

73550 **Radiologic examination, femur, two views** ☒
MED: 100-2, 15, 80; 100-4, 13, 10; 100-4, 13, 100
AMA: 2001, Sep, 4

73560 **Radiologic examination, knee; one or two views** ☒ ↵
MED: 100-2, 15, 80; 100-4, 13, 10; 100-4, 13, 100

73562 **three views** ☒ ↵
MED: 100-2, 15, 80; 100-4, 13, 10; 100-4, 13, 100

73564 **complete, four or more views** ☒ ↵
MED: 100-2, 15, 80; 100-4, 13, 10; 100-4, 13, 100
AMA: 1998, Nov, 21; 1998, Jun, 11

73565 **both knees, standing, anteroposterior** ☒ 80 ↵
MED: 100-2, 15, 80; 100-4, 13, 10; 100-4, 13, 100

73580 **Radiologic examination, knee, arthrography, radiological supervision and interpretation** Ⓢ ↵
MED: 100-2, 15, 80; 100-4, 13, 10; 100-4, 13, 100

Code 76003 cannot be reported with 73580.

To report injection procedure, consult CPT code 27370.

73590 Radiologic examination; tibia and fibula, two views ☒ ▣
MED: 100-2, 15, 80; 100-4, 13, 10; 100-4, 13, 100
AMA: 2001, Sep, 4

73592 lower extremity, infant, minimum of two views Ⓐ ☒
MED: 100-2, 15, 80; 100-4, 13, 10; 100-4, 13, 100

73600 Radiologic examination, ankle; two views ☒
MED: 100-2, 15, 80; 100-4, 13, 10; 100-4, 13, 100
AMA: 2001, Sep, 4

73610 complete, minimum of three views ☒ ▣
MED: 100-2, 15, 80; 100-4, 13, 10; 100-4, 13, 100

73615 Radiologic examination, ankle, arthrography, radiological supervision and
interpretation Ⓢ ▣
MED: 100-2, 15, 80; 100-4, 13, 10; 100-4, 13, 100

Code 76003 cannot be reported with 73615.

To report injection procedure, consult CPT code 27648.

73620 Radiologic examination, foot; two views ☒ ▣
MED: 100-2, 15, 80; 100-4, 13, 10; 100-4, 13, 100
AMA: 2001, Sep, 4

73630 complete, minimum of three views ☒ ▣
MED: 100-2, 15, 80; 100-4, 13, 10; 100-4, 13, 100

73650 Radiologic examination; calcaneus, minimum of two views ☒
MED: 100-2, 15, 80; 100-4, 13, 10; 100-4, 13, 100

73660 toe(s), minimum of two views ☒
MED: 100-2, 15, 80; 100-4, 13, 10; 100-4, 13, 100

73700 Computed tomography, lower extremity; without contrast material Ⓢ 80 ▣
MED: 100-2, 13, 30; 100-2, 15, 80; 100-3, 220.1; 100-4, 13, 10; 100-4, 13, 100

73701 with contrast material(s) Ⓢ 80 ▣
MED: 100-2, 13, 30; 100-2, 15, 80; 100-3, 220.1; 100-4, 13, 10; 100-4, 13, 100

73702 without contrast material, followed by contrast material(s) and further
sections Ⓢ 80 ▣
MED: 100-2, 13, 30; 100-2, 15, 80; 100-3, 220.1; 100-4, 13, 10; 100-4, 13, 100

If 3D rendering is performed, consult CPT codes 76376, 76377.

73706 Computed tomographic angiography, lower extremity, without contrast
material(s), followed by contrast material(s) and further sections, including
image post-processing Ⓢ 80 ▣
MED: 100-2, 15, 80; 100-4, 13, 10; 100-4, 13, 100
AMA: 2001, Jul, 3

To report CTA aorto-iliofemoral runoff, consult CPT code 75635.

73718 Magnetic resonance (eg, proton) imaging, lower extremity other than joint;
without contrast material(s) Ⓢ 80 ▣
MED: 100-2, 15, 80; 100-3, 220.2; 100-3, 220.3; 100-4, 13, 10; 100-4, 13, 100; 100-4, 13, 40
AMA: 2001, Jul, 3

73719 with contrast material(s) Ⓢ 80 ▣
MED: 100-2, 15, 80; 100-3, 220.2; 100-3, 220.3; 100-4, 13, 10; 100-4, 13, 100; 100-4, 13, 40
AMA: 2001, Jul, 3

Radiology

73720 — 74175

73720	without contrast material(s), followed by contrast material(s) and further sequences ⑤ 80 ↻

MED: 100-2, 15, 80; 100-3, 220.2; 100-3, 220.3; 100-4, 13, 10; 100-4, 13, 100; 100-4, 13, 40

AMA: 2001, Jul, 3

73721 Magnetic resonance (eg, proton) imaging, any joint of lower extremity; without contrast material ⑤ ↻

MED: 100-2, 15, 80; 100-3, 220.2; 100-3, 220.3; 100-4, 13, 10; 100-4, 13, 100; 100-4, 13, 40

AMA: 2001, Jul, 3

73722 with contrast material(s) ⑤ 80 ↻

MED: 100-2, 15, 80; 100-3, 220.2; 100-3, 220.3; 100-4, 13, 10; 100-4, 13, 100; 100-4, 13, 40

AMA: 2001, Jul, 3

73723 without contrast material(s), followed by contrast material(s) and further sequences ⑤ 80 ↻

MED: 100-2, 15, 80; 100-3, 220.2; 100-3, 220.3; 100-4, 13, 10; 100-4, 13, 100; 100-4, 13, 40

AMA: 2001, Jul, 3

73725 Magnetic resonance angiography, lower extremity, with or without contrast material(s) Ⓑ 80 ↻

MED: 100-2, 15, 80; 100-3, 220.2; 100-3, 220.3; 100-4, 13, 10; 100-4, 13, 100; 100-4, 13, 40.1; 100-4, 13, 40.1.1; 100-4, 18, 20.7

ABDOMEN

74000 Radiologic examination, abdomen; single anteroposterior view Ⓧ 80

MED: 100-2, 15, 80; 100-2, 15, 80.4; 100-4, 13, 10; 100-4, 13, 100; 100-4, 13, 90

AMA: 1998, Nov, 21

74010 anteroposterior and additional oblique and cone views Ⓧ 80 ↻

MED: 100-2, 15, 80; 100-4, 13, 10; 100-4, 13, 100

74020 complete, including decubitus and/or erect views Ⓧ 80 ↻

MED: 100-2, 15, 80; 100-4, 13, 10; 100-4, 13, 100

74022 complete acute abdomen series, including supine, erect, and/or decubitus views, single view chest Ⓧ 80 ↻

MED: 100-2, 15, 80; 100-4, 13, 10; 100-4, 13, 100

74150 Computed tomography, abdomen; without contrast material ⑤ 80 ↻

MED: 100-2, 15, 80; 100-3, 220.1; 100-4, 13, 10; 100-4, 13, 100; 100-4, 13, 30

AMA: 2002, Oct, 12

74160 with contrast material(s) ⑤ 80 ↻

MED: 100-2, 15, 80; 100-3, 220.1; 100-4, 13, 10; 100-4, 13, 100; 100-4, 13, 30

74170 without contrast material, followed by contrast material(s) and further sections ⑤ 80 ↻

MED: 100-2, 15, 80; 100-3, 220.1; 100-4, 13, 10; 100-4, 13, 100; 100-4, 13, 30

If 3D rendering is performed, consult CPT codes 76376, 76377.

For computed tomographic colonography, consult Category III codes 0066T, 0067T.

Codes 72192-72194 cannot be reported with Category III codes 0066T, 0067T.

74175 Computed tomographic angiography, abdomen, without contrast material(s), followed by contrast material(s) and further sections, including image post-processing ⑤ 80 ↻

MED: 100-2, 15, 80; 100-3, 220.1; 100-4, 13, 10; 100-4, 13, 100; 100-4, 13, 30

AMA: 2001, Jul, 3

To report CTA aorto-iliofemoral runoff, consult CPT code 75635.

74181 Magnetic resonance (eg, proton) imaging, abdomen; without contrast material(s) [S] [80] [↘]
MED: 100-2, 15, 80; 100-3, 220.2; 100-3, 220.3; 100-4, 13, 10; 100-4, 13, 100; 100-4, 13, 40
AMA: 2001, Jul, 3

74182 with contrast material(s) [S] [80] [↘]
MED: 100-2, 15, 80; 100-3, 220.2; 100-3, 220.3; 100-4, 13, 10; 100-4, 13, 100; 100-4, 13, 40
AMA: 2001, Jul, 3

74183 without contrast material(s), followed by with contrast material(s) and further sequences [S] [80] [↘]
MED: 100-2, 15, 80; 100-3, 220.2; 100-3, 220.3; 100-4, 13, 10; 100-4, 13, 100; 100-4, 13, 40
AMA: 2001, Jul, 3

74185 Magnetic resonance angiography, abdomen, with or without contrast material(s) [B] [80] [↘]
MED: 100-3, 220.2; 100-3, 220.3; 100-4, 13, 40.1; 100-4, 13, 40.1.1

74190 Peritoneogram (eg, after injection of air or contrast), radiological supervision and interpretation [X] [80] [↘]
MED: 100-2, 15, 80; 100-4, 13, 10; 100-4, 13, 100

If air or contrast is injected into the peritoneal cavity, consult CPT code 49400. If computed tomography is performed on the pelvis, consult CPT code 72192 or 74150.

GASTROINTESTINAL TRACT
If the gastrostomy tube is placed percutaneously, consult CPT code 43750.

74210 Radiologic examination; pharynx and/or cervical esophagus [S] [80]
MED: 100-2, 15, 80; 100-4, 13, 10; 100-4, 13, 100

74220 esophagus [S] [80] [↘]
MED: 100-2, 15, 80; 100-4, 13, 10; 100-4, 13, 100

74230 Swallowing function, with cineradiography/videoradiography [S] [80] [↘]
MED: 100-2, 15, 80; 100-4, 13, 10; 100-4, 13, 100

74235 Removal of foreign body(s), esophageal, with use of balloon catheter, radiological supervision and interpretation [S] [80] [↘]
MED: 100-2, 15, 80; 100-4, 13, 10; 100-4, 13, 100

To report esophagoscopy or upper gastrointestinal endoscopy procedure with removal of a foreign body, consult CPT codes 43215 and 43247.

74240 Radiologic examination, gastrointestinal tract, upper; with or without delayed films, without KUB [S] [80] [↘]
MED: 100-2, 15, 80; 100-4, 13, 10; 100-4, 13, 100

74241 with or without delayed films, with KUB [S] [80] [↘]
MED: 100-2, 15, 80; 100-4, 13, 10; 100-4, 13, 100

74245 with small intestine, includes multiple serial films [S] [80] [↘]
MED: 100-2, 15, 80; 100-4, 13, 10; 100-4, 13, 100

74246 Radiological examination, gastrointestinal tract, upper, air contrast, with specific high density barium, effervescent agent, with or without glucagon; with or without delayed films, without KUB [S] [80] [↘]
MED: 100-2, 15, 80; 100-4, 13, 10; 100-4, 13, 100

Moynihan test

Radiology

74247 — 74320

74247	with or without delayed films, with KUB	S 80 ⬛
	MED: 100-2, 15, 80; 100-4, 13, 10; 100-4, 13, 100	

74249	with small intestine follow-through	S 80 ⬛
	MED: 100-2, 15, 80; 100-4, 13, 10; 100-4, 13, 100	

74250	Radiologic examination, small intestine, includes multiple serial films;	S 80 ⬛
	MED: 100-2, 15, 80; 100-4, 13, 10; 100-4, 13, 100	

74251	via enteroclysis tube	S 80 ⬛
	MED: 100-2, 15, 80; 100-4, 13, 10; 100-4, 13, 100	

74260	Duodenography, hypotonic	S 80
	MED: 100-2, 15, 80; 100-4, 13, 10; 100-4, 13, 100	

74270	Radiologic examination, colon; barium enema, with or without KUB	S 80 ⬛
	MED: 100-2, 15, 80; 100-4, 13, 10; 100-4, 13, 100	

74280	air contrast with specific high density barium, with or without glucagon	S 80 ⬛
	MED: 100-2, 15, 80; 100-4, 13, 10; 100-4, 13, 100	

74283	Therapeutic enema, contrast or air, for reduction of intussusception or other intraluminal obstruction (eg, meconium ileus)	S 80
	MED: 100-2, 15, 80; 100-4, 13, 10; 100-4, 13, 100	
	AMA: 1997, Nov, 24	

74290	Cholecystography, oral contrast;	S 80
	MED: 100-2, 15, 80; 100-4, 13, 10; 100-4, 13, 100	

74291	additional or repeat examination or multiple day examination	S 80
	MED: 100-2, 15, 80; 100-4, 13, 10; 100-4, 13, 100	

74300	Cholangiography and/or pancreatography; intraoperative, radiological supervision and interpretation	X 80 ⬛
	MED: 100-2, 15, 80; 100-4, 13, 10; 100-4, 13, 100	
	AMA: 2000, Dec, 14; 1999, Nov, 41	

+ **74301**	additional set intraoperative, radiological supervision and interpretation (List separately in addition to code for primary procedure)	X 80 ⬛
	MED: 100-2, 15, 80; 100-4, 13, 10; 100-4, 13, 100	

Note that 74301 is an add-on code and must be used in conjunction with 74300.

74305	through existing catheter, radiological supervision and interpretation	X 80 ⬛
	MED: 100-2, 15, 80; 100-4, 13, 10; 100-4, 13, 100	
	AMA: 1999, Nov, 41	

To report procedure performed, consult CPT codes 47505, 47560-47561, 47563, and 48400. If a biliary duct stone extraction is performed percutaneously, consult CPT codes 47630 and 74327.

74320	Cholangiography, percutaneous, transhepatic, radiological supervision and interpretation	X 80 ⬛
	MED: 100-2, 15, 80; 100-4, 13, 10; 100-4, 13, 100	

To report procedure, consult CPT code 47500.

74327 **Postoperative biliary duct calculus removal, percutaneous via T-tube tract, basket, or snare (eg, Burhenne technique), radiological supervision and interpretation** $\boxed{S}$ $\boxed{80}$ $\boxed{\blacksquare}$
MED: 100-2, 15, 80; 100-4, 13, 10; 100-4, 13, 100

If a biliary duct stone extraction is performed percutaneously, consult CPT code 47630.

74328 **Endoscopic catheterization of the biliary ductal system, radiological supervision and interpretation** $\boxed{N}$ $\boxed{80}$ $\boxed{\blacksquare}$
MED: 100-2, 15, 80; 100-4, 13, 10; 100-4, 13, 100

To report endoscopic retrograde cholangiopancreatography (ECRP) procedure, consult CPT codes 43260-43272 as appropriate.

74329 **Endoscopic catheterization of the pancreatic ductal system, radiological supervision and interpretation** $\boxed{N}$ $\boxed{80}$ $\boxed{\blacksquare}$
MED: 100-2, 15, 80; 100-4, 13, 10; 100-4, 13, 100

To report endoscopic retrograde cholangiopancreatography (ECRP) procedure, consult CPT codes 43260-43272 as appropriate.

74330 **Combined endoscopic catheterization of the biliary and pancreatic ductal systems, radiological supervision and interpretation** $\boxed{N}$ $\boxed{80}$ $\boxed{\blacksquare}$
MED: 100-2, 15, 80; 100-4, 13, 10; 100-4, 13, 100

To report endoscopic retrograde cholangiopancreatography (ECRP) procedure, consult CPT codes 43260-43272 as appropriate.

74340 **Introduction of long gastrointestinal tube (eg, Miller-Abbott), including multiple fluoroscopies and films, radiological supervision and interpretation** $\boxed{X}$ $\boxed{80}$ $\boxed{\blacksquare}$
MED: 100-2, 15, 80; 100-4, 13, 10; 100-4, 13, 100

If tube is placed, consult CPT code 44500.

74350 **Percutaneous placement of gastrostomy tube, radiological supervision and interpretation** $\boxed{X}$ $\boxed{80}$ $\boxed{\blacksquare}$
MED: 100-2, 15, 80; 100-4, 13, 10; 100-4, 13, 100

74355 **Percutaneous placement of enteroclysis tube, radiological supervision and interpretation** $\boxed{X}$ $\boxed{80}$ $\boxed{\blacksquare}$
MED: 100-2, 15, 80; 100-4, 13, 10; 100-4, 13, 100

To report procedure, consult CPT code 44015.

74360 **Intraluminal dilation of strictures and/or obstructions (eg, esophagus), radiological supervision and interpretation** $\boxed{S}$ $\boxed{80}$ $\boxed{\blacksquare}$
MED: 100-2, 15, 80; 100-4, 13, 10; 100-4, 13, 100

AMA: 1994, Spring, 3

To report procedure, consult CPT codes 43220 or 43458.

74363 **Percutaneous transhepatic dilation of biliary duct stricture with or without placement of stent, radiological supervision and interpretation** $\boxed{S}$ $\boxed{80}$ $\boxed{\blacksquare}$
MED: 100-2, 15, 80; 100-4, 13, 10; 100-4, 13, 100

If a transhepatic catheter/stent is introduced percutaneously, consult CPT codes 47510 and 47511. If a biliary endoscopy is performed percutaneously via a T-tube or other tract with dilation of the biliary duct stricture(s), consult CPT codes 47555 and 47556.

| $\boxed{\blacksquare}$ CCI Comp | $\boxed{50}$ Bilateral Procedure | + CPT Add-on Code | $\bigcirc$ Modifier -51 Exempt | ♂ Male | ♀ Female |
| ● New Code | ▲ Revised Code | $\boxed{M}$ Maternity Edit | $\boxed{A}$ Age Edit | $\boxed{A}$–$\boxed{Y}$ APC Status Ind. | AMA: CPT Assistant |

© 2005 Ingenix, Inc. *(Blue Ink)* CPT only © 2005 American Medical Association. All Rights Reserved. *(Black Ink)* Radiology — 521

Radiology

74400 — 74475

URINARY TRACT

74400   Urography (pyelography), intravenous, with or without KUB, with or without
          tomography;   ⑤ ⑧⓪ 🔲
          MED: 100-2, 15, 80; 100-4, 13, 10; 100-4, 13, 100

74410   Urography, infusion, drip technique and/or bolus technique;   ⑤ ⑧⓪ 🔲
          MED: 100-2, 15, 80; 100-4, 13, 10; 100-4, 13, 100

74415   with nephrotomography   ⑤ ⑧⓪ 🔲
          MED: 100-2, 15, 80; 100-4, 13, 10; 100-4, 13, 100

74420   Urography, retrograde, with or without KUB   ⑤ ⑧⓪ 🔲
          MED: 100-2, 15, 80; 100-4, 13, 10; 100-4, 13, 100

          AMA: 2000, Sep, 11

74425   Urography, antegrade, (pyelostogram, nephrostogram, loopogram),
          radiological supervision and interpretation   ⑤ ⑧⓪ 🔲
          MED: 100-2, 15, 80; 100-4, 13, 10; 100-4, 13, 100

          AMA: 1997, Dec, 7; 1993, Fall, 14

          To report procedure, consult CPT codes 50394, 50684, and 50690.

74430   Cystography, minimum of three views, radiological supervision and
          interpretation   ⑤ ⑧⓪ 🔲
          MED: 100-2, 15, 80; 100-4, 13, 10; 100-4, 13, 100

          To report procedure, consult CPT codes 51600 and 51605.

74440   Vasography, vesiculography, or epididymography, radiological supervision
          and interpretation   ♂ ⑤ ⑧⓪ 🔲
          MED: 100-2, 15, 80; 100-4, 13, 10; 100-4, 13, 100

          To report procedure, consult CPT codes 52010 and 55300.

74445   Corpora cavernosography, radiological supervision and
          interpretation   ♂ ⑤ ⑧⓪ 🔲
          MED: 100-2, 15, 80; 100-4, 13, 10; 100-4, 13, 100

          To report procedure, consult CPT code 54230.

74450   Urethrocystography, retrograde, radiological supervision and
          interpretation   ⑤ ⑧⓪ 🔲
          MED: 100-2, 15, 80; 100-4, 13, 10; 100-4, 13, 100

          To report procedure, consult CPT code 51610.

74455   Urethrocystography, voiding, radiological supervision and
          interpretation   ⑤ ⑧⓪ 🔲
          MED: 100-2, 15, 80; 100-3, 230.2; 100-4, 13, 10; 100-4, 13, 100

          To report procedure, consult CPT code 51600.

74470   Radiologic examination, renal cyst study, translumbar, contrast
          visualization, radiological supervision and interpretation   Ⓧ ⑧⓪ 🔲
          MED: 100-2, 15, 80; 100-4, 13, 10; 100-4, 13, 100

          To report procedure, consult CPT code 50390.

74475   Introduction of intracatheter or catheter into renal pelvis for drainage
          and/or injection, percutaneous, radiological supervision and
          interpretation   ⑤ ⑧⓪ 🔲
          MED: 100-2, 15, 80; 100-4, 13, 10; 100-4, 13, 100

          AMA: 1997, Dec, 7

          To report procedure, consult CPT codes 50392 and 50396.

74480 Introduction of ureteral catheter or stent into ureter through renal pelvis for drainage and/or injection, percutaneous, radiological supervision and interpretation Ⓢ 80 🗎
MED: 100-2, 15, 80; 100-4, 13, 10; 100-4, 13, 100

AMA: 1993, Fall, 14

To report surgical procedure performed consult CPT codes 50393, 50395, and 50396 as appropriate. If transurethral surgery (ureter and pelvis) is performed, consult CPT codes 52320-52355.

74485 Dilation of nephrostomy, ureters, or urethra, radiological supervision and interpretation Ⓢ 80 🗎
MED: 100-2, 15, 80; 100-4, 13, 10; 100-4, 13, 100

If the ureter is dilated without radiological guidance, consult CPT codes 52341, 52344. If a nephrostomy or pyelostomy tube is changed, consult CPT code 50395.

To report procedure, consult CPT codes 50395 and 53600-53621.

GYNECOLOGICAL AND OBSTETRICAL

If radiological examination is performed on the abdomen and pelvis, consult CPT codes 72170-72190, 74000-74170.

74710 Pelvimetry, with or without placental localization ♀ ☒ 80
MED: 100-2, 15, 80; 100-4, 13, 10; 100-4, 13, 100

74740 Hysterosalpingography, radiological supervision and interpretation ♀ ☒ 80 🗎
MED: 100-2, 15, 80; 100-4, 13, 10; 100-4, 13, 100

AMA: 1999, Jul, 8; 1997, Nov, 24

If saline or contrast is introduced for hysterosalpingography, see 58340.

74742 Transcervical catheterization of fallopian tube, radiological supervision and interpretation ♀ ☒ 80 🗎
MED: 100-2, 15, 80; 100-4, 13, 10; 100-4, 13, 100

To report the transcervical introduction of a fallopian tube catheter with or without hysterosalpingography, consult CPT code 58345.

74775 Perineogram (eg, vaginogram, for sex determination or extent of anomalies) Ⓜ ♀ Ⓢ 80 🗎
MED: 100-2, 15, 80; 100-4, 13, 10; 100-4, 13, 100

HEART

To report cardiac catheterization procedures, consult CPT codes 93501-93556.

75552 Cardiac magnetic resonance imaging for morphology; without contrast material Ⓢ 80
MED: 100-2, 15, 80; 100-3, 220.2; 100-3, 220.3; 100-4, 13, 10; 100-4, 13, 100; 100-4, 13, 40

AMA: 1995, Fall, 1

75553 with contrast material Ⓢ 80 🗎
MED: 100-2, 15, 80; 100-3, 220.2; 100-3, 220.3; 100-4, 13, 10; 100-4, 13, 100; 100-4, 13, 40

AMA: 1995, Fall, 1

75554 Cardiac magnetic resonance imaging for funciton, with or without morphology; complete study Ⓢ 80 🗎
MED: 100-2, 15, 80; 100-3, 220.2; 100-3, 220.3; 100-4, 13, 10; 100-4, 13, 100; 100-4, 13, 40

AMA: 1995, Fall, 2

Radiology

75555	limited study	S 80

MED: 100-2, 15, 80; 100-3, 220.2; 100-3, 220.3; 100-4, 13, 10; 100-4, 13, 100; 100-4, 13, 40

AMA: 1995, Fall, 2

75556   Cardiac magnetic resonance imaging for velocity flow mapping   E

MED: 100-2, 15, 80; 100-3, 220.2; 100-3, 220.3; 100-4, 13, 10; 100-4, 13, 100; 100-4, 13, 40

AMA: 1995, Fall, 2

VASCULAR PROCEDURES

AORTA AND ARTERIES

Include introduction and all lesser order catheterization used in the approach. Additional order catheterization within the same family of arteries should be reported using codes in the 36000 range The following diagnostic angiography procedures include the work provided in the interventional procedure and should not be reported separately:

- Contrast injections, angiography, roadmapping, and/or fluoroscopy

- Vessel measurement

- Post angiography or stent angiography

Diagnostic codes may only be used in addition to the interventional procedure if the following are met:

- No previous angiographic study is available, and a full diagnostic study is performed that is the basis for the interventional procedure.

- A diagnostic study is documented in the medical records but the patient's condition has changed, there is not adequate visualization, or there is a clinical change during the procedure that requires reevaluation.

- The diagnostic study is performed in a different area from the interventional surgery

Do not separately report a diagnostic angiography performed at the same time as an interventional procedure if it specifically included in the interventional code procedure description.

To report intravenous procedures, consult CPT codes 36000-36013, 36400-36425 and 36100-36248 for intra-arterial procedures. To report radiological supervision and interpretation, consult CPT codes 75600-75978.

75600   **Aortography, thoracic, without serialography, radiological supervision and interpretation**   S 80

MED: 100-2, 15, 80; 100-4, 13, 10; 100-4, 13, 100

To report the injection procedure, consult CPT code 93544.

75605   **Aortography, thoracic, by serialography, radiological supervision and interpretation**   S 80

MED: 100-2, 15, 80; 100-4, 13, 10; 100-4, 13, 100

AMA: 1998, Dec, 9; 1994, Spring, 29

To report the injection procedure, consult CPT code 93544.

75625   **Aortography, abdominal, by serialography, radiological supervision and interpretation**   S 80

MED: 100-2, 15, 80; 100-4, 13, 10; 100-4, 13, 100

AMA: 2001, Jan, 14; 1993, Fall, 16

To report the injection procedure, consult CPT code 93544.

75555 — 75625

26 / TC Professional/Technical Component	80 / 80 Assist-at-Surgery Allowed/With Documentation	⊙ Conscious Sedation
Unlisted Not Covered **MED:** Pubs 100/NCD Reference 1 - 9 ASC Group	63 Modifier 63 Exempt

524 — Radiology   CPT only © 2005 American Medical Association. All Rights Reserved. (Black Ink)   © 2005 Ingenix, Inc. (Blue Ink)

75630   **Aortography, abdominal plus bilateral iliofemoral lower extremity, catheter, by serialography, radiological supervision and interpretation**   S 80 🖸
MED: 100-2, 15, 80; 100-4, 13, 10; 100-4, 13, 100

AMA: 2001, Jan, 14; 1993, Fall, 16

Include introduction and all lesser order catheterization used in the approach. Additional order catheterization within the same family of arteries should be reported using codes in the 36000s.

75635   **Computed tomographic angiography, abdominal aorta and bilateral iliofemoral lower extremity runoff, radiological supervision and interpretation, without contrast material(s), followed by contrast material(s) and further sections, including image post-processing**   S 80 🖸
MED: 100-2, 15, 80; 100-4, 13, 10; 100-4, 13, 100

AMA: 2001, Jul, 3

75650   **Angiography, cervicocerebral, catheter, including vessel origin, radiological supervision and interpretation**   S 80 🖸
MED: 100-2, 15, 80; 100-4, 13, 10; 100-4, 13, 100

AMA: 2000, Oct, 4; 1998, Apr, 3; 1994, Spring, 29

75658   **Angiography, brachial, retrograde, radiological supervision and interpretation**   S 80 🖸
MED: 100-2, 15, 80; 100-4, 13, 10; 100-4, 13, 100

75660   **Angiography, external carotid, unilateral, selective, radiological supervision and interpretation**   S 80 🖸
MED: 100-2, 15, 80; 100-4, 13, 10; 100-4, 13, 100

75662   **Angiography, external carotid, bilateral, selective, radiological supervision and interpretation**   S 80 🖸
MED: 100-2, 15, 80; 100-4, 13, 10; 100-4, 13, 100

75665   **Angiography, carotid, cerebral, unilateral, radiological supervision and interpretation**   S 80 🖸
MED: 100-2, 15, 80; 100-4, 13, 10; 100-4, 13, 100

75671   **Angiography, carotid, cerebral, bilateral, radiological supervision and interpretation**   S 80 🖸
MED: 100-2, 15, 80; 100-4, 13, 10; 100-4, 13, 100

AMA: 2000, Oct, 4

75676   **Angiography, carotid, cervical, unilateral, radiological supervision and interpretation**   S 80 🖸
MED: 100-2, 15, 80; 100-4, 13, 10; 100-4, 13, 100

75680   **Angiography, carotid, cervical, bilateral, radiological supervision and interpretation**   S 80 🖸
MED: 100-2, 15, 80; 100-4, 13, 10; 100-4, 13, 100

AMA: 2000, Oct, 4

75685   **Angiography, vertebral, cervical, and/or intracranial, radiological supervision and interpretation**   S 🖸
MED: 100-2, 15, 80; 100-4, 13, 10; 100-4, 13, 100

AMA: 2000, Oct, 4

75705   **Angiography, spinal, selective, radiological supervision and interpretation**   S 80 🖸
MED: 100-2, 15, 80; 100-4, 13, 10; 100-4, 13, 100

75710 — 75746

75710 Angiography, extremity, unilateral, radiological supervision and interpretation ⬜S⬜ ⬜80⬜ ⬜↴⬜
MED: 100-2, 15, 80; 100-4, 13, 10; 100-4, 13, 100

AMA: 2001, Jan, 14; 1999, Apr, 11

75716 Angiography, extremity, bilateral, radiological supervision and interpretation ⬜S⬜ ⬜80⬜ ⬜↴⬜
MED: 100-2, 15, 80; 100-4, 13, 10; 100-4, 13, 100

AMA: 2001, Jan, 14; 1993, Fall, 16

75722 Angiography, renal, unilateral, selective (including flush aortogram), radiological supervision and interpretation ⬜S⬜ ⬜80⬜ ⬜↴⬜
MED: 100-2, 15, 80; 100-4, 13, 10; 100-4, 13, 100

75724 Angiography, renal, bilateral, selective (including flush aortogram), radiological supervision and interpretation ⬜S⬜ ⬜80⬜ ⬜↴⬜
MED: 100-2, 15, 80; 100-4, 13, 10; 100-4, 13, 100

75726 Angiography, visceral, selective or supraselective, (with or without flush aortogram), radiological supervision and interpretation ⬜S⬜ ⬜80⬜ ⬜↴⬜
MED: 100-2, 15, 80; 100-4, 13, 10; 100-4, 13, 100

If selective angiography is performed, each additional visceral vessel studied after basic examination, consult CPT code 75774.

75731 Angiography, adrenal, unilateral, selective, radiological supervision and interpretation ⬜S⬜ ⬜80⬜ ⬜↴⬜
MED: 100-2, 15, 80; 100-4, 13, 10; 100-4, 13, 100

75733 Angiography, adrenal, bilateral, selective, radiological supervision and interpretation ⬜S⬜ ⬜80⬜ ⬜↴⬜
MED: 100-2, 15, 80; 100-4, 13, 10; 100-4, 13, 100

75736 Angiography, pelvic, selective or supraselective, radiological supervision and interpretation ⬜S⬜ ⬜80⬜ ⬜↴⬜
MED: 100-2, 15, 80; 100-4, 13, 10; 100-4, 13, 100

75741 Angiography, pulmonary, unilateral, selective, radiological supervision and interpretation ⬜S⬜ ⬜80⬜ ⬜↴⬜
MED: 100-2, 15, 80; 100-4, 13, 10; 100-4, 13, 100

To report an injection procedure during pulmonary angiography, consult CPT code 93541.

75743 Angiography, pulmonary, bilateral, selective, radiological supervision and interpretation ⬜S⬜ ⬜80⬜ ⬜↴⬜
MED: 100-2, 15, 80; 100-4, 13, 10; 100-4, 13, 100

AMA: 1998, Apr, 3; 1994, Spring, 29

For an injection procedure during pulmonary angiography, consult CPT code 93541.

75746 Angiography, pulmonary, by nonselective catheter or venous injection, radiological supervision and interpretation ⬜S⬜ ⬜80⬜ ⬜↴⬜
MED: 100-2, 15, 80; 100-4, 13, 10; 100-4, 13, 100

To report an injection procedure during cardiac catheterization To report pulmonary angiography, consult CPT code 93541. To report catheter introduction, injection procedure, consult CPT codes 93501-93533, 93539, 93540, 93545, and 93556.

If an intravenous procedure is reported, consult CPT codes 36000-36013, 36400-36425, and 36100-36248 To report an intra-arterial procedure.

26/**TC** Professional/Technical Component   **80**/**80** Assist-at-Surgery Allowed/With Documentation   ⊙ Conscious Sedation

 Unlisted   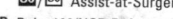 Not Covered   **MED:** Pubs 100/NCD Reference   **1**-**9** ASC Group   ⊛ Modifier 63 Exempt

526 — Radiology   CPT only © 2005 American Medical Association. All Rights Reserved. *(Black Ink)*   © 2005 Ingenix, Inc. *(Blue Ink)*

75756   **Angiography, internal mammary, radiological supervision and interpretation**   S 80 🗗
MED: 100-2, 15, 80; 100-4, 13, 10; 100-4, 13, 100

To report catheter introduction, injection procedure, consult CPT codes 93501-93533, 93545, and 93556.

+   **75774**   **Angiography, selective, each additional vessel studied after basic examination, radiological supervision and interpretation (List separately in addition to code for primary procedure)**   S 80 🗗
MED: 100-2, 15, 80; 100-4, 13, 10; 100-4, 13, 100

AMA: 1994, Spring, 29; 1993, Fall, 17

To report angiography, consult CPT code 75600-75790.

To report catheterizations, consult CPT codes 36215-36248.

To report introduction of catheter, injection procedure, consult CPT codes 93501-93533, 93545, 93555, 93556.

Note that 75774 is an add-on code that must be used in conjunction with the appropriate code To report the specific initial vessel studied. This code cannot be reported alone.

75790   **Angiography, arteriovenous shunt (eg, dialysis patient), radiological supervision and interpretation**   S 80 🗗
MED: 100-2, 15, 80; 100-4, 13, 10; 100-4, 13, 100

AMA: 2001, May, 1

To report catheter introduction, consult CPT codes 36140, 36145, 36215-36217, and 36245-36247.

VEINS AND LYMPHATICS

The following venography diagnostic procedures include the work provided in the interventional procedure and should not be reported separately:

* Contrast injections, venography, roadmapping, and/or fluoroscopy

* Vessel measurement

* Post venography or stent venography

Diagnostic procedure codes may only be used in addition to the interventional procedure if the following are met:

* No prior catheter-based venographic study is available and a full diagnostic study is performed, and the decision to intervene is based on that diagnostic study.

* A diagnostic study is documented in the medical records but the patient's condition has changed, there is not adequate visualization or there is a clinical change during the procedure that requires reevaluation.

* The diagnostic study is performed in a different area from the interventional surgery

Do not separately report a diagnostic venography performed at the same time as an interventional procedure if it specifically included in the interventional code procedure description.

The following procedures are included in a therapeutic transcatheter interventional procedure:

* Contrast injections, venography, roadmapping, and/or fluoroscopy

* Vessel measurement

* Except for services allowed by 75898, completion of angiography/venography

75756 — 75790

If an injection procedure is performed for the lymphatic system, consult CPT code 38790. If an injection procedure is performed for the venous system, consult CPT codes 36000-36015 and 36400-36510.

75801 **Lymphangiography, extremity only, unilateral, radiological supervision and interpretation** ⓧ 80 🔧
MED: 100-2, 15, 80; 100-4, 13, 10; 100-4, 13, 100

75803 **Lymphangiography, extremity only, bilateral, radiological supervision and interpretation** ⓧ 80 🔧
MED: 100-2, 15, 80; 100-4, 13, 10; 100-4, 13, 100

75805 **Lymphangiography, pelvic/abdominal, unilateral, radiological supervision and interpretation** ⓧ 80 🔧
MED: 100-2, 15, 80; 100-4, 13, 10; 100-4, 13, 100

75807 **Lymphangiography, pelvic/abdominal, bilateral, radiological supervision and interpretation** ⓧ 80 🔧
MED: 100-2, 15, 80; 100-4, 13, 10; 100-4, 13, 100

75809 **Shuntogram for investigation of previously placed indwelling nonvascular shunt (eg, LeVeen shunt, ventriculoperitoneal shunt, indwelling infusion pump), radiological supervision and interpretation** ⓧ 80 🔧
MED: 100-2, 15, 80; 100-4, 13, 10; 100-4, 13, 100

If an injection procedure is performed for the evaluation of a previously placed peritoneovenous shunt, consult CPT code 49427. For puncture of shunt tubing or reservoir for aspiration or injection procedure, consult CPT code 61070.

75810 **Splenoportography, radiological supervision and interpretation** Ⓢ 80 🔧
MED: 100-2, 15, 80; 100-4, 13, 10; 100-4, 13, 100

75820 **Venography, extremity, unilateral, radiological supervision and interpretation** Ⓢ 80 🔧
MED: 100-2, 15, 80; 100-4, 13, 10; 100-4, 13, 100
AMA: 1997, Oct, 10

75822 **Venography, extremity, bilateral, radiological supervision and interpretation** Ⓢ 80 🔧
MED: 100-2, 15, 80; 100-4, 13, 10; 100-4, 13, 100

75825 **Venography, caval, inferior, with serialography, radiological supervision and interpretation** Ⓢ 80 🔧
MED: 100-2, 15, 80; 100-4, 13, 10; 100-4, 13, 100

75827 **Venography, caval, superior, with serialography, radiological supervision and interpretation** Ⓢ 80 🔧
MED: 100-2, 15, 80; 100-4, 13, 10; 100-4, 13, 100
AMA: 1998, Apr, 3

75831 **Venography, renal, unilateral, selective, radiological supervision and interpretation** Ⓢ 80 🔧
MED: 100-2, 15, 80; 100-4, 13, 10; 100-4, 13, 100

75833 **Venography, renal, bilateral, selective, radiological supervision and interpretation** Ⓢ 80 🔧
MED: 100-2, 15, 80; 100-4, 13, 10; 100-4, 13, 100

75840 **Venography, adrenal, unilateral, selective, radiological supervision and interpretation** Ⓢ 80 🔧
MED: 100-2, 15, 80; 100-4, 13, 10; 100-4, 13, 100

75801 — 75840

75842   Venography, adrenal, bilateral, selective, radiological supervision and interpretation   ⓢ 80 ⮌
MED: 100-2, 15, 80; 100-4, 13, 10; 100-4, 13, 100

75860   Venography, venous sinus (eg, petrosal and inferior sagittal) or jugular, catheter, radiological supervision and interpretation   ⓢ 80 ⮌
MED: 100-2, 15, 80; 100-4, 13, 10; 100-4, 13, 100

75870   Venography, superior sagittal sinus, radiological supervision and interpretation   ⓢ 80 ⮌
MED: 100-2, 15, 80; 100-4, 13, 10; 100-4, 13, 100

75872   Venography, epidural, radiological supervision and interpretation   ⓢ 80 ⮌
MED: 100-2, 15, 80; 100-4, 13, 10; 100-4, 13, 100

75880   Venography, orbital, radiological supervision and interpretation   ⓢ 80 ⮌
MED: 100-2, 15, 80; 100-4, 13, 10; 100-4, 13, 100

75885   Percutaneous transhepatic portography with hemodynamic evaluation, radiological supervision and interpretation   ⓢ 80 ⮌
MED: 100-2, 15, 80; 100-4, 13, 10; 100-4, 13, 100

AMA: 2002, Mar, 10; 1996, Oct, 4

75887   Percutaneous transhepatic portography without hemodynamic evaluation, radiological supervision and interpretation   ⓢ 80 ⮌
MED: 100-2, 15, 80; 100-4, 13, 10; 100-4, 13, 100

AMA: 2002, Mar, 10

75889   Hepatic venography, wedged or free, with hemodynamic evaluation, radiological supervision and interpretation   ⓢ 80 ⮌
MED: 100-2, 15, 80; 100-4, 13, 10; 100-4, 13, 100

75891   Hepatic venography, wedged or free, without hemodynamic evaluation, radiological supervision and interpretation   ⓢ 80 ⮌
MED: 100-2, 15, 80; 100-4, 13, 10; 100-4, 13, 100

75893   Venous sampling through catheter, with or without angiography (eg, for parathyroid hormone, renin), radiological supervision and interpretation   Ⓝ 80 ⮌
MED: 100-2, 15, 80; 100-4, 13, 10; 100-4, 13, 100

If venous catheterization is performed for selective organ blood sampling, consult CPT code 36500.

TRANSCATHETER PROCEDURES

The following transcatheter procedures include the work provided in the interventional procedure and should not be reported separately:

- Contrast injections, venography, roadmapping, and/or fluoroscopy

- Vessel measurement

- Post venography or stent venography (except for those uses permitted by 75898).

Diagnostic angiography/venography performed at the same time as a transcatheter procedure is separately reportable unless it is specifically included in the descriptor. This includes instances when no prior catheter-based diagnostic angiography/venography study of the target vessel is available, prior diagnostic study is not adequate, or the patient's condition has changed since the previous study or during the intervention (see 75600-75893).

Codes 75956 and 75956 include all angiography of the thoracic aorta and its branches for diagnostic imaging prior to deployment of the primary endovascular devices, fluoroscopic guidance in the delivery of the endovascular components, and arterial angiography during the procedure.

CPT code 75958 includes the analogous services for placement of each proximal thoracic endovascular extension, and code 75959 includes the analogous services for placement of a distal thoracic endovascular extension(s) placed during a procedure after the primary repair.

75894 **Transcatheter therapy, embolization, any method, radiological supervision and interpretation** ⑤ 80 ⌐
MED: 100-2, 15, 80; 100-3, 20.28; 100-4, 13, 10; 100-4, 13, 100

AMA: 1998, Sep, 7

To report procedure, consult CPT codes 37204, 61624, and 61626.

75896 **Transcatheter therapy, infusion, any method (eg, thrombolysis other than coronary), radiological supervision and interpretation** ⑤ 80 ⌐
MED: 100-2, 15, 80; 100-4, 13, 10; 100-4, 13, 100

AMA: 2001, May, 1

To report injection procedure performed, consult CPT codes 37201, 37202. If coronary thrombolysis is performed, consult CPT codes 92975 and 92977.

75898 **Angiography through existing catheter for follow-up study for transcatheter therapy, embolization or infusion** ☒ 80 ⌐
MED: 100-2, 15, 80; 100-4, 13, 10; 100-4, 13, 100

▲ **75900** **Exchange of a previously placed intravascular catheter during thrombolytic therapy with contrast monitoring, radiological supervision and interpretation** ☐ 80 ⌐
MED: 100-2, 15, 80; 100-4, 13, 10; 100-4, 13, 100

If a previously placed arterial catheter is exchanged during thrombolytic therapy, consult CPT code 37209.

75901 **Mechanical removal of pericatheter obstructive material (eg, fibrin sheath) from central venous device via separate venous access, radiologic supervision and interpretation** ☒ 80 ⌐
MED: 100-2, 15, 80; 100-4, 13, 10; 100-4, 13, 100

To report procedure, consult CPT code 36595.

To report venous catheterization, consult CPT codes 36010-36012.

75902 **Mechanical removal of intraluminal (intracatheter) obstructive material from central venous device through device lumen, radiologic supervision and interpretation** ☒ 80 ⌐
MED: 100-2, 15, 80; 100-4, 13, 10; 100-4, 13, 100

To report procedure, consult CPT code 36596.

To report venous catheterization, consult CPT codes 36010-36012.

75940 **Percutaneous placement of IVC filter, radiological supervision and interpretation** ⑤ 80 ⌐
MED: 100-2, 15, 80; 100-4, 13, 10; 100-4, 13, 100

AMA: 2000, Nov, 11

To report procedure, consult CPT code 37620.

75945 **Intravascular ultrasound (non-coronary vessel), radiological supervision and interpretation; initial vessel** ⑤ 80 ⌐
MED: 100-3, 220.5; 100-4, 13, 10; 100-4, 13, 100

+ 75946   **each additional non-coronary vessel (List separately in addition to code for primary procedure)** ⑤ 80 🔾
MED: 100-2, 15, 80; 100-4, 13, 10; 100-4, 13, 100

To report placement of catheter, consult CPT codes 36215-36248. If transcatheter therapies are performed, consult CPT codes 37200-37208, 61624, and 61626. If an intravascular ultrasound is performed during a diagnostic evaluation and/or a therapeutic intervention, consult CPT codes 37250 and 37251.

Note that 75946 is an add-on code and must be used in conjunction with 75945.

75952   **Endovascular repair of infrarenal abdominal aortic aneurysm or dissection, radiological supervision and interpretation** © 80 🔾
MED: 100-2, 15, 80; 100-4, 13, 10; 100-4, 13, 100

To report implantation of endovascular grafts, consult CPT codes 38400-38408.

To report radiologic supervision and interpretation of endovascular repair of abdominal aortic aneurysm involving visceral vessels, consult Category III codes 0078T-0081T.

75953   **Placement of proximal or distal extension prosthesis for endovascular repair of infrarenal aortic or iliac artery aneurysm, pseudoaneurysm, or dissection, radiological supervision and interpretation** © 80 🔾
MED: 100-2, 15, 80; 100-4, 13, 10; 100-4, 13, 100

AMA: 2003, Feb, 1

To report implantation of endovascular extension prostheses, consult CPT codes 34825 and 34826.

75954   **Endovascular repair of iliac artery aneurysm, pseudoaneurysm, arteriovenous malformation, or trauma, radiological supervision and interpretation** © 80 🔾
MED: 100-2, 15, 80; 100-4, 13, 10; 100-4, 13, 100

AMA: 2003, Feb, 1

To report procedure, consult CPT code 34900.

● 75956   **Endovascular repair of descending thoracic aorta (eg, aneurysm, pseudoaneurysm, dissection, penetrating ulcer, intramural hematoma, or traumatic disruption); involving coverage of left subclavian artery origin, initial endoprosthesis plus descending thoracic aortic extension(s), if required, to level of celiac artery origin, radiological supervision and interpretation**

To report implantation of endovascular graft, consult CPT code 33880.

● 75957   **not involving coverage of left subclavian artery origin, initial endoprosthesis plus descending thoracic aortic extension(s), if required, to level of celiac artery origin, radiological supervision and interpretation**

To report implantation of endovascular graft, consult CPT code 33881.

● 75958   **Placement of proximal extension prosthesis for endovascular repair of descending thoracic aorta (eg, aneurysm, pseudoaneurysm, dissection, penetrating ulcer, intramural hematoma, or traumatic disruption), radiological supervision and interpretation**

Code 75958 should be reported for each proximal extension.

To report implantation of proximal endovascular extension, consult CPT codes 33883, 33884.

● **75959** **Placement of distal extension prosthesis(s) (delayed) after endovascular repair of descending thoracic aorta, as needed, to level of celiac origin, radiological supervision and interpretation**

Code 75959 cannot be reported with 75956, 57957.

Code 75959 should be reported only once, regardless of the number of modules deployed.

To report implantation of a distal endovascular extension, consult CPT code 33886.

75960 **Transcatheter introduction of intravascular stent(s), (except coronary, carotid, and vertebral vessel), percutaneous and/or open, radiological supervision and interpretation, each vessel** S 80
MED: 100-2, 15, 80; 100-4, 13, 10; 100-4, 13, 100

AMA: 2001, May, 1; 1996, Oct, 2; 1993, Fall, 18

To report procedure, consult CPT codes 37205-37208.

To report radiologic supervision and interpretation of transcatheter placement of extracranial vertebral or intrathoracic carotid artery stent(s), consult CPT Category III code 0075T, 0076T.

75961 **Transcatheter retrieval, percutaneous, of intravascular foreign body (eg, fractured venous or arterial catheter), radiological supervision and interpretation** S 80
MED: 100-2, 15, 80; 100-4, 13, 10; 100-4, 13, 100

To report procedure consult CPT code 37203.

75962 **Transluminal balloon angioplasty, peripheral artery, radiological supervision and interpretation** S 80
MED: 100-2, 15, 80; 100-4, 13, 10; 100-4, 13, 100

AMA: 2001, May, 1; 1993, Fall, 18

To report transluminal balloon angioplasty procedure consult CPT codes 35450-35460 or 35470-35476.

+ **75964** **Transluminal balloon angioplasty, each additional peripheral artery, radiological supervision and interpretation (List separately in addition to code for primary procedure)** S 80
MED: 100-3, 20.7; 100-3, 220.13; 100-4, 13, 10; 100-4, 13, 100

Note that 75964 is an add-on code and must be used in conjunction with 75962.

For transluminal balloon angioplasty procedure consult CPT codes 35450-35460 or 35470-35476.

75966 **Transluminal balloon angioplasty, renal or other visceral artery, radiological supervision and interpretation** S 80
MED: 100-3, 20.7; 100-3, 220.13; 100-4, 13, 10; 100-4, 13, 100

To report transluminal balloon angioplasty procedure consult CPT codes 35450-35460 or 35470-35476.

+ **75968** **Transluminal balloon angioplasty, each additional visceral artery, radiological supervision and interpretation (List separately in addition to code for primary procedure)** S 80
MED: 100-3, 20.7; 100-3, 220.13; 100-4, 13, 10; 100-4, 13, 100

Note that 75968 is an add-on code and must be used in conjunction with 75966. If a percutaneous transluminal coronary angioplasty is performed, consult CPT codes 92982-92984.

75970 **Transcatheter biopsy, radiological supervision and interpretation** S 80 ↻
MED: 100-2, 15, 80; 100-4, 13, 10; 100-4, 13, 100

If an injection procedure is performed for transcatheter therapy or for a biopsy, consult CPT codes 36100-36299. If a transcatheter renal and ureteral biopsy is performed, consult CPT code 52007. If a biopsy of the pancreas is performed through a percutaneous needle, consult CPT code 48102. If a biopsy of the abdominal or retroperitoneal mass is performed, consult CPT code 49180.

75978 **Transluminal balloon angioplasty, venous (eg, subclavian stenosis), radiological supervision and interpretation** S 80 ↻
MED: 100-2, 15, 80; 100-3, 20.7; 100-3, 220.13; 100-4, 13, 10; 100-4, 13, 100

AMA: 2001, May, 1; 1996, Oct, 4

To report procedures performed, consult CPT codes 35460 and 35476.

75980 **Percutaneous transhepatic biliary drainage with contrast monitoring, radiological supervision and interpretation** S 80 ↻
MED: 100-2, 15, 80; 100-4, 13, 10; 100-4, 13, 100

To report introduction procedure of percutaneous transhepatic catheter for bilary drainage, consult CPT code 47510.

75982 **Percutaneous placement of drainage catheter for combined internal and external biliary drainage or of a drainage stent for internal biliary drainage in patients with an inoperable mechanical biliary obstruction, radiological supervision and interpretation** S 80 ↻
MED: 100-2, 15, 80; 100-4, 13, 10; 100-4, 13, 100

To report procedures performed, consult CPT codes 47511 or 47556.

75984 **Change of percutaneous tube or drainage catheter with contrast monitoring (eg, gastrointestinal system, genitourinary system, abscess), radiological supervision and interpretation** X 80 ↻
MED: 100-2, 15, 80; 100-4, 13, 10; 100-4, 13, 100

To report procedure performed consult CPT codes 43760, 47525, 47530, 50398, 50688, 51705, 51710.

If a nephrostomy or pyelostomy tube is changed, consult CPT code 50398. If a percutaneous nephrostolithotomy or pyelostolithotomy is performed, consult CPT codes 50080 and 50081. To report percutaneous cholecystostomy, consult CPT code 47490.

To report introduction procedure only for percutaneous biliary drainage, consult CPT codes 47510 and 47511. To report change of percutaneous biliary drainage catheter only, consult CPT code 47525.

75989 **Radiological guidance (ie, fluoroscopy, ultrasound, or computed tomography), for percutaneous drainage (eg, abscess, specimen collection), with placement of catheter, radiological supervision and interpretation** N 80 ↻
MED: 100-2, 15, 80; 100-3, 220.1; 100-3, 220.5; 100-4, 13, 10; 100-4, 13, 100; 100-4, 13, 30

AMA: 1998, Mar, 8; 1997, Nov, 24

TRANSLUMINAL ATHERECTOMY

75992 **Transluminal atherectomy, peripheral artery, radiological supervision and interpretation** S 80 ↻
MED: 100-2, 15, 80; 100-4, 13, 10; 100-4, 13, 100

To report procedure performed, consult CPT codes 35481-35485, 35491-35495.

+   75993   Transluminal atherectomy, each additional peripheral artery, radiological supervision and interpretation (List separately in addition to code for primary procedure)   S 80 ↰
MED: 100-2, 15, 80; 100-4, 13, 10; 100-4, 13, 100

Note that 75993 is an add-on code and must be used in conjunction with 75992. If an open or a percutaneous transluminal peripheral atherectomy is performed, consult CPT codes 35481-35485 and 35491-35495.

75994   Transluminal atherectomy, renal, radiological supervision and interpretation   S 80 ↰
MED: 100-2, 15, 80; 100-4, 13, 10; 100-4, 13, 100

To report an open transluminal peripheral artherectomy consult CPT code 35480. To report a percutaneous transluminal peripheral atherectomy, consult CPT code 35490.

75995   Transluminal atherectomy, visceral, radiological supervision and interpretation   S 80 ↰
MED: 100-2, 15, 80; 100-4, 13, 10; 100-4, 13, 100

+   75996   Transluminal atherectomy, each additional visceral artery, radiological supervision and interpretation (List separately in addition to code for primary procedure)   S 80 ↰
MED: 100-2, 15, 80; 100-4, 13, 10; 100-4, 13, 100

Note that 75996 is an add-on code and must be used in conjunction with 75995.

OTHER PROCEDURES

If an arthrography is performed, of shoulder, consult CPT code 73040; elbow, consult CPT code 73085; wrist, consult CPT code 73115; hip, consult CPT code 73525; knee, consult CPT 73580; and ankle, consult CPT code 73615.

To report computed tomography cerebral perfusion analysis, consult Category III code 0042T.

+   75998   Fluoroscopic guidance for central venous access device placement, replacement (catheter only or complete), or removal (includes fluoroscopic guidance for vascular access and catheter manipulation, any necessary contrast injections through access site or catheter with related venography radiologic supervision and interpretation, and radiographic documentation of final catheter position) (List separately in addition to code for primary procedure)   N 80 ↰

Do not report 76003 in conjunction with CPT code 75998.

If a formal extremity venography is performed via a separate venous access and a separate interpretation is performed, consult CPT codes 36005 and 75820, 75822, 75825, or 75827.

76000   Fluoroscopy (separate procedure), up to one hour physician time, other than 71023 or 71034 (eg, cardiac fluoroscopy)   X 80 ↰
MED: 100-2, 15, 80; 100-4, 13, 10; 100-4, 13, 100

AMA: 2000, Dec, 14; 1999, Nov, 32; 1996, Apr, 10

76001   Fluoroscopy, physician time more than one hour, assisting a non-radiologic physician (eg, nephrostolithotomy, ERCP, bronchoscopy, transbronchial biopsy)   N 80 ↰
MED: 100-2, 15, 80; 100-4, 13, 10; 100-4, 13, 100

76003   **Fluoroscopic guidance for needle placement (eg, biopsy, aspiration, injection, localization device)**   N 80
MED: 100-2, 15, 80; 100-4, 13, 10; 100-4, 13, 100

AMA: 2001, Jul, 3; 1993, Fall, 14

Report the appropriate surgical code for the procedure.

Fluoroscopy 76003 is considered to be included in all radiographic arthrography except supervision and interpretation for CT and MR arthrography.

Code 76003 should not be used in conjunction with 70332, 73040, 73085, 73115, 73525, 73580, 73615.

Fluoroscopy 76003 is considered to be included in organ/anatomic specific radiological supervision and interpretation procedures 74320, 74350, 74355, 74445, 74470, 74475, 75809, 75810, 75885, 75887, 75980, 75982, 75989.

76005   **Fluoroscopic guidance and localization of needle or catheter tip for spine or paraspinous diagnostic or therapeutic injection procedures (epidural, transforaminal epidural, subarachnoid, paravertebral facet joint, paravertebral facet joint nerve or sacroiliac joint), including neurolytic agent destruction**   N
MED: 100-2, 15, 80; 100-4, 13, 10; 100-4, 13, 100

AMA: 2002, Sep, 11; 2000, Jan, 1; 2000, Feb, 4; 2000, Aug, 7; 1999, Nov, 32, 34, 41

Note that contrast injected during fluoroscopic guidance and localization is an inclusive component of CPT codes 62263-62264, 62270-62273, 62280-62282, 62310-62319. Note that fluoroscopic guidance of a subarachnoid puncture for diagnostic radiographic myelography is included in supervision and interpretation codes 72240, 72255, 72265, and 72270. If an epidural subarachnoid needle or catheter is placed and an injection made, consult CPT codes 62270-62273, 62280-62282, and 62310-62319. If arthrography is performed on the sacroiliac joint, consult CPT codes 27096 and 73542. If formal arthrography is not performed, recorded, and a formal radiographic report is not issued, consult CPT code 76005 for fluoroscopic guidance for sacroiliac joint injections. If a paravertebral facet joint is injected, consult CPT codes 64470-64476. If a transforaminal epidural needle is placed and an injection made, consult CPT codes 64479-64484. If destruction is performed by a neurolytic agent, consult CPT codes 64600-64680.

76006   **Manual application of stress performed by physician for joint radiography, including contralateral joint if indicated**   X
MED: 100-2, 15, 80; 100-4, 13, 10; 100-4, 13, 100

AMA: 1998, Nov, 21

To report interpretation of stressed images, consult appropriate radiology CPT code based on anatomic site and number of views.

76010   **Radiologic examination from nose to rectum for foreign body, single view, child**   A X 80
MED: 100-2, 15, 80; 100-4, 13, 10; 100-4, 13, 100

▲ **76012**   **Radiological supervision and interpretation, percutaneous vertebroplasty or vertebral augmentation including cavity creation, per vertebral body; under fluoroscopic guidance**   S 80
MED: 100-2, 15, 80; 100-4, 13, 10; 100-4, 13, 100

AMA: 2001, Mar, 1

To report percutaneous vertebroplasty consult CPT codes 22520-22522.

Radiology

76013 — 76082

▲ 76013   **under CT guidance**   S 80 ⤷
MED: 100-2, 15, 80; 100-4, 13, 10; 100-4, 13, 100
AMA: 2001, Mar, 1

To report percutaneous vertebroplasty consult CPT codes 22520-22522, 22523-22525.

76020   **Bone age studies**   X 80
MED: 100-2, 15, 80; 100-4, 13, 10; 100-4, 13, 100

76040   **Bone length studies (orthoroentgenogram, scanogram)**   X 80
MED: 100-2, 15, 80; 100-4, 13, 10; 100-4, 13, 100

76061   **Radiologic examination, osseous survey; limited (eg, for metastases)**   X 80
MED: 100-2, 15, 80; 100-4, 13, 10; 100-4, 13, 100

76062   **complete (axial and appendicular skeleton)**   X 80 ⤷
MED: 100-2, 15, 80; 100-4, 13, 10; 100-4, 13, 100

76065   **Radiologic examination, osseous survey, infant**   A X 80

76066   **Joint survey, single view, two or more joints (specify)**   X 80 ⤷
MED: 100-2, 15, 80; 100-4, 13, 10; 100-4, 13, 100

76070   **Computed tomography, bone mineral density study, one or more sites; axial skeleton (eg, hips, pelvis, spine)**   S 80
MED: 100-2, 15, 80; 100-3, 150.3; 100-3, 220.1; 100-4, 13, 10; 100-4, 13, 100; 100-4, 13, 30

76071   **appendicular skeleton (peripheral) (eg, radius, wrist, heel)**   S 80
MED: 100-2, 15, 80; 100-3, 150.3; 100-3, 220.1; 100-4, 13, 10; 100-4, 13, 100; 100-4, 13, 30

76075   **Dual energy x-ray absorptiometry (DXA), bone density study, one or more sites; axial skeleton (eg, hips, pelvis, spine)**   S 80
MED: 100-2, 15, 80; 100-3, 150.3; 100-4, 13, 10; 100-4, 13, 100
AMA: 1997, Nov, 24

76076   **appendicular skeleton (peripheral) (eg, radius, wrist, heel)**   S 80 ⤷
MED: 100-2, 15, 80; 100-3, 150.3; 100-4, 13, 10; 100-4, 13, 100
AMA: 1997, Nov, 24

76077   **vertebral fracture assessment**   X 80
To report dual energy x-ray absorptiometry (DXA) body composition study, consult CPT Category III code 0028T.

76078   **Radiographic absorptiometry (eg, photodensitometry, radiogrammetry), one or more sites**   X 80
MED: 100-2, 15, 80; 100-3, 150.3; 100-4, 13, 10; 100-4, 13, 100
AMA: 1997, Nov, 24

76080   **Radiologic examination, abscess, fistula or sinus tract study, radiological supervision and interpretation**   X 80 ⤷
MED: 100-2, 15, 80; 100-4, 13, 10; 100-4, 13, 100
AMA: 1998, Mar, 8; 1997, Nov, 24

To report procedure, consult CPT code 20501, 49424.

+ 76082   **Computer aided detection (computer algorithm analysis of digital image data for lesion detection) with further physician review for interpretation, with or without digitization of film radiographic images; diagnostic mammography (List separately in addition to code for primary procedure)**   A 80
Note that 76082 is an add-on code that must be used in conjunction with 76090 or 76091.

Radiology

+   76083   **screening mammography (List separately in addition to code for primary procedure)**   Ⓐ 🄤

Note that 76083 is an add-on code that must be used in conjunction with 76092.

76086   **Mammary ductogram or galactogram, single duct, radiological supervision and interpretation**   🆇 🄤
MED: 100-2, 15, 80; 100-4, 13, 10; 100-4, 13, 100

To report procedure, consult CPT code 19030.

76088   **Mammary ductogram or galactogram, multiple ducts, radiological supervision and interpretation**   🆇 🄤 🔁
MED: 100-2, 15, 80; 100-4, 13, 10; 100-4, 13, 100

To report procedure, consult CPT code 19030.

76090   **Mammography; unilateral**   Ⓐ 🄤 🔁
MED: 100-1, 5, 90.2; 100-2, 15, 80; 100-2, 15, 80.1; 100-3, 220.4; 100-4, 13, 10; 100-4, 13, 100; 100-4, 16, 10; 100-4, 16, 10.1; 100-4, 16, 110.4; 100-4, 18, 20.7

AMA: 1999, Jun, 10; 1996, Jul, 6

76091   **bilateral**   Ⓐ 🄤 🔁
MED: 100-1, 5, 90.2; 100-2, 15, 80; 100-2, 15, 80.1; 100-3, 220.4; 100-4, 13, 10; 100-4, 13, 100; 100-4, 16, 10; 100-4, 16, 10.1; 100-4, 16, 110.4; 100-4, 18, 20.7

AMA: 1996, Jul, 6

To report computer aided detection used in conjunction with a diagnostic mammography, consult CPT code 76082 and report with 76090 or 76091.

76092   **Screening mammography, bilateral (two view film study of each breast)**   Ⓐ 🄤 🔁
MED: 100-1, 5, 90.2; 100-2, 15, 80; 100-2, 15, 80.1; 100-3, 220.4; 100-4, 13, 10; 100-4, 13, 100; 100-4, 16, 10; 100-4, 16, 10.1; 100-4, 16, 110.4; 100-4, 18, 20; 100-4, 18, 20.7

AMA: 1999, Jun, 10; 1996, Jul, 6

To report computer aided detection applied to a screening mammogram, report CPT code 76085 with 76092.

To report computer aided detection used in conjunction with a screening mammography, consult CPT code 76083 and report with 76092.

If an electrical impedance scan of the breast, bilateral is performed, consult CPT Category III code 0060T.

76093   **Magnetic resonance imaging, breast, without and/or with contrast material(s); unilateral**   Ⓔ 🄤 🔁
MED: 100-2, 15, 80; 100-3, 220.2; 100-3, 220.3; 100-4, 13, 10; 100-4, 13, 100

76094   **bilateral**   Ⓔ 🄤 🔁
MED: 100-2, 15, 80; 100-4, 13, 10; 100-4, 13, 100

76095   **Stereotactic localization guidance for breast biopsy or needle placement (eg, for wire localization or for injection), each lesion, radiological supervision and interpretation**   🆇 🄤 🔁
MED: 100-2, 15, 80; 100-3, 20.7; 100-3, 220.13; 100-4, 13, 10; 100-4, 13, 100

AMA: 1997, Nov, 24; 1996, Apr, 9

Report the appropriate procedure with one of the following CPT codes 10022, 19000, 19001, 19102, 19103, 19290, 19291.

To report injection for sentinel node localization without lymphoscintigraphy, report CPT code 38792.

76083 — 76095

| 🔁 CCI Comp | 🔟 Bilateral Procedure | ✚ CPT Add-on Code | ⊘ Modifier -51 Exempt | ♂ Male | ♀ Female |
| ● New Code | ▲ Revised Code | Ⓜ Maternity Edit | Ⓐ Age Edit | Ⓐ–Ⓨ APC Status Ind. | AMA: CPT Assistant |

© 2005 Ingenix, Inc. *(Blue Ink)*   CPT only © 2005 American Medical Association. All Rights Reserved. *(Black Ink)*   Radiology — 537

76096 **Mammographic guidance for needle placement, breast (eg, for wire localization or for injection), each lesion, radiological supervision and interpretation** X 80 ⟲
MED: 100-3, 220.4

AMA: 2001, Jan, 8

To report the procedure, consult CPT codes 10022, 19000, 19102, 19103.

To report needle localization wire placement, consult CPT codes 19290 and 19291.

To report injection for sentinel node localization without lymphoscintigraphy, report CPT code 38792.

76098 **Radiological examination, surgical specimen** X 80
MED: 100-2, 15, 80; 100-4, 13, 10; 100-4, 13, 100

76100 **Radiologic examination, single plane body section (eg, tomography), other than with urography** X 80 ⟲
MED: 100-2, 15, 80; 100-4, 13, 10; 100-4, 13, 100

76101 **Radiologic examination, complex motion (ie, hypercycloidal) body section (eg, mastoid polytomography), other than with urography; unilateral** X 80
MED: 100-2, 15, 80; 100-4, 13, 10; 100-4, 13, 100

76102 **bilateral** X 80 ⟲
MED: 100-2, 15, 80; 100-4, 13, 10; 100-4, 13, 100

If a nephrotomography is performed, consult CPT code 74415.

76120 **Cineradiography/videoradiography, except where specifically included** X 80
MED: 100-2, 15, 80; 100-4, 13, 10; 100-4, 13, 100

AMA: 2000, Sep, 4

+ 76125 **Cineradiography/videoradiography to complement routine examination (List separately in addition to code for primary procedure)** X 80
MED: 100-2, 15, 80; 100-4, 13, 10; 100-4, 13, 100

AMA: 2000, Sep, 4

Note that 76125 is an add-on code that must be used in conjunction with the appropriate code for the primary procedure. This code cannot be reported alone.

76140 **Consultation on X-ray examination made elsewhere, written report** E
MED: 100-2, 15, 80; 100-4, 13, 10; 100-4, 13, 100

AMA: 1991, Summer, 13

76150 **Xeroradiography** X TC 80
MED: 100-2, 15, 80; 100-4, 13, 10; 100-4, 13, 100

Note that 76150 is to be used only for non-mammographic studies.

76350 **Subtraction in conjunction with contrast studies** N TC 80
MED: 100-2, 15, 80; 100-3, 220.1; 100-4, 13, 10; 100-4, 13, 100

76355 **Computed tomography guidance for stereotactic localization** S 80
MED: 100-2, 15, 80; 100-3, 220.1; 100-4, 13, 10; 100-4, 13, 100; 100-4, 13, 30

76360 **Computed tomography guidance for needle placement (eg, biopsy, aspiration, injection, localization device), radiological supervision and interpretation** S 80 ⟲
MED: 100-2, 15, 80; 100-3, 20.7; 100-3, 220.1; 100-3, 220.13; 100-4, 13, 10; 100-4, 13, 100

AMA: 2001, Jan, 8; 1993, Fall, 12

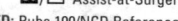

Radiology

76362   Computed tomography guidance for, and monitoring of, visceral tissue
ablation   ⑤ 80 🔲
MED: 100-2, 15, 80; 100-3, 220.1; 100-4, 13, 10; 100-4, 13, 100; 100-4, 13, 30

To report percutaneous radiofrequency ablation, consult CPT codes 47382 and
50592.

To report percutaneous cryotherapy ablation of renal tumors, consult CPT
Category III code 0135T.

76370   Computed tomography guidance for placement of radiation therapy
fields   ⑤ 80
MED: 100-2, 15, 80; 100-3, 220.1; 100-4, 13, 10; 100-4, 13, 100; 100-4, 13, 30

AMA: 1991, Fall, 12

If 3D rendering is performed, consult CPT codes 76376, 76377.

~~**76375** Coronal, sagittal, multiplanar, oblique, 3-dimensional and/or holographic
reconstruction of computed tomography, magnetic resonance imaging, or
other tomographic modality~~

● **76376**   3D rendering with interpretation and reporting of computed tomography,
magnetic resonance imaging, ultrasound, or other tomographic modality;
not requiring image postprocessing on an independent workstation

Report code 76376 in conjunction with code(s) for base imaging procedure(s).

Code 76376 cannot be reported with 70496, 70498, 70544-70549, 71275,
71555, 72159, 72191, 72198, 73206, 73225, 73706, 73725, 74175, 74185,
75635, 78814-78816, 0066T, 0067T.

● **76377**   requiring image postprocessing on an independent workstation

Report code 76377 in conjunction with code(s) for base imaging procedure(s).

Code 76377 cannot be used with 70496, 70498, 70544-70549, 71275, 71555,
72159, 72191, 72198, 73206, 73225, 73706, 73725, 74175, 74185, 75635,
78814-78816, 0066T, 0067T.

76380   Computed tomography, limited or localized follow-up study   ⑤ 80
MED: 100-2, 15, 80; 100-3, 220.1; 100-4, 13, 10; 100-4, 13, 100; 100-4, 13, 30

76390   Magnetic resonance spectroscopy   Ⓔ
MED: 100-2, 15, 80; 100-4, 13, 10; 100-4, 13, 100

AMA: 1997, Nov, 25

If magnetic resonance imaging is performed, consult the appropriate MRI body
site code.

76393   Magnetic resonance guidance for needle placement (eg, for biopsy, needle
aspiration, injection, or placement of localization device) radiological
supervision and interpretation   ⑤ 80 🔲
MED: 100-2, 15, 80; 100-3, 20.7; 100-3, 220.13; 100-3, 220.2; 100-3, 220.3; 100-4, 13, 10; 100-4,
13, 100; 100-4, 13, 40; 100-4, 13, 40.1

AMA: 2001, Jan, 8

To report procedure, see appropriate organ or site.

76362 — 76393

Radiology

76394   **Magnetic resonance guidance for, and monitoring of, visceral tissue ablation**   S 80
MED: 100-2, 15, 80; 100-3, 220.2; 100-3, 220.3; 100-4, 13, 10; 100-4, 13, 100; 100-4, 13, 40; 100-4, 13, 40.1

AMA: 2002, Oct, 1

To report percutaneous radiofrequency ablation, consult CPT codes 47382 and 50592.

For a focused ultrasound ablation treatment of uterine leiomyomata, consult Category III codes 0071T, 0072T.

To report percutaneous cryotherapy ablation of renal tumors, consult CPT Category III code 0135T.

76400   **Magnetic resonance (eg, proton) imaging, bone marrow blood supply** ☑ 80
MED: 100-2, 15, 80; 100-3, 220.2; 100-3, 220.3; 100-4, 13, 10; 100-4, 13, 100; 100-4, 13, 40; 100-4, 13, 40.1

76496   **Unlisted fluoroscopic procedure (eg, diagnostic, interventional)**   X 80
MED: 100-2, 15, 80; 100-4, 13, 10; 100-4, 13, 100

76497   **Unlisted computed tomography procedure (eg, diagnostic, interventional)**   S 80
MED: 100-2, 15, 80; 100-4, 13, 10; 100-4, 13, 100; 100-4, 13, 40; 100-4, 13, 40.1

76498   **Unlisted magnetic resonance procedure (eg, diagnostic, interventional)** S 80
MED: 100-2, 15, 80; 100-4, 13, 10; 100-4, 13, 100; 100-4, 13, 40; 100-4, 13, 40.1

76499   **Unlisted diagnostic radiographic procedure**   X 80
MED: 100-2, 15, 80; 100-4, 13, 10; 100-4, 13, 100

AMA: 2000, Sep, 4; 1999, Jul, 10

DIAGNOSTIC ULTRASOUND

Permanent records of ultrasound examinations such as description of anatomic region, measurements, obstructed view, and site to be localized for a guided surgical procedure are required. A written report of the exam should be included in the patient's medical record. Do not report an ultrasound without a thorough examination of the organ(s) or anatomic region, documentation of the image, and a final written report

HEAD AND NECK

To report diagnostic vascular ultrasound studies, consult 93875-93990. To report focused ultrasound ablation treatment of uterine leiomyomata, consult Category III codes 0071T, 0072T.

76506   **Echoencephalography, B-scan and/or real time with image documentation (gray scale) (for determination of ventricular size, delineation of cerebral contents and detection of fluid masses or other intracranial abnormalities), including A-mode encephalography as secondary component where indicated**   S 80
MED: 100-2, 15, 80; 100-3, 220.5

76510   **Ophthalmic ultrasound, diagnostic; B-scan and quantitative A-scan performed during the same patient encounter**   S 80

76511   **quantitative A-scan only**   S
MED: 100-2, 15, 80; 100-3, 10.1; 100-3, 220.5

AMA: 1999, Nov, 42; 1996, Oct, 9

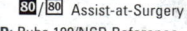
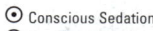

76512	**B-scan (with or without superimposed non-quantitative A-scan)** ⑤ 🖪
	MED: 100-2, 15, 80; 100-3, 10.1; 100-3, 220.5
	AMA: 1996, Oct, 9

76513	**anterior segment ultrasound, immersion (water bath) B-scan or high resolution biomicroscopy** ⑤ 🖪
	MED: 100-2, 15, 80; 100-3, 10.1; 100-3, 220.5
	AMA: 1999, Nov, 42

76514	**corneal pachymetry, unilateral or bilateral (determination of corneal thickness)** ⊠ 80

76516	**Ophthalmic biometry by ultrasound echography, A-scan;** ⑤ 80 🖪
	MED: 100-2, 15, 80; 100-3, 10.1; 100-3, 220.5

76519	**with intraocular lens power calculation** ⑤ 🖪
	MED: 100-2, 15, 80; 100-3, 10.1; 100-3, 220.5

To report partial coherence interferometry, consult CPT code 92136.

76529	**Ophthalmic ultrasonic foreign body localization** ⑤ 🖪
	MED: 100-2, 15, 80; 100-3, 220.5

76536	**Ultrasound, soft tissues of head and neck (eg, thyroid, parathyroid, parotid), B-scan and/or real time with image documentation** ⑤ 80 🖪
	MED: 100-2, 15, 80; 100-3, 220.5

CHEST

76604	**Ultrasound, chest, B-scan (includes mediastinum) and/or real time with image documentation** ⑤ 80 🖪
	MED: 100-2, 15, 80; 100-3, 220.5

76645	**Ultrasound, breast(s) (unilateral or bilateral), B-scan and/or real time with image documentation** ⑤ 80 🖪
	MED: 100-2, 15, 80; 100-3, 220.5

ABDOMEN AND RETROPERITONEUM

A complete ultrasound includes an examination of the abdomen (76700) and consists of B mode scans of: liver, gall bladder, common bile duct, pancreas, spleen, kidneys, upper abdominal aorta, and inferior vena cava including any demonstrated abdominal abnormality.

A complete ultrasound examination of the retroperitoneum (76770) includes B mode scans of: kidneys, abdominal aorta, common iliac artery origins, and inferior vena cava, including any demonstrated retroperitoneal abnormality. If clinical history points to urinary tract pathology, complete evaluation of the kidneys and urinary bladder also comprise a complete retroperitoneal ultrasound.

Do not report an ultrasound without a thorough examination of the organ(s) or anatomic region, documentation of the image, and a final written report.

76700	**Ultrasound, abdominal, B-scan and/or real time with image documentation; complete** ⑤ 80 🖪
	MED: 100-2, 15, 80; 100-3, 220.5
	AMA: 2001, Oct, 1; 1993, Fall, 13

76705	**limited (eg, single organ, quadrant, follow-up)** ⑤ 80 🖪
	MED: 100-2, 15, 80; 100-3, 220.5
	AMA: 2001, Oct, 1; 1993, Fall, 13

76770   Ultrasound, retroperitoneal (eg, renal, aorta, nodes), B-scan and/or real time with image documentation; complete   S 80 ⬚
MED: 100-2, 15, 80; 100-3, 220.5

AMA: 1999, May, 10; 1999, Jun, 10

76775   limited   S 80 ⬚
MED: 100-2, 15, 80; 100-3, 220.5

AMA: 1999, May, 10; 1999, Jun, 10

76778   Ultrasound, transplanted kidney, B-scan and/or real time with image documentation, with or without duplex Doppler study   S 80 ⬚
MED: 100-2, 15, 80; 100-3, 220.5

SPINAL CANAL

76800   Ultrasound, spinal canal and contents   S 80 ⬚
MED: 100-2, 15, 80; 100-3, 220.5

AMA: 1998, Apr, 15

PELVIS

OBSTETRICAL

76801   Ultrasound, pregnant uterus, real time with image documentation, fetal and maternal evaluation, first trimester (<14 weeks 0 days), transabdominal approach; single or first gestation   M ♀ S 80 ⬚
MED: 100-3, 220.5

+ **76802**   each additional gestation (List separately in addition to code for primary procedure)   M ♀ S 80 ⬚
MED: 100-3, 220.5

Note that 76802 is an add-0n code and must be used in conjunction with code 76801.

76805   Ultrasound, pregnant uterus, real time with image documentation, fetal and maternal evaluation, after first trimester (> or = 14 weeks 0 days), transabdominal approach; single or first gestation   M ♀ S 80 ⬚
MED: 100-2, 15, 80; 100-3, 220.5

AMA: 2001, Oct, 1; 1997, Nov, 25; 1997, Apr, 2

+ **76810**   each additional gestation (List separately in addition to code for primary procedure)   M ♀ S 80 ⬚
MED: 100-2, 15, 80; 100-3, 220.5

AMA: 2001, Oct, 1; 1997, Apr, 2

Note that 76810 is an add-on code and must be used in conjunction with CPT code 76805.

76811   Ultrasound, pregnant uterus, real time with image documentation, fetal and maternal evaluation plus detailed fetal anatomic examination, transabdominal approach; single or first gestation   M ♀ S 80 ⬚
MED: 100-3, 220.5

+ **76812**   each additional gestation (List separately in addition to code for primary procedure)   M ♀ S 80 ⬚
MED: 100-3, 220.5

Note that 76812 is an add-on code and must be used in conjunction with CPT code 76811.

76815   **Ultrasound, pregnant uterus, real time with image documentation, limited (eg, fetal heart beat, placental location, fetal position and/or qualitative amniotic fluid volume), one or more fetuses**   M ♀ S 80 ▣
MED: 100-2, 15, 80; 100-3, 220.5

AMA: 2001, Oct, 1; 2001, Dec, 6; 1997, Nov, 25; 1997, Apr, 2

Report 76815 only once per exam.

76816   **Ultrasound, pregnant uterus, real time with image documentation, follow-up (eg, re-evaluation of fetal size by measuring standard growth parameters and amniotic fluid volume, re-evaluation of organ system(s) suspected or confirmed to be abnormal on a previous scan), transabdominal approach, per fetus**   M ♀ S 80 ▣
MED: 100-2, 15, 80; 100-3, 220.5

AMA: 2001, Oct, 1; 1997, Apr, 2

To report each fetus examined in a multiple pregnancy, append modifier 59 to code 76816.

76817   **Ultrasound, pregnant uterus, real time with image documentation, transvaginal**   M ♀ S 80 ▣
MED: 100-3, 220.5

To report non-obstetrical transvaginal ultrasound, consult CPT code 76830.

To report transvaginal exam done at time of transabdominal obstetrical exam, report 76817 in addition to appropriate transabdominal obstetric ultrasound code.

76818   **Fetal biophysical profile; with non-stress testing**   M ♀ S 80 ▣
MED: 100-2, 15, 80; 100-3, 220.5

AMA: 2001, Sep, 4; 2001, Dec, 6; 1998, May, 10; 1997, Apr, 2

76819   **without non-stress testing**   M ♀ S 80 ▣
MED: 100-2, 15, 80; 100-3, 220.5

AMA: 2001, Sep, 4; 2001, Dec, 6

To report fetal biophysical profile assessments for any additional fetuses, modifier 59 should be appended.

To report amniotic fluid index without non-stress test, consult CPT code 76815.

76820   **Doppler velocimetry, fetal; umbilical artery**   ♀ S 80

76821   **middle cerebral artery**   ♀ S 80

76825   **Echocardiography, fetal, cardiovascular system, real time with image documentation (2D) with or without M-mode recording;**   M ♀ S 80 ▣
MED: 100-2, 15, 80; 100-3, 220.5

AMA: 1997, Apr, 2

76826   **follow-up or repeat study**   M ♀ S 80 ▣
MED: 100-2, 15, 80; 100-3, 220.5

AMA: 1997, Apr, 2

76827   **Doppler echocardiography, fetal, pulsed wave and/or continuous wave with spectral display; complete**   M ♀ S 80 ▣
MED: 100-2, 15, 80; 100-3, 220.5

AMA: 1997, Apr, 2

Radiology

76828 — 76872

| 76828 | follow-up or repeat study | ☐ ♀ ⑤ ⑧⁰ ☐ |

MED: 100-2, 15, 80; 100-3, 220.5

AMA: 1997, Apr, 2

If color mapping is performed, consult CPT code 93325.

NON-OBSTETRICAL

Code 76856 includes the complete evaluation of the female pelvis. Included in this exam is a description and measurement of the uterus and adnexal structures, measurement of the endometrium, measurement of the bladder (when applicable), and a description of any pelvic problems. This includes ovarian cysts, uterine leiomyomata, and free pelvic fluid.

Report 76856 for a complete evaluation of the male pelvis. This exam includes evaluation and measurement (when applicable) of the urinary bladder, evaluation of the prostate and seminal vesicles to the extent that they are visualized transabdominally, and any pelvic pathology. This includes bladder tumor, enlarged prostate, free pelvic fluid, and pelvic abscess.

Report 76857 for a focused limited examination of one or more pelvic abnormalities previously seen on ultrasound. Report 76857 rather than 76770 when for an examination of the urinary bladder alone (i.e., not including kidneys). Report 51798 for a bladder volume or post-void residual measurement is obtained without imaging the bladder.

Do not report an ultrasound without a thorough examination of the organ(s) or anatomic region, documentation of the image, and a final written report.

| 76830 | **Ultrasound, transvaginal** | ♀ ⑤ ⑧⁰ ☐ |

MED: 100-2, 15, 80; 100-3, 220.5

AMA: 1999, Jul, 8; 1996, Aug, 10

To report obstetrical transvaginal ultrasound, consult CPT code 76817.

To report non-obstetrical transvaginal exam performed at time of transabdominal non-obstetrical exam, report both 76830 and appropriate transabdominal code.

| 76831 | **Saline infusion sonohysterography (SIS), including color flow Doppler, when performed** | ♀ ⑤ ⑧⁰ ☐ |

MED: 100-2, 15, 80; 100-3, 220.5

AMA: 1999, Jul, 8; 1997, Nov, 25

To report the introduction of saline, consult CPT code 58340.

| 76856 | **Ultrasound, pelvic (nonobstetric), B-scan and/or real time with image documentation; complete** | ⑤ ⑧⁰ ☐ |

MED: 100-2, 15, 80; 100-3, 220.5

AMA: 2001, Oct, 1

| 76857 | **limited or follow-up (eg, for follicles)** | ⑤ ⑧⁰ ☐ |

MED: 100-2, 15, 80; 100-3, 220.5

AMA: 2001, Oct, 1; 1997, Jun, 10

GENITALIA

| 76870 | **Ultrasound, scrotum and contents** | ♂ ⑤ ⑧⁰ ☐ |

MED: 100-2, 15, 80; 100-3, 220.5

| 76872 | **Ultrasound, transrectal;** | ⑤ ⑧⁰ ☐ |

MED: 100-2, 15, 80; 100-3, 220.5

AMA: 1999, Nov, 42; 1996, May, 3

 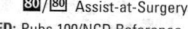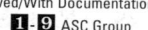

76873   prostate volume study for brachytherapy treatment planning (separate procedure) ♂ S ⬆

         MED: 100-2, 15, 80; 100-3, 220.5

         AMA: 1999, Nov, 42

EXTREMITIES

76880   Ultrasound, extremity, non-vascular, B-scan and/or real time with image documentation   S 80 ⬆

         MED: 100-2, 15, 80; 100-3, 220.5

76885   Ultrasound, infant hips, real time with imaging documentation; dynamic (requiring physician manipulation)   A S 80 ⬆

         MED: 100-2, 15, 80; 100-3, 220.5

         AMA: 1997, Nov, 25

76886   limited, static (not requiring physician manipulation)   A S 80 ⬆

         MED: 100-2, 15, 80; 100-3, 220.5

         AMA: 1997, Nov, 25

ULTRASONIC GUIDANCE PROCEDURES

76930   Ultrasonic guidance for pericardiocentesis, imaging supervision and interpretation   S 80 ⬆

         MED: 100-3, 220.5

         To report procedure, consult CPT codes 33010 and 33011.

76932   Ultrasonic guidance for endomyocardial biopsy, imaging supervision and interpretation   S 80 ⬆

         MED: 100-3, 220.5

         To report procedure, consult CPT code 93505.

76936   Ultrasound guided compression repair of arterial pseudo-aneurysm or arteriovenous fistulae (includes diagnostic ultrasound evaluation, compression of lesion and imaging)   S 80 ⬆

         MED: 100-3, 220.5

+   76937   Ultrasound guidance for vascular access requiring ultrasound evaluation of potential access sites, documentation of selected vessel patency, concurrent realtime ultrasound visualization of vascular needle entry, with permanent recording and reporting (List separately in addition to code for primary procedure)   N 80 ⬆

         Code 76937 cannot be reported in conjunction with 76942.

         To report a non-invasive extremity venous vascular diagnostic study performed separate from venous access guidance, consult CPT codes 93965, 93970 or 93971.

76940   Ultrasound guidance for, and monitoring of, visceral tissue ablation S 80 ⬆

         Code 76940 cannot be reported in conjunction with 76986.

         To report the ablation, consult CPT codes 47370-47382.

76941   Ultrasonic guidance for intrauterine fetal transfusion or cordocentesis, imaging supervision and interpretation   M ♀ S 80 ⬆

         MED: 100-3, 220.5

         To report fetal intrauterine transfusion procedure, consult CPT code 36460. If cordocentesis is performed, consult CPT code 59012.

Radiology

76942 — 76999

76942 **Ultrasonic guidance for needle placement (eg, biopsy, aspiration, injection, localization device), imaging supervision and interpretation** S 80 ▶
MED: 100-3, 20.7; 100-3, 220.13; 100-3, 220.5

AMA: 2001, Oct, 1; 1997, Jun, 5; 1996, May, 3; 1993, Fall, 12

Code 76942 cannot be reported in conjunction with 43232, 43237, 43242, 45341, 45342, or 76975.

To report microwave thermotherapy of the breast, consult CPT Category III code 0061T.

76945 **Ultrasonic guidance for chorionic villus sampling, imaging supervision and interpretation** M ♀ S 80 ▶
MED: 100-3, 220.5

To report chorionic villus sampling, consult CPT code 59015.

76946 **Ultrasonic guidance for amniocentesis, imaging supervision and interpretation** M ♀ S 80 ▶
MED: 100-3, 220.5

To report procedure, consult CPT code 59000.

76948 **Ultrasonic guidance for aspiration of ova, imaging supervision and interpretation** ♀ S 80 ▶
MED: 100-3, 220.5

To report procedure, consult CPT code 58970.

76950 **Ultrasonic guidance for placement of radiation therapy fields** S 80 ▶
MED: 100-3, 220.5

76965 **Ultrasonic guidance for interstitial radioelement application** S 80 ▶
MED: 100-3, 220.5

OTHER PROCEDURES

76970 **Ultrasound study follow-up (specify)** S 80 ▶
MED: 100-3, 220.5

76975 **Gastrointestinal endoscopic ultrasound, supervision and interpretation** S 80 ▶
MED: 100-3, 220.5; 100-4, 12, 30.1

AMA: 1994, Spring, 5

Code 76975 cannot be reported in conjunction with 43231, 43232, 43237, 43238, 43242, 43259, 45341, 45342, or 76942.

76977 **Ultrasound bone density measurement and interpretation, peripheral site(s), any method** X 80 ▶
MED: 100-3, 220.5

AMA: 1998, Nov, 21

76986 **Ultrasonic guidance, intraoperative** S 80
MED: 100-3, 220.5

Code 76986 should not be reported in conjunction with 47370-47382.

To report ultrasound guidance for open and laparoscopic radiofrequncey tissue ablation, consult CPT code 76490.

76999 **Unlisted ultrasound procedure (eg, diagnostic, interventional)** S 80
MED: 100-3, 220.5

RADIATION ONCOLOGY

CLINICAL TREATMENT PLANNING (EXTERNAL AND INTERNAL SOURCES)

The codes in this section provide for brachytherapy and teletherapy to include the initial consultation, clinical treatment planning, dosimetry, radiation physics, treatment devices and treatment management services. These codes also include follow-up care for up to three months following completion. Identify preliminary consultation and patient evaluation performed by the therapeutic radiologist by the evaluation and management code. Consult the glossary for terms and definitions and the front matter of this chapter for additional information.

77261   **Therapeutic radiology treatment planning; simple**   E 26 80 ⟳
       MED: 100-4, 12, 70; 100-4, 13, 20; 100-4, 13, 90
       AMA: 1997, Oct, 1

77262   **intermediate**   E 26 80 ⟳
       MED: 100-4, 12, 70; 100-4, 13, 20; 100-4, 13, 90
       AMA: 1997, Oct, 1

77263   **complex**   E 26 80 ⟳
       MED: 100-4, 12, 70; 100-4, 13, 20; 100-4, 13, 90
       AMA: 1997, Oct, 1; 1991, Fall, 12

77280   **Therapeutic radiology simulation-aided field setting; simple**   X 80 ⟳
       MED: 100-4, 12, 70; 100-4, 13, 20; 100-4, 13, 90
       AMA: 1997, Oct, 1; 1997, Nov, 26

77285   **intermediate**   X 80 ⟳
       MED: 100-4, 12, 70; 100-4, 13, 20; 100-4, 13, 90
       AMA: 1997, Oct, 1

77290   **complex**   X 80 ⟳
       MED: 100-4, 12, 70; 100-4, 13, 20; 100-4, 13, 90
       AMA: 1997, Oct, 1; 1991, Fall, 12

77295   **3-dimensional**   X 80 ⟳
       MED: 100-4, 12, 70; 100-4, 13, 20; 100-4, 13, 90
       AMA: 1997, Oct, 1; 1997, Nov, 26

77299   **Unlisted procedure, therapeutic radiology clinical treatment planning** E 80
       MED: 100-4, 12, 70; 100-4, 13, 20; 100-4, 13, 90

MEDICAL RADIATION PHYSICS, DOSIMETRY, TREATMENT DEVICES, AND SPECIAL SERVICES

77300   **Basic radiation dosimetry calculation, central axis depth dose calculation, TDF, NSD, gap calculation, off axis factor, tissue inhomogeneity factors, calculation of non-ionizing radiation surface and depth dose, as required during course of treatment, only when prescribed by the treating physician**   X 80 ⟳
       MED: 100-4, 12, 70; 100-4, 13, 20; 100-4, 13, 90
       AMA: 1997, Oct, 1; 1991, Fall, 13

77301   **Intensity modulated radiotherapy plan, including dose-volume histograms for target and critical structure partial tolerance specifications**   X 80 ⟳
       MED: 100-4, 12, 70; 100-4, 13, 20; 100-4, 13, 90

       Dose plan is optimized using inverse or forward planning technique for modulated beam delivery (eg, binary, dynamic MLC) to create highly conformal dose distribution. Computer plan distribution must be verified for positional accuracy based on dosimetric verification of the intensity map with verification of treatment set up and interpretation of verification methodology.

Radiology

77305 — 77334

77305 **Teletherapy, isodose plan (whether hand or computer calculated); simple (one or two parallel opposed unmodified ports directed to a single area of interest)** ☒ 80 ⬀
MED: 100-4, 12, 70; 100-4, 13, 20; 100-4, 13, 90

AMA: 1997, Oct, 1

77310 **intermediate (three or more treatment ports directed to a single area of interest)** ☒ 80 ⬀
MED: 100-4, 12, 70; 100-4, 13, 20; 100-4, 13, 90
AMA: 1997, Oct, 1

77315 **complex (mantle or inverted Y, tangential ports, the use of wedges, compensators, complex blocking, rotational beam, or special beam considerations)** ☒ 80 ⬀
MED: 100-4, 12, 70; 100-4, 13, 20; 100-4, 13, 90
AMA: 1997, Oct, 1; 1991, Fall, 13

Note that only one teletherapy isodose plan may be reported for a given course of therapy to a specific treatment area.

77321 **Special teletherapy port plan, particles, hemibody, total body** ☒ 80 ⬀
MED: 100-4, 12, 70; 100-4, 13, 20; 100-4, 13, 90

AMA: 1997, Oct, 1; 1991, Fall, 14

77326 **Brachytherapy isodose plan; simple (calculation made from single plane, one to four sources/ribbon application, remote afterloading brachytherapy, 1 to 8 sources)** ☒ 80 ⬀
MED: 100-4, 12, 70; 100-4, 13, 20; 100-4, 13, 90

AMA: 1991, Winter, 17

77327 **Brachytherapy isodose plan; intermediate (multiplane dosage calculations, application involving 5 to 10 sources/ribbons, remote afterloading brachytherapy, 9 to 12 sources)** ☒ 80 ⬀
AMA: 1991, Winter, 17

77328 **Brachytherapy isodose plan; complex (multiplane isodose plan, volume implant calculations, over 10 sources/ribbons used, special spatial reconstruction, remote afterloading brachytherapy, over 12 sources)** ☒ 80 ⬀
AMA: 1991, Winter, 17

77331 **Special dosimetry (eg, TLD, microdosimetry) (specify), only when prescribed by the treating physician** ☒ 80 ⬀
MED: 100-4, 12, 70; 100-4, 13, 20; 100-4, 13, 90

AMA: 1997, Oct, 1; 1991, Fall, 13

77332 **Treatment devices, design and construction; simple (simple block, simple bolus)** ☒ 80 ⬀
MED: 100-4, 12, 70; 100-4, 13, 20; 100-4, 13, 90

AMA: 1997, Oct, 1

77333 **intermediate (multiple blocks, stents, bite blocks, special bolus)** ☒ 80 ⬀
MED: 100-4, 12, 70; 100-4, 13, 20; 100-4, 13, 90

AMA: 1997, Oct, 1

77334 **complex (irregular blocks, special shields, compensators, wedges, molds or casts)** ☒ 80 ⬀
MED: 100-4, 12, 70; 100-4, 13, 20; 100-4, 13, 90

AMA: 1997, Oct, 1; 1991, Fall, 13

77336 Continuing medical physics consultation, including assessment of treatment parameters, quality assurance of dose delivery, and review of patient treatment documentation in support of the radiation oncologist, reported per week of therapy ☒ TC 80 ▣
MED: 100-4, 12, 70; 100-4, 13, 20; 100-4, 13, 90

AMA: 1998, Nov, 21; 1997, Oct, 1; 1991, Fall, 15

77370 Special medical radiation physics consultation ☒ TC 80 ▣
MED: 100-4, 12, 70; 100-4, 13, 20; 100-4, 13, 90

AMA: 1997, Oct, 1; 1991, Fall, 14

77399 Unlisted procedure, medical radiation physics, dosimetry and treatment devices, and special services ☒ 80
AMA: 1998, Nov, 21

RADIATION TREATMENT DELIVERY

Radiation treatment delivery codes 77401-77416 recognize the technical component and the assorted energy levels.

For stereotactic body radiation therapy treatment delivery, consult Category III code 0082.

77401 Radiation treatment delivery, superficial and/or ortho voltage ☒ TC 80 ▣
MED: 100-4, 12, 70; 100-4, 13, 20; 100-4, 13, 90

77402 Radiation treatment delivery, single treatment area, single port or parallel opposed ports, simple blocks or no blocks; up to 5 MeV ☒ TC 80 ▣
MED: 100-4, 12, 70; 100-4, 13, 20; 100-4, 13, 90

77403 6-10 MeV ☒ TC 80 ▣
MED: 100-4, 12, 70; 100-4, 13, 20; 100-4, 13, 90

77404 11-19 MeV ☒ TC 80 ▣
MED: 100-4, 12, 70; 100-4, 13, 20; 100-4, 13, 90

77406 20 MeV or greater ☒ TC 80 ▣
MED: 100-4, 12, 70; 100-4, 13, 20; 100-4, 13, 90

77407 Radiation treatment delivery, two separate treatment areas, three or more ports on a single treatment area, use of multiple blocks; up to 5 MeV ☒ TC 80 ▣
MED: 100-4, 12, 70; 100-4, 13, 20; 100-4, 13, 90

77408 6-10 MeV ☒ TC 80 ▣
MED: 100-4, 12, 70; 100-4, 13, 20; 100-4, 13, 90

77409 11-19 MeV ☒ TC 80 ▣
MED: 100-4, 12, 70; 100-4, 13, 20; 100-4, 13, 90

77411 20 MeV or greater ☒ TC 80 ▣
MED: 100-4, 12, 70; 100-4, 13, 20; 100-4, 13, 90

▲ **77412** Radiation treatment delivery, three or more separate treatment areas, custom blocking, tangential ports, wedges, rotational beam, compensators, electron beam; up to 5 MeV ☒ TC 80 ▣
MED: 100-4, 12, 70; 100-4, 13, 20; 100-4, 13, 90

▲ **77413** 6-10 MeV ☒ TC 80 ▣
MED: 100-4, 12, 70; 100-4, 13, 20; 100-4, 13, 90

AMA: 1991, Fall, 14

▲ **77414** 11-19 MeV ☒ TC 80 ▣
MED: 100-4, 12, 70; 100-4, 13, 20; 100-4, 13, 90

Radiology

▲ 77416   **20 MeV or greater**   S TC 80 �
               MED: 100-4, 12, 70; 100-4, 13, 20; 100-4, 13, 90

  77417   **Therapeutic radiology port film(s)**   X TC 80 ▦
               MED: 100-4, 12, 70; 100-4, 13, 20; 100-4, 13, 90

               AMA: 1997, Dec, 11; 1991, Fall, 14

  77418   **Intensity modulated treatment delivery, single or multiple fields/arcs, via
               narrow spatially and temporally modulated beams, binary, dynamic MLC,
               per treatment session**   S TC 80 ▦
               MED: 100-4, 12, 70; 100-4, 13, 20; 100-4, 13, 90

               To report intensity modulated treatment planning, consult CPT code 77301.
               To report compensator based beam modulation treatment delivery, consult
               Category III code 0073T.

● 77421   **Stereoscopic X-ray guidance for localization of target volume for the
               delivery of radiation therapy**

               Code 77421 cannot be reported with 77432, 0083T.

● 77422   **High energy neutron radiation treatment delivery; single treatment area
               using a single port or parallel-opposed ports with no blocks or simple
               blocking**

● 77423   **1 or more isocenter(s) with coplanar or non-coplanar geometry with
               blocking and/or wedge, and/or compensator(s)**

RADIATION TREATMENT MANAGEMENT

The codes in this section provide for brachytherapy and teletherapy to include the initial
consultation, clinical treatment planning, dosimetry, radiation physics, treatment devices and
treatment management services. These codes also include follow-up care for up to three months
following completion. Identify preliminary consultation and patient evaluation performed by the
therapeutic radiologist by the evaluation and management code. Consult the glossary for terms and
definitions and the front matter of this chapter for additional information.

For radiation treatment management, the professional services usually furnished consist of review of
patient treatment setup, port films, dosimetry, dose delivery and treatment parameters, and medical
evaluation and management services.

Report radiation treatment management in units of five treatment sessions; this is not reflective of
the actual time period in which the treatment are furnished. Treatment management consists of
review of dosimetry, dose delivery, and treatment parameters; review of port films; review of
treatment set-up; and examination of patient for medical evaluation and management.

  77427   **Radiation treatment management, five treatments**   E 26 ▦
               AMA: 2000, Feb, 7; 1999, Nov, 42

  77431   **Radiation therapy management with complete course of therapy consisting
               of one or two fractions only**   E 26 80 ▦
               MED: 100-4, 12, 70; 100-4, 13, 20; 100-4, 13, 90

               AMA: 1997, Oct, 1

               Note that 77431 is not to be used to fill in the last week of a long course of
               therapy.

  77432   **Stereotactic radiation treatment management of cerebral lesion(s)
               (complete course of treatment consisting of one session)**   E 26 80 ▦
               MED: 100-4, 12, 70; 100-4, 13, 20; 100-4, 13, 90

               AMA: 1997, Oct, 1

               To report stereotactic body radiation treatment management, consult Category
               III code 0083T.

77470   **Special treatment procedure (eg, total body irradiation, hemibody radiation, per oral, endocavitary or intraoperative cone irradiation)**   Ⓢ 80 Ⓡ
MED: 100-4, 12, 70; 100-4, 13, 20; 100-4, 13, 90

AMA: 1997, Oct, 1; 1991, Winter, 22

Note that 77470 assumes that this procedure is performed one or more times during the course of therapy, in addition to daily or weekly patient management.

77499   **Unlisted procedure, therapeutic radiology treatment management**   Ⓔ 80
MED: 100-4, 12, 70; 100-4, 13, 20; 100-4, 13, 90

AMA: 2000, Feb, 7; 1999, Nov, 42

PROTON BEAM TREATMENT DELIVERY

The codes in this section provide for brachytherapy and teletherapy to include the initial consultation, clinical treatment planning, dosimetry, radiation physics, treatment devices and treatment management services. These codes also include follow-up care for up to three months following completion. Identify preliminary consultation and patient evaluation performed by the therapeutic radiologist by the evaluation and management code. Consult the glossary for terms and definitions and the front matter of this chapter for additional information.

77520   **Proton treatment delivery; simple, without compensation**   Ⓢ ⓉⒸ
MED: 100-4, 12, 70; 100-4, 13, 20; 100-4, 13, 90

AMA: 1999, Nov, 43

77522   **simple, with compensation**   Ⓢ ⓉⒸ Ⓡ
MED: 100-4, 12, 70; 100-4, 13, 20; 100-4, 13, 90

77523   **intermediate**   Ⓢ ⓉⒸ Ⓡ
MED: 100-4, 12, 70; 100-4, 13, 20; 100-4, 13, 90

AMA: 1999, Nov, 43

77525   **complex**   Ⓢ ⓉⒸ Ⓡ
MED: 100-4, 12, 70; 100-4, 13, 20; 100-4, 13, 90

HYPERTHERMIA

The codes in this section provide for brachytherapy and teletherapy to include the initial consultation, clinical treatment planning, dosimetry, radiation physics, treatment devices and treatment management services. These codes also include follow-up care for up to three months following completion. Identify preliminary consultation and patient evaluation performed by the therapeutic radiologist by the evaluation and management code. Consult the glossary for terms and definitions and the front matter of this chapter for additional information.

Microwaves, ultrasound, probes, and radiofrequencies may be used in concert with radiation therapy to provide external, interstitial, and intracavitary hyperthermia. Include the management and follow-up care in the following codes; physics planning and insertion of the sources are also included.

⊙   77600   **Hyperthermia, externally generated; superficial (ie, heating to a depth of 4 cm or less)**   Ⓢ 80 Ⓡ
MED: 100-3, 110.1; 100-4, 12, 70; 100-4, 13, 20; 100-4, 13, 90

AMA: 1991, Winter, 22

⊙   77605   **deep (ie, heating to depths greater than 4 cm)**   Ⓢ 80 Ⓡ
MED: 100-3, 110.1; 100-4, 12, 70; 100-4, 13, 20; 100-4, 13, 90

AMA: 1991, Winter, 22

Radiology

⊙   77610   **Hyperthermia generated by interstitial probe(s); 5 or fewer interstitial applicators**   S 80 🗗
              MED: 100-3, 110.1; 100-4, 12, 70; 100-4, 13, 20; 100-4, 13, 90

              AMA: 1991, Winter, 22

⊙   77615   **more than 5 interstitial applicators**   S 80 🗗
              MED: 100-3, 110.1; 100-4, 12, 70; 100-4, 13, 20; 100-4, 13, 90

              AMA: 1991, Winter, 22

CLINICAL INTRACAVITARY HYPERTHERMIA

     77620   **Hyperthermia generated by intracavitary probe(s)**   S 80 🗗
              MED: 100-3, 110.1; 100-4, 12, 70; 100-4, 13, 20; 100-4, 13, 90

              AMA: 1991, Winter, 22

CLINICAL BRACHYTHERAPY

The codes in this section provide for brachytherapy and teletherapy to include the initial consultation, clinical treatment planning, dosimetry, radiation physics, treatment devices and treatment management services. These codes also include follow-up care for up to three months following completion. Identify preliminary consultation and patient evaluation performed by the therapeutic radiologist by the evaluation and management code. Consult the glossary for terms and definitions and the front matter of this chapter for additional information.

Man-made or natural radioactive elements are placed in or around the treatment field by a radiotherapist. CPT codes 77750-77799 include hospital admission and daily visits.

     77750   **Infusion or instillation of radioelement solution (includes 3 months follow-up care)**   S 80 🗗
              MED: 100-4, 12, 70; 100-4, 13, 20; 100-4, 13, 90

              To report the administration of radiolabeled monoclonal antibodies, consult CPT code 79403.

              To report non-antibody radiopharmaceutical therapy by IV administration, not including the three-month follow-up care, consult CPT code 79101.

     77761   **Intracavitary radiation source application; simple**   S 80 🗗
              MED: 100-4, 12, 70; 100-4, 13, 20; 100-4, 13, 90

              AMA: 1999, Mar, 3; 1996, Jan, 7; 1991, Winter, 23

     77762   **intermediate**   S 80 🗗
              MED: 100-4, 12, 70; 100-4, 13, 20; 100-4, 13, 90

              AMA: 1991, Winter, 23

     77763   **complex**   S 80 🗗
              MED: 100-4, 12, 70; 100-4, 13, 20; 100-4, 13, 90

              AMA: 1999, Mar, 3; 1991, Winter, 23

     77776   **Interstitial radiation source application; simple**   S 80 🗗
              MED: 100-4, 12, 70; 100-4, 13, 20; 100-4, 13, 90

              AMA: 1991, Winter, 23

     77777   **intermediate**   S 80 🗗
              MED: 100-4, 12, 70; 100-4, 13, 20; 100-4, 13, 90

              AMA: 1991, Winter, 23

     77778   **complex**   S 80 🗗
              MED: 100-4, 12, 70; 100-4, 13, 20; 100-4, 13, 90

              AMA: 1991, Winter, 23

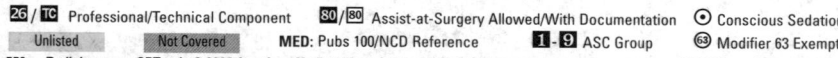

77610 — 77778

77781	**Remote afterloading high intensity brachytherapy; 1-4 source positions or catheters** MED: 100-4, 12, 70; 100-4, 13, 20; 100-4, 13, 90 AMA: 1999, Mar, 3; 1991, Winter, 23	S 80 ☐
77782	**5-8 source positions or catheters** MED: 100-4, 12, 70; 100-4, 13, 20; 100-4, 13, 90 AMA: 1999, Mar, 3; 1991, Winter, 23	S 80 ☐
77783	**9-12 source positions or catheters** MED: 100-4, 12, 70; 100-4, 13, 20; 100-4, 13, 90 AMA: 1999, Mar, 3; 1991, Winter, 23	S 80 ☐
77784	**over 12 source positions or catheters** MED: 100-4, 12, 70; 100-4, 13, 20; 100-4, 13, 90 AMA: 1999, Mar, 3; 1991, Winter, 23	S 80 ☐
77789	**Surface application of radiation source** MED: 100-4, 12, 70; 100-4, 13, 20; 100-4, 13, 90	S 80 ☐
77790	**Supervision, handling, loading of radiation source** MED: 100-4, 12, 70; 100-4, 13, 20; 100-4, 13, 90	N 80 ☐
77799	**Unlisted procedure, clinical brachytherapy** MED: 100-4, 12, 70; 100-4, 13, 20; 100-4, 13, 90	S 80

NUCLEAR MEDICINE

DIAGNOSTIC

ENDOCRINE SYSTEM

In Nuclear Medicine, the procedures can be listed separately or as part of the overall medical care of the patient. The provision of radium or other radioelements is not included in CPT codes 78000-79999. Report diagnostic and therapeutic radiopharmaceuticals supplied by the physician separately.

78000	**Thyroid uptake; single determination** MED: 100-2, 15, 80; 100-3, 220.8	S 80 ☐
78001	**multiple determinations** MED: 100-2, 15, 80; 100-3, 220.8	S 80 ☐

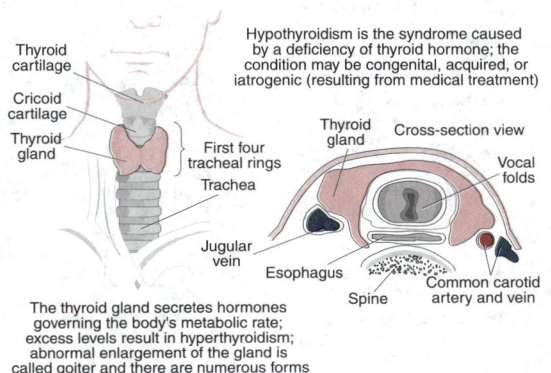

Hypothyroidism is the syndrome caused by a deficiency of thyroid hormone; the condition may be congenital, acquired, or iatrogenic (resulting from medical treatment)

Thyroid cartilage
Cricoid cartilage
Thyroid gland
First four tracheal rings
Trachea
Jugular vein
Esophagus
Spine
Thyroid gland — Cross-section view
Vocal folds
Common carotid artery and vein

The thyroid gland secretes hormones governing the body's metabolic rate; excess levels result in hyperthyroidism; abnormal enlargement of the gland is called goiter and there are numerous forms

Radiology

78003 — 78075

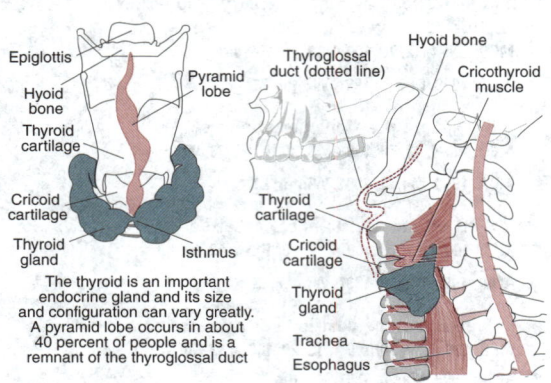

The thyroid is an important endocrine gland and its size and configuration can vary greatly. A pyramid lobe occurs in about 40 percent of people and is a remnant of the thyroglossal duct

78003	stimulation, suppression or discharge (not including initial uptake studies) ⓢ 80 ▣	
	MED: 100-2, 15, 80; 100-3, 220.8	
78006	Thyroid imaging, with uptake; single determination ⓢ 80 ▣	
	MED: 100-2, 15, 80; 100-3, 220.8	
78007	multiple determinations ⓢ 80 ▣	
	MED: 100-2, 15, 80; 100-3, 220.8	
78010	Thyroid imaging; only ⓢ 80 ▣	
	MED: 100-2, 15, 80; 100-3, 220.8	
78011	with vascular flow ⓢ 80 ▣	
	MED: 100-2, 15, 80; 100-3, 220.8	
78015	Thyroid carcinoma metastases imaging; limited area (eg, neck and chest only) ⓢ 80 ▣	
	MED: 100-2, 15, 80; 100-3, 220.8	
	AMA: 1998, Nov, 21	
78016	with additional studies (eg, urinary recovery) ⓢ 80 ▣	
	MED: 100-2, 15, 80; 100-3, 220.8	
78018	whole body ⓢ 80 ▣	
	MED: 100-2, 15, 80; 100-3, 220.8	
	AMA: 1999, Apr, 4	
+ **78020**	Thyroid carcinoma metastases uptake (List separately in addition to code for primary procedure) ⓢ 80 ▣	
	MED: 100-2, 15, 80; 100-3, 220.8	
	AMA: 1999, Apr, 4; 1998, Nov, 21	

Note that 78020 is an add-on code and must be used in conjunction with 78018.

78070	Parathyroid imaging ⓢ 80 ▣	
	MED: 100-2, 15, 80; 100-3, 220.8	
78075	Adrenal imaging, cortex and/or medulla ⓢ 80 ▣	
	MED: 100-2, 15, 80; 100-3, 220.8	

26 / TC Professional/Technical Component   80 / 80 Assist-at-Surgery Allowed/With Documentation   ☉ Conscious Sedation
Unlisted   Not Covered   MED: Pubs 100/NCD Reference   1 - 9 ASC Group   63 Modifier 63 Exempt
554 — Radiology   CPT only © 2005 American Medical Association. All Rights Reserved. (Black Ink)   © 2005 Ingenix, Inc. (Blue Ink)

78099	Unlisted endocrine procedure, diagnostic nuclear medicine	S 80
	MED: 100-2, 15, 80; 100-3, 220.8	

If a chemical analysis is needed, consult the Chemistry section of the CPT book.

HEMATOPOIETIC, RETICULOENDOTHELIAL AND LYMPHATIC SYSTEM

78102	Bone marrow imaging; limited area	S 80 ⌐
	MED: 100-2, 15, 80; 100-3, 220.8	
78103	multiple areas	S 80 ⌐
	MED: 100-2, 15, 80; 100-3, 220.8	
78104	whole body	S 80 ⌐
	MED: 100-2, 15, 80; 100-3, 220.8	
78110	Plasma volume, radiopharmaceutical volume-dilution technique (separate procedure); single sampling	S 80 ⌐
	MED: 100-2, 15, 80; 100-3, 220.8	
78111	multiple samplings	S 80 ⌐
	MED: 100-2, 15, 80; 100-3, 220.8	
78120	Red cell volume determination (separate procedure); single sampling	S 80 ⌐
	MED: 100-2, 15, 80; 100-3, 220.8	
78121	multiple samplings	S 80 ⌐
	MED: 100-2, 15, 80; 100-3, 220.8	
78122	Whole blood volume determination, including separate measurement of plasma volume and red cell volume (radiopharmaceutical volume-dilution technique)	S 80 ⌐
	MED: 100-2, 15, 80; 100-3, 220.8	
78130	Red cell survival study;	S 80 ⌐
	MED: 100-2, 15, 80; 100-3, 220.8	
78135	differential organ/tissue kinetics, (eg, splenic and/or hepatic sequestration)	S 80 ⌐
	MED: 100-2, 15, 80; 100-3, 220.8	
78140	Labeled red cell sequestration, differential organ/tissue, (eg, splenic and/or hepatic)	S 80 ⌐
	MED: 100-2, 15, 80; 100-3, 220.8	
78160	~~Plasma radioiron disappearance (turnover) rate~~	
78162	~~Radioiron oral absorption~~	
78170	~~Radioiron red cell utilization~~	
78172	~~Chelatable iron for estimation of total body iron~~	
78185	Spleen imaging only, with or without vascular flow	S 80 ⌐
	MED: 100-2, 15, 80; 100-3, 220.8	

If this procedure is combined with a liver study, consult CPT codes 78215 and 78216.

78190	Kinetics, study of platelet survival, with or without differential organ/tissue localization	S 80 ⌐
	MED: 100-2, 15, 80; 100-3, 220.8	
78191	Platelet survival study	S 80 ⌐
	MED: 100-2, 15, 80; 100-3, 220.8	

⌐ CCI Comp   50 Bilateral Procedure   + CPT Add-on Code   ⊘ Modifier -51 Exempt   ♂ Male   ♀ Female
● New Code   ▲ Revised Code   M Maternity Edit   A Age Edit   A—Y APC Status Ind.   AMA: CPT Assistant

© 2005 Ingenix, Inc. *(Blue Ink)*    CPT only © 2005 American Medical Association. All Rights Reserved. *(Black Ink)* 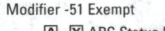   Radiology — 555

Radiology

78195 — 78262

78195   **Lymphatics and lymph nodes imaging**   S 80
MED: 100-2, 15, 80; 100-3, 220.8

AMA: 1999, Nov, 43; 1999, Dec, 8; 1998, Nov, 22

If sentinel node identification is performed without scintigraphy imaging, consult CPT code 38792. If the sentinel node is excised, consult CPT codes 38500-38542.

78199   **Unlisted hematopoietic, reticuloendothelial and lymphatic procedure, diagnostic nuclear medicine**   S 80
MED: 100-2, 15, 80; 100-3, 220.8

If chemical analysis is needed, consult the Chemistry section of CPT.

GASTROINTESTINAL SYSTEM

78201   **Liver imaging; static only**   S 80
MED: 100-2, 15, 80; 100-3, 220.8

78202   **with vascular flow**   S 80
MED: 100-2, 15, 80; 100-3, 220.8

If spleen imaging is performed by itself, consult CPT code 78185.

78205   **Liver imaging (SPECT)**   S 80
MED: 100-2, 15, 80; 100-3, 220.12; 100-3, 220.8

AMA: 1998, Nov, 22

78206   **with vascular flow**   S 80
MED: 100-2, 15, 80; 100-3, 220.8

AMA: 1998, Nov, 22

78215   **Liver and spleen imaging; static only**   S 80
MED: 100-2, 15, 80; 100-3, 220.8

78216   **with vascular flow**   S 80
MED: 100-2, 15, 80; 100-3, 220.8

78220   **Liver function study with hepatobiliary agents, with serial images**   S 80
MED: 100-2, 15, 80; 100-3, 220.8

78223   **Hepatobiliary ductal system imaging, including gallbladder, with or without pharmacologic intervention, with or without quantitative measurement of gallbladder function**   S 80
MED: 100-2, 15, 80; 100-3, 220.8

78230   **Salivary gland imaging;**   S 80
MED: 100-2, 15, 80; 100-3, 220.8

78231   **with serial images**   S 80
MED: 100-2, 15, 80; 100-3, 220.8

78232   **Salivary gland function study**   S 80
MED: 100-2, 15, 80; 100-3, 220.8

78258   **Esophageal motility**   S 80
MED: 100-2, 15, 80; 100-3, 220.8

78261   **Gastric mucosa imaging**   S 80
MED: 100-2, 15, 80; 100-3, 220.8

78262   **Gastroesophageal reflux study**   S 80
MED: 100-2, 15, 80; 100-3, 220.8

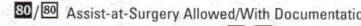

| 78264 | **Gastric emptying study** | S 80 🔲 |
| | MED: 100-2, 15, 80; 100-3, 220.8 | |

78267	**Urea breath test, C-14 (isotopic); acquisition for analysis**	A 🔲
	MED: 100-2, 15, 80; 100-3, 220.8	
	AMA: 1999, Nov, 43	

78268	**analysis**	A 🔲
	MED: 100-2, 15, 80; 100-3, 220.8	
	AMA: 1999, Nov, 43	

| 78270 | **Vitamin B-12 absorption study (eg, Schilling test); without intrinsic factor** | S 80 🔲 |
| | MED: 100-2, 15, 80; 100-3, 220.8 | |

| 78271 | **with intrinsic factor** | S 80 🔲 |
| | MED: 100-2, 15, 80; 100-3, 220.8 | |

| 78272 | **Vitamin B-12 absorption studies combined, with and without intrinsic factor** | S 80 🔲 |
| | MED: 100-2, 15, 80; 100-3, 220.8 | |

| 78278 | **Acute gastrointestinal blood loss imaging** | S 80 🔲 |
| | MED: 100-2, 15, 80; 100-3, 220.8 | |

| 78282 | **Gastrointestinal protein loss** | S 80 🔲 |
| | MED: 100-2, 15, 80; 100-3, 220.8 | |

| 78290 | **Intestine imaging (eg, ectopic gastric mucosa, Meckel's localization, volvulus)** | S 80 🔲 |
| | MED: 100-2, 15, 80; 100-3, 220.8 | |

| 78291 | **Peritoneal-venous shunt patency test (eg, for LeVeen, Denver shunt)** | S 80 🔲 |
| | MED: 100-2, 15, 80; 100-3, 220.8 | |

To report injection procedure, consult CPT code 49427.

| 78299 | **Unlisted gastrointestinal procedure, diagnostic nuclear medicine** | S 80 |
| | MED: 100-2, 15, 80; 100-3, 220.8 | |

If chemical analysis is needed, consult the Chemistry section of the CPT book.

MUSCULOSKELETAL SYSTEM

78300	**Bone and/or joint imaging; limited area**	S 80 🔲
	MED: 100-2, 15, 80; 100-3, 220.8	
	AMA: 1997, Mar, 11	

78305	**multiple areas**	S 80 🔲
	MED: 100-2, 15, 80; 100-3, 220.8	
	AMA: 1997, Mar, 11	

78306	**whole body**	S 80 🔲
	MED: 100-2, 15, 80; 100-3, 220.8; 100-4, 12, 70; 100-4, 13, 20; 100-4, 13, 90	
	AMA: 2002, Jan, 10; 1997, Mar, 11	

78315	**three phase study**	S 80 🔲
	MED: 100-2, 15, 80; 100-3, 220.8	
	AMA: 2002, Jan, 10	

78264 — 78315

Radiology

78320 — 78459

78320	**tomographic (SPECT)**	S 80
	MED: 100-2, 15, 80; 100-3, 220.12; 100-3, 220.8; 100-4, 12, 70; 100-4, 13, 20; 100-4, 13, 90	
	AMA: 1997, Mar, 11	

78350   **Bone density (bone mineral content) study, one or more sites; single photon asorptiometry**   X 80
    MED: 100-2, 15, 80; 100-3, 150.3; 100-3, 220.8

    AMA: 1997, Nov, 26

78351   **dual photon absorptiometry, one or more sites**   E
        MED: 100-2, 15, 80; 100-3, 150.3; 100-3, 220.8

        AMA: 1997, Nov, 26

        If radiographic bone density (photodensitometry) is performed, consult CPT code 76078.

78399   **Unlisted musculoskeletal procedure, diagnostic nuclear medicine**   S 80
    MED: 100-2, 15, 80; 100-3, 220.8

CARDIOVASCULAR SYSTEM

In Nuclear Medicine, the procedures can be listed separately or as part of the overall medical care of the patient. The provision of radium or other radioelements is not included in CPT codes 78000-79999. These materials should be reported separately.

Use stress testing codes from 93015-93018 series when the following procedures are performed during exercise or medication-induced stress. Infusion and blood pool imaging can be performed at rest or during stress.

78414   **Determination of central c-v hemodynamics (non-imaging) (eg, ejection fraction with probe technique) with or without pharmacologic intervention or exercise, single or multiple determinations**   S 80
    MED: 100-2, 15, 80; 100-3, 220.8

78428   **Cardiac shunt detection**   S 80
    MED: 100-2, 15, 80; 100-3, 220.8

78445   **Non-cardiac vascular flow imaging (ie, angiography, venography)**   S 80
    MED: 100-2, 15, 80; 100-3, 220.8

~~78455~~   ~~Venous thrombosis study (eg, radioactive fibrinogen)~~

78456   **Acute venous thrombosis imaging, peptide**   S
    MED: 100-2, 15, 80; 100-3, 220.8

    AMA: 1999, Nov, 43

78457   **Venous thrombosis imaging, venogram; unilateral**   S 80
    MED: 100-2, 15, 80; 100-3, 220.8

    AMA: 1999, Nov, 43

78458   **bilateral**   S 80
    MED: 100-2, 15, 80; 100-3, 220.8

    AMA: 1999, Nov, 43

78459   **Myocardial imaging, positron emission tomography (PET), metabolic evaluation**   S 80
    MED: 100-2, 15, 80; 100-3, 220.6; 100-3, 220.8

    AMA: 1997, Nov, 26; 1996, Jun, 5

    If a myocardial perfusion study is performed, consult CPT codes 78491-78492.

78460	**Myocardial perfusion imaging; (planar) single study, at rest or stress (exercise and/or pharmacologic), with or without quantification** ⑤ ⑧⓪ ⧉	

MED: 100-2, 15, 80; 100-3, 220.8

AMA: 2000, Apr, 1; 1999, Mar, 10

78461   **multiple studies, (planar) at rest and/or stress (exercise and/or pharmacologic), and redistribution and/or rest injection, with or without quantification** ⑤ ⑧⓪ ⧉
MED: 100-2, 15, 80; 100-3, 220.8

AMA: 1999, Mar, 10

78464   **tomographic (SPECT), single study (including attenuation correction when performed), at rest or stress (exercise and/or pharmacologic), with or without quantification** ⑤ ⑧⓪ ⧉
MED: 100-3, 220.8

AMA: 1999, Mar, 10

78465   **tomographic (SPECT), multiple studies (including attenuation correction when performed), at rest and/or stress (exercise and/or pharmacologic) and redistribution and/or rest injection, with or without quantification** ⑤ ⑧⓪ ⧉
MED: 100-2, 15, 80; 100-3, 220.12; 100-3, 220.8

AMA: 1999, Mar, 10; 1998, Aug, 11

78466   **Myocardial imaging, infarct avid, planar; qualitative or quantitative** ⑤ ⑧⓪ ⧉
MED: 100-2, 15, 80; 100-3, 220.8

78468   **with ejection fraction by first pass technique** ⑤ ⑧⓪ ⧉
MED: 100-2, 15, 80; 100-3, 220.8

78469   **tomographic SPECT with or without quantification** ⑤ ⑧⓪ ⧉
MED: 100-2, 15, 80; 100-3, 220.8

78472   **Cardiac blood pool imaging, gated equilibrium; planar, single study at rest or stress (exercise and/or pharmacologic), wall motion study plus ejection fraction, with or without additional quantitative processing** ⑤ ⑧⓪ ⧉
MED: 100-2, 15, 80; 100-3, 220.8

AMA: 1999, Nov, 44; 1999, Jun, 8; 1998, Nov, 22

To report assessment of right ventricular ejection fraction using first pass technique, consult CPT code 78496.

78473   **multiple studies, wall motion study plus ejection fraction, at rest and stress (exercise and/or pharmacologic), with or without additional quantification** ⑤ ⑧⓪ ⧉
MED: 100-2, 15, 80; 100-3, 220.8

AMA: 1999, Jun, 11

+   78478   **Myocardial perfusion study with wall motion, qualitative or quantitative study (List separately in addition to code for primary procedure)** ⑤ ⑧⓪ ⧉
MED: 100-2, 15, 80; 100-3, 220.8

AMA: 1999, Mar, 10

Note that 78478 is an add-on code and must be used in conjunction with 78460, 78461, 78464, and 78465.

⧉ CCI Comp	🔟 Bilateral Procedure	+ CPT Add-on Code ⊘ Modifier -51 Exempt ♂ Male ♀ Female
● New Code	▲ Revised Code	Ⓜ Maternity Edit Ⓐ Age Edit Ⓐ–Ⓨ APC Status Ind. AMA: CPT Assistant

© 2005 Ingenix, Inc. *(Blue Ink)*   CPT only © 2005 American Medical Association. All Rights Reserved. *(Black Ink)*   Radiology — 559

Radiology

78480 — 78585

+ **78480** **Myocardial perfusion study with ejection fraction (List separately in addition to code for primary procedure)** [S] [80] [▣]
MED: 100-2, 15, 80; 100-3, 220.8
AMA: 1997, Mar, 10

Note that 78480 is an add-on code and must be used in conjunction with 78460, 78461, 78464, and 78465.

78481 **Cardiac blood pool imaging, (planar), first pass technique; single study, at rest or with stress (exercise and/or pharmacologic), wall motion study plus ejection fraction, with or without quantification** [S] [80] [▣]
MED: 100-2, 15, 80; 100-3, 220.8

78483 **multiple studies, at rest and with stress (exercise and/or pharmacologic), wall motion study plus ejection fraction, with or without quantification** [S] [80] [▣]
MED: 100-2, 15, 80; 100-3, 220.8

If a cerebral blood flow study is conducted, consult CPT code 78615.

78491 **Myocardial imaging, positron emission tomography (PET), perfusion; single study at rest or stress** [S] [80] [▣]
MED: 100-2, 15, 80; 100-3, 220.6; 100-3, 220.8
AMA: 1997, Nov, 27

78492 **multiple studies at rest and/or stress** [S] [80] [▣]
MED: 100-2, 15, 80; 100-3, 220.6; 100-3, 220.8
AMA: 1997, Nov, 27

78494 **Cardiac blood pool imaging, gated equilibrium, SPECT, at rest, wall motion study plus ejection fraction, with or without quantitative processing** [S] [80] [▣]
MED: 100-2, 15, 80; 100-3, 220.8
AMA: 1999, Jun, 3; 1998, Nov, 22

+ **78496** **Cardiac blood pool imaging, gated equilibrium, single study, at rest, with right ventricular ejection fraction by first pass technique (List separately in addition to code for primary procedure)** [S] [80] [▣]
MED: 100-2, 15, 80; 100-3, 220.8
AMA: 1999, Jun, 3, 11; 1998, Nov, 22

Note that 78496 is an add-on code and must be used in conjunction with 78472.

78499 **Unlisted cardiovascular procedure, diagnostic nuclear medicine** [S] [80]
MED: 100-2, 15, 80; 100-3, 220.8

If chemical analysis is needed, consult the Chemistry section of the CPT book.

RESPIRATORY SYSTEM

78580 **Pulmonary perfusion imaging, particulate** [S] [80] [▣]
MED: 100-2, 15, 80; 100-3, 220.7; 100-3, 220.8
AMA: 1999, Mar, 4

78584 **Pulmonary perfusion imaging, particulate, with ventilation; single breath** [S] [80] [▣]
MED: 100-2, 15, 80; 100-3, 220.7; 100-3, 220.8
AMA: 1999, Mar, 4

78585 **rebreathing and washout, with or without single breath** [S] [80] [▣]
MED: 100-2, 15, 80; 100-3, 220.8
AMA: 1999, Mar, 4

Diagram of tomography principal (left)

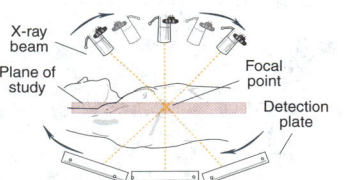

X-ray beam
Plane of study
Focal point
Detection plate

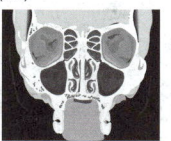

Schematic of frontal coronal CT section of skull

Tomogram is a general term for radiographic studies that focus on a single body plane, unimpeded by shadows cast by surrounding tissues and structures. The x-ray tube and the film are rotated around the patient during exposure of the focal point. Computed tomography (CT) offers a "slice" view of the study area and information is typically digitized and viewed on monitors. Magnetic resonance imaging (MRI) places a patient in the field of a powerful magnet while radio waves pass through the body; as with CT studies, views are usually of a "slice" of tissue. Ultrasound and nuclear imaging are other common radiological approaches

78586   **Pulmonary ventilation imaging, aerosol; single projection**   S 80 ⬚
              MED: 100-2, 15, 80; 100-3, 220.8
              AMA: 1999, Mar, 4

78587   **multiple projections (eg, anterior, posterior, lateral views)**   S 80 ⬚
              MED: 100-2, 15, 80; 100-3, 220.8
              AMA: 1999, Mar, 4

78588   **Pulmonary perfusion imaging, particulate, with ventilation imaging, aerosol, one or multiple projections**   S 80 ⬚
              MED: 100-2, 15, 80; 100-3, 220.7; 100-3, 220.8
              AMA: 1999, Mar, 4; 1998, Nov, 22

78591   **Pulmonary ventilation imaging, gaseous, single breath, single projection**   S 80 ⬚
              MED: 100-2, 15, 80; 100-3, 220.8
              AMA: 1999, Mar, 4

78593   **Pulmonary ventilation imaging, gaseous, with rebreathing and washout with or without single breath; single projection**   S 80 ⬚
              MED: 100-2, 15, 80; 100-3, 220.8
              AMA: 1999, Mar, 4

78594   **multiple projections (eg, anterior, posterior, lateral views)**   S 80 ⬚
              MED: 100-2, 15, 80; 100-3, 220.8

78596   **Pulmonary quantitative differential function (ventilation/perfusion) study**   S 80 ⬚
              MED: 100-2, 15, 80; 100-3, 220.8

78599   **Unlisted respiratory procedure, diagnostic nuclear medicine**   S 80
              MED: 100-2, 15, 80; 100-3, 220.8

NERVOUS SYSTEM

78600   **Brain imaging, limited procedure; static**   S 80 ⬚
              MED: 100-2, 15, 80; 100-3, 220.8

78601   **with vascular flow**   S 80 ⬚
              MED: 100-2, 15, 80; 100-3, 220.8

78605   **Brain imaging, complete study; static**   S 80 ⬚
              MED: 100-2, 15, 80; 100-3, 220.8

Radiology

| 78606 | with vascular flow | S 80 ⬚ |
| | MED: 100-2, 15, 80; 100-3, 220.8 | |

| 78607 | tomographic (SPECT) | S 80 ⬚ |
| | MED: 100-2, 15, 80; 100-3, 220.8 | |

| 78608 | Brain imaging, positron emission tomography (PET); metabolic evaluation | S 80 ⬚ |
| | MED: 100-2, 15, 80; 100-3, 220.6; 100-3, 220.8 | |

| 78609 | perfusion evaluation | S 80 ⬚ |
| | MED: 100-2, 15, 80; 100-3, 220.6; 100-3, 220.7; 100-3, 220.8 | |

| 78610 | Brain imaging, vascular flow only | S 80 ⬚ |
| | MED: 100-2, 15, 80; 100-3, 220.8 | |

| 78615 | Cerebral vascular flow | S 80 ⬚ |
| | MED: 100-2, 15, 80; 100-3, 220.8 | |

| 78630 | Cerebrospinal fluid flow, imaging (not including introduction of material); cisternography | S 80 ⬚ |
| | MED: 100-2, 15, 80; 100-3, 220.8 | |

If an injection procedure is performed, consult CPT codes 61000-61070 and 62270-62319.

| 78635 | ventriculography | S 80 ⬚ |
| | MED: 100-2, 15, 80; 100-3, 220.8 | |

If an injection procedure is performed, consult CPT codes 61000-61070 and 62270-62294.

| 78645 | shunt evaluation | S 80 ⬚ |
| | MED: 100-2, 15, 80; 100-3, 220.8 | |

If an injection procedure is performed, consult CPT codes 61000-61070 and 62270-62294.

| 78647 | tomographic (SPECT) | S 80 ⬚ |
| | MED: 100-2, 15, 80; 100-3, 220.12; 100-3, 220.8 | |

| 78650 | Cerebrospinal fluid leakage detection and localization | S 80 ⬚ |
| | MED: 100-2, 15, 80; 100-3, 220.8 | |

If an injection procedure is performed, consult CPT codes 61000-61070 and 62270-62294.

| 78660 | Radiopharmaceutical dacryocystography | S 80 ⬚ |
| | MED: 100-2, 15, 80; 100-3, 220.8 | |

| 78699 | Unlisted nervous system procedure, diagnostic nuclear medicine | S 80 |
| | MED: 100-2, 15, 80; 100-3, 220.8 | |

GENITOURINARY SYSTEM

| 78700 | Kidney imaging; static only | S 80 ⬚ |
| | MED: 100-2, 15, 80; 100-3, 220.8 | |

| 78701 | with vascular flow | S 80 ⬚ |
| | MED: 100-2, 15, 80; 100-3, 220.8 | |

| 78704 | with function study (ie, imaging renogram) | S 80 ⬚ |
| | MED: 100-2, 15, 80; 100-3, 220.8 | |

Radiology

78707   **Kidney imaging with vascular flow and function; single study without pharmacological intervention**   S 80 ⬚
MED: 100-2, 15, 80; 100-3, 220.8

AMA: 1997, Nov, 27

78708   **single study, with pharmacological intervention (eg, angiotensin converting enzyme inhibitor and/or diuretic**   S 80 ⬚
MED: 100-2, 15, 80; 100-3, 220.8

AMA: 1997, Nov, 27

78709   **multiple studies, with and without pharmacological intervention (eg, angiotensin converting enzyme inhibitor and/or diuretic)**   S 80 ⬚
MED: 100-2, 15, 80; 100-3, 220.8

AMA: 1997, Nov, 27

If a radioactive substance is introduced in association with renal endoscopy, consult CPT codes 50559 and 50578.

78710   **Kidney imaging, tomographic (SPECT)**   S 80 ⬚
MED: 100-2, 15, 80; 100-3, 220.12; 100-3, 220.8

AMA: 1997, Nov, 27

78715   **Kidney vascular flow only**   S 80 ⬚
MED: 100-2, 15, 80; 100-3, 220.8

78725   **Kidney function study, non-imaging radioisotopic study**   S 80 ⬚
MED: 100-2, 15, 80; 100-3, 220.8

AMA: 1998, Nov, 22

78730   **Urinary bladder residual study**   X 80 ⬚
MED: 100-2, 15, 80; 100-3, 220.8

If a radioactive substance is introduced in association with a cystotomy or a cystostomy, consult CPT code 51020. If a radioactive substance is introduced in association with a cystourethroscopy, consult CPT code 52250.

78740   **Ureteral reflux study (radiopharmaceutical voiding cystogram)**   S 80 ⬚
MED: 100-2, 15, 80; 100-3, 220.8; 100-3, 230.2

To report catheterization, consult CPT codes 51701, 51702, 51703.

78760   **Testicular imaging;**   ♂ S 80 ⬚
MED: 100-2, 15, 80; 100-3, 220.8

78761   **with vascular flow**   ♂ S 80 ⬚
MED: 100-2, 15, 80; 100-3, 220.8

To report introduction of radioactive substance with ureteral endoscopy, consult CPT codes 50959, 50978.

78799   **Unlisted genitourinary procedure, diagnostic nuclear medicine**   S 80
MED: 100-2, 15, 80; 100-3, 220.8

If chemistry analysis is needed, consult the Chemistry section of the CPT book.

78707 — 78799

OTHER PROCEDURES

See appropriate heading for specific organ sites.

78800 **Radiopharmaceutical localization of tumor or distribution of radiopharmaceutical agent(s); limited area** Ⓢ 80 🖽
MED: 100-2, 15, 80; 100-3, 220.8

Use 78800 to report radiophosphorus ocular tumor identification.

78801 **multiple areas** Ⓢ 80 🖽
MED: 100-2, 15, 80; 100-3, 220.8

78802 **whole body, single day imaging** Ⓢ 80 🖽
MED: 100-2, 15, 80; 100-3, 220.8; 100-4, 12, 70; 100-4, 13, 20; 100-4, 13, 90

78803 **tomographic (SPECT)** Ⓢ 80 🖽
MED: 100-2, 15, 80; 100-3, 220.12; 100-3, 220.8; 100-4, 12, 70; 100-4, 13, 20; 100-4, 13, 90

78804 **whole body, requiring two or more days imaging** Ⓢ 80 🖽

78805 **Radiopharmaceutical localization of inflammatory process; limited area** Ⓢ 80 🖽
MED: 100-2, 15, 80; 100-3, 220.8

AMA: 1999, Nov, 44

To report bone and/or joint imaging, consult CPT codes 78300, 78305, and 78306.

78806 **whole body** Ⓢ 80 🖽
MED: 100-2, 15, 80; 100-3, 220.8; 100-4, 12, 70; 100-4, 13, 20; 100-4, 13, 90

AMA: 1999, Nov, 44

78807 **tomographic (SPECT)** Ⓢ 80 🖽
MED: 100-2, 15, 80; 100-3, 220.12; 100-3, 220.8; 100-4, 12, 70; 100-4, 13, 20; 100-4, 13, 90

To report imaging bone infectious or inflammatory disease with a bone imaging radiopharmaceutical, consult 78300, 78305, 78306.

To report PET of brain, consult 78608, 78609. To report PET myocardial imaging, see 78491, 784992.

78811 **Tumor imaging, positron emission tomography (PET); limited area (eg, chest, head/neck)** Ⓢ 80 🖽

78812 **skull base to mid-thigh** Ⓢ 80 🖽

78813 **whole body** Ⓢ 80 🖽

78814 **Tumor imaging, positron emission tomography (PET) with concurrently acquired computed tomography (CT) for attenuation correction and anatomical localization; limited area (eg, chest, head/neck)** Ⓢ 80 🖽

78815 **skull base to mid-thigh** Ⓢ 80 🖽

78816 **whole body** Ⓢ 80 🖽

Codes 78811-78816 should be reported only once per session.

Report the CT scan code for other than attenuation correction and anatomical localization with the code for the specific site and append modifier 59.

78890 **Generation of automated data: interactive process involving nuclear physician and/or allied health professional personnel; simple manipulations and interpretation, not to exceed 30 minutes** Ⓝ
MED: 100-3, 220.8; 100-4, 12, 70; 100-4, 13, 20; 100-4, 13, 90

Report 78890 and 78891 in addition to primary procedure.

78891   **complex manipulations and interpretation, exceeding 30 minutes** [N]
MED: 100-3, 220.8; 100-4, 12, 70; 100-4, 13, 20; 100-4, 13, 90

Note that 78890 and 78891 should be used in addition to the primary procedure.

78999   **Unlisted miscellaneous procedure, diagnostic nuclear medicine** [S] [80]
MED: 100-3, 220.8

THERAPEUTIC

The oral and intravenous administration codes in this section include the method of administration. For intra-arterial, intra-cavitary, and intra-articular administration, also report the appropriate injection and/or procedure codes, as well as imaging guidance and radiological supervision and interpretation codes, when applicable.

79005   **Radiopharmaceutical therapy, by oral administration** [S] [80]

To report monoclonal antibody therrapy, consult 79403.

79101   **Radiopharmaceutical therapy, by intravenous administration** [S] [80] [CCI]

Code 79101 cannot be reported with CPT codes 36400, 36410, 79403, 90780, 96408.

To report radiolabeled monochlonal antibody by IV infusion, consult 79403.

To report infusion or instillation of non-antibody radioelement solution including three months after follow-up consult CPT code 77750.

79200   **Radiopharmaceutical therapy, by intracavitary administration** [S] [80] [CCI]
MED: 100-3, 220.8

79300   **Radiopharmaceutical therapy, by interstitial radioactive colloid administration** [S] [80] [CCI]
MED: 100-3, 220.8

79403   **Radiopharmaceutical therapy, radiolabeled monoclonal antibody by intravenous infusion** [S] [80] [CCI]

To report pre-treatment imaging, consult CPT codes 78802, 78804.

Code 79403 cannot be reported in conjunction with 79101.

79440   **Radiopharmaceutical therapy, by intra-articular administration** [S] [80] [CCI]
MED: 100-3, 220.8

79445   **Radiopharmaceutical therapy, by intra-arterial particulate administration** [S] [80] [CCI]

Code 79445 cannot be reported with 90783, 96420.

If angiography and interventional procedures are done, report the radiologic procedural codes for supervision and interpretation and the procedure before the intra-arterial radiopharmaceutical therapy.

79999   **Radiopharmaceutical therapy, unlisted procedure** [S] [80]
MED: 100-3, 220.8; 100-4, 12, 70; 100-4, 13, 20; 100-4, 13, 90

Pathology and Laboratory

CODING INFORMATION

ORGANIZATION

The pathology and laboratory (80048–89356) section of CPT is divided into 18 subsections. Subsections are as follows:

Organ or Disease Oriented Panels

Drug Testing

Therapeutic Drug Assays

Evocative/Suppression Testing

Consultations (Clinical Pathology)

Urinalysis

Chemistry

Hematology and Coagulation

Immunology

Transfusion Medicine

Microbiology

Anatomic Pathology

Cytopathology

Cytogenetic Studies

Surgical Pathology

Transcutaneous Procedures

Other Procedures

Reproductive Medicine Procedures

GUIDELINES

Inpatient coders are not required to code pathology or laboratory tests since they are not necessary in the assignment of diagnosis-related groups (DRGs). However, pathology and laboratory codes are itemized on chargemasters for reporting services and supplies to patients.

Outpatient coders frequently code pathology and laboratory tests. Coding instructions include listing each laboratory procedure separately, unless it is part of a panel. Never use modifier 51 Multiple procedures in pathology or laboratory coding.

Many lab tests can be performed by different methods. To choose the correct code, carefully review code descriptions as well as any notes. When in doubt, request information from the physician or laboratory for clarification, or consult an authoritative reference.

Pathology and laboratory services are provided by the physician or by technologists under the supervision of a physician. The majority of the codes represent a technical component only, but certain codes represent a global service-a combination of professional and technical components. If the pathologist reviews a test result or renders an opinion of a test that is represented by a global code, the code selected should be identified with modifier 26 to indicate that only the professional component was provided.

SUBSECTIONS

ORGAN OR DISEASE-ORIENTED PANELS

Nine codes (80048–80076) report panels listing definitive test components: basic metabolic; general health; electrolyte; comprehensive metabolic; obstetric; lipid; renal function; acute hepatitis; and hepatic function. These panels neither specify clinical parameters nor do they preclude performance of other tests. Tests performed in addition to the procedures defined in a panel can be reported separately. However, panel tests should not be reported separately on the same day as single test codes listed as part of the panel. For example, a hepatic function panel code 80076 includes codes 82040 (albumin), 82247 (bilirubin, total), 82248 (bilirubin, direct), 84075 (phosphatase, alkaline), 84155 (protein, total), 84460 (transferase, alanine amino (ALT) (SGBT), and 84450 (transferase, aspartate amino (AST) (SGOT).

DRUG TESTING

The drug testing subsection lists codes (80100–80101) for qualitative screens that are usually confirmed by a second technique. Thirteen drugs or classes of drugs are listed as examples of commonly assayed qualitative screens: alcohols; amphetamines; barbiturates; opiates; benzodiazepines; cocaine and metabolites; methadones; methaqualones; phencyclidines; phenothiazines; propoxyphenes; tetrahydrocannabinoids; and tricyclic antidepressants.

REPORTING DRUG SCREENS

Qualitative screens should be reported when a provider is testing for the presence of a particular substance or substances. Coding for qualitative screening tests is based on procedure, not method or analyte. For example, if confirmation of five drugs requires three procedures, 80102 Drug confirmation, each procedure is identified three times. Drugs that have been confirmed through qualitative testing may also be quantitated. Use codes from the chemistry section (82000–84999) or therapeutic drug assay section (80150–80299) to report quantitative testing.

THERAPEUTIC DRUG ASSAYS

The therapeutic drug assays subsection (80150–80299) lists codes for quantitative assays. Several of these codes were found in the chemistry and toxicology subsection in past editions of the CPT book and reported as either qualitative or quantitative tests.

CODING FOR DRUG ASSAYS

Codes listed under therapeutic drug assays or under chemistry are used when a drug is quantitated, or measured. Screening may be used to detect a substance, but it is not a prerequisite for quantitation. For example, screening is not necessary when a known drug has been overdosed. Coding for quantitative assays is based on the substance tested. Unless the code description notes otherwise, the examination material may be from any source.

EVOCATIVE/SUPPRESSION TESTING

These procedures (80400–80440) measure the effects of administered evocative (stimulating) or suppressive agents upon the patient and represent the technical component of the service. These panels measure levels of multiple constituents or the same constituent multiple times after administering the stimulating or suppressing agent. Most of these tests are performed to evaluate specific conditions stated in the code narrative. For example, 80400 ACTH stimulation panel (adrenocorticotropic hormone) is performed for adrenal insufficiency. The physician's administration of the agent is reported separately using 90780–90784. Supplies and drugs are reported separately, (99070 or HCPCS Level II codes). To report physician attendance and monitoring during the tests, refer to the appropriate evaluation and management codes. Prolonged physician care codes may be reported separately, except when testing is performed by prolonged infusion (90780–90781).

CONSULTATION (CLINICAL PATHOLOGY)

Two consultation codes (80500 and 80502) are reserved for the pathologist to indicate a service, not a test. The pathology consultation is performed at the request of an attending physician and requires a written report. Code 80500 is a limited service without review of the patient's history and medical records. Code 80502 is a comprehensive service for a complex diagnostic problem, with review of the patient's history and medical records.

URINALYSIS

Codes 81000–81099 are used for specific analysis of one or more components of the urine. Select the appropriate code based on method (e.g., dip stick, tablet reagent, qualitative, semiquantitative) purpose (e.g., pregnancy test, timed-volume, bacteriuria screen) and specific constituents evaluated (e.g., bilirubin, glucose, pH). Not all urine analyses are listed in this section. For other tests, see appropriate section. For example, urine chloride can be found in the chemistry section.

CHEMISTRY

Chemistry codes (82000–84999) report only quantitative tests unless the description specifies otherwise, as is the case with the chromatography codes (82486–82492). Qualitative screens are reported by the four drug testing codes (80100–80103).

An individual code or a series of codes may be required for appropriate reporting. Glucose testing is an example:

82947	Glucose; quantitative, blood (except reagent strip)
82948	blood, reagent strip
82950	post glucose dose (includes glucose)
82951	tolerance test (GTT), three specimens (includes glucose)
82952	tolerance test, each additional beyond three specimens

Code 82951 reports a three–specimen glucose tolerance test (GTT). This code includes obtaining the fasting blood sample, supplying and administering the oral glucose dose, and obtaining the next two samples (e.g., at one-half hour and one hour). Code 82952 reports additional samples beyond the first three. Report 82951 once and 82952 twice for a three-hour GTT in which specimens are obtained at zero, one-half, one, two, and three hours.

Multiple specimens from different sources as well as specimens obtained at different times should be reported separately. For example, total bilirubin levels (82247) obtained in the morning and afternoon would be reported twice on that date of service.

MOLECULAR DIAGNOSTICS

Tests in these series (83890–83912) are reported by procedure rather than analyte and should be coded separately for each procedure used in an analysis.

Pathology and Laboratory

HEMATOLOGY AND COAGULATION

The infectious agent antibodies subsection (85002–85999) lists those laboratory procedures specific to blood and blood-forming organs, including complete blood counts (CBC), clotting factors, clotting inhibitors, prothrombin and thrombin time, platelets, and sickling.

Code 85097 for bone marrow and smear interpretation is found in this subsection. However, when reporting interpretation services read procedure descriptions carefully as cell block interpretations and bone marrow biopsy interpretations should be reported with 88305.

IMMUNOLOGY

The immunology subsection (86000–86849) identifies codes for antigen and antibody studies. Detection of antibodies to infectious agents using multiple step qualitative or semiquantitative immunoassays should be reported with codes 86602–86804.

Specific tissue typing procedures are also found in the immunology subsection, see 86805–86822.

High-volume procedures include cardiolipin antibody; antigen complement; deoxyribonucleic acid antibody; hepatitis C antibody; delta agent hepatitis; heterophile antibodies; and streptococcus screening.

TRANSFUSION MEDICINE

Once listed in immunology, most blood bank codes are now grouped together under the transfusion medicine subsection (86850–86999). Since more blood bank procedures are likely to be performed on an outpatient basis, this subsection may expand in the future.

Be aware that the present codes do not report the supply of blood or blood products, and their cost may not be covered by insurance. Payers usually cover antibody screening, autologous blood or component collection, processing and storage, blood typing, and blood praeparata. Some payers require blood to be replaced (when the unit given is replaceable) instead of paid. Some payers will not cover the cost of blood components, such as albumin, plasma, or plasmanate. There may also be restrictions on procedures involving pheresis.

MICROBIOLOGY

These microbiology codes (87001–87999) identify services related to cultures, organism identification, and sensitivity studies. Many of the narratives are similar to those in the immunology section, so it is important to pay close attention to technique. Infectious agents identified by antigen detection, nucleic acid probe, or fluorescence microscopy is reported with codes 87260–87999 from microbiology. Infectious agents identified by antibody detection are reported with codes 86602–86804 from immunology. For example, cytomegalovirus (CMV) identified by infectious agent antigen detection by enzyme immunoassay technique, qualitative or semiquantitative, multiple step method is reported with 87332 from microbiology. However, CMV antibody detection by qualitative or semiquantitative immunoassay, multiple step method is reported with 86644.

ANATOMIC PATHOLOGY

Anatomic pathology (88000–88099) includes postmortem examinations (e.g., necropsy, autopsy), cytopathology (e.g., fluids, washing or brushing, Pap smears, fine needle aspirations, flow cytometry, etc.) and cytogenetic studies (e.g., tissue cultures for chromosome studies, etc.). Postmortem examination procedures report only the physician portion of the service. To report outside laboratory services, append modifier 90.

CYTOPATHOLOGY

Codes for reporting cervical and vaginal screening (Pap smears) (88141–88155, 88164–88167, 88174–88175) have undergone considerable revision and expansion in recent years. Codes 88142–88143 report cervical or vaginal specimens collected in a preservative fluid using automated thin layer preparation, with manual screening. Codes 88174–88175 report cervical or vaginal specimens collected in a preservative fluid using automated thin layer preparation, with automated screening. These specimens may then be examined by either Bethesda or non-Bethesda reporting systems. Codes 88150–88154 report cervical or vaginal specimens (Pap smears) prepared on slides and examined using non-Bethesda reporting systems. Codes 88164–88167 report cervical or vaginal specimens (Pap smears) prepared on slides and examined using Bethesda reporting systems. All of the above codes report manual screening and rescreening using various techniques under physician supervision. Cervical or vaginal cytopathology services requiring physician interpretation are reported separately with code 88141. Definitive hormonal evaluation is also reported separately with code 88155.

CYTOGENETIC STUDIES

Codes in this section (88230–88299) are related to the branch of genetics that studies cellular (cyto) structure and function as it relates to heredity (genetics). White blood cells, specifically T-lymphocytes, are the most commonly used specimen for chromosome analysis (88245–88289). Chromosome analysis for breakage syndromes (88245–88248) may be requested by the name of the specific syndrome being investigated, such as Fragile X, Xeroderma pigmentosum (XP), Ataxia-telangiectasia (A-T), and Fanconi anemia (FA), while 88249 reports a specific technique for the analysis of breakage syndromes involving clastogen stress. Other codes in this section include chromosome analysis for the presence of mosaicism (88263), malignant neoplasms (88264), and possible genetic abnormalities detectable within the cells of amniotic fluid (88269). Tissue and skin biopsies are reported separately using codes from the CPT surgery section. Physician interpretation and report are also reported separately, with 88291 from the cytogenetic studies section.

SURGICAL PATHOLOGY

The primary surgical pathology codes (88300–88309) describe gross and microscopic examination of specimens submitted for pathologic evaluation.

The specimen is the unit of service to report for surgical pathology. A specimen is defined as each tissue or tissues submitted for individual and separate evaluation. Each separate specimen requires individual examination and pathologic diagnosis. When two or more individual specimens are submitted from the same patient, each specimen is assigned an individual CPT code that should reflect the proper level of service.

The type of exam and the type of tissue define the level of service. CPT code 88300 should be reported for specimens requiring only gross examination. All other surgical pathology services require both gross and microscopic examination of the tissue and are defined by the type of specimen. The type of specimen included in each level is listed in the code description. For example, tissue submitted labeled "synovium knee" is examined by the pathologist and determined to be a synovial cyst. The surgical pathology code reported is 88304 because "bursa/synovial cyst" is listed under CPT code 88304.

Codes listed in 88300–88309 do not include any of the special services described by procedures 88311–88399. Procedures 88311–88399 describe additional services which may be reported separately and include the following: special stains, histochemistry, immunocytochemistry, immunofluorescent studies, electron microscopy, nerve teasing preparations, protein analysis by the western blot method, and pathology consultations during surgery.

TRANSCUTANEOUS PROCEDURES

This section (code 88400) describes the procedure to test bilirubin using a transdermal approach such as in a patch form applied to the skin.

OTHER PROCEDURES

Codes in this subsection (89050–89240) describe such procedures as crystal identification by light microscopy, duodenal intubation and aspiration, gastric intubation and aspiration, and nasal smear for eosinophils.

REPRODUCTIVE MEDICINE PROCEDURES

Reproductive laboratory services in this subsection include culture and co-culture of oocytes with coding options for extended culture and the use of microtechniques. There are codes for oocyte biopsies for pre-implantation genetic diagnoses, as well as coding options for storage and thawing of cryopreserved specimens.

LABORATORY CODING

Verify that all services performed have a signed physician order, are medically necessary and each is coded correctly, and supported by documentation in the medical record. Maintaining a current chargemaster or fee schedule is critical. Laboratories, (physician/clinic-based, hospital-based, or freestanding) must update their chargemasters and fee schedule annually and verify that the codes and descriptors match the services performed. Never report a service with a code that appears to be "close enough" to the actual service performed. If the descriptor does not match the service performed, review the CPT book to identify a more specific code. If a code cannot be identified, assign an unlisted procedure code and supply supporting documentation with the claim.

To avoid unbundling become familiar with the following subsections: Organ and Disease Oriented Panels (80048–80076), and Evocative/Suppression Testing (8040080440). Do not report individual codes when the individual laboratory procedures are included in a panel.

Pathology and Laboratory

80048 — 80061

ORGAN OR DISEASE ORIENTED PANELS

80048　**Basic metabolic panel**　　　　　　　　　　　　Ⓐ ▦
MED: 100-2, 15, 80

AMA: 2000, Jan, 7; 1999, Nov, 44; 1998, Jan, 6

This panel must include the following: Calcium (82310) Carbon dioxide (82374) Chloride (82435) Creatinine (82565) Glucose (82947) Potassium (84132) Sodium (84295) Urea nitrogen (BUN) (84520)

Code 80048 cannot be reported in conjunction with 80053.

80050　**General health panel**　　　　　　　　　　　　　Ⓔ
MED: 100-2, 15, 80

AMA: 1998, Jan, 6; 1997, Nov, 28; 1997, Jun, 10; 1993, Summer, 14; 1992, Winter, 14

This panel must include the following: Comprehensive metabolic panel (80053) Blood count, complete (CBC), automated and automated differential WBC count (85025 or 85027 and 85004) OR Blood count, complete (CBC), automated (85027) and appropriate manual differential WBC count (85007 or 85009) Thyroid stimulating hormone (TSH) (84443)

80051　**Electrolyte panel**　　　　　　　　　　　　　Ⓐ ▦
MED: 100-2, 15, 80

AMA: 1998, Jan, 6; 1997, Nov, 28

This panel must include the following: carbon dioxide (82374), chloride (82435), potassium (84132), sodium (84295)

80053　**Comprehensive metabolic panel**　　　　　　　Ⓐ ▦
MED: 100-2, 15, 80

AMA: 2000, May, 11; 2000, Jan, 7; 1999, Nov, 44; 1999, Dec, 1; 1998, Nov, 23; 1998, Jan, 6

This panel must include the following: Albumin (82040) Bilirubin, total (82247) Calcium (82310) Carbon dioxide (bicarbonate) (82374) Chloride (82435) Creatinine (82565) Glucose (82947) Phosphatase, alkaline (84075) Potassium (84132) Protein, total (84155) Sodium (84295) Transferase, alanine amino (ALT) (SGPT) (84460) Transferase, aspartate amino (AST) (SGOT) (84450) Urea nitrogen (BUN) (84520)

Note that 80053 cannot be used in addition to CPT codes 80048 and 80076.

80055　**Obstetric panel**　　　　　　　　　　　　Ⓜ ♀ Ⓔ
MED: 100-2, 15, 80

AMA: 1997, Jun, 10; 1993, Summer, 14; 1992, Winter, 14

This panel must include the following: Blood count, complete (CBC), automated and automated differential WBC count (85025 or 85027 and 85004) OR Blood count, complete (CBC), automated (85027) and appropriate manual differential WBC count (85007 or 85009) Hepatitis B surface antigen (HBsAg) (87340) Antibody, rubella (86762) Syphilis test, qualitative (eg, VDRL, RPR, ART) (86592) Antibody screen, RBC, each serum technique (86850) Blood typing, ABO (86900) AND Blood typing, Rh (D) (86901)

80061　**Lipid panel**　　　　　　　　　　　　　Ⓐ ✕ ▦
MED: 100-2, 15, 80; 100-3, 190.23

AMA: 2000, Mar, 11; 1997, Jun, 10; 1993, Summer, 14; 1992, Winter, 14

This panel must include the following: Cholesterol, serum, total (82465) Lipoprotein, direct measurement, high density cholesterol (HDL cholesterol) (83718) Triglycerides (84478)

 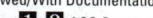 

80069	**Renal function panel**	Ⓐ 🔁

MED: 100-2, 15, 80; 100-3, 190.10

AMA: 2000, Jan, 7; 1999, Nov, 44

This panel must include the following: Albumin (82040) Calcium (82310) Carbon dioxide (bicarbonate) (82374) Chloride (82435) Creatinine (82565) Glucose (82947) Phosphorus inorganic (phosphate) (84100) Potassium (84132) Sodium (84295) Urea nitrogen (BUN) (84520)

80074	**Acute hepatitis panel**	Ⓐ 🔁

MED: 100-2, 15, 80; 100-3, 190.33

AMA: 2000, Jan, 7; 1999, Nov, 45

This panel must include the following: Hepatitis A antibody (HAAb), IgM antibody (86709) Hepatitis B core antibody (HBcAb), IgM antibody (86705) Hepatitis B surface antigen (HBsAg) (87340) Hepatitis C antibody (86803)

80076	**Hepatic function panel**	Ⓐ 🔁

MED: 100-2, 15, 80

AMA: 2000, Jan, 7; 1999, Nov, 45; 1999, Apr, 6; 1998, Jan, 6; 1997, Jun, 10; 1993, Summer, 14; 1992, Winter, 14

This panel must include the following: Albumin (82040) Bilirubin, total (82247) Bilirubin, direct (82248) Phosphatase, alkaline (84075) Protein, total (84155) Transferase, alanine amino (ALT) (SGPT) (84460) Transferase, aspartate amino (AST) (SGOT) (84450)

Note that 80076 cannot be used in addition to CPT code 80053.

DRUG TESTING

Consult CPT codes 82000-84999 (Chemistry) or 80150-80299 (Therapeutic drug assay) for quantitation of drugs screened.

80100	**Drug screen, qualitative; multiple drug classes chromatographic method, each procedure**	Ⓐ 🔁

MED: 100-2, 15, 80

AMA: 2000, Mar, 1; 1993, Fall, 26

80101	**single drug class method (eg, immunoassay, enzyme assay), each drug class**	Ⓐ ✖ 🔁

MED: 100-2, 15, 80; 100-3, 190.8

AMA: 2000, Mar, 1; 1993, Fall, 26

80102	**Drug confirmation, each procedure**	Ⓐ 🔁

MED: 100-2, 15, 80

AMA: 2000, Mar, 1; 1993, Fall, 26

80103	**Tissue preparation for drug analysis**	Ⓝ

MED: 100-2, 15, 80

AMA: 2000, Mar, 1

🔁 CCI Comp   🔟 Bilateral Proc.   ✚ CPT Add-on Code   ⊘ Modifier -51 Exempt   ♂/♀ Male/Female   ✖ CLIA Waived Test
● New Code   ▲ Revised Code   Ⓜ Maternity Edit   Ⓐ Age Edit   Ⓐ–Ⓨ APC Status Ind.   AMA: CPT Assistant

© 2005 Ingenix, Inc. *(Blue Ink)*   CPT only © 2005 American Medical Association. All Rights Reserved. *(Black Ink)*   Path/Lab — 571

THERAPEUTIC DRUG ASSAYS

For nonquantitative testing, consult CPT codes 80100-80103.

The specimen used for analysis may be from any source.

80150	**Amikacin**	A
	MED: 100-2, 15, 80	
	AMA: 2000, Mar, 1; 1993, Fall, 26; 1992, Winter, 14	
80152	**Amitriptyline**	A
	MED: 100-2, 15, 80	
	AMA: 2000, Mar, 1; 1993, Fall, 26; 1992, Winter, 14	
80154	**Benzodiazepines**	A
	MED: 100-2, 15, 80	
	AMA: 2000, Mar, 1; 1993, Fall, 26; 1992, Winter, 14	
80156	**Carbamazepine; total**	A
	MED: 100-2, 15, 80	
	AMA: 2000, Mar, 1; 1993, Fall, 26; 1992, Winter, 14	
80157	**free**	A
	MED: 100-2, 15, 80	
	AMA: 2000, Mar, 1; 1993, Fall, 26; 1992, Winter, 14	
80158	**Cyclosporine**	A
	MED: 100-2, 15, 80	
	AMA: 2000, Mar, 1; 1993, Fall, 26; 1992, Winter, 14	
80160	**Desipramine**	A
	MED: 100-2, 15, 80	
	AMA: 2000, Mar, 1; 1993, Fall, 26; 1992, Winter, 14	
80162	**Digoxin**	A
	MED: 100-2, 15, 80; 100-3, 190.24	
	AMA: 2000, Mar, 1; 1993, Fall, 26; 1992, Winter, 14	
80164	**Dipropylacetic acid (valproic acid)**	A
	MED: 100-2, 15, 80	
	AMA: 2000, Mar, 1; 1993, Fall, 26; 1992, Winter, 14	
80166	**Doxepin**	A
	MED: 100-2, 15, 80	
	AMA: 2000, Mar, 1; 1993, Fall, 26; 1992, Winter, 14	
80168	**Ethosuximide**	A
	MED: 100-2, 15, 80	
	AMA: 2000, Mar, 1; 1993, Fall, 26; 1992, Winter, 14	
80170	**Gentamicin**	A
	MED: 100-2, 15, 80	
	AMA: 2000, Mar, 1; 1993, Fall, 26; 1992, Winter, 14	
80172	**Gold**	A
	MED: 100-2, 15, 80	
	AMA: 2000, Mar, 1; 1993, Fall, 26; 1992, Winter, 14	

26 / TC Professional/Technical Component   80 / 80 Assist-at-Surgery Allowed/With Documentation   ⊙ Conscious Sedation
Unlisted   Not Covered   **MED:** Pubs 100/NCD Reference   1 - 9 ASC Group   63 Modifier 63 Exempt

80173 **Haloperidol** [A]
MED: 100-2, 15, 80

AMA: 2000, Mar, 1; 1993, Fall, 26; 1992, Winter, 14

80174 **Imipramine** [A]
MED: 100-2, 15, 80

AMA: 2000, Mar, 1; 1993, Fall, 26; 1992, Winter, 14

80176 **Lidocaine** [A]
MED: 100-2, 15, 80

AMA: 2000, Mar, 1; 1993, Fall, 26; 1992, Winter, 14

80178 **Lithium** [A]
MED: 100-2, 15, 80

AMA: 2000, Mar, 1; 1993, Fall, 26; 1992, Winter, 14

80182 **Nortriptyline** [A]
MED: 100-2, 15, 80

AMA: 2000, Mar, 1; 1993, Fall, 26; 1992, Winter, 14

80184 **Phenobarbital** [A]
MED: 100-2, 15, 80

AMA: 2000, Mar, 1; 1993, Fall, 26; 1992, Winter, 14

80185 **Phenytoin; total** [A]
MED: 100-2, 15, 80

AMA: 2000, Mar, 1; 1993, Fall, 26; 1992, Winter, 14

80186 **free** [A]
MED: 100-2, 15, 80

AMA: 2000, Mar, 1; 1993, Fall, 26; 1992, Winter, 14

80188 **Primidone** [A]
MED: 100-2, 15, 80

AMA: 2000, Mar, 1; 1993, Fall, 26; 1992, Winter, 14

80190 **Procainamide;** [A]
MED: 100-2, 15, 80

AMA: 2000, Mar, 1; 1993, Fall, 26; 1992, Winter, 14

80192 **with metabolites (eg, n-acetyl procainamide)** [A] [CCI]
MED: 100-2, 15, 80

AMA: 2000, Mar, 1; 1993, Fall, 26; 1992, Winter, 14

80194 **Quinidine** [A]
MED: 100-2, 15, 80

AMA: 2000, Mar, 1; 1993, Fall, 26; 1992, Winter, 14

● **80195** **Sirolimus**

80196 **Salicylate** [A]
MED: 100-2, 15, 80

AMA: 2000, Mar, 1; 1993, Fall, 26; 1992, Winter, 14

80197 **Tacrolimus** [A]
MED: 100-2, 15, 80

AMA: 2000, Mar, 1; 1993, Fall, 26; 1992, Winter, 14

Pathology and Laboratory

80198 — 80412

80198 **Theophylline** [A]
MED: 100-2, 15, 80

AMA: 2000, Mar, 1; 1993, Fall, 26; 1992, Winter, 14

80200 **Tobramycin** [A]
MED: 100-2, 15, 80

AMA: 2000, Mar, 1; 1993, Fall, 26; 1992, Winter, 14

80201 **Topiramate** [A]
MED: 100-2, 15, 80

AMA: 2000, Mar, 1; 1993, Fall, 26; 1992, Winter, 14

80202 **Vancomycin** [A]
MED: 100-2, 15, 80

AMA: 2000, Mar, 1; 1993, Fall, 26; 1992, Winter, 14

80299 **Quantitation of drug, not elsewhere specified** [A]
MED: 100-2, 15, 80

AMA: 2000, Mar, "1, 3"; 1993, Fall, 26; 1992, Winter, 14

EVOCATIVE/SUPPRESSION TESTING

80400 **ACTH stimulation panel; for adrenal insufficiency** [A] [↴]
MED: 100-2, 15, 80

AMA: 1994, Summer, 1

This panel must include the following: Cortisol (82533 x 2)

80402 **for 21 hydroxylase deficiency** [A] [↴]
MED: 100-2, 15, 80

AMA: 1994, Summer, 1

This panel must include the following: Cortisol (82533 x 2) 17 hydroxyprogesterone (83498 x 2)

80406 **for 3 beta-hydroxydehydrogenase deficiency** [A] [↴]
MED: 100-2, 15, 80

AMA: 1994, Summer, 1

This panel must include the following: Cortisol (82533 x 2) 17 hydroxypregnenolone (84143 x 2)

80408 **Aldosterone suppression evaluation panel (eg, saline infusion)** [A] [↴]
MED: 100-2, 15, 80

AMA: 1994, Summer, 1

This panel must include the following: Aldosterone (82088 x 2) Renin (84244 x 2)

80410 **Calcitonin stimulation panel (eg, calcium, pentagastrin)** [A] [↴]
MED: 100-2, 15, 80

AMA: 1994, Summer, 1

This panel must include the following: Calcitonin (82308 x 3)

80412 **Corticotropic releasing hormone (CRH) stimulation panel** [A] [↴]
MED: 100-2, 15, 80

AMA: 1994, Summer, 1

This panel must include the following: Cortisol (82533 x 6) Adrenocorticotropic hormone (ACTH) (82024 x 6)

[26] / [TC] Professional/Technical Component   [80] / [80] Assist-at-Surgery Allowed/With Documentation   ⊙ Conscious Sedation

Unlisted   Not Covered   MED: Pubs 100/NCD Reference   [1]-[9] ASC Group   ⑥³ Modifier 63 Exempt

574 — Path/Lab   CPT only © 2005 American Medical Association. All Rights Reserved. *(Black Ink)*   © 2005 Ingenix, Inc. *(Blue Ink)*

80414   **Chorionic gonadotropin stimulation panel; testosterone response** ♀ Ⓐ 🔲
MED: 100-2, 15, 80

AMA: 1994, Summer, 1

This panel must include the following: Testosterone (84403 x 2 on three pooled blood samples)

80415   **estradiol response** Ⓐ 🔲
MED: 100-2, 15, 80

AMA: 1994, Summer, 1

This panel must include the following: Estradiol (82670 x 2 on three pooled blood samples)

80416   **Renal vein renin stimulation panel (eg, captopril)** Ⓐ 🔲
MED: 100-2, 15, 80

AMA: 1994, Summer, 1

This panel must include the following: Renin (84244 x 6)

80417   **Peripheral vein renin stimulation panel (eg, captopril)** Ⓐ 🔲
MED: 100-2, 15, 80

This panel must include the following: Renin (84244 x 2)

80418   **Combined rapid anterior pituitary evaluation panel** Ⓐ 🔲
MED: 100-2, 15, 80

AMA: 1994, Summer, 1

This panel must include the following: Adrenocorticotropic hormone (ACTH) (82024 x 4) Luteinizing hormone (LH) (83002 x 4) Follicle stimulating hormone (FSH) (83001 x 4) Prolactin (84146 x 4) Human growth hormone (HGH) (83003 x 4) Cortisol (82533 x 4) Thyroid stimulating hormone (TSH) (84443 x 4)

80420   **Dexamethasone suppression panel, 48 hour** Ⓐ 🔲
MED: 100-2, 15, 80

AMA: 1994, Summer, 1

This panel must include the following: Free cortisol, urine (82530 x 2) Cortisol (82533 x 2) Volume measurement for timed collection (81050 x 2) (For single dose dexamethasone, use 82533)

If a single dose of dexamethasone is given, consult CPT code 82533.

80422   **Glucagon tolerance panel; for insulinoma** Ⓐ 🔲
MED: 100-2, 15, 80

AMA: 1994, Summer, 1

This panel must include the following: Glucose (82947 x 3) Insulin (83525 x 3)

80424   **for pheochromocytoma** Ⓐ 🔲
MED: 100-2, 15, 80

AMA: 1994, Summer, 1

This panel must include the following: Catecholamines, fractionated (82384 x 2)

80426   **Gonadotropin releasing hormone stimulation panel** Ⓐ 🔲
MED: 100-2, 15, 80

AMA: 1994, Summer, 1

This panel must include the following: Follicle stimulating hormone (FSH) (83001 x 4) Luteinizing hormone (LH) (83002 x 4)

🔲 CCI Comp	50 Bilateral Proc.	✚ CPT Add-on Code	⊘ Modifier -51 Exempt ♂/♀ Male/Female	❌ CLIA Waived Test
● New Code	▲ Revised Code	Ⓜ Maternity Edit	Ⓐ Age Edit Ⓐ—Ⓨ APC Status Ind.	AMA: CPT Assistant

Pathology and Laboratory

80428 — 80440

80428 **Growth hormone stimulation panel (eg, arginine infusion, l-dopa administration)** [A] [↵]
MED: 100-2, 15, 80

AMA: 1994, Summer, 1

This panel must include the following: Human growth hormone (HGH) (83003 x 4)

80430 **Growth hormone suppression panel (glucose administration)** [A] [↵]
MED: 100-2, 15, 80

AMA: 1994, Summer, 1

This panel must include the following: Glucose (82947 x 3) Human growth hormone (HGH) (83003 x 4)

80432 **Insulin-induced C-peptide suppression panel** [A] [↵]
MED: 100-2, 15, 80

AMA: 1994, Summer, 1

This panel must include the following: Insulin (83525) C-peptide (84681 x 5) Glucose (82947 x 5)

80434 **Insulin tolerance panel; for ACTH insufficiency** [A] [↵]
MED: 100-2, 15, 80

AMA: 1994, Summer, 1

This panel must include the following: Cortisol (82533 x 5) Glucose (82947 x 5)

80435 **for growth hormone deficiency** [A] [↵]
MED: 100-2, 15, 80

AMA: 1994, Summer, 1

This panel must include the following: Glucose (82947 x 5) Human growth hormone (HGH) (83003 x 5)

80436 **Metyrapone panel** [A] [↵]
MED: 100-2, 15, 80

AMA: 1994, Summer, 1

This panel must include the following: Cortisol (82533 x 2) 11 deoxycortisol (82634 x 2)

80438 **Thyrotropin releasing hormone (TRH) stimulation panel; one hour** [A] [↵]
MED: 100-2, 15, 80

AMA: 1994, Summer, 1

This panel must include the following: Thyroid stimulating hormone (TSH) (84443 x 3)

80439 **two hour** [A] [↵]
MED: 100-2, 15, 80

AMA: 1994, Summer, 1

This panel must include the following: Thyroid stimulating hormone (TSH) (84443 x 4)

80440 **for hyperprolactinemia** [A] [↵]
MED: 100-2, 15, 80

AMA: 1994, Summer, 1

This panel must include the following: Prolactin (84146 x 3)

[26] / [TC] Professional/Technical Component   [80] / [80] Assist-at-Surgery Allowed/With Documentation   ⊙ Conscious Sedation
 Unlisted   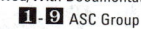 Not Covered   **MED:** Pubs 100/NCD Reference   [1]-[9] ASC Group   ⑥³ Modifier 63 Exempt
576 — Path/Lab   CPT only © 2005 American Medical Association. All Rights Reserved. *(Black Ink)*   © 2005 Ingenix, Inc. *(Blue Ink)*

CONSULTATIONS (CLINICAL PATHOLOGY)

80500 **Clinical pathology consultation; limited, without review of patient's history and medical records** ☒ 80
MED: 100-2, 15, 80; 100-4, 12, 60

AMA: 2002, Nov, 9; 1997, Apr, 9

80502 **comprehensive, for a complex diagnostic problem, with review of patient's history and medical records** ☒ 80 ⬚
MED: 100-2, 15, 80; 100-4, 12, 60

AMA: 2002, Nov, 9; 1997, Apr, 9

Note that 80502 may also be used for pharmacokinetic consultations. If a patient must be examined and evaluated, consult CPT codes 99241-99275.

URINALYSIS

To report urinalysis, infectious agent detection, semi-quantitative analysis of volatile compounds, consult Category III code 0041T.

81000 **Urinalysis, by dip stick or tablet reagent for bilirubin, glucose, hemoglobin, ketones, leukocytes, nitrite, pH, protein, specific gravity, urobilinogen, any number of these constituents; non-automated, with microscopy** Ⓐ ⬚
MED: 100-2, 15, 80

AMA: 1993, Fall, 25; 1990-1991, Winter, 10

81001 **automated, with microscopy** Ⓐ ⬚
MED: 100-2, 15, 80

81002 **non-automated, without microscopy** Ⓐ
MED: 100-2, 15, 80

AMA: 1998, Mar, 3

Mosenthal test

81003 **automated, without microscopy** Ⓐ ☒ ⬚
MED: 100-2, 15, 80

81005 **Urinalysis; qualitative or semiquantitative, except immunoassays** Ⓐ ⬚
MED: 100-2, 15, 80

AMA: 1993, Fall, 25; 1990-1991, Winter, 10

If urinalysis is performed of a non-immunoassay reagent strip, consult CPT codes 81000 and 81002. For qualitative or semiquantitative immunoassay, consult CPT code 83518.

To report microalbumin, consult CPT codes 82043, 82044.

Benedict test for dextrose

81007 **bacteriuria screen, except by culture or dipstick** Ⓐ ☒ ⬚
MED: 100-2, 15, 80

To report dipstick urinalysis consult CPT codes 81000 or 81002. To report urine culture, consult CPT codes 87086-87088.

81015 **microscopic only** Ⓐ
MED: 100-2, 15, 80

81020 **two or three glass test** Ⓐ ⬚
MED: 100-2, 15, 80

AMA: 1990-1991, Winter, 10

Valentine's test

81025   **Urine pregnancy test, by visual color comparison methods**   M ♀ A
        MED: 100-2, 15, 80
        AMA: 1998, Mar, 3

81050   **Volume measurement for timed collection, each**   A
        MED: 100-2, 15, 80

81099   **Unlisted urinalysis procedure**   A
        MED: 100-2, 15, 80

CHEMISTRY

82000   **Acetaldehyde, blood**   A
        MED: 100-2, 15, 80
        AMA: 2000, Mar, 1

82003   **Acetaminophen**   A
        MED: 100-2, 15, 80

82009   **Acetone or other ketone bodies, serum; qualitative**   A
        MED: 100-2, 15, 80

82010   **quantitative**   A ✖
        MED: 100-2, 15, 80

82013   **Acetylcholinesterase**   A
        MED: 100-2, 15, 80

        To report gastric acid, free and/or total, consult CPT codes 82926 and 82928.
        To report acid phosphatase, consult CPT codes 84060-84066.

82016   **Acylcarnitines; qualitative, each specimen**   A
        MED: 100-2, 15, 80
        AMA: 1998, Nov, 23

        Report quantitative carnitine (total and free) separately, consult CPT code 82379.

82017   **quantitative, each specimen**   A ▣
        MED: 100-2, 15, 80
        AMA: 1998, Nov, 23

82024   **Adrenocorticotropic hormone (ACTH)**   A ▣
        MED: 100-2, 15, 80; 100-3, 300.1

82030   **Adenosine, 5'-monophosphate, cyclic (cyclic AMP)**   A
        MED: 100-2, 15, 80

82040   **Albumin; serum**   A
        MED: 100-2, 15, 80; 100-3, 190.10
        AMA: 1999, Dec, 2

82042   **urine or other source, quantitative, each specimen**   A
        MED: 100-2, 15, 80

82043   **urine, microalbumin, quantitative**   A ▣
        MED: 100-2, 15, 80; 100-3, 190.10
        AMA: 1994, Summer, 2

82044   **urine, microalbumin, semiquantitative (eg, reagent strip assay)**   A ✖
        MED: 100-2, 15, 80; 100-3, 190.10
        AMA: 2002, Sep, 10; 1998, Mar, 3; 1994, Summer, 2

        To report prealbumin, consult CPT code 84134.

82045   **ischemia modified**   A

---

26 / TC Professional/Technical Component   80 / 80 Assist-at-Surgery Allowed/With Documentation   ⊙ Conscious Sedation
Unlisted   Not Covered   MED: Pubs 100/NCD Reference   1 - 9 ASC Group   63 Modifier 63 Exempt
578 — Path/Lab   CPT only © 2005 American Medical Association. All Rights Reserved. (Black Ink)   © 2005 Ingenix, Inc. (Blue Ink)

82055	**Alcohol (ethanol); any specimen except breath** MED: 100-2, 15, 80	A ☒

To report other volatiles including isopropyl alcohol and methanol, consult CPT code 84600.

82075	**breath** MED: 100-2, 15, 80	A
82085	**Aldolase** MED: 100-2, 15, 80	A
82088	**Aldosterone** MED: 100-2, 15, 80	A ↖

To report alkaline phosphatase, consult CPT codes 84075 and 84080.

82101	**Alkaloids, urine, quantitative** MED: 100-2, 15, 80	A

To report quantitative or qualitative acetone or other ketone bodies, serum, consult CPT codes 82009 and 82010. To report alpha tocopherol (Vitamin E), consult CPT code 84446.

82103	**Alpha-1-antitrypsin; total** MED: 100-2, 15, 80	A
82104	**phenotype** MED: 100-2, 15, 80	A
82105	**Alpha-fetoprotein; serum** MED: 100-2, 15, 80; 100-3, 190.25	A ↖
82106	**amniotic fluid** MED: 100-2, 15, 80	M ♀ A ↖
82108	**Aluminum** MED: 100-2, 15, 80; 100-3, 190.10	A
82120	**Amines, vaginal fluid, qualitative** MED: 100-2, 15, 80 AMA: 1999, Nov, 45	♀ A ☒

If a combined pH and amines test is performed for vaginitis, use 83986 in addition to 82120.

82127	**Amino acids; single, qualitative, each specimen** MED: 100-2, 15, 80 AMA: 1998, Nov, 24	A
82128	**multiple, qualitative, each specimen** MED: 100-2, 15, 80 AMA: 1998, Nov, 24	A ↖
82131	**single, quantitative, each specimen** MED: 100-2, 15, 80 AMA: 1998, Nov, 24; 1998, May, 11 Van Slyke method	A
82135	**Aminolevulinic acid, delta (ALA)** MED: 100-2, 15, 80	A

Pathology and Laboratory

82136 — 82180

82136   Amino acids, 2 to 5 amino acids, quantitative, each specimen   A
MED: 100-2, 15, 80

AMA: 1998, Nov, 24

82139   Amino acids, 6 or more amino acids, quantitative, each specimen   A
MED: 100-2, 15, 80

AMA: 1998, Nov, 24

82140   Ammonia   A
MED: 100-2, 15, 80

82143   Amniotic fluid scan (spectrophotometric)   M ♀ A
MED: 100-2, 15, 80

To report amniotic fluid L/S ratio, consult CPT code 83611. To report
amobarbital, consult CPT codes 80100-80103 to report qualitative analysis
and 82205 to report quantitative analysis.

82145   Amphetamine or methamphetamine   A
MED: 100-2, 15, 80

Prior to obtaining a quantitative analysis for amphetamine/methamphetamine,
a qualitative drug screen (80100-80101) and drug confirmation test (80102)
are normally performed.

82150   Amylase   A
MED: 100-2, 15, 80

82154   Androstanediol glucuronide   A
MED: 100-2, 15, 80

AMA: 1994, Summer, 5

82157   Androstenedione   A
MED: 100-2, 15, 80

82160   Androsterone   A
MED: 100-2, 15, 80

82163   Angiotensin II   A
MED: 100-2, 15, 80

82164   Angiotensin I - converting enzyme (ACE)   A
MED: 100-2, 15, 80

To report vasopressin (antidiuretic hormone, ADH), consult CPT code 84588.
To report heavy metal screening (arsenic, barium, beryllium, bismuth,
antimony, mercury), consult CPT code 83015. To report alpha-1-antitrypsin,
consult CPT codes 82103 and 82104.

82172   Apolipoprotein, each   A
MED: 100-2, 15, 80

82175   Arsenic   A
MED: 100-2, 15, 80

To report heavy metal screening (arsenic, barium, beryllium, bismuth,
antimony, mercury), consult CPT code 83015.

82180   Ascorbic acid (Vitamin C), blood   A
MED: 100-2, 15, 80

To report salicylate, consult CPT code 80196.

To report atherogenic index, blood, ultracentrifugation, quantitative, consult
CPT code 83716.

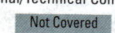

82190	**Atomic absorption spectroscopy, each analyte**		A
	MED: 100-2, 15, 80		
82205	**Barbiturates, not elsewhere specified**		A
	MED: 100-2, 15, 80		

Prior to obtaining a quantitative analysis for amphetamine/methamphetamine, a qualitative drug screen (80100-80101) and drug confirmation test (80102) are normally performed.

To report B-Natriuretic peptide, consult CPT code 83880.

82232	**Beta-2 microglobulin**		A
	MED: 100-2, 15, 80		

To report carbon dioxide (bicarbonate), consult CPT code 82374.

82239	**Bile acids; total**		A
	MED: 100-2, 15, 80		
82240	**cholylglycine**		A
	MED: 100-2, 15, 80		

To report urine bile pigments, consult CPT codes 81000-81005.

82247	**Bilirubin; total**		A
	MED: 100-2, 15, 80		

AMA: 2000, Jan, 7; 1999, Dec, 1; 1999, Apr, 6; 1998, Nov, 24

Van Den Bergh test

82248	**direct**		A
	MED: 100-2, 15, 80		

AMA: 1999, Dec, 1; 1999, Apr, 6; 1998, Nov, 24

82252	**feces, qualitative**		A
	MED: 100-2, 15, 80		
82261	**Biotinidase, each specimen**		A
	MED: 100-2, 15, 80		

AMA: 1998, Nov, 24

▲ 82270 **Blood, occult, by peroxidase activity (eg, guaiac), qualitative; feces, consecutive collected specimens with single determination, for colorectal neoplasm screening (ie, patient was provided three cards or single triple card for consecutive collection)** A
MED: 100-2, 15, 80; 100-3, 190.34

Day test

● 82271 **other sources**

● 82272 **Blood, occult, by peroxidase activity (eg, guaiac), qualitative, feces, single specimen (eg, from digital rectal exam)**

~~82273~~ ~~other sources~~

(Use 82271)

82274 **Blood, occult, by fecal hemoglobin determination by immunoassay, qualitative, feces, 1-3 simultaneous determinations** A ✖ ⤴
MED: 100-2, 15, 80

82286	**Bradykinin**		A
	MED: 100-2, 15, 80		
82300	**Cadmium**		A
	MED: 100-2, 15, 80		

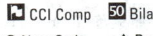 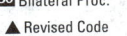

Pathology and Laboratory

82306 — 82379

82306	**Calcifediol (25-OH Vitamin D-3)**	A
	MED: 100-2, 15, 80	
82307	**Calciferol (Vitamin D)**	A
	MED: 100-2, 15, 80	

To report 1, 25-Dihydroxyvitamin D, consult CPT code 82652.

82308	**Calcitonin**	A
	MED: 100-2, 15, 80	
82310	**Calcium; total**	A
	MED: 100-2, 15, 80; 100-3, 190.10	
	AMA: 1999, Dec, 1	
82330	**ionized**	A
	MED: 100-2, 15, 80	
82331	**after calcium infusion test**	A
	MED: 100-2, 15, 80	
82340	**urine quantitative, timed specimen**	A
	MED: 100-2, 15, 80	
82355	**Calculus; qualitative analysis**	A
	MED: 100-2, 15, 80	
82360	**quantitative analysis, chemical**	A
	MED: 100-2, 15, 80	
82365	**infrared spectroscopy**	A
	MED: 100-2, 15, 80	
82370	**x-ray diffraction**	A
	MED: 100-2, 15, 80	

To report carbamates, see individual listings.

82373	**Carbohydrate deficient transferrin**	A
	MED: 100-2, 15, 80	
82374	**Carbon dioxide (bicarbonate)**	A
	MED: 100-2, 15, 80; 100-3, 190.10	
	AMA: 1999, Dec, 1	

Consult also CPT code 82803.

82375	**Carbon monoxide, (carboxyhemoglobin); quantitative**	A
	MED: 100-2, 15, 80	
82376	**qualitative**	A
	MED: 100-2, 15, 80	

To report end-tidal carbon monoxide, consult CPT Category III code 0043T.

82378	**Carcinoembryonic antigen (CEA)**	A
	MED: 100-2, 15, 80; 100-3, 190.26	
	AMA: 1996, Aug, 11; 1993, Fall, 25	
82379	**Carnitine (total and free), quantitative, each specimen**	A
	MED: 100-2, 15, 80	
	AMA: 1998, Nov, 24	

To report acylcarnitine, qualitative, consult CPT code 82016; quantitative, consult CPT code 82017.

82380   **Carotene**   A
        MED: 100-2, 15, 80

82382   **Catecholamines; total urine**   A
        MED: 100-2, 15, 80

82383   **blood**   A
        MED: 100-2, 15, 80

82384   **fractionated**   A ⊡
        MED: 100-2, 15, 80

        To report metanephrine, consult CPT code 83835. To report vanillylmandelic
        acid (VMA), consult CPT code 84585.

82387   **Cathepsin-D**   A
        MED: 100-2, 15, 80

82390   **Ceruloplasmin**   A
        MED: 100-2, 15, 80

82397   **Chemiluminescent assay**   A
        MED: 100-2, 15, 80

        AMA: 1993, Fall, 25

82415   **Chloramphenicol**   A
        MED: 100-2, 15, 80

82435   **Chloride; blood**   A
        MED: 100-2, 15, 80; 100-3, 190.10

        AMA: 1999, Dec, 1

82436   **urine**   A
        MED: 100-2, 15, 80

82438   **other source**   A
        MED: 100-2, 15, 80

        To report sweat collection by iontophoresis, consult CPT code 89230.

82441   **Chlorinated hydrocarbons, screen**   A
        MED: 100-2, 15, 80

        To report phenothiazine, consult CPT code 84022. To report calciferol (Vitamin
        D), consult CPT code 82307.

82465   **Cholesterol, serum or whole blood, total**   A ✕ ⊡
        MED: 100-2, 15, 80; 100-3, 190.23

        AMA: 2000, Mar, 11; 1999, Dec, 1

        To report high density lipoprotein (HDL) cholesterol, consult CPT code 83718.

82480   **Cholinesterase; serum**   A
        MED: 100-2, 15, 80

82482   **RBC**   A
        MED: 100-2, 15, 80

82485   **Chondroitin B sulfate, quantitative**   A
        MED: 100-2, 15, 80

        To report quantitative or qualitative chorionic gonadotropin (hCG), consult
        CPT codes 84702 and 84703.

82486 **Chromatography, qualitative; column (eg, gas liquid or HPLC), analyte not elsewhere specified** Ⓐ
MED: 100-2, 15, 80

AMA: 1998, Nov, 24-25

82487 **paper, 1-dimensional, analyte not elsewhere specified** Ⓐ
MED: 100-2, 15, 80

82488 **paper, 2-dimensional, analyte not elsewhere specified** Ⓐ
MED: 100-2, 15, 80

82489 **thin layer, analyte not elsewhere specified** Ⓐ
MED: 100-2, 15, 80

82491 **Chromatography, quantitative, column (eg, gas liquid or HPLC); single analyte not elsewhere specified, single stationary and mobile phase** Ⓐ
MED: 100-2, 15, 80

AMA: 2000, Mar, 1; 1998, Nov, 24-25; 1993, Fall, 25

82492 **multiple analytes, single stationary and mobile phase** Ⓐ ⬚
MED: 100-2, 15, 80

AMA: 2000, Mar, 1; 1998, Nov, 24-25

82495 **Chromium** Ⓐ
MED: 100-2, 15, 80; 100-3, 300.1

82507 **Citrate** Ⓐ
MED: 100-2, 15, 80

82520 **Cocaine or metabolite** Ⓐ
MED: 100-2, 15, 80

Prior to quantification, a drug screen is normally performed and is reported separately. For drug screen, consult CPT codes 80100-80103. For quantitative urine alkaloids, consult CPT code 82101. For complement, consult CPT codes 86160-86162.

82523 **Collagen cross links, any method** Ⓐ ✖
MED: 100-2, 15, 80; 100-3, 190.19

82525 **Copper** Ⓐ
MED: 100-2, 15, 80

To report urine porphyrins, consult CPT codes 84119 and 84120. To report hydroxycorticosteroids, 17- (17-OHCS), consult CPT code 83491.

82528 **Corticosterone** Ⓐ
MED: 100-2, 15, 80

Porter-Silber test

82530 **Cortisol; free** Ⓐ ⬚
MED: 100-2, 15, 80

AMA: 1994, Summer, 3

82533 **total** Ⓐ ⬚
MED: 100-2, 15, 80

AMA: 1994, Summer, 3

To report C-peptide, consult CPT code 84681.

82540 **Creatine** Ⓐ
MED: 100-2, 15, 80

82541   Column chromatography/mass spectrometry (eg, GC/MS, or HPLC/MS), analyte not elsewhere specified; qualitative, single stationary and mobile phase   A
> MED: 100-2, 15, 80
>
> AMA: 1998, Nov, 24-25

82542   quantitative, single stationary and mobile phase   A
> MED: 100-2, 15, 80
>
> AMA: 1998, Nov, 24-25

82543   stable isotope dilution, single analyte, quantitative, single stationary and mobile phase   A
> MED: 100-2, 15, 80
>
> AMA: 1998, Nov, 24-25

82544   stable isotope dilution, multiple analytes, quantitative, single stationary and mobile phase   A ⟲
> MED: 100-2, 15, 80
>
> AMA: 1999, Dec, 7; 1998, Nov, 24-25

82550   Creatine kinase (CK), (CPK); total   A ⟲
> MED: 100-2, 15, 80
>
> AMA: 1999, Dec, 1; 1998, Feb, 1

82552   isoenzymes   A ⟲
> MED: 100-2, 15, 80
>
> AMA: 1998, Feb, 1

82553   MB fraction only   A ⟲
> MED: 100-2, 15, 80
>
> AMA: 1998, Feb, 1

82554   isoforms   A ⟲
> MED: 100-2, 15, 80
>
> AMA: 1998, Feb, 1

82565   Creatinine; blood   A
> MED: 100-2, 15, 80; 100-3, 190.10
>
> AMA: 1999, Dec, 1

82570   other source   A ✖
> MED: 100-2, 15, 80

82575   clearance   A ⟲
> MED: 100-2, 15, 80
>
> **Holten test**

82585   Cryofibrinogen   A
> MED: 100-2, 15, 80

82595   Cryoglobulin, qualitative or semi-quantitative (eg, cryocrit)   A
> MED: 100-2, 15, 80

If quantitative cryoglobulin is performed consult CPT codes 82784, 82785.

If crystal is identified by light microscopy with or without polarizing lens analysis, any body fluid except urine, consult CPT code 89060.

82600   Cyanide   A
> MED: 100-2, 15, 80

82607   **Cyanocobalamin (Vitamin B-12);**   A ⟂
MED: 100-2, 15, 80

82608   **unsaturated binding capacity**   A
MED: 100-2, 15, 80

To report adenosine, 5-monophosphate, cyclic (cyclic AMP), consult CPT code 82030. To report guanosine monophosphate (GMP), cyclic, consult CPT code 83008. To report cyclosporine, consult CPT code 80158.

82615   **Cystine and homocystine, urine, qualitative**   A
MED: 100-2, 15, 80

82626   **Dehydroepiandrosterone (DHEA)**   A
MED: 100-2, 15, 80
AMA: 1994, Summer, 4

82627   **Dehydroepiandrosterone-sulfate (DHEA-S)**   A
MED: 100-2, 15, 80
AMA: 1994, Summer, 4

To report delta-aminolevulinic acid (ALA), consult CPT code 82135.

82633   **Desoxycorticosterone, 11-**   A
MED: 100-2, 15, 80

82634   **Deoxycortisol, 11-**   A ⟂
MED: 100-2, 15, 80

To report a dexamethasone suppression test, consult CPT code 80420. For amylase, consult CPT code 82150.

82638   **Dibucaine number**   A
MED: 100-2, 15, 80

To report volatiles (e.g., acetic anhydride, carbon tetrachloride, dichloroethane, dichloromethane, diethylether, isopropyl alcohol, methanol), consult CPT code 84600.

82646   **Dihydrocodeinone**   A
MED: 100-2, 15, 80

A drug screen (qualitative analysis) is normally performed prior to quantitative analysis. For drug screen, consult CPT codes 80100-80103.

82649   **Dihydromorphinone**   A
MED: 100-2, 15, 80

A drug screen (qualitative analysis) is normally performed prior to quantitative analysis. For drug screen, consult CPT codes 80100-80103.

82651   **Dihydrotestosterone (DHT)**   A
MED: 100-2, 15, 80

82652   **Dihydroxyvitamin D, 1,25-**   A ⟂
MED: 100-2, 15, 80

82654   **Dimethadione**   A
MED: 100-2, 15, 80

A drug screen (qualitative analysis) is normally performed prior to quantitative analysis. For drug screen, consult CPT codes 80100-80103. For total phenytoin, consult CPT code 80185. For dipropylacetic acid, consult CPT code 80164. For catecholamines, consult CPT codes 82382-82384. For duodenal intubation and aspiration, consult CPT code 89100. For endocrine receptor assays, consult CPT codes 84233-84235.

82656   **Elastase, pancreatic (EL-1), fecal, qualitative or semi-quantitative**   A

82657	Enzyme activity in blood cells, cultured cells, or tissue, not elsewhere specified; nonradioactive substrate, each specimen MED: 100-2, 15, 80 AMA: 1998, Nov, 25	Ⓐ
82658	radioactive substrate, each specimen MED: 100-2, 15, 80 AMA: 1998, Nov, 25	Ⓐ
82664	Electrophoretic technique, not elsewhere specified MED: 100-2, 15, 80	Ⓐ
82666	Epiandrosterone MED: 100-2, 15, 80	Ⓐ

To report catecholamines, consult CPT codes 82382-82384.

82668	Erythropoietin MED: 100-2, 15, 80	Ⓐ
82670	Estradiol MED: 100-2, 15, 80	Ⓐ ⚑
82671	Estrogens; fractionated MED: 100-2, 15, 80	Ⓐ
82672	total MED: 100-2, 15, 80	Ⓐ

To report estrogen receptor assay, consult CPT code 84233.

82677	Estriol MED: 100-2, 15, 80	Ⓐ
82679	Estrone MED: 100-2, 15, 80	Ⓐ ✖

To report alcohol (ethanol), consult CPT codes 82055 and 82075.

82690	Ethchlorvynol MED: 100-2, 15, 80	Ⓐ

To report alcohol (ethanol), consult CPT codes 82055 and 82075.

82693	Ethylene glycol MED: 100-2, 15, 80	Ⓐ
82696	Etiocholanolone MED: 100-2, 15, 80	Ⓐ

To report fractionation of ketosteroids, consult CPT code 83593.

82705	Fat or lipids, feces; qualitative MED: 100-2, 15, 80	Ⓐ
82710	quantitative MED: 100-2, 15, 80	Ⓐ
82715	Fat differential, feces, quantitative MED: 100-2, 15, 80	Ⓐ
82725	Fatty acids, nonesterified MED: 100-2, 15, 80	Ⓐ
82726	Very long chain fatty acids MED: 100-2, 15, 80 AMA: 1998, Nov, 25	Ⓐ

82728 **Ferritin** **A**
MED: 100-2, 15, 80; 100-3, 190.10; 100-4, 190.18

To report fetal hemoglobin, consult CPT codes 83030, 83033, and 85460. To report alpha-1 fetoprotein, consult CPT codes 82105 and 82106.

82731 **Fetal fibronectin, cervicovaginal secretions, semi-quantitative** **M ♀ A**
MED: 100-2, 15, 80

AMA: 1998, Nov, 25

82735 **Fluoride** **A**
MED: 100-2, 15, 80

82742 **Flurazepam** **A**
MED: 100-2, 15, 80

A drug screen (qualitative analysis) is normally performed prior to quantitative analysis. For drug screen, consult CPT codes 80100-80103. If a foam stability test is performed, consult CPT code 83662.

82746 **Folic acid; serum** **A**
MED: 100-2, 15, 80

82747 **RBC** **A**
MED: 100-2, 15, 80

To report gonadotropin; follicle stimulating hormone (FSH), consult CPT code 83001.

82757 **Fructose, semen** **♂ A**
MED: 100-2, 15, 80

To report fructosamine, consult CPT code 82985. To report sugars, chromatographic, TLC or paper chromatography, consult CPT code 84375.

82759 **Galactokinase, RBC** **A**
MED: 100-2, 15, 80

82760 **Galactose** **A**
MED: 100-2, 15, 80

82775 **Galactose-1-phosphate uridyl transferase; quantitative** **A**
MED: 100-2, 15, 80

82776 **screen** **A**
MED: 100-2, 15, 80

82784 **Gammaglobulin; IgA, IgD, IgG, IgM, each** **A ⟲**
MED: 100-2, 15, 80

AMA: 2000, Aug, 11; 1994, Spring, 31

Farr test

82785 **IgE** **A ⟲**
MED: 100-2, 15, 80

AMA: 1994, Spring, 31

To report allergen specific IgE, consult CPT code 86003 and 86005.
Farr test

82787 **immunoglobulin subclasses, (IgG1, 2, 3, or 4), each** **A ⟲**
MED: 100-2, 15, 80

To report Gamma-glutamyltransferase (GGT), consult CPT code 82977.

26/TC Professional/Technical Component   **80/80** Assist-at-Surgery Allowed/With Documentation   ⊙ Conscious Sedation
 Unlisted   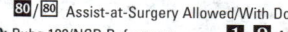 Not Covered   **MED:** Pubs 100/NCD Reference   **1-9** ASC Group   63 Modifier 63 Exempt
588 — Path/Lab   CPT only © 2005 American Medical Association. All Rights Reserved. *(Black Ink)*   © 2005 Ingenix, Inc. *(Blue Ink)*

| 82800 | **Gases, blood, pH only** | A 🔁 |
| | MED: 100-2, 15, 80 | |

| 82803 | **Gases, blood, any combination of pH, pCO_2, pO_2, CO_2, HCO_3 (including calculated O_2 saturation);** | A 🔁 |
| | MED: 100-2, 15, 80 | |

Note that 82803 is to be used for two or more of the following analytes: Gases, blood, any combination of pH, Carbon Dioxide, Hydrochloric acid, including calculated oxygen saturation.

| 82805 | **with O_2 saturation, by direct measurement, except pulse oximetry** | A 🔁 |
| | MED: 100-2, 15, 80 | |

| 82810 | **Gases, blood, O_2 saturation only, by direct measurement, except pulse oximetry** | A 🔁 |
| | MED: 100-2, 15, 80 | |

To report pulse oximetry, consult CPT code 94760.

| 82820 | **Hemoglobin-oxygen affinity (pO_2 for 50% hemoglobin saturation with oxygen)** | A 🔁 |
| | MED: 100-2, 15, 80 | |

| 82926 | **Gastric acid, free and total, each specimen** | A 🔁 |
| | MED: 100-2, 15, 80 | |

| 82928 | **Gastric acid, free or total, each specimen** | A |
| | MED: 100-2, 15, 80 | |

| 82938 | **Gastrin after secretin stimulation** | A |
| | MED: 100-2, 15, 80 | |

| 82941 | **Gastrin** | A |
| | MED: 100-2, 15, 80 | |

To report gentamicin, consult CPT code 80170. To report glutamyltransferase, gamma (GGT), consult CPT code 82977. To report gas liquid or HPLA chromatography, consult CPT code 82486.

| 82943 | **Glucagon** | A |
| | MED: 100-2, 15, 80 | |

| 82945 | **Glucose, body fluid, other than blood** | A |
| | MED: 100-2, 15, 80 | |

| 82946 | **Glucagon tolerance test** | A |
| | MED: 100-2, 15, 80 | |

82947	**Glucose; quantitative, blood (except reagent strip)**	A ❌ 🔁
	MED: 100-3, 190.20	
	AMA: 2002, Jun, 1; 1999, Sep, 10; 1999, Dec, 1; 1994, Summer, 5; 1993, Summer, 14	

82948	**blood, reagent strip**	A
	MED: 100-2, 15, 80; 100-3, 160.17; 100-3, 190.20	
	AMA: 1999, Jan, 10; 1994, Summer, 5	

82950	**post glucose dose (includes glucose)**	A ❌
	MED: 100-2, 15, 80; 100-3, 160.17	
	AMA: 2002, Jun, 1; 1999, Sep, 10	

82951   **tolerance test (GTT), three specimens (includes glucose)**   Ⓐ ☒ ↵
MED: 100-2, 15, 80

AMA: 2001, Feb, 10

82952   **tolerance test, each additional beyond three specimens**   Ⓐ ☒ ↵
MED: 100-2, 15, 80

AMA: 2001, Feb, 10

82953   **tolbutamide tolerance test**   Ⓐ ↵
MED: 100-2, 15, 80

If an insulin tolerance test is performed, consult CPT codes 80434 and 80435. If a leucine tolerance test is performed, consult CPT code 80428. For semiquantitative urine glucose, consult CPT codes 81000, 81002, 81005, and 81099.

82955   **Glucose-6-phosphate dehydrogenase (G6PD); quantitative**   Ⓐ
MED: 100-2, 15, 80

82960   **screen**   Ⓐ
MED: 100-2, 15, 80

If a glucose tolerance test is performed with medication, consult CPT code 90784 in addition.

82962   **Glucose, blood by glucose monitoring device(s) cleared by the FDA specifically for home use**   Ⓐ ☒
MED: 100-2, 15, 80; 100-3, 160.17; 100-3, 190.20

AMA: 1999, Jan, 10; 1994, Summer, 4

82963   **Glucosidase, beta**   Ⓐ
MED: 100-2, 15, 80

82965   **Glutamate dehydrogenase**   Ⓐ
MED: 100-2, 15, 80

82975   **Glutamine (glutamic acid amide)**   Ⓐ
MED: 100-2, 15, 80

82977   **Glutamyltransferase, gamma (GGT)**   Ⓐ
MED: 100-2, 15, 80; 100-3, 190.32

AMA: 1999, Dec, 1

82978   **Glutathione**   Ⓐ
MED: 100-2, 15, 80

82979   **Glutathione reductase, RBC**   Ⓐ
MED: 100-2, 15, 80

82980   **Glutethimide**   Ⓐ
MED: 100-2, 15, 80

To report glycohemoglobin, consult CPT code 83036.

82985   **Glycated protein**   Ⓐ ☒ ↵
MED: 100-2, 15, 80; 100-3, 190.21

AMA: 1994, Summer, 2

To report chorionic gonadotropin, consult CPT codes 84702 and 84703.

83001   **Gonadotropin; follicle stimulating hormone (FSH)**   Ⓐ ☒ ↵
MED: 100-2, 15, 80

26 / TC Professional/Technical Component   80 / 80 Assist-at-Surgery Allowed/With Documentation   ⊙ Conscious Sedation

Unlisted   Not Covered   **MED:** Pubs 100/NCD Reference   1 - 9 ASC Group   63 Modifier 63 Exempt

590 — Path/Lab   CPT only © 2005 American Medical Association. All Rights Reserved. *(Black Ink)*   © 2005 Ingenix, Inc. *(Blue Ink)*

83002   **luteinizing hormone (LH)** A ☒ ⤵
MED: 100-2, 15, 80

To report luteinizing releasing factor (LRH), consult CPT code 83727.

83003   **Growth hormone, human (HGH) (somatotropin)** A ⤵
MED: 100-2, 15, 80

To report antibody to human growth hormone, consult CPT code 86277.

83008   **Guanosine monophosphate (GMP), cyclic** A
MED: 100-2, 15, 80

83009   **Helicobacter pylori, blood test analysis for urease activity, non-radioactive isotope (eg, C-13)** A

To report H. pylori breath test analysis for urease activity, consult 83013, 83014.

83010   **Haptoglobin; quantitative** A
MED: 100-2, 15, 80

83012   **phenotypes** A
MED: 100-2, 15, 80

83013   **Helicobacter pylori; breath test analysis for urease activity, non-radioactive isotope (eg, C-13)** A ⤵
MED: 100-2, 15, 80

AMA: 1999, Nov, 45; 1999, Feb, 8; 1998, Nov, 25

To report H. pylori, stool, consult CPT code 87338. To report H. pylori, liquid scintillation counter, consult CPT codes 78267, 78268. To report H. pylori, enzyme immunoassay, consult CPT code 87339.

83014   **drug administration** A ⤵
MED: 100-2, 15, 80

AMA: 1999, Nov, 45; 1999, Feb, 8; 1998, Nov, 25

To report H. pylori, stool, consult CPT code 87338. To report H. pylori, liquid scintillation counter, consult CPT codes 78267, 78268. To report H. pylori, enzyme immunoassay, consult CPT code 87339.

To report H pylori, blood test analysis for urease activity, consult CPT code 83009.

83015   **Heavy metal (eg, arsenic, barium, beryllium, bismuth, antimony, mercury); screen** A
MED: 100-2, 15, 80

Reinsch test

83018   **quantitative, each** A
MED: 100-2, 15, 80

83020   **Hemoglobin fractionation and quantitation; electrophoresis (eg, A2, S, C, and/or F)** A ⤵
MED: 100-2, 15, 80; 100-4, 12, 60

AMA: 1998, Nov, 25

83021   **chromatography (eg, A2, S, C, and/or F)** A ⤵
MED: 100-2, 15, 80

AMA: 1999, Dec, 7; 1998, Nov, 25

83026   **Hemoglobin; by copper sulfate method, non-automated** A ☒
MED: 100-2, 15, 80

	83030	F (fetal), chemical	A ◪
		MED: 100-2, 15, 80	
	83033	F (fetal), qualitative	A ◪
		MED: 100-2, 15, 80	
▲	83036	glycosylated (A1C)	A ✖
		MED: 100-2, 15, 80; 100-3, 190.21	
		AMA: 1994, Summer, 2	

To report fecal hemoglobin detection by immunoassay, consult CPT code 82274.

	83037	glycosylated (A1C) by device cleared by FDA for home use	
	83045	methemoglobin, qualitative	A
		MED: 100-2, 15, 80	
	83050	methemoglobin, quantitative	A
		MED: 100-2, 15, 80	
	83051	plasma	A
		MED: 100-2, 15, 80	
	83055	sulfhemoglobin, qualitative	A
		MED: 100-2, 15, 80	
	83060	sulfhemoglobin, quantitative	A
		MED: 100-2, 15, 80	
	83065	thermolabile	A
		MED: 100-2, 15, 80	
	83068	unstable, screen	A ◪
		MED: 100-2, 15, 80	
	83069	urine	A
		MED: 100-2, 15, 80	
	83070	Hemosiderin; qualitative	A
		MED: 100-2, 15, 80	
	83071	quantitative	A
		MED: 100-2, 15, 80	

A drug screen (qualitative analysis) is normally performed prior to quantitative analysis. For drug screen, consult CPT codes 80100-80103. For hydroxyindoleacetic acid, 5- (HIAA), consult CPT code 83497. For high performance liquid chromatography HPLC, consult CPT code 82486.

	83080	b-Hexosaminidase, each assay	A
		MED: 100-2, 15, 80	
		AMA: 1998, Nov, 25	
	83088	Histamine	A
		MED: 100-2, 15, 80; 100-3, 110.10; 100-3, 250.3; 100-3, 30.6	

If a Hollander test is performed, consult CPT code 91052.

	83090	Homocysteine	A ◪
		MED: 100-2, 15, 80	
		AMA: 2001, Jan, 13	

83150	**Homovanillic acid (HVA)**	Ⓐ

MED: 100-2, 15, 80

If a hydrogen breath test is performed, consult CPT code 91065.

83491	**Hydroxycorticosteroids, 17- (17-OHCS)**	Ⓐ

MED: 100-2, 15, 80

To report cortisol, consult CPT code 82530, 82533. To report deoxycortisol, 11- consult CPT code 82634.

83497	**Hydroxyindolacetic acid, 5-(HIAA)**	Ⓐ

MED: 100-2, 15, 80

If a urine qualitative test is performed, consult CPT code 81005.
For 5-Hydroxytryptamine, consult CPT code 84260.

83498	**Hydroxyprogesterone, 17-d**	Ⓐ ◨

MED: 100-2, 15, 80

83499	**Hydroxyprogesterone, 20-**	Ⓐ

MED: 100-2, 15, 80

83500	**Hydroxyproline; free**	Ⓐ

MED: 100-2, 15, 80

83505	**total**	Ⓐ

MED: 100-2, 15, 80

83516	**Immunoassay for analyte other than infectious agent antibody or infectious agent antigen, qualitative or semiquantitative; multiple step method**	Ⓐ ◨

MED: 100-2, 15, 80

AMA: 1998, Nov, 25

83518	**single step method (eg, reagent strip)**	Ⓐ ✖

MED: 100-2, 15, 80

AMA: 1993, Fall, 26

83519	**Immunoassay, analyte, quantitative; by radiopharmaceutical technique (eg, RIA)**	Ⓐ ◨

MED: 100-2, 15, 80

AMA: 1994, Summer, 2; 1993, Fall, 26

83520	**not otherwise specified**	Ⓐ ◨

MED: 100-2, 15, 80

AMA: 1993, Fall, 26

To report qualitative or semi-quantitative immunoassay excluding infectious agent antibody or infectious agent antigen, multiple step method, consult CPT code 83516; single step method, consult CPT code 83518. For quantitative immunoassay by radiopharmaceutical immunoassay or radioimmunoassay (RIA), consult CPT code 83519. To report immunoassay for infectious agent antibody, qualitative or semi-quantitative, single step method (e.g., reagent strip), consult CPT code 86318. To report immunoassays for infectious agent antibody, qualitative or semi-quantitative multiple step method, consult CPT codes 86602-86804. To report infectious agent antigen detection by enzyme immunoassay, qualitative or semi-quantitative, consult CPT codes 87301-87899. For immunoassay for tumor antigen, consult CPT code 86316. To report immunoassay for infectious agent antibody not elsewhere specified, quantitative, consult CPT code 86317.

◪ CCI Comp 🔟 Bilateral Proc. ✚ CPT Add-on Code ⊘ Modifier -51 Exempt ♂/♀ Male/Female ✖ CLIA Waived Test
● New Code ▲ Revised Code Ⓜ Maternity Edit Ⓐ Age Edit Ⓐ-Ⓨ APC Status Ind. **AMA:** CPT Assistant

© 2005 Ingenix, Inc. *(Blue Ink)*   CPT only © 2005 American Medical Association. All Rights Reserved. *(Black Ink)*   Path/Lab — 593

Pathology and Laboratory

83525 — 83634

83525 Insulin; total   A ⊡
MED: 100-2, 15, 80

To report proinsulin, consult CPT code 84206.

83527   free   A
MED: 100-2, 15, 80

AMA: 1994, Summer, 5

83528 Intrinsic factor   A
MED: 100-2, 15, 80

To report intrinsic factor antibodies, consult CPT code 86340.

83540 Iron   A
MED: 100-2, 15, 80; 100-4, 190.18

AMA: 1993, Fall, 25

83550 Iron binding capacity   A
MED: 100-2, 15, 80; 100-4, 190.18

83570 Isocitric dehydrogenase (IDH)   A
MED: 100-2, 15, 80

To report isopropyl alcohol, consult CPT code 84600.

83582 Ketogenic steroids, fractionation   A
MED: 100-2, 15, 80

To report ketone bodies for serum, consult CPT codes 82009 and 82010. To
report ketone bodies for urine, consult CPT codes 81000-81003.

83586 Ketosteroids, 17- (17-KS); total   A
MED: 100-2, 15, 80

83593   fractionation   A
MED: 100-2, 15, 80

83605 Lactate (lactic acid)   A ☒
MED: 100-2, 15, 80

83615 Lactate dehydrogenase (LD), (LDH);   A
MED: 100-2, 15, 80; 100-3, 190.10

AMA: 1999, Dec, 1; 1998, Feb, 1; 1993, Fall, 25

83625   isoenzymes, separation and quantitation   A ⊡
MED: 100-2, 15, 80; 100-3, 190.10

AMA: 1998, Feb, 1; 1993, Fall, 25

▲ **83630** Lactoferrin, fecal; qualitative   A

● **83631**   quantitative

83632 Lactogen, human placental (HPL) human chorionic
somatomammotropin   M ♀ A
MED: 100-2, 15, 80

83633 Lactose, urine; qualitative   A
MED: 100-2, 15, 80

83634   quantitative   A
MED: 100-2, 15, 80

To report tolerance, consult CPT codes 82951 and 82952. If a breath hydrogen
test is performed to report lactase deficiency, consult CPT code 91065.

83655	**Lead** MED: 100-2, 15, 80	A
83661	**Fetal lung maturity assessment; lecithin sphingomyelin (L/S) ratio** MED: 100-2, 15, 80	M ♀ A ⬛
83662	**foam stability test** MED: 100-2, 15, 80	M ♀ A ⬛
83663	**fluorescence polarization** MED: 100-2, 15, 80	M ♀ A ⬛
83664	**lamellar body density** MED: 100-2, 15, 80	M ♀ A ⬛

To report phosphatidylglycerol, consult CPT code 84081.

83670	**Leucine aminopeptidase (LAP)** MED: 100-2, 15, 80	A
83690	**Lipase** MED: 100-2, 15, 80	A
● 83695	**Lipoprotein (a)**	
● 83700	**Lipoprotein, blood; electrophoretic separation and quantitation**	
● 83701	**high resolution fractionation and quantitation of lipoproteins including lipoprotein subclasses when performed (eg, electrophoresis, ultracentrifugation)**	
● 83704	**quantitation of lipoprotein particle numbers and lipoprotein particle subclasses (eg, by nuclear magnetic resonance spectroscopy)**	
~~83715~~	~~electrophoretic separation and quantitation~~	

(Use 83700, 83701)

~~83716~~	~~high resolution fractionation and quantitation of lipoproteins including lipoprotein subclasses when performed (eg, electrophoresis, nuclear magnetic resonance, ultracentrifugation)~~	

(Use 83700, 83701)

83718	**Lipoprotein, direct measurement; high density cholesterol (HDL cholesterol)** MED: 100-2, 15, 80; 100-3, 190.23 AMA: 1999, Oct, 11	A ❌ ⬛
83719	**VLDL cholesterol** MED: 100-2, 15, 80 AMA: 1999, Oct, 11	A ⬛
83721	**LDL cholesterol** MED: 100-2, 15, 80; 100-3, 190.23 AMA: 1999, Oct, 11; 1998, Nov, 25	A ⬛

To report fractionation by high resolution electrophoresis or ultracentrifugation, consult CPT code 83701.

To report lipoprotein paricle numbers and subclasses analysis by nuclear magnetic resonance spectroscopy, consult CPT code 83695.

For direct meaasurement, intermediate density lipoproteins (remnant lipoproteins), consult CPT Category III code 0026T.

83727   Luteinizing releasing factor (LRH)   A
   MED: 100-2, 15, 80

   If qualitative analysis is performed, consult CPT codes 80100-80103. For
   macroglobulins, alpha-2, consult CPT code 86329.

83735   Magnesium   A
   MED: 100-2, 15, 80

83775   Malate dehydrogenase   A
   MED: 100-2, 15, 80

   To report maltose tolerance, consult CPT codes 82951 and 82952. To report
   mammotropin, consult CPT code 84146.

83785   Manganese   A
   MED: 100-2, 15, 80

   To report marijuana, consult CPT codes 80100-80103.

83788   Mass spectrometry and tandem mass spectrometry (MS, MS/MS), analyte
   not elsewhere specified; qualitative, each specimen   A
   MED: 100-2, 15, 80

   AMA: 1998, Nov, 26

83789   quantitative, each specimen   A ▣
   MED: 100-2, 15, 80

   AMA: 1998, Nov, 26

83805   Meprobamate   A
   MED: 100-2, 15, 80

   A drug screen (qualitative analysis) is normally performed prior to quantitative
   analysis. For drug screen, consult CPT codes 80100-80103.

83825   Mercury, quantitative   A
   MED: 100-2, 15, 80

   To report mercury screen, consult CPT code 83015.

83835   Metanephrines   A
   MED: 100-2, 15, 80

   To report catecholamines, consult CPT codes 82382-82384.

83840   Methadone   A
   MED: 100-2, 15, 80

   A drug screen (qualitative analysis) is normally performed prior to quantitative
   analysis. For drug screen, consult CPT codes 80100-80103 and 82145. For
   methanol, consult CPT code 84600.

83857   Methemalbumin   A
   MED: 100-2, 15, 80

   To report methemoglobin, see hemoglobin CPT codes 83045 and 83050.

83858   Methsuximide   A
   MED: 100-2, 15, 80

   To report methyl alcohol, consult CPT code 84600. To report microalbumin,
   quantitative, consult CPT code 82043; semiquantitative, consult CPT code
   82044. To report microglobulin, beta-2, consult CPT code 82232.

83864   Mucopolysaccharides, acid; quantitative   A
   MED: 100-2, 15, 80

26 / TC Professional/Technical Component   80 / 80 Assist-at-Surgery Allowed/With Documentation   ⊙ Conscious Sedation
Unlisted   Not Covered   **MED:** Pubs 100/NCD Reference   1 - 9 ASC Group   63 Modifier 63 Exempt
596 — Path/Lab   CPT only © 2005 American Medical Association. All Rights Reserved. *(Black Ink)*   © 2005 Ingenix, Inc. *(Blue Ink)*
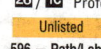

83866	**screen**	A
	MED: 100-2, 15, 80	

83872	**Mucin, synovial fluid (Ropes test)**	A
	MED: 100-2, 15, 80	

83873	**Myelin basic protein, cerebrospinal fluid**	A
	MED: 100-2, 15, 80	

To report oligoclonal bands, consult CPT code 83916.

83874	**Myoglobin**	A
	MED: 100-2, 15, 80	
	AMA: 1998, Feb, 1	

To report Nalorphine, consult CPT code 83925.

83880	**Natriuretic peptide**	A
83883	**Nephelometry, each analyte not elsewhere specified**	A
	MED: 100-2, 15, 80	

83885	**Nickel**	A
	MED: 100-2, 15, 80	

83887	**Nicotine**	A
	MED: 100-2, 15, 80	

Report codes 83890-83914 for use with molecular diagnostic techniques for analysis of nucleic acids.

Report codes 83890-83914 by procedure rather than analyte.

Report each procedure used in an analysis separately. For example, a procedure requiring isolation of DNA, restriction endonuclease digestion, electrophoresis, and nucleic acid probe amplification would be reported with codes 83890, 83892, 83894, and 83898.

Report the appropriate modifier when diagnostic procedures are performed to test for oncology, hematology, neurology, or inherited disorders.

83890	**Molecular diagnostics; molecular isolation or extraction**	A ⚫
	MED: 100-2, 15, 80	
	AMA: 1998, Nov, 26; 1993, Fall, 26	

To report microbial identification, consult CPT codes 87797 and 87798.

Code 83890-83912 separately for each procedure used in analysis rather than by analyte.

83891	**isolation or extraction of highly purified nucleic acid**	A ⚫
	MED: 100-2, 15, 80	
	AMA: 1998, Nov, 26	

83892	**enzymatic digestion**	A ⚫
	MED: 100-2, 15, 80	
	AMA: 1993, Fall, 26	

83893	**dot/slot blot production**	A ⚫
	MED: 100-2, 15, 80	
	AMA: 1998, Nov, 26	

83894	**separation by gel electrophoresis (eg, agarose, polyacrylamide)**	A ⚫
	MED: 100-2, 15, 80	
	AMA: 1998, Nov, 26; 1993, Fall, 25	

Pathology and Laboratory

83896 — 83912

83896   **nucleic acid probe, each**   A TC
MED: 100-2, 15, 80

AMA: 2002, Aug, 10; 1993, Fall, 26

83897   **nucleic acid transfer (eg, Southern, Northern)**   A TC
MED: 100-2, 15, 80

AMA: 1998, Nov, 26

▲   83898   **amplification of patient nucleic acid, each nucleic acid sequence** A TC
MED: 100-2, 15, 80

AMA: 1998, Nov, 26; 1993, Fall, 26

●   83900   **amplification of patient nucleic acid, multiplex, first two nucleic acid sequences**

+ ▲   83901   **amplification of patient nucleic acid, multiplex, each additional nucleic acid sequence (List separately in addition to code for primary procedure)**   A TC
MED: 100-2, 15, 80

AMA: 1998, Nov, 26

Note that 83901 is an add-on code and should be reported in conjunction with 83900.

83902   **reverse transcription**   A TC
MED: 100-2, 15, 80

83903   **mutation scanning, by physical properties (eg, single strand conformational polymorphisms (SSCP), heteroduplex, denaturing gradient gel electrophoresis (DGGE), RNA'ase A), single segment, each**   A TC

MED: 100-2, 15, 80

AMA: 1998, Nov, 26

83904   **mutation identification by sequencing, single segment, each segment**   A TC

MED: 100-2, 15, 80

AMA: 1998, Nov, 26

83905   **mutation identification by allele specific transcription, single segment, each segment**   A TC
MED: 100-2, 15, 80

AMA: 1998, Nov, 26

83906   **mutation identification by allele specific translation, single segment, each segment**   A TC
MED: 100-2, 15, 80

AMA: 1998, Nov, 26

●   83907   **lysis of cells prior to nucleic acid extraction (eg, stool specimens, paraffin embedded tissue)**

●   83908   **signal amplification of patient nucleic acid, each nucleic acid sequence**

To report multiplex amplification, consult CPT codes 83900, 83901.

●   83909   **separation and identification by high resolution technique (eg, capillary electrophoresis)**

83912   **interpretation and report**   A TC
MED: 100-2, 15, 80; 100-4, 12, 60

● 83914 **Mutation identification by enzymatic ligation or primer extension, single segment, each segment (eg, oligonucleotide ligation assay (OLA), single base chain extension (SBCE), or allele-specific primer extension (ASPE))**

83915 **Nucleotidase 5-** [A]
MED: 100-2, 15, 80

83916 **Oligoclonal immune (oligoclonal bands)** [A][⚷]
MED: 100-2, 15, 80

83918 **Organic acids; total, quantitative, each specimen** [A][⚷]
MED: 100-2, 15, 80

AMA: 1998, Nov, 26; 1996, Mar, 11

83919 **qualitative, each specimen** [A]
MED: 100-2, 15, 80

AMA: 1998, Nov, 26

83921 **Organic acid, single, quantitative** [A][⚷]
MED: 100-2, 15, 80

83925 **Opiates, (eg, morphine, meperidine)** [A]
MED: 100-2, 15, 80

83930 **Osmolality; blood** [A]
MED: 100-2, 15, 80

83935 **urine** [A]
MED: 100-2, 15, 80

83937 **Osteocalcin (bone gla protein)** [A]
MED: 100-2, 15, 80

AMA: 1994, Summer, 5

83945 **Oxalate** [A]
MED: 100-2, 15, 80

83950 **Oncoprotein, HER-2/neu** [A][⚷]
MED: 100-2, 15, 80

To report tissue analysis, consult CPT codes 88342, 88365.

83970 **Parathormone (parathyroid hormone)** [A]
MED: 100-2, 15, 80

To report screening for chlorinated hydrocarbons, consult CPT code 82441.

83986 **pH, body fluid, except blood** [A][✗]
MED: 100-2, 15, 80

To report blood pH, consult CPT codes 82800 and 82803.

83992 **Phencyclidine (PCP)** [A]
MED: 100-2, 15, 80

A drug screen (qualitative analysis) is normally performed prior to quantitative analysis. For drug screen, consult CPT codes 80100-80103. For phenobarbital, consult CPT code 80184.

84022 **Phenothiazine** [A]
MED: 100-2, 15, 80

A drug screen (qualitative analysis) is normally performed prior to quantitative analysis. For drug screen, consult CPT codes 80100-80101.

| [⚷] CCI Comp | [50] Bilateral Proc. | ✚ CPT Add-on Code | ⊘ Modifier -51 Exempt | ♂/♀ Male/Female | [✗] CLIA Waived Test |
| ● New Code | ▲ Revised Code | [M] Maternity Edit | [A] Age Edit | [A]–[Y] APC Status Ind. | AMA: CPT Assistant |

© 2005 Ingenix, Inc. *(Blue Ink)*   CPT only © 2005 American Medical Association. All Rights Reserved. *(Black Ink)*   Path/Lab — 599

Pathology and Laboratory

84030 — 84120

84030   **Phenylalanine (PKU), blood**   A
MED: 100-2, 15, 80

To report phenylalanine-tyrosine ratio, consult CPT codes 84030 and 84510.
Guthrie test

84035   **Phenylketones, qualitative**   A
MED: 100-2, 15, 80

84060   **Phosphatase, acid; total**   A
MED: 100-2, 15, 80

84061   **forensic examination**   A
MED: 100-2, 15, 80

84066   **prostatic**   ♂ A
MED: 100-2, 15, 80

84075   **Phosphatase, alkaline;**   A
MED: 100-2, 15, 80; 100-3, 160.17; 100-3, 190.10

AMA: 1999, Dec, 1

84078   **heat stable (total not included)**   A
MED: 100-2, 15, 80; 100-3, 160.17

84080   **isoenzymes**   A ◨
MED: 100-2, 15, 80; 100-3, 160.17

84081   **Phosphatidylglycerol**   A
MED: 100-2, 15, 80

To report inorganic phosphates, consult CPT code 84100. To report organic
phosphates, see code for specific method. For cholinesterase, consult CPT
codes 82480 and 82482.

84085   **Phosphogluconate, 6-, dehydrogenase, RBC**   A
MED: 100-2, 15, 80

84087   **Phosphohexose isomerase**   A
MED: 100-2, 15, 80

84100   **Phosphorus inorganic (phosphate);**   A
MED: 100-2, 15, 80; 100-3, 190.10

AMA: 1999, Dec, 1

84105   **urine**   A
MED: 100-2, 15, 80

To report pituitary gonadotropins, consult CPT codes 83001-83002. To report
PKU, consult CPT codes 84030 and 84035.

84106   **Porphobilinogen, urine; qualitative**   A
MED: 100-2, 15, 80

84110   **quantitative**   A
MED: 100-2, 15, 80

84119   **Porphyrins, urine; qualitative**   A
MED: 100-2, 15, 80

84120   **quantitation and fractionation**   A
MED: 100-2, 15, 80

84126	**Porphyrins, feces; quantitative**	A
	MED: 100-2, 15, 80	

84127	**qualitative**	A
	MED: 100-2, 15, 80	

To report porphyrin precursors, consult CPT codes 82135, 84106, and 84110. To report protoporphyrin, RBC, consult CPT codes 84202 and 84203.

84132	**Potassium; serum**	A
	MED: 100-2, 15, 80; 100-3, 190.10	
	AMA: 2002, Jun, 1; 1999, Dec, 1	

84133	**urine**	A
	MED: 100-2, 15, 80	

84134	**Prealbumin**	A
	MED: 100-2, 15, 80	

To report microalbumin, consult CPT codes 82043 and 82044.

84135	**Pregnanediol**	A
	MED: 100-2, 15, 80	

84138	**Pregnanetriol**	A
	MED: 100-2, 15, 80	

84140	**Pregnenolone**	A
	MED: 100-2, 15, 80	
	AMA: 1994, Summer, 6	

84143	**17-hydroxypregnenolone**	A
	MED: 100-2, 15, 80	
	AMA: 1994, Summer, 6	

84144	**Progesterone**	A
	MED: 100-2, 15, 80	

To report progesterone receptor assay, consult CPT code 84234. To report proinsulin, consult CPT code 84206.

84146	**Prolactin**	A ↵
	MED: 100-2, 15, 80	

84150	**Prostaglandin, each**	A
	MED: 100-2, 15, 80	

84152	**Prostate specific antigen (PSA); complexed (direct measurement)**	♂ A
	MED: 100-2, 15, 80; 100-3, 210.1; 100-4, 18, 50	

84153	**Prostate specific antigen (PSA); total**	♂ A
	MED: 100-2, 15, 80; 100-3, 190.31; 100-3, 210.1; 100-4, 18, 50	
	AMA: 1999, Dec, 10; 1999, Aug, 5; 1998, Nov, 26; 1997, Jan, 10; 1996, May, 10; 1996, Aug, 10; 1993, Fall, 26	

84154	**free**	♂ A
	MED: 100-3, 210.1	
	AMA: 1999, Dec, 10; 1999, Aug, 5; 1998, Nov, 26	

84155	**Protein, total, except by refractometry; serum**	A
	MED: 100-2, 15, 80; 100-3, 190.10	
	AMA: 2000, Jan, 7; 1999, Dec, 1	

 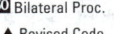  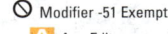 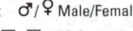

84156	urine	A
84157	other source (eg, synovial fluid, cerebrospinal fluid)	A
84160	Protein, total, by refractometry, any source MED: 100-2, 15, 80	A 🔁

To report urine total protein by dipstick method, consult CPT codes 81000-81003.

84163	Pregnancy-associated plasma protein-A (PAPP-A)	♀ A
84165	Protein; electrophoretic fractionation and quantitation, serum MED: 100-2, 15, 80; 100-4, 12, 60	A 🔁
84166	electrophoretic fractionation and quantitation, other fluids with concentration (eg, urine, CSF)	A 🔁
84181	Western Blot, with interpretation and report, blood or other body fluid MED: 100-2, 15, 80; 100-3, 190.9; 100-4, 12, 60	A 🔁
84182	Western Blot, with interpretation and report, blood or other body fluid, immunological probe for band identification, each MED: 100-2, 15, 80; 100-3, 190.9; 100-4, 12, 60	A 🔁

If a Western Blot tissue analysis is performed, consult CPT code 88371.

84202	Protoporphyrin, RBC; quantitative MED: 100-2, 15, 80	A
84203	screen MED: 100-2, 15, 80	A
84206	Proinsulin MED: 100-2, 15, 80	A

To report pseudocholinesterase, consult CPT code 82480.

84207	Pyridoxal phosphate (Vitamin B-6) MED: 100-2, 15, 80	A 🔁
84210	Pyruvate MED: 100-2, 15, 80	A
84220	Pyruvate kinase MED: 100-2, 15, 80	A
84228	Quinine MED: 100-2, 15, 80	A
84233	Receptor assay; estrogen MED: 100-2, 15, 80	A 🔁
84234	progesterone MED: 100-2, 15, 80	A 🔁
84235	endocrine, other than estrogen or progesterone (specify hormone) MED: 100-2, 15, 80	A 🔁
▲ 84238	non-endocrine (specify receptor) MED: 100-2, 15, 80	A 🔁
84244	Renin MED: 100-2, 15, 80	A 🔁

| 84252 | **Riboflavin (Vitamin B-2)** | A ⊡ |
| | MED: 100-2, 15, 80 | |

To report salicylates, consult CPT code 80196. If a secretin test is performed, consult CPT codes 99070, 89100 and appropriate analyses.

| 84255 | **Selenium** | A |
| | MED: 100-2, 15, 80 | |

| 84260 | **Serotonin** | A |
| | MED: 100-2, 15, 80 | |

To report urine metabolites (HIAA), consult CPT code 83497.

84270	**Sex hormone binding globulin (SHBG)**	A
	MED: 100-2, 15, 80	
	AMA: 1994, Summer, 4	

| 84275 | **Sialic acid** | A |
| | MED: 100-2, 15, 80 | |

To report sickle hemoglobin, consult CPT code 85660.

| 84285 | **Silica** | A |
| | MED: 100-2, 15, 80 | |

84295	**Sodium; serum**	A
	MED: 100-2, 15, 80; 100-3, 190.10	
	AMA: 1999, Dec, 1	

| 84300 | **urine** | A |
| | MED: 100-2, 15, 80 | |

| 84302 | **Sodium; other source** | A |

To report somatomammotropin, consult CPT code 83632. To report somatotropin, consult CPT code 83003.

84305	**Somatomedin**	A
	MED: 100-2, 15, 80	
	AMA: 1994, Summer, 4	

84307	**Somatostatin**	A
	MED: 100-2, 15, 80	
	AMA: 1994, Summer, 4	

| 84311 | **Spectrophotometry, analyte not elsewhere specified** | A |
| | MED: 100-2, 15, 80 | |

| 84315 | **Specific gravity (except urine)** | A |
| | MED: 100-2, 15, 80 | |

To report specific gravity, urine, consult CPT codes 81000-81003. If stone analysis is performed, consult CPT codes 82355-82370.

| 84375 | **Sugars, chromatographic, TLC or paper chromatography** | A |
| | MED: 100-2, 15, 80 | |

84376	**Sugars (mono-, di-, and oligosaccharides); single qualitative, each specimen**	A
	MED: 100-2, 15, 80	
	AMA: 1999, Dec, 7; 1998, Nov, 26-27	

Pathology and Laboratory

84252 — 84376

⊡ CCI Comp	50 Bilateral Proc.	✚ CPT Add-on Code	⊘ Modifier -51 Exempt	♂/♀ Male/Female	✗ CLIA Waived Test
● New Code	▲ Revised Code	M Maternity Edit	A Age Edit	A–Y APC Status Ind.	AMA: CPT Assistant
© 2005 Ingenix, Inc. *(Blue Ink)*		CPT only © 2005 American Medical Association. All Rights Reserved. *(Black Ink)*			Path/Lab — 603

84377	**multiple qualitative, each specimen**	Ⓐ 🔹
	MED: 100-2, 15, 80	
	AMA: 1998, Nov, 26-27	

84378	**single quantitative, each specimen**	Ⓐ 🔹
	MED: 100-2, 15, 80	
	AMA: 1998, Nov, 26-27	

84379	**multiple quantitative, each specimen**	Ⓐ 🔹
	MED: 100-2, 15, 80	
	AMA: 1999, Dec, 7; 1998, Nov, 26-27	

84392   **Sulfate, urine**   Ⓐ
MED: 100-2, 15, 80

To report T-3, consult CPT codes 84479-84481. To report T-4, consult CPT codes 84436-84439. To report sulfhemoglobin, see hemoglobin CPT codes 83055 and 83060.

84402   **Testosterone; free**   Ⓐ
MED: 100-2, 15, 80

84403   **total**   Ⓐ 🔹
MED: 100-2, 15, 80

84425   **Thiamine (Vitamin B-1)**   Ⓐ 🔹
MED: 100-2, 15, 80

84430   **Thiocyanate**   Ⓐ
MED: 100-2, 15, 80

84432   **Thyroglobulin**   Ⓐ
MED: 100-2, 15, 80
AMA: 1994, Summer, 2

Thyroglobulin, antibody, see 86800. If a thyrotropin releasing hormone (TRH) test is performed, consult CPT codes 80438 and 80439.

84436   **Thyroxine; total**   Ⓐ 🔹
MED: 100-2, 15, 80; 100-3, 190.22
AMA: 1994, Summer, 3; 1993, Fall, 25

84437   **requiring elution (eg, neonatal)**   Ⓐ
MED: 100-2, 15, 80

84439   **free**   Ⓐ 🔹
MED: 100-2, 15, 80; 100-3, 190.22

84442   **Thyroxine binding globulin (TBG)**   Ⓐ
MED: 100-2, 15, 80

84443   **Thyroid stimulating hormone (TSH)**   Ⓐ 🔹
MED: 100-2, 15, 80; 100-3, 190.22
AMA: 1994, Summer, 3

84445   **Thyroid stimulating immune globulins (TSI)**   Ⓐ 🔹
MED: 100-2, 15, 80
AMA: 1994, Summer, 3

To report tobramycin, consult CPT code 80200.

---

26 / **TC** Professional/Technical Component   **80**/**80** Assist-at-Surgery Allowed/With Documentation   ⊙ Conscious Sedation

Unlisted   Not Covered   **MED:** Pubs 100/NCD Reference   **1**-**9** ASC Group   63 Modifier 63 Exempt

604 — Path/Lab   CPT only © 2005 American Medical Association. All Rights Reserved. *(Black Ink)*   © 2005 Ingenix, Inc. *(Blue Ink)*

| 84446 | **Tocopherol alpha (Vitamin E)** | A ⟳ |
| | MED: 100-2, 15, 80 | |

To report tolbutamide tolerance, consult CPT code 82953.

84449	**Transcortin (cortisol binding globulin)**	A
	MED: 100-2, 15, 80	
	AMA: 1994, Summer, 6	

84450	**Transferase; aspartate amino (AST) (SGOT)**	A ✖
	MED: 100-2, 15, 80; 100-3, 160.17; 100-3, 190.10	
	AMA: 1999, Dec, 1	

84460	**alanine amino (ALT) (SGPT)**	A ✖
	MED: 100-2, 15, 80; 100-3, 160.17	
	AMA: 1999, Dec, 1	

84466	**Transferrin**	A ⟳
	MED: 100-2, 15, 80; 100-4, 190.18	
	AMA: 1994, Summer, 4	

To report iron binding capacity, consult CPT code 83550.

84478	**Triglycerides**	A ✖ ⟳
	MED: 100-2, 15, 80; 100-3, 190.23	
	AMA: 2000, Mar, 11; 1999, Dec, 1	

84479	**Thyroid hormone (T3 or T4) uptake or thyroid hormone binding ratio (THBR)**	A ⟳
	MED: 100-2, 15, 80; 100-3, 190.22	
	AMA: 1994, Summer, 3; 1993, Fall, 25	

| 84480 | **Triiodothyronine T3; total (TT-3)** | A ⟳ |
| | MED: 100-2, 15, 80 | |

| 84481 | **free** | A ⟳ |
| | MED: 100-2, 15, 80 | |

84482	**reverse**	A ⟳
	MED: 100-2, 15, 80	
	AMA: 1994, Summer, 2	

84484	**Troponin, quantitative**	A
	MED: 100-2, 15, 80	
	AMA: 1998, Jan, 6; 1998, Feb, 1; 1997, Nov, 29	

To report Troponin, qualitative assay, consult CPT code 84512.

| 84485 | **Trypsin; duodenal fluid** | A |
| | MED: 100-2, 15, 80 | |

| 84488 | **feces, qualitative** | A |
| | MED: 100-2, 15, 80 | |

| 84490 | **feces, quantitative, 24-hour collection** | A |
| | MED: 100-2, 15, 80 | |

| 84510 | **Tyrosine** | A |
| | MED: 100-2, 15, 80 | |

To report urate crystal identification, consult CPT code 89060.

84512   **Troponin, qualitative**   A
          MED: 100-2, 15, 80

          AMA: 1998, Jan, 6; 1998, Feb, 1; 1997, Nov, 29

          To report Troponin, quantitative assay, consult CPT code 84484.

84520   **Urea nitrogen; quantitative**   A
          MED: 100-2, 15, 80; 100-3, 160.17; 100-3, 190.10

          AMA: 1999, Dec, 1

84525   **semiquantitative (eg, reagent strip test)**   A
          MED: 100-2, 15, 80; 100-3, 160.17

          AMA: 1998, Mar, 3

          Patterson's test

84540   **Urea nitrogen, urine**   A
          MED: 100-2, 15, 80

84545   **Urea nitrogen, clearance**   A
          MED: 100-2, 15, 80

84550   **Uric acid; blood**   A
          MED: 100-2, 15, 80

          AMA: 1999, Dec, 1

84560   **other source**   A
          MED: 100-2, 15, 80

84577   **Urobilinogen, feces, quantitative**   A
          MED: 100-2, 15, 80

84578   **Urobilinogen, urine; qualitative**   A
          MED: 100-2, 15, 80

84580   **quantitative, timed specimen**   A ⬀
          MED: 100-2, 15, 80

84583   **semiquantitative**   A
          MED: 100-2, 15, 80

          To report uroporphyrins, consult CPT Code 84120. To report dipropylacetic
          acid (valproic acid), consult CPT code 80164.

84585   **Vanillylmandelic acid (VMA), urine**   A
          MED: 100-2, 15, 80

84586   **Vasoactive intestinal peptide (VIP)**   A
          MED: 100-2, 15, 80

          AMA: 1994, Summer, 6

84588   **Vasopressin (antidiuretic hormone, ADH)**   A
          MED: 100-2, 15, 80

84590   **Vitamin A**   A ⬀
          MED: 100-2, 15, 80

          To report thiamine (Vitamin B-1), consult CPT code 84425. To report
          Riboflavin (Vitamin B-2), consult CPT code 84252. To report pyridoxal
          phosphate (Vitamin B-6), consult CPT code 84207. To report cyanocobalamin
          (Vitamin B-12), consult CPT code 82607. If a Vitamin B-12 absorption study is
          performed, (e.g., Schilling test), consult CPT codes 78270 and 78271. To
          report ascorbic acid (Vitamin C), consult CPT code 82180. To report Vitamin
          D, consult CPT codes 82306, 82307, and 82652. To report tocopherol alpha
          (Vitamin E), consult CPT code 84446.

84591   **Vitamin, not otherwise specified**   [A]
MED: 100-2, 15, 80

84597   **Vitamin K**   [A] [◨]
MED: 100-2, 15, 80

To report vanillylmandelic acid (VMA), consult CPT code 84585.

84600   **Volatiles (eg, acetic anhydride, carbon tetrachloride, dichloroethane, dichloromethane, diethylether, isopropyl alcohol, methanol)**   [A]
MED: 100-2, 15, 80

To report acetaldehyde, consult CPT code 82000. To report plasma volume, radiopharmaceutical volume-dilution technique, consult CPT codes 78110 and 78111.

84620   **Xylose absorption test, blood and/or urine**   [A] [◨]
MED: 100-2, 15, 80

Administration of d-xylose is reported separately, consult CPT code 99070.

84630   **Zinc**   [A]
MED: 100-2, 15, 80

84681   **C-peptide**   [A] [◨]
MED: 100-2, 15, 80

84702   **Gonadotropin, chorionic (hCG); quantitative**   [A] [◨]
MED: 100-2, 15, 80; 100-3, 190.27

If a urine pregnancy test is conducted by visual color comparison, consult CPT code 81025.

84703   **qualitative**   [A] [✗]
MED: 100-2, 15, 80

If a urine pregnancy test is conducted by visual color comparison, consult CPT code 81025.

84830   **Ovulation tests, by visual color comparison methods for human luteinizing hormone**   ♀ [A] [✗]
MED: 100-2, 15, 80

84999   **Unlisted chemistry procedure**   [A]
MED: 100-2, 15, 80

AMA: 2000, Oct, 7

HEMATOLOGY AND COAGULATION

For agglutinins, see the Immunology section of the CPT book. For antiplasmin, consult CPT code 85410. For antithrombin III, consult CPT codes 85300 and 85301.

For blood banking procedures, see the Transfusion Medicine section.

85002   **Bleeding time**   [A]
MED: 100-2, 15, 80

85004   **Blood count; automated differential WBC count**   [A] [◨]
MED: 100-3, 190.15

85007   **blood smear, microscopic examination with manual differential WBC count**   [A] [◨]
MED: 100-2, 15, 80; 100-3, 190.15

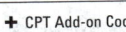
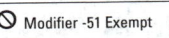

85008   **blood smear, microscopic examination without manual differential WBC count** ▣
MED: 100-2, 15, 80; 100-3, 190.15

To report other fluids (e.g., CSF), consult CPT codes 89050 and 89051.

85009   **manual differential WBC count, buffy coat** ▣ ▣
MED: 100-2, 15, 80

To report eosinophils, nasal smear, consult CPT code 89190.

85013   **spun microhematocrit** ▣ ▣
MED: 100-2, 15, 80; 100-3, 190.10; 100-3, 190.15

85014   **hematocrit (Hct)** ▣ ▣
MED: 100-2, 15, 80; 100-3, 190.15

85018   **hemoglobin (Hgb)** ▣ ▣
MED: 100-2, 15, 80; 100-3, 190.10; 100-3, 190.15

To report fecal hemoglobin detection by immunoassay, consult CPT code 82274.

To report other hemoglobin determinations, consult CPT codes 83020-83069.

85025   **Blood count; complete (CBC), automated (Hgb, Hct, RBC, WBC and platelet count) and automated differential WBC count** ▣ ▣
MED: 100-2, 15, 80; 100-3, 160.17; 100-3, 190.10; 100-3, 190.15

AMA: 2000, Jul, 11

85027   **complete (CBC), automated (Hgb, Hct, RBC, WBC and platelet count)** ▣ ▣
MED: 100-2, 15, 80; 100-3, 160.17; 100-3, 190.15

85032   **Blood count; manual cell count (erythrocyte, leukocyte, or platelet) each** ▣ ▣
MED: 100-3, 190.15

85041   **red blood cell (RBC), automated** ▣ ▣
MED: 100-2, 15, 80

Do not report 85041 with CPT codes 85025 or 85027.

85044   **reticulocyte, manual** ▣
MED: 100-2, 15, 80

85045   **reticulocyte, automated** ▣ ▣
MED: 100-2, 15, 80

85046   **reticulocytes, automated, including one or more cellular parameters (eg, reticulocyte hemoglobin content (CHr), immature reticulocyte fraction (IRF), reticulocyte volume (MRV), RNA content), direct measurement** ▣ ▣
MED: 100-2, 15, 80

AMA: 1998, Nov, 27

85048   **leukocyte (WBC), automated** ▣ ▣
MED: 100-2, 15, 80; 100-3, 190.15

85049   **platelet, automated** ▣ ▣
MED: 100-3, 190.15

85055   **Reticulated platelet assay** ▣

26 / **TC** Professional/Technical Component   **80** / **80** Assist-at-Surgery Allowed/With Documentation   ☉ Conscious Sedation
Unlisted   Not Covered   **MED:** Pubs 100/NCD Reference   **1**-**9** ASC Group   ⓺⓷ Modifier 63 Exempt
608 — Path/Lab   CPT only © 2005 American Medical Association. All Rights Reserved. *(Black Ink)*   © 2005 Ingenix, Inc. *(Blue Ink)*

85060   **Blood smear, peripheral, interpretation by physician with written report**   `B` `80`
MED: 100-2, 15, 80; 100-4, 12, 60

85097   **Bone marrow, smear interpretation**   `X` `80`
MED: 100-2, 15, 80; 100-4, 12, 60

AMA: 1998, Jul, 4; 1992, Winter, 17

To report special stains, consult CPT codes 85540, 88312, and 88313.

To report bone biopsy, consult CPT codes 20220, 20225, 20240, 20245, 20250, 20251.

85130   **Chromogenic substrate assay**   `A` `🔧`
MED: 100-2, 15, 80

To report circulating anti-coagulant screen (mixing studies), consult CPT codes 85611 and 85732.

85170   **Clot retraction**   `A` `🔧`
MED: 100-2, 15, 80

85175   **Clot lysis time, whole blood dilution**   `A` `🔧`
MED: 100-2, 15, 80

To report clotting factor I (fibrinogen), consult CPT codes 85384 and 85385.

85210   **Clotting; factor II, prothrombin, specific**   `A` `🔧`
MED: 100-2, 15, 80

Consult also CPT codes 85610-85613.

85220   **factor V (AcG or proaccelerin), labile factor**   `A` `🔧`
MED: 100-2, 15, 80

85230   **factor VII (proconvertin, stable factor)**   `A` `🔧`
MED: 100-2, 15, 80

85240   **factor VIII (AHG), one stage**   `A` `🔧`
MED: 100-2, 15, 80

85244   **factor VIII related antigen**   `A` `🔧`
MED: 100-2, 15, 80

85245   **factor VIII, VW factor, ristocetin cofactor**   `A` `🔧`
MED: 100-2, 15, 80

85246   **factor VIII, VW factor antigen**   `A` `🔧`
MED: 100-2, 15, 80

85247   **factor VIII, von Willebrand factor, multimetric analysis**   `A` `🔧`
MED: 100-2, 15, 80

85250   **factor IX (PTC or Christmas)**   `A` `🔧`
MED: 100-2, 15, 80

85260   **factor X (Stuart-Prower)**   `A` `🔧`
MED: 100-2, 15, 80

85270   **factor XI (PTA)**   `A` `🔧`
MED: 100-2, 15, 80

85280   **factor XII (Hageman)**   `A` `🔧`
MED: 100-2, 15, 80

85290	factor XIII (fibrin stabilizing)	A
	MED: 100-2, 15, 80	
85291	factor XIII (fibrin stabilizing), screen solubility	A
	MED: 100-2, 15, 80	
85292	prekallikrein assay (Fletcher factor assay)	A
	MED: 100-2, 15, 80	
85293	high molecular weight kininogen assay (Fitzgerald factor assay)	A
	MED: 100-2, 15, 80	
85300	Clotting inhibitors or anticoagulants; antithrombin III, activity	A
	MED: 100-2, 15, 80; 100-3, 110.3	
85301	antithrombin III, antigen assay	A
	MED: 100-2, 15, 80	
85302	protein C, antigen	A
	MED: 100-2, 15, 80	
85303	protein C, activity	A
	MED: 100-2, 15, 80	
85305	protein S, total	A
	MED: 100-2, 15, 80	
85306	protein S, free	A
	MED: 100-2, 15, 80	
85307	Activated Protein C (APC) resistance assay	A
	MED: 100-2, 15, 80	
85335	Factor inhibitor test	A
	MED: 100-2, 15, 80; 100-3, 110.3	
85337	Thrombomodulin	A
	MED: 100-2, 15, 80	

To report mixing studies for inhibitors, consult CPT code 85732.

85345	Coagulation time; Lee and White	A
	MED: 100-2, 15, 80	
85347	activated	A
	MED: 100-2, 15, 80	
85348	other methods	A
	MED: 100-2, 15, 80	

To report a differential count, consult CPT codes 85007 and subsequent codes. For duke bleeding time, consult CPT code 85002. For eosinophils, nasal smear, consult CPT code 89190.

| 85360 | Euglobulin lysis | A |
| | MED: 100-2, 15, 80 | |

To report fetal hemoglobin, consult CPT codes 83030, 83033, and 85460.

| 85362 | Fibrin(ogen) degradation (split) products (FDP)(FSP); agglutination slide, semiquantitative | A |
| | MED: 100-2, 15, 80 | |

To report immunoelectrophoresis, consult CPT code 86320.

26 / TC Professional/Technical Component   80 / 80 Assist-at-Surgery Allowed/With Documentation   ⊙ Conscious Sedation

Unlisted   Not Covered   MED: Pubs 100/NCD Reference   1 - 9 ASC Group   63 Modifier 63 Exempt

610 — Path/Lab   CPT only © 2005 American Medical Association. All Rights Reserved. *(Black Ink)*   © 2005 Ingenix, Inc. *(Blue Ink)*

85366	**paracoagulation**	A ⚡
	MED: 100-2, 15, 80	
85370	**quantitative**	A ⚡
	MED: 100-2, 15, 80	
85378	**Fibrin degradation products, D-dimer; qualitative or semiquantitative**	A ⚡
	MED: 100-2, 15, 80	
85379	**quantitative**	A ⚡
	MED: 100-2, 15, 80	

To report ultrasensitive and standard sensitivity quantitative D-dimer, consult CPT code 85379.

85380	**ultrasensitive (eg, for evaluation for venous thromboembolism), qualitative or semiquantitative**	A ⚡
85384	**Fibrinogen; activity**	A ⚡
	MED: 100-2, 15, 80	
85385	**antigen**	A ⚡
	MED: 100-2, 15, 80	
85390	**Fibrinolysins or coagulopathy screen, interpretation and report**	A ⚡
	MED: 100-2, 15, 80; 100-4, 12, 60	
85396	**Coagulation/fibrinolysis assay, whole blood (eg, viscoelastic clot assessment), including use of any pharmacologic additive(s), as indicated, including interpretation and written report, per day**	N 80
85400	**Fibrinolytic factors and inhibitors; plasmin**	A ⚡
	MED: 100-2, 15, 80	
85410	**alpha-2 antiplasmin**	A ⚡
	MED: 100-2, 15, 80	
85415	**plasminogen activator**	A ⚡
	MED: 100-2, 15, 80	
85420	**plasminogen, except antigenic assay**	A ⚡
	MED: 100-2, 15, 80	
85421	**plasminogen, antigenic assay**	A ⚡
	MED: 100-2, 15, 80	

To report fragility, red blood cell, consult CPT codes 85547 and 85555-85557.

85441	**Heinz bodies; direct**	A ⚡
	MED: 100-2, 15, 80	
85445	**induced, acetyl phenylhydrazine**	A ⚡
	MED: 100-2, 15, 80	

To report hematocrit (PCV), consult CPT codes 85014 and 85025, 85027. To report hemoglobin, consult CPT codes 83020-83068 and 85018, 85025, 85027.

85460	**Hemoglobin or RBCs, fetal, for fetomaternal hemorrhage; differential lysis (Kleihauer-Betke)**	M ♀ A ⚡
	MED: 100-2, 15, 80	
	AMA: 1993, Fall, 25	

Consult also CPT codes 83030 and 83033. For hemolysins, consult CPT codes 86940 and 86941.

85461   rosette   M ♀ A �
MED: 100-2, 15, 80

85475   Hemolysin, acid   A �
MED: 100-2, 15, 80

Consult also CPT codes 86940 and 86941.
Ham test

85520   Heparin assay   A �
MED: 100-2, 15, 80

85525   Heparin neutralization   A �
MED: 100-2, 15, 80

85530   Heparin-protamine tolerance test   A �
MED: 100-2, 15, 80

85536   Iron stain, peripheral blood   A �
MED: 100-2, 15, 80

To report iron stains on bone marrow or other tissues with physician evaluation, consult CPT code 88313.

85540   Leukocyte alkaline phosphatase with count   A �
MED: 100-2, 15, 80

85547   Mechanical fragility, RBC   A �
MED: 100-2, 15, 80

85549   Muramidase   A �
MED: 100-2, 15, 80

To report nitroblue tetrazolium dye test, consult CPT code 86384.

85555   Osmotic fragility, RBC; unincubated   A �
MED: 100-2, 15, 80

85557   incubated   A �
MED: 100-2, 15, 80

To report packed cell volume, consult CPT code 85013. To report partial throboplastin time, consult CPT codes 85730 and 85732. To report parasites, blood (e.g., malaria smears), consult CPT code 87207. To report plasmin, consult CPT code 85400. To report plasminogen, consult CPT code 85420. To report plasminogen factor, consult CPT code 85415.

85576   Platelet, aggregation (in vitro), each agent   A �
MED: 100-2, 15, 80; 100-4, 12, 60

AMA: 1996, Jul, 10

85597   Platelet neutralization   A �
MED: 100-2, 15, 80

85610   Prothrombin time;   A ✕ �
MED: 100-2, 15, 80; 100-3, 190.10; 100-3, 190.17

85611   substitution, plasma fractions, each   A �
MED: 100-2, 15, 80

85612   Russell viper venom time (includes venom); undiluted   A �
MED: 100-2, 15, 80

26 / TC Professional/Technical Component   80 / 80 Assist-at-Surgery Allowed/With Documentation   ⊙ Conscious Sedation
Unlisted   Not Covered   **MED:** Pubs 100/NCD Reference   1 - 9 ASC Group   63 Modifier 63 Exempt
612 — Path/Lab   CPT only © 2005 American Medical Association. All Rights Reserved. *(Black Ink)*   © 2005 Ingenix, Inc. *(Blue Ink)*

| 85613 | **diluted** | Ⓐ ▥ |
| | MED: 100-2, 15, 80 | |

To report red blood cell count, consult CPT codes 85025, 85027, and 85041.

| 85635 | **Reptilase test** | Ⓐ ▥ |
| | MED: 100-2, 15, 80 | |

To report reticulocyte count, consult CPT codes 85044 and 85045.

| 85651 | **Sedimentation rate, erythrocyte; non-automated** | Ⓐ ✖ |
| | MED: 100-2, 15, 80 | |

85652	**automated**	Ⓐ ▥
	MED: 100-2, 15, 80	
	Westergren test	

| 85660 | **Sickling of RBC, reduction** | Ⓐ ▥ |
| | MED: 100-2, 15, 80 | |

If hemoglobin electophoresis is performed, consult CPT codes 83020. For smears (e.g., for parasites, malaria), consult CPT code 87207.

| 85670 | **Thrombin time; plasma** | Ⓐ ▥ |
| | MED: 100-2, 15, 80 | |

| 85675 | **titer** | Ⓐ ▥ |
| | MED: 100-2, 15, 80 | |

| 85705 | **Thromboplastin inhibition, tissue** | Ⓐ ▥ |
| | MED: 100-2, 15, 80 | |

To report individual clotting factors, consult CPT codes 85245-85247.

85730	**Thromboplastin time, partial (PTT); plasma or whole blood**	Ⓐ ▥
	MED: 100-2, 15, 80; 100-3, 190.16	
	Hicks-Pitney test	

| 85732 | **substitution, plasma fractions, each** | Ⓐ ▥ |
| | MED: 100-2, 15, 80 | |

| 85810 | **Viscosity** | Ⓐ |
| | MED: 100-2, 15, 80 | |

To report Von Willebrand factor assay, consult CPT codes 85245-85247. To report a white blood cell (WBC) count, consult CPT codes 85025, 85027, 85048, and 89050.

| 85999 | **Unlisted hematology and coagulation procedure** | Ⓐ |
| | MED: 100-2, 15, 80 | |

IMMUNOLOGY

Acetylcholine receptor antibody, consult CPT codes 86255, 86256. Actinomyces to antibodies, consult CPT codes 86602. Adrenal cortex antibodies, consult CPT codes 86255, 86256. To report tuberculosis test, cell mediated immunity measurement of gamma interferon antigen response, consult CPT Category III code 0010T.

| 86000 | **Agglutinins, febrile (eg, Brucella, Francisella, Murine typhus, Q fever, Rocky Mountain spotted fever, scrub typhus), each antigen** | Ⓐ |
| | MED: 100-2, 15, 80 | |

To report antibodies to infectious agents, consult CPT codes 86602-86804.

▥ CCI Comp ⑤⓪ Bilateral Proc. ✚ CPT Add-on Code ⊘ Modifier -51 Exempt ♂/♀ Male/Female ✖ CLIA Waived Test
● New Code ▲ Revised Code Ⓜ Maternity Edit Ⓐ Age Edit Ⓐ–Ⓨ APC Status Ind. **AMA:** CPT Assistant

Pathology and Laboratory

86001 — 86078

86001   **Allergen specific IgG quantitative or semiquantitative, each allergen**   Ⓐ ⌐⌐
MED: 100-2, 15, 80

To report agglutinins and autohemolysins, consult CPT codes 86940 and 86941.

86003   **Allergen specific IgE; quantitative or semiquantitative, each allergen**   Ⓐ ⌐⌐
MED: 100-2, 15, 80

AMA: 1994, Spring, 31

To report total quantitative IgE, consult CPT code 82785.

86005   **qualitative, multiallergen screen (dipstick, paddle or disk)**   Ⓐ
MED: 100-2, 15, 80

AMA: 1994, Spring, 31

To report total qualitative IgE, consult CPT code 83518. To report alpha-1 antitrypsin, consult CPT codes 82103 and 82104. To report alpha-1 feto-protein, consult CPT codes 82105 and 82106. To report anti-AChR (acetylcholine receptor) antibody titer, consult CPT codes 86255 and 86256. To report anticardiolipin antibody, consult CPT code 86147. To report anti-DNA, consult CPT code 86225. To report anti-deoxyribonuclease titer, consult CPT code 86215.

86021   **Antibody identification; leukocyte antibodies**   Ⓐ ⌐⌐
MED: 100-2, 15, 80

86022   **platelet antibodies**   Ⓐ ⌐⌐
MED: 100-2, 15, 80

86023   **platelet associated immunoglobulin assay**   Ⓐ ⌐⌐
MED: 100-2, 15, 80

86038   **Antinuclear antibodies (ANA);**   Ⓐ ⌐⌐
MED: 100-2, 15, 80

86039   **titer**   Ⓐ ⌐⌐
MED: 100-2, 15, 80

To report antistreptococcal antibody (e.g., anti-DNAse), consult CPT code 86215. To report antistreptokinase titer, consult CPT code 86590.

86060   **Antistreptolysin O; titer**   Ⓐ ⌐⌐
MED: 100-2, 15, 80

To report antibodies to infectious agents, consult CPT codes 86602-86804.

86063   **screen**   Ⓐ
MED: 100-2, 15, 80

To report antibodies to infectious agents, consult CPT codes 86602-86804. To report antibodies to Blastomyces, consult CPT code 86612.

~~**86064**~~   ~~**B cells, total count**~~

(For B cells, total count, use 86355)

86077   **Blood bank physician services; difficult cross match and/or evaluation of irregular antibody(s), interpretation and written report**   ⓧ 80
MED: 100-2, 15, 80; 100-4, 12, 60

86078   **investigation of transfusion reaction including suspicion of transmissible disease, interpretation and written report**   ⓧ 80
MED: 100-2, 15, 80; 100-4, 12, 60

86079 authorization for deviation from standard blood banking procedures (eg, use of outdated blood, transfusion of Rh incompatible units), with written report ☒ 80
MED: 100-2, 15, 80; 100-4, 12, 60

To report antibodies to candida, consult CPT code 86628. To report skin testing, consult CPT code 86485. To report antibodies to brucella, consult CPT code 86622.

86140 C-reactive protein; Ⓐ
MED: 100-2, 15, 80

To report candidiasis, consult CPT code 86628.

86141   high sensitivity (hsCRP) Ⓐ ☒
MED: 100-2, 15, 80

86146 Beta 2 Glycoprotein I antibody, each Ⓐ
MED: 100-2, 15, 80

86147 Cardiolipin (phospholipid) antibody, each Ig class Ⓐ
MED: 100-2, 15, 80

86148 Anti-phosphatidylserine (phospholipid) antibody Ⓐ
MED: 100-2, 15, 80

AMA: 1997, Nov, 30

To report antiprothrombin (phopholipid cofactor) antibody, consult CPT Category III code 0030T.

86155 Chemotaxis assay, specify method Ⓐ
MED: 100-2, 15, 80

To report antibodies to coccidioides, consult CPT code 86635. To report skin testing, consult CPT code 86490.

To report clostridium difficile toxin, consult CPT code 87230.

86156 Cold agglutinin; screen Ⓐ
MED: 100-2, 15, 80

86157   titer Ⓐ ☒
MED: 100-2, 15, 80

86160 Complement; antigen, each component Ⓐ
MED: 100-2, 15, 80

86161   functional activity, each component Ⓐ
MED: 100-2, 15, 80

86162   total hemolytic (CH50) Ⓐ
MED: 100-2, 15, 80

86171 Complement fixation tests, each antigen Ⓐ
MED: 100-2, 15, 80

If a Coombs test is performed, consult CPT codes 86880-86886.

86185 Counterimmunoelectrophoresis, each antigen Ⓐ ☒
MED: 100-2, 15, 80

To report antibodies to cryptococcus, consult CPT code 86641.

● **86200** Cyclic citrullinated peptide (CCP), antibody

86215 Deoxyribonuclease, antibody Ⓐ ☒
MED: 100-2, 15, 80

86225   **Deoxyribonucleic acid (DNA) antibody; native or double stranded**   Ⓐ 🔲
MED: 100-2, 15, 80

To report antibodies to echinococcus, consult the appropriate code according to the specific method used. If an HIV antibody test is performed, consult CPT codes 86701-86703.

86226   **single stranded**   Ⓐ 🔲
MED: 100-2, 15, 80

To report fluorescent noninfectious agent antibody, consult CPT codes 86255 and 86256.

86235   **Extractable nuclear antigen, antibody to, any method (eg, nRNP, SS-A, SS-B, Sm, RNP, Sc170, J01), each antibody**   Ⓐ 🔲
MED: 100-2, 15, 80; 100-3, 220.8

86243   **Fc receptor**   Ⓐ
MED: 100-2, 15, 80

To report antibodies to filaria, consult the appropriate code according to the specific method used.

86255   **Fluorescent noninfectious agent antibody; screen, each antibody**   Ⓐ 🔲
MED: 100-2, 15, 80; 100-4, 12, 60

AMA: 1998, Nov, 27

86256   **titer, each antibody**   Ⓐ 🔲
MED: 100-2, 15, 80; 100-4, 12, 60

To report fluorescent technique for antigen identification in tissue, consult CPT code 88346; for indirect fluorescence, consult CPT code 88347. If a confirmatory test is performed for treponema pallidum, (e.g., FTA), consult CPT code 86781. To report gel (agar) diffusion tests, consult CPT code 86331.

86277   **Growth hormone, human (HGH), antibody**   Ⓐ
MED: 100-2, 15, 80

86280   **Hemagglutination inhibition test (HAI)**   Ⓐ
MED: 100-2, 15, 80

To report rubella, consult CPT code 86762. To report antibodies to infectious agents, consult CPT codes 86602-86804. To report hepatitis delta agent, antibody, consult CPT code 86692.

86294   **Immunoassay for tumor antigen, qualitative or semiquantitative (eg, bladder tumor antigen)**   Ⓐ ✖
MED: 100-2, 15, 80

86300   **Immunoassay for tumor antigen, quantitative; CA 15-3 (27.29)**   Ⓐ 🔲
MED: 100-2, 15, 80; 100-3, 190.29

86301   **CA 19-9**   Ⓐ 🔲
MED: 100-2, 15, 80; 100-3, 190.30

86304   **CA 125**   Ⓐ 🔲
MED: 100-2, 15, 80; 100-3, 190.28

To report measurement of serum HER-2/neu oncoprotein, consult CPT code 83950. For hepatitis delta agent, antibody, consult CPT code 86692.

86308   **Heterophile antibodies; screening**   Ⓐ ✖
MED: 100-2, 15, 80

To report antibodies to infectious agents, consult CPT codes 86602-86804.

26 / 🄣 Professional/Technical Component   **80**/**80** Assist-at-Surgery Allowed/With Documentation   ⊙ Conscious Sedation

Unlisted   Not Covered   **MED:** Pubs 100/NCD Reference   **1**-**9** ASC Group   ㊿ Modifier 63 Exempt

616 — Path/Lab   CPT only © 2005 American Medical Association. All Rights Reserved. *(Black Ink)*   © 2005 Ingenix, Inc. *(Blue Ink)*

| 86309 | titer | A |
| | MED: 100-2, 15, 80 | |

86310	titers after absorption with beef cells and guinea pig kidney	A
	MED: 100-2, 15, 80	
	AMA: 1993, Fall, 26	

To report antibodies to histoplasma, consult CPT code 86698. To report skin testing, consult CPT code 86510. To report antibodies to infectious agents, consult CPT codes 86602-86804. To report human growth hormone antibody, consult CPT code 86277.

86316	Immunoassay for tumor antigen, other antigen, quantitative (eg, CA 50, 72-4, 549), each	A ⚡
	MED: 100-2, 15, 80	
	AMA: 1999, Dec, 10; 1999, Aug, 5; 1998, Apr, 15; 1996, May, 11; 1996, Aug, 11	

86317	Immunoassay for infectious agent antibody, quantitative, not otherwise specified	A ⚡
	MED: 100-2, 15, 80	
	AMA: 1997, Nov, 30-31	

To report immunoassay techniques To report antigens, consult CPT codes 83516, 83518, 83519, 83520, 87301-87450, and 87810-87899. To report particle agglutination procedures, consult CPT code 86403.

| 86318 | Immunoassay for infectious agent antibody, qualitative or semiquantitative, single step method (eg, reagent strip) | A ❌ |
| | MED: 100-2, 15, 80 | |

| 86320 | Immunoelectrophoresis; serum | A ⚡ |
| | MED: 100-2, 15, 80; 100-4, 12, 60 | |

| 86325 | other fluids (eg, urine, cerebrospinal fluid) with concentration | A ⚡ |
| | MED: 100-2, 15, 80; 100-4, 12, 60 | |

| 86327 | crossed (2-dimensional assay) | A ⚡ |
| | MED: 100-2, 15, 80; 100-4, 12, 60 | |

86329	Immunodiffusion; not elsewhere specified	A ⚡
	MED: 100-2, 15, 80	
	AMA: 2000, Aug, 11	

| 86331 | gel diffusion, qualitative (Ouchterlony), each antigen or antibody | A ⚡ |
| | MED: 100-2, 15, 80 | |

| 86332 | Immune complex assay | A |
| | MED: 100-2, 15, 80 | |

| 86334 | Immunofixation electrophoresis; serum | A ⚡ |
| | MED: 100-2, 15, 80; 100-4, 12, 60 | |

| 86335 | other fluids with concentration (eg, urine, CSF) | A ⚡ |

| 86336 | Inhibin A | A |
| | MED: 100-2, 15, 80 | |

| 86337 | Insulin antibodies | A |
| | MED: 100-2, 15, 80 | |

| 86340 | Intrinsic factor antibodies | A |
| | MED: 100-2, 15, 80 | |

To report antibodies to leptospira, consult CPT code 86720. To report leukoagglutinins, consult CPT code 86021.

86341   **Islet cell antibody**   A
MED: 100-2, 15, 80

AMA: 1994, Summer, 6

86343   **Leukocyte histamine release test (LHR)**   A
MED: 100-2, 15, 80

86344   **Leukocyte phagocytosis**   A ☐
MED: 100-2, 15, 80

86353   **Lymphocyte transformation, mitogen (phytomitogen) or antigen induced blastogenesis**   A ☐
MED: 100-2, 15, 80; 100-3, 190.8

To report lymphocytes immunophenotyping, consult CPT codes 88182 and 88189 for cytometry and consult CPT codes 88342 and 88346 for microscopic techniques. To report malaria antibodies, consult CPT code 86750.

86353   **Lymphocyte transformation, mitogen (phytomitogen) or antigen induced blastogenesis**

● **86355**   **B cells, total count**

● **86357**   **Natural killer (NK) cells, total count**

86359   **T cells; total count**   A ☐
MED: 100-2, 15, 80

AMA: 1997, Nov, 30

86360   **absolute CD4 and CD8 count, including ratio**   A ☐
MED: 100-2, 15, 80

AMA: 1997, Nov, 30

86361   **absolute CD4 count**   A ☐
MED: 100-2, 15, 80

AMA: 1997, Nov, 30

● **86367**   **Stem cells (ie, CD34), total count**

To report flow cytometric immunophenotyping for the assessment of potential hematolymphoid neoplasia, consult CPT codes 88184-88189.

86376   **Microsomal antibodies (eg, thyroid or liver-kidney), each**   A ☐
MED: 100-2, 15, 80

86378   **Migration inhibitory factor test (MIF)**   A ☐
MED: 100-2, 15, 80

To report mitochondrial antibody, liver, consult CPT codes 86255 and 86256. To report mononucleosis, consult CPT codes 86308-86310.

86379   ~~Natural killer (NK) cells, total count~~

(For natural killer cells, total count, use 86357)

86382   **Neutralization test, viral**   A ☐
MED: 100-2, 15, 80

86384   **Nitroblue tetrazolium dye test (NTD)**   A ☐
MED: 100-2, 15, 80

To report Ouchterlony diffusion, consult CPT code 86331. To report platelet antibodies, consult CPT codes 86022 and 86023.

86403   **Particle agglutination; screen, each antibody**   A
MED: 100-2, 15, 80

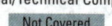

86406	**titer, each antibody**	A
	MED: 100-2, 15, 80	

If a pregnancy test is conducted, consult CPT codes 84702 and 84703. If a rapid plasma reagin test (RPR) is conducted, consult CPT codes 86592 and 86593.

86430	**Rheumatoid factor; qualitative**	A
	MED: 100-2, 15, 80	
86431	**quantitative**	A
	MED: 100-2, 15, 80	

If a serologic test is performed to test for syphilis, consult CPT codes 86592 and 86593.

● 86480 **Tuberculosis test, cell mediated immunity measurement of gamma interferon antigen response**

86485 **Skin test; candida**   X TC 80

MED: 100-2, 15, 80

To report antibody, candida, consult CPT code 86628.

86490 **coccidioidomycosis**   X TC 80

MED: 100-2, 15, 80

86510 **histoplasmosis**   X TC 80

MED: 100-2, 15, 80

To report histoplasma, antibody, consult CPT code 86698.

86580 **tuberculosis, intradermal**   X TC 80 ▣

MED: 100-2, 15, 80

Heaf test

~~86585~~   ~~tuberculosis, tine test~~

(For tuberculosis testing by intradermal (Mantoux) test use 86580)

86586 **Unlisted antigen, each**   X TC 80 ▣

MED: 100-2, 15, 80

AMA: 1998, Jul, 11

~~86587~~   ~~Stem cells (ie, CD34), total count~~

(For stem cells, total count, use 86367)

86590 **Streptokinase, antibody**   A

MED: 100-2, 15, 80

To report antibodies to infectious agents, consult CPT codes 86602-86804. To report streptolysin O antibody, see antistreptolysin O codes 86060 and 86063.

86592 **Syphilis test; qualitative (eg, VDRL, RPR, ART)**   A

MED: 100-2, 15, 80

To report antibodies to infectious agents, consult CPT codes 86602-86804.

Wasserman test

86593 **quantitative**   A

MED: 100-2, 15, 80

To report antibodies to infectious agents, consult CPT codes 86602-86804.

To report tetanus antibody, consult 86774. To report Thyroglobulin antibody, consult 86800. To report Thyroglobulin, consult 84432. To report Thyroid microsomal antibody, consult 86376. To report toxoplasma antibody, consult 86777-86778.

CPT codes 86602-86804 are qualitative or semiquantitative immunoassays performed by multiple step methods for the detection of antibodies to infectious agents. To report immunoassays by single step method such as reagent strips, consult code 86318. Report procedure codes for identification of antibodies as precisely as possible. When multiple tests are performed to detect antibodies to organisms classified more precisely than the specificity allowed by available codes, it is appropriate to code each as a separate service. To report assays that are performed for antibodies to Coxsackie A and B species, each assay should be reported separately. If multiple assays are performed for antibodies of different immunoglobulin classes, each assay should be reported separately.

To report the detection of antibodies other than those to infectious agents, consult specific antibody (e.g., 86021, 86022, 86023, 86376, 86800, 86850-86870) or specific method (e.g., 83516, 86255, 86256). To report infectious agent/antigen detection, consult 87260-87899

To report infectious agent/antigen detection, consult CPT codes 87620-87899.

86602	**Antibody; actinomyces**	A
	MED: 100-2, 15, 80	
	AMA: 1993, Fall, 26	
86603	**adenovirus**	A
	MED: 100-2, 15, 80	
	AMA: 1993, Fall, 26	
86606	**Aspergillus**	A
	MED: 100-2, 15, 80	
	AMA: 1993, Fall, 26	
86609	**bacterium, not elsewhere specified**	A
	MED: 100-2, 15, 80	
	AMA: 1993, Fall, 26	
86611	**Bartonella**	A
	MED: 100-2, 15, 80	
	AMA: 1993, Fall, 26	
86612	**Blastomyces**	A
	MED: 100-2, 15, 80	
	AMA: 1993, Fall, 26	

To report infectious agent/antigen detection, consult CPT codes 87620-87899.

86615	**Bordetella**	A
	MED: 100-2, 15, 80	
	AMA: 1993, Fall, 26	
86617	**Borrelia burgdorferi (Lyme disease) confirmatory test (eg, Western Blot or immunoblot)**	A
	MED: 100-2, 15, 80	
	AMA: 1993, Fall, 26	
86618	**Borrelia burgdorferi (Lyme disease)**	A ✖
	MED: 100-2, 15, 80	
	AMA: 1993, Fall, 26	
86619	**Borrelia (relapsing fever)**	A
	MED: 100-2, 15, 80	
	AMA: 1993, Fall, 26	

26 / **TC** Professional/Technical Component   **80** / **80** Assist-at-Surgery Allowed/With Documentation   ⊙ Conscious Sedation

Unlisted   Not Covered   **MED:** Pubs 100/NCD Reference   **1** - **9** ASC Group   ⑥³ Modifier 63 Exempt

620 — Path/Lab   CPT only © 2005 American Medical Association. All Rights Reserved. *(Black Ink)*   © 2005 Ingenix, Inc. *(Blue Ink)*

86622	**Brucella**	A

MED: 100-2, 15, 80

AMA: 1993, Fall, 26

86625	**Campylobacter**	A

MED: 100-2, 15, 80

AMA: 1993, Fall, 26

86628	**Candida**	A

MED: 100-2, 15, 80

AMA: 1993, Fall, 26

To report a skin test for candida, consult CPT code 86485.

86631	**Chlamydia**	A

MED: 100-2, 15, 80

AMA: 1993, Fall, 26

To report infectious agent/antigen detection, consult CPT codes 87620-87899.

86632	**Chlamydia, IgM**	A

MED: 100-2, 15, 80

AMA: 1997, Nov, 31; 1993, Fall, 26

To report chlamydia antigen, consult CPT codes 87270 and 87320. To report fluorescent antibody technique, consult CPT codes 86255 and 86256.

86635	**Coccidioides**	A

MED: 100-2, 15, 80

AMA: 1993, Fall, 26

To report infectious agent/antigen detection, consult CPT codes 87620-87899.

86638	**Coxiella burnetii (Q fever)**	A

MED: 100-2, 15, 80

AMA: 1993, Fall, 26

86641	**Cryptococcus**	A

MED: 100-2, 15, 80

AMA: 1993, Fall, 26

86644	**cytomegalovirus (CMV)**	A

MED: 100-2, 15, 80

AMA: 1993, Fall, 26

86645	**cytomegalovirus (CMV), IgM**	A

MED: 100-2, 15, 80

AMA: 1993, Fall, 26

To report infectious agent/antigen detection, consult CPT codes 87620-87899.

86648	**Diphtheria**	A

MED: 100-2, 15, 80

AMA: 1993, Fall, 26

86651	**encephalitis, California (La Crosse)**	A

MED: 100-2, 15, 80

AMA: 1993, Fall, 26

 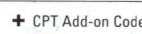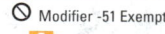

86652	encephalitis, Eastern equine	A
	MED: 100-2, 15, 80	
	AMA: 1993, Fall, 26	

86653	encephalitis, St. Louis	A
	MED: 100-2, 15, 80	
	AMA: 1993, Fall, 26	

86654	encephalitis, Western equine	A
	MED: 100-2, 15, 80	
	AMA: 1993, Fall, 26	

86658	enterovirus (eg, Coxsackie, echo, polio)	A
	MED: 100-2, 15, 80	
	AMA: 1993, Fall, 26	

To report antibodies to trichinella, consult CPT code 86784. To report antibodies to trypanosoma, consult the code appropriate for the specific method used. If skin testing is performed for tuberculosis, consult CPT code 86580. To report viral antibodies, consult the code appropriate for the specific method used.

86663	Epstein-Barr (EB) virus, early antigen (EA)	A
	MED: 100-2, 15, 80	
	AMA: 1993, Fall, 26	

86664	Epstein-Barr (EB) virus, nuclear antigen (EBNA)	A
	MED: 100-2, 15, 80; 100-3, 220.8	
	AMA: 1993, Fall, 26	

86665	Epstein-Barr (EB) virus, viral capsid (VCA)	A
	MED: 100-2, 15, 80	
	AMA: 1993, Fall, 26	

86666	Ehrlichia	A
	MED: 100-2, 15, 80	
	AMA: 1993, Fall, 26	

86668	Francisella tularensis	A
	MED: 100-2, 15, 80	
	AMA: 1993, Fall, 26	

86671	fungus, not elsewhere specified	A
	MED: 100-2, 15, 80	
	AMA: 1993, Fall, 26	

86674	Giardia lamblia	A
	MED: 100-2, 15, 80	
	AMA: 1993, Fall, 26	

86677	Helicobacter Pylori	A
	MED: 100-2, 15, 80	
	AMA: 1993, Fall, 26	

86682	helminth, not elsewhere specified	A
	MED: 100-2, 15, 80	
	AMA: 1993, Fall, 26	

26 / TC Professional/Technical Component   80/80 Assist-at-Surgery Allowed/With Documentation   ⊙ Conscious Sedation
Unlisted   Not Covered   MED: Pubs 100/NCD Reference   1-9 ASC Group   63 Modifier 63 Exempt
622 — Path/Lab   CPT only © 2005 American Medical Association. All Rights Reserved. (Black Ink)   © 2005 Ingenix, Inc. (Blue Ink)

86684	**Haemophilus influenza**	A

MED: 100-2, 15, 80

AMA: 1993, Fall, 26

86687	**HTLV-I**	A

MED: 100-2, 15, 80

AMA: 1993, Fall, 26

To report infectious agent/antigen detection, consult CPT codes 87620-87899.

86688	**HTLV-II**	A

MED: 100-2, 15, 80

AMA: 1993, Fall, 26

86689	**HTLV or HIV antibody, confirmatory test (eg, Western Blot)**	A

MED: 100-2, 15, 80; 100-3, 190.14; 100-3, 190.9

AMA: 1993, Fall, 26

86692	**hepatitis, delta agent**	A

MED: 100-2, 15, 80

AMA: 1997, Nov, 31; 1993, Fall, 26

To report hepatitis delta agent, antigen, consult CPT code 87380.

86694	**herpes simplex, non-specific type test**	A

MED: 100-2, 15, 80

AMA: 1993, Fall, 26

86695	**herpes simplex, type 1**	A

MED: 100-2, 15, 80

AMA: 1993, Fall, 26

86696	**herpes simplex, type 2**	A

MED: 100-2, 15, 80

AMA: 1997, Nov, 31; 1993, Fall, 26

86698	**histoplasma**	A

MED: 100-2, 15, 80

AMA: 1993, Fall, 26

86701	**HIV-1**	A ✕

MED: 100-2, 15, 80; 100-3, 190.14; 100-3, 190.9

AMA: 1993, Fall, 26

86702	**HIV-2**	A

MED: 100-2, 15, 80; 100-3, 190.14; 100-3, 190.9

AMA: 1993, Fall, 26

86703	**HIV-1 and HIV-2, single assay**	A

MED: 100-2, 15, 80; 100-3, 190.14; 100-3, 190.9

AMA: 1997, Nov, 31; 1993, Fall, 26

To report HIV-1 antigen, consult CPT code 87390. To report HIV-2 antigen, consult CPT code 87391. If a confirmatory test is conducted for the HIV antibody, (e.g., Western Blot), consult CPT code 86689.

86704	**Hepatitis B core antibody (HBcAb); total**	A

MED: 100-2, 15, 80

AMA: 1997, Nov, 31-32; 1993, Fall, 26

🅛 CCI Comp   50 Bilateral Proc.   ✚ CPT Add-on Code   ⊘ Modifier -51 Exempt   ♂/♀ Male/Female   ✕ CLIA Waived Test
● New Code   ▲ Revised Code   🅜 Maternity Edit   🅐 Age Edit   🅐–🆈 APC Status Ind.   **AMA:** CPT Assistant

© 2005 Ingenix, Inc. *(Blue Ink)*   CPT only © 2005 American Medical Association. All Rights Reserved. *(Black Ink)*   Path/Lab — 623

Pathology and Laboratory

86705 — 86735

86705   **IgM antibody**   A
        MED: 100-2, 15, 80

        AMA: 1997, Nov, 31-32; 1993, Fall, 26

86706   **Hepatitis B surface antibody (HBsAb)**   A
        MED: 100-2, 15, 80; 100-3, 190.10

        AMA: 1997, Nov, 31-32; 1993, Fall, 26

86707   **Hepatitis Be antibody (HBeAb)**   A
        MED: 100-2, 15, 80

        AMA: 1997, Nov, 31-32; 1993, Fall, 26

86708   **Hepatitis A antibody (HAAb); total**   A
        MED: 100-2, 15, 80

        AMA: 2000, Jun, 11; 1997, Nov, 31-32; 1993, Fall, 26

86709   **IgM antibody**   A
        MED: 100-2, 15, 80

        AMA: 2000, Jun, 11; 1997, Nov, 31-32; 1993, Fall, 26

86710   **Antibody; influenza virus**   A
        MED: 100-2, 15, 80

        AMA: 1993, Fall, 26

86713   **Legionella**   A
        MED: 100-2, 15, 80

        AMA: 1993, Fall, 26

86717   **Leishmania**   A
        MED: 100-2, 15, 80

        AMA: 1993, Fall, 26

86720   **Leptospira**   A
        MED: 100-2, 15, 80

        AMA: 1993, Fall, 26

86723   **Listeria monocytogenes**   A
        MED: 100-2, 15, 80

        AMA: 1993, Fall, 26

86727   **lymphocytic choriomeningitis**   A
        MED: 100-2, 15, 80

        AMA: 1993, Fall, 26

86729   **lymphogranuloma venereum**   A
        MED: 100-2, 15, 80

        AMA: 1993, Fall, 26

86732   **mucormycosis**   A
        MED: 100-2, 15, 80

        AMA: 1993, Fall, 26

86735   **mumps**   A
        MED: 100-2, 15, 80

        AMA: 1993, Fall, 26

86738   **mycoplasma**   Ⓐ
MED: 100-2, 15, 80
AMA: 1993, Fall, 26

86741   **Neisseria meningitidis**   Ⓐ
MED: 100-2, 15, 80
AMA: 1993, Fall, 26

86744   **Nocardia**   Ⓐ
MED: 100-2, 15, 80
AMA: 1993, Fall, 26

86747   **parvovirus**   Ⓐ
MED: 100-2, 15, 80
AMA: 1993, Fall, 26

86750   **Plasmodium (malaria)**   Ⓐ
MED: 100-2, 15, 80
AMA: 1993, Fall, 26

86753   **protozoa, not elsewhere specified**   Ⓐ
MED: 100-2, 15, 80
AMA: 1993, Fall, 26

86756   **respiratory syncytial virus**   Ⓐ
MED: 100-2, 15, 80
AMA: 1993, Fall, 26

86757   **Rickettsia**   Ⓐ
MED: 100-2, 15, 80
AMA: 1993, Fall, 26

86759   **rotavirus**   Ⓐ
MED: 100-2, 15, 80
AMA: 1993, Fall, 26

86762   **rubella**   Ⓐ
MED: 100-2, 15, 80
AMA: 1993, Fall, 26

86765   **rubeola**   Ⓐ
MED: 100-2, 15, 80
AMA: 1993, Fall, 26

86768   **Salmonella**   Ⓐ
MED: 100-2, 15, 80
AMA: 1993, Fall, 26

86771   **Shigella**   Ⓐ
MED: 100-2, 15, 80
AMA: 1993, Fall, 26

86774   **tetanus**   Ⓐ
MED: 100-2, 15, 80
AMA: 1993, Fall, 26

 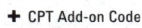

86777	**Toxoplasma**	A
	MED: 100-2, 15, 80	
	AMA: 1993, Fall, 26	

86778	**Toxoplasma, IgM**	A
	MED: 100-2, 15, 80	
	AMA: 1993, Fall, 26	

86781	**Treponema pallidum, confirmatory test (eg, FTA-abs)**	A
	MED: 100-2, 15, 80	
	AMA: 1993, Fall, 26	

86784	**Trichinella**	A
	MED: 100-2, 15, 80	
	AMA: 1993, Fall, 26	

86787	**varicella-zoster**	A
	MED: 100-2, 15, 80	
	AMA: 1993, Fall, 26	

86790	**virus, not elsewhere specified**	A
	MED: 100-2, 15, 80	
	AMA: 1993, Fall, 26	

86793	**Yersinia**	A
	MED: 100-2, 15, 80	
	AMA: 1993, Fall, 26	

86800	**Thyroglobulin antibody**	A
	MED: 100-2, 15, 80	
	AMA: 1993, Fall, 26	

To report thyroglobulin, consult CPT code 84432.

86803	**Hepatitis C antibody;**	A
	MED: 100-2, 15, 80	
	AMA: 1997, Nov, 31-32; 1993, Fall, 26	

86804	**confirmatory test (eg, immunoblot)**	A
	MED: 100-2, 15, 80	
	AMA: 1997, Nov, 31-32; 1993, Fall, 26	

TISSUE TYPING

| 86805 | **Lymphocytotoxicity assay, visual crossmatch; with titration** | A ⏩ |
| | MED: 100-2, 15, 80 | |

| 86806 | **without titration** | A |
| | MED: 100-2, 15, 80 | |

86807	**Serum screening for cytotoxic percent reactive antibody (PRA); standard method**	A
	MED: 100-2, 15, 80	
	AMA: 2001, Jun, 11	

86808	**quick method**	A
	MED: 100-2, 15, 80	
	AMA: 2001, Jun, 11	

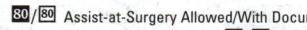

26 / **TC** Professional/Technical Component   **80** / **80** Assist-at-Surgery Allowed/With Documentation   ⊙ Conscious Sedation

Unlisted   Not Covered   **MED:** Pubs 100/NCD Reference   **1**-**9** ASC Group   63 Modifier 63 Exempt

626 — Path/Lab   CPT only © 2005 American Medical Association. All Rights Reserved. *(Black Ink)*   © 2005 Ingenix, Inc. *(Blue Ink)*

86812	**HLA typing; A, B, or C (eg, A10, B7, B27), single antigen** MED: 100-2, 15, 80; 100-3, 190.1	A
86813	**A, B, or C, multiple antigens** MED: 100-2, 15, 80; 100-3, 190.1	A 🔲
86816	**DR/DQ, single antigen** MED: 100-2, 15, 80; 100-3, 190.1	A
86817	**DR/DQ, multiple antigens** MED: 100-2, 15, 80; 100-3, 190.1	A 🔲
86821	**lymphocyte culture, mixed (MLC)** MED: 100-2, 15, 80; 100-3, 190.1; 100-3, 190.8	A
86822	**lymphocyte culture, primed (PLC)** MED: 100-2, 15, 80; 100-3, 190.1; 100-3, 190.8	A
86849	**Unlisted immunology procedure** MED: 100-2, 15, 80 AMA: 1998, Mar, 10	A

TRANSFUSION MEDICINE

For apheresis, consult CPT code 36511 or 36512. For therapeutic phlebotomy, consult CPT code 99195.

86850	**Antibody screen, RBC, each serum technique** MED: 100-2, 15, 80 AMA: 1993, Fall, 25	X
86860	**Antibody elution (RBC), each elution** MED: 100-2, 15, 80	X
86870	**Antibody identification, RBC antibodies, each panel for each serum technique** MED: 100-2, 15, 80 AMA: 2001, Mar, 10; 1993, Fall, 25	X
86880	**Antihuman globulin test (Coombs test); direct, each antiserum** MED: 100-2, 15, 80	X
86885	**indirect, qualitative, each antiserum** MED: 100-2, 15, 80	X
86886	**indirect, titer, each antiserum** MED: 100-2, 15, 80	X
86890	**Autologous blood or component, collection processing and storage; predeposited** MED: 100-1, 3, 20.5.2; 100-2, 15, 80; 100-3, 110.7; 100-3, 110.8 AMA: 1996, Apr, 2	X 🔲
86891	**intra- or postoperative salvage** MED: 100-1, 3, 20.5.2; 100-2, 15, 80; 100-3, 110.7; 100-3, 110.8	X 🔲
	To report physician services to autologous donors, consult CPT codes 99201-99204.	
86900	**Blood typing; ABO** MED: 100-2, 15, 80	X

🔲 CCI Comp   50 Bilateral Proc.   ✚ CPT Add-on Code   ⊘ Modifier -51 Exempt   ♂/♀ Male/Female   ❌ CLIA Waived Test

● New Code   ▲ Revised Code   M Maternity Edit   A Age Edit   Ⓐ—Ⓨ APC Status Ind.   **AMA:** CPT Assistant

86901	**Rh (D)**	☒

MED: 100-2, 15, 80

AMA: 1993, Fall, 25

86903	**antigen screening for compatible blood unit using reagent serum, per unit screened**	☒

MED: 100-2, 15, 80

86904	**antigen screening for compatible unit using patient serum, per unit screened**	☒

MED: 100-2, 15, 80

86905	**RBC antigens, other than ABO or Rh (D), each**	☒

MED: 100-2, 15, 80

86906	**Rh phenotyping, complete**	☒

MED: 100-2, 15, 80

86910	**Blood typing, for paternity testing, per individual; ABO, Rh and MN**	Ⓔ

MED: 100-2, 15, 80

86911	**each additional antigen system**	Ⓔ

MED: 100-2, 15, 80

86920	**Compatibility test each unit; immediate spin technique**	☒

MED: 100-2, 15, 80

86921	**incubation technique**	☒

MED: 100-2, 15, 80

86922	**antiglobulin technique**	☒

MED: 100-2, 15, 80

● 86923   **electronic**

Code 86923 cannot be reported with 86920-86922 for same unit crossmatch.

86927	**Fresh frozen plasma, thawing, each unit**	☒

MED: 100-2, 15, 80

86930	**Frozen blood, each unit; freezing (includes preparation)**	☒

MED: 100-2, 15, 80

AMA: 1996, Apr, 2

86931	**thawing**	☒ ⏎

MED: 100-2, 15, 80

86932	**freezing (includes preparation) and thawing**	☒ ⏎

MED: 100-2, 15, 80

86940	**Hemolysins and agglutinins; auto, screen, each**	Ⓐ

MED: 100-2, 15, 80

86941	**incubated**	Ⓐ

MED: 100-2, 15, 80

86945	**Irradiation of blood product, each unit**	☒

MED: 100-2, 15, 80

86950	**Leukocyte transfusion**	☒ ⏎

MED: 100-1, 3, 20.5.2; 100-1, 3, 20.5.3; 100-2, 15, 80; 100-3, 110.5; 100-3, 110.7

To report leukapheresis, consult CPT code 36511.

---

26 / TC Professional/Technical Component   **80 / 80** Assist-at-Surgery Allowed/With Documentation   ☉ Conscious Sedation

 Unlisted    Not Covered   **MED:** Pubs 100/NCD Reference   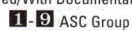 ASC Group   ⑥③ Modifier 63 Exempt

628 — Path/Lab   CPT only © 2005 American Medical Association. All Rights Reserved. *(Black Ink)*   © 2005 Ingenix, Inc. *(Blue Ink)*

● 86960 Volume reduction of blood or blood product (eg, red blood cells or platelets), each unit

86965 Pooling of platelets or other blood products ☒
MED: 100-2, 15, 80; 100-3, 110.8

86970 Pretreatment of RBCs for use in RBC antibody detection, identification, and/or compatibility testing; incubation with chemical agents or drugs, each ☒
MED: 100-2, 15, 80

86971 incubation with enzymes, each ☒
MED: 100-2, 15, 80

86972 by density gradient separation ☒
MED: 100-2, 15, 80

86975 Pretreatment of serum for use in RBC antibody identification; incubation with drugs, each ☒
MED: 100-2, 15, 80

86976 by dilution ☒
MED: 100-2, 15, 80

86977 incubation with inhibitors, each ☒
MED: 100-2, 15, 80

86978 by differential red cell absorption using patient RBCs or RBCs of known phenotype, each absorption ☒
MED: 100-2, 15, 80

86985 Splitting of blood or blood products, each unit ☒
MED: 100-2, 15, 80
AMA: 1996, Apr, 2

86999 Unlisted transfusion medicine procedure ☒
MED: 100-1, 3, 20.5; 100-1, 3, 20.5.2; 100-2, 15, 80

MICROBIOLOGY

87001 Animal inoculation, small animal; with observation Ⓐ
MED: 100-2, 15, 80

87003 with observation and dissection Ⓐ 🔁
MED: 100-2, 15, 80

87015 Concentration (any type), for infectious agents Ⓐ
MED: 100-2, 15, 80

CPT code 87015 should not be reported in conjunction with CPT code 87177.

87040 Culture, bacterial; blood, aerobic, with isolation and presumptive identification of isolates (includes anaerobic culture, if appropriate) Ⓐ 🔁
MED: 100-2, 15, 80
AMA: 2002, Jun, 1; 1997, Aug, 18

87045 stool, aerobic, with isolation and preliminary examination (eg, KIA, LIA), Salmonella and Shigella species Ⓐ 🔁
MED: 100-2, 15, 80

87046 stool, aerobic, additional pathogens, isolation and presumptive identification of isolates, each plate Ⓐ 🔁
MED: 100-2, 15, 80

87070　　　**any other source except urine, blood or stool, aerobic, with isolation and presumptive identification of isolates**　　Ⓐ
MED: 100-2, 15, 80

AMA: 2001, Nov, 10; 1997, Aug, 18

To report urine, consult CPT codes 87086-87088.

87071　　　**quantitative, aerobic with isolation and presumptive identification of isolates, any source except urine, blood or stool**　　Ⓐ ◪
MED: 100-2, 15, 80

To report urine, consult CPT codes 87086-87088.

87073　　　**quantitative, anaerobic with isolation and presumptive identification of isolates, any source except urine, blood or stool**　　Ⓐ ◪
MED: 100-2, 15, 80

To report definitive identification of isolates, consult CPT code 87076 or 87077. To report typing of isolates, consult CPT codes 87140-87158.

87075　　　**any source, except blood, anaerobic with isolation and presumptive identification of isolates**　　Ⓐ
MED: 100-2, 15, 80

87076　　　**anaerobic isolate, additional methods required for definitive identification, each isolate**　　Ⓐ
MED: 100-2, 15, 80

To report GLC (gas liquid chromatography) or HPLC (high pressure lipid chromatography consult CPT code 87143.

87077　　　**aerobic isolate, additional methods required for definitive identification, each isolate**　　Ⓐ ✖
MED: 100-2, 15, 80

AMA: 2001, Nov, 10

87081　　**Culture, presumptive, pathogenic organisms, screening only;**　　Ⓐ
MED: 100-2, 15, 80

AMA: 2001, Nov, 10

87084　　　**with colony estimation from density chart**　　Ⓐ
MED: 100-2, 15, 80

87086　　**Culture, bacterial; quantitative colony count, urine**　　Ⓐ ◪
MED: 100-2, 15, 80; 100-3, 190.12

87088　　　**with isolation and presumptive identification of isolates, urine**　　Ⓐ ◪
MED: 100-2, 15, 80; 100-3, 190.12

87101　　**Culture, fungi (mold or yeast) isolation, with presumptive identification of isolates; skin, hair, or nail**　　Ⓐ
MED: 100-2, 15, 80

AMA: 1999, Sep, 10

87102　　　**other source (except blood)**　　Ⓐ
MED: 100-2, 15, 80

87103　　　**blood**　　Ⓐ
MED: 100-2, 15, 80

87106　　**Culture, fungi, definitive identification, each organism; yeast**　　Ⓐ
MED: 100-2, 15, 80

Report CPT code 87106 in addition to CPT codes 87101, 87102 or 87103 when appropriate.

87107	mold	A
	MED: 100-2, 15, 80	

87109	**Culture, mycoplasma, any source**	A
	MED: 100-2, 15, 80	

87110	**Culture, chlamydia, any source**	A
	MED: 100-2, 15, 80	

To report immunofluorescence staining of shell vials, consult CPT code 87140.

87116 **Culture, tubercle or other acid-fast bacilli (eg, TB, AFB, mycobacteria) any source, with isolation and presumptive identification of isolates**   A
MED: 100-2, 15, 80

87118 **Culture, mycobacterial, definitive identification, each isolate**   A
MED: 100-2, 15, 80

To report nucleic acid probe identification, consult CPT code 87149. To report GLC or HPLC identification consult CPT code 87143.

87140 **Culture, typing; immunofluorescent method, each antiserum**   A ■
MED: 100-2, 15, 80

AMA: 2001, Nov, 10

87143 gas liquid chromatography (GLC) or high pressure liquid chromatography (HPLC) method   A ■
MED: 100-2, 15, 80

87147 immunologic method, other than immunofluoresence (eg, agglutination grouping), per antiserum   A ■
MED: 100-2, 15, 80

AMA: 2002, Apr, 18

87149 identification by nucleic acid probe   A ■
MED: 100-2, 15, 80

AMA: 2001, Nov, 10

87152 identification by pulse field gel typing   A
MED: 100-2, 15, 80

87158 other methods   A
MED: 100-2, 15, 80

AMA: 2001, Nov, 10

87164 **Dark field examination, any source (eg, penile, vaginal, oral, skin); includes specimen collection**   A ■
MED: 100-2, 15, 80; 100-4, 12, 60

87166 without collection   A ■
MED: 100-2, 15, 80

87168 **Macroscopic examination; arthropod**   A ■
MED: 100-2, 15, 80

87169 parasite   A ■
MED: 100-2, 15, 80

87172 **Pinworm exam (eg, cellophane tape prep)**   A ■
MED: 100-2, 15, 80

87176 Homogenization, tissue, for culture 🅰
MED: 100-2, 15, 80

87177 Ova and parasites, direct smears, concentration and identification 🅰 🗎
MED: 100-2, 15, 80

Do not report CPT code 87177 in conjunction with CPT code 87015. For coccidia or microsporidia exam, consult CPT code 87207. To report complex special stains including trichrome, iron hematoxylin, consult CPT code 87209. For nucleic acid probes in cytologic material, consult CPT code 88365. For molecular diagnostics, consult CPT codes 83890-83898 and 87470-87799.

To report direct smears from a primary source, consult CPT code 87207.

87181 Susceptibility studies, antimicrobial agent; agar dilution method, per agent (eg, antibiotic gradient strip) 🅰
MED: 100-2, 15, 80

AMA: 2001, Nov, 10

87184   disk method, per plate (12 or fewer agents) 🅰
MED: 100-2, 15, 80; 100-3, 190.12

AMA: 2001, Nov, 10

87185   enzyme detection (eg, beta lactamase), per enzyme 🅰
MED: 100-2, 15, 80

AMA: 2001, Nov, 10

87186   microdilution or agar dilution (minimum inhibitory concentration (MIC) or breakpoint), each multi-antimicrobial, per plate 🅰
MED: 100-2, 15, 80; 100-3, 190.12

AMA: 2001, Nov, 10

+ **87187**   microdilution or agar dilution, minimum lethal concentration (MLC), each plate (List separately in addition to code for primary procedure) 🅰
MED: 100-2, 15, 80

AMA: 2001, Nov, 10

Note that 87187 is an add-on code and must be used in conjunction with CPT code 87186 or 87188.

87188   macrobroth dilution method, each agent 🅰
MED: 100-2, 15, 80

AMA: 2001, Nov, 10

87190   mycobacteria, proportion method, each agent 🅰
MED: 100-2, 15, 80

To report other mycobacterial susceptibility studies, consult CPT codes 87181, 87184, 87186 87188. For fungal susceptibility studies, consult CPT codes 87181, 87184, 87187 or 87188.

87197 Serum bactericidal titer (Schlicter test) 🅰
MED: 100-2, 15, 80

87205 Smear, primary source with interpretation; Gram or Giemsa stain for bacteria, fungi, or cell types 🅰 🗎
MED: 100-2, 15, 80

87206   fluorescent and/or acid fast stain for bacteria, fungi, parasites, viruses or cell types 🅰 🗎
MED: 100-2, 15, 80

87207   **special stain for inclusion bodies or parasites (eg, malaria, coccidia, microsporidia, trypanosomes, herpes viruses)** 🄰 ▣
MED: 100-2, 15, 80; 100-4, 12, 60

To report direct smears with concentration and identification, consult CPT code 87177.

For thick smear preparation, consult CPT code 87015. For complex special stains, consult CPT codes 88312 and 88313. For fat, meat, fibers, nasal eosinophils and starch, see Other Procedures section.

Tzank smear

● **87209**   **complex special stain (eg, trichrome, iron hemotoxylin) for ova and parasites**

87210   **wet mount for infectious agents (eg, saline, India ink, KOH preps)** 🄰 ✖ ▣
MED: 100-2, 15, 80

To report KOH exam of skin, hair or nails, consult CPT code 87220.

87220   **Tissue examination by KOH slide of samples from skin, hair, or nails for fungi or ectoparasite ova or mites (eg, scabies)** 🄰 ▣
MED: 100-2, 15, 80

87230   **Toxin or antitoxin assay, tissue culture (eg, Clostridium difficile toxin)** 🄰
MED: 100-2, 15, 80

87250   **Virus isolation; inoculation of embryonated eggs, or small animal, includes observation and dissection** 🄰
MED: 100-2, 15, 80

87252   **tissue culture inoculation, observation, and presumptive identification by cytopathic effect** 🄰
MED: 100-2, 15, 80

87253   **tissue culture, additional studies or definitive identification (eg, hemabsorption, neutralization, immunofluorescence stain), each isolate** 🄰 ▣
MED: 100-2, 15, 80

To report electron microscopy, consult CPT code 88348. To report inclusion bodies in tissue sections, consult CPT codes 88304-88309; in smears, consult CPT codes 87207-87210; in fluids, consult CPT code 88106.

87254   **centrifuge enhanced (shell vial) technique, includes identification with immunofluorescence stain, each virus** 🄰 ▣
MED: 100-2, 15, 80

Report CPT code 87254 in addition to CPT code 87252 as appropriate.

87255   **including identification by non-immunologic method, other than by cytopathic effect (eg, virus specific enzymatic activity)** 🄰

87260   **Infectious agent antigen detection by immunofluorescent technique; adenovirus** 🄰 ▣
MED: 100-2, 15, 80

87265   **Bordetella pertussis/parapertussis** 🄰 ▣
MED: 100-2, 15, 80

AMA: 1997, Nov, 32

87267   **Enterovirus, direct fluorescent antibody (DFA)** 🄰 ▣

87269   **Giardia** 🄰 ▣

87270   **Chlamydia trachomatis**   Ⓐ ▣
MED: 100-2, 15, 80
AMA: 1997, Nov, 32

87271   **Cytomegalovirus, direct fluorescent antibody (DFA)**   Ⓐ ▣

87272   **cryptosporidium**   Ⓐ ▣
MED: 100-2, 15, 80
AMA: 1997, Nov, 32

87273   **Herpes simplex virus type 2**   Ⓐ ▣
MED: 100-2, 15, 80

87274   **Herpes simplex virus type 1**   Ⓐ ▣
MED: 100-2, 15, 80
AMA: 1997, Nov, 32

87275   **influenza B virus**   Ⓐ ▣
MED: 100-2, 15, 80

87276   **Influenza A virus**   Ⓐ ▣
MED: 100-2, 15, 80
AMA: 1997, Nov, 32

87277   **Legionella micdadei**   Ⓐ ▣
MED: 100-2, 15, 80

87278   **Legionella pneumophila**   Ⓐ ▣
MED: 100-2, 15, 80
AMA: 1997, Nov, 32

87279   **Parainfluenza virus, each type**   Ⓐ ▣
MED: 100-2, 15, 80

87280   **respiratory syncytial virus**   Ⓐ ▣
MED: 100-2, 15, 80
AMA: 1997, Nov, 32

87281   **Pneumocystis carinii**   Ⓐ ▣
MED: 100-2, 15, 80

87283   **Rubeola**   Ⓐ ▣
MED: 100-2, 15, 80

87285   **Treponema pallidum**   Ⓐ ▣
MED: 100-2, 15, 80
AMA: 1997, Nov, 32

87290   **Varicella zoster virus**   Ⓐ ▣
MED: 100-2, 15, 80
AMA: 1997, Nov, 32

87299   **not otherwise specified, each organism**   Ⓐ ▣
MED: 100-2, 15, 80
AMA: 2001, Nov, 10; 1997, Nov, 32

87300   **Infectious agent antigen detection by immunofluorescent technique, polyvalent for multiple organisms, each polyvalent antiserum**   Ⓐ ▣
MED: 100-2, 15, 80

To report physician evaluation of infectious disease agents by immunofluroescence, consult CPT code 88346.

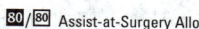

87301 **Infectious agent antigen detection by enzyme immunoassay technique, qualitative or semiquantitative, multiple step method; adenovirus enteric types 40/41** Ⓐ
MED: 100-2, 15, 80

AMA: 1999, Nov, 46; 1997, Nov, 32

87320 **Chlamydia trachomatis** Ⓐ
MED: 100-2, 15, 80

AMA: 1997, Nov, 32

87324 **Clostridium difficile toxin(s)** Ⓐ ⮌
MED: 100-2, 15, 80

AMA: 1997, Nov, 32

87327 **Cryptococcus neoformans** Ⓐ
MED: 100-2, 15, 80

To report Cryptococcus latex agglutination, consult CPT code 86403.

87328 **cryptosporidium** Ⓐ ⮌
MED: 100-2, 15, 80

AMA: 1997, Nov, 32

87329 **Giardia** Ⓐ ⮌

87332 **cytomegalovirus** Ⓐ
MED: 100-2, 15, 80

AMA: 1997, Nov, 32

87335 **Escherichia coli O157** Ⓐ
MED: 100-2, 15, 80

AMA: 1997, Nov, 32

To report Giardia antigen, consult CPT code 87329.

87336 **Entamoeba histolytica dispar group** Ⓐ
MED: 100-2, 15, 80

87337 **Entamoeba histolytica group** Ⓐ
MED: 100-2, 15, 80

87338 **Infectious agent antigen detection by enzyme immunoassay technique, qualitative or semiquantitative, multiple step method; Helicobacter pylori, stool** Ⓐ ⮌
MED: 100-2, 15, 80

AMA: 1999, Nov, 46

To report H. pylori, breath and blood by mass spectrometry, consult CPT codes 83013, 83014. To report H. pylori, liquid scintillation counter, consult CPT code 78267, 78268.

87339 **Helicobacter pylori** Ⓐ
MED: 100-2, 15, 80

To report H. pylori, breath and blood by mass spectrometry, consult CPT codes 83013, 83014. To report H. pylori, liquid scintillation counter, consult CPT code 78267, 78268.

To report H. pylori, stool, use CPT code 87338.

87340 **hepatitis B surface antigen (HBsAg)** Ⓐ ⮌
MED: 100-2, 15, 80; 100-3, 190.10

AMA: 2000, Jan, 11; 1997, Nov, 32

⮌ CCI Comp   50 Bilateral Proc.   ✚ CPT Add-on Code   ⊘ Modifier -51 Exempt   ♂/♀ Male/Female   ☒ CLIA Waived Test
● New Code   ▲ Revised Code   M Maternity Edit   A Age Edit   Ⓐ–Ⓨ APC Status Ind.   AMA: CPT Assistant
© 2005 Ingenix, Inc. *(Blue Ink)*   CPT only © 2005 American Medical Association. All Rights Reserved. *(Black Ink)*   Path/Lab — 635

87341   **hepatitis B surface antigen (HBsAg) neutralization**   Ⓐ
MED: 100-2, 15, 80

87350   **hepatitis Be antigen (HBeAg)**   Ⓐ 🔧
MED: 100-2, 15, 80

AMA: 1997, Nov, 32

87380   **hepatitis, delta agent**   Ⓐ
MED: 100-2, 15, 80

AMA: 1997, Nov, 32

87385   **Histoplasma capsulatum**   Ⓐ
MED: 100-2, 15, 80

AMA: 1997, Nov, 32

87390   **HIV-1**   Ⓐ
MED: 100-2, 15, 80; 100-3, 190.14

AMA: 1997, Nov, 32

87391   **HIV-2**   Ⓐ
MED: 100-2, 15, 80; 100-3, 190.14

AMA: 1997, Nov, 32

87400   **Influenza, A or B, each**   Ⓐ
MED: 100-2, 15, 80

AMA: 2001, Jun, 11; 2001, Dec, 6

87420   **respiratory syncytial virus**   Ⓐ
MED: 100-2, 15, 80

AMA: 1997, Nov, 32

87425   **rotavirus**   Ⓐ 🔧
MED: 100-2, 15, 80

AMA: 1997, Nov, 32

87427   **Shiga-like toxin**   Ⓐ
MED: 100-2, 15, 80

87430   **Streptococcus, group A**   Ⓐ
MED: 100-2, 15, 80

AMA: 1997, Nov, 32

87449   **Infectious agent antigen detection by enzyme immunoassay technique qualitative or semiquantitative; multiple step method, not otherwise specified, each organism**   Ⓐ ✖ 🔧
MED: 100-2, 15, 80

AMA: 2001, Nov, 10; 2000, Jan, 11; 1997, Nov, 32

87450   **single step method, not otherwise specified, each organism**   Ⓐ
MED: 100-2, 15, 80

AMA: 1997, Nov, 33

87451   **multiple step method, polyvalent for multiple organisms, each polyvalent antiserum**   Ⓐ
MED: 100-2, 15, 80

87470	Infectious agent detection by nucleic acid (DNA or RNA); Bartonella henselae and Bartonella quintana, direct probe technique	A CCI

MED: 100-2, 15, 80

AMA: 1997, Nov, 33-34

87471	Bartonella henselae and Bartonella quintana, amplified probe technique	A CCI

MED: 100-2, 15, 80

AMA: 1997, Nov, 33-34

87472	Bartonella henselae and Bartonella quintana, quantification	A CCI

MED: 100-2, 15, 80

AMA: 1997, Nov, 33-34

87475	Borrelia burgdorferi, direct probe technique	A CCI

MED: 100-2, 15, 80

AMA: 1997, Nov, 33-34

87476	Borrelia burgdorferi, amplified probe technique	A CCI

MED: 100-2, 15, 80

AMA: 1997, Nov, 33-34

87477	Borrelia burgdorferi, quantification	A CCI

MED: 100-2, 15, 80

AMA: 1997, Nov, 33-34

87480	Candida species, direct probe technique	A CCI

MED: 100-2, 15, 80

AMA: 1997, Nov, 33-34

87481	Candida species, amplified probe technique	A CCI

MED: 100-2, 15, 80

AMA: 1997, Nov, 33-34

87482	Candida species, quantification	A CCI

MED: 100-2, 15, 80

AMA: 1997, Nov, 33-34

87485	Chlamydia pneumoniae, direct probe technique	A CCI

MED: 100-2, 15, 80

AMA: 1997, Nov, 33-34

87486	Chlamydia pneumoniae, amplified probe technique	A CCI

MED: 100-2, 15, 80

AMA: 1997, Nov, 33-34

87487	Chlamydia pneumoniae, quantification	A CCI

MED: 100-2, 15, 80

AMA: 1997, Nov, 33-34

87490	Chlamydia trachomatis, direct probe technique	A CCI

MED: 100-2, 15, 80

AMA: 1997, Nov, 33-34

87491	Chlamydia trachomatis, amplified probe technique	A CCI

MED: 100-2, 15, 80

AMA: 1997, Nov, 33-34

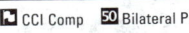

87492	**Chlamydia trachomatis, quantification**	Ⓐ 🔁
	MED: 100-2, 15, 80	
	AMA: 1997, Nov, 33-34	

87495	**cytomegalovirus, direct probe technique**	Ⓐ 🔁
	MED: 100-2, 15, 80	
	AMA: 1997, Nov, 33-34	

87496	**cytomegalovirus, amplified probe technique**	Ⓐ 🔁
	MED: 100-2, 15, 80	
	AMA: 1997, Nov, 33-34	

87497	**cytomegalovirus, quantification**	Ⓐ 🔁
	MED: 100-2, 15, 80	
	AMA: 1997, Nov, 33-34	

87510	**Gardnerella vaginalis, direct probe technique**	Ⓐ 🔁
	MED: 100-2, 15, 80	
	AMA: 1997, Nov, 33-34	

87511	**Gardnerella vaginalis, amplified probe technique**	Ⓐ 🔁
	MED: 100-2, 15, 80	
	AMA: 1997, Nov, 33-34	

87512	**Gardnerella vaginalis, quantification**	Ⓐ 🔁
	MED: 100-2, 15, 80	
	AMA: 1997, Nov, 33-34	

87515	**hepatitis B virus, direct probe technique**	Ⓐ 🔁
	MED: 100-2, 15, 80	
	AMA: 1997, Nov, 33-34	

87516	**hepatitis B virus, amplified probe technique**	Ⓐ 🔁
	MED: 100-2, 15, 80	
	AMA: 1997, Nov, 33-34	

87517	**hepatitis B virus, quantification**	Ⓐ 🔁
	MED: 100-2, 15, 80	
	AMA: 1997, Nov, 33-34	

87520	**hepatitis C, direct probe technique**	Ⓐ 🔁
	MED: 100-2, 15, 80	
	AMA: 1997, Nov, 33-34	

87521	**hepatitis C, amplified probe technique**	Ⓐ 🔁
	MED: 100-2, 15, 80	
	AMA: 1997, Nov, 33-34	

87522	**hepatitis C, quantification**	Ⓐ 🔁
	MED: 100-2, 15, 80	
	AMA: 1997, Nov, 33-34	

87525	**hepatitis G, direct probe technique**	Ⓐ 🔁
	MED: 100-2, 15, 80	
	AMA: 1997, Nov, 33-34	

87526	**hepatitis G, amplified probe technique**	A ◪
	MED: 100-2, 15, 80	
	AMA: 1997, Nov, 33-34	
87527	**hepatitis G, quantification**	A ◪
	MED: 100-2, 15, 80	
	AMA: 1997, Nov, 33-34	
87528	**Herpes simplex virus, direct probe technique**	A ◪
	MED: 100-2, 15, 80	
	AMA: 1997, Nov, 33-34	
87529	**Herpes simplex virus, amplified probe technique**	A ◪
	MED: 100-2, 15, 80	
	AMA: 1997, Nov, 33-34	
87530	**Herpes simplex virus, quantification**	A ◪
	MED: 100-2, 15, 80	
	AMA: 1997, Nov, 33-34	
87531	**Herpes virus-6, direct probe technique**	A ◪
	MED: 100-2, 15, 80	
	AMA: 1997, Nov, 33-34	
87532	**Herpes virus-6, amplified probe technique**	A ◪
	MED: 100-2, 15, 80	
	AMA: 1997, Nov, 33-34	
87533	**Herpes virus-6, quantification**	A ◪
	MED: 100-2, 15, 80	
	AMA: 1997, Nov, 33-34	
87534	**HIV-1, direct probe technique**	A ◪
	MED: 100-2, 15, 80; 100-3, 190.14	
	AMA: 1997, Nov, 33-34	
87535	**HIV-1, amplified probe technique**	A ◪
	MED: 100-2, 15, 80; 100-3, 190.14	
	AMA: 1997, Nov, 33-34	
87536	**HIV-1, quantification**	A ◪
	MED: 100-2, 15, 80; 100-3, 190.13	
	AMA: 1997, Nov, 33-34	
87537	**HIV-2, direct probe technique**	A ◪
	MED: 100-2, 15, 80; 100-3, 190.14	
	AMA: 1997, Nov, 33-34	
87538	**HIV-2, amplified probe technique**	A ◪
	MED: 100-2, 15, 80; 100-3, 190.14	
	AMA: 1997, Nov, 33-34	
87539	**HIV-2, quantification**	A ◪
	MED: 100-2, 15, 80; 100-3, 190.13	
	AMA: 1997, Nov, 33-34	

87540　　**Legionella pneumophila, direct probe technique**　　Ⓐ 🄽
MED: 100-2, 15, 80

AMA: 1997, Nov, 33-34

87541　　**Legionella pneumophila, amplified probe technique**　　Ⓐ 🄽
MED: 100-2, 15, 80

AMA: 1997, Nov, 33-34

87542　　**Legionella pneumophila, quantification**　　Ⓐ 🄽
MED: 100-2, 15, 80

AMA: 1997, Nov, 33-34

87550　　**Mycobacteria species, direct probe technique**　　Ⓐ 🄽
MED: 100-2, 15, 80

AMA: 1997, Nov, 33-34

87551　　**Mycobacteria species, amplified probe technique**　　Ⓐ 🄽
MED: 100-2, 15, 80

AMA: 1997, Nov, 33-34

87552　　**Mycobacteria species, quantification**　　Ⓐ 🄽
MED: 100-2, 15, 80

AMA: 1997, Nov, 33-34

87555　　**Mycobacteria tuberculosis, direct probe technique**　　Ⓐ 🄽
MED: 100-2, 15, 80

AMA: 1997, Nov, 33-34

87556　　**Mycobacteria tuberculosis, amplified probe technique**　　Ⓐ 🄽
MED: 100-2, 15, 80

AMA: 1997, Nov, 33-34

87557　　**Mycobacteria tuberculosis, quantification**　　Ⓐ 🄽
MED: 100-2, 15, 80

AMA: 1997, Nov, 33-34

87560　　**Mycobacteria avium-intracellulare, direct probe technique**　　Ⓐ 🄽
MED: 100-2, 15, 80

AMA: 1997, Nov, 33-34

87561　　**Mycobacteria avium-intracellulare, amplified probe technique**　　Ⓐ 🄽
MED: 100-2, 15, 80

AMA: 1997, Nov, 33-34

87562　　**Mycobacteria avium-intracellulare, quantification**　　Ⓐ 🄽
MED: 100-2, 15, 80

AMA: 1997, Nov, 33-34

87580　　**Mycoplasma pneumoniae, direct probe technique**　　Ⓐ 🄽
MED: 100-2, 15, 80

AMA: 1997, Nov, 33-34

87581　　**Mycoplasma pneumoniae, amplified probe technique**　　Ⓐ 🄽
MED: 100-2, 15, 80

AMA: 1997, Nov, 33-34

26 / **TC** Professional/Technical Component　　**80**/**80** Assist-at-Surgery Allowed/With Documentation　⊙ Conscious Sedation

Unlisted　　　Not Covered　　**MED**: Pubs 100/NCD Reference　　**1**-**9** ASC Group　　⊚ Modifier 63 Exempt

640 — Path/Lab　　CPT only © 2005 American Medical Association. All Rights Reserved. *(Black Ink)*　　© 2005 Ingenix, Inc. *(Blue Ink)*

87582 **Mycoplasma pneumoniae, quantification** Ⓐ 🔧
MED: 100-2, 15, 80

AMA: 1997, Nov, 33-34

87590 **Neisseria gonorrhoeae, direct probe technique** Ⓐ 🔧
MED: 100-2, 15, 80

AMA: 1997, Nov, 33-34

87591 **Neisseria gonorrhoeae, amplified probe technique** Ⓐ 🔧
MED: 100-2, 15, 80

AMA: 1997, Nov, 33-34

87592 **Neisseria gonorrhoeae, quantification** Ⓐ 🔧
MED: 100-2, 15, 80

AMA: 1997, Nov, 33-34

87620 **papillomavirus, human, direct probe technique** Ⓐ 🔧
MED: 100-2, 15, 80

AMA: 2002, Feb, 10; 1997, Nov, 33-34

87621 **papillomavirus, human, amplified probe technique** Ⓐ 🔧
MED: 100-2, 15, 80

AMA: 1997, Nov, 33-34

87622 **papillomavirus, human, quantification** Ⓐ 🔧
MED: 100-2, 15, 80

AMA: 1997, Nov, 33-34

87650 **Streptococcus, group A, direct probe technique** Ⓐ 🔧
MED: 100-2, 15, 80

AMA: 1997, Nov, 33-34

87651 **Streptococcus, group A, amplified probe technique** Ⓐ 🔧
MED: 100-2, 15, 80

AMA: 1997, Nov, 33-34

87652 **Streptococcus, group A, quantification** Ⓐ 🔧
MED: 100-2, 15, 80

AMA: 1997, Nov, 33-34

87660 **Trichomonas vaginalis, direct probe technique** Ⓐ 🔧

87797 **Infectious agent detection by nucleic acid (DNA or RNA), not otherwise
specified; direct probe technique, each organism** Ⓐ 🔧
MED: 100-2, 15, 80

AMA: 2001, Nov, 10; 1997, Nov, 34

87798 **amplified probe technique, each organism** Ⓐ 🔧
MED: 100-2, 15, 80

AMA: 2001, Nov, 10; 1997, Nov, 34

87799 **quantification, each organism** Ⓐ 🔧
MED: 100-2, 15, 80

AMA: 1997, Nov, 34

87800 **Infectious agent detection by nucleic acid (DNA or RNA), multiple
organisms; direct probe(s) technique** Ⓐ 🔧
MED: 100-2, 15, 80

🔧 CCI Comp 50 Bilateral Proc. ✚ CPT Add-on Code ⊘ Modifier -51 Exempt ♂/♀ Male/Female ☒ CLIA Waived Test
● New Code ▲ Revised Code Ⓜ Maternity Edit Ⓐ Age Edit Ⓐ–Ⓨ APC Status Ind. **AMA:** CPT Assistant

© 2005 Ingenix, Inc. *(Blue Ink)* CPT only © 2005 American Medical Association. All Rights Reserved. *(Black Ink)* Path/Lab — 641

87801   **amplified probe(s) technique**   A ▶
MED: 100-2, 15, 80

87802   **Infectious agent antigen detection by immunoassay with direct optical observation; Streptococcus, group B**   A ▶
MED: 100-2, 15, 80

87803   **Clostridium difficile toxin A**   A ▶
MED: 100-2, 15, 80

87804   **Influenza**   A ✖ ▶
MED: 100-2, 15, 80

87807   **respiratory syncytial virus**   A ▶

87810   **Infectious agent detection by immunoassay with direct optical observation; Chlamydia trachomatis**   A ▶
MED: 100-2, 15, 80

AMA: 1998, Jan, 6; 1997, Nov, 34

87850   **Neisseria gonorrhoeae**   A ▶
MED: 100-2, 15, 80

AMA: 1998, Jan, 6; 1997, Nov, 34

87880   **Streptococcus, group A**   A ✖ ▶
MED: 100-2, 15, 80

AMA: 1998, Jan, 6; 1998, Dec, 8; 1997, Nov, 34

87899   **not otherwise specified**   A ✖ ▶
MED: 100-2, 15, 80

AMA: 2001, Jun, 11

● 87900   **Infectious agent drug susceptibility phenotype prediction using regularly updated genotypic bioinformatics**

87901   **Infectious agent genotype analysis by nucleic acid (DNA or RNA), HIV 1, reverse transcriptase and protease**   A ▶
MED: 100-2, 15, 80

To report infectious agent drug susceptiblity phenotype prediction for HIV-1, consult CPT code 87900.

87902   **Hepatitis C virus**   A ▶
MED: 100-2, 15, 80

87903   **Infectious agent phenotype analysis by nucleic acid (DNA or RNA) with drug resistance tissue culture analysis, HIV 1; first through 10 drugs tested**   A ▶
MED: 100-2, 15, 80

+ ▲ 87904   **each additional drug tested (List separately in addition to code for primary procedure)**   A ▶
MED: 100-2, 15, 80

Note that 87904 is an add-on code and must be used in conjunction with CPT code 87903.

87999   **Unlisted microbiology procedure**   A
MED: 100-2, 15, 80

ANATOMIC PATHOLOGY

POSTMORTEM EXAMINATION

Codes 88000-88099 are used to report physician services only. For services performed by an outside laboratory, append modifier 90.

88000 Necropsy (autopsy), gross examination only; without CNS
MED: 100-1, 5, 90.2; 100-2, 15, 80; 100-2, 15, 80.1; 100-4, 16, 10; 100-4, 16, 10.1; 100-4, 16, 110.4
AMA: 1993, Fall, 26

88005 with brain
MED: 100-2, 15, 80
AMA: 1993, Fall, 26

88007 with brain and spinal cord
MED: 100-2, 15, 80
AMA: 1993, Fall, 26

88012 infant with brain
MED: 100-2, 15, 80
AMA: 1993, Fall, 26

88014 stillborn or newborn with brain
MED: 100-2, 15, 80
AMA: 1993, Fall, 26

88016 macerated stillborn
MED: 100-2, 15, 80
AMA: 1993, Fall, 26

88020 Necropsy (autopsy), gross and microscopic; without CNS
MED: 100-1, 5, 90.2; 100-2, 15, 80; 100-2, 15, 80.1; 100-4, 16, 10; 100-4, 16, 10.1; 100-4, 16, 110.4
AMA: 1993, Fall, 26

88025 with brain
MED: 100-2, 15, 80
AMA: 1993, Fall, 26

88027 with brain and spinal cord
MED: 100-2, 15, 80
AMA: 1993, Fall, 26

88028 infant with brain
MED: 100-2, 15, 80
AMA: 1993, Fall, 26

88029 stillborn or newborn with brain
MED: 100-2, 15, 80
AMA: 1993, Fall, 26

88036 Necropsy (autopsy), limited, gross and/or microscopic; regional
MED: 100-1, 5, 90.2; 100-2, 15, 80; 100-2, 15, 80.1; 100-4, 16, 10; 100-4, 16, 10.1; 100-4, 16, 110.4
AMA: 1993, Fall, 26

| 88037 | single organ | E |

MED: 100-2, 15, 80

AMA: 1993, Fall, 26

| 88040 | Necropsy (autopsy); forensic examination | E |

MED: 100-1, 5, 90.2; 100-2, 15, 80; 100-2, 15, 80.1; 100-4, 16, 10; 100-4, 16, 10.1; 100-4, 16, 110.4

AMA: 1993, Fall, 26

| 88045 | coroner's call | E |

MED: 100-2, 15, 80

AMA: 1993, Fall, 26

| 88099 | Unlisted necropsy (autopsy) procedure | E |

MED: 100-1, 5, 90.2; 100-2, 15, 80; 100-2, 15, 80.1; 100-4, 16, 10; 100-4, 16, 10.1; 100-4, 16, 110.4

AMA: 1993, Fall, 26

CYTOPATHOLOGY

To report cervicography, consult CPT Category III code 0003T.

To report cytology specimen collection via mammary duct catheter lavage, consult CPT Category III codes 0045T and 0046T.

| 88104 | Cytopathology, fluids, washings or brushings, except cervical or vaginal; smears with interpretation | X 80 |

MED: 100-2, 15, 80; 100-4, 12, 60

AMA: 1994, Fall, 3; 1991, Spring, 6

| 88106 | filter method only with interpretation | X 80 |

MED: 100-2, 15, 80; 100-4, 12, 60

AMA: 1994, Fall, 3

| 88107 | smears and filter preparation with interpretation | X 80 ▶ |

MED: 100-2, 15, 80; 100-4, 12, 60

AMA: 1994, Fall, 3

| 88108 | Cytopathology, concentration technique, smears and interpretation (eg, Saccomanno technique) | X 80 ▶ |

MED: 100-2, 15, 80; 100-4, 12, 60

AMA: 1998, Jan, 6; 1997, Nov, 34; 1994, Fall, 3

To report gastric intubation with lavage, consult CPT codes 89130-89141 and 91055. To report cervical or vaginal smears, consult CPT code 88150-88155. To report x-ray localization, consult CPT code 74340.

| 88112 | Cytopathology, selective cellular enhancement technique with interpretation (eg, liquid based slide preparation method), except cervical or vaginal | X 80 |

Code 88112 cannot be reported in conjunction with 88108.

| 88125 | Cytopathology, forensic (eg, sperm) | X 80 |

MED: 100-2, 15, 80; 100-4, 12, 60

| 88130 | Sex chromatin identification; Barr bodies | A |

MED: 100-2, 15, 80

26 / TC Professional/Technical Component　　**80/80** Assist-at-Surgery Allowed/With Documentation　　⊙ Conscious Sedation

Unlisted　　　Not Covered　　**MED:** Pubs 100/NCD Reference　　**1-9** ASC Group　　63 Modifier 63 Exempt

644 — Path/Lab　　CPT only © 2005 American Medical Association. All Rights Reserved. *(Black Ink)*　　© 2005 Ingenix, Inc. *(Blue Ink)*

88140   **peripheral blood smear, polymorphonuclear drumsticks**   Ⓐ
MED: 100-2, 15, 80

AMA: 1998, Nov, 27-28

To report Guard stain, consult CPT code 88313.

Report 88150–88154 for conventional Pap smears that are examined using the non-Bethesda method.

Report codes 88164–88167 for conventional Pap smears that are examined using the Bethesda method of reporting. Report 88142–88143 for liquid-based specimens processed as thin-layer preparations that are examined using any system of reporting. Report codes 88174–88175 for automated screening of liquid-based specimens. Report 88141 and 88155 in addition to the screening code selected when the additional services are provided. Manual rescreening requires a complete visual reassessment of the entire slide initially screened by either an automated or manual process. A manual review represents an assessment of selected cells or regions of a slide identified by an initial automated review.

▲ **88141**   **Cytopathology, cervical or vaginal (any reporting system), requiring interpretation by physician**   ♀ Ⓝ 26 80 ↲
MED: 100-2, 15, 80; 100-3, 190.2; 100-3, 210.2

AMA: 1999, Nov, 46; 1999, May, 6; 1999, Jan, 11; 1998, Jan, 6; 1997, Nov, 35

Note that 88141 is an add-on code and must be used in conjunction with 88142-88154, 88164-88167, and 88174-88175.

88142   **Cytopathology, cervical or vaginal (any reporting system), collected in preservative fluid, automated thin layer preparation; manual screening under physician supervision**   ♀ Ⓐ ↲
MED: 100-2, 15, 80; 100-3, 190.2; 100-3, 210.2

AMA: 1999, May, 6; 1998, Nov, 28; 1998, Jan, 6; 1997, Nov, 34-35

88143   **with manual screening and rescreening under physician supervision**   ♀ Ⓐ ↲
MED: 100-2, 15, 80; 100-3, 190.2; 100-3, 210.2

AMA: 1999, May, 6; 1998, Nov, 28; 1997, Nov, 34-35

To report automated screening of automated thin layer prep, consult CPT codes 88174, 88175.

88147   **Cytopathology smears, cervical or vaginal; screening by automated system under physician supervision**   ♀ Ⓐ ↲
MED: 100-2, 15, 80; 100-3, 190.2; 100-3, 210.2

AMA: 1999, Nov, 46; 1999, May, 6; 1999, Jan, 1; 1998, Nov, 28; 1997, Nov, 35

88148   **screening by automated system with manual rescreening under physician supervision**   ♀ Ⓐ ↲
MED: 100-2, 15, 80; 100-3, 190.2; 100-3, 210.2

AMA: 1999, Nov, 46; 1999, May, 6; 1999, Jan, 1

88150   **Cytopathology, slides, cervical or vaginal; manual screening under physician supervision**   ♀ Ⓐ ↲
MED: 100-2, 15, 80; 100-3, 190.2; 100-3, 210.2

AMA: 1999, May, 6; 1998, Nov, 28; 1997, Nov, 34-35; 1991, Winter, 19

88152   **with manual screening and computer-assisted rescreening under physician supervision**   ♀ Ⓐ ↲
MED: 100-2, 15, 80; 100-3, 190.2; 100-3, 210.2

AMA: 1999, May, 6; 1998, Jan, 6; 1997, Nov, 35

Pathology and Laboratory

88153 — 88172

88153   with manual screening and rescreening under physician supervision   ♀ A ⬆
MED: 100-2, 15, 80; 100-3, 190.2; 100-3, 210.2

AMA: 1999, May, 6; 1998, Nov, 28; 1997, Nov, 34-35

88154   with manual screening and computer-assisted rescreening using cell selection and review under physician supervision   ♀ A ⬆
MED: 100-2, 15, 80; 100-3, 190.2; 100-3, 210.2

AMA: 1999, May, 6; 1998, Nov, 28; 1997, Nov, 34-35

+   **88155**   Cytopathology, slides, cervical or vaginal, definitive hormonal evaluation (eg, maturation index, karyopyknotic index, estrogenic index) (List separately in addition to code(s) for other technical and interpretation services)   ♀ A ⬆
MED: 100-2, 15, 80; 100-3, 190.2; 100-3, 210.2

AMA: 1999, Nov, 46; 1999, May, 6; 1998, Nov, 28; 1997, Nov, 35

Note that 88155 is an add-on code and must be used in conjunction with 88142-88154, 88164-88167, and 88174-88175.

88160   Cytopathology, smears, any other source; screening and interpretation   X 80 ⬆
MED: 100-2, 15, 80; 100-4, 12, 60

88161   preparation, screening and interpretation   X 80 ⬆
MED: 100-2, 15, 80; 100-4, 12, 60

AMA: 1997, Aug, 18

88162   extended study involving over 5 slides and/or multiple stains   X 80 ⬆
MED: 100-2, 15, 80

If specimen needs to be obtained, consult percutaneous needle biopsy under the individual organ in the Surgery section of the CPT book. For aerosol collection of sputum, consult CPT code 89220. For special stains, consult CPT codes 88312-88314.

88164   Cytopathology, slides, cervical or vaginal (the Bethesda System); manual screening under physician supervision   ♀ A ⬆
MED: 100-2, 15, 80; 100-3, 190.2; 100-3, 210.2

AMA: 1999, May, 6; 1998, Nov, 28

88165   with manual screening and rescreening under physician supervision   ♀ A ⬆
MED: 100-2, 15, 80; 100-3, 190.2; 100-3, 210.2

AMA: 1999, May, 6; 1998, Nov, 28

88166   with manual screening and computer-assisted rescreening under physician supervision   ♀ A ⬆
MED: 100-2, 15, 80; 100-3, 190.2; 100-3, 210.2

AMA: 1999, May, 6; 1998, Nov, 28

88167   with manual screening and computer-assisted rescreening using cell selection and review under physician supervision   ♀ A ⬆
MED: 100-2, 15, 80; 100-3, 190.2; 100-3, 210.2

AMA: 1999, May, 6; 1998, Nov, 28

88172   Cytopathology, evaluation of fine needle aspirate; immediate cytohistologic study to determine adequacy of specimen(s)   X 80 ⬆
MED: 100-2, 15, 80; 100-4, 12, 60

AMA: 1998, Dec, 8; 1994, Fall, 2; 1993, Fall, 26

88173	interpretation and report	

88173   interpretation and report

MED: 100-2, 15, 80; 100-4, 12, 60

AMA: 1998, Dec, 8; 1994, Fall, 2; 1993, Fall, 26

To report fine needle aspirate, consult CPT codes 10021, 10022.

Codes 88172 and 88173 should not be reported with codes 88333 and 88334 for the same specimen.

88174   Cytopathology, cervical or vaginal (any reporting system), collected in preservative fluid, automated thin layer preparation; screening by automated system, under physician supervision

▲ **88175**   with screening by automated system and manual rescreening or review, under physician supervision

To report manual screening, consult CPT codes 88142, 88143.

▲ **88182**   Flow cytometry, cell cycle or DNA analysis

MED: 100-2, 15, 80; 100-4, 12, 60

To report tumor morphometry and DNA and ploidy analysis for imaging techniques, consult CPT code 88358.

88184   Flow cytometry, cell surface, cytoplasmic, or nuclear marker, technical component only; first marker

\+ **88185**   each additional marker (List separately in addition to code for first marker)

Note that 88185 is an add-on code and must be used in conjunction with code 88184.

88187   Flow cytometry, interpretation; 2 to 8 markers

88188   9 to 15 markers

88189   16 or more markers

88199   Unlisted cytopathology procedure

MED: 100-2, 15, 80

To report electron microscopy, consult CPT codes 88348 and 88349.

CYTOGENETIC STUDIES

Report the appropriate modifier when molecular diagnostic procedures are performed to test for oncologic or inherited disorder to specify probe type or condition tested.

For acetylcholinesterase, consult CPT code 82013. For alpha-fetoprotein, serum or amniotic fluid, consult CPT codes 82105 and 82106.

For laser microdissection of cells from tissue sample, consult CPT code 88380.

88230   Tissue culture for non-neoplastic disorders; lymphocyte

MED: 100-2, 15, 80; 100-3, 190.3; 100-3, 190.8

AMA: 1999, Oct, 1; 1998, Nov, 29

88233   skin or other solid tissue biopsy

MED: 100-2, 15, 80; 100-3, 190.3

AMA: 1999, Oct, 1; 1998, Nov, 29

88235   amniotic fluid or chorionic villus cells

MED: 100-2, 15, 80; 100-3, 190.3

AMA: 1999, Oct, 1; 1998, Nov, 29

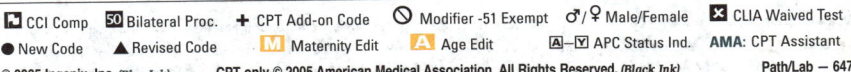

Pathology and Laboratory

88237 — 88269

88237   **Tissue culture for neoplastic disorders; bone marrow, blood cells**   Ⓐ
MED: 100-1, 5, 90.2; 100-2, 15, 80; 100-2, 15, 80.1; 100-3, 190.3; 100-4, 16, 10; 100-4, 16, 10.1; 100-4, 16, 110.4

AMA: 1999, Oct, 1; 1998, Nov, 29

88239   **solid tumor**   Ⓐ
MED: 100-2, 15, 80; 100-3, 190.3

AMA: 1999, Oct, 1; 1998, Nov, 29

88240   **Cryopreservation, freezing and storage of cells, each cell line**   Ⓐ
MED: 100-2, 15, 80; 100-3, 190.3

AMA: 1999, Oct, 1; 1998, Nov, 29

To report therapeutic cryopreservation and storage, consult CPT code 38207.

88241   **Thawing and expansion of frozen cells, each aliquot**   Ⓐ
MED: 100-2, 15, 80; 100-3, 190.3

AMA: 1999, Oct, 1; 1998, Nov, 29

To report therapeutic thawing of previous harvest, consult CPT code 38208.

88245   **Chromosome analysis for breakage syndromes; baseline Sister Chromatid Exchange (SCE), 20-25 cells**   Ⓐ ↔
MED: 100-2, 15, 80; 100-3, 190.3

AMA: 1999, Oct, 1; 1998, Nov, 29

88248   **baseline breakage, score 50-100 cells, count 20 cells, 2 karyotypes (eg, for ataxia telangiectasia, Fanconi anemia, fragile X)**   Ⓐ ↔
MED: 100-2, 15, 80; 100-3, 190.3

AMA: 1999, Oct, 1; 1998, Nov, 29

88249   **score 100 cells, clastogen stress (eg, diepoxybutane, mitomycin C, ionizing radiation, UV radiation)**   Ⓐ ↔
MED: 100-2, 15, 80; 100-3, 190.3

AMA: 1999, Oct, 1; 1998, Nov, 29

88261   **Chromosome analysis; count 5 cells, 1 karyotype, with banding**   Ⓐ ↔
MED: 100-2, 15, 80; 100-3, 190.3

AMA: 1999, Oct, 1; 1998, Nov, 29

88262   **count 15-20 cells, 2 karyotypes, with banding**   Ⓐ ↔
MED: 100-2, 15, 80; 100-3, 190.3

AMA: 1999, Oct, 1; 1998, Nov, 29

88263   **count 45 cells for mosaicism, 2 karyotypes, with banding**   Ⓐ ↔
MED: 100-2, 15, 80; 100-3, 190.3

AMA: 1999, Oct, 1; 1998, Nov, 29

88264   **analyze 20-25 cells**   Ⓐ ↔
MED: 100-2, 15, 80; 100-3, 190.3

AMA: 1999, Oct, 1; 1998, Nov, 29

88267   **Chromosome analysis, amniotic fluid or chorionic villus, count 15 cells, 1 karyotype, with banding**   Ⓜ ♀ Ⓐ ↔
MED: 100-2, 15, 80; 100-3, 190.3

88269   **Chromosome analysis, in situ for amniotic fluid cells, count cells from 6-12 colonies, 1 karyotype, with banding**   Ⓜ ♀ Ⓐ ↔
MED: 100-2, 15, 80; 100-3, 190.3

88271   Molecular cytogenetics; DNA probe, each (eg, FISH)   [A] [CCI]
     MED: 100-2, 15, 80; 100-3, 190.3

     AMA: 1999, Oct, 1; 1999, Mar, 10; 1998, Nov, 29

88272   chromosomal in situ hybridization, analyze 3-5 cells (eg, for derivatives and markers)   [A] [CCI]
     MED: 100-2, 15, 80; 100-3, 190.3

     AMA: 1999, Oct, 1; 1999, Mar, 10; 1998, Nov, 29

88273   chromosomal in situ hybridization, analyze 10-30 cells (eg, for microdeletions)   [A] [CCI]
     MED: 100-2, 15, 80; 100-3, 190.3

     AMA: 1999, Oct, 1; 1999, Mar, 10; 1998, Nov, 29

88274   interphase in situ hybridization, analyze 25-99 cells   [A] [CCI]
     MED: 100-2, 15, 80; 100-3, 190.3

     AMA: 1999, Oct, 1; 1999, Mar, 10; 1998, Nov, 29

88275   interphase in situ hybridization, analyze 100-300 cells   [A] [CCI]
     MED: 100-2, 15, 80; 100-3, 190.3

     AMA: 1999, Oct, 1; 1999, Mar, 10; 1998, Nov, 29

88280   Chromosome analysis; additional karyotypes, each study   [A] [CCI]
     MED: 100-2, 15, 80; 100-3, 190.3

88283   additional specialized banding technique (eg, NOR, C-banding)   [A] [CCI]
     MED: 100-2, 15, 80; 100-3, 190.3

88285   additional cells counted, each study   [A] [CCI]
     MED: 100-2, 15, 80; 100-3, 190.3

88289   additional high resolution study   [A] [CCI]
     MED: 100-2, 15, 80; 100-3, 190.3

     AMA: 1999, Oct, 1

88291   Cytogenetics and molecular cytogenetics, interpretation and report   [A] [26] [80] [CCI]
     MED: 100-2, 15, 80; 100-3, 190.3

     AMA: 1999, Oct, 1; 1998, Nov, 29

88299   Unlisted cytogenetic study   [X] [80]
     MED: 100-2, 15, 80; 100-3, 190.3

SURGICAL PATHOLOGY

88300   Level I - Surgical pathology, gross examination only   [X] [80]
     MED: 100-1, 5, 90.2; 100-2, 15, 80; 100-2, 15, 80.1; 100-4, 12, 60; 100-4, 16, 10; 100-4, 16, 10.1; 100-4, 16, 110.4

     AMA: 2000, Sep, 10; 1991, Winter, 18

88302   Level II - Surgical pathology, gross and microscopic examination   [X] [80]
     MED: 100-1, 5, 90.2; 100-2, 15, 80; 100-2, 15, 80.1; 100-4, 12, 60; 100-4, 16, 10; 100-4, 16, 10.1; 100-4, 16, 110.4

     AMA: 2000, Sep, 10; 1991, Winter, 18

     Appendix, Incidental; Fallopian Tube, Sterilization; Fingers/Toes, Amputation,Traumatic; Foreskin, Newborn, Hernia Sac, Any Location; Hydrocele Sac; Nerve; Skin, Plastic Repair; Sympathetic Ganglion; Testis, Castration; Vaginal Mucosa, Incidental; Vas Deferens, Sterilization

Pathology and Laboratory

88304 — 88305

88304 **Level III - Surgical pathology, gross and microscopic examination** ☒ 80 ▣
MED: 100-1, 5, 90.2; 100-2, 15, 80.1; 100-4, 12, 60; 100-4, 16, 10; 100-4, 16, 10.1; 100-4, 16, 110.4

AMA: 2000, Sep, 10; 1997, Aug, 18; 1991, Winter, 18; 1991, Spring, 2

Abortion, Induced Abscess Aneurysm - Arterial/Ventricular Anus, Tag Appendix, Other than Incidental Artery, Atheromatous Plaque Bartholin's Gland Cyst Bone Fragment(s), Other than Pathologic Fracture Bursa/Synovial Cyst Carpal Tunnel Tissue Cartilage, Shavings Cholesteatoma Colon, Colostomy Stoma Conjunctiva - Biopsy/Pterygium Cornea Diverticulum - Esophagus/Small Intestine Dupuytren's Contracture Tissue Femoral Head, Other than Fracture Fissure/Fistula Foreskin, Other than Newborn Gallbladder Ganglion Cyst Hematoma Hemorrhoids Hydatid of Morgagni Intervertebral Disc Joint, Loose Body Meniscus Mucocele, Salivary Neuroma - Morton's/Traumatic Pilonidal Cyst/Sinus Polyps, Inflammatory - Nasal/Sinusoidal Skin - Cyst/Tag/Debridement Soft Tissue, Debridement Soft Tissue, Lipoma Spermatocele Tendon/Tendon Sheath Testicular Appendage Thrombus or Embolus Tonsil and/or Adenoids Varicocele Vas Deferens, Other than Sterilization Vein, Varicosity

88305 **Level IV - Surgical pathology, gross and microscopic examination** ☒ 80 ▣
MED: 100-1, 5, 90.2; 100-2, 15, 80; 100-2, 15, 80.1; 100-4, 12, 60; 100-4, 16, 10; 100-4, 16, 10.1; 100-4, 16, 110.4

AMA: 2000, Sep, 10; 2000, Jul, 4; 2000, Dec, 15; 1998, Nov, 29-30; 1998, Jul, 4; 1997, Aug, 18; 1992, Winter, 17; 1991, Winter, 18; 1991, Spring, 6

Abortion - Spontaneous/Missed Artery, Biopsy Bone Marrow, Biopsy Bone Exostosis Brain/Meninges, Other than for Tumor Resection Breast, Biopsy, Not Requiring Microscopic Evaluation of Surgical Margins Breast, Reduction Mammoplasty Bronchus, Biopsy Cell Block, Any Source Cervix, Biopsy Colon, Biopsy Duodenum, Biopsy Endocervix, Curettings/Biopsy Endometrium, Curettings/Biopsy Esophagus, Biopsy Extremity, Amputation, Traumatic Fallopian Tube, Biopsy Fallopian Tube, Ectopic Pregnancy Femoral Head, Fracture Fingers/Toes, Amputation, Non-traumatic Gingiva/Oral Mucosa, Biopsy Heart Valve Joint, Resection Kidney, Biopsy Larynx, Biopsy Leiomyoma(s), Uterine Myomectomy - without Uterus Lip, Biopsy/Wedge Resection Lung, Transbronchial Biopsy Lymph Node, Biopsy Muscle, Biopsy Nasal Mucosa, Biopsy Nasopharynx/Oropharynx, Biopsy Nerve, Biopsy Odontogenic/Dental Cyst Omentum, Biopsy Ovary with or without Tube, Non-neoplastic Ovary, Biopsy/Wedge Resection Parathyroid Gland Peritoneum, Biopsy Pituitary Tumor Placenta, Other than Third Trimester Pleura/Pericardium - Biopsy/Tissue Polyp, Cervical/Endometrial Polyp, Colorectal Polyp, Stomach/Small Intestine Prostate, Needle Biopsy Prostate, TUR Salivary Gland, Biopsy Sinus, Paranasal Biopsy Skin, Other than Cyst/Tag/Debridement/Plastic Repair Small Intestine, Biopsy Soft Tissue, Other than Tumor/Mass/Lipoma/Debridement Spleen Stomach, Biopsy Synovium Testis, Other than Tumor/Biopsy/Castration Thyroglossal Duct/Brachial Cleft Cyst Tongue, Biopsy Tonsil, Biopsy Trachea, Biopsy Ureter, Biopsy Urethra, Biopsy Urinary Bladder, Biopsy Uterus, with or without Tubes and Ovaries, for Prolapse Vagina, Biopsy Vulva/Labia, Biopsy

88307   **Level V - Surgical pathology, gross and microscopic examination** ⊠ 80 ▣
MED: 100-1, 5, 90.2; 100-2, 15, 80; 100-2, 15, 80.1; 100-4, 12, 60; 100-4, 16, 10; 100-4, 16, 10.1; 100-4, 16, 110.4

AMA: 2000, Sep, 10; 2000, Jul, 4; 2000, Dec, 15; 1999, Jul, 10; 1998, Nov, 29-30; 1998, Jul, 4; 1992, Winter, 18; 1991, Winter, 18

Adrenal, Resection; Bone - Biopsy/Curettings; Bone Fragment(s), Pathologic Fracture; Brain, Biopsy; Brain/Meninges, Tumor Resection; Breast, Excision of Lesion, Requiring Microscopic Evaluation of Surgical Margins; Breast, Mastectomy - Partial/Simple; Cervix, Conization; Colon, Segmental Resection, Other than for Tumor; Extremity, Amputation, Non-Traumatic; Eye, Enucleation; Kidney, Partial/Total Nephrectomy; Larynx, Partial/Total Resection; Liver, Biopsy - Needle/Wedge; Liver, Partial Resection; Lung, Wedge Biopsy; Lymph Nodes, Regional Resection; Mediastinum, Mass; Myocardium, Biopsy; Odontogenic Tumor; Ovary with or without Tube, Neoplastic; Pancreas, Biopsy; Placenta, Third Trimester; Prostate, Except Radical Resection; Salivary Gland; Sentinel Lymph Node; Small Intestine; Resection, Other than for Tumor; Soft Tissue Mass (except Lipoma) - Biopsy/Simple Excision; Stomach - Subtotal/Total Resection, Other than for Tumor; Testis, Biopsy; Thymus, Tumor; Thyroid, Total/Lobe; Ureter, Resection; Urinary Bladder, TUR; Uterus, with or without Tubes and Ovaries, Other than Neoplastic/Prolapse

88309   **Level VI - Surgical pathology, gross and microscopic examination** ⊠ 80 ▣
MED: 100-1, 5, 90.2; 100-2, 15, 80; 100-2, 15, 80.1; 100-4, 12, 60; 100-4, 16, 10; 100-4, 16, 10.1; 100-4, 16, 110.4

AMA: 2000, Sep, 10; 2000, Jul, 4; 1993, Fall, "2, 26"; 1991, Winter, 18; 1991, Spring, 2

Bone Resection; Breast, Mastectomy - with Regional Lymph Nodes; Colon, Segmental Resection for Tumor; Colon, Total Resection; Esophagus, Partial/Total Resection; Extremity, Disarticulation; Fetus, with Dissection; Larynx, Partial/Total Resection - with Regional Lymph Nodes; Lung - Total/Lobe/Segment Resection; Pancreas, Total/Subtotal Resection; Prostate, Radical Resection; Small Intestine, Resection for Tumor; Soft Tissue Tumor, Extensive Resection; Stomach - Subtotal/Total Resection for Tumor; Testis, Tumor; Tongue/Tonsil - Resection for Tumor; Urinary Bladder, Partial/Total Resection; Uterus, with or without Tubes & Ovaries, Neoplastic; Vulva, Total/Subtotal Resection

To report fine needle aspiration, consult CPT codes 10021, 10022.

To report evaluation of fine needle aspirate, consult CPT codes 88172, 88173.

+   **88311**   **Decalcification procedure (List separately in addition to code for surgical pathology examination)** ⊠ 80
MED: 100-1, 5, 90.2; 100-2, 15, 80; 100-2, 15, 80.1; 100-4, 12, 60; 100-4, 16, 10; 100-4, 16, 10.1; 100-4, 16, 110.4

AMA: 2002, Jun, 11; 1998, Jul, 4; 1992, Winter, 18

+   **88312**   **Special stains (List separately in addition to code for primary service); Group I for microorganisms (eg, Gridley, acid fast, methenamine silver), each** ⊠ 80
MED: 100-4, 12, 60

AMA: 2002, Jun, 11

+   **88313**   **Group II, all other, (eg, iron, trichrome), except immunocytochemistry and immunoperoxidase stains, each** ⊠ 80 ▣
MED: 100-4, 12, 60

AMA: 2002, Jun, 11

If immunocytochemistry and immunoperoxidase tissue studies are performed, consult CPT code 88342.

 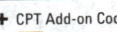 

+ **88314**   **histochemical staining with frozen section(s)**   X 80
MED: 100-1, 5, 90.2; 100-2, 15, 80; 100-2, 15, 80.1; 100-4, 12, 60; 100-4, 16, 10; 100-4, 16, 10.1; 100-4, 16, 110.4

88318   **Determinative histochemistry to identify chemical components (eg, copper, zinc)**   X 80
MED: 100-4, 12, 60

88319   **Determinative histochemistry or cytochemistry to identify enzyme constituents, each**   X 80
MED: 100-4, 12, 60

88321   **Consultation and report on referred slides prepared elsewhere**   X 80 ⟲
MED: 100-4, 12, 60

AMA: 2002, Dec, 10; 2000, Oct, 7; 1997, Apr, 9; 1991, Winter, 19

88323   **Consultation and report on referred material requiring preparation of slides**   X 80 ⟲
MED: 100-4, 12, 60

AMA: 2000, Oct, 7; 1997, Apr, 9; 1991, Winter, 19

88325   **Consultation, comprehensive, with review of records and specimens, with report on referred material**   X 80 ⟲
MED: 100-4, 12, 60

AMA: 1997, Apr, 9; 1991, Winter, 19

88329   **Pathology consultation during surgery;**   X 80 ⟲
MED: 100-4, 12, 60

AMA: 1997, Aug, 18; 1997, Apr, 12; 1991, Winter, 19

88331   **first tissue block, with frozen section(s), single specimen**   X 80 ⟲
MED: 100-1, 5, 90.2; 100-2, 15, 80; 100-2, 15, 80.1; 100-4, 12, 60; 100-4, 16, 10; 100-4, 16, 10.1; 100-4, 16, 110.4

AMA: 2002, Nov, 5; 2000, Jul, 4; 1997, Aug, 18; 1997, Apr, 12; 1991, Winter, 19; 1991, Spring, 2

88332   **each additional tissue block with frozen section(s)**   X 80 ⟲
MED: 100-1, 5, 90.2; 100-2, 15, 80; 100-2, 15, 80.1; 100-4, 12, 60; 100-4, 16, 10; 100-4, 16, 10.1; 100-4, 16, 110.4

AMA: 2000, Jul, 4; 1997, Aug, 18; 1997, Apr, 12; 1991, Winter, 19

● **88333**   **cytologic examination (eg, touch prep, squash prep), initial site**

● **88334**   **cytologic examination (eg, touch prep, squash prep), each additional site**

To report an intraoperative consultation on a specimen that requires both a frozen section and a cytologic evaluation, consult CPT codes 88331 and 88334.

To report a percutaneous needle biopsy that requires an intraprocedural cytologic examination, consult CPT code 88333.

Codes 88333 and 88334 cannot be reported for non-intraoperative cytologic examination; consult CPT codes 88160-88162.

Codes 88333 and 88334 cannot be reported for intraprocedural cytologic evaluation of fine needle aspirate; consult code 88172.

88342   **Immunohistochemistry (including tissue immunoperoxidase), each antibody**   X 80 ⟲
MED: 100-4, 12, 60

AMA: 2002, Nov, 5; 2000, Jul, 10

Code 88342 cannot be reported with CPT code 88360 or 88361 for the same antibody.

To report quantitative or semiquantitative immunohistochemistry, consult CPT codes 88360 and 88361.

88346   **Immunofluorescent study, each antibody; direct method**   ☒ 80
MED: 100-4, 12, 60

88347   **indirect method**   ☒ 80
MED: 100-4, 12, 60

88348   **Electron microscopy; diagnostic**   ☒ 80 ⊡
MED: 100-4, 12, 60

88349   **scanning**   ☒ 80
MED: 100-3, 190.4; 100-4, 12, 60

88355   **Morphometric analysis; skeletal muscle**   ☒ 80 ⊡
MED: 100-4, 12, 60

88356   **nerve**   ☒ 80 ⊡
MED: 100-4, 12, 60

88358   **tumor (eg, DNA ploidy)**   ☒ 80 ⊡
MED: 100-4, 12, 60

AMA: 2002, Jun, 11; 1999, Jul, 11; 1998, Jul, 4

Code 88358 should not be reported with 88313 unless each procedure is for a different special stain.

88360   **Morphometric analysis, tumor immunohistochemistry (eg, Her-2/neu, estrogen receptor/progesterone receptor), quantitative or semiquantitative, each antibody; manual**   ☒ 80 ⊡

88361   **using computer-assisted technology**   ☒ 80 ⊡

Codes 88360 and 88361 should not be reported with 88342 unless each procedure is for a different antibody.

To report morphometric analysis in situ hybridization, consult CPT codes 88367and 88368.

If semi-thin plastic-embedded sections are performed with morphometric analysis, only the analysis should be reported; if performed as an independent procedure, consult CPT codes 88300-88309.

88362   **Nerve teasing preparations**   ☒ 80 ⊡
MED: 100-4, 12, 60

88365   **In situ hybridization (eg, FISH), each probe**   ☒ 80 ⊡
AMA: 2002, Jun, 11

Code 88365 cannot be reported with CPT codes 88367, 88368, for the same probe.

88367   **Morphometric analysis, in situ hybridization, (quantitative or semi-quantitative) each probe; using computer-assisted technology**   ☒ 80 ⊡

88368   **manual**   ☒ 80 ⊡

88371   **Protein analysis of tissue by Western Blot, with interpretation and report;**   Ⓐ ⊡

88372   **immunological probe for band identification, each**   Ⓐ ⊡
MED: 100-3, 190.8; 100-4, 12, 60

88380   **Microdissection (eg, mechanical, laser capture)**   Ⓐ 80
AMA: 2002, Apr, 17

● **88384**   **Array-based evaluation of multiple molecular probes; 11 through 50 probes**

● **88385**   **51 through 250 probes**

● **88386**　**251 through 500 probes**

To report preparation of array-based evaluation, consult CPT codes 83890-83892, 83898-83901.

To report preparation and analyses of less than 11 probes, consult codes 83890-83914.

88399　**Unlisted surgical pathology procedure**　A 80
MED: 100-1, 5, 90.2; 100-2, 15, 80; 100-2, 15, 80.1; 100-4, 16, 10; 100-4, 16, 10.1; 100-4, 16, 110.4

TRANSCUTANEOUS PROCEDURES

88400　**Bilirubin, total, transcutaneous**　A

OTHER PROCEDURES

● **89049**　**Caffeine halothane contracture test (CHCT) for malignant hyperthermia susceptibility, including interpretation and report**

89050　**Cell count, miscellaneous body fluids (eg, cerebrospinal fluid, joint fluid), except blood;**　A ⏎
MED: 100-2, 15, 80

89051　　**with differential count**　A ⏎
MED: 100-2, 15, 80

89055　**Leukocyte assessment, fecal, qualitative or semiquantitative**　A

89060　**Crystal identification by light microscopy with or without polarizing lens analysis, any body fluid (except urine)**　A ⏎
MED: 100-2, 15, 80; 100-4, 12, 60

89100　**Duodenal intubation and aspiration; single specimen (eg, simple bile study or afferent loop culture) plus appropriate test procedure**　X 80 ⏎

89105　　**collection of multiple fractional specimens with pancreatic or gallbladder stimulation, single or double lumen tube**　X 80 ⏎

To report radiological localization, consult CPT code 74340. If chemical analyses are necessary, consult the Chemistry section of the CPT book. If an electrocardiogram is performed, consult CPT codes 93000-93268. If an esophagus acid perfusion test (Bernstein) is performed, consult CPT code 91030.

89125　**Fat stain, feces, urine, or respiratory secretions**　A ⏎

89130　**Gastric intubation and aspiration, diagnostic, each specimen, for chemical analyses or cytopathology;**　X 80 ⏎

89132　　**after stimulation**　X 80 ⏎

89135　**Gastric intubation, aspiration, and fractional collections (eg, gastric secretory study); one hour**　X 80 ⏎

89136　　**two hours**　X 80 ⏎

89140　　**two hours including gastric stimulation (eg, histalog, pentagastrin)**　X 80 ⏎

89141　　**three hours, including gastric stimulation**　X 80 ⏎

To report gastric lavage, therapeutic, consult CPT code 91105. To report radiologic localization of a gastric tube, consult CPT code 74340. If chemical analyses are necessary, consult CPT codes 82926 and 82928. To report joint fluid chemistry, consult the Chemistry section of the CPT book.

89160　**Meat fibers, feces**　A ⏎

89190	**Nasal smear for eosinophils**	Ⓐ ◪

To report occult blood, feces, consult CPT code 82270.

To report paternity tests, consult CPT code 86910.

89220	**Sputum, obtaining specimen, aerosol induced technique (separate procedure)**	⊠ ⒯⒞ ⑧⓪
89225	**Starch granules, feces**	Ⓐ ◪
89230	**Sweat collection by iontophoresis**	⊠ ⒯⒞ ⑧⓪ ◪
89235	**Water load test**	Ⓐ ◪
89240	**Unlisted miscellaneous pathology test**	Ⓐ ⑧⓪

If necessary to report basal metabolic rate, use CPT code 89240.

REPRODUCTIVE MEDICINE PROCEDURES

89250 Culture of oocyte(s)/embryo(s), less than 4 days; ♀ ⊠
AMA: 1998, Oct, 1; 1998, Jan, 6; 1997, Nov, 35-36

89251   with co-culture of oocyte(s)/embryos ♀ ⊠ ◪
AMA: 1998, Oct, 1; 1998, Jan, 6; 1997, Nov, 35-36

To report extended culture of oocyte(s)/embryo(s), consult CPT code 89272.

89253 Assisted embryo hatching, microtechniques (any method) ⊠
AMA: 1998, Oct, 1; 1998, Jan, 6; 1997, Nov, 35-36

89254 Oocyte identification from follicular fluid ♀ ⊠
AMA: 1998, Oct, 1; 1998, Jan, 6; 1997, Nov, 35-36

89255 Preparation of embryo for transfer (any method) ⊠
AMA: 1998, Oct, 1; 1998, Jan, 6; 1997, Nov, 35-36

89257 Sperm identification from aspiration (other than seminal fluid) ⊠ ◪
AMA: 1998, Oct, 1; 1998, Nov, 30; 1998, Jan, 6; 1997, Nov, 35-36

If semen is analyzed, consult CPT codes 89300-89320. If sperm is identified from testis tissue, consult CPT code 89264.

89258 Cryopreservation; embryo(s) ⊠
AMA: 1998, Oct, 1; 1998, Jan, 6; 1997, Nov, 36

89259   sperm ⊠
AMA: 1998, Oct, 1; 1998, Jan, 6; 1997, Nov, 36

To report cryopreservation of reproductive tissue, testicular, consult CPT code 89335.

To report cryopreservation of reproductive tissue, ovarian, consult CPT Category III code 0058T.

To report cryopreservation of oocyte(s), consult CPT Category III code 0059T.

89260 Sperm isolation; simple prep (eg, sperm wash and swim-up) for insemination or diagnosis with semen analysis ⊠ ◪
AMA: 1998, Oct, 1; 1998, Jan, 6; 1997, Nov, 36

89261   complex prep (eg, Percoll gradient, albumin gradient) for insemination or diagnosis with semen analysis ⊠ ◪
AMA: 1998, Oct, 1; 1998, Jan, 6; 1997, Nov, 36

If semen is analyzed without sperm wash or swim-up, consult CPT code 89320.

89264   **Sperm identification from testis tissue, fresh or cryopreserved**   ⊠ ▢
     AMA: 1998, Nov, 30

If the testis is biopsied, consult CPT codes 54500 and 54505. If sperm is identified from aspiration, consult CPT code 89257. If semen is analyzed, consult CPT codes 89300-89320.

89268   **Insemination of oocytes**   ♀ ⊠

89272   **Extended culture of oocyte(s)/embryo(s), 4-7 days**   ♀ ⊠

89280   **Assisted oocyte fertilization, microtechnique; less than or equal to 10 oocytes**   ♀ ⊠

89281   **Assisted oocyte fertilization, microtechnique; greater than 10 oocytes** ♀ ⊠

89290   **Biopsy, oocyte polar body or embryo blastomere, microtechnique (for pre-implantation genetic diagnosis); less than or equal to 5 embryos**   ♀ ⊠

89291   **Biopsy, oocyte polar body or embryo blastomere, microtechnique (for pre-implantation genetic diagnosis); greater than 5 embryos**   ♀ ⊠

89300   **Semen analysis; presence and/or motility of sperm including Huhner test (post coital)**   Ⓐ ⊠ ▢
     MED: 100-2, 15, 20.1

     AMA: 1998, Oct, 1; 1998, Jul, 10; 1997, Nov, 36

89310   **motility and count (not including Huhner test)**   Ⓐ ▢
     MED: 100-2, 15, 20.1

89320   **complete (volume, count, motility and differential)**   Ⓐ ▢
     MED: 100-2, 15, 20.1

To report skin tests, consult CPT codes 86485-86585 and 95010-95199.

89321   **Semen analysis, presence and/or motility of sperm**   Ⓐ
     MED: 100-2, 15, 20.1

To report Hyaluronan binding assay (HBA), consult Category III code 0087T.

89325   **Sperm antibodies**   Ⓐ ▢
     MED: 100-2, 15, 20.1

To report medicolegal identification of sperm, consult CPT code 88125.

89329   **Sperm evaluation; hamster penetration test**   Ⓐ ▢

89330   **cervical mucus penetration test, with or without spinnbarkeit test** Ⓐ ▢

89335   **Cryopreservation, reproductive tissue, testicular**   ⊠

To report cryopreservation of embryo(s), consult CPT code 89258. To report cryopreservation of sperm, consult CPT code 89259.

To report cryopreservation of reproductive tissue, ovarian, consult CPT Category III code 0058T.

To report cryopreservation of oocyte(s), consult CPT Category III code 0059T.

89342   **Storage, (per year); embryo(s)**   ⊠

89343   **sperm/semen**   ⊠

89344   **reproductive tissue, testicular/ovarian**   ⊠

89346   **oocyte(s)**   ♀ ⊠

89352   **Thawing of cryopreserved; embryo(s)**   ⊠

89353   **sperm/semen, each aliquot**   ⊠

89354   **reproductive tissue, testicular/ovarian**   ⊠

89356   **oocytes, each aliquot**   ⊠

Pathology and Laboratory

89264 — 89356

Medicine Services

CODING INFORMATION

ORGANIZATION

The medicine section (90281–99602) follows the pathology and laboratory section. The diagnostic and therapeutic services include immunizations, injections, specialty-specific codes, and special services.

Subsections within the medicine section are:

Immune Globulins

Immunization Administration for
    Vaccines/Toxoids

Vaccines/Toxoids

Hydration, Therapeutic, Prophylactic, and
    Diagnostic Injections and Infusions

Psychiatry

Biofeedback

Dialysis

Gastroenterology

Ophthalmology

Special Otorhinolaryngologic Services

Cardiovascular

Noninvasive Vascular Diagnostic Studies

Pulmonary

Allergy and Clinical Immunology

Endocrinology

Neurology and Neuromuscular Procedures

Central Nervous System Assessments/Tests (e.g.,
    Neuro-Cognitive, Mental Status, Speech
    Testing)

Health and Behavior Assessment/Intervention

Chemotherapy Administration

Photodynamic Therapy

Special Dermatological Procedures

Physical Medicine and Rehabilitation

Medical Nutrition Therapy

Osteopathic Manipulative Treatment

Chiropractic Manipulative Treatment

Special Services, Procedures and Reports

Qualifying Circumstances for Anesthesia

Sedation with or without Analgesia (Conscious
    Sedation)

Other Services and Procedures

Home Health Procedures/Services

Home Infusion Procedures

GUIDELINES

BUNDLED MEDICINE CODES

The process of coding integral services separately from a procedure or bundled service is called unbundling or fragmenting. If the component is considered part of the package or bundled service, do not code it individually. For example, 93015 includes all the components of a stress test and should be reported as such when the complete procedure is performed. If the components 93016, 93017 and 93018 are reported separately instead of the complete test (93015), the payer may rebundle the codes and reimburse for 93015. However, the payer may also simply deny the entire claim. It is important that you report only the services actually provided.

Medicine

IMMUNE GLOBULINS

Immune globulin codes (90281–90399) report only the supply of the immune globulin product that includes broad-spectrum and anti-infective immune globulins, antitoxins, and various other isoantibodies. Administration is reported separately with codes 90765–90768, 90772, 90774, 90775.

⊘   **90281**   **Immune globulin (IG), human, for intramuscular use**   E
MED: 100-2, 15, 50

AMA: 1999, Sep, 10; 1999, Jan, 1; 1998, Nov, 30

⊘   **90283**   **Immune globulin (IGIV), human, for intravenous use**   E
MED: 100-2, 15, 50

AMA: 1999, Jan, 1; 1998, Nov, 30

⊘   **90287**   **Botulinum antitoxin, equine, any route**   E
MED: 100-2, 15, 50

AMA: 1999, Jan, 1; 1998, Nov, 30

⊘   **90288**   **Botulism immune globulin, human, for intravenous use**   E
MED: 100-2, 15, 50

AMA: 1999, Jan, 1; 1998, Nov, 30

⊘   **90291**   **Cytomegalovirus immune globulin (CMV-IGIV), human, for intravenous use**   E
MED: 100-2, 15, 50

AMA: 1999, Jan, 1; 1998, Nov, 30

⊘   **90296**   **Diphtheria antitoxin, equine, any route**   N
MED: 100-2, 15, 50

AMA: 1999, Jan, 1; 1998, Nov, 30

⊘   **90371**   **Hepatitis B immune globulin (HBIG), human, for intramuscular use**   E
MED: 100-2, 15, 50

AMA: 1999, Jan, 1; 1998, Nov, 30

⊘   **90375**   **Rabies immune globulin (RIG), human, for intramuscular use and/or subcutaneous use**   K
MED: 100-2, 15, 50

AMA: 1999, Jan, 1; 1998, Nov, 30

⊘   **90376**   **Rabies immune globulin, heat-treated (RIG-HT), human, for intramuscular and/or subcutaneous use**   K
MED: 100-2, 15, 50

AMA: 1999, Jan, 1; 1998, Nov, 30

⊘   **90378**   **Respiratory syncytial virus immune globulin (RSV-IgIM), for intramuscular use, 50 mg, each**   E ⬙
MED: 100-2, 15, 50; 100-2, 16, 90

AMA: 1999, Jan, 1; 1998, Nov, 30

⊘   **90379**   **Respiratory syncytial virus immune globulin (RSV-IGIV), human, for intravenous use**   E
MED: 100-2, 15, 50; 100-2, 16, 90

AMA: 1999, Jan, 1; 1998, Nov, 30

⊘   **90384**   **Rho(D) immune globulin (RhIG), human, full-dose, for intramuscular use** E
MED: 100-2, 15, 50

AMA: 1999, Jan, 1; 1998, Nov, 30

90281 — 90384

⊘ **90385** **Rho(D) immune globulin (RhIG), human, mini-dose, for intramuscular use** Ⓝ
MED: 100-2, 15, 50

AMA: 1999, Jan, 1; 1998, Nov, 30

⊘ **90386** **Rho(D) immune globulin (RhIGIV), human, for intravenous use** Ⓔ
MED: 100-2, 15, 50

AMA: 1999, Jan, 1; 1998, Nov, 30

⊘ **90389** **Tetanus immune globulin (TIG), human, for intramuscular use** Ⓔ
MED: 100-2, 15, 50

AMA: 1999, Jan, 1; 1998, Nov, 30

⊘ **90393** **Vaccinia immune globulin, human, for intramuscular use** Ⓝ
MED: 100-2, 15, 50

AMA: 1999, Jan, 1; 1998, Nov, 30

⊘ **90396** **Varicella-zoster immune globulin, human, for intramuscular use** Ⓚ
MED: 100-2, 15, 50

AMA: 1999, Jan, 1; 1998, Nov, 30

⊘ **90399** **Unlisted immune globulin** Ⓔ
MED: 100-2, 15, 50

AMA: 1999, Sep, 10; 1999, Jan, 1; 1999, Feb, 11; 1998, Nov, 30

IMMUNIZATION ADMINISTRATION FOR VACCINES/TOXOIDS

IMMUNIZATION ADMINISTRATION FOR VACCINES/TOXOIDS

Immunization administration codes (90465–90474) are reported separately in addition to the code for the vaccine or toxoid supply (90476–90749). Significant, separately identifiable E/M services should also be reported.

Codes 90465-90468 should be reported only when the physician provides face-to-face counseling of the patient and the family during the administration of the vaccine. Report 90471-90474 when immunization administration is not accompanied by face-to-face physician contact.

If allergy tests are conducted, consult CPT codes 95004 and subsequent codes. For skin testing of bacterial, viral, fungal, extracts, consult CPT codes 86485-86586. If therapeutic or diagnostic injections are administered, consult CPT codes 90772–90779.

90465 **Immunization administration under 8 years of age (includes percutaneous, intradermal, subcutaneous, or intramuscular injections) when the physician counsels the patient/family; first injection (single or combination vaccine/toxoid), per day** Ⓐ Ⓑ 80 ▣

Code 90465 cannot be reported with CPT code 90467.

+ **90466** **each additional injection (single or combination vaccine/toxoid), per day (List separately in addition to code for primary procedure)** Ⓐ Ⓑ 80

Note that 90466 is an add-on code and must be used in conjunction with code 90465 or 90467 .

90467 **Immunization administration under age 8 years (includes intranasal or oral routes of administration) when the physician counsels the patient/family; first administration (single or combination vaccine/toxoid), per day** Ⓐ Ⓑ ▣

Code 90467 cannot be reported with CPT code 90465.

+ **90468** **each additional administration (single or combination vaccine/toxoid), per day (List separately in addition to code for primary procedure)** Ⓐ Ⓑ

Note that 90468 is an add-on code and must be used in conjunction with code 90465 or 90467.

Medicine

90471 — 90581

90471   **Immunization administration (includes percutaneous, intradermal, subcutaneous, or intramuscular injections); one vaccine (single or combination vaccine/toxoid)** ☒
MED: 100-2, 15, 50

AMA: 2002, Nov, 11; 2001, Jul, 1; 2001, Feb, 4; 2000, Nov, 10; 1999, Nov, 47-48; 1999, Jan, 1; 1999, Apr, 10; 1998, Nov, 31

Code 90471 cannot be reported with CPT code 90473.

+ **90472**   **each additional vaccine (single or combination vaccine/toxoid) (List separately in addition to code for primary procedure)** ☒
MED: 100-2, 15, 50

AMA: 2002, Nov, 11; 2001, Jul, 1; 2001, Feb, 4; 2000, Nov, 10; 1999, Nov, 47-48; 1999, Jan, 1; 1999, Apr, 10; 1998, Nov, 31

Note that 90472 is an add-on code and must be used in conjunction with 90471 or 90473.

If immune globulins are administered, use CPT codes 90780-90784 and consult CPT codes 90281-90399. For intravesical administration of BCG vaccine, use CPT code 51720, and consult CPT code 90586.

90473   **Immunization administration by intranasal or oral route; one vaccine (single or combination vaccine/toxoid)** ☒ ◪
MED: 100-2, 15, 50

AMA: 2002, Nov, 11

Code 90473 cannot be reported with CPT code 90471.

+ **90474**   **each additional vaccine (single or combination vaccine/toxoid) (List separately in addition to code for primary procedure)** ⓈS
MED: 100-2, 15, 50

AMA: 2002, Nov, 11

Note that 90474 is an add-on code and must be used in conjunction with code 90471 or 90473.

VACCINES, TOXOIDS

The AMA will be publishing new vaccine products before they have received FDA approval. The codes are identified with the ∕ symbol. Once they are approved, the symbol will be removed. Monitor the AMA internet website at www.ama-assn.org/ama/pub/category/10902.html for the most up-to-date information on these codes. The AMA will use this site to give CPT users updates of the CPT Editorial Panel actions regarding these products. Codes will also be made available twice a year, July 1 and January 1, on the website.

Report codes 90476-90748 recognize the vaccine product **only.** To report the administration of a vaccine/toxoid, the vaccine/toxoid product codes 90476-90749 must be used in addition to an immunization administration code(s) 90465-90474. Do not report modifier 51 to the vaccine/toxoid product code (90476-90749).

⊘ **90476**   **Adenovirus vaccine, type 4, live, for oral use** Ⓚ
MED: 100-2, 15, 50

AMA: 1999, Sep, 10; 1999, Nov, 48; 1999, Jan, 1; 1998, Nov, 31-33

⊘ **90477**   **Adenovirus vaccine, type 7, live, for oral use** Ⓝ
MED: 100-2, 15, 50

AMA: 1999, Nov, 48; 1999, Jan, 1; 1998, Nov, 31-33

⊘ **90581**   **Anthrax vaccine, for subcutaneous use** Ⓚ
MED: 100-2, 15, 50

AMA: 1999, Nov, 48; 1999, Jan, 1; 1998, Nov, 31-33

⊘ **90585** Bacillus Calmette-Guerin vaccine (BCG) for tuberculosis, live, for percutaneous use K ⤵

AMA: 1999, Nov, 48; 1999, Jan, 1; 1998, Nov, 31-33

⊘ **90586** Bacillus Calmette-Guerin vaccine (BCG) for bladder cancer, live, for intravesical use B

MED: 100-2, 15, 50

AMA: 1999, Nov, 48; 1999, Jan, 1; 1998, Nov, 31-33

⊘ **90632** Hepatitis A vaccine, adult dosage, for intramuscular use N

MED: 100-2, 15, 50; 100-2, 16, 90

AMA: 1999, Nov, 48; 1999, Jan, 1; 1998, Nov, 31-33

⊘ **90633** Hepatitis A vaccine, pediatric/adolescent dosage-2 dose schedule, for intramuscular use N

MED: 100-2, 15, 50; 100-2, 16, 90

AMA: 1999, Nov, 48; 1999, Jan, 1; 1998, Nov, 31-33

⊘ **90634** Hepatitis A vaccine, pediatric/adolescent dosage-3 dose schedule, for intramuscular use N

MED: 100-2, 15, 50; 100-2, 16, 90

AMA: 1999, Nov, 48; 1999, Jan, 1; 1998, Nov, 31-33

⊘ **90636** Hepatitis A and hepatitis B vaccine (HepA-HepB), adult dosage, for intramuscular use K

MED: 100-2, 15, 50

AMA: 1999, Nov, 48; 1999, Jan, 1; 1998, Nov, 31-33

⊘ **90645** Hemophilus influenza b vaccine (Hib), HbOC conjugate (4 dose schedule), for intramuscular use N ⤵

MED: 100-2, 15, 50

AMA: 1999, Nov, 48; 1999, Jan, 1; 1998, Nov, 31-33

⊘ **90646** Hemophilus influenza b vaccine (Hib), PRP-D conjugate, for booster use only, intramuscular use N ⤵

MED: 100-2, 15, 50

AMA: 1999, Nov, 48; 1999, Jan, 1; 1998, Nov, 31-33

⊘ **90647** Hemophilus influenza b vaccine (Hib), PRP-OMP conjugate (3 dose schedule), for intramuscular use N ⤵

MED: 100-2, 15, 50

AMA: 1999, Nov, 48; 1999, Jan, 1; 1998, Nov, 31-33

⊘ **90648** Hemophilus influenza b vaccine (Hib),PRP-T conjugate (4 dose schedule), for intramuscular use N ⤵

MED: 100-2, 15, 50

AMA: 1999, Nov, 48; 1999, Jan, 1; 1998, Nov, 31-33

⊘ ⁄ ● **90649** Human Papilloma virus (HPV) vaccine, types 6, 11, 16, 18 (quadrivalent), 3 dose schedule, for intramuscular use

⊘ **90655** Influenza virus vaccine, split virus, preservative free, for children 6-35 months of age, for intramuscular use A L ⤵

⊘ **90656** Influenza virus vaccine, split virus, preservative free, for use in individuals 3 years and above, for intramuscular use L ⤵

⁄ Drug Not Approved by FDA　　**50** Bilateral Procedure　　＋ CPT Add-on Code　　⊘ Modifier -51 Exempt　　♂ Male　　♀ Female
● New Code　　▲ Revised Code　　**M** Maternity Edit　　**A** Age Edit　　A—Y APC Status Ind.　　**AMA:** CPT Assistant

Medicine

90657 — 90698

⊘ 90657 Influenza virus vaccine, split virus, for children 6-35 months of age, for intramuscular use A L ▣
MED: 100-2, 15, 50

AMA: 2002, Feb, 10; 1999, Nov, 48; 1999, Jan, 1; 1998, Nov, 31-33

⊘ 90658 Influenza virus vaccine, split virus, for use in individuals 3 years of age and above, for intramuscular use L ▣
MED: 100-2, 15, 50

AMA: 1999, Nov, 48; 1999, Jan, 1; 1998, Nov, 31-33

⊘ 90660 Influenza virus vaccine, live, for intranasal use E
MED: 100-2, 15, 50

AMA: 1999, Nov, 48; 1999, Jan, 1; 1998, Nov, 31-33

⊘ 90665 Lyme disease vaccine, adult dosage, for intramuscular use N
MED: 100-2, 15, 50

AMA: 1999, Nov, 48; 1999, Jan, 1; 1998, Nov, 31-33

⊘ 90669 Pneumococcal conjugate vaccine, polyvalent, for children under 5 years, for intramuscular use E
MED: 100-2, 15, 50

AMA: 2000, Jun, 10; 1999, Nov, 48; 1999, Jan, 1; 1998, Nov, 31-33

⊘ 90675 Rabies vaccine, for intramuscular use K ▣
MED: 100-2, 15, 50

AMA: 1999, Nov, 48; 1999, Jan, 1; 1998, Nov, 31-33

⊘ 90676 Rabies vaccine, for intradermal use K
MED: 100-2, 15, 50

AMA: 1999, Nov, 48; 1999, Jan, 1; 1998, Nov, 31-33

⊘ ✂ ▲ 90680 Rotavirus vaccine, pentavalent, 3 dose schedule, live, for oral use N
MED: 100-2, 15, 50

AMA: 1999, Nov, 48; 1999, Jan, 1; 1998, Nov, 31-33

⊘ 90690 Typhoid vaccine, live, oral N
MED: 100-2, 15, 50

AMA: 1999, Nov, 48; 1999, Jan, 1; 1998, Nov, 31-33

⊘ 90691 Typhoid vaccine, Vi capsular polysaccharide (ViCPs), for intramuscular use N ▣
MED: 100-2, 15, 50

AMA: 1999, Nov, 48; 1999, Jan, 1; 1998, Nov, 31-33

⊘ 90692 Typhoid vaccine, heat- and phenol-inactivated (H-P), for subcutaneous or intradermal use N ▣
MED: 100-2, 15, 50

AMA: 1999, Nov, 48; 1999, Jan, 1; 1998, Nov, 31-33

⊘ 90693 Typhoid vaccine, acetone-killed, dried (AKD), for subcutaneous use (U.S. military) N ▣
MED: 100-2, 15, 50

AMA: 1999, Nov, 48; 1999, Jan, 1; 1998, Nov, 31-33

⊘ 90698 Diphtheria, tetanus toxoids, acellular pertussis vaccine, haemophilus influenza Type B, and poliovirus vaccine, inactivated (DTaP - Hib - IPV), for intramuscular use N

⊘ **90700** Diphtheria, tetanus toxoids, and acellular pertussis vaccine (DTaP), for use in individuals younger than 7 years, for intramuscular use Ⓐ Ⓝ ↺
MED: 100-2, 15, 50

AMA: 1999, Nov, 48; 1999, Jan, 1; 1998, Nov, 31-33; 1997, Feb, 9; 1996, Jan, 5

⊘ **90701** Diphtheria, tetanus toxoids, and whole cell pertussis vaccine (DTP), for intramuscular use Ⓝ ↺
MED: 100-2, 15, 50

AMA: 1999, Nov, 48; 1999, Jan, 1; 1998, Nov, 31-33; 1996, Jan, 6

⊘ **90702** Diphtheria and tetanus toxoids (DT) adsorbed for use in individuals younger than 7 years, for intramuscular use Ⓐ Ⓝ ↺
MED: 100-2, 15, 50

AMA: 2000, Jun, 10; 1999, Sep, 10; 1999, Nov, 48; 1999, Jan, 1; 1998, Nov, 31-33; 1996, Jan, 6

⊘ **90703** Tetanus toxoid adsorbed, for intramuscular use Ⓝ ↺
MED: 100-2, 15, 50

AMA: 1999, Sep, 10; 1999, Nov, 48; 1999, Jan, 1; 1998, Nov, 31-33; 1996, Jan, 6

⊘ **90704** Mumps virus vaccine, live, for subcutaneous use Ⓝ ↺
MED: 100-2, 15, 50; 100-2, 16, 90

AMA: 1999, Nov, 48; 1999, Jan, 1; 1998, Nov, 31-33

⊘ **90705** Measles virus vaccine, live, for subcutaneous use Ⓝ ↺
MED: 100-2, 15, 50; 100-2, 16, 90

AMA: 1999, Nov, 48; 1999, Jan, 1; 1998, Nov, 31-33

⊘ **90706** Rubella virus vaccine, live, for subcutaneous use Ⓝ ↺
MED: 100-2, 15, 50; 100-2, 16, 90

AMA: 1999, Nov, 48; 1999, Jan, 1; 1998, Nov, 31-33

⊘ **90707** Measles, mumps and rubella virus vaccine (MMR), live, for subcutaneous use Ⓝ ↺
MED: 100-2, 15, 50; 100-2, 16, 90

AMA: 1999, Nov, 48; 1999, Jan, 1; 1998, Nov, 31-33; 1997, Apr, 10; 1996, May, 10; 1996, Jan, 6

⊘ **90708** Measles and rubella virus vaccine, live, for subcutaneous use Ⓚ ↺
MED: 100-2, 15, 50; 100-2, 16, 90

AMA: 1999, Nov, 48; 1999, Jan, 1; 1998, Nov, 31-33

⊘ **90710** Measles, mumps, rubella, and varicella vaccine (MMRV), live, for subcutaneous use Ⓝ ↺
MED: 100-2, 15, 50; 100-2, 16, 90

AMA: 1999, Nov, 48; 1999, Jan, 1; 1998, Nov, 31-33; 1997, Apr, 10; 1996, May, 10

⊘ **90712** Poliovirus vaccine, (any type(s)) (OPV), live, for oral use Ⓝ
MED: 100-2, 15, 50; 100-2, 16, 90

AMA: 1999, Nov, 48; 1999, Jan, 1; 1998, Nov, 31-33; 1996, Jan, 6

⊘ ▲ **90713** Poliovirus vaccine, inactivated, (IPV), for subcutaneous or intramuscular use Ⓝ
MED: 100-2, 15, 50; 100-2, 16, 90

AMA: 1999, Nov, 48; 1999, Jan, 1; 1998, Nov, 31-33

Medicine

⊘ ● **90714** Tetanus and diphtheria toxoids (Td) adsorbed, preservative free, for use in individuals 7 years or older, for intramuscular use

⊘ ▲ **90715** Tetanus, diphtheria toxoids and acellular pertussis vaccine (Tdap), for use in individuals 7 years or older, for intramuscular use ⃞N

⊘ **90716** Varicella virus vaccine, live, for subcutaneous use ⃞K
MED: 100-2, 15, 50; 100-2, 16, 90

AMA: 1999, Nov, 48; 1999, Jan, 1; 1998, Nov, 31-33; 1997, Apr, 10; 1996, May, 10; 1996, Jan, 6

⊘ **90717** Yellow fever vaccine, live, for subcutaneous use ⃞N
AMA: 1999, Nov, 48; 1999, Jan, 1; 1998, Nov, 31-33

⊘ **90718** Tetanus and diphtheria toxoids (Td) adsorbed for use in individuals 7 years or older, for intramuscular use ⃞N ⃞
MED: 100-2, 15, 50; 100-2, 16, 90

AMA: 2000, Jun, 10; 1999, Nov, 48; 1999, Jan, 1; 1998, Nov, 31-33; 1996, Aug, 10

⊘ **90719** Diphtheria toxoid, for intramuscular use ⃞N ⃞
MED: 100-2, 15, 50; 100-2, 16, 90

AMA: 1999, Sep, 10; 1999, Nov, 48; 1999, Jan, 1; 1998, Nov, 31-33

⊘ **90720** Diphtheria, tetanus toxoids, and whole cell pertussis vaccine and Hemophilus influenza B vaccine (DTP-Hib), for intramuscular use ⃞N ⃞
MED: 100-2, 15, 50; 100-2, 16, 90

AMA: 1999, Nov, 48; 1999, Jan, 1; 1998, Nov, 31-33; 1996, Jan, 5

⊘ **90721** Diphtheria, tetanus toxoids, and acellular pertussis vaccine and Hemophilus influenza B vaccine (DtaP-Hib), for intramuscular use ⃞N ⃞
MED: 100-2, 15, 50; 100-2, 16, 90

AMA: 1999, Nov, 48; 1999, Jan, 1; 1998, Nov, 31-33; 1996, Jan, 5

⊘ **90723** Diphtheria, tetanus toxoids, acellular pertussis vaccine, Hepatitis B, and poliovirus vaccine, inactivated (DtaP-HepB-IPV), for intramuscular use ⃞E
MED: 100-2, 15, 50; 100-2, 16, 90

AMA: 1999, Nov, 48

⊘ **90725** Cholera vaccine for injectable use ⃞N
MED: 100-2, 15, 50

AMA: 1999, Nov, 48; 1999, Jan, 1; 1998, Nov, 31-33

⊘ **90727** Plague vaccine, for intramuscular use ⃞N
MED: 100-2, 15, 50

AMA: 1999, Nov, 48; 1999, Jan, 1; 1998, Nov, 31-33

⊘ **90732** Pneumococcal polysaccharide vaccine, 23-valent, adult or immunosuppressed patient dosage, for use in individuals 2 years or older, for subcutaneous or intramuscular use ⃞L
MED: 100-2, 15, 50

AMA: 1999, Nov, 48; 1999, Jan, 1; 1998, Nov, 31-33

⊘ **90733** Meningococcal polysaccharide vaccine (any group(s)), for subcutaneous use ⃞K
MED: 100-2, 15, 50

AMA: 1999, Nov, 48; 1999, Jan, 1; 1999, Dec, 7; 1998, Nov, 31-33

⊘ **90734** Meningococcal conjugate vaccine, serogroups A, C, Y and W-135 (tetravalent), for intramuscular use ⃞K

⊘ **90735** **Japanese encephalitis virus vaccine, for subcutaneous use** ⓚ
MED: 100-2, 15, 50
AMA: 1999, Nov, 48; 1999, Jan, 1; 1998, Nov, 31-33

⊘ ⚕ ● **90736** **Zoster (shingles) vaccine, live, for subcutaneous injection**

⊘ **90740** **Hepatitis B vaccine, dialysis or immunosuppressed patient dosage (3 dose schedule), for intramuscular use** Ⓕ
MED: 100-2, 15, 50; 100-3, 190.10
AMA: 2001, Apr, 10; 1999, Nov, 48

⊘ **90743** **Hepatitis B vaccine, adolescent (2 dose schedule), for intramuscular use** Ⓕ
MED: 100-2, 15, 50
AMA: 1999, Nov, 48

⊘ **90744** **Hepatitis B vaccine, pediatric/adolescent dosage (3 dose schedule), for intramuscular use** Ⓕ
MED: 100-2, 15, 50
AMA: 2000, Jun, 10; 1999, Nov, 48-49; 1999, Nov, 48; 1999, Jan, 1; 1998, Nov, 31-33; 1997, Jun, 10; 1996, Jan, 5

⊘ **90746** **Hepatitis B vaccine, adult dosage, for intramuscular use** Ⓕ
MED: 100-2, 15, 50
AMA: 1999, Nov, 48; 1999, Jan, 1; 1998, Nov, 31-33; 1996, Jan, 5

⊘ **90747** **Hepatitis B vaccine, dialysis or immunosuppressed patient dosage (4 dose schedule), for intramuscular use** Ⓕ
MED: 100-2, 15, 50; 100-3, 190.10
AMA: 2001, Apr, 10; 2000, Jun, 10; 1999, Nov, 48; 1999, Jan, 1; 1998, Nov, 31-33; 1997, Jun, 10; 1996, Jan, 5

⊘ **90748** **Hepatitis B and Hemophilus influenza b vaccine (HepB-Hib), for intramuscular use** Ⓔ
MED: 100-2, 15, 50
AMA: 1999, Sep, 10; 1999, Nov, 48; 1999, Jan, 1; 1998, Nov, 31-33; 1997, Nov, 37

⊘ **90749** **Unlisted vaccine/toxoid** Ⓝ
MED: 100-2, 15, 50
AMA: 2002, Nov, 11; 1999, Nov, 48; 1999, Jan, 1; 1998, Nov, 31-33; 1997, Feb, 9; 1996, Jan, 6

HYDRATION, THERAPEUTIC, PROPHYLACTIC, AND DIAGNOSTIC INJECTIONS AND INFUSIONS (EXCLUDES CHEMOTHERAPY)

Physician work involved in hydration, therapeutic, prophylactic, and diagnostic injections and infusion services includes verification of a plan of treatment and direction of personnel.

To report an evaluation and management service in addition to hydration, therapeutic, prophylactic, and diagnostic injections and infusion services, consult the appropriate evaluation and management code. Append modifier 25 to 90760–90779. A different diagnosis is not required.

The following codes are included in the infusion or injection:

- Local anesthesia

- Starting the IV

- Access to catheter, IV, or port

- Routine tubing, syringe, and supplies

- Flushing at the completion of the infusion

For declotting of a catheter or port, consult CPT code 36550.

Report the materials or drugs in addition to the injection or infusion codes.

If multiple infusions, injections, or combination services are performed, only the initial code should be reported unless the procedure requires the use of two separate IV sites. Report subsequent or concurrent services using the code that most closely describes the main reason for the procedure even if that is not the order in which the services are performed.

When reporting codes for which time is an issue, use the actual time for the administration of the infusion.

HYDRATION

The following codes are used to report infusion of prepacked fluids and electrolytes, and not drugs or other substances. These services usually require the supervision of a physician to include consent, safety oversight, and supervision of personnel. There is typically little special handling required to prepare, deliver, or dispose of the IV, and the administration does not require any special training for the staff. There is usually little patient risk after the initial set-up, and special patient monitoring is usually not required.

- **90760**   **Intravenous infusion, hydration; initial, up to 1 hour**

    Code 90760 cannot be reported when performed as a concurrent infusion service.

+ ● **90761**   **each additional hour, up to 8 hours (List separately in addition to code for primary procedure)**

    Note that 90761 is an add-on code and should be reported in conjunction with 90760.

    Code 90761 should be reported for hydration infusion intervals of greater than 30 minutes beyond 1-hour increments.

    Code 90761 should be reported to identify hydration if provided as a secondary or subsequent service after a different initial service [90760, 90765, 90774, 96409, 96413] is provided.

THERAPEUTIC, PROPHYLACTIC, AND DIAGNOSTIC INJECTIONS AND INFUSIONS

The following codes are used to describe a therapeutic, prophylactic, or diagnostic IV infusion or injection administered for other than hydration. These codes are used for the administration of drugs, and the fluid in which the drug is mixed is incidental and not separately reportable. These services usually require the supervision of a physician to include consent, patient assessment safety oversight, and the supervision of personnel. The staff usually requires training to include how to assess the patient and monitor the patient during the treatment.

An intravenous or intra-arterial push requires:

- The constant presence of the health care professional administering the substance or drug

- An infusion of 15 minutes or less

The first code (90765) is for infusions up to one hour and the second (90766) is for each additional hour up to eight hours. When reporting 90781, indicate the number of hours in the unit column on the CMS-1500 form or electronic bill. Remember that 90766 must be reported as a secondary code to 90765. Therapeutic or diagnostic injection codes (90782–90788) are for subcutaneous, intramuscular, intra-arterial, and intravenous injections of a therapeutic or diagnostic agent.

The materials injected are not included in the codes. When the drug is purchased and supplied by the physician, use 90281–90399 for immune globulin products, 99070 for supplies, including drugs, provided and not elsewhere listed, or the appropriate HCPCS Level II J code for other drugs. Medicare bundles the administration of the medication into the E/M service. Each Medicare and Medicaid carrier has individual requirements for HCPCS Level II codes to describe the drug administered. Some carriers require the use of the CPT code for the injection and the HCPCS Level II code for the drug; others use only the HCPCS Level II code and require a modifier to designate the method of administration.

● **90765** **Intravenous infusion, for therapy, prophylaxis, or diagnosis (specify substance or drug); initial, up to 1 hour**

+ ● **90766** **each additional hour, up to 8 hours (List separately in addition to code for primary procedure)**

Note that 90766 is an add-on code and should be reported in conjunction with 90765.

Code 90766 should be reported for additional hour(s) of sequential infusion.

Code 90766 should be reported for infusion intervals of greater than 30 minutes beyond 1-hour increments.

+ ● **90767** **additional sequential infusion, up to 1 hour (List separately in addition to code for primary procedure)**

Code 90767 should be reported in conjunction with 90765, 90774, 96409, 96413 when provided as a secondary or subsequent service after a different initial service. Report 90767 only once per sequential infusion of same infusate mix.

+ ● **90768** **concurrent infusion (List separately in addition to code for primary procedure)**

Code 90768 should be reported only once per encounter.

Note that 90768 is an add-on code and should be reported in conjunction with 90765, 96413.

● **90772** **Therapeutic, prophylactic or diagnostic injection (specify substance or drug); subcutaneous or intramuscular**

To report administration of vaccines/toxoids consult 90465-90466, 90471-90472.

Code 90772 should be reported for non-antineoplastic hormonal therapy injections.

Code 96401 should be reported for antineoplastic nonhormonal injection therapy.

Code 96402 should be reported for antineoplastic hormonal injection therapy.

Code 90772 cannot be reported for injections given without direct physician supervision; consult CPT code 99211.

● **90773** **intra-arterial**

● **90774** **intravenous push, single or initial substance/drug**

Codes 90772-90774 do not include injections for allergen immunotherapy; consult CPT codes 95115-95117.

+ ● **90775** **each additional sequential intravenous push of a new substance/drug (List separately in addition to code for primary procedure)**

Note that 90775 is an add-on code and must be used in conjunction with 90765, 90774, 96409, 96413.

Use code 90775 to report intravenous push of a new substance/drug when provided as a secondary or subsequent service after a different initial service has been provided.

● **90779** **Unlisted therapeutic, prophylactic or diagnostic intravenous or intra-arterial injection or infusion**

To report allergy immunizations, consult 95004 et seq.

THERAPEUTIC OR DIAGNOSTIC INFUSIONS (EXCLUDES CHEMOTHERAPY)

90780   ~~Intravenous infusion for therapy/diagnosis, administered by physician or under direct supervision of physician; up to one hour~~

90781   ~~each additional hour, up to eight (8) hours (List separately in addition to code for primary procedure)~~

(Use 90760, 90761, 90765-90768)

THERAPEUTIC, PROPHYLACTIC OR DIAGNOSTIC INJECTIONS

90782   ~~Therapeutic, prophylactic or diagnostic injection (specify material injected); subcutaneous or intramuscular~~

(Use 90772)

90783   ~~intra-arterial~~

(Use 90773)

90784   ~~intravenous~~

(Use 90774)

90788   ~~Intramuscular injection of antibiotic (specify)~~

(Use 90772)

90799   ~~Unlisted therapeutic, prophylactic or diagnostic injection~~

(Use 90779)

PSYCHIATRY

Psychiatry codes include psychiatric diagnostic or evaluation interview procedures (90801–90802), and psychiatric therapeutic procedures (90804–90899).

Psychiatric diagnostic interview exam (90801) includes a history, mental status, and disposition, and may include communication with family or other sources and ordering/interpretation of diagnostic studies. An interactive psychiatric diagnostic interview (90802) is furnished to children and older individuals lacking expressive and receptive communication skills. These procedure codes are normally reported only on the initial visit.

The most frequently reported services are therapeutic psychiatric service codes (90804–90829) for individual psychotherapy. Individual psychotherapy services are organized first by place of service (office/outpatient, inpatient/partial hospital/residential care). Codes within these two subcategories are organized by type of psychotherapy service (insight oriented, behavior modifying, supportive, interactive), face-to-face time, and the provision of additional medical evaluation or management services.

Other psychotherapy services (90845–90857) are used to report family and group psychotherapy services. Psychiatric services and procedures (90862–90899) are used to report medication management, electroconvulsive therapy, and hypnotherapy.

Hospital inpatient service codes (99221–99233) in the E/M section of the CPT book should be reported when the physician is involved in the medical management of an inpatient (e.g., when the attending physician reviews laboratory tests or initiates the patient's treatment plan). However, do not use hospital inpatient service codes when both psychotherapy and E/M services are provided on the same day. Combined E/M and psychotherapy services should be reported with codes designated as such in the psychiatry section (90804–90829).

To report repetitive transcranial magnetic stimulation for treatment of clinical depression, consult CPT Category III code 0018T.

PSYCHIATRIC DIAGNOSTIC OR EVALUATIVE INTERVIEW PROCEDURES

90801　**Psychiatric diagnostic interview examination**　S 80 ▸
MED: 100-3, 10.3; 100-3, 130.1; 100-4, 12, 100; 100-4, 12, 100.1.7; 100-4, 12, 100.1.8; 100-4, 12,
100.7; 100-4, 12, 110.2; 100-4, 12, 160; 100-4, 12, 160.1; 100-4, 12, 170

AMA: 2001, Mar, 5; 1997, Nov, 37-38; 1992, Summer, 12

90802　**Interactive psychiatric diagnostic interview examination using play
equipment, physical devices, language interpreter, or other mechanisms of
communication**　S 80 ▸
MED: 100-3, 10.3; 100-3, 130.1; 100-4, 12, 100; 100-4, 12, 100.1.7; 100-4, 12, 100.1.8; 100-4, 12,
110.2; 100-4, 12, 150; 100-4, 12, 160; 100-4, 12, 160.1; 100-4, 12, 170

AMA: 2001, Mar, 5; 1997, Nov, 37-38

PSYCHIATRIC THERAPEUTIC PROCEDURES

OFFICE OR OTHER OUTPATIENT FACILITY — INSIGHT ORIENTED, BEHAVIOR MODIFYING AND/OR SUPPORTIVE PSYCHOTHERAPY

90804　**Individual psychotherapy, insight oriented, behavior modifying and/or
supportive, in an office or outpatient facility, approximately 20 to 30
minutes face-to-face with the patient;**　S 80 ▸
MED: 100-3, 10.4; 100-3, 130.2; 100-3, 130.3; 100-3, 130.4; 100-3, 130.5; 100-3, 130.6; 100-3,
130.7; 100-3, 160.2; 100-3, 20.10; 100-3, 230.1; 100-3, 250.1; 100-3, 250.4; 100-3, 270.4; 100-3,
40.50; 100-4, 12, 100; 100-4, 12, 100.1.7; 100-4, 12, 100.1.8; 100-4, 12, 110.2; 100-4, 12, 150;
100-4, 12, 160; 100-4, 12, 160.1; 100-4, 12, 170

AMA: 2002, Oct, 11; 2001, Mar, 5; 1999, Jul, 10; 1997, Nov, 39

90805　　**with medical evaluation and management services**　S 80 ▸
MED: 100-3, 10.4; 100-3, 130.2; 100-3, 130.3; 100-3, 130.4; 100-3, 130.5; 100-3, 130.6; 100-3,
130.7; 100-3, 160.2; 100-3, 20.10; 100-3, 230.1; 100-3, 250.1; 100-3, 250.4; 100-3, 270.4; 100-3,
40.50; 100-4, 12, 100; 100-4, 12, 100.1.7; 100-4, 12, 100.1.8; 100-4, 12, 110.2; 100-4, 12, 150;
100-4, 12, 160; 100-4, 12, 160.1; 100-4, 12, 170

AMA: 2001, Mar, 5; 1999, Jul, 10; 1997, Nov, 39

90806　**Individual psychotherapy, insight oriented, behavior modifying and/or
supportive, in an office or outpatient facility, approximately 45 to 50
minutes face-to-face with the patient;**　S 80 ▸
MED: 100-3, 10.4; 100-3, 130.2; 100-3, 130.3; 100-3, 130.4; 100-3, 130.5; 100-3, 130.6; 100-3,
130.7; 100-3, 160.2; 100-3, 20.10; 100-3, 230.1; 100-3, 250.1; 100-3, 250.4; 100-3, 270.4; 100-3,
40.50; 100-4, 12, 100; 100-4, 12, 100.1.7; 100-4, 12, 100.1.8; 100-4, 12, 110.2; 100-4, 12, 150;
100-4, 12, 160; 100-4, 12, 160.1; 100-4, 12, 170

AMA: 2001, Mar, 5; 1999, Jul, 10; 1997, Nov, 39

90807　　**with medical evaluation and management services**　S 80 ▸
MED: 100-3, 10.4; 100-3, 130.2; 100-3, 130.3; 100-3, 130.4; 100-3, 130.5; 100-3, 130.6; 100-3,
130.7; 100-3, 160.2; 100-3, 20.10; 100-3, 230.1; 100-3, 250.1; 100-3, 250.4; 100-3, 270.4; 100-3,
40.50; 100-4, 12, 100; 100-4, 12, 100.1.7; 100-4, 12, 100.1.8; 100-4, 12, 110.2; 100-4, 12, 150;
100-4, 12, 160; 100-4, 12, 160.1; 100-4, 12, 170

AMA: 1999, Jul, 10; 1997, Nov, 39

90808　**Individual psychotherapy, insight oriented, behavior modifying and/or
supportive, in an office or outpatient facility, approximately 75 to 80
minutes face-to-face with the patient;**　S 80 ▸
MED: 100-3, 10.4; 100-3, 130.2; 100-3, 130.3; 100-3, 130.4; 100-3, 130.5; 100-3, 130.6; 100-3,
130.7; 100-3, 160.2; 100-3, 20.10; 100-3, 230.1; 100-3, 250.1; 100-3, 250.4; 100-3, 270.4; 100-3,
40.50; 100-4, 12, 100; 100-4, 12, 100.1.7; 100-4, 12, 100.1.8; 100-4, 12, 110.2; 100-4, 12, 150;
100-4, 12, 160; 100-4, 12, 160.1; 100-4, 12, 170

AMA: 2001, Mar, 5; 1999, Jul, 10; 1997, Nov, 39

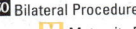  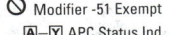

90809	with medical evaluation and management services Ⓢ 80 ▣

MED: 100-3, 10.4; 100-3, 130.2; 100-3, 130.3; 100-3, 130.4; 100-3, 130.5; 100-3, 130.6; 100-3, 130.7; 100-3, 160.2; 100-3, 20.10; 100-3, 250.1; 100-3, 250.4; 100-3, 270.4; 100-3, 40.50; 100-4, 12, 100; 100-4, 12, 100.1.7; 100-4, 12, 100.1.8; 100-4, 12, 110.2; 100-4, 12, 150; 100-4, 12, 160; 100-4, 12, 160.1; 100-4, 12, 170

AMA: 2001, Mar, 5; 1999, Jul, 10; 1997, Nov, 39

OFFICE OR OTHER OUTPATIENT FACILITY — INTERACTIVE PSYCHOTHERAPY

90810   **Individual psychotherapy, interactive, using play equipment, physical devices, language interpreter, or other mechanisms of nonverbal communication, in an office or outpatient facility, approximately 20 to 30 minutes face-to-face with the patient;**   Ⓢ 80 ▣

MED: 100-3, 10.4; 100-3, 130.2; 100-3, 130.3; 100-3, 130.4; 100-3, 130.5; 100-3, 130.6; 100-3, 130.7; 100-3, 160.2; 100-3, 20.10; 100-3, 230.1; 100-3, 250.1; 100-3, 250.4; 100-3, 270.4; 100-3, 40.50; 100-4, 12, 100; 100-4, 12, 100.1.7; 100-4, 12, 100.1.8; 100-4, 12, 110.2; 100-4, 12, 150; 100-4, 12, 160; 100-4, 12, 160.1; 100-4, 12, 170

AMA: 2001, Mar, 5; 1997, Nov, 39

90811   **with medical evaluation and management services**   Ⓢ 80 ▣

MED: 100-3, 10.4; 100-3, 130.2; 100-3, 130.3; 100-3, 130.4; 100-3, 130.5; 100-3, 130.6; 100-3, 130.7; 100-3, 160.2; 100-3, 20.10; 100-3, 230.1; 100-3, 250.1; 100-3, 250.4; 100-3, 270.4; 100-3, 40.50; 100-4, 12, 100; 100-4, 12, 100.1.7; 100-4, 12, 100.1.8; 100-4, 12, 110.2; 100-4, 12, 150; 100-4, 12, 160; 100-4, 12, 160.1; 100-4, 12, 170

AMA: 2001, Mar, 5

90812   **Individual psychotherapy, interactive, using play equipment, physical devices, language interpreter, or other mechanisms of nonverbal communication, in an office or outpatient facility, approximately 45 to 50 minutes face-to-face with the patient;**   Ⓢ 80 ▣

MED: 100-3, 10.4; 100-3, 130.2; 100-3, 130.3; 100-3, 130.4; 100-3, 130.5; 100-3, 130.6; 100-3, 130.7; 100-3, 160.2; 100-3, 20.10; 100-3, 230.1; 100-3, 250.1; 100-3, 250.4; 100-3, 270.4; 100-3, 40.50; 100-4, 12, 100; 100-4, 12, 100.1.7; 100-4, 12, 100.1.8; 100-4, 12, 110.2; 100-4, 12, 150; 100-4, 12, 160; 100-4, 12, 160.1; 100-4, 12, 170

AMA: 2001, Mar, 5; 1997, Nov, 39

90813   **with medical evaluation and management services**   Ⓢ 80 ▣

MED: 100-3, 10.4; 100-3, 130.2; 100-3, 130.3; 100-3, 130.4; 100-3, 130.5; 100-3, 130.6; 100-3, 130.7; 100-3, 160.2; 100-3, 20.10; 100-3, 230.1; 100-3, 250.1; 100-3, 250.4; 100-3, 270.4; 100-3, 40.50; 100-4, 12, 100; 100-4, 12, 100.1.7; 100-4, 12, 100.1.8; 100-4, 12, 110.2; 100-4, 12, 150; 100-4, 12, 160; 100-4, 12, 160.1; 100-4, 12, 170

AMA: 2001, Mar, 5; 1997, Nov, 39

90814   **Individual psychotherapy, interactive, using play equipment, physical devices, language interpreter, or other mechanisms of nonverbal communication, in an office or outpatient facility, approximately 75 to 80 minutes face-to-face with the patient;**   Ⓢ 80 ▣

MED: 100-3, 10.4; 100-3, 130.2; 100-3, 130.3; 100-3, 130.4; 100-3, 130.5; 100-3, 130.6; 100-3, 130.7; 100-3, 160.2; 100-3, 20.10; 100-3, 230.1; 100-3, 250.1; 100-3, 250.4; 100-3, 270.4; 100-3, 40.50; 100-4, 12, 100; 100-4, 12, 100.1.7; 100-4, 12, 100.1.8; 100-4, 12, 110.2; 100-4, 12, 150; 100-4, 12, 160; 100-4, 12, 160.1; 100-4, 12, 170

AMA: 2001, Mar, 5; 1997, Nov, 39

90815   **with medical evaluation and management services**   Ⓢ 80 ▣

MED: 100-3, 10.4; 100-3, 130.2; 100-3, 130.3; 100-3, 130.4; 100-3, 130.5; 100-3, 130.6; 100-3, 130.7; 100-3, 160.2; 100-3, 20.10; 100-3, 230.1; 100-3, 250.1; 100-3, 250.4; 100-3, 270.4; 100-3, 40.50; 100-4, 12, 100; 100-4, 12, 100.1.7; 100-4, 12, 100.1.8; 100-4, 12, 110.2; 100-4, 12, 150; 100-4, 12, 160; 100-4, 12, 160.1; 100-4, 12, 170

AMA: 2001, Mar, 5; 1997, Nov, 39

INPATIENT HOSPITAL, PARTIAL HOSPITAL OR RESIDENTIAL CARE FACILITY — INSIGHT ORIENTED, BEHAVIOR MODIFYING AND/OR SUPPORTIVE PSYCHOTHERAPY

90816   Individual psychotherapy, insight oriented, behavior modifying and/or supportive, in an inpatient hospital, partial hospital or residential care setting, approximately 20 to 30 minutes face-to-face with the patient;   [S] [80] [↑]
MED: 100-2, 15, 60.3; 100-3, 10.3; 100-3, 130.1; 100-3, 20.10; 100-4, 12, 100; 100-4, 12, 100.1.7; 100-4, 12, 100.1.8; 100-4, 12, 110.2; 100-4, 12, 150; 100-4, 12, 160; 100-4, 12, 160.1; 100-4, 12, 170

AMA: 2001, Mar, 5; 1997, Nov, 39-40

90817   with medical evaluation and management services   [S] [80] [↑]
MED: 100-2, 15, 60.3; 100-3, 10.3; 100-3, 130.1; 100-3, 20.10; 100-4, 12, 100; 100-4, 12, 100.1.7; 100-4, 12, 100.1.8; 100-4, 12, 110.2

AMA: 2001, Mar, 5; 1997, Nov, 39-40

90818   Individual psychotherapy, insight oriented, behavior modifying and/or supportive, in an inpatient hospital, partial hospital or residential care setting, approximately 45 to 50 minutes face-to-face with the patient;   [S] [80] [↑]
MED: 100-2, 15, 60.3; 100-3, 10.3; 100-3, 130.1; 100-3, 20.10; 100-4, 12, 100; 100-4, 12, 100.1.7; 100-4, 12, 100.1.8; 100-4, 12, 110.2; 100-4, 12, 150; 100-4, 12, 160; 100-4, 12, 160.1; 100-4, 12, 170

AMA: 2001, Mar, 5; 1997, Nov, 39-40

90819   with medical evaluation and management services   [S] [80] [↑]
MED: 100-2, 15, 60.3; 100-3, 10.3; 100-3, 130.1; 100-3, 20.10; 100-4, 12, 100; 100-4, 12, 100.1.7; 100-4, 12, 100.1.8; 100-4, 12, 110.2; 100-4, 12, 150; 100-4, 12, 160; 100-4, 12, 160.1; 100-4, 12, 170

AMA: 2001, Mar, 5

90821   Individual psychotherapy, insight oriented, behavior modifying and/or supportive, in an inpatient hospital, partial hospital or residential care setting, approximately 75 to 80 minutes face-to-face with the patient;   [S] [80] [↑]
MED: 100-2, 15, 60.3; 100-3, 10.3; 100-3, 130.1; 100-3, 20.10; 100-4, 12, 100; 100-4, 12, 100.1.7; 100-4, 12, 100.1.8; 100-4, 12, 110.2; 100-4, 12, 150; 100-4, 12, 160; 100-4, 12, 160.1; 100-4, 12, 170

AMA: 2001, Mar, 5; 1997, Nov, 39-40

90822   with medical evaluation and management services   [S] [80] [↑]
MED: 100-2, 15, 60.3; 100-3, 10.3; 100-3, 130.1; 100-3, 20.10; 100-4, 12, 100; 100-4, 12, 100.1.7; 100-4, 12, 100.1.8; 100-4, 12, 110.2; 100-4, 12, 150; 100-4, 12, 160; 100-4, 12, 160.1; 100-4, 12, 170

AMA: 2001, Mar, 5; 1997, Nov, 39-40

INPATIENT HOSPITAL, PARTIAL HOSPITAL OR RESIDENTIAL CARE FACILITY — INTERACTIVE PSYCHOTHERAPY

90823   Individual psychotherapy, interactive, using play equipment, physical devices, language interpreter, or other mechanisms of nonverbal communication, in an inpatient hospital, partial hospital or residential care setting, approximately 20 to 30 minutes face-to-face with the patient;   [S] [80] [↑]
MED: 100-2, 15, 60.3; 100-3, 10.3; 100-3, 130.1; 100-3, 20.10; 100-4, 12, 100; 100-4, 12, 100.1.7; 100-4, 12, 100.1.8; 100-4, 12, 110.2; 100-4, 12, 150; 100-4, 12, 160; 100-4, 12, 160.1; 100-4, 12, 170

AMA: 2001, Mar, 5; 1997, Nov, 40

Medicine

90824 — 90847

| 90824 | with medical evaluation and management services ⑤ 80 🔲
MED: 100-2, 15, 60.3; 100-3, 10.3; 100-3, 130.1; 100-3, 20.10; 100-4, 12, 100; 100-4, 12, 100.1.7; 100-4, 12, 100.1.8; 100-4, 12, 110.2; 100-4, 12, 150; 100-4, 12, 160; 100-4, 12, 160.1; 100-4, 12, 170

AMA: 2001, Mar, 5

90826 Individual psychotherapy, interactive, using play equipment, physical devices, language interpreter, or other mechanisms of nonverbal communication, in an inpatient hospital, partial hospital or residential care setting, approximately 45 to 50 minutes face-to-face with the patient; ⑤ 80 🔲
MED: 100-2, 15, 60.3; 100-3, 10.3; 100-3, 130.1; 100-3, 20.10; 100-4, 12, 100; 100-4, 12, 100.1.7; 100-4, 12, 100.1.8; 100-4, 12, 110.2; 100-4, 12, 150; 100-4, 12, 160; 100-4, 12, 160.1; 100-4, 12, 170

AMA: 2001, Mar, 5; 1997, Nov, 40

90827 with medical evaluation and management services ⑤ 80 🔲
MED: 100-2, 15, 60.3; 100-3, 10.3; 100-3, 130.1; 100-3, 20.10; 100-4, 12, 100; 100-4, 12, 100.1.7; 100-4, 12, 100.1.8; 100-4, 12, 110.2; 100-4, 12, 150; 100-4, 12, 160; 100-4, 12, 160.1; 100-4, 12, 170

AMA: 2001, Mar, 5; 1997, Nov, 40

90828 Individual psychotherapy, interactive, using play equipment, physical devices, language interpreter, or other mechanisms of nonverbal communication, in an inpatient hospital, partial hospital or residential care setting, approximately 75 to 80 minutes face-to-face with the patient; ⑤ 80 🔲
MED: 100-2, 15, 60.3; 100-3, 10.3; 100-3, 130.1; 100-3, 20.10; 100-4, 12, 100; 100-4, 12, 100.1.7; 100-4, 12, 100.1.8; 100-4, 12, 110.2; 100-4, 12, 150; 100-4, 12, 160; 100-4, 12, 160.1; 100-4, 12, 170

AMA: 2001, Mar, 5; 1997, Nov, 40

90829 with medical evaluation and management services ⑤ 80 🔲
MED: 100-2, 15, 60.3; 100-3, 10.3; 100-3, 130.1; 100-3, 20.10; 100-4, 12, 110.2; 100-4, 12, 150; 100-4, 12, 160; 100-4, 12, 160.1; 100-4, 12, 170

AMA: 2001, Mar, 5; 1997, Nov, 40

OTHER PSYCHOTHERAPY

90845 Psychoanalysis ⑤ 80 🔲
MED: 100-2, 15, 160; 100-3, 10.3; 100-3, 10.4; 100-3, 130.1; 100-3, 130.2; 100-3, 130.3; 100-3, 130.4; 100-3, 130.5; 100-3, 130.6; 100-3, 130.7; 100-3, 160.2; 100-3, 230.1; 100-3, 250.1; 100-3, 250.4; 100-3, 270.4; 100-3, 40.50; 100-4, 12, 110.2; 100-4, 12, 150; 100-4, 12, 160; 100-4, 12, 160.1; 100-4, 12, 170; 100-4, 12, 170.1

AMA: 2001, Mar, 5; 1997, Nov, 40-41; 1992, Summer, 15

90846 Family psychotherapy (without the patient present) ⑤ 80 🔲
MED: 100-2, 15, 160; 100-3, 10.3; 100-3, 10.4; 100-3, 130.1; 100-3, 130.2; 100-3, 130.3; 100-3, 130.4; 100-3, 130.5; 100-3, 130.6; 100-3, 130.7; 100-3, 160.2; 100-3, 230.1; 100-3, 250.1; 100-3, 250.4; 100-3, 270.4; 100-3, 40.50; 100-4, 12, 110.2; 100-4, 12, 150; 100-4, 12, 160; 100-4, 12, 160.1; 100-4, 12, 170; 100-4, 12, 170.1

AMA: 2001, Mar, 5; 1997, Nov, 40-41; 1992, Summer, 15

90847 Family psychotherapy (conjoint psychotherapy) (with patient present) ⑤ 80 🔲
MED: 100-3, 10.3; 100-3, 10.4; 100-3, 130.1; 100-3, 130.2; 100-3, 130.3; 100-3, 130.4; 100-3, 130.5; 100-3, 130.6; 100-3, 130.7; 100-3, 160.2; 100-3, 230.1; 100-3, 250.1; 100-3, 250.4; 100-3, 270.4; 100-3, 40.50; 100-4, 12, 110.2; 100-4, 12, 150; 100-4, 12, 160; 100-4, 12, 160.1; 100-4, 12, 170; 100-4, 12, 70; 100-4, 13, 20; 100-4, 13, 90

AMA: 2001, Mar, 5; 1997, Nov, 40-41; 1992, Summer, 15 |

Medicine

90849 — 90880

90849   **Multiple-family group psychotherapy**   S 80 🔄
         MED: 100-2, 15, 160; 100-3, 10.3; 100-3, 10.4; 100-3, 130.1; 100-3, 130.2; 100-3, 130.3; 100-3,
         130.4; 100-3, 130.5; 100-3, 130.6; 100-3, 130.7; 100-3, 160.2; 100-3, 230.1; 100-3, 250.1; 100-3,
         250.4; 100-3, 270.4; 100-3, 40.50; 100-4, 12, 110.2; 100-4, 12, 150; 100-4, 12, 160; 100-4, 12,
         160.1; 100-4, 12, 170; 100-4, 12, 170.1

         AMA: 2001, Mar, 5; 1997, Nov, 40-41; 1992, Summer, 15

90853   **Group psychotherapy (other than of a multiple-family group)**   S 80 🔄
         MED: 100-2, 15, 160; 100-3, 10.3; 100-3, 10.4; 100-3, 130.1; 100-3, 130.2; 100-3, 130.3; 100-3,
         130.4; 100-3, 130.5; 100-3, 130.6; 100-3, 130.7; 100-3, 160.2; 100-3, 230.1; 100-3, 250.1; 100-3,
         250.4; 100-3, 270.4; 100-3, 40.50; 100-4, 12, 110.2; 100-4, 12, 150; 100-4, 12, 160; 100-4, 12,
         160.1; 100-4, 12, 170; 100-4, 12, 170.1

         AMA: 2001, Mar, 5; 1997, Nov, 40-41; 1992, Summer, 15

90857   **Interactive group psychotherapy**   S 80 🔄
         MED: 100-2, 15, 160; 100-3, 10.3; 100-3, 10.4; 100-3, 130.1; 100-3, 130.2; 100-3, 130.3; 100-3,
         130.4; 100-3, 130.5; 100-3, 130.6; 100-3, 130.7; 100-3, 160.2; 100-3, 230.1; 100-3, 250.1; 100-3,
         250.4; 100-3, 270.4; 100-3, 40.50; 100-4, 12, 110.2; 100-4, 12, 150; 100-4, 12, 160; 100-4, 12,
         160.1; 100-4, 12, 170; 100-4, 12, 170.1

         AMA: 2001, Mar, 5; 1997, Nov, 40-41; 1992, Summer, 15

OTHER PSYCHIATRIC SERVICES OR PROCEDURES

90862   **Pharmacologic management, including prescription, use, and review of
         medication with no more than minimal medical psychotherapy**   X 80 🔄
         MED: 100-2, 15, 160; 100-3, 10.3; 100-3, 10.4; 100-3, 130.1; 100-3, 130.2; 100-3, 130.3; 100-3,
         130.4; 100-3, 130.5; 100-3, 130.6; 100-3, 130.7; 100-3, 160.2; 100-3, 230.1; 100-3, 250.1; 100-3,
         250.4; 100-3, 270.4; 100-3, 40.50; 100-4, 12, 160; 100-4, 12, 170; 100-4, 12, 170.1

         AMA: 2001, Mar, 5; 1997, Nov, 40-41; 1992, Summer, 16

90865   **Narcosynthesis for psychiatric diagnostic and therapeutic purposes (eg,
         sodium amobarbital (Amytal) interview)**   S 80 🔄
         MED: 100-1, 3, 30; 100-1, 3, 30.1; 100-1, 3, 30.2; 100-1, 3, 30.3; 100-2, 15, 160; 100-2, 15, 170;
         100-4, 12, 150; 100-4, 12, 160; 100-4, 12, 160.1; 100-4, 12, 170; 100-4, 12, 170.1; 100-4, 12, 210

         AMA: 2001, Mar, 5; 1997, Nov, 41

▲ 90870 **Electroconvulsive therapy (includes necessary monitoring)**   S 80 🔄
         MED: 100-1, 3, 30; 100-1, 3, 30.1; 100-1, 3, 30.2; 100-1, 3, 30.3; 100-2, 15, 160; 100-2, 15, 170;
         100-4, 12, 150; 100-4, 12, 160; 100-4, 12, 160.1; 100-4, 12, 170; 100-4, 12, 170.1; 100-4, 12, 210

         AMA: 2001, Mar, 5; 1992, Summer, 16

~~90871~~   ~~multiple seizures, per day~~

90875   **Individual psychophysiological therapy incorporating biofeedback training
         by any modality (face-to-face with the patient), with psychotherapy (eg,
         insight oriented, behavior modifying or supportive psychotherapy);
         approximately 20-30 minutes**   E
         MED: 100-3, 30.1; 100-3, 30.1.1

         AMA: 2001, Mar, 5; 1999, Jun, 5; 1998, Apr, 14; 1997, Sep, 11; 1997, Nov, 41

90876   **approximately 45-50 minutes**   E
         MED: 100-1, 3, 30; 100-1, 3, 30.1; 100-1, 3, 30.2; 100-1, 3, 30.3; 100-2, 15, 160; 100-2, 15, 170;
         100-3, 30.1; 100-3, 30.1.1; 100-4, 12, 150; 100-4, 12, 160; 100-4, 12, 160.1; 100-4, 12, 170; 100-
         4, 12, 170.1; 100-4, 12, 210

         AMA: 2001, Mar, 5; 1999, Jun, 5; 1997, Sep, 11; 1997, Nov, 41

90880   **Hypnotherapy**   S 80 🔄
         MED: 100-1, 3, 30; 100-1, 3, 30.1; 100-1, 3, 30.2; 100-1, 3, 30.3; 100-2, 15, 160; 100-2, 15, 170;
         100-4, 12, 150; 100-4, 12, 160; 100-4, 12, 160.1; 100-4, 12, 170; 100-4, 12, 170.1; 100-4, 12, 210

         AMA: 2001, Mar, 5; 1997, Nov, 41; 1992, Summer, 16

90882 Environmental intervention for medical management purposes on a psychiatric patient's behalf with agencies, employers, or institutions E
AMA: 2001, Mar, 5; 1992, Summer, 16

90885 Psychiatric evaluation of hospital records, other psychiatric reports, psychometric and/or projective tests, and other accumulated data for medical diagnostic purposes N
MED: 100-1, 3, 30; 100-1, 3, 30.1; 100-1, 3, 30.2; 100-1, 3, 30.3; 100-2, 15, 160; 100-2, 15, 170; 100-4, 12, 150; 100-4, 12, 160; 100-4, 12, 160.1; 100-4, 12, 170; 100-4, 12, 170.1; 100-4, 12, 210

AMA: 2001, Mar, 5; 1997, Nov, 41

90887 Interpretation or explanation of results of psychiatric, other medical examinations and procedures, or other accumulated data to family or other responsible persons, or advising them how to assist patient N
MED: 100-1, 3, 30; 100-1, 3, 30.1; 100-1, 3, 30.2; 100-1, 3, 30.3; 100-2, 15, 160; 100-2, 15, 170; 100-3, 70.1; 100-3, 70.2; 100-4, 12, 150; 100-4, 12, 160; 100-4, 12, 160.1; 100-4, 12, 170; 100-4, 12, 170.1; 100-4, 12, 210

AMA: 2002, Oct, 11; 2001, Mar, 5; 1992, Summer, 17

90889 Preparation of report of patient's psychiatric status, history, treatment, or progress (other than for legal or consultative purposes) for other physicians, agencies, or insurance carriers N
MED: 100-1, 3, 30; 100-1, 3, 30.1; 100-1, 3, 30.2; 100-1, 3, 30.3; 100-2, 15, 160; 100-2, 15, 170; 100-4, 12, 150; 100-4, 12, 160; 100-4, 12, 170; 100-4, 12, 170.1; 100-4, 12, 210

AMA: 2001, Mar, 5; 1992, Summer, 17

90899 Unlisted psychiatric service or procedure S 80
MED: 100-3, 30.5

AMA: 2001, Mar, 5

BIOFEEDBACK

Biofeedback codes (90901–90911) may require prior authorization. If the payer does not cover biofeedback, enlist the help of the medical director or prior authorization (or utilization) review nurses for service coverage. Documentation may be required, such as articles or printed research material about the benefits of biofeedback.

If psychophysiological therapy is performed incorporating biofeedback training, consult CPT codes 90875 and 90876.

90901 Biofeedback training by any modality A 80 ▯
MED: 100-3, 130.5; 100-3, 130.6; 100-3, 160.2; 100-3, 230.1; 100-3, 250.1; 100-3, 250.4; 100-3, 270.4; 100-3, 30.1; 100-3, 30.1.1; 100-3, 40.50

AMA: 2002, May, 18; 1999, Jun, 5; 1998, Jun, 10; 1998, Apr, 14; 1997, Sep, 11

90911 Biofeedback training, perineal muscles, anorectal or urethral sphincter, including EMG and/or manometry S 80 ▯
MED: 100-3, 130.5; 100-3, 130.6; 100-3, 160.2; 100-3, 230.1; 100-3, 250.1; 100-3, 250.4; 100-3, 270.4; 100-3, 30.1; 100-3, 30.1.1; 100-3, 40.50

AMA: 1999, Jun, 5; 1998, Jun, 10; 1997, Sep, 11; 1997, Nov, 41

To report pulsed magnetic neuromodulation to treat incontinence, consult CPT Category III code 0029T.

To report rectal sensation tone and compliance, consult 91120.

DIALYSIS

END STAGE RENAL DISEASE SERVICES

Dialysis services (90918–90999) are divided into end-stage renal disease (ESRD) services, hemodialysis, peritoneal dialysis, and miscellaneous dialysis procedures. Codes for the latter three services are selected according to whether the service includes single physician evaluations or repeated evaluations. Repeated evaluations are reported despite the lack of changes in the dialysis prescription.

Codes that report ESRD related services (90918–90921) are selected according to the age of the patient and reflect services for a full month. These services (90918–90921) should not be used if the physician is also submitting hospitalization codes during the month. For less than a full month, 90922–90925 are reported for each day ESRD service is provided. And the appropriate code from 90935–90947 should be reported for the inpatient dialysis services. Procedures for other medical problems and complications unrelated to ESRD are not included in the monthly ESRD service.

The dialysis procedure (90935–90947) includes all evaluation and management services related to the patient's ESRD rendered on a day dialysis is performed, as well as all other patient care services rendered during the dialysis procedure. Office and hospital visits are reported in addition to dialysis procedures only when they are unrelated to dialysis and cannot be rendered during a dialysis session.

For dialysis procedures other than hemodialysis provided during an inpatient hospital stay, consult CPT codes 90945-90947. For ESRD related services during an inpatient hospital stay, consult the appropriate Evaluation and Management codes.

Report CPT codes 90918-90921 one time per month for services performed in an outpatient setting. Do not use these codes if a hospitalization occurred during the month.

These procedures do not include dialysis treatment or services provided to the patient that are non-ESRD related. Report separately any non-ESRD related Evaluation and Management services that cannot be performed during the dialysis session.

90918   **End stage renal disease (ESRD) related services per full month; for patients under two years of age to include monitoring for the adequacy of nutrition, assessment of growth and development, and counseling of parents** Ⓐ Ⓔ
MED: 100-3, 110.15; 100-3, 190.10; 100-3, 230.14; 100-4, 8, 130; 100-4, 8, 140; 100-4, 8, 170; 100-4, 8, 60.4.4; 100-4, 8, 70; 100-4, 8, 80; 100-4, 8, 90; 100-4, 8, 90.1; 100-4, 8, 90.2; 100-4, 8, 90.2.2; 100-4, 8, 90.3.2

AMA: 2003, Jan, 22; 2002, May, 17; 1996, May, 4; 1993, Fall, 5

90919   **for patients between two and eleven years of age to include monitoring for the adequacy of nutrition, assessment of growth and development, and counseling of parents** Ⓐ Ⓔ
MED: 100-4, 8, 130; 100-4, 8, 140; 100-4, 8, 170; 100-4, 8, 60.4.4; 100-4, 8, 70; 100-4, 8, 80; 100-4, 8, 90; 100-4, 8, 90.1; 100-4, 8, 90.2; 100-4, 8, 90.2.2; 100-4, 8, 90.3.2

AMA: 2003, Jan, 22; 2002, May, 17; 1996, May, 5; 1993, Fall, 5

90920   **for patients between twelve and nineteen years of age to include monitoring for the adequacy of nutrition, assessment of growth and development, and counseling of parents** Ⓐ Ⓔ
MED: 100-4, 8, 130; 100-4, 8, 140; 100-4, 8, 170; 100-4, 8, 60.4.4; 100-4, 8, 70; 100-4, 8, 80; 100-4, 8, 90; 100-4, 8, 90.1; 100-4, 8, 90.2; 100-4, 8, 90.2.2; 100-4, 8, 90.3.2

AMA: 2003, Jan, 22; 2002, May, 17; 1996, May, 5; 1993, Fall, 5

90921   **for patients twenty years of age and over** Ⓔ
MED: 100-4, 8, 130; 100-4, 8, 60.4.4; 100-4, 8, 70; 100-4, 8, 80; 100-4, 8, 90; 100-4, 8, 90.1; 100-4, 8, 90.2; 100-4, 8, 90.2.2; 100-4, 8, 90.3.2

AMA: 2003, Jan, 22; 2002, May, 17; 1996, May, 5; 1993, Fall, 5

Medicine

90922 — 90939

90922   **End stage renal disease (ESRD) related services (less than full month), per day; for patients under two years of age**   A E
MED: 100-3, 110.15; 100-3, 190.10; 100-3, 230.14; 100-4, 8, 130; 100-4, 8, 140; 100-4, 8, 170; 100-4, 8, 60.4.4; 100-4, 8, 70; 100-4, 8, 80; 100-4, 8, 90; 100-4, 8, 90.1; 100-4, 8, 90.2; 100-4, 8, 90.2.2; 100-4, 8, 90.3.2

AMA: 2003, Jan, 22; 1996, May, 5; 1993, Fall, 5

90923   **for patients between two and eleven years of age**   A E
MED: 100-4, 8, 130; 100-4, 8, 140; 100-4, 8, 170; 100-4, 8, 60.4.4; 100-4, 8, 70; 100-4, 8, 80; 100-4, 8, 90; 100-4, 8, 90.1; 100-4, 8, 90.2; 100-4, 8, 90.2.2; 100-4, 8, 90.3.2

AMA: 2003, Jan, 22; 2002, May, 17; 1996, May, 5

90924   **for patients between twelve and nineteen years of age**   A E
MED: 100-4, 8, 130; 100-4, 8, 140; 100-4, 8, 170; 100-4, 8, 60.4.4; 100-4, 8, 70; 100-4, 8, 80; 100-4, 8, 90; 100-4, 8, 90.1; 100-4, 8, 90.2; 100-4, 8, 90.2.2; 100-4, 8, 90.3.2

AMA: 2003, Jan, 22; 2002, May, 17; 1996, May, 5

90925   **for patients twenty years of age and over**   E
MED: 100-4, 8, 130; 100-4, 8, 140; 100-4, 8, 170; 100-4, 8, 60.4.4; 100-4, 8, 70; 100-4, 8, 80; 100-4, 8, 90; 100-4, 8, 90.1; 100-4, 8, 90.2; 100-4, 8, 90.2.2; 100-4, 8, 90.3.2

AMA: 2003, Jan, 22; 2002, May, 17; 1996, May, 5

HEMODIALYSIS

Use CPT codes 90935-90937 for inpatient ESRD. Use CPT codes 90935-90937 to report the hemodialysis procedure and any Evaluation and Management service that is related to the patient's renal disorder provided on the day of the hemodialysis procedure.

For an unrelated Evaluation and Management service performed on the same day as hemodialysis, consult the appropriate Evaluation and Management code and append modifier 25 or code 09925.

For home visit hemodialysis services performed by a non-physician health care professional, use 99512.

If cannula declotting is performed, consult CPT codes 36831, 36833, 36860, and 36861. If a thrombolytic agent declots an implanted vascular access device or catheter, consult CPT code 36550. If the physician is in attendance for a prolonged period of time, consult CPT codes 99354-99360.

When collecting a blood specimen from a partially or completely implantable venous access device, consult CPT code 36540.

90935   **Hemodialysis procedure with single physician evaluation**   S 80
MED: 100-3, 130.8; 100-4, 8, 130; 100-4, 8, 140; 100-4, 8, 170; 100-4, 8, 60.4.4; 100-4, 8, 70; 100-4, 8, 80; 100-4, 8, 90; 100-4, 8, 90.1; 100-4, 8, 90.2; 100-4, 8, 90.2.2; 100-4, 8, 90.3.2

AMA: 2003, Jan, 22; 2002, May, 17; 1999, Nov, 49; 1993, Fall, 2

90937   **Hemodialysis procedure requiring repeated evaluation(s) with or without substantial revision of dialysis prescription**   E 80
MED: 100-3, 130.8; 100-4, 8, 130; 100-4, 8, 140; 100-4, 8, 170; 100-4, 8, 60.4.4; 100-4, 8, 70; 100-4, 8, 80; 100-4, 8, 90; 100-4, 8, 90.1; 100-4, 8, 90.2; 100-4, 8, 90.2.2; 100-4, 8, 90.3.2

AMA: 2003, Jan, 22; 2002, May, 17; 1999, Nov, 49; 1993, Fall, 2

~~90939~~   ~~Hemodialysis access flow study to determine blood flow in grafts and arteriovenous fistulae by an indicator dilution method, hook up; transcutaneous measurement and disconnection~~

(Use 90940)

▲ 90940   **Hemodialysis access flow study to determine blood flow in grafts and arteriovenous fistulae by an indicator method** Ⓝ ▣
MED: 100-4, 8, 130; 100-4, 8, 60.4.4; 100-4, 8, 70; 100-4, 8, 80; 100-4, 8, 90; 100-4, 8, 90.1; 100-4, 8, 90.2; 100-4, 8, 90.2.2; 100-4, 8, 90.3.2

AMA: 2003, Jan, 22; 1999, Nov, 49

Consult CPT code 93990 to report duplex scan of hemodialysis access.

MISCELLANEOUS DIALYSIS PROCEDURES
If the physician is in attendance for a prolonged period of time, consult CPT codes 99354-99360. If an intraperitoneal cannula or catheter is inserted, consult CPT codes 49420 and 49421.

90945   **Dialysis procedure other than hemodialysis (eg, peritoneal dialysis, hemofiltration, or other continuous renal replacement therapies), with single physician evaluation** Ⓢ 80 ▣
MED: 100-3, 110.15; 100-3, 190.10; 100-3, 230.14; 100-4, 8, 130; 100-4, 8, 140; 100-4, 8, 170; 100-4, 8, 60.4.4; 100-4, 8, 70; 100-4, 8, 80; 100-4, 8, 90; 100-4, 8, 90.1; 100-4, 8, 90.2; 100-4, 8, 90.2.2; 100-4, 8, 90.3.2

AMA: 2003, Jan, 22; 2001, Oct, 11; 1998, Jul, 10; 1997, Nov, 41; 1993, Fall, 2

To report home infusion of peritoneal dialysis, consult CPT codes 99601 and 99602.

90947   **Dialysis procedure other than hemodialysis (eg, peritoneal dialysis, hemofiltration, or other continuous renal replacement therapies) requiring repeated physician evaluations, with or without substantial revision of dialysis prescription** Ⓔ 80 ▣
MED: 100-3, 110.15; 100-3, 190.10; 100-3, 230.14; 100-4, 8, 130; 100-4, 8, 140; 100-4, 8, 170; 100-4, 8, 60.4.4; 100-4, 8, 70; 100-4, 8, 80; 100-4, 8, 90; 100-4, 8, 90.1; 100-4, 8, 90.2; 100-4, 8, 90.2.2; 100-4, 8, 90.3.2

AMA: 2003, Jan, 22; 2001, Oct, 11; 1998, Jul, 10; 1997, Nov, 41; 1993, Fall, 2

90989   **Dialysis training, patient, including helper where applicable, any mode, completed course** Ⓑ ▣
MED: 100-3, 190.10; 100-4, 8, 130; 100-4, 8, 140; 100-4, 8, 170; 100-4, 8, 60.4.4; 100-4, 8, 70; 100-4, 8, 80; 100-4, 8, 90; 100-4, 8, 90.1; 100-4, 8, 90.2; 100-4, 8, 90.2.2; 100-4, 8, 90.3.2

AMA: 2001, Jun, 10; 1993, Fall, 5

90993   **Dialysis training, patient, including helper where applicable, any mode, course not completed, per training session** Ⓑ ▣
MED: 100-3, 190.10; 100-4, 8, 130; 100-4, 8, 140; 100-4, 8, 170; 100-4, 8, 60.4.4; 100-4, 8, 70; 100-4, 8, 80; 100-4, 8, 90; 100-4, 8, 90.1; 100-4, 8, 90.2; 100-4, 8, 90.2.2; 100-4, 8, 90.3.2

AMA: 2001, Jun, 10; 1993, Fall, 5

90997   **Hemoperfusion (eg, with activated charcoal or resin)** Ⓔ 80 ▣
MED: 100-3, 110.15; 100-3, 230.14; 100-4, 8, 130; 100-4, 8, 140; 100-4, 8, 170; 100-4, 8, 60.4.4; 100-4, 8, 70; 100-4, 8, 80; 100-4, 8, 90; 100-4, 8, 90.1; 100-4, 8, 90.2; 100-4, 8, 90.2.2; 100-4, 8, 90.3.2

90999   **Unlisted dialysis procedure, inpatient or outpatient** Ⓑ 80
MED: 100-3, 190.10; 100-4, 8, 130; 100-4, 8, 140; 100-4, 8, 170; 100-4, 8, 60.4.4; 100-4, 8, 70; 100-4, 8, 80; 100-4, 8, 90; 100-4, 8, 90.1; 100-4, 8, 90.2; 100-4, 8, 90.2.2; 100-4, 8, 90.3.2

GASTROENTEROLOGY

The diagnostic procedures (91000–91299) are frequently performed with consultations or other E/M services that are reported separately. Even though gastroenterology is a medicine subspecialty, the majority of procedures performed by gastroenterologists are endoscopic and listed in the surgery section.

If duodenal intubation and aspiration are performed, consult CPT codes 89100-89105. If gastrointestinal radiologic procedures are performed, consult CPT codes 74210-74363. If esophagoscopy procedures are performed, consult CPT codes 43200-43228; upper GI endoscopy 43234-43259; endoscopy, small bowel and stomal 44360-44393; proctosigmoidoscopy 45300-45321; sigmoidoscopy 45330-45339; colonoscopy 45355-45385; and anoscopy 46600-46615.

91000	**Esophageal intubation and collection of washings for cytology, including preparation of specimens (separate procedure)**	⊠ 80 ⧠
91010	**Esophageal motility (manometric study of the esophagus and/or gastroesophageal junction) study;**	⊠ 80 ⧠
	MED: 100-3, 100.4	
	AMA: 1997, Nov, 42	
91011	**with mecholyl or similar stimulant**	⊠ 80 ⧠
91012	**with acid perfusion studies**	⊠ 80 ⧠
91020	**Gastric motility (manometric) studies**	⊠ 80 ⧠
	MED: 100-3, 100.4	
	AMA: 1997, Nov, 42	
● **91022**	**Duodenal motility (manometric) study**	

> To report if gastrointestinal endoscopy is performed, consult CPT code 43235.)

> To report fluoroscopy, consult CPT code 76000.

> To report a gastric motility study, consult 91020.

91030	**Esophagus, acid perfusion (Bernstein) test for esophagitis**	⊠ 80 ⧠
91034	**Esophagus, gastroesophageal reflux test; with nasal catheter pH electrode(s) placement, recording, analysis and interpretation**	⊠ 80 ⧠
91035	**with mucosal attached telemetry pH electrode placement, recording, analysis and interpretation**	⑤ 80 ⧠

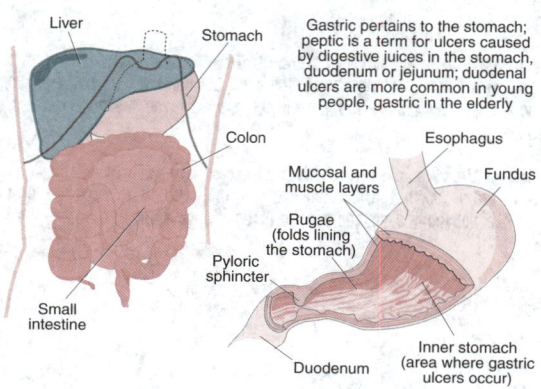

Gastric pertains to the stomach; peptic is a term for ulcers caused by digestive juices in the stomach, duodenum or jejunum; duodenal ulcers are more common in young people, gastric in the elderly

91037	Esophageal function test, gastroesophageal reflux test with nasal catheter intraluminal impedance electrode(s) placement, recording, analysis and interpretation; 🗷 80 🖵

91038	prolonged (greater than 1 hour, up to 24 hours) 🗷 80 🖵

91040	Esophageal balloon distension provocation study 🗷 80 🖵

To report balloon dilatation with endoscopy, consult CPT codes 43220, 43249, 43456, 43458.

91052	Gastric analysis test with injection of stimulant of gastric secretion (eg, histamine, insulin, pentagastrin, calcium and secretin) 🗷 80 🖵

MED: 100-3, 110.10; 100-3, 250.3; 100-3, 30.6; 100-3, 300.1

If the stomach is biopsied by capsule, peroral, or via tube, one or more specimens, consult CPT code 43600. If gastric laboratory procedures are performed, consult also CPT codes 89130-89141.

91055	Gastric intubation, washings, and preparing slides for cytology (separate procedure) 🗷 80 🖵

If therapeutic gastric lavage is performed, consult CPT code 91105.

Rehfuss' test

91060	Gastric saline load test 🗷 80 🖵

MED: 100-3, 100.5

If the small intestine is biopsied by capsule, peroral, or via tube (one or more specimens), consult CPT code 44100.

91065	Breath hydrogen test (eg, for detection of lactase deficiency, fructose intolerance, bacterial overgrowth, or oro-cecal gastrointestinal transit) 🗷 80 🖵

MED: 100-3, 100.5

To report H. pylori breath test analysis, consult 83013 for nonradioactive (C-13) isotope or 78268 for radioactive (C-14) isotope.

91100	Intestinal bleeding tube, passage, positioning and monitoring 🗷 80 🖵

91105	Gastric intubation, and aspiration or lavage for treatment (eg, for ingested poisons) 🗷 80 🖵

MED: 100-4, 12, 30.6.12

AMA: 1999, Nov, 49; 1996, Sep, 10; 1993, Spring, 34

If a cholangiography is performed, consult CPT codes 47500 and 74320. If abdominal paracentesis is performed, consult CPT codes 49080 and 49081; with instillation of medication, consult CPT codes 96440 and 96445. If peritoneoscopy is performed, consult CPT code 49320; with biopsy, consult CPT code 49321. If peritoneoscopy and guided transhepatic cholangiography is performed, consult CPT code 47560; with biopsy, consult CPT code 47561. If splenoportography is performed, consult CPT codes 38200 and 75810.

If gastric intubation is performed as part of critical care services (99291-99292) do not report separately.

91110	Gastrointestinal tract imaging, intraluminal (eg, capsule endoscopy), esophagus through ileum, with physician interpretation and report Ⓣ 80

Do not report visualization of the colon separately.

If the ileum is not visualized, append modifier 52.

91120	Rectal sensation, tone, and compliance test (ie, response to graded balloon distention) Ⓣ 80

To report biofeedback training, consult CPT code 90911.

To report anorectal manometry, consult CPT code 91122.

Medicine

91122 — 91299

91122	**Anorectal manometry**	T 80
91123	**Pulsed irrigation of fecal impaction**	N

GASTRIC PHYSIOLOGY

91132	**Electrogastrography, diagnostic, transcutaneous;**	X 80
91133	**with provocative testing**	X 80

OTHER PROCEDURES

91299	**Unlisted diagnostic gastroenterology procedure**	X 80

OPHTHALMOLOGY

The medical services of ophthalmologists are described in codes 92002 through 92499. General ophthalmological services (92002–92014) are divided into new and established patient categories that are further subdivided by level of service.

INTERMEDIATE LEVEL OF SERVICE

Intermediate service codes (92002 and 92012) report the evaluation of new or existing conditions that have been complicated by a new diagnostic or management problem. This new complaint may relate to the primary diagnosis. Included in the evaluation are:

- History
- General medical observation
- External examination
- Ophthalmoscopy
- Other diagnostic procedures as indicated:
— biomicroscopy
— mydriasis
— tonometry
- Initiation of diagnostic and treatment program

COMPREHENSIVE LEVEL OF SERVICE

Comprehensive service codes (92004 and 92014) report the evaluation of the complete visual system. This is a single service that need not be performed at one session. Included in this evaluation are:

- History
- General medical observation
- General evaluation of the complete visual system to include:
— external examination
— ophthalmoscopy
— gross visual field
— basic sensorimotor examination
- Other diagnostic procedures as indicated:
— biomicroscopy
— dilation (cycloplegia)
— mydriasis
— tonometry
- Initiation of a diagnostic treatment program

26 / TC Professional/Technical Component   80 / 80 Assist-at-Surgery Allowed/With Documentation   ⊙ Conscious Sedation

Unlisted   Not Covered   MED: Pubs 100/NCD Reference   1 - 9 ASC Group   63 Modifier 63 Exempt   CCI Comp

680 — Medicine   CPT only © 2005 American Medical Association. All Rights Reserved. *(Black Ink)*   © 2005 Ingenix, Inc. *(Blue Ink)*

SPECIAL OPHTHALMOLOGICAL SERVICES

Refractions (92015) should be reported additionally when performed at the time of a general ophthalmological service (92002–92014). Medicare allows the reporting of refractions, a noncovered service, to minimize patient confusion.

Gross visual field testing is integral to the general ophthalmic service and should not be reported separately. However, more extensive visual field examinations should be reported separately with codes 92081–92083. The CPT book recognizes three coding levels for visual field exams. The three specific visual field tests (limited, intermediate, and extended) are described as unilateral or bilateral.

Fitting and provision of contact lenses, glasses, and ocular prostheses are reported with the CPT codes 92310–92396. Use modifier 26 with 92391 or 92396 to report the service of fitting without supply. All the codes in this section are bilateral. For prescription or fitting of one eye, append modifier 52.

GENERAL OPHTHALMOLOGICAL SERVICES

NEW PATIENT

Consult the glossary for terms and definitions and the front matter of this chapter for additional information.

If surgical procedures are performed, consult Eye and Ocular Adnexa in the Surgery section (65091 and subsequent codes).

92002 **Ophthalmological services: medical examination and evaluation with initiation of diagnostic and treatment program; intermediate, new patient** V 80
  AMA: 1998, Aug, 1; 1997, Feb, 6

92004 **comprehensive, new patient, one or more visits** V 80
  AMA: 1998, Aug, 1; 1997, Feb, 6

ESTABLISHED PATIENT

92012 **Ophthalmological services: medical examination and evaluation, with initiation or continuation of diagnostic and treatment program; intermediate, established patient** V 80
  AMA: 1998, Aug, 1; 1997, Feb, 6

92014 **comprehensive, established patient, one or more visits** V 80
  AMA: 1999, Dec, 10; 1998, Aug, 1; 1997, Feb, 6

SPECIAL OPHTHALMOLOGICAL SERVICES

92015 **Determination of refractive state** E
  MED: 100-2, 16, 90

  AMA: 1998, Aug, 1; 1997, Feb, 6; 1996, Mar, 11

92018 **Ophthalmological examination and evaluation, under general anesthesia, with or without manipulation of globe for passive range of motion or other manipulation to facilitate diagnostic examination; complete** T 80
  AMA: 1997, Feb, 6

92019 **limited** T 80
  AMA: 1997, Feb, 6

92020 **Gonioscopy (separate procedure)** S 80
  AMA: 1997, Feb, 6

If gonioscopy is performed under general anesthesia, consult CPT cde 92018.

Medicine

92060 — 92135

92060   **Sensorimotor examination with multiple measurements of ocular deviation (eg, restrictive or paretic muscle with diplopia) with interpretation and report (separate procedure)** ⬛S ⬛80 ⬛
   AMA: 1997, Feb, 6

OTHER SPECIALIZED SERVICES

92065   **Orthoptic and/or pleoptic training, with continuing medical direction and evaluation** ⬛S ⬛80 ⬛
   AMA: 1998, Jun, 10; 1997, Feb, 6

92070   **Fitting of contact lens for treatment of disease, including supply of lens** ⬛N ⬛
   MED: 100-3, 80.1; 100-3, 80.4; 100-3, 80.9

   AMA: 1997, Feb, 6

92081   **Visual field examination, unilateral or bilateral, with interpretation and report; limited examination (eg, tangent screen, Autoplot, arc perimeter, or single stimulus level automated test, such as Octopus 3 or 7 equivalent)** ⬛S ⬛80 ⬛
   MED: 100-3, 80.9

   AMA: 1997, Feb, 6

92082   **intermediate examination (eg, at least 2 isopters on Goldmann perimeter, or semiquantitative, automated suprathreshold screening program, Humphrey suprathreshold automatic diagnostic test, Octopus program 33)** ⬛S ⬛80 ⬛
   MED: 100-3, 80.9

   AMA: 1997, Feb, 6

92083   **extended examination (eg, Goldmann visual fields with at least 3 isopters plotted and static determination within the central 30 degrees, or quantitative, automated threshold perimetry, Octopus programs G-1, 32 or 42, Humphrey visual field analyzer full threshold programs 30-2, 24-2, or 30/60-2)** ⬛S ⬛80 ⬛
   MED: 100-3, 80.9

   AMA: 1997, Feb, 6

   Note that gross visual field testing (e.g., confrontation testing) is a part of general ophthalmological services and is not reported separately.

92100   **Serial tonometry (separate procedure) with multiple measurements of intraocular pressure over an extended time period with interpretation and report, same day (eg, diurnal curve or medical treatment of acute elevation of intraocular pressure)** ⬛N ⬛80 ⬛
   AMA: 1998, Jun, 10; 1997, Feb, 6

92120   **Tonography with interpretation and report, recording indentation tonometer method or perilimbal suction method** ⬛S ⬛80 ⬛
   AMA: 1997, Feb, 6

92130   **Tonography with water provocation** ⬛S ⬛80 ⬛
   AMA: 1997, Feb, 6

92135   **Scanning computerized ophthalmic diagnostic imaging (eg, scanning laser) with interpretation and report, unilateral** ⬛S ⬛
   AMA: 1999, Mar, 10; 1999, Apr, 10; 1998, Nov, 33

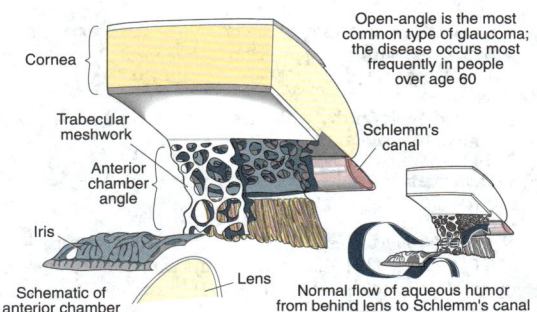

Glaucoma is caused by excessive intraocular pressure and abnormal accumulation of aqueous humor in the anterior chamber of the eye; pressure reduces blood supply to the optic nerve and causes nerve damage

92136 Ophthalmic biometry by partial coherence interferometry with intraocular lens power calculation S 80 ⬚
   MED: 100-3, 10.1

   AMA: 2002, Apr, 18

92140 Provocative tests for glaucoma, with interpretation and report, without tonography S 80 ⬚
   AMA: 1998, Aug, 1; 1997, Feb, 6

OPHTHALMOSCOPY
Routine ophthalmoscopy is considered part of special or general ophthalmologic services when indicated and therefore not separately reported.

92225 Ophthalmoscopy, extended, with retinal drawing (eg, for retinal detachment, melanoma), with interpretation and report; initial S ⬚
   AMA: 1999, Dec, 10; 1998, Aug, 1; 1997, Feb, 6

92226   subsequent S ⬚
   AMA: 1998, Aug, 1; 1997, Feb, 6

92230 Fluorescein angioscopy with interpretation and report T ⬚
   AMA: 1997, Feb, 6

92235 Fluorescein angiography (includes multiframe imaging) with interpretation and report S ⬚
   AMA: 1997, Feb, 6

92240 Indocyanine-green angiography (includes multiframe imaging) with interpretation and report) S ⬚
   MED: 100-3, 80.12; 100-3, 80.6

92250 Fundus photography with interpretation and report S 80 ⬚
   MED: 100-3, 80.12; 100-3, 80.6

   AMA: 1999, Apr, 10; 1997, Feb, 6

92260 Ophthalmodynamometry S 80 ⬚
   AMA: 1997, Feb, 6

   If ophthalmoscopy is performed under general anesthesia, consult CPT code 92018.

In the figure labels: Cornea, Trabecular meshwork, Anterior chamber angle, Iris, Schematic of anterior chamber, Lens, Schlemm's canal, Open-angle is the most common type of glaucoma; the disease occurs most frequently in people over age 60, Normal flow of aqueous humor from behind lens to Schlemm's canal

Medicine

92265 — 92312

OTHER SPECIALIZED SERVICES

92265 **Needle oculoelectromyography, one or more extraocular muscles, one or both eyes, with interpretation and report** S 80 ▯
AMA: 1997, Feb, 6

92270 **Electro-oculography with interpretation and report** S 80 ▯
AMA: 1997, Feb, 6

92275 **Electroretinography with interpretation and report** S 80 ▯
AMA: 1997, Feb, 6

If electronystagmography is performed for vestibular function studies, consult CPT codes 92541 and subsequent codes. If ophthalmic echography is performed (diagnostic ultrasound), consult CPT codes 76511-76529.

92283 **Color vision examination, extended, eg, anomaloscope or equivalent** S 80 ▯
AMA: 1997, Feb, 6

Note that color vision testing with pseudoisochromatic plates (such as HRR or Ishihara) is not reported separately. It is included in the appropriate general or ophthalmological service.
Farnsworth-Munsell color test

92284 **Dark adaptation examination, with interpretation and report** S 80 ▯
AMA: 1997, Feb, 6

92285 **External ocular photography with interpretation and report for documentation of medical progress (eg, close-up photography, slit lamp photography, goniophotography, stereo-photography)** S 80 ▯
MED: 100-3, 80.8

AMA: 1997, Sep, 10; 1997, Feb, 6

92286 **Special anterior segment photography with interpretation and report; with specular endothelial microscopy and cell count** S 80 ▯
AMA: 1997, Feb, 6

92287 **with fluorescein angiography** S 80 ▯
AMA: 1997, Feb, 6

CONTACT LENS SERVICES

Report the following contact lens codes separately from other ophthalmological services.

Fitting of contact lenses includes patient training and instruction as well as incidental revision of the contacts during the training period.

For therapeutic or surgical use of contact lens, consult CPT codes 68340 and 92970.

92310 **Prescription of optical and physical characteristics of and fitting of contact lens, with medical supervision of adaptation; corneal lens, both eyes, except for aphakia** E
MED: 100-3, 80.1; 100-3, 80.4

AMA: 1997, Feb, 6

To report prescription and fitting of one eye, append modifier 52.

92311 **corneal lens for aphakia, one eye** X 80 ▯
MED: 100-3, 80.1; 100-3, 80.4

AMA: 1997, Feb, 6

92312 **corneal lens for aphakia, both eyes** X 80 ▯
MED: 100-3, 80.1; 100-3, 80.4

AMA: 1997, Feb, 6

92313	**corneoscleral lens**	☒ 80 ↵

MED: 100-3, 80.1; 100-3, 80.4

AMA: 1997, Feb, 7

92314 **Prescription of optical and physical characteristics of contact lens, with medical supervision of adaptation and direction of fitting by independent technician; corneal lens, both eyes, except for aphakia** Ⓔ

MED: 100-3, 80.1; 100-3, 80.4

AMA: 1997, Feb, 7

To report prescription and fitting of one eye, append modifier 52.

92315	**corneal lens for aphakia, one eye**	☒ 80 ↵

MED: 100-3, 80.1; 100-3, 80.4

AMA: 1997, Feb, 7

92316	**corneal lens for aphakia, both eyes**	☒ 80 ↵

MED: 100-3, 80.1; 100-3, 80.4

AMA: 1997, Feb, 7

92317	**corneoscleral lens**	☒ 80 ↵

MED: 100-3, 80.1; 100-3, 80.4

AMA: 1997, Feb, 7

92325 **Modification of contact lens (separate procedure), with medical supervision of adaptation** ☒ ↵

MED: 100-3, 80.1; 100-3, 80.4

AMA: 1997, Feb, 7

To report therapeutic or surgical use of contact lens, consult CPT codes 68340 and 92970.

92326 **Replacement of contact lens** ☒ ↵

MED: 100-3, 80.1; 100-3, 80.4

AMA: 1997, Feb, 7

To report the prescription, fitting, and/or medical supervision of ocular prosthetic adaptation by the physician, consult the E/M codes or 92002-92004.

OCULAR PROSTHETICS, ARTIFICIAL EYE

If surgical procedures are performed, consult Eye and Ocular Adnexa in the Surgery section of the CPT book (65091 and subsequent codes).

If the supply is not included, append modifier 26. To report supply separately, consult CPT code 92393.

92330 ~~Prescription, fitting, and supply of ocular prosthesis (artificial eye), with medical supervision of adaptation~~

92335 ~~Prescription of ocular prosthesis (artificial eye) and direction of fitting and supply by independent technician, with medical supervision of adaptation~~

SPECTACLE SERVICES (INCLUDING PROSTHESIS FOR APHAKIA)

92340 **Fitting of spectacles, except for aphakia; monofocal** Ⓔ

AMA: 1998, Aug, 1; 1997, Feb, 7

92341 **bifocal** Ⓔ

AMA: 1997, Feb, 7

Medicine

92342 — 92499

92342	multifocal, other than bifocal	E
	AMA: 1997, Feb, 7	
92352	Fitting of spectacle prosthesis for aphakia; monofocal	X
	MED: 100-2, 15, 120; 100-4, 1, 30.3.5	
	AMA: 1997, Feb, 7	
92353	multifocal	X
	MED: 100-2, 15, 120; 100-4, 1, 30.3.5	
	AMA: 1997, Feb, 7	
92354	Fitting of spectacle mounted low vision aid; single element system	X
	AMA: 1997, Feb, 7	
92355	telescopic or other compound lens system	X
	AMA: 1997, Feb, 7	
92358	Prosthesis service for aphakia, temporary (disposable or loan, including materials)	X
	MED: 100-2, 15, 120; 100-4, 1, 30.3.5	
	AMA: 1997, Feb, 7	
92370	Repair and refitting spectacles; except for aphakia	E
	AMA: 1997, Feb, 7	
92371	spectacle prosthesis for aphakia	X
	MED: 100-2, 15, 120; 100-4, 1, 30.3.5	
	AMA: 1998, Aug, 1; 1997, Feb, 7	

Report the appropriate supply codes for spectacles or contact lenses.

SUPPLY OF MATERIALS

If surgical procedures are performed, consult CPT codes 65091 and subsequent codes.

92390	Supply of spectacles, except prosthesis for aphakia and low vision aids
92391	Supply of contact lenses, except prosthesis for aphakia
92392	Supply of low vision aids (A low vision aid is any lens or device used to aid or improve visual function in a person whose vision cannot be normalized by conventional spectacle correction. Includes reading additions up to 4D.)
92393	Supply of ocular prosthesis (artificial eye)
92395	Supply of permanent prosthesis for aphakia; spectacles
92396	contact lenses

OTHER PROCEDURES

92499	Unlisted ophthalmological service or procedure	S 80
	AMA: 1997, Feb, 7	

SPECIAL OTORHINOLARYNGOLOGIC SERVICES

Otorhinolaryngologic codes (92502–92700) identify the special diagnostic and treatment services not usually included in a comprehensive otorhinolaryngologic evaluation. Comprehensive ear, nose, and throat (ENT) evaluations include basic diagnostic procedures such as otoscopy and rhinoscopy. These services are an integral part of the evaluation and management service and are not itemized separately. Special services not generally included in this total evaluation are reported separately with 92502–92700, such as audiologic function tests (92551–92597). Hearing tests using calibrated electronic equipment are reportable; use of a tuning fork is not.

Hearing test codes are inherently bilateral (binaural, both ears). If only one ear is tested, the reduced service is reported with modifier 52. Codes 92590, 92592, and 92594 are the exceptions, identified in CPT as monaural (one ear). If binaural, report with 92591, 92593, or 92595.

If laryngoscopy is performed with stroboscopy, consult CPT code 31579.

	92502	**Otolaryngologic examination under general anesthesia**	T 80 ▚
	92504	**Binocular microscopy (separate diagnostic procedure)**	N 80 ▚
▲	92506	**Evaluation of speech, language, voice, communication, and/or auditory processing** MED: 100-2, 15, 230.3; 100-3, 170.3	A 80 ▚
▲	92507	**Treatment of speech, language, voice, communication, and/or auditory processing disorder; individual** MED: 100-2, 15, 230.3	A 80 ▚
▲	92508	**group, 2 or more individuals** MED: 100-2, 15, 230.3; 100-3, 50.3	A 80 ▚
	~~92510~~	~~**Aural rehabilitation following cochlear implant (includes evaluation of aural rehabilitation status and hearing, therapeutic services) with or without speech processor programming**~~	
	92511	**Nasopharyngoscopy with endoscope (separate procedure)**	T 80 ▚
	92512	**Nasal function studies (eg, rhinomanometry)**	X 80
	92516	**Facial nerve function studies (eg, electroneuronography)**	X 80
▲	92520	**Laryngeal function studies (ie, aerodynamic testing and acoustic testing)**	X 80

To report a single test, use modifier 52.

To report a flexible fiber optic laryngeal evaluation of swallowing and laryngeal sensory testing, consult CPT codes 92611-92617.

To report other testing of laryngeal function (eg. electroglottography), consult CPT code 92700.

	92526	**Treatment of swallowing dysfunction and/or oral function for feeding** MED: 100-3, 170.3	A 80 ▚

VESTIBULAR FUNCTION TESTS

WITH OBSERVATION AND EVALUATION BY PHYSICIAN, WITHOUT ELECTRICAL RECORDING

	92531	**Spontaneous nystagmus, including gaze**	N
	92532	**Positional nystagmus test**	N
	92533	**Caloric vestibular test, each irrigation (binaural, bithermal stimulation constitutes four tests)** AMA: 1996, May, 5	N
		Barany caloric test	
	92534	**Optokinetic nystagmus test**	N

WITH RECORDING (EG, ENG, PENG), AND MEDICAL DIAGNOSTIC EVALUATION

	92541	**Spontaneous nystagmus test, including gaze and fixation nystagmus, with recording**	X 80 ▚
	92542	**Positional nystagmus test, minimum of 4 positions, with recording**	X 80

92543 Caloric vestibular test, each irrigation (binaural, bithermal stimulation constitutes four tests), with recording   [X] [80] [CCI]
AMA: 1996, May, 5

92544 Optokinetic nystagmus test, bidirectional, foveal or peripheral stimulation, with recording   [X] [80]

92545 Oscillating tracking test, with recording   [X] [80]

92546 Sinusoidal vertical axis rotational testing   [X] [80]

+ **92547** Use of vertical electrodes (List separately in addition to code for primary procedure)   [X] [TC] [80]

Note that 92547 is an add-on code and must be used in conjunction with 92541-92546. If vestibular tests are unlisted, consult CPT code 92700.

92548 Computerized dynamic posturography   [X] [80]

AUDIOLOGIC FUNCTION TESTS WITH MEDICAL DIAGNOSTIC EVALUATION

The following codes describe the use of electronic equipment and differ from other otorhinolaryngologic services that include the use of tuning forks, clapping, whispering, and other stimuli. All CPT codes in this section are considered bilateral. Use modifier 52 if the test is performed on one ear only.

If speech, language, and/or hearing problems are evaluated through observation and assessment of performance, consult CPT code 92506.

92551 Screening test, pure tone, air only   [E]
MED: 100-2, 15, 80.3

92552 Pure tone audiometry (threshold); air only   [X] [TC] [80] [CCI]
MED: 100-2, 15, 80.3

92553   air and bone   [X] [TC] [80] [CCI]
MED: 100-2, 15, 80.3

92555 Speech audiometry threshold;   [X] [TC] [80] [CCI]
MED: 100-2, 15, 80.3

92556   with speech recognition   [X] [TC] [80] [CCI]
MED: 100-2, 15, 80.3

92557 Comprehensive audiometry threshold evaluation and speech recognition (92553 and 92556 combined)   [X] [TC] [80] [CCI]

To report hearing aid evaluation and selection, consult CPT codes 92590-92595.

92559 Audiometric testing of groups   [E]

92560 Bekesy audiometry; screening   [E]
MED: 100-2, 15, 80.3

92561   diagnostic   [X] [TC] [80] [CCI]
MED: 100-2, 15, 80.3

92562 Loudness balance test, alternate binaural or monaural   [X] [TC] [80] [CCI]

92563 Tone decay test   [X] [TC] [80] [CCI]

92564 Short increment sensitivity index (SISI)   [X] [TC] [80] [CCI]
AMA: 1996, Oct, 9

92565 Stenger test, pure tone   [X] [TC] [80] [CCI]

92567 Tympanometry (impedance testing)   [X] [TC] [80] [CCI]

▲ 92568   Acoustic reflex testing; threshold   X TC 80 ⮌

▲ 92569   decay   X TC 80 ⮌

92571   Filtered speech test   X TC 80 ⮌

92572   Staggered spondaic word test   X TC 80 ⮌

92573   Lombard test   X TC 80 ⮌

92575   Sensorineural acuity level test   X TC 80 ⮌

92576   Synthetic sentence identification test   X TC 80 ⮌

92577   Stenger test, speech   X TC 80 ⮌

92579   Visual reinforcement audiometry (VRA)   X TC 80 ⮌

92582   Conditioning play audiometry   X TC 80 ⮌

92583   Select picture audiometry   X TC 80 ⮌

92584   Electrocochleography   X TC 80 ⮌
         MED: 100-3, 50-31

92585   Auditory evoked potentials for evoked response audiometry and/or testing of the central nervous system; comprehensive   S 80 ⮌
         MED: 100-3, 50-31

92586   limited   S TC 80 ⮌
         MED: 100-3, 50-31

92587   Evoked otoacoustic emissions; limited (single stimulus level, either transient or distortion products)   X 80 ⮌

92588   comprehensive or diagnostic evaluation (comparison of transient and/or distortion product otoacoustic emissions at multiple levels and frequencies)   X 80 ⮌

92590   Hearing aid examination and selection; monaural   E
         MED: 100-2, 15, 80.3

92591   binaural   E
         MED: 100-2, 15, 80.3

92592   Hearing aid check; monaural   E
         MED: 100-2, 15, 80.3

92593   binaural   E
         MED: 100-2, 15, 80.3

92594   Electroacoustic evaluation for hearing aid; monaural   E
         MED: 100-2, 15, 80.3

92595   binaural   E
         MED: 100-2, 15, 80.3

92596   Ear protector attenuation measurements   X TC 80 ⮌
         MED: 100-2, 15, 80.3

92597   Evaluation for use and/or fitting of voice prosthetic device to supplement oral speech   A 80 ⮌

         To report augmentative and alternative communication device services, consult CPT codes 92605, 92607, and 92608.

✎ Drug Not Approved by FDA   50 Bilateral Procedure   + CPT Add-on Code   ⊘ Modifier -51 Exempt   ♂ Male   ♀ Female
● New Code   ▲ Revised Code   M Maternity Edit   A Age Edit   A—Y APC Status Ind.   AMA: CPT Assistant
© 2005 Ingenix, Inc. *(Blue Ink)*   CPT only © 2005 American Medical Association. All Rights Reserved. *(Black Ink)*   Medicine — 689

Medicine

92568 — 92597

Medicine

92601 — 92610

EVALUATIVE AND THERAPEUTIC SERVICES

CPT codes 92601 and 92603 are used to report post-operative analysis and fitting of previously placed external devices, connection to the cochlear implant, and stimulator programming. CPT codes 92602 and 92604 are used to report subsequent sessions for measurements and adjustments of the external transmitter and internal stimulator.

To report placement of cochlear implant, consult CPT code 69930.

92601   **Diagnostic analysis of cochlear implant, patient under 7 years of age; with programming**   A X 80 ↻
MED: 100-2, 15, 80.3; 100-3, 50.3

92602   **subsequent reprogramming**   A X 80 ↻
MED: 100-2, 15, 80.3; 100-3, 50.3

Do not report 92602 with CPT code 92601.

To report aural rehabilitation services after a cochlear implant consult CPT codes 92626-92627, 92630-92633.

92603   **Diagnostic analysis of cochlear implant, age 7 years or older; with programming**   X 80 ↻
MED: 100-2, 15, 80.3; 100-3, 50.3

92604   **subsequent reprogramming**   X 80 ↻
MED: 100-2, 15, 80.3; 100-3, 50.3

Do not report 92604 with CPT code 92603.

92605   **Evaluation for prescription of non-speech-generating augmentative and alternative communication device**   A
MED: 100-2, 15, 230.3; 100-3; 100-3, 50.3

92606   **Therapeutic service(s) for the use of non-speech-generating device, including programming and modification**   A
MED: 100-2, 15, 230.3; 100-3, 50.3

92607   **Evaluation for prescription for speech-generating augmentative and alternative communication device, face-to-face with the patient; first hour**   A 80 ↻
MED: 100-2, 15, 230.3; 100-3; 100-3, 50.1; 100-3, 50.3

To report evaluation for prescription of a non-speech generating device, consult CPT code 92605.

+   92608   **each additional 30 minutes (List separately in addition to code for primary procedure)**   A 80 ↻
MED: 100-2, 15, 230.3; 100-3; 100-3, 50.3

Note that 92608 is an add-on code and must be used in conjunction with CPT code 92607.

92609   **Therapeutic services for the use of speech-generating device, including programming and modification**   A 80 ↻
MED: 100-2, 15, 230.3; 100-3; 100-3, 50.1; 100-3, 50.3

To report therapeutic service(s) for the use of a non-speech generating device, consult CPT code 92606.

92610   **Evaluation of oral and pharyngeal swallowing function**   A 80 ↻
MED: 100-2, 15, 230.3; 100-3, 50.3

To report motion fluoroscopic evaluation of swallowing function, consult CPT code 92611.

To report flexible endoscopic examination, consult CPT codes 92612-92617.

92611   **Motion fluoroscopic evaluation of swallowing function by cine or video recording**   [A] [80] [⟳]
MED: 100-2, 15, 230.3; 100-3, 50.3

To report radiological supervision and interpretation, consult CPT code 74230.

To report evaluation of oral and pharyngeal swallowing functions, consult CPT code 92610.

92612   **Flexible fiberoptic endoscopic evaluation of swallowing by cine or video recording;**   [A] [80] [⟳]
MED: 100-2, 15, 230.3; 100-3, 50.3

To report flexible fiberoptic or endoscopic swallowing evaluation performed without cine or video recording, consult CPT code 92700.

To report flexible fiberoptic diagnostic laryngoscopy, consult CPT code 31575. Code 31575 cannot be reported with 92612-92617.

92613   **physician interpretation and report only**   [E] [80] [⟳]
MED: 100-2, 15, 230.3; 100-3, 50.3

To report evaluation of oral and pharyngeal swallowing function, consult CPT code 92610.

To report motion fluoroscopic evaluation of swallowing function, consult CPT code 92611.

92614   **Flexible fiberoptic endoscopic evaluation, laryngeal sensory testing by cine or video recording;**   [A] [80] [⟳]
MED: 100-2, 15, 230.3; 100-3, 50.3

If flexible fiberoptic or endoscopic evaluation of swallowing is performed without cine or video recording, use 92700

92615   **physician interpretation and report only**   [E] [80] [⟳]
MED: 100-2, 15, 230.3; 100-3, 50.3

92616   **Flexible fiberoptic endoscopic evaluation of swallowing and laryngeal sensory testing by cine or video recording;**   [A] [80] [⟳]
MED: 100-2, 15, 230.3; 100-3, 50.3

To report flexible fiberoptic or endoscopic swallowing evaluation performed without cine or video recording, consult CPT code 92700.

92617   **physician interpretation and report only**   [E] [80] [⟳]
MED: 100-2, 15, 230.3; 100-3, 50.3

92620   **Evaluation of central auditory function, with report; initial 60 minutes**   [X] [TC] [80] [⟳]

92621   **each additional 15 minutes**   [N] [TC] [80] [⟳]

Codes 92620, 92621 cannot be reported with CPT code 92506.

92625   **Assessment of tinnitus (includes pitch, loudness matching, and masking)**   [X] [TC] [80] [⟳]

Code 92625 cannot be reported with CPT code 92562.

If the procedure is performed unilaterally, append with modifier 52.

● **92626**   **Evaluation of auditory rehabilitation status; first hour**

● **92627**   **each additional 15 minutes (List separately in addition to code for primary procedure)**

Note that 92627 is an add-on code and must be used in conjunction with 92626.

Codes 92626, 92627are used to report the face-to-face time with the patient or family.

Medicine

- 92630   **Auditory rehabilitation; pre-lingual hearing loss**
- 92633   **post-lingual hearing loss**

OTHER PROCEDURES

92700   **Unlisted otorhinolaryngological service or procedure**   ☒ 80
MED: 100-2, 15, 230.3; 100-3, 50.3

CARDIOVASCULAR

Cardiovascular services (92950–93799) include diagnostic and therapeutic services.

THERAPEUTIC SERVICES

Therapeutic services are performed for treatment of a specific condition, disorder, or disease. Some of the more frequently performed services include percutaneous placement of intracoronary stents, percutaneous transluminal coronary angioplasty (PTCA), and percutaneous transluminal coronary arthrectomy.

Percutaneous placement of coronary stents (92980–92981) includes therapeutic procedures such as PTCA and arthrectomy. Do not report stent placements for procedures 92982, 92984, 92995, and 92996.

PTCA (92982–92984) is used to treat coronary artery obstruction. A balloon catheter is placed in the affected artery and the balloon is inflated to flatten the plaque against the wall of the artery and open the obstruction.

Percutaneous transluminal coronary arthrectomy (92995–92996) may be used instead of the PTCA to treat coronary artery obstruction. Arthrectomy involves placing a catheter into the affected artery and using a rotary cutter to remove the plaque. When arthrectomy is performed with a PTCA, the PTCA is not reported separately as it is included in procedures 92995 and 92996.

For non-surgical septal reduction therapy (e.g., alcohol ablation), consult CPT Category III code 0024T.

92950   **Cardiopulmonary resuscitation (eg, in cardiac arrest)**   Ⓢ 80 ▯
AMA: 1996, Jan, 7

Consult also critical care services 99291 and 99292.

⊙ 92953   **Temporary transcutaneous pacing**   Ⓢ 80 ▯
MED: 100-4, 12, 30.6.12

To report physician direction of ambulance or rescue personnel outside the hospital, consult CPT code 99288.

If temporary transcutaneous pacing is performed as part of critical care services (99291-99292) do not report separately.

⊙ 92960   **Cardioversion, elective, electrical conversion of arrhythmia; external**   Ⓢ 80 ▯
AMA: 2001, Jul, 11; 2000, Nov, 9; 2000, Jun, 5; 1999, Nov, 49; 1993, Summer, 13

⊙ 92961   **internal (separate procedure)**   Ⓢ ▯
AMA: 2000, Nov, 9; 2000, Jun, 5; 2000, Jul, 5; 1999, Nov, 49; 1993, Summer, 13

Note that 92961 cannot be reported in addition to CPT codes 93618-93624, 93631, 93640-93642, 93650-93652, 93662, and 93741-93744.

92970   **Cardioassist-method of circulatory assist; internal**   Ⓒ 80 ▯
92971   **external**   Ⓒ 80 ▯

If a balloon atrial-septostomy is performed, consult CPT code 92992. If catheters are placed for use in circulatory assist devices such as an intra-aortic balloon pump, consult CPT code 33970.

⊙ **+** **92973** **Percutaneous transluminal coronary thrombectomy (List separately in addition to code for primary procedure)** T 80 ◘
AMA: 2002, Mar, 10; 2002, Mar, 1

Note that 92973 is an add-on code and must be used in conjunction with codes 92980, 92982.

⊙ **+** **92974** **Transcatheter placement of radiation delivery device for subsequent coronary intravascular brachytherapy (List separately in addition to code for primary procedure)** T 80 ◘
AMA: 2002, Mar, 1

Note that 92974 is an add-on code and must be used in conjunction with codes 92980, 92982, 92995, 93508.

For intravascular radioelement application, see 77781-77784.

⊙ **92975** **Thrombolysis, coronary; by intracoronary infusion, including selective coronary angiography** C 80 ◘

92977 **by intravenous infusion** T ◘

If thrombolysis is performed of vessels other than coronary, consult CPT codes 37201 and 75896. If cerebral thrombolysis is performed, consult CPT code 37195.

⊙ **+** **92978** **Intravascular ultrasound (coronary vessel or graft) during diagnostic evaluation and/or therapeutic intervention including imaging supervision, interpretation and report; initial vessel (List separately in addition to code for primary procedure)** S 80 ◘
MED: 100-3, 220.5

AMA: 1999, Nov, 49; 1997, Nov, 43-44

Note that intravascular ultrasound services include all transducer manipulations and repositioning within the specific vessel being examined, both before and after therapeutic intervention (e.g., stent placement).

Note that 92978 is an add-on code that must be used in conjunction with the appropriate code for the primary procedure. This code cannot be reported alone.

⊙ **+** **92979** **each additional vessel (List separately in addition to code for primary procedure)** S 80
MED: 100-3, 220.5

AMA: 1999, Nov, 49; 1997, Nov, 43-44

Note that 92979 is an add-on code and must be used in conjunction with 92978.

⊙ **92980** **Transcatheter placement of an intracoronary stent(s), percutaneous, with or without other therapeutic intervention, any method; single vessel** T 80 ◘
AMA: 2001, Mar, 11; 2001, Apr, 10; 1998, Aug, 3; 1998, Apr, 9; 1996, Dec, 11; 1996, Aug, 2

Medicine

92973 — 92980

Medicine

⊙ **+   92981**   **each additional vessel (List separately in addition to code for primary procedure)**   T 80 ▣
MED: 100-3, 20.7; 100-3, 220.13

AMA: 2001, Mar, 11; 2001, Apr, 10

Note that 92981 is an add-on code and must be used in conjunction with 92980.

Use 92980, 92981 to report coronary artery stenting. If coronary angioplasty (92982, 92984) or atherectomy (92995, 92996) is performed in the same artery, it is considered part of the stenting procedure and should not be reported separately. Codes 92973 (percutaneous transluminal coronary thrombectomy), 92974 (coronary brachytherapy) and 92978, 92979 (intravascular ultrasound) should be used in addition to reporting the procedure for coronary stenting, atherectomy, and angioplasty and are not included in the therapeutic interventions in 92980.

If additional vessels are treated by angioplasty or atherectomy during the same session, consult CPT codes 92984 and 92996.

To report transcatheter placement of radiation delivery device for coronary intravascular brachytherapy, use 92974.

For intravascular radioelement application, consult CPT codes 77781-77784.

⊙   **92982**   **Percutaneous transluminal coronary balloon angioplasty; single vessel**   T 80 ▣
MED: 100-3, 20.7; 100-3, 220.13

AMA: 1997, Apr, 10; 1996, Aug, 2; 1992, Winter, 15

⊙ **+   92984**   **each additional vessel (List separately in addition to code for primary procedure)**   T 80 ▣
MED: 100-3, 20.7; 100-3, 220.13

AMA: 1997, Apr, 10; 1996, Dec, 11; 1996, Aug, 2; 1992, Winter, 15

Note that 92984 is an add-on code and must be used in conjunction with 92980, 92982, or 92995. If a stent is placed following the completion of angioplasty or atherectomy, consult CPT codes 92980 and 92981.

To report transcatheter placement of radiation delivery device for coronary intravascular brachytherapy, use 92974.

For intravascular radioelement application, see 77781-77784.

⊙   **92986**   **Percutaneous balloon valvuloplasty; aortic valve**   T 80 ▣
⊙   **92987**   **mitral valve**   T 80 ▣
       92990   **pulmonary valve**   T 80 ▣
       92992   **Atrial septectomy or septostomy; transvenous method, balloon, (eg, Rashkind type) (includes cardiac catheterization)**   C 80 ▣
AMA: 1998, Apr, 3, 10; 1997, Nov, 44

       92993   **blade method (Park septostomy) (includes cardiac catheterization)**   C 80 ▣
AMA: 1998, Apr, 3, 10

⊙   **92995**   **Percutaneous transluminal coronary atherectomy, by mechanical or other method, with or without balloon angioplasty; single vessel**   T 80 ▣
MED: 100-3, 20.7; 100-3, 220.13

AMA: 1992, Winter, 15

⊙ + **92996** **each additional vessel (List separately in addition to code for primary procedure)** T 80 🔲
AMA: 1998, Apr, 3; 1992, Winter, 15

> Note that 92996 is an add-on code and must be used in conjunction with 92980, 92982, or 92995. If a stent is placed following the completion of angioplasty or atherectomy, consult CPT codes 92980 and 92981. If additional vessels are treated by angioplasty or atherectomy during the same session, consult CPT code 92984.

92997 **Percutaneous transluminal pulmonary artery balloon angioplasty; single vessel** T 80 🔲
MED: 100-3, 20.7; 100-3, 220.13

AMA: 1997, Nov, 44

+ **92998** **each additional vessel (List separately in addition to code for primary procedure)** T 80 🔲
AMA: 1997, Nov, 44

> Note that 92998 is an add-on code and must be used in conjunction with 92997.

CARDIOGRAPHY

Cardiography services include electrocardiogram (ECG), cardiovascular stress tests, and electrocardiographic (Holter) monitoring. The Holter monitor is a diagnostic tool that creates a continuous record of the heart's electrical activity during the patient's normal activities for a 24-hour period. Cardiography codes include both a professional and a technical component. These codes have separate listings for the total component, the recording (technical component), and the review and interpretation (professional component). For example, code 93015 identifies the total service (global) for a cardiovascular stress test and includes the following components:

- Tracing (the technical component only (93017)

- Supervision of the procedure (a portion of the professional component) (93016)

- Interpretation and report (a portion of the professional component) (93018)

If echocardiography is performed, consult CPT codes 93303-93350.

93000 **Electrocardiogram, routine ECG with at least 12 leads; with interpretation and report** B 80 🔲
MED: 100-3, 160.17; 100-3, 20.15; 100-4, 12, 30.6.12; 100-4, 13, 100

AMA: 1997, Aug, 9

93005 **tracing only, without interpretation and report** S TC 80 🔲
MED: 100-3, 20.15; 100-4, 13, 100

AMA: 1997, Aug, 9

> If echocardiography is performed, consult CPT codes 93303-93350.

93010 **interpretation and report only** A 26 80 🔲
MED: 100-3, 20.15; 100-4, 12, 30.6.12; 100-4, 13, 100

AMA: 1997, Aug, 9

> If ECG monitoring is needed, consult CPT codes 99354-99360.

93012 **Telephonic transmission of post-symptom electrocardiogram rhythm strip(s), 24-hour attended monitoring, per 30 day period of time; tracing only** N TC 80 🔲
MED: 100-3, 20.15

AMA: 1996, Jun, 2

93014 **Telephonic transmission of post-symptom electrocardiogram rhythm strip(s), 24-hour attended monitoring, per 30 day period of time; physician review with interpretation and report only** B 26 80

MED: 100-3, 20.15

AMA: 1996, Jun, 2

If echocardiography is performed, consult CPT codes 93303-93350.

93015 **Cardiovascular stress test using maximal or submaximal treadmill or bicycle exercise, continous electrocardiographic monitoring, and/or pharmacological stress; with physician supervision, with interpretation and report** B 80 CCI

MED: 100-2, 15, 60.3; 100-3, 20.10; 100-3, 20.15

AMA: 2002, Aug, 10; 1996, Jun, 10; 1996, Apr, 11

93016 **physician supervision only, without interpretation and report** B 26 80 CCI

MED: 100-2, 15, 60.3; 100-3, 20.10; 100-3, 20.15

AMA: 2002, Aug, 10; 1996, Apr, 11

93017 **tracing only, without interpretation and report** X TC 80 CCI

MED: 100-2, 15, 60.3; 100-3, 20.10; 100-3, 20.15

AMA: 2002, Aug, 10

93018 **interpretation and report only** B 26 80 CCI

MED: 100-2, 15, 60.3; 100-3, 20.10; 100-3, 20.15

AMA: 1996, Jun, 10; 1996, Apr, 11

To report the inert gas rebreathing measurement, consult Category III codes 0104T, 0105T.

93024 **Ergonovine provocation test** X 80 CCI

MED: 100-3, 20.15

93025 **Microvolt T-wave alternans for assessment of ventricular arrhythmias** X 80 CCI

AMA: 2002, Mar, 1

93040 **Rhythm ECG, one to three leads; with interpretation and report** B 80 CCI

MED: 100-2, 15, 60.3; 100-3, 20.10; 100-3, 20.15; 100-4, 12, 30.6.12; 100-4, 13, 100

93041 **tracing only without interpretation and report** S TC 80

MED: 100-2, 15, 60.3; 100-3, 20.10; 100-3, 20.15; 100-4, 13, 100

93042 **interpretation and report only** B 26 80

MED: 100-2, 15, 60.3; 100-3, 20.10; 100-3, 20.15; 100-4, 12, 30.6.12; 100-4, 13, 100

93224 **Electrocardiographic monitoring for 24 hours by continuous original ECG waveform recording and storage, with visual superimposition scanning; includes recording, scanning analysis with report, physician review and interpretation** B 80 CCI

MED: 100-3, 20.15

93225 **recording (includes hook-up, recording, and disconnection)** X TC 80 CCI

MED: 100-3, 20.15

93226 **scanning analysis with report** X TC 80 CCI

MED: 100-3, 20.15

93227 **physician review and interpretation** B 26 80 CCI

MED: 100-3, 20.15

93230   Electrocardiographic monitoring for 24 hours by continuous original ECG waveform recording and storage without superimposition scanning utilizing a device capable of producing a full miniaturized printout; includes recording, microprocessor-based analysis with report, physician review and interpretation   B 80 ⌧
MED: 100-3, 20.15

93231   recording (includes hook-up, recording, and disconnection) ⌧ TC 80 ⌧
MED: 100-3, 20.15

93232   microprocessor-based analysis with report   ⌧ TC 80 ⌧
MED: 100-3, 20.15

93233   physician review and interpretation   B 26 80 ⌧
MED: 100-3, 20.15

93235   Electrocardiographic monitoring for 24 hours by continuous computerized monitoring and non-continuous recording, and real-time data analysis utilizing a device capable of producing intermittent full-sized waveform tracings, possibly patient activated; includes monitoring and real time data analysis with report, physician review and interpretation   B 80 ⌧
MED: 100-3, 20.15

Holter monitor procedure

93236   monitoring and real-time data analysis with report   ⌧ TC 80 ⌧
MED: 100-3, 20.15

93237   physician review and interpretation   B 26 80 ⌧
MED: 100-3, 20.15

93268   Patient demand single or multiple event recording with presymptom memory loop, 24-hour attended monitoring, per 30 day period of time; includes transmission, physician review and interpretation   B 80 ⌧
MED: 100-3, 20.15

AMA: 1999, Nov, 49-50; 1996, Jun, 2

If postsymptom recording is needed, consult CPT codes 93012 and 93014. If implanted patient activated cardiac event recording is needed, consult CPT codes 33282 and 93727.

93270   recording (includes hook-up, recording, and disconnection)   ⌧ TC 80 ⌧
MED: 100-3, 20.15

AMA: 1996, Jun, 2

93271   monitoring, receipt of transmissions, and analysis   ⌧ TC 80 ⌧
MED: 100-3, 20.15

AMA: 1996, Jun, 2

93272   physician review and interpretation only   B 26 80 ⌧
MED: 100-3, 20.15

AMA: 1999, Nov, 49-50; 1998, Apr, 14; 1996, Jun, 2

93278   Signal-averaged electrocardiography (SAECG), with or without ECG   S 80 ⌧
MED: 100-3, 20.15

To report only the interpretation and report, append modifier 26.

Medicine

93303 — 93313

ECHOCARDIOGRAPHY

This ultrasound technique of visualizing the heart and great arteries provides the physician with two-dimensional images and/or Doppler signals.

If fetal echocardiography is performed, consult CPT codes 76825-76828.

To report only the interpretation and report, append modifier 26. Report an echocardiography code for an ultrasound evaluation of the cardiac chambers and valves, the adjacent great vessels, and the pericardium. A complete transthoracic echocardiogram (93307) is a service that includes 2-dimensional and selected M-mode examination of the left and right atria, left and right ventricles, the aortic, mitral, and tricuspid valves, the pericardium, and adjacent portions of the aorta. These structures are evaluated using multiple views as required to obtain a complete functional and anatomic evaluation, and appropriate measurements are obtained and recorded. Identification and measurement of some structures may not always be possible in spite of significant effort. In these cases, the reason the a structure could not be visualized such as pulmonary veins, pulmonary artery, pulmonic valve, or inferior vena cava should be documented. Visualization of additional structures is included in this service.

Report a limited or follow-up study with code 93308. This is an examination that does not evaluate or document the attempt to evaluate all the structures that make up the complete echocardiography. When a repeat complete exam is not necessary, a follow up exam may be performed to do a more focused review. This is typically done in the follow up of a complete exam.

An echocardiography, either complete or limited must include an interpretation of all information obtained, documentation of all clinically relevant findings including quantitative measurements obtained, plus a description of any recognized abnormalities. The pertinent images, videotape, and/or digital data must be permanently stored and available for review. Do not separately report echocardiography that does not meet this criteria.

Do not report an ultrasound without a thorough examination of the organ(s) or anatomic region, documentation of the image, and a final written report.

93303	**Transthoracic echocardiography for congenital cardiac anomalies; complete**	S 80 ↰
	MED: 100-4, 12, 30.4	
	AMA: 1997, Nov, 44; 1997, Dec, 5	
93304	**follow-up or limited study**	S 80 ↰
	MED: 100-4, 12, 30.4	
	AMA: 1997, Nov, 44; 1997, Dec, 5	
93307	**Echocardiography, transthoracic, real-time with image documentation (2D) with or without M-mode recording; complete**	S 80 ↰
	MED: 100-4, 12, 30.4	
	AMA: 2000, Apr, 1; 1997, Dec, 5	
93308	**follow-up or limited study**	S 80 ↰
	MED: 100-4, 12, 30.4	
	AMA: 1997, Dec, 5	
⊙ **93312**	**Echocardiography, transesophageal, real time with image documentation (2D) (with or without M-mode recording); including probe placement, image acquisition, interpretation and report**	S 80 ↰
	MED: 100-4, 12, 30.4	
	AMA: 2000, Jan, 10; 1997, Dec, 5	
⊙ **93313**	**placement of transesophageal probe only**	S 80 ↰
	MED: 100-4, 12, 30.4	
	AMA: 1997, Dec, 5	

Medicine

⊙ 93314   image acquisition, interpretation and report only   N 80 ⌐
MED: 100-4, 12, 30.4

AMA: 2000, Jan, 10; 1997, Dec, 5

⊙ 93315   Transesophageal echocardiography for congential cardiac anomalies; including probe placement, image acquisisiton, interpretation and report   S 80 ⌐
MED: 100-4, 12, 30.4

AMA: 1997, Nov, 44; 1997, Dec, 5

⊙ 93316   placement of transesophageal probe only   S 80 ⌐
MED: 100-4, 12, 30.4

AMA: 1997, Nov, 44; 1997, Dec, 5

⊙ 93317   image acquisition, interpretation and report only   N 80 ⌐
MED: 100-4, 12, 30.4

AMA: 1997, Nov, 44; 1997, Dec, 5

⊙ 93318   Echocardiography, transesophageal (TEE) for monitoring purposes, including probe placement, real time 2-dimensional image acquisition and interpretation leading to ongoing (continuous) assessment of (dynamically changing) cardiac pumping function and to therapeutic measures on an immediate time basis   S 80 ⌐

+ 93320   Doppler echocardiography, pulsed wave and/or continuous wave with spectral display (List separately in addition to codes for echocardiographic imaging); complete   S 80 ⌐
MED: 100-3, 220.5; 100-4, 12, 30.4

AMA: 1997, Nov, 44; 1997, Dec, 5

Note that 93320 is an add-on code and must be used in conjunction with 93303, 93304, 93307, 93308, 93312, 93314, 93315, 93317, and 93350.

+ 93321   follow-up or limited study (List separately in addition to codes for echocardiographic imaging)   S 80 ⌐
MED: 100-4, 12, 30.4

AMA: 1997, Nov, 44; 1997, Dec, 5

Note that 93321 is an add-on code and must be used in conjunction with 93303, 93304, 93307, 93308, 93312, 93314, 93315, 93317, and 93350.

+ 93325   Doppler echocardiography color flow velocity mapping (List separately in addition to codes for echocardiography)   S 80 ⌐
MED: 100-3, 220.5; 100-4, 12, 30.4

AMA: 1997, Nov, 44; 1997, Dec, 5

Note that 93325 is an add-on code and must be used in conjunction with 76825, 76826, 76827, 76828, 93303, 93304, 93307, 93308, 93312, 93314, 93315, 93317, 93320, 93321, and 93350.

93350   Echocardiography, transthoracic, real-time with image documentation (2D, with or without M-mode recording) during rest and cardiovascular stress test using treadmill, bicycle exercise and/or pharmacologically induced stress, with interpretation and report   S 80 ⌐
MED: 100-4, 12, 30.4

AMA: 2002, Aug, 11

Consult CPT codes 93015-93018 for the appropriate stress testing code that needs to be reported in addition to 93350 to capture the exercise stress portion of the study.

93314 — 93350

Medicine

93501 — 93508

CARDIAC CATHETERIZATION

Cardiac catheterizations are invasive procedures used to visualize the heart chambers, valves, great vessels, and coronary arteries. Catheter procedures produce pressure measurements and blood volumes used to evaluate cardiac function and valve patency.

The three major components of cardiac catheterization include: introduction and positioning of the catheter (93501–93533) including repositioning, injection procedures (93539–93545) and imaging supervision, interpretation, and report (93555–93556).

Supervision and interpretation codes related to cardiac catheterization (93555 and 93556) are used with imaging performed as part of cardiac catheterization procedures. The plural presentation of the word "procedure(s)" as well as the "and/or" terminology in the descriptions of imaging services suggest the codes include imaging of one or more areas.

Aortic root aortography (93544) is the injection of a large bolus of dye into the proximal ascending aorta, just above the aortic valve. When thoracic aortography is performed without a cardiac catheterization, it should be reported using procedure 36200 and the appropriate radiologic supervision/interpretation (75600 or 75605).

A number of services rely on the following cardiac catheterization codes. The procedure itself includes introduction, positioning, gauging pressure, and procuring samples.

⊙ ⊘ **93501**   **Right heart catheterization**   T 80 ▣
MED: 100-3, 20.25

AMA: 2000, Apr, 10; 1998, Apr, 1; 1994, Spring, 24

To report bundle of His recording, consult CPT code 93600.

⊘ **93503**   **Insertion and placement of flow directed catheter (eg, Swan-Ganz) for monitoring purposes**   T 80 ▣
MED: 100-3, 20.25

AMA: 1998, Apr, 1; 1995, Fall, 8

If subsequent monitoring is needed, consult CPT codes 99356-99357.

ENDOMYOCARDIAL BIOPSY

Biopsy of the inside and middle layers of the heart is a separately reportable service. It may be performed in surgery or in the cardiac cath lab with the patient under local anesthesia. The sample is usually taken from the right or left ventricle. The patient is monitored constantly with both intracardiac and external ECG leads to record cardiac response.

⊙ ⊘ **93505**   **Endomyocardial biopsy**   T 80 ▣
MED: 100-3, 20.25

AMA: 2000, Apr, 10; 1998, Apr, 1

⊙ ⊘ **93508**   **Catheter placement in coronary artery(s), arterial coronary conduit(s), and/or venous coronary bypass graft(s) for coronary angiography without concomitant left heart catheterization**   T 80 ▣
MED: 100-3, 20.25

AMA: 2000, Aug, 11; 2000, Apr, 10; 1998, Apr, 1; 1997, Nov, 44-45

Note that 93508 is to be used only when left heart catheterization is not performed (CPT codes 93510, 93511, 93524, and 93526). Also note that 93508 is to be used only once per procedure.

To report transcatheter placement of radiation delivery device for coronary intravascular brachytherapy, consult CPT code 92974.

For intravascular radioelement application, consult CPT code 77781-77784.

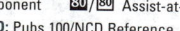

⊙ ⊘ 93510 Left heart catheterization, retrograde, from the brachial artery, axillary artery or femoral artery; percutaneous T 80 🖳
MED: 100-3, 20.25

AMA: 1998, Apr, 1; 1997, Nov, 44-45; 1994, Spring, 26

⊙ ⊘ 93511 by cutdown T 80 🖳
MED: 100-3, 20.25

AMA: 1998, Apr, 1; 1997, Nov, 44-45; 1994, Spring, 24

⊙ ⊘ 93514 Left heart catheterization by left ventricular puncture T 80 🖳
MED: 100-3, 20.25

AMA: 1998, Apr, 1; 1994, Spring, 24

⊙ ⊘ 93524 Combined transseptal and retrograde left heart catheterization T 80 🖳
MED: 100-3, 20.25

AMA: 1998, Apr, 1; 1997, Nov, 44-45; 1994, Spring, 24

⊙ ⊘ 93526 Combined right heart catheterization and retrograde left heart catheterization T 80 🖳
MED: 100-3, 20.25

AMA: 1998, Apr, 1; 1997, Nov, 44-45; 1994, Spring, 28

⊙ ⊘ 93527 Combined right heart catheterization and transseptal left heart catheterization through intact septum (with or without retrograde left heart catheterization) T 80 🖳
MED: 100-3, 20.25

AMA: 1998, Apr, 1

⊙ ⊘ 93528 Combined right heart catheterization with left ventricular puncture (with or without retrograde left heart catheterization) T 80 🖳
MED: 100-3, 20.25

AMA: 1998, Apr, 1

⊙ ⊘ 93529 Combined right heart catheterization and left heart catheterization through existing septal opening (with or without retrograde left heart catheterization) T 80 🖳
MED: 100-3, 20.25

AMA: 1998, Apr, 1

⊙ ⊘ 93530 Right heart catheterization, for congenital cardiac anomalies T 80 🖳
MED: 100-3, 20.25

AMA: 1998, Mar, 11; 1998, Apr, 3, 6-7; 1997, Nov, 45

⊘ 93531 Combined right heart catheterization and retrograde left heart catheterization, for congenital cardiac anomalies T 80 🖳
MED: 100-3, 20.25

AMA: 1998, Mar, 11; 1998, Apr, 8, 10-11; 1997, Nov, 45

⊘ 93532 Combined right heart catheterization and transseptal left heart catheterization through intact septum with or without retrograde left heart catheterization, for congenital cardiac anomalies T 80 🖳
MED: 100-3, 20.25

AMA: 1998, Mar, 11; 1998, Apr, 10-11; 1997, Nov, 45

Medicine

93533 — 93556

⊘ **93533** Combined right heart catheterization and transseptal left heart catheterization through existing septal opening, with or without retrograde left heart catheterization, for congenital cardiac anomalies ⊤ 80 🔲

MED: 100-3, 20.25

AMA: 1998, Mar, 11; 1998, Apr, 12, 13; 1997, Nov, 45

⊙ ⊘ **93539** Injection procedure during cardiac catheterization; for selective opacification of arterial conduits (eg, internal mammary), whether native or used for bypass ℕ 80 🔲

MED: 100-3, 20.25

AMA: 2001, Oct, 11; 1998, Apr, 3; 1997, Nov, 44-45; 1994, Spring, 27

When injection procedures are performed in conjunction with cardiac catheterization, these services do not include introduction of catheters but do include repositioning of catheters when necessary and use of automatic power injectors. Injection procedures represent separate identifiable services and may be coded in conjunction with one another when appropriate. The technical details of angiography, which include supervision of filming and processing and interpretation and report are not included. To report the technical details, consult CPT code 93555 and/or 93556. Note that modifier 51 should not be appended to these procedures.

⊙ ⊘ **93540** for selective opacification of aortocoronary venous bypass grafts, one or more coronary arteries ℕ 80 🔲

MED: 100-3, 20.25

AMA: 1998, Apr, 3; 1997, Nov, 44-45; 1994, Spring, 27

⊙ ⊘ **93541** for pulmonary angiography ℕ 80 🔲

MED: 100-3, 20.25

AMA: 1998, Apr, 3; 1997, Nov, 44-45; 1994, Spring, 28

⊙ ⊘ **93542** for selective right ventricular or right atrial angiography ℕ 80 🔲

MED: 100-3, 20.25

AMA: 1998, Apr, 3; 1997, Nov, 44-45; 1994, Spring, 24

⊙ ⊘ **93543** for selective left ventricular or left atrial angiography ℕ 80 🔲

MED: 100-3, 20.25

AMA: 1998, Apr, 3; 1997, Nov, 44-45; 1994, Spring, 28

⊙ ⊘ **93544** for aortography ℕ 80 🔲

MED: 100-3, 20.25

AMA: 1998, Apr, 3; 1997, Nov, 44-45; 1994, Spring, 28

⊙ ⊘ **93545** for selective coronary angiography (injection of radiopaque material may be by hand) ℕ 80 🔲

MED: 100-3, 20.25

AMA: 2002, Nov, 10; 1998, Apr, 3; 1997, Nov, 44-45; 1994, Spring, 28

⊙ ⊘ **93555** Imaging supervision, interpretation and report for injection procedure(s) during cardiac catheterization; ventricular and/or atrial angiography ℕ 80 🔲

MED: 100-3, 20.25

AMA: 1998, Apr, 3, 11, 12; 1997, Oct, 10; 1997, Nov, 44-45; 1994, Spring, 28

⊙ ⊘ **93556** pulmonary angiography, aortography, and/or selective coronary angiography including venous bypass grafts and arterial conduits (whether native or used in bypass) ℕ 80 🔲

MED: 100-3, 20.25

AMA: 1998, Apr, 3, 11, 12; 1997, Oct, 10; 1997, Nov, 44-45; 1994, Spring, 28

⊙ **93561** Indicator dilution studies such as dye or thermal dilution, including arterial and/or venous catheterization; with cardiac output measurement (separate procedure) N 80 ⬚

MED: 100-3, 20.25; 100-4, 12, 30.6.12

AMA: 1991, Winter, 25

If cardiac output measurements are done as part of critical care services (99291-99292), do not report separately.

Note that 93561 and 93562 are not to be used with cardiac catheterization codes. If radioisotope method is used for cardiac output, consult CPT code 78472, 78473, or 78481.

⊙ **93562** subsequent measurement of cardiac output N 80 ⬚

MED: 100-3, 20.25; 100-4, 12, 30.6.12

AMA: 1991, Winter, 25

⊙ + **93571** Intravascular Doppler velocity and/or pressure derived coronary flow reserve measurement (coronary vessel or graft) during coronary angiography including pharmacologically induced stress; initial vessel (List separately in addition to code for primary procedure) S 80 ⬚

MED: 100-3, 220.5

AMA: 2000, Apr, 1; 1998, Nov, 33

Note that 93571 is an add-on code that must be used in conjunction with the appropriate code for the primary procedure. This code cannot be reported alone.

⊙ + **93572** each additional vessel (List separately in addition to code for primary procedure) S 80

AMA: 2000, Apr, 1; 1998, Nov, 34

Note that measurements of intravascular distal coronary blood flow velocity include all Doppler transducer manipulations and repositioning within the specific vessel being examined, during coronary angiography or therapeutic intervention (e.g., angioplasty). If an unlisted cardiac catheterization procedure is performed, consult CPT code 93799.

Note that 93572 is an add-on code that must be used in conjunction with code 93571.

REPAIR OF SEPTAL DEFECT

To report echocardiographic services performed in conjunction with 93580-93581, consult CPT codes 93303-93317 and 93662 as appropriate.

93580 Percutaneous transcatheter closure of congenital interatrial communication (ie, Fontan fenestration, atrial septal defect) with implant T 80 ⬚

CPT code 93580 includes right heart catheterization and contrast injections for atrial and ventricular angiograms. Do not report 93501, 93529-93533, 93539, 93543 or 93555 in conjunction with CPT code 93580.

93581 Percutaneous transcatheter closure of a congenital ventricular septal defect with implant T 80 ⬚

CPT code 93581 includes right heart catheterization and contrast injections for atrial and ventricular angiograms. Do not report 93501, 93529-93533, 93539, 93543 or 93555 in conjunction with CPT code 93581.

Medicine

93600 — 93618

INTRACARDIAC ELECTROPHYSIOLOGICAL PROCEDURES/STUDIES

ELECTROPHYSIOLOGIC STUDIES (EPS)

EPS evaluate the electrical conduction system of the heart. An electrode is placed and the patient is monitored constantly with both intracardiac external ECG leads to record the cardiac response. Programmed electrical stimulation is delivered through an electrode catheter to evaluate electrical conduction pathways, formation of dysrhythmia, and automaticity and refractoriness of myocardial cells. These procedures may include induction of arrhythmia to isolate the origin of the conduction problem.

⊘ **93600** **Bundle of His recording** T 80 🔁
MED: 100-3, 20.12; 100-3, 20.13

AMA: 1997, Aug, 9; 1994, Summer, 12

⊘ **93602** **Intra-atrial recording** T 80 🔁
AMA: 1997, Aug, 9; 1994, Summer, 12

⊘ **93603** **Right ventricular recording** T 80 🔁
AMA: 1997, Aug, 9; 1994, Summer, 12

⊙ + **93609** **Intraventricular and/or intra-atrial mapping of tachycardia site(s) with catheter manipulation to record from multiple sites to identify origin of tachycardia (List separately in addition to code for primary procedure)** T 80 🔁
MED: 100-3, 20.12

AMA: 1997, Aug, 9; 1994, Summer, 12

Note that 93609 is an add-on code and must be used in conjunction with codes 93620, 93651, 93652.

Do not report 93609 in conjunction wit CPT code 93613.

⊘ **93610** **Intra-atrial pacing** T 80 🔁
MED: 100-3, 20.12

AMA: 1997, Aug, 9; 1994, Summer, 12

⊘ **93612** **Intraventricular pacing** T 80 🔁
MED: 100-3, 20.12

AMA: 1997, Aug, 9; 1994, Summer, 12

Do not report 93612 in conjunction with codes 93620, 93651, 93652.

⊙ **93613** **Intracardiac electrophysiologic 3-dimensional mapping (List separately in addition to code for primary procedure)** T 80 🔁
MED: 100-3, 20.12

Note that 93613 is an add-on code and must be used in conjunction with codes 93620, 93651, 93652.

Do not report 93613 in conjunction with CPT code 93609.

⊙ ⊘ **93615** **Esophageal recording of atrial electrogram with or without ventricular electrogram(s);** T 80 🔁
AMA: 1997, Aug, 9; 1994, Summer, 12

⊙ ⊘ **93616** **with pacing** T 80 🔁
AMA: 1997, Aug, 9; 1994, Summer, 12

⊙ ⊘ **93618** **Induction of arrhythmia by electrical pacing** T 80 🔁
AMA: 2000, Jun, 5; 1999, Apr, 10; 1997, Aug, 9; 1994, Summer, 12

If an intracardiac phonocardiogram is performed, consult CPT code 93799.

⊙ ⊘ **93619** Comprehensive electrophysiologic evaluation with right atrial pacing and recording, right ventricular pacing and recording, His bundle recording, including insertion and repositioning of multiple electrode catheters, without induction or attempted induction of arrhythmia T 80 ▣

MED: 100-3, 20.12

AMA: 1997, Aug, 9

Code 93619 should not be used in conjunction with codes 93600, 93602, 93610, 93612, 93618, or 93620-93622.

⊙ ⊘ **93620** Comprehensive electrophysiologic evaluation including insertion and repositioning of multiple electrode catheters with induction or attempted induction of arrhythmia; with right atrial pacing and recording, right ventricular pacing and recording, His bundle recording T 80 ▣

MED: 100-3, 20.12

AMA: 1998, Jul, 10; 1997, Oct, 10; 1997, Aug, 9; 1994, Summer, 12

Code 93620 should not be used in conjunction with codes 93600, 93602, 93610, 93612, 93618, or 93619.

⊙ **93621** with left atrial pacing and recording from coronary sinus or left atrium (List separately in addition to code for primary procedure) T 80 ▣

MED: 100-3, 20.12

AMA: 1998, Nov, 34; 1998, Jul, 10; 1997, Oct, 10; 1997, Aug, 9; 1994, Summer, 12

Note that 93621 is an add-on code and must be used in conjunction with 93620.

⊙ + **93622** with left ventricular pacing and recording (List separately in addition to code for primary procedure) T 80 ▣

MED: 100-3, 20.12

AMA: 1998, Nov, 34; 1998, Jul, 10; 1997, Oct, 10; 1997, Aug, 9; 1994, Summer, 14

Note that 93622 is an add-on code and must be used in conjunction with 93620.

+ **93623** Programmed stimulation and pacing after intravenous drug infusion (List separately in addition to code for primary procedure) T 80 ▣

MED: 100-3, 20.12

AMA: 1997, Aug, 9; 1994, Summer, 14

Note that 93623 is an add-on code and must be used in conjunction with 93619, 93620.

⊙ ⊘ **93624** Electrophysiologic follow-up study with pacing and recording to test effectiveness of therapy, including induction or attempted induction of arrhythmia T 80 ▣

MED: 100-3, 20.11; 100-3, 20.12

AMA: 1997, Aug, 9; 1994, Summer, 14

⊘ **93631** Intra-operative epicardial and endocardial pacing and mapping to localize the site of tachycardia or zone of slow conduction for surgical correction T 80 ▣

MED: 100-3, 20.11; 100-3, 20.12

AMA: 1997, Aug, 9; 1994, Summer, 14

Medicine

93640 — 93668

⊙ ⊘ **93640** **Electrophysiologic evaluation of single or dual chamber pacing cardioverter-defibrillator leads including defibrillation threshold evaluation (induction of arrhythmia, evaluation of sensing and pacing for arrhythmia termination) at time of initial implantation or replacement;** S 80 ▪

MED: 100-3, 20.12

AMA: 1999, Nov, 50; 1999, Apr, 10; 1997, Aug, 9; 1994, Summer, 14

If subsequent or periodic electronic analysis and/or reprogramming of single or dual-chamber pacing cardioverter-defibrillators is needed, consult CPT codes 93642 and 92741-93744.

⊙ ⊘ **93641** **with testing of single or dual chamber pacing cardioverter-defibrillator pulse generator** S 80 ▪

MED: 100-3, 20.12; 100-3, 20.8.2

AMA: 2000, Jun, 5; 2000, Jul, 5; 1999, Nov, 50; 1999, Apr, 10; 1997, Aug, 9; 1994, Summer, 14

⊙ ⊘ **93642** **Electrophysiologic evaluation of single or dual chamber pacing cardioverter-defibrillator (includes defibrillation threshold evaluation, induction of arrhythmia, evaluation of sensing and pacing for arrhythmia termination, and programming or reprogramming of sensing or therapeutic parameters)** S 80 ▪

MED: 100-3, 20.12; 100-3, 20.8.2

AMA: 2000, Jun, 5; 1999, Nov, 50; 1997, Aug, 9; 1994, Summer, 14

⊙ ⊘ **93650** **Intracardiac catheter ablation of atrioventricular node function, atrioventricular conduction for creation of complete heart block, with or without temporary pacemaker placement** T 80 ▪

AMA: 1997, Aug, 9; 1994, Summer, 15

⊙ ⊘ **93651** **Intracardiac catheter ablation of arrhythmogenic focus; for treatment of supraventricular tachycardia by ablation of fast or slow atrioventricular pathways, accessory atrioventricular connections or other atrial foci, singly or in combination** T 80 ▪

AMA: 1997, Aug, 9; 1994, Summer, 15

⊙ ⊘ **93652** **for treatment of ventricular tachycardia** T 80 ▪

AMA: 1997, Aug, 9; 1994, Summer, 15

⊘ **93660** **Evaluation of cardiovascular function with tilt table evaluation, with continuous ECG monitoring and intermittent blood pressure monitoring, with or without pharmacological intervention** S 80 ▪

If testing is performed of the autonomic nervous system function, consult CPT codes 95921-95923.

+ **93662** **Intracardiac echocardiography during therapeutic/diagnostic intervention, including imaging supervision and interpretation (List separately in addition to code for primary procedure)** S 80 ▪

Note that 93662 is an add-on code and must be used in conjunction with 93580, 93581, 93621, 93622, 93651 or 93652 as appropriate.

Do not report CPT code 92961 in addition to CPT code 93662.

PERIPHERAL ARTERIAL DISEASE REHABILITATION

Code 93668 identifies a service where the patient exercises under medical supervision for several sessions until symptoms of the disease abate. Each session is 45 to 60 minutes long.

93668 **Peripheral arterial disease (PAD) rehabilitation, per session** E

MED: 100-3, 20.14

OTHER VASCULAR STUDIES

If arterial cannulization and recording is performed of direct arterial pressure, consult CPT code 36620. If radiographic injection procedures are performed, consult CPT codes 36000-36299. If hemodialysis is performed for vascular cannulization, consult CPT codes 36800-36821. If chemotherapy is needed for a malignant disease, consult CPT codes 96408-96549. If penile plethysmography is performed, consult CPT code 54240.

93701   **Bioimpedance, thoracic, electrical**   S 80
    AMA: 2002, Mar, 1

93720   **Plethysmography, total body; with interpretation and report**   B 80 ↵
    MED: 100-3, 20.14

    AMA: 1999, Mar, 10

93721   **tracing only, without interpretation and report**   X TC 80
    MED: 100-3, 20.14

    AMA: 1999, Mar, 10

93722   **interpretation and report only**   B 26 80
    MED: 100-3, 20.14; 100-3, 20.8; 100-3, 20.8.1

    AMA: 1999, Mar, 10

If regional plethysmography is performed, consult CPT codes 93875-93931.

93724   **Electronic analysis of antitachycardia pacemaker system (includes electrocardiographic recording, programming of device, induction and termination of tachycardia via implanted pacemaker, and interpretation of recordings)**   S 80 ↵
    MED: 100-3, 20.15; 100-3, 20.8; 100-3, 20.8.1; 100-3, 20.8.2

    AMA: 1994, Summer, 23

93727   **Electronic analysis of implantable loop recorder (ILR) system (includes retrieval of recorded and stored ECG data, physician review and interpretation of retrieved ECG data and reprogramming)**   S 26 ↵
    MED: 100-3, 20.15; 100-3, 20.8; 100-3, 20.8.1

    AMA: 2000, Jul, 5; 1999, Nov, 50

93731   **Electronic analysis of dual-chamber pacemaker system (includes evaluation of programmable parameters at rest and during activity where applicable, using electrocardiographic recording and interpretation of recordings at rest and during exercise, analysis of event markers and device response); without reprogramming**   S 80 ↵
    MED: 100-3, 20.15; 100-3, 20.8; 100-3, 20.8.1; 100-3, 20.8.2

    AMA: 1998, Feb, 11; 1994, Summer, 23

93732   **with reprogramming**   S 80 ↵
    MED: 100-3, 20.15; 100-3, 20.8; 100-3, 20.8.1; 100-3, 20.8.2

    AMA: 2000, Mar, 10; 1998, Feb, 11; 1994, Summer, 23

93733   **Electronic analysis of dual chamber internal pacemaker system (may include rate, pulse amplitude and duration, configuration of wave form, and/or testing of sensory function of pacemaker), telephonic analysis**   S 80 ↵
    MED: 100-3, 20.15; 100-3, 20.8; 100-3, 20.8.1; 100-3, 20.8.2

    AMA: 1994, Summer, 23

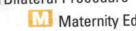 

Medicine

93734 — 93762

93734 Electronic analysis of single chamber pacemaker system (includes evaluation of programmable parameters at rest and during activity where applicable, using electrocardiographic recording and interpretation of recordings at rest and during exercise, analysis of event markers and device response); without reprogramming ⑤ 80 ◪
MED: 100-3, 20.15; 100-3, 20.8; 100-3, 20.8.1; 100-3, 20.8.2

AMA: 1998, Feb, 11; 1994, Summer, 23

93735 with reprogramming ⑤ 80 ◪
MED: 100-3, 20.15; 100-3, 20.8; 100-3, 20.8.1; 100-3, 20.8.2

AMA: 1998, Feb, 11; 1994, Summer, 23

93736 Electronic analysis of single chamber internal pacemaker system (may include rate, pulse amplitude and duration, configuration of wave form, and/or testing of sensory function of pacemaker), telephonic analysis ⑤ 80 ◪
MED: 100-3, 20.15; 100-3, 20.8; 100-3, 20.8.1; 100-3, 20.8.2

AMA: 1994, Summer, 23

93740 Temperature gradient studies Ⓧ

93741 Electronic analysis of pacing cardioverter-defibrillator (includes interrogation, evaluation of pulse generator status, evaluation of programmable parameters at rest and during activity where applicable, using electrocardiographic recording and interpretation of recordings at rest and during exercise, analysis of event markers and device response); single chamber or wearable cardioverter-defibrillator system, without reprogramming ⑤ ◪
MED: 100-3, 20.15

AMA: 2000, Jul, 5; 1999, Nov, 50-51

Code 93741 cannot be reported with CPT code 93745.

93742 single chamber or wearable cardioverter-defibrillator system, with reprogramming ⑤ ◪
MED: 100-3, 20.15

AMA: 2000, Jul, 5; 1999, Nov, 50-51

Code 93742 cannot be reported with CPT code 93745.

93743 dual chamber, without reprogramming ⑤ ◪
MED: 100-3, 20.15

AMA: 2000, Jul, 5; 1999, Nov, 50-51

93744 dual chamber, with reprogramming ⑤ ◪
MED: 100-3, 20.15; 100-3, 220.11

AMA: 2000, Jul, 5; 1999, Nov, 50-51

93745 Initial set-up and programming by a physician of wearable cardioverter-defibrillator includes initial programming of system, establishing baseline electronic ECG, transmission of data to data repository, patient instruction in wearing system and patient reporting of problems or events ⑤ 80 ◪
Code 93745 cannot be reported with 93741, 93742.

93760 Thermogram; cephalic Ⓔ
MED: 100-3, 220.11

93762 peripheral Ⓔ
MED: 100-3, 220.11

93770	**Determination of venous pressure**	N
	MED: 100-3, 20.19	

If central venous cannulization and pressure measurements are taken, consult CPT codes 36500 and 36555-36556.

93784	**Ambulatory blood pressure monitoring, utilizing a system such as magnetic tape and/or computer disk, for 24 hours or longer; including recording, scanning analysis, interpretation and report**	E 80 ↻
	MED: 100-3, 20.19	
93786	**recording only**	X TC 80
	MED: 100-3, 20.19	
93788	**scanning analysis with report**	X TC 80
	MED: 100-3, 20.19	
93790	**physician review with interpretation and report**	B 26 80
	MED: 100-3, 20.19	

OTHER PROCEDURES

93797	**Physician services for outpatient cardiac rehabilitation; without continuous ECG monitoring (per session)**	S 80 ↻
	MED: 100-2, 15, 60.3; 100-3, 20.10	
93798	**with continuous ECG monitoring (per session)**	S 80 ↻
	MED: 100-2, 15, 60.3; 100-3, 20.10	
93799	**Unlisted cardiovascular service or procedure**	S 80
	AMA: 1998, Mar, 11	

NON-INVASIVE VASCULAR DIAGNOSTIC STUDIES

Noninvasive vascular study codes (93875–93990) include the patient care required to supervise the studies and interpret the results.

A Duplex scan combines both two-dimensional structure of motion with time and Doppler ultrasonic signal documentation with spectral analysis and color flow velocity mapping or imaging to produce a real-time video display of organ structure and motion.

A vascular study must produce a hard copy with data analysis for the patient's record, including bidirectional vascular flow or imaging when provided. Simple hand-held (screening) devices do not meet these requirements and are not reported separately.

Report 93886 for a complete transcranial Doppler (TCD) study. A complete study includes an ultrasound evaluation of the right and left anterior circulation territories and the posterior circulation territories and the posterior circulation (which includes the vertebral arteries and the basilar artery). A limited TCD study (93888) is comprised of an ultrasound evaluation of two or fewer of these territories. For a TCD, ultrasound study is a reasonable and concerted attempt to identify arterial signals through an acoustic window.

CEREBROVASCULAR ARTERIAL STUDIES

93875	**Noninvasive physiologic studies of extracranial arteries, complete bilateral study (eg, periorbital flow direction with arterial compression, ocular pneumoplethysmography, Doppler ultrasound spectral analysis)**	S 80 ↻
	MED: 100-3, 20.14; 100-3, 20.17	
	AMA: 2000, Apr, 1; 1997, Dec, 10; 1996, Jun, 9	
93880	**Duplex scan of extracranial arteries; complete bilateral study**	S 80 ↻
	MED: 100-3, 20.17	
	AMA: 1996, Jun, 9	

Medicine

93882 — 93931

93882	unilateral or limited study	S 80 ⬛

MED: 100-3, 20.17

AMA: 1996, Jun, 9

93886	Transcranial Doppler study of the intracranial arteries; complete study	S 80 ⬛

MED: 100-3, 20.17

AMA: 1996, Jun, 9

93888	limited study	S 80 ⬛

MED: 100-3, 20.17

AMA: 1996, Jun, 9

93890	vasoreactivity study	S 80 ⬛

93892	emboli detection without intravenous microbubble injection	S 80 ⬛

93893	emboli detection with intravenous microbubble injection	S 80 ⬛

Codes 93890-93893 cannot be reported with CPT code 93888.

EXTREMITY ARTERIAL STUDIES (INCLUDING DIGITS)

93922	Noninvasive physiologic studies of upper or lower extremity arteries, single level, bilateral (eg, ankle/brachial indices, Doppler waveform analysis, volume plethysmography, transcutaneous oxygen tension measurement)	S 80 ⬛

MED: 100-3, 20.14

AMA: 1996, Jun, 9

93923	Non-invasive physiologic studies of upper or lower extremity arteries, multiple levels or with provocative functional maneuvers, complete bilateral study (eg, segmental blood pressure measurements, segmental Doppler waveform analysis, segmental volume plethysmography, segmental transcutaneous oxygen tension measurements, measurements with postural provocative tests, measurements with reactive hyperemia)	S 80 ⬛

MED: 100-3, 20.14

AMA: 2001, Jun, 10; 1996, Jun, 9

93924	Non-invasive physiologic studies of lower extremity arteries, at rest and following treadmill stress testing, complete bilateral study	S 80 ⬛

MED: 100-3, 20.14

AMA: 1996, Jun, 9

93925	Duplex scan of lower extremity arteries or arterial bypass grafts; complete bilateral study	S 80 ⬛

MED: 100-3, 20.14

AMA: 1996, Jun, 9

93926	unilateral or limited study	S 80 ⬛

MED: 100-3, 20.14

AMA: 2001, Oct, 1; 1996, Jun, 9

93930	Duplex scan of upper extremity arteries or arterial bypass grafts; complete bilateral study	S 80 ⬛

MED: 100-3, 20.14

AMA: 1996, Jun, 9

93931	unilateral or limited study	S 80 ⬛

MED: 100-3, 20.14

AMA: 2001, Oct, 1; 1996, Jun, 9

EXTREMITY VENOUS STUDIES (INCLUDING DIGITS)

93965 Non-invasive physiologic studies of extremity veins, complete bilateral study (eg, Doppler waveform analysis with responses to compression and other maneuvers, phleborheography, impedance plethysmography) S 80 🔲
MED: 100-3, 20.14

AMA: 1996, Jun, 9

93970 Duplex scan of extremity veins including responses to compression and other maneuvers; complete bilateral study S 80 🔲
AMA: 1996, Jun, 9

93971 unilateral or limited study S 80 🔲
AMA: 2001, Oct, 1; 1996, Jun, 9

VISCERAL AND PENILE VASCULAR STUDIES

93975 Duplex scan of arterial inflow and venous outflow of abdominal, pelvic, scrotal contents and/or retroperitoneal organs; complete study S 80 🔲
AMA: 1996, Jun, 9; 1996, Apr, 11

93976 limited study S 80 🔲
AMA: 1996, Jun, 9; 1996, Apr, 11

93978 Duplex scan of aorta, inferior vena cava, iliac vasculature, or bypass grafts; complete study S 80 🔲
AMA: 1996, Jun, 9

93979 unilateral or limited study S 80 🔲
AMA: 1996, Jun, 9

93980 Duplex scan of arterial inflow and venous outflow of penile vessels; complete study ♂ S 80 🔲
AMA: 1996, Jun, 9

93981 follow-up or limited study ♂ S 80 🔲
AMA: 1996, Jun, 9

EXTREMITY ARTERIAL-VENOUS STUDIES

93990 Duplex scan of hemodialysis access (including arterial inflow, body of access and venous outflow) S 80 🔲
AMA: 1996, Jun, 9

When using indicator dilution methods for measurement of hemodialysis access flow, consult CPT code 90940.

PULMONARY

Pulmonary codes (94010–94799) include both diagnostic and therapeutic services. All procedures include laboratory services, interpretation, and physician services. List hospital inpatient visits, consultations, emergency department services, or office visits separately when performed on the same date as a diagnostic pulmonary service. Specify the procedures that may be performed in requesting prior authorization for pulmonary testing. If ordering tests for a patient and unsure about which test should be performed, contact the pulmonary laboratory for clarification and CPT code numbers. Include that information in documentation for prior authorization and claim review.

CPT codes 94010-94799 include laboratory procedures and interpretation of results. Consult the appropriate Evaluation and Management CPT code and report it in addition to 94010-94799 when separate identifiable Evaluation and Management services are provided.

Medicine

94010 — 94250

SPIROMETRY/BRONCHOSPASM EVALUATION

Spirometry (94010–94070) measures lung capacity. Code 94010 refers to the measurement of the lung's capacity and flow measurements using a spirometer. Expiratory flow rate is calculated generally in terms of liters per second. Maximal voluntary ventilation is included in this service. The graphic record produced by the spirometer goes into the patient's record.

Codes 94014–94016 report patient initiated spirometric recording per 30 day time period.

Bronchospasm evaluation (94060) includes spirometry before and after the use of a bronchodilator. The final codes in this series report prolonged evaluation with multiple spirometric determinations.

94010 **Spirometry, including graphic record, total and timed vital capacity, expiratory flow rate measurement(s), with or without maximal voluntary ventilation** ☒ 80 ▣
AMA: 1999, Jan, 8; 1999, Feb, 9; 1998, Nov, 35; 1997, Nov, 45; 1996, Mar, 10; 1996, Feb, 9; 1995, Summer, 4

94014 **Patient-initiated spirometric recording per 30-day period of time; includes reinforced education, transmission of spirometric tracing, data capture, analysis of transmitted data, periodic recalibration and physician review and interpretation** ☒ 80 ▣
AMA: 1999, Jan, 8; 1999, Feb, 9; 1998, Nov, 34; 1996, Mar, 10; 1996, Feb, 9; 1995, Summer, 4

94015 **recording (includes hook-up, reinforced education, data transmission, data capture, trend analysis, and periodic recalibration)** ☒ TC 80 ▣
AMA: 1999, Jan, 8; 1999, Feb, 9; 1998, Nov, 34; 1996, Mar, 10; 1996, Feb, 9; 1995, Summer, 4

94016 **physician review and interpretation only** A 2G 80 ▣
AMA: 1999, Jan, 8; 1999, Feb, 9; 1998, Nov, 34; 1996, Mar, 10; 1996, Feb, 9; 1995, Summer, 4

94060 **Bronchodilation responsiveness, spirometry as in 94010, pre- and post-bronchodilator administration** ☒ 80 ▣
AMA: 1999, Jan, 8; 1999, Feb, 9; 1998, Nov, 34; 1997, Feb, 10; 1996, Mar, 10; 1996, Feb, 9; 1995, Summer, 4

If a bronchodilator supply is used, report with CPT code 99070 or applicable supply code.

If a prolonged exercise test is conducted for bronchospasm with pre- and post-spirometry, consult CPT code 94620.

94070 **Bronchospasm provocation evaluation, multiple spirometric determinations as in 94010, with administered agents (eg, antigen(s), cold air, methacholine)** ☒ 80 ▣
AMA: 1999, Jan, 8; 1999, Feb, 9; 1997, Nov, 45; 1996, Mar, 10; 1996, Feb, 9

Antigen administration should be reported separately with CPT code 99070 or applicable supply code.

94150 **Vital capacity, total (separate procedure)** ☒
AMA: 1999, Jan, 8; 1999, Feb, 9; 1996, Mar, 10; 1996, Feb, 9; 1995, Summer, 4

94200 **Maximum breathing capacity, maximal voluntary ventilation** ☒ 80
AMA: 1999, Jan, 8; 1999, Feb, 9; 1996, Mar, 10; 1996, Feb, 9; 1995, Summer, 4

94240 **Functional residual capacity or residual volume: helium method, nitrogen open circuit method, or other method** ☒ 80 ▣
AMA: 1999, Jan, 8; 1999, Feb, 9; 1996, Mar, 10; 1996, Feb, 9; 1995, Summer, 4

94250 **Expired gas collection, quantitative, single procedure (separate procedure)** ☒ 80
AMA: 1999, Jan, 8; 1999, Feb, 9; 1996, Mar, 10; 1996, Feb, 9; 1995, Summer, 4

94260   **Thoracic gas volume**   [X] [80] [↵]
AMA: 1999, Jan, 8; 1999, Feb, 9; 1996, Mar, 10; 1996, Feb, 9; 1995, Summer, 4

If plethysmography is performed, consult CPT codes 93720-93722.

94350   **Determination of maldistribution of inspired gas: multiple breath nitrogen washout curve including alveolar nitrogen or helium equilibration time**   [X] [80] [↵]
AMA: 1999, Jan, 8; 1999, Feb, 9; 1996, Mar, 10; 1996, Feb, 9; 1995, Summer, 4

94360   **Determination of resistance to airflow, oscillatory or plethysmographic methods**   [X] [80] [↵]
AMA: 1999, Jan, 8; 1999, Feb, 9; 1996, Mar, 10; 1996, Feb, 9; 1995, Summer, 4

94370   **Determination of airway closing volume, single breath tests**   [X] [80] [↵]
AMA: 1999, Jan, 8; 1999, Feb, 9; 1996, Mar, 10; 1996, Feb, 9; 1995, Summer, 4

94375   **Respiratory flow volume loop**   [X] [80] [↵]
AMA: 1999, Jan, 8; 1999, Feb, 9; 1996, Mar, 10; 1996, Feb, 9; 1995, Summer, 4

94400   **Breathing response to CO2 (CO2 response curve)**   [X] [80] [↵]
AMA: 1999, Jan, 8; 1999, Feb, 9; 1996, Mar, 10; 1996, Feb, 9; 1995, Summer, 4

94450   **Breathing response to hypoxia (hypoxia response curve)**   [X] [80] [↵]
AMA: 1999, Jan, 8; 1999, Feb, 9; 1996, Mar, 10; 1996, Feb, 9; 1995, Summer, 4

To report high altitude simulation test (HAST), consult CPT codes 94452, 94453.

94452   **High altitude simulation test (HAST), with physician interpretation and report;**   [X] [80] [↵]

To report obtaining arterial blood gases, consult CPT code 36600.

Code 94452 cannot be reported with CPT codes 94453, 94760, 94761.

94453   **with supplemental oxygen titration**   [X] [80] [↵]

To report obtaining arterial blood gases, consult CPT code 36600.

Code 94453 cannot be reported with CPT codes 94452, 94760, 94761.

94620   **Pulmonary stress testing; simple (eg, prolonged exercise test for bronchospasm with pre- and post-spirometry)**   [X] [80] [↵]
MED: 100-3, 240.7
AMA: 1999, Jan, 8; 1999, Feb, 9; 1998, Nov, 35; 1996, Mar, 10; 1996, Feb, 9; 1995, Summer, 4

94621   **complex (including measurements of CO2 production, O2 uptake, and electrocardiographic recordings)**   [X] [80] [↵]
MED: 100-3, 20.15
AMA: 2002, Aug, 10; 1999, Jan, 8; 1999, Feb, 9; 1998, Nov, 35; 1996, Mar, 10; 1996, Feb, 9; 1995, Summer, 4

94640   **Pressurized or nonpressurized inhalation treatment for acute airway obstruction or for sputum induction for diagnostic purposes (eg, with an aerosol generator, nebulizer, metered dose inhaler or intermittent positive pressure breathing (IPPB) device)**   [S] [↵]
AMA: 2000, Apr, 11; 1999, Jan, 8; 1999, Feb, 9; 1998, May, 10; 1996, Mar, 10; 1996, Feb, 9; 1995, Summer, 4

To report more than one inhalation treatment on the same day, append modifier 76 to code 94640.

94642   **Aerosol inhalation of pentamidine for pneumocystis carinii pneumonia treatment or prophylaxis**   [S] [↵]
AMA: 1999, Jan, 8; 1999, Feb, 9; 1996, Mar, 10; 1996, Feb, 9; 1995, Summer, 4

Medicine

94656 — 94720

94656 **Ventilation assist and management, initiation of pressure or volume preset ventilators for assisted or controlled breathing; first day** S 80
MED: 100-4, 12, 30.6.12

AMA: 1999, Jan, 8; 1999, Feb, 9; 1996, Mar, 10; 1996, Feb, 9; 1995, Summer, 4; 1992, Fall, 30

If ventilation assist and management is performed as part of critical care services (99291-99292) do not report separately.

94657 **subsequent days** S 80 🔲
MED: 100-4, 12, 30.6.12

AMA: 1999, Jan, 8; 1999, Feb, 9; 1996, Mar, 10; 1996, Feb, 9; 1995, Summer, 4; 1992, Fall, 30

If ventilation assist and management is performed as part of critical care services (99291-99292) do not report separately.

94660 **Continuous positive airway pressure ventilation (CPAP), initiation and management** S 80
MED: 100-4, 12, 30.6.12

AMA: 1999, Jan, 10; 1999, Feb, 9; 1996, Mar, 10; 1996, Feb, 9; 1995, Summer, 4; 1992, Fall, 30

If CPAP is performed as part of critical care services (99291-99292) do not report separately.

94662 **Continuous negative pressure ventilation (CNP), initiation and management** S 80
MED: 100-4, 12, 30.6.12

AMA: 1999, Jan, 8; 1999, Feb, 9; 1996, Mar, 10; 1996, Feb, 9; 1995, Summer, 4; 1992, Fall, 30

If CNP is performed as part of critical care services (99291-99292) do not report separately.

94664 **Demonstration and/or evaluation of patient utilization of an aerosol generator, nebulizer, metered dose inhaler or IPPB device** S 🔲
AMA: 2000, Apr, 11; 1999, Jan, 8; 1999, Feb, 9; 1998, May, 10; 1996, Mar, 10; 1996, Feb, 9; 1995, Summer, 4

Report 94664 only once per date of service.

94667 **Manipulation chest wall, such as cupping, percussing, and vibration to facilitate lung function; initial demonstration and/or evaluation** S 🔲
MED: 100-3, 150.1; 100-3, 240.7

AMA: 1999, Jan, 8; 1999, Feb, 9; 1996, Mar, 10; 1996, Feb, 9; 1995, Summer, 4

94668 **subsequent** S 🔲
MED: 100-3, 150.1; 100-3, 240.7

AMA: 1999, Jan, 8; 1999, Feb, 9; 1996, Mar, 10; 1996, Feb, 9; 1995, Summer, 4

94680 **Oxygen uptake, expired gas analysis; rest and exercise, direct, simple** X 80 🔲
AMA: 1999, Jan, 8; 1999, Feb, 9; 1996, Mar, 10; 1996, Feb, 9; 1995, Summer, 4

94681 **including CO2 output, percentage oxygen extracted** X 80 🔲
AMA: 1999, Jan, 8; 1999, Feb, 9; 1996, Mar, 10; 1996, Feb, 9; 1995, Summer, 4

To report blood gases consult CPT codes 82800-82810.

94690 **rest, indirect (separate procedure)** X 80 🔲
AMA: 1999, Jan, 8; 1999, Feb, 9; 1996, Mar, 10; 1996, Feb, 9; 1995, Summer, 4

If a single arterial procedure is performed, consult CPT code 36600.

94720 **Carbon monoxide diffusing capacity (eg, single breath, steady state)** X 80 🔲
AMA: 1999, Jan, 8; 1999, Feb, 9; 1996, Mar, 10; 1996, Feb, 9; 1995, Summer, 4

94725   **Membrane diffusion capacity**   ☒ 80 ↵
     AMA: 1999, Jan, 8; 1999, Feb, 9; 1996, Mar, 10; 1996, Feb, 9; 1995, Summer, 4

94750   **Pulmonary compliance study (eg, plethysmography, volume and pressure measurements)**   ☒ 80 ↵
     AMA: 1999, Jan, 8; 1999, Feb, 9; 1996, Mar, 10; 1996, Feb, 9; 1995, Summer, 4

94760   **Noninvasive ear or pulse oximetry for oxygen saturation; single determination**   Ⓝ TC 80 ↵
     MED: 100-4, 12, 30.6.12

     AMA: 1999, Jan, 8; 1999, Feb, 9; 1998, Jul, 1; 1997, Feb, 10; 1996, Mar, 10; 1996, Feb, 9; 1995, Summer, 4

     To report blood gases, consult CPT codes 82800-82810.

94761   **multiple determinations (eg, during exercise)**   Ⓝ TC 80 ↵
     AMA: 1999, Jun, 10; 1999, Jan, 8; 1999, Feb, 9; 1998, Jul, 1; 1996, Mar, 10; 1996, Feb, 9; 1995, Summer, 4

94762   **by continuous overnight monitoring (separate procedure)**   Ⓝ TC 80
     MED: 100-4, 12, 30.6.12

     AMA: 1999, Jan, 8; 1999, Feb, 9; 1998, Jul, 1; 1996, Mar, 10; 1996, Feb, 9; 1995, Summer, 4

94770   **Carbon dioxide, expired gas determination by infrared analyzer**   ☒ 80 ↵
     AMA: 1999, Jan, 8; 1999, Feb, 9; 1996, Mar, 10; 1996, Feb, 9; 1995, Summer, 4

     If bronchoscopy is performed, consult CPT codes 31622-31659. If a flow directed catheter is placed, consult CPT code 93503. If venipuncture is performed, consult CPT code 36410. If a central venous catheter is placed, consult CPT codes 36488-36491. If an arterial puncture is performed, consult CPT code 36600. If arterial catheterization is performed, consult CPT code 36620. If thoracentesis is performed, consult CPT code 32000. If a therapeutic phlebotomy is performed, consult CPT code 99195. If a needle biopsy is performed on the lung, consult CPT code 32405. If orotracheal or nasotracheal intubation is necessary, consult CPT code 31500.

94772   **Circadian respiratory pattern recording (pediatric pneumogram), 12 to 24 hour continuous recording, infant**   🅐 ☒ 80 ↵
     AMA: 1999, Jan, 8; 1999, Feb, 9; 1996, Mar, 10; 1996, Feb, 9; 1995, Summer, 4

     Separate procedure codes for electromyograms, EEG, ECG, and recordings of respiration cannot be reported with this procedural code.

94799   **Unlisted pulmonary service or procedure**   ☒ 80
     AMA: 1999, Jan, 8; 1999, Feb, 9; 1996, Mar, 10; 1996, Feb, 9; 1995, Summer, 4

ALLERGY AND CLINICAL IMMUNOLOGY

Allergy testing and immunology treatment (95004–95199) is performed according to the patient's history, physical findings, and clinical judgment of the provider. Specify the number of tests performed in the unit area of the claim or electronic billing form. Significant, separately identifiable E/M services should be reported in addition to allergen testing and immunotherapy.

Allergy sensitivity tests (95004–95078) reports the performance and evaluation of cutaneous and mucous membrane tests, the number of tests performed is based on clinical judgment, patient history and physical findings.

Immunotherapy (95115–95199) is the administration of allergenic extracts as antigens at periodic intervals in increasing dosages to a maintenance therapy level. If significant, separately identifiable evaluation and management services are provided in addition to immunotherapy, report the appropriate E/M code and append modifier 25.

✗ Drug Not Approved by FDA   50 Bilateral Procedure   ✚ CPT Add-on Code   ⊘ Modifier -51 Exempt   ♂ Male   ♀ Female
● New Code   ▲ Revised Code   M Maternity Edit   A Age Edit   Ⓐ—Ⓨ APC Status Ind.   AMA: CPT Assistant

© 2005 Ingenix, Inc. *(Blue Ink)*   CPT only © 2005 American Medical Association. All Rights Reserved. *(Black Ink)*   Medicine — 715

Medicine

95004 — 95065

ALLERGY TESTING

95004   Percutaneous tests (scratch, puncture, prick) with allergenic extracts, immediate type reaction, specify number of tests   ☒
MED: 100-2, 15, 20.2; 100-2, 15, 20.3; 100-4, 12, 200

AMA: 1991, Summer, 15

95010   Percutaneous tests (scratch, puncture, prick) sequential and incremental, with drugs, biologicals or venoms, immediate type reaction, specify number of tests   ☒ 80 ▣
MED: 100-2, 15, 20.2; 100-2, 15, 20.3; 100-4, 12, 200

AMA: 1991, Summer, 15

95015   Intracutaneous (intradermal) tests, sequential and incremental, with drugs, biologicals, or venoms, immediate type reaction, specify number of tests   ☒ 80 ▣
MED: 100-2, 15, 20.2; 100-2, 15, 20.3; 100-4, 12, 200

AMA: 1991, Summer, 15

95024   Intracutaneous (intradermal) tests with allergenic extracts, immediate type reaction, specify number of tests   ☒ ▣
MED: 100-2, 15, 20.2; 100-2, 15, 20.3; 100-4, 12, 200

AMA: 1991, Summer, 15

95027   Intracutaneous (intradermal) tests, sequential and incremental, with allergenic extracts for airborne allergens, immediate type reaction, specify number of tests   ☒ TC 80 ▣
MED: 100-2, 15, 20.2; 100-2, 15, 20.3; 100-4, 12, 200

AMA: 1997, Jun, 10; 1991, Summer, 15

95028   Intracutaneous (intradermal) tests with allergenic extracts, delayed type reaction, including reading, specify number of tests   ☒ TC 80 ▣
MED: 100-2, 15, 20.2; 100-2, 15, 20.3; 100-4, 12, 200

AMA: 1991, Summer, 14

95044   Patch or application test(s) (specify number of tests)   ☒ ▣
MED: 100-2, 15, 20.2; 100-2, 15, 20.3; 100-4, 12, 200

AMA: 1994, Spring, 31; 1991, Summer, 15

95052   Photo patch test(s) (specify number of tests)   ☒
MED: 100-2, 15, 20.2; 100-2, 15, 20.3; 100-4, 12, 200

AMA: 1994, Spring, 31

95056   Photo tests   ☒
MED: 100-2, 15, 20.2; 100-2, 15, 20.3; 100-4, 12, 200

AMA: 1991, Summer, 16

95060   Ophthalmic mucous membrane tests   ☒ TC 80
MED: 100-2, 15, 20.2; 100-2, 15, 20.3; 100-4, 12, 200

AMA: 1991, Summer, 16

95065   Direct nasal mucous membrane test   ☒ TC 80
MED: 100-2, 15, 20.2; 100-2, 15, 20.3; 100-4, 12, 200

AMA: 1991, Summer, 15

95070   Inhalation bronchial challenge testing (not including necessary pulmonary function tests); with histamine, methacholine, or similar compounds   ⓧ 🆃🅲 80 🔲

    MED: 100-2, 15, 20.2; 100-2, 15, 20.3; 100-4, 12, 200

    AMA: 1991, Summer, 16

95071   with antigens or gases, specify   ⓧ 🆃🅲 80 🔲

    MED: 100-2, 15, 20.2; 100-2, 15, 20.3; 100-3, 50-22; 100-4, 12, 200

    AMA: 1991, Summer, 16

If pulmonary function tests are performed, consult CPT codes 94060 and 94070.

95075   Ingestion challenge test (sequential and incremental ingestion of test items, eg, food, drug or other substance such as metabisulfite)   ⓧ 80

    MED: 100-2, 15, 20.2; 100-2, 15, 20.3; 100-3, 50-22; 100-4, 12, 200

    AMA: 2002, Oct, 11; 2001, Sep, 10; 1991, Summer, 16

95078   Provocative testing (eg, Rinkel test)   ⓧ 🆃🅲 80

    MED: 100-2, 15, 20.2; 100-2, 15, 20.3; 100-3, 110.11; 100-4, 12, 200

    AMA: 1991, Summer, 16

If allergy laboratory tests are conducted, consult CPT codes 86000-86999. If intravenous therapy is needed for severe or intractable allergic disease, consult CPT codes 90765-90768, 90772, 90774, 90775.

ALLERGEN IMMUNOTHERAPY

95115   Professional services for allergen immunotherapy not including provision of allergenic extracts; single injection   ⓧ 🔲

    MED: 100-2, 15, 20.2; 100-2, 15, 20.3; 100-4, 12, 200

    AMA: 2000, Apr, 4; 1998, Nov, 35; 1996, May, 1; 1995, Summer, 4; 1994, Spring, 30; 1991, Fall, 19

CPT codes 95115-95199 include all professional services needed for allergen immunotherapy. Office visits may be reported in addition to immunotherapy if other separately identifiable E/M services are rendered at the same time.

95117   two or more injections   ⓧ 🔲

    MED: 100-2, 15, 20.2; 100-2, 15, 20.3; 100-4, 12, 200

    AMA: 2000, Apr, 4; 1998, Nov, 35; 1996, May, 1; 1996, Aug, 10; 1994, Spring, 30; 1991, Fall, 19

95120   Professional services for allergen immunotherapy in prescribing physician's office or institution, including provision of allergenic extract; single injection   Ⓑ

    MED: 100-2, 15, 20.2; 100-2, 15, 20.3; 100-4, 12, 200

    AMA: 1998, Nov, 35; 1996, May, 2; 1994, Spring, 30; 1991, Fall, 19

95125   two or more injections   Ⓑ

    MED: 100-2, 15, 20.2; 100-2, 15, 20.3; 100-4, 12, 200

    AMA: 1998, Nov, 35; 1996, May, 2; 1996, Aug, 10; 1994, Spring, 30; 1991, Fall, 19

95130   single stinging insect venom   Ⓑ

    MED: 100-2, 15, 20.2; 100-2, 15, 20.3; 100-4, 12, 200

    AMA: 1999, Sep, 10; 1998, Nov, 35; 1996, May, 2; 1996, Jun, 10; 1991, Fall, 19

95131   two stinging insect venoms   Ⓑ

    MED: 100-2, 15, 20.2; 100-2, 15, 20.3; 100-4, 12, 200

    AMA: 1999, Sep, 10; 1998, Nov, 35; 1996, May, 2; 1996, Jun, 10; 1991, Fall, 19

95132   **three stinging insect venoms**   B
MED: 100-2, 15, 20.2; 100-2, 15, 20.3; 100-4, 12, 200

AMA: 1999, Sep, 11; 1998, Nov, 35; 1996, May, 2; 1991, Fall, 19

95133   **four stinging insect venoms**   B
MED: 100-2, 15, 20.2; 100-2, 15, 20.3; 100-4, 12, 200

AMA: 1999, Sep, 11; 1998, Nov, 35; 1996, May, 2; 1991, Fall, 19

95134   **five stinging insect venoms**   B
MED: 100-2, 15, 20.2; 100-2, 15, 20.3; 100-4, 12, 200

AMA: 1999, Sep, 11; 1998, Nov, 35; 1996, May, 2; 1991, Fall, 19

95144   **Professional services for the supervision of preparation and provision of antigens for allergen immunotherapy, single dose vial(s) (specify number of vials)**   X 80
MED: 100-2, 15, 20.2; 100-2, 15, 20.3; 100-3, 110.9; 100-4, 12, 200

AMA: 1998, Nov, 35; 1996, May, 10; 1994, Spring, 30; 1991, Fall, 19

A single dose vial is defined as a single dose of antigen administered in one injection.

95145   **Professional services for the supervision of preparation and provision of antigens for allergen immunotherapy (specify number of doses); single stinging insect venom**   X 80
MED: 100-2, 15, 20.2; 100-2, 15, 20.3; 100-3, 110.9; 100-4, 12, 200

AMA: 1998, Nov, 35; 1996, May, 1; 1991, Fall, 19

95146   **two single stinging insect venoms**   X 80
MED: 100-2, 15, 20.2; 100-2, 15, 20.3; 100-4, 12, 200

AMA: 1998, Nov, 35; 1996, May, 11; 1991, Fall, 19

95147   **three single stinging insect venoms**   X 80
MED: 100-2, 15, 20.2; 100-2, 15, 20.3; 100-3, 110.9; 100-4, 12, 200

AMA: 1998, Nov, 35; 1996, May, 11; 1991, Fall, 19

95148   **four single stinging insect venoms**   X 80
MED: 100-2, 15, 20.2; 100-2, 15, 20.3; 100-3, 110.9; 100-4, 12, 200

AMA: 1998, Nov, 35; 1996, May, 11; 1991, Fall, 19

95149   **five single stinging insect venoms**   X 80
MED: 100-2, 15, 20.2; 100-2, 15, 20.3; 100-3, 110.9; 100-4, 12, 200

AMA: 1998, Nov, 35; 1996, May, 11; 1991, Fall, 19

95165   **Professional services for the supervision of preparation and provision of antigens for allergen immunotherapy; single or multiple antigens (specify number of doses)**   X 80
MED: 100-2, 15, 20.2; 100-2, 15, 20.3; 100-3, 110.9; 100-4, 12, 200

AMA: 2001, Apr, 11; 2000, Apr, 4; 1998, Nov, 35; 1996, May, 11; 1994, Spring, 30; 1991, Fall, 19

95170   **whole body extract of biting insect or other arthropod (specify number of doses)**   X 80
MED: 100-2, 15, 20.2; 100-2, 15, 20.3; 100-3, 110.9; 100-4, 12, 200

AMA: 2001, Apr, 11; 1996, May, 12; 1994, Spring, 30; 1991, Fall, 19

When reporting allergy immunotherapy, a dose is the amount of antigen(s) administered in a single injection from a multiple dose vial.

95180   **Rapid desensitization procedure, each hour (eg, insulin, penicillin, equine serum)** ☒ 80 ⬏
     MED: 100-2, 15, 20.2; 100-2, 15, 20.3

95199   **Unlisted allergy/clinical immunologic service or procedure** ☒ 80
     MED: 100-2, 15, 20.2; 100-2, 15, 20.3; 100-3, 50-22

     AMA: 1998, Nov, 35; 1995, Summer, 4

If skin testing for bacterial, viral, and fungal extracts is performed, consult CPT codes 86485-86586 and 95028. If special reports are filed for an allergy patient, consult CPT code 99080. If testing procedures such as allergosorbent testing (RAST), rat mast cell technique (RMCT), mast cell degranulation test (MCDT), lymphocytic transformation test (LTT), leukocyte histamine release (LHR), migration inhibitory factor test (MIF), transfer factor test (TFT), or nitroblue tetrazolium dye test (NTD) are performed, consult the Immunology section in Pathology or use 95199.

ENDOCRINOLOGY

▲   95250   **Ambulatory continuous glucose monitoring of interstitial tissue fluid via a subcutaneous sensor for up to 72 hours; sensor placement, hook-up, calibration of monitor, patient training, removal of sensor, and printout of recording** ☒ TC 80 ⬏

     Code 95250 should not be used in conjunction with 99091.

     To report physician review, interpretation and written report associated with code 95250, see Evaluation and Management services section.

●   95251   **physician interpretation and report**

     Codes 95250, 95251 cannot be used in conjunction with 99091.

NEUROLOGY AND NEUROMUSCULAR PROCEDURES

Appropriate levels of consultation codes 99241-99255 may be used as neurologic services are typically consultative in nature.

In addition, services outlined in the evaluation and management guidelines applicable to a neurologic illness may be reported.

Included in the EEG is autonomic function, evoked potentials, reflex tests, EMG, NCV, and MEG services (codes 95812-95829 and 95860-95967). These include the recording, interpretation by a physician and report. For interpretation only, append modifier 26.

SLEEP TESTING

Sleep services (95805–95811) include sleep studies and polysomnography. Both types of services include continuous and simultaneous monitoring and recording of selected physiological and pathophysiological sleep parameters for a minimum of six hours. For studies of less than six hours append modifier 52. These services are global and include tracing, interpretation, and report. For interpretation only, append modifier 26. These studies are performed to diagnose a variety of sleep disorders and to evaluate a patient's response to therapies such as nasal continuous positive airway pressure (NCPAP).

Polysomnography is distinguished from sleep studies by the inclusion of sleep staging, which is defined to include:

- 1-4 lead electroencephalogram (EEG)

- Electro-oculogram (EOG)

- Submental electromyogram (EMG)

Additional parameters of sleep include:

Medicine

95805 — 95813

- Electrocardiogram (ECG)

- Airflow

- Ventilation and respiratory effort

- Gas exchange by oximetry, transcutaneous monitoring, or end tidal gas analysis

- Extremity muscle activity, motor activity-movement

- Extended electroencephalogram (EEG) monitoring

- Penile tumescence

- Gastroesophageal reflux

- Continuous blood pressure monitoring

- Snoring

- Body positions

95805 **Multiple sleep latency or maintenance of wakefulness testing, recording, analysis and interpretation of physiological measurements of sleep during multiple trials to assess sleepiness** ⓢ 80 🄲
AMA: 2002, Sep, 1; 2001, Dec, 3; 1998, Nov, 35; 1997, Nov, 45-46

95806 **Sleep study, simultaneous recording of ventilation, respiratory effort, ECG or heart rate, and oxygen saturation, unattended by a technologist** ⓢ 80 🄲
AMA: 1998, Nov, 35; 1998, Aug, 10; 1997, Nov, 45-46

95807 **Sleep study, simultaneous recording of ventilation, respiratory effort, ECG or heart rate, and oxygen saturation, attended by a technologist** ⓢ 80 🄲
AMA: 1998, Nov, 35; 1997, Nov, 46

95808 **Polysomnography; sleep staging with 1-3 additional parameters of sleep, attended by a technologist** ⓢ 80 🄲
AMA: 2002, Sep, 1; 1998, Nov, 35; 1998, Feb, 6; 1997, Nov, 46; 1996, Sep, 11

95810 **sleep staging with 4 or more additional parameters of sleep, attended by a technologist** ⓢ 80 🄲
AMA: 2002, Sep, 1; 1998, Nov, 35; 1998, Feb, 6

95811 **sleep staging with 4 or more additional parameters of sleep, with initiation of continuous positive airway pressure therapy or bilevel ventilation, attended by a technologist** ⓢ 80 🄲
AMA: 2002, Sep, 1; 1998, Nov, 35; 1998, Feb, 6; 1997, Nov, 46

ROUTINE ELECTROENCEPHALOGRAPHY (EEG)

CPT codes 95812-95822 include hyperventilation and/or photic stimulation procedures, do not report separately. Standard EEG services 95816-95822 include recording of 20-40 minutes. To report recordings of longer than 40 minutes, consult CPT codes 95812-95813.

95812 **Electroencephalogram (EEG) extended monitoring; 41-60 minutes** ⓢ 80 🄲
MED: 100-3, 160.21

AMA: 1998, Nov, 35; 1994, Winter, 18

95813 **greater than one hour** ⓢ 80 🄲
AMA: 1998, Nov, 35; 1994, Winter, 18

95816   **Electroencephalogram (EEG); including recording awake and drowsy** S 80 ⟳
MED: 100-3, 160.21

AMA: 2000, Jul, 1; 1999, Nov, 51; 1998, Nov, 35; 1996, Sep, 11

95819   **including recording awake and asleep** S 80 ⟳
MED: 100-3, 160.21

AMA: 2000, Jul, 1; 1999, Nov, 51; 1998, Nov, 35

95822   **recording in coma or sleep only** S 80
MED: 100-3, 160.21

AMA: 1998, Nov, 35

95824   **cerebral death evaluation only** S 80 ⟳
AMA: 1998, Nov, 35

95827   **all night recording** S 80 ⟳
AMA: 1998, Nov, 35

If ambulatory 24 hour EEG monitoring is needed, consult CPT code 95950-95953 or 95956. If an EEG is performed during nonintracranial surgery, consult CPT code 95955. If a Wada test is performed, consult CPT code 95958. If circadian respiratory patterns of infants are recorded, consult CPT code 94772.

To report digital analysis of EEG, consult CPT code 95957.

95829   **Electrocorticogram at surgery (separate procedure)** S 80 ⟳
AMA: 1998, Nov, 35

95830   **Insertion by physician of sphenoidal electrodes for electroencephalographic (EEG) recording** B 80 ⟳
MED: 100-3, 160.21

MUSCLE AND RANGE OF MOTION TESTING

95831   **Muscle testing, manual (separate procedure) with report; extremity (excluding hand) or trunk** A 80 ⟳
MED: 100-2, 15, 230.4

AMA: 2001, Nov, 4; 2000, Mar, 11; 2000, Jul, 1; 1999, Nov, 51; 1999, Dec, 10

95832   **hand, with or without comparison with normal side** A 80 ⟳
MED: 100-2, 15, 230.4

AMA: 2001, Nov, 4; 2000, Mar, 11; 2000, Jul, 1; 1999, Nov, 51; 1999, Dec, 10

95833   **total evaluation of body, excluding hands** A 80 ⟳
MED: 100-2, 15, 230.4

AMA: 2001, Nov, 4; 1999, Nov, 51; 1999, Dec, 10

95834   **total evaluation of body, including hands** A 80 ⟳
MED: 100-2, 15, 230.4

AMA: 2001, Nov, 4; 2000, Jul, 1; 1999, Nov, 51; 1999, Dec, 10

95851   **Range of motion measurements and report (separate procedure); each extremity (excluding hand) or each trunk section (spine)** A 80
MED: 100-2, 15, 230.4

AMA: 2001, Nov, 4; 1999, Sep, 10

95852   **hand, with or without comparison with normal side** A 80
MED: 100-2, 15, 230.4

AMA: 2001, Nov, 4

Medicine

95857 — 95873

95857   Tensilon test for myasthenia gravis   S 80 ▣

~~95858~~   ~~with electromyographic recording~~

ELECTROMYOGRAPHY AND NERVE CONDUCTION TESTS

95860   **Needle electromyography; one extremity with or without related paraspinal areas**   S 80 ▣
MED: 100-2, 15, 230.4; 100-2, 15, 80

AMA: 2002, Apr, 1; 2000, Jul, 1; 1997, Nov, 46

95861   **two extremities with or without related paraspinal areas**   S 80 ▣
MED: 100-2, 15, 230.4; 100-2, 15, 80

AMA: 2002, Apr, 1; 2000, Jul, 1; 1997, Nov, 46

To report dynamic electromyography performed during motion analysis studies, consult CPT code 96002-96003.

95863   **three extremities with or without related paraspinal areas**   S 80 ▣
MED: 100-2, 15, 230.4; 100-2, 15, 80

AMA: 2002, Apr, 1; 2000, Jul, 1; 1997, Nov, 46

95864   **four extremities with or without related paraspinal areas**   S 80 ▣
MED: 100-2, 15, 230.4; 100-2, 15, 80

AMA: 2002, Jan, 11; 2002, Apr, 1; 2000, Jul, 1; 1997, Nov, 46

● 95865   **larynx**

Modifier 50 cannot be used with 95865.

Report modifier 52 with 95865 to report a unilateral procedure.

● 95866   **hemidiaphragm**

95867   **cranial nerve supplied muscle(s), unilateral**   S 80 ▣
MED: 100-2, 15, 230.4; 100-2, 15, 80

AMA: 2002, Apr, 1

95868   **cranial nerve supplied muscles, bilateral**   S 80 ▣
MED: 100-2, 15, 230.4; 100-2, 15, 80

AMA: 2002, Apr, 1

95869   **thoracic paraspinal muscles (excluding T1 or T12)**   S 80 ▣
MED: 100-2, 15, 230.4; 100-2, 15, 80

AMA: 2002, Apr, 1; 1997, Nov, 46

95870   **limited study of muscles in one extremity or non-limb (axial) muscles (unilateral or bilateral), other than thoracic paraspinal, cranial nerve supplied muscles, or sphincters**   S 80
MED: 100-2, 15, 230.4; 100-2, 15, 80

AMA: 2002, Apr, 1; 2000, Jul, 1; 1999, Nov, 51; 1997, Nov, 46

Adson test

95872   **Needle electromyography using single fiber electrode, with quantitative measurement of jitter, blocking and/or fiber density, any/all sites of each muscle studied**   S 80
MED: 100-2, 15, 230.4; 100-2, 15, 80

AMA: 2002, Apr, 1

+ ● 95873   **Electrical stimulation for guidance in conjunction with chemodenervation (List separately in addition to code for primary procedure)**

+ ● **95874**   **Needle electromyography for guidance in conjunction with chemodenervation (List separately in addition to code for primary procedure)**

> Note that 95873, 95874 are add-on codes and must be used in conjunction with 64612-64614.
>
> Code 95874 cannot be used with 95873.
>
> Codes 95873, 95874 cannot be used with 95860-95870.

95875   **Ischemic limb exercise test with serial specimen(s) acquisition for muscle(s) metabolite(s)**   S 80 ◪
MED: 100-2, 15, 230.4; 100-2, 15, 80

⊘ **95900**   **Nerve conduction, amplitude and latency/velocity study, each nerve; motor, without F-wave study**   S 80
MED: 100-2, 15, 230.4

AMA: 2002, Apr, 1; 2000, Jul, 1; 2000, Jan, 10; 1999, Nov, 51-52; 1996, Jan, 2

⊘ **95903**   **motor, with F-wave study**   S 80 ◪
MED: 100-2, 15, 230.4; 100-2, 15, 80

AMA: 2002, Apr, 1; 2000, Jan, 10; 1999, Nov, 51-52; 1996, Jan, 2

⊘ **95904**   **sensory**   S 80
MED: 100-2, 15, 230.4; 100-2, 15, 80

AMA: 2002, Apr, 1; 1999, Sep, 11; 1999, Nov, 51-52; 1996, Jan, 2

> Note that 95900, 95903, and 95904 are to be reported only once when multiple sites on the same nerve are stimulated or recorded.

INTRAOPERATIVE NEUROPHYSIOLOGY

+ **95920**   **Intraoperative neurophysiology testing, per hour (List separately in addition to code for primary procedure)**   S 80 ◪
MED: 100-2, 15, 230.4; 100-2, 15, 80

AMA: 1999, Nov, 52; 1998, Nov, 35-36

> Note that 95920 is an add-on code and must be used in conjunction with the study performed 92585, 95822, 95860, 95861, 95867, 95868, 95870, 95900, 95904, 95925-95937.
>
> Code 95920 describes ongoing electrophysiologic testing and monitoring performed during surgical procedures. Code 95920 is reported per hour of service, and includes only the ongoing electrophysiologic monitoring time distinct from performance of specific type(s) of baseline electrophysiologic study(ies) (95860, 95861, 95867, 95868, 95870, 95900, 95904, 95928, 95929, 95933-95937) or interpretation of specific type(s) of baseline electrophysiologic study(ies) (92585, 95822, 95870, 95925-95928, 95929, 95930). The time spent performing or interpreting the baseline electrophysiologic study(ies) should not be counted as intraoperative monitoring, but represents separately reportable procedures. Code 95920 should be used once per hour even if multiple electrophysiologic studies are performed. The baseline electrophysiologic study(ies) should be used once per operative session.
>
> To report electrocorticography, consult CPT code 95829. To report intraoperative EEG during nonintracranial surgery, consult CPT code 95955.
>
> To report intraoperative functional cortical or subcortical mapping, consult CPT codes 95961-95962. To report intraoperative neurostimulator programming and analysis, consult CPT codes 95970-95975.

Medicine

AUTONOMIC FUNCTION TESTS

95921 **Testing of autonomic nervous system function; cardiovagal innervation (parasympathetic function), including two or more of the following; heart rate response to deep breathing with recorded R-R interval, Valsalva ratio, and 30:15 ratio** [S] [80] [⌐]

AMA: 2002, Apr, 1; 1998, Nov, 35-36

95922 **vasomotor adrenergic innervation (sympathetic adrenergic function), including beat-to-beat blood pressure and R-R interval changes during Valsalva maneuver and at least five minutes of passive tilt** [S] [80] [⌐]

AMA: 2002, Apr, 1; 1998, Nov, 35-36

95923 **sudomotor, including one or more of the following: quantitative sudomotor axon reflex test (QSART), silastic sweat imprint, thermoregulatory sweat test, and changes in sympathetic skin potential** [S] [80] [⌐]

MED: 100-3, 190.5

AMA: 2002, Apr, 1; 1998, Nov, 35-36

EVOKED POTENTIALS AND REFLEX TESTS

95925 **Short-latency somatosensory evoked potential study, stimulation of any/all peripheral nerves or skin sites, recording from the central nervous system; in upper limbs** [S] [80]

MED: 100-2, 15, 230.4; 100-2, 15, 80; 100-3, 50-31

AMA: 2002, Apr, 1; 1998, Nov, 35-36

95926 **in lower limbs** [S] [80]

MED: 100-2, 15, 230.4; 100-2, 15, 80; 100-3, 50-31

AMA: 2002, Apr, 1; 2001, May, 11

95927 **in the trunk or head** [S] [80]

MED: 100-2, 15, 230.4; 100-2, 15, 80; 100-3, 50-31

AMA: 2002, Apr, 1

If this procedure is performed unilaterally, append modifier 52 to the procedural code. If visual evoked potential testing is performed on the central nervous system, consult CPT code 95930. If brainstem evoked response recording takes place, consult CPT code 92585. If auditory evoked potentials testing is conducted on the central nervous system, consult CPT code 92585.

95928 **Central motor evoked potential study (transcranial motor stimulation); upper limbs** [S] [80]

95929 **lower limbs** [S] [80]

95930 **Visual evoked potential (VEP) testing central nervous system, checkerboard or flash** [S] [80]

MED: 100-2, 15, 230.4; 100-2, 15, 80; 100-3, 50-31

95933 **Orbicularis oculi (blink) reflex, by electrodiagnostic testing** [S] [80]

MED: 100-2, 15, 230.4; 100-2, 15, 80

AMA: 1998, Nov, 35-36

95934 **H-reflex, amplitude and latency study; record gastrocnemius/soleus muscle** [S] [50] [80]

MED: 100-2, 15, 230.4; 100-2, 15, 80

AMA: 2002, Apr, 1; 2001, Jul, 11; 1998, Nov, 35-36; 1996, Jan, 3

95936	record muscle other than gastrocnemius/soleus muscle	[S] [50] [80]
MED: 100-2, 15, 230.4; 100-2, 15, 80

AMA: 2002, Apr, 1; 1996, Jan, 3

If this procedure is performed bilaterally, append modifier 50 to the procedural code.

95937	**Neuromuscular junction testing (repetitive stimulation, paired stimuli), each nerve, any one method**	[S] [80] [↻]
MED: 100-2, 15, 230.4; 100-2, 15, 80

AMA: 2002, Apr, 1; 1998, Nov, 35-36

SPECIAL EEG TESTS

95950	**Monitoring for identification and lateralization of cerebral seizure focus, electroencephalographic (eg, 8 channel EEG) recording and interpretation, each 24 hours**	[S] [80] [↻]
MED: 100-3, 160.21; 100-3, 160.22

AMA: 1998, Nov, 35

95951	**Monitoring for localization of cerebral seizure focus by cable or radio, 16 or more channel telemetry, combined electroencephalographic (EEG) and video recording and interpretation (eg, for presurgical localization), each 24 hours**	[S] [80] [↻]
MED: 100-3, 160.21; 100-3, 160.22

AMA: 1998, Nov, 35

95953	**Monitoring for localization of cerebral seizure focus by computerized portable 16 or more channel EEG; electroencephalographic (EEG) recording and interpretation, each 24 hours**	[S] [80] [↻]
MED: 100-3, 160.21; 100-3, 160.22

AMA: 1998, Nov, 35

95954	**Pharmacological or physical activation requiring physician attendance during EEG recording of activation phase (eg, thiopental activation test)**	[S] [80] [↻]
AMA: 1998, Nov, 35; 1994, Winter, 18

If an EEG is analyzed digitally, consult CPT code 95957.

95955	**Electroencephalogram (EEG) during nonintracranial surgery (eg, carotid surgery)**	[S] [80] [↻]
MED: 100-3, 160.21; 100-3, 160.22; 100-3, 160.8; 100-3, 160.9

AMA: 1998, Nov, 35

95956	**Monitoring for localization of cerebral seizure focus by cable or radio, 16 or more channel telemetry, electroencephalographic (EEG) recording and interpretation, each 24 hours**	[S] [80] [↻]
MED: 100-3, 160.21; 100-3, 160.22

AMA: 1998, Nov, 35

95957	**Digital analysis of electroencephalogram (EEG) (eg, for epileptic spike analysis)**	[S] [80] [↻]
MED: 100-3, 160.21; 100-3, 160.22

AMA: 1998, Nov, 35; 1994, Winter, 18

Medicine

95958 — 95967

95958   **Wada activation test for hemispheric function, including electroencephalographic (EEG) monitoring**   S 80 ▣
MED: 100-3, 130.5; 100-3, 130.6; 100-3, 160.2; 100-3, 160.21; 100-3, 160.22; 100-3, 230.1; 100-3, 250.1; 100-3, 250.4; 100-3, 270.4; 100-3, 40.50

AMA: 1998, Nov, 35

95961   **Functional cortical and subcortical mapping by stimulation and/or recording of electrodes on brain surface, or of depth electrodes, to provoke seizures or identify vital brain structures; initial hour of physician attendance**   S 80 ▣
MED: 100-3, 130.5; 100-3, 130.6; 100-3, 160.2; 100-3, 160.7; 100-3, 230.1; 100-3, 250.1; 100-3, 250.4; 100-3, 270.4; 100-3, 40.50

AMA: 1999, Nov, 52-53; 1998, Nov, 35; 1994, Winter, 18

+ **95962**   **each additional hour of physician attendance (List separately in addition to code for primary procedure)**   S 80 ▣
AMA: 1999, Nov, 52-53; 1998, Nov, 35; 1994, Winter, 18

Note that 95962 is an add-on code and must be used in conjunction with 95961.

95965   **Magnetoencephalography (MEG), recording and analysis; for spontaneous brain magnetic activity (eg, epileptic cerebral cortex localization)**   T 80 ▣

95966   **for evoked magnetic fields, single modality (eg, sensory, motor, language, or visual cortex localization)**   T 80 ▣

+ **95967**   **for evoked magnetic fields, each additional modality (eg, sensory, motor, language, or visual cortex localization) (List separately in addition to code for primary procedure)**   T 80

Note that 95967 is an add-on code and must be used in conjunction with code 95966.

For electroencephalography performed in addition to magnetoencephalography, consult CPT codes 95812-95827.

For somatosensory evoked potentials, auditory evoked potentials, and visual evoked potentials performed in addition to magnetic evoked field responses, consult CPT codes 92585, 95925, 95926, and/or 95930.

For computed tomography performed in addition to magnetoencephalography, consult CPT codes 70450-70470, 70496.

To report MRI performed in addition to magnetoencephalography, consult CPT codes 70551-70553.

NEUROSTIMULATORS, ANALYSIS-PROGRAMMING

The following codes discuss the analysis and programming of neurostimulators. Neurostimulator pulse generators and transmitters affect pulse amplitude, duration, and frequency; more than eight electrode contacts; cycling; stimulation duration and spacing; number of programs and channels; phase angle; alternating polarities; configuration of wave form; and more than one clinical symptom.

CPT defines a simple neurostimulator as affecting up to three of these and a complex neurostimulator as affecting three or more.

Codes 95978 and 95979 describe initial or subsequent electronic analysis of an implanted brain neurostimulator pulse generator system, with programming.

If a neurostimulator pulse generator is inserted, consult CPT codes 61885, 63685, 63688, and 64590. If a neurostimulator pulse generator or receiver is revised or removed, consult CPT codes 61888, 63688, and 64595. If neurostimulator electrodes are implanted, consult CPT codes 61850-61875, 63650-63655, and 64553-64580. If neurostimulator electrodes are revised or removed, consult CPT codes 61880, 63660, and 64585.

95970   **Electronic analysis of implanted neurostimulator pulse generator system (eg, rate, pulse amplitude and duration, configuration of wave form, battery status, electrode selectability, output modulation, cycling, impedance and patient compliance measurements); simple or complex brain, spinal cord, or peripheral (ie, cranial nerve, peripheral nerve, autonomic nerve, neuromuscular) neurostimulator pulse generator/transmitter, without reprogramming**   S 80

MED: 100-3, 45-25

AMA: 1999, Sep, 1; 1999, Nov, 53-54; 1998, Nov, 36-37

95971   **simple spinal cord, or peripheral (ie, peripheral nerve, autonomic nerve, neuromuscular) neurostimulator pulse generator/transmitter, with intraoperative or subsequent programming**   S 80

MED: 100-3, 45-25

AMA: 1999, Sep, 1; 1999, Nov, 53-54; 1998, Nov, 36-37

95972   **complex spinal cord, or peripheral (except cranial nerve) neurostimulator pulse generator/transmitter, with intraoperative or subsequent programming, first hour**   S 80

AMA: 1999, Sep, 1; 1999, Nov, 53-54; 1998, Nov, 36-37

+ 95973   **complex spinal cord, or peripheral (except cranial nerve) neurostimulator pulse generator/transmitter, with intraoperative or subsequent programming, each additional 30 minutes after first hour (List separately in addition to code for primary procedure)**   S 80

AMA: 1999, Sep, 1; 1999, Nov, 53-54; 1998, Nov, 36-37

Note that 95973 is an add-on code and must be used in conjunction with 95972.

95974   **complex cranial nerve neurostimulator pulse generator/transmitter, with intraoperative or subsequent programming, with or without nerve interface testing, first hour**   S 80

AMA: 1999, Sep, 1; 1999, Nov, 53-54; 1998, Nov, 36-37

+ 95975   **complex cranial nerve neurostimulator pulse generator/transmitter, with intraoperative or subsequent programming, each additional 30 minutes after first hour (List separately in addition to code for primary procedure)**   S 80

AMA: 1999, Sep, 1; 1999, Nov, 53-54; 1998, Nov, 36-37

Note that 95975 is an add-on code and must be used in conjunction with 95974.

95978   **Electronic analysis of implanted neurostimulator pulse generator system (eg, rate, pulse amplitude and duration, battery status, electrode selectability and polarity, impedance and patient compliance measurements), complex deep brain neurostimulator pulse generator/transmitter, with initial or subsequent programming; first hour**   S 80

+ 95979   **each additional 30 minutes after first hour (List separately in addition to code for primary procedure)**   S 80

Note that 95979 os am add-on code and must be used in conjunction with 95978.

OTHER PROCEDURES

95990   **Refilling and maintenance of implantable pump or reservoir for drug delivery, spinal (intrathecal, epidural) or brain (intraventricular)**   [T]
MED: 100-3, 280.14

To report analysis and/or reprogramming of implantable infusion pump, consult CPT codes 62367-62368.

To report refill/maintenance of implanted infusion pump or reservoir for systemic drug therapy, consult CPT code 96530.

95991   **administered by physician**   [T] [80]

95999   **Unlisted neurological or neuromuscular diagnostic procedure**   [S] [80]
AMA: 1999, Feb, 11

MOTION ANALYSIS

Report codes 96000-96004 for services performed as part of major therapeutic or diagnostic decision making. Motion analysis is performed in a dedicated motion analysis department. This includes a facility capable of performing videotaping from the front, back and both sides, computerized 3-D kinematics, 3-D kinetics and dynamic electromyography. 3-D kinetics and stride characteristics may be included in code 96000.

96000   **Comprehensive computer-based motion analysis by video-taping and 3-D kinematics;**   [S] [80] [CCI]
MED: 100-2, 15, 230.4; 100-2, 15, 80
AMA: 2002, Aug, 5

96001   **with dynamic plantar pressure measurements during walking**   [S] [80] [CCI]
MED: 100-2, 15, 230.4; 100-2, 15, 80
AMA: 2002, Aug, 5

96002   **Dynamic surface electromyography, during walking or other functional activities, 1-12 muscles**   [S] [80] [CCI]
MED: 100-2, 15, 230.4; 100-2, 15, 80
AMA: 2002, Aug, 5

96003   **Dynamic fine wire electromyography, during walking or other functional activities, 1 muscle**   [S] [80] [CCI]
MED: 100-2, 15, 230.4; 100-2, 15, 80
AMA: 2002, Aug, 5

Codes 96002 and 96003 cannot be used with codes 95860-95864, 95869-95872.

96004   **Physician review and interpretation of comprehensive computer based motion analysis, dynamic plantar pressure measurements, dynamic surface electromyography during walking or other functional activities, and dynamic fine wire electromyography, with written report**   [E] [26] [80] [CCI]
AMA: 2002, Aug, 5

CENTRAL NERVOUS SYSTEM ASSESSMENTS/TESTS (EG, NEURO-COGNITIVE, MENTAL STATUS, SPEECH TESTING)

The reports resulting from the following tests address the cognitive function of the patient.

To report development of cognitive skills, consult CPT codes 97532 and 97533.

~~**96100**~~   ~~**Psychological testing (includes psychodiagnostic assessment of personality, psychopathology, emotionality, intellectual abilities, eg, WAIS R, Rorschach, MMPI) with interpretation and report, per hour**~~

(Use 96101, 96102, 96103)

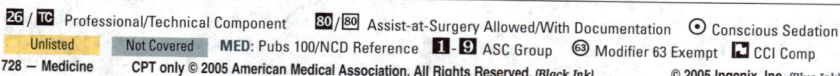

- 96101   Psychological testing (includes psychodiagnostic assessment of emotionality, intellectual abilities, personality and psychopathology, eg, MMPI, Rorshach, WAIS), per hour of the psychologist's or physician's time, both face-to-face time with the patient and time interpreting test results and preparing the report

- 96102   Psychological testing (includes psychodiagnostic assessment of emotionality, intellectual abilities, personality and psychopathology, eg, MMPI and WAIS), with qualified health care professional interpretation and report, administered by technician, per hour of technician time, face-to-face

- 96103   Psychological testing (includes psychodiagnostic assessment of emotionality, intellectual abilities, personality and psychopathology, eg, MMPI), administered by a computer, with qualified health care professional interpretation and report

   96105   Assessment of aphasia (includes assessment of expressive and receptive speech and language function, language comprehension, speech production ability, reading, spelling, writing, eg, by Boston Diagnostic Aphasia Examination) with interpretation and report, per hour   A 80
            MED: 100-1, 3, 30; 100-1, 3, 30.1; 100-1, 3, 30.2; 100-1, 3, 30.3; 100-2, 15, 160; 100-2, 15, 170; 100-2, 15, 80.2; 100-4, 12, 150; 100-4, 12, 160; 100-4, 12, 170; 100-4, 12, 170.1; 100-4, 12, 210

            AMA: 1996, Jul, 8

   96110   Developmental testing; limited (eg, Developmental Screening Test II, Early Language Milestone Screen), with interpretation and report   X
            MED: 100-1, 3, 30; 100-1, 3, 30.1; 100-1, 3, 30.2; 100-1, 3, 30.3; 100-2, 15, 160; 100-2, 15, 170; 100-2, 15, 80.2; 100-4, 12, 150; 100-4, 12, 160; 100-4, 12, 170; 100-4, 12, 170.1; 100-4, 12, 210

            AMA: 1996, Jul, 9

   96111   extended (includes assessment of motor, language, social, adaptive and/or cognitive functioning by standardized developmental instruments) with interpretation and report   X 80 ▶
            MED: 100-1, 3, 30; 100-1, 3, 30.1; 100-1, 3, 30.2; 100-1, 3, 30.3; 100-2, 15, 160; 100-2, 15, 170; 100-2, 15, 80.2; 100-4, 12, 150; 100-4, 12, 160; 100-4, 12, 170; 100-4, 12, 170.1; 100-4, 12, 210

            AMA: 1996, Jul, 9

   ~~96115~~   ~~Neurobehavorial status exam (clinical assessment of thinking, reasoning and judgment, eg, acquired knowledge, attention, memory, visual spatial abilities, language functions, planning) with interpretation and report, per hour~~

            (Use 96116)

- 96116   Neurobehavioral status exam (clinical assessment of thinking, reasoning and judgment, eg, acquired knowledge, attention, language, memory, planning and problem solving, and visual spatial abilities), per hour of the psychologist's or physician's time, both face-to-face time with the patient and time interpreting test results and preparing the report

   ~~96117~~   ~~Neuropsychological testing battery (eg, Halstead-Reitan, Luria, WAIS-R) with interpretation and report, per hour~~

            (Use 96118, 96119, 96120)

- 96118   Neuropsychological testing (eg, Halstead-Reitan Neuropsychological Battery, Wechsler Memory Scales and Wisconsin Card Sorting Test), per hour of the psychologist's or physician's time, both face-to-face time with the patient and time interpreting test results and preparing the report

Medicine

96119 — 96400

● 96119 **Neuropsychological testing (eg, Halstead-Reitan Neuropsychological Battery, Wechsler Memory Scales and Wisconsin Card Sorting Test), with qualified health care professional interpretation and report, administered by technician, per hour of technician time, face-to-face**

● 96120 **Neuropsychological testing (eg, Wisconsin Card Sorting Test), administered by a computer, with qualified health care professional interpretation and report**

HEALTH AND BEHAVIOR ASSESSMENT/INTERVENTION

Health and behavior assessment/intervention (96150–96155), are procedures used to identify the psychological, behavioral, emotional, cognitive, and social factors important to the prevention, treatment, or management of physical health problems. The codes include health and behavior assessment as well as health and behavior intervention, of which the latter is reported in 15-minute increments of direct face-to-face contact with the individual, a group, or the family of the individual.

For health and behavior assessment and/or intervention performed by a physician, consult Evaluation and Management or Preventive Medicine services codes.

96150 **Health and behavior assessment (eg, health-focused clinical interview, behavioral observations, psychophysiological monitoring, health-oriented questionnaires), each 15 minutes face-to-face with the patient; initial assessment** ⬛S⬛ ⬛80⬛ ⬛
AMA: 2002, Mar, 4

96151 **re-assessment** ⬛S⬛ ⬛80⬛ ⬛
AMA: 2002, Mar, 4

96152 **Health and behavior intervention, each 15 minutes, face-to-face; individual** ⬛S⬛ ⬛80⬛
AMA: 2002, Mar, 4

96153 **group (2 or more patients)** ⬛S⬛ ⬛80⬛
AMA: 2002, Mar, 4

96154 **family (with the patient present)** ⬛S⬛ ⬛80⬛
AMA: 2002, Mar, 4

96155 **family (without the patient present)** ⬛E⬛
AMA: 2002, Mar, 4

CHEMOTHERAPY ADMINISTRATION

~~96400~~ ~~Chemotherapy administration, subcutaneous or intramuscular, with or without local anesthesia~~

(Use 96401, 96402)

The following codes describe intravenous, subcutaneous, intramuscular, intra-arterial, and other than oral types of chemotherapy administration. This also includes administration of chemotherapy for noncancer diagnoses or monoclonal antibody agents, and other biologic response modifiers. These are complex services and usually require highly trained personnel to administer, mix, and dispose of the drug or substance. They require the direct supervision of the physician, including patient assessment, consent, supervision, and oversight during the procedure. The patient will usually require frequent monitoring during the infusion.

The following services are included in the administration codes:

· Use of a local anesthesia

· Starting the IV

· Access to IV, catheter, or port

- Routine tubing, syringe, and supplies

- Preparation of drug(s)

- Flushing at the completion of the infusion

- Hydration fluid

(For declotting of a catheter or port consult 36550.)

Report separate codes for each method of administration given by different techniques. For administration of other non-chemotherapy agents (e.g., antibiotics, analgesics, and steroids), consult CPT codes 90760, 90761, 90765, and 90779. These should be reported separately if administered as supportive management of the chemotherapy administration.

Report the drug separately. Fluid used for hydration is considered incidental.

If multiple infusions, injections, or combinations services are performed, only the initial code should be reported unless the procedure requires the use of two separate IV sites. Report the code that most closely describes the main reason for the procedure even if that is not the order in which the services are performed.

When reporting codes for which time is an issue, use the actual time for the administration of the infusion.

To report an evaluation and management service in addition to hydration, therapeutic, prophylactic, and diagnostic injections and infusion services, consult the appropriate evaluation and management codes. For an E/M service on the same day, append modifier 25 to 96401–96549. A different diagnosis is not required.

Report regional or isolation chemotherapy with codes for arterial infusion (96420–96425). Consult surgery codes from the Cardiovascular Surgery section to report placement of the catheter. To report placement of arterial and venous cannula(s) for extracorporeal circulation via a membrane oxygenator perfusion pump, consult 36823. This code includes dose calculation and the administration of chemotherapy by injection into the perfusate. Do not report codes 96409–96425 with 36823.

(For home infusion services, consult CPT codes 99601–99602.)

INJECTION AND INTRAVENOUS INFUSION CHEMOTHERAPY
An intravenous or intra-arterial push requires:

- The constant presence of the health care professional administering the substance or drug

- An infusion of 15 minutes or less

● **96401** **Chemotherapy administration, subcutaneous or intramuscular; non-hormonal anti-neoplastic**

● **96402** **hormonal anti-neoplastic**

▲ **96405** **Chemotherapy administration; intralesional, up to and including 7 lesions** Ⓢ 🔄

   MED: 100-3, 110.6; 100-4, 12, 30.5

   AMA: 2001, Jul, 1; 2001, Feb, 10; 1997, Aug, 19; 1996, Sep, 5

▲ **96406** **intralesional, more than 7 lesions** Ⓢ 🔄
   MED: 100-4, 12, 30.5

   AMA: 2001, Jul, 1; 2001, Feb, 10; 1997, Aug, 19; 1996, Sep, 5

~~96408~~ ~~Chemotherapy administration, intravenous; push technique~~

   (Use 96409)

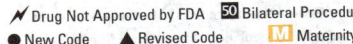

Medicine

96409 — 96423

● 96409   intravenous, push technique, single or initial substance/drug

~~96410~~   ~~infusion technique, up to one hour~~

(Use 96413)

+ ● 96411   intravenous, push technique, each additional substance/drug (List separately in addition to code for primary procedure)

Note that 96411 is an add-on code and must be used in conjunction with 96409, 96413.

~~96412~~   ~~infusion technique, one to 8 hours, each additional hour (List separately in addition to code for primary procedure)~~

(Use 96415)

● 96413   Chemotherapy administration, intravenous infusion technique; up to 1 hour, single or initial substance/drug

~~96414~~   ~~infusion technique, initiation of prolonged infusion (more than 8 hours), requiring the use of a portable or implantable pump~~

(Use 96416)

+ ● 96415   each additional hour, 1 to 8 hours (List separately in addition to code for primary procedure)

Note that 96415 is an add-on code and must be used in conjunction with 96413.

Code 96415 should be used for infusion intervals of greater than 30 minutes beyond 1-hour increments.

Code 90761 should be used to identify hydration, or 90766, 90767, 90775 to identify therapeutic, prophylactic, or diagnostic drug infusion or injection, if provided as a secondary or subsequent service in addition to 96413.

● 96416   initiation of prolonged chemotherapy infusion (more than 8 hours), requiring use of a portable or implantable pump

To report refilling and maintenance of a portable pump or an implantable infusion pump or reservoir for drug delivery, consult 96521-96523.

+ ● 96417   each additional sequential infusion (different substance/drug), up to 1 hour (List separately in addition to code for primary procedure)

Note that 96417 is an add-on code and must be used in conjunction with 96413.

This code should be used only once per sequential infusion. Report code 96415 for additional hour(s) of sequential infusion.

96420   **Chemotherapy administration, intra-arterial; push technique**   Ⓢ 🔲
     MED: 100-3, 110.2; 100-3, 110.6; 100-4, 12, 30.5

     AMA: 2001, Jul, 1; 2001, Feb, 10; 1999, Nov, 54; 1998, Nov, 37; 1997, Aug, 19

96422   **infusion technique, up to one hour**   Ⓢ 🔲
     MED: 100-3, 110.6; 100-4, 12, 30.5

     AMA: 2001, Jul, 1; 2001, Feb, 10; 1998, Nov, 37; 1997, Aug, 19; 1996, Dec, 10

+ ▲ 96423   **infusion technique, each additional hour up to 8 hours (List separately in addition to code for primary procedure)**   Ⓢ 🔲
     MED: 100-3, 110.6; 100-4, 12, 30.5

     AMA: 2001, Jul, 1; 2001, Feb, 10; 1998, Nov, 37; 1996, Dec, 10

Note that 96423 is an add-on code and must be used in conjunction with 96422.

Code 96423 should be reported for infusion intervals of greater than 30 minutes beyond 1-hour increments

---

26/**TC** Professional/Technical Component   **80**/**80** Assist-at-Surgery Allowed/With Documentation   ⊙ Conscious Sedation

Unlisted   Not Covered   **MED:** Pubs 100/NCD Reference   **1**-**9** ASC Group   ㉓ Modifier 63 Exempt   🔲 CCI Comp

732 — Medicine   CPT only © 2005 American Medical Association. All Rights Reserved. *(Black Ink)*   © 2005 Ingenix, Inc. *(Blue Ink)*

96425   infusion technique, initiation of prolonged infusion (more than 8 hours), requiring the use of a portable or implantable pump   S ⬜
MED: 100-3, 110.6; 100-4, 12, 30.5

AMA: 2001, Jul, 1; 2001, Feb, 10; 1999, Nov, 54

If an implanted pump or reservoir is refilled, consult CPT codes 96521-96523.

96440   **Chemotherapy administration into pleural cavity, requiring and including thoracentesis**   S 80 ⬜
MED: 100-3, 110.2; 100-3, 110.6; 100-4, 12, 30.5

AMA: 2001, Jul, 1; 2001, Feb, 10

96445   **Chemotherapy administration into peritoneal cavity, requiring and including peritoneocentesis**   S 80 ⬜
MED: 100-3, 110.2; 100-3, 110.6; 100-4, 12, 30.5

AMA: 2001, Jul, 1; 2001, Feb, 10

96450   **Chemotherapy administration, into CNS (eg, intrathecal), requiring and including spinal puncture**   S 80 ⬜
MED: 100-3, 110.2; 100-3, 110.6; 100-4, 12, 30.5

AMA: 2001, Jul, 1; 2001, Feb, 10

If intravesical (bladder) chemotherapy is administered, consult CPT code 51720. If a subarachnoid catheter and reservoir is inserted for drug infusion, consult CPT codes 62350, 62351, and 62360-62362. If an intraventricular catheter and reservoir is inserted, consult CPT codes 61210 and 61215.

~~**96520**~~   ~~**Refilling and maintenance of portable pump**~~

(Use 96521)

● **96521**   **Refilling and maintenance of portable pump**

● **96522**   **Refilling and maintenance of implantable pump or reservoir for drug delivery, systemic (eg, intravenous, intra-arterial)**

For refilling and maintenance of an implantable infusion pump for a spinal or brain drug infusion, use 95990-95991.

● **96523**   **Irrigation of implanted venous access device for drug delivery systems**

Code 96523 cannot be reported if an injection or infusion is provided on the same date of service.

~~**96530**~~   ~~**Refilling and maintenance of implantable pump or reservoir for drug delivery, systemic (eg, intravenous, intra-arterial)**~~

(Use 96522)

96542   **Chemotherapy injection, subarachnoid or intraventricular via subcutaneous reservoir, single or multiple agents**   S 80 ⬜
MED: 100-3, 110.2; 100-3, 110.6; 100-4, 12, 30.5

AMA: 2001, Jul, 1; 1997, Aug, 19

~~**96545**~~   ~~**Provision of chemotherapy agent**~~

96549   Unlisted chemotherapy procedure   S 80
MED: 100-3, 110.6; 100-4, 12, 30.5

AMA: 2001, Jul, 1; 1997, Aug, 19

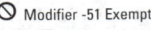

PHOTODYNAMIC THERAPY

These three codes (96567–96571) report photodynamic therapy either by external application of light to destroy malignancies or by endoscopic application of light that activates photosensitive drugs to destroy abnormal tissue.

For reporting ocular photodynamic therapy consult CPT code 67221.

96567   **Photodynamic therapy by external application of light to destroy premalignant and/or malignant lesions of the skin and adjacent mucosa (eg, lip) by activation of photosensitive drug(s), each phototherapy exposure session**   T ▣

   MED: 100-3, 45-30

+ **96570**   **Photodynamic therapy by endoscopic application of light to ablate abnormal tissue via activation of photosensitive drug(s); first 30 minutes (List separately in addition to code for endoscopy or bronchoscopy procedures of lung and esophagus)**   T ▣

   MED: 100-3, 100.2; 100-3, 45-30

   AMA: 2000, Sep, 5; 1999, Nov, 54

   Note that 96570 and 96571 are to be used in addition to bronchoscopy, endoscopy codes. Note that 96570-96571 are add-on codes and must be used in conjunction with 31641 or 43228 as appropriate.

+ **96571**   **each additional 15 minutes (List separately in addition to code for endoscopy or bronchoscopy procedures of lung and esophagus)**   T

   MED: 100-3, 100.2; 100-3, 45-30

   AMA: 2000, Sep, 5; 1999, Nov, 54

   Note that 96570 and 96571 are to be used in addition to bronchoscopy, endoscopy codes. Note that 96570-96571 are add-on codes and must be used in conjunction with 31641 or 43228 as appropriate.

SPECIAL DERMATOLOGICAL PROCEDURES

If intralesional injections are administered, consult CPT codes 11900 and 11901. If a Tzanck smear is performed, consult CPT code 87207. To report whole body photography, consult CPT Category III codes 0044T, 0045T.

96900   **Actinotherapy (ultraviolet light)**   S ▣

96902   **Microscopic examination of hairs plucked or clipped by the examiner (excluding hair collected by the patient) to determine telogen and anagen counts, or structural hair shaft abnormality**   N

   MED: 100-3, 190.6

   AMA: 1997, Nov, 46-47

96910   **Photochemotherapy; tar and ultraviolet B (Goeckerman treatment) or petrolatum and ultraviolet B**   S

   MED: 100-3, 130.5; 100-3, 130.6; 100-3, 160.2; 100-3, 230.1; 100-3, 250.1; 100-3, 250.4; 100-3, 270.4; 100-3, 40.50

96912   **psoralens and ultraviolet A (PUVA)**   S ▣

   MED: 100-3, 130.5; 100-3, 130.6; 100-3, 160.2; 100-3, 230.1; 100-3, 250.1; 100-3, 250.4; 100-3, 270.4; 100-3, 40.50

96913   **Photochemotherapy (Goeckerman and/or PUVA) for severe photoresponsive dermatoses requiring at least four to eight hours of care under direct supervision of the physician (includes application of medication and dressings)**   S ▣

   MED: 100-3, 130.5; 100-3, 130.6; 100-3, 160.2; 100-3, 230.1; 100-3, 250.1; 100-3, 250.4; 100-3, 270.4; 100-3, 40.50

96920	Laser treatment for inflammatory skin disease (psoriasis); total area less than 250 sq. cm	T 🔲
96921	250 sq. cm to 500 sq. cm	T 🔲
96922	over 500 sq. cm	T 🔲
96999	Unlisted special dermatological service or procedure	T 80

PHYSICAL MEDICINE AND REHABILITATION

EVALUATION SERVICES

Codes 97001–97006 report evaluation and re-evaluation services for physical, occupational, and athletic therapy. Codes 97001, 97003, and 97005 indicate the initial evaluation service. Re-evaluation services should be reported with codes 97002, 97004, and 97006.

MODALITIES

The modality range is organized into two groups. The first group (97010–97028) describes supervised procedures that do not require direct (one-on-one) patient contact. The second group (97032–97039) requires constant attendance and direct (one-on-one) patient contact.

The description for all treatment modalities specifies application of a modality to one or more areas. In other words, when hot or cold packs are applied to the arm, leg, and neck, code 97010 should be reported once. However, when different modalities are used, such as 97010 that reports the application of hot or cold pack, 97014 that reports the application of electrical stimulation, and 97022 for whirlpool therapy, each is reported separately.

Time should be reported in 15-minute increments for treatment modalities requiring constant attendance. If more than 15 minutes are required (i.e., 30 minutes) report two units on the CMS-1500 claim form. For less than 15 minutes, append the reduced service modifier 52 and adjust the usual cost of the code based on the time actually spent.

THERAPEUTIC PROCEDURES

Therapeutic procedures describe the application of clinical skills or services to improve function. These procedures require direct (one-on-one) patient contact. Some therapeutic procedures have a time component and should be reported once for each 15 minutes of treatment. Others do not have a time component and should be reported only once per visit. For work hardening/conditioning (97545–97546), report 97545 for the initial two hours and 97546 for each additional hour. Procedure 97546 is considered an "add on" procedure. "Add on" procedures are never reduced in value and modifier 51 multiple procedures should not be appended.

Report codes 97001-97555 for each distinct procedure performed. Modifier 51 should not be used with codes 97001-97555.

If muscles are tested for range of joint motion, electromyography, consult CPT codes 95831 and subsequent codes. For biofeedback training by EMG, consult CPT code 90901. For transcutaneous nerve stimulation (TNS), consult CPT code 64550.

97001	**Physical therapy evaluation**	A 80 🔲
	MED: 100-2, 15, 230.4; 100-2, 15, 60.3; 100-3, 20.10; 100-4, 5, 10	
	AMA: 2002, Oct, 11; 2001, Sep, 10; 2000, Feb, 11; 1997, Nov, 47	
97002	**Physical therapy re-evaluation**	A 80 🔲
	MED: 100-2, 15, 230.4; 100-2, 15, 60.3; 100-3, 20.10; 100-4, 5, 10	
	AMA: 2002, Oct, 11; 2001, Sep, 10; 2000, Feb, 11; 1997, Nov, 47	
97003	**Occupational therapy evaluation**	A 80 🔲
	MED: 100-2, 15, 230.4; 100-2, 15, 60.3; 100-3, 20.10; 100-4, 5, 10	
	AMA: 2002, Oct, 11; 1997, Nov, 47	

97004   **Occupational therapy re-evaluation**   A 80 ↻
MED: 100-2, 15, 230.4; 100-2, 15, 60.3; 100-3, 20.10; 100-4, 5, 10

AMA: 2002, Oct, 11; 1997, Nov, 47

97005   **Athletic training evaluation**   E
MED: 100-2, 15, 230.4; 100-4, 5, 10

AMA: 2002, Jun, 9

97006   **Athletic training re-evaluation**   E
MED: 100-2, 15, 230.4; 100-4, 5, 10

AMA: 2002, Jun, 9

MODALITIES

SUPERVISED

97010   **Application of a modality to one or more areas; hot or cold packs**   A
MED: 100-2, 15, 230; 100-2, 15, 230.1; 100-2, 15, 230.2; 100-2, 15, 230.4; 100-2, 15, 60.3; 100-3, 20.10; 100-4, 5, 10

AMA: 2002, Aug, 11; 2001, Nov, 4; 1998, Dec, 1; 1997, Nov, 47; 1996, Apr, 10; 1995, Summer, 5

97012   **traction, mechanical**   A 80 ↻
MED: 100-2, 15, 230; 100-2, 15, 230.1; 100-2, 15, 230.2; 100-2, 15, 230.4; 100-2, 15, 60.3; 100-3, 20.10; 100-4, 5, 10

AMA: 2002, Aug, 11; 2001, Nov, 4; 1998, Dec, 1; 1997, Nov, 47; 1995, Summer, 5

97014   **electrical stimulation (unattended)**   E
MED: 100-2, 15, 230; 100-2, 15, 60.3; 100-3, 160.12; 100-3, 160.15; 100-3, 20.10; 100-3, 35-102; 100-3, 35-98

AMA: 2002, Aug, 11; 2002, Apr, 18; 2001, Nov, 4; 1998, May, 10; 1997, Nov, 47; 1995, Summer, 5

To report acupuncture is performed with electrical stimulation, consult CPT code 97813, 97814.

97016   **vasopneumatic devices**   A 80 ↻
MED: 100-2, 15, 230; 100-2, 15, 230.1; 100-2, 15, 230.2; 100-2, 15, 230.4; 100-2, 15, 60.3; 100-3, 20.10; 100-4, 5, 10

AMA: 2002, Aug, 11; 2001, Nov, 4; 1998, Dec, 1; 1995, Summer, 6

97018   **paraffin bath**   A 80 ↻
MED: 100-2, 15, 230; 100-2, 15, 230.1; 100-2, 15, 230.2; 100-2, 15, 230.4; 100-2, 15, 60.3; 100-3, 20.10; 100-4, 5, 10

AMA: 2002, Aug, 11; 2001, Nov, 4; 1998, Dec, 1; 1995, Summer, 6

~~97020~~   ~~microwave~~
(Use 97024)

97022   **whirlpool**   A 80 ↻
MED: 100-2, 15, 230; 100-2, 15, 230.1; 100-2, 15, 60.3; 100-3, 130.5; 100-3, 130.6; 100-3, 150.5; 100-3, 160.2; 100-3, 20.10; 100-3, 230.1; 100-3, 250.1; 100-3, 250.4; 100-3, 270.4; 100-3, 40.50

AMA: 2002, Aug, 11; 2001, Nov, 4; 1998, May, 10; 1998, Dec, 1; 1995, Summer, 6

▲   97024   **diathermy (eg, microwave)**   A 80 ↻
MED: 100-2, 15, 230; 100-2, 15, 230.1; 100-2, 15, 60.3; 100-3, 150.5; 100-3, 20.10; 100-3, 240.3

AMA: 2002, Aug, 11; 2001, Nov, 4; 1998, Dec, 1; 1995, Summer, 6

97026   **infrared**   A 80
MED: 100-2, 15, 230; 100-2, 15, 230.1; 100-2, 15, 230.2; 100-2, 15, 230.4; 100-2, 15, 60.3; 100-3, 20.10; 100-4, 5, 10

AMA: 2002, Aug, 11; 2001, Nov, 4; 1998, Dec, 1; 1995, Summer, 6

97028   **ultraviolet**   A 80
MED: 100-2, 15, 230; 100-2, 15, 230.1; 100-2, 15, 230.2; 100-2, 15, 230.4; 100-2, 15, 60.3; 100-3, 20.10; 100-4, 5, 10

AMA: 2002, Aug, 11; 2001, Nov, 4; 1998, Dec, 1; 1996, Apr, 11; 1995, Summer, 6

CONSTANT ATTENDANCE

97032   **Application of a modality to one or more areas; electrical stimulation (manual), each 15 minutes**   A 80
MED: 100-2, 15, 230; 100-2, 15, 60.3; 100-3, 160.12; 100-3, 160.15; 100-3, 20.10; 100-3, 35-102; 100-3, 35-98

AMA: 2002, Apr, 18; 2001, Nov, 4; 1998, Dec, 1; 1995, Summer, 6

97033   **iontophoresis, each 15 minutes**   A 80
MED: 100-2, 15, 230; 100-2, 15, 230.1; 100-2, 15, 230.2; 100-2, 15, 230.4; 100-2, 15, 60.3; 100-3, 20.10; 100-4, 5, 10

AMA: 2001, Nov, 4; 1998, Dec, 1; 1995, Summer, 7

97034   **contrast baths, each 15 minutes**   A 80
MED: 100-2, 15, 230; 100-2, 15, 230.1; 100-2, 15, 230.2; 100-2, 15, 230.4; 100-2, 15, 60.3; 100-3, 20.10; 100-4, 5, 10

AMA: 2001, Nov, 4; 1998, Dec, 1; 1995, Summer, 7

97035   **ultrasound, each 15 minutes**   A 80
MED: 100-2, 15, 230; 100-2, 15, 230.1; 100-2, 15, 230.2; 100-2, 15, 60.3; 100-3, 20.10; 100-3, 240.3

AMA: 2001, Nov, 4; 1998, Dec, 1; 1996, Sep, 10; 1995, Summer, 7

97036   **Hubbard tank, each 15 minutes**   A 80
MED: 100-2, 15, 230; 100-2, 15, 230.1; 100-2, 15, 230.2; 100-2, 15, 60.3; 100-3, 130.5; 100-3, 130.6; 100-3, 160.2; 100-3, 20.10; 100-3, 230.1; 100-3, 250.1; 100-3, 250.4; 100-3, 270.4; 100-3, 40.50

AMA: 2001, Nov, 4; 1998, Dec, 1; 1995, Summer, 7

97039   **Unlisted modality (specify type and time if constant attendance)**   A 80
MED: 100-2, 15, 230; 100-2, 15, 230.1; 100-2, 15, 230.2; 100-2, 15, 230.4; 100-2, 15, 60.3; 100-3, 20.10; 100-4, 5, 10

AMA: 2001, Nov, 4; 2000, Jan, 10; 1998, May, 10; 1998, Dec, 1; 1995, Summer, 7

THERAPEUTIC PROCEDURES

97110   **Therapeutic procedure, one or more areas, each 15 minutes; therapeutic exercises to develop strength and endurance, range of motion and flexibility**   A 80
MED: 100-2, 15, 230; 100-2, 15, 230.1; 100-2, 15, 230.2; 100-2, 15, 230.4; 100-2, 15, 60.3; 100-3, 20.10; 100-4, 5, 10

AMA: 1999, Dec, 11; 1998, Nov, 37; 1995, Summer, 7

97112   **neuromuscular reeducation of movement, balance, coordination, kinesthetic sense, posture, and/or proprioception for sitting and/or standing activities**   A 80
MED: 100-2, 15, 230; 100-2, 15, 230.1; 100-2, 15, 230.2; 100-2, 15, 230.4; 100-2, 15, 60.3; 100-3, 20.10; 100-4, 5, 10

AMA: 1995, Summer, 7

Medicine

97113 — 97530

97113	**aquatic therapy with therapeutic exercises** A 80 ⚡

MED: 100-2, 15, 230; 100-2, 15, 230.1; 100-2, 15, 230.2; 100-2, 15, 230.4; 100-2, 15, 60.3; 100-3, 20.10; 100-4, 5, 10

AMA: 1995, Summer, 7

97116	**gait training (includes stair climbing)** A 80 ⚡

MED: 100-2, 15, 230; 100-2, 15, 230.1; 100-2, 15, 230.2; 100-2, 15, 230.4; 100-2, 15, 60.3; 100-3, 20.10; 100-4, 5, 10

AMA: 1996, Sep, 7; 1995, Summer, 8

To report comprehensive gait and motion analysis procedures, consult CPT codes 96000-96003.

97124	**massage, including effleurage, petrissage and/or tapotement (stroking, compression, percussion)** A 80 ⚡

MED: 100-2, 15, 230; 100-2, 15, 230.1; 100-2, 15, 230.2; 100-2, 15, 230.4; 100-2, 15, 60.3; 100-3, 20.10; 100-4, 5, 10

AMA: 1999, Dec, 7; 1996, May, 10; 1995, Summer, 8

To report myofascial release, consult CPT code 97140.

97139	**unlisted therapeutic procedure (specify)** A 80 ⚡

MED: 100-2, 15, 230; 100-2, 15, 230.1; 100-2, 15, 230.2; 100-2, 15, 230.4; 100-2, 15, 60.3; 100-3, 20.10; 100-4, 5, 10

AMA: 1995, Summer, 8

97140	**Manual therapy techniques (eg, mobilization/ manipulation, manual lymphatic drainage, manual traction), one or more regions, each 15 minutes** A 80 ⚡

MED: 100-2, 15, 230; 100-2, 15, 230.1; 100-2, 15, 230.2; 100-2, 15, 230.4; 100-2, 15, 60.3; 100-3, 20.10; 100-4, 5, 10

AMA: 2001, Aug, 10; 1999, Mar, 1; 1999, Jul, 11; 1999, Feb, 10; 1998, Nov, 37

97150	**Therapeutic procedure(s), group (2 or more individuals)** A 80 ⚡

MED: 100-2, 15, 230; 100-2, 15, 230.1; 100-2, 15, 230.2; 100-2, 15, 60.3; 100-3, 20.10

AMA: 1999, Oct, 10; 1999, Nov, 54-55; 1999, Dec, 11; 1997, Feb, 10; 1996, Dec, 10; 1995, Summer, 8

Note that 97150 is reported for each member of the group. Group therapy procedures involve constant attendance of the physician or therapist, but by definition do not require one-on-one patient contact by the physician or therapist. If manipulation under general anesthesia is performed, consult the appropriate anatomic section in Musculoskeletal System. If osteopathic manipulative treatment (OMT) is given, consult CPT codes 98925-98929.

~~97504~~	~~Orthotic(s) fitting and training, upper extremity(ies), lower extremity(ies), and/or trunk, each 15 minutes~~

(Use 97760)

~~97520~~	~~Prosthetic training, upper and/or lower extremities, each 15 minutes~~

(Use 97761)

97530	**Therapeutic activities, direct (one on one) patient contact by the provider (use of dynamic activities to improve functional performance), each 15 minutes** A 80 ⚡

MED: 100-2, 15, 230; 100-2, 15, 230.1; 100-2, 15, 230.2; 100-2, 15, 230.4; 100-2, 15, 60.3; 100-3, 20.10; 100-4, 5, 10

AMA: 2001, Dec, 6; 1995, Summer, 9

97532 Development of cognitive skills to improve attention, memory, problem solving, (includes compensatory training), direct (one-on-one) patient contact by the provider, each 15 minutes A 80
MED: 100-2, 15, 230; 100-2, 15, 230.1; 100-2, 15, 230.2; 100-2, 15, 230.4; 100-3, 20.10; 100-4, 5, 10

AMA: 2001, Dec, 1

97533 Sensory integrative techniques to enhance sensory processing and promote adaptive responses to environmental demands, direct (one-on-one) patient contact by the provider, each 15 minutes A 80
MED: 100-2, 15, 230; 100-2, 15, 230.1; 100-2, 15, 230.2; 100-2, 15, 230.4; 100-3, 20.10; 100-4, 5, 10

AMA: 2001, Dec, 1

97535 Self-care/home management training (eg, activities of daily living (ADL) and compensatory training, meal preparation, safety procedures, and instructions in use of assistive technology devices/adaptive equipment) direct one-on-one contact by provider, each 15 minutes A 80
MED: 100-2, 15, 230; 100-2, 15, 230.1; 100-2, 15, 230.2; 100-2, 15, 230.4; 100-2, 15, 60.3; 100-3, 20.10; 100-4, 5, 10

AMA: 2000, Apr, 11; 1996, Sep, 7

97537 Community/work reintegration training (eg, shopping, transportation, money management, avocational activities and/or work environment/modification analysis, work task analysis, use of assistive technology device/adaptive equipment), direct one-on-one contact by provider, each 15 minutes A 80
MED: 100-2, 15, 230; 100-2, 15, 230.1; 100-2, 15, 230.2; 100-2, 15, 230.4; 100-2, 15, 60.3; 100-3, 20.10; 100-4, 5, 10

AMA: 1996, Sep, 7

If wheelchair management/propulsion training is conducted, consult CPT code 97542.

▲ **97542** Wheelchair management (eg, assessment, fitting, training), each 15 minutes A 80
MED: 100-2, 15, 230; 100-2, 15, 230.1; 100-2, 15, 230.2; 100-2, 15, 230.4; 100-2, 15, 60.3; 100-3, 20.10; 100-4, 5, 10

AMA: 1996, Sep, 8

97545 Work hardening/conditioning; initial 2 hours A 80
MED: 100-2, 15, 230; 100-2, 15, 230.1; 100-2, 15, 230.2; 100-2, 15, 230.4; 100-2, 15, 60.3; 100-3, 20.10; 100-4, 5, 10

+ **97546** each additional hour (List separately in addition to code for primary procedure) A 80
MED: 100-2, 15, 230; 100-2, 15, 230.1; 100-2, 15, 230.2; 100-2, 15, 230.4; 100-2, 15, 60.3; 100-3, 20.10; 100-4, 5, 10

Note that 97546 is an add-on code and must be used in conjunction with 97545.

Medicine

ACTIVE WOUND CARE MANAGEMENT

Codes 97597–97606 report procedures that promote healing. Since the codes involve selective and nonselective debridement techniques, do not report codes 11040–11044 from the surgery section in addition to these codes.

97597 **Removal of devitalized tissue from wound(s), selective debridement, without anesthesia (eg, high pressure waterjet with/without suction, sharp selective debridement with scissors, scalpel and forceps), with or without topical application(s), wound assessment, and instruction(s) for ongoing care, may include use of a whirlpool, per session; total wound(s) surface area less than or equal to 20 square centimeters** A 80 C

Codes 97597-97602 cannot be reported with CPT codes 11040-11044.

97598 **total wound(s) surface area greater than 20 square centimeters** A 80 C

97602 **Removal of devitalized tissue from wound(s), non-selective debridement, without anesthesia (eg, wet-to-moist dressings, enzymatic, abrasion), including topical application(s), wound assessment, and instruction(s) for ongoing care, per session** A

MED: 100-2, 15, 230.4; 100-3, 130.5; 100-3, 130.6; 100-3, 160.2; 100-3, 230.1; 100-3, 250.1; 100-3, 250.4; 100-3, 270.2; 100-3, 270.4; 100-3, 35-102; 100-3, 35-98; 100-3, 40.50; 100-4, 5, 10

AMA: 2002, May, 5

Do not report CPT codes 97601, 97602 when reporting CPT codes 11040-11044.

97605 **Negative pressure wound therapy (eg, vacuum assisted drainage collection), including topical application(s), wound assessment, and instruction(s) for ongoing care, per session; total wound(s) surface area less than or equal to 50 square centimeters** A

97606 **total wound(s) surface area greater than 50 square centimeters** A

TESTS AND MEASUREMENTS

These services require direct on-on-one patient contact.

To report muscle testing, range of motion, electromyography or nerve velocity determinations, consult CPT codes 95831-95904.

97703 ~~Checkout for orthotic/prosthetic use, established patient, each 15 minutes~~
(Use 97762)

97750 **Physical performance test or measurement (eg, musculoskeletal, functional capacity), with written report, each 15 minutes** A 80 C

MED: 100-2, 15, 230; 100-2, 15, 230.1; 100-2, 15, 230.2; 100-3, 20.10; 100-4, 5, 10

AMA: 2002, May, 18; 2001, Nov, 4; 2000, Mar, 11; 1998, Aug, 11; 1997, Feb, 10; 1995, Summer, 5

97755 **Assistive technology assessment (eg, to restore, augment or compensate for existing function, optimize functional tasks and/or maximize environmental accessibility), direct one-on-one contact by provider, with written report, each 15 minutes** A 80 C

When reporting augmentative and alternative communication devices, consult CPT codes 92605 or 92607.

ORTHOTIC MANAGEMENT AND PROSTHETIC MANAGEMENT

●   **97760**   **Orthotic(s) management and training (including assessment and fitting when not otherwise reported), upper extremity(s), lower extremity(s) and/or trunk, each 15 minutes**

Code 97760 cannot be reported with 97116 for the same extremity.

●   **97761**   **Prosthetic training, upper and/or lower extremity(s), each 15 minutes**

●   **97762**   **Checkout for orthotic/prosthetic use, established patient, each 15 minutes**

OTHER PROCEDURES

For extracorporeal shock wave musculoskeletal therapy, consult CPT Category III code 0019T.

97799   **Unlisted physical medicine/rehabilitation service or procedure**   A 80
MED: 100-2, 15, 230.4; 100-4, 5, 10
AMA: 1999, Oct, 10; 1995, Summer, 5

MEDICAL NUTRITION THERAPY

Three codes, 97802–97804, report medical nutrition therapy face-to-face with the patient, each 15 minutes (97802) or a face-to-face reassessment and intervention, each 15 minutes (97803). Report 97804 for therapy involving two or more patients, each 30-minute period.

Consult Evaluation and Management or Preventive Medicine service codes for medical nutrition therapy assessment and/or intervention performed by physician.

97802   **Medical nutrition therapy; initial assessment and intervention, individual, face-to-face with the patient, each 15 minutes**   A 80 ▣
MED: 100-3, 130.5; 100-3, 130.6; 100-3, 160.2; 100-3, 180.1; 100-3, 230.1; 100-3, 250.1; 100-3, 250.4; 100-3, 270.4; 100-3, 35-26.1; 100-3, 40.1; 100-3, 40.50

97803   **re-assessment and intervention, individual, face-to-face with the patient, each 15 minutes**   A 80 ▣
MED: 100-3, 130.5; 100-3, 130.6; 100-3, 160.2; 100-3, 180.1; 100-3, 230.1; 100-3, 250.1; 100-3, 250.4; 100-3, 270.4; 100-3, 35-26.1; 100-3, 40.1; 100-3, 40.50

97804   **group (2 or more individual(s)), each 30 minutes**   A 80
MED: 100-3, 130.5; 100-3, 130.6; 100-3, 160.2; 100-3, 180.1; 100-3, 230.1; 100-3, 250.1; 100-3, 250.4; 100-3, 270.4; 100-3, 35-26.1; 100-3, 40.1; 100-3, 40.50

ACUPUNCTURE

Report acupuncture services based on 15-minute increments. This must be face-to-face contact with the patient and not the duration of the needle placement.

Report only one code per 15-minute increment. Report either 97810 or 97813 for the initial 15-minute increment. Use only one initial code per day.

Evaluation and management codes may be reported separately with modifier 25 if the patient's condition justifies the service.

97810   **Acupuncture, one or more needles; without electrical stimulation, initial 15 minutes of personal one-on-one contact with the patient**   E

+ ▲   **97811**   **without electrical stimulation, each additional 15 minutes of personal one-on-one contact with the patient, with re-insertion of needle(s) (List separately in addition to code for primary procedure)**   E

Note that 97811 is an add-on code and must be used in conjunction with 97810, 97813.

If evaluation and management services are performed separately, they can be coded with modifier 25 appended. The patient's condition must warrant such services. The time of the E/M service is not included in the time of the acupuncture.

✐ Drug Not Approved by FDA 50 Bilateral Procedure + CPT Add-on Code ⊘ Modifier -51 Exempt ♂Male ♀ Female
● New Code ▲ Revised Code M Maternity Edit A Age Edit A–Y APC Status Ind. AMA: CPT Assistant
© 2005 Ingenix, Inc. *(Blue Ink)*   CPT only © 2005 American Medical Association. All Rights Reserved. *(Black Ink)*   Medicine — 741

▲ 97813   **with electrical stimulation, initial 15 minutes of personal one-on-one contact with the patient**   Ⓔ

Code 97813 cannot be used in conjunction with 97810.

+ ▲ 97814   **with electrical stimulation, each additional 15 minutes of personal one-on-one contact with the patient, with re-insertion of needle(s) (List separately in addition to code for primary procedure)**   Ⓔ

Note that 97814 is an add-on code and must be used in conjunction with 97810, 97813.

If evaluation and management services are performed separately, they can be coded with modifier 25 appended. The patient's condition must warrant such services. The time of the E/M service is not included in the time of the acupuncture.

OSTEOPATHIC MANIPULATIVE TREATMENT

Codes 98925–98929 report inpatient or outpatient osteopathic manipulative treatment (OMT), which is a form of manual treatment applied by a physician to eliminate or alleviate somatic dysfunction and related disorders.

The number of body regions involved in the treatment differentiate the codes (i.e., head, cervical, thoracic, lumbar, sacral, pelvic, lower extremities, upper extremities, rib cage, and abdomen and viscera). OMT includes a component of E/M service to ascertain the effectiveness of the therapy and may be identified separately when:

    •   A physician diagnoses the condition requiring manipulative therapy and provides the therapy during the same visit.

    •   The condition requiring manipulative therapy fails to respond to the therapy or the condition significantly changes or intensifies and requires E/M services beyond the usual pre- and post-service work associated with the procedure.

    •   The physician treats a condition unrelated to the one requiring manipulative therapy during the same visit.

Consult the appropriate Evaluation and Management CPT code and append modifier 25 (or 09925) in addition to the code for OMT when separately identifiable Evaluation and Management services, above and beyond any pre or post service work associated with OMT, are provided.

Consult the glossary for terms and definitions and the front matter of this chapter for additional information.

98925   **Osteopathic manipulative treatment (OMT); one to two body regions involved**   Ⓢ 80 🔲

MED: 100-3, 150.1

AMA: 2000, Dec, 15; 2000, Aug, 11; 1998, Nov, 37-38; 1998, Jul, 10; 1997, Jan, 8, 10; 1996, May, 10

98926   **three to four body regions involved**   Ⓢ 80 🔲

MED: 100-3, 150.1

AMA: 2000, Dec, 15; 2000, Aug, 11; 1998, Nov, 37-38; 1997, Jan, 8; 1996, May, 10

98927   **five to six body regions involved**   Ⓢ 80 🔲

MED: 100-3, 150.1

AMA: 2000, Dec, 15; 2000, Aug, 11; 1998, Nov, 37-38; 1997, Jan, 8; 1996, May, 10

98928   **seven to eight body regions involved**   Ⓢ 80 🔲

MED: 100-3, 150.1

AMA: 2000, Dec, 15; 2000, Aug, 11; 1998, Nov, 37-38; 1997, Jan, 8; 1996, May, 10

98929   **nine to ten body regions involved**   Ⓢ 80 🔲

MED: 100-3, 150.1

AMA: 2000, Aug, 11; 1998, Nov, 37-38; 1997, Jan, 8,10; 1996, May, 10

CHIROPRACTIC MANIPULATIVE TREATMENT

Chiropractic manipulative treatment (CMT), reported with codes 98940–98943, is a form of manual treatment performed to influence joint and neurophysical function. CMT codes include a premanipulation patient assessment. Evaluation and management services should not be reported separately unless the patient's condition requires a separately identifiable E/M service beyond the usual pre- and post-service work normally associated with the procedure.

CMT codes are reported by region. The five spinal regions are cervical (includes atlanto-occipital joint); thoracic (includes costovertebral and costotransverse joints); lumbar, sacral; and pelvic (includes sacroiliac joint). The five extraspinal regions are defined as follows: head (including temporomandibular joint); lower extremities; upper extremities; rib cage, and abdomen.

Consult the appropriate Evaluation and Management CPT code and append modifier 25 (or 09925) in addition to the code for CMT when separately identifiable Evaluation and Management services, above and beyond any pre or post service work associated with CMT, are provided.

Consult the glossary for terms and definitions and the front matter of this chapter for additional information.

98940	**Chiropractic manipulative treatment (CMT); spinal, one to two regions**	S 80 ⬚
	MED: 100-1, 5, 70.6; 100-3, 150.1	
	AMA: 2000, Dec, 15; 1999, Feb, 10; 1998, Nov, 38; 1997, Jan, 7, 11	
98941	**spinal, three to four regions**	S 80 ⬚
	MED: 100-1, 5, 70.6; 100-3, 150.1	
	AMA: 2000, Dec, 15; 1999, Feb, 10; 1998, Nov, 38; 1997, Mar, 10; 1997, Jan, 7, 11	
98942	**spinal, five regions**	S 80 ⬚
	MED: 100-1, 5, 70.6; 100-3, 150.1	
	AMA: 2000, Dec, 15; 1999, Feb, 10; 1998, Nov, 38; 1997, Jan, 7, 11	
98943	**extraspinal, one or more regions**	E
	MED: 100-1, 5, 70.6; 100-3, 150.1	
	AMA: 2000, Dec, 15; 1999, Feb, 10; 1997, Mar, 10; 1997, Jan, 7, 11	

EDUCATION AND TRAINING FOR PATIENT SELF-MANAGEMENT

The education and training for patient self-management codes are used to report education and training services prescribed by a physician and provided by a qualified nonphysician health care provider. These codes may be used only when using a standardized curriculum that may be modified as necessary for the clinical needs, cultural norms, and health literacy of the patient(s).

The purpose of the educational and training services is to teach the patient how to manage the illness or delay the comorbidity(s).

●	**98960**	**Education and training for patient self-management by a qualified, nonphysician health care professional using a standardized curriculum, face-to-face with the patient (could include caregiver/family) each 30 minutes; individual patient**
●	**98961**	**2-4 patients**
●	**98962**	**5-8 patients**

SPECIAL SERVICES, PROCEDURES AND REPORTS

Special services and reports (99000–99091) allow supplemental reporting for services adjunct to the basic services provided. These services can be reported by both physicians and other qualified health care professionals. To justify use of these codes, identify the medical necessity of special circumstances. Document the information clearly and completely in the patient's medical record.

Medicine

99000 — 99056

Code 99024 reports a postoperative follow-up visit included in the global service period. Codes 99050–99058 identify emergency office calls and services provided after hours, on Sundays, or on holidays. Other codes in this category identify medical testimony, unusual travel requirements (e.g., escorting a patient on a trip of more than 10 miles), and educational services. Codes for transportation of specimens (99000–99001) should be reported only once per visit, regardless of the number of specimens. Code (99091) reports the collection and interpretation of physiologic data, with instructions to report the code only once in a 30-day period.

MISCELLANEOUS SERVICES

The following codes are for use for reporting services that are adjunct to the basic service performed.

99000   **Handling and/or conveyance of specimen for transfer from the physician's office to a laboratory**   B
       AMA: 2002, May, 19; 1999, Oct, 11; 1999, Feb, 10; 1994, Winter, 26

99001   **Handling and/or conveyance of specimen for transfer from the patient in other than a physician's office to a laboratory (distance may be indicated)**   B
       AMA: 2002, May, 19; 1994, Winter, 26

99002   **Handling, conveyance, and/or any other service in connection with the implementation of an order involving devices (eg, designing, fitting, packaging, handling, delivery or mailing) when devices such as orthotics, protectives, prosthetics are fabricated by an outside laboratory or shop but which items have been designed, and are to be fitted and adjusted by the attending physician**   B
       AMA: 1994, Winter, 26

       To report a routine collection of venous blood, consult CPT code 36415.

99024   **Postoperative follow-up visit, normally included in the surgical package, to indicate that an evaluation and management service was performed during a postoperative period for a reason(s) related to the original procedure**   B
       AMA: 2002, May, 19; 1997, Sep, 10; 1994, Winter, 26

       Note that 99024 is a component of a surgical package. Consult surgery guidelines.

99026   **Hospital mandated on call service; in-hospital, each hour**   E

99027   **out-of-hospital, each hour**   E

       To report physician standby services requiring prolonged attendance, consult CPT code 99360, as appropriate.

▲ **99050**   **Services provided in the office at times other than regularly scheduled office hours, or days when the office is normally closed (eg, holidays, Saturday or Sunday), in addition to basic service**   B
       MED: 100-4, 12, 70; 100-4, 13, 20; 100-4, 13, 90
       AMA: 2002, May, 19; 1994, Winter, 27

● **99051**   **Service(s) provided in the office during regularly scheduled evening, weekend, or holiday office hours, in addition to basic service**

~~99052~~   ~~Services requested between 10:00 PM and 8:00 AM in addition to basic service~~

● **99053**   **Service(s) provided between 10:00 PM and 8:00 AM at 24-hour facility, in addition to basic service**

~~99054~~   ~~Services requested on Sundays and holidays in addition to basic service~~

▲ **99056**   **Service(s) typically provided in the office, provided out of the office at request of patient, in addition to basic service**   B
       AMA: 2002, May, 19; 1994, Winter, 27

▲ 99058   **Service(s) provided on an emergency basis in the office, which disrupts other scheduled office services, in addition to basic service**   B
MED: 100-4, 12, 70; 100-4, 13, 20; 100-4, 13, 90

AMA: 2002, May, 19; 1994, Winter, 27

● 99060   **Service(s) provided on an emergency basis, out of the office, which disrupts other scheduled office services, in addition to basic service**

99070   **Supplies and materials (except spectacles), provided by the physician over and above those usually included with the office visit or other services rendered (list drugs, trays, supplies, or materials provided)**   B
AMA: 2002, May, 19; 2002, Aug, 11; 2001, Jul, 1, 3; 2000, Jun, 11; 1999, Jun, 10; 1998, May, 10; 1994, Winter, 28

To report a supply of spectacles, consult CPT codes 92390-92395.

99071   **Educational supplies, such as books, tapes, and pamphlets, provided by the physician for the patient's education at cost to physician**   B
MED: 100-2, 15, 60.3; 100-3, 20.10; 100-4, 12, 70; 100-4, 13, 20; 100-4, 13, 90

AMA: 2002, May, 19; 1994, Winter, 28

99075   **Medical testimony**   E
MED: 100-3, 40.1

AMA: 2002, May, 19; 1994, Winter, 28

99078   **Physician educational services rendered to patients in a group setting (eg, prenatal, obesity, or diabetic instructions)**   N
MED: 100-2, 15, 60.3; 100-3, 20.10; 100-3, 40.1

AMA: 2002, May, 19; 1998, Jan, 12; 1994, Winter, 28

99080   **Special reports such as insurance forms, more than the information conveyed in the usual medical communications or standard reporting form**   B
AMA: 2002, May, 19; 1994, Winter, 28

Code 99080 cannot be reported in conjunction with 99455, 99456 for the completion of Workmen's Compensation forms.

99082   **Unusual travel (eg, transportation and escort of patient)**   B 80
MED: 100-4, 12, 80.3

AMA: 2003, Jan, 24; 2002, May, 19

99090   **Analysis of clinical data stored in computers (eg, ECGs, blood pressures, hematologic data)**   B
MED: 100-4, 12, 30.6.12; 100-4, 12, 70; 100-4, 13, 20; 100-4, 13, 90

AMA: 2002, May, 19; 1994, Winter, 28

To report physician/health care professional collection and interpretation of physiologic data stored/transmitted by patient/caregiver, see 99091.

Do not report 99090 if other more specific CPT codes exist, e.g., 93014, 93227, 93233, 93272 for cardiographic services; 95250 for continuous glucose monitoring, 97750 for musculoskeletal function testing.

99091   **Collection and interpretation of physiologic data (eg, ECG, blood pressure, glucose monitoring) digitally stored and/or transmitted by the patient and/or caregiver to the physician or other qualified health care professional, requiring a minimum of 30 minutes of time**   E
AMA: 2002, May, 19

QUALIFYING CIRCUMSTANCES FOR ANESTHESIA

If an explanation is needed for these services, consult the Anesthesia guidelines.

+   **99100**   **Anesthesia for patient of extreme age, under 1 year and over 70 (List**
              separately in addition to code for primary anesthesia procedure)   ☐ B
              MED: 100-4, 12, 140; 100-4, 12, 140.2; 100-4, 12, 140.3.2; 100-4, 12, 50

              To report anesthesia for hernia repairs in the lower abdomen, infant one year
              of age or younger, consult CPT codes 00834, 00836.

+   **99116**   **Anesthesia complicated by utilization of total body hypothermia (List**
              separately in addition to code for primary anesthesia procedure)   ☐ B
              MED: 100-4, 12, 140; 100-4, 12, 140.2; 100-4, 12, 140.3.2; 100-4, 12, 50

+   **99135**   **Anesthesia complicated by utilization of controlled hypotension (List**
              separately in addition to code for primary anesthesia procedure)   ☐ B
              MED: 100-4, 12, 140; 100-4, 12, 140.2; 100-4, 12, 140.3.2; 100-4, 12, 50

+   **99140**   **Anesthesia complicated by emergency conditions (specify) (List separately**
              in addition to code for primary anesthesia procedure)   ☐ B
              MED: 100-4, 12, 140; 100-4, 12, 140.2; 100-4, 12, 140.3.2; 100-4, 12, 50

              AMA: 2001, Mar, 10

              An emergency exists when a delay in treatment would lead to a significant
              increase in the threat to life or body part.

SEDATION WITH OR WITHOUT ANALGESIA (CONSCIOUS SEDATION)

~~99141~~   ~~Sedation with or without analgesia (conscious sedation); intravenous,~~
           ~~intramuscular or inhalation~~

~~99142~~   ~~oral, rectal and/or intranasal~~

            (Use 99143-99145)

MODERATE (CONSCIOUS) SEDATON

Moderate (conscious) sedation includes the following services:

•   Patient assessment

•   IV access

•   Administration of medication

•   Maintenance of sedation

•   Monitoring of oxygen saturation, heart rate, and blood pressure

•   Recovery (not included in intraservice time)

Intraservice time begins when medication is given to start the sedation and requires continuous face-to-face attendance and ends when the physician is no longer in attendance.

Do not report 99143–99150 with 94760–94762.

When a physician other than a physician performing the procedure administers the moderate sedation in the facility setting, the second physician reports his/her services with codes 99148–99150. In the non-facility setting, codes 99148–99150 would not be used.

⊘ ● 99143   **Moderate sedation services (other than those services described by codes 00100-01999) provided by the same physician performing the diagnostic or therapeutic service that the sedation supports, requiring the presence of an independent trained observer to assist in the monitoring of the patients level of consciousness and physiological status; under 5 years of age, first 30 minutes intra-service time**

⊘ ● 99144   **age 5 years or older, first 30 minutes intra-service time**

+ ● 99145   **each additional 15 minutes intra-service time (List separately in addition to code for primary service)**

> Note that 99145 is an add-on code and must be used in conjunction with 99143, 99144.

⊘ ● 99148   **Moderate sedation services (other than those services described by codes 00100-01999), provided by a physician other than the health care professional performing the diagnostic or therapeutic service that the sedation supports; under 5 years of age, first 30 minutes intra-service time**

+ ● 99149   **age 5 years or older, first 30 minutes intra-service time**

   ● 99150   **each additional 15 minutes intra-service time (List separately in addition to code for primary service)**

> Note that 99150 is an add-on code and must be used in conjunction with 99148, 99149.

OTHER SERVICES AND PROCEDURES

Codes 99170–99199 report services such as anogenital examinations in cases of suspected child sexual abuse, medical intervention, and observation of patient following suspected cases of poisoning, and therapeutic phlebotomy.

99170   **Anogenital examination with colposcopic magnification in childhood for suspected trauma**   Ⓐ Ⓣ 🔁
     AMA: 1999, Nov, 55

99172   **Visual function screening, automated or semi-automated bilateral quantitative determination of visual acuity, ocular alignment, color vision by pseudoisochromatic plates, and field of vision (may include all or some screening of the determination(s) for contrast sensitivity, vision under glare)**   Ⓔ
     MED: 100-2, 16, 90

     AMA: 2001, Feb, 7

> This service MUST consist of graduated visual acuity stimuli that allow a quantitative determination of visual acuity (e.g., Snellen chart).

> This service may not be used in addition to a general opthalmological service or an E/M service.

> CPT code 99172 must not be used in conjunction with CPT code 99173.

99173   **Screening test of visual acuity, quantitative, bilateral**   Ⓔ
     MED: 100-2, 16, 90

     AMA: 1999, Nov, 55

> CPT code 99173 must not be used in conjunction with CPT code 99172.

99175   **Ipecac or similar administration for individual emesis and continued observation until stomach adequately emptied of poison**   Ⓝ

> If diagnostic intubation is needed, consult CPT codes 82926-82928 and 89130-89141. If gastric lavage is used for diagnostic purposes, consult CPT code 91055.

Medicine

99183 — 99511

99183	**Physician attendance and supervision of hyperbaric oxygen therapy, per session** ⒷⒷ⁸⁰	

MED: 100-3, 20.29

AMA: 2003, Jan, 23

Note that Evaluation and Management services and/or procedures (e.g., wound debridement) provided in a hyperbaric oxygen treatment facility in conjunction with a hyperbaric oxygen therapy session should be reported separately.

99185	**Hypothermia; regional** Ⓝ
	MED: 100-3, 110.6; 100-4, 12, 70; 100-4, 13, 20; 100-4, 13, 90

99186	**total body** Ⓝ🔁

99190	**Assembly and operation of pump with oxygenator or heat exchanger (with or without ECG and/or pressure monitoring); each hour** Ⓒ🔁

99191	**3/4 hour** Ⓒ🔁

99192	**1/2 hour** Ⓒ🔁

99195	**Phlebotomy, therapeutic (separate procedure)** Ⓧ🔁
	AMA: 1996, Jun, 10; 1996, Apr, 3

99199	**Unlisted special service, procedure or report** ⒷⒷ⁸⁰
	AMA: 1999, Nov, 55

HOME HEALTH PROCEDURES/SERVICES

Codes 99500–99600 report various home health procedures and services that are to be used by nonphysician health care providers. The codes report services delivered in the patient's home, which includes a private home, an assisted living apartment, a group home, a custodial care facility, or a school.

99500	**Home visit for prenatal monitoring and assessment to include fetal heart rate, non-stress test, uterine monitoring, and gestational diabetes monitoring** Ⓜ ♀ Ⓔ

99501	**Home visit for postnatal assessment and follow-up care** ♀ Ⓔ

99502	**Home visit for newborn care and assessment** Ⓐ Ⓔ

99503	**Home visit for respiratory therapy care (eg, bronchodilator, oxygen therapy, respiratory assessment, apnea evaluation)** Ⓔ

99504	**Home visit for mechanical ventilation care** Ⓔ

99505	**Home visit for stoma care and maintenance including colostomy and cystostomy** Ⓔ

99506	**Home visit for intramuscular injections** Ⓔ

99507	**Home visit for care and maintenance of catheter(s) (eg, urinary, drainage, and enteral)** Ⓔ

99509	**Home visit for assistance with activities of daily living and personal care** Ⓔ

To report self-care/home management training, see 97535.

To report home medical nutrition assessment and intervention services, see 97802-97804.

To report home speech therapy services, see 92507-92508.

99510	**Home visit for individual, family, or marriage counseling** Ⓔ

99511	**Home visit for fecal impaction management and enema administration** Ⓔ

| 99512 | **Home visit for hemodialysis** | E |

To report home infusion of peritoneal dialysis, consult CPT codes 99601 and 99602.

| 99600 | **Unlisted home visit service or procedure** | E |

HOME INFUSION PROCEDURES/SERVICES

The home infusion procedures (99601–99602) should be used to report the home administration of a variety of drugs and medications. These codes do not include the patient's self-administration of the medication.

These services are used to report home infusion, per visit. Any solutions, supplies, drugs or equipment provided the patient are not included in these codes and should be reported separately. To report more than two hours of home infusion, report 99601 for the first two hours and 99602 for each additional hour.

| 99601 | **Home infusion/specialty drug administration, per visit (up to 2 hours);** | E |
| + 99602 | **each additional hour (List separately in addition to primary procedure)** | E |

Note that 99602 is an add-on code that must be used in conjunction with code 99601.

CATEGORY II CODES

The following information is taken directly from the American Medical Association (AMA) *Physicians' Current Procedural Terminology* 2005.

The following section contains codes that describe services that may be considered parts of an evaluation and management service or clinical service and, as such, do not have a relative value associated with them. They may include results of a laboratory or radiology tests and other procedures, or safety practices or services reflecting compliance with state or federal law.

The codes include components that are usually part of another service and, do not have a relative value attached. The codes may also describe results from laboratory tests and other procedures, services intended to address patient safety practices, or services that demonstrate compliance with state or federal laws.

Codes are comprised of alpha numeric characters (i.e., 4 digits followed by the letter F).

Composite Measures	0001F-0005F
Patient Management	0500F-0503F
Patient History	1000F-1008F
Physical Examination	2000F-2004F
Diagnostic/Screening Processes or Results	3000F-3002F
Therapeutic, Preventive or Other Interventions	4000F-4018F
Follow-up or Other Outcomes	To begin with 500F (no codes at this time)
Patient Safety	To begin with 6000F (no codes at this time)

Category II codes are reviewed by the Performance Measurements Advisory Group (PMAG), which is an advisory body to the CPT Editorial Panel and the CPT/HCPAC Advisory Committee. The PMAG is comprised of performance measurement experts representing the Agency for Healthcare Research and Quality (AHRQ), the American Medical Association (AMA), the Centers for Medicare and Medicaid Services (CMS), the Joint Commission on Accreditation of Healthcare Organizations (JCAHO), the National Committee for Quality Assurance (NCQA), and the Physician Consortium for Performance Improvement. The PMAG may also seek advice and input from other national health care organizations, as needed, with regard to the development of Category II codes. Other sources may include national medical specialty societies, other national health care professional associations, accrediting bodies, and federal regulatory agencies.

The Category II codes are published twice a year: January 1 and July 1. Go to "www.ama-assn.org/go/cpt" for the most current listing.

MODIFIERS

The following performance measurement modifiers may be used for Category II codes to indicate that a service specified in the associate measure(s) was considered but not provided due to medical or patient circumstance(s) documented in the medical record. These modifiers function to exclude denominators from the performance measure.

Category II modifiers can be reported only with Category II codes; and cannot be reported with Category I or Category III codes. Unless otherwise noted in special guidelines, parenthetical notes, or code descriptor language, the modifiers included in the Category II section may be used with any code listed in the Category II section.

CATEGORY II CODES

1P Performance Measure Exclusion Modifier due to Medical Reasons:

Includes, for example:

- Patient allergic history

- Potential adverse drug interaction

- Acquired or congenital absence of organ or limb

- Other documented clinical contraindication

2P Performance Measure Exclusion Modifier due to Patient Choice:

Includes, for example:

- Patient refusal

- Economic

- Social

- Religious

COMPOSITE MEASURES

Composite measures codes combine several measures grouped within a single code descriptor to make possible reporting for clinical condition when all of the components have been met. If only some components are met, or if services are provided in addition to those that are included in the composite code, they may be reported individually using the appropriate CPT Category II codes for those services.

No measures at this time.

DIAGNOSTIC/SCREENING PROCESSES OR RESULTS

Diagnostic/screening processes or results codes describe the results of tests that are ordered such as clinical laboratory tests as well as radiological and other procedural examinations).

No codes at this time.

FOLLOW-UP OR OTHER OUTCOMES

Follow-up or other outcomes Category II codes designate the review and communication of test results to patients, patient satisfaction or experience with care, patient functional status, and patient morbidity and mortality.

No codes at this time.

PATIENT SAFETY

Category II codes that describe patient safety practices.

No codes at this time.

CATEGORY II CODES

PATIENT MANAGEMENT

The codes in this section describe encounters with healthcare professionals for the purpose of specific clinical indications, such as obstetrical care. The codes are used to track utilization of these services.

🔲 CCI Comp   50 Bilateral Procedure   ✚ CPT Add-on Code   ⊘ Modifier -51 Exempt   ♂Male   ♀ Female
● New Code   ▲ Revised Code   M Maternity Edit   A Age Edit   A–Y APC Status Ind.   AMA: CPT Assistant
© 2005 Ingenix, Inc. *(Blue Ink)*   CPT only © 2005 American Medical Association. All Rights Reserved. *(Black Ink)*   Category II — 751

Category II Codes

0001F — 2001F

● 0001F   Heart failure assessed (includes assessment of all the following components): Blood pressure measured (2000F) Level of activity assessed (1003F) Clinical symptoms of volume overload (excess) assessed (1004F) Weight, recorded (2001F) Auscultation of the heart performed (2003F) Clinical signs of volume overload (excess) assessed (2002F)

● 0005F   Osteoarthritis assessed Includes assessment of all the following components: Osteoarthritis symptoms and functional status assessed (1006F) Use of anti-inflammatory or over-the-counter (OTC) analgesic medications assessed (1007F) Initial examination of the involved joint(s) (includes visual inspection, palpation, range of motion) (2004F)

  0500F   Initial prenatal care visit (report at first prenatal encounter with health care professional providing obstetrical care. Report also date of visit and, in a separate field, the date of the last menstrual period - LMP)   M ♀ E

  0501F   Prenatal flow sheet documented in medical record by first prenatal visit (documentation includes at minimum blood pressure, weight, urine protein, uterine size, fetal heart tones, and estimated date of delivery). Report also: date of visit and, in a separate field, the date of the last menstrual period - LMP (Note: If reporting 0501F Prenatal flow sheet, it is not necessary to report 0500F Initial prenatal care visit)   M ♀ E

  0502F   Subsequent prenatal care visit [Excludes: patients who are seen for a condition unrelated to pregnancy or prenatal care (eg, an upper respiratory infection; patients seen for consultation only, not for continuing care)]   M ♀ E

  0503F   Postpartum care visit   M ♀ E

PATIENT HISTORY

This section of codes is used to describe measures for specific aspects of a patient history or for a review of systems.

  1000F   Tobacco use, smoking, assessed   E

  1001F   Tobacco use, non-smoking, assessed   E

  1002F   Anginal symptoms and level of activity, assessed   E

● 1003F   Level of activity assessed

● 1004F   Clinical symptoms of volume overload (excess) assessed

● 1005F   Asthma symptoms evaluated (includes physician documentation of numeric frequency of symptoms or patient completion of an asthma assessment tool/survey/questionnaire)

● 1006F   Osteoarthritis symptoms and functional status assessed (may include the use of a standardized scale or the completion of an assessment questionnaire, such as the SF-36, AAOS Hip & Knee Questionnaire) [Instructions: Report when osteoarthritis is addressed during the patient encounter]

● 1007F   Use of anti-inflammatory or analgesic over-the-counter (OTC) medications for symptom relief assessed

● 1008F   Gastrointestinal and renal risk factors assessed for patients on prescribed or OTC non-steroidal anti-inflammatory drug (NSAID)

PHYSICAL EXAMINATION

This section of codes is used to describe measures for specific aspects of a physical examination.

  2000F   Blood pressure, measured[1]   E

● 2001F   Weight recorded

- 2002F Clinical signs of volume overload (excess) assessed
- 2003F Auscultation of the heart performed
- 2004F Initial examination of the involved joint(s) (includes visual inspection, palpation, range of motion) [Instructions: Report only for initial osteoarthritis visit or for visits for new joint involvement]

DIAGNOSTIC/SCREENING PROCESSES OR RESULTS

- 3000F Blood pressure ≤ 140/90 mm Hg
- 3002F Blood pressure > 140/90 mm Hg

THERAPEUTIC, PREVENTIVE OR OTHER INTERVENTIONS

This section of codes is used to describe therapeutic, preventive or other interventions such as patient education and counseling for tobacco use and medication therapy.

4000F Tobacco use cessation intervention, counseling   E

4001F Tobacco use cessation intervention, pharmacologic therapy   E

4002F Statin therapy, prescribed   E

- 4003F Patient education, written/oral, appropriate for patients with heart failure performed

4006F Beta-blocker therapy, prescribed   E

4009F Angiotensin converting enzyme (ACE) inhibitor therapy, prescribed   E

▲ 4011F Oral antiplatelet therapy prescribed (eg, aspirin, clopidogrel/Plavix, or combination of aspirin and dipyridamole/Aggrenox)   E

- 4012F Warfarin therapy prescribed
- 4014F Written discharge instructions provided to heart failure patients discharged home. (Instructions include all of the following components: activity level, diet, discharge medications, follow-up appointment, weight monitoring, what to do if symptoms worsen) [Excludes patients 18 years of age]
- 4015F Persistent asthma, long term control medication [inhaled corticosteroids or an acceptable alternative treatment, (cromolyn sodium, leukotriene modifier, nedocromil, OR sustained release theophylline)], prescribed [Note: There are no medical exclusion criteria]

    Modifier 1P cannot be used with 4015F.

    Modifier 2P should be used to report patient reasons for not prescribing.

- 4016F Anti-inflammatory/analgesic agent prescribed [Use for prescribed or continued medication(s), including over-the-counter medication(s)]
- 4017F Gastrointestinal prophylaxis for NSAID use prescribed
- 4018F Therapeutic exercise for the involved joint(s) instructed or physical or occupational therapy prescribed

Category III Codes

0003T — 0021T

CATEGORY III CODES

The following is taken from information provided by the American Medical Association (AMA).

Category III codes are alphanumeric codes intended to allow data collection for the services and procedures below. This is an activity that is critically important in the evaluation of health care delivery and the formation of public and private policy. The use of the codes in this section will allow physicians and other qualified health care professionals, payers, health services researchers, and health policy experts to identify emerging technology, services, and procedures for clinical efficacy, utilization and outcomes.

Category I codes are the long-used, five-digit codes that make up the rest of the book. **If a Category III code is available for a given service or procedure, use the Category III code instead of a Category I unlisted code.**

The inclusion of a service or procedure in this section neither implies nor endorses clinical efficacy, safety or the applicability to clinical practice. The codes in this section do not conform to the usual requirements for CPT Category I codes. For Category I codes, the AMA requires that the service or procedure be performed by many health care professionals in clinical practice in multiple locations and that necessary FDA approval has already been received. The nature of emerging technology, services, and procedures is that these requirements may not be met. New temporary codes for emerging technology, services, and procedures have been placed in a separate section of the CPT book and the codes are differentiated from Category I CPT codes by the use of alphanumeric characters.

Since these are temporary codes, they may or may not receive placement in the CPT book; and, those not adopted as permanent codes will be archived by the AMA after five years unless it is believed the temporary code is still needed. If made a permanent code in the CPT book, the existing numbers do not imply where they will be placed.

CATEGORY III CODES

0003T	Cervicography	♀ S 80
0008T	Upper gastrointestinal endoscopy including esophagus, stomach, and either the duodenum and/or jejunum as appropriate, with suturing of the esophagogastric junction	T 80 ▣
~~0010T~~	~~Tuberculosis test, cell-mediated immunity measurement of gamma interferon antigen response~~	
	(Use 86480)	
0016T	Destruction of localized lesion of choroid (eg, choroidal neovascularization), transpupillary thermotherapy	T 50 80 ▣
0017T	Destruction of macular drusen, photocoagulation MED: 100-3, 45-30	E 50 80 ▣
0018T	Delivery of high power, focal magnetic pulses for direct stimulation to cortical neurons	S 80 ▣
▲ **0019T**	Extracorporeal shock wave involving musculoskeletal system, not otherwise specified, low energy	E
	To report the application of high energy extracorporeal shock wave involving the musculoskeletal system not otherwise specified, consult Category III code 0101T.	
	To report the application of high energy extracorporeal shock wave that involves the lateral humeral epicondyle, consult Category III code 0102T.	
~~0020T~~	~~involving plantar fascia~~	
	(Use 28890)	
0021T	Insertion of transcervical or transvaginal fetal oximetry sensor	♀ C 80 ▣

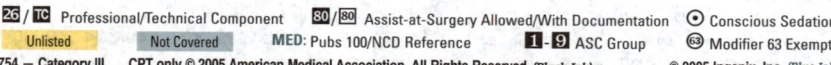

~~0023T   Infectious agent drug susceptibility phenotype prediction using genotypic comparison to known genotypic/phenotypic database, HIV-1~~

(Use 87900)

0024T   Non-surgical septal reduction therapy (eg, alcohol ablation), for hypertrophic obstructive cardiomyopathy, with coronary arteriograms, with or without temporary pacemaker ⓒ 80 🔧

0026T   Lipoprotein, direct measurement, intermediate density lipoproteins (IDL) (remnant lipoproteins) Ⓐ 80 🔧

0027T   Endoscopic lysis of epidural adhesions with direct visualization using mechanical means (eg, spinal endoscopic catheter system) or solution injection (eg, normal saline) including radiologic localization and epidurography Ⓣ 80 🔧

To report diagnostic epidurography, consult CPT code 64999.

0028T   Dual energy x-ray absorptiometry (DEXA) body composition study, one or more sites Ⓝ 80

0029T   Treatment(s) for incontinence, pulsed magnetic neuromodulation, per day Ⓐ 80 🔧

0030T   Antiprothrombin (phospholipid cofactor) antibody, each Ig class Ⓐ 80

0031T   Speculoscopy; ♀ Ⓝ 80

0032T   with directed sampling ♀ Ⓝ 80 🔧

~~0033T   Endovascular repair of descending thoracic aortic aneurysm, pseudoaneurysm or dissection; involving coverage of left subclavian artery origin, initial endoprosthesis~~

(For endovascular repair of descending thoracic aorta, involving coverage of left subclavian artery origin, use 33880)

~~0034T   not involving coverage of left subclavian artery origin, initial endoprosthesis~~

(For endovascular repair of descending thoracic aorta, not involving coverage of left subclavian artery origin, use 33881)

~~0035T   Placement of proximal or distal extension prosthesis for endovascular repair of descending thoracic aortic aneurysm, pseudoaneurysm or dissection; initial extension~~

(For proximal extension during endovascular repair of descending thoracic aorta, use 33883. Distal extensions are included in 33880, 33881. Distal extensions performed after endovascular repair of descending thoracic aorta are reported with 33886.)

~~0036T   each additional extension (List separately in addition to code for primary procedure)~~

(For additional proximal extensions use 33884. Additional distal extensions during endovascular repair of descending thoracic aorta are included in 33880, 33881. Additional distal extensions placed after endovascular repair of thoracic aorta are included in 33886.)

~~0037T   Open subclavian to carotid artery transposition performed in conjunction with endovascular thoracic aneurysm repair, by neck incision, unilateral~~

(For open subclavian to carotid artery transposition performed in conjunction with endovascular thoracic aortic repair by neck incision, use 33889.)

~~0038T~~   ~~Endovascular repair of descending thoracic aortic aneurysm, pseudoaneurysm or dissection involving coverage of left subclavian artery origin, initial endoprosthesis, radiological supervision and interpretation~~

(For endovascular repair of descending thoracic aorta, involving coverage of left subclavian artery origin, radiological supervision and interpretation, use 75956)

~~0039T~~   ~~Endovascular repair of descending thoracic aortic aneurysm, pseudoaneurysm or dissection not involving coverage of left subclavian artery origin, initial endoprosthesis, radiological supervision and interpretation~~

(For endovascular repair of descending thoracic aorta, not involving coverage of left subclavian artery origin, radiological supervision and interpretation, use 75957)

~~0040T~~   ~~Placement of proximal or distal extension prosthesis for endovascular repair of descending thoracic aortic aneurysm, pseudoaneurysm or dissection, each extension, radiological supervision and interpretation~~

(For placement of proximal extension prosthesis for endovascular repair of descending thoracic aorta, radiological supervision and interpretation, use 75958. For placement of distal extension prosthesis after thoracic endovascular repair of descending thoracic aorta, radiological supervision and interpretation, use 75959)

0041T   **Urinalysis infectious agent detection, semi-quantitative analysis of volatile compounds**   A 80

0042T   **Cerebral perfusion analysis using computed tomography with contrast administration, including post-processing of parametric maps with determination of cerebral blood flow, cerebral blood volume, and mean transit time**   N 80 ▣

0043T   **Carbon monoxide, expired gas analysis (eg, ETCOc/hemolysis breath test)**   A 80

0044T   **Whole body integumentary photography, at request of a physician, for monitoring of high-risk patients; with dysplastic nevus syndrome or familial melanoma**   N 80

0045T   **with history of dysplastic nevi or personal history of melanoma**   N 80

0046T   **Catheter lavage of a mammary duct(s) for collection of cytology specimen(s), in high risk individuals (Gail risk scoring or prior personal history of breast cancer), each breast; single duct**   ♀ T 80 ▣

0047T   **each additional duct**   ♀ T 80 ▣

0048T   **Implantation of a ventricular assist device, extracorporeal, percutaneous transseptal access, single or dual cannulation**   C 80 ▣

+   0049T   **Prolonged extracorporeal percutaneous transseptal ventricular assist device, greater than 24 hours, each subsequent 24 hour period (List separately in addition to code for primary procedure)**   C 80

Note that 0049T is an add-on code that must be used in conjunction with code 0048T.

0050T   **Removal of a ventricular assist device, extracorporeal, percutaneous transseptal access, single or dual cannulation**   C 80 ▣

0051T   **Implantation of a total replacement heart system (artificial heart) with recipient cardiectomy**   C 80 ▣

To report implantation of heart assist or ventricular assist device, consult CPT codes 33975, 33976.

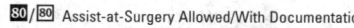

26 / TC Professional/Technical Component   80 / 80 Assist-at-Surgery Allowed/With Documentation   ⊙ Conscious Sedation
Unlisted   Not Covered   MED: Pubs 100/NCD Reference   1 - 9 ASC Group   63 Modifier 63 Exempt

0052T   **Replacement or repair of thoracic unit of a total replacement heart system (artificial heart)**   Ⓒ 80 🔲

To report replacement or repair of other implantable components in a total replacement heart system (artificial heart), consult CPT Category III code 0053T.

0053T   **Replacement or repair of implantable component or components of total replacement heart system (artificial heart) excluding thoracic unit** Ⓒ 80 🔲

To report replacement or repair of a thoracic unit of a total replacement heart system (artificial heart), consult CPT Category III code 0052T

＋   **0054T**   **Computer-assisted musculoskeletal surgical navigational orthopedic procedure, with image-guidance based on fluoroscopic images (List separately in addition to code for primary procedure)**   Ⓑ 80 🔲

Note that 0054T is an add-on code that must be used in conjunction with the appropriate code for the primary procedure. This code cannot be reported alone.

＋   **0055T**   **Computer-assisted musculoskeletal surgical navigational orthopedic procedure, with image-guidance based on CT/MRI images (List separately in addition to code for primary procedure)**   Ⓑ 80 🔲

Note that 0055T is an add-on code that must be used in conjunction with the appropriate code for the primary procedure. This code cannot be reported alone.

For CT or MRI guidance and localization for needle placement and annuloplasty together with 0062T, 0063T, consult CPT codes 76360, 76393.

＋   **0056T**   **Computer assisted musculoskeletal surgical navigational orthopedic procedure, image-less (List separately in addition to code for primary procedure)**   Ⓑ 80 🔲

Note that 0056T is an add-on code that must be used in conjunction with the appropriate code for the primary procedure. This code cannot be reported alone.

0058T   **Cryopreservation; reproductive tissue, ovarian**   Ⓧ 80

0059T   **oocyte(s)**   Ⓧ 80

To report cryopreservation of embryo(s), sperm and testicular reproductive tissue, consult CPT codes 89258, 89259, 89335.

0060T   **Electrical impedance scan of the breast, bilateral (risk assessment device for breast cancer)**   Ⓑ 80

0061T   **Destruction/reduction of malignant breast tumor including breast carcinoma cells in the margins, microwave phased array thermotherapy, disposable catheter with combined temperature monitoring probe and microwave sensor, externally applied microwave energy, including interstitial placement of sensor**   Ⓑ 80 🔲

To report imaging guidance, consult CPT codes 76942, 76986.

0062T   **Percutaneous intradiscal annuloplasty, any method, unilateral or bilateral including fluoroscopic guidance; single level**   Ⓣ 80 🔲

＋   **0063T**   **one or more additional levels (List separately in addition to 0062T for primary procedure)**   Ⓣ 80

To report CT or MRI guidance and localization for needle placement and annuloplasty in conjunction with 0062T, 0063T, consult CPT codes 76360, 76393.

0064T   **Spectroscopy, expired gas analysis (eg, nitric oxide/carbon dioxide test)**   Ⓐ 80

🔲 CCI Comp   🔢 Bilateral Procedure   ＋ CPT Add-on Code   ⊘ Modifier -51 Exempt   ♂ Male   ♀ Female
● New Code   ▲ Revised Code   Ⓜ Maternity Edit   Ⓐ Age Edit   Ⓐ–Ⓨ APC Status Ind.   AMA: CPT Assistant

| | **0065T** | **Ocular photoscreening, with interpretation and report, bilateral** | [A] [80] |

0065T — **Ocular photoscreening, with interpretation and report, bilateral** [A] [80]

Code 0065T cannot be reported with CPT code 99172 or 99173.

0066T — **Computed tomographic (CT) colonography (ie, virtual colonoscopy); screening** [E] [80]

0067T — **diagnostic** [S] [80]

Codes 0066T and 0067T cannot be reported with CPT codes 72192-72194, 74150-74170, 76375.

+ **0068T** — **Acoustic heart sound recording and computer analysis; with interpretation and report (List separately in addition to codes for electrocardiography)** [B] [80]

Note 0068T must be used with code 93000.

+ **0069T** — **acoustic heart sound recording and computer analysis only (List separately in addition to codes for electrocardiography)** [N]

Note 0069T must be used with code 93005.

+ **0070T** — **interpretation and report only (List separately in addition to codes for electrocardiography)** [N] [80]

0071T — **Focused ultrasound ablation of uterine leiomyomata, including MR guidance; total leiomyomata volume less than 200 cc of tissue** ♀ [T] [80] [C]

0072T — **total leiomyomata volume greater or equal to 200 cc of tissue** ♀ [T] [80] [C]

Code 0071T, 0072T cannot be reported with CPT codes 51702 or 76394.

0073T — **Compensator-based beam modulation treatment delivery of inverse planned treatment using three or more high resolution (milled or cast) compensator convergent beam modulated fields, per treatment session** [S] [80] [TC] [C]

To report treatment planning, consult code 77301.

Code 0073T cannot be reported with CPT codes 77401-77416, 77418.

ONLINE MEDICAL EVALUATION

A medical evaluation provided online is a service provided to a patient using internet resources. This service is provided as a response to a patient's inquiry online to a physician or a qualified healthcare professional. The physician or qualified healthcare professional must keep a permanent record of the encounter. These codes should not be to report routine services that would be included in other evaluation and management services. The codes include all communication including telephone calls, prescriptions, and laboratory orders related to the online evaluation.

0074T — **Online evaluation and management service, per encounter, provided by a physician, using the Internet or similar electronic communications network, in response to a patients request, established patient** [E] [80]

0075T — **Transcatheter placement of extracranial vertebral or intrathoracic carotid artery stent(s), including radiologic supervision and interpretation, percutaneous; initial vessel** [C] [80] [C]

+ **0076T** — **each additional vessel (List separately in addition to code for primary procedure)** [C] [80]

Note 0076T must be used with code 0075T.

When the ipsilateral extracranial vertebral or intrathoracic carotid arteriogram (including imaging and selective catheterization) confirms the need for stenting, then 0075T and 0076T include all the ipsilateral extracranial vertebral or intrathoracic selective carotid catheterization, all diagnostic imaging for ipsilateral extracranial vertebral or intrathoracic carotid artery stenting, and all related radiologic supervision and interpretation. Use the appropriate codes for selective catheterization and imaging instead of 0075T or 0076T if stenting is not indicated.

[26] / [TC] Professional/Technical Component   [80] / [80] Assist-at-Surgery Allowed/With Documentation   ⊙ Conscious Sedation

Unlisted   Not Covered   MED: Pubs 100/NCD Reference   [1] - [9] ASC Group   [63] Modifier 63 Exempt

758 — Category III   CPT only © 2005 American Medical Association. All Rights Reserved. *(Black Ink)*   © 2005 Ingenix, Inc. *(Blue Ink)*

0077T   Implanting and securing cerebral thermal perfusion probe, including twist drill or burr hole, to measure absolute cerebral tissue perfusion   C 80 ▣

Report 0078T-0081T according to the Endovascular Abdominal Aneurysm Repair guidelines set up for 34800-34826.

▲ **0078T**   Endovascular repair using prosthesis of abdominal aortic aneurysm, pseudoaneurysm or dissection, abdominal aorta involving visceral branches (superior mesenteric, celiac and/or renal artery(s))   C 80 ▣

Code 0078T cannot be reported with CPT codes 34800-34805, 35081, 35102, 35452, 35454, 35472, 37205-37208.

Note 0078T must be used with 35454, 37205-37208, when these procedures are performed outside the target zone of the endoprosthesis.

+ **0079T**   Placement of visceral extension prosthesis for endovascular repair of abdominal aortic aneurysm involving visceral vessels, each visceral branch (List separately in addition to code for primary procedure)   C 80 ▣

Note 0079T must be used with 0078T.

Code 0079T cannot be reported with 34800-34805, 35081, 35102, 35452, 35454, 35472, 37205-37208.

Note 0079T must be used with 35454, 37205-37208 when these procedures are performed outside the target zone of the endoprosthesis.

0080T   Endovascular repair of abdominal aortic aneurysm, pseudoaneurysm or dissection, abdominal aorta involving visceral vessels (superior mesenteric, celiac or renal), using fenestrated modular bifurcated prosthesis (two docking limbs), radiological supervision and interpretation   C 80 ▣

Code 0080T cannot be reported with CPT codes 34800-34805, 35801, 35102, 35452, 35472, 37205-37208.

Note 0080T must be used with 35454, 37205-37208, when these procedures are performed outside the target zone of the endoprosthesis.

+ **0081T**   Placement of visceral extension prosthesis for endovascular repair of abdominal aortic aneurysm involving visceral vessels, each visceral branch, radiological supervision and interpretation (List separately in addition to code for primary procedure)   C 80 ▣

Not 0081T must be used with 0080T.

Code 00081T cannot be used with CPT codes 34800-34805, 35081, 35102, 35452, 35454, 35472, 37205-37208.

Note 0081T must be used with 35454, 37205-37208, when these procedures are performed outside the target zone of the endoprosthesis

0082T   Stereotactic body radiation therapy, treatment delivery, one or more treatment areas, per day   B 80 ▣

Code 0082T cannot be reported with CPT codes 77401-77416, 77418.

0083T   Stereotactic body radiation therapy, treatment management, per day   N 80 ▣

Code 0083T cannot be reported with CPT codes 77427-77432.

0084T   Insertion of a temporary prostatic urethral stent   ♂ T 80 ▣

0085T   Breath test for heart transplant rejection   X 80

0086T   Left ventricular filling pressure indirect measurement by computerized calibration of the arterial waveform response to Valsalva maneuver   N 80

0087T   Sperm evaluation, Hyaluronan binding assay   X 80

Category III Codes

0088T — 0104T

	0088T	**Submucosal radiofrequency tissue volume reduction of tongue base, one or more sites, per session (ie, for treatment of obstructive sleep apnea syndrome)** T 80 ↻
●	**0089T**	**Actigraphy testing, recording, analysis and interpretation (minimum of three-day recording)**
●	**0090T**	**Total disc arthroplasty (artificial disc), anterior approach, including diskectomy to prepare interspace (other than for decompression); single interspace, cervical**
●	**0091T**	**single interspace, lumbar**
+ ●	**0092T**	**each additional interspace (List separately in addition to code for primary procedure)**

Note that 0092T is an add-on code and must be used in conjunction with 0090T, 0091T.

●	**0093T**	**Removal of total disc arthroplasty, anterior approach; single interspace, cervical**
●	**0094T**	**single interspace, lumbar**
+ ●	**0095T**	**each additional interspace (List separately in addition to code for primary procedure)**

Note that 0095T is an add-on code and must be used in conjunction with 0093T, 0094T.

●	**0096T**	**Revision of total disc arthroplasty, anterior approach; single interspace, cervical**

Code 0096T cannot be used with 0093T.

●	**0097T**	**single interspace, lumbar**

Code 0097T cannot be used with 0094T.

+ ●	**0098T**	**each additional interspace (List separately in addition to code for primary procedure)**

Note that 0098T is an add-on code and must be used in conjunction with 0096T, 0097T.

Code 0098T cannot be used with 0095T.

Code 0090T-0097T cannot be used with 22851, 49010 when performed at the same level.

Codes 0090T-0097T include fluoroscopy.

To report decompression, consult CPT codes 63001-63048.

●	**0099T**	**Implantation of intrastromal corneal ring segments**
●	**0100T**	**Placement of a subconjunctival retinal prosthesis receiver and pulse generator, and implantation of intra-ocular retinal electrode array, with vitrectomy**
●	**0101T**	**Extracorporeal shock wave involving musculoskeletal system, not otherwise specified, high energy**

To report the application of low energy musculoskeletal system extracorporeal shock wave, consult Category III code 0019T.

●	**0102T**	**Extracorporeal shock wave, high energy, performed by a physician, requiring anesthesia other than local, involving lateral humeral epicondyle**

To report the application of low energy musculoskeletal system extracorporeal shock wave, consult Category III code 0019T.

●	**0103T**	**Holotranscobalamin, quantitative**
●	**0104T**	**Inert gas rebreathing for cardiac output measurement; during rest**

- **0105T** during exercise
- **0106T** Quantitative sensory testing (QST), testing and interpretation per extremity; using touch pressure stimuli to assess large diameter sensation
- **0107T** using vibration stimuli to assess large diameter fiber sensation
- **0108T** using cooling stimuli to assess small nerve fiber sensation and hyperalgesia
- **0109T** using heat-pain stimuli to assess small nerve fiber sensation and hyperalgesia
- **0110T** using other stimuli to assess sensation
- **0111T** Long-chain (C20-22) omega-3 fatty acids in red blood cell (RBC) membranes

  To report very long chain fatty acids, consult CPT code 82726.

- **0115T** Medication therapy management service(s) provided by a pharmacist, individual, face-to-face with patient, initial 15 minutes, with assessment, and intervention if provided; initial encounter
- **0116T** subsequent encounter
+ • **0117T** each additional 15 minutes (List separately in addition to code for primary service)

  Note that 0117T is an add-on code and must be used in conjunction with 0115T, 0116T.

- **0120T** Ablation, cryosurgical, of fibroadenoma, including ultrasound guidance, each fibroadenoma

  Code 0120T cannot be used with 90772.

- **0123T** Fistulization of sclera for glaucoma, through ciliary body
- **0124T** Conjunctival incision with posterior juxtascleral placement of pharmacological agent (does not include supply of medication)
- **0126T** Common carotid intima-media thickness (IMT) study for evaluation of atherosclerotic burden or coronary heart disease risk factor assessment
- **0130T** Validated, statistically reliable, randomized, controlled, single-patient clinical investigation of FDA approved chronic care drugs, provided by a pharmacist, interpretation and report to the prescribing health care professional
- **0133T** Upper gastrointestinal endoscopy, including esophagus, stomach, and either the duodenum and/or jejunum as appropriate, with injection of implant material into and along the muscle of the lower esophageal sphincter (eg, for treatment of gastroesophageal reflux disease)
- **0135T** Ablation, renal tumor(s), unilateral, percutaneous, cryotherapy
- **0137T** Biopsy, prostate, needle, saturation sampling for prostate mapping

  Code 0137T cannot be used with 76942.

UNPUBLISHED CODES EFFECTIVE JANUARY 1, 2006

The following codes were announced by the AMA July 1, 2005 for implementation January 1, 2006, but were adopted too late for publication in the AMA's CPT manual. For more information, consult the AMA Web site, www.ama-assn.org. These codes are valid, but unpublished.

- **0140T** Exhaled breath condensate pH
- **0141T** Pancreatic islet cell transplantation through portal vein, percutaneous
- **0142T** Pancreatic islet cell transplantation through portal vein, open
- **0143T** Laparoscopy, surgical, pancreatic islet cell transplantation through portal vein

0105T — 0143T

- **0144T**   Computed tomography, heart, without contrast material, including image post processing and quantitative evaluation of coronary calcium

- **0145T**   Computed tomography, heart, without contrast material followed by contrast material(s) and further sections, including cardiac gating and 3D image post processing; cardiac structure and morphology

- **0146T**   Computed tomographic angiography of coronary arteries (including native and anomalous coronary arteries, coronary bypass grafts), without quantitative evaluation of coronary calcium

- **0147T**   Computed tomographic angiography of coronary arteries (including native and anomalous coronary arteries, coronary bypass grafts), with quantitative evaluation of coronary calcium

- **0148T**   Cardiac structure and morphology and computed tomographic angiography of coronary arteries (including native and anomalous coronary arteries, coronary bypass grafts), without quantitative evaluation of coronary calcium

- **0149T**   Cardiac structure and morphology and computed tomographic angiography of coronary arteries (including native and anomalous coronary arteries, coronary bypass grafts), with quantitative evaluation of coronary calcium

- **0150T**   Cardiac structure and morphology in congenital heart disease

- **0151T**   Computed tomography, heart, without contrast material followed by contrast material(s) and further sections, including cardiac gating and 3D image post processing; function evaluation (left and right ventricular function, ejection fraction and segmental wall motion)

- **0152T**   Computer aided detection (computer algorithm analysis of digital image data for lesion detection) with further physician review for interpretation, with or without digitization of film radiographic images; chest radiograph(s) (List separately in addition to code for primary procedure)

- **0153T**   Transcatheter placement of wireless physiologic sensor in aneurysmal sac during endovascular repair, including radiological supervision and interpretation and instrument calibration

- **0154T**   Non-invasive physiologic study of implanted wireless pressure sensor in aneurysmal sac following endovascular repair, complete study including recording, analysis of pressure and waveform tracings, interpretation and report

APPENDIX A — MODIFIERS

CPT MODIFIERS

This list includes all of the modifiers applicable to CPT codes.

21 Prolonged Evaluation and Management Services: When the face-to-face or floor/unit service(s) provided is prolonged or otherwise greater than that usually required for the highest level of evaluation and management service within a given category, it may be identified by adding modifier 21 to the evaluation and management code number. A report may also be appropriate.

22 Unusual Procedural Services: When the service(s) provided is greater than that usually required for the listed procedure, it may be identified by adding modifier 22 to the usual procedure number. A report may also be appropriate.

23 Unusual Anesthesia: Occasionally, a procedure, which usually requires either no anesthesia or local anesthesia, because of unusual circumstances must be done under general anesthesia. This circumstance may be reported by adding modifier 23 to the procedure code of the basic service.

24 Unrelated Evaluation and Management Service by the Same Physician During a Postoperative Period: The physician may need to indicate that an evaluation and management service was performed during a postoperative period for a reason(s) unrelated to the original procedure. This circumstance may be reported by adding modifier 24 to the appropriate level of E/M service.

25 Significant, Separately Identifiable Evaluation and Management Service by the Same Physician on the Same Day of the Procedure or Other Service: The physician may need to indicate that on the day a procedure or service identified by a CPT code was performed, the patient's condition required a significant, separately identifiable E/M service above and beyond the other service provided or beyond the usual preoperative and postoperative care associated with the procedure that was performed. A significant, separately identifiable E/M service is defined or substantiated by documentation that satisfies the relevant criteria for the respective E/M wervices to be reported (*see* **Evaluation and Management Services Guidelines** for instructions on determining level of E/M service.) The E/M service may be prompted by the symptom or condition for which the procedure and/or service was provided. As such, different diagnoses are not required for reporting of the E/M services on the same date. This circumstance may be reported by adding modifier 25 to the appropriate level of E/M service. **Note:** This modifier is not used to report an E/M service that resulted in a decision to perform surgery. See modifier 57.

26 Professional Component: Certain procedures are a combination of a physician component and a technical component. When the physician component is reported separately, the service may be identified by adding modifier 26 to the usual procedure number.

32 Mandated Services: Services related to mandated consultation and/or related services (eg, PRO, third party payer, governmental, legislative, or regulatory requirement) may be identified by adding modifier 32 to the basic procedure.

47 Anesthesia by Surgeon: Regional or general anesthesia provided by the surgeon may be reported by adding modifier 47 to the basic service. (This does not include local anesthesia.) **Note:** Modifier 47 would not be used as a modifier for the anesthesia procedures 00100-01999.

50 Bilateral Procedure: Unless otherwise identified in the listings, bilateral procedures that are performed at the same operative session should be identified by adding modifier 50 to the appropriate five digit code.

51 Multiple Procedures: When multiple procedures, other than Evaluation and Management Services, are performed at the same session by the same provider, the primary procedure or service may be reported as listed. The additional procedure(s) or service(s) may be identified by appending modifier 51 to the additional procedure or service code(s). **Note:** This modifier should not be appended to designated "add-on" codes.

52 Reduced Services: Under certain circumstances a service or procedure is partially reduced or eliminated at the physician's discretion. Under these circumstances the service provided can be identified by its usual procedure number and the addition of modifier 52, signifying that the service is reduced. This provides a means of reporting reduced services without disturbing the identification of the basic service. **Note:** For hospital outpatient reporting of a previously scheduled procedure/service that is partially reduced or cancelled as a result of extenuating circumstances or those that threaten the well-being of the patient prior to or after administration of anesthesia, see modifiers 73 and 74 (see modifiers approved for ASC hospital outpatient use).

53   Discontinued Procedure: Under certain circumstances, the physician may elect to terminate a surgical or diagnostic procedure. Due to extenuating circumstances or those that threaten the well being of the patient, it may be necessary to indicate that a surgical or diagnostic procedure was started but discontinued. This circumstance may be reported by adding modifier 53 to the code reported by the physician for the discontinued procedure. **Note:** This modifier is not used to report the elective cancellation of a procedure prior to the patient's anesthesia induction and/or surgical preparation in the operating suite. For outpatient hospital/ambulatory surgery center (ASC) reporting of a previously scheduled procedure/service that is partially reduced or cancelled as a result of extenuating circumstances or those that threaten the well being of the patient prior to or after administration of anesthesia, see modifiers 73 and 74 (see modifiers approved for ASC hospital outpatient use).

54   Surgical Care Only: When one physician performs a surgical procedure and another provides preoperative and/or postoperative management, surgical services may be identified by adding modifier 54 to the usual procedure number.

55   Postoperative Management Only: When one physician performs the postoperative management and another physician has performed the surgical procedure, the postoperative component may be identified by adding modifier 55 to the usual procedure number.

56   Preoperative Management Only: When one physician performs the preoperative care and evaluation and another physician performs the surgical procedure, the preoperative component may be identified by adding modifier 56 to the usual procedure number.

57   Decision for Surgery: An evaluation and management service that resulted in the initial decision to perform the surgery may be identified by adding modifier 57 to the appropriate level of E/M service.

58   Staged or Related Procedure or Service by the Same Physician During the Postoperative Period: The physician may need to indicate that the performance of a procedure or service during the postoperative period was: a) planned prospectively at the time of the original procedure (staged); b) more extensive than the original procedure; or c) for therapy following a diagnostic surgical procedure. This circumstance may be reported by adding modifier 58 to the staged or related procedure. **Note:** This modifier is not used to report the treatment of a problem that requires a return to the operating room. See modifier 78.

59   Distinct Procedural Service: Under certain circumstances, the physician may need to indicate that a procedure or service was distinct or independent from other services performed on the same day. Modifier 59 is used to identify procedures/services that are not normally reported together, but are appropriate under the circumstances. This may represent a different session or patient encounter, different procedure or surgery, different site or organ system, separate incision/excision, separate lesion, or separate injury (or area of injury in extensive injuries) not ordinarily encountered or performed on the same day by the same physician. However, when another already established modifier is appropriate it should be used rather than modifier 59. Only if no more descriptive modifier is available, and the use of modifier 59 best explains the circumstances, should modifier 59 be used.

62   Two Surgeons: When two surgeons work together as primary surgeons performing distinct part(s) of a procedure, each surgeon should report his/her distinct operative work by adding modifier 62 to the procedure code and any associated add-on code(s) for that procedure as long as both surgeons continue to work together as primary surgeons. Each surgeon should report the co-surgery once using the same procedure code. If an additional procedure(s) (including an add-on procedure(s)) is performed during the same surgical session, a separate code(s) may be reported with the modifier 62 added. **Note:** If a co-surgeon acts as an assistant in the performance of an additional procedure(s) during the same surgical session, the service(s) may be reported using a separate procedure code(s) with modifier 80 or modifier 82 added, as appropriate.

63   Procedure Performed on Infants less than 4 kg: Procedures performed on neonates and infants up to a present body weight of 4 kg may involve significantly increased complexity and physician work commonly associated with these patients. This circumstance may be reported by adding the modifier 63 to the procedure number. **Note:** Unless otherwise designated, this modifier may only be appended to procedures/services listed in the 20000-69999 code series. Modifier 63 should not be appended to any CPT codes in the E/M, Anesthesia, Radiology, Pathology/Laboratory or Medicine sections.

66 Surgical Team: Under some circumstances, highly complex procedures (requiring the concomitant services of several physicians, often of different specialties, plus other highly skilled, specially trained personnel, various types of complex equipment) are carried out under the "surgical team" concept. Such circumstances may be identified by each participating physician with the addition of modifier 66 to the basic procedure number used for reporting services.

76 Repeat Procedure by Same Physician: The physician may need to indicate that a procedure or service was repeated subsequent to the original procedure or service. This circumstance may be reported by adding modifier 76 to the repeated procedure/service.

77 Repeat Procedure by Another Physician: The physician may need to indicate that a basic procedure or service performed by another physician had to be repeated. This situation may be reported by adding modifier 77 to the repeated procedure/service.

78 Return to the Operating Room for a Related Procedure During the Postoperative Period: The physician may need to indicate that another procedure was performed during the postoperative period of the initial procedure. When this subsequent procedure is related to the first, and requires the use of the operating room, it may be reported by adding modifier 78 to the related procedure. (For repeat procedures on the same day, see modifier 76.)

79 Unrelated Procedure or Service by the Same Physician During the Postoperative Period: The physician may need to indicate that the performance of a procedure or service during the postoperative period was unrelated to the original procedure. This circumstance may be reported by using modifier 79. (For repeat procedures on the same day, see modifier 76.)

80 Assistant Surgeon: Surgical assistant services may be identified by adding modifier 80 to the usual procedure number(s).

81 Minimum Assistant Surgeon: Minimum surgical assistant services are identified by adding modifier 81 to the usual procedure number.

82 Assistant Surgeon (when qualified resident surgeon not available): The unavailability of a qualified resident surgeon is a prerequisite for use of modifier 82 appended to the usual procedure code number(s).

90 Reference (Outside) Laboratory: When laboratory procedures are performed by a party other than the treating or reporting physician, the procedure may be identified by adding modifier 90 to the usual procedure number.

91 Repeat Clinical Diagnostic Laboratory Test: In the course of treatment of the patient, it may be necessary to repeat the same laboratory test on the same day to obtain subsequent (multiple) test results. Under these circumstances, the laboratory test performed can be identified by its usual procedure number and the addition of modifier 91. **Note:** This modifier may not be used when tests are rerun to confirm initial results; due to testing problems with specimens or equipment; or for any other reason when a normal, one-time, reportable result is all that is required. This modifier may not be used when another code(s) describes a series of test results (eg, glucose tolerance tests, evocative/suppression testing). This modifier may only be used for a laboratory test(s) performed more than once on the same day on the same patient.

99 Multiple Modifiers: Under certain circumstances two or more modifiers may be necessary to completely delineate a service. In such situations, modifier 99 should be added to the basic procedure and other applicable modifiers may be listed as part of the description of the service.

ANESTHESIA PHYSICAL STATUS MODIFIERS

All anesthesia services are reported by use of the five-digit anesthesia procedure code with the appropriate physical status modifier appended.

P1 A normal healthy patient

P2 A patient with mild systemic disease

P3 A patient with severe systemic disease

P4 A patient with severe systemic disease that is a constant threat to life

P5 A moribund patient who is not expected to survive without the operation

P6 A declared brain-dead patient whose organs are being removed for donor purposes

MODIFIERS APPROVED FOR AMBULATORY SURGERY CENTER (ASC) HOSPITAL OUTPATIENT USE

CPT LEVEL I MODIFIERS

25 **Significant, Separately Identifiable Evaluation and Management Service by the Same Physician on the Same Day of the Procedure or Other Service:** The physician may need to indicate that on the day a procedure or service identified by a CPT code was performed, the patient's condition required a significant, separately identifiable E/M service above and beyond the other service provided or beyond the usual preoperative and postoperative care associated with the procedure that was performed. A significant, separately identifiable E/M service is defined or substantiated by documentationthat satisfies the relevant criteria for the respective E/M wervices to be reported (*see* **Evaluation and Management Services Guidelines** for instructions on determining level of E/M service.) The E/M service may be prompted by the symptom or condition for which the procedure and/or service was provided. As such, different diagnoses are not required for reporting of the E/M services on the same date. This circumstance may be reported by adding modifier 25 to the appropriate level of E/M service. **Note:** This modifier is not used to report an E/M service that resulted in a decision to perform surgery. See modifier 57.

27 **Multiple Outpatient Hospital E/M Encounters on the Same Date:** For hospital outpatient reporting purposes, utilization of hospital resources related to separate and distinct E/M encounters performed in multiple outpatient hospital settings on the same date may be reported by adding modifier 27 to each appropriate level outpatient and/or emergency department E/M code(s). This modifier provides a means of reporting circumstances involving evaluation and management services provided by a physician(s) in more than one (multiple) outpatient hospital setting(s) (eg, hospital emergency department, clinic). **Note:** This modifier is not to be used for physician reporting of multiple E/M services performed by the same physician on the same date. For physician reporting of all outpatient evaluation and management services provided by the same physician on the same date and performed in multiple outpatient settings (eg, hospital emergency department, clinic), see Evaluation and Management, Emergency Department, or Preventive Medicine Services codes.

50 **Bilateral Procedure:** Unless otherwise identified in the listings, bilateral procedures that are performed at the same operative session should be identified by adding modifier 50 to the appropriate five digit code.

52 **Reduced Services:** Under certain circumstances a service or procedure is partially reduced or eliminated at the physician's discretion. Under these circumstances the service provided can be identified by its usual procedure number and the addition of modifier 52, signifying that the service is reduced. This provides a means of reporting reduced services without disturbing the identification of the basic service. **Note:** For hospital outpatient reporting of a previously scheduled procedure/service that is partially reduced or cancelled as a result of extenuating circumstances or those that threaten the well-being of the patient prior to or after administration of anesthesia, see modifiers 73 and 74 (see modifiers approved for ASC hospital outpatient use).

58 **Staged or Related Procedure or Service by the Same Physician During the Postoperative Period:** The physician may need to indicate that the performance of a procedure or service during the postoperative period was: a) planned prospectively at the time of the original procedure (staged); b) more extensive than the original procedure; or c) for therapy following a diagnostic surgical procedure. This circumstance may be reported by adding modifier 58 to the staged or related procedure. **Note:** This modifier is not used to report the treatment of a problem that requires a return to the operating room. See modifier 78.

59 **Distinct Procedural Service:** Under certain circumstances, the physician may need to indicate that a procedure or service was distinct or independent from other services performed on the same day. Modifier 59 is used to identify procedures/services that are not normally reported together, but are appropriate under the circumstances. This may represent a different session or patient encounter, different procedure or surgery, different site or organ system, separate incision/excision, separate lesion, or separate injury (or area of injury in extensive injuries) not ordinarily encountered or performed on the same day by the same physician. However, when another already established modifier is appropriate it should be used rather than modifier 59. Only if no more descriptive modifier is available, and the use of modifier 59 best explains the circumstances, should modifier 59 be used.

73 **Discontinued Out-Patient Hospital/Ambulatory Surgery Center (ASC) Procedure Prior to the Administration of Anesthesia:** Due to extenuating circumstances or those that threaten the well being of the patient, the physician may cancel a surgical or diagnostic procedure subsequent to the patient's surgical preparation (including sedation when provided, and being taken to the room where the procedure is to be performed), but prior to the administration of anesthesia (local, regional block(s), or general). Under these circumstances, the intended service that is prepared for but cancelled can be reported by its usual procedure number and the addition of modifier 73. **Note:** The elective cancellation of a service prior to the administration of anesthesia and/or surgical preparation of the patient should not be reported. For physician reporting of a discontinued procedure, see modifier 53.

74 **Discontinued Out-Patient Hospital/Ambulatory Surgery Center (ASC) Procedure After Administration of Anesthesia:** Due to extenuating circumstances or those that threaten the well being of the patient, the physician may terminate a surgical or diagnostic procedure after the administration of anesthesia (local, regional block(s), general) or after the procedure was started (incision made, intubation started, scope inserted, etc.). Under these circumstances, the procedure started but terminated can be reported by its usual procedure number and the addition of modifier 74. **Note:** The elective cancellation of a service prior to the administration of anesthesia and/or surgical preparation of the patient should not be reported. For physician reporting of a discontinued procedure, see modifier 53.

76 **Repeat Procedure by Same Physician:** The physician may need to indicate that a procedure or service was repeated subsequent to the original procedure or service. This circumstance may be reported by adding modifier 76 to the repeated procedure/service.

77 **Repeat Procedure by Another Physician:** The physician may need to indicate that a basic procedure or service performed by another physician had to be repeated. This situation may be reported by adding modifier 77 to the repeated procedure/service.

78 **Return to the Operating Room for a Related Procedure During the**

Postoperative Period: The physician may need to indicate that another procedure was performed during the postoperative period of the initial procedure. When this subsequent procedure is related to the first, and requires the use of the operating room, it may be reported by adding modifier 78 to the related procedure. (For repeat procedures on the same day, see modifier 76.)

79 **Unrelated Procedure or Service by the Same Physician During the Postoperative Period:** The physician may need to indicate that the performance of a procedure or service during the postoperative period was unrelated to the original procedure. This circumstance may be reported by using modifier 79. (For repeat procedures on the same day, see modifier 76.)

91 **Repeat Clinical Diagnostic Laboratory Test:** In the course of treatment of the patient, it may be necessary to repeat the same laboratory test on the same day to obtain subsequent (multiple) test results. Under these circumstances, the laboratory test performed can be identified by its usual procedure number and the addition of modifier 91. **Note:** This modifier may not be used when tests are rerun to confirm initial results; due to testing problems with specimens or equipment; or for any other reason when a normal, one-time, reportable result is all that is required. This modifier may not be used when another code(s) describe a series of test results (eg, glucose tolerance tests, evocative/suppression testing). This modifier may only be used for a laboratory test(s) performed more than once on the same day on the same patient.

LEVEL II (HCPCS/NATIONAL) MODIFIERS

ANATOMICAL MODIFIERS

E1	Upper left, eyelid
E2	Lower left, eyelid
E3	Upper right, eyelid
E4	Lower right, eyelid
F1	Left hand, second digit
F2	Left hand, third digit
F3	Left hand, fourth digit
F4	Left hand, fifth digit
F5	Right hand, thumb
F6	Right hand, second digit
F7	Right hand, third digit
F8	Right hand, fourth digit
F9	Right hand, fifth digit

FA Left hand, thumb

LT Left side (used to identify procedures performed on the left side of the body)

RT Right side (used to identify procedures performed on the right side of the body)

T1 Left foot, second digit

T2 Left foot, third digit

T3 Left foot, fourth digit

T4 Left foot, fifth digit

T5 Right foot, great toe

T6 Right foot, second digit

T7 Right foot, third digit

T8 Right foot, fourth digit

T9 Right foot, fifth digit

TA Left foot, great toe

AMBULANCE MODIFIERS

GM Multiple patients on one ambulance trip

QM Ambulance service provided under arrangement by a provider of services

QN Ambulance service furnished directly by a provider of services

QL Patient pronounced dead after ambulance called

ANESTHESIA MODIFIERS

AA Anesthesia services performed personally by anesthesiologist

AD Medical supervision by a physician: more than four concurrent anesthesia procedures

G8 Monitored anesthesia care (MAC) for deep complex, complicated, or markedly invasive surgical procedure

G9 Monitored anesthesia care for patient who has history of severe cardio-pulmonary condition

QK Medical direction of two, three, or four concurrent anesthesia procedures involving qualified individuals

QS Monitored anesthesia care service

QY Medical direction of one certified registered nurse anesthetist (CRNA) by an anesthesiologist

QZ CRNA service: without medical direction by a physician

P1 A normal healthy patient

P2 A patient with mild systemic disease

P3 A patient with severe systemic disease

P4 A patient with severe systemic disease that is a constant threat to life

P5 A moribund patient who is not expected to survive without the operation

P6 A declared brain-dead patient whose organs are being removed for donor purposes

CORONARY ARTERY MODIFIERS

LC Left circumflex coronary artery (Hospitals use with codes 92980-92984, 92995, 92996)

LD Left anterior descending coronary artery (Hospitals use with codes 92980-92984, 92995, 92996)

RC Right coronary artery (Hospitals use with codes 92980-92984, 92995, 92996)

OPHTHALMOLOGY MODIFIERS

AP Determination of refractive state was not performed in the course of diagnostic ophthalmological examination

LS FDA-monitored intraocular lens implant

PL Progressive addition lenses

VP Aphakic patient

PROFESSIONAL SERVICES

AE Registered dietician

AF Specialty physician

AG Primary physician

AH Clinical psychologist

AJ Clinical social worker

AK Non participating physician

AM Physician, team member service

AQ Physician providing a service in an unlisted health professional shortage area (HPSA)

AR Physician provider services in a physician scarcity area

AS Physician assistant, nurse practitioner, or clinical nurse specialist services for assistant at surgery

AT Acute treatment (this modifier should be used when reporting service 98940, 98941, 98942)

CA Procedure payable only in the inpatient setting when performed emergently on an outpatient who expires prior to admission

CB Service ordered by a renal dialysis facility (RDF) physician as part of the esrd beneficiary's dialysis benefit, is not part of the composite rate, and is separately reimbursable

CC Procedure code change (use 'CC' when the procedure code submitted was changed either for administrative reasons or because an incorrect code was filed)

CG Innovator drug dispensed

CR Catastrophe/disaster related

EP	Service provided as part of medicaid early periodic screening diagnosis and treatment (EPSDT) program	GV	Attending physician not employed or paid under arrangement by the patient's hospice provider
ET	Emergency services	GW	Service not related to the hospice patient's terminal condition
FB	Item provided without cost to provider, supplier or practitioner (examples, but not limited to: covered under warranty, replaced due to defect, free samples)	GY	Item or service statutorily excluded or does not meet the definition of any medicare benefit
G7	Pregnancy resulted from rape or incest or pregnancy certified by physician as life threatening	GZ	Item or service expected to be denied as not reasonable and necessary
GA	Waiver of liability statement on file	H9	Court-ordered
GB	Claim being resubmitted for payment because it is no longer covered under a global payment demonstration	HA	Child/adolescent program
		HB	Adult program, non geriatric
		HC	Adult program, geriatric
GC	This service has been performed in part by a resident under the direction of a teaching physician	HD	Pregnant/parenting women's program
		HE	Mental health program
		HF	Substance abuse program
GE	This service has been performed by a resident without the presence of a teaching physician under the primary care exception	HG	Opioid addiction treatment program
		HH	Integrated mental health/substance abuse program
GF	Non-physician (e.g. nurse practitioner (NP), certified registered nurse anaesthetist (CRNA), certified registered nurse (CRN), clinical nurse specialist (CNS), physician assistant (PA)) services in a critical access hospital	HI	Integrated mental health and mental retardation/developmental disabilities program
		HJ	Employee assistance program
		HK	Specialized mental health programs for high-risk populations
GG	Performance and payment of a screening mammogram and diagnostic mammogram on the same patient, same day	HL	Intern
		HM	Less than bachelor degree level
GH	Diagnostic mammogram converted from screening mammogram on same day	HN	Bachelors degree level
		HO	Masters degree level
GJ	"OPT OUT" physician or practitioner emergency or urgent service	HP	Doctoral level
		HQ	Group setting
GK	Actual item/service ordered byphysician, item associated with GA or GZ modifier	HR	Family/couple with client present
		HS	Family/couple without client present
GL	Medically unnecessary upgrade provided instead of standard item, no charge, no advance beneficiary notice (ABN)	HT	Multi-disciplinary team
		HU	Funded by child welfare agency
GN	Service delivered personally by a speech-language pathologist or under an outpatient speech-language pathology plan of care	HV	Funded state addictions agency
		HW	Funded by state mental health agency
GO	Service delivered personally by an occupational therapist or under an outpatient occupational therapy plan of care	HX	Funded by county/local agency
		HY	Funded by juvenile justice agency
		HZ	Funded by criminal justice agency
GP	Service delivered personally by a physical therapist or under an outpatient physical therapy plan of care	KB	Beneficiary requested upgrade for ABN, more than four modifiers identified on claim
GQ	Via asynchronous telecommunications system	KC	Replacement of special power wheelchair interface
GR	This service was performed in whole or in part by a resident in a department of veterans affairs medical center or clinic, supervised in accordance with VA policy	KF	Item designated by FDA as class III device
		KX	Specific required documentation on file
		KZ	New coverage not implemented by managed care
GT	Via interactive audio and video telecommunication systems	Q4	Service for ordering/referring physician qualifies as a service exemption

Q5	Service furnished by a substitute physician under a reciprocal billing arrangement	SY	Persons who are in close contact with member of high-risk population (use only with codes for immunization)
Q6	Service furnished by a locum tenens physician	TC	Technical component. Under certain circumstances, a charge may be made for the technical component alone. Under those circumstances the technical component charge is identified by adding modifier 'TC' to the usual procedure number. Technical component charges are institutional charges and not billed separately by physicians. However, portable x-ray suppliers only bill for technical component and should utilize modifier TC. The charge data from portable x-ray suppliers will then be used to build customary and prevailing profiles.
QJ	Services/items provided to a prisoner or patient in state or local custody, however the state or local government, as applicable, meets the requirements in 42 cfr 411.4 (b)		
QP	Documentation is on file showing that the laboratory test(s) was ordered individually or ordered as a CPT-recognized panel other than automated profile codes 80002-80019, G0058, G0059, and G0060		
QQ	Claim submitted with a written statement of intent		
QR	Repeat laboratory test performed on the same day	TD	RN
QS	Monitored anesthesia care service	TE	LPN/LVN
QV	Item or service provided as routine care in a Medicare qualifying clinical trial	TF	Intermediate level of care
		TG	Complex/high level of care
QW	CLIA waived test	TH	Obstetrical treatment/services, prenatal or postpartum
QX	CRNA service: with medical direction by a physician	TJ	Program group, child and/or adolescent
QY	Medical direction of one certified registered nurse anesthetist (CRNA) by an anesthesiologist	TL	Early intervention/individualized family service plan (IFSP)
		TM	Individualized education program (IEP)
QZ	CRNA service: without medical direction by a physician	TN	Rural/outside providers' customary service area
SA	Nurse practitioner rendering service in collaboration with a physician	TP	Medical transport, unloaded vehicle
		TQ	Basic life support transport by a volunteer ambulance provider
SB	Nurse Midwife		
SC	Medically necessary service or supply	TS	Follow-up service
SD	Services provided by registered nurse with specialized, highly technical home infusion training	TT	Individualized service provided to more than one patient in same setting
		TU	Special payment rate, overtime
SE	State and/or federally funded programs/services	TV	Special payment rates, holidays/weekends
		U1	Medicaid level of care 1, as defined by each state
SG	Ambulatory surgical center (ASC) facility service	U2	Medicaid level of care 2, as defined by each state
SH	Second concurrently administered infusion therapy	U3	Medicaid level of care 3, as defined by each state
SJ	Third or more concurrently administered infusion therapy	U4	Medicaid level of care 4, as defined by each state
SK	Member of high risk population (use only with codes for immunization)	U5	Medicaid level of care 5, as defined by each state
SL	State supplied vaccine	U6	Medicaid level of care 6, as defined by each state
SM	Second surgical opinion		
SN	Third surgical opinion	U7	Medicaid level of care 7, as defined by each state
SQ	Item ordered by home health		
ST	Related to trauma or injury	U8	Medicaid level of care 8, as defined by each state
SU	Procedure performed in physician's office (to denote use of facility and equipment)		
SW	Services provided by a certified diabetic educator	U9	Medicaid level of care 9, as defined by each state

UA	Medicaid level of care 10, as defined by each state	0	Neoplasia (solid tumor, excluding sarcoma and lymphoma)
UB	Medicaid level of care 11, as defined by each state	1	Neoplasia (sarcoma)
UC	Medicaid level of care 12, as defined by each state	2	Neoplasia (lymphoid/hematopoietic)
		3	Non-neoplastic hematology/coagulation
UD	Medicaid level of care 13, as defined by each state	4	Histocompatibility/blood typing/identity/micorsatellite
UF	Services provided in the morning	5	Neurologic, non-neoplastic
UG	Services provided in the afternoon	6	Muscular, non-neoplastic
UH	Services provided in the evening	7	Metabolic, other
UJ	Services provided at night	8	Metabolic, transport
UK	Services provided on behalf of the client to someone other than the client (collateral relationship)	9	Metabolic-pharmacogenetics (9A-9L)
		9	Dysmorphology (9M-9Z)

The modifiers are:

UN	Two patients served
UP	Three patients served
UQ	Four patients served
UR	Five patients served
US	Six or more patients served

ESRD MODIFIERS

EJ	Subsequent claims for a defined course of therapy, e.g., EPO, sodium hyaluronate, infliximab
EM	Emergency reserve supply (for ESRD benefit only)
G1	Most recent urea reduction ratio (URR) reading of less than 60
G2	Most recent urea reduction ration (URR) reading of 60 to 64.9
G3	Most recent urea reduction ratio (URR) reading of 65 to 69.9
G4	Most recent urea reduction ratio (URR) reading of 70 to 74.9
G5	Most recent urea reduction ratio (URR) reading of 75 or greater
G6	ESRD patient for whom less than six dialysis sessions have been provided in a month
GS	Dosage of EPO or darbepoietin alfa has been reduced 25% of preceeding month's dosage
Q3	Live kidney donor: services associated with postoperative medical complications directly related to the donation

DENTAL MODIFIERS

ET	Emergency services (dental procedures performed in emergency situations should show the modifier 'ET')

GENETIC TESTING MODIFIERS

The ten disease categories are:

0A	BRCA1 (Hereditary breast/ovarian cancer)
0B	BRCA1 (Hereditary breast cancer)
0C	Neurofibromin (Neurofibromatosis, type 1)
0D	Merlin (Neurofibromatosis, type 2)
0E	c-RET (Multiple endocrine neoplasia, types 2A/B, familial medullary thyroid carcinoma)
0F	VHL (Von Hippel Lindau disease)
0G	SDHD (Hereditary paraganglioma)
0H	SDHB (Hereditary paraganglioma)
0I	ERRB2, commonly called Her-2/neu
0J	MLH1 (HNPCC mismatch repair genes)
0K	MSH2, MSH6, or PMS2 (HNPCC, mismatch repair genes)
0L	APC (Hereditary polyposis coli)
0M	Rb (Retinoblastoma)
0N	TP53, commonly called p53
0O	PTEN (Cowden's syndrome0
0P	KIT, also called CD 117 (gastrointestinal stromal tumor)
0Z	Solid tumor gene, not otherwise specified
1A	WT1 or WT2 (Wilm's tumor)
1B	PAX3, PAX7, or FOXO1A (Alveolar rhabdomyosarcoma)
1C	FLI1, ERG, ETV1, or EWSR1 (Ewing's sarcoma, desmoplastic round cell)
1D	DDIT3 or FUS (Myxoid liposarcoma)
1E	NR4A3, RBF56, or TCF12 (Myxoid chondrosarcoma)
1F	SSX1, SSX2, or SYT (Synovial sarcoma)
1G	MYCN (Neuroblastoma)
1H	COL1A1 or PDGFB (Dermatofibrosarcoma protuberans)
1I	TFE3 or ASPSCR1 (Alveolar soft parts sarcoma)
1J	JAZF1 or JJAZ1 (Endometrial stromal sarcoma)

1Z	Solid tumor, not otherwise specified
2A	RUNX1 or CBFA2T1, commonly called AML1 or ETO, (genes associated with t(8;21) AML1–also ETO (Acute myeloid leukemia)
2B	BCR–also ABL, genes associated with t(9;22) (Chronic myelogenous or acute leukemia)_ BCR—also ABL (Chronic myeloid, acute lymphoid leukemia)
2C	PBX1 or TCF3, genes associated with t(1;19) (Acaute lymphoblastic leukemia)CGF-1
2D	CBFB or MYH11, genes associated with inv 16 (AQcute myelogenous leukemia)CBF beta (Leukemia)
2E	MML (Leukemia)
2F	PML or RARAgenes associated with t(15;17) (Acute promyelocytic leukemia)PML/RAR alpha (Promyelocytic leukemia)
2G	ETV6, commonly called TEL, gene associated with t(12;210 (acute leukemia)TEL (Leukemia)
2H	BCL2 (B cell lymphoma, follicle center cell origin) bcl-2 (Lymphoma)
2I	CCND1, commonly called BCL1, cyclin D1 (Mantle cell lymphoma, myeloma) bcl-1 (Lymphoma)
2J	MYC (Burkitt lymphoma) c-myc (Lymphoma)
2K	IgH (Lymphoma/leukemia)
2L	IGK (Lymphoma/leukemia)
2M	TRB, T cell receptor beta (Lymphoma/leukemia)
2N	TRG, T cell receptor gamma (Lymphoma/leukemia)
2O	SIL or TAL1 (T cell leukemia)
2T	BCL6 (B cell lymphoma)
2Q	API1 or MALT1 (MALT lymphoma)
2R	NPM or ALK, genes associated with t(2;5)
2S	FLT3 (Acute myelogenous leukemia)
2Z	Lymphoid/hematopoetic neoplasia, not otherwise specified
3A	F5, commonly called Factor V (Leiden, others) (Hypercoagulable state)
3B	FACC (Fanconi anemia)
3C	FACD (Fanconi anemia)
3D	HBB, Beta globin (Thalassemia, Sickle cell anemia, other hemoglobinopathies)
3E	HBA, commonly called alpha globin (thalassemia)
3F	MTHFR (Elevated homocysteine)
3G	F2, commonly called prothrombin (20210, others) (Hypercoagulable state)Prothrombin (Factor II, 20210A) (Hypercoagulable state)
3H	F8, commonly called Factor VII (Hemophilia A/VWF)
3I	F9, commonly called Factor IX (Hemophilia B)
3K	F13, commonly called Factor XII (bleeding or hypercoagulable state) Beta globin
3Z	Non-neoplastic hematology/coagulation, not otherwise specified
4A	HLA-A
4B	HLA-B
4C	HLA-C
4D	HLA-D
4E	HLA-DR
4F	HLA-DQ
4G	HLA-DP
4H	Kell
4I	Fingerprint for engraftment (post-allogenic progenitor cell transplant)
4J	Fingerprint for donor allelotype (allogeneic transplant)
4K	Fingerprint for recipient allelotype (allogeneic transplant)
4L	fingerprint for leukocyte chimerism (allogeneic solid organ transplant)
4M	fingerprint for maternal versus fetal origin
4N	Microsatellite instability
4O	Microsatelite loss (loss of heterozygosity)
4Z	Histocompatibility/blood typing, not otherwise specified
5A	ASPA, commonly calledAspartoacylase A (Canavan disease)
5B	FMR-1 (Fragile X, FRAXA, syndrome)
5C	FRDA, commonly calledFrataxin (Freidreich's ataxia)
5D	HD, commonly called Huntington (Huntington's disease)
5E	GABRA, NIPA1, UBE3A, or ANCR GABRA (Prader Willi-Angelman syndrome)
5F	GJB2, commonly called Connexin-26 (Hereditary hearing loss) Connexin-26 (GJB2) (Hereditary deafness)
5G	GJB1, commonly calledConnexin-32 (X-linked Charcot-Marie-Tooth disease)
5H	SNRPN (Prader Willi-Angelman syndrome)
5I	SCA1, commonly called Ataxin-1 (Spinocerebellar ataxia, type 1)
5J	SCA2, commonly calledAtaxin-2 (Spinocerebellar ataxia, type 2)
5K	MJD, commonly called Ataxin-3 (Spinocerebellar ataxia, type 3, Machado-Joseph disease)
5L	CACNA1A (Spinocerebellar ataxia, type 6)
5M	ATXN7 Ataxin-7 (Spinocerebellar ataxia, type 7)

5N	PMP-22 (Charcot-Marie-Tooth disease, type 1A)	7Z	Metabolic, other, not otherwise specified
5O	MECP1 (Rett syndrome)	8A	CFTR (Cystic fibrosis)
5Z	Neurologic, non-neoplastic, not otherwise specified	8B	PRSS1 (Hereditary pancreatitis)
		8Z	Metabolic, transport, not otherwise specified)
6A	DMD, commonly called Dystrophin (Duchenne/Becker muscular dystrophy)	9A	TPMT (thiopurine methyltransferase) (patients on antimetabolite therapy)
6B	DMPK (Myotonic dystrophy, type 1)	9B	CYP2 genes, commonly called cytochrome p450 (drug metabolism)
6C	ZNF-9 (Myotonic dystrophy, type 2)		
6D	SMN1/SMN2 (Autosomal recessive spinal muscular atrophy)	9C	ABCB1, commonly called MDR1 or p-glycoprotein (drug transport)
6E	MTTK, commonly called tRNAlys (mytonic epilepsy, MERRF)	9D	NAT2 (drug metabolism)
		9L	Metabolic-pharmacogenetics, not otherwise specified
6F	MTTL1, commonly called tRNAleu (mitochondrial encephalomyopathy, MELAS)	9M	FGFR-1 (Pfeiffer and Kallmann syndromes)
6Z	Muscular, not otherwise specified	9N	FGFR2 (Crouzon, Jackson-Weiss, Apert, Saethre-Chotzen syndromes)
7A	APOE, commonly calledApolipoprotein E (Cardiovascular disease, Alzheimer's disease)	9O	FGFR3 (Achondroplasia, Hypochondroplasia, Thanatophoric dysplasia, types I and II, Crouzon syndrome with acanthosis nigricans, Muencke syndromes)
7B	NPC1 or NPC2, commonly called sphingomyelin phosphodiesterase (Nieman-Pick disease)		
7C	GBA, commonly called Acid Beta Glucosidase (Gaucher disease)	9P	TWIST (Saethre-Chotzen syndrome)
7D	HFE (Hemochromatosis)	9Q	DCGR, commonly called CATCH-22 (22q11 deletion syndromes)
7E	HEXA, commonly called Hexosaminidase A (Tay-Sachs disease)	9Z	Dysmorphology, not otherwise specified
7F	ACADM (medium chain acyl CoA dhydrogenase deficiency)		

APPENDIX B — NEW, CHANGED, DELETED, AND MODIFIED CODES

NEW CODES

0001F	0005F	0089T	0090T
0091T	0092T	0093T	0094T
0095T	0096T	0097T	0098T
0099T	0100T	0101T	0102T
0103T	0104T	0105T	0106T
0107T	0108T	0109T	0110T
0111T	0115T	0116T	0117T
0120T	0123T	0124T	0126T
0130T	0133T	0135T	0137T
0140T	0141T	0142T	0143T
0144T	0145T	0146T	0147T
0148T	0149T	0150T	0151T
0152T	0153T	0154T	01965
01966	1003F	1004F	1005F
1006F	1007F	1008F	15040
15110	15111	15115	15116
15130	15131	15135	15136
15150	15151	15152	15155
15156	15157	15170	15171
15175	15176	15300	15301
15320	15321	15330	15331
15335	15336	15340	15341
15360	15361	15365	15366
15420	15421	15430	15431
2001F	2002F	2003F	2004F
22010	22015	22523	22524
22525	28890	3000F	3002F
32503	32504	33507	33548
33768	33880	33881	33883
33884	33886	33889	33891
33925	33926	36598	37184
37185	37186	37187	37188
37718	37722	4003F	4012F
4014F	4015F	4016F	4017F
4018F	43770	43771	43772
43773	43774	43886	43887
43888	44180	44186	44187
44188	44213	44227	45395
45397	45400	45402	45499
45990	46505	46710	46712
50250	50382	50384	50387
50389	50592	51999	57295
58110	61630	61635	61640
61641	61642	64650	64653
75956	75957	75958	75959
76376	76377	77421	77422
77423	80195	82271	82272
83037	83631	83695	83700
83701	83704	83900	83907
83908	83909	83914	86200
86355	86357	86367	86480
86923	86960	87209	87900
88333	88334	88384	88385
88386	89049	90649	90714
90736	90760	90761	90765
90766	90767	90768	90772
90773	90774	90775	90779
91022	92626	92627	92630

92633	95251	95865	95866
95873	95874	96101	96102
96103	96116	96118	96119
96120	96401	96402	96409
96411	96413	96415	96416
96417	96521	96522	96523
97760	97761	97762	98960
98961	98962	99051	99053
99060	99143	99144	99145
99148	99149	99150	99300
99304	99305	99306	99307
99308	99309	99310	99318
99324	99325	99326	99327
99328	99334	99335	99336
99337	99339	99340	

CHANGED CODES

0019T	0078T	11440	11441
11442	11443	11444	11446
15000	15001	15100	15101
15120	15121	15400	15401
16020	16025	16030	28297
30130	30140	30801	30802
30930	31526	31531	31536
31541	31561	31571	33502
33503	33504	33505	33506
34833	34834	37209	4011F
43848	44202	44310	44320
45119	45540	45541	45550
50688	52647	52648	57421
64613	67901	67902	75900
76012	76013	76075	76076
76077	76140	76150	77295
77412	77413	77414	77416
77750	82270	83036	83090
83630	83719	83721	83898
83901	84238	87207	87904
88141	88175	88182	90680
90713	90715	90870	90918
90919	90920	90921	90922
90923	90924	90925	90940
91065	92506	92507	92508
92520	92568	92569	95250
95857	96405	96406	96423
97024	97542	97811	97813
97814	99050	99056	99058
99201	99202	99203	99204
99205	99221	99254	99602

DELETED CODES

0010T	0020T	0023T	0033T
0034T	0035T	0036T	0037T
0038T	0039T	0040T	01964
15342	15343	15350	15351
15810	15811	16010	16015
21493	21494	31585	31586
32520	32522	32525	33918
33919	37720	37730	42325
42326	43638	43639	44200
44201	44239	69410	76375
78160	78162	78170	78172
78455	82273	83715	83716

APPENDIX B

86064	86379	86585	86587
90780	90781	90782	90783
90784	90788	90799	90871
90939	92330	92335	92390
92391	92392	92393	92395
92396	92510	95858	96100
96115	96117	96400	96408
96410	96412	96414	96520
96530	96545	97020	97504
97520	97703	99052	99054
99141	99142	99261	99262
99263	99271	99272	99273
99274	99275	99301	99302
99303	99311	99312	99313
99321	99322	99323	99331
99332	99333		

ADD-ON CODES

0049T	0054T	0055T	0056T
0063T	0068T	0069T	0070T
0076T	0079T	0081T	0092T
0095T	0098T	0117T	01953
01968	01969	11001	11008
11101	11201	11732	11922
13102	13122	13133	13153
15001	15101	15111	15116
15121	15131	15136	15151
15152	15156	15157	15171
15176	15201	15221	15241
15261	15301	15321	15331
15336	15341	15361	15366
15401	15421	15431	15787
16036	17003	17310	19001
19126	19291	19295	19297
22103	22116	22216	22226
22328	22522	22525	22534
22585	22614	22632	26125
26861	26863	27358	27692
31620	31632	31633	31637
32501	33141	33225	33508
33530	33572	33768	33884
33924	33961	34808	34813
34826	35390	35400	35500
35572	35681	35682	35683
35685	35686	35697	35700
36218	36248	36476	36479
37185	37186	37206	37208
37250	37251	38746	38747
43635	44015	44121	44128
44139	44203	44213	44701
44955	47001	47550	48400
49568	49905	56606	57267
58110	58611	59525	60512
61316	61517	61609	61610
61611	61612	61641	61642
61795	61864	61868	62148
62160	63035	63043	63044
63048	63057	63066	63076
63078	63082	63086	63088
63091	63103	63295	63308
64472	64476	64480	64484
64623	64627	64727	64778
64783	64787	64832	64837
64859	64872	64874	64876
64901	64902	66990	67225
67320	67331	67332	67334
67335	67340	69990	74301
75774	75946	75964	75968
75993	75996	75998	76082
76083	76125	76802	76810
76812	76937	78020	78478
78480	78496	83901	87187
87904	88155	88185	88311
88312	88313	88314	90466
90468	90472	90474	90761
90766	90767	90768	90775
90781	92547	92608	92627
92973	92974	92978	92979
92981	92984	92996	92998
93320	93321	93325	93571
93572	93609	93613	93621
93622	93623	93662	95873
95874	95920	95962	95967
95973	95975	95979	96411
96412	96415	96417	96423
96570	96571	97546	97811
97814	99100	99116	99135
99140	99145	99150	99290
99292	99354	99355	99356
99357	99358	99359	99602

MODIFIER 51 EXEMPT CODES

17004	17304	17305	17306
17307	20660	20690	20692
20900	20902	20910	20912
20920	20922	20924	20926
20930	20931	20936	20937
20938	20974	20975	22840
22841	22842	22843	22844
22845	22846	22847	22848
22851	31500	32000	32002
32020	33517	33518	33519
33521	33522	33523	35600
36620	36660	38792	44500
61107	61210	62284	90281
90283	90287	90288	90291
90296	90371	90375	90376
90378	90379	90384	90385
90386	90389	90393	90396
90399	90476	90477	90581
90585	90586	90632	90633
90634	90636	90645	90646
90647	90648	90655	90656
90657	90658	90660	90665
90669	90675	90676	90680
90690	90691	90692	90693
90698	90700	90701	90702
90703	90704	90705	90706
90707	90708	90710	90712
90713	90714	90715	90716
90717	90718	90719	90720
90721	90723	90725	90727
90732	90733	90734	90735
90736	90740	90743	90744

90746	90747	90748	90749
93501	93503	93505	93508
93510	93511	93514	93524
93526	93527	93528	93529
93530	93531	93532	93533
93539	93540	93541	93542
93543	93544	93545	93555
93556	93600	93602	93603
93610	93612	93615	93616
93618	93619	93620	93624
93631	93640	93641	93642
93650	93651	93652	93660
95900	95903	95904	99143
99144	99148	99149	

MODIFIER 63 EXEMPT CODES

30545	31520	33401	33403
33470	33472	33502	33503
33505	33506	33610	33611
33619	33647	33670	33690
33694	33730	33732	33735
33736	33750	33755	33762
33778	33786	33922	33960
33961	36415	36420	36450
36460	36510	36660	39503
43313	43314	43520	43831
44055	44126	44127	44128
46070	46705	46715	46716
46730	46735	46740	46742
46744	47700	47701	49215
49491	49492	49495	49496
49600	49605	49606	49610
49611	53025	54000	54150
54160	63700	63702	63704
63706	65820		

CONSCIOUS SEDATION CODES

0018T	19298	20982	31615
31620	31622	31623	31624
31625	31628	31629	31635
31645	31646	31656	31725
32019	32020	32201	33010
33011	33206	33207	33208
33210	33211	33212	33213
33214	33216	33217	33218
33220	33222	33223	33233
33234	33235	33240	33241
33244	33249	35470	35471
35472	35473	35474	35475
35476	36555	36557	36558
36560	36561	36563	36565
36566	36568	36570	36571

36576	36578	36581	36582
36583	36585	36590	36870
37184	37185	37186	37187
37188	37203	37215	37216
43200	43201	43202	43204
43205	43215	43216	43217
43219	43220	43226	43227
43228	43231	43232	43234
43235	43236	43237	43238
43239	43240	43241	43242
43243	43244	43245	43246
43247	43248	43249	43250
43251	43255	43256	43257
43258	43259	43260	43261
43262	43263	43264	43265
43267	43268	43269	43271
43272	43453	43456	43458
44360	44361	44363	44364
44365	44366	44369	44370
44372	44373	44376	44377
44378	44379	44380	44382
44383	44385	44386	44388
44389	44390	44391	44392
44393	44394	44397	44500
44901	45303	45305	45307
45308	45309	45315	45317
45320	45321	45327	45332
45333	45334	45337	45338
45339	45340	45341	45342
45345	45355	45378	45379
45380	45381	45382	45383
45384	45385	45386	45387
45391	45392	47011	48511
49021	49041	49061	50021
50382	50384	50387	50592
58823	66720	77600	77605
77610	77615	92953	92960
92961	92973	92974	92975
92978	92979	92980	92981
92982	92984	92986	92987
92995	92996	93312	93313
93314	93315	93316	93317
93318	93501	93505	93508
93510	93511	93514	93524
93526	93527	93528	93529
93530	93539	93540	93541
93542	93543	93544	93545
93555	93556	93561	93562
93571	93572	93609	93613
93615	93616	93618	93619
93620	93621	93622	93624
93640	93641	93642	93650
93651	93652		

APPENDIX C — PLACE OF SERVICE AND TYPE OF SERVICE

PLACE OF SERVICE CODES FOR PROFESSIONAL CLAIMS

Database (last updated March 29, 2004)

Listed below are place of service codes and descriptions. These codes should be used on professional claims to specify the entity where service(s) were rendered. Check with individual payers (e.g., Medicare, Medicaid, other private insurance) for reimbursement policies regarding these codes. If you would like to comment on a code(s) or description(s), please send your request to posinfo@cms.hhs.gov.

01-02   UNASSIGNED
N/A

03   SCHOOL
A facility whose primary purpose is education.

04   HOMELESS SHELTER
A facility or location whose primary purpose is to provide temporary housing to homeless individuals (e.g., emergency shelters, individual or family shelters).

05   INDIAN HEALTH SERVICE FREE-STANDING FACILITY
A facility or location, owned and operated by the Indian Health Service, which provides diagnostic, therapeutic (surgical and non-surgical), and rehabilitation services to American Indians and Alaska Natives who do not require hospitalization.

06   INDIAN HEALTH SERVICE PROVIDER-BASED FACILITY
A facility or location, owned and operated by the Indian Health Service, which provides diagnostic, therapeutic (surgical and non-surgical), and rehabilitation services rendered by, or under the supervision of, physicians to American Indians and Alaska Natives admitted as inpatients or outpatients.

07   TRIBAL 638   FREE-STANDING FACILITY
A facility or location owned and operated by a federally recognized American Indian or Alaska Native tribe or tribal organization under a 638 agreement, which provides diagnostic, therapeutic (surgical and non-surgical), and rehabilitation services to tribal members who do not require hospitalization.

08   TRIBAL 638   PROVIDER-BASED FACILITY
A facility or location owned and operated by a federally recognized American Indian or Alaska Native tribe or tribal organization under a 638 agreement, which provides diagnostic, therapeutic (surgical and non-surgical), and rehabilitation services to tribal members admitted as inpatients or outpatients.

09-10   UNASSIGNED
N/A

11   OFFICE
Location, other than a hospital, skilled nursing facility (SNF), military treatment facility, community health center, State or local public health clinic, or intermediate care facility (ICF), where the health professional routinely provides health examinations, diagnosis, and treatment of illness or injury on an ambulatory basis.

12   HOME
Location, other than a hospital or other facility, where the patient receives care in a private residence.

13   ASSISTED LIVING FACILITY
Congregate residential facility with self-contained living units providing assessment of each resident's needs and on-site support 24 hours a day, 7 days a week, with the capacity to deliver or arrange for services including some health care and other services. (effective 10/1/03)

14   GROUP HOME *
A residence, with shared living areas, where clients receive supervision and other services such as social and/or behavioral services, custodial service, and minimal services (e.g., medication administration).

15   MOBILE UNIT
A facility/unit that moves from place-to-place equipped to provide preventive, screening, diagnostic, and/or treatment services.

16-19   UNASSIGNED
N/A

20   URGENT CARE FACILITY
Location, distinct from a hospital emergency room, an office, or a clinic, whose purpose is to diagnose and treat illness or injury for unscheduled, ambulatory patients seeking immediate medical attention.

21   INPATIENT HOSPITAL

A facility, other than psychiatric, which primarily provides diagnostic, therapeutic (both surgical and nonsurgical), and rehabilitation services by, or under, the supervision of physicians to patients admitted for a variety of medical conditions.

22   OUTPATIENT HOSPITAL

A portion of a hospital which provides diagnostic, therapeutic (both surgical and nonsurgical), and rehabilitation services to sick or injured persons who do not require hospitalization or institutionalization.

23   EMERGENCY ROOM - HOSPITAL

A portion of a hospital where emergency diagnosis and treatment of illness or injury is provided.

24   AMBULATORY SURGICAL CENTER

A freestanding facility, other than a physician's office, where surgical and diagnostic services are provided on an ambulatory basis.

25   BIRTHING CENTER

A facility, other than a hospital's maternity facilities or a physician's office, which provides a setting for labor, delivery, and immediate post-partum care as well as immediate care of new born infants.

26   MILITARY TREATMENT FACILITY

A medical facility operated by one or more of the Uniformed Services. Military Treatment Facility (MTF) also refers to certain former U.S. Public Health Service (USPHS) facilities now designated as Uniformed Service Treatment Facilities (USTF).

27-30   UNASSIGNED

N/A

31   SKILLED NURSING FACILITY

A facility which primarily provides inpatient skilled nursing care and related services to patients who require medical, nursing, or rehabilitative services but does not provide the level of care or treatment available in a hospital.

32   NURSING FACILITY

A facility which primarily provides to residents skilled nursing care and related services for the rehabilitation of injured, disabled, or sick persons, or, on a regular basis, health-related care services above the level of custodial care to other than mentally retarded individuals.

33   CUSTODIAL CARE FACILITY

A facility which provides room, board and other personal assistance services, generally on a long-term basis, and which does not include a medical component.

34   HOSPICE

A facility, other than a patient's home, in which palliative and supportive care for terminally ill patients and their families are provided.

35-40   UNASSIGNED

N/A

41   AMBULANCE - LAND

A land vehicle specifically designed, equipped and staffed for lifesaving and transporting the sick or injured.

42   AMBULANCE - AIR OR WATER

An air or water vehicle specifically designed, equipped and staffed for lifesaving and transporting the sick or injured.

43-48   UNASSIGNED

N/A

49   INDEPENDENT CLINIC

A location, not part of a hospital and not described by any other Place of Service code, that is organized and operated to provide preventive, diagnostic, therapeutic, rehabilitative, or palliative services to outpatients only. (effective 10/1/03)

50   FEDERALLY QUALIFIED HEALTH CENTER

A facility located in a medically underserved area that provides Medicare beneficiaries preventive primary medical care under the general direction of a physician.

51   INPATIENT PSYCHIATRIC FACILITY

A facility that provides inpatient psychiatric services for the diagnosis and treatment of mental illness on a 24-hour basis, by or under the supervision of a physician.

52   PSYCHIATRIC FACILITY-PARTIAL HOSPITALIZATION

A facility for the diagnosis and treatment of mental illness that provides a planned therapeutic program for patients who do not require full time hospitalization, but who need broader programs than are possible from outpatient visits to a hospital-based or hospital-affiliated facility.

53   COMMUNITY MENTAL HEALTH CENTER

A facility that provides the following services: outpatient services, including specialized outpatient services for children, the elderly, individuals who are chronically ill, and residents of the CMHC's mental health services area who have been discharged from inpatient treatment at a mental health facility; 24 hour a day emergency care services; day treatment, other partial hospitalization services, or psychosocial rehabilitation services; screening for patients being considered for admission to State mental health facilities to determine the appropriateness of such admission; and consultation and education services.

54   INTERMEDIATE CARE FACILITY/MENTALLY RETARDED

A facility which primarily provides health-related care and services above the level of custodial care to mentally retarded individuals but does not provide the level of care or treatment available in a hospital or SNF.

55   RESIDENTIAL SUBSTANCE ABUSE TREATMENT FACILITY

A facility which provides treatment for substance (alcohol and drug) abuse to live-in residents who do not require acute medical care. Services include individual and group therapy and counseling, family counseling, laboratory tests, drugs and supplies, psychological testing, and room and board.

56   PSYCHIATRIC RESIDENTIAL TREATMENT CENTER

A facility or distinct part of a facility for psychiatric care which provides a total 24-hour therapeutically planned and professionally staffed group living and learning environment.

57   NON-RESIDENTIAL SUBSTANCE ABUSE TREATMENT FACILITY

A location which provides treatment for substance (alcohol and drug) abuse on an ambulatory basis. Services include individual and group therapy and counseling, family counseling, laboratory tests, drugs and supplies, and psychological testing. (effective 10/1/03)

58-59   UNASSIGNED

N/A

60   MASS IMMUNIZATION CENTER

A location where providers administer pneumococcal pneumonia and influenza virus vaccinations and submit these services as electronic media claims, paper claims, or using the roster billing method. This generally takes place in a mass immunization setting, such as, a public health center, pharmacy, or mall but may include a physician office setting.

61   COMPREHENSIVE INPATIENT REHABILITATION FACILITY

A facility that provides comprehensive rehabilitation services under the supervision of a physician to inpatients with physical disabilities. Services include physical therapy, occupational therapy, speech pathology, social or psychological services, and orthotics and prosthetics services.

62   COMPREHENSIVE OUTPATIENT REHABILITATION FACILITY

A facility that provides comprehensive rehabilitation services under the supervision of a physician to outpatients with physical disabilities. Services include physical therapy, occupational therapy, and speech pathology services.

63-64   UNASSIGNED

N/A

65   END-STAGE RENAL DISEASE TREATMENT FACILITY

A facility other than a hospital, which provides dialysis treatment, maintenance, and/or training to patients or caregivers on an ambulatory or home-care basis.

66-70   UNASSIGNED

N/A

71   PUBLIC HEALTH CLINIC

A facility maintained by either State or local health departments that provides ambulatory primary medical care under the general direction of a physician. (effective 10/1/03)

72   RURAL HEALTH CLINIC

A certified facility which is located in a rural medically underserved area that provides ambulatory primary medical care under the general direction of a physician.

73-80   UNASSIGNED

N/A

81   INDEPENDENT LABORATORY

A laboratory certified to perform diagnostic and/or clinical tests independent of an institution or a physician's office.

82-98   UNASSIGNED

N/A

99   OTHER PLACE OF SERVICE

Other place of service not identified above.

* Revised, effective April 1, 2004.

TYPE OF SERVICE

COMMON WORKING FILE TYPE OF SERVICE (TOS) INDICATORS

For submitting a claim to the Common Working File (CWF), use the following table to assign the proper TOS. Some procedures may have more than one applicable TOS. For claims received on or after April 3, 1995, CWF will produce alerts on codes with incorrect TOS designations. Effective July 3, 1995, CWF is rejecting codes with incorrect TOS designations.

The only exceptions to this table are:

- Surgical services billed with the ASC facility service modifier SG must be reported as TOS F. The indicator F does not appear on the TOS table because its use is dependent upon the use of the SG modifier.

- Surgical services billed with an assistant-at-surgery modifier (80-82, AS,) must be reported with TOS 8. The 8 indicator does not appear on the TOS table because its use is dependent upon the use of the appropriate modifier. (See Medicare Claims Processing Manual, Chapter 12, "Physician/Practitioner Billing," for instructions on when assistant-at-surgery is allowable.)

- Psychiatric treatment services that are subject to the outpatient mental health treatment limitation should be reported with TOS T.

- TOS H appears in the list of descriptors. However, it does not appear in the table. In CWF, "H" is used only as an indicator for hospice. The carrier should not submit TOS H to CWF at this time.

- When these specific transfusion medicine codes appear on the claim (86880, 86885, 86886, 86900, 86903, 86904, 86905, and 86906 that also contains a blood product (P9010-P9022)), the transfusion medicine codes are paid under reasonable charge. When these services are to be paid under reasonable charge, use

TOS 1. When paid under reasonable charge, tests are paid at 80 percent. Coinsurance and deductible also apply.

NOTE: For injection codes with more than one possible TOS designation, use the following guidelines when assigning the TOS:

When the choice is L or 1,

- Use TOS L when the drug is used related to ESRD; or

- Use TOS 1 when the drug is not related to ESRD and is administered in the office.

When the choice is G or 1:

- Use TOS G when the drug is an immunosuppressive drug; or

- Use TOS 1 when the drug is used for other than immunosuppression.

When the choice is P or 1,

- Use TOS P if the drug is administered through durable medical equipment (DME); or

- Use TOS 1 if the drug is administered in the office.

The place of service or diagnosis may be considered when determining the appropriate TOS. The descriptors for each of the TOS codes listed in the following table are:

0	Whole Blood
1	Medical Care
2	Surgery
3	Consultation
4	Diagnostic Radiology
5	Diagnostic Laboratory
6	Therapeutic Radiology
7	Anesthesia
8	Assistant at Surgery
9	Other Medical Items or Services
A	Used DME
B	High Risk Screening Mammography
C	Low Risk Screening Mammography
D	Ambulance

E	Enteral/Parenteral Nutrients/Supplies	9.	M5A Specialist—Pathology
		10.	M5B Specialist—Psychiatry
F	Ambulatory Surgical Center (Facility Usage for Surgical Services)	11.	M5C Specialist—Ophthalmology
		12.	M5D Specialist—Other
		13.	M6 Consultations
G	Immunosuppressive Drugs		

2. Procedures

H	Hospice	1.	P0 Anesthesia
		2.	P1A Major Procedure—Breast
J	Diabetic Shoes	3.	P1B Major Procedure—Colectomy
		4.	P1C Major Procedure—Cholecystectomy
K	Hearing Items and Services	5.	P1D Major Procedure—Turp
L	ESRD Supplies	6.	P1E Major Procedure—Hysterectomy
		7.	P1F Major Procedure—Explor/Decompr/Excisdisc
M	Monthly Capitation Payment for Dialysis	8.	P1G Major Procedure—Other
		9.	P2A Major Procedure, Cardiovascular—CABG
N	Kidney Donor	10.	P2B Major Procedure, Cardiovascular—Aneurysm Repair
P	Lump Sum Purchase of DME, Prosthetics, Orthotics	11.	P2C Major Procedure, Cardiovascular—Thromboendarterectomy
		12.	P2D Major Procedure, Cardiovascular—Coronary Angioplasty (PTCA)
Q	Vision Items or Services	13.	P2E Major Procedure, Cardiovascular—Pacemaker Insertion
R	Rental of DME	14.	P2F Major Procedure, Cardiovascular—Other
S	Surgical Dressings or Other Medical Supplies	15.	P3Aa Major Procedure, Orthopedic—Hip Fracture Repair
		16.	P3B Major Procedure, Orthopedic—Hip Replacement
T	Outpatient Mental Health Treatment Limitation	17.	P3C Major Procedure, Orthopedic—Knee Replacement
		18.	P3D Major Procedure, Orthopedic—Other
U	Occupational Therapy	19.	P4A Eye Procedure—Corneal Transplant
V	Pneumococcal/Flu Vaccine	20.	P4B Eye Procedure—Cataract Removal/Lens Insertion
W	Physical Therapy	21.	P4C Eye Procedure—Retinal Detachment

BERENSON-EGGERS TYPE OF SERVICE (BETOS) CODES

The BETOS coding system was developed primarily for analyzing the growth in Medicare expenditures. The coding system covers all HCPCS codes; assigns a HCPCS code to only one BETOS code; consists of readily understood clinical categories (as opposed to statistical or financial categories); consists of categories that permit objective assignment; is stable over time; and is relatively immune to minor changes in technology or practice patterns.

BETOS CODES AND DESCRIPTIONS:

1. Evaluation And Management

1.	M1A Office Visits—New
2.	M1B Office Visits—Established
3.	M2A Hospital Visit—Initial
4.	M2B Hospital Visit—Subsequent
5.	M2C Hospital Visit—Critical Care
6.	M3 Emergency Room Visit
7.	M4A Home Visit
8.	M4B Nursing Home Visit

22.	P4D Eye Procedure—Treatment Of Retinal Lesions
23.	P4E Eye Procedure—Other
24.	P5A Ambulatory Procedures—Skin
25.	P5B Ambulatory Procedures—Musculoskeletal
26.	P5C Ambulatory Procedures—Inguinal Hernia Repair
27.	P5D Ambulatory Procedures—Lithotripsy
28.	P5E Ambulatory Procedures—Other
29.	P6A Minor Procedures—Skin
30.	P6B Minor Procedures—Musculoskeletal

31. P6C Minor Procedures—Other (Medicare Fee Schedule)
32. P6D Minor Procedures—Other (Non-Medicare Fee Schedule)
33. P7A Oncology—Radiation Therapy
34. P7B Oncology—Other
35. P8A Endoscopy—Arthroscopy
36. P8B Endoscopy—Upper Gastrointestinal
37. P8C Endoscopy—Sigmoidoscopy
38. P8D Endoscopy—Colonoscopy
39. P8E Endoscopy—Cystoscopy
40. P8F Endoscopy—Bronchoscopy
41. P8G Endoscopy—Laparoscopic Cholecystectomy
42. P8H Endoscopy—Laryngoscopy
43. P8I Endoscopy—Other
44. P9A Dialysis Services (Medicare Fee Schedule)
45. P9B Dialysis Services (Non-Medicare Fee Schedule)

3. Imaging

1. I1A Standard Imaging—Chest
2. I1B Standard Imaging—Musculoskeletal
3. I1C Standard Imaging—Breast
4. I1D Standard Imaging—Contrast Gastrointestinal
5. I1E Standard Imaging—Nuclear Medicine
6. I1F Standard Imaging—Other
7. I2A Advanced Imaging—CAT: Head
8. I2B Advanced Imaging—CAT: Other
9. I2C Advanced Imaging—MRI: Brain
10. I2D Advanced Imaging—MRI: Other
11. I3A Echography—Eye
12. I3B Echography—Abdomen/Pelvis
13. I3C Echography—Heart
14. I3D Echography—Carotid Arteries
15. I3E Echography—Prostate, Transrectal
16. I3F Echography—Other
17. I4A Imaging/Procedure—Heart,Including Cardiac Catheterization
18. I4B Imaging/Procedure—Other

4. Tests

1. T1A Lab Tests—Routine Venipuncture (Non-Medicare Fee Schedule)
2. T1B Lab Tests—Automated General Profiles
3. T1C Lab Tests—Urinalysis
4. T1D Lab Tests—Blood Counts
5. T1E Lab Tests—Glucose
6. T1F Lab Tests—Bacterial Cultures
7. T1G Lab Tests—Other (Medicare Fee Schedule)
8. T1H Lab Tests—Other (Non-Medicare Fee Schedule)
9. T2A Other Tests—Electrocardiograms
10. T2B Other Tests—Cardiovascular Stress Tests
11. T2C Other Tests—Ekg Monitoring
12. T2D Other Tests—Other

5. Durable Medical Equipment

1. D1A Medical/Surgical Supplies
2. D1B Hospital Beds
3. D1C Oxygen And Supplies
4. D1D Wheelchairs
5. D1E Other DME
6. D1F Orthotic Devices

6. Other

1. O1A Ambulance
2. O1B Chiropractic
3. O1C Enteral And Parenteral
4. O1D Chemotherapy
5. O1E Other Drugs
6. O1F Vision, Hearing And Speech Services
7. O1G Influenza Immunization

7. Exceptions/Unclassified

1. Y1 Other—Medicare Fee Schedule
2. Y2 Other—Non-Medicare Fee Schedule
3. Z1 Local Codes
4. Z2 Undefined Codes

APPENDIX D

APPENDIX D — PUB100/NCD REFERENCES

REVISIONS TO THE CMS MANUAL SYSTEM

The Centers for Medicare and Medicaid Services (CMS) initiated its long awaited transition from a paper-based manual system to a Web-based system on October 1, 2003, which updates and restructures all manual instructions. The new system, called the online CMS Manual system, combines all of the various program instructions into an electronic manual, which can be found at http://www.cms.hhs.gov/manuals.

Effective September 30, 2003, the former method of publishing program memoranda (PMs) to communicate program instructions was replaced by the following four templates:

- One-time notification
- Manual revisions
- Business requirement
- Confidential requirements

The Office of Strategic Operations and Regulatory Affairs (OSORA), Division of Issuances, will continue to communicate advanced program instructions to the regions and contractor community every Friday as it currently does. These instructions will also contain a transmittal sheet to identify changes pertaining to a specific manual, requirement, or notification.

The Web-based system has been organized by functional area (e.g., eligibility, entitlement, claims processing, benefit policy, program integrity) in an effort to eliminate redundancy within the manuals, simplify the updating process, and make CMS program instructions available in a more timely manner. The initial release will include Pub. 100, Pub. 100-02, Pub. 100-03, Pub. 100-04, Pub. 100-05, Pub. 100-09, Pub. 100-15, and Pub. 100-20.

The Web-based system contains the functional areas included in the table below:

Publication #	Title
Pub. 100	Introduction
Pub. 100-1	Medicare General Information, Eligibility, and Entitlement
Pub. 100-2	Medicare Benefit Policy (basic coverage rules)
Pub. 100-3	Medicare National Coverage Determinations (national coverage decisions)
Pub. 100-4	Medicare Claims Processing (includes appeals, contractor interface with CWF, and MSN)
Pub. 100-5	Medicare Secondary Payer
Pub. 100-6	Medicare Financial Management (includes Intermediary Desk Review and Audit)
Pub. 100-7	Medicare State Operations
Pub. 100-8	Medicare Program Integrity
Pub. 100-9	Medicare Contractor Beneficiary and Provider Communications
Pub. 100-10	Medicare Quality Improvement Organization
Pub. 100-11	Reserved
Pub. 100-12	State Medicaid
Pub. 100-13	Medicaid State Children's Health Insurance Program
Pub. 100-14	Medicare End Stage Renal Disease Network
Pub. 100-15	Medicare State Buy-In
Pub. 100-16	Medicare Managed Care
Pub. 100-17	Medicare Business Partners Systems Security
Pub. 100-18	Medicare Business Partners Security Oversight
Pub. 100-19	Demonstrations
Pub. 100-20	One-Time Notification

Table of Contents

The table below shows the paper-based manuals used to construct the Web-based system. Although this is just an overview, CMS is in the process of developing detailed crosswalks to guide you from a specific section of the old manuals to the appropriate area of the new manual, as well as to show how the information in each section was derived.

Paper-Based Manuals	Internet-Only Manuals
Pub. 06—Medicare Coverage Issues	Pub. 100-01—Medicare General Information, Eligibility, and Entitlement
Pub. 09—Medicare Outpatient Physical Therapy	Pub. 100-02—Medicare Benefit Policy
Pub. 10—Medicare Hospital	Pub. 100-03—Medicare National Coverage Determinations
Pub. 11—Medicare Home Health Agency	Pub. 100-04—Medicare Claims Processing
Pub. 12—Medicare Skilled Nursing Facility	Pub. 100-05—Medicare Secondary Payer
Pub. 13—Medicare Intermediary Manual, Parts 1, 2, 3, and 4	Pub. 100-06—Medicare Financial Management
Pub. 14—Medicare Carriers Manual, Parts 1, 2, 3, and 4	Pub. 100-08—Medicare Program Integrity
Pub. 21—Medicare Hospice	Pub. 100-09—Medicare Contractor Beneficiary and Provider Communications
Pub. 27—Medicare Rural Health Clinic and Federally Qualified Health Center	
Pub. 29--Medicare Renal Dialysis Facility	
Program Memoranda	
Pub. 60A—Intermediaries	

© 2005 Ingenix, Inc.

Pub. 60B—Carriers

Pub. 60AB—Intermediaries/Carriers

NOTE: Information derived from Pub. 06 to Pub. 60AB was used to develop Pub. 100-01 to Pub. 100-09 for the Internet-only manual.

Pub. 19—Medicare Peer Review	Pub. 100-10—Medicare Quality Organization Improvement Organization
Pub. 07—Medicare State Operations	Pub. 100-07—Medicare State Operations
Pub. 45—State Medicaid	Pub. 100-12—State Medicaid
Pub. 81—Medicare End Stage Renal Disease	Pub. 100-13—Medicaid State Children's Health Insurance Program
Pub. 24—Medicare State Buy-In	Pub. 100-14—Medicare End Stage Renal Disease Network Organizations Network Organizations
Pub. 75—Health Maintenance Organization/Competitive Medical Plan Care	Pub. 100-15—Medicare State Buy-In
Pub. 76—Health Maintenance Organization/Competitive Medical Plan (PM)	Pub. 100-16—Medicare Managed
Pub. 77—Manual for Federally Qualified Health Maintenance Organizations	Pub. 100-17—Business Partners Systems Security
Pub. 13—Medicare Intermediaries Manual, Part 2	Pub. 100-18—Business Partners Security Oversight
Pub. 14—Medicare Carriers Manual, Part 2	Pub 100-19—Demonstrations
Pub. 13—Medicare Intermediaries Manual, Part 2	Pub 100-20—One-Time
Pub. 14—Medicare Carriers Manual, Part 2	
Demonstrations (PMs)	
Program instructions that impact multiple manuals or have no manual impact.	

NATIONAL COVERAGE DETERMINATIONS MANUAL

The National Coverage Determinations Manual (NCD), which is the electronic replacement for the Coverage Issues Manual (CIM), is organized according to categories such as diagnostic services, supplies, and medical procedures. The table of contents lists each category and subject within that category. A revision transmittal sheet will identify any new material and recap the changes as well as provide an effective date for the change and any background information. At any time, one can refer to a transmittal indicated on the page of the manual to view this information.

By the time it is complete, the book will contain two chapters. Chapter 1 includes a description of national coverage

determinations that have been made by CMS. When available, chapter 2 will contain a list of HCPCS codes related to each coverage determination. To make the manual easier to use, it is organized in accordance with CPT category sequences. Where there is no national coverage determination that affects a particular CPT category, the category is listed as reserved in the table of contents.

The following table is the crosswalk of the NCD to the CIM. However, at this time, many of the NCD policies are not yet available. The CMS Web site also contains a crosswalk of the CIM to the NCD.

MEDICARE BENEFIT POLICY MANUAL

The Medicare Benefit Policy Manual replaces current Medicare general coverage instructions that are not national coverage determinations. As a general rule, in the past these instructions have been found in chapter II of the Medicare Carriers Manual, the Medicare Intermediary Manual, other provider manuals, and program memoranda. New instructions will be published in this manual. As new transmittals are included they will be identified.

On the CMS Web site, a crosswalk from the new manual to the source manual is provided with each chapter and may be accessed from the chapter table of contents. In addition, the crosswalk for each section is shown immediately under the section heading.

The list below is the table of contents for the Medicare Benefit Policy Manual:

Chapter	Title
One	Inpatient Hospital Services
Two	Inpatient Psychiatric Hospital Services
Three	Duration of Covered Inpatient Services
Four	Inpatient Psychiatric Benefit Days Reduction and Lifetime Limitation
Five	Lifetime Reserve Days
Six	Hospital Services Covered Under Part B
Seven	Home Health Services
Eight	Coverage of Extended Care (SNF) Services Under Hospital Insurance
Nine	Coverage of Hospice Services Under Hospital Insurance
Ten	Ambulance Services
Eleven	End Stage Renal Disease (ESRD)
Twelve	Comprehensive Outpatient Rehabilitation Facility (CORF) Coverage
Thirteen	Rural Health Clinic (RHC) and Federally Qualified Health Center (FQHC) Services
Fourteen	Medical Devices

© 2005 Ingenix, Inc.

| Fifteen | Covered Medical and Other Health Services |
| Sixteen | General Exclusions from Coverage |

MCM/CIM CROSSWALK TO PUB 100 REFERENCE

MCM	PUB 100
15016	100-4,12,100; 100-4,12,100.1.7; 100-4,12,100.1.8
15018	100-4,12,50; 100-4,12,140.3.2
15020	100-4,12,60
15021.1	100-4,13,10
15022	100-4,12,70; 100-4,13,20; 100-4,13,90
15023	100-4,13,100
15026	100-4,12,80.3
15038	100-4,12,40.6
15050	100-4,12,200
15100	100-4,12,30.1
15200	100-4,12,30.2
15350	100-4,8,140; 100-4,8,170
15360	100-4,12,30.4
15400	100-4,12,30.5
15501	100-4,12,30.6
15504	100-4,12,30.6.8
15505	100-4,12,30.6.9
15505.1	100-4,12,30.6.9
15505.2	100-4,12,30.6.9
15506	100-4,12,30.6.10
15507	100-4,12,30.6.11
15508	100-4,12,30.6.12
15509	100-4,12,30.6.13
15509.1	100-4,12,30.6.13
15510	100-4,12,30.6.14
15511.1	100-4,12,30.6.15
15511.2	100-4,12,30.6.15
15511.3	100-4,12,30.6.15
15512	100-4,12,30.6.16
15514	100-4,12,30.6
2005.1	100-2,15,20.1
2005.2	100-2,15,20.2
2005.3	100-2,15,20.3
2020	100-1,5,70; 100-2,15,30; 100-4,12,10
2020.26	100-1,5,70.6
2049	100-2,15,50
2050.3	100-2,15,60.3
2070	100-2,15,80
2070.1	100-1,5,90.2; 100-2,15,80.1; 100-4,16,10; 100-4,16,10.1; 100-4,16,110.4
2070.2	100-2,15,80.2; 100-4,12,160
2070.3	100-2,15,80.3
2070.4	100-4,13,90
2079	100-2,15,100
2130	100-2,15,120
2136	100-2,15,150
2150	100-2,15,160; 100-4,12,160; 100-4,12,170; 100-4,12,170.1
2152	100-2,15,170; 100-4,12,150
2154	100-2,15,180
2210	100-2,15,230
2210.1	100-2,15,230.1
2210.2	100-2,15,230.2
2215	100-2,15,230.4; 100-4,5,10
2216	100-2,15,230.3
2265	100-2,15,260; 100-4,12,90.3; 100-4,14,10
2300	100-2,16,10

MCM	PUB 100
2300.1	100-2,16,180
2320	100-2,16,90
2329	100-2,16,120
2455	100-1,3,20.5; 100-1,3,20.5.2; 100-1,3,20.5.3
2470	100-1,3,30; 100-1,3,30.1; 100-1,3,30.2; 100-1,3,30.3; 100-4,12,210
2472.4	100-4,12,110.2
3045.4	100-4,1,30.3.5
3324	100-4,20,50.3; 100-4,20,100.2.2
4137	100-4,12,50
4141	100-2,15,30
4142	100-4,12,30.6.10
4146	100-1,3,30.2
4161	100-2,15,230.4
4172	100-4,12,140
4175	100-4,11,10; 100-4,11,40.1.3
4180	100-4,18,60
4182	100-4,18,50
4270	100-4,8,70; 100-4,8,80; 100-4,8,90; 100-4,8,90.1; 100-4,8,90.3.2; 100-4,8,130
4270.1	100-4,8,60.4.4; 100-4,8,90.1; 100-4,8,90.2; 100-4,8,90.2.2
4450	100-4,20,100.2.2
4471.2	100-2,15,50.5
4601	100-4,18,20
4602	100-4,13,40; 100-4,13,40.1; 100-4,13,40.1.1; 100-4,18,20.7
4826	100-4,12,40.6
4827	100-4,12,40.7
4830	100-4,12,140.2
5112	100-4,12,160.1
5112.1	100-4,12,170
5249	100-4,8,120.1

CIM	NCD
20.9	100-3,20.9
240.1	100-3,240.1
35-10	100-3,20.29
35-101	100-3,250.4; 100-3,130.5; 100-3,270.4; 100-3,130.6; 100-3,230.1; 100-3,160.2; 100-3,40.5; 100-3,250.1
35-102	100-3,270.1
35-104	100-3,260.5
35-11	100-3,230.3
35-12	100-3,140.4
35-13	100-3,150.7
35-14	100-3,70.2; 100-3,70.1
35-15	100-3,240.7
35-16	100-3,80.11
35-17	100-3,160.1
35-19	100-3,30.6; 100-3,250.3; 100-3,110.10
35-2	100-3,150.1
35-20	100-3,250.4; 100-3,130.5; 100-3,270.4; 100-3,130.6; 100-3,230.1; 100-3,160.2; 100-3,40.5; 100-3,250.1
35-21	100-3,10.3; 100-3,130.1
35-21.1	100-3,10.4; 100-3,130.2
35-22	100-3,10.3; 100-3,130.1
35-22.1	100-3,10.4; 100-3,130.2
35-22.2	100-3,250.4; 100-3,130.5; 100-3,270.4; 100-3,130.6; 100-3,230.1; 100-3,160.2; 100-3,40.5; 100-3,250.1
35-22.3	100-3,250.4; 100-3,130.5; 100-3,270.4; 100-3,130.6; 100-3,230.1; 100-3,160.2; 100-3,40.5; 100-3,250.1
35-23	100-3,130.3
35-23.1	100-3,130.4
35-24	100-3,230.4
35-25	100-3,20.10
35-26	100-3,250.4; 100-3,130.5; 100-3,270.4; 100-3,130.6; 100-3,230.1; 100-3,160.2; 100-3,40.5; 100-3,250.1
35-27	100-3,30.1; 100-3,30.1.1

35-27.1	100-3,30.1; 100-3,30.1.1
35-3	100-3,240.3
35-30	100-3,110.8
35-30.1	100-3,110.8.1
35-31	100-3,250.4; 100-3,130.5; 100-3,270.4; 100-3,130.6; 100-3,230.1; 100-3,160.2; 100-3,40.5; 100-3,250.1
35-32	100-3,20.1
35-33	100-3,100.8
35-34	100-3,20.23
35-35	100-3,20.28
35-38	100-3,230.14; 100-3,110.15
35-39	100-3,80.12; 100-3,80.6
35-40	100-3,100.1
35-41	100-3,150.5
35-42	100-3,130.7
35-44	100-3,10.1
35-45	100-3,20.25
35-46	100-3,160.7.1
35-47	100-3,140.2
35-48	100-3,150.2
35-49	100-3,110.1
35-51	100-3,130.8
35-52	100-3,140.5
35-53	100-3,260.1
35-53.1	100-3,260.2
35-54	100-3,80.7
35-55	100-3,240.6
35-57	100-3,160.8
35-57.1	100-3,160.9
35-58	100-3,20.3
35-59	100-3,100.2
35-60	100-3,110.14
35-61	100-3,140.3
35-66	100-3,250.4; 100-3,130.5; 100-3,270.4; 100-3,130.6; 100-3,230.1; 100-3,160.2; 100-3,40.5; 100-3,250.1
35-69	100-3,100.9; 100-3,20.4
35-7	100-3,20.18
35-71	100-3,110.16
35-72	100-3,160.15
35-73	100-3,100.10
35-75	100-3,20.11
35-77	100-3,160.12
35-78	100-3,20.12
35-79	100-3,20.8.3
35-81	100-3,250.4; 100-3,130.5; 100-3,270.4; 100-3,130.6; 100-3,230.1; 100-3,160.2; 100-3,40.5; 100-3,250.1
35-82	100-3,260.3
35-84	100-3,160.4
35-85	100-3,100.9; 100-3,20.4
35-87	100-3,260.9
35-88	100-3,20.5; 100-3,110.4
35-89	100-3,170.3
35-9	100-3,80.10
35-90	100-3,20.5; 100-3,110.4
35-91	100-3,100.13
35-92	100-3,30.5
35-94	100-3,20.6
35-95	100-3,20.26
35-96	100-3,230.9
35-98	100-3,270.1
35-99	100-3,140.1
40-1	100-3,190.12
40-10	100-3,190.21
40-11	100-3,190.22
40-12	100-3,190.23
40-13	100-3,190.24
40-14	100-3,190.25
40-15	100-3,190.26
40-16	100-3,190.27
40-17	100-3,190.28; 100-3,190.29; 100-3,190.30
40-18	100-3,190.28; 100-3,190.29; 100-3,190.30
40-19	100-3,190.28; 100-3,190.29; 100-3,190.30
40-2	100-3,190.13; 100-3,190.14
40-20	100-3,190.31
40-21	100-3,190.32
40-22	100-3,190.33
40-23	100-3,190.34
40-3	100-3,190.14; 100-3,190.13
40-4	100-3,190.15
40-5	100-3,190.16
40-6	100-3,190.17
40-8	100-3,190.19
40-9	100-3,190.20
45-1	100-3,160.17
45-11	100-3,10.5
45-12	100-3,270.5
45-16	100-3,110.2
45-17	100-3,160.20
45-18	100-3,110.5
45-19	100-3,10.2; 100-3,280.13
45-21	100-3,110.6
45-22	100-3,260.7
45-23	100-3,230.12
45-25	100-3,160.13
45-27	100-3,110.7
45-28	100-3,110.9
45-29	100-3,30.6; 100-3,250.3; 100-3,110.10
45-31	100-3,30.6; 100-3,250.3; 100-3,110.10
45-4	100-3,150.6
45-7	100-3,80.1; 100-3,80.4
50-1	100-3,20.8.1; 100-3,20.8
50-10	100-3,230.6
50-12	100-3,220.1
50-13	100-3,220.3; 100-3,220.2
50-14	100-3,220.3; 100-3,220.2
50-15	100-3,20.15
50-17	100-3,190.10
50-18	100-3,190.4
50-2	100-3,110.3
50-20	100-3,190.2
50-20.1	100-3,210.2
50-21	100-3,220.4
50-22	100-3,110.12
50-23	100-3,190.1
50-24	100-3,190.6
50-25	100-3,100.4
50-26	100-3,260.6
50-27	100-3,220.7
50-29	100-3,190.3
50-3	100-3,20.13
50-30	100-3,220.8
50-31	100-3,160.10
50-32	100-3,220.13; 100-3,20.7
50-33	100-3,230.2
50-34	100-3,300.1
50-35	100-3,190.5
50-36	100-3,220.6
50-37	100-3,20.17
50-38	100-3,80.8
50-39	100-3,160.21
50-39.1	100-3,160.22
50-40	100-3,160.5

© 2005 Ingenix, Inc.

Appendixes

50-42	100-3,20.19
50-44	100-3,150.3
50-45	100-3,190.8
50-49	100-3,80.9
50-5	100-3,220.11
50-51	100-3,100.5
50-52	100-3,190.9
50-53	100-3,110.11
50-55	100-3,210.1
50-58	100-3,220.12
50-59	100-3,220.13; 100-3,20.7
50-6	100-3,20.14
50-7	100-3,220.5
50-8	100-3,70.2; 100-3,70.1
50-8.1	100-3,70.2.1
50-9	100-3,100.12
55-3	100-3,230.14; 100-3,110.15
60-14	100-3,280.14
60-20	100-3,10.2; 100-3,280.13
60-22	100-3,160.18
60-23	100-3,50.1
60-25	100-3,270.2
60-7	100-3,20.8.2
65-1	100-3,80.1; 100-3,80.4
65-14	100-3,50.3
65-4	100-3,160.6
65-5	100-3,50.2
65-6	100-3,20.8.1; 100-3,20.8
65-7	100-3,80.12; 100-3,80.6
65-8	100-3,160.7
65-9	100-3,230.10
80-2	100-3,40.1
80-3	100-3,180.1
80.2.1	100-3,80.2
80.3.1	100-3,80.3

PUB 100 REFERENCES

Pub. 100-1, Chapter 3, Section 20.5
Blood Deductibles (Part A and Part B)

Program payment may not be made for the first 3 pints of whole blood or equivalent units of packed red cells received under Part A and Part B combined in a calendar year. However, blood processing (e.g., administration, storage) is not subject to the deductible.

The blood deductibles are in addition to any other applicable deductible and coinsurance amounts for which the patient is responsible.

The deductible applies only to the first 3 pints of blood furnished in a calendar year, even if more than one provider furnished blood.

Pub. 100-1, Chapter 3, Section 20.5.2
Part B Blood Deductible

Blood is furnished on an outpatient basis or is subject to the Part B blood deductible and is counted toward the combined limit. It should be noted that payment for blood may be made to the hospital under Part B only for blood furnished in an outpatient setting. Blood is not covered for inpatient Part B services.

Pub. 100-1, Chapter 3, Section 20.5.3
Items Subject to Blood Deductibles

The blood deductibles apply only to whole blood and packed red cells. The term whole blood means human blood from which none of the liquid or cellular components have been removed. Where packed red cells are furnished, a unit of packed red cells is considered equivalent to a pint of whole blood. Other components of blood such as platelets, fibrinogen, plasma, gamma globulin, and serum albumin are not subject to the blood deductible. However, these components of blood are covered as biologicals.

Refer to Pub. 100-04, Medicare Claims Processing Manual, chapter 4, §231 regarding billing for blood and blood products under the Hospital Outpatient Prospective Payment System (OPPS).

Pub. 100-1, Chapter 3, Section 30
Outpatient Mental Health Treatment Limitation

Regardless of the actual expenses a beneficiary incurs for treatment of mental, psychoneurotic, and personality disorders while the beneficiary is not an inpatient of a hospital at the time such expenses are incurred, the amount of those expenses that may be recognized for Part B deductible and payment purposes is limited to 62.5 percent of the Medicare allowed amount for these services. The limitation is called the outpatient mental health treatment limitation. Since Part B deductible also applies the program pays for about half of the allowed amount recognized for mental health therapy services.

Expenses for diagnostic services (e.g., psychiatric testing and evaluation to diagnose the patient's illness) are not subject to this limitation. This limitation applies only to therapeutic services and to services performed to evaluate the progress of a course of treatment for a diagnosed condition.

Pub. 100-1, Chapter 3, Section 30.1
Application of Mental Health Limitation - Status of Patient

The limitation is applicable to expenses incurred in connection with the treatment of an individual who is not an inpatient of a hospital. Thus, the limitation applies to mental health services furnished to a person in a physician's office, in the patient's home, in a skilled nursing facility, as an outpatient, and so forth. The term "hospital" in this context means an institution which is primarily engaged in providing to inpatients, by or under the supervision of a physician(s):

- Diagnostic and therapeutic services for medical diagnosis, and treatment, and care of injured, disabled, or sick persons;
- Rehabilitation services for injured, disabled, or sick persons; or
- Psychiatric services for the diagnosis and treatment of mentally ill patients.

Pub. 100-1, Chapter 3, Section 30.2
Disorders Subject to Mental Health Limitation

The term "mental, psychoneurotic, and personality disorders" is defined as the specific psychiatric conditions described in the American Psychiatric Association's Diagnostic and Statistical Manual of Mental Disorders, Third Edition - Revised (DSM-III-R).

If the treatment services rendered are for both a psychiatric condition and one or more nonpsychiatric conditions, the charges are separated to apply the limitation only to the mental health charge. Normally HCPCS code and diagnoses

Appendixes

are used. Where HCPCS code is not available on the claim, revenue code is used.

If the service is primarily on the basis of a diagnosis of Alzheimer's Disease (coded 331.0 in the International Classification of Diseases, 9th Revision) or Alzheimer's or other disorders (coded 290.XX in DSM-III-R), treatment typically represents medical management of the patient's condition (rather than psychiatric treatment) and is not subject to the limitation.

Pub. 100-1, Chapter 3, Section 30.3
Diagnostic Services

The mental health limitation does not apply to tests and evaluations performed to establish or confirm the patient's diagnosis. Diagnostic services include psychiatric or psychological tests and interpretations, diagnostic consultations, and initial evaluations. However, testing services performed to evaluate a patient's progress during treatment are considered part of treatment and are subject to the limitation.

Pub. 100-1, Chapter 5, Section 70
Physician Defined

Physician means doctor of medicine, doctor of osteopathy (including osteopathic practitioner), doctor of dental surgery or dental medicine (within the limitations in subsection §70.2), doctor of podiatric medicine (within the limitations in subsection §70.3), or doctor of optometry (within the limitations of subsection §70.5), and, with respect to certain specified treatment, a doctor of chiropractic legally authorized to practice by a State in which he/she performs this function. The services performed by a physician within these definitions are subject to any limitations imposed by the State on the scope of practice.

The issuance by a State of a license to practice medicine constitutes legal authorization. Temporary State licenses also constitute legal authorization to practice medicine. If State law authorizes local political subdivisions to establish higher standards for medical practitioners than those set by the State licensing board, the local standards determine whether a particular physician has legal authorization. If State licensing law limits the scope of practice of a particular type of medical practitioner, only the services within the limitations are covered.

The issuance by a State of a license to practice medicine constitutes legal authorization. Temporary State licenses also constitute legal authorization to practice medicine. If State law authorizes local political subdivisions to establish higher standards for medical practitioners than those set by the State licensing board, the local standards determine whether a particular physician has legal authorization. If State licensing law limits the scope of practice of a particular type of medical practitioner, only the services within the limitations are covered.

NOTE: The term physician does not include such practitioners as a Christian Science practitioner or naturopath.

Pub. 100-1, Chapter 5, Section 70.6
Chiropractors

A. General

A licensed chiropractor who meets uniform minimum standards (see subsection C) is a physician for specified services. Coverage extends only to treatment by means of manual manipulation of the spine to correct a subluxation demonstrated by X-ray, provided such treatment is legal in the State where performed. All other services furnished or ordered by chiropractors are not covered. An X-ray obtained by a chiropractor for his or her own diagnostic purposes before commencing treatment may suffice for claims documentation purposes. This means that if a chiropractor orders, takes, or interprets an X-ray to demonstrate a subluxation of the spine, the X-ray can be used for claims processing purposes. However, there is no coverage or payment for these services or for any other diagnostic or therapeutic service ordered or furnished by the chiropractor.

In addition, in performing manual manipulation of the spine, some chiropractors use manual devices that are hand-held with the thrust of the force of the device being controlled manually. While such manual manipulation may be covered, there is no separate payment permitted for use of this device.

B. Licensure and Authorization to Practice

A chiropractor must be licensed or legally authorized to furnish chiropractic services by the State or jurisdiction in which the services are furnished.

C. Uniform Minimum Standards

I. Prior to July 1, 1974, Chiropractors licensed or authorized to practice prior to July 1, 1974, and those individuals who commenced their studies in a chiropractic college before that date must meet all of the following minimum standards to render payable services under the program:

a. Preliminary education equal to the requirements for graduation from an accredited high school or other secondary school;

b. Graduation from a college of chiropractic approved by the State's chiropractic examiners that included the completion of a course of study covering a period of not less than 3 school years of 6 months each year in actual continuous attendance covering adequate course of study in the subjects of anatomy, physiology, symptomatology and diagnosis, hygiene and sanitation, chemistry, histology, pathology, and principles and practice of chiropractic, including clinical instruction in vertebral palpation, nerve tracing and adjusting; and

c. Passage of an examination prescribed by the State's chiropractic examiners covering the subjects listed in subsection b.

2. After June 30, 1974 - Individuals commencing their studies in a chiropractic college after June 30, 1974, must meet all of the following additional requirements:

a. Satisfactory completion of 2 years of pre-chiropractic study at the college level;

b. Satisfactory completion of a 4-year course of 8 months each year (instead of a 3-year course of 6 months each year) at a college or school of chiropractic that includes not less than 4,000 hours in the scientific and chiropractic courses specified in subsection 1.b, plus courses in the use and effect of X-ray and chiropractic analysis; and

c. The practitioner must be over 21 years of age.

Pub. 100-1, Chapter 5, Section 90.2
Laboratory Defined

© 2005 Ingenix, Inc.

Laboratory means a facility for the biological, microbiological, serological, chemical, immuno-hematological, hematological, biophysical, cytological, pathological, or other examination of materials derived from the human body for the purpose of providing information for the diagnosis, prevention, or treatment of any disease or impairment of, or the assessment of the health of, human beings. These examinations also include procedures to determine, measure, or otherwise describe the presence or absence of various substances or organisms in the body. Facilities only collecting or preparing specimens (or both) or only serving as a mailing service and not performing testing are not considered laboratories.

Pub. 100-2, Chapter 13, Section 30
Rural Health Clinic and Federally Qualified Health Center Service Defined

A3-3192.2, A3-3643, RHC-400, RHC-500

Payments for covered RHC/FQHC services furnished to Medicare beneficiaries are made on the basis of an all-inclusive rate per covered visit (except for pneumococcal and influenza vaccines and their administration, which is paid at 100 percent of reasonable cost). The term "visit" is defined as a face-to-face encounter between the patient and a physician, physician assistant, nurse practitioner, certified nurse midwife, visiting nurse, clinical psychologist, or clinical social worker during which an RHC/FQHC service is rendered. Encounters with (1) more than one health professional; and (2) multiple encounters with the same health professional which take place on the same day and at a single location, constitute a single visit. An exception occurs in cases in which the patient, subsequent to the first encounter, suffers an illness or injury requiring additional diagnosis or treatment.

Pub. 100-2, Chapter 15, Section 20.1
Physician Expense for Surgery, Childbirth, and Treatment for Infertility

B3-2005.I

A. Surgery and Childbirth

Skilled medical management is covered throughout the events of pregnancy, beginning with diagnosis, continuing through delivery and ending after the necessary postnatal care. Similarly, in the event of termination of pregnancy, regardless of whether terminated spontaneously or for therapeutic reasons (i.e., where the life of the mother would be endangered if the fetus were brought to term), the need for skilled medical management and/or medical services is equally important as in those cases carried to full term. After the infant is delivered and is a separate individual, items and services furnished to the infant are not covered on the basis of the mother's eligibility.

Most surgeons and obstetricians bill patients an all-inclusive package charge intended to cover all services associated with the surgical procedure or delivery of the child. All expenses for surgical and obstetrical care, including preoperative/prenatal examinations and tests and post-operative/postnatal services, are considered incurred on the date of surgery or delivery, as appropriate. This policy applies whether the physician bills on a package charge basis, or itemizes the bill separately for these items.

Occasionally, a physician's bill may include charges for additional services not directly related to the surgical procedure or the delivery. Such charges are considered incurred on the date the additional services are furnished.

The above policy applies only where the charges are imposed by one physician or by a clinic on behalf of a group of physicians. Where more than one physician imposes charges for surgical or obstetrical services, all preoperative/prenatal and post-operative/postnatal services performed by the physician who performed the surgery or delivery are considered incurred on the date of the surgery or delivery. Expenses for services rendered by other physicians are considered incurred on the date they were performed.

B. Treatment for Infertility

Reasonable and necessary services associated with treatment for infertility are covered under Medicare. Infertility is a condition sufficiently at variance with the usual state of health to make it appropriate for a person who normally is expected to be fertile to seek medical consultation and treatment.

Pub. 100-2, Chapter 15, Section 20.2
Physician Expense for Allergy Treatment

B3-2005.2, B3-4145

Allergists commonly bill separately for the initial diagnostic workup and for the treatment (See §60.2). Where it is necessary to provide treatment over an extended period, the allergist may submit a single bill for all of the treatments, or may bill periodically. In either case the Form CMS-1500 claim shows the Healthcare Common Procedure Coding System (HCPCS) codes and from and through dates of service, or the Form CMS-1450 outpatient claim shows the HCPCS code and date of service (except for critical access hospital (CAH) claims).

Pub. 100-2, Chapter 15, Section 20.3
Artificial Limbs, Braces, and Other Custom Made Items Ordered But Not Furnished

B3-2005.3

A. Date of Incurred Expense

If a custom-made item was ordered but not furnished to a beneficiary because the individual died or because the order was canceled by the beneficiary or because the beneficiary's condition changed and the item was no longer reasonable and necessary or appropriate, payment can be made based on the supplier's expenses. (See subsection B for determination of the allowed amount.) In such cases, the expense is considered incurred on the date the beneficiary died or the date the supplier learned of the cancellation or that the item was no longer reasonable and necessary or appropriate for the beneficiary's condition. If the beneficiary died or the beneficiary's condition changed and the item was no longer reasonable and necessary or appropriate, payment can be made on either an assigned or unassigned claim. If the beneficiary, for any other reason, canceled the order, payment can be made to the supplier only.

B. Determination of Allowed Amount

The allowed amount is based on the services furnished and materials used, up to the date the supplier learned of the beneficiary's death or of the cancellation of the order or that the item was no longer reasonable and necessary or appropriate. The Durable Medical Equipment Regional Carrier (DMERC), carrier or intermediary, as appropriate, determines the services performed and the allowable amount appropriate in the particular situation. It takes into account any salvage value of the device to the supplier.

Where a supplier breaches an agreement to make a prosthesis, brace, or other custom-made device for a Medicare beneficiary, e.g., an unexcused failure to provide the article within the time specified in the contract, payment may not be made for any work or material expended on the item. Whether a particular supplier has lived up to its agreement, of course, depends on the facts in the individual case.

Pub. 100-2, Chapter 15, Section 30
Physician Services

B3-2020, B3-4142

A. General

Physician services are the professional services performed by a physician or physicians for a patient including diagnosis, therapy, surgery, consultation, and care plan oversight. The physician must render the service for the service to be covered. (See Publication 100-1, the Medicare General Information, Eligibility, and Entitlement Manual, Chapter 5, §70, for definition of physician.) A service may be considered to be a physician's service where the physician either examines the patient in person or is able to visualize some aspect of the patient's condition without the interposition of a third person's judgment. Direct visualization would be possible by means of x-rays, electrocardiogram and electroencephalogram tapes, tissue samples, etc.

For example, the interpretation by a physician of an actual electrocardiogram or electroencephalogram reading that has been transmitted via telephone (i.e., electronically rather than by means of a verbal description) is a covered service.

Professional services of the physician are covered if provided within the United States, and may be performed in a home, office, institution, or at the scene of an accident. A patient's home, for this purpose, is anywhere the patient makes his or her residence, e.g., home for the aged, a nursing home, a relative's home.

B. Telephone Services

Services by means of a telephone call between a physician and a beneficiary, or between a physician and a member of a beneficiary's family, are covered under Medicare, but carriers may not make separate payment for these services under the program. The physician work resulting from telephone calls is considered to be an integral part of the prework and postwork of other physician services, and the fee schedule amount for the latter services already includes payment for the telephone calls. See the Medicare Benefit Policy Manual, Chapter 15, "Covered Medical and Other Health Services," §270, for coverage of telehealth services.

C. Consultations

A consultation may be paid when the consulting physician initiates treatment on the same day as the consultation. It is only after a transfer of care has occurred that evaluation and management (E&M) services may not be billed as consultations; they must be billed as subsequent office/outpatient visits

Therefore, if covered, a consultation is reimbursable when it is a professional service furnished a patient by a second physician at the request of the attending physician. Such a consultation includes the history and examination of the patient as well as the written report, which is furnished to the attending physician for inclusion in the patient's permanent medical record. These reports must be prepared and submitted to the provider for retention when they involve patients of institutions responsible for maintaining such records, and submitted to the attending physician's office for other patients.

To reimburse laboratory consultations, the services must:

Be requested by the patient's attending physician;

Relate to a test result that lies outside of the clinically significant normal or expected/established range relative to the condition of the patient;

Result in a written narrative report included in the patient's medical record; and

Require medical judgment by the consultant physician.

A consultation must involve a medical judgment that ordinarily requires a physician. Where a nonphysician laboratory specialist could furnish the information, the service of the physician is not a consultation payable under Part B.

The following indicators can ordinarily distinguish attending physician's claims:

Therapeutic services are included on the bill in addition to an examination;

The patient's history is before the examiner while the claim is reviewed and the billing physician has previously rendered other services to the patient; or

Information in the file indicates that the patient was not referred.

The attending physician may remove himself from the care of the patient and turn the patient over to the person who performed a consultation service. In this situation, the initial examination would be a consultation if the above requirements were met at that time.

D. Patient-Initiated Second Opinions

Patient-initiated second opinions that relate to the medical need for surgery or for major nonsurgical diagnostic and therapeutic procedures (e.g., invasive diagnostic techniques such as cardiac catheterization and gastroscopy) are covered under Medicare. In the event that the recommendation of the first and second physician differs regarding the need for surgery (or other major procedure), a third opinion is also covered. Second and third opinions are covered even though the surgery or other procedure, if performed, is determined not covered. Payment may be made for the history and examination of the patient, and for other covered diagnostic services required to properly evaluate the patient's need for a procedure and to render a professional opinion. In some cases, the results of tests done by the first physician may be available to the second physician.

E. Concurrent Care

Concurrent care exists where more than one physician renders services more extensive than consultative services during a period of time. The reasonable and necessary services of each physician rendering concurrent care could be covered where each is required to play an active role in the patient's treatment, for example, because of the

© 2005 Ingenix, Inc.

existence of more than one medical condition requiring diverse specialized medical services.

In order to determine whether concurrent physicians' services are reasonable and necessary, the carrier must decide the following:

1. Whether the patient's condition warrants the services of more than one physician on an attending (rather than consultative) basis, and
2. Whether the individual services provided by each physician are reasonable and necessary.

In resolving the first question, the carrier should consider the specialties of the physicians as well as the patient's diagnosis, as concurrent care is usually (although not always) initiated because of the existence of more than one medical condition requiring diverse specialized medical or surgical services. The specialties of the physicians are an indication of the necessity for concurrent services, but the patient's condition and the inherent reasonableness and necessity of the services, as determined by the carrier's medical staff in accordance with locality norms, must also be considered. For example, although cardiology is a sub-specialty of internal medicine, the treatment of both diabetes and of a serious heart condition might require the concurrent services of two physicians, each practicing in internal medicine but specializing in different sub-specialties.

While it would not be highly unusual for concurrent care performed by physicians in different specialties (e.g., a surgeon and an internist) or by physicians in different sub-specialties of the same specialty (e.g., an allergist and a cardiologist) to be found medically necessary, the need for such care by physicians in the same specialty or sub-specialty (e.g., two internists or two cardiologists) would occur infrequently since in most cases both physicians would possess the skills and knowledge necessary to treat the patient. However, circumstances could arise which would necessitate such care. For example, a patient may require the services of two physicians in the same specialty or sub-specialty when one physician has further limited his or her practice to some unusual aspect of that specialty, e.g., tropical medicine. Similarly, concurrent services provided by a family physician and an internist may or may not be found to be reasonable and necessary, depending on the circumstances of the specific case. If it is determined that the services of one of the physicians are not warranted by the patient's condition, payment may be made only for the other physician's (or physicians') services.

Once it is determined that the patient requires the active services of more than one physician, the individual services must be examined for medical necessity, just as where a single physician provides the care. For example, even if it is determined that the patient requires the concurrent services of both a cardiologist and a surgeon, payment may not be made for any services rendered by either physician which, for that condition, exceed normal frequency or duration unless there are special circumstances requiring the additional care.

The carrier must also assure that the services of one physician do not duplicate those provided by another, e.g., where the family physician visits during the post-operative period primarily as a courtesy to the patient.

Hospital admission services performed by two physicians for the same beneficiary on the same day could represent reasonable and necessary services, provided, as stated above, that the patient's condition necessitates treatment by both physicians. The level of difficulty of the service provided may vary between the physicians, depending on the severity of the complaint each one is treating and that physician's prior contact with the patient. For example, the admission services performed by a physician who has been treating a patient over a period of time for a chronic condition would not be as involved as the services performed by a physician who has had no prior contact with the patient and who has been called in to diagnose and treat a major acute condition.

Carriers should have sufficient means for identifying concurrent care situations. A correct coverage determination can be made on a concurrent care case only where the claim is sufficiently documented for the carrier to determine the role each physician played in the patient's care (i.e., the condition or conditions for which the physician treated the patient). If, in any case, the role of each physician involved is not clear, the carrier should request clarification.

F. Completion of Claims Forms

Separate charges for the services of a physician in completing a Form CMS-1500, a statement in lieu of a Form CMS-1500, or an itemized bill are not covered. Payment for completion of the Form CMS-1500 claim form is considered included in the fee schedule amount.

G. Care Plan Oversight Services

Care plan oversight is supervision of patients under care of home health agencies or hospices that require complex and multidisciplinary care modalities involving regular physician development and/or revision of care plans, review of subsequent reports of patient status, review of laboratory and other studies, communication with other health professionals not employed in the same practice who are involved in the patient's care, integration of new information into the care plan, and/or adjustment of medical therapy.

Such services are covered for home health and hospice patients, but are not covered for patients of skilled nursing facilities (SNFs), nursing home facilities, or hospitals.

These services are covered only if all the following requirements are met:

1. The beneficiary must require complex or multi-disciplinary care modalities requiring ongoing physician involvement in the patient's plan of care;

2. The care plan oversight (CPO) services should be furnished during the period in which the beneficiary was receiving Medicare covered HHA or hospice services;

3. The physician who bills CPO must be the same physician who signed the home health or hospice plan of care;

4. The physician furnished at least 30 minutes of care plan oversight within the calendar month for which payment is claimed. Time spent by a physician's nurse or the time spent consulting with one's nurse is not countable toward the 30-minute threshold. Low-intensity services included as part of other evaluation and management services are not included as part of the 30 minutes required for coverage;

5. The work included in hospital discharge day management (codes 99238-99239) and discharge from observation (code 99217) is not countable toward the 30 minutes per month required for work on the same day as discharge but only for those services separately documented as occurring after

the patient is actually physically discharged from the hospital;

6. The physician provided a covered physician service that required a face-to-face encounter with the beneficiary within the six months immediately preceding the first care plan oversight service. Only evaluation and management services are acceptable prerequisite face-to-face encounters for CPO. EKG, lab, and surgical services are not sufficient face-to-face services for CPO;

7. The care plan oversight billed by the physician was not routine post-operative care provided in the global surgical period of a surgical procedure billed by the physician;

8. If the beneficiary is receiving home health agency services, the physician did not have a significant financial or contractual interest in the home health agency. A physician who is an employee of a hospice, including a volunteer medical director, should not bill CPO services. Payment for the services of a physician employed by the hospice is included in the payment to the hospice;

9. The physician who bills the care plan oversight services is the physician who furnished them;

10. Services provided incident to a physician's service do not qualify as CPO and do not count toward the 30-minute requirement;

11. The physician is not billing for the Medicare end stage renal disease (ESRD) capitation payment for the same beneficiary during the same month; and

12. The physician billing for CPO must document in the patient's record the services furnished and the date and length of time associated with those services.

Pub. 100-2, Chapter 15, Section 50
Drugs and Biologicals

B3-2049, A3-3112.4.B, HO-230.4.B

The Medicare program provides limited benefits for outpatient drugs. The program covers drugs that are furnished "incident to" a physician's service provided that the drugs are not usually self-administered by the patients who take them.

Generally, drugs and biologicals are covered only if all of the following requirements are met:

They meet the definition of drugs or biologicals (see §50.1);

They are of the type that are not usually self-administered. (see §50.2);

They meet all the general requirements for coverage of items as incident to a physician's services (see §§50.1 and 50.3);

They are reasonable and necessary for the diagnosis or treatment of the illness or injury for which they are administered according to accepted standards of medical practice (see §50.4);

They are not excluded as noncovered immunizations (see §50.4.2); and

They have not been determined by the FDA to be less than effective. (See §§50.4.4).

Medicare Part B does generally not cover drugs that can be self-administered, such as those in pill form, or are used for self-injection. However, the statute provides for the coverage of some self-administered drugs. Examples of

self-administered drugs that are covered include blood-clotting factors, drugs used in immunosuppressive therapy, erythropoietin for dialysis patients, osteoporosis drugs for certain homebound patients, and certain oral cancer drugs. (See §110.3 for coverage of drugs, which are necessary to the effective use of Durable Medical Equipment (DME) or prosthetic devices.)

Pub. 100-2, Chapter 15, Section 50.5
Self-Administered Drugs and Biologicals

B3-2049.5

Medicare Part B does not cover drugs that are usually self-administered by the patient unless the statute provides for such coverage. The statute explicitly provides coverage, for blood clotting factors, drugs used in immunosuppressive therapy, erythropoietin for dialysis patients, certain oral anti-cancer drugs and anti-emetics used in certain situations.

Pub. 100-2, Chapter 15, Section 60.3
Incident to Physician's Service in Clinic

B3-2050.3

Services and supplies incident to a physician's service in a physician directed clinic or group association are generally the same as those described above.

A physician directed clinic is one where:

1. A physician (or a number of physicians) is present to perform medical (rather than administrative) services at all times the clinic is open;

2. Each patient is under the care of a clinic physician; and

3. The nonphysician services are under medical supervision.

In highly organized clinics, particularly those that are departmentalized, direct physician supervision may be the responsibility of several physicians as opposed to an individual attending physician. In this situation, medical management of all services provided in the clinic is assured. The physician ordering a particular service need not be the physician who is supervising the service. Therefore, services performed by auxiliary personnel and other aides are covered even though they are performed in another department of the clinic.

Supplies provided by the clinic during the course of treatment are also covered. When the auxiliary personnel perform services outside the clinic premises, the services are covered only if performed under the direct supervision of a clinic physician. If the clinic refers a patient for auxiliary services performed by personnel who are not supervised by clinic physicians, such services are not incident to a physician's service.

Pub. 100-2, Chapter 15, Section 80
Requirements for Diagnostic X-Ray, Diagnostic Laboratory, and Other Diagnostic Tests

B3-2070

This section describes the levels of physician supervision required for furnishing the technical component of diagnostic tests for a Medicare beneficiary who is not a hospital inpatient or outpatient. Section 410.32(b) of the Code of Federal Regulations (CFR) requires that diagnostic tests covered under §1861(s)(3) of the Act (the Act) and payable under the physician fee schedule, with certain exceptions listed in the regulation, have to be performed under the supervision of an individual meeting the definition of a physician (§1861(r) of the Act) to be considered reasonable and necessary and, therefore, covered under Medicare. The regulation defines these levels of physician supervision for diagnostic tests as follows:

General Supervision - means the procedure is furnished under the physician's overall direction and control, but the physician's presence is not required during the performance of the procedure. Under general supervision, the training of the nonphysician personnel who actually performs the diagnostic procedure and the maintenance of the necessary equipment and supplies are the continuing responsibility of the physician.

Direct Supervision - in the office setting means the physician must be present in the office suite and immediately available to furnish assistance and direction throughout the performance of the procedure. It does not mean that the physician must be present in the room when the procedure is performed.

Personal Supervision - means a physician must be in attendance in the room during the performance of the procedure.

One of the following numerical levels is assigned to each CPT or HCPCS code in the Medicare Physician Fee Schedule Database:

0   Procedure is not a diagnostic test or procedure is a diagnostic test which is not subject to the physician supervision policy.

1   Procedure must be performed under the general supervision of a physician.

2   Procedure must be performed under the direct supervision of a physician.

3   Procedure must be performed under the personal supervision of a physician.

4   Physician supervision policy does not apply when procedure is furnished by a qualified, independent psychologist or a clinical psychologist; otherwise must be performed under the general supervision of a physician.

5   Physician supervision policy does not apply when procedure is furnished by a qualified audiologist; otherwise must be performed under the general supervision of a physician.

6   Procedure must be performed by a physician or by a physical therapist (PT) who is certified by the American Board of Physical Therapy Specialties (ABPTS) as a qualified electrophysiologic clinical specialist and is permitted to provide the procedure under State law.

6a   Supervision standards for level 66 apply; in addition, the PT with ABPTS certification may supervise another PT but only the PT with ABPTS certification may bill.

7a   Supervision standards for level 77 apply; in addition, the PT with ABPTS certification may supervise another PT but only the PT with ABPTS certification may bill.

9   Concept does not apply.

21   Procedure must be performed by a technician with certification under general supervision of a physician; otherwise must be performed under direct supervision of a physician.

22   Procedure may be performed by a technician with on-line real-time contact with physician.

66   Procedure must be performed by a physician or by a PT with ABPTS certification and certification in this specific procedure.

77   Procedure must be performed by a PT with ABPTS certification or by a PT without certification under direct supervision of a physician, or by a technician with certification under general supervision of a physician.

Nurse practitioners, clinical nurse specialists, and physician assistants are not defined as physicians under §1861(r) of the Act. Therefore, they may not function as supervisory physicians under the diagnostic tests benefit (§1861(s)(3) of the Act). However, when these practitioners personally perform diagnostic tests as provided under §1861(s)(2)(K) of the Act, §1861(s)(3) does not apply and they may perform diagnostic tests pursuant to State scope of practice laws and under the applicable State requirements for physician supervision or collaboration.

Because the diagnostic tests benefit set forth in §1861(s)(3) of the Act is separate and distinct from the incident to benefit set forth in §1861(s)(2) of the Act, diagnostic tests need not meet the incident to requirements. Diagnostic tests may be furnished under situations that meet the incident to requirements but this is not required. However, carriers must not scrutinize claims for diagnostic tests utilizing the incident to requirements.

Pub. 100-2, Chapter 15, Section 80.1
Clinical Laboratory Services

B3-2070.1

Section 1833 and 1861 of the Act provides for payment of clinical laboratory services under Medicare Part B. Clinical laboratory services involve the biological, microbiological, serological, chemical, immunohematological, hematological, biophysical, cytological, pathological, or other examination of materials derived from the human body for the diagnosis, prevention, or treatment of a disease or assessment of a medical condition. Laboratory services must meet all applicable requirements of the Clinical Laboratory Improvement Amendments of 1988 (CLIA), as set forth at 42 CFR part 493. Section 1862(a)(1)(A) of the Act provides that Medicare payment may not be made for services that are not reasonable and necessary. Clinical laboratory services must be ordered and used promptly by the physician who is treating the beneficiary as described in 42 CFR 410.32(a), or by a qualified nonphysician practitioner, as described in 42 CFR 410.32(a)(3).

See the Medicare Claims Processing Manual Chapter 16 for related claims processing instructions.

Pub. 100-2, Chapter 15, Section 80.2
Psychological Tests

B3-2070.2

The diagnostic testing services performed by a psychologist (who is not a clinical psychologist as defined in §160.A) practicing independently of an institution, agency, or physician's office are covered as other diagnostic tests if a physician orders such testing. Medicare covers this type of testing as an outpatient service if furnished by any psychologist who is licensed or certified to practice psychology in the State or jurisdiction where the psychologist is furnishing services or, if the jurisdiction does not issue licenses, if provided by any practicing psychologist. (It is CMS' understanding that all States, the District of Columbia, and Puerto Rico license psychologists, but that some trust territories do not. Examples of psychologists, other than clinical psychologists, whose services are covered under this provision include, but are not limited to, educational psychologists and counseling psychologists.)

To determine whether the diagnostic psychological testing services of a particular independent psychologist are covered under Part B in States that have statutory licensure or certification, the carrier secures from the appropriate State agency a current listing of psychologists holding the required credentials. In States or territories that lack statutory licensing and certification, the carrier checks individual qualifications when provider numbers are issued. Possible reference sources are the national directory of membership of the American Psychological Association, which provides data about the educational background of individuals and indicates which members are board-certified, and records and directories of the State or territorial psychological association. If qualification is dependent on a doctoral degree from a currently accredited program, the carrier verifies the date of accreditation of the school involved, since such accreditation is not retroactive. If the reference sources listed above do not provide enough information (e.g., the psychologist is not a member of the association), the carrier contacts the psychologist personally for the required information. Generally, carriers maintain a continuing list of psychologists whose qualifications have been verified.

NOTE: Diagnostic psychological testing services performed by persons who meet these requirements are covered as other diagnostic tests. When, however, the psychologist is not practicing independently, but is on the staff of an institution, agency, or clinic, that entity bills for the diagnostic services.

Expenses for such testing are not subject to the payment limitation on treatment for mental, psychoneurotic, and personality disorders. Independent psychologists are not required by law to accept assignment when performing psychological tests. However, regardless of whether the psychologist accepts assignment, the psychologist must report on the claim form the name and address of the physician who ordered the test.

The carrier considers psychologists as practicing independently when:

They render services on their own responsibility, free of the administrative and professional control of an employer such as a physician, institution, agency;

- The persons they treat are their own patients; and
- They have the right to bill directly, collect and retain the fee for their services.

A psychologist practicing in an office located in an institution may be considered an independently practicing psychologist when both of the following conditions exist:

The office is confined to a separately-identified part of the facility which is used solely as the psychologist's office and cannot be construed as extending throughout the entire institution; and

The psychologist conducts a private practice, i.e., services are rendered to patients from outside the institution as well as to institutional patients

Pub. 100-2, Chapter 15, Section 80.3
Otologic Evaluations

B3-2070.3, PM-B-01-34, B-02-004, PM AB-02-080

Diagnostic testing, including hearing and balance assessment services, performed by a qualified audiologist is covered as "other diagnostic tests" under §1861(s)(3) of the Act when a physician orders such testing for the purpose of obtaining information necessary for the physician's diagnostic evaluation or to determine the appropriate medical or surgical treatment of a hearing deficit or related medical problem. Services are excluded by virtue of §1862(a)(7) of the Act when the diagnostic information required to determine the appropriate medial or surgical treatment is already known to the physician, or the diagnostic services are performed only to determine the need for or the appropriate type of hearing aid.

Diagnostic services performed by a qualified audiologist and meeting the above requirements are payable as "other diagnostic tests". The payment for these services is determined by the reason the tests were performed, rather than the diagnosis or the patient's condition. Payment for these services is based on the physician fee schedule amount except for audiology services furnished in a hospital outpatient department which are paid under the Outpatient Prospective Payment System. Nonhospital entities billing for the audiologist's services may accept assignment under the usual procedure or, if not accepting assignment, may charge the patient and submit a nonassigned claim on their behalf.

If a physician refers a beneficiary to an audiologist for evaluation of signs or symptoms associated with hearing loss or ear injury, the audiologist's diagnostic services should be covered even if the only outcome is the prescription of a hearing aid. If a beneficiary undergoes diagnostic testing performed by an audiologist without a physician referral, the tests are not covered even if the audiologist discovers a pathologic condition.

Pub. 100-2, Chapter 15, Section 100
Surgical Dressings, Splints, Casts, and Other Devices Used for Reductions of Fractures and Dislocations

B3-2079, A3-3110.3, HO-228.3,

Surgical dressings are limited to primary and secondary dressings required for the treatment of a wound caused by, or treated by, a surgical procedure that has been performed by a physician or other health care professional to the extent permissible under State law. In addition, surgical dressings required after debridement of a wound are also covered, irrespective of the type of debridement, as long as the debridement was reasonable and necessary and was performed by a health care professional acting within the scope of his/her legal authority when performing this function. Surgical dressings are covered for as long as they are medically necessary.

Primary dressings are therapeutic or protective coverings applied directly to wounds or lesions either on the skin or caused by an opening to the skin. Secondary dressing materials that serve a therapeutic or protective function and that are needed to secure a primary dressing are also

© 2005 Ingenix, Inc.

covered. Items such as adhesive tape, roll gauze, bandages, and disposable compression material are examples of secondary dressings. Elastic stockings, support hose, foot coverings, leotards, knee supports, surgical leggings, gauntlets, and pressure garments for the arms and hands are examples of items that are not ordinarily covered as surgical dressings. Some items, such as transparent film, may be used as a primary or secondary dressing.

If a physician, certified nurse midwife, physician assistant, nurse practitioner, or clinical nurse specialist applies surgical dressings as part of a professional service that is billed to Medicare, the surgical dressings are considered incident to the professional services of the health care practitioner. (See §§60.1, 180, 190, 200, and 210.) When surgical dressings are not covered incident to the services of a health care practitioner and are obtained by the patient from a supplier (e.g., a drugstore, physician, or other health care practitioner that qualifies as a supplier) on an order from a physician or other health care professional authorized under State law or regulation to make such an order, the surgical dressings are covered separately under Part B.

Splints and casts, and other devices used for reductions of fractures and dislocations are covered under Part B of Medicare. This includes dental splints.

Pub. 100-2, Chapter 15, Section 120
Prosthetic Devices

B3-2130, A3-3110.4, HO-228.4, A3-3111, HO-229

A. General

Prosthetic devices (other than dental) which replace all or part of an internal body organ (including contiguous tissue), or replace all or part of the function of a permanently inoperative or malfunctioning internal body organ are covered when furnished on a physician's order. This does not require a determination that there is no possibility that the patient's condition may improve sometime in the future. If the medical record, including the judgment of the attending physician, indicates the condition is of long and indefinite duration, the test of permanence is considered met. (Such a device may also be covered under §60.I as a supply when furnished incident to a physician's service.)

Examples of prosthetic devices include artificial limbs, parenteral and enteral (PEN) nutrition, cardiac pacemakers, prosthetic lenses (see subsection B), breast prostheses (including a surgical brassiere) for postmastectomy patients, maxillofacial devices, and devices which replace all or part of the ear or nose. A urinary collection and retention system with or without a tube is a prosthetic device replacing bladder function in case of permanent urinary incontinence. The foley catheter is also considered a prosthetic device when ordered for a patient with permanent urinary incontinence. However, chucks, diapers, rubber sheets, etc., are supplies that are not covered under this provision. Although hemodialysis equipment is a prosthetic device, payment for the rental or purchase of such equipment in the home is made only for use under the provisions for payment applicable to durable medical equipment.

An exception is that if payment cannot be made on an inpatient's behalf under Part A, hemodialysis equipment, supplies, and services required by such patient could be covered under Part B as a prosthetic device, which replaces the function of a kidney. See the Medicare Benefit Policy Manual, Chapter 11, "End Stage Renal Disease," for payment for hemodialysis equipment used in the home. See the Medicare Benefit Policy Manual, Chapter 1, "Inpatient Hospital Services," §10, for additional instructions on hospitalization for renal dialysis.

NOTE: Medicare does not cover a prosthetic device dispensed to a patient prior to the time at which the patient undergoes the procedure that makes necessary the use of the device. For example, the carrier does not make a separate Part B payment for an intraocular lens (IOL) or pacemaker that a physician, during an office visit prior to the actual surgery, dispenses to the patient for his or her use. Dispensing a prosthetic device in this manner raises health and safety issues. Moreover, the need for the device cannot be clearly established until the procedure that makes its use possible is successfully performed. Therefore, dispensing a prosthetic device in this manner is not considered reasonable and necessary for the treatment of the patient's condition.

Colostomy (and other ostomy) bags and necessary accouterments required for attachment are covered as prosthetic devices. This coverage also includes irrigation and flushing equipment and other items and supplies directly related to ostomy care, whether the attachment of a bag is required.

Accessories and/or supplies which are used directly with an enteral or parenteral device to achieve the therapeutic benefit of the prosthesis or to assure the proper functioning of the device may also be covered under the prosthetic device benefit subject to the additional guidelines in the Medicare National Coverage Determinations Manual.

Covered items include catheters, filters, extension tubing, infusion bottles, pumps (either food or infusion), intravenous (I.V.) pole, needles, syringes, dressings, tape, Heparin Sodium (parenteral only), volumetric monitors (parenteral only), and parenteral and enteral nutrient solutions. Baby food and other regular grocery products that can be blenderized and used with the enteral system are not covered. Note that some of these items, e.g., a food pump and an I.V. pole, qualify as DME. Although coverage of the enteral and parenteral nutritional therapy systems is provided on the basis of the prosthetic device benefit, the payment rules relating to lump sum or monthly payment for DME apply to such items.

The coverage of prosthetic devices includes replacement of and repairs to such devices as explained in subsection D.

Finally, the Benefits Improvement and Protection Act of 2000 amended §1834(h)(1) of the Act by adding a provision (1834 (h)(1)(G)(i)) that requires Medicare payment to be made for the replacement of prosthetic devices which are artificial limbs, or for the replacement of any part of such devices, without regard to continuous use or useful lifetime restrictions if an ordering physician determines that the replacement device, or replacement part of such a device, is necessary.

Payment may be made for the replacement of a prosthetic device that is an artificial limb, or replacement part of a device if the ordering physician determines that the replacement device or part is necessary because of any of the following:

1. A change in the physiological condition of the patient;

2. An irreparable change in the condition of the device, or in a part of the device; or

3. The condition of the device, or the part of the device, requires repairs and the cost of such repairs would be more than 60 percent of the cost of a replacement device, or, as the case may be, of the part being replaced.

This provision is effective for items replaced on or after April 1, 2001. It supersedes any rule that that provided a 5-year or other replacement rule with regard to prosthetic devices.

B. Prosthetic Lenses

The term "internal body organ" includes the lens of an eye. Prostheses replacing the lens of an eye include post-surgical lenses customarily used during convalescence from eye surgery in which the lens of the eye was removed. In addition, permanent lenses are also covered when required by an individual lacking the organic lens of the eye because of surgical removal or congenital absence. Prosthetic lenses obtained on or after the beneficiary's date of entitlement to supplementary medical insurance benefits may be covered even though the surgical removal of the crystalline lens occurred before entitlement.

1. Prosthetic Cataract Lenses

One of the following prosthetic lenses or combinations of prosthetic lenses furnished by a physician (see §30.4 for coverage of prosthetic lenses prescribed by a doctor of optometry) may be covered when determined to be reasonable and necessary to restore essentially the vision provided by the crystalline lens of the eye:

Prosthetic bifocal lenses in frames;

Prosthetic lenses in frames for far vision, and prosthetic lenses in frames for near vision; or

When a prosthetic contact lens(es) for far vision is prescribed (including cases of binocular and monocular aphakia), make payment for the contact lens(es) and prosthetic lenses in frames for near vision to be worn at the same time as the contact lens(es), and prosthetic lenses in frames to be worn when the contacts have been removed.

Lenses which have ultraviolet absorbing or reflecting properties may be covered, in lieu of payment for regular (untinted) lenses, if it has been determined that such lenses are medically reasonable and necessary for the individual patient.

Medicare does not cover cataract sunglasses obtained in addition to the regular (untinted) prosthetic lenses since the sunglasses duplicate the restoration of vision function performed by the regular prosthetic lenses.

2. Payment for Intraocular Lenses (IOLs) Furnished in Ambulatory Surgical Centers (ASCs)

Effective for services furnished on or after March 12, 1990, payment for intraocular lenses (IOLs) inserted during or subsequent to cataract surgery in a Medicare certified ASC is included with the payment for facility services that are furnished in connection with the covered surgery.

Refer to the Medicare Claims Processing Manual, Chapter 14, "Ambulatory Surgical Centers," for more information.

3. Limitation on Coverage of Conventional Lenses

One pair of conventional eyeglasses or conventional contact lenses furnished after each cataract surgery with insertion of an IOL is covered.

C. Dentures

Dentures are excluded from coverage. However, when a denture or a portion of the denture is an integral part (built-in) of a covered prosthesis (e.g., an obturator to fill an opening in the palate), it is covered as part of that prosthesis.

D. Supplies, Repairs, Adjustments, and Replacement

Supplies are covered that are necessary for the effective use of a prosthetic device (e.g., the batteries needed to operate an artificial larynx). Adjustment of prosthetic devices required by wear or by a change in the patient's condition is covered when ordered by a physician. General provisions relating to the repair and replacement of durable medical equipment in §110.2 for the repair and replacement of prosthetic devices are applicable. (See the Medicare Benefit Policy Manual, Chapter 16, "General Exclusions from Coverage," §40.4, for payment for devices replaced under a warranty.) Replacement of conventional eyeglasses or contact lenses furnished in accordance with §120.B.3 is not covered.

Necessary supplies, adjustments, repairs, and replacements are covered even when the device had been in use before the user enrolled in Part B of the program, so long as the device continues to be medically required.

Pub. 100-2, Chapter 15, Section 150
Dental Services

B3-2136

As indicated under the general exclusions from coverage, items and services in connection with the care, treatment, filling, removal, or replacement of teeth or structures directly supporting the teeth are not covered. "Structures directly supporting the teeth" means the periodontium, which includes the gingivae, dentogingival junction, periodontal membrane, cementum of the teeth, and alveolar process.

In addition to the following, see Pub 100-1, the Medicare General Information, Eligibility, and Entitlement Manual, Chapter 5, Definitions and Pub 3, the Medicare National Coverage Determinations Manual for specific services which may be covered when furnished by a dentist. If an otherwise noncovered procedure or service is performed by a dentist as incident to and as an integral part of a covered procedure or service performed by the dentist, the total service performed by the dentist on such an occasion is covered.

EXAMPLE 1:

The reconstruction of a ridge performed primarily to prepare the mouth for dentures is a noncovered procedure. However, when the reconstruction of a ridge is performed as a result of and at the same time as the surgical removal of a tumor (for other than dental purposes), the totality of surgical procedures is a covered service.

EXAMPLE 2:

Medicare makes payment for the wiring of teeth when this is done in connection with the reduction of a jaw fracture.

The extraction of teeth to prepare the jaw for radiation treatment of neoplastic disease is also covered. This is an exception to the requirement that to be covered, a noncovered procedure or service performed by a dentist must be an incident to and an integral part of a covered procedure or service performed by the dentist. Ordinarily, the dentist extracts the patient's teeth, but another physician, e.g., a radiologist, administers the radiation treatments.

When an excluded service is the primary procedure involved, it is not covered, regardless of its complexity or difficulty. For example, the extraction of an impacted tooth is not covered. Similarly, an alveoplasty (the surgical improvement of the shape and condition of the alveolar process) and a frenectomy are excluded from coverage when either of these procedures is performed in connection with an excluded service, e.g., the preparation of the mouth for dentures. In a like manner, the removal of a torus palatinus (a bony protuberance of the hard palate) may be a covered service. However, with rare exception, this surgery is performed in connection with an excluded service, i.e., the preparation of the mouth for dentures. Under such circumstances, Medicare does not pay for this procedure.

Dental splints used to treat a dental condition are excluded from coverage under 1862(a)(12) of the Act. On the other hand, if the treatment is determined to be a covered medical condition (i.e., dislocated upper/lower jaw joints), then the splint can be covered.

Whether such services as the administration of anesthesia, diagnostic x-rays, and other related procedures are covered depends upon whether the primary procedure being performed by the dentist is itself covered. Thus, an x-ray taken in connection with the reduction of a fracture of the jaw or facial bone is covered. However, a single x-ray or x-ray survey taken in connection with the care or treatment of teeth or the periodontium is not covered.

Medicare makes payment for a covered dental procedure no matter where the service is performed. The hospitalization or nonhospitalization of a patient has no direct bearing on the coverage or exclusion of a given dental procedure.

Payment may also be made for services and supplies furnished incident to covered dental services. For example, the services of a dental technician or nurse who is under the direct supervision of the dentist or physician are covered if the services are included in the dentist's or physician's bill.

Pub. 100-2, Chapter 15, Section 160
Clinical Psychologist Services

B3-2150

A. Clinical Psychologist (CP) Defined

To qualify as a clinical psychologist (CP), a practitioner must meet the following requirements:

Hold a doctoral degree in psychology;

Be licensed or certified, on the basis of the doctoral degree in psychology, by the State in which he or she practices, at the independent practice level of psychology to furnish diagnostic, assessment, preventive, and therapeutic services directly to individuals.

B. Qualified Clinical Psychologist Services Defined

Effective July 1, 1990, the diagnostic and therapeutic services of CPs and services and supplies furnished incident to such services are covered as the services furnished by a physician or as incident to physician's services are covered. However, the CP must be legally authorized to perform the

services under applicable licensure laws of the State in which they are furnished.

C. Types of Clinical Psychologist Services That May Be Covered

The CPs may provide the following services:

Diagnostic and therapeutic services that the CP is legally authorized to perform in accordance with State law and/or regulation. Carriers pay all qualified CPs based on the physician fee schedule for the diagnostic and therapeutic services. (Psychological tests by practitioners who do not meet the requirements for a CP may be covered under the provisions for diagnostic tests as described in §80.2.

Services and supplies furnished incident to a CP's services are covered if the requirements that apply to services incident to a physician's services, as described in §60 are met. These services must be:

o Mental health services that are commonly furnished in CPs' offices;

o An integral, although incidental, part of professional services performed by the CP;

o Performed under the direct personal supervision of the CP; i.e., the CP must be physically present and immediately available; and

o Furnished without charge or included in the CP's bill.

Any person involved in performing the service must be an employee of the CP (or an employee of the legal entity that employs the supervising CP) under the common law control test of the Act, as set forth in 20 CFR 404.1007 and §RS 2101.020 of the Retirement and Survivors Insurance part of the Social Security Program Operations Manual System.

Carriers are required to familiarize themselves with appropriate State laws and/or regulations governing a CP's scope of practice.

D. Noncovered Services

The services of CPs are not covered if the service is otherwise excluded from Medicare coverage even though a clinical psychologist is authorized by State law to perform them. For example, §1862(a)(1)(A) of the Act excludes from coverage services that are not "reasonable and necessary for the diagnosis or treatment of an illness or injury or to improve the functioning of a malformed body member." Therefore, even though the services are authorized by State law, the services of a CP that are determined to be not reasonable and necessary are not covered. Additionally, any therapeutic services that are billed by CPs under CPT psychotherapy codes that include medical evaluation and management services are not covered.

E. Requirement for Consultation

When applying for a Medicare provider number, a CP must submit to the carrier a signed Medicare provider/supplier enrollment form that indicates an agreement to the effect that, contingent upon the patient's consent, the CP will attempt to consult with the patient's attending or primary care physician in accordance with accepted professional ethical norms, taking into consideration patient confidentiality.

If the patient assents to the consultation, the CP must attempt to consult with the patient's physician within a reasonable time after receiving the consent. If the CP's attempts to consult directly with the physician are not successful, the CP must notify the physician within a reasonable time that he or she is furnishing services to the patient. Additionally, the CP must document, in the patient's medical record, the date the patient consented or declined consent to consultations, the date of consultation, or, if attempts to consult did not succeed, that date and manner of notification to the physician.

The only exception to the consultation requirement for CPs is in cases where the patient's primary care or attending physician refers the patient to the CP. Also, neither a CP nor a primary care nor attending physician may bill Medicare or the patient for this required consultation.

F. Outpatient Mental Health Services Limitation

All covered therapeutic services furnished by qualified CPs are subject to the outpatient mental health services limitation in Pub 100-1, Medicare General Information, Eligibility, and Entitlement Manual, Chapter 3, "Deductibles, Coinsurance Amounts, and Payment Limitations," §30, (i.e., only 62 1/2 percent of expenses for these services are considered incurred expenses for Medicare purposes). The limitation does not apply to diagnostic services.

G. Assignment Requirement

Assignment is required.

Pub. 100-2, Chapter 15, Section 170
Clinical Social Worker (CSW) Services

B3-2152

See the Medicare Claims Processing Manual Chapter 12, Physician/Nonphysician Practitioners, §150, "Clinical Social Worker Services," for payment requirements.

A. Clinical Social Worker Defined

Section 1861(hh) of the Act defines a "clinical social worker" as an individual who:

Possesses a master's or doctor's degree in social work;

Has performed at least two years of supervised clinical social work; and

Is licensed or certified as a clinical social worker by the State in which the services are performed; or

In the case of an individual in a State that does not provide for licensure or certification, has completed at least 2 years or 3,000 hours of post master's degree supervised clinical social work practice under the supervision of a master's level social worker in an appropriate setting such as a hospital, SNF, or clinic.

B. Clinical Social Worker Services Defined

Section 1861(hh)(2) of the Act defines "clinical social worker services" as those services that the CSW is legally authorized to perform under State law (or the State regulatory mechanism provided by State law) of the State in which such services are performed for the diagnosis and treatment of mental illnesses. Services furnished to an inpatient of a hospital or an inpatient of a SNF that the SNF is required to provide as a requirement for participation are not included. The services that are covered are those that are otherwise covered if furnished by a physician or as incident to a physician's professional service.

C. Covered Services

Coverage is limited to the services a CSW is legally authorized to perform in accordance with State law (or State regulatory mechanism established by State law). The services of a CSW may be covered under Part B if they are:

The type of services that are otherwise covered if furnished by a physician, or as incident to a physician's service. (See §30 for a description of physicians' services and §70 of Pub 100-1, the Medicare General Information, Eligibility, and Entitlement Manual, Chapter 5, for the definition of a physician.);

Performed by a person who meets the definition of a CSW (See subsection A.); and

Not otherwise excluded from coverage.

Carriers should become familiar with the State law or regulatory mechanism governing a CSW's scope of practice in their service area.

D. Noncovered Services

Services of a CSW are not covered when furnished to inpatients of a hospital or to inpatients of a SNF if the services furnished in the SNF are those that the SNF is required to furnish as a condition of participation in Medicare. In addition, CSW services are not covered if they are otherwise excluded from Medicare coverage even though a CSW is authorized by State law to perform them. For example, the Medicare law excludes from coverage services that are not "reasonable and necessary for the diagnosis or treatment of an illness or injury or to improve the functioning of a malformed body member."

E. Outpatient Mental Health Services Limitation

All covered therapeutic services furnished by qualified CSWs are subject to the outpatient psychiatric services limitation in Pub 100-1, Medicare General Information, Eligibility, and Entitlement Manual, Chapter 3, "Deductibles, Coinsurance Amounts, and Payment Limitations," §30, (i.e., only 62 1/2 percent of expenses for these services are considered incurred expenses for Medicare purposes). The limitation does not apply to diagnostic services.

F. Assignment Requirement

Assignment is required.

Pub. 100-2, Chapter 15, Section 180
Nurse-Midwife (CNM) Services

B3-2154

A. General

Effective on or after July 1, 1988, the services provided by a certified nurse-midwife or incident to the certified nurse-midwife's services are covered. Payment is made under assignment only.

See the Medicare Claims Processing Manual, Chapter 12, "Physician and Nonphysician Practitioners," §130, for payment methodology for nurse midwife services.

B. Certified Nurse-Midwife Defined

A certified nurse-midwife is a registered nurse who has successfully completed a program of study and clinical experience in nurse-midwifery, meeting guidelines prescribed by the Secretary, or who has been certified by an organization recognized by the Secretary. The Secretary has recognized certification by the American College of Nurse-Midwives and State qualifying requirements in those

States that specify a program of education and clinical experience for nurse-midwives for these purposes. A nurse-midwife must:

Be currently licensed to practice in the State as a registered professional nurse; and

Meet one of the following requirements:

1. Be legally authorized under State law or regulations to practice as a nurse-midwife and have completed a program of study and clinical experience for nurse-midwives, as specified by the State; or

2. If the State does not specify a program of study and clinical experience that nurse-midwives must complete to practice in that State, the nurse-midwife must:

a. Be currently certified as a nurse-midwife by the American College of Nurse-Midwives;

b. Have satisfactorily completed a formal education program (of at least one academic year) that, upon completion, qualifies the nurse to take the certification examination offered by the American College of Nurse-Midwives; or

c. Have successfully completed a formal education program for preparing registered nurses to furnish gynecological and obstetrical care to women during pregnancy, delivery, and the postpartum period, and care to normal newborns, and have practiced as a nurse-midwife for a total of 12 months during any 18-month period from August 8, 1976, to July 16, 1982.

C. Covered Services

1. General - Effective January 1, 1988, through December 31, 1993, the coverage of nurse-midwife services was restricted to the maternity cycle. The maternity cycle is a period that includes pregnancy, labor, and the immediate postpartum period.

Beginning with services furnished on or after January 1, 1994, coverage is no longer limited to the maternity cycle. Coverage is available for services furnished by a nurse-midwife that he or she is legally authorized to perform in the State in which the services are furnished and that would otherwise be covered if furnished by a physician, including obstetrical and gynecological services.

2. Incident To - Services and supplies furnished incident to a nurse midwife's service are covered if they would have been covered when furnished incident to the services of a doctor of medicine or osteopathy, as described in §60.

D. Noncovered Services

The services of nurse-midwives are not covered if they are otherwise excluded from Medicare coverage even though a nurse-midwife is authorized by State law to perform them. For example, the Medicare program excludes from coverage routine physical checkups and services that are not reasonable and necessary for the diagnosis or treatment of an illness or injury or to improve the functioning of a malformed body member.

Coverage of service to the newborn continues only to the point that the newborn is or would normally be treated medically as a separate individual. Items and services furnished the newborn from that point are not covered on the basis of the mother's eligibility.

E. Relationship With Physician

Most States have licensure and other requirements applicable to nurse-midwives. For example, some require that the nurse-midwife have an arrangement with a physician for the referral of the patient in the event a problem develops that requires medical attention. Others may require that the nurse-midwife function under the general supervision of a physician. Although these and similar State requirements must be met in order for the nurse-midwife to provide Medicare covered care, they have no effect on the nurse-midwife's right to personally bill for and receive direct Medicare payment. That is, billing does not have to flow through a physician or facility.

See §60.2 for coverage of services performed by nurse-midwives incident to the service of physicians.

F. Place of Service

There is no restriction on place of service. Therefore, nurse-midwife services are covered if provided in the nurse-midwife's office, in the patient's home, or in a hospital or other facility, such as a clinic or birthing center owned or operated by a nurse-midwife.

G. Assignment Requirement

Assignment is required.

Pub. 100-2, Chapter 15, Section 230
Practice of Physical Therapy, Occupational Therapy, and Speech-Language Pathology

Pub. 100-2, Chapter 15, Section 230.1
Practice of Physical Therapy

A. General

Physical therapy services are those services provided within the scope of practice of physical therapists and necessary for the diagnosis and treatment of impairments, functional limitations, disabilities or changes in physical function and health status. (See Pub. 100-03, the Medicare National Coverage Determinations Manual, for specific conditions or services.)

B. Qualified Physical Therapist Defined

Reference: 42CFR484.4

A qualified physical therapist for program coverage purposes is a person who is licensed as a physical therapist by the state in which he or she is practicing and meets one of the following requirements:

Has graduated from a physical therapy curriculum approved by (1) the American Physical Therapy Association, or by (2) the Committee on Allied Health Education and Accreditation of the American Medical Association, or (3) Council on Medical Education of the American Medical Association, and the American Physical Therapy Association; or

Prior to January 1, 1966, (1) was admitted to membership by the American Physical Therapy Association, or (2) was admitted to registration by the American Registry of Physical Therapists, or (3) has graduated from a physical therapy curriculum in a 4-year college or university approved by a state department of education; or

Has 2 years of appropriate experience as a physical therapist and has achieved a satisfactory grade on a proficiency examination conducted, approved or sponsored by the Public Health Service, except that such determinations of proficiency do not apply with respect to persons initially licensed by a state or seeking qualification as a physical therapist after December 31, 1977; or

Was licensed or registered prior to January 1, 1966, and prior to January 1, 1970, had 15 years of full-time experience in the treatment of illness or injury through the practice of physical therapy in which services were rendered under the order and direction of attending and referring doctors of medicine or osteopathy; or

If trained outside the United States, (1) was graduated since 1928 from a physical therapy curriculum approved in the country in which the curriculum was located and in which there is a member organization of the World Confederation for Physical Therapy, (2) meets the requirements for membership in a member organization of the World Confederation for Physical Therapy.

C. Services of Physical Therapy Support Personnel

Reference: 42CFR 484.4

A physical therapist assistant (PTA) is a person who is licensed as a physical therapist assistant, if applicable, by the State in which practicing, and

- Has graduated from a 2-year college-level program approved by the American Physical Therapy Association; or
- Has 2 years of appropriate experience as a physical therapist assistant, and has achieved a satisfactory grade on a proficiency examination conducted, approved, or sponsored by the U.S. Public Health Service, except that these determinations of proficiency do not apply with respect to persons initially licensed by a State or seeking initial qualification as a PTA after December 31, 1977.

The services of PTAs used when providing covered therapy benefits are included as part of the covered service. These services are billed by the supervising physical therapist. PTAs may not provide evaluation services, make clinical judgments or decisions or take responsibility for the service. They act at the direction and under the supervision of the treating physical therapist and in accordance with state laws.

A physical therapist must supervise PTAs. The level and frequency of supervision differs by setting (and by state or local law). General supervision is required for PTAs in all settings except private practice (which requires direct supervision) unless state practice requirements are more stringent, in which case state or local requirements must be followed. See specific settings for details. For example, in clinics, rehabilitation agencies, and public health agencies, 42CFR485.713 indicates that when a PTA provides services, either on or off the organization's premises, those services are supervised by a qualified physical therapist who makes an onsite supervisory visit at least once every 30 days or more frequently if required by state or local laws or regulation.

The services of a PTA shall not be billed as services incident to a physician/NPP's service, because they do not meet the qualifications of a therapist.

The cost of supplies (e.g., theraband, hand putty, electrodes) used in furnishing covered therapy care is included in the payment for the HCPCS codes billed by the physical therapist, and are, therefore, not separately billable.

Separate coverage and billing provisions apply to items that meet the definition of brace in §130.

Services provided by aides, even if under the supervision of a therapist, are not therapy services in the outpatient setting and are not covered by Medicare. Although an aide may help the therapist by providing unskilled services, those services that are unskilled are not covered by Medicare and shall be denied as not reasonable and necessary if they are billed as therapy services.

D. Application of Medicare Guidelinesto PT Services

This subsection will be used in the future to illustrate the application of the above guidelines to some of the physical therapy modalities and procedures utilized in the treatment of patients.

Pub. 100-2, Chapter 15, Section 230.2
Practice of Occupational Therapy

A. General

Occupational therapy services are those services provided within the scope of practice of occupational therapists and necessary for the diagnosis and treatment of impairments, functional disabilities or changes in physical function and health status. (See Pub. 100-03, the Medicare National Coverage Determinations Manual, for specific conditions or services.)

Occupational therapy is medically prescribed treatment concerned with improving or restoring functions which have been impaired by illness or injury or, where function has been permanently lost or reduced by illness or injury, to improve the individual's ability to perform those tasks required for independent functioning. Such therapy may involve:

The evaluation, and reevaluation as required, of a patient's level of function by administering diagnostic and prognostic tests;

The selection and teaching of task-oriented therapeutic activities designed to restore physical function; e.g., use of woodworking activities on an inclined table to restore shoulder, elbow, and wrist range of motion lost as a result of burns;

The planning, implementing, and supervising of individualized therapeutic activity programs as part of an overall "active treatment" program for a patient with a diagnosed psychiatric illness; e.g., the use of sewing activities which require following a pattern to reduce confusion and restore reality orientation in a schizophrenic patient;

The planning and implementing of therapeutic tasks and activities to restore sensory-integrative function; e.g., providing motor and tactile activities to increase sensory input and improve response for a stroke patient with functional loss resulting in a distorted body image;

The teaching of compensatory technique to improve the level of independence in the activities of daily living, for example:

o Teaching a patient who has lost the use of an arm how to pare potatoes and chop vegetables with one hand;

o Teaching an upper extremity amputee how to functionally utilize a prosthesis;

o Teaching a stroke patient new techniques to enable the patient to perform feeding, dressing, and other activities as independently as possible; or

o Teaching a patient with a hip fracture/hip replacement techniques of standing tolerance and balance to enable the patient to perform such functional activities as dressing and homemaking tasks.

The designing, fabricating, and fitting of orthotics and self-help devices; e.g., making a hand splint for a patient with rheumatoid arthritis to maintain the hand in a functional position or constructing a device which would enable an individual to hold a utensil and feed independently; or

Vocational and prevocational assessment and training, subject to the limitations specified in item B below.

Only a qualified occupational therapist has the knowledge, training, and experience required to evaluate and, as necessary, reevaluate a patient's level of function, determine whether an occupational therapy program could reasonably be expected to improve, restore, or compensate for lost function and, where appropriate, recommend to the physician/NPP a plan of treatment.

B. Qualified Occupational Therapist Defined

Reference: 42CFR484.4

A qualified occupational therapist for program coverage purposes is an individual who meets one of the following requirements:

Is a graduate of an occupational therapy curriculum accredited jointly by the Committee on Allied Health Education of the American Medical Association and the American Occupational Therapy Association;

Is eligible for the National Registration Examination of the American Occupational Therapy Association; or

Has 2 years of appropriate experience as an occupational therapist, and has achieved a satisfactory grade on a proficiency examination conducted, approved, or sponsored by the U.S. Public Health Service, except that such determinations of proficiency do not apply with respect to persons initially licensed by a State or seeking initial qualification as an occupational therapist after December 31, 1977.

C. Services of Occupational Therapy Support Personnel

Reference: 42CFR 484.4

An occupational therapy assistant (OTA) is a person who:

- Meets the requirements for certification as an occupational therapy assistant established by the American Occupational Therapy Association; or
- Has 2 years of appropriate experience as an occupational therapy assistant and has achieved a satisfactory grade on a proficiency examination conducted, approved, or sponsored by the U.S. Public Health Service, except that such determinations of proficiency do not apply with respect to persons initially licensed by a State or seeking initial qualification as an occupational therapy assistant after December 31, 1977.

The services of OTAs used when providing covered therapy benefits are included as part of the covered service. These services are billed by the supervising occupational therapist.

OTAs may not provide evaluation services, make clinical judgments or decisions or take responsibility for the service. They act at the direction and under the supervision of the treating occupational therapist and in accordance with state laws.

An occupational therapist must supervise OTAs. The level and frequency of supervision differs by setting (and by state or local law). General supervision is required for OTAs in all settings except private practice (which requires direct supervision) unless state practice requirements are more stringent, in which case state or local requirements must be followed. See specific settings for details. For example, in clinics, rehabilitation agencies, and public health agencies, 42CFR485.713 indicates that when an OTA provides services, either on or off the organization's premises, those services are supervised by a qualified occupational therapist who makes an onsite supervisory visit at least once every 30 days or more frequently if required by state or local laws or regulation.

The services of an OTA shall not be billed as services incident to a physician/NPP's service, because they do not meet the qualifications of a therapist.

The cost of supplies (e.g., looms, ceramic tiles, or leather) used in furnishing covered therapy care is included in the payment for the HCPCS codes billed by the occupational therapist and are, therefore, not separately billable. Separate coverage and billing provisions apply to items that meet the definition of brace in §130 of this manual.

Services provided by aides, even if under the supervision of a therapist, are not therapy services in the outpatient setting and are not covered by Medicare. Although an aide may help the therapist by providing unskilled services, those services that are unskilled are not covered by Medicare and shall be denied as not reasonable and necessary if they are billed as therapy services.

D. Application of Medicare Guidelines to Occupational Therapy Services

Occupational therapy may be required for a patient with a specific diagnosed psychiatric illness. If such services are required, they are covered assuming the coverage criteria are met. However, where an individual's motivational needs are not related to a specific diagnosed psychiatric illness, the meeting of such needs does not usually require an individualized therapeutic program. Such needs can be met through general activity programs or the efforts of other professional personnel involved in the care of the patient. Patient motivation is an appropriate and inherent function of all health disciplines, which is interwoven with other functions performed by such personnel for the patient. Accordingly, since the special skills of an occupational therapist are not required, an occupational therapy program for individuals who do not have a specific diagnosed psychiatric illness is not to be considered reasonable and necessary for the treatment of an illness or injury. Services furnished under such a program are not covered.

Occupational therapy may include vocational and prevocational assessment and training. When services provided by an occupational therapist are related solely to specific employment opportunities, work skills, or work settings, they are not reasonable or necessary for the diagnosis or treatment of an illness or injury and are not covered. However, carriers and intermediaries exercise care in applying this exclusion, because the assessment of level of function and the teaching of compensatory techniques to improve the level of function, especially in activities of daily living, are services which occupational therapists provide for both vocational and nonvocational purposes. For example, an assessment of sitting and standing tolerance might be nonvocational for a mother of young children or a retired individual living alone, but could also be a vocational test for a sales clerk. Training an amputee in the use of prosthesis for telephoning is necessary for everyday activities as well as for employment purposes. Major changes in life style may be mandatory for an individual with a substantial disability. The techniques of adjustment cannot be considered exclusively vocational or nonvocational.

Pub. 100-2, Chapter 15, Section 230.3
Practice of Speech-Language Pathology

A. General

Speech-language pathology services are those services provided within the scope of practice of speech-language pathologists and necessary for the diagnosis and treatment of speech and language disorders, which result in communication disabilities and for the diagnosis and treatment of swallowing disorders (dysphagia), regardless of the presence of a communication disability. (See Pub. 100-03, chapter 1, §170.3)

B. Qualified Speech-Language Pathologist Defined

A qualified speech-language pathologist for program coverage purposes meets one of the following requirements:

- The education and experience requirements for a Certificate of Clinical Competence in (speech-language pathology or audiology) granted by the American Speech-Language Hearing Association; or
- Meets the educational requirements for certification and is in the process of accumulating the supervised experience required for certification.

Speech-language pathologists may not enroll and submit claims directly to Medicare. The services of speech-language pathologists may be billed by providers such as rehabilitation agencies, HHAs, CORFs, hospices, outpatient departments of hospitals, and suppliers such as physicians, NPPs, physical and occupational therapists in private practice.

C. Services of Speech-Language Pathology Support Personnel

Services of speech-language pathology assistants are not recognized for Medicare coverage. Services provided by speech-language pathology assistants, even if they are licensed to provide services in their states, will be considered unskilled services and denied as not reasonable and necessary if they are billed as therapy services.

Services provided by aides, even if under the supervision of a therapist, are not therapy services and are not covered by Medicare. Although an aide may help the therapist by providing unskilled services, those services are not covered by Medicare and shall be denied as not reasonable and necessary if they are billed as therapy services.

D. Application of Medicare Guidelines to Speech-Language Pathology Services

1. Evaluation Services

Speech-language pathology evaluation services are covered if they are reasonable and necessary and not excluded as routine screening by §1862(a)(7) of the Act. The speech-language pathologist employs a variety of formal and informal speech, language, and dysphagia assessment tests to ascertain the type, causal factor(s), and severity of the speech and language or swallowing disorders. Reevaluation of patients for whom speech, language and swallowing were previously contraindicated is covered only if the patient exhibits a change in medical condition. However, monthly reevaluations; e.g., a Western Aphasia Battery, for a patient undergoing a rehabilitative speech-language pathology program, are considered a part of the treatment session and shall not be covered as a separate evaluation for billing purposes. Although hearing screening by the speech-language pathologist may be part of an evaluation, it is not billable as a separate service.

2. Therapeutic Services

The following are examples of common medical disorders and resulting communication deficits, which may necessitate active rehabilitative therapy. This list is not all-inclusive:

Cerebrovascular disease such as cerebral vascular accidents presenting with dysphagia, aphasia/dysphasia, apraxia, and dysarthria;

Neurological disease such as Parkinsonism or Multiple Sclerosis with dysarthria, dysphagia, inadequate respiratory volume/control, or voice disorder; or

Laryngeal carcinoma requiring laryngectomy resulting in aphonia.

3. Aural Rehabilitation

Aural rehabilitation may be covered and medically necessary when it has been determined by a speech-language pathologist in collaboration with an audiologist that the beneficiary's current amplification options (hearing aid, other amplification device or cochlear implant) will not sufficiently meet the patient's functional communication needs.

Assessment for the need for aural rehabilitation may be done by a speech language pathologist and includes evaluation of comprehension and production of language in oral, signed or written modalities, speech and voice production, listening skills, speech reading, communications strategies, and the impact of the hearing loss on the patient/client and family.

Aural rehabilitation consists of treatment that focuses on comprehension, and production of language in oral, signed or written modalities; speech and voice production, auditory training, speech reading, multimodal (e.g., visual, auditory-visual, and tactile) training, communication strategies, education and counseling. In determining the necessity for treatment, the beneficiary's performance in both clinical and natural environment should be considered.

4. Dysphagia

Dysphagia, or difficulty in swallowing, can cause food to enter the airway, resulting in coughing, choking, pulmonary problems, aspiration or inadequate nutrition and hydration with resultant weight loss, failure to thrive, pneumonia and death. It is most often due to complex neurological and/or structural impairments including head and neck trauma, cerebrovascular accident, neuromuscular degenerative diseases, head and neck cancer, dementias, and encephalopathies. For these reasons, it is important that

© 2005 Ingenix, Inc.

only qualified professionals with specific training and experience in this disorder provide evaluation and treatment.

The speech-language pathologist performs clinical and instrumental assessments and analyzes and integrates the diagnostic information to determine candidacy for intervention as well as appropriate compensations and rehabilitative therapy techniques. The equipment that is used in the examination may be fixed, mobile or portable. Professional guidelines recommend that the service be provided in a team setting with a physician/NPP who provides supervision of the radiological examination and interpretation of medical conditions revealed in it.

Swallowing assessment and rehabilitation are highly specialized services. The professional rendering care must have education, experience and demonstrated competencies. Competencies include but are not limited to: identifying abnormal upper aerodigestive tract structure and function; conducting an oral, pharyngeal, laryngeal and respiratory function examination as it relates to the functional assessment of swallowing; recommending methods of oral intake and risk precautions; and developing a treatment plan employing appropriate compensations and therapy techniques.

Pub. 100-2, Chapter 15, Section 230.4
Services Furnished by a Physical or Occupational Therapist in Private Practice

A. General

In order to qualify to bill Medicare directly as a therapist, each individual must be enrolled as a private practitioner and employed in one of the following practice types: an unincorporated solo practice, unincorporated partnership, unincorporated group practice, physician/NPP group or groups that are not professional corporations, if allowed by state and local law. Physician/NPP group practices may employ physical therapists in private practice (PTPP) and/or occupational therapists in private practice (OTPP) if state and local law permits this employee relationship.

For purposes of this provision, a physician/NPP group practice is defined as one or more physicians/NPPs enrolled with Medicare who may bill as one entity. For further details on issues concerning enrollment, see the provider enrollment Web site at www.cms.hhs.gov/providers/enrollment.

Private practice also includes therapists who are practicing therapy as employees of another supplier, of a professional corporation or other incorporated therapy practice. Private practice does not include individuals when they are working as employees of an institutional provider.

Services should be furnished in the therapist's or group's office or in the patient's home. The office is defined as the location(s) where the practice is operated, in the state(s) where the therapist (and practice, if applicable) is legally authorized to furnish services, during the hours that the therapist engages in the practice at that location. If services are furnished in a private practice office space, that space shall be owned, leased, or rented by the practice and used for the exclusive purpose of operating the practice. For example, a therapist in private practice may furnish aquatic therapy in a community center pool. As required in other settings (such as rehabilitation agencies and CORFs), the practice would have to rent or lease the pool for those hours, and the use of the pool during that time would have to be restricted to the therapist's patients, in order to recognize

the pool as part of the therapist's own practice office during those hours. Therapists in private practice must be approved as meeting certain requirements, but do not execute a formal provider agreement with the Secretary.

If therapists who have their own Medicare Personal Identification number (PIN) or National Provider Identifier (NPI) are employed by therapist groups, physician/NPP groups, or groups that are not professional organizations, the requirement that therapy space be owned, leased, or rented may be satisfied by the group that employs the therapist. Each physical or occupational therapist employed by a group should enroll as a PT or OT in private practice.

When therapists with a Medicare PIN/NPI provide services in the physician's/NPP's office in which they are employed, and bill using their PIN/NPI for each therapy service, then the direct supervision requirement for PTAs and OTAs apply.

When the PT or OT who has a Medicare PIN/ NPI is employed in a physician's/NPP's office the services are ordinarily billed as services of the PT or OT, with the PT or OT identified on the claim as the supplier of services. However, services of the PT or OT who has a Medicare PIN/NPI may also be billed by the physician/NPP as services incident to the physician's/NPP's service. (See §230.5 for rules related to PTA and OTA services incident to a physician.) In that case, the physician/NPP is the supplier of service, the Unique Provider Identification Number (UPIN) or NPI of the physician/NPP (ordering or supervising, as indicated) is reported on the claim with the service and all the rules for incident to services (§230.5) must be followed.

B. Private Practice Defined

Reference:**Federal Register** November, 1998, pages 58863-58869; 42CFR 410.38(b)

The carrier considers a therapist to be in private practice if the therapist maintains office space at his or her own expense and furnishes services only in that space or the patient's home. Or, a therapist is employed by another supplier and furnishes services in facilities provided at the expense of that supplier.

The therapist need not be in full-time private practice but must be engaged in private practice on a regular basis; i.e., the therapist is recognized as a private practitioner and for that purpose has access to the necessary equipment to provide an adequate program of therapy.

The physical or occupational therapy services must be provided either by or under the direct supervision of the therapist in private practice. Each physical or occupational therapist in a practice should be enrolled as a Medicare provider. If a physical or occupational therapist is not enrolled, the services of that therapist must be directly supervised by an enrolled physical or occupational therapist. Direct supervision requires that the supervising private practice therapist be present in the office suite at the time the service is performed. These direct supervision requirements apply only in the private practice setting and only for physical therapists and occupational therapists and their assistants. In other outpatient settings, supervision rules differ. The services of support personnel must be included in the therapist's bill. The supporting personnel, including other therapists, must be W-2 or 1099 employees of the therapist in private practice or other qualified employer.

Coverage of outpatient physical therapy and occupational therapy under Part B includes the services of a qualified therapist in private practice when furnished in the therapist's office or the beneficiary's home. For this purpose, "home" includes an institution that is used as a home, but not a hospital, CAH or SNF, (**Federal Register** Nov. 2, 1998, pg 58869). Place of Service (POS) includes:

- 03/School, only if residential,
- 04/Homeless Shelter,
- 12/Home, other than a facility that is a private residence,
- 14/Group Home,
- 33/Custodial Care Facility.

C. Assignment

Reference: Nov. 2, 1998 **Federal Register**, pg. 58863

See also Pub. 100-04 chapter 1, 30.2.

When physicians, NPPs, PTPPs or OTPPs obtain provider numbers, they have the option of accepting assignment (participating) or not accepting assignment (nonparticipating). In contrast, providers, such as outpatient hospitals, SNFs, rehabilitation agencies, and CORFs, do not have the option. For these providers, assignment is mandatory.

If physicians/NPPs, PTPPs or OTPPs accept assignment (are participating), they must accept the Medicare Physician Fee Schedule amount as payment. Medicare pays 80% and the patient is responsible for 20%. In contrast, if they do not accept assignment, Medicare will only pay 95% of the fee schedule amount. However, when these services are not furnished on an assignment-related basis, the limiting charge applies. (See §1848(g)(2)(c) of the Act.)

NOTE: Services furnished by a therapist in the therapist's office under arrangements with hospitals in rural communities and public health agencies (or services provided in the beneficiary's home under arrangements with a provider of outpatient physical or occupational therapy services) are not covered under this provision. See section 230.6.

Pub. 100-2, Chapter 15, Section 260
Ambulatory Surgical Center Services

B3-2265

Facility services furnished by ambulatory surgical centers (ASCs) in connection with certain surgical procedures are covered under Part B. To receive coverage of and payment for its services under this provision, a facility must be certified as meeting the requirements for an ASC and enter into a written agreement with CMS. Medicare periodically updates the list of covered procedures and related payment amounts through release of regulations and Program Memoranda. The ASC must accept Medicare's payment for such procedures as payment in full with respect to those services defined as ASC facility services.

Where services are performed in an ASC, the physician and others who perform covered services may also be paid for his/her professional services; however, the "professional" rate is then adjusted since the ASC incurs the facility costs.

Pub. 100-2, Chapter 16, Section 10
General Exclusions From Coverage

A3-3150, HO-260, HHA-232, B3-2300

No payment can be made under either the hospital insurance or supplementary medical insurance program for certain items and services, when the following conditions exist:

- Not reasonable and necessary (§20);
- No legal obligation to pay for or provide (§40);
- Paid for by a governmental entity (§50);
- Not provided within United States (§60);
- Resulting from war (§70);
- Personal comfort (§80);
- Routine services and appliances (§90);
- Custodial care (§110);
- Cosmetic surgery (§120);
- Charges by immediate relatives or members of household (§130);
- Dental services (§140);
- Paid or expected to be paid under workers' compensation (§150);
- Nonphysician services provided to a hospital inpatient that were not provided directly or arranged for by the hospital (§170);
- Services Related to and Required as a Result of Services Which are not Covered Under Medicare (§180);
- Excluded foot care services and supportive devices for feet (§30); or
- Excluded investigational devices (See Chapter 14, §30).

Pub. 100-2, Chapter 16, Section 90
Routine Services and Appliances

A3-3157, HO-260.7, B3-2320, R-1797A3 - 5/00

Routine physical checkups; eyeglasses, contact lenses, and eye examinations for the purpose of prescribing, fitting, or changing eyeglasses; eye refractions by whatever practitioner and for whatever purpose performed; hearing aids and examinations for hearing aids; and immunizations are not covered.

The routine physical checkup exclusion applies to (a) examinations performed without relationship to treatment or diagnosis for a specific illness, symptom, complaint, or injury; and (b) examinations required by third parties such as insurance companies, business establishments, or Government agencies.

If the claim is for a diagnostic test or examination performed solely for the purpose of establishing a claim under title IV of Public Law 91-173, "Black Lung Benefits," the service is not covered under Medicare and the claimant should be advised to contact their Social Security office regarding the filing of a claim for reimbursement under the "Black Lung" program.

The exclusions apply to eyeglasses or contact lenses, and eye examinations for the purpose of prescribing, fitting, or changing eyeglasses or contact lenses for refractive errors. The exclusions do not apply to physicians' services (and services incident to a physicians' service) performed in conjunction with an eye disease, as for example, glaucoma or cataracts, or to post-surgical prosthetic lenses which are customarily used during convalescence from eye surgery in which the lens of the eye was removed, or to permanent prosthetic lenses required by an individual lacking the

© 2005 Ingenix, Inc.

organic lens of the eye, whether by surgical removal or congenital disease. Such prosthetic lens is a replacement for an internal body organ - the lens of the eye. (See the Medicare Benefit Policy Manual, Chapter 15, "Covered Medical and Other Health Services," §120).

Expenses for all refractive procedures, whether performed by an ophthalmologist (or any other physician) or an optometrist and without regard to the reason for performance of the refraction, are excluded from coverage.

A - Immunizations

Vaccinations or inoculations are excluded as immunizations unless they are either

- Directly related to the treatment of an injury or direct exposure to a disease or condition, such as antirabies treatment, tetanus antitoxin or booster vaccine, botulin antitoxin, antivenin sera, or immune globulin.(In the absence of injury or direct exposure, preventive immunization (vaccination or inoculation) against such diseases as smallpox, polio, diphtheria, etc., is not covered.); or
- Specifically covered by statute, as described in the Medicare Benefit Policy Manual, Chapter 15, "Covered Medical and Other Health Services," §50.

B - Antigens

Prior to the Omnibus Reconciliation Act of 1980, a physician who prepared an antigen for a patient could not be reimbursed for that service unless the physician also administered the antigen to the patient. Effective January 1, 1981, payment may be made for a reasonable supply of antigens that have been prepared for a particular patient even though they have not been administered to the patient by the same physician who prepared them if:

- The antigens are prepared by a physician who is a doctor of medicine or osteopathy, and
- The physician who prepared the antigens has examined the patient and has determined a plan of treatment and a dosage regimen.

A reasonable supply of antigens is considered to be not more than a 12-week supply of antigens that has been prepared for a particular patient at any one time. The purpose of the reasonable supply limitation is to assure that the antigens retain their potency and effectiveness over the period in which they are to be administered to the patient. (See the Medicare Benefit Policy Manual, Chapter 15, "Covered Medical and Other Health Services," §50.4.4.2)

Pub. 100-2, Chapter 16, Section 100
Hearing Aids and Cochlear Implants

Section 1862(a)(7) of the Social Security Act states that no payment may be made under part A or part B for any expenses incurred for items or services "where such expenses are for . . . hearing aids or examinations therefore. . . "This policy is further reiterated at 42 CFR 411.15(d) which specifically states that "hearing aids or examination for the purpose of prescribing, fitting, or changing hearing aids" are excluded from coverage.

Any device that does not produce as its output an electrical signal that directly stimulates the auditory nerve is a hearing aid for the purposes of Medicare payment policy. Examples of hearing aids are devices that produce air-conducted sound into the external auditory canal, devices that produce sound by mechanically vibrating bone, or devices that produce sound by vibrating the cochlear fluid through stimulation of the round window.

Devices such as cochlear implants, which produce as their output an electrical signal that directly stimulates the auditory nerve, are not considered to be hearing aids for purposes of Medicare payment policy. (See National Coverage Determinations Manual).

Medicare contractors deny payment for an item or service that is associated with any hearing aid as defined above. See §180 for policy for the medically necessary treatment of complications of implantable hearing aids, such as medically necessary removals of implantable hearing aids due to infection.

Pub. 100-2, Chapter 16, Section 120
Cosmetic Surgery

A3-3160, HO-260.11, B3-2329

Cosmetic surgery or expenses incurred in connection with such surgery is not covered. Cosmetic surgery includes any surgical procedure directed at improving appearance, except when required for the prompt (i.e., as soon as medically feasible) repair of accidental injury or for the improvement of the functioning of a malformed body member. For example, this exclusion does not apply to surgery in connection with treatment of severe burns or repair of the face following a serious automobile accident, or to surgery for therapeutic purposes which coincidentally also serves some cosmetic purpose.

Pub. 100-2, Chapter 16, Section 180
Services Related to and Required as a Result of Services Which Are Not Covered Under Medicare

B3-2300.1, A3-3101.14, HO-210.12

Medical and hospital services are sometimes required to treat a condition that arises as a result of services that are not covered because they are determined to be not reasonable and necessary or because they are excluded from coverage for other reasons. Services "related to" noncovered services (e.g., cosmetic surgery, noncovered organ transplants, noncovered artificial organ implants, etc.), including services related to follow-up care and complications of noncovered services which require treatment during a hospital stay in which the noncovered service was performed, are not covered services under Medicare. Services "not related to" noncovered services are covered under Medicare.

Following are examples of services "related to" and "not related to" noncovered services while the beneficiary is an inpatient:

- A beneficiary was hospitalized for a noncovered service and broke a leg while in the hospital. Services related to care of the broken leg during this stay is a clear example of "not related to" services and are covered under Medicare.
- A beneficiary was admitted to the hospital for covered services, but during the course of hospitalization became a candidate for a noncovered transplant or implant and actually received the transplant or implant during that hospital stay. When the original admission was

entirely unrelated to the diagnosis that led to a recommendation for a noncovered transplant or implant, the services related to the admitting condition would be covered.

- A beneficiary was admitted to the hospital for covered services related to a condition which ultimately led to identification of a need for transplant and receipt of a transplant during the same hospital stay. If, on the basis of the nature of the services and a comparison of the date they are received with the date on which the beneficiary is identified as a transplant candidate, the services could reasonably be attributed to preparation for the noncovered transplant, the services would be "related to" noncovered services and would also be noncovered.

Following is an example of services received subsequent to a noncovered inpatient stay:

After a beneficiary has been discharged from the hospital stay in which the beneficiary received noncovered services, medical and hospital services required to treat a condition or complication that arises as a result of the prior noncovered services may be covered when they are reasonable and necessary in all other respects. Thus, coverage could be provided for subsequent inpatient stays or outpatient treatment ordinarily covered by Medicare, even if the need for treatment arose because of a previous noncovered procedure. Some examples of services that may be found to be covered under this policy are the reversal of intestinal bypass surgery for obesity, repair of complications from transsexual surgery or from cosmetic surgery, removal of a noncovered bladder stimulator, or treatment of any infection at the surgical site of a noncovered transplant that occurred following discharge from the hospital.

However, any subsequent services that could be expected to have been incorporated into a global fee are considered to have been paid in the global fee, and may not be paid again. Thus, where a patient undergoes cosmetic surgery and the treatment regimen calls for a series of postoperative visits to the surgeon for evaluating the patient's progress, these visits are not paid.

Pub. 100-3, Section 10.1
Use of Visual Tests Prior to and General Anesthesia During Cataract Surgery

A. Pre-Surgery Evaluations (Effective for Services Performed On or After 09-14-88).-- Cataract surgery with an intraocular lens (IOL) implant is a high volume Medicare procedure. Along with the surgery, a substantial number of preoperative tests are available to the surgeon. In most cases, a comprehensive eye examination (ocular history and ocular examination) and a single scan to determine the appropriate pseudophakic power of the IOL are sufficient. In most cases involving a simple cataract, a diagnostic ultrasound A-scan is used. For patients with a dense cataract, an ultrasound B-scan may be used.

Accordingly, where the only diagnosis is cataract(s), Medicare does not routinely cover testing other than one comprehensive eye examination (or a combination of a brief/intermediate examination not to exceed the charge of a comprehensive examination) and an A-scan or, if medically

justified, a B-scan. Claims for additional tests are denied as not reasonable and necessary unless there is an additional diagnosis and the medical need for the additional tests is fully documented.

Because cataract surgery is an elective procedure, the patient may decide not to have the surgery until later, or to have the surgery performed by a physician other than the diagnosing physician. In these situations, it may be medically appropriate for the operating physician to conduct another examination. To the extent the additional tests are considered reasonable and necessary by the carrier's medical staff, they are covered.

B. General Anesthesia.--The use of general anesthesia in cataract surgery may be considered reasonable and necessary if, for particular medical indications, it is the accepted procedure among ophthalmologists in the local community to use general anesthesia. In the claims review process, do not front-end" reject any claims for the use of general anesthesia in cataract surgery. Obtain advice from your medical consultants before deciding whether to deny a claim involving use of general anesthesia in cataract surgery. Where regular postpayment review discloses a questionable utilization pattern, obtain case documentation.

Pub. 100-3, Section 10.2
Transcutaneous Electrical Nerve Stimulation (TENS) for Acute Post-Operative Pain

The use of transcutaneous electrical nerve stimulation (TENS) for the relief of acute post-operative pain is covered under Medicare. TENS may be covered whether used as an adjunct to the use of drugs, or as an alternative to drugs, in the treatment of acute pain resulting from surgery.

TENS devices, whether durable or disposable, may be used in furnishing this service. When used for the purpose of treating acute post-operative pain, TENS devices are considered supplies. As such they may be hospital supplies furnished inpatients covered under Part A, or supplies incident to a physician's service when furnished in connection with surgery done on an outpatient basis, and covered under Part B.

It is expected that TENS, when used for acute post-operative pain, will be necessary for relatively short periods of time, usually 30 days or less. In cases when TENS is used for longer periods, contractors should attempt to ascertain whether TENS is no longer being used for acute pain but rather for chronic pain, in which case the TENS device may be covered as durable medical equipment as described in §60-20.

Pub. 100-3, Section 10.3
Inpatient Hospital Pain Rehabilitation Programs

Since pain rehabilitation programs of a lesser scope than that described above would raise a question as to whether the program could be provided in a less intensive setting than on an inpatient hospital basis, carefully evaluate such programs to determine whether the program does, in fact, necessitate a hospital level of care. Some pain rehabilitation programs may utilize services and devices which are excluded from coverage, e.g., acupuncture (see §35-8), biofeedback (see §35-27), dorsal column stimulator (see

§65-8), and family counseling services (see §35-l4). In determining whether the scope of a pain program does necessitate inpatient hospital care, evaluate only those services and devices which are covered. Although diagnostic tests may be an appropriate part of pain rehabilitation programs, such tests would be covered in an individual case only where they can be reasonably related to a patient's illness, complaint, symptom, or injury and where they do not represent an unnecessary duplication of tests previously performed.

An inpatient program of 4 weeks' duration is generally required to modify pain behavior. After this period it would be expected that any additional rehabilitation services which might be required could be effectively provided on an outpatient basis under an outpatient pain rehabilitation program (see §10.4 of the NCD Manual) or other outpatient program. The first 7-l0 days of such an inpatient program constitute, in effect, an evaluation period. If a patient is unable to adjust to the program within this period, it is generally concluded that it is unlikely that the program will be effective and the patient is discharged from the program. On occasions a program longer than 4 weeks may be required in a particular case. In such a case there should be documentation to substantiate that inpatient care beyond a 4-week period was reasonable and necessary. Similarly, where it appears that a patient participating in a program is being granted frequent outside passes, a question would exist as to whether an inpatient program is reasonable and necessary for the treatment of the patient's condition.

An inpatient hospital stay for the purpose of participating in a pain rehabilitation program would be covered as reasonable and necessary to the treatment of a patient's condition where the pain is attributable to a physical cause, the usual methods of treatment have not been successful in alleviating it, and a significant loss of ability to function independently has resulted from the pain. Chronic pain patients often have psychological problems which accompany or stem from the physical pain and it is appropriate to include psychological treatment in the multidisciplinary approach. However, patients whose pain symptoms result from a mental condition, rather than from any physical cause, generally cannot be succesfully treated in a pain rehabilitation program.

Pub. 100-3, Section 10.4
Outpatient Hospital Pain Rehabilitation Programs

Coverage of services furnished under outpatient hospital pain rehabilitation programs, including services furnished in group settings under individualized plans of treatment, is available if the patient's pain is attributable to a physical cause, the usual methods of treatment have not been successful in alleviating it, and a significant loss of ability by the patient to function independently has resulted from the pain. If a patient meets these conditions and the program provides services of the types described in 10.3 of the NCD Manual, the services provided under the program may be covered. Noncovered services (e.g., vocational counseling, meals for outpatients, or acupuncture) continue to be excluded from coverage, and intermediaries would not be precluded from finding, in the case of particular patients, that the pain rehabilitation program is not reasonable and necessary under §1862(a)(1) of the Act for the treatment of their conditions.

Pub. 100-3, Section 10.5

Autogenous Epidural Blood Graft

Autogenous epidural blood grafts are considered a safe and effective remedy for severe headaches that may occur after performance of spinal anesthesia, spinal taps or myelograms, and are covered.

Pub. 100-3, Section 20.1
Vertebral Artery Surgery

Obstructions which block the flow of blood through the vertebral artery can cause vertigo, visual or speech defects, ataxia, mental confusion, or stroke. These symptoms in patients result from reduction in blood flow to the brain and range from symptoms of transient basilar ischemia to mental deterioration or completed stroke.

Five types of surgical procedures are performed to relieve obstructions to vertebral artery blood flow. They are:

- Vertebral artery endarterectomy, a procedure which cleans out arteriosclerotic plaques which are inside the vertebral artery;
- Vertebral artery by-pass or resection with anastomosis or graft;
- Subclavian artery resection with or without endarterectomy;
- Removal of laterally located osteophytes anywhere in the C6(C7)-C2 course of the vertebral artery; and
- Arteriolysis which frees the artery from surrounding tissue, with or without arteriopexy (fixation of the vessel).

These procedures can be medically reasonable and necessary, but only if each of the following conditions is met:

- Symptoms of vertebral artery obstruction exist;
- Other causes have been considered and ruled out;
- There is radiographic evidence of a valid vertebral artery obstruction; and
- Contraindications to the procedure do not exist, such as coexistent obstructions of multiple cerebral vessels.

Angiograms documenting a valid obstruction should show not only the aortic arch with the vessels off the arch, but also show the vessels in the neck and head (providing biplane views of the carotid and vertebral vascular system). In addition, serial views are needed to diagnose "subclavian steal," the condition in which subclavian artery obstruction causes the symptoms of vertebral artery obstruction. Because the symptoms are not specific for vertebral artery obstruction, other causes must be considered. In addition to vertebral artery obstruction, the differential diagnosis should include various degenerative disorders of the brain, orthostatic hypotension, acoustic neuroma, labyrinthitis, diabetes mellitus and hypoglycemia related disorders.

Obstructions which can cause symptoms of blocked vertebral artery blood flow and which can be documented by an angiogram include:

- Intravascular obstructions - arteriosclerotic lesions within the vertebral artery or in other arteries.
- Extravascular obstructions
- Bony tissue or osteophytes, located laterally in the C6(C7)-C2 cervical vertebral area course of the vertebral artery, most commonly at C5 -C6.

- Anatomical variations - Anomalous location of the origin of the vertebral artery, a congenital aberration, and tortuosity and kinks of the vertebral artery.
- Fibrous tissue - Tissue changed as a result of manipulation of the neck for neck pain or injury associated with hematoma; external bands, tendinous slings, and fibrous bands.

The most controversial obstructions include vertebral artery tortuosity and kinks and connective tissue along the course of the vertebral artery, and variously called external bands, tendinous slings and fibrous bands. In the absence of symptoms of vertebral artery obstruction, vascular surgeons feel such abnormalities are insignificant. Vascular surgery experts, however, agree that these abnormalities in very rare cases do cause symptoms of vertebral artery obstruction and do necessitate surgical correction.

Vertebral artery construction and vertebral artery surgery are phrases which most physicians interpret to include only surgical cleaning (endarterectomy) and bypass (resection) procedures. However, some physicians who use these terms mean all operative manipulations which remove vertebral artery blood flow obstructions. Also, some physicians use general terms of vascular surgery, such as endarterectomy when vertebral artery related surgery is performed. Use of the above terminology specifies neither the surgical procedure performed nor its relationship to the vertebral artery. Therefore, in developing claims for this type of procedure, require specific identification of the obstruction in question and the surgical procedure performed. Also, in view of the specific coverage criteria given, develop all claims for vertebral artery surgery on a case-by-case basis.

Make payment for a surgical procedure listed above if: (1) it is reasonable and necessary for the individual patient to have the surgery performed to remove or relieve an obstruction to vertebral artery flow, and (2) the four conditions noted are met.

In all other cases, these procedures cannot be considered reasonable and necessary within the meaning of §1862(a)(1) of the Act and are not reimbursable under the program.

Pub. 100-3, Section 20.3
Thoracic Duct Drainage (TDD) in Renal Transplants

TDD is performed on an inpatient basis, and the inpatient stay is covered for patients admitted for treatment in advance of a kidney transplant as well as for those receiving it post-transplant. TDD is a covered technique when furnished to a kidney transplant recipient or an individual approved to receive kidney transplantation in a hospital approved to perform kidney transplantation.

Pub. 100-3, Section 20.4
Implantation of Automatic Defibrillators

A. Covered Indications

1) Documented episode of cardiac arrest due to ventricular fibrillation (VF), not due to a transient or reversible cause (effective July 1, 1991);

2) Documented sustained ventricular tachyarrhythmia (VT), either spontaneous or induced by an electrophysiology (EP) study, not associated with an acute myocardial infarction (MI) and not due to a transient or reversible cause (effective July 1, 1999);

3) Documented familial or inherited conditions with a high risk of life-threatening VT, such as long QT syndrome or hypertrophic cardiomyopathy (effective July 1, 1999);

Additional indications effective for services performed on or after October 1, 2003:

4) Coronary artery disease with a documented prior MI, a measured left ventricular ejection fraction 0.35, and inducible, sustained VT or VF at EP study. (The MI must have occurred more than 4 weeks prior to defibrillator insertion. The EP test must be performed more than 4 weeks after the qualifying MI.);

5) Documented prior MI and a measured left ventricular ejection fraction 0.30 and a QRS duration of >120 milliseconds. Patients must not have:

a. New York Heart Association classification IV;

b. Cardiogenic shock or symptomatic hypotension while in a stable baseline rhythm;

c. Had a coronary artery bypass graft (CABG) or percutaneous transluminal coronary angioplasty (PTCA) within past 3 months;

d. Had an enzyme-positive MI within past month;

e. Clinical symptoms or findings that would make them a candidate for coronary revascularization; or

f. Any disease, other than cardiac disease (e.g.cancer, uremia, liver failure), associated with a likelihood of survival less than 1 year.

B. All patients considered for implantation of a defibrillator must not have irreversible brain damage, disease or dysfunction that precludes the ability to give informed consent.

C. MIs must be documented by elevated cardiac enzymes or Q-waves on an electrocardiogram. Ejection fractions must be measured by angiography, radionuclide scanning,or echocardiography.

D. All other indications remain noncovered except in Category B IDE clinical trials (60 CFR 48417) or as a routine cost in clinical trials defined under section 310.1 of the NCD Manual.

See Defibrillator Flow Chart.

Pub. 100-3, Section 20.5
Extracorporeal Immunoadsorption (ECI) Using Protein A Columns

For claims with dates of service on or after January 1, 2001, Medicare covers the use of Protein A columns for the treatment of ITP. In addition, Medicare will cover Protein A columns for the treatment of rheumatoid arthritis (RA) under the following conditions:

1. Patient has severe RA. Patient disease is active, having >5 swollen joints, >20 tender joints, and morning stiffness >60 minutes.
2. Patient has failed an adequate course of a minimum of 3 Disease Modifying Anti-Rheumatic Drugs (DMARDs). Failure does not include intolerance.

Other uses of these columns are currently considered to be investigational and, therefore, not reasonable and necessary under the Medicare law. (See §1862(a)(1)(A) of the Act.)

APPENDIX D

Pub. 100-3, Section 20.6
Transmyocardial Revascularization (TMR)

CMS therefore covers TMR as a late or last resort for patients with severe (Canadian Cardiovascular Society classification Classes III or IV) angina (stable or unstable), which has been found refractory to standard medical therapy, including drug therapy at the maximum tolerated or maximum safe dosages. In addition, the angina symptoms must be caused by areas of the heart not amenable to surgical therapies such as percutaneous transluminal coronary angioplasty, stenting, coronary atherectomy or coronary bypass. Coverage is further limited to those uses of the laser used in performing the procedure which have been approved by the Food and Drug Administration for the purpose for which they are being used.

Patients would have to meet the following additional selection guidelines:

1. An ejection fraction of 25% or greater;
2. Have areas of viable ischemic myocardium (as demonstrated by diagnostic study) which are not capable of being revascularized by direct coronary intervention; and
3. Have been stabilized, or have had maximal efforts to stabilize acute conditions such as severe ventricular arrhythmias, decompensated congestive heart failure or acute myocardial infarction.

Coverage is limited to physicians who have been properly trained in the procedure. Providers of this service is performed must also document that all ancillary personnel, including physicians, nurses, operating room personnel and technicians, are trained in the procedure and the proper use of the equipment involved. Coverage is further limited to providers which have dedicated cardiac care units, including the diagnostic and support services necessary for care of patients undergoing this therapy. In addition, these providers must conform to the standards for laser safety set by the American National Standards Institute, ANSIZ1363.

Pub. 100-3, Section 20.7
Percutaneous Transluminal Angioplasty (PTA)

B. Nationally Covered Indications

PTA is covered to treat the following indications:

1. Atherosclerotic obstructive lesions:

   - In the lower extremities, i.e., the iliac, femoral, and popliteal arteries, or in the upper extremities, i.e., the innominate, subclavian, axillary, and brachial arteries. The upper extremities do not include head or neck vessels.
   - Of a single coronary artery for patients for whom the likely alternative treatment is coronary bypass surgery and who exhibit the following characteristics:

     Angina refractory to optimal medical management;

     Objective evidence of myocardial ischemia; and

     Lesions amenable to angioplasty;

   - Of the renal arteries for patients in whom there is inadequate response to a thorough medical management of symptoms and for whom surgery is the likely alternative. PTA for this group of patients is an alternative to surgery, not simply an addition to medical management.
   - Of arteriovenous dialysis fistulas and grafts when performed through either a venous of arterial approach.

2. Effective July 1, 2001, Medicare will cover PTA of the carotid artery concurrent with carotid stent placement when furnished in accordance with the Food and Drug Administration (FDA) approved protocols governing Category B Investigational Device Exemption (IDE) clinical trials. PTA of the carotid artery, when provided solely for the purpose of carotid artery dilation concurrent with carotid stent placement, is considered to be a reasonable and necessary service only when provided in the context of such a clinical trial.

3. Effective October 12, 2004, Medicare covers PTA of the carotid artery concurrent with the placement of an FDA-approved carotid stent for an FDA-approved indication when furnished in accordance with FDA-approved protocols governing post-approval studies. CMS determines that coverage of PTA of the carotid artery is reasonable and necessary under these circumstances.

C. Nationally Noncovered Indications

1. Performance of PTA in the carotid artery when used to treat obstructive lesions outside of FDA-approved protocols governing Category B IDE clinical trials and outside of FDA-required post approval studies remains a noncovered service.

2. Performance of PTA to treat obstructive lesions of the vertebral and cerebral arteries remains noncovered. The safety and efficacy of these procedures are not established.

D. Other

All other indications for PTA for which CMS has not specifically indicated coverage remain noncovered.

(This NCD last reviewed September 2004.)

Pub. 100-3, Section 20.8
Cardiac Pacemakers

Cardiac pacemakers are covered as prosthetic devices under the Medicare program, subject to the following conditions and limitations. While cardiac pacemakers have been covered under Medicare for many years, there were no specific guidelines for their use other than the general Medicare requirement that covered services be reasonable and necessary for the treatment of the condition. Services rendered for cardiac pacing on or after the effective dates of this instruction are subject to these guidelines, which are based on certain assumptions regarding the clinical goals of cardiac pacing. While some uses of pacemakers are relatively certain or unambiguous, many other uses require considerable expertise and judgment.

Consequently, the medical necessity for permanent cardiac pacing must be viewed in the context of overall patient management. The appropriateness of such pacing may be conditional on other diagnostic or therapeutic modalities having been undertaken. Although significant complications and adverse side effects of pacemaker use are relatively rare, they cannot be ignored when considering the use of pacemakers for dubious medical conditions, or marginal clinical benefit.

These guidelines represent current concepts regarding medical circumstances in which permanent cardiac pacing may be appropriate or necessary. As with other areas of medicine, advances in knowledge and techniques in cardiology are expected. Consequently, judgments about the medical necessity and acceptability of new uses for cardiac pacing in new classes of patients may change as more more conclusive evidence becomes available. This instruction applies only to permanent cardiac pacemakers, and does not address the use of temporary, non-implanted pacemakers.

The two groups of conditions outlined below deal with the necessity for cardiac pacing for patients in general. These are intended as guidelines in assessing the medical necessity for pacing therapies, taking into account the particular circumstances in each case. However, as a general rule, the two groups of current medical concepts may be viewed as representing:

Group I: Single-Chamber Cardiac Pacemakers – a) conditions under which single chamber pacemaker claims may be considered covered without further claims development; and b) conditions under which single-chamber pacemaker claims would be denied unless further claims development shows that they fall into the covered category, or special medical circumstances exist of the sufficiency to convince the contractor that the claim should be paid.

Group II: Dual-Chamber Cardiac Pacemakers - a) conditions under which dual-chamber pacemaker claims may be considered covered without further claims development, and b) conditions under which dual-chamber pacemaker claims would be denied unless further claims development shows that they fall into the covered categories for single- and dual-chamber pacemakers, or special medical circumstances exist sufficient to convince the contractor that the claim should be paid.

CMS opened the NCD on Cardiac Pacemakers to afford the public an opportunity to comment on the proposal to revise the language contained in the instruction. The revisions transfer the focus of the NCD from the actual pacemaker implantation procedure itself to the reasonable and necessary medical indications that justify cardiac pacing. This is consistent with our findings that pacemaker implantation is no longer considered routinely harmful or an experimental procedure.

Group I: Single-Chamber Cardiac Pacemakers (Effective March 16, 1983)

A. Nationally Covered Indications

Conditions under which cardiac pacing is generally considered acceptable or necessary, provided that the conditions are chronic or recurrent and not due to transient causes such as acute myocardial infarction, drug toxicity, or electrolyte imbalance. (In cases where there is a rhythm disturbance, if the rhythm disturbance is chronic or recurrent, a single episode of a symptom such as syncope or seizure is adequate to establish medical necessity.)

1. Acquired complete (also referred to as third-degree) AV heart block.
2. Congenital complete heart block with severe bradycardia (in relation to age), or significant physiological deficits or significant symptoms due to the bradycardia.
3. Second-degree AV heart block of Type II (i.e., no progressive prolongation of P-R interval prior to each blocked beat. P-R interval indicates the time taken for an impulse to travel from the atria to the ventricles on an electrocardiogram).
4. Second-degree AV heart block of Type I (i.e., progressive prolongation of P-R interval prior to each blocked beat) with significant symptoms due to hemodynamic instability associated with the heart block.
5. Sinus bradycardia associated with major symptoms (e.g., syncope, seizures, congestive heart failure); or substantial sinus bradycardia (heart rate less than 50) associated with dizziness or confusion. The correlation between symptoms and bradycardia must be documented, or the symptoms must be clearly attributable to the bradycardia rather than to some other cause.
6. In selected and few patients, sinus bradycardia of lesser severity (heart rate 50-59) with dizziness or confusion. The correlation between symptoms and bradycardia must be documented, or the symptoms must be clearly attributable to the bradycardia rather than to some other cause.
7. Sinus bradycardia is the consequence of long-term necessary drug treatment for which there is no acceptable alternative when accompanied by significant symptoms (e.g., syncope, seizures, congestive heart failure, dizziness or confusion). The correlation between symptoms and bradycardia must be documented, or the symptoms must be clearly attributable to the bradycardia rather than to some other cause.
8. Sinus node dysfunction with or without tachyarrhythmias or AV conduction block (i.e., the bradycardia-tachycardia syndrome, sino-atrial block, sinus arrest) when accompanied by significant symptoms (e.g., syncope, seizures, congestive heart failure, dizziness or confusion).
9. Sinus node dysfunction with or without symptoms when there are potentially life-threatening ventricular arrhythmias or tachycardia secondary to the bradycardia (e.g., numerous premature ventricular contractions, couplets, runs of premature ventricular contractions, or ventricular tachycardia).
10. Bradycardia associated with supraventricular tachycardia (e.g., atrial fibrillation, atrial flutter, or paroxysmal atrial tachycardia) with high-degree AV block which is unresponsive to appropriate pharmacological management and when the bradycardia is associated with significant symptoms (e.g., syncope, seizures, congestive heart failure, dizziness or confusion).
11. The occasional patient with hypersensitive carotid sinus syndrome with syncope due to bradycardia and unresponsive to prophylactic medical measures.
12. Bifascicular or trifascicular block accompanied by syncope which is attributed to transient complete heart block after other plausible causes of syncope have been reasonably excluded.
13. Prophylactic pacemaker use following recovery from acute myocardial infarction during which there

was temporary complete (third-degree) and/or Mobitz Type II second-degree AV block in association with bundle branch block.

14. In patients with recurrent and refractory ventricular tachycardia, "overdrive pacing" (pacing above the basal rate) to prevent ventricular tachycardia.

(Effective May 9, 1985)

15. Second-degree AV heart block of Type I with the QRS complexes prolonged.

B. Nationally Noncovered Indications

Conditions which, although used by some physicians as a basis for permanent cardiac pacing, are considered unsupported by adequate evidence of benefit and therefore should not generally be considered appropriate uses for single-chamber pacemakers in the absence of the above indications. Contractors should review claims for pacemakers with these indications to determine the need for further claims development prior to denying the claim, since additional claims development may be required. The object of such further development is to establish whether the particular claim actually meets the conditions in a) above. In claims where this is not the case or where such an event appears unlikely, the contractor may deny the claim

1. Syncope of undetermined cause.
2. Sinus bradycardia without significant symptoms.
3. Sino-atrial block or sinus arrest without significant symptoms.
4. Prolonged P-R intervals with atrial fibrillation (without third-degree AV block) or with other causes of transient ventricular pause.
5. Bradycardia during sleep.
6. Right bundle branch block with left axis deviation (and other forms of fascicular or bundle branch block) without syncope or other symptoms of intermittent AV block).
7. Asymptomatic second-degree AV block of Type I unless the QRS complexes are prolonged or electrophysiological studies have demonstrated that the block is at or beyond the level of the His bundle (a component of the electrical conduction system of the heart).

Effective October 1, 2001

8. Asymptomatic bradycardia in post-mycardial infarction patients about to initiate long-term beta-blocker drug therapy.

Group II: Dual-Chamber Cardiac Pacemakers – (Effective May 9, 1985)

A. Nationally Covered Indications

Conditions under dual-chamber cardiac pacing are considered acceptable or necessary in the general medical community unless conditions 1 and 2 under Group II. B., are present:

1. Patients in who single-chamber (ventricular pacing) at the time of pacemaker insertion elicits a definite drop in blood pressure, retrograde conduction, or discomfort.
2. Patients in whom the pacemaker syndrome (atrial ventricular asynchrony), with significant symptoms,

has already been experienced with a pacemaker that is being replaced.
3. Patients in whom even a relatively small increase in cardiac efficiency will importantly improve the quality of life, e.g., patients with congestive heart failure despite adequate other medical measures.
4. Patients in whom the pacemaker syndrome can be anticipated, e.g., in young and active people, etc.

Dual-chamber pacemakers may also be covered for the conditions, as listed in Group I. A., if the medical necessity is sufficiently justified through adequate claims development. Expert physicians differ in their judgments about what constitutes appropriate criteria for dual-chamber pacemaker use. The judgment that such a pacemaker is warranted in the patient meeting accepted criteria must be based upon the individual needs and characteristics of that patient, weighing the magnitude and likelihood of anticipated benefits against the magnitude and likelihood of disadvantages to the patient.

B. Nationally Noncovered Indications

Whenever the following conditions (which represent overriding contraindications) are present, dual-chamber pacemakers are not covered:

1. Ineffective atrial contractions (e.g., chronic atrial fibrillation or flutter, or giant left atrium.
2. Frequent or persistent supraventricular tachycardias, except where the pacemaker is specifically for the control of the tachycardia.
3. A clinical condition in which pacing takes place only intermittently and briefly, and which is not associated with a reasonable likelihood that pacing needs will become prolonged, e.g., the occasional patient with hypersensitive carotid sinus syndrome with syncope due to bradycardia and unresponsive to prophylactic medical measures.
4. Prophylactic pacemaker use following recovery from acute myocardial infarction during which there was temporary complete (third-degree) and/or Type II second-degree AV block in association with bundle branch block.

C. Other

All other indications for dual-chamber cardiac pacing for which CMS has not specifically indicated coverage remain nationally noncovered, ecept for Category B IDE clinical trails, or as routine costs of dual-chamber cardiac pacing associated with clinical trials, in accordance with section 310.1 of the NCD Manual..

(This NCD last reviewed June 2004.)

Pub. 100-3, Section 20.8.1
Cardiac Pacemaker Evaluation Services

Medicare covers a variety of services for the post-implant follow-up and evaluation of implanted cardiac pacemakers. The following guidelines are designed to assist contractors in identifying and processing claims for such services.

NOTE: These new guidelines are limited to lithium battery-powered pacemakers, because mercury-zinc battery-powered pacemakers are no longer being manufactured and virtually all have been replaced by lithium units. Contractors still receiving claims for monitoring such units should continue to apply the guidelines published in 1980 to those units until they are replaced.

One fact of which contractors should be aware is that many dual-chamber units may be programmed to pace only the ventricles; this may be done either at the time the pacemaker is implanted or at some time afterward. In such cases, a dual-chamber unit, when programmed or reprogrammed for ventricular pacing, should be treated as a single-chamber pacemaker in applying screening guidelines.

The decision as to how often any patient's pacemaker should be monitored is the responsibility of the patient's physician who is best able to take into account the condition and circumstances of the individual patient. These may vary over time, requiring modifications of the frequency with which the patient should be monitored. In cases where monitoring is done by some entity other than the patient's physician, such as a commercial monitoring service or hospital outpatient department, the physician's prescription for monitoring is required and should be periodically renewed (at least annually) to assure that the frequency of monitoring is proper for the patient. When a patient is monitered both during clinica visits and transtelephonically, the contractor should be sure to include frequency data on both ypes of monitoring in evaluating the reasonableness of the frequency of monitoring services received by the patient.

Since there are over 200 pacemaker models in service at any given point, and a variety of patient conditions that give rise to the need for pacemakers, the question of the appropriate frequency of monitorings is a complex one. Nevertheless, it is possible to develop guidelines within which the vast majority of pacemaker monitorings will fall and contractors should do this, using their own data and experience, as well as the frequency guidelines which follow, in order to limit extensive claims development to those cases requiring special attention.

Pub. 100-3, Section 20.8.2
Self-Contained Pacemaker Monitors

Self-contained pacemaker monitors are accepted devices for monitoring cardiac pacemakers. Accordingly, program payment may be made for the rental or purchase of either of the following pacemaker monitors when it is prescribed by a physician for a patient with a cardiac pacemaker:

A. Digital Electronic Pacemaker Monitor.--This device provides the patient with an instantaneous digital readout of his pacemaker pulse rate. Use of this device does not involve professional services until there has been a change of five pulses (or more) per minute above or below the initial rate of the pacemaker; when such change occurs, the patient contacts his physician.

B. Audible/Visible Signal Pacemaker Monitor.--This device produces an audible and visible signal which indicates the pacemaker rate. Use of this device does not involve professional services until a change occurs in these signals; at such time, the patient contacts his physician.

NOTE: The design of the self-contained pacemaker monitor makes it possible for the patient to monitor his pacemaker periodically and minimizes the need for regular visits to the outpatient department of the provider.
Therefore, documentation of the medical necessity for pacemaker evaluation in the outpatient department of the provider should be obtained where such evaluation is

employed in addition to the self-contained pacemaker monitor used by the patient in his home.

Pub. 100-3, Section 20.8.3
Anesthesia in Cardiac Pacemaker Surgery

The use of general or monitored anesthesia during transvenous cardiac pacemaker surgery may be reasonable and necessary and therefore covered under Medicare only if adequate documentation of medical necessity is provided on a case-by-case basis. Obtain advice from your medical consultants or from appropriate specialty physicians or groups in your locality regarding the adequacy of documentation before deciding whether a particular claim should be covered.

A second type of pacemaker surgery that is sometimes performed involves the use of the thoracic method of implantation, which requires open surgery. Where the thoracic method is employed, general anesthesia is always used and should not require special medical documentation.

Pub. 100-3, Section 20.9
Artificial Hearts and Related Devices

A. Covered Indications

1. Post-cardiotomy (effective for services performed on or after October 18, 1993)

Post-cardiotomy is the period following open-heart surgery. VADs used for support of blood circulation post-cardiotomy are covered only if they have received approval from the Food and Drug Administration (FDA) for that purpose, and the VADs are used according to the FDA-approved labeling instructions.

2. Bridge-to-Transplant (effective for services performed on or after January 22, 1996)

VADs used for bridge-to-transplant are covered only if they have received approval from the FDA for that purpose, and the VADs are used according to the FDA-approved labeling instructions. All of the following criteria must be fulfilled in order for Medicare coverage to be provided for a VAD used as a bridge-to-transplant:

> a. The patient is approved and listed as a candidate for heart transplantation by a Medicare-approved heart transplant center; and,
>
> b. The implanting site, if different than the Medicare-approved transplant center, must receive written permission from the Medicare-approved heart transplant center under which the patient is listed prior to implantation of the VAD.

The Medicare-approved heart transplant center should make every reasonable effort to transplant patients on such devices as soon as medically reasonable. Ideally, the Medicare-approved heart transplant centers should determine patient-specific timetables for transplantation, and should not maintain such patients on VADs if suitable hearts become available.

3. Destination Therapy (effective for services performed on or after October 1, 2003)

Destination therapy is for patients that require permanent mechanical cardiac support. VADs used for destination therapy are covered only if they have received approval from the FDA for that purpose, and the device is used according to the FDA-approved labeling instructions. VADs are covered for patients who have chronic end-stage heart failure (New York Heart Association Class IV end-stage left ventricular failure for at least 90 days with a life expectancy of less than 2 years), are not candidates for heart transplantation, and meet **all** of the following conditions:

    a. The patient's Class IV heart failure symptoms have failed to respond to optimal medical management, including dietary salt restriction, diuretics, digitalis, beta-blockers, and ACE inhibitors (if tolerated) for at least 60 of the last 90 days;

    b. The patient has a left ventricular ejection fraction (LVEF) < 25%;

    c. The patient has demonstrated functional limitation with a peak oxygen consumption of < 12 ml/kg/min; **or** the patient has a continued need for intravenous inotropic therapy owing to symptomatic hypotension, decreasing renal function, or worsening pulmonary congestion; **and**

    d. The patient has the appropriate body size > to support the VAD implantation.

In addition, the Centers for Medicare & Medicaid Services (CMS) has determined that VAD implantation as destination therapy is reasonable and necessary only when the procedure is performed in a Medicare-approved heart transplant facility that, between January 1, 2001, and September 30, 2003, implanted at least 15 VADs as a bridge-to-transplant or as destination therapy. These devices must have been approved by the FDA for destination therapy or as a bridge-to-transplant, or have been implanted as part of an FDA investigational device exemption (IDE) trial for one of these two indications. VADs implanted for other investigational indications or for support of blood circulation post-cardiotomy do not satisfy the volume requirement for this purpose. Since the relationship between volume and outcomes has not been well-established for VAD use, facilities that have minimal deficiencies in meeting this standard may apply and include a request for an exception based upon additional factors. Some of the factors CMS will consider are geographic location of the center, number of destination procedures performed, and patient outcomes from VAD procedures completed.

Also, this facility must be an active, continuous member of a national, audited registry that requires submission of health data on all VAD destination therapy patients from the date of implantation throughout the remainder of their lives. This registry must have the ability to accommodate data related to any device approved by the FDA for destination therapy regardless of manufacturer. The registry must also provide such routine reports as may be specified by CMS, and must have standards for data quality and timeliness of data submissions such that hospitals failing to meet them will be removed from membership. CMS believes that the registry sponsored by the International Society for Heart and Lung Transplantation is an example of a registry that meets these characteristics.

Hospitals also must have in place staff and procedures that ensure that prospective VAD recipients receive all information necessary to assist them in giving appropriate informed consent for the procedure so that they and their families are fully aware of the aftercare requirements and potential limitations, as well as benefits, following VAD implantation.

CMS plans to develop accreditation standards for facilities that implant VADs and, when implemented, VAD implantation will be considered reasonable and necessary only at accredited facilities.

A list of facilities eligible for Medicare reimbursement for VADs as destination therapy will be maintained on our website and available at www.cms.hhs.gov/coverage/lvadfacility.asp. In order to be placed on this list, facilities must submit a letter to the Director, Coverage and Analysis Group, 7500 Security Blvd, Mailstop C1-09-06, Baltimore, MD 21244. This letter must be received by CMS within 90 days of the issue date on this transmittal. The letter must include the following information

- Facility's name and complete address;
- Facility's Medicare provider number;
- List of all implantations between Jan. 1, 2001, and Sept. 30, 2003, with the following information:
  - Date of implantation,
  - Indication for implantation (only destination and bridge-to-transplant can be reported; post-cardiotomy VAD implants are not to be included),
  - Device name and manufacturer, and,
  - Date of device removal and reason (e.g., transplantation, recovery, device malfunction), or date and cause of patient's death;
- Point-of-contact for questions with telephone number
- Registry to which patient information will be submitted; **and**
- Signature of a senior facility administrative official.

Facilities not meeting the minimal standards and requesting exception should, in addition to supplying the information above, include the factors that they deem critical in requesting the exception to the standards.

CMS will review the information contained in the above letters. When the review is complete, all necessary information is received, and criteria are met, CMS will include the name of the newly Medicare-approved facility on the CMS web site. No reimbursement for destination therapy will be made for implantations performed before the date the facility is added to the CMS web site. Each newly approved facility will also receive a formal letter from CMS stating the official approval date it was added to the list.

B. **Noncovered Indications (effective for services performed on or after May 19, 1986)**

1.Artificial Heart

Since there is no authoritative evidence substantiating the safety and effectiveness of a VAD used as a replacement for the human heart, Medicare does not cover this device when used as an artificial heart.

2. All other indications for the use of VADs not otherwise listed remain noncovered, except in the context of Category B IDE clinical trials (42 CFR 405) or as a routine cost in clinical

trials defined under section 310.1 of the NCD manual (old CIM 30-1).

(This NCD last reviewed October 2003.)

Pub. 100-3, Section 20.10
Cardiac Rehabilitation Programs

Medicare coverage of cardiac rehabilitation programs are considered reasonable and necessary only for patients with a clear medical need, who are referred by their attending physician and (1) have a documented diagnosis of acute myocardial infarction within the preceding 12 months; or (2) have had coronary bypass surgery; and/or (3) have stable angina pectoris.

Cardiac rehabilitation programs may be provided either by the outpatient department of a hospital or in a physician-directed clinic. Coverage for either program is subject to the following conditions:

- The facility meets the definition of a hospital outpatient department or a physician-directed clinic, i.e., a physician is on the premises available to perform medical duties at all times the facility is open, and each patient is under the care of a hospital or clinic physician;
- The facility has available for immediate use all the necessary cardio-pulmonary emergency diagnostic and therapeutic life saving equipment accepted by the medical community as medically necessary, e.g., oxygen, cardiopulmonary resuscitation equipment, or defibrillator;
- The program is conducted in an area set aside for the exclusive use of the program while it is in session;
- The program is staffed by personnel necessary to conduct the program safely and effectively, who are trained in both basic and advanced life support techniques and in exercise therapy for coronary disease. Services of nonphysician personnel must be furnished under the direct supervision of a physician. Direct supervision means that a physician must be in the exercise program area and immediately available and accessible for an emergency at all times the exercise program is conducted. It does not require that a physician be physically present in the exercise room itself, provided the contractor does not determine that the physician is too remote from the patients' exercise area to be considered immediately available and accessible. The examples below are for illustration purposes only. They are not meant to limit the discretion of the contractor to make determinations in this regard.
  - The case in which a contractor determines that the presence of a physician in an office across the hall from the exercise room who is available at all times for an emergency meets the requirement that the physician is immediately available and accessible; or
  - The case in which a contractor determines that the presence of a physician in a building other than that containing the exercise room does not meet the requirement that the physician is immediately available and accessible; and

- The nonphysician personnel are employees of either the physician, hospital, or clinic conducting the program and their services are "incident-to a physician's professional services

Contractors need not undertake elaborate or costly monitoring activities to determine whether these requirements are met, but need only satisfy themselves to the extent that they ordinarily do in connection with, for example, the requirements for coverage of services in physician-directed clinics.

In addition to the conditions listed above, coverage for cardiac rehabilitation programs furnished by hospitals to outpatients are also subject to the rules described in the Medicare Benefit Policy Manual, Chapter 6, "Hospital Services Covered Under Part B" §20.4.1

B. Diagnostic Testing - Stress Testing.

A prospective candidate for a cardiac rehabilitation program must be evaluated for his suitability to participate. A valuable diagnostic test for this purpose is the stress test. The program need not necessarily include a stress test, but may accept one performed by the patient's attending physician. Stress testing performed in the outpatient department of a hospital or in a physician-directed clinic may be covered when reasonable and necessary for one or more of the following:

- Evaluation of chest pain, especially atypical chest pain;
- Development of exercise prescriptions for patients with known cardiac disease; and/or
- Pre and postoperative evaluation of patients undergoing coronary artery by-pass procedures.

Refer to subsection E, Utilization Screens, for the acceptable frequency of stress testing performed during an individual's exercise program.

ECG Rhythm Strips. ECG rhythm strips (and other ECG monitoring) constitute an important and necessary procedure which should be done periodically while a cardiac patient is engaged in a physician-controlled exercise program. See subsection E, Utilization Screens, for allowable screens.C. Other Diagnostic and Therapeutic Services

A freestanding or hospital based cardiac rehabilitation clinic may also provide diagnostic and therapeutic services other than stress testing and ECG monitoring. Any such other services must meet the usual coverage requirements for the specific service, e.g., the incident-to, and reasonable and necessary requirements.

1. Psychotherapy and Psychological Testing

It would not normally be considered reasonable and necessary to provide psychotherapy to all cardiac rehabilitation patients, or even to test all such patients to determine whether they may have a mental, psychoneurotic, or personality disorder. However, where a patient has a diagnosed mental, psychoneurotic, or personality disorder, psychotherapy furnished by a psychiatrist--or by a psychologist rendering such services incident to a physician's professional service--may be covered. Similarly, diagnostic testing of a cardiac rehabilitation patient for a mental problem may be covered where the patient shows appropriate symptoms, e.g., excessive anxiety or fear associated with the cardiac disease.

APPENDIX D

2. Physical and Occupational Therapy.

Physical therapy and occupational therapy would not be covered when furnished in connection with cardiac rehabilitation exercise program services covered under this section unless there also is a diagnosed noncardiac condition requiring such therapy, e.g., where a patient who is just recuperating from an acute phase of heart disease may have had a stroke which would require physical and/or occupational therapy. (While the cardiac rehabilitation exercise program may by some be considered a form of physical therapy, it is a specialized program conducted and/or supervised by specially trained personnel whose services are performed under the direct supervision of a physician.) Restrictions on coverage of physical therapy and occupational therapy under this section do not affect rules regarding coverage or noncoverage of such services when furnished in a hospital inpatient or outpatient setting. (See Medicare Benefit Policy Manual, Chapter 1, "Inpatient Hospital Services", §90.)

3. Patient Education Services

Many cardiac rehabilitation programs provide health education in the form of lectures or counseling in which patients and/or family members are given information, e.g., on diet, nutrition, and sexual activity to assist them in adjusting their living habits because of the cardiac condition. However, the same kind of information would have been furnished to a patient and/or family members by the attending physician following the patient's acute cardiac episode. Therefore, formal lectures and counseling on these subjects are not considered reasonable and necessary as a separately identifiable service when provided as a part of a cardiac rehabilitation exercise program. In addition, where a free-standing cardiac rehabilitation clinic provides board and room for the patient (and in some cases family members), these services are not covered under Medicare.

D. Duration of the Program

Services provided in connection with a cardiac rehabilitation exercise program may be considered reasonable and necessary for up to 36 sessions, usually 3 sessions a week in a single 12 week period. Coverage for continued participation in cardiac exercise programs beyond 12 weeks would be allowed only on a case-by-case basis with exit criteria taken into consideration.

Although firm exit criteria for terminating the therapeutic outpatient exercise treatment and rehabilitation program have not been established, the following guidelines have been identified as acceptable:

- The patient has achieved a stable level of exercise tolerance without ischemia or dysrhythmia;
- Symptoms of angina or dyspnea are stable at the patient's maximum exercise level;
- Patient's resting blood pressure and heart rate are within normal limits; or
- The stress test is not positive during exercise. (A positive test in this context implies an ECG with a junctional depression of 2mm or more associated with slowly rising, horizontal, or down sloping ST segment.)

Accordingly, claims for coverage of cardiac rehabilitation exercise programs beyond 12 weeks are reviewed by the contractors' medical consultants. When claims are accompanied by acceptable documentation that the patient

has not reached an exit level, coverage may be extended, but should not exceed a maximum of 24 weeks.

E. Utilization Screens

Patients who participate in cardiac rehabilitation programs will require certain services more frequently than other patients being treated on an outpatient basis. Therefore, in order to provide coverage in a uniform manner, the following utilization screens should be implemented in addition to existing screens for any cardiac rehabilitation services not listed:

1-Group 1 Services

Continuous ECG telemetric monitoring during exercise; New patient comprehensive evaluation, including history, physical, and preparation of initial exercise prescription.

ECG rhythm strip with interpretation and physician's revision of exercise prescription; and

Limited examination for physician followup to adjust medication or other treatment changes.

A visit including one or more of this range of routine services is considered as one routine cardiac rehabilitation visit. In order for the visit to be reimbursable, at least one of the Group 1 services must be performed. The same rate of reimbursement would be allowed for each visit, but not all the services need be performed at each visit.

Allow a maximum of three visits per week.

2-Group 2 Services

Allow one at the beginning of the program if not already performed by the patient's attending physician, or if that performed by the patient's attending physician is not acceptable to the program's director.

- ECG stress test (treadmill or bicycle ergometer) with physician monitoring and report.

Allow one at the beginning of the program and one after 3 months (usually the completion of the program).

- Other physician services, as needed.

Pub. 100-3, Section 20.11
Intraoperative Ventricular Mapping

The intraoperative ventricular mapping procedure is covered under Medicare only for the uses and medical conditions described below:

- Localize accessory pathways associated with the Wolff-Parkinson-White (WPW) and other preexcitation syndromes;
- Map the sequence of atrial and ventricular activation for drug-resistant supraventricular tachycardias;
- Delineate the anatomical course of His bundle and/or bundle branches during corrective cardiac surgery for congenital heart diseases; and
- Direct the surgical treatment of patients with refractory ventricular tachyarrhythmias.

Pub. 100-3, Section 20.12
Diagnostic Endocardial Electrical Stimulation (Pacing)

Diagnostic endocardial electrical stimulation (EES), also called programmed electrical stimulation of the heart, is

© 2005 Ingenix, Inc.

Appendixes — 53

covered under Medicare when used for patients with severe cardiac arrhythmias.

Pub. 100-3, Section 20.13
HIS Bundle Study

Medicare coverage of the procedure would be limited to selected patients: those with complex ongoing acute arrhythmias, those with intermittent or permanent heart block in whom pacemaker implantation is being considered, and those patients who have recently developed heart block secondary to a myocardial infarction. When heart catheterization and the His Bundle Study are performed at the same time, the program will cover only one catheterization and a small adtitional charge for the study.

When a His bundle cardiogram is obtained as part of a diagnostic endocardial electrical stimulation, no separate charge will be recognized for the His bundle study. (See 35-78, Diagnostic Endocardial Electrical Stimulation.)

Pub. 100-3, Section 20.14
Plethysmography

Medicare coverage is extended to those procedures listed in Category I below when used for the accepted medical indications mentioned above. The procedures in Category II are still considered experimental and are not covered at this time. Denial of claims because a noncovered procedure was used or because there was no medical indication for plethysmographic evaluation of any type should be based on §1862(a)(1) of the Act.

CATEGORY I

Segmental Plethysmography.--Included under this procedure are services performed with a regional plethysmograph, differential plethysmograph, recording oscillometer, and a pulse volume recorder.

Electrical Impedance Plethysmography

Ultrasonic Measurement of Blood Flow (Doppler).--While not strictly a plethysmographic method, this is also a useful tool in the evaluation of suspected peripheral vascular disease or preoperative screening of podiatric patients with suspected peripheral vascular compromise. (See §50-7 for the applicable coverage policy on this procedure.)

Oculoplethysmography--See §50-37, Noninvasive Tests of Carotid Function.

Strain Gauge Plethysmography--This test is based on recording the non-pulsatile aspects of inflowing blood at various points on an extremity by a mercury-in-silastic strain gauge sensor. The instrument consists of a chart recorder, an automatic cuff inflation and deflation system, and a recording manometer.

CATEGORY II

The following methods have not yet reached a level of development such as to allow their routine use in the evaluation of suspected peripheral vascular disease.

Inductance Plethysmography--This method is considered experimental and does not provide reproducible results.

Capacitance Plethysmography--This method is considered experimental and does not provide reproducible results.

Mechanical Oscillometry--This is a non-standardized method which offers poor sensitivity and is not considered superior to the simple measurement of peripheral blood pressure.

Photoelectric Plethysmography--This method is considered useful only in determining whether or not a pulse is present and does not provide reproducible measurements of blood flow.

Differential plethysmography, on the other hand, is a system which uses an impedance technique to compare pulse pressures at various points along a limb, with a reference pressure at the mid-brachial or wrist level. It is not clear whether this technique, as usually performed in the physician's office, meets the definition of plethysmography because quantitative measurements of blood flow are usually not made. It has been concluded, in any event, that the differential plethysmography system is a blood pulse recorder of undetermined value, which has the potential for significant overutilization. Therefore, reimbursement for studies done by techniques other than venous occlusive pneumoplethysmography should be denied, at least until additional data on these devices, including controlled clinical studies, become available.

Pub. 100-3, Section 20.15
Electrocardiographic Services

Reimbursement may be made under Part B for electrocardiographic (EKG) services rendered by a physician or incident to his/her services or by an approved laboratory or an approved supplier of portable X-ray services. Since there is no coverage for EKG services of any type rendered on a screening basis or as part of a routine examination, the claim must indicate the signs and symptoms or other clinical reason necessitating the services.

A separate charge by an attending or consulting physician for EKG interpretation is allowed only when it is the normal practice to make such charge in addition to the regular office visit charge. No payment is made for EKG interpretations by individuals other than physicians.

On a claim involving EKG services furnished by a laboratory or portable x-ray supplier, identify the physician ordering the service and, when the charge includes both the taking of the tracing and its interpretation, include the identity of the physician making the interpretation. No separate bill for the services of a physician is paid unless it is clear that he/she was the patient's attending physician or was acting as a consulting physician. The taking of an EKG in an emergency, i.e., when the patient is or may be experiencing what is commonly referred to as a heart attack, is covered as a laboratory service or a diagnostic service by a portable X-ray supplier only when the evidence shows that a physician was in attendance at the time the service was performed or immediately thereafter.

The documentation required in the various situations mentioned above must be furnished not only when the laboratory or portable X-ray supplier bills the patient or carrier for its service, but also when such a facility bills the attending physician who, in turn, bills the patient or carrier for the EKG services.(In addition to the evidence required to document the claim, the laboratory or portable x-ray supplier must maintain in its records the referring physician 's written order and the identity of the employee taking the tracing.)

Long Term EKG Monitoring, also referred to as long-term EKG recording, Holter recording, or dynamic electrocardiography, is a diagnostic procedure which provides a continuous record of the electrocardiographic activity of a patient's heart while he is engaged in his daily activities.

The basic components of the long-term EKG monitoring systems are a sensing element, the design of which may provide either for the recording of electrocardiographic information on magnetic tape or for detecting significant variations in rate or rhythm as they occur, and a component for either graphically recording the electrocardiographic data or for visual or computer assisted analysis of the information recorded on magnetic tape. The long-term EKG permits the examination in the ambulant or potentially ambulant patient of as many as 70,000 heartbeats in a 12-hour recording while the standard EKG which is obtained in the recumbent position, yields information on only 50 to 60 cardiac cycles and provides only a limited data base on which diagnostic judgments may be made.

Many patients with cardiac arrhythmias are unaware of the presence of an irregularity in heart rhythm. Due to the transient nature of many arrhythmias and the short intervals in which the rhythm of the heart is observed by conventional standard EKG techniques, the offending arrhythmias can go undetected. With the extended examination provided by the long-term EKG, the physician is able not only to detect but also to classify various types of rhythm disturbances and waveform abnormalities and note the frequency of their occurrence. The knowledge of the reaction of the heart to daily activities with respect to rhythm, rate, conduction disturbances, and changes are of great assistance in directing proper therapy and

This modality is valuable in both inpatient and outpatient diagnosis and therapy. Long-term monitoring of ambulant or potentially ambulant inpatients provides significant potential for reducing the length of stay for post-coronary infarct patients in the intensive care setting and may result in earlier discharge from the hospital with greater assurance of safety to the patients. The indications for the use of this technique, noted below, are similar for both inpatients and outpatients.

The long-term EKG has proven effective in detecting transient episodes of cardiac dysrhythmia and in permitting the correlation of these episodes with cardiovascular symptomatology.It is also useful for patients who have symptoms of obscure etiology suggestive of cardiac arrhythmia.Examples of such symptoms include palpitations, chest pain, dizziness, light-headedness, near syncope, syncope, transient ischemic episodes, dyspnea, and shortness of breath.

This technique would also be appropriate at the time of institution of any arrhythmic drug therapy and may be performed during the course of therapy to evaluate response.It is also appropriate for evaluating a change of dosage and may be indicated shortly before and after the discontinuation of anti-arrhythemic medication.The therapeutic response to a drug whose duration of action and peak of effectiveness is defined in hours cannot be properly assessed by examining 30-40 cycles on a standard EKG rhythm strip.The knowledge that all patients placed on anti-arrhythmic medication do not respond to therapy and the known toxicity of anti-arrhythmic agents clearly indicate that proper assessment should be made on an individual basis to determine whether medication should be continued and at what dosage level.

The long-term EKG is also valuable in the assessment of patients with coronary artery disease. It enables the documentation of etiology of such symptoms as chest pain and shortness of breath.Since the standard EKG is often normal during the intervals between the episodes of precordial pain, it is essential to obtain EKG information while the symptoms are occurring. The long-term EKG has enabled the correlation of chest symptoms with the objective evidence of ST-segment abnormalities.It is appropriate for patients who are recovering from an acute mycardial infarction or coronary insufficiency before and after discharge from the hospital, since it is impossible to predict which of these patients is subject to ventricular arrhythmias on the basis of the presence or absence of rhythm disturbances during the period of initial coronary care. The long-term EKG enables the physician to identify patients who are at a higher risk of dying suddenly in the period following an acute myocardial infarction.It may also be reasonable and necessary where the high-risk patient with known cardiovascular disease advances to a substantially higher level of activity which might trigger increased or new types of arrhythmias necessitating treatment. Such a high-risk case would be one in which there is documentation that acute phase arrhythmias have not totally disappeared during the period of convalescence.

The use of the long-term EKG for routine assessment of pacemaker function can no longer be justified (see §20.8.1). Its use for the patient with an internal pacemaker would be covered only when he has symptoms suggestive of arrhythmia not revealed by the standard EKG or rhythm strip.

These guidelines are intended as a general outline of the circumstances under which the use of this diagnostic procedure would be warranted. Each patient receiving a long-term EKG should be evaluated completely, prior to performance of this diagnostic study. A complete history and physical examination should be obtained and the referring physician should review the indications for use of the long-term EKG.

The performance of a long-term EKG does not necessarily require the prior performance of a standard EKG. Nor does the demonstration of a normal standard EKG preclude the need for a long- term EKG. Finally, the demonstration of an abnormal standard EKG does not obviate the need for a long-term EKG if there is suspicion that the dysrhythmia is transient in nature.

A period of recording of up to 24 hours would normally be adequate to detect most transient arrhythmias and provide essential diagnostic information. The medical necessity for longer periods of monitoring must be documented.

Medical documentation for adjudicating claims for the use of the long-term EKG should be similar to other EKG services, X-ray services, and laboratory procedures. Generally, a statement of the diagnostic impression of the referring physician with an indication of the patient's relevant signs and symptoms should be sufficient for purposes of making a determination regarding the reasonableness and medical necessity for the use of this procedure. However, the intermediaries or carriers should require whatever additional documentation their medical consultants deem necessary to properly adjudicate the individual claim where the information submitted is not adequate.

It should be noted that the recording device furnished to the patient is simply one component of the diagnostic system and a separate charge for it will not be recognized under the durable medical equipment benefit.

Patient-Activated EKG Recorders, distributed under a variety of brand names, permit the patient to record an EKG upon manifestation of symptoms, or in response to a physician's order (e.g., immediately following strong exertion).Most such devices also permit the patient to simultaneously voice-record in order to describe symptoms and/or activity. In addition, some of these devices permit transtelephonic transmission of the recording to a physician's office, clinic, hospital, etc., having a decoder/recorder for review and analysis, thus eliminating the need to physically transport the tape. Some of these devices also permit a "time sampling" mode of operation. However, the "time sampling" mode is not covered--only the patient-activated mode of operation, when used for the indications described below, is covered at this time.

Services in connection with patient-activated EKG recorders are covered when used as an alternative to the long-term EKG monitoring (described above) for similar indications--detecting and characterizing symptomatic arrhythmias, regulation of anti-arrhythmic drug therapy, etc. Like long- term EKG monitoring, use of these devices is covered for evaluating patients with symptoms of obscure etiology suggestive of cardiac arrhythmia such as palpitations, chest pain, dizziness, lightheadedness, near syncope, syncope, transient ischemic episodes, dyspnea and shortness of breath.

As with long-term EKG monitors, patient-activated EKG recorders may be useful for both inpatient and outpatient diagnosis and therapy.While useful for assessing some post-coronary infarct patients in the hospital setting, these devices should not, however, be covered for outpatient monitoring of recently discharged post-infarct patients.

Computer Analyzed Electrocardiograms-Computer interpretation of EKG's is recognized as a valid and effective technique which will improve the quality and availability of cardiology services. Reimbursement may be made for such computer service when furnished in the setting and under the circumstances required for coverage of other electrocardiographic services. Where either a laboratory's or a portable x-ray supplier's charge for EKG services includes the physician review and certification of the printout as well as the computer interpretation, the certifying physician must be identified on the HCFA-1490 before the entire charge can be considered a reimbursable charge. Where the laboratory's (or portable x-ray supplier's) reviewing physician is not identified, the carrier should conclude that no professional component is involved and make its charge determination accordingly. If the supplying laboratory (or portable x-ray supplier when supplied by such a facility) does not include professional review and certification of the hard copy, a charge by the patient's physician may be recognized for the service. In any case the charge for the physician component should be substantially less than that for physician interpretation of the conventional EKG tracing in view of markedly reduced demand on the physician's time where computer interpretation is involved. Considering the unit cost reduction expected of this innovation, the total charge for the complete EKG service (taking of tracing and interpretation) when computer interpretation is employed should never exceed that considered reasonable for the service when physician interpretation is involved.

Transtelephonic Electrocardiographic Transmissions (Formerly Referred to as EKG Telephone Reporter Systems) is extended to include the use of transtelephonic electrocardiographic (EKG) transmissions as a diagnostic service for the indications described below, when performed with equipment meeting the standards described below, subject to the limitations and conditions specified below. Coverage is further limited to the amounts payable with respect to the physician's service in interpreting the results of such transmissions, including charges for rental of the equipment. The device used by the beneficiary is part of a total diagnostic system and is not considered durable medical equipment.

1. Covered Uses

The use of transtelephonic EKGs is covered for the following uses:

- To detect, characterize, and document <u>symptomatic</u> transient arrhythmias;
- To overcome problems in regulating antiarrhythmic drug dosage;
- To carry out early posthospital monitoring of patients discharged after myocardial infarction; (only if 24-hour coverage is provided, see 4. below).

Since cardiology is a rapidly changing field, some uses other than those specified above may be covered if, in the judgment of the contractor's medical consultants, such a use was justifiable in the particular case.The enumerated uses above represent uses for which a firm coverage determination has been made, and for which contractors may make payment without extensive claims development or review.

2. Specifications for Devices

The devices used by the patient are highly portable (usually pocket-sized) and detect and convert the normal EKG signal so that it can be transmitted via ordinary telephone apparatus to a receiving station. At the receiving end, the signal is decoded and transcribed into a conventional EKG. There are numerous devices available which transmit EKG readings in this fashion. For purposes of Medicare coverage, however, the transmitting devices must meet at least the following criteria:

- They must be capable of transmitting EKG Leads, I, II, or III;
- These lead transmissions must be sufficiently comparable to readings obtained by a conventional EKG to permit proper interpretation of abnormal cardiac rhythms.

3.Potential for Abuse - Need for Screening Guidelines

While the use of these devices may often compare favorably with more costly alternatives, this is the case only where the information they contribute is actively utilized by a knowledgeable practitioner as part of overall medical management of the patient. Consequently, it is vital that contractors be aware of the potential for abuse of these devices, and adopt necessary screening and physician education policies to detect and halt potentially abusive situations. For example, use of these devices to diagnose and treat suspected arrhythmias as a routine substitute for more conventional methods of diagnosis, such as a careful history, physical examination, and standard EKG and rhythm strip would not be appropriate. Moreover, contractors should require written justification for use of such devices in excess of 30 consecutive days in cases involving detection of transient arrhythmias.

Contractors may find it useful to review claims for these devices with a view toward detecting patterns of practice which may be useful in developing schedules which may be adopted for screening such claims in the future.

4. Twenty-four Hour Coverage

No payment may be made for the use of these devices to carry out early posthospital monitoring of patients discharged after myocardial infarction unless provision is made for 24 hour coverage in the manner described below.

Twenty-four hour coverage means that there must be, at the monitoring site (or sites) an experienced EKG technician receiving calls; tape recording devices do not meet this requirement. Further, such technicians should have immediate access to a physician, and have been instructed in when and how to contact available facilities to assist the patient in case of emergencies.

Pub. 100-3, Section 20.17
Noninvasive Tests of Carotid Function

It is important to note that the names of these tests are not standardized. Following are some of the acceptable tests, recognizing that this list is not inclusive and that determinations should be made by local medical consultants:

DIRECT TESTS
Carotid Phonoangiography
Direct Bruit Analysis
Spectral Bruit Analysis
Doppler Flow Velocity
Ultrasound Imaging including Real Time
B-Scan and Doppler Devices

INDIRECT TESTS
Periorbital Directional Doppler Ultrasonography
Oculoplethysmography
Ophthalmodynamometry

Pub. 100-3, Section 20.18
Carotid Body Resection/Carotid Body Denervation

Carotid body resection is occasionally used to relieve pulmonary symptoms, including asthma, but has been shown to lack general acceptance of the professional medical community. In addition, controlled clinical studies establishing the safety and effectiveness of this procedure are needed. Therefore, all carotid body resections to relieve pulmonary symptoms must be considered investigational and cannot be considered reasonable and necessary within the meaning of section 1862(a)(l) of the law. No program reimbursement may be made in such cases.

There is, however, one instance where carotid body resection has been accepted by the medical community as effective. That instance is when evidence of a mass in the carotid body,with or without symptoms, indicates the need for surgery to remove the carotid body tumor.

Denervation of a carotid sinus to treat hypersensitive carotid sinus reflex is another procedure performed in the area of the carotid body. In the case of hypersensitive carotid sinus, light pressure on the upper part of the neck (such as might be experienced when turning or raising one's head) results in symptoms such as dizziness or syncope due to hypotension and slowed heart rate. Failure of medical

therapy and continued deterioration in the condition of the patient in such cases may indicate need for surgery. Denervation of the carotid sinus is rarely performed, but when elected as the therapy of choice with the above indications, this procedure may be considered reasonable and necessary.

Pub. 100-3, Section 20.19
Ambulatory Blood Pressure Monitoring

ABPM must be performed for at least 24 hours to meet coverage criteria.

ABPM is only covered for those patients with suspected white coat hypertension. Suspected white coat hypertension is defined as

1) office blood pressure >140/90 mm Hg on at least three separate clinic/office visits with two separate measurements made at each visit;

2) at least two documented blood pressure measurements taken outside the office which are <140/90 mm Hg; and

3) no evidence of end-organ damage.

The information obtained by ABPM is necessary in order to determine the appropriate management of the patient. ABPM is not covered for any other uses. In the rare circumstance that ABPM needs to be performed more than once in a patient, the qualifying criteria described above must be met for each subsequent ABPM test.

For those patients that undergo ABPM and have an ambulatory blood pressure of <135/85 with no evidence of end-organ damage, it is likely that their cardiovascular risk is similar to that of normotensives. They should be followed over time. Patients for which ABPM demonstrates a blood pressure of >135/85 may be at increased cardiovascular risk, and a physician may wish to consider antihypertensive therapy.

Pub. 100-3, Section 20.23
Fabric Wrapping of Abdominal Aneurysms

Fabric wrapping of abdominal aneurysms is not a covered Medicare procedure. This is a treatment for abdominal aneurysms which involves wrapping aneurysms with cellophane or fascia lata. This procedure has not been shown to prevent eventual rupture. In extremely rare instances, external wall reinforcement may be indicated when the current accepted treatment (excision of the aneurysm and reconstruction with synthetic materials) is not a viable alternative, but external wall reinforcement is not fabric wrapping. Accordingly, fabric wrapping of abdominal aneurysms is not considered reasonable and necessary within the meaning of §1862(a)(1) of the Act.

Pub. 100-3, Section 20.25
Cardiac Catheterization Performed in Other than a Hospital Setting

Cardiac catheterization performed in a hospital setting for either inpatients or outpatients is a covered service. The procedure may also be covered when performed in a freestanding clinic when the carrier, in consultation with the appropriate Quality Improvement Organization (QIO), determines that the procedure can be performed safely in all respects in the particular facility. Prior to approving Medicare payment for cardiac catheterizations performed in freestanding clinics, carriers must request QIO review of the clinic.

Pub. 100-3, Section 20.26
Partial Ventriculectomy

Since the mortality rate is high and there are no published scientific articles or clinical studies regarding partial ventriculectomy, this procedure cannot be considered reasonable and necessary within the meaning of §1862(a)(1) of the Act. Therefore, partial ventriculectomy is not covered by Medicare.

Pub. 100-3, Section 20.28
Therapeutic Embolization

Therapeutic embolization is covered when done for hemorrhage, and for other conditions amenable to treatment by the procedure, when reasonable and necessary for the individual patient. Renal embolization for the treatment of renal adenocarcinoma continues to be covered, effective December 15, 1978, as one type of therapeutic embolization, to:

- Reduce tumor vascularity preoperatively;
- Reduce tumor bulk in inoperable cases; or
- Palliate specific symptoms.

Pub. 100-3, Section 20.29
Hyperbaric Oxygen Therapy

A. Covered Conditions.--Program reimbursement for HBO therapy will be limited to that which is administered in a chamber (including the one man unit) and is limited to the following conditions:
  1. Acute carbon monoxide intoxication, (ICD-9-CM diagnosis 986).
  2. Decompression illness, (ICD-9-CM diagnosis 993.2, 993.3).
  3. Gas embolism, (ICD-9-CM diagnosis 958.0, 999.1).
  4. Gas gangrene, (ICD-9-CM diagnosis 0400).
  5. Acute traumatic peripheral ischemia. HBO therapy is a valuable adjunctive treatment to be used in combination with accepted standard therapeutic measures when loss of function, limb, or life is threatened. (ICD-9-CM diagnosis 902.53, 903.01, 903.1, 904.0, 904.41.)
  6. Crush injuries and suturing of severed limbs. As in the previous conditions, HBO therapy would be an adjunctive treatment when loss of function, limb, or life is threatened. (ICD-9-CM diagnosis 927.00-927.03, 927.09-927.11, 927.20-927.21, 927.8-927.9, 928.00-928.01, 928.10-928.11, 928.20-928.21, 928.3, 928.8-928.9, 929.0, 929.9, 996.90- 996.99.)
  7. Progressive necrotizing infections (necrotizing fasciitis), (ICD-9-CM diagnosis 728.86).
  8. Acute peripheral arterial insufficiency, (ICD-9-CM diagnosis 444.21, 444.22, 81).
  9. Preparation and preservation of compromised skin grafts (not for primary management of wounds), (ICD-9CM diagnosis 996.52; excludes artificial skin graft).
  10. Chronic refractory osteomyelitis, unresponsive to conventional medical and surgical management, (ICD-9-CM diagnosis 730.10-730.19).
  11. Osteoradionecrosis as an adjunct to conventional treatment, (ICD-9-CM diagnosis 526.89).
  12. Soft tissue radionecrosis as an adjunct to conventional treatment, (ICD-9-CM diagnosis 990).
  13. Cyanide poisoning, (ICD-9-CM diagnosis 987.7, 989.0).
  14. Actinomycosis, only as an adjunct to conventional therapy when the disease process is refractory to antibiotics and surgical treatment, (ICD-9-CM diagnosis 039.0-039.4, 039.8, 039.9).
  15. Diabetic wounds of the lower extremities in patients who meet the following three criteria:
      a. Patient has type I or type II diabetes and has a lower extremity wound that is due to diabetes;
      b. Patient has a wound classified as Wagner grade III or higher; and
      c. Patient has failed an adequate course of standard wound therapy.

The use of HBO therapy is covered as adjunctive therapy only after there are no measurable signs of healing for at least 30 –days of treatment with standard wound therapy and must be used in addition to standard wound care. Standard wound care in patients with diabetic wounds includes: assessment of a patient's vascular status and correction of any vascular problems in the affected limb if possible, optimization of nutritional status, optimization of glucose control, debridement by any means to remove devitalized tissue, maintenance of a clean, moist bed of granulation tissue with appropriate moist dressings, appropriate off-loading, and necessary treatment to resolve any infection that might be present. Failure to respond to standard wound care occurs when there are no measurable signs of healing for at least 30 consecutive days. Wounds must be evaluated at least every 30 days during administration of HBO therapy. Continued treatment with HBO therapy is not covered if measurable signs of healing have not been demonstrated within any 30-day period of treatment.

B. Noncovered Conditions.--All other indications not specified under §35-10(A) are not covered under the Medicare program. No program payment may be made for any conditions other than those listed in §35-10 (A).

No program payment may be made for HBO in the treatment of the following conditions:
  1. Cutaneous, decubitus, and stasis ulcers.
  2. Chronic peripheral vascular insufficiency.
  3. Anaerobic septicemia and infection other than clostridial.

4. Skin burns (thermal).
5. Senility.
6. Myocardial infarction.
7. Cardiogenic shock.
8. Sickle cell anemia.
9. Acute thermal and chemical pulmonary damage, i.e., smoke inhalation with pulmonary insufficiency.
10. Acute or chronic cerebral vascular insufficiency.
11. Hepatic necrosis.
12. Aerobic septicemia.
13. Nonvascular causes of chronic brain syndrome (Pick's disease, Alzheimer's disease, Korsakoff's disease).
14. Tetanus.
15. Systemic aerobic infection.
16. Organ transplantation.
17. Organ storage.
18. Pulmonary emphysema.
19. Exceptional blood loss anemia.
20. Multiple Sclerosis.
21. Arthritic Diseases.
22. Acute cerebral edema.

C. Topical Application of Oxygen.

This method of administering oxygen does not meet the definition of HBO therapy as stated above. Also, its clinical efficacy has not been established. Therefore, no Medicare reimbursement may be made for the topical application of oxygen.

Pub. 100-3, Section 30.1
Biofeedback Therapy

Biofeedback therapy is covered under Medicare only when it is reasonable and necessary for the individual patient for muscle re-education of specific muscle groups or for treating pathological muscle abnormalities of spasticity, incapacitating muscle spasm, or weakness, and more conventional treatments (heat, cold, massage, exercise, support) have not been successful. This therapy is not covered for treatment of ordinary muscle tension states or for psychosomatic conditions. (See the Medicare Benefit Policy Manual, Chapter 15, for general coverage requirements about physical therapy requirements.)

Pub. 100-3, Section 30.1.1
Biofeedback Therapy for the Treatment of Urinary Incontinence

This policy applies to biofeedback therapy rendered by a practitioner in an office or other facility setting.

Biofeedback is covered for the treatment of stress and/or urge incontinence in cognitively intact patients who have failed a documented trial of pelvic muscle exercise (PME)training. Biofeedback is not a treatment, per se, but a tool to help patients learn how to perform PME. Biofeedback-assisted PME incorporates the use of an electronic or mechanical device to relay visual and/or auditory evidence of pelvic floor muscle tone, in order to improve awareness of pelvic floor musculature and to assist patients in the performance of PME.

A failed trial of PME training is defined as no clinically significant improvement in urinary incontinence after completing 4 weeks of an ordered plan of pelvic muscle exercises to increase periurethral muscle strength.

Contractors may decide whether or not to cover biofeedback as an initial treatment modality.

Home use of biofeedback therapy is not covered.

Pub. 100-3, Section 30.5
Transcendental Meditation

After review of this issue, HCFA has concluded that the evidence concerning the medical efficacy of TM is incomplete at best and does not demonstrate effectiveness and that a professional level of skill is not required for the training of patients to engage in TM.

Although many articles have been written about application of TM for patients with certain forms of hypertension and anxiety, there are no rigorous scientific studies that demonstrate the effectiveness of TM for use as an adjunct medical therapy for such conditions. Accordingly, neither TM nor the training of patients for its use are covered under the Medicare program.

Pub. 100-3, Section 30.6
Intravenous Histamine Therapy

However, there is no scientifically valid clinical evidence that histamine therapy is effective for any condition regardless of the method of administration, nor is it accepted or widely used by the medical profession. Therefore, histamine therapy cannot be considered reasonable and necessary, and program payment for such therapy is not made.

Pub. 100-3, Section 40.1
Diabetes Outpatient Self-Management Training

Please refer to 42 CFR 410.140 - 410.146 for conditions that must be met for Medicare coverage.

Pub. 100-3, Section 40.5
Treatment of Obesity

B. Nationally Covered Indications

Service performed in connection with the treatment of obesity are covered by medicare when such servcies are an integral and necessary aprt of a course of treatment for diseases such as hypothryroidism, Cushing's disease, hypothalamic lesions, cardiovascular diseases, respiratory diseases, diabetes, and hypertension.

C. Nationally Noncovered Indications

1. The treatment of obesity unrelated to such a medical condition (see section B above) is not considered reasonable and necessary and is not covered under the Medicare program.
2. Supplemented fasting is not covered under the Medicare program as a general treatment for obesity (see section D below for discretionary local coverage).

D.Other

Where weight loss is necessary before surgery in order to ameliorate the complications posed by obesity when it coexists with pathological conditions such as cardiac and respiratory diseases, diabetes, or hypertension (and other more conservative techniques to achieve this end are not regarded as appropriate), supplemented fasting with adequate monitoring of the patient is eligible for local coverage determination through individual contractor discretion. The risks associated with the achievement of rapid weight loss must be carefully balanced against the risk posed by the condition requiring the surgical treatment.

(This NCD last reviewed September 2004.)

Cross-reference §100.1, 100.8, 100.11

Pub. 100-3, Section 50.1
Speech Generating Devices

Effective January 1, 2001, augmentative and alternative communication devices or communicators, which are hereafter referred to as "speech generating devices" are now considered to fall within the DME benefit category established by §1861(n) of the Social Security Act. They may be covered if the contractor's medical staff determines that the patient suffers from a severe speech impairment and that the medical condition warrants the use of a device based on the following definitions.

Pub. 100-3, Section 50.2
Electronic Speech Aids

Electronic speech aids are covered under Part B as prosthetic devices when the patient has had a laryngectomy or his larynx is permanently inoperative.

Pub. 100-3, Section 50.3
Cochlear Implantation

B. Nationally Covered Indications

1. Effective for services performed on or after April 4, 2005, cochlear implantation may be covered for treatment of bilateral pre- or -post- linguistic, sensorineural, moderate-to-profound hearing loss in individuals who demonstrate limited benefit from amplification. Limited benefit from amplification is defined by test scores of les than or equal to 40% correct in the best aided listening condition on tape recorded tests of open-set sentence cognition. Medicare coverage is provided only for those patients who meet all of the following selection guidelines.

- Diagnosis of bilateral severe-to-profound sensorineural hearing impairment with limited benefit from appropriate hearing (or vibrotactile) aids;
- Cognitive ability to use auditory clues and a willingness to undergo an extended program of rehabilitation;
- Freedom from middle ear infection, an accessible cochlear lumen that is structurally suited to implantation, and freedom from lesions in the auditory nerve and acoustic areas of the central nervous system;
- No contraindications to surgery; and
- The device must be used in accordance withe the FDA-approved labeling.

2. Effective for services performed on or after April 4, 2005, cochlear implantation may be covered for individuals meeting the selection guidelines above and with hearing test scores of greater than 40% and less than or equal to 60% only when the provider is participating in, and patients are enrolled in, either an FDA-approved category B investigational device exemption clinical trial as defined at 42 CFR 405.201, a trial under the Centers for Medicare & Medicaid (CMS) Clinical Trial Policy as defined at section

310.1 of the National Coverage Determinations Manual, or a prospective, controlled comparative trial approved by CMS as consistent with the evidentiary requirements for National Coverage Analyses and meeting specific quality standards.

C. Nationally Noncovered Indications

Medicare beneficiaries not meeting all of the coverage criteria for cochlear iimplantation listed are deemed not eligible for Medicare coverage under section 1862(a)(1)(A) of the Social Security Act.

D. Other

All other indications for cochlear implantation not otherwise indicated as nationally covered on non-covered above remain at local contractor discretion.

Pub. 100-3, Section 70.1
Consultations with a Beneficiary's Family and Associates

In certain types of medical conditions, including when a patient is withdrawn and uncommunicative due to a mental disorder or comatose, the physician may contact relatives and close associates to secure background information to assist in diagnosis and treatment planning. When a physician contacts his patient's relatives or associates for this purpose, expenses of such interviews are properly chargeable as physician's services to the patient on whose behalf the information was secured. If the beneficiary is not an inpatient of a hospital, Part B reimbursement for such an interview is subject to the special limitation on payments for physicians' services in connection with mental, psychoneurotic, and personality disorders.

A physician may also have contacts with a patient's family and associates for purposes other than securing background information. In some cases, the physician will provide counseling to members of the household. Family counseling services are covered only where the primary purpose of such counseling is the treatment of the patient's condition. For example, two situations where family counseling services would be appropriate are as follows: (1) where there is a need to observe the patient's interaction with family members; and/or (2) where there is a need to assess the capability of and assist the family members in aiding in the management of the patient. Counseling principally concerned with the effects of the patient's condition on the individual being interviewed would not be reimbursable as part of the physician's personal services to the patient. While to a limited degree, the counseling described in the second situation may be used to modify the behavior of the family members, such services nevertheless are covered because they relate primarily to the management of the patient's problems and not to the treatment of the family member's problems.

Pub. 100-3, Section 70.2
Consultation Services Rendered by a Podiatrist in a Skilled Nursing Facility

Consultation services rendered by a podiatrist in a skilled nursing facility are covered if the services are reasonable and necessary and do not come within any of the specific statutory exclusions. Section l862(a)(13) of the Act excludes payment for the treatment of flat foot conditions, the treatment of subluxations of the foot, and routine foot care. To determine whether the consultation comes within the foot care exclusions, apply the same rule as for initial diagnostic examinations, i.e., where services are performed

APPENDIX D

in connection with specific symptoms or complaints which suggest the need for covered services, the services are covered regardless of the resulting diagnosis. The exclusion of routine physician examinations is also pertinent and would generally exclude podiatric consultation performed on all patients in a skilled nursing facility on a routine basis for screening purposes, except in those cases where a specific foot ailment is involved. Section 1862(a)(7) of the Act excludes payment for routine physical checkups.

Pub. 100-3, Section 70.2.1
Services Provided for the Diagnosis and Treatment of Diabetic Sensory Neuropathy with Loss of Protective Sensation (AKA Diabetic Peripheral Neuropathy

Diabetic sensory neuropathy with LOPS is a localized illness of the feet and falls within the regulation's exception to the general exclusionary rule [see 42 CFR §411.15(l)(1)(i)]. Foot exams for people with diabetic sensory neuropathy with LOPS are reasonable and necessary to allow for early intervention in serious complications that typically afflict diabetics with the disease.

Effective for services furnished on or after July 1, 2002, Medicare covers, as a physician service, an evaluation (examination and treatment) of the feet no more often than every six months for individuals with a documented diagnosis of diabetic sensory neuropathy and LOPS, as long as the beneficiary has not seen a foot care specialist for some other reason in the interim. LOPS shall be diagnosed through sensory testing with the 5.07 monofilament using established guidelines, such as those developed by the National Institute of Diabetes and Digestive and Kidney Diseases guidelines. Five sites should be tested on the plantar surface of each foot, according to the National Institute of Diabetes and Digestive and Kidney Diseases guidelines. The areas must be tested randomly since the loss of protective sensation may be patchy in distribution, and the patient may get clues if the test is done rhythmically. Heavily callused areas should be avoided. As suggested by the American Podiatric Medicine Association, an absence of sensation at two or more sites out of 5 tested on either foot when tested with the 5.07 Semmes-Weinstein monofilament must be present and documented to diagnose peripheral neuropathy with loss of protective sensation.

  A. The examination includes:

    1) a patient history, and

    2) a physical examination that must consist of at least the following elements:
      a. visual inspection of forefoot and hindfoot (including toe web spaces);
      b. evaluation of protective sensation;
      c. evaluation of foot structure and biomechanics;
      d. evaluation of vascular status and skin integrity;
      e. evaluation of the need for special footwear; and

    3) patient education.

  B. Treatment includes, but is not limited to:

    1) local care of superficial wounds;

    2) debridement of corns and calluses; and

    3) trimming and debridement of nails.

The diagnosis of diabetic sensory neuropathy with LOPS should be established and documented prior to coverage of foot care. Other causes of peripheral neuropathy should be considered and investigated by the primary care physician prior to initiating or referring for foot care for persons with LOPS.

Pub. 100-3, Section 80.1
Hydrophilic Contact Lens For Corneal Bandage

Payment may be made under §1861(s)(2) of the Act for a hydrophilic contact les approved by the Food and Drug Administration (FDA) and used as a supply incident to a pphysician's service. Payment for the lens is included in the payment for the physician's service to which the lens is incident. Contractors are authorized to accept an FDA letter of approval or other FDA published material as evidence of FDA approval. (See §80.4 of the NCD Manual for coverage of a hydrophilic contact lens as prosthetic device.)

Pub. 100-3, Section 80.2
Ocular Photodynamic Therapy

OPT is only covered when used in conjunction with verteporfin.

Effective July 1, 2001, OPT with verteporfin was approved for a diagnosis of neovascular AMD with predominately classic subfoveal choroidal neovascularization (CNV) lesions (where the area of classic CNV occupies >= 50% of the area of the entire lesion) at the initial visit as determined by a fluorescein angiogram.

On October 17, 2001, CMS announced its "intent to cover" OPT with verteporfin for AMD patients with occult and no classic subfoveal CNV as determined by a fluorescein angiogram. The October 17, 2001, decision was never implemented.

On March 28, 2002, after thorough review and reconsideration of the October 17, 2001, intent to cover policy, CMS determined that the current noncoverage policy for OPT for verteporfin for AMD patients with occult and no classic subfoveal CNV as determined by a fluorescein angiogram should remain in effect.

Effective August 20, 2002, CMS issued a noncovered instruction for OPT with verteporfin for AMD patients with occult and no classic subfoveal CNV as determined by a fluorescein angiogram.

Covered Indications

Effective April 1, 2004, OPT with verteporfin continues to be approved for a diagnosis of neovascular AMD with predominately classic subfoveal CNV lesions (where the area of classic CNV occupies >= 50% of the area of the entire lesion) at the initial visit as determined by a fluorescein angiogram. (CNV lesions are comprised of classic and/or occult components.) Subsequent follow-up visits require a fluorescein angiogram prior to treatment. There are no requirements regarding visual acuity, lesion size, and number of re-treatments when treating predominantly classic lesions.

In addition, after thorough review and reconsideration of the August 20, 2002, noncoverage policy, CMS determines that the evidence is adequate to conclude that OPT with verteporfin is reasonable and necessary for treating:

    1. Subfoveal occult with no classic CNV associated with AMD; and,

CPT only © 2005 American Medical Association. All Rights Reserved.
© 2005 Ingenix, Inc.
Appendixes — 61

2. Subfoveal minimally classic CNV (where the area of classic CNV occupies <50% of the area of the entire lesion) associated with AMD.

The above 2 indications are considered reasonable and necessary only when:

1. The lesions are small (4 disk areas or less in size) at the time of initial treatment or within the 3 months prior to initial treatment; and,
2. The lesions have shown evidence of progression within the 3 months prior to initial treatment. Evidence of progression must be documented by deterioration of visual acuity (at least 5 letters on a standard eye examination chart), lesion growth (an increase in at least 1 disk area), or the appearance of blood associated with the lesion.

Noncovered Indications

Other uses of OPT with verteporfin to treat AMD not already addressed by CMS will continue to be noncovered. These include, but are not limited to, the following AMD indications:

- Juxtafoveal or extrafoveal CNV lesions (lesions outside the fovea),
- Inability to obtain a fluorescein angiogram,
- Atrophic or "dry" AMD.

Other

OPT with verteporfin for other ocular indications, such as pathologic myopia or presumed ocular histoplasmosis syndrome, continue to be eligible for local coverage determinations through individual contractor discretion.

(This NCD last reviewed March 2004.)

Pub. 100-3, Section 80.3
Verteporfin

Covered Indications

Effective April 1, 2004, OPT with verteporfin is covered for patients with a diagnosis of neovascular age-related macular degeneration (AMD) with:

- Predominately classic subfoveal choroidal neovascularization (CNV) lesions (where the area of classic CNV occupies >= 50% of the area of the entire lesion) at the initial visit as determined by a fluorescein angiogram. (CNV lesions are comprised of classic and/or occult components.) Subsequent follow-up visits require a fluorescein angiogram prior to treatment. There are no requirements regarding visual acuity, lesion size, and number of retreatments when treating predominantly classic lesions.
- Subfoveal occult with no classic associated with AMD.
- Subfoveal minimally classic CNV CNV (where the area of classic CNV occupies <50% of the area of the entire lesion) associated with AMD.

The above 2 indications are considered reasonable and necessary only when:

1. The lesions are small (4 disk areas or less in size) at the time of initial treatment or within the 3 months prior to initial treatment; and,

2. The lesions have shown evidence of progression within the 3 months prior to initial treatment. Evidence of progression must be documented by deterioration of visual acuity (at least 5 letters on a standard eye examination chart), lesion growth (an increase in at least 1 disk area), or the appearance of blood associated with the lesion.

Noncovered Indications

Other uses of OPT with verteporfin to treat AMD not already addressed by CMS will continue to be noncovered. These include, but are not limited to, the following AMD indications: juxtafoveal or extrafoveal CNV lesions (lesions outside the fovea), inability to obtain a fluorescein angiogram, or atrophic or "dry" AMD.

Other

OPT with verteporfin for other ocular indications, such as pathologic myopia or presumed ocular histoplasmosis syndrome, continue to be eligible for local coverage determinations through individual contractor discretion.

(This NCD last reviewed March 2004.)

Pub. 100-3, Section 80.4
Hydrophilic Contact Lenses

Hydrophilic contact lenses are eyeglasses within the meaning of the exclusion in §1862(a)(7) of the Act and are not covered when used in the treatment of nondiseased eyes with spherical ametropia, refractive astigmatism, and/or corneal astigmatism. Payment may be made under the prosthetic device benefit, however, for hydrophilic contact lenses when prescribed for an aphakic patient.

Contractors are authorized to accept an FDA letter of approval or other FDA published material as evidence of FDA approval. (See §80.1 of the NCD Manual for coverage of a hydrophilic lens as a corneal bandage.)

Pub. 100-3, Section 80.6
Intraocular Photography

Intraocular photography is covered when used for the diagnosis of such conditions as macular degeneration, retinal neoplasms, choroid disturbances and diabetic retinopathy, or to identify glaucoma, multiple sclerosis and other central nervous system abnormalities. Make Medicare payment for the use of this procedure by an opthalmologist in these situations when it is reasonable and necessary for the individual patient to receive these services.

Pub. 100-3, Section 80.7
Refractive Keratoplasty

The correction of common refractive errors by eyeglasses, contact lenses or other prosthetic devices is specifically excluded from coverage. The use of radial keratotomy and/or keratoplasty for the purpose of refractive error compensation is considered a substitute or alternative to eye glasses or contact lenses, which are specifically excluded by §1862 (a)(7) of the Act (except in certain cases in connection with cataract surgery). In addition, many in the medical community consider such procedures cosmetic surgery, which is excluded by section §1862(a)(10) of the Act. Therefore, radial keratotomy and keratoplasty to treat refractive defects are not covered.

APPENDIX D

Keratoplasty that treats specific lesions of the cornea, such as phototherapeutic keratectomy that removes scar tissue from the visual field, deals with an abnormality of the eye and is not cosmetic surgery. Such cases may be covered under §1862(a)(1)(A) of the Act.

The use of lasers to treat ophthalmic disease constitutes opthalmalogic surgery. Coverage is restricted to practitioners who have completed an approved training program in ophthalmologic surgery.

Pub. 100-3, Section 80.8
Endothelial Cell Photography

Endothelial cell photography is a covered procedure under Medicare when reasonable and necessary for patients who meet one or more of the following criteria:

- Have slit lamp evidence of endothelial dystrophy (cornea guttata),
- Have slit lamp evidence of corneal edema (unilateral or bilateral),
- Are about to undergo a secondary intraocular lens implantation,
- Have had previous intraocular surgery and require cataract surgery,
- Are about to undergo a surgical procedure associated with a higher risk to corneal endothelium; i.e., phacoemulsification, or refractive surgery (see §35-54 for excluded refractive procedures),
- With evidence of posterior polymorphous dystrophy of the cornea or irido-corneal-endothelium syndrome, or
- Are about to be fitted with extended wear contact lenses after intraocular surgery.

When a pre-surgical examination for cataract surgery is performed and the conditions of this section are met, if the only visual problem is cataracts, endothelial cell photography is covered as part of the presurgical comprehensive eye examination or combination brief/intermediate examination provided prior to cataract surgery, and not in addition to it. (See §10.1)

Pub. 100-3, Section 80.9
Computer Enhanced Perimetry

It is a covered service when used in assessing visual fields in patients with glaucoma or other neuropathologic defects.

Pub. 100-3, Section 80.10
Phaco-Emulsification procedure - cataract extraction

In view of recommendations of authoritative sources in the field of ophthalmology, the subject technique is viewed as an accepted procedure for removal of cataracts. Accordingly, program reimbursement may be made for necessary services furnished in connection with cataract extraction utilizing the phaco-emulsification procedure.

Pub. 100-3, Section 80.11
Vitrectomy

Vitrectomy may be considered reasonable and necessary for the following conditions: vitreous loss incident to cataract surgery, vitreous opacities due to vitreous hemorrhage or other causes, retinal detachments secondary to vitreous strands, proliferative retinopathy, and vitreous retraction.

See chapter 15 of the Medicare Carriers Manual for how to determine payment for physician vitrectomy services and §5243 of the Medicare Carriers Manual for how to determine payment for ASC facility vitrectomy services. Also, see §4630 of the Medicare Carriers Manual to identify when, for Medicare payment purposes, certain vitrectomy codes are included in other codes or when codes for other services include vitrectomy codes. The CPT codes for vitrectomy services are 67005, 67010, 67036, 67038, 67039, and 67040.

Pub. 100-3, Section 80.12
Intraocular Lenses (IOLs)

Intraocular lens implantation services, as well as the lens itself, may be covered if reasonable and necessary for the individual. Implantation services may include hospital, surgical, and other medical services, including pre-implantation ultrasound (A-scan) eye measurement of one or both eyes.

Pub. 100-3, Section 100.1
Gastric Bypass Surgery for Obesity

Gastric bypass surgery for extreme obesity is covered under the program if (1) it is medically appropriate for the individual to have such surgery; and (2) the surgery is to correct an illness which caused the obesity or was aggravated by the obesity.

Pub. 100-3, Section 100.2
Endoscopy

Endoscopic procedures are covered when reasonable and necessary for the individual patient.

Pub. 100-3, Section 100.4
Esophageal Manometry

Esophageal manometry is covered under Medicare where it is determined to be reasonable and necessary for the individual patient.

Pub. 100-3, Section 100.5
Diagnostic Breath Analyses

The Following Breath Test is Covered:

- Lactose breath hydrogen to detect lactose malabsorption .

The Following Breath Tests are Excluded from Coverage;

- Lactulose breath hydrogen for diagnosing small bowel bacterial overgrowth and measuring small bowel transit time.
- CO_2 for diagnosing bile acid malabsorption.
- CO_2 for diagnosing fat malabsorption.

Pub. 100-3, Section 100.8
Intestinal By-Pass Surgery

The safety of intestinal bypass surgery for treatment of obesity has not been demonstrated. Severe adverse reactions such as steatorrhea, electrolyte depletion, liver failure, arthralgia, hypoplasia of bone marrow, and avitaminosis have sometimes occurred as a result of this procedure. It does not meet the reasonable and necessary provisions of §1862(a)(1) of the Act and is not a covered Medicare procedure.

Pub. 100-3, Section 100.9
Implantation of Anti-Gastroesophageal Reflux Device

The implantation of this device may be considered reasonable and necessary in specific clinical situations where a conventional valvuloplasty procedure is contraindicated. The implantation of an anti-gastroesophageal reflux device is covered only for patients with documented severe or life threatening gastroesophageal reflux disease whose conditions have been resistant to medical treatment and who also:

- have esophageal involvement with progressive systemic sclerosis; or
- have foreshortening of the esophagus such that insufficient tissue exists to permit a valve reconstruction; or
- are poor surgical risks for a valvuloplasty procedure; or
- have failed previous attempts at surgical treatment with valvuloplasty procedures.

Pub. 100-3, Section 100.10
Injection Sclerotherapy for Esophageal Variceal Bleeding

This procedure is covered under Medicare.

Pub. 100-3, Section 100.12
Gastrophotography

Gastrophotography is an accepted procedure for diagnosis and treatment of gastrointestinal disorders. The photographic record provided by this procedure is often necessary for consultation and/or followup purposes and when required for such purposes, is more valuable than a conventional gastroscopic examination. Such a record facilitates the documentation and evaluation (healing or worsening) of lesions such as the gastric ulcer, facilitates consultation between physicians concerning difficult-to-interpret lesions, provides preoperative characterization for the surgeon, and permits better diagnosis of postoperative gastric bleeding to help determine whether there is a need for reoperation. Therefore, program reimbursement may be made for this procedure.

Pub. 100-3, Section 100.13
Laparoscopic Cholecystectomy

Laparoscopic cholecystectomy is a covered surgical procedure in which a diseased gall bladder is removed through the use of instruments introduced via cannulae, with vision of the operative field maintained by use of a high-resolution television camera-monitor system (video laparoscope). For inpatient claims, use ICD-9-CM code 51.23, Laparoscopic cholecystectomy. For all other claims, use CPT codes 49310 for laparoscopy, surgical; cholecystectomy (any method), and 49311 for laparoscopy, surgical: cholecystectomy with cholangiography.

Pub. 100-3, Section 110.1
Hyperthermia for Treatment of Cancer

Local hyperthermia is covered under Medicare when used in connection with radiation therapy for the treatment of primary or metastatic cutaneous or subcutaneous superficial malignancies. It is not covered when used alone or in connection with chemotherapy.

Pub. 100-3, Section 110.2

Certain Drugs Distributed by the National Cancer Institute

A physician is eligible to receive Group C drugs from the Divison of Cancer Treatment only if the following requirements are met:

- A physician must be registered with the NCI as an investigator by having completed an FD-Form 1573;
- A written request for the drug, indicating the disease to be treated, must be submitted to the NCI;
- The use of the drug must be limited to indications outlined in the NCI's guidelines; and
- All adverse reactions must be reported to the Investigational Drug Branch of the Division of Cancer Treatment.

In view of these NCI controls on distribution and use of Group C drugs, intermediaries may assume, in the absence of evidence to the contrary, that a Group C drug and the related hospital stay are covered if all other applicable coverage requirements are satisfied.

If there is reason to question coverage in a particular case, the matter should be resolved with the assistance of the Quality improvemetn organization (QIO), or if there is none, the assistance of your medical consultants.

Information regarding those drugs which are classified as Group C drugs may be obtained from:

Office of the Chief, Investigational Drug Branch
Division of Cancer Treatment, CTEP, Landow Building
Room 4C09, National Cancer Institute
Bethesda, Maryland 20205

Pub. 100-3, Section 110.3
Cytotoxic Food Tests

Prior to August 5, 1985, Medicare covered cytotoxic food tests as an adjunct to in vivo clinical allergy tests in complex food allergy problems. Effective August 5, l985, cytotoxic leukocyte tests for food allergies are excluded from Medicare coverage because available evidence does not show that these tests are safe and effective. This exclusion was published as a CMS Ruling in the "Federal Register" on July 5, 1985.

Pub. 100-3, Section 110.4
Extracorporeal Photopheresis

Extracorporeal photopheresis is covered by Medicare only when used in the palliative treatment of the skin manifestations of CTCL that has not responded to other therapy.

Pub. 100-3, Section 110.5
Granulocyte Transfusions

Granulocyte transfusions to patients suffering from severe infection and granulocytopenia are a covered service under Medicare.

Pub. 100-3, Section 110.6
Scalp Hypothermia During Chemotherapy, to Prevent Hair Loss

While ice-filled bags or bandages or other devices used for scalp hypothermia during chemotherapy may be covered as supplies of the kind commonly furnished without a separate charge, no separate charge for them would be recognized.

Pub. 100-3, Section 110.7
Blood Transfusions

B. Policy Governing Transfusions

For Medicare coverage purposes, it is important to distinguish between a transfusion itself and preoperative blood services; e.g., collection, processing, storage. Medically necessary transfusion of blood, regardless of the type, may generally be a covered service under both Part A and Part B of Medicare. Coverage does not make a distinction between the transfusion of homologous, autologous, or donor-directed blood. With respect to the coverage of the services associated with the preoperative collection, processing, and storage of autologous and donor-directed blood, the following policies apply.

1. Hospital Part A and B Coverage and Payment

Under §1862(a)(14) of the Act, non-physician services furnished to hospital patients are covered and paid for as hospital services. As provided in §1886 of the Act, under the prospective [payment system (PPS), the diagnosis related group (DRG) payment to the hospital includes all covered blood and blood processing expenses, whether or not the blood is eventually used.

Under its provider agreement, a hospital is required to furnish or arrange for all covered services furnished to hospital patients. medicare payment is made to the hospital, under PPS or cost reimbursement, for covered inpatient services, and it is intended to reflect payment for all costs of furnishing those services.

2. Nonhospital Part B Coverage

Under Part B, to be eligible for separate coverage, a service must fit the definition of one of the services authorized by §1832 of the Act. These services are defined in 42 CFR 410.10 and do not include a separate category for a supplier's services associated with blood donation services, either autologous or donor-directed. That is, the collection, processing, and storage of blood for later transfusion into the beneficiary is not recognized as a separate service under Part B. Therefore, there is no avenue through which a blood supplier can receive direct payment under Part B for blood donation services.

C..Perioperative Blood Salvage

When the perioperative blood salvage process is used in surgery on a hospital patient, payment made to the hospital (under PPS or through cost reimbursement) for the procedure in which that process is used is intended to encompass payment for all costs relating to that process.

Pub. 100-3, Section 110.8
Blood Platelet Transfusions

Blood platelet transplants are safe and effective for the correction of thrombocytopenia and other blood defects. It is covered under Medicare when treatment is reasonable and necessary for the individual patient.

Pub. 100-3, Section 110.8.1
Stem Cell Transplantation

1. Allogeneic Stem Cell Transplantation.

Allogeneic stem cell transplantation is a procedure in which a portion of a healthy donor's stem cell or bone marrow is obtained and prepared for intravenous infusion.

a. Covered Conditions.--The following uses of allogeneic bone marrow transplantation are covered under Medicare:

- Effective for services performed on or after August 1, 1978, for the treatment of leukemia, leukemia in remission, or aplasti anemia when it is reasonable and necessary; and

- Effective for services performed on or after June 3, 1985, for the treatment of severe combined immunodeficiency disease (SCID) , and for the treatment of Wiskott - Aldrich syndrome.

b. Noncovered Conditions

Effective for services performed on or after May 24, 1996, allogeneic stem cell transplantation is not covered as treatment for multiple myeloma.

Allogeneic stem cell transplantation is not covered as treatment for multiple myeloma.

2. Autologous Stem Cell Transplantation

Autologous stem cell transplantation is a technique for restoring stem cells using the patient's own previously stored cells.

1. Covered Conditions

Effective for services performed on or after April 28, 1989, AuSCT is considered reasonable and necessary under §1862(a)(1)(A) of the Social Security Act for the following conditions and is covered under Medicare for patients with:

- Acute leukemia in remission who have a high probability of relapse and who have no human leucocyte antigens (HLA)-matched;
- Resistant non-Hodgkin's lymphomas or those presenting with poor prognostic features following an initial response;
- Recurrent or refractory neuroblastoma (; or
- Advanced Hodgkin's disease who have failed conventional therapy and haveno HLA-matched donor;

Effective October 1, 2000, single AuSCT is only covered for Durie-Salmon Stage II or III patients that fit the following requirement:

- Newly diagnosed or responsive multiple myeloma. This includes those patients wipreviously untreated disease, those with at least a partial response to prior chemotherapy (defined as a 50 percent decrease either in measurable paraprotein [serum and/or urine] or in bone marrow infiltration, sustained for at least 1 month), and those in responsive relapse; and
- Adequate cardiac, renal, pulmonary, and hepatic function.

Effective for services performed on or after March 15, 2005, when recognized clinical risk factors are emplloyed to select patients for transplantation, high dose melphalan (HDM) together with AuSCT is reasonable and necessary for Medicare beneficiaries of any age group with primary amyloid light chain (AL) amyloidosis who meet the folling criteria:

- Amylloid deposition in 2 or fewer organs; and,

- Cardiac left ventricular ejection fraction (EF) greater than 45%.

b. Noncovered Indications

Insufficient data exist to establish definite conclusions regarding the efficacy of AuSCT for the following conditions:

- Acute leukemia not in remission
- Chronic granulocytic leukemia;
- Solid tumors (other than neuroblastoma);
- Up to October 1, 2000, multiple myeloma;
- Tandem transplantation (multiple rounds of AuSCT) for patients with multiple myelooma;
- Effective October 1, 2000, non primary AL amyloidosis; and,
- Effective October 1, 2000, thru March 14, 2005, primary AL amyloidosis for Medicare beneficiaries age 64 or older.

In these cases, AuSCT is not considered reasonable and necessary within the meaning of §1862(a)(1)(A) of the Act and is not covered under Medicare.

B. Other

All other indications for stem cell transplantation not otherwise noted above as covered or noncovered nationally remain at local contractor discretion.

(This NCD last reviewed March 2005)

Pub. 100-3, Section 110.9
Antigens Prepared for Sublingual Administration

For antigens provided to patients on or after November 17, 1996, Medicare does not cover such antigens if they are to be administered sublingually, i.e., by placing drops under the patient's tongue. This kind of allergy therapy has not been proven to be safe and effective. Antigens are covered only if they are administered by injection.

Pub. 100-3, Section 110.10
Intravenous Iron Therapy

A. Effective December 1, 2000, Medicare covers sodium ferric gluconate complex in sucrose injection as a first line treatment of iron deficiency anemia when furnished intravenously to patients undergoing chronic hemodialysis who are receiving supplemental erythropoeitin therapy.
B. Effective October 1, 2001, Medicare also covers iron sucrose injection as a first line treatment of iron deficiency anemia when furnished intravenously to patients undergoing chronic hemodialysis who are receiving supplemental erythropoeitin therapy.

Pub. 100-3, Section 110.11
Food Allergy Testing and Treatment

Effective October 31, 1988, sublingual intracutaneous and subcutaneous provocative and neutralization testing and neutralization therapy for food allergies are excluded from Medicare coverage because available evidence does not show that these tests and therapies are effective. This exclusion was published as a Final Notice in the "Federal Register" on September 29, 1988.

Pub. 100-3, Section 110.12
Challenge Ingestion Food Testing

This procedure is covered when it is used on an outpatient basis if it is reasonable and necessary for the individual patient.

Challenge ingestion food testing has not been proven to be effective in the diagnosis of rheumatoid arthritis, depression, or respiratory disorders. Accordingly, its use in the diagnosis of these conditions is not reasonable and necessary within the meaning of section 1862(a)(1) of the Medicare law, and no program payment is made for this procedure when it is so used.

Pub. 100-3, Section 110.14
Apheresis (Therapeutic Pheresis)

B. Indications

Apheresis is covered for the following indications:

- Plasma exchange for acquired myasthenia gravis;
- Leukapheresis in the treatment of leukemekia
- Plasmapheresis in the treatment of primary macroglobulinemia (Waldenstrom);
- Treatment of hyperglobulinemias, including (but not limited to) multiple myelomas, cryoglobulinemia and hyperviscosity syndromes;
- Plasmapheresis or plasma exchange as a last resort treatment of thrombotic thrombocytopenic purpura (TTP);
- Plasmapheresis or plasma exchange in the last resort treatment of life threatening rheumatoid vasculitis;
- Plasma perfusion of charcoal filters for treatment of pruritis of cholestatic liver disease;
- Plasma exchange in the treatment of Goodpasture's Syndrome;
- Plasma exchange in the treatment of glomerulonephritis associated with antiglomerular basement membrane antibodies and advancing renal failure or pulmonary hemorrhage;
- Treatment of chronic relapsing polyneuropathy for patients with severe or life threatening symptoms who have failed to respond to conventional therapy;
- Treatment of life threatening scleroderma and polymyositis when the patient is unresponsive to conventional therapy;
- Treatment of Guillain-Barre Syndrome; and
- Treatment of last resort for life threatening systemic lupus erythematosus (SLE) when conventional therapy has failed to prevent clinical deterioration.

C. Settings

Apheresis is covered only when performed in a hospital setting (either inpatient or outpatient). or in a nonhospital setting. e.g. physician directed clinic when the following conditions are met:

- A physician (or a number of physicians) is present to perform medical services and to respond to medical emergencies at all times during patient care hours;
- Each patient is under the care of a physician; and
- All nonphysician services are furnished under the direct, personal supervision of a physician.

Pub. 100-3, Section 110.15
Ultrafiltration, Hemoperfusion and Hemofiltration

A. Ultrafiltration.--This is a process for removing excess fluid from the blood through the dialysis membrane by means of pressure. It is not a substitute for dialysis. Ultrafiltration is utilized in cases where excess fluid cannot be removed easily during the regular course of hemodialysis. When it is performed, it is commonly done during the first hour or two of each hemodialysis on patients who, e.g., have refractory edema. Ultrafiltration is a covered procedure under the Medicare program (effective for services performed on and after 9/1/79).

Predialysis Ultrafiltration.--While this procedure requires additional staff care, the facility dialysis rate is intended to cover the full range of complicated and uncomplicated nonacute dialysis treatments. Therefore, no additional facility charge is recognized for predialysis ultrafiltration. The physician's role in ultrafiltration varies with the stability of the patient's condition. In unstable patients, the physician may need to be present at the initiation of dialysis, and available either in- house or in close proximity to monitor the patient carefully. In patients who are relatively stable, but who seem to accumulate excessive weight gain, the procedure requires only a modest increase in physician involvement over routine outpatient hemodialysis.

Occasionally, medical complications may occur which require that ultrafiltration be performed separate from the dialysis treatment, and in these cases an additional charge can be recognized. However, the claim must be documented as to why the ultrafiltration could not have been performed at the same time as the dialysis.

B. Hemoperfusion.--This is a process which removes substances from the blood using a charcoal or resin artificial kidney. When used in the treatment of life threatening drug overdose, hemoperfusion is a covered service for patients with or without renal failure (effective for services performed on and after 9/1/79). Hemoperfusion generally requires a physician to be present to initiate treatment and to be present in the hospital or an adjacent medical office during the entire procedure, as changes may be sudden. Special staff training and equipment are required.

Develop charges for hemoperfusion in the same manner as for any new or unusual service. One or two treatments are usually all that is necessary to remove the toxic compound; document additional treatments. Hemoperfusion may be performed concurrently with dialysis, and in those cases payment for the hemoperfusion reflects only the additional care rendered over and above the care given with dialysis.

The effects of using hemoperfusion to improve the results of chronic hemodialysis are not known. Therefore, hemoperfusion is not a covered service when used to improve the results of hemodialysis. In addition, it has not been demonstrated that the use of hemoperfusion in conjunction with deferoxamine (DFO), in treating symptomatic patients with iron overload, is efficacious. There is also a paucity of data regarding its efficacy in treating asymptomatic patients with iron overload. Therefore, hemoperfusion used in conjunction with DFO in treating patients with iron overload is not a covered service; i.e., it is not considered reasonable and necessary within the meaning of §1862(a)(1) of the Act.

However, the use of hemoperfusion in conjunction with DFO for the treatment of patients with aluminum toxicity has been demonstrated to be clinically efficacious and is therefore regarded as a covered service.

C. Hemofiltration.--This is a process which removes fluid, electrolytes and other low molecular weight toxic substances from the blood by filtration through hollow artificial membranes and may be routinely performed in 3 weekly sessions. Hemofiltration (which is also known as diafiltration) is a covered procedure under Medicare and is a safe and effective technique for the treatment of ESRD patients and an alternative to peritoneal dialysis and hemodialysis (effective for services performed on and after August 20, 1987). In contrast to both hemodialysis and peritoneal dialysis treatments, which eliminate dissolved substances via diffusion across semipermeable membranes, hemofiltration mimics the filtration process of the normal kidney. The technique requires an arteriovenous access. Hemofiltration may be performed either in facility or at home.

The procedure is most advantageous when applied to high-risk unstable patients, such as older patients with cardiovascular diseases or diabetes, because there are fewer side effects such as hypotension, hypertension or volume overload.

Pub. 100-3, Section 110.16
Nonselective (Random) Transfusions and Living Related Donor Specific Transfusions (DST) in Kidney Transplantation

These pretransplant transfusions are covered under Medicare without a specific limitation on the number of transfusions, subject to the normal Medicare blood deductible provisions. Where blood is given directly to the transplant patient; e.g., in the case of donor specific transfusions, the blood is considered replaced for purposes of the blood deductible provisions.

Pub. 100-3, Section 130.1
Inpatient Hospital Stays for the Treatment of Alcoholism

A. Inpatient Hospital Stay for Alcohol Detoxification

Many hospitals provide detoxification services during the more acute stages of alcoholism or alcohol withdrawal. When the high probability or occurrence of medical complications (e.g., delirium, confusion, trauma, or unconsciousness) during detoxification for acute alcoholism or alcohol withdrawal necessitates the constant availability of physicians and/or complex medical equipment found only in the hospital setting, inpatient hospital care during this period is considered reasonable and necessary and is therefore covered under the program. Generally, detoxification can be accomplished within 2-3 days with an occasional need for up to 5 days where the patient's condition dictates. This limit (5 days) may be extended in an individual case where there is a need for a longer period for detoxification for a particular patient. In such cases, however, there should be documentation by a physician which substantiates that a longer period of detoxification was reasonable and necessary. When the detoxification needs of an individual no longer require an inpatient hospital setting, coverage should be denied on the basis that inpatient hospital care is not reasonable and necessary as required by section 1862(a)(l) of the Act. Following detoxification a patient may be transferred to an inpatient rehabilitation unit or discharged to a residential treatment program or outpatient treatment setting.

B. Inpatient Hospital Stay for Alcohol Rehabilitation

Hospitals may also provide structured inpatient alcohol rehabilitation programs to the chronic alcoholic. These programs are composed primarily of coordinated educational and psychotherapeutic services provided on a group basis. Depending on the subject matter, a series of lectures, discussions, films, and group therapy sessions are led by either physicians, psychologists, or alcoholism counselors from the hospital or various outside organizations. In addition, individual psychotherapy and family counseling (see §70.1 of the NCD Manual) may be provided in selected cases. These programs are conducted under the supervision and direction of a physician. Patients may directly enter an inpatient hospital rehabilitation program after having undergone detoxification in the same hospital or in another hospital or may enter an inpatient hospital rehabilitation program without prior hospitalization for detoxification. Alcohol rehabilitation can be provided in a variety of settings other than the hospital setting. In order for an inpatient hospital stay for alcohol rehabilitation to be covered under Medicare it must be medically necessary for the care to be provided in the inpatient hospital setting rather than in a less costly facility or on an outpatient basis. Inpatient hospital care for receipt of an alcohol rehabilitation program would generally be medically necessary where either (l) there is documentation by the physician that recent alcohol rehabilitation services in a less intensive setting or on an outpatient basis have proven unsuccessful and, as a consequence, the patient requires the supervision and intensity of services which can only be found in the controlled environment of the hospital, or (2) only the hospital environment can assure the medical management or control of the patient's concomitant conditions during the course of alcohol rehabilitation. (However, a patient's concomitant condition may make the use of certain alcohol treatment modalities medically inappropriate.) In addition, the "active treatment" criteria (see the Medicare Benefit Policy Manual, Chapter 2, "Inpatient Psychiatric Hospital Services," §20) should be applied to psychiatric care in the general hospital as well as to psychiatric care in a psychiatric hospital. Since alcoholism is classifiable as a psychiatric condition the "active treatment" criteria must also be met in order for alcohol rehabilitation services to be covered under Medicare. (Thus, it is the combined need for "active treatment" and for covered care which can only be provided in the inpatient hospital setting, rather than the fact that rehabilitation immediately follows a period of detoxification, which provides the basis for coverage of inpatient hospital alcohol rehabilitation programs.)

Generally 16-19 days of rehabilitation services are sufficient to bring a patient to a point where care could be continued in other than an inpatient hospital setting. An inpatient hospital stay for alcohol rehabilitation may be extended beyond this limit in an individual case where a longer period of alcohol rehabilitation is medically necessary. In such cases, however, there should be documentation by a physician which substantiates the need for such care. Where the rehabilitation needs of an individual no longer require an inpatient hospital setting, coverage should be denied on the basis that inpatient hospital care is not reasonable and necessary as required by section 1862(a)(l) of the Act..

Subsequent admissions to the inpatient hospital setting for alcohol rehabilitation followup, reinforcement, or "recap" treatments are considered to be readmissions (rather than an extension of the original stay) and must meet the requirements of this section for coverage under Medicare. Prior admissions to the inpatient hospital setting--either in the same hospital or in a different hospital--may be an indication that the "active treatment" requirements are not met (i.e., there is no reasonable expectation of improvement) and the stay should not be covered. Accordingly, there should be documentation to establish that "readmission" to the hospital setting for alcohol rehabilitation services can reasonably be expected to result in improvement of the patient's condition. For example, the documentation should indicate what changes in the patient's medical condition, social or emotional status, or treatment plan make improvement likely, or why the patient's initial hospital treatment was not sufficient.

C. Combined Alcohol Detoxification/Rehabilitation Programs.--

Fiscal intermediaries should apply the guidelines in A. and B. above to both phases of a combined inpatient hospital alcohol detoxification/rehabilitation program. Not all patients who require the inpatient hospital setting for detoxification also need the inpatient hospital setting for rehabilitation. (See §130.1 of the NCD Manual for coverage of outpatient hospital alcohol rehabilitation services.) Where the inpatient hospital setting is medically necessary for both alcohol detoxification and rehabilitation, generally a 3-week period is reasonable and necessary to bring the patient to the point where care can be continued in other than an inpatient hospital setting.

Decisions regarding reasonableness and necessity of treatment, the need for an inpatient hospital level of care, and length of treatment should be made by intermediaries based on accepted medical practice with the advice of their medical consultant. (In hospitals under PSRO review, PSRO determinations of medical necessity of services and appropriateness of the level of care at which services are provided are binding on the title XVIII fiscal intermediaries for purposes of adjudicating claims for payment.)

Pub. 100-3, Section 130.2
Outpatient Hospital Services for Treatment of Alcoholism

Coverage is available for both diagnostic and therapeutic services furnished for the treatment of alcoholism by the hospital to outpatients subject to the same rules applicable to outpatient hospital services in general. While there is no coverage for day hospitalization programs, per se, individual services which meet the requirements in the Medicare Benefit Policy Manual, Chapter 6, §20 may be covered. (Meals, transportation and recreational and social activities do not fall within the scope of covered outpatient hospital services under Medicare.)

All services must be reasonable and necessary for diagnosis or treatment of the patient's condition (see the Medicare Benefit Policy Manual, chapter 16 §20). Thus, educational services and family counseling would only be covered where they are directly related to treatment of the patient's condition. The frequency of treatment and period of time over which it occurs must also be reasonable and necessary.

Pub. 100-3, Section 130.3
Chemical AversionTherapy for Treatment of Alcoholism

Available evidence indicates that chemical aversion therapy may be an effective component of certain alcoholism treatment programs, particularly as part of multimodality treatment programs which include other behavioral techniques and therapies, such as psychotherapy. Based on this evidence, HCFA's medical consultants have recommended that chemical aversion therapy be covered under Medicare. However, since chemical aversion therapy is a demanding therapy which may not be appropriate for all Medicare beneficiaries needing treatment for alcoholism, a physician should certify to the appropriateness of chemical aversion therapy in the individual case. Therefore, if chemical aversion therapy for treatment of alcoholism is determined to be reasonable and necessary for an individual patient, it is covered under Medicare.

When it is medically necessary for a patient to receive chemical aversion therapy as a hospital inpatient, coverage for care in that setting is available. (See §35-22 regarding coverage of multimodality treatment programs.) Followup treatments for chemical aversion therapy can generally be provided on an outpatient basis. Thus, where a patient is admitted as an inpatient for receipt of chemical aversion therapy, there must be documentation by the physician of the need in the individual case for the inpatient hospital admission.

Decisions regarding reasonableness and necessity of treatment and the need for an inpatient hospital level of care should be made by intermediaries based on accepted medical practice with the advice of their medical consultant. (In hospitals under PSRO review, PSRO determinations of medical necessity of services and appropriateness of the level of care at which services are provided are binding on the title XVIII fiscal intermediaries for purposes of adjudicating claims for payment.)

Pub. 100-3, Section 130.4
Electrical Aversion Therapy for Treatment of Alcoholism

Electrical aversion therapy has not been shown to be safe and effective and therefore is excluded from coverage.

Pub. 100-3, Section 130.5
Treatment of Alcoholism and Drug Abuse in a Freestanding Clinic

Coverage is available for alcoholism or drug abuse treatment services (such as drug therapy, psychotherapy, and patient education) that are provided incident to a physician's professional service in a freestanding clinic to patients who, for example, have been discharged from an inpatient hospital stay for the treatment of alcoholism or drug abuse or to individuals who are not in the acute stages of alcoholism or drug abuse but require treatment. The coverage available for these services is subject to the same rules generally applicable to the coverage of clinic services. (See HCFA-Pub. 14-3, §§2020ff., and §§2050 ff.) Of course, the services also must be reasonable and necessary for the diagnosis or treatment of the individual's alcoholism or drug abuse. The Part B psychiatric limitation (see HCFA-Pub. 14-3, §2470) would apply to alcoholism or drug abuse treatment services furnished by physicians to individuals who are not hospital inpatients.

Pub. 100-3, Section 130.6
Treatment of Drug Abuse (Chemical Dependency)

Accordingly, when it is medically necessary for a patient to receive detoxification and/or rehabilitation for drug substance abuse as a hospital inpatient, coverage for care in that setting is available. Coverage is also available for treatment services that are provided in the outpatient department of a hospital to patients who, for example, have been discharged from an inpatient stay for the treatment of drug substance abuse or who require treatment but do not require the availability and intensity of services found only in the inpatient hospital setting. The coverage available for these services is subject to the same rules generally applicable to the coverage of outpatient hospital services. The services must also be reasonable and necessary for treatment of the individual's condition. Decisions regarding reasonableness and necessity of treatment, the need for an inpatient hospital level of care, and length of treatment should be made by intermediaries based on accepted medical practice with the advice of their medical consultant. (In hospitals under PSRO review, PSRO determinations of medical necessity of services and appropriateness of the level of care at which services are provided are binding on the title XVIII fiscal intermediaries for purposes of adjudicating claims for payment.)

Pub. 100-3, Section 130.7
Withdrawal Treatments for Narcotic Addictions

Withdrawal is an accepted treatment for narcotic addiction, and Part B payment can be made for these services if they are provided by the physician directly or under his personal supervision and if they are reasonable and necessary. In reviewing claims, reasonableness and necessity are determined with the aid of the contractor's medical staff.

Drugs that the physician provides in connection with this treatment are also covered if they cannot be self-administered and meet all other statutory requirements.

Pub. 100-3, Section 130.8
Hemodialysis for Treatment of Schizophrenia

Scientific evidence supporting use of hemodialysis as a safe and effective means of treatment for schizophrenia is inconclusive at this time. Accordingly, Medicare does not cover hemodialysis for treatment of schizophrenia.

Pub. 100-3, Section 140.1
Abortion

Abortions are not covered Medicare procedures except:

1. If the pregnancy is the result of an act of rape or incest; or
2. In the case where a woman suffers from a physical disorder, physical injury, or physical illness, including a life-endangering physical condition caused by or arising from the pregnancy itself, that would, as certified by a physician, place the woman in danger of death unless an abortion is performed.

This restricted coverage applies to CPT codes 59840, 59841, 59850, 59851, 59852, 59855, 59856, 59857, and 59866.

Pub. 100-3, Section 140.2
Breast Reconstruction Following Mastectomy

Reconstruction of the affected and the contralateral unaffected breast following a medically necessary mastectomy is considered a relatively safe and effective

Appendixes

noncosmetic procedure. Accordingly, program payment may be made for breast reconstruction surgery following removal of a breast for any medical reason.

Program payment may not be made for breast reconstruction for cosmetic reasons. (Cosmetic surgery is excluded from coverage under §1862(a)(10) of the Social Security Act.)

Pub. 100-3, Section 140.3
Transsexual Surgery

Transsexual surgery for sex reassignment of transsexuals is controversial. Because of the lack of well controlled, long term studies of the safety and effectiveness of the surgical procedures and attendant therapies for transsexualism, the treatment is considered experimental. Moreover, there is a high rate of serious complications for these surgical procedures. For these reasons, transsexual surgery is not covered.

Pub. 100-3, Section 140.4
Plastic Surgery to Correct "Moon Face"

The cosmetic surgery exclusion precludes payment for any surgical procedure directed at improving appearance. The condition giving rise to the patient's preoperative appearance is generally not a consideration. The only exception to the exclusion is surgery for the prompt repair of an accidental injury or for the improvement of a malformed body member which coincidentally serves some cosmetic purpose. Since surgery to correct a condition of "moon face" which developed as a side effect of cortisone therapy does not meet the exception to the exclusion, it is not covered under Medicare (§1862(a)(10) of the Act).

Pub. 100-3, Section 140.5
Laser Procedures

Medicare recognizes the use of lasers for many medical indications. Procedures performed with lasers are sometimes used in place of more conventional techniques. In the absence of a specific noncoverage instruction, and where a laser has been approved for marketing by the Food and Drug Administration, contractor discretion may be used to determine whether a procedure performed with a laser is reasonable and necessary and, therefore, covered.

The determination of coverage for a procedure performed using a laser is made on the basis that the use of lasers to alter, revise, or destroy tissue is a surgical procedure. Therefore, coverage of laser procedures is restricted to practitioners with training in the surgical management of the disease or condition being treated.

Pub. 100-3, Section 150.1
Manipulation

A. Manipulation of the Rib Cage.--Manual manipulation of the rib cage contributes to the treatment of respiratory conditions such as bronchitis, emphysema, and asthma as part of a regimen which includes other elements of therapy, and is covered only under such circumstances.

B. Manipulation of the Head.--Manipulation of the occipitocervical or temporomandibular regions of the head when indicated for conditions affecting those portions of the head and neck is a covered service.

Pub. 100-3, Section 150.2
Osteogenic Stimulation

Electrical Osteogenic Stimulators

B. Nationally Covered Indications

1. Noninvasive Stimulator.

The noninvasive stimulator device is covered only for the following indications:

- Nonunion of long bone fractures;
- Failed fusion, where a minimum of nine months has elapsed since the last surgery;
- Congenital pseudarthroses; and
- Effective July 1, 1996, as an adjunct to spinal fusion surgery for patients at high risk of pseudarthrosis due to previously failed spinal fusion at the same site or for those undergoing multiple level fusion. A multiple level fusion involves 3 or more vertebrae (e.g., L3-L5, L4-S1, etc).
- Effective September 15, 1980, nonunion of long bone fractures is considered to exist only after 6 or more months have elapsed without healing of the fracture.
- Effective April 1, 2000, nonunion of long bone fractures is considered to exist only when serial radiographs have confirmed that fracture healing has ceased for 3 or more months prior to starting treatment with the electrical osteogenic stimulator. Serial radiographs must include a minimum of 2 sets of radiographs, each including multiple views of the fracture site, separated by a minimum of 90 days.

2. Invasive (Implantable) Stimulator.

The invasive stimulator device is covered only for the following indications:

- Nonunion of long bone fractures
- Effective July 1, 1996, as an adjunct to spinal fusion surgery for patients at high risk of pseudarthrosis due to previously failsed spinal fusion at the same site or for those undergoing multiple level fusion. A multiple level fusion involves 3 or more vertebrae (e.g., L3-5, L4-S1, etc.)
- Effective September 15, 1980, nonunion of long bone fractures is considered to exist only after 6 or more months have elapsed without healing of the fracture.
- Effective April 1, 2000, non union of long bone fractures is considered to exist only when serial radiographs have confirmed that fracture healing has ceased for 3 or more months prior to starting treatment with the electrical osteogenic stimulator. Serial radiographs must include a minimum of 2 sets of radiographs, each including multiple views of the fracture site, separated by a minimum of 90 days.

Effective for services performed on or after January 1, 2001, ultrasonic osteogenic stimulators are covered as medically reasonable and necessary for the treatment of non-union fractures. In demonstrating nonunion of fractures, we would expect:

- A minimum of two sets of radiographs obtained prior to starting treatment with the osteogenic stimulator, separated by a minimum of 90 days. Each radiograph must include multiple views of the fracture site accompanied with a written interpretation by a physician stating that there has been no clinically significant evidence of fracture healing between the two sets of radiographs.

- Indications that the patient failed at least one surgical intervention for the treatment of the fracture.

- Effective April 27, 2005, upon the recommendation of the ultrasound stimulation for nonunion fracture healing, CMS determins that the evidence is adequate to condlude that noninvasive ultrasound stimulation for the treatment of nonunion bone fractures prior to surfical intervention is reasonable and necessary. In demonstrating non-union fracturs, CMS expects:

- A minimum of 2 sets of radiographs, obtained prior to starting treating with the osteogenic stimulator, separated by a minimum of 90 days. Each radiograph set must include multiple views of the fracture site accompanied with a written interpretation by a physician stating that there has been no clinically significant evidence of fracture healing between the 2 sets of radiographs.

C. Nationally Non-Covered Indications

Nonunion fractures of the skull, vertebrae and those that are tumor-related are excluded from coverage.

Ultrasonic osteogenic stimulators may not be used concurrently with other non-invasive osteogenic devices.

Ultrasonic osteogenic stimulators for fresh fracturs and delayed unions remain non-covered.

(This NCD last reviewed June 2005)

Pub. 100-3, Section 150.3
Bone (Mineral) Density Studies

The Following Bone (Mineral) Density Studies Are Covered Under Medicare:

A. Single Photon Absorptiometry

A non-invasive radiological technique that measures absorption of a monochromatic photon beam by bone material. The device is placed directly on the patient, uses a low dose of radionuclide, and measures the mass absorption efficiency of the energy used. It provides a quantitative measurement of the bone mineral of cortical and trabecular bone, and is used in assessing an individual's treatment response at appropriate intervals.

Single photon absorptiometry is covered under Medicare when used in assessing changes in bone density of patients with osteodystrophy or osteoporosis when performed on the same individual at intervals of 6 to 12 months.

B. Bone Biopsy

A physiologic test which is a surgical, invasive procedure. A small sample of bone (usually from the ilium) is removed, generally by a biopsy needle. The biopsy sample is then examined histologically, and provides a qualitative measurement of the bone mineral of trabecular bone. This procedure is used in ascertaining a differential diagnosis of bone disorders and is used primarily to differentiate osteomalacia from osteoporosis.

Bone biopsy is covered under Medicare when used for the qualitative evaluation of bone no more than four times per patient, unless there is special justification given. When used more than four times on a patient, bone biopsy leaves a defect in the pelvis and may produce some patient discomfort.

C. Photodensitometry(radiographic absorptiometry)

A noninvasive radiological procedure that attempts to assess bone mass by measuring the optical density of extremity radiographs with a photodensitometer, usually with a reference to a standard density wedge placed on the film at the time of exposure. This procedure provides a quantitative measurement of the bone mineral of bone, and is used for monitoring gross bone change.

The Following Bone (Mineral) Density Study Is Not Covered Under Medicare:

D. Dual Photon Absorptiometry

A noninvasive radiological technique that measures absorption of a dichromatic beam by bone material. This procedure is not covered under Medicare because it is still considered to be in the investigational stage.

Pub. 100-3, Section 150.5
Diathermy Treatment

High energy pulsed wave diathermy machines have been found to produce some degree of therapeutic benefit for essentially the same conditions and to the same extent as standard diathermy. Accordingly, where the contractor's medical staff has determined that the pulsed wave diathermy apparatus used is one which is considered therapeutically effective, the treatments are considered a covered service, but only for those conditions for which standard diathermy is medically indicated and only when rendered by a physician or incident to a physician's professional services. Further, when the charge for covered pulsed wave diathermy treatment is substantially in excess of that which is reasonable for standard diathermy, payment is based on the reasonable charge for standard diathermy (CPT-4 code 97024, ICD-9-CM code 93.34).

Pub. 100-3, Section 150.6
Vitamin B12 Injections to Strengthen Tendons, Ligaments, ETC., of the Foot

Vitamin B12 injections to strengthen tendons, ligaments, etc., of the foot are not covered under Medicare because (1) there is no evidence that vitamin B12 injections are effective for the purpose of strengthening weakened tendons and ligaments, and (2) this is nonsurgical treatment under the subluxation exclusion. Accordingly, vitamin B12 injections are not considered reasonable and necessary within the meaning of §1862(a)(1) of the Act.

Pub. 100-3, Section 150.7
Prolotherapy, Joint Sclerotherapy, and Ligamentous Injections with Sclerosing Agents

The medical effectiveness of the above therapies has not been verified by scientifically controlled studies. Accordingly, reimbursement for these modalities should be denied on the ground that they are not reasonable and necessary as required by §1862(a)(1) of the Act.

Pub. 100-3, Section 160.1
Induced Lesions of Nerve Tracts

Accordingly, program payment may be made for these denervation procedures when used in selected cases (concurred in by contractor's medical staff) to treat chronic pain.

Pub. 100-3, Section 160.2
Treatment of Motor Function Disorders with Electric Nerve Stimulation

Where electric nerve stimulation is employed to treat motor function disorders, no reimbursement may be made for the stimulator or for the services related to its implantation since this treatment cannot be considered reasonable and necessary.

NOTE: For Medicare coverage of deep brain stimulation for essential tremor and Parkinson's disease, see §65-19.

Pub. 100-3, Section 160.4
Stereotactic Cingulotomy as a Means of Psychosurgery

Stereotactic cingulotomy is not covered under Medicare because the procedure is considered to be investigational.

Pub. 100-3, Section 160.5
Stereotaxic Depth Electrode Implantation

Stereotaxic depth electrode implantation prior to surgical treatment of focal epilepsy for patients who are unresponsive to anticonvulsant medications has been found both safe and effective for diagnosing resectable seizure foci that may go undetected by conventional scalp electroencephalographs (EEGs).

Pub. 100-3, Section 160.6
Carotid Sinus Nerve Stimulator

Implantation of the carotid sinus nerve stimulator is indicated for relief of angina pectoris in carefully selected patients who are refractory to medical therapy and who after undergoing coronary angiography study either are poor candidates for or refuse to have coronary bypass surgery. In such cases, Medicare reimbursement may be made for this device and for the related services required for its implantation.

However, the use of the carotid sinus nerve stimulator in the treatment of paroxysmal supraventricular tachycardia is considered investigational and is not in common use by the medical community. The device and related services in such cases cannot be considered as reasonable and necessary for the treatment of an illness or injury or to improve the functioning of a malformed body member as required by §1862(a)(1) of the law.

Pub. 100-3, Section 160.7
Electrical Nerve Stimulators

Two general classifications of electrical nerve stimulators are employed to treat chronic intractable pain: peripheral nerve stimulators and central nervous system stimulators.

A-Implanted Peripheral Nerve Stimulators

Payment may be made under the prosthetic device benefit for implanted peripheral nerve stimulators. Use of this stimulator involves implantation of electrodes around a selected peripheral nerve. The stimulating electrode is connected by an insulated lead to a receiver unit which is implanted under the skin at a depth not greater than 1/2 inch. Stimulation is induced by a generator connected to an antenna unit which is attached to the skin surface over the receiver unit. Implantation of electrodes requires surgery and usually necessitates an operating room.

NOTE: Peripheral nerve stimulators may also be employed to assess a patient's suitability for continued treatment with an electric nerve stimulator. As explained in §160.7.1, such use of the stimulator is covered as part of the total diagnostic service furnished to the beneficiary rather than as a prosthesis.

B-Central Nervous System Stimulators (Dorsal Column and Depth Brain Stimulators).The implantation of central nervous system stimulators may be covered as therapies for the relief of chronic intractable pain, subject to the following conditions:

1-Types of Implantations

There are two types of implantations covered by this instruction:

- Dorsal Column (Spinal Cord) Neurostimulation.--The surgical implantation of neurostimulator electrodes within the dura mater (endodural) or the percutaneous insertion of electrodes in the epidural space is covered.
- Depth Brain Neurostimulation.--The stereotactic implantation of electrodes in the deep brain (e.g., thalamus and periaqueductal gray matter) is covered.

2-Conditions for Coverage

No payment may be made for the implantation of dorsal column or depth brain stimulators or services and supplies related to such implantation, unless all of the conditions listed below have been met:

- The implantation of the stimulator is used only as a late resort (if not a last resort) for patients with chronic intractable pain;
- With respect to item a, other treatment modalities (pharmacological, surgical, physical, or psychological therapies) have been tried and did not prove satisfactory, or are judged to be unsuitable or contraindicated for the given patient;
- Patients have undergone careful screening, evaluation and diagnosis by a multidisciplinary team prior to implantation. (Such screening must include psychological, as well as physical evaluation);
- All the facilities, equipment, and professional and support personnel required for the proper diagnosis, treatment training, and followup of the patient (including that required to satisfy item c) must be available; and
- Demonstration of pain relief with a temporarily implanted electrode precedes permanent implantation.

Contractors may find it helpful to work with QIOs to obtain the information needed to apply these conditions to claims.

Pub. 100-3, Section 160.7.1
Assessing Patient's Suitability for Electrical Nerve Stimulation Therapy

Electrical nerve stimulation is an accepted modality for assessing a patient's suitability for ongoing treatment with a transcutaneous or an implanted nerve stimulator.

Accordingly, program payment may be made for the following techniques when used to determine the potential therapeutic usefulness of an electrical nerve stimulator:

A. Transcutaneous Electrical Nerve Stimulation (TENS).

This technique involves attachment of a transcutaneous nerve stimulator to the surface of the skin over the peripheral nerve to be stimulated. It is used by the patient on a trial basis and its effectiveness in modulating pain is monitored by the physician, or physical therapist. Generally, the physician or physical therapist is able to determine whether the patient is likely to derive a significant therapeutic benefit from continuous use of a transcutaneous stimulator within a trial period of 1 month; in a few cases this determination may take longer to make. Document the medical necessity for such services which are furnished beyond the first month. (See §45-25 for an explanation of coverage of medically necessary supplies for the effective use of TENS.)

If TENS significantly alleviates pain, it may be considered as primary treatment; if it produces no relief or greater discomfort than the original pain electrical nerve stimulation therapy is ruled out. However, where TENS produces incomplete relief, further evaluation with percutaneous electrical nerve stimulation may be considered to determine whether an implanted peripheral nerve stimulator would provide significant relief from pain. (See §35-46B.)

Usually, the physician or physical therapist providing the services will furnish the equipment necessary for assessment. Where the physician or physical therapist advises the patient to rent the TENS from a supplier during the trial period rather than supplying it himself/herself, program payment may be made for rental of the TENS as well as for the services of the physician or physical therapist who is evaluating its use. However, the combined program payment which is made for the physician's or physical therapist's services and the rental of the stimulator from a supplier should not exceed the amount which would be payable for the total service, including the stimulator, furnished by the physician or physical therapist alone.

B. Percutaneous Electrical Nerve Stimulation (PEN)

This diagnostic procedure which involves stimulation of peripheral nerves by a needle electrode inserted through the skin is performed only in a physician's office, clinic, or hospital outpatient department. Therefore, it is covered only when performed by a physician or incident to physician's service. If pain is effectively controlled by percutaneous stimulation, implantation of electrodes is warranted.

As in the case of TENS (described in subsection A), generally the physician should be able to determine whether the patient is likely to derive a significant therapeutic benefit from continuing use of an implanted nerve stimulator within a trial period of 1 month. In a few cases, this determination may take longer to make. The medical necessity for such diagnostic services which are furnished beyond the first month must be documented.

NOTE: Electrical nerve stimulators do not prevent pain but only alleviate pain as it occurs. A patient can be taught how to employ the stimulator, and once this is done, can use it safely and effectively without direct physician supervision. Consequently, it is inappropriate for a patient to visit his/her physician, physical therapist, or an outpatient clinic on a continuing basis for treatment of pain with electrical nerve stimulation. Once it is determined that electrical nerve

stimulation should be continued as therapy and the patient has been trained to use the stimulator, it is expected that a stimulator will be implanted or the patient will employ the TENS on a continual basis in his/her home. Electrical nerve stimulation treatments furnished by a physician in his/her office, by a physical therapist or outpatient clinic are excluded from coverage by §1862(a)(1) of the Act. (See §65-8 for an explanation of coverage of the therapeutic use of implanted peripheral nerve stimulators under the prosthetic devices benefit. See §60-20 for an explanation of coverage of the therapeutic use of TENS under the durable medical equipment benefit.)

Pub. 100-3, Section 160.8
Electroencephalographic Monitoring During Surgical Procedures Involving the Cerebral Vasculature

Electroencephalographic (EEG) monitoring is a safe and reliable technique for the assessment of gross cerebral blood flow during general anesthesia and is covered under Medicare. Very characteristic changes in the EEG occur when cerebral perfusion is inadequate for cerebral function. EEG monitoring as an indirect measure of cerebral perfusion requires the expertise of an electroencephalographer, a neurologist trained in EEG, or an advanced EEG technician for its proper interpretation.

The EEG monitoring may be covered routinely in carotid endarterectomies and in other neurological procedures where cerebral perfusion could be reduced. Such other procedures might include aneurysm surgery where hypotensive anesthesia is used or other cerebral vascular procedures where cerebral blood flow may be interrupted.

Pub. 100-3, Section 160.9
Electronecephalographic (EEG) Monitoring during Open-Heart Surgery

The value of EEG monitoring during open heart surgery and in the immediate post-operative period is debatable because there are little published data based on well designed studies regarding its clinical effectiveness. The procedure is not frequently used and does not enjoy widespread acceptance of benefit.

Accordingly, Medicare does not cover EEG monitoring during open heart surgery and during the immediate post-operative period.

Pub. 100-3, Section 160.10
Evoked Response Tests

Evoked response tests, including brain stem evoked response and visual evoked response tests, are generally accepted as safe and effective diagnostic tools. Program payment may be made for these procedures.

Pub. 100-3, Section 160.12
Neuromuscular Electrical Stimulaton (NMES)

Treatment of Muscle Atrophy

Coverage of NMES to treat muscle atrophy is limited to the treatment of patients with disuse atrophy where the nerve supply to the muscle is intact, including brain, spinal cord and peripheral nerves and other non-neurological reasons for disuse atrophy. Examples include casting or splinting of a limb, contracture due to scarring of soft tissue as in burn lesions, and hip replacement surgery (until orthotic training begins). (See CIM 45-25 for an explanation of coverage of medically necessary supplies for the effective use of NMES).

Use for Walking in Patients with Spinal Cord Injury (SCI)

The type of NMES that is used to enhance the ability to walk of SCI patients is commonly referred to as functional electrical stimulation (FES). These devices are surface units that use electrical impulses to activate paralyzed or weak muscles in precise sequence. Coverage for the use of NMES/FES is limited to SCI patients, for walking, who have completed a training program, which consists of at least 32 physical therapy sessions with the device over a period of 3 months. The trial period of physical therapy will enable the physician treating the patient for his or her spinal cord injury to properly evaluate the person's ability to use these devices frequently and for the long term. Physical therapy sessions are only covered in the inpatient hospital, outpatient hospital, comprehensive outpatient rehabilitation facilities, and outpatient rehabilitation facilities. The physical therapy necessary to perform this training must be directly performed by the physical therapist as part of a one-on-one training program; this service cannot be done unattended.

The goal of physical therapy must be to train SCI patients on the use of NMES/FES devices to achieve walking, not to reverse or retard muscle atrophy.

Coverage for NMES/FES for walking will be limited to SCI patients with all of the following characteristics:

1) persons with intact lower motor units (L1 and below) (both muscle and peripheral nerve);

2) persons with muscle and joint stability for weight bearing at upper and lower extremities that can demonstrate balance and control to maintain an upright support posture independently;

3) persons that demonstrate brisk muscle contraction to NMES and have sensory perception of electrical stimulation sufficient for muscle contraction;

4) persons that possess high motivation, commitment and cognitive ability to use such devices for walking;

5) persons that can transfer independently and can demonstrate independent standing tolerance for at least 3 minutes;

6) persons that can demonstrate hand and finger function to manipulate controls;

7) persons with at least 6-month post recovery spinal cord injury and restorative surgery;

8) persons without hip and knee degenerative disease and no history of long bone fracture secondary to osteoporosis; and

9) persons who have demonstrated a willingness to use the device long-term.

NMES/FES for walking will not be covered in SCI patients with any of the following:

1) persons with cardiac pacemakers;

2) severe scoliosis or severe osteoporosis;

3) skin disease or cancer at area of stimulation;

4) irreversible contracture; or

5) autonomic dysreflexia.

The only settings where therapists with the sufficient skills to provide these services are employed, are inpatient hospitals, outpatient hospitals, comprehensive outpatient rehabilitation facilities and outpatient rehabilitation facilities. The physical therapy necessary to perform this training must be part of a one-on-one training program.

Additional therapy after the purchase of the DME would be limited by our general policies on coverage of skilled physical therapy.

All other uses of NMES remain non-covered.

Pub. 100-3, Section 160.13
Supplies Used in the Delivery of Transcutaneous Electrical Nerve Stimulation (TENS) and Neuromuscular Electrical Stimulation (NMES)

A form-fitting conductive garment (and medically necessary related supplies) may be covered under the program only when:

1. It has received permission or approval for marketing by the Food and Drug Administration;

2. It has been prescribed by a physician for use in delivering covered TENS or NMES treatment; and

3. One of the medical indications outlined below is met:

- The patient cannot manage without the conductive garment because there is such a large area or so many sites to be stimulated and the stimulation would have to be delivered so frequently that it is not feasible to use conventional electrodes, adhesive tapes and lead wires;
- The patient cannot manage without the conductive garment for the treatment of chronic intractable pain because the areas or sites to be stimulated are inaccessible with the use of conventional electrodes, adhesive tapes and lead wires;
- The patient has a documented medical condition such as skin problems that preclude the application of conventional electrodes, adhesive tapes and lead wires;
- The patient requires electrical stimulation beneath a cast either to treat disuse atrophy, where the nerve supply to the muscle is intact, or to treat chronic intractable pain; or
- The patient has a medical need for rehabilitation strengthening (pursuant to a written plan of rehabilitation) following an injury where the nerve supply to the muscle is intact.

A conductive garment is not covered for use with a TENS device during the trial period specified in §35-46 unless:

4. The patient has a documented skin problem prior to the start of the trial period; and

5. The carrier's medical consultants are satisfied that use of such an item is medically necessary for the patient.

Pub. 100-3, Section 160.15
Electrotherapy for Treatment of Facial Nerve Paralysis (Bell's Palsy)

Electrotherapy for the treatment of facial nerve paralysis, commonly known as Bell's Palsy, is not covered under Medicare because its clinical effectiveness has not been established.

© 2005 Ingenix, Inc.

APPENDIX D

Pub. 100-3, Section 160.17
L-DOPA

A. Part A Payment for L-Dopa and Associated Inpatient Hospital Services.--A hospital stay and related ancillary services for the administration of L-Dopa are covered if medically required for this purpose. Whether a drug represents an allowable inpatient hospital cost during such stay depends on whether it meets the definition of a drug in §1861(t) of the Act; i.e., on its inclusion in the compendia named in the Act or approval by the hospital's pharmacy and drug therapeutics (P&DT) or equivalent committee. (Levodopa (L-Dopa) has been favorably evaluated for the treatment of Parkinsonism by A.M.A. Drug Evaluations, First Edition 1971, the replacement compendia for "New Drugs.")

Inpatient hospital services are frequently not required in many cases when L-Dopa therapy is initiated. Therefore, determine the medical need for inpatient hospital services on the basis of medical facts in the individual case. It is not necessary to hospitalize the typical, well-functioning, ambulatory Parkinsonian patient who has no concurrent disease at the start of L-Dopa treatment. It is reasonable to provide inpatient hospital services for Parkinsonism patients with concurrent diseases, particularly of the cardiovascular, gastrointestinal, and neuropsychiatric systems. Although many patients require hospitalization for a period of under 2 weeks, a 4-week period of inpatient care is not unreasonable.

Laboratory tests in connection with the administration of L-Dopa.--The tests medically warranted in connection with the achievement of optimal dosage and the control of the side effects of L-Dopa include a complete blood count, liver function tests such as SGOT, SGPT, and/or alkaline phosphatase, BUN or creatinine and urinalysis, blood sugar, and electrocardiogram.

Whether or not the patient is hospitalized, laboratory tests in certain cases are reasonable at weekly intervals although some physicians prefer to perform the tests much less frequently.

Physical therapy furnished in connection with administration of L-Dopa.--Where, following administration of the drug, the patient experiences a reduction of rigidity which permits the reestablishment of a restorative goal for him/her, physical therapy services required to enable him/her to achieve this goal are payable provided they require the skills of a qualified physical therapist and are furnished by or under the supervision of such a therapist. However, once the individual's restoration potential has been achieved, the services required to maintain him/her at this level do not generally require the skills of a qualified physical therapist. In such situations, the role of the therapist is to evaluate the patient's needs in consultation with his/her physician and design a program of exercise appropriate to the capacity and tolerance of the patient and treatment objectives of the physician, leaving to others the actual carrying out of the program. While the evaluative services rendered by a qualified physical therapist are payable as physical therapy, services furnished by others in connection with the carrying out of the maintenance program established by the therapist are not.

B. Part A Reimbursement for L-Dopa Therapy in SNFs.--Initiation of L-Dopa therapy can be appropriately carried out in the SNF setting, applying the same guidelines used for initiation of L-Dopa therapy in the hospital, including the types of patients who should be covered for inpatient services, the role of physical therapy, and the use of laboratory tests. (See subsection A.)

Where inpatient care is required and L-Dopa therapy is initiated in the SNF, limit the stay to a maximum of 4 weeks; but in many cases the need may be no longer than 1 or 2 weeks, depending upon the patient's condition. However, where L-Dopa therapy is begun in the hospital and the patient is transferred to an SNF for continuation of the therapy, a combined length of stay in hospital and SNF of no longer than 4 weeks is reasonable (i.e., 1 week hospital stay followed by 3 weeks SNF stay; or 2 weeks hospital stay followed by 2 weeks SNF stay; etc.). Medical need must be demonstrated in cases where the combined length of stay in hospital and SNF is longer than 4 weeks. The choice of hospital or SNF, and the decision regarding the relative length of time spent in each, should be left to the medical judgment of the treating physician.

C. L-Dopa Coverage Under Part B.--Part B reimbursement may not be made for the drug L-Dopa since it is a self-administrable drug. (See Intermediary Manual, §3112.4B; Carriers Manual, §2050.5B; and Hospital Manual, §230.4B.) However, physician services rendered in connection with its administration and control of its side effects are covered if determined to be reasonable and necessary. Initiation of L-Dopa therapy on an outpatient basis is possible in most cases. Visit frequency ranging from every week to every 2 or 3 months is acceptable. However, after half a year of therapy, visits more frequent than every month would usually not be reasonable.

Pub. 100-3, Section 160.18
Vagus Nerve Stimulation for Treatment of Seizures

Clinical evidence has shown that vagus nerve stimulation is safe and effective treatment for patients with medically refractory partial onset seizures, for whom surgery is not recommended or for whom surgery has failed. Vagus nerve stimulation is not covered for patients with other types of seizure disorders which are medically refractory and for whom surgery is not recommended or for whom surgery has failed.

A partial onset seizure has a focal onset in one area of the brain and may or may not involve a loss of motor control or alteration of consciousness. Partial onset seizures may be simple, complex, or complex partial seizures, secondarily generalized.

Pub. 100-3, Section 160.20
Transfer Factor for Treatment of Multiple Sclerosis

Transfer factor is the dialysate of an extract from sensitized leukocytes which increases cellular immune activity in the recipient. It is not covered as a treatment for multiple sclerosis because its use for the purpose is still experimental.

Pub. 100-3, Section 160.21

Telephone Transmission of Electroencephalograms

Telephone transmission of electroencephalograms (EEGs) is covered as a physician's service or as incident to a physician's service when reasonable and necessary for the individual patient, under appropriate circumstances. The service is safe, and may save time and cost in sending EEGs from remote areas without special competence in neurology, neurosurgery, and electroencephalography, by avoiding the need to transport patients to large medical centers for standard EEG testing.

Pub. 100-3, Section 160.22
Ambulatory Electroencephalographic (EEG) Monitoring

Ambulatory EEG monitoring is a diagnostic procedure for patients in whom a seizure diathesis is suspected but not defined by history, physical or resting EEG. Ambulatory EEG can be utilized in the differential diagnosis of syncope and transient ischemic attacks if not elucidated by conventional studies. Ambulatory EEG should always be preceded by a resting EEG.

Ambulatory EEG monitoring is considered an established technique and covered under Medicare for the above purposes.

Pub. 100-3, Section 170.3
Speech Pathology Services for the Treatment of Dysphagia

Speech pathology services are covered under Medicare for the treatment of dysphagia, regardless of the presence of a communication disability.

Patients who are motivated, moderately alert, and have some degree of deglutition and swallowing functions are appropriate candidates for dysphagia therapy. Elements of the therapy program can include thermal stimulation to heighten the sensitivity of the swallowing reflex, exercises to improve oral-motor control, training in laryngeal adduction and compensatory swallowing techniques, and positioning and dietary modifications. Design all programs to ensure swallowing safety of the patient during oral feedings and maintain adequate nutrition.

Pub. 100-3, Section 180.1
Medical Nutrition Therapy

Effective October 1, 2002, basic coverage of MNT for the first year a beneficiary receives MNT with either a diagnosis of renal disease or diabetes as defined at 42 CFR §410.130 is 3 hours. Also effective October 1, 2002, basic coverage in subsequent years for renal disease or diabetes is 2 hours. The dietitian/nutritionist may choose how many units are performed per day as long as all of the other requirements in this NCD and 42 CFR §§410.130-410.134 are met. Pursuant to the exception at 42 CFR §410.132(b)(5), additional hours are considered to be medically necessary and covered if the treating physician determines that there is a change in medical condition, diagnosis, or treatment regimen that requires a change in MNT and orders additional hours during that episode of care.

Effective October 1, 2002, if the treating physician determines that receipt of both MNT and DSMT is medically necessary in the same episode of care, Medicare will cover both DSMT and MNT initial and subsequent years without decreasing either benefit as long as DSMT and MNT are not provided on the same date of service. The dietitian/nutritionist may choose how many units are performed per day as long as

all of the other requirements in the NCD and 42 CFR §§410.130-410.134 are met. Pursuant to the exception at 42 CFR 410.132(b)(5), additional hours are considered to be medically necessary and covered if the treating physician determines that there is a change in medical condition, diagnosis, or treatment regimen that requires a change in MNT and orders additional hours during that episode of care.

Pub. 100-3, Section 190.1
Histocompatibility Testing

This testing is safe and effective when it is performed on patients:

A. In preparation for a kidney transplant;
B. In preparation for bone marrow transplantation;
C. In preparation for blood platelet transfusions (particularly where multiple infusions are involved); or
D. Who are suspected of having ankylosing spondylitis.

This testing is covered under Medicare when used for any of the indications listed in A, B, and C and if it is reasonable and necessary for the patient.

It is covered for ankylosing spondylitis in cases where other methods of diagnosis would not be appropriate or have yielded inconclusive results. Request documentation supporting the medical necessity of the test from the physician in all cases where ankylosing spondylitis is indicated as the reason for the test.

Pub. 100-3, Section 190.2
Diagnostic Pap Smears

A diagnostic pap smear and related medically necessary services are covered under Medicare Part B when ordered by a physician under one of the following conditions:

- Previous cancer of the cervix, uterus, or vagina that has been or is presently being treated;
- Previous abnormal pap smear;
- Any abnormal findings of the vagina, cervix, uterus, ovaries, or adnexa;
- Any significant complaint by the patient referable to the female reproductive system; or
- Any signs or symptoms that might in the physician's judgment reasonably be related to a gynecologic disorder.

Screening Pap Smears and Pelvic Examinations for Early Detection of Cervical or Vaginal Cancer

(For screening pap smears, effective for services performed on or after July 1, 1990. For pelvic examinations including clinical breast examination, effective for services furnished on or after January 1, 1998.)

A screening pap smear (use HCPCS code P3000 Screening Papanicolaou smear, cervical or vaginal, up to three smears; by technician under physician supervision or P3001 Screening Papanicolaou smear, cervical or vaginal, up to three smears requiring interpretation by physician). (Use HCPCS codes G0123 Screening Cytopathology, cervical or vaginal (any reporting system), collected in preservative fluid, automated thin layer preparation, screening by cytotechnologist under physician supervision or G0124 Screening Cytopathology, cervical or vaginal (any reporting system) collected in preservative fluid, automated thin layer preparation, requiring interpretation by physician) and related medically necessary services provided to a woman for the early detection of cervical cancer (including collection of the sample of cells and a physician's interpretation of the test results) and pelvic examination (including clinical breast examination) (use HCPCS code G0101 cervical or vaginal cancer screening; pelvic and clinical breast examination) are covered under Medicare Part B when ordered by a physician (or authorized practitioner) under one of the following conditions

She has not had such a test during the preceding three years or is a woman of childbearing age (§1861(nn) of the Act).

- There is evidence (on the basis of her medical history or other findings) that she is at high risk of developing cervical cancer and her physician (or authorized practitioner) recommends that she have the test performed more frequently than every 3 years.

High risk factors for cervical and vaginal cancer are:

- Early onset of sexual activity (under 16 years of age);
- Multiple sexual partners (five or more in a lifetime);
- History of sexually transmitted disease (including HIV infection);
- Fewer than three negative or any pap smears within the previous seven years; and
- DES (diethylstilbestrol) - exposed daughters of women who took DES during pregnancy.

NOTE: Claims for pap smears must indicate the beneficiary's low or high risk status by including the appropriate ICD-9-CM diagnosis code as required by claims processing instructions.

Definitions

A woman as described in §1861(nn) of the Act is a woman who is of childbearing age and has had a pap smear test during any of the preceding three years that indicated the presence of cervical or vaginal cancer or other abnormality, or is at high risk of developing cervical or vaginal cancer.

A woman of childbearing age is one who is premenopausal and has been determined by a physician or other qualified practitioner to be of childbearing age, based upon the medical history or other findings.

Other "qualified practitioner," as defined in 42 CFR 410.56(a) includes a certified nurse midwife (as defined in §1861(gg) of the Act), or a physician assistant, nurse practitioner, or clinical nurse specialist (as defined in §1861(aa) of the Act) who is authorized under State law to perform the examination.

Screening Pelvic Examination

Section 4102 of the Balanced Budget Act of 1997 provides for coverage of screening pelvic examinations (including a clinical breast examination) for all female beneficiaries, subject to certain frequency and other limitations. A screening pelvic examination (including a clinical breast examination) should include at least seven of the following eleven elements:

- Inspection and palpation of breasts for masses or lumps, tenderness, symmetry, or nipple discharge

- Digital rectal examination including sphincter tone, presence of hemorrhoids, and rectal masses. Pelvic examination (with or without specimen collection for smears and cultures) including:
  - External genitalia (for example, general appearance, hair distribution, or lesions).
  - Urethral meatus (for example, size, location, lesions, or prolapse).
  - Urethra (for example, masses, tenderness, or scarring).
  - Bladder (for example, fullness, masses, or tenderness).
  - Vagina (for example, general appearance, estrogen effect, discharge lesions, pelvic support, cystocele, or rectocele).
  - Cervix (for example, general appearance, lesions, or discharge).
  - Uterus (for example, size, contour, position, mobility, tenderness, consistency, descent, or support).
  - Adnexa/parametria (for example, masses, tenderness, organomegaly, or nodularity).
  - Anus and perineum.

This description is from Documentation Guidelines for Evaluation and Management Services, published in May 1997 and was developed by the Centers for Medicare & Medicaid Services and the American Medical Association.

Pub. 100-3, Section 190.3
Cytogenetic Studies

Medicare covers these tests when they are reasonable and necessary for the diagnosis or treatment of the following conditions:

- Genetic disorders (e.g., mongolism) in a fetus (See Medicare Benefit Policy Manual, Chapter 15, "Covered medical and Other health Services," §20.1)
- Failure of sexual development;
- Chronic myelogenous leukemia;
- Acute leukemias lymphoid (FAB L1-L3), myeloid (FAB M0-M7), and unclassified; or
- Mylodysplasia

Pub. 100-3, Section 190.4
Electron Microscope

The electron microscope has been used in the examination of biopsies for years; its efficacy, and therefore its Medicare coverage, is not being questioned. However, there are less expensive methods for examining biopsies which are normally adequate. The additional expense for the electron microscope is normally warranted only when distinguishing different types of nephritis from renal needle biopsies or when there is an uncertain diagnosis from the pathologist. When an uncertain diagnosis from the pathologists results from a less expensive method of examination and an electron microscope examination is therefore necessary, both biopsy examinations are covered. Where the additional expense for an electron microscope examination is not warranted, payment is based upon the less costly methods of examining biopsies.

Pub. 100-3, Section 190.5
Sweat Test

The sweat test is an important diagnostic tool in cystic fibrosis and may be covered when used for that purpose. Usage of the sweat test as a predictor of efficacy of sympathectomy in peripheral vascular disease is unproven and, therefore, is not covered.

Pub. 100-3, Section 190.6
Hair Analysis

Hair analysis to detect mineral traces as an aid in diagnosing human disease is not a covered service under Medicare.

The correlation of hair analysis to the chemical state of the whole body is not possible at this time, and therefore this diagnostic procedure cannot be considered to be reasonable and necessary under §1862(a)(1) of the Act.

Pub. 100-3, Section 190.8
Lymphocyte Mitogen Response Assays

It is a covered test under Medicare when it is medically necessary to assess lymphocytic function in diagnosed immunodeficiency diseases and to monitor immunotherapy.

It is not covered when it is used to monitor the treatment of cancer, because its use for that purpose is experimental.

Pub. 100-3, Section 190.9
Serologic Testing for Acquired Immunodeficiency Syndrome (AIDS)

These tests may be covered when performed to help determine a diagnosis for symptomatic patients. They are not covered when furnished as part of a screening program for asymptomatic persons.

NOTE:	Two enzyme-linked immunosorbent assay (ELISA) tests that were conducted on the same specimen must be both positive before Medicare will cover the Western blot test.

Pub. 100-3, Section 190.10
Laboratory Tests - CRD Patients

A. Laboratory tests are essential to monitor the progress of CRD patients. The following list and frequencies of tests constitute the level and types of routine laboratory tests that are covered. Bills for other types of tests are considered nonroutine. Routine tests at greater frequencies must include medical justification. Nonroutine tests generally are justified by the diagnosis. The routinely covered regimen includes the following tests:

Per Dialysis

All hematocrit or hemoglobin and clotting time tests furnished incident to dialysis treatments.

Per Week

Prothrombin time for patients on anticoagulant therapy

Serum Creatinine

Per Week or Thirteen Per Quarter

BUN

Monthly

CBC	Serum Calcium
Serum Potassium	Serum Chloride
Serum Bicarbonate	Serum Phosphorous
Total Protein	Serum Albumin
Alkaline Phospatase	AST, SGOT
LDH	

Guidelines for tests other than those routinely performed include:

Serum Aluminum - one every 3 months

Serum Ferritin - one every 3 months

The following tests for hepatitis B are covered when patients first enter a dialysis facility: hepatitis B surface antigen (HBsAg) and Anti-HBs. Coverage of future testing in these patients depends on their serologic status and on whether they have been successfully immunized against hepatitis B virus. The following table summarizes the frequency of serologic surveillance for hepatitis B. Tests furnished according to this table do not require additional documentation and are paid separately because payment for maintenance dialysis treatments does not take them into account.

	Frequency of Screening	
Vaccination and Serologic Status	HBsAg Patients	Anti-HBs Patients
UNVACCINATED Susceptible		
HBsAg Carrier	Monthly	Semiannually
Anti-HBs-Positive	Annually	None
(1)	None	Annually
VACCINATED Anti-HBs-Positive (1)		
Low Level or No	None	Annually
Anti-HBs	Monthly	Semiannually

(1) At least 10 sample ration units by radioimmunoassay or positive by enzyme immunoassay.

Patients who are in the process of receiving hepatitis B vaccines, but have not received the complete series, should continue to be routinely screened as susceptible. Between one and six months after the third dose, all vaccines should be tested for anti-HBs to confirm their response to the vaccine. Patients who have a level of anti-HBs of at least 10 sample ratio units (SRUs) by radioimmunoassay (RIA) or who are positive by enzyme immunoassay (EIA) are considered adequate responders to vaccine and need only be tested

APPENDIX D

for anti-HBs annually to verify their immune status. If anti-HBs drops below 10 SRUs by RIA or is negative by EIA, a booster dose of hepatitis B vaccine should be given.

B. Laboratory tests are subject to the normal coverage requirements. If the laboratory services are performed by a free-standing facility, be sure it meets the conditions of coverage for independent laboratories.

Pub. 100-3, Section 190.12
Urine Culture, Bacterial

Indications

1. A patient's urinalysis is abnormal suggesting urinary tract infection, for example, abnormal microscopic (hematuria, pyuria, bacteriuria); abnormal biochemical urinalysis (positive leukocyte esterase, nitrite, protein, blood); a Gram's stain positive for microorganisms; positive bacteriuria screen by a non culture technique; or other significant abnormality of a urinalysis. While it is not essential to evaluate a urine specimen by one of these methods before a urine culture is performed, certain clinical presentations with highly suggestive signs and symptoms may lend themselves to an antecedent urinalysis procedure where follow-up culture depends upon an initial positive or abnormal test result.

2. A patient has clinical signs and symptoms indicative of a possible urinary tract infection (UTI). Acute lower UTI may present with urgency, frequency, nocturia, dysuria, discharge or incontinence. These findings may also be noted in upper UTI with additional systemic symptoms (for example, fever, chills, lethargy); or pain in the costovertebral, abdominal, or pelvic areas. Signs and symptoms may overlap considerably with other inflammatory conditions of the genitourinary tract (for example, prostatitis, urethritis, vaginitis, or cervicitis). Elderly or immunocompromised patients, or patients with neurologic disorders may present atypically (for example, general debility, acute mental status changes, declining functional status).

3. The patient is being evaluated for suspected urosepsis, fever of unknown origin, or other systemic manifestations of infection but without a known source. Signs and symptoms used to define sepsis have been well-established.

4. A test-of cure is generally not indicated in an uncomplicated infection. However, it may be indicated if the patient is being evaluated for response to therapy and there is a complicating co-existing urinary abnormality including structural or functional abnormalities, calculi, foreign bodies, or ureteral/renal stents or there is clinical or laboratory evidence of failure to respond as described in Indications 1 and 2.

5. In surgical procedures involving major manipulations of the genitourinary tract, preoperative examination to detect occult infection may be indicated in selected cases (for example, prior to renal transplantation, manipulation or removal of kidney stones, or transurethral surgery of the bladder or prostate).

6. Urine culture may be indicated to detect occult infection in renal transplant recipients on immunosuppressive therapy.

Limitations

1. CPT 87086 may be used one time per encounter.

2. Colony count restrictions on coverage of CPT 87088 do not apply as they may be highly variable according to syndrome or other clinical circumstances (for example, antecedent therapy, collection time, degree of hydration).

3. CPT 87088, 87184, and 87186 may be used multiple times in association with or independent of 87086, as urinary tract infections may be polymicrobial.

4. Testing for asymptomatic bacteriuria as part of a prenatal evaluation may be medically appropriate but is considered screening and, therefore, not covered by Medicare. The US Preventive Services Task Force has concluded that screening for asymptomatic bacteriuria outside of the narrow indication for pregnant women is generally not indicated. There are insufficient data to recommend screening in ambulatory elderly patients including those with diabetes. Testing may be clinically indicated on other grounds including likelihood of recurrence or potential adverse effects of antibiotics, but is considered screening in the absence of clinical or laboratory evidence of infection.

Pub. 100-3, Section 190.13
Human Immunodeficiency Virus Testing (Prognosis Including Monitoring)

Indications:

1. A plasma HIV RNA baseline level may be medically necessary in any patient with confirmed HIV infection.

2. Regular periodic measurement of plasma HIV RNA levels may be medically necessary to determine risk for disease progression in an HIV-infected individual and to determine when to initiate or modify antiretroviral treatment regimens.

3. In clinical situations where the risk of HIV infection is significant and initiation of therapy is anticipated, a baseline HIV quantification may be performed. These situations include:

a. Persistence of borderline or equivocal serologic reactivity in an at-risk individual.

b. Signs and symptoms of acute retroviral syndrome characterized by fever, malaise, lymphadenopathy and rash in an at-risk individual.

Limitations:

1. Viral quantification may be appropriate for prognostic use including baseline determination, periodic monitoring, and monitoring of response to therapy. Use as a diagnostic test method is not indicated.

2. Measurement of plasma HIV RNA levels should be performed at the time of establishment of an HIV infection diagnosis. For an accurate baseline, 2 specimens in a 2-week period are appropriate.

3. For prognosis including anti-retroviral therapy monitoring, regular, periodic measurements are appropriate. The frequency of viral load testing should be consistent with the most current Centers for Disease Control and Prevention guidelines for use of anti-retroviral agents in adults and adolescents or pediatrics.

4. Because differences in absolute HIV copy number are known to occur using different assays, plasma HIV RNA levels should be measured by the same analytical method. A change in assay method may necessitate re-establishment of a baseline.

5. Nucleic acid quantification techniques are representative of rapidly emerging and evolving new technologies. As such, users are advised to remain current on FDA-approval status.

Appendixes

Pub. 100-3, Section 190.14
Human Immunodeficiency Virus Testing (Diagnosis)

Indications:

Diagnostic testing to establish HIV infection may be indicated when there is a strong clinical suspicion supported by one or more of the following clinical findings:

1. The patient has a documented, otherwise unexplained, AIDS-defining or AIDS-associated opportunistic infection.

2. The patient has another documented sexually transmitted disease which identifies significant risk of exposure to HIV and the potential for an early or subclinical infection.

3. The patient has documented acute or chronic hepatitis B or C infection that identifies significant risk of exposure to HIV and the potential for an early or subclinical infection.

4. The patient has a documented AIDS-defining or AIDS-associated neoplasm.

5. The patient has a documented AIDS-associated neurologic disorder or otherwise unexplained dementia.

6. The patient has another documented AIDS-defining clinical condition, or a history of other severe, recurrent, or persistent conditions which suggest an underlying immune deficiency (for example, cutaneous or mucosal disorders).

7. The patient has otherwise unexplained generalized signs and symptoms suggestive of a chronic process with an underlying immune deficiency (for example, fever, weight loss, malaise, fatigue, chronic diarrhea, failure to thrive, chronic cough, hemoptysis, shortness of breath, or lymphadenopathy).

8. The patient has otherwise unexplained laboratory evidence of a chronic disease process with an underlying immune deficiency (for example, anemia, leukopenia, pancytopenia, lymphopenia, or low CD4+ lymphocyte count).

9. The patient has signs and symptoms of acute retroviral syndrome with fever, malaise, lymphadenopathy, and skin rash.

10. The patient has documented exposure to blood or body fluids known to be capable of transmitting HIV (for example, needlesticks and other significant blood exposures) and antiviral therapy is initiated or anticipated to be initiated.

11. The patient is undergoing treatment for rape. (HIV testing is a part of the rape treatment protocol.)

For a comprehensive tabulation of AIDS-defining and AIDS associated conditions, refer to Rhame, R.S. 1994. Acquired immunodeficiency syndrome, p. 628-652. Infectious Diseases; P.D. Hoeprich, M.C. Jordan, and A.R. Ronald (J.B. Lippincott Co., Philadelphia).

Limitations:

1. HIV antibody testing in the United States is usually performed using HIV-1 or HIV-½ combination tests. HIV-2 testing is indicated if clinical circumstances suggest HIV-2 is likely (that is, compatible clinical findings and HIV-1 test negative). HIV-2 testing may also be indicated in areas of the country where there is greater prevalence of HIV-2 infections.

2. The Western Blot test should be performed only after documentation that the initial EIA tests are repeatedly positive or equivocal on a single sample.

3. The HIV antigen tests currently have no defined diagnostic usage.

4. Direct viral RNA detection may be performed in those situations where serologic testing does not establish a diagnosis but strong clinical suspicion persists (for example, acute retroviral syndrome, nonspecific serologic evidence of HIV, or perinatal HIV infection).

5. If initial serologic tests confirm an HIV infection, repeat testing is not indicated.

6. If initial serologic tests are HIV EIA negative and there is no indication for confirmation of infection by viral RNA detection, the interval prior to retesting is 3-6 months.

7. Testing for evidence of HIV infection using serologic methods may be medically appropriate in situations where there is a risk of exposure to HIV. However, in the absence of a documented AIDS defining or HIV associated disease, an HIV associated sign or symptom, or documented exposure to a known HIV-infected source, the testing is considered by Medicare to be screening and thus is not covered by Medicare (for example, history of multiple blood component transfusions, exposure to blood or body fluids not resulting in consideration of therapy, history of transplant, history of illicit drug use, multiple sexual partners, same-sex encounters, prostitution, or contact with prostitutes).

8. The CPT Editorial Panel has issued a number of codes for infectious agent detection by direct antigen or nucleic acid probe techniques that have not yet been developed or are only being used on an investigational basis. Laboratory providers are advised to remain current on FDA-approval status for these tests.

Pub. 100-3, Section 190.15
Blood Counts

Indications:

Indications for a CBC or hemogram include red cell, platelet, and white cell disorders. Examples of these indications are enumerated individually below.

1. Indications for a CBC generally include the evaluation of bone marrow dysfunction as a result of neoplasms, therapeutic agents, exposure to toxic substances, or pregnancy. The CBC is also useful in assessing peripheral destruction of blood cells, suspected bone marrow failure or bone marrow infiltrate, suspected myeloproliferative, myelodysplastic, or lymphoproliferative processes, and immune disorders.

2. Indications for hemogram or CBC related to red cell (RBC) parameters of the hemogram include signs, symptoms, test results, illness, or disease that can be associated with anemia or other red blood cell disorder (e.g., pallor, weakness, fatigue, weight loss, bleeding, acute injury associated with blood loss or suspected blood loss, abnormal menstrual bleeding, hematuria, hematemesis, hematochezia, positive fecal occult blood test, malnutrition, vitamin deficiency, malabsorption, neuropathy, known malignancy, presence of acute or chronic disease that may have associated anemia, coagulation or hemostatic disorders, postural dizziness, syncope, abdominal pain, change in bowel habits, chronic marrow hypoplasia or decreased RBC production, tachycardia, systolic heart murmur, congestive heart failure, dyspnea, angina, nailbed deformities, growth

retardation, jaundice, hepatomegaly, splenomegaly, lymphadenopathy, ulcers on the lower extremities).

3. Indications for hemogram or CBC related to red cell (RBC) parameters of the hemogram include signs, symptoms, test results, illness, or disease that can be associated with polycythemia (for example, fever, chills, ruddy skin, conjunctival redness, cough, wheezing, cyanosis, clubbing of the fingers, orthopnea, heart murmur, headache, vague cognitive changes including memory changes, sleep apnea, weakness, pruritus, dizziness, excessive sweating, visual symptoms, weight loss, massive obesity, gastrointestinal bleeding, paresthesias, dyspnea, joint symptoms, epigastric distress, pain and erythema of the fingers or toes, venous or arterial thrombosis, thromboembolism, myocardial infarction, stroke, transient ischemic attacks, congenital heart disease, chronic obstructive pulmonary disease, increased erythropoietin production associated with neoplastic, renal or hepatic disorders, androgen or diuretic use, splenomegaly, hepatomegaly, diastolic hypertension.)

4. Specific indications for CBC with differential count related to the WBC include signs, symptoms, test results, illness, or disease associated with leukemia, infections or inflammatory processes, suspected bone marrow failure or bone marrow infiltrate, suspected myeloproliferative, myelodysplastic or lymphoproliferative disorder, use of drugs that may cause leukopenia, and immune disorders (e.g., fever, chills, sweats, shock, fatigue, malaise, tachycardia, tachypnea, heart murmur, seizures, alterations of consciousness, meningismus, pain such as headache, abdominal pain, arthralgia, odynophagia, or dysuria, redness or swelling of skin, soft tissue bone, or joint, ulcers of the skin or mucous membranes, gangrene, mucous membrane discharge, bleeding, thrombosis, respiratory failure, pulmonary infiltrate, jaundice, diarrhea, vomiting, hepatomegaly, splenomegaly, lymphadenopathy, opportunistic infection such as oral candidiasis.)

5. Specific indications for CBC related to the platelet count include signs, symptoms, test results, illness, or disease associated with increased or decreased platelet production and destruction, or platelet dysfunction(e.g., gastrointestinal bleeding, genitourinary tract bleeding, bilateral epistaxis, thrombosis, ecchymosis, purpura, jaundice, petechiae, fever, heparin therapy, suspected DIC, shock, pre-eclampsia, neonate with maternal ITP, massive transfusion, recent platelet transfusion, cardiopulmonary bypass, hemolytic uremic syndrome, renal diseases, lymphadenopathy, hepatomegaly, splenomegaly, hypersplenism, neurologic abnormalities, viral or other infection, myeloproliferative, myelodysplastic, or lymphoproliferative disorder, thrombosis, exposure to toxic agents, excessive alcohol ingestion, autoimmune disorders (SLE, RA and other).

6. Indications for hemogram or CBC related to red cell (RBC) parameters of the hemogram include, in addition to those already listed, thalassemia, suspected hemoglobinopathy, lead poisoning, arsenic poisoning, and spherocytosis.

7. Specific indications for CBC with differential count related to the WBC include, in addition to those already listed, storage diseases/mucopolysaccharidoses, and use of drugs that cause leukocytosis such as G-CSF or GM-CSF.

8. Specific indications for CBC related to platelet count include, in addition to those already listed, May-Hegglin syndrome and Wiskott-Aldrich syndrome.

Limitations:

1. Testing of patients who are asymptomatic, or who do not have a condition that could be expected to result in a hematological abnormality, is screening and is not a covered service.

2. In some circumstances it may be appropriate to perform only a hemoglobin or hematocrit to assess the oxygen carrying capacity of the blood. When the ordering provider requests only a hemoglobin or hematocrit, the remaining components of the CBC are not covered.

3. When a blood count is performed for an end-stage renal disease (ESRD) patient, and is billed outside the ESRD rate, documentation of the medical necessity for the blood count must be submitted with the claim.

4. In some patients presenting with certain signs, symptoms or diseases, a single CBC may be appropriate. Repeat testing may not be indicated unless abnormal results are found, or unless there is a change in clinical condition. If repeat testing is performed, a more descriptive diagnosis code (e.g., anemia) should be reported to support medical necessity. However, repeat testing may be indicated where results are normal in patients with conditions where there is a continued risk for the development of hematologic abnormality.

Pub. 100-3, Section 190.16
Partial Thromboplastin Time (PTT)

Indications:

1. The PTT is most commonly used to quantitate the effect of therapeutic unfractionated heparin and to regulate its dosing. Except during transitions between heparin and warfarin therapy, in general both the PTT and PT are not necessary together to assess the effect of anticoagulation therapy. PT and PTT must be justified separately. (See "Limitations" section for further discussion.)

2. A PTT may be used to assess patients with signs or symptoms of hemorrhage or thrombosis. For example:

> a. abnormal bleeding, hemorrhage or hematoma petechiae or other signs of thrombocytopenia that could be due to Disseminated Intravascular Coagulation;

> b. swollen extremity with or without prior trauma

3. A PTT may be useful in evaluating patients who have a history of a condition known to be associated with the risk of hemorrhage or thrombosis that is related to the intrinsic coagulation pathway. Such abnormalities may be genetic or acquired. For example:

> a. dysfibrinogenemia;

> b. afibrinogenemia (complete);

> c. acute or chronic liver dysfunction or failure, including Wilson's disease;

> d. hemophilia;

> e. liver disease and failure;

> f. infectious processes;

> g. bleeding disorders;

> h. disseminated intravascular coagulation;

> i. lupus erythematosus or other conditions associated with circulating inhibitors, e.g.,

Factor VIII Inhibitor, lupus-like anticoagulant, etc.;

j. sepsis;

k. von Willebrand's disease;

l. arterial and venous thrombosis, including the evaluation of hypercoagulable states;

m. clinical conditions associated with nephrosis or renal failure;

n. other acquired and congenital coagulopathies as well as thrombotic states.

4. A PTT may be used to assess the risk of thrombosis or hemorrhage in patients who are going to have a medical intervention known to be associated with increased risk of bleeding or thrombosis. An example is as follows: evaluation prior to invasive procedures or operations of patients with personal or family history of bleeding or who are on heparin therapy

Limitations:

1. The PTT is not useful in monitoring the effects of warfarin on a patient's coagulation routinely. However, a PTT may be ordered on a patient being treated with warfarin as heparin therapy is being discontinued. (See coding guidelines for instructions on the use of code V58.61 in this situation.) A PTT may also be indicated when the PT is markedly prolonged due to warfarin toxicity.

2. The need to repeat this test is determined by changes in the underlying medical condition and/or the dosing of heparin.

3. Testing prior to any medical intervention associated with a risk of bleeding and thrombosis (other than thrombolytic therapy) will generally be considered medically necessary only where there are signs or symptoms of a bleeding or thrombotic abnormality or a personal history of bleeding, thrombosis or a condition associated with a coagulopathy. Hospital/clinic-specific policies, protocols, etc., in and of themselves, cannot alone justify coverage.

Pub. 100-3, Section 190.17
Prothrombin Time (PT)

Indications:

1. A PT may be used to assess patients taking warfarin. The prothrombin time is generally not useful in monitoring patients receiving heparin who are not taking warfarin.

2. A PT may be used to assess patients with signs or symptoms of abnormal bleeding or thrombosis. For example:

a. swollen extremity with or without prior trauma;

b. unexplained bruising;

c. abnormal bleeding, hemorrhage or hematoma;

d. petechiae or other signs of thrombocytopenia that could be due to Disseminated Intravascular Coagulation.

3. A PT may be useful in evaluating patients who have a history of a condition known to be associated with the risk of bleeding or thrombosis that is related to the extrinsic

coagulation pathway. Such abnormalities may be genetic or acquired. For example:

a. dysfibrinogenemia;

b. afibrinogenemia (complete);

c. acute or chronic liver dysfunction or failure, including

d. Wilson's disease and Hemochromatosis;

e. disseminated intravascular coagulation (DIC);

f. congenital and acquired deficiencies of factors II, V, VII, X;

g. vitamin K deficiency;

h. lupus erythematosus;

i. hypercoagulable state;

j. paraproteinemia;

k. lymphoma;

l. amyloidosis;

m. acute and chronic leukemias;

n. plasma cell dyscrasia;

o. HIV infection;

p. malignant neoplasms;

q. hemorrhagic fever;

r. salicylate poisoning;

s. obstructive jaundice;

t. intestinal fistula;

u. malabsorption syndrome;

v. colitis;

w. chronic diarrhea;

x. presence of peripheral venous or arterial thrombosis or pulmonary emboli or myocardial infarction;

y. patients with bleeding or clotting tendencies;

z. organ transplantation;

aa. presence of circulating coagulation inhibitors.

4. A PT may be used to assess the risk of hemorrhage or thrombosis in patients who are going to have a medical intervention known to be associated with increased risk of bleeding or thrombosis. For example:

a. evaluation prior to invasive procedures or operations of patients with personal history of bleeding or a condition associated with coagulopathy

b. prior to the use of thrombolytic medication.

Limitations:

1. When an ESRD patient is tested for PT, testing more frequently than weekly (the frequency authorized by 3171.2, Fiscal Intermediary Manual, or 2231.3 Medicare Carrier

© 2005 Ingenix, Inc.

APPENDIX D

Manual) requires documentation of medical necessity (e.g. other than a diagnosis of "Chronic Renal Failure" or "Renal Failure, Unspecified").

2. The need to repeat this test is determined by changes in the underlying medical condition and/or the dosing of warfarin. In a patient on stable warfarin therapy, it is ordinarily not necessary to repeat testing more than every two to three weeks. When testing is performed to evaluate a patient with signs or symptoms of abnormal bleeding or thrombosis and the initial test result is normal, it is ordinarily not necessary to repeat testing unless there is a change in the patient's medical status.

3. Since the INR is a calculation, it will not be paid in addition to the PT when expressed in seconds, and is considered part of the conventional prothrombin time.

4. Testing prior to any medical intervention associated with a risk of bleeding and thrombosis (other than thrombolytic therapy) will generally be considered medically necessary only where there are signs or symptoms of a bleeding or thrombotic abnormality or a personal history of bleeding, thrombosis or a condition associated with a coagulopathy. Hospital/clinic-specific policies, protocols, etc., in and of themselves, cannot alone justify coverage.

Pub. 100-3, Section 190.19
Collagen Crosslinks, Any Method

Indications:

Generally speaking, collagen crosslink testing is useful mostly in "fast losers" of bone. The age when these bone markers can help direct therapy is often pre-Medicare. By the time a fast loser of bone reaches age 65, she will most likely have been stabilized by appropriate therapy or have lost so much bone mass that further testing is useless. Coverage for bone marker assays may be established, however, for younger Medicare beneficiaries and for those men and women who might become fast losers because of some other therapy such as glucocorticoids. Safeguards should be incorporated to prevent excessive use of tests in patients for whom they have no clinical relevance.

Collagen crosslinks testing is used to:

1. Identify individuals with elevated bone resorption, who have osteoporosis in whom response to treatment is being monitored;
2. Predict response (as assessed by bone mass measurements) to FDA approved antiresorptive therapy in postmenopausal women; and
3. Assess response to treatment of patients with osteoporosis, Paget's disease of the bone, or risk for osteoporosis where treatment may include FDA approved antiresorptive agents, anti-estrogens or selective estrogen receptor moderators.

Limitations:

Because of significant specimen to specimen collagen crosslink physiologic variability (15-20%), current recommendations for appropriate utilization include: one or two base-line assays from specified urine collections on separate days; followed by a repeat assay about three months after starting anti-resorptive therapy; followed by a repeat assay in 12 months after the three-month assay; and thereafter not more than annually, unless there is a change

in therapy in which circumstance an additional test may be indicated three months after the initiation of new therapy.

Some collagen crosslink assays may not be appropriate for use in some disorders, according to FDA labeling restrictions.

Pub. 100-3, Section 190.20
Blood Glucose Testing

Indications:

Blood glucose values are often necessary for the management of patients with diabetes mellitus, where hyperglycemia and hypoglycemia are often present. They are also critical in the determination of control of blood glucose levels in the patient with impaired fasting glucose (FPG 110-125 mg/dL), the patient with insulin resistance syndrome and/or carbohydrate intolerance (excessive rise in glucose following ingestion of glucose or glucose sources of food), in the patient with a hypoglycemia disorder such as nesidioblastosis or insulinoma, and in patients with a catabolic or malnutrition state. In addition to those conditions already listed, glucose testing may be medically necessary in patients with tuberculosis, unexplained chronic or recurrent infections, alcoholism, coronary artery disease (especially in women), or unexplained skin conditions (including pruritis, local skin infections, ulceration and gangrene without an established cause).

Many medical conditions may be a consequence of a sustained elevated or depressed glucose level. These include comas, seizures or epilepsy, confusion, abnormal hunger, abnormal weight loss or gain, and loss of sensation. Evaluation of glucose may also be indicated in patients on medications known to affect carbohydrate metabolism.

Effective January 1, 2005, the Medicare law expanded coverage to diabetic screening services. Some forms of blood glucode testing covered under this national coverage determination may be covered for screening purposes subject to specified frequencies. See 42 CFR 410.18 and section 90, chapter 18 of the **Claims Processing** Manual, for a full description of this screening benefit.

Limitations:

Frequent home blood glucose testing by diabetic patients should be encouraged. In stable, non-hospitalized patients who are unable or unwilling to do home monitoring, it may be reasonable and necessary to measure quantitative blood glucose up to four times annually.

Depending upon the age of the patient, type of diabetes, degree of control, complications of diabetes, and other co-morbid conditions, more frequent testing than four times annually may be reasonable and necessary.

In some patients presenting with nonspecific signs, symptoms, or diseases not normally associated with disturbances in glucose metabolism, a single blood glucose test may be medically necessary. Repeat testing may not be indicated unless abnormal results are found or unless there is a change in clinical condition. If repeat testing is performed, a specific diagnosis code (e.g., diabetes) should be reported to support medical necessity. However, repeat testing may be indicated where results are normal in patients with conditions where there is a confirmed continuing risk of glucose metabolism abnormality (e.g., monitoring glucocorticoid therapy).

Pub. 100-3, Section 190.21

Appendixes

Glycated Hemoglobin/Glycated Protein

Indications:

Glycated hemoglobin/protein testing is widely accepted as medically necessary for the management and control of diabetes. It is also valuable to assess hyperglycemia, a history of hyperglycemia or dangerous hypoglycemia. Glycated protein testing may be used in place of glycated hemoglobin in the management of diabetic patients, and is particularly useful in patients who have abnormalities of erythrocytes such as hemolytic anemia or hemoglobinopathies.

Limitations:

It is not considered reasonable and necessary to perform glycated hemoglobin tests more often than every three months on a controlled diabetic patient to determine whether the patient's metabolic control has been on average within the target range. It is not considered reasonable and necessary for these tests to be performed more frequently than once a month for diabetic pregnant women. Testing for uncontrolled type one or two diabetes mellitus may require testing more than four times a year. The above Description Section provides the clinical basis for those situations in which testing more frequently than four times per annum is indicated, and medical necessity documentation must support such testing in excess of the above guidelines.

Many methods for the analysis of glycated hemoglobin show significant interference from elevated levels of fetal hemoglobin or by variant hemoglobin molecules. When the glycated hemoglobin assay is initially performed in these patients, the laboratory may inform the ordering physician of a possible analytical interference. Alternative testing, including glycated protein, for example, fructosamine, may be indicated for the monitoring of the degree of glycemic control in this situation. It is therefore conceivable that a patient will have both a glycated hemoglobin and glycated protein ordered on the same day. This should be limited to the initial assay of glycated hemoglobin, with subsequent exclusive use of glycated protein. These tests are not considered to be medically necessary for the diagnosis of diabetes.

Pub. 100-3, Section 190.22
Thyroid Testing

Indications:

Thyroid function tests are used to define hyper function, euthyroidism, or hypofunction of thyroid disease. Thyroid testing may be reasonable and necessary to:

distinguish between primary and secondary hypothyroidism; confirm or rule out primary hypothyroidism; monitor thyroid hormone levels (for example, patients with goiter, thyroid nodules, or thyroid cancer); monitor drug therapy in patients with primary hypothyroidism; confirm or rule out primary hyperthyroidism; and monitor therapy in patients with hyperthyroidism.

Thyroid function testing may be medically necessary in patients with disease or neoplasm of the thyroid and other endocrine glands. Thyroid function testing may also be medically necessary in patients with metabolic disorders; malnutrition; hyperlipidemia; certain types of anemia; psychosis and non-psychotic personality disorders; unexplained depression; ophthalmologic disorders; various cardiac arrhythmias; disorders of menstruation; skin conditions; myalgias; and a wide array of signs and symptoms, including alterations in consciousness; malaise; hypothermia; symptoms of the nervous and musculoskeletal system; skin and integumentary system; nutrition and metabolism; cardiovascular; and gastrointestinal system.

It may be medically necessary to do follow-up thyroid testing in patients with a personal history of malignant neoplasm of the endocrine system and in patients on long-term thyroid drug therapy.

Limitations:

Testing may be covered up to two times a year in clinically stable patients; more frequent testing may be reasonable and necessary for patients whose thyroid therapy has been altered or in whom symptoms or signs of hyperthyroidism or hypothyroidism are noted.

Pub. 100-3, Section 190.23
Lipid Testing

Indications:

The medical community recognizes lipid testing as appropriate for evaluating atherosclerotic cardiovascular disease. Conditions in which lipid testing may be indicated include:

- Assessment of patients with atherosclerotic cardiovascular disease
- Evaluation of primary dyslipidemia
- Any form of atherosclerotic disease, or any disease leading to the formation of atherosclerotic disease
- Diagnostic evaluation of diseases associated with altered lipid metabolism, such as: nephrotic syndrome, pancreatitis, hepatic disease, and hypo and hyperthyroidism
- Secondary dyslipidemia, including diabetes mellitus, disorders of gastrointestinal absorption, chronic renal failure
- Signs or symptoms of dyslipidemias, such as skin lesions
- As follow-up to the initial screen for coronary heart disease (total cholesterol + HDL cholesterol) when total cholesterol is determined to be high (>240 mg/dL), or borderline-high (200-240 mg/dL) plus two or more coronary heart disease risk factors, or an HDL cholesterol <35 mg/dl.

To monitor the progress of patients on anti-lipid dietary management and pharmacologic therapy for the treatment of elevated blood lipid disorders, total cholesterol, HDL cholesterol and LDL cholesterol may be used. Triglycerides may be obtained if this lipid fraction is also elevated or if the patient is put on drugs (for example, thiazide diuretics, beta blockers, estrogens, glucocorticoids, and tamoxifen) which may raise the triglyceride level.

When monitoring long term anti-lipid dietary or pharmacologic therapy and when following patients with borderline high total or LDL cholesterol levels, it may be reasonable to perform the lipid panel annually. A lipid panel at a yearly interval will usually be adequate while measurement of the serum total cholesterol or a measured LDL should suffice for interim visits if the patient does not have hypertriglyceridemia.

Any one component of the panel or a measured LDL may be reasonable and necessary up to six times the first year for monitoring dietary or pharmacologic therapy. More frequent total cholesterol HDL cholesterol, LDL cholesterol and triglyceride testing may be indicated for marked elevations or for changes to anti-lipid therapy due to inadequate initial patient response to dietary or pharmacologic therapy. The LDL cholesterol or total cholesterol may be measured three times yearly after treatment goals have been achieved.

Electrophoretic or other quantitation of lipoproteins may be indicated if the patient has a primary disorder of lipoid metabolism.

Effective January 1, 2005, the Medicare law expanded coverage to cardiovascular screening services. Several of the procedures included in this NCD may be covered for screening purposes subject to specified frequencies. See 42 CFR 410.17 and section 100, chapter 18, of the Claims Processing Manual, for a full description of this benefit.

Limitations:

Lipid panel and hepatic panel testing may be used for patients with severe psoriasis which has not responded to conventional therapy and for which the retinoid etretinate has been prescribed and who have developed hyperlipidemia or hepatic toxicity. Specific examples include erythrodermia and generalized pustular type and psoriasis associated with arthritis.

Routine screening and prophylactic testing for lipid disorder are not covered by Medicare. While lipid screening may be medically appropriate, Medicare by statute does not pay for it. Lipid testing in asymptomatic individuals is considered to be screening regardless of the presence of other risk factors such as family history, tobacco use, etc.

Once a diagnosis is established, one or several specific tests are usually adequate for monitoring the course of the disease. Less specific diagnoses (for example, other chest pain) alone do not support medical necessity of these tests.

When monitoring long term anti-lipid dietary or pharmacologic therapy and when following patients with borderline high total or LDL cholesterol levels, it is reasonable to perform the lipid panel annually. A lipid panel at a yearly interval will usually be adequate while measurement of the serum total cholesterol or a measured LDL should suffice for interim visits if the patient does not have hypertriglyceridemia.

Any one component of the panel or a measured LDL may be medically necessary up to six times the first year for monitoring dietary or pharmacologic therapy. More frequent total cholesterol HDL cholesterol, LDL cholesterol and triglyceride testing may be indicated for marked elevations or for changes to anti-lipid therapy due to inadequate initial patient response to dietary or pharmacologic therapy. The LDL cholesterol or total cholesterol may be measured three times yearly after treatment goals have been achieved.

If no dietary or pharmacological therapy is advised, monitoring is not necessary.

When evaluating non-specific chronic abnormalities of the liver (for example, elevations of transaminase, alkaline phosphatase, abnormal imaging studies, etc.), a lipid panel would generally not be indicated more than twice per year.

Pub. 100-3, Section 190.24
Digoxin Therapeutic Drug Assay

Indications:

Digoxin levels may be performed to monitor drug levels of individuals receiving digoxin therapy because the margin of safety between side effects and toxicity is narrow or because the blood level may not be high enough to achieve the desired clinical effect.

Clinical indications may include individuals on digoxin:

- With symptoms, signs or electrocardiogram (ECG) suggestive of digoxin toxicity;
- Taking medications that influence absorption, bioavailability, distribution, and/or elimination of digoxin;
- With impaired renal, hepatic, gastrointestinal, or thyroid function;
- With pH and/or electrolyte abnormalities;
- With unstable cardiovascular status, including myocarditis;
- Requiring monitoring of patient compliance.

Clinical indications may include individuals:

- Suspected of accidental or intended overdose.
- Who have an acceptable cardiac diagnosis (as listed) and for whom an accurate history of use of digoxin is unobtainable

The value of obtaining regular serum digoxin levels is uncertain, but it may be reasonable to check levels once yearly after a steady state is achieved. In addition, it may be reasonable to check the level if:

- Heart failure status worsens;
- Renal function deteriorates;
- Additional medications are added that could affect the digoxin level;
- Signs or symptoms of toxicity develop.

Steady state will be reached in approximately 1 week in patients with normal renal function, although 2 3 weeks may be needed in patients with renal impairment. After changes in dosages or the addition of a medication that could affect the digoxin level, it is reasonable to check the digoxin level one week after the change or addition. Based on the clinical situation, in cases of digoxin toxicity, testing may need to be done more than once a week.

Digoxin is indicated for the treatment of patients with heart failure due to systolic dysfunction and for reduction of the ventricular response in patients with atrial fibrillation or flutter. Digoxin may also be indicated for the treatment of other supraventricular arrhythmias, particularly in the presence of heart failure.

Limitations:

This test is not appropriate for patients on digitoxin or treated with digoxin FAB (fragment antigen binding) antibody.

Pub. 100-3, Section 190.25
Alpha-Fetoprotein

Indications:

AFP is useful for the diagnosis of hepatocellular carcinoma in high-risk patients (such as alcoholic cirrhosis, cirrhosis of viral etiology, hemochromatosis, and alpha 1-antitrypsin deficiency) and in separating patients with benign

Appendixes

hepatocellular neoplasms or metastases from those with hepatocellular carcinoma and, as a non-specific tumor associated antigen, serves in marking germ cell neoplasms of the testis, ovary, retro peritoneum, and mediastinum.

Pub. 100-3, Section 190.26
Carcinoembryonic Antigen

Indications

CEA may be medically necessary for follow-up of patients with colorectal carcinoma. It would however only be medically necessary at treatment decision making points. In some clinical situations (e.g. adenocarcinoma of the lung, small cell carcinoma of the lung, and some gastrointestinal carcinomas) when a more specific marker is not expressed by the tumor, CEA may be a medically necessary alternative marker for monitoring. Preoperative CEA may also be helpful in determining the post operative adequacy of surgical resection and subsequent medical management. In general, a single tumor marker will suffice in following patients with colorectal carcinoma or other malignancies that express such tumor markers.

In following patients who have had treatment for colorectal carcinoma, ASCO guideline suggests that if resection of liver metastasis would be indicated, it is recommended that post-operative CEA testing be performed every two to three months in patients with initial stage II or stage III disease for at least two years after diagnosis.

For patients with metastatic solid tumors which express CEA, CEA may be measured at the start of the treatment and with subsequent treatment cycles to assess the tumor's response to therapy.

Limitations:

Serum CEA determinations are generally not indicated more frequently than once per chemotherapy treatment cycle for patients with metastatic solid tumors which express CEA or every two months post-surgical treatment for patients who have had colorectal carcinoma. However, it may be proper to order the test more frequently in certain situations, for example, when there has been a significant change from prior CEA level or a significant change in patient status which could reflect disease progression or recurrence.

Testing with a diagnosis of an in situ carcinoma is not reasonably done more frequently than once, unless the result is abnormal, in which case the test may be repeated once.

Pub. 100-3, Section 190.27
Human Chorionic Gonadotropin

Indications:

hCG is useful for monitoring and diagnosis of germ cell neoplasms of the ovary, testis, mediastinum, retroperitoneum, and central nervous system. In addition, hCG is useful for monitoring pregnant patients with vaginal bleeding, hypertension and/or suspected fetal loss.

Limitations:

Not more than once per month for diagnostic purposes. As needed for monitoring of patient progress and treatment. Qualitative hCG assays are not appropriate for medically managing patients with known or suspected germ cell neoplasms.

Pub. 100-3, Section 190.28

Tumor Antigen by Immunoassay - CA125

Indications:

CA 125 is a high molecular weight serum tumor marker elevated in 80% of patients who present with epithelial ovarian carcinoma. It is also elevated in carcinomas of the fallopian tube, endometrium, and endocervix. An elevated level may also be associated with the presence of a malignant mesothelioma.

A CA125 level may be obtained as part of the initial pre-operative work-up for women presenting with a suspicious pelvic mass to be used as a baseline for purposes of post-operative monitoring. Initial declines in CA 125 after initial surgery and/or chemotherapy for ovarian carcinoma are also measured by obtaining three serum levels during the first month post treatment to determine the patient's CA 125 half-life, which has significant prognostic implications.

CA 125 levels are again obtained at the completion of chemotherapy as an index of residual disease. Surveillance CA125 measurements are generally obtained every 3 months for 2 years, every 6 months for the next 3 years, and yearly thereafter. CA 125 levels are also an important indicator of a patient's response to therapy in the presence of advanced or recurrent disease. In this setting, CA 125 levels may be obtained prior to each treatment cycle.

Limitations:

These services are not covered for the evaluation of patients with signs or symptoms suggestive of malignancy. The service may be ordered at times necessary to assess either the presence of recurrent disease or the patient's response to treatment with subsequent treatment cycles.

CA 125 is specifically not covered for aiding in the differential diagnosis of patients with a pelvic mass as the sensitivity and specificity of the test is not sufficient. In general, a single "tumor marker" will suffice in following a patient with one of these malignancies.

Pub. 100-3, Section 190.29
Tumor Antigen by Immunoassay CA 15-3/CA 27.29

Indications:

Multiple tumor markers are available for monitoring the response of certain malignancies to therapy and assessing whether residual tumor exists post-surgical therapy.

CA 15-3 is often medically necessary to aid in the management of patients with breast cancer. Serial testing must be used in conjunction with other clinical methods for monitoring breast cancer. For monitoring, if medically necessary, use consistently either CA 15-3 or CA 27.29, not both.

CA 27.29 is equivalent to CA 15-3 in its usage in management of patients with breast cancer.

Limitations:

These services are not covered for the evaluation of patients with signs or symptoms suggestive of malignancy. The service may be ordered at times necessary to assess either the presence of recurrent disease or the patient's response to treatment with subsequent treatment cycles.

Pub. 100-3, Section 190.30
Tumor Antigen by Immunoassay CA 19-9

Indications:

Multiple tumor markers are available for monitoring the response of certain malignancies to therapy and assessing whether residual tumor exists post-surgical therapy.

Levels are useful in following the course of patients with established diagnosis of pancreatic and biliary ductal carcinoma. The test is not indicated for diagnosing these two diseases.

Limitations:

These services are not covered for the evaluation of patients with signs or symptoms suggestive of malignancy. The service may be ordered at times necessary to assess either the presence of recurrent disease or the patient's response to treatment with subsequent treatment cycles.

Pub. 100-3, Section 190.31
Prostate Specific Antigen

Indications:

PSA is of proven value in differentiating benign from malignant disease in men with lower urinary tract signs and symptoms (e.g., hematuria, slow urine stream, hesitancy, urgency, frequency, nocturia and incontinence) as well as with patients with palpably abnormal prostate glands on physician exam, and in patients with other laboratory or imaging studies that suggest the possibility of a malignant prostate disorder. PSA is also a marker used to follow the progress of prostate cancer once a diagnosis has been established, such as in detecting metastatic or persistent disease in patients who may require additional treatment. PSA testing may also be useful in the differential diagnosis of men presenting with as yet undiagnosed disseminated metastatic disease.

Limitations:

Generally, for patients with lower urinary tract signs or symptoms, the test is performed only once per year unless there is a change in the patient's medical condition.

Testing with a diagnosis of in situ carcinoma is not reasonably done more frequently than once, unless the result is abnormal, in which case the test may be repeated once.

Pub. 100-3, Section 190.32
Gamma Glutamyl Transferase

Indications:

1. To provide information about known or suspected hepatobiliary disease, for example:
   a. following chronic alcohol or drug ingestion;
   b. following exposure to hepatotoxins;
   c. when using medication known to have a potential for causing liver toxicity (e.g., following the drug manufacturer's recommendations); or
   d. following infection (e.g., viral hepatitis and other specific infections such as amoebiasis, tuberculosis, psittacosis, and similar infections)
2. To assess liver injury/function following diagnosis of primary or secondary malignant neoplasms
3. To assess liver injury/function in a wide variety of disorders and diseases known to cause liver involvement (e.g., diabetes mellitus, malnutrition, disorders of iron and mineral metabolism, sarcoidosis, amyloidosis, lupus, and hypertension)

4. To assess liver function related to gastrointestinal disease
5. To assess liver function related to pancreatic disease
6. To assess liver function in patients subsequent to liver transplantation
7. To differentiate between the different sources of elevated alkaline phosphatase activity

Limitations:

When used to assess liver dysfunction secondary to existing non-hepatobiliary disease with no change in signs, symptoms, or treatment, it is generally not necessary to repeat a GGT determination after a normal result has been obtained unless new indications are present.

If the GGT is the only "liver" enzyme abnormally high, it is generally not necessary to pursue further evaluation for liver disease for this specific indication.

When used to determine if other abnormal enzyme tests reflect liver abnormality rather than other tissue, it generally is not necessary to repeat a GGT more than one time per week.

Because of the extreme sensitivity of GGT as a marker for cytochrome oxidase induction or cell membrane permeability, it is generally not useful in monitoring patients with known liver disease.

Pub. 100-3, Section 190.33
Hepatitis Panel/Acute Hepatitis Panel

Indications:

1. To detect viral hepatitis infection when there are abnormal liver function test results, with or without signs or symptoms of hepatitis.
2. Prior to and subsequent to liver transplantation.

Limitations:

After a hepatitis diagnosis has been established, only individual tests, rather than the entire panel, are needed.

Pub. 100-3, Section 190.34
Fecal Occult Blood

Indications:

1. To evaluate known or suspected alimentary tract conditions that might cause bleeding into the intestinal tract.
2. To evaluate unexpected anemia.
3. To evaluate abnormal signs, symptoms, or complaints that might be associated with loss of blood.
4. To evaluate patient complaints of black or red-tinged stools.

Limitations:

1. Code 82270 is reported once for the testing of up to three separate specimens (comprising either one or two tests per specimen).
2. In patients who are taking non-steroidal anti-inflammatory drugs and have a history of gastrointestinal bleeding but no other signs, symptoms, or complaints associated with gastrointestinal blood loss, testing for occult blood

may generally be appropriate no more than once every three months.

3. When testing is done for the purpose of screening for colorectal cancer in the absence of signs, symptoms, conditions, or complaints associated with gastrointestinal blood loss, HCPCS code G0107 (Colorectal cancer screening; fecal-occult blood test, 1-3 simultaneous determinations) should be used.

Pub. 100-3, Section 210.1
Prostate Cancer Screening Tests

A. General.--Section 4103 of the Balanced Budget Act of 1997 provides for coverage of certain prostate cancer screening tests subject to certain coverage, frequency, and payment limitations. Effective for services furnished on or after January 1, 2000. Medicare will cover prostate cancer screening tests/procedures for the early detection of prostate cancer. Coverage of prostate cancer screening tests includes the following procedures furnished to an individual for the early detection of prostate cancer:

- Screening digital rectal examination; and

- Screening prostate specific antigen blood test

B. Screening Digital Rectal Examinations.--Screening digital rectal examinations (HCPCS code G0102) are covered at a frequency of once every 12 months for men who have attained age 50 (at least 11 months have passed following the month in which the last Medicare-covered screening digital rectal examination was performed). Screening digital rectal examination means a clinical examination of an individual's prostate for nodules or other abnormalities of the prostate. This screening must be performed by a doctor of medicine or osteopathy (as defined in §1861(r)(1) of the Act), or by a physician assistant, nurse practitioner, clinical nurse specialist, or certified nurse midwife (as defined in §1861(aa) and §1861(gg) of the Act) who is authorized under State law to perform the examination, fully knowledgeable about the beneficiary's medical condition, and would be responsible for using the results of any examination performed in the overall management of the beneficiary's specific medical problem.

C. Screening Prostate Specific Antigen Tests.--Screening prostate specific antigen tests (code G0103) are covered at a frequency of once every 12 months for men who have attained age 50 (at least 11 months have passed following the month in which the last Medicare-covered screening prostate specific antigen test was performed). Screening prostate specific antigen tests (PSA) means a test to detect the marker for adenocarcinoma of prostate. PSA is a reliable immunocytochemical marker for primary and metastatic adenocarcinoma of prostate. This screening must be ordered by the beneficiary's physician or by the beneficiary's physician assistant, nurse practitioner, clinical nurse specialist, or certified nurse midwife (the term "attending physician" is defined in §1861(r)(1) of the Act to mean a doctor of medicine or osteopathy and the terms "physician assistant, nurse practitioner, clinical nurse specialist, or certified nurse midwife" are defined in §1861(aa) and §1861(gg) of the Act) who is fully knowledgeable about the beneficiary's medical condition, and who would be responsible for using the results of any examination (test) performed in the overall management of the beneficiary's specific medical problem.

Pub. 100-3, Section 210.2
Screening Pap Smears and Pelvic Examinations for Early Detection of Cervical or Vaginal Cancer

A screening pap smear and related medically necessary services provided to a woman for the early detection of cervical cancer (including collection of the sample of cells and a physician's interpretation of the test results) and pelvic examination (including clinical breast examination) are covered under Medicare Part B when ordered by a physician (or authorized practitioner) under one of the following conditions:

- She has not had such a test during the preceding 3 years or is a woman of childbearing age (§1861(nn) of the Act).
- There is evidence (on the basis of her medical history or other findings) that she is at high risk of developing cervical cancer and her physician (or authorized practitioner) recommends that she have the test performed more frequently than every 3 years.
- High risk factors for cervical and vaginal cancer are:
- Early onset of sexual activity (under 16 years of age)
- Multiple sexual partners (five or more in a lifetime)
- History of sexually transmitted disease (including HIV infection)
- Fewer than three negative or any pap smears within the previous 7 years; and
- DES (diethylstilbestrol) - exposed daughters of women who took DES during pregnancy.
- V76.2, special screening for malignant neoplasms of the cervix, indicates low risk;
- V15.89, other specified personal history presenting hazards to health, indicates high risk.

If pap smear or pelvic exam claims do not point to one of these diagnosis codes, the claim will reject in the Common Working File. Claims can contain up to four diagnosis codes, but the one pointed to on the line item must be either V76.2 or V15.89.

Definitions:

A woman as described in §1861(nn) of the Act is a woman who is of childbearing age and has had a pap smear test during any of the preceding 3 years that indicated the presence of cervical or vaginal cancer or other abnormality, or is at high risk of developing cervical or vaginal cancer.

A woman of childbearing age is one who is premenopausal and has been determined by a physician or other qualified practitioner to be of childbearing age, based upon the medical history or other findings.

Other qualified practitioner", as defined in 42 CFR 410.56(a) includes a certified nurse midwife (as defined in §1861(gg) of the Act), or a physician assistant, nurse practitioner, or clinical nurse specialist (as defined in §1861(aa) of the Act) who is authorized under State law to perform the examination.

Screening Pelvic Examination:

Section 4102 of the Balanced Budget Act of 1997 provides for coverage of screening pelvic examinations (including a clinical breast examination) for all female beneficiaries, effective January 1, 1998, subject to certain frequency and other limitations. A screening pelvic examination (including a clinical breast examination) should include at least seven of the following eleven elements:

- Inspection and palpation of breasts for masses or lumps, tenderness, symmetry, or nipple discharge.
- Digital rectal examination including sphincter tone, presence of hemorrhoids, and rectal masses. Pelvic examination (with or without specimen collection for smears and cultures) including:
- External genitalia (for example, general appearance, hair distribution, or lesions).
- Urethral maetus (for example, size, location, lesions, or prolapse).
- Urethra (for example, masses, tenderness, or scarring).
- Bladder (for example, fullness, masses, or tenderness).
- Vagina (for example, general appearance, estrogen effect, discharge lesions, pelvic support, cystocele, or rectocele).
- Cervix (for example, general appearance, lesions, or discharge).
- Uterus (for example, size, contour, position, mobility, tenderness, consistency, descent, or support).
- Adnexa/parametria (for example, masses, tenderness, organomegaly, or nodularity).
- Anus and perineum.

This description is from Documentation Guidelines for Evaluation and Management Services, published in May 1997 and was developed by the Health Care Financing Administration and the American Medical Association.

Pub. 100-3, Section 220.1
Computerized Tomography

A. General

Diagnostic examinations of the head (head scans) and of other parts of the body (body scans) performed by computerized tomography (CT) scanners are covered if you find that the medical and scientific literature and opinion support the effective use of a scan for the condition, and the scan is: (1) reasonable and necessary for the individual patient; and (2) performed on a model of CT equipment that meets the criteria in C below.

CT scans have become the primary diagnostic tool for many conditions and symptoms. CT scanning used as the primary diagnostic tool can be cost effective because it can eliminate the need for a series of other tests, is non-invasive and thus virtually eliminates complications, and does not require hospitalization.

B. Determining Whether a CT Scan Is Reasonable and Necessary

Sufficient information must be provided with claims to differentiate CT scans from other radiology services and to make coverage determinations. Carefully review claims to insure that a scan is reasonable and necessary for the individual patient; i.e., the use must be found to be medically

appropriate considering the patient's symptoms and preliminary diagnosis.

There is no general rule that requires other diagnostic tests to be tried before CT scanning is used. However, in an individual case the contractor's medical staff may determine that use of a CT scan as the initial diagnostic test was not reasonable and necessary because it was not supported by the patient's symptoms or complaints stated on the claim form; e.g., "periodic headaches."

Claims for CT scans are reviewed for evidence of abuse which might include the absence of reasonable indications for the scans, an excessive number of scans or unnecessarily expensive types of scans considering the facts in the particular cases.

C-Approved Models of CT Equipment

1. Criteria for Approval

In the absence of evidence to the contrary, you may assume that a CT scan for which payment is requested has been performed on equipment that meets the following criteria:

a. The model must be known to the Food and Drug Administration, and

b. Must be in the full market release phase of development.

Should it be necessary to confirm that those criteria are met, ask the manufacturer to submit the information in subsection C.2. If manufacturers inquire about obtaining Medicare approval for their equipment, inform them of the foregoing criteria.

2. Evidence of Approval

a. The letter sent by the Bureau of Radiological Health, Food and Drug Administration (FDA), to the manufacturer acknowledging the FDA's receipt of information on the specific CT scanner system model submitted as required under Public Law 90-602, "The Radiation Control for Health and Safety Act of 1968."

b. A letter signed by the chief executive officer or other officer acting in a similar capacity for the manufacturer which:

1. Furnishes the CT scanner system model number, all names that hospitals and physicians' offices may use to refer to the CT scanner system on claims, and the accession number assigned by FDA to the specific model;

2. Specifies whether the scanner performs head scans only, body scans only (i.e., scans of parts of the body other than the head), or head and body scans;

3. States that the company or corporation is satisfied with the results of the developmental stages that preceded the full market release phase of the equipment, that the equipment is in the full market release phase, and the date on which it was decided to put the product into the full market release phase.

D-Mobile Ct Equipment

CT scans performed on mobile units are subject to the same Medicare coverage requirements applicable to scans performed on stationary units, as well as certain health and safety requirements recommended by PHS. As with scans performed on stationary units, the scans must be determined medically necessary for the individual patient. The scans must be performed on types of CT scanning equipment that have been approved for use as stationary units (see C above), and must be in compliance with applicable State laws and regulations for control of radiation.

1. Hospital Setting

The hospital must assume responsibility for the quality of the scan furnished to inpatients and outpatients and must assure that a radiologist or other qualified physician is in charge of the procedure. The radiologist or other physician (i.e., one who is with the mobile unit) who is responsible for the procedure must be approved by the hospital for similar privileges.

2. Ambulatory Setting

If mobile CT scan services are furnished at an ambulatory health care facility other than a hospital-based facility, e.g., a freestanding physician-directed clinic, the diagnostic procedure must be performed by or under the direct personal supervision of a radiologist or other qualified physician. In addition, the facility must maintain a record of the attending physician's order for a scan performed on a mobile unit.

3. Billing for Mobile CT Scans

Hospitals, hospital-associated radiologists, ambulatory health care facilities, and physician owner/operators of mobile units may bill for mobile scans as they would for scans performed on stationary equipment.

4. Claims Review

Evidence of compliance with applicable State laws and regulations for control of radiation should be requested from owners of mobile CT scan units upon receipt of the first claims. All mobile scan claims should be reviewed very carefully in accordance with instructions applicable to scans performed on fixed units, with particular emphasis on the medical necessity for scans performed in an ambulatory setting.

E-Multi-Planar Diagnostic Imaging (MPDI)

In usual computerized tomography (CT) scanning procedures, a series of transverse or axial images are reproduced. These transverse images are routinely translated into coronal and/or sagittal views. Multiplanar

diagnostic imaging (MPDI) is a process which further translates the data produced by CT scanning by providing reconstructed oblique images which can contribute to diagnostic information. MPDI, also known as planar image reconstruction or reformatted imaging, is covered under Medicare when provided as a service to an entity performing a covered CT scan.

Pub. 100-3, Section 220.2
Magnetic Resonance Imaging

Magnetic resonance imaging (MRI), formerly called nuclear magnetic resonance (NMR), is covered under Medicare when furnished as described below for the types of covered conditions described in this instruction.

A. General
1. Method of Operation.--Magnetic resonance imaging is a noninvasive method of graphically representing the distribution of water and other hydrogen-rich molecules in the human body. In contrast to conventional radiographs or CT scans, in which the image is produced by X-ray beam attenuation by an object, MRI is capable of producing images by several techniques. In fact, various combinations of MR image production methods may be employed to emphasize particular characteristics of the tissue or body part being examined. The basic elements by which MRI produces an image are the density of hydrogen nuclei in the object being examined, their motion, and the relaxation times, the period of time required for the nuclei to return to their original states in the main, static magnetic field after being subjected to a brief additional magnetic field. These relaxation times reflect the physical-chemical properties of tissue and the molecular environment of its hydrogen nuclei. Only hydrogen atoms are present in human tissues in sufficient concentration for current use in clinical MRI.
2. General Clinical Utility.--Overall, MRI is a useful diagnostic imaging modality that is capable of demonstrating a wide variety of soft-tissue lesions with contrast resolution equal or superior to CT scanning in various parts of the body.

Among the advantages of MRI are the absence of ionizing radiation and the ability to achieve high levels of tissue contrast resolution without injected iodinated radiological contrast agents. Recent advances in technology have resulted in development and FDA approval of new paramagnetic contrast agents for MRI which allow even better visualization in some instances. Multislice imaging and the ability to image in multiple planes, especially sagittal and coronal, have provided a flexibility not easily available with other modalities. Because cortical (outer layer) bone and metallic prostheses do not cause distortion of MR images, it has been possible to visualize certain lesions and body regions with greater certainty than has been possible with CT. The use of MRI on certain soft tissue structures for the purpose of detecting disruptive, neoplastic, degenerative, or inflammatory lesions has now become established in medical practice.

B. Covered Clinical Applications.--Although several uses of MRI are still considered investigational and some uses are clearly contraindicated (see subsection D), MRI is considered medically efficacious for a number of uses. Use the following descriptions as general guidelines or examples of what may be considered covered rather than as a restrictive list of specific coverages. Coverage is limited to MRI units which have received FDA premarket approval, and such units must be operated within the parameters specified by the approval. As with all items and services, the services must be reasonable and necessary for the diagnosis or treatment of the specific patient involved.

MRI is useful in examining the head, central nervous system, and spine. Multiple sclerosis can be diagnosed with MRI and the contents of the posterior fossa are visible. The inherent tissue contrast resolution of MRI makes it an appropriate standard diagnostic modality for general neuroradiology.

MRI can assist in the differential diagnosis of mediastinal and retroperitoneal masses, including abnormalities of the large vessels such as aneurysms and dissection. When a clinical need exists to visualize the parenchyma of solid organs to detect anatomic disruption or neoplasia, this can be accomplished in the liver, urogenital system, adrenals, and pelvic organs without the use of radiological contrast materials. When MRI is considered reasonable and necessary, the use of paramagnetic contrast materials may be covered as part of the study. MRI may also be used to detect and stage pelvic and retroperitoneal neoplasms and to evaluate disorders of cancellous bone and soft tissues. It may also be used in the detection of pericardial thickening. Primary and secondary bone neoplasm and aseptic necrosis can be detected at an early stage and monitored with MRI. Patients with metallic prostheses, especially of the hip, can be imaged in order to detect the early stages of infection of the bone to which the prothesis is attached.

Effective for services provided on or after March 22, 1994, MRI may also be covered to diagnose disc disease without regard to whether radiological imaging has been tried first to diagnose the problem.

C. Gating Devices and Surface Coils (Effective for Services On or After March 4, 1991).-- Gating devices which eliminate distorted images caused by cardiac and respiratory movement cycles are now considered state of the art techniques and may be covered. Surface and other specialty coils may also be covered, as they are used routinely for high resolution imaging where small limited regions of the body are studied. They produce high signal-to-noise ratios resulting in images of enhanced anatomic detail.

D. Contraindications and Noncovered Uses.--
  a. Contraindications.--MRI is not covered when the following patient-specific contraindications are present. It is not covered for patients with cardiac pacemakers or with metallic clips on vascular aneurysms. MRI during a viable pregnancy is also contraindicated at this time. The danger inherent in bringing ferromagnetic materials within range of MRI units generally constrains the use of MRI on acutely ill patients requiring life support systems and monitoring devices which employ ferromagnetic materials. In addition, the long imaging time and the enclosed position of the patient may result in claustrophobia, making patients who have a history of claustrophobia unsuitable candidates for MRI procedures.

  b. Noncovered Uses.--Several uses of MRI have been identified as investigational and are not covered. These include measurement of blood flow and spectroscopy. In addition, MRI is not suitable for the imaging of cortical bone and calcifications and for procedures involving spatial resolution of bone or calcifications.

Pub. 100-3, Section 220.2.1
Magnetic Resonance Spectroscopy (MRS)

B. Nationally Covered Indications

Not applicable.

C. Nationally Noncovered Indications

After thorough review and reconsideration of the existing national noncoverage determination for MRS, as well as the available evidence for the use of MRS as a diagnostic tool for distinguishing indeterminate brain lesions, and/or as an aid in conducting brain biopsies, CMS has determined that the evidence is not adequate to conclude that MRS is reasonable and necessary within the meaning of section 1862(a)(1)(A) of the Social Security Act, for use in the diagnosis of brain tumors. Therefore, CMS reaffirms its current national noncoverage determination for all indications of MRS.

D. Other

Not applicable.

(This NCD last reviewed September 2004.)

Pub. 100-3, Section 220.3
Magnetic Resonance Angiography

In a National Coverage Analysis decision memorandum (#CAG-00142N), issued on April 15, 2003, CMS reviewed scientific and clinical literature on MRA, and set forth its basis for the following coverage policy. Below are the only indications for which Medicare coverage is allowed for MRA. All other uses of MRA not listed in this manual are not covered.

A. Head and Neck.--Studies have proven that MRA is effective for evaluating flow in internal carotid vessels of the head and neck. However, not all potential applications of MRA have been proven effective. As a result, all of the following criteria must apply in order for Medicare to provide coverage for MRA of the head and neck:
  a. MRA is used to evaluate the carotid arteries, the circle of Willis, the anterior, middle or posterior cerebral arteries, the

vertebral or basilar arteries or the venous sinuses;

b. MRA is performed on patients with conditions of the head and neck for which surgery is anticipated and may be found to be appropriate based on the MRA. These conditions include, but are not limited to, tumor, aneurysm, vascular malformations, vascular occlusion or thrombosis. Within this broad category of disorders, medical necessity is the underlying determinant of the need for an MRA in specific diseases. The medical records should clearly justify and demonstrate the existence of medical necessity.

c. MRA and contrast angiography (CA) are not expected to be performed on the same patient for diagnostic purposes prior to the application of anticipated therapy. Only one of these tests will be covered routinely unless the physician can demonstrate the medical need to perform both tests.

B. Peripheral Arteries of Lower Extremities.--Studies have proven that MRA of peripheral arteries is useful in determining the presence and extent of peripheral vascular disease in lower extremities. This procedure is non-invasive and has been shown to find occult vessels in some patients for which those vessels were not apparent when CA was performed. Medicare will cover either MRA or CA to evaluate peripheral arteries of the lower extremities. However, both MRA and CA may be useful is some cases, such as:

a. A patient has had CA and this test was unable to identify a viable run-off vessel for bypass. When exploratory surgery is not believed to be a reasonable medical course of action for this patient, MRA may be performed to identify the viable runoff vessel.

b. A patient has had MRA, but the results are inconclusive.

C. Abdomen and Pelvis. -- Effective for dates of service on or after July 1, 1999, MRA is covered for pre-operative evaluation of patients undergoing elective abdominal aortic aneurysm (AAA) repair. Scientific evidence reveals MRA is considered comparable to CA in determining the extent of AAA, as well as evaluating aortoiliac occlusion disease and renal artery pathology that may be necessary in the surgical planning of AAA repair. These studies also reveal that MRA could provide a net benefit to the patient. If preoperative CA is avoided, then patients are not exposed to the risks associated with invasive procedures, contrast media, end-organ damage, or arterial injury.

Effective for dates of service on or after July 1, 2003, MRA coverage has been expanded to include imaging the renal arteries and the aortoiliac arteries in the absence of AAA or aortic dissection. MRA should be obtained in those circumstances in which using MRA is expected to avoid obtaining CA, when physician history, physical examination, and standard assessment tools provide insufficient information for patient management, and obtaining an MRA has a high probability of positively affecting

patient management. However, CA may be ordered after obtaining the results of an MRA in those rare instances where medical necessity is demonstrated.

D. Chest.--

1. Diagnosis of Pulmonary Embolism.--Current scientific data has shown that diagnostic pulmonary MRAs are improving due to recent developments such as faster imaging capabilities and gadolinium-enhancement. However, these advances in MRA are not significant enough to warrant replacement of pulmonary angiography in the diagnosis of pulmonary embolism for patients who have no contraindication to receiving intravenous iodinated contrast material. Patients who are allergic to iodinated contrast material face a high risk of developing complications if they undergo pulmonary angiography or computed tomography angiography. Therefore, Medicare will cover MRA of the chest for diagnosing a suspected pulmonary embolism when it is contraindicated for the patient to receive intravascular iodinated contrast material.

2. Evaluation of Thoracic Aortic Dissection and Aneurysm.--Studies have shown that MRA of the chest has a high level of diagnostic accuracy for pre-operative and post-operative evaluation of aortic dissection of aneurysm. Depending on the clinical presentation, MRA may be used as an alternative to other non-invasive imaging technologies, such as transesophageal echocardiography and CT. Generally, Medicare will provide coverage only for MRA or for CA when used as a diagnostic test. However, if both MRA and CA of the chest are used, the physician must demonstrate the medical need for performing these tests.

While the intent of this policy is to provide reimbursement for either MRA or CA, HCFA is also allowing flexibility for physicians to make appropriate decisions concerning the use of these tests based on the needs of individual patients. HCFA anticipates, however, low utilization of the combined use of MRA and CA. As a result, HCFA encourages contractors to monitor the use of these tests and, where indicated, requires evidence of the need to perform both MRA and CA.

Pub. 100-3, Section 220.4
Mammograms

A diagnostic mammography is a covered service if it is ordered by a doctor of medicine or osteopathy as defined in §1861(r)(1) of the Act.

Payment may not be made for screening mammography performed on a woman under age 35. Payment may be made for only one screening mammography performed on a woman over age 34, but under age 40. For an asymptomatic woman over age 39, payment may be made for a screening mammography performed after at least 11 months have passed following the month in which the last screening mammography was performed.

APPENDIX D

A radiological mammogram is a covered diagnostic test under the following conditions:

- A patient has distinct signs and symptoms for which a mammogram is indicated;
- A patient has a history of breast cancer; or
- A patient is asymptomatic but, on the basis of the patient's history and other factors the physician considers significant, the physician's judgment is that a mammogram is appropriate.

Use of mammograms in routine screening of (1) asymptomatic women aged 50 and over, and (2) asymptomatic women aged 40 or over whose mothers or sisters have had the disease, is considered medically appropriate, but would not be covered for Medicare purposes.

Pub. 100-3, Section 220.5
Ultrasound Diagnostic Procedures

Coverage.--Ultrasound diagnostic procedures utilizing low energy sound waves are being widely employed to determine the composition and contours of nearly all body tissues except bone and air-filled spaces. This technique permits noninvasive visualization of even the deepest structures in the body. The use of the ultrasound technique is sufficiently developed that it can be considered essential to good patient care in diagnosing a wide variety of conditions.

Ultrasound diagnostic procedures are listed below and are divided into two categories. Medicare coverage is extended to the procedures listed in Category I. Periodic claims review by the intermediary's medical consultants should be conducted to insure that the techniques are medically appropriate and the general indications specified in these categories are met.

Techniques in Category II are considered experimental and should not be covered at this time.

CATEGORY I (Clinically effective, usually part of initial patient evaluation, may be an adjunct to radiologic and nuclear medicine diagnostic technique).

Echoencephalography, (Diencephalic Midline) (A-Mode)

Echoencephalography, Complete (Diencephalic Midline and Ventricular Size)

Ocular and Orbital Echography (A-Mode)

Covered procedures include efforts to determine the suitability of aphakic patients for implantation of an artificial lens (pseudophakoi) following cataract surgery.

Ocular and Orbital Sonography (B-Mode)

Echocardiography, Pericardial Effusion (M-Mode)

Pericardiocentesis, by Ultrasonic Guidance

Echocardiography, Cardiac Valve(s) (M-Mode)

Echocardiography, Complete (M-Mode)

Echocardiography, limited (e.g., follow-up or limited study) (M-Mode)

Pleural Effusion Echography

Thoracentesis, by Ultrasonic Guidance

Abdominal Sonography, complete survey study (B-Scan)

Abdominal Sonography, limited (e.g., follow-up or limited study) (B-Scan)

Abdominal sonography is not synonymous with ultrasound examination of individual organs.

Renal Cyst Aspiration, by Ultrasonic Guidance

Renal Biopsy, by Ultrasonic Guidance

Pancreas Sonography (B-Scan)

Pancreatic sonography has proven effective in diagnosing pseudocysts.

Spleen Sonography (B-Scan)

Abdominal Aorta Echography (A-Mode)

Abdominal Aorta Sonography (B-Scan)

Retroperitoneal Sonography (B-Scan)

Retroperitoneal sonography does not include planning of fields for radiation therapy.

Urinary Bladder Sonography (B-Scan)

Urinary bladder sonography does not include staging of bladder tumors.

Pregnancy Diagnosis sonography (B-Scan)

Fetal Age Determination (Biparietal Diameter) Sonography (B-Scan)

Fetal Growth Rate Sonography (B-Scan)

Placenta Localization Sonography (B-Scan)

Pregnancy Sonography, Complete (B-Scan)

Molar Pregnancy Diagnosis Sonography (B-Scan)

Ectopic Pregnancy Diagnosis sonography (B-Scan)

Passive Testing (Antepartum Monitoring of Fetal Heart Rate In the Resting Fetus)

Intrauterine Contraceptive Device Sonography (B-Scan)

Pelvic Mass Diagnosis Sonography (B-Scan)

Amniocentesis, by Ultrasonic Guidance

Arterial Flow Study, Peripheral (Doppler)

Venous Flow Study, Peripheral (Doppler)

Arterial Aneurysm, Peripheral (B-Scan)

Radiation Therapy Planning Sonography (B-Scan)

Thyroid Echography (A-Mode)

Thyroid Sonography (B-Scan)

Breast Echography (A-Mode)

Breast Sonography (B-Scan)

Hepatic Sonography (B-Scan)

Gallbladder Sonography

Renal Sonography

Two-Dimensional Echocardiography (B-Mode)

CATEGORY II (Clinical reliability and efficacy not proven).

B-Scan for atherosclerotic narrowing of peripheral arteries.

Monitoring of cardiac output (Doppler)

NOTE:

In view of the rapid changes in the field of ultrasound diagnosis, uses for ultrasound diagnostic procedures other than those listed under Categories I and II should be carefully reviewed before payment. Medical justification may be required. When appropriate, new uses for ultrasound diagnostic procedures should be forwarded to the Bureau of Eligibility, Reimbursement and Coverage, HCFA, so that revisions may be made in the coverage policy when appropriate.

Pub. 100-3, Section 220.6
PET Scans

The following indications may be covered for PET under certain circumstances. Details of Medicare PET coverage are discussed later in this section. Unless otherwise indicated, the clinical conditions below are covered when PET utilizes FDG as a tracer.

NOTE: This manual section lists all Medicare-covered uses of PET scans. A particular use of PET scans is not covered unless this manual specifically provides that such use is covered. Although this section lists some non-covered uses of PET scans, it does not constitute an exhaustive list of all non-covered uses.

Clinical Condition	Effective Date	Coverage
Solitary Pulmonary Nodules (SPNs)	January 1, 1998	Characterization
Lung Cancer (Non Small Cell)	January 1, 1998	Initial staging
Lung Cancer (Non Small Cell)	July 1, 2001	Diagnosis, staging and restaging
Esophageal Cancer	July 1, 2001	Diagnosis, staging and restaging
Colorectal Cancer	July 1, 1999	Determining location of tumors if rising CEA level suggests recurrence
Colorectal Cancer	July 1, 2001	Diagnosis, staging and restaging
Lymphoma	July 1, 1999	Staging and restaging only when used as an alternative to Gallium scan
Lymphoma	July 1, 2001	Diagnosis, staging and restaging
Melanoma	July 1, 1999	Evaluating recurrence prior to surgery as an alternative to a Gallium scan
Melanoma	July 1, 2001	Diagnosis, staging and restaging; Non-covered for evaluating regional nodes
Breast Cancer	October 1, 2002	As an adjunct to standard imaging modalities for staging patients with distant metastasis or restaging patients with locoregional recurrence or metastasis; as an adjunct to standard imaging modalities for monitoring tumor response to treatment for women with locally advanced and metastatic breast cancer when a change in therapy is anticipated.
Head and Neck Cancers (excluding CNS and thyroid)	July 1, 2001	Diagnosis, staging and restaging
Thyroid Cancer	October 1, 2003	Restaging of recurrent or residual thyroid cancers of follicular cell origin that have been previously treated by thyroidectomy and radioiodine ablation and have a serum thyroglobulin >10ng/ml and negative I-131 whole body scan performed
Myocardial Viability	July 1, 2001 to September 30, 2002	Covered only following inconclusive SPECT
Myocardial Viability	October 1, 2001	Primary or initial diagnosis, or following an inconclusive SPECT prior to revascularization. SPECT may not be used following an inconclusive PET scan
Refractory Seizures	July 1, 2001	Covered for pre-surgical evaluation only

© 2005 Ingenix, Inc.

Perfusion of the heart using Rubidium 82* tracer	March 14, 1995	Covered for noninvasive imaging of the perfusion of the heart
Perfusion of the heart using ammonia N-13* tracer	October 1, 2003	Covered for noninvasive imaging of the perfusion of the heart

*Not FDG-PET.

EFFECTIVE JANUARY 28, 2005: This manual section lists Medicare-covered uses of PET scans effective for services performed on or after January 28, 2005. Except as set forth below in cancer indications listed as "covereage with evidence development", a particular use of PET scans is not covered unless this manual specifically provides that such use is covered. Although this section 220.6 lists some non-covered uses of PET scans, it does not constitute an exhaustive list of all non-covered uses.

For cancer indications listed as "coverage with evidence development" CMS determines that the evidence is sufficient to conclude that an FDG PET scan is reasonable and necessary only when the provider is participating in, and patients are enrolled in, one of the following types of prospective clinical studies that is designed to collect additional information at the time of the scan to assist in patient management:

- A cliinical trial of FDG PET that meets the requirements of Food and Drug Administration (FDA) category B investigational device exemption (42 CFR 405.201);
- An FDG PET clinical study that is designed to collect additional information at the time of the scan to assist in patient management. Qualifying clinical studies must ensure that specific hypotheses are addressed; appropriate data elements are collected; hospitals and providers are qualified to provide the PET scan and interpret the results; participating hospitals and providers accurately report data on all enrolled patients not included in other qualifying trials through adequate auditing mechanisms; and, all patient confidentiality, privacy, and other Federal laws must be followed.

Effective January 28, 2005: For PET services identified as "Coverage with Evidence Development. Medicare shall notify providers and beneficiaries where theses services can be accessed, as they become available, via the following:

- Federal Register Notice
- CMS coverage Web site at: www.cms.gov/coverage

Indication	Covered[1]	Nationally Non-Covered[2]	Coverage with Evidence Development[3]
Brain			X
Breast	X	X	
-Diagnosis	X	X	
-Initial staging of axillary nodes			
-Staging of distant metastasis			
-Restaging, monitoring*			
Cervical			
-Staging as adjunct to conventional imaging	X		X
-Other staging			X
-Diagnosis, restaging, monitoring*			
Colorectal			
-Diagnosis, staging, restaging	X		X
-Monitoring*			
Esophagus			
-Diagnosis, staging, restaging	X		X
-Monitoring*			
Head and Neck (non-CNS/thyroid			
-Diagnosis, staging, restaging	X		X
-Monitoring*			
Lymphoma			
-Diagnosis, staging, restaging	X		X
-Monitoring*			
Melanoma			
-Diagnosis, staging, restaging	X		X
-Monitoring*			
Non-small Cell Lung			
-Diagnosis, staging, restaging	X		X
-Monitoring*			
Ovarian			X
Pancreatic			X

Small Cell Lung			X
Soft Tissue Sarcoma			S
Solitary Pulmonary Nodule (characterization)	X		
Thyroid -Staging of follicular cell tumors -Restaging of medullary cell tumors -Diagnosis, other staging & restaging -Monitoring*	X		X X X
Testicular			X
All other cancers not listed herein (all indications)			X

[1] Covered nationally based on evidence of benefit. Refer to National Coverage Determination Manual Section 220.6 in its entirety for specific coverage language and limitations for each indication.

[2] Non-covered nationally based on evidence of harm or no benefit.

[3] Covered only in specific settings discussed above if certain patient safeguards are provided. Otherwise, non-covered nationally based on lack of evidence sufficient to establish either benefit or harm or no prior decision addressing this cancer. Medicare shall notify providers and beneficiaries where these services can be accessed, as they become available, via the following:

- Federal Register Notice

CMS coverage Web site at: www.cms.gov/coverage

*Monitoring = monitoring response to treatment when a change in therapy is anticipated.

II. General Conditions of Coverage for FDG PET

    A. Allowable FDG PET Systems
        1. Definitions: For purposes of this section,
            a. "Any FDA approved" means all systems approved or cleared for marketing by the FDA to image radionuclides in the body.
            b. "FDA approved" means that the system indicated has been approved or cleared for marketing by the FDA to image radionuclides in the body.

            c. "Certain coincidence systems" refers to the systems that have all the following features:
                  • Crystal at least 5/8-inch thick
                  • Techniques to minimize or correct for scatter and/or randoms, and
                  • Digital detectors and iterative reconstruction.
            Scans performed with gamma camera PET systems with crystals thinner than 5/8-inch will not be covered by Medicare. In addition, scans performed with systems with crystals greater than or equal to 5/8-inch in thickness, but that do not meet the other listed design characteristics are not covered by Medicare.
        2. Allowable PET systems by covered clinical indication:

	Allowable Type of FDG PET System		
Covered Clinical Condition	Prior to July 1, 2001	July 1, 2001 through December 31, 2001	On or after January 1, 2002
Characterization of single pulmonary nodules	Effective 1/1/1998, any FDA approved	Any FDA approved	FDA approved: Full ring Partial ring Certain coincidence systems
Initial staging of lung cancer (non small cell)	Effective 1/1/1998, any FDA approved	Any FDA approved	FDA approved: Full ring Partial ring Certain coincidence systems
Evaluating recurrence of melanoma prior to surgery as an alternative to a gallium scan	Effective 7/1/1999, any FDA approved.	Any FDA approved	FDA approved: Full ring Partial ring Certain coincidence systems
Diagnosis, staging, and restaging of colorectal cancer	Not covered by Medicare	Full ring	FDA approved: Full ring Partial ring
Diagnosis, staging, and restaging of esophageal cancer	Not covered by Medicare	Full ring	FDA approved: Full ring Partial ring

© 2005 Ingenix, Inc.

Diagnosis, staging, and restaging of head and neck cancers (excluding CNS and thyroid)	Not covered by Medicare	Full ring	FDA approved: Full ring Partial ring
Diagnosis, staging, and restaging of lung cancer (non small cell)	Not covered by Medicare	Full ring	FDA approved: Full ring Partial ring
Diagnosis, staging, and restaging of lymphoma	Not covered by Medicare	Full ring	FDA approved: Full ring Partial ring
Diagnosis, staging, and restaging of melanoma (noncovered for evaluating regional nodes)	Not covered by Medicare	Full ring	FDA approved: Full ring Partial ring
Determination of myocardial viability only following an inconclusive SPECT	Not covered by Medicare	Full ring	FDA approved: Full ring Partial ring
Presurgical evaluation of refractory seizures	Not covered by Medicare	Full ring	FDA approved: Full ring Partial ring
Breast Cancer	Not covered	Not covered	Effective October 1, 2002, full and partial ring
Thyroid Cancer	Not covered	Not covered	Effective October 1, 2003, full and partial ring
Myocardial Viability Primary or initial diagnosis prior to revascularization	Not covered	Not covered	Effective October 1, 2002, full and partial ring

B. Regardless of any other terms or conditions, all uses of FDG PET scans, in order to be covered by the Medicare program, must meet the following general conditions prior to June 30, 2001:
  1. Submission of claims for payment must include any information Medicare requires

to assure that the PET scans performed were: (a) medically necessary, (b) did not unnecessarily duplicate other covered diagnostic tests, and (c) did not involve investigational drugs or procedures using investigational drugs, as determined by the Food and Drug Administration (FDA).
  2. The PET scan entity submitting claims for payment must keep such patient records as Medicare requires on file for each patient for whom a PET scan claim is made.

C. Regardless of any other terms or conditions, all uses of FDG PET scans, in order to be covered by the Medicare program, must meet the following general conditions as of July 1, 2001:
  1. The provider of the PET scan should maintain on file the doctor's referral and documentation that the procedure involved only FDA approved drugs and devices, as is normal business practice.
  2. The ordering physician is responsible for documenting the medical necessity of the study and that it meets the conditions specified in the instructions. The physician should have documentation in the beneficiary's medical record to support the referral to the PET scan provider.

III. Covered Indications for PET Scans and Limitations/Requirements for Usage

For all uses of PET relating to malignancies the following conditions apply:

1. Diagnosis: PET is covered only in clinical situations in which the PET results may assist in avoiding an invasive diagnostic procedure, or in which the PET results may assist in determining the optimal anatomical location to perform an invasive diagnostic procedure. In general, for most solid tumors, a tissue diagnosis is made prior to the performance of PET scanning. PET scans following a tissue diagnosis are performed for the purpose of staging, not diagnosis. Therefore, the use of PET in the diagnosis of lymphoma, esophageal, and colorectal cancers as well as in melanoma should be rare. PET is not covered for other diagnostic uses, and is not covered for screening (testing of patients without specific signs and symptoms of disease).

2. Staging and or Restaging: PET is covered in clinical situations in which 1) (a) the stage of the cancer remains in doubt after completion of a standard diagnostic workup, including conventional imaging (computed tomography, magnetic resonance imaging, or ultrasound) or (b) the use of PET would also be considered reasonable and necessary if it could potentially replace one or more conventional imaging studies when it is expected that conventional study information is insufficient for the clinical management of the patient and 2) clinical management of the patient would differ depending on the stage of the cancer identified. PET will be covered for restaging

after the completion of treatment for the purpose of detecting residual disease, for detecting suspected recurrence or to determine the extent of a known recurrence. Use of PET would also be considered reasonable and necessary if it could potentially replace one or more conventional imaging studies when it is expected that conventional study information is insufficient for the clinical management of the patient.

3. <u>Monitoring</u>: Use of PET to monitor tumor response during the planned course of therapy (i.e. when no change in therapy is being contemplated) is <u>not covered</u> except for breast cancer. Restaging only occurs after a course of treatment is completed, and this is covered, subject to the conditions above.

NOTE: In the absence of national frequency limitations, contractors, should, if necessary, develop frequency requirements on any or all of the indications covered on and after July 1, 2001.

(This NCD last reviewed December 2004.)

Pub. 100-3, Section 220.7
Xenon Scan

Program payment may be made for this diagnostic procedure which involves perfusion lung imaging with 133 xenon. However, review for evidence of abuse which might include absence of reasonable indications, inappropriate sequence, or excessive number or kinds of procedures used in the care of individual patients.

Pub. 100-3, Section 220.8
Nuclear Radiology Procedure

Nuclear radiology procedures, including nuclear examinations performed with mobile radiological equipment, are covered if reasonable and necessary for the individual patient. Although these procedures may not be widely used, they are generally accepted. Review claims for these procedures for evidence of abuse which might absence of reasonable indications, inappropriate sequence, or excessive number or kinds of procedures used in the care of individual patients.

Pub. 100-3, Section 220.11
Thermography

Thermography for any indication (including breast lesions which were excluded from Medicare coverage on July 20, 1984) is excluded from Medicare coverage because the available evidence does not support this test as a useful aid in the diagnosis or treatment of illness or injury. Therefore, it is not considered effective. This exclusion was published as a HCFA Final Notice in the **Federal Register** on **November 20, 1992.**

Pub. 100-3, Section 220.12
Single Photon Emission Tomography - Covered

Frequency limitations: Contractor discretion.

In the case of myocardial viability, FDG PET may be used following a SPECT that was found to be inconclusive. However, SPECT may not be used following an inconclusive FDG PET performed to evaluate myocardial viability.

Pub. 100-3, Section 220.13
Percutaneous Image-Guided Breast Biopsy

The Breast Imaging Reporting and Data System (or BIRADS system) employed by the American College of Radiology provides a standardized lexicon with which radiologists may report their interpretation of a mammogram. The BIRADS grading of mammograms is as follows: Grade I-Negative, Grade II-Benign finding, Grade III-Probably benign, Grade IV-Suspicious abnormality, and Grade V-Highly suggestive of malignant neoplasm.

A. Nonpalpable Breast Lesions.--

Effective January 1, 2003, Medicare covers percutaneous image-guided breast biopsy using stereotactic or ultrasound imaging for a radiographic abnormality that is nonpalpable and is graded as a BIRADS III, IV, or V.

B. Palpable Breast Lesions.--

Effective January 1, 2003, Medicare covers percutaneous image guided breast biopsy using stereotactic or ultrasound imaging for palpable lesions that are difficult to biopsy using palpation alone. Contractors have the discretion to decide what types of palpable lesions are difficult to biopsy using palpation.

Pub. 100-3, Section 230.1
Treatment of Kidney Stones

In addition to the traditional surgical/endoscopic techniques for the treatment of kidney stones, the following lithotripsy techniques are also covered for services rendered on or after March 15, 1985.

A. Extracorporeal Shock Wave Lithotripsy.--Extracorporeal Shock Wave Lithotripsy (ESWL) is a non-invasive method of treating kidney stones using a device called a lithotriptor. The lithotriptor uses shock waves generated outside of the body to break up upper urinary tract stones. It focuses the shock waves specifically on stones under X-ray visualization, pulverizing them by repeated shocks. ESWL is covered under Medicare for use in the treatment of upper urinary tract kidney stones.

B. Percutaneous Lithotripsy.--Percutaneous lithotripsy (or nephrolithotomy) is an invasive method of treating kidney stones by using ultrasound, electrohydraulic or mechanical lithotripsy. A probe is inserted through an incision in the skin directly over the kidney and applied to the stone. A form of lithotripsy is then used to fragment the stone. Mechanical or electrohydraulic lithotripsy may be used as an alternative or adjunct to ultrasonic lithotripsy. Percutaneous lithotripsy of kidney stones by ultrasound or by the related techniques of electrohydraulic or mechanical lithotripsy is covered under Medicare.

The following is covered for services rendered on or after January 16, 1988.

C. Transurethral Ureteroscopic Lithotripsy.--Transurethral ureteroscopic lithotripsy is a method of fragmenting and removing ureteral

© 2005 Ingenix, Inc.

and renal stones through a cystoscope. The cystoscope is inserted through the urethra into the bladder. Catheters are passed through the scope into the opening where the ureters enter the bladder. Instruments passed through this opening into the ureters are used to manipulate and ultimately disintegrate stones, using either mechanical crushing, transcystoscopic electrohydraulic shock waves, ultrasound or laser. Transurethral ureteroscopic lithotripsy for the treatment of urinary tract stones of the kidney or ureter is covered under Medicare.

Pub. 100-3, Section 230.2
Uroflowmetric Evaluations

Uroflowmetric evaluations (also referred to as urodynamic voiding or urodynamic flow studies) are covered under Medicare for diagnosing various urological dysfunctions, including bladder outlet obstructions.

Pub. 100-3, Section 230.3
Sterilization

A. Covered Conditions.--
- Payment may be made only where sterilization is a necessary part of the treatment of an illness or injury, e.g., removal of a uterus because of a tumor, removal of diseased ovaries (bilateral oophorectomy), or bilateral orchidectomy in a case of cancer of the prostate. Deny claims when the pathological evidence of the necessity to perform any such procedures to treat an illness or injury is absent; and
- Sterilization of a mentally retarded beneficiary is covered if it is a necessary part of the treatment of an illness or injury. Monitor such surgeries closely and obtain the information needed to determine whether in fact the surgery was performed as a means of treating an illness or injury or only to achieve sterilization.

B. NonCovered Conditions.--
- Elective hysterectomy, tubal ligation, and vasectomy, if the stated reason for these procedures is sterilization;
- A sterilization that is performed because a physician believes another pregnancy would endanger the overall general health of the woman is not considered to be reasonable and necessary for the diagnosis or treatment of illness or injury within the meaning of §1862(a)(1) of the law. The same conclusion would apply where the sterilization is performed only as a measure to prevent the possible development of, or effect on, a mental condition should the individual become pregnant; and
- Sterilization of a mentally retarded person where the purpose is to prevent conception, rather than the treatment of an illness or injury.

Pub. 100-3, Section 230.4

Diagnosis and Treatment of Impotence

Program payment may be made for diagnosis and treatment of sexual impotence. Since causes and, therefore, appropriate treatment vary, if abuse is suspected it may be necessary to request documentation of appropriateness in individual cases. If treatment is furnished to patients (other than hospital inpatients) in connection with a mental condition, apply the psychiatric service limitation described in the Medicare General Information, Eligibility, and Entitlement Manual, Chapter 3.

Pub. 100-3, Section 230.6
Vabra Aspirator

Program payment cannot be made for the aspirator or the related diagnostic services when furnished in connection with the examination of an asymptomatic patient. Payment for routine physical checkups is precluded under the statute (§1862(a)(7) of the Act).

Pub. 100-3, Section 230.9
Cryosurgery of Prostate

Cryosurgery of the prostate as a salvage therapy is not covered for any services performed prior to June 30, 2001.

Salvage cryosurgery of the prostate for recurrent cancer is medically necessary and appropriate only for those patients with localized disease who:

a. Have failed a trial of radiation therapy as their primary treatment; and
b. Meet one of the following conditions: Stage T2B or below, Gleason score < 9, PSA < 8 ng/mL.

Cryosurgery as salvage therapy is therefore not covered under Medicare after failure of other therapies as the primary treatment. Cryosurgery as salvage is only covered after the failure of a trial of radiation therapy, under the conditions noted above.

Pub. 100-3, Section 230.10
Incontinence Control Devices

A. Mechanical/Hydraulic Incontinence Control Devices.--Mechanical/hydraulic incontinence control devices are accepted as safe and effective in the management of urinary incontinence in patients with permanent anatomic and neurologic dysfunctions of the bladder. This class of devices achieves control of urination by compression of the urethra. The materials used and the success rate may vary somewhat from device to device. Such a device is covered when its use is reasonable and necessary for the individual patient.

B. Collagen Implant.--A collagen implant, which is injected into the submucosal tissues of the urethra and/or the bladder neck and into tissues adjacent to the urethra, is a prosthetic device used in the treatment of stress urinary incontinence resulting from intrinsic sphincter deficiency (ISD). ISD is a cause of stress urinary incontinence in which the urethral sphincter is unable to contract and generate sufficient resistance in the bladder, especially during stress maneuvers.

Appendixes

Prior to collagen implant therapy, a skin test for collagen sensitivity must be administered and evaluated over a 4 week period.

In male patients, the evaluation must include a complete history and physical examination and a simple cystometrogram to determine that the bladder fills and stores properly. The patient then is asked to stand upright with a full bladder and to cough or otherwise exert abdominal pressure on his bladder. If the patient leaks, the diagnosis of ISD is established.

In female patients, the evaluation must include a complete history and physical examination (including a pelvic exam) and a simple cystometrogram to rule out abnormalities of bladder compliance and abnormalities of urethral support. Following that determination, an abdominal leak point pressure (ALLP) test is performed. Leak point pressure, stated in cm H2O, is defined as the intra-abdominal pressure at which leakage occurs from the bladder (around a catheter) when the bladder has been filled with a minimum of 150 cc fluid. If the patient has an ALLP of less than 100 cm H2O, the diagnosis of ISD is established.

To use a collagen implant, physicians must have urology training in the use of a cystoscope and must complete a collagen implant training program.

Coverage of a collagen implant, and the procedure to inject it, is limited to the following types of patients with stress urinary incontinence due to ISD:

- Male or female patients with congenital sphincter weakness secondary to conditions such as myelomeningocele or epispadias;
- Male or female patients with acquired sphincter weakness secondary to spinal cord lesions;
- Male patients following trauma, including prostatectomy and/or radiation; and
- Female patients without urethral hypermobility and with abdominal leak point pressures of 100 cm H2O or less.

Patients whose incontinence does not improve with 5 injection procedures (5 separate treatment sessions) are considered treatment failures, and no further treatment of urinary incontinence by collagen implant is covered. Patients who have a reoccurrence of incontinence following successful treatment with collagen implants in the past (e.g., 6-12 months previously) may benefit from additional treatment sessions. Coverage of additional sessions may be allowed but must be supported by medical justification.

C. Non-Implantable Pelvic Floor Electrical Stimulator.--(See §60-24.)

Pub. 100-3, Section 230.12
Dimethyl Sulfoxide (DMSO)

The Food and Drug Administration has determined that the only purpose for which DMSO is safe and effective for humans is in the treatment of the bladder condition, interstitial cystitis. Therefore, the use of DMSO for all other indications is not considered to be reasonable and necessary. Payment may be made for its use only when reasonable and necessary for a patient in the treatment of interstitial cystitis.

Pub. 100-3, Section 230.14

Ultrafiltration Monitor

Covered:

Ultrafiltration and ultrafiltration monitoring as a component of hemodialysis has an established and critical role in maintaining the well-being of ESRD patients and is a covered service. The Ultrafiltration Monitor is covered under the Medicare program when it is used to calculate fluid rates for those recipients who present difficult fluid management problems. Determine the medical necessity of this device on a case-by-case basis.

Not Covered:

Ultrafiltration, independent of conventional dialysis, is considered experimental, and technology exclusively designed for this purpose is not covered under Medicare.

Pub. 100-3, Section 240.1
Lung Volume Reduction Surgery (Reduction Pneumoplasty)

A. Covered Indications

Medicare-covered LVRS approaches are limited to bilateral excision of a damaged lung with stapling performed via median sternotomy or video-assisted thoracoscopic surgery.

1. National Emphysema Treatment Trial (NETT) participants (effective for services performed on or after August 11, 1997):

    Medicare provides coverage to those beneficiaries who are participating in the NETT trial for all services integral to the study and for which the Medicare statute does not prohibit coverage.

2. Medicare will only consider LVRS reasonable and necessary when all of the following requirements are met (effective for services performed on or after January 1, 2004):

    a. The patient satisfies all the criteria outlined below:

Assessment	Criteria
History and physical examination	Consistent with emphysema
	BMI, $<= 31.1$ kg/m^2 (men) or $<= 32.3$ kg/m^2 (women)
	Stable with $<=20$ mg prednisone (or equivalent) qd
Radiographic	High Resolution Computer Tomography (HRCT) scan evidence of bilateral emphysema
Pulmonary function (pre-rehabilitation)	Forced expiratory volume in one second (FEV$_1$) $<=$ 45% predicted ($>= 15$% predicted if age $>=70$ years)
	Total lung capacity (TLC) $>=100$% predicted post-bronchodilator

	Residual volume (RV) >=150% predicted post-bronchodilator
Arterial blood gas level (pre-rehabilitation)	PCO_2, <= 60 mm Hg (PCO_2, <= 55 mm Hg if 1-mile above sea level)
	PO_2, >= 45 mm Hg on room air (PO_2, >= 30 mm Hg if 1-mile above sea level)
Cardiac assessment	Approval for surgery by cardiologist if any of the following are present: Unstable angina; left-ventricular ejection fraction (LVEF) cannot be estimated from the echocardiogram; LVEF < 45%; dobutamine-radionuclide cardiac scan indicates coronary artery disease or ventricular dysfunction; arrhythmia (> 5 premature ventricular contractions per minute; cardiac rhythm other than sinus; premature ventricular contractions on EKG at rest)
Surgical assessment	Approval for surgery by pulmonary physician, thoracic surgeon, and anesthesiologist post-rehabilitation
Exercise	Post-rehabilitation 6-min walk of >=140 m; able to complete 3 min unloaded pedaling in exercise tolerance test (pre- and post-rehabilitation)
Consent	Signed consents for screening and rehabilitation
Smoking	Plasma cotinine level <= 13.7 ng/mL (or arterial carboxyhemoglobin <= 2.5% if using nicotine products)
	Nonsmoking for 4 months prior to initial interview and throughout evaluation for surgery
Preoperative diagnostic and therapeutic program adherence	Must complete assessment for and program of preoperative services in preparation for surgery

b. In addition, the patient must have:

- Severe upper lobe predominant emphysema (as defined by radiologist assessment of upper lobe predominance on CT scan), **or**
- Severe non-upper lobe emphysema with low exercise capacity.

Patients with low exercise capacity are those whose maximal exercise capacity is at or below 25 watts for women and 40 watts (w) for men after completion of the preoperative therapeutic program in preparation for LVRS. Exercise capacity is measured by incremental, maximal, symptom-limited exercise with a cycle ergometer utilizing 5 or 10 watt/minute ramp on 30% oxygen after 3 minutes of unloaded pedaling.

c. The surgery must be performed at facilities that were identified by the National Heart, Lung, and Blood Institute to meet the thresholds for participation in the NETT, **and** at sites that have been approved by Medicare as lung transplant facilities. These facilities are listed on our Web site at www.cms.hhs.gov/coverage/lvrsfacility.pdf. The CMS is currently working to develop accreditation standards for facilities to perform LVRS and when implemented, will consider LVRS to be reasonable and necessary only at accredited facilities.

d. The surgery must be preceded and followed by a program of diagnostic and therapeutic services consistent with those provided in the NETT and designed to maximize the patient's potential to successfully undergo and recover from surgery. The program must include a 6- to 10-week series of at least 16, and no more than 20, preoperative sessions, each lasting a minimum of 2 hours. It must also include at least 6, and no more than 10, postoperative sessions, each lasting a minimum of 2 hours, within 8 to 9 weeks of the LVRS. This program must be consistent with the care plan developed by the treating physician following performance of a comprehensive evaluation of the patient's medical, psychosocial and nutritional needs, be consistent with the preoperative and postoperative services provided in the NETT, and arranged, monitored, and performed under the coordination of the facility where the surgery takes place.

B. **Noncovered Indications**

1. LVRS is not covered in **any** of the following clinical circumstances:

a. Patient characteristics carry a high risk for perioperative morbidity and/or mortality;
b. The disease is unsuitable for LVRS;
c. Medical conditions or other circumstances make it likely that the patient will be unable to complete the preoperative and postoperative pulmonary diagnostic and therapeutic program required for surgery;
d. The patient presents with FEVō <20% of predicted value, and either homogeneous distribution of emphysema on CT scan, **or** carbon monoxide diffusing capacity of < 20% of predicted value (high-risk group identified October 2001 by the NETT); or

e. The patient satisfies the criteria outlined above in section 2(a), and has severe, non-upper lobe emphysema with high exercise capacity. High exercise capacity is defined as a maximal workload at the completion of the preoperative diagnostic and therapeutic program that is above 25 w for women and 40 w for men (under the measurement conditions for cycle ergometry specified above).

2. All other indications for LVRS not otherwise specified remain noncovered.

Pub. 100-3, Section 240.3
Heat Treatment, including the Use of Diathermy and Ultrasound for Pulmonary Conditions

There is no physiological rationale or valid scientific documentation of effectiveness of diathermy or ultrasound heat treatments for asthma, bronchitis, or any other pulmonary condition and for such purpose this treatment cannot be considered reasonable and necessary within the meaning of section 1862(a)(1) of the Act.

Pub. 100-3, Section 240.6
Transvenous (Catheter) Pulmonary Embolectomy

Transvenous (catheter) pulmonary embolectomy is a procedure for removing pulmonary emboli by passing a catheter through the femoral vein. It is not covered under Medicare because it is still experimental.

Pub. 100-3, Section 240.7
Postural Drainage Procedures and Pulmonary Exercises

In most cases, postural drainage procedures and pulmonary exercises can be carried out safely and effectively by nursing personnel. However, in some cases patients may have acute or severe pulmonary conditions involving complex situations in which these procedures or exercises require the knowledge and skills of a physical therapist or a respiratory therapist. Therefore, if the attending physician determines as part of his/her plan of treatment that for the safe and effective administration of such services the procedures or exercises in question need to be performed by a physical therapist, the services of such a therapist constitute covered physical therapy when provided as an inpatient hospital service, extended care service, home health service, or outpatient physical therapy service.

NOTE: Physical therapy furnished in the outpatient department of a hospital is covered under the outpatient physical therapy benefit.

If the attending physician determines that the services should be performed by a respiratory therapist, the services of such a therapist constitute covered respiratory therapy when provided as an inpatient hospital service, outpatient hospital service, or extended care service, assuming that such services are furnished to the skilled nursing facility by a hospital with which the facility has a transfer agreement. Since the services of a respiratory therapist are not covered under the home health benefit, payment may not be made under the home health benefit for visits by a respiratory therapist to a patient's home to provide such services. Postural drainage procedures and pulmonary exercises are also covered when furnished by a physical therapist or a respiratory therapist as incident to a physician's professional service.

Pub. 100-3, Section 250.1
Treatment of Psoriasis

Psoriasis is a chronic skin disease, for which several conventional methods of treatment have been recognized as covered. These include topical application of steroids or other drugs; ultraviolet light (actinotherapy); and coal tar alone or in combination with ultraviolet B light (Goeckerman treatment).

A newer treatment for psoriasis uses a psoralen derivative drug in combination with ultraviolet A light, known as PUVA. PUVA therapy is covered for treatment of intractable, disabling psoriasis, but only after the psoriasis has not responded to more conventional treatment. The contractor should document this before paying for PUVA therapy.

In addition, reimbursement for PUVA therapy should be limited to amounts paid for other types of photochemotherapy; ordinarily, payment should not be allowed for more than 30 days of treatment, unless improvement is documented.

Pub. 100-3, Section 250.3
Intravenous Immune Globulin for the Treatment of Autoimmune Mucocutaneous Blistering Diseases

Effective October 1, 2002, IVIg is covered for the treatment of biopsy-proven (1) Pemphigus Vulgaris, (2) Pemphigus Foliaceus, (3) Bullous Pemphigoid, (4) Mucous Membrane Pemphigoid (a.k.a., Cicatricial Pemphigoid), and (5) Epidermolysis Bullosa Acquisita for the following patient subpopulations:

1. Patients who have failed conventional therapy. Contractors have the discretion to define what constitutes failure of conventional therapy;
2. Patients in whom conventional therapy is otherwise contraindicated. Contractors have the discretion to define what constitutes contraindications to conventional therapy; or
3. Patients with rapidly progressive disease in whom a clinical response could not be affected quickly enough using conventional agents. In such situations IVIg therapy would be given along with conventional treatment(s) and the IVIg would be used only until the conventional therapy could take effect.

In addition, IVIg for the treatment of autoimmune mucocutaneous blistering diseases must be used only for short-term therapy and not as a maintenance therapy. Contractors have the discretion to decide what constitutes short-term therapy.

Pub. 100-3, Section 250.4
Treatment of Actinic Keratosis

Medicare covers the destruction of actinic keratoses without restrictions based on lesion or patient characteristics.

Pub. 100-3, Section 260.1
Adult Liver Transplantation

A. General

Effective July 15, 1996, adult liver transplantation when performed on beneficiaries with end stage liver disease other than hepatitis B or malignancies is covered under

Medicare when performed in a facility which is approved by CMS as meeting institutional coverage criteria.

Effective December 10, 1999, adult liver transplantation when performed on beneficiaries with end stage liver disease other than malignancies is covered under Medicare when performed in a facility which is approved by CMS as meeting institutional coverage criteria.

Effective September 1, 2001, Medicare covers adult liver transplantation for hepatocellular carcinoma when the following conditions are met:

1. The patient is not a candidate for subtotal liver resection;
2. The patient's tumor(s) is less than or equal to 5 cm in diameter;
3. There is no macrovascular involvement;
4. There is no identifiable extrahepatic spread of tumor to surrounding lymph nodes, lungs, abdominal organs or bone; and
5. The transplant is furnished in a facility which is approved by CMS as meeting institutional coverage criteria for liver transplants (See 65 FR 15006).

Adult liver transplantation for other malignancies remains excluded from coverage.

Coverage of adult liver transplantation is effective as of the date of the facility's approval, but for applications received before July 13, 1991, can be effective as early as March 8, 1990. (See *Federal Register* 56 FR 15006 dated April 12, 1991.)

B. Follow-up Care

Follow-up care or retransplantation (ICD-9-M 996.82, Complications of Transplanted Organ, Liver required as a result of a covered liver transplant is covered, provided such services are otherwise reasonable and necessary. Follow-up care is also covered for patients who have been discharged from a hospital after receiving noncoverd liver transplant. Coverage for follow-up care is for items and services that are reasonable and necessary as determined by Medicare guidelines. (See Intermediary Manual, §3101.14 and Carriers Manual, §2300.1.)

C. Immunosuppressive Drugs.--See Intermediary Manual, §3600.8 and Carriers Manual; §§2050.5, 4471, and 5249.

Pub. 100-3, Section 260.2
Pediatric Liver Transplantation

Effective for services performed on or after February 9, 1984, liver transplantation is covered for children (under age 18) with extrahepatic biliary atresia or any other form of end stage liver disease, except that coverage is not provided for children with a malignancy extending beyond the margins of the liver or those with persistent viremia.

Effective for services performed on or after April 12, 1991, liver transplantation is covered for Medicare beneficiaries when performed in a pediatric hospital that performs pediatric liver transplants if the hospital submits an application which CMS approves documenting that:

- The hospital's pediatric liver transplant program is operated jointly by the hospital and another facility that has been found by CMS to meet the institutional coverage criteria in the *Federal Register* notice of April 12, 1991;

- The unified program shares the same transplant surgeons and quality assurance program (including oversight committee, patient protocol, and patient selection criteria); and
- The hospital is able to provide the specialized facilities, services, and personnel that are required by pediatric liver transplant patients.

Pub. 100-3, Section 260.3
Pancreas Transplants

B. National Covered Indications

CMS determines that whole organ pancreas transplantation will be nationally covered by Medicare only when performed siumltaneous with or after a kidney transplant. If the pancreas transplant occurs after the kidney transplant, immunosuppressive therapy will begin with the date of discharge from the inpatient stay for the pancrease transplant.

C. Nationally Noncovered Indications

CMS determines that the following procedures are not considered reasonable and necessary within the meaning of section 1862(a)(1)(A) of the Social Security Act:

1. Pancreas transplantation for diabetic patients who have not experienced end stage renal failure secondary to diabetes.

2. Transplantation of partial pancreatic tissue or islet cells (except in the context of a clinical trial (see section 260.3.1 of the NCD Manual)).

D. Other

Not applicable

(This NCD last reviewed July 2004.)

Pub. 100-3, Section 260.5
Intestinal and Multi-Visceral Transplantation

Medicare covers intestinal and multi-visceral transplantation for the purpose of restoring intestinal function in patients with irreversible intestinal failure. Intestinal failure is defined as the loss of absorptive capacity of the small bowel secondary to severe primary gastrointestinal disease or surgically induced short bowel syndrome. It may be associated with both mortality and profound morbidity. Multi-visceral transplantation includes organs in the digestive system (stomach, duodenum, pancreas, liver and intestine).

The evidence supports the fact that aged patients generally do not survive as well as younger patients receiving intestinal transplantation. Nonetheless, some older patients who are free from other contraindications have received the procedure and are progressing well, as evidenced by the United Network for Organ Sharing (UNOS) data. Thus, it is not appropriate to include specific exclusions from coverage, such as an age limitation, in the national coverage policy.

This procedure is covered **only** when performed for patients who have failed total parenteral nutrition (TPN) and only when performed in centers that meet approval criteria.

Failed TPN

TPN delivers nutrients intravenously, avoiding the need for absorption through the small bowel. TPN failure includes the following:

- Impending or overt liver failure due to TPN induced liver injury. The clinical manifestations include elevated serum bilirubin and/or liver enzymes, splenomegaly, thrombocytopenia, gastroesophageal varices, coagulopathy, stomal bleeding or hepatic fibrosis/cirrhosis.
- Thrombosis of the major central venous channels; jugular, subclavian, and femoral veins. Thrombosis of two or more of these vessels is considered a life threatening complication and failure of TPN therapy. The sequelae of central venous thrombosis are lack of access for TPN infusion, fatal sepsis due to infected thrombi, pulmonary embolism, Superior Vena Cava syndrome, or chronic venous insufficiency.
- Frequent line infection and sepsis. The development of two or more episodes of systemic sepsis secondary to line infection per year that requires hospitalization indicates failure of TPN therapy. A single episode of line related fungemia, septic shock and/or Acute Respiratory Distress Syndrome are considered indicators of TPN failure.
- Frequent episodes of severe dehydration despite intravenous fluid supplement in addition to TPN. Under certain medical conditions such as secretory diarrhea and non-constructable gastrointestinal tract, the loss of the gastrointestinal and pancreatobiliary secretions exceeds the maximum intravenous infusion rates that can be tolerated by the cardiopulmonary system. Frequent episodes of dehydration are deleterious to all body organs particularly kidneys and the central nervous system with the development of multiple kidney stones, renal failure, and permanent brain damage.

Approved Transplant Facilities

Intestinal transplantation is covered by Medicare if performed in an approved facility. The criteria for approval of centers will be based on a volume of 10 intestinal transplants per year with a 1-year actuarial survival of 65 percent using the Kaplan-Meier technique. More specific criteria can be found at:
http://www.cms.hhs.gov/providers/transplant/default.asp.

Pub. 100-3, Section 260.6
Dental Examination Prior to Kidney Transplantation

Despite the "dental services exclusion" in §1862(a)(12) of the Act (see the Medicare Benefit Policy Manual, Chapter 16, "General Exclusions from Coverage" §140), an oral or dental examination performed on an inpatient basis as part of a comprehensive workup prior to renal transplant surgery is a covered service. This is because the purpose of the examination is not for the care of the teeth or structures directly supporting the teeth. Rather, the examination is for the identification, prior to a complex surgical procedure, of existing medical problems where the increased possibility of infection would not only reduce the chances for successful surgery but would also expose the patient to additional risks in undergoing such surgery.

Such a dental or oral examination would be covered under Part A of the program if performed by a dentist on the hospital's staff, or under Part B if performed by a physician. (When performing a dental or oral examination, a dentist is not recognized as a physician under §1861(r) of the law.)(See the Mediacre Geneal Information, Eligibility and Entitlement Manual, Chapter 15, "Covered Medical and Other Health Services," §150)

Pub. 100-3, Section 260.7
Lymphocyte Immune Globulin, Anti-Thymocyte Globulin (Equine)

The FDA has approved one lymphocyte immune globulin preparation for marketing, lymphocyte immune globulin, anti-thymocyte globulin (equine). This drug is indicated for the management of allograft rejection episodes in renal transplantation. It is covered under Medicare when used for this purpose. Other forms of lymphocyte globulin preparation which the FDA approves for this indication in the future may be covered under Medicare.

Pub. 100-3, Section 260.9
Heart Transplants

A. General.--Cardiac transplantation is covered under Medicare when performed in a facility which is approved by Medicare as meeting institutional coverage criteria. (See HCFA Ruling 87-1.)

B. Exceptions.--In certain limited cases, exceptions to the criteria may be warranted if there is justification and if the facility ensures our objectives of safety and efficacy. Under no circumstances will exceptions be made for facilities whose transplant programs have been in existence for less than two years, and applications from consortia will not be approved.

Although consortium arrangements will not be approved for payment of Medicare transplants, consideration will be given to applications from heart transplant facilities that consist of more than one hospital where all of the following conditions exist:

- The hospitals are under the common control or have a formal affiliation arrangement with each other under the auspices of an organization such as a university or a legally-constituted medical research institute; and
- The hospitals share resources by routinely using the same personnel or services in their transplant programs. The sharing of resources must be supported by the submission of operative notes or other information that documents the routine use of the same personnel and services in all of the individual hospitals. At a minimum, shared resources means:
  - The individual members of the transplant team, consisting of the cardiac transplant surgeons, cardiologists and pathologists, must practice in all the hospitals and it can be documented that they otherwise function as members of the transplant team; and
  - The same organ procurement organization, immunology, and tissue-typing services must be used by all the hospitals; and
- The hospitals submit, in the manner required (Kaplan-Meier method) their

individual and pooled experience and survival data; and

- The hospitals otherwise meet the remaining Medicare criteria for heart transplant facilities; that is, the criteria regarding patient selection, patient management, program commitment, etc.

C. Pediatric Hospitals.--Cardiac transplantation is covered for Medicare beneficiaries when performed in a pediatric hospital that performs pediatric heart transplants if the hospital submits an application which HCFA approves as documenting that:

- The hospital's pediatric heart transplant program is operated jointly by the hospital and another facility that has been found by HCFA to meet the institutional coverage criteria in HCFA Ruling 87-1;
- The unified program shares the same transplant surgeons and quality assurance program (including oversight committee, patient protocol, and patient selection criteria); and
- The hospital is able to provide the specialized facilities, services, and personnel that are required by pediatric heart transplant patients.

D. Follow-up Care.--

Follow-up care required as a result of a covered heart transplant is covered, provided such services are otherwise reasonable and necessary. Follow-up care is also covered for patients who have been discharged from a hospital after receiving a noncovered heart transplant. Coverage for follow-up care would be for items and services that are reasonable and necessary, as determined by Medicare guidelines. (See Medicare Benefit Policy Manual, chapter 16, "General Exclusions from Coverage," §180.)

E. Immunosuppressive Drugs.

See the Medicare Claims Processing Manual, Chapter 17, "Drugs and Biologicals," §80.3.1, and Chapter 8, "Outpatient ESRD Hospital, Independent Facility, and Physician/Supplier Claims," §120.1.

F. Artificial Hearts

Medicare does not cover the use of artificial hearts as a permanent replacement for a human heart or as a temporary life-support system until a human heart becomes available for transplant (often referred to as a "bridge to transplant"). Medicare does cover a ventricular assist device (VAD) when used in conjunction with specific criteria listed in §20.9 of the NCD Manual..

Pub. 100-3, Section 270.1
Electrical Stimulation (ES) and Electromagnetic Therapy for the Treatment of Wounds

A. *Nationally Covered Indications*

The use of ES and electromagnetic therapy for the treatment of wounds are considered adjunctive therapies, and will only be covered for chronic Stage III or Stage IV pressure ulcers, arterial ulcers, diabetic ulcers, and venous stasis ulcers. Chronic ulcers are defined as ulcers that have not

healed within 30 days of occurrence. ES or electromagnetic therapy will be covered only after appropriate standard wound therapy has been tried for at least 30 days and there are no measurable signs of improved healing. This 30-day period may begin while the wound is acute.

Standard wound care includes: optimization of nutritional status, debridement by any means to remove devitalized tissue, maintenance of a clean, moist bed of granulation tissue with appropriate moist dressings, and necessary treatment to resolve any infection that may be present. Standard wound care based on the specific type of wound includes: frequent repositioning of a patient with pressure ulcers (usually every 2 hours), offloading of pressure and good glucose control for diabetic ulcers, establishment of adequate circulation for arterial ulcers, and the use of a compression system for patients with venous ulcers.

Measurable signs of improved healing include: a decrease in wound size (either surface area or volume), decrease in amount of exudates, and decrease in amount of necrotic tissue. ES or electromagnetic therapy must be discontinued when the wound demonstrates 100% epitheliliazed wound bed.

ES and electromagnetic therapy services can only be covered when performed by a physician, physical therapist, or incident to a physician service. Evaluation of the wound is an integral part of wound therapy. When a physician, physical therapist, or a clinician incident to a physician, performs ES or electromagnetic therapy, the practitioner must evaluate the wound and contact the treating physician if the wound worsens. If ES or electromagnetic therapy is being used, wounds must be evaluated at least monthly by the treating physician.

B. *Nationally Noncovered Indications*

1. ES and electromagnetic therapy will not be covered as an initial treatment modality.

2. Continued treatment with ES or electromagnetic therapy is not covered if measurable signs of healing have not been demonstrated within any 30-day period of treatment.

3. Unsupervised use of ES or electromagnetic therapy for wound therapy will not be covered, as this use has not been found to be medically reasonable and necessary.

C. *Other*

All other uses of ES and electromagnetic therapy not otherwise specified for the treatment of wounds remain at local contractor discretion.

(This NCD last reviewed March 2004.)

Pub. 100-3, Section 270.2
Noncontact Normothermic Wound Therapy (NNWT)

There is insufficient scientific or clinical evidence to consider this device as reasonable and necessary for the treatment of wounds within the meaning of §1862(a)(1)(A) of the Social Security Act and will not be covered by Medicare.

Pub. 100-3, Section 270.4
Treatment of Decubitus Ulcers

An accepted procedure for healing decubitus ulcers is to remove dead tissue from the lesions and to keep them clean to promote the growth of new tissue. This may be accomplished by hydrotherapy (whirlpool) treatments. Hydrotherapy (whirlpool) treatment for decubitus ulcers is a covered service under Medicare for patients when treatment is reasonable and necessary. Some other methods of treating decubitus ulcers, the safety and effectiveness of which have not been established, are not covered under the Medicare program. Some examples of these types of treatments are: ultraviolet light, low intensity direct current, topical application of oxygen, and topical dressings with Balsam of Peru in castor oil.

Pub. 100-3, Section 270.5
Porcine Skin and Gradient Pressure Dressings

Porcine (pig) skin dressings are covered, if reasonable and necessary for the individual patient as an occlusive dressing for burns, donor sites of a homograft, and decubiti and other ulcers.

Gradient pressure dressings are Jobst elasticized heavy duty dressings used to reduce hypertrophic scarring and joint contractures following burn injury. They are covered when used for that purpose.

Pub. 100-3, Section 280.13
Transcutaneous Electrical Nerve Stimulators (TENS)

Payment for TENS may be made under the durable medical equipment benefit. (See §45-25 for an explanation of coverage of medically necessary supplies for the effective use of TENS and §45-19 for an explanation of coverage of TENS for acute post-operative pain.)

Pub. 100-3, Section 280.14
Infusion Pumps

B. Nationally Covered Indications

THE FOLLOWING INDICATIONS FOR TREATMENT USING INFUSION PUMPS ARE COVERED UNDER MEDICARE:

1. External Infusion Pumps.--

a. Iron Poisoning (Effective for Services Performed On or After September 26, 1984).--When used in the administration of deferoxamine for the treatment of acute iron poisoning and iron overload, only external infusion pumps are covered.

b. Thromboembolic Disease (Effective for Services Performed On or After September 26, 1984).--When used in the administration of heparin for the treatment of thromboembolic disease and/or pulmonary embolism, only external infusion pumps used in an institutional setting are covered.

c. Chemotherapy for Liver Cancer (Effective for Services Performed On or After January 29, 1985).--The external chemotherapy infusion pump is covered when used in the treatment of primary hepatocellular carcinoma or colorectal cancer where this disease is unresectable or where the patient refuses surgical excision of the tumor.

d. Morphine for Intractable Cancer Pain (Effective for Services Performed On or After April 22, 1985).--Morphine infusion via an external infusion pump is covered when used in the treatment of intractable pain caused by cancer (in either an inpatient or outpatient setting, including a hospice).

e. Continuous subcutaneous Insulin Infusion (CSII) Pumps (Effective for Services Performed On or After December 17, 2004)

Continuous subcutaneous insuline infusion (CSII) and related drugs/supplies are covered as medically reasonable and necessary in the home setting for the treatment of diabetic patients who: (1) either meet the updated fasting C-Peptide

testing requirement, or, are beta cell autoantibody podsitive; and, (2) satisfy the remaining criteria for insulin pump therapy as described below. Patients must meet either Criterion A or B as follows:

Criterion A: The patient has completed a comprehensive diabetes education program, and has been on a program of multiple daily injections of insulin (i.e. at least 3 injections per day), with frequent self-adjustments of insulin dose for at least 6 months prior to initiation of the insulin pump, and has documented frequency of glucose self-testing an average of at least 4 times per day during the 2 months prior to initiation of the insulin pump, and meets one or more of the following criteria while on the multiple daily injection regimen:

- Glycosylated hemoglobin level (HbAlc) > 7.0 percent
- History of recurring hypoglycemia
- Wide fluctuations in blood glucose before mealtime
- Dawn phenomenon with fasting blood sugars frequently exceeding 200 mg/dl
- History of severe glycemic excursions

Criterion B The patient with diabetes has been on a pump prior to enrollment in Medicare and has documented frequency of glucose self-testing an average of at least 4 times per day during the month prior to Medicare enrollment.

General CSII Criteria

In addition to meeting Criterion A or B above, the following general requirements must be met:

The patient with diabetes must be insulinopenic per the updated fasting C-peptide testing requirement, or, as an alternative, must be beta cell autoantibody positive.

Update fasting C-peptide testing requirment:

- Insuliopenia is defined as a fasting C-peptide level that is less than or equal to 110% of the lower limit of normal of the laboratory's measurement method.
- For patients with renal insufficiency and creatinine clearance (actual or calculated from age, gender, weight, and serum creatinine) <50 ml/minue, insulinopenia is defined as a fasting C-peptide level that is less than or equal to 200% of the lower limit of normal of the laboratory's measurement method.
- Fasting C-peptide levels will only be considered valid with a concurrently obtained fasting glucose <225 mg/dl.
- Levels only need to be documented once in the medical records.

Continued coverage of the insulin pump would require that the patient has been seen and evaluated the treating physician at least every 3 months.

The pump must be ordered by and follow-up care of the patient must be managed by a physician who manages multiple patients with CSII and who works closely with a team including nurses, diabetes educators, and dietitians who are knowledgeable in the use of CSII.

Other Uses of CSII

The CMS will continue to allow coverage of all other uses of CSII in accordance with the Category B investigational device exemption (IDE) clilnical trials regulation (42 CFR 405.201) or as a routine cost umder the clinical trials policy

APPENDIX D

(Medicare National Coverage Determination (NCD) Manual 310.1).

f. Other uses of external infusion pumps <u>are covered</u> if the contractor's medical staff verifies the appropriateness of the therapy and of the prescribed pump for the individual patient.

NOTE: Payment may also be made for drugs necessary for the effective use of an external infusion pump as long as the drug being used with the pump is itself reasonable and necessary for the patient's treatment.

<u>2. Implantable Infusion Pumps.</u>--

<u>a. Chemotherapy for Liver Cancer (Effective for Services Performed On or AfterSeptember 26, 1984)</u>

<u>The implantable infusion pump is covered for intra-arterial infusion of 5-FUdR for the treatment of liver cancer for patients with primary hepatocellular carcinoma or Duke's Class D colorectal cancer, in whom the metastases are limited to the liver, and where (1) the disease is unresectable or (2) where the patient refuses surgical excision of the tumor.</u>

<u>b. Anti-Spasmodic Drugs for Severe Spasticity.</u>

An implantable infusion pump is covered when used to administer anti-spasmodic drugs intrathecally (e.g., baclofen) to treat chronic intractable spasticity in patients who have proven unresponsive to less invasive medical therapy as determined by the following criteria:

As indicated by at least a 6-week trial, the patient cannot be maintained on noninvasive methods of spasm control, such as oral anti-spasmodic drugs, either because these methods fail to control adequately the spasticity or produce intolerable side effects, and prior to pump implantation, the patient must have responded favorably to a trial intrathecal dose of the anti-spasmodic drug.

<u>c. Opioid Drugs for Treatment of Chronic Intractable Pain.</u>

An implantable infusion pump is covered when used to administer opioid drugs (e.g., morphine) intrathecally or epidurally for treatment of severe chronic intractable pain of malignant or nonmalignant origin in patients who have a life expectancy of at least 3 months and who have proven unresponsive to less invasive medical therapy as determined by the following criteria:

The patient's history must indicate that he/she would not respond adequately to non-invasive methods of pain control, such as systemic opioids (including attempts to eliminate physical and behavioral abnormalities which may cause an exaggerated reaction to pain); and a preliminary trial of intraspinal opioid drug administration must be undertaken with a temporary intrathecal/epidural catheter to substantiate adequately acceptable pain relief and degree of side effects (including effects on the activities of daily living) and patient acceptance.

<u>d. Coverage of Other Uses of Implanted Infusion Pumps</u>

<u>Determinations may be made on coverage of other uses of implanted infusion pumps if the contractor's medical staff verifies that:</u>

- The drug is reasonable and necessary for the treatment of the individual patient;
- It is medically necessary that the drug be administered by an implanted infusion pump; and
- The Food and Drug Administration (FDA)- approved labelling for the pump must specify that the drug being administered and the purpose for which it is administered is an indicated use for the pump.

<u>e. Implantation of Infusion Pump Is Contraindicated.</u>

The implantation of an infusion pump is contraindicated in the following patients:

- with a known allergy or hypersensitivity to the drug being used (e.g., oral baclofen, morphine, etc.);
- who have an infection;
- whose body size is insufficient to support the weight and bulk of the device; andwith other implanted programmable devices since crosstalk between devices may inadvertently change the prescription.

NOTE: Payment may also be made for drugs necessary for the effective use of an implantable infusion pump as long as the drug being used with the pump is itself reasonable and necessary for the patient's treatment.

C. Nationall Noncovered Indications

THE FOLLOWING INDICATIONS FOR TREATMENT USING INFUSION PUMPS ARE <u>NOT</u> COVERED UNDER MEDICARE:
<u>1. External Infusion Pumps.</u>--
<u>a. Vancomycin (Effective for Services Beginning On or After September 1, 1996).</u>

Medicare coverage of vancomycin as a durable medical equipment infusion pump benefit is not covered. There is insufficient evidence to support the necessity of using an external infusion pump, instead of a disposable elastomeric pump or the gravity drip method, to administer vancomycin in a safe and appropriate manner.

<u>2. Implantable Infusion Pump.</u>--

<u>a. Thromboembolic Disease (Effective for Services Performed On or After September 26, 1984).</u>

According to the Public Health Service, there is insufficient published clinical data to support the safety and effectiveness of the heparin implantable pump. Therefore, the use of an implantable infusion pump for infusion of heparin in the treatment of recurrent thromboembolic disease is not covered.
<u>b. Diabetes</u>

<u>Implanted infusion pumps for the infusion of insulin to treat diabetes is not covered. The data do not demonstrate that the pump provides effective administration of insulin.</u>

D. Other

Not applicable

(This NCD last reviewed January 2005.)

Pub. 100-3, Section 300.1
Obsolete or Unreliable Diagnostic Tests

A. Diagnostic Tests (Effective for services performed on or after May 15, 1980).--Do not routinely pay for the following diagnostic tests because they are obsolete and have been replaced by more advanced procedures. The listed tests may be paid for only if the medical need for the procedure is satisfactorily justified by the physician who performs it. When the services are subject to PRO review, the PRO is responsible for determining that satisfactory medical justification exists. When the services are not subject to PRO review, the intermediary or carrier is responsible for determining that satisfactory medical justification exists. This includes:
- Amylase, blood isoenzymes, electrophoretic,
- Chromium, blood,
- Guanase, blood,
- Zinc sulphate turbidity, blood,
- Skin test, cat scratch fever,
- Skin test, lymphopathia venereum,
- Circulation time, one test,
- Cephalin flocculation,
- Congo red, blood,
- Hormones, adrenocorticotropin quantitative animal tests,
- Hormones, adrenocorticotropin quantitative bioassay,
- Thymol turbidity, blood,
- Skin test, actinomycosis,
- Skin test, brucellosis,
- Skin test, psittacosis,
- Skin test, trichinosis,
- Calcium, feces, 24-hour quantitative,
- Starch, feces, screening,
- Chymotrypsin, duodenal contents,
- Gastric analysis, pepsin,
- Gastric analysis, tubeless,
- Calcium saturation clotting time,
- Capillary fragility test (Rumpel-Leede),
- Colloidal gold,
- Bendien's test for cancer and tuberculosis,
- Bolen's test for cancer,
- Rehfuss test for gastric acidity, and
- Serum seromucoid assay for cancer and other diseases.

B. Cardiovascular Tests (Effective for services performed on or after January 1, 1997).--Do not pay for the following phonocardiography and vectorcardiography diagnostic tests because they have been determined to be outmoded and of little clinical value. They include:
- CPT code 93201, Phonocardiogram with or without ECG lead; with supervision during recording with interpretation and report (when equipment is supplied by the physician),
- CPT code 93202, Phonocardiogram; tracing only, without interpretation and report (e.g., when equipment is supplied by the hospital, clinic),
- CPT code 93204, Phonocardiogram; interpretation and report,
- CPT code 93205, Phonocardiogram with ECG lead, with indirect carotid artery and/or jugular vein tracing, and/or apex cardiogram; with interpretation and report,
- CPT code 93208, Phonocardiogram; without interpretation and report,
- CPT code 93209, Phonocardiogram; interpretation and report only,
- CPT code 93210, Intracardiac,
- CPT code 93220, Vectorcardiogram (VCG), with or without ECG; with interpretation and report,
- CPT code 93221, Vectorcardiogram; tracing only, without interpretation and report, and
- CPT code 93222, Vectorcardiogram; interpretation and report only.

Pub. 100-4, Chapter 1, Section 30.3.5
Effect of Assignment Upon Purchase of Cataract Glasses From Participating Physician or Supplieron Claims Submitted to Carriers

B3-3045.4

A pair of cataract glasses is comprised of two distinct products: a professional product (the prescribed lenses) and a retail commercial product (the frames). The frames serve not only as a holder of lenses but also as an article of personal apparel. As such, they are usually selected on the basis of personal taste and style. Although Medicare will pay only for standard frames, most patients want deluxe frames. Participating physicians and suppliers cannot profitably furnish such deluxe frames unless they can make an extra (noncovered) charge for the frames even though they accept assignment.

Therefore, a participating physician or supplier (whether an ophthalmologist, optometrist, or optician) who accepts assignment on cataract glasses with deluxe frames may charge the Medicare patient the difference between his/her usual charge to private pay patients for glasses with standard frames and his/her usual charge to such patients for glasses with deluxe frames, in addition to the applicable deductible and coinsurance on glasses with standard frames, if all of the following requirements are met:

A. The participating physician or supplier has standard frames available, offers them for sale to the patient, and issues and ABN to the patient that explains the price and other differences between standard and deluxe frames. Refer to Chapter 30.

B. The participating physician or supplier obtains from the patient (or his/her representative) and keeps on file the following signed and dated statement:

_____

Name of Patient   Medicare Claim Number

Having been informed that an extra charge is being made by the physician or supplier for deluxe frames, that this extra charge is not covered by Medicare, and that standard frames are available for purchase from the physician or supplier at no extra charge, I have chosen to purchase deluxe frames.

_____

Signature   Date

© 2005 Ingenix, Inc.

C. The participating physician or supplier itemizes on his/her claim his/her actual charge for the lenses, his/her actual charge for the standard frames, and his/her actual extra charge for the deluxe frames (charge differential).

Once the assigned claim for deluxe frames has been processed, the carrier will follow the ABN instructions as described in §60.

Pub. 100-4, Chapter 1, Section 60.4.5
Clarification of Liability for Preventive Screening Benefits Subject to Frequency Limits

Some Medicare preventive benefits are subject to frequency limits, and are also specifically cited at §1862 (a)(1) (F) ff. of the Act as subject to "medical necessity." There has been some confusion as to the basis of denial and how such services are adjudicated. When medical necessity is the basis for denial (i.e., §1862 (a)(1) (F) ff. of the Act), a ABN is necessary in order to shift the liability to the beneficiary, and special ABN-related billing must be used (see III. E. above). Services above frequency limits, however, had been erroneously considered noncovered services by some, and billed as such, not requiring ABNs. In these cases default liability in Medicare systems is the provider, unless specific billing methods and modifiers were used to signal beneficiary liability (see sections III A. and B. above).

Medicare FIs systems had been programmed with frequency as the primary reason for denial at one time, and Medicare carrier systems have used medical necessity. FI systems have changed so that medical necessity is the primary reason for denial.

It may be contrary to provider practices to submit services over the frequency limit as covered charges, as ABN billing requires. However, it can be pointed out that existing Common Working File (CWF) frequency edits should still result in the denial of these services. Remittance denial reason codes and MSN messages to be used in this situation are listed below for beneficiary and provider liability should either circumstance occur:

TABLE 10:

Appendixes

Preventive Benefit	HCPCS Code(s)	PROVIDER LIABLE (ANSI) Remittance Group and Reason Code	PROVIDER LIABLE MSN Message	BENE. LIABLE (ANSI) Remittance Group and Reason Code	BENE. LIABLE MSN Message
Screening mammography	G0202, 76092, 76083	CO – 57 [57: Payment denied/redu-ced because the payer deems the information submitted does not support this level of service, this many services, this length of service, this dosage, or this day's supply.]	15.21 The information provided does not support the need for this many services or items in this period of time but you do not have to pay this amount. [Le informacion proporciona-da no justifica la necesidad do esta cantidad de servicios o articulos an este periodo de tiempo pero usted no tiene que pagar esta cantidad.]	PR – 57* [57: Payment denied/redu-ced because the payer deems the information submitted does not support this level of service, this many services, this length of service, this dosage, or this day's supply.]	15.22 The information provided does not support the need for this many services or items in this period of time so pay for this item or service. [Le informacion proporcio-nada no justifica la necesidad do esta cantidad de servicios o articulos an este periodo de tiempo por lo cual Medicare no pagara por este articulo o servicio.]
Screening pap smear	G0123, G0143, G0144, G0145, G0147, G0148, P3000, Q0091	CO - 57	Ditto above	PR – 57*	Ditto above
Screening pelvic exam	G0101	CO - 57	Ditto above	PR – 57*	Ditto above
Screening glaucoma	G0117, G0118	CO - 57	Ditto above	PR – 57*	Ditto above
Prostate cancer screening test	G0102, G0103	CO - 57	Ditto above	PR – 57*	Ditto above
Colorectal cancer screening test	G0104, G0106, G0107, G0120, G0122	CO - 57	Ditto above	PR – 57*	Ditto above

© 2005 Ingenix, Inc.

APPENDIX D

This ANSI ASC X12 reason code becomes obsolete with implementation of the 835 remittance version 4050. For the purpose of this table, use of 57 in the 835 version 4050 and subsequent versions can be crosswalked to code 151: "Payment adjusted because the payer deems the information submitted does not support this many services".

Pub. 100-4, Chapter 3, Section 90.3
Stem Cell Transplantation

A3-3614, HO-416.1

Stem cell transplantation is a process in which stem cells are harvested from either a patient's or donor's bone marrow or peripheral blood for intravenous infusion. The transplant can be used to effect hematopoietic reconstitution following severely myelotoxic doses of chemotherapy (HDCT) and/or radiotherapy used to treat various malignancies. Allogeneic stem cell transplant may also be used to restore function in recipients having an inherited or acquired deficiency or defect.

Allogeneic and autologous stem cell transplants are covered under Medicare for specific diagnoses. Effective October 1, 1990, these cases were assigned to the DRG 481, Bone Marrow Transplant.

The FI's Medicare Code Editor (MCE) will edit stem cell transplant procedure codes against diagnosis codes to determine which cases meet specified coverage criteria. Cases with a diagnosis code for a covered condition will pass (as covered) the MCE noncovered procedure edit. When a stem cell transplant case is selected for review based on the random selection of beneficiaries, the QIO will review the case on a post-payment basis to assure proper coverage decisions

Procedure code 41.00 (bone marrow transplant, not otherwise specified) will be classified as noncovered and the claim will be returned to the hospital for a more specific procedure code.

Pub. 100-4, Chapter 3, Section 90.4
Liver Transplants

A3-3615, A3-3615.5, HO-416.5

A - Background

For Medicare coverage purposes, liver transplants are considered medically reasonable and necessary for specified conditions when performed in facilities that meet specific criteria.

To review the current list of Approved Liver Transplant Centers, see http://www.cms.hhs.gov/providers/transplant/livrlist.asp

Pub. 100-4, Chapter 3, Section 90.6
Intestinal and Multi-Visceral Transplants

A3-3615.7, Transmittal R1878A3

A. Background

Effective for services on or after April 1, 2001, Medicare covers intestinal and multi-visceral transplantation for the purpose of restoring intestinal function in patients with irreversible intestinal failure. Intestinal failure is defined as the loss of absorptive capacity of the small bowel secondary to severe primary gastrointestinal disease or surgically induced short bowel syndrome. Intestinal failure prevents oral nutrition and may be associated with both mortality and profound morbidity. Multi-Visceral transplantation includes organs in the digestive system (stomach, duodenum, liver, and intestine). See the National Coverage Determinations Manual for further information.

B. Approved Transplant Facilities

Medicare will cover intestinal transplantation if performed in an approved facility. The approved facilities are located at http://cms.hhs.gov/providers/transplant/default.asp.

C. Billing

ICD-9-CM procedure code 46.97 is effective for discharges on or after April 1, 2001. The Medicare Code Editor (MCE) lists this code as a non-covered procedure with no exceptions. The FI is to override the MCE when this procedure code is listed and the coverage criteria are met in an approved transplant facility.

For this procedure where the provider is approved as transplant facility, and the service is performed on or after the transplant approval date, the FI must suspend the claim for clerical review of the operative report to determine whether the beneficiary has at least one of the covered conditions listed when the diagnosis code is for a covered condition.

This review is not part of the FI's medical review workload. Instead, the FI should complete this review as part of it's claims processing workload.

Charges for ICD-9-CM procedure code 46.97 should be billed under revenue code 0360, Operating Room Services.

For discharge dates on or after October 1, 2001, acquisition charges are billed under revenue code 081X, Organ Acquisition. For discharge dates between April 1, 2001, and September 30, 2001, hospitals were to report the acquisition charges on the claim, but there was no interim pass-through payment made for these costs.

Bill the procedure used to obtain the donor's organ on the same claim, using appropriate ICD-9-CM procedure codes.

The 11X bill type should be used when billing for intestinal transplants.

Immunosuppressive therapy for intestinal transplantation is covered and should be billed consistent with other organ transplants under the current rules.

There is no specific ICD-9-CM diagnosis code for intestinal failure. Diagnosis codes exist to capture the causes of intestinal failure. Some examples of intestinal failure include, but are not limited to:

Volvulus 560.2,

Volvulus gastroschisis 756.79, other [congenital] anomalies of abdominal wall,

Volvulus gastroschisis 569.89, other specified disorders of intestine,

Necrotizing enterocolitis 777.5, necrotizing enterocolitis in fetus or newborn,

Necrotizing enterocolitis 014.8, other tuberculosis of intestines, peritoneum, and mesenteric,

Necrotizing enterocolitis and splanchnic vascular thrombosis 557.0, acute vascular insufficiency of intestine,

Inflammatory bowel disease 569.9, unspecified disorder of intestine,

Radiation enteritis 777.5, necrotizing enterocolitis in fetus or newborn, and

Radiation enteritis 558.1.

D. Acquisition Costs

A separate organ acquisition cost center was established for acquisition costs incurred on or after October 1, 2001. The Medicare Cost Report will include a separate line to account for these transplantation costs. For intestinal and multi-visceral transplants performed between April 1, 2001, and October 1, 2001, the DRG payment was payment in full for all hospital services related to this procedure.

E. Medicare Summary Notices (MSN), Remittance Advice Messages, and Notice of Utilization Notices (NOU)

If an intestinal transplant is billed by an unapproved facility after April 1, 2001, the FI must deny the claim and use MSN message 21.6, "This item or service is not covered when performed, referred, or ordered by this provider;" 21.18, "This item or service is not covered when performed or ordered by this provider;" or, 16.2, "This service cannot be paid when provided in this location/facility;" and Remittance Advice Message, Claim Adjustment Reason Code 52, "The referring/prescribing/rendering provider is not eligible to refer/prescribe/order/perform the service billed."

Pub. 100-4, Chapter 3, Section 100.1
Billing for Abortion Services

A3-3652

Effective October 1, 1998, abortions are not covered under the Medicare program except for instances where the pregnancy is a result of an act of rape or incest; or the woman suffers from a physical disorder, physical injury, or physical illness, including a life endangering physical condition caused by the pregnancy itself that would, as certified by a physician, place the woman in danger of death unless an abortion is performed.

A - "G" Modifier

The "G7" modifier is defined as "the pregnancy resulted from rape or incest, or pregnancy certified by physician as life threatening."

Beginning July 1, 1999, providers should bill for abortion services using the new Modifier G7. This modifier can be used on claims with dates of services October 1, 1998, and after. CWF will be able to recognize the modifier beginning July 1, 1999.

B - FI Billing Instructions

1 - Hospital Inpatient Billing

Hospitals will bill the FI on Form CMS-1450 using bill type 11X. Medicare will pay only when condition code A7 or A8 is used in FLs 24-30 of UB92 along with an appropriate ICD-9-CM principal diagnosis code that will group to DRG 380 or with an appropriate ICD-9-CM principal diagnosis code and one of the four appropriate ICD-9-CM operating room procedure codes listed below that will group to DRG 381.

69.01	69.02	69.51	74.91

Providers must use ICD-9-CM codes 69.01 and 69.02 to describe exactly the procedure or service performed.

The FI must manually review claims with the above ICD-9-CM procedure codes to verify that all of the above conditions are met.

2 - Outpatient Billing

Hospitals will bill the FI on Form CMS-1450 using bill type 13X, 83X and 85X. Medicare will pay only if one of the following CPT codes is used with the "G7" modifier.

59840	59851	59856
59841	59852	59857
59850	59855	59866

C - Common Working File (CWF) Edits

For hospital outpatient claims, CWF will bypass its edits for a managed care beneficiary who is having an abortion outside their plan and the claim is submitted with the "G7" modifier and one of the above CPT codes.

For hospital inpatient claims, CWF will bypass its edits for a managed care beneficiary who is having an abortion outside their plan and the claim is submitted with one of the above ICD-9-CM procedure codes.

D - Medicare Summary Notices (MSN)/Explanation of Your Medicare Benefits Remittance Advice Message

If a claim is submitted with one of the above CPT procedure codes but no "G7" modifier, the claim is denied. The FI states on the MSN the following message:

This service was denied because Medicare covers this service only under certain circumstances." (MSN Message 21.21).

For the remittance advice the FI uses existing American National Standard Institute (ANSI) X12-835 claim adjustment reason code B5, "Claim/service denied/reduced because coverage guidelines were not met or were exceeded."

Pub. 100-4, Chapter 3, Section 100.7
Lung Volume Reduction Surgery

Lung Volume Reduction Surgery (LVRS) (also known as reduction pneumoplasty, lung shaving, or lung contouring) is an invasive surgical procedure to reduce the volume of a hyperinflated lung in order to allow the underlying compressed lung to expand, and thus, establish improved respiratory function.

Effective for discharges on or after January 1, 2004, Medicare will cover LVRS under certain conditions as described in §240 of Pub. 100-03, "National Coverage Determinations".

The Medicare Code Editor (MCE) creates a Limited Coverage edit for procedure code 32.22. This procedure code has limited coverage due to the stringent conditions that must be met by hospitals. Where this procedure code is identified by MCE, the FI shall determine if coverage criteria is met and override the MCE if appropriate.

The LVRS can only be performed in the facilities listed on the following Web site:www.cms.hhs.gov/coverage/lvrsfacility.pdf

Medicare previously only covered LVRS as part of the National Emphysema Treatment Trial (NETT). The study is limited to 18 hospitals, and patients are randomized into two arms, either medical management and LVRS or medical management. The study is conducted by The National Heart, Lung, and Blood Institute of the National Institutes of Health

© 2005 Ingenix, Inc.

and coordinated by Johns Hopkins University (JHU). Claims for patients in the NETT are identified by the presence of Condition Code EY. The JHU instructs hospitals of the correct billing procedures for billing claims under the NETT. Claims processing procedures in place for the NETT remain the same.

Pub. 100-4, Chapter 4, Section 180.3
Unlisted Service or Procedure

This section does not apply to OPPS hospitals.

There may be services or procedures performed that are not found in HCPCS. These are typically services that are rarely provided, unusual, variable, or new. A number of specific code numbers have been designated for reporting unlisted procedures. When an unlisted procedure code is used, a report describing the service is submitted with the claim. Pertinent information includes a definition or description of the nature, extent, and need for the procedure and the time, effort, and equipment necessary to provide the service.

When an FI receives a claim with an unlisted procedure code, it reviews it to verify that there is no existing code that adequately describes the procedure. If it determines that an adequately descriptive code is contained in HCPCS, it advises the hospital of the proper code and processes the claim. If it determines that no existing code is sufficiently descriptive, it pays the claim using the unlisted procedure code. If the frequency of the procedure warrants assignment of a local code, the FI forwards a copy and the operative report to the RO HCPCS coordinator for a code determination. When it receives a determination, the FI informs the hospital of the correct code for future reporting. Local codes are not accepted under OPPS and line items for local codes are no longer paid on cost.

NOTE: If the claim is submitted via EMC or identified after the bill has been processed, an operative report, the provider number, revenue codes, and charges are sufficient.

The "Unlisted Procedures" and codes for surgery are:

HCPCS code	Unlisted Procedure
15999	Unlisted procedure, excision pressure ulcer
17999	Unlisted procedure, skin, mucous membrane and subcutaneous tissue
19499	Unlisted procedure, breast
20999	Unlisted procedure, musculoskeletal system, general
21299	Unlisted craniofacial and maxillofacial procedures
21499	Unlisted orthopedic procedure, head
21899	Unlisted procedure, neck or thorax
22899	Unlisted procedure, spine
22999	Unlisted procedure, abdomen, musculoskeletal system
23929	Unlisted procedure, shoulder

HCPCS code	Unlisted Procedure
24999	Unlisted procedure, humerus or elbow
25999	Unlisted procedure, forearm or wrist
26989	Unlisted procedure, hands or fingers
27299	Unlisted procedure, pelvis or hip joint
27599	Unlisted procedure, femur or knee
27899	Unlisted procedure, leg or ankle
28899	Unlisted procedure, foot or toes
29799	Unlisted procedure, casting or strapping
29909	Unlisted procedure, arthroscopy
30999	Unlisted procedure, nose
31299	Unlisted procedure, accessory sinuses
31599	Unlisted procedure, larynx
31899	Unlisted procedure, trachea, bronchi
32999	Unlisted procedure, lungs, and pleura
33999	Unlisted procedure, cardiac surgery
36299	Unlisted procedure, vascular injection
37799	Unlisted procedure, vascular surgery
38999	Unlisted procedure, hemic or lymphatic system
39499	Unlisted procedure, mediastinum
39599	Unlisted procedure, diaphragm
40799	Unlisted procedure, lips
40899	Unlisted procedure, vestibule of mouth
41599	Unlisted procedure, tongue, floor of mouth
41899	Unlisted procedure, dentoalveolar structures
42299	Unlisted procedure, palate, uvula
42699	Unlisted procedure, salivary glands or ducts
42999	Unlisted procedure, pharynx, adenoids, or tonsils
43499	Unlisted procedure, esophag
43999	Unlisted procedure, stomach
44799	Unlisted procedure, intestine

HCPCS code	Unlisted Procedure
44899	Unlisted procedure, Meckel's diverticulum and the mesentery
45999	Unlisted procedure, rectum
46999	Unlisted procedure, anus
47399	Unlisted procedure, liver
47999	Unlisted procedure, biliary tract
48999	Unlisted procedure, pancreas
49999	Unlisted procedure, abdomen, peritoneum, and omentum
53899	Unlisted procedure, urinary system
55899	Unlisted procedure, male genital system
56399	Unlisted procedure, laparoscopy, hysteroscopy
58999	Unlisted procedure, female genital system non-obstetrical
59899	Unlisted procedure, maternity care and delivery
60699	Unlisted procedure, endocrine system
64999	Unlisted procedure, nervous system
66999	Unlisted procedure, anterior segment of eye
67299	Unlisted procedure, posterior segment
67399	Unlisted procedure, ocular muscle
67599	Unlisted procedure, orbit
67999	Unlisted procedure, eyelids
68399	Unlisted procedure, conjunctiva
68899	Unlisted procedure, lacrimal system
69399	Unlisted procedure, external ear
69799	Unlisted procedure, middle ear
69949	Unlisted procedure, inner ear
69979	Unlisted procedure, temporal bone, middle fossa approach

Pub. 100-4, Chapter 5, Section 10

Part B Outpatient Rehabilitation and Comprehensive Outpatient Rehabilitation Facility (CORF) Services - General

Section 4541(a)(2) of the Balanced Budget Act (BBA) (P.L. 105-33), which added§1834(k)(5) to the Social Security Act (the Act), required that all claims for outpatient rehabilitation, certain audiology services and comprehensive outpatient rehabilitation facility (CORF) services, be reported using a uniform coding system. The CMS chose HCPCS (Healthcare Common Procedure Coding System) as the coding system to be used for the reporting of these services. This coding requirement is effective for all claims for outpatient rehabilitation services including certain audiology services and CORF services submitted on or after April 1, 1998.

The BBA also required payment under a prospective payment system for outpatient rehabilitation services including audiology and CORF services. Effective for claims with dates of service on or after January 1, 1999, the Medicare Physician Fee Schedule (MPFS) became the method of payment for outpatient physical therapy (which includes outpatient speech-language pathology) services furnished by:

Comprehensive Outpatient Rehabilitation Facilities (CORFs);

Outpatient Physical Therapy Providers (OPTs);

Other Rehabilitation Facilities (ORFs);

Hospitals (to outpatients and inpatients who are not in a covered Part A stay);

Skilled Nursing Facilities (SNFs) (to residents not in a covered Part A stay and to nonresidents who receive outpatient rehabilitation services from the SNF); and

Home Health Agencies (HHAs) (to individuals who are not homebound or otherwise are not receiving services under a home health plan of care (POC)).

The MPFS is used as a method of payment for outpatient rehabilitation services furnished under arrangement with any of these providers.

In addition, the MPFS is used as the payment system for audiology and CORF services identified by the HCPCS codes in §20Assignment is mandatory.

The Medicare **allowed charge** for the services is the lower of the actual charge or the MPFS amount. The Medicare payment for the services is 80 percent of the allowed charge after the Part B deductible is met. Coinsurance is made at 20 percent of the lower of the actual charge or the MPFS amount. The general coinsurance rule (20 percent of the actual charges) does not apply when making payment under the MPFS. This is a final payment.

The MPFS does **not** apply to outpatient rehabilitation services furnished by critical access hospitals (CAHs). CAHs are to be paid on a reasonable cost basis.

Intermediaries (FIs) process outpatient rehabilitation claims from hospitals, including CAHs, SNFs, CORFs, outpatient rehabilitation agencies, and outpatient physical therapy providers for which they have received a tie in notice from the RO. Carriers process claims from physicians, certain nonphysician practitioners (NPPs), and physical and occupational therapists in private practice (PTPPs and OTPPs). A physician-directed clinic that bills for services furnished incident to a physician's service (see Chapter 15 in the Medicare Benefit Policy Manual for a definition of "incident to") bills the carrier.

There are different fee rates for nonfacility and facility services. Chapter 23 describes the differences in these two rates. (See fields 28 and 29 of the record therein described). Facility rates apply to professional services performed in a facility other than the professional's office. Nonfacility rates apply when the service is performed in the professional's office. The nonfacility rate (that paid when the provider performs the services in its own facility) accommodates overhead and indirect expenses the provider incurs by operating its own facility. Thus it is somewhat higher than the facility rate.

FIs pay the nonfacility rate for services performed in the provider's facility. Carriers may pay the facility or nonfacility rate depending upon where the service is performed (place of service on the claim), and the provider specialty.

Carriers pay the codes in *§20*under the MPFS regardless of whether they may be considered rehabilitation services. However, FIs must use this list to determine whether to pay under outpatient rehabilitation rules or whether payment rules for other types of service may apply, e.g., OPPS for hospitals, reasonable costs for CAHs.

Note that because a service is considered an outpatient rehabilitation service does not automatically imply payment for that service. Additional criteria, including coverage, plan of care and physician certification must also be met. These criteria are described in the Medicare Benefit Policy Manual, Chapters 1 and 15.

Payment for rehabilitation services provided to Part A inpatients of hospitals or SNFs is included in the respective PPS rate. Also, for SNFs (but not hospitals), if the beneficiary has Part B, but not Part A coverage (e.g., Part A benefits are exhausted), the SNF must bill the FI for any rehabilitation service (except audiologic function services). Independent audiologists may bill the carrier directly for services rendered to Part B Medicare entitled beneficiaries residing in a SNF, but not in a SNF Part A covered stay. Payment is made based on the MPFS, whether by the carrier or the FI (FI). For beneficiaries not in a covered Part A SNF stay, who are sometimes referred to as beneficiaries in a Part B SNF stay, audiologic function tests are payable under Part B when billed by the SNF as type of bill 22X, or when billed directly to the carrier by the provider or supplier of the service. For tests that include both a professional component and technical component, the SNF may elect to bill the technical component to the FI, but is not required to bill the service. (The professional component of a service is the direct patient care provided by the physician or *audiologist*, e.g., the interpretation of a test.)

Payment for rehabilitation services provided by home health agencies under a home health plan of care is included in the home health PPS rate. HHAs may submit bill type 34X and be paid under the MPFS if there are no home health services billed under a home health plan of care at the same time, and there is a valid rehabilitation Plan of Care (e.g., the patient is not homebound).

An institutional employer (other than a SNF) of the physical therapists in private practice (PTPPs), occupational therapists in private practice (OTPPs), or physician performing outpatient services, (e.g., hospital, CORF, etc.), or a clinic billing on behalf of the physician or therapist may bill the carrier on Form CMS-1500.

The MPFS is the basis of payment for outpatient rehabilitation services furnished by PTPPs and OTPPs, physicians, and certain nonphysician practitioners or for diagnostic tests provided incident to the services of such physicians or nonphysician practitioners. (See the Medicare Benefit Policy Manual, Chapter 15, for a definition of "incident to.") Such services are billed to the Part B carrier. Assignment is mandatory.

The following table identifies the provider types or physician/nonphysician and to which contractor they may submit bills.

Appendixes

"Provider/Service" Type	Bill to	Bill Type	Comment
Inpatient hospital Part A	FI	11X	Included in PPS
Inpatient SNF Part A	FI	21X	Included in PPS
Inpatient hospital Part B	FI	12X	Hospital may obtain services under arrangements and bill, or rendering provider may bill.
Inpatient SNF Part B except for audiology function tests.	FI	22X	SNF must provide and bill, or obtain under arrangements and bill.
Inpatient SNF Part B audiology function tests only.	FI	22X	SNF may bill the FI or provider of service may bill the carrier.
Outpatient hospital	FI	13X	Hospital may provide and bill or obtain under arrangements and bill, or rendering provider may bill
Outpatient SNF	FI	23X	SNF must provide and bill or obtain under arrangements and bill
HHA billing for services rendered under a Part A or Part B home health plan of care.	FI	32X	Service is included in PPS rate. CMS determines whether payment is from Part A or Part B trust fund.
HHA billing for services not rendered under a Part A or Part B home health plan of care, but rendered under a therapy plan of care.	FI	34X	Service not under home health plan of care.
Other Rehabilitation Facility (ORF) with 6-digit provider number assigned by CMS RO	FI	74X	Paid MPFS for outpatient rehabilitation services effective January 1, 1999, and all other services except drugs effective July 1, 2000. Starting April 1, 2002, drugs are paid 95% of the AWP. For claims with dates of service on or after July 1, 2003, drugs and biologicals do not apply in an OPT setting. Therefore, FIs are to advise their OPTs not to bill for them.
CORF with 6-digit provider number assigned by CMS RO	FI	75X	Paid MPFS for outpatient rehabilitation services effective January 1, 1999, and all other services except drugs effective July 1, 2000. Starting April 1, 2002, drugs are paid 95% of the AWP.
Physician, NPPs, PTPPs, OTPPs, and, for diagnostic tests only, audiologists (service in hospital or SNF)	Carrier	See Chapter 26 for place of service, and type of service coding.	Payment may not be made for therapy services to Part A inpatients of hospitals or SNFs, or for Part B SNF residents. Otherwise, carrier billing. Note that physician/ NPP/PTPP/OTPP employee of facility may assign benefits to the facility, enabling the facility to bill for physician/therapist to carrier
Physician/NPP/PTPP/OTPP office, independent clinic or patient's home	Carrier	See Chapter 26 for place of service, and type of service coding.	Paid via Physician fee schedule.
Practicing audiologist for services defined as diagnostic tests only	Carrier	See Chapter 26 for place of service, and type of service coding.	Some audiologists tests provided in hospitals are considered other diagnostic tests and are subject to HOPPS instead of MPFS for outpatient therapy fee schedule.
Critical Access Hospital - inpatient Part A	FI	85X	Rehabilitation services are paid cost.
Critical Access Hospital - inpatient Part B	FI	85X	Rehabilitation services are paid cost.
Critical Access Hospital – outpatient Part B	FI	85X	Rehabilitation services are paid cost.

Complete Claim form completion requirements are contained in Chapters 25 and 26.

For a list of the outpatient rehabilitation HCPCS codes see *§20*

If an FI receives a claim for one of the these HCPCS codes with dates of service on or after July 1, 2003, that does not appear on the supplemental file it currently uses to pay the therapy claims, it contacts its local carrier to obtain the price in order to pay the claim. When requesting the pricing data, it advises the carrier to provide it with the nonfacility fee.

NOTE: The list of codes in *§20*contains commonly utilized codes for outpatient rehabilitation services. FIs may consider other codes for payment under the MPFS as outpatient rehabilitation services to the extent that such codes are determined to be medically reasonable and necessary and those that could be performed within the scope of practice of the therapist *providing the service.*

Pub. 100-4, Chapter 5, Section 20
HCPCS Coding Requirement

A. Uniform Coding

Section 1834(k)(5) of the Act requires that all claims for outpatient rehabilitation, certain audiology services and CORF services be reported using a uniform coding system. The HCPCS is the coding system used for the reporting of these services.

Effective for claims submitted on or after April 1, 1998, providers that had not previously reported HCPCS for outpatient rehabilitation and CORF services began using HCPCS to report these services and certain audiology services. This requirement does not apply to outpatient rehabilitation and audiology services provided by:

Critical Access Hospitals, which are paid on a cost basis, not MPFS;

RHCs, and FQHCs for which therapy is included in the all-inclusive rate; or

Providers that do not furnish therapy services.

The following "providers of services" must bill the FI for outpatient rehabilitation services using HCPCS codes:

Hospitals (to outpatients and inpatients who are not in a covered Part A stay);

Skilled nursing facilities (SNFs) (to residents not in a covered Part A stay and to nonresidents who receive outpatient rehabilitation services from the SNF);

Home health agencies (HHAs) (to individuals who are not homebound or otherwise are not receiving services under a home health plan of care (POC));

Comprehensive outpatient rehabilitation agencies (CORFs); and

Outpatient physical therapy providers (OPTs), i.e., outpatient physical therapy facilities.

Note that the requirements for hospitals and SNFs apply to inpatient Part B and outpatient services only. Inpatient Part A is included in the respective PPS rate and not billed separately.

For HHAs, HCPCS coding for outpatient rehabilitation services is required only when the HHA provides such service to individuals that are not homebound and; therefore, not under a Home Health plan of care.

Providers billing to intermediaries shall report:

- *The date the therapy plan of care was either established or last reviewed (see §220.1.3B) in Occurrence Code 17, 29, or 30.*
- *The first day of treatment in Occurrence Code 35, 44, or 45.*

B - Applicable Outpatient Rehabilitation HCPCS Codes

Regardless of *the presence of a* financial limitation, CMS identifies the following codes as therapy services. *Therapy services include only physical therapy, occupational therapy and speech-language pathology services. Therapist means only a physical therapist, occupational therapist or speech-language pathologist.Therapy modifiers are GP for physical therapy, GO for occupational therapy, and GN for speech-language pathology. Check the notes below the chart for details about each code.*

The financial limits (when in effect) apply to services represented by the following codes, except as noted below. (NOTE: Listing of the following codes does not imply that services are covered.)

64550+	90901+	92506	92507	92508	92526
92597	92605****	92606****	92607	92608	92609
92610+	92611+	92612+	92614+	92616+	95831+
95832+	95833+	95834+	95851+	95852+	96105+
96110+w	96111+	96115+	97001	97002	97003
97004	97010****	97012	97016	97018	97020
97022	97024	97026	97028	97032	97033
97034	97035	97036	97039	97110	97112
97113	97116	97124	97139	97140	97150
97504**	97520	97530	97532+	97533	97535
97537	97542	97597+	97598+	97602****	97605****
97606****	97703	97750	97755	97799*	G0279+***
G0280+***	G0281	G0283	G0329	0029T+***	

* The physician fee schedule abstract file does not contain a price for codes 96110, or 97799, since the carrier prices them. Therefore, the FI must contact the carrier to obtain the appropriate fee schedule amount in order to make proper payment for these codes.

w Effective January 1, 2004, 96110 will be an active code on the physician fee schedule. Carriers shall no longer price this code.

** Code 97504 should not be reported with code 97116. However, if code 97504 was performed on an upper extremity and code 97116 (gait training) was also performed, both codes may be billed with modifier 59 to denote a separate anatomic site.

*** The physician fee schedule abstract file does not contain a price for codes G0279, G0280, *or* 0029T since they are priced by the carrier. In addition, the carrier determines coverage for these codes. Therefore, the FI contacts the carrier to obtain the appropriate fee schedule amount.

****Codes are bundled. They are bundled with any therapy codes. Regardless of whether they are billed alone or in conjunction with another therapy code, never make payment separately for these codes. If billed alone, code*s marked* ****should be denied using the existing EOMB/MSN language. For remittance advice notices, use group code

CO and claim adjustment reason code 97 that says: "Payment is included in the allowance for another service/procedure." Use reason code 97 to deny a procedure code that should have been bundled. Alternatively, reason code B15, which has the same intent, may also be used.

If billed by an outpatient hospital department, these are paid using the Outpatient Prospective Payment system (OPPS).

Underlined codes are always therapy services, regardless of who performs them. These codes always require therapy modifiers (GP, GO, GN).

+ Codes sometimes represent therapy services. These codes and all codes on the above list always represent therapy services when performed by therapists.

There are some circumstances when these codes will not be considered representative of therapy services and therapy limits (when they are in effect) will not apply. Codes marked + are not therapy services when:

- It is not appropriate to bill the service under a therapy plan of care, _and_
- _They are billed by providers of services who are not therapists, i.e., physicians, clinical nurse specialists, nurse practitioners and psychologists._

The Codes marked + on the above list may not be used by _therapists, or by_ practitioners _who are not therapists_ without a therapy modifier in situations where the service provided is integral to an outpatient rehabilitation therapy service. _For example, when the service is rendered with the goal of rehabilitation and the service is within the scope of practice of a therapist as defined by State or local law, a modifier is required. When there is doubt about whether a service should be part of a therapy plan of care, the contractor shall make that determination._

"Outpatient rehabilitation therapy" refers to skilled _therapy_ services, requiring the skills of qualified therapists, performed for restorative purposes and generally involving ongoing treatments. In contrast, a non-therapy service (usually a one-time service) is a service performed by non-therapist practitioners, without rehabilitative plan or goals, e.g., _application of a surface (Transcutaneous) neurostimulator – 64550, and biofeedback training by any modality – 90901 may be non-therapy services when not done by therapists. When performed by therapists, these are therapy services._ Contractors have discretion to determine whether circumstances require a plan or describe a therapy service.

Codes on the above list that do not have a + sign are considered "always therapy" codes and always require a therapy modifier. Therapy services, whether represented by "always therapy" codes, or + codes in the above list performed as outpatient rehabilitation therapy services, must follow all the policies for therapy services (e.g., Pub. 100-04, Chapter 5; Pub. 100-02, Chapter 15).

C - Additional HCPCS Codes

Codes that are not on the list of therapy services should not be billed with a modifier. For example, the following outpatient non-rehabilitation HCPCS codes _should be billed without modifiers:_ 95860, 95861, 95863, 95864, 95867, 95869, 95870, 95900, 95903, 95904, 95934, G0237, G0238, and G0239.

Some codes that were previously on this list have been removed (e.g., cast and splint services). We have determined that these services are most often performed outside a therapy plan of care and have removed them from the list. Codes that are not on the list may be billed when the services are furnished by therapists if the services are covered and appropriately delivered (e.g., the therapist is qualified to provide the service).

NOTE: The above list_s_ of codes are intended to facilitate the _contractor's_ ability to pay claims under the MPFS. It is not intended to be a list of all covered OPT services and does not assure coverage of these services.

Pub. 100-4, Chapter 5, Section 100.10
Group Therapy Services (Code 97150)

CR 2225, A3-1872 Dated 1-24-03, A3-3653, B3-15302-15304

Carriers pay for outpatient physical therapy services (which includes outpatient speech-language pathology services) and outpatient occupational therapy services provided simultaneously to two or more individuals by a practitioner as group therapy services. The individuals can be, but need not be performing the same activity. The physician or therapist involved in group therapy services must be in constant attendance, but one-on-one patient contact is not required.

Pub. 100-4, Chapter 8, Section 60.4.4
Epoetin Alfa (EPO) Furnished to Home Patients

Medicare covers EPO for dialysis patients who use EPO in the home, when requirements for a patient care plan and patient selection as described in the Medicare Benefit Policy Manual, Chapter 11, are met.

When EPO is prescribed for a home patient, it may be either administered in a facility, e.g., the one shown on the Form CMS-382 (ESRD Beneficiary Method Selection Form) or furnished by a facility or Method II supplier for self-administration to a home patient determined to be competent to administer this drug. For EPO furnished for self-administration to Method I and Method II home patients determined to be competent, the renal facility bills its FI and the Method II supplier bills its DMERC. No additional payment is made for training a prospective self-administering patient or retraining an existing home patient to self-administer EPO.

Method II patients who self-administer may obtain EPO only from either their Method II supplier, or a Medicare certified ESRD facility.

In this case, the DMERC makes payment at the same rate that applies to facilities. Program payment may not be made for EPO furnished by a physician to a patient for self-administration.

DMERCs pay for EPO for Method II ESRD beneficiaries only. DMERCs shall deny claims for EPO where the beneficiary is not a Method II home dialysis patient.

When denying line items for patients that are not Method II, use the following message on the remittance advice:

ANSI message 7011: Claim not covered by this payer contractor. You must send the claim to the correct payer contractor.

When denying line items for patients that are not Method II, use the following message on the Medicare Summary Notice (MSN):

English: 8.59- Durable Medical Equipment Regional Carriers pay for Epoetin Alfa and Darbepoetin Alfa only for Method II End Stage Renal Disease home dialysis patients.

Spanish: 8.59- Las Empresas Regionales de Equipo Médico Duradero pagan por los medicamentos Epoetina Alfa y

Darbepoetina Alfa s lo a pacientes del M todo II de di lisis con enfermedad renal en etapa final que est n confinados al hogar.

Pub. 100-4, Chapter 8, Section 70
Payment for Home Dialysis

A3-3644, PRM-1-2706.1.E, PRM-1-2706.2, A3-3169, RO-2 3440.2, B3-4270.1

Home dialysis is dialysis performed by an appropriately trained dialysis patient at home. Hemodialysis, CCPD, IPD and CAPD may be performed at home. For all dialysis services furnished by an ESRD facility, the facility must accept assignment, and only the facility may be paid by the Medicare program. Method II suppliers can receive payment for patients selecting Method II. The Method II supplier must accept assignment. Method II suppliers receive payment for supplies and equipment only.

For purposes of home dialysis, a skilled nursing facility (SNF) may qualify as a beneficiary's home. The services are excluded from SNF consolidated billing for its inpatients. The home dialysis services are billed either by the ESRD facility or the supplier depending on the Method selection made by the beneficiary.

Pub. 100-4, Chapter 8, Section 80
Home Dialysis Method I Billing to the Intermediary

A3-3644.A, PRM-1-2710, PRM-1-2710.4, A3-3169, RDF-318, RO2-3440, B3-4270, B3-4271

If the Medicare home dialysis patient chooses Method I, the dialysis facility with which the Medicare home patient is associated assumes responsibility for providing all home dialysis equipment and supplies, and home support services. For these services, the facility receives the same Medicare dialysis payment rate as it would receive for an in-facility patient under the composite rate system. The beneficiary is responsible for paying any unmet Part B deductible and the 20-percent coinsurance. After the beneficiary's Part B deductible is met, the FI pays 80 percent of the specific facility's composite rate for each in-facility outpatient maintenance dialysis treatment.

Under Method I items and services included in the composite rate must be furnished by the facility, either directly or under arrangement. The cost of an item or service is included under the composite rate unless specifically excluded. Therefore, the determination as to whether an item or service is covered under the composite rate payment does not depend on the frequency that dialysis patients require the item or service, or the number of patients who require it. If the facility fails to provide (either directly or under arrangement) any part of the items and services covered under the rate, the facility cannot be paid any amount for the items and services that it does furnish.

New items or services developed after the rate applicable for that particular year was computed are included in the composite rate payments. As such, ESRD facilities assume the responsibility for providing a dialysis service and must decide whether a particular item or service is medically appropriate and cost effective. Since the composite rate is adjusted, as necessary, based on the most recent cost data available to CMS, the costs of new items and services are taken into account in setting future rates. Similarly, any savings attributable to advancements in the treatment of

ESRD accrue to the facility because no adjustment to any individual facility's rate is made.

Pub. 100-4, Chapter 8, Section 90
Method II Billing

A3-3644.A, RO-2-3440.C, B3-4270, B3-4271, B3-4270.1, B3-4270.2, B3-34271, PRM-1-2740, A3-3644.3

Physicians and independent laboratories, must submit claims (Form CMS-1500 or electronic equivalent) to their local carrier for services furnished to end stage renal disease (ESRD) beneficiaries. Suppliers of Method II dialysis equipment and supplies will submit their claims (Form CMS-1500 or electronic equivalent) to the appropriate Durable Medical Equipment Regional Carriers (DMERCs). All ESRD facilities must submit their claims to their appropriate FI.

The amount of Medicare payment under Method II for home dialysis equipment and supplies may NOT exceed $1974.45 for continuous cycling peritoneal dialysis (CCPD) and $1490.85 for all other methods of dialysis.

All laboratory tests furnished to home dialysis patients who have selected payment Method II (see §70.1 above), are billed to and paid by the carrier at the fee schedule, if the tests are performed by an independent dialysis facility for an independent dialysis facility patient.

If the beneficiary elects to deal directly with a supplier and make arrangements for securing the necessary supplies and equipment to dialyze at home, and chooses Method II, he/she deals directly with a supplier of home dialysis equipment and supplies (this supplier is not a dialysis facility). A supplier other than a facility bills the DMERC. There can be only one supplier per beneficiary, and the supplier must accept assignment. The beneficiary is responsible for any unmet Part B deductible and the 20 percent coinsurance.

Only a supplier that is not a dialysis facility may submit a claim to a DMERC for home dialysis supplies and equipment. Suppliers will submit these claims on Form CMS-1500, or electronic equivalent. Under Method II, beneficiaries may not submit any claims and cannot receive payment for any benefits for home dialysis equipment and supplies.

The supplier must have a written agreement with a Medicare approved dialysis facility that will provide all necessary support, backup, and emergency dialysis services. The dialysis facility will not receive a regular per treatment payment for a patient who chooses Method II.

However, if the facility provides any support services, backup, and emergency dialysis services to a beneficiary who selects this option, the facility is reimbursed for the items or services it furnishes. Hospital-based facilities are paid the reasonable cost of support services, subject to the lesser of cost or charges provisions of §1833(a)(2)(A) of the Act. Independent facilities are paid on a reasonable charge basis for any home dialysis support services they furnish.

A - Description of Support Services

Support services specifically applicable to home patients include but are not limited to:

- Surveillance of the patient's home adaptation, including provisions for visits to the home in accordance with a written plan prepared and periodically reviewed by a team that includes the patient's physician and other professionals familiar with the patient's condition;

- Furnishing dialysis-related emergency services;
- Consultation for the patient with a qualified social worker and a qualified dietician;
- Maintaining a record-keeping system which assures continuity of care;
- Maintaining and submitting all required documentation to the ESRD network;
- Assuring that the water supply is of the appropriate quality;
- Assuring that the appropriate supplies are ordered on an ongoing basis;
- Arranging for the provision of all ESRD laboratory tests;
- Testing and appropriate treatment of water used in dialysis;
- Monitoring the functioning of dialysis equipment;
- All other necessary dialysis services as required under the ESRD conditions for coverage;
- Watching the patient perform CAPD and assuring that it is done correctly, and reviewing with the patient any aspects of the technique he/she may have forgotten, or informing the patient of modification in apparatus or technique;
- Documenting whether the patient has or has not had peritonitis that requires physician intervention or hospitalization, (unless there is evidence of peritonitis, a culture for peritonitis is not necessary);
- Inspection of the catheter site; and
- Since home dialysis support services include maintaining a medical record for each home dialysis patient, the Method II supplier must report to the support service dialysis facility within 30 days all items and services that it furnished to the patient so that the facility can record this information in the patient's medical record.

The services must be furnished in accordance with the written plan required for home dialysis patients. See the Medicare Benefit Policy Manual, Chapter 15, for coverage of telehealth services, and this manual, Chapter 12 for billing telehealth.

Each of the support services may be paid routinely at a frequency of once per month. Any support services furnished in excess of this frequency must be documented for being reasonable and necessary. For example, the patient may contract peritonitis and require an unscheduled connecting tube change.

B - Reasonableness Determinations

Support services (which include the laboratory services included under the composite rate for in-facility patients) are paid on a reasonable charge basis to independent facilities and a reasonable cost basis to hospital-based facilities, subject to the Method II payment cap (refer to §140). A reasonable cost/charge determination must be made for each individual support service furnished to home patients. With respect to the connecting tube change, facilities may bill Medicare for the personnel services required to change the connecting tube, but must look to the Method II supplier for payment for the connecting tube itself.

The payment cap is not a payment rate that is paid automatically each month. Accordingly, in no case may the FI routinely pay any monthly amount for support services without a claim that shows the services actually furnished.

Pub. 100-4, Chapter 8, Section 90.1
DMERC Denials for Beneficiary Submitted Claims Under Method II

A3-3170.6, A3-3644.3, A3-3644.3.A - E, HO-238.2.C, HO-238.3, HO-238.3.A, B32231.3.A and B, B3-2231, B3-4270.1, PRM-1-2709.2.A

Under Method II, beneficiaries may not submit any claims and cannot receive payment for any benefits for home dialysis equipment and supplies. DMERCs must deny unassigned and beneficiary submitted claims with the following MSN messages.

MSN # 16.6: "This item or service cannot be paid unless the provider accepts assignment."

Spanish: "Este articulo o servicio no se pagar a menos de que el proveedor acepte asignaci n."

MSN # 16.7: "Your provider must complete and submit your claim."

Spanish: "Su proveedor debe completar y someter su reclamaci n."

MSN # 16.36: "If you have already paid it, you are entitled to a refund from this provider."

Spanish: "Si usted ya lo ha pagado, tiene derecho a un reebolso de su proveedor."

Pub. 100-4, Chapter 8, Section 90.2
Requirements for Payment by the DMERC

B3-4270.1, B3-3045.7

DMERCS may make payment to home dialysis suppliers only if all of the following conditions are met:

- The beneficiary has elected Method II and to receive home dialysis equipment and supplies from an independent supplier. (Method II);
- The supplier is not a Medicare approved dialysis facility;
- The supplier accepts assignment for all Method II equipment and supplies;
- The supplier agrees to be the beneficiary's sole supplier for all home dialysis equipment and supplies;
- The supplier agrees to bill on a monthly basis for the quantity of supplies appropriate for that period. (However, there is one exception to this rule. Beneficiaries are permitted to have one month's supplies in reserve in case of emergency.);
- The supplier maintains a written certification in its files that it has a written agreement with a Medicare approved dialysis facility under which the facility will furnish all necessary support, backup, and emergency dialysis services, for each beneficiary the supplier services. (For Medicare beneficiaries who are also entitled to military or veterans benefits, a military or Veteran's Administration (VA) hospital satisfies this requirement.) As of July 1, 2002, suppliers are required to use a modifier (Specific required documentation on file) on any claim for services requiring such a backup agreement. See §90.4 for more information. The supplier may not provide supplies or services to the beneficiary, or

submit a claim to the DMERC, until they have a valid written support service facility agreement for that beneficiary. The dialysis facility must be a reasonable distance from the beneficiary's home in order to furnish these services. Determine a reasonable distance by considering such variables as terrain, whether the patient's home is located in a rural or urban area, and the usual distances traveled and time in transit by patients in the area in obtaining health care services;

- In cases where a supplier cannot establish an agreement with a support service facility that is within a reasonable distance from the patient's home, the supplier must establish a written agreement with a support service facility outside of the geographic area of the patient's home. However, in this situation, the support service facility must establish a written agreement with a dialysis facility within the beneficiary's geographic region to provide any required in-facility dialysis treatments. In this situation, the support service facility will be responsible for providing all other necessary services for the patient, and must provide for the coordination of the patient's care and monitor the patient through frequent visits to the patient's home. The signed agreement with the Method II supplier must stipulate how the support services facility will provide each of the required support services. The written agreement must include documentation to support the arrangement with the local facility for any needed in-facility services;
- The supplier reports to the backup facility within 30 days all items and services that it furnishes to the patient so that the facility can record this information in the patient's medical record; and
- The supplies and equipment are reasonable and necessary for that patient.

Pub. 100-4, Chapter 8, Section 90.2.2
DMERC Letter Explaining Requirements to Method II Supplier

B3-4270.1 updated with transmittal B3-1729 (11-01)

DMERCs must explain the Medicare requirements to every Method II supplier they service. Below is a sample letter to use.

Dear Method II Supplier:

Our records show that you supply home dialysis equipment and/or supplies to Medicare home dialysis beneficiaries who have chosen payment Method II. Effective February 1, 1990, there is a limit on the amount that a dialysis supplier may be paid under Method II.

The payment limit for Method II benefits for all forms of dialysis except continuous cycling peritoneal dialysis (CCPD) cannot exceed the median composite rate for hospital-based dialysis facilities. This rate is $1,974.45 for continuous cycling peritoneal dialysis (CCPD) and $1,490.85 for all other methods of dialysis. These limits are subject to the usual Medicare Part B deductible and coinsurance amounts.

There are additional requirements for Method II benefits. Each Method II beneficiary that did not choose Method II before February 1, 1990 must certify in writing that he/she deals with a single supplier for all home dialysis equipment

and supplies. Beneficiaries who chose Method II before February 1, 1990, are presumed to meet this requirement and need not submit this certification. If a beneficiary chooses Method II on or after February 1, 1990, the beneficiary (or the dialysis facility or the supplier on the beneficiary's behalf) must write the following in Block 8 of the Form CMS382:

"I certify that I have only one Method II supplier."

As a Method II home dialysis supplier, in order to be paid Medicare benefits, the supplier must:

- Be the beneficiary's sole supplier for all home dialysis equipment and supplies needed by the beneficiary;
- Accept assignment of Medicare benefits for home dialysis equipment and supplies. If the supplier does not accept assignment, inform your Medicare beneficiaries that the supplier does not accept assignment and that, therefore, Medicare CANNOT pay for his/her home dialysis equipment or supplies;
- Maintain written certifications that there is a written agreement with a Medicare approved dialysis facility under which the facility will furnish all necessary support, backup, and emergency dialysis services for each beneficiary you serve. Support services include, but are not limited to, maintaining the patient's medical record and providing information required by the ESRD network. For each Medicare beneficiaries, there must be an agreement with a dialysis facility that is a reasonable distance from the beneficiary's home. The CMS determines a reasonable distance by considering such variables as terrain, whether the beneficiary's home is in an urban or rural area, and the usual distances traveled and time in transit by patients in the area when obtaining health services. In cases where an agreement with a support service facility cannot be established that is within a reasonable distance from the patient's home, a written agreement with a support service facility outside of the geographic area of the patient's home must be established. In this situation, the support service facility must establish a written arrangement with a dialysis facility within the beneficiary's geographic region to provide any required in-facility dialysis treatments. In this situation, the support service facility will be responsible for providing all other necessary services for the beneficiary and must provide for the coordination of the patient's care and monitor the patient through frequent visits to the patient's home. The signed agreement with the Method II supplier must stipulate how the support services facility will provide each of the required support services. The written agreement must include documentation to support the arrangement with the local facility for any needed in-facility services. Suppliers may not provide services or submit a claim to Medicare before this agreement is obtained. They need not identify individual beneficiaries.
- Report to the support service dialysis facility within 30 days all items and services that are furnished to the patient so that this information can be recorded by the facility in the medical record; and
- Agree to generally bill once a month and for only one month's quantity of supplies at a time. In the

event that a beneficiary becomes a hospital inpatient for at least three days (not counting the day of admission or discharge), suppliers must prorate the following month's supply bills to account for supplies the beneficiary did not use while an inpatient.

Pub. 100-4, Chapter 8, Section 90.3.2
Home Dialysis Supplies and Equipment HCPCS Codes Used to Bill the DMERC

PM B-01-56, B3-4270 updated 11-16-01(CR 1799)

A - HCPCS Codes

Prior to January 1, 2002, suppliers billed for dialysis supplies using codes describing "kits" of supplies. The use of kit codes such as A4820, A4900, A4901, A4905, and A4914 allows suppliers to bill for supply items without separately identifying the supplies that are being furnished to the patient. Effective January 1, 2002, these kit codes were deleted and suppliers are now required to bill for dialysis supplies using existing and newly developed HCPCS codes for individual dialysis items. Refer to the LMRP for the HCPCS codes for dialysis supplies and equipment that are effective for claims received on or after January 1, 2002.

A4651 A4652 A4656 A4657 A4660 A4663 A4680 A4690 A4706 A4707 A4708 A4709 A4712 A4714 A4719 A4720 A4721 A4722 A4723 A4724 A4725 A4726 A4730 A4736 A4737 A4740 A4750 A4755 A4760 A4765 A4766 A4770 A4771 A4772 A4773 A4774 A4801 A4802 A4860 A4870 A4911 A4913 A4918 A4927 A4928 A4929 E1500 E1510 E1520 E1530 E1540 E1550 E1560 E1570 E1575 E1580 E1590 E1592 E1594 E1600 E1610 E1615 E1620 E1625 E1630 E1632 E1635 E1636 E1637 E1638 E1639 E1699

DMERCs gap-fill reasonable charge amounts for 2002 for all of the applicable codes other than codes A4913 and E1699, the codes used for miscellaneous supplies and equipment that do not fall under any of the other HCPCS codes. The gap-filled amounts should be established using price lists in effect as of December 31, 2000 if available. These gap-filled payment amounts will apply to all claims with dates of service from January 1, 2002, through December 31, 2002.

Codes A4650 - A4927 and E1510 - E1702 may be used only for supplies and equipment relating to home dialysis. In particular, items not related to dialysis should not be included in the supply kit codes (A4820, A4900, A4901, A4905) or listed in the miscellaneous codes (A4910, A4913, E1699). Conversely, supplies and equipment relating to home dialysis should not be billed using other HCPCS codes.

Dialysis supply kits (A4820, A4900, A4901, A4905) billed by an individual supplier must contain the same type and quantity of supplies each time that it is billed. One unit of service would represent the typical amount of supplies needed for one month of dialysis. The content of the kit may not vary from patient to patient or in a single patient from month to month unless the 52 modifier is used (see below). If more than this typical amount of supplies is needed in one month, the excess supplies should be billed using other dialysis supply codes. If significantly less than the usual amount is needed for 1 month, the 52 modifier should be added to the code and the submitted charge reduced accordingly. A listing of the components of each kit billed by a supplier must be available for review by the DMERC.

For items before January 1, 2002, dialysis solutions (A4700, A4705) should not be included in the supply kit but should

be separately billed. One unit of service for these codes is for one liter of dialysis solution.

For items before January 1, 2002, items not included in kits must be billed separately, using either a specific code (A4650 - A4927) or miscellaneous code (A4910, A4913, E1699).

Code A4901 and/or E1594 should be billed for each month that the patient receives CCPD.

An EM modifier should be added to a dialysis supply code when it represents emergency reserve supplies over and above the typical monthly amount.

B - Modifiers

Method II suppliers must maintain documentation to support the existence of a written agreement with a Medicare certified support service facility within a reasonable distance from the beneficiary's home.

Effective July 1, 2002, suppliers must use "KX" modifier on the line item level for all Method II home dialysis claims to indicate that they have this documentation on file, and must provide it to the DMERC upon request. As of July 1, 2002, DMERCs must front end reject any Method II claims that do not have the "KX" modifier at the line level. The supplier may correct and resubmit the claim with the appropriate modifier. DMERCs and the shared systems must make all systems changes necessary to reject Method II claims that do not have the "KX" modifier.

The following listed modifiers are frequently used to identify the service/charges billed for Dialysis Supplies.

CC-Procedure code change - Used by the carrier when the procedure code submitted was changed either for administrative reasons or because an incorrect procedure code was filed. Do not use this modifier when filing claims to Palmetto GBA.

EJ-Subsequent Claim (for Erythropoietin Alpha-EPO injection only)

EM-Emergency reserve supply [for End Stage Renal Disease (ESRD) benefit only]

KY-Specific requirements found in the Documentation section of the Medical Policy have been met and evidence of this is available in the supplier's record. Effective July 1, 2002, suppliers must use the " KY" modifier on the line item level for all Method II home dialysis claims.

NU-New Equipment - Used when purchasing new equipment.

RR-Initial Rental - Rental (use the -RR modifier when DME is to be rented).

UE-Used durable medical equipment

ZU-Advance notice of possible medical necessity denial on file (this modifier will be discontinued with the implementation of HIPAA)

ZY-Potentially noncovered item or service billed for denial or at the beneficiary's request (not to be used for medical necessity denials) (this modifier will be discontinued with the implementation of HIPAA)

Pub. 100-4, Chapter 8, Section 120.1
Payment for Immunosuppressive Drugs Furnished to Transplant Patients

PRM-1-2711.5, B3-4471, AB-01-10

A. General

Effective January 1, 1987, Medicare pays for FDA approved self-administered immunosuppressive drugs. Generally, under this benefit, payment is made for self-administered immunosuppressive drugs that are specifically labeled and approved for marketing as such by the FDA, as well as those prescription drugs, such as prednisone, that are used in conjunction with immunosuppressive drugs as part of a therapeutic regimen reflected in FDA approved labeling for immunosuppressive drugs. This benefit is subject to the Part B deductible and coinsurance provision. There is no time limitation on the coverage of these drugs; however, if a beneficiary loses Medicare coverage as a result of the transplant, the drugs are no longer covered. When the beneficiary reaches the age of 65 and becomes entitled, that person can have the drugs covered again. The hospital pharmacy must ask the physician to furnish the patient with a non-refillable 30-day prescription for the immunosuppressive drugs. This is because the dosage of these drugs frequently diminishes over a period of time, and it is not uncommon for the physician to change the prescription from one drug to another because of the patient's needs. Also, these drugs are expensive, and the coinsurance liability on unused drugs could be a financial burden to the beneficiary. Unless there are special circumstances, the FI and carrier do not consider a supply of drugs in excess of 30 days to be reasonable and necessary and limits payment accordingly.

B. Payment

Payment is made on a reasonable cost basis if the beneficiary is the outpatient of a participating hospital. In all other cases, payment is made on an allowable charge basis.

C. FDA Approved Drugs

Some of the most commonly prescribed immunosuppressive drugs are:

- Sandimmune (cyclosporine), Sandoz Pharmaceutical (oral or parenteral),
- Imuran (azathioprine), Burroughs Wellcome Vial (oral),
- Atgam (antithymocyte/globulin), Upjohn (parenteral); and
- Orthoclone OKT3 (muromonab - CD3) Ortho Pharmaceutical (parenteral).

Also covered are prescription drugs used in conjunction with immunosuppressive drugs as part of a therapeutic regimen reflected in FDA approved labeling for immunosuppressive drugs.

The payment for the drug is limited to the cost of the most frequently administered dosage of the drug (adjusted for medical factors as determined by the physician).

Consult such sources as the Drug Topics Red Book, American Druggists Blue Book, and Medispan, realizing that substantial discounts are available.

Pub. 100-4, Chapter 8, Section 130
Physicians and Supplier (Nonfacility) Billing for ESRD Services - General

B3-4270 updated with Transmittal 1729

Payment for renal-related physicians' services to ESRD patients is made in either of the following ways:

- Under the Monthly Capitation Payment (MCP) (see §140 below for an explanation of the MCP); or
- Using the daily codes for ESRD services (CPT codes 90922-90925) with units that represent the number of days services were furnished.
- Under the Initial method (IM)

The carrier receives bills (Form CMS-1500 or electronic equivalent) from physicians for services furnished ESRD beneficiaries. DMERCs receive bills for equipment and supplies for Method II beneficiaries. Intermediaries receive bills from ESRD facilities. Lab bills from CLIA certified independent dialysis facilities were billed to the carrier before September 1, 1997, and to the FI beginning on that date. Other certified labs continue to bill the carrier.

Pub. 100-4, Chapter 8, Section 140
Monthly Capitation Payment Method for Physicians' Services Furnished to Patients on Maintenance Dialysis

B3-15060, B3-15060.1, B3-15060.2, B3-15060.3, B3-15060.4, B3-15060.5, B3-15350, B3-2230.3, B3-2230.6, B3-4272, B3-4272.1, B3-4272.2

The monthly capitation payment is a payment for most dialysis-related physician services furnished to Medicare ESRD patients is through the monthly capitation payment (MCP). The same monthly amount is paid to the physician for each patient supervised regardless of whether the patient dialyzes at home or as an outpatient in an approved ESRD facility. The Medicare program pays 80 percent of the MCP after the beneficiary's Part B deductible is met. The beneficiary is responsible for the Part B deductible amounts and the 20 percent coinsurance.

Pub. 100-4, Chapter 8, Section 140.1
Services Included in Monthly Capitation Payment

B3-4272.1

The following physician services are included in the MCP:

- Assessment of the need for a specified diet and the need for nutritional supplementation for the control of chronic renal failure. Specification of the quantity of total protein, high biologic protein, sodium, potassium, and amount of fluids to be allowed during a given time period. For diabetic patients with chronic renal failure, the prescription usually specifies the number of calories in the diet.
- Assessment of which mode(s) of chronic dialysis (types of hemodialysis or peritoneal dialysis) are suitable for a given patient and recommendation of the type(s) of therapy for a given patient.
- Assessment and determination of which type of dialysis access is best suited for a given patient and arrangement for creation of dialysis access.
- Assessment of whether the patient meets preliminary criteria as a renal transplant candidate and presentation of this assessment to the patient and family.
- Prescription of the parameters of intradialytic management. For chronic hemodialysis therapies, this includes the type of dialysis access, the type and amount of anticoagulant to be employed, blood flow rates, dialysate flow rate, ultrafiltration rate, dialysate temperature, type of dialysate (acetate versus bicarbonate) and composition of the electrolytes in the dialysate, size of hemodialyzer

(surface area) and composition of the dialyzer membrane (conventional versus high flux), duration and frequency of treatments, the type and frequency of measuring indices of clearance, and intradialytic medications to be administered. For chronic peritoneal dialysis therapies, this includes the type of peritoneal dialysis, the volume of dialysate, concentration of dextrose in the dialysate, electrolyte composition of the dialysate, duration of each exchange, and addition of medication to the dialysate, such as heparin, and the type and frequency of measuring indices of clearance. For diabetics, the quantity of insulin to be added to each exchange is prescribed.

- Assessment of whether the patient has significant renal failure-related anemia, determination of the etiology(ies) for the anemia based on diagnostic tests, and prescription of therapy for correction of the anemia, such as vitamins, oral or parenteral iron, and hormonal therapy such as erythropoietin.
- Assessment of whether the patient has hyperparathyroidism and/or renal osteodystrophy secondary to chronic renal failure and prescription of appropriate therapy, such as calcium and phosphate binders for control of hyperphosphatemia. Based upon assessment of parahormone levels, serum calcium levels, and evaluation for the presence of metabolic bone disease, the physician determines whether oral or parenteral therapy with vitamin D or its analogs is indicated and prescribes the appropriate therapy. Based upon assessment and diagnosis of bone disease, the physician may prescribe specific chelation therapy with deferoxamine and the use of hemoperfusion for removal or aluminum and the chelation.
- Assessment of whether the patient has dialysis-related arthropathy or neuropathy and adjustment of the patient's prescription accordingly. Referral of the patient for any additional needed specialist evaluation and management of these end-organ problems.
- Assessment of whether the patient has fluid overload resulting from renal failure and establishment of an estimated "ideal (dry) weight." The physician determines the need for fluid removal independent of the dialysis prescription and implements these measures when indicated.
- Determination of the need for and prescription of antihypertensive medications and their timing relative to dialysis when the patient is hypertensive in spite of correction of fluid overload.
- Periodic review of the dialysis records to ascertain whether the patient is receiving the prescribed amount of dialysis and ordering of indices of clearance, such as urea kinetics, in order to ascertain whether the dialysis prescription is producing adequate dialysis. If the indices of clearance suggest that the prescription requires alteration, the physician orders changes in the hemodialysis prescription, such as blood flow rate, dialyzer surface area, dialysis frequency, and/or dialysis duration (length of treatment). For peritoneal dialysis patients, the physician may order changes in the volume of dialysate, dextrose concentration of the dialysate, and duration of the exchanges.

- Periodic visits to the patient during dialysis to ascertain whether the dialysis is working well and whether the patient is tolerating the procedure well (physiologically and psychologically). During these visits, the physician determines whether alteration in any aspect of a given patient's prescription is indicated, such as changes in the estimate of the patient's dry weight. Review of the treatment with the nurse or technician performing the therapy is also included. The frequency of these visits will vary depending upon the patient's medical status, complicating conditions, and other determinants.
- Performance of periodic physical assessments, based upon the patient's clinical stability, in order to determine the necessity for alterations in various aspects of the patient's prescription. Similarly, the physician reviews the results of periodic laboratory testing in order to determine the need for alterations in the patient's prescription, such as changes in the amount and timing of phosphate binders or dose of erythropoietin.
- Periodic assessment of the adequacy and function of the patient's dialysis access appropriate tests and antibiotic therapy.
- Interpretations of the following tests:

o Bone mineral density studies (CPT codes 76070, 76075, 78350, and 78351);

o Noninvasive vascular diagnostic studies of hemodialysis access (CPT codes 93925, 93926, 93930, 93931, and 93990);

o Nerve conduction studies (CPT codes 95900, 95903, 95904, 95925, 95926, 95927, 95934, 95935, and 95936);

o Electromyography studies (CPT codes 95860, 95861, 95863, 95864, 95867, 95867, 95869, and 95872).

Periodic review and update of the patient's short-term and long-term care plans with staff.

Coordination and direction of the care of patients by other professional staff, such as dieticians and social workers.

Certification of the need for items and services such as durable medical equipment and home health care services. Care plan oversight services described by CPT code 99375 are included in the MCP and may not be separately reported.

Pub. 100-4, Chapter 8, Section 140.5
Determining Monthly Capitation Payment Amount for Physician's Services to Maintenance Dialysis Patients

B3-15060.3

Effective with services rendered on January 1, 1995, the MCP is paid in accordance with the Medicare physician fee schedule. For adult patients, providers bill CPT code 90921. To bill for a month of services for pediatric patients, providers bill the appropriate monthly code (CPT codes 90918, 90919, or 90920). Because the services described by the care plan oversight codes (CPT codes 99375 and 99376) are included in the MCP, physicians may not bill for care plan oversight in the same month as they bill for the MCP.

Pub. 100-4, Chapter 8, Section 170
Billing Physician Dialysis Services (codes 90935 - 90999) and Related Payment

B3-15350.B.3

© 2005 Ingenix, Inc.

APPENDIX D

Except when the MCP applies claims for physicians' inpatient dialysis services furnished to ESRD or acute dialysis patients are processed using physicians' inpatient dialysis services procedure codes 90935, 90937, 90945, and 90947. All carriers must use these codes for these services.

Carriers make payment on the basis of ESRD procedure codes, i.e., codes 90935, 90937, 90945, or 90947, only if the place of service on the claim is inpatient hospital. This is because all physicians' outpatient renal-related services are included in payment made under the monthly capitation payment.

A. ESRD Monthly Capitation Payments

Effective January 1, 1995, monthly capitation payments are made under the physician fee schedule. For their adult patients, physicians may bill either the monthly code (CPT code 90921) or the daily code (CPT code 90922) with units that represent the number of days in a single month, but may not bill both.

To bill for a month of services for pediatric patients, providers should bill the appropriate monthly code (CPT codes 90919, 90920, or 90921). To bill for less than a month of service, providers bill the appropriate daily code (CPT codes 90923-90925) and units that represent the number of days. Providers may bill either the monthly code or the daily code, but not both. Since billing is done at the conclusion of the month, the patient's age at the end of month is the age of the patient for billing purposes.

B - Inpatient and Outpatient Dialysis Services On Same Date As An Evaluation and Management Service

CPT codes 90935 and 90937 are used to report inpatient ESRD hemodialysis and outpatient hemodialysis performed on non-ESRD patients (e.g., patients in acute renal failure requiring a brief period of dialysis prior to recovery). CPT codes 90945 and 90947 are used to report all non-hemodialysis procedures. All four of these codes include payment for any evaluation and management services related to the patients renal disease that are provided on the same date as the dialysis service. Therefore, payment for all evaluation and management services is bundled into the payment for 90935, 90937, 90945, and 90947, except for the following evaluation and management services which may be reported on the same date as a dialysis service with the use of the –25 modifier and they are significant and separately identifiable and met any medical necessity requirements:

99201-99205	Office or Other Outpatient Visit for a New Patient
99211-99215	Office or Other Outpatient Visit for an Established Patient
99221-99223	Initial Hospital Care for a New or Established Patient
99238-99239	Hospital Discharge Day Management Services
99241-99245	Office or Other Outpatient Consultations, New or Established Patient
99251-99255	Initial Inpatient Consultations, New or Established Patient
99291-99292	Critical Care Services

In the absence of one of these codes being reported with the –25 modifier and meeting the other requirements listed above, pay only the dialysis service and deny the evaluation and management service. Furthermore, payment is not allowed for more than one dialysis service per day.

Pub. 100-4, Chapter 11, Section 10
Overview

Medicare beneficiaries entitled to hospital insurance (Part A) who have terminal illnesses and a life expectancy of six months or less have the option of electing hospice benefits in lieu of standard Medicare coverage for treatment and management of their terminal condition. Only care provided by a Medicare certified hospice is covered under the hospice benefit provisions.

Hospice care is available for two 90-day periods and an unlimited number of 60-day periods during the remainder of the hospice patient's lifetime. However, abeneficiary may voluntarily terminate his hospice election period. Election/termination dates are retained onCWF.

When hospice coverage is elected, the beneficiary waives all rights to Medicare Part B payments for services that are related to the treatment and management of his/her terminal illness during any period his/her hospice benefit election is in force, except for professional services of an attending physician, which may include a nurse practitioner. If the attending physician, who may be a nurse practitioner, is an employee of the designated hospice, he or she may not receive compensation from the hospice for those services under Part B. These physician professional services are billed to Medicare Part A by the hospice.

To be covered, hospice services must be reasonable and necessary for the palliation or management of the terminal illness and related conditions. The individual must elect hospice care and a certification that the individual is terminally ill must be completed by the patient's attending physician (if there is one), and the Medical Director (or the physician member of the Interdisciplinary Group (IDG)). Nurse practitioners serving as the attending physician may not certify or re-certify the terminal illness. A plan of care must be established before services are provided. To be covered, services must be consistent with the plan of care. Certification of terminal illness is based on the physician's or medical director's clinical judgment regarding the normal course of an individual's illness. It should be noted that predicting life expectancy is not always exact.

See the Medicare Benefit Policy Manual, Chapter 9, for additional general information about the Hospice benefit.

See Chapter 29 of this manual for information on the appeals process that should be followed when an entity is dissatisfied with the determination made on a claim.

See Chapter 9 of the Medicare Benefit Policy Manual for hospice eligibility requirements and election of hospice care.

Pub. 100-4, Chapter 11, Section 40.1.3
Attending Physician Services

When hospice coverage is elected, the beneficiary waives all rights toMedicare Part Bpayments for professional services that are related to the treatment and management of his/her terminal illness during any period his/her hospice benefit election isin force, except for professional services of an"attending physician," who is not an employee of the designated hospice nor receives compensation from the hospice for those services. For purposes of administering the hospice benefit provisions, an "attending physician" means an individual who:

- Is a doctor of medicine or osteopathy or
- A nurse practitioner (for professional services related to the terminal illness that are furnished on or after December 8, 2003); and
- Is identified by the individual, at the time he/she elects hospice coverage, as having the most significant role in the determination and delivery of their medical care.

Even though a beneficiary elects hospice coverage, he/she may designate and use an attending physician, who is not employed by nor receives compensation from the hospice for professional services furnished, in addition to the services of hospice-employed physicians. The professional services of an attending physician, who may be a nurse practitioner as defined in Chapter 9, that are reasonable and necessary for the treatment and management of a hospice patient's terminal illness are not considered hospice services.

Where the service is considered a hospice service (i.e., a service related to the hospice patient's terminal illness that was furnished by someone other than the designated "attending physician" [or a physician substituting for the attending physician]) the physician or other provider must look to the hospice for payment.

Professional services related to the hospice patient's terminal condition that were furnished by the "attending physician", who may be a nurse practitioner, are billed to carriers. When the attending physician furnishes a terminal illness related service that includes both a professional and technical component (e.g., x-rays), he/she bills the professional component of such services to the carrier and looks to the hospice for payment for the technical component. Likewise, the attending physician, who may be a nurse practitioner, would look to the hospice for payment for terminal illness related services furnished that have no professional component (e.g., clinical lab tests). The remainder of this section explains this in greater detail.

When a Medicare beneficiary elects hospice coverage he/she may designate an attending physician, who may be a nurse practitioner, not employed by the hospice, in addition to receiving care from hospice-employed physicians. The professional services of a non-hospice affiliated attending physician for the treatment and management of a hospice patient's terminal illness are not considered "hospice services." These attending physician services are billed to the carrier, provided they were not furnished under a payment arrangement with the hospice. The attending physician codes services with the GV modifier "Attending physician not employed or paid under agreement by the patient's hospice provider" when billing his/her professional services furnished for the treatment and management of a hospice patient's terminal condition. Carriers make payment to the attending physician or beneficiary, as appropriate, based on the payment and deductible rules applicable to each covered service.

Payments for the services of attending physician are not counted in determining whether the hospice cap amount has been exceeded because services provided by an independent attending physician are not part of the hospice's care.

Services provided by an independent attending physician who may be a nurse practitioner must be coordinated with any direct care services provided by hospice physicians.

Only the direct professional services of an independent attending physician, who may be a nurse practitioner, to a patient may be billed; the costs for services such as lab or x-rays are not to be included in the bill.

If another physician covers for a hospice patient's designated attending physician, the services of the substituting physician are billed by the designated attending physician under the reciprocal or locum tenens billing instructions. In such instances, the attending physician bills using the GV modifier in conjunction with either the Q5 or Q6 modifier.

When services related to a hospice patient's terminal condition are furnished under a payment arrangement with the hospice by the designated attending physician who may be a nurse practitioner, the physician must look to the hospice for payment. In this situation the physicians' services are hospice services and are billed by the hospice to its FI.

Carriers must process and pay for covered, medically necessary Part B services that physicians furnish to patients after their hospice benefits are revoked even if the patient remains under the care of the hospice. Such services are billed without the GV or GW modifiers. Make payment based on applicable Medicare payment and deductible rules for each covered service even if the beneficiary continues to be treated by the hospice after hospice benefits are revoked.

The CWF response contains the period of hospice entitlement. This information is a permanent part of the notice and is furnished on all CWF replies and automatic notices. Carriers use the CWF reply for validating dates of hospice coverage and to research, examine and adjudicate services coded with the GV or GW modifiers.

Pub. 100-4, Chapter 12, Section 10
General

B3-2020

This chapter provides claims processing instructions for physician and nonphysician practitioner services.

Most physician services are paid according to the Medicare Physician Fee Schedule. Section 20 below offers additional information on the fee schedule application. Chapter 23 includes the fee schedule format and payment localities, and identifies services that are paid at reasonable charge rather than based on the fee schedule. In addition:

- Chapter 13 describes billing and payment for radiology services.
- Chapter 16 outlines billing and payment under the laboratory fee schedule.
- Chapter 17 provides a description of billing and payment for drugs.
- Chapter 18 describes billing and payment for preventive services and screening tests.

The Medicare Manual Pub 100-1, Medicare General Information, Eligibility, and Entitlement Manual, Chapter 5, provides definitions for the following:

Physician;

Doctors of Medicine and Osteopathy;

Dentists;

Doctors of Podiatric Medicine;

Optometrists;

Chiropractors (but only for spinal manipulation); and

Interns and Residents.

The Medicare Benefit Policy Manual, Chapter 15, provides coverage policy for the following services.

Telephone services;

Consultations;

Patient initiated second opinions; and

Concurrent care.

Chapter 26 provides guidance on completing and submitting Medicare claims.

Pub. 100-4, Chapter 12, Section 30.1
Digestive System (Codes 40000 - 49999)

B3-15100

A - Upper Gastrointestinal Endoscopy Including Endoscopic Ultrasound (EUS) (Code 43259)

If the person performing the original diagnostic endoscopy has access to the EUS and the clinical situation requires an EUS, the EUS may be done at the same time. The procedure, diagnostic and EUS, is reported under the same code, CPT 43259. This code conforms to CPT guidelines for the indented codes. The service represented by the indented code, in this case code 43259 for EUS, includes the service represented by the unintended code preceding the list of indented codes. Therefore, when a diagnostic examination of the upper gastrointestinal tract "including esophagus, stomach, and either the duodenum or jejunum as appropriate," includes the use of endoscopic ultrasonography, the service is reported by a single code, namely 43259.

Interpretation, whether by a radiologist or endoscopist, is reported under CPT code 76975-26. These codes may both be reported on the same day.

B - Incomplete Colonoscopies (Codes 45330 and 45378)

An incomplete colonoscopy, e.g., the inability to extend beyond the splenic flexure, is billed and paid using colonoscopy code 45378 with modifier "-53." The Medicare physician fee schedule database has specific values for code 45378-53. These values are the same as for code 45330, sigmoidoscopy, as failure to extend beyond the splenic flexure means that a sigmoidoscopy rather than a colonoscopy has been performed. However, code 45378-53 should be used when an incomplete colonoscopy has been done because other MPFSDB indicators are different for codes 45378 and 45330.

Pub. 100-4, Chapter 12, Section 30.2
Urinary and Male Genital Systems (Codes 50010 - 55899)

B3-15200

A - Cystourethroscopy With Ureteral Catheterization (Code 52005)

Code 52005 has a zero in the bilateral field (payment adjustment for bilateral procedure does not apply) because the basic procedure is an examination of the bladder and urethra (cystourethroscopy), which are not paired organs.

The work RVUs assigned take into account that it may be necessary to examine and catheterize one or both ureters. No additional payment is made when the procedure is billed with bilateral modifier "-50." Neither is any additional payment made when both ureters are examined and code 52005 is billed with multiple surgery modifier "-51." It is inappropriate to bill code 52005 twice, once by itself and once with modifier "-51," when both ureters are examined.

B - Cystourethroscopy With Fulgration and/or Resection of Tumors (Codes 52234, 52235, and 52240)

The descriptors for codes 52234 through 52240 include the language "tumor(s)."

This means that regardless of the number of tumors removed, only one unit of a single code can be billed on a given date of service. It is inconsistent to allow payment for removal of a small (code 52234) and a large (code 52240) tumor using two codes when only one code is allowed for the removal of more than one large tumor. For these three codes only one unit may be billed for any of these codes, only one of the codes may be billed, and the billed code reflects the size of the largest tumor removed.

Pub. 100-4, Chapter 12, Section 30.4
Echocardiography Services (Codes 93303 - 93350)

B3-15360

Effective October 1, 2000, physicians may separately bill for contrast agents used in echocardiography. Physicians should use HCPCS Code A9700 (Supply of injectable contrast material for use in echocardiography, per study). The type of service code is 9. This code will be carrier-priced.

Pub. 100-4, Chapter 12, Section 30.5
Chemotherapy Administration (Codes 96400 - 96549)And Non Chemotherapy Drug Infusions (Codes 90780-90781)

A - General Use of Codes

Chemotherapy administration codes, 96400 through 96450, 96542, 96545, and 96549, are only to be used when reporting chemotherapy administration when the drug being used is an anti-neoplastic **and** the diagnosis is cancer. The administration of other drugs, such as growth factors, saline, and diuretics, to patients with cancer, or the administration of anti-neoplastics to patients with a diagnosis other than cancer, are reported with codes 90780 through 90784 as appropriate. For services furnished on or after January, 1, 2004, do not allow payment for CPT code 99211, with or without modifier 25, if it is billed with a nonchemotherapy drug infusion code, 90780 or 90781, or a chemotherapy administration code, 96400, 96408 to 96425, 96520, or 96530.

Physicians providing chemotherapy drug administration services (or nonchemotherapy drug infusion services) and evaluation and management services, other than CPT code 99211, on the same day must bill in accordance with section 30.6.6 using modifier "25". Carriers pay for evaluation and management services provided on the same day as the chemotherapy drug administration (or nonchemotherapy drug infusion services) if the evaluation and management service meets the requirements of section 30.6.6 even though the underlying codes do not have global periods.

B - Chemotherapy Administration by Push and Infusion on Same Day

Separate payment is allowed for chemotherapy administration by push and by infusion technique on the same day. Only one push administration is paid on a single day. For services furnished on or after January 1, 2004, allow code 96408 to be reported and paid once per day for each drug administered.

C - Chemotherapy Infusion and Hydration Therapy Infusion on Same Day

Separate payment is not allowed for the infusion of saline, an anti-emetic, or any other nonchemotherapy drug under CPT codes 90780 and 90781 when administered at the same time as chemotherapy infusion (CPT codes 96410, 96412, or 96414). Separate payment is allowed for these two services on the same day when they are provided sequentially, rather than at the same time. Physicians use the modifier "-59" to indicate when CPT codes 90780 and 90781 are provided sequentially with CPT codes 96410, 96412, and 96414.

Pub. 100-4, Chapter 12, Section 30.6
Evaluation and Management Service Codes - General (Codes 99201 - 99499)

B3-15501-15501.1

Pub. 100-4, Chapter 12, Section 30.6.2
Billing for Medically Necessary Visit on Same Occasion as Preventive Medicine Service

See Chapter 18 for payment for covered preventive services.

When a physician furnishes a Medicare beneficiary a covered visit at the same place and on the same occasion as a noncovered preventive medicine service (CPT codes 99381-99397), consider the covered visit to be provided in lieu of a part of the preventive medicine service of equal value to the visit. A preventive medicine service (CPT codes 99381-99397) is a noncovered service. The physician may charge the beneficiary, as a charge for the noncovered remainder of the service, the amount by which the physician's current established charge for the preventive medicine service exceeds his/her current established charge for the covered visit. Pay for the covered visit based on the lesser of the fee schedule amount or the physician's actual charge for the visit. The physician is not required to give the beneficiary written advance notice of noncoverage of the part of the visit that constitutes a routine preventive visit. However, the physician is responsible for notifying the patient in advance of his/her liability for the charges for services that are not medically necessary to treat the illness or injury.

There could be covered and noncovered procedures performed during this encounter (e.g., screening x-ray, EKG, lab tests.). These are considered individually. Those procedures which are for screening for asymptomatic conditions are considered noncovered and, therefore, no payment is made. Those procedures ordered to diagnose or monitor a symptom, medical condition, or treatment are evaluated for medical necessity and, if covered, are paid.

Pub. 100-4, Chapter 12, Section 30.6.7
Payment for Office/Outpatient Visits (Codes 99201 - 99215)

B3-15502

A - Definition of New Patient for Selection of Visit Code

Carriers must interpret the phrase "new patient" to mean a patient who has not received any professional services from the physician **or physician group practice** within the previous three years.

If no evaluation and management service is performed, the patient may continue to be treated as a new patient. For example, if a professional component of a previous procedure is billed in a 3-year time-period, e.g., a lab interpretation is billed and no evaluation and management service is performed, then this patient remains a new patient for the initial visit. An interpretation of a diagnostic test, reading an x-ray or EKG etc., in the absence of an evaluation and management service does not affect the designation of a new patient.

B - Office/Outpatient Visits Provided on Same Day for Unrelated Problems

Carriers may not pay two office visits billed by a physician for the same beneficiary on the same day unless the physician documents that the visits were for unrelated problems in the office or outpatient setting which could not be provided during the same encounter (e.g., office visit for blood pressure medication evaluation, followed five hours later by a visit for evaluation of leg pain following an accident).

C - Office/Outpatient or Emergency Department Visit on Day of Admission to Nursing Facility

Carriers may not pay a physician for an emergency department visit or an office visit **and** a comprehensive nursing facility assessment on the same day. They bundle evaluation and management services on the same date provided in sites other than the nursing facility into the initial nursing facility care code when performed on the same date as the nursing facility admission by the same physician.

D - Injection and Evaluation and Management Code Billed Separately on Same Day of Service

Carriers must advise physicians that CPT code 99211 cannot be used to report a visit solely for the purpose of receiving an injection which meets the definition of CPT codes 90782, 90783, 90784, or 90788. Carriers may not pay CPT codes 90782, 90783, 90784, or 90788 if any other physician fee schedule service was rendered.

The drug is billed as a J code, whether the injection is separately billable or not.

If no evaluation and management service or other service is provided on the same day as the injection, the injection code is billed.

Pub. 100-4, Chapter 12, Section 30.6.8
Payment for Hospital Observation Services (Codes 99217 - 99220)

B3-15504

A - Who May Bill Initial Observation Care

Carriers pay for initial observation care billed by only the physician who admitted the patient to hospital observation and was responsible for the patient during his/her stay in observation. A physician who does not have inpatient admitting privileges but who is authorized to admit a patient to observation status may bill these codes.

For a physician to bill the initial observation care codes, there must be a medical observation record for the patient which contains dated and timed physician's admitting orders regarding the care the patient is to receive while in observation, nursing notes, and progress notes prepared by the physician while the patient was in observation status. This record must be in addition to any record prepared as a

© 2005 Ingenix, Inc.

result of an emergency department or outpatient clinic encounter.

Payment for an initial observation care code is for all the care rendered by the admitting physician on the date the patient was admitted to observation. All other physicians who see the patient while he or she is in observation must bill the office and other outpatient service codes or outpatient consultation codes as appropriate when they provide services to the patient.

For example, if an internist admits a patient to observation and asks an allergist for a consultation on the patient's condition, only the internist may bill the initial observation care code. The allergist must bill using the outpatient consultation code that best represents the services he or she provided. The allergist cannot bill an inpatient consultation since the patient was not a hospital inpatient.

B - Physician Billing for Observation Care Following Admission to Observation

If the patient is discharged on the same date as admission to observation, pay only the initial observation care code because that code represents a full day of care.

If the patient remains in observation after the first date following the admission to observation, it is expected that the patient would be discharged on that second calendar date. The physician bills CPT code 99217 for observation care discharge services provided on the second date.

In the rare circumstance when a patient is held in observation status for more than two calendar dates, the physician must bill subsequent services furnished before the date of discharge using the outpatient/office visit codes. The physician may not use the subsequent hospital care codes since the patient is not an inpatient of the hospital.

C - Admission to Inpatient Status from Observation

If the same physician who admitted a patient to observation status also admits the patient to inpatient status from observation before the end of the date on which the patient was admitted to observation, pay only an initial hospital visit for the evaluation and management services provided on that date. Medicare payment for the initial hospital visit includes all services provided to the patient on the date of admission by that physician, regardless of the site of service. The physician may not bill an initial observation care code for services on the date that he or she admits the patient to inpatient status. If the patient is admitted to inpatient status from observation subsequent to the date of admission to observation, the physician must bill an initial hospital visit for the services provided on that date. The physician may not bill the hospital observation discharge management code (code 99217) or an outpatient/office visit for the care provided in observation on the date of admission to inpatient status.

D - Hospital Observation During Global Surgical Period

The global surgical fee includes payment for hospital observation (codes 99217, 99218, 99219, and 99220, 99234, 99235, 99236) services unless the criteria for use of CPT modifiers "-24," "-25," or "-57" are met. Carriers must pay for these services in addition to the global surgical fee only if both of the following requirements are met:

- The hospital observation service meets the criteria needed to justify billing it with CPT modifiers "-24," "-25," or "-57" (decision for major surgery); and

- The hospital observation service furnished by the surgeon meets all of the criteria for the hospital observation code billed.

Examples of the decision for surgery during a hospital observation period are:

- A patient is admitted by an emergency department physician to an observation unit for observation of a head injury. A neurosurgeon is called in to do a consultation on the need for surgery while the patient is in the observation unit and decides that the patient requires surgery. The surgeon would bill an outpatient consultation with the "-57" modifier to indicate that the decision for surgery was made during the consultation. The surgeon must bill an outpatient consultation because the patient in an observation unit is not an inpatient of the hospital. Only the physician who admitted the patient to hospital observation may bill for initial observation care.

- A patient is admitted by a neurosurgeon to a hospital observation unit for observation of a head injury. During the observation period, the surgeon makes the decision for surgery. The surgeon would bill the appropriate level of hospital observation code with the "-57" modifier to indicate that the decision for surgery was made while the surgeon was providing hospital observation care.

Examples of hospital observation services during the postoperative period of a surgery are:

- A patient at the 80th day following a TURP is admitted to observation by the surgeon who performed the procedure with abdominal pain from a kidney stone. The surgeon decides that the patient does not require surgery. The surgeon would bill the observation code with CPT modifier "24" and documentation to support that the observation services are unrelated to the surgery.

- A patient at the 80th day following a TURP is admitted to observation with abdominal pain by the surgeon who performed the procedure. While the patient is in hospital observation, the surgeon decides that the patient requires kidney surgery. The surgeon would bill the observation code with HCPCS modifier "57" to indicate that the decision for surgery was made while the patient was in hospital observation. The subsequent surgical procedure would be reported with modifier "-79."

- A patient at the 20th day following a resection of the colon is admitted to observation for abdominal pain by the surgeon who performed the surgery. The surgeon determines that the patient requires no further colon surgery and discharges the patient. The surgeon may not bill for the observation services furnished during the global period because they were related to the previous surgery.

An example of a billable hospital observation service on the same day as a procedure is a patient is admitted to the hospital observation unit for observation of a head injury by a physician who repaired a laceration of the scalp in the emergency department. The physician would bill the observation code with a CPT modifier 25 and the procedure code.

Pub. 100-4, Chapter 12, Section 30.6.9
Payment for Inpatient Hospital Visits - General (Codes 99221 - 99239)

B3-15505-15505.2

A - Hospital Visit and Critical Care on Same Day

See §30.6.12.E for billing of critical care on the day of another evaluation and management service.

B - Two Hospital Visits Same Day

Carriers pay a physician for only one hospital visit per day for the same patient, whether the problems seen during the encounters are related or not. The inpatient hospital visit descriptors contain the phrase "per day" which means that the code and the payment established for the code represent all services provided on that date. The physician should select a code that reflects all services provided during the date of the service.

C - Hospital Visits Same Day But by Different Physicians

In a hospital inpatient situation involving one physician covering for another, if physician A sees the patient in the morning and physician B, who is covering for A, sees the same patient in the evening, carriers do not pay physician B for the second visit. The hospital visit descriptors include the phrase "per day" meaning care for the day.

If the physicians are each responsible for a different aspect of the patient's care, pay both visits if the physicians are in different specialties and the visits are billed with different diagnoses. There are circumstances where concurrent care may be billed by physicians of the same specialty.

D - Visits to Patients in Swing Beds

If the inpatient care is being billed by the hospital as inpatient hospital care, the hospital care codes apply. If the inpatient care is being billed by the hospital as nursing facility care, then the nursing facility codes apply.

Pub. 100-4, Chapter 12, Section 30.6.10
Consultations (Codes 99241 - 99275)

B3-15506

A - Consultation Versus Visit

Carriers pay for a consultation when all of the criteria for the use of a consultation code are met:

- Specifically, a consultation is distinguished from a visit because it is provided by a physician whose opinion or advice regarding evaluation and/or management of a specific problem is requested by another physician or other appropriate source (unless it is a patient-generated confirmatory consultation);
- A request for a consultation from an appropriate source and the need for consultation must be documented in the patient's medical record; and
- After the consultation is provided, the consultant prepares a written report of his/her findings, which is provided to the referring physician.

Consultations may be billed for time if the counseling/coordination of care constitutes more than 50 percent of the face-to-face encounter between the physician and the patient. The preceding requirements must also be met.

B - Consultation Followed by Treatment

Carriers must pay for an initial consultation if all the criteria for a consultation are satisfied. Payment may be made regardless of treatment initiation unless a transfer of care occurs. A transfer of care occurs when the referring physician transfers the responsibility for the patient's complete care to the receiving physician at the time of referral, and the receiving physician documents approval of care in advance. The receiving physician would report a new or established patient visit depending on the situation (a new patient is one who has not received any professional services from the physician or another physician of the same specialty who belongs to the same group practice within the past three years) and setting (e.g., office or inpatient).

A physician consultant may initiate diagnostic and/or therapeutic services at an initial or subsequent visit. Subsequent visits (not performed to complete the initial consultation) to manage a portion or all of the patient's condition should be reported as established patient office visit or subsequent hospital care, depending on the setting.

C - Consultations Requested by Members of Same Group

Carriers pay for a consultation if one physician in a group practice requests a consultation from another physician in the same group practice as long as all of the requirements for use of the CPT consultation codes are met.

Limited licensed practitioners, e.g., nurse practitioners or physician assistants, may request a consultation. They may perform other services within the scope of practice for limited licensed practitioners in the State in which they practice. Applicable collaboration and general supervision rules apply as well as billing rules.

D - Documentation for Consultations

A request for a consultation from an appropriate source and the need for consultation must be documented in the patient's medical record. A written report must be furnished to the requesting physician.

In an emergency department or an inpatient or outpatient setting in which the medical record is shared between the referring physician and the consultant, the request may be documented as part of a plan written in the requesting physician's progress note, an order in the medical record, or a specific written request for the consultation. In these settings, the report may consist of an appropriate entry in the common medical record. In an office setting, the documentation requirement may be met by a specific written request for the consultation from the requesting physician or if the consultant's records show a specific reference to the request. In this setting, the consultation report is a separate document communicated to the requesting physician.

E - Consultation for Preoperative Clearance

Preoperative consultations are payable for new or established patients performed by any physician at the request of a surgeon, as long as all of the requirements for billing the consultation codes are met.

F - Postoperative Care by Physician Who Did Preoperative Clearance Consultation

If subsequent to the completion of a preoperative consultation in the office or hospital, the consultant assumes responsibility for the management of a portion or all of the patient's condition(s) during the postoperative period, the consultation codes should not be used. In the hospital setting, the physician who has performed a preoperative consultation and assumes responsibility for the management of a portion or all of the patient's condition(s) during the postoperative period should use the appropriate subsequent hospital care codes (not follow-up consultation codes) to bill for the concurrent care he or she is providing. In the office setting, the appropriate established patient visit code should be used during the postoperative period.

A physician (primary care or specialist) who performs a postoperative evaluation of a new or established patient at the request of the surgeon may bill the appropriate consultation code for evaluation and management services furnished during the postoperative period following surgery as long as all of the criteria for the use of the consultation codes are met and that same physician has not already performed a preoperative consultation.

G - Surgeon's Request That Another Physician Participate In Postoperative Care

If the surgeon asks a physician who had not seen the patient for a preoperative consultation to take responsibility for the management of an aspect of the patient's condition during the postoperative period, the physician may not bill a consultation because the surgeon is not asking the physician's opinion or advice for the surgeon's use in treating the patient. The physician's services would constitute concurrent care and should be billed using the appropriate level visit codes.

H - Examples of Consultations

EXAMPLE 1

An internist sees a patient that he has followed for 20 years for mild hypertension and diabetes mellitus. The patient exhibits a new skin lesion and the internist sends the patient to a dermatologist for further evaluation. The dermatologist examines the patient and removes the lesion which is determined to be an early melanoma. The dermatologist dictates and forwards a report to the internist regarding his evaluation and treatment of the patient.

EXAMPLE 2

A general ophthalmologist diagnoses a patient with a retinal detachment. He sends the patient to a retinal subspecialist to evaluate the patient because the general ophthalmologist does not treat this specific problem. The retinal subspecialist evaluates the patient and subsequently schedules surgery. He sends a report to the referring physician explaining his findings and the treatment option selected.

EXAMPLE 3

A family physician diagnoses a patient with diabetes mellitus. The family physician asks the ophthalmologist for a base line evaluation to rule out diabetic retinopathy. The ophthalmologist examines the patient and sends a report to the family physician on his findings. The ophthalmologist tells the patient at the time of service to return in one year for a follow-up visit. This subsequent follow-up visit should be billed as an established patient visit in the office or other outpatient setting, as appropriate.

EXAMPLE 4

A rural family practice physician examines a patient who has been under his care for 20 years and diagnoses a new onset of atrial fibrillation. The family practitioner sends the patient to a cardiologist at an urban cardiology center for advice on his care and management. The cardiologist examines the patient, suggests a cardiac catheterization and other diagnostic tests which he schedules and then sends a written report to the requesting physician. The cardiologist subsequently routinely sees the patient once a year as follow-up. Subsequent visits provided by the cardiologist should be billed as an established patient visit in the office or other outpatient setting, as appropriate. Other routine care continues to be followed by the family practice physician.

EXAMPLE 5

A family practice physician examines a female patient who has been under his care for some time and diagnoses a breast mass. The family practitioner sends the patient to a general surgeon for advice and management of the mass and related patient care. The general surgeon examines the patient and recommends a breast biopsy, which he schedules, and then sends a written report to the requesting physician. The general surgeon subsequently performs a biopsy and then routinely sees the patient once a year as follow-up. Subsequent visits provided by the surgeon should be billed as an established patient visit in the office or other outpatient setting, as appropriate. Other routine care continues to be followed by the family practice physician.

EXAMPLE 6

An internist examines a patient who has been under his care for some time, and diagnoses a thyroid mass. The internist sends the patient to a general surgeon for advice on management of the mass and related patient care. The general surgeon examines the patient, orders diagnostic tests, and suggests a needle biopsy of the mass. The surgeon then schedules the procedure and sends a written report to the requesting physician. The general surgeon subsequently performs a thin needle biopsy and then routinely sees the patient twice as follow-up for the mass. Subsequent visits provided by the surgeon should be billed as an established patient visit in the office or other or other outpatient setting, as appropriate. Other routine care continues to be followed by the internist.

EXAMPLE 7

A patient with underlying diabetes mellitus and renal insufficiency is seen in the emergency room for the evaluation of fever, cough and purulent sputum. Since it is not clear whether the patient needs to be admitted, the emergency room physician requests an opinion by the on-call internist. The internist may bill a consultation regardless if the patient is discharged from the emergency room or whether the patient is admitted to the hospital as long as the criteria for consultation have been met. If the internist admits the patient to the hospital, he/she may bill either an initial inpatient consultation or initial hospital care code but not both for the same date of service.

I - Examples That Do Not Satisfy the Criteria for Consultations

EXAMPLE 1: Standing orders in the medical record for consultations.

EXAMPLE 2: No order for a consultation.

EXAMPLE 3: No written report of a consultation.

EXAMPLE 4: After hours, an internist receives a call from her patient about a complaint of abdominal pain. The internist believes this requires immediate evaluation and advises the patient to go to the emergency room where she meets the patient and evaluates him. The emergency room physician does not see the patient. The internist should bill for the appropriate level of emergency department service, or if the patient is admitted to the hospital she would bill this visit as an inpatient admission.

Pub. 100-4, Chapter 12, Section 30.6.11
Emergency Department Visits (Codes 99281 - 99288)

B3-15507

A - Use of Emergency Department Codes by Physicians Not Assigned to Emergency Department

Any physician seeing a patient registered in the emergency department may use emergency department visit codes (for services matching the code description). It is not required that the physician be assigned to the emergency department.

B - Use of Emergency Department Codes In Office

Emergency department coding is not appropriate if the site of service is an office or outpatient setting or any sight of service other than an emergency department. The emergency department codes should only be used if the patient is seen in the emergency department and the services described by the HCPCS code definition are provided. The emergency department is defined as an organized hospital-based facility for the provision of unscheduled or episodic services to patients who present for immediate medical attention.

C - Use of Emergency Department Codes to Bill Nonemergency Services

Services in the emergency department may not be emergencies. However the codes (99281 - 99288) are payable if the described services are provided.

However, if the physician asks the patient to meet him or her in the emergency department as an alternative to the physician's office and the patient is not registered as a patient in the emergency department, the physician should bill the appropriate office/outpatient visit codes. Normally a lower level emergency department code would be reported for a nonemergency condition.

D - Emergency Department or Office/Outpatient Visits on Same Day As Nursing Facility Admission

Emergency department visit provided on the same day as a comprehensive nursing facility assessment are not paid. Payment for evaluation and management services on the same date provided in sites other than the nursing facility are included in the payment for initial nursing facility care when performed on the same date as the nursing facility admission.

E - Physician Billing for Emergency Department Services Provided to Patient by Both Patient's Personal Physician and Emergency Department Physician

If a physician advises his/her own patient to go to an emergency department (ED) of a hospital for care and the physician subsequently is asked by the ED physician to come to the hospital to evaluate the patient and to advise the ED physician as to whether the patient should be admitted to the hospital or be sent home, the physicians should bill as follows:

- If the patient is admitted to the hospital by the patient's personal physician, then the patient's regular physician should bill only the appropriate level of the initial hospital care (codes 99221 - 99223) because all evaluation and management services provided by that physician in conjunction with that admission are considered part of the initial hospital care when performed on the same date as the admission. The ED physician who saw the patient in the emergency department should bill the appropriate level of the ED codes.

- If the ED physician, based on the advice of the patient's personal physician who came to the emergency department to see the patient, sends the patient home, then the ED physician should bill the appropriate level of emergency department service. The patient's personal physician should also bill the level of emergency department code that describes the service he or she provided in the emergency department. The patient's personal physician would not bill a consultation because he or she is not providing information to the emergency department physician for his or her use in treating the patient. If the patient's personal physician does not come to the hospital to see the patient, but only advises the emergency department physician by telephone, then the patient's personal physician may not bill.

F - Emergency Department Physician Requests Another Physician to See the Patient in Emergency Department or Office/Outpatient Setting

If the emergency department physician requests that another physician evaluate a given patient, the other physician should bill a consultation if the criteria for consultation are met. If the criteria for a consultation are not met and the patient is discharged from the Emergency Department or admitted to the hospital by another physician, the physician contacted by the Emergency Department physician should bill an emergency department visit. If the consulted physician admits the patient to the hospital and the criteria for a consultation are not met, he/she should bill an initial hospital care code.

Pub. 100-4, Chapter 12, Section 30.6.12
Critical Care Visits and Neonatal Intensive Care (Codes 99291 - 99292)

B3-15508

A - Use of Critical Care (Code 99292) in Cases Which are Not Medical Emergencies

Critical care includes the care of critically ill and unstable patients who require constant physician attention, whether the patient is in the course of a medical emergency or not. It involves decision making of high complexity to assess, manipulate, and support circulatory, respiratory, central nervous, metabolic, or other vital system function to prevent or treat single or multiple vital organ system failure. It often also requires extensive interpretation of multiple databases and the application of advanced technology to manage the critically ill patient.

Critical care is usually, but not always, given in a critical care area such is the coronary care unit, intensive care unit, respiratory care unit, or the emergency department. However, payment may be made for critical care services provided in any location as long as the care provided meets the definition of critical care. Services for a patient who is not critically ill and unstable but who happens to be in a critical care, intensive care, or other specialized care unit are reported using subsequent hospital care codes (99231-99233) or hospital consultation codes (99251 - 99263). Critical care may include neonatal intensive care.

B - Constant Attendance or Constant Attention as Prerequisite for Use of Critical Care Codes

The duration of critical care time to be reported is the time the physician spent working on the critical care patient's case, whether that time was spent at the immediate bedside or elsewhere on the floor, but immediately available to the patient.

For example, time spent reviewing laboratory test results or discussing the critically ill patient's care with other medical staff in the unit or at the nursing station on the floor would be reported as critical care, even if it does not occur at the bedside.

Time spent in activities that occur outside of the unit or off the floor (e.g., telephone calls, whether taken at home, in the office, or elsewhere in the hospital) may not be reported as critical care since the physician is not immediately available to the patient. This work is the typical pre and post-service work that accompanies any evaluation and management service. Time spent in activities that do not directly contribute to the treatment of the patient may not be reported as critical care, even if they are performed in the critical care unit at a patient's bedside (e.g., telephone calls to discuss other patients, reviewing literature).

For critical care to be billed, the physician must devote his or her full attention to the patient and, therefore, cannot render evaluation and management services to any other patient during the same period of time.

The time spent with the individual patient and the service rendered should be recorded in the patient's record to support the claim for critical care services.

C - Hours and Days of Critical Care

Payment for critical care is not restricted to a fixed number of days. As long as the critical care criteria are met and the services are reasonable and necessary to treat illness or injury, payment for critical care services is appropriate. However, claims for seemingly improbable amounts of critical care on the same date are subjected to review to determine if the physician has filed a false claim.

D - Counting of Units of Critical Care Services

Code 99291 (critical care, first hour) is used to report the services of a physician providing constant attention to a critically ill patient for a total of 30 to 74 minutes on a given day. Only one unit of code 99291 may be billed by a physician for a patient on a given date.

If the total duration of critical care provided by the physician on a given day is less than 30 minutes, the appropriate evaluation and management code should be used. In the hospital setting, it is expected that the Level 3 subsequent hospital care code 99233 would most often be used.

Code 99292 (critical care, each additional 30 minutes) is used to report the services of a physician providing constant attention to the critically ill patient for 15 to 30 minutes beyond the first 74 minutes of critical care on a given day.

The following illustrates the correct reporting of critical care services:

Total Duration of Critical Care	Code(s)
Less than 30 minutes	99232 or 99233
30-74 minutes	99291 x 1
75-104 minutes	99291 x 1 and 99292 x 1
105-134 minutes	99291 x 1 and 99292 x 2
135-164 minutes	99291 x 1 and 99292 x 3
165-194 minutes	99291 x 1 and 99292 x 4

E - Critical Care Service and other Evaluation and Management Services Provided on Same Day

If critical care is required upon the patient's presentation to the emergency department, only critical care codes 99291-99292 may be reported. Emergency department codes will not be paid for the same day. If there is a hospital or office/outpatient evaluation and management service furnished early in the day and at that time the patient does not require critical care, but the patient requires critical care later in the day, both critical care and the evaluation and management service may be paid.

Physicians must submit supporting documentation when critical care is billed on the same day as other evaluation and management services.

F - Critical Care Services Provided During Preoperative Portion of Global Period of Procedure With 90 Day Global Period in Trauma and Burn Cases

Preoperative critical care may be paid in addition to a global fee if the patient is critically ill and requires the constant attendance of the physician, **and** the critical care is unrelated to the specific anatomic injury or general surgical procedure performed. Such patients are potentially unstable or have conditions that could pose a significant threat to life or risk of prolonged impairment.

In order for these services to be paid, two reporting requirements must be met. Codes 99291/99292 **and** modifier "25" (significant, separately identifiable evaluation and management services by the same physician on the day of the procedure) must be used, and documentation that the critical care was unrelated to the specific anatomic injury or general surgical procedure performed must be submitted. An ICD-9-CM code in the range 800.0 through 959.9 (except 930-939), which clearly indicates that the critical care was unrelated to the surgery, is acceptable documentation.

G - Critical Care Services Provided During Postoperative Period of Procedure With Global Period in Trauma and Burn Cases

Postoperative critical care may be paid in addition to a global fee if the patient is critically ill and requires the constant attendance of the physician, **and** the critical care is unrelated to the specific anatomic injury or general surgical procedure performed. Such patients are potentially unstable or have conditions that could pose a significant threat to life or risk of prolonged impairment.

In order for these services to be paid, two reporting requirements must be met. Codes 99291/99292 **and** modifier "24" (Unrelated evaluation and management service by the same physician during a postoperative period) must be used, and documentation that the critical care was unrelated to the specific anatomic injury or general surgical procedure performed must be submitted. An ICD-9-CM code in the range 800.0 through 959.9 (except 930-939), which clearly

Appendixes

indicates that the critical care was unrelated to the surgery, is acceptable documentation.

Pub. 100-4, Chapter 12, Section 30.6.13
Nursing Facility Visits (Codes 99301 - 99313)

B3-15509-15509.1

A - Visits to Perform Resident Assessments

Visits necessary to perform all Medicare required assessments are payable. Physicians use the CPT codes for comprehensive nursing facility assessments (99301-99303) to report evaluation and management services involving comprehensive resident assessments. Evaluation and Management documentation guidelines apply.

B - Visits to Comply With Federal Regulations (42 CFR 483.40)

Payment is made for visits required to monitor and evaluate residents at least once every 30 days for the first 90 days after admission and at least once every 60 days thereafter. These visits and all other medically necessary visits for the diagnosis or treatment of illness or injury or to improve the functioning of a malformed body member are covered under Medicare Part B. Physicians use CPT codes for subsequent nursing facility care (99311-99313) when reporting evaluation and management services that do not involve resident assessments. Medicare does not pay for additional visits required by State law for an admission unless the visits are necessary to meet the medical needs of the individual resident.

C - Medically Complex Care

Payment is made for visits to residents in a SNF who are receiving services for medically complex care upon discharge from an acute care facility when the visits are medically necessary and documented in the medical record. Physicians use CPT codes for subsequent nursing facility care (99311-99313) when reporting evaluation and management services.

D - Visits by Nonphysician Practitioners

Visits to comply with Federal Regulations in SNFs after the initial visit by the physician may, at the option of the physician, be provided by a nonphysician practitioner, i.e., physician assistant (PA), nurse practitioner (NP) or clinical nurse specialist (CNS). (Refer to 42 CFR 483.40(4) and (e) and B3-45-15.)

Any medically necessary physician task in a NF (including tasks which the regulations specify must be performed personally by the physician) may also be satisfied, when performed by a nurse practitioner (NP), physician assistant (PA), or clinical nurse specialist (CNS) (at the option of the State) who is not an employee of the facility in which they practice. (Refer to 42 CFR 483.40 (f).)

Where a physician establishes an office in a SNF/NF, the "incident to" services and requirements are confined to this discrete part of the facility designated as his/her office. "Incident to" services may not be billed in a hospital setting. Thus, services performed outside the "office" area would be subject to the coverage rules applicable to services provided outside the office setting, i.e., nursing home.

Services provided by physician-employed or independent nonphysician practitioners must meet Medicare requirements and fall within the scope of services that practitioners are licensed to perform. A physician assistant must be under the general supervision of the physician.

These visits and all other medically necessary visits for the diagnosis or treatment of illness or injury or to improve the functioning of a malformed body member are covered under Medicare Part B.

E - Gang Visits

Although the selection of the level of service for an evaluation and management encounter is not based on time, the CPT codes provide an approximate time typically spent with a resident. The level of service and code billed must be medically necessary (§§1862 (a)(1)(A) of the Act) for each resident. Claims for an unreasonable number of visits to residents at a facility within a 24-hour period may indicate aberrancy and result in medical review to determine medical necessity. Medical records must document the specific services to each individual resident.

Pub. 100-4, Chapter 12, Section 30.6.14
Home Care and Domiciliary Care Visits (Codes 99321 - 99350)

B3-15510

A - Physician Visits to Patients Residing in Various Places of Service

Current Procedural Terminology (CPT) codes 99321 through 99333, Domiciliary, Rest Home (e.g., Boarding Home), or Custodial Care Services, are used to report evaluation and management (E/M) services to residents residing in a facility which provides, room, board, and other personal assistance services, generally on a long- term basis. These codes are limited to the specific two digit places of service (POS) 33 (Custodial Care Facility) and 55 (Residential Substance Abuse Facility). These facilities, also, often referred to as adult living facilities or assisted living facilities.

Physicians and providers furnishing E/M services to residents in a living arrangement described by one of the POS listed above must use the level of service code in the range of codes 99321- 99333 to report the service they provide.

CPT codes 99341 through 99350, Home Services codes, are used to report E/M services furnished to a patient residing in his or her own private residence and not any type of facility. These codes apply only to the specific two digit POS 12 (Patient's Home). Home Services codes, CPT codes 99341 through 99350, may not be used for billing for E/M services provided other than in the private residence of an individual.

E/M services provided to patients residing in a Skilled Nursing Facility (SNF) (CPT definition formerly identified as SNFs, intermediate care facilities (ICFs), or long term care facilities (LTCFs) must be reported using the appropriate level of service code within the range identified for Comprehensive Nursing Facility Assessments and Subsequent Nursing Facility Care services. Codes range from 99301 through 99303 for the former and 99311 through 99313 for the latter, and Nursing Facility Discharge Services codes 99315 - 99316. These codes are limited to the specific two digit POS 31 (SNF), 32 (Nursing Home/Nursing Facility), 54 (Intermediate Care Facility/Mentally Retarded) and 56 (Psychiatric Residential Treatment Center).

The nursing facility codes should be used with POS 31 if the patient is in a Part A SNF stay and POS 32 if the patient does not have Part A SNF benefits.

Pub. 100-4, Chapter 12, Section 30.6.15

© 2005 Ingenix, Inc.

Prolonged Services and Standby Services (Codes 99354 - 99360)

B3-15511-15511.3

Pub. 100-4, Chapter 12, Section 30.6.16
Case Management Services (Codes 99362 and 99371 - 99373)

B3-15512

A - Team Conferences

Team conferences (codes 99361-99362) may not be paid separately. Payment for these services is included in the payment for the services to which they relate.

B - Telephone Calls

Telephone calls (codes 99371-99373) may not be paid separately. Payment for telephone calls is included in payment for billable services (e.g., visit, surgery, diagnostic procedure results).

Pub. 100-4, Chapter 12, Section 40.6
Claims for Multiple Surgeries

B3-4826, B3-15038, B3-15056

A - General

Multiple surgeries are separate procedures performed by a single physician or physicians in the same group practice on the same patient at the same operative session or on the same day for which separate payment may be allowed. Co-surgeons, surgical teams, or assistants-at-surgery may participate in performing multiple surgeries on the same patient on the same day.

Multiple surgeries are distinguished from procedures that are components of or incidental to a primary procedure. These intra-operative services, incidental surgeries, or components of more major surgeries are not separately billable. See Chapter 23 for a description of mandatory edits to prevent separate payment for those procedures. Major surgical procedures are determined based on the MFSDB approved amount and not on the submitted amount from the providers. The major surgery, as based on the MFSDB, may or may not be the one with the larger submitted amount.

Also, see subsection D below for a description of the standard payment policy on multiple surgeries. However, these standard payment rules are not appropriate for certain procedures. Field 21 of the MFSDB indicates whether the standard payment policy rules apply to a multiple surgery, or whether special payment rules apply. Site of service payment adjustments (codes with an indicator of "1" in Field 27 of the MFSDB) should be applied before multiple surgery payment adjustments.

B - Billing Instructions

The following procedures apply when billing for multiple surgeries by the same physician on the same day.

- Report the more major surgical procedure without the multiple procedures modifier "-51."
- Report additional surgical procedures performed by the surgeon on the same day with modifier "-51."

There may be instances in which two or more physicians each perform distinctly different, unrelated surgeries on the same patient on the same day (e.g., in some multiple trauma cases). When this occurs, the payment adjustment rules for multiple surgeries may not be appropriate. In such cases, the physician does not use modifier "-51" unless one of the surgeons individually performs multiple surgeries.

C - Carrier Claims Processing System Requirements

Carriers must be able to:

1. Identify multiple surgeries by both of the following methods:

The presence on the claim form or electronic submission of the "51" modifier; and

The billing of more than one separately payable surgical procedure by the same physician performed on the same patient on the same day, whether on different lines or with a number greater than 1 in the units column on the claim form or inappropriately billed with modifier "78" (i.e., after the global period has expired);

2. Access Field 34 of the MFSDB to determine the Medicare fee schedule payment amount for each surgery;

3. Access Field 21 for each procedure of the MFSDB to determine if the payment rules for multiple surgeries apply to any of the multiple surgeries billed on the same day;

4. If Field 21 for any of the multiple procedures contains an indicator of "0," the multiple surgery rules do not apply to that procedure. Base payment on the lower of the billed amount or the fee schedule amount (Field 34 or 35) for each code unless other payment adjustment rules apply;

5. For dates of service prior to January 1, 1995, if Field 21 contains an indicator of "1," the standard rules for pricing multiple surgeries apply (see items 68 below);

6. Rank the surgeries subject to the standard multiple surgery rules (indicator "1") in descending order by the Medicare fee schedule amount;

7. Base payment for each ranked procedure on the lower of the billed amount, or:

100 percent of the fee schedule amount (Field 34 or 35) for the highest valued procedure;

50 percent of the fee schedule amount for the second highest valued procedure; and

25 percent of the fee schedule amount for the third through the fifth highest valued procedures;

8. If more than five procedures are billed, pay for the first five according to the rules listed in 5, 6, and 7 above and suspend the sixth and subsequent procedures for manual review and payment, if appropriate, "by report." Payment determined on a "by report" basis for these codes should never be lower than 25 percent of the full payment amount;

9. For dates of service on or after January 1, 1995, new standard rules for pricing multiple surgeries apply. If Field 21 contains an indicator of "2," these new standard rules apply (see items 10-12 below);

10. Rank the surgeries subject to the multiple surgery rules (indicator "2") in descending order by the Medicare fee schedule amount;

11. Base payment for each ranked procedure (indicator "2") on the lower of the billed amount:

100 percent of the fee schedule amount (Field 34 or 35) for the highest valued procedure; and

Appendixes

50 percent of the fee schedule amount for the second through the fifth highest valued procedures; or

12. If more than five procedures with an indicator of "2" are billed, pay for the first five according to the rules listed in 9, 10, and 11 above and suspend the sixth and subsequent procedures for manual review and payment, if appropriate, "by report." Payment determined on a "by report" basis for these codes should never be lower than 50 percent of the full payment amount. Pay by the unit for services that are already reduced (e.g., 17003). Pay for 17340 only once per session, regardless of how many lesions were destroyed;

NOTE: For dates of service prior to January 1, 1995, the multiple surgery indicator of "2" indicated that special dermatology rules applied. The payment rules for these codes have not changed. The rules were expanded, however, to all codes that previously had a multiple surgery indicator of "1." For dates of service prior to January 1, 1995, if a dermatological procedure with an indicator of "2" was billed with the "-51" modifier with other procedures that are **not** dermatological procedures (procedures with an indicator of "1" in Field 21), the standard multiple surgery rules applied. Pay no less than 50 percent for the dermatological procedures with an indicator of "2." See §§40.6.C.6-8 for required actions.

13. If Field 21 contains an indicator of "3," and multiple endoscopies are billed, the special rules for multiple endoscopic procedures apply. Pay the full value of the highest valued endoscopy, plus the difference between the next highest and the base endoscopy. Access Field 31A of the MFSDB to determine the base endoscopy.

EXAMPLE

In the course of performing a fiber optic colonoscopy (CPT code 45378), a physician performs a biopsy on a lesion (code 45380) and removes a polyp (code 45385) from a different part of the colon. The physician bills for codes 45380 and 45385. The value of codes 45380 and 45385 have the value of the diagnostic colonoscopy (45378) built in. Rather than paying 100 percent for the highest valued procedure (45385) and 50 percent for the next (45380), pay the full value of the higher valued endoscopy (45385), plus the difference between the next highest endoscopy (45380) and the base endoscopy (45378).

Carriers assume the following fee schedule amounts for these codes:

45378 - $255.40

45380 - $285.98

45385 - $374.56

Pay the full value of 45385 ($374.56), plus the difference between 45380 and 45378 ($30.58), for a total of $405.14.

NOTE: If an endoscopic procedure with an indicator of "3" is billed with the "-51" modifier with other procedures that are **not** endoscopies (procedures with an indicator of "1" in Field 21), the standard multiple surgery rules apply. See §§40.6.C.6-8 for required actions.

14. Apply the following rules where endoscopies are performed on the same day as unrelated endoscopies or other surgical procedures:

Two unrelated endoscopies (e.g., 46606 and 43217): Apply the usual multiple surgery rules;

Two sets of unrelated endoscopies (e.g., 43202 and 43217; 46606 and 46608): Apply the special endoscopy rules to each series and then apply the multiple surgery rules. Consider the total payment for each set of endoscopies as one service;

Two related endoscopies and a third, unrelated procedure: Apply the special endoscopic rules to the related endoscopies, and, then apply the multiple surgery rules. Consider the total payment for the related endoscopies as one service and the unrelated endoscopy as another service.

15. If two or more multiple surgeries are of equal value, rank them in descending dollar order billed and base payment on the percentages listed above (i.e., 100 percent for the first billed procedure, 50 percent for the second, etc.);

16. If any of the multiple surgeries are bilateral surgeries, consider the bilateral procedure at 150 percent as one payment amount, rank this with the remaining procedures, and apply the appropriate multiple surgery reductions. See §40.7 for bilateral surgery payment instructions.);

17. Round all adjusted payment amounts to the nearest cent;

18. If some of the surgeries are subject to special rules while others are subject to the standard rules, automate pricing to the extent possible. If necessary, price manually;

19. In cases of multiple interventional radiological procedures, both the radiology code and the primary surgical code are paid at 100 percent of the fee schedule amount. The subsequent surgical procedures are paid at the standard multiple surgical percentages (50 percent, 50 percent, 50 percent and 50 percent);

20. Apply the requirements in §§40 on global surgeries to multiple surgeries;

21. Retain the "-51" modifier in history for any multiple surgeries paid at less than the full global amount; and

22. Follow the instructions on adjudicating surgery claims submitted with the "22" modifier. Review documentation to determine if full payment should be made for those distinctly different, unrelated surgeries performed by different physicians on the same day.

D - Ranking of Same Day Multiple Surgeries When One Surgery Has a "22" Modifier and Additional Payment is Allowed

(Rev. 1, 10-01-03)

B3-4826

If the patient returns to the operating room after the initial operative session on the same day as a result of complications from the original surgery, the complications rules apply to each procedure required to treat the complications from the original surgery. The multiple surgery rules would not apply.

However, if the patient is returned to the operating room during the postoperative period of the original surgery, not on the same day of the original surgery, for multiple procedures that are required as a result of complications from the original surgery, the complications rules would apply. The multiple surgery rules would also not apply.

Multiple surgeries are defined as separate procedures performed by a single physician or physicians in the same group practice on the same patient at the same operative session or on the same day for which separate payment may be allowed. Cosurgeons, surgical teams, or

© 2005 Ingenix, Inc.

assistants-at-surgery may participate in performing multiple surgeries on the same patient on the same day.

Multiple surgeries are distinguished from procedures that are components of or incidental to a primary procedure. These intra-operative services, incidental surgeries, or components of more major surgeries are not separately billable. See Chapter 23 for a description of mandatory edits to prevent separate payment for those procedures.

Pub. 100-4, Chapter 12, Section 40.7
Claims for Bilateral Surgeries

B3-4827, B3-15040

A - General

Bilateral surgeries are procedures performed on both sides of the body during the same operative session or on the same day.

The terminology for some procedure codes includes the terms "bilateral" (e.g., code 27395; Lengthening of the hamstring tendon; multiple, bilateral.) or "unilateral or bilateral" (e.g., code 52290; cystourethroscopy; with ureteral meatotomy, unilateral or bilateral). The payment adjustment rules for bilateral surgeries do not apply to procedures identified by CPT as "bilateral" or "unilateral or bilateral" since the fee schedule reflects any additional work required for bilateral surgeries.

Field 22 of the MFSDB indicates whether the payment adjustment rules apply to a surgical procedure.

B - Billing Instructions for Bilateral Surgeries

If a procedure is not identified by its terminology as a bilateral procedure (or unilateral or bilateral), physicians must report the procedure with modifier "50." They report such procedures as a single line item. (**NOTE**: This differs from the CPT coding guidelines which indicate that bilateral procedures should be billed as two line items.)

If a procedure is identified by the terminology as bilateral (or unilateral or bilateral), as in codes 27395 and 52290, physicians do not report the procedure with modifier "50."

C - Claims Processing System Requirements

Carriers must be able to:

1. Identify bilateral surgeries by the presence on the claim form or electronic submission of the "-50" modifier **or** of the same code on separate lines reported once with modifier "-LT" and once with modifier "-RT";

2. Access Field 34 or 35 of the MFSDB to determine the Medicare payment amount;

3. Access Field 22 of the MFSDB:

If Field 22 contains an indicator of "0," "2," or "3," the payment adjustment rules for bilateral surgeries do not apply. Base payment on the lower of the billed amount or 100 percent of the fee schedule amount (Field 34 or 35) unless other payment adjustment rules apply.

NOTE: Some codes which have a bilateral indicator of "0" in the MFSDB may be performed more than once on a given day. These are services that would never be considered bilateral and thus should not be billed with modifier "-50." Where such a code is billed on multiple line items or with more than 1 in the units field and carriers have determined that the code may be reported more than once, bypass the

"0" bilateral indicator and refer to the multiple surgery field for pricing;

If Field 22 contains an indicator of "1," the standard adjustment rules apply. Base payment on the lower of the billed amount or 150 percent of the fee schedule amount (Field 34 or 35). (Multiply the payment amount in Field 34 or 35 for the surgery by 150 percent and round to the nearest cent.)

4. Apply the requirements §§40 - 40.4 on global surgeries to bilateral surgeries; and

5. Retain the "-50" modifier in history for any bilateral surgeries paid at the adjusted amount.

(**NOTE**: The "-50" modifier is not retained for surgeries which are bilateral by definition such as code 27395.)

Pub. 100-4, Chapter 12, Section 50
Payment for Anesthesiology Services

B3-15018

A - General Payment Rule

The fee schedule amount for physician anesthesia services furnished on or after January 1, 1992 is, with the exceptions noted, based on allowable base and time units multiplied by an anesthesia conversion factor specific to that locality. The base unit for each anesthesia procedure is listed in §50.K, Exhibit 1. The way in which time units are calculated is described in §50.G. CMS releases the conversion factor annually. Carriers may not allow separate payment for the anesthesia service performed by the physician who also furnishes the medical or surgical service. In that case, payment for the anesthesia service is made through the payment for the medical or surgical service. For example, carriers may not allow separate payment for the surgeon's performance of a local or surgical anesthesia if the surgeon also performs the surgical procedure. Similarly, separate payment is not allowed for the psychiatrist's performance of the anesthesia service associated with the electroconvulsive therapy if the psychiatrist performs the electroconvulsive therapy.

B - Payment at Personally Performed Rate

Carriers must determine the fee schedule payment, recognizing the base unit for the anesthesia code and one time unit per 15 minutes of anesthesia time if:

- The physician personally performed the entire anesthesia service alone;
- The physician is involved with one anesthesia case with a resident, the physician is a teaching physician as defined in §100, and the service is furnished on or after January 1, 1996;

The physician is continuously involved in a single case involving a student nurse anesthetist;

- The physician is continuously involved in one anesthesia case involving a CRNA (or AA) and the service was furnished prior to January 1, 1998. If the physician is involved with a single case with a CRNA (or AA) and the service is furnished on or after January 1, 1998, carriers may pay the physician service and the CRNA (or AA) service in accordance with the medical direction payment policy; or

- The physician and the CRNA (or AA) are involved in one anesthesia case and the services of each are found to be medically necessary. Documentation must be submitted by both the CRNA and the physician to support payment of the full fee for each of the two providers. The physician reports the "AA" modifier and the CRNA reports the "QZ" modifier for a nonmedically directed case.

C - Payment at the Medically Directed Rate

Carriers determine payment for the physician's medical direction service furnished on or after January 1, 1998 on the basis of 50 percent of the allowance for the service performed by the physician alone. Medical direction occurs if the physician medically directs qualified individuals in two, three, or four concurrent cases and the physician performs the following activities.

- Performs a pre-anesthetic examination and evaluation;
- Prescribes the anesthesia plan;
- Personally participates in the most demanding procedures in the anesthesia plan, including induction and emergence;
- Ensures that any procedures in the anesthesia plan that he or she does not perform are performed by a qualified anesthetist;
- Monitors the course of anesthesia administration at frequent intervals;
- Remains physically present and available for immediate diagnosis and treatment of emergencies; and
- Provides indicated-post-anesthesia care.

Prior to January 1, 1999 the physician was required to participate in the most demanding procedures of the anesthesia plan, including induction and emergence.

For medical direction services furnished on or after January 1, 1999, the physician must participate only in the most demanding procedures of the anesthesia plan, including, if applicable, induction and emergence. Also for medical direction services furnished on or after January 1, 1999, the physician must document in the medical record that he or she performed the pre-anesthetic examination and evaluation. Physicians must also document that they provided indicated post-anesthesia care, were present during some portion of the anesthesia monitoring, and were present during the most demanding procedures, including induction and emergence, where indicated.

For services furnished on or after January 1, 1994, the physician can medically direct two, three, or four concurrent procedures involving qualified individuals, all of whom could be CRNAs, AAs, interns, residents or combinations of these individuals. The medical direction rules apply to cases involving student nurse anesthetists if the physician directs two concurrent cases, each of which involves a student nurse anesthetist, or the physician directs one case involving a student nurse anesthetist and another involving a CRNA, AA, intern or resident.

If anesthesiologists are in a group practice, one physician member may provide the pre-anesthesia examination and evaluation while another fulfills the other criteria. Similarly, one physician member of the group may provide post-anesthesia care while another member of the group furnishes the other component parts of the anesthesia service. However, the medical record must indicate that the services were furnished by physicians and identify the physicians who furnished them.

A physician who is concurrently directing the administration of anesthesia to not more than four surgical patients cannot ordinarily be involved in furnishing additional services to other patients. However, addressing an emergency of short duration in the immediate area, administering an epidural or caudal anesthetic to ease labor pain, or periodic, rather than continuous, monitoring of an obstetrical patient does not substantially diminish the scope of control exercised by the physician in directing the administration of anesthesia to surgical patients. It does not constitute a separate service for the purpose of determining whether the medical direction criteria are met. Further, while directing concurrent anesthesia procedures, a physician may receive patients entering the operating suite for the next surgery, check or discharge patients in the recovery room, or handle scheduling matters without affecting fee schedule payment.

However, if the physician leaves the immediate area of the operating suite for other than short durations or devotes extensive time to an emergency case or is otherwise not available to respond to the immediate needs of the surgical patients, the physician's services to the surgical patients are supervisory in nature. Carriers may not make payment under the fee schedule.

See §50.J for a definition of concurrent anesthesia procedures.

D - Payment at Medically Supervised Rate

Carriers may allow only three base units per procedure when the anesthesiologist is involved in furnishing more than four procedures concurrently or is performing other services while directing the concurrent procedures. An additional time unit may be recognized if the physician can document he or she was present at induction.

E - Billing and Payment for Multiple Anesthesia Procedures

B3-4830.C and D

Physicians bill for the anesthesia services associated with multiple bilateral surgeries by reporting the anesthesia procedure with the highest base unit value with the multiple procedure modifier "-51." They report the total time for all procedures in the line item with the highest base unit value.

If the same anesthesia CPT code applies to two or more of the surgical procedures, billers enter the anesthesia code with the "-51" modifier and the number of surgeries to which the modified CPT code applies.

Payment can be made under the fee schedule for anesthesia services associated with multiple surgical procedures or multiple bilateral procedures. Payment is determined based on the base unit of the anesthesia procedure with the highest base unit value and time units based on the actual anesthesia time of the multiple procedures. See §§40.6.40.7 for a definition and appropriate billing and claims processing instructions for multiple and bilateral surgeries.

F - Payment for Medical and Surgical Services Furnished in Addition to Anesthesia Procedure

Payment may be made under the fee schedule for specific medical and surgical services furnished by the anesthesiologist as long as these services are reasonable and medically necessary or provided that other rebundling provisions (see §30 and Chapter 23) do not preclude separate

© 2005 Ingenix, Inc.

payment. These services may be furnished in conjunction with the anesthesia procedure to the patient or may be furnished as single services, e.g., during the day of or the day before the anesthesia service. These services include the insertion of a Swan Ganz catheter, the insertion of central venous pressure lines, emergency intubation, and critical care visits.

G - Anesthesia Time and Calculation of Anesthesia Time Units

Anesthesia time is defined as the period during which an anesthesia practitioner is present with the patient. It starts when the anesthesia practitioner begins to prepare the patient for anesthesia services in the operating room or an equivalent area and ends when the anesthesia practitioner is no longer furnishing anesthesia services to the patient, that is, when the patient may be placed safely under postoperative care. Anesthesia time is a continuous time period from the start of anesthesia to the end of an anesthesia service. In counting anesthesia time for services furnished on or after January 1, 2000, the anesthesia practitioner can add blocks of time around an interruption in anesthesia time as long as the anesthesia practitioner is furnishing continuous anesthesia care within the time periods around the interruption.

Actual anesthesia time in minutes is reported on the claim. For anesthesia services furnished on or after January 1, 1994, carriers compute time units by dividing reported anesthesia time by 15 minutes. Round the time unit to one decimal place. Carriers do not recognize time units for CPT codes 01995 or 01996.

For purposes of this section, anesthesia practitioner means a physician who performs the anesthesia service alone, a CRNA who is not medically directed, or a CRNA or AA, who is medically directed. The physician who medically directs the CRNA or AA would ordinarily report the same time as the CRNA or AA reports for the CRNA service.

H - Base Unit Reduction for Concurrent Medically Directed Procedures

If the physician medically directs concurrent medically directed procedures prior to January 1, 1994, reduce the number of base units for each concurrent procedure as follows.

- For two concurrent procedures, the base unit on each procedure is reduced 10 percent.
- For three concurrent procedures, the base unit on each procedure is reduced 25 percent.
- For four concurrent procedures, the base on each concurrent procedure is reduced 40 percent.
- If the physician medically directs concurrent procedures prior to January 1, 1994, and any of the concurrent procedures are cataract or iridectomy anesthesia, reduce the base units for each cataract or iridectomy procedure by 10 percent.

I - Monitored Anesthesia Care

Carriers pay for reasonable and medically necessary monitored anesthesia care services on the same basis as other anesthesia services. Anesthesiologists use modifier QS to report monitored anesthesia care cases. Monitored anesthesia care involves the intra-operative monitoring by a physician or qualified individual under the medical direction of a physician or of the patient's vital physiological signs in anticipation of the need for administration of general anesthesia or of the development of adverse physiological patient reaction to the surgical procedure. It also includes the performance of a pre-anesthetic examination and evaluation, prescription of the anesthesia care required, administration of any necessary oral or parenteral medications (e.g., etropine, demerol, valium) and provision of indicated postoperative anesthesia care.

Payment is made under the fee schedule using the payment rules in subsection B if the physician personally performs the monitored anesthesia care case or under the rules in subsection C if the physician medically directs four or fewer concurrent cases and monitored anesthesia care represents one or more of these concurrent cases.

J - Definition of Concurrent Medically Directed Anesthesia Procedures

Concurrency is defined with regard to the maximum number of procedures that the physician is medically directing within the context of a single procedure and whether these other procedures overlap each other. Concurrency is not dependent on each of the cases involving a Medicare patient. For example, if an anesthesiologist directs three concurrent procedures, two of which involve non-Medicare patients and the remaining a Medicare patient, this represents three concurrent cases. The following example illustrates this concept and guides physicians in determining how many procedures they are directing.

EXAMPLE

Procedures A through E are medically directed procedures involving CRNAs and furnished between January 1, 1992 and December 31, 1997 (1998 concurrent instructions can be found in subsection C.) The starting and ending times for each procedure represent the periods during which anesthesia time is counted. Assume that none of the procedures were cataract or iridectomy anesthesia.

Procedure A begins at 8:00 a.m. and lasts until 8:20 a.m.

Procedure B begins at 8:10 a.m. and lasts until 8:45 a.m.

Procedure C begins at 8:30 a.m. and lasts until 9:15 a.m.

Procedure D begins at 9:00 a.m. and lasts until 12:00 noon.

Procedure E begins at 9:10 a.m. and lasts until 9:55 a.m.

Procedure	Number of Concurrent Medically Directed Procedures	Base Unit Reduction Percentage
A	2	10%
B	2	10%
C	3	25%
D	3	25%
E	3	25%

From 8:00 a.m. to 8:20 a.m., the length of procedure A, the anesthesiologist medically directed two concurrent procedures, A and B.

From 8:10 a.m. to 8:45 a.m., the length of procedure B, the anesthesiologist medically directed two concurrent procedures. From 8:10 to 8:20 a.m., the anesthesiologist medically directed procedures A and B. From 8:20 to 8:30 a.m., the anesthesiologist medically directed only procedure B. From 8:30 to 8:45 a.m., the anesthesiologist medically directed procedures B and C. Thus, during procedure B, the anesthesiologist medically directed, at most, two concurrent procedures.

From 8:30 a.m. to 9:15 a.m., the length of procedure C, the anesthesiologist medically directed three concurrent procedures. From 8:30 to 8:45 a.m., the anesthesiologist medically directed procedures B and C. From 8:45 to 9:00 a.m., the anesthesiologist medically directed procedure C. From 9:00 to 9:10 a.m., the anesthesiologist medically directed procedures C and D. From 9:10 to 9:15 a.m., the anesthesiologist medically directed procedures C, D and E. Thus, during procedure C, the anesthesiologist medically directed, at most, three concurrent procedures.

The same analysis shows that during procedure D or E, the anesthesiologist medically directed, at most, three concurrent procedures.

K - Anesthesia Claims Modifiers

B3-4830, B3-15018.K

Physicians report the appropriate anesthesia modifier to denote whether the service was personally performed, medically directed, or medically supervised.

Specific anesthesia modifiers include:

AA - Anesthesia Services performed personally by the anesthesiologist

AD - Medical Supervision by a physician; more than 4 concurrent anesthesia procedures;

G8 - Monitored anesthesia care (MAC) for deep complex complicated, or markedly invasive surgical procedures;

G9 - Monitored anesthesia care for patient who has a history of severe cardio-pulmonary condition

QK - Medical direction of two, three or four concurrent anesthesia procedures involving qualified individuals

QS - Monitored anesthesia care service

QX - CRNA service; with medical direction by a physician

QY - Medical direction of one certified registered nurse anesthetist by an anesthesiologist

QZ - CRNA service: Without medical direction by a physician.

The QS modifier is for informational purposes. Providers must report actual anesthesia time on the claim.

Carriers must determine payment for anesthesia in accordance with these instructions. They must be able to determine the uniform base unit that is assigned to the anesthesia code and apply the appropriate reduction where the anesthesia procedures is medically directed. They must also be able to determine the number of anesthesia time units from actual anesthesia time reported on the claim, differentiating 15 minute time unit intervals for personally performed anesthesia procedures and 30 minute time unit intervals for medically directed procedures. Carriers must multiply allowable units by the anesthesia-specific conversion factor used to determine fee schedule payment for the payment area.

Exhibit 1: Base Unit for Each Anesthesia Procedure

CPT Anesthesia Code	Anesthesia Procedure	Base Units
HEAD		
00100	Anesthesia for procedures on Integumentary system of head and/or salivary glands, including biopsy; not otherwise specified	5
00102	Plastic repair of cleft lip	6
00103	Anesthesia for procedures in eye, blepharoplasty	5
00104	Anesthesia for electroconvulsive therapy	4
00120	Anesthesia for procedures on external, middle, and inner ear, including biopsy; not otherwise specified	5
00124	Otoscopy	4
00126	Tympanotomy	4
00140	Anesthesia for procedures on eye; not otherwise specified	5
00142	Lens surgery	4
00144	Corneal transplant	6
00145	Vitrectomy	6
00147	Iridectomy	4
00148	Ophthalmoscopy	4
00160	Anesthesia for procedures on nose and accessory sinuses; not otherwise specified	5
00162	Radical surgery	7
00164	Biopsy, soft tissue	4
00170	Anesthesia for intraoral procedures, including biopsy; not otherwise specified	5
00172	Repair of cleft palate	6
00174	Excision of retropharyngeal tumor	6
00176	Radical surgery	7
00190	Anesthesia for procedures on facial bones; not otherwise specified	5
00192	Radical surgery (including prognathism)	7
00210	Anesthesia for intracranial procedures; not otherwise specified	11
00212	Subdural taps	5
00214	Burr holes (For burr holes for ventriculography, see 01902.)	9
00215	Anesthesia for intracranial procedures; elevation of depressed skull fracture, extradural (simple or compound)	9
00216	Vascular procedures	15
00218	Procedures in sitting position	13
00220	Spinal fluid shunting procedures	10
00222	Electrocoagulation of intracranial nerve	6
NECK		
00300	Anesthesia for all procedures on integumentary system of neck, including subcutaneous tissue	5
00320	Anesthesia for all procedures on esophagus, thyroid, larynx, trachea and lymphatic system of neck; not otherwise specified	6

CPT Anesthesia Code	Anesthesia Procedure	Base Units
HEAD		
00322	Needle biopsy of thyroid (For procedures on cervical spine and cord see 00600, 00604, 00670)	3
00350	Anesthesia for procedures on major vessels of neck; not otherwise specified	10
00352	Simple ligation (For arteriography; see radiologic procedure 01916)	5
THORAX (CHEST WALL AND SHOULDER GIRDLE)		
00400	Anesthesia for procedures on anterior integumentary system of chest, including subcutaneous tissue; not otherwise specified	3
00402	Reconstructive procedures on breast (e.g.,reduction or augmentation mammoplasty, muscle flaps)	5
00404	Radical or modified radical procedures on breast	5
00406	Radical or modified radical procedures on breast with internal mammary node dissection	
00410	Electrical conversion of arrhythmias	4
00420	Anesthesia for procedures on posterior integumentary system of chest, including subcutaneous tissue	5
00450	Anesthesia for procedures on clavicle and scapula; not otherwise specified	5
00452	Radical surgery	6
00454	Biopsy of clavicle	3
00470	Anesthesia for partial rib resection; not otherwise specified	6
00472	Thoracoplasty (any type)	10
00474	Radical procedures, (e.g., pectus excavatum)	13
INTRATHORACIC		
00500	Anesthesia for all procedures on esophagus	15
00520	Anesthesia for closed chest procedures (including esophagoscopy, bronchoscopy, thoracoscopy); not otherwise specified	6
00522	Needle biopsy of pleura	4
00524	Pneumocentesis	4
00528	Mediastinoscopy	8
00530	Anesthesia for transvenous pacemaker insertion	4
00532	Anesthesia for vascular access to central venous circulation	4
00534	Anesthesia for thoracotomy procedures involving lungs, pleura, diaphragm, and mediastinum; not otherwise specified	7
00537	Anesthesia for cardiac electrophys	7
00540	Anesthesia for thoracotomy procedures involving lungs, pleura, diaphragm, and mediastinum; not otherwise specified	13

CPT Anesthesia Code	Anesthesia Procedure	Base Units
HEAD		
00542	Decortication	15
00544	Pleurectomy	15
00546	Pulmonary resection with thoracoplasty	15
00548	Intrathoracic repair of trauma to trachea and bronchi	15
00550	Anesthesia for sternal debridement	
00560	Anesthesia for procedures on heart, pericardium, and great vessels of chest; without pump oxygenator	15
00562	With pump oxygenator	20
00563	Anesthesia for heart proc with pump	25
00566	Anesthesia for cabg without pump	25
00580	Anesthesia for heart or heart/lung transplant	20
SPINE AND SPINAL CORD		
00600	Anesthesia for procedures on cervical spine and cord; not otherwise specified (For myelography and discography, see radiological procedures 01906-01914.)	10
00604	Posterior cervical laminectomy in sitting position	
00620	Anesthesia for procedures on thoracic spine and cord; not otherwise specified	10
00622	Thoracolumbar sympathectomy	13
00630	Anesthesia for procedures in lumbar region; not otherwise specified	8
00632	Lumbar sympathectomy	7
00634	Chemonucleolysis	10
00635	Anesthesia for lumbar puncture	4
00670	Anesthesia for extensive spine and spinal cord procedures (e.g., Harrington rod technique)	13
UPPER ABDOMEN		
00700	Anesthesia for procedures on upper anterior abdominal wall; not otherwise specified	3
00702	Percutaneous liver biopsy	4
00730	Anesthesia for procedures on upper posterior abdominal wall	5
00740	Anesthesia for upper gastrointestinal endoscopic procedures	5
00750	Anesthesia for hernia repairs in upper abdomen; not otherwise specified	4
00752	Lumbar and ventral (incisional) hernias and/or wound dehiscence	6
00754	Omphalocele	7
00756	Transabdominal repair of diaphragmatic hernia	7
00770	Anesthesia for all procedures on major abdominal blood vessels	15
00790	Anesthesia for intraperitoneal procedures in upper abdomen including laparoscopy; not otherwise specified	7
00792	Partial hepatectomy (excluding liver biopsy)	13

CPT Anesthesia Code	Anesthesia Procedure	Base Units	CPT Anesthesia Code	Anesthesia Procedure	Base Units
HEAD			**HEAD**		
00794	Pancreatectomy, partial or total (e.g., Whipple procedure)	8	00910	Anesthesia for transurethral procedures (including urethrocystoscopy); not otherwise specified	3
00796	Liver transplant (recipient)	30	00912	Transurethral resection of bladder tumor(s)	5
00797	Anesthesia, surgery for obesity	8	00914	Transurethral resection of prostate	5
LOWER ABDOMEN			00916	Post-transurethral resection bleeding	5
00800	Anesthesia for procedures on lower anterior abdominal wall; not otherwise specified	3	00918	With fragmentation and/or fragmentation removal of ureteral calculus	5
00802	Panniculectomy	5	00920	Anesthesia for procedures on male external genitalia; not otherwise specified	3
00810	Anesthesia for intestinal endoscopic procedures	6	00922	Seminal vesicles	6
00820	Anesthesia for procedures on lower posterior abdominal wall	5	00924	Undescended testis, unilateral or bilateral	4
00830	Anesthesia for hernia repairs in lower abdomen; not otherwise specified	4	00926	Radical orchiectomy, inguinal	4
00832	Ventral and incisional hernias		00928	Radical orchiectomy, abdominal	6
00840	Anesthesia for intraperitoneal procedures in lower abdomen including laparoscopy; not otherwise specified	6	00930	Orchiopexy, unilateral and bilateral	4
			00932	Complete amputation of penis	4
			00934	Radical amputation of penis with bilateral inguinal lymphadenectomy	6
00842	Amniocentesis	4	00936	Radical amputation of penis with bilateral inguinal and iliac lymphadenectomy	8
00844	Abdominoperineal resection	7			
00846	Radical hysterectomy	8			
00848	Pelvic exenteration	8	00938	Insertion of penile prosthesis (perineal approach)	4
00851	Anestheisa, tubal ligation	6	00940	Anesthesia for vaginal procedures (including biopsy of labia, vagina, cervix or endometrium); not otherwise specified	3
00860	Anesthesia for extraperitoneal procedures in lower abdomen, including urinary tract; not otherwise specified	6			
00862	Renal procedures, including upper 1/3 of ureter or donor nephrectomy	7	00942	Colpotomy, colpectomy, colporrhaphy	4
00864	Total cystectomy	8	00944	Vaginal hysterectomy	6
00865	Anesthesia for removal of prostate	7	00948	Cervical cerlage	4
00866	Adrenalectomy		00950	Culdoscopy	5
00868	Renal transplant (recipient)	10	00952	Hysteroscopy	4
	(For donor nephrectomy, use 00862.)		00955	Continuous epidural and analgesic for labor and vaginal delivery	5
	(For harvesting kidney from brain-dead patient, use 01990.)		**PELVIS (EXCEPT HIP)**		
00869	Anesthesia for vasectomy	3	01000	Anesthesia for procedures on anterior integumentary system of pelvis (anterior to iliac crest), except external genitalia	3
00870	Cystolithotomy	5			
00872	Anesthesia for lithotripsy, extracorporeal shock wave; with water bath	7	01110	Anesthesia for procedures on posterior integumentary system of pelvis (posterior to iliac crest), except perineum	5
00873	Without water bath	5			
00880	Anesthesia for procedures on major lower abdominal vessels; not otherwise specified	15	01112	Anesthesia for bone aspirate/bx	5
			01120	Anesthesia for procedures on bony pelvis	6
00882	Inferior vena cava ligation	10	01130	Anesthesia for body cast application or revision	3
00884	Transvenous umbrella insertion	5			
PERINEUM			01140	Anesthesia for interpelviabdominal (hind quarter) amputation	15
00902	Anorectal procedure (including endoscopy and/or biopsy)	4			
00904	Radical perineal procedure	7			
00906	Vulvectomy	4			
00908	Perineal prostatectomy	6			

APPENDIX D

CPT Anesthesia Code	Anesthesia Procedure	Base Units
HEAD		
01150	Anesthesia for radical procedures for tumor of pelvis, except hind quarter amputation	8
01160	Anesthesia for closed procedures involving symphysis pubis or sacroiliac joint	4
01170	Anesthesia for open procedures involving symphysis pubis or sacroiliac joint	8
01180	Anesthesia for obturator neurectomy; extrapelvic	3
01190	Intrapelvic	4
UPPER LEG (EXCEPT KNEE)		
01200	Anesthesia for all closed procedures involving hip joint	4
01202	Anesthesia for arthroscopic procedures of hip joint	4
01210	Anesthesia for open procedures involving hip joint; not otherwise specified	6
01212	Hip disarticulation	10
01214	Total hip replacement or revision	10
01215	Anesthesia for revise hip repair	10
01220	Anesthesia for all closed procedures involving upper 2/3 of femur	4
01230	Anesthesia for open procedures involving upper 2/3 of femur; not otherwise specified	6
01232	Amputation	5
01234	Radical resection	8
01240	Anesthesia for all procedures on integumentary system of upper leg	3
01250	Anesthesia for all procedures on nerves, muscles, tendons, fascia, and bursae of upper leg	4
01260	Anesthesia for all procedures involving veins of upper leg, including exploration	3
01270	Anesthesia for procedures involving arteries of upper leg, including bypass graft; not otherwise specified	8
01272	Femoral artery ligation	4
01274	Femoral artery embolectomy	6
KNEE AND POPLITEAL AREA		
01320	Anesthesia for all procedures on nerves, muscles, tendons, fascia and bursae of knee and/or popliteal area	4
01340	Anesthesia for all closed procedures on lower 1/3 of femur	4
01360	Anesthesia for all open procedures on lower 1/3 of femur	5
01380	Anesthesia for all closed procedures on knee joint	3
01382	Anesthesia for arthroscopic procedures of knee joint	3

CPT Anesthesia Code	Anesthesia Procedure	Base Units
HEAD		
01390	Anesthesia for all closed procedures on upper ends of tibia and fibula, and/or patella	3
01392	Anesthesia for all open procedures on upper ends of tibia and fibula and/or patella	4
01400	Anesthesia for open procedures on knee joint; not otherwise specified	4
01402	Total knee replacement	7
01404	Disarticulation at knee	5
01420	Anesthesia for all cast applications, removal, or repair involving knee joint	3
01430	Anesthesia for procedures on veins of knee and popliteal area; not otherwise specified	3
01432	Arteriovenous fistula	5
01440	Anesthesia for procedures on arteries of knee and Popliteal area; not otherwise specified	5
01442	Popliteal thromboendarterectomy, with or without patch graft	8
01444	Popliteal excision and graft or repair for occlusion or aneurysm	8
LOWER LEG		
(Below knee - includes ankle and foot)		
01462	Anesthesia for all closed procedures on lower leg, ankle, and foot	3
01464	Anesthesia for arthroscopic procedures of ankle joint	3
01470	Anesthesia for procedures on nerves, muscles, tendons, and fascia of lower leg, ankle, and foot; not otherwise specified	3
01472	Repair of ruptured Achilles tendon, with or without graft	5
01474	Gastrocnemius recession (e.g., Strayer procedure)	5
01480	Anesthesia for open procedures on bones of lower leg, ankle, and foot; not otherwise specified	3
01482	Radical resection	4
01484	Osteotomy or osteoplasty of tibia and/or fibula	4
01486	Total ankle replacement	7
01490	Anesthesia for lower leg cast application, removal, or repair	3
01500	Anesthesia for procedures on arteries of lower leg, including bypass graft; not otherwise specified	8
01502	Embolectomy, direct or catheter	6
01520	Anesthesia for procedures on veins of lower leg; not otherwise specified	3
01522	Venous thrombectomy, direct or catheter	5

Appendixes

CPT Anesthesia Code	Anesthesia Procedure	Base Units
	SHOULDER AND AXILLA	
	(Includes humeral head and neck, sternoclavicular joint, acromioclavicular joint, and shoulder joint)	
01610	Anesthesia for all procedures on nerves, muscles, tendons, fascia, and bursae of shoulder and axilla	5
	(Includes humeral head and neck, sternoclavicular joint, acromioclavicular joint, and shoulder joint)	
01620	Anesthesia for all closed procedures on humeral head and neck, sternoclavicular joint, and shoulder joint	4
01622	Anesthesia for arthroscopic procedures of shoulder joint	4
01630	Anesthesia for open procedures on humeral head and neck, sternoclavicular joint, acromioclavicular oint, and shoulder joint; not otherwise specified	5
01632	Radical resection	6
01634	Shoulder disarticulation	9
01636	Interthoracoscapular (forequarter) amputation	15
01638	Total shoulder replacement	10
01650	Anesthesia for procedures on arteries of shoulder and axilla; not otherwise specified	6
01652	Axillary-brachial aneurysm	10
01654	Bypass graft	8
01656	Axillary-femoral bypass graft	10
01670	Anesthesia for all procedures on veins of shoulder and axilla	4
01680	Anesthesia for shoulder cast application, removal or repair; not otherwise specified	3
01682	Shoulder spica	4

CPT Anesthesia Code	Anesthesia Procedure	Base Units
	UPPER ARM AND ELBOW	
01710	Anesthesia for procedures on nerves, muscles, tendons, fascia, bursae of upper arm and elbow; not otherwise specified	3
01712	Tenotomy, elbow to shoulder, open	5
01714	Tenoplasty, elbow to shoulder	5
01716	Tenodesis, rupture of long tendon of biceps	5
01730	Anesthesia for all closed procedures on humerus and elbow	3
01732	Anesthesia for arthroscopic procedures of elbow joint	3
01740	Anesthesia for open procedures on humerus and elbow; not otherwise specified	4

CPT Anesthesia Code	Anesthesia Procedure	Base Units
01742	Osteotomy of humerus	5
01744	Repair of nonunion or malunion of humerus	5
01756	Radical procedures	6
01758	Excision of cyst or tumor of humerus	5
01760	Total elbow replacement	7
01770	Anesthesia for procedures on arteries of upper arm; not otherwise specified	8
01772	Embolectomy	6
01780	Anesthesia for procedures on veins of upper arm and elbow; not otherwise specified	3
01782	Phleborrhaphy	4
	FOREARM, WRIST AND HAND	
01810	Anesthesia for all procedures on nerves, muscles, tendons, fascia, bursae of forearm, wrist, and hand	3
01820	Anesthesia for all closed procedures on radius, ulna, wrist, or hand bones	3
01830	Anesthesia for open procedures on radius, ulna, wrist, or hand bones; not otherwise specified	3
01832	Total wrist replacement	6
01840	Anesthesia for procedures on arteries of forearm, wrist, and hand; not otherwise specified	6
01842	Embolectomy	6
01844	Anesthesia for vascular shunt, or shunt revision, any type (e.g., dialysis)	6
01850	Anesthesia for procedures on veins of forearm, wrist, and hand; not otherwise specified	3
01852	Phleborrhaphy	4
01860	Anesthesia for forearm, wrist, or hand cast application, removal or repair	3
	RADIOLOGICAL PROCEDURES	
01905		5
01916	Anesthesia for arteriograms, needle; carotid, or vertebral	5
01920	Anesthesia for cardiac catheterization including coronary arteriography and ventriculography (not to include Swan-Ganz catheter)	7
01922	Anesthesia for noninvasive imaging or radiation therapy	7
01924	Anesthesia, ther intervene rad, art	5
01925	Anesthesia, ther intervene rad, car	7
01926	Anesthesia, tx interv rad hrt/cran	8
	MISCELLANEOUS PROCEDURE(S)	
01930	Anesthesia, ther intervene rad, vein	5
01931	Anesthesia, ther intervene rad, tip	7
01932	Anesthesia, tx interv rad, th vein	6
01952	Anesthesia, burn, less 4 percent	5
01953	Anesthesia, burn 4-9 percent	5
01960	Anesthesia, vaginal delivery	5
01961	Anesthesia, caesarean delivery	7

© 2005 Ingenix, Inc.

01962	Anesthesia, emergency hysterectomy	8
01963	Anesthesia, caesarean hysterectomy	8
01964	Anesthesia, abortion procedures	4
01967	Anesthesia/analg, vaginal delivery	5
01968	Anesthesia/analg caesarean delivery add-on	2
01969	Anesthesia/analg caesarean hysterectomy add-on	5
01990	Physiological support for harvesting of organ(s) from brain-dead patient	7
01995	Region IV administration of local anesthetic agent (upper or lower extremity)	5
01996	Daily management of epidural or subarachnoid drug administration	3
01999	Unlisted anesthesia procedure(s)	I.C.*
*Individual Consideration		

Pub. 100-4, Chapter 12, Section 60
Payment for Pathology Services

B3-15020, AB-01-47 (CR1499)

A - General Payment Rule

Payment may be made under the fee schedule for the professional component of physician laboratory or physician pathology services furnished to hospital inpatients or outpatients by hospital physicians or by independent laboratories, if they qualify as the reassignee for the physician service.. Payment may be made under the fee schedule, as noted below, for the technical component (TC) of pathology services furnished by an independent laboratory to hospital inpatients or outpatients. Payment may be made under the fee schedule for the technical component of physician pathology services furnished by an independent laboratory, or a hospital if it is acting as an independent laboratory, to non-hospital patients. The Medicare physician fee schedule identifies those physician laboratory or physician pathology services that have a technical component service.

CMS published a final regulation in 1999 that would no longer allow independent laboratories to bill under the physician fee schedule for the TC of physician pathology services. The implementation of this regulation was delayed by Section 542 of the Benefits and Improvement and Protection Act of 2000 (BIPA). Section 542 allows the Medicare carrier to continue to pay for the TC of physician pathology services when an independent laboratory furnishes this service to an inpatient or outpatient of a covered hospital. This provision is applicable to TC services furnished in 2001, 2002, 2003, 2004, 2005 or 2006.

For this provision, a covered hospital is a hospital that had an arrangement with an independent laboratory that was in effect as of July 22, 1999, under which a laboratory furnished the TC of physician pathology services to fee-for-service Medicare beneficiaries who were hospital inpatients or outpatients, and submitted claims for payment for the TC to a carrier. The TC could have been submitted separately or combined with the professional component and reported as a combined service.

The term, fee-for-service Medicare beneficiary, means an individual who:

Is entitled to benefits under Part A or enrolled under Part B of title XVIII or both; and

Is not enrolled in any of the following: A Medicare + Choice plan under Part C of such title; a plan offered by an eligible organization under §1876 of the Social Security Act; a program of all-inclusive care for the elderly under §1894; or a social health maintenance organization demonstration project established under Section 4108 of the Omnibus Budget Reconciliation Act of 1987.

In implementing Section 542, the carriers should consider as independent laboratories those entities that it has previously recognized as independent laboratories.

An independent laboratory that has acquired another independent laboratory that had an arrangement of July 22, 1999, with a covered hospital, can bill the TC of physician pathology services for that hospital's inpatients and outpatients under the physician fee schedule.

An independent laboratory that furnishes the TC of physician pathology services to inpatients or outpatients of a hospital that is not a covered hospital may not bill the carrier for the TC of physician pathology services during the time §542 is in effect.

If the arrangement between the independent laboratory and the covered hospital limited the provision of TC physician pathology services to certain situations or at particular times, then the independent laboratory can bill the carrier only for these limited services.

The carrier shall require independent laboratories that had an arrangement, on or prior to July 22, 1999 with a covered hospital, to bill for the technical component of physician pathology services to provide a copy of this agreement, or other documentation substantiating that an arrangement was in effect between the hospital and the independent laboratory as of this date. The independent laboratory must submit this documentation for each covered hospital that the independent laboratory services.

See Chapter 16 for additional instruction on laboratory services including clinical diagnostic laboratory services.

Physician laboratory and pathology services are limited to:

- Surgical pathology services;
- Specific cytopathology, hematology and blood banking services that have been identified to require performance by a physician and are listed below;
- Clinical consultation services that meet the requirements in subsection D below; and
- Clinical laboratory interpretation services that meet the requirements and which are specifically listed in subsection E below.

B - Surgical Pathology Services

Surgical pathology services include the gross and microscopic examination of organ tissue performed by a physician, except for autopsies, which are not covered by Medicare. Surgical pathology services paid under the physician fee schedule are reported under the following CPT codes:

88300, 88302, 88304, 88305, 88307, 88309, 88311, 88312, 88313, 88314, 88318, 88319, 88321, 88323, 88325, 88329, 88331, 88332, 88342, 88346, 88347, 88348, 88349, 88355, 88356, 88358, 88361, 88362, 88365, 88380.

Depending upon circumstances and the billing entity, the carriers may pay professional component, technical component or both.

C - Specific Hematology, Cytopathology and Blood Banking Services

Cytopathology services include the examination of cells from fluids, washings, brushings or smears, but generally excluding hematology. Examining cervical and vaginal smears are the most common service in cytopathology. Cervical and vaginal smears do not require interpretation by a physician unless the results are or appear to be abnormal. In such cases, a physician personally conducts a separate microscopic evaluation to determine the nature of an abnormality. This microscopic evaluation ordinarily does require performance by a physician. When medically necessary and when furnished by a physician, it is paid under the fee schedule.

These codes include 88104, 88106, 88107, 88108, 88112, 88125, 88141, 88160, 88161, 88162, 88172, 88173, 88180, 88182.

For services furnished prior to January 1, 1999, carriers pay separately under the physician fee schedule for the interpretation of an abnormal pap smear furnished to a hospital inpatient by a physician. They must pay under the clinical laboratory fee schedule for pap smears furnished in all other situations. This policy also applies to screening pap smears requiring a physician interpretation. For services furnished on or after January 1, 1999, carriers allow separate payment for a physician's interpretation of a pap smear to any patient (i.e., hospital or non-hospital) as long as: (1) the laboratory's screening personnel suspect an abnormality; and (2) the physician reviews and interprets the pap smear.

This policy also applies to screening pap smears requiring a physician interpretation and described in the National Coverage Determination Manual and Chapter 18. These services are reported under codes P3000 or P3001.

Physician hematology services include microscopic evaluation of bone marrow aspirations and biopsies. It also includes those limited number of peripheral blood smears which need to be referred to a physician to evaluate the nature of an apparent abnormality identified by the technologist. These codes include 85060, 38220, 85097, and 38221.

Carriers pay the professional component for the interpretation of an abnormal blood smear (code 85060) furnished to a hospital inpatient by a hospital physician or an independent laboratory.

For the other listed hematology codes, payment may be made for the professional component if the service is furnished to a patient by a hospital physician or independent laboratory. In addition, payment may be made for these services furnished to patients by an independent laboratory.

Codes 38220 and 85097 represent professional-only component services and have no technical component values.

Blood banking services of hematologists and pathologists are paid under the physician fee schedule when analyses are performed on donor and/or patient blood to determine compatible donor units for transfusion where cross matching is difficult or where contamination with transmissible disease of donor is suspected.

The blood banking codes are 86077, 86078, and 86079 and represent professional component only services. These codes do not have a technical component.

D - Clinical Consultation Services

Clinical consultations are paid under the physician fee schedule only if they:

Are requested by the patient's attending physician;

Relate to a test result that lies outside the clinically significant normal or expected range in view of the condition of the patient;

Result in a written narrative report included in the patient's medical record; and

Require the exercise of medical judgment by the consultant physician.

Clinical consultations are professional component services only. There is no technical component. The clinical consultation codes are 80500 and 80502.

Routine conversations held between a laboratory director and an attending physician about test orders or results do not qualify as consultations unless all four requirements are met. Laboratory personnel, including the director, may from time to time contact attending physicians to report test results or to suggest additional testing or be contacted by attending physicians on similar matters. These contacts do not constitute clinical consultations. However, if in the course of such a contact, the attending physician requests a consultation from the pathologist, and if that consultation meets the other criteria and is properly documented, it is paid under the fee schedule.

EXAMPLE

A pathologist telephones a surgeon about a patient's suitability for surgery based on the results of clinical laboratory test results. During the course of their conversation, the surgeon ask the pathologist whether, based on test results, patient history and medical records, the patient is a candidate for surgery. The surgeon's request requires the pathologist to render a medical judgment and provide a consultation. The pathologist follows up his/her oral advice with a written report and the surgeon notes in the patient's medical record that he/she requested a consultation. This consultation is paid under the fee schedule.

In any case, if the information could ordinarily be furnished by a nonphysician laboratory specialist, the service of the physician is not a consultation payable under the fee schedule.

See the Program Integrity Manual for guidelines for related data analysis to identify inappropriate patterns of billing for consultations.

E - Clinical Laboratory Interpretation Services

Only clinical laboratory interpretation services listed below and which meet the criteria in subsections D.1, D.3, and D.4 for clinical consultations and, as a result, are billable under the fee schedule. These services are reported under the clinical laboratory code with modifier 26. These services can be paid under the physician fee schedule if they are furnished to a patient by a hospital pathologist or an independent laboratory. Note that a hospital's standing order policy can be used as a substitute for the individual request by the patient's attending physician. Carriers are not allowed to revise CMS's list to accommodate local medical practice. The CMS periodically reviews this list and adds or deletes clinical laboratory codes as warranted.

Clinical Laboratory Interpretation Services

Code	Definition
83020	Hemoglobin; electrophoresis
83912	Nucleic acid probe, with electrophoresis, with examination and report
84165	Protein, total, serum; electrophoretic fractionation and quantitation
84181	Protein; Western Blot with interpretation and report, blood or other body fluid
84182	Protein; Western Blot, with interpretation and report, blood or other body fluid, immunological probe for band identification; each
85390	Fibrinolysin; screening
85576	Platelet; aggregation (in vitro), any agent
86255	Fluorescent antibody; screen
86256	Fluorescent antibody; titer
86320	Immunoelectrophoresis; serum, each specimen
86325	Immunoelectrophoresis; other fluids (e.g.urine) with concentra tion, each specimen
86327	Immunoelectrophoresis; crossed (2 dimensional assay)
86334	Immunofixation electrophoresis
87164	Dark field examination, any source (e.g. penile, vaginal, oral, skin); includes specimen collection
87207	Smear, primary source, with interpretation; special stain for inclusion bodies or intracellular parasites (e.g. malaria, kala azar, herpes)
88371	Protein analysis of tissue by Western Blot, with interpretation and report.
88372	Protein analysis of tissue by Western Blot, immunological probe for band identification, each
89060	Crystal identification by light microscopy with or without polarizing lens analysis, any body fluid (except urine)

Pub. 100-4, Chapter 12, Section 70
Payment Conditions for Radiology Services

B3-15022

See Chapter 13 for claims processing instructions for radiology.

Pub. 100-4, Chapter 12, Section 80.3
Unusual Travel (CPT Code 99082)

B3-15026

In general, travel has been incorporated in the MPFSDB individual fees and is thus not separately payable. Carriers must pay separately for unusual travel (CPT code 99082) only when the physician submits documentation to demonstrate that the travel was very unusual.

Pub. 100-4, Chapter 12, Section 90.3
Physicians' Services Performed in Ambulatory Surgical Centers (ASC)

B3-2265, B3-2265.4

See Chapter 14, for a description of services that may be billed by an ASC and services separately billed by physicians.

The ASC payment does not include the professional services of the physician. These are billed separately by the physician. Physicians' services include the services of anesthesiologists administering or supervising the administration of anesthesia to ASC patients and the patients' recovery from the anesthesia. The term physicians' services also includes any routine pre- or postoperative services, such as office visits, consultations, diagnostic tests, removal of stitches, changing of dressings, and other services which the individual physician usually performs.

The physician must enter the place of service code (POS) 24 on the claim to show that the procedure was performed in an ASC.

The carrier pays the "facility" fee from the MPFSDB to the physician. The facility fee is for services done in a facility other than the physician's office and is less then the nonfacility fee for services performed in the physician's office.

Pub. 100-4, Chapter 12, Section 100
Teaching Physician Services

B3-2020.7, B3-8201, B3-15016

A - General

Medical insurance covers the services attending physicians (other than interns and residents) render in the teaching setting to individual patients.

The following guidelines and instructions relate primarily to hospitals, but to the extent they are applicable, also govern payment for services of attending physicians supervising interns and residents in skilled nursing facilities.

Payment under the MPFSDB may be made for the professional services rendered to a beneficiary by his/her attending physician where the attending physician provides personal and identifiable direction to interns or residents who are participating in the care of the patient. In the case of major surgical procedures and other complex and dangerous procedures or situations, such personal direction must include supervision in person by the attending physician. A charge is recognized under Part B for the services of an attending physician who involves residents and interns in the care of his/her patient only if his/her services to the patient are of the same character, in terms of responsibilities to the patient that are assumed and fulfilled, as the service he/she renders to other paying patients.

The carrying out by the physician of these responsibilities is demonstrated by such actions as:

- Reviewing the patient's history and physical examination;
- Personally examining the patient within a reasonable period after admission;
- Confirming or revising diagnosis;
- Determining the course of treatment to be followed;
- Assuring that any supervision needed by the interns and residents was furnished; and
- By making frequent review of the patient's progress.

As evidence that a covered service was rendered by the supervisory physician, the medical record must contain signed or countersigned notes by the supervisory physician that show he/she personally reviewed the patients medical history, gave a physical examination, confirmed or revised the diagnosis, visited the patient during the more critical period of the illness, and discharged the patient. For all other individual occasions of service billed, notes in the medical record by interns, residents, or nurses which indicate that the physician was physically present when the service was rendered are sufficient documentation of the physician's involvement.

B - Definitions

For purposes of this section, the following definitions apply.

Resident - An individual who participates in an approved graduate medical education (GME) program or a physician who is not in an approved GME program but who is authorized to practice only in a hospital setting. The term includes interns and fellows in GME programs recognized as approved for purposes of direct GME payments made by the FI.

The fact that an individual hospital does not choose to include an eligible individual in its full-time equivalency count of residents does not change that individual's status as a resident in an approved GME program.

A medical student is never considered to be a resident. Any contribution of a medical student to the performance of a service or billable procedure (other than the taking of a history in the case of an E/M service) must be performed in the physical presence of a physician or jointly with a resident in a service meeting the requirements set forth below for teaching physician billing.

Teaching Physician - A physician (other than another resident) who involves residents in the care of his or her patients.

Direct Medical and Surgical Services - Services to individual beneficiaries that are either personally furnished by a physician or furnished by a resident under the supervision of a physician in a teaching hospital making the reasonable cost election for physician services furnished in teaching hospitals. All payments for such services are made by the FI for the hospital.

Teaching Hospital - A hospital engaged in an approved GME residency program in medicine, osteopathy, dentistry, or podiatry.

Teaching Setting - Any provider, hospital-based provider, or nonprovider setting in which Medicare payment for the services of residents is made by the FI under the direct graduate medical education payment methodology or

freestanding SNF or HHA in which such payments are made on a reasonable cost basis.

Pub. 100-4, Chapter 12, Section 100.1.7
Assistants at Surgery in Teaching Hospitals

B3-15016.D

A - General

Carriers do not pay for the services of assistants at surgery furnished in a teaching hospital which has a training program related to the medical specialty required for the surgical procedure and has a qualified resident available to perform the service unless the requirements of one of subsections C, D, or E are met. Each teaching hospital has a different situation concerning numbers of residents, qualifications of residents, duties of residents, and types of surgeries performed.

The FI should provide the carrier with a list of teaching physicians and hospitals. There may be some teaching hospitals in which carriers can apply a presumption about the availability of a qualified resident in a training program related to the medical specialty required for the surgical procedures, but there are other teaching hospitals in which there are often no qualified residents available. This may be due to their involvement in other activities, complexity of the surgery, numbers of residents in the program, or other valid reasons. Carriers process assistant at surgery claims for services furnished in teaching hospitals on the basis of the following certification by the assistant, or through the use of modifier -82 which indicates that a qualified resident surgeon was not available. This certification is for use only when the basis for payment is the unavailability of qualified residents.

I understand that §1842(b)(7)(D) of the Act generally prohibits Medicare physician fee schedule payment for the services of assistants at surgery in teaching hospitals when qualified residents are available to furnish such services. I certify that the services for which payment is claimed were medically necessary and that no qualified resident was available to perform the services. I further understand that these services are subject to post-payment review by the Medicare carrier.

Carriers retain the claim and certification for four years and conduct post-payment reviews as necessary. For example, carriers investigate situations in which it is always certified that there are no qualified residents available, and undertake recovery if warranted.

Assistant at surgery claims denied based on these instructions do not qualify for payment under the limitation on liability provision.

B - Definition

An assistant at surgery is a physician who actively assists the physician in charge of a case in performing a surgical procedure. The conditions for coverage of such services in teaching hospitals are more restrictive than those in other settings because of the availability of residents who are qualified to perform this type of service.

C - Exceptional Circumstances

Payment may be made for the services of assistants at surgery in teaching hospitals, subject to the special limitation in §20.4.3 not withstanding the availability of a qualified resident to furnish the services. There may be exceptional medical circumstances, e.g., emergency, life-threatening

© 2005 Ingenix, Inc.

situations such as multiple traumatic injuries which require immediate treatment. There may be other situations in which the medical staff may find that exceptional medical circumstances justify the services of a physician assistant at surgery even though a qualified resident is available.

D - Physicians Who Do Not Involve Residents in Patient Care

Payment may be made for the services of assistants at surgery in teaching hospitals, subject to the limitations in §20.4.3, above, if the primary surgeon has an across-the-board policy of never involving residents in the preoperative, operative, or postoperative care of his or her patients. Generally, this exception is applied to community physicians who have no involvement in the hospital's GME program. In such situations, payment may be made for reasonable and necessary services on the same basis as would be the case in a nonteaching hospital. However, if the assistant is not a physician primarily engaged in the field of surgery, no payment is made unless either of the criteria of subsection E is met.

E - Multiple Physician Specialties Involved in Surgery

Complex medical procedures, including multistage transplant surgery and coronary bypass, may require a team of physicians. In these situations, each of the physicians performs a unique, discrete function requiring special skills integral to the total procedure. Each physician is engaged in a level of activity different from assisting the surgeon in charge of the case. The special payment limitation in §20.4.3 is not applied. If payment is made on the basis of a single team fee, additional claims are denied. The carrier will determine which procedures performed in the service area require a team approach to surgery. Team surgery is paid for on a "By Report" basis.

The services of physicians of different specialties may be necessary during surgery when each specialist is required to play an active role in the patient's treatment because of the existence of more than one medical condition requiring diverse, specialized medical services. For example, a patient's cardiac condition may require the a cardiologist be present to monitor the patient's condition during abdominal surgery. In this type of situation, the physician furnishing the concurrent care is functioning at a different level than that of an assistant at surgery, and payment is made on a regular fee schedule basis.

Pub. 100-4, Chapter 12, Section 100.1.8
Physician Billing in the Teaching Setting

B3-8204, B3-15016

A - Reimbursement to the Hospital

When a hospital is billing the carrier, as opposed to the physician billing the carrier, for covered services, it must bill the carrier on the Form CMS1500 or equivalent electronic format. It no longer has the option to establish any other type of agreement with the carrier.

B - Carrier Claims

The method by which services performed in a teaching setting must be billed is determined by the manner in which reimbursement is made for such services. For carriers, the shared system suspends claims submitted by a teaching physician, for review.

Pub. 100-4, Chapter 12, Section 110.2

Outpatient Mental Health Limitation

B3-4112, B3-2472.4

The carrier must apply the outpatient mental health limitation to all covered mental health therapeutic services furnished by PAs. The reduction is 62.5 percent applied after the 85 percent.

Refer to §210 below for a complete discussion of the outpatient mental health limitation.

Pub. 100-4, Chapter 12, Section 140
Certified Registered Nurse Anesthetist (CRNA) Services

B3-16003, B3-16003 A, B3-3040.4, B3-4172

Section 9320 of OBRA 1986 provides for payment under a fee schedule to certified registered nurse anesthetists (CRNAs) and anesthesia assistants (AAs). CRNAs and AAs may bill Medicare directly for their services or have payment made to an employer or an entity under which they have a contract. This could be a hospital, physician or ASC. This provision is effective for services rendered on or after January 1, 1989.

Anesthesia services are subject to the usual Part B coinsurance and deductible and when furnished on or after January 1, 1992 by a qualified nurse anesthetist and are paid at the lesser of the actual charge, the physician fee schedule, or the CRNA fee schedule. Payment for CRNA services is made only on an assignment basis.

Pub. 100-4, Chapter 12, Section 140.2
Entity or Individual to Whom CRNA Fee Schedule is Payable

B3-16003.C, B3-4830.A

Payment for the services of a CRNA may be made to the CRNA who furnished the anesthesia services or to a hospital, physician, group practice, or ASC with which the CRNA has an employment or contractual relationship.

Pub. 100-4, Chapter 12, Section 140.3.2
Anesthesia Time and Calculation of Anesthesia Time Units

B3-15018.G

Anesthesia time means the time during which a CRNA is present with the patient. It starts when the CRNA begins to prepare the patient for anesthesia services in the operating room or an equivalent area and ends when the CRNA is no longer furnishing anesthesia services to the patient, that is, when the patient may be placed safely under postoperative care. Anesthesia time is a continuous time period from the start of anesthesia to the end of an anesthesia service. In counting anesthesia time for services furnished on or after January 1, 2000, the CRNA can add blocks of time around an interruption in anesthesia time as long as the CRNA is furnishing continuous anesthesia care within the time periods around the interruption.

Pub. 100-4, Chapter 12, Section 150
Clinical Social Worker (CSW) Services

B3-2152, B3-17000

See Medicare Benefit Policy Manual, Chapter 15, for coverage requirements.

Assignment of benefits is required.

Payment is at 75 percent of the physician fee schedule.

CSWs are identified on the provider file by specialty code 80 and provider type 56.

Medicare applies the outpatient mental health limitation to all covered therapeutic services furnished by qualified CSWs. Refer to §210, below, for a discussion of the outpatient mental health limitation. The modifier "AJ" must be applied on CSN services.

Pub. 100-4, Chapter 12, Section 160
Independent Psychologist Services

B3-2150, B3-2070.2

See the Medicare Benefit Policy Manual, Chapter 15, for coverage requirements.

There are a number of types of psychologists. Educational psychologists engage in identifying and treating education-related issues. In contrast, counseling psychologists provide services that include a broader realm including phobias, familial issues, etc. Psychometrists are psychologists who have been trained to administer and interpret tests. However, clinical psychologists are defined as a provider of diagnostic and therapeutic services. Because of the differences in services provided, services provided by psychologists who do not provide clinical services are subject to different billing guidelines. One service often provided by nonclinical psychologist is diagnostic testing.

NOTE: Diagnostic psychological testing services performed by persons who meet these requirements are covered as other diagnostic tests. When, however, the psychologist is not practicing independently, but is on the staff of an institution, agency, or clinic, that entity bills for the diagnostic services.

Expenses for such testing are not subject to the payment limitation on treatment for mental, psychoneurotic, and personality disorders. Independent psychologists are not required by law to accept assignment when performing psychological tests. However, regardless of whether the psychologist accepts assignment, he or she must report on the claim form the name and address of the physician who ordered the test.

Pub. 100-4, Chapter 12, Section 160.1
Payment

Diagnostic testing services are not subject to the outpatient mental health limitation. Refer to §210, below, for a discussion of the outpatient mental health limitation.

The diagnostic testing services performed by a psychologist (who is not a clinical psychologist) practicing independently of an institution, agency, or physician's office are covered as other diagnostic tests if a physician orders such testing. Medicare covers this type of testing as an outpatient service if furnished by any psychologist who is licensed or certified to practice psychology in the State or jurisdiction where he or she is furnishing services or, if the jurisdiction does not issue licenses, if provided by any practicing psychologist. (It is CMS' understanding that all States, the District of Columbia, and Puerto Rico license psychologists, but that some trust territories do not. Examples of psychologists, other than clinical psychologists, whose services are covered under this provision include, but are not limited to, educational psychologists and counseling psychologists.)

To determine whether the diagnostic psychological testing services of a particular independent psychologist are covered under Part B in States which have statutory licensure or certification, carriers must secure from the appropriate State agency a current listing of psychologists holding the required credentials. In States or territories which lack statutory licensing and certification, carriers must check individual qualifications as claims are submitted. Possible reference sources are the national directory of membership of the American Psychological Association, which provides data about the educational background of individuals and indicates which members are board-certified, and records and directories of the State or territorial psychological association. If qualification is dependent on a doctoral degree from a currently accredited program, carriers must verify the date of accreditation of the school involved, since such accreditation is not retroactive. If the reference sources listed above do not provide enough information (e.g., the psychologist is not a member of the association), carriers must contact the psychologist personally for the required information. Carriers may wish to maintain a continuing list of psychologists whose qualifications have been verified.

Medicare excludes expenses for diagnostic testing from the payment limitation on treatment for mental/psychoneurotic/personality disorders.

Carriers must identify the independent psychologist's choice whether or not to accept assignment when performing psychological tests.

Carriers must accept an independent psychologist claim only if the psychologist reports the name/UPIN of the physician who ordered a test.

Carriers pay nonparticipating independent psychologists at 95 percent of the physician fee schedule allowed amount. Carriers pay participating independent psychologists at 100 percent of the physician fee schedule allowed amount.

Independent psychologists are identified on the provider file by specialty code 62 and provider type 35.

Pub. 100-4, Chapter 12, Section 170
Clinical Psychologist Services

B3-2150

See Medicare Benefit Policy Manual, Chapter 15, for general coverage requirements.

Direct payment may be made under Part B for professional services. However, services furnished incident to the professional services of CPs to hospital patients remain bundled. Therefore, payment must continue to be made to the hospital (by the FI) for such "incident to" services.

Pub. 100-4, Chapter 12, Section 170.1
Payment

B3-2150, B3-17001.1

All covered therapeutic services furnished by qualified CPs are subject to the outpatient mental health services limitation (i.e., only 62 1/2 percent of expenses for these services are considered incurred expenses for Medicare purposes). The limitation does not apply to diagnostic services. Refer to §210 below for a discussion of the outpatient mental health limitation.

Payment for the services of CPs is made on the basis of a fee schedule or the actual charge, whichever is less, and only on the basis of assignment.

CPs are identified by specialty code 68 and provider type 27. Modifier "AH" is required on CP services.

Pub. 100-4, Chapter 12, Section 190.7
Carrier Editing of Telehealth Claims

Effective October 1, 2001, covered telehealth services include CPT codes 99241 – 99275, 99201 – 99215, 90801 (effective March 1, 2003), 90804 - 90809, and 90862. *Effective January 1, 2005, covered telehealth services also include HCPCS codes G0308, G0309, G0311, G0312, G0314, G0315, G0317, and G0318.* When furnished as telehealth services these codes are billed with either the "GT" or "GQ" modifier.

The carrier shall approve covered telehealth services if the physician or practitioner is licensed under State law to provide the service. Carriers must familiarize themselves with licensure provisions of States for which they process claims and disallow telehealth services furnished by physicians or practitioners who are not authorized to furnish the applicable telehealth service under State law. For example, if a nurse practitioner is not licensed to provide individual psychotherapy under State law, he or she would not be permitted to receive payment for individual psychotherapy under Medicare. The carrier shall install edits to ensure that only properly licensed physicians and practitioners are paid for covered telehealth services.

If a carrier receives claims for professional telehealth services coded with the "GQ" modifier (representing "via asynchronous telecommunications system"), it shall approve/pay for these services only if the physician or practitioner is affiliated with a Federal telemedicine demonstration conducted in Alaska or Hawaii. The carrier may require the physician or practitioner at the distant site to document his or her participation in a Federal telemedicine demonstration program conducted in Alaska or Hawaii prior to paying for telehealth services provided via asynchronous, store and forward technologies.

If a carrier denies telehealth services because the physician or practitioner may not bill for them, the carrier uses MSN message 21.18: "This item or service is not covered when performed or ordered by this practitioner." The carrier uses remittance advice message 52 when denying the claim based upon MSN message 21.18.

If a service is billed with one of the telehealth modifiers and the procedure code is not designated as a covered telehealth service, the carrier denies the service using MSN message 9.4: "This item or service was denied because information required to make payment was incorrect." The remittance advice message depends on what is incorrect, e.g., B18 if procedure code or modifier is incorrect, 125 for submission billing errors, 412 for difference inconsistencies. The carrier uses B18 as the explanation for the denial of the claim.

Pub. 100-4, Chapter 12, Section 200
Allergy Testing and Immunotherapy

B3-15050

A - Allergy Testing

The MPFSDB fee amounts for allergy testing services billed under codes 95004-95078 are established for single tests. Therefore, the number of tests must be shown on the claim.

EXAMPLE

If a physician performs 25 percutaneous tests (scratch, puncture, or prick) with allergenic extract, the physician must bill code 95004 and specify 25 in the units field of Form CMS1500 (paper claims or electronic format). To compute payment, the Medicare carrier multiplies the payment for one test (i.e., the payment listed in the fee schedule) by the quantity listed in the units field.

B - Allergy Immunotherapy

For services rendered on or after January 1, 1995, all antigen/allergy immunotherapy services are paid for under the Medicare physician fee schedule. Prior to that date, only the antigen injection services, i.e., only codes 95115 and 95117, were paid for under the fee schedule. Codes representing antigens and their preparation and single codes representing both the antigens and their injection were paid for under the Medicare reasonable charge system. A legislative change brought all of these services under the fee schedule at the beginning of 1995 and the following policies are effective as of January 1, 1995:

1 - CPT codes 95120 through 95134 are not valid for Medicare. Codes 95120 through 95134 represent complete services, i.e., services that include both the injection service as well as the antigen and its preparation.

2 - Separate coding for injection only codes (i.e., codes 95115 and 95117) and/or the codes representing antigens and their preparation (i.e., codes 95144 through 95170) must be used.

If both services are provided both codes are billed.

This includes allergists who provide both services through the use of treatment boards.

3 - If a physician bills both an injection code plus either codes 95165 or 95144, carriers pay the appropriate injection code (i.e., code 95115 or code 95117) plus the code 95165 rate. When a provider bills for codes 95115 or 95117 plus code 95144, carriers change 95144 to 95165 and pay accordingly. Code 95144 (single dose vials of antigen) should be billed only if the physician providing the antigen is providing it to be injected by some other entity. Single dose vials, which should be used only as a means of insuring proper dosage amounts for injections, are more costly than multiple dose vials (i.e., code 95165) and therefore their payment rate is higher. Allergists who prepare antigens are assumed to be able to administer proper doses from the less costly multiple dose vials. Thus, regardless of whether they use or bill for single or multiple dose vials at the same time that they are billing for an injection service, they are paid at the multiple dose vial rate.

4 - The fee schedule amounts for the antigen codes (95144 through 95170) are for a single dose. When billing those codes, physicians are to specify the number of doses provided. When making payment, carriers multiply the fee schedule amount by the number of doses specified in the units field.

5 - If a patient's doses are adjusted, e.g., because of patient reaction, and the antigen provided is actually more or fewer doses than originally anticipated, the physician is to make no change in the number of doses for which he or she bills. The number of doses anticipated at the time of the antigen preparation is the number of doses to be billed. This is consistent with the notes on page 30 of the Spring 1994 issue of the American Medical Association's CPT Assistant. Those

notes indicate that the antigen codes mean that the physician is to identify the number of doses "prospectively planned to be provided." The physician is to "identify the number of doses scheduled when the vial is provided." This means that in cases where the patient actually gets more doses than originally anticipated (because dose amounts were decreased during treatment) and in cases where the patient gets fewer doses (because dose amounts were increased), no change is to be made in the billing. In the first case, carriers are not to pay more because the number of doses provided in the original vial(s) increased. In the second case, carriers are not to seek recoupment (if carriers have already made payment) because the number of doses is less than originally planned. This is the case for both venom and nonvenom antigen codes.

6 - Venom Doses and Catch-Up Billing - Venom doses are prepared in separate vials and not mixed together - except in the case of the three vespid mix (white and yellow hornets and yellow jackets). A dose of code 95146 (the two-venom code) means getting some of two venoms. Similarly, a dose of code 95147 means getting some of three venoms; a dose of code 95148 means getting some of four venoms; and a dose of 95149 means getting some of five venoms. Some amount of each of the venoms must be provided. Questions arise when the administration of these venoms does not remain synchronized because of dosage adjustments due to patient reaction. For example, a physician prepares ten doses of code 95148 (the four venom code) in two vials - one containing 10 doses of three vespid mix and another containing 10 doses of wasp venom. Because of dose adjustment, the three vespid mix doses last longer, i.e., they last for 15 doses. Consequently, questions arise regarding the amount of "replacement" wasp venom antigen that should be prepared and how it should be billed. Medicare pricing amounts have savings built into the use of the higher venom codes. Therefore, if a patient is in two venom, three venom, four venom or five venom therapy, the carrier objective is to pay at the highest venom level possible. This means that, to the greatest extent possible, code 95146 is to be billed for a patient in two venom therapy, code 95147 is to be billed for a patient in three venom therapy, code 95148 is to be billed for a patient in four venom therapy, and code 95149 is to be billed for a patient in five venom therapy. Thus, physicians are to be instructed that the venom antigen preparation, after dose adjustment, must be done in a manner that, as soon as possible, synchronizes the preparation back to the highest venom code possible. In the above example, the physician should prepare and bill for only 5 doses of "replacement" wasp venom - billing five doses of code 95145 (the one venom code). This will permit the physician to get back to preparing the four venoms at one time and therefore billing the doses of the "cheaper" four venom code. Use of a code below the venom treatment number for the particular patient should occur only for the purpose of "catching up."

7 - **Code 95165 Doses**. - Code 95165 represents preparation of vials of non-venom antigens. As in the case of venoms, some non-venom antigens cannot be mixed together, i.e., they must be prepared in separate vials. An example of this is mold and pollen. Therefore, some patients will be injected at one time from one vial – containing in one mixture all of the appropriate antigens – while other patients will be injected at one time from more than one vial. In establishing the practice expense component for mixing a multidose vial of antigens, we observed that the most common practice

was to prepare a 10 cc vial; we also observed that the most common use was to remove aliquots with a volume of 1 cc. Our PE computations were based on those facts. Therefore, a physician's removing 10 1cc aliquot doses captures the entire PE component for the service.

This does not mean that the physician must remove 1 cc aliquot doses from a multidose vial. It means that the practice expenses payable for the preparation of a 10cc vial remain the same irrespective of the size or number of aliquots removed from the vial. Therefore, a physician may not bill this vial preparation code for more than 10 doses per vial; paying more than 10 doses per multidose vial would significantly overpay the practice expense component attributable to this service. (Note that this code does not include the injection of antigen(s); injection of antigen(s) is separately billable.)

When a multidose vial contains less than 10cc, physicians should bill Medicare for the number of 1 cc aliquots that may be removed from the vial. That is, a physician may bill Medicare up to a maximum of 10 doses per multidose vial, but should bill Medicare for fewer than 10 doses per vial when there is less than 10cc in the vial.

If it is medically necessary, physicians may bill Medicare for preparation of more than one multidose vial.

EXAMPLES:

(1) If a 10cc multidose vial is filled to 6cc with antigen, the physician may bill Medicare for 6 doses since six 1cc aliquots may be removed from the vial.

If a 5cc multidose vial is filled completely, the physician may bill Medicare for 5 doses for this vial.

(3) If a physician removes cc aliquots from a 10cc multidose vial for a total of 20 doses from one vial, he/she may only bill Medicare for 10 doses. Billing for more than 10 doses would mean that Medicare is overpaying for the practice expense of making the vial.

(4) If a physician prepares two 10cc multidose vials, he/she may bill Medicare for 20 doses. However, he/she may remove aliquots of any amount from those vials. For example, the physician may remove aliquots from one vial, and 1cc aliquots from the other vial, but may bill no more than a total of 20 doses.

(5) If a physician prepares a 20cc multidose vial, he/she may bill Medicare for 20 doses, since the practice expense is calculated based on the physician's removing 1cc aliquots from a vial. If a physician removes 2cc aliquots from this vial, thus getting only 10 doses, he/she may nonetheless bill Medicare for 20 doses because the PE for 20 doses reflects the actual practice expense of preparing the vial.

(6) If a physician prepares a 5cc multidose vial, he may bill Medicare for 5 doses, based on the way that the practice expense component is calculated. However, if the physician removes ten cc aliquots from the vial, he/she may still bill only 5 doses because the practice expense of preparing the vial is the same, without regard to the number of additional doses that are removed from the vial.

C - Allergy Shots and Visit Services on the Same Day

At the outset of the physician fee schedule, the question was posed as to whether visits should be billed on the same day as an allergy injection (CPT codes 95115-95117), since these codes have status indicators of A rather than T. Visits should not be billed

APPENDIX D

with allergy injection services 95115 or 95117 unless the visit represents another separately identifiable service. This language parallels CPT editorial language that accompanies the allergen immunotherapy codes, which include codes 9515 and 95117. Prior to January 1, 1995, you appeared to be enforcing this policy through three (3) different means:

- *Advising physician to use modifier 25 with the visit service;*
- *Denying payment for the visit unless documentation has been provided; and*
- *Paying for both the visit and the allergy shot if both are billed for.*

For services rendered on or after January 1, 1995, you are to enforce the requirement that visits not be billed and paid for on the same day as an allergy injection through the following means. Effective for services rendered on or after that date, the global surgery policies will apply to all codes in the allergen immunotherapy series, including the allergy shot codes 95115 and 95117. To accomplish this, CMS changed the global surgery indicator for allergen immunotherapy codes from XXX, which meant that the global surgery concept did not apply to those codes, to 000, which means that the global surgery concept applies, but that there are no days in the postoperative global period. Now that the global surgery policies apply to these services, you are to rely on the use of modifier 25 as the only means through which you can make payment for visit services provided on the same day as allergen immunotherapy services. In order for a physician to receive payment for a visit service provided on the same day that the physician also provides a service in the allergen immunotherapy series (i.e., any service in the series from 95115 through 95199), the physician is to bill a modifier 25 with the visit code, indicating that the patient's condition required a significant, separately identifiable visit service above and beyond the allergen immunotherapy service provided.

D - Reasonable Supply of Antigens

See CMS Manual System, Internet Only Manual, Medicare Benefits Policy Manual, CMS Pub. 100-02 Chapter 15, section 50.4.4, regarding the coverage of antigens, including what constitutes a reasonable supply of antigens.

Pub. 100-4, Chapter 12, Section 210
Outpatient Mental Health Limitation

B3-2470

Regardless of the actual expenses a beneficiary incurs for treatment of mental, psychoneurotic, and personality disorders while the beneficiary is not an inpatient of a hospital at the time such expenses are incurred, the amount of those expenses that may be recognized for Part B deductible and payment purposes is limited to 62.5 percent of the Medicare allowed amount for those services. This limitation is called the outpatient mental health treatment limitation. Expenses for diagnostic services (e.g., psychiatric testing and evaluation to diagnose the patient's illness) are not subject to this limitation. This limitation applies only to therapeutic services and to services performed to evaluate the progress of a course of treatment for a diagnosed condition.

Pub. 100-4, Chapter 13, Section 10
ICD -9-CM Coding for Diagnostic Tests

B3-15021.1

The ICD-9-CM Coding Guidelines for Outpatient Services (hospital-based and physician office) have instructed physicians to report diagnoses based on test results. Instructions and examples for coding specialists, contractors, physicians, hospitals, and other health care providers to use in determining the use of ICD-9-CM codes for coding diagnostic test results is found in Chapter 23.

Pub. 100-4, Chapter 13, Section 20
Payment Conditions for Radiology Services

B3-15022

Pub. 100-4, Chapter 13, Section 30
Computerized Axial Tomography (CT) Procedures

Carriers do not reduce or deny payment for medically necessary multiple CT scans of different areas of the body that are performed on the same day.

The TC RVUs for CT procedures that specify "with contrast" include payment for high osmolar contrast media. When separate payment is made for low osmolar contrast media under the conditions set forth in §30.1.1, reduce payment for the contrast media as set forth in §30.1.2.

Pub. 100-4, Chapter 13, Section 40
Magnetic Resonance Imaging (MRI) Procedures

Carriers do not make additional payments for three or more MRI sequences. The RVUs reflect payment levels for two sequences.

The TC RVUs for MRI procedures that specify "with contrast" include payment for paramagnetic contrast media. Carriers do not make separate payment under code A4647.

A diagnostic technique has been developed under which an MRI of the brain or spine is first performed without contrast material, then another MRI is performed with a standard (0.1mmol/kg) dose of contrast material and, based on the need to receive a better image, a third MRI is performed with an additional double dosage (0.2mmol/kg) of contrast material. When the high-dose contrast technique is utilized, carriers:

Do not pay separately for the contrast material used in the second MRI procedure;

Pay for the contrast material given for the third MRI procedure through supply code A4643 when billed with CPT codes 70553, 72156, 72157, and 72158;

Do not pay for the third MRI procedure. For example, in the case of an MRI of the brain, if CPT code 70553 (without contrast material, followed by with contrast material(s) and further sequences) is billed, make no payment for CPT code 70551 (without contrast material(s)), the additional procedure given for the purpose of administering the double dosage, furnished during the same session. Medicare does not pay for the third procedure (as distinguished from the contrast material) because the CPT definition of code 70553 includes all further sequences; and

Do not apply the payment criteria for low osmolar contrast media in §30.1.2 to billings for code A4643.

Pub. 100-4, Chapter 13, Section 40.1
Magnetic Resonance Angiography

R1 795B3, B3-4602, R1 883A3, A3-3665

Pub. 100-4, Chapter 13, Section 40.1.1
Magnetic Resonance Angiography Coverage Summary

Section 1861(s)(2)(C) of the Act provides for coverage of diagnostic testing. Coverage of magnetic resonance angiography (MRA) of the head and neck, and MRA of the peripheral vessels of the lower extremities is limited as described in the Medicare National Coverage Determinations Manual. This instruction has been revised as of July 1, 2003, based on a determination that coverage is reasonable and necessary in additional circumstances. Under that instruction, MRA is generally covered only to the extent that it is used as a substitute for contrast angiography, except to the extent that there are documented circumstances consistent with that instruction that demonstrate the medical necessity of both tests. There is no coverage of MRA outside of the indications and circumstances described in that instruction.

Because the status codes for HCPCS codes 71555, 71555-TC, 71555-26, 74185, 74185-TC, and 74185-26 were changed in the MPFSDB from N to R on April 1, 1998, any MRA claims with those HCPCS codes with dates of service between April 1, 1998, and June 30, 1999, are to be processed according to the contractor's discretionary authority to determine payment in the absence of national policy.

40.1.2 HCPCS Coding Requirements

(Rev. 1, 10-01-03)

Providers must report HCPCS codes when submitting claims for MRA of the chest, abdomen, head, neck or peripheral vessels of lower extremities. The following HCPCS codes should be used to report these services:

MRA of head	70544, 70544-26, 70544-TC
MRA of head	70545, 70545-26, 70545-TC
MRA of head	70546, 70546-26, 70546-TC
MRA of neck	70547, 70547-26, 70547-TC
MRA of neck	70548, 70548-26, 70548-TC
MRA of neck	70549, 70549-26, 70549-TC
MRA of chest	71555, 71555-26, 71555-TC
MRA of pelvis	72198, 72198-26, 72198-TC
MRA of abdomen (dates of service on or after July 1, 2003) – see below.	74185, 74185-26, 74185-TC
MRA of peripheral vessels of lower extremities	73725, 73725-26, 73725-TC

Hospitals subject to OPPS should report the following C codes in place of the above HCPCS codes as follows:

MRA of chest 71555: C8909 – C8911

MRA of abdomen 74185: C8900 – C8902

MRA of peripheral vessels of lower extremities 73725: C8912 – C8914

For claims with dates of service on or after July 1, 2003, coverage under this benefit has been expanded for the use of MRA for diagnosing pathology in the renal or aortoiliac arteries. The following HCPCS code should be used to report this expanded coverage of MRA:

- MRA, pelvis, with or without contrast material(s) 72198, 72198-26, 72198-TC

Hospitals subject to OPPS report the following C codes in place of HCPCS code 72198:

- MRA, pelvis, with or without contrast material(s) 72198: C8918 - C8920

Providers utilizing the UB-92 flat file, use record type 61, HCPCS code (Field No. 6) to report HCPCS/CPT code. Providers utilizing the hard copy UB-92, report the HCPCS/CPT code in FL 44 "HCPCS/Rates." Providers utilizing the Medicare A 837 Health Care Claim version 3051 implementations 3A.01 and 1A.C1, report the HCPCS/CPT in 2-395-SV202-02.

Pub. 100-4, Chapter 13, Section 60
Positron Emission Tomography (PET) Scans– GeneralInformation

Positron emission tomography (PET) is a noninvasive imaging procedure that assesses perfusion and the level of metabolic activity in various organ systems of the human body. A positron camera (tomograph) is used to produce cross-sectional tomographic images which are obtained by detecting radioactivity from a radioactive tracer substance (radiopharmaceutical) that emits a radioactive tracer substance (radiopharmaceutical FDG) such as 2 –[F-18] flouro-D-glucose FDG, that is administered intravenously to the patient.

The Medicare National Coverage Determinations *(NCD)* Manual, Chapter 1, §220.6, contains additional coverage instructions to indicate the conditions under which a PET scan is performed.

A – Definitions

For all uses of PET, excluding Rubidium 82 for perfusion of the heart, myocardial viability and refractory seizures, the following definitions apply:

Diagnosis: PET is covered only in clinical situations in which the PET results may assist in avoiding an invasive diagnostic procedure, or in which the PET results may assist in determining the optimal anatomical location to perform an invasive diagnostic procedure. In general, for most solid tumors, a tissue diagnosis is made prior to the performance of PET scanning. PET scans following a tissue diagnosis are *generally* performed for the purpose of staging, *rather than* diagnosis. Therefore, the use of PET in the diagnosis of lymphoma, esophageal and colorectal cancers, as well as in melanoma, should be rare. PET is not covered for other diagnostic uses, and is not covered for screening (testing of patients without specific signs and symptoms of disease).

Staging: PET is covered in clinical situations in which (1) (a) the stage of the cancer remains in doubt after completion of a standard diagnostic workup, including conventional imaging (computed tomography, magnetic resonance imaging, or ultrasound) or, (b) the use of PET would also be considered reasonable and necessary if it could potentially replace one or more conventional imaging studies when it is expected that conventional study information is insufficient for the clinical management of the patient and, (2) clinical management of the patient would differ depending on the stage of the cancer identified.

Restaging: PET will be covered for restaging: *(1)* after the completion of treatment for the purpose of detecting residual disease, *(2)* for detecting suspected recurrence, *or metastasis*, *(3)* to determine the extent of a known recurrence, or *(4)* if it

© 2005 Ingenix, Inc.

could potentially replace one or more conventional imaging studies when it is expected that conventional study information isto determine the extent of a known recurrence, or if study information is insufficient for the clinical management of the patient. Restaging applies to testing after a course of treatment is completed and is covered subject to the conditions above.

Monitoring: Use of PET to monitor tumor response to treatment during the planned course of therapy (i.e., when a change in therapy is *anticipated*).

B - Limitations

For staging and restaging: PET is covered in either/or both of the following circumstances:

The stage of the cancer remains in doubt after completion of a standard diagnostic workup, including conventional imaging (computed tomography, magnetic resonance imaging, or ultrasound); and/or

The clinical management of the patient would differ depending on the stage of the cancer identified. PET will be covered for restaging after the completion of treatment for the purpose of detecting residual disease, for detecting suspected recurrence, or to determine the extent of a known recurrence. Use of PET would also be considered reasonable and necessary if it could potentially replace one or more conventional imaging studies when it is expected that conventional study information is insufficient for the clinical management of the patient.

The PET is not covered for other diagnostic uses, and is not covered for screening (testing of patients without specific symptoms). Use of PET to monitor tumor response during the planned course of therapy (i.e. when no change in therapy is being contemplated) is not covered.

Pub. 100-4, Chapter 13, Section 60.1
Billing Instructions

A - Billing and Payment Instructions or Responsibilities for Carriers

Claims for PET scan services must be billed on Form-CMS 1500 or the electronic equivalent with the appropriate HCPCS *or CPT* code and diagnosis codes to the local carrier. Effective for claims received on or after July 1, 2001, PET modifiers were discontinued and are no longer a claims processing requirement for PET scan claims. Therefore, July 1, 2001, and after the MSN messages regarding the use of PET modifiers can be discontinued. The type of service (TOS) for the new PET scan procedure codes is TOS 4, Diagnostic Radiology. Payment is based on the Medicare Physician Fee Schedule.

B - Billing and Payment Instructions or Responsibilities for FIs

Claims for PET scan procedures must be billed to the FI on Form CMS-1450 (UB-92) or the electronic equivalent with the appropriate diagnosis and HCPCS "G" code *or CPT cod*e to indicate the conditions under which a PET scan was done. These codes represent the technical component costs associated with these procedures when furnished to hospital and SNF outpatients. They are paid as follows:

under OPPS for hospitals subject to OPPS

under current payment methodologies for hospitals not subject to OPPS

on a reasonable cost basis for critical access hospitals.

on a reasonable cost basis for skilled nursing facilities.

Institutional providers bill these codes under Revenue Code 0404 (PET Scan).

Medicare contractors shall pay claims submitted for services provided by a critical access hospital (CAH) as follows: Method I technical services are paid at 101% of reasonable cost; Method II technical services are paid at 101% of reasonable cost, and professional services are paid at 115% of the Medicare Physician Fee Schedule Data Base.

C - Frequency

In the absence of national frequency limitations, for all indications covered on and after July 1, 2001, contractors can, if necessary, develop frequency limitations on any or all covered PET scan services.

D - Post-Payment Review for PET Scans

As with any claim, but particularly in view of the limitations on this coverage, Medicare may decide to conduct post-payment reviews to determine that the use of PET scans is consistent with coverage instructions. Pet scanning facilities must keep patient record information on file for each Medicare patient for whom a PET scan claim is made. These medical records can be used in any post-payment reviews and must include the information necessary to substantiate the need for the PET scan. These records must include standard information (e.g., age, sex, and height) along with sufficient patient histories to allow determination that the steps required in the coverage instructions were followed. Such information must include, but is not limited to, the date, place and results of previous diagnostic tests (e.g., cytopathology and surgical pathology reports, CT), as well as the results and reports of the PET scan(s) performed at the center. If available, such records should include the prognosis derived from the PET scan, together with information regarding the physician or institution to which the patient proceeded following the scan for treatment or evaluation. The ordering physician is responsible for forwarding appropriate clinical data to the PET scan facility.

Effective for claims received on or after July 1, 2001, CMS no longer requires paper documentation to be submitted up front with PET scan claims. Contractors shall be aware and advise providers of the specific documentation requirements for PET scans for dementia and neurodegenerative diseases. This information is outlined in section 60.12. Documentation requirements such as physician referral and medical necessity determination are to be maintained by the provider as part of the beneficiary's medical record. This information must be made available to the carrier or FI upon request of additional documentation to determine appropriate payment of an individual claim.

Pub. 100-4, Chapter 13, Section 60.2
Use of Gamma Cameras and Full Ring and Partial Ring PET Scanners for PET Scans

See the Medicare *NCD* Manual, Section 220.6, concerning 2-[F-18] Fluoro-D-Glucose (FDG) PET scanners and details about coverage.

On July 1, 2001, HCPCS codes G0210 - G0230 were added to allow billing for all currently covered indications for FDG PET. Although the codes do not indicate the type of PET scanner, these codes were used until January 1, 2002, by providers to bill for services in a manner consistent with the coverage policy.

Appendixes

Effective January 1, 2002, HCPCS codes G0210 – G0230 were updated with new descriptors to properly reflect the type of PET scanner used. In addition, four new HCPCS codes became effective for dates of service on and after January 1, 2002, (G0231, G0232, G0233, G0234) for covered conditions that may be billed if a gamma camera is used for the PET scan. *For services performed from January 1, 2002, through January 27, 2005, providers should bill using the revised HCPCS codes G0210 - G0234. Beginning January 28, 2005 providers should bill using the appropriate CPT code.*

Pub. 100-4, Chapter 13, Section 60.3
PET Scan Qualifying Conditions and HCPCS Code Chart

Below is a summary of all covered PET scan conditions, with effective dates.

NOTE: The G codes below except those a # can be used to bill for PET Scan services through January 27, 2005. Effective for dates of service on or after January 28, 2005, providers must bill for PET Scan services using the appropriate CPT codes. See section 60.3.1. The G codes with a # can continue to be used for billing after January 28, 2005 and these remain non-covered by Medicare. (**NOTE:** PET Scanners must be FDA-approved.)

Conditions	Coverage Effective Date	****HCPCS/CPT
*Myocardial perfusion imaging (following previous PET G0030-G0047) single study, rest or stress (exercise and/or pharmacologic)	3/14/95	G0030
*Myocardial perfusion imaging (following previous PET G0030-G0047) multiple studies, rest or stress (exercise and/or pharmacologic)	3/14/95	G0031
*Myocardial perfusion imaging (following rest SPECT, 78464); single study, rest or stress (exercise and/or pharmacologic)	3/14/95	G0032
*Myocardial perfusion imaging (following rest SPECT 78464); multiple studies, rest or stress (exercise and/or pharmacologic)	3/14/95	G0033
*Myocardial perfusion (following stress SPECT 78465); single study, rest or stress (exercise and/or pharmacologic)	3/14/95	G0034
*Myocardial Perfusion Imaging (following stress SPECT 78465); multiple studies, rest or stress (exercise and/or pharmacologic)	3/14/95	G0035
*Myocardial Perfusion Imaging (following coronary angiography 93510-93529); single study, rest or stress (exercise and/or pharmacologic)	3/14/95	G0036
*Myocardial Perfusion Imaging, (following coronary angiography), 93510-93529); multiple studies, rest or stress (exercise and/or pharmacologic)	3/14/95	G0037
*Myocardial Perfusion Imaging (following stress planar myocardial perfusion, 78460); single study, rest or stress (exercise and/or pharmacologic)		G0038

Conditions	Coverage Effective Date	****HCPCS/CPT
*Myocardial Perfusion Imaging (following stress planar myocardial perfusion, 78460); multiple studies, rest or stress (exercise and/or pharmacologic)	3/14/95	G0039
*Myocardial Perfusion Imaging (following stress echocardiogram 93350); single study, rest or stress (exercise and/or pharmacologic)	3/14/95	G0040
*Myocardial Perfusion Imaging (following stress echocardiogram, 93350); multiple studies, rest or stress (exercise and/or pharmacologic)	3/14/95	G0041
*Myocardial Perfusion Imaging (following stress nuclear ventriculogram 78481 or 78483); single study, rest or stress (exercise and/or pharmacologic)	3/14/95	G0042
*Myocardial Perfusion Imaging (following stress nuclear ventriculogram 78481 or 78483); multiple studies, rest or stress (exercise and/or pharmacologic)	3/14/95	G0043
*Myocardial Perfusion Imaging (following stress ECG, 93000); single study, rest or stress (exercise and/or pharmacologic)	3/14/95	G0044
*Myocardial perfusion (following stress ECG, 93000), multiple studies; rest or stress (exercise and/or pharmacologic)	3/14/95	G0045
*Myocardial perfusion (following stress ECG, 93015), single study; rest or stress (exercise and/or pharmacologic)	3/14/95	G0046
*Myocardial perfusion (following stress ECG, 93015); multiple studies, rest or stress (exercise and/or pharmacologic)	3/14/95	G0047

Conditions	Coverage Effective Date	****HCPCS/CPT
PET imaging regional or whole body; single pulmonary nodule	1/1/98	G0125
Lung cancer, non-small cell (PET imaging whole body) Diagnosis, Initial Staging, Restaging	7/1/01	G0210 G0211 G0212
Colorectal cancer (PET imaging whole body) Diagnosis, Initial Staging, Restaging	7/1/01	G0213 G0214 G0215
Melanoma (PET imaging whole body) Diagnosis, Initial Staging, Restaging	7/1/01	G0216 G0217 G0218

Melanoma for non-covered indications	7/1/01	#G0219
Lymphoma (PET imaging whole body) Diagnosis, Initial Staging, Restaging	7/1/01	G0220 G0221 G0222
Head and neck cancer; excluding thyroid and CNS cancers (PET imaging whole body or regional) Diagnosis, Initial Staging, Restaging	7/1/01	G0223 G0224 G0225
Conditions	**Coverage Effective Date**	****HCPCS/CPT**
Esophageal cancer (PET imaging whole body) Diagnosis, Initial Staging, Restaging	7/1/01	G0226 G0227 G0228
Metabolic brain imaging for pre-surgical evaluation of refractory seizures	7/1/01	G0229
Metabolic assessment for myocardial viability following inconclusive SPECT study	7/1/01	G0230
Recurrence of colorectal or colorectal metastatic cancer (PET whole body, gamma cameras only)	1/1/02	G0231
Staging and characterization of lymphoma (PET whole body, gamma cameras only)	1/1/02	G0232
Recurrence of melanoma or melanoma metastatic cancer (PET whole body, gamma cameras only)	1/1/02	G0233
Regional or whole body, for solitary pulmonary nodule following CT, or for initial staging of non-small cell lung cancer (gamma cameras only)	1/1/02	G0234
Non-Covered Service *PET imaging, any site not otherwise specified*	*1/28/05*	*#G0235*
Non-Covered Service Initial diagnosis of breast cancer and/or surgical planning for breast cancer (e.g., initial staging of axillary lymph nodes), not covered (full- and partial-ring PET scanners only)	10/1/02	#G0252
Breast cancer, staging/restaging of local regional recurrence or distant metastases, i.e., staging/restaging after or prior to course of treatment (full- and partial-ring PET scanners only)	10/1/02	G0253
Conditions	**Coverage Effective Date**	****HCPCS/CPT**
Breast cancer, evaluation of responses to treatment, performed during course of treatment (full- and partial-ring PET scanners only)	10/1/02	G0254
Myocardial imaging, positron emission tomography (PET), metabolic evaluation)	10/1/02	78459
Restaging or previously treated thyroid cancer of follicular cell origin following negative I-131 whole body scan (full- and partial-ring PET scanner only)	10/1/03	G0296
Tracer Rubidium**82 (Supply of Radiopharmaceutical Diagnostic Imaging Agent) (This is only billed through Outpatient Perspective Payment System, OPPS.) (Carriers must use HCPCS Code A4641).	10/1/03	Q3000
Supply of Radiopharmaceutical Diagnostic Imaging Agent, Ammonia N-13	01/1/04	A9526
PET imaging, brain imaging for the differential diagnosis of Alzheimer's disease with aberrant features vs. fronto-temporal dementia	09/15/04	*Appropriate CPT Code from section 60.3.1*
PET Cervical Cancer *Staging as adjunct to conventional imaging, other staging, diagnosis, restaging, monitoring*	*1/28/05*	*Appropriate CPT Code from section 60.3.1*

***NOTE:** Carriers must report A4641 for the tracer Rubidium 82 when used with PET scan codes G0030 through G0047 for services performed on or before January 27, 2005

****NOTE:** Not FDG PET

*****NOTE:** For dates of service October 1, 2003, through December 31, 2003, use temporary code Q4078 for billing this radiopharmaceutical.

Pub. 100-4, Chapter 13, Section 60.4
PET Scans for Imaging of the Perfusion of the Heart Using Rubidium 82 (Rb 82)

For dates of service on or after March 14, 1995, Medicare covers one PET scan for imaging of the perfusion of the heart using Rubidium 82 (Rb 82), provided that the following conditions are met:

The PET is done at a PET imaging center with a PET scanner that has been approved by the FDA;

The PET scan is a rest alone or rest with pharmacologic stress PET scan, used for noninvasive imaging of the perfusion of the heart for the diagnosis and management of patients with known or suspected coronary artery disease, using Rb 82; and

Either the PET scan is used in place of, but not in addition to, a single photon emission computed tomography (SPECT) or the PET scan is used following a SPECT that was found inconclusive.

Pub. 100-4, Chapter 13, Section 60.9
Coverage of PET Scans for Myocardial Viability

FDG PET is covered for the determination of myocardial viability following an inconclusive single photon computed tomography test (SPECT) from July 1, 2001, through September 30, 2002. Only full ring scanners are covered as the scanning medium for this service from July 1, 2001, through December 31, 2001. However, as of January 1, 2002, full and partial ring scanners are covered for myocardial viability following an inconclusive SPECT.

Beginning October 1, 2002, Medicare will cover FDG PET for the determination of myocardial viability as a primary or initial diagnostic study prior to revascularization, and will continue to cover FDG PET when used as a follow-up to an inconclusive SPECT. However, if a patient received a FDG PET study with inconclusive results, a follow-up SPECT is not covered. FDA full and partial ring PET scanners are covered. In the event that a patient receives a SPECT with inconclusive results, a PET scan may be performed and covered by Medicare. However, a SPECT is not covered following a FDG PET with inconclusive results. See the Medicare National Coverage Determinations Manual, Section 220.6 for specific frequency limitations for Myocardial Viability following an inconclusive SPECT.

Documentation that these conditions are met should be maintained by the referring provider as part of the beneficiary's medical record.

HCPCS Code for PET Scan for Myocardial Viability

78459 - Myocardial imaging, positron emission tomography (PET), metabolic evaluation

Pub. 100-4, Chapter 13, Section 60.11
Coverage of PET Scans for Perfusion of the Heart Using Ammonia N-13

Effective for service performed on or after October 1, 2003, PET scans performed at rest or with pharmacological stress used for noninvasive imaging of the perfusion of the heart for the diagnosis and management of patients with known or suspected coronary artery disease using the FDA-approved radiopharmaceutical ammonia N-13 are covered, provided the following requirements are met.

Pub. 100-4, Chapter 13, Section 60.12
Coverage for PET Scans for Dementia and Neurodegenerative Diseases

Effective for dates of service on or after September 15, 2004, Medicare will cover FDG PET scans for a differential diagnosis of fronto-temporal dementia (FTD) and Alzheimer's disease OR; its use in a CMS-approved practical clinical trial focused on the utility of FDG-PET in the diagnosis or treatment of dementing neurodegenerative diseases. Refer to Pub. 100-03, NCD Manual, section 220.6.13, for complete coverage conditions and clinical trial requirements.

A. Carrier and FI Billing Requirements for PET Scan Claims for FDG-PET for the Differential Diagnosis of Fronto-temporal Dementia and Alzheimer's Disease:

- ***CPT*** Code for PET Scans for Dementia and Neurodegenerative Diseases

Contractors shall advise providers to use the appropriate CPT code from section 60.3.1 for dementia and neurodegenerative diseases for services performed on or after January 28, 2005.

- Diagnosis Codes for PET Scans for Dementia and Neurodegenerative Diseases

The contractor shall ensure one of the following appropriate diagnosis codes is present on claims for PET Scans for AD:

-- 290.0, 290.10 - 290.13, 290.20 - 290, 21, 290.3, 331.0, 331.11, 331.19, 331.2, 331.9, 780.93

Medicare contractors shall use an appropriate Medicare Summary Notice (MSN) message such as 16.48, "Medicare does not pay for this item or service for this condition" to deny claims when submitted with *an appropriate CPT code from section 60.3.1 and* with a diagnosis code other than the range of codes listed above. Also, contractors shall use an appropriate Remittance Advice (RA) such as 11, "The diagnosis is inconsistent with the procedure."

Medicare contractors shall instruct providers to issue an Advanced Beneficiary Notice to beneficiaries advising them of potential financial liability *prior to delivering the service* if one of the appropriate diagnosis codes will not be present on the claim.

- Provider Documentation Required with the PET Scan Claim

Medicare contractors shall inform providers to ensure the conditions mentioned in the NCD Manual, section 220.6.13, have been met. The information must also be maintained in the beneficiary's medical record:

-- Date of onset of symptoms;

-- Diagnosis of clinical syndrome (normal aging, mild cognitive impairment or MCI: mild, moderate, or severe dementia);

-- Mini mental status exam (MMSE) or similar test score;

-- Presumptive cause (possible, probably, uncertain AD);

-- Any neuropsychological testing performed;

-- Results of any structural imaging (MRI, CT) performed;

-- Relevant laboratory tests (B12, thyroid hormone); and,

-- Number and name of prescribed medications.

B. Carrier and FI Billing Requirements for FDG-PET Scans Claims for CMS-approved Neurodegenerative Disease Practical Clinical Trials

- Carriers and FIs

Contractors should not receive claims for this service until the clinical trial centers have been identified. Once these centers are identified, CMS will list the centers on the CMS Web site.

- **Carriers Only**

Carriers shall pay claims for PET scans for beneficiaries participating in a CMS-approved clinical trial submitted with the **QV** modifier. Refer to Pub. 100-03, NCD Manual, section 220.6.13, for complete policy and clinical trial requirements.

- **FIs Only**

In order to pay claims for PET scans on behalf of beneficiaries participating in a CMS-approved clinical trial, FIs require providers to submit claims with ICD-9 code V70.7 in the second diagnosis position on the Form CMS-1450 (UB-92), or the electronic equivalent, with the appropriate principal diagnosis code *and an appropriate CPT code from section 60.3.1*. Refer to Publication 100-03, NCD Manual, section 220.6.13.

Pub. 100-4, Chapter 13, Section 70.3
Radiation Treatment Delivery (CPT 77401 - 77417)

Carriers pay for these TC services on a daily basis under CPT codes 77401-77416 for radiation treatment delivery. They do not use local codes and RVUs in paying for the TC of radiation oncology services. Multiple treatment sessions on

© 2005 Ingenix, Inc.

the same day are payable as long as there has been a distinct break in therapy services, and the individual sessions are of the character usually furnished on different days. Carriers pay for CPT code 77417 (Therapeutic radiology port film(s)) on a weekly (five fractions) basis.

Pub. 100-4, Chapter 13, Section 70.4
Clinical Brachytherapy (CPT Codes 77750 - 77799)

Carriers must apply the bundled services policy to procedures in this family of codes other than CPT code 77776. For procedures furnished in settings in which TC payments are made, carriers must pay separately for the expendable source associated with these procedures under CPT code 79900 except in the case of remote after-loading high intensity brachytherapy procedures (CPT codes 77781-77784). In the four codes cited, the expendable source is included in the RVUs for the TC of the procedures.

Pub. 100-4, Chapter 13, Section 90
Services of Portable X-Ray Suppliers

B3-2070.4, B3-15022.G, B3-4131, B3-4831

Services furnished by portable x-ray suppliers may have as many as four components. Carriers must follow the following rules.

Pub. 100-4, Chapter 13, Section 100
Interpretation of Diagnostic Tests

B3-15023

Pub. 100-4, Chapter 13, Section 140.2
Frequency Standard

SNF-533.5.B, B3-4181.2, A3-3631.n

Medicare pays for a bone mass measurement meeting the criteria as stated above once every two years (at least 23 months have passed since the month the last bone mass measurement was performed). However, if it is medically necessary, Medicare may pay for a bone mass measurement for a beneficiary more frequently than every two years. Examples of situations where more frequent bone mass measurement procedures may be medically necessary include, but are not limited to, the following medical circumstances:

- Monitoring beneficiaries on long-term glucocorticoid (steroid) therapy of more than three months; and
- Allowing for a confirmatory baseline bone mass measurement (either central or peripheral) to permit monitoring of beneficiaries in the future if the initial test was performed with a technique that is different from the proposed monitoring method (for example, if the initial test was performed using bone sonometry and monitoring is anticipated using bone densitometry, cover the baseline measurement using bone densitometry).

Pub. 100-4, Chapter 13, Section 140.3
Payment Methodology and HCPCS Coding

Carriers pay for bone mass measurement procedures based on the Medicare physician fee schedule. Claims from physicians, other practitioners, or suppliers where assignment was not taken are subject to the Medicare limiting charge.

FIs pay for bone mass measurement procedures under the current payment methodologies for radiology services according to the type of provider.

Deductible and coinsurance apply.

Any of the following codes may be used when billing for bone mass measurements. All of these codes are bone densitometry measurements except code 76977 which is bone sonometry measurements. Codes are applicable to billing FIs and carriers.

76070 76071 76075 76076 76078 76977 78350 G0130

FIs are billed using Form CMS-1450 or its electronic equivalent. The appropriate bill types are: 12X, 13X, 14X, 22X, 23X, 34X, 71X (Provider-based and independent), 72X, 73X (Provider-based and freestanding), 83X, and 85X.

Providers using the UB-92 flat file use record type 40 to report bill type. Record type (Field No. 1), sequence number (Field No. 2), patient control number (Field No. 3), and type of bill (Field No. 4) are required.

Providers who use the hard copy UB-92 (Form CMS-1450) report the applicable bill type in Form Locator (FL) 4, Type of Bill.

Providers must report HCPCS codes for bone mass measurements under revenue code 320 with number of units and line item dates of service per revenue code line for each bone mass measurement reported.

Carriers are billed for bone mass measurement procedures using Form CMS-1500 or its electronic equivalent.

Pub. 100-4, Chapter 14, Section 10
General

B3-2265

Payment is made under Part B for certain surgical procedures that are furnished in ASCs and are approved for being furnished in an ASC. These procedures are those that generally do not exceed 90 minutes in length and do not require more than four hours recovery or convalescent time.

To be paid under this provision, a facility must be certified as meeting the requirements for an ASC and must enter into a written agreement with the Centers for Medicare & Medicaid Services (CMS). The certification process is described in the State Operations Manual.

Medicare will not pay an ASC for those procedures that require more than an ASC level of care, or for minor procedures that are normally performed in a physician's office.

The CMS publishes updates to the list of procedures for which an ASC may be paid each year. The complete list of procedures is available through the Public Use files (PUF) at http://www.cms.hhs.gov/researchers/. This includes applicable codes, payment groups, and payment amounts for each ASC group before adjustments for regional wage variations. Applicable wage indices are also published via program memorandum.

ASCs must accept Medicare's payment for such procedures as payment in full for the facility service with respect to those services defined as ASC facility services. The physician and anesthesiologist may bill and be paid for the professional component of the service also.

Certain other services may be performed in an ASC facility, billed by the appropriate certified provider/supplier, or in certain cases by the ASC facility itself, and paid outside of the facility rate.

Pub. 100-4, Chapter 16, Section 10
Background

B3-2070, B3-2070.1, B3-4110.3, B3-5114

Diagnostic X-ray, laboratory, and other diagnostic tests, including materials and the services of technicians, are covered under the Medicare program. Some clinical laboratory procedures or tests require Food and Drug Administration (FDA) approval before coverage is provided.

A diagnostic laboratory test is considered a laboratory service for billing purposes, regardless of whether it is performed in:

A physician's office, by an independent laboratory;

By a hospital laboratory for its outpatients or nonpatients;

In a rural health clinic; or

In an HMO or Health Care Prepayment Plan (HCPP) for a patient who is not a member.

When a hospital laboratory performs laboratory tests for nonhospital patients, the laboratory is functioning as an independent laboratory, and still bills the fiscal intermediary (FI). Also, when physicians and laboratories perform the same test, whether manually or with automated equipment, the services are deemed similar.

Laboratory services furnished by an independent laboratory are covered under SMI if the laboratory is an approved Independent Clinical Laboratory. However, as is the case of all diagnostic services, in order to be covered these services must be related to a patient's illness or injury (or symptom or complaint) and ordered by a physician. A small number of laboratory tests can be covered as a preventive screening service.

See the Medicare Benefit Policy Manual, Chapter 15, for detailed coverage requirements.

See the Medicare Program Integrity Manual, Chapter 10, for laboratory/supplier enrollment guidelines.

See the Medicare State Operations Manual for laboratory/supplier certification requirements.

Pub. 100-4, Chapter 16, Section 10.1
Definitions

B3-2070.1, B3-2070.1.B, RHC-406.4

"Independent Laboratory" - An independent laboratory is one that is independent both of an attending or consulting physician's office and of a hospital that meets at least the requirements to qualify as an emergency hospital as defined in §1861(e) of the Social Security Act (the Act). (See the Medicare Benefits Policy Manual, Chapter 15, for detailed discussion.)

"Physician Office Laboratory" – A physician office laboratory is a laboratory maintained by a physician or group of physicians for performing diagnostic tests in connection with the physician practice.

"Clinical Laboratory"- See the Medicare Benefits Policy Manual, Chapter 15.

"Qualified Hospital Laboratory" - A qualified hospital laboratory is one that provides some clinical laboratory tests 24 hours a day, 7 days a week, to serve a hospital's emergency room that is also available to provide services 24 hours a day, 7 days a week. For the qualified hospital laboratory to meet this requirement, the hospital must have physicians physically present or available within 30 minutes through a medical staff call roster to handle emergencies 24 hours a day, 7 days a week; and hospital laboratory technologists must be on duty or on call at all times to provide testing for the emergency room.

"Hospital Outpatient" - See the Medicare Benefit Policy Manual, Chapter 2.

"Referring laboratory" - A Medicare-approved laboratory that receives a specimen to be tested and that refers the specimen to another laboratory for performance of the laboratory test.

"Reference laboratory" - A Medicare-enrolled laboratory that receives a specimen from another, referring laboratory for testing and that actually performs the test.

"Billing laboratory" - The laboratory that submits a bill or claim to Medicare.

"Service" - A clinical diagnostic laboratory test. Service and test are synonymous.

"Test" - A clinical diagnostic laboratory service. Service and test are synonymous.

"CLIA" - The Clinical Laboratory Improvement Act and CMS implementing regulations and processes.

"Certification" - A laboratory that has met the standards specified in the CLIA.

"Draw Station' - A place where a specimen is collected but no Medicare-covered clinical laboratory testing is performed on the drawn specimen.

"Medicare-approved laboratory - A laboratory that meets all of the enrollment standards as a Medicare provider including the certification by a CLIA certifying authority.

Pub. 100-4, Chapter 16, Section 110.4
Carrier Contacts With Independent Clinical Laboratories

B3-2070.1.F

An important role of the carrier is as a communicant of necessary information to independent clinical laboratories. Failure to inform independent laboratories of Medicare regulations and claims processing procedures may have an adverse effect on prosecution of laboratories suspected of fraudulent activities with respect to tests performed by, or billed on behalf of, independent laboratories. United States Attorneys often must prosecute under a handicap or may refuse to prosecute cases where there is no evidence that a laboratory has been specifically informed of Medicare regulations and claims processing procedures.

To assure that laboratories are aware of Medicare regulations and carrier's policy, notification must be sent to independent laboratories when any changes are made in coverage policy or claims processing procedures. Additionally, to completely document efforts to fully inform independent laboratories of Medicare policy and the laboratory's responsibilities, previously issued newsletters should be periodically re-issued to remind laboratories of existing requirements.

APPENDIX D

Some items which should be discussed are the requirements to have the same charges for Medicare and private patients, to document fully the medical necessity for collection of specimens from a skilled nursing facility or a beneficiary's home, and, in cases when a laboratory service is referred from one independent laboratory to another independent laboratory, to identify the laboratory actually performing the test.

Additionally, when carrier professional relations representatives make personal contacts with particular laboratories, they should prepare and retain reports of contact indicating dates, persons present, and issues discussed.

Pub. 100-4, Chapter 18, Section 20
Screening MammographyServices

A – Screening Mammography

Beginning January 1, 1991, Medicare provides Part B coverage of screening mammographies for women. Screening mammographies are radiologic procedures for early detection of breast cancer and include a physician's interpretation of the results. A doctor's prescription or referral is not necessary for the procedure to be covered. Whether payment can be made is determined by a woman's age and statutory frequency parameter. See Pub 100-02 Medicare Benefit Policy Manual, chapter 15, section 280.3 for additional coverage information for a screening mammography.

Section 4101 of the Balanced Budget Act (BBA) of 1997 provides for annual screening mammographies for women over age 39 and waives the Part B deductible. Coverage applies as follows:

Age Groups	Screening Period
Under age 35	No payment allowed for screening mammography.
35-39	Baseline (pay for only one screening mammography performed on a woman between her 35th and 40th birthday)
Over age 39	Annual (11 full months have elapsed following the month of last screening

NOTE: Count months between screening mammographies beginning the month after the date of the examination. For example, if Mrs. Smith received a screening mammography examination in January 2005, begin counting the next month (February 2005) until 11 months have elapsed. Payment can be made for another screening mammography in January 2006.

B - Diagnostic Mammography

A diagnostic mammography is a radiological mammogram and is a covered diagnostic test under the following conditions:

A patient has distinct signs and symptoms for which a mammogram is indicated;

A patient has a history of breast cancer; or

A patient is asymptomatic, but based on the patient's history and other factors the physician considers significant, the physician's judgment is that a mammogram is appropriate.

Beginning January 1, 2005, Medicare Prescription Drug, Improvement, and Modernization Act (MMA) of 2003, § 644, Public Law 108-173 has changed the way Medicare pays for

diagnostic mammography. Medicare will pay based on the MPFS in lieu of OPPS or the lower of the actual change.

Pub. 100-4, Chapter 18, Section 20.2
HCPCS and Diagnosis Codes for Mammography Services

The following HCPCS and TOS codes are used to bill for mammography services.

HCPCS Code	TOS	Definition
76082	4	Computer aided detection (computer algorithm analysis of digital image data for lesion detection) with further physician review for interpretation, with or without digitization of film radiographic images, diagnostic mammography (list separately in addition to code for primary procedure). **Effective January 1, 2004.**
76083	1	Computer aided detection (computer algorithm analysis of digital image data for lesion detection) with further physician review for interpretation, with or without digitization of film radiographic images, screening mammography (list separately in addition to code for primary procedure). **Effective January 1, 2004.**
76085	1	Digitization of film radiographic images with computer analysis for lesion detection and further physician review for interpretation screening mammography (list separately in addition to code for primary procedure). Use with CPT code 76092 **Code 76085 was effective 1-1-2002 for all claims submitted to a carrier or an FI, except hospital outpatient prospective payment (OPPS) claims, which are billed to the FI.** For OPPS claims billed to the FI, this code is effective 4-1-2002. Deleted as of December 31, 2003.
76090	1	Diagnostic mammography, unilateral.
76091	1	Diagnostic mammography, bilateral.
76092	1, B, C	Screening mammography, bilateral (two view film study of each breast).
G0202	1	Screening mammography, producing direct digital image, bilateral, all views. **Code Effective 4-1-2001.**
G0203		Screening mammography film processed to produce digital images analyzed for potential abnormalities, bilateral all views; **Code Effective 4-1-2001 and terminated 12-31-2001, with the exception of hospitals subject to OPPS, who may bill this code through 3-31-02.**
G0204	4	Diagnostic mammography, direct digital image, bilateral, all views; **Code Effective 4-1-2001.**
G0205		Diagnostic mammography, film processed to produce digital image analyzed for potential abnormalities, bilateral, all views; **Code Effective 4-1-2001 and terminated 12-31-2001, with the exception of hospitals subject to OPPS, who may bill this code through 3-31-02.**

HCPCS Code	TOS	Definition
G0206	1	Diagnostic mammography, producing direct digital image, unilateral, all views; **Code Effective 4-1-2001.**
G0207		Diagnostic mammography, film processed to produce digital image analyzed for potential abnormalities, unilateral, all views; **Code Effective 4-1-2001 and terminated 12-31-2001, with the exception of hospitals subject to OPPS, who may bill this code through 3-31-02.**
G0236		Digitization of film radiographic images with computer analysis for lesion detection and further physician review for interpretation, diagnostic mammography (List separately in addition to code for primary procedure). Use with CPT Codes 76090 or 76091. **Code G0236 was effective 1-1-2002 for all claims submitted to a carrier or an FI except hospital OPPS claims, which are billed to the FI.** For OPPS claims billed to the FI, the code is effective 4-1-2002. Deleted as of December 31, 2003.

New Modifier "-GG": Performance and payment of a screening mammography and diagnostic mammography on same patient same day - This is billed with the Diagnostic Mammography code to show the test changed from a screening test to a diagnostic test. Contractors will pay both the screening and diagnostic mammography tests. This modifier is for tracking purposes only. This applies to claims with dates of service on or after January 1, 2002.

A - Diagnosis for Services On or After January 1, 1998

The BBA of 1997 eliminated payment based on high-risk indicators. However, to assure proper coding, one of the following diagnosis codes should be reported on screening mammography claims as appropriate:

V76.11 – "Special screening for malignant neoplasm, screening mammogram for high-risk patients" or;

V76.12 - "Special screening for malignant neoplasm, other screening mammography."

Beginning October 1, 2003, carriers are no longer permitted to plug the ICD-9-CM code for a screening mammography when the screening mammography claim has no diagnosis code. Screening mammography claims with no diagnosis code must be returned as unprocessable for assigned claims. For unassigned claims, deny the claim.

FI claims receive the diagnosis in FL 67, "Principal Diagnosis Code" *of Form CMS-1450.* Carriers receive this diagnosis in field 21 of Form CMS-1500.

Diagnosis codes for a diagnostic mammography will vary according to diagnosis.

B - Diagnoses for Services October 1, 1997 Through December 31, 1997

On every screening mammography claim where the patient is not a high-risk individual, diagnosis code V76.12 is reported on the claim.

If the screening is for a high risk individual, the provider reports the principal diagnosis code as V76.11 - "Screening mammogram for high risk patient."

In addition, for high-risk individuals, one of the following applicable diagnoses codes is reported as "Other Diagnoses codes" (Form CMS-1450, FL 68)

- V10.3 "Personal history - Malignant neoplasm female breast";
- V16.3 "Family history - Malignant neoplasm breast"; or
- V15.89 "Other specified personal history representing hazards to health."

The following chart indicates the ICD-9 diagnosis codes reported for each high-risk category:

High Risk Category	Appropriate Diagnosis Code
A personal history of breast cancer	V10.3
A mother, sister, or daughter who has breast cancer	V16.3
Not given birth prior to age 30	V15.89
A personal history of biopsy-proven benign breast disease	V15.89

Pub. 100-4, Chapter 18, Section 20.5 Carrier Processing Requirements

B3-4601.3, B3-4601.3.A

Carriers complete the following activities in processing mammography claims:

Process the claim to the point of payment based on the information provided on the claim and in carrier claims history.

Identify the claim as a screening mammography claim by the CPT-4 code listed in field 24D and the diagnosis code(s) listed in field 21 of Form CMS-1500.

Confirm that the facility listed on the claim is certified to perform the service for Medicare beneficiaries.

Assigned physician specialty code 45 to facilities who are certified to perform only screening mammography.

Ensure that entities that bill globally for screening mammography contain a blank in modifier position #1.

Ensure that entities that bill for the technical component use only HCPCS modifier "-TC."

Ensure that physicians who bill the professional component separately use HCPCS modifier "-26."

Send the mammography modifier to CWF in the first modifier position on the claim. If more than one modifier is necessary, e.g., if the service was performed in a rural Health Manpower Shortage Area (HMSA) facility, instruct providers to bill the mammography modifier in modifier position 1 and the rural (or other) modifier in modifier position 2.

Ensure all those who are qualified include the 6-digit FDA assigned certification number of the screening center in field 32 of Form CMS-1500 and in field 31 on the electronic NSF. Carriers retain this number in their provider files.

Handle a claim according to current rules if it is determined that a facility is not FDA-certified. A provider/facility must have FDA certification to be reimbursed by Medicare. FDA

© 2005 Ingenix, Inc.

certification number must be on the claim and match the FDA file forwarded to contractors.

Waive Part B deductible and apply coinsurance for a screening mammography.

Add diagnosis code V76.12 if a claim comes in for screening mammography without a diagnosis and the carrier file data shows this is appropriate. If there are other diagnoses on the claim, but not code V76.12, add it. (Do not change or overlay code V76.12 but ADD it). At a minimum, edit for age, frequency, and place of service (POS).

NOTE: Beginning October 1, 2003, carriers are no longer permitted to plug the ICD-9 code for a screening mammography when the screening mammography claim has no diagnosis code. Screening mammography claims with no diagnosis code must be returned as unprocessable for assigned claims. For unassigned claims, deny the claim.

Carrier Provider Education

Educate providers that when a screening mammography turns to a diagnostic mammography on the same day for the same beneficiary, add the "-GG" modifier to the diagnostic code and bill both codes on the same claim. Both services are reimbursable by Medicare.

Educate providers that they cannot bill an add-on code without also billing for the appropriate mammography code. If just the add-on code is billed, the service will be denied. Both the add-on code and the appropriate mammography code should be on the same claim.

Pub. 100-4, Chapter 18, Section 20.7
Mammograms Performed With New Technologies

Section 104 of the Benefits Improvement and Protection Act 2000, (BIPA) entitled Modernization of Screening Mammography Benefit, provides for new payment methodologies for both diagnostic and screening mammograms that utilize advanced new technologies for the period April 1, 2001, to December 31, 2001 (to March 31, 2002 for hospitals subject to OPPS). Under this provision, payment for technologies that directly take digital images would equal 150 percent of the amount that would otherwise be paid for a bilateral diagnostic mammography. For technologies that convert standard film images to digital form, payment will be derived from the statutory screening mammography limit plus an additional payment of $15.00 for carrier claims and $10.20 for FI (technical component only) claims.

Payment restrictions for digital screening and diagnostic mammography apply to those facilities that meet all FDA certifications as provided under the Mammography Quality Standards Act. However, CAD codes billed in conjunction with digital mammographies or film mammographies are not subject to FDA certification requirements.

Mammography related CAD equipmentdoes not require FDA certification.

Mammography utilizes a direct x-ray of the breast. By contrast, the CAD process uses laser beam to scan the mammography film from a film (analog) mammography, converts it into digital data for the computer, and analyzes the video display for areas suspicious for cancer. The CAD process used with digital mammography analyzes the data from the mammography on a video display for suspicious areas. The patient is not required to be present for the CAD process.

Only one screening mammogram, either 76092 or G0202, may be billed in a calendar year. Therefore, providers/suppliers must not submit claims reflecting both a film screening mammography (76092) and a digital screening mammography G0202. Also, they must not submit claims reflecting HCPCS codes 76090 or 76091 (diagnostic mammography-film) and G0204 or G0206 (diagnostic mammography-digital). Contractors deny the claim when both a film and digital screening or diagnostic mammography is reported. However, a screening and diagnostic mammography can be billed together.

A - Payment Requirements for FI Claims With Dates of Service On or After April 1, 2001 Through December 31, 2001 (Through March 31, 2002 for Hospitals Subject to OPPS).

Providers bill the FI for the technical component of screening and diagnostic mammographies that utilize advanced technologies with one of six new HCPCS codes, G0202 - G0207. See payment methodology below for each of the codes during the period April 1, 2001 through December 31, 2001 (or March 31, 2002 for hospitals subject to OPPS). Payments for codes G0202 through G0205 are based, in part, on the MPFS payment amounts. The amounts that are based on the MPFS that both carriers and FIs use in calculating the payments for these codes were furnished in a BIPA mammography benefit pricing file for implementation on April 1, 2001.

HCPCS   Definition
G0202   Screening mammography producing direct digital image, bilateral, all views

Payment Method:

Payment will be the lesser of the provider's charge or the amount that will be provided for this code in the pricing file. (That amount is 150 percent of the locality specific technical component payment amount under the physician fee schedule for CPT code 76091, the code for bilateral diagnostic mammogram, during 2001.) Part B deductible does not apply. Coinsurance will equal 20 percent of the lesser of the actual charge or 150 percent of the locality specific payment of CPT code 76091.

HCPCS   Definition
G0203   Screening mammography, film processed to produce digital image analyzed for potential abnormalities, bilateral, all views

Payment Method:

Payment will be equal to the lesser of the actual charge for the procedure, the amount that is provided in the pricing file (which represents 68 percent of the locality specific global payment amount for a bilateral diagnostic mammography (CPT 76091) under the physician fee schedule), or $57.28 (which represents the amount of the 2001 statutory limit for a screening mammography attributable to the technical component of the service, plus the technical portion of the $15.00 add-on for 2001 which is provided under the new legislation). Part B deductible does not apply. Coinsurance is 20 percent of the charge.

HCPCS   Definition
G0204   Diagnostic mammography, direct digital image, bilateral, all views

Payment Method:

Payment will be the lesser of the provider's charge or the amount that will be provided for this code in the pricing file. (That amount is 150 percent of the locality specific amount paid under the physician fee schedule for the technical component (TC) of CPT code 76091, the code for a bilateral diagnostic mammogram.) Deductible is applicable. Coinsurance will equal 20 percent of the lesser of the actual charge or 150 percent of the locality specific payment of CPT code 76091.

NOTE: Effective January 1, 2005 payment will be made under MPFS for claims from hospitals subject to OPPS.

HCPCS	Definition
G0205	Diagnostic mammography, film processed to produce digital image analyzed for potential abnormalities, bilateral, all views.

Payment Method:

Payment will be equal to the lesser of the actual charge for the procedure, the amount that will be provided in the pricing file (which represents 68 percent of the locality specific global payment amount for a bilateral diagnostic mammography (CPT 76091) under the physician fee schedule), or $57.28 (which represents the amount of the 2001 statutory limit for a screening mammography attributable to the technical component of the service, plus the technical portion of the $15.00 add-on for 2001 which is provided under the new legislation). Deductible applies. Coinsurance is 20 percent of the charge.

HCPCS	Definition
G0206	Diagnostic mammography, direct digital image, unilateral, all views.

Payment Method:

Payment will be made based on the same amount that is paid to the provider, under the payment method applicable to the specific provider type (e.g., hospital, rural health clinic, etc.) for CPT code 76090, the code for a mammogram, and one breast. For example, this service, when furnished as a hospital outpatient service, will be paid the amount under the outpatient prospective payment system (OPPS) for CPT code 76090. Deductible applies. Coinsurance is the national unadjusted coinsurance for the APC wage adjusted for the specific hospital.

NOTE: Effective January 1, 2005 payment will be made under MPFS for claims from hospitals subject to OPPS.

HCPCS	Definition
G0207	Diagnostic mammography, film processed to produce digital image analyzed for potential abnormalities, unilateral, all views.

Payment Method:

Payment will be based on the same amount that is paid to the provider, under the payment method applicable to the specific provider type (e.g., hospital, rural health clinic, etc.) for CPT code 76090, the code for mammogram, and one breast. For example, this service, when furnished as a hospital outpatient service, will be paid the amount payable under the OPPS for CPT code 76090. Deductible applies. Coinsurance is the national unadjusted coinsurance for the APC wage adjusted for the specific hospital.

B - Payment Requirements for Claims with Dates of Service on or After January 1, 2002 (April 1, 2002 for hospitals subject to OPPS).

Codes G0203, G0205 and G0207 are not billable codes for claims with dates of service on or after January 1, 2002 (April 1, 2002 for hospitals subject to OPPS).

FI Payment

Code	Payment
G0202	Payment will be equal to the lower of the actual charge or the locality specific technical component payment amount under the MPFS when performed in a hospital outpatient department, CAH, or SNF. Coinsurance is 20 percent of the lower amount; the Program pays 80 percent.

Deductible does not apply.

G0204	Payment will be made under OPPS for hospital outpatient departments. Coinsurance is the national unadjusted coinsurance for the APC wage adjusted for the specific hospital. Payment will be made on a reasonable cost basis for CAHs and coinsurance is based on charges. Payment is made under the MPFS when performed in a SNF and coinsurance is 20 percent of the lower of the actual charge or the MPFS amount.

Deductible applies.

NOTE: Effective January 1, 2005 payment will be made under MPFS for claims from hospitals subject to OPPS.

G0206	Payment will be made under OPPS for hospital outpatient departments. Coinsurance is the national unadjusted coinsurance for the APC wage adjusted for the specific hospital. Payment will be made on a reasonable cost basis for CAHs and coinsurance is based on charges. Payment is made under the MPFS when performed in a SNF. Coinsurance is 20 percent of the lower of the actual charge or the MPFS amount.

Deductible applies.

NOTE: Effective January 1, 2005 payment will be made under MPFS for claims from hospitals subject to OPPS.

Providers bill for the technical portion of screening and diagnostic mammograms on Form CMS-1450 under bill type 13X, 22X, 23X, or 85X. The professional component is billed to the carrier on Form CMS-1500 (or electronic equivalent).

Providers bill for digital screening mammographies on Form CMS-1450, utilizing revenue code 0403 and HCPCS G0202 or G0203.

Providers bill for digital diagnostic mammographies on Form CMS-1450, utilizing revenue code 0401 and HCPCS G0204, G0205, G0206 or G0207.

NOTE: Codes G0203, G0205 and G0207 are not billable codes for claims with dates of service on or after January 1, 2002.

CAHs electing the optional method of payment for outpatient services are paid according to §20.3.2.3 of this chapter.

Carrier Payment

All codes paid by the carrier are based on the Medicare Physician Fee Schedule (MPFS).

© 2005 Ingenix, Inc.

APPENDIX D

Code	Payment
G0202	Payment is the lesser of the provider's charge or the MPFS amount provided for this code in the pricing file.
	Part B deductible does not apply, however, coinsurance applies.
G0204	Payment is the lesser of the provider's charge or the MPFS amount provided for this code in the pricing file.
	Deductible and coinsurance apply.
G0206	Payment is the lesser of the provider's charge or the MPFS amount provided for this code in the pricing file.
	Deductible and coinsurance apply.

Contractors were furnished a mammography benefit pricing file to pay claims containing the above codes.

Pub. 100-4, Chapter 18, Section 50
Prostate Cancer Screening Tests and Procedures

B3-4182, A3-3616

Sections 1861(s)(2)(P) and 1861(oo) of the Act (as added by §4103 of the Balanced Budget Act of 1997), provide for Medicare Part B coverage of certain prostate cancer screening tests subject to certain coverage, frequency, and payment limitations. Effective for services furnished on or after January 1, 2000, Medicare Part B covers prostate cancer screening tests/procedures for the early detection of prostate cancer. Coverage of prostate cancer screening tests includes the following procedures furnished to an individual for the early detection of prostate cancer:

Screening digital rectal examination, and

Screening prostate specific antigen (PSA) blood test.

Each test may be paid at a frequency of once every 12 months for men who have attained age 50 (i.e., starting at least one day after they have attained age 50), if at least 11 months have passed following the month in which the last Medicare-covered screening digital rectal examination was performed (for digital rectal exams) or PSA test was performed (for PSA tests).

Pub. 100-4, Chapter 18, Section 60
Colorectal Cancer Screening

B3-4180, B3-4180.6, A3-3660.17

See the Medicare Benefit Policy Manual, Chapter 1, for Medicare Part B coverage and effective dates of colorectal rectal screening services.

Effective for services furnished on or after January 1, 1998, payment may be made for colorectal cancer screening for the early detection of cancer. For screening colonoscopy services (one of the types of services included in this benefit) prior to July 2001, coverage was limited to high-risk individuals. For services July 1, 2001, and later screening colonoscopies are covered for individuals not at high risk.

The following services are considered colorectal cancer screening services:

Fecal-occult blood test, 1-3 simultaneous determinations (guaiac-based);

Flexible sigmoidoscopy;

Colonoscopy; and,

Barium enema

Effective for services on or after January 1, 2004, payment may be made for the following colorectal cancer screening service as an alternative for the guaiac-based fecal-occult blood test, 1-3 simultaneous determinations:

Fecal-occult blood test, immunoassay, 1-3 simultaneous determinations

Pub. 100-4, Chapter 18, Section 100
Cardiovascular Disease Screening

Pub. 100-4, Chapter 20, Section 50.3
Payment for Replacement of Parenteral and Enteral Pumps

B3-3324

Payment for replacement of PEN pumps purchased more than eight years prior to the current date may be considered, with documentation that indicates proof of purchase date. Medicare will consider payment for either a replacement by purchase or 15 months of rental.

Pub. 100-4, Chapter 20, Section 100.2.2
Evidence of Medical Necessity for Parenteral and Enteral Nutrition (PEN) Therapy

B3-3324, B3-4450

PEN coverage is determined by information provided by the treating physician and the PEN supplier. A completed certification of medical necessity (CMN) must accompany and support initial claims for PEN to establish whether coverage criteria are met and to ensure that the PEN therapy provided is consistent with the attending or ordering physician's prescription. Contractors ensure that the CMN contains pertinent information from the treating physician. Uniform specific medical data facilitate the review and promote consistency in coverage determinations and timelier claims processing.

The medical and prescription information on a PEN CMN can be most appropriately completed by the treating physician or from information in the patient's records by an employee of the physician for the physician's review and signature. Although PEN suppliers sometimes may assist in providing the PEN services, they cannot complete the CMN since they do not have the same access to patient information needed to properly enter medical or prescription information. Contractors use appropriate professional relations issuances, training sessions, and meetings to ensure that all persons and PEN suppliers are aware of this limitation of their role.

When properly completed, the PEN CMN includes the elements of a prescription as well as other data needed to determine whether Medicare coverage is possible. This practice will facilitate prompt delivery of PEN services and timely submittal of the related claim.

Pub. 100-4, Chapter 32, Section 10.1
Ambulatory Blood Pressure Monitoring (ABPM) Billing Requirements

A. Coding Applicable to Local Carriers & Fiscal Intermediaries (FIs)

Effective April 1, 2002, a National Coverage Decision was made to allow for Medicare coverage of ABPM for those beneficiaries with suspected "white coat hypertension" (WCH). ABPM involves the use of a non-invasive device, which is used to measure blood pressure in 24-hour cycles. These 24-hour measurements are stored in the device and are later interpreted by a physician. Suspected "WCH" is defined as: (1) Clinic/office blood pressure >140/90 mm Hg on at least three separate clinic/office visits with two separate measurements made at each visit; (2) At least two documented separate blood pressure measurements taken outside the clinic/office which are < 140/90 mm Hg; and (3) No evidence of end-organ damage. ABPM is not covered for any other uses. Coverage policy can be found in Medicare National Coverage Determinations Manual, Chapter 1, Section 20.19. (www.cms.hhs.gov/masnuals/103 cov determ/ncd103index.asp)

The ABPM must be performed for at least 24 hours to meet coverage criteria. Payment is not allowed for institutionalized beneficiaries, such as those receiving Medicare covered skilled nursing in a facility. In the rare circumstance that ABPM needs to be performed more than once for a beneficiary, the qualifying criteria described above must be met for each subsequent ABPM test.

Effective dates for applicable Common Procedure Coding System (HCPCS) codes for ABPM for suspected WCH and their covered effective dates are as follows:

HCPCS	Definition	Effective Date
93784	ABPM, utilizing a system such as magnetic tape and/or computer disk, for 24 hours or longer; including recording, scanning analysis, interpretation and report.	04/01/2002
93786	ABPM, utilizing a system such as magnetic tape and/or computer disk, for 24 hours or longer; recording only.	04/01/2002
93788	ABPM, utilizing a system such as magnetic tape and/or computer disk, for 24 hours or longer; scanning analysis with report.	01/01/2004
93790	ABPM, utilizing a system such as magnetic tape and/or computer disk, for 24 hours or longer; physician review with interpretation and report.	04/01/2002

In addition, the following diagnosis code must be present:

Diagnosis Code	Description
796.2	Elevated blood pressure reading without diagnosis of hypertension.

B. FI Billing Instructions

The applicable types of bills acceptable when billing for ABPM services are 13X, 14X, 23X, 71X, 73X, 75X, and 85X. Chapter 25 of this manual provides general billing instructions that must be followed for bills submitted to FIs. The FIs pay for hospital outpatient ABPM services billed on a 13x and 14x type of bill with HCPCS 93786 and/or 93788 as follows: (1) Outpatient Prospective Payment System (OPPS) hospitals pay based on the Ambulatory Payment Classification (APC); (2) non-OPPS hospitals (Indian Health Services Hospitals, Hospitals that provide Part B services only, and hospitals located in American Samoa, Guam, Saipan and the Virgin Islands) pay based on reasonable cost, except for Maryland Hospitals which are paid based on a percentage of cost.

The FIs pay for comprehensive outpatient rehabilitation facility (CORF) ABPM services billed on a 75x type of bill with HCPCS code 93786 and/or 93788 based on the Medicare Physician Fee Schedule (MPFS) amount for that HCPCS code.

The FIs pay for ABPM services for critical access hospitals (CAHs) billed on a 85x type of bill as follows: (1) for CAHs that elected the Standard Method and billed HCPCS code 93786 and/or 93788, pay based on reasonable cost for that HCPCS code; and (2) for CAHs that elected the Optional Method and billed any combination of HCPCS codes 93786, 93788 and 93790 pay based on reasonable cost for HCPCS 93786 and 93788 and pay 115% of the MPFS amount for HCPCS 93790.

The FIs pay for ABPM services for skilled nursing facility (SNF) outpatients billed on a 23x type of bill with HCPCS code 93786 and/or 93788, based on the MPFS.

The FIs accept independent and provider-based rural health clinic (RHC) bills for visits under the all-inclusive rate when the RHC bills on a 71x type of bill with revenue code 052x for providing the professional component of ABPM services. The FIs should not make a separate payment to a RHC for the professional component of ABPM services in addition to the all-inclusive rate. RHCs are not required to use ABPM HCPCS codes for professional services covered under the all-inclusive rate.

The FIs accept free-standing and provider-based federally qualified health center (FQHC) bills for visits under the all-inclusive rate when the FQHC bills on a 73x type of bill with revenue code 052x for providing the professional component of ABPM services. The FIs should not make a separate payment to a FQHC for the professional component of ABPM services in addition to the all-inclusive rate. FQHCs are not required to use ABPM HCPCS codes for professional services covered under the all-inclusive rate.

The FIs pay provider-based RHCs/FQHCs for the technical component of ABPM services when billed under the base provider's number using the above requirements for that particular base provider type, i.e., a OPPS hospital based RHC would be paid for the ABPM technical component services under the OPPS using the APC for code 93786 and/or 93788 when billed on a 13x type of bill.

Independent and free-standing RHC/FQHC practitioners are only paid for providing the technical component of ABPM

© 2005 Ingenix, Inc.

services when billed to the carrier following the carrier instructions.

C. Carrier Claims

Local carriers pay for ABPM services billed with diagnosis code 796.2 and HCPCS codes 93784 or for any combination of 93786, 93788 and 93790, based on the MPFS for the specific HCPCS code billed.

D. Coinsurance and Deductible

The FIs and local carriers shall apply coinsurance and deductible to payments for ABPM services except for services billed to the FI by FQHCs. For FQHCs only co-insurance applies.

Pub. 100-4, Chapter 32, Section 30
Hyperbaric Oxygen (HBO) Therapy

Pub. 100-4, Chapter 32, Section 40
Sacral Nerve Stimulation

A sacral nerve stimulator is a pulse generator that transmits electrical impulses to the sacral nerves through an implanted wire. These impulses cause the bladder muscles to contract, which gives the patient ability to void more properly.

Pub. 100-4, Chapter 32, Section 50
Deep Brain Stimulation for Essential Tremor and Parkinson's Disease

Deep brain stimulation (DBS) refers to high-frequency electrical stimulation of anatomic regions deep within the brain utilizing neurosurgically implanted electrodes. These DBS electrodes are stereotactically placed within targeted nuclei on one (unilateral) or both (bilateral) sides of the brain. There are currently three targets for DBS -- the thalamic ventralis intermedius nucleus (VIM), subthalamic nucleus (STN) and globus pallidus interna (GPi).

Essential tremor (ET) is a progressive, disabling tremor most often affecting the hands. ET may also affect the head, voice and legs. The precise pathogenesis of ET is unknown. While it may start at any age, ET usually peaks within the second and sixth decades. Beta-adrenergic blockers and anticonvulsant medications are usually the first line treatments for reducing the severity of tremor. Many patients, however, do not adequately respond or cannot tolerate these medications. In these medically refractory ET patients, thalamic VIM DBS may be helpful for symptomatic relief of tremor.

Parkinson's disease (PD) is an age-related progressive neurodegenerative disorder involving the loss of dopaminergic cells in the substantia nigra of the midbrain. The disease is characterized by tremor, rigidity, bradykinesia and progressive postural instability. Dopaminergic medication is typically used as a first line treatment for reducing the primary symptoms of PD. However, after prolonged use, medication can become less effective and can produce significant adverse events such as dyskinesias and other motor function complications. For patients who become unresponsive to medical treatments and/or have intolerable side effects from medications, DBS for symptom relief may be considered.

APPENDIX E — HCPCS TO CPT CROSSWALK

CPT (HCPCS Level I)	PM/Transmittal	Source	HCPCS Level II
21077			L8042
21087			L8040
21088			L8041, L8042, L8044, L8046
38210-38213	AB-02-163		G0267
45300-45387 (mutually exclusive)		CCI	Comprehensive code G0105
45300-45387, 46604, 46608, 46614 (mutually exclusive)		CCI	Comprehensive code G0104
69210 for non-Medicare only	A-02-129		G0268
71555		Medicare Claims Processing Manual, Ch. 13, Sec. 40.1.2 (Rev. 10/1/03)	C8909-C8911
72198	A-03-051	Medicare Claims Processing Manual, Ch. 13, Sec. 40.1.2 (Rev. 10/1/03)	C8918-C8920
74270, 74280 (mutually exclusive)		CCI	Comprehensive code G0106
76090	Hospital Manual, Ch. 10, Sec. 458	—	G0206
76091	Hospital Manual, Ch. 10, Sec. 458	—	G0202-G0206
82270	R80CP	Pub 100-04	G0328
82270 (mutually exclusive)		CCI	Comprehensive code G0107
84153, 84154 (mutually exclusive)		CCI	Comprehensive code G0103
88160-88161		Transmittal 800, CCI	Comprehensive code P3000
88174	AB-02-163		G0144
88175	AB-02-163		G0145
88240	AB-02-163		G0265
88241	AB-02-163		G0266
90471-90472	B-03-001		G0008, G0009, G0010
90919, 90920, 90921		68FR63216	G0308-G0327
99183 (carrier requires) hyperbaric oxygen therapy)	AB-702-183		C1300 (report for hospital outpatient)
Included in E & M code 99201-99456 & 99499		CCI	G0102

APPENDIX F — GLOSSARY

Abdominal lymphadenectomy — Cutting out (removing) the lymph node grouping, with or without para-aortic and vena caval nodes, and dissecting away from the surrounding tissue, nerves, and blood vessels.

Absorbable sutures — Strands prepared from collagen or a synthetic polymer and capable of being absorbed by tissue over time. Examples include surgical gut, collagen sutures, or synthetics like polydioxanone (PDS), polyglactin 910 (Vicryl), polylecapron 25 (Monocryl), polyglyconate (Maxon), and polyglycolic acid (Dexon).

Acetabuloplasty — Plastic repair/reconstruction of the acetabulum. The acetabulum is the rounded cavity on the external surface of the innominate bone that receives the head of the femur.

Air conduction — The transportation of sound from the air, through the external auditory canal, to the tympanic membrane, and ossicular chain, ending at, but not including the cochlea. Testing air conduction establishes the patency or nonpatency of these mechanisms.

Air puff device — Measures intraocular pressure by evaluating the force of a reflected amount of air blown against the cornea. A valuable screening tool, but less precise than other methods.

Allograft — Tissue obtained from a nonidentical individual of the same species. Other terms used to identify allografts include: allogenic graft, homologous graft, homoplastic graft.

Amniocentesis — Amniocentesis provides an accurate source of chromosomal information about the fetus. It is usually performed between 16 and 20 weeks gestation.

Anastomosis — Surgically created connection between ducts, blood vessels, or bowel segments to allow flow from one to the other.

Angioplasty — Reconstruction or repair of a diseased or damaged blood vessel.

Annuloplasty — The annuli are thick, fibrous rings and one is found surrounding each of the cardiac chambers. The atrial and ventricular muscle fibers attach to the annuli. In annuloplasty, weakened annuli may be surgically plicated, or tucked, to improve muscular functions.

Anorectal anometry — Measurement of pressure generated by anal sphincter to help treat incontinence.

Anterior chamber lenses — These are inserted in conjunction with intracapsular cataract extraction and posterior chamber lenses are inserted in conjunction with extracapsular cataract extraction. Anterior chamber lenses are commonly used for secondary insertion.

Applanation tomometer — Measures intraocular pressure by recording the force required to flatten an area of the cornea. It is attached to a slit lamp and is considered the most accurate methodology.

Aspirate — Physician uses a syringe or a suction device to withdraw fluid or air from a cavity.

Atrial septal defect — An atrial septal defect allows oxygenated blood to return to the lungs instead of circulating throughout the rest of the body. This can increase pulmonary blood flow, causing pulmonary hypertension if the defect is not closed.

Auricle — The external ear, or auricle, is a single elastic cartilage covered in skin and normal adnexal features (hair follicles, sweat glands, and sebaceous glands). The ridged nature of the auricle is to channel sounds into the acoustic meatus. The semicircular depression leading into the ear is named the concha, Latin for shell. The lining of the acoustic meatus is skin with ceruminous glands that secrete ear wax.

Autogenous transplant — Transplanted from one part of the patient's body to another. Autogenous bone may be freshly harvested, or preserved and stored in a bone bank for later grafting. Most commonly, the bone is cryogenically preserved. Other terms for autograft include: autogenic graft, autologous graft, autotransplant.

Bankart procedure — This procedure is also referred to as a capsulolabral reconstruction. The procedure is used to treat recurrent dislocation of the shoulder requiring reconstruction of the avulsed capsule and labrum at the glenoid lip.

Bartholin's gland — Gland on either side of vaginal opening. Also called vestibular glands.

Bartholin's gland abscess — An abscess of the Bartholin's gland is a pocket of pus and surrounding cellulitis caused by infection of the Bartholin's gland. Symptoms include localized swelling and pain in the posterior labia majora. The pain may extend into the lower vagina.

Basic value or base uUnit (anesthesia services) — The basic value, also referred to as the base unit or relative value, has two components. One component reflects all usual services included in the anesthesia service, including pre-operative and post-operative visits, administration of fluids and/or blood products incident to the procedure, and interpretation of non-invasive monitoring (ECG, temperature, blood pressure, oximetry, capnography, and mass spectrometry). The second component reflects the relative work or cost of the specific anesthesia service. Cost in this context refers to the physician's cost of doing business. For anesthesiologists, the majority of the cost goes to malpractice insurance.

Berman locator — Small, sensitive tool for detecting location of a metallic foreign body.

Bifurcated — Having two branches or divisions, such as the left pulmonary veins that split off from the left atrium to carry oxygenated blood away from the heart.

Biopsy — Tissue or fluid removed for diagnosis. A pathologist confirms a diagnosis through analysis of the cells in the biopsy material.

Blalock-Hanlon procedure — A segment of the right atrium is excised, creating an atrial septal defect. This is a palliative procedure for transposition of great vessels.

Blalock-Taussig procedure — An end-to-side anastomosis of right subclavian artery to right pulmonary artery allows arterial and venous blood to mix and flow through the shunt to the pulmonary artery and into the lungs for oxygenation.

Blepharorrhaphy — Synonym of tarsorrhaphy. See tarsorrhaphy.

Blue baby — A term commonly used for infants that are cyanotic due to oxygen deprivation.

Body positions — There are several body positions for patients during surgical procedures. These include:

- Fowler's position. Position assumed by patient when the head of the bed is raised 18 or 20 inches and the individual's knees are elevated.

- Prone. Lying horizontally when lying face downward.

- Supine. Lying horizontally on the back (also called dorsal decubitus position).

- Trendelenburg position. Position by the patient when the patient's head is lower in relation to the inclined plane of the body and legs.

Bone conduction —The transportation of sound through bone. The source of sound is placed on the skull or teeth, and the vibration stimulates the cochlea, bypassing normal air conduction routes. Bone conduction requires operational sensorineural hearing mechanisms.

Bone mass measurement — The term means a radiologic or radioisotopic procedure or other procedure approved by the FDA for identifying bone mass, detecting bone loss. or determining bone quality. The procedure includes a physician's interpretation of the results. Qualifying individuals must be an estrogen-deficient woman at clinical risk for osteoporosis with vertebral abnormalities.

Bristow procedure — This procedure transfers the tip of the coracoid process with its muscle attachments across the anteroinferior

glenohumeral joint creating a musculotendinous sling.

Buccal mucosa — The mucous membrane on the inside of the cheek.

Caldwell-Luc — A large nasoantral window is created above the canine tooth in this intraoral approach to surgery. This antrostomy is usually limited to adults because of the unerupted teeth in children.

Cardiopulmonary bypass — Venous blood is diverted to a heart-lung machine, which mechanically pumps and oxygenates the blood temporarily so that the heart can be bypassed while an open procedure on the heart or coronary arteries is performed. During bypass, the lungs are deflated and immobile.

Cardioverter-defibrillator — A cardioverter-defibrillator device uses both low energy cardioversion or defibrillating shocks and antitachycardia pacing to treat ventricular tachycardia or ventricular fibrillation. It may be either a single or dual chamber device. Cardioverter-defibrillators may require the placement of multiple leads even for single chamber devices.

Care plan oversight services — The term describes the services of a physician providing ongoing review and revision of a patient's care plan involving complex or multidisciplinary care modalities. Care plan oversight services are reported separately from any necessary office/outpatient, hospital, home, nursing facility, or domiciliary services.

Case management services — Physician case management is a process of involving direct patient care as well as coordinating and controlling access to the patient or initiating and/or supervising other necessary health care services.

Cataract extraction — The most common surgical procedure performed on adults. Most ophthalmologists perform cataract surgery in an ambulatory surgical setting. Anterior chamber lenses are inserted in conjunction with intracapsular cataract extraction and posterior chamber lenses are inserted in conjunction with extracapsular cataract extraction.

Certified nurse midwife — The term means a registered nurse who has successfully completed a program of study and clinical experience or has been certified by a recognized organization.

Cervical cap — Cervical cap is similar in form and function to the diaphragm, however, it can be left in place for up to 48 hours.

Cervical intraepithelial neoplasia — This classification system is used to report abnormalities in the epithelial cell:

- CIN I. Cervical intraepithelial neoplasia I; low-grade abnormality; mild dysplasia

- CIN II. Cervical intraepithelial neoplasia II; high-grade abnormality; moderate dysplasia

- CIN III. Cervical intraepithelial neoplasia III; carcinoma in situ; severe dysplasia

Choanal atresis — A potentially dangerous congenital defect. Infants unable to breathe through their noses cannot feed properly and have difficulty keeping their air passages clear.

Cholecystectomy — The removal of the gallbladder and its contents is the most common major operation in the United States, and performed as the definitive treatment for gallstones.

Chorionic villi sampling — Chorionic villi sampling provides a rich source of fetal genetic information. Obtained between the eighth week and the twelfth week of gestation, it can provide information to diagnose some enzymatic defects.

Chronic pain management services — The term describes distinct services frequently performed by anesthesiologists who have additional training in pain management procedures. Pain management services include initial and subsequent evaluation and management (E/M) services, trigger point injections, spine and spinal cord injections, and nerve blocks.

Cineplastic amputation — This type of amputation may also be referred to as a cinematic amputation or a kineplasty procedure. In this type of amputation, the muscles and tendons of the remaining portion of the extremity are arranged so that they may be utilized for motor functions. Following this type of amputation, a specially constructed prosthetic device allows the individual to execute more complex movements because the muscles and tendons are able to communicate independent movements to the device.

Circadian — Refers to the 24 hour period.

Classification of surgical wound — Surgical wounds fall into four categories that determine methods of treatment and outcomes:

- Clean wound. No inflammation and procedure performed under sterile operating room conditions with no break in sterile technique. No alimentary, respiratory, oropharyngeal, or genitourinary tracts are involved in the surgery. Infection rate: up to 5 percent.

- Clean-contaminated wound. No inflammation and procedure performed with minor break in surgical technique. No unusual contamination found in alimentary, respiratory, genitourinary, or oropharyngeal

cavity entered. Infection rate: up to 11 percent.

- Contaminated wound. Acute nonpurulent inflammation noted and procedure performed with major break in surgical technique. Open wound less than four hours old. Gross contamination from gastrointestinal tract. Infection rate: up to 20 percent.

- Dirty and infected wound. Existing infection and inflammation prior to surgery in a dirty traumatic wound more than four hours old, or an old abscess and/or existing surgical infection. In either case abscess, and nonsterile conditions were present. Wound older than four hours. Perforated viscus, fecal contamination, necrotic tissue, or foreign body may be present. Infection rate: up to 40 percent.

Clinical social worker — The term means an individual who possesses a master's or doctor's degree in social work and, after obtaining the degree, has performed at least two years of supervised clinical social work. A clinical social worker must be licensed by the state or, in the case of states without licensure, must completed at least two years or 3,000 hours of post-master's degree supervised clinical social work practice under the supervision of a master's level social worker.

CO$_2$ laser — A carbon dioxide laser that emits an invisible beam and vaporizes water-rich tissue. The vapor is suctioned from the site.

Colorectal cancer screening tests — The term means any of the following procedures furnished to an individual for the purpose of early detection of colorectal cancer:

- Screening fecal-occult blood test

- Screening flexible sigmoidoscopy

- In the case of an individual at high risk for colorectal cancer, screening colonoscopy

- Other tests or procedures, and modifications to tests and procedures, with such frequency and payment limits

- Individuals are considered at high risk for colorectal cancer because of family history, prior experience of cancer or precursor neoplastic polyps, history of chronic digestive disease condition (i.e., inflammatory bowel disease, Crohn's Disease, or ulcerative colitis), or the presence of any appropriate recognized gene markers for colorectal cancer.

Colostomy — Artificial surgical opening anywhere along the length of the colon to the skin surface for the diversion of feces.

Appendixes

Colpocleisis — Vaginal canal closure.

Commissurotomy — Surgical division or opening of a band of fibrous tissue.

Community mental health center, partial hospitalization services — The term means the services prescribed and supervised by a physician pursuant to an individualized, written plan of treatment that sets forth the diagnosis and the type, amount, frequency, and duration of care for a patient in a community mental health center. Services must be reasonable and necessary for the diagnosis or active treatment of the individual's condition and to prevent relapse or hospitalization. The items and services include the following:

- Individual and group therapy with physicians, psychologists, or other mental health professionals

- Occupational therapy requiring the skills of a qualified occupational therapist

- Services of social workers, trained psychiatric nurses, and other staff trained to work with psychiatric patients

- Drugs and biologicals for therapeutic purposes that cannot be self-administered)

- Individualized activity therapies that are not primarily recreational or diversionary

- Family counseling

- Patient training and education

- Diagnostic services, and

- Other items and services, excluding meals and transportation

Comprehensive outpatient rehabilitation facility (CORF) — The term describes a facility that provides (by or under the supervision of physicians) diagnostic, therapeutic, and restorative services to outpatients. Patients must be under the supervision of a physician and the facility must maintain the medical record of each patient. The following items and services provided by a physician or other qualified professional to an outpatient of a comprehensive outpatient rehabilitation facility under a plan established and periodically reviewed by a physician:

- Physicians' services

- Physical therapy, occupational therapy, speech-language pathology services, and respiratory therapy

- Prosthetic and orthotic devices, including testing, fitting, or training in the use of prosthetic and orthotic devices

- Social and psychological services

- Nursing care provided by or under the supervision of a registered professional nurse

- Drugs and biologicals that cannot be self-administered

- Supplies and durable medical equipment

- Other supplies and services necessary for the rehabilitation of the patient that are ordinarily available through the CORF

A CORF must provide a surety bond in an amount that is not less than $50,000 to ensure the efficiency and effectiveness of its programs.

Conjunctivodacryocystostomy — Surgical connection of the lacrimal sac directly to the conjunctival sac.

Conjunctivorhinostomy — Correction of an obstruction of the lacrimal canal

Consultations — The term describes consulting services provided at the request of another physician or other appropriate source for the purpose of rendering an opinion or advice regarding the evaluation and management of a specific problem. Consultations in CPT fall under four subcategories: office or other outpatient consultations, initial inpatient consultations, follow-up inpatient consultations, and confirmatory consultations.

Costochondral — Pertains to the ribs and the scapula.

Covered osteoporosis drug — The term means an injectable drug approved for the treatment of post-menopausal osteoporosis provided to an individual by a home health agency if the individual's attending physician certifies that the individual has suffered a bone fracture related to post-menopausal osteoporosis. The individual must be unable to learn the skills needed to self-administer such drug or is otherwise physically or mentally incapable of self-administering the drug and be confined to home.

Core needle biopsy — A large-bore biopsy needle is inserted into a mass and a core of tissue is removed for diagnostic study.

Craterization — Excision of a portion of bone to create a crater-like depression to facilitate drainage from infected areas of bone.

Cricoid — The circular cartilage around the trachea.

Cryolathe — Tool for reshaping a button of corneal tissue.

Cryosurgery — Local freezing of diseased tissue without causing harm to adjacent tissue. The cold causes tissue necrosis. Frozen tissue may be removed without significant bleeding during the surgical procedure, even in highly vascular tissue. Liquid nitrogen is the most commonly used source for the cold.

Cutdown — The technique of creating a small, incised opening for venipuncture.

Cytogenetic studies — The term refers to the procedures in CPT 2001 that are related to the branch of genetics that studies cellular (cyto) structure and function as it relates to heredity (genetics). White blood cells, specifically T-lymphocytes, are the most commonly used specimen for chromosome analysis.

Dacryocystorhinostomy — Performed by suturing the posterior flaps while the lacrimal obstruction is removed, preserving the conjunctiva.

Dacryocystotome — Instrument for incising lacrimal duct strictures, also spelled dacryocystitome.

Dacryorhinocystostomy — Synonym to dacryocystorhinostomy.

Debride — Procedure involves the removal of all foreign objects and damaged tissue from a burn or a wound to prevent infection and promote healing.

Dermis graft — Skin graft that has been separated from the epidermal tissue and the underlying subcutaneous fat. Used primarily as a substitute for fascia grafts in plastic surgery.

Desensitization — Administration of extracts of allergens periodically to build immunity in the patient.

Destruction — The term describes the ablation of benign, premalignant, or malignant tissue by any of the following methods used alone or in combination: electrosurgery, cryosurgery, laser, and chemical treatment.

Diabetes outpatient self-management training services — The term means educational and training services furnished by a certified provider in an outpatient setting. The physician managing the individual's diabetic condition must certify that the services are needed under a comprehensive plan of care provide the patient with the skills and knowledge necessary for therapeutic program compliance (including skills related to the self-administration of injectable drugs). The provider must meet applicable standards established by the National Diabetes Advisory or be recognized by an organization that represents individuals with diabetes as meeting standards for furnishing the services.

Diagnostic procedures — Terms describes the procedures performed to evaluate the patient's complaints or symptoms. These procedures help the physician establish the nature of the patient's disease or condition so that definitive care can be provided. Diagnostic procedures include endoscopy, arthroscopy, injection procedures, and biopsies.

Diaphragm — Flexible, dome-shaped rubber cap that fits over the cervix and acts as a barrier to sperm. It must be used in conjunction with spermicidal cream or jelly. It is generally left in place for eight hours after coitus.

Diaphysectomy — Partial removal of a portion of bone, usually a portion of the shaft of a long bone, to facilitate drainage from infected bone.

Diathermy — Heating of tissue using microwave radiation, ultrasound, or electric currents.

Dilation — Artificial increase in the diameter of an opening made by medication or by instrumentation.

Discharge planning process — The term defines a plan applicable to services furnished by the hospital to individuals entitled to medical benefits. Upon the request of a patient's physician, the hospital must arrange for the development and initial implementation of a discharge plan for the patient. The discharge planning evaluation must be included in the patient's medical record for use in establishing an appropriate discharge plan and the results of the evaluation must be discussed with the patient or the patient's representative). Plan guidelines and standards should address the following:

- Patients who are likely to suffer adverse health consequences upon discharge in the absence of adequate discharge planning and patients, their physicians, and their representatives requesting a discharge plan

- Appropriate arrangements for post-hospital care made before discharge and to avoid unnecessary delays in discharge

- An evaluation of a patient's likely need for appropriate post-hospital services, including hospice services and the availability of those services, including the availability of home health services

Dissect — A scalpel, a probe, or scissors is used to cut apart tissues for visual or microscopic study.

Dorsal — Pertaining to the back or posterior aspect.

Drugs and biologicals — The term covers drugs and biologicals included - or approved for inclusion - in the United States Pharmacopoeia, the National Formulary, the United States Homeopathic Pharmacopoeia, in New Drugs or Accepted Dental Remedies, or approved by the pharmacy and drug therapeutics committee of the medical staff of the hospital. Drugs also include those used in an anticancer chemotherapeutic regimen for a medically accepted approved by the FDA. The carrier determines medical acceptance based on supportive clinical evidence.

Durable medical equipment (DME) — The term includes iron lungs, oxygen tents, hospital beds, and wheelchairs used in the patient's home, including an institution considered the patient's home. DME also blood-testing strips and blood glucose monitors for individuals with diabetes without regard to Type I or Type II diabetes or use of insulin.

DuToit staple capsulorrhaphy — Reattachment of the capsule and glenoid labrum to the glenoid lip using staples to anchor the avulsed capsule and glenoid labrum.

Eden-Hybinette — This anterior repair utilizes an anterior bone block to augment the bony anterior glenoid lip.

EDTA — Drug used to inhibit damage to the cornea by collagenase. EDTA is especially effective in alkali burns as it neutralizes soluable alkali, including lye.

Effusion — Escape of fluid from within a body cavity.

Electrocautery — Destruction of tissue using high-frequency electrical current. The current produces heat, which destroys cells.

Emergency — A serious medical condition or symptom (including severe pain) resulting from injury, sickness, or mental illness that arises suddenly and requires immediate care and treatment, generally received within 24 hours of onset, to avoid jeopardy to the life, limb, or health of a covered person.

Endarterectomy — Removal of the endothelial lining of a diseased or damaged artery.

Epiphysiodesis — Surgical fusion of an epiphysis performed to prematurely stop further bone growth.

Escharotomy — Removal of the scab caused by the burn, which is constricting blood flow. The procedure allows the edges to separate and restore blood flow to the unburned tissues.

Established patient — Evaluation and Management guidelines define an established patient as one who has received professional services from the physician, or another physician of the same specialty who belongs to the same group practice, within the past three years.

Exenteration — Radical excision of the contents of a body cavity (e.g., orbit).

Extended care services — The term defines the items and services provided to an inpatient of a skilled nursing facility, including nursing care, physical or occupational therapy, speech pathology, drugs and supplies, and medical social services.

External electrical capacitor device — External electrical stimulation device designed to promote bone healing. This device may also promote neural regeneration, revascularization, epiphyseal growth, and ligament maturation.

External pulsating electromagnetic field — External stimulation device designed to promote bone healing. This device may also promote neural regeneration, revascularization, epiphyseal growth, and ligament maturation.

Evaluation and management (E/M) codes — E/M codes encompass services that are part of the 99000 series of CPT codes and represent the services most frequently performed by physicians (e.g., office, emergency department, inpatient visits).

Evaluation and management service components — The components of history, examination, and medical decision making are keys to selecting the correct E/M codes. In most cases, all three components must be addressed in the documentation. However, in established, subsequent, and follow-up categories, only two of the three must be met or exceeded for a given code.

Eyre-Brook capsulorrhaphy — Reattachment of the capsule and glenoid labrum to the glenoid lip.

Fascia — The fibrous tissue that envelopes the muscle.

Fasciectomy — Surgical incision through the fascia.

Fasciotomy — Excision of the fascia or strips of fascial tissue.

Fat graft — A graft composed of fatty tissue completely freed from surrounding tissue. Used primarily to fill in depressions.

Fine needle aspiration (FNA) — A 22- or through 25-gauge needle attached to a syringe is inserted into a lesion/tissue and a few cells are aspirated for diagnostic study. Aspiration is also used to remove fluid from a benign cyst.

Fluoroscopy — Radiology technique that allows visual examination of part of the body or a function of an organ using a device that projects an x-ray image on a fluorescent screen.

Focal length — Distance between the object in focus and the lens.

Free flap — Tissue that is completely detached from the donor site and reattached to the recipient site. It receives its blood supply from capillary ingrowth at the recipient site.

Free microvascular flap — Tissue that is completely detached from the donor site following careful dissection and preservation of the blood vessels. The tissue is attached to the recipient site and the transfered blood vessels are anastomosed to vessels in the recipient site.

Fulguration — Destruction of living tissue by sparks from electric current.

Gas tamponade — Absorbable gas may be injected to force the retina against the choroid. Common gases include room air, short-acting sulfahexafluoride, intermediate-acting perfluoroethane, or long-acting perfluorooctane.

Hemilaminectomy — Excision of the right or left lamina.

Hemoperitoneum — The effusion of blood into the peritoneal cavity.

Heterologous transplant — Nonhuman biotissue transplanted into the patient.

Heterotopic transplant — Tissue transplanted from a different anatomical site for usage as is natural for that tissue, for example, buccal mucosa to a conjunctival site.

Home health agency — The term means a public agency or private organization providing skilled nursing services and other therapeutic services. Home health agencies receiving federal funds must have policies governing it services and the medical services of a physician or registered professional nurse. According to law, home health agencies must maintain clinical reports of all patients. Provisions of the Balanced Budget Act of 1997, home health agencies must provide, on a continuing basis, surety bonds of $50,000 to guarantee the efficient and effective operation of the agency. The term home health agency does not include any agency or organization that is primarily for the care and treatment of mental diseases.

Home health services — The term encompasses the items and services a home health agency provides to an individual, according to a plan developed and reviewed by the patient's physician. Services may include:

- Part-time or intermittent nursing care provided by or under the supervision of a registered professional nurse
- Physical or occupational therapy or speech-language pathology services
- Medical social services under the direction of a physician
- Part-time or intermittent services of a home health aide who has successfully completed a training program
- Medical supplies (including catheters, catheter supplies, ostomy bags, and supplies related to ostomy care, and a covered osteoporosis drug and durable medical equipment
- Medical services provided by an intern or resident-in-training of a hospital affiliated with the home health agency

Homogenous transplant (homograft) — Tissue from another human transplanted to the patient. For bone transplants, the tissue is usually obtained from a cadaver.

Hospice care — The term specifies the following items and services provided to a terminally ill individual by a hospice program under a written plan established and periodically reviewed by the individual's attending physician and by the medical director:

- Nursing care provided by or under the supervision of a registered professional nurse
- Physical or occupational therapy or speech-language pathology services
- Medical social services under the direction of a physician
- Services of a home health aide who has successfully completed a training program
- Medical supplies (including drugs and biologicals) and the use of medical appliances
- Physicians' services
- Short-term inpatient care (including both respite care and procedures necessary for pain control and acute and chronic symptom management) in an inpatient facility on an intermittent basis and not consecutively over longer than five days
- Counseling (including dietary counseling) with respect to care of the terminally ill individual and adjustment to his death
- Any item or service which is specified in the plan and for which payment may be made

Hospice program — An Hospice program establishes the care and service plan and ensures that the services are available (as needed) on a 24-hour basis and also provides bereavement counseling for the immediate family of terminally ill individuals. The services may be delivered in an individual's home, on an outpatient basis, and on a short-term inpatient basis, directly or under arrangements made by the agency or organization. The Hospice agency is responsible for all services in an aggregate number of days of inpatient care provided in any 12-month period, as overseen by an interdisciplinary group of personnel that includes at least one physician, one registered professional nurse, and one social worker. A central clinical record must be maintained for each patient.

According to federal law, an Hospice cannot discontinue its services with respect to a patient because of the inability of the patient to pay for care. Volunteers may provide care and services as long as the program maintains records on the cost savings and expansion of care and services achieved through volunteers.

Hospital — The term means an institution that provides, under the supervision of physicians, diagnostic, therapeutic, and rehabilitation services for medical diagnosis, treatment, and care of patients. Hospitals receiving federal funds must maintain clinical records on all patients, provides 24-hour nursing services, and have a discharge planning process in place. The term "hospital" also includes religious nonmedical health care institutions and facilities of 50 beds or less located in rural areas.

Ileostomy — Proximal end of transected ileum is brought out through the peritoneum and muscle of the abdominal wall to the skin. Liquid or semisolid discharge is collected in a bag over the stoma.

Infundibulectomy — Excision of the anterosuperior portion of the right ventricle of the heart.

Institutional planning — The terms describes the overall plan and budget of a hospital, skilled nursing facility, comprehensive outpatient rehabilitation facility, or home health agency. Plans must be prepared by a governing and submitted to the state health agency. Plans must include:

- An annual operating budget
- A capital expenditures plan for at least a three-year period

Internal direct current stimulator — Electrostimulation device designed to promote bone regeneration by encouraging cellular response in bone and ligaments. It is placed directly into the surgical site.

Intramedullary implants — An intramedullary nail, rod, or pin is placed into the intramedullary canal at the fracture site. Intramedullary implants not only provide a method of aligning the fracture, they also act as a splint and may reduce fracture pain. Implants may be rigid or flexible. Rigid implants are preferred for prophylactic treatment of diseased bone, while flexible implants are preferred for traumatic injuries.

Irrigation — To wash out or cleanse a body cavity wound with water or other fluid.

Jatene procedure — This corrective measure for transposition of the great vessels is used when subaortic stenosis and narrowing of the left aortic ventricular junction are present requiring reconstruction of these sites as well as surgical correction of the transposed aortic and pulmonary arteries. This technique may be used in cases where the transposition is accompanied by a ventricular septal defect or a large patent ductus arteriosus.

Krypton laser — Because the krypton spectrum (red-yellow) is poorly absorbed by hemoglobin, it can be used effectively to treat retinal bleeding, macular lesions, and vessel aberrations of the choroid.

Lacrimal punctum — The opening of the lacrimal papilla of the eyelid through which tears flow to the canaliculi to the lacrimal sac.

Lacrimotome — Knife for cutting the lacrimal sac or duct.

Lacrimotomy — Incision of the lacrimal sac or duct.

Larynx — The larynx is the air passage of the neck area, serving as the voice mechanism as well as the valve to prevent food and other particles from entering the respiratory tract. The larynx is composed of three single cartilages: cricoid, epiglottis, and thyroid; and three paired cartilages: arytenoid, corniculate, and cuneiform.

Laser surgery — Laser beams deliver a sharply defined burn, and the color and wavelength of the laser determines which tissues it can best treat. The argon laser is effective in coagulating blood-rich tissue with heat. CO_2 lasers are used to vaporize tissue. Potassium titanyl phosphate (KTP) lasers coagulate tissues. Nd:YAG lasers cut and cauterize.

LEEP — Loop electrosurgical excision prcocedure. This uses a stainless steel or tungsten loop electrode to excise a central core of cervical tissue. This is a therapeutic technique for treatment of premalignant lesions in women of child-bearing age, since future childbearing is unaffected.

Levonorgestrel — Drug inhibiting ovulation and preventing sperm from penetrating cervical mucus. It is delivered subcutaneously in polysiloxone capsules. The capsules can be effective for up to five years, and provide a cumulative pregnancy rate of less than 2 percent. The capsules are not biodegradable, and therefore must be removed. Removal is more difficult than insertion of levonorgestrel capsules because fibrosis develops around the capsules. Normal hormonal activity and a return to fertility begins immediately upon removal.

Appendixes

Ligation — This procedure involves tying off a blood vessel or duct with a suture or a soft, thin wire (ligature wire).

Magnuson-Stack procedure — Recurrent anterior dislocation is treated by tightening and realigning the subscapularis tendon.

Marsupialization — Suturing of cyst walls to the edge of a wound, following evacuation of the wound, so cavity may close by granulation.

Mastectomy — The surgical removal of one or both breasts and is most often performed to remove a malignant tumor. The types of mastectomy include:

- Radical. The breast, all lymph nodes in the axilla, and some muscles of the chest wall are removed.

- Modified radical. The large muscles of the chest that move the arm are preserved.

- Simple. Only breast tissue, nipple, and a small portion of overlying skin are removed.

McDonald procedure — Polyester tape is placed around the cervix with a running stitch to assist in the prevention of pre-term delivery. Tape is removed at term for vaginal delivery.

Mitral valve — The mitral valve is located between the left atrium and left ventricle of the heart. It has two cusps and is, therefore, frequently referred to as the bicuspid valve.

Mohs micrographic surgery — This is a special technique used to treat complex or ill-defined skin cancer and requires a single physician to provide two distinct services. The first service is surgical and involves the destruction of the lesion by a combination of chemosurgery and excision. The second service is that of a pathologist and includes mapping, color coding of specimens, microscopic examination of specimens, and complete histopathologic preparation.

Mustard procedure — This corrective measure for transposition of great vessels involves an intra-atrial baffle made of pericardial tissue or synthetic material. The baffle is secured between pulmonary veins and mitral valve and between mitral and tricuspid valves. The baffle directs systemic venous flow into the left ventricle and lungs and pulmonary venous flow into the right ventricle and aorta.

Myasthenia gravis — Neuromuscular disorder with symptoms of fatigue and exhaustion with fluctuating severity.

Myotomy — Cutting of a muscle to gain access to underlying tissues or to relieve constriction in a sphincter.

Nasal polyps — Polyps usually are bilateral, but they can be unilateral. Polyps, soft, edematous growths, project from nasal or sinus mucosa and may obstruct the posterior choanae. In addition to obstructing ventilation, they may affect the sense of smell if the olfactory epithelium is blocked. The KTP laser or the CO_2 laser is sometimes used in reducing or eliminating polyps.

Nasal sinus — The nasal sinuses are air-filled cavities in the crainal bones that earn their names; all are lined with mucous membrane continuous with the nasal cavity and all drain fluids into the nasal cavity. The ethmoid cells vary in size and number and feature very thin septa, or walls. The maxillary sinuses are the largest and are the most frequently infected.

Nasopharynx — The nasopharynx is the membranous passage above the level of the soft palate; the oropharynx is the region between the soft palate and the edge of the epiglottis; the hypopharynx is the region of the epiglottis to the juncture of the larynx and esophagus; the three regions collectively are called the pharynx.

Nd:YAG laser — Invisible pulsed neodyminum is used for cataract extraction and lysis of vitreous strands. The light used by the Nd:YAG laser does not require the tissues that are being treated to be pigmented.

Neurectomy — The removal of part of a nerve.

New patient — Evaluation and Management guidelines define a new patient as one who has not received any professional services from the physician, or another physician of the same specialty who belongs to the same group practice, within the past three years.

Nissen fundoplasty — Fundus of the stomach is wrapped around the lower end of the esophagus to treat reflux esophagitis.

Nonabsorable sutures — Strands of natural or synthetic material that resist absorption into living tissue. Skin is usually closed with nonabsorbable sutures. Examples include surgical silk, surgical cotton, linen, stainless steel, surgical nylon, polyester fiber, polybutester (Novafil), polyethylene (Dermalene), and polypropylene (Prolene, Surilene).

Nystagmus — Uncontrolled rapid movement of the eye.

Oophorectomy — Removal of ovary.

Outpatient physical therapy services — The term means the physical therapy services provided to an outpatient of a clinic, rehabilitation agency, or public health agency. The attending physician must establish a plan of physical therapy or periodically review a plan developed by a qualified physical therapist. A group of professional personnel, including one or more physicians (associated with the clinic or rehabilitation agency) and one or more qualified physical therapists must govern services and maintain clinical records of all patients. Outpatient clinics must provide a surety bond of $50,000 to guarantee the efficiency and effectiveness of programs. The term outpatient physical therapy services also includes physical therapy services provided by a physical therapist in office or at the patient's home and speech-language pathology services.

Pacemaker — A pacemaker device is used to artificially stimulate the heart muscle by the use of electric impulses that aid in maintaining normal sinus rhythm.

Paratenon graft — A graft composed of the fatty tissue found between a tendon and its sheath.

Pedicle flap — Tissue that remains partially attached to the donor site by a pedicle or stem. The blood supply is provided by vessels that remain intact in the pedicle or stem of the flap.

Percutaneous skeletal fixation — Treatment that is neither open nor closed. In this procedure, the injury site is not directly visualized. Instead fixation devices (pins, screws) are placed to stabilize the dislocation using x-ray guidance.

Percutaneous transluminal coronary angioplasty (PTCA) — The term describes the procedure used to treat coronary artery obstruction. A balloon catheter is placed in the affected artery and the balloon is inflated to flatten the plaque against the wall of the artery and open the obstruction.

Pericardium — The pericardium is the thin and slippery case in which the heart lies. It is lined with fluid so that the heart is free to pulse and move as it beats.

Physical status modifiers (anesthesia services) — Physical status modifiers reflect the patient's state of health. Individuals undergoing surgery may be healthy or may have varying degrees of systemic disease. A patient's health status affects the work related to providing the anesthesia service.

Pleurodesis — The production of adhesions between the parietal and visceral pleura.

Plication — Operation involving folding, shortening, or decreasing the size of a muscle or hollow organ by taking in tucks.

Potts-Smith-Gibson procedure — A side-to-side anastomosis of the aorta and left pulmonary artery creating a shunt that enlarges as the child grows.

Profunda — Denotes a part of a structure that is deeper from the surface of the body than the rest of the structure.

Prolonged physician services — Extended pre- or post-operative care provided to a patient whose condition requires services beyond the usual.

Prostate cancer screening tests — The term means a test that consists of any (or all) of the procedures provided for the early detection of prostate cancer to a man over 50 years of age who has not had a test during the preceding year. The procedures are as follows:

- A digital rectal examination
- A prostate-specific antigen blood test

After 2002, the list of procedures may be expanded as appropriate for the early detection of prostate cancer, taking into account changes in technology and standards of medical practice, availability, effectiveness, costs, and other factors.

Provider of services — The term means a hospital, critical access hospital, skilled nursing facility, comprehensive outpatient rehabilitation facility, home health agency, hospice program.

Psychiatric hospital — The term means an institution that provides, under the supervision of physicians, services for the diagnosis and treatment of mentally ill persons. Psychiatric hospitals receiving federal funds must maintain clinical records sufficient to determine the type of treatment provided to patients.

Pulmonary artery banding — In this palliative procedure for transposition of great vessels, the pulmonary artery is surgically constricted to prevent irreversible pulmonary vascular obstructive changes. Banding is often performed when a large ventricular septal defect is present.

Putti-Platt procedure — This procedure treats recurrent anterior dislocation by tightening and realigning the subscapularis tendon, thereby partially eliminating external rotation. The anterior capsule is also tightened and reinforced.

Pyloroplasty — Enlargement of the opening between the stomach and duodenum that may be performed in patients with an obstructing pyloric ulcer in combination with a vagotomy to treat bleeding duodenal ulcers.

Appendixes

Radiological examination — The term in CPT refers to plain films of specific sites. Other terms used to describe plain films include standard or conventional films. Services employing other modalities and additional techniques include the following:

- Computerized Axial Tomography (CT or CAT scan) is a type of imaging that employs basic tomographic technique enhanced by computer imaging. Computer enhancement synthesizes the images obtained from different directions in a given plane, effectively reconstructing a cross-sectional plane of the body.

- Computerized Tomography Angiography (CTA) provides multiple rapid thin section CT scans, a series of x-ray beams taken from different angles to create cross-sectional images of organs, bones, and tissues.

- Magnetic Resonance Imaging (MRI) involves the application of an external magnetic field that forces a uniform alignment of hydrogen atom nuclei in the soft tissue. The nuclei emit radiofrequency signals that are converted into sets of tomographic images and displayed on a computer screen for three-dimensional visualization of the soft tissue structure.

Rashkind procedure — A balloon catheter is inserted into the left atrium, inflated, and pulled across the septum to enlarge the foramen ovale, thus creating an atrial septal defect. This is a palliative procedure for transposition of great vessels.

Repair — Repair is the surgical closure of a wound. The wound may be a result of injury/trauma or it may be a surgically created defect. Repairs are divided into three categories: simple, intermediate, and complex. Simple repair is performed when the wound is superficial and only requires simple, one layer, primary suturing. Intermediate repair is performed for wounds and lacerations in which one or more of the deeper layers of subcutaneous tissue and non-muscle fascia are repaired in addition to the skin and subcutaneous tissue. Complex repair includes repair of wounds requiring more than layered closure. See also Wound repair.

Rural health clinic — The term defines a clinic in an area where there is a shortage of health services. The clinic must provide routine diagnostic services, including clinical laboratory services and have prompt access to additional diagnostic services from facilities meeting requirements (i.e., agreements with one or more hospitals for the referral and admission of patients requiring inpatient, diagnostic, or other specialized services not available at the clinic). In addition, the clinic must be able to administer drugs and biologicals as necessary for the treatment of emergency cases and have appropriate procedures or arrangements for storing, administering, and dispensing any drugs and biologicals. Staff must include a nurse practitioner, a physician assistant, or a certified nurse-midwife available for patient care not less than 50 percent of the time the clinic operates. In the case of a facility that is not a physician-directed clinic, there must be an arrangement with one or more physicians for the periodic review of covered services furnished by physician assistants and nurse practitioners.

Saucerization — Creation of a shallow, saucer-like depression in the bone to facilitate drainage from infected areas of bone.

Schiotz tonometer — Measures intraocular pressure by recording the depth of an indentation on the cornea by a plunger of known weight. The degree of indentation is calibrated on the tonometer to correspond to the intraocular pressure.

Screening mammography — The term means a radiologic procedure provided to a woman for the purpose of early detection of breast cancer and includes a physician's interpretation of the results of the procedure.

Screening pap smear; screening pelvic exam — The term means a diagnostic laboratory test consisting of a routine exfoliative cytology test (Papanicolaou test) provided to a woman for the purpose of early detection of cervical or vaginal cancer. The exam includes a clinical breast examination and a physician's interpretation of the results. Coverage depends on several factors, including the results of an exam during the preceding three years that indicated the presence of cervical or vaginal cancer or other abnormality or is at high risk of developing cervical or vaginal cancer.

Senning procedure — Flaps of intra-atrial septum and right atrial wall are used to create two interatrial channels to divert the systemic and pulmonary venous circulation.

Sensitivity Tests — Describes a number of methods of applying selective suspected allergens to the skin or mucous.

Sensorineural conduction — The transportation of sound from the cochlea to the acoustic nerve and central auditory pathway to the brain.

Separate procedures — Term in CPT describes services that are commonly carried out as an integral part of a larger service, and as such do not warrant separate identification. These services are noted in CPT with the parenthetical phrase (separate procedure). When this phrase appears before the semicolon, all indented descriptions that follow are covered by it.

Shirodkar procedure — Mersilene tape is drawn around the internal os and tied. This requires a small incision in the vaginal mucosa and usually predicates cesarean section.

Sinus of valsalva — Small cavity in the aorta just superior to the aortic valve. It is the origin of the coronary arteries. This area may also be referred to as the aortic sinus.

Speech-language pathology services; audiology services — The term means such speech, language, and related function assessment and rehabilitation services furnished by a qualified speech-language pathologist. Audiology services include hearing and balance assessment services furnished by a qualified audiologist. A qualified speech pathologist and audiologist must have a master's or doctoral degree in their respective fields and be licensed to serve in the state. Speech pathologists and audiologists practicing in states without licensure must complete 350 hours of supervised clinical work and perform at least nine months of supervised full-time service after earning their degrees.

Speech prosthetics — Electronic speech aids are covered by Medicare under Part B as prosthetic devices when the patient has had a laryngectomy. One operates by placing a vibrating head against the throat; the other amplifies sound waves through a tube which is inserted into the user's mouth.

Sphinteroplasty — Plastic surgery done to correct, augment, or improve the function of the muscular sphincter fibers founds in organs such as the anus or intestines.

Spirometry — Measurement of the lungs' breathing capacity.

Staghorn calculus — A concretion of the renal pelvis that often fills several calices.

Surgical package — The majority of the CPT surgical codes are "package" services; they include the actual surgical procedure, local infiltration, metacarpal and digital block or topical anesthesia (when used), and the normal, uncomplicated postoperative care.

Suture — There are numerous suturing techniques employed in wound closure. Among these are:

- Buried suture. A suture placed under the skin for a layered closure. It may be continuous or interrupted.

- Continuous suture. A running stitch with tension evenly distributed across the single strand so that it provides a leak proof suture line.

- Interrupted suture. A series of single stitches with tension isolated at each stitch. If one stitch loosens, the others may not be affected, and in the presence of infection, the isolated sutures cannot act as a wick to transport the infection.

- Purse-string suture. A continuous suture placed around a lumen and tightened to reduce or close the lumen.

- Retention suture. A secondary suture bridging the primary suture. Functionally, it provides support to the primary repair. A plastic or rubber bolster may be placed over the primary repair and under the retention sutures.

Tarsocheiloplasty — Plastic operation upon the edge of the eyelid for the treatment of trichiasis.

Tarsorrhaphy — Suture of a portion or all of the opposing eyelids for the purpose of shortening the palpebral fissure, or closing it entirely. External tarsorrhaphy involves the suture of the outer edges of the eyelid margins; median tarsorraphy involves the middle eyelid margins; and internal tarsorrhaphy involves the inner eyelid margins.

Tendon allograft — Allografts are tissues obtained from another individual of the same species. Tendon allografts are usually obtained from cadavers and frozen or freeze dried for later use in soft tissue repairs where the physician elects not to obtain an autogenous graft (a graft obtained from the individual on whom the surgery is being performed).

Tendon suture material — Tendons are composed of fibrous tissue consisting primarily of collagen and containing few cells or blood vessels. This tissue heals more slowly than tissues with more vascularization. Because of this, tendons are usually repaired with nonabsorbable suture material. Examples include surgical silk, surgical cotton, linen, stainless steel, surgical nylon, polyester fiber, polybutester (Novafil), polyethylene (Dermalene), and polypropylene (Prolene, Surilene).

Tenon's capsule — Connective tissue that forms the capsule enclosing the posterior eyeball, extending from the conjunctival fornix and continuous with the muscular fascia of the eye, also called the bulbar fascia, capsula bulbi, bulbar sheath, Bonnet's ocular, or sheath of eyeball.

Tensilon — Edrophonium chloride. An agent used for evaluation and treatment of myasthenia gravis.

Terminally Ill — An individual is considered to be "terminally ill" if the medical prognosis for life expectancy is six months or less.

Tetralogy of Fallot — A combination of congenital cardiac defects that include interventricular defect, pulmonary stenosis, right ventricular hypertrophy, and malpositioning of the aorta so that it receives venous as well as arterial blood.

Therapeutic Services — Term describes the procedures performed for treatment of a specific diagnosis. These services include performance of the procedure, various incidental elements, and normal, related follow-up care.

Thoracentesis — Using a needle to perforate the chest wall and pleural space for the aspiration of fluid for diagnostic or therapeutic purposes, or for biopsy.

Thoracic lymphadenectomy — Procedure to cut out the lymph nodes near the lungs, around the heart, and behind the trachea.

Thoracostomy — Making an incision into the chest wall to provide an opening for drainage.

Thyroglossal duct — An embryonic duct through which the thyroid gland descends during fetal development. The duct may form a cyst or sinus in adulthood. It is found at the front of the neck, within the hyoid bone.

Total shoulder replacement — Prosthetic replacement of the entire shoulder joint, including the humeral head and the glenoid fossa.

Trabeculae carneae cordis — Bands of muscular tissue that line the walls of the ventricles in the heart.

Tracheostomy — Formation of a tracheal opening to create a path for respiration. This is performed to relieve obstruction or improve patency of an airway. This is generally a more long-term measure.

Tracheotomy — Incision into the trachea below the larynx. This may be a controlled procedure or an emergency procedure, but is generally considered a temporary measure.

Trephine — A saw for removing a circular disk of bone used on the skull.

Tricuspid atresia — Tricuspid atresia is the congenital absence of the valve and it may occur with other defects, such as atrial septal defect, pulmonary atresia, and transposition of great vessels.

Tympanic membrane — The tympanic membrane is a thin, sensitive tissue and is the gateway to the middle ear. The membrane vibrates in response to sound waves and the movement is transmitted via the ossicular chain to the internal ear. The tympanic membrane may be punctured and tympanum penetrated by objects placed in the ear canal or entering the canal accidentally.

Urodynamics — The term describes a diagnostic service performed to evaluate the storage of urine and urine flow through the urinary tract.

Vagotomy — Division of the vagus nerves in the treatment of chronic gastric, pyloric, and duodenal ulcers that can cause severe pain and difficulties in eating and sleeping. Procedure interrupts nerve impulses to lower gastric acid production and hastens gastric emptying.

Vasectomy — Male sterilization achieved through removal of a portion of the vas deferens (route spermatozoa must take).

VBAC — (Vaginal Birth After Cesarean) Denotes a successful vaginal delivery after a previous cesarean delivery.

Ventricular septal defect — In a large ventricular septal defect, oxygenated blood flows back into the lungs, causing pulmonary hypertension. Small defects may be asymptomatic, and treatment may be unnecessary.

Vertebral interspace — The non-bony space between two vertebral bodies containing the intervertebral disk. It includes the nucleus pulposus, annulus, fibrosus, and the two cartilagenous endplates.

Volar — Pertaining to the palm of the hand or sole of the foot. Also may refer to the flexor surface of the forearm, wrist, or hand.

Waterston procedure — Anastomosis of aorta and right pulmonary artery placed on the posterior aspect of the aorta.

Wharton's ducts — The salivary ducts below the mandible.

Wick catheter — A device used to monitor interstitial fluid pressure. It provides continuous measurement of interstitial fluid pressure. It may also be used intraoperatively during fasciotomy procedures to evaluate the effectiveness of the decompression.

Wound repair — Repairs in CPT are divided into three categories: simple, intermediate, and complex. They are further described by anatomic site and wound size.

- Simple repair is performed when the wound is superficial, e.g., involving partial or full-thickness damage to the skin and/or subcutaneous tissues. No deeper structures are involved and only simple, one layer, primary suturing is required. This procedure includes local anesthetic and chemical or electrocauterization of wounds not closed.

- Intermediate repair is performed for wounds and lacerations in which one or more of the deeper layers of subcutaneous tissue and non-muscle fascia are repaired in addition to the skin and subcutaneous tissue. Single-layer closure can also be coded as an intermediate repair if the wound is heavily contaminated and requires extensive cleaning or removal of particulate matter.

- Complex repair includes repair of wounds requiring more than layered closure. Wounds coded from this category include those requiring revision, debridement, extensive undermining, and placement of stents or retention sutures. Complex repairs also include those requiring creation of a defect (e.g., extending excision) and special preparation of the site.

Xenograft — Tissue obtained from an animal of another species. Other terms for xenograft include heterograft, heterologous graft, xenogeneic graft.

Z-plasty — A plastic surgery technique used primarily to release tension or elongate contractured scar tissue. A Z-shaped incision is made with the middle line of the Z crossing the area of greatest tension. The triangular flaps are then rotated so that they cross the incision line in the opposite direction creating a reversed Z.

Notes

Notes

Notes

Notes

Notes

Notes

Notes

Notes

Notes

Notes